The Directory of

Local Court and County Record Retrievers

The Definitive Guide to Searching for Public Record Information at the State Level

2007 Edition

BRB Publications, Inc.

www.brbpub.com

Dedicated to the Searching & Understanding of Public Records

THE DIRECTORY OF LOCAL COURT AND COUNTY RECORD RETRIEVERS

2007 Edition

Edited by: Peter J. Weber, Annette Jackson, and Michael Sankey

Post Office Box 27869
Tempe, AZ 85285 U.S.A.
Telephone: 800-929-3811 Fax: 800-929-3810

www.brbpub.com

ISBN 1-879792-88-5 or 978-1-879792-88-3

Publisher's Cataloging-in-Publications
(Provided by Quality Books, Inc.)

The directory of local court and county record retrievers : the definitive guide to searching for public record information at the state level / [edited by Peter J. Weber, Annette Jackson, and Michael Sankey]. -- 2007 ed.
p. cm.
Includes index.
ISBN 1-879792-88-5
1. Court records--Research--United States--Directories. 2. Public records--Research--United States --Directories. 3. Legal research--United States--Directories. I. Weber, Peter J. (Peter Julius, 1952- II. Jackson, Annette, 1955-. III. Sankey, Michael L., 1949- IV. BRB Publications. V. Title: Local court and county record retrievers.

KF8700.A19D572 2007 342.73'0662'02573
QBI06-600698

This Directory includes elements of *The Public Record Retriever Network (PRRN)* 

Contents

Introduction

Simply put, this directory is a resource for local, hands-on document retrievers who search for public record information at source government agencies.

Who Are These Firms?

Public Record Retrievers physically visit government agencies—such as a court or recorder's office—to search within specific requested categories of public records. Usually the purpose is to obtain documentation for hiring, for lending, for litigation, or for legal compliance (e.g., incorporations). The individual goes directly to the agency to "look up" the information. Retrievers do *not* review or interpret the results or issue reports in the sense that investigators do, but rather return copies of existing documents resulting from the search.

The act of retrieving public record documents can be a stand-alone profession, or it can be a function or service offered by a private investigator, a public record search firm, a screening company, a title company, a process server, or a genealogist. Record retrievers may also be known as **abstractors, document retrievers,** or **record researchers.** In many states, abstractors perform services commonly associated with real estate title and ownership research.

These Record Retrievers Are Experts

In this directory, local record retrievers are indexed and profiled with only one qualification: **that they provide hands-on document searching and retrieval.** Based on the information they've provided about themselves, we feel they can fulfill your particular public record searching needs in an accurate and legal manner.

Those retrievers who are members of the **Public Record Retriever Network (PRRN)** are indicated throughout the book by the icon. PRRN is the first group to adopt *Industry Standards* specifically for the retrieval of public record documents. Members also must abide by a *Code of Professional Conduct*. More information regarding PRRN is found at the end of this book.

While record retrievers tend to be localized, there are many retrieval companies that offer state or national coverage. These larger retrieval companies hire other local retrievers as independent contractors to cover jurisdictions beyond their own local area. A retriever company's "other retrievers" are commonly referred to as **correspondents**. In fact, many of the retrievers listed in this directory act as correspondents for larger firms. Some entries in the directory prefer to work primarily as correspondents on an ongoing basis in a "wholesale" manner. Others prefer to only work the "retail" side of the business for the true end-users of the records. Accordingly, the fees retrievers charge can vary based on the volume of the client's needs.

> **Note:** The County Index section in this book will **only** indicate a county where a record retriever does an in-person search by himself or herself, or by a payroll employee.
>
> Many retrievers also maintain a network of correspondents and provide services in additional counties not listed within the County Index. This additional coverage is indicated in the Profiles section under Correspondent Relationships.

The Information in This Directory is Based on Surveys

All of the information contained in this directory is based upon responses to surveys conducted by the BRB Publications staff. The geographic coverage and profile information listed for each entry is based upon that company's or that individual's own responses to our survey. While trying to reflect these responses correctly, we are not responsible for the accuracy of their answers. If inaccuracies are readily apparent or coverage issues have been noticed, our staff has conducted phone interviews in an effort to find a resolution.

We are selective about the entries. We have removed companies profiled in previous works when multiple complaints about their services have been brought to our attention. Also, we will not include a start-up company with no proven record-searching experience. We have tried our best to make this directory as inclusive of professional retrievers as possible. If you have a problem with an entry in this book, let BRB know by using the Retriever Satisfaction Survey found in the back of this book.

What is Out There? Keep in Mind These Truths About Public Records...

Retrievers are your link to public records. Keep in mind that the public record search process is complicated. One must know where to search, how to search, and the degree of restrictions placed by government agencies on record access. Consider the following—

- Just because records are maintained in a certain way in your state or county, do not assume that any other county or state does things the same way.
- Not all public records are online; in fact only about one third of all records defined as "public" are available online today, and much of that is by subscription rather than free.
- An information chain exists between the record repository and the record's final end-user. A record retriever is an important link in this information chain.

Other Research Tools

Having knowledge about a jurisdiction's record-keeping policies and retrieval procedures is always a plus when you need to obtain information from that office. For example, if you already know facts about the office—such as that the records in a court are indexed only by defendant, or that a public terminal is available at the court office—you can better determine whether the retriever really knows what they're talking about. BRB Publications maintains extensive reference materials that feature this kind of information about state agencies, state and federal courts, county recorders' offices, and other public and private institutions where you may want to search. This useful information is available online in the *Public Record Research System,* a subscription web product updated weekly. BRB also offers the same information as an annual publication titled *The Sourcebook to Public Record Information*. Visit www.brbpub.com for more information.

How To Be Listed In This Directory

If you or your firm provides hands-on record retrieval service at the county level, you are eligible to be listed. There is no charge to be listed in this directory.

You can call BRB Publications at 800-929-3811 to obtain a questionnaire and additional information about being listed in this Directory. We would be glad to answer any questions you have. You can also visit www.brbpub.com/prrn/join.asp to download the Retriever Questionnaire, as well as information about PRRN membership.

There is a membership fee involved if you choose to join the Public Record Retriever Network (PRRN). Members are indicated in this Directory by the ▣ icon. New members are listed immediately on the PRRN website. Membership in PRRN is also open to Associate Members. See the PRRN membership information at the rear of this book.

As mentioned above, BRB Publications' policy is not to include an individual or company in this book if we have received complaints about them. Also, our editors may, at their discretion, cancel the listing of any company that, in their opinion, is not conducting business in a highly ethical manner.

Some Advice If You Solicit Firms in this Directory

One of the objectives of this Directory is to promote the vendors. Also, a stated objective of PRRN is to promote improved marketing and sales practices within the industry. As a result, entries in this book realize they will receive solicitations from other retrievers or from entities hiring retrievers.

If you wish to let a company know that you provide retrieval services in a certain geographic area and want to see if they may be interested in using you, first consider the following:

- Does the firm use outside sources? (outside sources are called "Correspondents" in the profile)
- Does this firm offer to its own clientele the type for public record you wish to provide?

For example, if you provide criminal record searches, do not send an information sheet about your services to a firm in the book that only searches real estate records in three counties. When you do wish to see if a firm is interested in your services, we suggest to **first call and ask** if you can fax or mail your information.

If You Fax, Be Aware of the Law

If you fax to someone in this book, we strongly urge you pre-qualify the entity and be careful with the wording of your message.

The Telephone Consumer Protection Act of 1991 (A Federal Law) states "...It shall be unlawful for any person within the U.S. to use a (c) telephone facsimile machine, computer, or other device to send an unsolicited advertisement to a telephone facsimile machine..." and "A person or entity may … bring in an appropriate Court of that State (B) an action to recover ... or to receive $500 in damages for each violation … plus up to three times that amount…" etc.

A Guide to Working With Record Retrievers

What Makes a Retriever Competent?

The four most significant attributes of the kind of record retriever you want on your side are—

1. Local Experience and Expertise

- Knows exactly where to go to obtain the information you need
- Knows personally the people who work at the government agency
- Knows exactly what the records look like and what the contents mean

2. Searching Time Frame

- Knows just how long the project will take
- Knows whether it is possible to expedite the project
- Completes the project as promised

3. Delivery of Document

- Can deliver the document when and where required
- Will only conduct a search of records that are legally available to you
- Knows and explains the possible pitfalls involved in obtaining the information you need

4. Cost

- Knows the basis for the costs—copy fee, certification fee, etc.
- Can reasonably estimate the total fee

The rest of this chapter is devoted to guidelines that will help you choose a quality retriever for your needs and also to instruct you on how to place an order.

By following these steps, you should be able to minimize problems and insure you are obtaining the correct information you need.

Ten Questions to Ask a Retriever

You have a right to expect that a local record retriever will be conversant with all the nuances of the type of record search you need performed. You should also expect that the retriever is able to educate you about exactly what can be searched and if there are any limitations.

The **Ten Questions to Ask a Retriever** illustrates the various questions you want answered before committing your project to a record retriever and will help you determine the quality of a retriever.

	Questions to Ask:			
1.	What is your expertise in the type of information I need?	HIGH	MEDIUM	LOW
2.	What is your expertise in dealing with the agency where the information is stored?	HIGH	MEDIUM	LOW
3.	How frequently do you access the agency where the information I need is stored?	DAILY	WEEKLY	OTHER
4.	How frequently do you access the specific information I need?	DAILY	WEEKLY	OTHER
5.	Are the original documents stored at this agency?	YES	NO	DON'T KNOW
6.	In what form will I receive the information?	AS YOU WISH	VERBAL ONLY	DOCS ONLY
7.	Will you explain what the information means for me (e.g., what does an internal motor vehicle code mean)?	YES	NO	NO
8.	Will my search be legal and remain confidential?	YES	NOT FULLY EXPLAINED	DON'T KNOW
9.	What are all the costs I will (may) incur to obtain the information?	EXPLAINED	NOT FULLY EXPLAINED	DON'T KNOW
10.	Do you serve other clients who have needs like mine and may I talk to a few of them?	YES	UNSURE	NO
	If you circled a preponderance of answers in one column, you should—	Consider This Retriever	Consider Other Retriever	Do Not Use This Retriever

Hands-on Versus Online

There are many, many web pages that offer online access to public records. Many government sites provide an online search to an index of public records. Many retrievers, especially those who are private investigators, have the means and wherewithal to perform these online searches. This book is not a forum to discuss when to perform an online search or the pluses and minuses associated with an online search versus a hands-on search. However, when you call a record retriever because you need an in person search at a court or recorder's office, make sure that you are clear on your expectations.

The next section covers specific topics that you need to consider before you hire a retriever.

Before You Place An Order With A Retriever ... Read This

If you are not clear at the outset of what you expect a record retriever to do for you, you are asking for trouble. Perhaps the number one reason we receive a complaint call about a retriever is that there was a major misunderstanding about expectations between the retriever and the client.

Here are ten aspects of a search we think are essential **to review before you hire a retriever.** Of course, the one big question not on this list that you will want to ask the retriever – what is the cost? The reason is that the answer cannot be determined until the ten items below are clear to both parties.

1. Determine Exactly What Type of Records You Want Searched

You must always be crystal clear about what information you need. Do not give the retriever vague instructions. For example—

Criminal Searches

An order to do a "criminal record search," is not an adequate description. Is it for felonies only, for felonies and misdemeanors, or for both? If misdemeanors are desired, should the search include DWI's? Is a federal court search also required?

Civil Searches

Many counties have two or three levels or tiers where civil cases are filed. The level is usually determined by the dollar amount associated with the case. For example, in some counties there may be as many as 20 courts with authority to try small claims cases, or multiple courts with claims limits under a certain figure. Some counties also have geographic divisions for upper end cases. A search of each court can each incur a separate fee. Be sure to ask what is required if you wish someone to search "all civil cases" in a county.

UCC Searches

If you need a UCC search, do you wish to have the search include tax liens, and if so, just federal or both federal and state tax liens? What about abstracts of judgment or judgment liens? Do you want to search only in a central office, or should a local filing office search also be conducted? Is your client aware of the different types of search methods necessary to overcome the limitations of searches under revised Article 9 of the UCC in most central filing offices? Do you know how to determine what state to search in?

Real Estate Searches

There are many kinds of real estate searches, some of which may be requested together. For example, if you indicate you wish to know if a subject owns any property in a county you might also want to know whether any of the properties are mortgaged.

Whatever the type of search you desire, it is best to explore the options available at the outset, and not to assume the searching procedures are the same you experienced in a different county or state.

2. Determine Where Do You Want to Search

Frequently this question is associated with the previous question. Simply make sure to ask if there is more than one location where the information requested might be obtained. Court locations provide a complex example in a number of states and counties. A county may have two courts with the same jurisdictions, but without a combined index to search, or municipal courts in a county may have overlapping jurisdiction with the state court in the county with respect to misdemeanors. You must determine if you wish the retriever to search all or only part of the county court structure.

Another example, all real estate searches take place at a county recorder's (or equivalent) office. However, the location for other types of public information can get more complicated, especially under revised Article 9 of the UCC. For example, if the subject is organized in one state but has its chief executive office in another, and the client asks for UCC and federal tax lien searches, it would be necessary to perform searches in two separate locations.

Another consideration is which county to search. There are over 8,000 ZIP Codes that cross county lines. Your may wish to independently check which county is correct for the given address or ZIP Code of the subject. When asked, the retriever can perform a more thorough job by searching in highly populous contiguous counties where additional records might be located.

> **Note:** The word "county" is frequently used in this chapter to describe a local geographic area. The use of this term is also meant to recognize and include the parishes in Louisiana as well as many independent cities that have either separate jurisdictional recording offices, courts, or both. For example, while there are 3,141 counties and parishes in the U.S., there are over 3,600 local entities in the U.S. that hold recorded documents.

3. Decide the Time Period to Search

When hiring a retriever to search public records, you need to give specific instructions on how far back to make the search. Better yet, ask what is the retriever's norm or standard search period for that particular county. Many local jurisdictions have computerized an index to records, but the index may only go back a limited number of years. If the date range of the index does not meet your needs, the retriever will need to perform a separate, manual search of the older records.

Even in UCC searching, where the usual period is "All," your client may only want to update her records from a certain date.

4. Know the Subject's Name

You should develop standards to determine if the subject name you give a retriever is adequate for searching.

Individual names such as "Carl Ernst" may be adequate for your purposes, or you may want to ask whether the middle initial is known, especially if the name is common. Also, "C. Alexander Ernst" may create real search problems for the retriever if you don't know what the "C" stands for.

Business entity names usually have endings such as "Corp." or "Inc." You might want to ask about the retriever's standard procedure – if they search to include the ending or if they ignore all business entity endings. Some names involve additional complexities. For example, which should be searched – "UCC Guide Inc.," or "The UCC Guide Inc.," or both?

You will need to state clearly in your request the names you wish to be searched and any constraints or limitations on search procedures due to the form of the name. A retriever may be expected to find common variations of the subject name, but cannot, nor is responsible to, determine all the weird variations that a keypuncher might inflict on a name.

5. Let the Retriever Know if You Anticipate Records or Hits

Public record searching is not a test. It always helps the retriever to know if you are aware of any records that now exist on the subject. You may say, "That's none of his or her business, the retriever is hired to do the search." That's OK, but you realize that public records can be mis-indexed by the filing officers or court personnel. Most retrievers will extend their search procedures beyond their usual thorough methods if they did not get a hit when one was anticipated.

Another consideration is when a government office charges a lot for copies, and automatically makes copies for all searches. If you know the subject has hundreds of filings, you may ask the retriever to advise a more cost-efficient way to search the records without incurring substantial copy charges.

6. Prepare to Ask How the Search Will be Conducted

Has anyone ever asked this question? Everyone should ask.

Public record searches are performed at the actual court or recorder records office, by human beings. Keep in mind the methods of storage and retrieval of public records can vary from one government agency to another. Who performs that actual search? Some agencies require that the names to be searched for be handed over to the clerk who performs the actual search. Some agencies have computer terminals that a researcher can view in person. The researcher may have to type in each name, or the researcher may review a list of names to see if the applicant's name appears. Some agencies index names in other searchable formats such as ledgers, microfiche, or microfilm. Further, it is now common for indexes to be made available to the general public on the Internet, either from a government agency or a database vendor who has purchased the data from the government agency.

Thus, there may be a number of ways that public information can be searched out. Some of these ways may be official, some unofficial but provided by the agency, and some provided by private vendors.

Therefore, it is incumbent upon you to ask the retriever about the possible search methods and clarify how you wish the search to be performed. In agencies where either the retriever or the agency may perform the search, you should decide which way to go. If for legal reasons you require an "official" search, one done by the government office itself and certified, make that requirement clear at the outset.

In those jurisdictions where a retriever has the option of searching on a private, third party database rather than on the official database of the agency, the retriever should never conduct a search on the private database without your express permission.

7. Know What Documents You Want to Obtain

This aspect of an order can be quite costly. Perhaps you think you are asking for a list or index of public records on a subject and the retriever hands you copies of 500 UCC filings. Make sure you find out first if you have no choice but to obtain documents as part of a search. The retriever should inform you of the possibility of excessive copy costs in advance of performing the search.

8. Know Your Deadline

Let the retriever know when you need the results and ask if you have a reasonable time expectation. In those jurisdictions where government personnel must perform the search you need to know if the normal turnaround time does not fit your needs. In those situations, ask if the government agency offers an expedited service (which is usually for an additional fee) or you will need to adjust your expectations.

9. Determine How You Want the Results Given to You

Be clear on how you expect the form of delivery of the search results. Do you want them by fax, by telephone, email, overnight courier, or just by regular mail? Ask the retriever if there are different fees for different delivery methods.

10. Keep a Written Log of the Request

The nine items summarized above should indicate your complete instructions. If you have an ongoing relationship with a retriever, that retriever should maintain a standard set of client instructions for your orders. If you are working with a new or relatively new retriever, you will lose nothing by being comprehensive with your instructions. Keep a log with the date and time the order was placed, the time and method of expected delivery, and whom you spoke if you placed the order by telephone. Using standard, written procedures will minimize the chances of making a mistake and help insure your instructions are legible and complete.

How to Use This Book

How This Book is Organized

This directory consists of two main sections. To help you know "who" has access to "what" public record information, see **the Local Retriever County Index**. Located in the front two-thirds of this book, see **the Local Retriever County Index** is a county-by-county index showing which firms visit the courthouse or recorder's office within a particular county.

To learn more about a particular retriever, review **the Local Retriever Profiles** section located in the back one-third of the book. All retrievers are listed in alphabetical order there.

Also, the far back of this book contains the following: **1. Profiles of PRRN Associate Members** (firms that provide public record and public record services other than hands-on record retrieval); **2. PRRN membership materials** including the PRRN **Code of Public Record Retriever Standards; 3. a Reader Satisfaction Survey** form to use to register a complaint about an entity in this Directory.

Also, we strongly urge readers to read previous chapter carefully. The proven hints and suggestions will make your public record searching tasks and choice of a retriever more efficient.

About The County Index

Retrievers Shown County by County

There are 3,561 counties, parishes, independent cities and equivalent jurisdictions in the United States listed here in alphabetical order within each state. Note that there are entries for North America (Canada and Bermuda) in the front of the Index. You will find Puerto Rico and the Virgin Islands listed alphabetically among the states.

Icons and Bullet Items

Each retriever that accesses government offices in a county is listed under that county name with a bullet (black dot) to signify each category of data the company retrieves.

Retrievers who **serve process** are indicated with the designation "**[SOP]**".

Retrievers that are members of the **Public Record Retriever Network (PRRN)** are indicated by the PRRN logo ▦.

Nine Types of Data Included

Each county heading indicates the types of records available in that jurisdiction. The left side of the page indicates records available from the county or municipal court system. The right side of the page indicates records available from the recorder or other courthouse offices.

On page 12, the **Summary of Codes** explains the meaning of each abbreviation used.

About The Retrievers Profile Section Index

Information Found in the 2,597 Profiles...

- Retriever name and the logo if a PRRN Member in 2007 at time this Directory printed
- Address and telephone numbers, including fax when available
- Web page address; email address
- Summary of types of records retrieved
- Local retrieval area—a list of counties each services directly
- Other geographic areas serviced through correspondents
- Year established
- Project turnaround times
- Billing and payment terms
- If they perform service of process
- Additional information, including special areas of expertise

Although the usual billing practices used by each of the retrieval companies are indicated, no information about actual pricing is included. Fees are subject to private negotiation and depend on the type and extent of any given project.

Hints and Tips on Using the Profiles Section

Alphabetical Rules

As mentioned above, individual names are alphabetized by last name first, unless the name appears as part of a company name, in which case it is alphabetized by the first letter of the company name.

If the word "The" appears to be a definitive connected part of the company name, you may find the company in the "T" section.

Branch offices of larger retriever firms are listed individually. Usually the firm name is followed by the branch office name or locale in parenthesis, along with that branch's corresponding retrieval area.

Read for Specialties and Expertise

Each retriever was given the opportunity to submit a twenty-five word statement indicating what they do best. Take a moment and read this statement before calling a retriever. This will give you a much better idea of their service and expertise.

Listed at the end of this section are PRRN Associate Members who offer regional or national search or screening services only.

Some Retrievers Are Mobile

Don't be alarmed if you don't get a live person when calling a retriever. Many retrievers are on the job at the local courthouse or recorder's office. Some may carry a cell phone. As a general rule, retrievers will return calls as they are able. We provide all the telephone numbers for each entry in this Profile section. The previous section—the Index—only had the main telephone number.

Only Call a Retriever for the Records They Retrieve

Please review which categories of records are retrieved by a company prior to making a telephone call. For example, if a company only searches records at the recorder's office, you are wasting your time and the retriever's time to ask for a criminal or civil record from a court record repository.

Coverage Area Claimed in the County Index

Entries in this publication are based on the responses of each retrieval company. A county entry is shown when a retriever states to us that he, she or a true payroll employee visits that particular jurisdiction, and not a friend, another retriever, or correspondent.

Companies that offer only online indexing to these counties have been excluded, to the best of our knowledge. However, there are many companies that offer both hands-on and electronic retrieval.

Coverage Area By Correspondents or Networks

Keep in mind that many companies provide service in areas beyond the counties listed. When a retriever has the capability of offering expanded geographic coverage, the area is indicated in its Retriever Profile under **Correspondent Relationships**.

Searching Records at State Agencies

The retrievers located in or near a state capital often offer expertise in searching records at state agencies, for example where corporate and UCC records are located. If you need records retrieved or searched from a state agency, start with those firms with a physical presence in the capital, or if the firm states this expertise in the profile.

Summary of Codes

Court Records

CODE	Government Agency	Type of Information
CR	Criminal Court	Municipal, county and state level criminal cases
CV	Civil Court	Municipal, county and state level civil cases
PR	Probate Court	Wills and estate cases
US	US District Court	Federal civil and criminal cases
BK	Bankruptcy Court	United States bankruptcy cases

County Records - Recordings

CODE	Government Agency	Type of Information
UC	UCC Filing Office	Uniform Commercial Code and other personal property liens
RE	Real Estate Recording Office	Real property transactions and liens
TX	Tax Filing Office(s)	Federal and state tax liens, judgment liens
VS	Vital Records Office	Vital statistics—birth, death, marriage, divorce

- "CODE" designates the agency and type of information obtainable in each county from a retriever.
- —This symbol designates a Public Record Retriever Network member.
- "[SOP]" after the retriever name designates Service of Process.
- Individual retrievers without a company name are listed in order of their last name.

North America

Canada

COURT RECORDS RETRIEVED — CAPITAL - ONTARIO PROVINCE — RECORDED RECORDS RETRIEVED

CR	CV	PR	US	BK	←COURTS	ALBERTA	RECORDER→	UC	RE	TX	VS
•	•				Accurate Source.com Inc		877-635-8551				
•	•			•	Bison Security Group [SOP]		800-661-2245, 866-245-2083		•	•	•
•	•				Shepp Johnman & Associates Inv [SOP]		877-258-9073				

CR	CV	PR	US	BK	←COURTS	BRITISH COLUMBIA	RECORDER→	UC	RE	TX	VS
•	•				Accurate Source.com Inc		877-635-8551				
•	•		•		FBIG Investigations [SOP]		866-245-2082, 888-540-0456		•	•	
•	•	•		•	Mercury Service Inc.		604-228-9993	•	•		
•	•	•		•	Sterling Pacific Investigations Ltd [SOP]		250-652-0541				

CR	CV	PR	US	BK	←COURTS	MANITOBA	RECORDER→	UC	RE	TX	VS
•	•				Accurate Source.com Inc		877-635-8551				
•	•	•	•		Oliver, Yaskiw & Associates [SOP]		866-245-5045		•	•	•

CR	CV	PR	US	BK	←COURTS	NEW BRUNSWICK	RECORDER→	UC	RE	TX	VS
•	•				Accurate Source.com Inc		877-635-8551				
•	•	•	•		CSI Investigations [SOP]		866-245-2089, 888-818-5251	•	•	•	
•	•				InfoFax		902-425-4444		•	•	

CR	CV	PR	US	BK	←COURTS	NEWFOUNDLAND	RECORDER→	UC	RE	TX	VS
•	•				Accurate Source.com Inc		877-635-8551				
•	•	•	•		CSI Investigations [SOP]		866-245-2089, 888-818-5251	•	•	•	
•	•				InfoFax		902-425-4444		•	•	

CR	CV	PR	US	BK	←COURTS	NORTHWEST TERRITORIES	RECORDER→	UC	RE	TX	VS
•	•				Accurate Source.com Inc		877-635-8551				

CR	CV	PR	US	BK	←COURTS	NOVA SCOTIA	RECORDER→	UC	RE	TX	VS
•	•				Accurate Source.com Inc		877-635-8551				
•	•	•	•		CSI Investigations [SOP]		866-245-2089, 888-818-5251	•	•	•	
•	•				InfoFax		902-425-4444		•	•	

CR	CV	PR	US	BK	←COURTS	ONTARIO	RECORDER→	UC	RE	TX	VS
	•	•			Aberdeen Investigations, Inc [SOP]		807-626-4074		•	•	
•	•				Accurate Source.com Inc		877-635-8551				
	•			•	Idealogic [SOP]		866-506-9900	•	•	•	•
	•	•	•	•	King-Reed & Assoc Ltd.		877-695-6575	•		•	•

CR	CV	PR	US	BK	←COURTS PRINCE EDWARD ISLAND	RECORDER→	UC	RE	TX	VS
•	•				Accurate Source.com Inc	877-635-8551				
•	•	•	•		CSI Investigations [SOP]	866-245-2089, 888-818-5251	•	•	•	
•	•				InfoFax	902-425-4444		•	•	

CR	CV	PR	US	BK	←COURTS SASKATCHEWAN	RECORDER→	UC	RE	TX	VS
•	•				Accurate Source.com Inc	877-635-8551				
•	•		•		Evident [SOP]	866-245-2084		•		

CR	CV	PR	US	BK	←COURTS YUKON	RECORDER→	UC	RE	TX	VS
•	•				Accurate Source.com Inc	877-635-8551				

[SOP] = PERFORMS SERVICE OF PROCESS

Bermuda, Domincan Republic

COURT RECORDS RETRIEVED — CAPITAL - HAMILTON — RECORDED RECORDS RETRIEVED

CR	CV	PR	US	BK	←COURTS BERMUDA	RECORDER→	UC	RE	TX	VS
•	•	•		•	Caribbean Investigative Network [SOP]	441-292-2626		•		•

CR	CV	PR	US	BK	←COURTS DOMINICAN REPUBLIC	RECORDER→	UC	RE	TX	VS
•	•		•	•	Rucar Business Information Center	787-645-1659	•	•	•	•

Note: Puerto Rico and the **Virgin Islands** are listed with the US States, which follow alphabetically.

COURT RECORDS

CODE	GOVERNMENT AGENCY	TYPE OF INFORMATION
CR	Criminal Court	Municipal, county and state level criminal cases
CV	Civil Court	Municipal, county and state level civil cases
PR	Probate Court	Wills and estate cases
US	US District Court	Federal civil and criminal cases
BK	Bankruptcy Court	United States bankruptcy cases

COUNTY RECORDS - RECORDINGS

CODE	GOVERNMENT AGENCY	TYPE OF INFORMATION
UC	UCC Filing Office	Uniform Commercial Code and other personal property liens
RE	Real Estate Recording Office	Real property transactions and liens
TX	Tax Filing Office(s)	Federal and state tax liens, judgment liens
VS	Vital Records Office	Vital statistics—birth, death, marriage, divorce

Alabama

COURT RECORDS RETRIEVED — CAPITAL - MONTGOMERY COUNTY — RECORDED RECORDS RETRIEVED

CR	CV	PR	US	BK	←COURTS	AUTAUGA	RECORDER→	UC	RE	TX	VS
	•	•			AlaDocs Inc		205-251-8200	•	•	•	
		•			Autauga Abstract		334-361-0606	•	•	•	
•	•	•	•	•	Public Record Services [SOP]		334-262-0350	•	•	•	•

CR	CV	PR	US	BK	←COURTS	BALDWIN	RECORDER→	UC	RE	TX	VS
•	•	•	•	•	A & A Screening Solutions LLC [SOP]		877-999-9318	•		•	
	•	•			AlaDocs Inc		205-251-8200	•	•	•	
	•	•	•		Brabston Legal Investigations Inc [SOP]		251-666-5666	•		•	
	•	•			Guiles & O'Hear LLC		251-478-8245	•	•	•	•
•	•	•	•	•	Ike L Hoy PE (Control Systems)		850-259-4650	•	•	•	•
•	•	•			Alice S Mosley [SOP]		251-937-8468	•	•	•	
•	•	•	•	•	Parker Legal Services [SOP]		251-476-7464	•	•	•	•
•	•	•	•	•	🏛Parrish Research		850-936-1240	•	•	•	•
•	•	•	•	•	Public Record Services [SOP]		334-262-0350	•	•	•	•

CR	CV	PR	US	BK	←COURTS	BARBOUR	RECORDER→	UC	RE	TX	VS
	•	•			AlaDocs Inc		205-251-8200	•	•	•	
•	•	•	•	•	Public Record Services [SOP]		334-262-0350	•	•	•	•

CR	CV	PR	US	BK	←COURTS	BIBB	RECORDER→	UC	RE	TX	VS
	•	•			AlaDocs Inc		205-251-8200	•	•	•	
•	•	•	•	•	Public Record Services [SOP]		334-262-0350	•	•	•	•

CR	CV	PR	US	BK	←COURTS	BLOUNT	RECORDER→	UC	RE	TX	VS
	•	•			AlaDocs Inc		205-251-8200	•	•	•	
•	•	•	•	•	🏛Charles F Edgar & Associates Inc [SOP]		256-539-7761	•	•	•	
•	•	•			Johnston & Associates		256-673-0855	•	•	•	
•	•	•	•	•	Public Record Services [SOP]		334-262-0350	•	•	•	•

CR	CV	PR	US	BK	←COURTS	BULLOCK	RECORDER→	UC	RE	TX	VS
	•	•			AlaDocs Inc		205-251-8200	•	•	•	
•	•	•	•	•	Public Record Services [SOP]		334-262-0350	•	•	•	•

CR	CV	PR	US	BK	←COURTS	BUTLER	RECORDER→	UC	RE	TX	VS
	•	•			AlaDocs Inc		205-251-8200	•	•	•	
•	•	•	•	•	Public Record Services [SOP]		334-262-0350	•	•	•	•

CR	CV	PR	US	BK	←COURTS	CALHOUN	RECORDER→	UC	RE	TX	VS
	•	•			AlaDocs Inc		205-251-8200	•	•	•	
•	•	•	•	•	🏛B & B Reporting Inc [SOP]		256-574-2524	•	•	•	•
•	•	•	•	•	🏛Charles F Edgar & Associates Inc [SOP]		256-539-7761	•	•	•	
•	•	•	•	•	Public Record Services [SOP]		334-262-0350	•	•	•	•
	•	•	•	•	Southern Land & Title LLC		256-543-1361	•	•	•	

CR	CV	PR	US	BK	←COURTS	CHAMBERS	RECORDER→	UC	RE	TX	VS
	•	•			AlaDocs Inc		205-251-8200	•	•	•	
•	•			•	Attorneys Services & Legal Inv [SOP]		706-322-3554 or 322-3224	•	•	•	
•	•	•	•	•	Public Record Services [SOP]		334-262-0350	•	•	•	•

CR	CV	PR	US	BK	←Courts CHEROKEE	Recorder→	UC	RE	TX	VS
	•	•			AlaDocs Inc	205-251-8200	•	•	•	
•	•	•	•	•	Charles F Edgar & Associates Inc [SOP]	256-539-7761	•	•	•	
•	•	•	•	•	Public Record Services [SOP]	334-262-0350	•	•	•	•
	•	•	•	•	Southern Land & Title LLC	256-543-1361	•	•	•	
	•	•	•	•	Title Guaranty & Trust of Chattanooga	423-266-5751	•	•	•	

CR	CV	PR	US	BK	←Courts CHILTON	Recorder→	UC	RE	TX	VS
	•	•			AlaDocs Inc	205-251-8200	•	•	•	
•	•	•	•	•	Public Record Services [SOP]	334-262-0350	•	•	•	•

CR	CV	PR	US	BK	←Courts CHOCTAW	Recorder→	UC	RE	TX	VS
	•	•			AlaDocs Inc	205-251-8200	•	•	•	
•	•	•	•	•	Public Record Services [SOP]	334-262-0350	•	•	•	•

CR	CV	PR	US	BK	←Courts CLARKE	Recorder→	UC	RE	TX	VS
	•	•			AlaDocs Inc	205-251-8200	•	•	•	
	•	•	•	•	Brabston Legal Investigations Inc [SOP]	251-666-5666	•		•	
•	•	•	•	•	Parrish Research	850-936-1240	•	•	•	•
	•	•	•		Presley's Title & Abstract Co, Inc	888-544-8006	•	•	•	•
•	•	•	•		Public Record Services [SOP]	334-262-0350	•	•	•	•

CR	CV	PR	US	BK	←Courts CLAY	Recorder→	UC	RE	TX	VS
	•	•			AlaDocs Inc	205-251-8200	•	•	•	
•	•	•	•	•	Public Record Services [SOP]	334-262-0350	•	•	•	•

CR	CV	PR	US	BK	←Courts CLEBURNE	Recorder→	UC	RE	TX	VS
	•	•			AlaDocs Inc	205-251-8200	•	•	•	
•	•	•	•	•	Public Record Services [SOP]	334-262-0350	•	•	•	•
	•	•	•	•	Southern Land & Title LLC	256-543-1361	•	•	•	

CR	CV	PR	US	BK	←Courts COFFEE	Recorder→	UC	RE	TX	VS
	•	•			AlaDocs Inc	205-251-8200	•	•	•	
•	•	•	•	•	Parrish Research	850-936-1240	•	•	•	•
•	•	•	•	•	Public Record Services [SOP]	334-262-0350	•	•	•	•
		•			V & A Research LLC	334-774-7092	•	•	•	

CR	CV	PR	US	BK	←Courts COLBERT	Recorder→	UC	RE	TX	VS
	•	•			AlaDocs Inc	205-251-8200	•	•	•	
•	•	•	•	•	Charles F Edgar & Associates Inc [SOP]	256-539-7761	•	•	•	
•	•	•			Freelance Abstracting Service [SOP]	662-424-3636	•	•		•
	•	•	•		Maureen H Poole	931-294-2988	•	•	•	
•	•	•	•	•	Public Record Services [SOP]	334-262-0350	•	•	•	•
•	•	•	•	•	Risk Mitigation Services Inc [SOP]	866-633-9339	•		•	

CR	CV	PR	US	BK	←Courts CONECUH	Recorder→	UC	RE	TX	VS
	•	•			AlaDocs Inc	205-251-8200	•	•	•	
	•	•			Melissa F Morris	334-222-1986	•	•	•	
•	•	•	•	•	Parrish Research	850-936-1240	•	•	•	•
	•	•	•		Presley's Title & Abstract Co, Inc	888-544-8006	•	•	•	•
•	•	•	•	•	Public Record Services [SOP]	334-262-0350	•	•	•	•

CR	CV	PR	US	BK	←Courts COOSA	Recorder→	UC	RE	TX	VS
	•	•			AlaDocs Inc	205-251-8200	•	•	•	
•	•	•	•	•	Public Record Services [SOP]	334-262-0350	•	•	•	•

CR	CV	PR	US	BK	←Courts COVINGTON	Recorder→	UC	RE	TX	VS
	•	•			AlaDocs Inc	205-251-8200	•	•	•	
•	•	•	•	•	Ike L Hoy PE (Control Systems)	850-259-4650	•	•	•	•
	•	•			Melissa F Morris	334-222-1986	•	•	•	
•	•	•	•	•	Parrish Research	850-936-1240	•	•	•	•

CR	CV	PR	US	BK	←Courts	Recorder→	UC	RE	TX	VS
	•	•	•		Presley's Title & Abstract Co, Inc	888-544-8006	•	•	•	•
•	•	•	•	•	Public Record Services [SOP]	334-262-0350	•	•	•	•

CR	CV	PR	US	BK	←Courts CRENSHAW	Recorder→	UC	RE	TX	VS
	•	•			AlaDocs Inc	205-251-8200	•	•	•	
•	•	•	•	•	Public Record Services [SOP]	334-262-0350	•	•	•	•

CR	CV	PR	US	BK	←Courts CULLMAN	Recorder→	UC	RE	TX	VS
	•	•			AlaDocs Inc	205-251-8200	•	•	•	
•	•	•	•	•	Charles F Edgar & Associates Inc [SOP]	256-539-7761	•	•	•	
•	•	•	•	•	Public Record Services [SOP]	334-262-0350	•	•	•	•

CR	CV	PR	US	BK	←Courts DALE	Recorder→	UC	RE	TX	VS
	•	•			AlaDocs Inc	205-251-8200	•	•	•	
•	•	•	•	•	Parrish Research	850-936-1240	•	•	•	•
•	•	•	•	•	Public Record Services [SOP]	334-262-0350	•	•	•	•
		•			V & A Research LLC	334-774-7092	•	•	•	

CR	CV	PR	US	BK	←Courts DALLAS	Recorder→	UC	RE	TX	VS
	•	•			AlaDocs Inc	205-251-8200	•	•	•	
•	•	•	•	•	Public Record Services [SOP]	334-262-0350	•	•	•	•

CR	CV	PR	US	BK	←Courts DE KALB	Recorder→	UC	RE	TX	VS
•	•	•	•	•	A All State Tracers Company	423-605-0155	•	•	•	•
	•	•			AlaDocs Inc	205-251-8200	•	•	•	
•	•	•	•	•	B & B Reporting Inc [SOP]	256-574-2524	•	•	•	•
•	•	•	•	•	Charles F Edgar & Associates Inc [SOP]	256-539-7761	•	•	•	
•	•	•	•	•	Public Record Services [SOP]	334-262-0350	•	•	•	•
	•	•	•	•	Southern Land & Title LLC	256-543-1361	•	•	•	
	•	•	•	•	Title Guaranty & Trust of Chattanooga	423-266-5751	•	•	•	

CR	CV	PR	US	BK	←Courts ELMORE	Recorder→	UC	RE	TX	VS
	•	•			AlaDocs Inc	205-251-8200	•	•	•	
		•			Autauga Abstract	334-361-0606	•	•	•	
•	•	•	•	•	Public Record Services [SOP]	334-262-0350	•	•	•	•

CR	CV	PR	US	BK	←Courts ESCAMBIA	Recorder→	UC	RE	TX	VS
	•	•			AlaDocs Inc	205-251-8200	•	•	•	
•	•	•	•	•	Ike L Hoy PE (Control Systems)	850-259-4650	•	•	•	•
	•	•			Melissa F Morris	334-222-1986	•	•	•	
•	•	•	•	•	Parrish Research	850-936-1240	•	•	•	•
	•	•	•		Presley's Title & Abstract Co, Inc	888-544-8006	•	•	•	•
•	•	•	•	•	Public Record Services [SOP]	334-262-0350	•	•	•	•

CR	CV	PR	US	BK	←Courts ETOWAH	Recorder→	UC	RE	TX	VS
	•	•			AlaDocs Inc	205-251-8200	•	•	•	
•	•	•	•	•	Charles F Edgar & Associates Inc [SOP]	256-539-7761	•	•	•	
•	•	•			Johnston & Associates	256-673-0855	•	•	•	
•	•	•	•	•	Public Record Services [SOP]	334-262-0350	•	•	•	•
	•	•	•	•	Southern Land & Title LLC	256-543-1361	•	•	•	

CR	CV	PR	US	BK	←Courts FAYETTE	Recorder→	UC	RE	TX	VS
	•	•			AlaDocs Inc	205-251-8200	•	•	•	
•	•	•	•	•	Public Record Services [SOP]	334-262-0350	•	•	•	•

CR	CV	PR	US	BK	←Courts FRANKLIN	Recorder→	UC	RE	TX	VS
	•	•			AlaDocs Inc	205-251-8200	•	•	•	
•	•	•	•	•	Charles F Edgar & Associates Inc [SOP]	256-539-7761	•	•	•	
	•	•	•		Maureen H Poole	931-294-2988	•	•	•	
•	•	•	•	•	Public Record Services [SOP]	334-262-0350	•	•	•	•

CR	CV	PR	US	BK	←Courts	Geneva	Recorder→	UC	RE	TX	VS
	•	•			AlaDocs Inc		205-251-8200	•	•	•	
•	•	•	•	•	Ike L Hoy PE (Control Systems)		850-259-4650	•	•	•	•
•	•	•	•	•	Parrish Research		850-936-1240	•	•	•	•
•	•	•	•	•	Public Record Services [SOP]		334-262-0350	•	•	•	•
		•			V & A Research LLC		334-774-7092	•	•	•	

CR	CV	PR	US	BK	←Courts	Greene	Recorder→	UC	RE	TX	VS
	•	•			AlaDocs Inc		205-251-8200	•	•	•	
•	•	•	•	•	Public Record Services [SOP]		334-262-0350	•	•	•	•

CR	CV	PR	US	BK	←Courts	Hale	Recorder→	UC	RE	TX	VS
	•	•			AlaDocs Inc		205-251-8200	•	•	•	
•	•	•	•	•	Public Record Services [SOP]		334-262-0350	•	•	•	•

CR	CV	PR	US	BK	←Courts	Henry	Recorder→	UC	RE	TX	VS
	•	•			AlaDocs Inc		205-251-8200	•	•	•	
•	•	•	•	•	Parrish Research		850-936-1240	•	•	•	•
•	•	•	•	•	Public Record Services [SOP]		334-262-0350	•	•	•	•
		•			V & A Research LLC		334-774-7092	•	•	•	

CR	CV	PR	US	BK	←Courts	Houston	Recorder→	UC	RE	TX	VS
	•	•			AlaDocs Inc		205-251-8200	•	•	•	
•	•	•	•	•	Parrish Research		850-936-1240	•	•	•	•
•	•	•	•	•	Public Record Services [SOP]		334-262-0350	•	•	•	•
	•	•	•	•	Title Guaranty & Trust of Chattanooga		423-266-5751	•	•	•	
		•			V & A Research LLC		334-774-7092	•	•	•	

CR	CV	PR	US	BK	←Courts	Jackson	Recorder→	UC	RE	TX	VS
•	•	•	•		A All State Tracers Company		423-605-0155	•	•	•	•
	•	•			AlaDocs Inc		205-251-8200	•	•	•	
•	•	•	•	•	B & B Reporting Inc [SOP]		256-574-2524	•	•	•	•
•	•	•	•	•	Charles F Edgar & Associates Inc [SOP]		256-539-7761	•	•	•	
•	•	•	•	•	Public Record Services [SOP]		334-262-0350	•	•	•	•

CR	CV	PR	US	BK	←Courts	Jefferson	Recorder→	UC	RE	TX	VS
•			•	•	ADM & Associates Inc		800-242-5999				
	•	•			AlaDocs Inc		205-251-8200	•	•	•	
•	•	•	•	•	Charles F Edgar & Associates Inc [SOP]		256-539-7761	•	•	•	
•	•	•	•	•	Confidential Background Services [SOP]		205-447-1539	•	•	•	•
•	•	•	•	•	Mid-South Legal Services [SOP]		800-340-9855	•		•	•
•	•	•	•	•	Parrish Research		850-936-1240	•	•	•	•
•	•	•	•	•	Public Record Services [SOP]		334-262-0350	•	•	•	•
		•			Faith Simpson [SOP]		205-381-0788	•	•	•	
	•	•	•	•	Southern Land & Title LLC		256-543-1361	•	•	•	

CR	CV	PR	US	BK	←Courts	Lamar	Recorder→	UC	RE	TX	VS
	•	•			AlaDocs Inc		205-251-8200	•	•	•	
•	•	•	•	•	Aldridge & Associates [SOP]		662-651-7376	•	•	•	•
•	•	•	•	•	Public Record Services [SOP]		334-262-0350	•	•	•	•

CR	CV	PR	US	BK	←Courts	Lauderdale	Recorder→	UC	RE	TX	VS
	•	•			AlaDocs Inc		205-251-8200	•	•	•	
•	•	•	•	•	Charles F Edgar & Associates Inc [SOP]		256-539-7761	•	•	•	
	•	•	•		Maureen H Poole		931-294-2988	•	•	•	
•	•	•	•	•	Public Record Services [SOP]		334-262-0350	•	•	•	•
•	•	•	•	•	Risk Mitigation Services Inc [SOP]		866-633-9339	•		•	

CR	CV	PR	US	BK	←Courts	Lawrence	Recorder→	UC	RE	TX	VS
	•	•			AlaDocs Inc		205-251-8200	•	•	•	
•	•	•	•	•	Charles F Edgar & Associates Inc [SOP]		256-539-7761	•	•	•	
•	•	•	•	•	Public Record Services [SOP]		334-262-0350	•	•	•	•
•	•	•	•	•	Risk Mitigation Services Inc [SOP]		866-633-9339	•		•	

CR	CV	PR	US	BK	←Courts	Lee	Recorder→	UC	RE	TX	VS
	•	•			AlaDocs Inc		205-251-8200	•	•	•	
•	•			•	Attorneys Services & Legal Inv [SOP]		706-322-3554 or 322-3224	•	•	•	
•	•	•	•	•	Public Record Services [SOP]		334-262-0350	•	•	•	•

CR	CV	PR	US	BK	←Courts	Limestone	Recorder→	UC	RE	TX	VS
	•	•			AlaDocs Inc		205-251-8200	•	•	•	
•	•	•	•	•	Charles F Edgar & Associates Inc [SOP]		256-539-7761	•	•	•	
	•	•	•		Maureen H Poole		931-294-2988	•	•	•	
•	•	•	•	•	Public Record Services [SOP]		334-262-0350	•	•	•	•

CR	CV	PR	US	BK	←Courts	Lowndes	Recorder→	UC	RE	TX	VS
	•	•			AlaDocs Inc		205-251-8200	•	•	•	
•	•	•	•	•	Public Record Services [SOP]		334-262-0350	•	•	•	•

CR	CV	PR	US	BK	←Courts	Macon	Recorder→	UC	RE	TX	VS
	•	•			AlaDocs Inc		205-251-8200	•	•	•	
•	•	•	•	•	Public Record Services [SOP]		334-262-0350	•	•	•	•

CR	CV	PR	US	BK	←Courts	Madison	Recorder→	UC	RE	TX	VS
	•	•			AlaDocs Inc		205-251-8200	•	•	•	
•	•	•	•	•	B & B Reporting Inc [SOP]		256-574-2524	•	•	•	•
•	•	•	•	•	Charles F Edgar & Associates Inc [SOP]		256-539-7761	•	•	•	
•	•	•			Johnston & Associates		256-673-0855	•	•	•	
	•	•	•		Maureen H Poole		931-294-2988	•	•	•	
•	•	•	•	•	Public Record Services [SOP]		334-262-0350	•	•	•	•
	•	•	•	•	Southern Land & Title LLC		256-543-1361	•	•	•	

CR	CV	PR	US	BK	←Courts	Marengo	Recorder→	UC	RE	TX	VS
	•	•			AlaDocs Inc		205-251-8200	•	•	•	
•	•	•	•	•	Public Record Services [SOP]		334-262-0350	•	•	•	•

CR	CV	PR	US	BK	←Courts	Marion	Recorder→	UC	RE	TX	VS
	•	•			AlaDocs Inc		205-251-8200	•	•	•	
	•	•	•		Maureen H Poole		931-294-2988	•	•	•	
•	•	•	•	•	Public Record Services [SOP]		334-262-0350	•	•	•	•

CR	CV	PR	US	BK	←Courts	Marshall	Recorder→	UC	RE	TX	VS
	•	•			AlaDocs Inc		205-251-8200	•	•	•	
•	•	•	•	•	B & B Reporting Inc [SOP]		256-574-2524	•	•	•	•
•	•	•	•	•	Charles F Edgar & Associates Inc [SOP]		256-539-7761	•	•	•	
•	•	•			Johnston & Associates		256-673-0855	•	•	•	
•	•	•	•	•	Public Record Services [SOP]		334-262-0350	•	•	•	•
	•	•	•	•	Southern Land & Title LLC		256-543-1361	•	•	•	

CR	CV	PR	US	BK	←Courts	Mobile	Recorder→	UC	RE	TX	VS
•	•	•	•	•	A & A Screening Solutions LLC [SOP]		877-999-9318	•		•	
	•	•			AlaDocs Inc		205-251-8200	•	•	•	
	•	•	•	•	Brabston Legal Investigations Inc [SOP]		251-666-5666	•		•	
	•	•			Guiles & O'Hear LLC		251-478-8245	•	•	•	•
•	•	•	•	•	Ike L Hoy PE (Control Systems)		850-259-4650	•	•	•	•
•	•	•	•	•	Parker Legal Services [SOP]		251-476-7464	•	•	•	•
•	•	•	•	•	Parrish Research		850-936-1240	•	•	•	•
•	•	•	•	•	Public Record Services [SOP]		334-262-0350	•	•	•	•

CR	CV	PR	US	BK	←COURTS	MONROE	RECORDER→	UC	RE	TX	VS
	•	•			AlaDocs Inc		205-251-8200	•	•	•	
•	•	•	•	•	Parrish Research		850-936-1240	•	•	•	•
	•	•	•		Presley's Title & Abstract Co, Inc		888-544-8006	•	•	•	•
•	•	•	•	•	Public Record Services [SOP]		334-262-0350	•	•	•	•
CR	**CV**	**PR**	**US**	**BK**	**←COURTS**	**MONTGOMERY**	**RECORDER→**	**UC**	**RE**	**TX**	**VS**
	•	•			AlaDocs Inc		205-251-8200	•	•	•	
•	•	•	•	•	Public Record Services [SOP]		334-262-0350	•	•	•	•
CR	**CV**	**PR**	**US**	**BK**	**←COURTS**	**MORGAN**	**RECORDER→**	**UC**	**RE**	**TX**	**VS**
	•	•			AlaDocs Inc		205-251-8200	•	•	•	
•	•	•	•	•	Charles F Edgar & Associates Inc [SOP]		256-539-7761	•	•	•	
	•	•	•		Maureen H Poole		931-294-2988	•	•	•	
•	•	•	•	•	Public Record Services [SOP]		334-262-0350	•	•	•	•
CR	**CV**	**PR**	**US**	**BK**	**←COURTS**	**PERRY**	**RECORDER→**	**UC**	**RE**	**TX**	**VS**
	•	•			AlaDocs Inc		205-251-8200	•	•	•	
•	•	•			James M Barnes Jr [SOP]		334-683-6060	•	•	•	•
•	•	•	•	•	Public Record Services [SOP]		334-262-0350	•	•	•	•
CR	**CV**	**PR**	**US**	**BK**	**←COURTS**	**PICKENS**	**RECORDER→**	**UC**	**RE**	**TX**	**VS**
	•	•			AlaDocs Inc		205-251-8200	•	•	•	
•	•	•	•	•	Public Record Services [SOP]		334-262-0350	•	•	•	•
CR	**CV**	**PR**	**US**	**BK**	**←COURTS**	**PIKE**	**RECORDER→**	**UC**	**RE**	**TX**	**VS**
	•	•			AlaDocs Inc		205-251-8200	•	•	•	
•	•	•	•	•	Parrish Research		850-936-1240	•	•	•	•
•	•	•	•	•	Public Record Services [SOP]		334-262-0350	•	•	•	•
CR	**CV**	**PR**	**US**	**BK**	**←COURTS**	**RANDOLPH**	**RECORDER→**	**UC**	**RE**	**TX**	**VS**
	•	•			AlaDocs Inc		205-251-8200	•	•	•	
•	•	•	•	•	Public Record Services [SOP]		334-262-0350	•	•	•	•
	•	•	•	•	Southern Land & Title LLC		256-543-1361	•	•	•	
CR	**CV**	**PR**	**US**	**BK**	**←COURTS**	**RUSSELL**	**RECORDER→**	**UC**	**RE**	**TX**	**VS**
	•	•			AlaDocs Inc		205-251-8200	•	•	•	
•	•			•	Attorneys Services & Legal Inv [SOP]		706-322-3554 or 322-3224	•	•	•	
•	•	•	•	•	Public Record Services [SOP]		334-262-0350	•	•	•	•
CR	**CV**	**PR**	**US**	**BK**	**←COURTS**	**SHELBY**	**RECORDER→**	**UC**	**RE**	**TX**	**VS**
•			•	•	ADM & Associates Inc		800-242-5999				
	•	•			AlaDocs Inc		205-251-8200	•	•	•	
•	•	•	•	•	Charles F Edgar & Associates Inc [SOP]		256-539-7761	•	•	•	
•	•	•	•	•	Confidential Background Services [SOP]		205-447-1539	•	•	•	•
•	•	•	•	•	Mid-South Legal Services [SOP]		800-340-9855	•		•	•
•	•	•	•	•	Parrish Research		850-936-1240	•	•	•	•
•	•	•	•	•	Public Record Services [SOP]		334-262-0350	•	•	•	•
	•	•	•	•	Southern Land & Title LLC		256-543-1361	•	•	•	
CR	**CV**	**PR**	**US**	**BK**	**←COURTS**	**ST CLAIR**	**RECORDER→**	**UC**	**RE**	**TX**	**VS**
	•	•			AlaDocs Inc		205-251-8200	•	•	•	
•	•	•	•	•	Charles F Edgar & Associates Inc [SOP]		256-539-7761	•	•	•	
•	•	•	•	•	Confidential Background Services [SOP]		205-447-1539	•	•	•	•
•	•	•	•	•	Mid-South Legal Services [SOP]		800-340-9855	•		•	•
•	•	•	•	•	Parrish Research		850-936-1240	•	•	•	•
•	•	•	•	•	Public Record Services [SOP]		334-262-0350	•	•	•	•
	•	•	•	•	Southern Land & Title LLC		256-543-1361	•	•	•	
CR	**CV**	**PR**	**US**	**BK**	**←COURTS**	**SUMTER**	**RECORDER→**	**UC**	**RE**	**TX**	**VS**
	•	•			AlaDocs Inc		205-251-8200	•	•	•	

CR	CV	PR	US	BK	Retriever	Phone	UC	RE	TX	VS
•	•	•	•	•	Public Record Services [SOP]	334-262-0350	•	•	•	•

CR	CV	PR	US	BK	←COURTS TALLADEGA	RECORDER→	UC	RE	TX	VS
	•	•			AlaDocs Inc	205-251-8200	•	•	•	
•	•	•	•	•	Charles F Edgar & Associates Inc [SOP]	256-539-7761	•	•	•	
•	•	•	•	•	Mid-South Legal Services [SOP]	800-340-9855	•		•	•
•	•	•	•	•	Public Record Services [SOP]	334-262-0350	•	•	•	•
	•	•	•	•	Southern Land & Title LLC	256-543-1361	•	•	•	

CR	CV	PR	US	BK	←COURTS TALLAPOOSA	RECORDER→	UC	RE	TX	VS
	•	•			AlaDocs Inc	205-251-8200	•	•	•	
•	•	•	•	•	Public Record Services [SOP]	334-262-0350	•	•	•	•

CR	CV	PR	US	BK	←COURTS TUSCALOOSA	RECORDER→	UC	RE	TX	VS
	•	•			AlaDocs Inc	205-251-8200	•	•	•	
•	•	•	•	•	Charles F Edgar & Associates Inc [SOP]	256-539-7761	•	•	•	
•	•	•	•	•	Mid-South Legal Services [SOP]	800-340-9855	•		•	•
•	•	•	•	•	Parrish Research	850-936-1240	•	•	•	•
•	•	•	•	•	Public Record Services [SOP]	334-262-0350	•	•	•	•

CR	CV	PR	US	BK	←COURTS WALKER	RECORDER→	UC	RE	TX	VS
	•	•			AlaDocs Inc	205-251-8200	•	•	•	
•	•	•	•	•	Charles F Edgar & Associates Inc [SOP]	256-539-7761	•	•	•	
•	•	•	•	•	Mid-South Legal Services [SOP]	800-340-9855	•		•	•
•	•	•	•	•	Public Record Services [SOP]	334-262-0350	•	•	•	•

CR	CV	PR	US	BK	←COURTS WASHINGTON	RECORDER→	UC	RE	TX	VS
	•	•			AlaDocs Inc	205-251-8200	•	•	•	
•	•	•	•	•	Public Record Services [SOP]	334-262-0350	•	•	•	•

CR	CV	PR	US	BK	←COURTS WILCOX	RECORDER→	UC	RE	TX	VS
	•	•			AlaDocs Inc	205-251-8200	•	•	•	
•	•	•	•	•	Public Record Services [SOP]	334-262-0350	•	•	•	•

CR	CV	PR	US	BK	←COURTS WINSTON	RECORDER→	UC	RE	TX	VS
	•	•			AlaDocs Inc	205-251-8200	•	•	•	
•	•	•	•	•	Charles F Edgar & Associates Inc [SOP]	256-539-7761	•	•	•	
•	•	•	•	•	Public Record Services [SOP]	334-262-0350	•	•	•	•

[SOP] = PERFORMS SERVICE OF PROCESS

Editor's Note: The County Index section in this book will **only** indicate a county where a record retriever does an in-person search by himself or herself, or by a payroll employee.

Many retrievers also maintain a network of correspondents and provide services in additional counties not listed within the County Index. This additional coverage is indicated in the Profiles section under Correspondent Relationships.

Alaska

Alaskan jurisdiction boundaries of court districts do not match jurisdictional boundaries of recording offices. In this directory, the court jurisdictional district names are used, which are based on the federal FIPS Code.

COURT RECORDS RETRIEVED — CAPITAL - JUNEAU BOROUGH — RECORDED RECORDS RETRIEVED

CR	CV	PR	US	BK	<Courts	Aleutian Islands, East	Recording>	UC	RE	TX	VS
•	•		•	•		Alaska Public Records Search LLC [SOP]	800-808-5105	•	•	•	

CR	CV	PR	US	BK	←Courts	Aleutians Islands, West	Recorder→	UC	RE	TX	VS
•	•		•	•		Alaska Public Records Search LLC [SOP]	800-808-5105	•	•	•	

CR	CV	PR	US	BK	←Courts	Anchorage	Recorder→	UC	RE	TX	VS
•	•	•	•	•		Alaska Court Services [SOP]	907-258-3211				
•	•		•	•		Alaska Public Records Search LLC [SOP]	800-808-5105	•	•	•	
•	•	•	•	•		Complete Corporate Services of Alaska [SOP]	907-790-4956	•	•	•	
•	•	•	•	•		North Country Process Inc [SOP]	907-274-2023	•	•	•	
						Pacific NW Title of Alaska	907-561-5122		•	•	
•	•	•	•	•		Research by Robin	907-929-7850	•	•	•	•

CR	CV	PR	US	BK	←Courts	Bethel	Recorder→	UC	RE	TX	VS
						Pacific NW Title of Alaska	907-561-5122		•	•	

CR	CV	PR	US	BK	←Courts	Bristol Bay	Recorder→	UC	RE	TX	VS
•	•		•	•		Alaska Public Records Search LLC [SOP]	800-808-5105	•	•	•	
						Pacific NW Title of Alaska	907-561-5122		•	•	

CR	CV	PR	US	BK	←Courts	Fairbanks North Star	Recorder→	UC	RE	TX	VS
•	•	•	•	•		Alaska Court Services [SOP]	907-258-3211				
•	•		•	•		Alaska Public Records Search LLC [SOP]	800-808-5105	•	•	•	
						Fairbanks Title Agency	907-456-6626		•	•	
•	•	•	•	•		Fort Enterprises Process Srv & Investigation [SOP]	907-488-7766	•	•	•	•
•	•	•	•	•		North Country Process Inc [SOP]	907-274-2023	•	•	•	

CR	CV	PR	US	BK	←Courts	Haines	Recorder→	UC	RE	TX	VS
•	•	•	•	•		Civil Claims Service [SOP]	907-364-2714	•	•	•	•
•	•	•	•	•		Complete Corporate Services of Alaska [SOP]	907-790-4956	•	•	•	

CR	CV	PR	US	BK	←Courts	Juneau	Recorder→	UC	RE	TX	VS
•	•		•	•		Alaska Public Records Search LLC [SOP]	800-808-5105	•	•	•	
•	•	•	•	•		Civil Claims Service [SOP]	907-364-2714	•	•	•	•
•	•	•	•	•		Complete Corporate Services of Alaska [SOP]	907-790-4956	•	•	•	

CR	CV	PR	US	BK	←Courts	Kenai Peninsula	Recorder→	UC	RE	TX	VS
•	•	•	•	•		Alaska Court Services [SOP]	907-258-3211				
•	•		•	•		Alaska Public Records Search LLC [SOP]	800-808-5105	•	•	•	
•	•	•	•	•		North Country Process Inc [SOP]	907-274-2023	•	•	•	
						South Central Title Agency Inc	907-262-4494		•	•	

CR	CV	PR	US	BK	←Courts	Ketchikan Gateway	Recorder→	UC	RE	TX	VS
•	•	•	•	•		Civil Claims Service [SOP]	907-364-2714	•	•	•	•
•	•	•	•	•		Complete Corporate Services of Alaska [SOP]	907-790-4956	•	•	•	
•	•	•	•	•		North Country Process Inc [SOP]	907-274-2023	•	•	•	

CR	CV	PR	US	BK	←Courts	Kodiak Island	Recorder→	UC	RE	TX	VS
•	•	•	•	•		Alaska Court Services [SOP]	907-258-3211				

CR	CV	PR	US	BK	←Courts **MATANUSKA-SUSITNA**	Recorder→	UC	RE	TX	VS
•	•		•	•	Alaska Public Records Search LLC [SOP]	800-808-5105	•	•	•	
•	•	•	•	•	North Country Process Inc [SOP]	907-274-2023	•	•	•	

CR	CV	PR	US	BK	←Courts **NOME**	Recorder→	UC	RE	TX	VS
					Fairbanks Title Agency	907-456-6626		•	•	

CR	CV	PR	US	BK	←Courts **NORTH SLOPE**	Recorder→	UC	RE	TX	VS
•	•		•	•	Alaska Public Records Search LLC [SOP]	800-808-5105	•	•	•	

CR	CV	PR	US	BK	←Courts **NORTHWEST ARCTIC**	Recorder→	UC	RE	TX	VS
					See adjoining counties for retrievers or call court/recorder directly.					

CR	CV	PR	US	BK	←Courts **PRINCE OF WALES-OUTER KETCHIKAN**	Recorder→	UC	RE	TX	VS
•	•	•	•	•	Complete Corporate Services of Alaska [SOP]	907-790-4956	•	•	•	

CR	CV	PR	US	BK	←Courts **SITKA**	Recorder→	UC	RE	TX	VS
•	•	•	•	•	Civil Claims Service [SOP]	907-364-2714	•	•	•	•
•	•	•	•	•	Complete Corporate Services of Alaska [SOP]	907-790-4956	•	•	•	

CR	CV	PR	US	BK	←Courts **SKAGWAY-HOONAH-ANGOON**	Recorder→	UC	RE	TX	VS
•	•	•	•	•	Civil Claims Service [SOP]	907-364-2714	•	•	•	•
•	•	•	•	•	Complete Corporate Services of Alaska [SOP]	907-790-4956	•	•	•	

CR	CV	PR	US	BK	←Courts **SOUTHEAST FAIRBANKS**	Recorder→	UC	RE	TX	VS
					See adjoining counties for retrievers or call court/recorder directly.					

CR	CV	PR	US	BK	←Courts **VALDEZ-CORDOVA**	Recorder→	UC	RE	TX	VS
•	•	•	•	•	Alaska Court Services [SOP]	907-258-3211				
•	•		•	•	Alaska Public Records Search LLC [SOP]	800-808-5105	•	•	•	
					Pacific NW Title of Alaska	907-561-5122		•	•	

CR	CV	PR	US	BK	←Courts **WADE HAMPTON**	Recorder→	UC	RE	TX	VS
					See adjoining counties for retrievers or call court/recorder directly.					

CR	CV	PR	US	BK	←Courts **WRANGELL-PETERSBURG**	Recorder→	UC	RE	TX	VS
•	•	•	•	•	Civil Claims Service [SOP]	907-364-2714	•	•	•	•
•	•	•	•	•	Complete Corporate Services of Alaska [SOP]	907-790-4956	•	•	•	

CR	CV	PR	US	BK	←Courts **YUKON-KOYUKUK**	Recorder→	UC	RE	TX	VS
					See adjoining counties for retrievers or call court/recorder directly.					

Arizona

COURT RECORDS RETRIEVED — CAPITAL - MARICOPA COUNTY — RECORDED RECORDS RETRIEVED

Apache

CR	CV	PR	US	BK	←Courts	Recorder→	UC	RE	TX	VS
•	•				Access Information Services, Inc - AZ Katie Anderson	520-405-8737				
•	•	•	•	•	AccuSearch Inc	800-462-7019	•	•	•	
•	•	•	•	•	Arizona Research & Retrieval Services Inc	888-500-7767	•	•	•	•
•	•				Attorney Service New Mexico [SOP]	505-326-7486				
•	•	•	•	•	MacIntire & Associates (Tucson)	800-641-2737	•		•	
•					PDQ Legal Services Inc	480-556-6660				
•	•	•		•	Raban's Record Search & Inv [SOP]	928-337-4250	•	•	•	
•	•	•			The Public Record Source	623-773-3997	•		•	•

Cochise

CR	CV	PR	US	BK	←Courts	Recorder→	UC	RE	TX	VS
•	•				Access Information Services, Inc - AZ Katie Anderson	520-405-8737				
•	•	•	•	•	Arizona Research & Retrieval Services Inc	888-500-7767	•	•	•	•
•	•	•	•	•	E-Z Messenger Attorney Service Inc [SOP]	800-264-8436	•	•	•	
•	•	•			Holifield Investigation Agency	800-427-1294		•	•	
•	•	•	•	•	MacIntire & Associates (Tucson)	800-641-2737	•		•	
•					PDQ Legal Services Inc	480-556-6660				
•	•	•	•	•	Research Unlimited LLC	520-624-7024	•	•	•	•
•	•	•	•	•	South East Arizona Legal Support	520-432-9032	•	•	•	•
•	•	•			The Public Record Source	623-773-3997	•		•	•
•	•	•			Valley Security Inc [SOP]	928-428-2142		•	•	•

Coconino

CR	CV	PR	US	BK	←Courts	Recorder→	UC	RE	TX	VS
•	•				Access Information Services, Inc - AZ Katie Anderson	520-405-8737				
•	•	•	•	•	AccuSearch Inc	800-462-7019	•	•	•	
•	•	•	•	•	Arizona Research & Retrieval Services Inc	888-500-7767	•	•	•	•
•	•	•			Frontier Private Process Service (Flagstaff) [SOP]	800-711-8511	•	•	•	
•	•	•	•	•	Hawkins & EZmessenger Inc [SOP]	602-452-1800	•	•	•	•
•	•	•	•	•	MacIntire & Associates (Tucson)	800-641-2737	•		•	
					Nationwide Environmental Title Research	800-324-4956		•		
•	•	•			Northern Arizona Investigations [SOP]	800-657-2747	•	•	•	
•					PDQ Legal Services Inc	480-556-6660				
•	•				Public Records Info Service	520-797-0486				
•	•	•			The Public Record Source	623-773-3997	•		•	•

Gila

CR	CV	PR	US	BK	←Courts	Recorder→	UC	RE	TX	VS
•	•				Access Information Services, Inc - AZ Katie Anderson	520-405-8737				
•	•	•	•	•	AccuSearch Inc	800-462-7019	•	•	•	
•	•	•	•	•	Arizona Research & Retrieval Services Inc	888-500-7767	•	•	•	•
•	•	•			Barnone Bailbonds & Investigations [SOP]	800-607-8200	•	•	•	•
•	•	•	•	•	MacIntire & Associates (Tucson)	800-641-2737	•		•	
•					PDQ Legal Services Inc	480-556-6660				
•	•	•			The Public Record Source	623-773-3997	•		•	•

Graham

CR	CV	PR	US	BK	←Courts	Recorder→	UC	RE	TX	VS
•	•				Access Information Services, Inc - AZ Katie Anderson	520-405-8737				
•	•	•	•	•	AccuSearch Inc	800-462-7019	•	•	•	
•	•	•	•	•	Arizona Research & Retrieval Services Inc	888-500-7767	•	•	•	•
•	•	•	•	•	MacIntire & Associates (Tucson)	800-641-2737	•		•	
•					PDQ Legal Services Inc	480-556-6660				

CR	CV	PR	US	BK	←Courts	Recorder→	UC	RE	TX	VS
•	•	•			The Public Record Source	623-773-3997	•		•	•
•	•	•			Valley Security Inc [SOP]	928-428-2142		•	•	•

Greenlee

CR	CV	PR	US	BK	←Courts	Recorder→	UC	RE	TX	VS
•	•				Access Information Services, Inc - AZ Katie Anderson	520-405-8737				
•	•	•	•	•	AccuSearch Inc	800-462-7019	•	•	•	
•	•	•	•	•	Arizona Research & Retrieval Services Inc	888-500-7767	•	•	•	•
•	•	•	•	•	MacIntire & Associates (Tucson)	800-641-2737	•		•	
•					PDQ Legal Services Inc	480-556-6660				
•	•	•			The Public Record Source	623-773-3997	•		•	•
•	•	•			Valley Security Inc [SOP]	928-428-2142		•	•	•

La Paz

CR	CV	PR	US	BK	←Courts	Recorder→	UC	RE	TX	VS
•	•				Access Information Services, Inc - AZ Katie Anderson	520-405-8737				
•	•	•	•	•	AccuSearch Inc	800-462-7019	•	•	•	
•	•	•	•	•	Arizona Research & Retrieval Services Inc	888-500-7767	•	•	•	•
•	•	•	•	•	MacIntire & Associates (Tucson)	800-641-2737	•		•	
•					PDQ Legal Services Inc	480-556-6660				
•	•	•			The Public Record Source	623-773-3997	•		•	•

Maricopa

CR	CV	PR	US	BK	←Courts	Recorder→	UC	RE	TX	VS
•	•	•	•	•	A Very Private Eye Research & Investigations Corp	623-572-2665	•	•	•	
•	•				Access Information Services, Inc - AZ Katie Anderson	520-405-8737				
•	•		•		Accurate Background Inc	800-784-3911				
•	•	•	•	•	AccuSearch Inc	800-462-7019	•	•	•	
•	•	•	•	•	Arizona Research & Retrieval Services Inc	888-500-7767	•	•	•	•
•	•	•	•	•	Capital City Assurance Group [SOP]	602-728-0100		•	•	•
	•	•	•	•	Capitol Corporate Services Inc (AZ)	800-255-4052	•		•	
•					Clarifacts Inc	800-318-0553				
•	•		•		Contemporary Information Corp	800-754-0009			•	
•	•	•	•	•	DL Investigations & Attorney Support [SOP]	602-285-9901	•	•	•	•
					Document Research Service	480-947-5493	•	•	•	•
•	•	•	•	•	E-Z Messenger Attorney Service Inc [SOP]	800-380-8081	•			•
•	•	•	•	•	Fleming Attorney Service [SOP]	800-776-3301	•	•	•	
•	•	•	•	•	Frontier Private Process Service (Phoenix) [SOP]	800-860-0858	•	•	•	•
•	•	•	•	•	Guardian Investigations & Document Svc Inc	602-257-0897	•	•	•	
•	•	•	•	•	Hawkins & EZmessenger Inc [SOP]	602-452-1800	•	•	•	•
					HK Partners Research	808-291-2071	•	•	•	•
•	•		•	•	Infotrack Information Services Inc	800-275-5594	•	•	•	
•	•	•	•	•	MacIntire & Associates (Tucson)	800-641-2737	•		•	
	•			•	Maricopa Research	623-935-0572	•	•	•	•
•	•	•	•	•	Paul Kevin McGriff	602-309-7138	•	•	•	•
•	•	•	•	•	National Document	800-829-5578	•	•	•	
					Nationwide Environmental Title Research	800-324-4956		•		
•	•	•	•	•	NU West Investigations [SOP]	623-937-9676	•	•	•	•
•					PDQ Legal Services Inc	480-556-6660				
•			•	•	Phelps Employer Services	800-347-9918		•		
•	•				Public Records Info Service	520-797-0486				
					Reliance Abstract Company - AZ	800-207-1523	•	•	•	
•					Risk Assessment Group	866-777-1114				
•					Screencorp Inc	602-739-7289				
•	•	•	•	•	Sebia LLC Investigations [SOP]	877-814-0307	•	•	•	
•	•	•	•		Slover Investigations	480-917-3708	•		•	
•	•	•			The Public Record Source	623-773-3997	•		•	•

Mohave

CR	CV	PR	US	BK	←Courts	Recorder→	UC	RE	TX	VS
•	•				Access Information Services, Inc - AZ Katie Anderson	520-405-8737				
•	•	•	•	•	AccuSearch Inc	800-462-7019	•	•	•	
•	•	•	•	•	Arizona Research & Retrieval Services Inc	888-500-7767	•	•	•	•
•	•	•	•	•	Bodo PI [SOP]	877-381-7009	•	•	•	•

CR	CV	PR	US	BK	←Courts		Recorder→	UC	RE	TX	VS
•	•	•	•	•	MacIntire & Associates (Tucson)		800-641-2737	•		•	
•	•				Mohave County Process Service [SOP]		800-692-5881			•	
					Nationwide Environmental Title Research		800-324-4956		•		
•					PDQ Legal Services Inc		480-556-6660				
					Reliance Abstract Company - AZ		800-207-1523	•	•	•	
•	•	•			The Public Record Source		623-773-3997	•		•	•

CR	CV	PR	US	BK	←Courts	Navajo	Recorder→	UC	RE	TX	VS
•	•				Access Information Services, Inc - AZ Katie Anderson		520-405-8737				
•	•	•	•	•	AccuSearch Inc		800-462-7019	•	•	•	
•	•	•	•	•	Arizona Research & Retrieval Services Inc		888-500-7767	•	•	•	•
•	•	•	•	•	MacIntire & Associates (Tucson)		800-641-2737	•		•	
•	•	•			Northern Arizona Investigations [SOP]		800-657-2747	•	•	•	
•					PDQ Legal Services Inc		480-556-6660				
•	•	•			The Public Record Source		623-773-3997	•		•	•

CR	CV	PR	US	BK	←Courts	Pima	Recorder→	UC	RE	TX	VS
•	•				Access Information Services, Inc - AZ Katie Anderson		520-405-8737				
•	•	•	•	•	AccuSearch Inc		800-462-7019	•	•	•	
•	•	•	•	•	ACMS Process Service [SOP]		520-629-0303	•	•	•	•
•	•	•	•	•	Arizona Research & Retrieval Services Inc		888-500-7767	•	•	•	•
•	•	•	•	•	E-Z Messenger Attorney Service Inc [SOP]		800-264-8436	•	•	•	
•	•	•	•	•	Linda Gonzales		520-603-6360	•	•	•	•
•	•		•	•	Infotrack Information Services Inc		800-275-5594	•	•	•	
•	•	•	•	•	Kroes Detective Agency [SOP]		800-249-0694	•	•	•	
•	•	•	•	•	MacIntire & Associates (Tucson)		800-641-2737	•		•	
•	•	•	•	•	Molloy & Company Inc dba Judicial Courier [SOP]		520-792-0250	•	•	•	•
					Nationwide Environmental Title Research		800-324-4956		•		
•					PDQ Legal Services Inc		480-556-6660				
•	•				Public Records Info Service		520-797-0486				
					Reliance Abstract Company - AZ		800-207-1523	•	•	•	
•	•	•	•	•	Research Unlimited LLC		520-624-7024	•	•	•	•
•	•	•			The Public Record Source		623-773-3997	•		•	•
•	•	•	•	•	Kathy Wolken		520-615-7665			•	

CR	CV	PR	US	BK	←Courts	Pinal	Recorder→	UC	RE	TX	VS
•	•				Access Information Services, Inc - AZ Katie Anderson		520-405-8737				
•	•	•	•	•	AccuSearch Inc		800-462-7019	•	•	•	
•	•	•	•	•	ACMS Process Service [SOP]		520-629-0303	•	•	•	•
•	•	•	•	•	Arizona Research & Retrieval Services Inc		888-500-7767	•	•	•	•
•	•		•		Contemporary Information Corp		800-754-0009			•	
•	•		•	•	Infotrack Information Services Inc		800-275-5594	•	•	•	
•	•	•	•	•	MacIntire & Associates (Tucson)		800-641-2737	•		•	
					Nationwide Environmental Title Research		800-324-4956		•		
•					PDQ Legal Services Inc		480-556-6660				
					Reliance Abstract Company - AZ		800-207-1523	•	•	•	
•	•	•	•	•	Sebia LLC Investigations [SOP]		877-814-0307	•	•	•	
•	•	•			The Public Record Source		623-773-3997	•		•	•

CR	CV	PR	US	BK	←Courts	Santa Cruz	Recorder→	UC	RE	TX	VS
•	•				Access Information Services, Inc - AZ Katie Anderson		520-405-8737				
•	•	•	•	•	ACMS Process Service [SOP]		520-629-0303	•	•	•	•
•	•	•	•	•	Arizona Research & Retrieval Services Inc		888-500-7767	•	•	•	•
•	•	•	•	•	E-Z Messenger Attorney Service Inc [SOP]		800-264-8436	•	•	•	
•	•	•	•	•	MacIntire & Associates (Tucson)		800-641-2737	•		•	
•					PDQ Legal Services Inc		480-556-6660				
•	•	•	•	•	Research Unlimited LLC		520-624-7024	•	•	•	•
•	•	•			The Public Record Source		623-773-3997	•		•	•

CR	CV	PR	US	BK	←COURTS YAVAPAI	RECORDER→	UC	RE	TX	VS
•	•				Access Information Services, Inc - AZ Katie Anderson	520-405-8737				
•	•	•	•	•	AccuSearch Inc	800-462-7019	•	•	•	
•	•	•	•	•	Arizona Research & Retrieval Services Inc	888-500-7767	•	•	•	•
•	•				Kim Estrada	928-273-2835	•		•	
•	•	•	•	•	MacIntire & Associates (Tucson)	800-641-2737	•		•	
					Nationwide Environmental Title Research	800-324-4956		•		
•	•	•	•	•	Palmer Investigative Services [SOP]	800-280-2951	•	•	•	
•					PDQ Legal Services Inc	480-556-6660				
					Reliance Abstract Company - AZ	800-207-1523	•	•	•	
•	•	•			The Public Record Source	623-773-3997	•		•	•

CR	CV	PR	US	BK	←COURTS YUMA	RECORDER→	UC	RE	TX	VS
•	•				Access Information Services, Inc - AZ Katie Anderson	520-405-8737				
•	•	•	•	•	Arizona Research & Retrieval Services Inc	888-500-7767	•	•	•	•
•	•	•	•	•	Certified Process & Information Services [SOP]	928-341-0756	•	•	•	•
			•	•	JRW Documents & Lien Services LLC	928-314-3993	•	•	•	
•	•	•	•	•	MacIntire & Associates (Tucson)	800-641-2737	•		•	
•					PDQ Legal Services Inc	480-556-6660				
•	•	•			The Public Record Source	623-773-3997	•		•	•

COURT RECORDS

CODE	GOVERNMENT AGENCY	TYPE OF INFORMATION
CR	Criminal Court	Municipal, county and state level criminal cases
CV	Civil Court	Municipal, county and state level civil cases
PR	Probate Court	Wills and estate cases
US	US District Court	Federal civil and criminal cases
BK	Bankruptcy Court	United States bankruptcy cases

COUNTY RECORDS - RECORDINGS

CODE	GOVERNMENT AGENCY	TYPE OF INFORMATION
UC	UCC Filing Office	Uniform Commercial Code and other personal property liens
RE	Real Estate Recording Office	Real property transactions and liens
TX	Tax Filing Office(s)	Federal and state tax liens, judgment liens
VS	Vital Records Office	Vital statistics—birth, death, marriage, divorce

Editor's Tip: This section of the directory is not organized to promote search firms that are statewide, regional, or national in coverage.

An expanded resource of search firms, distributors, and screening firms is BRB Publication's website at www.brbpub.com. Click the "Find A Vendor" tab. Both sources contain information on firms that use online resources to obtain public record index information.

Arkansas

Arkansas has 75 counties. 10 counties contain two separate recording offices. They are Arkansas, Carroll, Clay, Craighead, Franklin, Logan, Mississippi, Prairie, Sebastian, and Yell.

COURT RECORDS RETRIEVED — CAPITAL - PULASKI COUNTY — RECORDED RECORDS RETRIEVED

CR	CV	PR	US	BK	←Courts	ARKANSAS	Recorder→	UC	RE	TX	VS
•	•			•	Christy Corley		cell- 870-672-2957, 870-357-8714; fax-same		•	•	•
•	•	•	•	•	Quest Research (Arkansas)		501-374-4712	•	•	•	•
	•	•	•	•	Record Data Inc (Arkansas)		501-223-0949	•	•	•	
	•	•	•	•	River Enterprises		870-672-1732	•	•	•	•

CR	CV	PR	US	BK	←Courts	ASHLEY	Recorder→	UC	RE	TX	VS
•	•	•			AAA Research		870-310-3528	•	•	•	•
	•	•	•	•	Record Data Inc (Arkansas)		501-223-0949	•	•	•	

CR	CV	PR	US	BK	←Courts	BAXTER	Recorder→	UC	RE	TX	VS
•	•				Roy Adams		870-741-0489		•	•	
		•			Baxter County Abstract Co		870-425-8989		•		
	•	•	•	•	Record Data Inc (Arkansas)		501-223-0949	•	•	•	

CR	CV	PR	US	BK	←Courts	BENTON	Recorder→	UC	RE	TX	VS
•	•				Roy Adams		870-741-0489		•	•	
•	•		•	•	Advantage Research Corporation		501-262-5575	•	•	•	•
•	•	•	•	•	Courthouse Concepts Inc		877-750-3660	•	•	•	•
•	•	•	•	•	CourthouseData		479-582-0900	•	•	•	
•	•	•	•	•	North Winds Investigations Inc [SOP]		800-530-4514	•	•	•	•
	•	•	•	•	Record Data Inc (Arkansas)		501-223-0949	•	•	•	
•	•		•	•	Ridgerunner Record Search Inc		479-443-4928	•		•	
	•	•			Stewart Title of Arkansas		479-273-2111	•	•	•	

CR	CV	PR	US	BK	←Courts	BOONE	Recorder→	UC	RE	TX	VS
•	•				Roy Adams		870-741-0489		•	•	
•	•	•	•	•	CourthouseData		479-582-0900	•	•	•	
	•	•	•	•	Record Data Inc (Arkansas)		501-223-0949	•	•	•	

CR	CV	PR	US	BK	←Courts	BRADLEY	Recorder→	UC	RE	TX	VS
•	•	•			AAA Research		870-310-3528	•	•	•	•
•	•			•	Christy Corley		cell- 870-672-2957, 870-357-8714; fax-same		•	•	•
•	•	•			Martin Abstract Co (Warren)		870-226-7487	•	•	•	
	•	•	•	•	Record Data Inc (Arkansas)		501-223-0949	•	•	•	

CR	CV	PR	US	BK	←Courts	CALHOUN	Recorder→	UC	RE	TX	VS
•	•	•			AAA Research		870-310-3528	•	•	•	•
	•	•	•	•	Record Data Inc (Arkansas)		501-223-0949	•	•	•	

CR	CV	PR	US	BK	←Courts	CARROLL	Recorder→	UC	RE	TX	VS
•	•				Roy Adams		870-741-0489		•	•	
•	•	•	•	•	Courthouse Concepts Inc		877-750-3660	•	•	•	•
•	•	•	•	•	CourthouseData		479-582-0900	•	•	•	
	•	•	•	•	Record Data Inc (Arkansas)		501-223-0949	•	•	•	

CR	CV	PR	US	BK	←Courts	CHICOT	Recorder→	UC	RE	TX	VS
•	•	•			AAA Research		870-310-3528	•	•	•	•
	•	•	•	•	Record Data Inc (Arkansas)		501-223-0949	•	•	•	

CR	CV	PR	US	BK	←Courts	CLARK	Recorder→	UC	RE	TX	VS
•	•	•			AAA Research		870-310-3528	•	•	•	•
•	•		•	•	Advantage Research Corporation		501-262-5575	•	•	•	•
•	•	•			Clark County Abstract & Title Co Inc		870-246-2821	•	•	•	
•	•	•	•	•	CourthouseData		479-582-0900	•	•	•	
•	•	•	•	•	Quest Research (Arkansas)		501-374-4712	•	•	•	•
	•	•	•	•	Record Data Inc (Arkansas)		501-223-0949	•	•	•	

CR	CV	PR	US	BK	←Courts	CLAY	Recorder→	UC	RE	TX	VS
	•	•	•	•	Record Data Inc (Arkansas)		501-223-0949	•	•	•	

CR	CV	PR	US	BK	←Courts	CLEBURNE	Recorder→	UC	RE	TX	VS
•	•	•	•	•	CourthouseData		479-582-0900	•	•	•	
	•	•	•	•	Record Data Inc (Arkansas)		501-223-0949	•	•	•	

CR	CV	PR	US	BK	←Courts	CLEVELAND	Recorder→	UC	RE	TX	VS
•	•	•			AAA Research		870-310-3528	•	•	•	•
•	•			•	Christy Corley		cell- 870-672-2957, 870-357-8714; fax-same		•	•	•
•	•	•			Martin Abstract Co (Warren)		870-226-7487	•	•	•	
	•	•	•	•	Record Data Inc (Arkansas)		501-223-0949	•	•	•	

CR	CV	PR	US	BK	←Courts	COLUMBIA	Recorder→	UC	RE	TX	VS
•	•	•			AAA Research		870-310-3528	•	•	•	•
	•		•		Joe Gillenwater [SOP]		870-772-2923	•	•	•	
	•	•	•		Record Data Inc (Arkansas)		501-223-0949	•	•	•	
	•	•			Security Abstract Co (Arkansas)		870-234-1291	•	•	•	

CR	CV	PR	US	BK	←Courts	CONWAY	Recorder→	UC	RE	TX	VS
•	•	•	•	•	Courthouse Concepts Inc		877-750-3660	•	•	•	•
•	•	•	•	•	CourthouseData		479-582-0900	•	•	•	
	•	•			Morrilton Abstract Co		501-354-2611	•	•	•	
•	•	•	•	•	Quest Research (Arkansas)		501-374-4712	•	•	•	•
	•	•	•	•	Record Data Inc (Arkansas)		501-223-0949	•	•	•	

CR	CV	PR	US	BK	←Courts	CRAIGHEAD	Recorder→	UC	RE	TX	VS
	•	•	•	•	Record Data Inc (Arkansas)		501-223-0949	•	•	•	

CR	CV	PR	US	BK	←Courts	CRAWFORD	Recorder→	UC	RE	TX	VS
•	•	•	•		AL McLeroy Inv [SOP]		479-484-0444, Fax- same	•	•		•
•	•	•	•	•	Courthouse Concepts Inc		877-750-3660	•	•	•	•
•	•	•	•	•	CourthouseData		479-582-0900	•	•	•	
•	•	•			Crawford County Abstract Co Inc (Arkansas)		479-474-2711		•	•	
	•	•			Hebert Land Services		918-647-9524	•	•	•	•
					Mosley Abstract & Title Insurance Co		479-782-3054		•	•	
•	•	•	•	•	North Winds Investigations Inc [SOP]		800-530-4514	•	•	•	•
	•	•	•	•	Record Data Inc (Arkansas)		501-223-0949	•	•	•	

CR	CV	PR	US	BK	←Courts	CRITTENDEN	Recorder→	UC	RE	TX	VS
•					Blue Line Investigations		901-266-7100				
	•	•	•	•	Record Data Inc (Arkansas)		501-223-0949	•	•	•	
•	•	•			Marilyn Stewart		870-633-0149, cell 870-270-7286		•	•	
•	•	•	•	•	The Discovery Group Inc		662-280-1576	•		•	•

CR	CV	PR	US	BK	←Courts	CROSS	Recorder→	UC	RE	TX	VS
	•	•	•	•	Record Data Inc (Arkansas)		501-223-0949	•	•	•	
•	•	•			Marilyn Stewart		870-633-0149, cell 870-270-7286		•	•	

CR	CV	PR	US	BK	←Courts	DALLAS	Recorder→	UC	RE	TX	VS
•	•	•			AAA Research		870-310-3528	•	•	•	•
	•	•	•	•	Record Data Inc (Arkansas)		501-223-0949	•	•	•	

CR	CV	PR	US	BK	←COURTS	DESHA	RECORDER→	UC	RE	TX	VS
•	•	•			Desha Abstract & Title Co LLC		870-222-5001	•	•	•	
	•	•	•	•	Record Data Inc (Arkansas)		501-223-0949	•	•	•	

CR	CV	PR	US	BK	←COURTS	DREW	RECORDER→	UC	RE	TX	VS
•	•	•			AAA Research		870-310-3528	•	•	•	•
•	•			•	Christy Corley		cell- 870-672-2957, 870-357-8714; fax-same		•	•	•
•	•	•			Drew County Abstract & Title Co		870-367-6607	•	•	•	
	•	•	•	•	Record Data Inc (Arkansas)		501-223-0949	•	•	•	

CR	CV	PR	US	BK	←COURTS	FAULKNER	RECORDER→	UC	RE	TX	VS
•	•		•	•	Advantage Research Corporation		501-262-5575	•	•	•	•
•	•		•	•	Arkansas Corporate Research & Service Co		501-374-3843	•			
•	•	•	•	•	Courthouse Concepts Inc		877-750-3660	•	•	•	•
•	•	•	•	•	CourthouseData		479-582-0900	•	•	•	
•	•		•	•	Data-Search of Arkansas		501-868-4814	•			
•	•		•	•	Pro Facto Inc		501-988-5340	•	•	•	
•	•	•	•	•	Quest Research (Arkansas)		501-374-4712	•	•	•	•
	•	•	•	•	Record Data Inc (Arkansas)		501-223-0949	•	•	•	

CR	CV	PR	US	BK	←COURTS	FRANKLIN	RECORDER→	UC	RE	TX	VS
•	•	•	•	•	Courthouse Concepts Inc		877-750-3660	•	•	•	•
•	•	•	•	•	CourthouseData		479-582-0900	•	•	•	
	•	•			Hebert Land Services		918-647-9524	•	•	•	•
					Mosley Abstract & Title Insurance Co		479-782-3054		•	•	
	•	•	•		Record Data Inc (Arkansas)		501-223-0949	•	•	•	

CR	CV	PR	US	BK	←COURTS	FULTON	RECORDER→	UC	RE	TX	VS
	•	•	•	•	Record Data Inc (Arkansas)		501-223-0949	•	•	•	

CR	CV	PR	US	BK	←COURTS	GARLAND	RECORDER→	UC	RE	TX	VS
•	•		•	•	Advantage Research Corporation		501-262-5575	•	•	•	•
•	•	•	•	•	CourthouseData		479-582-0900	•	•	•	
•	•		•	•	Data-Search of Arkansas		501-868-4814	•			
•	•	•	•	•	Quest Research (Arkansas)		501-374-4712	•	•	•	•
	•	•	•	•	Record Data Inc (Arkansas)		501-223-0949	•	•	•	

CR	CV	PR	US	BK	←COURTS	GRANT	RECORDER→	UC	RE	TX	VS
•	•	•			AAA Research		870-310-3528	•	•	•	•
•	•			•	Christy Corley		cell- 870-672-2957, 870-357-8714; fax-same		•	•	•
•	•	•	•	•	CourthouseData		479-582-0900	•	•	•	
•	•	•	•	•	Quest Research (Arkansas)		501-374-4712	•	•	•	•
	•	•	•	•	Record Data Inc (Arkansas)		501-223-0949	•	•	•	
•	•	•			Spears & Jones Attorneys		501-315-5335	•	•	•	

CR	CV	PR	US	BK	←COURTS	GREENE	RECORDER→	UC	RE	TX	VS
	•	•	•	•	Record Data Inc (Arkansas)		501-223-0949	•	•	•	

CR	CV	PR	US	BK	←COURTS	HEMPSTEAD	RECORDER→	UC	RE	TX	VS
•	•	•			AAA Research		870-310-3528	•	•	•	•
	•		•	•	Joe Gillenwater [SOP]		870-772-2923	•	•	•	
•					Alex Greene		903-794-1371			•	
•	•	•			Hempstead County Abstract & Title		870-777-2351		•	•	
	•	•	•	•	Record Data Inc (Arkansas)		501-223-0949	•	•	•	

CR	CV	PR	US	BK	←COURTS	HOT SPRING	RECORDER→	UC	RE	TX	VS
•	•		•	•	Advantage Research Corporation		501-262-5575	•	•	•	•
					Central Arkansas Title		501-332-3770	•	•	•	•
•	•	•	•	•	CourthouseData		479-582-0900	•	•	•	
•	•		•	•	Pro Facto Inc		501-988-5340	•	•	•	
•	•	•	•	•	Quest Research (Arkansas)		501-374-4712	•	•	•	•

CR	CV	PR	US	BK	←Courts		Recorder→	UC	RE	TX	VS
	•	•	•	•	Record Data Inc (Arkansas)		501-223-0949	•	•	•	

CR	CV	PR	US	BK	←Courts	**Howard**	Recorder→	UC	RE	TX	VS
•	•	•			AAA Research		870-310-3528	•	•	•	•
	•		•	•	Joe Gillenwater [SOP]		870-772-2923	•	•	•	
	•	•	•	•	Record Data Inc (Arkansas)		501-223-0949	•	•	•	

CR	CV	PR	US	BK	←Courts	**Independence**	Recorder→	UC	RE	TX	VS
		•			Independence County Abstract Co		870-793-3333	•	•	•	
	•	•	•	•	Record Data Inc (Arkansas)		501-223-0949	•	•	•	

CR	CV	PR	US	BK	←Courts	**Izard**	Recorder→	UC	RE	TX	VS
		•			Izard County Abstract Co		870-368-4818	•	•	•	
	•	•	•	•	Record Data Inc (Arkansas)		501-223-0949	•	•	•	

CR	CV	PR	US	BK	←Courts	**Jackson**	Recorder→	UC	RE	TX	VS
•	•		•	•	Data-Search of Arkansas		501-868-4814	•			
	•	•			Jackson County Land Title Services, Inc		870-523-8976	•	•	•	
	•	•	•	•	Record Data Inc (Arkansas)		501-223-0949	•	•	•	

CR	CV	PR	US	BK	←Courts	**Jefferson**	Recorder→	UC	RE	TX	VS
•	•		•	•	Advantage Research Corporation		501-262-5575	•	•	•	•
•	•			•	Christy Corley		cell- 870-672-2957, 870-357-8714; fax-same		•	•	•
•	•	•	•	•	CourthouseData		479-582-0900	•	•	•	
•	•		•	•	Data-Search of Arkansas		501-868-4814	•			
•	•	•			Molly Ply Investigations		501-397-2620, Fax-same			•	
•	•	•	•	•	Quest Research (Arkansas)		501-374-4712	•	•	•	•
	•	•	•	•	Record Data Inc (Arkansas)		501-223-0949	•	•	•	
	•	•	•	•	River Enterprises		870-672-1732	•	•	•	•

CR	CV	PR	US	BK	←Courts	**Johnson**	Recorder→	UC	RE	TX	VS
•	•	•	•	•	Courthouse Concepts Inc		877-750-3660	•	•	•	•
•	•	•	•	•	CourthouseData		479-582-0900	•	•	•	
	•	•	•	•	Record Data Inc (Arkansas)		501-223-0949	•	•	•	

CR	CV	PR	US	BK	←Courts	**Lafayette**	Recorder→	UC	RE	TX	VS
•	•	•			AAA Research		870-310-3528	•	•	•	•
	•		•	•	Joe Gillenwater [SOP]		870-772-2923	•	•	•	
•	•	•			Lafayette County Abstract & Title Inc		870-921-4263	•	•	•	•
	•	•	•	•	Record Data Inc (Arkansas)		501-223-0949	•	•	•	

CR	CV	PR	US	BK	←Courts	**Lawrence**	Recorder→	UC	RE	TX	VS
•	•	•			Mullen Abstract Co		870-886-2452	•	•	•	
	•	•	•	•	Record Data Inc (Arkansas)		501-223-0949	•	•	•	

CR	CV	PR	US	BK	←Courts	**Lee**	Recorder→	UC	RE	TX	VS
•	•	•			Daggett Abstract Co		870-295-3434 x16	•	•	•	
•	•		•	•	Data-Search of Arkansas		501-868-4814	•			
	•	•	•	•	Record Data Inc (Arkansas)		501-223-0949	•	•	•	
•	•	•			Marilyn Stewart		870-633-0149, cell 870-270-7286		•	•	

CR	CV	PR	US	BK	←Courts	**Lincoln**	Recorder→	UC	RE	TX	VS
•	•	•			AAA Research		870-310-3528	•	•	•	•
•	•			•	Christy Corley		cell- 870-672-2957, 870-357-8714; fax-same		•	•	•
		•			Lincoln Abstract Co		870-628-3144	•	•	•	
	•	•	•	•	Record Data Inc (Arkansas)		501-223-0949	•	•	•	

CR	CV	PR	US	BK	←Courts	**Little River**	Recorder→	UC	RE	TX	VS
•	•	•			AAA Research		870-310-3528	•	•	•	•
	•		•	•	Joe Gillenwater [SOP]		870-772-2923	•	•	•	
•					Alex Greene		903-794-1371			•	
					McIver Abstract & Title Co		870-898-3502		•		

CR	CV	PR	US	BK	←Courts	Recorder→	UC	RE	TX	VS
	•	•	•	•	Record Data Inc (Arkansas)	501-223-0949	•	•	•	

CR	CV	PR	US	BK	←Courts LOGAN	Recorder→	UC	RE	TX	VS
•	•	•	•		AL McLeroy Inv [SOP]	479-484-0444, Fax- same	•	•		•
•	•	•	•	•	CourthouseData	479-582-0900	•	•	•	
	•	•			Hebert Land Services	918-647-9524	•	•	•	•
	•	•	•	•	Record Data Inc (Arkansas)	501-223-0949	•	•	•	

CR	CV	PR	US	BK	←Courts LONOKE	Recorder→	UC	RE	TX	VS
•	•		•	•	Arkansas Corporate Research & Service Co.	501-374-3843	•			
•	•	•	•	•	CourthouseData	479-582-0900	•	•	•	
•	•		•	•	Data-Search of Arkansas	501-868-4814	•			
	•	•			First State Abstract	501-676-2486	•	•	•	
•	•		•	•	Pro Facto Inc	501-988-5340	•	•	•	
•	•	•	•	•	Quest Research (Arkansas)	501-374-4712	•	•	•	•
	•	•	•	•	Record Data Inc (Arkansas)	501-223-0949	•	•	•	
	•	•	•	•	River Enterprises	870-672-1732	•	•	•	•

CR	CV	PR	US	BK	←Courts MADISON	Recorder→	UC	RE	TX	VS
•	•				Roy Adams	870-741-0489		•	•	
•	•	•	•	•	Courthouse Concepts Inc	877-750-3660	•	•	•	•
•	•	•	•	•	CourthouseData	479-582-0900	•	•	•	
	•	•	•	•	Record Data Inc (Arkansas)	501-223-0949	•	•	•	
		•			Town & Country Abstract Co (Arkansas)	479-738-2055	•	•	•	

CR	CV	PR	US	BK	←Courts MARION	Recorder→	UC	RE	TX	VS
•	•	•			Marion County Abstract Co (Arkansas)	870-449-4218	•	•	•	
	•	•	•	•	Record Data Inc (Arkansas)	501-223-0949	•	•	•	

CR	CV	PR	US	BK	←Courts MILLER	Recorder→	UC	RE	TX	VS
•	•		•	•	Advantage Research Corporation	501-262-5575	•	•	•	•
	•		•	•	Joe Gillenwater [SOP]	870-772-2923	•	•	•	
•					Alex Greene	903-794-1371			•	
	•	•	•	•	Record Data Inc (Arkansas)	501-223-0949	•	•	•	

CR	CV	PR	US	BK	←Courts MISSISSIPPI	Recorder→	UC	RE	TX	VS
	•	•			Prewitt-Rogers Abstract Co	870-563-2137	•	•	•	
	•	•	•	•	Record Data Inc (Arkansas)	501-223-0949	•	•	•	

CR	CV	PR	US	BK	←Courts MONROE	Recorder→	UC	RE	TX	VS
•	•	•			Menard Title & Abstract Co Inc	870-747-3712		•	•	•
•	•	•	•	•	Quest Research (Arkansas)	501-374-4712	•	•	•	•
	•	•	•	•	Record Data Inc (Arkansas)	501-223-0949	•	•	•	
	•	•	•	•	River Enterprises	870-672-1732	•	•	•	•

CR	CV	PR	US	BK	←Courts MONTGOMERY	Recorder→	UC	RE	TX	VS
•	•	•	•	•	CourthouseData	479-582-0900	•	•	•	
•	•	•	•	•	Quest Research (Arkansas)	501-374-4712	•	•	•	•
	•	•	•	•	Record Data Inc (Arkansas)	501-223-0949	•	•	•	

CR	CV	PR	US	BK	←Courts NEVADA	Recorder→	UC	RE	TX	VS
•	•	•			AAA Research	870-310-3528	•	•	•	•
	•		•	•	Joe Gillenwater [SOP]	870-772-2923	•	•	•	
	•	•	•	•	Record Data Inc (Arkansas)	501-223-0949	•	•	•	

CR	CV	PR	US	BK	←Courts NEWTON	Recorder→	UC	RE	TX	VS
•	•				Roy Adams	870-741-0489		•	•	
•	•	•	•	•	CourthouseData	479-582-0900	•	•	•	
	•	•	•	•	Record Data Inc (Arkansas)	501-223-0949	•	•	•	

CR	CV	PR	US	BK	←Courts OUACHITA	Recorder→	UC	RE	TX	VS
•	•	•			AAA Research	870-310-3528	•	•	•	•

CR	CV	PR	US	BK	←Courts	Recorder→	UC	RE	TX	VS
•	•		•	•	Data-Search of Arkansas	501-868-4814	•			
	•	•	•	•	Record Data Inc (Arkansas)	501-223-0949	•	•	•	

CR	CV	PR	US	BK	←Courts PERRY	Recorder→	UC	RE	TX	VS
•	•	•	•	•	CourthouseData	479-582-0900	•	•	•	
•	•	•	•	•	Quest Research (Arkansas)	501-374-4712	•	•	•	•
	•	•	•	•	Record Data Inc (Arkansas)	501-223-0949	•	•	•	

CR	CV	PR	US	BK	←Courts PHILLIPS	Recorder→	UC	RE	TX	VS
	•	•			East Arkansas Title Co	870-338-8306	•	•	•	
	•	•	•	•	Record Data Inc (Arkansas)	501-223-0949	•	•	•	

CR	CV	PR	US	BK	←Courts PIKE	Recorder→	UC	RE	TX	VS
•	•	•			AAA Research	870-310-3528	•	•	•	•
	•	•	•	•	Record Data Inc (Arkansas)	501-223-0949	•	•	•	

CR	CV	PR	US	BK	←Courts POINSETT	Recorder→	UC	RE	TX	VS
•	•	•			Poinsett County Abstract Co	870-578-5914	•	•	•	
	•	•	•	•	Record Data Inc (Arkansas)	501-223-0949	•	•	•	

CR	CV	PR	US	BK	←Courts POLK	Recorder→	UC	RE	TX	VS
•	•	•	•	•	CourthouseData	479-582-0900	•	•	•	
•	•	•			Martin Title & Closing Services	479-394-1963	•	•	•	
	•	•	•	•	Record Data Inc (Arkansas)	501-223-0949	•	•	•	

CR	CV	PR	US	BK	←Courts POPE	Recorder→	UC	RE	TX	VS
•	•	•	•	•	Courthouse Concepts Inc	877-750-3660	•	•	•	•
•	•	•	•	•	CourthouseData	479-582-0900	•	•	•	
	•	•			Hebert Land Services	918-647-9524	•	•	•	•
	•	•	•	•	Record Data Inc (Arkansas)	501-223-0949	•	•	•	

CR	CV	PR	US	BK	←Courts PRAIRIE	Recorder→	UC	RE	TX	VS
•	•	•	•	•	Quest Research (Arkansas)	501-374-4712	•	•	•	•
	•	•	•	•	Record Data Inc (Arkansas)	501-223-0949	•	•	•	
	•	•	•	•	River Enterprises	870-672-1732	•	•	•	•

CR	CV	PR	US	BK	←Courts PULASKI	Recorder→	UC	RE	TX	VS
•	•		•	•	Advantage Research Corporation	501-262-5575	•	•	•	•
•	•		•	•	Arkansas Corporate Research & Service Co	501-374-3843	•			
•	•	•	•	•	Attorney's Services Inc [SOP]	888-376-6267	•	•	•	•
•					Blue Line Investigations	901-266-7100				
•	•	•	•	•	Courthouse Concepts Inc	877-750-3660	•	•	•	•
•	•	•	•	•	CourthouseData	479-582-0900	•	•	•	
•	•		•	•	Data-Search of Arkansas	501-868-4814	•			
•	•	•			Molly Ply Investigations	501-397-2620, Fax-same	•		•	
•	•	•	•	•	North Winds Investigations Inc [SOP]	800-530-4514	•	•	•	•
•	•		•	•	Pro Facto Inc	501-988-5340	•	•	•	
•	•	•	•	•	Quest Research (Arkansas)	501-374-4712	•	•	•	•
	•	•	•	•	Record Data Inc (Arkansas)	501-223-0949	•	•	•	

CR	CV	PR	US	BK	←Courts RANDOLPH	Recorder→	UC	RE	TX	VS
	•	•	•	•	Record Data Inc (Arkansas)	501-223-0949	•	•	•	
•	•	•			Service Abstract Company of Randolph County [SOP]	870-892-4538	•	•	•	

CR	CV	PR	US	BK	←Courts SALINE	Recorder→	UC	RE	TX	VS
•	•		•	•	Advantage Research Corporation	501-262-5575	•	•	•	•
•	•		•	•	Arkansas Corporate Research & Service Co	501-374-3843	•			
•	•	•	•	•	CourthouseData	479-582-0900	•	•	•	
•	•		•	•	Data-Search of Arkansas	501-868-4814	•			
•	•		•	•	Pro Facto Inc	501-988-5340	•	•	•	
•	•	•	•	•	Quest Research (Arkansas)	501-374-4712	•	•	•	•
	•	•	•	•	Record Data Inc (Arkansas)	501-223-0949	•	•	•	

CR	CV	PR	US	BK	←Courts		Recorder→	UC	RE	TX	VS
•	•	•			Spears & Jones Attorneys		501-315-5335	•	•	•	

CR	CV	PR	US	BK	←Courts	Scott	Recorder→	UC	RE	TX	VS
•	•	•	•		AL McLeroy Inv [SOP]		479-484-0444, Fax- same	•	•		•
•	•	•	•	•	CourthouseData		479-582-0900	•	•	•	
	•	•			Hebert Land Services		918-647-9524	•	•	•	•
	•	•	•	•	Record Data Inc (Arkansas)		501-223-0949	•	•	•	

CR	CV	PR	US	BK	←Courts	Searcy	Recorder→	UC	RE	TX	VS
	•	•	•	•	Record Data Inc (Arkansas)		501-223-0949	•	•	•	

CR	CV	PR	US	BK	←Courts	Sebastian	Recorder→	UC	RE	TX	VS
•	•		•	•	Advantage Research Corporation		501-262-5575	•	•	•	•
•	•	•	•		AL McLeroy Inv [SOP]		479-484-0444, Fax- same	•	•		•
•	•	•	•	•	Courthouse Concepts Inc		877-750-3660	•	•	•	•
•	•	•	•	•	CourthouseData		479-582-0900	•	•	•	
	•	•			Hebert Land Services		918-647-9524	•	•	•	•
					Mosley Abstract & Title Insurance Co		479-782-3054		•	•	
•	•	•	•	•	North Winds Investigations Inc [SOP]		800-530-4514	•	•	•	•
	•	•	•	•	Record Data Inc (Arkansas)		501-223-0949	•	•	•	

CR	CV	PR	US	BK	←Courts	Sevier	Recorder→	UC	RE	TX	VS
•	•	•			AAA Research		870-310-3528	•	•	•	•
	•	•	•	•	Record Data Inc (Arkansas)		501-223-0949	•	•	•	

CR	CV	PR	US	BK	←Courts	Sharp	Recorder→	UC	RE	TX	VS
	•	•	•	•	Record Data Inc (Arkansas)		501-223-0949	•	•	•	
•	•	•			Sharp County Abstract Co Inc		870-994-7314	•	•	•	

CR	CV	PR	US	BK	←Courts	St Francis	Recorder→	UC	RE	TX	VS
	•	•	•	•	Record Data Inc (Arkansas)		501-223-0949	•	•	•	
•	•	•			Marilyn Stewart		870-633-0149, cell 870-270-7286		•	•	

CR	CV	PR	US	BK	←Courts	Stone	Recorder→	UC	RE	TX	VS
	•	•			Mountain View Abstract Co		870-269-8410	•	•	•	
	•	•	•	•	Record Data Inc (Arkansas)		501-223-0949	•	•	•	

CR	CV	PR	US	BK	←Courts	Union	Recorder→	UC	RE	TX	VS
•	•	•			AAA Research		870-310-3528	•	•	•	•
	•	•	•	•	Record Data Inc (Arkansas)		501-223-0949	•	•	•	
	•	•			Union Abstract Co		870-863-6053	•	•	•	

CR	CV	PR	US	BK	←Courts	Van Buren	Recorder→	UC	RE	TX	VS
•	•	•	•	•	CourthouseData		479-582-0900	•	•	•	
	•	•	•	•	Record Data Inc (Arkansas)		501-223-0949	•	•	•	

CR	CV	PR	US	BK	←Courts	Washington	Recorder→	UC	RE	TX	VS
•	•				Roy Adams		870-741-0489		•	•	
•	•		•	•	Advantage Research Corporation		501-262-5575	•	•	•	•
•	•	•	•	•	Courthouse Concepts Inc		877-750-3660	•	•	•	•
•	•	•	•	•	CourthouseData		479-582-0900	•	•	•	
•	•	•	•	•	North Winds Investigations Inc [SOP]		800-530-4514	•	•	•	•
	•	•	•	•	Record Data Inc (Arkansas)		501-223-0949	•	•	•	
•	•		•	•	Ridgerunner Record Search Inc		479-443-4928	•		•	
	•	•			Stewart Title of Arkansas		479-273-2111	•	•	•	

CR	CV	PR	US	BK	←Courts	White	Recorder→	UC	RE	TX	VS
•	•	•			Citizen's Title Co		501-268-5571	•	•	•	
•	•	•	•	•	CourthouseData		479-582-0900	•	•	•	
•	•		•	•	Data-Search of Arkansas		501-868-4814	•			
	•	•	•	•	Record Data Inc (Arkansas)		501-223-0949	•	•	•	
	•	•			Strother-Wilbourn Land Title Co		501-268-8273	•	•	•	

CR	CV	PR	US	BK	←COURTS WOODRUFF	RECORDER→	UC	RE	TX	VS
	•	•	•	•	Record Data Inc (Arkansas)	501-223-0949	•	•	•	

CR	CV	PR	US	BK	←COURTS YELL	RECORDER→	UC	RE	TX	VS
•	•	•	•	•	CourthouseData	479-582-0900	•	•	•	
	•	•			Hebert Land Services	918-647-9524	•	•	•	•
	•	•	•	•	Record Data Inc (Arkansas)	501-223-0949	•	•	•	

[SOP] = PERFORMS SERVICE OF PROCESS

 = PRRN Member. *A retriever you can trust!*

COURT RECORDS

CODE	GOVERNMENT AGENCY	TYPE OF INFORMATION
CR	Criminal Court	Municipal, county and state level criminal cases
CV	Civil Court	Municipal, county and state level civil cases
PR	Probate Court	Wills and estate cases
US	US District Court	Federal civil and criminal cases
BK	Bankruptcy Court	United States bankruptcy cases

COUNTY RECORDS - RECORDINGS

CODE	GOVERNMENT AGENCY	TYPE OF INFORMATION
UC	UCC Filing Office	Uniform Commercial Code and other personal property liens
RE	Real Estate Recording Office	Real property transactions and liens
TX	Tax Filing Office(s)	Federal and state tax liens, judgment liens
VS	Vital Records Office	Vital statistics—birth, death, marriage, divorce

Editor's Note: The County Index section in this book will **only** indicate a county where a record retriever does an in-person search by himself or herself, or by a payroll employee.

Many retrievers also maintain a network of correspondents and provide services in additional counties not listed within the County Index. This additional coverage is indicated in the Profiles section under Correspondent Relationships.

California

CR	CV	PR	US	BK	←COURTS — CAPITAL - SACRAMENTO COUNTY — ALAMEDA	RECORDER→	UC	RE	TX	VS
					COURT RECORDS RETRIEVED / **RECORDED RECORDS RETRIEVED**					
•	•	•	•	•	A & A Legal Service Inc [SOP]	650-697-9431	•	•	•	•
•	•		•		A-1 Unisource Screening & Information	800-525-6972				
•	•	•	•	•	Access Research	619-231-8947	•		•	•
•	•	•			AD Services (ADS) [SOP]	800-827-9101		•	•	•
•	•		•		Advantage Background Services Inc	800-355-2650				
•	•		•		Atlas Research Services Inc	818-920-6376				
•	•	•	•	•	Attorney's Aid Inc of Sacramento [SOP]	916-648-1559	•	•		•
•	•	•	•	•	Attorney's Diversified Services-Oakland [SOP]	800-800-6788	•	•	•	•
•	•		•	•	Baxter Research Inc	415-333-5402				
•	•	•	•	•	Bay Area Records [SOP]	888-934-3848	•	•	•	
					BirthCertificate.com	888-934-3848				•
•	•	•	•	•	C & S Research	530-415-3161	•	•	•	•
•	•	•	•	•	Cal Search	858-488-7572	•		•	•
•	•		•		Contemporary Information Corp	800-754-0009			•	
•	•	•	•	•	Court Record Consultants [SOP]	818-366-1906	•	•	•	
•	•		•	•	Laura Cross	510-336-0865			•	•
•	•	•			Equity Title Search [SOP]	323-965-0759		•		•
•	•	•	•	•	Espy Investigative Services	877-843-3779	•	•	•	•
•	•				Huffman Research	510-537-4261				
•	•				Inquest	408-395-1300				
•	•	•	•	•	Lone Star Legal	415-255-8550	•	•	•	•
•	•	•		•	Maggie M & Associates	707-778-7304	•	•	•	•
					Models with Brains	925-838-3899	•	•	•	
•	•	•	•	•	One Legal, Inc [SOP]	800-938-8815				
•	•	•	•	•	Pacific Corporate & Title Services (Sacramento)	800-230-4988	•	•	•	•
•	•	•	•	•	Pacific Research & Retrieval Inc [SOP]	800-222-7040	•	•	•	•
•	•	•	•	•	PFC Information Services Inc	510-653-5061	•	•	•	•
•	•	•	•	•	Powell Court Service	888-976-9355	•	•	•	•
•	•				Private Eyes Inc	877-292-3330	•	•	•	
•	•	•	•	•	Probus Research [SOP]	888-934-3848	•	•	•	•
	•	•	•	•	Quest Discovery Service [SOP]	408-441-7000	•	•	•	•
•	•	•	•	•	Rapid Document Service	209-745-0999	•	•	•	•
•	•				Rapid Research	510-777-9461				
•	•	•	•	•	RJI Services Inc [SOP]	800-344-4754	•	•	•	•
					Leslie or Mike Sosa	916-984-7654	•	•	•	
•	•				Sumpter & Associates LLC	925-671-7755	•	•	•	•
•	•	•	•	•	Swift Attorney Service [SOP]	800-987-9438	•	•	•	•
•	•	•	•	•	The Amherst Group	800-521-0237	•	•	•	•
	•	•	•	•	Title Court Service	510-763-0975	•	•	•	•
•	•	•	•	•	Universal Information Research [SOP]	800-363-9813	•	•		•
•	•	•	•	•	Wakeman Process Service Inc [SOP]	510-886-7667				
•	•	•	•	•	Western Attorney Services	415-487-4140				
	•	•	•	•	Wheels of Justice Inc [SOP]	800-649-1198	•	•	•	•
•	•	•	•	•	WP Mortensen & Associates	925-828-6440	•	•	•	•
•	•	•	•	•	Zook Search Inc California	415-387-1029	•	•	•	•

CR	CV	PR	US	BK	←Courts	ALPINE	Recorder→	UC	RE	TX	VS
•	•	•	•	•	Attorney's Diversified Services-Sacramento [SOP]		800-266-4624	•	•	•	•
•	•	•	•	•	DCW & Associates [SOP]		800-899-0442	•	•	•	•
	•	•	•	•	Quest Discovery Service [SOP]		408-441-7000	•	•	•	•
	•	•	•	•	Title Court Service		510-763-0975	•	•	•	•

CR	CV	PR	US	BK	←Courts	AMADOR	Recorder→	UC	RE	TX	VS
•	•	•	•	•	Ahern Research		209-754-9709	•	•	•	•
•	•	•	•	•	Attorney's Diversified Services-Stockton [SOP]		800-343-2108	•	•	•	•
•	•		•	•	DLS Background Services Inc		951-301-8584	•		•	
•	•				Quality Business Information		916-684-0444				
	•	•	•	•	Quest Discovery Service [SOP]		408-441-7000	•	•	•	•
•	•	•	•	•	Rapid Document Service		209-745-0999	•	•	•	•
	•	•	•	•	Title Court Service		510-763-0975	•	•	•	•

CR	CV	PR	US	BK	←Courts	BUTTE	Recorder→	UC	RE	TX	VS
•	•	•			A.D.I. Litigation Support Services [SOP]		530-743-4245		•	•	•
•	•	•	•	•	Access Research		619-231-8947	•		•	•
•	•	•	•	•	Attorney's Diversified Services-Redding [SOP]		800-473-1228	•	•	•	•
•	•		•	•	Business Connections [SOP]		530-527-6229	•		•	•
•	•	•	•	•	C & S Research		530-415-3161	•	•	•	•
•	•	•	•	•	Cal Search		858-488-7572	•		•	•
•	•	•			Nina N Cooper		707-758-6165	•		•	•
•	•				Nor-Cal Court Research		530-865-3525				
	•	•	•	•	Quest Discovery Service [SOP]		408-441-7000	•	•	•	•
•	•				The Legal Source Attorney Services		800-786-8163				
	•	•	•	•	Title Court Service		510-763-0975	•	•	•	•

CR	CV	PR	US	BK	←Courts	CALAVERAS	Recorder→	UC	RE	TX	VS
•	•	•	•	•	Ahern Research		209-754-9709	•	•	•	•
•	•		•		Atlas Research Services Inc		818-920-6376				
•	•	•	•	•	Attorney's Diversified Services-Stockton [SOP]		800-343-2108	•	•	•	•
•	•				Quality Business Information		916-684-0444				
	•	•	•	•	Quest Discovery Service [SOP]		408-441-7000	•	•	•	•
•	•	•	•	•	Rapid Document Service		209-745-0999	•	•	•	•
	•	•	•	•	Title Court Service		510-763-0975	•	•	•	•

CR	CV	PR	US	BK	←Courts	COLUSA	Recorder→	UC	RE	TX	VS
•	•	•			A.D.I. Litigation Support Services [SOP]		530-743-4245		•	•	•
•	•	•	•	•	Attorney's Diversified Services-Sacramento [SOP]		800-266-4624	•	•	•	•
•	•	•	•	•	C & S Research		530-415-3161	•	•	•	•
	•	•	•	•	Quest Discovery Service [SOP]		408-441-7000	•	•	•	•
•	•				The Legal Source Attorney Services		800-786-8163				
	•	•	•	•	Title Court Service		510-763-0975	•	•	•	•

CR	CV	PR	US	BK	←Courts	CONTRA COSTA	Recorder→	UC	RE	TX	VS
•	•	•	•	•	A & A Legal Service Inc [SOP]		650-697-9431	•	•	•	•
•	•	•	•	•	Access Research		619-231-8947	•		•	•
•	•	•			AD Services (ADS) [SOP]		800-827-9101		•	•	•
•	•		•		Atlas Research Services Inc		818-920-6376				
•	•	•	•	•	Attorney's Aid Inc of Sacramento [SOP]		916-648-1559	•	•		•
•	•	•	•	•	Attorney's Diversified Services-Oakland [SOP]		800-800-6788	•	•	•	•
•	•		•	•	Baxter Research Inc		415-333-5402				
•	•	•	•	•	Bay Area Records [SOP]		888-934-3848	•	•	•	
					BirthCertificate.com		888-934-3848				•
•	•	•	•	•	C & S Research		530-415-3161	•	•	•	•
•	•	•	•	•	Cal Search		858-488-7572	•		•	•
•	•		•		Contemporary Information Corp		800-754-0009			•	
•	•	•	•	•	Court Record Consultants [SOP]		818-366-1906	•	•	•	
•	•		•	•	Laura Cross		510-336-0865			•	•

CR	CV	PR	US	BK	←Courts	Recorder→	UC	RE	TX	VS
•	•	•	•	•	Espy Investigative Services	877-843-3779	•	•	•	•
•	•	•			GMV Research	707-228-8708			•	•
•	•				Inquest	408-395-1300				
•	•	•			Jean Randall Process Service [SOP]	866-386-5777	•	•	•	
•	•	•		•	Maggie M & Associates	707-778-7304	•	•	•	•
					Models with Brains	925-838-3899	•	•	•	
•	•	•	•	•	One Legal, Inc [SOP]	800-938-8815				
•	•	•	•	•	Pacific Corporate & Title Services (Sacramento)	800-230-4988	•	•	•	•
•	•	•	•	•	Pacific Research & Retrieval Inc [SOP]	800-222-7040	•	•	•	•
•	•				Private Eyes Inc	877-292-3330	•	•	•	
•	•	•	•	•	Probus Research [SOP]	888-934-3848	•	•	•	•
•	•				Pryamid Research	530-867-1568			•	
	•	•	•	•	Quest Discovery Service [SOP]	408-441-7000	•	•	•	•
•	•	•	•	•	Rapid Document Service	209-745-0999	•	•	•	•
•	•	•	•	•	RJI Services Inc [SOP]	800-344-4754	•	•	•	•
•	•				Sumpter & Associates LLC	925-671-7755	•	•	•	•
•	•	•	•	•	Swift Attorney Service [SOP]	800-987-9438	•	•	•	•
•	•	•	•	•	The Amherst Group	800-521-0237	•	•	•	•
	•	•	•	•	Title Court Service	510-763-0975	•	•	•	•
•	•	•	•	•	Wakeman Process Service Inc [SOP]	510-886-7667				
•	•	•	•	•	West Coast MCI [SOP]	925-372-8909	•	•	•	•
•	•	•	•	•	Western Attorney Services	415-487-4140				
	•	•	•	•	Wheels of Justice Inc [SOP]	800-649-1198	•	•	•	•
•	•	•	•	•	WP Mortensen & Associates	925-828-6440	•	•	•	•
CR	**CV**	**PR**	**US**	**BK**	**←Courts — DEL NORTE**	**Recorder→**	**UC**	**RE**	**TX**	**VS**
•	•	•	•	•	Attorney's Diversified Services-Redding [SOP]	800-473-1228	•	•	•	•
	•	•	•	•	Quest Discovery Service [SOP]	408-441-7000	•	•	•	•
•	•				Red's Rapid Research	707-764-8836	•	•	•	•
•	•	•			Research & Investigative Associates [SOP]	707-444-8767	•	•	•	•
	•	•	•	•	Title Court Service	510-763-0975	•	•	•	•
CR	**CV**	**PR**	**US**	**BK**	**←Courts — EL DORADO**	**Recorder→**	**UC**	**RE**	**TX**	**VS**
•	•		•		A-1 Unisource Screening & Information	800-525-6972				
•	•	•	•	•	Attorney's Aid Inc of Sacramento [SOP]	916-648-1559	•	•		•
•	•	•	•	•	Attorney's Diversified Services-Sacramento [SOP]	800-266-4624	•	•	•	•
•	•	•	•	•	C & S Research	530-415-3161	•	•	•	•
•	•	•	•	•	DCW & Associates [SOP]	800-899-0442	•	•	•	•
•	•	•	•	•	Legalese [SOP]	916-453-2860	•	•	•	•
•	•	•		•	Maggie M & Associates	707-778-7304	•	•	•	•
					Mobile Abstracting Services	916-965-6544	•	•	•	
•	•	•	•	•	Pacific Corporate & Title Services (Sacramento)	800-230-4988	•	•	•	•
•	•				Quality Business Information	916-684-0444				
	•	•	•	•	Quest Discovery Service [SOP]	408-441-7000	•	•	•	•
•	•	•	•	•	Rapid Document Service	209-745-0999	•	•	•	•
					Reliable Document Retrieval Inc	916-438-3000	•	•	•	
•	•	•	•	•	Seyfried Support Services	916-359-5275	•	•	•	•
					Leslie or Mike Sosa	916-984-7654	•	•	•	
	•	•	•	•	Title Court Service	510-763-0975	•	•	•	•
CR	**CV**	**PR**	**US**	**BK**	**←Courts — FRESNO**	**Recorder→**	**UC**	**RE**	**TX**	**VS**
•	•	•	•	•	Access Research	619-231-8947	•		•	•
•	•	•	•	•	Accessible Document Retrieval	559-779-5491	•	•	•	•
•	•	•	•	•	Action Legal Support Services [SOP]	559-432-3337				
•	•	•	•	•	Affordable Pearlegal Inc	800-958-2144	•	•	•	•
•	•				Alpha Information Inc	800-900-1471				
•	•		•		Atlas Research Services Inc	818-920-6376				
•	•	•	•	•	Attorney's Aid Inc of Sacramento [SOP]	916-648-1559	•	•		•
•	•	•	•	•	Attorney's Diversified Services-Fresno [SOP]	800-842-2695	•	•	•	•

CR	CV	PR	US	BK	←Courts	Recorder→	UC	RE	TX	VS
•	•		•	•	Business Connections [SOP]	530-527-6229	•		•	•
•	•	•	•	•	Cal Search	858-488-7572	•		•	•
•					California Backgrounds	559-274-9784				
•	•	•	•	•	Court Record Consultants [SOP]	818-366-1906	•	•	•	
•	•	•	•	•	DCW & Associates [SOP]	800-899-0442	•	•	•	•
•					InVision Research	559-271-3170				
•	•		•	•	Keppler Legal Research	559-431-2591				
•	•	•		•	Maggie M & Associates	707-778-7304	•	•	•	•
•	•	•	•	•	One Legal, Inc [SOP]	800-938-8815				
•	•	•	•	•	Dora Orum	559-251-5193	•	•	•	•
•	•	•	•	•	Pacific Corporate & Title Services (Sacramento)	800-230-4988	•	•	•	•
	•	•	•	•	Quest Discovery Service [SOP]	408-441-7000	•	•	•	•
•	•	•	•	•	Rapid Document Service	209-745-0999	•	•	•	•
	•	•	•	•	Title Court Service	510-763-0975	•	•	•	•
•	•			•	Total Access	559-325-1169	•		•	•
•	•	•	•	•	Vio-Com-Data Research	559-438-1058		•		

CR	CV	PR	US	BK	←Courts — GLENN	Recorder→	UC	RE	TX	VS
•	•		•		A-1 Unisource Screening & Information	800-525-6972				
•	•	•	•	•	Attorney's Diversified Services-Redding [SOP]	800-473-1228	•	•	•	•
•	•		•	•	Business Connections [SOP]	530-527-6229	•		•	•
•	•				Nor-Cal Court Research	530-865-3525				
	•	•	•	•	Quest Discovery Service [SOP]	408-441-7000	•	•	•	•
•	•				The Legal Source Attorney Services	800-786-8163				
	•	•	•	•	Title Court Service	510-763-0975	•	•	•	•

CR	CV	PR	US	BK	←Courts — HUMBOLDT	Recorder→	UC	RE	TX	VS
•	•		•		Atlas Research Services Inc	818-920-6376				
•	•	•	•	•	Attorney's Diversified Services-Santa Rosa [SOP]	800-473-5455	•	•	•	•
•	•				Nor-Cal Court Research	530-865-3525				
	•	•	•	•	Quest Discovery Service [SOP]	408-441-7000	•	•	•	•
•	•				Red's Rapid Research	707-764-8836	•	•	•	•
•	•	•			Research & Investigative Associates [SOP]	707-444-8767	•	•	•	•
•	•	•			SafeHire	707-442-5043	•		•	•
	•	•	•	•	Title Court Service	510-763-0975	•	•	•	•

CR	CV	PR	US	BK	←Courts — IMPERIAL	Recorder→	UC	RE	TX	VS
•	•	•	•	•	Access Research	619-231-8947	•		•	•
•	•	•	•	•	Attorney's Diversified Services-San Diego [SOP]	800-566-9501	•	•	•	•
•	•	•	•	•	Bollinger Attorney Service [SOP]	760-329-2504	•	•	•	•
•	•		•		Contemporary Information Corp	800-754-0009			•	
•	•	•	•	•	One Legal, Inc [SOP]	800-938-8815				
	•	•	•	•	Quest Discovery Service [SOP]	408-441-7000	•	•	•	•
•	•	•	•	•	The Amherst Group	800-521-0237	•	•	•	•
	•	•	•	•	Title Court Service	510-763-0975	•	•	•	•

CR	CV	PR	US	BK	←Courts — INYO	Recorder→	UC	RE	TX	VS
•	•	•			Sharron Andrews	760-878-2038	•	•	•	•
•	•	•	•	•	Attorney's Diversified Services-Fresno [SOP]	800-842-2695	•	•	•	•
	•	•	•	•	Quest Discovery Service [SOP]	408-441-7000	•	•	•	•
	•	•	•	•	Title Court Service	510-763-0975	•	•	•	•
•	•			•	W.E. Works Office/Attorney Support [SOP]	760-873-3788		•	•	•

CR	CV	PR	US	BK	←Courts — KERN	Recorder→	UC	RE	TX	VS
•	•		•		A-1 Unisource Screening & Information	800-525-6972				
•	•	•	•	•	Access Research	619-231-8947	•		•	•
•	•	•			Accurate Research & Closing Services [SOP]	661-302-5110 or 5105	•	•	•	
•	•	•	•	•	Action Legal Support Services [SOP]	559-432-3337				
•	•	•	•	•	APSCREEN Inc	800-277-2733	•	•	•	•
•	•		•		Atlas Research Services Inc	818-920-6376				

CR	CV	PR	US	BK	←Courts	Recorder→	UC	RE	TX	VS
•	•	•	•	•	Attorney's Diversified Services-Bakersfield [SOP]	800-842-6334	•		•	
•					California Backgrounds	559-274-9784				
•	•				Coastal Research	805-710-4926		•	•	
•	•		•		Contemporary Information Corp	800-754-0009			•	
•	•	•	•	•	Court Record Consultants [SOP]	818-366-1906	•	•	•	
•	•	•	•	•	DCW & Associates [SOP]	800-899-0442	•	•	•	•
•	•	•			For The Record Title & Court Services	661-703-9610	•	•	•	•
•					InVision Research	559-271-3170				
•	•	•	•	•	One Legal, Inc [SOP]	800-938-8815				
	•	•			Pebble Beach Enterprises	661-301-7979		•	•	•
	•	•	•	•	Quest Discovery Service [SOP]	408-441-7000	•	•	•	•
	•	•		•	The Daily Report	800-803-6127	•	•	•	•
	•	•	•	•	Title Court Service	510-763-0975	•	•	•	•
•	•			•	Total Access	559-325-1169	•		•	•
•	•	•	•	•	Vio-Com-Data Research	559-438-1058		•		

CR	CV	PR	US	BK	←Courts — **Kings**	Recorder→	UC	RE	TX	VS
•	•	•	•	•	Affordable Pearlegal Inc	800-958-2144	•	•	•	•
•	•	•	•	•	Attorney's Diversified Services-Fresno [SOP]	800-842-2695	•	•	•	•
•					California Backgrounds	559-274-9784				
•					InVision Research	559-271-3170				
•	•		•	•	Keppler Legal Research	559-431-2591				
•	•	•	•	•	One Legal, Inc [SOP]	800-938-8815				
•	•	•			Marilyn Peterson [SOP]	559-732-2135	•	•	•	•
	•	•	•	•	Quest Discovery Service [SOP]	408-441-7000	•	•	•	•
					Leslie or Mike Sosa	916-984-7654	•	•	•	
	•	•	•	•	Title Court Service	510-763-0975	•	•	•	•
•	•			•	Total Access	559-325-1169	•		•	•
•	•	•	•	•	Vio-Com-Data Research	559-438-1058		•		

CR	CV	PR	US	BK	←Courts — **Lake**	Recorder→	UC	RE	TX	VS
•	•	•	•	•	Access Research	619-231-8947	•		•	•
•	•	•	•	•	Attorney's Diversified Services-Santa Rosa [SOP]	800-473-5455	•	•	•	•
•	•	•	•	•	DCW & Associates [SOP]	800-899-0442	•	•	•	•
•	•	•			Mendo-Lake Paralegals	707-263-8755	•	•	•	•
	•	•	•	•	Quest Discovery Service [SOP]	408-441-7000	•	•	•	•
	•	•	•	•	Title Court Service	510-763-0975	•	•	•	•

CR	CV	PR	US	BK	←Courts — **Lassen**	Recorder→	UC	RE	TX	VS
•	•	•	•	•	Attorney's Diversified Services-Redding [SOP]	800-473-1228	•	•	•	•
•	•				Lassen Attorney/Investigative Services [SOP]	530-251-2399				
	•	•	•	•	Quest Discovery Service [SOP]	408-441-7000	•	•	•	•
•	•				The Legal Source Attorney Services	800-786-8163				
	•	•	•	•	Title Court Service	510-763-0975	•	•	•	•

CR	CV	PR	US	BK	←Courts — **Los Angeles**	Recorder→	UC	RE	TX	VS
•	•	•	•	•	A & M Attorney Services Inc [SOP]	562-426-8306				
•	•	•	•	•	A California Process & Attorney Service [SOP]	909-381-5185	•	•	•	•
•	•		•		A-1 Unisource Screening & Information	800-525-6972				
•	•	•	•	•	Access Research	619-231-8947	•		•	•
•	•		•		Accurate Background Inc	800-784-3911				
•	•		•	•	Accurate Source.com Inc [SOP]	800-978-8950	•		•	
•	•				Alpha Information Inc	800-900-1471				
•	•	•	•	•	Alpha Record Search & Retrieval	323-851-5701	•	•	•	•
•	•	•	•	•	Alternative Investigative & Attorney Services [SOP]	818-402-0800	•	•	•	•
•	•	•	•	•	APSCREEN Inc	800-277-2733	•	•	•	•
•	•	•	•	•	Assist Investigations	310-451-2204	•	•	•	•
•	•		•		Atlas Research Services Inc	818-920-6376				
•	•	•	•	•	Attorney's Diversified Services-Ventura [SOP]	800-933-8014	•	•	•	•
				•	Banko Document Retrieval	800-969-2377				

					Retriever	Phone				
•	•	•	•	•	Benchmark Investigations [SOP]	800-248-7721	•	•	•	•
•	•	•	•	•	Bergman Records Access [SOP]	323-939-1632	•	•	•	•
•	•	•	•	•	Cal Info Inc	213-687-8710	•	•	•	•
•	•	•	•	•	Cal Search	858-488-7572	•		•	•
•					California Criminal Research [SOP]	909-590-9177				
•	•	•	•	•	Collective Intelligence Inc [SOP]	800-436-1969				•
•	•		•		Contemporary Information Corp	800-754-0009			•	
•	•		•	•	Corporate Research Solutions Inc	800-486-0757	•	•	•	•
•	•	•	•	•	Court Record Consultants [SOP]	818-366-1906	•	•	•	
•	•				Crutchfield & Associates [SOP]	818-349-4836	•	•	•	
•	•	•	•	•	Daily Journal Corporation	800-952-5232	•	•		•
•	•	•	•	•	DCW & Associates [SOP]	800-899-0442	•	•	•	•
•	•		•	•	DLS Background Services Inc	951-301-8584	•		•	
					Document Depot Express	562-860-2907, cell- 562-706-2031		•	•	•
•	•	•	•	•	Docu-Search California	800-466-9450	•	•	•	•
					Dr Dave's Docs	818-246-3087		•		
	•	•	•	•	EAGLE i Communications	702-658-3912	•	•	•	
•	•	•	•	•	English Research & Retrieval Inc [SOP]	951-328-9995	•	•	•	•
•	•	•			Equity Title Search [SOP]	323-965-0759		•		•
•	•	•	•	•	Executive Attorney Service Inc [SOP]	213-482-6680				
•	•	•	•	•	First Investigative Consultants, PI# 6949 [SOP]	800-900-4342	•	•	•	•
•	•	•	•	•	Kern Attorney Service Inc [SOP]	800-675-5376		•	•	•
	•	•	•	•	Patrick King [SOP]	626-452-0838	•	•	•	•
•	•	•	•	•	Legal Research Associates Inc [SOP]	714-734-9337	•	•	•	•
•	•	•	•	•	LegalNet Inc [SOP]	888-530-3100	•	•	•	•
•	•				Liberty Alliance [SOP]	800-630-2880				
					Los Angeles County Document Services Inc	818-241-1990		•	•	
•	•	•	•	•	Loss Prevention Associates Inc	714-593-2323				
•	•		•	•	Metropolis Group	818-861-7099				
•	•	•	•	•	Net Check Investigations	888-638-2432	•	•		
•	•	•	•	•	Theresa Olaires	714-595-4729	•	•	•	•
•	•	•	•	•	One Legal, Inc [SOP]	800-938-8815				
•	•	•	•	•	Pacific Corporate & Title Services (Sacramento)	800-230-4988	•	•	•	•
•	•	•	•	•	Pacificsearch & Information	619-702-3334	•	•	•	•
•	•	•	•	•	Parasec (California)	800-533-7272	•	•	•	•
•	•	•	•	•	Powell Court Service	888-976-9355	•	•	•	•
•	•	•	•	•	Process Service Network [SOP]	800-417-7623		•	•	•
	•	•	•	•	Quest Discovery Service [SOP]	408-441-7000	•	•	•	•
•	•	•	•	•	Record Access	888-621-1491	•		•	
•	•	•	•	•	Research & Retrieval Inc	800-707-8771	•	•	•	•
•	•	•	•	•	Research For You	626-974-4484	•	•	•	•
•	•	•	•	•	RJI Services Inc [SOP]	800-344-4754	•	•	•	•
•	•	•	•	•	Southern California Strategic Research	323-257-4472	•	•	•	•
•	•	•	•	•	Specialized Investigations [SOP]	800-714-3728			•	
•	•	•	•	•	The Amherst Group	800-521-0237	•	•	•	•
	•	•	•	•	Title Court Service	510-763-0975	•	•	•	•
•	•	•	•	•	Triwest Investigative Services [SOP]	323-254-5151			•	•
					Tseng Document Retrieval	562-863-3415	•	•	•	
•	•	•	•	•	Universal Information Research [SOP]	800-363-9813	•	•		•
•	•				US Background Screening Inc	866-777-1322				
•			•	•	Welliver & Associates LLC [SOP]	800-569-5677				
•	•	•	•	•	Westlaw Court Express	800-766-3320	•	•	•	•
•	•		•	•	WestLaw CourtEXPRESS (DC) [SOP]	800-542-3320				
•	•	•	•	•	XL Professional Services Inc [SOP]		•	•	•	•
•	•	•	•	•	Zook Search Inc	562-484-1638	•	•	•	•

CR	CV	PR	US	BK	←Courts	Madera	Recorder→	UC	RE	TX	VS
•	•	•	•	•	Accessible Document Retrieval		559-779-5491	•	•	•	•
•	•	•	•	•	Action Legal Support Services [SOP]		559-432-3337				
•	•	•	•	•	Affordable Pearlegal Inc		800-958-2144	•	•	•	•
•	•	•	•	•	Attorney Service of Merced [SOP]		209-383-3233	•	•	•	•
•	•	•	•		Attorney's Diversified Services-Fresno [SOP]		800-842-2695	•	•	•	•
•					California Backgrounds		559-274-9784				
•					InVision Research		559-271-3170				
•	•		•	•	Keppler Legal Research		559-431-2591				
•	•	•	•	•	One Legal, Inc [SOP]		800-938-8815				
	•	•	•	•	Quest Discovery Service [SOP]		408-441-7000	•	•	•	•
•	•	•	•	•	Rapid Document Service		209-745-0999	•	•	•	•
	•	•	•	•	Title Court Service		510-763-0975	•	•	•	•
•	•			•	Total Access		559-325-1169	•		•	•
•	•	•	•	•	Vio-Com-Data Research		559-438-1058		•		

CR	CV	PR	US	BK	←Courts	Marin	Recorder→	UC	RE	TX	VS
•	•	•	•	•	A & A Legal Service Inc [SOP]		650-697-9431	•	•	•	•
•	•	•	•	•	Access Research		619-231-8947	•		•	•
•	•				Alpha Information Inc		800-900-1471				
•	•	•	•	•	Attorney's Diversified Services-Santa Rosa [SOP]		800-473-5455	•	•	•	•
•	•		•	•	Baxter Research Inc		415-333-5402				
•	•	•	•	•	Bay Area Records [SOP]		888-934-3848	•	•	•	
					BirthCertificate.com		888-934-3848				•
•	•	•	•	•	Cal Search		858-488-7572	•		•	•
•	•	•	•	•	Court Record Consultants [SOP]		818-366-1906	•	•	•	
•	•		•	•	Laura Cross		510-336-0865			•	•
•	•		•	•	DLS Background Services Inc		951-301-8584	•		•	
•	•	•			Jean Randall Process Service [SOP]		866-386-5777	•	•	•	
•	•	•		•	Maggie M & Associates		707-778-7304	•	•	•	•
•	•	•	•	•	One Legal, Inc [SOP]		800-938-8815				
•	•	•	•	•	Pacific Corporate & Title Services (Sacramento)		800-230-4988	•	•	•	•
•	•	•	•	•	Pacific Research & Retrieval Inc [SOP]		800-222-7040	•	•	•	•
•	•	•	•	•	Probus Research [SOP]		888-934-3848	•	•	•	•
	•	•	•	•	Quest Discovery Service [SOP]		408-441-7000	•	•	•	•
•	•	•		•	Rapid Document Service		209-745-0999	•	•	•	•
					Leslie or Mike Sosa		916-984-7654	•	•	•	
•	•	•	•	•	The Amherst Group		800-521-0237	•	•	•	•
	•	•	•	•	Title Court Service		510-763-0975	•	•	•	•
•	•	•	•	•	Universal Information Research [SOP]		800-363-9813	•	•		•
•	•	•	•	•	Western Attorney Services		415-487-4140				
	•	•	•	•	Wheels of Justice Inc [SOP]		800-649-1198	•	•	•	•
•	•	•	•	•	Zook Search Inc California		415-387-1029	•	•	•	•

CR	CV	PR	US	BK	←Courts	Mariposa	Recorder→	UC	RE	TX	VS
•	•	•	•	•	Attorney Service of Merced [SOP]		209-383-3233	•	•	•	•
•	•	•	•	•	Attorney's Diversified Services-Fresno [SOP]		800-842-2695	•	•	•	•
	•	•	•	•	Quest Discovery Service [SOP]		408-441-7000	•	•	•	•
	•	•	•	•	Title Court Service		510-763-0975	•	•	•	•

CR	CV	PR	US	BK	←Courts	Mendocino	Recorder→	UC	RE	TX	VS
•	•	•	•	•	Attorney's Diversified Services-Santa Rosa [SOP]		800-473-5455	•	•	•	•
•	•	•			Frazier & Associates		707-462-8559	•		•	•
•	•				Kamber Agency [SOP]		707-961-5464				
	•	•	•	•	Quest Discovery Service [SOP]		408-441-7000	•	•	•	•
	•	•	•	•	Title Court Service		510-763-0975	•	•	•	•

CR	CV	PR	US	BK	←COURTS — MERCED	RECORDER→	UC	RE	TX	VS
•	•	•	•	•	Action Legal Support Services [SOP]	559-432-3337				
•	•	•	•	•	Attorney Service of Merced [SOP]	209-383-3233	•	•	•	•
•	•	•	•	•	Attorney's Diversified Services-Fresno [SOP]	800-842-2695	•	•	•	•
•	•		•	•	Business Connections [SOP]	530-527-6229	•		•	•
•	•	•	•	•	Cal Search	858-488-7572	•		•	•
•	•			•	Central Valley Records Service Inc	209-524-3849	•		•	•
•	•	•		•	Maggie M & Associates	707-778-7304	•	•	•	•
•	•	•	•	•	One Legal, Inc [SOP]	800-938-8815				
	•	•	•	•	Quest Discovery Service [SOP]	408-441-7000	•	•	•	•
•	•	•	•	•	Rapid Document Service	209-745-0999	•	•	•	•
					Leslie or Mike Sosa	916-984-7654	•	•	•	
	•	•	•	•	Title Court Service	510-763-0975	•	•	•	•

CR	CV	PR	US	BK	←COURTS — MODOC	RECORDER→	UC	RE	TX	VS
•	•	•	•	•	Attorney's Diversified Services-Redding [SOP]	800-473-1228	•	•	•	•
•	•		•	•	Business Connections [SOP]	530-527-6229	•		•	•
•	•				Lassen Attorney/Investigative Services [SOP]	530-251-2399				
	•	•	•	•	Quest Discovery Service [SOP]	408-441-7000	•	•	•	•
	•	•	•	•	Title Court Service	510-763-0975	•	•	•	•

CR	CV	PR	US	BK	←COURTS — MONO	RECORDER→	UC	RE	TX	VS
•	•	•	•	•	Attorney's Diversified Services-Fresno [SOP]	800-842-2695	•	•	•	•
	•	•	•	•	Quest Discovery Service [SOP]	408-441-7000	•	•	•	•
	•	•	•	•	Title Court Service	510-763-0975	•	•	•	•
•	•			•	W.E. Works Office/Attorney Support [SOP]	760-873-3788		•	•	•

CR	CV	PR	US	BK	←COURTS — MONTEREY	RECORDER→	UC	RE	TX	VS
•	•	•	•	•	Access Research	619-231-8947	•		•	•
•	•		•		Atlas Research Services Inc	818-920-6376				
•	•	•			Attorney Service of California-Monterey [SOP]	888-306-2194	•	•	•	•
•	•	•			Attorney Service of California-Santa Cruz [SOP]	888-306-2194	•	•	•	•
•	•	•	•	•	Attorney's Diversified Services-Fresno [SOP]	800-842-2695	•	•	•	•
•	•		•	•	Baxter Research Inc	415-333-5402				
•	•				Bit O' Blarney	831-663-6945				
•	•	•	•	•	Cal Search	858-488-7572	•		•	•
•	•		•		Contemporary Information Corp	800-754-0009			•	
•	•	•	•	•	Court Record Consultants [SOP]	818-366-1906	•	•	•	
•	•	•			Lincoln Investigations Inc DBA Bay Point Legal Service [SOP]	800-383-0897	•	•	•	•
•	•	•	•	•	One Legal, Inc [SOP]	800-938-8815				
•	•	•	•	•	Pacific Corporate & Title Services (Sacramento)	800-230-4988	•	•	•	•
	•	•	•	•	Quest Discovery Service [SOP]	408-441-7000	•	•	•	•
					Leslie or Mike Sosa	916-984-7654	•	•	•	
•	•	•			Stan Duby Investigations [SOP]	800-953-0435	•		•	•
	•	•	•	•	Title Court Service	510-763-0975	•	•	•	•
•	•	•			Tri County Investigations	831-758-3124	•	•	•	•
•	•	•	•	•	Western Attorney Services	415-487-4140				

CR	CV	PR	US	BK	←COURTS — NAPA	RECORDER→	UC	RE	TX	VS
•	•	•			A David Research	707-479-2779	•	•	•	•
•	•				Annette Sanders Research	707-449-3620				
•	•		•		Atlas Research Services Inc	818-920-6376				
•	•	•	•	•	Attorney's Diversified Services-Santa Rosa [SOP]	800-473-5455	•	•	•	•
•	•	•			Nina N Cooper	707-758-6165	•		•	•
•	•	•			GMV Research	707-228-8708			•	•
•	•	•		•	Maggie M & Associates	707-778-7304	•	•	•	•
•	•	•			Napa-Sonoma Connection	707-952-6426	•	•	•	•
•	•	•	•	•	One Legal, Inc [SOP]	800-938-8815				
•	•	•	•	•	Pacific Corporate & Title Services (Sacramento)	800-230-4988	•	•	•	•

CR	CV	PR	US	BK	←Courts		Recorder→	UC	RE	TX	VS
	•	•	•	•	Quest Discovery Service [SOP]		408-441-7000	•	•	•	•
•	•	•	•	•	Rapid Document Service		209-745-0999	•	•	•	•
•	•	•	•	•	The Amherst Group		800-521-0237	•	•	•	•
	•	•	•	•	Title Court Service		510-763-0975	•	•	•	•

CR	CV	PR	US	BK	←Courts	Nevada	Recorder→	UC	RE	TX	VS
•	•	•	•	•	Attorney's Diversified Services-Sacramento [SOP]		800-266-4624	•	•	•	•
•	•	•	•	•	C & S Research		530-415-3161	•	•	•	•
•	•	•			Nina N Cooper		707-758-6165	•		•	•
•	•	•	•	•	DCW & Associates [SOP]		800-899-0442	•	•	•	•
•	•				Norcal Public Records Service		408-221-6654	•	•	•	
•	•				Quality Business Information		916-684-0444				
	•	•	•	•	Quest Discovery Service [SOP]		408-441-7000	•	•	•	•
•	•				The Legal Source Attorney Services		800-786-8163				
	•	•	•	•	Title Court Service		510-763-0975	•	•	•	•

CR	CV	PR	US	BK	←Courts	Orange	Recorder→	UC	RE	TX	VS
•	•				A & C Research		951-301-6956				
•	•	•	•	•	A & M Attorney Services Inc [SOP]		562-426-8306				
•	•	•	•	•	A California Process & Attorney Service [SOP]		909-381-5185	•	•	•	•
•	•		•		A-1 Unisource Screening & Information		800-525-6972				
•	•	•	•	•	Access Research		619-231-8947	•		•	•
•	•		•		Accurate Background Inc		800-784-3911				
•	•		•	•	Accurate Source.com Inc [SOP]		800-978-8950	•		•	
•	•				Alpha Information Inc		800-900-1471				
•	•	•	•	•	Alternative Investigative & Attorney Services [SOP]		818-402-0800	•	•	•	•
•	•	•	•	•	APSCREEN Inc		800-277-2733	•	•	•	•
•	•	•	•	•	Assist Investigations		310-451-2204	•	•	•	•
•	•		•		Atlas Research Services Inc		818-920-6376				
•	•	•	•	•	Attorney's Diversified Services-San Diego [SOP]		800-566-9501	•	•	•	•
•	•	•	•	•	Benchmark Investigations [SOP]		800-248-7721	•	•	•	•
•	•	•	•	•	Bergman Records Access [SOP]		323-939-1632	•	•	•	•
•	•	•			Bosic & Bosic [SOP]		951-788-1988; Fax- same		•	•	•
•	•	•	•	•	Cal Info Inc		213-687-8710	•	•	•	•
•	•	•	•	•	Cal Search		858-488-7572	•		•	•
•					California Criminal Research [SOP]		909-590-9177				
•	•	•	•	•	Collective Intelligence Inc [SOP]		800-436-1969				•
•	•		•		Contemporary Information Corp		800-754-0009			•	
•	•		•	•	Corporate Research Solutions Inc		800-486-0757	•	•	•	•
•	•	•	•	•	Court Record Consultants [SOP]		818-366-1906	•	•	•	
•	•				Crutchfield & Associates [SOP]		818-349-4836	•	•	•	
	•		•	•	Crystal Clear Copy Service [SOP]		760-947-5699				
•	•	•	•	•	Daily Journal Corporation		800-952-5232	•	•		•
•	•	•	•	•	DCW & Associates [SOP]		800-899-0442	•	•	•	•
					Document Depot Express		562-860-2907, cell- 562-706-2031		•	•	•
•	•	•	•	•	Docu-Search California		800-466-9450	•	•	•	•
					Dr Dave's Docs		818-246-3087		•		
	•	•	•	•	EAGLE i Communications		702-658-3912	•	•	•	
•	•	•	•	•	English Research & Retrieval Inc [SOP]		951-328-9995	•	•	•	•
•	•	•			Equity Title Search [SOP]		323-965-0759		•		•
•	•	•	•	•	Executive Attorney Service Inc [SOP]		213-482-6680				
•	•	•	•	•	First Investigative Consultants, PI# 6949 [SOP]		800-900-4342	•	•	•	•
•	•		•		Insight Public Record Research Corp		800-615-8111				
•	•	•	•	•	Kern Attorney Service Inc [SOP]		800-675-5376		•	•	•
•	•				Deborah Labhart		714-993-0185				
•	•	•	•	•	Legal Research Associates Inc [SOP]		714-734-9337	•	•	•	•
•	•	•	•	•	LegalNet Inc [SOP]		888-530-3100	•	•	•	•
•	•				Liberty Alliance [SOP]		800-630-2880				
					Los Angeles County Document Services Inc		818-241-1990		•	•	

CR	CV	PR	US	BK	←Courts	Recorder→	UC	RE	TX	VS
•	•	•	•	•	Loss Prevention Associates Inc	714-593-2323				
•	•	•	•	•	Theresa Olaires	714-595-4729	•	•	•	•
•	•	•	•	•	One Legal, Inc [SOP]	800-938-8815				
•	•	•	•	•	Pacific Corporate & Title Services (Sacramento)	800-230-4988	•	•	•	•
•	•	•	•	•	Pacificsearch & Information	619-702-3334	•	•	•	•
•	•	•	•	•	Parasec (California)	800-533-7272	•	•	•	•
•	•	•	•	•	Powell Court Service	888-976-9355	•	•	•	•
•	•	•	•	•	Process Service Network [SOP]	800-417-7623		•	•	•
	•	•	•	•	Quest Discovery Service [SOP]	408-441-7000	•	•	•	•
•	•	•	•	•	RAM Services [SOP]	714-792-2860	•	•	•	•
•	•	•	•	•	Record Access	888-621-1491	•		•	
•	•	•	•	•	Research & Retrieval Inc	800-707-8771	•	•	•	
•	•	•	•	•	Research For You	626-974-4484	•	•	•	•
•	•	•	•	•	RJI Services Inc [SOP]	800-344-4754	•	•	•	•
•	•	•	•	•	Rogers Investigations & Research	800-935-6654	•	•	•	•
•	•	•	•	•	Southern California Strategic Research	323-257-4472	•	•	•	•
•	•	•	•	•	The Amherst Group	800-521-0237	•	•	•	•
	•	•	•	•	Title Court Service	510-763-0975	•	•	•	•
					Tseng Document Retrieval	562-863-3415	•	•	•	
•	•	•	•	•	Universal Information Research [SOP]	800-363-9813	•	•		•
•			•	•	Welliver & Associates LLC [SOP]	800-569-5677				
•	•	•	•	•	Westlaw Court Express	800-766-3320	•	•	•	•
•	•	•	•	•	Zook Search Inc	562-484-1638	•	•	•	•

CR	CV	PR	US	BK	←Courts PLACER	Recorder→	UC	RE	TX	VS
•	•	•	•	•	A Data Source	916-726-4636	•	•		•
•	•		•		Atlas Research Services Inc	818-920-6376				
•	•	•	•	•	Attorney's Aid Inc of Sacramento [SOP]	916-648-1559	•	•		•
•	•	•	•	•	Attorney's Diversified Services-Sacramento [SOP]	800-266-4624	•	•	•	•
•	•	•	•	•	C & S Research	530-415-3161	•	•	•	•
•	•	•	•	•	DCW & Associates [SOP]	800-899-0442	•	•	•	•
•	•		•	•	DLS Background Services Inc	951-301-8584	•		•	
•					InVision Research	559-271-3170				
•	•	•	•	•	Legalese [SOP]	916-453-2860	•	•	•	•
					Mobile Abstracting Services	916-965-6544	•	•	•	
					Models with Brains	925-838-3899	•	•	•	
•	•				Norcal Public Records Service	408-221-6654	•	•	•	
•	•	•	•	•	One Legal, Inc [SOP]	800-938-8815				
•	•	•	•	•	Pacific Corporate & Title Services (Sacramento)	800-230-4988	•	•	•	•
•	•				Quality Business Information	916-684-0444				
	•	•	•	•	Quest Discovery Service [SOP]	408-441-7000	•	•	•	•
•	•	•	•	•	Rapid Document Service	209-745-0999	•	•	•	•
					Reliable Document Retrieval Inc	916-438-3000	•	•	•	
•	•	•	•	•	Seyfried Support Services	916-359-5275	•	•	•	•
					Leslie or Mike Sosa	916-984-7654	•	•	•	
	•	•	•	•	Title Court Service	510-763-0975	•	•	•	•
•	•	•	•	•	United Attorneys' Services	916-457-3000	•	•	•	•

CR	CV	PR	US	BK	←Courts PLUMAS	Recorder→	UC	RE	TX	VS
•	•	•	•	•	Attorney's Diversified Services-Redding [SOP]	800-473-1228	•	•	•	•
•	•				Lassen Attorney/Investigative Services [SOP]	530-251-2399				
	•	•	•	•	Quest Discovery Service [SOP]	408-441-7000	•	•	•	•
•	•				The Legal Source Attorney Services	800-786-8163				
	•	•	•	•	Title Court Service	510-763-0975	•	•	•	•

CR	CV	PR	US	BK	←COURTS RIVERSIDE	RECORDER→	UC	RE	TX	VS
•	•				A & C Research	951-301-6956				
•	•	•	•	•	A California Process & Attorney Service [SOP]	909-381-5185	•	•	•	•
•	•		•		A-1 Unisource Screening & Information	800-525-6972				
•	•	•	•	•	Access Research	619-231-8947	•		•	•
•	•		•		Accurate Background Inc	800-784-3911				
•	•		•	•	Accurate Source.com Inc [SOP]	800-978-8950	•		•	
•	•				Alpha Information Inc	800-900-1471				
•	•	•	•	•	Alternative Investigative & Attorney Services [SOP]	818-402-0800	•	•	•	•
•	•	•	•	•	American Legal Services [SOP]	760-323-5445		•	•	
•	•	•	•	•	APSCREEN Inc	800-277-2733	•	•	•	•
•	•		•		Atlas Research Services Inc	818-920-6376				
•	•	•	•	•	Attorney's Diversified Services-San Diego [SOP]	800-566-9501	•	•	•	•
•	•	•	•	•	Bollinger Attorney Service [SOP]	760-329-2504	•	•	•	•
•	•	•			Bosic & Bosic [SOP]	951-788-1988; Fax- same		•	•	•
•	•	•	•	•	Cal Search	858-488-7572	•		•	•
•	•	•			Cheri's Court Service	951-684-6499, cell- 951-233-1037				
•	•				Coastal Research	805-710-4926		•	•	
•	•	•	•	•	Collective Intelligence Inc [SOP]	800-436-1969				•
•	•		•		Contemporary Information Corp	800-754-0009			•	
•	•	•	•	•	Court Record Consultants [SOP]	818-366-1906	•	•	•	
	•		•	•	Crystal Clear Copy Service [SOP]	760-947-5699				
•	•	•	•	•	Daily Journal Corporation	800-952-5232	•	•		•
•	•	•	•	•	DCW & Associates [SOP]	800-899-0442	•	•	•	•
•	•		•	•	DLS Background Services Inc	951-301-8584	•		•	
					Document Depot Express	562-860-2907, cell- 562-706-2031		•	•	•
•	•	•	•	•	Docu-Search California	800-466-9450	•	•	•	•
					Dr Dave's Docs	818-246-3087		•		
•	•	•	•	•	English Research & Retrieval Inc [SOP]	951-328-9995	•	•	•	•
•	•	•			Equity Title Search [SOP]	323-965-0759		•		•
•	•	•	•	•	Executive Attorney Service Inc [SOP]	213-482-6680				
•	•	•	•	•	First Investigative Consultants, PI# 6949 [SOP]	800-900-4342	•	•	•	•
•	•		•		Insight Public Record Research Corp	800-615-8111				
•	•	•	•	•	Kay's Rapid Record Research	909-790-2073	•	•	•	•
•	•	•	•	•	Kern Attorney Service Inc [SOP]	800-675-5376		•	•	•
•	•	•	•	•	Legal Research Associates Inc [SOP]	714-734-9337	•	•	•	•
•	•				Liberty Alliance [SOP]	800-630-2880				
					Los Angeles County Document Services Inc	818-241-1990		•	•	
•	•	•	•	•	Loss Prevention Associates Inc	714-593-2323				
•	•	•	•	•	Joe Y Nerio	909-824-9358				•
•	•	•	•	•	One Legal, Inc [SOP]	800-938-8815				
•	•	•	•	•	Pacific Corporate & Title Services (Sacramento)	800-230-4988	•	•	•	•
•	•	•	•	•	Powell Court Service	888-976-9355	•	•	•	•
•	•	•	•	•	Precision Research & Information	951-244-8118	•		•	•
•	•	•	•	•	Process Service Network [SOP]	800-417-7623		•	•	•
	•	•	•	•	Quest Discovery Service [SOP]	408-441-7000	•	•	•	•
•	•	•			RASCAL [SOP]	951-693-0165		•	•	
•	•	•	•	•	Research & Retrieval Inc	800-707-8771	•	•	•	
•	•	•	•	•	RJI Services Inc [SOP]	800-344-4754	•	•	•	•
•	•	•	•	•	Southern California Strategic Research	323-257-4472	•	•	•	•
•	•	•	•	•	The Amherst Group	800-521-0237	•	•	•	•
	•	•	•	•	Title Court Service	510-763-0975	•	•	•	•
					Tseng Document Retrieval	562-863-3415	•	•	•	
•	•	•	•	•	Universal Information Research [SOP]	800-363-9813	•	•		•
•			•	•	Welliver & Associates LLC [SOP]	800-569-5677				
•	•	•	•	•	XL Professional Services Inc [SOP]		•	•	•	•

CR	CV	PR	US	BK	←COURTS **SACRAMENTO**	RECORDER→	UC	RE	TX	VS
•	•	•	•	•	A Data Source	916-726-4636	•	•		•
•	•		•		A-1 Unisource Screening & Information	800-525-6972				
•	•	•	•	•	Access Research	619-231-8947	•		•	•
•	•	•	•	•	Attorney's Aid Inc of Sacramento [SOP]	916-648-1559	•	•		•
•	•	•	•	•	Attorney's Diversified Services-Sacramento [SOP]	800-266-4624	•	•	•	•
•	•	•	•	•	C & S Research	530-415-3161	•	•	•	•
•	•	•	•	•	Cal Search	858-488-7572	•		•	•
	•	•	•	•	Cal Title-Search Inc	800-482-1497	•	•	•	•
•	•	•	•	•	Capitol City Network	916-395-2917	•	•	•	•
	•		•	•	Capitol Corporate Services Inc (California)	800-327-4842	•		•	
					Capitol Services (California)	916-443-0657	•			
•	•	•	•	•	Confi-Chek	800-821-7404	•	•	•	•
•	•		•		Contemporary Information Corp	800-754-0009			•	
•	•	•			Nina N Cooper	707-758-6165	•		•	•
•	•	•	•	•	Court Record Consultants [SOP]	818-366-1906	•	•	•	
•	•	•	•	•	DataSearch Inc	800-452-3282	•	•	•	•
•	•				Inquest	408-395-1300				
•					InVision Research	559-271-3170				
•	•	•	•	•	Legalese [SOP]	916-453-2860	•	•	•	•
					Logan Registration Service Inc	916-457-5787	•			
•	•				McCoy Investigations (CAPI# 18621)	800-287-6789				
					Mobile Abstracting Services	916-965-6544	•	•	•	
					Models with Brains	925-838-3899	•	•	•	
•	•	•	•	•	One Legal, Inc [SOP]	800-938-8815				
•	•	•	•	•	Pacific Corporate & Title Services (Sacramento)	800-230-4988	•	•	•	•
•	•	•	•	•	Parasec (California)	800-533-7272	•	•	•	•
•	•				Quality Business Information	916-684-0444				
	•	•	•	•	Quest Discovery Service [SOP]	408-441-7000	•	•	•	•
•	•	•	•	•	Rapid Document Service	209-745-0999	•	•	•	•
•	•				Records Research Inc (California)	800-952-5766	•	•	•	
					Reliable Document Retrieval Inc	916-438-3000	•	•	•	
•	•	•	•	•	Research & Retrieval Inc	800-707-8771	•	•	•	
					Searching Registration Service	800-488-0238	•	•		•
•	•	•	•	•	Seyfried Support Services	916-359-5275	•	•	•	•
					Leslie or Mike Sosa	916-984-7654	•	•	•	
•	•	•	•	•	The Amherst Group	800-521-0237	•	•	•	•
•	•				The Legal Source Attorney Services	800-786-8163				
	•	•	•	•	Title Court Service	510-763-0975	•	•	•	•
•	•		•	•	Unisearch Inc (California)	800-769-1864	•		•	
•	•	•	•	•	United Attorneys' Services	916-457-3000	•	•	•	•
•	•	•	•	•	Westlaw Court Express	800-766-3320	•	•	•	•

CR	CV	PR	US	BK	←COURTS **SAN BENITO**	RECORDER→	UC	RE	TX	VS
•	•	•	•	•	Attorney's Diversified Services-Fresno [SOP]	800-842-2695	•	•	•	•
•	•		•		Contemporary Information Corp	800-754-0009			•	
•	•	•	•	•	Court Record Consultants [SOP]	818-366-1906	•	•	•	
•	•	•			Lincoln Investigations Inc DBA Bay Point Legal Service [SOP]	800-383-0897	•	•	•	•
	•	•	•	•	Quest Discovery Service [SOP]	408-441-7000	•	•	•	•
	•	•	•	•	Title Court Service	510-763-0975	•	•	•	•
•	•	•			Tri County Investigations	831-758-3124	•	•	•	•

CR	CV	PR	US	BK	←COURTS **SAN BERNARDINO**	RECORDER→	UC	RE	TX	VS
•	•				A & C Research	951-301-6956				
•	•	•	•	•	A California Process & Attorney Service [SOP]	909-381-5185	•	•	•	•
•	•		•		A-1 Unisource Screening & Information	800-525-6972				
•	•	•	•	•	Access Research	619-231-8947	•		•	•
•	•		•		Accurate Background Inc	800-784-3911				
•	•		•	•	Accurate Source.com Inc [SOP]	800-978-8950	•		•	

CR	CV	PR	US	BK	Retriever	Phone	UC	RE	TX	VS
•	•				Alpha Information Inc	800-900-1471				
•	•	•	•	•	Alternative Investigative & Attorney Services [SOP]	818-402-0800	•	•	•	•
•	•	•	•	•	APSCREEN Inc	800-277-2733	•	•	•	•
•	•		•		Atlas Research Services Inc	818-920-6376				
•	•	•	•	•	Bollinger Attorney Service [SOP]	760-329-2504	•	•	•	•
•	•	•			Bosic & Bosic [SOP]	951-788-1988; Fax- same		•	•	•
•	•	•	•	•	Cal Search	858-488-7572	•		•	•
•	•	•			Cheri's Court Service	951-684-6499, cell- 951-233-1037				
•	•				Coastal Research	805-710-4926		•	•	
•	•	•	•	•	Collective Intelligence Inc [SOP]	800-436-1969				•
•	•		•		Contemporary Information Corp.	800-754-0009			•	
•	•	•	•	•	Court Record Consultants [SOP]	818-366-1906	•	•	•	
•	•				Crutchfield & Associates [SOP]	818-349-4836	•	•	•	
	•		•	•	Crystal Clear Copy Service [SOP]	760-947-5699				
•	•	•	•	•	Daily Journal Corporation	800-952-5232	•	•		•
•	•	•	•	•	DCW & Associates [SOP]	800-899-0442	•	•	•	•
					Document Depot Express	562-860-2907, cell- 562-706-2031		•	•	•
•	•	•	•	•	Docu-Search California	800-466-9450	•	•	•	•
					Dr Dave's Docs	818-246-3087		•		
•	•	•	•	•	English Research & Retrieval Inc [SOP]	951-328-9995	•	•	•	•
•	•	•	•	•	Executive Attorney Service Inc [SOP]	213-482-6680				
•	•	•	•	•	First Investigative Consultants, PI# 6949 [SOP]	800-900-4342	•	•	•	•
•	•		•		Insight Public Record Research Corp	800-615-8111				
•	•	•	•	•	Kay's Rapid Record Research	909-790-2073	•	•	•	•
•	•	•	•	•	Kern Attorney Service Inc [SOP]	800-675-5376		•	•	•
•	•	•	•	•	Legal Research Associates Inc [SOP]	714-734-9337	•	•	•	•
•	•				Liberty Alliance [SOP]	800-630-2880				
					Los Angeles County Document Services Inc	818-241-1990		•	•	
•	•	•	•	•	Loss Prevention Associates Inc	714-593-2323				
•	•	•	•	•	Joe Y Nerio	909-824-9358				•
•	•	•	•	•	One Legal, Inc [SOP]	800-938-8815				
•	•	•	•	•	Pacific Corporate & Title Services (Sacramento)	800-230-4988	•	•	•	•
•	•	•	•	•	Powell Court Service	888-976-9355	•	•	•	•
•	•	•	•	•	Precision Research & Information	951-244-8118	•		•	•
•	•	•	•	•	Process Service Network [SOP]	800-417-7623		•	•	•
	•	•	•	•	Quest Discovery Service [SOP]	408-441-7000	•	•	•	•
•	•	•	•	•	Research & Retrieval Inc	800-707-8771	•	•	•	
•	•	•	•	•	Southern California Strategic Research	323-257-4472	•	•	•	•
•	•	•	•	•	The Amherst Group	800-521-0237	•	•	•	•
	•	•	•		Title Court Service	510-763-0975	•	•	•	•
					Tseng Document Retrieval	562-863-3415	•	•	•	
•	•	•	•	•	Universal Information Research [SOP]	800-363-9813	•	•		•
•			•	•	Welliver & Associates LLC [SOP]	800-569-5677				

San Diego

CR	CV	PR	US	BK	←Courts	Recorder→	UC	RE	TX	VS
•	•		•		A-1 Unisource Screening & Information	800-525-6972				
•	•		•	•	Aaron Anderson Agency	760-751-0101			•	
•	•	•	•	•	Access Research	619-231-8947	•		•	•
•	•		•		Accurate Background Inc	800-784-3911				
•	•		•	•	Accurate Source.com Inc [SOP]	800-978-8950	•		•	
•	•	•	•	•	AccuTech Legal Support Services [SOP]	800-275-7189	•	•	•	•
•	•	•	•	•	Alpha Attorney Service [SOP]	619-235-8008	•	•	•	•
•	•				Alpha Information Inc	800-900-1471				
•	•	•	•	•	APSCREEN Inc	800-277-2733	•	•	•	•
•	•		•		Atlas Research Services Inc	818-920-6376				
•	•	•	•	•	Attorney's Diversified Services-San Diego [SOP]	800-566-9501	•	•	•	•
				•	Banko Document Retrieval	800-969-2377				
•	•	•	•	•	Benchmark Investigations [SOP]	800-248-7721	•	•	•	•
	•				Budget Document Retrieval & Information Service	866-805-6288		•	•	•

CR	CV	PR	US	BK	Courts / Recorder	Phone	UC	RE	TX	VS
•	•	•	•	•	Cal Search	858-488-7572	•		•	•
•					California Criminal Research [SOP]	909-590-9177				
•	•				Coastal Research	805-710-4926		•	•	
•	•	•	•	•	Collective Intelligence Inc [SOP]	800-436-1969				•
•	•		•		Contemporary Information Corp	800-754-0009			•	
					County Court Retrievers Inc	909-307-0814		•		
•	•	•	•	•	Court Record Consultants [SOP]	818-366-1906	•	•	•	
•	•				Crutchfield & Associates [SOP]	818-349-4836	•	•	•	
•	•	•	•	•	Daily Journal Corporation	800-952-5232	•	•		•
•	•	•	•	•	DCW & Associates [SOP]	800-899-0442	•	•	•	•
					Document Depot Express	562-860-2907, cell- 562-706-2031		•	•	•
•	•	•	•	•	Docu-Search California	800-466-9450	•	•	•	•
					Dr Dave's Docs	818-246-3087		•		
•	•	•	•	•	File Finders Public Record Research Inc/dba Filefinders	619-656-6068	•	•	•	•
•	•	•	•	•	First Investigative Consultants, PI# 6949 [SOP]	800-900-4342	•	•	•	•
•	•	•	•	•	Fred Phillips Research Inc	858-735-3431	•	•	•	
•	•		•	•	Insight Public Record Research Corp	800-615-8111				
•	•	•	•	•	Kern Attorney Service Inc [SOP]	800-675-5376		•	•	•
•	•		•	•	L & J Research	619-829-2083	•		•	•
•	•	•	•	•	Law In Motion [SOP]	619-232-1291	•	•	•	•
•	•				Liberty Alliance [SOP]	800-630-2880				
					Los Angeles County Document Services Inc	818-241-1990		•	•	
•	•	•	•	•	Loss Prevention Associates Inc	714-593-2323				
•	•		•	•	Metropolis Group	818-861-7099				
•	•	•	•	•	Joe Y Nerio	909-824-9358				•
•	•	•	•	•	One Legal, Inc [SOP]	800-938-8815				
•	•	•	•	•	Owens & Associates Inv [SOP]	800-297-1343	•	•	•	•
•	•	•	•	•	Pacific Corporate & Title Services (Sacramento)	800-230-4988	•	•	•	•
•	•	•	•	•	Pacificsearch & Information	619-702-3334	•	•	•	•
	•	•	•	•	Quest Discovery Service [SOP]	408-441-7000	•	•	•	•
•	•	•			RASCAL [SOP]	951-693-0165		•	•	
•	•	•	•	•	Research & Retrieval Inc	800-707-8771	•	•	•	
•	•	•	•	•	RJI Services Inc [SOP]	800-344-4754	•	•	•	•
•	•	•	•	•	Rogers Investigations & Research	800-935-6654	•	•	•	•
	•	•	•	•	Seva Services	619-253-7932		•	•	•
•	•	•	•	•	Sutherlin Associated Services	760-433-1555	•	•	•	
•	•	•	•	•	The Amherst Group	800-521-0237	•	•	•	•
	•	•	•	•	Title Court Service	510-763-0975	•	•	•	•
					Tseng Document Retrieval	562-863-3415	•	•	•	
•	•	•	•	•	Universal Information Research [SOP]	800-363-9813	•	•		•
•			•	•	Welliver & Associates LLC [SOP]	800-569-5677				
•	•	•	•	•	Westlaw Court Express	800-766-3320	•	•	•	•
•	•	•	•	•	XL Professional Services Inc [SOP]		•	•	•	•

CR	CV	PR	US	BK	←Courts — SAN FRANCISCO	Recorder→	UC	RE	TX	VS
•	•	•	•	•	A & A Legal Service Inc [SOP]	650-697-9431	•	•	•	•
•	•		•		A-1 Unisource Screening & Information	800-525-6972				
•	•	•	•	•	Access Research	619-231-8947	•		•	•
•	•		•		Accurate Background Inc	800-784-3911				
•	•		•		Advantage Background Services Inc	800-355-2650				
•	•	•	•	•	Attorney's Diversified Services-San Francisco [SOP]	800-775-3455	•	•	•	•
•	•		•	•	Baxter Research Inc	415-333-5402				
•	•	•	•	•	Bay Area Records [SOP]	888-934-3848	•	•	•	
					BirthCertificate.com	888-934-3848				•
•	•	•	•	•	Cal Search	858-488-7572	•		•	•
•	•		•		Contemporary Information Corp	800-754-0009			•	
•	•	•	•	•	Court Record Consultants [SOP]	818-366-1906	•	•	•	
•	•		•	•	Laura Cross	510-336-0865			•	•

CR	CV	PR	US	BK	Courts	Recorder	UC	RE	TX	VS
•	•	•	•		Edith Wiggins & Marvin Singer	415-771-9369	•		•	
•	•	•			Equity Title Search [SOP]	323-965-0759		•		•
•					InVision Research	559-271-3170				
•	•	•	•	•	Lone Star Legal	415-255-8550	•	•	•	•
•	•	•		•	Maggie M & Associates	707-778-7304	•	•	•	•
					Models with Brains	925-838-3899	•	•	•	
•	•	•	•	•	One Legal, Inc [SOP]	800-938-8815				
•	•	•	•	•	Pacific Corporate & Title Services (Sacramento)	800-230-4988	•	•	•	•
•	•	•	•	•	Pacific Research & Retrieval Inc [SOP]	800-222-7040	•	•	•	•
•	•	•	•	•	PFC Information Services Inc	510-653-5061	•	•	•	•
•	•	•	•	•	Probus Research [SOP]	888-934-3848	•	•	•	•
	•	•	•	•	Quest Discovery Service [SOP]	408-441-7000	•	•	•	•
•	•	•	•	•	Rapid Document Service	209-745-0999	•	•	•	•
•	•	•	•	•	Research & Retrieval Inc	800-707-8771	•	•	•	
•	•	•	•	•	RJI Services Inc [SOP]	800-344-4754	•	•	•	•
•	•	•	•	•	Swift Attorney Service [SOP]	800-987-9438	•	•	•	•
•	•	•	•	•	The Amherst Group	800-521-0237	•	•	•	•
•	•				Deborah W Thompson	415-272-5773	•	•	•	
	•	•	•	•	Title Court Service	510-763-0975	•	•	•	•
•	•	•	•	•	Universal Information Research [SOP]	800-363-9813	•	•		•
•	•	•	•	•	Wakeman Process Service Inc [SOP]	510-886-7667				
•	•	•	•	•	Western Attorney Services	415-487-4140				
•	•	•	•	•	Westlaw Court Express	800-766-3320	•	•	•	•
	•	•	•	•	Wheels of Justice Inc [SOP]	800-649-1198	•	•	•	•
•	•	•	•	•	Zook Search Inc California	415-387-1029	•	•	•	•

CR	CV	PR	US	BK	←Courts	San Joaquin Recorder→	UC	RE	TX	VS
•	•	•			AD Services (ADS) [SOP]	800-827-9101		•	•	•
•	•		•		Atlas Research Services Inc	818-920-6376				
•	•	•	•	•	Attorney Service of Merced [SOP]	209-383-3233	•	•	•	•
•	•	•	•	•	Attorney's Aid Inc of Sacramento [SOP]	916-648-1559	•	•		•
•	•	•	•	•	Attorney's Diversified Services-Stockton [SOP]	800-343-2108	•	•	•	•
•					California Backgrounds	559-274-9784				
•	•			•	Central Valley Records Service Inc	209-524-3849	•		•	•
•	•	•	•	•	Espy Investigative Services	877-843-3779	•	•	•	•
•					InVision Research	559-271-3170				
•	•	•	•	•	Legalese [SOP]	916-453-2860	•	•	•	•
•	•	•	•	•	One Legal, Inc [SOP]	800-938-8815				
•	•	•	•	•	Pacific Corporate & Title Services (Sacramento)	800-230-4988	•	•	•	•
•	•				Quality Business Information	916-684-0444				
	•	•	•	•	Quest Discovery Service [SOP]	408-441-7000	•	•	•	•
•	•	•	•	•	Rapid Document Service	209-745-0999	•	•	•	•
					Reliable Document Retrieval Inc	916-438-3000	•	•	•	
	•	•	•	•	Title Court Service	510-763-0975	•	•	•	•
•	•	•	•	•	United Attorneys' Services	916-457-3000	•	•	•	•

CR	CV	PR	US	BK	←Courts	San Luis Obispo Recorder→	UC	RE	TX	VS
•	•	•	•	•	Attorney Service of San Luis Obispo [SOP]	850-543-8919	•	•	•	•
•	•	•	•	•	Attorney's Diversified Services-Ventura [SOP]	800-933-8014	•	•	•	•
•	•	•			Leslie Bearce	805-704-5699	•	•	•	•
•	•				Coastal Research	805-710-4926		•	•	
•	•	•	•	•	Collective Intelligence Inc [SOP]	800-436-1969				•
•	•	•	•	•	Court Record Consultants [SOP]	818-366-1906	•	•	•	
•	•	•		•	CourtCheckers [SOP]	805-898-7084	•	•	•	•
•	•	•	•	•	DCW & Associates [SOP]	800-899-0442	•	•	•	•
•	•	•	•	•	English Research & Retrieval Inc [SOP]	951-328-9995	•	•	•	•
•	•	•	•	•	One Legal, Inc [SOP]	800-938-8815				
	•	•	•	•	Quest Discovery Service [SOP]	408-441-7000	•	•	•	•
	•	•	•	•	Title Court Service	510-763-0975	•	•	•	•

CR	CV	PR	US	BK	←COURTS SAN MATEO	RECORDER→	UC	RE	TX	VS
•	•	•	•	•	A & A Legal Service Inc [SOP]	650-697-9431	•	•	•	•
•	•		•		A-1 Unisource Screening & Information	800-525-6972				
•	•	•	•	•	Access Research	619-231-8947	•		•	•
•	•		•		Accurate Background Inc	800-784-3911				
•	•	•			AD Services (ADS) [SOP]	800-827-9101		•	•	•
•	•	•	•	•	Attorney's Diversified Services-San Francisco [SOP]	800-775-3455	•	•	•	•
•	•		•	•	Baxter Research Inc	415-333-5402				
•	•	•	•	•	Bay Area Records [SOP]	888-934-3848	•	•	•	
•	•	•	•	•	Bayshore Research & Retrieval [SOP]	408-298-1354	•	•	•	•
					BirthCertificate.com	888-934-3848				•
•	•	•	•	•	Cal Search	858-488-7572	•		•	•
•	•		•		Contemporary Information Corp	800-754-0009			•	
•	•		•	•	Laura Cross	510-336-0865			•	•
•	•	•	•		Edith Wiggins & Marvin Singer	415-771-9369	•		•	
•	•				Incognito Services [SOP]	650-363-9100		•		
•	•				Inquest	408-395-1300				
•					InVision Research	559-271-3170				
•	•	•	•	•	Jess Barker Document Research/Retrieval	888-316-3773	•	•	•	•
•	•				Legal Document Search & Signing Services [SOP]	408-483-0061			•	•
•	•	•	•	•	Lone Star Legal	415-255-8550	•	•	•	•
					Models with Brains	925-838-3899	•	•	•	
•	•	•	•	•	One Legal, Inc [SOP]	800-938-8815				
•	•	•	•	•	Pacific Corporate & Title Services (Sacramento)	800-230-4988	•	•	•	•
•	•	•	•	•	Pacific Research & Retrieval Inc [SOP]	800-222-7040	•	•	•	•
•	•	•	•	•	Probus Research [SOP]	888-934-3848	•	•	•	•
	•	•	•	•	Quest Discovery Service [SOP]	408-441-7000	•	•	•	•
•	•	•	•	•	Rapid Document Service	209-745-0999	•	•	•	•
•	•				Rapid Research	510-777-9461				
					Leslie or Mike Sosa	916-984-7654	•	•	•	
•	•	•	•	•	Swift Attorney Service [SOP]	800-987-9438	•	•	•	•
	•	•	•	•	Title Court Service	510-763-0975	•	•	•	•
•	•	•	•	•	Wakeman Process Service Inc [SOP]	510-886-7667				
•	•	•	•	•	Western Attorney Services	415-487-4140				
•	•	•	•	•	Westlaw Court Express	800-766-3320	•	•	•	•
	•	•	•	•	Wheels of Justice Inc [SOP]	800-649-1198	•	•	•	•

CR	CV	PR	US	BK	←COURTS SANTA BARBARA	RECORDER→	UC	RE	TX	VS
•	•		•		A-1 Unisource Screening & Information	800-525-6972				
•	•	•	•	•	Abstrax	805-683-9606	•	•	•	•
•	•	•	•	•	APSCREEN Inc	800-277-2733	•	•	•	•
•	•	•	•	•	Associated Attorney Services [SOP]	805-898-0022	•	•	•	•
•	•		•		Atlas Research Services Inc	818-920-6376				
•	•	•	•	•	Attorney Service of San Luis Obispo [SOP]	850-543-8919	•	•	•	•
•	•	•	•	•	Attorney's Diversified Services-Ventura [SOP]	800-933-8014	•	•	•	•
•	•				Todd Boehr	805-452-7579				
•	•	•	•	•	Cal Search	858-488-7572	•		•	•
•	•				Coastal Research	805-710-4926		•	•	
•	•	•	•	•	Collective Intelligence Inc [SOP]	800-436-1969				•
•	•	•		•	Commercial Process Serving Inc [SOP]	800-382-0088				
•	•		•		Contemporary Information Corp	800-754-0009			•	
•	•	•	•	•	Court Record Consultants [SOP]	818-366-1906	•	•	•	
•	•	•		•	CourtCheckers [SOP]	805-898-7084	•	•	•	•
•	•	•	•	•	DCW & Associates [SOP]	800-899-0442	•	•	•	•
					Dr Dave's Docs	818-246-3087		•		
•	•	•	•	•	English Research & Retrieval Inc [SOP]	951-328-9995	•	•	•	•
•	•	•	•	•	One Legal, Inc [SOP]	800-938-8815				
	•	•	•	•	Quest Discovery Service [SOP]	408-441-7000	•	•	•	•

CR	CV	PR	US	BK	←Courts		Recorder→	UC	RE	TX	VS
•	•	•	•	•	Southern California Strategic Research		323-257-4472	•	•	•	•
•	•	•	•	•	The Amherst Group		800-521-0237	•	•	•	•
	•	•	•	•	Title Court Service		510-763-0975	•	•	•	•
				•	Title Runners		805-569-6939	•	•	•	•

CR	CV	PR	US	BK	←Courts	Santa Clara	Recorder→	UC	RE	TX	VS
•	•	•	•	•	A & A Legal Service Inc [SOP]		650-697-9431	•	•	•	•
•	•	•	•	•	Access Research		619-231-8947	•		•	•
•	•		•		Accurate Background Inc		800-784-3911				
•	•	•			AD Services (ADS) [SOP]		800-827-9101		•	•	•
•	•		•		Advantage Background Services Inc		800-355-2650				
•	•		•		Atlas Research Services Inc		818-920-6376				
•	•	•	•	•	Attorney's Diversified Services-San Francisco [SOP]		800-775-3455	•	•	•	•
•	•		•	•	Baxter Research Inc		415-333-5402				
•	•	•	•	•	Bay Area Records [SOP]		888-934-3848	•	•	•	
•	•	•	•	•	Bayshore Research & Retrieval [SOP]		408-298-1354	•	•	•	•
					BirthCertificate.com		888-934-3848				•
•	•	•	•	•	Cal Search		858-488-7572	•		•	•
•	•		•		Contemporary Information Corp.		800-754-0009			•	
•	•	•	•	•	Court Record Consultants [SOP]		818-366-1906	•	•	•	
•	•		•	•	Laura Cross		510-336-0865			•	•
•	•		•	•	DLS Background Services Inc		951-301-8584	•		•	
•	•	•	•	•	Espy Investigative Services		877-843-3779	•	•	•	•
•	•	•	•	•	Haber Investigations [SOP]		800-382-6333	•	•	•	•
•	•				Inquest		408-395-1300				
•	•	•	•	•	Jess Barker Document Research/Retrieval		888-316-3773	•	•	•	•
•	•				Legal Document Search & Signing Services [SOP]		408-483-0061			•	•
•	•	•		•	Maggie M & Associates		707-778-7304	•	•	•	•
					Models with Brains		925-838-3899	•	•	•	
•	•	•	•	•	One Legal, Inc [SOP]		800-938-8815				
•	•	•	•	•	PAC Research		831-475-7780	•		•	•
•	•	•	•	•	Pacific Corporate & Title Services (Sacramento)		800-230-4988	•	•	•	•
•	•	•	•	•	Pacific Research & Retrieval Inc [SOP]		800-222-7040	•	•	•	•
•	•	•	•	•	Powell Court Service		888-976-9355	•	•	•	•
•	•	•	•	•	Probus Research [SOP]		888-934-3848	•	•	•	•
	•		•	•	Quest Discovery Service [SOP]		408-441-7000	•	•	•	•
•	•	•	•	•	Rapid Document Service		209-745-0999	•	•	•	•
•	•	•	•	•	Research & Retrieval Inc		800-707-8771	•	•	•	
					Leslie or Mike Sosa		916-984-7654	•	•	•	
•	•	•	•	•	Swift Attorney Service [SOP]		800-987-9438	•	•	•	•
•	•	•	•	•	The Amherst Group		800-521-0237	•	•	•	•
	•	•	•	•	Title Court Service		510-763-0975	•	•	•	•
•	•	•	•	•	Universal Information Research [SOP]		800-363-9813	•	•		•
•	•	•	•	•	Wakeman Process Service Inc [SOP]		510-886-7667				
•	•	•	•	•	Western Attorney Services		415-487-4140				
•	•	•	•	•	Westlaw Court Express		800-766-3320	•	•	•	•
	•	•	•	•	Wheels of Justice Inc [SOP]		800-649-1198	•	•	•	•

CR	CV	PR	US	BK	←Courts	Santa Cruz	Recorder→	UC	RE	TX	VS
•	•		•		Atlas Research Services Inc		818-920-6376				
•	•	•			Attorney Service of California-Santa Cruz [SOP]		888-306-2194	•	•	•	•
•	•	•	•	•	Attorney's Diversified Services-Fresno [SOP]		800-842-2695	•	•	•	•
•	•		•	•	Baxter Research Inc		415-333-5402				
•	•	•	•	•	Cal Search		858-488-7572	•		•	•
•	•		•		Contemporary Information Corp.		800-754-0009			•	
•	•				Inquest		408-395-1300				
•	•	•			Lincoln Investigations Inc DBA Bay Point Legal Service [SOP]		800-383-0897	•	•	•	•
•	•	•	•	•	One Legal, Inc [SOP]		800-938-8815				
•	•	•	•	•	PAC Research		831-475-7780	•		•	•

CR	CV	PR	US	BK	←Courts	Recorder→	UC	RE	TX	VS
•	•	•	•	•	Pacific Corporate & Title Services (Sacramento)	800-230-4988	•	•	•	•
	•	•	•	•	Quest Discovery Service [SOP]	408-441-7000	•	•	•	•
					Leslie or Mike Sosa	916-984-7654	•	•	•	
	•	•	•	•	Title Court Service	510-763-0975	•	•	•	•
•	•	•			Tri County Investigations	831-758-3124	•	•	•	•

CR	CV	PR	US	BK	←Courts **SHASTA**	Recorder→	UC	RE	TX	VS
•	•	•	•	•	Attorney's Aid Inc of Sacramento [SOP]	916-648-1559	•	•		•
•	•	•	•	•	Attorney's Diversified Services-Redding [SOP]	800-473-1228	•	•	•	•
•	•		•	•	Business Connections [SOP]	530-527-6229	•		•	•
•	•	•	•	•	C & S Research	530-415-3161	•	•	•	•
•	•				Carmona & Associates [SOP]	530-246-1010	•	•	•	•
•	•	•			GMV Research	707-228-8708			•	•
•	•	•		•	Maggie M & Associates	707-778-7304	•	•	•	•
•	•				Nor-Cal Court Research	530-865-3525				
	•	•	•	•	Quest Discovery Service [SOP]	408-441-7000	•	•	•	•
•	•				The Legal Source Attorney Services	800-786-8163				
	•	•	•	•	Title Court Service	510-763-0975	•	•	•	•

CR	CV	PR	US	BK	←Courts **SIERRA**	Recorder→	UC	RE	TX	VS
•	•	•	•	•	Attorney's Diversified Services-Sacramento [SOP]	800-266-4624	•	•	•	•
•	•	•	•	•	C & S Research	530-415-3161	•	•	•	•
•	•	•			Nina N Cooper	707-758-6165	•		•	•
•	•	•	•	•	DCW & Associates [SOP]	800-899-0442	•	•	•	•
•	•				Lassen Attorney/Investigative Services [SOP]	530-251-2399				
	•	•	•	•	Quest Discovery Service [SOP]	408-441-7000	•	•	•	•
	•	•	•	•	Title Court Service	510-763-0975	•	•	•	•

CR	CV	PR	US	BK	←Courts **SISKIYOU**	Recorder→	UC	RE	TX	VS
•	•		•		Atlas Research Services Inc	818-920-6376				
•	•	•	•	•	Attorney's Diversified Services-Redding [SOP]	800-473-1228	•	•	•	•
•	•				Carmona & Associates [SOP]	530-246-1010	•	•	•	•
•	•	•	•	•	Cleveland & Carl Inv [SOP]	800-888-6629	•	•	•	•
	•	•	•	•	Quest Discovery Service [SOP]	408-441-7000	•	•	•	•
					Leslie or Mike Sosa	916-984-7654	•	•	•	
	•	•	•	•	Title Court Service	510-763-0975	•	•	•	•

CR	CV	PR	US	BK	←Courts **SOLANO**	Recorder→	UC	RE	TX	VS
•	•				Annette Sanders Research	707-449-3620				
•	•		•		Atlas Research Services Inc	818-920-6376				
•	•	•	•	•	Attorney's Diversified Services-Sacramento [SOP]	800-266-4624	•	•	•	•
•	•	•			Nina N Cooper	707-758-6165	•		•	•
•	•		•	•	DLS Background Services Inc	951-301-8584	•		•	
•	•	•			GMV Research	707-228-8708			•	•
•	•	•			Jean Randall Process Service [SOP]	866-386-5777	•	•	•	
					Models with Brains	925-838-3899	•	•	•	
•	•	•	•	•	One Legal, Inc [SOP]	800-938-8815				
•	•	•	•	•	Pacific Corporate & Title Services (Sacramento)	800-230-4988	•	•	•	•
•	•				Private Eyes Inc	877-292-3330	•	•	•	
•	•				Pryamid Research	530-867-1568			•	
•	•				Quality Business Information	916-684-0444				
	•	•	•	•	Quest Discovery Service [SOP]	408-441-7000	•	•	•	•
•	•	•	•	•	Rapid Document Service	209-745-0999	•	•	•	•
					Leslie or Mike Sosa	916-984-7654	•	•	•	
•	•				Sumpter & Associates LLC	925-671-7755	•	•	•	•
	•	•	•	•	Title Court Service	510-763-0975	•	•	•	•
•	•	•	•	•	West Coast MCI [SOP]	925-372-8909	•	•	•	•
•	•	•	•	•	Western Attorney Services	415-487-4140				

CR	CV	PR	US	BK	←COURTS SONOMA	RECORDER→	UC	RE	TX	VS
•	•	•			A David Research	707-479-2779	•	•	•	•
•					Alpha Omega USA Information Brokers LLC [SOP]	866-636-6342				
•	•		•		Atlas Research Services Inc	818-920-6376				
•	•	•	•	•	Attorney's Aid Inc of Sacramento [SOP]	916-648-1559	•	•		•
•	•	•	•	•	Attorney's Diversified Services-Santa Rosa [SOP]	800-473-5455	•	•	•	•
•	•		•	•	Baxter Research Inc	415-333-5402				
•	•	•	•	•	DCW & Associates [SOP]	800-899-0442	•	•	•	•
•	•	•			Jean Randall Process Service [SOP]	866-386-5777	•	•	•	
•	•	•		•	Maggie M & Associates	707-778-7304	•	•	•	•
•	•	•			Napa-Sonoma Connection	707-952-6426	•	•	•	•
•	•				Norcal Public Records Service	408-221-6654	•	•	•	
•	•	•	•	•	One Legal, Inc [SOP]	800-938-8815				
•	•	•	•	•	Pacific Corporate & Title Services (Sacramento)	800-230-4988	•	•	•	•
	•	•	•	•	Quest Discovery Service [SOP]	408-441-7000	•	•	•	•
•	•	•			SRS Private Investigations Inc [SOP]	707-537-1091	•	•	•	•
•	•	•	•	•	The Amherst Group	800-521-0237	•	•	•	•
	•	•	•	•	Title Court Service	510-763-0975	•	•	•	•
•	•	•	•	•	Western Attorney Services	415-487-4140				

CR	CV	PR	US	BK	←COURTS STANISLAUS	RECORDER→	UC	RE	TX	VS
•	•	•	•	•	Action Legal Support Services [SOP]	559-432-3337				
•	•	•			AD Services (ADS) [SOP]	800-827-9101		•	•	•
•	•	•	•	•	Attorney Service of Merced [SOP]	209-383-3233	•	•	•	•
•	•	•	•	•	Attorney's Aid Inc of Sacramento [SOP]	916-648-1559	•	•		•
•	•	•	•	•	Attorney's Diversified Services-Modesto [SOP]	800-473-0273	•	•	•	•
•	•	•	•	•	Cal Search	858-488-7572	•		•	•
•	•			•	Central Valley Records Service Inc	209-524-3849	•		•	•
•	•	•	•	•	Court Record Consultants [SOP]	818-366-1906	•	•	•	
•	•	•	•	•	Espy Investigative Services	877-843-3779	•	•	•	•
•	•	•	•	•	One Legal, Inc [SOP]	800-938-8815				
•	•	•	•	•	Pacific Corporate & Title Services (Sacramento)	800-230-4988	•	•	•	•
•	•				Quality Business Information	916-684-0444				
	•	•	•	•	Quest Discovery Service [SOP]	408-441-7000	•	•	•	•
•	•	•	•	•	Rapid Document Service	209-745-0999	•	•	•	•
	•	•	•	•	Title Court Service	510-763-0975	•	•	•	•

CR	CV	PR	US	BK	←COURTS SUTTER	RECORDER→	UC	RE	TX	VS
•	•	•			A.D.I. Litigation Support Services [SOP]	530-743-4245		•	•	•
•	•	•	•	•	Attorney's Aid Inc of Sacramento [SOP]	916-648-1559	•	•		•
•	•	•	•	•	Attorney's Diversified Services-Sacramento [SOP]	800-266-4624	•	•	•	•
•	•	•	•	•	C & S Research	530-415-3161	•	•	•	•
•	•	•			Nina N Cooper	707-758-6165	•		•	•
•	•	•	•	•	Legalese [SOP]	916-453-2860	•	•	•	•
					Mobile Abstracting Services	916-965-6544	•	•	•	
	•	•	•	•	Quest Discovery Service [SOP]	408-441-7000	•	•	•	•
•	•	•	•	•	Rapid Document Service	209-745-0999	•	•	•	•
•	•	•	•	•	Seyfried Support Services	916-359-5275	•	•	•	•
•	•				The Legal Source Attorney Services	800-786-8163				
	•	•	•	•	Title Court Service	510-763-0975	•	•	•	•

CR	CV	PR	US	BK	←COURTS TEHAMA	RECORDER→	UC	RE	TX	VS
•	•	•	•	•	Attorney's Diversified Services-Redding [SOP]	800-473-1228	•	•	•	•
•	•		•	•	Business Connections [SOP]	530-527-6229	•		•	•
•	•				Carmona & Associates [SOP]	530-246-1010	•	•	•	•
•	•		•	•	DLS Background Services Inc	951-301-8584	•		•	
•	•				Nor-Cal Court Research	530-865-3525				
	•	•	•	•	Quest Discovery Service [SOP]	408-441-7000	•	•	•	•

continued

CR	CV	PR	US	BK	←Courts	Recorder→	UC	RE	TX	VS
•	•				The Legal Source Attorney Services	800-786-8163				
	•	•	•	•	Title Court Service	510-763-0975	•	•	•	•

CR	CV	PR	US	BK	←Courts **Trinity**	Recorder→	UC	RE	TX	VS
•	•	•	•	•	Attorney's Diversified Services-Redding [SOP]	800-473-1228	•	•	•	•
	•	•	•	•	Quest Discovery Service [SOP]	408-441-7000	•	•	•	•
	•	•	•	•	Title Court Service	510-763-0975	•	•	•	•

CR	CV	PR	US	BK	←Courts **Tulare**	Recorder→	UC	RE	TX	VS
•	•	•	•	•	Action Legal Support Services [SOP]	559-432-3337				
•	•	•	•	•	Affordable Pearlegal Inc	800-958-2144	•	•	•	•
•	•	•	•	•	Attorney's Diversified Services-Fresno [SOP]	800-842-2695	•	•	•	•
•					California Backgrounds	559-274-9784				
•	•		•	•	DLS Background Services Inc	951-301-8584	•		•	
•					InVision Research	559-271-3170				
•	•	•	•	•	Jess Barker Document Research/Retrieval	888-316-3773	•	•	•	•
•	•		•	•	Keppler Legal Research	559-431-2591				
•	•	•	•	•	One Legal, Inc [SOP]	800-938-8815				
•	•	•			Marilyn Peterson [SOP]	559-732-2135	•	•	•	•
	•	•	•	•	Quest Discovery Service [SOP]	408-441-7000	•	•	•	•
	•	•	•	•	Title Court Service	510-763-0975	•	•	•	•
•	•			•	Total Access	559-325-1169	•		•	•
•	•	•	•	•	Vio-Com-Data Research	559-438-1058		•		

CR	CV	PR	US	BK	←Courts **Tuolumne**	Recorder→	UC	RE	TX	VS
•	•	•	•	•	Attorney's Diversified Services-Modesto [SOP]	800-473-0273	•	•	•	•
•	•		•	•	DLS Background Services Inc	951-301-8584	•		•	
	•	•	•	•	Quest Discovery Service [SOP]	408-441-7000	•	•	•	•
	•	•	•	•	Title Court Service	510-763-0975	•	•	•	•

CR	CV	PR	US	BK	←Courts **Ventura**	Recorder→	UC	RE	TX	VS
•	•		•		A-1 Unisource Screening & Information	800-525-6972				
•	•	•	•	•	Abstrax	805-683-9606	•	•	•	•
•	•	•	•	•	Access Research	619-231-8947	•		•	•
•	•		•		Accurate Background Inc	800-784-3911				
•	•		•	•	Accurate Source.com Inc [SOP]	800-978-8950	•		•	
•	•				Alpha Information Inc	800-900-1471				
•	•	•	•	•	Alternative Investigative & Attorney Services [SOP]	818-402-0800	•	•	•	•
•	•	•	•	•	APSCREEN Inc	800-277-2733	•	•	•	•
•	•		•		Atlas Research Services Inc	818-920-6376				
•	•	•	•	•	Attorney's Diversified Services-Ventura [SOP]	800-933-8014	•	•	•	•
•	•				Todd Boehr	805-452-7579				
•	•	•	•	•	Cal Search	858-488-7572	•		•	•
•	•				Coastal Research	805-710-4926		•	•	
•	•	•	•	•	Collective Intelligence Inc [SOP]	800-436-1969				•
•	•	•		•	Commercial Process Serving Inc [SOP]	800-382-0088				
•	•		•		Contemporary Information Corp	800-754-0009			•	
•	•	•	•	•	Court Record Consultants [SOP]	818-366-1906	•	•	•	
•	•	•		•	CourtCheckers [SOP]	805-898-7084	•	•	•	•
•	•				Crutchfield & Associates [SOP]	818-349-4836	•	•	•	
•	•	•	•	•	Daily Journal Corporation	800-952-5232	•	•		•
•	•	•	•	•	DCW & Associates [SOP]	800-899-0442	•	•	•	•
					Dr Dave's Docs	818-246-3087		•		
•	•	•	•	•	English Research & Retrieval Inc [SOP]	951-328-9995	•	•	•	•
•	•	•	•	•	Executive Attorney Service Inc [SOP]	213-482-6680				
•	•	•	•	•	First Investigative Consultants, PI# 6949 [SOP]	800-900-4342	•	•	•	•
•	•	•	•	•	Kern Attorney Service Inc [SOP]	800-675-5376		•	•	•
•	•				Liberty Alliance [SOP]	800-630-2880				
					Los Angeles County Document Services Inc	818-241-1990		•	•	
•	•		•	•	Metropolis Group	818-861-7099				

CR	CV	PR	US	BK	←Courts	Recorder→	UC	RE	TX	VS
•	•	•	•	•	One Legal, Inc [SOP]	800-938-8815				
•	•	•	•	•	Process Service Network [SOP]	800-417-7623		•	•	•
	•	•	•	•	Quest Discovery Service [SOP]	408-441-7000	•	•	•	•
•	•	•		•	RJI Services Inc [SOP]	800-344-4754	•	•	•	•
•	•	•	•	•	Southern California Strategic Research	323-257-4472	•	•	•	•
•	•	•	•	•	The Amherst Group	800-521-0237	•	•	•	•
	•	•	•	•	Title Court Service	510-763-0975	•	•	•	•
					Tseng Document Retrieval	562-863-3415	•	•	•	
•	•	•	•	•	Universal Information Research [SOP]	800-363-9813	•	•		•
•	•	•	•	•	Vio-Com-Data Research	559-438-1058		•		
•			•	•	Welliver & Associates LLC [SOP]	800-569-5677				

CR	CV	PR	US	BK	←Courts	Yolo	Recorder→	UC	RE	TX	VS
•	•		•		Atlas Research Services Inc		818-920-6376				
•	•	•	•	•	Attorney's Aid Inc of Sacramento [SOP]		916-648-1559	•	•		•
•	•	•	•	•	Attorney's Diversified Services-Sacramento [SOP]		800-266-4624	•	•	•	•
•	•	•	•	•	C & S Research		530-415-3161	•	•	•	•
•	•	•			Nina N Cooper		707-758-6165	•		•	•
•					InVision Research		559-271-3170				
•	•	•	•	•	Legalese [SOP]		916-453-2860	•	•	•	•
					Mobile Abstracting Services		916-965-6544	•	•	•	
•	•	•	•	•	One Legal, Inc [SOP]		800-938-8815				
•	•	•	•	•	Pacific Corporate & Title Services (Sacramento)		800-230-4988	•	•	•	•
					Pryamid Research		530-867-1568			•	
•	•				Quality Business Information		916-684-0444				
	•	•	•	•	Quest Discovery Service [SOP]		408-441-7000	•	•	•	•
•	•	•	•	•	Rapid Document Service		209-745-0999	•	•	•	•
					Reliable Document Retrieval Inc		916-438-3000	•	•	•	
•	•	•	•	•	Seyfried Support Services		916-359-5275	•	•	•	•
	•	•		•	Title Court Service		510-763-0975	•	•	•	•
•	•	•	•	•	United Attorneys' Services		916-457-3000	•	•	•	•

CR	CV	PR	US	BK	←Courts	Yuba	Recorder→	UC	RE	TX	VS
•	•	•			A.D.I. Litigation Support Services [SOP]		530-743-4245		•	•	•
•	•	•	•	•	Attorney's Diversified Services-Sacramento [SOP]		800-266-4624	•	•	•	•
•	•	•	•	•	C & S Research		530-415-3161	•	•	•	•
•	•	•			Nina N Cooper		707-758-6165	•		•	•
•	•	•	•	•	Legalese [SOP]		916-453-2860	•	•	•	•
					Mobile Abstracting Services		916-965-6544	•	•	•	
	•	•	•	•	Quest Discovery Service [SOP]		408-441-7000	•	•	•	•
•	•	•	•	•	Seyfried Support Services		916-359-5275	•	•	•	•
•	•				The Legal Source Attorney Services		800-786-8163				
	•	•	•	•	Title Court Service		510-763-0975	•	•	•	•

Editor's Note: The County Index section in this book will **only** indicate a county where a record retriever does an in-person search by himself or herself, or by a payroll employee.

Many retrievers also maintain a network of correspondents and provide services in additional counties not listed within the County Index. This additional coverage is indicated in the Profiles section under Correspondent Relationships.

Colorado

Court Records Retrieved | **Capital - Denver County** | **Recorded Records Retrieved**

CR	CV	PR	US	BK	←Courts	Adams	Recorder→	UC	RE	TX	VS
•	•	•	•	•	Centennial Coverages Inc (Colorado)		800-338-8221	•	•	•	•
•	•	•	•	•	Colorado Records Search Inc [SOP]		800-645-7712	•	•	•	•
	•				Colorado Records Sooner		303-494-2132	•	•	•	
•	•	•	•	•	Condello Associates, Accusearch [SOP]		888-756-9687	•	•	•	•
					Documents 5280		303-438-8967	•	•	•	
•	•	•	•	•	Barbara K Henritze		303-499-3750	•	•	•	•
•	•	•	•	•	Independent Research LLC		303-969-8608	•	•	•	•
•	•	•	•	•	Peregrine Investigation & Research [SOP]		303-324-7442	•	•	•	•
•	•	•	•	•	R A Heales & Associates Ltd		800-225-7043	•	•	•	•
					Records Quest		303-369-0693	•	•	•	•
•	•		•		RIQ and Associates Inc		720-529-5736	•	•	•	•
•	•	•	•	•	Search Company International [SOP]		800-727-2120	•	•	•	
					Title Company of Denver		303-369-5443		•	•	
•	•	•	•	•	Wolz Corporate USA		303-655-9659	•		•	

CR	CV	PR	US	BK	←Courts	Alamosa	Recorder→	UC	RE	TX	VS
•	•	•	•	•	Independent Research LLC		303-969-8608	•	•	•	•

CR	CV	PR	US	BK	←Courts	Arapahoe	Recorder→	UC	RE	TX	VS
•	•		•	•	ABA Services		720-344-1259	•	•	•	
•	•	•	•	•	Access Information		800-827-7607	•	•	•	•
•	•	•	•	•	Centennial Coverages Inc (Colorado)		800-338-8221	•	•	•	•
•	•	•	•	•	Colorado Records Search Inc [SOP]		800-645-7712	•	•	•	•
	•				Colorado Records Sooner		303-494-2132	•	•	•	
•	•	•	•	•	Condello Associates, Accusearch [SOP]		888-756-9687	•	•	•	•
					Documents 5280		303-438-8967	•	•	•	
•	•	•	•	•	Independent Research LLC		303-969-8608	•	•	•	•
•	•	•	•	•	Peregrine Investigation & Research [SOP]		303-324-7442	•	•	•	•
•	•	•	•	•	R A Heales & Associates Ltd		800-225-7043	•	•	•	•
					Records Quest		303-369-0693	•	•	•	•
•	•		•		RIQ and Associates Inc		720-529-5736	•	•	•	•
•	•	•	•	•	Search and Retrieve		303-587-7852	•	•	•	•
•	•	•	•	•	Search Company International [SOP]		800-727-2120	•	•	•	
					Title Company of Denver		303-369-5443		•	•	
•	•	•	•	•	Wolz Corporate USA		303-655-9659	•		•	

CR	CV	PR	US	BK	←Courts	Archuleta	Recorder→	UC	RE	TX	VS
•	•				Attorney Service New Mexico [SOP]		505-326-7486				
•	•	•	•	•	Colorado Records Search Inc [SOP]		800-645-7712	•	•	•	•
•	•	•			Finney Land Co		970-259-5691	•	•	•	•
		•			Great Divide Title		970-731-7700	•	•	•	
•	•	•	•	•	Independent Research LLC		303-969-8608	•	•	•	•

CR	CV	PR	US	BK	←Courts	Baca	Recorder→	UC	RE	TX	VS
•	•	•	•	•	Colorado Records Search Inc [SOP]		800-645-7712	•	•	•	•
•	•	•	•	•	Independent Research LLC		303-969-8608	•	•	•	•

CR	CV	PR	US	BK	←Courts **Bent**	Recorder→	UC	RE	TX	VS
					Bent County Abstract & Title	719-456-0381		•		
		•			Guaranty Abstract Co (Colorado)	719-336-3261	•	•	•	
•	•	•	•	•	Independent Research LLC	303-969-8608	•	•	•	•

CR	CV	PR	US	BK	←Courts **Boulder**	Recorder→	UC	RE	TX	VS
•	•	•	•	•	Access Information	800-827-7607	•	•	•	•
•	•	•	•	•	Alpha-Omega Investigations [SOP]	866-510-8200	•	•	•	•
•	•		•		Background Information Services	303-442-3960	•			
•	•	•	•	•	Centennial Coverages Inc (Colorado)	800-338-8221	•	•	•	•
•	•	•	•	•	Colorado Records Search Inc [SOP]	800-645-7712	•	•	•	•
	•				Colorado Records Sooner	303-494-2132	•	•	•	
•	•	•	•	•	Condello Associates, Accusearch [SOP]	888-756-9687	•	•	•	•
					Documents 5280	303-438-8967	•	•	•	
•	•	•	•	•	Barbara K Henritze	303-499-3750	•	•	•	•
•	•	•	•	•	Independent Research LLC	303-969-8608	•	•	•	•
•	•	•	•	•	Milestone Legal Support [SOP]	800-317-9221	•	•	•	•
•	•	•	•	•	Peregrine Investigation & Research [SOP]	303-324-7442	•	•	•	•
•	•	•	•	•	R A Heales & Associates Ltd	800-225-7043	•	•	•	•
					Records Quest	303-369-0693	•	•	•	•
•	•		•	•	RIQ and Associates Inc	720-529-5736	•	•	•	•
•	•	•	•	•	Search Company International [SOP]	800-727-2120	•	•	•	
•	•	•	•	•	The Paper Chase - CO [SOP]	970-350-1008	•	•	•	•
					Title Company of Denver	303-369-5443		•	•	
•	•	•	•	•	Wolz Corporate USA	303-655-9659	•		•	

CR	CV	PR	US	BK	←Courts **Broomfield**	Recorder→	UC	RE	TX	VS
•	•	•	•	•	Access Information	800-827-7607	•	•	•	•
•	•	•	•	•	Colorado Records Search Inc [SOP]	800-645-7712	•	•	•	•
	•				Colorado Records Sooner	303-494-2132	•	•	•	
•	•	•	•	•	Condello Associates, Accusearch [SOP]	888-756-9687	•	•	•	•
					Documents 5280	303-438-8967	•	•	•	
•	•	•	•	•	Barbara K Henritze	303-499-3750	•	•	•	•
•	•	•	•	•	Independent Research LLC	303-969-8608	•	•	•	•
					Records Quest	303-369-0693	•	•	•	•
•	•		•	•	RIQ and Associates Inc	720-529-5736	•	•	•	•
•	•	•	•	•	Search Company International [SOP]	800-727-2120	•	•	•	
					Title Company of Denver	303-369-5443		•	•	
•	•	•	•	•	Wolz Corporate USA	303-655-9659	•		•	

CR	CV	PR	US	BK	←Courts **Chaffee**	Recorder→	UC	RE	TX	VS
					Chaffee Title and Escrow Inc	719-539-2215	•	•	•	
					CIBMS	800-922-0002		•	•	
•	•	•	•	•	Independent Research LLC	303-969-8608	•	•	•	•

CR	CV	PR	US	BK	←Courts **Cheyenne**	Recorder→	UC	RE	TX	VS
		•			Cheyenne County Abstract Co	719-767-5585	•	•	•	
•	•	•	•	•	Colorado Records Search Inc [SOP]	800-645-7712	•	•	•	•
•	•	•	•	•	Independent Research LLC	303-969-8608	•	•	•	•

CR	CV	PR	US	BK	←Courts **Clear Creek**	Recorder→	UC	RE	TX	VS
		•			Clear Creek-Gelpin Abstract & Title Corp	303-569-2391		•		
•	•	•	•	•	Colorado Records Search Inc [SOP]	800-645-7712	•	•	•	•
					Documents 5280	303-438-8967	•	•	•	
•	•	•	•	•	Independent Research LLC	303-969-8608	•	•	•	•
•	•				McCormick Detective Agency [SOP]	970-453-6378	•	•	•	
•	•		•		RIQ and Associates Inc	720-529-5736	•	•	•	•
•	•	•	•	•	Search Company International [SOP]	800-727-2120	•	•	•	

CR	CV	PR	US	BK	←Courts	Conejos	Recorder→	UC	RE	TX	VS
•	•	•	•	•	Independent Research LLC		303-969-8608	•	•	•	•

CR	CV	PR	US	BK	←Courts	Costilla	Recorder→	UC	RE	TX	VS
•	•	•	•	•	Independent Research LLC		303-969-8608	•	•	•	•

CR	CV	PR	US	BK	←Courts	Crowley	Recorder→	UC	RE	TX	VS
•	•	•	•	•	Independent Research LLC		303-969-8608	•	•	•	•

CR	CV	PR	US	BK	←Courts	Custer	Recorder→	UC	RE	TX	VS
•	•	•	•	•	Independent Research LLC		303-969-8608	•	•	•	•
•	•		•		RIQ and Associates Inc		720-529-5736	•	•	•	•
					Security Title Canon City		800-526-7805		•		

CR	CV	PR	US	BK	←Courts	Delta	Recorder→	UC	RE	TX	VS
•	•	•	•	•	Colorado Records Search Inc [SOP]		800-645-7712	•	•	•	•
					Comparable Sales Research		970-249-2118	•	•	•	
					First American Title Co (Colorado)		970-874-8286	•	•	•	
•	•	•			Grand Valley Associates [SOP]		970-256-9300	•	•	•	
•	•	•	•	•	Independent Research LLC		303-969-8608	•	•	•	•
•	•	•	•	•	Search Company International [SOP]		800-727-2120	•	•	•	

CR	CV	PR	US	BK	←Courts	Denver	Recorder→	UC	RE	TX	VS
•	•		•	•	ABA Services		720-344-1259	•	•	•	
•	•	•	•	•	Access Information		800-827-7607	•	•	•	•
•	•	•	•	•	Centennial Coverages Inc (Colorado)		800-338-8221	•	•	•	•
•	•	•	•	•	Colorado Records Search Inc [SOP]		800-645-7712	•	•	•	•
	•				Colorado Records Sooner		303-494-2132	•	•	•	
•	•	•	•	•	Condello Associates, Accusearch [SOP]		888-756-9687	•	•	•	•
•	•	•	•		Kathleen Demmitt		303-781-0605, Fax- same				•
					Documents 5280		303-438-8967	•	•	•	
•	•	•	•	•	Gryder Express Tracking Service Inc		561-535-1495, cell- 561-584 2079	•	•	•	•
•	•	•	•	•	Barbara K Henritze		303-499-3750	•	•	•	•
•					HR Plus		800-332-7587				
•	•	•	•	•	Independent Research LLC		303-969-8608	•	•	•	•
•	•	•	•	•	Milestone Legal Support [SOP]		800-317-9221	•	•	•	•
				•	NACM/Colorado		800-451-7868	•			
•	•	•	•	•	Peregrine Investigation & Research [SOP]		303-324-7442	•	•	•	•
•	•	•	•	•	R A Heales & Associates Ltd		800-225-7043	•	•	•	•
					Records Quest		303-369-0693	•	•	•	•
•	•		•		RIQ and Associates Inc		720-529-5736	•	•	•	•
•	•	•	•	•	Search and Retrieve		303-587-7852	•	•	•	•
•	•	•	•	•	Search Company International [SOP]		800-727-2120	•	•	•	
					Title Company of Denver		303-369-5443		•	•	
•	•	•	•	•	Wolz Corporate USA		303-655-9659	•		•	

CR	CV	PR	US	BK	←Courts	Dolores	Recorder→	UC	RE	TX	VS
•	•	•	•	•	Independent Research LLC		303-969-8608	•	•	•	•
					Montezuma-Dolores Title Co		970-565-8491	•	•	•	

CR	CV	PR	US	BK	←Courts	Douglas	Recorder→	UC	RE	TX	VS
•	•		•	•	ABA Services		720-344-1259	•	•	•	
•	•	•	•	•	Access Information		800-827-7607	•	•	•	•
•	•	•	•	•	Centennial Coverages Inc (Colorado)		800-338-8221	•	•	•	•
•	•	•	•	•	Colorado Records Search Inc [SOP]		800-645-7712	•	•	•	•
	•				Colorado Records Sooner		303-494-2132	•	•	•	
					Documents 5280		303-438-8967	•	•	•	
•	•	•	•	•	Independent Research LLC		303-969-8608	•	•	•	•
•	•	•	•	•	Peregrine Investigation & Research [SOP]		303-324-7442	•	•	•	•
•	•	•	•	•	R A Heales & Associates Ltd		800-225-7043	•	•	•	•

CR	CV	PR	US	BK	←Courts	Recorder→	UC	RE	TX	VS
					Records Quest	303-369-0693	•	•	•	•
•	•		•		RIQ and Associates Inc	720-529-5736	•	•	•	•
•	•	•	•	•	Search and Retrieve	303-587-7852	•	•	•	•
•	•	•	•	•	Search Company International [SOP]	800-727-2120	•	•	•	
					Title Company of Denver	303-369-5443		•	•	

Eagle

CR	CV	PR	US	BK	←Courts	Recorder→	UC	RE	TX	VS
•	•	•	•	•	Colorado Records Search Inc [SOP]	800-645-7712	•	•	•	•
•	•	•	•	•	Eagle Process Servers [SOP]	970-331-7712	•	•	•	•
•	•	•	•	•	Independent Research LLC	303-969-8608	•	•	•	•
•	•		•		RIQ and Associates Inc	720-529-5736	•	•	•	•
•	•	•	•	•	Search Company International [SOP]	800-727-2120	•	•	•	

El Paso

CR	CV	PR	US	BK	←Courts	Recorder→	UC	RE	TX	VS
•	•	•	•	•	Centennial Coverages Inc (Colorado)	800-338-8221	•	•	•	•
•	•	•	•	•	Colorado Records Search Inc [SOP]	800-645-7712	•	•	•	•
	•				Colorado Records Sooner	303-494-2132	•	•	•	
					Documents 5280	303-438-8967	•	•	•	
•	•	•	•	•	Independent Research LLC	303-969-8608	•	•	•	•
•	•	•			Legal Express [SOP]	719-578-0407		•	•	•
•					PreSearch Background Services	719-533-1880				
•	•	•		•	R A Heales & Associates Ltd	800-225-7043		•	•	•
					Records Quest	303-369-0693	•	•	•	•
•	•		•		RIQ and Associates Inc	720-529-5736	•	•	•	•
•	•	•	•	•	Search Company International [SOP]	800-727-2120	•	•	•	
					Title Company of Denver	303-369-5443		•	•	

Elbert

CR	CV	PR	US	BK	←Courts	Recorder→	UC	RE	TX	VS
•	•	•	•	•	Centennial Coverages Inc (Colorado)	800-338-8221	•	•	•	•
•	•	•	•	•	Colorado Records Search Inc [SOP]	800-645-7712	•	•	•	•
					Documents 5280	303-438-8967	•	•	•	
•	•	•	•	•	Independent Research LLC	303-969-8608	•	•	•	•
•	•		•		RIQ and Associates Inc	720-529-5736	•	•	•	•
•	•	•	•	•	Search Company International [SOP]	800-727-2120	•	•	•	
					Title Company of Denver	303-369-5443		•	•	

Fremont

CR	CV	PR	US	BK	←Courts	Recorder→	UC	RE	TX	VS
•	•	•	•	•	Colorado Records Search Inc [SOP]	800-645-7712	•	•	•	•
•	•	•	•	•	Independent Research LLC	303-969-8608	•	•	•	•
•	•		•		RIQ and Associates Inc	720-529-5736	•	•	•	•
•	•	•	•	•	Search Company International [SOP]	800-727-2120	•	•	•	
					Security Title Canon City	800-526-7805		•		

Garfield

CR	CV	PR	US	BK	←Courts	Recorder→	UC	RE	TX	VS
•	•	•	•	•	Colorado Records Search Inc [SOP]	800-645-7712	•	•	•	•
•	•	•			Grand Valley Associates [SOP]	970-256-9300	•	•	•	
•	•		•	•	Independent Research LLC	303-969-8608	•	•	•	•
•	•	•	•		Search Company International [SOP]	800-727-2120	•	•	•	

Gilpin

CR	CV	PR	US	BK	←Courts	Recorder→	UC	RE	TX	VS
		•			Clear Creek-Gelpin Abstract & Title Corp	303-569-2391		•		
•	•	•	•		Colorado Records Search Inc [SOP]	800-645-7712	•	•	•	•
					Documents 5280	303-438-8967	•	•	•	
•	•	•	•		Independent Research LLC	303-969-8608	•	•	•	•
•	•		•		RIQ and Associates Inc	720-529-5736	•	•	•	•
•	•	•	•		Search Company International [SOP]	800-727-2120	•	•	•	

Grand

CR	CV	PR	US	BK	←Courts	Recorder→	UC	RE	TX	VS
	•				Colorado Records Sooner	303-494-2132	•	•	•	
•	•	•	•	•	Independent Research LLC	303-969-8608	•	•	•	•

CR	CV	PR	US	BK	←Courts	**Gunnison**	Recorder→	UC	RE	TX	VS
•	•	•	•	•	Colorado Records Search Inc [SOP]		800-645-7712	•	•	•	•
					First Gunnison Title & Escrow		800-530-9598		•	•	
•	•	•	•	•	Independent Research LLC		303-969-8608	•	•	•	•

CR	CV	PR	US	BK	←Courts	**Hinsdale**	Recorder→	UC	RE	TX	VS
					First Gunnison Title & Escrow		800-530-9598		•	•	
		•			Hinsdale Title Co		970-944-2614		•	•	
•	•	•	•	•	Independent Research LLC		303-969-8608	•	•	•	•

CR	CV	PR	US	BK	←Courts	**Huerfano**	Recorder→	UC	RE	TX	VS
					Dotter Abstract & Associates		719-738-1730	•	•	•	•
•	•	•	•	•	Independent Research LLC		303-969-8608	•	•	•	•

CR	CV	PR	US	BK	←Courts	**Jackson**	Recorder→	UC	RE	TX	VS
•	•	•	•	•	Independent Research LLC		303-969-8608	•	•	•	•

CR	CV	PR	US	BK	←Courts	**Jefferson**	Recorder→	UC	RE	TX	VS
•	•		•	•	ABA Services		720-344-1259	•	•	•	
•	•	•	•	•	Access Information		800-827-7607	•	•	•	•
•	•	•	•	•	Centennial Coverages Inc (Colorado)		800-338-8221	•	•	•	•
•	•	•	•	•	Colorado Records Search Inc [SOP]		800-645-7712	•	•	•	•
	•				Colorado Records Sooner		303-494-2132	•	•	•	
•	•	•	•	•	Condello Associates, Accusearch [SOP]		888-756-9687	•	•	•	•
					Documents 5280		303-438-8967	•	•	•	
•	•	•	•	•	Barbara K Henritze		303-499-3750	•	•	•	•
•	•	•	•	•	Independent Research LLC		303-969-8608	•	•	•	•
•	•	•	•	•	Peregrine Investigation & Research [SOP]		303-324-7442	•	•	•	•
•	•	•	•	•	R A Heales & Associates Ltd		800-225-7043	•	•	•	•
					Records Quest		303-369-0693	•	•	•	•
•	•		•		RIQ and Associates Inc		720-529-5736	•	•	•	•
•	•	•	•	•	Search and Retrieve		303-587-7852	•	•	•	•
•	•	•	•	•	Search Company International [SOP]		800-727-2120	•	•	•	
					Title Company of Denver		303-369-5443		•	•	
•	•	•	•	•	Wolz Corporate USA		303-655-9659	•		•	

CR	CV	PR	US	BK	←Courts	**Kiowa**	Recorder→	UC	RE	TX	VS
•	•	•	•	•	Independent Research LLC		303-969-8608	•	•	•	•
		•			Kiowa County Abstract Co		719-438-5811		•	•	•

CR	CV	PR	US	BK	←Courts	**Kit Carson**	Recorder→	UC	RE	TX	VS
•	•	•	•	•	Independent Research LLC		303-969-8608	•	•	•	•

CR	CV	PR	US	BK	←Courts	**La Plata**	Recorder→	UC	RE	TX	VS
•	•				Attorney Service New Mexico [SOP]		505-326-7486				
•	•	•	•	•	Colorado Records Search Inc [SOP]		800-645-7712	•	•	•	•
•	•	•			Finney Land Co		970-259-5691	•	•	•	•
•	•	•	•	•	Independent Research LLC		303-969-8608	•	•	•	•
					Information Services (Colorado)		970-385-4897	•	•	•	•

CR	CV	PR	US	BK	←Courts	**Lake**	Recorder→	UC	RE	TX	VS
•	•	•	•	•	Independent Research LLC		303-969-8608	•	•	•	•
•	•				McCormick Detective Agency [SOP]		970-453-6378	•	•	•	
		•			Stewart Title Co		719-486-2688	•	•	•	•

CR	CV	PR	US	BK	←Courts	**Larimer**	Recorder→	UC	RE	TX	VS
•	•	•	•	•	Alpha-Omega Investigations [SOP]		866-510-8200	•	•	•	•
	•				Lyndalee Berger		970-669-7691		•	•	
•	•	•	•	•	Centennial Coverages Inc (Colorado)		800-338-8221	•	•	•	•
•	•	•	•	•	Colorado Records Search Inc [SOP]		800-645-7712	•	•	•	•
	•				Colorado Records Sooner		303-494-2132	•	•	•	

CR	CV	PR	US	BK	←Courts	Recorder→	UC	RE	TX	VS
•	•	•	•	•	Condello Associates, Accusearch [SOP]	888-756-9687	•	•	•	•
					Documents 5280	303-438-8967	•	•	•	
•					HR Plus	800-332-7587				
•	•	•	•	•	Independent Research LLC	303-969-8608	•	•	•	•
	•	•	•	•	Daniel E Peel	970-377-8500	•	•	•	
					Records Quest	303-369-0693	•	•	•	•
•	•		•		RIQ and Associates Inc	720-529-5736	•	•	•	•
•	•	•	•	•	Search Company International [SOP]	800-727-2120	•	•	•	
•	•	•	•	•	The Berkana Firm LLC [SOP]	970-669-2179	•	•	•	•
•	•	•	•	•	The Paper Chase - CO [SOP]	970-350-1008	•	•	•	•
					Title Company of Denver	303-369-5443		•	•	

CR	CV	PR	US	BK	←Courts **Las Animas**	Recorder→	UC	RE	TX	VS
•	•	•	•	•	Colorado Records Search Inc [SOP]	800-645-7712	•	•	•	•
					Dotter Abstract & Associates	719-738-1730	•	•	•	•
•	•	•	•	•	Independent Research LLC	303-969-8608	•	•	•	•

CR	CV	PR	US	BK	←Courts **Lincoln**	Recorder→	UC	RE	TX	VS
	•				Hedlund Abstract	719-743-2353	•	•	•	
•	•	•	•	•	Independent Research LLC	303-969-8608	•	•	•	•

CR	CV	PR	US	BK	←Courts **Logan**	Recorder→	UC	RE	TX	VS
•	•	•	•	•	Independent Research LLC	303-969-8608	•	•	•	•
•	•				Northeast Colorado Title Co LLC	970-522-7130	•	•	•	

CR	CV	PR	US	BK	←Courts **Mesa**	Recorder→	UC	RE	TX	VS
•	•	•	•	•	Colorado Records Search Inc [SOP]	800-645-7712	•	•	•	•
•	•	•			Grand Valley Associates [SOP]	970-256-9300	•	•	•	
•	•	•	•	•	Independent Research LLC	303-969-8608	•	•	•	•
					Information Services (Colorado)	970-385-4897	•	•	•	•
					Records Quest	303-369-0693	•	•	•	•
•	•	•	•	•	Records Research of Mesa County [SOP]	866-321-6611	•	•	•	•
•	•	•	•	•	Search Company International [SOP]	800-727-2120	•	•	•	

CR	CV	PR	US	BK	←Courts **Mineral**	Recorder→	UC	RE	TX	VS
•	•	•	•	•	Independent Research LLC	303-969-8608	•	•	•	•
					Rio Grande Mineral Title	719-657-3366	•	•	•	

CR	CV	PR	US	BK	←Courts **Moffat**	Recorder→	UC	RE	TX	VS
•	•	•	•	•	Independent Research LLC	303-969-8608	•	•	•	•
					Quality Research Service Inc	970-824-4144, cell- 970-629-0388	•	•	•	

CR	CV	PR	US	BK	←Courts **Montezuma**	Recorder→	UC	RE	TX	VS
•	•				Attorney Service New Mexico [SOP]	505-326-7486				
•	•	•	•	•	Colorado Records Search Inc [SOP]	800-645-7712	•	•	•	•
•	•	•			Finney Land Co	970-259-5691	•	•	•	•
•	•	•	•	•	Independent Research LLC	303-969-8608	•	•	•	•
					Montezuma-Dolores Title Co	970-565-8491	•	•	•	

CR	CV	PR	US	BK	←Courts **Montrose**	Recorder→	UC	RE	TX	VS
•	•	•	•	•	Colorado Records Search Inc [SOP]	800-645-7712	•	•	•	•
					Comparable Sales Research	970-249-2118	•	•	•	
					First American Title Co (Colorado)	970-874-8286	•	•	•	
•	•	•			Grand Valley Associates [SOP]	970-256-9300	•	•	•	
•	•	•	•	•	Independent Research LLC	303-969-8608	•	•	•	•

CR	CV	PR	US	BK	←Courts **Morgan**	Recorder→	UC	RE	TX	VS
•	•	•	•	•	Colorado Records Search Inc [SOP]	800-645-7712	•	•	•	•
					Documents 5280	303-438-8967	•	•	•	
•	•	•	•	•	Independent Research LLC	303-969-8608	•	•	•	•
•	•		•		RIQ and Associates Inc	720-529-5736	•	•	•	•

CR	CV	PR	US	BK	←Courts	**OTERO**	Recorder→	UC	RE	TX	VS
•	•	•	•	•	Independent Research LLC		303-969-8608	•	•	•	•

CR	CV	PR	US	BK	←Courts	**OURAY**	Recorder→	UC	RE	TX	VS
•	•	•	•	•	Colorado Records Search Inc [SOP]		800-645-7712	•	•	•	•
					Comparable Sales Research		970-249-2118	•	•	•	
					First American Title Co (Colorado)		970-874-8286	•	•	•	
•	•	•	•	•	Independent Research LLC		303-969-8608	•	•	•	•

CR	CV	PR	US	BK	←Courts	**PARK**	Recorder→	UC	RE	TX	VS
•	•	•	•	•	Colorado Records Search Inc [SOP]		800-645-7712	•	•	•	•
•	•	•	•	•	Independent Research LLC		303-969-8608	•	•	•	•
•	•				McCormick Detective Agency [SOP]		970-453-6378	•	•	•	
•	•		•		RIQ and Associates Inc		720-529-5736	•	•	•	•

CR	CV	PR	US	BK	←Courts	**PHILLIPS**	Recorder→	UC	RE	TX	VS
•	•	•	•	•	Independent Research LLC		303-969-8608	•	•	•	•

CR	CV	PR	US	BK	←Courts	**PITKIN**	Recorder→	UC	RE	TX	VS
•	•	•	•	•	Colorado Records Search Inc [SOP]		800-645-7712	•	•	•	•
•	•	•	•	•	Independent Research LLC		303-969-8608	•	•	•	•
					Land Title Guarantee Co		970-925-1678	•	•	•	•

CR	CV	PR	US	BK	←Courts	**PROWERS**	Recorder→	UC	RE	TX	VS
					Bent County Abstract & Title		719-456-0381		•		
		•			Guaranty Abstract Co (Colorado)		719-336-3261	•	•	•	
•	•	•	•	•	Independent Research LLC		303-969-8608	•	•	•	•

CR	CV	PR	US	BK	←Courts	**PUEBLO**	Recorder→	UC	RE	TX	VS
•	•	•	•	•	Colorado Records Search Inc [SOP]		800-645-7712	•	•	•	•
•	•	•	•	•	Independent Research LLC		303-969-8608	•	•	•	•
•	•		•		RIQ and Associates Inc		720-529-5736	•	•	•	•
•	•	•	•	•	Search Company International [SOP]		800-727-2120	•	•	•	

CR	CV	PR	US	BK	←Courts	**RIO BLANCO**	Recorder→	UC	RE	TX	VS
•	•	•	•	•	Independent Research LLC		303-969-8608	•	•	•	•
					Quality Research Service Inc		970-824-4144, cell- 970-629-0388	•	•	•	

CR	CV	PR	US	BK	←Courts	**RIO GRANDE**	Recorder→	UC	RE	TX	VS
•	•	•	•	•	Colorado Records Search Inc [SOP]		800-645-7712	•	•	•	•
•	•	•	•	•	Independent Research LLC		303-969-8608	•	•	•	•
					Rio Grande Mineral Title		719-657-3366	•	•	•	

CR	CV	PR	US	BK	←Courts	**ROUTT**	Recorder→	UC	RE	TX	VS
•	•	•	•	•	Colorado Records Search Inc [SOP]		800-645-7712	•	•	•	•
•	•	•	•	•	Independent Research LLC		303-969-8608	•	•	•	•
					Quality Research Service Inc		970-824-4144, cell- 970-629-0388	•	•	•	

CR	CV	PR	US	BK	←Courts	**SAGUACHE**	Recorder→	UC	RE	TX	VS
•	•	•	•	•	Independent Research LLC		303-969-8608	•	•	•	•
					Saguache County Abstract & Investment		719-655-2611		•	•	

CR	CV	PR	US	BK	←Courts	**SAN JUAN**	Recorder→	UC	RE	TX	VS
•	•	•	•	•	Independent Research LLC		303-969-8608	•	•	•	•

CR	CV	PR	US	BK	←Courts	**SAN MIGUEL**	Recorder→	UC	RE	TX	VS
•	•	•	•	•	Colorado Records Search Inc [SOP]		800-645-7712	•	•	•	•
•	•	•	•	•	Independent Research LLC		303-969-8608	•	•	•	•

CR	CV	PR	US	BK	←Courts	**SEDGWICK**	Recorder→	UC	RE	TX	VS
•	•	•	•	•	Independent Research LLC		303-969-8608	•	•	•	•
					Sedgwick County Title Co		970-474-2696	•	•	•	

CR	CV	PR	US	BK	←COURTS	SUMMIT	RECORDER→	UC	RE	TX	VS
•	•	•	•	•	Colorado Records Search Inc [SOP]		800-645-7712	•	•	•	•
•	•	•	•	•	Independent Research LLC		303-969-8608	•	•	•	•
•	•				McCormick Detective Agency [SOP]		970-453-6378	•	•	•	
•	•		•		RIQ and Associates Inc		720-529-5736	•	•	•	•

CR	CV	PR	US	BK	←COURTS	TELLER	RECORDER→	UC	RE	TX	VS
•	•	•	•	•	Colorado Records Search Inc [SOP]		800-645-7712	•	•	•	•
•	•	•	•	•	Independent Research LLC		303-969-8608	•	•	•	•
•	•	•			Legal Express [SOP]		719-578-0407		•	•	•
•	•		•		RIQ and Associates Inc		720-529-5736	•	•	•	•
•	•	•	•	•	Search Company International [SOP]		800-727-2120	•	•	•	

CR	CV	PR	US	BK	←COURTS	WASHINGTON	RECORDER→	UC	RE	TX	VS
•	•	•	•	•	Independent Research LLC		303-969-8608	•	•	•	•
					Washington County Title Co		970-345-2256	•		•	

CR	CV	PR	US	BK	←COURTS	WELD	RECORDER→	UC	RE	TX	VS
•	•	•	•	•	Alpha-Omega Investigations [SOP]		866-510-8200	•	•	•	•
	•				Lyndalee Berger		970-669-7691		•	•	
•	•	•	•	•	Colorado Records Search Inc [SOP]		800-645-7712	•	•	•	•
	•				Colorado Records Sooner		303-494-2132	•	•	•	
•	•	•	•	•	Condello Associates, Accusearch [SOP]		888-756-9687	•	•	•	•
					Documents 5280		303-438-8967	•	•	•	
•	•	•	•	•	Independent Research LLC		303-969-8608	•	•	•	•
	•	•	•	•	Daniel E Peel		970-377-8500	•	•	•	•
•	•	•	•	•	Peregrine Investigation & Research [SOP]		303-324-7442	•	•	•	•
					Records Quest		303-369-0693	•	•	•	•
•	•		•		RIQ and Associates Inc		720-529-5736	•	•	•	•
•	•	•	•	•	Search Company International [SOP]		800-727-2120	•	•	•	•
•	•	•	•	•	The Berkana Firm LLC [SOP]		970-669-2179	•	•	•	•
•	•	•	•	•	The Paper Chase - CO [SOP]		970-350-1008	•	•	•	•
					Title Company of Denver		303-369-5443		•	•	

CR	CV	PR	US	BK	←COURTS	YUMA	RECORDER→	UC	RE	TX	VS
•	•	•	•	•	Independent Research LLC		303-969-8608	•	•	•	•

COURT RECORDS

CODE	GOVERNMENT AGENCY	TYPE OF INFORMATION
CR	Criminal Court	Municipal, county and state level criminal cases
CV	Civil Court	Municipal, county and state level civil cases
PR	Probate Court	Wills and estate cases
US	US District Court	Federal civil and criminal cases
BK	Bankruptcy Court	United States bankruptcy cases

COUNTY RECORDS - RECORDINGS

CODE	GOVERNMENT AGENCY	TYPE OF INFORMATION
UC	UCC Filing Office	Uniform Commercial Code and other personal property liens
RE	Real Estate Recording Office	Real property transactions and liens
TX	Tax Filing Office(s)	Federal and state tax liens, judgment liens
VS	Vital Records Office	Vital statistics—birth, death, marriage, divorce

Connecticut

…has 8 counties and 169 towns/cities. There is no county recording in Connecticut, all recording is done at the town/city level. The recording officer is the Town/City Clerk. Be careful not to confuse searching in the following towns/cities that each bear the same name as a county as equivalent to a countywide search for recorded documents: Fairfield, Hartford, Litchfield, New Haven, New London, Tolland, Windham.

COURT RECORDS RETRIEVED — CAPITAL - HARTFORD COUNTY — RECORDED RECORDS RETRIEVED

CR	CV	PR	US	BK	←COURTS FAIRFIELD	RECORDER→	UC	RE	TX	VS
•	•	•	•	•	🏛ATT Loss Prevention Inc	877-556-9613	•	•	•	•
					BSG Connecticut Search, LLC	203-758-2493	•	•	•	
					CIBMS	800-922-0002		•	•	
•	•		•	•	🏛CN Search LLC	860-349-3772	•	•	•	
•	•	•	•	•	🏛Connecticut Investigative Services	888-676-1472	•	•	•	•
•	•	•	•	•	Data Reporting Corp [SOP]	800-570-7750	•	•	•	
•	•	•			Genealogical Researcher	860-365-0580		•	•	•
•	•	•	•	•	🏛Information Management Systems Inc [SOP]	888-403-8347	•	•	•	•
•	•	•	•	•	🏛Lutek Investigations LLC [SOP]	860-729-3310	•	•	•	•
•	•	•	•	•	🏛National Research Associates Inc	860-529-3006	•	•	•	•
	•	•	•	•	🏛New England Abstract LLC	203-430-7712	•	•	•	•
					Pro Search Inc	203-348-6994	•	•	•	
•	•	•	•	•	🏛The Docket Clerk LLC	866-758-2683	•	•	•	•
•	•	•	•	•	TJM & Associates	800-749-4254	•	•	•	•

CR	CV	PR	US	BK	←COURTS HARTFORD	RECORDER→	UC	RE	TX	VS
					🏛Advanced Title Co LLC	203-634-0721	•	•	•	
•	•	•	•	•	🏛ATT Loss Prevention Inc	877-556-9613	•	•	•	•
					BSG Connecticut Search, LLC	203-758-2493	•	•	•	
					CIBMS	800-922-0002		•	•	
•	•		•	•	🏛CN Search LLC	860-349-3772	•	•	•	
•	•	•	•	•	Data Reporting Corp [SOP]	800-570-7750	•	•	•	
•	•	•			Genealogical Researcher	860-365-0580		•	•	•
•	•	•	•	•	🏛Information Management Systems Inc [SOP]	888-403-8347	•	•	•	•
•	•	•	•	•	🏛Lutek Investigations LLC [SOP]	860-729-3310	•	•	•	•
•	•	•	•	•	🏛National Research Associates Inc	860-529-3006	•	•	•	•
	•	•	•	•	🏛New England Abstract LLC	203-430-7712	•	•	•	•
•	•	•	•	•	🏛The Docket Clerk LLC	866-758-2683	•	•	•	•
•	•	•	•	•	TJM & Associates	800-749-4254	•	•	•	•

CR	CV	PR	US	BK	←COURTS LITCHFIELD	RECORDER→	UC	RE	TX	VS
•	•	•	•	•	🏛ATT Loss Prevention Inc	877-556-9613	•	•	•	•
					BSG Connecticut Search, LLC	203-758-2493	•	•	•	
					CIBMS	800-922-0002		•	•	
•	•		•	•	🏛CN Search LLC	860-349-3772	•	•	•	
•	•	•	•	•	Data Reporting Corp [SOP]	800-570-7750	•	•	•	
•	•	•			Genealogical Researcher	860-365-0580		•	•	•
•	•	•	•	•	🏛Information Management Systems Inc [SOP]	888-403-8347	•	•	•	•
•	•	•	•	•	🏛Lutek Investigations LLC [SOP]	860-729-3310	•	•	•	•
•	•	•	•	•	🏛National Research Associates Inc	860-529-3006	•	•	•	•
	•	•	•	•	🏛New England Abstract LLC	203-430-7712	•	•	•	•
•	•	•	•	•	🏛The Docket Clerk LLC	866-758-2683	•	•	•	•
•	•	•	•	•	TJM & Associates	800-749-4254	•	•	•	•

CR	CV	PR	US	BK	←COURTS MIDDLESEX	RECORDER→	UC	RE	TX	VS
					🏛Advanced Title Co LLC	203-634-0721	•	•	•	
•	•	•	•	•	🏛ATT Loss Prevention Inc	877-556-9613	•	•	•	•
					CIBMS	800-922-0002		•	•	
•	•		•	•	🏛CN Search LLC	860-349-3772	•	•	•	

CR	CV	PR	US	BK	←Courts	Recorder→	UC	RE	TX	VS
•	•	•	•	•	Data Reporting Corp [SOP]	800-570-7750	•	•	•	
•	•	•			Genealogical Researcher	860-365-0580		•	•	•
•	•	•	•	•	Information Management Systems Inc [SOP]	888-403-8347	•	•	•	•
•	•	•	•	•	Lutek Investigations LLC [SOP]	860-729-3310	•	•	•	•
•	•	•	•	•	National Research Associates Inc	860-529-3006	•	•	•	•
	•	•	•	•	New England Abstract LLC	203-430-7712	•	•	•	•
	•	•			Valerie Shickel	860-767-2269	•	•	•	•
•	•	•	•	•	The Docket Clerk LLC	866-758-2683	•	•	•	•
•	•	•	•	•	TJM & Associates	800-749-4254	•	•	•	•

CR	CV	PR	US	BK	←Courts **New Haven**	Recorder→	UC	RE	TX	VS
					Advanced Title Co LLC	203-634-0721	•	•	•	
•	•	•	•	•	ATT Loss Prevention Inc	877-556-9613	•	•	•	•
					BSG Connecticut Search, LLC	203-758-2493	•	•	•	
					CIBMS	800-922-0002		•	•	
•	•		•	•	CN Search LLC	860-349-3772	•	•	•	
•	•	•	•	•	Connecticut Investigative Services	888-676-1472	•	•	•	•
•	•	•	•	•	Data Reporting Corp [SOP]	800-570-7750	•	•	•	
•	•	•			Genealogical Researcher	860-365-0580		•	•	•
•	•	•	•	•	Information Management Systems Inc [SOP]	888-403-8347	•	•	•	•
•	•	•	•	•	Lutek Investigations LLC [SOP]	860-729-3310	•	•	•	•
•	•	•	•	•	National Research Associates Inc	860-529-3006	•	•	•	•
	•	•	•	•	New England Abstract LLC	203-430-7712	•	•	•	•
	•	•			Valerie Shickel	860-767-2269	•	•	•	•
•	•	•	•	•	The Docket Clerk LLC	866-758-2683	•	•	•	•
•	•	•	•	•	TJM & Associates	800-749-4254	•	•	•	•

CR	CV	PR	US	BK	←Courts **New London**	Recorder→	UC	RE	TX	VS
•	•	•	•	•	ATT Loss Prevention Inc	877-556-9613	•	•	•	•
					CIBMS	800-922-0002		•	•	
•	•		•	•	CN Search LLC	860-349-3772	•	•	•	
•	•	•	•	•	Data Reporting Corp [SOP]	800-570-7750	•	•	•	
•	•	•			Genealogical Researcher	860-365-0580		•	•	•
•	•	•	•	•	Information Management Systems Inc [SOP]	888-403-8347	•	•	•	•
•	•	•	•	•	Lutek Investigations LLC [SOP]	860-729-3310	•	•	•	•
•	•	•	•	•	National Research Associates Inc	860-529-3006	•	•	•	•
	•	•			Valerie Shickel	860-767-2269	•	•	•	•
•	•	•	•	•	The Docket Clerk LLC	866-758-2683	•	•	•	•

CR	CV	PR	US	BK	←Courts **Tolland**	Recorder→	UC	RE	TX	VS
•	•	•	•	•	ATT Loss Prevention Inc	877-556-9613	•	•	•	•
					CIBMS	800-922-0002		•	•	
•	•		•	•	CN Search LLC	860-349-3772	•	•	•	
•	•	•	•	•	Data Reporting Corp [SOP]	800-570-7750	•	•	•	
•	•	•			Genealogical Researcher	860-365-0580		•	•	•
•	•	•	•	•	Information Management Systems Inc [SOP]	888-403-8347	•	•	•	•
•	•	•	•	•	Lutek Investigations LLC [SOP]	860-729-3310	•	•	•	•
•	•	•	•	•	National Research Associates Inc	860-529-3006	•	•	•	•
•	•	•	•	•	The Docket Clerk LLC	866-758-2683	•	•	•	•

CR	CV	PR	US	BK	←Courts **Windham**	Recorder→	UC	RE	TX	VS
•	•	•	•	•	ATT Loss Prevention Inc	877-556-9613	•	•	•	•
					CIBMS	800-922-0002		•	•	
•	•		•	•	CN Search LLC	860-349-3772	•	•	•	
•	•	•	•	•	Data Reporting Corp [SOP]	800-570-7750	•	•	•	
•	•	•			Genealogical Researcher	860-365-0580		•	•	•
•	•	•	•	•	Information Management Systems Inc [SOP]	888-403-8347	•	•	•	•
•	•	•	•	•	Lutek Investigations LLC [SOP]	860-729-3310	•	•	•	•
•	•	•	•	•	National Research Associates Inc	860-529-3006	•	•	•	•
•	•	•	•	•	The Docket Clerk LLC	866-758-2683	•	•	•	•

Delaware

COURT RECORDS RETRIEVED — CAPITAL - KENT COUNTY — RECORDED RECORDS RETRIEVED

CR	CV	PR	US	BK	←COURTS KENT	RECORDER→	UC	RE	TX	VS
•	•		•	•	Accufax: Authentic Document Retrieval	800-336-1001	•	•	•	•
•	•		•	•	Blue Marble Logistics LLC [SOP]	302-661-4390	•	•	•	
•	•				CorpAmerica Inc - Corp. Service Co	888-736-4300	•	•	•	
•	•	•	•	•	CSC - Corporation Service Company [SOP]	800-927-9800	•	•	•	•
•	•	•	•	•	DDR (Delaware Document Retrieval) [SOP]	800-343-1742	•	•	•	
•	•		•	•	Delaware Attorney Services [SOP]	800-457-9560	•	•	•	•
•	•	•	•	•	Hylind Search Company Inc (Delaware) [SOP]	888-243-6857	•	•	•	•
	•		•	•	Incorporating Services Ltd	800-346-4646	•	•	•	•
•	•		•	•	InfoRetrieval Services [SOP]	302-337-0548				
•	•		•		Know It All Background Research Services Inc	888-281-9535				
•	•				Legal Research Services	302-672-9411	•	•	•	•
•	•		•	•	National Background Investigations Inc	800-798-0079			•	
	•		•	•	National Corporate Research Ltd	800-483-1140	•	•	•	
•	•		•	•	Research Specialists Inc	610-358-2507 or 724-5353	•		•	

CR	CV	PR	US	BK	←COURTS NEW CASTLE	RECORDER→	UC	RE	TX	VS
•	•		•	•	Accufax: Authentic Document Retrieval	800-336-1001	•	•	•	•
•	•	•	•	•	Assured Inquiries LLC [SOP]	888-644-0004		•		
•	•		•	•	Blue Marble Logistics LLC [SOP]	302-661-4390	•	•	•	
•	•				CorpAmerica Inc - Corp. Service Co	888-736-4300	•	•	•	
•	•	•	•	•	DDR (Delaware Document Retrieval) [SOP]	800-343-1742	•	•	•	
•	•		•	•	Delaware Attorney Services [SOP]	800-457-9560	•	•	•	•
•	•	•	•	•	Hylind Search Company Inc (Delaware) [SOP]	888-243-6857	•	•	•	•
	•		•	•	Incorporating Services Ltd	800-346-4646	•	•	•	•
•	•		•	•	InfoRetrieval Services [SOP]	302-337-0548				
•	•		•		Know It All Background Research Services Inc	888-281-9535				
•	•	•	•	•	Legal Beagles Inc [SOP]	800-743-9897	•	•	•	•
•	•				Legal Research Services	302-672-9411	•	•	•	•
•	•		•	•	National Background Investigations Inc	800-798-0079			•	
•	•		•	•	Research Specialists Inc	610-358-2507 or 724-5353	•		•	
	•		•	•	Security Search & Abstract Co Inc	800-345-9494	•	•	•	
•	•		•	•	TriState Courier [SOP]	800-783-0945	•	•	•	

CR	CV	PR	US	BK	←COURTS SUSSEX	RECORDER→	UC	RE	TX	VS
•	•		•	•	Accufax: Authentic Document Retrieval	800-336-1001	•	•	•	•
•	•				CorpAmerica Inc - Corp. Service Co	888-736-4300	•	•	•	
•	•	•	•	•	CSC - Corporation Service Company [SOP]	800-927-9800	•	•	•	•
•	•	•	•	•	DDR (Delaware Document Retrieval) [SOP]	800-343-1742	•	•	•	
•	•		•	•	Delaware Attorney Services [SOP]	800-457-9560	•	•	•	•
•	•	•	•	•	Hylind Search Company Inc (Delaware) [SOP]	888-243-6857	•	•	•	•
	•		•	•	Incorporating Services Ltd	800-346-4646	•	•	•	•
•	•		•	•	InfoRetrieval Services [SOP]	302-337-0548				
•	•		•		Know It All Background Research Services Inc	888-281-9535				
•	•				Legal Research Services	302-672-9411	•	•	•	•
•	•		•	•	National Background Investigations Inc	800-798-0079			•	
•	•		•	•	Research Specialists Inc	610-358-2507 or 724-5353	•		•	

District of Columbia

COURT RECORDS RETRIEVED					CAPITAL - WASHINGTON		RECORDED RECORDS RETRIEVED			
CR	CV	PR	US	BK	←COURTS DISTRICT OF COLUMBIA	RECORDER→	UC	RE	TX	VS
•	•		•	•	ABA Services	720-344-1259	•	•	•	
•	•	•	•	•	ALIASS [SOP]	800-747-0820	•	•	•	•
•	•		•	•	Asset Control Inc	877-277-3812	•	•	•	•
•	•	•	•	•	Cal Info Inc	202-537-8901				
•	•	•	•	•	Capitol District Information [SOP]	800-494-5225	•	•	•	
•	•	•	•	•	CorpAssist Inc - DC Office	800-438-2996	•	•	•	•
•	•	•	•	•	CSC - Corporation Service Company [SOP]	800-927-9800	•	•	•	•
					Direct Title Solutions Inc	540-450-0740	•	•	•	
•	•	•	•	•	Docu-Search of Washington DC	202-737-5707	•	•	•	•
•	•	•	•	•	Enterprise Title Company Inc	703-351-8066	•	•	•	•
					Estate Title & Escrow Inc	703-385-5850	•	•	•	
	•	•	•	•	Federal Research LLC [SOP]	800-846-3190	•	•	•	•
•	•	•	•	•	Fitzgerald Servaites Inc	202-257-7775	•	•	•	•
•	•	•	•	•	Global Securities Information	202-572-1997				
•	•	•	•	•	Hylind Search Company Inc (Maryland) [SOP]	888-449-5463	•	•	•	•
•	•	•	•	•	Infoline Inc	888-284-4581	•	•	•	•
•	•	•	•	•	Investigative Consultants Inc	202-237-1500	•	•	•	•
	•	•	•	•	M & M Search Service	301-251-9545	•	•	•	•
•	•	•	•	•	Mohr Information Services LLC	540-678-8775	•	•	•	
•	•		•	•	National Background Investigations Inc	800-798-0079			•	
	•		•	•	ResearchSource for Hard-to-Find Information	202-778-0002				
•	•	•	•	•	Security Consultants Inc	202-686-3953			•	•
•	•	•	•	•	Torri's Legal Services [SOP]	800-990-7378				
	•	•		•	Tri-County Title Abstracts Inc	202-737-6116	•	•	•	
•	•	•	•	•	Washington Document Service (DC)	800-728-5201	•	•	•	•
•	•		•	•	WestLaw CourtEXPRESS (DC) [SOP]	800-542-3320				

Editor's Note: The County Index section in this book will **only** indicate a county where a record retriever does an in-person search by himself or herself, or by a payroll employee.

Many retrievers also maintain a network of correspondents and provide services in additional counties not listed within the County Index. This additional coverage is indicated in the Profiles section under Correspondent Relationships.

Florida

COURT RECORDS RETRIEVED — CAPITAL - LEON COUNTY — RECORDED RECORDS RETRIEVED

CR	CV	PR	US	BK	←COURTS	ALACHUA	RECORDER→	UC	RE	TX	VS
	•	•			AAA Search Excellence Inc		352-688-6751	•	•	•	
•	•	•	•	•	Accurate Background Check [SOP]		877-611-2277		•	•	•
•	•	•	•	•	Direct Corporate Services Inc		800-783-7904	•	•	•	
•	•	•	•	•	First Choice Research		888-878-1595	•		•	
•	•	•	•		Lehr's Process Service [SOP]		352-331-1010	•	•	•	•
	•		•	•	Phoenix Document Service Inc		727-581-2552	•	•	•	
		•			The Searchers-NKA Hackman Abstracts Inc		352-493-0101	•	•	•	
•	•	•			Twin Oaks Research		352-465-7844	•	•	•	

CR	CV	PR	US	BK	←COURTS	BAKER	RECORDER→	UC	RE	TX	VS
•	•	•	•	•	First Choice Research		888-878-1595	•		•	
•	•	•	•	•	Mulholland Investigations & Security [SOP]		904-354-7989	•	•	•	•
•	•	•	•	•	Pacific Photocopy & Research (Jacksonville) [SOP]		904-355-1062	•	•	•	•
	•		•	•	Phoenix Document Service Inc		727-581-2552	•	•	•	

CR	CV	PR	US	BK	←COURTS	BAY	RECORDER→	UC	RE	TX	VS
	•	•			AAA Search Excellence Inc		352-688-6751	•	•	•	
•	•	•	•	•	Corporate Access Inc [SOP]		800-969-1666	•	•	•	•
•	•	•	•	•	Direct Corporate Services Inc		800-783-7904	•	•	•	
•	•	•	•	•	Emerald Coast Protective Services Inc [SOP]		877-234-6252	•	•	•	•
•	•	•	•	•	First Choice Research		888-878-1595	•		•	
•	•				First Quality Research Co		813-862-2778				
•	•	•	•	•	Ike L Hoy PE (Control Systems)		850-259-4650	•	•	•	•
•	•	•	•	•	Pacific Photocopy & Research (Pensacola) [SOP]		850-435-3183	•	•	•	•
•	•	•	•	•	Parrish Research		850-936-1240	•	•	•	•
	•		•	•	Phoenix Document Service Inc		727-581-2552	•	•	•	
					Research Express		850-926-5665		•		

CR	CV	PR	US	BK	←COURTS	BRADFORD	RECORDER→	UC	RE	TX	VS
•	•	•	•	•	First Choice Research		888-878-1595	•		•	
	•	•			Dudley P Hardy PA		904-964-5701	•	•	•	
•	•	•	•	•	Pacific Photocopy & Research (Jacksonville) [SOP]		904-355-1062	•	•	•	•

CR	CV	PR	US	BK	←COURTS	BREVARD	RECORDER→	UC	RE	TX	VS
•	•	•	•	•	A Very Private Eye Inc [SOP]		407-273-6646	•	•	•	•
	•	•			AAA Search Excellence Inc		352-688-6751	•	•	•	
•	•	•	•	•	Andrews Agency Inc [SOP]		407-649-2085	•	•	•	•
•	•	•	•	•	Bell Investigative Services Inc		954-454-4859	•	•	•	•
•	•	•			Crummey Investigations Inc [SOP]		321-724-0518	•	•	•	•
•	•	•	•	•	Direct Corporate Services Inc		800-783-7904	•	•	•	
	•	•	•	•	First American Title Ins Co		407-740-7131	•	•	•	•
•	•	•	•	•	First Choice Research		888-878-1595	•		•	
•	•	•	•	•	Hale Investigative Services/Process [SOP]		800-882-5137	•	•	•	•
	•	•	•	•	ICDI Inc		407-622-2532	•	•	•	
	•	•	•	•	Independent Research Assoc		407-832-8580	•	•	•	
					L L Lesko Inc		772-879-2625	•	•	•	
•	•	•		•	National Information Agency [SOP]		321-543-9381	•	•	•	•
	•		•	•	Phoenix Document Service Inc		727-581-2552	•	•	•	
					Source Documents & Information Inc		727-447-8844	•	•	•	

CR	CV	PR	US	BK	←COURTS BROWARD	RECORDER→	UC	RE	TX	VS
•	•	•	•	•	Accurate Confidential Research Inc	305-386-6677	•	•	•	•
•	•	•	•	•	All American Document Services	954-761-7292	•	•	•	•
•	•	•	•	•	American Legal Solution Inc	954-791-1415	•	•	•	•
•	•	•	•	•	ATT Investigations Inc	800-733-4405	•	•	•	•
•	•	•	•	•	Bell Investigative Services Inc	954-454-4859	•	•	•	•
•	•	•	•	•	Compass Investigations [SOP]	954-527-5722	•	•	•	•
•	•				Deception Control Inc	800-776-1660		•	•	•
•	•	•	•	•	Direct Corporate Services Inc	800-783-7904	•	•	•	
•	•	•	•	•	Esquire Express Inc [SOP]	800-439-8744	•	•	•	•
•	•	•	•	•	First Choice Research	888-878-1595	•		•	
					Ft Lauderdale-Miami Courthouse Research Inc	954-434-6819	•	•	•	
	•		•	•	IGB Associates Inc	813-226-8810	•	•	•	
•	•		•	•	Infotrack Information Services Inc	800-275-5594	•	•	•	
•	•	•	•	•	JM Search Services Inc	800-393-7563	•	•	•	
•	•	•	•	•	Judicial Process & Support Inc [SOP]	800-852-5002				
•	•	•	•	•	Judicial Research & Retrieval Services (Ft Lauderdale)	954-832-0111	•	•	•	•
•	•	•	•	•	Legal 1 Document Retrieval [SOP]	954-455-5220	•	•	•	•
				•	Johanna E Malki	305-899-0273	•	•	•	
•	•	•	•	•	Medina Retrieval Service	954-560-9077		•		
•	•	•	•	•	Pacific Photocopy & Research (Ft. Lauderdale)	954-764-5646	•	•	•	•
•	•	•	•	•	Premiere Investigations [SOP]	954-974-1139	•	•	•	•
•	•		•	•	Professional Background Searches LLC	954-394-8680				
•	•	•	•	•	R T Boxold & Associates LLC [SOP]	561-371-3855	•	•	•	•
					Source Documents & Information Inc	727-447-8844	•	•	•	
					South Florida Title Research Inc dba SFTR	866-398-7387	•	•	•	
•	•	•	•	•	Sugarbaker Investigations	352-684-9388	•			•
•	•	•	•	•	The Records Reviewer Inc	305-934-4920	•	•	•	
•	•				Variety International Processing Inc	877-245-6994				
•	•	•	•	•	WF Greenberg & Co LLC [SOP]	888-770-9008	•	•	•	•

CR	CV	PR	US	BK	←COURTS CALHOUN	RECORDER→	UC	RE	TX	VS
•	•	•	•	•	Corporate Access Inc [SOP]	800-969-1666	•	•	•	•
•	•	•	•	•	First Choice Research	888-878-1595	•		•	
•	•	•	•	•	Parrish Research	850-936-1240	•	•	•	•
					Research Express	850-926-5665		•		

CR	CV	PR	US	BK	←COURTS CHARLOTTE	RECORDER→	UC	RE	TX	VS
•	•		•	•	A Public Record Expert Inc	941-504-7734	•	•		•
	•	•			AAA Search Excellence Inc	352-688-6751	•	•	•	
•	•	•	•	•	Direct Corporate Services Inc	800-783-7904	•	•	•	
•	•	•	•	•	First Choice Research	888-878-1595	•		•	
	•	•			Guzman Title Research Inc	941-423-5310	•	•	•	
•	•		•	•	Infotrack Information Services Inc	800-275-5594	•	•	•	
•	•	•	•	•	Pacific Photocopy & Research (Tampa)	813-221-6828	•	•	•	•
•	•	•			Palo Verde Research	239-481-9434	•	•	•	
	•		•	•	Phoenix Document Service Inc	727-581-2552	•	•	•	
•	•	•	•	•	South Florida Legal Services of Naples [SOP]	239-332-7000		•	•	•
•	•	•	•	•	SWF Private Inv [SOP]	941-764-9156	•	•	•	•

CR	CV	PR	US	BK	←COURTS CITRUS	RECORDER→	UC	RE	TX	VS
	•	•			AAA Search Excellence Inc	352-688-6751	•	•	•	
•	•	•	•	•	Accurate Background Check [SOP]	877-611-2277		•	•	•
		•			Coast to Coast Abstracting	813-748-3699	•	•	•	
•	•	•	•	•	First Choice Research	888-878-1595	•		•	
•	•		•	•	GPS & Associates - Florida	866-813-8131	•		•	•
•	•	•	•	•	Pacific Photocopy & Research (Jacksonville) [SOP]	904-355-1062	•	•	•	•
	•		•	•	Phoenix Document Service Inc	727-581-2552	•	•	•	
•	•	•	•	•	Prestige Legal Services [SOP]	800-784-7572	•	•	•	•

CR	CV	PR	US	BK	←Courts	Recorder→	UC	RE	TX	VS
		•			The Searchers-NKA Hackman Abstracts Inc	352-493-0101	•	•	•	
•	•	•			Twin Oaks Research	352-465-7844	•	•	•	

CR	CV	PR	US	BK	←Courts **CLAY**	Recorder→	UC	RE	TX	VS
	•	•			AAA Search Excellence Inc	352-688-6751	•	•	•	
•	•	•	•	•	First Choice Research	888-878-1595	•		•	
•	•	•	•	•	First Coast Inv [SOP]	904-398-4076			•	•
					Ft Lauderdale-Miami Courthouse Research Inc	954-434-6819	•	•	•	
•	•		•	•	G & L Research Associates	904-743-4116	•	•	•	
		•			Land Title of America Group	904-797-9600	•	•	•	•
•	•	•	•	•	Millennial Investigative Agency	888-299-7574	•	•	•	•
•	•	•	•	•	Mulholland Investigations & Security [SOP]	904-354-7989	•	•	•	•
•	•	•	•	•	Pacific Photocopy & Research (Jacksonville) [SOP]	904-355-1062	•	•	•	•

CR	CV	PR	US	BK	←Courts **COLLIER**	Recorder→	UC	RE	TX	VS
	•	•			AAA Search Excellence Inc	352-688-6751	•	•	•	
•	•	•	•	•	American Legal Solution Inc	954-791-1415	•	•	•	•
	•				Attorney's Title Ins. Fund Inc	239-774-2627	•	•	•	•
•	•	•	•	•	Bell Investigative Services Inc	954-454-4859	•	•	•	•
•	•	•	•	•	Direct Corporate Services Inc	800-783-7904	•	•	•	
•	•	•	•	•	First Choice Research	888-878-1595	•		•	
•	•	•	•	•	Florida Records Research	239-435-1189	•	•	•	•
•	•		•	•	Infotrack Information Services Inc	800-275-5594	•	•	•	
•	•	•	•	•	MEM Consulting [SOP]	239-394-2893	•	•	•	•
•	•	•	•	•	Pacific Photocopy & Research (Tampa)	813-221-6828	•	•	•	•
•	•	•			Palo Verde Research	239-481-9434	•	•	•	
	•		•	•	Phoenix Document Service Inc	727-581-2552	•	•	•	
•	•	•	•	•	South Florida Legal Services of Naples [SOP]	239-332-7000		•	•	•

CR	CV	PR	US	BK	←Courts **COLUMBIA**	Recorder→	UC	RE	TX	VS
•	•	•	•	•	First Choice Research	888-878-1595	•		•	
•	•				First Quality Research Co	813-862-2778				
•	•	•	•	•	Pacific Photocopy & Research (Jacksonville) [SOP]	904-355-1062	•	•	•	•
					Research Express	850-926-5665		•		

CR	CV	PR	US	BK	←Courts **DADE (MIAMI-DADE)**	Recorder→	UC	RE	TX	VS
•	•	•	•	•	Accurate Confidential Research Inc	305-386-6677	•	•	•	•
•	•	•	•	•	All American Document Services	954-761-7292	•	•	•	•
•	•	•	•	•	American Legal Solution Inc	954-791-1415	•	•	•	•
•	•	•	•	•	ATT Investigations Inc	800-733-4405	•	•	•	•
				•	Banko Document Retrieval	800-969-2377				
•	•	•	•	•	Bell Investigative Services Inc	954-454-4859	•	•	•	•
•	•	•	•	•	Compass Investigations [SOP]	954-527-5722	•	•	•	•
•	•				Deception Control Inc	800-776-1660		•	•	•
•	•	•	•	•	Direct Corporate Services Inc	800-783-7904	•	•	•	
•	•	•	•	•	Esquire Express Inc [SOP]	800-439-8744	•	•	•	•
•	•	•	•	•	First Choice Research	888-878-1595	•		•	
•	•		•	•	GPS & Associates - Florida	866-813-8131	•		•	•
	•		•	•	IGB Associates Inc	813-226-8810	•	•	•	
•	•		•	•	Infotrack Information Services Inc	800-275-5594	•	•	•	
•	•	•	•	•	JM Search Services Inc	800-393-7563	•	•	•	
•	•	•	•	•	Judicial Process & Support Inc [SOP]	800-852-5002				
•	•	•	•	•	Judicial Research & Retrieval Services (Miami) [SOP]	305-379-3900	•	•	•	•
•	•	•	•	•	Legal 1 Document Retrieval [SOP]	954-455-5220	•	•	•	•
				•	Johanna E Malki	305-899-0273	•	•	•	
•	•	•	•	•	Medina Retrieval Service	954-560-9077		•		
•	•	•	•	•	Pacific Photocopy & Research (Miami)	305-371-7694	•	•	•	•
	•		•	•	Phoenix Document Service Inc	727-581-2552	•	•	•	
•	•	•	•	•	Premiere Investigations [SOP]	954-974-1139	•	•	•	•
•	•		•	•	Professional Background Searches LLC	954-394-8680				

CR	CV	PR	US	BK	Name	Phone	UC	RE	TX	VS
•	•	•	•	•	R T Boxold & Associates LLC [SOP]	561-371-3855	•	•	•	•
					Source Documents & Information Inc	727-447-8844	•	•	•	
					South Florida Title Research Inc dba SFTR	866-398-7387	•	•	•	
•	•	•	•	•	Sugarbaker Investigations	352-684-9388	•			•
•	•	•	•	•	The Records Reviewer Inc	305-934-4920	•	•	•	
•	•				Variety International Processing Inc	877-245-6994				
•	•	•	•	•	Robert Vollrath [SOP]	305-343-9344	•	•	•	•
•	•	•	•	•	WF Greenberg & Co LLC [SOP]	888-770-9008	•	•	•	•

CR	CV	PR	US	BK	←Courts — De Soto	Recorder→	UC	RE	TX	VS
•	•	•	•	•	A Public Record Expert Inc	941-504-7734	•	•		•
•	•	•			DeSoto Abstract & Title Co (FL)	863-494-3656	•	•	•	•
•	•	•	•	•	Direct Corporate Services Inc	800-783-7904	•	•	•	
•	•	•	•	•	First Choice Research	888-878-1595	•		•	
	•	•			Guzman Title Research Inc	941-423-5310	•	•	•	
•	•	•	•	•	Pacific Photocopy & Research (Tampa)	813-221-6828	•	•	•	•

CR	CV	PR	US	BK	←Courts — Dixie	Recorder→	UC	RE	TX	VS
•	•	•	•	•	First Choice Research	888-878-1595	•		•	
					Research Express	850-926-5665		•		
		•			The Searchers-NKA Hackman Abstracts Inc	352-493-0101	•	•	•	

CR	CV	PR	US	BK	←Courts — Duval	Recorder→	UC	RE	TX	VS
	•	•			AAA Search Excellence Inc	352-688-6751	•	•	•	
	•	•	•	•	First American Title Ins Co	407-740-7131	•	•	•	•
•	•	•	•	•	First Choice Research	888-878-1595	•		•	
•	•	•	•	•	First Coast Inv [SOP]	904-398-4076			•	•
•	•		•	•	G & L Research Associates	904-743-4116	•	•	•	
	•		•	•	IGB Associates Inc	813-226-8810	•	•	•	
•	•		•	•	Infotrack Information Services Inc	800-275-5594	•	•	•	
•	•	•	•	•	Judicial Research & Retrieval Services (Jacksonville)	904-356-9110	•	•	•	•
		•			Land Title of America Group	904-797-9600	•	•	•	•
•	•	•	•	•	Millennial Investigative Agency	888-299-7574	•	•	•	•
•	•	•	•	•	Mulholland Investigations & Security [SOP]	904-354-7989	•	•	•	•
•	•	•	•	•	Pacific Photocopy & Research (Jacksonville) [SOP]	904-355-1062	•	•	•	•
•	•				SingleSource Services Corp	800-713-3412	•		•	

CR	CV	PR	US	BK	←Courts — Escambia	Recorder→	UC	RE	TX	VS
•	•	•	•	•	BraveWolf's Background Investigations	850-791-6279	•	•		
•	•	•	•	•	Coastal Office Dimensions	850-637-1058	•	•	•	•
•	•	•	•	•	Direct Corporate Services Inc	800-783-7904	•	•	•	
•	•	•	•	•	First Choice Research	888-878-1595	•		•	
•	•		•	•	Infotrack Information Services Inc	800-275-5594	•	•	•	
•	•	•	•	•	Judicial Research & Retrieval Services (Miami) [SOP]	305-379-3900	•	•	•	•
•	•	•	•	•	Pacific Photocopy & Research (Pensacola) [SOP]	850-435-3183	•	•	•	•
•	•	•	•	•	Parrish Research	850-936-1240	•	•	•	•
	•		•	•	Phoenix Document Service Inc	727-581-2552	•	•	•	

CR	CV	PR	US	BK	←Courts — Flagler	Recorder→	UC	RE	TX	VS
•	•	•	•	•	Direct Corporate Services Inc	800-783-7904	•	•	•	
	•	•	•	•	First American Title Ins Co	407-740-7131	•	•	•	•
•	•	•	•	•	First Choice Research	888-878-1595	•		•	
		•			Flagler County Abstract Co [SOP]	386-437-4151	•	•	•	
		•			Land Title of America Group	904-797-9600	•	•	•	•
•					LNS Research Co.	386-428-1936				
•	•	•			Lowry Document Service	386-789-6193	•	•	•	•
•	•	•	•	•	Pacific Photocopy & Research (Jacksonville) [SOP]	904-355-1062	•	•	•	•
	•		•	•	Phoenix Document Service Inc	727-581-2552	•	•	•	
•		•	•	•	XpertSearch Inc	732-229-6688	•	•	•	•

CR	CV	PR	US	BK	←COURTS **FRANKLIN**	RECORDER→	UC	RE	TX	VS
•	•	•	•	•	Corporate Access Inc [SOP]	800-969-1666	•	•	•	•
•	•	•	•	•	First Choice Research	888-878-1595	•		•	
•	•	•	•	•	Parrish Research	850-936-1240	•	•	•	•
					Research Express	850-926-5665		•		

CR	CV	PR	US	BK	←COURTS **GADSDEN**	RECORDER→	UC	RE	TX	VS
•	•		•	•	Capital Connection [SOP]	850-224-8870	•	•	•	
•	•	•	•	•	Corporate Access Inc [SOP]	800-969-1666	•	•	•	•
•	•	•	•	•	First Choice Research	888-878-1595	•		•	
	•		•	•	Florida Filing & Search Services Inc	800-435-9371	•		•	
	•	•			Gadsden Abstract Co	850-627-6811		•	•	
•	•	•	•	•	Judicial Research & Retrieval Services (Miami) [SOP]	305-379-3900	•	•	•	•
•	•	•	•	•	Parrish Research	850-936-1240	•	•	•	•
					Research Express	850-926-5665		•		
•	•	•	•	•	State Information Bureau [SOP]	800-881-1742	•	•	•	•
•	•	•	•	•	Sunstate Research Associates Inc	800-621-7234	•		•	

CR	CV	PR	US	BK	←COURTS **GILCHRIST**	RECORDER→	UC	RE	TX	VS
•	•	•	•	•	First Choice Research	888-878-1595	•		•	
					Research Express	850-926-5665		•		
		•			The Searchers-NKA Hackman Abstracts Inc	352-493-0101	•	•	•	

CR	CV	PR	US	BK	←COURTS **GLADES**	RECORDER→	UC	RE	TX	VS
•	•	•	•	•	First Choice Research	888-878-1595	•		•	
•	•	•			Okeechobee Abstract & Title Ins Inc	863-763-3710	•	•	•	
•	•	•	•	•	Pacific Photocopy & Research (Tampa)	813-221-6828	•	•	•	•

CR	CV	PR	US	BK	←COURTS **GULF**	RECORDER→	UC	RE	TX	VS
•	•	•	•	•	Corporate Access Inc [SOP]	800-969-1666	•	•	•	•
•	•	•	•	•	Emerald Coast Protective Services Inc [SOP]	877-234-6252	•	•	•	•
•	•	•	•	•	First Choice Research	888-878-1595	•		•	
•	•	•	•	•	Parrish Research	850-936-1240	•	•	•	•
					Research Express	850-926-5665		•		

CR	CV	PR	US	BK	←COURTS **HAMILTON**	RECORDER→	UC	RE	TX	VS
•	•	•			API	229-559-4717			•	
•	•	•	•	•	First Choice Research	888-878-1595	•		•	
•	•	•	•	•	Pacific Photocopy & Research (Jacksonville) [SOP]	904-355-1062	•	•	•	•
					Research Express	850-926-5665		•		

CR	CV	PR	US	BK	←COURTS **HARDEE**	RECORDER→	UC	RE	TX	VS
•	•	•	•	•	A Public Record Expert Inc	941-504-7734	•	•		•
•	•	•			Al Smith Private Inv [SOP]	863-295-1375	•	•	•	•
•	•	•	•	•	First Choice Research	888-878-1595	•		•	
•	•	•	•	•	Pacific Photocopy & Research (Tampa)	813-221-6828	•	•	•	•

CR	CV	PR	US	BK	←COURTS **HENDRY**	RECORDER→	UC	RE	TX	VS
•	•	•	•	•	Direct Corporate Services Inc	800-783-7904	•	•	•	
•	•	•	•	•	First Choice Research	888-878-1595	•		•	
•	•	•	•	•	Florida Records Research	239-435-1189	•	•	•	•
•	•	•	•	•	Pacific Photocopy & Research (Tampa)	813-221-6828	•	•	•	•
•	•	•			Palo Verde Research	239-481-9434	•	•	•	
•	•	•	•	•	R T Boxold & Associates LLC [SOP]	561-371-3855	•	•	•	•
•	•	•	•	•	South Florida Legal Services of Naples [SOP]	239-332-7000		•	•	•

CR	CV	PR	US	BK	←COURTS **HERNANDO**	RECORDER→	UC	RE	TX	VS
	•	•			AAA Search Excellence Inc	352-688-6751	•	•	•	
		•			Coast to Coast Abstracting	813-748-3699	•	•	•	
•	•	•	•	•	Direct Corporate Services Inc	800-783-7904	•	•	•	
•	•	•	•	•	First Choice Research	888-878-1595	•		•	

CR	CV	PR	US	BK	←Courts	Recorder→	UC	RE	TX	VS
•	•		•	•	GPS & Associates - Florida	866-813-8131	•		•	•
•	•	•	•	•	Gulf Coast Records	727-580-4873	•	•	•	•
•	•	•	•	•	Mohr Information Services LLC	540-678-8775	•	•	•	
•	•	•	•	•	Pacific Photocopy & Research (Tampa)	813-221-6828	•	•	•	•
	•		•	•	Phoenix Document Service Inc	727-581-2552	•	•	•	
•	•	•	•	•	Prestige Legal Services [SOP]	800-784-7572	•	•	•	•
					Source Documents & Information Inc	727-447-8844	•	•	•	
•	•	•	•	•	Sugarbaker Investigations	352-684-9388	•			•
		•			The Searchers-NKA Hackman Abstracts Inc	352-493-0101	•	•	•	

CR	CV	PR	US	BK	←Courts	**Highlands** Recorder→	UC	RE	TX	VS
•	•	•			Al Smith Private Inv [SOP]	863-295-1375	•	•	•	•
•	•	•	•	•	First Choice Research	888-878-1595	•		•	
•	•	•	•	•	Pacific Photocopy & Research (Miami)	305-371-7694	•	•	•	•
	•		•	•	Phoenix Document Service Inc	727-581-2552	•	•	•	
	•	•			South Ridge Abstract & Title Co	863-385-2521	•	•	•	

CR	CV	PR	US	BK	←Courts	**Hillsborough** Recorder→	UC	RE	TX	VS
•	•	•	•	•	A Public Record Expert Inc	941-504-7734	•	•		•
•	•	•	•	•	All Phase Reports [SOP]	813-885-9822	•	•	•	•
•	•	•	•	•	ATT Investigations Inc	800-733-4405	•	•	•	•
•	•	•	•	•	Bell Investigative Services Inc	954-454-4859	•	•	•	•
		•			Coast to Coast Abstracting	813-748-3699	•	•	•	
•	•	•	•	•	Colton & Associates Inc [SOP]	800-704-6699	•	•	•	•
•	•		•	•	Criminal Research & Inv	888-243-5252			•	
•	•	•	•	•	Direct Corporate Services Inc	800-783-7904	•	•	•	
					Doc Hunters	727-518-6700	•	•	•	
•	•			•	Employee Assurance Inc	888-640-9847				
•	•	•	•	•	EX-CEL Investigations [SOP]	800-317-7626	•	•	•	•
•	•	•	•	•	First Choice Research	888-878-1595	•		•	
•	•				First Quality Research Co	813-862-2778				
•	•	•	•	•	Gietzen & Associates Inc [SOP]	813-223-3233		•	•	
•	•		•	•	GPS & Associates - Florida	866-813-8131	•		•	•
•	•	•	•	•	Gulf Coast Records	727-580-4873	•	•	•	•
	•		•	•	IGB Associates Inc	813-226-8810	•	•	•	
•	•		•	•	Infotrack Information Services Inc	800-275-5594	•	•	•	
•	•	•	•	•	Judicial Research & Retrieval Services (Tampa)	813-228-7200	•	•	•	•
•	•	•	•	•	Mohr Information Services LLC	540-678-8775	•	•	•	
	•				O & E Specialties Inc	813-948-1354	•	•	•	•
•	•	•	•	•	Pacific Photocopy & Research (Tampa)	813-221-6828	•	•	•	•
	•		•	•	Phoenix Document Service Inc	727-581-2552	•	•	•	
•	•	•	•	•	Prestige Legal Services [SOP]	800-784-7572	•	•	•	•
					Source Documents & Information Inc	727-447-8844	•	•	•	
•	•	•	•	•	Sugarbaker Investigations	352-684-9388	•			•
•	•		•		Sunshine Research Inc	888-786-1242	•			

CR	CV	PR	US	BK	←Courts	**Holmes** Recorder→	UC	RE	TX	VS
•	•	•	•	•	First Choice Research	888-878-1595	•		•	
•	•	•	•	•	Ike L Hoy PE (Control Systems)	850-259-4650	•	•	•	•
•	•	•	•	•	Parrish Research	850-936-1240	•	•	•	•
					Research Express	850-926-5665		•		

CR	CV	PR	US	BK	←Courts	**Indian River** Recorder→	UC	RE	TX	VS
	•	•			AAA Search Excellence Inc	352-688-6751	•	•	•	
•	•	•			Crummey Investigations Inc [SOP]	321-724-0518	•	•	•	•
•	•	•	•	•	Direct Corporate Services Inc	800-783-7904	•	•	•	
•	•	•	•	•	First Choice Research	888-878-1595	•		•	
•	•		•	•	Infotrack Information Services Inc	800-275-5594	•	•	•	
					L L Lesko Inc	772-879-2625	•	•	•	
•	•	•	•	•	Pacific Photocopy & Research (Miami)	305-371-7694	•	•	•	•

CR	CV	PR	US	BK	Name	Phone	UC	RE	TX	VS
	•		•	•	Phoenix Document Service Inc	727-581-2552	•	•	•	
					Reliable Title Search Inc	772-489-9650	•	•	•	
		•			Treasure Coast Title Co	772-461-7190	•	•	•	

CR	CV	PR	US	BK	←COURTS JACKSON	RECORDER→	UC	RE	TX	VS
•	•	•	•	•	Emerald Coast Protective Services Inc [SOP]	877-234-6252	•	•	•	•
•	•	•	•	•	First Choice Research	888-878-1595	•		•	
	•		•	•	Florida Filing & Search Services Inc	800-435-9371	•		•	
•	•	•	•	•	Parrish Research	850-936-1240	•	•	•	•
					Research Express	850-926-5665		•		

CR	CV	PR	US	BK	←COURTS JEFFERSON	RECORDER→	UC	RE	TX	VS
•	•	•			API	229-559-4717			•	
•	•		•	•	Capital Connection [SOP]	850-224-8870	•	•	•	
•	•	•	•	•	Corporate Access Inc [SOP]	800-969-1666	•	•	•	•
•	•	•	•	•	First Choice Research	888-878-1595	•		•	
	•		•	•	Florida Filing & Search Services Inc	800-435-9371	•		•	
•	•	•			North Florida Abstract & Title Company	850-997-2670	•	•	•	•
					Research Express	850-926-5665		•		
•	•	•	•	•	State Information Bureau [SOP]	800-881-1742	•	•	•	•
	•		•	•	Sunstate Research Associates Inc	800-621-7234	•		•	

CR	CV	PR	US	BK	←COURTS LAFAYETTE	RECORDER→	UC	RE	TX	VS
•	•	•	•	•	First Choice Research	888-878-1595	•		•	
					Research Express	850-926-5665		•		

CR	CV	PR	US	BK	←COURTS LAKE	RECORDER→	UC	RE	TX	VS
•	•	•	•	•	A Very Private Eye Inc [SOP]	407-273-6646	•	•	•	•
•	•	•	•	•	Andrews Agency Inc [SOP]	407-649-2085	•	•	•	•
•	•	•	•	•	ATT Investigations Inc	800-733-4405	•	•	•	•
•	•	•	•	•	CIV, Inc	407-352-4188, 407-433-1612	•	•	•	•
•	•	•	•	•	Direct Corporate Services Inc	800-783-7904	•	•	•	
•	•				Elman Resources	407-834-5344, cell- 407-221-8485				
	•	•	•	•	First American Title Ins Co	407-740-7131	•	•	•	•
•	•	•	•	•	First Choice Research	888-878-1595	•		•	
•	•	•	•	•	Hale Investigative Services/Process [SOP]	800-882-5137	•	•	•	•
•	•		•	•	Infotrack Information Services Inc	800-275-5594	•	•	•	
•	•	•	•	•	Investigative Legal Services Inc [SOP]	888-426-7436	•	•	•	•
	•		•	•	Phoenix Document Service Inc	727-581-2552	•	•	•	

CR	CV	PR	US	BK	←COURTS LEE	RECORDER→	UC	RE	TX	VS
	•	•			AAA Search Excellence Inc	352-688-6751	•	•	•	
•	•	•	•	•	Bell Investigative Services Inc	954-454-4859	•	•	•	•
		•			Coast to Coast Abstracting	813-748-3699	•	•	•	
•	•	•	•	•	Direct Corporate Services Inc	800-783-7904	•	•	•	
•	•	•	•	•	First Choice Research	888-878-1595	•		•	
•	•	•	•	•	Florida Records Research	239-435-1189	•	•	•	•
	•	•			Guzman Title Research Inc	941-423-5310	•	•	•	
•	•		•	•	Infotrack Information Services Inc	800-275-5594	•	•	•	
•	•	•	•	•	Judicial Research & Retrieval Services (Miami) [SOP]	305-379-3900	•	•	•	•
•	•	•	•	•	Pacific Photocopy & Research (Tampa)	813-221-6828	•	•	•	•
•	•	•			Palo Verde Research	239-481-9434	•	•	•	
	•		•	•	Phoenix Document Service Inc	727-581-2552	•	•	•	
•	•	•	•	•	South Florida Legal Services of Naples [SOP]	239-332-7000		•	•	•
•	•	•	•	•	SWF Private Inv [SOP]	941-764-9156	•	•	•	•

CR	CV	PR	US	BK	←COURTS LEON	RECORDER→	UC	RE	TX	VS
•	•	•			API	229-559-4717			•	
•	•		•	•	Capital Connection [SOP]	850-224-8870	•	•	•	
•	•	•	•	•	Corporate Access Inc [SOP]	800-969-1666	•	•	•	•

CR	CV	PR	US	BK	Courts / Name	Phone	UC	RE	TX	VS
•	•	•	•	•	Direct Corporate Services Inc	800-783-7904	•	•	•	
•	•	•	•	•	First Choice Research	888-878-1595	•		•	
•	•				First Quality Research Co	813-862-2778				
	•		•	•	Florida Filing & Search Services Inc	800-435-9371	•		•	
	•		•	•	Florida Information Associates Inc	850-878-0188				
	•		•	•	Florida Research & Filing Services Inc	850-656-6446	•	•	•	
•	•		•	•	Infotrack Information Services Inc	800-275-5594	•	•	•	
•	•	•	•	•	Judicial Research & Retrieval Services (Miami) [SOP]	305-379-3900	•	•	•	•
•	•	•	•	•	Parrish Research	850-936-1240	•	•	•	•
	•		•	•	Phoenix Document Service Inc	727-581-2552	•	•	•	
					Research Express	850-926-5665		•		
•	•	•	•	•	State Information Bureau [SOP]	800-881-1742	•	•	•	•
	•		•	•	Sunstate Research Associates Inc	800-621-7234	•		•	

CR	CV	PR	US	BK	←Courts **LEVY**	Recorder→	UC	RE	TX	VS
•	•	•	•	•	Accurate Background Check [SOP]	877-611-2277		•	•	•
•	•	•	•	•	First Choice Research	888-878-1595	•		•	
		•			The Searchers-NKA Hackman Abstracts Inc	352-493-0101	•	•	•	
•	•	•			Twin Oaks Research	352-465-7844	•	•	•	

CR	CV	PR	US	BK	←Courts **LIBERTY**	Recorder→	UC	RE	TX	VS
•	•	•	•	•	Corporate Access Inc [SOP]	800-969-1666	•	•	•	•
•	•	•	•	•	First Choice Research	888-878-1595	•		•	
•	•	•	•	•	Parrish Research	850-936-1240	•	•	•	•
					Research Express	850-926-5665		•		

CR	CV	PR	US	BK	←Courts **MADISON**	Recorder→	UC	RE	TX	VS
•	•	•			API	229-559-4717			•	
•	•	•	•	•	First Choice Research	888-878-1595	•		•	
					Research Express	850-926-5665		•		

CR	CV	PR	US	BK	←Courts **MANATEE**	Recorder→	UC	RE	TX	VS
•	•	•	•	•	A Public Record Expert Inc	941-504-7734	•	•		•
•	•	•			Chambers Investigations	800-792-1107	•	•	•	•
		•			Coast to Coast Abstracting	813-748-3699	•	•	•	
•	•	•	•	•	Direct Corporate Services Inc	800-783-7904	•	•	•	
•	•	•	•	•	First Choice Research	888-878-1595	•		•	
•	•	•	•	•	Gulf Coast Records	727-580-4873	•	•	•	•
	•		•	•	IGB Associates Inc	813-226-8810	•	•	•	
•	•		•	•	Infotrack Information Services Inc	800-275-5594	•	•	•	
•	•	•	•	•	Pacific Photocopy & Research (Tampa)	813-221-6828	•	•	•	•
	•		•	•	Phoenix Document Service Inc	727-581-2552	•	•	•	
					Source Documents & Information Inc	727-447-8844	•	•	•	
•	•	•			Steele Investigation Agency [SOP]	941-758-5890	•	•	•	•
•	•	•	•	•	Sugarbaker Investigations	352-684-9388	•			•
•	•		•		Sunshine Research Inc	888-786-1242	•			

CR	CV	PR	US	BK	←Courts **MARION**	Recorder→	UC	RE	TX	VS
	•	•			AAA Search Excellence Inc	352-688-6751	•	•	•	
•	•	•	•	•	Accurate Background Check [SOP]	877-611-2277		•	•	•
•	•	•	•	•	ATT Investigations Inc	800-733-4405	•	•	•	•
•	•	•	•	•	Direct Corporate Services Inc	800-783-7904	•	•	•	
•	•				Elman Resources	407-834-5344, cell- 407-221-8485				
	•	•	•	•	First American Title Ins Co	407-740-7131	•	•	•	•
•	•	•	•	•	First Choice Research	888-878-1595	•		•	
•	•	•	•		Lehr's Process Service [SOP]	352-331-1010	•	•	•	•
•	•	•	•	•	Pacific Photocopy & Research (Jacksonville) [SOP]	904-355-1062	•	•	•	•
	•		•	•	Phoenix Document Service Inc	727-581-2552	•	•	•	
•	•	•	•	•	Sugarbaker Investigations	352-684-9388	•			•
		•			The Searchers-NKA Hackman Abstracts Inc	352-493-0101	•	•	•	

CR	CV	PR	US	BK	←Courts **MARTIN**	Recorder→	UC	RE	TX	VS
•	•	•	•	•	Direct Corporate Services Inc	800-783-7904	•	•	•	
•	•	•	•	•	First Choice Research	888-878-1595	•		•	
•	•				First Quality Research Co	813-862-2778				
•	•	•	•	•	Information Search Inc	561-624-5115	•	•	•	•
					L L Lesko Inc	772-879-2625	•	•	•	
•	•	•	•	•	Pacific Photocopy & Research (Miami)	305-371-7694	•	•	•	•
•	•	•			Patton Investigative Agency Inc [SOP]	772-398-1227	•	•	•	•
	•		•	•	Phoenix Document Service Inc	727-581-2552	•	•	•	
•	•	•	•	•	Public Records Research Inc (Florida)	561-746-0850	•	•	•	
•	•	•	•	•	R T Boxold & Associates LLC [SOP]	561-371-3855	•	•	•	•
					Reliable Title Search Inc	772-489-9650	•	•	•	
					South Florida Title Research Inc dba SFTR	866-398-7387	•	•	•	
		•			Treasure Coast Title Co	772-461-7190	•	•	•	

CR	CV	PR	US	BK	←Courts **MONROE**	Recorder→	UC	RE	TX	VS
	•	•			AAA Search Excellence Inc	352-688-6751	•	•	•	
•	•	•	•	•	American Legal Solution Inc	954-791-1415	•	•	•	•
•	•	•	•	•	Bell Investigative Services Inc	954-454-4859	•	•	•	•
•	•	•	•	•	Coastal Office Dimensions	850-637-1058	•	•	•	•
•	•	•	•	•	Direct Corporate Services Inc	800-783-7904	•	•	•	
•	•	•	•	•	First Choice Research	888-878-1595	•		•	
•	•	•			Independent Abstract & Title	305-294-5105	•	•	•	
•	•	•	•	•	Pacific Photocopy & Research (Miami)	305-371-7694	•	•	•	•
	•		•	•	Phoenix Document Service Inc	727-581-2552	•	•	•	

CR	CV	PR	US	BK	←Courts **NASSAU**	Recorder→	UC	RE	TX	VS
•	•	•	•	•	First Choice Research	888-878-1595	•		•	
•	•	•	•	•	First Coast Inv [SOP]	904-398-4076			•	•
•	•				First Quality Research Co	813-862-2778				
					Ft Lauderdale-Miami Courthouse Research Inc	954-434-6819	•	•	•	
•	•		•	•	G & L Research Associates	904-743-4116	•	•	•	
•	•		•	•	Infotrack Information Services Inc	800-275-5594	•	•	•	
•	•	•	•	•	Judicial Research & Retrieval Services (Jacksonville)	904-356-9110	•	•	•	•
		•			Land Title of America Group	904-797-9600	•	•	•	•
•	•	•	•	•	Mulholland Investigations & Security [SOP]	904-354-7989	•	•	•	•
•	•	•	•	•	Pacific Photocopy & Research (Jacksonville) [SOP]	904-355-1062	•	•	•	•
	•		•	•	Phoenix Document Service Inc	727-581-2552	•	•	•	

CR	CV	PR	US	BK	←Courts **OKALOOSA**	Recorder→	UC	RE	TX	VS
	•	•			AAA Search Excellence Inc	352-688-6751	•	•	•	
•	•	•	•	•	Direct Corporate Services Inc	800-783-7904	•	•	•	
•	•	•	•	•	First Choice Research	888-878-1595	•		•	
•	•	•	•	•	Ike L Hoy PE (Control Systems)	850-259-4650	•	•	•	•
•	•		•	•	Infotrack Information Services Inc	800-275-5594	•	•	•	
•	•	•	•	•	Pacific Photocopy & Research (Pensacola) [SOP]	850-435-3183	•	•	•	•
•	•	•	•	•	Parrish Research	850-936-1240	•	•	•	•
	•		•	•	Phoenix Document Service Inc	727-581-2552	•	•	•	

CR	CV	PR	US	BK	←Courts **OKEECHOBEE**	Recorder→	UC	RE	TX	VS
•	•	•	•	•	Direct Corporate Services Inc	800-783-7904	•	•	•	
•	•	•	•	•	First Choice Research	888-878-1595	•		•	
•	•	•			Okeechobee Abstract & Title Ins Inc	863-763-3710	•	•	•	
•	•	•	•	•	Pacific Photocopy & Research (Miami)	305-371-7694	•	•	•	•
•	•	•			Patton Investigative Agency Inc [SOP]	772-398-1227	•	•	•	•
•	•	•	•	•	R T Boxold & Associates LLC [SOP]	561-371-3855	•	•	•	•
					Reliable Title Search Inc	772-489-9650	•	•	•	
		•			Treasure Coast Title Co	772-461-7190	•	•	•	

CR	CV	PR	US	BK	←COURTS ORANGE RECORDER→		UC	RE	TX	VS
•	•	•	•	•	A Very Private Eye Inc [SOP]	407-273-6646	•	•	•	•
•	•	•	•	•	Andrews Agency Inc [SOP]	407-649-2085	•	•	•	•
•	•	•	•	•	ATT Investigations Inc	800-733-4405	•	•	•	•
•	•	•	•	•	Bell Investigative Services Inc	954-454-4859	•	•	•	•
•	•	•	•	•	CIV, Inc	407-352-4188, 407-433-1612	•	•	•	•
•	•	•			Crummey Investigations Inc [SOP]	321-724-0518	•	•	•	•
•	•	•	•	•	Direct Corporate Services Inc	800-783-7904	•	•	•	
•	•				Elman Resources	407-834-5344, cell- 407-221-8485				
	•	•	•	•	First American Title Ins Co	407-740-7131	•	•	•	•
•	•	•	•	•	First Choice Research	888-878-1595	•		•	
•	•				First Quality Research Co	813-862-2778				
					Ft Lauderdale-Miami Courthouse Research Inc	954-434-6819	•	•	•	
•	•		•	•	GPS & Associates - Florida	866-813-8131	•		•	•
•	•	•	•	•	Hale Investigative Services/Process [SOP]	800-882-5137	•	•	•	•
	•		•	•	ICDI Inc	407-622-2532	•	•	•	
	•		•	•	IGB Associates Inc	813-226-8810	•	•	•	
	•	•	•	•	Independent Research Assoc	407-832-8580	•	•	•	
•	•		•	•	Infotrack Information Services Inc	800-275-5594	•	•	•	
•	•	•	•	•	Investigative Legal Services Inc [SOP]	888-426-7436	•	•	•	•
•	•	•	•	•	Judicial Research & Retrieval Services (Orlando)	407-999-7717	•	•	•	•
•	•	•	•	•	Legal 1 Document Retrieval [SOP]	954-455-5220	•	•	•	•
•	•	•	•	•	Liquori Investigations	386-423-4235	•	•	•	•
•	•	•	•	•	Pacific Photocopy & Research (Orlando)	407-425-7234	•	•	•	•
	•		•	•	Phoenix Document Service Inc	727-581-2552	•	•	•	
					Source Documents & Information Inc	727-447-8844	•	•	•	
•	•	•	•	•	Sugarbaker Investigations	352-684-9388	•			•
•		•	•	•	XpertSearch Inc	732-229-6688	•	•	•	•

CR	CV	PR	US	BK	←COURTS OSCEOLA RECORDER→		UC	RE	TX	VS
•	•	•	•	•	A Very Private Eye Inc [SOP]	407-273-6646	•	•	•	•
•	•	•	•	•	Andrews Agency Inc [SOP]	407-649-2085	•	•	•	•
•	•	•	•	•	ATT Investigations Inc	800-733-4405	•	•	•	•
•	•	•	•	•	CIV, Inc	407-352-4188, 407-433-1612	•	•	•	•
•	•	•	•	•	Direct Corporate Services Inc	800-783-7904	•	•	•	
•	•				Elman Resources	407-834-5344, cell- 407-221-8485				
	•	•	•	•	First American Title Ins Co	407-740-7131	•	•	•	•
•	•	•	•	•	First Choice Research	888-878-1595	•		•	
•	•	•	•	•	Hale Investigative Services/Process [SOP]	800-882-5137	•	•	•	•
	•	•	•	•	ICDI Inc	407-622-2532	•	•	•	
	•	•	•	•	Independent Research Assoc	407-832-8580	•	•	•	
•	•		•	•	Infotrack Information Services Inc	800-275-5594	•	•	•	
•	•	•	•	•	Investigative Legal Services Inc [SOP]	888-426-7436	•	•	•	•
•	•	•	•	•	Judicial Research & Retrieval Services (Orlando)	407-999-7717	•	•	•	•
•	•	•	•	•	Pacific Photocopy & Research (Orlando)	407-425-7234	•	•	•	•
	•		•	•	Phoenix Document Service Inc	727-581-2552	•	•	•	

CR	CV	PR	US	BK	←COURTS PALM BEACH RECORDER→		UC	RE	TX	VS
•	•	•	•	•	Accurate Confidential Research Inc	305-386-6677	•	•	•	•
•	•	•	•	•	All American Document Services	954-761-7292	•	•	•	•
•	•	•	•	•	American Legal Solution Inc	954-791-1415	•	•	•	•
•	•	•	•	•	ATT Investigations Inc	800-733-4405	•	•	•	•
•	•	•	•	•	Barry Shuster Information Services, A Div of Search-It Inc	877-852-2507	•	•	•	•
•	•	•	•	•	Bell Investigative Services Inc	954-454-4859	•	•	•	•
•	•	•	•	•	Compass Investigations [SOP]	954-527-5722	•	•	•	•
•	•				Deception Control Inc	800-776-1660		•	•	•
•	•	•	•	•	Direct Corporate Services Inc	800-783-7904	•	•	•	
•	•	•	•	•	Esquire Express Inc [SOP]	800-439-8744	•	•	•	•
•	•	•	•	•	First Choice Research	888-878-1595	•		•	

CR	CV	PR	US	BK	←Courts	Recorder→	UC	RE	TX	VS
•	•				First Quality Research Co	813-862-2778				
					Ft Lauderdale-Miami Courthouse Research Inc	954-434-6819	•	•	•	
•	•		•	•	GPS & Associates - Florida	866-813-8131	•		•	•
•	•	•	•	•	Gryder Express Tracking Service Inc	561-535-1495, cell- 561-584 2079	•	•	•	•
•	•	•	•	•	Information Search Inc	561-624-5115	•	•	•	•
•	•		•	•	Infotrack Information Services Inc	800-275-5594	•	•	•	
•	•	•	•	•	JM Search Services Inc	800-393-7563	•	•	•	
•	•	•	•	•	Judicial Research & Retrieval Services (Palm Beach)	561-659-7677	•	•	•	•
					L L Lesko Inc	772-879-2625	•	•	•	
•	•	•	•	•	Legal 1 Document Retrieval [SOP]	954-455-5220	•	•	•	•
•	•	•	•	•	Medina Retrieval Service	954-560-9077		•		
•	•	•	•	•	David Mulberry [SOP]	800-704-1287	•	•	•	•
•	•	•	•	•	Pacific Photocopy & Research (West Palm Beach)	561-832-3878	•	•	•	•
•	•	•	•	•	Paralegal Field Research Service [SOP]	800-256-7459				
	•		•	•	Phoenix Document Service Inc	727-581-2552	•	•	•	
•	•	•	•	•	Premiere Investigations [SOP]	954-974-1139	•	•	•	•
•	•		•	•	Professional Background Searches LLC	954-394-8680				
•	•	•	•	•	Public Records Research Inc (Florida)	561-746-0850	•	•	•	
•	•	•	•	•	R T Boxold & Associates LLC [SOP]	561-371-3855	•	•	•	•
					Reliable Title Search Inc	772-489-9650	•	•	•	
•	•	•	•	•	Paul Scholtes [SOP]	561-385-8163	•	•	•	•
					Source Documents & Information Inc	727-447-8844	•	•	•	
					South Florida Title Research Inc dba SFTR	866-398-7387	•	•	•	
•	•	•	•	•	The Records Reviewer Inc	305-934-4920	•	•	•	
•	•				Variety International Processing Inc	877-245-6994				
•	•	•	•	•	WF Greenberg & Co LLC [SOP]	888-770-9008	•	•	•	•

CR	CV	PR	US	BK	←Courts	Pasco	Recorder→	UC	RE	TX	VS
	•	•			AAA Search Excellence Inc		352-688-6751	•	•	•	
•	•	•	•	•	Accurate Background Check [SOP]		877-611-2277		•	•	•
•	•	•	•	•	All Phase Reports [SOP]		813-885-9822	•	•	•	•
•	•		•	•	Applicant Insight Ltd		800-771-7703	•			
•	•	•	•	•	ATT Investigations Inc		800-733-4405	•	•	•	•
		•			Coast to Coast Abstracting		813-748-3699	•	•	•	
•	•	•	•	•	Colton & Associates Inc [SOP]		800-704-6699	•	•	•	•
•	•		•	•	Criminal Research & Inv		888-243-5252			•	
•	•	•	•	•	Direct Corporate Services Inc		800-783-7904	•	•	•	
•	•			•	Employee Assurance Inc		888-640-9847				
•	•	•	•	•	First Choice Research		888-878-1595	•		•	
•	•				First Quality Research Co		813-862-2778				
•	•	•	•	•	Gietzen & Associates Inc [SOP]		813-223-3233		•	•	
•	•		•	•	GPS & Associates - Florida		866-813-8131	•		•	•
•	•	•	•	•	Gulf Coast Records		727-580-4873	•	•	•	•
	•		•	•	IGB Associates Inc		813-226-8810	•	•	•	
•	•		•	•	Infotrack Information Services Inc		800-275-5594	•	•	•	
•	•	•	•	•	Judicial Research & Retrieval Services (Tampa)		813-228-7200	•	•	•	•
•	•	•	•	•	Mohr Information Services LLC		540-678-8775	•	•	•	
	•				O & E Specialties Inc		813-948-1354	•	•	•	•
•	•	•	•	•	Pacific Photocopy & Research (Tampa)		813-221-6828	•	•	•	•
	•		•	•	Phoenix Document Service Inc		727-581-2552	•	•	•	
•	•	•	•	•	Prestige Legal Services [SOP]		800-784-7572	•	•	•	•
					Source Documents & Information Inc		727-447-8844	•	•	•	
•	•	•	•	•	Sugarbaker Investigations		352-684-9388	•			•
•	•		•		Sunshine Research Inc		888-786-1242	•			
		•			The Searchers-NKA Hackman Abstracts Inc		352-493-0101	•	•	•	

CR	CV	PR	US	BK	←Courts PINELLAS	Recorder→	UC	RE	TX	VS
•	•	•	•	•	A Public Record Expert Inc	941-504-7734	•	•		•
	•	•			AAA Search Excellence Inc	352-688-6751	•	•	•	
•	•	•	•	•	All Phase Reports [SOP]	813-885-9822	•	•	•	•
•	•		•	•	Applicant Insight Ltd	800-771-7703	•			
•	•	•	•	•	ATT Investigations Inc	800-733-4405	•	•	•	•
•	•	•	•	•	Bell Investigative Services Inc	954-454-4859	•	•	•	•
		•			Coast to Coast Abstracting	813-748-3699	•	•	•	
•	•	•	•	•	Colton & Associates Inc [SOP]	800-704-6699	•	•	•	•
•	•		•	•	Criminal Research & Inv	888-243-5252			•	
•	•	•	•	•	Direct Corporate Services Inc	800-783-7904	•	•	•	
					Doc Hunters	727-518-6700	•	•	•	
•	•			•	Employee Assurance Inc	888-640-9847				
•	•	•	•	•	EX-CEL Investigations [SOP]	800-317-7626	•	•	•	•
•	•	•	•	•	First Choice Research	888-878-1595	•		•	
•	•	•	•	•	Gietzen & Associates Inc [SOP]	813-223-3233		•	•	
•	•		•	•	GPS & Associates - Florida	866-813-8131	•		•	•
•	•	•	•	•	Gulf Coast Records	727-580-4873	•	•	•	•
	•		•	•	IGB Associates Inc	813-226-8810	•	•	•	
•	•		•	•	Infotrack Information Services Inc	800-275-5594	•	•	•	
•	•	•	•	•	Judicial Research & Retrieval Services (Tampa)	813-228-7200	•	•	•	•
•	•	•	•	•	Mohr Information Services LLC	540-678-8775	•	•	•	
	•				O & E Specialties Inc	813-948-1354	•	•	•	•
•	•	•	•	•	Pacific Photocopy & Research (Tampa)	813-221-6828	•	•	•	•
	•		•	•	Phoenix Document Service Inc	727-581-2552	•	•	•	
•	•	•	•	•	Prestige Legal Services [SOP]	800-784-7572	•	•	•	•
					Source Documents & Information Inc	727-447-8844	•	•	•	
•	•	•	•	•	Sugarbaker Investigations	352-684-9388	•			•
•	•		•		Sunshine Research Inc	888-786-1242	•			
•	•				We Search Information Retrieval	727-656-6977		•		

CR	CV	PR	US	BK	←Courts POLK	Recorder→	UC	RE	TX	VS
•	•	•	•	•	A Very Private Eye Inc [SOP]	407-273-6646	•	•	•	•
	•	•			AAA Search Excellence Inc	352-688-6751	•	•	•	
•	•	•			Al Smith Private Inv [SOP]	863-295-1375	•	•	•	•
•	•	•	•	•	All Phase Reports [SOP]	813-885-9822	•	•	•	•
		•			Coast to Coast Abstracting	813-748-3699	•	•	•	
•	•		•	•	Criminal Research & Inv	888-243-5252			•	
•	•	•	•	•	Direct Corporate Services Inc	800-783-7904	•	•	•	
	•	•	•	•	First American Title Ins Co	407-740-7131	•	•	•	•
•	•	•	•	•	First Choice Research	888-878-1595	•		•	
•	•				First Quality Research Co	813-862-2778				
•	•	•	•	•	Gietzen & Associates Inc [SOP]	813-223-3233		•	•	
•	•		•	•	GPS & Associates - Florida	866-813-8131	•		•	•
•	•	•	•	•	Gulf Coast Records	727-580-4873	•	•	•	•
•	•	•	•	•	Hale Investigative Services/Process [SOP]	800-882-5137	•	•	•	•
	•		•	•	IGB Associates Inc	813-226-8810	•	•	•	
•	•		•	•	Infotrack Information Services Inc	800-275-5594	•	•	•	
•	•	•	•	•	Judicial Research & Retrieval Services (Tampa)	813-228-7200	•	•	•	•
•	•	•	•	•	Mohr Information Services LLC	540-678-8775	•	•	•	
	•				O & E Specialties Inc	813-948-1354	•	•	•	•
•	•	•	•	•	Pacific Photocopy & Research (Tampa)	813-221-6828	•	•	•	•
	•		•	•	Phoenix Document Service Inc	727-581-2552	•	•	•	
					Source Documents & Information Inc	727-447-8844	•	•	•	
•	•	•	•	•	Sugarbaker Investigations	352-684-9388	•			•

CR	CV	PR	US	BK	←Courts	Putnam	Recorder→	UC	RE	TX	VS
•	•	•	•	•	First Choice Research		888-878-1595	•		•	
•	•				First Quality Research Co		813-862-2778				
		•			Land Title of America Group		904-797-9600	•	•	•	•
•	•	•	•	•	Pacific Photocopy & Research (Jacksonville) [SOP]		904-355-1062	•	•	•	•
	•		•	•	Phoenix Document Service Inc		727-581-2552	•	•	•	

CR	CV	PR	US	BK	←Courts	Santa Rosa	Recorder→	UC	RE	TX	VS
•	•	•	•	•	Coastal Office Dimensions		850-637-1058	•	•	•	•
•	•	•	•	•	Direct Corporate Services Inc		800-783-7904	•	•	•	
•	•	•	•	•	First Choice Research		888-878-1595	•		•	
•	•	•	•	•	Ike L Hoy PE (Control Systems)		850-259-4650	•	•	•	•
•	•	•	•	•	Pacific Photocopy & Research (Pensacola) [SOP]		850-435-3183	•	•	•	•
•	•	•	•	•	Parrish Research		850-936-1240	•	•	•	•
	•		•	•	Phoenix Document Service Inc		727-581-2552	•	•	•	

CR	CV	PR	US	BK	←Courts	Sarasota	Recorder→	UC	RE	TX	VS
•	•	•	•	•	A Public Record Expert Inc		941-504-7734	•	•		•
	•	•			AAA Search Excellence Inc		352-688-6751	•	•	•	
•	•	•			Chambers Investigations		800-792-1107	•	•	•	•
		•			Coast to Coast Abstracting		813-748-3699	•	•	•	
•	•	•	•	•	Direct Corporate Services Inc		800-783-7904	•	•	•	
•	•	•	•	•	First Choice Research		888-878-1595	•		•	
•	•	•	•	•	Gulf Coast Records		727-580-4873	•	•	•	•
	•	•			Guzman Title Research Inc		941-423-5310	•	•	•	
	•		•	•	IGB Associates Inc		813-226-8810	•	•	•	
•	•		•	•	Infotrack Information Services Inc		800-275-5594	•	•	•	
•	•	•	•	•	Pacific Photocopy & Research (Tampa)		813-221-6828	•	•	•	•
	•		•	•	Phoenix Document Service Inc		727-581-2552	•	•	•	
					Source Documents & Information Inc		727-447-8844	•	•	•	
•	•	•			Steele Investigation Agency [SOP]		941-758-5890	•	•	•	•
•	•	•	•	•	Sugarbaker Investigations		352-684-9388	•			•
•	•	•	•	•	SWF Private Inv [SOP]		941-764-9156	•	•	•	•

CR	CV	PR	US	BK	←Courts	Seminole	Recorder→	UC	RE	TX	VS
•	•	•	•	•	A Very Private Eye Inc [SOP]		407-273-6646	•	•	•	•
	•	•			AAA Search Excellence Inc		352-688-6751	•	•	•	
•	•	•	•	•	Andrews Agency Inc [SOP]		407-649-2085	•	•	•	•
•	•	•	•	•	ATT Investigations Inc		800-733-4405	•	•	•	•
•	•	•	•	•	Bell Investigative Services Inc		954-454-4859	•	•	•	•
•	•	•	•	•	CIV, Inc		407-352-4188, 407-433-1612	•	•	•	•
•	•	•	•	•	Direct Corporate Services Inc		800-783-7904	•	•	•	
•	•				Elman Resources		407-834-5344, cell- 407-221-8485				
	•	•	•	•	First American Title Ins Co		407-740-7131	•	•	•	•
•	•	•	•	•	First Choice Research		888-878-1595	•		•	
•	•				First Quality Research Co		813-862-2778				
•	•	•	•	•	Hale Investigative Services/Process [SOP]		800-882-5137	•	•	•	•
	•	•	•	•	ICDI Inc		407-622-2532	•	•	•	
	•	•	•	•	Independent Research Assoc		407-832-8580	•	•	•	
•	•	•	•	•	Investigative Legal Services Inc [SOP]		888-426-7436	•	•	•	•
•	•	•	•	•	Judicial Research & Retrieval Services (Orlando)		407-999-7717	•	•	•	•
•	•	•	•	•	Legal 1 Document Retrieval [SOP]		954-455-5220	•	•	•	•
•	•	•	•	•	Liquori Investigations		386-423-4235	•	•	•	•
•					LNS Research Co.		386-428-1936				
•	•	•			Lowry Document Service		386-789-6193	•	•	•	•
•	•	•	•	•	Pacific Photocopy & Research (Orlando)		407-425-7234	•	•	•	•
	•		•	•	Phoenix Document Service Inc		727-581-2552	•	•	•	
•	•	•	•	•	Sugarbaker Investigations		352-684-9388	•			•
•		•	•	•	XpertSearch Inc		732-229-6688	•	•	•	•

CR	CV	PR	US	BK	←COURTS	ST. JOHNS	RECORDER→	UC	RE	TX	VS
•	•	•	•	•	First Choice Research		888-878-1595	•		•	
•	•				First Quality Research Co		813-862-2778				
		•			Flagler County Abstract Co [SOP]		386-437-4151	•	•	•	
•	•		•	•	G & L Research Associates		904-743-4116	•	•	•	
•	•	•	•	•	Judicial Research & Retrieval Services (Jacksonville)		904-356-9110	•	•	•	•
		•			Land Title of America Group		904-797-9600	•	•	•	•
•	•	•	•	•	Millennial Investigative Agency		888-299-7574	•	•	•	•
•	•	•	•	•	Mulholland Investigations & Security [SOP]		904-354-7989	•	•	•	•
•	•	•	•	•	Pacific Photocopy & Research (Jacksonville) [SOP]		904-355-1062	•	•	•	•
	•		•	•	Phoenix Document Service Inc		727-581-2552	•	•	•	
•		•	•	•	XpertSearch Inc		732-229-6688	•	•	•	•

CR	CV	PR	US	BK	←COURTS	ST. LUCIE	RECORDER→	UC	RE	TX	VS
•	•	•	•	•	Bell Investigative Services Inc		954-454-4859	•	•	•	•
•	•	•	•	•	Direct Corporate Services Inc		800-783-7904	•	•	•	
•	•	•	•	•	First Choice Research		888-878-1595	•		•	
•	•				First Quality Research Co		813-862-2778				
•	•	•	•	•	Information Search Inc		561-624-5115	•	•	•	•
•	•	•	•	•	Judicial Research & Retrieval Services (Palm Beach)		561-659-7677	•	•	•	•
					L L Lesko Inc		772-879-2625	•	•	•	
•	•	•	•	•	Pacific Photocopy & Research (Miami)		305-371-7694	•	•	•	•
•	•	•			Patton Investigative Agency Inc [SOP]		772-398-1227	•	•	•	•
	•		•	•	Phoenix Document Service Inc		727-581-2552	•	•	•	
					Reliable Title Search Inc		772-489-9650	•	•	•	
		•			Treasure Coast Title Co		772-461-7190	•	•	•	
•	•				Variety International Processing Inc		877-245-6994				

CR	CV	PR	US	BK	←COURTS	SUMTER	RECORDER→	UC	RE	TX	VS
•	•	•	•	•	Accurate Background Check [SOP]		877-611-2277		•	•	•
		•			Coast to Coast Abstracting		813-748-3699	•	•	•	
•	•	•	•	•	Direct Corporate Services Inc		800-783-7904	•	•	•	
•	•	•	•	•	First Choice Research		888-878-1595	•		•	
•	•	•	•	•	Pacific Photocopy & Research (Jacksonville) [SOP]		904-355-1062	•	•	•	•
•	•	•	•	•	Prestige Legal Services [SOP]		800-784-7572	•	•	•	•
		•			The Searchers-NKA Hackman Abstracts Inc		352-493-0101	•	•	•	

CR	CV	PR	US	BK	←COURTS	SUWANNEE	RECORDER→	UC	RE	TX	VS
•	•	•			API		229-559-4717			•	
•	•	•	•	•	First Choice Research		888-878-1595	•		•	
•	•	•	•	•	Pacific Photocopy & Research (Jacksonville) [SOP]		904-355-1062	•	•	•	•
					Research Express		850-926-5665		•		

CR	CV	PR	US	BK	←COURTS	TAYLOR	RECORDER→	UC	RE	TX	VS
•	•	•	•	•	First Choice Research		888-878-1595	•		•	
					Research Express		850-926-5665		•		
		•			The Searchers-NKA Hackman Abstracts Inc		352-493-0101	•	•	•	

CR	CV	PR	US	BK	←COURTS	UNION	RECORDER→	UC	RE	TX	VS
•	•	•	•	•	First Choice Research		888-878-1595	•		•	
•	•				First Quality Research Co		813-862-2778				
•	•	•	•	•	Pacific Photocopy & Research (Jacksonville) [SOP]		904-355-1062	•	•	•	•
					Research Express		850-926-5665		•		

CR	CV	PR	US	BK	←COURTS	VOLUSIA	RECORDER→	UC	RE	TX	VS
•	•	•	•	•	Andrews Agency Inc [SOP]		407-649-2085	•	•	•	•
•	•	•	•	•	ATT Investigations Inc		800-733-4405	•	•	•	•
•	•	•	•	•	Bell Investigative Services Inc		954-454-4859	•	•	•	•
•	•	•	•	•	Direct Corporate Services Inc		800-783-7904	•	•	•	
•	•				Elman Resources		407-834-5344, cell- 407-221-8485				

CR	CV	PR	US	BK	←Courts	Recorder→	UC	RE	TX	VS
	•	•	•	•	First American Title Ins Co	407-740-7131	•	•	•	•
•	•	•	•	•	First Choice Research	888-878-1595	•		•	
		•			Flagler County Abstract Co [SOP]	386-437-4151	•	•	•	
•	•	•	•	•	Hale Investigative Services/Process [SOP]	800-882-5137	•	•	•	•
	•	•	•	•	ICDI Inc	407-622-2532	•	•	•	
	•	•	•	•	Independent Research Assoc	407-832-8580	•	•	•	
•	•		•	•	Infotrack Information Services Inc	800-275-5594	•	•	•	
•	•	•	•	•	Legal 1 Document Retrieval [SOP]	954-455-5220	•	•	•	•
•	•	•	•	•	Liquori Investigations	386-423-4235	•	•	•	•
•					LNS Research Co.	386-428-1936				
•	•	•			Lowry Document Service	386-789-6193	•	•	•	•
	•		•	•	Phoenix Document Service Inc	727-581-2552	•	•	•	
•	•	•	•	•	Sugarbaker Investigations	352-684-9388	•			•
		•			The Searchers-NKA Hackman Abstracts Inc	352-493-0101	•	•	•	
•		•	•	•	XpertSearch Inc	732-229-6688	•	•	•	•
CR	**CV**	**PR**	**US**	**BK**	**←Courts — WAKULLA**	**Recorder→**	**UC**	**RE**	**TX**	**VS**
•	•		•	•	Capital Connection [SOP]	850-224-8870	•	•	•	
•	•	•	•	•	Corporate Access Inc [SOP]	800-969-1666	•	•	•	•
•	•	•	•	•	First Choice Research	888-878-1595	•		•	
	•		•	•	Florida Filing & Search Services Inc	800-435-9371	•		•	
•	•	•	•	•	Parrish Research	850-936-1240	•	•	•	•
					Research Express	850-926-5665		•		
•	•	•	•	•	State Information Bureau [SOP]	800-881-1742	•	•	•	•
	•		•	•	Sunstate Research Associates Inc	800-621-7234	•		•	
CR	**CV**	**PR**	**US**	**BK**	**←Courts — WALTON**	**Recorder→**	**UC**	**RE**	**TX**	**VS**
	•	•			AAA Search Excellence Inc	352-688-6751	•	•	•	
•	•	•	•	•	Direct Corporate Services Inc	800-783-7904	•	•	•	
•	•	•	•	•	Emerald Coast Protective Services Inc [SOP]	877-234-6252	•	•	•	•
•	•	•	•	•	First Choice Research	888-878-1595	•		•	
•	•				First Quality Research Co	813-862-2778				
•	•	•	•	•	Ike L Hoy PE (Control Systems)	850-259-4650	•	•	•	•
•	•		•	•	Infotrack Information Services Inc	800-275-5594	•	•	•	
•	•	•	•	•	Pacific Photocopy & Research (Pensacola) [SOP]	850-435-3183	•	•	•	•
•	•	•	•	•	Parrish Research	850-936-1240	•	•	•	•
	•		•	•	Phoenix Document Service Inc	727-581-2552	•	•	•	
CR	**CV**	**PR**	**US**	**BK**	**←Courts — WASHINGTON**	**Recorder→**	**UC**	**RE**	**TX**	**VS**
•	•	•	•	•	First Choice Research	888-878-1595	•		•	
•	•	•	•	•	Ike L Hoy PE (Control Systems)	850-259-4650	•	•	•	•
•	•	•	•	•	Pacific Photocopy & Research (Pensacola) [SOP]	850-435-3183	•	•	•	•
•	•	•	•	•	Parrish Research	850-936-1240	•	•	•	•
					Research Express	850-926-5665		•		

[SOP] = PERFORMS SERVICE OF PROCESS

 = PRRN Member. *A retriever you can trust!*

Georgia

Court Records Retrieved — Capital - Fulton County — Recorded Records Retrieved

Appling

CR	CV	PR	US	BK	←Courts	Recorder→	UC	RE	TX	VS
•	•				Background Research Agency Inc	770-788-1885			•	
•	•		•	•	Lighthouse Information Services [SOP]	770-516-9152				
•	•				National Pre-Employment Research [SOP]	770-389-6607				

Atkinson

CR	CV	PR	US	BK	←Courts	Recorder→	UC	RE	TX	VS
•	•	•			API	229-559-4717			•	
•	•		•	•	Lighthouse Information Services [SOP]	770-516-9152				

Bacon

CR	CV	PR	US	BK	←Courts	Recorder→	UC	RE	TX	VS
•	•				Background Research Agency Inc	770-788-1885			•	
•	•		•	•	Lighthouse Information Services [SOP]	770-516-9152				
					Lenn R Lynch	229-942-7331		•	•	

Baker

CR	CV	PR	US	BK	←Courts	Recorder→	UC	RE	TX	VS
•	•				Background Research Agency Inc	770-788-1885			•	

Baldwin

CR	CV	PR	US	BK	←Courts	Recorder→	UC	RE	TX	VS
•	•				Background Research Agency Inc	770-788-1885			•	
•	•				Karen Jackson	478-452-9390; Fax- same			•	
•	•		•	•	Lighthouse Information Services [SOP]	770-516-9152				
•	•				National Pre-Employment Research [SOP]	770-389-6607				
	•			•	Southern Courthouse Ventures	678-413-4697	•	•	•	

Banks

CR	CV	PR	US	BK	←Courts	Recorder→	UC	RE	TX	VS
•	•				Background Research Agency Inc	770-788-1885			•	
	•			•	Southern Courthouse Ventures	678-413-4697	•	•	•	
•	•				Turek Paralegal Services	770-540-7891 cell, 706-548-6842		•	•	

Barrow

CR	CV	PR	US	BK	←Courts	Recorder→	UC	RE	TX	VS
•	•				Able Atlanta Research	404-502-2024	•		•	
	•	•	•	•	Atlanta Title Abstractors	770-267-2727	•	•	•	
•	•				Background Research Agency Inc	770-788-1885			•	
	•		•	•	Courthouse Abstractors	770-271-9002	•	•	•	
•	•	•	•	•	Excel Search Inc	770-844-1201	•	•	•	•
•	•		•	•	G.A. Public Record Services Inc	800-760-2468 x314				
•	•				Professional Paralegal Services Inc [SOP]	706-783-2648		•		
	•			•	Southern Courthouse Ventures	678-413-4697	•	•	•	
•	•				Turek Paralegal Services	770-540-7891 cell, 706-548-6842		•	•	

Bartow

CR	CV	PR	US	BK	←Courts	Recorder→	UC	RE	TX	VS
•	•	•	•	•	A All State Tracers Company	423-605-0155	•	•	•	•
•	•	•	•	•	Axis Research Inc	877-795-1005	•	•	•	
•	•				Background Research Agency Inc	770-788-1885			•	
	•		•	•	Courthouse Abstractors	770-271-9002	•	•	•	
•	•		•	•	Lighthouse Information Services [SOP]	770-516-9152				
					Majestic Research Services Inc	678-355-5393	•	•	•	
•	•		•	•	Public Chex Inc	770-889-5662	•	•	•	
	•			•	Southern Courthouse Ventures	678-413-4697	•	•	•	
•	•	•	•	•	Southern Research Enterprises [SOP]	770-387-9439	•	•	•	•

CR	CV	PR	US	BK	←Courts	Ben Hill	Recorder→	UC	RE	TX	VS
•	•				Background Research Agency Inc		770-788-1885			•	
•	•		•	•	Lighthouse Information Services [SOP]		770-516-9152				
					Morris Abstracting		229-831-7535, cell-229-848-2709		•	•	

CR	CV	PR	US	BK	←Courts	Berrien	Recorder→	UC	RE	TX	VS
•	•	•			API		229-559-4717			•	
•	•				Background Research Agency Inc		770-788-1885			•	
•	•		•	•	Lighthouse Information Services [SOP]		770-516-9152				
					Morris Abstracting		229-831-7535, cell-229-848-2709		•	•	

CR	CV	PR	US	BK	←Courts	Bibb	Recorder→	UC	RE	TX	VS
•	•				Background Research Agency Inc		770-788-1885			•	
•	•	•	•	•	Glaze Research		478-476-0539, 478-256-6696		•	•	•
•	•	•	•	•	Graystone Investigations Inc [SOP]		478-743-5551	•	•	•	•
•	•				National Pre-Employment Research [SOP]		770-389-6607				
	•			•	Southern Courthouse Ventures		678-413-4697	•	•	•	

CR	CV	PR	US	BK	←Courts	Bleckley	Recorder→	UC	RE	TX	VS
•	•				Background Research Agency Inc		770-788-1885			•	
•	•		•	•	Lighthouse Information Services [SOP]		770-516-9152				
•	•				National Pre-Employment Research [SOP]		770-389-6607				

CR	CV	PR	US	BK	←Courts	Brantley	Recorder→	UC	RE	TX	VS
•	•				Background Research Agency Inc		770-788-1885			•	
•	•		•		Lighthouse Information Services [SOP]		770-516-9152				
					Michael's Legal Research		912-269-5532	•	•		
•	•				National Pre-Employment Research [SOP]		770-389-6607				
	•	•			Betty M Rowell, CLA		912-449-0849	•	•	•	

CR	CV	PR	US	BK	←Courts	Brooks	Recorder→	UC	RE	TX	VS
•	•	•			API		229-559-4717			•	
•	•				Background Research Agency Inc		770-788-1885			•	

CR	CV	PR	US	BK	←Courts	Bryan	Recorder→	UC	RE	TX	VS
•	•				Background Research Agency Inc		770-788-1885			•	
•	•	•	•	•	Crisp & Associates [SOP]		912-898-9973	•		•	
•	•				National Pre-Employment Research [SOP]		770-389-6607				

CR	CV	PR	US	BK	←Courts	Bulloch	Recorder→	UC	RE	TX	VS
•	•				Background Research Agency Inc		770-788-1885			•	
•	•		•	•	Lighthouse Information Services [SOP]		770-516-9152				
•	•				National Pre-Employment Research [SOP]		770-389-6607				

CR	CV	PR	US	BK	←Courts	Burke	Recorder→	UC	RE	TX	VS
•	•				Background Research Agency Inc		770-788-1885			•	
•	•	•	•	•	CSRA Background Verification Inc		706-869-8882	•	•	•	
•	•	•	•	•	David Smith Detective Agency [SOP]		877-793-9426	•		•	
•	•				National Pre-Employment Research [SOP]		770-389-6607				
					Thompson Research		706-860-4181		•	•	
•	•		•		Verifi LLC		423-344-0133	•	•	•	•
					David V Weber, Attorney		706-860-8160		•		

CR	CV	PR	US	BK	←Courts	Butts	Recorder→	UC	RE	TX	VS
•	•				Background Research Agency Inc		770-788-1885			•	
•	•	•			Reba Jones		478-994-4501				
•	•				National Pre-Employment Research [SOP]		770-389-6607				
	•	•			Reliable Abstract		678-614-0715		•	•	
	•			•	Southern Courthouse Ventures		678-413-4697	•	•	•	

CR	CV	PR	US	BK	←Courts	CALHOUN	Recorder→	UC	RE	TX	VS
•	•				Background Research Agency Inc		770-788-1885			•	

CR	CV	PR	US	BK	←Courts	CAMDEN	Recorder→	UC	RE	TX	VS
•	•				Background Research Agency Inc		770-788-1885			•	
•	•		•	•	Lighthouse Information Services [SOP]		770-516-9152				
•	•		•		Troy Lindsey		912-265-4405; Fax- same				
					Michael's Legal Research		912-269-5532	•	•		
•	•				National Pre-Employment Research [SOP]		770-389-6607				

CR	CV	PR	US	BK	←Courts	CANDLER	Recorder→	UC	RE	TX	VS
•	•				Background Research Agency Inc		770-788-1885			•	
		•	•	•	John E Jones Jr Land Title & Appraisal		912-685-3047	•	•	•	•
•	•		•	•	Lighthouse Information Services [SOP]		770-516-9152				

CR	CV	PR	US	BK	←Courts	CARROLL	Recorder→	UC	RE	TX	VS
•	•				Background Research Agency Inc		770-788-1885			•	
•	•				KYMRON Research LLC [SOP]		770-703-7301				
•	•				Shelia Pettit		770-832-9273				
	•			•	Southern Courthouse Ventures		678-413-4697	•	•	•	
•	•		•	•	Specialty Services [SOP]		770-942-8264	•	•	•	

CR	CV	PR	US	BK	←Courts	CATOOSA	Recorder→	UC	RE	TX	VS
•	•	•	•	•	A All State Tracers Company		423-605-0155	•	•	•	•
•	•				Background Research Agency Inc		770-788-1885			•	
					DocuSearch Services		423-894-2425	•	•	•	
•	•				Kim Osborne		706-935-4202				
•	•				Search & Find		706-884-9801			•	
	•			•	Southern Courthouse Ventures		678-413-4697	•	•	•	
•	•	•	•	•	Southern Research Enterprises [SOP]		770-387-9439	•	•	•	•
	•	•	•	•	Title Guaranty & Trust of Chattanooga		423-266-5751	•	•	•	
•	•		•	•	Verifi LLC		423-344-0133	•	•	•	

CR	CV	PR	US	BK	←Courts	CHARLTON	Recorder→	UC	RE	TX	VS
•	•				Background Research Agency Inc		770-788-1885			•	
•	•		•	•	Lighthouse Information Services [SOP]		770-516-9152				

CR	CV	PR	US	BK	←Courts	CHATHAM	Recorder→	UC	RE	TX	VS
•	•				Background Research Agency Inc		770-788-1885			•	
•	•	•	•	•	Crisp & Associates [SOP]		912-898-9973	•		•	
•	•		•	•	R L Ferrelle		912-330-9923				
•	•		•	•	Lighthouse Information Services [SOP]		770-516-9152				
•	•				National Pre-Employment Research [SOP]		770-389-6607				

CR	CV	PR	US	BK	←Courts	CHATTAHOOCHEE	Recorder→	UC	RE	TX	VS
•	•			•	Attorneys Services & Legal Inv [SOP]		706-322-3554 or 322-3224	•	•	•	
•	•				Background Research Agency Inc		770-788-1885			•	

CR	CV	PR	US	BK	←Courts	CHATTOOGA	Recorder→	UC	RE	TX	VS
•	•	•	•	•	A All State Tracers Company		423-605-0155	•	•	•	•
•	•				Background Research Agency Inc		770-788-1885			•	
					DocuSearch Services		423-894-2425	•	•	•	
	•			•	Southern Courthouse Ventures		678-413-4697	•	•	•	
•	•	•	•	•	Southern Research Enterprises [SOP]		770-387-9439	•	•	•	•
	•	•	•	•	Title Guaranty & Trust of Chattanooga		423-266-5751	•	•	•	
•	•		•	•	Verifi LLC		423-344-0133	•	•	•	

CR	CV	PR	US	BK	←Courts	CHEROKEE	Recorder→	UC	RE	TX	VS
•	•	•	•	•	A All State Tracers Company		423-605-0155	•	•	•	•
•	•	•	•	•	Archives Retrieval Service of GA		770-252-5510	•	•	•	•
•	•	•	•	•	Axis Research Inc		877-795-1005	•	•	•	

CR	CV	PR	US	BK	←Courts	Recorder→	UC	RE	TX	VS
•	•				Background Research Agency Inc	770-788-1885			•	
	•		•	•	Courthouse Abstractors	770-271-9002	•	•	•	
					DocuSearch Services	423-894-2425	•	•	•	
•	•	•	•	•	Excel Search Inc	770-844-1201	•	•	•	•
•	•				KYMRON Research LLC [SOP]	770-703-7301				
•	•		•	•	Lighthouse Information Services [SOP]	770-516-9152				
					Majestic Research Services Inc.	678-355-5393	•	•	•	
•	•		•	•	Public Chex Inc	770-889-5662	•	•	•	
	•			•	Southern Courthouse Ventures	678-413-4697	•	•	•	
•	•	•	•	•	Southern Research Enterprises [SOP]	770-387-9439	•	•	•	•
CR	**CV**	**PR**	**US**	**BK**	**←Courts CLARKE**	**Recorder→**	**UC**	**RE**	**TX**	**VS**
	•	•	•	•	Atlanta Title Abstractors	770-267-2727	•	•	•	
•	•				Background Research Agency Inc	770-788-1885			•	
•	•	•	•	•	Excel Search Inc	770-844-1201	•	•	•	•
•	•				National Pre-Employment Research [SOP]	770-389-6607				
•	•				Professional Paralegal Services Inc [SOP]	706-783-2648		•		
	•			•	Southern Courthouse Ventures	678-413-4697	•	•	•	
•	•	•			Taya Gordon Research	706-546-6598	•	•	•	
•	•				Turek Paralegal Services	770-540-7891 cell, 706-548-6842		•	•	
•	•	•	•		John Wilmot	706-546-7411	•	•	•	•
CR	**CV**	**PR**	**US**	**BK**	**←Courts CLAY**	**Recorder→**	**UC**	**RE**	**TX**	**VS**
•	•				Background Research Agency Inc	770-788-1885			•	
CR	**CV**	**PR**	**US**	**BK**	**←Courts CLAYTON**	**Recorder→**	**UC**	**RE**	**TX**	**VS**
•	•	•	•	•	A All State Tracers Company	423-605-0155	•	•	•	•
•					Able Atlanta Research	404-502-2024	•			
•	•	•	•	•	Archives Retrieval Service of GA	770-252-5510	•	•	•	•
•	•	•	•	•	Atlanta Attorney Services [SOP]	800-804-4078	•		•	
•	•	•	•	•	Atlanta Legal Services Inc [SOP]	877-302-4136	•	•	•	•
	•	•	•	•	Atlanta Title Abstractors	770-267-2727	•	•	•	
•	•	•	•	•	Attorneys' Personal Services [SOP]	800-245-0122	•	•	•	•
•	•	•	•	•	Axis Research Inc	877-795-1005	•	•	•	
•	•				Background Research Agency Inc	770-788-1885			•	
	•		•	•	Courthouse Abstractors	770-271-9002	•	•	•	
•	•	•	•	•	Ed Knight Information Service	800-282-6418	•	•	•	
•	•	•	•	•	Excel Search Inc	770-844-1201	•	•	•	•
•	•	•	•	•	John Roberson Inv [SOP]	800-325-0914	•	•	•	•
•		•	•	•	Judicial Research & Retrieval Services (Georgia)	800-529-1338	•	•	•	•
•	•				KYMRON Research LLC [SOP]	770-703-7301				
					Majestic Research Services Inc.	678-355-5393	•	•	•	
•	•				Minor Services Inc - Excel Legal Search	770-987-0942, 770-789-8543	•		•	
•	•				Search & Find	706-884-9801			•	
	•			•	Southern Courthouse Ventures	678-413-4697	•	•	•	
•	•				TPQ Associates	770-475-0743	•	•	•	
CR	**CV**	**PR**	**US**	**BK**	**←Courts CLINCH**	**Recorder→**	**UC**	**RE**	**TX**	**VS**
•	•	•			API	229-559-4717			•	
•	•				Background Research Agency Inc	770-788-1885			•	
•	•		•	•	Lighthouse Information Services [SOP]	770-516-9152				
CR	**CV**	**PR**	**US**	**BK**	**←Courts COBB**	**Recorder→**	**UC**	**RE**	**TX**	**VS**
•	•	•	•	•	A All State Tracers Company	423-605-0155	•	•	•	•
•	•	•	•	•	Atlanta Attorney Services [SOP]	800-804-4078	•		•	
•	•	•	•	•	Atlanta Legal Services Inc [SOP]	877-302-4136	•	•	•	•
	•	•	•	•	Atlanta Title Abstractors	770-267-2727	•	•	•	
•	•	•	•	•	Attorneys' Personal Services [SOP]	800-245-0122	•	•	•	•
•	•	•	•	•	Axis Research Inc	877-795-1005	•	•	•	
•	•				Background Research Agency Inc	770-788-1885			•	

CR	CV	PR	US	BK	←Courts		Recorder→	UC	RE	TX	VS
	•		•	•	Courthouse Abstractors		770-271-9002	•	•	•	
•	•				Dayton Hayes Inc		404-418-8323	•	•	•	
					DocuSearch Services		423-894-2425	•	•	•	
					Docx		866-729-8099	•	•		
•	•	•	•	•	Excel Search Inc		770-844-1201	•	•	•	•
•	•	•	•	•	John Roberson Inv [SOP]		800-325-0914	•	•	•	•
•		•	•	•	Judicial Research & Retrieval Services (Georgia)		800-529-1338	•	•	•	•
•	•				KYMRON Research LLC [SOP]		770-703-7301				
•	•		•	•	Lighthouse Information Services [SOP]		770-516-9152				
					Majestic Research Services Inc.		678-355-5393	•	•	•	
•	•	•	•	•	Marathon Research LLC		678-570-7163	•	•	•	•
•	•	•	•	•	MLQ Attorney Services [SOP]		800-446-8794	•	•	•	•
•	•		•	•	Public Chex Inc		770-889-5662	•	•	•	
	•			•	Southern Courthouse Ventures		678-413-4697	•	•	•	
•	•	•	•	•	Southern Research Enterprises [SOP]		770-387-9439	•	•	•	•
•	•				TPQ Associates		770-475-0743	•	•	•	

CR	CV	PR	US	BK	←Courts	Coffee	Recorder→	UC	RE	TX	VS
•	•				Background Research Agency Inc		770-788-1885			•	
•	•		•	•	Lighthouse Information Services [SOP]		770-516-9152				

CR	CV	PR	US	BK	←Courts	Colquitt	Recorder→	UC	RE	TX	VS
•	•	•			API		229-559-4717			•	
•	•				Background Research Agency Inc		770-788-1885			•	
•	•		•	•	Lighthouse Information Services [SOP]		770-516-9152				
					Morris Abstracting		229-831-7535, cell-229-848-2709		•	•	

CR	CV	PR	US	BK	←Courts	Columbia	Recorder→	UC	RE	TX	VS
•	•				Background Research Agency Inc		770-788-1885			•	
•	•	•	•		CSRA Background Verification Inc		706-869-8882	•	•	•	
•	•	•	•		David Smith Detective Agency [SOP]		877-793-9426	•		•	
•	•				National Pre-Employment Research [SOP]		770-389-6607				
•	•		•	•	Verifi LLC		423-344-0133	•	•	•	
					David V Weber, Attorney		706-860-8160		•		

CR	CV	PR	US	BK	←Courts	Cook	Recorder→	UC	RE	TX	VS
•	•	•			API		229-559-4717			•	
•	•				Background Research Agency Inc		770-788-1885			•	
•	•		•	•	Lighthouse Information Services [SOP]		770-516-9152				
					Morris Abstracting		229-831-7535, cell-229-848-2709		•	•	

CR	CV	PR	US	BK	←Courts	Coweta	Recorder→	UC	RE	TX	VS
•	•	•	•	•	Archives Retrieval Service of GA		770-252-5510	•	•	•	•
•	•				Background Research Agency Inc		770-788-1885			•	
•	•	•	•	•	John Roberson Inv [SOP]		800-325-0914	•	•	•	•
					Majestic Research Services Inc.		678-355-5393	•	•	•	
•	•				National Pre-Employment Research [SOP]		770-389-6607				
•	•				Shelia Pettit		770-832-9273				
	•			•	Southern Courthouse Ventures		678-413-4697	•	•	•	
•	•	•	•	•	Southern Research Enterprises [SOP]		770-387-9439	•	•	•	•
•	•		•	•	Specialty Services [SOP]		770-942-8264	•	•	•	

CR	CV	PR	US	BK	←Courts	Crawford	Recorder→	UC	RE	TX	VS
•	•				Background Research Agency Inc		770-788-1885			•	
•	•	•	•	•	Glaze Research		478-476-0539, 478-256-6696		•	•	•
•	•	•	•	•	Graystone Investigations Inc [SOP]		478-743-5551	•	•	•	•
	•			•	Southern Courthouse Ventures		678-413-4697	•	•	•	

CR	CV	PR	US	BK	←Courts	Crisp	Recorder→	UC	RE	TX	VS
•	•				Background Research Agency Inc		770-788-1885			•	

CR	CV	PR	US	BK	←Courts	DADE	Recorder→	UC	RE	TX	VS
•	•				Background Research Agency Inc		770-788-1885			•	
•	•	•	•	•	Southern Research Enterprises [SOP]		770-387-9439	•	•	•	•
	•	•	•	•	Title Guaranty & Trust of Chattanooga		423-266-5751	•	•	•	
•	•		•	•	Verifi LLC		423-344-0133	•	•	•	

CR	CV	PR	US	BK	←Courts	DAWSON	Recorder→	UC	RE	TX	VS
•	•	•	•	•	A All State Tracers Company		423-605-0155	•	•	•	•
	•				AFX Corp Inc		706-867-6794		•	•	
•	•				Background Research Agency Inc		770-788-1885			•	
	•		•	•	Courthouse Abstractors		770-271-9002	•	•	•	
•	•	•	•	•	Excel Search Inc		770-844-1201	•	•	•	•
•					Intricate Solutions Inc		866-640-5210				
•	•	•	•	•	John Roberson Inv [SOP]		800-325-0914	•	•	•	•
•	•		•	•	Public Chex Inc		770-889-5662	•	•	•	
	•			•	Southern Courthouse Ventures		678-413-4697	•	•	•	
•	•	•	•	•	Southern Research Enterprises [SOP]		770-387-9439	•	•	•	•
•	•				Turek Paralegal Services		770-540-7891 cell, 706-548-6842		•	•	

CR	CV	PR	US	BK	←Courts	DE KALB	Recorder→	UC	RE	TX	VS
•	•	•	•	•	A All State Tracers Company		423-605-0155	•	•	•	•
•	•				Able Atlanta Research		404-502-2024	•		•	
•	•	•	•	•	Archives Retrieval Service of GA		770-252-5510	•	•	•	•
•	•	•	•	•	Atlanta Attorney Services [SOP]		800-804-4078	•		•	
•	•	•	•	•	Atlanta Legal Services Inc [SOP]		877-302-4136	•	•	•	•
	•	•	•	•	Atlanta Title Abstractors		770-267-2727	•	•	•	
•	•	•	•	•	Atlantic Investigations [SOP]		800-216-9877	•	•	•	•
•	•	•	•	•	Attorneys' Personal Services [SOP]		800-245-0122	•	•	•	•
•	•	•	•	•	Axis Research Inc		877-795-1005	•	•	•	
•	•				Background Research Agency Inc		770-788-1885			•	
	•		•	•	Courthouse Abstractors		770-271-9002	•	•	•	
•	•				Dayton Hayes Inc		404-418-8323	•	•	•	
					Docx		866-729-8099	•	•		
•	•	•	•	•	Excel Search Inc		770-844-1201	•	•	•	•
•	•	•	•	•	John Roberson Inv [SOP]		800-325-0914	•	•	•	•
•		•	•	•	Judicial Research & Retrieval Services (Georgia)		800-529-1338	•	•	•	•
•	•				KYMRON Research LLC [SOP]		770-703-7301				
•	•		•	•	Lighthouse Information Services [SOP]		770-516-9152				
					Majestic Research Services Inc		678-355-5393	•	•	•	
•	•	•	•	•	Marathon Research LLC		678-570-7163	•	•	•	•
•	•				Minor Services Inc - Excel Legal Search		770-987-0942, 770-789-8543	•		•	
•	•	•	•	•	MLQ Attorney Services [SOP]		800-446-8794	•	•	•	•
•	•		•	•	Public Chex Inc		770-889-5662	•	•	•	
	•			•	Southern Courthouse Ventures		678-413-4697	•	•	•	
•	•		•	•	Specialty Services [SOP]		770-942-8264	•	•	•	
•	•				TPQ Associates		770-475-0743	•	•	•	

CR	CV	PR	US	BK	←Courts	DECATUR	Recorder→	UC	RE	TX	VS
•	•				Background Research Agency Inc		770-788-1885			•	

CR	CV	PR	US	BK	←Courts	DODGE	Recorder→	UC	RE	TX	VS
•	•				Background Research Agency Inc		770-788-1885			•	
•	•		•	•	Lighthouse Information Services [SOP]		770-516-9152				

CR	CV	PR	US	BK	←Courts	DOOLY	Recorder→	UC	RE	TX	VS
•	•				Background Research Agency Inc		770-788-1885			•	

CR	CV	PR	US	BK	←Courts	DOUGHERTY	Recorder→	UC	RE	TX	VS
•	•				Background Research Agency Inc		770-788-1885			•	
•	•		•	•	Lighthouse Information Services [SOP]		770-516-9152				

CR	CV	PR	US	BK	←Courts	County / Retriever	Phone	Recorder→	UC	RE	TX	VS
						Lenn R Lynch	229-942-7331			•	•	
CR	**CV**	**PR**	**US**	**BK**	**←Courts**	**DOUGLAS**		**Recorder→**	**UC**	**RE**	**TX**	**VS**
•	•	•	•	•		A All State Tracers Company	423-605-0155		•	•	•	•
•	•	•	•	•		Atlanta Legal Services Inc [SOP]	877-302-4136		•	•	•	•
	•	•	•	•		Atlanta Title Abstractors	770-267-2727		•	•	•	
•	•	•	•	•		Axis Research Inc	877-795-1005		•	•	•	
•	•					Background Research Agency Inc	770-788-1885				•	
	•		•	•		Courthouse Abstractors	770-271-9002		•	•	•	
•	•	•				Terri Irwin	770-920-9957				•	
•	•					KYMRON Research LLC [SOP]	770-703-7301					
						Majestic Research Services Inc	678-355-5393		•	•	•	
	•			•		Southern Courthouse Ventures	678-413-4697		•	•	•	
•	•	•	•	•		Southern Research Enterprises [SOP]	770-387-9439		•	•	•	•
•	•		•	•		Specialty Services [SOP]	770-942-8264		•	•	•	
CR	**CV**	**PR**	**US**	**BK**	**←Courts**	**EARLY**		**Recorder→**	**UC**	**RE**	**TX**	**VS**
•	•					Background Research Agency Inc	770-788-1885				•	
•	•					Tom Baxley Law Office	229-723-3426					
CR	**CV**	**PR**	**US**	**BK**	**←Courts**	**ECHOLS**		**Recorder→**	**UC**	**RE**	**TX**	**VS**
•	•	•				API	229-559-4717				•	
CR	**CV**	**PR**	**US**	**BK**	**←Courts**	**EFFINGHAM**		**Recorder→**	**UC**	**RE**	**TX**	**VS**
•	•					Background Research Agency Inc	770-788-1885				•	
•	•	•	•	•		Crisp & Associates [SOP]	912-898-9973		•		•	
•	•		•	•		R L Ferrelle	912-330-9923					
•	•					National Pre-Employment Research [SOP]	770-389-6607					
CR	**CV**	**PR**	**US**	**BK**	**←Courts**	**ELBERT**		**Recorder→**	**UC**	**RE**	**TX**	**VS**
•	•					Background Research Agency Inc	770-788-1885				•	
•	•					Professional Paralegal Services Inc [SOP]	706-783-2648			•		
•	•					Turek Paralegal Services	770-540-7891 cell, 706-548-6842			•	•	
CR	**CV**	**PR**	**US**	**BK**	**←Courts**	**EMANUEL**		**Recorder→**	**UC**	**RE**	**TX**	**VS**
•	•					Background Research Agency Inc	770-788-1885				•	
•	•		•	•		Lighthouse Information Services [SOP]	770-516-9152					
CR	**CV**	**PR**	**US**	**BK**	**←Courts**	**EVANS**		**Recorder→**	**UC**	**RE**	**TX**	**VS**
•	•					Background Research Agency Inc	770-788-1885				•	
•	•					National Pre-Employment Research [SOP]	770-389-6607					
CR	**CV**	**PR**	**US**	**BK**	**←Courts**	**FANNIN**		**Recorder→**	**UC**	**RE**	**TX**	**VS**
•	•	•	•	•		John Roberson Inv [SOP]	800-325-0914		•	•	•	•
	•			•		Southern Courthouse Ventures	678-413-4697		•	•	•	
•	•	•	•	•		Southern Research Enterprises [SOP]	770-387-9439		•	•	•	•
	•	•	•	•		Title Guaranty & Trust of Chattanooga	423-266-5751		•	•	•	
CR	**CV**	**PR**	**US**	**BK**	**←Courts**	**FAYETTE**		**Recorder→**	**UC**	**RE**	**TX**	**VS**
•	•	•	•	•		Archives Retrieval Service of GA	770-252-5510		•	•	•	•
	•	•	•	•		Atlanta Title Abstractors	770-267-2727		•	•	•	
•	•	•	•	•		Axis Research Inc	877-795-1005		•	•	•	
•	•					Background Research Agency Inc	770-788-1885				•	
•	•	•	•	•		John Roberson Inv [SOP]	800-325-0914		•	•	•	•
•	•					KYMRON Research LLC [SOP]	770-703-7301					
						Majestic Research Services Inc	678-355-5393		•	•	•	
•	•					Search & Find	706-884-9801				•	
	•			•		Southern Courthouse Ventures	678-413-4697		•	•	•	
CR	**CV**	**PR**	**US**	**BK**	**←Courts**	**FLOYD**		**Recorder→**	**UC**	**RE**	**TX**	**VS**
•	•	•	•	•		A All State Tracers Company	423-605-0155		•	•	•	•
•	•					Background Research Agency Inc	770-788-1885				•	

CR	CV	PR	US	BK	←Courts	Recorder→	UC	RE	TX	VS
					DocuSearch Services	423-894-2425	•	•	•	
•	•	•	•		Euchner Research LLC	678-614-1816	•	•	•	•
	•			•	Southern Courthouse Ventures	678-413-4697	•	•	•	
•	•	•	•	•	Southern Research Enterprises [SOP]	770-387-9439	•	•	•	•

CR	CV	PR	US	BK	←Courts **Forsyth**	Recorder→	UC	RE	TX	VS
•	•	•	•	•	A All State Tracers Company	423-605-0155	•	•	•	•
•	•	•	•	•	Atlanta Attorney Services [SOP]	800-804-4078	•		•	
•	•	•	•	•	Atlanta Legal Services Inc [SOP]	877-302-4136	•	•	•	•
•	•	•	•	•	Axis Research Inc	877-795-1005	•	•	•	
•	•				Background Research Agency Inc	770-788-1885			•	
	•		•	•	Courthouse Abstractors	770-271-9002	•	•	•	
•	•	•	•	•	Excel Search Inc	770-844-1201	•	•	•	•
•	•	•	•	•	Graystone Investigations Inc [SOP]	478-743-5551	•	•	•	•
•	•	•			Penny Harmon	404-580-3099	•	•	•	
•	•		•	•	Public Chex Inc	770-889-5662	•	•	•	
	•			•	Southern Courthouse Ventures	678-413-4697	•	•	•	
•	•				TPQ Associates	770-475-0743	•	•	•	

CR	CV	PR	US	BK	←Courts **Franklin**	Recorder→	UC	RE	TX	VS
•	•				Background Research Agency Inc	770-788-1885			•	
•	•				Jean McCullough	706-491-9595		•	•	
	•			•	Southern Courthouse Ventures	678-413-4697	•	•	•	

CR	CV	PR	US	BK	←Courts **Fulton**	Recorder→	UC	RE	TX	VS
•	•	•	•	•	A All State Tracers Company	423-605-0155	•	•	•	•
•	•				Able Atlanta Research	404-502-2024	•		•	
•	•	•	•	•	Archives Retrieval Service of GA	770-252-5510	•	•	•	•
•	•	•	•	•	Atlanta Attorney Services [SOP]	800-804-4078	•		•	
•	•	•	•	•	Atlanta Legal Services Inc [SOP]	877-302-4136	•	•	•	•
	•	•	•	•	Atlanta Title Abstractors	770-267-2727	•	•	•	
•	•	•	•	•	Attorneys' Personal Services [SOP]	800-245-0122	•	•	•	•
•	•	•	•	•	Axis Research Inc	877-795-1005	•	•	•	
•	•				Background Research Agency Inc	770-788-1885			•	
	•		•	•	Courthouse Abstractors	770-271-9002	•	•	•	
•	•				Dayton Hayes Inc	404-418-8323	•	•	•	
					Docx	866-729-8099	•	•		
•	•	•	•	•	Excel Search Inc	770-844-1201	•	•	•	•
•	•	•	•	•	John Roberson Inv [SOP]	800-325-0914	•	•	•	•
•		•	•	•	Judicial Research & Retrieval Services (Georgia)	800-529-1338	•	•	•	•
•	•				KYMRON Research LLC [SOP]	770-703-7301				
•	•		•	•	Lighthouse Information Services [SOP]	770-516-9152				
					Majestic Research Services Inc.	678-355-5393	•	•	•	
•	•	•	•	•	Marathon Research LLC	678-570-7163	•	•	•	•
•	•				Minor Services Inc - Excel Legal Search	770-987-0942, 770-789-8543	•		•	
•	•	•	•	•	MLQ Attorney Services [SOP]	800-446-8794	•	•	•	•
•	•		•	•	Public Chex Inc	770-889-5662	•	•	•	
	•			•	Southern Courthouse Ventures	678-413-4697	•	•	•	
•	•	•	•	•	Southern Research Enterprises [SOP]	770-387-9439	•	•	•	•
•	•		•	•	Specialty Services [SOP]	770-942-8264	•	•	•	
•	•				TPQ Associates	770-475-0743	•	•	•	

CR	CV	PR	US	BK	←Courts **Gilmer**	Recorder→	UC	RE	TX	VS
•	•	•	•	•	A All State Tracers Company	423-605-0155	•	•	•	•
•	•				Background Research Agency Inc	770-788-1885			•	
•	•	•	•	•	John Roberson Inv [SOP]	800-325-0914	•	•	•	•
	•			•	Southern Courthouse Ventures	678-413-4697	•	•	•	
•	•	•	•	•	Southern Research Enterprises [SOP]	770-387-9439	•	•	•	•
	•	•	•	•	Title Guaranty & Trust of Chattanooga	423-266-5751	•	•	•	
•	•		•	•	Verifi LLC	423-344-0133	•	•	•	

CR	CV	PR	US	BK	←COURTS	GLASCOCK	RECORDER→	UC	RE	TX	VS
•	•				Mahaffey Law Office		706-547-4090				
•	•				National Pre-Employment Research [SOP]		770-389-6607				

CR	CV	PR	US	BK	←COURTS	GLYNN	RECORDER→	UC	RE	TX	VS
•	•				Background Research Agency Inc		770-788-1885			•	
•	•		•	•	(icon) Lighthouse Information Services [SOP]		770-516-9152				
•	•		•		Troy Lindsey		912-265-4405; Fax- same				
					(icon) Michael's Legal Research		912-269-5532	•	•		
•	•				National Pre-Employment Research [SOP]		770-389-6607				

CR	CV	PR	US	BK	←COURTS	GORDON	RECORDER→	UC	RE	TX	VS
•	•	•	•	•	(icon) A All State Tracers Company		423-605-0155	•	•	•	•
•	•				Background Research Agency Inc		770-788-1885			•	
	•		•	•	Courthouse Abstractors		770-271-9002	•	•	•	
					DocuSearch Services		423-894-2425	•	•	•	
•	•	•	•		(icon) Euchner Research LLC		678-614-1816	•	•	•	•
	•			•	(icon) Southern Courthouse Ventures		678-413-4697	•	•	•	
•	•	•	•	•	Southern Research Enterprises [SOP]		770-387-9439	•	•	•	•
	•	•	•	•	Title Guaranty & Trust of Chattanooga		423-266-5751	•	•	•	

CR	CV	PR	US	BK	←COURTS	GRADY	RECORDER→	UC	RE	TX	VS
•	•				Background Research Agency Inc		770-788-1885			•	

CR	CV	PR	US	BK	←COURTS	GREENE	RECORDER→	UC	RE	TX	VS
•	•	•			Merritt & Henry LLC		706-342-9668	•	•	•	
•	•				National Pre-Employment Research [SOP]		770-389-6607				
•	•				Professional Paralegal Services Inc [SOP]		706-783-2648		•		
•	•	•	•		Bill Scholly		706-342-4166; Fax- same			•	
	•			•	(icon) Southern Courthouse Ventures		678-413-4697	•	•	•	

CR	CV	PR	US	BK	←COURTS	GWINNETT	RECORDER→	UC	RE	TX	VS
•	•	•	•	•	(icon) A All State Tracers Company		423-605-0155	•	•	•	•
•	•				Able Atlanta Research		404-502-2024	•		•	
•	•	•	•	•	(icon) Archives Retrieval Service of GA		770-252-5510	•	•	•	•
•	•	•	•	•	(icon) Atlanta Attorney Services [SOP]		800-804-4078	•		•	
•	•	•	•	•	Atlanta Legal Services Inc [SOP]		877-302-4136	•	•	•	•
	•	•	•	•	Atlanta Title Abstractors		770-267-2727	•	•	•	
•	•	•	•	•	Attorneys' Personal Services [SOP]		800-245-0122	•	•	•	•
•	•	•	•	•	(icon) Axis Research Inc		877-795-1005	•	•	•	
•	•				Background Research Agency Inc		770-788-1885			•	
	•		•	•	Courthouse Abstractors		770-271-9002	•	•	•	
•	•				(icon) Dayton Hayes Inc		404-418-8323	•	•	•	
•	•	•	•	•	Excel Search Inc		770-844-1201	•	•	•	•
•	•	•	•	•	John Roberson Inv [SOP]		800-325-0914	•	•	•	•
•		•	•	•	Judicial Research & Retrieval Services (Georgia)		800-529-1338	•	•	•	•
•	•				(icon) KYMRON Research LLC [SOP]		770-703-7301				
•	•		•	•	(icon) Lighthouse Information Services [SOP]		770-516-9152				
					Majestic Research Services Inc		678-355-5393	•	•	•	
•	•	•	•	•	(icon) MLQ Attorney Services [SOP]		800-446-8794	•	•	•	•
•	•		•	•	(icon) Public Chex Inc		770-889-5662	•	•	•	
	•			•	(icon) Southern Courthouse Ventures		678-413-4697	•	•	•	
•	•				(icon) TPQ Associates		770-475-0743	•	•	•	

CR	CV	PR	US	BK	←COURTS	HABERSHAM	RECORDER→	UC	RE	TX	VS
•	•				Background Research Agency Inc		770-788-1885			•	
•	•				National Pre-Employment Research [SOP]		770-389-6607				
	•			•	(icon) Southern Courthouse Ventures		678-413-4697	•	•	•	
•	•				Turek Paralegal Services		770-540-7891 cell, 706-548-6842		•	•	

CR	CV	PR	US	BK	←COURTS	HALL	RECORDER→	UC	RE	TX	VS
•	•				Able Atlanta Research		404-502-2024	•		•	
	•	•	•	•	Atlanta Title Abstractors		770-267-2727	•	•	•	
•	•	•	•	•	Axis Research Inc		877-795-1005	•	•	•	
•	•				Background Research Agency Inc		770-788-1885			•	
	•		•	•	Courthouse Abstractors		770-271-9002	•	•	•	
•	•	•	•	•	Excel Search Inc		770-844-1201	•	•	•	•
•	•	•			Penny Harmon		404-580-3099	•	•	•	
•	•	•	•	•	John Roberson Inv [SOP]		800-325-0914	•	•	•	•
•	•		•	•	Public Chex Inc		770-889-5662	•	•	•	
	•			•	Southern Courthouse Ventures		678-413-4697	•	•	•	
•	•				TPQ Associates		770-475-0743	•	•	•	
•	•				Turek Paralegal Services		770-540-7891 cell, 706-548-6842		•	•	

CR	CV	PR	US	BK	←COURTS	HANCOCK	RECORDER→	UC	RE	TX	VS
•	•				Background Research Agency Inc		770-788-1885			•	
	•			•	Southern Courthouse Ventures		678-413-4697	•	•	•	

CR	CV	PR	US	BK	←COURTS	HARALSON	RECORDER→	UC	RE	TX	VS
•	•				Background Research Agency Inc		770-788-1885			•	
•	•				Shelia Pettit		770-832-9273				
	•			•	Southern Courthouse Ventures		678-413-4697	•	•	•	

CR	CV	PR	US	BK	←COURTS	HARRIS	RECORDER→	UC	RE	TX	VS
•	•			•	Attorneys Services & Legal Inv [SOP]		706-322-3554 or 322-3224	•	•	•	
•	•				Background Research Agency Inc		770-788-1885			•	
•	•				Search & Find		706-884-9801			•	

CR	CV	PR	US	BK	←COURTS	HART	RECORDER→	UC	RE	TX	VS
•	•				Background Research Agency Inc		770-788-1885			•	

CR	CV	PR	US	BK	←COURTS	HEARD	RECORDER→	UC	RE	TX	VS
•	•				Background Research Agency Inc		770-788-1885			•	
•	•				Shelia Pettit		770-832-9273				

CR	CV	PR	US	BK	←COURTS	HENRY	RECORDER→	UC	RE	TX	VS
•	•	•	•	•	A All State Tracers Company		423-605-0155	•	•	•	•
•	•				Able Atlanta Research		404-502-2024	•		•	
•	•	•	•	•	Archives Retrieval Service of GA		770-252-5510	•	•	•	•
•	•	•	•	•	Axis Research Inc		877-795-1005	•	•	•	
•	•				Background Research Agency Inc		770-788-1885			•	
•	•	•	•	•	Ed Knight Information Service		800-282-6418	•	•	•	
•	•	•	•	•	Excel Search Inc		770-844-1201	•	•	•	•
•	•	•	•	•	John Roberson Inv [SOP]		800-325-0914	•	•	•	•
					Majestic Research Services Inc		678-355-5393	•	•	•	
•	•				Minor Services Inc - Excel Legal Search		770-987-0942, 770-789-8543	•		•	
•	•				National Pre-Employment Research [SOP]		770-389-6607				
	•	•			Reliable Abstract		678-614-0715		•	•	
•	•				Search & Find		706-884-9801			•	
	•			•	Southern Courthouse Ventures		678-413-4697	•	•	•	

CR	CV	PR	US	BK	←COURTS	HOUSTON	RECORDER→	UC	RE	TX	VS
•	•				Background Research Agency Inc		770-788-1885			•	
•	•	•	•	•	Glaze Research		478-476-0539, 478-256-6696		•	•	•
•	•	•	•	•	Graystone Investigations Inc [SOP]		478-743-5551	•	•	•	•

CR	CV	PR	US	BK	←COURTS	IRWIN	RECORDER→	UC	RE	TX	VS
•	•				Background Research Agency Inc		770-788-1885			•	
•	•		•	•	Lighthouse Information Services [SOP]		770-516-9152				
					Morris Abstracting		229-831-7535, cell-229-848-2709		•	•	

CR	CV	PR	US	BK	←Courts	Jackson	Recorder→	UC	RE	TX	VS
	•	•	•	•	Atlanta Title Abstractors		770-267-2727	•	•	•	
•	•				Background Research Agency Inc		770-788-1885			•	
•	•	•	•	•	Excel Search Inc		770-844-1201	•	•	•	•
	•			•	Southern Courthouse Ventures		678-413-4697	•	•	•	
•	•	•			Taya Gordon Research		706-546-6598	•	•	•	
•	•				Turek Paralegal Services		770-540-7891 cell, 706-548-6842		•	•	
•	•	•	•		John Wilmot		706-546-7411	•	•	•	•

CR	CV	PR	US	BK	←Courts	Jasper	Recorder→	UC	RE	TX	VS
•	•				Background Research Agency Inc		770-788-1885			•	
•	•				National Pre-Employment Research [SOP]		770-389-6607				
•	•	•	•		Bill Scholly		706-342-4166; Fax- same			•	
	•			•	Southern Courthouse Ventures		678-413-4697	•	•	•	

CR	CV	PR	US	BK	←Courts	Jeff Davis	Recorder→	UC	RE	TX	VS
•	•		•	•	Lighthouse Information Services [SOP]		770-516-9152				

CR	CV	PR	US	BK	←Courts	Jefferson	Recorder→	UC	RE	TX	VS
•	•				Background Research Agency Inc		770-788-1885			•	
•	•	•	•	•	David Smith Detective Agency [SOP]		877-793-9426	•		•	
•	•		•	•	Lighthouse Information Services [SOP]		770-516-9152				

CR	CV	PR	US	BK	←Courts	Jenkins	Recorder→	UC	RE	TX	VS
•	•				Background Research Agency Inc		770-788-1885			•	
•	•		•	•	Lighthouse Information Services [SOP]		770-516-9152				

CR	CV	PR	US	BK	←Courts	Johnson	Recorder→	UC	RE	TX	VS
•	•				Background Research Agency Inc		770-788-1885			•	
•	•		•	•	Lighthouse Information Services [SOP]		770-516-9152				

CR	CV	PR	US	BK	←Courts	Jones	Recorder→	UC	RE	TX	VS
•	•				Background Research Agency Inc		770-788-1885			•	
•	•	•	•	•	Glaze Research		478-476-0539, 478-256-6696		•	•	•
•	•	•	•	•	Graystone Investigations Inc [SOP]		478-743-5551	•	•	•	•
	•			•	Southern Courthouse Ventures		678-413-4697	•	•	•	

CR	CV	PR	US	BK	←Courts	Lamar	Recorder→	UC	RE	TX	VS
•	•				Background Research Agency Inc		770-788-1885			•	
•	•	•			Reba Jones		478-994-4501				
•	•				National Pre-Employment Research [SOP]		770-389-6607				
	•			•	Southern Courthouse Ventures		678-413-4697	•	•	•	

CR	CV	PR	US	BK	←Courts	Lanier	Recorder→	UC	RE	TX	VS
•	•	•			API		229-559-4717			•	
•	•		•	•	Lighthouse Information Services [SOP]		770-516-9152				

CR	CV	PR	US	BK	←Courts	Laurens	Recorder→	UC	RE	TX	VS
•	•				Background Research Agency Inc		770-788-1885			•	
•	•	•			LG Services LLC		478-290-3808, 478-274-8622				
•	•		•	•	Lighthouse Information Services [SOP]		770-516-9152				
•	•				National Pre-Employment Research [SOP]		770-389-6607				

CR	CV	PR	US	BK	←Courts	Lee	Recorder→	UC	RE	TX	VS
•	•				Background Research Agency Inc		770-788-1885			•	
•	•		•	•	Lighthouse Information Services [SOP]		770-516-9152				
					Lenn R Lynch		229-942-7331		•	•	

CR	CV	PR	US	BK	←Courts	Liberty	Recorder→	UC	RE	TX	VS
•	•				Background Research Agency Inc		770-788-1885			•	
•	•	•	•	•	Crisp & Associates [SOP]		912-898-9973	•		•	
•	•				National Pre-Employment Research [SOP]		770-389-6607				

CR	CV	PR	US	BK	←Courts	Lincoln	Recorder→	UC	RE	TX	VS
•	•	•	•	•	David Smith Detective Agency [SOP]		877-793-9426	•		•	
					Thompson Research		706-860-4181		•	•	

CR	CV	PR	US	BK	←Courts	Long	Recorder→	UC	RE	TX	VS
•	•				Background Research Agency Inc		770-788-1885			•	
					Michael's Legal Research		912-269-5532	•	•		

CR	CV	PR	US	BK	←Courts	Lowndes	Recorder→	UC	RE	TX	VS
•	•	•			API		229-559-4717			•	
•	•				Background Research Agency Inc		770-788-1885			•	
•	•		•	•	Lighthouse Information Services [SOP]		770-516-9152				

CR	CV	PR	US	BK	←Courts	Lumpkin	Recorder→	UC	RE	TX	VS
•	•				Background Research Agency Inc		770-788-1885			•	
	•		•	•	Courthouse Abstractors		770-271-9002	•	•	•	
•					Intricate Solutions Inc		866-640-5210				
	•			•	Southern Courthouse Ventures		678-413-4697	•	•	•	
•	•	•	•	•	Southern Research Enterprises [SOP]		770-387-9439	•	•	•	•
•	•				Turek Paralegal Services		770-540-7891 cell, 706-548-6842		•	•	

CR	CV	PR	US	BK	←Courts	Macon	Recorder→	UC	RE	TX	VS
	•			•	Southern Courthouse Ventures		678-413-4697	•	•	•	

CR	CV	PR	US	BK	←Courts	Madison	Recorder→	UC	RE	TX	VS
	•	•	•	•	Atlanta Title Abstractors		770-267-2727	•	•	•	
•	•				Background Research Agency Inc		770-788-1885			•	
•	•	•	•	•	Excel Search Inc		770-844-1201	•	•	•	•
•	•				National Pre-Employment Research [SOP]		770-389-6607				
•	•				Professional Paralegal Services Inc [SOP]		706-783-2648		•		
	•			•	Southern Courthouse Ventures		678-413-4697	•	•	•	
•	•	•			Taya Gordon Research		706-546-6598	•	•	•	
•	•				Turek Paralegal Services		770-540-7891 cell, 706-548-6842		•	•	
•	•	•	•		John Wilmot		706-546-7411	•	•	•	•

CR	CV	PR	US	BK	←Courts	Marion	Recorder→	UC	RE	TX	VS
•	•			•	Attorneys Services & Legal Inv [SOP]		706-322-3554 or 322-3224	•	•	•	
•	•				Background Research Agency Inc		770-788-1885			•	
•	•				National Pre-Employment Research [SOP]		770-389-6607				

CR	CV	PR	US	BK	←Courts	McDuffie	Recorder→	UC	RE	TX	VS
•	•				Background Research Agency Inc		770-788-1885			•	
•	•	•	•	•	CSRA Background Verification Inc		706-869-8882	•	•	•	
•	•	•	•	•	David Smith Detective Agency [SOP]		877-793-9426	•		•	
•	•				National Pre-Employment Research [SOP]		770-389-6607				
					Thompson Research		706-860-4181		•	•	
•	•		•	•	Verifi LLC		423-344-0133	•	•	•	

CR	CV	PR	US	BK	←Courts	McIntosh	Recorder→	UC	RE	TX	VS
•	•				Background Research Agency Inc		770-788-1885			•	
•	•		•	•	Lighthouse Information Services [SOP]		770-516-9152				
					Michael's Legal Research		912-269-5532	•	•		
•	•				National Pre-Employment Research [SOP]		770-389-6607				
•	•		•		Troy Lindsey		912-265-4405; Fax- same				

CR	CV	PR	US	BK	←Courts	Meriwether	Recorder→	UC	RE	TX	VS
•	•				Background Research Agency Inc		770-788-1885			•	
•	•				National Pre-Employment Research [SOP]		770-389-6607				

CR	CV	PR	US	BK	←Courts	Miller	Recorder→	UC	RE	TX	VS
•	•				Background Research Agency Inc		770-788-1885			•	

CR	CV	PR	US	BK	←Courts **MITCHELL** Recorder→		UC	RE	TX	VS
•	•				Background Research Agency Inc	770-788-1885			•	

CR	CV	PR	US	BK	←Courts **MONROE** Recorder→		UC	RE	TX	VS
•	•				Background Research Agency Inc	770-788-1885			•	
•	•	•	•	•	Glaze Research	478-476-0539, 478-256-6696		•	•	•
•	•	•	•	•	Graystone Investigations Inc [SOP]	478-743-5551	•	•	•	•
•	•	•			Reba Jones	478-994-4501				
•	•				National Pre-Employment Research [SOP]	770-389-6607				
	•			•	Southern Courthouse Ventures	678-413-4697	•	•	•	

CR	CV	PR	US	BK	←Courts **MONTGOMERY** Recorder→		UC	RE	TX	VS
•	•				Background Research Agency Inc	770-788-1885			•	
•	•		•	•	Lighthouse Information Services [SOP]	770-516-9152				

CR	CV	PR	US	BK	←Courts **MORGAN** Recorder→		UC	RE	TX	VS
	•	•	•	•	Atlanta Title Abstractors	770-267-2727	•	•	•	
•	•				Background Research Agency Inc	770-788-1885			•	
•	•	•	•	•	Excel Search Inc	770-844-1201	•	•	•	•
•	•	•			Merritt & Henry LLC	706-342-9668	•	•	•	
•	•				National Pre-Employment Research [SOP]	770-389-6607				
•	•				Professional Paralegal Services Inc [SOP]	706-783-2648		•		
•	•	•	•		Bill Scholly	706-342-4166; Fax- same			•	
	•			•	Southern Courthouse Ventures	678-413-4697	•	•	•	

CR	CV	PR	US	BK	←Courts **MURRAY** Recorder→		UC	RE	TX	VS
•	•	•	•	•	A All State Tracers Company	423-605-0155	•	•	•	•
•	•				Background Research Agency Inc	770-788-1885			•	
					DocuSearch Services	423-894-2425	•	•	•	
	•			•	Southern Courthouse Ventures	678-413-4697	•	•	•	
•	•	•	•	•	Southern Research Enterprises [SOP]	770-387-9439	•	•	•	•
	•	•	•	•	Title Guaranty & Trust of Chattanooga	423-266-5751	•	•	•	
•	•		•	•	Verifi LLC	423-344-0133	•	•	•	

CR	CV	PR	US	BK	←Courts **MUSCOGEE** Recorder→		UC	RE	TX	VS
•	•			•	Attorneys Services & Legal Inv [SOP]	706-322-3554 or 322-3224	•	•	•	
•	•				Background Research Agency Inc	770-788-1885			•	
•	•				KYMRON Research LLC [SOP]	770-703-7301				
•	•				National Pre-Employment Research [SOP]	770-389-6607				
•	•				Search & Find	706-884-9801			•	

CR	CV	PR	US	BK	←Courts **NEWTON** Recorder→		UC	RE	TX	VS
	•	•	•	•	Atlanta Title Abstractors	770-267-2727	•	•	•	
•	•				Background Research Agency Inc	770-788-1885			•	
•	•	•	•	•	Excel Search Inc	770-844-1201	•	•	•	•
•	•	•			Roger Gladden Law Office [SOP]	404-550-0749; Fax- same	•	•	•	
•	•				National Pre-Employment Research [SOP]	770-389-6607				
•	•				Search & Find	706-884-9801			•	
	•			•	Southern Courthouse Ventures	678-413-4697	•	•	•	

CR	CV	PR	US	BK	←Courts **OCONEE** Recorder→		UC	RE	TX	VS
	•	•	•	•	Atlanta Title Abstractors	770-267-2727	•	•	•	
•	•				Background Research Agency Inc	770-788-1885			•	
	•	•			Clear Title Search Inc	706-340-6278		•	•	
•	•	•	•	•	Excel Search Inc	770-844-1201	•	•	•	•
•	•				National Pre-Employment Research [SOP]	770-389-6607				
•	•				Professional Paralegal Services Inc [SOP]	706-783-2648		•		
	•			•	Southern Courthouse Ventures	678-413-4697	•	•	•	
•	•	•			Taya Gordon Research	706-546-6598	•	•	•	
•	•				Turek Paralegal Services	770-540-7891 cell, 706-548-6842		•	•	

CR	CV	PR	US	BK	Courts	Phone	UC	RE	TX	VS
•	•	•	•		John Wilmot	706-546-7411	•	•	•	•

Oglethorpe

CR	CV	PR	US	BK	←Courts	Recorder→	UC	RE	TX	VS
	•	•	•	•	Atlanta Title Abstractors	770-267-2727	•	•	•	
•	•				Background Research Agency Inc	770-788-1885			•	
	•	•			Clear Title Search Inc	706-340-6278		•	•	
•	•	•	•	•	Excel Search Inc	770-844-1201	•	•	•	•
•	•				Professional Paralegal Services Inc [SOP]	706-783-2648		•		
	•			•	Southern Courthouse Ventures	678-413-4697	•	•	•	
•	•	•			Taya Gordon Research	706-546-6598	•	•	•	
•	•				Turek Paralegal Services	770-540-7891 cell, 706-548-6842		•	•	
•	•	•	•		John Wilmot	706-546-7411	•	•	•	•

Paulding

CR	CV	PR	US	BK	←Courts	Recorder→	UC	RE	TX	VS
•	•	•	•	•	A All State Tracers Company	423-605-0155	•	•	•	•
•	•	•	•	•	Atlanta Legal Services Inc [SOP]	877-302-4136	•	•	•	•
•	•	•	•	•	Axis Research Inc	877-795-1005	•	•	•	
•	•				Background Research Agency Inc	770-788-1885			•	
					Majestic Research Services Inc	678-355-5393	•	•	•	
	•			•	Southern Courthouse Ventures	678-413-4697	•	•	•	
•	•	•	•	•	Southern Research Enterprises [SOP]	770-387-9439	•	•	•	•
•	•		•	•	Specialty Services [SOP]	770-942-8264	•	•	•	

Peach

CR	CV	PR	US	BK	←Courts	Recorder→	UC	RE	TX	VS
•	•				Background Research Agency Inc	770-788-1885			•	
•	•	•	•	•	Glaze Research	478-476-0539, 478-256-6696		•	•	•
•	•	•	•	•	Graystone Investigations Inc [SOP]	478-743-5551	•	•	•	•
•	•				National Pre-Employment Research [SOP]	770-389-6607				
	•			•	Southern Courthouse Ventures	678-413-4697	•	•	•	

Pickens

CR	CV	PR	US	BK	←Courts	Recorder→	UC	RE	TX	VS
•	•	•	•	•	A All State Tracers Company	423-605-0155	•	•	•	•
•	•	•	•	•	Axis Research Inc	877-795-1005	•	•	•	
•	•				Background Research Agency Inc	770-788-1885			•	
•	•	•	•	•	John Roberson Inv [SOP]	800-325-0914	•	•	•	•
	•			•	Southern Courthouse Ventures	678-413-4697	•	•	•	
•	•	•	•	•	Southern Research Enterprises [SOP]	770-387-9439	•	•	•	•

Pierce

CR	CV	PR	US	BK	←Courts	Recorder→	UC	RE	TX	VS
•	•				Background Research Agency Inc	770-788-1885			•	
•	•		•	•	Lighthouse Information Services [SOP]	770-516-9152				
•	•				National Pre-Employment Research [SOP]	770-389-6607				
	•	•			Betty M Rowell, CLA	912-449-0849	•	•	•	

Pike

CR	CV	PR	US	BK	←Courts	Recorder→	UC	RE	TX	VS
•	•				Background Research Agency Inc	770-788-1885			•	
•	•	•			Reba Jones	478-994-4501				
•	•				National Pre-Employment Research [SOP]	770-389-6607				
	•			•	Southern Courthouse Ventures	678-413-4697	•	•	•	

Polk

CR	CV	PR	US	BK	←Courts	Recorder→	UC	RE	TX	VS
•	•	•	•	•	A All State Tracers Company	423-605-0155	•	•	•	•
•	•				Background Research Agency Inc	770-788-1885			•	
•	•				Shelia Pettit	770-832-9273				
	•			•	Southern Courthouse Ventures	678-413-4697	•	•	•	

Pulaski

CR	CV	PR	US	BK	←Courts	Recorder→	UC	RE	TX	VS
•	•				Background Research Agency Inc	770-788-1885			•	
•	•		•	•	Lighthouse Information Services [SOP]	770-516-9152				

CR	CV	PR	US	BK	←Courts	**Putnam**	Recorder→	UC	RE	TX	VS
•	•				Background Research Agency Inc		770-788-1885			•	
•	•	•			Merritt & Henry LLC		706-342-9668	•	•	•	
•	•				National Pre-Employment Research [SOP]		770-389-6607				
•	•				Professional Paralegal Services Inc [SOP]		706-783-2648		•		
•	•	•	•		Bill Scholly		706-342-4166; Fax- same			•	
	•			•	Southern Courthouse Ventures		678-413-4697	•	•	•	

CR	CV	PR	US	BK	←Courts	**Quitman**	Recorder→	UC	RE	TX	VS
•	•				Background Research Agency Inc		770-788-1885			•	

CR	CV	PR	US	BK	←Courts	**Rabun**	Recorder→	UC	RE	TX	VS
	•			•	Southern Courthouse Ventures		678-413-4697	•	•	•	

CR	CV	PR	US	BK	←Courts	**Randolph**	Recorder→	UC	RE	TX	VS
					Lenn R Lynch		229-942-7331		•	•	

CR	CV	PR	US	BK	←Courts	**Richmond**	Recorder→	UC	RE	TX	VS
•	•				Background Research Agency Inc		770-788-1885			•	
•	•	•	•	•	CSRA Background Verification Inc		706-869-8882	•	•	•	
•	•	•	•	•	David Smith Detective Agency [SOP]		877-793-9426	•		•	
•	•				National Pre-Employment Research [SOP]		770-389-6607				
					Thompson Research		706-860-4181		•	•	
					David V Weber, Attorney		706-860-8160				

CR	CV	PR	US	BK	←Courts	**Rockdale**	Recorder→	UC	RE	TX	VS
•	•				Able Atlanta Research		404-502-2024	•		•	
•	•	•	•	•	Atlanta Legal Services Inc [SOP]		877-302-4136	•	•	•	•
	•	•	•	•	Atlanta Title Abstractors		770-267-2727	•	•	•	
•	•				Background Research Agency Inc		770-788-1885			•	
•	•	•	•	•	Excel Search Inc		770-844-1201	•	•	•	•
•	•	•			Roger Gladden Law Office [SOP]		404-550-0749; Fax- same	•	•	•	
•	•				Minor Services Inc - Excel Legal Search		770-987-0942, 770-789-8543	•		•	
•	•				National Pre-Employment Research [SOP]		770-389-6607				
•	•				Search & Find		706-884-9801			•	
	•			•	Southern Courthouse Ventures		678-413-4697	•	•	•	
•	•				Turek Paralegal Services		770-540-7891 cell, 706-548-6842		•	•	

CR	CV	PR	US	BK	←Courts	**Schley**	Recorder→	UC	RE	TX	VS
					Lenn R Lynch		229-942-7331		•	•	

CR	CV	PR	US	BK	←Courts	**Screven**	Recorder→	UC	RE	TX	VS
•	•		•	•	Lighthouse Information Services [SOP]		770-516-9152				

CR	CV	PR	US	BK	←Courts	**Seminole**	Recorder→	UC	RE	TX	VS
•	•				Background Research Agency Inc		770-788-1885			•	

CR	CV	PR	US	BK	←Courts	**Spalding**	Recorder→	UC	RE	TX	VS
	•	•	•	•	Atlanta Title Abstractors		770-267-2727	•	•	•	
•	•	•	•	•	Axis Research Inc		877-795-1005	•	•	•	
•	•				Background Research Agency Inc		770-788-1885			•	
•	•	•	•	•	John Roberson Inv [SOP]		800-325-0914	•	•	•	•
•	•				National Pre-Employment Research [SOP]		770-389-6607				
	•	•			Reliable Abstract		678-614-0715		•	•	
	•			•	Southern Courthouse Ventures		678-413-4697	•	•	•	

CR	CV	PR	US	BK	←Courts	**Stephens**	Recorder→	UC	RE	TX	VS
•	•				Background Research Agency Inc		770-788-1885			•	
•	•		•	•	Lighthouse Information Services [SOP]		770-516-9152				
	•			•	Southern Courthouse Ventures		678-413-4697	•	•	•	

CR	CV	PR	US	BK	←Courts	Stewart	Recorder→	UC	RE	TX	VS
•	•			•	Attorneys Services & Legal Inv [SOP]		706-322-3554 or 322-3224	•	•	•	

CR	CV	PR	US	BK	←Courts	Sumter	Recorder→	UC	RE	TX	VS
•	•				Background Research Agency Inc		770-788-1885			•	
					Lenn R Lynch		229-942-7331		•	•	

CR	CV	PR	US	BK	←Courts	Talbot	Recorder→	UC	RE	TX	VS
•	•				Background Research Agency Inc		770-788-1885			•	
•	•				National Pre-Employment Research [SOP]		770-389-6607				

CR	CV	PR	US	BK	←Courts	Taliaferro	Recorder→	UC	RE	TX	VS
•	•				Background Research Agency Inc		770-788-1885			•	
•	•				National Pre-Employment Research [SOP]		770-389-6607				

CR	CV	PR	US	BK	←Courts	Tattnall	Recorder→	UC	RE	TX	VS
•	•				Background Research Agency Inc		770-788-1885			•	
•	•				National Pre-Employment Research [SOP]		770-389-6607				

CR	CV	PR	US	BK	←Courts	Taylor	Recorder→	UC	RE	TX	VS
•	•				Background Research Agency Inc		770-788-1885			•	
•	•				Lisa McDonald		478-862-5594 (courthouse)			•	
•	•				National Pre-Employment Research [SOP]		770-389-6607				

CR	CV	PR	US	BK	←Courts	Telfair	Recorder→	UC	RE	TX	VS
•	•				Background Research Agency Inc		770-788-1885			•	
•	•		•	•	Lighthouse Information Services [SOP]		770-516-9152				

CR	CV	PR	US	BK	←Courts	Terrell	Recorder→	UC	RE	TX	VS
•	•				Background Research Agency Inc		770-788-1885			•	
•	•		•	•	Lighthouse Information Services [SOP]		770-516-9152				
					Lenn R Lynch		229-942-7331		•	•	

CR	CV	PR	US	BK	←Courts	Thomas	Recorder→	UC	RE	TX	VS
•	•	•			API		229-559-4717			•	
•	•				Background Research Agency Inc		770-788-1885			•	
•	•	•	•	•	Corporate Access Inc [SOP]		800-969-1666	•	•	•	•
•	•				MJS Inv		229-226-1292				

CR	CV	PR	US	BK	←Courts	Tift	Recorder→	UC	RE	TX	VS
•	•	•			API		229-559-4717			•	
•	•				Background Research Agency Inc		770-788-1885			•	
•	•		•	•	Lighthouse Information Services [SOP]		770-516-9152				
					Morris Abstracting		229-831-7535, cell-229-848-2709		•	•	

CR	CV	PR	US	BK	←Courts	Toombs	Recorder→	UC	RE	TX	VS
•	•				Background Research Agency Inc		770-788-1885			•	

CR	CV	PR	US	BK	←Courts	Towns	Recorder→	UC	RE	TX	VS
	•			•	Southern Courthouse Ventures		678-413-4697	•	•	•	

CR	CV	PR	US	BK	←Courts	Treutlen	Recorder→	UC	RE	TX	VS
•	•				Background Research Agency Inc		770-788-1885			•	
•	•		•	•	Lighthouse Information Services [SOP]		770-516-9152				

CR	CV	PR	US	BK	←Courts	Troup	Recorder→	UC	RE	TX	VS
•	•				Background Research Agency Inc		770-788-1885			•	
•	•				National Pre-Employment Research [SOP]		770-389-6607				
•	•				Shelia Pettit		770-832-9273				
•	•				Search & Find		706-884-9801			•	

CR	CV	PR	US	BK	←COURTS	TURNER	RECORDER→	UC	RE	TX	VS
•	•				Background Research Agency Inc		770-788-1885			•	
•	•		•	•	Lighthouse Information Services [SOP]		770-516-9152				
					Morris Abstracting		229-831-7535, cell-229-848-2709		•	•	

CR	CV	PR	US	BK	←COURTS	TWIGGS	RECORDER→	UC	RE	TX	VS
•	•				Background Research Agency Inc		770-788-1885			•	
•	•	•	•	•	Glaze Research		478-476-0539, 478-256-6696		•	•	•
•	•		•	•	Lighthouse Information Services [SOP]		770-516-9152				
•	•				National Pre-Employment Research [SOP]		770-389-6607				

CR	CV	PR	US	BK	←COURTS	UNION	RECORDER→	UC	RE	TX	VS
•	•				Background Research Agency Inc		770-788-1885			•	
	•			•	Southern Courthouse Ventures		678-413-4697	•	•	•	

CR	CV	PR	US	BK	←COURTS	UPSON	RECORDER→	UC	RE	TX	VS
•	•				Background Research Agency Inc		770-788-1885			•	
•	•	•			Reba Jones		478-994-4501				
•	•				National Pre-Employment Research [SOP]		770-389-6607				

CR	CV	PR	US	BK	←COURTS	WALKER	RECORDER→	UC	RE	TX	VS
•	•				Background Research Agency Inc		770-788-1885			•	
					DocuSearch Services		423-894-2425	•	•	•	
•	•				Search & Find		706-884-9801			•	
	•			•	Southern Courthouse Ventures		678-413-4697	•	•	•	
•	•	•	•	•	Southern Research Enterprises [SOP]		770-387-9439	•	•	•	•
	•	•	•	•	Title Guaranty & Trust of Chattanooga		423-266-5751	•	•	•	
•	•		•	•	Verifi LLC		423-344-0133	•	•	•	

CR	CV	PR	US	BK	←COURTS	WALTON	RECORDER→	UC	RE	TX	VS
•	•				Able Atlanta Research		404-502-2024	•		•	
•	•				Background Research Agency Inc		770-788-1885			•	
•	•	•	•	•	Excel Search Inc		770-844-1201	•	•	•	•
•	•	•			Roger Gladden Law Office [SOP]		404-550-0749; Fax- same	•	•	•	
•	•				National Pre-Employment Research [SOP]		770-389-6607				
•	•				Professional Paralegal Services Inc [SOP]		706-783-2648		•		
•	•				Search & Find		706-884-9801			•	
	•			•	Southern Courthouse Ventures		678-413-4697	•	•	•	
•	•				Turek Paralegal Services		770-540-7891 cell, 706-548-6842		•	•	

CR	CV	PR	US	BK	←COURTS	WARE	RECORDER→	UC	RE	TX	VS
•	•				Background Research Agency Inc		770-788-1885			•	
•	•		•	•	Lighthouse Information Services [SOP]		770-516-9152				
•	•				National Pre-Employment Research [SOP]		770-389-6607				
	•	•			Betty M Rowell, CLA		912-449-0849	•	•	•	

CR	CV	PR	US	BK	←COURTS	WARREN	RECORDER→	UC	RE	TX	VS
•	•				Background Research Agency Inc		770-788-1885			•	
•	•		•	•	Verifi LLC		423-344-0133	•	•	•	

CR	CV	PR	US	BK	←COURTS	WASHINGTON	RECORDER→	UC	RE	TX	VS
•	•				Background Research Agency Inc		770-788-1885			•	
•	•		•	•	Lighthouse Information Services [SOP]		770-516-9152				

CR	CV	PR	US	BK	←COURTS	WAYNE	RECORDER→	UC	RE	TX	VS
•	•				Background Research Agency Inc		770-788-1885			•	
•	•				National Pre-Employment Research [SOP]		770-389-6607				

CR	CV	PR	US	BK	←COURTS	WEBSTER	RECORDER→	UC	RE	TX	VS
•	•				Background Research Agency Inc		770-788-1885			•	
					Lenn R Lynch		229-942-7331		•	•	

CR	CV	PR	US	BK	←COURTS	WHEELER	RECORDER→	UC	RE	TX	VS
•	•				Background Research Agency Inc		770-788-1885			•	
•	•		•	•	Lighthouse Information Services [SOP]		770-516-9152				

CR	CV	PR	US	BK	←COURTS	WHITE	RECORDER→	UC	RE	TX	VS
•	•				Background Research Agency Inc		770-788-1885			•	
	•			•	Southern Courthouse Ventures		678-413-4697	•	•	•	
•	•				Turek Paralegal Services		770-540-7891 cell, 706-548-6842		•	•	

CR	CV	PR	US	BK	←COURTS	WHITFIELD	RECORDER→	UC	RE	TX	VS
•	•	•	•	•	A All State Tracers Company		423-605-0155	•	•	•	•
•	•				Background Research Agency Inc		770-788-1885			•	
	•		•	•	Courthouse Abstractors		770-271-9002	•	•	•	
					DocuSearch Services		423-894-2425	•	•	•	
	•			•	Southern Courthouse Ventures		678-413-4697	•	•	•	
•	•	•	•	•	Southern Research Enterprises [SOP]		770-387-9439	•	•	•	•
	•	•	•	•	Title Guaranty & Trust of Chattanooga		423-266-5751	•	•	•	
•	•		•	•	Verifi LLC		423-344-0133	•	•	•	

CR	CV	PR	US	BK	←COURTS	WILCOX	RECORDER→	UC	RE	TX	VS
•	•		•	•	Lighthouse Information Services [SOP]		770-516-9152				

CR	CV	PR	US	BK	←COURTS	WILKES	RECORDER→	UC	RE	TX	VS
•	•				Background Research Agency Inc		770-788-1885			•	
•	•				Turek Paralegal Services		770-540-7891 cell, 706-548-6842		•	•	

CR	CV	PR	US	BK	←COURTS	WILKINSON	RECORDER→	UC	RE	TX	VS
•	•				Background Research Agency Inc		770-788-1885			•	

CR	CV	PR	US	BK	←COURTS	WORTH	RECORDER→	UC	RE	TX	VS
•	•				Background Research Agency Inc		770-788-1885			•	
•	•		•	•	Lighthouse Information Services [SOP]		770-516-9152				
					Morris Abstracting		229-831-7535, cell-229-848-2709		•	•	

Editor's Note: The County Index section in this book will **only** indicate a county where a record retriever does an in-person search by himself or herself, or by a payroll employee.

Many retrievers also maintain a network of correspondents and provide services in additional counties not listed within the County Index. This additional coverage is indicated in the Profiles section under Correspondent Relationships.

Hawaii

Court Records Retrieved — Capital - Honolulu County — Recorded Records Retrieved

CR	CV	PR	US	BK	←Courts **Hawaii**	Recorder→	UC	RE	TX	VS
•	•		•	•	Doc-U-Search Hawaii	808-523-1200	•	•	•	
•	•	•	•	•	Judith A Fitzgerald	808-263-2120	•	•	•	
		•	•	•	Hawaii Real Property Research	808-396-7581	•	•	•	•
•	•	•	•	•	Honolulu Information Service, Inc [SOP]	808-524-4488	•	•	•	•
•	•	•	•	•	Island Legal	808-756-7404	•	•	•	•
•	•	•	•	•	Wood & Tait Inc [SOP]	800-774-8585		•		

CR	CV	PR	US	BK	←Courts **Honolulu**	Recorder→	UC	RE	TX	VS
•	•		•	•	Doc-U-Search Hawaii	808-523-1200	•	•	•	
•	•	•	•	•	Judith A Fitzgerald	808-263-2120	•	•	•	
		•	•	•	Hawaii Real Property Research	808-396-7581	•	•	•	•
					HK Partners Research	808-291-2071	•	•	•	•
•	•	•	•	•	Honolulu Information Service, Inc [SOP]	808-524-4488	•	•	•	•
•	•	•	•	•	Island Legal	808-756-7404	•	•	•	•
•	•		•	•	National Information Access Bureau (NIAB) [SOP]	800-787-6422		•		•
•	•	•	•	•	Wood & Tait Inc [SOP]	800-774-8585		•		

CR	CV	PR	US	BK	←Courts **Kalawao**	Recorder→	UC	RE	TX	VS
•	•		•	•	Doc-U-Search Hawaii	808-523-1200	•	•	•	
		•	•	•	Hawaii Real Property Research	808-396-7581	•	•	•	•

CR	CV	PR	US	BK	←Courts **Kauai**	Recorder→	UC	RE	TX	VS
•	•		•	•	Doc-U-Search Hawaii	808-523-1200	•	•	•	
•	•	•	•	•	Judith A Fitzgerald	808-263-2120	•	•	•	
		•	•	•	Hawaii Real Property Research	808-396-7581	•	•	•	•
•	•	•	•	•	Honolulu Information Service, Inc [SOP]	808-524-4488	•	•	•	•
•	•	•	•	•	Island Legal	808-756-7404	•	•	•	•
•	•	•	•	•	Wood & Tait Inc [SOP]	800-774-8585		•		

CR	CV	PR	US	BK	←Courts **Maui**	Recorder→	UC	RE	TX	VS
•	•		•	•	Doc-U-Search Hawaii	808-523-1200	•	•	•	
•	•	•	•	•	Judith A Fitzgerald	808-263-2120	•	•	•	
		•	•	•	Hawaii Real Property Research	808-396-7581	•	•	•	•
•	•	•	•	•	Honolulu Information Service, Inc [SOP]	808-524-4488	•	•	•	•
•	•	•	•	•	Island Legal	808-756-7404	•	•	•	•
•	•	•	•	•	Wood & Tait Inc [SOP]	800-774-8585		•		

Editor's Tip: Simply because your state or county has certain rules, regulations and practices regarding the accessibility and content of public records, does not mean those same rules apply elsewhere.

Idaho

COURT RECORDS RETRIEVED — CAPITAL - ADA COUNTY — RECORDED RECORDS RETRIEVED

CR	CV	PR	US	BK	←COURTS — ADA	RECORDER→	UC	RE	TX	VS
•	•		•		Accurate Records Research LLC	208-888-2857	•	•	•	
•	•	•	•	•	Attorneys Messenger Service [SOP]	208-345-2905	•	•	•	•
•	•	•	•	•	Burr Investigation [SOP]	800-582-5441	•	•	•	•
•	•		•	•	CB Research [SOP]	208-376-3312	•	•	•	•
•	•	•	•	•	Integrity Check LLC	877-887-1226	•	•	•	•
•	•	•	•	•	Lord Investigations, LLC [SOP]	208-939-4040	•			
•	•	•	•	•	Record Search America Inc	208-375-1906	•	•	•	
•	•		•	•	Shadow Trackers Investigative Services Inc [SOP]	208-895-0074			•	
•	•	•	•	•	Tri-County Process Serving [SOP]	800-473-3454	•	•	•	
•	•	•			Wright Research	208-455-2450	•		•	•

CR	CV	PR	US	BK	←COURTS — ADAMS	RECORDER→	UC	RE	TX	VS
•	•	•	•	•	Burr Investigation [SOP]	800-582-5441	•	•	•	•

CR	CV	PR	US	BK	←COURTS — BANNOCK	RECORDER→	UC	RE	TX	VS
•	•		•		Accurate Records Research LLC	208-888-2857	•	•	•	
•	•	•	•	•	Attorneys Messenger Service [SOP]	208-345-2905	•	•	•	•
•	•	•	•	•	Carter Investigations [SOP]	208-232-3592	•	•	•	•
•	•	•	•	•	Record Search America Inc	208-375-1906	•	•	•	

CR	CV	PR	US	BK	←COURTS — BEAR LAKE	RECORDER→	UC	RE	TX	VS
	•	•			First Idaho Title Co	208-847-1300	•	•	•	

CR	CV	PR	US	BK	←COURTS — BENEWAH	RECORDER→	UC	RE	TX	VS
•	•	•	•	•	Gem State Inv [SOP]	208-746-4152	•	•	•	•

CR	CV	PR	US	BK	←COURTS — BINGHAM	RECORDER→	UC	RE	TX	VS
•	•	•	•	•	Carter Investigations [SOP]	208-232-3592	•	•	•	•
•	•	•			Reliable Record Research	208-522-9886; cell-208-569-5825	•	•	•	•

CR	CV	PR	US	BK	←COURTS — BLAINE	RECORDER→	UC	RE	TX	VS
•	•	•	•	•	Burr Investigation [SOP]	800-582-5441	•	•	•	•
•	•	•			Mower Services [SOP]	888-317-7458	•	•	•	
•	•	•			Northern Intermountain Security Inc [SOP]	208-726-2705	•	•	•	•
•	•				Lori Stroebel	208-481-0806			•	

CR	CV	PR	US	BK	←COURTS — BOISE	RECORDER→	UC	RE	TX	VS
•	•		•		Accurate Records Research LLC	208-888-2857	•	•	•	
•	•	•			Heidi Ambrose	208-392-6709; Fax- same		•	•	•
•	•	•	•	•	Burr Investigation [SOP]	800-582-5441	•	•	•	•
•	•	•	•	•	Integrity Check LLC	877-887-1226	•	•	•	•
•	•	•	•	•	Lord Investigations, LLC [SOP]	208-939-4040	•			
•	•	•	•	•	Tri-County Process Serving [SOP]	800-473-3454	•	•	•	

CR	CV	PR	US	BK	←COURTS — BONNER	RECORDER→	UC	RE	TX	VS
•	•				Debra Smith Research [SOP]	208-267-5605	•	•	•	•

CR	CV	PR	US	BK	←COURTS — BONNEVILLE	RECORDER→	UC	RE	TX	VS
•	•	•	•	•	Carter Investigations [SOP]	208-232-3592	•	•	•	•
•	•				Keys Paper Chase	208-523-9680; Fax- same	•	•	•	
•	•	•			Reliable Record Research	208-522-9886; cell-208-569-5825	•	•	•	•

CR	CV	PR	US	BK	←Courts **Boundary**	Recorder→	UC	RE	TX	VS
•	•				Debra Smith Research [SOP]	208-267-5605	•	•	•	•

CR	CV	PR	US	BK	←Courts **Butte**	Recorder→	UC	RE	TX	VS
	•	•			Idaho Title & Trust Co [SOP]	208-527-8517	•	•	•	

CR	CV	PR	US	BK	←Courts **Camas**	Recorder→	UC	RE	TX	VS
•	•	•			Northern Intermountain Security Inc [SOP]	208-726-2705	•	•	•	•

CR	CV	PR	US	BK	←Courts **Canyon**	Recorder→	UC	RE	TX	VS
•	•				Accurate Records Research LLC	208-888-2857	•	•	•	
•	•	•	•	•	Attorneys Messenger Service [SOP]	208-345-2905	•	•	•	•
•	•	•	•	•	Burr Investigation [SOP]	800-582-5441	•	•	•	•
•	•		•		CB Research [SOP]	208-376-3312	•	•	•	•
•	•	•	•	•	Integrity Check LLC	877-887-1226	•	•	•	•
•	•	•	•	•	Lord Investigations, LLC [SOP]	208-939-4040	•			
•	•	•	•	•	Record Search America Inc	208-375-1906	•	•	•	
•	•		•	•	Shadow Trackers Investigative Services Inc [SOP]	208-895-0074			•	
•	•	•	•	•	Tri-County Process Serving [SOP]	800-473-3454	•	•	•	
•	•	•			Wright Research	208-455-2450	•		•	•

CR	CV	PR	US	BK	←Courts **Caribou**	Recorder→	UC	RE	TX	VS
•	•	•	•	•	Record Search America Inc	208-375-1906	•	•	•	

CR	CV	PR	US	BK	←Courts **Cassia**	Recorder→	UC	RE	TX	VS
•	•	•	•	•	Burr Investigation [SOP]	800-582-5441	•	•	•	•
		•			Cassia County Abstract Co	208-678-8347	•	•	•	

CR	CV	PR	US	BK	←Courts **Clark**	Recorder→	UC	RE	TX	VS

See adjoining counties for retrievers or call court/recorder directly.

CR	CV	PR	US	BK	←Courts **Clearwater**	Recorder→	UC	RE	TX	VS
•	•	•	•	•	Gem State Inv [SOP]	208-746-4152	•	•	•	•

CR	CV	PR	US	BK	←Courts **Custer**	Recorder→	UC	RE	TX	VS

See adjoining counties for retrievers or call court/recorder directly.

CR	CV	PR	US	BK	←Courts **Elmore**	Recorder→	UC	RE	TX	VS
•	•	•	•	•	Attorneys Messenger Service [SOP]	208-345-2905	•	•	•	•
•	•	•	•	•	Burr Investigation [SOP]	800-582-5441	•	•	•	•
•	•	•	•	•	Integrity Check LLC	877-887-1226	•	•	•	•
•	•	•	•	•	Lord Investigations, LLC [SOP]	208-939-4040	•			
•	•	•	•	•	Tri-County Process Serving [SOP]	800-473-3454	•	•	•	

CR	CV	PR	US	BK	←Courts **Franklin**	Recorder→	UC	RE	TX	VS
	•	•			First American Title of Preston	208-852-2810	•	•	•	•

CR	CV	PR	US	BK	←Courts **Fremont**	Recorder→	UC	RE	TX	VS
•	•				Keys Paper Chase	208-523-9680; Fax- same	•	•	•	

CR	CV	PR	US	BK	←Courts **Gem**	Recorder→	UC	RE	TX	VS
•	•		•		Accurate Records Research LLC	208-888-2857	•	•	•	
•	•	•	•	•	Attorneys Messenger Service [SOP]	208-345-2905	•	•	•	•
•	•	•	•	•	Burr Investigation [SOP]	800-582-5441	•	•	•	•
•	•	•	•	•	Integrity Check LLC	877-887-1226	•	•	•	•
•	•	•	•	•	Lord Investigations, LLC [SOP]	208-939-4040	•			
•	•	•	•	•	Record Search America Inc	208-375-1906	•	•	•	
•	•	•	•	•	Tri-County Process Serving [SOP]	800-473-3454	•	•	•	

CR	CV	PR	US	BK	←Courts **Gooding**	Recorder→	UC	RE	TX	VS
•	•	•	•	•	Burr Investigation [SOP]	800-582-5441	•	•	•	•
•	•	•			Northern Intermountain Security Inc [SOP]	208-726-2705	•	•	•	•

CR	CV	PR	US	BK	←Courts	Idaho	Recorder→	UC	RE	TX	VS
•	•	•	•	•	Gem State Inv [SOP]		208-746-4152	•	•	•	•
•	•	•			Betty O'Brien		208-983-2751				

CR	CV	PR	US	BK	←Courts	Jefferson	Recorder→	UC	RE	TX	VS
•	•				Keys Paper Chase		208-523-9680; Fax- same	•	•	•	
•	•	•			Reliable Record Research		208-522-9886; cell-208-569-5825	•	•	•	•

CR	CV	PR	US	BK	←Courts	Jerome	Recorder→	UC	RE	TX	VS
•	•	•			Northern Intermountain Security Inc [SOP]		208-726-2705	•	•	•	•

CR	CV	PR	US	BK	←Courts	Kootenai	Recorder→	UC	RE	TX	VS
					Rat Dog Research LLC		208-765-4598	•	•	•	
•	•				Alice E Sackman		208-964-0209	•	•	•	

CR	CV	PR	US	BK	←Courts	Latah	Recorder→	UC	RE	TX	VS
•	•		•		Accurate Records Research LLC		208-888-2857	•	•	•	
•	•	•	•	•	Gem State Inv [SOP]		208-746-4152	•	•	•	•
•	•		•	•	Carrie J Myers		208-883-7963	•	•	•	
•	•		•	•	Ryan Myers		208-882-6678	•	•	•	
•	•	•	•	•	Record Search America Inc		208-375-1906	•	•	•	

CR	CV	PR	US	BK	←Courts	Lemhi	Recorder→	UC	RE	TX	VS

See adjoining counties for retrievers or call court/recorder directly.

CR	CV	PR	US	BK	←Courts	Lewis	Recorder→	UC	RE	TX	VS
•	•	•	•	•	Gem State Inv [SOP]		208-746-4152	•	•	•	•
•	•	•			Lewis County Abstract (Idaho) d/b/a Lewis County Title		208-937-2621		•	•	

CR	CV	PR	US	BK	←Courts	Lincoln	Recorder→	UC	RE	TX	VS
•	•	•			Northern Intermountain Security Inc [SOP]		208-726-2705	•	•	•	•

CR	CV	PR	US	BK	←Courts	Madison	Recorder→	UC	RE	TX	VS
•	•				Davenport Background Searches		208-356-5036		•	•	
•	•				Keys Paper Chase		208-523-9680; Fax- same	•	•	•	
•	•	•			Reliable Record Research		208-522-9886; cell-208-569-5825	•	•	•	•

CR	CV	PR	US	BK	←Courts	Minidoka	Recorder→	UC	RE	TX	VS
•	•	•	•	•	Burr Investigation [SOP]		800-582-5441	•	•	•	•

CR	CV	PR	US	BK	←Courts	Nez Perce	Recorder→	UC	RE	TX	VS
•	•	•	•	•	Gem State Inv [SOP]		208-746-4152	•	•	•	•
•	•		•	•	Ryan Myers		208-882-6678	•	•	•	

CR	CV	PR	US	BK	←Courts	Oneida	Recorder→	UC	RE	TX	VS
•	•	•			Mower Services [SOP]		888-317-7458	•	•	•	

CR	CV	PR	US	BK	←Courts	Owyhee	Recorder→	UC	RE	TX	VS
•	•	•	•	•	Attorneys Messenger Service [SOP]		208-345-2905	•	•	•	•
•	•	•	•	•	Burr Investigation [SOP]		800-582-5441	•	•	•	•

CR	CV	PR	US	BK	←Courts	Payette	Recorder→	UC	RE	TX	VS
•	•		•		Accurate Records Research LLC		208-888-2857	•	•	•	
•	•	•	•	•	Record Search America Inc		208-375-1906	•	•	•	
•	•	•	•	•	Tri-County Process Serving [SOP]		800-473-3454	•	•	•	

CR	CV	PR	US	BK	←Courts	Power	Recorder→	UC	RE	TX	VS
•	•	•	•	•	Carter Investigations [SOP]		208-232-3592	•	•	•	•

CR	CV	PR	US	BK	←Courts	Shoshone	Recorder→	UC	RE	TX	VS

See adjoining counties for retrievers or call court/recorder directly.

CR	CV	PR	US	BK	←Courts	Teton	Recorder→	UC	RE	TX	VS
			•	•	Alliance Title & Escrow Corp		800-214-1418	•	•	•	

CR	CV	PR	US	BK	←COURTS TWIN FALLS	RECORDER→	UC	RE	TX	VS
•	•	•	•		Attorneys Messenger Service [SOP]	208-345-2905	•	•	•	•
•	•				Sharisa Barnes	208-308-5496; Fax- same				
•	•	•		•	Burr Investigation [SOP]	800-582-5441	•	•	•	•
•	•	•			Northern Intermountain Security Inc [SOP]	208-726-2705	•	•	•	•

CR	CV	PR	US	BK	←COURTS VALLEY	RECORDER→	UC	RE	TX	VS
•	•	•		•	Burr Investigation [SOP]	800-582-5441	•	•	•	•
•	•	•	•	•	Lord Investigations, LLC [SOP]	208-939-4040	•			
•	•	•	•	•	Tri-County Process Serving [SOP]	800-473-3454	•	•	•	

CR	CV	PR	US	BK	←COURTS WASHINGTON	RECORDER→	UC	RE	TX	VS
•	•	•	•	•	Lord Investigations, LLC [SOP]	208-939-4040	•			
•	•	•			Washington County Title	208-414-1455	•	•	•	

[SOP] = PERFORMS SERVICE OF PROCESS

COURT RECORDS

CODE	GOVERNMENT AGENCY	TYPE OF INFORMATION
CR	Criminal Court	Municipal, county and state level criminal cases
CV	Civil Court	Municipal, county and state level civil cases
PR	Probate Court	Wills and estate cases
US	US District Court	Federal civil and criminal cases
BK	Bankruptcy Court	United States bankruptcy cases

COUNTY RECORDS - RECORDINGS

CODE	GOVERNMENT AGENCY	TYPE OF INFORMATION
UC	UCC Filing Office	Uniform Commercial Code and other personal property liens
RE	Real Estate Recording Office	Real property transactions and liens
TX	Tax Filing Office(s)	Federal and state tax liens, judgment liens
VS	Vital Records Office	Vital statistics—birth, death, marriage, divorce

= PRRN Member. *A retriever you can trust!*

Illinois

COURT RECORDS RETRIEVED | **CAPITAL - SANGAMON COUNTY** | **RECORDED RECORDS RETRIEVED**

CR	CV	PR	US	BK	←COURTS ADAMS	RECORDER→	UC	RE	TX	VS
•	•	•			Bi-State Title Search (Div of Bi-State Ind.)	866-450-7399	•	•	•	
•	•	•			Ferret Diversified Services Inc	847-579-0007		•		
•	•		•	•	Infotrack Information Services Inc	800-275-5594	•	•	•	
•	•	•			Marion County Abstract Co (Missouri)	800-952-5314	•	•	•	•
•	•	•	•	•	PII Inc [SOP]	217-483-8845	•	•	•	•
•	•	•	•	•	Woelfel & Assoc Inc [SOP]	888-297-7180	•	•	•	

CR	CV	PR	US	BK	←COURTS ALEXANDER	RECORDER→	UC	RE	TX	VS
•	•	•	•	•	Heartland Investigations Inc [SOP]	877-684-6313	•	•	•	•

CR	CV	PR	US	BK	←COURTS BOND	RECORDER→	UC	RE	TX	VS
•	•	•			Bi-State Title Search (Div of Bi-State Ind.)	866-450-7399	•	•	•	
	•	•		•	Bond Title	618-664-1872		•	•	•
•	•		•	•	Infotrack Information Services Inc	800-275-5594	•	•	•	
•	•	•	•	•	Woelfel & Assoc Inc [SOP]	888-297-7180	•	•	•	

CR	CV	PR	US	BK	←COURTS BOONE	RECORDER→	UC	RE	TX	VS
•	•				Angel P I's [SOP]	800-973-3832				
•	•		•	•	Infotrack Information Services Inc	800-275-5594	•	•	•	
•	•	•		•	Security First Title Co.	815-235-2900	•	•	•	
•	•	•	•	•	Stewart & Associates Inc - Rockford [SOP]	815-961-0150	•	•	•	•
•	•				Julie L Thomas	815-234-4172				

CR	CV	PR	US	BK	←COURTS BROWN	RECORDER→	UC	RE	TX	VS
•	•		•	•	Infotrack Information Services Inc	800-275-5594	•	•	•	

CR	CV	PR	US	BK	←COURTS BUREAU	RECORDER→	UC	RE	TX	VS
•	•				Angel P I's [SOP]	800-973-3832				
•	•		•	•	Infotrack Information Services Inc	800-275-5594	•	•	•	

CR	CV	PR	US	BK	←COURTS CALHOUN	RECORDER→	UC	RE	TX	VS
•	•		•	•	Infotrack Information Services Inc	800-275-5594	•	•	•	
•	•	•	•	•	Woelfel & Assoc Inc [SOP]	888-297-7180	•	•	•	

CR	CV	PR	US	BK	←COURTS CARROLL	RECORDER→	UC	RE	TX	VS
•	•	•			Ferret Diversified Services Inc	847-579-0007		•		
•	•		•	•	Infotrack Information Services Inc	800-275-5594	•	•	•	
•	•	•		•	Security First Title Co.	815-235-2900	•	•	•	
•	•	•	•	•	Stewart & Associates Inc - Rockford [SOP]	815-961-0150	•	•	•	•

CR	CV	PR	US	BK	←COURTS CASS	RECORDER→	UC	RE	TX	VS
•	•	•			Exacta Search & Document Retrieval	217-528-3677	•	•	•	
	•	•			First American Title Insurance Company (IL)	309-347-6126	•	•	•	•
•	•		•	•	Infotrack Information Services Inc	800-275-5594	•	•	•	
•	•	•	•	•	PII Inc [SOP]	217-483-8845	•	•	•	•

CR	CV	PR	US	BK	←COURTS CHAMPAIGN	RECORDER→	UC	RE	TX	VS
•	•	•	•	•	Diligent Detective Agency Inc [SOP]	877-694-3332		•	•	•
•	•	•			Exacta Search & Document Retrieval	217-528-3677	•	•	•	
•	•	•			Ferret Diversified Services Inc	847-579-0007		•		
•	•		•	•	Infotrack Information Services Inc	800-275-5594	•	•	•	

CR	CV	PR	US	BK	Retriever	Phone	UC	RE	TX	VS
•	•	•	•	•	Jacobs & Associates CPD Inc [SOP]	800-445-1675	•	•	•	•
•	•	•	•	•	United Risk Partners LLC	877-593-9995	•	•	•	•

CR	CV	PR	US	BK	←COURTS CHRISTIAN	RECORDER→	UC	RE	TX	VS
•	•	•			Exacta Search & Document Retrieval	217-528-3677	•	•	•	
•	•		•	•	Infotrack Information Services Inc	800-275-5594	•	•	•	
•	•	•	•	•	PII Inc [SOP]	217-483-8845	•	•	•	•

CR	CV	PR	US	BK	←COURTS CLARK	RECORDER→	UC	RE	TX	VS
					Abstract & Title Co.	618-445-2554		•		
•	•				Crossroads Research	812-299-0809				
					Everhart & Everhart Abstractors	217-849-2671	•	•	•	

CR	CV	PR	US	BK	←COURTS CLAY	RECORDER→	UC	RE	TX	VS
					Abstract & Title Co.	618-445-2554		•		
•	•	•	•	•	Nancy Durbin Court Research [SOP]	618-267-0472 cell; 618-548-8296	•	•	•	•
•	•	•	•	•	Woelfel & Assoc Inc [SOP]	888-297-7180	•	•	•	

CR	CV	PR	US	BK	←COURTS CLINTON	RECORDER→	UC	RE	TX	VS
•	•	•			Bi-State Title Search (Div of Bi-State Ind.)	866-450-7399	•	•	•	
	•	•		•	Bond Title	618-664-1872		•	•	•
•	•		•	•	Infotrack Information Services Inc	800-275-5594	•	•	•	
•	•	•	•	•	Kevin W McClain Investigations Ltd [SOP]	877-532-1152	•	•	•	•
•	•	•	•	•	Nancy Durbin Court Research [SOP]	618-267-0472 cell; 618-548-8296	•	•	•	•
					Sharp Law Firm	618-242-0246		•	•	
•	•	•	•	•	Woelfel & Assoc Inc [SOP]	888-297-7180	•	•	•	

CR	CV	PR	US	BK	←COURTS COLES	RECORDER→	UC	RE	TX	VS
					Abstract & Title Co.	618-445-2554		•		
					Everhart & Everhart Abstractors	217-849-2671	•	•	•	
•	•	•			Ferret Diversified Services Inc	847-579-0007		•		
•	•		•	•	Infotrack Information Services Inc	800-275-5594	•	•	•	
•	•	•	•	•	Jacobs & Associates CPD Inc [SOP]	800-445-1675	•	•	•	•
•	•	•	•	•	PII Inc [SOP]	217-483-8845	•	•	•	•

CR	CV	PR	US	BK	←COURTS COOK	RECORDER→	UC	RE	TX	VS
•	•	•	•	•	AAA VTS Investigations [SOP]	800-203-4160	•	•	•	•
					ARC Document Research Inc	312-346-4895	•	•	•	
•	•	•	•	•	Argus Services Inc [SOP]	800-297-3377			•	•
•	•		•	•	Asset Control Inc	877-277-3812	•	•	•	•
			•	•	Aurico Reports Inc [SOP]	866-255-1852	•	•	•	•
•	•	•	•	•	Chicagoland Detective Services Inc [SOP]	877-426-4278	•	•	•	•
					Concord Commercial Services	972-931-7431		•		
•	•	•	•	•	CSC - Corporation Service Company [SOP]	800-927-9800	•	•	•	•
•			•	•	George L Dickinson	708-307-4792				
•	•	•			Ferret Diversified Services Inc	847-579-0007		•		
•	•		•	•	Infotrack Information Services Inc	800-275-5594	•	•	•	
•	•				Investigative Research Consultants Inc [SOP]	888-578-8600				
•	•	•	•	•	JG Weiss Research & Retrieval	773-241-6923	•	•	•	•
•	•	•		•	Kevin W McClain Investigations Ltd [SOP]	877-532-1152	•	•	•	•
•	•	•	•	•	LaSalle Process Servers LP [SOP]	800-815-3801		•	•	
•	•	•	•	•	Legal Data Resources	800-735-9207	•	•	•	•
•	•	•	•	•	Lynne J Cox Paralegal	800-510-3009	•	•	•	
•	•	•	•	•	Metro Clerking Inc	312-263-2977	•	•	•	•
•					Professional Services of America Inc	304-485-1278				
					R & B Research & Recording Inc	847-477-7510	•	•		
•	•	•	•	•	Record Information Services	630-557-1000	•	•	•	•
•	•		•	•	SPI [SOP]	773-581-1400				
•	•	•	•	•	Spyglass Research [SOP]	773-581-0180	•	•	•	•
•	•	•	•	•	United Risk Partners LLC	877-593-9995	•	•	•	•

CR	CV	PR	US	BK			UC	RE	TX	VS
					The Wilki Group Inc	847-204-7339	•	•		

CR	CV	PR	US	BK	←Courts **CRAWFORD**	Recorder→	UC	RE	TX	VS
					Abstract & Title Co	618-445-2554		•		
•	•				Crossroads Research	812-299-0809				
•	•	•			Lawrence County Title	618-943-4464	•	•	•	•

CR	CV	PR	US	BK	←Courts **CUMBERLAND**	Recorder→	UC	RE	TX	VS
					Abstract & Title Co	618-445-2554		•		
					Everhart & Everhart Abstractors	217-849-2671	•	•	•	
•	•		•	•	Infotrack Information Services Inc	800-275-5594	•	•	•	

CR	CV	PR	US	BK	←Courts **DE KALB**	Recorder→	UC	RE	TX	VS
•	•	•	•	•	AAA VTS Investigations [SOP]	800-203-4160	•	•	•	•
•	•				Angel P I's [SOP]	800-973-3832				
•	•	•	•	•	Argus Services Inc [SOP]	800-297-3377			•	•
•	•	•			AV Investigations Inc [SOP]	630-443-3617	•	•	•	•
•	•	•			Cynthia Ellis	815-895-9527				
•	•	•			Ferret Diversified Services Inc	847-579-0007		•		
•	•		•	•	Infotrack Information Services Inc	800-275-5594	•	•	•	
•	•	•	•	•	Record Information Services	630-557-1000	•	•	•	•
•	•	•	•	•	Stewart & Associates Inc - Rockford [SOP]	815-961-0150	•	•	•	•
•	•				Julie L Thomas	815-234-4172				
•	•	•	•	•	United Risk Partners LLC	877-593-9995	•	•	•	•
•	•	•	•	•	Yahnke Professional Services & Investigations [SOP]	630-966-9774; Fax- same	•	•	•	•

CR	CV	PR	US	BK	←Courts **DE WITT**	Recorder→	UC	RE	TX	VS
•	•	•			Exacta Search & Document Retrieval	217-528-3677	•	•	•	
•	•				Margaret Flowers	217-877-2105				
•	•		•	•	Infotrack Information Services Inc	800-275-5594	•	•	•	
•	•	•	•	•	Jacobs & Associates CPD Inc [SOP]	800-445-1675	•	•	•	•

CR	CV	PR	US	BK	←Courts **DOUGLAS**	Recorder→	UC	RE	TX	VS
		•			Douglas County Abstract Co Inc	217-253-3214	•	•	•	
•	•		•	•	Infotrack Information Services Inc	800-275-5594	•	•	•	
•	•	•	•	•	Jacobs & Associates CPD Inc [SOP]	800-445-1675	•	•	•	•

CR	CV	PR	US	BK	←Courts **DU PAGE**	Recorder→	UC	RE	TX	VS
•	•	•	•	•	AAA VTS Investigations [SOP]	800-203-4160	•	•	•	•
					ARC Document Research Inc	312-346-4895	•	•	•	
•	•	•	•	•	Argus Services Inc [SOP]	800-297-3377			•	•
•	•	•			AV Investigations Inc [SOP]	630-443-3617	•	•	•	•
•	•	•	•	•	Chicagoland Detective Services Inc [SOP]	877-426-4278	•	•	•	•
•	•	•			Ferret Diversified Services Inc	847-579-0007		•		
•	•		•	•	Infotrack Information Services Inc	800-275-5594	•	•	•	
•	•				Investigative Research Consultants Inc [SOP]	888-578-8600				
•	•	•	•	•	JG Weiss Research & Retrieval	773-241-6923	•	•	•	•
•	•	•	•	•	LaSalle Process Servers LP [SOP]	800-815-3801		•	•	
•	•	•	•	•	Legal Data Resources	800-735-9207	•	•	•	•
•	•	•	•	•	Metro Clerking Inc	312-263-2977	•	•	•	•
•					Professional Services of America Inc	304-485-1278				
					R & B Research & Recording Inc	847-477-7510	•	•		
•	•	•	•	•	Record Information Services	630-557-1000	•	•	•	•
•	•		•	•	SPI [SOP]	773-581-1400				
•	•	•	•	•	Spyglass Research [SOP]	773-581-0180	•	•	•	•
•	•	•	•	•	United Risk Partners LLC	877-593-9995	•	•	•	•
					The Wilki Group Inc	847-204-7339	•	•		
•	•	•	•	•	Yahnke Professional Services & Investigations [SOP]	630-966-9774; Fax- same	•	•	•	•

CR	CV	PR	US	BK	←COURTS	EDGAR	RECORDER→	UC	RE	TX	VS
•	•				Crossroads Research		812-299-0809				
	•	•			Edgar County Title Co		217-465-5821	•	•	•	•
•	•		•	•	Infotrack Information Services Inc		800-275-5594	•	•	•	

CR	CV	PR	US	BK	←COURTS	EDWARDS	RECORDER→	UC	RE	TX	VS
					Abstract & Title Co		618-445-2554		•		
					Sharp Law Firm		618-242-0246		•	•	

CR	CV	PR	US	BK	←COURTS	EFFINGHAM	RECORDER→	UC	RE	TX	VS
					Abstract & Title Co		618-445-2554		•		
					Everhart & Everhart Abstractors		217-849-2671	•	•	•	
•	•		•	•	Infotrack Information Services Inc		800-275-5594	•	•	•	
•	•	•	•	•	Kevin W McClain Investigations Ltd [SOP]		877-532-1152	•	•	•	•
•	•	•	•	•	PII Inc [SOP]		217-483-8845	•	•	•	•

CR	CV	PR	US	BK	←COURTS	FAYETTE	RECORDER→	UC	RE	TX	VS
	•	•		•	Bond Title		618-664-1872		•	•	•
•	•		•	•	Infotrack Information Services Inc		800-275-5594	•	•	•	
•	•	•	•	•	Nancy Durbin Court Research [SOP]		618-267-0472 cell; 618-548-8296	•	•	•	•
•	•	•	•	•	Woelfel & Assoc Inc [SOP]		888-297-7180	•	•	•	

CR	CV	PR	US	BK	←COURTS	FORD	RECORDER→	UC	RE	TX	VS
•	•	•	•	•	Diligent Detective Agency Inc [SOP]		877-694-3332		•	•	•
•	•				Margaret Fiorillo [SOP]		217-379-3359	•	•	•	•
•	•		•	•	Infotrack Information Services Inc		800-275-5594	•	•	•	

CR	CV	PR	US	BK	←COURTS	FRANKLIN	RECORDER→	UC	RE	TX	VS
					Abstract & Title Co		618-445-2554		•		
•	•	•	•	•	Heartland Investigations Inc [SOP]		877-684-6313	•	•	•	•
•	•		•	•	Infotrack Information Services Inc		800-275-5594	•	•	•	
•	•	•	•	•	Kevin W McClain Investigations Ltd [SOP]		877-532-1152	•	•	•	•
			•	•	Midwest Backgrounds Inc		618-942-8808				
•	•	•	•	•	William J O'Shea, PI [SOP]		618-937-3895	•	•	•	•
					Palmer & Murrie Abstract Co Inc		618-993-3866	•	•	•	
					Real Estate Data Inc		618-964-1907	•	•	•	
					Sharp Law Firm		618-242-0246		•	•	

CR	CV	PR	US	BK	←COURTS	FULTON	RECORDER→	UC	RE	TX	VS
•	•	•			Exacta Search & Document Retrieval		217-528-3677	•	•	•	
	•	•			First American Title Insurance Company (IL)		309-347-6126	•	•	•	•
•	•		•	•	Infotrack Information Services Inc		800-275-5594	•	•	•	
•	•		•	•	Security Services Inc (SSI) [SOP]		800-383-4312				
		•			Wilson Abstract Co		309-833-2049	•	•	•	•

CR	CV	PR	US	BK	←COURTS	GALLATIN	RECORDER→	UC	RE	TX	VS
					Abstract & Title Co		618-445-2554		•		
•	•	•	•	•	Heartland Investigations Inc [SOP]		877-684-6313	•	•	•	•

CR	CV	PR	US	BK	←COURTS	GREENE	RECORDER→	UC	RE	TX	VS
•	•		•	•	Infotrack Information Services Inc		800-275-5594	•	•	•	
•	•	•			O H Vivell Title Co		217-942-3733	•	•	•	•

CR	CV	PR	US	BK	←COURTS	GRUNDY	RECORDER→	UC	RE	TX	VS
•	•				Angel P I's [SOP]		800-973-3832				
•	•		•	•	Infotrack Information Services Inc		800-275-5594	•	•	•	

CR	CV	PR	US	BK	←COURTS	HAMILTON	RECORDER→	UC	RE	TX	VS
					Abstract & Title Co		618-445-2554		•		
•	•	•	•	•	Heartland Investigations Inc [SOP]		877-684-6313	•	•	•	•
					Sharp Law Firm		618-242-0246		•	•	

CR	CV	PR	US	BK	←Courts	HANCOCK	Recorder→	UC	RE	TX	VS
•	•		•	•	Infotrack Information Services Inc		800-275-5594	•	•	•	
		•			Wilson Abstract Co		309-833-2049	•	•	•	•

CR	CV	PR	US	BK	←Courts	HARDIN	Recorder→	UC	RE	TX	VS
•	•	•			Hardin County Abstract Co		618-287-7944	•	•	•	•
•	•	•	•	•	Heartland Investigations Inc [SOP]		877-684-6313	•	•	•	•

CR	CV	PR	US	BK	←Courts	HENDERSON	Recorder→	UC	RE	TX	VS
•	•		•	•	Infotrack Information Services Inc		800-275-5594	•	•	•	
		•			Wilson Abstract Co		309-833-2049	•	•	•	•

CR	CV	PR	US	BK	←Courts	HENRY	Recorder→	UC	RE	TX	VS
•	•	•			Ferret Diversified Services Inc		847-579-0007		•		
•	•		•	•	Infotrack Information Services Inc		800-275-5594	•	•	•	
•	•				SAS Associates Inc [SOP]		800-373-0727				

CR	CV	PR	US	BK	←Courts	IROQUOIS	Recorder→	UC	RE	TX	VS
•	•	•	•	•	Diligent Detective Agency Inc [SOP]		877-694-3332		•	•	•
•	•		•	•	Infotrack Information Services Inc		800-275-5594	•	•	•	

CR	CV	PR	US	BK	←Courts	JACKSON	Recorder→	UC	RE	TX	VS
					Abstract & Title Co		618-445-2554		•		
•	•	•			Bi-State Title Search (Div of Bi-State Ind.)		866-450-7399	•	•	•	
•	•	•			Ferret Diversified Services Inc		847-579-0007		•		
•	•	•	•	•	Heartland Investigations Inc [SOP]		877-684-6313	•	•	•	•
•	•		•	•	Infotrack Information Services Inc		800-275-5594	•	•	•	
•	•	•			Search & Genealogy Services		618-529-1024	•	•	•	•

CR	CV	PR	US	BK	←Courts	JASPER	Recorder→	UC	RE	TX	VS
					Abstract & Title Co		618-445-2554		•		
•	•	•			Eaton Abstract Company		618-783-8474	•	•	•	

CR	CV	PR	US	BK	←Courts	JEFFERSON	Recorder→	UC	RE	TX	VS
					Abstract & Title Co		618-445-2554		•		
•	•	•	•	•	Heartland Investigations Inc [SOP]		877-684-6313	•	•	•	•
•	•		•	•	Infotrack Information Services Inc		800-275-5594	•	•	•	
•	•	•	•	•	Kevin W McClain Investigations Ltd [SOP]		877-532-1152	•	•	•	•
•	•	•	•	•	Nancy Durbin Court Research [SOP]		618-267-0472 cell; 618-548-8296	•	•	•	•
					Palmer & Murrie Abstract Co Inc		618-993-3866	•	•	•	
					Sharp Law Firm		618-242-0246		•	•	

CR	CV	PR	US	BK	←Courts	JERSEY	Recorder→	UC	RE	TX	VS
					Bi-State Title Search (Div of Bi-State Ind.)		866-450-7399	•	•	•	
•	•		•	•	Infotrack Information Services Inc		800-275-5594	•	•	•	
•	•	•	•	•	Woelfel & Assoc Inc [SOP]		888-297-7180	•	•	•	

CR	CV	PR	US	BK	←Courts	JO DAVIESS	Recorder→	UC	RE	TX	VS
•	•	•			Ferret Diversified Services Inc		847-579-0007		•		
•	•		•	•	Infotrack Information Services Inc		800-275-5594	•	•	•	
•	•	•			Security First Title Co		815-235-2900	•	•	•	
•	•	•	•	•	Stewart & Associates Inc - Rockford [SOP]		815-961-0150	•	•	•	•
•	•				Julie L Thomas		815-234-4172				

CR	CV	PR	US	BK	←Courts	JOHNSON	Recorder→	UC	RE	TX	VS
					Abstract & Title Co		618-445-2554		•		
•	•	•	•	•	Heartland Investigations Inc [SOP]		877-684-6313	•	•	•	•
•	•		•	•	Infotrack Information Services Inc		800-275-5594	•	•	•	
	•	•			Johnson County Abstract		618-658-3721	•	•	•	•
					Palmer & Murrie Abstract Co Inc		618-993-3866	•	•	•	
					Real Estate Data Inc		618-964-1907	•	•	•	

CR	CV	PR	US	BK	←Courts KANE Recorder→	UC	RE	TX	VS
•	•	•	•	•	AAA VTS Investigations [SOP] 800-203-4160	•	•	•	•
					ARC Document Research Inc 312-346-4895	•	•	•	
•	•	•	•	•	Argus Services Inc [SOP] 800-297-3377			•	•
•	•	•			AV Investigations Inc [SOP] 630-443-3617	•	•	•	•
•	•	•	•	•	Chicagoland Detective Services Inc [SOP] 877-426-4278	•	•	•	•
•	•	•			Cynthia Ellis 815-895-9527				
•	•	•			Ferret Diversified Services Inc 847-579-0007		•		
•	•		•	•	Infotrack Information Services Inc 800-275-5594	•	•	•	
•	•	•	•	•	JG Weiss Research & Retrieval 773-241-6923	•	•	•	•
•	•	•	•	•	LaSalle Process Servers LP [SOP] 800-815-3801		•	•	
•	•	•	•	•	Metro Clerking Inc 312-263-2977	•	•	•	•
					R & B Research & Recording Inc 847-477-7510	•	•		
•	•	•	•	•	Record Information Services 630-557-1000	•	•	•	•
•	•	•	•	•	Spyglass Research [SOP] 773-581-0180	•	•	•	•
•	•				Julie L Thomas 815-234-4172				
•	•	•	•	•	United Risk Partners LLC 877-593-9995	•	•	•	•
					The Wilki Group Inc 847-204-7339	•	•		
•	•	•	•	•	Yahnke Professional Services & Investigations [SOP] ....630-966-9774; Fax- same	•	•	•	•

CR	CV	PR	US	BK	←Courts KANKAKEE Recorder→	UC	RE	TX	VS
•	•	•	•	•	Diligent Detective Agency Inc [SOP] 877-694-3332		•	•	•
•	•		•	•	Infotrack Information Services Inc 800-275-5594	•	•	•	
•	•	•			Skimerhorn Inv [SOP] 815-933-0843	•	•	•	•

CR	CV	PR	US	BK	←Courts KENDALL Recorder→	UC	RE	TX	VS
•	•	•	•	•	AAA VTS Investigations [SOP] 800-203-4160	•	•	•	•
•	•				Angel P I's [SOP] 800-973-3832				
•	•	•	•	•	Argus Services Inc [SOP] 800-297-3377			•	•
•	•	•			AV Investigations Inc [SOP] 630-443-3617	•	•	•	•
•	•	•			Cynthia Ellis 815-895-9527				
•	•	•			Ferret Diversified Services Inc 847-579-0007		•		
•	•		•	•	Infotrack Information Services Inc 800-275-5594	•	•	•	
•	•	•	•	•	Record Information Services 630-557-1000	•	•	•	•
•	•				Julie L Thomas 815-234-4172				
•	•	•	•	•	United Risk Partners LLC 877-593-9995	•	•	•	•
•	•	•	•	•	Yahnke Professional Services & Investigations [SOP] ....630-966-9774; Fax- same	•	•	•	•

CR	CV	PR	US	BK	←Courts KNOX Recorder→	UC	RE	TX	VS
•	•		•	•	Infotrack Information Services Inc 800-275-5594	•	•	•	
•	•		•	•	Security Services Inc (SSI) [SOP] 800-383-4312				

CR	CV	PR	US	BK	←Courts LA SALLE Recorder→	UC	RE	TX	VS
•	•				Angel P I's [SOP] 800-973-3832				
•	•		•	•	Infotrack Information Services Inc 800-275-5594	•	•	•	

CR	CV	PR	US	BK	←Courts LAKE Recorder→	UC	RE	TX	VS
•	•	•	•	•	AAA VTS Investigations [SOP] 800-203-4160	•	•	•	•
					ARC Document Research Inc 312-346-4895	•	•	•	
•	•	•	•	•	Argus Services Inc [SOP] 800-297-3377			•	•
•	•	•	•	•	Chicagoland Detective Services Inc [SOP] 877-426-4278	•	•	•	•
•	•	•			Ferret Diversified Services Inc 847-579-0007		•		
•	•		•	•	Infotrack Information Services Inc 800-275-5594	•	•	•	
•	•	•	•	•	JG Weiss Research & Retrieval 773-241-6923	•	•	•	•
•	•	•	•	•	LaSalle Process Servers LP [SOP] 800-815-3801		•	•	
•	•	•			Lawyer's Resource 888-218-8361	•	•	•	•
•	•	•	•	•	Legal Data Resources 800-735-9207	•	•	•	•
•	•	•	•	•	Metro Clerking Inc 312-263-2977	•	•	•	•
•	•	•			PeopleSearch 877-835-1983	•	•	•	•
					R & B Research & Recording Inc 847-477-7510	•	•		

CR	CV	PR	US	BK	←Courts	Recorder→	UC	RE	TX	VS
•	•	•	•	•	Record Information Services	630-557-1000	•	•	•	•
•	•	•	•	•	Spyglass Research [SOP]	773-581-0180	•	•	•	•
•	•	•			Dona Szymaszek	847-540-7425	•	•	•	•
•	•	•	•	•	United Risk Partners LLC	877-593-9995	•	•	•	•

LAWRENCE

CR	CV	PR	US	BK	←Courts	Recorder→	UC	RE	TX	VS
					Abstract & Title Co.	618-445-2554		•		
•	•				Crossroads Research	812-299-0809				
•	•	•			Lawrence County Title	618-943-4464	•	•	•	•

LEE

CR	CV	PR	US	BK	←Courts	Recorder→	UC	RE	TX	VS
•	•				Angel P I's [SOP]	800-973-3832				
•	•	•			Ferret Diversified Services Inc	847-579-0007		•		
•	•		•	•	Infotrack Information Services Inc	800-275-5594	•	•	•	
•	•	•		•	Security First Title Co.	815-235-2900	•	•	•	
•	•	•	•	•	Stewart & Associates Inc - Rockford [SOP]	815-961-0150	•	•	•	•

LIVINGSTON

CR	CV	PR	US	BK	←Courts	Recorder→	UC	RE	TX	VS
•	•				Angel P I's [SOP]	800-973-3832				
•	•		•	•	Infotrack Information Services Inc	800-275-5594	•	•	•	

LOGAN

CR	CV	PR	US	BK	←Courts	Recorder→	UC	RE	TX	VS
•	•				Angel P I's [SOP]	800-973-3832				
•	•	•			Exacta Search & Document Retrieval	217-528-3677	•	•	•	
•	•	•			Ferret Diversified Services Inc	847-579-0007		•		
•	•				Margaret Flowers	217-877-2105				
•	•		•	•	Infotrack Information Services Inc	800-275-5594	•	•	•	
•	•	•	•	•	Jacobs & Associates CPD Inc [SOP]	800-445-1675	•	•	•	•
•	•	•	•	•	Meador Investigations [SOP]	888-688-9944	•	•	•	•
•	•	•	•	•	PII Inc [SOP]	217-483-8845	•	•	•	•

MACON

CR	CV	PR	US	BK	←Courts	Recorder→	UC	RE	TX	VS
•	•	•			Exacta Search & Document Retrieval	217-528-3677	•	•	•	
•	•				Margaret Flowers	217-877-2105				
•	•		•	•	Infotrack Information Services Inc	800-275-5594	•	•	•	
•	•	•	•	•	Jacobs & Associates CPD Inc [SOP]	800-445-1675	•	•	•	•
•	•	•	•	•	Meador Investigations [SOP]	888-688-9944	•	•	•	•
•	•	•	•	•	PII Inc [SOP]	217-483-8845	•	•	•	•

MACOUPIN

CR	CV	PR	US	BK	←Courts	Recorder→	UC	RE	TX	VS
•	•	•			Bi-State Title Search (Div of Bi-State Ind.)	866-450-7399	•	•	•	
	•	•		•	Bond Title	618-664-1872		•	•	•
•	•	•			Exacta Search & Document Retrieval	217-528-3677	•	•	•	
•	•		•	•	Infotrack Information Services Inc	800-275-5594	•	•	•	
•	•	•	•	•	Jess Barker Document Research/Retrieval	888-316-3773	•	•	•	•
•	•	•	•	•	PII Inc [SOP]	217-483-8845	•	•	•	•
•	•	•	•	•	Woelfel & Assoc Inc [SOP]	888-297-7180	•	•	•	

MADISON

CR	CV	PR	US	BK	←Courts	Recorder→	UC	RE	TX	VS
•	•	•	•	•	AAA Process Service Inc [SOP]	888-350-5809	•	•	•	•
•	•	•			Bi-State Title Search (Div of Bi-State Ind.)	866-450-7399	•	•	•	
	•	•		•	Bond Title	618-664-1872		•	•	•
•	•	•	•	•	Brad Clarkson	618-288-7599	•	•	•	•
•	•	•			Compu-Fact Research Inc	636-477-1115, 618-239-0677	•	•	•	
•	•	•			Cynthia Ellis	815-895-9527				
•	•	•			Ferret Diversified Services Inc	847-579-0007		•		
					GHI Abstracting Inc	618-971-5780 or 618-654-7253	•	•	•	
•	•		•	•	Infotrack Information Services Inc	800-275-5594	•	•	•	
•	•	•	•	•	Jess Barker Document Research/Retrieval	888-316-3773	•	•	•	•
•	•	•	•	•	Kellerman Investigations Ltd [SOP]	888-402-6662				
•	•	•	•	•	Kevin W McClain Investigations Ltd [SOP]	877-532-1152	•	•	•	•

CR	CV	PR	US	BK	←Courts	Recorder→	UC	RE	TX	VS
	•	•	•	•	Master File Inc [SOP]	866-242-0469	•	•	•	
•	•	•	•	•	Services Rendered Inc [SOP]	888-434-8200	•		•	•
•	•	•	•	•	United Risk Partners LLC	877-593-9995	•	•	•	•
•	•	•	•	•	Woelfel & Assoc Inc [SOP]	888-297-7180	•	•	•	

CR	CV	PR	US	BK	←Courts **Marion**	Recorder→	UC	RE	TX	VS
					Abstract & Title Co.	618-445-2554		•		
•	•		•	•	Infotrack Information Services Inc	800-275-5594	•	•	•	
•	•	•	•	•	Kevin W McClain Investigations Ltd [SOP]	877-532-1152	•	•	•	•
•	•	•	•	•	Nancy Durbin Court Research [SOP]	618-267-0472 cell; 618-548-8296	•	•	•	•
					Sharp Law Firm	618-242-0246		•		
•	•	•	•		Woelfel & Assoc Inc [SOP]	888-297-7180	•	•	•	

CR	CV	PR	US	BK	←Courts **Marshall**	Recorder→	UC	RE	TX	VS
•	•				Angel P I's [SOP]	800-973-3832				
•	•		•	•	Infotrack Information Services Inc	800-275-5594	•	•	•	
•	•		•	•	Security Services Inc (SSI) [SOP]	800-383-4312				

CR	CV	PR	US	BK	←Courts **Mason**	Recorder→	UC	RE	TX	VS
•	•	•			Exacta Search & Document Retrieval	217-528-3677	•	•	•	
	•	•			First American Title Insurance Company (IL)	309-347-6126	•	•	•	•
•	•		•	•	Infotrack Information Services Inc	800-275-5594	•	•	•	
•	•	•	•	•	Jacobs & Associates CPD Inc [SOP]	800-445-1675	•	•	•	•
•	•	•	•	•	PII Inc [SOP]	217-483-8845	•	•	•	•

CR	CV	PR	US	BK	←Courts **Massac**	Recorder→	UC	RE	TX	VS
					Abstract & Title Co.	618-445-2554		•		
•	•	•	•	•	Heartland Investigations Inc [SOP]	877-684-6313	•	•	•	•
					Palmer & Murrie Abstract Co Inc	618-993-3866	•	•	•	

CR	CV	PR	US	BK	←Courts **McDonough**	Recorder→	UC	RE	TX	VS
				•	Infotrack Information Services Inc	800-275-5594	•	•	•	
		•			Wilson Abstract Co	309-833-2049	•	•	•	•

CR	CV	PR	US	BK	←Courts **McHenry**	Recorder→	UC	RE	TX	VS
•	•	•	•	•	AAA VTS Investigations [SOP]	800-203-4160	•	•	•	•
					ARC Document Research Inc	312-346-4895	•	•	•	
•	•	•	•	•	Argus Services Inc [SOP]	800-297-3377			•	•
•	•		•	•	Infotrack Information Services Inc	800-275-5594	•	•	•	
				•	LaSalle Process Servers LP [SOP]	800-815-3801				
•	•	•	•	•	Metro Clerking Inc	312-263-2977	•	•	•	•
•	•				Quickfacts	815-236-8874	•	•	•	
					R & B Research & Recording Inc	847-477-7510		•		
•	•	•	•	•	Record Information Services	630-557-1000	•	•	•	•
•	•	•			Dona Szymaszek	847-540-7425	•	•	•	•
•	•	•	•	•	United Risk Partners LLC	877-593-9995	•	•	•	•
					The Wilki Group Inc	847-204-7339	•	•		

CR	CV	PR	US	BK	←Courts **McLean**	Recorder→	UC	RE	TX	VS
•	•	•			Exacta Search & Document Retrieval	217-528-3677	•	•	•	
•	•	•			Foster Inv [SOP]	800-526-0307	•	•	•	•
•	•		•	•	Infotrack Information Services Inc	800-275-5594	•	•	•	
•	•	•	•	•	Jacobs & Associates CPD Inc [SOP]	800-445-1675	•	•	•	•
•	•		•	•	Security Services Inc (SSI) [SOP]	800-383-4312				

CR	CV	PR	US	BK	←Courts **Menard**	Recorder→	UC	RE	TX	VS
•	•				Angel P I's [SOP]	800-973-3832				
•	•	•			Exacta Search & Document Retrieval	217-528-3677	•	•	•	
	•	•			First American Title Insurance Company (IL)	309-347-6126	•	•	•	•
•	•		•	•	Infotrack Information Services Inc	800-275-5594	•	•	•	
•	•	•	•	•	Meador Investigations [SOP]	888-688-9944	•	•	•	•

CR	CV	PR	US	BK	←Courts	Recorder→	UC	RE	TX	VS
•	•	•	•	•	PII Inc [SOP]	217-483-8845	•	•	•	•

Mercer

CR	CV	PR	US	BK	←Courts	Recorder→	UC	RE	TX	VS
•	•	•			Ferret Diversified Services Inc	847-579-0007		•		
•	•		•	•	Infotrack Information Services Inc	800-275-5594	•	•	•	
•	•				SAS Associates Inc [SOP]	800-373-0727				

Monroe

CR	CV	PR	US	BK	←Courts	Recorder→	UC	RE	TX	VS
•	•	•	•	•	AAA Process Service Inc [SOP]	888-350-5809	•	•	•	•
•	•	•			Bi-State Title Search (Div of Bi-State Ind.)	866-450-7399	•	•	•	
•	•		•	•	Infotrack Information Services Inc	800-275-5594	•	•	•	
					Monroe County Title Co	618-939-8292		•		
•	•	•	•	•	Services Rendered Inc [SOP]	888-434-8200	•		•	•

Montgomery

CR	CV	PR	US	BK	←Courts	Recorder→	UC	RE	TX	VS
•	•	•			Bi-State Title Search (Div of Bi-State Ind.)	866-450-7399	•	•	•	
	•	•		•	Bond Title	618-664-1872		•	•	•
•	•	•			Exacta Search & Document Retrieval	217-528-3677	•	•	•	
•	•		•	•	Infotrack Information Services Inc	800-275-5594	•	•	•	
•	•	•	•	•	PII Inc [SOP]	217-483-8845	•	•	•	•

Morgan

CR	CV	PR	US	BK	←Courts	Recorder→	UC	RE	TX	VS
•	•	•			Exacta Search & Document Retrieval	217-528-3677	•	•	•	
•	•		•	•	Infotrack Information Services Inc	800-275-5594	•	•	•	
•				•	Legal Research Solutions	217-585-0668			•	
•	•	•	•	•	PII Inc [SOP]	217-483-8845	•	•	•	•

Moultrie

CR	CV	PR	US	BK	←Courts	Recorder→	UC	RE	TX	VS
•	•				Margaret Flowers	217-877-2105				
•	•		•	•	Infotrack Information Services Inc	800-275-5594	•	•	•	
•	•	•	•	•	Jacobs & Associates CPD Inc [SOP]	800-445-1675	•	•	•	•
•	•	•	•	•	PII Inc [SOP]	217-483-8845	•	•	•	•

Ogle

CR	CV	PR	US	BK	←Courts	Recorder→	UC	RE	TX	VS
•	•				Angel P I's [SOP]	800-973-3832				
•	•	•			Ferret Diversified Services Inc	847-579-0007		•		
•	•		•	•	Infotrack Information Services Inc	800-275-5594	•	•	•	
•	•	•		•	Security First Title Co.	815-235-2900	•	•	•	
•	•	•	•	•	Stewart & Associates Inc - Rockford [SOP]	815-961-0150	•	•	•	•
•	•				Julie L Thomas	815-234-4172				

Peoria

CR	CV	PR	US	BK	←Courts	Recorder→	UC	RE	TX	VS
•	•				Angel P I's [SOP]	800-973-3832				
•	•	•	•	•	Dana Caughey Document Retrieval Service	309-694-4407	•	•	•	
•	•	•			Exacta Search & Document Retrieval	217-528-3677	•	•	•	
•	•		•	•	Infotrack Information Services Inc	800-275-5594	•	•	•	
•	•	•	•	•	Meador Investigations [SOP]	888-688-9944	•	•	•	•
•	•		•	•	Reality Check Inc	309-699-1846	•	•	•	
•	•		•	•	Security Services Inc (SSI) [SOP]	800-383-4312				

Perry

CR	CV	PR	US	BK	←Courts	Recorder→	UC	RE	TX	VS
					Abstract & Title Co.	618-445-2554		•		
•	•	•			Bi-State Title Search (Div of Bi-State Ind.)	866-450-7399	•	•	•	
•	•	•	•	•	Heartland Investigations Inc [SOP]	877-684-6313	•	•	•	•
•	•		•	•	Infotrack Information Services Inc	800-275-5594	•	•	•	
•	•	•			Search & Genealogy Services	618-529-1024	•	•	•	•

Piatt

CR	CV	PR	US	BK	←Courts	Recorder→	UC	RE	TX	VS
•	•	•			Exacta Search & Document Retrieval	217-528-3677	•	•	•	
•	•		•	•	Infotrack Information Services Inc	800-275-5594	•	•	•	
•	•	•	•	•	Jacobs & Associates CPD Inc [SOP]	800-445-1675	•	•	•	•

CR	CV	PR	US	BK	←Courts	Pike	Recorder→	UC	RE	TX	VS
•	•	•			Ferret Diversified Services Inc		847-579-0007		•		
•	•		•	•	Infotrack Information Services Inc		800-275-5594	•	•	•	
•	•	•			Marion County Abstract Co (Missouri)		800-952-5314	•	•	•	•

CR	CV	PR	US	BK	←Courts	Pope	Recorder→	UC	RE	TX	VS
					Abstract & Title Co.		618-445-2554		•		
•	•	•	•	•	Heartland Investigations Inc [SOP]		877-684-6313	•	•	•	•

CR	CV	PR	US	BK	←Courts	Pulaski	Recorder→	UC	RE	TX	VS
•	•	•	•	•	Heartland Investigations Inc [SOP]		877-684-6313	•	•	•	•
	•	•			Pulaski County Abstract Company - IL		618-748-9233, Fax- same	•	•	•	•

CR	CV	PR	US	BK	←Courts	Putnam	Recorder→	UC	RE	TX	VS
•	•				Angel P I's [SOP]		800-973-3832				
•	•		•	•	Infotrack Information Services Inc		800-275-5594	•	•	•	

CR	CV	PR	US	BK	←Courts	Randolph	Recorder→	UC	RE	TX	VS
					Abstract & Title Co.		618-445-2554		•		
•	•	•			Bi-State Title Search (Div of Bi-State Ind.)		866-450-7399	•	•	•	
•	•	•	•	•	Heartland Investigations Inc [SOP]		877-684-6313	•	•	•	•
•	•		•	•	Infotrack Information Services Inc		800-275-5594	•	•	•	
•	•	•	•	•	Woelfel & Assoc Inc [SOP]		888-297-7180	•	•	•	

CR	CV	PR	US	BK	←Courts	Richland	Recorder→	UC	RE	TX	VS
					Abstract & Title Co.		618-445-2554		•		
•	•	•			Lawrence County Title		618-943-4464	•	•	•	•

CR	CV	PR	US	BK	←Courts	Rock Island	Recorder→	UC	RE	TX	VS
•	•	•	•	•	Cynthia-Renee's Professional Business Svc [SOP]		563-324-9445	•	•	•	•
•	•	•	•	•	DocumentServe Express [SOP]		309-786-2220	•	•	•	•
•	•	•			Ferret Diversified Services Inc		847-579-0007		•		
•	•	•	•	•	FYII Acct [SOP]		563-299-5683	•	•	•	•
•	•		•	•	Infotrack Information Services Inc		800-275-5594	•	•	•	
•	•	•	•	•	James M Sweeney & Associates Inc [SOP]		800-494-5922	•		•	•
•	•				SAS Associates Inc [SOP]		800-373-0727				
•	•	•	•	•	United Risk Partners LLC		877-593-9995	•	•	•	•

CR	CV	PR	US	BK	←Courts	Saline	Recorder→	UC	RE	TX	VS
					Abstract & Title Co.		618-445-2554		•		
•	•	•	•	•	Heartland Investigations Inc [SOP]		877-684-6313	•	•	•	•
	•	•			Kotner Abstract & Title		618-273-7611	•	•	•	
					Palmer & Murrie Abstract Co Inc		618-993-3866	•	•	•	

CR	CV	PR	US	BK	←Courts	Sangamon	Recorder→	UC	RE	TX	VS
•	•				Angel P I's [SOP]		800-973-3832				
					ARC Document Research Inc		312-346-4895	•	•	•	
•	•	•			Bi-State Title Search (Div of Bi-State Ind.)		866-450-7399	•	•	•	
•	•	•			Cynthia Ellis		815-895-9527				
•	•	•			Exacta Search & Document Retrieval		217-528-3677	•	•	•	
•	•	•	•	•	Faxxon Legal Information Services Inc		800-932-9966	•	•	•	•
•	•	•			Ferret Diversified Services Inc		847-579-0007		•		
•	•				Margaret Flowers		217-877-2105				
•	•		•	•	Infotrack Information Services Inc		800-275-5594	•	•	•	
•	•	•	•	•	Jacobs & Associates CPD Inc [SOP]		800-445-1675	•	•	•	•
•	•	•	•	•	Jess Barker Document Research/Retrieval		888-316-3773	•	•	•	•
•				•	Legal Research Solutions		217-585-0668			•	
•	•	•	•	•	Meador Investigations [SOP]		888-688-9944	•	•	•	•
•	•	•	•	•	PII Inc [SOP]		217-483-8845	•	•	•	•
•	•	•	•	•	ProCom Services Corp		217-525-7600	•		•	•
•	•	•	•	•	United Risk Partners LLC		877-593-9995	•	•	•	•

CR	CV	PR	US	BK	←COURTS SCHUYLER RECORDER→	UC	RE	TX	VS
•	•	•			Exacta Search & Document Retrieval........217-528-3677	•	•	•	
	•				First American Title Insurance Company (IL)........309-347-6126	•	•	•	•
•	•		•	•	Infotrack Information Services Inc........800-275-5594	•	•	•	
		•			Wilson Abstract Co........309-833-2049	•	•	•	•

CR	CV	PR	US	BK	←COURTS SCOTT RECORDER→	UC	RE	TX	VS
•	•	•			Exacta Search & Document Retrieval........217-528-3677	•	•	•	
•	•		•	•	Infotrack Information Services Inc........800-275-5594	•	•	•	
•	•	•	•	•	PII Inc [SOP]........217-483-8845	•	•	•	•

CR	CV	PR	US	BK	←COURTS SHELBY RECORDER→	UC	RE	TX	VS
•	•		•	•	Infotrack Information Services Inc........800-275-5594	•	•	•	
•	•	•	•	•	Jacobs & Associates CPD Inc [SOP]........800-445-1675	•	•	•	•
•	•	•	•	•	PII Inc [SOP]........217-483-8845	•	•	•	•
•	•	•			Shelby County Land Title Corp........217-774-2623	•	•	•	•

CR	CV	PR	US	BK	←COURTS ST. CLAIR RECORDER→	UC	RE	TX	VS
•	•	•	•	•	AAA Process Service Inc [SOP]........888-350-5809	•	•	•	•
•	•	•			Bi-State Title Search (Div of Bi-State Ind.)........866-450-7399	•	•	•	
	•	•		•	Bond Title........618-664-1872		•	•	•
•	•	•	•	•	Brad Clarkson........618-288-7599	•	•	•	•
•	•	•			Compu-Fact Research Inc........636-477-1115, 618-239-0677	•	•	•	
					GHI Abstracting Inc........618-971-5780 or 618-654-7253	•	•	•	
•	•		•	•	Infotrack Information Services Inc........800-275-5594	•	•	•	
•	•	•	•	•	Jess Barker Document Research/Retrieval........888-316-3773	•	•	•	•
•	•	•	•	•	Kellerman Investigations Ltd [SOP]........888-402-6662				
•	•	•	•	•	Kevin W McClain Investigations Ltd [SOP]........877-532-1152	•	•	•	•
•	•				KLK Research........636-366-7055				
	•	•	•	•	Master File Inc [SOP]........866-242-0469	•	•	•	
•	•	•	•	•	Services Rendered Inc [SOP]........888-434-8200	•		•	•
•	•	•	•	•	Woelfel & Assoc Inc [SOP]........888-297-7180	•	•	•	

CR	CV	PR	US	BK	←COURTS STARK RECORDER→	UC	RE	TX	VS
•	•		•	•	Infotrack Information Services Inc........800-275-5594	•	•	•	
•	•		•	•	Security Services Inc (SSI) [SOP]........800-383-4312				

CR	CV	PR	US	BK	←COURTS STEPHENSON RECORDER→	UC	RE	TX	VS
•	•	•			Ferret Diversified Services Inc........847-579-0007		•		
•	•		•	•	Infotrack Information Services Inc........800-275-5594	•	•	•	
•	•	•		•	Security First Title Co........815-235-2900	•	•	•	
•	•	•	•	•	Stewart & Associates Inc - Rockford [SOP]........815-961-0150	•	•	•	•
•	•				Julie L Thomas........815-234-4172				

CR	CV	PR	US	BK	←COURTS TAZEWELL RECORDER→	UC	RE	TX	VS
•	•				Angel P I's [SOP]........800-973-3832				
•	•	•	•	•	Dana Caughey Document Retrieval Service........309-694-4407	•	•	•	
•	•	•			Exacta Search & Document Retrieval........217-528-3677	•	•	•	
•	•		•	•	Infotrack Information Services Inc........800-275-5594	•	•	•	
•	•	•	•	•	Meador Investigations [SOP]........888-688-9944	•	•	•	•
•	•		•	•	Reality Check Inc........309-699-1846	•	•	•	
•	•				Secretarial Outsource Services........309-347-3736				
•	•		•	•	Security Services Inc (SSI) [SOP]........800-383-4312				

CR	CV	PR	US	BK	←COURTS UNION RECORDER→	UC	RE	TX	VS
					Abstract & Title Co........618-445-2554		•		
•	•	•			Bi-State Title Search (Div of Bi-State Ind.)........866-450-7399	•	•	•	
•	•	•			Ferret Diversified Services Inc........847-579-0007		•		
•	•	•	•	•	Heartland Investigations Inc [SOP]........877-684-6313	•	•	•	•
•	•		•	•	Infotrack Information Services Inc........800-275-5594	•	•	•	

CR	CV	PR	US	BK	←Courts		Recorder→	UC	RE	TX	VS
					Palmer & Murrie Abstract Co Inc		618-993-3866	•	•	•	
•	•	•			Search & Genealogy Services		618-529-1024	•	•	•	•
CR	**CV**	**PR**	**US**	**BK**	**←Courts**	**VERMILION**	**Recorder→**	**UC**	**RE**	**TX**	**VS**
•	•	•	•	•	Diligent Detective Agency Inc [SOP]		877-694-3332		•	•	•
•	•		•	•	Infotrack Information Services Inc		800-275-5594	•	•	•	
CR	**CV**	**PR**	**US**	**BK**	**←Courts**	**WABASH**	**Recorder→**	**UC**	**RE**	**TX**	**VS**
					Abstract & Title Co.		618-445-2554		•		
•	•	•			Lawrence County Title		618-943-4464	•	•	•	•
CR	**CV**	**PR**	**US**	**BK**	**←Courts**	**WARREN**	**Recorder→**	**UC**	**RE**	**TX**	**VS**
•	•		•	•	Infotrack Information Services Inc		800-275-5594	•	•	•	
		•			Wilson Abstract Co.		309-833-2049	•	•	•	•
CR	**CV**	**PR**	**US**	**BK**	**←Courts**	**WASHINGTON**	**Recorder→**	**UC**	**RE**	**TX**	**VS**
•	•	•			Bi-State Title Search (Div of Bi-State Ind.)		866-450-7399	•	•	•	
•	•		•	•	Infotrack Information Services Inc		800-275-5594	•	•	•	
•	•	•	•	•	Kevin W McClain Investigations Ltd [SOP]		877-532-1152	•	•	•	•
CR	**CV**	**PR**	**US**	**BK**	**←Courts**	**WAYNE**	**Recorder→**	**UC**	**RE**	**TX**	**VS**
					Abstract & Title Co.		618-445-2554		•		
					Sharp Law Firm		618-242-0246		•	•	
CR	**CV**	**PR**	**US**	**BK**	**←Courts**	**WHITE**	**Recorder→**	**UC**	**RE**	**TX**	**VS**
					Abstract & Title Co.		618-445-2554		•		
•	•	•	•	•	Heartland Investigations Inc [SOP]		877-684-6313	•	•	•	•
CR	**CV**	**PR**	**US**	**BK**	**←Courts**	**WHITESIDE**	**Recorder→**	**UC**	**RE**	**TX**	**VS**
•	•	•			Ferret Diversified Services Inc		847-579-0007		•		
•	•		•	•	Infotrack Information Services Inc		800-275-5594	•	•	•	
•	•	•		•	Security First Title Co.		815-235-2900	•	•	•	
•	•	•	•	•	Stewart & Associates Inc - Rockford [SOP]		815-961-0150	•	•	•	•
CR	**CV**	**PR**	**US**	**BK**	**←Courts**	**WILL**	**Recorder→**	**UC**	**RE**	**TX**	**VS**
•	•	•	•	•	AAA VTS Investigations [SOP]		800-203-4160	•	•	•	•
					ARC Document Research Inc		312-346-4895	•	•	•	
•	•	•	•	•	Argus Services Inc [SOP]		800-297-3377			•	•
•	•	•			Cynthia Ellis		815-895-9527				
•	•				Jo Ann Entwistle		815-838-2871				
•	•	•			Ferret Diversified Services Inc		847-579-0007		•		
•	•		•	•	Infotrack Information Services Inc		800-275-5594	•	•	•	
•	•	•	•	•	JG Weiss Research & Retrieval		773-241-6923	•	•	•	•
•	•	•	•	•	LaSalle Process Servers LP [SOP]		800-815-3801		•	•	
•	•	•	•	•	Legal Data Resources		800-735-9207	•	•	•	•
•	•	•	•	•	Metro Clerking Inc		312-263-2977	•	•	•	•
					R & B Research & Recording Inc		847-477-7510	•	•		
•	•	•	•	•	Record Information Services		630-557-1000	•	•	•	•
•	•		•	•	SPI [SOP]		773-581-1400				
•	•	•	•	•	Spyglass Research [SOP]		773-581-0180	•	•	•	•
•	•	•	•	•	United Risk Partners LLC		877-593-9995	•	•	•	•
					The Wilki Group Inc		847-204-7339	•	•		
•	•	•	•	•	Yahnke Professional Services & Investigations [SOP]		630-966-9774; Fax- same	•	•	•	•
CR	**CV**	**PR**	**US**	**BK**	**←Courts**	**WILLIAMSON**	**Recorder→**	**UC**	**RE**	**TX**	**VS**
					Abstract & Title Co.		618-445-2554		•		
•	•	•	•	•	Rebecca Bulls		731-799-3066; Fax- same				
•	•	•	•	•	Heartland Investigations Inc [SOP]		877-684-6313	•	•	•	•
•	•		•	•	Infotrack Information Services Inc		800-275-5594	•	•	•	
•	•	•	•	•	Kevin W McClain Investigations Ltd [SOP]		877-532-1152	•	•	•	•
•			•	•	Midwest Backgrounds Inc		618-942-8808				

CR	CV	PR	US	BK	Name	Phone	UC	RE	TX	VS
•	•	•	•	•	William J O'Shea, PI [SOP]	618-937-3895	•	•	•	•
					Palmer & Murrie Abstract Co Inc	618-993-3866	•	•	•	
					Real Estate Data Inc	618-964-1907	•	•	•	
					Sharp Law Firm	618-242-0246		•	•	

CR	CV	PR	US	BK	←COURTS WINNEBAGO	RECORDER→	UC	RE	TX	VS
•	•				Angel P I's [SOP]	800-973-3832				
					ARC Document Research Inc	312-346-4895	•	•	•	
•	•	•	•	•	Argus Services Inc [SOP]	800-297-3377			•	•
•	•	•			Cynthia Ellis	815-895-9527				
•	•	•			Ferret Diversified Services Inc	847-579-0007		•		
•	•	•	•	•	Gregg Investigations, Inc of Rockford [SOP]	800-866-1976	•		•	•
•	•		•	•	Infotrack Information Services Inc	800-275-5594	•	•	•	
•	•	•		•	Security First Title Co.	815-235-2900	•	•	•	
•	•	•	•	•	Stewart & Associates Inc - Rockford [SOP]	815-961-0150	•	•	•	•
•	•				Julie L Thomas	815-234-4172				

CR	CV	PR	US	BK	←COURTS WOODFORD	RECORDER→	UC	RE	TX	VS
•	•				Angel P I's [SOP]	800-973-3832				
•	•	•	•	•	Dana Caughey Document Retrieval Service	309-694-4407	•	•	•	
•	•	•			Exacta Search & Document Retrieval	217-528-3677	•	•	•	
•	•		•	•	Infotrack Information Services Inc	800-275-5594	•	•	•	
•	•		•	•	Security Services Inc (SSI) [SOP]	800-383-4312				

Editor's Note: The County Index section in this book will **only** indicate a county where a record retriever does an in-person search by himself or herself, or by a payroll employee.

Many retrievers also maintain a network of correspondents and provide services in additional counties not listed within the County Index. This additional coverage is indicated in the Profiles section under Correspondent Relationships.

Indiana

COURT RECORDS RETRIEVED — CAPITAL - MARION COUNTY — RECORDED RECORDS RETRIEVED

CR	CV	PR	US	BK	←COURTS **ADAMS**	RECORDER→	UC	RE	TX	VS
•	•				Advanced Collection Services Inc	260-827-8189		•	•	•
•	•				Dean Research Group	260-485-4648	•	•	•	
	•		•	•	McGinley Search & File Service Corp	317-807-0760	•	•	•	
•	•				Schurger Land Title Co.	260-724-4408	•	•	•	
	•	•			Tri-County Land Title	260-589-3139	•	•	•	•
•	•	•	•	•	We Search ReSearch Inc	800-251-8167	•	•	•	

CR	CV	PR	US	BK	←COURTS **ALLEN**	RECORDER→	UC	RE	TX	VS
•	•		•	•	ASK Services Inc (Indiana)	888-416-1313	•	•	•	
•					Teresa L Coty	260-420-1015	•	•	•	
•	•				Dean Research Group	260-485-4648	•	•	•	
	•	•		•	Kings Title & Closing Services	800-860-2990	•	•	•	•
	•		•	•	McGinley Search & File Service Corp	317-807-0760	•	•	•	
•	•	•	•	•	We Search ReSearch Inc	800-251-8167	•	•	•	

CR	CV	PR	US	BK	←COURTS **BARTHOLOMEW**	RECORDER→	UC	RE	TX	VS
	•				Hotopp Public Record Searches	812-342-2163	•	•	•	
•	•				Chet Kylander	812-988-9522			•	
	•		•	•	McGinley Search & File Service Corp	317-807-0760	•	•	•	
•	•	•			McPheron Info Services	765-482-1650, cell- 765-894-0107	•	•	•	•
•	•				Myers Investigations Inc [SOP]	800-788-8018	•		•	•
•	•				PAC Data LLC	812-654-3207		•	•	•
	•				Parsley Enterprises Inc	317-878-9979		•	•	

CR	CV	PR	US	BK	←COURTS **BENTON**	RECORDER→	UC	RE	TX	VS
•	•	•		•	County Courthouse Retrieval	765-485-0233	•	•	•	
•	•	•			Held Abstract & Title Co Inc	765-762-2457	•	•	•	
	•		•	•	McGinley Search & File Service Corp	317-807-0760	•	•	•	
•	•	•			Tippecanoe Title Services Inc	888-423-2457	•	•	•	
•	•	•	•	•	We Search ReSearch Inc	800-251-8167	•	•	•	

CR	CV	PR	US	BK	←COURTS **BLACKFORD**	RECORDER→	UC	RE	TX	VS
	•	•		•	Kings Title & Closing Services	800-860-2990	•	•	•	•
	•		•	•	McGinley Search & File Service Corp	317-807-0760	•	•	•	
•	•	•	•	•	We Search ReSearch Inc	800-251-8167	•	•	•	

CR	CV	PR	US	BK	←COURTS **BOONE**	RECORDER→	UC	RE	TX	VS
•	•		•		Checkered Past Inc.	765-474-3905	•	•	•	
•	•	•		•	County Courthouse Retrieval	765-485-0233	•	•	•	
•	•	•	•	•	International Investigators Inc [SOP]	800-403-8111	•	•	•	•
	•	•			Land America Lawyers Title	260-424-2929	•	•	•	•
•	•		•		LC Limited Inc.	317-887-9688				
	•		•	•	McGinley Search & File Service Corp	317-807-0760	•	•	•	
•	•	•			McPheron Info Services	765-482-1650, cell- 765-894-0107	•	•	•	•
					Mill Creek Title Service	317-714-7190	•	•	•	•
•	•				Myers Investigations Inc [SOP]	800-788-8018	•		•	•
•	•				Paper Trail Information Services Inc	866-623-7238				
•	•				Royal Title Services	800-773-7279	•	•	•	•
•	•	•	•	•	Special Investigations Inc [SOP]	317-773-7900	•	•	•	•
•	•	•			Tippecanoe Title Services Inc	888-423-2457	•	•	•	
•	•	•	•	•	We Search ReSearch Inc	800-251-8167	•	•	•	

CR	CV	PR	US	BK	←COURTS	BROWN RECORDER→	UC	RE	TX	VS
	•				Hotopp Public Record Searches	812-342-2163	•	•	•	
•	•				Chet Kylander	812-988-9522			•	
	•		•	•	McGinley Search & File Service Corp	317-807-0760	•	•	•	
•	•	•			McPheron Info Services	765-482-1650, cell- 765-894-0107	•	•	•	•
•	•				PAC Data LLC	812-654-3207		•	•	•
	•				Parsley Enterprises Inc	317-878-9979		•	•	
•	•				Priority Process Service [SOP]	866-464-2192	•	•	•	

CR	CV	PR	US	BK	←COURTS	CARROLL RECORDER→	UC	RE	TX	VS
	•		•	•	McGinley Search & File Service Corp	317-807-0760	•	•	•	
•	•	•			McPheron Info Services	765-482-1650, cell- 765-894-0107	•	•	•	•
					Mill Creek Title Service	317-714-7190	•		•	•
•	•	•			Tippecanoe Title Services Inc	888-423-2457	•	•	•	
•	•	•	•	•	We Search ReSearch Inc	800-251-8167	•	•	•	

CR	CV	PR	US	BK	←COURTS	CASS RECORDER→	UC	RE	TX	VS
•	•				Don Martin & Assoc. [SOP]	765-452-1760				
	•		•	•	McGinley Search & File Service Corp	317-807-0760	•	•	•	
•	•	•			Tippecanoe Title Services Inc	888-423-2457	•	•	•	
•	•	•	•	•	We Search ReSearch Inc	800-251-8167	•	•	•	

CR	CV	PR	US	BK	←COURTS	CLARK RECORDER→	UC	RE	TX	VS
					Virginia Balentine	812-267-5497-cell		•		
•	•				Tracy A Gabehart, Paralegal	502-957-6459				
•	•	•	•	•	Rick Hessig [SOP]	502-583-2453	•		•	•
	•		•	•	McGinley Search & File Service Corp	317-807-0760	•	•	•	
					Salem Title Corporation	812-883-5806	•	•	•	
•	•	•	•	•	Steve Knight Services	812-364-4461	•	•	•	•
•	•				Xpress Research	812-923-7202; cell- 812-207-4284				

CR	CV	PR	US	BK	←COURTS	CLAY RECORDER→	UC	RE	TX	VS
•	•				Crossroads Research	812-299-0809				
•	•		•	•	JB Acree Research	812-443-2443	•	•	•	
	•		•	•	McGinley Search & File Service Corp	317-807-0760	•	•	•	
•	•				Priority Process Service [SOP]	866-464-2192	•	•	•	

CR	CV	PR	US	BK	←COURTS	CLINTON RECORDER→	UC	RE	TX	VS
•	•	•		•	County Courthouse Retrieval	765-485-0233	•	•	•	
	•	•			Land America Lawyers Title	260-424-2929	•	•	•	•
	•		•	•	McGinley Search & File Service Corp	317-807-0760	•	•	•	
•	•	•			McPheron Info Services	765-482-1650, cell- 765-894-0107	•	•	•	•
					Mill Creek Title Service	317-714-7190	•	•	•	•
•	•	•			Tippecanoe Title Services Inc	888-423-2457	•	•	•	
•	•	•	•	•	We Search ReSearch Inc	800-251-8167	•	•	•	

CR	CV	PR	US	BK	←COURTS	CRAWFORD RECORDER→	UC	RE	TX	VS
	•		•	•	McGinley Search & File Service Corp	317-807-0760	•	•	•	
					Salem Title Corporation	812-883-5806	•	•	•	

CR	CV	PR	US	BK	←COURTS	DAVIESS RECORDER→	UC	RE	TX	VS
					BMC Abstract	812-661-2484		•	•	
	•	•			James F Havill Attorney at Law PC	812-254-0050	•	•	•	•
	•		•	•	McGinley Search & File Service Corp	317-807-0760	•	•	•	
•	•				Priority Process Service [SOP]	866-464-2192	•	•	•	

CR	CV	PR	US	BK	←COURTS	DEARBORN RECORDER→	UC	RE	TX	VS
•	•	•			AM Search & Retrieve	812-689-0672	•	•	•	
•	•	•	•	•	DDI Inc [SOP]	866-954-3000	•	•	•	•
•	•				Michelle Gump	812-537-8877				
	•		•	•	McGinley Search & File Service Corp	317-807-0760	•	•	•	

CR	CV	PR	US	BK	←Courts	Recorder→	UC	RE	TX	VS
•	•				PAC Data LLC	812-654-3207		•	•	•
•					Phoenix Research Inc	800-260-1092				

CR	CV	PR	US	BK	←Courts **DECATUR**	Recorder→	UC	RE	TX	VS
	•	•			Ford Abstract Corp	812-663-2190	•	•	•	
	•	•		•	Kings Title & Closing Services	800-860-2990	•	•	•	•
•	•				Chet Kylander	812-988-9522			•	
	•		•	•	McGinley Search & File Service Corp	317-807-0760	•	•	•	
•	•	•			McPheron Info Services	765-482-1650, cell- 765-894-0107	•	•	•	•
•	•	•			McPheron Info Services	765-482-1650, cell- 765-894-0107	•	•	•	•
•	•				PAC Data LLC	812-654-3207		•	•	•
	•				Parsley Enterprises Inc	317-878-9979		•	•	

CR	CV	PR	US	BK	←Courts **DEKALB**	Recorder→	UC	RE	TX	VS
•	•		•	•	ASK Services Inc (Indiana)	888-416-1313	•	•	•	
•	•				Dean Research Group	260-485-4648	•	•	•	
	•	•			Land America Lawyers Title	260-424-2929	•	•	•	•
	•		•	•	McGinley Search & File Service Corp	317-807-0760	•	•	•	
•	•	•	•	•	We Search ReSearch Inc	800-251-8167	•	•	•	

CR	CV	PR	US	BK	←Courts **DELAWARE**	Recorder→	UC	RE	TX	VS
	•	•			Kings Title & Abstract Co (Muncie)	800-294-1566	•	•	•	
	•	•		•	Kings Title & Closing Services	800-860-2990	•	•	•	•
	•		•	•	McGinley Search & File Service Corp	317-807-0760	•	•	•	
•	•				Myers Investigations Inc [SOP]	800-788-8018	•		•	•
•	•	•	•	•	We Search ReSearch Inc	800-251-8167	•	•	•	

CR	CV	PR	US	BK	←Courts **DUBOIS**	Recorder→	UC	RE	TX	VS
					BMC Abstract	812-661-2484		•	•	
•	•			•	Patricia Lynch	812-678-4416 or 812-678-4809		•	•	
	•		•	•	McGinley Search & File Service Corp	317-807-0760	•	•	•	
•	•				Priority Process Service [SOP]	866-464-2192	•	•	•	

CR	CV	PR	US	BK	←Courts **ELKHART**	Recorder→	UC	RE	TX	VS
	•	•	•	•	Abstract & Data Search Services	888-457-5344	•	•	•	•
•					Acme Research	219-878-9950, fax-same				
•	•		•	•	ASK Services Inc (Indiana)	888-416-1313	•	•	•	
•	•	•	•	•	Case Services Inc [SOP]	877-291-6868	•	•	•	
	•	•	•	•	Land Grant Title Group Inc	888-563-4768	•	•	•	
	•		•	•	McGinley Search & File Service Corp	317-807-0760	•	•	•	
					McKesson Title Corp [SOP]	800-261-8437	•	•	•	
•	•	•		•	Michiana Info LLC	574-277-8909			•	
	•				Michiana Searches Inc	574-266-4652, 574-536-7135	•	•	•	
•					Midwest Security Group LLC	800-311-5498			•	
•	•		•	•	MJT Research	219-326-7637 or 219-363-2070	•	•	•	•
•	•	•	•	•	We Search ReSearch Inc	800-251-8167	•	•	•	

CR	CV	PR	US	BK	←Courts **FAYETTE**	Recorder→	UC	RE	TX	VS
•					Jack Gilland	765-825-6461; Fax- same			•	
	•	•		•	Kings Title & Closing Services	800-860-2990	•	•	•	•
	•		•	•	McGinley Search & File Service Corp	317-807-0760	•	•	•	
•	•	•			McPheron Info Services	765-482-1650, cell- 765-894-0107	•	•	•	•
•	•				PAC Data LLC	812-654-3207		•	•	•
	•				Union County Title Co	765-458-7148	•	•	•	
•	•	•	•	•	We Search ReSearch Inc	800-251-8167	•	•	•	

CR	CV	PR	US	BK	←Courts **FLOYD**	Recorder→	UC	RE	TX	VS
					Virginia Balentine	812-267-5497-cell		•		
•	•				Tracy A Gabehart, Paralegal	502-957-6459				
•	•	•	•	•	Rick Hessig [SOP]	502-583-2453	•		•	•
	•		•	•	McGinley Search & File Service Corp	317-807-0760	•	•	•	

CR	CV	PR	US	BK	Courts	Recorder	UC	RE	TX	VS
					Salem Title Corporation	812-883-5806	•	•	•	
•	•	•	•	•	Steve Knight Services	812-364-4461	•	•	•	•
•	•				Xpress Research	812-923-7202; cell- 812-207-4284				

CR	CV	PR	US	BK	←COURTS **FOUNTAIN**	RECORDER→	UC	RE	TX	VS
•	•	•			Held Abstract & Title Co Inc	765-762-2457	•	•	•	
•	•		•	•	JB Acree Research	812-443-2443	•	•	•	
	•	•			Massey Abstract Inc	765-793-3451	•	•	•	
	•		•	•	McGinley Search & File Service Corp	317-807-0760	•	•	•	
•	•	•			McPheron Info Services	765-482-1650, cell- 765-894-0107	•	•	•	•
					Mill Creek Title Service	317-714-7190	•	•	•	•
•	•	•			Tippecanoe Title Services Inc	888-423-2457	•	•	•	
•	•	•	•	•	We Search ReSearch Inc	800-251-8167	•	•	•	

CR	CV	PR	US	BK	←COURTS **FRANKLIN**	RECORDER→	UC	RE	TX	VS
•					Jack Gilland	765-825-6461; Fax- same			•	
	•	•		•	Kings Title & Closing Services	800-860-2990	•	•	•	•
	•		•	•	McGinley Search & File Service Corp	317-807-0760	•	•	•	
•	•				PAC Data LLC	812-654-3207		•	•	•
	•				Union County Title Co	765-458-7148	•	•	•	
•	•	•	•	•	We Search ReSearch Inc	800-251-8167	•	•	•	

CR	CV	PR	US	BK	←COURTS **FULTON**	RECORDER→	UC	RE	TX	VS
	•		•	•	McGinley Search & File Service Corp	317-807-0760	•	•	•	
					McKesson Title Corp [SOP]	800-261-8437	•	•	•	
•	•	•	•	•	We Search ReSearch Inc	800-251-8167	•	•	•	

CR	CV	PR	US	BK	←COURTS **GIBSON**	RECORDER→	UC	RE	TX	VS
•	•	•	•	•	BBI LLC	812-985-0832; cell- 812-774-7500	•	•	•	•
•	•		•	•	Hi-Tech Investigative [SOP]	812-477-1400				
	•		•	•	McGinley Search & File Service Corp	317-807-0760	•	•	•	

CR	CV	PR	US	BK	←COURTS **GRANT**	RECORDER→	UC	RE	TX	VS
•	•				Don Martin & Assoc. [SOP]	765-452-1760				
	•	•			Grant County Abstract Co (Indiana)	765-664-7371	•	•	•	
	•	•			Kings Title & Abstract Co (Marion)	800-662-1299	•	•	•	
	•	•		•	Kings Title & Closing Services	800-860-2990	•	•	•	•
	•		•	•	McGinley Search & File Service Corp	317-807-0760	•	•	•	
•	•	•	•	•	We Search ReSearch Inc	800-251-8167	•	•	•	

CR	CV	PR	US	BK	←COURTS **GREENE**	RECORDER→	UC	RE	TX	VS
	•		•	•	McGinley Search & File Service Corp	317-807-0760	•	•	•	
•	•				PAC Data LLC	812-654-3207		•	•	•
•	•				Priority Process Service [SOP]	866-464-2192	•	•	•	
•	•				Starhill Technical Services	812-384-7840	•	•	•	

CR	CV	PR	US	BK	←COURTS **HAMILTON**	RECORDER→	UC	RE	TX	VS
•	•		•	•	ASK Services Inc (Indiana)	888-416-1313	•	•	•	
•	•		•		Checkered Past Inc	765-474-3905	•	•	•	
•	•	•	•	•	Info Search Inc	317-251-6290	•	•	•	•
•	•	•	•	•	International Investigators Inc [SOP]	800-403-8111	•	•	•	•
	•		•	•	Land America Lawyers Title	260-424-2929	•	•	•	•
•	•		•	•	LC Limited Inc	317-887-9688				
	•		•	•	McGinley Search & File Service Corp	317-807-0760	•	•	•	
•	•	•			McPheron Info Services	765-482-1650, cell- 765-894-0107	•	•	•	•
•	•				Myers Investigations Inc [SOP]	800-788-8018	•		•	•
•	•	•	•	•	National Service Information Inc (Indiana) [SOP]	317-266-0040	•	•	•	•
•	•				PAC Data LLC	812-654-3207		•	•	•
•	•				Paper Trail Information Services Inc	866-623-7238				
•	•	•	•	•	Special Investigations Inc [SOP]	317-773-7900	•	•	•	•
•	•	•			Tippecanoe Title Services Inc	888-423-2457	•	•	•	

CR	CV	PR	US	BK	←Courts		Recorder→	UC	RE	TX	VS
•	•	•	•	•	We Search ReSearch Inc		800-251-8167	•	•	•	
CR	**CV**	**PR**	**US**	**BK**	**←Courts**	**Hancock**	**Recorder→**	**UC**	**RE**	**TX**	**VS**
•	•	•	•	•	International Investigators Inc [SOP]		800-403-8111	•	•	•	•
	•	•			Kings Title & Abstract Co (Shelbyville)		317-398-0424	•	•	•	
	•	•			Land America Lawyers Title		260-424-2929	•	•	•	•
	•		•	•	McGinley Search & File Service Corp		317-807-0760	•	•	•	
•	•	•			McPheron Info Services		765-482-1650, cell- 765-894-0107	•	•	•	•
•	•				Myers Investigations Inc [SOP]		800-788-8018	•		•	•
•	•	•	•	•	National Service Information Inc (Indiana) [SOP]		317-266-0040	•	•	•	•
	•				Parsley Enterprises Inc		317-878-9979		•	•	
•	•	•	•	•	We Search ReSearch Inc		800-251-8167	•	•	•	
CR	**CV**	**PR**	**US**	**BK**	**←Courts**	**Harrison**	**Recorder→**	**UC**	**RE**	**TX**	**VS**
					Virginia Balentine		812-267-5497-cell				
	•		•	•	McGinley Search & File Service Corp		317-807-0760	•	•	•	
					Salem Title Corporation		812-883-5806	•	•	•	
•	•	•	•	•	Steve Knight Services		812-364-4461	•	•	•	•
•	•				Xpress Research		812-923-7202; cell- 812-207-4284				
CR	**CV**	**PR**	**US**	**BK**	**←Courts**	**Hendricks**	**Recorder→**	**UC**	**RE**	**TX**	**VS**
•	•		•	•	ASK Services Inc (Indiana)		888-416-1313	•	•	•	
•	•		•		Checkered Past Inc		765-474-3905	•	•	•	
•	•	•		•	County Courthouse Retrieval		765-485-0233	•	•	•	
•	•	•	•	•	Info Search Inc		317-251-6290	•	•	•	•
•	•	•	•	•	International Investigators Inc [SOP]		800-403-8111	•	•	•	•
•	•		•		LC Limited Inc		317-887-9688				
	•		•	•	McGinley Search & File Service Corp		317-807-0760	•	•	•	
•	•	•			McPheron Info Services		765-482-1650, cell- 765-894-0107	•	•	•	•
					Mill Creek Title Service		317-714-7190	•	•	•	•
•	•				Myers Investigations Inc [SOP]		800-788-8018	•		•	•
•	•	•	•	•	National Service Information Inc (Indiana) [SOP]		317-266-0040	•	•	•	•
•	•				Paper Trail Information Services Inc		866-623-7238				
•	•	•			Tippecanoe Title Services Inc		888-423-2457	•	•	•	
•	•	•	•	•	We Search ReSearch Inc		800-251-8167	•	•	•	
CR	**CV**	**PR**	**US**	**BK**	**←Courts**	**Henry**	**Recorder→**	**UC**	**RE**	**TX**	**VS**
	•	•		•	Kings Title & Closing Services		800-860-2990	•	•	•	•
	•	•			Land America Lawyers Title		260-424-2929	•	•	•	•
	•		•	•	McGinley Search & File Service Corp		317-807-0760	•	•	•	
•	•	•			McPheron Info Services		765-482-1650, cell- 765-894-0107	•	•	•	•
•	•	•	•	•	We Search ReSearch Inc		800-251-8167	•	•	•	
CR	**CV**	**PR**	**US**	**BK**	**←Courts**	**Howard**	**Recorder→**	**UC**	**RE**	**TX**	**VS**
•	•				Don Martin & Assoc. [SOP]		765-452-1760				
	•		•	•	McGinley Search & File Service Corp		317-807-0760	•	•	•	
•	•	•			McPheron Info Services		765-482-1650, cell- 765-894-0107	•	•	•	•
	•	•			Moore Title & Escrow Inc		888-289-1301	•	•	•	•
•	•	•			Tippecanoe Title Services Inc		888-423-2457	•	•	•	
•	•	•	•	•	We Search ReSearch Inc		800-251-8167	•	•	•	
CR	**CV**	**PR**	**US**	**BK**	**←Courts**	**Huntington**	**Recorder→**	**UC**	**RE**	**TX**	**VS**
•	•				Advanced Collection Services Inc		260-827-8189		•	•	•
•	•				Dean Research Group		260-485-4648	•	•	•	
	•	•			Jones Abstract & Title Co Inc		866-356-5663	•	•	•	
	•	•			Land America Lawyers Title		260-424-2929	•	•	•	•
	•		•	•	McGinley Search & File Service Corp		317-807-0760	•	•	•	
•	•	•	•	•	We Search ReSearch Inc		800-251-8167	•	•	•	
CR	**CV**	**PR**	**US**	**BK**	**←Courts**	**Jackson**	**Recorder→**	**UC**	**RE**	**TX**	**VS**
	•				Hotopp Public Record Searches		812-342-2163	•	•	•	

CR	CV	PR	US	BK	←Courts	Recorder→	UC	RE	TX	VS
•	•				Chet Kylander	812-988-9522			•	
	•		•	•	McGinley Search & File Service Corp	317-807-0760	•	•	•	
•	•				PAC Data LLC	812-654-3207		•	•	•
	•				Parsley Enterprises Inc	317-878-9979		•	•	
					Salem Title Corporation	812-883-5806	•	•	•	

CR	CV	PR	US	BK	←Courts **Jasper**	Recorder→	UC	RE	TX	VS
	•		•	•	McGinley Search & File Service Corp	317-807-0760	•	•	•	
•	•		•	•	Star Security & Inv [SOP]	219-554-0100	•	•	•	•
•	•	•			Tippecanoe Title Services Inc	888-423-2457	•	•	•	
•	•	•	•	•	We Search ReSearch Inc	800-251-8167	•	•	•	

CR	CV	PR	US	BK	←Courts **Jay**	Recorder→	UC	RE	TX	VS
	•	•			Jay Portland Abstract Inc Co	260-726-6466	•	•	•	•
	•	•		•	Kings Title & Closing Services	800-860-2990	•	•	•	•
	•		•	•	McGinley Search & File Service Corp	317-807-0760	•	•	•	
	•	•			Tri-County Land Title	260-589-3139	•	•	•	•
•	•	•	•	•	We Search ReSearch Inc	800-251-8167	•	•	•	

CR	CV	PR	US	BK	←Courts **Jefferson**	Recorder→	UC	RE	TX	VS
	•		•	•	McGinley Search & File Service Corp	317-807-0760	•	•	•	
•	•				PAC Data LLC	812-654-3207		•	•	•
•	•				Xpress Research	812-923-7202; cell- 812-207-4284				

CR	CV	PR	US	BK	←Courts **Jennings**	Recorder→	UC	RE	TX	VS
•	•				Chet Kylander	812-988-9522			•	
	•		•	•	McGinley Search & File Service Corp	317-807-0760	•	•	•	
	•	•			North Vernon Abstract Co Inc	812-346-2259	•	•	•	
•	•				PAC Data LLC	812-654-3207		•	•	•
	•				Parsley Enterprises Inc	317-878-9979		•	•	

CR	CV	PR	US	BK	←Courts **Johnson**	Recorder→	UC	RE	TX	VS
•	•		•	•	ASK Services Inc (Indiana)	888-416-1313	•	•	•	
	•				Hotopp Public Record Searches	812-342-2163	•	•	•	
•	•	•	•	•	International Investigators Inc [SOP]	800-403-8111	•	•	•	•
•	•				Chet Kylander	812-988-9522			•	
	•	•			Land America Lawyers Title	260-424-2929	•	•	•	
	•		•	•	McGinley Search & File Service Corp	317-807-0760	•	•	•	
•	•	•			McPheron Info Services	765-482-1650, cell- 765-894-0107	•	•	•	•
					Mill Creek Title Service	317-714-7190	•	•	•	•
•	•				Myers Investigations Inc [SOP]	800-788-8018		•	•	•
•	•	•	•	•	National Service Information Inc (Indiana) [SOP]	317-266-0040	•	•	•	•
•	•				PAC Data LLC	812-654-3207		•	•	•
	•				Parsley Enterprises Inc	317-878-9979		•	•	
•	•	•	•	•	We Search ReSearch Inc	800-251-8167	•	•	•	

CR	CV	PR	US	BK	←Courts **Knox**	Recorder→	UC	RE	TX	VS
•	•				Crossroads Research	812-299-0809				
	•	•			L Fay Hedden Abstract Office Inc	812-882-5273	•	•	•	•
	•		•	•	McGinley Search & File Service Corp	317-807-0760	•	•	•	
•	•				Priority Process Service [SOP]	866-464-2192	•	•	•	

CR	CV	PR	US	BK	←Courts **Kosciusko**	Recorder→	UC	RE	TX	VS
•	•				Dean Research Group	260-485-4648	•	•	•	
	•	•			Land America Lawyers Title	260-424-2929	•	•	•	•
	•	•	•	•	Land Grant Title Group Inc	888-563-4768	•	•	•	
	•		•	•	McGinley Search & File Service Corp	317-807-0760	•	•	•	
					McKesson Title Corp [SOP]	800-261-8437	•	•	•	
•	•	•	•	•	We Search ReSearch Inc	800-251-8167	•	•	•	

CR	CV	PR	US	BK	←Courts LA PORTE	Recorder→	UC	RE	TX	VS
	•	•	•	•	Abstract & Data Search Services	888-457-5344	•	•	•	•
•	•		•	•	ASK Services Inc (Indiana)	888-416-1313	•	•	•	
•	•	•	•	•	Case Services Inc [SOP]	877-291-6868	•	•	•	•
•	•		•	•	Infotrack Information Services Inc	800-275-5594	•	•	•	
	•		•	•	McGinley Search & File Service Corp	317-807-0760	•	•	•	
					McKesson Title Corp [SOP]	800-261-8437	•	•	•	
•	•		•	•	Merola Services (Indiana)	219-878-9699	•	•	•	•
•	•	•		•	Michiana Info LLC	574-277-8909			•	
•					Midwest Security Group LLC	800-311-5498			•	
•	•		•	•	MJT Research	219-326-7637 or 219-363-2070	•	•	•	•
•					S & G Information Services	219-898-5610-cell, 219-325-3473; Fax- same				
•	•		•	•	Star Security & Inv [SOP]	219-554-0100	•	•	•	•
•	•	•	•	•	We Search ReSearch Inc	800-251-8167	•	•	•	

CR	CV	PR	US	BK	←Courts LAGRANGE	Recorder→	UC	RE	TX	VS
•	•				Dean Research Group	260-485-4648	•	•	•	
•	•	•			LaGrange Title Company	260-463-3232	•	•	•	•
	•	•			Land America Lawyers Title	260-424-2929	•	•	•	•
	•	•	•	•	Land Grant Title Group Inc	888-563-4768	•	•	•	
	•		•	•	McGinley Search & File Service Corp	317-807-0760	•	•	•	
•	•				Colleen Tracy	260-463-4044		•	•	•
•	•	•	•	•	We Search ReSearch Inc	800-251-8167	•	•	•	

CR	CV	PR	US	BK	←Courts LAKE	Recorder→	UC	RE	TX	VS
•	•		•	•	ASK Services Inc (Indiana)	888-416-1313	•	•	•	
•	•		•	•	Infotrack Information Services Inc	800-275-5594	•	•	•	
•	•	•	•	•	Lynne J Cox Paralegal	800-510-3009	•	•	•	
	•		•	•	McGinley Search & File Service Corp	317-807-0760	•	•	•	
•					Midwest Security Group LLC	800-311-5498			•	
•	•		•	•	MJT Research	219-326-7637 or 219-363-2070	•	•	•	•
•			•		S & G Information Services	219-898-5610-cell, 219-325-3473; Fax- same				
•	•		•	•	Star Security & Inv [SOP]	219-554-0100	•	•	•	•
•	•	•	•	•	We Search ReSearch Inc	800-251-8167	•	•	•	

CR	CV	PR	US	BK	←Courts LAWRENCE	Recorder→	UC	RE	TX	VS
•	•	•			Joyce Beasley	812-325-2379	•		•	
	•		•	•	McGinley Search & File Service Corp	317-807-0760	•	•	•	
•	•				PAC Data LLC	812-654-3207		•	•	•
•	•				Priority Process Service [SOP]	866-464-2192	•	•	•	
					Salem Title Corporation	812-883-5806	•	•	•	
•	•				Starhill Technical Services	812-384-7840	•	•	•	

CR	CV	PR	US	BK	←Courts MADISON	Recorder→	UC	RE	TX	VS
	•	•			Kings Title & Abstract Co (Anderson)	800-317-1515	•	•	•	
	•	•		•	Kings Title & Closing Services	800-860-2990		•	•	•
	•	•			Land America Lawyers Title	260-424-2929	•	•	•	•
	•		•	•	McGinley Search & File Service Corp	317-807-0760	•	•	•	
•	•	•			McPheron Info Services	765-482-1650, cell- 765-894-0107	•	•	•	•
•	•				Myers Investigations Inc [SOP]	800-788-8018	•		•	•
•	•	•	•	•	We Search ReSearch Inc	800-251-8167	•	•	•	

CR	CV	PR	US	BK	←Courts MARION	Recorder→	UC	RE	TX	VS
	•	•	•	•	Abstract & Data Search Services	888-457-5344	•	•	•	•
•	•		•	•	Advanced Background Services	317-884-4600		•	•	
•	•		•	•	ASK Services Inc (Indiana)	888-416-1313	•	•	•	
	•	•	•	•	Central Indiana Paralegal Service Inc	317-636-1311	•		•	
•	•	•	•	•	Info Search Inc	317-251-6290	•	•	•	•
•	•		•	•	Infotrack Information Services Inc	800-275-5594	•	•	•	
•	•	•	•	•	International Investigators Inc [SOP]	800-403-8111	•	•	•	•

CR	CV	PR	US	BK	←Courts	Recorder→	UC	RE	TX	VS
	•	•			Land America Lawyers Title	260-424-2929	•	•	•	•
•	•		•		LC Limited Inc	317-887-9688				
	•		•	•	McGinley Search & File Service Corp	317-807-0760	•	•	•	
•	•	•			McPheron Info Services	765-482-1650, cell- 765-894-0107	•	•	•	•
•	•				Myers Investigations Inc [SOP]	800-788-8018	•		•	•
•	•	•	•	•	National Service Information Inc (Indiana) [SOP]	317-266-0040	•	•	•	•
•	•				PAC Data LLC	812-654-3207		•	•	•
	•				Parsley Enterprises Inc	317-878-9979		•	•	
•	•	•	•	•	Record Retrieval of Indianapolis [SOP]	317-383-1306	•	•	•	•
•	•	•	•	•	Special Investigations Inc [SOP]	317-773-7900	•	•	•	•
•	•	•			Tippecanoe Title Services Inc	888-423-2457	•	•	•	
•	•	•	•	•	We Search ReSearch Inc	800-251-8167	•	•	•	

CR	CV	PR	US	BK	←Courts **MARSHALL**	Recorder→	UC	RE	TX	VS
•					Acme Research	219-878-9950, fax-same				
•	•	•	•	•	Case Services Inc [SOP]	877-291-6868	•	•	•	•
	•	•	•	•	Land Grant Title Group Inc	888-563-4768	•	•	•	
	•		•	•	McGinley Search & File Service Corp	317-807-0760	•	•	•	
					McKesson Title Corp [SOP]	800-261-8437	•	•	•	
•	•		•	•	MJT Research	219-326-7637 or 219-363-2070	•	•	•	•
•	•	•	•	•	We Search ReSearch Inc	800-251-8167	•	•	•	

CR	CV	PR	US	BK	←Courts **MARTIN**	Recorder→	UC	RE	TX	VS
•				•	Patricia Lynch	812-678-4416 or 812-678-4809		•	•	
	•		•	•	McGinley Search & File Service Corp	317-807-0760	•	•	•	
•	•				Priority Process Service [SOP]	866-464-2192	•	•	•	

CR	CV	PR	US	BK	←Courts **MIAMI**	Recorder→	UC	RE	TX	VS
•	•				Dean Research Group	260-485-4648	•	•	•	
•	•				Don Martin & Assoc. [SOP]	765-452-1760				
	•		•	•	McGinley Search & File Service Corp	317-807-0760	•	•	•	
	•	•			Wabash Valley Abstract Co Inc	765-472-4351	•	•	•	
•	•	•	•	•	We Search ReSearch Inc	800-251-8167	•	•	•	

CR	CV	PR	US	BK	←Courts **MONROE**	Recorder→	UC	RE	TX	VS
•	•	•			Joyce Beasley	812-325-2379	•		•	
•	•	•			Daniel E Gardner, dba SCIPRIS	812-335-0746	•	•	•	•
	•				Hotopp Public Record Searches	812-342-2163	•	•	•	
	•		•	•	McGinley Search & File Service Corp	317-807-0760	•	•	•	
					Mill Creek Title Service	317-714-7190	•	•	•	•
•	•				Myers Investigations Inc [SOP]	800-788-8018	•		•	•
•	•				PAC Data LLC	812-654-3207		•	•	•
•	•				Priority Process Service [SOP]	866-464-2192	•	•	•	
•					Starhill Technical Services	812-384-7840	•	•	•	
•	•	•			Trace Investigations [SOP]	812-334-8857	•	•	•	•

CR	CV	PR	US	BK	←Courts **MONTGOMERY**	Recorder→	UC	RE	TX	VS
•	•	•		•	County Courthouse Retrieval	765-485-0233	•	•	•	
	•		•	•	McGinley Search & File Service Corp	317-807-0760	•	•	•	
•	•	•			McPheron Info Services	765-482-1650, cell- 765-894-0107	•	•	•	•
					Mill Creek Title Service	317-714-7190	•	•	•	•
•	•	•			Tippecanoe Title Services Inc	888-423-2457	•	•	•	
•	•	•	•	•	We Search ReSearch Inc	800-251-8167	•	•	•	

CR	CV	PR	US	BK	←Courts **MORGAN**	Recorder→	UC	RE	TX	VS
•	•		•	•	ASK Services Inc (Indiana)	888-416-1313	•	•	•	
•	•	•			Joyce Beasley	812-325-2379	•		•	
	•	•			Land America Lawyers Title	260-424-2929	•	•	•	•
	•		•	•	McGinley Search & File Service Corp	317-807-0760	•	•	•	
					Mill Creek Title Service	317-714-7190	•	•	•	•

CR	CV	PR	US	BK	←Courts **NEWTON**	Recorder→	UC	RE	TX	VS
	•		•	•	McGinley Search & File Service Corp	317-807-0760	•	•	•	
•	•		•	•	Star Security & Inv [SOP]	219-554-0100	•	•	•	•
•	•	•			Tippecanoe Title Services Inc	888-423-2457	•	•	•	
•	•	•	•	•	We Search ReSearch Inc	800-251-8167	•	•	•	

CR	CV	PR	US	BK	←Courts **NOBLE**	Recorder→	UC	RE	TX	VS
•	•				Dean Research Group	260-485-4648	•	•	•	
	•	•			Land America Lawyers Title	260-424-2929	•	•	•	•
	•		•	•	McGinley Search & File Service Corp	317-807-0760	•	•	•	
•	•				Colleen Tracy	260-463-4044		•	•	•
•	•	•	•	•	We Search ReSearch Inc	800-251-8167	•	•	•	

CR	CV	PR	US	BK	←Courts **OHIO**	Recorder→	UC	RE	TX	VS
•	•	•			AM Search & Retrieve	812-689-0672	•	•	•	
	•		•	•	McGinley Search & File Service Corp	317-807-0760	•	•	•	
•	•				PAC Data LLC	812-654-3207		•	•	•

CR	CV	PR	US	BK	←Courts **ORANGE**	Recorder→	UC	RE	TX	VS
	•		•	•	McGinley Search & File Service Corp	317-807-0760	•	•	•	
	•	•			Orange County Abstract & Title Co Inc	812-723-3044	•	•	•	
•	•				Priority Process Service [SOP]	866-464-2192	•	•	•	
					Salem Title Corporation	812-883-5806	•	•	•	

CR	CV	PR	US	BK	←Courts **OWEN**	Recorder→	UC	RE	TX	VS
•	•	•			Joyce Beasley	812-325-2379	•		•	
	•		•	•	McGinley Search & File Service Corp	317-807-0760	•	•	•	
					Mill Creek Title Service	317-714-7190	•	•	•	•
•	•				Priority Process Service [SOP]	866-464-2192	•	•	•	
•	•				Starhill Technical Services	812-384-7840	•	•	•	

CR	CV	PR	US	BK	←Courts **PARKE**	Recorder→	UC	RE	TX	VS
•	•				Crossroads Research	812-299-0809				
•	•		•	•	JB Acree Research	812-443-2443	•	•	•	
	•		•	•	McGinley Search & File Service Corp	317-807-0760	•	•	•	
					Mill Creek Title Service	317-714-7190	•	•	•	•
•	•	•			Tippecanoe Title Services Inc	888-423-2457	•	•	•	

CR	CV	PR	US	BK	←Courts **PERRY**	Recorder→	UC	RE	TX	VS
					BMC Abstract	812-661-2484		•	•	
	•		•	•	McGinley Search & File Service Corp	317-807-0760	•	•	•	
•	•				PAC Data LLC	812-654-3207		•	•	•
•	•	•	•	•	Summit Documents	270-281-5406	•	•	•	•

CR	CV	PR	US	BK	←Courts **PIKE**	Recorder→	UC	RE	TX	VS
					BMC Abstract	812-661-2484		•	•	
	•		•	•	McGinley Search & File Service Corp	317-807-0760	•	•	•	
•	•				Priority Process Service [SOP]	866-464-2192	•	•	•	

CR	CV	PR	US	BK	←Courts **PORTER**	Recorder→	UC	RE	TX	VS
•	•		•	•	ASK Services Inc (Indiana)	888-416-1313	•	•	•	
•	•		•	•	Infotrack Information Services Inc	800-275-5594	•	•	•	
	•		•	•	McGinley Search & File Service Corp	317-807-0760	•	•	•	
•	•		•	•	MJT Research	219-326-7637 or 219-363-2070	•	•	•	•
•	•				PAC Data LLC	812-654-3207		•	•	•
•			•		S & G Information Services	219-898-5610-cell, 219-325-3473; Fax- same				
•	•		•	•	Star Security & Inv [SOP]	219-554-0100	•	•	•	•
•	•	•	•	•	We Search ReSearch Inc	800-251-8167	•	•	•	

CR	CV	PR	US	BK	←Courts **POSEY**	Recorder→	UC	RE	TX	VS
•	•	•	•	•	BBI LLC	812-985-0832; cell- 812-774-7500	•	•	•	•

CR	CV	PR	US	BK	←Courts	Recorder→	UC	RE	TX	VS
•	•		•	•	D.G.I. LLC [SOP]	812-853-3222	•	•	•	•
•	•		•	•	Hi-Tech Investigative [SOP]	812-477-1400				
	•		•	•	McGinley Search & File Service Corp	317-807-0760	•	•	•	
•	•		•	•	RightTrack Services	812-421-0866	•	•	•	

CR	CV	PR	US	BK	←Courts **Pulaski**	Recorder→	UC	RE	TX	VS
	•		•	•	McGinley Search & File Service Corp	317-807-0760	•	•	•	
					McKesson Title Corp [SOP]	800-261-8437	•	•	•	
•	•				Pulaski County Abstract - IN	574-946-3841		•	•	
•	•	•	•	•	We Search ReSearch Inc	800-251-8167	•	•	•	

CR	CV	PR	US	BK	←Courts **Putnam**	Recorder→	UC	RE	TX	VS
•	•		•	•	JB Acree Research	812-443-2443	•	•	•	
	•		•	•	McGinley Search & File Service Corp	317-807-0760	•	•	•	
					Mill Creek Title Service	317-714-7190	•	•	•	•
•	•				Myers Investigations Inc [SOP]	800-788-8018	•		•	•
•	•				Paper Trail Information Services Inc	866-623-7238				

CR	CV	PR	US	BK	←Courts **Randolph**	Recorder→	UC	RE	TX	VS
	•	•			Kings Title & Abstract Co (Winchester)	800-280-6322	•	•	•	
	•	•		•	Kings Title & Closing Services	800-860-2990	•	•	•	•
	•		•	•	McGinley Search & File Service Corp	317-807-0760	•	•	•	
•	•	•			McPheron Info Services	765-482-1650, cell- 765-894-0107	•	•	•	•
•	•	•	•	•	We Search ReSearch Inc	800-251-8167	•	•	•	

CR	CV	PR	US	BK	←Courts **Ripley**	Recorder→	UC	RE	TX	VS
•	•	•			AM Search & Retrieve	812-689-0672	•	•	•	
	•		•	•	McGinley Search & File Service Corp	317-807-0760	•	•	•	
•	•				PAC Data LLC	812-654-3207		•	•	•

CR	CV	PR	US	BK	←Courts **Rush**	Recorder→	UC	RE	TX	VS
	•				Kings Title & Abstract Co (Rushville)	877-932-5757	•	•	•	
	•	•		•	Kings Title & Closing Services	800-860-2990	•	•	•	•
	•		•	•	McGinley Search & File Service Corp	317-807-0760	•	•	•	
•	•	•			McPheron Info Services	765-482-1650, cell- 765-894-0107	•	•	•	•
•	•	•			Mullins Abstract	765-932-3182; Fax- same		•	•	
•	•				PAC Data LLC	812-654-3207		•	•	•
•	•	•	•	•	We Search ReSearch Inc	800-251-8167	•	•	•	

CR	CV	PR	US	BK	←Courts **Scott**	Recorder→	UC	RE	TX	VS
	•		•	•	McGinley Search & File Service Corp	317-807-0760	•	•	•	
•	•				PAC Data LLC	812-654-3207		•	•	•
	•				Parsley Enterprises Inc	317-878-9979		•	•	
					Salem Title Corporation	812-883-5806	•	•	•	
•	•				Xpress Research	812-923-7202; cell- 812-207-4284				

CR	CV	PR	US	BK	←Courts **Shelby**	Recorder→	UC	RE	TX	VS
•	•	•	•	•	International Investigators Inc [SOP]	800-403-8111	•	•	•	•
	•	•			Kings Title & Abstract Co (Shelbyville)	317-398-0424	•	•	•	
	•	•		•	Kings Title & Closing Services	800-860-2990	•	•	•	•
•	•				Chet Kylander	812-988-9522			•	
	•		•	•	McGinley Search & File Service Corp	317-807-0760	•	•	•	
•	•	•			McPheron Info Services	765-482-1650, cell- 765-894-0107	•	•	•	•
•	•				Myers Investigations Inc [SOP]	800-788-8018	•		•	•
•	•				PAC Data LLC	812-654-3207		•	•	•
	•				Parsley Enterprises Inc	317-878-9979		•	•	
•	•	•	•	•	We Search ReSearch Inc	800-251-8167	•	•	•	

CR	CV	PR	US	BK	←Courts **SPENCER**	Recorder→	UC	RE	TX	VS
					BMC Abstract	812-661-2484		•	•	
•	•		•	•	D.G.I. LLC [SOP]	812-853-3222	•	•	•	•
•	•		•	•	Hi-Tech Investigative [SOP]	812-477-1400				
•	•			•	Patricia Lynch	812-678-4416 or 812-678-4809		•	•	
	•		•	•	McGinley Search & File Service Corp	317-807-0760	•	•	•	
•	•	•	•	•	Summit Documents	270-281-5406	•	•	•	•
•	•	•			Wetherill Law Office	812-649-2221	•	•	•	•

CR	CV	PR	US	BK	←Courts **ST. JOSEPH**	Recorder→	UC	RE	TX	VS
	•	•	•	•	Abstract & Data Search Services	888-457-5344	•	•	•	•
•					Acme Research	219-878-9950, fax-same				
•	•		•	•	ASK Services Inc (Indiana)	888-416-1313	•	•	•	
•	•	•	•	•	Case Services Inc [SOP]	877-291-6868	•	•	•	•
	•	•	•	•	Land Grant Title Group Inc	888-563-4768	•	•	•	
	•		•	•	McGinley Search & File Service Corp	317-807-0760	•	•	•	
					McKesson Title Corp [SOP]	800-261-8437	•	•	•	
•	•	•		•	Michiana Info LLC	574-277-8909			•	
	•				Michiana Searches Inc	574-266-4652, 574-536-7135	•	•	•	
•					Midwest Security Group LLC	800-311-5498			•	
•	•		•	•	MJT Research	219-326-7637 or 219-363-2070	•	•	•	•
•			•		S & G Information Services	219-898-5610-cell, 219-325-3473; Fax- same				
•	•	•	•	•	We Search ReSearch Inc	800-251-8167	•	•	•	

CR	CV	PR	US	BK	←Courts **STARKE**	Recorder→	UC	RE	TX	VS
	•		•	•	McGinley Search & File Service Corp	317-807-0760	•	•	•	
					McKesson Title Corp [SOP]	800-261-8437	•	•	•	
•	•	•			Starke County Abstract Title & Guaranty	574-772-3733	•	•	•	
•	•	•	•	•	We Search ReSearch Inc	800-251-8167	•	•	•	

CR	CV	PR	US	BK	←Courts **STEUBEN**	Recorder→	UC	RE	TX	VS
•	•		•	•	ASK Services Inc (Indiana)	888-416-1313	•	•	•	
•	•				Dean Research Group	260-485-4648	•	•	•	
	•	•			Land America Lawyers Title	260-424-2929	•	•	•	•
	•		•	•	McGinley Search & File Service Corp	317-807-0760	•	•	•	
•	•				PAC Data LLC	812-654-3207		•	•	•
•	•				Colleen Tracy	260-463-4044		•	•	•
•	•	•	•	•	We Search ReSearch Inc	800-251-8167	•	•	•	

CR	CV	PR	US	BK	←Courts **SULLIVAN**	Recorder→	UC	RE	TX	VS
•	•				Crossroads Research	812-299-0809				
	•		•	•	McGinley Search & File Service Corp	317-807-0760	•	•	•	
•	•				Priority Process Service [SOP]	866-464-2192	•	•	•	

CR	CV	PR	US	BK	←Courts **SWITZERLAND**	Recorder→	UC	RE	TX	VS
•	•				PAC Data LLC	812-654-3207		•	•	•
	•	•			Valley Title Services Inc	812-427-2135	•	•	•	

CR	CV	PR	US	BK	←Courts **TIPPECANOE**	Recorder→	UC	RE	TX	VS
•	•		•		Checkered Past Inc	765-474-3905	•	•	•	
•	•	•		•	County Courthouse Retrieval	765-485-0233	•	•	•	
	•		•	•	McGinley Search & File Service Corp	317-807-0760	•	•	•	
•	•	•			McPheron Info Services	765-482-1650, cell- 765-894-0107	•	•	•	•
					Mill Creek Title Service	317-714-7190	•	•	•	•
•	•				Paper Trail Information Services Inc	866-623-7238				
•	•	•			Tippecanoe Title Services Inc	888-423-2457	•	•	•	
•	•	•	•	•	We Search ReSearch Inc	800-251-8167	•	•	•	

CR	CV	PR	US	BK	←Courts	TIPTON	Recorder→	UC	RE	TX	VS
•	•				Don Martin & Assoc. [SOP]		765-452-1760				
	•		•	•	McGinley Search & File Service Corp		317-807-0760	•	•	•	
•	•	•			McPheron Info Services		765-482-1650, cell- 765-894-0107	•	•	•	•
	•	•			Moore Title & Escrow Inc		888-289-1301	•	•	•	•
•	•	•	•	•	We Search ReSearch Inc		800-251-8167	•	•	•	

CR	CV	PR	US	BK	←Courts	UNION	Recorder→	UC	RE	TX	VS
•					Jack Gilland		765-825-6461; Fax- same			•	
	•		•	•	McGinley Search & File Service Corp		317-807-0760	•	•	•	
•	•	•			McPheron Info Services		765-482-1650, cell- 765-894-0107	•	•	•	•
•	•				PAC Data LLC		812-654-3207		•	•	•
	•				Union County Title Co		765-458-7148	•	•	•	
•	•	•	•	•	We Search ReSearch Inc		800-251-8167	•	•	•	

CR	CV	PR	US	BK	←Courts	VANDERBURGH	Recorder→	UC	RE	TX	VS
•	•	•	•	•	BBI LLC		812-985-0832; cell- 812-774-7500	•	•	•	•
•	•		•	•	D.G.I. LLC [SOP]		812-853-3222	•	•	•	•
•	•		•	•	Hi-Tech Investigative [SOP]		812-477-1400				
	•		•	•	McGinley Search & File Service Corp		317-807-0760	•	•	•	
•	•		•	•	RightTrack Services		812-421-0866	•	•	•	

CR	CV	PR	US	BK	←Courts	VERMILLION	Recorder→	UC	RE	TX	VS
•	•				Crossroads Research		812-299-0809				
•	•		•	•	JB Acree Research		812-443-2443	•	•	•	
	•	•			Massey Abstract Inc		765-793-3451	•	•	•	
	•		•	•	McGinley Search & File Service Corp		317-807-0760	•	•	•	
					Mill Creek Title Service		317-714-7190	•	•	•	•
•	•	•			Tippecanoe Title Services Inc		888-423-2457	•	•	•	

CR	CV	PR	US	BK	←Courts	VIGO	Recorder→	UC	RE	TX	VS
•	•				Crossroads Research		812-299-0809				
•	•		•	•	JB Acree Research		812-443-2443	•	•	•	
	•		•	•	McGinley Search & File Service Corp		317-807-0760	•	•	•	
•	•				Priority Process Service [SOP]		866-464-2192	•	•	•	

CR	CV	PR	US	BK	←Courts	WABASH	Recorder→	UC	RE	TX	VS
•	•				Dean Research Group		260-485-4648	•	•	•	
•	•				Don Martin & Assoc. [SOP]		765-452-1760				
	•	•			Land America Lawyers Title		260-424-2929	•	•	•	•
	•		•	•	McGinley Search & File Service Corp		317-807-0760	•	•	•	
•	•	•	•	•	We Search ReSearch Inc		800-251-8167	•	•	•	

CR	CV	PR	US	BK	←Courts	WARREN	Recorder→	UC	RE	TX	VS
•	•	•			Held Abstract & Title Co Inc		765-762-2457	•	•	•	
	•	•			Massey Abstract Inc		765-793-3451	•	•	•	
	•		•	•	McGinley Search & File Service Corp		317-807-0760	•	•	•	
					Mill Creek Title Service		317-714-7190	•	•	•	•
•	•	•			Tippecanoe Title Services Inc		888-423-2457	•	•	•	
•	•	•	•	•	We Search ReSearch Inc		800-251-8167	•	•	•	

CR	CV	PR	US	BK	←Courts	WARRICK	Recorder→	UC	RE	TX	VS
•	•	•	•	•	BBI LLC		812-985-0832; cell- 812-774-7500	•	•	•	•
•	•		•	•	D.G.I. LLC [SOP]		812-853-3222	•	•	•	•
•	•		•	•	Hi-Tech Investigative [SOP]		812-477-1400				
•	•			•	Patricia Lynch		812-678-4416 or 812-678-4809		•	•	
	•		•	•	McGinley Search & File Service Corp		317-807-0760	•	•	•	
•	•		•	•	RightTrack Services		812-421-0866	•	•	•	
•	•	•	•	•	Summit Documents		270-281-5406	•	•	•	•

CR	CV	PR	US	BK	←Courts	WASHINGTON	Recorder→	UC	RE	TX	VS
	•		•	•	McGinley Search & File Service Corp		317-807-0760	•	•	•	
					Salem Title Corporation		812-883-5806	•	•	•	
•	•				Xpress Research		812-923-7202; cell- 812-207-4284				

CR	CV	PR	US	BK	←Courts	WAYNE	Recorder→	UC	RE	TX	VS
	•	•			Kings Title & Abstract Co (Richmond)		800-757-7762	•	•	•	
	•	•		•	Kings Title & Closing Services		800-860-2990	•	•	•	•
	•		•	•	McGinley Search & File Service Corp		317-807-0760	•	•	•	
•	•	•			McPheron Info Services		765-482-1650, cell- 765-894-0107	•	•	•	•
•	•				PAC Data LLC		812-654-3207		•	•	•
	•				Union County Title Co		765-458-7148	•	•	•	
•	•	•	•	•	We Search ReSearch Inc		800-251-8167	•	•	•	

CR	CV	PR	US	BK	←Courts	WELLS	Recorder→	UC	RE	TX	VS
•	•				Advanced Collection Services Inc		260-827-8189		•	•	•
•	•				Dean Research Group		260-485-4648	•	•	•	
	•	•			Land America Lawyers Title		260-424-2929	•	•	•	•
	•		•	•	McGinley Search & File Service Corp		317-807-0760	•	•	•	
	•	•			Tri-County Land Title		260-589-3139	•	•	•	•
•	•	•	•	•	We Search ReSearch Inc		800-251-8167	•	•	•	

CR	CV	PR	US	BK	←Courts	WHITE	Recorder→	UC	RE	TX	VS
	•		•	•	McGinley Search & File Service Corp		317-807-0760	•	•	•	
•	•				Tim McQuinn		574-583-9360				
•	•	•			Tippecanoe Title Services Inc		888-423-2457	•	•	•	
•	•	•	•	•	We Search ReSearch Inc		800-251-8167	•	•	•	

CR	CV	PR	US	BK	←Courts	WHITLEY	Recorder→	UC	RE	TX	VS
•	•				Dean Research Group		260-485-4648	•	•	•	
	•	•			Gates Land Title Corp		260-244-5127	•	•	•	•
	•	•			Land America Lawyers Title		260-424-2929	•	•	•	•
	•		•	•	McGinley Search & File Service Corp		317-807-0760	•	•	•	
•	•	•	•	•	We Search ReSearch Inc		800-251-8167	•	•	•	

[SOP] = Performs service of process

Court Records

CODE	Government Agency	Type of Information
CR	Criminal Court	Municipal, county and state level criminal cases
CV	Civil Court	Municipal, county and state level civil cases
PR	Probate Court	Wills and estate cases
US	US District Court	Federal civil and criminal cases
BK	Bankruptcy Court	United States bankruptcy cases

County Records - Recordings

CODE	Government Agency	Type of Information
UC	UCC Filing Office	Uniform Commercial Code and other personal property liens
RE	Real Estate Recording Office	Real property transactions and liens
TX	Tax Filing Office(s)	Federal and state tax liens, judgment liens
VS	Vital Records Office	Vital statistics—birth, death, marriage, divorce

Iowa

Lee County in **Iowa** has two recording offices.

COURT RECORDS RETRIEVED | **CAPITAL - POLK COUNTY** | **RECORDED RECORDS RETRIEVED**

CR	CV	PR	US	BK	←COURTS	RECORDER→	UC	RE	TX	VS
					ADAIR					
	•	•			Adair County Abstract Company	800-798-6129	•	•	•	
	•				Court Services of Iowa Inc	515-965-5722	•	•	•	
	•	•	•	•	The Title Co Inc (Prairie Du Chien WI)	888-918-4853	•	•	•	•
		•			Williamson Abstract Co	641-743-2175	•	•	•	•
					ADAMS					
	•				Court Services of Iowa Inc	515-965-5722	•	•	•	
	•	•	•	•	The Title Co Inc (Prairie Du Chien WI)	888-918-4853	•	•	•	•
					ALLAMAKEE					
	•				Court Services of Iowa Inc	515-965-5722	•	•	•	
•	•	•			Palmer Abstract Inc	563-568-3488	•	•	•	•
	•	•	•	•	The Title Co Inc (Prairie Du Chien WI)	888-918-4853	•	•	•	•
					APPANOOSE					
	•				Court Services of Iowa Inc	515-965-5722	•	•	•	
	•	•	•	•	The Title Co Inc (Prairie Du Chien WI)	888-918-4853	•	•	•	•
					AUDUBON					
	•				Court Services of Iowa Inc	515-965-5722	•	•	•	
	•	•	•	•	The Title Co Inc (Prairie Du Chien WI)	888-918-4853	•	•	•	•
					BENTON					
•	•	•	•		Benton County Title Co	319-472-2369	•	•	•	•
	•				Court Services of Iowa Inc	515-965-5722	•	•	•	
	•	•	•	•	The Title Co Inc (Prairie Du Chien WI)	888-918-4853	•	•	•	•
					BLACK HAWK					
	•	•			Black Hawk County Abstract Co	319-291-4000	•	•	•	
	•				Court Services of Iowa Inc	515-965-5722	•	•	•	
	•	•	•	•	The Title Co Inc (Prairie Du Chien WI)	888-918-4853	•	•	•	•
					BOONE					
•	•	•	•	•	Applicant Profile Services [SOP]	515-727-7964	•	•	•	•
•	•	•			Boone County Abstract Co	515-432-3633	•	•	•	•
	•				Court Services of Iowa Inc	515-965-5722	•	•	•	
	•	•	•	•	The Title Co Inc (Prairie Du Chien WI)	888-918-4853	•	•	•	•
					BREMER					
	•	•	•		Bremer County Abstract Co	319-352-2710	•	•	•	•
	•				Court Services of Iowa Inc	515-965-5722	•	•	•	
	•	•	•	•	The Title Co Inc (Prairie Du Chien WI)	888-918-4853	•	•	•	•
					BUCHANAN					
	•				Court Services of Iowa Inc	515-965-5722	•	•	•	
	•	•	•	•	The Title Co Inc (Prairie Du Chien WI)	888-918-4853	•	•	•	•

CR	CV	PR	US	BK	←Courts	Buena Vista	Recorder→	UC	RE	TX	VS
	•				Court Services of Iowa Inc		515-965-5722	•	•	•	
•	•	•			Fritcher Abstract Co.		712-732-2732		•	•	•
•	•	•	•		R & D Research Services [SOP]		712-737-8741	•	•	•	•
	•	•	•	•	The Title Co Inc (Prairie Du Chien WI)		888-918-4853	•	•	•	•

CR	CV	PR	US	BK	←Courts	Butler	Recorder→	UC	RE	TX	VS
	•				Court Services of Iowa Inc		515-965-5722	•	•	•	
	•	•	•	•	The Title Co Inc (Prairie Du Chien WI)		888-918-4853	•	•	•	•

CR	CV	PR	US	BK	←Courts	Calhoun	Recorder→	UC	RE	TX	VS
	•				Court Services of Iowa Inc		515-965-5722	•	•	•	
	•	•	•	•	The Title Co Inc (Prairie Du Chien WI)		888-918-4853	•	•	•	•

CR	CV	PR	US	BK	←Courts	Carroll	Recorder→	UC	RE	TX	VS
	•				Court Services of Iowa Inc		515-965-5722	•	•	•	
	•	•	•	•	The Title Co Inc (Prairie Du Chien WI)		888-918-4853	•	•	•	•

CR	CV	PR	US	BK	←Courts	Cass	Recorder→	UC	RE	TX	VS
•	•	•	•	•	Cass County Abstract Co Inc (Iowa)		712-243-2136	•	•	•	•
	•				Court Services of Iowa Inc		515-965-5722	•	•	•	
	•	•	•	•	The Title Co Inc (Prairie Du Chien WI)		888-918-4853	•	•	•	•
•					Beth Young		712-767-2510		•	•	

CR	CV	PR	US	BK	←Courts	Cedar	Recorder→	UC	RE	TX	VS
•	•	•	•	•	ASAP Process Service [SOP]		877-455-2490		•		•
	•				Court Services of Iowa Inc		515-965-5722	•	•	•	
•	•	•	•	•	FYII Acct [SOP]		563-299-5683	•	•	•	•
		•			Land Title Corp		563-886-6915	•	•	•	
	•	•	•	•	The Title Co Inc (Prairie Du Chien WI)		888-918-4853	•	•	•	•

CR	CV	PR	US	BK	←Courts	Cerro Gordo	Recorder→	UC	RE	TX	VS
•	•	•	•	•	Cerro Gordo Abstract Co		641-423-1145	•	•	•	•
	•				Court Services of Iowa Inc		515-965-5722	•	•	•	
	•	•	•	•	The Title Co Inc (Prairie Du Chien WI)		888-918-4853	•	•	•	•

CR	CV	PR	US	BK	←Courts	Cherokee	Recorder→	UC	RE	TX	VS
	•				Court Services of Iowa Inc		515-965-5722	•	•	•	
•	•	•			First Abstract & Loan Co.		712-225-3612	•	•	•	
•	•	•	•		R & D Research Services [SOP]		712-737-8741	•	•	•	•
	•	•	•	•	The Title Co Inc (Prairie Du Chien WI)		888-918-4853	•	•	•	•

CR	CV	PR	US	BK	←Courts	Chickasaw	Recorder→	UC	RE	TX	VS
	•				Court Services of Iowa Inc		515-965-5722	•	•	•	
	•	•	•	•	The Title Co Inc (Prairie Du Chien WI)		888-918-4853	•	•	•	•

CR	CV	PR	US	BK	←Courts	Clarke	Recorder→	UC	RE	TX	VS
					Banta Abstract Co.		641-342-2029, Fax- same		•	•	
	•				Court Services of Iowa Inc		515-965-5722	•	•	•	
	•	•	•	•	The Title Co Inc (Prairie Du Chien WI)		888-918-4853	•	•	•	•

CR	CV	PR	US	BK	←Courts	Clay	Recorder→	UC	RE	TX	VS
	•				Court Services of Iowa Inc		515-965-5722	•	•	•	
•	•	•	•		R & D Research Services [SOP]		712-737-8741	•	•	•	•
•	•	•			Security Land Title Co.		712-262-1074	•	•	•	
	•	•	•	•	The Title Co Inc (Prairie Du Chien WI)		888-918-4853	•	•	•	•

CR	CV	PR	US	BK	←Courts	Clayton	Recorder→	UC	RE	TX	VS
•	•	•			Clayton County Abstract Co		563-245-1430	•	•	•	•
	•				Court Services of Iowa Inc		515-965-5722	•	•	•	
	•	•	•	•	The Title Co Inc (Prairie Du Chien WI)		888-918-4853	•	•	•	•

CR	CV	PR	US	BK	←COURTS	CLINTON	RECORDER→	UC	RE	TX	VS
•	•	•			Abstract & Title Guaranty Co		563-243-2027	•	•	•	•
	•				Court Services of Iowa Inc		515-965-5722	•	•	•	
•	•	•	•	•	Cynthia-Renee's Professional Business Svc [SOP]		563-324-9445	•	•	•	•
	•	•	•	•	The Title Co Inc (Prairie Du Chien WI)		888-918-4853	•	•	•	•

CR	CV	PR	US	BK	←COURTS	CRAWFORD	RECORDER→	UC	RE	TX	VS
	•				Court Services of Iowa Inc		515-965-5722	•	•	•	
•	•	•			Crawford County Abstract Co (Iowa)		712-263-5626	•	•	•	•
	•	•	•	•	The Title Co Inc (Prairie Du Chien WI)		888-918-4853	•	•	•	•

CR	CV	PR	US	BK	←COURTS	DALLAS	RECORDER→	UC	RE	TX	VS
•	•	•	•	•	Adams Investigations [SOP]		888-844-0624	•	•	•	•
•	•	•	•	•	Applicant Profile Services [SOP]		515-727-7964	•	•	•	•
	•				Court Services of Iowa Inc		515-965-5722	•	•	•	
•	•	•	•	•	Hawkeye Legal Services [SOP]		515-276-3984	•			•
	•	•	•	•	The Title Co Inc (Prairie Du Chien WI)		888-918-4853	•	•	•	•

CR	CV	PR	US	BK	←COURTS	DAVIS	RECORDER→	UC	RE	TX	VS
	•				Court Services of Iowa Inc		515-965-5722	•	•	•	
•	•	•			Lynch Abstracting		641-664-3188	•	•	•	•
	•	•	•	•	The Title Co Inc (Prairie Du Chien WI)		888-918-4853	•	•	•	•

CR	CV	PR	US	BK	←COURTS	DECATUR	RECORDER→	UC	RE	TX	VS
	•				Court Services of Iowa Inc		515-965-5722	•	•	•	
•	•	•			Elson & Fulton Abstractors		641-446-4621	•	•	•	•

CR	CV	PR	US	BK	←COURTS	DELAWARE	RECORDER→	UC	RE	TX	VS
	•				Court Services of Iowa Inc		515-965-5722	•	•	•	
•	•	•			Delaware County Abstract Co (Iowa)		563-927-4858	•	•	•	•
	•	•	•	•	The Title Co Inc (Prairie Du Chien WI)		888-918-4853	•	•	•	•

CR	CV	PR	US	BK	←COURTS	DES MOINES	RECORDER→	UC	RE	TX	VS
	•				Court Services of Iowa Inc		515-965-5722	•	•	•	
	•	•	•	•	The Title Co Inc (Prairie Du Chien WI)		888-918-4853	•	•	•	•

CR	CV	PR	US	BK	←COURTS	DICKINSON	RECORDER→	UC	RE	TX	VS
		•			Cornell Abstract Co		712-336-3845	•	•	•	
	•				Court Services of Iowa Inc		515-965-5722	•	•	•	
•	•	•	•		R & D Research Services [SOP]		712-737-8741	•	•	•	•
	•	•	•	•	The Title Co Inc (Prairie Du Chien WI)		888-918-4853	•	•	•	•

CR	CV	PR	US	BK	←COURTS	DUBUQUE	RECORDER→	UC	RE	TX	VS
	•	•			Abeln Abstract & Title Co		563-582-7148		•	•	•
	•				Court Services of Iowa Inc		515-965-5722	•	•	•	
	•	•	•	•	The Title Co Inc (Prairie Du Chien WI)		888-918-4853	•	•	•	•

CR	CV	PR	US	BK	←COURTS	EMMET	RECORDER→	UC	RE	TX	VS
	•				Court Services of Iowa Inc		515-965-5722	•	•	•	
•	•	•			Estherville Abstract Co		712-362-3148	•	•	•	•
	•	•	•	•	The Title Co Inc (Prairie Du Chien WI)		888-918-4853	•	•	•	•

CR	CV	PR	US	BK	←COURTS	FAYETTE	RECORDER→	UC	RE	TX	VS
	•				Court Services of Iowa Inc		515-965-5722	•	•	•	
	•	•	•	•	The Title Co Inc (Prairie Du Chien WI)		888-918-4853	•	•	•	•

CR	CV	PR	US	BK	←COURTS	FLOYD	RECORDER→	UC	RE	TX	VS
	•				Court Services of Iowa Inc		515-965-5722	•	•	•	
		•			Iowa Title & Realty Co		641-228-1515	•	•	•	•
	•	•	•	•	The Title Co Inc (Prairie Du Chien WI)		888-918-4853	•	•	•	•

CR	CV	PR	US	BK	←Courts	FRANKLIN	Recorder→	UC	RE	TX	VS
	•				Court Services of Iowa Inc		515-965-5722	•	•	•	
•	•	•			Franklin County Abstract Co (Iowa)		641-456-4551	•	•	•	•
	•	•	•	•	The Title Co Inc (Prairie Du Chien WI)		888-918-4853	•	•	•	•

CR	CV	PR	US	BK	←Courts	FREMONT	Recorder→	UC	RE	TX	VS
	•				Court Services of Iowa Inc		515-965-5722	•	•	•	

CR	CV	PR	US	BK	←Courts	GREENE	Recorder→	UC	RE	TX	VS
•	•	•	•	•	Applicant Profile Services [SOP]		515-727-7964	•	•	•	•
	•				Court Services of Iowa Inc		515-965-5722	•	•	•	
•	•				Greene County Abstract Company Inc		515-386-2191	•	•	•	
•	•	•	•	•	Hawkeye Legal Services [SOP]		515-276-3984	•			•
	•	•	•	•	The Title Co Inc (Prairie Du Chien WI)		888-918-4853	•	•	•	•

CR	CV	PR	US	BK	←Courts	GRUNDY	Recorder→	UC	RE	TX	VS
•	•	•	•	•	Applicant Profile Services [SOP]		515-727-7964	•	•	•	•
	•				Court Services of Iowa Inc		515-965-5722	•	•	•	
	•	•	•	•	The Title Co Inc (Prairie Du Chien WI)		888-918-4853	•	•	•	•

CR	CV	PR	US	BK	←Courts	GUTHRIE	Recorder→	UC	RE	TX	VS
•	•	•	•	•	Applicant Profile Services [SOP]		515-727-7964	•	•	•	•
	•				Court Services of Iowa Inc		515-965-5722	•	•	•	
	•	•			Guthrie County Abstract		641-332-2339; Fax- 641-332-2340	•	•	•	•
	•	•	•	•	The Title Co Inc (Prairie Du Chien WI)		888-918-4853	•	•	•	•

CR	CV	PR	US	BK	←Courts	HAMILTON	Recorder→	UC	RE	TX	VS
•	•	•	•	•	Applicant Profile Services [SOP]		515-727-7964	•	•	•	•
	•				Court Services of Iowa Inc		515-965-5722	•	•	•	
•	•	•			Tim Neuroth		515-832-3156	•	•	•	•
	•	•	•	•	The Title Co Inc (Prairie Du Chien WI)		888-918-4853	•	•	•	•

CR	CV	PR	US	BK	←Courts	HANCOCK	Recorder→	UC	RE	TX	VS
	•				Court Services of Iowa Inc		515-965-5722	•	•	•	
		•			Hancock County Abstract Co		641-923-2454	•	•	•	
	•	•	•	•	The Title Co Inc (Prairie Du Chien WI)		888-918-4853	•	•	•	•

CR	CV	PR	US	BK	←Courts	HARDIN	Recorder→	UC	RE	TX	VS
•	•	•	•	•	Applicant Profile Services [SOP]		515-727-7964	•	•	•	•
	•				Court Services of Iowa Inc		515-965-5722	•	•	•	
	•	•	•	•	The Title Co Inc (Prairie Du Chien WI)		888-918-4853	•	•	•	•

CR	CV	PR	US	BK	←Courts	HARRISON	Recorder→	UC	RE	TX	VS
	•				Court Services of Iowa Inc		515-965-5722	•	•	•	
•	•	•			Harrison County Title & Guaranty		712-644-2703		•	•	
	•	•	•	•	The Title Co Inc (Prairie Du Chien WI)		888-918-4853	•	•	•	•
•	•		•	•	Thomas Research Services [SOP]		402-339-7291	•		•	

CR	CV	PR	US	BK	←Courts	HENRY	Recorder→	UC	RE	TX	VS
	•				Court Services of Iowa Inc		515-965-5722	•	•	•	
•	•	•		•	Henry County Abstract Co (Iowa)		319-385-9017	•	•	•	•
	•	•	•	•	The Title Co Inc (Prairie Du Chien WI)		888-918-4853	•	•	•	•

CR	CV	PR	US	BK	←Courts	HOWARD	Recorder→	UC	RE	TX	VS
	•				Court Services of Iowa Inc		515-965-5722	•	•	•	
•	•	•	•		Howard County Abstract & Title Co		563-547-4944	•	•	•	
	•	•	•	•	The Title Co Inc (Prairie Du Chien WI)		888-918-4853	•	•	•	•

CR	CV	PR	US	BK	←Courts	HUMBOLDT	Recorder→	UC	RE	TX	VS
	•				Court Services of Iowa Inc		515-965-5722	•	•	•	
•	•	•			Olson & Humboldt County Abstract		515-332-1593	•	•	•	•
	•	•	•	•	The Title Co Inc (Prairie Du Chien WI)		888-918-4853	•	•	•	•

CR	CV	PR	US	BK	←Courts	Ida	Recorder→	UC	RE	TX	VS
	•				Court Services of Iowa Inc		515-965-5722	•	•	•	
	•	•	•	•	The Title Co Inc (Prairie Du Chien WI)		888-918-4853	•	•	•	•

CR	CV	PR	US	BK	←Courts	Iowa	Recorder→	UC	RE	TX	VS
•	•	•	•	•	ASAP Process Service [SOP]		877-455-2490		•		•
	•				Court Services of Iowa Inc		515-965-5722	•	•	•	
•	•	•			Iowa County Abstract Company		319-642-7321	•	•	•	
	•	•	•	•	The Title Co Inc (Prairie Du Chien WI)		888-918-4853	•	•	•	•

CR	CV	PR	US	BK	←Courts	Jackson	Recorder→	UC	RE	TX	VS
•	•	•			Abstract & Title Guaranty Co		563-243-2027	•	•	•	•
•	•	•	•	•	ASAP Process Service [SOP]		877-455-2490		•		•
	•				Court Services of Iowa Inc		515-965-5722	•	•	•	
	•	•			Iowa Title & Guaranty Co		563-652-6081	•	•	•	•
•	•				SAS Associates Inc [SOP]		800-373-0727				
	•	•	•	•	The Title Co Inc (Prairie Du Chien WI)		888-918-4853	•	•	•	•

CR	CV	PR	US	BK	←Courts	Jasper	Recorder→	UC	RE	TX	VS
•	•	•	•	•	Applicant Profile Services [SOP]		515-727-7964	•	•	•	•
	•				Court Services of Iowa Inc		515-965-5722	•	•	•	
•	•	•	•	•	Hawkeye Legal Services [SOP]		515-276-3984	•			•
•	•	•	•	•	JR Investigations [SOP]		515-288-4682	•	•	•	•
	•	•	•	•	The Title Co Inc (Prairie Du Chien WI)		888-918-4853	•	•	•	•

CR	CV	PR	US	BK	←Courts	Jefferson	Recorder→	UC	RE	TX	VS
	•				Court Services of Iowa Inc		515-965-5722	•	•	•	
•	•	•			Jefferson County Abstract		641-472-5052	•	•	•	•
	•	•	•	•	The Title Co Inc (Prairie Du Chien WI)		888-918-4853	•	•	•	•

CR	CV	PR	US	BK	←Courts	Johnson	Recorder→	UC	RE	TX	VS
•	•	•	•	•	ASAP Process Service [SOP]		877-455-2490		•		•
	•				Court Services of Iowa Inc		515-965-5722	•	•	•	
•	•	•	•	•	FYII Acct [SOP]		563-299-5683	•	•	•	•
•	•	•			Reliance Title Services		319-354-6505	•	•	•	•
	•	•	•	•	The Title Co Inc (Prairie Du Chien WI)		888-918-4853	•	•	•	•

CR	CV	PR	US	BK	←Courts	Jones	Recorder→	UC	RE	TX	VS
•	•	•			Abstract & Title Services Inc		319-462-4828	•	•	•	•
•	•	•	•	•	ASAP Process Service [SOP]		877-455-2490		•		•
	•				Court Services of Iowa Inc		515-965-5722	•	•	•	
	•	•	•	•	The Title Co Inc (Prairie Du Chien WI)		888-918-4853	•	•	•	•

CR	CV	PR	US	BK	←Courts	Keokuk	Recorder→	UC	RE	TX	VS
	•				Court Services of Iowa Inc		515-965-5722	•	•	•	
	•	•	•	•	The Title Co Inc (Prairie Du Chien WI)		888-918-4853	•	•	•	•

CR	CV	PR	US	BK	←Courts	Kossuth	Recorder→	UC	RE	TX	VS
	•				Court Services of Iowa Inc		515-965-5722	•	•	•	
	•	•			Kossuth Abstract & Title Co		515-295-3745		•	•	
	•	•	•	•	The Title Co Inc (Prairie Du Chien WI)		888-918-4853	•	•	•	•

CR	CV	PR	US	BK	←Courts	Lee	Recorder→	UC	RE	TX	VS
					Lee County in **Iowa** has two recording offices.						
	•	•			American Abstract & Title		319-372-8110	•	•	•	•
	•				Court Services of Iowa Inc		515-965-5722	•	•	•	
	•	•	•	•	The Title Co Inc (Prairie Du Chien WI)		888-918-4853	•	•	•	•

CR	CV	PR	US	BK	←Courts	Linn	Recorder→	UC	RE	TX	VS
•	•	•	•	•	ASAP Process Service [SOP]		877-455-2490		•		•
	•				Court Services of Iowa Inc		515-965-5722	•	•	•	
•	•	•	•	•	FYII Acct [SOP]		563-299-5683	•	•	•	•

CR	CV	PR	US	BK	←Courts	Recorder→	UC	RE	TX	VS
•	•	•	•	•	Iowa Title Co	319-365-1478	•	•	•	•
	•	•	•	•	The Title Co Inc (Prairie Du Chien WI)	888-918-4853	•	•	•	•

CR	CV	PR	US	BK	←Courts **Louisa**	Recorder→	UC	RE	TX	VS
	•				Court Services of Iowa Inc	515-965-5722	•	•	•	
	•	•	•	•	The Title Co Inc (Prairie Du Chien WI)	888-918-4853	•	•	•	•

CR	CV	PR	US	BK	←Courts **Lucas**	Recorder→	UC	RE	TX	VS
	•				Court Services of Iowa Inc	515-965-5722	•	•	•	
	•	•	•	•	The Title Co Inc (Prairie Du Chien WI)	888-918-4853	•	•	•	•

CR	CV	PR	US	BK	←Courts **Lyon**	Recorder→	UC	RE	TX	VS
	•				Court Services of Iowa Inc	515-965-5722	•	•	•	
		•			Lyon County Title Co Inc	712-472-3758		•	•	
•	•	•	•		R & D Research Services [SOP]	712-737-8741	•	•	•	•

CR	CV	PR	US	BK	←Courts **Madison**	Recorder→	UC	RE	TX	VS
•	•	•	•	•	Applicant Profile Services [SOP]	515-727-7964	•	•	•	•
	•				Court Services of Iowa Inc	515-965-5722	•	•	•	
•	•	•	•	•	Hawkeye Legal Services [SOP]	515-276-3984	•			•
•	•	•	•	•	JR Investigations [SOP]	515-288-4682	•	•	•	•
•	•	•			Security Abstract & Title Inc	515-462-1691	•	•	•	•
	•	•	•	•	The Title Co Inc (Prairie Du Chien WI)	888-918-4853	•	•	•	•

CR	CV	PR	US	BK	←Courts **Mahaska**	Recorder→	UC	RE	TX	VS
	•				Court Services of Iowa Inc	515-965-5722	•	•	•	
•	•	•	•	•	Hawkeye Legal Services [SOP]	515-276-3984	•			•
•	•	•			Mahaska Title - Johnson Abstract Co	641-673-5666	•	•	•	•
	•	•	•	•	The Title Co Inc (Prairie Du Chien WI)	888-918-4853	•	•	•	•

CR	CV	PR	US	BK	←Courts **Marion**	Recorder→	UC	RE	TX	VS
	•				Court Services of Iowa Inc	515-965-5722	•	•	•	
•	•	•	•	•	Hawkeye Legal Services [SOP]	515-276-3984	•			•
•	•	•			Marion County Title Services	641-842-3518	•	•	•	•
	•	•	•	•	The Title Co Inc (Prairie Du Chien WI)	888-918-4853	•	•	•	•

CR	CV	PR	US	BK	←Courts **Marshall**	Recorder→	UC	RE	TX	VS
•	•	•	•	•	Applicant Profile Services [SOP]	515-727-7964	•	•	•	•
	•				Court Services of Iowa Inc	515-965-5722	•	•	•	
•	•	•	•	•	Marshall County Abstract Company	641-752-5358	•	•	•	•
	•	•	•	•	The Title Co Inc (Prairie Du Chien WI)	888-918-4853	•	•	•	•

CR	CV	PR	US	BK	←Courts **Mills**	Recorder→	UC	RE	TX	VS
•	•	•	•	•	Coit Enterprises	402-451-0462		•	•	
	•				Court Services of Iowa Inc	515-965-5722	•	•	•	
	•	•	•	•	The Title Co Inc (Prairie Du Chien WI)	888-918-4853	•	•	•	•
•	•		•	•	Thomas Research Services [SOP]	402-339-7291	•		•	

CR	CV	PR	US	BK	←Courts **Mitchell**	Recorder→	UC	RE	TX	VS
	•				Court Services of Iowa Inc	515-965-5722	•	•	•	
•	•	•			Mitchell County Abstract Co	641-732-4571	•	•	•	
	•	•	•	•	The Title Co Inc (Prairie Du Chien WI)	888-918-4853	•	•	•	•

CR	CV	PR	US	BK	←Courts **Monona**	Recorder→	UC	RE	TX	VS
	•				Court Services of Iowa Inc	515-965-5722	•	•	•	
	•	•	•	•	The Title Co Inc (Prairie Du Chien WI)	888-918-4853	•	•	•	•

CR	CV	PR	US	BK	←Courts **Monroe**	Recorder→	UC	RE	TX	VS
	•				Court Services of Iowa Inc	515-965-5722	•	•	•	
	•	•	•	•	The Title Co Inc (Prairie Du Chien WI)	888-918-4853	•	•	•	•

CR	CV	PR	US	BK	←Courts	MONTGOMERY	Recorder→	UC	RE	TX	VS
	•				Court Services of Iowa Inc		515-965-5722	•	•	•	
	•	•	•	•	The Title Co Inc (Prairie Du Chien WI)		888-918-4853	•	•	•	•
•					Beth Young		712-767-2510		•	•	

CR	CV	PR	US	BK	←Courts	MUSCATINE	Recorder→	UC	RE	TX	VS
	•				Court Services of Iowa Inc		515-965-5722	•	•	•	
•	•	•	•	•	Cynthia-Renee's Professional Business Svc [SOP]		563-324-9445	•	•	•	•
•	•	•	•	•	FYII Acct [SOP]		563-299-5683	•	•	•	•
	•	•			Legal Abstract Co		563-263-3171	•	•	•	•
	•	•	•	•	The Title Co Inc (Prairie Du Chien WI)		888-918-4853	•	•	•	•

CR	CV	PR	US	BK	←Courts	O'BRIEN	Recorder→	UC	RE	TX	VS
	•				Court Services of Iowa Inc		515-965-5722	•	•	•	
•	•	•	•		R & D Research Services [SOP]		712-737-8741	•	•	•	•

CR	CV	PR	US	BK	←Courts	OSCEOLA	Recorder→	UC	RE	TX	VS
	•				Court Services of Iowa Inc		515-965-5722	•	•	•	
•	•	•	•		R & D Research Services [SOP]		712-737-8741	•	•	•	•
		•	•		The Title Co Inc (Iowa)		712-754-2284	•	•	•	

CR	CV	PR	US	BK	←Courts	PAGE	Recorder→	UC	RE	TX	VS
	•				Court Services of Iowa Inc		515-965-5722	•	•	•	
	•	•			Page County Abstract & Title Company		712-542-3613	•	•	•	

CR	CV	PR	US	BK	←Courts	PALO ALTO	Recorder→	UC	RE	TX	VS
	•				Court Services of Iowa Inc		515-965-5722	•	•	•	
•	•	•	•		Palo Alto County Abstract Co		712-852-4313	•	•	•	
	•	•	•	•	The Title Co Inc (Prairie Du Chien WI)		888-918-4853	•	•	•	•

CR	CV	PR	US	BK	←Courts	PLYMOUTH	Recorder→	UC	RE	TX	VS
	•				Court Services of Iowa Inc		515-965-5722	•	•	•	
		•			Plymouth County Abstract		712-546-4564	•	•	•	
•	•	•	•		R & D Research Services [SOP]		712-737-8741	•	•	•	•
	•	•	•	•	The Title Co Inc (Prairie Du Chien WI)		888-918-4853	•	•	•	•

CR	CV	PR	US	BK	←Courts	POCAHONTAS	Recorder→	UC	RE	TX	VS
	•				Court Services of Iowa Inc		515-965-5722	•	•	•	
	•	•	•	•	The Title Co Inc (Prairie Du Chien WI)		888-918-4853	•	•	•	•

CR	CV	PR	US	BK	←Courts	POLK	Recorder→	UC	RE	TX	VS
•	•	•	•	•	Adams Investigations [SOP]		888-844-0624	•	•	•	•
•	•	•	•	•	Applicant Profile Services [SOP]		515-727-7964	•	•	•	•
	•				Court Services of Iowa Inc		515-965-5722	•	•	•	
•	•	•	•	•	FYII Acct [SOP]		563-299-5683	•	•	•	•
•	•	•	•	•	Hawkeye Legal Services [SOP]		515-276-3984	•			•
•	•	•	•	•	JR Investigations [SOP]		515-288-4682	•	•	•	•
•	•				SAS Associates Inc [SOP]		800-373-0727				
	•		•	•	Search Network Ltd (Iowa)		800-383-5050	•	•	•	
	•	•	•	•	The Title Co Inc (Prairie Du Chien WI)		888-918-4853	•	•	•	•

CR	CV	PR	US	BK	←Courts	POTTAWATTAMIE	Recorder→	UC	RE	TX	VS
•	•	•	•	•	Coit Enterprises		402-451-0462		•	•	
	•				Court Services of Iowa Inc		515-965-5722	•	•	•	
•	•	•	•	•	Legal Eagle Inc / Eagle Search & Service [SOP]		402-342-4427	•	•	•	•
	•	•	•	•	The Title Co Inc (Prairie Du Chien WI)		888-918-4853	•	•	•	•
•	•		•	•	Thomas Research Services [SOP]		402-339-7291	•		•	

CR	CV	PR	US	BK	←Courts	POWESHIEK	Recorder→	UC	RE	TX	VS
	•				Court Services of Iowa Inc		515-965-5722	•	•	•	
•	•	•	•	•	Poweshiek Abstract Co Inc		641-236-8668	•	•	•	•

CR	CV	PR	US	BK	←Courts	Recorder→	UC	RE	TX	VS
	•	•	•	•	The Title Co Inc (Prairie Du Chien WI)	888-918-4853	•	•	•	•

CR	CV	PR	US	BK	←Courts **Ringgold**	Recorder→	UC	RE	TX	VS
	•				Court Services of Iowa Inc	515-965-5722	•	•	•	
•	•	•			Ringgold County Abstract Co Inc	641-464-3902	•	•	•	•
	•	•	•	•	The Title Co Inc (Prairie Du Chien WI)	888-918-4853	•	•	•	•

CR	CV	PR	US	BK	←Courts **Sac**	Recorder→	UC	RE	TX	VS
	•				Court Services of Iowa Inc	515-965-5722	•	•	•	
•	•	•			Sac County Abstract Co	712-662-7317	•	•	•	•
	•	•	•	•	The Title Co Inc (Prairie Du Chien WI)	888-918-4853	•	•	•	•

CR	CV	PR	US	BK	←Courts **Scott**	Recorder→	UC	RE	TX	VS
•	•	•			Bettendorf Abstract Co [SOP]	563-359-3646	•	•	•	•
	•				Court Services of Iowa Inc	515-965-5722	•	•	•	
•	•	•	•	•	Cynthia-Renee's Professional Business Svc [SOP]	563-324-9445	•	•	•	•
•	•	•	•	•	DocumentServe Express [SOP]	309-786-2220	•	•	•	•
•	•	•	•	•	FYII Acct [SOP]	563-299-5683	•	•	•	•
•	•	•	•	•	James M Sweeney & Associates Inc [SOP]	800-494-5922	•		•	•
•	•				SAS Associates Inc [SOP]	800-373-0727				
	•	•	•	•	The Title Co Inc (Prairie Du Chien WI)	888-918-4853	•	•	•	•

CR	CV	PR	US	BK	←Courts **Shelby**	Recorder→	UC	RE	TX	VS
	•				Court Services of Iowa Inc	515-965-5722	•	•	•	
		•			Ouren Title Inc	712-755-2174		•	•	•
	•	•	•	•	The Title Co Inc (Prairie Du Chien WI)	888-918-4853	•	•	•	•

CR	CV	PR	US	BK	←Courts **Sioux**	Recorder→	UC	RE	TX	VS
	•				Court Services of Iowa Inc	515-965-5722	•	•	•	
•	•	•	•		R & D Research Services [SOP]	712-737-8741	•	•	•	•

CR	CV	PR	US	BK	←Courts **Story**	Recorder→	UC	RE	TX	VS
•	•	•	•	•	Applicant Profile Services [SOP]	515-727-7964	•	•	•	•
	•				Court Services of Iowa Inc	515-965-5722	•	•	•	
•	•	•	•	•	Hawkeye Legal Services [SOP]	515-276-3984	•			•
					Story Countpile Co	515-382-4127	•	•	•	
	•	•	•	•	The Title Co Inc (Prairie Du Chien WI)	888-918-4853	•	•	•	•

CR	CV	PR	US	BK	←Courts **Tama**	Recorder→	UC	RE	TX	VS
	•				Court Services of Iowa Inc	515-965-5722	•	•	•	
•	•	•	•		Tama County Abstract	888-561-9061	•	•	•	•
	•	•	•	•	The Title Co Inc (Prairie Du Chien WI)	888-918-4853	•	•	•	•

CR	CV	PR	US	BK	←Courts **Taylor**	Recorder→	UC	RE	TX	VS
	•				Court Services of Iowa Inc	515-965-5722	•	•	•	

CR	CV	PR	US	BK	←Courts **Union**	Recorder→	UC	RE	TX	VS
	•				Court Services of Iowa Inc	515-965-5722	•	•	•	
	•	•	•	•	The Title Co Inc (Prairie Du Chien WI)	888-918-4853	•	•	•	•

CR	CV	PR	US	BK	←Courts **Van Buren**	Recorder→	UC	RE	TX	VS
	•				Court Services of Iowa Inc	515-965-5722	•	•	•	
	•	•	•	•	The Title Co Inc (Prairie Du Chien WI)	888-918-4853	•	•	•	•
•	•	•			Van Buren Abstract Co	319-293-7760	•	•	•	•

CR	CV	PR	US	BK	←Courts **Wapello**	Recorder→	UC	RE	TX	VS
	•				Court Services of Iowa Inc	515-965-5722	•	•	•	
	•	•	•	•	The Title Co Inc (Prairie Du Chien WI)	888-918-4853	•	•	•	•

CR	CV	PR	US	BK	←Courts **Warren**	Recorder→	UC	RE	TX	VS
•	•	•	•	•	Applicant Profile Services [SOP]	515-727-7964	•	•	•	•
	•				Court Services of Iowa Inc	515-965-5722	•	•	•	

CR	CV	PR	US	BK	←Courts		Recorder→	UC	RE	TX	VS
•	•	•	•	•	Hawkeye Legal Services [SOP]		515-276-3984	•			•
•	•	•	•	•	JR Investigations [SOP]		515-288-4682	•	•	•	•
	•	•	•	•	The Title Co Inc (Prairie Du Chien WI)		888-918-4853	•	•	•	•
		•			Warren County Abstract Company		515-961-7479	•	•	•	•
CR	**CV**	**PR**	**US**	**BK**	**←Courts**	**WASHINGTON**	**Recorder→**	**UC**	**RE**	**TX**	**VS**
	•				Court Services of Iowa Inc		515-965-5722	•	•	•	
	•	•	•	•	The Title Co Inc (Prairie Du Chien WI)		888-918-4853	•	•	•	•
CR	**CV**	**PR**	**US**	**BK**	**←Courts**	**WAYNE**	**Recorder→**	**UC**	**RE**	**TX**	**VS**
	•				Court Services of Iowa Inc		515-965-5722	•	•	•	
•	•	•			John H Rider Abstracts of Title		641-872-1966	•	•	•	
	•	•	•	•	The Title Co Inc (Prairie Du Chien WI)		888-918-4853	•	•	•	•
CR	**CV**	**PR**	**US**	**BK**	**←Courts**	**WEBSTER**	**Recorder→**	**UC**	**RE**	**TX**	**VS**
•	•	•	•	•	Applicant Profile Services [SOP]		515-727-7964	•	•	•	•
	•				Court Services of Iowa Inc		515-965-5722	•	•	•	
	•	•	•	•	The Title Co Inc (Prairie Du Chien WI)		888-918-4853	•	•	•	•
•	•	•			Webster County-Butler & Rhodes Abstract		515-573-3341	•	•	•	•
CR	**CV**	**PR**	**US**	**BK**	**←Courts**	**WINNEBAGO**	**Recorder→**	**UC**	**RE**	**TX**	**VS**
	•				Court Services of Iowa Inc		515-965-5722	•	•	•	
	•	•	•	•	The Title Co Inc (Prairie Du Chien WI)		888-918-4853	•	•	•	•
CR	**CV**	**PR**	**US**	**BK**	**←Courts**	**WINNESHIEK**	**Recorder→**	**UC**	**RE**	**TX**	**VS**
	•				Court Services of Iowa Inc		515-965-5722	•	•	•	
	•	•	•	•	The Title Co Inc (Prairie Du Chien WI)		888-918-4853	•	•	•	•
CR	**CV**	**PR**	**US**	**BK**	**←Courts**	**WOODBURY**	**Recorder→**	**UC**	**RE**	**TX**	**VS**
	•				Court Services of Iowa Inc		515-965-5722	•	•	•	
•	•		•		Intra-Lex Investigations Inc [SOP]		712-233-1639	•	•	•	
•	•	•	•		Professional Support Services of Siouxland		712-233-2383	•	•	•	•
•	•	•	•		R & D Research Services [SOP]		712-737-8741	•	•	•	•
	•	•	•	•	The Title Co Inc (Prairie Du Chien WI)		888-918-4853	•	•	•	•
CR	**CV**	**PR**	**US**	**BK**	**←Courts**	**WORTH**	**Recorder→**	**UC**	**RE**	**TX**	**VS**
	•				Court Services of Iowa Inc		515-965-5722	•	•	•	
	•	•	•	•	The Title Co Inc (Prairie Du Chien WI)		888-918-4853	•	•	•	•
	•	•			Worth County Abstract Co Inc		641-324-1761	•	•	•	•
CR	**CV**	**PR**	**US**	**BK**	**←Courts**	**WRIGHT**	**Recorder→**	**UC**	**RE**	**TX**	**VS**
•	•	•	•	•	Applicant Profile Services [SOP]		515-727-7964	•	•	•	•
	•				Court Services of Iowa Inc		515-965-5722	•	•	•	
	•	•	•	•	The Title Co Inc (Prairie Du Chien WI)		888-918-4853	•	•	•	•

[SOP] = Performs service of process

= PRRN Member. *A retriever you can trust!*

Kansas

COURT RECORDS RETRIEVED | **CAPITAL - SHAWNEE COUNTY** | **RECORDED RECORDS RETRIEVED**

CR	CV	PR	US	BK	←COURTS	ALLEN	RECORDER→	UC	RE	TX	VS
•	•		•	•	Research Information Services LLC		800-522-3884	•		•	
•	•	•			Street Abstract Co		620-625-2421	•	•	•	

CR	CV	PR	US	BK	←COURTS	ANDERSON	RECORDER→	UC	RE	TX	VS
•	•		•	•	Research Information Services LLC		800-522-3884	•		•	

CR	CV	PR	US	BK	←COURTS	ATCHISON	RECORDER→	UC	RE	TX	VS
•	•	•			Bi-State Title Search (Div of Bi-State Ind.)		866-450-7399	•	•	•	
•	•	•			David and Marvin Criqui		785-889-4659		•	•	•
•	•		•	•	Research Information Services LLC		800-522-3884	•		•	

CR	CV	PR	US	BK	←COURTS	BARBER	RECORDER→	UC	RE	TX	VS
•	•		•	•	Research Information Services LLC		800-522-3884	•		•	

CR	CV	PR	US	BK	←COURTS	BARTON	RECORDER→	UC	RE	TX	VS
	•	•			Barton County Abstract & Title Co		620-793-3781	•	•	•	
•	•		•	•	Research Information Services LLC		800-522-3884	•		•	

CR	CV	PR	US	BK	←COURTS	BOURBON	RECORDER→	UC	RE	TX	VS
•	•	•			American Research Unlimited Inc		417-358-6494	•	•	•	•
•	•				Becky Headrick		417-321-0745				
•	•	•			Linn County Abstract Co		888-795-2949	•	•	•	
•	•		•	•	Research Information Services LLC		800-522-3884	•		•	

CR	CV	PR	US	BK	←COURTS	BROWN	RECORDER→	UC	RE	TX	VS
•	•	•			Brown County Title Co		785-742-4194	•	•	•	
•	•	•			David and Marvin Criqui		785-889-4659		•	•	•
•	•		•	•	Research Information Services LLC		800-522-3884	•		•	

CR	CV	PR	US	BK	←COURTS	BUTLER	RECORDER→	UC	RE	TX	VS
•	•	•	•	•	Branda Agency [SOP]		800-310-8174	•	•	•	•
•	•	•	•	•	Kansas Investigative Services Inc [SOP]		888-889-3340	•	•	•	•
•	•		•	•	Research Information Services LLC		800-522-3884	•		•	
•	•	•	•	•	Walters Document Service [SOP]		316-682-5629	•	•	•	

CR	CV	PR	US	BK	←COURTS	CHASE	RECORDER→	UC	RE	TX	VS
	•	•			Moon Abstract Co		620-342-1917	•	•	•	
•	•		•	•	Research Information Services LLC		800-522-3884	•		•	

CR	CV	PR	US	BK	←COURTS	CHAUTAUQUA	RECORDER→	UC	RE	TX	VS
•	•	•			Chautauqua County Abstract Co inc		620-725-3215	•	•	•	•
•	•		•	•	Research Information Services LLC		800-522-3884	•		•	

CR	CV	PR	US	BK	←COURTS	CHEROKEE	RECORDER→	UC	RE	TX	VS
•	•	•			American Research Unlimited Inc		417-358-6494	•	•	•	•
•	•	•			Barrett Title Co		620-856-3531	•	•	•	•
•	•		•	•	Research Information Services LLC		800-522-3884	•		•	

CR	CV	PR	US	BK	←COURTS	CHEYENNE	RECORDER→	UC	RE	TX	VS
•	•		•	•	Research Information Services LLC		800-522-3884	•		•	
•	•	•	•		The R M Jaqua Abstract Co		785-332-3041	•	•	•	
•	•	•			Wilma Whitney		785-852-4932		•	•	

CR	CV	PR	US	BK	←Courts **Clark**	Recorder→	UC	RE	TX	VS
•		•			High Plains Land & Title	620-225-6574		•	•	
	•	•			Meade County Title Clark County	800-725-7802	•	•	•	•
•	•		•	•	Research Information Services LLC	800-522-3884	•		•	

CR	CV	PR	US	BK	←Courts **Clay**	Recorder→	UC	RE	TX	VS
•	•	•			Attorney's Title Co	785-243-1357	•	•	•	
•	•		•	•	Research Information Services LLC	800-522-3884	•		•	

CR	CV	PR	US	BK	←Courts **Cloud**	Recorder→	UC	RE	TX	VS
•	•	•			Attorney's Title Co	785-243-1357	•	•	•	
•	•		•	•	Research Information Services LLC	800-522-3884	•		•	

CR	CV	PR	US	BK	←Courts **Coffey**	Recorder→	UC	RE	TX	VS
	•	•			Moon Abstract Co	620-342-1917	•	•	•	
•	•		•	•	Research Information Services LLC	800-522-3884	•		•	
•	•	•			Street Abstract Co	620-625-2421	•	•	•	

CR	CV	PR	US	BK	←Courts **Comanche**	Recorder→	UC	RE	TX	VS
•	•	•			Comanche Abstract & Title Co	620-582-2125	•	•	•	
•	•		•	•	Research Information Services LLC	800-522-3884	•		•	

CR	CV	PR	US	BK	←Courts **Cowley**	Recorder→	UC	RE	TX	VS
•	•	•			Barbour Title Co	866-379-0430	•	•	•	•
•	•		•	•	Research Information Services LLC	800-522-3884	•		•	
•	•	•	•	•	Walters Document Service [SOP]	316-682-5629	•	•	•	

CR	CV	PR	US	BK	←Courts **Crawford**	Recorder→	UC	RE	TX	VS
•	•	•			American Research Unlimited Inc	417-358-6494	•	•	•	•
•	•		•	•	Research Information Services LLC	800-522-3884	•		•	

CR	CV	PR	US	BK	←Courts **Decatur**	Recorder→	UC	RE	TX	VS
•	•	•			Decatur County Abstract	785-626-3885	•	•	•	•
•	•	•	•		First Insurance Agency of Hoxie Inc	800-569-0198	•	•	•	
•	•		•	•	Research Information Services LLC	800-522-3884	•		•	

CR	CV	PR	US	BK	←Courts **Dickinson**	Recorder→	UC	RE	TX	VS
•	•				Al Bernardi Backgrounds Process Service	785-456-8821	•	•	•	
•	•				Capital Investigative Services Inc	800-633-7136				
•	•		•	•	Research Information Services LLC	800-522-3884	•		•	

CR	CV	PR	US	BK	←Courts **Doniphan**	Recorder→	UC	RE	TX	VS
•	•	•			David and Marvin Criqui	785-889-4659		•	•	•
•	•	•			Euler Abstract & Title Co [SOP]	785-985-3562		•	•	
•	•		•	•	Research Information Services LLC	800-522-3884	•		•	

CR	CV	PR	US	BK	←Courts **Douglas**	Recorder→	UC	RE	TX	VS
•	•	•			Bi-State Title Search (Div of Bi-State Ind.)	866-450-7399	•	•	•	
•	•				Capital Investigative Services Inc	800-633-7136				
•	•	•	•	•	Credit Bureau of Eudora Inc (CBE) [SOP]	785-542-1771	•	•	•	•
•	•	•			David and Marvin Criqui	785-889-4659		•	•	•
•	•		•	•	Executive Investigative Services [SOP]	800-764-9484	•	•	•	
•	•		•	•	Future Security Concepts	800-398-3051	•		•	
•	•	•	•	•	Hatfield Process Service [SOP]	816-842-9800	•	•	•	•
•	•	•	•	•	Heartland Document Retrieval	888-221-2778 orders only	•	•	•	•
•					LLG Enterprises	816-625-0947				
•	•		•	•	Research Information Services LLC	800-522-3884	•		•	
	•		•	•	SearchWorks Inc	913-383-0940	•	•	•	

CR	CV	PR	US	BK	←Courts EDWARDS	Recorder→	UC	RE	TX	VS
•		•			High Plains Land & Title	620-225-6574		•	•	
•	•		•	•	Research Information Services LLC	800-522-3884	•		•	
•	•	•			Richardson Abstract Co Inc	620-659-2592	•	•	•	

CR	CV	PR	US	BK	←Courts ELK	Recorder→	UC	RE	TX	VS
•	•	•			Elk County Abstract & Title Co	620-374-2500	•	•	•	•
•	•		•	•	Research Information Services LLC	800-522-3884	•		•	

CR	CV	PR	US	BK	←Courts ELLIS	Recorder→	UC	RE	TX	VS
•	•	•			Ellis County Abstract & Title Co.	785-625-2316	•	•	•	•
•	•		•	•	Research Information Services LLC	800-522-3884	•		•	

CR	CV	PR	US	BK	←Courts ELLSWORTH	Recorder→	UC	RE	TX	VS
•	•				Capital Investigative Services Inc	800-633-7136				
•	•		•	•	Research Information Services LLC	800-522-3884	•		•	

CR	CV	PR	US	BK	←Courts FINNEY	Recorder→	UC	RE	TX	VS
•					Pat Brown	620-277-2065				
	•	•			Campbell Abstract Inc	620-275-7441	•	•	•	
•	•		•	•	Research Information Services LLC	800-522-3884	•		•	

CR	CV	PR	US	BK	←Courts FORD	Recorder→	UC	RE	TX	VS
	•	•			Ford County Title Co Inc	620-227-2349	•	•	•	
•		•			High Plains Land & Title	620-225-6574		•	•	
•	•		•	•	Research Information Services LLC	800-522-3884	•		•	

CR	CV	PR	US	BK	←Courts FRANKLIN	Recorder→	UC	RE	TX	VS
•	•	•			Bi-State Title Search (Div of Bi-State Ind.)	866-450-7399	•	•	•	
•	•				Capital Investigative Services Inc	800-633-7136				
•	•		•	•	Executive Investigative Services [SOP]	800-764-9484	•	•	•	
•	•	•			Haley Title Co Inc	785-242-2457	•	•	•	
•	•	•	•	•	Heartland Document Retrieval	888-221-2778 orders only	•	•	•	•
•	•		•	•	Research Information Services LLC	800-522-3884	•		•	

CR	CV	PR	US	BK	←Courts GEARY	Recorder→	UC	RE	TX	VS
•	•				Al Bernardi Backgrounds Process Service	785-456-8821	•	•	•	
•	•				Capital Investigative Services Inc	800-633-7136				
•	•		•	•	Research Information Services LLC	800-522-3884	•		•	

CR	CV	PR	US	BK	←Courts GOVE	Recorder→	UC	RE	TX	VS
•	•	•	•		First Insurance Agency of Hoxie Inc	800-569-0198	•	•	•	
•	•		•	•	Research Information Services LLC	800-522-3884	•		•	

CR	CV	PR	US	BK	←Courts GRAHAM	Recorder→	UC	RE	TX	VS
•	•	•	•		First Insurance Agency of Hoxie Inc	800-569-0198	•	•	•	
•	•		•	•	Research Information Services LLC	800-522-3884	•		•	

CR	CV	PR	US	BK	←Courts GRANT	Recorder→	UC	RE	TX	VS
•	•	•			American Title & Abstract Specialists Inc.	620-624-9111	•	•	•	•
•	•	•			Frazee Abstract & Title, Inc.	800-736-7832	•	•	•	•
•	•		•	•	Research Information Services LLC	800-522-3884	•		•	

CR	CV	PR	US	BK	←Courts GRAY	Recorder→	UC	RE	TX	VS
	•	•			Ford County Title Co Inc	620-227-2349	•	•	•	
•		•			High Plains Land & Title	620-225-6574		•	•	
•	•		•	•	Research Information Services LLC	800-522-3884	•		•	

CR	CV	PR	US	BK	←Courts GREELEY	Recorder→	UC	RE	TX	VS
•	•				Martha's Retrieval	620-375-2251		•		
•	•				Martha Myers	620-375-2251; Fax- same			•	
•	•		•	•	Research Information Services LLC	800-522-3884	•		•	

CR	CV	PR	US	BK	←COURTS **GREENWOOD**	RECORDER→	UC	RE	TX	VS
	•	•			Moon Abstract Co	620-342-1917	•	•	•	
•	•		•	•	Research Information Services LLC	800-522-3884	•		•	
•	•	•			Street Abstract Co	620-625-2421	•	•	•	

CR	CV	PR	US	BK	←COURTS **HAMILTON**	RECORDER→	UC	RE	TX	VS
•	•	•			Frazee Abstract & Title, Inc.	800-736-7832	•	•	•	•
•	•		•	•	Research Information Services LLC	800-522-3884	•		•	
•	•	•			Wayne K Westblade, Attny	620-384-5352				

CR	CV	PR	US	BK	←COURTS **HARPER**	RECORDER→	UC	RE	TX	VS
•	•				Couch Title and Abstract	620-842-5512, Fax- same		•	•	
•	•		•	•	Research Information Services LLC	800-522-3884	•		•	

CR	CV	PR	US	BK	←COURTS **HARVEY**	RECORDER→	UC	RE	TX	VS
•	•	•	•	•	Branda Agency [SOP]	800-310-8174	•	•	•	•
•	•				Capital Investigative Services Inc	800-633-7136				
	•	•			Regier Title Co	316-283-2750	•	•	•	
•	•		•	•	Research Information Services LLC	800-522-3884	•		•	
•	•	•			SumData	620-241-5448	•	•	•	
•	•	•	•	•	Walters Document Service [SOP]	316-682-5629	•	•	•	

CR	CV	PR	US	BK	←COURTS **HASKELL**	RECORDER→	UC	RE	TX	VS
•	•	•			American Title & Abstract Specialists Inc.	620-624-9111	•	•	•	•
•	•	•			Haskell County Abstract & Title	620-675-2322	•	•	•	•
•	•	•			Gwen Meairs	620-629-0551				
•	•		•	•	Research Information Services LLC	800-522-3884	•		•	

CR	CV	PR	US	BK	←COURTS **HODGEMAN**	RECORDER→	UC	RE	TX	VS
•		•			High Plains Land & Title	620-225-6574		•	•	
•	•	•			Hodgeman County Abstract & Title Ins Co Inc	620-357-8328	•	•	•	
•	•		•	•	Research Information Services LLC	800-522-3884	•		•	

CR	CV	PR	US	BK	←COURTS **JACKSON**	RECORDER→	UC	RE	TX	VS
•	•				Capital Investigative Services Inc	800-633-7136				
•	•	•			David and Marvin Criqui	785-889-4659		•	•	•
•	•		•	•	Research Information Services LLC	800-522-3884	•		•	

CR	CV	PR	US	BK	←COURTS **JEFFERSON**	RECORDER→	UC	RE	TX	VS
•	•	•			Bi-State Title Search (Div of Bi-State Ind.)	866-450-7399	•	•	•	
•	•				Capital Investigative Services Inc	800-633-7136				
•	•	•			David and Marvin Criqui	785-889-4659		•	•	•
•	•	•			Finley Abstract & Title Co	785-863-2271	•	•	•	
•	•		•	•	Research Information Services LLC	800-522-3884	•		•	

CR	CV	PR	US	BK	←COURTS **JEWELL**	RECORDER→	UC	RE	TX	VS
•	•	•			Gail L Miller	785-378-3128			•	
•	•		•	•	Research Information Services LLC	800-522-3884	•		•	
•	•	•			Weltner Phillips Law Office	785-378-3172	•	•	•	

CR	CV	PR	US	BK	←COURTS **JOHNSON**	RECORDER→	UC	RE	TX	VS
•					Affirm Background Screening Inc	715-682-2601				
•	•	•			American Title & Abstract Specialists Inc.	620-624-9111	•	•	•	•
•	•		•	•	Armstrong Document Retrieval	913-341-1991	•	•	•	
•	•	•			Bi-State Title Search (Div of Bi-State Ind.)	866-450-7399	•	•	•	
•	•	•	•	•	Credit Bureau of Eudora Inc (CBE) [SOP]	785-542-1771	•	•	•	•
•	•	•	•	•	D & B Legal Services Inc [SOP]	913-963-1279	•	•	•	•
•	•		•	•	Executive Investigative Services [SOP]	800-764-9484	•	•	•	
•	•		•	•	Future Security Concepts	800-398-3051	•		•	
•	•	•	•	•	Hatfield Process Service [SOP]	816-842-9800	•	•	•	•
•	•	•	•	•	Heartland Document Retrieval	888-221-2778 orders only	•	•	•	•

CR	CV	PR	US	BK	←Courts	Recorder→	UC	RE	TX	VS
•	•	•	•	•	KC Court Research Inc	913-239-8995	•	•	•	
•					LLG Enterprises	816-625-0947				
	•	•	•		M & J Abstractors	913-727-3588	•	•	•	
•	•	•	•	•	Medlin Research Company	913-206-4615	•	•	•	
•	•		•	•	Research Information Services LLC	800-522-3884	•		•	
•	•		•	•	Rigoli Searches	913-908-8863	•	•	•	
	•		•	•	SearchWorks Inc	913-383-0940	•	•	•	
CR	**CV**	**PR**	**US**	**BK**	**←Courts — KEARNY**	**Recorder→**	**UC**	**RE**	**TX**	**VS**
•	•	•			Frazee Abstract & Title, Inc.	800-736-7832	•	•	•	•
•	•		•	•	Research Information Services LLC	800-522-3884	•		•	
CR	**CV**	**PR**	**US**	**BK**	**←Courts — KINGMAN**	**Recorder→**	**UC**	**RE**	**TX**	**VS**
•	•	•	•	•	Branda Agency [SOP]	800-310-8174	•	•	•	•
	•	•			Kingman Abstract & Title Co Inc	620-532-2011		•	•	
•	•		•	•	Research Information Services LLC	800-522-3884	•		•	
CR	**CV**	**PR**	**US**	**BK**	**←Courts — KIOWA**	**Recorder→**	**UC**	**RE**	**TX**	**VS**
•	•		•	•	Research Information Services LLC	800-522-3884	•		•	
CR	**CV**	**PR**	**US**	**BK**	**←Courts — LABETTE**	**Recorder→**	**UC**	**RE**	**TX**	**VS**
•	•	•			American Research Unlimited Inc	417-358-6494	•	•	•	•
•	•				Realty Inc	620-795-4511		•	•	
•	•		•	•	Research Information Services LLC	800-522-3884	•		•	
CR	**CV**	**PR**	**US**	**BK**	**←Courts — LANE**	**Recorder→**	**UC**	**RE**	**TX**	**VS**
•	•		•	•	Research Information Services LLC	800-522-3884	•		•	
CR	**CV**	**PR**	**US**	**BK**	**←Courts — LEAVENWORTH**	**Recorder→**	**UC**	**RE**	**TX**	**VS**
•	•	•			Bi-State Title Search (Div of Bi-State Ind.)	866-450-7399	•	•	•	
•	•	•	•	•	Credit Bureau of Eudora Inc (CBE) [SOP]	785-542-1771	•	•	•	•
•	•	•			David and Marvin Criqui	785-889-4659		•	•	•
•	•		•	•	Executive Investigative Services [SOP]	800-764-9484	•	•	•	
•	•		•	•	Future Security Concepts	800-398-3051	•		•	
•	•	•	•	•	Heartland Document Retrieval	888-221-2778 orders only	•	•	•	•
	•	•	•		M & J Abstractors	913-727-3588	•	•	•	
•	•		•	•	Research Information Services LLC	800-522-3884	•		•	
•	•				Rigoli Searches	913-908-8863	•	•	•	
CR	**CV**	**PR**	**US**	**BK**	**←Courts — LINCOLN**	**Recorder→**	**UC**	**RE**	**TX**	**VS**
	•	•			Lincoln Home Title (KS)	785-524-4228	•	•	•	
•	•		•	•	Research Information Services LLC	800-522-3884	•		•	
CR	**CV**	**PR**	**US**	**BK**	**←Courts — LINN**	**Recorder→**	**UC**	**RE**	**TX**	**VS**
•	•	•			Linn County Abstract Co	888-795-2949	•	•	•	
•	•		•	•	Research Information Services LLC	800-522-3884	•		•	
CR	**CV**	**PR**	**US**	**BK**	**←Courts — LOGAN**	**Recorder→**	**UC**	**RE**	**TX**	**VS**
•	•				Jodi Moellering	785-672-3979				
•	•				Pyramid Abstract	785-672-4285		•		•
•	•		•	•	Research Information Services LLC	800-522-3884	•		•	
•	•	•			Wilma Whitney	785-852-4932		•	•	
CR	**CV**	**PR**	**US**	**BK**	**←Courts — LYON**	**Recorder→**	**UC**	**RE**	**TX**	**VS**
•	•				Capital Investigative Services Inc	800-633-7136				
	•	•			Moon Abstract Co	620-342-1917	•	•	•	
•	•		•	•	Research Information Services LLC	800-522-3884	•		•	
CR	**CV**	**PR**	**US**	**BK**	**←Courts — MARION**	**Recorder→**	**UC**	**RE**	**TX**	**VS**
•	•				Capital Investigative Services Inc	800-633-7136				
•	•	•			Hannaford Abstract & Title Co.	620-382-2130	•	•	•	•
•	•		•	•	Research Information Services LLC	800-522-3884	•		•	

CR	CV	PR	US	BK		Phone	UC	RE	TX	VS
●	●	●			SumData	620-241-5448	●	●	●	

CR	CV	PR	US	BK	←COURTS MARSHALL	RECORDER→	UC	RE	TX	VS
●	●	●			David and Marvin Criqui	785-889-4659		●	●	●
●	●		●	●	Research Information Services LLC	800-522-3884	●		●	

CR	CV	PR	US	BK	←COURTS MCPHERSON	RECORDER→	UC	RE	TX	VS
●	●	●	●	●	Branda Agency [SOP]	800-310-8174	●	●	●	●
●	●				Capital Investigative Services Inc	800-633-7136				
●	●		●	●	Research Information Services LLC	800-522-3884	●		●	
●	●	●			SumData	620-241-5448	●	●	●	
●	●				Jacquie Willems	785-227-4775				

CR	CV	PR	US	BK	←COURTS MEADE	RECORDER→	UC	RE	TX	VS
●		●			High Plains Land & Title	620-225-6574		●	●	
	●	●			Meade County Title	620-873-2756	●	●	●	
●	●		●	●	Research Information Services LLC	800-522-3884	●		●	

CR	CV	PR	US	BK	←COURTS MIAMI	RECORDER→	UC	RE	TX	VS
●	●	●			Bi-State Title Search (Div of Bi-State Ind.)	866-450-7399	●	●	●	
●	●		●	●	Executive Investigative Services [SOP]	800-764-9484	●	●	●	
●	●	●	●	●	Heartland Document Retrieval	888-221-2778 orders only	●	●	●	●
●	●	●	●	●	Medlin Research Company	913-206-4615	●	●	●	
●	●		●	●	Research Information Services LLC	800-522-3884	●		●	

CR	CV	PR	US	BK	←COURTS MITCHELL	RECORDER→	UC	RE	TX	VS
●	●	●			Attorney's Title Co	785-243-1357	●	●	●	
●	●		●	●	Research Information Services LLC	800-522-3884	●		●	

CR	CV	PR	US	BK	←COURTS MONTGOMERY	RECORDER→	UC	RE	TX	VS
	●	●			Montgomery County Abstract Co	620-331-1440	●	●	●	
●	●		●	●	Research Information Services LLC	800-522-3884	●		●	

CR	CV	PR	US	BK	←COURTS MORRIS	RECORDER→	UC	RE	TX	VS
	●	●			Moon Abstract Co	620-342-1917	●	●	●	
●	●		●	●	Research Information Services LLC	800-522-3884	●		●	

CR	CV	PR	US	BK	←COURTS MORTON	RECORDER→	UC	RE	TX	VS
●	●	●			American Title & Abstract Specialists Inc	620-624-9111	●	●	●	●
●	●		●	●	Research Information Services LLC	800-522-3884	●		●	
●	●				Southwest Tax & Accounting	620-697-2422				

CR	CV	PR	US	BK	←COURTS NEMAHA	RECORDER→	UC	RE	TX	VS
●	●	●			David and Marvin Criqui	785-889-4659		●	●	●
	●	●			Nemaha County Abstract & Title Co	785-336-2137	●	●	●	●
●	●		●	●	Research Information Services LLC	800-522-3884	●		●	

CR	CV	PR	US	BK	←COURTS NEOSHO	RECORDER→	UC	RE	TX	VS
	●	●	●	●	Locke-Neosho Abstracts Inc	620-244-3641	●	●	●	
●	●		●	●	Research Information Services LLC	800-522-3884	●		●	
●	●	●			Street Abstract Co	620-625-2421	●	●	●	

CR	CV	PR	US	BK	←COURTS NESS	RECORDER→	UC	RE	TX	VS
●	●				Ness County Abstract	785-798-3846		●		
●	●		●	●	Research Information Services LLC	800-522-3884	●		●	

CR	CV	PR	US	BK	←COURTS NORTON	RECORDER→	UC	RE	TX	VS
●	●		●	●	Research Information Services LLC	800-522-3884	●		●	
●	●	●			Security Abstract Company	785-877-2141	●	●	●	●

CR	CV	PR	US	BK	←COURTS OSAGE	RECORDER→	UC	RE	TX	VS
●	●				Capital Investigative Services Inc	800-633-7136				
●	●		●	●	Research Information Services LLC	800-522-3884	●		●	

CR	CV	PR	US	BK	←COURTS **OSBORNE** RECORDER→	Phone	UC	RE	TX	VS
•	•	•			Gregory Abstract & Title Co Inc	785-346-5445	•	•	•	
•	•		•	•	Research Information Services LLC	800-522-3884	•		•	

CR	CV	PR	US	BK	←COURTS **OTTAWA** RECORDER→	Phone	UC	RE	TX	VS
•	•	•			Attorney's Title Co.	785-243-1357	•	•	•	
•	•		•	•	Research Information Services LLC	800-522-3884	•		•	

CR	CV	PR	US	BK	←COURTS **PAWNEE** RECORDER→	Phone	UC	RE	TX	VS
•	•		•	•	Research Information Services LLC	800-522-3884	•		•	
•	•	•			Taylor Abstract & Title Inc	620-285-2026	•	•	•	

CR	CV	PR	US	BK	←COURTS **PHILLIPS** RECORDER→	Phone	UC	RE	TX	VS
•	•		•	•	Research Information Services LLC	800-522-3884	•		•	

CR	CV	PR	US	BK	←COURTS **POTTAWATOMIE** RECORDER→	Phone	UC	RE	TX	VS
•	•				Capital Investigative Services Inc	800-633-7136				
•	•	•			David and Marvin Criqui	785-889-4659		•	•	•
	•	•			Pottawatomie County Abstract Co.	785-457-3441	•	•	•	•
•	•		•	•	Research Information Services LLC	800-522-3884	•		•	

CR	CV	PR	US	BK	←COURTS **PRATT** RECORDER→	Phone	UC	RE	TX	VS
	•	•			Centennial Abstract of Pratt	620-672-5928	•	•	•	
•	•		•	•	Research Information Services LLC	800-522-3884	•		•	

CR	CV	PR	US	BK	←COURTS **RAWLINS** RECORDER→	Phone	UC	RE	TX	VS
•	•	•			Brown, Creighton & Peckham Attorneys	785-626-3295				
•	•	•			Decatur County Abstract	785-626-3885	•	•	•	•
•	•		•	•	Research Information Services LLC	800-522-3884	•		•	

CR	CV	PR	US	BK	←COURTS **RENO** RECORDER→	Phone	UC	RE	TX	VS
•	•	•	•	•	Branda Agency [SOP]	800-310-8174	•	•	•	•
•	•	•	•	•	Kansas Investigative Services Inc [SOP]	888-889-3340	•	•	•	•
•	•		•	•	Research Information Services LLC	800-522-3884	•		•	
•	•	•			SumData	620-241-5448	•	•	•	
•	•	•	•	•	Walters Document Service [SOP]	316-682-5629	•	•	•	

CR	CV	PR	US	BK	←COURTS **REPUBLIC** RECORDER→	Phone	UC	RE	TX	VS
•	•	•			Attorney's Title Co.	785-243-1357	•	•	•	
•	•	•			Gail L Miller	785-378-3128			•	
•	•		•	•	Research Information Services LLC	800-522-3884	•		•	

CR	CV	PR	US	BK	←COURTS **RICE** RECORDER→	Phone	UC	RE	TX	VS
•	•				Capital Investigative Services Inc	800-633-7136				
•	•		•	•	Research Information Services LLC	800-522-3884	•		•	
•	•	•			SumData	620-241-5448	•	•	•	

CR	CV	PR	US	BK	←COURTS **RILEY** RECORDER→	Phone	UC	RE	TX	VS
•	•				Al Bernardi Backgrounds Process Service	785-456-8821	•	•	•	
•	•				Capital Investigative Services Inc	800-633-7136				
	•	•			Charlson & Wilson Bonded Abstractors	785-537-2900	•	•	•	
•	•	•			David and Marvin Criqui	785-889-4659		•	•	•
•	•		•	•	Research Information Services LLC	800-522-3884	•		•	

CR	CV	PR	US	BK	←COURTS **ROOKS** RECORDER→	Phone	UC	RE	TX	VS
•	•	•			Ellis County Abstract & Title Co.	785-625-2316	•	•	•	•
•	•		•	•	Research Information Services LLC	800-522-3884	•		•	

CR	CV	PR	US	BK	←COURTS **RUSH** RECORDER→	Phone	UC	RE	TX	VS
•	•	•			LaCrosse Abstract & Title LLC	800-256-6911	•	•	•	
•	•		•	•	Research Information Services LLC	800-522-3884	•		•	

CR	CV	PR	US	BK	←Courts	RUSSELL	Recorder→	UC	RE	TX	VS
•	•		•	•	Research Information Services LLC		800-522-3884	•		•	

CR	CV	PR	US	BK	←Courts	SALINE	Recorder→	UC	RE	TX	VS
	•	•			C W Lynn Abstract Co Inc		785-823-3706	•	•	•	
•	•				Capital Investigative Services Inc		800-633-7136				
•	•		•	•	Research Information Services LLC		800-522-3884	•		•	
•	•	•			SumData		620-241-5448	•	•	•	
•	•				Jacquie Willems		785-227-4775				

CR	CV	PR	US	BK	←Courts	SCOTT	Recorder→	UC	RE	TX	VS
•	•		•	•	Research Information Services LLC		800-522-3884	•		•	
	•	•	•		Scott County Abstract & Title Co Inc		620-872-3470	•	•	•	•

CR	CV	PR	US	BK	←Courts	SEDGWICK	Recorder→	UC	RE	TX	VS
•	•	•	•	•	Branda Agency [SOP]		800-310-8174	•	•	•	•
•	•	•	•	•	Kansas Investigative Services Inc [SOP]		888-889-3340	•	•	•	•
•					LLG Enterprises		816-625-0947				
•	•		•	•	Research Information Services LLC		800-522-3884	•		•	
•	•	•	•	•	Walters Document Service [SOP]		316-682-5629	•	•	•	

CR	CV	PR	US	BK	←Courts	SEWARD	Recorder→	UC	RE	TX	VS
•	•	•			American Title & Abstract Specialists Inc		620-624-9111	•	•	•	•
•	•		•	•	Research Information Services LLC		800-522-3884	•		•	

CR	CV	PR	US	BK	←Courts	SHAWNEE	Recorder→	UC	RE	TX	VS
•	•				Capital Investigative Services Inc		800-633-7136				
•	•	•	•	•	Credit Bureau of Eudora Inc (CBE) [SOP]		785-542-1771	•	•	•	•
•	•	•			David and Marvin Criqui		785-889-4659		•	•	•
•	•		•	•	Future Security Concepts		800-398-3051	•		•	
•	•	•	•	•	Hatfield Process Service [SOP]		816-842-9800	•	•	•	•
•	•	•	•	•	Heartland Document Retrieval		888-221-2778 orders only	•	•	•	•
•					LLG Enterprises		816-625-0947				
•	•		•	•	Research Information Services LLC		800-522-3884	•		•	
	•		•	•	Search Network Ltd (Kansas)		800-338-3618	•	•	•	•

CR	CV	PR	US	BK	←Courts	SHERIDAN	Recorder→	UC	RE	TX	VS
•	•	•	•		First Insurance Agency of Hoxie Inc		800-569-0198	•	•	•	
•	•		•	•	Research Information Services LLC		800-522-3884	•		•	

CR	CV	PR	US	BK	←Courts	SHERMAN	Recorder→	UC	RE	TX	VS
•	•				Northwest Kansas Abstract & Title Co Inc		785-899-5641, cell- 785-821-3748		•	•	
•	•		•	•	Research Information Services LLC		800-522-3884	•		•	
•	•				Sherman County Abstract		785-890-7507		•	•	
	•	•			Teeters Abstract & Title Co		785-890-7138	•	•	•	
•	•	•			Wilma Whitney		785-852-4932		•	•	

CR	CV	PR	US	BK	←Courts	SMITH	Recorder→	UC	RE	TX	VS
	•	•			Collier Abstracts Inc		785-282-3351	•	•	•	
•	•		•	•	Research Information Services LLC		800-522-3884	•		•	

CR	CV	PR	US	BK	←Courts	STAFFORD	Recorder→	UC	RE	TX	VS
•	•		•	•	Research Information Services LLC		800-522-3884	•		•	
	•	•			Stafford County Abstract & Title Co		620-549-3579	•	•	•	•
•	•	•			Taylor Abstract & Title Inc		620-285-2026	•	•	•	

CR	CV	PR	US	BK	←Courts	STANTON	Recorder→	UC	RE	TX	VS
•	•	•			Frazee Abstract & Title, Inc.		800-736-7832	•	•	•	•
•	•		•	•	Research Information Services LLC		800-522-3884	•		•	

CR	CV	PR	US	BK	←Courts STEVENS	Recorder→	UC	RE	TX	VS
•	•	•			American Title & Abstract Specialists Inc	620-624-9111	•	•	•	•
•	•	•			McQueen Abstract Company	620-544-2311	•	•	•	
•	•		•	•	Research Information Services LLC	800-522-3884	•		•	

CR	CV	PR	US	BK	←Courts SUMNER	Recorder→	UC	RE	TX	VS
•	•	•			Barbour Title Co	866-379-0430	•	•	•	•
•	•	•	•	•	Branda Agency [SOP]	800-310-8174	•	•	•	•
•	•		•	•	Research Information Services LLC	800-522-3884	•		•	
•	•	•	•	•	Walters Document Service [SOP]	316-682-5629	•	•	•	

CR	CV	PR	US	BK	←Courts THOMAS	Recorder→	UC	RE	TX	VS
•	•				Traci Collins	785-672-2719				
•	•	•	•		First Insurance Agency of Hoxie Inc	800-569-0198	•	•	•	
•	•		•	•	Research Information Services LLC	800-522-3884	•		•	
•	•	•			The Gordon Company of Colby	785-462-7555	•	•	•	
•	•	•			Wilma Whitney	785-852-4932		•	•	

CR	CV	PR	US	BK	←Courts TREGO	Recorder→	UC	RE	TX	VS
•	•	•			Fowler Abstract & Title Inc	785-743-6422	•	•	•	•
•	•		•	•	Research Information Services LLC	800-522-3884	•		•	

CR	CV	PR	US	BK	←Courts WABAUNSEE	Recorder→	UC	RE	TX	VS
•	•				Capital Investigative Services Inc	800-633-7136				
•	•	•			David and Marvin Criqui	785-889-4659		•	•	•
•	•		•	•	Research Information Services LLC	800-522-3884	•		•	

CR	CV	PR	US	BK	←Courts WALLACE	Recorder→	UC	RE	TX	VS
•	•				Martha's Retrieval	620-375-2251		•		
•	•				Martha Myers	620-375-2251; Fax- same			•	
•	•		•	•	Research Information Services LLC	800-522-3884	•		•	
•	•	•			Wilma Whitney	785-852-4932		•	•	

CR	CV	PR	US	BK	←Courts WASHINGTON	Recorder→	UC	RE	TX	VS
•	•	•			Attorney's Title Co	785-243-1357	•	•	•	
•	•		•	•	Research Information Services LLC	800-522-3884	•		•	

CR	CV	PR	US	BK	←Courts WICHITA	Recorder→	UC	RE	TX	VS
•	•				Martha's Retrieval	620-375-2251		•		
•	•				Martha Myers	620-375-2251; Fax- same			•	
•	•		•	•	Research Information Services LLC	800-522-3884	•		•	

CR	CV	PR	US	BK	←Courts WILSON	Recorder→	UC	RE	TX	VS
	•	•			Fink Abstract Co	620-378-2351	•	•	•	•
•	•		•	•	Research Information Services LLC	800-522-3884	•		•	
•	•	•			Street Abstract Co	620-625-2421	•	•	•	

CR	CV	PR	US	BK	←Courts WOODSON	Recorder→	UC	RE	TX	VS
•	•		•	•	Research Information Services LLC	800-522-3884	•		•	
•	•	•			Street Abstract Co	620-625-2421	•	•	•	

CR	CV	PR	US	BK	←Courts WYANDOTTE	Recorder→	UC	RE	TX	VS
•	•		•	•	Armstrong Document Retrieval	913-341-1991	•	•	•	
•	•	•			Bi-State Title Search (Div of Bi-State Ind.)	866-450-7399	•	•	•	
•	•	•	•	•	D & B Legal Services Inc [SOP]	913-963-1279	•	•	•	•
•	•		•	•	Executive Investigative Services [SOP]	800-764-9484	•	•	•	
•	•		•	•	Future Security Concepts	800-398-3051	•		•	
	•	•	•	•	Connie Giandalia	816-217-1849	•	•	•	
•	•	•	•	•	Hatfield Process Service [SOP]	816-842-9800	•	•	•	•
•	•	•	•	•	Heartland Document Retrieval	888-221-2778 orders only	•	•	•	•
•	•	•	•	•	KC Court Research Inc	913-239-8995	•	•	•	

•					LLG Enterprises	816-625-0947			
	•	•	•		M & J Abstractors	913-727-3588	•	•	•
•	•		•	•	Research Information Services LLC	800-522-3884	•		•
	•		•	•	SearchWorks Inc	913-383-0940	•	•	•

[SOP] = PERFORMS SERVICE OF PROCESS

Editor's Tip: Remember the first rule about public record searching-- Simply because your state or county has certain rules, regulations and practices regarding the accessibility and content of public records, does not mean that another state or county adheres to the same rules.

COURT RECORDS

CODE	GOVERNMENT AGENCY	TYPE OF INFORMATION
CR	Criminal Court	Municipal, county and state level criminal cases
CV	Civil Court	Municipal, county and state level civil cases
PR	Probate Court	Wills and estate cases
US	US District Court	Federal civil and criminal cases
BK	Bankruptcy Court	United States bankruptcy cases

COUNTY RECORDS - RECORDINGS

CODE	GOVERNMENT AGENCY	TYPE OF INFORMATION
UC	UCC Filing Office	Uniform Commercial Code and other personal property liens
RE	Real Estate Recording Office	Real property transactions and liens
TX	Tax Filing Office(s)	Federal and state tax liens, judgment liens
VS	Vital Records Office	Vital statistics—birth, death, marriage, divorce

Editor's Tip: At the back of this directory is a short list of search firms who are Public Record Retriever Network "Associate Members." These Associate Members utilize retrievers to obtain documents outside their local area of coverage. The Associate Members are statewide, regional, or national in scope, and are not listed in the county sections.

 = PRRN Member. *A retriever you can trust!*

Kentucky

Kentucky has 120 counties and 122 recording offices. Kenton County has two recording offices. Jefferson County has a separate office for UCC filing until June 30, 2001; that office now only handles extensions, terminations and amendments to exisiting filings and will searches for those filings.

COURT RECORDS RETRIEVED — CAPITAL - FRANKLIN COUNTY — RECORDED RECORDS RETRIEVED

CR	CV	PR	US	BK	←Courts ADAIR	Recorder→	UC	RE	TX	VS
					A & S Abstracting	270-250-1203		•	•	
					South Eastern Data	606-679-1688		•	•	

CR	CV	PR	US	BK	←Courts ALLEN	Recorder→	UC	RE	TX	VS
•	•				Hayes Inv [SOP]	270-781-7488				

CR	CV	PR	US	BK	←Courts ANDERSON	Recorder→	UC	RE	TX	VS
	•		•	•	Equisearch	859-268-1206		•	•	
	•		•	•	KY Search & Retrieval Services	859-252-6874	•	•	•	

CR	CV	PR	US	BK	←Courts BALLARD	Recorder→	UC	RE	TX	VS
•	•	•	•	•	Rebecca Bulls	731-799-3066; Fax- same				
•	•				Jonathan Duke	270-596-7509				
					Western Kentucky Title	270-898-9666		•	•	

CR	CV	PR	US	BK	←Courts BARREN	Recorder→	UC	RE	TX	VS
					Jeanetta, Conner	270-746-4465		•	•	
•	•				Hayes Inv [SOP]	270-781-7488				
	•	•			Attorney Reed Moore Jr	270-487-6262	•	•	•	

CR	CV	PR	US	BK	←Courts BATH	Recorder→	UC	RE	TX	VS
					All Search Title Co	606-474-4253		•	•	
•	•				Price One Inv	859-881-4452, cell- 859-608-5100		•		

CR	CV	PR	US	BK	←Courts BELL	Recorder→	UC	RE	TX	VS
					Vance Title Research	606-574-1912, cell- 606-273-2460		•	•	

CR	CV	PR	US	BK	←Courts BOONE	Recorder→	UC	RE	TX	VS
•	•	•	•	•	Active Detective Bureau Inc [SOP]	800-405-4006		•	•	•
•	•				Sherry Conley	859-824-6001, Fax- same				
•	•				Criminal Information Network Inc	888-923-0271				
•	•	•	•	•	DDI Inc [SOP]	866-954-3000	•	•	•	•
•				•	Document Retrieval Network Inc	859-654-2890	•	•	•	
					FarVision Consulting Title Co	304-733-5086		•	•	
•	•	•	•	•	General Corporate Investigations - GCI [SOP]	800-735-7992	•	•	•	•
•					Phoenix Research Inc	800-260-1092				
	•	•			Real Land Abstract Inc	859-291-1140	•	•	•	
•	•		•	•	Search International Inc	859-342-0456	•	•	•	
•	•		•		Xpedite Wholesale Criminal Research	800-325-3609				

CR	CV	PR	US	BK	←Courts BOURBON	Recorder→	UC	RE	TX	VS
	•		•	•	Equisearch	859-268-1206	•	•	•	
	•		•	•	KY Search & Retrieval Services	859-252-6874	•	•	•	
•	•				Price One Inv	859-881-4452, cell- 859-608-5100		•		

CR	CV	PR	US	BK	←Courts BOYD	Recorder→	UC	RE	TX	VS
					All Search Title Co	606-474-4253		•	•	
•	•	•	•		Daniel Agency	606-324-6029	•	•	•	•

CR	CV	PR	US	BK	←Courts		UC	RE	TX	VS
•	•	•	•	•	McBrayer McGinnis Leslie & Kirkland	606-473-7303	•	•	•	•
•	•				Search 4 U	606-739-5050			•	

CR	CV	PR	US	BK	←Courts BOYLE	Recorder→	UC	RE	TX	VS
					Adams Freelance Title	606-365-8108		•	•	
	•		•	•	Equisearch	859-268-1206	•	•	•	
	•		•	•	KY Search & Retrieval Services	859-252-6874	•	•	•	

CR	CV	PR	US	BK	←Courts BRACKEN	Recorder→	UC	RE	TX	VS
					FarVision Consulting Title Co	304-733-5086		•	•	
•	•				Price One Inv	859-881-4452, cell- 859-608-5100		•		

CR	CV	PR	US	BK	←Courts BREATHITT	Recorder→	UC	RE	TX	VS
					Irene Friend	606-464-2638	•	•	•	

CR	CV	PR	US	BK	←Courts BRECKENRIDGE	Recorder→	UC	RE	TX	VS
		•			Jerry Guffey	270-259-4828	•	•	•	•

CR	CV	PR	US	BK	←Courts BULLITT	Recorder→	UC	RE	TX	VS
				•	Accurate Abstracting Services LLC	502-585-4017	•	•	•	
•	•	•	•	•	Attorney Services of Kentucky [SOP]	502-327-6677	•	•	•	•
•	•				Tracy A Gabehart, Paralegal	502-957-6459				
	•		•		KY Data Search Inc	502-637-4658	•	•	•	
•	•				Xpress Research	812-923-7202; cell- 812-207-4284				

CR	CV	PR	US	BK	←Courts BUTLER	Recorder→	UC	RE	TX	VS
		•			Jerry Guffey	270-259-4828	•	•	•	•
•	•				Hayes Inv [SOP]	270-781-7488				

CR	CV	PR	US	BK	←Courts CALDWELL	Recorder→	UC	RE	TX	VS
		•			William R Young Law Office Inc	270-388-0807		•	•	

CR	CV	PR	US	BK	←Courts CALLOWAY	Recorder→	UC	RE	TX	VS
•	•	•	•	•	Rebecca Bulls	731-799-3066; Fax- same				
					Western Kentucky Title	270-898-9666		•	•	

CR	CV	PR	US	BK	←Courts CAMPBELL	Recorder→	UC	RE	TX	VS
•	•	•	•	•	Active Detective Bureau Inc [SOP]	800-405-4006		•	•	•
•	•				Sherry Conley	859-824-6001, Fax- same				
•	•				Criminal Information Network Inc	888-923-0271				
•	•	•	•	•	DDI Inc [SOP]	866-954-3000	•	•	•	•
•				•	Document Retrieval Network Inc	859-654-2890	•	•	•	
•	•	•	•	•	General Corporate Investigations - GCI [SOP]	800-735-7992	•	•	•	•
•					Phoenix Research Inc	800-260-1092				
	•	•			Real Land Abstract Inc	859-291-1140	•	•	•	
•	•		•	•	Search International Inc	859-342-0456	•	•	•	
•	•		•		Xpedite Wholesale Criminal Research	800-325-3609				

CR	CV	PR	US	BK	←Courts CARLISLE	Recorder→	UC	RE	TX	VS
•	•	•	•	•	Rebecca Bulls	731-799-3066; Fax- same				
					Dawn Curran Letcher	859-289-3745		•	•	
					Western Kentucky Title	270-898-9666		•	•	

CR	CV	PR	US	BK	←Courts CARROLL	Recorder→	UC	RE	TX	VS

See adjoining counties for retrievers or call court/recorder directly.

CR	CV	PR	US	BK	←Courts CARTER	Recorder→	UC	RE	TX	VS
					All Search Title Co	606-474-4253		•	•	
•	•	•	•		Daniel Agency	606-324-6029	•	•	•	•
•	•	•	•	•	McBrayer McGinnis Leslie & Kirkland	606-473-7303	•	•	•	•

CR	CV	PR	US	BK	←Courts CASEY	Recorder→	UC	RE	TX	VS
					South Eastern Data	606-679-1688		•	•	

CR	CV	PR	US	BK	←Courts	CHRISTIAN	Recorder→	UC	RE	TX	VS
•	•				The Paper Chase - KY		270-886-0367; Fax-same				

CR	CV	PR	US	BK	←Courts	CLARK	Recorder→	UC	RE	TX	VS
				•	Accurate Abstracting Services LLC		502-585-4017	•	•	•	
	•		•	•	Equisearch		859-268-1206	•	•	•	
	•		•	•	KY Search & Retrieval Services		859-252-6874	•	•	•	

CR	CV	PR	US	BK	←Courts	CLAY	Recorder→	UC	RE	TX	VS
					South Eastern Data		606-679-1688		•	•	
					Vance Title Research		606-574-1912, cell- 606-273-2460	•	•	•	

CR	CV	PR	US	BK	←Courts	CLINTON	Recorder→	UC	RE	TX	VS
•	•				David Cross		606-387-6638		•	•	
					South Eastern Data		606-679-1688		•	•	

CR	CV	PR	US	BK	←Courts	CRITTENDEN	Recorder→	UC	RE	TX	VS
•	•	•			Undercover LLC		270-784-2070		•	•	
		•			William R Young Law Office Inc		270-388-0807		•	•	
	•				Jerry Wright		270-965-2721				

CR	CV	PR	US	BK	←Courts	CUMBERLAND	Recorder→	UC	RE	TX	VS
					Judd Law Office		270-864-3144		•	•	

CR	CV	PR	US	BK	←Courts	DAVIESS	Recorder→	UC	RE	TX	VS
	•	•			Attorney John O Hicks III		270-273-5749	•	•	•	
•	•	•	•		Lindsey and Suyak Investigations LLC [SOP]		270-281-0213	•	•	•	
•	•	•	•	•	Summit Documents		270-281-5406	•	•	•	•

CR	CV	PR	US	BK	←Courts	EDMONSON	Recorder→	UC	RE	TX	VS
		•			Jerry Guffey		270-259-4828	•	•	•	•
•	•				Hayes Inv [SOP]		270-781-7488				

CR	CV	PR	US	BK	←Courts	ELLIOTT	Recorder→	UC	RE	TX	VS
					All Search Title Co		606-474-4253		•	•	
•	•	•	•		Daniel Agency		606-324-6029	•	•	•	•

CR	CV	PR	US	BK	←Courts	ESTILL	Recorder→	UC	RE	TX	VS
					Irene Friend		606-464-2638	•	•	•	

CR	CV	PR	US	BK	←Courts	FAYETTE	Recorder→	UC	RE	TX	VS
•	•	•	•	•	Attorney Services of Kentucky [SOP]		502-327-6677	•	•	•	•
•	•				Sherry Conley		859-824-6001, Fax- same				
•				•	Document Retrieval Network Inc		859-654-2890	•	•	•	
	•		•	•	Equisearch		859-268-1206	•	•	•	
	•		•	•	KY Search & Retrieval Services		859-252-6874	•	•	•	
•	•	•	•	•	McBrayer McGinnis Leslie & Kirkland		606-473-7303	•	•	•	•
•	•				Price One Inv		859-881-4452, cell- 859-608-5100		•		
•	•				VeriCorp Inc		502-413-5313				
•	•				Xpress Research		812-923-7202; cell- 812-207-4284				

CR	CV	PR	US	BK	←Courts	FLEMING	Recorder→	UC	RE	TX	VS
					All Search Title Co		606-474-4253		•	•	
	•		•	•	KY Search & Retrieval Services		859-252-6874	•	•	•	
•	•				Price One Inv		859-881-4452, cell- 859-608-5100		•		

CR	CV	PR	US	BK	←Courts	FLOYD	Recorder→	UC	RE	TX	VS
					All Search Title Co		606-474-4253		•	•	
•	•	•	•		Daniel Agency		606-324-6029	•	•	•	•

CR	CV	PR	US	BK	←Courts	FRANKLIN	Recorder→	UC	RE	TX	VS
•	•	•	•	•	Attorney Services of Kentucky [SOP]		502-327-6677	•	•	•	•
	•		•	•	Equisearch		859-268-1206	•	•	•	

CR	CV	PR	US	BK	←Courts		UC	RE	TX	VS
	•		•		KY Data Search Inc	502-637-4658	•	•	•	
	•		•	•	KY Search & Retrieval Services	859-252-6874	•	•	•	
•	•	•	•	•	McBrayer McGinnis Leslie & Kirkland	606-473-7303	•	•	•	•
•	•	•	•	•	National Service Information Inc (Ohio)	800-235-0337	•		•	•

CR	CV	PR	US	BK	←Courts	**Fulton** Recorder→	UC	RE	TX	VS
	•	•	•	•	Susan Parker	731-884-9994	•	•	•	

CR	CV	PR	US	BK	←Courts	**Gallatin** Recorder→	UC	RE	TX	VS
		•			Huddleston & Huddleston Law Firm	859-567-2818	•	•	•	

CR	CV	PR	US	BK	←Courts	**Garrard** Recorder→	UC	RE	TX	VS
					Adams Freelance Title	606-365-8108		•	•	
	•		•	•	Equisearch	859-268-1206	•	•	•	
	•		•	•	KY Search & Retrieval Services	859-252-6874	•	•	•	
					South Eastern Data	606-679-1688		•	•	

CR	CV	PR	US	BK	←Courts	**Grant** Recorder→	UC	RE	TX	VS
•	•				Sherry Conley	859-824-6001, Fax- same				
•				•	Document Retrieval Network Inc	859-654-2890	•	•	•	
•				•	Search International Inc	859-342-0456	•	•	•	

CR	CV	PR	US	BK	←Courts	**Graves** Recorder→	UC	RE	TX	VS
•	•	•	•	•	Rebecca Bulls	731-799-3066; Fax- same				
					Western Kentucky Title	270-898-9666		•	•	

CR	CV	PR	US	BK	←Courts	**Grayson** Recorder→	UC	RE	TX	VS
		•			Jerry Guffey	270-259-4828	•	•	•	•

CR	CV	PR	US	BK	←Courts	**Green** Recorder→	UC	RE	TX	VS
					See adjoining counties for retrievers or call court/recorder directly.					

CR	CV	PR	US	BK	←Courts	**Greenup** Recorder→	UC	RE	TX	VS
					All Search Title Co	606-474-4253		•	•	
•	•	•	•		Daniel Agency	606-324-6029	•	•	•	•
•	•	•	•	•	McBrayer McGinnis Leslie & Kirkland	606-473-7303	•	•	•	•

CR	CV	PR	US	BK	←Courts	**Hancock** Recorder→	UC	RE	TX	VS
•	•	•	•		Lindsey and Suyak Investigations LLC [SOP]	270-281-0213	•	•	•	
•	•	•	•	•	Summit Documents	270-281-5406	•	•	•	•

CR	CV	PR	US	BK	←Courts	**Hardin** Recorder→	UC	RE	TX	VS
•	•	•	•	•	Attorney Services of Kentucky [SOP]	502-327-6677	•	•	•	•
•	•				Tracy A Gabehart, Paralegal	502-957-6459				
		•			Jerry Guffey	270-259-4828	•	•	•	•
	•		•		KY Data Search Inc	502-637-4658	•	•	•	
	•	•			Lincoln Trail Title Services Inc	270-765-5566	•	•	•	
•	•				Xpress Research	812-923-7202; cell- 812-207-4284				

CR	CV	PR	US	BK	←Courts	**Harlan** Recorder→	UC	RE	TX	VS
					Vance Title Research	606-574-1912, cell- 606-273-2460	•	•	•	

CR	CV	PR	US	BK	←Courts	**Harrison** Recorder→	UC	RE	TX	VS
•				•	Document Retrieval Network Inc	859-654-2890	•	•	•	
	•	•			Hood & Whalen	859-234-4321; Fax- same	•	•	•	•
	•		•	•	KY Search & Retrieval Services	859-252-6874	•	•	•	
•	•				Price One Inv	859-881-4452, cell- 859-608-5100		•		

CR	CV	PR	US	BK	←Courts	**Hart** Recorder→	UC	RE	TX	VS
		•			Jerry Guffey	270-259-4828	•	•	•	•

CR	CV	PR	US	BK	←Courts	**Henderson** Recorder→	UC	RE	TX	VS
•	•	•	•	•	BBI LLC	812-985-0832; cell- 812-774-7500	•	•	•	•

CR	CV	PR	US	BK	Retriever	Phone	UC	RE	TX	VS
•	•		•	•	D.G.I. LLC [SOP]	812-853-3222	•	•	•	•
•	•	•			Randy Fish	270-822-4412; cell- 270-952-0731				
•	•	•			Susan Hicks	270-724-2093				
•	•	•	•	•	Summit Documents	270-281-5406	•	•	•	•
•	•				West Star Inv	270-826-4030, cell- 270-869-4071				

CR	CV	PR	US	BK	←Courts HENRY	Recorder→	UC	RE	TX	VS
	•		•		KY Data Search Inc	502-637-4658	•	•	•	
•	•				Xpress Research	812-923-7202; cell- 812-207-4284				

CR	CV	PR	US	BK	←Courts HICKMAN	Recorder→	UC	RE	TX	VS
•	•	•	•	•	Rebecca Bulls	731-799-3066; Fax- same				
	•	•	•	•	Susan Parker	731-884-9994	•	•	•	

CR	CV	PR	US	BK	←Courts HOPKINS	Recorder→	UC	RE	TX	VS
•	•				West Star Inv	270-826-4030, cell- 270-869-4071				

CR	CV	PR	US	BK	←Courts JACKSON	Recorder→	UC	RE	TX	VS
					Tommy Hayes	606-287-8891		•		
					South Eastern Data	606-679-1688		•	•	

CR	CV	PR	US	BK	←Courts JEFFERSON	Recorder→	UC	RE	TX	VS
				•	Accurate Abstracting Services LLC	502-585-4017	•	•	•	
•	•	•	•	•	Attorney Services of Kentucky [SOP]	502-327-6677	•	•	•	•
•				•	Document Retrieval Network Inc	859-654-2890	•	•	•	
•	•				Tracy A Gabehart, Paralegal	502-957-6459				
•	•	•	•	•	Rick Hessig [SOP]	502-583-2453	•		•	•
	•		•		KY Data Search Inc	502-637-4658	•	•	•	
•	•				VeriCorp Inc	502-413-5313				
•	•				Xpress Research	812-923-7202; cell- 812-207-4284				

CR	CV	PR	US	BK	←Courts JESSAMINE	Recorder→	UC	RE	TX	VS
	•		•	•	Equisearch	859-268-1206	•	•	•	
	•		•	•	KY Search & Retrieval Services	859-252-6874	•	•	•	
•	•				Price One Inv	859-881-4452, cell- 859-608-5100		•		

CR	CV	PR	US	BK	←Courts JOHNSON	Recorder→	UC	RE	TX	VS
					All Search Title Co	606-474-4253		•	•	
•	•	•	•		Daniel Agency	606-324-6029	•	•	•	•

CR	CV	PR	US	BK	←Courts KENTON	Recorder→	UC	RE	TX	VS
•	•	•	•	•	Active Detective Bureau Inc [SOP]	800-405-4006		•	•	•
•	•	•	•	•	Attorney Services of Kentucky [SOP]	502-327-6677	•	•	•	•
•	•				Sherry Conley	859-824-6001, Fax- same				
•	•				Criminal Information Network Inc	888-923-0271				
•	•	•	•	•	DDI Inc [SOP]	866-954-3000	•	•	•	•
•				•	Document Retrieval Network Inc	859-654-2890	•	•	•	
•	•	•	•	•	General Corporate Investigations - GCI [SOP]	800-735-7992	•	•	•	•
•					Phoenix Research Inc	800-260-1092				
	•	•			Real Land Abstract Inc	859-291-1140	•	•	•	
•	•		•	•	Search International Inc	859-342-0456	•	•	•	
•	•		•		Xpedite Wholesale Criminal Research	800-325-3609				

CR	CV	PR	US	BK	←Courts KNOTT	Recorder→	UC	RE	TX	VS
					Vance Title Research	606-574-1912, cell- 606-273-2460	•	•	•	

CR	CV	PR	US	BK	←Courts KNOX	Recorder→	UC	RE	TX	VS
					William Patrick Hauser	606-546-3811		•	•	
					South Eastern Data	606-679-1688		•	•	
					Vance Title Research	606-574-1912, cell- 606-273-2460	•	•	•	

CR	CV	PR	US	BK	←Courts	**Larue**	Recorder→	UC	RE	TX	VS
					Lincoln Trail Title		270-765-5566		●	●	
●	●				Xpress Research		812-923-7202; cell- 812-207-4284				

CR	CV	PR	US	BK	←Courts	**Laurel**	Recorder→	UC	RE	TX	VS
					South Eastern Data		606-679-1688		●	●	
					Vance Title Research		606-574-1912, cell- 606-273-2460	●	●	●	

CR	CV	PR	US	BK	←Courts	**Lawrence**	Recorder→	UC	RE	TX	VS
					All Search Title Co		606-474-4253		●	●	
●	●	●	●		Daniel Agency		606-324-6029	●	●	●	●
●	●	●	●	●	McBrayer McGinnis Leslie & Kirkland		606-473-7303	●	●	●	●

CR	CV	PR	US	BK	←Courts	**Lee**	Recorder→	UC	RE	TX	VS
					Irene Friend		606-464-2638	●	●	●	

CR	CV	PR	US	BK	←Courts	**Leslie**	Recorder→	UC	RE	TX	VS
●	●	●			Attorney Leonard Brashear		606-672-3577	●	●	●	
					Vance Title Research		606-574-1912, cell- 606-273-2460	●	●	●	

CR	CV	PR	US	BK	←Courts	**Letcher**	Recorder→	UC	RE	TX	VS
					Vance Title Research		606-574-1912, cell- 606-273-2460	●	●	●	

CR	CV	PR	US	BK	←Courts	**Lewis**	Recorder→	UC	RE	TX	VS
					All Search Title Co		606-474-4253		●	●	
●	●	●	●	●	McBrayer McGinnis Leslie & Kirkland		606-473-7303	●	●	●	●

CR	CV	PR	US	BK	←Courts	**Lincoln**	Recorder→	UC	RE	TX	VS
					Adams Freelance Title		606-365-8108		●	●	
	●		●	●	Equisearch		859-268-1206	●	●	●	
	●		●	●	KY Search & Retrieval Services		859-252-6874	●	●	●	
					South Eastern Data		606-679-1688		●	●	

CR	CV	PR	US	BK	←Courts	**Livingston**	Recorder→	UC	RE	TX	VS
					Richard Peek Jr Attny		270-928-4523		●	●	
		●			William R Young Law Office Inc		270-388-0807		●	●	

CR	CV	PR	US	BK	←Courts	**Logan**	Recorder→	UC	RE	TX	VS
●					Diane Crawley		270-847-0177				
●	●				Hayes Inv [SOP]		270-781-7488				

CR	CV	PR	US	BK	←Courts	**Lyon**	Recorder→	UC	RE	TX	VS
		●			William R Young Law Office Inc		270-388-0807		●	●	

CR	CV	PR	US	BK	←Courts	**Madison**	Recorder→	UC	RE	TX	VS
	●		●	●	Equisearch		859-268-1206	●	●	●	
	●		●	●	KY Search & Retrieval Services		859-252-6874	●	●	●	
					South Eastern Data		606-679-1688		●	●	

CR	CV	PR	US	BK	←Courts	**Magoffin**	Recorder→	UC	RE	TX	VS
					See adjoining counties for retrievers or call court/recorder directly.						

CR	CV	PR	US	BK	←Courts	**Marion**	Recorder→	UC	RE	TX	VS
	●	●			Avritt & Avritt		270-692-4270	●	●	●	●

CR	CV	PR	US	BK	←Courts	**Marshall**	Recorder→	UC	RE	TX	VS
●	●	●	●	●	Rebecca Bulls		731-799-3066; Fax- same				
					Western Kentucky Title		270-898-9666		●	●	
		●			William R Young Law Office Inc		270-388-0807		●	●	

CR	CV	PR	US	BK	←Courts	**Martin**	Recorder→	UC	RE	TX	VS
					All Search Title Co		606-474-4253		●	●	
●	●	●	●		Daniel Agency		606-324-6029	●	●	●	●

CR	CV	PR	US	BK	←COURTS MASON	RECORDER→	UC	RE	TX	VS
					All Search Title Co	606-474-4253		•	•	

CR	CV	PR	US	BK	←COURTS MC CRACKEN	RECORDER→	UC	RE	TX	VS
•	•	•	•	•	Rebecca Bulls	731-799-3066; Fax- same				
•	•				Jonathan Duke	270-596-7509				
					Western Kentucky Title	270-898-9666		•	•	

CR	CV	PR	US	BK	←COURTS MC CREARY	RECORDER→	UC	RE	TX	VS
					Vickie King Paralegal	606-376-5931		•		
					South Eastern Data	606-679-1688		•	•	

CR	CV	PR	US	BK	←COURTS MC LEAN	RECORDER→	UC	RE	TX	VS
	•	•			Attorney John O Hicks III	270-273-5749	•	•	•	

CR	CV	PR	US	BK	←COURTS MEADE	RECORDER→	UC	RE	TX	VS
•	•	•	•	•	Attorney Services of Kentucky [SOP]	502-327-6677	•	•	•	•
	•		•		KY Data Search Inc	502-637-4658	•	•	•	

CR	CV	PR	US	BK	←COURTS MENIFEE	RECORDER→	UC	RE	TX	VS
					All Search Title Co	606-474-4253		•	•	

CR	CV	PR	US	BK	←COURTS MERCER	RECORDER→	UC	RE	TX	VS
	•		•	•	Equisearch	859-268-1206	•	•	•	
	•		•	•	KY Search & Retrieval Services	859-252-6874	•	•	•	

CR	CV	PR	US	BK	←COURTS METCALFE	RECORDER→	UC	RE	TX	VS
					Jeanetta, Conner	270-746-4465		•	•	

CR	CV	PR	US	BK	←COURTS MONROE	RECORDER→	UC	RE	TX	VS
	•	•			Attorney Reed Moore Jr	270-487-6262	•	•	•	

CR	CV	PR	US	BK	←COURTS MONTGOMERY	RECORDER→	UC	RE	TX	VS
					All Search Title Co	606-474-4253		•	•	
	•		•	•	Equisearch	859-268-1206	•	•	•	
	•		•	•	KY Search & Retrieval Services	859-252-6874	•	•	•	

CR	CV	PR	US	BK	←COURTS MORGAN	RECORDER→	UC	RE	TX	VS
					All Search Title Co	606-474-4253		•	•	
•	•	•	•		Daniel Agency	606-324-6029	•	•	•	•

CR	CV	PR	US	BK	←COURTS MUHLENBERG	RECORDER→	UC	RE	TX	VS
	•	•			Attorney John O Hicks III	270-273-5749	•	•	•	

CR	CV	PR	US	BK	←COURTS NELSON	RECORDER→	UC	RE	TX	VS
				•	Accurate Abstracting Services LLC	502-585-4017	•	•	•	
•	•	•	•	•	Attorney Services of Kentucky [SOP]	502-327-6677	•	•	•	•
•	•				Tracy A Gabehart, Paralegal	502-957-6459				
	•		•		KY Data Search Inc	502-637-4658	•	•	•	
•	•				Xpress Research	812-923-7202; cell- 812-207-4284				

CR	CV	PR	US	BK	←COURTS NICHOLAS	RECORDER→	UC	RE	TX	VS
•	•				Price One Inv	859-881-4452, cell- 859-608-5100				

CR	CV	PR	US	BK	←COURTS OHIO	RECORDER→	UC	RE	TX	VS
		•			Jerry Guffey	270-259-4828	•	•	•	•
•	•	•	•		Lindsey and Suyak Investigations LLC [SOP]	270-281-0213	•	•	•	
•	•	•	•	•	Summit Documents	270-281-5406	•	•	•	•

CR	CV	PR	US	BK	←COURTS OLDHAM	RECORDER→	UC	RE	TX	VS
				•	Accurate Abstracting Services LLC	502-585-4017	•	•	•	
•	•	•	•	•	Attorney Services of Kentucky [SOP]	502-327-6677	•	•	•	•
	•		•		KY Data Search Inc	502-637-4658	•	•	•	

CR	CV	PR	US	BK	←Courts		UC	RE	TX	VS
•	•				VeriCorp Inc	502-413-5313				
•	•				Xpress Research	812-923-7202; cell- 812-207-4284				

CR	CV	PR	US	BK	←Courts **OWEN**	Recorder→	UC	RE	TX	VS
•	•				Sherry Conley	859-824-6001, Fax- same				

CR	CV	PR	US	BK	←Courts **OWSLEY**	Recorder→	UC	RE	TX	VS
					Irene Friend	606-464-2638	•	•	•	

CR	CV	PR	US	BK	←Courts **PENDLETON**	Recorder→	UC	RE	TX	VS
•				•	Document Retrieval Network Inc	859-654-2890	•	•	•	
•	•		•	•	Search International Inc	859-342-0456	•	•	•	
•	•				Sherry Conley	859-824-6001, Fax- same				

CR	CV	PR	US	BK	←Courts **PERRY**	Recorder→	UC	RE	TX	VS
					Vance Title Research	606-574-1912, cell- 606-273-2460	•	•	•	

CR	CV	PR	US	BK	←Courts **PIKE**	Recorder→	UC	RE	TX	VS
•	•	•	•		Daniel Agency	606-324-6029	•	•	•	•

CR	CV	PR	US	BK	←Courts **POWELL**	Recorder→	UC	RE	TX	VS
					Irene Friend	606-464-2638	•	•	•	
•	•	•			Melinda Nolan	606-663-4141	•	•	•	

CR	CV	PR	US	BK	←Courts **PULASKI**	Recorder→	UC	RE	TX	VS
					South Eastern Data	606-679-1688		•	•	

CR	CV	PR	US	BK	←Courts **ROBERTSON**	Recorder→	UC	RE	TX	VS
					Jesse Melcher, Attny	606-724-5322		•	•	

CR	CV	PR	US	BK	←Courts **ROCKCASTLE**	Recorder→	UC	RE	TX	VS
					Adams Freelance Title	606-365-8108		•	•	
					South Eastern Data	606-679-1688		•	•	

CR	CV	PR	US	BK	←Courts **ROWAN**	Recorder→	UC	RE	TX	VS
					All Search Title Co	606-474-4253		•	•	
•	•	•	•		Daniel Agency	606-324-6029	•	•	•	•

CR	CV	PR	US	BK	←Courts **RUSSELL**	Recorder→	UC	RE	TX	VS
					Courtesy Title	270-343-4486		•	•	
					South Eastern Data	606-679-1688		•	•	

CR	CV	PR	US	BK	←Courts **SCOTT**	Recorder→	UC	RE	TX	VS
•	•				Sherry Conley	859-824-6001, Fax- same				
	•		•	•	Equisearch	859-268-1206	•	•	•	
	•		•	•	KY Search & Retrieval Services	859-252-6874	•	•	•	

CR	CV	PR	US	BK	←Courts **SHELBY**	Recorder→	UC	RE	TX	VS
•	•	•	•	•	Attorney Services of Kentucky [SOP]	502-327-6677	•	•	•	•
	•		•		KY Data Search Inc	502-637-4658	•	•	•	
•	•				VeriCorp Inc	502-413-5313				
•	•				Xpress Research	812-923-7202; cell- 812-207-4284				

CR	CV	PR	US	BK	←Courts **SIMPSON**	Recorder→	UC	RE	TX	VS
•	•				Hayes Inv [SOP]	270-781-7488				

CR	CV	PR	US	BK	←Courts **SPENCER**	Recorder→	UC	RE	TX	VS
				•	Accurate Abstracting Services LLC	502-585-4017	•	•	•	
	•		•		KY Data Search Inc	502-637-4658	•	•	•	
•	•				Xpress Research	812-923-7202; cell- 812-207-4284				

CR	CV	PR	US	BK	←Courts **TAYLOR**	Recorder→	UC	RE	TX	VS
					Cumberland Title	606-787-8743		•	•	

Todd

See adjoining counties for retrievers or call court/recorder directly.

Trigg

CR	CV	PR	US	BK	Courts / Recorder	Phone	UC	RE	TX	VS
					Quinn and Woodall Attnys	270-522-3481		•	•	
		•			William R Young Law Office Inc	270-388-0807		•	•	

Trimble

CR	CV	PR	US	BK	Courts / Recorder	Phone	UC	RE	TX	VS
•	•				Xpress Research	812-923-7202; cell- 812-207-4284				

Union

CR	CV	PR	US	BK	Courts / Recorder	Phone	UC	RE	TX	VS
•	•	•			Randy Fish	270-822-4412; cell- 270-952-0731				
•					Phoenix Research Inc	800-260-1092				

Warren

CR	CV	PR	US	BK	Courts / Recorder	Phone	UC	RE	TX	VS
					Jeanetta, Conner	270-746-4465		•	•	
•	•				Hayes Inv [SOP]	270-781-7488				
•	•	•			Undercover LLC	270-784-2070		•	•	

Washington

CR	CV	PR	US	BK	Courts / Recorder	Phone	UC	RE	TX	VS
					Theresa Marrinan	859-336-5425		•	•	

Wayne

CR	CV	PR	US	BK	Courts / Recorder	Phone	UC	RE	TX	VS
					Terry Kirkland	606-348-8645				
					South Eastern Data	606-679-1688		•	•	

Webster

CR	CV	PR	US	BK	Courts / Recorder	Phone	UC	RE	TX	VS
•	•	•	•	•	Summit Documents	270-281-5406	•	•	•	•
•	•				West Star Inv	270-826-4030, cell- 270-869-4071				

Whitley

CR	CV	PR	US	BK	Courts / Recorder	Phone	UC	RE	TX	VS
					South Eastern Data	606-679-1688		•	•	
					Vance Title Research	606-574-1912, cell- 606-273-2460	•	•	•	

Wolfe

CR	CV	PR	US	BK	Courts / Recorder	Phone	UC	RE	TX	VS
					Irene Friend	606-464-2638	•	•	•	

Woodford

CR	CV	PR	US	BK	Courts / Recorder	Phone	UC	RE	TX	VS
	•		•	•	Equisearch	859-268-1206	•	•	•	
	•		•	•	KY Search & Retrieval Services	859-252-6874	•	•	•	

Editor's Tip: Sending an unsolicited fax is not recommended, and it is not legal. So, before faxing to a potential new retriever contact, we recommend that you first make a courtesy call, and ask for permission to fax to them.

Louisiana

COURT RECORDS RETRIEVED — CAPITAL - EAST BATON ROUGE PARISH — RECORDED RECORDS RETRIEVED

CR	CV	PR	US	BK	←Courts **Acadia**	Recorder→	UC	RE	TX	VS
•	•	•	•	•	ABC Investigators Inc [SOP]	800-738-7300	•	•	•	
•	•		•	•	Bayou Investigations Inc [SOP]	800-256-9009	•			
•	•	•	•	•	Sittig Services [SOP]	337-580-3334				
•	•	•	•	•	TENSTAR Corporation (Crowley) [SOP]	800-960-2214	•	•	•	•

CR	CV	PR	US	BK	←Courts **Allen**	Recorder→	UC	RE	TX	VS
•	•	•	•	•	Abstracting & Legal Research Inc	318-473-9979	•	•	•	•
•	•	•	•	•	TENSTAR Corporation (Main Office) [SOP]	800-960-2214	•	•	•	•

CR	CV	PR	US	BK	←Courts **Ascension**	Recorder→	UC	RE	TX	VS
	•	•	•	•	Abstracts by Godail	800-660-7318	•	•	•	
	•	•			Ascension Title Services Inc	225-647-8051	•	•	•	
•	•	•	•	•	Bombet Cashio & Associates [SOP]	800-256-5333	•	•	•	•
•	•	•			Faith to Faith Legal Productions LLC	225-751-9202	•	•	•	
•	•		•	•	Global Investigative & Legal Service [SOP]	888-644-2066				
•	•		•	•	P & A Research Service [SOP]	225-279-2118	•	•	•	
•	•	•	•	•	TENSTAR Corporation (Baton Rouge) [SOP]	800-864-5154	•	•	•	•

CR	CV	PR	US	BK	←Courts **Assumption**	Recorder→	UC	RE	TX	VS
	•	•	•	•	Abstracts by Godail	800-660-7318	•	•	•	
•	•	•			Faith to Faith Legal Productions LLC	225-751-9202	•	•	•	
•	•		•	•	Global Investigative & Legal Service [SOP]	888-644-2066				
•	•	•	•	•	TENSTAR Corporation (New Orleans) [SOP]	800-864-5154	•	•	•	•

CR	CV	PR	US	BK	←Courts **Avoyelles**	Recorder→	UC	RE	TX	VS
•	•	•	•	•	Abstracting & Legal Research Inc	318-473-9979	•	•	•	•
•	•		•	•	Global Investigative & Legal Service [SOP]	888-644-2066				
•	•	•	•	•	TENSTAR Corporation (Baton Rouge) [SOP]	800-864-5154	•	•	•	•

CR	CV	PR	US	BK	←Courts **Beauregard**	Recorder→	UC	RE	TX	VS
		•			Beauregard Abstract Co	337-463-7090	•	•	•	
•	•		•	•	Global Investigative & Legal Service [SOP]	888-644-2066				
•	•	•	•	•	TENSTAR Corporation (Main Office) [SOP]	800-960-2214	•	•	•	•
•	•	•	•	•	Wise Land & Abstract Co Inc	337-436-3419	•	•	•	•

CR	CV	PR	US	BK	←Courts **Bienville**	Recorder→	UC	RE	TX	VS
	•	•	•	•	Access Louisiana Inc	800-489-5620	•	•	•	•
	•	•			M & M Title / Mitchell Co	318-798-1198	•	•	•	
•	•	•	•	•	TENSTAR Corporation (Shreveport) [SOP]	800-960-2214	•	•	•	•

CR	CV	PR	US	BK	←Courts **Bossier**	Recorder→	UC	RE	TX	VS
	•	•	•	•	Access Louisiana Inc	800-489-5620	•	•	•	•
•	•	•	•	•	All The Facts [SOP]	866-401-5676	•	•	•	•
•	•	•	•	•	Bombet Cashio & Associates [SOP]	800-256-5333	•	•	•	•
•	•	•	•	•	Bradley Enterprises LLC	318-868-4906	•	•	•	
•	•				J & J Research	318-752-8320				
	•	•			M & M Title / Mitchell Co	318-798-1198	•	•	•	
•	•	•	•	•	Southern Research Company	888-772-6952	•	•	•	
•	•	•	•	•	TENSTAR Corporation (Shreveport) [SOP]	800-960-2214	•	•	•	•

CR	CV	PR	US	BK	←Courts	Caddo	Recorder→	UC	RE	TX	VS
	•	•	•	•	Access Louisiana Inc		800-489-5620	•	•	•	•
•	•	•	•	•	All The Facts [SOP]		866-401-5676	•	•	•	•
•	•	•	•	•	Bombet Cashio & Associates [SOP]		800-256-5333	•	•	•	•
•	•	•	•	•	Bradley Enterprises LLC		318-868-4906	•	•	•	
•	•				J & J Research		318-752-8320				
	•	•			M & M Title / Mitchell Co		318-798-1198	•	•	•	
•	•	•	•	•	Southern Research Company		888-772-6952	•	•	•	
•	•	•	•	•	TENSTAR Corporation (Shreveport) [SOP]		800-960-2214	•	•	•	•

CR	CV	PR	US	BK	←Courts	Calcasieu	Recorder→	UC	RE	TX	VS
•					Donna Eccles		337-558-6627				
•					Infopoint Research		888-457-0501, 409-729-1944				
•	•	•	•	•	Tactical Private Inv [SOP]		800-779-4893	•	•	•	•
•	•	•	•	•	TENSTAR Corporation (Main Office) [SOP]		800-960-2214	•	•	•	•
•	•	•	•	•	Wise Land & Abstract Co Inc		337-436-3419	•		•	•

CR	CV	PR	US	BK	←Courts	Caldwell	Recorder→	UC	RE	TX	VS
•	•	•	•	•	TENSTAR Corporation (Main Office) [SOP]		800-960-2214	•	•	•	•

CR	CV	PR	US	BK	←Courts	Cameron	Recorder→	UC	RE	TX	VS
•	•	•	•	•	TENSTAR Corporation (Main Office) [SOP]		800-960-2214	•	•	•	•

CR	CV	PR	US	BK	←Courts	Catahoula	Recorder→	UC	RE	TX	VS
•	•	•	•	•	TENSTAR Corporation (Main Office) [SOP]		800-960-2214	•	•	•	•

CR	CV	PR	US	BK	←Courts	Claiborne	Recorder→	UC	RE	TX	VS
•	•	•			AAA Research		870-310-3528	•	•	•	•
	•	•	•	•	Access Louisiana Inc		800-489-5620	•	•	•	•
	•	•			M & M Title / Mitchell Co		318-798-1198	•	•	•	
•	•	•	•	•	TENSTAR Corporation (Shreveport) [SOP]		800-960-2214	•	•	•	•

CR	CV	PR	US	BK	←Courts	Concordia	Recorder→	UC	RE	TX	VS
•	•	•	•	•	TENSTAR Corporation (Baton Rouge) [SOP]		800-864-5154	•	•	•	•

CR	CV	PR	US	BK	←Courts	DeSoto	Recorder→	UC	RE	TX	VS
	•	•	•	•	Access Louisiana Inc		800-489-5620	•	•	•	•
	•	•			M & M Title / Mitchell Co		318-798-1198	•	•	•	
•	•	•	•	•	TENSTAR Corporation (Shreveport) [SOP]		800-960-2214	•	•	•	•

CR	CV	PR	US	BK	←Courts	East Baton Rouge	Recorder→	UC	RE	TX	VS
	•	•	•	•	Abstracts by Godail		800-660-7318	•	•	•	
•	•				AccuScreen Systems [SOP]		800-383-6476				
•	•	•	•	•	Judy J Badon/Public Records Specialists		225-291-5537	•	•	•	•
•	•	•	•	•	Bombet Cashio & Associates [SOP]		800-256-5333	•	•	•	•
	•		•		Capitol Corporate Services Inc (Louisiana)		800-408-1262	•		•	
•	•	•			Faith to Faith Legal Productions LLC		225-751-9202	•	•	•	
•	•	•	•	•	Genco Services [SOP]		225-218-4511	•	•	•	•
•	•		•	•	Global Investigative & Legal Service [SOP]		888-644-2066				
•	•				KJB Court Services		225-274-6453				
•	•		•	•	P & A Research Service [SOP]		225-279-2118	•	•	•	
•	•	•	•	•	TENSTAR Corporation (Baton Rouge) [SOP]		800-864-5154	•	•	•	•

CR	CV	PR	US	BK	←Courts	East Carroll	Recorder→	UC	RE	TX	VS
•	•	•	•	•	TENSTAR Corporation (Main Office) [SOP]		800-960-2214	•	•	•	•

CR	CV	PR	US	BK	←Courts	East Feliciana	Recorder→	UC	RE	TX	VS
•	•	•	•	•	TENSTAR Corporation (Baton Rouge) [SOP]		800-864-5154	•	•	•	•

CR	CV	PR	US	BK	←Courts	Evangeline	Recorder→	UC	RE	TX	VS
•	•	•	•	•	Abstracting & Legal Research Inc		318-473-9979	•	•	•	•
•	•		•	•	Bayou Investigations Inc [SOP]		800-256-9009	•			

CR	CV	PR	US	BK	←Courts	Recorder→	UC	RE	TX	VS
•	•	•	•	•	Sittig Services [SOP]	337-580-3334				
•	•	•	•	•	TENSTAR Corporation (Main Office) [SOP]	800-960-2214	•	•	•	•

CR	CV	PR	US	BK	←Courts **Franklin**	Recorder→	UC	RE	TX	VS
•	•	•	•	•	TENSTAR Corporation (Main Office) [SOP]	800-960-2214	•	•	•	•

CR	CV	PR	US	BK	←Courts **Grant**	Recorder→	UC	RE	TX	VS
•	•	•	•	•	Abstracting & Legal Research Inc	318-473-9979	•	•	•	•
•	•		•	•	Global Investigative & Legal Service [SOP]	888-644-2066				
•	•	•	•	•	TENSTAR Corporation (Main Office) [SOP]	800-960-2214	•	•	•	•

CR	CV	PR	US	BK	←Courts **Iberia**	Recorder→	UC	RE	TX	VS
•	•		•	•	Bayou Investigations Inc [SOP]	800-256-9009	•			
•	•		•	•	Global Investigative & Legal Service [SOP]	888-644-2066				
•	•				Sarah B Migues	337-364-8509				
•	•	•	•	•	TENSTAR Corporation (Main Office) [SOP]	800-960-2214	•	•	•	•

CR	CV	PR	US	BK	←Courts **Iberville**	Recorder→	UC	RE	TX	VS
	•	•			Ascension Title Services Inc	225-647-8051	•	•	•	
•	•	•	•	•	Bombet Cashio & Associates [SOP]	800-256-5333	•	•	•	•
•	•	•			Faith to Faith Legal Productions LLC	225-751-9202	•	•	•	
•	•	•	•	•	Genco Services [SOP]	225-218-4511	•	•	•	•
•	•				KJB Court Services	225-274-6453				
•	•	•	•	•	TENSTAR Corporation (Baton Rouge) [SOP]	800-864-5154	•	•	•	•

CR	CV	PR	US	BK	←Courts **Jackson**	Recorder→	UC	RE	TX	VS
•	•	•	•	•	TENSTAR Corporation (Main Office) [SOP]	800-960-2214	•	•	•	•

CR	CV	PR	US	BK	←Courts **Jefferson**	Recorder→	UC	RE	TX	VS
•	•	•	•	•	Bombet Cashio & Associates [SOP]	800-256-5333	•	•	•	•
	•		•	•	Darren J Harper & Associates [SOP]	800-962-4907		•	•	
•	•		•	•	Global Investigative & Legal Service [SOP]	888-644-2066				
•	•		•		Powell's Backtracking [SOP]	504-342-2052				
•	•	•	•	•	TENSTAR Corporation (New Orleans) [SOP]	800-864-5154	•	•	•	•

CR	CV	PR	US	BK	←Courts **Jefferson Davis**	Recorder→	UC	RE	TX	VS
•	•	•	•	•	ABC Investigators Inc [SOP]	800-738-7300	•	•	•	
•	•		•	•	Bayou Investigations Inc [SOP]	800-256-9009	•			
•	•		•	•	Global Investigative & Legal Service [SOP]	888-644-2066				
•	•	•	•	•	TENSTAR Corporation (Crowley) [SOP]	800-960-2214	•	•	•	•
•	•	•	•	•	Wise Land & Abstract Co Inc	337-436-3419	•	•	•	•

CR	CV	PR	US	BK	←Courts **La Salle**	Recorder→	UC	RE	TX	VS
•	•	•	•	•	TENSTAR Corporation (Main Office) [SOP]	800-960-2214	•	•	•	•

CR	CV	PR	US	BK	←Courts **Lafayette**	Recorder→	UC	RE	TX	VS
•	•	•	•	•	ABC Investigators Inc [SOP]	800-738-7300	•	•	•	
•	•		•	•	Bayou Investigations Inc [SOP]	800-256-9009	•			
•	•	•	•	•	Sittig Services [SOP]	337-580-3334				
•	•	•	•	•	TENSTAR Corporation (Main Office) [SOP]	800-960-2214	•	•	•	•

CR	CV	PR	US	BK	←Courts **Lafourche**	Recorder→	UC	RE	TX	VS
•	•	•	•		Jerry M Braud	985-447-1227	•	•	•	
•	•		•	•	Global Investigative & Legal Service [SOP]	888-644-2066				
•	•		•	•	P & A Research Service [SOP]	225-279-2118	•	•	•	
•	•	•	•	•	TENSTAR Corporation (New Orleans) [SOP]	800-864-5154	•	•	•	•

CR	CV	PR	US	BK	←Courts **Lincoln**	Recorder→	UC	RE	TX	VS
	•	•			M & M Title / Mitchell Co	318-798-1198	•	•	•	
•	•	•	•	•	TENSTAR Corporation (Main Office) [SOP]	800-960-2214	•	•	•	•

CR	CV	PR	US	BK	←Courts	LIVINGSTON	Recorder→	UC	RE	TX	VS
	•	•	•	•		Abstracts by Godail	800-660-7318	•	•	•	
•	•	•				Faith to Faith Legal Productions LLC	225-751-9202	•	•	•	
•	•		•	•		Global Investigative & Legal Service [SOP]	888-644-2066				
•	•					KJB Court Services	225-274-6453				
•	•	•				Professional Choice Services	225-294-3703	•	•	•	•
•	•	•	•	•		TENSTAR Corporation (Baton Rouge) [SOP]	800-864-5154	•	•	•	•

CR	CV	PR	US	BK	←Courts	MADISON	Recorder→	UC	RE	TX	VS
•	•	•	•	•		TENSTAR Corporation (Main Office) [SOP]	800-960-2214	•	•	•	•

CR	CV	PR	US	BK	←Courts	MOREHOUSE	Recorder→	UC	RE	TX	VS
•	•	•				AAA Research	870-310-3528	•	•	•	•
•	•	•	•	•		TENSTAR Corporation (Main Office) [SOP]	800-960-2214	•	•	•	•

CR	CV	PR	US	BK	←Courts	NATCHITOCHES	Recorder→	UC	RE	TX	VS
•	•	•	•	•		Abstracting & Legal Research Inc	318-473-9979	•	•	•	•
•	•		•	•		Global Investigative & Legal Service [SOP]	888-644-2066				
•	•	•	•	•		TENSTAR Corporation (Shreveport) [SOP]	800-960-2214	•	•	•	•

CR	CV	PR	US	BK	←Courts	ORLEANS	Recorder→	UC	RE	TX	VS
•	•	•	•	•		Bombet Cashio & Associates [SOP]	800-256-5333	•	•	•	•
	•		•	•		Darren J Harper & Associates [SOP]	800-962-4907		•	•	
•	•		•	•		Global Investigative & Legal Service [SOP]	888-644-2066				
•	•					KJB Court Services	225-274-6453				
•	•		•			Powell's Backtracking [SOP]	504-342-2052				
•	•	•	•	•		TENSTAR Corporation (New Orleans) [SOP]	800-864-5154	•	•	•	•

CR	CV	PR	US	BK	←Courts	OUACHITA	Recorder→	UC	RE	TX	VS
•	•	•				AAA Research	870-310-3528	•	•	•	•
•	•	•	•	•		TENSTAR Corporation (Main Office) [SOP]	800-960-2214	•	•	•	•

CR	CV	PR	US	BK	←Courts	PLAQUEMINES	Recorder→	UC	RE	TX	VS
•	•					Glenn A Fleming	504-393-0988	•	•	•	
•	•	•	•	•		TENSTAR Corporation (New Orleans) [SOP]	800-864-5154	•	•	•	•

CR	CV	PR	US	BK	←Courts	POINTE COUPEE	Recorder→	UC	RE	TX	VS
	•	•	•	•		Abstracts by Godail	800-660-7318	•	•	•	
•	•	•				Faith to Faith Legal Productions LLC	225-751-9202	•	•	•	
•	•	•	•	•		TENSTAR Corporation (Baton Rouge) [SOP]	800-864-5154	•	•	•	•

CR	CV	PR	US	BK	←Courts	RAPIDES	Recorder→	UC	RE	TX	VS
•	•	•	•	•		Abstracting & Legal Research Inc	318-473-9979	•	•	•	•
	•	•	•	•		Abstracts by Godail	800-660-7318	•	•	•	
•	•		•	•		Global Investigative & Legal Service [SOP]	888-644-2066				
•	•	•	•	•		TENSTAR Corporation (Main Office) [SOP]	800-960-2214	•	•	•	•

CR	CV	PR	US	BK	←Courts	RED RIVER	Recorder→	UC	RE	TX	VS
	•	•	•	•		Access Louisiana Inc	800-489-5620	•	•	•	•
•	•	•	•	•		TENSTAR Corporation (Shreveport) [SOP]	800-960-2214	•	•	•	•

CR	CV	PR	US	BK	←Courts	RICHLAND	Recorder→	UC	RE	TX	VS
•	•	•	•	•		TENSTAR Corporation (Main Office) [SOP]	800-960-2214	•	•	•	•

CR	CV	PR	US	BK	←Courts	SABINE	Recorder→	UC	RE	TX	VS
•	•	•	•	•		Abstracting & Legal Research Inc	318-473-9979	•	•	•	•
•	•		•	•		Global Investigative & Legal Service [SOP]	888-644-2066				
•	•	•	•	•		TENSTAR Corporation (Shreveport) [SOP]	800-960-2214	•	•	•	•

CR	CV	PR	US	BK	←Courts	ST. BERNARD	Recorder→	UC	RE	TX	VS
•	•		•			Powell's Backtracking [SOP]	504-342-2052				
•	•	•	•	•		TENSTAR Corporation (New Orleans) [SOP]	800-864-5154	•	•	•	•

CR	CV	PR	US	BK	←Courts	St. Charles	Recorder→	UC	RE	TX	VS
•	•	•	•	•	Bombet Cashio & Associates [SOP]		800-256-5333	•	•	•	•
•	•		•	•	Global Investigative & Legal Service [SOP]		888-644-2066				
•	•		•	•	P & A Research Service [SOP]		225-279-2118	•	•	•	
•	•	•	•	•	TENSTAR Corporation (New Orleans) [SOP]		800-864-5154	•	•	•	•

CR	CV	PR	US	BK	←Courts	St. Helena	Recorder→	UC	RE	TX	VS
•	•	•	•	•	TENSTAR Corporation (Baton Rouge) [SOP]		800-864-5154	•	•	•	•

CR	CV	PR	US	BK	←Courts	St. James	Recorder→	UC	RE	TX	VS
	•	•			Ascension Title Services Inc		225-647-8051	•	•	•	
•	•		•	•	Global Investigative & Legal Service [SOP]		888-644-2066				
•	•		•	•	P & A Research Service [SOP]		225-279-2118	•	•	•	
•	•	•	•	•	TENSTAR Corporation (New Orleans) [SOP]		800-864-5154	•	•	•	•

CR	CV	PR	US	BK	←Courts	St. John the Baptist	Recorder→	UC	RE	TX	VS
•	•	•	•	•	Bombet Cashio & Associates [SOP]		800-256-5333	•	•	•	•
•	•		•	•	Global Investigative & Legal Service [SOP]		888-644-2066				
•	•		•	•	P & A Research Service [SOP]		225-279-2118	•	•	•	
•	•	•	•	•	TENSTAR Corporation (New Orleans) [SOP]		800-864-5154	•	•	•	•

CR	CV	PR	US	BK	←Courts	St. Landry	Recorder→	UC	RE	TX	VS
•	•	•	•	•	ABC Investigators Inc [SOP]		800-738-7300	•	•	•	
•	•	•	•	•	Abstracting & Legal Research Inc		318-473-9979	•	•	•	•
	•	•	•	•	Abstracts by Godail		800-660-7318	•	•	•	
•	•		•	•	Bayou Investigations Inc [SOP]		800-256-9009	•			
•	•	•	•	•	Sittig Services [SOP]		337-580-3334				
•	•	•	•	•	TENSTAR Corporation (Main Office) [SOP]		800-960-2214	•	•	•	•

CR	CV	PR	US	BK	←Courts	St. Martin	Recorder→	UC	RE	TX	VS
•	•		•	•	Bayou Investigations Inc [SOP]		800-256-9009	•			
•	•				Sarah B Migues		337-364-8509				
•	•				Camelia Soprano		337-923-4273			•	
•	•	•	•	•	TENSTAR Corporation (Main Office) [SOP]		800-960-2214	•	•	•	•

CR	CV	PR	US	BK	←Courts	St. Mary	Recorder→	UC	RE	TX	VS
•	•		•	•	Bayou Investigations Inc [SOP]		800-256-9009	•			
•	•				Linda Lucia		337-923-4271; Fax- same				
•	•				Sarah B Migues		337-364-8509				
•	•				Camelia Soprano		337-923-4273			•	
•	•	•	•	•	TENSTAR Corporation (Main Office) [SOP]		800-960-2214	•	•	•	•

CR	CV	PR	US	BK	←Courts	St. Tammany	Recorder→	UC	RE	TX	VS
	•	•			A Public Record Search Inc		985-892-5194	•	•	•	
•	•	•	•	•	Bombet Cashio & Associates [SOP]		800-256-5333	•	•	•	•
•	•		•		Powell's Backtracking [SOP]		504-342-2052				
•	•	•			Professional Choice Services		225-294-3703	•	•	•	•
•	•	•			Kathy Swenson, PI [SOP]		985-863-8151	•	•	•	
•	•	•	•	•	TENSTAR Corporation (New Orleans) [SOP]		800-864-5154	•	•	•	•

CR	CV	PR	US	BK	←Courts	Tangipahoa	Recorder→	UC	RE	TX	VS
•	•	•			Professional Choice Services		225-294-3703	•	•	•	•
•	•	•	•	•	TENSTAR Corporation (New Orleans) [SOP]		800-864-5154	•	•	•	•

CR	CV	PR	US	BK	←Courts	Tensas	Recorder→	UC	RE	TX	VS
•	•	•	•	•	TENSTAR Corporation (Main Office) [SOP]		800-960-2214	•	•	•	•

CR	CV	PR	US	BK	←Courts	Terrebonne	Recorder→	UC	RE	TX	VS
•	•		•	•	Global Investigative & Legal Service [SOP]		888-644-2066				
•	•	•	•	•	TENSTAR Corporation (New Orleans) [SOP]		800-864-5154	•	•	•	•

CR	CV	PR	US	BK	←Courts UNION Recorder→	Phone	UC	RE	TX	VS
•	•	•			AAA Research	870-310-3528	•	•	•	•
•	•	•	•	•	TENSTAR Corporation (Main Office) [SOP]	800-960-2214	•	•	•	•

CR	CV	PR	US	BK	←Courts VERMILION Recorder→	Phone	UC	RE	TX	VS
•	•	•	•	•	ABC Investigators Inc [SOP]	800-738-7300	•	•	•	
•	•		•	•	Bayou Investigations Inc [SOP]	800-256-9009	•			
•	•		•	•	Global Investigative & Legal Service [SOP]	888-644-2066				
•	•				Sarah B Migues	337-364-8509				
•	•	•	•	•	TENSTAR Corporation (Main Office) [SOP]	800-960-2214	•	•	•	•

CR	CV	PR	US	BK	←Courts VERNON Recorder→	Phone	UC	RE	TX	VS
•	•	•	•	•	Abstracting & Legal Research Inc	318-473-9979	•	•	•	•
•	•		•	•	Global Investigative & Legal Service [SOP]	888-644-2066				
•	•	•	•	•	TENSTAR Corporation (Main Office) [SOP]	800-960-2214	•	•	•	•

CR	CV	PR	US	BK	←Courts WASHINGTON Recorder→	Phone	UC	RE	TX	VS
•	•	•	•	•	TENSTAR Corporation (New Orleans) [SOP]	800-864-5154	•	•	•	•

CR	CV	PR	US	BK	←Courts WEBSTER Recorder→	Phone	UC	RE	TX	VS
	•	•	•	•	Access Louisiana Inc	800-489-5620	•	•	•	•
	•	•			M & M Title / Mitchell Co	318-798-1198	•	•	•	
•	•	•	•	•	TENSTAR Corporation (Shreveport) [SOP]	800-960-2214	•	•	•	•

CR	CV	PR	US	BK	←Courts WEST BATON ROUGE Recorder→	Phone	UC	RE	TX	VS
	•	•	•	•	Abstracts by Godail	800-660-7318	•	•	•	
•	•				AccuScreen Systems [SOP]	800-383-6476				
•	•	•	•	•	Judy J Badon/Public Records Specialists	225-291-5537	•	•	•	•
•	•	•	•	•	Bombet Cashio & Associates [SOP]	800-256-5333	•	•	•	•
•	•	•			Faith to Faith Legal Productions LLC	225-751-9202	•	•	•	
•	•	•	•	•	Genco Services [SOP]	225-218-4511	•	•	•	•
•	•		•	•	Global Investigative & Legal Service [SOP]	888-644-2066				
•	•				KJB Court Services	225-274-6453				
•	•	•	•	•	TENSTAR Corporation (Baton Rouge) [SOP]	800-864-5154	•	•	•	•

CR	CV	PR	US	BK	←Courts WEST CARROLL Recorder→	Phone	UC	RE	TX	VS
•	•	•	•	•	TENSTAR Corporation (Main Office) [SOP]	800-960-2214	•	•	•	•

CR	CV	PR	US	BK	←Courts WEST FELICIANA Recorder→	Phone	UC	RE	TX	VS
•	•				KJB Court Services	225-274-6453				
•	•	•	•	•	TENSTAR Corporation (Baton Rouge) [SOP]	800-864-5154	•	•	•	•

CR	CV	PR	US	BK	←Courts WINN Recorder→	Phone	UC	RE	TX	VS
•	•	•	•	•	TENSTAR Corporation (Main Office) [SOP]	800-960-2214	•	•	•	•

Maine

Maine has 16 counties and 18 recording offices. Aroostook and Oxford Counties each have two recording offices.

COURT RECORDS RETRIEVED — CAPITAL - KENNEBEC COUNTY — RECORDED RECORDS RETRIEVED

CR	CV	PR	US	BK	←COURTS	ANDROSCOGGIN	RECORDER→	UC	RE	TX	VS
•	•	•	•	•	Lawyers Investigating Service [SOP]	888-244-5685		•	•	•	•
•	•	•	•	•	Pearl Information Services	207-775-5889		•	•	•	•
•	•	•	•	•	Public Information Resource	800-675-6350		•	•	•	•
•	•	•			Surette Investigations [SOP]	207-268-3419		•	•	•	•
•	•	•	•	•	Toby Nason Detective & Security Agency [SOP]	207-873-7512					

CR	CV	PR	US	BK	←COURTS	AROOSTOOK	RECORDER→	UC	RE	TX	VS
•	•	•	•	•	Toby Nason Detective & Security Agency [SOP]	207-873-7512					

CR	CV	PR	US	BK	←COURTS	CUMBERLAND	RECORDER→	UC	RE	TX	VS
			•		A/M Investigations [SOP]	207-838-3111					
•	•	•	•	•	Lawyers Investigating Service [SOP]	888-244-5685		•	•	•	•
	•	•	•		Maine Public Record Services	207-646-9065		•	•	•	
•	•	•	•	•	NR&C	207-791-2852		•	•	•	
•	•	•	•	•	Pearl Information Services	207-775-5889		•	•	•	•
•	•	•	•	•	Public Information Resource	800-675-6350		•	•	•	•
•	•	•		•	Records Research & Retrieval	207-737-2903; cell- 207-504-2444		•	•	•	•
•	•				Serunian Inv [SOP]	207-773-2660					
•	•	•	•	•	Toby Nason Detective & Security Agency [SOP]	207-873-7512					

CR	CV	PR	US	BK	←COURTS	FRANKLIN	RECORDER→	UC	RE	TX	VS
•	•	•	•	•	NR&C	207-791-2852		•	•	•	
•	•	•	•	•	Public Information Resource	800-675-6350		•	•	•	•
•	•	•	•	•	Toby Nason Detective & Security Agency [SOP]	207-873-7512					

CR	CV	PR	US	BK	←COURTS	HANCOCK	RECORDER→	UC	RE	TX	VS
•	•	•	•	•	Acadia Legal Support [SOP]	207-223-5285			•	•	•
		•			Fraser Abstracting	207-947-6344		•	•	•	
•	•	•			Froese Title Research	207-483-2282		•	•	•	
•	•	•	•	•	Toby Nason Detective & Security Agency [SOP]	207-873-7512					

CR	CV	PR	US	BK	←COURTS	KENNEBEC	RECORDER→	UC	RE	TX	VS
•	•	•	•	•	Lawyers Investigating Service [SOP]	888-244-5685		•	•	•	•
•	•	•	•	•	NR&C	207-791-2852		•	•	•	
•	•	•	•	•	Pearl Information Services	207-775-5889		•	•	•	•
•	•	•	•	•	Public Information Resource	800-675-6350		•	•	•	•
•	•	•		•	Records Research & Retrieval	207-737-2903; cell- 207-504-2444		•	•	•	•
•	•	•			Surette Investigations [SOP]	207-268-3419		•	•	•	•
•	•	•	•	•	Toby Nason Detective & Security Agency [SOP]	207-873-7512					

CR	CV	PR	US	BK	←COURTS	KNOX	RECORDER→	UC	RE	TX	VS
•	•	•	•	•	Pearl Information Services	207-775-5889		•	•	•	•
•	•	•	•	•	Public Information Resource	800-675-6350		•	•	•	•
•	•	•	•	•	Toby Nason Detective & Security Agency [SOP]	207-873-7512					

CR	CV	PR	US	BK	←COURTS	LINCOLN	RECORDER→	UC	RE	TX	VS
•	•	•	•	•	Lawyers Investigating Service [SOP]	888-244-5685		•	•	•	•
•	•	•	•	•	Public Information Resource	800-675-6350		•	•	•	•
•	•	•		•	Records Research & Retrieval	207-737-2903; cell- 207-504-2444		•	•	•	•

CR	CV	PR	US	BK	←Courts		Recorder→	UC	RE	TX	VS
•	•	•			Surette Investigations [SOP]		207-268-3419	•	•	•	•
•	•	•	•	•	Toby Nason Detective & Security Agency [SOP]		207-873-7512				

CR	CV	PR	US	BK	←Courts	Oxford	Recorder→	UC	RE	TX	VS
•	•	•	•	•	Lawyers Investigating Service [SOP]		888-244-5685	•	•	•	•
•	•	•	•	•	NR&C		207-791-2852	•	•	•	
•	•	•	•	•	Public Information Resource		800-675-6350	•	•	•	•
•	•	•	•	•	Toby Nason Detective & Security Agency [SOP]		207-873-7512				

CR	CV	PR	US	BK	←Courts	Penobscot	Recorder→	UC	RE	TX	VS
•	•	•	•	•	Acadia Legal Support [SOP]		207-223-5285		•	•	•
		•			Fraser Abstracting		207-947-6344	•	•	•	
•	•	•			Froese Title Research		207-483-2282	•	•	•	
•	•	•	•	•	Public Information Resource		800-675-6350	•	•	•	•
•	•	•	•	•	Toby Nason Detective & Security Agency [SOP]		207-873-7512				

CR	CV	PR	US	BK	←Courts	Piscataquis	Recorder→	UC	RE	TX	VS
		•			Fraser Abstracting		207-947-6344	•	•	•	
•	•	•	•	•	Toby Nason Detective & Security Agency [SOP]		207-873-7512				

CR	CV	PR	US	BK	←Courts	Sagadahoc	Recorder→	UC	RE	TX	VS
•	•	•	•	•	Lawyers Investigating Service [SOP]		888-244-5685	•	•	•	•
•	•	•	•	•	Pearl Information Services		207-775-5889	•	•	•	•
•	•	•	•	•	Public Information Resource		800-675-6350	•	•	•	•
•	•	•		•	Records Research & Retrieval		207-737-2903; cell- 207-504-2444	•	•	•	•
•	•	•			Surette Investigations [SOP]		207-268-3419	•	•	•	•
•	•	•	•	•	Toby Nason Detective & Security Agency [SOP]		207-873-7512				

CR	CV	PR	US	BK	←Courts	Somerset	Recorder→	UC	RE	TX	VS
•	•	•	•	•	Public Information Resource		800-675-6350	•	•	•	•
•	•	•	•	•	Toby Nason Detective & Security Agency [SOP]		207-873-7512				

CR	CV	PR	US	BK	←Courts	Waldo	Recorder→	UC	RE	TX	VS
•	•	•	•	•	Acadia Legal Support [SOP]		207-223-5285		•	•	•
		•			Fraser Abstracting		207-947-6344	•	•	•	
•	•	•	•	•	Public Information Resource		800-675-6350	•	•	•	•
•	•	•	•	•	Toby Nason Detective & Security Agency [SOP]		207-873-7512				

CR	CV	PR	US	BK	←Courts	Washington	Recorder→	UC	RE	TX	VS
•	•	•			Froese Title Research		207-483-2282	•	•	•	
•	•	•	•	•	Toby Nason Detective & Security Agency [SOP]		207-873-7512				

CR	CV	PR	US	BK	←Courts	York	Recorder→	UC	RE	TX	VS
•	•	•	•	•	Lawyers Investigating Service [SOP]		888-244-5685	•	•	•	•
	•	•	•		Maine Public Record Services		207-646-9065	•	•	•	
•	•	•	•	•	NR&C		207-791-2852	•	•	•	
•	•	•	•	•	Pearl Information Services		207-775-5889	•	•	•	•
•	•	•	•	•	Public Information Resource		800-675-6350	•	•	•	•
•	•				Serunian Inv [SOP]		207-773-2660				
•	•	•	•	•	Toby Nason Detective & Security Agency [SOP]		207-873-7512				

Maryland

Maryland has 23 counties and one independent city, Baltimore City, with both a court structure and recording office.

COURT RECORDS RETRIEVED — CAPITAL - ANNE ARUNDEL COUNTY — RECORDED RECORDS RETRIEVED

CR	CV	PR	US	BK	←COURTS ALLEGANY	RECORDER→	UC	RE	TX	VS
•	•		•	•	Accufax: Authentic Document Retrieval	800-336-1001	•	•	•	•
					First Choice Title Service LLC	410-960-6493		•		
•	•	•	•	•	Hylind Search Company Inc (Maryland) [SOP]	888-449-5463	•	•	•	•
•	•		•	•	National Background Investigations Inc	800-798-0079			•	

CR	CV	PR	US	BK	←COURTS ANNE ARUNDEL	RECORDER→	UC	RE	TX	VS
•	•	•	•	•	A P Legal Support Services [SOP]	800-273-9928	•	•	•	•
•	•		•	•	Accufax: Authentic Document Retrieval	800-336-1001	•	•	•	•
•			•		Arrow Background Services LLC	301-475-7802				
•	•		•	•	Background Hound LLC	410-484-6887	•		•	
•	•	•	•	•	Capitol District Information [SOP]	800-494-5225	•	•	•	
•	•	•			Chesapeake Services [SOP]	800-834-7938	•	•	•	•
•	•		•	•	CorpAssist Inc - Baltimore	800-536-9778	•	•	•	
					Document Retrieval Inc [SOP]	443-995-7488		•		
	•	•	•	•	Federal Research LLC [SOP]	800-846-3190	•	•	•	•
					First Choice Title Service LLC	410-960-6493		•		
	•	•	•	•	Harbor City Research Inc	800-445-6029	•	•	•	
•	•	•	•	•	Hylind Search Company Inc (Maryland) [SOP]	888-449-5463	•	•	•	•
•	•	•	•	•	Infoline Inc	888-284-4581	•	•	•	•
•	•	•	•	•	MLQ Attorney Services [SOP]	800-446-8794	•	•	•	•
•	•	•	•	•	Mohr Information Services LLC	540-678-8775	•	•	•	
•	•		•	•	National Background Investigations Inc	800-798-0079			•	
•	•	•	•	•	Rosemary O'Brien [SOP]	301-434-4044; cell- 301-807-1809	•	•	•	•
					Runnymeade Research Inc	410-998-9886		•		
•	•	•	•	•	Security Consultants Inc	202-686-3953			•	•

CR	CV	PR	US	BK	←COURTS BALTIMORE	RECORDER→	UC	RE	TX	VS
•	•	•	•	•	A P Legal Support Services [SOP]	800-273-9928	•	•	•	•
•	•		•	•	Accufax: Authentic Document Retrieval	800-336-1001	•	•	•	•
•			•		Arrow Background Services LLC	301-475-7802				
•	•		•	•	Background Hound LLC	410-484-6887	•		•	
•	•	•	•	•	Capitol District Information [SOP]	800-494-5225	•	•	•	
•	•		•	•	CorpAssist Inc - Baltimore	800-536-9778	•	•	•	
					Document Retrieval Inc [SOP]	443-995-7488		•		
	•	•	•	•	Federal Research LLC [SOP]	800-846-3190	•	•	•	•
					First Choice Title Service LLC	410-960-6493		•		
•	•	•			FYI Investigations	877-475-7083	•	•	•	
	•	•	•	•	Harbor City Research Inc	800-445-6029	•	•	•	
•	•	•	•	•	Hylind Search Company Inc (Maryland) [SOP]	888-449-5463	•	•	•	•
•	•	•	•	•	Infoline Inc	888-284-4581	•	•	•	•
•					Kroll Background America	800-697-7189		•	•	
	•	•			Maryland Research & Abstract Co	410-823-1944	•	•		
•	•	•	•	•	Mohr Information Services LLC	540-678-8775	•	•	•	
•	•		•	•	National Background Investigations Inc	800-798-0079			•	
					R Frier Title Services	city- 410-627-1991; county- 410-977-6667		•	•	
					Runnymeade Research Inc	410-998-9886		•		
•	•	•	•	•	Security Consultants Inc	202-686-3953			•	•
•	•		•	•	Wieder Young Research	301-681-7206			•	

CR	CV	PR	US	BK	←Courts	Baltimore City	Recorder→	UC	RE	TX	VS
•	•	•	•	•	A P Legal Support Services [SOP]		800-273-9928	•	•	•	•
•	•		•	•	Accufax: Authentic Document Retrieval		800-336-1001	•	•	•	•
•			•		Arrow Background Services LLC		301-475-7802				
•	•		•	•	Background Hound LLC		410-484-6887	•		•	
•	•	•	•	•	Capitol District Information [SOP]		800-494-5225	•	•	•	
•	•		•	•	CorpAssist Inc - Baltimore		800-536-9778	•	•	•	
					Document Retrieval Inc [SOP]		443-995-7488		•		
	•	•	•	•	Federal Research LLC [SOP]		800-846-3190	•	•	•	•
					First Choice Title Service LLC		410-960-6493		•		
	•			•	Harbor City Research Inc		800-445-6029		•	•	
•	•	•	•	•	Hylind Search Company Inc (Maryland) [SOP]		888-449-5463	•	•	•	•
•	•	•	•	•	Infoline Inc.		888-284-4581	•	•	•	•
•					Kroll Background America		800-697-7189		•	•	
•	•	•	•	•	Mohr Information Services LLC		540-678-8775	•	•	•	
•	•		•	•	National Background Investigations Inc		800-798-0079			•	
					R Frier Title Services		city- 410-627-1991; county- 410-977-6667		•	•	
					Runnymeade Research Inc.		410-998-9886		•		
•	•	•	•	•	Torri's Legal Services [SOP]		800-990-7378				
•	•		•	•	Wieder Young Research		301-681-7206			•	

CR	CV	PR	US	BK	←Courts	Calvert	Recorder→	UC	RE	TX	VS
•	•		•	•	Accufax: Authentic Document Retrieval		800-336-1001	•	•	•	•
					Document Retrieval Inc [SOP]		443-995-7488		•		
					First Choice Title Service LLC		410-960-6493		•		
•	•	•	•	•	Hylind Search Company Inc (Maryland) [SOP]		888-449-5463	•	•	•	•
•	•	•	•	•	Infoline Inc.		888-284-4581	•	•	•	•
•	•		•	•	National Background Investigations Inc		800-798-0079			•	
•	•		•	•	Wieder Young Research		301-681-7206			•	

CR	CV	PR	US	BK	←Courts	Caroline	Recorder→	UC	RE	TX	VS
•	•		•	•	Accufax: Authentic Document Retrieval		800-336-1001	•	•	•	•
•	•	•			Chesapeake Services [SOP]		800-834-7938	•	•	•	•
•	•	•			Delmarva Abstractors [SOP]		410-228-6044	•	•	•	
					First Choice Title Service LLC		410-960-6493		•		
•	•	•	•	•	Hylind Search Company Inc (Maryland) [SOP]		888-449-5463	•	•	•	•
•	•		•	•	National Background Investigations Inc		800-798-0079			•	
•	•	•			Shore One Title Abstract Services		410-943-8637		•	•	

CR	CV	PR	US	BK	←Courts	Carroll	Recorder→	UC	RE	TX	VS
•	•	•	•	•	A P Legal Support Services [SOP]		800-273-9928	•	•	•	•
•	•		•	•	Accufax: Authentic Document Retrieval		800-336-1001	•	•	•	•
•			•		Arrow Background Services LLC		301-475-7802				
•	•		•	•	Background Hound LLC		410-484-6887	•		•	
					Document Retrieval Inc [SOP]		443-995-7488		•		
					First Choice Title Service LLC		410-960-6493		•		
•	•	•	•	•	Hylind Search Company Inc (Maryland) [SOP]		888-449-5463	•	•	•	•
•					Kroll Background America		800-697-7189		•	•	
•	•		•	•	National Background Investigations Inc		800-798-0079			•	
					Runnymeade Research Inc.		410-998-9886		•		
•	•		•	•	Wieder Young Research		301-681-7206			•	

CR	CV	PR	US	BK	←Courts	Cecil	Recorder→	UC	RE	TX	VS
•	•		•	•	Accufax: Authentic Document Retrieval		800-336-1001	•	•	•	•
					Document Retrieval Inc [SOP]		443-995-7488		•		
					First Choice Title Service LLC		410-960-6493		•		
•	•	•	•	•	Hylind Search Company Inc (Maryland) [SOP]		888-449-5463	•	•	•	•
•	•		•	•	National Background Investigations Inc		800-798-0079			•	

CR	CV	PR	US	BK	←Courts	CHARLES	Recorder→	UC	RE	TX	VS
•	•		•	•	Accufax: Authentic Document Retrieval		800-336-1001	•	•	•	•
					Document Retrieval Inc [SOP]		443-995-7488		•		
					First Choice Title Service LLC		410-960-6493		•		
•	•	•	•	•	Hylind Search Company Inc (Maryland) [SOP]		888-449-5463	•	•	•	•
•	•	•	•	•	Infoline Inc.		888-284-4581	•	•	•	•
•	•		•	•	National Background Investigations Inc		800-798-0079			•	
•	•		•	•	Wieder Young Research		301-681-7206			•	

CR	CV	PR	US	BK	←Courts	DORCHESTER	Recorder→	UC	RE	TX	VS
•	•		•	•	Accufax: Authentic Document Retrieval		800-336-1001	•	•	•	•
•	•	•			Delmarva Abstractors [SOP]		410-228-6044	•	•	•	
					First Choice Title Service LLC		410-960-6493		•		
•	•	•	•	•	Hylind Search Company Inc (Maryland) [SOP]		888-449-5463	•	•	•	•
•	•		•	•	National Background Investigations Inc		800-798-0079			•	
•	•	•			Shore One Title Abstract Services		410-943-8637	•	•	•	

CR	CV	PR	US	BK	←Courts	FREDERICK	Recorder→	UC	RE	TX	VS
•	•		•	•	Accufax: Authentic Document Retrieval		800-336-1001	•	•	•	•
					Document Retrieval Inc [SOP]		443-995-7488		•		
					First Choice Title Service LLC		410-960-6493		•		
•	•	•	•	•	Hylind Search Company Inc (Maryland) [SOP]		888-449-5463	•	•	•	•
•	•	•	•	•	Infoline Inc.		888-284-4581	•	•	•	•
•	•	•	•	•	MLQ Attorney Services [SOP]		800-446-8794	•	•	•	•
•	•	•	•	•	Mohr Information Services LLC		540-678-8775	•	•	•	
•	•		•	•	National Background Investigations Inc		800-798-0079			•	
•	•	•			Quality Abstractors Inc		301-695-9329	•	•	•	
•	•	•	•	•	Resource Reporting Ltd [SOP]		877-268-7810	•	•	•	
•	•		•	•	Wieder Young Research		301-681-7206			•	

CR	CV	PR	US	BK	←Courts	GARRETT	Recorder→	UC	RE	TX	VS
•	•		•	•	Accufax: Authentic Document Retrieval		800-336-1001	•	•	•	•
					First Choice Title Service LLC		410-960-6493		•		
•	•	•	•	•	Hylind Search Company Inc (Maryland) [SOP]		888-449-5463	•	•	•	•
•	•		•	•	National Background Investigations Inc		800-798-0079			•	

CR	CV	PR	US	BK	←Courts	HARFORD	Recorder→	UC	RE	TX	VS
•	•	•	•	•	A P Legal Support Services [SOP]		800-273-9928	•	•	•	•
•	•		•	•	Accufax: Authentic Document Retrieval		800-336-1001	•	•	•	•
•			•		Arrow Background Services LLC		301-475-7802				
					Document Retrieval Inc [SOP]		443-995-7488		•		
	•	•	•	•	Federal Research LLC [SOP]		800-846-3190	•	•	•	•
					First Choice Title Service LLC		410-960-6493		•		
•	•	•			FYI Investigations		877-475-7083	•	•	•	
	•	•	•	•	Harbor City Research Inc		800-445-6029	•	•	•	
•	•	•	•	•	Hylind Search Company Inc (Maryland) [SOP]		888-449-5463	•	•	•	•
•					Kroll Background America		800-697-7189		•	•	
	•	•			Maryland Research & Abstract Co		410-823-1944	•	•		
•	•		•	•	National Background Investigations Inc		800-798-0079			•	
•	•	•	•	•	Security Consultants Inc		202-686-3953			•	•
•	•		•	•	Wieder Young Research		301-681-7206			•	

CR	CV	PR	US	BK	←Courts	HOWARD	Recorder→	UC	RE	TX	VS
•	•	•	•	•	A P Legal Support Services [SOP]		800-273-9928	•	•	•	•
•	•		•	•	Accufax: Authentic Document Retrieval		800-336-1001	•	•	•	•
•			•		Arrow Background Services LLC		301-475-7802				
•	•		•	•	Background Hound LLC		410-484-6887	•		•	
•	•		•	•	CorpAssist Inc - Baltimore		800-536-9778	•	•	•	
					Document Retrieval Inc [SOP]		443-995-7488		•		
	•	•	•	•	Federal Research LLC [SOP]		800-846-3190	•	•	•	•

CR	CV	PR	US	BK	←Courts		Recorder→	UC	RE	TX	VS
					First Choice Title Service LLC		410-960-6493		•		
	•	•	•	•	Harbor City Research Inc		800-445-6029	•	•	•	
•	•	•	•	•	Hylind Search Company Inc (Maryland) [SOP]		888-449-5463	•	•	•	•
•	•	•	•	•	Infoline Inc		888-284-4581	•	•	•	•
•	•	•	•	•	Investigative Consultants Inc		202-237-1500	•	•	•	•
•	•	•	•	•	Mohr Information Services LLC		540-678-8775	•	•	•	
•	•		•	•	National Background Investigations Inc		800-798-0079			•	
•	•	•	•	•	Rosemary O'Brien [SOP]		301-434-4044; cell- 301-807-1809	•	•	•	•
					Runnymede Research Inc		410-998-9886		•		
•	•	•	•	•	Security Consultants Inc		202-686-3953			•	•
•	•		•	•	Wieder Young Research		301-681-7206			•	
CR	**CV**	**PR**	**US**	**BK**	**←Courts**	**Kent**	**Recorder→**	**UC**	**RE**	**TX**	**VS**
•	•		•	•	Accufax: Authentic Document Retrieval		800-336-1001	•	•	•	•
•	•	•			Chesapeake Services [SOP]		800-834-7938	•	•	•	•
					First Choice Title Service LLC		410-960-6493		•		
•	•	•	•	•	Hylind Search Company Inc (Maryland) [SOP]		888-449-5463	•	•	•	•
•	•		•	•	National Background Investigations Inc		800-798-0079			•	
CR	**CV**	**PR**	**US**	**BK**	**←Courts**	**Montgomery**	**Recorder→**	**UC**	**RE**	**TX**	**VS**
•	•	•	•	•	A P Legal Support Services [SOP]		800-273-9928	•	•	•	•
•	•		•	•	Accufax: Authentic Document Retrieval		800-336-1001	•	•	•	•
•	•	•	•	•	ALIASS [SOP]		800-747-0820	•	•	•	•
•			•		Arrow Background Services LLC		301-475-7802				
•	•	•	•	•	Capitol District Information [SOP]		800-494-5225	•	•	•	
•	•	•	•	•	CorpAssist Inc - DC Office		800-438-2996	•	•	•	•
					Document Retrieval Inc [SOP]		443-995-7488		•		
•	•	•	•	•	Docu-Search of Washington DC		202-737-5707	•	•	•	•
•	•	•	•	•	Elder & Ryan Abstracts LLC		301-854-1200	•	•	•	•
•	•	•	•	•	Enterprise Title Company Inc		703-351-8066	•	•	•	•
					First Choice Title Service LLC		410-960-6493		•		
•	•	•	•	•	Fitzgerald Servaites Inc		202-257-7775	•	•	•	•
	•	•	•	•	Harbor City Research Inc		800-445-6029	•	•	•	
•	•	•	•	•	Hylind Search Company Inc (Maryland) [SOP]		888-449-5463	•	•	•	•
•	•	•	•	•	Infoline Inc		888-284-4581	•	•	•	•
•	•	•	•	•	Investigative Consultants Inc		202-237-1500	•	•	•	•
	•	•	•	•	M & M Search Service		301-251-9545	•	•	•	•
•	•	•	•	•	MLQ Attorney Services [SOP]		800-446-8794	•	•	•	•
•	•	•	•	•	Mohr Information Services LLC		540-678-8775	•	•	•	
•	•		•	•	National Background Investigations Inc		800-798-0079			•	
•	•	•	•	•	Rosemary O'Brien [SOP]		301-434-4044; cell- 301-807-1809	•	•	•	•
•	•	•	•	•	Resource Reporting Ltd [SOP]		877-268-7810	•	•	•	
•	•	•	•	•	Security Consultants Inc		202-686-3953			•	•
•	•	•	•	•	Washington Document Service (DC)		800-728-5201	•	•	•	•
•	•		•	•	WestLaw CourtEXPRESS (DC) [SOP]		800-542-3320				
•	•		•	•	Wieder Young Research		301-681-7206			•	
CR	**CV**	**PR**	**US**	**BK**	**←Courts**	**Prince George's**	**Recorder→**	**UC**	**RE**	**TX**	**VS**
•	•	•	•	•	A P Legal Support Services [SOP]		800-273-9928	•	•	•	•
•	•		•	•	Accufax: Authentic Document Retrieval		800-336-1001	•	•	•	•
•	•	•	•	•	ALIASS [SOP]		800-747-0820	•	•	•	•
•			•		Arrow Background Services LLC		301-475-7802				
•	•		•	•	Background Hound LLC		410-484-6887	•		•	
•	•	•	•	•	Capitol District Information [SOP]		800-494-5225	•	•	•	
•	•	•	•	•	CorpAssist Inc - DC Office		800-438-2996	•	•	•	•
					Document Retrieval Inc [SOP]		443-995-7488		•		
•	•	•	•	•	Docu-Search of Washington DC		202-737-5707	•	•	•	•
•	•	•	•	•	Enterprise Title Company Inc		703-351-8066	•	•	•	•
					First Choice Title Service LLC		410-960-6493		•		

CR	CV	PR	US	BK	←Courts	Recorder→	UC	RE	TX	VS
●	●	●	●	●	Fitzgerald Servaites Inc	202-257-7775	●	●	●	●
	●	●	●	●	Harbor City Research Inc	800-445-6029	●	●	●	
●	●	●	●	●	Hylind Search Company Inc (Maryland) [SOP]	888-449-5463	●	●	●	●
●	●	●	●	●	Infoline Inc	888-284-4581	●	●	●	●
●	●	●	●	●	Investigative Consultants Inc	202-237-1500	●	●	●	●
	●	●	●	●	M & M Search Service	301-251-9545	●	●	●	●
●	●	●	●	●	MLQ Attorney Services [SOP]	800-446-8794	●	●	●	●
●	●	●	●	●	Mohr Information Services LLC	540-678-8775	●	●	●	
●	●		●	●	National Background Investigations Inc	800-798-0079			●	
●	●	●	●	●	Rosemary O'Brien [SOP]	301-434-4044; cell- 301-807-1809	●	●	●	●
●	●	●	●	●	Security Consultants Inc	202-686-3953			●	●
●	●		●	●	WestLaw CourtEXPRESS (DC) [SOP]	800-542-3320				
●	●		●	●	Wieder Young Research	301-681-7206			●	

CR	CV	PR	US	BK	←Courts **Queen Anne's**	Recorder→	UC	RE	TX	VS
●	●		●	●	Accufax: Authentic Document Retrieval	800-336-1001	●	●	●	●
●	●	●			Chesapeake Services [SOP]	800-834-7938	●	●	●	●
●	●	●			Delmarva Abstractors [SOP]	410-228-6044	●	●	●	
					Document Retrieval Inc [SOP]	443-995-7488		●		
					First Choice Title Service LLC	410-960-6493		●		
●	●		●	●	National Background Investigations Inc	800-798-0079			●	

CR	CV	PR	US	BK	←Courts **Somerset**	Recorder→	UC	RE	TX	VS
●	●		●	●	Accufax: Authentic Document Retrieval	800-336-1001	●	●	●	●
●	●	●			Judith Ayres	757-336-5313	●	●	●	●
					First Choice Title Service LLC	410-960-6493		●		
●	●		●	●	National Background Investigations Inc	800-798-0079			●	

CR	CV	PR	US	BK	←Courts **St. Mary's**	Recorder→	UC	RE	TX	VS
●	●		●	●	Accufax: Authentic Document Retrieval	800-336-1001	●	●	●	●
					Document Retrieval Inc [SOP]	443-995-7488		●		
					First Choice Title Service LLC	410-960-6493		●		
●	●	●	●	●	Hylind Search Company Inc (Maryland) [SOP]	888-449-5463	●	●	●	●
●	●		●	●	National Background Investigations Inc	800-798-0079			●	

CR	CV	PR	US	BK	←Courts **Talbot**	Recorder→	UC	RE	TX	VS
●	●		●	●	Accufax: Authentic Document Retrieval	800-336-1001	●	●	●	●
●	●	●			Chesapeake Services [SOP]	800-834-7938	●	●	●	●
●	●	●			Delmarva Abstractors [SOP]	410-228-6044	●	●	●	
					First Choice Title Service LLC	410-960-6493		●		
●	●	●	●	●	Hylind Search Company Inc (Maryland) [SOP]	888-449-5463	●	●	●	●
●	●		●	●	National Background Investigations Inc	800-798-0079			●	
●	●	●			Shore One Title Abstract Services	410-943-8637	●	●	●	

CR	CV	PR	US	BK	←Courts **Washington**	Recorder→	UC	RE	TX	VS
●	●		●	●	Accufax: Authentic Document Retrieval	800-336-1001	●	●	●	●
					First Choice Title Service LLC	410-960-6493		●		
●	●	●	●	●	Hylind Search Company Inc (Maryland) [SOP]	888-449-5463	●	●	●	●
●	●	●	●	●	Mohr Information Services LLC	540-678-8775	●	●	●	
●	●		●	●	National Background Investigations Inc	800-798-0079			●	
●	●	●			Quality Abstractors Inc	301-695-9329	●	●	●	
●	●	●	●	●	Resource Reporting Ltd [SOP]	877-268-7810	●	●	●	
●	●		●	●	Wieder Young Research	301-681-7206			●	

CR	CV	PR	US	BK	←Courts **Wicomico**	Recorder→	UC	RE	TX	VS
●	●		●	●	Accufax: Authentic Document Retrieval	800-336-1001	●	●	●	●
●	●	●			Judith Ayres	757-336-5313	●	●	●	●
					First Choice Title Service LLC	410-960-6493		●		
●	●	●	●	●	Hylind Search Company Inc (Maryland) [SOP]	888-449-5463	●	●	●	●
●	●		●	●	National Background Investigations Inc	800-798-0079			●	

CR	CV	PR	US	BK	←COURTS	WORCESTER	RECORDER→	UC	RE	TX	VS
•	•		•	•		Accufax: Authentic Document Retrieval	800-336-1001	•	•	•	•
•	•	•				Judith Ayres	757-336-5313	•	•	•	•
						First Choice Title Service LLC	410-960-6493		•		
•	•	•	•	•		Hylind Search Company Inc (Maryland) [SOP]	888-449-5463	•	•	•	•
•	•		•	•		National Background Investigations Inc	800-798-0079			•	

[SOP] = PERFORMS SERVICE OF PROCESS

COURT RECORDS

CODE	GOVERNMENT AGENCY	TYPE OF INFORMATION
DT	US District Court	Federal civil and criminal cases
BK	Bankruptcy Court	United States bankruptcy cases
CV	Civil Court	Municipal, county and state level civil cases
CR	Criminal Court	Municipal, county and state level criminal cases
PR	Probate Court	Wills and estate cases

COUNTY RECORDS - RECORDINGS

CODE	GOVERNMENT AGENCY	TYPE OF INFORMATION
UC	UCC Filing Office	Uniform Commercial Code and other personal property liens
RE	Real Estate Recording Office	Real property transactions and liens
TX	Tax Filing Office(s)	Federal and state tax liens, judgment liens
VS	Vital Records Office	Vital statistics—birth, death, marriage, divorce

Editor's Tip: Remember the first rule about public record searching-- Simply because your state or county has certain rules, regulations and practices regarding the accessibility and content of public records, does not mean that another state or county adheres to the same rules.

Massachusetts

Massachusetts has 14 counties and 21 recording offices. Berkshire and Bristol counties each have three recording offices. Essex, Middlesex, and Worcester counties each have two recording offices. Cities/towns bearing the same name as a county are Barnstable, Essex, Franklin, Hampden, Nantucket, Norfolk, Plymouth, and Worcester.

COURT RECORDS RETRIEVED — CAPITAL - SUFFOLK COUNTY — RECORDED RECORDS RETRIEVED

Barnstable

CR	CV	PR	US	BK	←Courts	Recorder→	UC	RE	TX	VS
•	•	•	•	•	Associated Professional Services [SOP]	800-849-7870	•	•	•	•
•	•	•	•	•	Barry Shuster Information Services, A Div of Search-It Inc	877-852-2507	•	•	•	•
•	•	•	•	•	Bearak Reports	800-331-5677	•	•	•	•
•	•	•			Brenda L Gaskill	508-759-3156	•	•	•	•
•	•	•	•	•	Len Page Paralegal/Research Services	508-967-2504	•	•	•	•
•	•	•	•	•	Northshore Paralegal Services Inc [SOP]	800-883-6020	•	•	•	•
•	•	•	•	•	R & R Search Inc	508-359-2400	•	•	•	•
•	•				Rapid Record Retrieval	508-759-8622				
•	•	•	•	•	Simmons Agency Inc [SOP]	800-237-8230		•	•	•

Berkshire

CR	CV	PR	US	BK	←Courts	Recorder→	UC	RE	TX	VS
•	•	•	•	•	Barry Shuster Information Services, A Div of Search-It Inc	877-852-2507	•	•	•	•
•	•	•	•	•	Bearak Reports	800-331-5677	•	•	•	•
•	•	•	•	•	Northshore Paralegal Services Inc [SOP]	800-883-6020	•	•	•	•
•	•	•	•	•	R & R Search Inc	508-359-2400	•	•	•	•
		•			Registry Research	413-528-3919		•		
•	•	•	•		Seyler Retrieval		•			

Bristol

CR	CV	PR	US	BK	←Courts	Recorder→	UC	RE	TX	VS
•	•	•	•	•	Associated Professional Services [SOP]	800-849-7870	•	•	•	•
•	•	•	•	•	Barry Shuster Information Services, A Div of Search-It Inc	877-852-2507	•	•	•	•
•	•	•	•	•	Bearak Reports	800-331-5677	•	•	•	•
•	•	•	•	•	D & D Retrieval Services	781-297-0933	•	•	•	
•	•	•	•	•	Data Quest Ltd [SOP]	800-292-9797	•	•	•	•
•	•	•			Brenda L Gaskill	508-759-3156	•	•	•	•
•	•	•	•	•	LegalTrieve Information Services	508-238-4227	•	•	•	
•	•	•	•	•	Len Page Paralegal/Research Services	508-967-2504	•	•	•	•
•	•	•	•	•	Northshore Paralegal Services Inc [SOP]	800-883-6020	•	•	•	•
•	•	•	•	•	R & R Search Inc	508-359-2400	•	•	•	•
•	•				Rapid Record Retrieval	508-759-8622				

Dukes

CR	CV	PR	US	BK	←Courts	Recorder→	UC	RE	TX	VS
•	•	•	•	•	Barry Shuster Information Services, A Div of Search-It Inc	877-852-2507	•	•	•	•
•	•	•	•	•	R & R Search Inc	508-359-2400	•	•	•	•

Essex

CR	CV	PR	US	BK	←Courts	Recorder→	UC	RE	TX	VS
•	•	•	•	•	Barry Shuster Information Services, A Div of Search-It Inc	877-852-2507	•	•	•	•
•	•	•	•	•	Bearak Reports	800-331-5677	•	•	•	•
•	•	•	•	•	D & D Retrieval Services	781-297-0933	•	•	•	
•	•	•	•	•	Data Quest Ltd [SOP]	800-292-9797	•	•	•	•
	•	•	•	•	Essex County Paralegals Inc	800-922-4752	•	•	•	
•	•	•			JMB Title Abstracting	603-505-1910		•		
•	•	•	•	•	LegalTrieve Information Services	508-238-4227	•	•	•	
•	•	•	•	•	Michael B Fixman & Associates [SOP]	800-434-9626	•	•	•	•
•	•	•	•	•	Northshore Paralegal Services Inc [SOP]	800-883-6020	•	•	•	•
•	•	•	•	•	P.S.P.S. Legal Support Services Inc [SOP]	617-846-7130	•	•	•	•

CR	CV	PR	US	BK	←Courts	Recorder→	UC	RE	TX	VS
•	•	•	•	•	Paralegal Resource Center Inc	866-742-1939	•	•	•	•
•	•				Primetime Research Inc	866-737-2714				
•	•	•	•	•	R & R Search Inc	508-359-2400	•	•	•	•
•	•				The Wethersfield Group	978-388-5551				

CR	CV	PR	US	BK	←Courts FRANKLIN	Recorder→	UC	RE	TX	VS
•	•	•	•	•	Barry Shuster Information Services, A Div of Search-It Inc	877-852-2507	•	•	•	•
•	•	•	•	•	Bearak Reports	800-331-5677	•	•	•	•
•	•	•	•	•	Northshore Paralegal Services Inc [SOP]	800-883-6020	•	•	•	•
•	•				Primetime Research Inc	866-737-2714				
•	•	•	•	•	R & R Search Inc	508-359-2400	•	•	•	•
•	•	•	•		Seyler Retrieval		•			
•	•	•	•	•	Worcester Record Search Inc	508-842-7282	•	•	•	•

CR	CV	PR	US	BK	←Courts HAMPDEN	Recorder→	UC	RE	TX	VS
•	•	•	•	•	Barry Shuster Information Services, A Div of Search-It Inc	877-852-2507	•	•	•	•
	•		•	•	Forbes Public Research Inc	518-732-2961	•	•	•	
•	•	•	•	•	Northshore Paralegal Services Inc [SOP]	800-883-6020	•	•	•	•
•	•				Primetime Research Inc	866-737-2714				
•	•	•	•	•	R & R Search Inc	508-359-2400	•	•	•	•
•	•	•	•		Seyler Retrieval		•			
•	•	•	•	•	Worcester Record Search Inc	508-842-7282	•	•	•	•

CR	CV	PR	US	BK	←Courts HAMPSHIRE	Recorder→	UC	RE	TX	VS
•	•	•	•	•	Barry Shuster Information Services, A Div of Search-It Inc	877-852-2507	•	•	•	•
•	•	•	•	•	Bearak Reports	800-331-5677	•	•	•	•
•	•	•	•	•	Northshore Paralegal Services Inc [SOP]	800-883-6020	•	•	•	•
•	•				Primetime Research Inc	866-737-2714				
•	•	•	•	•	R & R Search Inc	508-359-2400	•	•	•	•
•	•	•	•		Seyler Retrieval		•			
•	•	•	•	•	Worcester Record Search Inc	508-842-7282	•	•	•	•

CR	CV	PR	US	BK	←Courts MIDDLESEX	Recorder→	UC	RE	TX	VS
•	•	•	•	•	A Scott Broadhurst Associates	617-536-3486	•	•	•	
•	•	•	•	•	Barry Shuster Information Services, A Div of Search-It Inc	877-852-2507	•	•	•	•
	•	•	•	•	Bay State Corporate Services Inc	617-742-8484	•	•	•	•
•	•	•	•	•	Bearak Reports	800-331-5677	•	•	•	•
•	•	•	•	•	CSC - Corporation Service Company [SOP]	800-927-9800	•	•	•	•
•	•	•	•	•	D & D Retrieval Services	781-297-0933	•	•	•	
•	•	•	•	•	Data Quest Ltd [SOP]	800-292-9797	•	•	•	•
	•	•	•	•	Essex County Paralegals Inc	800-922-4752	•	•	•	
•	•	•			JMB Title Abstracting	603-505-1910		•		
•	•	•	•	•	LegalTrieve Information Services	508-238-4227	•	•	•	
	•	•		•	Massachusetts Document Retrieval	617-249-0323		•		•
•	•		•	•	Masscourtresearch	617-696-2178			•	
•	•	•	•	•	Michael B Fixman & Associates [SOP]	800-434-9626	•	•	•	•
•	•	•	•	•	NH Background Investigations LLC	603-598-4106	•	•	•	•
•	•	•	•	•	Northshore Paralegal Services Inc [SOP]	800-883-6020	•	•	•	•
•	•	•	•	•	P.S.P.S. Legal Support Services Inc [SOP]	617-846-7130	•	•	•	•
•	•				Walter J Pace	617-389-6730				
•	•	•	•	•	Paralegal Resource Center Inc	866-742-1939	•	•	•	•
•	•				Primetime Research Inc	866-737-2714				
		•			Quirk Associates	781-326-1202	•	•	•	•
•	•	•	•	•	R & R Search Inc	508-359-2400	•	•	•	•
•	•	•	•	•	RCC & Associates Inc	508-839-3234			•	
•	•	•	•	•	Simmons Agency Inc [SOP]	800-237-8230		•	•	•
•	•	•	•	•	Suburban Record Research	617-536-3486	•	•	•	
					Veritas Information Services	781-643-7811		•		
•	•				The Wethersfield Group	978-388-5551				

CR	CV	PR	US	BK	←Courts	NANTUCKET	Recorder→	UC	RE	TX	VS
•	•	•	•	•	Barry Shuster Information Services, A Div of Search-It Inc		877-852-2507	•	•	•	•
•	•	•	•	•	Northshore Paralegal Services Inc [SOP]		800-883-6020	•	•	•	•
•	•	•	•	•	R & R Search Inc		508-359-2400	•	•	•	•

CR	CV	PR	US	BK	←Courts	NORFOLK	Recorder→	UC	RE	TX	VS
•	•	•	•	•	A Scott Broadhurst Associates		617-536-3486	•	•	•	
•	•	•	•	•	Barry Shuster Information Services, A Div of Search-It Inc		877-852-2507	•	•	•	•
•	•	•	•	•	Bearak Reports		800-331-5677	•	•	•	•
•	•	•	•	•	D & D Retrieval Services		781-297-0933	•	•	•	
•	•	•	•	•	Data Quest Ltd [SOP]		800-292-9797	•	•	•	•
•	•	•	•	•	LegalTrieve Information Services		508-238-4227	•	•	•	
•	•	•	•	•	Len Page Paralegal/Research Services		508-967-2504	•	•	•	•
•	•	•	•	•	Northshore Paralegal Services Inc [SOP]		800-883-6020	•	•	•	•
•	•	•	•	•	Paralegal Resource Center Inc		866-742-1939	•	•	•	•
•	•				Primetime Research Inc		866-737-2714				
		•			Quirk Associates		781-326-1202	•	•	•	•
•	•	•	•	•	R & R Search Inc		508-359-2400	•	•	•	•
•	•				Rapid Record Retrieval		508-759-8622				
•	•	•	•	•	Simmons Agency Inc [SOP]		800-237-8230		•	•	•
•	•	•	•	•	Suburban Record Research		617-536-3486	•	•	•	
					Veritas Information Services		781-643-7811		•		

CR	CV	PR	US	BK	←Courts	PLYMOUTH	Recorder→	UC	RE	TX	VS
•	•	•	•	•	Associated Professional Services [SOP]		800-849-7870	•	•	•	•
•	•	•	•	•	Barry Shuster Information Services, A Div of Search-It Inc		877-852-2507	•	•	•	•
•	•	•	•	•	Bearak Reports		800-331-5677	•	•	•	•
•	•	•	•	•	D & D Retrieval Services		781-297-0933	•	•	•	
•	•	•	•	•	Data Quest Ltd [SOP]		800-292-9797	•	•	•	•
•	•	•			Brenda L Gaskill		508-759-3156	•	•	•	•
•	•	•	•	•	LegalTrieve Information Services		508-238-4227	•	•	•	
•	•	•	•	•	Len Page Paralegal/Research Services		508-967-2504	•	•	•	•
•	•	•	•	•	Northshore Paralegal Services Inc [SOP]		800-883-6020	•	•	•	•
•	•	•	•	•	Paralegal Resource Center Inc		866-742-1939	•	•	•	•
•	•	•	•	•	R & R Search Inc		508-359-2400	•	•	•	•
•	•				Rapid Record Retrieval		508-759-8622				
•	•	•	•	•	Simmons Agency Inc [SOP]		800-237-8230		•	•	•

CR	CV	PR	US	BK	←Courts	SUFFOLK	Recorder→	UC	RE	TX	VS
•	•	•	•	•	A Scott Broadhurst Associates		617-536-3486	•	•	•	
•	•	•	•	•	Barry Shuster Information Services, A Div of Search-It Inc		877-852-2507	•	•	•	•
	•	•	•	•	Bay State Corporate Services Inc		617-742-8484	•	•	•	•
•	•	•	•	•	Bearak Reports		800-331-5677	•	•	•	•
•	•	•	•	•	CSC - Corporation Service Company [SOP]		800-927-9800	•	•	•	•
•	•	•	•	•	D & D Retrieval Services		781-297-0933	•	•	•	
•	•	•	•	•	Data Quest Ltd [SOP]		800-292-9797	•	•	•	•
•	•	•	•	•	LegalTrieve Information Services		508-238-4227	•	•	•	
	•	•		•	Massachusetts Document Retrieval		617-249-0323		•		•
•	•		•	•	Masscourtresearch		617-696-2178			•	
•	•	•	•	•	Michael B Fixman & Associates [SOP]		800-434-9626	•	•	•	•
•	•	•	•	•	NH Background Investigations LLC		603-598-4106	•	•	•	•
•	•	•	•	•	Northshore Paralegal Services Inc [SOP]		800-883-6020	•	•	•	•
•	•	•	•	•	P.S.P.S. Legal Support Services Inc [SOP]		617-846-7130	•	•	•	•
•	•				Walter J Pace		617-389-6730				
•	•	•	•	•	Paralegal Resource Center Inc		866-742-1939	•	•	•	•
•	•				Primetime Research Inc		866-737-2714				
		•			Quirk Associates		781-326-1202	•	•	•	•
•	•	•	•	•	R & R Search Inc		508-359-2400	•	•	•	•
•	•	•	•	•	RCC & Associates Inc		508-839-3234			•	

CR	CV	PR	US	BK	←Courts		Recorder→	UC	RE	TX	VS
•	•	•	•	•	Simmons Agency Inc [SOP]		800-237-8230		•	•	•
•	•	•	•	•	Suburban Record Research		617-536-3486	•	•	•	
					Veritas Information Services		781-643-7811		•		

CR	CV	PR	US	BK	←Courts	Worcester	Recorder→	UC	RE	TX	VS
•	•	•	•	•	A Scott Broadhurst Associates		617-536-3486	•	•	•	
•	•	•	•	•	Barry Shuster Information Services, A Div of Search-It Inc		877-852-2507	•	•	•	•
•	•	•	•	•	Bearak Reports		800-331-5677	•	•	•	•
•	•	•	•	•	Data Quest Ltd [SOP]		800-292-9797	•	•	•	•
	•	•	•	•	Essex County Paralegals Inc		800-922-4752	•	•	•	
	•	•	•	•	Marcia A Gazoorian		508-754-9503	•	•	•	
•	•	•	•	•	Northshore Paralegal Services Inc [SOP]		800-883-6020	•	•	•	•
•	•	•	•		Paralegal Resource Center Inc		866-742-1939	•	•	•	•
•	•				Primetime Research Inc		866-737-2714				
•	•	•	•	•	R & R Search Inc		508-359-2400	•	•	•	•
•	•	•	•	•	RCC & Associates Inc		508-839-3234			•	
•	•	•	•	•	Suburban Record Research		617-536-3486	•	•	•	
•	•	•	•	•	Worcester Record Search Inc		508-842-7282	•	•	•	•

[SOP] = Performs service of process

= PRRN Member. *A retriever you can trust!*

Court Records

CODE	Government Agency	Type of Information
CR	Criminal Court	Municipal, county and state level criminal cases
CV	Civil Court	Municipal, county and state level civil cases
PR	Probate Court	Wills and estate cases
US	US District Court	Federal civil and criminal cases
BK	Bankruptcy Court	United States bankruptcy cases

County Records - Recordings

CODE	Government Agency	Type of Information
UC	UCC Filing Office	Uniform Commercial Code and other personal property liens
RE	Real Estate Recording Office	Real property transactions and liens
TX	Tax Filing Office(s)	Federal and state tax liens, judgment liens
VS	Vital Records Office	Vital statistics—birth, death, marriage, divorce

Editor's Tip: At the back of this directory is a short list of search firms who are Public Record Retriever Network "Associate Members." These Associate Members utilize retrievers to obtain documents outside their local area of coverage. The Associate Members are statewide, regional, or national in scope, and are not listed in the county sections.

Michigan

COURT RECORDS RETRIEVED — CAPITAL - INGHAM COUNTY — RECORDED RECORDS RETRIEVED

CR	CV	PR	US	BK	←COURTS	RECORDER→	UC	RE	TX	VS
					ALCONA					
•	•		•	•	ASK Services Inc (Michigan)	888-416-1313	•	•	•	•
	•	•			Mt Pleasant Abstract & Title Inc	989-773-3651	•	•	•	
					ALGER					
•	•		•	•	ASK Services Inc (Michigan)	888-416-1313	•	•	•	•
					ALLEGAN					
•	•		•	•	ASK Services Inc (Michigan)	888-416-1313	•	•	•	•
		•			Lake Michigan Title Co	269-637-8595	•	•	•	
	•		•	•	Michigan Search Company	734-427-7224	•	•	•	
•	•	•	•	•	ProSearch Information Retrieval	269-637-5145	•	•	•	•
•	•	•	•	•	SWP Searches [SOP]	616-847-6989	•	•	•	•
					ALPENA					
•	•		•	•	ASK Services Inc (Michigan)	888-416-1313	•	•	•	•
		•			Huron Shores Abstract & Title	989-734-3344	•	•	•	
	•	•			Mt Pleasant Abstract & Title Inc	989-773-3651	•	•	•	
•	•	•	•	•	Research North Inc of Alpena [SOP]	888-876-1010	•	•	•	•
					ANTRIM					
•	•		•	•	ASK Services Inc (Michigan)	888-416-1313	•	•	•	•
	•	•			Mt Pleasant Abstract & Title Inc	989-773-3651	•	•	•	
					ARENAC					
•	•	•			Arenae Abstract & Title Co	989-846-6560	•	•	•	•
•	•		•	•	ASK Services Inc (Michigan)	888-416-1313	•	•	•	•
		•			Bay County Abstract Co	989-895-9910	•	•	•	
•	•	•			Ogemaw Title Co	989-345-7240	•	•	•	•
					BARAGA					
•	•		•	•	ASK Services Inc (Michigan)	888-416-1313	•	•	•	•
		•			Copper Range Abstract & Title Agency	906-482-7903	•	•	•	•
					BARRY					
•	•		•	•	ASK Services Inc (Michigan)	888-416-1313	•	•	•	•
•	•	•			Metropolitan Title Co (Hastings)	269-945-9447	•	•	•	•
	•		•	•	Michigan Search Company	734-427-7224	•	•	•	
•	•	•	•	•	The Fatman Intl Private Detective Service [SOP]	616-949-1790	•	•	•	•
					BAY					
•	•		•	•	ASK Services Inc (Michigan)	888-416-1313	•	•	•	•
		•			Bay County Abstract Co	989-895-9910	•	•	•	
	•	•	•	•	Paul Maisano Designs	248-625-6366	•	•	•	
•	•	•	•	•	Records Retrieval Service	810-220-0810	•	•	•	•
•	•	•	•	•	Teter Security Assoc Inc	800-726-5959			•	
					BENZIE					
•	•		•	•	ASK Services Inc (Michigan)	888-416-1313	•	•	•	•

CR	CV	PR	US	BK	←Courts	Berrien	Recorder→	UC	RE	TX	VS
•	•		•	•	ASK Services Inc (Michigan)		888-416-1313	•	•	•	•
•	•	•	•	•	Case Services Inc [SOP]		877-291-6868	•	•	•	•
•	•				Independent Research Inc		269-429-9873				
		•			Lake Michigan Title Co		269-637-8595	•	•	•	
	•		•	•	Michigan Search Company		734-427-7224	•	•	•	
•	•	•	•	•	ProSearch Information Retrieval		269-637-5145	•	•	•	•

CR	CV	PR	US	BK	←Courts	Branch	Recorder→	UC	RE	TX	VS
•	•		•	•	ASK Services Inc (Michigan)		888-416-1313	•	•	•	•
	•		•	•	Michigan Search Company		734-427-7224	•	•	•	
		•			The Talon Group		517-437-7345		•	•	•

CR	CV	PR	US	BK	←Courts	Calhoun	Recorder→	UC	RE	TX	VS
•	•		•	•	ASK Services Inc (Michigan)		888-416-1313	•	•	•	•
	•		•	•	Michigan Search Company		734-427-7224	•	•	•	
	•	•	•	•	Paul Maisano Designs		248-625-6366	•	•	•	
•	•	•	•	•	Records Retrieval Service		810-220-0810	•	•	•	•
		•			The Talon Group		517-437-7345		•	•	•
•	•	•	•	•	The Fatman Intl Private Detective Service [SOP]		616-949-1790	•	•	•	•

CR	CV	PR	US	BK	←Courts	Cass	Recorder→	UC	RE	TX	VS
•	•		•	•	ASK Services Inc (Michigan)		888-416-1313	•	•	•	•
•	•	•	•	•	Case Services Inc [SOP]		877-291-6868	•	•	•	•
	•		•	•	Michigan Search Company		734-427-7224	•	•	•	
•	•	•	•	•	ProSearch Information Retrieval		269-637-5145	•	•	•	•
•	•	•			St Joseph County Abstract Office Inc		269-467-6075	•	•	•	•

CR	CV	PR	US	BK	←Courts	Charlevoix	Recorder→	UC	RE	TX	VS
•	•		•	•	ASK Services Inc (Michigan)		888-416-1313	•	•	•	•
•	•	•	•	•	Research North Inc of Petoskey [SOP]		888-876-1010	•	•	•	•

CR	CV	PR	US	BK	←Courts	Cheboygan	Recorder→	UC	RE	TX	VS
•	•		•	•	ASK Services Inc (Michigan)		888-416-1313	•	•	•	•
					Cheboygan Title		866-627-7150	•	•	•	•
	•	•			Mt Pleasant Abstract & Title Inc		989-773-3651	•	•	•	

CR	CV	PR	US	BK	←Courts	Chippewa	Recorder→	UC	RE	TX	VS
•	•		•	•	ASK Services Inc (Michigan)		888-416-1313	•	•	•	•
		•			Mackinac Abstract & Title		906-643-7452	•	•	•	

CR	CV	PR	US	BK	←Courts	Clare	Recorder→	UC	RE	TX	VS
•	•		•	•	ASK Services Inc (Michigan)		888-416-1313	•	•	•	•
		•			Bay County Abstract Co		989-895-9910	•	•	•	
					Isabella County Abstract		989-773-3241	•	•	•	•
		•			Land Title & Abstract		989-426-0011	•	•	•	•
	•	•			Mt Pleasant Abstract & Title Inc		989-773-3651	•	•	•	

CR	CV	PR	US	BK	←Courts	Clinton	Recorder→	UC	RE	TX	VS
•	•		•	•	ASK Services Inc (Michigan)		888-416-1313	•	•	•	•
	•	•	•	•	Paul Maisano Designs		248-625-6366	•	•	•	

CR	CV	PR	US	BK	←Courts	Crawford	Recorder→	UC	RE	TX	VS
•	•		•	•	ASK Services Inc (Michigan)		888-416-1313	•	•	•	•
					Crawford Cty Title, Roscommon Cty Title		989-348-9832	•	•	•	
	•	•			Mt Pleasant Abstract & Title Inc		989-773-3651	•	•	•	

CR	CV	PR	US	BK	←Courts	Delta	Recorder→	UC	RE	TX	VS
•	•		•	•	ASK Services Inc (Michigan)		888-416-1313	•	•	•	•
•	•	•	•	•	Research North Inc of Marquette [SOP]		888-876-1010	•	•	•	•

CR	CV	PR	US	BK	←Courts	**Dickinson**	Recorder→	UC	RE	TX	VS
•	•		•	•	ASK Services Inc (Michigan)		888-416-1313	•	•	•	•
•	•	•			Great Lake Search		906-774-4654				
	•		•	•	Michigan Search Company		734-427-7224	•	•	•	
					Superior Title & Abstract		906-774-9010		•	•	

CR	CV	PR	US	BK	←Courts	**Eaton**	Recorder→	UC	RE	TX	VS
•	•		•	•	ASK Services Inc (Michigan)		888-416-1313	•	•	•	•
	•		•	•	Michigan Search Company		734-427-7224	•	•	•	
	•	•	•	•	Paul Maisano Designs		248-625-6366	•	•	•	

CR	CV	PR	US	BK	←Courts	**Emmet**	Recorder→	UC	RE	TX	VS
•	•		•	•	ASK Services Inc (Michigan)		888-416-1313	•	•	•	•
•	•	•	•	•	Research North Inc of Petoskey [SOP]		888-876-1010	•	•	•	•

CR	CV	PR	US	BK	←Courts	**Genesee**	Recorder→	UC	RE	TX	VS
•	•	•	•	•	Advanced Surveillance Group Inc [SOP]		888-677-9700	•	•		•
•	•		•	•	ASK Services Inc (Michigan)		888-416-1313	•	•	•	•
					Centennial Title & Abstract Co		810-238-5100		•	•	
•	•				Independent Research Inc		269-429-9873				
•	•				Investigative Information Inc		586-491-6125		•	•	
•	•				Michigan Court Reports		810-210-4741				
	•		•	•	Michigan Search Company		734-427-7224	•	•	•	
	•	•	•	•	Paul Maisano Designs		248-625-6366	•	•	•	
•	•	•	•	•	Records Retrieval Service		810-220-0810	•	•	•	•
					Sargents Title Co		810-767-2355		•		

CR	CV	PR	US	BK	←Courts	**Gladwin**	Recorder→	UC	RE	TX	VS
•	•		•	•	ASK Services Inc (Michigan)		888-416-1313	•	•	•	•
		•			Bay County Abstract Co		989-895-9910	•	•	•	
		•			Gladwin County Abstract Company		989-426-7411	•	•	•	
		•			Land Title & Abstract		989-426-0011	•	•	•	•
	•	•			Mt Pleasant Abstract & Title Inc		989-773-3651	•	•	•	

CR	CV	PR	US	BK	←Courts	**Gogebic**	Recorder→	UC	RE	TX	VS
•					Affirm Background Screening Inc		715-682-2601				
•	•		•	•	ASK Services Inc (Michigan)		888-416-1313	•	•	•	•
	•	•			Associate Title - Iron County		906-932-6340	•	•	•	
					Guardian Title		906-932-3244		•		

CR	CV	PR	US	BK	←Courts	**Grand Traverse**	Recorder→	UC	RE	TX	VS
•	•		•	•	ASK Services Inc (Michigan)		888-416-1313	•	•	•	•
		•			Grand Traverse Title Co		231-946-5686	•	•	•	
	•		•	•	Michigan Search Company		734-427-7224	•	•	•	
•	•	•			Research North Inc of Traverse City [SOP]		888-876-1010	•	•	•	•

CR	CV	PR	US	BK	←Courts	**Gratiot**	Recorder→	UC	RE	TX	VS
		•			Alma Abstract & Title Co		989-463-8325	•	•	•	•
•	•		•	•	ASK Services Inc (Michigan)		888-416-1313	•	•	•	•
	•	•			Mt Pleasant Abstract & Title Inc		989-773-3651	•	•	•	

CR	CV	PR	US	BK	←Courts	**Hillsdale**	Recorder→	UC	RE	TX	VS
•	•		•	•	ASK Services Inc (Michigan)		888-416-1313	•	•	•	•
	•		•	•	Michigan Search Company		734-427-7224	•	•	•	
		•			The Talon Group		517-437-7345		•	•	•

CR	CV	PR	US	BK	←Courts	**Houghton**	Recorder→	UC	RE	TX	VS
•	•		•	•	ASK Services Inc (Michigan)		888-416-1313	•	•	•	•
		•			Copper Range Abstract & Title Agency		906-482-7903	•	•	•	•

CR	CV	PR	US	BK	←Courts	**Huron** Recorder→	UC	RE	TX	VS
•	•		•	•	ASK Services Inc (Michigan)	888-416-1313	•	•	•	•
		•			Bay County Abstract Co	989-895-9910	•	•	•	

CR	CV	PR	US	BK	←Courts	**Ingham** Recorder→	UC	RE	TX	VS
•	•		•	•	ASK Services Inc (Michigan)	888-416-1313	•	•	•	•
•	•				Independent Research Inc	269-429-9873				
	•		•	•	Michigan Search Company	734-427-7224	•	•	•	
	•	•	•	•	Paul Maisano Designs	248-625-6366	•	•	•	
•	•	•	•	•	Records Retrieval Service	810-220-0810	•	•	•	•

CR	CV	PR	US	BK	←Courts	**Ionia** Recorder→	UC	RE	TX	VS
•	•		•	•	ASK Services Inc (Michigan)	888-416-1313	•	•	•	•

CR	CV	PR	US	BK	←Courts	**Iosco** Recorder→	UC	RE	TX	VS
•	•		•	•	ASK Services Inc (Michigan)	888-416-1313	•	•	•	•
	•	•			Iosco County Abstract Office Ltd	989-362-3231	•	•	•	•
	•	•			Mt Pleasant Abstract & Title Inc	989-773-3651	•	•	•	

CR	CV	PR	US	BK	←Courts	**Iron** Recorder→	UC	RE	TX	VS
•	•		•	•	ASK Services Inc (Michigan)	888-416-1313	•	•	•	•
		•			Copper Range Abstract & Title Agency	906-482-7903	•	•	•	•
•	•	•			Great Lake Search	906-774-4654				
					Penninsula Title & Abstract Corp	906-875-6618	•	•	•	

CR	CV	PR	US	BK	←Courts	**Isabella** Recorder→	UC	RE	TX	VS
•	•		•	•	ASK Services Inc (Michigan)	888-416-1313	•	•	•	•
		•			Bay County Abstract Co	989-895-9910	•	•	•	
					Isabella County Abstract	989-773-3241		•	•	•
	•		•	•	Michigan Search Company	734-427-7224	•	•	•	
	•	•	•	•	Midland Title and Abstract Co	989-839-1003	•	•	•	•
	•	•			Mt Pleasant Abstract & Title Inc	989-773-3651	•	•	•	

CR	CV	PR	US	BK	←Courts	**Jackson** Recorder→	UC	RE	TX	VS
•	•		•	•	ASK Services Inc (Michigan)	888-416-1313	•	•	•	•
	•		•	•	Michigan Search Company	734-427-7224	•	•	•	
	•	•	•	•	Paul Maisano Designs	248-625-6366	•	•	•	

CR	CV	PR	US	BK	←Courts	**Kalamazoo** Recorder→	UC	RE	TX	VS
•	•		•	•	ASK Services Inc (Michigan)	888-416-1313	•	•	•	•
•	•				Independent Research Inc	269-429-9873				
	•		•	•	Michigan Search Company	734-427-7224	•	•	•	
	•	•	•	•	Paul Maisano Designs	248-625-6366	•	•	•	
•	•	•	•	•	ProSearch Information Retrieval	269-637-5145	•	•	•	•
•	•	•	•	•	Records Retrieval Service	810-220-0810	•	•	•	•

CR	CV	PR	US	BK	←Courts	**Kalkaska** Recorder→	UC	RE	TX	VS
•	•		•	•	ASK Services Inc (Michigan)	888-416-1313	•	•	•	•
					Crawford Cty Title, Roscommon Cty Title	989-348-9832	•	•	•	
	•	•			Mt Pleasant Abstract & Title Inc	989-773-3651	•	•	•	

CR	CV	PR	US	BK	←Courts	**Kent** Recorder→	UC	RE	TX	VS
•	•		•	•	ASK Services Inc (Michigan)	888-416-1313	•	•	•	•
•	•				Independent Research Inc	269-429-9873				
	•		•	•	Michigan Search Company	734-427-7224	•	•	•	
	•	•	•	•	Paul Maisano Designs	248-625-6366	•	•	•	
•	•		•	•	Professional Courier Service	616-451-4445	•			•
•	•	•	•	•	ProSearch Information Retrieval	269-637-5145	•	•	•	•
•	•	•	•	•	Records Retrieval Service	810-220-0810	•	•	•	•
		•	•	•	Special Private Investigations Inc	800-577-3783				
		•	•	•	SPI [SOP]	800-577-3783				

CR	CV	PR	US	BK	←Courts		Recorder→	UC	RE	TX	VS
•	•	•	•	•	SWP Searches [SOP]		616-847-6989	•	•	•	•
•	•	•	•	•	The Fatman Intl Private Detective Service [SOP]		616-949-1790	•	•	•	•

CR	CV	PR	US	BK	←Courts	Keweenaw	Recorder→	UC	RE	TX	VS
•	•		•	•	ASK Services Inc (Michigan)		888-416-1313	•	•	•	•
		•			Copper Range Abstract & Title Agency		906-482-7903	•	•	•	•

CR	CV	PR	US	BK	←Courts	Lake	Recorder→	UC	RE	TX	VS
•	•		•	•	ASK Services Inc (Michigan)		888-416-1313	•	•	•	•
•	•	•			Lake County Abstract Co Inc		231-745-3432	•	•	•	•
	•	•			Mt Pleasant Abstract & Title Inc		989-773-3651	•	•	•	

CR	CV	PR	US	BK	←Courts	Lapeer	Recorder→	UC	RE	TX	VS
•	•		•	•	ASK Services Inc (Michigan)		888-416-1313	•	•	•	•
		•			Bay County Abstract Co		989-895-9910	•	•	•	
		•			LaPeer County Abstract & Title Co Inc		810-664-9951	•	•	•	•
•	•				Michigan Court Reports		810-210-4741				
	•	•	•	•	Paul Maisano Designs		248-625-6366	•	•	•	

CR	CV	PR	US	BK	←Courts	Leelanau	Recorder→	UC	RE	TX	VS
•	•		•	•	ASK Services Inc (Michigan)		888-416-1313	•	•	•	•
		•			Leelanau Title Co		231-271-6191	•	•	•	
•	•	•			Research North Inc of Traverse City [SOP]		888-876-1010	•	•	•	•

CR	CV	PR	US	BK	←Courts	Lenawee	Recorder→	UC	RE	TX	VS
					American Title Company of Lenawee		517-263-4040		•		
•	•		•	•	ASK Services Inc (Michigan)		888-416-1313	•	•	•	•

CR	CV	PR	US	BK	←Courts	Livingston	Recorder→	UC	RE	TX	VS
•	•		•	•	ASK Services Inc (Michigan)		888-416-1313	•	•	•	•
					Centennial Title & Abstract Co		810-238-5100		•	•	
	•	•			Landmark Title Service		810-227-1733	•	•	•	•
•	•	•	•	•	Michael Anderson Company		800-992-9936	•	•	•	•
	•		•	•	Michigan Search Company		734-427-7224	•	•	•	
	•	•	•	•	Paul Maisano Designs		248-625-6366	•	•	•	
•	•	•	•	•	Records Retrieval Service		810-220-0810	•	•	•	•

CR	CV	PR	US	BK	←Courts	Luce	Recorder→	UC	RE	TX	VS
•	•		•	•	ASK Services Inc (Michigan)		888-416-1313	•	•	•	•
		•			Mackinac Abstract & Title		906-643-7452	•	•	•	

CR	CV	PR	US	BK	←Courts	Mackinac	Recorder→	UC	RE	TX	VS
•	•		•	•	ASK Services Inc (Michigan)		888-416-1313	•	•	•	•
		•			Mackinac Abstract & Title		906-643-7452	•	•	•	
		•			Whiteside Abstract & Title Insurance		906-643-9292	•	•	•	

CR	CV	PR	US	BK	←Courts	Macomb	Recorder→	UC	RE	TX	VS
	•	•	•	•	Abstractor Associates Inc		586-778-7554	•	•	•	•
•	•	•	•	•	Advanced Surveillance Group Inc [SOP]		888-677-9700	•	•		•
•	•	•	•	•	ASK Services Inc (Michigan)		888-416-1313	•	•	•	•
•	•	•	•	•	Barnes Information Svcs LLC		248-232-3842	•	•	•	•
•	•	•	•	•	Ruth Joane Carson		888-895-3697		•	•	•
•	•				Independent Research Inc		269-429-9873				
•	•				Investigative Information Inc		586-491-6125		•	•	
•	•	•	•	•	Jackson Information Services Inc		586-242-4122	•	•	•	
•	•	•	•	•	Michael Anderson Company		800-992-9936	•	•	•	•
	•			•	Michigan Search Company		734-427-7224	•	•	•	
	•	•	•	•	Paul Maisano Designs		248-625-6366	•	•	•	
•					Pure Again		586-465-4359, cell- 586-484-3242	•	•	•	
•	•	•	•	•	Records Retrieval Service		810-220-0810	•	•	•	•
•	•	•	•	•	VISTA Inc [SOP]		248-559-3500	•	•	•	•

CR	CV	PR	US	BK	←Courts	MANISTEE	Recorder→	UC	RE	TX	VS
•	•		•	•	ASK Services Inc (Michigan)		888-416-1313	•	•	•	•
•	•	•			Manistee Abstract & Title Co		231-723-3397	•	•	•	•

CR	CV	PR	US	BK	←Courts	MARQUETTE	Recorder→	UC	RE	TX	VS
•	•		•	•	ASK Services Inc (Michigan)		888-416-1313	•	•	•	•
		•			Copper Range Abstract & Title Agency		906-482-7903	•	•	•	•
		•			Great Northern Title & Abstract Inc		906-228-6100	•	•	•	
•	•	•	•	•	Research North Inc of Marquette [SOP]		888-876-1010	•	•	•	•

CR	CV	PR	US	BK	←Courts	MASON	Recorder→	UC	RE	TX	VS
•	•		•	•	ASK Services Inc (Michigan)		888-416-1313	•	•	•	•
					Mason County Abstract & Title Inc		231-843-2645	•	•	•	

CR	CV	PR	US	BK	←Courts	MECOSTA	Recorder→	UC	RE	TX	VS
•	•		•	•	ASK Services Inc (Michigan)		888-416-1313	•	•	•	•
					Isabella County Abstract		989-773-3241		•	•	•
	•	•			Mt Pleasant Abstract & Title Inc		989-773-3651	•	•	•	

CR	CV	PR	US	BK	←Courts	MENOMINEE	Recorder→	UC	RE	TX	VS
•	•		•	•	ASK Services Inc (Michigan)		888-416-1313	•	•	•	•
•	•	•			Associated Peninsula Title & Abstract Co		906-863-7871	•	•	•	•

CR	CV	PR	US	BK	←Courts	MIDLAND	Recorder→	UC	RE	TX	VS
•	•		•	•	ASK Services Inc (Michigan)		888-416-1313	•	•	•	•
		•			Bay County Abstract Co		989-895-9910	•	•	•	
	•		•	•	Michigan Search Company		734-427-7224	•	•	•	
	•	•	•	•	Midland Title and Abstract Co		989-839-1003	•	•	•	•
	•	•			Mt Pleasant Abstract & Title Inc		989-773-3651	•	•	•	
•	•	•	•	•	Records Retrieval Service		810-220-0810	•	•	•	•
•	•	•	•	•	Teter Security Assoc Inc		800-726-5959			•	

CR	CV	PR	US	BK	←Courts	MISSAUKEE	Recorder→	UC	RE	TX	VS
•	•		•	•	ASK Services Inc (Michigan)		888-416-1313	•	•	•	•
					Missaukee Title Co		231-839-4563		•		
	•	•			Mt Pleasant Abstract & Title Inc		989-773-3651	•	•	•	

CR	CV	PR	US	BK	←Courts	MONROE	Recorder→	UC	RE	TX	VS
•	•		•	•	ASK Services Inc (Michigan)		888-416-1313	•	•	•	•
	•	•	•	•	Paul Maisano Designs		248-625-6366	•	•	•	
•	•	•	•	•	Records Retrieval Service		810-220-0810	•	•	•	•
•	•	•	•	•	VISTA Inc [SOP]		248-559-3500	•	•	•	•

CR	CV	PR	US	BK	←Courts	MONTCALM	Recorder→	UC	RE	TX	VS
		•			Alma Abstract & Title Co		989-463-8325	•	•	•	•
•	•		•	•	ASK Services Inc (Michigan)		888-416-1313	•	•	•	•
					Isabella County Abstract		989-773-3241		•	•	•
	•	•			Mt Pleasant Abstract & Title Inc		989-773-3651	•	•	•	

CR	CV	PR	US	BK	←Courts	MONTMORENCY	Recorder→	UC	RE	TX	VS
•	•		•	•	ASK Services Inc (Michigan)		888-416-1313	•	•	•	•
	•	•			Mt Pleasant Abstract & Title Inc		989-773-3651	•	•	•	

CR	CV	PR	US	BK	←Courts	MUSKEGON	Recorder→	UC	RE	TX	VS
•	•		•	•	ASK Services Inc (Michigan)		888-416-1313	•	•	•	•
•	•	•	•	•	SWP Searches [SOP]		616-847-6989	•	•	•	•

CR	CV	PR	US	BK	←Courts	NEWAYGO	Recorder→	UC	RE	TX	VS
•	•		•	•	ASK Services Inc (Michigan)		888-416-1313	•	•	•	•
	•	•			Mt Pleasant Abstract & Title Inc		989-773-3651	•	•	•	

CR	CV	PR	US	BK	←Courts	OAKLAND	Recorder→	UC	RE	TX	VS
•	•	•	•	•	Advanced Surveillance Group Inc [SOP]		888-677-9700	•	•		•
•	•		•	•	ASK Services Inc (Michigan)		888-416-1313	•	•	•	•
•	•	•	•	•	Barnes Information Svcs LLC		248-232-3842	•	•	•	•
•	•	•	•	•	Ruth Joane Carson		888-895-3697		•	•	•
•	•				Independent Research Inc		269-429-9873				
•	•				Investigative Information Inc		586-491-6125		•	•	
•	•	•	•	•	Jackson Information Services Inc		586-242-4122	•	•	•	
	•	•			Landmark Title Service		810-227-1733	•	•	•	•
	•		•		Lightning Records Inc		734-285-2495	•	•	•	
•	•	•	•	•	Michael Anderson Company		800-992-9936	•	•	•	•
	•		•	•	Michigan Search Company		734-427-7224	•	•	•	
	•	•	•	•	Paul Maisano Designs		248-625-6366	•	•	•	
•					Pure Again		586-465-4359, cell- 586-484-3242	•	•	•	
•	•	•	•	•	Records Retrieval Service		810-220-0810	•	•	•	•
•	•	•	•	•	VISTA Inc [SOP]		248-559-3500	•	•	•	•

CR	CV	PR	US	BK	←Courts	OCEANA	Recorder→	UC	RE	TX	VS
•	•		•	•	ASK Services Inc (Michigan)		888-416-1313	•	•	•	•

CR	CV	PR	US	BK	←Courts	OGEMAW	Recorder→	UC	RE	TX	VS
•	•		•	•	ASK Services Inc (Michigan)		888-416-1313	•	•	•	•
	•	•			Mt Pleasant Abstract & Title Inc		989-773-3651	•	•	•	
					Ogemaw County Abstract Co		989-345-0110		•	•	
•	•	•			Ogemaw Title Co		989-345-7240	•	•	•	•

CR	CV	PR	US	BK	←Courts	ONTONAGON	Recorder→	UC	RE	TX	VS
•	•		•	•	ASK Services Inc (Michigan)		888-416-1313	•	•	•	•
		•			Copper Range Abstract & Title Agency		906-482-7903	•	•	•	•
					Guardian Title		906-932-3244		•		
					Penninsula Title & Abstract Corp		906-875-6618	•	•	•	

CR	CV	PR	US	BK	←Courts	OSCEOLA	Recorder→	UC	RE	TX	VS
•	•		•	•	ASK Services Inc (Michigan)		888-416-1313	•	•	•	•
•	•	•			Lake County Abstract Co Inc		231-745-3432	•	•	•	•
	•	•			Mt Pleasant Abstract & Title Inc		989-773-3651	•	•	•	

CR	CV	PR	US	BK	←Courts	OSCODA	Recorder→	UC	RE	TX	VS
•	•		•	•	ASK Services Inc (Michigan)		888-416-1313	•	•	•	•
	•	•			Oscoda County Abstract Inc		989-826-5832	•	•	•	

CR	CV	PR	US	BK	←Courts	OTSEGO	Recorder→	UC	RE	TX	VS
•	•		•	•	ASK Services Inc (Michigan)		888-416-1313	•	•	•	•
	•	•			Mt Pleasant Abstract & Title Inc		989-773-3651	•	•	•	

CR	CV	PR	US	BK	←Courts	OTTAWA	Recorder→	UC	RE	TX	VS
•	•		•	•	ASK Services Inc (Michigan)		888-416-1313	•	•	•	•
	•		•	•	Michigan Search Company		734-427-7224	•	•	•	
	•	•	•	•	Paul Maisano Designs		248-625-6366	•	•	•	
•	•	•	•	•	Records Retrieval Service		810-220-0810	•	•	•	•
•	•	•	•	•	SWP Searches [SOP]		616-847-6989	•	•	•	•
•	•	•	•	•	The Fatman Intl Private Detective Service [SOP]		616-949-1790	•	•	•	•

CR	CV	PR	US	BK	←Courts	PRESQUE ISLE	Recorder→	UC	RE	TX	VS
•	•		•	•	ASK Services Inc (Michigan)		888-416-1313	•	•	•	•
		•			Huron Shores Abstract & Title		989-734-3344	•	•	•	
	•	•			Mt Pleasant Abstract & Title Inc		989-773-3651	•	•	•	
	•	•			Presque Isle Title Inc		989-734-2816	•	•	•	
•	•	•	•	•	Research North Inc of Alpena [SOP]		888-876-1010	•	•	•	•

CR	CV	PR	US	BK	←Courts **ROSCOMMON** Recorder→	UC	RE	TX	VS
•	•		•	•	ASK Services Inc (Michigan) 888-416-1313	•	•	•	•
					Crawford Cty Title, Roscommon Cty Title 989-348-9832	•	•	•	
	•	•			Mt Pleasant Abstract & Title Inc 989-773-3651	•	•	•	

CR	CV	PR	US	BK	←Courts **SAGINAW** Recorder→	UC	RE	TX	VS
•	•		•	•	ASK Services Inc (Michigan) 888-416-1313	•	•	•	•
		•			Bay County Abstract Co 989-895-9910	•	•	•	
					Centennial Title & Abstract Co 810-238-5100		•	•	
•	•				Independent Research Inc 269-429-9873				
•	•				Investigative Information Inc 586-491-6125		•	•	
	•		•	•	Michigan Search Company 734-427-7224	•	•	•	
	•	•	•		Paul Maisano Designs 248-625-6366	•	•	•	
•	•	•	•	•	Records Retrieval Service 810-220-0810	•	•	•	•
•	•	•	•		Teter Security Assoc Inc 800-726-5959			•	

CR	CV	PR	US	BK	←Courts **SANILAC** Recorder→	UC	RE	TX	VS
•	•		•	•	ASK Services Inc (Michigan) 888-416-1313	•	•	•	•
		•			Bay County Abstract Co 989-895-9910	•	•	•	

CR	CV	PR	US	BK	←Courts **SCHOOLCRAFT** Recorder→	UC	RE	TX	VS
•	•		•	•	ASK Services Inc (Michigan) 888-416-1313	•	•	•	•

CR	CV	PR	US	BK	←Courts **SHIAWASSEE** Recorder→	UC	RE	TX	VS
•	•		•	•	ASK Services Inc (Michigan) 888-416-1313	•	•	•	•
					Centennial Title & Abstract Co 810-238-5100		•	•	
	•	•	•	•	Paul Maisano Designs 248-625-6366	•	•	•	

CR	CV	PR	US	BK	←Courts **ST. CLAIR** Recorder→	UC	RE	TX	VS
	•	•	•	•	Abstractor Associates Inc. 586-778-7554	•	•	•	•
•	•		•	•	ASK Services Inc (Michigan) 888-416-1313	•	•	•	•
	•	•			Huron Title Co (Michigan) 800-878-4853	•	•	•	
•	•				Investigative Information Inc 586-491-6125		•	•	
•	•	•	•	•	Jackson Information Services Inc 586-242-4122	•	•	•	
•	•				Michigan Court Reports 810-210-4741				
	•	•	•	•	Paul Maisano Designs 248-625-6366	•	•	•	

CR	CV	PR	US	BK	←Courts **ST. JOSEPH** Recorder→	UC	RE	TX	VS
•	•		•	•	ASK Services Inc (Michigan) 888-416-1313	•	•	•	•
	•		•	•	Michigan Search Company 734-427-7224	•	•	•	
•	•	•			St Joseph County Abstract Office Inc 269-467-6075	•	•	•	•

CR	CV	PR	US	BK	←Courts **TUSCOLA** Recorder→	UC	RE	TX	VS
•	•		•	•	ASK Services Inc (Michigan) 888-416-1313	•	•	•	•
		•			Bay County Abstract Co 989-895-9910	•	•	•	
					Centennial Title & Abstract Co 810-238-5100		•	•	

CR	CV	PR	US	BK	←Courts **VAN BUREN** Recorder→	UC	RE	TX	VS
•	•		•	•	ASK Services Inc (Michigan) 888-416-1313	•	•	•	•
		•			Lake Michigan Title Co 269-637-8595	•	•	•	
	•		•	•	Michigan Search Company 734-427-7224	•	•	•	
•	•	•	•	•	ProSearch Information Retrieval 269-637-5145	•	•	•	•
•	•	•			Van Buren County Abstract Office 269-657-4250	•	•	•	•

CR	CV	PR	US	BK	←Courts **WASHTENAW** Recorder→	UC	RE	TX	VS
	•	•	•	•	Abstractor Associates Inc. 586-778-7554	•	•	•	•
•	•		•	•	ASK Services Inc (Michigan) 888-416-1313	•	•	•	•
•	•				Independent Research Inc 269-429-9873				
	•	•			Landmark Title Service 810-227-1733	•	•	•	•
	•		•		Lightning Records Inc. 734-285-2495	•	•	•	
•	•	•	•	•	Michael Anderson Company 800-992-9936	•	•	•	•

CR	CV	PR	US	BK	←Courts	Recorder→	UC	RE	TX	VS
	•		•	•	Michigan Search Company	734-427-7224	•	•	•	
	•	•	•	•	Paul Maisano Designs	248-625-6366	•	•	•	
•	•	•	•	•	Records Retrieval Service	810-220-0810	•	•	•	•
•	•	•	•	•	VISTA Inc [SOP]	248-559-3500	•	•	•	•

CR	CV	PR	US	BK	←Courts WAYNE	Recorder→	UC	RE	TX	VS
	•	•	•	•	Abstractor Associates Inc	586-778-7554	•	•	•	•
•	•	•	•	•	Advanced Surveillance Group Inc [SOP]	888-677-9700	•	•		•
•	•		•	•	ASK Services Inc (Michigan)	888-416-1313	•	•	•	•
•	•	•	•	•	Barnes Information Svcs LLC	248-232-3842	•	•	•	•
•	•	•	•	•	Ruth Joane Carson	888-895-3697		•	•	•
•	•				Independent Research Inc	269-429-9873				
•	•				Investigative Information Inc	586-491-6125		•	•	
•	•	•	•	•	Jackson Information Services Inc	586-242-4122	•	•	•	
	•		•		Lightning Records Inc	734-285-2495	•	•	•	
•	•	•	•	•	Michael Anderson Company	800-992-9936	•	•	•	•
	•		•	•	Michigan Search Company	734-427-7224	•	•	•	
	•	•	•	•	Paul Maisano Designs	248-625-6366	•	•	•	
•					Pure Again	586-465-4359, cell- 586-484-3242	•	•	•	
•	•	•	•	•	Records Retrieval Service	810-220-0810	•	•	•	•
•	•	•	•	•	VISTA Inc [SOP]	248-559-3500	•	•	•	•

CR	CV	PR	US	BK	←Courts WEXFORD	Recorder→	UC	RE	TX	VS
•	•		•	•	ASK Services Inc (Michigan)	888-416-1313	•	•	•	•
	•		•	•	Michigan Search Company	734-427-7224	•	•	•	

[SOP] = Performs service of process

Court Records

CODE	Government Agency	Type of Information
DT	US District Court	Federal civil and criminal cases
BK	Bankruptcy Court	United States bankruptcy cases
CV	Civil Court	Municipal, county and state level civil cases
CR	Criminal Court	Municipal, county and state level criminal cases
PR	Probate Court	Wills and estate cases

County Records - Recordings

CODE	Government Agency	Type of Information
UC	UCC Filing Office	Uniform Commercial Code and other personal property liens
RE	Real Estate Recording Office	Real property transactions and liens
TX	Tax Filing Office(s)	Federal and state tax liens, judgment liens
VS	Vital Records Office	Vital statistics—birth, death, marriage, divorce

Minnesota

COURT RECORDS RETRIEVED — CAPITAL - RAMSEY COUNTY — RECORDED RECORDS RETRIEVED

CR	CV	PR	US	BK	←COURTS **AITKIN**	RECORDER→	UC	RE	TX	VS
•	•		•	•	ABC Services Inc Court Services	507-357-6320				
	•	•	•	•	Abstract & Title Services of Carlton Inc [SOP]	888-331-3966	•	•	•	
•	•	•	•	•	Capitol Lien Records & Research [SOP]	800-845-4077	•	•	•	•
•	•		•		Omni Data Retrieval Inc	952-985-7220			•	
•	•		•	•	Paragon Document Research Inc [SOP]	800-892-4235	•	•	•	

CR	CV	PR	US	BK	←COURTS **ANOKA**	RECORDER→	UC	RE	TX	VS
•	•		•	•	ABC Services Inc Court Services	507-357-6320				
•	•		•	•	ABC Services Inc Real Estate Svcs	507-357-6320	•	•	•	
•	•	•	•	•	Accountable Process Servers Inc [SOP]	612-991-7849		•	•	
•	•	•	•	•	Adit Research Inc	888-721-5220	•	•	•	•
•					Alpha Court Records & Research	651-699-2222				
	•		•	•	Associated Abstracting Services of MN	612-819-6115	•		•	
•	•	•	•	•	Avalon Information Services	715-222-4095		•	•	•
•	•	•	•	•	Capitol Lien Records & Research [SOP]	800-845-4077	•	•	•	•
	•	•	•	•	CSC Minnesota	800-327-1886	•	•	•	•
•	•			•	Dovolos & Associates [SOP]	952-920-9999	•		•	
•	•				GHS Inc - Record Research	763-566-2125, cell- 612-210-9716			•	
•	•	•	•	•	Heartland Information Services [SOP]	800-967-1882	•	•	•	•
•	•				Horvath Enterprises Inc	320-982-3253			•	
		•		•	Independent Abstracting Service Inc	763-792-6800	•	•	•	•
•	•	•	•	•	Information Reporting Services Inc	612-870-8770			•	
	•			•	Land Title Inc	651-638-1900		•	•	
•	•	•	•	•	Metro Legal Services [SOP]	800-488-8994	•	•	•	•
•	•		•		Omni Data Retrieval Inc	952-985-7220			•	
•	•		•	•	Paragon Document Research Inc [SOP]	800-892-4235	•	•	•	
•	•	•	•	•	Twin Cities Research	651-714-0002	•	•	•	•
•	•	•	•	•	Verified Credentials Inc	800-473-4934	•	•	•	•
•	•	•	•	•	Patricia Wolff [SOP]	952-270-0095	•	•	•	•

CR	CV	PR	US	BK	←COURTS **BECKER**	RECORDER→	UC	RE	TX	VS
•	•	•	•	•	Capitol Lien Records & Research [SOP]	800-845-4077	•	•	•	•
•	•				Horvath Enterprises Inc	320-982-3253			•	
•	•		•		Omni Data Retrieval Inc	952-985-7220			•	
•	•		•	•	Paragon Document Research Inc [SOP]	800-892-4235	•	•	•	

CR	CV	PR	US	BK	←COURTS **BELTRAMI**	RECORDER→	UC	RE	TX	VS
•	•		•	•	ABC Services Inc Court Services	507-357-6320				
•	•	•	•	•	ACME Research [SOP]	218-224-3239	•	•	•	•
•	•	•	•	•	Capitol Lien Records & Research [SOP]	800-845-4077	•	•	•	•
•	•		•		Omni Data Retrieval Inc	952-985-7220			•	
•	•		•	•	Paragon Document Research Inc [SOP]	800-892-4235	•	•	•	
					Sathre Title & Abstracting Inc	218-751-4565	•	•	•	

CR	CV	PR	US	BK	←COURTS **BENTON**	RECORDER→	UC	RE	TX	VS
•	•		•	•	ABC Services Inc Court Services	507-357-6320				
•					Alpha Court Records & Research	651-699-2222				
	•		•	•	Associated Abstracting Services of MN	612-819-6115	•	•	•	
	•	•	•		Benton County Abstract Co	320-968-7278	•	•	•	•
•	•	•	•	•	Capitol Lien Records & Research [SOP]	800-845-4077	•	•	•	•

CR	CV	PR	US	BK	←Courts	Recorder→	UC	RE	TX	VS
•	•				Horvath Enterprises Inc	320-982-3253			•	
•	•		•		Omni Data Retrieval Inc	952-985-7220			•	
•	•		•	•	Paragon Document Research Inc [SOP]	800-892-4235	•	•	•	
•	•	•			Scott Investigation [SOP]	800-357-7862	•	•	•	•
					Tri-County Abstract & Title Guaranty	800-892-2399	•	•	•	
•	•	•	•	•	Twin Cities Research	651-714-0002	•	•	•	•
CR	**CV**	**PR**	**US**	**BK**	**←Courts** **BIG STONE**	**Recorder→**	**UC**	**RE**	**TX**	**VS**
•	•		•	•	ABC Services Inc Court Services	507-357-6320				
•					Alpha Court Records & Research	651-699-2222				
•	•	•	•	•	Capitol Lien Records & Research [SOP]	800-845-4077	•	•	•	•
•	•		•		Omni Data Retrieval Inc	952-985-7220			•	
•	•		•	•	Paragon Document Research Inc [SOP]	800-892-4235	•	•	•	
CR	**CV**	**PR**	**US**	**BK**	**←Courts** **BLUE EARTH**	**Recorder→**	**UC**	**RE**	**TX**	**VS**
•	•		•	•	ABC Services Inc Court Services	507-357-6320				
•	•		•	•	ABC Services Inc Real Estate Svcs	507-357-6320	•	•	•	
•					Alpha Court Records & Research	651-699-2222				
	•		•	•	Associated Abstracting Services of MN	612-819-6115	•	•	•	
•	•	•	•	•	Capitol Lien Records & Research [SOP]	800-845-4077	•	•	•	•
•	•	•	•	•	Information Reporting Services Inc	612-870-8770			•	
•	•		•		Omni Data Retrieval Inc	952-985-7220			•	
•	•		•	•	Paragon Document Research Inc [SOP]	800-892-4235	•	•	•	
•	•	•	•	•	Twin Cities Research	651-714-0002	•	•	•	•
CR	**CV**	**PR**	**US**	**BK**	**←Courts** **BROWN**	**Recorder→**	**UC**	**RE**	**TX**	**VS**
•	•		•	•	ABC Services Inc Court Services	507-357-6320				
•	•		•	•	ABC Services Inc Real Estate Svcs	507-357-6320	•	•	•	
•					Alpha Court Records & Research	651-699-2222				
•	•	•	•	•	Capitol Lien Records & Research [SOP]	800-845-4077	•	•	•	•
•	•		•		Omni Data Retrieval Inc	952-985-7220			•	
•	•		•	•	Paragon Document Research Inc [SOP]	800-892-4235	•	•	•	
•	•	•	•	•	Twin Cities Research	651-714-0002	•	•	•	•
CR	**CV**	**PR**	**US**	**BK**	**←Courts** **CARLTON**	**Recorder→**	**UC**	**RE**	**TX**	**VS**
•	•		•	•	ABC Services Inc Court Services	507-357-6320				
	•	•	•	•	Abstract & Title Services of Carlton Inc [SOP]	888-331-3966	•	•	•	
•					Alpha Court Records & Research	651-699-2222				
•	•	•	•	•	Capitol Lien Records & Research [SOP]	800-845-4077	•	•	•	•
•	•		•		Omni Data Retrieval Inc	952-985-7220			•	
•	•		•	•	Paragon Document Research Inc [SOP]	800-892-4235	•	•	•	
•	•	•	•	•	Twin Cities Research	651-714-0002	•	•	•	•
CR	**CV**	**PR**	**US**	**BK**	**←Courts** **CARVER**	**Recorder→**	**UC**	**RE**	**TX**	**VS**
•	•		•	•	ABC Services Inc Court Services	507-357-6320				
•	•		•	•	ABC Services Inc Real Estate Svcs	507-357-6320	•	•	•	
•	•	•	•	•	Adit Research Inc	888-721-5220	•	•	•	•
•					Alpha Court Records & Research	651-699-2222				
	•		•	•	Associated Abstracting Services of MN	612-819-6115	•	•	•	
•	•	•	•	•	Avalon Information Services	715-222-4095		•	•	•
•	•	•	•	•	Capitol Lien Records & Research [SOP]	800-845-4077	•	•	•	•
	•	•	•	•	CSC Minnesota	800-327-1886	•	•	•	•
•	•			•	Dovolos & Associates [SOP]	952-920-9999	•		•	
•	•				GHS Inc - Record Research	763-566-2125, cell- 612-210-9716		•	•	
•	•	•	•	•	Heartland Information Services [SOP]	800-967-1882	•	•	•	•
		•		•	Independent Abstracting Service Inc	763-792-6800	•	•	•	•
•	•	•	•	•	Information Reporting Services Inc	612-870-8770			•	
•	•		•	•	INPRO [SOP]	952-891-3617	•		•	•
•	•	•	•	•	Metro Legal Services [SOP]	800-488-8994	•	•	•	•
•	•		•		Omni Data Retrieval Inc	952-985-7220			•	

CR	CV	PR	US	BK	←Courts	Recorder→	UC	RE	TX	VS
•	•		•	•	Paragon Document Research Inc [SOP]	800-892-4235	•	•	•	
•	•	•	•	•	Twin Cities Research	651-714-0002	•	•	•	•
•	•	•	•	•	Verified Credentials Inc	800-473-4934	•	•	•	•
•	•	•	•	•	Patricia Wolff [SOP]	952-270-0095	•	•	•	•

Cass

CR	CV	PR	US	BK	←Courts	Recorder→	UC	RE	TX	VS
•	•		•	•	ABC Services Inc Court Services	507-357-6320				
•	•	•	•	•	ACME Research [SOP]	218-224-3239	•	•	•	•
•					Alpha Court Records & Research	651-699-2222				
•	•	•	•	•	Capitol Lien Records & Research [SOP]	800-845-4077	•	•	•	•
•		•			Cygneture Title Inc	218-828-0122	•	•	•	
•	•		•		Omni Data Retrieval Inc	952-985-7220			•	
•	•		•	•	Paragon Document Research Inc [SOP]	800-892-4235	•	•	•	

Chippewa

CR	CV	PR	US	BK	←Courts	Recorder→	UC	RE	TX	VS
•	•		•	•	ABC Services Inc Court Services	507-357-6320				
•					Alpha Court Records & Research	651-699-2222				
•	•	•	•	•	Capitol Lien Records & Research [SOP]	800-845-4077	•	•	•	•
•	•		•		Omni Data Retrieval Inc	952-985-7220			•	
•	•		•	•	Paragon Document Research Inc [SOP]	800-892-4235	•	•	•	
•	•	•	•	•	Twin Cities Research	651-714-0002	•	•	•	•

Chisago

CR	CV	PR	US	BK	←Courts	Recorder→	UC	RE	TX	VS
•	•		•	•	ABC Services Inc Court Services	507-357-6320				
•	•	•	•	•	Accountable Process Servers Inc [SOP]	612-991-7849		•	•	
•					Alpha Court Records & Research	651-699-2222				
	•		•	•	Associated Abstracting Services of MN	612-819-6115	•	•	•	
•	•	•	•	•	Capitol Lien Records & Research [SOP]	800-845-4077	•	•	•	•
•	•				GHS Inc - Record Research	763-566-2125, cell- 612-210-9716		•	•	
•	•				Horvath Enterprises Inc	320-982-3253			•	
		•		•	Independent Abstracting Service Inc	763-792-6800	•	•	•	•
	•			•	Land Title Inc	651-638-1900	•	•	•	
•	•		•		Omni Data Retrieval Inc	952-985-7220			•	
•	•		•	•	Paragon Document Research Inc [SOP]	800-892-4235	•	•	•	
•	•	•	•	•	Twin Cities Research	651-714-0002	•	•	•	•
•	•	•	•	•	Verified Credentials Inc	800-473-4934	•	•	•	•

Clay

CR	CV	PR	US	BK	←Courts	Recorder→	UC	RE	TX	VS
•	•	•	•	•	Butcher & Associates Ltd [SOP]	701-224-1541	•	•	•	•
•	•	•	•	•	C.C.I. [SOP]	701-235-4842	•	•	•	
•	•	•	•	•	Capitol Lien Records & Research [SOP]	800-845-4077	•	•	•	•
					Cass County Abstract Co (North Dakota)	701-232-3341	•	•	•	
	•	•	•	•	Clay County Abstract Co [SOP]	218-233-1358	•	•	•	
•	•				Horvath Enterprises Inc	320-982-3253			•	
•	•		•		Omni Data Retrieval Inc	952-985-7220			•	
•	•		•	•	Paragon Document Research Inc [SOP]	800-892-4235	•	•	•	

Clearwater

CR	CV	PR	US	BK	←Courts	Recorder→	UC	RE	TX	VS
•	•		•	•	ABC Services Inc Court Services	507-357-6320				
•	•	•	•	•	Capitol Lien Records & Research [SOP]	800-845-4077	•	•	•	•
•	•		•		Omni Data Retrieval Inc	952-985-7220			•	
•	•		•	•	Paragon Document Research Inc [SOP]	800-892-4235	•	•	•	

Cook

CR	CV	PR	US	BK	←Courts	Recorder→	UC	RE	TX	VS
•	•		•	•	ABC Services Inc Court Services	507-357-6320				
•					Alpha Court Records & Research	651-699-2222				
•	•	•	•	•	Capitol Lien Records & Research [SOP]	800-845-4077	•	•	•	•
•	•		•		Omni Data Retrieval Inc	952-985-7220			•	
•	•		•	•	Paragon Document Research Inc [SOP]	800-892-4235	•	•	•	
•	•	•	•	•	Twin Cities Research	651-714-0002	•	•	•	•

CR	CV	PR	US	BK	←COURTS **COTTONWOOD**	RECORDER→	UC	RE	TX	VS
•	•		•	•	ABC Services Inc Court Services	507-357-6320				
•					Alpha Court Records & Research	651-699-2222				
•	•	•	•	•	Capitol Lien Records & Research [SOP]	800-845-4077	•	•	•	•
					Cottonwood County Abstract Company	507-831-1504		•	•	
•	•		•		Omni Data Retrieval Inc	952-985-7220			•	
•	•		•	•	Paragon Document Research Inc [SOP]	800-892-4235	•	•	•	
•	•	•	•	•	Twin Cities Research	651-714-0002	•	•	•	•

CR	CV	PR	US	BK	←COURTS **CROW WING**	RECORDER→	UC	RE	TX	VS
•	•		•	•	ABC Services Inc Court Services	507-357-6320				
•	•	•	•	•	Capitol Lien Records & Research [SOP]	800-845-4077	•	•	•	•
					Crow Wing County Abstract Co	218-829-7368	•	•	•	
•		•			Cygneture Title Inc	218-828-0122	•	•	•	
•	•		•		Omni Data Retrieval Inc	952-985-7220			•	
•	•		•	•	Paragon Document Research Inc [SOP]	800-892-4235	•	•	•	

CR	CV	PR	US	BK	←COURTS **DAKOTA**	RECORDER→	UC	RE	TX	VS
•	•		•	•	ABC Services Inc Court Services	507-357-6320				
•	•		•	•	ABC Services Inc Real Estate Svcs	507-357-6320	•	•	•	
•	•	•	•	•	Adit Research Inc	888-721-5220	•	•	•	•
•					Alpha Court Records & Research	651-699-2222				
•	•	•	•	•	Avalon Information Services	715-222-4095		•	•	•
•	•	•	•	•	Capitol Lien Records & Research [SOP]	800-845-4077	•	•	•	•
	•	•	•	•	CSC Minnesota	800-327-1886	•	•	•	•
		•			Dakota County Abstract Co	651-437-5600	•	•	•	
•	•			•	Dovolos & Associates [SOP]	952-920-9999	•		•	
•	•				GHS Inc - Record Research	763-566-2125, cell- 612-210-9716		•	•	
•	•	•	•	•	Heartland Information Services [SOP]	800-967-1882	•	•	•	•
		•		•	Independent Abstracting Service Inc	763-792-6800	•	•	•	•
•	•	•	•	•	Information Reporting Services Inc	612-870-8770			•	
•	•		•	•	INPRO [SOP]	952-891-3617	•		•	•
	•			•	Land Title Inc	651-638-1900	•	•	•	
•	•	•	•	•	Metro Legal Services [SOP]	800-488-8994	•	•	•	•
•	•		•		Omni Data Retrieval Inc	952-985-7220			•	
•	•		•	•	Paragon Document Research Inc [SOP]	800-892-4235	•	•	•	
•	•	•	•	•	The McDowell Agency Inc [SOP]	651-644-3880	•	•	•	•
•	•	•	•	•	Twin Cities Research	651-714-0002	•	•	•	•
•	•	•	•	•	Verified Credentials Inc	800-473-4934	•	•	•	•
•	•	•	•	•	Patricia Wolff [SOP]	952-270-0095	•	•	•	•

CR	CV	PR	US	BK	←COURTS **DODGE**	RECORDER→	UC	RE	TX	VS
•	•		•	•	ABC Services Inc Court Services	507-357-6320				
•	•		•	•	ABC Services Inc Real Estate Svcs	507-357-6320	•	•	•	
•					Alpha Court Records & Research	651-699-2222				
•	•	•	•	•	Capitol Lien Records & Research [SOP]	800-845-4077	•	•	•	•
•	•		•		Omni Data Retrieval Inc	952-985-7220			•	
•	•		•	•	Paragon Document Research Inc [SOP]	800-892-4235	•	•	•	
•	•	•	•	•	Twin Cities Research	651-714-0002	•	•	•	•

CR	CV	PR	US	BK	←COURTS **DOUGLAS**	RECORDER→	UC	RE	TX	VS
•	•	•	•	•	Capitol Lien Records & Research [SOP]	800-845-4077	•	•	•	•
	•	•			Douglas County Abstract Co	320-763-3426		•	•	
•	•				Horvath Enterprises Inc	320-982-3253			•	
•	•		•		Omni Data Retrieval Inc	952-985-7220			•	
•	•		•	•	Paragon Document Research Inc [SOP]	800-892-4235	•	•	•	
•	•				West Central Process Service [SOP]	320-239-2665, cell- 320-808-6968				

CR	CV	PR	US	BK	←Courts	Faribault	Recorder→	UC	RE	TX	VS
•	•		•	•	ABC Services Inc Court Services		507-357-6320				
•					Alpha Court Records & Research		651-699-2222				
•	•	•	•	•	Capitol Lien Records & Research [SOP]		800-845-4077	•	•	•	•
					Sharon K Hannaman Abstracter		507-526-5144		•	•	
•	•		•		Omni Data Retrieval Inc		952-985-7220			•	
•	•		•	•	Paragon Document Research Inc [SOP]		800-892-4235	•	•	•	
•	•	•	•	•	Twin Cities Research		651-714-0002	•	•	•	•

CR	CV	PR	US	BK	←Courts	Fillmore	Recorder→	UC	RE	TX	VS
•	•		•	•	ABC Services Inc Court Services		507-357-6320				
•					Alpha Court Records & Research		651-699-2222				
•	•	•	•	•	Capitol Lien Records & Research [SOP]		800-845-4077	•	•	•	•
•	•		•		Omni Data Retrieval Inc		952-985-7220			•	
•	•		•	•	Paragon Document Research Inc [SOP]		800-892-4235	•	•	•	

CR	CV	PR	US	BK	←Courts	Freeborn	Recorder→	UC	RE	TX	VS
•	•		•	•	ABC Services Inc Court Services		507-357-6320				
•	•		•	•	ABC Services Inc Real Estate Svcs		507-357-6320	•	•	•	
		•			Albert Lea Abstract Co		507-373-9001	•	•	•	•
•					Alpha Court Records & Research		651-699-2222				
•	•	•	•	•	Capitol Lien Records & Research [SOP]		800-845-4077	•	•	•	•
•	•				GHS Inc - Record Research		763-566-2125, cell- 612-210-9716		•	•	
•	•		•		Omni Data Retrieval Inc		952-985-7220			•	
•	•		•	•	Paragon Document Research Inc [SOP]		800-892-4235	•	•	•	

CR	CV	PR	US	BK	←Courts	Goodhue	Recorder→	UC	RE	TX	VS
•	•		•	•	ABC Services Inc Court Services		507-357-6320				
•					Alpha Court Records & Research		651-699-2222				
•	•	•	•	•	Capitol Lien Records & Research [SOP]		800-845-4077	•	•	•	•
•	•	•	•	•	Information Reporting Services Inc		612-870-8770			•	
•	•		•		Omni Data Retrieval Inc		952-985-7220			•	
•	•		•	•	Paragon Document Research Inc [SOP]		800-892-4235	•	•	•	
•	•	•	•	•	Twin Cities Research		651-714-0002	•	•	•	•
•	•	•	•	•	Verified Credentials Inc		800-473-4934	•	•	•	•

CR	CV	PR	US	BK	←Courts	Grant	Recorder→	UC	RE	TX	VS
•	•		•	•	ABC Services Inc Court Services		507-357-6320				
•					Alpha Court Records & Research		651-699-2222				
•	•	•	•	•	Capitol Lien Records & Research [SOP]		800-845-4077	•	•	•	•
•	•		•		Omni Data Retrieval Inc		952-985-7220			•	
•	•		•	•	Paragon Document Research Inc [SOP]		800-892-4235	•	•	•	
•	•				West Central Process Service [SOP]		320-239-2665, cell- 320-808-6968				

CR	CV	PR	US	BK	←Courts	Hennepin	Recorder→	UC	RE	TX	VS
•	•		•	•	ABC Services Inc Court Services		507-357-6320				
•	•		•	•	ABC Services Inc Real Estate Svcs		507-357-6320	•	•	•	
•	•	•	•	•	Accountable Process Servers Inc [SOP]		612-991-7849		•	•	
•	•	•	•	•	Adit Research Inc		888-721-5220	•	•	•	•
•					Alpha Court Records & Research		651-699-2222				
	•		•	•	Associated Abstracting Services of MN		612-819-6115	•	•	•	
•	•	•	•	•	Avalon Information Services		715-222-4095		•	•	•
•	•	•	•	•	Capitol Lien Records & Research [SOP]		800-845-4077	•	•	•	•
	•	•	•	•	CSC Minnesota		800-327-1886	•	•	•	•
•	•			•	Dovolos & Associates [SOP]		952-920-9999	•		•	
•	•				GHS Inc - Record Research		763-566-2125, cell- 612-210-9716		•	•	
•	•	•	•	•	Heartland Information Services [SOP]		800-967-1882	•	•	•	•
		•		•	Independent Abstracting Service Inc		763-792-6800	•	•	•	•
•	•	•	•	•	Information Reporting Services Inc		612-870-8770			•	
•	•		•	•	INPRO [SOP]		952-891-3617	•		•	•

CR	CV	PR	US	BK	←Courts	Recorder→	UC	RE	TX	VS
	•			•	Land Title Inc	651-638-1900	•	•	•	
•	•	•	•	•	Metro Legal Services [SOP]	800-488-8994	•	•	•	•
•	•		•		Omni Data Retrieval Inc	952-985-7220			•	
•	•		•	•	Paragon Document Research Inc [SOP]	800-892-4235	•	•	•	
•	•		•	•	Premier Corporate Services MN	800-227-1256	•	•	•	
•	•	•	•	•	The McDowell Agency Inc [SOP]	651-644-3880	•	•	•	•
•	•	•	•	•	Twin Cities Research	651-714-0002	•	•	•	•
•	•	•	•	•	Verified Credentials Inc	800-473-4934	•	•	•	•

CR	CV	PR	US	BK	←Courts **HOUSTON**	Recorder→	UC	RE	TX	VS
•	•		•	•	ABC Services Inc Court Services	507-357-6320				
•					Alpha Court Records & Research	651-699-2222				
•	•	•	•	•	Capitol Lien Records & Research [SOP]	800-845-4077	•	•	•	•
•	•		•		Omni Data Retrieval Inc	952-985-7220			•	
•	•		•	•	Paragon Document Research Inc [SOP]	800-892-4235	•	•	•	
		•	•	•	The Title Co Inc (La Crosse)	800-788-4853	•	•	•	

CR	CV	PR	US	BK	←Courts **HUBBARD**	Recorder→	UC	RE	TX	VS
•	•	•	•	•	ACME Research [SOP]	218-224-3239	•	•	•	•
•	•	•	•	•	Capitol Lien Records & Research [SOP]	800-845-4077	•	•	•	•
•	•		•		Omni Data Retrieval Inc	952-985-7220			•	
•	•		•	•	Paragon Document Research Inc [SOP]	800-892-4235	•	•	•	

CR	CV	PR	US	BK	←Courts **ISANTI**	Recorder→	UC	RE	TX	VS
•	•		•	•	ABC Services Inc Court Services	507-357-6320				
•	•	•	•	•	Accountable Process Servers Inc [SOP]	612-991-7849		•	•	
•					Alpha Court Records & Research	651-699-2222				
	•		•	•	Associated Abstracting Services of MN	612-819-6115	•	•	•	
•	•	•	•	•	Capitol Lien Records & Research [SOP]	800-845-4077	•	•	•	•
•	•				Horvath Enterprises Inc	320-982-3253			•	
		•		•	Independent Abstracting Service Inc	763-792-6800	•	•	•	•
•	•		•		Omni Data Retrieval Inc	952-985-7220			•	
•	•		•	•	Paragon Document Research Inc [SOP]	800-892-4235	•	•	•	
•	•	•	•	•	Twin Cities Research	651-714-0002	•	•	•	•

CR	CV	PR	US	BK	←Courts **ITASCA**	Recorder→	UC	RE	TX	VS
•	•		•	•	ABC Services Inc Court Services	507-357-6320				
•					Alpha Court Records & Research	651-699-2222				
•	•	•	•	•	Capitol Lien Records & Research [SOP]	800-845-4077	•	•	•	•
	•	•			Itasca County Abstract Co	218-326-9601	•	•	•	•
•	•		•		Omni Data Retrieval Inc	952-985-7220			•	
•	•		•	•	Paragon Document Research Inc [SOP]	800-892-4235	•	•	•	
•	•	•	•	•	Twin Cities Research	651-714-0002	•	•	•	•

CR	CV	PR	US	BK	←Courts **JACKSON**	Recorder→	UC	RE	TX	VS
•	•		•	•	ABC Services Inc Court Services	507-357-6320				
•					Alpha Court Records & Research	651-699-2222				
•	•	•	•	•	Capitol Lien Records & Research [SOP]	800-845-4077	•	•	•	•
•	•		•		Omni Data Retrieval Inc	952-985-7220			•	
•	•		•	•	Paragon Document Research Inc [SOP]	800-892-4235	•	•	•	
•	•	•	•	•	Twin Cities Research	651-714-0002	•	•	•	•

CR	CV	PR	US	BK	←Courts **KANABEC**	Recorder→	UC	RE	TX	VS
•	•		•	•	ABC Services Inc Court Services	507-357-6320				
•					Alpha Court Records & Research	651-699-2222				
•	•	•	•	•	Capitol Lien Records & Research [SOP]	800-845-4077	•	•	•	•
•	•				Horvath Enterprises Inc	320-982-3253			•	
•	•		•		Omni Data Retrieval Inc	952-985-7220			•	
•	•		•	•	Paragon Document Research Inc [SOP]	800-892-4235	•	•	•	
•	•	•	•	•	Twin Cities Research	651-714-0002	•	•	•	•

CR	CV	PR	US	BK	←Courts	Kandiyohi	Recorder→	UC	RE	TX	VS
•	•		•	•	ABC Services Inc Court Services		507-357-6320				
•					Alpha Court Records & Research		651-699-2222				
•	•	•	•	•	Capitol Lien Records & Research [SOP]		800-845-4077	•	•	•	•
•	•		•		Omni Data Retrieval Inc		952-985-7220			•	
•	•		•	•	Paragon Document Research Inc [SOP]		800-892-4235	•	•	•	
•	•	•	•	•	Twin Cities Research		651-714-0002	•	•	•	•

CR	CV	PR	US	BK	←Courts	Kittson	Recorder→	UC	RE	TX	VS
•	•		•	•	ABC Services Inc Court Services		507-357-6320				
•					Alpha Court Records & Research		651-699-2222				
•	•	•	•	•	Capitol Lien Records & Research [SOP]		800-845-4077	•	•	•	•
•	•		•		Omni Data Retrieval Inc		952-985-7220			•	
•	•		•	•	Paragon Document Research Inc [SOP]		800-892-4235	•	•	•	

CR	CV	PR	US	BK	←Courts	Koochiching	Recorder→	UC	RE	TX	VS
•	•		•	•	ABC Services Inc Court Services		507-357-6320				
•	•	•	•	•	Capitol Lien Records & Research [SOP]		800-845-4077	•	•	•	•
•	•		•		Omni Data Retrieval Inc		952-985-7220			•	
•	•		•	•	Paragon Document Research Inc [SOP]		800-892-4235	•	•	•	

CR	CV	PR	US	BK	←Courts	Lac Qui Parle	Recorder→	UC	RE	TX	VS
•	•		•	•	ABC Services Inc Court Services		507-357-6320				
•					Alpha Court Records & Research		651-699-2222				
•	•	•	•	•	Capitol Lien Records & Research [SOP]		800-845-4077	•	•	•	•
•	•		•		Omni Data Retrieval Inc		952-985-7220			•	
•	•		•	•	Paragon Document Research Inc [SOP]		800-892-4235	•	•	•	
•	•	•	•	•	Twin Cities Research		651-714-0002	•	•	•	•

CR	CV	PR	US	BK	←Courts	Lake	Recorder→	UC	RE	TX	VS
•	•		•	•	ABC Services Inc Court Services		507-357-6320				
•					Alpha Court Records & Research		651-699-2222				
•	•	•	•	•	Capitol Lien Records & Research [SOP]		800-845-4077	•	•	•	•
•	•		•		Omni Data Retrieval Inc		952-985-7220			•	
•	•		•	•	Paragon Document Research Inc [SOP]		800-892-4235	•	•	•	
•	•	•	•	•	Twin Cities Research		651-714-0002	•	•	•	•

CR	CV	PR	US	BK	←Courts	Lake of the Woods	Recorder→	UC	RE	TX	VS
•	•	•	•	•	Capitol Lien Records & Research [SOP]		800-845-4077	•	•	•	•
•	•		•		Omni Data Retrieval Inc		952-985-7220			•	
•	•		•	•	Paragon Document Research Inc [SOP]		800-892-4235	•	•	•	

CR	CV	PR	US	BK	←Courts	Le Sueur	Recorder→	UC	RE	TX	VS
•	•		•	•	ABC Services Inc Court Services		507-357-6320				
•	•		•	•	ABC Services Inc Real Estate Svcs		507-357-6320				
•					Alpha Court Records & Research		651-699-2222				
	•		•	•	Associated Abstracting Services of MN		612-819-6115	•	•	•	
•	•	•	•	•	Capitol Lien Records & Research [SOP]		800-845-4077	•	•	•	•
•	•		•		Omni Data Retrieval Inc		952-985-7220			•	
•	•		•	•	Paragon Document Research Inc [SOP]		800-892-4235	•	•	•	
•	•	•	•	•	Twin Cities Research		651-714-0002	•	•	•	•

CR	CV	PR	US	BK	←Courts	Lincoln	Recorder→	UC	RE	TX	VS
•	•		•	•	ABC Services Inc Court Services		507-357-6320				
•					Alpha Court Records & Research		651-699-2222				
•	•	•	•	•	Capitol Lien Records & Research [SOP]		800-845-4077	•	•	•	•
•	•		•		Omni Data Retrieval Inc		952-985-7220			•	
•	•		•	•	Paragon Document Research Inc [SOP]		800-892-4235	•	•	•	

CR	CV	PR	US	BK	←COURTS **LYON** RECORDER→		UC	RE	TX	VS
•	•		•	•	ABC Services Inc Court Services	507-357-6320				
•					Alpha Court Records & Research	651-699-2222				
•	•	•	•	•	Capitol Lien Records & Research [SOP]	800-845-4077	•	•	•	•
•	•		•		Omni Data Retrieval Inc	952-985-7220			•	
•	•		•	•	Paragon Document Research Inc [SOP]	800-892-4235	•	•	•	

CR	CV	PR	US	BK	←COURTS **MAHNOMEN** RECORDER→		UC	RE	TX	VS
•	•		•	•	ABC Services Inc Court Services	507-357-6320				
•					Alpha Court Records & Research	651-699-2222				
•	•	•	•	•	Capitol Lien Records & Research [SOP]	800-845-4077	•	•	•	•
					Mahnomen County Abstract Co	218-935-5227		•		
•	•		•		Omni Data Retrieval Inc	952-985-7220			•	
•	•		•	•	Paragon Document Research Inc [SOP]	800-892-4235	•	•	•	

CR	CV	PR	US	BK	←COURTS **MARSHALL** RECORDER→		UC	RE	TX	VS
•	•		•	•	ABC Services Inc Court Services	507-357-6320				
•					Alpha Court Records & Research	651-699-2222				
•	•	•	•	•	Capitol Lien Records & Research [SOP]	800-845-4077	•	•	•	•
•	•		•		Omni Data Retrieval Inc	952-985-7220			•	
•	•		•	•	Paragon Document Research Inc [SOP]	800-892-4235	•	•	•	
			•	•	Pennington County Abstract Co	218-681-2527		•	•	

CR	CV	PR	US	BK	←COURTS **MARTIN** RECORDER→		UC	RE	TX	VS
•	•		•	•	ABC Services Inc Court Services	507-357-6320				
•					Alpha Court Records & Research	651-699-2222				
•	•	•	•	•	Capitol Lien Records & Research [SOP]	800-845-4077	•	•	•	•
•	•		•		Omni Data Retrieval Inc	952-985-7220			•	
•	•		•	•	Paragon Document Research Inc [SOP]	800-892-4235	•	•	•	
•	•	•	•	•	Twin Cities Research	651-714-0002	•	•	•	•

CR	CV	PR	US	BK	←COURTS **MCLEOD** RECORDER→		UC	RE	TX	VS
•	•		•	•	ABC Services Inc Court Services	507-357-6320				
•	•		•	•	ABC Services Inc Real Estate Svcs	507-357-6320	•	•	•	
•					Alpha Court Records & Research	651-699-2222				
•	•	•	•	•	Capitol Lien Records & Research [SOP]	800-845-4077	•	•	•	•
•	•		•		Omni Data Retrieval Inc	952-985-7220			•	
•	•		•	•	Paragon Document Research Inc [SOP]	800-892-4235	•	•	•	
•	•	•	•	•	Twin Cities Research	651-714-0002	•	•	•	•

CR	CV	PR	US	BK	←COURTS **MEEKER** RECORDER→		UC	RE	TX	VS
•	•		•	•	ABC Services Inc Court Services	507-357-6320				
•					Alpha Court Records & Research	651-699-2222				
•	•	•	•	•	Capitol Lien Records & Research [SOP]	800-845-4077	•	•	•	•
•	•		•		Omni Data Retrieval Inc	952-985-7220			•	
•	•		•	•	Paragon Document Research Inc [SOP]	800-892-4235	•	•	•	
•	•	•	•	•	Twin Cities Research	651-714-0002	•	•	•	•

CR	CV	PR	US	BK	←COURTS **MILLE LACS** RECORDER→		UC	RE	TX	VS
•	•		•	•	ABC Services Inc Court Services	507-357-6320				
•					Alpha Court Records & Research	651-699-2222				
	•		•	•	Associated Abstracting Services of MN	612-819-6115	•	•	•	
•	•	•	•	•	Capitol Lien Records & Research [SOP]	800-845-4077	•	•	•	•
•	•				Horvath Enterprises Inc	320-982-3253			•	
•	•		•		Omni Data Retrieval Inc	952-985-7220			•	
•	•		•	•	Paragon Document Research Inc [SOP]	800-892-4235	•	•	•	
					Tri-County Abstract & Title Guaranty	800-892-2399	•	•	•	
•	•	•	•	•	Twin Cities Research	651-714-0002	•	•	•	•

Morrison

CR	CV	PR	US	BK	←Courts	Recorder→	UC	RE	TX	VS
•	•		•	•	ABC Services Inc Court Services	507-357-6320				
•	•	•	•	•	Capitol Lien Records & Research [SOP]	800-845-4077	•	•	•	•
•		•			Cygneture Title Inc	218-828-0122	•	•	•	
•	•				Horvath Enterprises Inc	320-982-3253			•	
		•			Larson Abstract Co	320-632-5667	•	•	•	•
•	•		•		Omni Data Retrieval Inc	952-985-7220			•	
•	•		•	•	Paragon Document Research Inc [SOP]	800-892-4235	•	•	•	
					Tri-County Abstract & Title Guaranty	800-892-2399	•	•	•	

Mower

CR	CV	PR	US	BK	←Courts	Recorder→	UC	RE	TX	VS
•	•		•	•	ABC Services Inc Court Services	507-357-6320				
•	•		•	•	ABC Services Inc Real Estate Svcs	507-357-6320	•	•	•	
		•			Albert Lea Abstract Co	507-373-9001	•	•	•	•
•					Alpha Court Records & Research	651-699-2222				
•	•	•	•	•	Capitol Lien Records & Research [SOP]	800-845-4077	•	•	•	•
•	•				GHS Inc - Record Research	763-566-2125, cell- 612-210-9716		•	•	
•	•		•		Omni Data Retrieval Inc	952-985-7220			•	
•	•		•	•	Paragon Document Research Inc [SOP]	800-892-4235	•	•	•	

Murray

CR	CV	PR	US	BK	←Courts	Recorder→	UC	RE	TX	VS
•	•		•	•	ABC Services Inc Court Services	507-357-6320				
•					Alpha Court Records & Research	651-699-2222				
•	•	•	•	•	Capitol Lien Records & Research [SOP]	800-845-4077	•	•	•	•
•	•		•		Omni Data Retrieval Inc	952-985-7220			•	
•	•		•	•	Paragon Document Research Inc [SOP]	800-892-4235	•	•	•	

Nicollet

CR	CV	PR	US	BK	←Courts	Recorder→	UC	RE	TX	VS
•	•		•	•	ABC Services Inc Court Services	507-357-6320				
•	•		•	•	ABC Services Inc Real Estate Svcs	507-357-6320	•	•	•	
•					Alpha Court Records & Research	651-699-2222				
	•		•	•	Associated Abstracting Services of MN	612-819-6115	•	•	•	
•	•	•	•	•	Capitol Lien Records & Research [SOP]	800-845-4077	•	•	•	•
•	•				GHS Inc - Record Research	763-566-2125, cell- 612-210-9716		•	•	
•	•		•		Omni Data Retrieval Inc	952-985-7220			•	
•	•		•	•	Paragon Document Research Inc [SOP]	800-892-4235	•	•	•	
•	•	•	•	•	Twin Cities Research	651-714-0002	•	•	•	•

Nobles

CR	CV	PR	US	BK	←Courts	Recorder→	UC	RE	TX	VS
•	•		•	•	ABC Services Inc Court Services	507-357-6320				
•					Alpha Court Records & Research	651-699-2222				
•	•	•	•	•	Capitol Lien Records & Research [SOP]	800-845-4077	•	•	•	•
•	•		•		Omni Data Retrieval Inc	952-985-7220			•	
•	•		•	•	Paragon Document Research Inc [SOP]	800-892-4235	•	•	•	

Norman

CR	CV	PR	US	BK	←Courts	Recorder→	UC	RE	TX	VS
•	•		•	•	ABC Services Inc Court Services	507-357-6320				
•					Alpha Court Records & Research	651-699-2222				
•	•	•	•	•	Capitol Lien Records & Research [SOP]	800-845-4077	•	•	•	•
•	•		•		Omni Data Retrieval Inc	952-985-7220			•	
•	•		•	•	Paragon Document Research Inc [SOP]	800-892-4235	•	•	•	

Olmsted

CR	CV	PR	US	BK	←Courts	Recorder→	UC	RE	TX	VS
•	•		•	•	ABC Services Inc Court Services	507-357-6320				
•	•		•	•	ABC Services Inc Real Estate Svcs	507-357-6320	•	•	•	
•					Alpha Court Records & Research	651-699-2222				
•	•	•	•	•	Capitol Lien Records & Research [SOP]	800-845-4077	•	•	•	•
•	•				GHS Inc - Record Research	763-566-2125, cell- 612-210-9716		•	•	
•	•	•	•	•	Information Reporting Services Inc	612-870-8770			•	
•	•		•		Omni Data Retrieval Inc	952-985-7220			•	

CR	CV	PR	US	BK	Courts	Phone	UC	RE	TX	VS
•	•		•	•	Paragon Document Research Inc [SOP]	800-892-4235	•	•	•	

CR	CV	PR	US	BK	←Courts — OTTER TAIL — Recorder→		UC	RE	TX	VS
•	•	•	•	•	Capitol Lien Records & Research [SOP]	800-845-4077	•	•	•	•
•	•				Horvath Enterprises Inc	320-982-3253			•	
	•	•			N F Field Abstract Co	218-736-6844	•	•	•	
•	•		•		Omni Data Retrieval Inc	952-985-7220			•	
•	•		•	•	Paragon Document Research Inc [SOP]	800-892-4235	•	•	•	
		•			West Central Abstracting Co	218-736-5685	•	•	•	•

CR	CV	PR	US	BK	←Courts — PENNINGTON — Recorder→		UC	RE	TX	VS
•	•		•	•	ABC Services Inc Court Services	507-357-6320				
•					Alpha Court Records & Research	651-699-2222				
•	•	•	•	•	Capitol Lien Records & Research [SOP]	800-845-4077	•	•	•	•
	•				Grand Forks Abstract & Title Co	701-772-3484	•	•	•	
•	•		•		Omni Data Retrieval Inc	952-985-7220			•	
•	•		•	•	Paragon Document Research Inc [SOP]	800-892-4235	•	•	•	
			•	•	Pennington County Abstract Co	218-681-2527		•	•	

CR	CV	PR	US	BK	←Courts — PINE — Recorder→		UC	RE	TX	VS
•	•		•	•	ABC Services Inc Court Services	507-357-6320				
	•	•	•	•	Abstract & Title Services of Carlton Inc [SOP]	888-331-3966	•	•	•	
•					Alpha Court Records & Research	651-699-2222				
•	•	•	•	•	Capitol Lien Records & Research [SOP]	800-845-4077	•	•	•	•
•	•				Horvath Enterprises Inc	320-982-3253			•	
•	•		•		Omni Data Retrieval Inc	952-985-7220			•	
•	•		•	•	Paragon Document Research Inc [SOP]	800-892-4235	•	•	•	
•	•	•	•	•	Twin Cities Research	651-714-0002	•	•	•	•

CR	CV	PR	US	BK	←Courts — PIPESTONE — Recorder→		UC	RE	TX	VS
•	•		•	•	ABC Services Inc Court Services	507-357-6320				
•					Alpha Court Records & Research	651-699-2222				
•	•	•	•	•	Capitol Lien Records & Research [SOP]	800-845-4077	•	•	•	•
•	•		•		Omni Data Retrieval Inc	952-985-7220			•	
•	•		•	•	Paragon Document Research Inc [SOP]	800-892-4235	•	•	•	
•	•	•			Pipestone County Abstract Co LLC	507-825-5833	•	•	•	

CR	CV	PR	US	BK	←Courts — POLK — Recorder→		UC	RE	TX	VS
•	•		•	•	ABC Services Inc Court Services	507-357-6320				
•					Alpha Court Records & Research	651-699-2222				
•	•	•	•	•	Capitol Lien Records & Research [SOP]	800-845-4077	•	•	•	•
•	•		•		Omni Data Retrieval Inc	952-985-7220			•	
•	•		•	•	Paragon Document Research Inc [SOP]	800-892-4235	•	•	•	
					Strander Abstract Inc	218-281-1191		•	•	

CR	CV	PR	US	BK	←Courts — POPE — Recorder→		UC	RE	TX	VS
•	•		•	•	ABC Services Inc Court Services	507-357-6320				
•					Alpha Court Records & Research	651-699-2222				
•	•	•	•	•	Capitol Lien Records & Research [SOP]	800-845-4077	•	•	•	•
	•	•			Douglas County Abstract Co	320-763-3426		•	•	
•	•		•		Omni Data Retrieval Inc	952-985-7220			•	
•	•		•	•	Paragon Document Research Inc [SOP]	800-892-4235	•	•	•	
•	•				West Central Process Service [SOP]	320-239-2665, cell-320-808-6968				

CR	CV	PR	US	BK	←Courts — RAMSEY — Recorder→		UC	RE	TX	VS
•	•		•	•	ABC Services Inc Court Services	507-357-6320				
•	•		•	•	ABC Services Inc Real Estate Svcs	507-357-6320	•	•	•	
•	•	•	•	•	Accountable Process Servers Inc [SOP]	612-991-7849		•	•	
•	•	•	•	•	Adit Research Inc	888-721-5220	•	•	•	•
•					Alpha Court Records & Research	651-699-2222				
•	•	•	•	•	Avalon Information Services	715-222-4095		•	•	•

CR	CV	PR	US	BK	←Courts	Recorder→	UC	RE	TX	VS
•	•	•	•	•	Capitol Lien Records & Research [SOP]	800-845-4077	•	•	•	•
	•	•	•	•	CSC Minnesota	800-327-1886	•	•	•	•
•	•			•	Dovolos & Associates [SOP]	952-920-9999	•		•	
•	•				GHS Inc - Record Research	763-566-2125, cell- 612-210-9716		•	•	
•	•	•	•	•	Heartland Information Services [SOP]	800-967-1882	•	•	•	•
		•		•	Independent Abstracting Service Inc	763-792-6800	•	•	•	•
•	•	•	•	•	Information Reporting Services Inc	612-870-8770			•	
•	•		•	•	INPRO [SOP]	952-891-3617	•		•	•
	•			•	Land Title Inc	651-638-1900	•	•	•	
•	•	•	•	•	Metro Legal Services [SOP]	800-488-8994	•	•	•	•
•	•		•		Omni Data Retrieval Inc	952-985-7220			•	
•	•		•	•	Paragon Document Research Inc [SOP]	800-892-4235	•	•	•	
•	•		•	•	Premier Corporate Services MN	800-227-1256	•	•	•	
•	•	•	•	•	The McDowell Agency Inc [SOP]	651-644-3880	•	•	•	•
•	•	•	•	•	Twin Cities Research	651-714-0002	•	•	•	•
•	•	•	•	•	Verified Credentials Inc	800-473-4934	•	•	•	•

CR	CV	PR	US	BK	←Courts **Red Lake**	Recorder→	UC	RE	TX	VS
•					Alpha Court Records & Research	651-699-2222				
•	•	•	•	•	Capitol Lien Records & Research [SOP]	800-845-4077	•	•	•	•
•	•		•		Omni Data Retrieval Inc	952-985-7220			•	
•	•		•	•	Paragon Document Research Inc [SOP]	800-892-4235	•	•	•	

CR	CV	PR	US	BK	←Courts **Redwood**	Recorder→	UC	RE	TX	VS
•	•		•	•	ABC Services Inc Court Services	507-357-6320				
•					Alpha Court Records & Research	651-699-2222				
•	•	•	•	•	Capitol Lien Records & Research [SOP]	800-845-4077	•	•	•	•
•	•		•		Omni Data Retrieval Inc	952-985-7220			•	
•	•		•	•	Paragon Document Research Inc [SOP]	800-892-4235	•	•	•	
					Renville County Abstract Co	320-523-5328		•	•	
•	•	•	•	•	Twin Cities Research	651-714-0002	•	•	•	•

CR	CV	PR	US	BK	←Courts **Renville**	Recorder→	UC	RE	TX	VS
•	•		•	•	ABC Services Inc Court Services	507-357-6320				
•					Alpha Court Records & Research	651-699-2222				
•	•	•	•	•	Capitol Lien Records & Research [SOP]	800-845-4077	•	•	•	•
•	•		•		Omni Data Retrieval Inc	952-985-7220			•	
•	•		•	•	Paragon Document Research Inc [SOP]	800-892-4235	•	•	•	
					Renville County Abstract Co	320-523-5328		•	•	
•	•	•	•	•	Twin Cities Research	651-714-0002	•	•	•	•

CR	CV	PR	US	BK	←Courts **Rice**	Recorder→	UC	RE	TX	VS
•	•		•	•	ABC Services Inc Court Services	507-357-6320				
•	•		•	•	ABC Services Inc Real Estate Svcs	507-357-6320	•	•	•	
•					Alpha Court Records & Research	651-699-2222				
	•		•	•	Associated Abstracting Services of MN	612-819-6115	•	•	•	
•	•	•	•	•	Capitol Lien Records & Research [SOP]	800-845-4077	•	•	•	•
•	•				GHS Inc - Record Research	763-566-2125, cell- 612-210-9716		•	•	
•	•		•		Omni Data Retrieval Inc	952-985-7220			•	
•	•		•	•	Paragon Document Research Inc [SOP]	800-892-4235	•	•	•	
•	•	•	•	•	Verified Credentials Inc	800-473-4934	•	•	•	•

CR	CV	PR	US	BK	←Courts **Rock**	Recorder→	UC	RE	TX	VS
•	•		•	•	ABC Services Inc Court Services	507-357-6320				
•					Alpha Court Records & Research	651-699-2222				
•	•	•	•	•	Capitol Lien Records & Research [SOP]	800-845-4077	•	•	•	•
•	•		•		Omni Data Retrieval Inc	952-985-7220			•	
•	•		•	•	Paragon Document Research Inc [SOP]	800-892-4235	•	•	•	

CR	CV	PR	US	BK	←COURTS **ROSEAU** RECORDER→		UC	RE	TX	VS
•	•		•	•	ABC Services Inc Court Services	507-357-6320				
•					Alpha Court Records & Research	651-699-2222				
•	•	•	•		Capitol Lien Records & Research [SOP]	800-845-4077	•	•	•	•
•	•		•		Omni Data Retrieval Inc	952-985-7220			•	
•	•		•	•	Paragon Document Research Inc [SOP]	800-892-4235	•	•	•	

CR	CV	PR	US	BK	←COURTS **SCOTT** RECORDER→		UC	RE	TX	VS
•	•		•	•	ABC Services Inc Court Services	507-357-6320				
•	•		•	•	ABC Services Inc Real Estate Svcs	507-357-6320	•	•	•	
•	•	•	•	•	Adit Research Inc.	888-721-5220	•	•	•	•
•					Alpha Court Records & Research	651-699-2222				
	•		•	•	Associated Abstracting Services of MN	612-819-6115	•	•	•	
•	•	•	•	•	Avalon Information Services	715-222-4095		•	•	•
•	•	•	•	•	Capitol Lien Records & Research [SOP]	800-845-4077	•	•	•	•
	•	•	•	•	CSC Minnesota	800-327-1886	•	•	•	•
•	•			•	Dovolos & Associates [SOP]	952-920-9999	•		•	
•	•				GHS Inc - Record Research	763-566-2125, cell- 612-210-9716		•	•	
•	•	•	•	•	Heartland Information Services [SOP]	800-967-1882	•	•	•	•
		•		•	Independent Abstracting Service Inc	763-792-6800	•	•	•	•
•	•	•	•	•	Information Reporting Services Inc	612-870-8770			•	
•	•		•	•	INPRO [SOP]	952-891-3617	•		•	•
•	•	•	•	•	Metro Legal Services [SOP]	800-488-8994	•	•	•	•
•	•		•		Omni Data Retrieval Inc	952-985-7220			•	
•	•		•	•	Paragon Document Research Inc [SOP]	800-892-4235	•	•	•	
•	•	•	•	•	Twin Cities Research	651-714-0002	•	•	•	•
•	•	•	•	•	Verified Credentials Inc	800-473-4934	•	•	•	•
•	•	•	•	•	Patricia Wolff [SOP]	952-270-0095	•	•	•	•

CR	CV	PR	US	BK	←COURTS **SHERBURNE** RECORDER→		UC	RE	TX	VS
•	•		•	•	ABC Services Inc Court Services	507-357-6320				
•	•		•	•	ABC Services Inc Real Estate Svcs	507-357-6320	•	•	•	
•	•	•	•	•	Accountable Process Servers Inc [SOP]	612-991-7849		•	•	
•	•	•	•	•	Adit Research Inc.	888-721-5220	•	•	•	•
•					Alpha Court Records & Research	651-699-2222				
	•		•	•	Associated Abstracting Services of MN	612-819-6115	•	•	•	
•	•	•	•	•	Avalon Information Services	715-222-4095		•	•	•
•	•	•	•	•	Capitol Lien Records & Research [SOP]	800-845-4077	•	•	•	•
	•	•	•	•	CSC Minnesota	800-327-1886	•	•	•	•
•	•				GHS Inc - Record Research	763-566-2125, cell- 612-210-9716		•	•	
•	•				Horvath Enterprises Inc	320-982-3253			•	
		•		•	Independent Abstracting Service Inc	763-792-6800	•	•	•	•
•	•	•	•	•	Metro Legal Services [SOP]	800-488-8994	•	•	•	•
•	•		•		Omni Data Retrieval Inc	952-985-7220			•	
•	•		•	•	Paragon Document Research Inc [SOP]	800-892-4235	•	•	•	
					Tri-County Abstract & Title Guaranty	800-892-2399	•	•	•	
•	•	•	•	•	Twin Cities Research	651-714-0002	•	•	•	•
•	•	•	•	•	Verified Credentials Inc	800-473-4934	•	•	•	•

CR	CV	PR	US	BK	←COURTS **SIBLEY** RECORDER→		UC	RE	TX	VS
•	•		•	•	ABC Services Inc Court Services	507-357-6320				
•	•		•	•	ABC Services Inc Real Estate Svcs	507-357-6320	•	•	•	
•					Alpha Court Records & Research	651-699-2222				
•	•	•	•	•	Capitol Lien Records & Research [SOP]	800-845-4077	•	•	•	•
•	•		•		Omni Data Retrieval Inc	952-985-7220			•	
•	•		•	•	Paragon Document Research Inc [SOP]	800-892-4235	•	•	•	
•	•	•	•	•	Twin Cities Research	651-714-0002	•	•	•	•

CR	CV	PR	US	BK	←COURTS ST. LOUIS	RECORDER→	UC	RE	TX	VS
•	•		•	•	ABC Services Inc Court Services	507-357-6320				
	•	•	•	•	Abstract & Title Services of Carlton Inc [SOP]	888-331-3966	•	•	•	
•					Alpha Court Records & Research	651-699-2222				
•	•	•	•	•	Capitol Lien Records & Research [SOP]	800-845-4077	•	•	•	•
•	•		•		Omni Data Retrieval Inc	952-985-7220			•	
•	•		•	•	Paragon Document Research Inc [SOP]	800-892-4235	•	•	•	
•	•		•	•	Twin Cities Research	651-714-0002	•	•	•	•

CR	CV	PR	US	BK	←COURTS STEARNS	RECORDER→	UC	RE	TX	VS
	•		•	•	Associated Abstracting Services of MN	612-819-6115	•	•	•	
•	•	•	•	•	Capitol Lien Records & Research [SOP]	800-845-4077	•	•	•	•
•	•				Horvath Enterprises Inc	320-982-3253			•	
•	•		•		Omni Data Retrieval Inc	952-985-7220			•	
•	•		•	•	Paragon Document Research Inc [SOP]	800-892-4235	•	•	•	
•	•	•			Scott Investigation [SOP]	800-357-7862	•	•	•	•
					Tri-County Abstract & Title Guaranty	800-892-2399	•	•	•	
•	•	•	•	•	Verified Credentials Inc	800-473-4934	•	•	•	•

CR	CV	PR	US	BK	←COURTS STEELE	RECORDER→	UC	RE	TX	VS
•	•		•	•	ABC Services Inc Court Services	507-357-6320				
•	•		•	•	ABC Services Inc Real Estate Svcs	507-357-6320	•	•	•	
•					Alpha Court Records & Research	651-699-2222				
	•		•	•	Associated Abstracting Services of MN	612-819-6115	•	•	•	
•	•	•	•	•	Capitol Lien Records & Research [SOP]	800-845-4077	•	•	•	•
•	•		•		Omni Data Retrieval Inc	952-985-7220			•	
•	•		•	•	Paragon Document Research Inc [SOP]	800-892-4235	•	•	•	
					Steele County Abstract Co	507-451-6487		•	•	

CR	CV	PR	US	BK	←COURTS STEVENS	RECORDER→	UC	RE	TX	VS
•	•		•	•	ABC Services Inc Court Services	507-357-6320				
•					Alpha Court Records & Research	651-699-2222				
•	•	•	•	•	Capitol Lien Records & Research [SOP]	800-845-4077	•	•	•	•
•	•		•		Omni Data Retrieval Inc	952-985-7220			•	
•	•		•	•	Paragon Document Research Inc [SOP]	800-892-4235	•	•	•	
•	•				West Central Process Service [SOP]	320-239-2665, cell- 320-808-6968				

CR	CV	PR	US	BK	←COURTS SWIFT	RECORDER→	UC	RE	TX	VS
•	•		•	•	ABC Services Inc Court Services	507-357-6320				
•					Alpha Court Records & Research	651-699-2222				
•	•	•	•	•	Capitol Lien Records & Research [SOP]	800-845-4077	•	•	•	•
•	•		•		Omni Data Retrieval Inc	952-985-7220			•	
•	•		•	•	Paragon Document Research Inc [SOP]	800-892-4235	•	•	•	

CR	CV	PR	US	BK	←COURTS TODD	RECORDER→	UC	RE	TX	VS
•	•		•	•	ABC Services Inc Court Services	507-357-6320				
•	•	•	•	•	Capitol Lien Records & Research [SOP]	800-845-4077	•	•	•	•
•		•			Cygneture Title Inc	218-828-0122	•	•	•	
•	•				Horvath Enterprises Inc	320-982-3253			•	
•	•		•		Omni Data Retrieval Inc	952-985-7220			•	
•	•		•	•	Paragon Document Research Inc [SOP]	800-892-4235	•	•	•	

CR	CV	PR	US	BK	←COURTS TRAVERSE	RECORDER→	UC	RE	TX	VS
•	•		•	•	ABC Services Inc Court Services	507-357-6320				
•					Alpha Court Records & Research	651-699-2222				
•	•	•	•	•	Capitol Lien Records & Research [SOP]	800-845-4077	•	•	•	•
•	•		•		Omni Data Retrieval Inc	952-985-7220			•	
•	•		•	•	Paragon Document Research Inc [SOP]	800-892-4235	•	•	•	

CR	CV	PR	US	BK	←COURTS WABASHA	RECORDER→	UC	RE	TX	VS
•	•		•	•	ABC Services Inc Court Services	507-357-6320				
•					Alpha Court Records & Research	651-699-2222				
•	•	•	•	•	Capitol Lien Records & Research [SOP]	800-845-4077	•	•	•	•
•	•		•		Omni Data Retrieval Inc	952-985-7220			•	
•	•		•	•	Paragon Document Research Inc [SOP]	800-892-4235	•	•	•	
	•	•	•	•	Wabasha County Abstract Co	651-565-3391	•	•	•	•

CR	CV	PR	US	BK	←COURTS WADENA	RECORDER→	UC	RE	TX	VS
•	•		•	•	ABC Services Inc Court Services	507-357-6320				
•	•	•	•	•	Capitol Lien Records & Research [SOP]	800-845-4077	•	•	•	•
•		•			Cygneture Title Inc	218-828-0122	•	•	•	
•	•				Horvath Enterprises Inc	320-982-3253			•	
•	•		•		Omni Data Retrieval Inc	952-985-7220			•	
•	•		•	•	Paragon Document Research Inc [SOP]	800-892-4235	•	•	•	

CR	CV	PR	US	BK	←COURTS WASECA	RECORDER→	UC	RE	TX	VS
•	•		•	•	ABC Services Inc Court Services	507-357-6320				
•	•		•	•	ABC Services Inc Real Estate Svcs	507-357-6320	•	•	•	
•					Alpha Court Records & Research	651-699-2222				
•	•	•	•	•	Capitol Lien Records & Research [SOP]	800-845-4077	•	•	•	•
•	•		•		Omni Data Retrieval Inc	952-985-7220			•	
•	•		•	•	Paragon Document Research Inc [SOP]	800-892-4235	•	•	•	

CR	CV	PR	US	BK	←COURTS WASHINGTON	RECORDER→	UC	RE	TX	VS
•	•		•	•	ABC Services Inc Court Services	507-357-6320				
•	•		•	•	ABC Services Inc Real Estate Svcs	507-357-6320	•	•	•	
•	•	•	•	•	Accountable Process Servers Inc [SOP]	612-991-7849		•	•	
•	•	•	•	•	Adit Research Inc.	888-721-5220	•	•	•	•
•					Alpha Court Records & Research	651-699-2222				
•	•	•	•	•	Avalon Information Services	715-222-4095		•	•	•
•	•	•	•	•	Capitol Lien Records & Research [SOP]	800-845-4077	•	•	•	•
	•	•	•	•	CSC Minnesota	800-327-1886	•	•	•	•
•	•			•	Dovolos & Associates [SOP]	952-920-9999	•		•	
•	•			•	GHS Inc - Record Research	763-566-2125, cell- 612-210-9716		•	•	
•	•	•	•	•	Heartland Information Services [SOP]	800-967-1882	•	•	•	•
•	•				Horvath Enterprises Inc	320-982-3253			•	
		•		•	Independent Abstracting Service Inc	763-792-6800	•	•	•	•
•	•	•	•	•	Information Reporting Services Inc	612-870-8770			•	
	•			•	Land Title Inc	651-638-1900	•	•	•	
•	•	•	•	•	Metro Legal Services [SOP]	800-488-8994	•	•	•	•
•	•		•		Omni Data Retrieval Inc	952-985-7220			•	
•	•		•	•	Paragon Document Research Inc [SOP]	800-892-4235	•	•	•	
•	•	•	•	•	The McDowell Agency Inc [SOP]	651-644-3880	•	•	•	•
•	•	•	•	•	Twin Cities Research	651-714-0002	•	•	•	•
•	•	•	•	•	Verified Credentials Inc	800-473-4934	•	•	•	•

CR	CV	PR	US	BK	←COURTS WATONWAN	RECORDER→	UC	RE	TX	VS
•	•		•	•	ABC Services Inc Court Services	507-357-6320				
•					Alpha Court Records & Research	651-699-2222				
•	•	•	•	•	Capitol Lien Records & Research [SOP]	800-845-4077	•	•	•	•
•	•		•		Omni Data Retrieval Inc	952-985-7220			•	
•	•		•	•	Paragon Document Research Inc [SOP]	800-892-4235	•	•	•	
•	•	•	•	•	Twin Cities Research	651-714-0002	•	•	•	•

CR	CV	PR	US	BK	←COURTS WILKIN	RECORDER→	UC	RE	TX	VS
•	•		•	•	ABC Services Inc Court Services	507-357-6320				
•					Alpha Court Records & Research	651-699-2222				
•	•	•	•	•	Capitol Lien Records & Research [SOP]	800-845-4077	•	•	•	•
•	•		•		Omni Data Retrieval Inc	952-985-7220			•	

•	•		•	•	Paragon Document Research Inc [SOP]	800-892-4235	•	•	•	
•	•	•			PRN Abstract & Title Co	701-642-3781	•	•	•	•
•	•	•			Wilkin County Abstract	701-642-3781	•	•	•	

CR	CV	PR	US	BK	←COURTS — WINONA	RECORDER→	UC	RE	TX	VS
•	•		•	•	ABC Services Inc Court Services	507-357-6320				
•					Alpha Court Records & Research	651-699-2222				
•	•	•	•	•	Capitol Lien Records & Research [SOP]	800-845-4077	•	•	•	•
•	•	•	•	•	Information Reporting Services Inc	612-870-8770			•	
•	•		•		Omni Data Retrieval Inc	952-985-7220			•	
•	•		•	•	Paragon Document Research Inc [SOP]	800-892-4235	•	•	•	

CR	CV	PR	US	BK	←COURTS — WRIGHT	RECORDER→	UC	RE	TX	VS
•	•		•	•	ABC Services Inc Court Services	507-357-6320				
•					Alpha Court Records & Research	651-699-2222				
	•		•	•	Associated Abstracting Services of MN	612-819-6115	•	•	•	
	•	•	•	•	Campbell Abstract Co	763-682-1252		•	•	
•	•	•	•	•	Capitol Lien Records & Research [SOP]	800-845-4077	•	•	•	•
	•	•	•	•	CSC Minnesota	800-327-1886	•	•	•	•
•	•				Horvath Enterprises Inc	320-982-3253			•	
		•		•	Independent Abstracting Service Inc	763-792-6800	•	•	•	•
•	•	•	•	•	Information Reporting Services Inc	612-870-8770			•	
•	•	•	•	•	Metro Legal Services [SOP]	800-488-8994	•	•	•	•
•	•		•		Omni Data Retrieval Inc	952-985-7220			•	
•	•		•	•	Paragon Document Research Inc [SOP]	800-892-4235	•	•	•	
					Tri-County Abstract & Title Guaranty	800-892-2399	•	•	•	
•	•	•	•	•	Twin Cities Research	651-714-0002	•	•	•	•
•	•	•	•	•	Verified Credentials Inc	800-473-4934	•	•	•	•
•	•	•	•	•	Patricia Wolff [SOP]	952-270-0095	•	•	•	•

CR	CV	PR	US	BK	←COURTS — YELLOW MEDICINE	RECORDER→	UC	RE	TX	VS
•	•		•	•	ABC Services Inc Court Services	507-357-6320				
•					Alpha Court Records & Research	651-699-2222				
•	•	•	•	•	Capitol Lien Records & Research [SOP]	800-845-4077	•	•	•	•
•	•		•		Omni Data Retrieval Inc	952-985-7220			•	
•	•		•	•	Paragon Document Research Inc [SOP]	800-892-4235	•	•	•	
•	•	•	•	•	Twin Cities Research	651-714-0002	•	•	•	•

 = PRRN Member. *A retriever you can trust!*

Mississippi

Mississippi has 82 counties and 92 recording offices. Ten counties have two separate recording offices - Bolivar, Carroll, Chickasaw, Craighead, Harrison, Hinds, Jasper, Jones, Panola, Tallahatchie, and Yalobusha.

COURT RECORDS RETRIEVED — CAPITAL - HINDS COUNTY — RECORDED RECORDS RETRIEVED

CR	CV	PR	US	BK	←COURTS		RECORDER→	UC	RE	TX	VS
						ADAMS					
•	•	•	•	•	TENSTAR Corporation (Jackson) [SOP]		800-864-5154	•	•	•	•
						ALCORN					
•	•	•			Freelance Abstracting Service [SOP]		662-424-3636	•	•		•
	•	•	•	•	Mitchell McNutt & Sams PA		662-842-3871	•	•	•	•
•	•	•			Segars & Holly [SOP]		662-423-1006	•	•	•	•
						AMITE					
•	•	•			Conrad Mord		601-876-2611	•	•	•	•
						ATTALA					
					See adjoining counties for retrievers or call court/recorder directly.						
						BENTON					
•	•	•			Freelance Abstracting Service [SOP]		662-424-3636	•	•		•
•	•	•	•	•	Record-Check Services Inc		800-530-7226	•	•	•	•
						BOLIVAR					
•	•	•			Barbara Tweedle		662-759-3048, 662-759-3762	•	•	•	
						CALHOUN					
•	•	•	•	•	Aldridge & Associates [SOP]		662-651-7376	•	•	•	•
						CARROLL					
					See adjoining counties for retrievers or call court/recorder directly.						
						CHICKASAW					
•	•	•	•	•	Aldridge & Associates [SOP]		662-651-7376	•	•	•	•
•	•	•	•	•	TENSTAR Corporation (Tupelo) [SOP]		800-864-5154	•	•	•	•
						CHOCTAW					
•	•	•			Joe C Griffin		662-285-6080	•	•	•	•
•	•				Newell & Associates Inc [SOP]		601-693-7700	•	•	•	
						CLAIBORNE					
•	•	•	•	•	TENSTAR Corporation (Jackson) [SOP]		800-864-5154	•	•	•	•
						CLARKE					
•	•	•	•	•	Pro-Tech Investigations LLC		877-685-5655		•	•	
•	•	•			George Williams		601-776-2111	•	•	•	
						CLAY					
•	•	•	•	•	Aldridge & Associates [SOP]		662-651-7376	•	•	•	•
						COAHOMA					
•	•	•	•	•	The Discovery Group Inc		662-280-1576	•		•	•
						COPIAH					
•	•	•	•	•	TENSTAR Corporation (Jackson) [SOP]		800-864-5154	•	•	•	•

CR	CV	PR	US	BK	←Courts	County / Retriever	Recorder→	UC	RE	TX	VS
CR	CV	PR	US	BK	←Courts	**COVINGTON**	Recorder→	UC	RE	TX	VS
						B Scott Buffington	601-849-4267	•	•	•	
•	•	•	•	•		Pro-Tech Investigations LLC	877-685-5655		•	•	
CR	CV	PR	US	BK	←Courts	**DE SOTO**	Recorder→	UC	RE	TX	VS
•						Blue Line Investigations	901-266-7100				
		•				Landmark Abstract & Information Services	901-268-3200	•	•	•	
•	•	•	•	•		Lenow International Inc [SOP]	901-726-0735	•		•	•
•	•	•				Mid-America Reporting Co LLC	662-487-0932	•	•	•	•
•	•	•	•	•		Record-Check Services Inc	800-530-7226	•	•	•	•
•	•	•	•	•		Schaeffer Papers [SOP]	800-848-6119		•	•	•
•	•	•	•	•		The Discovery Group Inc	662-280-1576	•		•	•
CR	CV	PR	US	BK	←Courts	**FORREST**	Recorder→	UC	RE	TX	VS
						B Scott Buffington	601-849-4267	•	•	•	
•	•	•	•	•		Pro-Tech Investigations LLC	877-685-5655		•	•	
						TSI - Title Services LLC	800-736-9331	•	•	•	
CR	CV	PR	US	BK	←Courts	**FRANKLIN**	Recorder→	UC	RE	TX	VS
•	•	•				K Maxwell Graves Jr [SOP]	601-384-2733	•	•	•	
CR	CV	PR	US	BK	←Courts	**GEORGE**	Recorder→	UC	RE	TX	VS
•	•	•				Jerry Axton [SOP]	228-475-1739		•	•	•
•	•	•	•	•		TENSTAR Corporation (Jackson) [SOP]	800-864-5154	•	•	•	•
CR	CV	PR	US	BK	←Courts	**GREENE**	Recorder→	UC	RE	TX	VS
•	•	•	•	•		Pro-Tech Investigations LLC	877-685-5655		•	•	
CR	CV	PR	US	BK	←Courts	**GRENADA**	Recorder→	UC	RE	TX	VS
•	•	•	•	•		TENSTAR Corporation (Tupelo) [SOP]	800-864-5154	•	•	•	•
CR	CV	PR	US	BK	←Courts	**HANCOCK**	Recorder→	UC	RE	TX	VS
•	•	•	•	•		Advanced Research & Inv. LLC [SOP]	888-896-9305	•	•	•	•
•	•	•	•	•		Pro-Tech Investigations LLC	877-685-5655		•	•	
•	•	•	•	•		TENSTAR Corporation (Jackson) [SOP]	800-864-5154	•	•	•	•
CR	CV	PR	US	BK	←Courts	**HARRISON**	Recorder→	UC	RE	TX	VS
•	•	•	•	•		Advanced Research & Inv. LLC [SOP]	888-896-9305	•	•	•	•
•	•	•	•	•		Pro-Tech Investigations LLC	877-685-5655		•	•	
•	•	•	•	•		TENSTAR Corporation (Jackson) [SOP]	800-864-5154	•	•	•	•
CR	CV	PR	US	BK	←Courts	**HINDS**	Recorder→	UC	RE	TX	VS
•	•	•	•	•		McAllister & Associates Inc [SOP]	601-977-0406			•	•
•	•	•	•	•		Mr Holmes Inv [SOP]	601-859-7955	•	•	•	•
•	•					SRA Investigations Inc [SOP]	800-530-7115 x4197				
•	•	•	•	•		TENSTAR Corporation (Jackson) [SOP]	800-864-5154	•	•	•	•
CR	CV	PR	US	BK	←Courts	**HOLMES**	Recorder→	UC	RE	TX	VS
•	•	•	•	•		TENSTAR Corporation (Jackson) [SOP]	800-864-5154	•	•	•	•
CR	CV	PR	US	BK	←Courts	**HUMPHREYS**	Recorder→	UC	RE	TX	VS
						See adjoining counties for retrievers or call court/recorder directly.					
CR	CV	PR	US	BK	←Courts	**ISSAQUENA**	Recorder→	UC	RE	TX	VS
•	•	•				Weissinger & Hunter	662-873-6258	•	•	•	•
CR	CV	PR	US	BK	←Courts	**ITAWAMBA**	Recorder→	UC	RE	TX	VS
•	•	•	•	•		Aldridge & Associates [SOP]	662-651-7376	•	•	•	•
•	•	•				Freelance Abstracting Service [SOP]	662-424-3636	•	•		•
•	•	•	•	•		TENSTAR Corporation (Tupelo) [SOP]	800-864-5154	•		•	•
CR	CV	PR	US	BK	←Courts	**JACKSON**	Recorder→	UC	RE	TX	VS
•	•	•	•	•		Advanced Research & Inv. LLC [SOP]	888-896-9305	•	•	•	•

CR	CV	PR	US	BK	←Courts	Recorder→	UC	RE	TX	VS
•	•	•			Jerry Axton [SOP]	228-475-1739		•	•	•
•	•	•	•		TENSTAR Corporation (Jackson) [SOP]	800-864-5154	•	•	•	•

CR	CV	PR	US	BK	←Courts **Jasper**	Recorder→	UC	RE	TX	VS
•	•	•	•	•	Pro-Tech Investigations LLC	877-685-5655		•	•	

CR	CV	PR	US	BK	←Courts **Jefferson**	Recorder→	UC	RE	TX	VS
•	•	•	•	•	TENSTAR Corporation (Jackson) [SOP]	800-864-5154	•	•	•	•

CR	CV	PR	US	BK	←Courts **Jefferson Davis**	Recorder→	UC	RE	TX	VS
					B Scott Buffington	601-849-4267	•	•	•	
•	•	•	•	•	Pro-Tech Investigations LLC	877-685-5655		•	•	

CR	CV	PR	US	BK	←Courts **Jones**	Recorder→	UC	RE	TX	VS
•	•	•	•	•	Pro-Tech Investigations LLC	877-685-5655		•	•	
•	•	•	•	•	TENSTAR Corporation (Jackson) [SOP]	800-864-5154	•	•	•	•

CR	CV	PR	US	BK	←Courts **Kemper**	Recorder→	UC	RE	TX	VS
					See adjoining counties for retrievers or call court/recorder directly.					

CR	CV	PR	US	BK	←Courts **Lafayette**	Recorder→	UC	RE	TX	VS
•	•	•			Mid-America Reporting Co LLC	662-487-0932	•	•	•	•
	•	•	•	•	Mitchell McNutt & Sams PA	662-842-3871	•	•	•	•
•	•	•	•	•	The Discovery Group Inc	662-280-1576	•		•	•

CR	CV	PR	US	BK	←Courts **Lamar**	Recorder→	UC	RE	TX	VS
					B Scott Buffington	601-849-4267	•	•	•	
•	•	•	•	•	Pro-Tech Investigations LLC	877-685-5655		•	•	
					TSI - Title Services LLC	800-736-9331	•	•	•	

CR	CV	PR	US	BK	←Courts **Lauderdale**	Recorder→	UC	RE	TX	VS
•	•				Newell & Associates Inc [SOP]	601-693-7700	•	•	•	

CR	CV	PR	US	BK	←Courts **Lawrence**	Recorder→	UC	RE	TX	VS
•	•	•	•	•	TENSTAR Corporation (Jackson) [SOP]	800-864-5154	•	•	•	•

CR	CV	PR	US	BK	←Courts **Leake**	Recorder→	UC	RE	TX	VS
					See adjoining counties for retrievers or call court/recorder directly.					

CR	CV	PR	US	BK	←Courts **Lee**	Recorder→	UC	RE	TX	VS
•	•	•	•	•	Aldridge & Associates [SOP]	662-651-7376	•	•	•	•
•	•	•			Freelance Abstracting Service [SOP]	662-424-3636	•	•		•
	•	•	•	•	Mitchell McNutt & Sams PA	662-842-3871	•	•	•	•
•	•	•	•	•	TENSTAR Corporation (Tupelo) [SOP]	800-864-5154	•	•	•	•

CR	CV	PR	US	BK	←Courts **Leflore**	Recorder→	UC	RE	TX	VS
					See adjoining counties for retrievers or call court/recorder directly.					

CR	CV	PR	US	BK	←Courts **Lincoln**	Recorder→	UC	RE	TX	VS
•	•	•	•	•	TENSTAR Corporation (Jackson) [SOP]	800-864-5154	•	•	•	•

CR	CV	PR	US	BK	←Courts **Lowndes**	Recorder→	UC	RE	TX	VS
•	•	•	•	•	Aldridge & Associates [SOP]	662-651-7376	•	•	•	•
	•	•	•	•	Mitchell McNutt & Sams PA	662-842-3871	•	•	•	•
•	•				Newell & Associates Inc [SOP]	601-693-7700	•	•	•	

CR	CV	PR	US	BK	←Courts **Madison**	Recorder→	UC	RE	TX	VS
•	•	•	•	•	McAllister & Associates Inc [SOP]	601-977-0406			•	•
•	•	•	•	•	Mr Holmes Inv [SOP]	601-859-7955	•	•	•	•
•	•				SRA Investigations Inc [SOP]	800-530-7115 x4197				
•	•	•	•	•	TENSTAR Corporation (Jackson) [SOP]	800-864-5154	•	•	•	•

CR	CV	PR	US	BK	←Courts **Marion**	Recorder→	UC	RE	TX	VS
•	•	•	•	•	Pro-Tech Investigations LLC	877-685-5655		•	•	

CR	CV	PR	US	BK	←COURTS MARSHALL	RECORDER→	UC	RE	TX	VS
•					Blue Line Investigations	901-266-7100				
•	•	•	•	•	Record-Check Services Inc	800-530-7226	•	•	•	•
•	•	•	•	•	The Discovery Group Inc	662-280-1576	•		•	•

CR	CV	PR	US	BK	←COURTS MONROE	RECORDER→	UC	RE	TX	VS
•	•	•	•	•	Aldridge & Associates [SOP]	662-651-7376	•	•	•	•
•	•	•	•	•	TENSTAR Corporation (Tupelo) [SOP]	800-864-5154	•	•	•	•
					The Copy Shop of Aberdeen	662-369-4428				

CR	CV	PR	US	BK	←COURTS MONTGOMERY	RECORDER→	UC	RE	TX	VS
•	•	•	•	•	TENSTAR Corporation (Tupelo) [SOP]	800-864-5154	•	•	•	•

CR	CV	PR	US	BK	←COURTS NESHOBA	RECORDER→	UC	RE	TX	VS
•	•				Newell & Associates Inc [SOP]	601-693-7700	•	•	•	

CR	CV	PR	US	BK	←COURTS NEWTON	RECORDER→	UC	RE	TX	VS
					See adjoining counties for retrievers or call court/recorder directly.					

CR	CV	PR	US	BK	←COURTS NOXUBEE	RECORDER→	UC	RE	TX	VS
					See adjoining counties for retrievers or call court/recorder directly.					

CR	CV	PR	US	BK	←COURTS OKTIBBEHA	RECORDER→	UC	RE	TX	VS
•					Blue Line Investigations	901-266-7100				

CR	CV	PR	US	BK	←COURTS PANOLA	RECORDER→	UC	RE	TX	VS
•					Blue Line Investigations	901-266-7100				
•	•	•			Mid-America Reporting Co LLC	662-487-0932	•	•	•	•

CR	CV	PR	US	BK	←COURTS PEARL RIVER	RECORDER→	UC	RE	TX	VS
•	•	•	•	•	Advanced Research & Inv. LLC [SOP]	888-896-9305	•	•	•	•
•	•	•	•	•	Pro-Tech Investigations LLC	877-685-5655		•	•	

CR	CV	PR	US	BK	←COURTS PERRY	RECORDER→	UC	RE	TX	VS
•	•	•	•	•	Pro-Tech Investigations LLC	877-685-5655		•	•	
					TSI - Title Services LLC	800-736-9331	•	•	•	

CR	CV	PR	US	BK	←COURTS PIKE	RECORDER→	UC	RE	TX	VS
•	•	•			Conrad Mord	601-876-2611	•	•	•	•

CR	CV	PR	US	BK	←COURTS PONTOTOC	RECORDER→	UC	RE	TX	VS
•	•	•	•	•	Aldridge & Associates [SOP]	662-651-7376	•	•	•	•
•	•	•			Freelance Abstracting Service [SOP]	662-424-3636	•	•		•
	•	•	•	•	Mitchell McNutt & Sams PA	662-842-3871	•	•	•	•
•	•	•	•	•	TENSTAR Corporation (Tupelo) [SOP]	800-864-5154	•	•	•	•

CR	CV	PR	US	BK	←COURTS PRENTISS	RECORDER→	UC	RE	TX	VS
•	•	•			Freelance Abstracting Service [SOP]	662-424-3636	•	•		•
•	•	•			Attorney John A Hatcher [SOP]	662-728-9444	•	•	•	•
•	•	•			Segars & Holly [SOP]	662-423-1006	•	•	•	•
•	•	•	•	•	TENSTAR Corporation (Tupelo) [SOP]	800-864-5154	•	•	•	•

CR	CV	PR	US	BK	←COURTS QUITMAN	RECORDER→	UC	RE	TX	VS
•	•	•	•	•	The Discovery Group Inc	662-280-1576	•		•	•

CR	CV	PR	US	BK	←COURTS RANKIN	RECORDER→	UC	RE	TX	VS
•	•	•	•	•	McAllister & Associates Inc [SOP]	601-977-0406			•	•
•	•	•	•	•	Mr Holmes Inv [SOP]	601-859-7955	•	•	•	•
•	•				SRA Investigations Inc [SOP]	800-530-7115 x4197				
•	•	•	•	•	TENSTAR Corporation (Jackson) [SOP]	800-864-5154	•	•	•	•

CR	CV	PR	US	BK	←COURTS SCOTT	RECORDER→	UC	RE	TX	VS
•	•	•			Thompson & Hollingsworth PA	601-469-3411	•	•	•	•

CR	CV	PR	US	BK	←Courts SHARKEY	Recorder→	UC	RE	TX	VS
•	•	•			Weissinger & Hunter	662-873-6258	•	•	•	•

CR	CV	PR	US	BK	←Courts SIMPSON	Recorder→	UC	RE	TX	VS
					B Scott Buffington	601-849-4267	•	•	•	
•	•	•	•	•	TENSTAR Corporation (Jackson) [SOP]	800-864-5154	•	•	•	•

CR	CV	PR	US	BK	←Courts SMITH	Recorder→	UC	RE	TX	VS
					B Scott Buffington	601-849-4267	•	•	•	
•	•	•	•	•	Pro-Tech Investigations LLC	877-685-5655		•	•	
•	•	•			Thompson & Hollingsworth PA	601-469-3411	•	•	•	•

CR	CV	PR	US	BK	←Courts STONE	Recorder→	UC	RE	TX	VS
•	•	•	•	•	Advanced Research & Inv. LLC [SOP]	888-896-9305	•	•	•	•
•	•	•	•	•	Pro-Tech Investigations LLC	877-685-5655		•	•	

CR	CV	PR	US	BK	←Courts SUNFLOWER	Recorder→	UC	RE	TX	VS
					See adjoining counties for retrievers or call court/recorder directly.					

CR	CV	PR	US	BK	←Courts TALLAHATCHIE	Recorder→	UC	RE	TX	VS
					See adjoining counties for retrievers or call court/recorder directly.					

CR	CV	PR	US	BK	←Courts TATE	Recorder→	UC	RE	TX	VS
•					Blue Line Investigations	901-266-7100				
•	•	•	•	•	The Discovery Group Inc	662-280-1576	•		•	•

CR	CV	PR	US	BK	←Courts TIPPAH	Recorder→	UC	RE	TX	VS
•	•	•			Freelance Abstracting Service [SOP]	662-424-3636	•	•		•
•	•	•	•	•	TENSTAR Corporation (Tupelo) [SOP]	800-864-5154	•	•	•	•

CR	CV	PR	US	BK	←Courts TISHOMINGO	Recorder→	UC	RE	TX	VS
	•	•			Carly J Carman Abstracting Service [SOP]	662-424-2233	•	•	•	
•	•	•			Freelance Abstracting Service [SOP]	662-424-3636	•	•		•
•	•	•			Segars & Holly [SOP]	662-423-1006	•	•	•	•

CR	CV	PR	US	BK	←Courts TUNICA	Recorder→	UC	RE	TX	VS
•					Blue Line Investigations	901-266-7100				
•	•	•			Mid-America Reporting Co LLC	662-487-0932	•	•	•	•
•	•	•	•	•	Schaeffer Papers [SOP]	800-848-6119		•	•	•
•	•	•	•	•	The Discovery Group Inc	662-280-1576	•		•	•

CR	CV	PR	US	BK	←Courts UNION	Recorder→	UC	RE	TX	VS
•	•	•	•	•	Aldridge & Associates [SOP]	662-651-7376	•	•	•	•
	•	•	•	•	Mitchell McNutt & Sams PA	662-842-3871	•	•	•	•
•	•	•	•	•	TENSTAR Corporation (Tupelo) [SOP]	800-864-5154	•	•	•	•

CR	CV	PR	US	BK	←Courts WALTHALL	Recorder→	UC	RE	TX	VS
•	•	•			Conrad Mord	601-876-2611	•	•	•	•

CR	CV	PR	US	BK	←Courts WARREN	Recorder→	UC	RE	TX	VS
•	•	•	•	•	TENSTAR Corporation (Jackson) [SOP]	800-864-5154	•	•	•	•

CR	CV	PR	US	BK	←Courts WASHINGTON	Recorder→	UC	RE	TX	VS
					See adjoining counties for retrievers or call court/recorder directly.					

CR	CV	PR	US	BK	←Courts WAYNE	Recorder→	UC	RE	TX	VS
•	•	•	•	•	Pro-Tech Investigations LLC	877-685-5655		•	•	

CR	CV	PR	US	BK	←Courts WEBSTER	Recorder→	UC	RE	TX	VS
•	•	•	•	•	TENSTAR Corporation (Tupelo) [SOP]	800-864-5154	•	•	•	•

CR	CV	PR	US	BK	←Courts WILKINSON	Recorder→	UC	RE	TX	VS
					See adjoining counties for retrievers or call court/recorder directly.					

CR	CV	PR	US	BK	←Courts	Winston	Recorder→	UC	RE	TX	VS
	•	•			Taylor Tucker		662-773-9254	•	•	•	•

CR	CV	PR	US	BK	←Courts	Yalobusha	Recorder→	UC	RE	TX	VS
•	•	•	•	•	TENSTAR Corporation (Tupelo) [SOP]		800-864-5154	•	•	•	•

CR	CV	PR	US	BK	←Courts	Yazoo	Recorder→	UC	RE	TX	VS
•	•	•	•	•	TENSTAR Corporation (Jackson) [SOP]		800-864-5154	•	•	•	•

[SOP] = Performs service of process

Court Records

CODE	Government Agency	Type of Information
CR	Criminal Court	Municipal, county and state level criminal cases
CV	Civil Court	Municipal, county and state level civil cases
PR	Probate Court	Wills and estate cases
US	US District Court	Federal civil and criminal cases
BK	Bankruptcy Court	United States bankruptcy cases

County Records - Recordings

CODE	Government Agency	Type of Information
UC	UCC Filing Office	Uniform Commercial Code and other personal property liens
RE	Real Estate Recording Office	Real property transactions and liens
TX	Tax Filing Office(s)	Federal and state tax liens, judgment liens
VS	Vital Records Office	Vital statistics—birth, death, marriage, divorce

 = PRRN Member. *A retriever you can trust!*

Editor's Tip: Remember the first rule about public record searching-- Simply because your state or county has certain rules, regulations and practices regarding the accessibility and content of public records, does not mean that another state or county adheres to the same rules.

Missouri

Missouri has 114 counties and one independent city, City of St. Louis, with both a separate court structure and recording office.

COURT RECORDS RETRIEVED — CAPITAL - COLE COUNTY — RECORDED RECORDS RETRIEVED

Adair

CR	CV	PR	US	BK	←Courts / Recorder→	Phone	UC	RE	TX	VS
					North Missouri Title	660-665-4711		•	•	

Andrew

CR	CV	PR	US	BK	←Courts / Recorder→	Phone	UC	RE	TX	VS
•	•	•			Hollis Search	660-446-2730		•	•	
•	•	•	•	•	NW Missouri Information Services [SOP]	816-233-4779	•	•	•	•

Atchison

CR	CV	PR	US	BK	←Courts / Recorder→	Phone	UC	RE	TX	VS
•	•	•			Hollis Search	660-446-2730		•	•	
•	•	•	•	•	NW Missouri Information Services [SOP]	816-233-4779	•	•	•	•

Audian

CR	CV	PR	US	BK	←Courts / Recorder→	Phone	UC	RE	TX	VS
•	•	•			Bi-State Title Search (Div of Bi-State Ind.)	866-450-7399	•	•	•	

Audrain

CR	CV	PR	US	BK	←Courts / Recorder→	Phone	UC	RE	TX	VS
	•	•			Audrain County Title Co	573-581-5136	•	•	•	
	•	•			Guaranty Land Title	573-874-4912	•	•	•	•
					Real Data	573-893-4898		•	•	
•	•	•			Wells Abstract Co	573-221-0644	•	•	•	

Barry

CR	CV	PR	US	BK	←Courts / Recorder→	Phone	UC	RE	TX	VS
		•			Barry County Abstract & Title	417-847-3224	•	•	•	
•	•	•	•	•	National Investigative Services Inc [SOP]	417-831-2500	•	•	•	•

Barton

CR	CV	PR	US	BK	←Courts / Recorder→	Phone	UC	RE	TX	VS
•	•	•			American Research Unlimited Inc	417-358-6494	•	•	•	•
•	•	•			Barton County Title Co.	417-682-3100	•	•	•	•
•					LLG Enterprises	816-625-0947				
•	•	•	•	•	National Investigative Services Inc [SOP]	417-831-2500	•	•	•	•

Bates

CR	CV	PR	US	BK	←Courts / Recorder→	Phone	UC	RE	TX	VS
•	•	•			American Research Unlimited Inc	417-358-6494	•	•	•	•
•	•	•			Bi-State Title Search (Div of Bi-State Ind.)	866-450-7399	•	•	•	

Benton

CR	CV	PR	US	BK	←Courts / Recorder→	Phone	UC	RE	TX	VS
	•	•			Drake Land Title Co	660-438-5188	•	•	•	
•	•	•			General Investigations LLC [SOP]	660-747-8900	•	•	•	•
•	•				Ozark Inv [SOP]	888-685-5366				
	•	•			The Right Search	417-852-7097	•	•	•	

Bollinger

CR	CV	PR	US	BK	←Courts / Recorder→	Phone	UC	RE	TX	VS
•	•	•			Bollinger County Abstract Co	573-238-2823	•	•	•	
					Collier Connections	573-576-3035	•	•	•	

Boone

CR	CV	PR	US	BK	←Courts / Recorder→	Phone	UC	RE	TX	VS
				•	G-Docs Abstracting LLC	636-586-4242	•	•	•	
	•	•			Guaranty Land Title	573-874-4912	•	•	•	•
•	•		•		Harmon Document Retrieval Service [SOP]	573-635-6690				
•	•		•		J & J Enterprises - MO [SOP]	573-395-4205	•	•	•	
•					LLG Enterprises	816-625-0947				
					Real Data	573-893-4898		•	•	

CR	CV	PR	US	BK	←COURTS **BUCHANAN** RECORDER→	UC	RE	TX	VS
•	•	•			Bi-State Title Search (Div of Bi-State Ind.)....866-450-7399	•	•	•	
•	•	•	•	•	Hatfield Process Service [SOP]....816-842-9800	•	•	•	•
•	•	•			Hollis Search....660-446-2730		•	•	
•					LLG Enterprises....816-625-0947				
•	•	•	•	•	NW Missouri Information Services [SOP]....816-233-4779	•	•	•	•

CR	CV	PR	US	BK	←COURTS **BUTLER** RECORDER→	UC	RE	TX	VS
	•	•			First American Title Co....573-686-1495	•	•	•	

CR	CV	PR	US	BK	←COURTS **CALDWELL** RECORDER→	UC	RE	TX	VS
	•	•			Daviess County Land Title LLC....660-663-2155		•		
	•	•			Guaranty Land Title....573-874-4912	•	•	•	•
•	•	•			Hollis Search....660-446-2730		•	•	

CR	CV	PR	US	BK	←COURTS **CALLAWAY** RECORDER→	UC	RE	TX	VS
•	•	•			Bi-State Title Search (Div of Bi-State Ind.)....866-450-7399	•	•	•	
	•	•			Guaranty Land Title....573-874-4912	•	•	•	•
•	•		•		Harmon Document Retrieval Service [SOP]....573-635-6690				
•	•		•		J & J Enterprises - MO [SOP]....573-395-4205	•	•	•	
•					LLG Enterprises....816-625-0947				
					Real Data....573-893-4898		•	•	

CR	CV	PR	US	BK	←COURTS **CAMDEN** RECORDER→	UC	RE	TX	VS
				•	G-Docs Abstracting LLC....636-586-4242	•	•	•	
	•	•			Guaranty Land Title....573-874-4912	•	•	•	•
•	•		•		Harmon Document Retrieval Service [SOP]....573-635-6690				
•	•	•			Mozark Investigations [SOP]....866-308-1411	•	•	•	•
•	•				Ozark Inv [SOP]....888-685-5366				
					Real Data....573-893-4898		•	•	

CR	CV	PR	US	BK	←COURTS **CAPE GIRARDEAU** RECORDER→	UC	RE	TX	VS
	•	•	•		Cape Girardeau County Abstract & Title....573-335-5890	•	•	•	
					Collier Connections....573-576-3035	•	•	•	
•	•		•	•	Interquest Information Services....800-455-1655	•	•	•	•
•					LLG Enterprises....816-625-0947				

CR	CV	PR	US	BK	←COURTS **CARROLL** RECORDER→	UC	RE	TX	VS
•	•	•			Carroll Abstract Co....660-542-1364		•	•	

CR	CV	PR	US	BK	←COURTS **CARTER** RECORDER→	UC	RE	TX	VS
•	•	•			Mozark Investigations [SOP]....866-308-1411	•	•	•	•

CR	CV	PR	US	BK	←COURTS **CASS** RECORDER→	UC	RE	TX	VS
•					Affirm Background Screening Inc....715-682-2601				
	•	•	•	•	Andrea's Abstracting aka ASAP Services [SOP]....816-987-6300		•	•	
	•				Arbuckle Searches....816-550-9106		•	•	
•	•	•			Bi-State Title Search (Div of Bi-State Ind.)....866-450-7399	•	•	•	
•	•	•	•	•	D & B Legal Services Inc [SOP]....913-963-1279	•	•	•	•
•	•	•	•	•	Hatfield Process Service [SOP]....816-842-9800	•	•	•	•
•	•	•	•	•	Medlin Research Company....913-206-4615	•	•	•	
	•		•	•	SearchWorks Inc....913-383-0940	•	•	•	

CR	CV	PR	US	BK	←COURTS **CEDAR** RECORDER→	UC	RE	TX	VS
•	•	•			American Research Unlimited Inc....417-358-6494	•	•	•	•
•	•	•	•	•	National Investigative Services Inc [SOP]....417-831-2500	•	•	•	•

CR	CV	PR	US	BK	←COURTS **CHARITON** RECORDER→	UC	RE	TX	VS
	•	•			Guaranty Land Title....573-874-4912	•	•	•	•

CR	CV	PR	US	BK	←COURTS CHRISTIAN	RECORDER→	UC	RE	TX	VS
•	•	•			American Research Unlimited Inc	417-358-6494	•	•	•	•
	•	•			Hogan Land Title Co	417-882-3000		•	•	
•	•		•	•	Kolling & Associates	417-889-4092				
					Lincoln-Evans Advanced Land & Title	417-581-8251	•	•	•	
	•				MO Data Inc	417-299-2469	•	•	•	
•	•	•	•	•	National Investigative Services Inc [SOP]	417-831-2500	•	•	•	•
					Sparks Searches	417-725-4851		•	•	

CR	CV	PR	US	BK	←COURTS CLARK	RECORDER→	UC	RE	TX	VS
•	•	•			Bi-State Title Search (Div of Bi-State Ind.)	866-450-7399	•	•	•	
		•			Lewis County Abstract (Missouri)	573-288-4461	•	•	•	
•	•	•			Marion County Abstract Co (Missouri)	800-952-5314	•	•	•	•
		•			Scotland County Abstract & Title Inc	660-465-7052		•	•	

CR	CV	PR	US	BK	←COURTS CLAY	RECORDER→	UC	RE	TX	VS
	•	•	•	•	Andrea's Abstracting aka ASAP Services [SOP]	816-987-6300		•	•	
•	•		•	•	Armstrong Document Retrieval	913-341-1991	•	•	•	
•	•	•			Bi-State Title Search (Div of Bi-State Ind.)	866-450-7399	•	•	•	
•	•	•	•	•	D & B Legal Services Inc [SOP]	913-963-1279	•	•	•	•
•	•		•	•	Executive Investigative Services [SOP]	800-764-9484	•	•	•	
	•	•	•	•	Connie Giandalia	816-217-1849	•	•	•	
•	•	•	•	•	Hatfield Process Service [SOP]	816-842-9800	•	•	•	•
•	•	•			Hollis Search	660-446-2730		•	•	
•					LLG Enterprises	816-625-0947				
	•	•	•		M & J Abstractors	913-727-3588	•	•	•	
•	•	•	•	•	NW Missouri Information Services [SOP]	816-233-4779	•	•	•	•
•	•				Rigoli Searches	913-908-8863	•	•	•	
	•		•	•	SearchWorks Inc	913-383-0940	•	•	•	

CR	CV	PR	US	BK	←COURTS CLINTON	RECORDER→	UC	RE	TX	VS
•	•	•			Bi-State Title Search (Div of Bi-State Ind.)	866-450-7399	•	•	•	
	•	•			Daviess County Land Title LLC	660-663-2155	•	•	•	
	•	•			Guaranty Land Title	573-874-4912	•	•	•	•
•	•	•			Hollis Search	660-446-2730		•	•	
•	•	•	•	•	NW Missouri Information Services [SOP]	816-233-4779	•	•	•	•

CR	CV	PR	US	BK	←COURTS COLE	RECORDER→	UC	RE	TX	VS
	•	•			Guaranty Land Title	573-874-4912	•	•	•	•
•	•		•		Harmon Document Retrieval Service [SOP]	573-635-6690				
•	•		•		J & J Enterprises - MO [SOP]	573-395-4205	•	•	•	
•	•	•			Jeff City Filing Inc [SOP]	573-634-3894	•	•	•	•
					Real Data	573-893-4898		•	•	

CR	CV	PR	US	BK	←COURTS COOPER	RECORDER→	UC	RE	TX	VS
	•	•			Guaranty Land Title	573-874-4912	•	•	•	•
					Real Data	573-893-4898		•	•	

CR	CV	PR	US	BK	←COURTS CRAWFORD	RECORDER→	UC	RE	TX	VS
•	•	•			Bi-State Title Search (Div of Bi-State Ind.)	866-450-7399	•	•	•	
					Crawford County Title Co	573-885-6470		•	•	
				•	G-Docs Abstracting LLC	636-586-4242	•	•	•	
	•	•			Guaranty Land Title	573-874-4912	•	•	•	•
•	•	•			Mozark Investigations [SOP]	866-308-1411	•	•	•	•
					Real Data	573-893-4898		•	•	

CR	CV	PR	US	BK	←COURTS DADE	RECORDER→	UC	RE	TX	VS
•	•	•			American Research Unlimited Inc	417-358-6494	•	•	•	•
•	•	•	•	•	National Investigative Services Inc [SOP]	417-831-2500	•	•	•	•
		•			Russell Abstract	417-637-2414		•	•	

CR	CV	PR	US	BK	←Courts DALLAS	Recorder→	UC	RE	TX	VS
•	•	•	•	•	National Investigative Services Inc [SOP]	417-831-2500	•	•	•	•
•	•				Ozark Inv [SOP]	888-685-5366				

CR	CV	PR	US	BK	←Courts DAVIESS	Recorder→	UC	RE	TX	VS
	•	•			Daviess County Land Title LLC	660-663-2155	•	•	•	
	•	•			Guaranty Land Title	573-874-4912	•	•	•	•
•	•	•			Hollis Search	660-446-2730		•	•	
					Trenton Abstract and Title Co LLC	660-359-2100		•	•	

CR	CV	PR	US	BK	←Courts DEKALB	Recorder→	UC	RE	TX	VS
	•	•			Daviess County Land Title LLC	660-663-2155	•	•	•	
	•	•			Guaranty Land Title	573-874-4912	•	•	•	•
•	•	•			Hollis Search	660-446-2730		•	•	
•	•	•	•	•	NW Missouri Information Services [SOP]	816-233-4779	•	•	•	•

CR	CV	PR	US	BK	←Courts DENT	Recorder→	UC	RE	TX	VS
•	•	•			Bi-State Title Search (Div of Bi-State Ind.)	866-450-7399	•	•	•	
	•	•			Guaranty Land Title	573-874-4912	•	•	•	•
•	•	•			Mozark Investigations [SOP]	866-308-1411	•	•	•	•
	•	•			Steelman Abstracting Co	573-729-6183		•	•	

CR	CV	PR	US	BK	←Courts DOUGLAS	Recorder→	UC	RE	TX	VS
•	•	•			Douglas County Abstract & Title Co	417-683-4701		•	•	
•	•	•	•	•	National Investigative Services Inc [SOP]	417-831-2500	•	•	•	•
	•	•			South Central Missouri Title Co	417-926-6163	•	•	•	
					Sparks Searches	417-725-4851		•	•	

CR	CV	PR	US	BK	←Courts DUNKLIN	Recorder→	UC	RE	TX	VS
•					LLG Enterprises	816-625-0947				

CR	CV	PR	US	BK	←Courts FRANKLIN	Recorder→	UC	RE	TX	VS
•	•	•	•	•	AAA Process Service Inc [SOP]	888-350-5809	•	•	•	•
•	•	•			Assured Title Company	636-240-0833	•	•	•	
•	•	•			Bi-State Title Search (Div of Bi-State Ind.)	866-450-7399	•	•	•	
•	•				David Lung & Assoc [SOP]	888-477-2664				
				•	G-Docs Abstracting LLC	636-586-4242	•	•	•	
•	•		•	•	Infotrack Information Services Inc	800-275-5594	•	•	•	
•	•	•	•	•	Lenmark Personal Services [SOP]	636-677-3831		•		
•	•	•			Mozark Investigations [SOP]	866-308-1411	•	•	•	•
•	•	•	•	•	Services Rendered Inc [SOP]	888-434-8200	•		•	•
•	•	•	•	•	St Vrain Resources [SOP]	314-645-1710			•	•
•	•	•			TRI-County Title LLC	636-239-7800	•	•	•	

CR	CV	PR	US	BK	←Courts GASCONADE	Recorder→	UC	RE	TX	VS
•	•	•			Bi-State Title Search (Div of Bi-State Ind.)	866-450-7399	•	•	•	
				•	G-Docs Abstracting LLC	636-586-4242	•	•	•	
•	•		•		J & J Enterprises - MO [SOP]	573-395-4205	•	•	•	
•	•	•			Mozark Investigations [SOP]	866-308-1411	•	•	•	•
•	•	•			Donna Mundwiller	573-486-2925	•	•	•	•
					Real Data	573-893-4898		•	•	

CR	CV	PR	US	BK	←Courts GENTRY	Recorder→	UC	RE	TX	VS
	•	•			Holden Abstract Co	660-726-3417	•	•	•	
•	•	•			Hollis Search	660-446-2730		•	•	

CR	CV	PR	US	BK	←Courts GREENE	Recorder→	UC	RE	TX	VS
•	•	•			American Research Unlimited Inc	417-358-6494	•	•	•	•
•	•	•			Compu-Fact Research Inc	636-477-1115, 618-239-0677	•	•	•	
	•	•			Hogan Land Title Co	417-882-3000		•	•	
					J & A Land Searching	417-887-1049		•		

CR	CV	PR	US	BK			UC	RE	TX	VS
•	•		•	•	Kolling & Associates	417-889-4092				
					Lincoln-Evans Advanced Land & Title	417-581-8251	•	•	•	
	•				MO Data Inc	417-299-2469	•	•	•	
•	•	•	•	•	National Investigative Services Inc [SOP]	417-831-2500	•	•	•	•
•					Jacqueline Schoeneberg	417-889-6390				
	•	•			The Right Search	417-852-7097	•	•	•	

CR	CV	PR	US	BK	←COURTS **GRUNDY**	RECORDER→	UC	RE	TX	VS
					Trenton Abstract and Title Co LLC	660-359-2100		•	•	

CR	CV	PR	US	BK	←COURTS **HARRISON**	RECORDER→	UC	RE	TX	VS
	•	•			Harrison County Title	660-425-3523	•	•	•	
•	•	•			Hollis Search	660-446-2730		•	•	

CR	CV	PR	US	BK	←COURTS **HENRY**	RECORDER→	UC	RE	TX	VS
•	•	•			Bi-State Title Search (Div of Bi-State Ind.)	866-450-7399	•	•	•	
•	•	•			General Investigations LLC [SOP]	660-747-8900	•	•	•	•
		•			Henry County Abstract Co (Missouri)	660-885-6168		•		

CR	CV	PR	US	BK	←COURTS **HICKORY**	RECORDER→	UC	RE	TX	VS
					Bentley Title Co	417-745-6626	•	•	•	
•	•	•	•	•	National Investigative Services Inc [SOP]	417-831-2500	•	•	•	•
•	•				Ozark Inv [SOP]	888-685-5366				
	•	•			The Right Search	417-852-7097	•	•	•	

CR	CV	PR	US	BK	←COURTS **HOLT**	RECORDER→	UC	RE	TX	VS
•	•	•			Hollis Search	660-446-2730		•	•	
					Holt County Title Co	660-446-2371		•	•	
•	•	•	•	•	NW Missouri Information Services [SOP]	816-233-4779	•	•	•	•

CR	CV	PR	US	BK	←COURTS **HOWARD**	RECORDER→	UC	RE	TX	VS
•	•	•			Geo G Smith & Son Inc	660-248-2467	•	•	•	•
	•	•			Guaranty Land Title	573-874-4912	•	•	•	•

CR	CV	PR	US	BK	←COURTS **HOWELL**	RECORDER→	UC	RE	TX	VS
	•	•			Brill Title Company	417-256-2951	•	•	•	
				•	G-Docs Abstracting LLC	636-586-4242	•	•	•	
•					LLG Enterprises	816-625-0947				

CR	CV	PR	US	BK	←COURTS **IRON**	RECORDER→	UC	RE	TX	VS
	•	•			American Heritage Abstract	573-431-1359	•	•	•	
•	•	•			Mozark Investigations [SOP]	866-308-1411	•	•	•	•

CR	CV	PR	US	BK	←COURTS **JACKSON**	RECORDER→	UC	RE	TX	VS
	•	•	•	•	Andrea's Abstracting aka ASAP Services [SOP]	816-987-6300		•	•	
•	•		•	•	Armstrong Document Retrieval	913-341-1991	•	•	•	
•	•	•			Bi-State Title Search (Div of Bi-State Ind.)	866-450-7399	•	•	•	
•	•	•	•	•	D & B Legal Services Inc [SOP]	913-963-1279	•	•	•	•
	•	•	•	•	Connie Giandalia	816-217-1849	•	•	•	
•	•	•	•	•	Hatfield Process Service [SOP]	816-842-9800	•	•	•	•
•	•	•	•	•	Jess Barker Document Research/Retrieval	888-316-3773	•	•	•	•
•	•	•	•	•	KC Court Research Inc	913-239-8995	•	•	•	
•					LLG Enterprises	816-625-0947				
	•	•	•		M & J Abstractors	913-727-3588	•	•	•	
•	•	•	•	•	NW Missouri Information Services [SOP]	816-233-4779	•	•	•	•
	•		•	•	SearchWorks Inc	913-383-0940	•	•	•	

CR	CV	PR	US	BK	←COURTS **JASPER**	RECORDER→	UC	RE	TX	VS
•	•	•			American Research Unlimited Inc	417-358-6494	•	•	•	•
				•	G-Docs Abstracting LLC	636-586-4242	•	•	•	
•	•	•	•	•	National Investigative Services Inc [SOP]	417-831-2500	•	•	•	•

CR	CV	PR	US	BK	←COURTS	JEFFERSON	RECORDER→	UC	RE	TX	VS
•	•	•	•	•	AAA Process Service Inc [SOP]		888-350-5809	•	•	•	•
•	•	•			Assured Title Company		636-240-0833	•	•	•	
•	•	•			Bi-State Title Search (Div of Bi-State Ind.)		866-450-7399	•	•	•	
•	•				David Lung & Assoc [SOP]		888-477-2664				
				•	G-Docs Abstracting LLC		636-586-4242	•	•	•	
•	•		•	•	Infotrack Information Services Inc		800-275-5594	•	•	•	
	•	•			Integrity Abstracting [SOP]		314-807-6359	•	•	•	
•	•	•	•	•	Lenmark Personal Services [SOP]		636-677-3831		•		
			•	•	Master File Inc [SOP]		866-242-0469	•	•	•	
•	•	•	•	•	Services Rendered Inc [SOP]		888-434-8200	•		•	•
•	•	•	•	•	St Vrain Resources [SOP]		314-645-1710			•	•

CR	CV	PR	US	BK	←COURTS	JOHNSON	RECORDER→	UC	RE	TX	VS
	•				Arbuckle Searches		816-550-9106		•	•	
•	•	•			Bi-State Title Search (Div of Bi-State Ind.)		866-450-7399	•	•	•	
•	•	•			General Investigations LLC [SOP]		660-747-8900	•	•	•	•
	•		•	•	SearchWorks Inc		913-383-0940	•	•	•	

CR	CV	PR	US	BK	←COURTS	KNOX	RECORDER→	UC	RE	TX	VS
•	•	•			Bi-State Title Search (Div of Bi-State Ind.)		866-450-7399	•	•	•	
	•				Knox County Abstract		660-397-3259		•	•	
		•			Scotland County Abstract & Title Inc		660-465-7052		•	•	
•	•	•			Wells Abstract Co		573-221-0644	•	•	•	

CR	CV	PR	US	BK	←COURTS	LACLEDE	RECORDER→	UC	RE	TX	VS
				•	G-Docs Abstracting LLC		636-586-4242	•	•	•	
	•	•			Guaranty Land Title		573-874-4912	•	•	•	•
•	•	•	•	•	National Investigative Services Inc [SOP]		417-831-2500	•	•	•	•
•	•				Ozark Inv [SOP]		888-685-5366				

CR	CV	PR	US	BK	←COURTS	LAFAYETTE	RECORDER→	UC	RE	TX	VS
•	•	•			Bi-State Title Search (Div of Bi-State Ind.)		866-450-7399	•	•	•	
		•			Lafayette County Land Title Co		660-259-4631		•		

CR	CV	PR	US	BK	←COURTS	LAWRENCE	RECORDER→	UC	RE	TX	VS
•	•	•			American Research Unlimited Inc		417-358-6494	•	•	•	•
•	•	•	•	•	National Investigative Services Inc [SOP]		417-831-2500	•	•	•	•

CR	CV	PR	US	BK	←COURTS	LEWIS	RECORDER→	UC	RE	TX	VS
•	•	•			Bi-State Title Search (Div of Bi-State Ind.)		866-450-7399	•	•	•	
		•			Lewis County Abstract (Missouri)		573-288-4461	•	•	•	
•	•	•			Marion County Abstract Co (Missouri)		800-952-5314	•	•	•	•
•	•	•			Wells Abstract Co		573-221-0644	•	•	•	

CR	CV	PR	US	BK	←COURTS	LINCOLN	RECORDER→	UC	RE	TX	VS
•	•	•			Assured Title Company		636-240-0833	•	•	•	
•	•	•			Bi-State Title Search (Div of Bi-State Ind.)		866-450-7399	•	•	•	
•	•				David Lung & Assoc [SOP]		888-477-2664				
				•	G-Docs Abstracting LLC		636-586-4242	•	•	•	
•	•		•	•	Infotrack Information Services Inc		800-275-5594	•	•	•	
	•	•			Troy Title Co LLC		636-528-2220		•	•	

CR	CV	PR	US	BK	←COURTS	LINN	RECORDER→	UC	RE	TX	VS
					Linn County Title		660-258-2260		•	•	

CR	CV	PR	US	BK	←COURTS	LIVINGSTON	RECORDER→	UC	RE	TX	VS
	•	•			Guaranty Land Title		573-874-4912	•	•	•	•
	•	•			Staton Abstract & Title Co		660-646-1421	•	•	•	•
					Trenton Abstract and Title Co LLC		660-359-2100		•	•	

CR	CV	PR	US	BK	←Courts **Macon**	Recorder→	UC	RE	TX	VS
	•	•			Guaranty Land Title	573-874-4912	•	•	•	•
	•	•			Macon County Title	660-385-6474	•	•	•	•
•	•	•			Marion County Abstract Co (Missouri)	800-952-5314	•	•	•	•
•	•	•			Wells Abstract Co	573-221-0644	•	•	•	

CR	CV	PR	US	BK	←Courts **Madison**	Recorder→	UC	RE	TX	VS
	•	•			American Heritage Abstract	573-431-1359	•	•	•	
		•			Preferred Land Title	800-310-6721	•	•	•	

CR	CV	PR	US	BK	←Courts **Maries**	Recorder→	UC	RE	TX	VS
	•	•			Guaranty Land Title	573-874-4912	•	•	•	•
		•			Hollenbeck Title Co	573-422-3633	•	•	•	
•	•		•		J & J Enterprises - MO [SOP]	573-395-4205	•	•	•	
•	•	•			Mozark Investigations [SOP]	866-308-1411	•	•	•	•
					Real Data	573-893-4898		•	•	

CR	CV	PR	US	BK	←Courts **Marion**	Recorder→	UC	RE	TX	VS
•	•	•			Bi-State Title Search (Div of Bi-State Ind.)	866-450-7399	•	•	•	
		•			Lewis County Abstract (Missouri)	573-288-4461	•	•	•	
•	•	•			Marion County Abstract Co (Missouri)	800-952-5314	•	•	•	•
					Real Data	573-893-4898		•	•	
•	•	•			Wells Abstract Co	573-221-0644	•	•	•	

CR	CV	PR	US	BK	←Courts **McDonald**	Recorder→	UC	RE	TX	VS
•	•	•			American Research Unlimited Inc	417-358-6494	•	•	•	•
•	•	•	•	•	National Investigative Services Inc [SOP]	417-831-2500	•	•	•	•

CR	CV	PR	US	BK	←Courts **Mercer**	Recorder→	UC	RE	TX	VS
					Trenton Abstract and Title Co LLC	660-359-2100		•	•	

CR	CV	PR	US	BK	←Courts **Miller**	Recorder→	UC	RE	TX	VS
				•	G-Docs Abstracting LLC	636-586-4242	•	•	•	
	•	•			Guaranty Land Title	573-874-4912	•	•	•	•
•	•		•		Harmon Document Retrieval Service [SOP]	573-635-6690				
•	•		•		J & J Enterprises - MO [SOP]	573-395-4205	•	•	•	
•	•	•			Mozark Investigations [SOP]	866-308-1411	•	•	•	•
•	•	•	•	•	National Investigative Services Inc [SOP]	417-831-2500	•	•	•	•
•	•				Ozark Inv [SOP]	888-685-5366				

CR	CV	PR	US	BK	←Courts **Mississippi**	Recorder→	UC	RE	TX	VS
	•	•			Mississippi County Abstract & Loan Co	573-683-4671		•	•	

CR	CV	PR	US	BK	←Courts **Moniteau**	Recorder→	UC	RE	TX	VS
	•	•			Guaranty Land Title	573-874-4912	•	•	•	•
•	•		•		Harmon Document Retrieval Service [SOP]	573-635-6690				

CR	CV	PR	US	BK	←Courts **Monroe**	Recorder→	UC	RE	TX	VS
•	•	•			Bi-State Title Search (Div of Bi-State Ind.)	866-450-7399	•	•	•	
	•	•			Guaranty Land Title	573-874-4912	•	•	•	•
•	•	•			Marion County Abstract Co (Missouri)	800-952-5314	•	•	•	•
•	•	•			Monroe County Abstract & Title Co Inc	660-327-4109	•	•	•	
•	•	•			Wells Abstract Co	573-221-0644	•	•	•	

CR	CV	PR	US	BK	←Courts **Montgomery**	Recorder→	UC	RE	TX	VS
•	•	•			Assured Title Company	636-240-0833	•	•	•	
•	•	•			Bi-State Title Search (Div of Bi-State Ind.)	866-450-7399	•	•	•	
•					LLG Enterprises	816-625-0947				
•	•	•			Montgomery County Abstract & Title Co	573-564-2298	•	•	•	
	•	•			Troy Title Co LLC	636-528-2220		•	•	

CR	CV	PR	US	BK	←COURTS	MORGAN	RECORDER→	UC	RE	TX	VS
	•	•			Guaranty Land Title		573-874-4912	•	•	•	•
•	•		•		Harmon Document Retrieval Service [SOP]		573-635-6690				
	•	•			Hubbard-Kavanaugh Title Co		573-378-4411	•	•	•	•
•	•				Ozark Inv [SOP]		888-685-5366				
					Real Data		573-893-4898		•	•	

CR	CV	PR	US	BK	←COURTS	NEW MADRID	RECORDER→	UC	RE	TX	VS
•	•	•			Security Abstract Co (Missouri)		573-748-2372		•	•	•

CR	CV	PR	US	BK	←COURTS	NEWTON	RECORDER→	UC	RE	TX	VS
•	•	•			American Research Unlimited Inc		417-358-6494	•	•	•	•
				•	G-Docs Abstracting LLC		636-586-4242	•	•	•	
•	•	•	•	•	National Investigative Services Inc [SOP]		417-831-2500	•	•	•	•

CR	CV	PR	US	BK	←COURTS	NODAWAY	RECORDER→	UC	RE	TX	VS
•	•	•			Hollis Search		660-446-2730		•	•	
	•	•			Nodaway County Abstract Co		660-582-2332		•	•	
•	•	•	•	•	NW Missouri Information Services [SOP]		816-233-4779	•	•	•	•

CR	CV	PR	US	BK	←COURTS	OREGON	RECORDER→	UC	RE	TX	VS
					Allen Abstract & Title		417-778-6665		•	•	

CR	CV	PR	US	BK	←COURTS	OSAGE	RECORDER→	UC	RE	TX	VS
	•	•			Guaranty Land Title		573-874-4912	•	•	•	•
•	•		•		Harmon Document Retrieval Service [SOP]		573-635-6690				
•	•		•		J & J Enterprises - MO [SOP]		573-395-4205	•	•	•	
•					LLG Enterprises		816-625-0947				
					Real Data		573-893-4898		•	•	

CR	CV	PR	US	BK	←COURTS	OZARK	RECORDER→	UC	RE	TX	VS
•	•	•	•	•	National Investigative Services Inc [SOP]		417-831-2500	•	•	•	•

CR	CV	PR	US	BK	←COURTS	PEMISCOT	RECORDER→	UC	RE	TX	VS
	•	•			DeReign & DeReign Attorneys at Law		573-333-4666	•	•	•	

CR	CV	PR	US	BK	←COURTS	PERRY	RECORDER→	UC	RE	TX	VS
					Collier Connections		573-576-3035	•	•	•	
		•			Kiefer Title Co		573-547-7755		•	•	
•					LLG Enterprises		816-625-0947				

CR	CV	PR	US	BK	←COURTS	PETTIS	RECORDER→	UC	RE	TX	VS
•	•	•			General Investigations LLC [SOP]		660-747-8900	•	•	•	•
	•	•			Guaranty Land Title		573-874-4912	•	•	•	•
•					LLG Enterprises		816-625-0947				
					Real Data		573-893-4898		•	•	

CR	CV	PR	US	BK	←COURTS	PHELPS	RECORDER→	UC	RE	TX	VS
				•	G-Docs Abstracting LLC		636-586-4242	•	•	•	
	•	•			Guaranty Land Title		573-874-4912	•	•	•	•
•	•		•		J & J Enterprises - MO [SOP]		573-395-4205	•	•	•	
•	•	•			Mozark Investigations [SOP]		866-308-1411	•	•	•	•
•	•	•	•	•	National Investigative Services Inc [SOP]		417-831-2500	•	•	•	•
					Real Data		573-893-4898		•	•	

CR	CV	PR	US	BK	←COURTS	PIKE	RECORDER→	UC	RE	TX	VS
•	•	•			Bi-State Title Search (Div of Bi-State Ind.)		866-450-7399	•	•	•	
•	•	•			Marion County Abstract Co (Missouri)		800-952-5314	•	•	•	•
	•	•			Troy Title Co LLC		636-528-2220		•	•	

CR	CV	PR	US	BK	←COURTS PLATTE	RECORDER→	UC	RE	TX	VS
•	•		•	•	Armstrong Document Retrieval	913-341-1991	•	•	•	
•	•	•			Bi-State Title Search (Div of Bi-State Ind.)	866-450-7399	•	•	•	
•	•	•	•	•	D & B Legal Services Inc [SOP]	913-963-1279	•	•	•	•
•	•		•	•	Executive Investigative Services [SOP]	800-764-9484	•	•	•	
•	•	•	•	•	Hatfield Process Service [SOP]	816-842-9800	•	•	•	•
•	•	•			Hollis Search	660-446-2730		•	•	
•					LLG Enterprises	816-625-0947				
	•	•	•		M & J Abstractors	913-727-3588	•	•	•	
•	•	•	•	•	NW Missouri Information Services [SOP]	816-233-4779	•	•	•	•
•	•				Rigoli Searches	913-908-8863	•	•	•	
	•		•	•	SearchWorks Inc	913-383-0940	•	•	•	

CR	CV	PR	US	BK	←COURTS POLK	RECORDER→	UC	RE	TX	VS
•	•	•	•	•	National Investigative Services Inc [SOP]	417-831-2500	•	•	•	•
	•	•			The Right Search	417-852-7097	•	•	•	

CR	CV	PR	US	BK	←COURTS PULASKI	RECORDER→	UC	RE	TX	VS
				•	G-Docs Abstracting LLC	636-586-4242	•	•	•	
	•	•			Guaranty Land Title	573-874-4912	•	•	•	•
•	•		•		J & J Enterprises - MO [SOP]	573-395-4205	•	•	•	
•	•	•			Mozark Investigations [SOP]	866-308-1411	•	•	•	•
•	•				Ozark Inv [SOP]	888-685-5366				
					Real Data	573-893-4898		•	•	

CR	CV	PR	US	BK	←COURTS PUTNAM	RECORDER→	UC	RE	TX	VS
					Putnam County Abstract	660-947-3105	•	•	•	

CR	CV	PR	US	BK	←COURTS RALLS	RECORDER→	UC	RE	TX	VS
•	•	•			Bi-State Title Search (Div of Bi-State Ind.)	866-450-7399	•	•	•	
		•			Lewis County Abstract (Missouri)	573-288-4461	•	•	•	
•	•	•			Marion County Abstract Co (Missouri)	800-952-5314	•	•	•	•
					Real Data	573-893-4898		•	•	
•	•	•			Wells Abstract Co	573-221-0644	•	•	•	

CR	CV	PR	US	BK	←COURTS RANDOLPH	RECORDER→	UC	RE	TX	VS
	•	•			Guaranty Land Title	573-874-4912	•	•	•	•
•					LLG Enterprises	816-625-0947				
					Real Data	573-893-4898		•	•	
	•	•			Town & Country Abstract Co (Missouri)	660-277-3467	•	•	•	
•	•	•			Wells Abstract Co	573-221-0644	•	•	•	

CR	CV	PR	US	BK	←COURTS RAY	RECORDER→	UC	RE	TX	VS
•	•	•			Bi-State Title Search (Div of Bi-State Ind.)	866-450-7399	•	•	•	
					Ray County Land Title	816-470-6500		•	•	

CR	CV	PR	US	BK	←COURTS REYNOLDS	RECORDER→	UC	RE	TX	VS
•	•	•			Mozark Investigations [SOP]	866-308-1411	•	•	•	•

CR	CV	PR	US	BK	←COURTS RIPLEY	RECORDER→	UC	RE	TX	VS
					Current River Abstract	573-996-2907		•	•	
	•				Ripley County Abstract	573-996-3115		•	•	

CR	CV	PR	US	BK	←COURTS SALINE	RECORDER→	UC	RE	TX	VS
•	•	•			General Investigations LLC [SOP]	660-747-8900	•	•	•	•
	•	•			Guaranty Land Title	573-874-4912	•	•	•	•

CR	CV	PR	US	BK	←COURTS SCHUYLER	RECORDER→	UC	RE	TX	VS
		•			Scotland County Abstract & Title Inc	660-465-7052		•	•	

CR	CV	PR	US	BK	←COURTS SCOTLAND	RECORDER→	UC	RE	TX	VS
•	•	•			Bi-State Title Search (Div of Bi-State Ind.)	866-450-7399	•	•	•	
		•			Scotland County Abstract & Title Inc	660-465-7052		•	•	

CR	CV	PR	US	BK	←COURTS SCOTT	RECORDER→	UC	RE	TX	VS
					Collier Connections	573-576-3035	•	•	•	

CR	CV	PR	US	BK	←COURTS SHANNON	RECORDER→	UC	RE	TX	VS
•	•	•			Mozark Investigations [SOP]	866-308-1411	•	•	•	•

CR	CV	PR	US	BK	←COURTS SHELBY	RECORDER→	UC	RE	TX	VS
•	•	•			Bi-State Title Search (Div of Bi-State Ind.)	866-450-7399	•	•	•	
•	•	•			Marion County Abstract Co (Missouri)	800-952-5314	•	•	•	•
•	•	•			Wells Abstract Co	573-221-0644	•	•	•	

CR	CV	PR	US	BK	←COURTS ST. CHARLES	RECORDER→	UC	RE	TX	VS
•	•	•	•	•	AAA Process Service Inc [SOP]	888-350-5809	•	•	•	•
•	•	•			Assured Title Company	636-240-0833	•	•	•	
•	•	•			Bi-State Title Search (Div of Bi-State Ind.)	866-450-7399	•	•	•	
•	•				Cardinal Title LLC	636-397-4300		•		
•	•	•	•	•	Brad Clarkson	618-288-7599	•	•	•	•
•	•				David Lung & Assoc [SOP]	888-477-2664				
				•	G-Docs Abstracting LLC	636-586-4242	•	•	•	
•	•		•	•	Infotrack Information Services Inc	800-275-5594	•	•	•	
•	•		•	•	Infotrack Information Services Inc	800-275-5594	•	•	•	
	•	•			Integrity Abstracting [SOP]	314-807-6359	•	•	•	
•	•	•	•	•	Jess Barker Document Research/Retrieval	888-316-3773	•	•	•	•
•	•				KLK Research	636-366-7055				
•	•	•	•	•	Kyle & Kyle (Michelle Kyle)	314-846-7728	•	•	•	
•	•	•	•	•	Lenmark Personal Services [SOP]	636-677-3831		•		
•					LLG Enterprises	816-625-0947				
	•	•	•	•	Master File Inc [SOP]	866-242-0469	•	•	•	
•	•	•		•	Quick Search Title Services	636-723-1888		•	•	•
•	•	•	•	•	Services Rendered Inc [SOP]	888-434-8200	•		•	•
•	•	•	•	•	SMS Searches	314-691-1593	•	•	•	•
•	•	•	•	•	St Vrain Resources [SOP]	314-645-1710			•	•
•	•	•	•	•	Woelfel & Assoc Inc [SOP]	888-297-7180	•	•	•	
•	•	•			Elaine Wolf	314-731-1839				•

CR	CV	PR	US	BK	←COURTS ST. CLAIR	RECORDER→	UC	RE	TX	VS
	•	•			The Right Search	417-852-7097	•	•	•	

CR	CV	PR	US	BK	←COURTS ST. FRANCOIS	RECORDER→	UC	RE	TX	VS
	•	•			American Heritage Abstract	573-431-1359	•	•	•	
•	•	•			Bi-State Title Search (Div of Bi-State Ind.)	866-450-7399	•	•	•	
					Collier Connections	573-576-3035	•	•	•	
•	•	•			Mozark Investigations [SOP]	866-308-1411	•	•	•	•
		•			Preferred Land Title	800-310-6721	•	•	•	

CR	CV	PR	US	BK	←COURTS ST. LOUIS	RECORDER→	UC	RE	TX	VS
•	•	•	•	•	AAA Process Service Inc [SOP]	888-350-5809	•	•	•	•
•	•	•			Assured Title Company	636-240-0833	•	•	•	
•	•	•			Bi-State Title Search (Div of Bi-State Ind.)	866-450-7399	•	•	•	
•	•				Cardinal Title LLC	636-397-4300		•		
•	•	•	•	•	Brad Clarkson	618-288-7599	•	•	•	•
•	•				David Lung & Assoc [SOP]	888-477-2664				
				•	G-Docs Abstracting LLC	636-586-4242	•	•	•	
	•	•			Guaranty Land Title	573-874-4912	•	•	•	•
•	•		•	•	Infotrack Information Services Inc	800-275-5594	•	•	•	
	•	•			Integrity Abstracting [SOP]	314-807-6359	•	•	•	

CR	CV	PR	US	BK	←Courts	Recorder→	UC	RE	TX	VS
•	•	•	•	•	Jess Barker Document Research/Retrieval	888-316-3773	•	•	•	•
•	•				KLK Research	636-366-7055				
•	•	•	•	•	Kyle & Kyle (Michelle Kyle)	314-846-7728	•	•	•	
•	•	•	•	•	Lenmark Personal Services [SOP]	636-677-3831		•		
•	•	•	•	•	Lueken Document Research Inc	314-631-5928	•	•	•	•
	•	•	•	•	Master File Inc [SOP]	866-242-0469	•	•	•	
•	•	•		•	Quick Search Title Services	636-723-1888		•	•	•
•	•	•	•	•	Services Rendered Inc [SOP]	888-434-8200	•		•	•
•	•	•	•	•	SMS Searches	314-691-1593	•	•	•	•
•	•	•	•	•	St Vrain Resources [SOP]	314-645-1710			•	•
•	•	•	•	•	Woelfel & Assoc Inc [SOP]	888-297-7180	•	•	•	
•	•	•			Elaine Wolf	314-731-1839				•

CR	CV	PR	US	BK	←Courts **ST. LOUIS CITY**	Recorder→	UC	RE	TX	VS
•	•	•	•	•	AAA Process Service Inc [SOP]	888-350-5809	•	•	•	•
•	•	•			Assured Title Company	636-240-0833	•	•	•	
•	•	•			Bi-State Title Search (Div of Bi-State Ind.)	866-450-7399	•	•	•	
•	•				Cardinal Title LLC	636-397-4300		•		
•	•	•	•	•	Brad Clarkson	618-288-7599	•	•	•	•
				•	G-Docs Abstracting LLC	636-586-4242	•	•	•	
	•	•			Guaranty Land Title	573-874-4912	•	•	•	•
•	•		•	•	Infotrack Information Services Inc	800-275-5594	•	•	•	
•	•				KLK Research	636-366-7055				
•	•	•	•	•	Kyle & Kyle (Michelle Kyle)	314-846-7728	•	•	•	
•	•	•	•	•	Lueken Document Research Inc	314-631-5928	•	•	•	•
	•	•	•	•	Master File Inc [SOP]	866-242-0469	•	•	•	
•	•	•		•	Quick Search Title Services	636-723-1888		•	•	•
•	•	•	•	•	Services Rendered Inc [SOP]	888-434-8200	•		•	•
•	•	•	•	•	SMS Searches	314-691-1593	•	•	•	•
•	•	•	•	•	St Vrain Resources [SOP]	314-645-1710			•	•

CR	CV	PR	US	BK	←Courts **STE. GENEVIEVE**	Recorder→	UC	RE	TX	VS
•	•	•			Bi-State Title Search (Div of Bi-State Ind.)	866-450-7399	•	•	•	
					Collier Connections	573-576-3035	•	•	•	
				•	G-Docs Abstracting LLC	636-586-4242	•	•	•	
		•			Preferred Land Title	800-310-6721	•	•	•	

CR	CV	PR	US	BK	←Courts **STODDARD**	Recorder→	UC	RE	TX	VS
					Collier Connections	573-576-3035	•	•	•	
		•			County Wide Abstract & Title Co Inc	573-624-2436	•	•	•	
•					LLG Enterprises	816-625-0947				

CR	CV	PR	US	BK	←Courts **STONE**	Recorder→	UC	RE	TX	VS
	•	•			Hogan Land Title Co	417-882-3000		•	•	
	•				MO Data Inc	417-299-2469	•	•	•	
•	•	•	•	•	National Investigative Services Inc [SOP]	417-831-2500	•	•	•	•
					Sparks Searches	417-725-4851		•	•	

CR	CV	PR	US	BK	←Courts **SULLIVAN**	Recorder→	UC	RE	TX	VS
					Putnam County Abstract	660-947-3105	•	•	•	
•	•	•	•	•	Sullivan County Abstract Co	660-265-3744	•	•	•	•

CR	CV	PR	US	BK	←Courts **TANEY**	Recorder→	UC	RE	TX	VS
	•	•			Hogan Land Title Co	417-882-3000		•	•	
					Lincoln-Evans Advanced Land & Title	417-581-8251	•	•	•	
	•				MO Data Inc	417-299-2469	•	•	•	
•	•	•	•	•	National Investigative Services Inc [SOP]	417-831-2500	•	•	•	•
					Sparks Searches	417-725-4851		•	•	

CR	CV	PR	US	BK	←COURTS TEXAS	RECORDER→	UC	RE	TX	VS
				•	G-Docs Abstracting LLC	636-586-4242	•	•	•	
•	•	•			Mozark Investigations [SOP]	866-308-1411	•	•	•	•

CR	CV	PR	US	BK	←COURTS VERNON	RECORDER→	UC	RE	TX	VS
•	•	•			American Research Unlimited Inc	417-358-6494	•	•	•	•
•	•	•	•	•	National Investigative Services Inc [SOP]	417-831-2500	•	•	•	•

CR	CV	PR	US	BK	←COURTS WARREN	RECORDER→	UC	RE	TX	VS
•	•	•			Assured Title Company	636-240-0833	•	•	•	
•	•	•			Bi-State Title Search (Div of Bi-State Ind.)	866-450-7399	•	•	•	
•	•				David Lung & Assoc [SOP]	888-477-2664				
•	•		•	•	Infotrack Information Services Inc	800-275-5594	•	•	•	
	•	•			Troy Title Co LLC	636-528-2220		•	•	

CR	CV	PR	US	BK	←COURTS WASHINGTON	RECORDER→	UC	RE	TX	VS
	•	•			American Heritage Abstract	573-431-1359	•	•	•	
•	•	•			Bi-State Title Search (Div of Bi-State Ind.)	866-450-7399	•	•	•	
				•	G-Docs Abstracting LLC	636-586-4242	•	•	•	
•	•	•			Mozark Investigations [SOP]	866-308-1411	•	•	•	•
		•			Preferred Land Title	800-310-6721	•	•	•	

CR	CV	PR	US	BK	←COURTS WAYNE	RECORDER→	UC	RE	TX	VS
	•	•			Wayne County Abstract	573-224-3616		•	•	

CR	CV	PR	US	BK	←COURTS WEBSTER	RECORDER→	UC	RE	TX	VS
	•	•			D D Hamilton Title Co	417-859-2078	•	•	•	
	•				MO Data Inc	417-299-2469	•	•	•	
•	•	•	•	•	National Investigative Services Inc [SOP]	417-831-2500	•	•	•	•

CR	CV	PR	US	BK	←COURTS WORTH	RECORDER→	UC	RE	TX	VS
•	•	•			Hollis Search	660-446-2730		•	•	

CR	CV	PR	US	BK	←COURTS WRIGHT	RECORDER→	UC	RE	TX	VS
	•	•			D D Hamilton Title Co	417-859-2078	•	•	•	
•	•	•	•	•	National Investigative Services Inc [SOP]	417-831-2500	•	•	•	•

COURT RECORDS

CODE	GOVERNMENT AGENCY	TYPE OF INFORMATION
CR	Criminal Court	Municipal, county and state level criminal cases
CV	Civil Court	Municipal, county and state level civil cases
PR	Probate Court	Wills and estate cases
US	US District Court	Federal civil and criminal cases
BK	Bankruptcy Court	United States bankruptcy cases

COUNTY RECORDS - RECORDINGS

CODE	GOVERNMENT AGENCY	TYPE OF INFORMATION
UC	UCC Filing Office	Uniform Commercial Code and other personal property liens
RE	Real Estate Recording Office	Real property transactions and liens
TX	Tax Filing Office(s)	Federal and state tax liens, judgment liens
VS	Vital Records Office	Vital statistics—birth, death, marriage, divorce

Montana

Court Records Retrieved | **Capital - Lewis And Clark County** | **Recorded Records Retrieved**

CR	CV	PR	US	BK	←Courts	Recorder→	UC	RE	TX	VS
					BEAVERHEAD					
•	•	•		•	J B Data & Research, LLC	406-585-3323	•	•	•	
	•	•			Southern Montana Abstract & Title	406-683-4445	•	•	•	•
•	•	•	•	•	Washington Court Records Service	509-448-5012	•	•	•	•
CR	CV	PR	US	BK	←Courts **BIG HORN**	Recorder→	UC	RE	TX	VS
	•	•			American Title & Escrow of Big Horn County	406-665-3797	•	•	•	
CR	CV	PR	US	BK	←Courts **BLAINE**	Recorder→	UC	RE	TX	VS
•	•	•			Blaine County Title Co	406-357-3884	•	•	•	•
•	•	•	•	•	Washington Court Records Service	509-448-5012	•	•	•	•
CR	CV	PR	US	BK	←Courts **BROADWATER**	Recorder→	UC	RE	TX	VS
•	•	•	•	•	AEGIS Consulting & Investigations Inc	888-742-3447	•		•	•
•	•	•		•	J B Data & Research, LLC	406-585-3323	•	•	•	
•	•				Mountain States Title Services	406-443-0521	•	•	•	
•	•	•	•	•	MT Corporate Services	406-227-7665	•	•	•	
•	•	•	•		Titleworks	406-442-4450		•	•	
•	•	•	•	•	Washington Court Records Service	509-448-5012	•	•	•	•
CR	CV	PR	US	BK	←Courts **CARBON**	Recorder→	UC	RE	TX	VS
					Carbon County Abstract & Title	406-446-1090	•	•	•	
•	•	•	•	•	Washington Court Records Service	509-448-5012	•	•	•	•
CR	CV	PR	US	BK	←Courts **CARTER**	Recorder→	UC	RE	TX	VS
	•	•			Security Abstract & Title Co	800-728-5022	•	•	•	
•	•	•	•	•	Washington Court Records Service	509-448-5012	•	•	•	•
CR	CV	PR	US	BK	←Courts **CASCADE**	Recorder→	UC	RE	TX	VS
•	•	•	•	•	AEGIS Consulting & Investigations Inc	888-742-3447	•		•	•
•	•	•	•	•	Equity Process Management [SOP]	888-721-3337	•		•	•
•	•	•		•	J B Data & Research, LLC	406-585-3323	•	•	•	
•	•				Statewide Recovery Inc [SOP]	406-761-4843				
•	•	•	•		Statewide Recovery Inc [SOP]	406-761-4843	•	•	•	•
•	•	•	•	•	Washington Court Records Service	509-448-5012	•	•	•	•
CR	CV	PR	US	BK	←Courts **CHOUTEAU**	Recorder→	UC	RE	TX	VS
	•	•			Chouteau County Abstract Co	406-622-3221		•	•	
•	•				Statewide Recovery Inc [SOP]	406-761-4843				
CR	CV	PR	US	BK	←Courts **CUSTER**	Recorder→	UC	RE	TX	VS
	•	•			Security Abstract & Title Co	800-728-5022	•	•	•	
CR	CV	PR	US	BK	←Courts **DANIELS**	Recorder→	UC	RE	TX	VS
	•	•	•	•	Montana Abstract Co Inc	406-487-5961		•	•	•
					Jake Nichols	406-765-1651 (Fax- same), alt phone- 406-765-1806		•	•	
CR	CV	PR	US	BK	←Courts **DAWSON**	Recorder→	UC	RE	TX	VS
	•	•			First American Title Co of Montana Inc	406-365-5482	•	•	•	
•	•	•	•	•	Washington Court Records Service	509-448-5012	•	•	•	•

CR	CV	PR	US	BK	←COURTS **DEER LODGE**	RECORDER→	UC	RE	TX	VS
•	•	•	•	•	Equity Process Management [SOP]	888-721-3337	•		•	•
•	•	•	•	•	Montana Abstract & Title Co	406-533-0433	•	•	•	•
•	•	•	•		Titleworks	406-442-4450		•	•	

CR	CV	PR	US	BK	←COURTS **FALLON**	RECORDER→	UC	RE	TX	VS
					Fallon County Abstractor	406-778-3929		•	•	

CR	CV	PR	US	BK	←COURTS **FERGUS**	RECORDER→	UC	RE	TX	VS
•	•	•		•	J B Data & Research, LLC	406-585-3323	•	•	•	
•	•	•			Realty Title Co Inc	406-535-2326	•	•	•	•
•	•	•	•	•	Washington Court Records Service	509-448-5012	•	•	•	•

CR	CV	PR	US	BK	←COURTS **FLATHEAD**	RECORDER→	UC	RE	TX	VS
•	•	•	•	•	Equity Process Management [SOP]	888-721-3337	•		•	•
•	•	•		•	J B Data & Research, LLC	406-585-3323	•	•	•	
•	•				Statewide Recovery Inc [SOP]	406-761-4843				
•	•	•	•	•	Washington Court Records Service	509-448-5012	•	•	•	•

CR	CV	PR	US	BK	←COURTS **GALLATIN**	RECORDER→	UC	RE	TX	VS
•	•	•	•	•	AEGIS Consulting & Investigations Inc	888-742-3447	•		•	•
•	•			•	All Secure Inc	406-388-7505; cell- 406-920-1931	•	•	•	
•	•	•	•	•	Equity Process Management [SOP]	888-721-3337	•		•	•
•	•	•		•	J B Data & Research, LLC	406-585-3323	•	•	•	
•	•	•	•	•	Washington Court Records Service	509-448-5012	•	•	•	•

CR	CV	PR	US	BK	←COURTS **GARFIELD**	RECORDER→	UC	RE	TX	VS
	•	•			Security Abstract & Title Co	800-728-5022	•	•	•	

CR	CV	PR	US	BK	←COURTS **GLACIER**	RECORDER→	UC	RE	TX	VS
•	•				Statewide Recovery Inc [SOP]	406-761-4843				

CR	CV	PR	US	BK	←COURTS **GOLDEN VALLEY**	RECORDER→	UC	RE	TX	VS
	•	•			Sweet Grass Title Co	406-932-4888		•	•	

CR	CV	PR	US	BK	←COURTS **GRANITE**	RECORDER→	UC	RE	TX	VS
•	•	•	•	•	Montana Abstract & Title Co	406-533-0433	•	•	•	•

CR	CV	PR	US	BK	←COURTS **HILL**	RECORDER→	UC	RE	TX	VS
•	•	•	•	•	Equity Process Management [SOP]	888-721-3337	•		•	•
	•	•			Hill County Title Co	406-265-7624	•	•	•	•
•	•				Statewide Recovery Inc [SOP]	406-761-4843				

CR	CV	PR	US	BK	←COURTS **JEFFERSON**	RECORDER→	UC	RE	TX	VS
•	•	•	•	•	AEGIS Consulting & Investigations Inc	888-742-3447	•		•	•
•	•	•		•	J B Data & Research, LLC	406-585-3323	•	•	•	
•	•				Mountain States Title Services	406-443-0521	•	•	•	
•	•	•	•		Titleworks	406-442-4450		•	•	

CR	CV	PR	US	BK	←COURTS **JUDITH BASIN**	RECORDER→	UC	RE	TX	VS
•	•	•			Realty Title Co Inc	406-535-2326	•	•	•	•

CR	CV	PR	US	BK	←COURTS **LAKE**	RECORDER→	UC	RE	TX	VS
•	•	•	•	•	Equity Process Management [SOP]	888-721-3337	•		•	•
•	•	•			First American Title & Escrow (Polson)	800-331-2349	•	•	•	
•	•	•		•	J B Data & Research, LLC	406-585-3323	•	•	•	
	•	•			Lake County Abstract & Title Co	800-823-6225	•	•	•	•

CR	CV	PR	US	BK	←COURTS **LEWIS AND CLARK**	RECORDER→	UC	RE	TX	VS
•	•	•	•	•	AEGIS Consulting & Investigations Inc	888-742-3447	•		•	•
•	•	•	•	•	Equity Process Management [SOP]	888-721-3337	•		•	•
	•	•	•	•	Helena Abstract & Title Co	406-442-5080	•	•	•	
•	•	•		•	J B Data & Research, LLC	406-585-3323	•	•	•	

CR	CV	PR	US	BK	←Courts	Phone	UC	RE	TX	VS
•	•				Mountain States Title Services	406-443-0521	•	•	•	
•	•	•	•	•	MT Corporate Services	406-227-7665	•	•	•	
•	•	•	•		Statewide Recovery Inc [SOP]	406-761-4843	•	•	•	•
•	•	•	•		Titleworks	406-442-4450		•	•	

CR	CV	PR	US	BK	←Courts: **Liberty**	Recorder→	UC	RE	TX	VS
	•	•			Marias Title Company	406-434-5156	•	•	•	•

CR	CV	PR	US	BK	←Courts: **Lincoln**	Recorder→	UC	RE	TX	VS
					First American Title & Escrow (Libby)	800-282-5630		•	•	
•	•	•		•	J B Data & Research, LLC	406-585-3323	•	•	•	

CR	CV	PR	US	BK	←Courts: **Madison**	Recorder→	UC	RE	TX	VS
					First American Title Co	800-570-5337		•		
•	•	•		•	J B Data & Research, LLC	406-585-3323	•	•	•	

CR	CV	PR	US	BK	←Courts: **McCone**	Recorder→	UC	RE	TX	VS
	•	•			First American Title Co of Montana Inc	406-365-5482	•	•	•	

CR	CV	PR	US	BK	←Courts: **Meagher**	Recorder→	UC	RE	TX	VS
•	•	•			Potter & Co	406-547-3355	•	•	•	•
•	•	•	•		Titleworks	406-442-4450		•	•	

CR	CV	PR	US	BK	←Courts: **Mineral**	Recorder→	UC	RE	TX	VS
	•	•			First American Title Mineral County	406-822-3391		•	•	

CR	CV	PR	US	BK	←Courts: **Missoula**	Recorder→	UC	RE	TX	VS
•	•	•	•	•	AEGIS Consulting & Investigations Inc	888-742-3447	•		•	•
•	•	•	•	•	Equity Process Management [SOP]	888-721-3337	•		•	•
		•			Insured Titles Inc	406-728-7900	•	•	•	
•	•	•		•	J B Data & Research, LLC	406-585-3323	•	•	•	
•	•	•	•		Titleworks	406-442-4450		•	•	

CR	CV	PR	US	BK	←Courts: **Musselshell**	Recorder→	UC	RE	TX	VS
					American Title & Escrow of Musselshell County	406-323-3165	•	•	•	

CR	CV	PR	US	BK	←Courts: **Park**	Recorder→	UC	RE	TX	VS
•	•	•		•	J B Data & Research, LLC	406-585-3323	•	•	•	

CR	CV	PR	US	BK	←Courts: **Petroleum**	Recorder→	UC	RE	TX	VS
•	•	•			Realty Title Co Inc	406-535-2326	•	•	•	•

CR	CV	PR	US	BK	←Courts: **Phillips**	Recorder→	UC	RE	TX	VS
					Phillips County Abstract Co	406-654-1413		•	•	

CR	CV	PR	US	BK	←Courts: **Pondera**	Recorder→	UC	RE	TX	VS
•	•				Statewide Recovery Inc [SOP]	406-761-4843				

CR	CV	PR	US	BK	←Courts: **Powder River**	Recorder→	UC	RE	TX	VS
•	•	•			Sheri McDowell	406-436-2885				

CR	CV	PR	US	BK	←Courts: **Powell**	Recorder→	UC	RE	TX	VS
•	•	•	•	•	Equity Process Management [SOP]	888-721-3337	•		•	•
•	•				Mountain States Title Services	406-443-0521	•	•	•	
•	•	•	•		Titleworks	406-442-4450		•	•	

CR	CV	PR	US	BK	←Courts: **Prairie**	Recorder→	UC	RE	TX	VS
•	•	•			Prairie Abstract & Title	406-635-5472	•	•	•	•

CR	CV	PR	US	BK	←Courts: **Ravalli**	Recorder→	UC	RE	TX	VS
					Bitterroot Research	406-363-4408	•	•	•	
•	•	•	•	•	Equity Process Management [SOP]	888-721-3337	•		•	•
•	•	•		•	J B Data & Research, LLC	406-585-3323	•	•	•	

Richland

CR	CV	PR	US	BK	←Courts	Recorder→	UC	RE	TX	VS
					See adjoining counties for retrievers or call court/recorder directly.					

Roosevelt

CR	CV	PR	US	BK	←Courts	Recorder→	UC	RE	TX	VS
					Jake Nichols	406-765-1651 (Fax- same), alt phone- 406-765-1806		•	•	
	•	•			Roosevelt County Abstract Co Inc	406-653-2800	•	•	•	

Rosebud

CR	CV	PR	US	BK	←Courts	Recorder→	UC	RE	TX	VS
					See adjoining counties for retrievers or call court/recorder directly.					

Sanders

CR	CV	PR	US	BK	←Courts	Recorder→	UC	RE	TX	VS
		•	•		First American Title Co (Thomspon Falls)	406-827-3591	•	•	•	
•	•	•		•	J B Data & Research, LLC	406-585-3323	•	•	•	

Sheridan

CR	CV	PR	US	BK	←Courts	Recorder→	UC	RE	TX	VS
					Jake Nichols	406-765-1651 (Fax- same), alt phone- 406-765-1806		•	•	

Silver Bow

CR	CV	PR	US	BK	←Courts	Recorder→	UC	RE	TX	VS
•	•	•	•	•	Equity Process Management [SOP]	888-721-3337	•		•	•
•	•	•		•	J B Data & Research, LLC	406-585-3323	•	•	•	
•	•	•	•	•	Montana Abstract & Title Co	406-533-0433	•	•	•	•

Stillwater

CR	CV	PR	US	BK	←Courts	Recorder→	UC	RE	TX	VS
	•	•			Stillwater Abstract	406-322-5216	•	•	•	

Sweet Grass

CR	CV	PR	US	BK	←Courts	Recorder→	UC	RE	TX	VS
	•	•			Sweet Grass Title Co	406-932-4888		•	•	

Teton

CR	CV	PR	US	BK	←Courts	Recorder→	UC	RE	TX	VS
•	•				Statewide Recovery Inc [SOP]	406-761-4843				

Toole

CR	CV	PR	US	BK	←Courts	Recorder→	UC	RE	TX	VS
	•	•			Marias Title Company	406-434-5156	•	•	•	•
•	•				Statewide Recovery Inc [SOP]	406-761-4843				

Treasure

CR	CV	PR	US	BK	←Courts	Recorder→	UC	RE	TX	VS
					See adjoining counties for retrievers or call court/recorder directly.					

Valley

CR	CV	PR	US	BK	←Courts	Recorder→	UC	RE	TX	VS
•	•	•			Valley County Abstract Company	406-228-2350	•	•	•	•

Wheatland

CR	CV	PR	US	BK	←Courts	Recorder→	UC	RE	TX	VS
	•	•			Sweet Grass Title Co	406-932-4888		•	•	

Wibaux

CR	CV	PR	US	BK	←Courts	Recorder→	UC	RE	TX	VS
•	•	•	•	•	Washington Court Records Service	509-448-5012	•	•	•	•

Yellowstone

CR	CV	PR	US	BK	←Courts	Recorder→	UC	RE	TX	VS
•	•	•	•	•	AEGIS Consulting & Investigations Inc	888-742-3447	•	•	•	•
•	•	•		•	J B Data & Research, LLC	406-585-3323	•	•	•	
•	•	•	•		PHB Minerals	406-248-8838	•	•	•	•
	•	•			Title Information Services	800-443-7874	•	•	•	•

Yellowstone National Park (part)

CR	CV	PR	US	BK	←Courts	Recorder→	UC	RE	TX	VS
					See adjoining counties for retrievers or call court/recorder directly. The Park is largely in Wyoming but court administration section is out of Gardiner, MT, Park County.					

Nebraska

COURT RECORDS RETRIEVED — CAPITAL - LANCASTER COUNTY — RECORDED RECORDS RETRIEVED

CR	CV	PR	US	BK	←COURTS / County / RECORDER→	Phone	UC	RE	TX	VS
					ADAMS					
		•			Adams Land Title (Hastings)	402-463-4198		•	•	
•	•				Fact Finders of Nebraska	308-534-8956	•	•	•	
		•	•		St Paul Abstract & Title	308-754-4922		•	•	
					ANTELOPE					
•	•				Susan K Rosenbaum	888-459-8700			•	
					ARTHUR					
	•	•			Southwestern Title Agency of Western Nebraska	308-284-4001		•	•	
	•	•	•	•	Thalken Title Co	308-284-3972	•	•	•	
					BANNER					
					City Abstract	308-632-4021		•		
					BLAINE					
	•	•			Brown County Abstract Co (Nebraska)	402-387-2718	•	•	•	
					BOONE					
•	•				Susan K Rosenbaum	888-459-8700			•	
					BOX BUTTE					
					See adjoining counties for retrievers or call court/recorder directly.					
					BOYD					
		•			McCarthy Abstract Co	402-336-2860	•	•	•	
					BROWN					
	•	•			Brown County Abstract Co (Nebraska)	402-387-2718	•	•	•	
•	•	•			Sandhills Title	402-376-2639		•	•	
					BUFFALO					
		•			Adams Land Title (Hastings)	402-463-4198		•	•	
	•	•			Barney Abstract & Title Co	308-234-5548	•	•	•	•
•	•				Fact Finders of Nebraska	308-534-8956	•	•	•	
•					Resource Management Specialists	877-476-3337				
		•	•		St Paul Abstract & Title	308-754-4922		•	•	
					BURT					
•	•	•			Anderson Abstract Co	402-374-1476	•	•	•	
					BUTLER					
	•	•			Colfax County Title & Abstract Co	402-352-2027		•	•	
•	•				Susan K Rosenbaum	888-459-8700			•	
					CASS					
		•	•	•	Nebraska Default & Title Services Inc	866-866-5100		•	•	
•	•	•			Otoe County Title Co	402-873-5501	•	•	•	
•	•		•	•	Thomas Research Services [SOP]	402-339-7291	•		•	
					CEDAR					
		•	•		Merkel Abstract & Title	402-254-3547		•		
					CHASE					
	•	•			Southwestern Title Agency of Western Nebraska	308-284-4001		•	•	

CR	CV	PR	US	BK	←Courts	Recorder→	UC	RE	TX	VS
	•	•	•	•	Thalken Title Co	308-284-3972	•	•	•	
CR	**CV**	**PR**	**US**	**BK**	**←Courts CHERRY**	**Recorder→**	**UC**	**RE**	**TX**	**VS**
•	•	•			Sandhills Abstracting	308-282-1140	•	•	•	•
•	•	•			Sandhills Title	402-376-2639		•	•	
	•	•	•	•	Thalken Title Co	308-284-3972	•	•	•	
CR	**CV**	**PR**	**US**	**BK**	**←Courts CHEYENNE**	**Recorder→**	**UC**	**RE**	**TX**	**VS**
	•	•	•	•	Cheyenne County Abstract	308-254-5636	•	•	•	
	•	•			Deuel County Abstract Co (Nebraska) [SOP]	308-874-2212	•	•	•	
CR	**CV**	**PR**	**US**	**BK**	**←Courts CLAY**	**Recorder→**	**UC**	**RE**	**TX**	**VS**
					Abstract & Title Inc	402-729-2771	•	•	•	
		•			Adams Land Title (Hastings)	402-463-4198		•	•	
CR	**CV**	**PR**	**US**	**BK**	**←Courts COLFAX**	**Recorder→**	**UC**	**RE**	**TX**	**VS**
	•	•			Colfax County Title & Abstract Co	402-352-2027		•	•	
•	•				Susan K Rosenbaum	888-459-8700			•	
CR	**CV**	**PR**	**US**	**BK**	**←Courts CUMING**	**Recorder→**	**UC**	**RE**	**TX**	**VS**
					See adjoining counties for retrievers or call court/recorder directly.					
CR	**CV**	**PR**	**US**	**BK**	**←Courts CUSTER**	**Recorder→**	**UC**	**RE**	**TX**	**VS**
•					Western Nebraska Inv [SOP]	308-534-9003	•	•	•	
CR	**CV**	**PR**	**US**	**BK**	**←Courts DAKOTA**	**Recorder→**	**UC**	**RE**	**TX**	**VS**
•	•	•	•	•	Professional Support Services of Siouxland	712-233-2383	•	•	•	•
•	•		•	•	Intra-Lex Investigations Inc [SOP]	712-233-1639	•	•	•	
CR	**CV**	**PR**	**US**	**BK**	**←Courts DAWES**	**Recorder→**	**UC**	**RE**	**TX**	**VS**
		•			Dawes County Abstract Co.	308-432-4840	•	•	•	
CR	**CV**	**PR**	**US**	**BK**	**←Courts DAWSON**	**Recorder→**	**UC**	**RE**	**TX**	**VS**
•	•				Fact Finders of Nebraska	308-534-8956	•	•	•	
•	•				Western Nebraska Inv [SOP]	308-534-9003	•	•	•	
CR	**CV**	**PR**	**US**	**BK**	**←Courts DEUEL**	**Recorder→**	**UC**	**RE**	**TX**	**VS**
	•	•			Deuel County Abstract Co (Nebraska) [SOP]	308-874-2212	•	•	•	
	•	•	•	•	Thalken Title Co	308-284-3972	•	•	•	
CR	**CV**	**PR**	**US**	**BK**	**←Courts DIXON**	**Recorder→**	**UC**	**RE**	**TX**	**VS**
					See adjoining counties for retrievers or call court/recorder directly.					
CR	**CV**	**PR**	**US**	**BK**	**←Courts DODGE**	**Recorder→**	**UC**	**RE**	**TX**	**VS**
•	•	•	•	•	Coit Enterprises	402-451-0462		•	•	
		•	•	•	Nebraska Default & Title Services Inc	866-866-5100		•	•	
•	•	•			Jean Peck [SOP]	402-721-4143	•	•	•	•
•	•				Susan K Rosenbaum	888-459-8700			•	
CR	**CV**	**PR**	**US**	**BK**	**←Courts DOUGLAS**	**Recorder→**	**UC**	**RE**	**TX**	**VS**
•	•	•	•	•	Coit Enterprises	402-451-0462		•	•	
•	•	•	•	•	Legal Eagle Inc / Eagle Search & Service [SOP]	402-342-4427	•	•	•	•
		•	•	•	Nebraska Default & Title Services Inc	866-866-5100		•	•	
•					Resource Management Specialists	877-476-3337				
•	•		•		Thomas Research Services [SOP]	402-339-7291	•		•	
CR	**CV**	**PR**	**US**	**BK**	**←Courts DUNDY**	**Recorder→**	**UC**	**RE**	**TX**	**VS**
	•	•			Southwestern Title Agency of Western Nebraska	308-284-4001		•	•	
CR	**CV**	**PR**	**US**	**BK**	**←Courts FILLMORE**	**Recorder→**	**UC**	**RE**	**TX**	**VS**
					Abstract & Title Inc	402-729-2771	•	•	•	
		•			Adams Land Title (Hastings)	402-463-4198		•	•	

CR	CV	PR	US	BK	←Courts	FRANKLIN	Recorder→	UC	RE	TX	VS
		•			Adams Land Title (Hastings)		402-463-4198		•	•	

CR	CV	PR	US	BK	←Courts	FRONTIER	Recorder→	UC	RE	TX	VS
•	•	•			Scott Abstract		308-532-8535	•	•	•	•
•	•				Western Nebraska Inv [SOP]		308-534-9003	•	•	•	

CR	CV	PR	US	BK	←Courts	FURNAS	Recorder→	UC	RE	TX	VS
•	•	•			Furnas Valley Title		308-824-3304		•	•	

CR	CV	PR	US	BK	←Courts	GAGE	Recorder→	UC	RE	TX	VS
					Abstract & Title Inc		402-729-2771	•	•	•	
	•	•	•		Nebraska Title Company		402-228-2233	•	•	•	

CR	CV	PR	US	BK	←Courts	GARDEN	Recorder→	UC	RE	TX	VS
	•	•			Deuel County Abstract Co (Nebraska) [SOP]		308-874-2212	•	•	•	
	•	•	•	•	Thalken Title Co		308-284-3972	•	•	•	

CR	CV	PR	US	BK	←Courts	GARFIELD	Recorder→	UC	RE	TX	VS
					See adjoining counties for retrievers or call court/recorder directly.						

CR	CV	PR	US	BK	←Courts	GOSPER	Recorder→	UC	RE	TX	VS
•	•				Fact Finders of Nebraska		308-534-8956	•	•	•	
•	•	•	•	•	Todd Wilson PC		308-785-2550	•	•	•	

CR	CV	PR	US	BK	←Courts	GRANT	Recorder→	UC	RE	TX	VS
	•	•	•	•	Thalken Title Co		308-284-3972	•	•	•	

CR	CV	PR	US	BK	←Courts	GREELEY	Recorder→	UC	RE	TX	VS
	•	•			Janke Abstract Co		308-754-4251	•	•	•	

CR	CV	PR	US	BK	←Courts	HALL	Recorder→	UC	RE	TX	VS
		•			Adams Land Title (Hastings)		402-463-4198		•	•	
•	•				Fact Finders of Nebraska		308-534-8956	•	•	•	
	•	•			Janke Abstract Co		308-754-4251	•	•	•	
•					Resource Management Specialists		877-476-3337				
•	•				Susan K Rosenbaum		888-459-8700			•	
		•	•		St Paul Abstract & Title		308-754-4922		•	•	

CR	CV	PR	US	BK	←Courts	HAMILTON	Recorder→	UC	RE	TX	VS
		•			Adams Land Title (Hastings)		402-463-4198		•	•	
•	•	•			First Securities Corp in Aurora		402-694-6926	•	•	•	•
•	•				Susan K Rosenbaum		888-459-8700			•	

CR	CV	PR	US	BK	←Courts	HARLAN	Recorder→	UC	RE	TX	VS
•	•	•			Furnas Valley Title		308-824-3304		•	•	
					Harlan County Abstract		308-928-2343		•	•	

CR	CV	PR	US	BK	←Courts	HAYES	Recorder→	UC	RE	TX	VS
•	•	•			Scott Abstract		308-532-8535	•	•	•	•

CR	CV	PR	US	BK	←Courts	HITCHCOCK	Recorder→	UC	RE	TX	VS
					See adjoining counties for retrievers or call court/recorder directly.						

CR	CV	PR	US	BK	←Courts	HOLT	Recorder→	UC	RE	TX	VS
		•			McCarthy Abstract Co		402-336-2860	•	•	•	

CR	CV	PR	US	BK	←Courts	HOOKER	Recorder→	UC	RE	TX	VS
•	•	•			Scott Abstract		308-532-8535	•	•	•	•

CR	CV	PR	US	BK	←Courts	HOWARD	Recorder→	UC	RE	TX	VS
	•	•			Janke Abstract Co		308-754-4251	•	•	•	
•	•				Susan K Rosenbaum		888-459-8700			•	
		•	•		St Paul Abstract & Title		308-754-4922		•	•	

CR	CV	PR	US	BK	←Courts		Recorder→	UC	RE	TX	VS
CR	CV	PR	US	BK	←Courts	**Jefferson**	Recorder→	UC	RE	TX	VS
					Abstract & Title Inc		402-729-2771	•	•	•	
CR	CV	PR	US	BK	←Courts	**Johnson**	Recorder→	UC	RE	TX	VS
					Morrissey Morrissey & Dalluge		402-335-3344		•		
CR	CV	PR	US	BK	←Courts	**Kearney**	Recorder→	UC	RE	TX	VS
		•			Adams Land Title (Hastings)		402-463-4198		•	•	
•	•				Fact Finders of Nebraska		308-534-8956	•	•	•	
		•			Miller Abstract & Title Co		308-832-0969	•	•	•	
CR	CV	PR	US	BK	←Courts	**Keith**	Recorder→	UC	RE	TX	VS
	•	•			Deuel County Abstract Co (Nebraska) [SOP]		308-874-2212	•	•	•	
	•	•			Southwestern Title Agency of Western Nebraska		308-284-4001			•	
	•	•	•	•	Thalken Title Co		308-284-3972	•	•	•	
•	•				Western Nebraska Inv [SOP]		308-534-9003	•	•	•	
CR	CV	PR	US	BK	←Courts	**Keya Paha**	Recorder→	UC	RE	TX	VS
	•	•			Brown County Abstract Co (Nebraska)		402-387-2718	•	•	•	
•	•	•			Sandhills Title		402-376-2639		•	•	
CR	CV	PR	US	BK	←Courts	**Kimball**	Recorder→	UC	RE	TX	VS
	•	•			Deuel County Abstract Co (Nebraska) [SOP]		308-874-2212	•	•	•	
CR	CV	PR	US	BK	←Courts	**Knox**	Recorder→	UC	RE	TX	VS
	•	•			Northeast Nebraska Title & Escrow		402-371-1221	•	•	•	•
•	•				Susan K Rosenbaum		888-459-8700			•	
•	•	•			Valverde Abstract Co Inc		402-288-4466		•	•	
CR	CV	PR	US	BK	←Courts	**Lancaster**	Recorder→	UC	RE	TX	VS
		•	•	•	Nebraska Default & Title Services Inc		866-866-5100		•	•	
			•	•	Records Research Inc (Nebraska) [SOP]		402-476-3869, 402-323-3828- direct line	•		•	
•					Resource Management Specialists		877-476-3337				
•	•				Susan K Rosenbaum		888-459-8700			•	
•	•		•		Searches by SKW		402-786-2184			•	
CR	CV	PR	US	BK	←Courts	**Lincoln**	Recorder→	UC	RE	TX	VS
•	•				Fact Finders of Nebraska		308-534-8956	•	•	•	
•					Resource Management Specialists		877-476-3337				
•	•	•			Scott Abstract		308-532-8535	•	•	•	•
•	•				Western Nebraska Inv [SOP]		308-534-9003	•	•	•	
CR	CV	PR	US	BK	←Courts	**Logan**	Recorder→	UC	RE	TX	VS
•	•	•			Scott Abstract		308-532-8535	•	•	•	•
•	•				Western Nebraska Inv [SOP]		308-534-9003	•	•	•	
CR	CV	PR	US	BK	←Courts	**Loup**	Recorder→	UC	RE	TX	VS
					See adjoining counties for retrievers or call court/recorder directly.						
CR	CV	PR	US	BK	←Courts	**Madison**	Recorder→	UC	RE	TX	VS
•	•				Northeast Nebraska Court Research		402-439-2469		•	•	•
	•	•			Northeast Nebraska Title & Escrow		402-371-1221	•	•	•	•
•	•				Susan K Rosenbaum		888-459-8700			•	
CR	CV	PR	US	BK	←Courts	**McPherson**	Recorder→	UC	RE	TX	VS
•	•	•			Scott Abstract		308-532-8535	•	•	•	•
CR	CV	PR	US	BK	←Courts	**Merrick**	Recorder→	UC	RE	TX	VS
	•	•			Janke Abstract Co		308-754-4251	•	•	•	
•	•				Susan K Rosenbaum		888-459-8700			•	

CR	CV	PR	US	BK	←COURTS	MORRILL	RECORDER→	UC	RE	TX	VS
	•	•			Deuel County Abstract Co (Nebraska) [SOP]		308-874-2212	•	•	•	

CR	CV	PR	US	BK	←COURTS	NANCE	RECORDER→	UC	RE	TX	VS
	•	•			Janke Abstract Co		308-754-4251	•	•	•	
•	•				Susan K Rosenbaum		888-459-8700			•	

CR	CV	PR	US	BK	←COURTS	NEMAHA	RECORDER→	UC	RE	TX	VS
		•			Auburn Abstract & Title Company LLC		402-274-4321	•	•	•	
•	•	•			Otoe County Title Co		402-873-5501	•	•	•	

CR	CV	PR	US	BK	←COURTS	NUCKOLLS	RECORDER→	UC	RE	TX	VS
		•			Adams Land Title (Hastings)		402-463-4198		•	•	

CR	CV	PR	US	BK	←COURTS	OTOE	RECORDER→	UC	RE	TX	VS
•	•	•			Otoe County Title Co		402-873-5501	•	•	•	
•	•		•	•	Thomas Research Services [SOP]		402-339-7291	•		•	

CR	CV	PR	US	BK	←COURTS	PAWNEE	RECORDER→	UC	RE	TX	VS
•	•	•			Pawnee County Abstract Co		402-852-2035	•	•	•	
•	•	•			Stehlik Law Office		402-852-2973	•	•	•	

CR	CV	PR	US	BK	←COURTS	PERKINS	RECORDER→	UC	RE	TX	VS
	•	•			Southwestern Title Agency of Western Nebraska		308-284-4001		•	•	
	•	•	•	•	Thalken Title Co		308-284-3972	•	•	•	
•	•				Western Nebraska Inv [SOP]		308-534-9003	•	•	•	

CR	CV	PR	US	BK	←COURTS	PHELPS	RECORDER→	UC	RE	TX	VS
		•			Dealey Abstract & Title Company		308-995-4622	•	•	•	
•	•				Fact Finders of Nebraska		308-534-8956	•	•	•	

CR	CV	PR	US	BK	←COURTS	PIERCE	RECORDER→	UC	RE	TX	VS
		•			Chilvers Abstract & Title Co		402-329-4525	•	•	•	
	•	•			Northeast Nebraska Title & Escrow		402-371-1221	•	•	•	•
•	•				Susan K Rosenbaum		888-459-8700			•	

CR	CV	PR	US	BK	←COURTS	PLATTE	RECORDER→	UC	RE	TX	VS
•	•	•			Platte County Title & Escrow Co		402-563-4519	•	•	•	
•	•				Susan K Rosenbaum		888-459-8700			•	
		•			Tri County Title & Escrow Co.		402-747-2141	•	•	•	

CR	CV	PR	US	BK	←COURTS	POLK	RECORDER→	UC	RE	TX	VS
•	•				Susan K Rosenbaum		888-459-8700			•	
		•			Tri County Title & Escrow Co.		402-747-2141	•	•	•	

CR	CV	PR	US	BK	←COURTS	RED WILLOW	RECORDER→	UC	RE	TX	VS
•	•				Fact Finders of Nebraska		308-534-8956	•	•	•	
•	•				Western Nebraska Inv [SOP]		308-534-9003	•	•	•	

CR	CV	PR	US	BK	←COURTS	RICHARDSON	RECORDER→	UC	RE	TX	VS
•	•	•			Southeast Nebraska Abstract		402-245-4222	•	•	•	

CR	CV	PR	US	BK	←COURTS	ROCK	RECORDER→	UC	RE	TX	VS
	•	•			Brown County Abstract Co (Nebraska)		402-387-2718	•	•	•	

CR	CV	PR	US	BK	←COURTS	SALINE	RECORDER→	UC	RE	TX	VS
					Abstract & Title Inc		402-729-2771	•	•	•	

CR	CV	PR	US	BK	←COURTS	SARPY	RECORDER→	UC	RE	TX	VS
•	•	•	•	•	Coit Enterprises		402-451-0462		•	•	
•	•	•	•	•	Legal Eagle Inc / Eagle Search & Service [SOP]		402-342-4427	•	•	•	•
		•	•	•	Nebraska Default & Title Services Inc		866-866-5100		•	•	
•					Resource Management Specialists		877-476-3337				

CR	CV	PR	US	BK	Retriever	Phone	UC	RE	TX	VS
•	•		•	•	Thomas Research Services [SOP]	402-339-7291	•		•	

CR	CV	PR	US	BK	←Courts SAUNDERS	Recorder→	UC	RE	TX	VS
		•			Hamilton & Johnson Abstract Inc	402-443-3081	•	•	•	
		•	•	•	Nebraska Default & Title Services Inc	866-866-5100		•	•	
•	•	•			Jean Peck [SOP]	402-721-4143	•	•	•	•
•	•				Susan K Rosenbaum	888-459-8700			•	

CR	CV	PR	US	BK	←Courts SCOTTS BLUFF	Recorder→	UC	RE	TX	VS
					City Abstract	308-632-4021		•	•	
	•	•			Deuel County Abstract Co (Nebraska) [SOP]	308-874-2212	•	•	•	

CR	CV	PR	US	BK	←Courts SEWARD	Recorder→	UC	RE	TX	VS
					Abstract & Title Inc	402-729-2771	•	•	•	
•	•				Susan K Rosenbaum	888-459-8700			•	

CR	CV	PR	US	BK	←Courts SHERIDAN	Recorder→	UC	RE	TX	VS
		•			Dawes County Abstract Co	308-432-4840	•	•	•	
•	•	•			Sandhills Abstracting	308-282-1140	•	•	•	•
	•	•	•	•	Thalken Title Co	308-284-3972	•	•	•	

CR	CV	PR	US	BK	←Courts SHERMAN	Recorder→	UC	RE	TX	VS
	•	•			Janke Abstract Co	308-754-4251	•	•		

CR	CV	PR	US	BK	←Courts SIOUX	Recorder→	UC	RE	TX	VS
		•			Dawes County Abstract Co	308-432-4840	•	•	•	

CR	CV	PR	US	BK	←Courts STANTON	Recorder→	UC	RE	TX	VS
•	•				Northeast Nebraska Court Research	402-439-2469		•	•	•
					Stanton Co Abstract	402-439-2142		•	•	

CR	CV	PR	US	BK	←Courts THAYER	Recorder→	UC	RE	TX	VS
					Abstract & Title Inc	402-729-2771	•	•	•	

CR	CV	PR	US	BK	←Courts THOMAS	Recorder→	UC	RE	TX	VS
•	•	•			Sandhills Title	402-376-2639		•	•	
•	•	•			Scott Abstract	308-532-8535	•	•	•	•

CR	CV	PR	US	BK	←Courts THURSTON	Recorder→	UC	RE	TX	VS
					See adjoining counties for retrievers or call court/recorder directly.					

CR	CV	PR	US	BK	←Courts VALLEY	Recorder→	UC	RE	TX	VS
					Springdale Realty	308-728-3569		•	•	

CR	CV	PR	US	BK	←Courts WASHINGTON	Recorder→	UC	RE	TX	VS
•	•	•	•	•	Coit Enterprises	402-451-0462		•	•	
		•	•	•	Nebraska Default & Title Services Inc	866-866-5100		•	•	
•	•	•			Jean Peck [SOP]	402-721-4143	•	•	•	•
•	•		•	•	Thomas Research Services [SOP]	402-339-7291	•		•	

CR	CV	PR	US	BK	←Courts WAYNE	Recorder→	UC	RE	TX	VS
		•			Chilvers Abstract & Title Co	402-329-4525	•	•	•	

CR	CV	PR	US	BK	←Courts WEBSTER	Recorder→	UC	RE	TX	VS
		•			Adams Land Title (Hastings)	402-463-4198		•	•	

CR	CV	PR	US	BK	←Courts WHEELER	Recorder→	UC	RE	TX	VS
		•			McCarthy Abstract Co	402-336-2860	•	•	•	

CR	CV	PR	US	BK	←Courts YORK	Recorder→	UC	RE	TX	VS
		•			Adams Land Title (Hastings)	402-463-4198		•	•	
•	•				Susan K Rosenbaum	888-459-8700			•	
•	•	•			York County Title Co	402-362-4405	•	•	•	

Nevada

Nevada has an independent city with its own court structure and recording office – Carson City.

COURT RECORDS RETRIEVED — CAPITAL - CARSON CITY COUNTY — RECORDED RECORDS RETRIEVED

CR	CV	PR	US	BK	←COURTS	CARSON CITY	RECORDER→	UC	RE	TX	VS
•	•	•	•	•	Avalon/Tracy Bowers		775-853-3003	•	•	•	•
					Capitol Corporate Services Inc (Nevada)		800-899-0490	•		•	
			•	•	Coyote		775-972-6530	•	•	•	
•	•	•	•	•	CSC - Corporation Service Company [SOP]		800-927-9800	•	•	•	•
•	•	•	•	•	High Sierra Courier Service [SOP]		877-812-8444	•		•	•
•	•	•	•	•	Pacific Security Intelligence		530-832-0259	•	•	•	•
	•		•		Parasec (Nevada)		888-972-7273	•		•	
•	•	•	•	•	Reno/Carson Messenger Service Inc [SOP]		800-222-4249	•	•	•	•
					Top Flight Solutions		775-331-6490	•	•	•	•
•	•	•	•	•	Unisearch Inc (Nevada) [SOP]		800-260-1131	•		•	

CR	CV	PR	US	BK	←COURTS	CHURCHILL	RECORDER→	UC	RE	TX	VS
•	•	•	•	•	Avalon/Tracy Bowers		775-853-3003	•	•	•	•
					Nevada Land Services		800-233-4999	•	•	•	
•	•	•	•	•	Pacific Security Intelligence		530-832-0259	•	•	•	•
•	•	•	•	•	Reno/Carson Messenger Service Inc [SOP]		800-222-4249	•	•	•	•
					Top Flight Solutions		775-331-6490	•	•	•	•

CR	CV	PR	US	BK	←COURTS	CLARK	RECORDER→	UC	RE	TX	VS
•	•		•		Accurate Background Inc		800-784-3911				
•	•	•	•	•	Arizona Research & Retrieval Services Inc		888-500-7767	•	•	•	•
•	•	•	•	•	Avalon/Tracy Bowers		775-853-3003	•	•	•	•
•	•	•	•	•	Bodo PI [SOP]		877-381-7009	•	•	•	•
•	•	•	•	•	Deines Inc		702-453-9859	•	•	•	
	•	•	•	•	Diamond Abstractors Inc		702-355-0364	•	•	•	•
					Document Recording & Retrieval Services		702-558-6207		•		•
	•	•	•	•	EAGLE i Communications		702-658-3912	•	•	•	
					Global Title Reporting Services Inc		702-248-0593	•	•	•	
•	•	•	•	•	Infotrackers Inc		702-948-7055	•	•	•	
•	•	•	•	•	Integrity Records Access		702-296-9145	•	•	•	•
•	•	•	•	•	National Search Solutions LLC		702-431-9100	•	•	•	•
•	•	•	•	•	Pacific Security Intelligence		530-832-0259	•	•	•	•
•	•	•	•	•	Pete Costanzo Private Inv		702-459-1640	•	•	•	
•	•				Public Records Info Service		520-797-0486				

CR	CV	PR	US	BK	←COURTS	DOUGLAS	RECORDER→	UC	RE	TX	VS
•	•	•	•	•	Avalon/Tracy Bowers		775-853-3003	•	•	•	•
•	•	•	•	•	High Sierra Courier Service [SOP]		877-812-8444	•		•	•
•	•	•	•	•	Pacific Security Intelligence		530-832-0259	•	•	•	•
	•		•		Parasec (Nevada)		888-972-7273	•		•	
•	•	•	•	•	Reno/Carson Messenger Service Inc [SOP]		800-222-4249	•	•	•	•
					Top Flight Solutions		775-331-6490	•	•	•	•
•	•	•	•	•	Unisearch Inc (Nevada) [SOP]		800-260-1131	•		•	

CR	CV	PR	US	BK	←COURTS	ELKO	RECORDER→	UC	RE	TX	VS
•	•	•	•	•	Avalon/Tracy Bowers		775-853-3003	•	•	•	•
•	•	•	•	•	Pacific Security Intelligence		530-832-0259	•	•	•	•

CR	CV	PR	US	BK	←COURTS	ESMERALDA	RECORDER→	UC	RE	TX	VS
					Nevada Land Services		800-233-4999	•	•	•	
•	•	•	•	•	Pacific Security Intelligence		530-832-0259	•	•	•	•

CR	CV	PR	US	BK	←Courts	EUREKA	Recorder→	UC	RE	TX	VS
					Nevada Land Services		800-233-4999	•	•	•	
•	•	•	•	•	Pacific Security Intelligence		530-832-0259	•	•	•	•

CR	CV	PR	US	BK	←Courts	HUMBOLDT	Recorder→	UC	RE	TX	VS
•	•	•	•	•	Avalon/Tracy Bowers		775-853-3003	•	•	•	•
					Nevada Land Services		800-233-4999	•	•	•	
•	•	•	•	•	Pacific Security Intelligence		530-832-0259	•	•	•	•

CR	CV	PR	US	BK	←Courts	LANDER	Recorder→	UC	RE	TX	VS
					Nevada Land Services		800-233-4999	•	•	•	
•	•	•	•	•	Pacific Security Intelligence		530-832-0259	•	•	•	•

CR	CV	PR	US	BK	←Courts	LINCOLN	Recorder→	UC	RE	TX	VS
					Nevada Land Services		800-233-4999	•	•	•	
•	•	•	•	•	Pacific Security Intelligence		530-832-0259	•	•	•	•

CR	CV	PR	US	BK	←Courts	LYON	Recorder→	UC	RE	TX	VS
•	•	•	•	•	Avalon/Tracy Bowers		775-853-3003	•	•	•	•
•	•	•	•	•	Pacific Security Intelligence		530-832-0259	•	•	•	•
•	•	•	•	•	Reno/Carson Messenger Service Inc [SOP]		800-222-4249	•	•	•	•

CR	CV	PR	US	BK	←Courts	MINERAL	Recorder→	UC	RE	TX	VS
					Nevada Land Services		800-233-4999	•	•	•	
•	•	•	•	•	Pacific Security Intelligence		530-832-0259	•	•	•	•

CR	CV	PR	US	BK	←Courts	NYE	Recorder→	UC	RE	TX	VS
					Nevada Land Services		800-233-4999	•	•	•	
•	•	•	•	•	Pacific Security Intelligence		530-832-0259	•	•	•	•

CR	CV	PR	US	BK	←Courts	PERSHING	Recorder→	UC	RE	TX	VS
					Nevada Land Services		800-233-4999	•	•	•	
•	•	•	•	•	Pacific Security Intelligence		530-832-0259	•	•	•	•

CR	CV	PR	US	BK	←Courts	STOREY	Recorder→	UC	RE	TX	VS
•	•	•	•	•	Avalon/Tracy Bowers		775-853-3003	•	•	•	•
			•	•	Coyote		775-972-6530	•	•	•	
•	•	•	•	•	Pacific Security Intelligence		530-832-0259	•	•	•	•
•	•	•	•	•	Reno/Carson Messenger Service Inc [SOP]		800-222-4249	•	•	•	•
					Top Flight Solutions		775-331-6490	•	•	•	•
•	•	•	•	•	Unisearch Inc (Nevada) [SOP]		800-260-1131	•		•	

CR	CV	PR	US	BK	←Courts	WASHOE	Recorder→	UC	RE	TX	VS
	•	•	•	•	A-1 Document Service LLC		775-544-7993	•	•	•	•
•	•	•	•	•	Avalon/Tracy Bowers		775-853-3003	•	•	•	•
			•	•	Coyote		775-972-6530	•	•	•	
•	•	•	•	•	Deines Inc		702-453-9859	•	•	•	
•	•	•	•	•	Diamond Abstractors Inc		702-355-0364	•	•	•	•
					Document Recording & Retrieval Services		702-558-6207		•		•
•	•	•	•	•	Dody Fuhrmann-Private Investigator		775-544-7993	•	•	•	•
•	•	•	•	•	High Sierra Courier Service [SOP]		877-812-8444	•		•	•
•	•	•	•	•	Pacific Security Intelligence		530-832-0259	•	•	•	•
•	•	•	•	•	Reno/Carson Messenger Service Inc [SOP]		800-222-4249	•	•	•	•
					Top Flight Solutions		775-331-6490	•	•	•	•
•	•	•	•	•	Unisearch Inc (Nevada) [SOP]		800-260-1131	•		•	

CR	CV	PR	US	BK	←Courts	WHITE PINE	Recorder→	UC	RE	TX	VS
•	•	•	•	•	Pacific Security Intelligence		530-832-0259	•	•	•	•

New Hampshire

New Hampshire has 10 recording offices. There are 233 cities/town which previously handled the filing of UCCs. The recording officers are Register of Deeds (for real estate only) and Town/City Clerk (for UCCs). Be careful to distinguish the following names that are identical for both a town/city and a county - Grafton, Hillsborough, Merrimack, Strafford, and Sullivan. The following unincorporated towns do not have a Town Clerk, so all liens are located at the corresponding county: Cambridge (Coos), Dicksville (Coos), Green's Grant (Coos), Hale's Location (Carroll), Millsfield (Coos), and Wentworth's Location (Coos).

COURT RECORDS RETRIEVED — CAPITAL - MERRIMACK COUNTY — RECORDED RECORDS RETRIEVED

CR	CV	PR	US	BK	←COURTS BELKNAP	RECORDER→	UC	RE	TX	VS
	•		•	•	Abstracting US Inc	603-598-4106 x208	•	•	•	•
•	•	•	•	•	Coast to Coast Research Network	603-776-5985	•	•	•	•
	•	•	•	•	Concord Search & Retrieval Inc	877-273-1119	•	•	•	•
•	•	•	•	•	Doc*U*Search Inc	800-332-3034	•	•	•	•
•	•				MSI Inv [SOP]	603-298-8060				
•	•	•	•	•	NH Background Investigations LLC	603-598-4106	•	•	•	•
•	•				Primetime Research Inc	866-737-2714				
•	•		•	•	The Research Connection Inc of NH	800-540-5064	•	•	•	•

CR	CV	PR	US	BK	←COURTS CARROLL	RECORDER→	UC	RE	TX	VS
	•		•	•	Abstracting US Inc	603-598-4106 x208	•	•	•	•
•	•	•	•	•	Coast to Coast Research Network	603-776-5985	•	•	•	•
•	•	•	•	•	Doc*U*Search Inc	800-332-3034	•	•	•	•
•	•	•	•	•	NH Background Investigations LLC	603-598-4106	•	•	•	•
•	•	•	•	•	NR&C	207-791-2852	•	•	•	
•	•		•	•	The Research Connection Inc of NH	800-540-5064	•	•	•	•

CR	CV	PR	US	BK	←COURTS CHESHIRE	RECORDER→	UC	RE	TX	VS
	•		•	•	Abstracting US Inc	603-598-4106 x208	•	•	•	•
•	•	•	•	•	Coast to Coast Research Network	603-776-5985	•	•	•	•
	•	•	•	•	Concord Search & Retrieval Inc	877-273-1119	•	•	•	•
•	•	•	•	•	Doc*U*Search Inc	800-332-3034	•	•	•	•
•	•				MSI Inv [SOP]	603-298-8060				
•	•	•	•	•	NH Background Investigations LLC	603-598-4106	•	•	•	•
•	•	•	•	•	NR&C	207-791-2852	•	•	•	
•	•				Primetime Research Inc	866-737-2714				
•	•		•	•	The Research Connection Inc of NH	800-540-5064	•	•	•	•

CR	CV	PR	US	BK	←COURTS COOS	RECORDER→	UC	RE	TX	VS
	•		•	•	Abstracting US Inc	603-598-4106 x208	•	•	•	•
•	•	•	•	•	Coast to Coast Research Network	603-776-5985	•	•	•	•
	•	•	•	•	Concord Search & Retrieval Inc	877-273-1119	•	•	•	•
•	•	•	•	•	Doc*U*Search Inc	800-332-3034	•	•	•	•
•	•	•	•	•	NH Background Investigations LLC	603-598-4106	•	•	•	•
•	•		•	•	The Research Connection Inc of NH	800-540-5064	•	•	•	•

CR	CV	PR	US	BK	←COURTS GRAFTON	RECORDER→	UC	RE	TX	VS
	•		•	•	Abstracting US Inc	603-598-4106 x208	•	•	•	•
•	•	•	•	•	Coast to Coast Research Network	603-776-5985	•	•	•	•
•	•	•	•	•	Doc*U*Search Inc	800-332-3034	•	•	•	•
•	•				MSI Inv [SOP]	603-298-8060				
•	•	•	•	•	NH Background Investigations LLC	603-598-4106	•	•	•	•
•	•		•	•	The Research Connection Inc of NH	800-540-5064	•	•	•	•

CR	CV	PR	US	BK	←COURTS HILLSBOROUGH	RECORDER→	UC	RE	TX	VS
	•		•	•	Abstracting US Inc	603-598-4106 x208	•	•	•	•
•	•	•	•	•	Coast to Coast Research Network	603-776-5985	•	•	•	•
	•	•	•	•	Concord Search & Retrieval Inc	877-273-1119	•	•	•	•
•	•	•	•	•	Doc*U*Search Inc	800-332-3034	•	•	•	•
•	•	•			JMB Title Abstracting	603-505-1910		•		
•	•	•	•	•	NH Background Investigations LLC	603-598-4106	•	•	•	•
•	•	•	•	•	Northeast Criminal Research	603-880-6805				•
•	•	•	•	•	NR&C	207-791-2852	•	•	•	
•	•				Primetime Research Inc	866-737-2714				
•	•		•	•	The Research Connection Inc of NH	800-540-5064	•	•	•	•

CR	CV	PR	US	BK	←COURTS MERRIMACK	RECORDER→	UC	RE	TX	VS
	•		•	•	Abstracting US Inc	603-598-4106 x208	•	•	•	•
•	•	•	•	•	Coast to Coast Research Network	603-776-5985	•	•	•	•
	•	•	•	•	Concord Search & Retrieval Inc	877-273-1119	•	•	•	•
•	•	•	•	•	Doc*U*Search Inc	800-332-3034	•	•	•	•
•	•	•	•	•	NH Background Investigations LLC	603-598-4106	•	•	•	•
•	•	•	•	•	Northeast Criminal Research	603-880-6805				•
•	•	•	•		NR&C	207-791-2852	•	•	•	
•	•				Primetime Research Inc	866-737-2714				
•	•		•	•	The Research Connection Inc of NH	800-540-5064	•	•	•	•

CR	CV	PR	US	BK	←COURTS ROCKINGHAM	RECORDER→	UC	RE	TX	VS
	•		•	•	Abstracting US Inc	603-598-4106 x208	•	•	•	•
•	•	•	•	•	Coast to Coast Research Network	603-776-5985	•	•	•	•
	•	•	•	•	Concord Search & Retrieval Inc	877-273-1119	•	•	•	•
•	•	•	•	•	Doc*U*Search Inc	800-332-3034	•	•	•	•
•	•	•			JMB Title Abstracting	603-505-1910		•		
•	•	•	•	•	NH Background Investigations LLC	603-598-4106	•	•	•	•
•	•	•	•	•	Northeast Criminal Research	603-880-6805				•
•	•	•	•	•	NR&C	207-791-2852	•	•	•	
•	•				Primetime Research Inc	866-737-2714				
		•			Reliable Title Co of NH	603-798-5230	•	•	•	
•	•		•	•	The Research Connection Inc of NH	800-540-5064	•	•	•	•

CR	CV	PR	US	BK	←COURTS STRAFFORD	RECORDER→	UC	RE	TX	VS
	•		•	•	Abstracting US Inc	603-598-4106 x208	•	•	•	•
•	•	•	•	•	Coast to Coast Research Network	603-776-5985	•	•	•	•
	•	•	•	•	Concord Search & Retrieval Inc	877-273-1119	•	•	•	•
•	•	•	•	•	Doc*U*Search Inc	800-332-3034	•	•	•	•
•	•	•	•	•	NH Background Investigations LLC	603-598-4106	•	•	•	•
•	•	•	•	•	Northeast Criminal Research	603-880-6805				•
•	•				Primetime Research Inc	866-737-2714				
•	•		•	•	The Research Connection Inc of NH	800-540-5064	•	•	•	•

CR	CV	PR	US	BK	←COURTS SULLIVAN	RECORDER→	UC	RE	TX	VS
	•		•	•	Abstracting US Inc	603-598-4106 x208	•	•	•	•
•	•	•	•	•	Coast to Coast Research Network	603-776-5985	•	•	•	•
	•	•	•	•	Concord Search & Retrieval Inc	877-273-1119	•	•	•	•
•	•	•	•	•	Doc*U*Search Inc	800-332-3034	•	•	•	•
•	•				MSI Inv [SOP]	603-298-8060				
•	•	•	•	•	NH Background Investigations LLC	603-598-4106	•	•	•	•
•	•		•	•	The Research Connection Inc of NH	800-540-5064	•	•	•	•

New Jersey

COURT RECORDS RETRIEVED — **CAPITAL - MERCER COUNTY** — **RECORDED RECORDS RETRIEVED**

CR	CV	PR	US	BK	←COURTS **ATLANTIC** RECORDER→		UC	RE	TX	VS
•	•		•	•	Accufax: Authentic Document Retrieval	800-336-1001	•	•	•	•
		•			Accurate Abstracts by Delores Dios	201-207-0628	•	•	•	
	•	•	•	•	Charles Jones Inc	800-792-8888	•	•	•	
•	•				Detailed Investigations	609-704-1801				
•	•	•	•	•	Fidelifacts	800-678-0007	•	•	•	•
•	•		•	•	Flink Findzum Lawyers Service [SOP]	800-380-5434	•	•	•	•
					Peg Fuoti	609-625-9401	•	•	•	
•	•	•	•	•	Inquisitive Research Corporation	732-321-0041	•	•	•	•
	•	•			Liberty Record Search of NJ Inc	973-887-8808	•	•	•	
•	•		•	•	National Background Investigations Inc	800-798-0079			•	
•	•	•	•	•	Searcher Girls	800-292-2757	•	•	•	
	•		•	•	Superior Information Services, LLC	800-848-0489	•		•	
•					TenantSafe Inc	888-502-0135				
•	•	•	•	•	US Document Retrieval Service Inc	800-595-0145		•	•	•

CR	CV	PR	US	BK	←COURTS **BERGEN** RECORDER→		UC	RE	TX	VS
•	•		•	•	Accufax: Authentic Document Retrieval	800-336-1001	•	•	•	•
		•			Accurate Abstracts by Delores Dios	201-207-0628	•	•	•	
•	•	•	•	•	Callahan Lawyers Service [SOP]	877-767-2245				•
•	•	•	•	•	Certified Judicial Process Service & Legal Support [SOP]	877-217-3783	•	•	•	•
	•	•	•	•	Charles Jones Inc	800-792-8888	•	•	•	
•	•				Court Data Search	973-770-1170				
			•	•	Credit Lenders Service Agency Inc	856-787-9005	•	•	•	
•	•				Detailed Investigations	609-704-1801				
•	•	•	•	•	DLS (Demovsky Lawyer Service - New York) [SOP]	800-443-1058	•	•	•	•
•	•	•	•	•	Fidelifacts	800-678-0007	•	•	•	•
•	•		•	•	Flink Findzum Lawyers Service [SOP]	800-380-5434	•	•	•	•
•	•	•	•	•	Gamma Investigative Research Inc [SOP]	800-878-9393	•	•	•	
•	•	•	•	•	In Search of Inc	201-224-3063	•	•	•	•
•	•	•	•	•	Inquisitive Research Corporation	732-321-0041	•	•	•	•
	•	•			Liberty Record Search of NJ Inc	973-887-8808	•	•	•	
•	•		•	•	National Background Investigations Inc	800-798-0079			•	
	•		•	•	Phoenix Document Service Inc	727-581-2552	•	•	•	
•	•	•	•	•	Searcher Girls	800-292-2757	•	•	•	
	•		•	•	Superior Information Services, LLC	800-848-0489	•		•	
•					TenantSafe Inc	888-502-0135				
•	•	•	•	•	US Document Retrieval Service Inc	800-595-0145		•	•	•

CR	CV	PR	US	BK	←COURTS **BURLINGTON** RECORDER→		UC	RE	TX	VS
•	•		•	•	Accufax: Authentic Document Retrieval	800-336-1001	•	•	•	•
		•			Accurate Abstracts by Delores Dios	201-207-0628	•	•	•	
					Atlantic Coast Abstract Co	732-431-1099		•		
•	•		•	•	Best Legal Services Inc [SOP]	800-562-9620	•	•	•	•
	•	•	•	•	Charles Jones Inc	800-792-8888	•	•	•	
•	•	•	•	•	Coyne Search Service Inc	215-547-1853	•	•	•	•
			•	•	Credit Lenders Service Agency Inc	856-787-9005	•	•	•	
•	•				Detailed Investigations	609-704-1801				
•	•	•	•	•	Fidelifacts	800-678-0007	•	•	•	•
•	•		•	•	Flink Findzum Lawyers Service [SOP]	800-380-5434	•	•	•	•

CR	CV	PR	US	BK	Retriever	Phone	UC	RE	TX	VS
					Infiniti Title Agency Inc	856-727-0818		•	•	
•	•	•	•	•	Inquisitive Research Corporation	732-321-0041	•	•	•	•
	•	•			Liberty Record Search of NJ Inc	973-887-8808	•	•	•	
•	•		•	•	National Background Investigations Inc	800-798-0079			•	
•	•	•	•	•	Searcher Girls	800-292-2757	•	•	•	
	•	•	•	•	Searchtec	877-2SEARCH	•	•	•	
	•		•	•	Superior Information Services, LLC	800-848-0489	•		•	
•	•	•	•	•	Talone & Associates [SOP]	800-553-5189	•	•	•	•
•					TenantSafe Inc	888-502-0135				

CR	CV	PR	US	BK	←Courts CAMDEN	Recorder→	UC	RE	TX	VS
•	•		•	•	Accufax: Authentic Document Retrieval	800-336-1001	•	•	•	•
		•			Accurate Abstracts by Delores Dios	201-207-0628	•	•	•	
•	•				Eileen Augatis	609-472-6513	•	•	•	
•	•		•	•	Best Legal Services Inc [SOP]	800-562-9620	•	•	•	•
	•	•	•	•	Charles Jones Inc	800-792-8888	•	•	•	
•	•		•	•	County House Research Inc	866-594-1177			•	
•	•	•	•	•	Coyne Search Service Inc	215-547-1853	•	•	•	•
			•	•	Credit Lenders Service Agency Inc	856-787-9005	•	•	•	
•	•				Detailed Investigations	609-704-1801				
•	•	•	•	•	Fidelifacts	800-678-0007	•	•	•	•
•	•		•	•	Flink Findzum Lawyers Service [SOP]	800-380-5434	•	•	•	•
•	•	•	•	•	Inquisitive Research Corporation	732-321-0041	•	•	•	•
•	•	•	•	•	Keystone Intelligence Network Inc	215-545-1111	•	•	•	•
	•	•			Liberty Record Search of NJ Inc	973-887-8808	•	•	•	
•	•		•	•	National Background Investigations Inc	800-798-0079			•	
•	•	•	•	•	Searcher Girls	800-292-2757	•	•	•	
	•	•	•	•	Searchtec	877-2SEARCH	•	•	•	
	•		•	•	Superior Information Services, LLC	800-848-0489	•		•	
•	•	•	•	•	Talone & Associates [SOP]	800-553-5189	•	•	•	•
•					TenantSafe Inc	888-502-0135				
•	•	•	•	•	US Document Retrieval Service Inc	800-595-0145		•	•	•

CR	CV	PR	US	BK	←Courts CAPE MAY	Recorder→	UC	RE	TX	VS
•	•		•	•	Accufax: Authentic Document Retrieval	800-336-1001	•	•	•	•
		•			Accurate Abstracts by Delores Dios	201-207-0628	•	•	•	
	•	•	•	•	Charles Jones Inc	800-792-8888	•	•	•	
•	•				Crossland Abstract	609-465-2220		•	•	
•	•				Detailed Investigations	609-704-1801				
•	•	•	•	•	Fidelifacts	800-678-0007	•	•	•	•
•	•		•	•	Flink Findzum Lawyers Service [SOP]	800-380-5434	•	•	•	•
•	•	•	•	•	Inquisitive Research Corporation	732-321-0041	•	•	•	•
	•	•			Liberty Record Search of NJ Inc	973-887-8808	•	•	•	
•	•		•	•	National Background Investigations Inc	800-798-0079			•	
	•		•	•	Superior Information Services, LLC	800-848-0489	•		•	
•					TenantSafe Inc	888-502-0135				

CR	CV	PR	US	BK	←Courts CUMBERLAND	Recorder→	UC	RE	TX	VS
•	•		•	•	Accufax: Authentic Document Retrieval	800-336-1001	•	•	•	•
		•			Accurate Abstracts by Delores Dios	201-207-0628	•	•	•	
	•	•	•	•	Charles Jones Inc	800-792-8888	•	•	•	
•	•				Detailed Investigations	609-704-1801				
•	•	•	•	•	Fidelifacts	800-678-0007	•	•	•	•
•	•		•	•	Flink Findzum Lawyers Service [SOP]	800-380-5434	•	•	•	•
•	•	•	•	•	Inquisitive Research Corporation	732-321-0041	•	•	•	•
	•	•			Liberty Record Search of NJ Inc	973-887-8808	•	•	•	
•	•		•	•	National Background Investigations Inc	800-798-0079			•	
	•		•	•	Superior Information Services, LLC	800-848-0489	•		•	
•					TenantSafe Inc	888-502-0135				

CR	CV	PR	US	BK	←COURTS	ESSEX	RECORDER→	UC	RE	TX	VS
•	•		•	•	Accufax: Authentic Document Retrieval		800-336-1001	•	•	•	•
		•			Accurate Abstracts by Delores Dios		201-207-0628	•	•	•	
•	•				B & B Investigative Services		732-446-7482				
•	•	•	•	•	Callahan Lawyers Service [SOP]		877-767-2245				•
•	•	•	•	•	Certified Judicial Process Service & Legal Support [SOP]		877-217-3783	•	•	•	•
	•	•	•	•	Charles Jones Inc		800-792-8888	•	•	•	
•	•				Court Data Search		973-770-1170				
•	•				Detailed Investigations		609-704-1801				
•	•	•	•	•	DLS (Demovsky Lawyer Service - New York) [SOP]		800-443-1058	•	•	•	•
•	•	•	•	•	Fidelifacts		800-678-0007	•	•	•	•
•	•		•	•	Flink Findzum Lawyers Service [SOP]		800-380-5434	•	•	•	•
•	•	•	•	•	In Search of Inc		201-224-3063	•	•	•	•
•	•	•	•	•	Inquisitive Research Corporation		732-321-0041	•	•	•	•
	•	•			Liberty Record Search of NJ Inc		973-887-8808	•	•	•	
•	•		•	•	National Background Investigations Inc		800-798-0079			•	
	•		•	•	Phoenix Document Service Inc		727-581-2552	•	•	•	
•	•	•	•	•	Searcher Girls		800-292-2757	•	•	•	
	•		•	•	Superior Information Services, LLC		800-848-0489	•		•	
•	•	•	•	•	Superior Subpoena Service [SOP]		908-392-6229	•	•	•	
•					TenantSafe Inc		888-502-0135				
•	•	•	•	•	US Document Retrieval Service Inc		800-595-0145		•	•	•

CR	CV	PR	US	BK	←COURTS	GLOUCESTER	RECORDER→	UC	RE	TX	VS
•	•		•	•	Accufax: Authentic Document Retrieval		800-336-1001	•	•	•	•
		•			Accurate Abstracts by Delores Dios		201-207-0628	•	•	•	
•	•				Eileen Augatis		609-472-6513	•	•	•	
•	•		•	•	Best Legal Services Inc [SOP]		800-562-9620	•	•	•	•
	•	•	•	•	Charles Jones Inc		800-792-8888	•	•	•	
•	•				Detailed Investigations		609-704-1801				
•	•	•	•	•	Fidelifacts		800-678-0007	•	•	•	•
•	•		•	•	Flink Findzum Lawyers Service [SOP]		800-380-5434	•	•	•	•
•	•	•	•	•	Inquisitive Research Corporation		732-321-0041	•	•	•	•
•	•	•	•	•	Keystone Intelligence Network Inc		215-545-1111	•	•	•	•
	•	•			Liberty Record Search of NJ Inc		973-887-8808	•	•	•	
•	•		•	•	National Background Investigations Inc		800-798-0079			•	
•	•	•	•	•	Searcher Girls		800-292-2757	•	•	•	
	•	•	•	•	Searchtec		877-2SEARCH	•	•	•	
	•		•	•	Superior Information Services, LLC		800-848-0489	•		•	
•	•	•	•	•	Talone & Associates [SOP]		800-553-5189	•	•	•	•
•					TenantSafe Inc		888-502-0135				

CR	CV	PR	US	BK	←COURTS	HUDSON	RECORDER→	UC	RE	TX	VS
•	•		•	•	Accufax: Authentic Document Retrieval		800-336-1001	•	•	•	•
		•			Accurate Abstracts by Delores Dios		201-207-0628	•	•	•	
•	•				B & B Investigative Services		732-446-7482				
•	•	•	•	•	Callahan Lawyers Service [SOP]		877-767-2245				•
•	•	•	•	•	Certified Judicial Process Service & Legal Support [SOP]		877-217-3783	•	•	•	•
	•	•	•	•	Charles Jones Inc		800-792-8888	•	•	•	
•	•				Court Data Search		973-770-1170				
•	•				Detailed Investigations		609-704-1801				
•	•	•	•	•	Fidelifacts		800-678-0007	•	•	•	•
•	•		•	•	Flink Findzum Lawyers Service [SOP]		800-380-5434	•	•	•	•
•	•	•	•	•	Gamma Investigative Research Inc [SOP]		800-878-9393	•	•	•	
•	•	•	•	•	In Search of Inc		201-224-3063	•	•	•	•
•	•	•	•	•	Inquisitive Research Corporation		732-321-0041	•	•	•	•
	•	•			Liberty Record Search of NJ Inc		973-887-8808	•	•	•	
•	•		•	•	National Background Investigations Inc		800-798-0079			•	
•	•	•	•	•	Searcher Girls		800-292-2757	•	•	•	

CR	CV	PR	US	BK	Retriever	Phone	UC	RE	TX	VS
	•		•	•	Superior Information Services, LLC	800-848-0489	•		•	
•	•	•	•	•	Superior Subpoena Service [SOP]	908-392-6229	•	•	•	
•					TenantSafe Inc	888-502-0135				
•	•	•	•	•	US Document Retrieval Service Inc	800-595-0145		•	•	•

CR	CV	PR	US	BK	←COURTS HUNTERDON	RECORDER→	UC	RE	TX	VS
•	•		•	•	Accufax: Authentic Document Retrieval	800-336-1001	•	•	•	•
		•			Accurate Abstracts by Delores Dios	201-207-0628	•	•	•	
•	•	•			Dan & Jackie Buck	908-537-2475	•	•	•	•
	•	•	•	•	Charles Jones Inc	800-792-8888	•	•	•	
•	•				Detailed Investigations	609-704-1801				
•	•	•	•	•	Fidelifacts	800-678-0007	•	•	•	•
•	•		•	•	Flink Findzum Lawyers Service [SOP]	800-380-5434	•	•	•	•
•	•	•	•	•	Inquisitive Research Corporation	732-321-0041	•	•	•	•
	•	•			Liberty Record Search of NJ Inc	973-887-8808	•	•	•	
•	•		•	•	National Background Investigations Inc	800-798-0079			•	
•	•	•	•	•	Searcher Girls	800-292-2757	•	•	•	
	•		•	•	Superior Information Services, LLC	800-848-0489	•		•	
•					TenantSafe Inc	888-502-0135				

CR	CV	PR	US	BK	←COURTS MERCER	RECORDER→	UC	RE	TX	VS
•	•		•	•	Accufax: Authentic Document Retrieval	800-336-1001	•	•	•	•
		•			Accurate Abstracts by Delores Dios	201-207-0628	•	•	•	
					Atlantic Coast Abstract Co	732-431-1099		•		
•	•				B & B Investigative Services	732-446-7482				
•	•	•	•	•	Certified Judicial Process Service & Legal Support [SOP]	877-217-3783	•	•	•	•
	•	•	•	•	Charles Jones Inc	800-792-8888	•	•	•	
•	•	•	•	•	Coyne Search Service Inc	215-547-1853	•	•	•	•
			•	•	Credit Lenders Service Agency Inc	856-787-9005	•	•	•	
•	•	•	•	•	CSC - Corporation Service Company [SOP]	800-927-9800	•	•	•	•
•	•				Detailed Investigations	609-704-1801				
•	•				Ethical Equations	732-928-4130				
•	•	•	•	•	Fidelifacts	800-678-0007	•	•	•	•
•	•		•	•	Flink Findzum Lawyers Service [SOP]	800-380-5434	•	•	•	•
•	•	•	•	•	Inquisitive Research Corporation	732-321-0041	•	•	•	•
•	•				Intelysis Corp (Ziegler & Assoc.)	800-489-1239		•		•
	•		•	•	Kaufman Information Resources Inc	732-438-1967	•	•	•	•
	•	•			Liberty Record Search of NJ Inc	973-887-8808	•	•	•	
•	•		•	•	National Background Investigations Inc	800-798-0079			•	
•	•	•	•	•	Searcher Girls	800-292-2757	•	•	•	
	•	•	•	•	Searchtec	877-2SEARCH	•	•	•	
			•	•	State Capital Title & Abstract Co	800-876-8994				
	•		•	•	Superior Information Services, LLC	800-848-0489	•		•	
•					TenantSafe Inc	888-502-0135				

CR	CV	PR	US	BK	←COURTS MIDDLESEX	RECORDER→	UC	RE	TX	VS
•	•		•	•	Accufax: Authentic Document Retrieval	800-336-1001	•	•	•	•
		•			Accurate Abstracts by Delores Dios	201-207-0628	•	•	•	
					Atlantic Coast Abstract Co	732-431-1099		•		
•	•				B & B Investigative Services	732-446-7482				
•	•	•	•	•	Certified Judicial Process Service & Legal Support [SOP]	877-217-3783	•	•	•	•
	•	•	•	•	Charles Jones Inc	800-792-8888	•	•	•	
•	•				Court Data Search	973-770-1170				
			•	•	Credit Lenders Service Agency Inc	856-787-9005	•	•	•	
•	•				Detailed Investigations	609-704-1801				
•	•	•	•	•	Fidelifacts	800-678-0007	•	•	•	•
•	•		•	•	Flink Findzum Lawyers Service [SOP]	800-380-5434	•	•	•	•
•	•	•	•	•	Inquisitive Research Corporation	732-321-0041	•	•	•	•
	•		•	•	Kaufman Information Resources Inc	732-438-1967	•	•	•	•

CR	CV	PR	US	BK	Name	Phone	UC	RE	TX	VS
	•	•			Liberty Record Search of NJ Inc	973-887-8808	•	•	•	
•	•		•	•	National Background Investigations Inc	800-798-0079			•	
	•		•	•	Phoenix Document Service Inc	727-581-2552	•	•	•	
•	•	•	•	•	Searcher Girls	800-292-2757	•	•	•	
	•		•	•	Superior Information Services, LLC	800-848-0489	•		•	
•	•	•	•	•	Superior Subpoena Service [SOP]	908-392-6229	•	•	•	
•					TenantSafe Inc	888-502-0135				
•	•	•	•	•	US Document Retrieval Service Inc	800-595-0145		•	•	•

CR	CV	PR	US	BK	←COURTS MONMOUTH	RECORDER→	UC	RE	TX	VS
•	•		•	•	Accufax: Authentic Document Retrieval	800-336-1001	•	•	•	•
		•			Accurate Abstracts by Delores Dios	201-207-0628	•	•	•	
					Atlantic Coast Abstract Co	732-431-1099		•		
•	•				B & B Investigative Services	732-446-7482				
	•	•	•	•	Charles Jones Inc	800-792-8888	•	•	•	
•	•				Court Data Search	973-770-1170				
•	•				Detailed Investigations	609-704-1801				
•	•				Ethical Equations	732-928-4130				
•	•	•	•	•	Fidelifacts	800-678-0007	•	•	•	•
•	•		•	•	Flink Findzum Lawyers Service [SOP]	800-380-5434	•	•	•	•
•	•	•	•	•	Inquisitive Research Corporation	732-321-0041	•	•	•	•
	•		•	•	Kaufman Information Resources Inc	732-438-1967	•	•	•	•
	•	•			Liberty Record Search of NJ Inc	973-887-8808	•	•	•	
•	•		•	•	National Background Investigations Inc	800-798-0079			•	
	•		•	•	Phoenix Document Service Inc	727-581-2552	•	•	•	
•	•	•	•	•	Searcher Girls	800-292-2757	•	•	•	
	•		•	•	Security Search & Abstract Co Inc	800-345-9494	•	•	•	
	•		•	•	Superior Information Services, LLC	800-848-0489	•		•	
•					TenantSafe Inc	888-502-0135				
•	•	•	•	•	US Document Retrieval Service Inc	800-595-0145		•	•	•
•		•	•	•	XpertSearch Inc	732-229-6688	•	•	•	•

CR	CV	PR	US	BK	←COURTS MORRIS	RECORDER→	UC	RE	TX	VS
•	•		•	•	Accufax: Authentic Document Retrieval	800-336-1001	•	•	•	•
		•			Accurate Abstracts by Delores Dios	201-207-0628	•	•	•	
		•			Ronald J Axelrod	973-538-4606	•	•	•	
•	•	•			Dan & Jackie Buck	908-537-2475	•	•	•	•
•	•	•	•	•	Callahan Lawyers Service [SOP]	877-767-2245				•
•	•	•	•	•	Certified Judicial Process Service & Legal Support [SOP]	877-217-3783	•	•	•	•
	•	•	•	•	Charles Jones Inc	800-792-8888	•	•	•	
•	•				Court Data Search	973-770-1170				
			•	•	Credit Lenders Service Agency Inc	856-787-9005	•	•	•	
•	•				Detailed Investigations	609-704-1801				
•	•	•	•	•	Fidelifacts	800-678-0007	•	•	•	•
•	•		•	•	Flink Findzum Lawyers Service [SOP]	800-380-5434	•	•	•	•
•	•	•	•	•	Inquisitive Research Corporation	732-321-0041	•	•	•	•
	•	•			Liberty Record Search of NJ Inc	973-887-8808	•	•	•	
•	•		•	•	National Background Investigations Inc	800-798-0079			•	
	•		•	•	Phoenix Document Service Inc	727-581-2552	•	•	•	
•	•	•	•	•	Searcher Girls	800-292-2757	•	•	•	
	•		•	•	Superior Information Services, LLC	800-848-0489	•		•	
•					TenantSafe Inc	888-502-0135				
•	•	•	•	•	US Document Retrieval Service Inc	800-595-0145		•	•	•

CR	CV	PR	US	BK	←COURTS OCEAN	RECORDER→	UC	RE	TX	VS
•	•		•	•	Accufax: Authentic Document Retrieval	800-336-1001	•	•	•	•
		•			Accurate Abstracts by Delores Dios	201-207-0628	•	•	•	
					Atlantic Coast Abstract Co	732-431-1099		•		
•	•				B & B Investigative Services	732-446-7482				

CR	CV	PR	US	BK	Courts	Recorder	UC	RE	TX	VS
	•	•	•	•	Charles Jones Inc	800-792-8888	•	•	•	
			•	•	Credit Lenders Service Agency Inc	856-787-9005	•	•	•	
•	•				Detailed Investigations	609-704-1801				
•	•				Ethical Equations	732-928-4130				
	•	•			Faithful Abstract	908-351-9398	•	•	•	
•	•	•	•	•	Fidelifacts	800-678-0007	•	•	•	•
•	•		•	•	Flink Findzum Lawyers Service [SOP]	800-380-5434	•	•	•	•
•	•	•	•	•	Inquisitive Research Corporation	732-321-0041	•	•	•	•
		•			Margaret Laratta	732-349-1301	•	•	•	
	•	•			Liberty Record Search of NJ Inc	973-887-8808	•	•	•	
•	•		•	•	National Background Investigations Inc	800-798-0079			•	
	•		•	•	Phoenix Document Service Inc	727-581-2552	•	•	•	
•	•	•	•	•	Searcher Girls	800-292-2757	•	•	•	
	•		•	•	Security Search & Abstract Co Inc	800-345-9494	•	•	•	
	•		•	•	Superior Information Services, LLC	800-848-0489	•		•	
•					TenantSafe Inc	888-502-0135				
•	•	•	•	•	US Document Retrieval Service Inc	800-595-0145		•	•	•
•		•	•	•	XpertSearch Inc	732-229-6688	•	•	•	•

CR	CV	PR	US	BK	←Courts PASSAIC	Recorder→	UC	RE	TX	VS
•	•		•	•	Accufax: Authentic Document Retrieval	800-336-1001	•	•	•	•
		•			Accurate Abstracts by Delores Dios	201-207-0628	•	•	•	
•	•	•	•	•	Callahan Lawyers Service [SOP]	877-767-2245				•
•	•	•	•	•	Certified Judicial Process Service & Legal Support [SOP]	877-217-3783	•	•	•	•
	•	•	•	•	Charles Jones Inc	800-792-8888	•	•	•	
•	•				Court Data Search	973-770-1170				
•	•				Detailed Investigations	609-704-1801				
•	•	•	•	•	Fidelifacts	800-678-0007	•	•	•	•
•	•		•	•	Flink Findzum Lawyers Service [SOP]	800-380-5434	•	•	•	•
•	•	•	•	•	Gamma Investigative Research Inc [SOP]	800-878-9393	•	•	•	
•	•	•	•	•	In Search of Inc	201-224-3063	•	•	•	•
•	•	•	•	•	Inquisitive Research Corporation	732-321-0041	•	•	•	•
	•	•			Liberty Record Search of NJ Inc	973-887-8808	•	•	•	
•	•		•	•	National Background Investigations Inc	800-798-0079			•	
	•		•	•	Phoenix Document Service Inc	727-581-2552	•	•	•	
•	•	•	•	•	Searcher Girls	800-292-2757	•	•	•	
	•		•	•	Superior Information Services, LLC	800-848-0489	•		•	
•					TenantSafe Inc	888-502-0135				

CR	CV	PR	US	BK	←Courts SALEM	Recorder→	UC	RE	TX	VS
•	•		•	•	Accufax: Authentic Document Retrieval	800-336-1001	•	•	•	•
		•			Accurate Abstracts by Delores Dios	201-207-0628	•	•	•	
	•	•	•	•	Charles Jones Inc	800-792-8888	•	•	•	
•	•				Detailed Investigations	609-704-1801				
•	•	•	•	•	Fidelifacts	800-678-0007	•	•	•	•
•	•		•	•	Flink Findzum Lawyers Service [SOP]	800-380-5434	•	•	•	•
•	•	•	•	•	Inquisitive Research Corporation	732-321-0041	•	•	•	•
	•	•			Liberty Record Search of NJ Inc	973-887-8808	•	•	•	
•	•		•	•	National Background Investigations Inc	800-798-0079			•	
	•		•	•	Superior Information Services, LLC	800-848-0489	•		•	
•					TenantSafe Inc	888-502-0135				

CR	CV	PR	US	BK	←Courts SOMERSET	Recorder→	UC	RE	TX	VS
•	•		•	•	Accufax: Authentic Document Retrieval	800-336-1001	•	•	•	•
		•			Accurate Abstracts by Delores Dios	201-207-0628	•	•	•	
					Atlantic Coast Abstract Co	732-431-1099		•		
		•			Ronald J Axelrod	973-538-4606	•	•	•	
•	•				B & B Investigative Services	732-446-7482				
•	•	•			Dan & Jackie Buck	908-537-2475	•	•	•	•

CR	CV	PR	US	BK	←Courts		Recorder→	UC	RE	TX	VS
	•	•	•	•	Charles Jones Inc		800-792-8888	•	•	•	
		•			CMT Abstract		908-722-6565	•	•	•	
•	•				Court Data Search		973-770-1170				
			•	•	Credit Lenders Service Agency Inc		856-787-9005	•	•	•	
•	•				Detailed Investigations		609-704-1801				
•	•	•	•	•	Fidelifacts		800-678-0007	•	•	•	•
•	•		•	•	Flink Findzum Lawyers Service [SOP]		800-380-5434	•	•	•	•
•	•	•	•	•	Inquisitive Research Corporation		732-321-0041	•	•	•	•
	•		•	•	Kaufman Information Resources Inc		732-438-1967	•	•	•	•
					KJK Abstract Co		908-725-6336	•	•	•	
	•	•			Liberty Record Search of NJ Inc		973-887-8808	•	•	•	
•					Lucy and Tyler Public Records Services		908-725-4356		•		
•	•		•	•	National Background Investigations Inc		800-798-0079			•	
•	•	•	•	•	Searcher Girls		800-292-2757	•	•	•	
	•		•	•	Superior Information Services, LLC		800-848-0489	•		•	
•					TenantSafe Inc		888-502-0135				

CR	CV	PR	US	BK	←Courts	Sussex	Recorder→	UC	RE	TX	VS
•	•		•	•	Accufax: Authentic Document Retrieval		800-336-1001	•	•	•	•
		•			Accurate Abstracts by Delores Dios		201-207-0628	•	•	•	
•	•	•	•	•	Callahan Lawyers Service [SOP]		877-767-2245				•
	•	•	•	•	Charles Jones Inc		800-792-8888	•	•	•	
•	•				Court Data Search		973-770-1170				
•	•				Detailed Investigations		609-704-1801				
•	•	•	•	•	Fidelifacts		800-678-0007	•	•	•	•
•	•		•	•	Flink Findzum Lawyers Service [SOP]		800-380-5434	•	•	•	•
•	•	•	•	•	Gamma Investigative Research Inc [SOP]		800-878-9393	•	•	•	
•	•	•	•	•	Inquisitive Research Corporation		732-321-0041	•	•	•	•
•	•	•			LaPrade Services Inc [SOP]		845-473-0468	•	•	•	•
	•	•			Liberty Record Search of NJ Inc		973-887-8808	•	•	•	
•	•		•	•	National Background Investigations Inc		800-798-0079			•	
	•		•	•	Superior Information Services, LLC		800-848-0489	•		•	
•					TenantSafe Inc		888-502-0135				

CR	CV	PR	US	BK	←Courts	Union	Recorder→	UC	RE	TX	VS
•	•		•	•	Accufax: Authentic Document Retrieval		800-336-1001	•	•	•	•
		•			Accurate Abstracts by Delores Dios		201-207-0628	•	•	•	
					Atlantic Coast Abstract Co		732-431-1099		•		
•	•				B & B Investigative Services		732-446-7482				
•	•	•	•	•	Certified Judicial Process Service & Legal Support [SOP]		877-217-3783	•	•	•	•
	•	•	•	•	Charles Jones Inc		800-792-8888	•	•	•	
•	•				Court Data Search		973-770-1170				
•	•				Detailed Investigations		609-704-1801				
	•	•			Faithful Abstract		908-351-9398	•	•	•	
•	•	•	•	•	Fidelifacts		800-678-0007	•	•	•	•
•	•		•	•	Flink Findzum Lawyers Service [SOP]		800-380-5434	•	•	•	•
•	•	•	•	•	Gamma Investigative Research Inc [SOP]		800-878-9393	•	•	•	
•	•	•	•	•	In Search of Inc		201-224-3063	•	•	•	•
•	•	•	•	•	Inquisitive Research Corporation		732-321-0041	•	•	•	•
	•		•	•	Kaufman Information Resources Inc		732-438-1967	•	•	•	•
	•	•			Liberty Record Search of NJ Inc		973-887-8808	•	•	•	
•	•		•	•	National Background Investigations Inc		800-798-0079			•	
	•		•	•	Phoenix Document Service Inc		727-581-2552	•	•	•	
•	•	•	•	•	Searcher Girls		800-292-2757	•	•	•	
	•		•	•	Superior Information Services, LLC		800-848-0489	•		•	
•	•	•	•	•	Superior Subpoena Service [SOP]		908-392-6229	•	•	•	
•					TenantSafe Inc		888-502-0135				
•	•	•	•	•	US Document Retrieval Service Inc		800-595-0145		•	•	•

CR	CV	PR	US	BK	←Courts	WARREN	Recorder→	UC	RE	TX	VS
•	•		•	•		Accufax: Authentic Document Retrieval	800-336-1001	•	•	•	•
		•				Accurate Abstracts by Delores Dios	201-207-0628	•	•	•	
•	•	•				Dan & Jackie Buck	908-537-2475	•	•	•	•
	•	•	•	•		Charles Jones Inc	800-792-8888	•	•	•	
•	•					Detailed Investigations	609-704-1801				
•	•	•	•	•		Fidelifacts	800-678-0007	•	•	•	•
•	•		•	•		Flink Findzum Lawyers Service [SOP]	800-380-5434	•	•	•	•
•	•	•	•	•		Gamma Investigative Research Inc [SOP]	800-878-9393	•	•	•	
•	•	•	•	•		Inquisitive Research Corporation	732-321-0041	•	•	•	•
•	•	•				LaPrade Services Inc [SOP]	845-473-0468	•	•	•	•
	•	•				Liberty Record Search of NJ Inc	973-887-8808	•	•	•	
•	•		•	•		National Background Investigations Inc	800-798-0079			•	
	•		•	•		Superior Information Services, LLC	800-848-0489	•		•	
•						TenantSafe Inc	888-502-0135				

[SOP] = PERFORMS SERVICE OF PROCESS

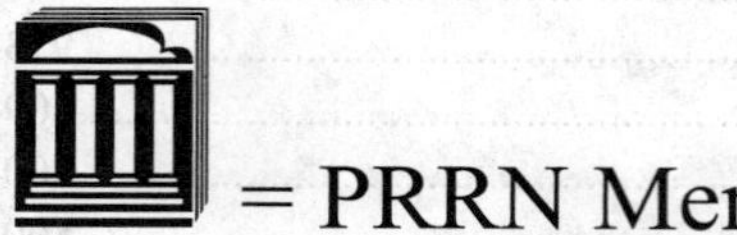 = PRRN Member. *A retriever you can trust!*

COURT RECORDS

CODE	GOVERNMENT AGENCY	TYPE OF INFORMATION
CR	Criminal Court	Municipal, county and state level criminal cases
CV	Civil Court	Municipal, county and state level civil cases
PR	Probate Court	Wills and estate cases
US	US District Court	Federal civil and criminal cases
BK	Bankruptcy Court	United States bankruptcy cases

COUNTY RECORDS - RECORDINGS

CODE	GOVERNMENT AGENCY	TYPE OF INFORMATION
UC	UCC Filing Office	Uniform Commercial Code and other personal property liens
RE	Real Estate Recording Office	Real property transactions and liens
TX	Tax Filing Office(s)	Federal and state tax liens, judgment liens
VS	Vital Records Office	Vital statistics—birth, death, marriage, divorce

New Mexico

COURT RECORDS RETRIEVED — CAPITAL - SANTA FE COUNTY — RECORDED RECORDS RETRIEVED

CR	CV	PR	US	BK	←COURTS BERNALILLO RECORDER→	Phone	UC	RE	TX	VS
•	•	•	•	•	Duke City Process Service & Inv [SOP]	888-335-9889		•	•	•
•	•	•	•	•	Infomax	505-994-0370	•	•	•	•
•		•	•	•	Professional Services of New Mexico Inc	505-271-2291				
•	•	•	•	•	R Miller & Associates LLC [SOP]	800-395-1992	•	•	•	
	•	•			Real Property Resources	505-232-3555	•	•	•	
					Carol Seewald [SOP]	505-831-5713	•	•	•	

CR	CV	PR	US	BK	←COURTS CATRON RECORDER→	UC	RE	TX	VS

See adjoining counties for retrievers or call court/recorder directly.

CR	CV	PR	US	BK	←COURTS CHAVES RECORDER→	Phone	UC	RE	TX	VS
•	•	•	•	•	Infomax	505-994-0370	•	•	•	•
	•	•			Landmark Title Roswell	505-622-5340	•	•	•	

CR	CV	PR	US	BK	←COURTS CIBOLA RECORDER→	Phone	UC	RE	TX	VS
•	•				Attorney Service New Mexico [SOP]	505-326-7486				
•	•	•	•	•	Duke City Process Service & Inv [SOP]	888-335-9889		•	•	•
•	•	•	•	•	Infomax	505-994-0370	•	•	•	•
	•	•			Real Property Resources	505-232-3555	•	•	•	

CR	CV	PR	US	BK	←COURTS COLFAX RECORDER→	Phone	UC	RE	TX	VS
•	•	•	•	•	Infomax	505-994-0370	•	•	•	•

CR	CV	PR	US	BK	←COURTS CURRY RECORDER→	Phone	UC	RE	TX	VS
•	•	•	•		Clovis Title & Abstract Ltd	505-762-4403	•	•	•	
•	•	•	•	•	Davick Services	800-658-6656	•	•	•	
•	•	•	•	•	Infomax	505-994-0370	•	•	•	•
	•	•			Landmark Title Inc (Clovis NM)	505-763-3904	•	•	•	

CR	CV	PR	US	BK	←COURTS DE BACA RECORDER→	Phone	UC	RE	TX	VS
•	•	•	•	•	Davick Services	800-658-6656	•	•	•	
	•	•			De Baca Abstract Inc	505-355-2431	•	•		
•	•	•	•	•	Infomax	505-994-0370	•	•	•	•

CR	CV	PR	US	BK	←COURTS DONA ANA RECORDER→	Phone	UC	RE	TX	VS
•	•	•			A.G.O. Legal Process Service [SOP]	505-526-4303	•	•	•	•
•	•	•	•	•	Duke City Process Service & Inv [SOP]	888-335-9889		•	•	•
•	•		•		Nancy Harris [SOP]	877-461-6700	•		•	
•	•	•	•	•	Infomax	505-994-0370	•	•	•	•
•	•	•	•	•	Legal Net Process Service [SOP]	915-532-7871	•		•	•
	•	•			Real Property Resources	505-232-3555	•	•	•	

CR	CV	PR	US	BK	←COURTS EDDY RECORDER→	Phone	UC	RE	TX	VS
	•	•			Caprock Title Co	432-687-3232		•	•	
	•	•			Currier Abstract Company	505-746-9823	•	•	•	
•	•				Lorina Dominquez	505-887-3489; Fax- same				
	•	•			Eddy County Abstract Co	800-348-1232	•	•	•	
	•	•			Guaranty Title Co (New Mexico)	505-887-3593	•	•	•	
•	•	•	•	•	Infomax	505-994-0370	•	•	•	•

CR	CV	PR	US	BK	←Courts	Grant	Recorder→	UC	RE	TX	VS
•	•	•			A.G.O. Legal Process Service [SOP]		505-526-4303	•	•	•	•
•	•	•	•	•	Infomax		505-994-0370	•	•	•	•

CR	CV	PR	US	BK	←Courts	Guadalupe	Recorder→	UC	RE	TX	VS
•	•	•	•	•	Infomax		505-994-0370	•	•	•	•
		•	•		John The Abstractor		505-472-1197	•	•	•	
		•			Territorial Title		505-425-3563	•	•	•	•

CR	CV	PR	US	BK	←Courts	Harding	Recorder→	UC	RE	TX	VS
					CuTitle Services Inc		505-374-8517		•	•	
					First Title Services		505-461-1300		•	•	

CR	CV	PR	US	BK	←Courts	Hidalgo	Recorder→	UC	RE	TX	VS
•	•	•			A.G.O. Legal Process Service [SOP]		505-526-4303	•	•	•	•
					Hidalgo County Abstract		505-542-9181		•	•	
•	•	•	•	•	Infomax		505-994-0370	•	•	•	•

CR	CV	PR	US	BK	←Courts	Lea	Recorder→	UC	RE	TX	VS
	•	•			Caprock Title Co.		432-687-3232		•	•	
•	•	•	•	•	Davick Services		800-658-6656	•	•	•	
	•	•			Elliott & Waldron Title & Abstract		505-393-7706	•	•	•	
•	•	•	•	•	Infomax		505-994-0370	•	•	•	•

CR	CV	PR	US	BK	←Courts	Lincoln	Recorder→	UC	RE	TX	VS
•	•	•			A.G.O. Legal Process Service [SOP]		505-526-4303	•	•	•	•
•	•	•	•	•	Infomax		505-994-0370	•	•	•	•
	•	•			Lincoln County Abstract & Title Co (NM)		800-635-4692	•	•	•	

CR	CV	PR	US	BK	←Courts	Los Alamos	Recorder→	UC	RE	TX	VS
•	•	•	•	•	Duke City Process Service & Inv [SOP]		888-335-9889		•	•	•
•	•		•		Nancy Harris [SOP]		877-461-6700	•		•	
•	•	•	•	•	Infomax		505-994-0370	•	•	•	•
	•	•			Real Property Resources		505-232-3555	•	•	•	

CR	CV	PR	US	BK	←Courts	Luna	Recorder→	UC	RE	TX	VS
•	•	•			A.G.O. Legal Process Service [SOP]		505-526-4303	•	•	•	•
•	•	•	•	•	Infomax		505-994-0370	•	•	•	•
•	•	•			Mimbres Valley Abstract & Title Co		505-546-8896	•	•	•	•

CR	CV	PR	US	BK	←Courts	McKinley	Recorder→	UC	RE	TX	VS
•	•				Attorney Service New Mexico [SOP]		505-326-7486				
•	•	•	•	•	Infomax		505-994-0370	•	•	•	•
	•	•			Real Property Resources		505-232-3555	•	•	•	

CR	CV	PR	US	BK	←Courts	Mora	Recorder→	UC	RE	TX	VS
		•			Territorial Title		505-425-3563	•	•	•	•

CR	CV	PR	US	BK	←Courts	Otero	Recorder→	UC	RE	TX	VS
•	•	•	•	•	Infomax		505-994-0370	•	•	•	•

CR	CV	PR	US	BK	←Courts	Quay	Recorder→	UC	RE	TX	VS
•	•	•	•	•	Davick Services		800-658-6656	•	•	•	
•	•	•	•	•	Infomax		505-994-0370	•	•	•	•

CR	CV	PR	US	BK	←Courts	Rio Arriba	Recorder→	UC	RE	TX	VS
•	•				Attorney Service New Mexico [SOP]		505-326-7486				
	•	•			Espanola Abstract Co.		505-753-2248	•	•	•	•
•	•		•		Nancy Harris [SOP]		877-461-6700	•		•	
•	•	•	•	•	Infomax		505-994-0370	•	•	•	•

CR	CV	PR	US	BK	←Courts	Roosevelt	Recorder→	UC	RE	TX	VS
•	•	•	•	•	Davick Services		800-658-6656	•	•	•	

CR	CV	PR	US	BK	Retriever	Phone	UC	RE	TX	VS
	•	•	•	•	Graham Abstract & Title Co	505-356-8505	•	•	•	
•	•	•	•	•	Infomax	505-994-0370	•	•	•	•

CR	CV	PR	US	BK	←COURTS SAN JUAN	RECORDER→	UC	RE	TX	VS
•	•				Attorney Service New Mexico [SOP]	505-326-7486				
•	•	•	•	•	Infomax	505-994-0370	•	•	•	•
	•	•			Real Property Resources	505-232-3555	•	•	•	
•	•	•			San Juan County Abstract & Title	505-325-2808	•	•	•	•

CR	CV	PR	US	BK	←COURTS SAN MIGUEL	RECORDER→	UC	RE	TX	VS
•	•		•		Nancy Harris [SOP]	877-461-6700	•		•	
•	•	•	•	•	Infomax	505-994-0370	•	•	•	•
		•			Territorial Title	505-425-3563	•	•	•	•

CR	CV	PR	US	BK	←COURTS SANDOVAL	RECORDER→	UC	RE	TX	VS
•	•	•	•	•	Duke City Process Service & Inv [SOP]	888-335-9889		•	•	•
•	•	•	•	•	Infomax	505-994-0370	•	•	•	•
•		•	•	•	Professional Services of New Mexico Inc	505-271-2291				
	•	•			Real Property Resources	505-232-3555	•	•	•	
					Carol Seewald [SOP]	505-831-5713	•	•	•	

CR	CV	PR	US	BK	←COURTS SANTA FE	RECORDER→	UC	RE	TX	VS
•	•	•	•	•	Duke City Process Service & Inv [SOP]	888-335-9889		•	•	•
•	•		•		Nancy Harris [SOP]	877-461-6700	•		•	
•	•	•	•	•	Infomax	505-994-0370	•	•	•	•
	•	•			Real Property Resources	505-232-3555	•	•	•	
					Carol Seewald [SOP]	505-831-5713	•	•	•	
	•		•	•	UCC Search Inc	800-453-9404	•	•	•	

CR	CV	PR	US	BK	←COURTS SIERRA	RECORDER→	UC	RE	TX	VS
•	•	•	•	•	Infomax	505-994-0370	•	•	•	•

CR	CV	PR	US	BK	←COURTS SOCORRO	RECORDER→	UC	RE	TX	VS
•	•	•	•	•	Infomax	505-994-0370	•	•	•	•
					Carol Seewald [SOP]	505-831-5713	•	•	•	

CR	CV	PR	US	BK	←COURTS TAOS	RECORDER→	UC	RE	TX	VS
•	•	•	•	•	Duke City Process Service & Inv [SOP]	888-335-9889		•	•	•
•	•	•	•	•	Infomax	505-994-0370	•	•	•	•
•	•	•			PLM Court Research [SOP]	505-758-4467				

CR	CV	PR	US	BK	←COURTS TORRANCE	RECORDER→	UC	RE	TX	VS
•	•	•	•	•	Duke City Process Service & Inv [SOP]	888-335-9889		•	•	•
•	•	•	•	•	Infomax	505-994-0370	•	•	•	•
					Carol Seewald [SOP]	505-831-5713	•	•	•	

CR	CV	PR	US	BK	←COURTS UNION	RECORDER→	UC	RE	TX	VS
	•	•			Clayton Title Services Inc	505-374-9789	•	•	•	•
•	•	•	•	•	Infomax	505-994-0370	•	•	•	•

CR	CV	PR	US	BK	←COURTS VALENCIA	RECORDER→	UC	RE	TX	VS
•	•	•	•	•	Duke City Process Service & Inv [SOP]	888-335-9889		•	•	•
•	•	•	•	•	Infomax	505-994-0370	•	•	•	•
	•	•			Real Property Resources	505-232-3555	•	•	•	
					Carol Seewald [SOP]	505-831-5713	•	•	•	

New York

Capital - Albany County

Court Records Retrieved | Recorded Records Retrieved

Albany

CR	CV	PR	US	BK	←Courts / Recorder→	Phone	UC	RE	TX	VS
•	•		•	•	Access Information Services Inc - NY [SOP]	800-388-1598	•	•	•	
	•		•	•	Attorney's Process & Research Service Inc [SOP]	800-640-7863	•	•	•	
•	•	•	•	•	Blumberg Excelsior Corporate Services Inc [SOP]	800-999-0850	•	•	•	•
			•	•	Capitol Services Inc (New York)	800-662-0171	•		•	
•	•	•	•	•	Credit Control Inc/Resource Confidential [SOP]	800-886-7407	•	•	•	•
•	•	•	•	•	DLS (Demovsky Lawyer Service - Albany) [SOP]	518-449-8411	•	•	•	
	•		•	•	Forbes Public Research Inc	518-732-2961	•	•	•	
		•		•	Four Corners Abstract	800-724-3668	•	•	•	
		•	•	•	Lightning Legal Services LLC [SOP]	518-463-1049	•		•	•
•	•		•	•	Merola Services	219-878-9699	•	•	•	•
			•	•	Monroe Title Insurance Corp (Albany)	800-966-6763	•	•	•	
		•	•	•	Monroe Title Insurance Corp (Rochester)	800-966-6763	•	•	•	
•	•	•	•	•	Nationwide Information Services Inc [SOP]	800-873-3482	•	•	•	•
•	•	•	•	•	Northeast Investigations Inc [SOP]	888-796-1051	•	•	•	•
•	•	•	•	•	Relyea Services Inc [SOP]	800-854-4111	•	•	•	•
	•	•		•	Ryco Information Services Inc	800-240-7926	•	•	•	
•	•	•	•	•	SearchLink LLC	716-873-8315	•	•	•	
•	•	•	•	•	Servico Inc [SOP]	518-463-4179	•	•	•	•
	•		•	•	UCC Direct Services - Albany	800-342-3676	•	•	•	
	•		•	•	Zap! Courier Service	518-449-3361				

Allegany

CR	CV	PR	US	BK	←Courts / Recorder→	Phone	UC	RE	TX	VS
		•	•	•	Monroe Title Insurance Corp (Rochester)	800-966-6763	•	•	•	
	•	•		•	Ryco Information Services Inc	800-240-7926	•	•	•	
•	•	•	•	•	SearchLink LLC	716-873-8315	•	•	•	
•	•		•	•	Synerfax Inc	800-245-3013				

Bronx

CR	CV	PR	US	BK	←Courts / Recorder→	Phone	UC	RE	TX	VS
	•		•	•	Abstract Art Corporation	212-228-1850	•	•	•	
•	•	•	•	•	Alstate Process Service Inc [SOP]	631-667-1800	•	•	•	•
			•	•	American Abstract	631-262-1826	•	•	•	•
•	•	•	•	•	ASSIST International [SOP]	800-382-7747	•	•	•	•
				•	Blumberg Excelsior Corporate Services Inc (NYC, NY)	800-221-2972	•		•	
	•	•	•	•	Bridge Service Corp	800-225-2736	•	•	•	
•	•	•	•	•	Court Explorers Inc [SOP]	212-608-1585	•	•	•	•
•	•	•	•	•	DLS (Demovsky Lawyer Service - New York) [SOP]	800-443-1058	•	•	•	•
•				•	Document Retrieval Network Inc	859-654-2890	•	•	•	
•	•	•	•	•	Fidelifacts	800-678-0007	•	•	•	•
•	•		•	•	G.A. Public Record Services Inc	800-760-2468 x314				
•	•	•	•	•	Inquisitive Research Corporation	732-321-0041	•	•	•	•
•	•		•	•	Investigative Resources [SOP]	212-571-2500	•	•	•	
	•	•	•	•	Keating & Walker [SOP]	800-466-2730				
	•	•	•	•	LegalEase Inc [SOP]	800-393-1277			•	
				•	Mutual Abstract Corporation	212-964-4686	•	•	•	
•	•	•			Pallorium Inc [SOP]	212-969-0286		•	•	•
•	•	•	•	•	Priority Abstract LLC [SOP]	888-941-1234	•	•	•	•
	•	•		•	Ryco Information Services Inc	800-240-7926	•	•	•	
•	•	•	•	•	Search NY Inc [SOP]	212-608-2546	•	•	•	•

CR	CV	PR	US	BK	←Courts	Recorder→	UC	RE	TX	VS
•	•	•	•	•	SearchLink LLC	716-873-8315	•	•	•	
•	•		•	•	Synerfax Inc	800-245-3013				
•	•	•	•	•	US Document Retrieval Service Inc	800-595-0145		•	•	•
•	•	•	•	•	Zook Search Inc NYC	718-369-3879	•	•	•	•

Broome

CR	CV	PR	US	BK	←Courts	Recorder→	UC	RE	TX	VS
•	•	•	•	•	Credit Control Inc/Resource Confidential [SOP]	800-886-7407	•	•	•	•
•	•	•	•	•	Crump Investigative Services [SOP]	607-785-2661	•	•	•	•
		•		•	Four Corners Abstract	800-724-3668	•	•	•	
		•	•	•	Monroe Title Insurance Corp (Rochester)	800-966-6763	•	•	•	
•	•	•	•	•	Northeast Investigations Inc [SOP]	888-796-1051	•	•	•	•
	•	•		•	Ryco Information Services Inc	800-240-7926	•	•	•	
•	•	•	•	•	SearchLink LLC	716-873-8315	•	•	•	

Cattaraugus

CR	CV	PR	US	BK	←Courts	Recorder→	UC	RE	TX	VS
	•	•			Cattaraugus Abstract Corp	800-559-1242	•	•	•	
					Thomas E Corsi	716-863-7797		•		
	•	•		•	Ryco Information Services Inc	800-240-7926	•	•	•	
•	•	•	•	•	SearchLink LLC	716-873-8315	•	•	•	

Cayuga

CR	CV	PR	US	BK	←Courts	Recorder→	UC	RE	TX	VS
•	•	•			24 Hour Record Retriever & Abstract Inc [SOP]	800-294-3740	•	•	•	
	•	•			Central New York Abstract Corp	315-724-1614	•	•	•	
		•		•	Four Corners Abstract	800-724-3668	•	•	•	
		•	•	•	Monroe Title Insurance Corp (Rochester)	800-966-6763	•	•	•	
•	•	•	•	•	Northeast Investigations Inc [SOP]	888-796-1051	•	•	•	•
	•	•		•	Ryco Information Services Inc	800-240-7926	•	•	•	
•	•	•	•	•	SearchLink LLC	716-873-8315	•	•	•	
•	•		•	•	Synerfax Inc	800-245-3013				

Chautauqua

CR	CV	PR	US	BK	←Courts	Recorder→	UC	RE	TX	VS
					Thomas E Corsi	716-863-7797		•		
		•	•	•	Monroe Title Insurance Corp (Rochester)	800-966-6763	•	•	•	
	•	•		•	Ryco Information Services Inc	800-240-7926	•	•	•	
•	•	•	•	•	SearchLink LLC	716-873-8315	•	•	•	

Chemung

CR	CV	PR	US	BK	←Courts	Recorder→	UC	RE	TX	VS
•	•	•	•	•	Crump Investigative Services [SOP]	607-785-2661	•	•	•	•
		•	•	•	Monroe Title Insurance Corp (Rochester)	800-966-6763	•	•	•	
	•	•		•	Ryco Information Services Inc	800-240-7926	•	•	•	
•	•	•	•	•	SearchLink LLC	716-873-8315	•	•	•	

Chenango

CR	CV	PR	US	BK	←Courts	Recorder→	UC	RE	TX	VS
		•		•	Four Corners Abstract	800-724-3668	•	•	•	
	•	•		•	Ryco Information Services Inc	800-240-7926	•	•	•	
•	•	•	•	•	SearchLink LLC	716-873-8315	•	•	•	

Clinton

CR	CV	PR	US	BK	←Courts	Recorder→	UC	RE	TX	VS
	•	•		•	Ryco Information Services Inc	800-240-7926	•	•	•	
•	•	•	•	•	SearchLink LLC	716-873-8315	•	•	•	

Columbia

CR	CV	PR	US	BK	←Courts	Recorder→	UC	RE	TX	VS
	•		•	•	Attorney's Process & Research Service Inc [SOP]	800-640-7863	•	•	•	
•	•	•	•	•	Blumberg Excelsior Corporate Services Inc [SOP]	800-999-0850	•	•	•	•
		•		•	Four Corners Abstract	800-724-3668	•	•	•	
•	•	•			Onistagrawa Abstracting Corp	518-827-8088		•	•	
	•	•		•	Ryco Information Services Inc	800-240-7926	•	•	•	
•	•	•	•	•	SearchLink LLC	716-873-8315	•	•	•	
•	•	•	•	•	Walsh Investigative Services [SOP]	845-896-3566	•	•	•	•

CR	CV	PR	US	BK	←Courts	Cortland	Recorder→	UC	RE	TX	VS
•	•	•	•	•	Northeast Investigations Inc [SOP]		888-796-1051	•	•	•	•
	•	•		•	Ryco Information Services Inc		800-240-7926	•	•	•	
•	•	•	•	•	SearchLink LLC		716-873-8315	•	•	•	
•	•		•	•	Synerfax Inc		800-245-3013				

CR	CV	PR	US	BK	←Courts	Delaware	Recorder→	UC	RE	TX	VS
		•		•	Four Corners Abstract		800-724-3668	•	•	•	
	•	•	•	•	Harry W Hawley Inc		607-746-3860	•	•	•	
•	•	•			Onistagrawa Abstracting Corp		518-827-8088		•	•	
	•	•		•	Ryco Information Services Inc		800-240-7926	•	•	•	
•	•	•	•	•	SearchLink LLC		716-873-8315	•	•	•	

CR	CV	PR	US	BK	←Courts	Dutchess	Recorder→	UC	RE	TX	VS
•	•				1st Choice Abstracting		845-313-6437	•	•	•	
•	•	•	•	•	Court Explorers Inc [SOP]		212-608-1585	•	•	•	•
•	•	•	•	•	Fidelifacts		800-678-0007	•	•	•	•
•	•	•			LaPrade Services Inc [SOP]		845-473-0468	•	•	•	•
•	•	•			Orange Paper Placers Inc [SOP]		845-294-7810	•	•	•	•
•					PC Abstracting		845-699-6107	•	•	•	
	•	•		•	Ryco Information Services Inc		800-240-7926	•	•	•	
•	•	•	•	•	Search NY Inc [SOP]		212-608-2546	•	•	•	•
•	•	•	•	•	SearchLink LLC		716-873-8315	•	•	•	
•	•				Sure Search		845-744-4243	•	•	•	
•	•	•	•	•	Walsh Investigative Services [SOP]		845-896-3566	•	•	•	•

CR	CV	PR	US	BK	←Courts	Erie	Recorder→	UC	RE	TX	VS
•	•	•	•	•	Action Services & Research Inc [SOP]		877-553-7504	•	•	•	•
					Thomas E Corsi		716-863-7797		•		
		•		•	Four Corners Abstract		800-724-3668	•	•	•	
•	•		•	•	G.A. Public Record Services Inc		800-760-2468 x314				
					Karl Iggers		716-812-2587	•	•	•	•
•	•	•	•	•	Investigate-Claims.com [SOP]		716-689-6577	•	•	•	•
		•	•	•	Monroe Title Insurance Corp (Rochester)		800-966-6763	•	•	•	
•	•	•	•	•	Northeast Investigations Inc [SOP]		888-796-1051	•	•	•	•
•	•	•	•	•	Paralegal Services of Buffalo		716-822-3279	•	•	•	•
•	•		•	•	Philip D Smith & Associates [SOP]		716-631-2100	•		•	
	•	•		•	Ryco Information Services Inc		800-240-7926	•	•	•	
•	•	•	•	•	SearchLink LLC		716-873-8315	•	•	•	
•	•		•	•	Synerfax Inc		800-245-3013				

CR	CV	PR	US	BK	←Courts	Essex	Recorder→	UC	RE	TX	VS
	•	•		•	Ryco Information Services Inc		800-240-7926	•	•	•	
•	•	•	•	•	SearchLink LLC		716-873-8315	•	•	•	

CR	CV	PR	US	BK	←Courts	Franklin	Recorder→	UC	RE	TX	VS
		•			Etna Abstract Corp		518-483-7204	•	•	•	
	•	•		•	Ryco Information Services Inc		800-240-7926	•	•	•	
•	•	•	•	•	SearchLink LLC		716-873-8315	•	•	•	

CR	CV	PR	US	BK	←Courts	Fulton	Recorder→	UC	RE	TX	VS
•	•	•	•	•	Credit Control Inc/Resource Confidential [SOP]		800-886-7407	•	•	•	•
		•		•	Four Corners Abstract		800-724-3668	•	•	•	
		•	•	•	Monroe Title Insurance Corp (Rochester)		800-966-6763	•	•	•	
•	•	•			Onistagrawa Abstracting Corp		518-827-8088		•	•	
	•	•		•	Ryco Information Services Inc		800-240-7926	•	•	•	
		•			Sacandaga Abstract Corp		518-773-2828	•	•	•	
•	•	•	•	•	SearchLink LLC		716-873-8315	•	•	•	

CR	CV	PR	US	BK	←Courts GENESEE Recorder→		UC	RE	TX	VS
					Thomas E Corsi	716-863-7797		•		
		•		•	Four Corners Abstract	800-724-3668	•	•	•	
		•	•	•	Monroe Title Insurance Corp (Rochester)	800-966-6763	•	•	•	
	•	•		•	Ryco Information Services Inc	800-240-7926	•	•	•	
•	•	•	•	•	SearchLink LLC	716-873-8315	•	•	•	

CR	CV	PR	US	BK	←Courts GREENE Recorder→		UC	RE	TX	VS
•	•	•	•	•	Blumberg Excelsior Corporate Services Inc [SOP]	800-999-0850	•	•	•	•
		•		•	Four Corners Abstract	800-724-3668	•	•	•	
•	•	•			Onistagrawa Abstracting Corp	518-827-8088		•	•	
	•	•		•	Ryco Information Services Inc	800-240-7926	•	•	•	
•	•	•	•	•	SearchLink LLC	716-873-8315	•	•	•	

CR	CV	PR	US	BK	←Courts HAMILTON Recorder→		UC	RE	TX	VS
	•	•		•	Ryco Information Services Inc	800-240-7926	•	•	•	
•	•	•	•	•	SearchLink LLC	716-873-8315	•	•	•	
•	•		•	•	Synerfax Inc	800-245-3013				

CR	CV	PR	US	BK	←Courts HERKIMER Recorder→		UC	RE	TX	VS
	•	•			Central New York Abstract Corp	315-724-1614	•	•	•	
•	•	•	•	•	Credit Control Inc/Resource Confidential [SOP]	800-886-7407	•	•	•	•
		•		•	Four Corners Abstract	800-724-3668	•	•	•	
•	•	•	•	•	LegalWorks Inc [SOP]	800-853-6756	•	•	•	•
•	•	•	•	•	Northeast Investigations Inc [SOP]	888-796-1051	•	•	•	•
	•	•		•	Ryco Information Services Inc	800-240-7926	•	•	•	
•	•	•	•	•	SearchLink LLC	716-873-8315	•	•	•	

CR	CV	PR	US	BK	←Courts JEFFERSON Recorder→		UC	RE	TX	VS
•	•	•			24 Hour Record Retriever & Abstract Inc [SOP]	800-294-3740	•	•	•	
•	•	•	•	•	MS Document Services Inc	800-292-3868	•	•	•	•
•	•	•	•	•	Northeast Investigations Inc [SOP]	888-796-1051	•	•	•	•
	•	•		•	Ryco Information Services Inc	800-240-7926	•	•	•	
•	•	•	•	•	SearchLink LLC	716-873-8315	•	•	•	

CR	CV	PR	US	BK	←Courts KINGS Recorder→		UC	RE	TX	VS
	•		•	•	Abstract Art Corporation	212-228-1850	•	•	•	
•	•	•	•	•	Alstate Process Service Inc [SOP]	631-667-1800	•	•	•	•
			•	•	American Abstract	631-262-1826	•	•	•	•
•	•	•	•	•	ASSIST International [SOP]	800-382-7747	•	•	•	•
				•	Blumberg Excelsior Corporate Services Inc (NYC, NY)	800-221-2972	•		•	
	•	•	•	•	Bridge Service Corp	800-225-2736	•	•	•	
•	•	•	•	•	Business Intelligence Inc [SOP]	516-938-1525 x107	•	•	•	•
•	•	•	•	•	Court Explorers Inc [SOP]	212-608-1585	•	•	•	•
•	•	•	•	•	CSC New York City	800-221-0770	•	•	•	•
•	•	•	•	•	DLS (Demovsky Lawyer Service - New York) [SOP]	800-443-1058	•	•	•	•
•				•	Document Retrieval Network Inc	859-654-2890	•	•	•	
•	•	•	•	•	Fidelifacts	800-678-0007	•	•	•	•
•	•		•	•	G.A. Public Record Services Inc	800-760-2468 x314				
•	•	•	•	•	Inquisitive Research Corporation	732-321-0041	•	•	•	•
•	•	•	•	•	Introspect Investigations USA Inc [SOP]	800-847-7177	•	•	•	
•	•		•	•	Investigative Resources [SOP]	212-571-2500	•	•	•	
	•	•	•	•	Keating & Walker [SOP]	800-466-2730				
	•	•	•	•	LegalEase Inc [SOP]	800-393-1277			•	
				•	Mutual Abstract Corporation	212-964-4686	•	•	•	
•	•	•			Pallorium Inc [SOP]	212-969-0286		•	•	•
•	•	•	•	•	Priority Abstract LLC [SOP]	888-941-1234	•	•	•	•
	•	•		•	Ryco Information Services Inc	800-240-7926	•	•	•	
•	•	•	•	•	Search NY Inc [SOP]	212-608-2546	•	•	•	•
•	•	•	•	•	SearchLink LLC	716-873-8315	•	•	•	

CR	CV	PR	US	BK	←Courts	Recorder→	UC	RE	TX	VS
•	•		•	•	Synerfax Inc	800-245-3013				
•	•				Deborah W Thompson	415-272-5773	•	•	•	
•	•	•	•	•	US Document Retrieval Service Inc	800-595-0145		•	•	•
•	•	•	•	•	Zook Search Inc NYC	718-369-3879	•	•	•	•

CR	CV	PR	US	BK	←Courts **Lewis**	Recorder→	UC	RE	TX	VS
	•	•		•	National Abstract	800-535-3477	•	•	•	
•	•	•	•	•	Northeast Investigations Inc [SOP]	888-796-1051	•	•	•	•
	•	•		•	Ryco Information Services Inc	800-240-7926	•	•	•	
•	•	•	•	•	SearchLink LLC	716-873-8315	•	•	•	

CR	CV	PR	US	BK	←Courts **Livingston**	Recorder→	UC	RE	TX	VS
					Thomas E Corsi	716-863-7797		•		
		•		•	Four Corners Abstract	800-724-3668	•	•	•	
		•	•	•	Monroe Title Insurance Corp (Rochester)	800-966-6763	•	•	•	
	•	•		•	Ryco Information Services Inc	800-240-7926	•	•	•	
•	•	•	•	•	SearchLink LLC	716-873-8315	•	•	•	

CR	CV	PR	US	BK	←Courts **Madison**	Recorder→	UC	RE	TX	VS
	•	•			Central New York Abstract Corp	315-724-1614	•	•	•	
•	•	•	•	•	Credit Control Inc/Resource Confidential [SOP]	800-886-7407	•	•	•	•
		•		•	Four Corners Abstract	800-724-3668	•	•	•	
•	•	•	•	•	LegalWorks Inc [SOP]	800-853-6756	•	•	•	•
		•	•	•	Monroe Title Insurance Corp (Rochester)	800-966-6763	•	•	•	
•	•	•	•	•	Northeast Investigations Inc [SOP]	888-796-1051	•	•	•	•
		•			Oneida Valley Abstract	315-363-1444	•	•	•	
	•	•		•	Ryco Information Services Inc	800-240-7926	•	•	•	
•	•	•	•	•	SearchLink LLC	716-873-8315	•	•	•	

CR	CV	PR	US	BK	←Courts **Monroe**	Recorder→	UC	RE	TX	VS
•	•	•			24 Hour Record Retriever & Abstract Inc [SOP]	800-294-3740	•	•	•	
•	•	•	•	•	Balkin Information Services	585-482-1506	•	•	•	
		•		•	Four Corners Abstract	800-724-3668	•	•	•	
					Karl Iggers	716-812-2587	•	•	•	•
•	•	•	•	•	Legal Recording of Rochester Inc	585-232-6710	•	•	•	
		•	•	•	Monroe Title Insurance Corp (Rochester)	800-966-6763	•	•	•	
•	•	•	•	•	MS Document Services Inc	800-292-3868	•	•	•	•
•	•	•	•	•	Northeast Investigations Inc [SOP]	888-796-1051	•	•	•	•
•	•		•	•	Philip D Smith & Associates [SOP]	716-631-2100	•		•	
	•	•		•	Ryco Information Services Inc	800-240-7926	•	•	•	
•	•	•	•	•	SearchLink LLC	716-873-8315	•	•	•	
•	•		•	•	Synerfax Inc	800-245-3013				

CR	CV	PR	US	BK	←Courts **Montgomery**	Recorder→	UC	RE	TX	VS
		•		•	Four Corners Abstract	800-724-3668	•	•	•	
		•	•	•	Monroe Title Insurance Corp (Rochester)	800-966-6763	•	•	•	
•	•	•			Onistagrawa Abstracting Corp	518-827-8088		•	•	
	•	•		•	Ryco Information Services Inc	800-240-7926	•	•	•	
		•			Sacandaga Abstract Corp	518-773-2828	•	•	•	
•	•	•	•	•	SearchLink LLC	716-873-8315	•	•	•	
•	•		•	•	Synerfax Inc	800-245-3013				

CR	CV	PR	US	BK	←Courts **Nassau**	Recorder→	UC	RE	TX	VS
•	•	•	•	•	Alstate Process Service Inc [SOP]	631-667-1800	•	•	•	•
			•	•	American Abstract	631-262-1826	•	•	•	•
•	•	•	•	•	Business Intelligence Inc [SOP]	516-938-1525 x107	•	•	•	•
					Contemporary Realty Solutions Inc	631-979-5677	•	•	•	•
•	•	•	•	•	Court Explorers Inc [SOP]	212-608-1585	•	•	•	•
•	•	•	•	•	DLS (Demovsky Lawyer Service - New York) [SOP]	800-443-1058	•	•	•	•
•				•	Document Retrieval Network Inc	859-654-2890	•	•	•	

CR	CV	PR	US	BK	←Courts	Recorder→	UC	RE	TX	VS
•	•	•	•	•	Fidelifacts	800-678-0007	•	•	•	•
•	•	•	•	•	Gotcha Attorney Services Inc [SOP]	800-698-2748	•	•	•	
•	•	•	•	•	Inquisitive Research Corporation	732-321-0041	•	•	•	•
•	•	•	•	•	Introspect Investigations USA Inc [SOP]	800-847-7177	•	•	•	
	•	•	•	•	Keating & Walker [SOP]	800-466-2730				
	•	•	•	•	LegalEase Inc [SOP]	800-393-1277			•	
•	•	•	•	•	LIDA Credit Agency Inc	516-678-4600	•	•	•	•
				•	Mutual Abstract Corporation	212-964-4686	•	•	•	
•	•	•			Pallorium Inc [SOP]	212-969-0286		•	•	•
•	•	•	•	•	Priority Abstract LLC [SOP]	888-941-1234	•	•	•	•
	•	•	•	•	PST Abstracting Inc	631-744-0759	•	•	•	
•					Reda's Attorney Service	631-331-0700	•	•	•	
	•	•		•	Ryco Information Services Inc	800-240-7926	•	•	•	
•	•	•	•	•	Search NY Inc [SOP]	212-608-2546	•	•	•	•
•	•	•	•	•	SearchLink LLC	716-873-8315	•	•	•	
•	•	•	•	•	Security Enforcement Inc [SOP]	800-924-2896 (NY)	•	•	•	•
•	•		•	•	Synerfax Inc	800-245-3013				
•	•	•	•	•	US Document Retrieval Service Inc	800-595-0145		•	•	

CR	CV	PR	US	BK	←Courts **New York - Manhattan**	Recorder→	UC	RE	TX	VS
•	•	•	•	•	A J Info	732-766-9268 or 732-353-6835	•	•	•	•
	•		•	•	Abstract Art Corporation	212-228-1850	•	•	•	
•	•	•	•	•	Alstate Process Service Inc [SOP]	631-667-1800	•	•	•	•
			•	•	American Abstract	631-262-1826	•	•	•	•
•	•	•	•	•	ASSIST International [SOP]	800-382-7747	•	•	•	•
				•	Blumberg Excelsior Corporate Services Inc (NYC, NY)	800-221-2972	•		•	
	•	•	•	•	Bridge Service Corp	800-225-2736	•	•	•	
•	•	•	•	•	Business Intelligence Inc [SOP]	516-938-1525 x107	•	•	•	•
•	•	•	•	•	Court Explorers Inc [SOP]	212-608-1585	•	•	•	•
•	•	•	•	•	CSC New York City	800-221-0770	•	•	•	•
•	•	•	•	•	DLS (Demovsky Lawyer Service - New York) [SOP]	800-443-1058	•	•	•	•
•	•	•	•	•	EHS Research Services [SOP]	914-472-5848	•	•	•	
•	•	•	•	•	Fidelifacts	800-678-0007	•	•	•	•
•	•		•	•	G.A. Public Record Services Inc	800-760-2468 x314				
•	•	•	•	•	Inquisitive Research Corporation	732-321-0041	•	•	•	•
•	•	•	•	•	Introspect Investigations USA Inc [SOP]	800-847-7177	•	•	•	
•	•	•	•	•	Investigative Resources [SOP]	212-571-2500	•	•	•	
	•	•	•	•	Keating & Walker [SOP]	800-466-2730				
	•	•	•	•	LegalEase Inc [SOP]	800-393-1277			•	
				•	Mutual Abstract Corporation	212-964-4686	•	•	•	
•	•	•			Pallorium Inc [SOP]	212-969-0286		•	•	•
•	•	•	•	•	Priority Abstract LLC [SOP]	888-941-1234	•	•	•	•
	•	•		•	Ryco Information Services Inc	800-240-7926	•	•	•	
•	•	•	•	•	Search NY Inc [SOP]	212-608-2546	•	•	•	•
•	•	•	•	•	SearchLink LLC	716-873-8315	•	•	•	
•	•		•	•	Synerfax Inc	800-245-3013				
•	•				Deborah W Thompson	415-272-5773	•	•	•	
•	•	•	•	•	US Document Retrieval Service Inc	800-595-0145		•	•	•
•	•		•	•	WestLaw CourtEXPRESS (DC) [SOP]	800-542-3320				
•	•	•	•	•	Derrick Wetherell	646-216-9831	•	•	•	•
•	•	•	•	•	Zook Search Inc NYC	718-369-3879	•	•	•	•

CR	CV	PR	US	BK	←Courts **Niagara**	Recorder→	UC	RE	TX	VS
•	•	•	•	•	Action Services & Research Inc [SOP]	877-553-7504	•	•	•	•
					Thomas E Corsi	716-863-7797		•		
		•		•	Four Corners Abstract	800-724-3668	•	•	•	
					Karl Iggers	716-812-2587	•	•	•	•
•	•	•	•	•	Investigate-Claims.com [SOP]	716-689-6577	•	•	•	•
		•	•	•	Monroe Title Insurance Corp (Rochester)	800-966-6763	•	•	•	

CR	CV	PR	US	BK	←Courts	Recorder→	UC	RE	TX	VS
•	•	•	•	•	Paralegal Services of Buffalo	716-822-3279	•	•	•	•
•	•		•	•	Philip D Smith & Associates [SOP]	716-631-2100	•		•	
	•	•		•	Ryco Information Services Inc	800-240-7926	•	•	•	
•	•	•	•	•	SearchLink LLC	716-873-8315	•	•	•	
•	•		•	•	Synerfax Inc	800-245-3013				
CR	**CV**	**PR**	**US**	**BK**	**←Courts — ONEIDA**	**Recorder→**	**UC**	**RE**	**TX**	**VS**
	•	•			Central New York Abstract Corp	315-724-1614	•	•	•	
•	•	•	•	•	Credit Control Inc/Resource Confidential [SOP]	800-886-7407	•	•	•	•
		•		•	Four Corners Abstract	800-724-3668	•	•	•	
•	•	•	•	•	LegalWorks Inc [SOP]	800-853-6756	•	•	•	•
•	•	•	•	•	Midstate Legal Support Services [SOP]	315-797-8609	•	•	•	•
		•	•	•	Monroe Title Insurance Corp (Rochester)	800-966-6763	•	•	•	
•	•	•	•	•	Northeast Investigations Inc [SOP]	888-796-1051	•	•	•	•
•	•	•	•	•	Shirley Perrone	315-733-6126			•	
	•	•		•	Ryco Information Services Inc	800-240-7926	•	•	•	
•	•	•	•	•	SearchLink LLC	716-873-8315	•	•	•	
CR	**CV**	**PR**	**US**	**BK**	**←Courts — ONONDAGA**	**Recorder→**	**UC**	**RE**	**TX**	**VS**
•	•	•			24 Hour Record Retriever & Abstract Inc [SOP]	800-294-3740	•	•	•	
•	•	•	•	•	Credit Control Inc/Resource Confidential [SOP]	800-886-7407	•	•	•	•
		•		•	Four Corners Abstract	800-724-3668	•	•	•	
•	•		•	•	Merola Services	219-878-9699	•	•	•	•
		•	•	•	Monroe Title Insurance Corp (Rochester)	800-966-6763	•	•	•	
•	•	•	•	•	MS Document Services Inc	800-292-3868	•	•	•	•
•	•	•	•	•	Northeast Investigations Inc [SOP]	888-796-1051	•	•	•	•
	•	•		•	Ryco Information Services Inc	800-240-7926	•	•	•	
•	•	•	•	•	SearchLink LLC	716-873-8315	•	•	•	
•	•		•	•	Synerfax Inc	800-245-3013				
CR	**CV**	**PR**	**US**	**BK**	**←Courts — ONTARIO**	**Recorder→**	**UC**	**RE**	**TX**	**VS**
		•		•	Four Corners Abstract	800-724-3668	•	•	•	
		•	•	•	Monroe Title Insurance Corp (Rochester)	800-966-6763	•	•	•	
	•	•		•	Ryco Information Services Inc	800-240-7926	•	•	•	
•	•	•	•	•	SearchLink LLC	716-873-8315	•	•	•	
•	•		•	•	Synerfax Inc	800-245-3013				
CR	**CV**	**PR**	**US**	**BK**	**←Courts — ORANGE**	**Recorder→**	**UC**	**RE**	**TX**	**VS**
•	•				1st Choice Abstracting	845-313-6437	•	•	•	
•	•	•	•	•	ASSIST International [SOP]	800-382-7747	•	•	•	•
•	•	•	•	•	Attorney Service Bureau [SOP]	845-638-1323	•	•	•	•
•	•	•	•	•	Court Explorers Inc [SOP]	212-608-1585	•	•	•	•
•	•		•	•	Fidelifacts	800-678-0007	•	•	•	•
					Hill-N-Dale Abstracters Inc	845-294-5110		•		
•	•	•			LaPrade Services Inc [SOP]	845-473-0468	•	•	•	•
•	•	•	•	•	Orange Abstractor Services Co	845-294-3331	•	•	•	
•	•	•			Orange Paper Placers Inc [SOP]	845-294-7810	•	•	•	•
•	•				PC Abstracting	845-699-6107	•	•	•	
	•	•		•	Ryco Information Services Inc	800-240-7926	•	•	•	
•	•	•	•	•	Search NY Inc [SOP]	212-608-2546	•	•	•	•
•	•	•	•	•	SearchLink LLC	716-873-8315	•	•	•	
•	•				Sure Search	845-744-4243	•	•	•	
•	•	•	•	•	US Document Retrieval Service Inc	800-595-0145		•	•	•
•	•		•	•	Walsh Investigative Services [SOP]	845-896-3566	•	•	•	•
CR	**CV**	**PR**	**US**	**BK**	**←Courts — ORLEANS**	**Recorder→**	**UC**	**RE**	**TX**	**VS**
					Thomas E Corsi	716-863-7797		•		
		•		•	Four Corners Abstract	800-724-3668	•	•	•	
		•	•	•	Monroe Title Insurance Corp (Rochester)	800-966-6763	•	•	•	
	•	•		•	Ryco Information Services Inc	800-240-7926	•	•	•	

CR	CV	PR	US	BK	←Courts	Recorder→	UC	RE	TX	VS
•	•	•	•	•	SearchLink LLC	716-873-8315	•	•	•	
•	•		•	•	Synerfax Inc	800-245-3013				

CR	CV	PR	US	BK	←Courts **Oswego**	Recorder→	UC	RE	TX	VS
•	•	•	•	•	24 Hour Record Retriever & Abstract Inc [SOP]	800-294-3740	•	•	•	
•	•	•	•	•	Credit Control Inc/Resource Confidential [SOP]	800-886-7407	•	•	•	•
		•		•	Four Corners Abstract	800-724-3668	•	•	•	
		•	•	•	Monroe Title Insurance Corp (Rochester)	800-966-6763	•	•	•	
•	•	•	•	•	MS Document Services Inc	800-292-3868	•	•	•	•
•	•	•	•	•	Northeast Investigations Inc [SOP]	888-796-1051	•	•	•	•
	•	•		•	Ryco Information Services Inc	800-240-7926	•	•	•	
•	•	•	•	•	SearchLink LLC	716-873-8315	•	•	•	

CR	CV	PR	US	BK	←Courts **Otsego**	Recorder→	UC	RE	TX	VS
		•	•	•	Monroe Title Insurance Corp (Rochester)	800-966-6763	•	•	•	
•	•	•			Onistagrawa Abstracting Corp	518-827-8088		•	•	
	•	•		•	Ryco Information Services Inc	800-240-7926	•	•	•	
•	•	•	•	•	SearchLink LLC	716-873-8315	•	•	•	

CR	CV	PR	US	BK	←Courts **Putnam**	Recorder→	UC	RE	TX	VS
•	•			•	1st Choice Abstracting	845-313-6437	•	•	•	
•	•	•	•	•	ASSIST International [SOP]	800-382-7747	•	•	•	•
•	•	•	•	•	EHS Research Services [SOP]	914-472-5848	•	•	•	
•	•	•	•	•	Fidelifacts	800-678-0007	•	•	•	•
•	•	•			LaPrade Services Inc [SOP]	845-473-0468	•	•	•	•
•	•	•			Orange Paper Placers Inc [SOP]	845-294-7810	•	•	•	•
•	•				PC Abstracting	845-699-6107	•	•	•	
	•	•		•	Ryco Information Services Inc	800-240-7926	•	•	•	
•	•	•	•	•	SearchLink LLC	716-873-8315	•	•	•	
•	•				Sure Search	845-744-4243	•	•	•	
•	•	•	•	•	Walsh Investigative Services [SOP]	845-896-3566	•	•	•	•
•	•	•	•	•	Derrick Wetherell	646-216-9831	•	•	•	•

CR	CV	PR	US	BK	←Courts **Queens**	Recorder→	UC	RE	TX	VS
	•		•	•	Abstract Art Corporation	212-228-1850	•	•	•	
•	•	•	•	•	Alstate Process Service Inc [SOP]	631-667-1800	•	•	•	•
			•	•	American Abstract	631-262-1826	•	•	•	•
•	•	•	•	•	ASSIST International [SOP]	800-382-7747	•	•	•	•
				•	Blumberg Excelsior Corporate Services Inc (NYC, NY)	800-221-2972	•			
	•	•	•	•	Bridge Service Corp	800-225-2736	•	•	•	
•	•	•	•	•	Business Intelligence Inc [SOP]	516-938-1525 x107	•	•	•	•
•	•	•	•	•	Court Explorers Inc [SOP]	212-608-1585	•	•	•	
•	•	•	•	•	CSC New York City	800-221-0770	•	•	•	
•	•	•	•	•	DLS (Demovsky Lawyer Service - New York) [SOP]	800-443-1058	•	•	•	•
•				•	Document Retrieval Network Inc	859-654-2890	•	•	•	
•	•	•	•	•	Fidelifacts	800-678-0007	•	•	•	•
•	•		•	•	G.A. Public Record Services Inc	800-760-2468 x314				
•	•	•	•	•	Inquisitive Research Corporation	732-321-0041	•	•	•	•
•	•	•	•	•	Introspect Investigations USA Inc [SOP]	800-847-7177	•	•	•	
•	•		•	•	Investigative Resources [SOP]	212-571-2500	•	•	•	
	•	•	•	•	Keating & Walker [SOP]	800-466-2730	•	•	•	
	•	•	•	•	LegalEase Inc [SOP]	800-393-1277			•	
•	•	•	•	•	LIDA Credit Agency Inc	516-678-4600	•	•	•	•
				•	Mutual Abstract Corporation	212-964-4686	•	•	•	
•	•	•			Pallorium Inc [SOP]	212-969-0286		•	•	•
•	•	•	•	•	Priority Abstract LLC [SOP]	888-941-1234	•	•	•	•
	•	•		•	Ryco Information Services Inc	800-240-7926	•	•	•	
•	•	•	•	•	Search NY Inc [SOP]	212-608-2546	•	•	•	•
•	•	•	•	•	SearchLink LLC	716-873-8315	•	•	•	
•	•		•	•	Synerfax Inc	800-245-3013				

CR	CV	PR	US	BK			UC	RE	TX	VS
•	•				Deborah W Thompson	415-272-5773	•	•	•	
•	•	•	•	•	US Document Retrieval Service Inc	800-595-0145		•	•	•
•	•	•	•	•	Zook Search Inc NYC	718-369-3879	•	•	•	•

CR	CV	PR	US	BK	←COURTS RENSSELAER	RECORDER→	UC	RE	TX	VS
•	•		•	•	Access Information Services Inc - NY [SOP]	800-388-1598	•	•	•	
	•		•	•	Attorney's Process & Research Service Inc [SOP]	800-640-7863	•	•	•	
•	•	•	•	•	Blumberg Excelsior Corporate Services Inc [SOP]	800-999-0850	•	•	•	•
			•	•	Capitol Services Inc (New York)	800-662-0171	•		•	
•	•	•	•	•	Credit Control Inc/Resource Confidential [SOP]	800-886-7407	•	•	•	•
•	•	•	•	•	DLS (Demovsky Lawyer Service - Albany) [SOP]	518-449-8411	•	•	•	
		•		•	Four Corners Abstract	800-724-3668	•	•	•	
		•	•	•	Lightning Legal Services LLC [SOP]	518-463-1049	•	•	•	
			•	•	Monroe Title Insurance Corp (Albany)	800-966-6763	•	•	•	
		•	•	•	Monroe Title Insurance Corp (Rochester)	800-966-6763	•	•	•	
•	•	•	•	•	Relyea Services Inc [SOP]	800-854-4111	•	•	•	•
	•	•		•	Ryco Information Services Inc	800-240-7926	•	•	•	
•	•	•	•	•	SearchLink LLC	716-873-8315	•	•	•	
			•	•	Zap! Courier Service	518-449-3361	•	•	•	

CR	CV	PR	US	BK	←COURTS RICHMOND	RECORDER→	UC	RE	TX	VS
•	•	•	•	•	A J Info	732-766-9268 or 732-353-6835	•	•	•	•
	•		•	•	Abstract Art Corporation	212-228-1850	•	•	•	
•	•	•	•	•	Alstate Process Service Inc [SOP]	631-667-1800	•	•	•	•
			•	•	American Abstract	631-262-1826	•	•	•	•
•	•	•	•	•	ASSIST International [SOP]	800-382-7747	•	•	•	•
			•	•	Blumberg Excelsior Corporate Services Inc (NYC, NY)	800-221-2972	•		•	
•	•	•	•	•	Court Explorers Inc [SOP]	212-608-1585	•	•	•	•
•	•	•	•	•	DLS (Demovsky Lawyer Service - New York) [SOP]	800-443-1058	•	•	•	•
•	•	•	•	•	Fidelifacts	800-678-0007	•	•	•	•
•	•	•	•	•	Inquisitive Research Corporation	732-321-0041	•	•	•	•
•	•		•	•	Investigative Resources [SOP]	212-571-2500	•	•	•	
•	•	•	•	•	Keating & Walker [SOP]	800-466-2730	•	•	•	
•	•			•	Pallorium Inc [SOP]	212-969-0286		•	•	•
•	•	•	•	•	Priority Abstract LLC [SOP]	888-941-1234	•	•	•	•
	•	•		•	Ryco Information Services Inc	800-240-7926	•	•	•	
•	•	•	•	•	Search NY Inc [SOP]	212-608-2546	•	•	•	•
•	•	•	•	•	SearchLink LLC	716-873-8315	•	•	•	
•	•		•	•	Synerfax Inc	800-245-3013				
•	•	•	•	•	US Document Retrieval Service Inc	800-595-0145		•	•	•

CR	CV	PR	US	BK	←COURTS ROCKLAND	RECORDER→	UC	RE	TX	VS
•	•				1st Choice Abstracting	845-313-6437	•	•	•	
•	•	•	•	•	ASSIST International [SOP]	800-382-7747	•	•	•	•
•	•	•	•	•	Attorney Service Bureau [SOP]	845-638-1323	•	•	•	•
•	•	•	•	•	DLS (Demovsky Lawyer Service - New York) [SOP]	800-443-1058	•	•	•	•
•	•	•	•	•	EHS Research Services [SOP]	914-472-5848	•	•	•	
•	•	•	•	•	Fidelifacts	800-678-0007	•	•	•	•
•	•	•			Marilyn Smolinsky & Associates	845-634-5770	•	•	•	
•	•	•			Orange Paper Placers Inc [SOP]	845-294-7810	•	•	•	•
•	•				PC Abstracting	845-699-6107	•	•	•	
	•	•			Ryco Information Services Inc	800-240-7926	•	•	•	
•	•	•	•	•	Search NY Inc [SOP]	212-608-2546	•	•	•	•
•	•	•	•	•	SearchLink LLC	716-873-8315	•	•	•	
•	•				Sure Search	845-744-4243	•	•	•	
•	•	•	•	•	US Document Retrieval Service Inc	800-595-0145		•	•	•
•	•	•	•	•	Walsh Investigative Services [SOP]	845-896-3566	•	•	•	•
•	•	•	•	•	Westchester Court Services-Fox Advertising Inc [SOP]	914-948-5200	•	•	•	

CR	CV	PR	US	BK	←Courts **SARATOGA**	Recorder→	UC	RE	TX	VS
•	•		•	•	Access Information Services Inc - NY [SOP]	800-388-1598	•	•	•	
	•		•	•	Attorney's Process & Research Service Inc [SOP]	800-640-7863	•	•	•	
•	•	•	•	•	Credit Control Inc/Resource Confidential [SOP]	800-886-7407	•	•	•	•
	•		•	•	Forbes Public Research Inc	518-732-2961	•	•	•	
		•		•	Four Corners Abstract	800-724-3668	•	•	•	
		•	•	•	Lightning Legal Services LLC [SOP]	518-463-1049	•		•	•
		•	•	•	Monroe Title Insurance Corp (Rochester)	800-966-6763	•	•	•	
•	•	•	•	•	Relyea Services Inc [SOP]	800-854-4111	•	•	•	•
	•	•		•	Ryco Information Services Inc	800-240-7926	•	•	•	
•	•	•	•	•	SearchLink LLC	716-873-8315	•	•	•	
	•		•	•	Zap! Courier Service	518-449-3361				

CR	CV	PR	US	BK	←Courts **SCHENECTADY**	Recorder→	UC	RE	TX	VS
•	•		•	•	Access Information Services Inc - NY [SOP]	800-388-1598	•	•	•	
	•		•	•	Attorney's Process & Research Service Inc [SOP]	800-640-7863	•	•	•	
•	•	•	•	•	Blumberg Excelsior Corporate Services Inc [SOP]	800-999-0850	•	•	•	•
•	•	•	•	•	Credit Control Inc/Resource Confidential [SOP]	800-886-7407	•	•	•	•
•	•	•	•	•	DLS (Demovsky Lawyer Service - Albany) [SOP]	518-449-8411	•	•	•	
	•		•	•	Forbes Public Research Inc	518-732-2961	•	•	•	
		•		•	Four Corners Abstract	800-724-3668	•	•	•	
		•	•	•	Lightning Legal Services LLC [SOP]	518-463-1049	•		•	•
		•	•	•	Monroe Title Insurance Corp (Rochester)	800-966-6763	•	•	•	
•	•	•			Onistagrawa Abstracting Corp	518-827-8088		•	•	
•	•	•	•	•	Relyea Services Inc [SOP]	800-854-4111	•	•	•	•
	•	•		•	Ryco Information Services Inc	800-240-7926	•	•	•	
•	•	•	•	•	SearchLink LLC	716-873-8315	•	•	•	
•	•	•	•	•	Servico Inc [SOP]	518-463-4179	•	•	•	•
	•		•	•	Zap! Courier Service	518-449-3361				

CR	CV	PR	US	BK	←Courts **SCHOHARIE**	Recorder→	UC	RE	TX	VS
•	•	•			Onistagrawa Abstracting Corp	518-827-8088		•	•	
	•	•		•	Ryco Information Services Inc	800-240-7926	•	•	•	
•	•	•	•	•	SearchLink LLC	716-873-8315	•	•	•	

CR	CV	PR	US	BK	←Courts **SCHUYLER**	Recorder→	UC	RE	TX	VS
		•	•	•	Monroe Title Insurance Corp (Rochester)	800-966-6763	•	•	•	
	•	•		•	Ryco Information Services Inc	800-240-7926	•	•	•	
•	•	•	•	•	SearchLink LLC	716-873-8315	•	•	•	

CR	CV	PR	US	BK	←Courts **SENECA**	Recorder→	UC	RE	TX	VS
		•		•	Four Corners Abstract	800-724-3668	•	•	•	
		•	•	•	Monroe Title Insurance Corp (Rochester)	800-966-6763	•	•	•	
	•	•		•	Ryco Information Services Inc	800-240-7926	•	•	•	
•	•	•	•	•	SearchLink LLC	716-873-8315	•	•	•	

CR	CV	PR	US	BK	←Courts **ST. LAWRENCE**	Recorder→	UC	RE	TX	VS
	•	•		•	Ryco Information Services Inc	800-240-7926	•	•	•	
•	•	•	•	•	SearchLink LLC	716-873-8315	•	•	•	

CR	CV	PR	US	BK	←Courts **STEUBEN**	Recorder→	UC	RE	TX	VS
		•	•	•	Monroe Title Insurance Corp (Rochester)	800-966-6763	•	•	•	
	•	•		•	Ryco Information Services Inc	800-240-7926	•	•	•	
•	•	•	•	•	SearchLink LLC	716-873-8315	•	•	•	

CR	CV	PR	US	BK	←Courts **SUFFOLK**	Recorder→	UC	RE	TX	VS
•	•	•	•	•	Alstate Process Service Inc [SOP]	631-667-1800	•	•	•	•
			•	•	American Abstract	631-262-1826	•	•	•	•
•	•	•	•	•	ASSIST International [SOP]	800-382-7747	•	•	•	•
•	•	•	•	•	Business Intelligence Inc [SOP]	516-938-1525 x107	•	•	•	•

CR	CV	PR	US	BK	Retriever	Phone	UC	RE	TX	VS
					Contemporary Realty Solutions Inc	631-979-5677	•	•	•	
•	•	•	•	•	Court Explorers Inc [SOP]	212-608-1585	•	•	•	•
•				•	Document Retrieval Network Inc	859-654-2890	•	•	•	
•	•	•	•	•	Fidelifacts	800-678-0007	•	•	•	•
•	•		•	•	G.A. Public Record Services Inc	800-760-2468 x314				
•	•	•	•	•	Gotcha Attorney Services Inc [SOP]	800-698-2748	•	•	•	
•	•	•	•	•	Inquisitive Research Corporation	732-321-0041	•	•	•	•
•	•	•	•	•	LIDA Credit Agency Inc	516-678-4600	•	•	•	•
•	•	•			Pallorium Inc [SOP]	212-969-0286		•	•	•
•	•	•	•	•	Priority Abstract LLC [SOP]	888-941-1234	•	•	•	•
	•	•	•	•	PST Abstracting Inc	631-744-0759	•	•	•	
•					Reda's Attorney Service	631-331-0700	•	•	•	
	•	•		•	Ryco Information Services Inc	800-240-7926	•	•	•	
•	•	•	•	•	Search NY Inc [SOP]	212-608-2546	•	•	•	
•	•	•	•	•	SearchLink LLC	716-873-8315	•	•	•	
•	•	•	•	•	Security Enforcement Inc [SOP]	800-924-2896 (NY)	•	•	•	•
•	•				Donna Stovall [SOP]	631-744-5834	•	•	•	
•	•				Sure Search	845-744-4243	•	•	•	
•	•	•	•	•	US Document Retrieval Service Inc	800-595-0145		•	•	•

CR	CV	PR	US	BK	←Courts **SULLIVAN**	Recorder→	UC	RE	TX	VS
•	•				1st Choice Abstracting	845-313-6437	•	•	•	
					Hill-N-Dale Abstracters Inc	845-294-5110		•		
•	•	•			Orange Paper Placers Inc [SOP]	845-294-7810	•	•	•	•
•	•				PC Abstracting	845-699-6107	•	•	•	
	•	•		•	Ryco Information Services Inc	800-240-7926	•	•	•	
•	•	•	•	•	SearchLink LLC	716-873-8315	•	•	•	
•	•				Sure Search	845-744-4243	•	•	•	
•	•	•	•	•	Walsh Investigative Services [SOP]	845-896-3566	•	•	•	•

CR	CV	PR	US	BK	←Courts **TIOGA**	Recorder→	UC	RE	TX	VS
•	•	•	•	•	Crump Investigative Services [SOP]	607-785-2661	•	•	•	•
		•		•	Four Corners Abstract	800-724-3668	•	•	•	
		•	•	•	Monroe Title Insurance Corp (Rochester)	800-966-6763	•	•	•	
	•	•		•	Ryco Information Services Inc	800-240-7926	•	•	•	
•	•	•	•	•	SearchLink LLC	716-873-8315	•	•	•	

CR	CV	PR	US	BK	←Courts **TOMPKINS**	Recorder→	UC	RE	TX	VS
•	•	•	•	•	Crump Investigative Services [SOP]	607-785-2661	•	•	•	•
		•	•	•	Monroe Title Insurance Corp (Rochester)	800-966-6763	•	•	•	
	•	•		•	Ryco Information Services Inc	800-240-7926	•	•	•	
•	•	•	•	•	SearchLink LLC	716-873-8315	•	•	•	

CR	CV	PR	US	BK	←Courts **ULSTER**	Recorder→	UC	RE	TX	VS
•	•	•			Data-Find	845-246-3263	•	•	•	
•	•	•	•	•	Fidelifacts	800-678-0007	•	•	•	•
					Hill-N-Dale Abstracters Inc	845-294-5110		•		
•	•	•			LaPrade Services Inc [SOP]	845-473-0468	•	•	•	•
•	•	•			Orange Paper Placers Inc [SOP]	845-294-7810	•	•	•	•
•	•	•			Ranger Recovery [SOP]	845-679-2957	•	•	•	•
	•	•		•	Ryco Information Services Inc	800-240-7926	•	•	•	
•	•	•	•	•	SearchLink LLC	716-873-8315	•	•	•	
•	•	•	•	•	Walsh Investigative Services [SOP]	845-896-3566	•	•	•	•

CR	CV	PR	US	BK	←Courts **WARREN**	Recorder→	UC	RE	TX	VS
	•		•	•	Attorney's Process & Research Service Inc [SOP]	800-640-7863	•	•	•	
•	•	•	•	•	Credit Control Inc/Resource Confidential [SOP]	800-886-7407	•	•	•	•
	•		•	•	Forbes Public Research Inc	518-732-2961	•	•	•	
		•	•	•	Monroe Title Insurance Corp (Rochester)	800-966-6763	•	•	•	
	•	•		•	Ryco Information Services Inc	800-240-7926	•	•	•	

CR	CV	PR	US	BK			UC	RE	TX	VS
•	•	•	•	•	SearchLink LLC	716-873-8315	•	•	•	

CR	CV	PR	US	BK	←Courts **WASHINGTON**	Recorder→	UC	RE	TX	VS
	•		•	•	Attorney's Process & Research Service Inc [SOP]	800-640-7863	•	•	•	
•	•	•	•	•	Credit Control Inc/Resource Confidential [SOP]	800-886-7407	•	•	•	•
		•	•	•	Monroe Title Insurance Corp (Rochester)	800-966-6763	•	•	•	
	•	•		•	Ryco Information Services Inc	800-240-7926	•	•	•	
•	•	•	•	•	SearchLink LLC	716-873-8315	•	•	•	

CR	CV	PR	US	BK	←Courts **WAYNE**	Recorder→	UC	RE	TX	VS
		•		•	Four Corners Abstract	800-724-3668	•	•	•	
		•	•	•	Monroe Title Insurance Corp (Rochester)	800-966-6763	•	•	•	
	•	•		•	Ryco Information Services Inc	800-240-7926	•	•	•	
•	•	•	•	•	SearchLink LLC	716-873-8315	•	•	•	
•	•		•	•	Synerfax Inc	800-245-3013				

CR	CV	PR	US	BK	←Courts **WESTCHESTER**	Recorder→	UC	RE	TX	VS
•	•				1st Choice Abstracting	845-313-6437	•	•	•	
			•	•	American Abstract	631-262-1826	•	•	•	•
•	•	•	•	•	ASSIST International [SOP]	800-382-7747	•	•	•	•
•	•	•	•	•	Attorney Service Bureau [SOP]	845-638-1323	•	•	•	•
•	•	•	•	•	Business Intelligence Inc [SOP]	516-938-1525 x107	•	•	•	•
•	•	•	•	•	Court Explorers Inc [SOP]	212-608-1585	•	•	•	•
•	•	•	•	•	DLS (Demovsky Lawyer Service - New York) [SOP]	800-443-1058	•	•	•	•
•	•	•	•	•	EHS Research Services [SOP]	914-472-5848	•	•	•	•
•	•	•	•	•	Fidelifacts	800-678-0007	•	•	•	•
•	•	•	•	•	Inquisitive Research Corporation	732-321-0041	•	•	•	•
	•	•	•	•	Keating & Walker [SOP]	800-466-2730				
	•	•	•	•	LegalEase Inc [SOP]	800-393-1277			•	
				•	Mutual Abstract Corporation	212-964-4686	•	•	•	
•	•	•			Pallorium Inc [SOP]	212-969-0286		•	•	•
•	•				PC Abstracting	845-699-6107	•	•	•	
	•	•		•	Ryco Information Services Inc	800-240-7926	•	•	•	
•	•	•	•	•	Search NY Inc [SOP]	212-608-2546	•	•	•	•
•	•	•	•	•	SearchLink LLC	716-873-8315	•	•	•	
•	•	•	•	•	Sure Search	845-744-4243	•	•	•	
•	•	•	•	•	US Document Retrieval Service Inc	800-595-0145		•	•	•
•	•	•	•	•	Walsh Investigative Services [SOP]	845-896-3566	•	•	•	•
•	•	•	•	•	Westchester Court Services-Fox Advertising Inc [SOP]	914-948-5200	•		•	
•	•	•	•	•	Derrick Wetherell	646-216-9831	•	•	•	•

CR	CV	PR	US	BK	←Courts **WYOMING**	Recorder→	UC	RE	TX	VS
					Thomas E Corsi	716-863-7797		•		
		•	•	•	Monroe Title Insurance Corp (Rochester)	800-966-6763	•	•	•	
	•	•		•	Ryco Information Services Inc	800-240-7926	•	•	•	
•	•	•	•	•	SearchLink LLC	716-873-8315	•	•	•	

CR	CV	PR	US	BK	←Courts **YATES**	Recorder→	UC	RE	TX	VS
		•		•	Four Corners Abstract	800-724-3668	•	•	•	
		•	•	•	Monroe Title Insurance Corp (Rochester)	800-966-6763	•	•	•	
	•	•		•	Ryco Information Services Inc	800-240-7926	•	•	•	
•	•	•	•	•	SearchLink LLC	716-873-8315	•	•	•	

North Carolina

COURT RECORDS RETRIEVED — CAPITAL - WAKE COUNTY — RECORDED RECORDS RETRIEVED

CR	CV	PR	US	BK	←COURTS	RECORDER→	UC	RE	TX	VS
					ALAMANCE					
•	•	•	•	•	NC Corporate Connection Inc	888-844-8360	•	•	•	•
•	•	•	•	•	Paralegal Services of North Carolina Inc [SOP]	919-821-7762	•	•	•	•
•	•	•	•	•	Searchtec (Carolinas) [SOP]	800-528-8790	•	•	•	•
					ALEXANDER					
•	•	•	•	•	Track' Um Private Investigations [SOP]	877-634-9106	•	•	•	•
					ALLEGHANY					
•	•	•	•	•	Searchtec (Carolinas) [SOP]	800-528-8790	•	•	•	•
•	•	•	•	•	Track' Um Private Investigations [SOP]	877-634-9106	•	•	•	•
					ANSON					
•	•	•	•	•	Searchtec (Carolinas) [SOP]	800-528-8790	•	•	•	•
					ASHE					
	•	•			Miller & Johnson PLLC	828-264-1125	•	•	•	
•	•	•	•	•	Searchtec (Carolinas) [SOP]	800-528-8790	•	•	•	•
•	•	•	•	•	Track' Um Private Investigations [SOP]	877-634-9106	•	•	•	•
					AVERY					
	•	•			Miller & Johnson PLLC	828-264-1125	•	•	•	
					BEAUFORT					
	•				Sue P Hamm	252-322-5015	•	•	•	•
•	•	•	•	•	Searchtec (Carolinas) [SOP]	800-528-8790	•	•	•	•
					BERTIE					
•	•	•	•	•	Searchtec (Carolinas) [SOP]	800-528-8790	•	•	•	•
					BLADEN					
•	•	•	•	•	Searchtec (Carolinas) [SOP]	800-528-8790	•	•	•	•
					BRUNSWICK					
•	•	•	•	•	Searchtec (Carolinas) [SOP]	800-528-8790	•	•	•	•
					BUNCOMBE					
•	•	•			Carolina Investigative Research Inc [SOP]	800-328-8981	•	•	•	•
•	•	•	•	•	Paralegal Services Inc	828-606-8297	•	•	•	•
•	•	•	•	•	Ramsey Paralegal/Process [SOP]	828-687-9974; send faxes to Attn. Don Ramsey	•	•	•	•
•	•		•	•	WNC Search Service	828-768-0062	•	•	•	
					BURKE					
•	•	•	•	•	Ramsey Paralegal/Process [SOP]	828-687-9974; send faxes to Attn. Don Ramsey	•	•	•	•
					CABARRUS					
	•			•	Victoria J Armes	704-663-4085	•	•	•	
•	•	•	•	•	Axis Research Inc	877-795-1005	•	•	•	
•	•	•	•	•	NC Corporate Connection Inc	888-844-8360	•	•	•	•
•	•		•	•	Reynolds Professional Service Inc [SOP]	800-814-8662				•
•	•	•	•	•	Searchtec (Carolinas) [SOP]	800-528-8790	•	•	•	•
•	•	•	•		The Henry Agency [SOP]	704-526-5030	•	•	•	•

CR	CV	PR	US	BK	←Courts	**Caldwell**	Recorder→	UC	RE	TX	VS
•	•	•	•	•	Track' Um Private Investigations [SOP]		877-634-9106	•	•	•	•

CR	CV	PR	US	BK	←Courts	**Camden**	Recorder→	UC	RE	TX	VS
•	•	•	•	•	Hornthal Riley Ellis & Maland		252-335-0871	•	•	•	•
•	•	•	•	•	Searchtec (Carolinas) [SOP]		800-528-8790	•	•	•	•

CR	CV	PR	US	BK	←Courts	**Carteret**	Recorder→	UC	RE	TX	VS
•	•	•	•	•	Searchtec (Carolinas) [SOP]		800-528-8790	•	•	•	•

CR	CV	PR	US	BK	←Courts	**Caswell**	Recorder→	UC	RE	TX	VS
•	•	•	•	•	Searchtec (Carolinas) [SOP]		800-528-8790	•	•	•	•

CR	CV	PR	US	BK	←Courts	**Catawba**	Recorder→	UC	RE	TX	VS
	•			•	Victoria J Armes		704-663-4085	•	•	•	
•	•	•	•	•	Axis Research Inc		877-795-1005	•	•	•	
•	•	•	•	•	NC Corporate Connection Inc.		888-844-8360	•	•	•	•
•	•	•	•	•	Track' Um Private Investigations [SOP]		877-634-9106	•	•	•	•

CR	CV	PR	US	BK	←Courts	**Chatham**	Recorder→	UC	RE	TX	VS
•	•	•	•	•	ASK Services Inc (North Carolina)		888-416-1313	•	•	•	•
•	•	•			Carolina Investigative Research Inc [SOP]		800-328-8981	•	•	•	•
•	•	•	•	•	NC Corporate Connection Inc.		888-844-8360	•	•	•	•
•	•	•	•	•	Paralegal Services of North Carolina Inc [SOP]		919-821-7762	•	•	•	•
•	•				Poindexter & Associates Inc [SOP]		800-373-2804				
•	•	•	•	•	Searchtec (Carolinas) [SOP]		800-528-8790	•	•	•	•

CR	CV	PR	US	BK	←Courts	**Cherokee**	Recorder→	UC	RE	TX	VS
•	•	•	•	•	Ramsey Paralegal/Process [SOP]		828-687-9974; send faxes to Attn. Don Ramsey	•	•	•	•

CR	CV	PR	US	BK	←Courts	**Chowan**	Recorder→	UC	RE	TX	VS
•	•	•	•	•	Hornthal Riley Ellis & Maland		252-335-0871	•	•	•	•
•	•	•	•	•	Searchtec (Carolinas) [SOP]		800-528-8790	•	•	•	•

CR	CV	PR	US	BK	←Courts	**Clay**	Recorder→	UC	RE	TX	VS
					See adjoining counties for retrievers or call court/recorder directly.						

CR	CV	PR	US	BK	←Courts	**Cleveland**	Recorder→	UC	RE	TX	VS
•	•	•	•	•	Ramsey Paralegal/Process [SOP]		828-687-9974; send faxes to Attn. Don Ramsey	•	•	•	•
•	•		•	•	Reynolds Professional Service Inc [SOP]		800-814-8662				•

CR	CV	PR	US	BK	←Courts	**Columbus**	Recorder→	UC	RE	TX	VS
	•	•			Accurate Data		910-862-4949	•		•	
•	•	•	•	•	Searchtec (Carolinas) [SOP]		800-528-8790	•	•	•	•

CR	CV	PR	US	BK	←Courts	**Craven**	Recorder→	UC	RE	TX	VS
	•				Sue P Hamm		252-322-5015	•	•	•	•
•	•	•	•	•	Searchtec (Carolinas) [SOP]		800-528-8790	•	•	•	•
					Cheryl Smith		252-633-3890	•	•		

CR	CV	PR	US	BK	←Courts	**Cumberland**	Recorder→	UC	RE	TX	VS
					Abstract Art Inc		910-592-2972	•	•	•	•
	•	•			Accurate Data		910-862-4949	•		•	
•	•	•			Carolina Investigative Research Inc [SOP]		800-328-8981	•	•	•	•
•	•	•	•	•	Paralegal Services of North Carolina Inc [SOP]		919-821-7762	•	•	•	•
•	•				Poindexter & Associates Inc [SOP]		800-373-2804				
•	•	•	•	•	Searchtec (Carolinas) [SOP]		800-528-8790	•	•	•	•

CR	CV	PR	US	BK	←Courts	**Currituck**	Recorder→	UC	RE	TX	VS
•	•	•	•	•	Searchtec (Carolinas) [SOP]		800-528-8790	•	•	•	•

CR	CV	PR	US	BK	←Courts	**Dare**	Recorder→	UC	RE	TX	VS
•	•	•	•	•	Hornthal Riley Ellis & Maland		252-335-0871	•	•	•	•

CR	CV	PR	US	BK	←Courts	Recorder→	UC	RE	TX	VS
•	•	•	•	•	Searchtec (Carolinas) [SOP]	800-528-8790	•	•	•	•
CR	**CV**	**PR**	**US**	**BK**	**←Courts — DAVIDSON**	**Recorder→**	**UC**	**RE**	**TX**	**VS**
•	•		•		Agency-One Inv [SOP]	800-557-5500	•	•	•	•
•	•		•	•	Reynolds Professional Service Inc [SOP]	800-814-8662				•
•	•	•	•	•	Searchtec (Carolinas) [SOP]	800-528-8790	•	•	•	•
CR	**CV**	**PR**	**US**	**BK**	**←Courts — DAVIE**	**Recorder→**	**UC**	**RE**	**TX**	**VS**
•	•		•		Agency-One Inv [SOP]	800-557-5500	•	•	•	•
•	•	•	•	•	Searchtec (Carolinas) [SOP]	800-528-8790	•	•	•	•
CR	**CV**	**PR**	**US**	**BK**	**←Courts — DUPLIN**	**Recorder→**	**UC**	**RE**	**TX**	**VS**
•	•	•	•	•	Searchtec (Carolinas) [SOP]	800-528-8790	•	•	•	•
CR	**CV**	**PR**	**US**	**BK**	**←Courts — DURHAM**	**Recorder→**	**UC**	**RE**	**TX**	**VS**
•	•	•	•	•	ASK Services Inc (North Carolina)	888-416-1313	•	•	•	•
•	•	•			Carolina Investigative Research Inc [SOP]	800-328-8981	•	•	•	•
•	•	•	•	•	NC Corporate Connection Inc.	888-844-8360	•	•	•	•
•	•	•	•	•	Paralegal Services of North Carolina Inc [SOP]	919-821-7762	•	•	•	•
•	•				Poindexter & Associates Inc [SOP]	800-373-2804				
	•		•	•	Search Services	919-801-3010	•		•	•
•	•	•	•	•	Searchtec (Carolinas) [SOP]	800-528-8790	•	•	•	•
•	•	•	•	•	Title Searches by Liz Aulis	919-878-0227; cell- 919-395-7433	•	•	•	•
CR	**CV**	**PR**	**US**	**BK**	**←Courts — EDGECOMBE**	**Recorder→**	**UC**	**RE**	**TX**	**VS**
•	•	•	•	•	Searchtec (Carolinas) [SOP]	800-528-8790	•	•	•	•
CR	**CV**	**PR**	**US**	**BK**	**←Courts — FORSYTH**	**Recorder→**	**UC**	**RE**	**TX**	**VS**
•	•		•		Agency-One Inv [SOP]	800-557-5500	•	•	•	•
•	•	•	•	•	Searchtec (Carolinas) [SOP]	800-528-8790	•	•	•	•
CR	**CV**	**PR**	**US**	**BK**	**←Courts — FRANKLIN**	**Recorder→**	**UC**	**RE**	**TX**	**VS**
•	•	•	•	•	NC Corporate Connection Inc.	888-844-8360	•	•	•	•
•	•	•	•	•	Paralegal Services of North Carolina Inc [SOP]	919-821-7762	•	•	•	•
•	•				Poindexter & Associates Inc [SOP]	800-373-2804				
•	•	•	•	•	Searchtec (Carolinas) [SOP]	800-528-8790	•	•	•	•
•	•	•	•	•	Title Searches by Liz Aulis	919-878-0227; cell- 919-395-7433	•	•	•	•
CR	**CV**	**PR**	**US**	**BK**	**←Courts — GASTON**	**Recorder→**	**UC**	**RE**	**TX**	**VS**
•	•	•	•	•	Axis Research Inc	877-795-1005	•	•	•	
•	•	•	•	•	Barefoot Private Investigations [SOP]	704-377-1000	•	•	•	
•	•	•	•	•	NC Corporate Connection Inc.	888-844-8360	•	•	•	•
•	•		•	•	Reynolds Professional Service Inc [SOP]	800-814-8662				•
•	•	•	•	•	Searchtec (Carolinas) [SOP]	800-528-8790	•	•	•	•
•	•	•	•		The Henry Agency [SOP]	704-526-5030				
CR	**CV**	**PR**	**US**	**BK**	**←Courts — GATES**	**Recorder→**	**UC**	**RE**	**TX**	**VS**
•	•	•	•	•	Hornthal Riley Ellis & Maland	252-335-0871	•	•	•	•
•	•	•	•	•	Searchtec (Carolinas) [SOP]	800-528-8790	•	•	•	•
CR	**CV**	**PR**	**US**	**BK**	**←Courts — GRAHAM**	**Recorder→**	**UC**	**RE**	**TX**	**VS**
					See adjoining counties for retrievers or call court/recorder directly.					
CR	**CV**	**PR**	**US**	**BK**	**←Courts — GRANVILLE**	**Recorder→**	**UC**	**RE**	**TX**	**VS**
•	•	•	•	•	NC Corporate Connection Inc.	888-844-8360	•	•	•	•
•	•				Poindexter & Associates Inc [SOP]	800-373-2804				
•	•	•	•	•	Searchtec (Carolinas) [SOP]	800-528-8790	•	•	•	•
•	•	•	•	•	Title Searches by Liz Aulis	919-878-0227; cell- 919-395-7433	•	•	•	•
CR	**CV**	**PR**	**US**	**BK**	**←Courts — GREENE**	**Recorder→**	**UC**	**RE**	**TX**	**VS**
	•	•			Paralegal Enterprises Inc	252-758-6622				
•	•	•	•	•	Searchtec (Carolinas) [SOP]	800-528-8790	•	•	•	•

CR	CV	PR	US	BK	←Courts	**Guilford**	Recorder→	UC	RE	TX	VS
•	•		•		Agency-One Inv [SOP]		800-557-5500	•	•	•	•
•	•	•	•	•	Paralegal Services of North Carolina Inc [SOP]		919-821-7762	•	•	•	•
•	•	•	•	•	Searchtec (Carolinas) [SOP]		800-528-8790	•	•	•	•

CR	CV	PR	US	BK	←Courts	**Halifax**	Recorder→	UC	RE	TX	VS
•	•	•	•	•	Searchtec (Carolinas) [SOP]		800-528-8790	•	•	•	•
•	•	•			Ward Abstracting Services		252-535-3440	•	•	•	•

CR	CV	PR	US	BK	←Courts	**Harnett**	Recorder→	UC	RE	TX	VS
					Abstract Art Inc		910-592-2972	•	•	•	•
•	•	•	•	•	ASK Services Inc (North Carolina)		888-416-1313	•	•	•	•
•	•	•			Carolina Investigative Research Inc [SOP]		800-328-8981	•	•	•	•
•	•	•	•	•	NC Corporate Connection Inc.		888-844-8360	•	•	•	•
•	•	•	•	•	Paralegal Services of North Carolina Inc [SOP]		919-821-7762	•	•	•	•
•	•				Poindexter & Associates Inc [SOP]		800-373-2804				
•	•	•	•	•	Searchtec (Carolinas) [SOP]		800-528-8790	•	•	•	•

CR	CV	PR	US	BK	←Courts	**Haywood**	Recorder→	UC	RE	TX	VS
•	•	•	•	•	Ramsey Paralegal/Process [SOP]		828-687-9974; send faxes to Attn. Don Ramsey	•	•	•	•
•	•	•			Kathi Watson		828-648-5830	•	•	•	•
•	•		•	•	WNC Search Service		828-768-0062	•	•	•	

CR	CV	PR	US	BK	←Courts	**Henderson**	Recorder→	UC	RE	TX	VS
•	•	•	•	•	Paralegal Services Inc		828-606-8297	•	•	•	•
•	•	•	•	•	Ramsey Paralegal/Process [SOP]		828-687-9974; send faxes to Attn. Don Ramsey	•	•	•	•
•	•		•	•	WNC Search Service		828-768-0062	•	•	•	

CR	CV	PR	US	BK	←Courts	**Hertford**	Recorder→	UC	RE	TX	VS
•	•	•	•	•	Hornthal Riley Ellis & Maland		252-335-0871	•	•	•	•
•	•	•	•	•	Searchtec (Carolinas) [SOP]		800-528-8790	•	•	•	•

CR	CV	PR	US	BK	←Courts	**Hoke**	Recorder→	UC	RE	TX	VS
•	•	•			Carolina Investigative Research Inc [SOP]		800-328-8981	•	•	•	•
•	•	•	•	•	Searchtec (Carolinas) [SOP]		800-528-8790	•	•	•	•

CR	CV	PR	US	BK	←Courts	**Hyde**	Recorder→	UC	RE	TX	VS
•	•	•	•	•	Searchtec (Carolinas) [SOP]		800-528-8790	•	•	•	•

CR	CV	PR	US	BK	←Courts	**Iredell**	Recorder→	UC	RE	TX	VS
	•			•	Victoria J Armes		704-663-4085	•	•	•	
•	•		•	•	Reynolds Professional Service Inc [SOP]		800-814-8662				•
•	•	•	•	•	Searchtec (Carolinas) [SOP]		800-528-8790	•	•	•	•
•	•	•	•		The Henry Agency [SOP]		704-526-5030	•	•	•	•
•	•	•	•	•	Track' Um Private Investigations [SOP]		877-634-9106	•	•	•	•

CR	CV	PR	US	BK	←Courts	**Jackson**	Recorder→	UC	RE	TX	VS
•	•	•	•	•	Ramsey Paralegal/Process [SOP]		828-687-9974; send faxes to Attn. Don Ramsey	•	•	•	•
•	•	•			Kathi Watson		828-648-5830	•	•	•	•

CR	CV	PR	US	BK	←Courts	**Johnston**	Recorder→	UC	RE	TX	VS
					Abstract Art Inc		910-592-2972	•	•	•	•
•	•	•	•	•	ASK Services Inc (North Carolina)		888-416-1313	•	•	•	•
•	•	•			Carolina Investigative Research Inc [SOP]		800-328-8981	•	•	•	•
•	•	•	•	•	NC Corporate Connection Inc.		888-844-8360	•	•	•	•
•	•	•	•	•	Paralegal Services of North Carolina Inc [SOP]		919-821-7762	•	•	•	•
•	•				Poindexter & Associates Inc [SOP]		800-373-2804				
•	•	•	•	•	Searchtec (Carolinas) [SOP]		800-528-8790	•	•	•	•

CR	CV	PR	US	BK	←Courts	**Jones**	Recorder→	UC	RE	TX	VS
•	•	•	•	•	Searchtec (Carolinas) [SOP]		800-528-8790	•	•	•	•
					Cheryl Smith		252-633-3890	•	•		

CR	CV	PR	US	BK	←Courts	Lee	Recorder→	UC	RE	TX	VS
•	•	•	•	•	ASK Services Inc (North Carolina)		888-416-1313	•	•	•	•
•	•	•			Carolina Investigative Research Inc [SOP]		800-328-8981	•	•	•	•
•	•	•	•	•	Searchtec (Carolinas) [SOP]		800-528-8790	•	•	•	•

CR	CV	PR	US	BK	←Courts	Lenoir	Recorder→	UC	RE	TX	VS
	•				Sue P Hamm		252-322-5015	•	•	•	•
•	•	•	•	•	Searchtec (Carolinas) [SOP]		800-528-8790	•	•	•	•

CR	CV	PR	US	BK	←Courts	Lincoln	Recorder→	UC	RE	TX	VS
	•			•	Victoria J Armes		704-663-4085	•	•	•	
•	•	•	•	•	Axis Research Inc		877-795-1005	•	•	•	
•	•	•	•	•	NC Corporate Connection Inc.		888-844-8360	•	•	•	•
•	•		•	•	Reynolds Professional Service Inc [SOP]		800-814-8662				•
•	•	•	•		The Henry Agency [SOP]		704-526-5030	•	•	•	•

CR	CV	PR	US	BK	←Courts	Macon	Recorder→	UC	RE	TX	VS
•	•	•	•	•	Ramsey Paralegal/Process [SOP]		828-687-9974; send faxes to Attn. Don Ramsey	•	•	•	•

CR	CV	PR	US	BK	←Courts	Madison	Recorder→	UC	RE	TX	VS
•	•	•	•	•	Ramsey Paralegal/Process [SOP]		828-687-9974; send faxes to Attn. Don Ramsey	•	•	•	•
•	•		•	•	WNC Search Service		828-768-0062	•	•	•	

CR	CV	PR	US	BK	←Courts	Martin	Recorder→	UC	RE	TX	VS
•	•	•	•	•	Searchtec (Carolinas) [SOP]		800-528-8790	•	•	•	•

CR	CV	PR	US	BK	←Courts	McDowell	Recorder→	UC	RE	TX	VS
•	•	•	•	•	Paralegal Services Inc		828-606-8297	•	•	•	•
•	•	•	•	•	Ramsey Paralegal/Process [SOP]		828-687-9974; send faxes to Attn. Don Ramsey	•	•	•	•
•	•		•	•	WNC Search Service		828-768-0062	•	•	•	

CR	CV	PR	US	BK	←Courts	Mecklenburg	Recorder→	UC	RE	TX	VS
•	•	•	•	•	Axis Research Inc		877-795-1005	•	•	•	
•	•	•	•	•	Barefoot Private Investigations [SOP]		704-377-1000	•	•	•	
	•	•			DiSearch		704-846-6335	•	•	•	
•	•	•	•	•	NC Corporate Connection Inc.		888-844-8360	•	•	•	•
•	•		•	•	Reynolds Professional Service Inc [SOP]		800-814-8662				•
•	•	•	•	•	Searchtec (Carolinas) [SOP]		800-528-8790	•	•	•	•
•	•	•	•		The Henry Agency [SOP]		704-526-5030	•	•	•	•

CR	CV	PR	US	BK	←Courts	Mitchell	Recorder→	UC	RE	TX	VS
•	•				Asset Protection Associates Inc		828-765-9359				
•	•	•	•	•	Paralegal Services Inc		828-606-8297	•	•	•	•
•	•	•	•	•	Searchtec (Carolinas) [SOP]		800-528-8790	•	•	•	•

CR	CV	PR	US	BK	←Courts	Montgomery	Recorder→	UC	RE	TX	VS
•	•	•	•	•	Searchtec (Carolinas) [SOP]		800-528-8790	•	•	•	•

CR	CV	PR	US	BK	←Courts	Moore	Recorder→	UC	RE	TX	VS
•	•	•			Carolina Investigative Research Inc [SOP]		800-328-8981	•	•	•	•
•	•	•	•	•	Searchtec (Carolinas) [SOP]		800-528-8790	•	•	•	•

CR	CV	PR	US	BK	←Courts	Nash	Recorder→	UC	RE	TX	VS
•	•	•	•	•	NC Corporate Connection Inc.		888-844-8360	•	•	•	•
•	•	•	•	•	Paralegal Services of North Carolina Inc [SOP]		919-821-7762	•	•	•	•
•	•	•	•	•	Searchtec (Carolinas) [SOP]		800-528-8790	•	•	•	•

CR	CV	PR	US	BK	←Courts	New Hanover	Recorder→	UC	RE	TX	VS
•	•	•	•	•	Searchtec (Carolinas) [SOP]		800-528-8790	•	•	•	•

CR	CV	PR	US	BK	←Courts	Northampton	Recorder→	UC	RE	TX	VS
•	•	•	•	•	Searchtec (Carolinas) [SOP]		800-528-8790	•	•	•	•
•	•	•			Ward Abstracting Services		252-535-3440	•	•	•	•

CR	CV	PR	US	BK	←Courts ONSLOW	Recorder→	UC	RE	TX	VS
•	•	•	•	•	Searchtec (Carolinas) [SOP]	800-528-8790	•	•	•	•

CR	CV	PR	US	BK	←Courts ORANGE	Recorder→	UC	RE	TX	VS
•	•	•	•	•	ASK Services Inc (North Carolina)	888-416-1313	•	•	•	•
•	•	•	•	•	NC Corporate Connection Inc	888-844-8360	•	•	•	•
•	•	•	•	•	Paralegal Services of North Carolina Inc [SOP]	919-821-7762	•	•	•	•
•	•	•	•	•	Searchtec (Carolinas) [SOP]	800-528-8790	•	•	•	•
•	•	•	•	•	Title Searches by Liz Aulis	919-878-0227; cell- 919-395-7433	•	•	•	•

CR	CV	PR	US	BK	←Courts PAMLICO	Recorder→	UC	RE	TX	VS
	•				Sue P Hamm	252-322-5015	•	•	•	•
•	•	•	•	•	Searchtec (Carolinas) [SOP]	800-528-8790	•	•	•	•
					Cheryl Smith	252-633-3890	•	•		

CR	CV	PR	US	BK	←Courts PASQUOTANK	Recorder→	UC	RE	TX	VS
•	•	•	•	•	Hornthal Riley Ellis & Maland	252-335-0871	•	•	•	•
•	•	•	•	•	Searchtec (Carolinas) [SOP]	800-528-8790	•	•	•	•

CR	CV	PR	US	BK	←Courts PENDER	Recorder→	UC	RE	TX	VS
•	•	•	•	•	Searchtec (Carolinas) [SOP]	800-528-8790	•	•	•	•

CR	CV	PR	US	BK	←Courts PERQUIMANS	Recorder→	UC	RE	TX	VS
•	•	•	•	•	Hornthal Riley Ellis & Maland	252-335-0871	•	•	•	•
•	•	•	•	•	Searchtec (Carolinas) [SOP]	800-528-8790	•	•	•	•

CR	CV	PR	US	BK	←Courts PERSON	Recorder→	UC	RE	TX	VS
•	•	•	•	•	Searchtec (Carolinas) [SOP]	800-528-8790	•	•	•	•
•	•	•	•	•	Title Searches by Liz Aulis	919-878-0227; cell- 919-395-7433	•	•	•	•

CR	CV	PR	US	BK	←Courts PITT	Recorder→	UC	RE	TX	VS
	•				Sue P Hamm	252-322-5015	•	•	•	•
	•	•			Paralegal Enterprises Inc	252-758-6622	•	•	•	•
•	•	•	•	•	Searchtec (Carolinas) [SOP]	800-528-8790	•	•	•	•

CR	CV	PR	US	BK	←Courts POLK	Recorder→	UC	RE	TX	VS
•	•	•	•	•	Paralegal Services Inc	828-606-8297	•	•	•	•
•	•	•	•	•	Ramsey Paralegal/Process [SOP]	828-687-9974; send faxes to Attn. Don Ramsey	•	•	•	•
•	•		•	•	WNC Search Service	828-768-0062	•	•	•	

CR	CV	PR	US	BK	←Courts RANDOLPH	Recorder→	UC	RE	TX	VS
•	•	•	•	•	Searchtec (Carolinas) [SOP]	800-528-8790	•	•	•	•

CR	CV	PR	US	BK	←Courts RICHMOND	Recorder→	UC	RE	TX	VS
•	•	•	•	•	Searchtec (Carolinas) [SOP]	800-528-8790	•	•	•	•

CR	CV	PR	US	BK	←Courts ROBESON	Recorder→	UC	RE	TX	VS
	•	•			Accurate Data	910-862-4949	•		•	
•	•	•	•	•	Searchtec (Carolinas) [SOP]	800-528-8790	•	•	•	•

CR	CV	PR	US	BK	←Courts ROCKINGHAM	Recorder→	UC	RE	TX	VS
•	•		•		Agency-One Inv [SOP]	800-557-5500	•	•	•	•
•	•	•	•	•	Searchtec (Carolinas) [SOP]	800-528-8790	•	•	•	•

CR	CV	PR	US	BK	←Courts ROWAN	Recorder→	UC	RE	TX	VS
•	•		•		Agency-One Inv [SOP]	800-557-5500	•	•	•	•
	•			•	Victoria J Armes	704-663-4085	•	•	•	
•	•	•	•	•	Axis Research Inc	877-795-1005	•	•	•	
•	•	•	•	•	NC Corporate Connection Inc	888-844-8360	•	•	•	•
•	•				Poindexter & Associates Inc [SOP]	800-373-2804				
•	•		•	•	Reynolds Professional Service Inc [SOP]	800-814-8662				•
•	•	•	•	•	Searchtec (Carolinas) [SOP]	800-528-8790	•	•	•	

CR	CV	PR	US	BK	←Courts **Rutherford**	Recorder→	UC	RE	TX	VS
•	•	•	•	•	Paralegal Services Inc	828-606-8297	•	•	•	•
•	•	•	•	•	Ramsey Paralegal/Process [SOP]	828-687-9974; send faxes to Attn. Don Ramsey	•	•	•	•
•	•		•	•	WNC Search Service	828-768-0062	•	•	•	

CR	CV	PR	US	BK	←Courts **Sampson**	Recorder→	UC	RE	TX	VS
					Abstract Art Inc	910-592-2972	•	•	•	•
	•	•			Accurate Data	910-862-4949	•		•	
•	•	•	•	•	Searchtec (Carolinas) [SOP]	800-528-8790	•	•	•	•

CR	CV	PR	US	BK	←Courts **Scotland**	Recorder→	UC	RE	TX	VS
•	•		•	•	Searchtec (Carolinas) [SOP]	800-528-8790	•	•	•	•

CR	CV	PR	US	BK	←Courts **Stanly**	Recorder→	UC	RE	TX	VS
•	•		•	•	Reynolds Professional Service Inc [SOP]	800-814-8662				•
•	•	•	•	•	Searchtec (Carolinas) [SOP]	800-528-8790	•	•	•	•
•	•	•	•		The Henry Agency [SOP]	704-526-5030	•	•	•	•

CR	CV	PR	US	BK	←Courts **Stokes**	Recorder→	UC	RE	TX	VS
•	•		•		Agency-One Inv [SOP]	800-557-5500	•	•	•	•
•	•	•	•	•	Searchtec (Carolinas) [SOP]	800-528-8790	•	•	•	•

CR	CV	PR	US	BK	←Courts **Surry**	Recorder→	UC	RE	TX	VS
•	•		•		Agency-One Inv [SOP]	800-557-5500	•	•	•	•
•	•	•	•	•	Searchtec (Carolinas) [SOP]	800-528-8790	•	•	•	•
•	•	•	•	•	Track' Um Private Investigations [SOP]	877-634-9106	•	•	•	•

CR	CV	PR	US	BK	←Courts **Swain**	Recorder→	UC	RE	TX	VS
•	•	•	•	•	Ramsey Paralegal/Process [SOP]	828-687-9974; send faxes to Attn. Don Ramsey	•	•	•	•

CR	CV	PR	US	BK	←Courts **Transylvania**	Recorder→	UC	RE	TX	VS
•	•	•	•	•	Ramsey Paralegal/Process [SOP]	828-687-9974; send faxes to Attn. Don Ramsey	•	•	•	•
•	•		•	•	WNC Search Service	828-768-0062	•	•	•	

CR	CV	PR	US	BK	←Courts **Tyrrell**	Recorder→	UC	RE	TX	VS
•	•	•	•	•	Hornthal Riley Ellis & Maland	252-335-0871	•	•	•	•
•	•	•	•	•	Searchtec (Carolinas) [SOP]	800-528-8790	•	•	•	•

CR	CV	PR	US	BK	←Courts **Union**	Recorder→	UC	RE	TX	VS
•	•	•	•	•	Axis Research Inc	877-795-1005	•	•	•	
	•	•			DiSearch	704-846-6335	•	•	•	
•	•	•	•	•	NC Corporate Connection Inc.	888-844-8360	•	•	•	•
•	•	•	•	•	Searchtec (Carolinas) [SOP]	800-528-8790	•	•	•	•
•	•	•	•		The Henry Agency [SOP]	704-526-5030	•	•	•	•

CR	CV	PR	US	BK	←Courts **Vance**	Recorder→	UC	RE	TX	VS
•	•				Poindexter & Associates Inc [SOP]	800-373-2804				
•	•	•	•	•	Searchtec (Carolinas) [SOP]	800-528-8790	•	•	•	•
•	•	•	•	•	Title Searches by Liz Aulis	919-878-0227; cell- 919-395-7433	•	•	•	•

CR	CV	PR	US	BK	←Courts **Wake**	Recorder→	UC	RE	TX	VS
•	•	•	•	•	ASK Services Inc (North Carolina)	888-416-1313	•	•	•	•
•	•	•			Carolina Investigative Research Inc [SOP]	800-328-8981	•	•	•	•
•	•		•	•	For The Record Inc	919-836-7559				
•	•		•	•	NC Corporate Connection Inc.	888-844-8360	•	•	•	•
•	•	•	•	•	Paralegal Services of North Carolina Inc [SOP]	919-821-7762	•	•	•	•
•	•				Poindexter & Associates Inc [SOP]	800-373-2804				
	•		•	•	Search Services	919-801-3010	•		•	•
•	•	•	•	•	Searchtec (Carolinas) [SOP]	800-528-8790	•	•	•	•
•	•	•	•	•	Title Searches by Liz Aulis	919-878-0227; cell- 919-395-7433	•	•	•	•

CR	CV	PR	US	BK	←Courts	WARREN	Recorder→	UC	RE	TX	VS
•	•				Poindexter & Associates Inc [SOP]		800-373-2804				
•	•	•	•	•	Searchtec (Carolinas) [SOP]		800-528-8790	•	•	•	•
•	•	•	•	•	Title Searches by Liz Aulis		919-878-0227; cell- 919-395-7433	•	•	•	•
•	•	•			Ward Abstracting Services		252-535-3440	•	•	•	•

CR	CV	PR	US	BK	←Courts	WASHINGTON	Recorder→	UC	RE	TX	VS
•	•	•	•	•	Hornthal Riley Ellis & Maland		252-335-0871	•	•	•	•
•	•	•	•	•	Searchtec (Carolinas) [SOP]		800-528-8790	•	•	•	•

CR	CV	PR	US	BK	←Courts	WATAUGA	Recorder→	UC	RE	TX	VS
	•	•			Miller & Johnson PLLC		828-264-1125	•	•	•	
•	•	•	•	•	Searchtec (Carolinas) [SOP]		800-528-8790	•	•	•	•
•	•	•	•	•	Track' Um Private Investigations [SOP]		877-634-9106	•	•	•	•

CR	CV	PR	US	BK	←Courts	WAYNE	Recorder→	UC	RE	TX	VS
					Abstract Art Inc		910-592-2972	•	•	•	•
•	•	•	•	•	Paralegal Services of North Carolina Inc [SOP]		919-821-7762	•	•	•	•
•	•	•	•	•	Searchtec (Carolinas) [SOP]		800-528-8790	•	•	•	•

CR	CV	PR	US	BK	←Courts	WILKES	Recorder→	UC	RE	TX	VS
•	•	•	•	•	Searchtec (Carolinas) [SOP]		800-528-8790	•	•	•	•
•	•	•	•	•	Track' Um Private Investigations [SOP]		877-634-9106	•	•	•	•

CR	CV	PR	US	BK	←Courts	WILSON	Recorder→	UC	RE	TX	VS
•	•	•	•	•	Searchtec (Carolinas) [SOP]		800-528-8790	•	•	•	•

CR	CV	PR	US	BK	←Courts	YADKIN	Recorder→	UC	RE	TX	VS
•	•		•		Agency-One Inv [SOP]		800-557-5500	•	•	•	•
•	•	•	•	•	Searchtec (Carolinas) [SOP]		800-528-8790	•	•	•	•
•	•	•	•	•	Track' Um Private Investigations [SOP]		877-634-9106	•	•	•	•

CR	CV	PR	US	BK	←Courts	YANCEY	Recorder→	UC	RE	TX	VS
•	•				Asset Protection Associates Inc		828-765-9359				
•	•	•	•	•	Ramsey Paralegal/Process [SOP]		828-687-9974; send faxes to Attn. Don Ramsey	•	•	•	•

[SOP] = Performs service of process

Editor's Tip: In the interest of compiling a concise index with less than 5,000 pages, the Local Retrievers County Index does not indicate counties where a firm provides document retrieval services using hired correspondents and non-employees. Correspondent Relationships are indicated in a Retriever's Profile.

North Dakota

Court Records Retrieved — Capital - Burleigh County — Recorded Records Retrieved

CR	CV	PR	US	BK	←Courts	Adams	Recorder→	UC	RE	TX	VS
					Adams County Abstract Co		701-567-2224	•	•	•	
•	•	•			Gion Law Office		701-563-4354	•	•	•	•

CR	CV	PR	US	BK	←Courts	Barnes	Recorder→	UC	RE	TX	VS
•	•	•			Credit Bureau of Valley City		701-845-3912	•	•	•	•
•	•				Hons Investigations [SOP]		800-450-4667				

CR	CV	PR	US	BK	←Courts	Benson	Recorder→	UC	RE	TX	VS
•	•				Hons Investigations [SOP]		800-450-4667				
	•	•			Surety Title Co		701-947-2446	•	•	•	

CR	CV	PR	US	BK	←Courts	Billings	Recorder→	UC	RE	TX	VS
					See adjoining counties for retrievers or call court/recorder directly.						

CR	CV	PR	US	BK	←Courts	Bottineau	Recorder→	UC	RE	TX	VS
•	•				Hons Investigations [SOP]		800-450-4667				

CR	CV	PR	US	BK	←Courts	Bowman	Recorder→	UC	RE	TX	VS
•	•	•			Gion Law Office		701-563-4354	•	•	•	•
•	•				Hons Investigations [SOP]		800-450-4667				
	•	•	•		Southwest Abstract & Title Company		701-523-2922	•	•	•	

CR	CV	PR	US	BK	←Courts	Burke	Recorder→	UC	RE	TX	VS
	•	•	•		Mountrail County Abstract & Title Co		701-628-2886	•	•	•	
	•				Northwest Abstract & Title Inc		800-798-6723	•	•	•	

CR	CV	PR	US	BK	←Courts	Burleigh	Recorder→	UC	RE	TX	VS
•	•	•			Bismarck Title Co		701-222-4247	•	•	•	
•	•	•	•	•	Butcher & Associates Ltd [SOP]		701-224-1541	•	•	•	•
•	•				Hons Investigations [SOP]		800-450-4667				
•	•	•	•	•	Search Company of North Dakota LLC [SOP]		701-223-1848	•	•	•	•

CR	CV	PR	US	BK	←Courts	Cass	Recorder→	UC	RE	TX	VS
•	•	•	•	•	Butcher & Associates Ltd [SOP]		701-224-1541	•	•	•	•
•	•	•	•	•	C.C.I. [SOP]		701-235-4842	•	•	•	
					Cass County Abstract Co (North Dakota)		701-232-3341	•	•	•	
	•	•	•	•	Clay County Abstract Co [SOP]		218-233-1358	•	•	•	
•	•				Hons Investigations [SOP]		800-450-4667				
•	•	•	•	•	Search Company of North Dakota LLC [SOP]		701-223-1848	•	•	•	•

CR	CV	PR	US	BK	←Courts	Cavalier	Recorder→	UC	RE	TX	VS
•	•				Hons Investigations [SOP]		800-450-4667				
	•		•	•	McHugh Abstract Co		701-256-2851	•	•	•	•
•	•	•			Welch & Ekman		701-284-7833	•	•	•	•

CR	CV	PR	US	BK	←Courts	Dickey	Recorder→	UC	RE	TX	VS
•	•	•	•	•	Dickey County Abstract & Title		701-349-3450	•	•	•	•
•	•				Hons Investigations [SOP]		800-450-4667				

CR	CV	PR	US	BK	←Courts	Divide	Recorder→	UC	RE	TX	VS
					Divide Abstract Co		701-965-6352, 701-965-2222		•	•	

CR	CV	PR	US	BK	←Courts	Dunn	Recorder→	UC	RE	TX	VS
•	•				Hons Investigations [SOP]		800-450-4667				
	•				Northwest Abstract & Title Inc		800-798-6723	•	•	•	

CR	CV	PR	US	BK	←Courts	Eddy	Recorder→	UC	RE	TX	VS
•	•				Hons Investigations [SOP]		800-450-4667				
	•	•			Surety Title Co		701-947-2446	•	•	•	

CR	CV	PR	US	BK	←Courts	Emmons	Recorder→	UC	RE	TX	VS
					Emmons County Abstract & Title		701-254-4261	•	•	•	
•	•				Hons Investigations [SOP]		800-450-4667				

CR	CV	PR	US	BK	←Courts	Foster	Recorder→	UC	RE	TX	VS
	•	•			Foster County Abstract & Title		701-652-3164	•	•	•	•

CR	CV	PR	US	BK	←Courts	Golden Valley	Recorder→	UC	RE	TX	VS
					See adjoining counties for retrievers or call court/recorder directly.						

CR	CV	PR	US	BK	←Courts	Grand Forks	Recorder→	UC	RE	TX	VS
	•				Grand Forks Abstract & Title Co		701-772-3484	•	•	•	
•	•				Hons Investigations [SOP]		800-450-4667				

CR	CV	PR	US	BK	←Courts	Grant	Recorder→	UC	RE	TX	VS
•	•	•			Gion Law Office		701-563-4354	•	•	•	•

CR	CV	PR	US	BK	←Courts	Griggs	Recorder→	UC	RE	TX	VS
	•	•			Surety Title Co		701-947-2446	•	•	•	

CR	CV	PR	US	BK	←Courts	Hettinger	Recorder→	UC	RE	TX	VS
•	•	•			Gion Law Office		701-563-4354	•	•	•	•
	•		•	•	Hettinger-Sioux County Abstractors Inc		701-824-3148	•	•	•	•

CR	CV	PR	US	BK	←Courts	Kidder	Recorder→	UC	RE	TX	VS
					Kidder County Abstract Co		701-475-2432	•	•	•	

CR	CV	PR	US	BK	←Courts	La Moure	Recorder→	UC	RE	TX	VS
					LaMoure County Abstract Co		701-883-4246		•	•	
					Stutsman County Abstract		701-252-4870	•	•	•	

CR	CV	PR	US	BK	←Courts	Logan	Recorder→	UC	RE	TX	VS
	•				Logan County Abstract Co		701-754-2200	•	•	•	

CR	CV	PR	US	BK	←Courts	McHenry	Recorder→	UC	RE	TX	VS
•	•	•	•		McHenry County Abstract & Title Co		701-537-5723	•	•	•	

CR	CV	PR	US	BK	←Courts	McIntosh	Recorder→	UC	RE	TX	VS
•	•	•			Abstracts of McIntosh County Inc		701-288-3618	•	•	•	•
	•				Ashley Abstract Co		701-288-3584	•	•	•	•

CR	CV	PR	US	BK	←Courts	McKenzie	Recorder→	UC	RE	TX	VS
	•	•			Abstract &Title Co		701-842-3366	•	•	•	
	•	•	•	•	Mountrail County Abstract & Title Co		701-628-2886	•	•	•	

CR	CV	PR	US	BK	←Courts	McLean	Recorder→	UC	RE	TX	VS
•	•				Hons Investigations [SOP]		800-450-4667				
•	•	•	•	•	McLean County Abstract Inc		701-462-3244	•	•	•	•

CR	CV	PR	US	BK	←Courts	Mercer	Recorder→	UC	RE	TX	VS
•	•				Hons Investigations [SOP]		800-450-4667				
	•				Mercer County Abstract Co Inc		701-748-2190		•	•	
	•	•	•	•	Oliver County Abstract		701-794-3496	•	•	•	

CR	CV	PR	US	BK	←Courts	Morton	Recorder→	UC	RE	TX	VS
•	•	•			Bismarck Title Co		701-222-4247	•	•	•	

CR	CV	PR	US	BK	←Courts		Recorder→	UC	RE	TX	VS
•	•	•	•	•	Butcher & Associates Ltd [SOP]		701-224-1541	•	•	•	•
•	•				Hons Investigations [SOP]		800-450-4667				
•	•	•	•	•	🏛Search Company of North Dakota LLC [SOP]		701-223-1848	•	•	•	•
CR	**CV**	**PR**	**US**	**BK**	**←Courts**	**MOUNTRAIL**	**Recorder→**	**UC**	**RE**	**TX**	**VS**
•	•				Hons Investigations [SOP]		800-450-4667				
	•	•	•	•	Mountrail County Abstract & Title Co		701-628-2886	•	•	•	
CR	**CV**	**PR**	**US**	**BK**	**←Courts**	**NELSON**	**Recorder→**	**UC**	**RE**	**TX**	**VS**
					See adjoining counties for retrievers or call court/recorder directly.						
CR	**CV**	**PR**	**US**	**BK**	**←Courts**	**OLIVER**	**Recorder→**	**UC**	**RE**	**TX**	**VS**
	•	•	•	•	Oliver County Abstract		701-794-3496	•	•	•	
CR	**CV**	**PR**	**US**	**BK**	**←Courts**	**PEMBINA**	**Recorder→**	**UC**	**RE**	**TX**	**VS**
					A Short Abstract Co		701-265-4176		•	•	
•	•				Hons Investigations [SOP]		800-450-4667				
•	•	•			Welch & Ekman		701-284-7833	•	•	•	•
CR	**CV**	**PR**	**US**	**BK**	**←Courts**	**PIERCE**	**Recorder→**	**UC**	**RE**	**TX**	**VS**
•	•				Hons Investigations [SOP]		800-450-4667				
	•	•			Pierce County Abstract		701-776-7777, Fax-same	•	•	•	
CR	**CV**	**PR**	**US**	**BK**	**←Courts**	**RAMSEY**	**Recorder→**	**UC**	**RE**	**TX**	**VS**
•	•				Hons Investigations [SOP]		800-450-4667				
CR	**CV**	**PR**	**US**	**BK**	**←Courts**	**RANSOM**	**Recorder→**	**UC**	**RE**	**TX**	**VS**
					Ransom County Title Co		701-683-5511; Fax- same		•	•	
CR	**CV**	**PR**	**US**	**BK**	**←Courts**	**RENVILLE**	**Recorder→**	**UC**	**RE**	**TX**	**VS**
					Myaer & Co Inc		701-756-6487	•	•	•	
CR	**CV**	**PR**	**US**	**BK**	**←Courts**	**RICHLAND**	**Recorder→**	**UC**	**RE**	**TX**	**VS**
•	•				Hons Investigations [SOP]		800-450-4667				
•	•	•			PRN Abstract & Title Co		701-642-3781	•	•	•	•
CR	**CV**	**PR**	**US**	**BK**	**←Courts**	**ROLETTE**	**Recorder→**	**UC**	**RE**	**TX**	**VS**
•	•				Hons Investigations [SOP]		800-450-4667				
•	•	•			Rolette County Abstract Inc		701-477-3149	•	•	•	•
CR	**CV**	**PR**	**US**	**BK**	**←Courts**	**SARGENT**	**Recorder→**	**UC**	**RE**	**TX**	**VS**
					See adjoining counties for retrievers or call court/recorder directly.						
CR	**CV**	**PR**	**US**	**BK**	**←Courts**	**SHERIDAN**	**Recorder→**	**UC**	**RE**	**TX**	**VS**
•	•	•	•		McHenry County Abstract & Title Co		701-537-5723	•	•	•	
CR	**CV**	**PR**	**US**	**BK**	**←Courts**	**SIOUX**	**Recorder→**	**UC**	**RE**	**TX**	**VS**
	•		•	•	Hettinger-Sioux County Abstractors Inc		701-824-3148	•	•	•	•
CR	**CV**	**PR**	**US**	**BK**	**←Courts**	**SLOPE**	**Recorder→**	**UC**	**RE**	**TX**	**VS**
•	•	•			Gion Law Office		701-563-4354	•	•	•	•
	•	•	•		Southwest Abstract & Title Company		701-523-2922	•	•	•	
CR	**CV**	**PR**	**US**	**BK**	**←Courts**	**STARK**	**Recorder→**	**UC**	**RE**	**TX**	**VS**
•	•	•			Gion Law Office		701-563-4354	•	•	•	•
•	•				Hons Investigations [SOP]		800-450-4667				
CR	**CV**	**PR**	**US**	**BK**	**←Courts**	**STEELE**	**Recorder→**	**UC**	**RE**	**TX**	**VS**
	•				M B Cassell		701-524-1961		•	•	
CR	**CV**	**PR**	**US**	**BK**	**←Courts**	**STUTSMAN**	**Recorder→**	**UC**	**RE**	**TX**	**VS**
•	•				Hons Investigations [SOP]		800-450-4667				
					Stutsman County Abstract		701-252-4870			•	

CR	CV	PR	US	BK	←COURTS TOWNER	RECORDER→	UC	RE	TX	VS
					Towner County Abstract Co	701-968-3006		•	•	

CR	CV	PR	US	BK	←COURTS TRAILL	RECORDER→	UC	RE	TX	VS
	•				Traill County Abstract	701-636-4880	•	•	•	

CR	CV	PR	US	BK	←COURTS WALSH	RECORDER→	UC	RE	TX	VS
•	•				Hons Investigations [SOP]	800-450-4667				
•	•	•			Welch & Ekman	701-284-7833	•	•	•	•

CR	CV	PR	US	BK	←COURTS WARD	RECORDER→	UC	RE	TX	VS
•	•	•	•		Devine & Co Inc	701-852-6800		•	•	
•	•				Hons Investigations [SOP]	800-450-4667				
	•	•	•	•	Mountrail County Abstract & Title Co	701-628-2886	•	•	•	

CR	CV	PR	US	BK	←COURTS WELLS	RECORDER→	UC	RE	TX	VS
					Wells County Abstract	701-547-3433			•	

CR	CV	PR	US	BK	←COURTS WILLIAMS	RECORDER→	UC	RE	TX	VS
•	•				Hons Investigations [SOP]	800-450-4667				
	•	•	•	•	Mountrail County Abstract & Title Co	701-628-2886	•	•	•	
	•				Northwest Abstract & Title Inc	800-798-6723	•	•	•	

[SOP] = PERFORMS SERVICE OF PROCESS

= PRRN Member. *A retriever you can trust!*

COURT RECORDS

CODE	GOVERNMENT AGENCY	TYPE OF INFORMATION
CR	Criminal Court	Municipal, county and state level criminal cases
CV	Civil Court	Municipal, county and state level civil cases
PR	Probate Court	Wills and estate cases
US	US District Court	Federal civil and criminal cases
BK	Bankruptcy Court	United States bankruptcy cases

COUNTY RECORDS - RECORDINGS

CODE	GOVERNMENT AGENCY	TYPE OF INFORMATION
UC	UCC Filing Office	Uniform Commercial Code and other personal property liens
RE	Real Estate Recording Office	Real property transactions and liens
TX	Tax Filing Office(s)	Federal and state tax liens, judgment liens
VS	Vital Records Office	Vital statistics—birth, death, marriage, divorce

Ohio

COURT RECORDS RETRIEVED — CAPITAL - FRANKLIN COUNTY — RECORDED RECORDS RETRIEVED

CR	CV	PR	US	BK	←COURTS	ADAMS	RECORDER→	UC	RE	TX	VS
						See adjoining counties for retrievers or call court/recorder directly.					

CR	CV	PR	US	BK	←COURTS	ALLEN	RECORDER→	UC	RE	TX	VS
•	•					A1 Inv [SOP]	419-229-1955, 419-229-2872				
	•	•				Oberdier Search Services	740-361-7530	•	•	•	

CR	CV	PR	US	BK	←COURTS	ASHLAND	RECORDER→	UC	RE	TX	VS
•	•	•	•	•		Investigative Solutions	330-947-2911	•		•	•
•	•	•	•	•		On the Record Inc	330-652-4109	•	•	•	•
	•	•	•	•		Provest - Ohio [SOP]	800-519-6331		•	•	
•	•					Judi Sampson	740-439-1202	•	•	•	
•	•	•				Urban Title Search Services Inc	419-289-0437	•	•	•	•

CR	CV	PR	US	BK	←COURTS	ASHTABULA	RECORDER→	UC	RE	TX	VS
•	•	•	•	•		Ace Background Check Inc	800-731-9221	•	•	•	•
•	•	•	•	•		Allington International	866-729-8555	•	•	•	•
•	•	•	•	•		Eagle Communications [SOP]	216-297-3200	•	•	•	•
•	•	•	•	•		Investigative Solutions	330-947-2911	•		•	•
•	•		•			Management Information Services	216-241-4282				
•	•	•	•	•		On the Record Inc	330-652-4109	•	•	•	•
•	•		•			Pre-Check, The Pre-Check Company	800-268-2435				

CR	CV	PR	US	BK	←COURTS	ATHENS	RECORDER→	UC	RE	TX	VS
•	•	•	•	•		Boerger Investigative Services LLC [SOP]	877-754-8295	•	•	•	•
•	•	•	•	•		Confidential Services [SOP]	800-752-4581	•	•	•	•
						Liberty Record Search Inc	304-863-5542	•	•	•	
•	•					Judi Sampson	740-439-1202	•	•	•	

CR	CV	PR	US	BK	←COURTS	AUGLAIZE	RECORDER→	UC	RE	TX	VS
•	•					A1 Inv [SOP]	419-229-1955, 419-229-2872				
•	•	•	•	•		CCB Researchers Ltd	937-653-4466	•	•	•	
•	•	•				Steven P Mielke	419-586-2323	•	•	•	

CR	CV	PR	US	BK	←COURTS	BELMONT	RECORDER→	UC	RE	TX	VS
•	•	•	•	•		Ace Background Check Inc	800-731-9221	•	•	•	•
•	•	•				Dora Doty	740-695-4917	•	•	•	•
•	•	•	•	•		On the Record Inc	330-652-4109	•	•	•	•
•	•					Judi Sampson	740-439-1202	•	•	•	

CR	CV	PR	US	BK	←COURTS	BROWN	RECORDER→	UC	RE	TX	VS
•	•	•				Ginger Galloway	937-241-8442	•	•	•	
	•	•	•	•		Provest - Ohio [SOP]	800-519-6331		•	•	

CR	CV	PR	US	BK	←COURTS	BUTLER	RECORDER→	UC	RE	TX	VS
•	•	•	•	•		Active Detective Bureau Inc [SOP]	800-405-4006		•	•	•
•	•	•	•	•		Advanced Background Check Inc	888-264-4018	•	•	•	•
•	•		•			Advantage Background Services Inc	800-355-2650				
	•					Cynthia H Miller, Paralegal	513-368-2855	•	•	•	
•				•		Document Retrieval Network Inc	859-654-2890	•	•	•	
•	•	•	•	•		General Corporate Investigations - GCI [SOP]	800-735-7992	•	•	•	•
•						Phoenix Research Inc	800-260-1092				

CR	CV	PR	US	BK	←Courts	Recorder→	UC	RE	TX	VS
	•	•	•	•	Provest - Ohio [SOP]	800-519-6331		•	•	
	•	•			Queen City Paralegal	513-984-4345		•	•	
	•				Union County Title Co	765-458-7148	•	•	•	
	•	•			Urban Abstract Inc	513-755-8527	•	•		
•	•		•		Xpedite Wholesale Criminal Research	800-325-3609				

CR	CV	PR	US	BK	←Courts CARROLL	Recorder→	UC	RE	TX	VS
•	•	•	•	•	Ace Background Check Inc	800-731-9221	•	•	•	•
					Liberty Record Search Inc	304-863-5542	•	•	•	
•	•	•	•	•	On the Record Inc	330-652-4109	•	•	•	•
•	•	•		•	David M Rumancik	330-837-7737	•	•	•	
•	•				Judi Sampson	740-439-1202	•	•	•	
•	•	•			Woodard & Bohse Law Office [SOP]	330-343-8848 or 8849	•	•	•	•

CR	CV	PR	US	BK	←Courts CHAMPAIGN	Recorder→	UC	RE	TX	VS
•	•	•	•	•	CCB Researchers Ltd	937-653-4466	•	•	•	
•	•	•			Ginger Galloway	937-241-8442	•	•	•	

CR	CV	PR	US	BK	←Courts CLARK	Recorder→	UC	RE	TX	VS
•	•	•	•	•	CCB Researchers Ltd	937-653-4466	•	•	•	
•	•	•			Ginger Galloway	937-241-8442	•	•	•	
•	•		•		North American Security Solutions	888-898-6277		•	•	

CR	CV	PR	US	BK	←Courts CLERMONT	Recorder→	UC	RE	TX	VS
•	•	•	•	•	Active Detective Bureau Inc [SOP]	800-405-4006		•	•	•
	•	•			Stephanie Allen	513-658-1647	•	•	•	
•	•	•	•	•	Confidential Services [SOP]	800-752-4581	•	•	•	•
•	•				Criminal Information Network Inc	888-923-0271				
	•				Cynthia H Miller, Paralegal	513-368-2855	•	•	•	
•				•	Document Retrieval Network Inc	859-654-2890		•	•	
•	•	•	•		General Corporate Investigations - GCI [SOP]	800-735-7992	•	•	•	•
•					Phoenix Research Inc	800-260-1092				
	•	•	•	•	Provest - Ohio [SOP]	800-519-6331		•	•	
	•	•			Queen City Paralegal	513-984-4345		•	•	
	•	•			Real Land Abstract Inc	859-291-1140	•	•	•	
•	•		•		Search International Inc	859-342-0456	•	•	•	
	•	•			Urban Abstract Inc	513-755-8527	•	•		
•	•		•		Xpedite Wholesale Criminal Research	800-325-3609				

CR	CV	PR	US	BK	←Courts CLINTON	Recorder→	UC	RE	TX	VS
•	•	•			Ginger Galloway	937-241-8442	•	•	•	

CR	CV	PR	US	BK	←Courts COLUMBIANA	Recorder→	UC	RE	TX	VS
•	•	•	•	•	Ace Background Check Inc	800-731-9221	•	•	•	•
•	•	•			Applied Research & Investigation	800-594-0008				
•	•	•	•	•	Gary Grusha	330-544-9424	•	•	•	•
•	•	•	•	•	Investigative Solutions	330-947-2911	•		•	•
					Liberty Record Search Inc	304-863-5542	•	•	•	
•	•	•	•	•	On the Record Inc	330-652-4109	•	•	•	•
•	•		•		Pre-Check, The Pre-Check Company	800-268-2435				

CR	CV	PR	US	BK	←Courts COSHOCTON	Recorder→	UC	RE	TX	VS
•	•	•	•	•	Ace Background Check Inc	800-731-9221	•	•	•	•
•	•	•			Tina Campbell	740-492-0228, cell- 740-260-1194	•	•	•	
•	•				Judi Sampson	740-439-1202	•	•	•	
•	•	•			Woodard & Bohse Law Office [SOP]	330-343-8848 or 8849	•	•	•	•

CR	CV	PR	US	BK	←Courts CRAWFORD	Recorder→	UC	RE	TX	VS
	•	•			Oberdier Search Services	740-361-7530	•	•	•	
•	•	•			Precision Quest [SOP]	740-383-3753	•	•	•	•
	•	•	•	•	Provest - Ohio [SOP]	800-519-6331		•	•	

CR	CV	PR	US	BK	←COURTS	CUYAHOGA	RECORDER→	UC	RE	TX	VS
•	•		•	•	A1 Background Screening		330-940-2454				
•	•	•	•	•	A1 Cleveland Service Agency Inc [SOP]		888-212-5614	•	•	•	•
•	•	•	•	•	Ace Background Check Inc		800-731-9221	•	•	•	•
•	•	•	•	•	Advanced Background Check Inc		888-264-4018	•	•	•	•
•	•		•		Advantage Background Services Inc		800-355-2650				
•	•	•	•	•	Allington International		866-729-8555	•	•	•	•
•	•		•	•	ASK Services Inc		888-416-1313	•	•	•	
•	•	•	•	•	Attorney Services of Northeast Ohio [SOP]		800-804-7787		•	•	•
•	•	•	•	•	Boerger Investigative Services LLC [SOP]		877-754-8295	•	•	•	•
•	•	•	•	•	Confidential Services [SOP]		800-752-4581	•	•	•	•
•	•	•	•	•	Corporate Screening Services		800-229-8606	•			
•	•	•	•	•	Eagle Communications [SOP]		216-297-3200	•	•	•	•
•	•	•	•	•	Investigative Solutions		330-947-2911	•		•	•
•	•		•	•	J H L Enterprises		440-845-2823	•	•	•	
	•	•		•	KasparNet LLC		800-886-7534	•	•	•	
	•	•			Lorain County Title Co		440-284-5100	•	•	•	•
•	•				Management Information Services		216-241-4282				
•	•	•	•		National Service Information Inc (Ohio)		800-235-0337	•		•	•
•	•	•	•	•	On the Record Inc		330-652-4109	•	•	•	•
•	•		•		Pre-Check, The Pre-Check Company		800-268-2435				
	•	•	•	•	Provest - Ohio [SOP]		800-519-6331		•	•	
•	•				Quantum Recording Services		440-327-5604, 440-554-0040		•	•	•
•	•	•	•	•	Research Associates		800-225-9693	•	•	•	•
	•		•	•	Search One Services		614-834-5603	•	•	•	
•	•		•	•	Security Essentials LLC		440-247-7808			•	
•	•	•	•	•	Sherlock Research		330-882-4690	•	•	•	•

CR	CV	PR	US	BK	←COURTS	DARKE	RECORDER→	UC	RE	TX	VS
•	•	•	•	•	CCB Researchers Ltd		937-653-4466	•	•	•	
•	•		•	•	North American Security Solutions		888-898-6277		•	•	
	•	•	•	•	Provest - Ohio [SOP]		800-519-6331		•	•	
•	•				Kevin Van Tilburg		419-733-0478		•	•	

CR	CV	PR	US	BK	←COURTS	DEFIANCE	RECORDER→	UC	RE	TX	VS
•	•				Kevin Van Tilburg		419-733-0478		•	•	

CR	CV	PR	US	BK	←COURTS	DELAWARE	RECORDER→	UC	RE	TX	VS
•	•	•	•	•	Accurate Background Services LLC		614-205-0743	•	•	•	•
•	•	•	•	•	Advanced Background Check Inc		888-264-4018	•	•	•	•
•	•		•	•	ASK Services Inc		888-416-1313	•	•	•	
•	•	•	•	•	Boerger Investigative Services LLC [SOP]		877-754-8295	•	•	•	•
•	•	•	•	•	CCB Researchers Ltd		937-653-4466	•	•	•	
•	•	•	•	•	Confidential Services [SOP]		800-752-4581	•	•	•	•
•	•	•	•	•	InfoCorp Investigative Services LLC [SOP]		866-657-8003	•		•	•
•	•	•	•	•	M C Associates [SOP]		740-366-1922	•	•	•	•
	•	•			G Scott Miller		740-363-1324	•	•	•	
•	•	•	•	•	National Service Information Inc (Ohio)		800-235-0337	•		•	•
•	•	•			Precision Quest [SOP]		740-383-3753	•	•	•	•
	•	•	•	•	Provest - Ohio [SOP]		800-519-6331		•	•	
	•	•			Research Information Consultants		614-286-6303	•	•	•	
	•		•	•	Search One Services		614-834-5603	•	•	•	

CR	CV	PR	US	BK	←COURTS	ERIE	RECORDER→	UC	RE	TX	VS
•	•	•	•	•	Ace Background Check Inc		800-731-9221	•	•	•	•
•	•	•	•	•	Investigative Solutions		330-947-2911	•		•	•
	•	•			Lorain County Title Co		440-284-5100	•	•	•	•
•	•	•	•	•	On the Record Inc		330-652-4109	•	•	•	•
	•	•	•	•	Provest - Ohio [SOP]		800-519-6331		•	•	

CR	CV	PR	US	BK	←Courts	FAIRFIELD	Recorder→	UC	RE	TX	VS
•	•	•	•	•	Accurate Background Services LLC		614-205-0743	•	•	•	•
•	•		•	•	ASK Services Inc		888-416-1313	•	•	•	
•	•	•	•	•	Boerger Investigative Services LLC [SOP]		877-754-8295	•	•	•	•
•	•	•	•	•	M C Associates [SOP]		740-366-1922	•	•	•	•
	•	•	•	•	Provest - Ohio [SOP]		800-519-6331		•	•	
	•		•	•	Search One Services		614-834-5603	•	•	•	

CR	CV	PR	US	BK	←Courts	FAYETTE	Recorder→	UC	RE	TX	VS
•	•	•			Ginger Galloway		937-241-8442	•	•	•	
	•	•	•	•	Provest - Ohio [SOP]		800-519-6331		•	•	

CR	CV	PR	US	BK	←Courts	FRANKLIN	Recorder→	UC	RE	TX	VS
•	•	•	•	•	Accurate Background Services LLC		614-205-0743	•	•	•	•
•	•	•	•	•	Advanced Background Check Inc		888-264-4018	•	•	•	•
•	•		•	•	ASK Services Inc		888-416-1313	•	•	•	
•	•	•	•	•	Boerger Investigative Services LLC [SOP]		877-754-8295	•	•	•	•
•	•	•	•	•	CCB Researchers Ltd		937-653-4466	•	•	•	
•	•	•	•	•	Confidential Services [SOP]		800-752-4581	•	•	•	•
•	•	•	•	•	Eagle Communications [SOP]		216-297-3200	•	•	•	•
•					FYI Screening Inc		800-809-2419				
•	•	•	•	•	InfoCorp Investigative Services LLC [SOP]		866-657-8003	•		•	•
•	•	•	•	•	M C Associates [SOP]		740-366-1922	•	•	•	•
		•	•	•	MBK Consulting		614-239-8977	•	•	•	•
•	•	•	•	•	National Service Information Inc (Ohio)		800-235-0337	•		•	•
•	•		•		Pre-Check, The Pre-Check Company		800-268-2435				
•	•	•			Precision Quest [SOP]		740-383-3753	•	•	•	•
	•	•	•	•	Provest - Ohio [SOP]		800-519-6331		•	•	
	•	•			RecordSearch Inc		614-905-0085	•	•	•	
	•	•			Research Information Consultants		614-286-6303	•	•	•	
•	•				Right Staff Ltd		614-833-3401				
	•		•	•	Search One Services		614-834-5603	•	•	•	
	•		•	•	Unisearch Inc (Ohio)		877-208-7783	•		•	
•	•		•		Xpedite Wholesale Criminal Research		800-325-3609				

CR	CV	PR	US	BK	←Courts	FULTON	Recorder→	UC	RE	TX	VS
•	•				Kevin Van Tilburg		419-733-0478		•	•	

CR	CV	PR	US	BK	←Courts	GALLIA	Recorder→	UC	RE	TX	VS
					Liberty Record Search Inc		304-863-5542	•	•	•	
•	•				Judi Sampson		740-439-1202	•	•	•	

CR	CV	PR	US	BK	←Courts	GEAUGA	Recorder→	UC	RE	TX	VS
•	•	•	•	•	Ace Background Check Inc		800-731-9221	•	•	•	•
•	•		•		Advantage Background Services Inc		800-355-2650				
•	•	•	•	•	Allington International		866-729-8555	•	•	•	•
•	•	•	•	•	Attorney Services of Northeast Ohio [SOP]		800-804-7787		•	•	•
•	•	•	•	•	Chreyton Research		440-354-0316	•	•	•	•
•	•	•	•	•	Eagle Communications [SOP]		216-297-3200	•	•	•	•
•	•	•	•	•	Investigative Solutions		330-947-2911	•			•
•	•		•		Management Information Services		216-241-4282				
•	•	•	•	•	On the Record Inc		330-652-4109	•	•	•	•
•	•		•		Pre-Check, The Pre-Check Company		800-268-2435				
	•	•	•	•	Provest - Ohio [SOP]		800-519-6331		•	•	
•	•		•	•	Security Essentials LLC		440-247-7808			•	

CR	CV	PR	US	BK	←Courts	GREENE	Recorder→	UC	RE	TX	VS
•	•	•	•	•	CCB Researchers Ltd		937-653-4466	•	•	•	
•	•	•			Ginger Galloway		937-241-8442	•	•	•	
•					Linda Catherine Hill		937-294-7961				

CR	CV	PR	US	BK	Retriever	Phone	UC	RE	TX	VS
•	•		•	•	Midwest Investigative Services Inc [SOP]	800-227-9740				•
•	•		•	•	North American Security Solutions	888-898-6277		•	•	
•	•		•		Pre-Check, The Pre-Check Company	800-268-2435				
	•	•	•	•	Provest - Ohio [SOP]	800-519-6331		•	•	
	•		•	•	Search One Services	614-834-5603	•	•	•	

CR	CV	PR	US	BK	←COURTS GUERNSEY RECORDER→		UC	RE	TX	VS
•	•	•	•	•	Ace Background Check Inc	800-731-9221	•	•	•	•
•	•	•			Tina Campbell	740-492-0228, cell- 740-260-1194	•	•	•	
•	•	•			Dora Doty	740-695-4917	•	•	•	•
•	•				Judi Sampson	740-439-1202	•	•	•	

CR	CV	PR	US	BK	←COURTS HAMILTON RECORDER→		UC	RE	TX	VS
•	•	•	•	•	Active Detective Bureau Inc [SOP]	800-405-4006		•	•	•
•	•	•	•	•	Advanced Background Check Inc.	888-264-4018	•	•	•	•
•	•		•		Advantage Background Services Inc	800-355-2650				
•	•		•	•	ASK Services Inc	888-416-1313	•	•	•	
•	•	•	•	•	Confidential Services [SOP]	800-752-4581	•	•	•	•
•	•				Criminal Information Network Inc	888-923-0271				
	•				Cynthia H Miller, Paralegal	513-368-2855	•	•	•	
•	•	•	•	•	DDI Inc [SOP]	866-954-3000	•	•	•	•
•				•	Document Retrieval Network Inc	859-654-2890	•	•	•	
•	•	•	•	•	Eagle Communications [SOP]	216-297-3200	•	•	•	•
•	•	•	•	•	General Corporate Investigations - GCI [SOP]	800-735-7992	•	•	•	•
•	•	•	•	•	M C Associates [SOP]	740-366-1922	•	•	•	•
•	•	•	•	•	National Service Information Inc (Ohio)	800-235-0337	•		•	•
•					Phoenix Research Inc	800-260-1092				
	•	•	•	•	Provest - Ohio [SOP]	800-519-6331		•	•	
	•	•			Queen City Paralegal	513-984-4345		•	•	
	•	•			Real Land Abstract Inc	859-291-1140	•	•	•	
•	•		•	•	Search International Inc	859-342-0456	•	•	•	
	•		•	•	Search One Services	614-834-5603	•	•	•	
	•	•			Urban Abstract Inc	513-755-8527	•	•		
•	•		•		Xpedite Wholesale Criminal Research	800-325-3609				

CR	CV	PR	US	BK	←COURTS HANCOCK RECORDER→		UC	RE	TX	VS
•	•				A1 Inv [SOP]	419-229-1955, 419-229-2872				
•	•		•		Pre-Check, The Pre-Check Company	800-268-2435				
•	•				Kevin Van Tilburg	419-733-0478		•	•	

CR	CV	PR	US	BK	←COURTS HARDIN RECORDER→		UC	RE	TX	VS
•	•				A1 Inv [SOP]	419-229-1955, 419-229-2872				
•	•				Kevin Van Tilburg	419-733-0478		•	•	

CR	CV	PR	US	BK	←COURTS HARRISON RECORDER→		UC	RE	TX	VS
•	•	•	•	•	Ace Background Check Inc	800-731-9221	•	•	•	•
•	•	•			Dora Doty	740-695-4917	•	•	•	•
•	•	•	•	•	On the Record Inc	330-652-4109	•	•	•	•
•	•				River Research Service	304-670-3622	•	•	•	
•	•				Judi Sampson	740-439-1202	•	•	•	
•	•	•			Woodard & Bohse Law Office [SOP]	330-343-8848 or 8849	•	•	•	•

CR	CV	PR	US	BK	←COURTS HENRY RECORDER→		UC	RE	TX	VS
•	•				Kevin Van Tilburg	419-733-0478		•	•	

CR	CV	PR	US	BK	←COURTS HIGHLAND RECORDER→		UC	RE	TX	VS
•	•	•			Ginger Galloway	937-241-8442	•	•	•	

CR	CV	PR	US	BK	←COURTS HOCKING RECORDER→		UC	RE	TX	VS
•	•	•			Tina Campbell	740-492-0228, cell- 740-260-1194	•	•	•	
•	•				Judi Sampson	740-439-1202	•	•	•	

CR	CV	PR	US	BK	←COURTS **HOLMES**	RECORDER→	UC	RE	TX	VS
•	•	•	•	•	Ace Background Check Inc	800-731-9221	•	•	•	•
•	•	•	•	•	Investigative Solutions	330-947-2911	•		•	•
•	•	•	•	•	On the Record Inc	330-652-4109	•	•	•	•
•	•	•		•	David M Rumancik	330-837-7737	•	•	•	
•	•	•			Urban Title Search Services Inc	419-289-0437	•	•	•	•
•	•	•			Woodard & Bohse Law Office [SOP]	330-343-8848 or 8849	•	•	•	•

CR	CV	PR	US	BK	←COURTS **HURON**	RECORDER→	UC	RE	TX	VS
•	•	•	•	•	Ace Background Check Inc	800-731-9221	•	•	•	•
•	•	•	•	•	Investigative Solutions	330-947-2911	•		•	•
•	•	•	•	•	On the Record Inc	330-652-4109	•	•	•	•
	•	•	•	•	Provest - Ohio [SOP]	800-519-6331		•	•	

CR	CV	PR	US	BK	←COURTS **JACKSON**	RECORDER→	UC	RE	TX	VS
•	•	•			Salyer & Assoc.	740-596-5291	•	•	•	•
•	•				Judi Sampson	740-439-1202	•	•	•	

CR	CV	PR	US	BK	←COURTS **JEFFERSON**	RECORDER→	UC	RE	TX	VS
•	•	•	•	•	Ace Background Check Inc	800-731-9221	•	•	•	•
•	•	•			Dora Doty	740-695-4917	•	•	•	•
					Liberty Record Search Inc	304-863-5542	•	•	•	
•	•	•	•	•	On the Record Inc	330-652-4109	•	•	•	•
•	•				River Research Service	304-670-3622	•	•	•	
•	•				Judi Sampson	740-439-1202	•	•	•	

CR	CV	PR	US	BK	←COURTS **KNOX**	RECORDER→	UC	RE	TX	VS
•	•	•	•	•	Ace Background Check Inc	800-731-9221	•	•	•	•
•	•	•	•	•	M C Associates [SOP]	740-366-1922	•	•	•	•
	•	•	•	•	Provest - Ohio [SOP]	800-519-6331		•	•	
•	•				Judi Sampson	740-439-1202	•	•	•	

CR	CV	PR	US	BK	←COURTS **LAKE**	RECORDER→	UC	RE	TX	VS
•	•	•	•	•	A1 Cleveland Service Agency Inc [SOP]	888-212-5614	•	•	•	•
•	•	•	•	•	Ace Background Check Inc	800-731-9221	•	•	•	•
•	•		•		Advantage Background Services Inc	800-355-2650				
•	•	•	•	•	Allington International	866-729-8555	•	•	•	•
•	•	•	•	•	Attorney Services of Northeast Ohio [SOP]	800-804-7787		•	•	•
•	•	•	•	•	Boerger Investigative Services LLC [SOP]	877-754-8295	•	•	•	•
•	•	•	•	•	Chreyton Research	440-354-0316	•	•	•	•
•	•	•	•	•	Corporate Screening Services	800-229-8606	•			
•	•	•	•	•	Eagle Communications [SOP]	216-297-3200	•	•	•	•
•	•	•	•	•	Investigative Solutions	330-947-2911	•		•	•
•	•		•		Management Information Services	216-241-4282				
•	•	•	•	•	On the Record Inc	330-652-4109	•	•	•	•
•	•		•		Pre-Check, The Pre-Check Company	800-268-2435				
	•	•	•	•	Provest - Ohio [SOP]	800-519-6331		•	•	
•	•	•	•	•	Research Associates	800-225-9693	•	•	•	•
•	•		•	•	Security Essentials LLC	440-247-7808			•	

CR	CV	PR	US	BK	←COURTS **LAWRENCE**	RECORDER→	UC	RE	TX	VS

See adjoining counties for retrievers or call court/recorder directly.

CR	CV	PR	US	BK	←COURTS **LICKING**	RECORDER→	UC	RE	TX	VS
•	•	•	•	•	Accurate Background Services LLC	614-205-0743	•	•	•	•
•	•	•	•	•	Ace Background Check Inc	800-731-9221	•	•	•	•
•	•		•	•	ASK Services Inc	888-416-1313	•	•	•	
•	•	•	•	•	Boerger Investigative Services LLC [SOP]	877-754-8295	•	•	•	•
•	•	•			Tina Campbell	740-492-0228, cell- 740-260-1194	•	•	•	
•	•	•	•	•	M C Associates [SOP]	740-366-1922	•	•	•	•

CR	CV	PR	US	BK	←Courts	Recorder→	UC	RE	TX	VS
	•	•	•	•	Provest - Ohio [SOP]	800-519-6331		•	•	
•	•				Judi Sampson	740-439-1202	•	•	•	
	•		•	•	Search One Services	614-834-5603	•	•	•	

CR	CV	PR	US	BK	←Courts **LOGAN**	Recorder→	UC	RE	TX	VS
•	•	•	•	•	CCB Researchers Ltd	937-653-4466	•	•	•	

CR	CV	PR	US	BK	←Courts **LORAIN**	Recorder→	UC	RE	TX	VS
•	•	•	•	•	Ace Background Check Inc	800-731-9221	•	•	•	•
•	•	•	•	•	Advanced Background Check Inc	888-264-4018	•	•	•	•
•	•	•	•	•	Allington International	866-729-8555	•	•	•	•
•	•	•	•	•	Attorney Services of Northeast Ohio [SOP]	800-804-7787		•	•	•
•	•	•	•	•	Corporate Screening Services	800-229-8606	•			
•	•	•	•	•	Eagle Communications [SOP]	216-297-3200	•	•	•	•
	•			•	Investigative Solutions	330-947-2911	•		•	•
	•	•			Lorain County Title Co	440-284-5100	•	•	•	•
•	•		•		Management Information Services	216-241-4282				
•	•	•	•	•	On the Record Inc	330-652-4109	•	•	•	•
•	•		•		Pre-Check, The Pre-Check Company	800-268-2435				
	•	•	•	•	Provest - Ohio [SOP]	800-519-6331		•	•	
•	•				Quantum Recording Services	440-327-5604, 440-554-0040		•	•	•
•	•	•	•	•	Research Associates	800-225-9693	•	•	•	•

CR	CV	PR	US	BK	←Courts **LUCAS**	Recorder→	UC	RE	TX	VS
•	•	•	•	•	Advanced Background Check Inc	888-264-4018	•	•	•	•
•	•		•	•	ASK Services Inc	888-416-1313	•	•	•	
•	•	•	•	•	Confidential Services [SOP]	800-752-4581	•	•	•	•
•	•	•	•	•	M & D Records Research	419-693-5649	•	•	•	•
•	•	•	•	•	National Service Information Inc (Ohio)	800-235-0337	•		•	•
•	•		•		Pre-Check, The Pre-Check Company	800-268-2435				
	•	•	•	•	Provest - Ohio [SOP]	800-519-6331		•	•	

CR	CV	PR	US	BK	←Courts **MADISON**	Recorder→	UC	RE	TX	VS
•	•		•	•	ASK Services Inc	888-416-1313	•	•	•	
•	•	•	•	•	Boerger Investigative Services LLC [SOP]	877-754-8295	•	•	•	•
•	•	•	•	•	CCB Researchers Ltd	937-653-4466	•	•	•	
•	•	•			Ginger Galloway	937-241-8442	•	•	•	
•	•		•		Pre-Check, The Pre-Check Company	800-268-2435				
	•	•	•	•	Provest - Ohio [SOP]	800-519-6331		•	•	

CR	CV	PR	US	BK	←Courts **MAHONING**	Recorder→	UC	RE	TX	VS
•	•	•	•	•	Attorney Services of Northeast Ohio [SOP]	800-804-7787		•	•	•
•	•	•	•	•	Eagle Communications [SOP]	216-297-3200	•	•	•	•
•	•	•	•	•	Gary Grusha	330-544-9424	•	•	•	•
•	•	•	•	•	Investigative Solutions	330-947-2911	•		•	•
•	•	•	•	•	On the Record Inc	330-652-4109	•	•	•	•
•	•		•		Pre-Check, The Pre-Check Company	800-268-2435				

CR	CV	PR	US	BK	←Courts **MARION**	Recorder→	UC	RE	TX	VS
•	•	•	•	•	Boerger Investigative Services LLC [SOP]	877-754-8295	•	•	•	•
•	•	•	•	•	National Service Information Inc (Ohio)	800-235-0337	•		•	•
	•	•			Oberdier Search Services	740-361-7530	•	•	•	
•	•	•			Precision Quest [SOP]	740-383-3753	•	•	•	•
	•	•		•	Provest - Ohio [SOP]	800-519-6331		•	•	

CR	CV	PR	US	BK	←Courts **MEDINA**	Recorder→	UC	RE	TX	VS
•	•		•	•	A1 Background Screening	330-940-2454				
•	•	•	•	•	Ace Background Check Inc	800-731-9221	•	•	•	•
•	•	•	•	•	Allington International	866-729-8555	•	•	•	•
•	•	•	•	•	Attorney Services of Northeast Ohio [SOP]	800-804-7787		•	•	•
•	•	•	•	•	Confidential Services [SOP]	800-752-4581	•	•	•	•

CR	CV	PR	US	BK	←Courts	Recorder→	UC	RE	TX	VS
•	•	•	•	•	Corporate Screening Services	800-229-8606	•			
•	•	•	•	•	Investigative Solutions	330-947-2911	•		•	•
•	•		•	•	J H L Enterprises	440-845-2823	•	•	•	
	•	•		•	KasparNet LLC	800-886-7534	•	•	•	
•	•	•	•	•	On the Record Inc	330-652-4109	•	•	•	•
•	•		•		Pre-Check, The Pre-Check Company	800-268-2435				
	•	•	•	•	Provest - Ohio [SOP]	800-519-6331		•	•	
•	•				Quantum Recording Services	440-327-5604, 440-554-0040		•	•	•
•	•	•	•	•	Sherlock Research	330-882-4690	•	•	•	•

CR	CV	PR	US	BK	←Courts **Meigs**	Recorder→	UC	RE	TX	VS
					Liberty Record Search Inc	304-863-5542	•	•	•	
•	•				Judi Sampson	740-439-1202	•	•	•	

CR	CV	PR	US	BK	←Courts **Mercer**	Recorder→	UC	RE	TX	VS
•	•				A1 Inv [SOP]	419-229-1955, 419-229-2872				
•	•	•	•	•	CCB Researchers Ltd	937-653-4466	•	•	•	
•	•	•			Steven P Mielke	419-586-2323	•	•	•	

CR	CV	PR	US	BK	←Courts **Miami**	Recorder→	UC	RE	TX	VS
•	•	•	•	•	CCB Researchers Ltd	937-653-4466	•	•	•	
•	•		•	•	Midwest Investigative Services Inc [SOP]	800-227-9740				•
•	•		•	•	North American Security Solutions	888-898-6277		•	•	
	•		•	•	Search One Services	614-834-5603	•	•	•	

CR	CV	PR	US	BK	←Courts **Monroe**	Recorder→	UC	RE	TX	VS
•	•	•			Dora Doty	740-695-4917	•	•	•	•
•	•				Judi Sampson	740-439-1202	•	•	•	

CR	CV	PR	US	BK	←Courts **Montgomery**	Recorder→	UC	RE	TX	VS
•	•	•	•	•	Advanced Background Check Inc	888-264-4018	•	•	•	•
•	•		•		Advantage Background Services Inc	800-355-2650				
•	•	•	•	•	CCB Researchers Ltd	937-653-4466	•	•	•	
•				•	Document Retrieval Network Inc	859-654-2890	•	•	•	
•	•	•	•	•	General Corporate Investigations - GCI [SOP]	800-735-7992	•	•	•	•
•					Linda Catherine Hill	937-294-7961				
•	•	•	•	•	M C Associates [SOP]	740-366-1922	•	•	•	•
					Midwest Abstract Co	800-606-9488	•	•	•	
•	•		•	•	Midwest Investigative Services Inc [SOP]	800-227-9740				•
•	•	•	•	•	National Service Information Inc (Ohio)	800-235-0337	•		•	•
•	•		•	•	North American Security Solutions	888-898-6277		•	•	
	•	•	•	•	Provest - Ohio [SOP]	800-519-6331		•	•	
	•	•			Urban Abstract Inc	513-755-8527	•	•		

CR	CV	PR	US	BK	←Courts **Morgan**	Recorder→	UC	RE	TX	VS
•	•	•			Tina Campbell	740-492-0228, cell- 740-260-1194	•	•	•	

CR	CV	PR	US	BK	←Courts **Morrow**	Recorder→	UC	RE	TX	VS
	•	•			Oberdier Search Services	740-361-7530	•	•	•	
•	•	•			Precision Quest [SOP]	740-383-3753	•	•	•	•
	•	•	•	•	Provest - Ohio [SOP]	800-519-6331		•	•	

CR	CV	PR	US	BK	←Courts **Muskingum**	Recorder→	UC	RE	TX	VS
•	•	•	•	•	Ace Background Check Inc	800-731-9221	•	•	•	•
•	•	•			Tina Campbell	740-492-0228, cell- 740-260-1194	•	•	•	
•	•	•	•	•	M C Associates [SOP]	740-366-1922	•	•	•	•
•	•				Judi Sampson	740-439-1202	•	•	•	

CR	CV	PR	US	BK	←COURTS	NOBLE	RECORDER→	UC	RE	TX	VS
•	•	•			Tina Campbell		740-492-0228, cell- 740-260-1194	•	•	•	
•	•	•			Dora Doty		740-695-4917	•	•	•	•
•	•				Judi Sampson		740-439-1202	•	•	•	

CR	CV	PR	US	BK	←COURTS	OTTAWA	RECORDER→	UC	RE	TX	VS
•	•	•	•	•	Investigative Solutions		330-947-2911	•		•	•
	•	•	•	•	Provest - Ohio [SOP]		800-519-6331		•	•	

CR	CV	PR	US	BK	←COURTS	PAULDING	RECORDER→	UC	RE	TX	VS
					Kevin Van Tilburg		419-733-0478		•	•	

CR	CV	PR	US	BK	←COURTS	PERRY	RECORDER→	UC	RE	TX	VS
•	•	•			Tina Campbell		740-492-0228, cell- 740-260-1194	•	•	•	
•					Judi Sampson		740-439-1202	•	•	•	

CR	CV	PR	US	BK	←COURTS	PICKAWAY	RECORDER→	UC	RE	TX	VS
•	•	•	•	•	Accurate Background Services LLC		614-205-0743	•	•	•	•
•	•	•	•	•	M C Associates [SOP]		740-366-1922	•	•	•	•
					Pre-Check, The Pre-Check Company		800-268-2435				
	•	•	•	•	Provest - Ohio [SOP]		800-519-6331		•	•	
	•		•	•	Search One Services		614-834-5603	•	•	•	

CR	CV	PR	US	BK	←COURTS	PIKE	RECORDER→	UC	RE	TX	VS
					See adjoining counties for retrievers or call court/recorder directly.						

CR	CV	PR	US	BK	←COURTS	PORTAGE	RECORDER→	UC	RE	TX	VS
•	•		•	•	A1 Background Screening		330-940-2454				
•	•	•	•	•	Ace Background Check Inc		800-731-9221	•	•	•	•
•	•	•	•	•	Attorney Services of Northeast Ohio [SOP]		800-804-7787		•	•	•
•	•	•	•	•	Eagle Communications [SOP]		216-297-3200	•	•	•	•
•	•	•	•	•	Investigative Solutions		330-947-2911	•		•	•
	•	•		•	KasparNet LLC		800-886-7534	•	•	•	
	•	•			Ohio Title		330-297-7003	•	•	•	•
•	•	•	•	•	On the Record Inc		330-652-4109	•	•	•	•
•	•		•		Pre-Check, The Pre-Check Company		800-268-2435				
	•	•	•	•	Provest - Ohio [SOP]		800-519-6331		•	•	
•	•	•	•	•	Sherlock Research		330-882-4690	•	•	•	•

CR	CV	PR	US	BK	←COURTS	PREBLE	RECORDER→	UC	RE	TX	VS
•	•	•	•	•	CCB Researchers Ltd		937-653-4466	•	•	•	
•	•		•	•	North American Security Solutions		888-898-6277		•	•	
	•	•	•	•	Provest - Ohio [SOP]		800-519-6331		•	•	
	•				Union County Title Co		765-458-7148	•	•	•	

CR	CV	PR	US	BK	←COURTS	PUTNAM	RECORDER→	UC	RE	TX	VS
•	•				A1 Inv [SOP]		419-229-1955, 419-229-2872				
•	•				Kevin Van Tilburg		419-733-0478		•	•	

CR	CV	PR	US	BK	←COURTS	RICHLAND	RECORDER→	UC	RE	TX	VS
•	•	•	•	•	Ace Background Check Inc		800-731-9221	•	•	•	•
•	•	•	•	•	Boerger Investigative Services LLC [SOP]		877-754-8295	•	•	•	•
					Lori A Day		419-544-4740		•		
•	•	•	•	•	On the Record Inc		330-652-4109	•	•	•	•
	•	•	•	•	Provest - Ohio [SOP]		800-519-6331		•	•	
•	•				Judi Sampson		740-439-1202	•	•	•	
•	•	•			Urban Title Search Services Inc		419-289-0437	•	•	•	•

CR	CV	PR	US	BK	←Courts	Ross	Recorder→	UC	RE	TX	VS
•	•	•	•	•	M C Associates [SOP]		740-366-1922	•	•	•	•

CR	CV	PR	US	BK	←Courts	Sandusky	Recorder→	UC	RE	TX	VS
•	•	•	•	•	Investigative Solutions		330-947-2911	•		•	•
	•	•	•	•	Provest - Ohio [SOP]		800-519-6331		•	•	

CR	CV	PR	US	BK	←Courts	Scioto	Recorder→	UC	RE	TX	VS
					See adjoining counties for retrievers or call court/recorder directly.						

CR	CV	PR	US	BK	←Courts	Seneca	Recorder→	UC	RE	TX	VS
	•	•	•	•	Provest - Ohio [SOP]		800-519-6331		•	•	

CR	CV	PR	US	BK	←Courts	Shelby	Recorder→	UC	RE	TX	VS
•	•	•	•	•	CCB Researchers Ltd		937-653-4466	•	•	•	
•	•				Kevin Van Tilburg		419-733-0478		•	•	

CR	CV	PR	US	BK	←Courts	Stark	Recorder→	UC	RE	TX	VS
•	•		•	•	A1 Background Screening		330-940-2454				
•	•	•	•	•	Ace Background Check Inc		800-731-9221	•	•	•	•
•	•	•	•	•	Allington International		866-729-8555	•	•	•	•
•	•	•	•	•	Attorney Services of Northeast Ohio [SOP]		800-804-7787		•	•	•
•	•	•	•	•	Boerger Investigative Services LLC [SOP]		877-754-8295	•	•	•	•
•	•	•	•	•	Eagle Communications [SOP]		216-297-3200	•	•	•	•
•	•	•	•	•	Investigative Solutions		330-947-2911	•		•	•
•	•	•	•	•	On the Record Inc		330-652-4109	•	•	•	•
•	•		•		Pre-Check, The Pre-Check Company		800-268-2435				
	•	•	•	•	Provest - Ohio [SOP]		800-519-6331		•	•	
•	•	•		•	David M Rumancik		330-837-7737	•	•	•	
•	•				Judi Sampson		740-439-1202	•	•	•	
•	•	•	•	•	Sherlock Research		330-882-4690	•	•	•	•

CR	CV	PR	US	BK	←Courts	Summit	Recorder→	UC	RE	TX	VS
•	•		•	•	A1 Background Screening		330-940-2454				
•	•	•	•	•	Advanced Background Check Inc		888-264-4018	•	•	•	•
•	•		•		Advantage Background Services Inc		800-355-2650				
•	•	•	•	•	Allington International		866-729-8555	•	•	•	•
•	•	•	•	•	Attorney Services of Northeast Ohio [SOP]		800-804-7787		•	•	•
•	•	•	•	•	Boerger Investigative Services LLC [SOP]		877-754-8295	•	•	•	•
•	•	•	•	•	Eagle Communications [SOP]		216-297-3200	•	•	•	•
•	•	•	•	•	Investigative Solutions		330-947-2911	•		•	•
	•	•		•	KasparNet LLC		800-886-7534	•	•	•	
•	•	•	•	•	National Service Information Inc (Ohio)		800-235-0337	•		•	•
•	•	•	•	•	On the Record Inc		330-652-4109	•	•	•	•
•	•		•		Pre-Check, The Pre-Check Company		800-268-2435				
	•	•	•	•	Provest - Ohio [SOP]		800-519-6331		•	•	
•	•	•	•	•	Research Associates		800-225-9693	•	•	•	•
•	•	•		•	David M Rumancik		330-837-7737	•	•	•	
•	•		•	•	Security Essentials LLC		440-247-7808			•	
•	•	•	•	•	Sherlock Research		330-882-4690	•	•	•	•

CR	CV	PR	US	BK	←Courts	Trumbull	Recorder→	UC	RE	TX	VS
•	•	•	•	•	Ace Background Check Inc		800-731-9221	•	•	•	•
•	•	•	•	•	Allington International		866-729-8555	•	•	•	•
•	•	•	•	•	Attorney Services of Northeast Ohio [SOP]		800-804-7787		•	•	•
•	•	•	•	•	Eagle Communications [SOP]		216-297-3200	•	•	•	•
•	•	•	•	•	Gary Grusha		330-544-9424	•	•	•	•
•	•	•	•	•	Investigative Solutions		330-947-2911	•		•	•
•	•	•	•	•	On the Record Inc		330-652-4109	•	•	•	•
•	•		•		Pre-Check, The Pre-Check Company		800-268-2435				

CR	CV	PR	US	BK	Retriever	Phone	UC	RE	TX	VS
•	•	•		•	David M Rumancik	330-837-7737	•	•	•	
		•			Trumbull County Abstract Co	330-399-1891		•	•	

CR	CV	PR	US	BK	←Courts **Tuscarawas**	Recorder→	UC	RE	TX	VS
•	•	•	•	•	Ace Background Check Inc	800-731-9221	•	•	•	•
•	•	•	•	•	Investigative Solutions	330-947-2911	•		•	•
•	•	•	•	•	On the Record Inc	330-652-4109	•	•	•	•
•	•	•		•	David M Rumancik	330-837-7737	•	•	•	
•	•				Judi Sampson	740-439-1202	•	•	•	
•	•	•			Woodard & Bohse Law Office [SOP]	330-343-8848 or 8849	•	•	•	•

CR	CV	PR	US	BK	←Courts **Union**	Recorder→	UC	RE	TX	VS
•	•	•	•	•	Boerger Investigative Services LLC [SOP]	877-754-8295	•	•	•	•
•	•	•	•	•	CCB Researchers Ltd	937-653-4466	•	•	•	
•	•	•	•	•	M C Associates [SOP]	740-366-1922	•	•	•	•
•	•	•			Precision Quest [SOP]	740-383-3753	•	•	•	•
	•	•	•	•	Provest - Ohio [SOP]	800-519-6331		•	•	

CR	CV	PR	US	BK	←Courts **Van Wert**	Recorder→	UC	RE	TX	VS
•	•				A1 Inv [SOP]	419-229-1955, 419-229-2872				
•	•	•			Steven P Mielke	419-586-2323	•	•	•	
•	•				Kevin Van Tilburg	419-733-0478		•	•	

CR	CV	PR	US	BK	←Courts **Vinton**	Recorder→	UC	RE	TX	VS
•	•	•			Salyer & Assoc.	740-596-5291	•	•	•	•
•	•				Judi Sampson	740-439-1202	•	•	•	

CR	CV	PR	US	BK	←Courts **Warren**	Recorder→	UC	RE	TX	VS
•	•	•	•	•	Active Detective Bureau Inc [SOP]	800-405-4006		•	•	•
•	•	•	•	•	Advanced Background Check Inc	888-264-4018	•	•	•	•
	•				Cynthia H Miller, Paralegal	513-368-2855	•	•	•	
•				•	Document Retrieval Network Inc	859-654-2890	•	•	•	
•	•	•	•	•	General Corporate Investigations - GCI [SOP]	800-735-7992	•	•	•	•
•	•		•	•	Midwest Investigative Services Inc [SOP]	800-227-9740				•
•					Phoenix Research Inc	800-260-1092				
	•	•	•	•	Provest - Ohio [SOP]	800-519-6331		•	•	
	•	•			Queen City Paralegal	513-984-4345		•	•	
	•	•			Urban Abstract Inc	513-755-8527	•	•		
•	•		•		Xpedite Wholesale Criminal Research	800-325-3609				

CR	CV	PR	US	BK	←Courts **Washington**	Recorder→	UC	RE	TX	VS
•	•		•		Accu-Check Information Services	304-375-4802	•		•	
					Liberty Record Search Inc	304-863-5542	•	•	•	
•	•				Judi Sampson	740-439-1202	•	•	•	

CR	CV	PR	US	BK	←Courts **Wayne**	Recorder→	UC	RE	TX	VS
•	•	•	•	•	Ace Background Check Inc	800-731-9221	•	•	•	•
•	•	•	•	•	Attorney Services of Northeast Ohio [SOP]	800-804-7787		•	•	•
•	•	•	•	•	Investigative Solutions	330-947-2911	•		•	•
•	•		•	•	J H L Enterprises	440-845-2823	•	•	•	
•	•	•	•	•	On the Record Inc	330-652-4109	•	•	•	•
	•	•	•	•	Provest - Ohio [SOP]	800-519-6331		•	•	
•	•	•		•	David M Rumancik	330-837-7737	•	•	•	
•	•				Judi Sampson	740-439-1202	•	•	•	
•	•	•	•	•	Sherlock Research	330-882-4690	•	•	•	•
•	•	•			Urban Title Search Services Inc	419-289-0437	•	•	•	•

CR	CV	PR	US	BK	←Courts WILLIAMS	Recorder→	UC	RE	TX	VS
					See adjoining counties for retrievers or call court/recorder directly.					

CR	CV	PR	US	BK	←Courts WOOD	Recorder→	UC	RE	TX	VS
•	•	•	•	•	M & D Records Research	419-693-5649	•	•	•	•
•	•		•		Pre-Check, The Pre-Check Company	800-268-2435				
	•	•	•	•	Provest - Ohio [SOP]	800-519-6331		•	•	
•	•				Kevin Van Tilburg	419-733-0478		•	•	

CR	CV	PR	US	BK	←Courts WYANDOT	Recorder→	UC	RE	TX	VS
•	•	•	•	•	Boerger Investigative Services LLC [SOP]	877-754-8295	•	•	•	•
	•	•			Oberdier Search Services	740-361-7530	•	•	•	
	•	•	•	•	Provest - Ohio [SOP]	800-519-6331		•	•	

[SOP] = Performs service of process

Court Records

CODE	Government Agency	Type of Information
CR	Criminal Court	Municipal, county and state level criminal cases
CV	Civil Court	Municipal, county and state level civil cases
PR	Probate Court	Wills and estate cases
US	US District Court	Federal civil and criminal cases
BK	Bankruptcy Court	United States bankruptcy cases

County Records - Recordings

CODE	Government Agency	Type of Information
UC	UCC Filing Office	Uniform Commercial Code and other personal property liens
RE	Real Estate Recording Office	Real property transactions and liens
TX	Tax Filing Office(s)	Federal and state tax liens, judgment liens
VS	Vital Records Office	Vital statistics—birth, death, marriage, divorce

Oklahoma

COURT RECORDS RETRIEVED — CAPITAL - OKLAHOMA COUNTY — RECORDED RECORDS RETRIEVED

CR	CV	PR	US	BK	←COURTS ADAIR RECORDER→	UC	RE	TX	VS
•	•	•	•	•	AAA Abstract Co Inc (Oklahoma) 918-696-2770	•	•	•	•
•	•	•	•	•	Document Retrieval Service 877-902-9377	•	•	•	•
•	•		•	•	Information Searches Inc 918-369-8126				
		•	•	•	Records Search & Report Service....918-885-4724, 918-885-9955	•	•	•	•
•	•				Redi-Info Information Services....888-320-6805				

CR	CV	PR	US	BK	←COURTS ALFALFA RECORDER→	UC	RE	TX	VS
	•	•			Alfalfa Guaranty Abstract Co 580-596-3394	•	•	•	•
•	•	•	•	•	Document Retrieval Service 877-902-9377	•	•	•	•
•	•				Redi-Info Information Services....888-320-6805				

CR	CV	PR	US	BK	←COURTS ATOKA RECORDER→	UC	RE	TX	VS
					Atoka Abstract Co Inc 580-889-7316	•	•	•	
•	•	•	•	•	Document Retrieval Service 877-902-9377	•	•	•	•
•	•		•	•	Information Searches Inc 918-369-8126				
					Moore Mowdy & Youngblood 580-889-5656		•		
•	•				Redi-Info Information Services....888-320-6805				

CR	CV	PR	US	BK	←COURTS BEAVER RECORDER→	UC	RE	TX	VS
	•	•			Beaver County Abstract Co 580-625-4423	•	•	•	•
•	•	•	•	•	Document Retrieval Service 877-902-9377	•	•	•	•
•	•				Redi-Info Information Services....888-320-6805				

CR	CV	PR	US	BK	←COURTS BECKHAM RECORDER→	UC	RE	TX	VS
•	•	•			Beckham County Abstract 580-928-3143	•	•	•	•
•	•	•	•	•	Document Retrieval Service 877-902-9377	•	•	•	•
•	•				Redi-Info Information Services....888-320-6805				

CR	CV	PR	US	BK	←COURTS BLAINE RECORDER→	UC	RE	TX	VS
	•	•			Blaine County Abstract....580-623-7248 or 7257	•	•	•	
•	•	•	•	•	Document Retrieval Service 877-902-9377	•	•	•	•
•	•				Redi-Info Information Services....888-320-6805				

CR	CV	PR	US	BK	←COURTS BRYAN RECORDER→	UC	RE	TX	VS
•	•	•	•	•	Clarke Investigations Inc [SOP] 405-844-7300	•	•	•	•
•	•	•	•	•	Document Retrieval Service 877-902-9377	•	•	•	•
					Moore Mowdy & Youngblood 580-889-5656		•		
•	•				Redi-Info Information Services....888-320-6805				
		•	•	•	Pat Stephens....903-583-5215	•	•	•	

CR	CV	PR	US	BK	←COURTS CADDO RECORDER→	UC	RE	TX	VS
•	•	•	•	•	Clarke Investigations Inc [SOP] 405-844-7300	•	•	•	•
•	•	•	•	•	Document Retrieval Service 877-902-9377	•	•	•	•
•	•	•			Lacey Pioneer Abstract Company Inc 405-247-5152	•	•	•	•
•	•				Redi-Info Information Services....888-320-6805				
•	•		•	•	Tammy L Listen Investigations [SOP] 405-340-4843	•	•	•	•

CR	CV	PR	US	BK	←COURTS CANADIAN RECORDER→	UC	RE	TX	VS
•	•	•	•	•	American Detective Agency [SOP] 800-219-9120	•	•	•	•
•	•	•	•	•	Clarke Investigations Inc [SOP] 405-844-7300	•	•	•	•

CR	CV	PR	US	BK	←Courts	Recorder→	UC	RE	TX	VS
•	•	•	•	•	Document Retrieval Service	877-902-9377	•	•	•	•
					Noel D Law Jr	918-599-0988	•	•		
•	•	•	•	•	Mark McKee, PI [SOP]	405-636-1976	•	•	•	•
•	•				Redi-Info Information Services	888-320-6805				
•	•	•	•		Rus B Robison & Associates Inc [SOP]	405-603-2932	•	•	•	
•	•		•	•	Tammy L Listen Investigations [SOP]	405-340-4843	•	•	•	•
•	•	•	•	•	United Legal Services [SOP]	888-232-8432	•	•	•	

CR	CV	PR	US	BK	←Courts — CARTER	Recorder→	UC	RE	TX	VS
•	•	•	•	•	Clarke Investigations Inc [SOP]	405-844-7300	•	•	•	•
•	•	•	•	•	Document Retrieval Service	877-902-9377	•	•	•	•
•	•		•	•	Information Searches Inc	918-369-8126				
					Marshall County Abstract Co	580-795-7388		•		
•	•				Redi-Info Information Services	888-320-6805				

CR	CV	PR	US	BK	←Courts — CHEROKEE	Recorder→	UC	RE	TX	VS
•	•	•			Cherokee Capitol Abstract Title & Closing	918-456-8851	•	•	•	•
•	•	•	•	•	Clarke Investigations Inc [SOP]	405-844-7300	•	•	•	•
•	•	•	•	•	Document Retrieval Service	877-902-9377	•	•	•	•
					Noel D Law Jr	918-599-0988	•	•		
•	•		•	•	Oklahoma Court Explorers	918-360-4798		•	•	
		•	•	•	Records Search & Report Service	918-885-4724, 918-885-9955	•	•	•	•
•	•				Redi-Info Information Services	888-320-6805				

CR	CV	PR	US	BK	←Courts — CHOCTAW	Recorder→	UC	RE	TX	VS
	•	•			Choctaw County Abstract & Title	580-326-9616	•	•	•	
•	•	•	•	•	Document Retrieval Service	877-902-9377	•	•	•	•

CR	CV	PR	US	BK	←Courts — CIMARRON	Recorder→	UC	RE	TX	VS
•	•	•	•	•	Document Retrieval Service	877-902-9377	•	•	•	•
•	•				Redi-Info Information Services	888-320-6805				

CR	CV	PR	US	BK	←Courts — CLEVELAND	Recorder→	UC	RE	TX	VS
•	•	•	•	•	American Detective Agency [SOP]	800-219-9120	•	•	•	•
	•	•			American-First Abstract Co	405-321-7577	•	•	•	
•	•	•	•	•	Clarke Investigations Inc [SOP]	405-844-7300	•	•	•	•
•	•	•	•	•	Document Retrieval Service	877-902-9377	•	•	•	•
					Noel D Law Jr	918-599-0988	•	•		
•	•	•	•	•	Mark McKee, PI [SOP]	405-636-1976	•	•	•	•
•	•				Redi-Info Information Services	888-320-6805				
•	•	•	•		Rus B Robison & Associates Inc [SOP]	405-603-2932	•	•	•	
•	•		•	•	Tammy L Listen Investigations [SOP]	405-340-4843	•	•	•	•
•	•	•	•	•	United Legal Services [SOP]	888-232-8432	•	•	•	

CR	CV	PR	US	BK	←Courts — COAL	Recorder→	UC	RE	TX	VS
•	•	•	•	•	Document Retrieval Service	877-902-9377	•	•	•	•
					Moore Mowdy & Youngblood	580-889-5656		•		

CR	CV	PR	US	BK	←Courts — COMANCHE	Recorder→	UC	RE	TX	VS
•	•	•	•	•	H Ray Anderson	580-355-4450	•	•	•	
•	•	•	•	•	Clarke Investigations Inc [SOP]	405-844-7300	•	•	•	•
•	•	•	•	•	Document Retrieval Service	877-902-9377	•	•	•	•
•	•	•			King Investigations Inc	580-477-1676		•	•	
•	•	•	•	•	Mendenhall Information Services	940-696-0758	•	•	•	•
•	•				Redi-Info Information Services	888-320-6805				
	•	•			Southwest Abstract & Title Co	405-355-3680	•	•	•	
•	•	•			T.A.B.B.S. Investigations & Process Service [SOP]	580-477-3292	•	•	•	•

CR	CV	PR	US	BK	←Courts — COTTON	Recorder→	UC	RE	TX	VS
•	•	•	•	•	H Ray Anderson	580-355-4450	•	•	•	
•	•	•	•	•	Document Retrieval Service	877-902-9377	•	•	•	•

CR	CV	PR	US	BK	Retriever	Phone	UC	RE	TX	VS
•	•	•	•	•	Mendenhall Information Services	940-696-0758	•	•	•	•
•	•				Redi-Info Information Services	888-320-6805				

CR	CV	PR	US	BK	←COURTS CRAIG	RECORDER→	UC	RE	TX	VS
•	•				Davis and Assoc. [SOP]	918-825-5223				
•	•	•	•	•	Document Retrieval Service	877-902-9377	•	•	•	•
					Noel D Law Jr	918-599-0988	•	•		
		•	•	•	Records Search & Report Service	918-885-4724, 918-885-9955	•	•	•	•
•	•				Redi-Info Information Services	888-320-6805				
					Vinita Title Co	918-256-2617	•	•	•	•

CR	CV	PR	US	BK	←COURTS CREEK	RECORDER→	UC	RE	TX	VS
•	•	•	•	•	Clarke Investigations Inc [SOP]	405-844-7300	•	•	•	•
					Docu-File USA Inc	877-742-4994		•		
•	•	•	•	•	Document Retrieval Service	877-902-9377	•	•	•	•
•	•			•	Information Searches Inc	918-369-8126				
					Noel D Law Jr	918-599-0988	•	•		
		•	•	•	Records Search & Report Service	918-885-4724, 918-885-9955	•	•	•	•
•	•				Redi-Info Information Services	888-320-6805				
					SRT Investigations	918-481-6045		•	•	
	•	•			Union-Speer Abstract Co	918-224-4540	•	•	•	
•	•	•	•	•	Zero Investigations Inc [SOP]	866-400-9376	•	•	•	•

CR	CV	PR	US	BK	←COURTS CUSTER	RECORDER→	UC	RE	TX	VS
•	•	•	•	•	Clarke Investigations Inc [SOP]	405-844-7300	•	•	•	•
	•	•			Clinton Abstract Co Inc	580-323-3025	•	•	•	
•	•	•	•	•	Document Retrieval Service	877-902-9377	•	•	•	•
•	•				Redi-Info Information Services	888-320-6805				

CR	CV	PR	US	BK	←COURTS DELAWARE	RECORDER→	UC	RE	TX	VS
•	•	•	•		Clarke Investigations Inc [SOP]	405-844-7300	•	•	•	•
•	•				Davis and Assoc. [SOP]	918-825-5223				
	•	•			Delaware County Abstract Co (Oklahoma)	918-253-4425	•	•	•	
•	•	•	•	•	Document Retrieval Service	877-902-9377	•	•	•	•
					Noel D Law Jr	918-599-0988	•	•		
		•	•	•	Records Search & Report Service	918-885-4724, 918-885-9955	•	•	•	•
•	•				Redi-Info Information Services	888-320-6805				

CR	CV	PR	US	BK	←COURTS DEWEY	RECORDER→	UC	RE	TX	VS
•	•	•	•	•	Clarke Investigations Inc [SOP]	405-844-7300	•	•	•	•
•	•	•	•	•	Dewey County Abstract Co	580-328-5556	•	•	•	
•	•	•	•	•	Document Retrieval Service	877-902-9377	•	•	•	•
•	•				Redi-Info Information Services	888-320-6805				

CR	CV	PR	US	BK	←COURTS ELLIS	RECORDER→	UC	RE	TX	VS
•	•	•	•	•	Clarke Investigations Inc [SOP]	405-844-7300	•	•	•	•
•	•	•	•	•	Document Retrieval Service	877-902-9377	•	•	•	•
•	•				Redi-Info Information Services	888-320-6805				

CR	CV	PR	US	BK	←COURTS GARFIELD	RECORDER→	UC	RE	TX	VS
•	•	•	•	•	Clarke Investigations Inc [SOP]	405-844-7300	•	•	•	•
•	•	•	•	•	Document Retrieval Service	877-902-9377	•	•	•	•
	•	•			J C Humphrey Abstract Co	580-237-3136	•	•	•	
•	•				Redi-Info Information Services	888-320-6805				

CR	CV	PR	US	BK	←COURTS GARVIN	RECORDER→	UC	RE	TX	VS
•	•	•	•	•	Clarke Investigations Inc [SOP]	405-844-7300	•	•	•	•
•	•	•	•	•	Document Retrieval Service	877-902-9377	•	•	•	•
•	•				Redi-Info Information Services	888-320-6805				

CR	CV	PR	US	BK	←Courts	**Grady** Recorder→	UC	RE	TX	VS
•	•	•	•	•	Clarke Investigations Inc [SOP]	405-844-7300	•	•	•	•
•	•	•	•	•	Document Retrieval Service	877-902-9377	•	•	•	•
•	•		•	•	Information Searches Inc	918-369-8126				
•	•		•	•	Tammy L Listen Investigations [SOP]	405-340-4843	•	•	•	•
•	•	•	•	•	United Legal Services [SOP]	888-232-8432	•	•	•	
	•	•			Washita Valley Abstract Co.	405-224-6111	•	•	•	

CR	CV	PR	US	BK	←Courts	**Grant** Recorder→	UC	RE	TX	VS
•	•	•	•	•	Document Retrieval Service	877-902-9377	•	•	•	•
	•	•			Grant County Abstract Co (Oklahoma)	580-395-2854	•	•	•	
•	•				Redi-Info Information Services	888-320-6805				

CR	CV	PR	US	BK	←Courts	**Greer** Recorder→	UC	RE	TX	VS
•	•	•	•	•	Clarke Investigations Inc [SOP]	405-844-7300	•	•	•	•
•	•	•	•	•	Document Retrieval Service	877-902-9377	•	•	•	•
	•	•			Greer Guaranty Abstract Co	580-782-3121	•	•	•	•
•	•	•			King Investigations Inc	580-477-1676		•	•	
•	•				Redi-Info Information Services	888-320-6805				
•	•	•			T.A.B.B.S. Investigations & Process Service [SOP]	580-477-3292	•	•	•	•

CR	CV	PR	US	BK	←Courts	**Harmon** Recorder→	UC	RE	TX	VS
•	•	•	•	•	Clarke Investigations Inc [SOP]	405-844-7300	•	•	•	•
•	•	•	•	•	Document Retrieval Service	877-902-9377	•	•	•	•
•	•	•			King Investigations Inc	580-477-1676		•	•	
•	•				Redi-Info Information Services	888-320-6805				
•	•	•			T.A.B.B.S. Investigations & Process Service [SOP]	580-477-3292	•	•	•	•

CR	CV	PR	US	BK	←Courts	**Harper** Recorder→	UC	RE	TX	VS
•	•	•	•	•	Clarke Investigations Inc [SOP]	405-844-7300	•	•	•	•
•	•	•	•	•	Document Retrieval Service	877-902-9377	•	•	•	•
•	•				Redi-Info Information Services	888-320-6805				
	•	•			Woodward County Abstract Co	580-256-3344	•	•	•	

CR	CV	PR	US	BK	←Courts	**Haskell** Recorder→	UC	RE	TX	VS
•	•	•	•	•	Document Retrieval Service	877-902-9377	•	•	•	•
	•	•			Guaranty Abstract of Stigler	918-967-8876	•	•	•	
	•	•			Hebert Land Services	918-647-9524	•	•	•	•
		•	•	•	Records Search & Report Service	918-885-4724, 918-885-9955	•	•	•	•
•	•				Redi-Info Information Services	888-320-6805				

CR	CV	PR	US	BK	←Courts	**Hughes** Recorder→	UC	RE	TX	VS
	•	•			Atlas Abstract Co	405-379-3311		•	•	
•	•	•	•	•	Document Retrieval Service	877-902-9377	•	•	•	•
•	•				Redi-Info Information Services	888-320-6805				

CR	CV	PR	US	BK	←Courts	**Jackson** Recorder→	UC	RE	TX	VS
•	•	•	•	•	Clarke Investigations Inc [SOP]	405-844-7300	•	•	•	•
•	•	•	•	•	Document Retrieval Service	877-902-9377	•	•	•	•
	•	•			Jackson County Abstract Co	580-482-1235	•	•	•	
•	•	•			King Investigations Inc	580-477-1676		•	•	
•	•	•	•	•	Mendenhall Information Services	940-696-0758	•	•	•	•
•	•				Redi-Info Information Services	888-320-6805				
•	•	•			T.A.B.B.S. Investigations & Process Service [SOP]	580-477-3292	•	•	•	•

CR	CV	PR	US	BK	←Courts	**Jefferson** Recorder→	UC	RE	TX	VS
•	•	•	•	•	H Ray Anderson	580-355-4450	•	•	•	
•	•	•	•	•	Document Retrieval Service	877-902-9377	•	•	•	•
•	•				Redi-Info Information Services	888-320-6805				

CR	CV	PR	US	BK	←Courts	Johnston	Recorder→	UC	RE	TX	VS
	•	•			Buffalo Land Abstract Inc		800-631-1880	•	•	•	
•	•	•	•	•	Document Retrieval Service		877-902-9377	•	•	•	•
					Marshall County Abstract Co		580-795-7388		•		
					Moore Mowdy & Youngblood		580-889-5656		•		
•	•				Redi-Info Information Services		888-320-6805				

CR	CV	PR	US	BK	←Courts	Kay	Recorder→	UC	RE	TX	VS
					Albright Abstract & Title Guaranty		877-362-2525			•	
•	•	•	•	•	Clarke Investigations Inc [SOP]		405-844-7300	•	•	•	•
•	•	•	•	•	Document Retrieval Service		877-902-9377	•	•	•	•
		•	•	•	Records Search & Report Service		918-885-4724, 918-885-9955	•	•	•	•
•	•				Redi-Info Information Services		888-320-6805				

CR	CV	PR	US	BK	←Courts	Kingfisher	Recorder→	UC	RE	TX	VS
•	•	•	•	•	Clarke Investigations Inc [SOP]		405-844-7300	•	•	•	•
•	•	•	•	•	Document Retrieval Service		877-902-9377	•	•	•	•
•	•				Redi-Info Information Services		888-320-6805				

CR	CV	PR	US	BK	←Courts	Kiowa	Recorder→	UC	RE	TX	VS
•	•	•	•	•	Clarke Investigations Inc [SOP]		405-844-7300	•	•	•	•
•	•	•	•	•	Document Retrieval Service		877-902-9377	•	•	•	•
•	•	•			King Investigations Inc		580-477-1676		•	•	
	•	•			Kiowa County Abstract Company		580-726-5283	•	•	•	
•	•				Redi-Info Information Services		888-320-6805				
•	•	•			T.A.B.B.S. Investigations & Process Service [SOP]		580-477-3292	•	•	•	•

CR	CV	PR	US	BK	←Courts	Latimer	Recorder→	UC	RE	TX	VS
•	•	•	•	•	Document Retrieval Service		877-902-9377	•	•	•	•
	•	•			Hebert Land Services		918-647-9524	•	•	•	•
•	•				Redi-Info Information Services		888-320-6805				

CR	CV	PR	US	BK	←Courts	Leflore	Recorder→	UC	RE	TX	VS
•	•	•	•	•	Document Retrieval Service		877-902-9377	•	•	•	•
	•	•			Hebert Land Services		918-647-9524	•	•	•	•
•	•				Redi-Info Information Services		888-320-6805				

CR	CV	PR	US	BK	←Courts	Lincoln	Recorder→	UC	RE	TX	VS
	•	•			Abstract & Guaranty Co		405-258-1244	•	•	•	
•	•	•	•	•	Clarke Investigations Inc [SOP]		405-844-7300	•	•	•	•
•	•	•	•	•	Document Retrieval Service		877-902-9377	•	•	•	•
					Noel D Law Jr		918-599-0988	•	•		
		•	•	•	Records Search & Report Service		918-885-4724, 918-885-9955	•	•	•	•
•	•				Redi-Info Information Services		888-320-6805				
•	•		•	•	Tammy L Listen Investigations [SOP]		405-340-4843	•	•	•	•
•	•	•	•	•	United Legal Services [SOP]		888-232-8432	•	•	•	

CR	CV	PR	US	BK	←Courts	Logan	Recorder→	UC	RE	TX	VS
•	•	•	•	•	Clarke Investigations Inc [SOP]		405-844-7300	•	•	•	•
•	•	•	•	•	Document Retrieval Service		877-902-9377	•	•	•	•
					Noel D Law Jr		918-599-0988	•	•		
		•	•	•	Records Search & Report Service		918-885-4724, 918-885-9955	•	•	•	•
•	•				Redi-Info Information Services		888-320-6805				
•	•		•	•	Tammy L Listen Investigations [SOP]		405-340-4843	•	•	•	•
•	•	•	•	•	United Legal Services [SOP]		888-232-8432	•	•	•	

CR	CV	PR	US	BK	←Courts	Love	Recorder→	UC	RE	TX	VS
•	•	•	•	•	Document Retrieval Service		877-902-9377	•	•	•	•
	•	•			Marietta Abstract Co		580-276-2231	•	•	•	•
•	•				Redi-Info Information Services		888-320-6805				

CR	CV	PR	US	BK	←Courts MAJOR	Recorder→	UC	RE	TX	VS
•	•	•	•	•	Document Retrieval Service	877-902-9377	•	•	•	•
•	•	•			Fairview Abstract Co	580-227-4524	•	•	•	•
•	•				Redi-Info Information Services	888-320-6805				

CR	CV	PR	US	BK	←Courts MARSHALL	Recorder→	UC	RE	TX	VS
•	•	•	•	•	Document Retrieval Service	877-902-9377	•	•	•	•
					Marshall County Abstract Co	580-795-7388		•		
•	•				Redi-Info Information Services	888-320-6805				

CR	CV	PR	US	BK	←Courts MAYES	Recorder→	UC	RE	TX	VS
•	•	•	•	•	Clarke Investigations Inc [SOP]	405-844-7300	•	•	•	•
•	•				Davis and Assoc. [SOP]	918-825-5223				
•	•	•	•	•	Document Retrieval Service	877-902-9377	•	•	•	•
•	•		•	•	Information Searches Inc	918-369-8126				
					Noel D Law Jr	918-599-0988	•	•		
	•	•			Mayes County Abstract	918-825-3074	•	•	•	•
•	•		•	•	Oklahoma Court Explorers	918-360-4798		•	•	
		•	•	•	Records Search & Report Service	918-885-4724, 918-885-9955	•	•	•	•
•	•				Redi-Info Information Services	888-320-6805				

CR	CV	PR	US	BK	←Courts MCCLAIN	Recorder→	UC	RE	TX	VS
	•	•			American Abstract Company	405-527-7575	•	•	•	
•	•	•	•	•	Clarke Investigations Inc [SOP]	405-844-7300	•	•	•	•
•	•	•	•	•	Document Retrieval Service	877-902-9377	•	•	•	•
					Noel D Law Jr	918-599-0988	•	•		
•	•	•	•	•	Mark McKee, PI [SOP]	405-636-1976	•	•	•	•
•	•				Redi-Info Information Services	888-320-6805				
•	•	•	•		Rus B Robison & Associates Inc [SOP]	405-603-2932	•	•	•	
•	•		•	•	Tammy L Listen Investigations [SOP]	405-340-4843	•	•	•	•
•	•	•	•	•	United Legal Services [SOP]	888-232-8432	•	•	•	

CR	CV	PR	US	BK	←Courts MCCURTAIN	Recorder→	UC	RE	TX	VS
•	•	•	•	•	Document Retrieval Service	877-902-9377	•	•	•	•
•	•				Redi-Info Information Services	888-320-6805				
	•	•			Southern Abstract & Title Co	580-286-2288	•	•	•	•

CR	CV	PR	US	BK	←Courts MCINTOSH	Recorder→	UC	RE	TX	VS
•	•	•	•	•	Document Retrieval Service	877-902-9377	•	•	•	•
					Eufaula Abstract & Title Co Inc	918-689-2241	•	•	•	
•	•		•	•	Information Searches Inc	918-369-8126				
•	•		•	•	Oklahoma Court Explorers	918-360-4798		•	•	
		•	•	•	Records Search & Report Service	918-885-4724, 918-885-9955	•	•	•	•
•	•				Redi-Info Information Services	888-320-6805				

CR	CV	PR	US	BK	←Courts MURRAY	Recorder→	UC	RE	TX	VS
•	•	•	•	•	Document Retrieval Service	877-902-9377	•	•	•	•
	•	•			Murray County Abstract Inc	800-687-2988	•	•	•	
•	•				Redi-Info Information Services	888-320-6805				

CR	CV	PR	US	BK	←Courts MUSKOGEE	Recorder→	UC	RE	TX	VS
•	•	•	•	•	Clarke Investigations Inc [SOP]	405-844-7300	•	•	•	•
•	•	•	•	•	Document Retrieval Service	877-902-9377	•	•	•	•
•	•		•	•	Information Searches Inc	918-369-8126				
					Noel D Law Jr	918-599-0988	•	•		
•	•		•	•	Oklahoma Court Explorers	918-360-4798		•	•	
		•	•	•	Records Search & Report Service	918-885-4724, 918-885-9955	•	•	•	•
•	•				Redi-Info Information Services	888-320-6805				
					SRT Investigations	918-481-6045		•	•	

CR	CV	PR	US	BK	←COURTS **NOBLE**	RECORDER→	UC	RE	TX	VS
•	•	•	•	•	Clarke Investigations Inc [SOP]	405-844-7300	•	•	•	•
•	•	•	•	•	Document Retrieval Service	877-902-9377	•	•	•	•
					Noel D Law Jr	918-599-0988	•	•		
•	•	•	•		Powers Abstract Co Inc	580-336-4068	•	•	•	
		•	•	•	Records Search & Report Service	918-885-4724, 918-885-9955	•	•	•	•
•	•				Redi-Info Information Services	888-320-6805				

CR	CV	PR	US	BK	←COURTS **NOWATA**	RECORDER→	UC	RE	TX	VS
•	•	•	•	•	Document Retrieval Service	877-902-9377	•	•	•	•
•	•		•	•	Information Searches Inc	918-369-8126				
					Noel D Law Jr	918-599-0988	•	•		
		•	•	•	Records Search & Report Service	918-885-4724, 918-885-9955	•	•	•	•
•	•				Redi-Info Information Services	888-320-6805				
					SRT Investigations	918-481-6045		•	•	

CR	CV	PR	US	BK	←COURTS **OKFUSKEE**	RECORDER→	UC	RE	TX	VS
•	•	•	•	•	Document Retrieval Service	877-902-9377	•	•	•	•
	•	•			Okfusee Abstract & Title Co	918-623-0565	•	•	•	•
		•	•	•	Records Search & Report Service	918-885-4724, 918-885-9955	•	•	•	•
•	•				Redi-Info Information Services	888-320-6805				

CR	CV	PR	US	BK	←COURTS **OKLAHOMA**	RECORDER→	UC	RE	TX	VS
•	•	•	•	•	American Detective Agency [SOP]	800-219-9120	•	•	•	•
•	•	•	•	•	Clarke Investigations Inc [SOP]	405-844-7300	•	•	•	•
•	•	•	•	•	Document Retrieval Service	877-902-9377	•	•	•	•
					Noel D Law Jr	918-599-0988	•	•		
•	•	•	•	•	Mark McKee, PI [SOP]	405-636-1976	•	•	•	•
•	•				Redi-Info Information Services	888-320-6805				
•	•	•	•		Rus B Robison & Associates Inc [SOP]	405-603-2932	•	•	•	
					SRT Investigations	918-481-6045		•	•	
•	•		•	•	Tammy L Listen Investigations [SOP]	405-340-4843	•	•	•	•
•	•	•	•	•	United Legal Services [SOP]	888-232-8432	•	•	•	

CR	CV	PR	US	BK	←COURTS **OKMULGEE**	RECORDER→	UC	RE	TX	VS
•	•	•	•	•	Clarke Investigations Inc [SOP]	405-844-7300	•	•	•	•
•	•	•	•	•	Document Retrieval Service	877-902-9377	•	•	•	•
•	•		•	•	Information Searches Inc	918-369-8126				
					Noel D Law Jr	918-599-0988	•	•		
		•	•	•	Records Search & Report Service	918-885-4724, 918-885-9955	•	•	•	•
•	•				Redi-Info Information Services	888-320-6805				
					SRT Investigations	918-481-6045		•	•	

CR	CV	PR	US	BK	←COURTS **OSAGE**	RECORDER→	UC	RE	TX	VS
•	•	•	•	•	Document Retrieval Service	877-902-9377	•	•	•	•
•	•		•	•	Information Searches Inc	918-369-8126				
					Noel D Law Jr	918-599-0988	•	•		
		•	•	•	Records Search & Report Service	918-885-4724, 918-885-9955	•	•	•	•
•	•				Redi-Info Information Services	888-320-6805				
					SRT Investigations	918-481-6045		•	•	

CR	CV	PR	US	BK	←COURTS **OTTAWA**	RECORDER→	UC	RE	TX	VS
•	•	•	•	•	Document Retrieval Service	877-902-9377	•	•	•	•
					Noel D Law Jr	918-599-0988	•	•		
	•	•			Photo Abstract Co	918-542-1871	•	•	•	•
		•	•	•	Records Search & Report Service	918-885-4724, 918-885-9955	•	•	•	•
•	•				Redi-Info Information Services	888-320-6805				

CR	CV	PR	US	BK	←Courts	**Pawnee** Recorder→	UC	RE	TX	VS
•	•	•	•	•	Document Retrieval Service	877-902-9377	•	•	•	•
					Noel D Law Jr	918-599-0988	•	•		
		•	•	•	Records Search & Report Service	918-885-4724, 918-885-9955	•	•	•	•
•	•				Redi-Info Information Services	888-320-6805				

CR	CV	PR	US	BK	←Courts	**Payne** Recorder→	UC	RE	TX	VS
•	•	•	•	•	Clarke Investigations Inc [SOP]	405-844-7300	•	•	•	•
•	•	•	•	•	Document Retrieval Service	877-902-9377	•	•	•	•
					Noel D Law Jr	918-599-0988	•	•		
		•	•	•	Records Search & Report Service	918-885-4724, 918-885-9955	•	•	•	•
•	•				Redi-Info Information Services	888-320-6805				

CR	CV	PR	US	BK	←Courts	**Pittsburg** Recorder→	UC	RE	TX	VS
•	•	•	•	•	Document Retrieval Service	877-902-9377	•	•	•	•
	•	•			Hebert Land Services	918-647-9524	•	•	•	•
•	•	•			Pioneer Abstract Co of McAlester Inc	918-423-0817		•	•	
•	•				Redi-Info Information Services	888-320-6805				

CR	CV	PR	US	BK	←Courts	**Pontotoc** Recorder→	UC	RE	TX	VS
•	•	•	•	•	Document Retrieval Service	877-902-9377	•	•	•	•
•	•				Redi-Info Information Services	888-320-6805				

CR	CV	PR	US	BK	←Courts	**Pottawatomie** Recorder→	UC	RE	TX	VS
•	•	•	•	•	Document Retrieval Service	877-902-9377	•	•	•	•
•	•				Pott County Researchers	405-395-4460				
•	•				Redi-Info Information Services	888-320-6805				
•	•		•	•	Tammy L Listen Investigations [SOP]	405-340-4843	•	•	•	•
•	•	•	•	•	United Legal Services [SOP]	888-232-8432	•	•	•	

CR	CV	PR	US	BK	←Courts	**Pushmataha** Recorder→	UC	RE	TX	VS
•	•	•	•	•	Document Retrieval Service	877-902-9377	•	•	•	•
					Moore Mowdy & Youngblood	580-889-5656		•		
	•	•			Pushmataha County Abstract Co	580-298-3189		•	•	
•	•				Redi-Info Information Services	888-320-6805				

CR	CV	PR	US	BK	←Courts	**Roger Mills** Recorder→	UC	RE	TX	VS
•	•	•	•	•	Clarke Investigations Inc [SOP]	405-844-7300	•	•	•	•
•	•	•	•	•	Document Retrieval Service	877-902-9377	•	•	•	•
•	•				Redi-Info Information Services	888-320-6805				

CR	CV	PR	US	BK	←Courts	**Rogers** Recorder→	UC	RE	TX	VS
•	•	•	•	•	Clarke Investigations Inc [SOP]	405-844-7300	•	•	•	•
•	•	•	•	•	Court Data Research Services	918-745-2231	•	•	•	
•	•				Davis and Assoc. [SOP]	918-825-5223				
					Docu-File USA Inc	877-742-4994		•		
•	•	•	•	•	Document Retrieval Service	877-902-9377	•	•	•	•
•	•		•	•	Information Searches Inc	918-369-8126				
					Noel D Law Jr	918-599-0988	•	•		
•	•		•	•	Oklahoma Court Explorers	918-360-4798		•	•	
		•	•	•	Records Search & Report Service	918-885-4724, 918-885-9955	•	•	•	•
•	•				Redi-Info Information Services	888-320-6805				
	•	•			Rogers County Abstract Co	918-341-0525	•	•	•	•
					SRT Investigations	918-481-6045		•	•	
•	•	•	•	•	Zero Investigations Inc [SOP]	866-400-9376	•	•	•	•

CR	CV	PR	US	BK	←Courts	**Seminole** Recorder→	UC	RE	TX	VS
•	•	•	•	•	Document Retrieval Service	877-902-9377	•	•	•	•
•	•				Redi-Info Information Services	888-320-6805				

CR	CV	PR	US	BK	←COURTS SEQUOYAH	RECORDER→	UC	RE	TX	VS
•	•	•	•	•	Document Retrieval Service	877-902-9377	•	•	•	•
	•	•			Hebert Land Services	918-647-9524	•	•	•	•
		•	•	•	Records Search & Report Service	918-885-4724, 918-885-9955	•	•	•	•
•	•				Redi-Info Information Services	888-320-6805				

CR	CV	PR	US	BK	←COURTS STEPHENS	RECORDER→	UC	RE	TX	VS
•	•	•	•	•	H Ray Anderson	580-355-4450	•	•	•	
•	•	•	•	•	Document Retrieval Service	877-902-9377	•	•	•	•
•	•	•	•	•	Mendenhall Information Services	940-696-0758	•	•	•	•
•	•				Redi-Info Information Services	888-320-6805				
	•	•			Stephens County Abstract Co	580-255-2525	•	•	•	

CR	CV	PR	US	BK	←COURTS TEXAS	RECORDER→	UC	RE	TX	VS
•	•	•	•	•	Clarke Investigations Inc [SOP]	405-844-7300	•	•	•	•
•	•	•	•	•	Document Retrieval Service	877-902-9377	•	•	•	•
•	•				Redi-Info Information Services	888-320-6805				

CR	CV	PR	US	BK	←COURTS TILLMAN	RECORDER→	UC	RE	TX	VS
•	•	•	•	•	H Ray Anderson	580-355-4450	•	•	•	
•	•	•	•	•	Clarke Investigations Inc [SOP]	405-844-7300	•	•	•	•
•	•	•	•	•	Document Retrieval Service	877-902-9377	•	•	•	•
•	•	•			King Investigations Inc	580-477-1676		•	•	
•	•	•	•	•	Mendenhall Information Services	940-696-0758	•	•	•	•
•	•				Redi-Info Information Services	888-320-6805				
•	•	•			T.A.B.B.S. Investigations & Process Service [SOP]	580-477-3292	•	•	•	•

CR	CV	PR	US	BK	←COURTS TULSA	RECORDER→	UC	RE	TX	VS
•	•	•	•	•	Clarke Investigations Inc [SOP]	405-844-7300	•	•	•	•
•	•	•	•	•	Court Data Research Services	918-745-2231	•	•	•	
					Docu-File USA Inc	877-742-4994		•		
•	•	•	•	•	Document Retrieval Service	877-902-9377	•	•	•	•
•	•		•	•	Indepth Profiles Inc	800-364-8319				
•	•		•	•	Information Searches Inc	918-369-8126				
•	•	•	•	•	Jones & Associates Inc [SOP]	918-583-4779	•	•	•	•
					Noel D Law Jr	918-599-0988	•	•		
•	•		•	•	Oklahoma Court Explorers	918-360-4798		•	•	
		•	•	•	Records Search & Report Service	918-885-4724, 918-885-9955	•	•	•	•
•	•				Redi-Info Information Services	888-320-6805				
					SRT Investigations	918-481-6045		•	•	
•	•	•	•	•	Zero Investigations Inc [SOP]	866-400-9376	•	•	•	•

CR	CV	PR	US	BK	←COURTS WAGONER	RECORDER→	UC	RE	TX	VS
•	•	•	•	•	Clarke Investigations Inc [SOP]	405-844-7300	•	•	•	•
•	•	•	•	•	Document Retrieval Service	877-902-9377	•	•	•	•
					Noel D Law Jr	918-599-0988	•	•		
•	•		•	•	Oklahoma Court Explorers	918-360-4798		•	•	
		•	•	•	Records Search & Report Service	918-885-4724, 918-885-9955	•	•	•	•
•	•				Redi-Info Information Services	888-320-6805				
					SRT Investigations	918-481-6045		•	•	
	•	•			Wagoner County Abstract Co	918-485-2215	•	•	•	

CR	CV	PR	US	BK	←COURTS WASHINGTON	RECORDER→	UC	RE	TX	VS
•	•	•	•	•	Clarke Investigations Inc [SOP]	405-844-7300	•	•	•	•
•	•	•	•	•	Document Retrieval Service	877-902-9377	•	•	•	•
•	•		•	•	Information Searches Inc	918-369-8126				
					Noel D Law Jr	918-599-0988	•	•		
	•	•			Musselman Abstract Co	918-336-6410	•	•	•	
		•	•	•	Records Search & Report Service	918-885-4724, 918-885-9955	•	•	•	•
•	•				Redi-Info Information Services	888-320-6805				

CR	CV	PR	US	BK	←Courts		Recorder→	UC	RE	TX	VS
					SRT Investigations		918-481-6045		•	•	

CR	CV	PR	US	BK	←Courts	Washita	Recorder→	UC	RE	TX	VS
•	•	•	•	•	Document Retrieval Service		877-902-9377	•	•	•	•
•	•				Redi-Info Information Services		888-320-6805				

CR	CV	PR	US	BK	←Courts	Woods	Recorder→	UC	RE	TX	VS
•	•	•	•	•	Document Retrieval Service		877-902-9377	•	•	•	•
•	•				Redi-Info Information Services		888-320-6805				
•	•	•			Woods County Abstract Corp		580-327-1746	•	•	•	

CR	CV	PR	US	BK	←Courts	Woodward	Recorder→	UC	RE	TX	VS
•	•	•	•	•	Clarke Investigations Inc [SOP]		405-844-7300	•	•	•	•
•	•	•	•	•	Document Retrieval Service		877-902-9377	•	•	•	•
•	•				Redi-Info Information Services		888-320-6805				
	•	•			Woodward County Abstract Co		580-256-3344	•	•	•	

Court Records

Code	Government Agency	Type of Information
CR	Criminal Court	Municipal, county and state level criminal cases
CV	Civil Court	Municipal, county and state level civil cases
PR	Probate Court	Wills and estate cases
US	US District Court	Federal civil and criminal cases
BK	Bankruptcy Court	United States bankruptcy cases

County Records - Recordings

Code	Government Agency	Type of Information
UC	UCC Filing Office	Uniform Commercial Code and other personal property liens
RE	Real Estate Recording Office	Real property transactions and liens
TX	Tax Filing Office(s)	Federal and state tax liens, judgment liens
VS	Vital Records Office	Vital statistics—birth, death, marriage, divorce

Editor's Tip: Sending an unsolicited fax is not recommended, and it is not legal. So, before faxing to a potential new retriever contact, we recommend that you first make a courtesy call and ask for permission to fax to them.

Oregon

COURT RECORDS RETRIEVED — CAPITAL - MARION COUNTY — RECORDED RECORDS RETRIEVED

CR	CV	PR	US	BK	←COURTS BAKER	RECORDER→	UC	RE	TX	VS
•	•	•			M & M Legal Services [SOP]	541-963-8219; Fax- same		•	•	•
•	•	•	•	•	Quik Check Records Inc	503-876-6477	•	•	•	•
•	•	•	•	•	Washington Court Records Service	509-448-5012	•	•	•	•

CR	CV	PR	US	BK	←COURTS BENTON	RECORDER→	UC	RE	TX	VS
•	•	•	•	•	Data Research Inc (Oregon)	800-992-1983	•	•	•	
•	•	•	•	•	Quik Check Records Inc	503-876-6477	•	•	•	•
•	•	•	•	•	Washington Court Records Service	509-448-5012	•	•	•	•

CR	CV	PR	US	BK	←COURTS CLACKAMAS	RECORDER→	UC	RE	TX	VS
•	•	•	•	•	Barrister Support Service [SOP]	503-246-8934				
•	•	•	•	•	Burton-Dukes Legal Support LLC [SOP]	360-254-0878	•	•	•	•
•	•	•	•	•	Data Research Inc (Oregon)	800-992-1983	•	•	•	
•	•	•	•	•	Lawyer's Legal Service LLC [SOP]	800-224-7911	•	•	•	•
					Linda's Property Information Service	503-659-6186	•	•	•	
•	•	•	•	•	Quik Check Records Inc	503-876-6477	•	•	•	•
	•	•			Timely Documents	360-944-1082	•	•	•	
•	•		•	•	Vancouver Legal Messengers Inc [SOP]	888-695-3654	•	•	•	•
•	•	•	•	•	Washington Court Records Service	509-448-5012	•	•	•	•

CR	CV	PR	US	BK	←COURTS CLATSOP	RECORDER→	UC	RE	TX	VS
•	•	•	•	•	Lawyer's Legal Service LLC [SOP]	800-224-7911	•	•	•	•
•	•	•	•	•	Quik Check Records Inc	503-876-6477	•	•	•	•
•	•	•	•	•	Washington Court Records Service	509-448-5012	•	•	•	•

CR	CV	PR	US	BK	←COURTS COLUMBIA	RECORDER→	UC	RE	TX	VS
•	•	•	•	•	Data Research Inc (Oregon)	800-992-1983	•	•	•	
•	•	•	•	•	Lawyer's Legal Service LLC [SOP]	800-224-7911	•	•	•	•
•	•	•	•	•	Quik Check Records Inc	503-876-6477	•	•	•	•
•	•	•	•	•	Washington Court Records Service	509-448-5012	•	•	•	•

CR	CV	PR	US	BK	←COURTS COOS	RECORDER→	UC	RE	TX	VS
•	•	•	•	•	Data Research Inc (Oregon)	800-992-1983	•	•	•	
	•	•			First American Title Insurance of Oregon	800-235-0119	•	•	•	•
•	•	•			North Pacific Legal [SOP]	541-888-5118			•	
•	•	•	•	•	Quik Check Records Inc	503-876-6477	•	•	•	•
•	•	•	•	•	Washington Court Records Service	509-448-5012	•	•	•	•

CR	CV	PR	US	BK	←COURTS CROOK	RECORDER→	UC	RE	TX	VS
•	•	•			Central Legal Services [SOP]	800-599-8133	•	•	•	•
•	•	•	•	•	Data Research Inc (Oregon)	800-992-1983	•	•	•	
•	•	•	•	•	Quik Check Records Inc	503-876-6477	•	•	•	•
•	•				Tri-County Legal Process Service [SOP]	800-600-6315				
•	•	•	•	•	Washington Court Records Service	509-448-5012	•	•	•	•

CR	CV	PR	US	BK	←COURTS CURRY	RECORDER→	UC	RE	TX	VS
•	•	•	•	•	Data Research Inc (Oregon)	800-992-1983	•	•	•	
•	•	•	•	•	Quik Check Records Inc	503-876-6477	•	•	•	•
•	•	•	•	•	Washington Court Records Service	509-448-5012	•	•	•	•

CR	CV	PR	US	BK	←Courts	Deschutes	Recorder→	UC	RE	TX	VS
•	•	•			Central Legal Services [SOP]		800-599-8133	•	•	•	•
•	•	•	•	•	Data Research Inc (Oregon)		800-992-1983	•	•	•	
•	•	•	•	•	Quik Check Records Inc		503-876-6477	•	•	•	•
•	•				Tri-County Legal Process Service [SOP]		800-600-6315				
•	•	•	•	•	Washington Court Records Service		509-448-5012	•	•	•	•

CR	CV	PR	US	BK	←Courts	Douglas	Recorder→	UC	RE	TX	VS
•	•	•	•	•	Data Research Inc (Oregon)		800-992-1983	•	•	•	
•	•	•			Douglas County Title Co (Oregon)		541-672-3388	•	•	•	•
•	•	•	•	•	Quik Check Records Inc		503-876-6477	•	•	•	•
•	•	•			Ticor Title Roseburg		800-660-1146	•	•	•	
•	•	•	•	•	Washington Court Records Service		509-448-5012	•	•	•	•

CR	CV	PR	US	BK	←Courts	Gilliam	Recorder→	UC	RE	TX	VS
•	•	•	•	•	Quik Check Records Inc		503-876-6477	•	•	•	•
•	•	•	•	•	Washington Court Records Service		509-448-5012	•	•	•	•

CR	CV	PR	US	BK	←Courts	Grant	Recorder→	UC	RE	TX	VS
•	•	•	•	•	Quik Check Records Inc		503-876-6477	•	•	•	•
•	•	•	•	•	Washington Court Records Service		509-448-5012	•	•	•	•

CR	CV	PR	US	BK	←Courts	Harney	Recorder→	UC	RE	TX	VS
•	•	•	•	•	Quik Check Records Inc		503-876-6477	•	•	•	•

CR	CV	PR	US	BK	←Courts	Hood River	Recorder→	UC	RE	TX	VS
•	•	•	•	•	Data Research Inc (Oregon)		800-992-1983	•	•	•	
•	•	•	•	•	Lawyer's Legal Service LLC [SOP]		800-224-7911	•	•	•	•
•	•	•	•	•	Quik Check Records Inc		503-876-6477	•	•	•	•
•	•	•	•	•	Washington Court Records Service		509-448-5012	•	•	•	•

CR	CV	PR	US	BK	←Courts	Jackson	Recorder→	UC	RE	TX	VS
•	•	•	•	•	Cleveland & Carl Inv [SOP]		800-888-6629	•	•	•	•
•	•	•	•	•	Data Research Inc (Oregon)		800-992-1983	•	•	•	
•	•	•	•	•	Quik Check Records Inc		503-876-6477	•	•	•	•
•	•	•	•	•	Washington Court Records Service		509-448-5012	•	•	•	•

CR	CV	PR	US	BK	←Courts	Jefferson	Recorder→	UC	RE	TX	VS
•	•	•			Central Legal Services [SOP]		800-599-8133	•	•	•	•
•	•	•	•	•	Data Research Inc (Oregon)		800-992-1983	•	•	•	
•	•	•	•	•	Quik Check Records Inc		503-876-6477	•	•	•	•
•	•				Tri-County Legal Process Service [SOP]		800-600-6315				
•	•	•	•	•	Washington Court Records Service		509-448-5012	•	•	•	•

CR	CV	PR	US	BK	←Courts	Josephine	Recorder→	UC	RE	TX	VS
•	•	•	•	•	Cleveland & Carl Inv [SOP]		800-888-6629	•	•	•	•
•	•	•	•	•	Quik Check Records Inc		503-876-6477	•	•	•	•
•	•	•	•	•	Washington Court Records Service		509-448-5012	•	•	•	•

CR	CV	PR	US	BK	←Courts	Klamath	Recorder→	UC	RE	TX	VS
•	•	•	•	•	Cleveland & Carl Inv [SOP]		800-888-6629	•	•	•	•
•	•	•	•	•	Data Research Inc (Oregon)		800-992-1983	•	•	•	
•	•	•	•	•	Quik Check Records Inc		503-876-6477	•	•	•	•
•	•	•	•	•	Washington Court Records Service		509-448-5012	•	•	•	•

CR	CV	PR	US	BK	←Courts	Lake	Recorder→	UC	RE	TX	VS
•	•	•	•	•	Quik Check Records Inc		503-876-6477	•	•	•	•

CR	CV	PR	US	BK	←Courts	Lane	Recorder→	UC	RE	TX	VS
•	•	•	•	•	B & J/Barristers' Aide Inc [SOP]		541-687-0747				•
•	•	•	•	•	Cleveland & Carl Inv [SOP]		800-888-6629	•	•	•	•
•	•	•	•	•	Data Research Inc (Oregon)		800-992-1983	•	•	•	

CR	CV	PR	US	BK	←Courts	Recorder→	UC	RE	TX	VS
•	•	•	•	•	Quik Check Records Inc	503-876-6477	•	•	•	•
•	•				Thomas Legal Support Service [SOP]	541-563-3345				
•	•	•	•	•	Washington Court Records Service	509-448-5012	•	•	•	•

CR	CV	PR	US	BK	←Courts Lincoln	Recorder→	UC	RE	TX	VS
•	•	•	•	•	Data Research Inc (Oregon)	800-992-1983	•	•	•	
•	•	•	•	•	Quik Check Records Inc	503-876-6477	•	•	•	•
•	•				Thomas Legal Support Service [SOP]	541-563-3345				
•	•	•	•	•	Washington Court Records Service	509-448-5012	•	•	•	•

CR	CV	PR	US	BK	←Courts Linn	Recorder→	UC	RE	TX	VS
•	•	•	•	•	Data Research Inc (Oregon)	800-992-1983	•	•	•	
•	•	•	•	•	Quik Check Records Inc	503-876-6477	•	•	•	•
•	•	•	•	•	Washington Court Records Service	509-448-5012	•	•	•	•

CR	CV	PR	US	BK	←Courts Malheur	Recorder→	UC	RE	TX	VS
•	•	•	•	•	Quik Check Records Inc	503-876-6477	•	•	•	•

CR	CV	PR	US	BK	←Courts Marion	Recorder→	UC	RE	TX	VS
•	•	•	•	•	CSC - Corporation Service Company [SOP]	800-927-9800	•	•	•	•
•	•	•	•	•	Data Research Inc (Oregon)	800-992-1983	•	•	•	
•	•	•	•	•	Lawyer's Legal Service LLC [SOP]	800-224-7911	•	•	•	•
•	•	•			Mill Creek Investigation Agency PC	877-378-1581		•		
•	•	•	•	•	Quik Check Records Inc	503-876-6477	•	•	•	•
	•				Unisearch Inc (Oregon)	800-554-3113	•		•	
•	•	•	•	•	Washington Court Records Service	509-448-5012	•	•	•	•

CR	CV	PR	US	BK	←Courts Morrow	Recorder→	UC	RE	TX	VS
•	•	•	•	•	Quik Check Records Inc	503-876-6477	•	•	•	•
•	•	•	•	•	Washington Court Records Service	509-448-5012	•	•	•	•

CR	CV	PR	US	BK	←Courts Multnomah	Recorder→	UC	RE	TX	VS
•	•	•	•	•	Barrister Support Service [SOP]	503-246-8934				
•	•	•	•	•	Burton-Dukes Legal Support LLC [SOP]	360-254-0878	•	•	•	•
•	•	•	•	•	Data Research Inc (Oregon)	800-992-1983	•	•	•	
•	•	•	•	•	Jess Barker Document Research/Retrieval	888-316-3773	•	•	•	•
•	•	•	•	•	Lawyer's Legal Service LLC [SOP]	800-224-7911	•	•	•	•
					Linda's Property Information Service	503-659-6186	•	•	•	
•	•				Prospective Renters Verification Service	503-655-0888	•	•	•	•
•	•	•	•	•	Quik Check Records Inc	503-876-6477	•	•	•	•
	•	•			Timely Documents	360-944-1082	•	•	•	
•	•		•	•	Vancouver Legal Messengers Inc [SOP]	888-695-3654	•	•	•	•
•	•	•	•	•	Washington Court Records Service	509-448-5012	•	•	•	•

CR	CV	PR	US	BK	←Courts Polk	Recorder→	UC	RE	TX	VS
•	•	•	•	•	Cleveland & Carl Inv [SOP]	800-888-6629	•	•	•	•
•	•	•	•	•	Data Research Inc (Oregon)	800-992-1983	•	•	•	
•	•	•			Mill Creek Investigation Agency PC	877-378-1581		•		
•	•	•	•	•	Quik Check Records Inc	503-876-6477	•	•	•	•
•	•	•	•	•	Washington Court Records Service	509-448-5012	•	•	•	•

CR	CV	PR	US	BK	←Courts Sherman	Recorder→	UC	RE	TX	VS
•	•	•	•	•	Quik Check Records Inc	503-876-6477	•	•	•	•
•	•	•	•	•	Washington Court Records Service	509-448-5012	•	•	•	•

CR	CV	PR	US	BK	←Courts Tillamook	Recorder→	UC	RE	TX	VS
•	•	•	•	•	Quik Check Records Inc	503-876-6477	•	•	•	•
•	•				Thomas Legal Support Service [SOP]	541-563-3345				
•	•	•	•	•	Washington Court Records Service	509-448-5012	•	•	•	•

CR	CV	PR	US	BK	←Courts	UMATILLA	Recorder→	UC	RE	TX	VS
•	•	•	•	•	Quik Check Records Inc		503-876-6477	•	•	•	•
•	•	•	•	•	Washington Court Records Service		509-448-5012	•	•	•	•

CR	CV	PR	US	BK	←Courts	UNION	Recorder→	UC	RE	TX	VS
•	•				Eastern Oregon Title Inc		541-963-8561	•	•	•	
•	•	•			M & M Legal Services [SOP]		541-963-8219; Fax- same		•	•	•
•	•	•	•	•	Quik Check Records Inc		503-876-6477	•	•	•	•
•	•	•	•	•	Washington Court Records Service		509-448-5012	•	•	•	•

CR	CV	PR	US	BK	←Courts	WALLOWA	Recorder→	UC	RE	TX	VS
•	•	•			M & M Legal Services [SOP]		541-963-8219; Fax- same		•	•	•
•	•	•	•	•	Quik Check Records Inc		503-876-6477	•	•	•	•
•	•	•	•	•	Washington Court Records Service		509-448-5012	•	•	•	•

CR	CV	PR	US	BK	←Courts	WASCO	Recorder→	UC	RE	TX	VS
•	•	•	•	•	Data Research Inc (Oregon)		800-992-1983	•	•	•	

CR	CV	PR	US	BK	←Courts	WASHINGTON	Recorder→	UC	RE	TX	VS
•	•	•	•	•	Barrister Support Service [SOP]		503-246-8934				
•	•		•	•	Burton-Dukes Legal Support LLC [SOP]		360-254-0878	•	•	•	•
•	•	•	•	•	Data Research Inc (Oregon)		800-992-1983	•	•	•	
•	•	•	•	•	Jess Barker Document Research/Retrieval		888-316-3773	•	•	•	•
•	•	•	•	•	Lawyer's Legal Service LLC [SOP]		800-224-7911	•	•	•	•
					Linda's Property Information Service		503-659-6186	•	•	•	
•	•	•	•	•	Quik Check Records Inc		503-876-6477	•	•	•	•
	•	•			Timely Documents		360-944-1082	•	•	•	
•	•		•	•	Vancouver Legal Messengers Inc [SOP]		888-695-3654	•	•	•	•
•	•	•	•	•	Washington Court Records Service		509-448-5012	•	•	•	•

CR	CV	PR	US	BK	←Courts	WHEELER	Recorder→	UC	RE	TX	VS
•	•	•	•	•	Quik Check Records Inc		503-876-6477	•	•	•	•
•	•	•	•	•	Washington Court Records Service		509-448-5012	•	•	•	•

CR	CV	PR	US	BK	←Courts	YAMHILL	Recorder→	UC	RE	TX	VS
•	•	•		•	Data Research Inc (Oregon)		800-992-1983	•	•	•	
•	•	•	•	•	Lawyer's Legal Service LLC [SOP]		800-224-7911	•	•	•	•
•	•	•	•	•	Quik Check Records Inc		503-876-6477	•	•	•	•
•	•	•	•	•	Washington Court Records Service		509-448-5012	•	•	•	•

Editor's Tip: This section of the directory is not organized to promote search firms that are statewide, regional, or national in coverage.

An expanded resource of search firms, distributors, and screening firms is BRB Publication's website at www.brbpub.com. Click the "Find A Vendor" tab. Both sources contain information on firms that use online resources to obtain public record index information.

Pennsylvania

COURT RECORDS RETRIEVED | **CAPITAL - DAUPHIN COUNTY** | **RECORDED RECORDS RETRIEVED**

CR	CV	PR	US	BK	←COURTS ADAMS	RECORDER→	UC	RE	TX	VS
•	•		•	•	Accufax: Authentic Document Retrieval	800-336-1001	•	•	•	•
					Colonial Valley Abstract Co	717-848-2871	•	•	•	
•	•				Docket Detective LLC	717-249-7053				
•	•	•	•	•	Franklin Civil Process [SOP]	717-263-0041	•	•	•	•

CR	CV	PR	US	BK	←COURTS ALLEGHENY	RECORDER→	UC	RE	TX	VS
•	•		•	•	Accufax: Authentic Document Retrieval	800-336-1001	•	•	•	•
•	•	•			Applied Research & Investigation	800-594-0008				
	•	•	•	•	Cfacts	800-233-4747	•	•	•	
•	•		•	•	Financial Dimensions	800-858-9808	•	•	•	
•	•	•	•	•	Hawk Investigations [SOP]	412-487-9274	•	•	•	•
•					Justifacts Credential Verification Inc	800-356-6885				
•	•	•			Miller Abstracts	412-607-4952	•	•	•	
•	•	•	•	•	Pittsburgh Information & Research Co [SOP]	412-766-3832	•	•	•	•
•	•	•	•	•	Quest & Assoc Inc	412-563-1007	•	•	•	

CR	CV	PR	US	BK	←COURTS ARMSTRONG	RECORDER→	UC	RE	TX	VS
•	•		•	•	Accufax: Authentic Document Retrieval	800-336-1001	•	•	•	•
•	•	•		•	Falcon Research & Settlement	800-828-4081	•	•	•	
•	•	•	•	•	Hawk Investigations [SOP]	412-487-9274	•	•	•	•
•	•	•	•	•	ILS Research Inc [SOP]	570-454-3535	•	•	•	•
	•	•			Jireh Business Information Solutions Inc	724-863-7270		•	•	
•					Justifacts Credential Verification Inc	800-356-6885				
	•	•			Lawyers' Abstract Co	724-283-3510	•	•	•	

CR	CV	PR	US	BK	←COURTS BEAVER	RECORDER→	UC	RE	TX	VS
•	•		•	•	Accufax: Authentic Document Retrieval	800-336-1001	•	•	•	•
•	•	•			Applied Research & Investigation	800-594-0008				
	•	•	•	•	Cfacts	800-233-4747	•	•	•	
•	•				Docket Detective LLC	717-249-7053				
•	•	•	•	•	Hawk Investigations [SOP]	412-487-9274	•	•	•	•
•	•	•	•	•	ILS Research Inc [SOP]	570-454-3535	•	•	•	•
	•	•			Jireh Business Information Solutions Inc	724-863-7270		•	•	
•	•	•	•	•	Pittsburgh Information & Research Co [SOP]	412-766-3832	•	•	•	•

CR	CV	PR	US	BK	←COURTS BEDFORD	RECORDER→	UC	RE	TX	VS
•	•		•	•	Accufax: Authentic Document Retrieval	800-336-1001	•	•	•	•
•	•	•			B & G Ltd of Hollidaysburg	814-695-8414	•	•	•	
•	•		•	•	Excel Abstract Services	814-623-5213	•	•	•	
•	•	•	•	•	ILS Research Inc [SOP]	570-454-3535	•	•	•	•
	•	•			Jireh Business Information Solutions Inc	724-863-7270		•	•	

CR	CV	PR	US	BK	←COURTS BERKS	RECORDER→	UC	RE	TX	VS
		•			Abstract Associates of Lancaster Inc [SOP]	717-581-5841	•	•	•	•
•	•		•	•	Accufax: Authentic Document Retrieval	800-336-1001	•	•	•	•
					ATACO Inc	800-220-2039		•		
•	•		•	•	Best Legal Services Inc [SOP]	800-562-9620	•	•	•	•
•	•	•	•	•	Commonwealth Investigative Agency	610-433-2325	•	•	•	•
•	•		•	•	Confidential Investigations [SOP]	800-969-4827	•	•	•	•
•					MBE	610-395-2202				
•	•	•	•	•	Pittsburgh Information & Research Co [SOP]	412-766-3832	•	•	•	•

CR	CV	PR	US	BK	Retriever	Phone	UC	RE	TX	VS
•	•		•	•	Public Records Abstract	484-256-6416	•	•	•	•
	•		•	•	Security Search & Abstract Co Inc	800-345-9494	•	•	•	
•	•	•			William C Brown & Co	610-373-1516	•	•	•	

CR	CV	PR	US	BK	←Courts BLAIR	Recorder→	UC	RE	TX	VS
•	•		•	•	Accufax: Authentic Document Retrieval	800-336-1001	•	•	•	•
•	•	•			B & G Ltd of Hollidaysburg	814-695-8414	•	•	•	
	•	•			Jireh Business Information Solutions Inc	724-863-7270		•	•	
•	•	•	•	•	Pittsburgh Information & Research Co [SOP]	412-766-3832	•	•	•	•

CR	CV	PR	US	BK	←Courts BRADFORD	Recorder→	UC	RE	TX	VS
•	•		•	•	Accufax: Authentic Document Retrieval	800-336-1001	•	•	•	•
					Deeds Plus Abstract Services Inc	570-746-3844	•	•	•	
•	•				Krayer Detective Agency Inc [SOP]	800-249-3704				

CR	CV	PR	US	BK	←Courts BUCKS	Recorder→	UC	RE	TX	VS
•	•		•	•	Accufax: Authentic Document Retrieval	800-336-1001	•	•	•	•
					ATACO Inc	800-220-2039		•		
•	•	•	•	•	B & R Services for Professionals [SOP]	800-503-7400	•	•	•	•
•	•	•	•	•	Background Data Services LLC	610-284-2834, cell- 610-529-2200	•		•	•
•	•		•	•	Best Legal Services Inc [SOP]	800-562-9620	•	•	•	•
•	•	•	•	•	Commonwealth Investigative Agency	610-433-2325	•	•	•	•
•	•	•	•	•	Coyne Search Service Inc	215-547-1853	•	•	•	•
•	•	•	•	•	ICORP Services & Solutions [SOP]	888-512-8257	•	•	•	•
•	•	•	•	•	Inquisitive Research Corporation	732-321-0041	•	•	•	•
•					MBE	610-395-2202				
•	•	•	•	•	Pittsburgh Information & Research Co [SOP]	412-766-3832	•	•	•	•
•	•		•	•	Research Specialists Inc	610-358-2507 or 724-5353	•		•	
	•	•	•	•	Searchtec	877-2SEARCH	•	•	•	
	•		•	•	Security Search & Abstract Co Inc	800-345-9494	•	•	•	
•	•	•	•	•	Talone & Associates [SOP]	800-553-5189	•	•	•	•

CR	CV	PR	US	BK	←Courts BUTLER	Recorder→	UC	RE	TX	VS
•	•		•	•	Accufax: Authentic Document Retrieval	800-336-1001	•	•	•	•
	•	•	•	•	Cfacts	800-233-4747	•	•	•	
•	•	•		•	Falcon Research & Settlement	800-828-4081	•	•	•	
•	•	•	•	•	Hawk Investigations [SOP]	412-487-9274	•	•	•	•
•	•	•	•	•	ILS Research Inc [SOP]	570-454-3535	•	•	•	•
	•	•			Jireh Business Information Solutions Inc	724-863-7270		•	•	
•					Justifacts Credential Verification Inc	800-356-6885				
	•	•			Lawyers' Abstract Co	724-283-3510	•	•	•	
•	•	•	•	•	Pittsburgh Information & Research Co [SOP]	412-766-3832	•	•	•	•

CR	CV	PR	US	BK	←Courts CAMBRIA	Recorder→	UC	RE	TX	VS
•	•		•	•	Accufax: Authentic Document Retrieval	800-336-1001	•	•	•	•
•	•	•			B & G Ltd of Hollidaysburg	814-695-8414	•	•	•	
•	•				Docket Detective LLC	717-249-7053				
•	•	•	•	•	ILS Research Inc [SOP]	570-454-3535	•	•	•	•
	•	•			Jireh Business Information Solutions Inc	724-863-7270		•	•	
•	•				Mainline Researchers Inc	814-472-7913	•	•	•	

CR	CV	PR	US	BK	←Courts CAMERON	Recorder→	UC	RE	TX	VS
•	•		•	•	Accufax: Authentic Document Retrieval	800-336-1001	•	•	•	•
•	•	•		•	Falcon Research & Settlement	800-828-4081	•	•	•	
•	•	•	•	•	ILS Research Inc [SOP]	570-454-3535	•	•	•	•
•	•	•			David Reed [SOP]	814-486-9327	•	•	•	•

CR	CV	PR	US	BK	←Courts CARBON	Recorder→	UC	RE	TX	VS
•	•				ACBS	866-530-2227	•	•	•	
•	•		•	•	Accufax: Authentic Document Retrieval	800-336-1001	•	•	•	•
•	•		•	•	Confidential Investigations [SOP]	800-969-4827	•	•	•	•

CR	CV	PR	US	BK	←COURTS		RECORDER→	UC	RE	TX	VS
	•	•			Fidelity Home Abstract Inc		800-224-5601	•	•	•	
•	•	•	•	•	ILS Research Inc [SOP]		570-454-3535	•	•	•	•
	•	•			Toma Abstract Inc		570-454-7899	•	•	•	
CR	**CV**	**PR**	**US**	**BK**	**←COURTS**	**CENTRE**	**RECORDER→**	**UC**	**RE**	**TX**	**VS**
•	•		•	•	Accufax: Authentic Document Retrieval		800-336-1001	•	•	•	•
•	•	•			B & G Ltd of Hollidaysburg		814-695-8414	•	•	•	
CR	**CV**	**PR**	**US**	**BK**	**←COURTS**	**CHESTER**	**RECORDER→**	**UC**	**RE**	**TX**	**VS**
		•			Abstract Associates of Lancaster Inc [SOP]		717-581-5841	•	•	•	•
	•		•	•	Accufax: Authentic Document Retrieval		800-336-1001	•	•	•	•
•	•	•	•	•	American Abstractors Inc [SOP]		610-353-5375	•	•	•	•
					ATACO Inc		800-220-2039		•		
•	•	•	•	•	B & R Services for Professionals [SOP]		800-503-7400	•	•	•	•
•	•	•	•	•	Background Data Services LLC		610-284-2834, cell- 610-529-2200	•		•	•
•	•	•	•	•	Background Data Services LLC		610-284-2834, cell- 610-529-2200	•		•	•
•	•		•	•	Best Legal Services Inc [SOP]		800-562-9620	•	•	•	•
•	•		•	•	Blue Marble Logistics LLC [SOP]		302-661-4390	•	•	•	
•	•	•	•	•	Coyne Search Service Inc		215-547-1853	•	•	•	•
•	•	•	•	•	Inquisitive Research Corporation		732-321-0041	•	•	•	•
•	•	•	•	•	Pittsburgh Information & Research Co [SOP]		412-766-3832	•	•	•	•
•	•		•	•	Research Specialists Inc		610-358-2507 or 724-5353	•		•	
	•	•	•	•	Searchtec		877-2SEARCH	•	•	•	
	•		•	•	Security Search & Abstract Co Inc		800-345-9494	•	•	•	
•	•		•	•	Services For Lawyers		610-566-9165		•	•	•
•	•	•	•	•	Talone & Associates [SOP]		800-553-5189	•	•	•	•
CR	**CV**	**PR**	**US**	**BK**	**←COURTS**	**CLARION**	**RECORDER→**	**UC**	**RE**	**TX**	**VS**
•	•		•	•	Accufax: Authentic Document Retrieval		800-336-1001	•	•	•	•
•	•	•		•	Falcon Research & Settlement		800-828-4081	•	•	•	
•	•	•	•	•	ILS Research Inc [SOP]		570-454-3535	•	•	•	•
CR	**CV**	**PR**	**US**	**BK**	**←COURTS**	**CLEARFIELD**	**RECORDER→**	**UC**	**RE**	**TX**	**VS**
•	•		•	•	Accufax: Authentic Document Retrieval		800-336-1001	•	•	•	•
•	•	•			B & G Ltd of Hollidaysburg		814-695-8414	•	•	•	
•	•	•		•	Falcon Research & Settlement		800-828-4081	•	•	•	
CR	**CV**	**PR**	**US**	**BK**	**←COURTS**	**CLINTON**	**RECORDER→**	**UC**	**RE**	**TX**	**VS**
•	•		•	•	Accufax: Authentic Document Retrieval		800-336-1001	•	•	•	•
CR	**CV**	**PR**	**US**	**BK**	**←COURTS**	**COLUMBIA**	**RECORDER→**	**UC**	**RE**	**TX**	**VS**
•	•		•	•	Accufax: Authentic Document Retrieval		800-336-1001	•	•	•	•
•	•	•	•	•	ILS Research Inc [SOP]		570-454-3535	•	•	•	•
•	•				Krayer Detective Agency Inc [SOP]		800-249-3704				
	•	•			Toma Abstract Inc		570-454-7899	•	•	•	
CR	**CV**	**PR**	**US**	**BK**	**←COURTS**	**CRAWFORD**	**RECORDER→**	**UC**	**RE**	**TX**	**VS**
•	•		•	•	Accufax: Authentic Document Retrieval		800-336-1001	•	•	•	•
•	•	•	•	•	ILS Research Inc [SOP]		570-454-3535	•	•	•	•
	•				Realty Settlement Inc		814-336-1802	•	•	•	
•	•	•		•	David M Rumancik		330-837-7737	•	•	•	
CR	**CV**	**PR**	**US**	**BK**	**←COURTS**	**CUMBERLAND**	**RECORDER→**	**UC**	**RE**	**TX**	**VS**
•	•		•	•	Accufax: Authentic Document Retrieval		800-336-1001	•	•	•	•
•	•	•	•	•	Associated Services [SOP]		717-938-1550	•	•	•	
•	•				Docket Detective LLC		717-249-7053				
•	•	•	•	•	Franklin Civil Process [SOP]		717-263-0041	•	•	•	•
•	•	•	•	•	ILS Research Inc [SOP]		570-454-3535	•	•	•	•
•	•	•	•	•	Information Network Associates Inc [SOP]		800-443-0824	•	•	•	•
	•	•	•	•	Penncorp Service Group Inc		800-544-9050	•	•	•	•
•	•	•	•	•	Pittsburgh Information & Research Co [SOP]		412-766-3832	•	•	•	•

CR	CV	PR	US	BK	←COURTS DAUPHIN	RECORDER→	UC	RE	TX	VS
		•			Abstract Associates of Lancaster Inc [SOP]	717-581-5841	•	•	•	•
•	•		•	•	Accufax: Authentic Document Retrieval	800-336-1001	•	•	•	•
•	•	•	•	•	Associated Services [SOP]	717-938-1550	•	•	•	
•	•		•	•	Best Legal Services Inc [SOP]	800-562-9620	•	•	•	•
•	•				Docket Detective LLC	717-249-7053				
•	•	•	•	•	Esquire Assist Ltd	717-232-9398	•	•	•	
	•	•			HomeHistories.com	717-754-0283		•		•
•	•		•	•	Information Network Associates Inc [SOP]	800-443-0824	•	•	•	•
	•	•	•	•	Penncorp Service Group Inc	800-544-9050	•	•	•	•
•	•	•	•	•	Pittsburgh Information & Research Co [SOP]	412-766-3832	•	•	•	•
•	•	•	•	•	Shinkowsky Investigations	800-276-0202	•	•	•	•

CR	CV	PR	US	BK	←COURTS DELAWARE	RECORDER→	UC	RE	TX	VS
•	•		•	•	Accufax: Authentic Document Retrieval	800-336-1001	•	•	•	•
•	•	•	•	•	American Abstractors Inc [SOP]	610-353-5375	•	•	•	•
					ATACO Inc	800-220-2039		•		
•	•	•	•	•	B & R Services for Professionals [SOP]	800-503-7400	•	•	•	•
•	•	•	•	•	Background Data Services LLC	610-284-2834, cell- 610-529-2200	•		•	•
•	•		•	•	Best Legal Services Inc [SOP]	800-562-9620	•	•	•	•
•	•		•	•	Blue Marble Logistics LLC [SOP]	302-661-4390	•	•	•	
•	•	•	•	•	Coyne Search Service Inc	215-547-1853	•	•	•	•
•	•	•	•	•	ICORP Services & Solutions [SOP]	888-512-8257	•	•	•	•
•	•	•	•	•	Inquisitive Research Corporation	732-321-0041	•	•	•	•
•	•	•	•	•	Pittsburgh Information & Research Co [SOP]	412-766-3832	•	•	•	•
•	•		•	•	Research Specialists Inc	610-358-2507 or 724-5353	•		•	
	•	•	•	•	Searchtec	877-2SEARCH	•	•	•	
	•		•	•	Security Search & Abstract Co Inc	800-345-9494	•	•	•	
•	•	•	•	•	Services For Lawyers	610-566-9165		•	•	•
•	•	•	•	•	Talone & Associates [SOP]	800-553-5189	•	•	•	•

CR	CV	PR	US	BK	←COURTS ELK	RECORDER→	UC	RE	TX	VS
•	•		•	•	Accufax: Authentic Document Retrieval	800-336-1001	•	•	•	•
•	•	•		•	Falcon Research & Settlement	800-828-4081	•	•	•	
•	•	•	•	•	ILS Research Inc [SOP]	570-454-3535	•	•	•	•
•	•	•			David Reed [SOP]	814-486-9327	•	•	•	•

CR	CV	PR	US	BK	←COURTS ERIE	RECORDER→	UC	RE	TX	VS
•	•		•	•	Accufax: Authentic Document Retrieval	800-336-1001	•	•	•	•
•	•		•	•	Darlene Chiota	814-454-7589	•	•	•	
•	•	•	•	•	Pittsburgh Information & Research Co [SOP]	412-766-3832	•	•	•	•

CR	CV	PR	US	BK	←COURTS FAYETTE	RECORDER→	UC	RE	TX	VS
•	•		•	•	Accufax: Authentic Document Retrieval	800-336-1001	•	•	•	•
•	•	•			Fayette Professional Services	412-439-1450	•	•	•	
•	•	•	•	•	Hawk Investigations [SOP]	412-487-9274	•	•	•	•
•	•	•			Heather L Gilbert Title Abstract & Closing Service	724-998-5954	•	•	•	•
•	•	•	•	•	ILS Research Inc [SOP]	570-454-3535	•	•	•	•
	•	•			Jireh Business Information Solutions Inc	724-863-7270		•	•	

CR	CV	PR	US	BK	←COURTS FOREST	RECORDER→	UC	RE	TX	VS
•	•		•	•	Accufax: Authentic Document Retrieval	800-336-1001	•	•	•	•
•	•	•		•	Falcon Research & Settlement	800-828-4081	•	•	•	
•	•	•	•	•	ILS Research Inc [SOP]	570-454-3535	•	•	•	•

CR	CV	PR	US	BK	←COURTS FRANKLIN	RECORDER→	UC	RE	TX	VS
•	•		•	•	Accufax: Authentic Document Retrieval	800-336-1001	•	•	•	•
					Colonial Valley Abstract Co	717-848-2871	•	•	•	
•	•	•	•	•	Franklin Civil Process [SOP]	717-263-0041	•	•	•	•

CR	CV	PR	US	BK	←Courts **FULTON** Recorder→	Phone	UC	RE	TX	VS
•	•		•	•	Accufax: Authentic Document Retrieval	800-336-1001	•	•	•	•
•	•	•	•	•	Franklin Civil Process [SOP]	717-263-0041	•	•	•	•

CR	CV	PR	US	BK	←Courts **GREENE** Recorder→	Phone	UC	RE	TX	VS
•	•		•	•	Accufax: Authentic Document Retrieval	800-336-1001	•	•	•	•
•	•	•			Fayette Professional Services	412-439-1450	•	•	•	
•	•	•			Heather L Gilbert Title Abstract & Closing Service	724-998-5954	•	•	•	•
•	•	•	•	•	ILS Research Inc [SOP]	570-454-3535	•	•	•	•
	•	•			Jireh Business Information Solutions Inc.	724-863-7270		•	•	

CR	CV	PR	US	BK	←Courts **HUNTINGDON** Recorder→	Phone	UC	RE	TX	VS
•	•		•	•	Accufax: Authentic Document Retrieval	800-336-1001	•	•	•	•
•	•	•			B & G Ltd of Hollidaysburg	814-695-8414	•	•	•	

CR	CV	PR	US	BK	←Courts **INDIANA** Recorder→	Phone	UC	RE	TX	VS
•	•		•	•	Accufax: Authentic Document Retrieval	800-336-1001	•	•	•	•
•	•	•		•	Falcon Research & Settlement	800-828-4081	•	•	•	
•	•	•	•	•	Hawk Investigations [SOP]	412-487-9274	•	•	•	•
•	•	•	•	•	ILS Research Inc [SOP]	570-454-3535	•	•	•	•
	•	•			Jireh Business Information Solutions Inc.	724-863-7270		•	•	
•	•	•			Schillinger & Keith Abstract & Settlement	800-275-2959	•	•	•	

CR	CV	PR	US	BK	←Courts **JEFFERSON** Recorder→	Phone	UC	RE	TX	VS
•	•		•	•	Accufax: Authentic Document Retrieval	800-336-1001	•	•	•	•
•	•	•		•	Falcon Research & Settlement	800-828-4081	•	•	•	
•	•	•	•	•	ILS Research Inc [SOP]	570-454-3535	•	•	•	•

CR	CV	PR	US	BK	←Courts **JUNIATA** Recorder→	Phone	UC	RE	TX	VS
•	•		•	•	Accufax: Authentic Document Retrieval	800-336-1001	•	•	•	•

CR	CV	PR	US	BK	←Courts **LACKAWANNA** Recorder→	Phone	UC	RE	TX	VS
	•	•			Abstract Enterprises Inc	570-963-5290	•	•	•	•
•	•		•	•	Accufax: Authentic Document Retrieval	800-336-1001	•	•	•	•
			•	•	Credit Lenders Service Agency Inc	856-787-9005	•	•	•	
•	•	•	•	•	ILS Research Inc [SOP]	570-454-3535	•	•	•	•
•	•				Krayer Detective Agency Inc [SOP]	800-249-3704				
•	•	•	•	•	Pittsburgh Information & Research Co [SOP]	412-766-3832	•	•	•	•
	•		•		Marg Strein	570-457-3939	•		•	•

CR	CV	PR	US	BK	←Courts **LANCASTER** Recorder→	Phone	UC	RE	TX	VS
		•			Abstract Associates of Lancaster Inc [SOP]	717-581-5841	•	•	•	•
•	•		•	•	Accufax: Authentic Document Retrieval	800-336-1001	•	•	•	•
			•	•	American Abstractors Inc [SOP]	610-353-5375	•	•	•	•
•	•		•	•	Best Legal Services Inc [SOP]	800-562-9620	•	•	•	•
					Colonial Valley Abstract Co	717-848-2871	•	•	•	
•	•				Docket Detective LLC	717-249-7053				
•	•	•	•	•	Pittsburgh Information & Research Co [SOP]	412-766-3832	•	•	•	•
	•		•	•	Security Search & Abstract Co Inc	800-345-9494	•	•	•	
•	•	•	•	•	Shinkowsky Investigations	800-276-0202	•	•	•	•
•	•	•	•	•	Talone & Associates [SOP]	800-553-5189	•	•	•	•

CR	CV	PR	US	BK	←Courts **LAWRENCE** Recorder→	Phone	UC	RE	TX	VS
•	•		•	•	Accufax: Authentic Document Retrieval	800-336-1001	•	•	•	•
•	•	•	•	•	Hawk Investigations [SOP]	412-487-9274	•	•	•	•
•	•	•	•	•	ILS Research Inc [SOP]	570-454-3535	•	•	•	•
	•	•			Jireh Business Information Solutions Inc.	724-863-7270		•	•	

CR	CV	PR	US	BK	←COURTS **LEBANON** RECORDER→	UC	RE	TX	VS
		•			Abstract Associates of Lancaster Inc [SOP] 717-581-5841	•	•	•	•
•	•		•	•	Accufax: Authentic Document Retrieval 800-336-1001	•	•	•	•
•	•				Docket Detective LLC 717-249-7053				
	•	•			HomeHistories.com 717-754-0283		•		•
•	•	•	•	•	Information Network Associates Inc [SOP] 800-443-0824	•	•	•	•

CR	CV	PR	US	BK	←COURTS **LEHIGH** RECORDER→	UC	RE	TX	VS
•	•				ACBS 866-530-2227	•	•	•	
•	•		•	•	Accufax: Authentic Document Retrieval 800-336-1001	•	•	•	•
•	•	•	•		Associated Investigative Services Inc [SOP] 610-351-9911	•	•	•	
•	•	•	•	•	Commonwealth Investigative Agency 610-433-2325	•	•	•	•
•	•		•	•	Confidential Investigations [SOP] 800-969-4827	•	•	•	•
•					MBE 610-395-2202				
•	•	•	•	•	Pittsburgh Information & Research Co [SOP] 412-766-3832	•	•	•	•
	•		•	•	Security Search & Abstract Co Inc 800-345-9494	•	•	•	
•	•	•	•	•	Talone & Associates [SOP] 800-553-5189	•	•	•	•
	•	•			John A Zapf 610-868-5101	•	•	•	

CR	CV	PR	US	BK	←COURTS **LUZERNE** RECORDER→	UC	RE	TX	VS
•	•		•	•	Accufax: Authentic Document Retrieval 800-336-1001	•	•	•	•
		•			All Penn Abstract Co 570-823-5410	•	•	•	
•	•	•	•	•	Commonwealth Investigative Agency 610-433-2325	•	•	•	•
•	•	•	•	•	ILS Research Inc [SOP] 570-454-3535	•	•	•	•
•	•				Krayer Detective Agency Inc [SOP] 800-249-3704				
•	•	•	•	•	Pittsburgh Information & Research Co [SOP] 412-766-3832	•	•	•	•
	•	•	•		Marg Strein 570-457-3939	•	•	•	•
	•	•			Toma Abstract Inc 570-454-7899	•	•	•	

CR	CV	PR	US	BK	←COURTS **LYCOMING** RECORDER→	UC	RE	TX	VS
•	•		•	•	Accufax: Authentic Document Retrieval 800-336-1001	•	•	•	•

CR	CV	PR	US	BK	←COURTS **MCKEAN** RECORDER→	UC	RE	TX	VS
•	•		•	•	Accufax: Authentic Document Retrieval 800-336-1001	•	•	•	•
•	•	•		•	Falcon Research & Settlement 800-828-4081	•	•	•	
•	•	•			David Reed [SOP] 814-486-9327	•	•	•	•

CR	CV	PR	US	BK	←COURTS **MERCER** RECORDER→	UC	RE	TX	VS
•	•		•	•	Accufax: Authentic Document Retrieval 800-336-1001	•	•	•	•
•	•	•			DRP Paralegal Services Inc 724-699-5528	•	•	•	
•	•	•		•	Falcon Research & Settlement 800-828-4081	•	•	•	
	•				Realty Settlement Inc 814-336-1802	•	•	•	
•	•	•		•	David M Rumancik 330-837-7737	•	•	•	

CR	CV	PR	US	BK	←COURTS **MIFFLIN** RECORDER→	UC	RE	TX	VS
•	•		•	•	Accufax: Authentic Document Retrieval 800-336-1001	•	•	•	•

CR	CV	PR	US	BK	←COURTS **MONROE** RECORDER→	UC	RE	TX	VS
•	•		•	•	Accufax: Authentic Document Retrieval 800-336-1001	•	•	•	•
•	•		•	•	Confidential Investigations [SOP] 800-969-4827	•	•	•	•
			•		Credit Lenders Service Agency Inc 856-787-9005	•	•	•	
	•	•			Fidelity Home Abstract Inc 800-224-5601	•	•	•	
•	•				Krayer Detective Agency Inc [SOP] 800-249-3704				
•	•	•	•	•	Pittsburgh Information & Research Co [SOP] 412-766-3832	•	•	•	•
	•	•			Toma Abstract Inc 570-454-7899	•	•	•	

CR	CV	PR	US	BK	←COURTS **MONTGOMERY** RECORDER→	UC	RE	TX	VS
•	•		•	•	Accufax: Authentic Document Retrieval 800-336-1001	•	•	•	•
•	•	•	•	•	American Abstractors Inc [SOP] 610-353-5375	•	•	•	•
•	•	•	•	•	B & R Services for Professionals [SOP] 800-503-7400	•	•	•	•
•	•	•	•	•	Background Data Services LLC ....610-284-2834, cell- 610-529-2200	•		•	•

CR	CV	PR	US	BK	←Courts	Recorder→	UC	RE	TX	VS
•	•		•	•	Best Legal Services Inc [SOP]	800-562-9620	•	•	•	•
•	•	•	•	•	Coyne Search Service Inc	215-547-1853	•	•	•	•
•	•	•	•	•	ICORP Services & Solutions [SOP]	888-512-8257	•	•	•	•
•	•	•	•	•	Inquisitive Research Corporation	732-321-0041	•	•	•	•
•	•	•	•	•	Keystone Intelligence Network Inc	215-545-1111	•	•	•	•
•					MBE	610-395-2202				
•	•		•	•	Research Specialists Inc	610-358-2507 or 724-5353	•		•	
	•	•		•	Searchtec	877-2SEARCH	•	•	•	
	•		•	•	Security Search & Abstract Co Inc	800-345-9494	•	•	•	
•	•	•	•	•	Services For Lawyers	610-566-9165		•	•	•
•	•	•	•	•	Talone & Associates [SOP]	800-553-5189	•	•	•	•
•	•	•	•	•	Walt J Grant Title Services	610-631-7672	•	•	•	•

CR	CV	PR	US	BK	←Courts MONTOUR	Recorder→	UC	RE	TX	VS
•	•		•	•	Accufax: Authentic Document Retrieval	800-336-1001	•	•	•	•
•	•	•			ST Sayers & MS Chiarkas	570-286-9831		•	•	
	•	•			Toma Abstract Inc	570-454-7899	•	•	•	

CR	CV	PR	US	BK	←Courts NORTHAMPTON	Recorder→	UC	RE	TX	VS
•	•				ACBS	866-530-2227	•	•	•	
•	•		•	•	Accufax: Authentic Document Retrieval	800-336-1001	•	•	•	•
•	•	•	•	•	Commonwealth Investigative Agency	610-433-2325	•	•	•	•
•	•		•	•	Confidential Investigations [SOP]	800-969-4827	•	•	•	•
	•	•			Fidelity Home Abstract Inc	800-224-5601	•	•	•	
•	•	•	•	•	Inquisitive Research Corporation	732-321-0041	•	•	•	•
•					MBE	610-395-2202				
	•		•	•	Security Search & Abstract Co Inc	800-345-9494	•	•	•	
	•	•			John A Zapf	610-868-5101	•	•	•	

CR	CV	PR	US	BK	←Courts NORTHUMBERLAND	Recorder→	UC	RE	TX	VS
•	•		•	•	Accufax: Authentic Document Retrieval	800-336-1001	•	•	•	•
•	•	•	•	•	Shinkowsky Investigations	800-276-0202	•	•	•	•
•	•	•			ST Sayers & MS Chiarkas	570-286-9831		•	•	

CR	CV	PR	US	BK	←Courts PERRY	Recorder→	UC	RE	TX	VS
•	•		•	•	Accufax: Authentic Document Retrieval	800-336-1001	•	•	•	•
•	•				Docket Detective LLC	717-249-7053				

CR	CV	PR	US	BK	←Courts PHILADELPHIA	Recorder→	UC	RE	TX	VS
•	•		•	•	Accufax: Authentic Document Retrieval	800-336-1001	•	•	•	•
•	•	•	•	•	American Abstractors Inc [SOP]	610-353-5375	•	•	•	•
•	•	•	•	•	B & R Services for Professionals [SOP]	800-503-7400	•	•	•	•
•	•		•	•	Best Legal Services Inc [SOP]	800-562-9620	•	•	•	•
•	•		•	•	Blue Marble Logistics LLC [SOP]	302-661-4390	•	•	•	
•	•		•	•	County House Research Inc	866-594-1177				
•	•	•	•	•	Coyne Search Service Inc	215-547-1853	•	•	•	•
•	•				Ethical Equations	732-928-4130				
•	•	•	•	•	ICORP Services & Solutions [SOP]	888-512-8257	•	•	•	•
•					Iles & Bond Inc	856-854-9580	•	•		
•	•	•	•	•	Inquisitive Research Corporation	732-321-0041	•	•	•	•
•	•	•	•	•	Keystone Intelligence Network Inc	215-545-1111	•	•	•	•
•	•		•		Know It All Background Research Services Inc	888-281-9535				
•					MBE	610-395-2202				
•	•	•	•	•	Pittsburgh Information & Research Co [SOP]	412-766-3832	•	•	•	•
	•	•	•	•	Searchtec	877-2SEARCH	•	•	•	
	•		•	•	Security Search & Abstract Co Inc	800-345-9494	•	•	•	
•	•	•	•	•	Talone & Associates [SOP]	800-553-5189	•	•	•	•

CR	CV	PR	US	BK	←Courts	Pike	Recorder→	UC	RE	TX	VS
•	•		•	•		Accufax: Authentic Document Retrieval	800-336-1001	•	•	•	•
•	•	•				Arbor Abstracting Co	570-253-0472	•	•	•	
			•	•		Credit Lenders Service Agency Inc	856-787-9005	•	•	•	
	•	•				Fidelity Home Abstract Inc	800-224-5601	•	•	•	
•	•					Krayer Detective Agency Inc [SOP]	800-249-3704				

CR	CV	PR	US	BK	←Courts	Potter	Recorder→	UC	RE	TX	VS
•	•		•	•		Accufax: Authentic Document Retrieval	800-336-1001	•	•	•	•
•	•	•		•		Falcon Research & Settlement	800-828-4081	•	•	•	
•	•	•				David Reed [SOP]	814-486-9327	•	•	•	•

CR	CV	PR	US	BK	←Courts	Schuylkill	Recorder→	UC	RE	TX	VS
						ACBS	866-530-2227	•	•	•	
•	•		•	•		Accufax: Authentic Document Retrieval	800-336-1001	•	•	•	•
	•	•				Assured Realty	570-622-1366	•	•	•	
•	•	•	•	•		ILS Research Inc [SOP]	570-454-3535	•	•	•	•
•	•	•				Pellish & Pellish Attorneys at Law	570-622-2338	•	•	•	•
	•		•	•		Security Search & Abstract Co Inc	800-345-9494	•	•	•	
	•	•				Toma Abstract Inc	570-454-7899	•	•	•	

CR	CV	PR	US	BK	←Courts	Snyder	Recorder→	UC	RE	TX	VS
•	•		•	•		Accufax: Authentic Document Retrieval	800-336-1001	•	•	•	•
•	•	•				ST Sayers & MS Chiarkas	570-286-9831		•	•	

CR	CV	PR	US	BK	←Courts	Somerset	Recorder→	UC	RE	TX	VS
•	•		•	•		Accufax: Authentic Document Retrieval	800-336-1001	•	•	•	•
	•	•				Jireh Business Information Solutions Inc	724-863-7270		•	•	
	•					Somerset Abstract Co Ltd	814-445-9525		•	•	

CR	CV	PR	US	BK	←Courts	Sullivan	Recorder→	UC	RE	TX	VS
•	•		•	•		Accufax: Authentic Document Retrieval	800-336-1001	•	•	•	•
•	•					Docket Detective LLC	717-249-7053				

CR	CV	PR	US	BK	←Courts	Susquehanna	Recorder→	UC	RE	TX	VS
•	•		•	•		Accufax: Authentic Document Retrieval	800-336-1001	•	•	•	•
•	•	•				Cindy Bartkis	570-756-3093	•	•	•	•
•	•					Krayer Detective Agency Inc [SOP]	800-249-3704				

CR	CV	PR	US	BK	←Courts	Tioga	Recorder→	UC	RE	TX	VS
•	•		•	•		Accufax: Authentic Document Retrieval	800-336-1001	•	•	•	•

CR	CV	PR	US	BK	←Courts	Union	Recorder→	UC	RE	TX	VS
•	•		•	•		Accufax: Authentic Document Retrieval	800-336-1001	•	•	•	•
•	•					Docket Detective LLC	717-249-7053				
•	•	•				ST Sayers & MS Chiarkas	570-286-9831		•	•	

CR	CV	PR	US	BK	←Courts	Venango	Recorder→	UC	RE	TX	VS
•	•		•	•		Accufax: Authentic Document Retrieval	800-336-1001	•	•	•	•
•	•	•		•		Falcon Research & Settlement	800-828-4081	•	•	•	
•	•	•		•		ILS Research Inc [SOP]	570-454-3535	•	•	•	•
	•					Realty Settlement Inc	814-336-1802	•	•	•	
•	•	•		•		David M Rumancik	330-837-7737	•	•	•	

CR	CV	PR	US	BK	←Courts	Warren	Recorder→	UC	RE	TX	VS
•	•		•	•		Accufax: Authentic Document Retrieval	800-336-1001	•	•	•	•
•	•	•		•		Falcon Research & Settlement	800-828-4081	•	•	•	

CR	CV	PR	US	BK	←Courts	Washington	Recorder→	UC	RE	TX	VS
•	•		•	•		Accufax: Authentic Document Retrieval	800-336-1001	•	•	•	•
	•	•	•	•		Cfacts	800-233-4747	•	•	•	
•	•	•				Fayette Professional Services	412-439-1450	•	•	•	

CR	CV	PR	US	BK	←Courts		Recorder→	UC	RE	TX	VS
•	•	•	•	•	Hawk Investigations [SOP]		412-487-9274	•	•	•	•
•	•	•			Heather L Gilbert Title Abstract & Closing Service		724-998-5954	•	•	•	•
	•	•			Jireh Business Information Solutions Inc		724-863-7270		•	•	
•	•	•	•	•	Pittsburgh Information & Research Co [SOP]		412-766-3832	•	•	•	•

CR	CV	PR	US	BK	←Courts	Wayne	Recorder→	UC	RE	TX	VS
•	•		•	•	Accufax: Authentic Document Retrieval		800-336-1001	•	•	•	•
•	•	•			Arbor Abstracting Co		570-253-0472	•	•	•	
			•	•	Credit Lenders Service Agency Inc		856-787-9005	•	•	•	
	•	•			Fidelity Home Abstract Inc		800-224-5601	•	•	•	
	•				Inter-County Abstract		570-253-4734		•		
•	•				Krayer Detective Agency Inc [SOP]		800-249-3704				
•	•	•			Kathleen Schloesser		570-253-5368	•	•	•	

CR	CV	PR	US	BK	←Courts	Westmoreland	Recorder→	UC	RE	TX	VS
•	•		•	•	Accufax: Authentic Document Retrieval		800-336-1001	•	•	•	•
	•	•	•	•	Cfacts		800-233-4747	•	•	•	
•	•	•			Fayette Professional Services		412-439-1450	•	•	•	
•	•	•	•	•	Hawk Investigations [SOP]		412-487-9274	•	•	•	•
•	•	•	•	•	ILS Research Inc [SOP]		570-454-3535	•	•	•	•
	•	•			Jireh Business Information Solutions Inc		724-863-7270		•	•	
•					Justifacts Credential Verification Inc		800-356-6885				
	•	•			Lawyers' Abstract Co		724-283-3510	•	•	•	
•	•	•			Miller Abstracts		412-607-4952	•	•	•	
•	•	•	•	•	Pittsburgh Information & Research Co [SOP]		412-766-3832	•	•	•	•

CR	CV	PR	US	BK	←Courts	Wyoming	Recorder→	UC	RE	TX	VS
•	•		•	•	Accufax: Authentic Document Retrieval		800-336-1001	•	•	•	•
•	•	•			Catherine J Garbus		570-836-6749	•	•	•	•
•	•				Krayer Detective Agency Inc [SOP]		800-249-3704				

CR	CV	PR	US	BK	←Courts	York	Recorder→	UC	RE	TX	VS
		•			Abstract Associates of Lancaster Inc [SOP]		717-581-5841	•	•	•	•
•	•	•			Abstract One		302-732-9027	•	•	•	•
•	•		•	•	Accufax: Authentic Document Retrieval		800-336-1001	•	•	•	•
•	•	•	•	•	Associated Services [SOP]		717-938-1550	•	•	•	
					Colonial Valley Abstract Co		717-848-2871	•	•	•	
•	•				Docket Detective LLC		717-249-7053				
•	•	•	•	•	Information Network Associates Inc [SOP]		800-443-0824	•	•	•	•
•	•	•	•	•	Pittsburgh Information & Research Co [SOP]		412-766-3832	•	•	•	•

[SOP] = Performs service of process

Editor's Tip: Only Call a Retriever For the Records They Retrieve.
If you call for a criminal record from a retriever who only does work at the recorder's office, then you are wasting your time and the retriever's time.

Puerto Rico

Court Records Retrieved					Capital - San Juan	Recorded Records Retrieved				
CR	CV	PR	US	BK	←Courts Puerto Rico Recorder→		UC	RE	TX	VS
•	•		•	•	Cestero & Co Inc [SOP]	866-456-6672	•	•	•	•
•	•		•	•	GPS & Associates - Florida	866-813-8131	•		•	•
•	•		•	•	Rucar Business Information Center	787-645-1659	•	•	•	•

[SOP] = Performs service of process

Editor's Tip: At the back of this directory is a short list of search firms who are Public Record Retriever Network "Associate Members." These Associate Members utilize retrievers to obtain documents outside their local area of coverage. The Associate Members are statewide, regional, or national in scope, and are not listed in the county sections.

Court Records

Code	Government Agency	Type of Information
CR	Criminal Court	Municipal, county and state level criminal cases
CV	Civil Court	Municipal, county and state level civil cases
PR	Probate Court	Wills and estate cases
US	US District Court	Federal civil and criminal cases
BK	Bankruptcy Court	United States bankruptcy cases

County Records - Recordings

Code	Government Agency	Type of Information
UC	UCC Filing Office	Uniform Commercial Code and other personal property liens
RE	Real Estate Recording Office	Real property transactions and liens
TX	Tax Filing Office(s)	Federal and state tax liens, judgment liens
VS	Vital Records Office	Vital statistics—birth, death, marriage, divorce

Rhode Island

Rhode Island has 5 counties and 39 towns with 39 recording offices. There is **no county recording** in this state. All recording is done at the city/town level. Be aware that 3 sites bear the same name as their respective counties. Therefore, the recordings within the counties of Bristol, Newport, and Providence can relate to property located in cities/towns other than the individual cities of Bristol, Newport, and Providence.

COURT RECORDS RETRIEVED — CAPITAL - PROVIDENCE COUNTY — RECORDED RECORDS RETRIEVED

CR	CV	PR	US	BK	←COURTS BRISTOL RECORDER→	Phone	UC	RE	TX	VS
•	•	•	•	•	Access RI Public Information [SOP]	877-999-7474	•		•	•
•	•	•	•	•	Barry Shuster Information Services, A Div of Search-It Inc	877-852-2507	•	•	•	•
•	•	•	•	•	Hughes Legal Support [SOP]	800-783-7690	•	•	•	
•	•	•	•	•	McGuire Research Associates	401-647-7881	•	•	•	
•	•				Primetime Research Inc	866-737-2714				
•	•	•	•	•	Professional Background Services Inc	401-714-8433	•	•	•	•
•	•				Rapid Record Retrieval	508-759-8622				
•	•	•	•	•	Trax [SOP]	401-245-3004	•	•	•	•

CR	CV	PR	US	BK	←COURTS KENT RECORDER→	Phone	UC	RE	TX	VS
•	•	•	•	•	Access RI Public Information [SOP]	877-999-7474	•		•	•
•	•	•	•	•	Barry Shuster Information Services, A Div of Search-It Inc	877-852-2507	•	•	•	•
•	•	•	•	•	Hughes Legal Support [SOP]	800-783-7690	•	•	•	
•	•	•	•	•	McGuire Research Associates	401-647-7881	•	•	•	
•	•	•	•	•	Parasearch Inc	401-732-2490	•	•	•	
•	•				Primetime Research Inc	866-737-2714				
•	•	•	•	•	Professional Background Services Inc	401-714-8433	•	•	•	•
•	•				Rapid Record Retrieval	508-759-8622				
•	•	•	•	•	Trax [SOP]	401-245-3004	•	•	•	•

CR	CV	PR	US	BK	←COURTS NEWPORT RECORDER→	Phone	UC	RE	TX	VS
•	•	•	•	•	Access RI Public Information [SOP]	877-999-7474	•		•	•
•	•	•	•	•	Barry Shuster Information Services, A Div of Search-It Inc	877-852-2507	•	•	•	•
•	•	•	•	•	Hughes Legal Support [SOP]	800-783-7690	•	•	•	
•	•	•	•	•	McGuire Research Associates	401-647-7881	•	•	•	
•	•	•	•	•	Parasearch Inc	401-732-2490	•	•	•	
•	•				Primetime Research Inc	866-737-2714				
•	•	•	•	•	Professional Background Services Inc	401-714-8433	•	•	•	•
•	•				Rapid Record Retrieval	508-759-8622				
•	•	•	•	•	Trax [SOP]	401-245-3004	•	•	•	•

CR	CV	PR	US	BK	←COURTS PROVIDENCE RECORDER→	Phone	UC	RE	TX	VS
•	•	•	•	•	Access RI Public Information [SOP]	877-999-7474	•		•	•
•	•	•	•	•	Barry Shuster Information Services, A Div of Search-It Inc	877-852-2507	•	•	•	•
•	•	•	•	•	Hughes Legal Support [SOP]	800-783-7690	•	•	•	
•	•	•	•	•	McGuire Research Associates	401-647-7881	•	•	•	
•	•	•	•	•	Parasearch Inc	401-732-2490	•	•	•	
•	•				Primetime Research Inc	866-737-2714				
•	•	•	•	•	Professional Background Services Inc	401-714-8433	•	•	•	•
•	•				Rapid Record Retrieval	508-759-8622				
•	•	•	•	•	Trax [SOP]	401-245-3004	•	•	•	•

CR	CV	PR	US	BK	←COURTS WASHINGTON	RECORDER→	UC	RE	TX	VS
•	•	•	•	•	Access RI Public Information [SOP]	877-999-7474	•		•	•
•	•	•	•	•	Barry Shuster Information Services, A Div of Search-It Inc	877-852-2507	•	•	•	•
•	•	•	•	•	Hughes Legal Support [SOP]	800-783-7690	•	•	•	
•	•	•	•	•	McGuire Research Associates	401-647-7881	•	•	•	
•	•	•	•	•	Parasearch Inc	401-732-2490	•	•	•	
•	•				Primetime Research Inc	866-737-2714				
•	•	•	•	•	Professional Background Services Inc	401-714-8433	•	•	•	•
•	•				Rapid Record Retrieval	508-759-8622				
•	•	•	•	•	Trax [SOP]	401-245-3004	•	•	•	•

[SOP] = PERFORMS SERVICE OF PROCESS

Editor's Tip: Remember the first rule about public record searching-- Simply because your state or county has certain rules, regulations and practices regarding the accessibility and content of public records, does not mean that another state or county adheres to the same rules.

South Carolina

COURT RECORDS RETRIEVED | **CAPITAL - RICHLAND COUNTY** | **RECORDED RECORDS RETRIEVED**

CR	CV	PR	US	BK	←COURTS **ABBEVILLE** RECORDER→		UC	RE	TX	VS
•	•	•	•	•	Carolina Investigative Research (SC)	800-328-8981	•	•	•	•
•	•				Cedar Ridge Abstracts	864-366-9239		•	•	
	•	•	•	•	Liberty Corporate Services Inc	888-875-1280	•	•	•	
•	•	•	•	•	Searchtec (Carolinas) [SOP]	800-528-8790	•	•	•	•
		•			Upper State Title Corp	864-260-4649 or 864-260-4063	•	•	•	
•	•				Upstate Investigations [SOP]	864-277-0757			•	

CR	CV	PR	US	BK	←COURTS **AIKEN** RECORDER→		UC	RE	TX	VS
•	•	•	•	•	CSRA Background Verification Inc	706-869-8882	•	•	•	
•	•	•	•	•	David Smith Detective Agency [SOP]	877-793-9426	•		•	
	•	•			Lexington Title Corp	803-957-1243	•	•	•	
	•	•	•	•	Liberty Corporate Services Inc	888-875-1280	•	•	•	
	•	•			SCC Information Services Inc	803-957-1243	•	•	•	
•	•	•	•	•	Searchtec (Carolinas) [SOP]	800-528-8790	•	•	•	•
•	•	•	•	•	Title Abstracts & Document Services	803-649-2500, Fax- same	•	•	•	•
•	•		•	•	Verifi LLC	423-344-0133	•	•	•	

CR	CV	PR	US	BK	←COURTS **ALLENDALE** RECORDER→		UC	RE	TX	VS
•	•	•	•	•	Searchtec (Carolinas) [SOP]	800-528-8790	•	•	•	•
•	•	•	•	•	Title Abstracts & Document Services	803-649-2500, Fax- same	•	•	•	•
•	•		•	•	Verifi LLC	423-344-0133	•	•	•	

CR	CV	PR	US	BK	←COURTS **ANDERSON** RECORDER→		UC	RE	TX	VS
•	•				Allied Investigative Services [SOP]	800-302-0861				
•	•	•	•	•	Carolina Investigative Research (SC)	800-328-8981	•	•	•	•
•	•				Corley Research	803-331-3309				
	•	•	•	•	Liberty Corporate Services Inc	888-875-1280	•	•	•	
•	•	•	•	•	Searchtec (Carolinas) [SOP]	800-528-8790	•	•	•	•
•	•	•	•	•	Sutton & Associates Investigations Inc [SOP]	864-232-9007	•	•	•	•
		•			Upper State Title Corp	864-260-4649 or 864-260-4063	•	•	•	

CR	CV	PR	US	BK	←COURTS **BAMBERG** RECORDER→		UC	RE	TX	VS
	•	•	•	•	Horger Barnwell & Reid LLP	803-531-3000	•	•	•	•
•	•	•	•	•	Searchtec (Carolinas) [SOP]	800-528-8790	•	•	•	•
•	•	•	•	•	Title Abstracts & Document Services	803-649-2500, Fax- same	•	•	•	•
•	•	•	•	•	VIP Services LLC	888-249-9947	•	•	•	

CR	CV	PR	US	BK	←COURTS **BARNWELL** RECORDER→		UC	RE	TX	VS
•	•	•	•	•	Searchtec (Carolinas) [SOP]	800-528-8790	•	•	•	•
•	•	•	•	•	Title Abstracts & Document Services	803-649-2500, Fax- same	•	•	•	•
•	•		•	•	Verifi LLC	423-344-0133	•	•	•	

CR	CV	PR	US	BK	←COURTS **BEAUFORT** RECORDER→		UC	RE	TX	VS
•	•	•			Amma H General Ltd	843-263-5677 or 843-525-9890	•	•	•	
•	•	•			Asset Protection Investigations, Inc [SOP]	843-525-9664		•	•	
•	•				Corley Research	803-331-3309				
	•	•	•	•	Liberty Corporate Services Inc	888-875-1280	•	•	•	
•	•	•	•	•	Searchtec (Carolinas) [SOP]	800-528-8790	•	•	•	•

CR	CV	PR	US	BK	←Courts	Berkeley	Recorder→	UC	RE	TX	VS
	•	•	•	•	Liberty Corporate Services Inc		888-875-1280	•	•	•	
•	•	•	•	•	Searchtec (Carolinas) [SOP]		800-528-8790	•	•	•	•
•	•	•	•	•	VIP Services LLC		888-249-9947	•	•	•	

CR	CV	PR	US	BK	←Courts	Calhoun	Recorder→	UC	RE	TX	VS
	•	•	•	•	Horger Barnwell & Reid LLP		803-531-3000	•	•	•	•
	•	•			Lexington Title Corp		803-957-1243	•	•	•	
	•	•	•	•	Liberty Corporate Services Inc		888-875-1280	•	•	•	
•	•	•	•	•	Searchtec (Carolinas) [SOP]		800-528-8790	•	•	•	•
•	•	•	•	•	VIP Services LLC		888-249-9947	•	•	•	

CR	CV	PR	US	BK	←Courts	Charleston	Recorder→	UC	RE	TX	VS
•	•				Corley Research		803-331-3309				
	•	•	•	•	Liberty Corporate Services Inc		888-875-1280	•	•	•	
•	•		•		Process Serving Unlimited [SOP]		843-728-2732				
•	•	•	•	•	Searchtec (Carolinas) [SOP]		800-528-8790	•	•	•	•
					Seve Company		843-762-4520	•	•	•	
•	•	•	•	•	VIP Services LLC		888-249-9947	•	•	•	

CR	CV	PR	US	BK	←Courts	Cherokee	Recorder→	UC	RE	TX	VS
•	•	•	•	•	Carolina Investigative Research (SC)		800-328-8981	•	•	•	•
•	•	•	•	•	Searchtec (Carolinas) [SOP]		800-528-8790	•	•	•	•

CR	CV	PR	US	BK	←Courts	Chester	Recorder→	UC	RE	TX	VS
•	•	•	•	•	Searchtec (Carolinas) [SOP]		800-528-8790	•	•	•	•

CR	CV	PR	US	BK	←Courts	Chesterfield	Recorder→	UC	RE	TX	VS
•	•	•	•	•	Searchtec (Carolinas) [SOP]		800-528-8790	•	•	•	•

CR	CV	PR	US	BK	←Courts	Clarendon	Recorder→	UC	RE	TX	VS
•	•	•	•	•	Searchtec (Carolinas) [SOP]		800-528-8790	•	•	•	•

CR	CV	PR	US	BK	←Courts	Colleton	Recorder→	UC	RE	TX	VS
•	•	•			Asset Protection Investigations, Inc [SOP]		843-525-9664		•	•	
	•	•	•	•	Liberty Corporate Services Inc		888-875-1280	•	•	•	
•	•	•	•	•	Searchtec (Carolinas) [SOP]		800-528-8790	•	•	•	•

CR	CV	PR	US	BK	←Courts	Darlington	Recorder→	UC	RE	TX	VS
	•	•	•	•	Liberty Corporate Services Inc		888-875-1280	•	•	•	
•	•	•	•	•	Searchtec (Carolinas) [SOP]		800-528-8790	•	•	•	•

CR	CV	PR	US	BK	←Courts	Dillon	Recorder→	UC	RE	TX	VS
•	•	•	•	•	Searchtec (Carolinas) [SOP]		800-528-8790	•	•	•	•

CR	CV	PR	US	BK	←Courts	Dorchester	Recorder→	UC	RE	TX	VS
	•	•	•	•	Horger Barnwell & Reid LLP		803-531-3000	•	•	•	•
	•	•	•	•	Liberty Corporate Services Inc		888-875-1280	•	•	•	
•	•	•	•	•	Searchtec (Carolinas) [SOP]		800-528-8790	•	•	•	•
•	•	•	•	•	VIP Services LLC		888-249-9947	•	•	•	

CR	CV	PR	US	BK	←Courts	Edgefield	Recorder→	UC	RE	TX	VS
•	•	•	•	•	David Smith Detective Agency [SOP]		877-793-9426	•		•	
	•	•			Lexington Title Corp		803-957-1243	•	•	•	
	•	•			SCC Information Services Inc		803-957-1243	•	•	•	
•	•	•	•	•	Searchtec (Carolinas) [SOP]		800-528-8790	•	•	•	•
•	•	•	•	•	Title Abstracts & Document Services		803-649-2500, Fax- same	•	•	•	•
•	•	•	•	•	Verifi LLC		423-344-0133	•	•	•	

CR	CV	PR	US	BK	←Courts	Fairfield	Recorder→	UC	RE	TX	VS
	•	•			Lexington Title Corp		803-957-1243	•	•	•	
•	•	•	•	•	Searchtec (Carolinas) [SOP]		800-528-8790	•	•	•	•

CR	CV	PR	US	BK	←COURTS	FLORENCE	RECORDER→	UC	RE	TX	VS
•	•	•	•	•	Carolina Investigative Research (SC)		800-328-8981	•	•	•	•
•	•				Corley Research		803-331-3309				
	•	•	•	•	Liberty Corporate Services Inc		888-875-1280	•	•	•	
•	•	•	•	•	Searchtec (Carolinas) [SOP]		800-528-8790	•	•	•	•

CR	CV	PR	US	BK	←COURTS	GEORGETOWN	RECORDER→	UC	RE	TX	VS
	•	•	•	•	Liberty Corporate Services Inc		888-875-1280	•	•	•	
•	•	•	•	•	Searchtec (Carolinas) [SOP]		800-528-8790	•	•	•	•

CR	CV	PR	US	BK	←COURTS	GREENVILLE	RECORDER→	UC	RE	TX	VS
•	•	•	•	•	Carolina Investigative Research (SC)		800-328-8981	•	•	•	•
•	•				Corley Research		803-331-3309				
	•	•	•	•	Liberty Corporate Services Inc		888-875-1280	•	•	•	
•	•	•	•	•	Searchtec (Carolinas) [SOP]		800-528-8790	•	•	•	•
•	•	•	•	•	Sutton & Associates Investigations Inc [SOP]		864-232-9007	•	•	•	•
		•			Upper State Title Corp		864-260-4649 or 864-260-4063	•	•	•	

CR	CV	PR	US	BK	←COURTS	GREENWOOD	RECORDER→	UC	RE	TX	VS
•	•	•	•	•	Carolina Investigative Research (SC)		800-328-8981	•	•	•	•
	•	•	•	•	Liberty Corporate Services Inc		888-875-1280	•	•	•	
•	•	•	•	•	Searchtec (Carolinas) [SOP]		800-528-8790	•	•	•	•
		•			Upper State Title Corp		864-260-4649 or 864-260-4063	•	•	•	
•	•				Upstate Investigations [SOP]		864-277-0757			•	

CR	CV	PR	US	BK	←COURTS	HAMPTON	RECORDER→	UC	RE	TX	VS
•	•	•			Amma H General Ltd		843-263-5677 or 843-525-9890	•	•	•	
•	•	•			Asset Protection Investigations, Inc [SOP]		843-525-9664		•	•	
	•	•	•	•	Liberty Corporate Services Inc		888-875-1280	•	•	•	
•	•	•	•	•	Searchtec (Carolinas) [SOP]		800-528-8790	•	•	•	•

CR	CV	PR	US	BK	←COURTS	HORRY	RECORDER→	UC	RE	TX	VS
•					Info Quest Inc		800-507-9628				•
	•	•	•	•	Liberty Corporate Services Inc		888-875-1280	•	•	•	
•	•	•	•	•	Searchtec (Carolinas) [SOP]		800-528-8790	•	•	•	•

CR	CV	PR	US	BK	←COURTS	JASPER	RECORDER→	UC	RE	TX	VS
•	•	•			Amma H General Ltd		843-263-5677 or 843-525-9890	•	•	•	
•	•	•			Asset Protection Investigations, Inc [SOP]		843-525-9664		•	•	
	•	•	•	•	Liberty Corporate Services Inc		888-875-1280	•	•	•	
•	•	•	•	•	Searchtec (Carolinas) [SOP]		800-528-8790	•	•	•	•

CR	CV	PR	US	BK	←COURTS	KERSHAW	RECORDER→	UC	RE	TX	VS
	•	•			Lexington Title Corp		803-957-1243	•	•	•	
	•	•	•	•	Liberty Corporate Services Inc		888-875-1280	•	•	•	
•	•	•	•	•	Searchtec (Carolinas) [SOP]		800-528-8790	•	•	•	•

CR	CV	PR	US	BK	←COURTS	LANCASTER	RECORDER→	UC	RE	TX	VS
•	•	•	•	•	Carolina Investigative Research (SC)		800-328-8981	•	•	•	•
•	•	•	•	•	Searchtec (Carolinas) [SOP]		800-528-8790	•	•	•	•

CR	CV	PR	US	BK	←COURTS	LAURENS	RECORDER→	UC	RE	TX	VS
•	•	•	•	•	Carolina Investigative Research (SC)		800-328-8981	•	•	•	•
	•	•	•	•	Liberty Corporate Services Inc		888-875-1280	•	•	•	
•	•	•	•	•	Searchtec (Carolinas) [SOP]		800-528-8790	•	•	•	•
		•			Upper State Title Corp		864-260-4649 or 864-260-4063	•	•	•	

CR	CV	PR	US	BK	←COURTS	LEE	RECORDER→	UC	RE	TX	VS
	•	•	•	•	Liberty Corporate Services Inc		888-875-1280	•	•	•	
•	•	•	•	•	Searchtec (Carolinas) [SOP]		800-528-8790	•	•	•	•

CR	CV	PR	US	BK	←Courts	LEXINGTON	Recorder→	UC	RE	TX	VS
•	•				Corley Research		803-331-3309				
•	•	•	•	•	Charles M Kneisley		803-936-1200	•	•	•	
	•	•			Lexington Title Corp		803-957-1243	•	•	•	
	•	•	•	•	Liberty Corporate Services Inc		888-875-1280	•	•	•	
	•	•			SCC Information Services Inc		803-957-1243	•	•	•	
•	•	•	•	•	Searchtec (Carolinas) [SOP]		800-528-8790	•	•	•	•
•	•	•	•	•	Bobbie Slice		803-932-7013	•	•	•	
•	•	•	•	•	Title Abstracts & Document Services		803-649-2500, Fax- same	•	•	•	•
•	•		•	•	Verifi LLC		423-344-0133	•	•	•	
•	•	•	•	•	VIP Services LLC		888-249-9947	•	•	•	

CR	CV	PR	US	BK	←Courts	MARION	Recorder→	UC	RE	TX	VS
•	•	•	•	•	Searchtec (Carolinas) [SOP]		800-528-8790	•	•	•	•

CR	CV	PR	US	BK	←Courts	MARLBORO	Recorder→	UC	RE	TX	VS
•	•	•	•	•	Searchtec (Carolinas) [SOP]		800-528-8790	•	•	•	•

CR	CV	PR	US	BK	←Courts	McCORMICK	Recorder→	UC	RE	TX	VS
•	•	•	•	•	Searchtec (Carolinas) [SOP]		800-528-8790	•	•	•	•
		•			Upper State Title Corp		864-260-4649 or 864-260-4063	•	•	•	
•	•				Upstate Investigations [SOP]		864-277-0757			•	

CR	CV	PR	US	BK	←Courts	NEWBERRY	Recorder→	UC	RE	TX	VS
	•	•			Lexington Title Corp		803-957-1243	•	•	•	
	•	•	•	•	Liberty Corporate Services Inc		888-875-1280	•	•	•	
	•	•			SCC Information Services Inc		803-957-1243	•	•	•	
•	•	•	•	•	Searchtec (Carolinas) [SOP]		800-528-8790	•	•	•	•
•	•	•	•	•	Bobbie Slice		803-932-7013	•	•	•	
•	•	•	•	•	Title Abstracts & Document Services		803-649-2500, Fax- same	•	•	•	•

CR	CV	PR	US	BK	←Courts	OCONEE	Recorder→	UC	RE	TX	VS
	•	•	•	•	Liberty Corporate Services Inc		888-875-1280	•	•	•	
•	•	•	•	•	Searchtec (Carolinas) [SOP]		800-528-8790	•	•	•	•
		•			Upper State Title Corp		864-260-4649 or 864-260-4063	•	•	•	

CR	CV	PR	US	BK	←Courts	ORANGEBURG	Recorder→	UC	RE	TX	VS
	•	•	•	•	Horger Barnwell & Reid LLP		803-531-3000	•	•	•	•
	•	•			Lexington Title Corp		803-957-1243	•	•	•	
	•	•	•	•	Liberty Corporate Services Inc		888-875-1280	•	•	•	
•	•	•	•	•	Searchtec (Carolinas) [SOP]		800-528-8790	•	•	•	•
•	•	•	•	•	Title Abstracts & Document Services		803-649-2500, Fax- same	•	•	•	•
•	•	•	•	•	VIP Services LLC		888-249-9947	•	•	•	

CR	CV	PR	US	BK	←Courts	PICKENS	Recorder→	UC	RE	TX	VS
•	•				Corley Research		803-331-3309				
	•	•	•	•	Liberty Corporate Services Inc		888-875-1280	•	•	•	
•	•	•	•	•	Searchtec (Carolinas) [SOP]		800-528-8790	•	•	•	•
•	•	•	•	•	Sutton & Associates Investigations Inc [SOP]		864-232-9007	•	•	•	•
		•			Upper State Title Corp		864-260-4649 or 864-260-4063	•	•	•	

CR	CV	PR	US	BK	←Courts	RICHLAND	Recorder→	UC	RE	TX	VS
•	•	•	•	•	Carolina Investigative Research (SC)		800-328-8981	•	•	•	•
•	•				Corley Research		803-331-3309				
•	•	•	•	•	Charles M Kneisley		803-936-1200	•	•	•	
	•	•			Lexington Title Corp		803-957-1243	•	•	•	
	•	•	•	•	Liberty Corporate Services Inc		888-875-1280	•	•	•	
•	•	•	•	•	Searchtec (Carolinas) [SOP]		800-528-8790	•	•	•	•
•	•	•	•	•	Bobbie Slice		803-932-7013	•	•	•	
•	•	•	•	•	Title Abstracts & Document Services		803-649-2500, Fax- same	•	•	•	•
•	•	•	•	•	Verifi LLC		423-344-0133	•	•	•	

CR	CV	PR	US	BK	←COURTS SALUDA RECORDER→		UC	RE	TX	VS
•	•	•	•	•	David Smith Detective Agency [SOP]	877-793-9426	•		•	
	•	•			Lexington Title Corp	803-957-1243	•	•	•	
	•	•	•	•	Liberty Corporate Services Inc	888-875-1280	•	•	•	
	•	•			SCC Information Services Inc	803-957-1243	•	•	•	
•	•	•	•	•	Searchtec (Carolinas) [SOP]	800-528-8790	•	•	•	•

CR	CV	PR	US	BK	←COURTS SPARTANBURG RECORDER→		UC	RE	TX	VS
•	•	•	•	•	Carolina Investigative Research (SC)	800-328-8981	•	•	•	•
	•	•	•	•	Liberty Corporate Services Inc	888-875-1280	•	•	•	
•	•	•	•	•	Searchtec (Carolinas) [SOP]	800-528-8790	•	•	•	•
•	•	•	•	•	Sutton & Associates Investigations Inc [SOP]	864-232-9007	•	•	•	•
		•			Upper State Title Corp	864-260-4649 or 864-260-4063	•	•	•	

CR	CV	PR	US	BK	←COURTS SUMTER RECORDER→		UC	RE	TX	VS
•	•				Corley Research	803-331-3309				
	•	•	•	•	Liberty Corporate Services Inc	888-875-1280	•	•	•	
•	•	•	•	•	Searchtec (Carolinas) [SOP]	800-528-8790	•	•	•	•

CR	CV	PR	US	BK	←COURTS UNION RECORDER→		UC	RE	TX	VS
•	•	•	•	•	Searchtec (Carolinas) [SOP]	800-528-8790	•	•	•	•

CR	CV	PR	US	BK	←COURTS WILLIAMSBURG RECORDER→		UC	RE	TX	VS
•	•	•	•	•	Searchtec (Carolinas) [SOP]	800-528-8790	•	•	•	•

CR	CV	PR	US	BK	←COURTS YORK RECORDER→		UC	RE	TX	VS
•	•	•	•	•	Carolina Investigative Research (SC)	800-328-8981	•	•	•	•
•	•				Corley Research	803-331-3309				
	•	•	•	•	Liberty Corporate Services Inc	888-875-1280	•	•	•	
•	•		•	•	Reynolds Professional Service Inc [SOP]	800-814-8662				•
•	•	•	•	•	Searchtec (Carolinas) [SOP]	800-528-8790	•	•	•	•

COURT RECORDS

CODE	GOVERNMENT AGENCY	TYPE OF INFORMATION
CR	Criminal Court	Municipal, county and state level criminal cases
CV	Civil Court	Municipal, county and state level civil cases
PR	Probate Court	Wills and estate cases
US	US District Court	Federal civil and criminal cases
BK	Bankruptcy Court	United States bankruptcy cases

COUNTY RECORDS - RECORDINGS

CODE	GOVERNMENT AGENCY	TYPE OF INFORMATION
UC	UCC Filing Office	Uniform Commercial Code and other personal property liens
RE	Real Estate Recording Office	Real property transactions and liens
TX	Tax Filing Office(s)	Federal and state tax liens, judgment liens
VS	Vital Records Office	Vital statistics—birth, death, marriage, divorce

South Dakota

COURT RECORDS RETRIEVED — CAPITAL - HUGHES COUNTY — RECORDED RECORDS RETRIEVED

CR	CV	PR	US	BK	←COURTS	AURORA	RECORDER→	UC	RE	TX	VS
•	•	•		•	Aurora County Land Title Company		605-942-7558		•	•	

CR	CV	PR	US	BK	←COURTS	BEADLE	RECORDER→	UC	RE	TX	VS
	•	•			Huron Title Co		605-352-6157	•	•	•	

CR	CV	PR	US	BK	←COURTS	BENNETT	RECORDER→	UC	RE	TX	VS
	•				Home Abstract Co		605-685-6525		•	•	

CR	CV	PR	US	BK	←COURTS	BONHOMME	RECORDER→	UC	RE	TX	VS
					Bon Homme Title Co		605-589-3572		•	•	

CR	CV	PR	US	BK	←COURTS	BROOKINGS	RECORDER→	UC	RE	TX	VS
•	•	•	•	•	Decker Document Retrieval		605-336-8402	•	•	•	•

CR	CV	PR	US	BK	←COURTS	BROWN	RECORDER→	UC	RE	TX	VS
•	•	•	•	•	Legal Support Services Inc		800-583-0365	•	•	•	•

CR	CV	PR	US	BK	←COURTS	BRULE	RECORDER→	UC	RE	TX	VS
	•	•			Brule County Abstract Co.		605-734-4275, fax-same		•	•	

CR	CV	PR	US	BK	←COURTS	BUFFALO	RECORDER→	UC	RE	TX	VS
	•	•			Brule County Abstract Co.		605-734-4275, fax-same		•	•	

CR	CV	PR	US	BK	←COURTS	BUTTE	RECORDER→	UC	RE	TX	VS
•	•	•	•	•	Adit Research Inc.		888-721-5220	•	•	•	•
•	•	•	•	•	Webster's Research Inc		605-718-5472	•	•	•	

CR	CV	PR	US	BK	←COURTS	CAMPBELL	RECORDER→	UC	RE	TX	VS
					Campbell County Abstract & Title		605-437-2222, Fax- same		•	•	

CR	CV	PR	US	BK	←COURTS	CHARLES MIX	RECORDER→	UC	RE	TX	VS
					Platte Title Co		605-337-3824		•	•	

CR	CV	PR	US	BK	←COURTS	CLARK	RECORDER→	UC	RE	TX	VS
		•			Clark Abstract & Title Co.		605-532-3812	•	•	•	•

CR	CV	PR	US	BK	←COURTS	CLAY	RECORDER→	UC	RE	TX	VS
					Clay County Title		605-624-2068		•	•	

CR	CV	PR	US	BK	←COURTS	CODINGTON	RECORDER→	UC	RE	TX	VS
		•			Watertown Title & Escrow Co.		605-886-8406	•	•	•	•

CR	CV	PR	US	BK	←COURTS	CORSON	RECORDER→	UC	RE	TX	VS

See adjoining counties for retrievers or call court/recorder directly.

CR	CV	PR	US	BK	←COURTS	CUSTER	RECORDER→	UC	RE	TX	VS
•	•	•	•	•	Adit Research Inc.		888-721-5220	•	•	•	•
•	•	•	•	•	Webster's Research Inc		605-718-5472	•	•	•	

CR	CV	PR	US	BK	←COURTS	DAVISON	RECORDER→	UC	RE	TX	VS
	•				The Title Company		605-996-4900		•	•	

CR	CV	PR	US	BK	←COURTS	DAY	RECORDER→	UC	RE	TX	VS
	•	•			Grue Abstract Co		605-345-3891	•	•	•	•

CR	CV	PR	US	BK	←Courts		Recorder→	UC	RE	TX	VS
						DEUEL					
•	•	•			Deuel County Abstract Co		605-874-8597	•	•	•	•
						DEWEY					
•	•	•			Titles of Dakota Inc (Dupree)		605-365-5247	•	•	•	
	•	•			Titles of Dakota Inc (Timber Lake)		605-365-5247		•	•	
						DOUGLAS					
	•	•			Douglas County Title Inc (South Dakota)		605-724-2235		•	•	
						EDMUNDS					
	•	•			Edmunds County Abstract Co.		605-426-6041		•	•	
						FALL RIVER					
•	•	•	•	•	Adit Research Inc.		888-721-5220	•	•	•	•
		•			Fall River Abstract Co		605-745-5187		•	•	
•	•	•	•	•	Webster's Research Inc		605-718-5472	•	•	•	
						FAULK					
					See adjoining counties for retrievers or call court/recorder directly.						
						GRANT					
	•	•			Grant County Abstract & Title Co		605-432-5461	•	•	•	
						GREGORY					
	•	•			Gregory County Title Co		605-775-2943; Fax- same		•	•	
						HAAKON					
					Haakon County Abstract Co		605-859-2461	•	•	•	
						HAMLIN					
					See adjoining counties for retrievers or call court/recorder directly.						
						HAND					
					Hand County Abstract & Title Co		605-853-2194	•	•	•	
						HANSON					
	•				The Title Company		605-996-4900		•	•	
						HARDING					
					Harding County Abstract		605-375-3422		•	•	
						HUGHES					
•	•	•	•	•	Marilyn Person		605-224-8168	•		•	•
						HUTCHINSON					
•	•	•			Oplinger Abstract & Title Inc		605-387-2335	•	•	•	•
						HYDE					
					See adjoining counties for retrievers or call court/recorder directly.						
						JACKSON					
	•	•			Brule County Abstract Co.		605-734-4275, fax-same		•	•	
•	•	•			Jones County Title Company		605-669-3004	•	•	•	
						JERAULD					
	•	•			Jerauld County Abstract Co Inc		605-539-1541	•	•	•	
						JONES					
•	•	•			Jones County Title Company		605-669-3004	•	•	•	•
						KINGSBURY					
		•			Purintun Abstract		605-854-3401; Fax- same	•	•	•	

CR	CV	PR	US	BK	←COURTS	LAKE	RECORDER→	UC	RE	TX	VS
	•	•			Weber Abstract Co		605-256-4640	•	•	•	•

CR	CV	PR	US	BK	←COURTS	LAWRENCE	RECORDER→	UC	RE	TX	VS
•	•	•	•	•	Adit Research Inc		888-721-5220	•	•	•	•
•	•	•	•	•	Legal Support Services Inc		800-583-0365	•	•	•	•
•	•	•	•	•	Webster's Research Inc		605-718-5472	•	•	•	

CR	CV	PR	US	BK	←COURTS	LINCOLN	RECORDER→	UC	RE	TX	VS
•	•				Action Professional Services [SOP]		888-335-3090	•	•	•	
•	•	•	•	•	Decker Document Retrieval		605-336-8402	•	•	•	•

CR	CV	PR	US	BK	←COURTS	LYMAN	RECORDER→	UC	RE	TX	VS
	•	•			Brule County Abstract Co		605-734-4275, fax-same		•	•	
	•	•			Lyman County Title Co		605-869-2269	•	•	•	

CR	CV	PR	US	BK	←COURTS	MARSHALL	RECORDER→	UC	RE	TX	VS
		•	•		Marshall Land & Title Co Inc		605-448-5796	•	•	•	•

CR	CV	PR	US	BK	←COURTS	MCCOOK	RECORDER→	UC	RE	TX	VS
•	•	•			McCook County Abstract & Title Ins		605-425-2612	•	•	•	•

CR	CV	PR	US	BK	←COURTS	MCPHERSON	RECORDER→	UC	RE	TX	VS
					See adjoining counties for retrievers or call court/recorder directly.						

CR	CV	PR	US	BK	←COURTS	MEADE	RECORDER→	UC	RE	TX	VS
•	•	•	•	•	Adit Research Inc		888-721-5220	•	•	•	•
•	•	•	•	•	Legal Support Services Inc		800-583-0365	•	•	•	•
•	•	•	•	•	Webster's Research Inc		605-718-5472	•	•	•	

CR	CV	PR	US	BK	←COURTS	MELLETTE	RECORDER→	UC	RE	TX	VS
					See adjoining counties for retrievers or call court/recorder directly.						

CR	CV	PR	US	BK	←COURTS	MINER	RECORDER→	UC	RE	TX	VS
	•	•			Fidelity Abstract & Title Co		605-772-5632	•	•	•	

CR	CV	PR	US	BK	←COURTS	MINNEHAHA	RECORDER→	UC	RE	TX	VS
•	•				Action Professional Services [SOP]		888-335-3090	•	•	•	
•	•	•	•	•	Decker Document Retrieval		605-336-8402	•	•	•	•
•	•	•	•	•	Legal Support Services Inc		800-583-0365	•	•	•	•

CR	CV	PR	US	BK	←COURTS	MOODY	RECORDER→	UC	RE	TX	VS
	•	•			Moody County Abstract Co		605-997-3723	•	•	•	

CR	CV	PR	US	BK	←COURTS	PENNINGTON	RECORDER→	UC	RE	TX	VS
•	•	•	•	•	Adit Research Inc		888-721-5220	•	•	•	•
•	•	•	•	•	Legal Support Services Inc		800-583-0365	•	•	•	•
•	•	•	•	•	Webster's Research Inc		605-718-5472	•	•	•	

CR	CV	PR	US	BK	←COURTS	PERKINS	RECORDER→	UC	RE	TX	VS
•	•	•			Perkins County Abstract Co		605-244-5544, Fax-same	•	•	•	

CR	CV	PR	US	BK	←COURTS	POTTER	RECORDER→	UC	RE	TX	VS
•	•	•			Potter County Land & Abstract Inc		605-765-2858		•	•	•

CR	CV	PR	US	BK	←COURTS	ROBERTS	RECORDER→	UC	RE	TX	VS
					Roberts County Title		605-698-7272		•	•	

CR	CV	PR	US	BK	←COURTS	SANBORN	RECORDER→	UC	RE	TX	VS
	•	•			Sanborn County Realty & Title		605-796-4417		•	•	

CR	CV	PR	US	BK	←COURTS	SHANNON	RECORDER→	UC	RE	TX	VS
•	•	•	•	•	Adit Research Inc		888-721-5220	•	•	•	•
		•			Fall River Abstract Co		605-745-5187		•	•	

CR	CV	PR	US	BK	← Courts **SPINK** Recorder →	UC	RE	TX	VS
					Spink County Abstract 605-472-2011		•	•	

CR	CV	PR	US	BK	← Courts **STANLEY** Recorder →	UC	RE	TX	VS
•	•	•	•		Marilyn Person 605-224-8168	•		•	•
		•			Titles of Dakota Inc (Fort Pierre) 800-794-2725	•	•	•	

CR	CV	PR	US	BK	← Courts **SULLY** Recorder →	UC	RE	TX	VS
•	•	•	•	•	Marilyn Person 605-224-8168	•		•	•
		•			Titles of Dakota Inc (Fort Pierre) 800-794-2725	•	•	•	

CR	CV	PR	US	BK	← Courts **TODD** Recorder →	UC	RE	TX	VS
	•	•			Tripp & Todd Title Company 605-842-0334	•	•	•	•

CR	CV	PR	US	BK	← Courts **TRIPP** Recorder →	UC	RE	TX	VS
	•	•			Tripp & Todd Title Company 605-842-0334	•	•	•	•

CR	CV	PR	US	BK	← Courts **TURNER** Recorder →	UC	RE	TX	VS
					Turner County Abstract 605-297-5555		•	•	

CR	CV	PR	US	BK	← Courts **UNION** Recorder →	UC	RE	TX	VS
•	•	•	•	•	Professional Support Services of Siouxland 712-233-2383	•	•	•	•
					Union County Abstract & Title Co 605-356-3180	•	•	•	•

CR	CV	PR	US	BK	← Courts **WALWORTH** Recorder →	UC	RE	TX	VS
	•	•			Walworth County Abstract & Title 605-649-7772	•	•	•	

CR	CV	PR	US	BK	← Courts **YANKTON** Recorder →	UC	RE	TX	VS
					See adjoining counties for retrievers or call court/recorder directly.				

CR	CV	PR	US	BK	← Courts **ZIEBACH** Recorder →	UC	RE	TX	VS
•	•	•			Titles of Dakota Inc (Dupree) 605-365-5247	•	•	•	

[SOP] = Performs service of process

Court Records

CODE	GOVERNMENT AGENCY	TYPE OF INFORMATION
DT	US District Court	Federal civil and criminal cases
BK	Bankruptcy Court	United States bankruptcy cases
CV	Civil Court	Municipal, county and state level civil cases
CR	Criminal Court	Municipal, county and state level criminal cases
PR	Probate Court	Wills and estate cases

 = PRRN Member. *A retriever you can trust!*

Tennessee

Sullivan County in **Tennessee** has two separate recording offices.

COURT RECORDS RETRIEVED					CAPITAL - DAVIDSON COUNTY	RECORDED RECORDS RETRIEVED				
CR	CV	PR	US	BK	←COURTS **ANDERSON**	RECORDER→	UC	RE	TX	VS
		•			Thomas E Ewinger Jr	423-614-5290	•	•	•	•
•	•		•	•	Gamble Legal Research	865-966-3364	•		•	
•	•	•	•	•	Bill Hundemer	865-670-1740, 670-604-6031	•	•	•	
		•			NNBS Inc	865-977-8808	•	•	•	•
	•	•	•	•	Record Data Inc (Tennessee)	615-221-0021	•	•	•	
•	•		•	•	Records Research of Knoxville	865-693-3589	•	•	•	
•	•	•	•	•	Stallings Search Services	615-781-2323	•	•	•	•
•	•	•	•	•	TMC	865-609-7675	•	•	•	•
•	•		•	•	Verifi LLC	423-344-0133	•	•	•	
•	•	•	•	•	Vinson Detective Agency TN [SOP]	888-525-5047	•	•	•	•
CR	CV	PR	US	BK	←COURTS **BEDFORD**	RECORDER→	UC	RE	TX	VS
•	•	•	•	•	A All State Tracers Company	423-605-0155	•	•	•	•
•	•				Rachel Arnold	931-684-1672			•	
•	•	•	•	•	Charles F Edgar & Associates Inc [SOP]	256-539-7761	•	•	•	
	•	•	•		Maureen H Poole	931-294-2988	•	•	•	
	•	•	•	•	Record Data Inc (Tennessee)	615-221-0021	•	•	•	
CR	CV	PR	US	BK	←COURTS **BENTON**	RECORDER→	UC	RE	TX	VS
	•	•	•	•	D K Abstract	731-686-9363	•	•	•	•
•	•				Patricia L Estes-Howell	731-784-1050				
	•	•	•	•	Susan Parker	731-884-9994	•	•	•	
	•	•	•	•	Record Data Inc (Tennessee)	615-221-0021	•	•	•	
CR	CV	PR	US	BK	←COURTS **BLEDSOE**	RECORDER→	UC	RE	TX	VS
•	•	•	•	•	A All State Tracers Company	423-605-0155	•	•	•	•
		•			Thomas E Ewinger Jr	423-614-5290	•	•	•	•
	•	•			Real Estate Loan Services	423-855-0581	•	•	•	
	•	•	•	•	Record Data Inc (Tennessee)	615-221-0021	•	•	•	
	•	•	•	•	Title Guaranty & Trust of Chattanooga	423-266-5751	•	•	•	
•	•		•	•	Verifi LLC	423-344-0133	•	•	•	
CR	CV	PR	US	BK	←COURTS **BLOUNT**	RECORDER→	UC	RE	TX	VS
•	•	•	•	•	A All State Tracers Company	423-605-0155	•	•	•	•
		•			Thomas E Ewinger Jr	423-614-5290	•	•	•	•
•	•		•	•	Gamble Legal Research	865-966-3364	•		•	
•	•	•	•	•	Bill Hundemer	865-670-1740, 670-604-6031	•	•	•	
					William "Bill" H Maynard	423-472-9858	•	•	•	
		•			NNBS Inc	865-977-8808	•	•	•	•
•	•	•	•	•	Profile Information Services	512-472-9380	•	•	•	•
	•	•	•	•	Record Data Inc (Tennessee)	615-221-0021	•	•	•	
•	•		•	•	Records Research of Knoxville	865-693-3589	•	•	•	
•	•	•	•	•	Schaeffer Papers [SOP]	800-848-6119		•	•	•
•	•	•	•	•	TMC	865-609-7675	•	•	•	•
•	•		•	•	Verifi LLC	423-344-0133	•	•	•	
•	•	•	•	•	Vinson Detective Agency TN [SOP]	888-525-5047	•	•	•	•

CR	CV	PR	US	BK	←Courts BRADLEY	Recorder→	UC	RE	TX	VS
•	•	•	•	•	A All State Tracers Company	423-605-0155	•	•	•	•
•	•		•	•	Botts & Assoc [SOP]	423-479-7714	•	•	•	•
		•			Thomas E Ewinger Jr	423-614-5290	•	•	•	•
					William "Bill" H Maynard	423-472-9858	•	•	•	
	•	•			Real Estate Loan Services	423-855-0581	•	•	•	
	•	•	•	•	Record Data Inc (Tennessee)	615-221-0021	•	•	•	
	•	•	•	•	Title Guaranty & Trust of Chattanooga	423-266-5751	•	•	•	
•	•		•	•	Verifi LLC	423-344-0133	•	•	•	

CR	CV	PR	US	BK	←Courts CAMPBELL	Recorder→	UC	RE	TX	VS
	•	•	•	•	Record Data Inc (Tennessee)	615-221-0021	•	•	•	

CR	CV	PR	US	BK	←Courts CANNON	Recorder→	UC	RE	TX	VS
•	•	•	•	•	A All State Tracers Company	423-605-0155	•	•	•	•
	•	•	•	•	Real Estate Loan Services of TN Inc	800-475-2334	•	•	•	
	•	•	•	•	Record Data Inc (Tennessee)	615-221-0021	•	•	•	
•	•				Pam Smith	931-686-2804			•	

CR	CV	PR	US	BK	←Courts CARROLL	Recorder→	UC	RE	TX	VS
	•	•	•	•	D K Abstract	731-686-9363	•	•	•	•
	•	•	•	•	Susan Parker	731-884-9994	•	•	•	
	•	•	•	•	Record Data Inc (Tennessee)	615-221-0021	•	•	•	
	•	•	•	•	Stallings Search Services	615-781-2323	•	•	•	•

CR	CV	PR	US	BK	←Courts CARTER	Recorder→	UC	RE	TX	VS
•	•				Shelly and James Dobler	423-753-4885				
•	•				National Pre-Employment Research [SOP]	770-389-6607				
	•	•	•	•	Record Data Inc (Tennessee)	615-221-0021	•	•	•	

CR	CV	PR	US	BK	←Courts CHEATHAM	Recorder→	UC	RE	TX	VS
•					DataSearch	866-645-2562			•	
•	•	•	•	•	Kroll Document Filing & Retrieval Services [SOP]	800-324-2050	•	•	•	•
	•	•	•	•	Real Estate Loan Services of TN Inc	800-475-2334	•	•	•	
	•	•	•	•	Record Data Inc (Tennessee)	615-221-0021	•	•	•	
		•		•	Right On Time Documents Inc	615-885-8672	•	•	•	
•	•	•	•	•	Stallings Search Services	615-781-2323	•	•	•	•

CR	CV	PR	US	BK	←Courts CHESTER	Recorder→	UC	RE	TX	VS
	•	•	•	•	D K Abstract	731-686-9363	•	•	•	•
•	•				Patricia L Estes-Howell	731-784-1050				
	•	•	•	•	Record Data Inc (Tennessee)	615-221-0021	•	•	•	

CR	CV	PR	US	BK	←Courts CLAIBORNE	Recorder→	UC	RE	TX	VS
	•	•	•	•	Record Data Inc (Tennessee)	615-221-0021	•	•	•	
•	•	•			Title Express Inc	423-587-9886	•	•	•	

CR	CV	PR	US	BK	←Courts CLAY	Recorder→	UC	RE	TX	VS
					Jimmie Kirby	931-858-8786, cell- 931-267-2418				
	•	•	•	•	Record Data Inc (Tennessee)	615-221-0021	•	•	•	
•					Larry M Warner	931-484-1611		•	•	

CR	CV	PR	US	BK	←Courts COCKE	Recorder→	UC	RE	TX	VS
•	•				Datalink Investigative Services [SOP]	865-674-0030				
	•	•	•	•	Record Data Inc (Tennessee)	615-221-0021	•	•	•	
•	•	•			Title Express Inc	423-587-9886	•	•	•	

CR	CV	PR	US	BK	←Courts COFFEE	Recorder→	UC	RE	TX	VS
•	•	•	•	•	A All State Tracers Company	423-605-0155	•	•	•	•
•	•	•	•	•	Charles F Edgar & Associates Inc [SOP]	256-539-7761	•	•	•	
	•	•	•		Maureen H Poole	931-294-2988	•	•	•	

CR	CV	PR	US	BK	←Courts	Recorder→	UC	RE	TX	VS
	•	•	•	•	Record Data Inc (Tennessee)	615-221-0021	•	•	•	
•	•				Pam Smith	931-686-2804			•	
	•	•	•	•	Title Guaranty & Trust of Chattanooga	423-266-5751	•	•	•	

CR	CV	PR	US	BK	←Courts **CROCKETT**	Recorder→	UC	RE	TX	VS
•	•	•	•	•	Bryant Information Services	901-475-1276	•	•	•	
	•	•	•	•	D K Abstract	731-686-9363	•	•	•	•
•	•				Patricia L Estes-Howell	731-784-1050				
	•	•	•	•	Susan Parker	731-884-9994	•	•	•	
	•	•	•	•	Record Data Inc (Tennessee)	615-221-0021	•	•	•	

CR	CV	PR	US	BK	←Courts **CUMBERLAND**	Recorder→	UC	RE	TX	VS
•	•	•	•	•	A All State Tracers Company	423-605-0155	•	•	•	•
•	•	•	•	•	Bill Hundemer	865-670-1740, 670-604-6031	•	•	•	
•	•				National Pre-Employment Research [SOP]	770-389-6607				
•	•	•	•	•	Public Records Research	931-520-8902	•	•	•	•
	•	•	•	•	Real Estate Loan Services of TN Inc	800-475-2334	•	•	•	
	•	•	•	•	Record Data Inc (Tennessee)	615-221-0021	•	•	•	
•	•	•	•	•	Source Resources [SOP]	800-678-8774	•	•	•	
•	•		•	•	Verifi LLC	423-344-0133	•	•	•	
•					Larry M Warner	931-484-1611		•	•	

CR	CV	PR	US	BK	←Courts **DAVIDSON**	Recorder→	UC	RE	TX	VS
•	•	•	•	•	A All State Tracers Company	423-605-0155	•	•	•	•
					Lisa Bracey-Farris [SOP]	615-859-7135; cell- 615-943-4118		•	•	
•	•		•	•	Guaranty Research Svcs Inc	800-697-8534			•	
•	•	•	•		Information Inc	615-884-8000			•	•
•	•	•	•	•	Investigative Consultant Service	615-885-1126	•			•
•	•	•	•	•	Investigative Survelliance Group [SOP]	615-895-0268	•	•	•	•
					Judi Knecht	615-832-8255	•	•	•	
•					Kroll Background America	800-697-7189		•	•	
•	•	•	•	•	Kroll Document Filing & Retrieval Services [SOP]	800-324-2050	•	•	•	•
•					Lucy and Tyler Public Records Services	908-725-4356		•		
•	•				National Pre-Employment Research [SOP]	770-389-6607				
	•	•	•		Maureen H Poole	931-294-2988	•	•	•	
	•	•	•	•	Real Estate Loan Services of TN Inc	800-475-2334	•	•	•	
	•	•	•	•	Record Data Inc (Tennessee)	615-221-0021	•	•	•	
		•		•	Right On Time Documents Inc	615-885-8672	•	•	•	
•	•	•	•	•	Schaeffer Papers [SOP]	800-848-6119		•	•	•
•	•	•	•	•	Stallings Search Services	615-781-2323	•	•	•	•

CR	CV	PR	US	BK	←Courts **DECATUR**	Recorder→	UC	RE	TX	VS
•	•	•	•	•	A All State Tracers Company	423-605-0155	•	•	•	•
	•	•	•	•	D K Abstract	731-686-9363	•	•	•	•
•	•				Mashburn's Background Screening	931-852-2713			•	
	•	•	•	•	Record Data Inc (Tennessee)	615-221-0021	•	•	•	

CR	CV	PR	US	BK	←Courts **DEKALB**	Recorder→	UC	RE	TX	VS
•	•	•	•	•	A All State Tracers Company	423-605-0155	•	•	•	•
•	•	•	•	•	Public Records Research	931-520-8902	•	•	•	•
	•	•	•	•	Real Estate Loan Services of TN Inc	800-475-2334	•	•	•	
	•	•	•	•	Record Data Inc (Tennessee)	615-221-0021	•	•	•	
•	•				Pam Smith	931-686-2804			•	
•	•	•	•	•	Source Resources [SOP]	800-678-8774	•	•	•	

CR	CV	PR	US	BK	←Courts **DICKSON**	Recorder→	UC	RE	TX	VS
	•	•	•	•	Real Estate Loan Services of TN Inc	800-475-2334	•	•	•	
	•	•	•	•	Record Data Inc (Tennessee)	615-221-0021	•	•	•	
		•		•	Right On Time Documents Inc	615-885-8672	•	•	•	
•	•	•	•	•	Stallings Search Services	615-781-2323	•	•	•	•

CR	CV	PR	US	BK	←Courts	Dyer	Recorder→	UC	RE	TX	VS
•					Blue Line Investigations		901-266-7100				
	•	•	•	•	D K Abstract		731-686-9363	•	•	•	•
•	•				Patricia L Estes-Howell		731-784-1050				
	•	•	•	•	Susan Parker		731-884-9994	•	•	•	
	•	•	•	•	Record Data Inc (Tennessee)		615-221-0021	•	•	•	

CR	CV	PR	US	BK	←Courts	Fayette	Recorder→	UC	RE	TX	VS
•					Blue Line Investigations		901-266-7100				
•	•	•	•	•	Bryant Information Services		901-475-1276	•	•	•	
	•	•	•	•	D K Abstract		731-686-9363	•	•	•	•
•	•	•			The Daily News & Chandler Reports		901-523-1561		•		
•	•	•		•	Mid-South Subpoena Service [SOP]		800-737-8542	•	•	•	•
•	•				National Pre-Employment Research [SOP]		770-389-6607				
	•	•	•	•	Record Data Inc (Tennessee)		615-221-0021	•	•	•	
•	•	•	•	•	Record-Check Services Inc		800-530-7226	•	•	•	•

CR	CV	PR	US	BK	←Courts	Fentress	Recorder→	UC	RE	TX	VS
					Jimmie Kirby		931-858-8786, cell- 931-267-2418				
	•	•	•	•	Real Estate Loan Services of TN Inc		800-475-2334	•	•	•	
	•	•	•	•	Record Data Inc (Tennessee)		615-221-0021	•	•	•	
•					Larry M Warner		931-484-1611		•	•	

CR	CV	PR	US	BK	←Courts	Franklin	Recorder→	UC	RE	TX	VS
•	•	•	•	•	A All State Tracers Company		423-605-0155	•	•	•	•
•	•	•			J Stephen Broadway		931-433-5979	•	•	•	•
•	•	•	•	•	Charles F Edgar & Associates Inc [SOP]		256-539-7761	•	•	•	
•	•				National Pre-Employment Research [SOP]		770-389-6607				
	•	•	•		Maureen H Poole		931-294-2988	•	•	•	
	•	•	•	•	Record Data Inc (Tennessee)		615-221-0021	•	•	•	
	•	•	•	•	Title Guaranty & Trust of Chattanooga		423-266-5751	•	•	•	

CR	CV	PR	US	BK	←Courts	Gibson	Recorder→	UC	RE	TX	VS
•	•	•	•	•	Bryant Information Services		901-475-1276	•	•	•	
	•	•	•	•	D K Abstract		731-686-9363	•	•	•	•
•	•				Patricia L Estes-Howell		731-784-1050				
•	•				I L Research		731-686-0526				
	•	•	•	•	Susan Parker		731-884-9994	•	•	•	
	•	•	•	•	Record Data Inc (Tennessee)		615-221-0021	•	•	•	

CR	CV	PR	US	BK	←Courts	Giles	Recorder→	UC	RE	TX	VS
•	•	•			J Stephen Broadway		931-433-5979	•	•	•	•
•	•	•	•	•	Charles F Edgar & Associates Inc [SOP]		256-539-7761	•	•	•	
•	•				Mashburn's Background Screening		931-852-2713			•	
•	•				National Pre-Employment Research [SOP]		770-389-6607				
	•	•	•		Maureen H Poole		931-294-2988	•	•	•	
	•	•	•	•	Real Estate Loan Services of TN Inc		800-475-2334	•	•	•	
	•	•	•	•	Record Data Inc (Tennessee)		615-221-0021	•	•	•	

CR	CV	PR	US	BK	←Courts	Grainger	Recorder→	UC	RE	TX	VS
	•	•	•	•	Record Data Inc (Tennessee)		615-221-0021	•	•	•	

CR	CV	PR	US	BK	←Courts	Greene	Recorder→	UC	RE	TX	VS
	•	•	•	•	Record Data Inc (Tennessee)		615-221-0021	•	•	•	
•	•	•			Title Express Inc		423-587-9886	•	•	•	

CR	CV	PR	US	BK	←Courts GRUNDY	Recorder→	UC	RE	TX	VS
•	•	•	•	•	A All State Tracers Company	423-605-0155	•	•	•	•
	•	•			Real Estate Loan Services	423-855-0581	•	•	•	
	•	•	•	•	Record Data Inc (Tennessee)	615-221-0021	•	•	•	
•	•				Pam Smith	931-686-2804			•	
	•	•	•	•	Title Guaranty & Trust of Chattanooga	423-266-5751	•	•	•	

CR	CV	PR	US	BK	←Courts HAMBLEN	Recorder→	UC	RE	TX	VS
•	•				Datalink Investigative Services [SOP]	865-674-0030				
	•	•	•	•	Record Data Inc (Tennessee)	615-221-0021	•	•	•	
•	•	•			Title Express Inc	423-587-9886	•	•	•	

CR	CV	PR	US	BK	←Courts HAMILTON	Recorder→	UC	RE	TX	VS
•	•	•	•	•	A All State Tracers Company	423-605-0155	•	•	•	•
					DocuSearch Services	423-894-2425	•	•	•	
		•			Thomas E Ewinger Jr	423-614-5290	•	•	•	•
					Judi Knecht	615-832-8255	•	•	•	
•					Lucy and Tyler Public Records Services	908-725-4356		•		
					William "Bill" H Maynard	423-472-9858	•	•	•	
	•	•			Real Estate Loan Services	423-855-0581	•	•	•	
	•	•	•	•	Record Data Inc (Tennessee)	615-221-0021	•	•	•	
		•		•	Right On Time Documents Inc	615-885-8672	•	•	•	
•	•	•	•	•	Stallings Search Services	615-781-2323	•	•	•	•
	•	•		•	Title Guaranty & Trust of Chattanooga	423-266-5751	•	•	•	
•	•		•	•	Verifi LLC	423-344-0133	•	•	•	

CR	CV	PR	US	BK	←Courts HANCOCK	Recorder→	UC	RE	TX	VS
	•	•	•	•	Record Data Inc (Tennessee)	615-221-0021	•	•	•	

CR	CV	PR	US	BK	←Courts HARDEMAN	Recorder→	UC	RE	TX	VS
•	•	•	•	•	Bryant Information Services	901-475-1276	•	•	•	
	•	•	•	•	D K Abstract	731-686-9363	•	•	•	•
•	•				Patricia L Estes-Howell	731-784-1050				
•	•	•	•	•	Mid-South Subpoena Service [SOP]	800-737-8542	•	•	•	•
	•	•	•	•	Record Data Inc (Tennessee)	615-221-0021	•	•	•	

CR	CV	PR	US	BK	←Courts HARDIN	Recorder→	UC	RE	TX	VS
	•	•	•	•	D K Abstract	731-686-9363	•	•	•	•
•	•	•			Freelance Abstracting Service [SOP]	662-424-3636	•	•		•
•	•				Mashburn's Background Screening	931-852-2713			•	
	•	•	•	•	Record Data Inc (Tennessee)	615-221-0021	•	•	•	

CR	CV	PR	US	BK	←Courts HAWKINS	Recorder→	UC	RE	TX	VS
•	•				Terry Carpenter	423-357-1125	•		•	
•	•				National Pre-Employment Research [SOP]	770-389-6607				
	•	•	•	•	Record Data Inc (Tennessee)	615-221-0021	•	•	•	
•	•	•			Title Express Inc	423-587-9886	•	•	•	

CR	CV	PR	US	BK	←Courts HAYWOOD	Recorder→	UC	RE	TX	VS
•	•	•	•	•	Bryant Information Services	901-475-1276	•	•	•	
	•	•	•	•	D K Abstract	731-686-9363	•	•	•	•
•	•				Patricia L Estes-Howell	731-784-1050				
•	•				National Pre-Employment Research [SOP]	770-389-6607				
	•	•	•	•	Susan Parker	731-884-9994	•	•	•	
	•	•	•	•	Record Data Inc (Tennessee)	615-221-0021	•	•	•	

CR	CV	PR	US	BK	←Courts HENDERSON	Recorder→	UC	RE	TX	VS
•					Blue Line Investigations	901-266-7100				
	•	•	•	•	D K Abstract	731-686-9363	•	•	•	•
•	•				Patricia L Estes-Howell	731-784-1050				
	•	•	•	•	Record Data Inc (Tennessee)	615-221-0021	•	•	•	

CR	CV	PR	US	BK	←Courts	Henry	Recorder→	UC	RE	TX	VS
•	•	•	•	•	Rebecca Bulls		731-799-3066; Fax- same				
	•	•	•	•	D K Abstract		731-686-9363	•	•	•	•
	•	•	•	•	Susan Parker		731-884-9994	•	•	•	
	•	•	•	•	Record Data Inc (Tennessee)		615-221-0021	•	•	•	

CR	CV	PR	US	BK	←Courts	Hickman	Recorder→	UC	RE	TX	VS
					Larry R Dorning PC		931-796-5959	•	•	•	
•	•				Mashburn's Background Screening		931-852-2713			•	
	•	•	•		Maureen H Poole		931-294-2988	•	•	•	
	•	•	•	•	Real Estate Loan Services of TN Inc		800-475-2334	•	•	•	
	•	•	•	•	Record Data Inc (Tennessee)		615-221-0021	•	•	•	

CR	CV	PR	US	BK	←Courts	Houston	Recorder→	UC	RE	TX	VS
•	•				Heather Moore		931-413-5594; cell- 931-721-7284		•	•	
	•	•	•	•	Real Estate Loan Services of TN Inc		800-475-2334	•	•	•	
	•	•	•	•	Record Data Inc (Tennessee)		615-221-0021	•	•	•	

CR	CV	PR	US	BK	←Courts	Humphreys	Recorder→	UC	RE	TX	VS
	•	•	•	•	D K Abstract		731-686-9363	•	•	•	•
	•	•	•	•	Susan Parker		731-884-9994	•	•	•	
	•	•	•	•	Real Estate Loan Services of TN Inc		800-475-2334	•	•	•	
	•	•	•	•	Record Data Inc (Tennessee)		615-221-0021	•	•	•	

CR	CV	PR	US	BK	←Courts	Jackson	Recorder→	UC	RE	TX	VS
					Jimmie Kirby		931-858-8786, cell- 931-267-2418				
	•	•	•	•	Real Estate Loan Services of TN Inc		800-475-2334	•	•	•	
	•	•	•	•	Record Data Inc (Tennessee)		615-221-0021	•	•	•	
•	•	•	•	•	Source Resources [SOP]		800-678-8774	•	•	•	

CR	CV	PR	US	BK	←Courts	Jefferson	Recorder→	UC	RE	TX	VS
•	•				Datalink Investigative Services [SOP]		865-674-0030				
		•			NNBS Inc		865-977-8808	•	•	•	•
	•	•	•	•	Record Data Inc (Tennessee)		615-221-0021	•	•	•	
•	•	•			Title Express Inc		423-587-9886	•	•	•	
•	•	•	•	•	Vinson Detective Agency TN [SOP]		888-525-5047	•	•	•	•

CR	CV	PR	US	BK	←Courts	Johnson	Recorder→	UC	RE	TX	VS
	•	•	•	•	Record Data Inc (Tennessee)		615-221-0021	•	•	•	

CR	CV	PR	US	BK	←Courts	Knox	Recorder→	UC	RE	TX	VS
•	•	•	•	•	A All State Tracers Company		423-605-0155	•	•	•	•
		•			Thomas E Ewinger Jr		423-614-5290	•	•	•	•
•	•		•	•	Gamble Legal Research		865-966-3364	•		•	
•	•	•	•	•	Bill Hundemer		865-670-1740, 670-604-6031	•	•	•	
					Judi Knecht		615-832-8255	•	•	•	
•	•	•	•	•	Legal Investigations [SOP]		865-970-4444	•	•		
•					Lucy and Tyler Public Records Services		908-725-4356		•		
					William "Bill" H Maynard		423-472-9858	•	•	•	
		•			NNBS Inc		865-977-8808	•	•	•	•
•	•	•	•	•	Profile Information Services		512-472-9380	•	•	•	•
	•	•	•	•	Record Data Inc (Tennessee)		615-221-0021	•	•	•	
•	•		•	•	Records Research of Knoxville		865-693-3589	•	•	•	
		•		•	Right On Time Documents Inc		615-885-8672	•	•	•	
•	•	•	•	•	Schaeffer Papers [SOP]		800-848-6119		•	•	•
•	•	•	•	•	Southern Process Service [SOP]		865-525-3124		•		
•	•	•	•	•	Stallings Search Services		615-781-2323	•	•	•	•
•	•	•	•	•	TMC		865-609-7675	•	•	•	•
•	•		•	•	Verifi LLC		423-344-0133	•	•	•	
•	•	•	•	•	Vinson Detective Agency TN [SOP]		888-525-5047	•	•	•	•

CR	CV	PR	US	BK	←Courts	LAKE	Recorder→	UC	RE	TX	VS
	•	•	•	•	D K Abstract		731-686-9363	•	•	•	•
•	•				Patricia L Estes-Howell		731-784-1050				
	•	•	•	•	Susan Parker		731-884-9994	•	•	•	
	•	•	•	•	Record Data Inc (Tennessee)		615-221-0021	•	•	•	

CR	CV	PR	US	BK	←Courts	LAUDERDALE	Recorder→	UC	RE	TX	VS
•					Blue Line Investigations		901-266-7100				
•	•	•	•	•	Bryant Information Services		901-475-1276	•	•	•	
	•	•	•	•	D K Abstract		731-686-9363	•	•	•	•
•	•				Patricia L Estes-Howell		731-784-1050				
•	•	•	•	•	Mid-South Subpoena Service [SOP]		800-737-8542	•	•	•	•
•	•				National Pre-Employment Research [SOP]		770-389-6607				
	•	•	•	•	Susan Parker		731-884-9994	•	•	•	
	•	•	•	•	Record Data Inc (Tennessee)		615-221-0021	•	•	•	

CR	CV	PR	US	BK	←Courts	LAWRENCE	Recorder→	UC	RE	TX	VS
•	•	•			J Stephen Broadway		931-433-5979	•	•	•	•
•	•	•	•	•	Charles F Edgar & Associates Inc [SOP]		256-539-7761	•	•	•	
					Larry R Dorning PC		931-796-5959	•	•	•	
•	•				Mashburn's Background Screening		931-852-2713			•	
•	•				National Pre-Employment Research [SOP]		770-389-6607				
	•	•	•		Maureen H Poole		931-294-2988	•	•	•	
	•	•	•	•	Real Estate Loan Services of TN Inc		800-475-2334	•	•	•	
	•	•	•	•	Record Data Inc (Tennessee)		615-221-0021	•	•	•	

CR	CV	PR	US	BK	←Courts	LEWIS	Recorder→	UC	RE	TX	VS
					Larry R Dorning PC		931-796-5959	•	•	•	
•	•				Mashburn's Background Screening		931-852-2713			•	
•	•				National Pre-Employment Research [SOP]		770-389-6607				
	•	•	•		Maureen H Poole		931-294-2988	•	•	•	
	•	•	•	•	Real Estate Loan Services of TN Inc		800-475-2334	•	•	•	
	•	•	•	•	Record Data Inc (Tennessee)		615-221-0021	•	•	•	
•	•	•			Lori Stewart		931-796-2565				

CR	CV	PR	US	BK	←Courts	LINCOLN	Recorder→	UC	RE	TX	VS
•	•	•	•	•	A All State Tracers Company		423-605-0155	•	•	•	•
•	•	•			J Stephen Broadway		931-433-5979	•	•	•	•
•	•	•	•	•	Charles F Edgar & Associates Inc [SOP]		256-539-7761	•	•	•	
•	•				Mashburn's Background Screening		931-852-2713			•	
	•	•	•		Maureen H Poole		931-294-2988	•	•	•	
	•	•	•	•	Record Data Inc (Tennessee)		615-221-0021	•	•	•	

CR	CV	PR	US	BK	←Courts	LOUDON	Recorder→	UC	RE	TX	VS
•	•	•	•	•	A All State Tracers Company		423-605-0155	•	•	•	•
•	•		•	•	Botts & Assoc [SOP]		423-479-7714	•	•	•	•
		•			Thomas E Ewinger Jr		423-614-5290	•	•	•	•
•	•		•	•	Gamble Legal Research		865-966-3364	•		•	
•	•	•	•	•	Bill Hundemer		865-670-1740, 670-604-6031	•	•	•	
					William "Bill" H Maynard		423-472-9858	•		•	
		•			NNBS Inc		865-977-8808	•	•	•	•
•	•	•	•	•	Profile Information Services		512-472-9380	•	•	•	•
	•	•	•	•	Record Data Inc (Tennessee)		615-221-0021	•	•	•	
	•	•	•	•	Title Guaranty & Trust of Chattanooga		423-266-5751	•	•	•	
•	•		•	•	Verifi LLC		423-344-0133	•	•	•	

CR	CV	PR	US	BK	←Courts	MACON	Recorder→	UC	RE	TX	VS
•	•				Cumberland Research		615-735-6558				
	•	•	•	•	Real Estate Loan Services of TN Inc		800-475-2334	•	•	•	
	•	•	•	•	Record Data Inc (Tennessee)		615-221-0021	•	•	•	

CR	CV	PR	US	BK	Retriever	Phone	UC	RE	TX	VS
•	•	•	•	•	Source Resources [SOP]	800-678-8774	•	•	•	
CR	**CV**	**PR**	**US**	**BK**	**←COURTS MADISON**	**RECORDER→**	**UC**	**RE**	**TX**	**VS**
	•	•	•	•	D K Abstract	731-686-9363	•	•	•	•
•	•				Patricia L Estes-Howell	731-784-1050				
•	•				I L Research	731-686-0526				
•	•	•	•	•	Mid-South Subpoena Service [SOP]	800-737-8542	•	•	•	•
•	•				Robert Osborne	731-664-6234			•	
	•	•	•	•	Susan Parker	731-884-9994	•	•	•	
	•	•	•	•	Record Data Inc (Tennessee)	615-221-0021	•	•	•	
CR	**CV**	**PR**	**US**	**BK**	**←COURTS MARION**	**RECORDER→**	**UC**	**RE**	**TX**	**VS**
•	•	•	•	•	A All State Tracers Company	423-605-0155	•	•	•	•
•	•	•	•	•	Charles F Edgar & Associates Inc [SOP]	256-539-7761	•	•	•	
		•			Thomas E Ewinger Jr	423-614-5290	•	•	•	•
•	•				National Pre-Employment Research [SOP]	770-389-6607				
	•	•			Real Estate Loan Services	423-855-0581	•	•	•	
	•	•	•	•	Record Data Inc (Tennessee)	615-221-0021	•	•	•	
	•	•	•	•	Title Guaranty & Trust of Chattanooga	423-266-5751	•	•	•	
•	•		•	•	Verifi LLC	423-344-0133	•	•	•	
CR	**CV**	**PR**	**US**	**BK**	**←COURTS MARSHALL**	**RECORDER→**	**UC**	**RE**	**TX**	**VS**
•	•	•			J Stephen Broadway	931-433-5979	•	•	•	•
•	•	•	•	•	Charles F Edgar & Associates Inc [SOP]	256-539-7761	•	•	•	
	•	•	•		Maureen H Poole	931-294-2988	•	•	•	
	•	•	•	•	Real Estate Loan Services of TN Inc	800-475-2334	•	•	•	
	•	•	•	•	Record Data Inc (Tennessee)	615-221-0021	•	•	•	
CR	**CV**	**PR**	**US**	**BK**	**←COURTS MAURY**	**RECORDER→**	**UC**	**RE**	**TX**	**VS**
•	•	•	•	•	Charles F Edgar & Associates Inc [SOP]	256-539-7761	•		•	
					Larry R Dorning PC	931-796-5959	•	•	•	
•	•				Mashburn's Background Screening	931-852-2713			•	
•	•				National Pre-Employment Research [SOP]	770-389-6607				
	•	•	•		Maureen H Poole	931-294-2988	•	•	•	
	•	•	•	•	Real Estate Loan Services of TN Inc	800-475-2334	•	•	•	
	•	•	•	•	Record Data Inc (Tennessee)	615-221-0021	•	•	•	
•	•				Patricia Winters	615-595-2670			•	
CR	**CV**	**PR**	**US**	**BK**	**←COURTS MCMINN**	**RECORDER→**	**UC**	**RE**	**TX**	**VS**
•	•	•	•	•	A All State Tracers Company	423-605-0155	•	•	•	•
•	•		•	•	Botts & Assoc [SOP]	423-479-7714	•	•	•	•
		•			Thomas E Ewinger Jr	423-614-5290	•	•	•	•
•	•	•	•	•	Bill Hundemer	865-670-1740, 670-604-6031	•	•	•	
					William "Bill" H Maynard	423-472-9858	•	•	•	
•	•				National Pre-Employment Research [SOP]	770-389-6607				
	•	•			Real Estate Loan Services	423-855-0581	•	•	•	
	•	•	•	•	Record Data Inc (Tennessee)	615-221-0021	•	•	•	
	•	•	•	•	Title Guaranty & Trust of Chattanooga	423-266-5751	•	•	•	
•	•		•	•	Verifi LLC	423-344-0133	•	•	•	
CR	**CV**	**PR**	**US**	**BK**	**←COURTS MCNAIRY**	**RECORDER→**	**UC**	**RE**	**TX**	**VS**
	•	•	•	•	D K Abstract	731-686-9363	•	•	•	•
•	•				Patricia L Estes-Howell	731-784-1050				
•	•	•			Freelance Abstracting Service [SOP]	662-424-3636	•	•		•
	•	•	•	•	Record Data Inc (Tennessee)	615-221-0021	•	•	•	
CR	**CV**	**PR**	**US**	**BK**	**←COURTS MEIGS**	**RECORDER→**	**UC**	**RE**	**TX**	**VS**
•	•	•	•	•	A All State Tracers Company	423-605-0155	•	•	•	•
•	•		•	•	Botts & Assoc [SOP]	423-479-7714	•	•	•	•
		•			Thomas E Ewinger Jr	423-614-5290	•	•	•	•
					William "Bill" H Maynard	423-472-9858	•	•	•	

CR	CV	PR	US	BK	←Courts	Recorder→	UC	RE	TX	VS
•	•	•	•	•	Mid-South Subpoena Service [SOP]	800-737-8542	•	•	•	•
•	•				National Pre-Employment Research [SOP]	770-389-6607				
	•	•			Real Estate Loan Services	423-855-0581	•	•	•	
	•	•	•	•	Record Data Inc (Tennessee)	615-221-0021	•	•	•	
	•	•	•	•	Title Guaranty & Trust of Chattanooga	423-266-5751	•	•	•	
•	•		•	•	Verifi LLC	423-344-0133	•	•	•	

MONROE

CR	CV	PR	US	BK	←Courts	Recorder→	UC	RE	TX	VS
•	•	•	•	•	A All State Tracers Company	423-605-0155	•	•	•	•
•	•		•	•	Botts & Assoc [SOP]	423-479-7714	•	•	•	•
		•			Thomas E Ewinger Jr	423-614-5290	•	•	•	•
•	•	•	•	•	Bill Hundemer	865-670-1740, 670-604-6031	•	•	•	
					William "Bill" H Maynard	423-472-9858	•	•	•	
	•	•			Real Estate Loan Services	423-855-0581	•	•	•	
	•	•	•	•	Record Data Inc (Tennessee)	615-221-0021	•	•	•	
	•	•	•	•	Title Guaranty & Trust of Chattanooga	423-266-5751	•	•	•	
•	•		•	•	Verifi LLC	423-344-0133	•	•	•	

MONTGOMERY

CR	CV	PR	US	BK	←Courts	Recorder→	UC	RE	TX	VS
•					DataSearch	866-645-2562			•	
	•	•	•	•	Real Estate Loan Services of TN Inc	800-475-2334	•	•	•	
	•	•	•	•	Record Data Inc (Tennessee)	615-221-0021	•	•	•	
		•		•	Right On Time Documents Inc	615-885-8672	•	•	•	
•	•	•	•	•	Stallings Search Services	615-781-2323	•	•	•	•

MOORE

CR	CV	PR	US	BK	←Courts	Recorder→	UC	RE	TX	VS
•	•	•			J Stephen Broadway	931-433-5979	•	•	•	•
•	•	•	•	•	Charles F Edgar & Associates Inc [SOP]	256-539-7761	•	•	•	
	•	•	•		Maureen H Poole	931-294-2988	•	•	•	
	•	•	•	•	Record Data Inc (Tennessee)	615-221-0021	•	•	•	

MORGAN

CR	CV	PR	US	BK	←Courts	Recorder→	UC	RE	TX	VS
•	•	•	•	•	Bill Hundemer	865-670-1740, 670-604-6031	•	•	•	
•	•				National Pre-Employment Research [SOP]	770-389-6607				
	•	•	•	•	Record Data Inc (Tennessee)	615-221-0021	•	•	•	
•	•		•	•	Verifi LLC	423-344-0133	•	•	•	

OBION

CR	CV	PR	US	BK	←Courts	Recorder→	UC	RE	TX	VS
•					Blue Line Investigations	901-266-7100				
•	•	•	•	•	Bryant Information Services	901-475-1276	•	•	•	
•	•	•	•	•	Rebecca Bulls	731-799-3066; Fax- same				
	•	•	•	•	D K Abstract	731-686-9363	•	•	•	•
•	•				Patricia L Estes-Howell	731-784-1050				
	•	•	•	•	Susan Parker	731-884-9994	•	•	•	
	•	•	•	•	Record Data Inc (Tennessee)	615-221-0021	•	•	•	

OVERTON

CR	CV	PR	US	BK	←Courts	Recorder→	UC	RE	TX	VS
					Jimmie Kirby	931-858-8786, cell- 931-267-2418				
•	•	•	•	•	Public Records Research	931-520-8902	•	•	•	•
	•	•	•	•	Real Estate Loan Services of TN Inc	800-475-2334	•	•	•	
	•	•	•	•	Record Data Inc (Tennessee)	615-221-0021	•	•	•	
•	•				Pam Smith	931-686-2804			•	
•	•	•	•	•	Source Resources [SOP]	800-678-8774	•	•	•	
•					Larry M Warner	931-484-1611		•	•	

PERRY

CR	CV	PR	US	BK	←Courts	Recorder→	UC	RE	TX	VS
	•	•	•	•	D K Abstract	731-686-9363	•	•	•	•
					Larry R Dorning PC	931-796-5959	•	•	•	
•	•				Mashburn's Background Screening	931-852-2713			•	
	•	•	•	•	Real Estate Loan Services of TN Inc	800-475-2334	•	•	•	
	•	•	•	•	Record Data Inc (Tennessee)	615-221-0021	•	•	•	

CR	CV	PR	US	BK	←Courts PICKETT	Recorder→	UC	RE	TX	VS
	●	●	●	●	Real Estate Loan Services of TN Inc	800-475-2334	●	●	●	
	●	●	●	●	Record Data Inc (Tennessee)	615-221-0021	●	●	●	
●					Larry M Warner	931-484-1611		●	●	

CR	CV	PR	US	BK	←Courts POLK	Recorder→	UC	RE	TX	VS
●	●	●	●	●	A All State Tracers Company	423-605-0155	●	●	●	●
●	●		●	●	Botts & Assoc [SOP]	423-479-7714	●	●	●	●
		●			Thomas E Ewinger Jr	423-614-5290	●	●	●	●
●	●	●	●	●	Bill Hundemer	865-670-1740, 670-604-6031	●	●	●	
					William "Bill" H Maynard	423-472-9858	●	●	●	
●	●				National Pre-Employment Research [SOP]	770-389-6607				
	●	●			Real Estate Loan Services	423-855-0581	●	●	●	
	●	●	●	●	Record Data Inc (Tennessee)	615-221-0021	●	●	●	
	●	●	●	●	Title Guaranty & Trust of Chattanooga	423-266-5751	●	●	●	
●	●		●	●	Verifi LLC	423-344-0133	●	●	●	

CR	CV	PR	US	BK	←Courts PUTNAM	Recorder→	UC	RE	TX	VS
●	●	●	●	●	Bill Hundemer	865-670-1740, 670-604-6031	●	●	●	
					Jimmie Kirby	931-858-8786, cell- 931-267-2418				
●	●	●	●	●	Public Records Research	931-520-8902	●	●	●	●
●	●	●			Rapid Documents	931-372-6948		●	●	●
	●	●	●	●	Real Estate Loan Services of TN Inc	800-475-2334	●	●	●	
	●	●	●	●	Record Data Inc (Tennessee)	615-221-0021	●	●	●	
●	●				Pam Smith	931-686-2804			●	
●	●	●	●	●	Source Resources [SOP]	800-678-8774	●	●	●	
●	●		●	●	Verifi LLC	423-344-0133	●	●	●	
●					Larry M Warner	931-484-1611		●	●	

CR	CV	PR	US	BK	←Courts RHEA	Recorder→	UC	RE	TX	VS
●	●	●	●	●	A All State Tracers Company	423-605-0155	●	●	●	●
●	●		●	●	Botts & Assoc [SOP]	423-479-7714	●	●	●	●
		●			Thomas E Ewinger Jr	423-614-5290	●	●	●	●
					William "Bill" H Maynard	423-472-9858	●	●	●	
	●	●			Real Estate Loan Services	423-855-0581	●	●	●	
	●	●	●	●	Record Data Inc (Tennessee)	615-221-0021	●	●	●	
	●	●	●	●	Title Guaranty & Trust of Chattanooga	423-266-5751	●	●	●	
●	●		●	●	Verifi LLC	423-344-0133	●	●	●	

CR	CV	PR	US	BK	←Courts ROANE	Recorder→	UC	RE	TX	VS
●	●	●	●	●	A All State Tracers Company	423-605-0155	●	●	●	●
		●			Thomas E Ewinger Jr	423-614-5290	●	●	●	●
●	●		●	●	Gamble Legal Research	865-966-3364	●		●	
●	●	●	●	●	Bill Hundemer	865-670-1740, 670-604-6031	●	●	●	
					William "Bill" H Maynard	423-472-9858	●	●	●	
		●			NNBS Inc	865-977-8808	●	●	●	●
	●	●	●	●	Record Data Inc (Tennessee)	615-221-0021	●	●	●	
●	●	●	●	●	Source Resources [SOP]	800-678-8774	●	●	●	
●	●		●	●	Verifi LLC	423-344-0133	●	●	●	

CR	CV	PR	US	BK	←Courts ROBERTSON	Recorder→	UC	RE	TX	VS
●					DataSearch	866-645-2562			●	
●	●	●	●	●	Kroll Document Filing & Retrieval Services [SOP]	800-324-2050	●	●	●	●
	●	●	●	●	Real Estate Loan Services of TN Inc	800-475-2334	●	●	●	
	●	●	●	●	Record Data Inc (Tennessee)	615-221-0021	●	●	●	
		●		●	Right On Time Documents Inc	615-885-8672	●	●	●	
●	●	●	●	●	Stallings Search Services	615-781-2323	●	●	●	●

CR	CV	PR	US	BK	←COURTS	RUTHERFORD RECORDER→	UC	RE	TX	VS
•	•	•	•	•	A All State Tracers Company	423-605-0155	•	•	•	•
•	•				Crime Checkers	615-735-0010	•		•	
•	•		•	•	Guaranty Research Svcs Inc	800-697-8534			•	
•	•	•	•	•	Investigative Surveillance Group [SOP]	615-895-0268	•	•	•	•
					Judi Knecht	615-832-8255	•	•	•	
•					Kroll Background America	800-697-7189		•	•	
•	•	•	•	•	Kroll Document Filing & Retrieval Services [SOP]	800-324-2050	•	•	•	•
•	•				Mid-State Records	615-791-1123			•	
	•	•	•		Maureen H Poole	931-294-2988	•	•	•	
	•	•	•	•	Real Estate Loan Services of TN Inc	800-475-2334	•	•	•	
	•	•	•	•	Record Data Inc (Tennessee)	615-221-0021	•	•	•	
		•		•	Right On Time Documents Inc	615-885-8672	•	•	•	
•	•		•	•	Stallings Search Services	615-781-2323	•	•	•	•
•	•	•	•	•	TMC	865-609-7675	•	•	•	•

CR	CV	PR	US	BK	←COURTS	SCOTT RECORDER→	UC	RE	TX	VS
	•	•	•	•	Record Data Inc (Tennessee)	615-221-0021	•	•	•	

CR	CV	PR	US	BK	←COURTS	SEQUATCHIE RECORDER→	UC	RE	TX	VS
•	•	•	•	•	A All State Tracers Company	423-605-0155	•	•	•	•
		•			Thomas E Ewinger Jr	423-614-5290	•	•	•	•
	•	•			Real Estate Loan Services	423-855-0581	•	•	•	
	•	•	•	•	Record Data Inc (Tennessee)	615-221-0021	•	•	•	
	•	•	•	•	Title Guaranty & Trust of Chattanooga	423-266-5751	•	•	•	
•	•		•	•	Verifi LLC	423-344-0133	•	•	•	

CR	CV	PR	US	BK	←COURTS	SEVIER RECORDER→	UC	RE	TX	VS
•	•		•	•	Gamble Legal Research	865-966-3364	•		•	
•	•	•	•	•	Bill Hundemer	865-670-1740, 670-604-6031	•	•	•	
•	•				National Pre-Employment Research [SOP]	770-389-6607				
		•			NNBS Inc	865-977-8808	•	•	•	•
	•	•	•	•	Record Data Inc (Tennessee)	615-221-0021	•	•	•	
•	•		•	•	Records Research of Knoxville	865-693-3589	•	•	•	
•	•	•			Title Express Inc	423-587-9886	•	•	•	
•	•		•	•	Verifi LLC	423-344-0133	•	•	•	
•	•	•	•	•	Vinson Detective Agency TN [SOP]	888-525-5047	•	•	•	•

CR	CV	PR	US	BK	←COURTS	SHELBY RECORDER→	UC	RE	TX	VS
•	•	•	•	•	B & B Reporting Inc [SOP]	256-574-2524	•	•	•	•
•	•		•	•	Backgrounds Express LLC [SOP]	888-811-4667				
•					Blue Line Investigations	901-266-7100				
•	•	•	•	•	Bryant Information Services	901-475-1276	•	•	•	
•	•	•			The Daily News & Chandler Reports	901-523-1561		•		
•					DJ Records	901-795-6450				
					Judi Knecht	615-832-8255	•	•	•	
•	•	•	•	•	Lenow International Inc [SOP]	901-726-0735	•		•	•
•	•	•	•	•	Mid-South Subpoena Service [SOP]	800-737-8542	•	•	•	•
•	•				Pinnacle Records	901-324-9163				
	•	•	•	•	Record Data Inc (Tennessee)	615-221-0021	•	•	•	
•	•	•	•	•	Record-Check Services Inc	800-530-7226	•	•	•	•
		•		•	Right On Time Documents Inc	615-885-8672	•	•	•	
•	•	•	•	•	Schaeffer Papers [SOP]	800-848-6119		•	•	•
•	•	•	•	•	Stallings Search Services	615-781-2323	•	•	•	•
•	•	•	•	•	The Discovery Group Inc	662-280-1576	•		•	•

Smith

CR	CV	PR	US	BK	←Courts / Smith	Recorder→	UC	RE	TX	VS
•	•				Cumberland Research	615-735-6558				
					Jimmie Kirby	931-858-8786, cell- 931-267-2418				
	•	•	•	•	Real Estate Loan Services of TN Inc	800-475-2334	•	•	•	
	•	•	•	•	Record Data Inc (Tennessee)	615-221-0021	•	•	•	
•	•	•	•	•	Source Resources [SOP]	800-678-8774	•	•	•	

Stewart

CR	CV	PR	US	BK	←Courts / Stewart	Recorder→	UC	RE	TX	VS
	•	•	•	•	D K Abstract	731-686-9363	•	•	•	•
•					DataSearch	866-645-2562			•	
	•	•	•	•	Susan Parker	731-884-9994	•	•	•	
	•	•	•	•	Real Estate Loan Services of TN Inc	800-475-2334	•	•	•	
	•	•	•	•	Record Data Inc (Tennessee)	615-221-0021	•	•	•	

Sullivan

CR	CV	PR	US	BK	←Courts / Sullivan	Recorder→	UC	RE	TX	VS
•	•				Terry Carpenter	423-357-1125	•		•	
•	•				Shelly and James Dobler	423-753-4885				
	•	•	•	•	Record Data Inc (Tennessee)	615-221-0021	•	•	•	
		•		•	Right On Time Documents Inc	615-885-8672	•	•	•	
•	•	•		•	Spencer Investigations LLC [SOP]	423-323-1100	•	•	•	

Sumner

CR	CV	PR	US	BK	←Courts / Sumner	Recorder→	UC	RE	TX	VS
					Lisa Bracey-Farris [SOP]	615-859-7135; cell- 615-943-4118		•	•	
•	•				Cumberland Research	615-735-6558				
•	•		•	•	Guaranty Research Svcs Inc	800-697-8534			•	
•	•	•	•	•	Kroll Document Filing & Retrieval Services [SOP]	800-324-2050	•	•	•	•
	•	•	•	•	Real Estate Loan Services of TN Inc	800-475-2334	•	•	•	
	•	•	•	•	Record Data Inc (Tennessee)	615-221-0021	•	•	•	
		•		•	Right On Time Documents Inc	615-885-8672	•	•	•	
•	•	•	•	•	Schaeffer Papers [SOP]	800-848-6119		•	•	•
•	•	•	•	•	Stallings Search Services	615-781-2323	•	•	•	•

Tipton

CR	CV	PR	US	BK	←Courts / Tipton	Recorder→	UC	RE	TX	VS
•					Blue Line Investigations	901-266-7100				
•	•	•	•	•	Bryant Information Services	901-475-1276	•	•	•	
	•	•	•	•	D K Abstract	731-686-9363	•	•	•	•
•	•	•			The Daily News & Chandler Reports	901-523-1561		•		
•	•	•	•	•	Mid-South Subpoena Service [SOP]	800-737-8542	•	•	•	•
•	•				National Pre-Employment Research [SOP]	770-389-6607				
	•	•	•	•	Susan Parker	731-884-9994	•	•	•	
	•	•	•	•	Record Data Inc (Tennessee)	615-221-0021	•	•	•	
•	•	•	•	•	Record-Check Services Inc	800-530-7226	•	•	•	•

Trousdale

CR	CV	PR	US	BK	←Courts / Trousdale	Recorder→	UC	RE	TX	VS
•	•				Cumberland Research	615-735-6558				
	•	•	•	•	Real Estate Loan Services of TN Inc	800-475-2334	•	•	•	
	•	•	•	•	Record Data Inc (Tennessee)	615-221-0021	•	•	•	

Unicoi

CR	CV	PR	US	BK	←Courts / Unicoi	Recorder→	UC	RE	TX	VS
•	•				Shelly and James Dobler	423-753-4885				
	•	•	•	•	Record Data Inc (Tennessee)	615-221-0021	•	•	•	

Union

CR	CV	PR	US	BK	←Courts / Union	Recorder→	UC	RE	TX	VS
•	•				National Pre-Employment Research [SOP]	770-389-6607				
		•			NNBS Inc	865-977-8808	•	•	•	•
	•	•	•	•	Record Data Inc (Tennessee)	615-221-0021	•	•	•	
•	•		•	•	Records Research of Knoxville	865-693-3589	•	•	•	
•	•	•	•	•	TMC	865-609-7675	•	•	•	•

CR	CV	PR	US	BK	←Courts	Van Buren	Recorder→	UC	RE	TX	VS
•	•	•	•	•		A All State Tracers Company	423-605-0155	•	•	•	•
	•	•	•	•		Record Data Inc (Tennessee)	615-221-0021	•	•	•	
•	•					Pam Smith	931-686-2804			•	
	•	•	•	•		Title Guaranty & Trust of Chattanooga	423-266-5751	•	•	•	

CR	CV	PR	US	BK	←Courts	Warren	Recorder→	UC	RE	TX	VS
•	•	•	•	•		A All State Tracers Company	423-605-0155	•	•	•	•
	•	•	•	•		Record Data Inc (Tennessee)	615-221-0021	•	•	•	
•	•					Pam Smith	931-686-2804			•	

CR	CV	PR	US	BK	←Courts	Washington	Recorder→	UC	RE	TX	VS
•	•					Terry Carpenter	423-357-1125	•		•	
•	•					Shelly and James Dobler	423-753-4885				
	•	•	•	•		Record Data Inc (Tennessee)	615-221-0021	•	•	•	
•	•	•		•		Spencer Investigations LLC [SOP]	423-323-1100	•	•	•	
•	•	•	•	•		Stallings Search Services	615-781-2323	•	•	•	•
•	•	•	•	•		TMC	865-609-7675	•	•	•	•

CR	CV	PR	US	BK	←Courts	Wayne	Recorder→	UC	RE	TX	VS
						Larry R Dorning PC	931-796-5959	•	•	•	
•	•					Mashburn's Background Screening	931-852-2713			•	
	•	•	•			Maureen H Poole	931-294-2988	•	•	•	
	•	•	•	•		Real Estate Loan Services of TN Inc	800-475-2334	•	•	•	
	•	•	•	•		Record Data Inc (Tennessee)	615-221-0021	•	•	•	

CR	CV	PR	US	BK	←Courts	Weakley	Recorder→	UC	RE	TX	VS
•						Blue Line Investigations	901-266-7100				
•	•	•	•	•		Rebecca Bulls	731-799-3066; Fax- same				
	•	•	•	•		D K Abstract	731-686-9363	•	•	•	•
•	•					Patricia L Estes-Howell	731-784-1050				
	•	•	•	•		Susan Parker	731-884-9994	•	•	•	
	•	•	•	•		Record Data Inc (Tennessee)	615-221-0021	•	•	•	
•	•					Dawn Richards	731-364-2456				

CR	CV	PR	US	BK	←Courts	White	Recorder→	UC	RE	TX	VS
•	•	•	•	•		A All State Tracers Company	423-605-0155	•	•	•	•
						Jimmie Kirby	931-858-8786, cell- 931-267-2418				
•	•	•				Rapid Documents	931-372-6948		•	•	•
	•	•	•	•		Real Estate Loan Services of TN Inc	800-475-2334	•	•	•	
	•	•	•	•		Record Data Inc (Tennessee)	615-221-0021	•	•	•	
•	•					Pam Smith	931-686-2804			•	
•	•	•	•	•		Source Resources [SOP]	800-678-8774	•	•	•	
•						Larry M Warner	931-484-1611		•	•	

CR	CV	PR	US	BK	←Courts	Williamson	Recorder→	UC	RE	TX	VS
•	•	•	•	•		A All State Tracers Company	423-605-0155	•	•	•	•
•	•		•	•		Guaranty Research Svcs Inc	800-697-8534			•	
						Judi Knecht	615-832-8255	•	•	•	
•	•	•	•	•		Kroll Document Filing & Retrieval Services [SOP]	800-324-2050	•	•	•	•
•						Lucy and Tyler Public Records Services	908-725-4356		•		
•	•					Mid-State Records	615-791-1123			•	
	•	•	•			Maureen H Poole	931-294-2988	•	•	•	
	•	•	•	•		Real Estate Loan Services of TN Inc	800-475-2334	•	•	•	
	•	•	•	•		Record Data Inc (Tennessee)	615-221-0021	•	•	•	
		•		•		Right On Time Documents Inc	615-885-8672	•	•	•	
•	•	•	•	•		Stallings Search Services	615-781-2323	•	•	•	•

CR	CV	PR	US	BK	←COURTS WILSON	RECORDER→	UC	RE	TX	VS
•	•	•	•	•	A All State Tracers Company	423-605-0155	•	•	•	•
•	•				Crime Checkers	615-735-0010	•		•	
•	•		•	•	Guaranty Research Svcs Inc	800-697-8534			•	
•	•	•	•		Investigative Consultant Service	615-885-1126	•			•
•	•	•	•	•	Investigative Surveillance Group [SOP]	615-895-0268	•	•	•	•
					Jimmie Kirby	931-858-8786, cell- 931-267-2418				
•	•	•	•	•	Kroll Document Filing & Retrieval Services [SOP]	800-324-2050	•	•	•	•
	•	•	•		Maureen H Poole	931-294-2988	•	•	•	
	•	•	•	•	Real Estate Loan Services of TN Inc	800-475-2334	•	•	•	
	•	•	•	•	Record Data Inc (Tennessee)	615-221-0021	•	•	•	
		•			Right On Time Documents Inc	615-885-8672	•	•	•	
•	•	•	•	•	Stallings Search Services	615-781-2323	•	•	•	•

[SOP] = PERFORMS SERVICE OF PROCESS

= PRRN Member. *A retriever you can trust!*

COURT RECORDS

CODE	GOVERNMENT AGENCY	TYPE OF INFORMATION
CR	Criminal Court	Municipal, county and state level criminal cases
CV	Civil Court	Municipal, county and state level civil cases
PR	Probate Court	Wills and estate cases
US	US District Court	Federal civil and criminal cases
BK	Bankruptcy Court	United States bankruptcy cases

COUNTY RECORDS - RECORDINGS

CODE	GOVERNMENT AGENCY	TYPE OF INFORMATION
UC	UCC Filing Office	Uniform Commercial Code and other personal property liens
RE	Real Estate Recording Office	Real property transactions and liens
TX	Tax Filing Office(s)	Federal and state tax liens, judgment liens
VS	Vital Records Office	Vital statistics—birth, death, marriage, divorce

Texas

Court Records Retrieved — Capital - Travis County — Recorded Records Retrieved

CR	CV	PR	US	BK	←Courts	ANDERSON	Recorder→	UC	RE	TX	VS
						Anderson County Abstract Co	903-729-5871	•	•	•	•
•	•		•			Dataprompt Corporation	214-395-2530				
		•				DeedSearcher Title Research Services	281-375-8480	•	•	•	
•	•	•	•	•		Profile Information Services	512-472-9380	•	•	•	•

CR	CV	PR	US	BK	←Courts	ANDREWS	Recorder→	UC	RE	TX	VS
•	•	•	•	•		Davick Services	800-658-6656	•	•	•	

CR	CV	PR	US	BK	←Courts	ANGELINA	Recorder→	UC	RE	TX	VS
•	•	•				Community Title Co	936-559-7900	•	•	•	•
•	•					Crimecheck Research Services	281-288-6930				
		•				DeedSearcher Title Research Services	281-375-8480	•	•	•	
•	•	•	•			East Tex Records Research	936-414-1193	•	•	•	
						East Texas Public Records	936-632-7385		•		
						Record Time Research	936-632-5150		•		

CR	CV	PR	US	BK	←Courts	ARANSAS	Recorder→	UC	RE	TX	VS
•	•	•	•	•		Condor Inv [SOP]	361-881-8977	•	•	•	•
•	•	•	•	•		Corpus Christi Court Services	361-815-8202	•	•	•	
•	•	•	•	•		Shawver & Associates	800-364-2333	•	•	•	•
•	•	•	•	•		Texas Civil Process [SOP]	800-976-9595	•	•	•	•

CR	CV	PR	US	BK	←Courts	ARCHER	Recorder→	UC	RE	TX	VS
•	•	•	•	•		Mendenhall Information Services	940-696-0758	•	•	•	•
•	•	•	•	•		Superior Process Service [SOP]	888-230-2663				
•	•	•	•	•		Texas Detective.com [SOP]	940-592-7000	•	•	•	•

CR	CV	PR	US	BK	←Courts	ARMSTRONG	Recorder→	UC	RE	TX	VS
•	•	•	•	•		Davick Services	800-658-6656	•	•	•	
	•	•	•	•		Rollins Research Ltd	806-353-7886, cell- 806-654-2376	•	•	•	
•	•	•				Security Abstract Co	806-874-3511	•	•	•	•

CR	CV	PR	US	BK	←Courts	ATASCOSA	Recorder→	UC	RE	TX	VS
		•		•		Abstracts/Trustees of Texas	888-452-0331	•	•	•	
•	•	•	•	•		Best Process Service [SOP]	210-930-7417	•	•	•	•
•	•					Crimecheck Research Services	281-288-6930				
		•				DeedSearcher Title Research Services	281-375-8480	•	•	•	
		•				Land Records of Texas	800-678-8016	•	•	•	
•	•	•	•	•		Property Research & Documentation Service Inc	210-520-7884	•	•	•	•

CR	CV	PR	US	BK	←Courts	AUSTIN	Recorder→	UC	RE	TX	VS
		•		•		Abstracts/Trustees of Texas	888-452-0331	•	•	•	
•	•	•	•	•		All State Document Services	888-246-8180	•	•	•	•
		•				Botts Title Co	254-697-6962	•	•	•	•
		•				DeedSearcher Title Research Services	281-375-8480	•	•	•	
		•				Land Records of Texas	800-678-8016	•	•	•	
•	•	•	•	•		Professional Civil Process (Austin) [SOP]	800-950-7493	•	•	•	•
•	•	•	•	•		The Research Staff Inc	800-822-3584	•	•	•	

CR	CV	PR	US	BK	←Courts	Bailey	Recorder→	UC	RE	TX	VS
•	•	•	•	•	Davick Services		800-658-6656	•	•	•	
•	•	•			Farwell Abstract Co Inc		806-481-9992		•	•	

CR	CV	PR	US	BK	←Courts	Bandera	Recorder→	UC	RE	TX	VS
•	•	•	•	•	Best Process Service [SOP]		210-930-7417	•	•	•	•
•	•				Crimecheck Research Services		281-288-6930				
		•			Land Records of Texas		800-678-8016	•	•	•	
•	•	•	•	•	Property Research & Documentation Service Inc		210-520-7884	•	•	•	•

CR	CV	PR	US	BK	←Courts	Bastrop	Recorder→	UC	RE	TX	VS
		•		•	Abstracts/Trustees of Texas		888-452-0331	•	•	•	
•	•	•	•	•	Americorp Research Inc		800-620-0015	•	•	•	•
	•		•		Carma Austin		254-634-1701	•		•	
	•	•	•	•	Central Tejas Research & Title Services		512-469-6026	•	•	•	
		•			DeedSearcher Title Research Services		281-375-8480	•	•	•	
					Executec Services		512-345-5402	•	•	•	
•	•	•	•	•	John C Dunaway & Company [SOP]		512-835-5888	•	•	•	•
		•			Land Records of Texas		800-678-8016	•	•	•	
•	•	•	•	•	MS Document Services Inc		800-292-3868	•	•	•	•
•	•	•	•	•	Promesa Enterprises Inc		800-474-4420	•	•	•	•
•	•	•	•	•	Research Network		512-469-1740	•	•	•	•

CR	CV	PR	US	BK	←Courts	Baylor	Recorder→	UC	RE	TX	VS
•	•	•	•	•	Mendenhall Information Services		940-696-0758	•	•	•	•
•	•	•	•	•	Superior Process Service [SOP]		888-230-2663				

CR	CV	PR	US	BK	←Courts	Bee	Recorder→	UC	RE	TX	VS
•	•	•	•	•	Condor Inv [SOP]		361-881-8977	•	•	•	•
•	•	•	•	•	Corpus Christi Court Services		361-815-8202	•	•	•	
•	•		•		Dataprompt Corporation		214-395-2530				
		•			DeedSearcher Title Research Services		281-375-8480	•	•	•	
•	•	•	•	•	Shawver & Associates		800-364-2333	•	•	•	•
•	•	•	•	•	Texas Civil Process [SOP]		800-976-9595	•	•	•	•
•	•	•			Texas Research		325-646-2890	•	•	•	

CR	CV	PR	US	BK	←Courts	Bell	Recorder→	UC	RE	TX	VS
		•			American Abstract & Title Co Inc		254-526-9525		•	•	•
•	•	•	•	•	Americorp Research Inc		800-620-0015	•	•	•	•
•	•	•	•	•	Attorney Civil Process Service [SOP]		254-755-6447				
	•		•	•	Carma Austin		254-634-1701	•		•	
•	•		•		Bar Nunn Research Specialists		512-497-5584				
•	•		•	•	BG Criminal Research		254-755-6808	•		•	
	•	•	•		John Blackburn		210-867-0399	•	•	•	
•	•	•	•	•	Countywide Research Services [SOP]		512-922-1676	•	•	•	•
•	•				Crimecheck Research Services		281-288-6930				
•	•		•		Dataprompt Corporation		214-395-2530				
		•			DeedSearcher Title Research Services		281-375-8480	•	•	•	
•	•	•	•	•	Harvey Public Records Inc		254-662-6265	•	•	•	•
					Heart O' Texas Research		254-752-2057		•	•	
•	•	•		•	Research N More		512-868-5828	•	•	•	•
•	•		•	•	Sterling Research		512-670-9334	•	•	•	•
•	•	•	•	•	Taylor Research & Investigations [SOP]		972-991-5045	•	•	•	•
•	•		•	•	Texsearch #A09479 [SOP]		903-786-4636	•	•	•	

CR	CV	PR	US	BK	←Courts	Bexar	Recorder→	UC	RE	TX	VS
		•		•	Abstracts/Trustees of Texas		888-452-0331	•	•	•	
•	•				Accu-Source Inc		940-627-4944				
•	•		•	•	Asset Control Inc		877-277-3812	•	•	•	•
•	•	•	•	•	Best Process Service [SOP]		210-930-7417	•	•	•	•

CR	CV	PR	US	BK	←Courts	Recorder→	UC	RE	TX	VS
•	•	•	•	•	Bexar Professional [SOP]	210-228-0083	•	•	•	•
	•	•	•		John Blackburn	210-867-0399	•	•	•	
•	•	•			Cornerstone Title Research	210-354-7102	•	•	•	•
•	•	•	•	•	Countywide Research Services [SOP]	512-922-1676	•	•	•	•
•	•		•		Dataprompt Corporation	214-395-2530				
		•			DeedSearcher Title Research Services	281-375-8480	•	•	•	
•	•	•	•	•	DFW Court Services [SOP]	800-436-0516	•	•	•	
•	•				First Advantage	800-687-0894				
•	•		•		FP Resources	866-989-8999				
•	•	•	•	•	Hollerbach and Assoc Inc	800-580-8485	•	•	•	•
		•			Land Records of Texas	800-678-8016	•	•	•	
		•	•	•	Morgan/Brooks Resources Inc	210-476-0500	•	•	•	
•	•	•	•	•	MS Document Services Inc	800-292-3868	•	•	•	•
•					PI Inc	800-359-5131				
•	•	•	•	•	Professional Civil Process (Austin) [SOP]	800-950-7493	•	•	•	•
•	•	•	•	•	Property Research & Documentation Service Inc	210-520-7884	•	•	•	•
•	•				Spearhead Research - On Target Information	512-295-7298				
•	•		•	•	Spectrum Screening Inc	800-222-8199	•		•	
•	•	•	•	•	Texas Industrial Security Inc	214-634-2791			•	
•	•	•			TexDirect	830-964-5233	•	•	•	
•	•		•	•	Texsearch #A09479 [SOP]	903-786-4636	•	•	•	

CR	CV	PR	US	BK	←Courts **Blanco**	Recorder→	UC	RE	TX	VS
		•		•	Abstracts/Trustees of Texas	888-452-0331	•	•	•	
•	•	•	•	•	MS Document Services Inc	800-292-3868	•	•	•	•

CR	CV	PR	US	BK	←Courts **Borden**	Recorder→	UC	RE	TX	VS
•	•	•	•	•	Davick Services	800-658-6656	•	•	•	
		•	•		Snyder Abstract & Title Co Inc	325-573-6339	•	•	•	

CR	CV	PR	US	BK	←Courts **Bosque**	Recorder→	UC	RE	TX	VS
•	•	•	•	•	Attorney Civil Process Service [SOP]	254-755-6447				
•	•	•			B & B Info Search	817-774-1310				
	•	•	•		John Blackburn	210-867-0399	•	•	•	
•	•				Crimecheck Research Services	281-288-6930				
					Heart O' Texas Research	254-752-2057		•	•	

CR	CV	PR	US	BK	←Courts **Bowie**	Recorder→	UC	RE	TX	VS
•	•		•		Dataprompt Corporation	214-395-2530				
	•		•	•	Joe Gillenwater [SOP]	870-772-2923	•	•	•	
	•	•			Twin City Title Co Inc	903-793-7671	•	•	•	

CR	CV	PR	US	BK	←Courts **Brazoria**	Recorder→	UC	RE	TX	VS
		•		•	Abstracts/Trustees of Texas	888-452-0331	•	•	•	
•	•	•	•	•	All State Document Services	888-246-8180	•	•	•	•
•	•	•	•	•	Ameritex Legal Support	888-670-7575				
	•	•	•	•	Ameritite Abstract & Research Inc	800-856-1228	•	•	•	
	•	•	•	•	BAST Research Services Inc	713-721-7077	•	•	•	
•	•	•	•	•	Court Record Research Inc [SOP]	800-552-3353	•	•	•	•
•	•	•		•	Courthouse Specialists	800-925-4225	•	•	•	
•	•				Criminal Background Investigations	979-848-0632				
		•			DeedSearcher Title Research Services	281-375-8480	•	•	•	
					Fox Hunt	713-772-8018	•	•	•	
	•	•	•	•	Garza-McNamee Agency Inc	888-262-6221	•	•	•	
•	•	•	•	•	Gulf Coast AccuSearch	713-228-6600; cell- 713-542-3047	•	•	•	•
•	•	•	•	•	Houston Court Services Inc [SOP]	713-655-0555	•	•	•	•
•	•	•	•	•	John V Eriksson Group Inc	281-488-0018	•	•	•	•
•	•	•	•	•	Kimmons Security Services Inc [SOP]	281-679-0070	•	•	•	•
		•			Land Records of Texas	800-678-8016	•	•	•	
•	•		•	•	Mach 5 Couriers Inc [SOP]	800-593-2023				

CR	CV	PR	US	BK	←Courts		UC	RE	TX	VS
•	•	•	•	•	PM Clinton International Investigation [SOP]	866-686-6864	•	•	•	
•	•				Research & Demographic Solutions LLC	817-706-7726				
•	•	•	•	•	The Research Staff Inc	800-822-3584	•	•	•	

CR	CV	PR	US	BK	←Courts	Brazos Recorder→	UC	RE	TX	VS
		•		•	Abstracts/Trustees of Texas	888-452-0331	•	•	•	
•	•	•	•	•	Airborn Civil Process & Inv [SOP]	888-933-6863	•	•	•	•
•	•	•	•	•	All State Document Services	888-246-8180	•	•	•	•
	•		•	•	Carma Austin	254-634-1701	•		•	
•	•				Crimecheck Research Services	281-288-6930				
•	•		•		Dataprompt Corporation	214-395-2530				
		•			DeedSearcher Title Research Services	281-375-8480	•	•	•	
•	•	•	•	•	Houston Court Services Inc [SOP]	713-655-0555	•	•	•	•
		•			Land Records of Texas	800-678-8016	•	•	•	
•	•	•	•	•	Matrix Info Services [SOP]	979-846-3593	•	•	•	•
•	•				Research & Demographic Solutions LLC	817-706-7726				
•	•	•	•	•	The Research Staff Inc	800-822-3584	•	•	•	

CR	CV	PR	US	BK	←Courts	Brewster Recorder→	UC	RE	TX	VS
	•	•			Ellyson Abstract & Title Co of Brewster	432-837-5801	•	•	•	•
•	•	•	•	•	Presidio County Abstract	432-729-4264	•	•	•	

CR	CV	PR	US	BK	←Courts	Briscoe Recorder→	UC	RE	TX	VS
•	•	•	•	•	Davick Services	800-658-6656	•	•	•	
	•	•			Guaranty Abstract Co (Silverton)	806-823-2354	•	•	•	

CR	CV	PR	US	BK	←Courts	Brooks Recorder→	UC	RE	TX	VS
					Border Title Group	956-791-5810	•	•	•	
•	•	•	•	•	Condor Inv [SOP]	361-881-8977	•	•	•	•
		•			DeedSearcher Title Research Services	281-375-8480	•	•	•	
•	•	•	•	•	Shawver & Associates	800-364-2333	•	•	•	•

CR	CV	PR	US	BK	←Courts	Brown Recorder→	UC	RE	TX	VS
	•	•			Brown County Abstract Co (Texas)	325-646-6591	•	•	•	
		•			Heartland Title Company	325-646-0509		•	•	
•	•	•	•	•	MS Document Services Inc	800-292-3868	•	•	•	•
•	•	•			Texas Research	325-646-2890	•	•	•	

CR	CV	PR	US	BK	←Courts	Burleson Recorder→	UC	RE	TX	VS
		•		•	Abstracts/Trustees of Texas	888-452-0331	•	•	•	
	•		•	•	Carma Austin	254-634-1701	•		•	
		•			Botts Title Co	254-697-6962	•	•	•	•
		•			DeedSearcher Title Research Services	281-375-8480	•	•	•	

CR	CV	PR	US	BK	←Courts	Burnet Recorder→	UC	RE	TX	VS
		•		•	Abstracts/Trustees of Texas	888-452-0331	•	•	•	
	•		•	•	Carma Austin	254-634-1701	•		•	
•	•	•	•	•	Countywide Research Services [SOP]	512-922-1676	•	•	•	•
		•			DeedSearcher Title Research Services	281-375-8480	•	•	•	
•	•	•	•	•	MS Document Services Inc	800-292-3868	•	•	•	•

CR	CV	PR	US	BK	←Courts	Caldwell Recorder→	UC	RE	TX	VS
		•		•	Abstracts/Trustees of Texas	888-452-0331	•	•	•	
	•		•	•	Carma Austin	254-634-1701	•		•	
	•	•	•	•	Central Tejas Research & Title Services	512-469-6026	•	•	•	
•	•				Crimecheck Research Services	281-288-6930				
		•			DeedSearcher Title Research Services	281-375-8480	•	•	•	
		•			Land Records of Texas	800-678-8016	•	•	•	
•	•	•	•	•	MS Document Services Inc	800-292-3868	•	•	•	•
•					PI Inc	800-359-5131				
•	•	•	•	•	Property Research & Documentation Service Inc	210-520-7884	•	•	•	•

CR	CV	PR	US	BK	←Courts	Recorder→	UC	RE	TX	VS
•	•	•			TexDirect	830-964-5233	•	•	•	

CR	CV	PR	US	BK	←Courts CALHOUN	Recorder→	UC	RE	TX	VS
•	•	•	•	•	All State Document Services	888-246-8180	•	•	•	•
	•	•			Bedgood Abstract & Title Co (Port Lavaca)	361-552-6761, 361-573-1785	•	•	•	
•	•	•	•	•	Condor Inv [SOP]	361-881-8977	•	•	•	•
		•			DeedSearcher Title Research Services	281-375-8480	•	•	•	

CR	CV	PR	US	BK	←Courts CALLAHAN	Recorder→	UC	RE	TX	VS
		•			Big Country Title	325-698-9195	•	•	•	•
•	•	•	•	•	MS Document Services Inc	800-292-3868	•	•	•	•
•	•	•			Russell-Surles Title Inc	325-854-1115	•	•	•	

CR	CV	PR	US	BK	←Courts CAMERON	Recorder→	UC	RE	TX	VS
		•			DeedSearcher Title Research Services	281-375-8480	•	•	•	
•	•		•		Murray Research	817-295-4820				
•	•	•	•	•	Professional Civil Process (Austin) [SOP]	800-950-7493	•	•	•	•
•	•	•	•	•	Professional Civil Process (McAllen) [SOP]	800-880-4223	•	•	•	•
•	•	•	•	•	Record Finders	956-571-5378	•	•	•	•
•	•				Research & Demographic Solutions LLC	817-706-7726				
•	•	•	•	•	Shawver & Associates	800-364-2333	•	•	•	•
•	•	•	•	•	South Texas Title and Trustee Services	956-412-3413	•	•	•	•
•	•		•	•	Texsearch #A09479 [SOP]	903-786-4636	•	•	•	
	•	•	•	•	Valley Abstract & Trustee Services	956-571-1119	•	•	•	

CR	CV	PR	US	BK	←Courts CAMP	Recorder→	UC	RE	TX	VS
	•	•			Camp County Land Abstract Co	903-856-3676	•	•		•
		•			DeedSearcher Title Research Services	281-375-8480	•	•	•	

CR	CV	PR	US	BK	←Courts CARSON	Recorder→	UC	RE	TX	VS
	•	•	•	•	Rollins Research Ltd	806-353-7886, cell- 806-654-2376	•	•	•	

CR	CV	PR	US	BK	←Courts CASS	Recorder→	UC	RE	TX	VS
	•		•	•	Joe Gillenwater [SOP]	870-772-2923	•	•	•	
	•	•			M & M Title / Mitchell Co	318-798-1198	•	•	•	

CR	CV	PR	US	BK	←Courts CASTRO	Recorder→	UC	RE	TX	VS
•	•	•	•	•	Davick Services	800-658-6656	•	•	•	
	•	•	•	•	Rollins Research Ltd	806-353-7886, cell- 806-654-2376	•	•	•	

CR	CV	PR	US	BK	←Courts CHAMBERS	Recorder→	UC	RE	TX	VS
•	•	•	•	•	All State Document Services	888-246-8180	•	•	•	•
•	•	•			Don W Caskey	281-422-7527	•	•	•	•
•	•	•		•	Courthouse Specialists	800-925-4225	•	•	•	
•	•	•	•	•	ELH Contracting Inc Independent Land & Title Abstractor	409-832-5793	•	•	•	•
•	•				Integrity Check	409-962-1991				
		•			Land Records of Texas	800-678-8016	•	•	•	
•	•		•	•	Mach 5 Couriers Inc [SOP]	800-593-2023				
•	•	•	•	•	PM Clinton International Investigation [SOP]	866-686-6864	•	•	•	
•	•	•	•	•	The Research Staff Inc	800-822-3584	•	•	•	

CR	CV	PR	US	BK	←Courts CHEROKEE	Recorder→	UC	RE	TX	VS
		•			DeedSearcher Title Research Services	281-375-8480	•	•	•	

CR	CV	PR	US	BK	←Courts CHILDRESS	Recorder→	UC	RE	TX	VS
	•	•			H S Black Abstractor Inc	940-937-3681	•	•	•	•
•	•	•	•	•	Mendenhall Information Services	940-696-0758	•	•	•	•

CR	CV	PR	US	BK	←Courts CLAY	Recorder→	UC	RE	TX	VS
•	•	•	•	•	Mendenhall Information Services	940-696-0758	•	•	•	•
•	•	•	•	•	Superior Process Service [SOP]	888-230-2663				
•	•	•	•	•	Texas Detective.com [SOP]	940-592-7000	•	•	•	•

CR	CV	PR	US	BK	←Courts	COCHRAN	Recorder→	UC	RE	TX	VS
•	•	•	•	•	Davick Services		800-658-6656	•	•	•	

CR	CV	PR	US	BK	←Courts	COKE	Recorder→	UC	RE	TX	VS
•	•	•			Coke County Abstract Co		325-453-2049	•	•	•	•

CR	CV	PR	US	BK	←Courts	COLEMAN	Recorder→	UC	RE	TX	VS
		•			Coleman County Title Co		325-625-4628	•	•	•	
•	•	•	•	•	MS Document Services Inc		800-292-3868	•	•	•	•

CR	CV	PR	US	BK	←Courts	COLLIN	Recorder→	UC	RE	TX	VS
•	•	•	•	•	A+ Super Search Inc		800-687-5553	•	•	•	•
		•		•	Abstracts/Trustees of Texas		888-452-0331	•	•	•	
•	•				Accu-Source Inc		940-627-4944				
	•	•			Ameristar Information Network		800-920-9270		•	•	•
	•	•	•	•	Ameritítle Abstract & Research Inc		800-856-1228	•	•	•	
•	•	•	•	•	ASA (Attorney Service Associates) [SOP]		972-394-1175	•	•	•	•
•	•		•	•	Asset Control Inc		877-277-3812	•	•	•	•
•	•	•	•	•	Attorney's Service Bureau of Texas [SOP]		888-522-5297	•	•	•	•
					David C Bayoud		214-824-9944		•		
•	•	•	•	•	Bray & Freeman LP [SOP]		817-596-9255	•	•	•	•
•	•	•	•	•	Certified Process Service [SOP]		800-717-3463	•	•	•	•
					Concord Commercial Services		972-931-7431		•		
•	•	•		•	Courthouse Specialists		800-925-4225	•	•	•	
•	•				Crimecheck Research Services		281-288-6930				
•	•	•	•	•	CRRG Inc		800-687-9030	•	•	•	•
•	•		•		Dataprompt Corporation		214-395-2530				
		•			DeedSearcher Title Research Services		281-375-8480	•	•	•	
•	•	•	•	•	DFW Court Services [SOP]		800-436-0516	•	•	•	
•	•				First Advantage		800-687-0894				
•	•		•		FP Resources		866-989-8999				
•	•			•	G.A. Public Record Services Inc		800-760-2468 x314				
•	•		•	•	General Information Services		800-447-0798	•	•		
•	•				Inquest Investigations, LLC		903-893-2020	•		•	
		•			Land Records of Texas		800-678-8016	•	•	•	
•	•		•	•	Lone Star Investigations & Recovery Inc		800-887-3890	•	•	•	•
•	•	•	•	•	Mendenhall Information Services		940-696-0758	•	•	•	•
•	•	•	•	•	MS Document Services Inc		800-292-3868	•	•	•	•
•	•	•	•	•	PADIC Inc [SOP]		940-665-6130	•	•	•	•
•	•	•	•	•	Quick Search		214-358-2840	•	•	•	•
•	•				Record Retrieval Services Inc		866-569-8343		•	•	
•	•				Research & Demographic Solutions LLC		817-706-7726				
•	•	•	•	•	Security Information Service Inc [SOP]		214-637-4055	•	•	•	•
•	•		•	•	Spectrum Screening Inc		800-222-8199	•		•	
		•	•	•	Pat Stephens		903-583-5215	•	•	•	
•	•	•	•	•	Taylor Research & Investigations [SOP]		972-991-5045	•	•	•	•
•	•				Tex Research		817-472-5997, cell- 682-551-5306				
•	•		•	•	Texsearch #A09479 [SOP]		903-786-4636	•	•	•	
		•			Title Info		817-244-7757		•	•	
					TOB Public Records Research		214-358-4744	•	•	•	

CR	CV	PR	US	BK	←Courts	COLLINGSWORTH	Recorder→	UC	RE	TX	VS
					See adjoining counties for retrievers or call court/recorder directly.						

CR	CV	PR	US	BK	←Courts	COLORADO	Recorder→	UC	RE	TX	VS
		•		•	Abstracts/Trustees of Texas		888-452-0331	•	•	•	
•	•	•	•	•	All State Document Services		888-246-8180	•	•	•	•
		•			Botts Title Co		254-697-6962	•	•	•	•
					Colorado County Abstract Co		979-732-2213	•	•	•	
		•			DeedSearcher Title Research Services		281-375-8480	•	•	•	

CR	CV	PR	US	BK	←Courts	COMAL	Recorder→	UC	RE	TX	VS
		•		•	Abstracts/Trustees of Texas		888-452-0331	•	•	•	
•	•	•	•	•	Best Process Service [SOP]		210-930-7417	•	•	•	•
•	•	•			Cornerstone Title Research		210-354-7102	•	•	•	•
•	•				Crimecheck Research Services		281-288-6930				
		•			DeedSearcher Title Research Services		281-375-8480	•	•	•	
		•	•	•	Morgan/Brooks Resources Inc		210-476-0500	•	•	•	
•	•	•	•	•	MS Document Services Inc		800-292-3868	•	•	•	•
•					PI Inc		800-359-5131				
•	•	•	•	•	Property Research & Documentation Service Inc		210-520-7884	•	•	•	•
•	•				Research & Demographic Solutions LLC		817-706-7726				
•	•				Spearhead Research - On Target Information		512-295-7298				
•	•	•			TexDirect		830-964-5233	•	•	•	
•	•		•	•	Texsearch #A09479 [SOP]		903-786-4636	•	•	•	

CR	CV	PR	US	BK	←Courts	COMANCHE	Recorder→	UC	RE	TX	VS
•	•	•			Comanche County Abstract Co		325-356-2564	•	•	•	•
•	•	•	•	•	MS Document Services Inc		800-292-3868	•	•	•	•

CR	CV	PR	US	BK	←Courts	CONCHO	Recorder→	UC	RE	TX	VS

See adjoining counties for retrievers or call court/recorder directly.

CR	CV	PR	US	BK	←Courts	COOKE	Recorder→	UC	RE	TX	VS
•	•		•		Dataprompt Corporation		214-395-2530				
•	•	•	•	•	ETC Investigations		888-560-4001	•	•	•	
•	•	•	•	•	Mendenhall Information Services		940-696-0758	•	•	•	•
•	•	•	•	•	PADIC Inc [SOP]		940-665-6130	•	•	•	•
•	•	•	•	•	Quick Search		214-358-2840	•	•	•	•
•	•	•	•	•	Security Information Service Inc [SOP]		214-637-4055	•	•	•	•
•	•		•	•	Texsearch #A09479 [SOP]		903-786-4636	•	•	•	

CR	CV	PR	US	BK	←Courts	CORYELL	Recorder→	UC	RE	TX	VS
		•		•	Abstracts/Trustees of Texas		888-452-0331	•	•	•	
		•			American Abstract & Title Co Inc		254-526-9525		•	•	•
	•		•	•	Carma Austin		254-634-1701	•		•	
•	•		•	•	BG Criminal Research		254-755-6808	•		•	
•	•		•		Dataprompt Corporation		214-395-2530				
		•			DeedSearcher Title Research Services		281-375-8480	•	•	•	
					Heart O' Texas Research		254-752-2057		•	•	

CR	CV	PR	US	BK	←Courts	COTTLE	Recorder→	UC	RE	TX	VS
•	•	•	•	•	Davick Services		800-658-6656	•	•	•	
		•			Jones & Renfrow Abstracters		806-492-3573	•	•	•	•

CR	CV	PR	US	BK	←Courts	CRANE	Recorder→	UC	RE	TX	VS

See adjoining counties for retrievers or call court/recorder directly.

CR	CV	PR	US	BK	←Courts	CROCKETT	Recorder→	UC	RE	TX	VS
					Crockett County Abstract Co		325-392-2232	•	•	•	

CR	CV	PR	US	BK	←Courts	CROSBY	Recorder→	UC	RE	TX	VS
•	•	•	•	•	Davick Services		800-658-6656	•	•	•	

CR	CV	PR	US	BK	←Courts	CULBERSON	Recorder→	UC	RE	TX	VS
	•	•	•	•	Stewart Title of Midland Inc		432-687-3355		•		

CR	CV	PR	US	BK	←Courts	DALLAM	Recorder→	UC	RE	TX	VS
	•	•			Hunter & Oelke		800-350-1288		•	•	
	•	•	•	•	Rollins Research Ltd		806-353-7886, cell- 806-654-2376	•	•	•	

CR	CV	PR	US	BK	←Courts	DALLAS	Recorder→	UC	RE	TX	VS
•	•	•	•	•	A+ Super Search Inc		800-687-5553	•	•	•	•

CR	CV	PR	US	BK	←Courts	Recorder→	UC	RE	TX	VS
		•		•	Abstracts/Trustees of Texas	888-452-0331	•	•	•	
•	•				Accu-Source Inc	940-627-4944				
	•	•			Ameristar Information Network	800-920-9270		•	•	•
	•	•	•	•	Amerititle Abstract & Research Inc	800-856-1228	•	•	•	
•	•	•	•	•	ASA (Attorney Service Associates) [SOP]	972-394-1175	•	•	•	•
•	•		•	•	Asset Control Inc	877-277-3812	•	•	•	•
•	•	•	•	•	Attorney's Service Bureau of Texas [SOP]	888-522-5297	•	•	•	•
					David C Bayoud	214-824-9944		•		
•	•	•	•	•	Bray & Freeman LP [SOP]	817-596-9255	•	•	•	•
	•		•	•	Capitol Services Inc (Texas)	800-345-4647	•		•	
•	•	•	•	•	Certified Process Service [SOP]	800-717-3463	•	•	•	•
•	•				CLUSO Inc	866-30-CLUSO				
					Concord Commercial Services	972-931-7431		•		
•	•	•		•	Courthouse Specialists	800-925-4225	•	•	•	
•	•	•	•	•	CRRG Inc	800-687-9030	•	•	•	•
•	•		•	•	Dataprompt Corporation	214-395-2530				
		•			DeedSearcher Title Research Services	281-375-8480	•	•	•	
•	•	•	•	•	DFW Court Services [SOP]	800-436-0516	•	•	•	
•	•				First Advantage	800-687-0894				
•	•		•		FP Resources	866-989-8999				
•	•		•	•	G.A. Public Record Services Inc	800-760-2468 x314				
•	•		•	•	General Information Services	800-447-0798	•	•		
•	•		•		Hart & Associates Inc	866-429-4044				
•	•	•	•	•	Hollerbach and Assoc Inc	800-580-8485	•	•	•	•
•	•	•	•	•	Info2go	817-656-1997	•	•	•	•
•	•				Inquest Investigations, LLC	903-893-2020	•		•	
•	•	•	•	•	Kimmons Security Services Inc [SOP]	281-679-0070	•	•	•	•
		•			Land Records of Texas	800-678-8016	•	•	•	
•	•		•	•	Lone Star Investigations & Recovery Inc	800-887-3890	•	•	•	•
•	•	•	•	•	Mendenhall Information Services	940-696-0758	•	•	•	•
•	•	•	•	•	MS Document Services Inc	800-292-3868	•	•	•	•
•	•		•		Murray Research	817-295-4820				
•	•	•			Nell Watkins & Associates	972-226-8811	•	•	•	•
•	•	•		•	PADIC Inc [SOP]	940-665-6130	•	•	•	•
•		•			Princeton Data Search Inc	469-474-1025		•	•	
•	•	•	•	•	Private Eyes	903-882-5697	•	•	•	•
•	•	•	•	•	Professional Civil Process (Austin) [SOP]	800-950-7493	•	•	•	•
•	•	•	•	•	Quick Search	214-358-2840	•	•	•	•
•	•				Record Retrieval Services Inc	866-569-8343		•	•	
•	•	•	•	•	Reliable Courier [SOP]	214-637-4800			•	•
•	•				Research & Demographic Solutions LLC	817-706-7726				
•	•	•	•	•	Secrest Legal Services	214-696-3959	•	•	•	
•	•	•	•	•	Security Information Service Inc [SOP]	214-637-4055	•	•	•	•
•	•	•	•	•	Segovia & Associates [SOP]	877-573-7833		•		•
•	•		•	•	Spectrum Screening Inc	800-222-8199	•		•	
•	•	•	•	•	Taylor Research & Investigations [SOP]	972-991-5045	•	•	•	•
•	•	•	•	•	Texas Industrial Security Inc	214-634-2791			•	
•	•		•	•	Texsearch #A09479 [SOP]	903-786-4636	•	•	•	
		•			Title Info	817-244-7757		•	•	
					TOB Public Records Research	214-358-4744	•	•	•	
•	•	•			Watkins Investigations [SOP]	972-926-6011	•	•	•	

CR	CV	PR	US	BK	←Courts **Dawson**	Recorder→	UC	RE	TX	VS
•	•	•	•	•	Davick Services	800-658-6656	•	•	•	
					South Plains Abstract Co	806-872-3023	•	•	•	

CR	CV	PR	US	BK	←Courts **De Witt**	Recorder→	UC	RE	TX	VS
		•			DeedSearcher Title Research Services	281-375-8480	•	•	•	
•	•	•	•	•	Property Research & Documentation Service Inc	210-520-7884	•	•	•	•

CR	CV	PR	US	BK	←COURTS DEAF SMITH	RECORDER→	UC	RE	TX	VS
•	•	•	•	•	Davick Services	800-658-6656	•	•	•	
•	•	•	•	•	Patricia Chambers Inv [SOP]	806-258-7555, cell- 806-671-5221	•	•	•	
	•	•	•	•	Rollins Research Ltd	806-353-7886, cell- 806-654-2376	•	•	•	

CR	CV	PR	US	BK	←COURTS DELTA	RECORDER→	UC	RE	TX	VS
•	•	•			Delta County Title Co [SOP]	903-395-4116	•	•	•	•
•	•	•			SanDiver & Associates	903-886-2909	•	•	•	•

CR	CV	PR	US	BK	←COURTS DENTON	RECORDER→	UC	RE	TX	VS
•	•	•	•	•	A+ Super Search Inc	800-687-5553	•	•	•	•
		•		•	Abstracts/Trustees of Texas	888-452-0331	•	•	•	
•	•				Accu-Source Inc	940-627-4944				
	•	•			Ameristar Information Network	800-920-9270		•	•	•
	•	•	•	•	Amerititle Abstract & Research Inc	800-856-1228	•	•	•	
•	•	•	•	•	ASA (Attorney Service Associates) [SOP]	972-394-1175	•	•	•	•
•	•		•	•	Asset Control Inc	877-277-3812	•	•	•	•
•	•	•	•	•	Attorney's Service Bureau of Texas [SOP]	888-522-5297	•	•	•	•
					David C Bayoud	214-824-9944		•		
•	•	•	•	•	Bray & Freeman LP [SOP]	817-596-9255	•	•	•	•
•	•	•		•	Courthouse Specialists	800-925-4225	•	•	•	
•	•	•	•	•	CRRG Inc	800-687-9030	•	•	•	•
•	•		•		Dataprompt Corporation	214-395-2530				
		•			DeedSearcher Title Research Services	281-375-8480	•	•	•	
•	•	•	•	•	DFW Court Services [SOP]	800-436-0516	•	•	•	
•	•	•	•	•	ETC Investigations	888-560-4001	•	•	•	
•	•				First Advantage	800-687-0894				
•	•		•		FP Resources	866-989-8999				
•	•		•	•	G.A. Public Record Services Inc	800-760-2468 x314				
•	•		•	•	General Information Services	800-447-0798	•	•		
•	•				Hart & Associates Inc	866-429-4044				
•	•	•	•	•	Info2go	817-656-1997	•	•	•	•
•	•				Inquest Investigations, LLC	903-893-2020	•		•	
		•			Land Records of Texas	800-678-8016	•	•	•	
•	•		•	•	Lone Star Investigations & Recovery Inc	800-887-3890	•	•	•	•
•	•	•	•	•	Mendenhall Information Services	940-696-0758	•	•	•	•
•	•	•	•	•	MS Document Services Inc	800-292-3868	•	•	•	•
•	•		•		Murray Research	817-295-4820				
•	•	•	•	•	PADIC Inc [SOP]	940-665-6130	•	•	•	•
•	•	•	•	•	Professional Civil Process (Austin) [SOP]	800-950-7493	•	•	•	•
•	•	•	•	•	Quick Search	214-358-2840	•	•	•	•
•	•				Research & Demographic Solutions LLC	817-706-7726				
•	•	•	•	•	Security Information Service Inc [SOP]	214-637-4055	•	•	•	•
•	•		•	•	Spectrum Screening Inc	800-222-8199	•		•	
•	•	•	•	•	Taylor Research & Investigations [SOP]	972-991-5045	•	•	•	•
•	•		•	•	Texsearch #A09479 [SOP]	903-786-4636	•	•	•	
		•			Title Info	817-244-7757		•	•	
					TOB Public Records Research	214-358-4744	•	•	•	

CR	CV	PR	US	BK	←COURTS DICKENS	RECORDER→	UC	RE	TX	VS
	•	•			Caprock Title Co.	432-687-3232		•	•	
•	•	•	•	•	Davick Services	800-658-6656	•	•	•	

CR	CV	PR	US	BK	←COURTS DIMMIT	RECORDER→	UC	RE	TX	VS
•	•	•			Border Legal Services [SOP]	830-773-0525			•	•
					Border Title Group	956-791-5810	•	•	•	
					Border Title Group, FKA Elliott & Waldron Abstract	830-876-2926		•	•	

CR	CV	PR	US	BK	←Courts DONLEY	Recorder→	UC	RE	TX	VS
	•	•	•	•	Rollins Research Ltd	806-353-7886, cell- 806-654-2376	•	•	•	
•	•	•			Security Abstract Co	806-874-3511	•	•	•	•

CR	CV	PR	US	BK	←Courts DUVAL	Recorder→	UC	RE	TX	VS
•	•	•	•	•	Condor Inv [SOP]	361-881-8977	•	•	•	•
•	•	•	•	•	Corpus Christi Court Services	361-815-8202	•	•	•	
•	•	•	•	•	Shawver & Associates	800-364-2333	•	•	•	•
•	•	•	•	•	Texas Civil Process [SOP]	800-976-9595	•	•	•	•

CR	CV	PR	US	BK	←Courts EASTLAND	Recorder→	UC	RE	TX	VS
•	•	•	•	•	MS Document Services Inc	800-292-3868	•	•	•	•

CR	CV	PR	US	BK	←Courts ECTOR	Recorder→	UC	RE	TX	VS
		•		•	Abstracts/Trustees of Texas	888-452-0331	•	•	•	
•	•	•	•	•	Davick Services	800-658-6656	•	•	•	
		•			DeedSearcher Title Research Services	281-375-8480	•	•	•	
•	•		•	•	Permian Court Reporters Inc [SOP]	432-683-3032				
•	•		•	•	Texsearch #A09479 [SOP]	903-786-4636	•	•	•	

CR	CV	PR	US	BK	←Courts EDWARDS	Recorder→	UC	RE	TX	VS
	•	•			Rocksprings Abstract & Title Co	830-683-2185	•	•	•	•

CR	CV	PR	US	BK	←Courts EL PASO	Recorder→	UC	RE	TX	VS
•	•	•			A.G.O. Legal Process Service [SOP]	505-526-4303	•	•	•	•
		•			DeedSearcher Title Research Services	281-375-8480	•	•	•	
•	•		•	•	Human Arts Consulting	800-493-2641				
•	•	•	•	•	Legal Net Process Service [SOP]	915-532-7871	•		•	•
•	•	•	•	•	Professional Civil Process (Austin) [SOP]	800-950-7493	•	•	•	•
•	•	•	•	•	Quick Search	214-358-2840	•	•	•	•
•	•				Research & Demographic Solutions LLC	817-706-7726				

CR	CV	PR	US	BK	←Courts ELLIS	Recorder→	UC	RE	TX	VS
•	•	•	•	•	A+ Super Search Inc	800-687-5553	•	•	•	•
•	•	•			B & B Info Search	817-774-1310				
					David C Bayoud	214-824-9944		•		
•	•				Sallie Blount	972-824-1414				
•	•				Crimecheck Research Services	281-288-6930				
•	•	•	•	•	CRRG Inc	800-687-9030	•	•	•	•
		•			DeedSearcher Title Research Services	281-375-8480	•	•	•	
•	•	•	•	•	ETC Investigations	888-560-4001	•	•	•	
		•			Land Records of Texas	800-678-8016	•	•	•	
•	•	•	•	•	PADIC Inc [SOP]	940-665-6130	•	•	•	•
•	•	•	•	•	Quick Search	214-358-2840	•	•	•	•
•	•	•	•	•	Reliable Courier [SOP]	214-637-4800			•	•
•	•	•	•	•	Security Information Service Inc [SOP]	214-637-4055	•	•	•	•
•	•	•	•	•	Taylor Research & Investigations [SOP]	972-991-5045	•	•	•	•
					TOB Public Records Research	214-358-4744	•	•	•	

CR	CV	PR	US	BK	←Courts ERATH	Recorder→	UC	RE	TX	VS
•	•	•			B & B Info Search	817-774-1310				
•	•		•		Dataprompt Corporation	214-395-2530				
•	•	•	•	•	ETC Investigations	888-560-4001	•	•	•	
•	•	•	•	•	Mendenhall Information Services	940-696-0758	•	•	•	•

CR	CV	PR	US	BK	←Courts FALLS	Recorder→	UC	RE	TX	VS
		•		•	Abstracts/Trustees of Texas	888-452-0331	•	•	•	
•	•	•	•	•	Attorney Civil Process Service [SOP]	254-755-6447				
	•		•	•	Carma Austin	254-634-1701	•		•	
	•	•			Falls County Title Co Inc	254-883-2112	•	•	•	•
					Heart O' Texas Research	254-752-2057		•	•	

CR	CV	PR	US	BK	←COURTS	FANNIN	RECORDER→	UC	RE	TX	VS
•	•		•		Dataprompt Corporation		214-395-2530				
		•			DeedSearcher Title Research Services		281-375-8480	•	•	•	
•	•	•	•	•	Quick Search		214-358-2840	•	•	•	•
		•	•	•	Pat Stephens		903-583-5215	•	•	•	
•	•		•	•	Texsearch #A09479 [SOP]		903-786-4636	•	•	•	

CR	CV	PR	US	BK	←COURTS	FAYETTE	RECORDER→	UC	RE	TX	VS
		•		•	Abstracts/Trustees of Texas		888-452-0331	•	•	•	
		•			Botts Title Co		254-697-6962	•	•	•	•
•	•	•			Clear Title Co		979-968-5885	•	•	•	•
		•			DeedSearcher Title Research Services		281-375-8480	•	•	•	
		•			Land Records of Texas		800-678-8016	•	•	•	

CR	CV	PR	US	BK	←COURTS	FISHER	RECORDER→	UC	RE	TX	VS
•	•	•	•	•	Davick Services		800-658-6656	•	•	•	
	•	•			Fisher/Jones Title Co (Roby)		325-776-2471	•	•	•	•
•	•	•	•	•	MS Document Services Inc		800-292-3868	•	•	•	•

CR	CV	PR	US	BK	←COURTS	FLOYD	RECORDER→	UC	RE	TX	VS
•	•	•	•	•	Davick Services		800-658-6656	•	•	•	

CR	CV	PR	US	BK	←COURTS	FOARD	RECORDER→	UC	RE	TX	VS
•	•	•	•	•	Mendenhall Information Services		940-696-0758	•	•	•	•
•	•	•	•	•	Superior Process Service [SOP]		888-230-2663				

CR	CV	PR	US	BK	←COURTS	FORT BEND	RECORDER→	UC	RE	TX	VS
		•		•	Abstracts/Trustees of Texas		888-452-0331	•	•	•	
•	•	•	•	•	Airborn Civil Process & Inv [SOP]		888-933-6863	•	•	•	•
•	•	•	•	•	All State Document Services		888-246-8180	•	•	•	•
•	•	•	•	•	Ameritex Legal Support		888-670-7575				
	•	•	•	•	Ameritite Abstract & Research Inc		800-856-1228	•	•	•	
	•	•	•	•	BAST Research Services Inc		713-721-7077	•	•	•	
•	•	•	•	•	Compex Legal Services [SOP]		713-861-3900				•
•	•	•	•	•	Court Record Research Inc [SOP]		800-552-3353	•	•	•	•
•	•	•		•	Courthouse Specialists		800-925-4225	•	•	•	
		•			DeedSearcher Title Research Services		281-375-8480	•	•	•	
•	•				Ford Data Research		281-238-9400				
					Fox Hunt		713-772-8018	•	•	•	
•	•		•		FP Resources		866-989-8999				
	•	•	•	•	Garza-McNamee Agency Inc		888-262-6221	•	•	•	
•	•	•	•	•	Gulf Coast AccuSearch		713-228-6600; cell- 713-542-3047	•	•	•	•
•	•	•	•	•	Houston Court Services Inc [SOP]		713-655-0555	•	•	•	•
•	•				Information Protective Services Inc (IPS)		888-720-3784				
•	•	•	•	•	John V Eriksson Group Inc		281-488-0018			•	•
•	•	•	•	•	Kimmons Security Services Inc [SOP]		281-679-0070	•	•	•	•
		•			Land Records of Texas		800-678-8016	•	•	•	
•	•		•	•	Mach 5 Couriers Inc [SOP]		800-593-2023				
•	•	•	•	•	PM Clinton International Investigation [SOP]		866-686-6864	•	•	•	
•	•	•	•	•	Professional Civil Process (Austin) [SOP]		800-950-7493	•	•	•	•
•	•		•	•	Spectrum Screening Inc		800-222-8199	•		•	
		•			Texas Abstract Services		866-290-3743		•	•	
•	•	•	•	•	The Research Staff Inc		800-822-3584	•	•	•	

CR	CV	PR	US	BK	←COURTS	FRANKLIN	RECORDER→	UC	RE	TX	VS
	•		•	•	Joe Gillenwater [SOP]		870-772-2923	•	•	•	

CR	CV	PR	US	BK	←COURTS	FREESTONE	RECORDER→	UC	RE	TX	VS
		•		•	Abstracts/Trustees of Texas		888-452-0331	•	•	•	

CR	CV	PR	US	BK	←COURTS	FRIO	RECORDER→	UC	RE	TX	VS
		•		•	Abstracts/Trustees of Texas		888-452-0331	•	•	•	
•	•	•	•	•	Best Process Service [SOP]		210-930-7417	•	•	•	•
		•			Land Records of Texas		800-678-8016	•	•	•	

CR	CV	PR	US	BK	←COURTS	GAINES	RECORDER→	UC	RE	TX	VS
•	•	•	•	•	Davick Services		800-658-6656	•	•	•	

CR	CV	PR	US	BK	←COURTS	GALVESTON	RECORDER→	UC	RE	TX	VS
		•		•	Abstracts/Trustees of Texas		888-452-0331	•	•	•	
•	•	•	•	•	All State Document Services		888-246-8180	•	•	•	•
•	•	•	•	•	Ameritex Legal Support		888-670-7575				
	•	•	•	•	Ameritile Abstract & Research Inc		800-856-1228	•	•	•	
	•	•	•	•	BAST Research Services Inc		713-721-7077	•	•	•	
•	•	•	•	•	Compex Legal Services [SOP]		713-861-3900				•
•	•	•	•	•	Court Record Research Inc [SOP]		800-552-3353	•	•	•	•
•	•	•		•	Courthouse Specialists		800-925-4225	•	•	•	
•	•				Criminal Background Investigations		979-848-0632				
		•			DeedSearcher Title Research Services		281-375-8480	•	•	•	
	•	•	•	•	Garza-McNamee Agency Inc		888-262-6221	•	•	•	
•	•	•	•	•	John V Eriksson Group Inc		281-488-0018	•	•	•	•
•	•	•	•	•	Kimmons Security Services Inc [SOP]		281-679-0070	•	•	•	•
•	•		•	•	Mach 5 Couriers Inc [SOP]		800-593-2023				
•	•	•	•	•	PM Clinton International Investigation [SOP]		866-686-6864	•	•	•	
•	•	•	•	•	Professional Civil Process (Austin) [SOP]		800-950-7493	•	•	•	•
•	•		•	•	Spectrum Screening Inc		800-222-8199	•		•	
•	•		•		The Partnership [SOP]		877-558-9928	•		•	
•	•	•	•	•	The Research Staff Inc		800-822-3584	•	•	•	

CR	CV	PR	US	BK	←COURTS	GARZA	RECORDER→	UC	RE	TX	VS
•	•	•	•	•	Davick Services		800-658-6656	•	•	•	

CR	CV	PR	US	BK	←COURTS	GILLESPIE	RECORDER→	UC	RE	TX	VS
		•		•	Abstracts/Trustees of Texas		888-452-0331	•	•	•	
•	•	•			Fredericksburg Titles Inc		830-997-3852	•	•	•	

CR	CV	PR	US	BK	←COURTS	GLASSCOCK	RECORDER→	UC	RE	TX	VS
		•			Big Spring Abstract & Title Co Inc		432-267-1604		•	•	
•	•	•	•	•	Davick Services		800-658-6656				

CR	CV	PR	US	BK	←COURTS	GOLIAD	RECORDER→	UC	RE	TX	VS
	•	•			Bedgood Abstract & Title Co (Goliad)		361-645-3145	•	•	•	
•	•	•	•	•	Corpus Christi Court Services		361-815-8202	•	•	•	
		•			DeedSearcher Title Research Services		281-375-8480	•	•	•	

CR	CV	PR	US	BK	←COURTS	GONZALES	RECORDER→	UC	RE	TX	VS
		•		•	Abstracts/Trustees of Texas		888-452-0331	•	•	•	
•	•				Crimecheck Research Services		281-288-6930				
•	•	•	•	•	Property Research & Documentation Service Inc		210-520-7884	•	•	•	•
•	•	•			TexDirect		830-964-5233	•	•	•	

CR	CV	PR	US	BK	←COURTS	GRAY	RECORDER→	UC	RE	TX	VS
	•	•	•	•	Rollins Research Ltd		806-353-7886, cell- 806-654-2376	•	•	•	

CR	CV	PR	US	BK	←COURTS	GRAYSON	RECORDER→	UC	RE	TX	VS
		•		•	Abstracts/Trustees of Texas		888-452-0331	•	•	•	
•	•				Accu-Source Inc		940-627-4944				
•	•		•		Dataprompt Corporation		214-395-2530				
		•			DeedSearcher Title Research Services		281-375-8480	•	•	•	
•	•	•	•	•	DFW Court Services [SOP]		800-436-0516	•	•	•	
•	•				Inquest Investigations, LLC		903-893-2020	•		•	

CR	CV	PR	US	BK	←Courts	Recorder→	UC	RE	TX	VS
•	•	•	•	•	Mendenhall Information Services	940-696-0758	•	•	•	•
•	•	•	•	•	PADIC Inc [SOP]	940-665-6130	•	•	•	•
•	•	•	•	•	Quick Search	214-358-2840	•	•	•	•
•	•				Research & Demographic Solutions LLC	817-706-7726				
•	•	•	•	•	Security Information Service Inc [SOP]	214-637-4055	•	•	•	•
		•	•	•	Pat Stephens	903-583-5215	•	•	•	
•	•		•	•	Texsearch #A09479 [SOP]	903-786-4636	•	•	•	

CR	CV	PR	US	BK	←Courts **Gregg**	Recorder→	UC	RE	TX	VS
•	•				Accu-Source Inc	940-627-4944				
•	•		•		Dataprompt Corporation	214-395-2530				
		•			DeedSearcher Title Research Services	281-375-8480	•	•	•	
•	•				Inquest Investigations, LLC	903-893-2020	•		•	
•	•				Research & Demographic Solutions LLC	817-706-7726				
•	•		•	•	Texsearch #A09479 [SOP]	903-786-4636	•	•	•	

CR	CV	PR	US	BK	←Courts **Grimes**	Recorder→	UC	RE	TX	VS
		•		•	Abstracts/Trustees of Texas	888-452-0331	•	•	•	
		•			DeedSearcher Title Research Services	281-375-8480	•	•	•	
	•	•			Guaranty Title Co of Grimes County	936-825-7322	•	•	•	
		•			Land Records of Texas	800-678-8016	•	•	•	

CR	CV	PR	US	BK	←Courts **Guadalupe**	Recorder→	UC	RE	TX	VS
		•		•	Abstracts/Trustees of Texas	888-452-0331	•	•	•	
•	•		•		Bar Nunn Research Specialists	512-497-5584				
•	•	•	•	•	Best Process Service [SOP]	210-930-7417	•	•	•	•
•	•				Crimecheck Research Services	281-288-6930				
		•			DeedSearcher Title Research Services	281-375-8480	•	•	•	
		•			Land Records of Texas	800-678-8016	•	•	•	
•					PI Inc	800-359-5131				
•	•	•	•	•	Property Research & Documentation Service Inc	210-520-7884	•	•	•	•
•	•	•			TexDirect	830-964-5233	•	•	•	
•	•		•	•	Texsearch #A09479 [SOP]	903-786-4636	•	•	•	

CR	CV	PR	US	BK	←Courts **Hale**	Recorder→	UC	RE	TX	VS
•	•	•	•	•	Davick Services	800-658-6656	•	•	•	

CR	CV	PR	US	BK	←Courts **Hall**	Recorder→	UC	RE	TX	VS
•	•	•			Security Abstract Co	806-874-3511	•	•	•	•

CR	CV	PR	US	BK	←Courts **Hamilton**	Recorder→	UC	RE	TX	VS
					See adjoining counties for retrievers or call court/recorder directly.					

CR	CV	PR	US	BK	←Courts **Hansford**	Recorder→	UC	RE	TX	VS
					See adjoining counties for retrievers or call court/recorder directly.					

CR	CV	PR	US	BK	←Courts **Hardeman**	Recorder→	UC	RE	TX	VS
•	•	•	•	•	Mendenhall Information Services	940-696-0758	•	•	•	•
•	•	•	•	•	Superior Process Service [SOP]	888-230-2663				
•	•	•			T.A.B.B.S. Investigations & Process Service [SOP]	580-477-3292	•	•	•	•

CR	CV	PR	US	BK	←Courts **Hardin**	Recorder→	UC	RE	TX	VS
•	•	•	•	•	All State Document Services	888-246-8180	•	•	•	•
•	•	•	•	•	ELH Contracting Inc Independent Land & Title Abstractor	409-832-5793	•	•	•	•
	•	•			Hooks Title & Abstract	409-246-3447	•	•	•	
•					Infopoint Research	888-457-0501, 409-729-1944				
•	•				Integrity Check	409-962-1991				
•	•		•	•	The Partnership [SOP]	877-558-9928	•		•	
•	•	•	•	•	The Research Staff Inc	800-822-3584	•	•	•	

CR	CV	PR	US	BK	←Courts	Harris	Recorder→	UC	RE	TX	VS
		•		•	Abstracts/Trustees of Texas		888-452-0331	•	•	•	
•	•				Accu-Source Inc		940-627-4944				
•	•	•	•	•	Airborn Civil Process & Inv [SOP]		888-933-6863	•	•	•	•
•	•	•	•	•	All State Document Services		888-246-8180	•	•	•	•
•	•	•	•	•	Ameritex Legal Support		888-670-7575				
	•	•	•	•	Ameritite Abstract & Research Inc		800-856-1228	•	•	•	
•	•		•	•	Asset Control Inc		877-277-3812	•	•	•	•
	•	•	•	•	BAST Research Services Inc		713-721-7077	•	•	•	
	•		•	•	Capitol Services Inc (Texas)		800-345-4647	•		•	
•	•	•	•	•	Compex Legal Services [SOP]		713-861-3900				•
•	•	•	•	•	Court Record Research Inc [SOP]		800-552-3353	•	•	•	•
•	•	•		•	Courthouse Specialists		800-925-4225	•	•	•	
•	•		•		Dataprompt Corporation		214-395-2530				
•	•		•	•	DBU Investigations		281-564-9043 or 832-283-6518	•		•	
		•			DeedSearcher Title Research Services		281-375-8480	•	•	•	
•	•	•	•	•	DFW Court Services [SOP]		800-436-0516	•	•	•	
•	•				First Advantage		800-687-0894				
					Fox Hunt		713-772-8018	•	•	•	
•	•		•		FP Resources		866-989-8999				
•	•		•	•	G.A. Public Record Services Inc		800-760-2468 x314				
	•	•	•	•	Garza-McNamee Agency Inc		888-262-6221	•	•	•	
•	•		•	•	General Information Services		800-447-0798	•	•		
•	•	•	•	•	Gulf Coast AccuSearch		713-228-6600; cell- 713-542-3047	•	•	•	•
•	•	•	•	•	Hollerbach and Assoc Inc		800-580-8485	•	•	•	•
•	•	•	•	•	Houston Court Services Inc [SOP]		713-655-0555	•	•	•	•
•	•				Information Protective Services Inc (IPS)		888-720-3784				
•	•	•	•	•	John V Eriksson Group Inc		281-488-0018	•	•	•	•
•	•	•	•	•	Kimmons Security Services Inc [SOP]		281-679-0070	•	•	•	•
		•			Land Records of Texas		800-678-8016	•	•	•	
•	•		•	•	Mach 5 Couriers Inc [SOP]		800-593-2023				
•	•	•			Metro Research & Inv [SOP]		936-441-2294	•	•	•	•
•	•	•	•	•	MS Document Services Inc		800-292-3868	•	•	•	•
•					PI Inc		800-359-5131				
•	•	•	•	•	PM Clinton International Investigation [SOP]		866-686-6864	•	•	•	
•	•	•	•	•	Professional Civil Process (Austin) [SOP]		800-950-7493	•	•	•	•
•	•		•	•	Spectrum Screening Inc		800-222-8199	•		•	
		•			Texas Abstract Services		866-290-3743		•	•	
•	•		•	•	Texsearch #A09479 [SOP]		903-786-4636	•	•	•	
•	•		•		The Partnership [SOP]		877-558-9928	•		•	
•	•	•	•	•	The Research Staff Inc		800-822-3584	•	•	•	
•	•	•	•	•	Varoga & Shallett		713-522-0101	•	•	•	•

CR	CV	PR	US	BK	←Courts	Harrison	Recorder→	UC	RE	TX	VS
	•	•			M & M Title / Mitchell Co		318-798-1198	•	•	•	

CR	CV	PR	US	BK	←Courts	Hartley	Recorder→	UC	RE	TX	VS
	•	•			Hunter & Oelke		800-350-1288		•	•	
	•	•	•	•	Rollins Research Ltd		806-353-7886, cell- 806-654-2376	•	•	•	

CR	CV	PR	US	BK	←Courts	Haskell	Recorder→	UC	RE	TX	VS
•	•	•			Haskell Abstract & TItle Co		940-864-2604	•	•	•	•
•	•	•	•	•	Mendenhall Information Services		940-696-0758	•	•	•	•
•	•	•	•	•	Superior Process Service [SOP]		888-230-2663				

CR	CV	PR	US	BK	←Courts	Hays	Recorder→	UC	RE	TX	VS
		•		•	Abstracts/Trustees of Texas		888-452-0331	•	•	•	
•	•	•	•	•	Americorp Research Inc		800-620-0015	•	•	•	•
	•		•	•	Carma Austin		254-634-1701	•		•	

CR	CV	PR	US	BK	←Courts	Recorder→	UC	RE	TX	VS
•	•		•		Bar Nunn Research Specialists	512-497-5584				
	•	•	•		John Blackburn	210-867-0399	•	•	•	
	•	•	•	•	Central Tejas Research & Title Services	512-469-6026	•	•	•	
•	•				Crimecheck Research Services	281-288-6930				
		•			DeedSearcher Title Research Services	281-375-8480	•	•	•	
•	•	•	•	•	John C Dunaway & Company [SOP]	512-835-5888	•	•	•	•
		•			Land Records of Texas	800-678-8016	•	•	•	
•	•	•	•	•	MS Document Services Inc	800-292-3868	•	•	•	•
•					PI Inc	800-359-5131				
•	•	•	•	•	Promesa Enterprises Inc	800-474-4420	•	•	•	•
•	•	•	•	•	Property Research & Documentation Service Inc	210-520-7884	•	•	•	•
•	•				Research & Demographic Solutions LLC	817-706-7726				
•	•	•	•	•	Research Network	512-469-1740	•	•	•	•
•	•				Spearhead Research - On Target Information	512-295-7298				
•	•		•	•	Spectrum Screening Inc	800-222-8199	•		•	
•	•	•			TexDirect	830-964-5233	•	•	•	
•	•		•	•	Texsearch #A09479 [SOP]	903-786-4636	•	•	•	

CR	CV	PR	US	BK	←Courts	**Hemphill**	Recorder→	UC	RE	TX	VS

See adjoining counties for retrievers or call court/recorder directly.

CR	CV	PR	US	BK	←Courts **Henderson**	Recorder→	UC	RE	TX	VS
•	•		•		Dataprompt Corporation	214-395-2530				
	•	•			M & M Title / Mitchell Co	318-798-1198	•	•	•	
•		•			Princeton Data Search Inc	469-474-1025		•	•	
•	•	•	•	•	Private Eyes	903-882-5697	•	•	•	•

CR	CV	PR	US	BK	←Courts **Hidalgo**	Recorder→	UC	RE	TX	VS
		•		•	Abstracts/Trustees of Texas	888-452-0331	•	•	•	
•	•		•	•	Asset Control Inc	877-277-3812	•	•	•	•
		•			DeedSearcher Title Research Services	281-375-8480	•	•	•	
•	•		•		Murray Research	817-295-4820				
•	•	•			Jean Peck [SOP]	402-721-4143	•	•	•	•
•	•	•	•	•	Professional Civil Process (McAllen) [SOP]	800-880-4223	•	•	•	•
•	•	•	•	•	Record Finders	956-571-5378	•	•	•	•
•	•				Research & Demographic Solutions LLC	817-706-7726				
•	•	•	•	•	Shawver & Associates	800-364-2333	•	•	•	•
•	•	•	•	•	South Texas Title and Trustee Services	956-412-3413	•	•	•	•
•	•		•	•	Texsearch #A09479 [SOP]	903-786-4636	•	•	•	
	•	•	•	•	Valley Abstract & Trustee Services	956-571-1119	•	•	•	

CR	CV	PR	US	BK	←Courts **Hill**	Recorder→	UC	RE	TX	VS
		•		•	Abstracts/Trustees of Texas	888-452-0331	•	•	•	
•	•	•	•	•	Attorney Civil Process Service [SOP]	254-755-6447				
•	•	•			B & B Info Search	817-774-1310				
•	•				Crimecheck Research Services	281-288-6930				
•	•	•			Eastland Title Co	254-582-2762	•	•	•	•
•	•	•	•	•	ETC Investigations	888-560-4001	•	•	•	
		•			Land Records of Texas	800-678-8016	•	•	•	
•	•		•		Murray Research	817-295-4820				
•	•	•	•	•	Private Eyes	903-882-5697	•	•	•	•

CR	CV	PR	US	BK	←Courts **Hockley**	Recorder→	UC	RE	TX	VS
•	•	•	•	•	Davick Services	800-658-6656	•	•	•	

CR	CV	PR	US	BK	←Courts **Hood**	Recorder→	UC	RE	TX	VS
•	•	•	•	•	A+ Super Search Inc	800-687-5553	•	•	•	•
•	•	•			B & B Info Search	817-774-1310				
•	•	•	•	•	Bray & Freeman LP [SOP]	817-596-9255	•	•	•	•
•	•				Crimecheck Research Services	281-288-6930				

CR	CV	PR	US	BK	Name	Phone	UC	RE	TX	VS
		•			DeedSearcher Title Research Services	281-375-8480	•	•	•	
•	•	•	•	•	ETC Investigations	888-560-4001	•	•	•	
•	•	•	•	•	Mendenhall Information Services	940-696-0758	•	•	•	•

CR	CV	PR	US	BK	←COURTS HOPKINS	RECORDER→	UC	RE	TX	VS
•	•		•		Dataprompt Corporation	214-395-2530				
•	•	•			SanDiver & Associates	903-886-2909	•	•	•	•

CR	CV	PR	US	BK	←COURTS HOUSTON	RECORDER→	UC	RE	TX	VS
		•			DeedSearcher Title Research Services	281-375-8480	•	•	•	
•	•	•	•	•	Professional Civil Process (Austin) [SOP]	800-950-7493	•	•	•	•

CR	CV	PR	US	BK	←COURTS HOWARD	RECORDER→	UC	RE	TX	VS
		•		•	Abstracts/Trustees of Texas	888-452-0331	•	•	•	
		•			Big Spring Abstract & Title Co Inc	432-267-1604		•	•	
•	•		•		Dataprompt Corporation	214-395-2530				
•	•	•	•	•	Davick Services	800-658-6656	•	•	•	

CR	CV	PR	US	BK	←COURTS HUDSPETH	RECORDER→	UC	RE	TX	VS
•	•	•	•	•	Legal Net Process Service [SOP]	915-532-7871	•		•	•

CR	CV	PR	US	BK	←COURTS HUNT	RECORDER→	UC	RE	TX	VS
•	•				Accu-Source Inc	940-627-4944				
•	•		•		Dataprompt Corporation	214-395-2530				
		•			Land Records of Texas	800-678-8016	•	•	•	
•		•			Princeton Data Search Inc	469-474-1025		•	•	
•	•	•	•	•	Quick Search	214-358-2840	•	•	•	•
•	•	•			SanDiver & Associates	903-886-2909	•	•	•	•
•	•	•	•	•	Security Information Service Inc [SOP]	214-637-4055	•	•	•	•
		•	•	•	Pat Stephens	903-583-5215	•	•	•	
•	•	•	•	•	Taylor Research & Investigations [SOP]	972-991-5045	•	•	•	•

CR	CV	PR	US	BK	←COURTS HUTCHINSON	RECORDER→	UC	RE	TX	VS
	•	•	•	•	Rollins Research Ltd	806-353-7886, cell- 806-654-2376	•	•	•	
•	•	•		•	Stroud Research & Sales	806-878-3195; cell- 806-886-3731			•	•

CR	CV	PR	US	BK	←COURTS IRION	RECORDER→	UC	RE	TX	VS
					See adjoining counties for retrievers or call court/recorder directly.					

CR	CV	PR	US	BK	←COURTS JACK	RECORDER→	UC	RE	TX	VS
•	•	•	•	•	Bray & Freeman LP [SOP]	817-596-9255	•	•	•	•
•	•	•	•	•	ETC Investigations	888-560-4001	•	•	•	
•	•	•	•	•	Mendenhall Information Services	940-696-0758	•	•	•	•
	•	•			Spiller Abstract	940-567-2271	•	•	•	
•	•	•	•	•	Superior Process Service [SOP]	888-230-2663				

CR	CV	PR	US	BK	←COURTS JACKSON	RECORDER→	UC	RE	TX	VS
•	•	•	•	•	All State Document Services	888-246-8180	•	•	•	•
		•			DeedSearcher Title Research Services	281-375-8480	•	•	•	
	•	•			Guaranty Abstract Co of Jackson County Inc	361-782-3591	•	•	•	

CR	CV	PR	US	BK	←COURTS JASPER	RECORDER→	UC	RE	TX	VS
		•			Garland Smith Abstract Co	409-384-2571	•	•	•	•

CR	CV	PR	US	BK	←COURTS JEFF DAVIS	RECORDER→	UC	RE	TX	VS
	•	•			Ellyson Abstract & Title Co of Brewster	432-837-5801	•	•	•	•
	•	•			Jeff Davis County Abstract Co	432-426-3288	•	•	•	

CR	CV	PR	US	BK	←COURTS JEFFERSON	RECORDER→	UC	RE	TX	VS
		•		•	Abstracts/Trustees of Texas	888-452-0331	•	•	•	
•	•	•	•	•	All State Document Services	888-246-8180	•	•	•	•
•	•	•	•	•	Compex Legal Services [SOP]	713-861-3900				•

CR	CV	PR	US	BK	Retriever	Phone	UC	RE	TX	VS
		•			DeedSearcher Title Research Services	281-375-8480	•	•	•	
•	•	•	•	•	ELH Contracting Inc Independent Land & Title Abstractor	409-832-5793	•	•	•	•
•					Infopoint Research	888-457-0501, 409-729-1944				
•	•				Integrity Check	409-962-1991				
•	•		•	•	Mach 5 Couriers Inc [SOP]	800-593-2023				
•	•		•		The Partnership [SOP]	877-558-9928	•		•	
•	•	•	•	•	The Research Staff Inc	800-822-3584	•	•	•	

CR	CV	PR	US	BK	←COURTS **JIM HOGG**	RECORDER→	UC	RE	TX	VS
					Border Title Group	956-791-5810	•	•	•	
		•			DeedSearcher Title Research Services	281-375-8480	•	•	•	

CR	CV	PR	US	BK	←COURTS **JIM WELLS**	RECORDER→	UC	RE	TX	VS
					Border Title Group	956-791-5810	•	•	•	
•	•	•	•	•	Condor Inv [SOP]	361-881-8977	•	•	•	•
•	•	•	•	•	Corpus Christi Court Services	361-815-8202	•	•	•	
		•			DeedSearcher Title Research Services	281-375-8480	•	•	•	
•	•				Information Protective Services Inc (IPS)	888-720-3784				
•	•	•	•	•	Shawver & Associates	800-364-2333	•	•	•	•
•	•	•	•	•	Texas Civil Process [SOP]	800-976-9595	•	•	•	•

CR	CV	PR	US	BK	←COURTS **JOHNSON**	RECORDER→	UC	RE	TX	VS
•	•	•	•	•	A+ Super Search Inc	800-687-5553	•	•	•	•
		•		•	Abstracts/Trustees of Texas	888-452-0331	•	•	•	
•	•				Accu-Source Inc	940-627-4944				
•	•	•			B & B Info Search	817-774-1310				
•	•	•	•	•	Bray & Freeman LP [SOP]	817-596-9255	•	•	•	•
•	•				Crimecheck Research Services	281-288-6930				
•	•	•	•	•	CRRG Inc	800-687-9030	•	•	•	•
•	•		•		Dataprompt Corporation	214-395-2530				
		•			DeedSearcher Title Research Services	281-375-8480	•	•	•	
•	•	•	•	•	ETC Investigations	888-560-4001	•	•	•	
		•			Land Records of Texas	800-678-8016	•	•	•	
•	•	•	•	•	Mendenhall Information Services	940-696-0758	•	•	•	•
•	•		•		Murray Research	817-295-4820				
•	•	•	•	•	Quick Search	214-358-2840	•	•	•	•
•	•				Research & Demographic Solutions LLC	817-706-7726				
•	•	•	•	•	Security Information Service Inc [SOP]	214-637-4055	•	•	•	•
•	•	•	•	•	Taylor Research & Investigations [SOP]	972-991-5045	•	•	•	•
		•			Title Info	817-244-7757		•	•	

CR	CV	PR	US	BK	←COURTS **JONES**	RECORDER→	UC	RE	TX	VS
	•	•			Fisher/Jones Title Co (Anson)	325-823-3236	•	•	•	•
•	•	•	•	•	MS Document Services Inc	800-292-3868	•	•	•	•

CR	CV	PR	US	BK	←COURTS **KARNES**	RECORDER→	UC	RE	TX	VS
		•		•	Abstracts/Trustees of Texas	888-452-0331	•	•	•	
	•	•			Karnes Land Title Co Inc	830-780-2221	•	•	•	•

CR	CV	PR	US	BK	←COURTS **KAUFMAN**	RECORDER→	UC	RE	TX	VS
		•		•	Abstracts/Trustees of Texas	888-452-0331	•	•	•	
•	•				Accu-Source Inc	940-627-4944				
•	•	•	•	•	CRRG Inc	800-687-9030	•	•	•	•
•	•		•		Dataprompt Corporation	214-395-2530				
		•			DeedSearcher Title Research Services	281-375-8480	•	•	•	
		•			Land Records of Texas	800-678-8016	•	•	•	
•	•	•			Nell Watkins & Associates	972-226-8811	•	•	•	•
		•			Princeton Data Search Inc	469-474-1025	•	•	•	
•	•	•	•	•	Private Eyes	903-882-5697	•	•	•	•
•	•	•	•	•	Quick Search	214-358-2840	•	•	•	•

CR	CV	PR	US	BK	Retriever	Phone	UC	RE	TX	VS
•	•	•	•	•	Security Information Service Inc [SOP]	214-637-4055	•	•	•	•
•	•	•	•	•	Taylor Research & Investigations [SOP]	972-991-5045	•	•	•	•
•	•		•		Texsearch #A09479 [SOP]	903-786-4636	•	•	•	
					TOB Public Records Research	214-358-4744	•	•	•	
•	•	•			Watkins Investigations [SOP]	972-926-6011	•	•	•	

CR	CV	PR	US	BK	←Courts **Kendall**	Recorder→	UC	RE	TX	VS
		•		•	Abstracts/Trustees of Texas	888-452-0331	•	•	•	
		•			DeedSearcher Title Research Services	281-375-8480	•	•	•	
•	•	•	•		Property Research & Documentation Service Inc	210-520-7884	•	•	•	•

CR	CV	PR	US	BK	←Courts **Kenedy**	Recorder→	UC	RE	TX	VS
					See adjoining counties for retrievers or call court/recorder directly.					

CR	CV	PR	US	BK	←Courts **Kent**	Recorder→	UC	RE	TX	VS
	•	•			Caprock Title Co.	432-687-3232		•	•	
•	•	•	•	•	Davick Services	800-658-6656	•	•	•	

CR	CV	PR	US	BK	←Courts **Kerr**	Recorder→	UC	RE	TX	VS
		•		•	Abstracts/Trustees of Texas	888-452-0331	•	•	•	
•	•	•	•	•	Best Process Service [SOP]	210-930-7417	•	•	•	•
•	•	•	•		Property Research & Documentation Service Inc	210-520-7884	•	•	•	•

CR	CV	PR	US	BK	←Courts **Kimble**	Recorder→	UC	RE	TX	VS
					See adjoining counties for retrievers or call court/recorder directly.					

CR	CV	PR	US	BK	←Courts **King**	Recorder→	UC	RE	TX	VS
	•	•			Caprock Title Co.	432-687-3232		•	•	
•	•	•	•	•	Davick Services	800-658-6656	•	•	•	
		•			Jones & Renfrow Abstracters	806-492-3573	•	•	•	•

CR	CV	PR	US	BK	←Courts **Kinney**	Recorder→	UC	RE	TX	VS
					See adjoining counties for retrievers or call court/recorder directly.					

CR	CV	PR	US	BK	←Courts **Kleberg**	Recorder→	UC	RE	TX	VS
•	•	•	•	•	Condor Inv [SOP]	361-881-8977	•	•	•	•
•	•	•	•	•	Corpus Christi Court Services	361-815-8202	•	•	•	
•	•		•		Dataprompt Corporation	214-395-2530				
•	•				Information Protective Services Inc (IPS)	888-720-3784				
•	•		•		Murray Research	817-295-4820				
•	•	•	•	•	Shawver & Associates	800-364-2333	•	•	•	•
•	•	•	•	•	Texas Civil Process [SOP]	800-976-9595	•	•	•	•

CR	CV	PR	US	BK	←Courts **Knox**	Recorder→	UC	RE	TX	VS
•	•	•	•	•	Davick Services	800-658-6656	•	•	•	
		•			DeedSearcher Title Research Services	281-375-8480	•	•	•	
•	•	•	•	•	Mendenhall Information Services	940-696-0758	•	•	•	•
•	•	•	•	•	Superior Process Service [SOP]	888-230-2663				

CR	CV	PR	US	BK	←Courts **La Salle**	Recorder→	UC	RE	TX	VS
					Border Title Group	956-791-5810	•	•	•	
		•			DeedSearcher Title Research Services	281-375-8480	•	•	•	

CR	CV	PR	US	BK	←Courts **Lamar**	Recorder→	UC	RE	TX	VS
•	•				Accu-Source Inc	940-627-4944				
•	•		•		Dataprompt Corporation	214-395-2530				
•	•		•		Murray Research	817-295-4820				
		•	•	•	Pat Stephens	903-583-5215	•	•	•	

CR	CV	PR	US	BK	←Courts **Lamb**	Recorder→	UC	RE	TX	VS
•	•	•	•	•	Davick Services	800-658-6656	•	•	•	

CR	CV	PR	US	BK	←COURTS	LAMPASAS RECORDER→	UC	RE	TX	VS
		•		•	Abstracts/Trustees of Texas	888-452-0331	•	•	•	
	•		•	•	Carma Austin	254-634-1701	•		•	

CR	CV	PR	US	BK	←COURTS	LAVACA RECORDER→	UC	RE	TX	VS
		•		•	Abstracts/Trustees of Texas	888-452-0331	•	•	•	
		•			DeedSearcher Title Research Services	281-375-8480	•	•	•	
•	•	•	•	•	Property Research & Documentation Service Inc	210-520-7884	•	•	•	•

CR	CV	PR	US	BK	←COURTS	LEE RECORDER→	UC	RE	TX	VS
		•		•	Abstracts/Trustees of Texas	888-452-0331	•	•	•	
	•	•	•		Botts Title Co	979-542-3636		•	•	
•	•	•	•	•	MS Document Services Inc	800-292-3868	•	•	•	•

CR	CV	PR	US	BK	←COURTS	LEON RECORDER→	UC	RE	TX	VS
	•	•			Guaranty Title Co (Centerville)	903-536-2133	•	•	•	•

CR	CV	PR	US	BK	←COURTS	LIBERTY RECORDER→	UC	RE	TX	VS
•	•	•	•	•	All State Document Services	888-246-8180	•	•	•	•
•	•	•	•	•	Ameritex Legal Support	888-670-7575				
•	•	•			Don W Caskey	281-422-7527	•	•	•	•
•	•	•		•	Courthouse Specialists	800-925-4225	•	•	•	
•	•	•	•	•	ELH Contracting Inc Independent Land & Title Abstractor	409-832-5793	•	•	•	•
•	•	•	•	•	The Research Staff Inc	800-822-3584	•	•	•	

CR	CV	PR	US	BK	←COURTS	LIMESTONE RECORDER→	UC	RE	TX	VS
		•		•	Abstracts/Trustees of Texas	888-452-0331	•	•	•	
•	•		•		Dataprompt Corporation	214-395-2530				
		•			Groesbeck Abstract & Title Co d/b/a Limestone County Title Company	254-729-3806	•	•	•	•

CR	CV	PR	US	BK	←COURTS	LIPSCOMB RECORDER→	UC	RE	TX	VS
					See adjoining counties for retrievers or call court/recorder directly.					

CR	CV	PR	US	BK	←COURTS	LIVE OAK RECORDER→	UC	RE	TX	VS
•	•	•	•	•	Corpus Christi Court Services	361-815-8202	•	•	•	
•	•	•	•	•	Texas Civil Process [SOP]	800-976-9595	•	•	•	•

CR	CV	PR	US	BK	←COURTS	LLANO RECORDER→	UC	RE	TX	VS
		•		•	Abstracts/Trustees of Texas	888-452-0331	•	•	•	

CR	CV	PR	US	BK	←COURTS	LOVING RECORDER→	UC	RE	TX	VS
	•	•	•	•	Stewart Title of Midland Inc	432-687-3355		•		

CR	CV	PR	US	BK	←COURTS	LUBBOCK RECORDER→	UC	RE	TX	VS
•	•		•		Dataprompt Corporation	214-395-2530				
•	•	•	•	•	Davick Services	800-658-6656	•	•	•	
		•			DeedSearcher Title Research Services	281-375-8480	•	•	•	
•	•	•			Texas Research	325-646-2890	•	•	•	
•	•	•	•	•	US Legal Support of Lubbock [SOP]	877-947-8500	•	•	•	•

CR	CV	PR	US	BK	←COURTS	LYNN RECORDER→	UC	RE	TX	VS
•	•	•	•	•	Davick Services	800-658-6656	•	•	•	

CR	CV	PR	US	BK	←COURTS	MADISON RECORDER→	UC	RE	TX	VS
		•			DeedSearcher Title Research Services	281-375-8480	•	•	•	
	•	•			Landmark Title Co of Madison County	936-348-5618	•	•	•	

CR	CV	PR	US	BK	←COURTS	MARION RECORDER→	UC	RE	TX	VS
		•			DeedSearcher Title Research Services	281-375-8480	•	•	•	
	•	•			M & M Title / Mitchell Co	318-798-1198	•	•	•	

CR	CV	PR	US	BK	←Courts **Martin**	Recorder→	UC	RE	TX	VS
•	•	•	•	•	Davick Services	800-658-6656	•	•	•	
	•	•	•	•	Stewart Title of Midland Inc	432-687-3355		•		

CR	CV	PR	US	BK	←Courts **Mason**	Recorder→	UC	RE	TX	VS
	•	•			First Mason Title Co	325-347-6388	•	•	•	•

CR	CV	PR	US	BK	←Courts **Matagorda**	Recorder→	UC	RE	TX	VS
•	•	•	•	•	All State Document Services	888-246-8180	•	•	•	•
		•			Bay City Abstract & Title	979-245-6321	•	•	•	
		•			DeedSearcher Title Research Services	281-375-8480	•	•	•	
•	•	•	•	•	Gulf Coast AccuSearch	713-228-6600; cell- 713-542-3047	•	•	•	•
•	•	•	•	•	The Research Staff Inc	800-822-3584	•	•	•	

CR	CV	PR	US	BK	←Courts **Maverick**	Recorder→	UC	RE	TX	VS
•	•	•			Border Legal Services [SOP]	830-773-0525			•	•
		•			Border Title Group	830-773-0555	•	•	•	
					Border Title Group	956-791-5810	•	•	•	

CR	CV	PR	US	BK	←Courts **McCulloch**	Recorder→	UC	RE	TX	VS
					See adjoining counties for retrievers or call court/recorder directly.					

CR	CV	PR	US	BK	←Courts **McLennan**	Recorder→	UC	RE	TX	VS
		•		•	Abstracts/Trustees of Texas	888-452-0331	•	•	•	
•	•	•	•	•	Attorney Civil Process Service [SOP]	254-755-6447				
	•		•	•	Carma Austin	254-634-1701			•	
•	•		•	•	BG Criminal Research	254-755-6808	•		•	
	•	•	•		John Blackburn	210-867-0399	•	•	•	
•	•		•		Dataprompt Corporation	214-395-2530				
		•			DeedSearcher Title Research Services	281-375-8480	•	•	•	
•	•	•	•	•	Harvey Public Records Inc	254-662-6265	•	•	•	•
					Heart O' Texas Research	254-752-2057		•	•	
•	•		•	•	Texsearch #A09479 [SOP]	903-786-4636	•	•	•	

CR	CV	PR	US	BK	←Courts **McMullen**	Recorder→	UC	RE	TX	VS
					See adjoining counties for retrievers or call court/recorder directly.					

CR	CV	PR	US	BK	←Courts **Medina**	Recorder→	UC	RE	TX	VS
		•		•	Abstracts/Trustees of Texas	888-452-0331	•	•	•	
•	•	•	•	•	Best Process Service [SOP]	210-930-7417	•	•	•	•
		•			Land Records of Texas	800-678-8016	•	•	•	
•	•	•	•	•	Property Research & Documentation Service Inc	210-520-7884	•	•	•	•

CR	CV	PR	US	BK	←Courts **Menard**	Recorder→	UC	RE	TX	VS
					See adjoining counties for retrievers or call court/recorder directly.					

CR	CV	PR	US	BK	←Courts **Midland**	Recorder→	UC	RE	TX	VS
		•		•	Abstracts/Trustees of Texas	888-452-0331	•	•	•	
•	•	•	•	•	Davick Services	800-658-6656	•	•	•	
		•			DeedSearcher Title Research Services	281-375-8480	•	•	•	
•	•		•	•	Permian Court Reporters Inc [SOP]	432-683-3032				
	•	•	•	•	Stewart Title of Midland Inc	432-687-3355		•		
•	•		•	•	Texsearch #A09479 [SOP]	903-786-4636	•	•	•	

CR	CV	PR	US	BK	←Courts **Milam**	Recorder→	UC	RE	TX	VS
		•		•	Abstracts/Trustees of Texas	888-452-0331	•	•	•	
	•		•	•	Carma Austin	254-634-1701	•		•	
		•			Botts Title Co	254-697-6962	•	•	•	•
		•			DeedSearcher Title Research Services	281-375-8480	•	•	•	

CR	CV	PR	US	BK	←Courts **Mills**	Recorder→	UC	RE	TX	VS
					See adjoining counties for retrievers or call court/recorder directly.					

CR	CV	PR	US	BK	←Courts	MITCHELL	Recorder→	UC	RE	TX	VS
•	•	•	•	•	Davick Services		800-658-6656	•	•	•	
•	•	•	•	•	MS Document Services Inc		800-292-3868	•	•	•	•

CR	CV	PR	US	BK	←Courts	MONTAGUE	Recorder→	UC	RE	TX	VS
•	•	•	•	•	ETC Investigations		888-560-4001	•	•	•	
•	•	•	•	•	Mendenhall Information Services		940-696-0758	•	•	•	•
•	•	•	•	•	Quick Search		214-358-2840	•	•	•	•
•	•	•	•	•	Superior Process Service [SOP]		888-230-2663				

CR	CV	PR	US	BK	←Courts	MONTGOMERY	Recorder→	UC	RE	TX	VS
		•		•	Abstracts/Trustees of Texas		888-452-0331	•	•	•	
•	•	•	•	•	All State Document Services		888-246-8180	•	•	•	•
•	•	•	•	•	Ameritex Legal Support		888-670-7575				
	•	•	•	•	Ameritite Abstract & Research Inc		800-856-1228	•	•	•	
	•	•	•	•	BAST Research Services Inc		713-721-7077	•	•	•	
•	•	•	•	•	Compex Legal Services [SOP]		713-861-3900				•
•	•	•	•	•	Court Record Research Inc [SOP]		800-552-3353	•	•	•	•
•	•	•			Courthouse Filings Inc		936-273-6427	•	•	•	•
•	•	•		•	Courthouse Specialists		800-925-4225	•	•	•	
•	•				Crimecheck Research Services		281-288-6930				
		•			DeedSearcher Title Research Services		281-375-8480	•	•	•	
					Fox Hunt		713-772-8018	•	•	•	
•	•		•		FP Resources		866-989-8999				
	•	•	•	•	Garza-McNamee Agency Inc		888-262-6221	•	•	•	
•	•	•	•	•	Gulf Coast AccuSearch		713-228-6600; cell- 713-542-3047	•	•	•	•
•	•	•	•	•	Houston Court Services Inc [SOP]		713-655-0555	•	•	•	•
•	•	•	•	•	John V Eriksson Group Inc		281-488-0018	•	•	•	•
•	•	•	•	•	Kimmons Security Services Inc [SOP]		281-679-0070	•	•	•	•
•	•		•	•	Mach 5 Couriers Inc [SOP]		800-593-2023				
•	•	•			Metro Research & Inv [SOP]		936-441-2294	•	•	•	•
•	•	•	•	•	PM Clinton International Investigation [SOP]		866-686-6864	•	•	•	
•	•		•		The Partnership [SOP]		877-558-9928	•		•	
•	•	•	•	•	The Research Staff Inc		800-822-3584	•	•	•	

CR	CV	PR	US	BK	←Courts	MOORE	Recorder→	UC	RE	TX	VS
	•	•	•	•	Rollins Research Ltd		806-353-7886, cell- 806-654-2376	•	•	•	

CR	CV	PR	US	BK	←Courts	MORRIS	Recorder→	UC	RE	TX	VS
	•		•	•	Joe Gillenwater [SOP]		870-772-2923	•	•	•	

CR	CV	PR	US	BK	←Courts	MOTLEY	Recorder→	UC	RE	TX	VS
•	•	•	•	•	Davick Services		800-658-6656	•	•	•	
		•			Jones & Renfrow Abstracters		806-492-3573	•	•	•	•

CR	CV	PR	US	BK	←Courts	NACOGDOCHES	Recorder→	UC	RE	TX	VS
•	•	•			Community Title Co		936-559-7900	•	•	•	•
		•			DeedSearcher Title Research Services		281-375-8480	•	•	•	
•	•	•	•		East Tex Records Research		936-414-1193	•	•	•	
					Record Time Research		936-632-5150		•		

CR	CV	PR	US	BK	←Courts	NAVARRO	Recorder→	UC	RE	TX	VS
•	•	•			B & B Info Search		817-774-1310				
		•			Navarro County Abstract Co		903-874-3768		•	•	

CR	CV	PR	US	BK	←Courts	NEWTON	Recorder→	UC	RE	TX	VS
		•			Garland Smith Abstract Co		409-384-2571	•	•	•	•

CR	CV	PR	US	BK	←Courts	NOLAN	Recorder→	UC	RE	TX	VS
•	•	•	•	•	Davick Services		800-658-6656	•	•	•	
•	•	•	•	•	MS Document Services Inc		800-292-3868	•	•	•	•

CR	CV	PR	US	BK	←Courts	Nueces	Recorder→	UC	RE	TX	VS
•	•				Accu-Source Inc		940-627-4944				
•	•	•	•	•	Condor Inv [SOP]		361-881-8977	•	•	•	•
•	•	•	•	•	Corpus Christi Court Services		361-815-8202	•	•	•	
•	•		•		Dataprompt Corporation		214-395-2530				
		•			DeedSearcher Title Research Services		281-375-8480	•	•	•	
•	•	•	•	•	FYII Acct [SOP]		563-299-5683	•	•	•	•
•	•				Inquest Investigations, LLC		903-893-2020	•		•	
•	•	•	•	•	Professional Civil Process (Austin) [SOP]		800-950-7493	•	•	•	•
•	•				Research & Demographic Solutions LLC		817-706-7726				
•	•	•	•	•	Shawver & Associates		800-364-2333	•	•	•	•
•	•	•	•	•	Texas Civil Process [SOP]		800-976-9595	•	•	•	•
•	•		•	•	Texsearch #A09479 [SOP]		903-786-4636	•	•	•	

CR	CV	PR	US	BK	←Courts	Ochiltree	Recorder→	UC	RE	TX	VS
		•			DeedSearcher Title Research Services		281-375-8480	•	•	•	

CR	CV	PR	US	BK	←Courts	Oldham	Recorder→	UC	RE	TX	VS
•	•	•	•	•	Davick Services		800-658-6656	•	•	•	
	•	•	•	•	Rollins Research Ltd		806-353-7886, cell- 806-654-2376	•	•	•	

CR	CV	PR	US	BK	←Courts	Orange	Recorder→	UC	RE	TX	VS
•	•	•	•	•	All State Document Services		888-246-8180	•	•	•	•
		•			DeedSearcher Title Research Services		281-375-8480	•	•	•	
•	•	•	•	•	ELH Contracting Inc Independent Land & Title Abstractor		409-832-5793	•	•	•	•
•					Infopoint Research		888-457-0501, 409-729-1944				
•	•				Integrity Check		409-962-1991				
•	•		•		The Partnership [SOP]		877-558-9928	•		•	
•	•	•	•	•	The Research Staff Inc		800-822-3584	•	•	•	

CR	CV	PR	US	BK	←Courts	Palo Pinto	Recorder→	UC	RE	TX	VS
•	•	•			B & B Info Search		817-774-1310				
•	•	•	•	•	Bray & Freeman LP [SOP]		817-596-9255	•	•	•	•
		•			DeedSearcher Title Research Services		281-375-8480	•	•	•	
		•			Elliott & Waldron Abstr Co of Palo Pinto		940-325-6564	•	•	•	
•	•	•	•	•	ETC Investigations		888-560-4001	•	•	•	
•	•	•	•	•	Mendenhall Information Services		940-696-0758	•	•	•	•
•	•	•	•	•	MS Document Services Inc		800-292-3868	•	•	•	•
•	•	•	•	•	Private Eyes		903-882-5697	•	•	•	•

CR	CV	PR	US	BK	←Courts	Panola	Recorder→	UC	RE	TX	VS
		•			DeedSearcher Title Research Services		281-375-8480	•	•	•	
	•	•			M & M Title / Mitchell Co		318-798-1198	•	•	•	

CR	CV	PR	US	BK	←Courts	Parker	Recorder→	UC	RE	TX	VS
•	•				Accu-Source Inc		940-627-4944				
•	•	•			B & B Info Search		817-774-1310				
•	•	•	•	•	Bray & Freeman LP [SOP]		817-596-9255	•	•	•	•
•	•	•	•	•	CRRG Inc		800-687-9030	•	•	•	•
•	•		•		Dataprompt Corporation		214-395-2530				
		•			DeedSearcher Title Research Services		281-375-8480	•	•	•	
•	•	•	•	•	ETC Investigations		888-560-4001	•	•	•	
		•			Land Records of Texas		800-678-8016	•	•	•	
•	•	•	•	•	Mendenhall Information Services		940-696-0758	•	•	•	•
•	•	•	•	•	MS Document Services Inc		800-292-3868	•	•	•	•
•	•		•		Murray Research		817-295-4820				
•	•	•	•	•	Private Eyes		903-882-5697	•	•	•	•
•	•				Research & Demographic Solutions LLC		817-706-7726				
•	•	•	•	•	Taylor Research & Investigations [SOP]		972-991-5045	•	•	•	•
		•			Title Info		817-244-7757		•	•	

CR	CV	PR	US	BK	←Courts **PARMER**	Recorder→	UC	RE	TX	VS
•	•	•	•	•	Davick Services	800-658-6656	•	•	•	
•	•	•			Farwell Abstract Co Inc	806-481-9992		•	•	
•	•				Research & Demographic Solutions LLC	817-706-7726				

CR	CV	PR	US	BK	←Courts **PECOS**	Recorder→	UC	RE	TX	VS
		•			DeedSearcher Title Research Services	281-375-8480	•	•	•	
					Elliott & Waldron Abstract Co - Pecos	432-336-5214	•	•	•	

CR	CV	PR	US	BK	←Courts **POLK**	Recorder→	UC	RE	TX	VS
					See adjoining counties for retrievers or call court/recorder directly.					

CR	CV	PR	US	BK	←Courts **POTTER**	Recorder→	UC	RE	TX	VS
		•		•	Abstracts/Trustees of Texas	888-452-0331	•	•	•	
•	•				Crimecheck Research Services	281-288-6930				
•	•	•	•	•	Davick Services	800-658-6656	•	•	•	
		•			DeedSearcher Title Research Services	281-375-8480	•	•	•	
•	•	•	•	•	Patricia Chambers Inv [SOP]	806-258-7555, cell- 806-671-5221	•	•	•	
	•	•	•	•	Rollins Research Ltd	806-353-7886, cell- 806-654-2376	•	•	•	
•	•		•	•	Texsearch #A09479 [SOP]	903-786-4636	•	•	•	

CR	CV	PR	US	BK	←Courts **PRESIDIO**	Recorder→	UC	RE	TX	VS
	•	•			Ellyson Abstract & Title Co of Brewster	432-837-5801	•	•	•	•
•	•	•	•	•	Presidio County Abstract	432-729-4264	•	•	•	

CR	CV	PR	US	BK	←Courts **RAINS**	Recorder→	UC	RE	TX	VS
	•	•			AAA Abstract & Title Co Inc (Texas) [SOP]	903-473-2233		•	•	

CR	CV	PR	US	BK	←Courts **RANDALL**	Recorder→	UC	RE	TX	VS
•	•				Crimecheck Research Services	281-288-6930				
•	•	•	•	•	Davick Services	800-658-6656	•	•	•	
		•			DeedSearcher Title Research Services	281-375-8480	•	•	•	
•	•	•	•	•	Patricia Chambers Inv [SOP]	806-258-7555, cell- 806-671-5221	•	•	•	
	•	•	•	•	Rollins Research Ltd	806-353-7886, cell- 806-654-2376	•	•	•	
•	•		•	•	Texsearch #A09479 [SOP]	903-786-4636	•	•	•	

CR	CV	PR	US	BK	←Courts **REAGAN**	Recorder→	UC	RE	TX	VS
	•	•	•	•	Stewart Title of Midland Inc	432-687-3355		•		

CR	CV	PR	US	BK	←Courts **REAL**	Recorder→	UC	RE	TX	VS
	•	•			Real County Title Co	830-232-5303	•	•	•	

CR	CV	PR	US	BK	←Courts **RED RIVER**	Recorder→	UC	RE	TX	VS
	•		•	•	Joe Gillenwater [SOP]	870-772-2923	•	•	•	

CR	CV	PR	US	BK	←Courts **REEVES**	Recorder→	UC	RE	TX	VS
	•	•	•	•	Stewart Title of Midland Inc	432-687-3355		•		

CR	CV	PR	US	BK	←Courts **REFUGIO**	Recorder→	UC	RE	TX	VS
•	•	•	•	•	Condor Inv [SOP]	361-881-8977	•	•	•	•
•	•	•	•	•	Corpus Christi Court Services	361-815-8202	•	•	•	
		•			DeedSearcher Title Research Services	281-375-8480	•	•	•	
•	•	•	•	•	Shawver & Associates	800-364-2333	•	•	•	•
•	•	•	•	•	Texas Civil Process [SOP]	800-976-9595	•	•	•	•

CR	CV	PR	US	BK	←Courts **ROBERTS**	Recorder→	UC	RE	TX	VS
	•	•	•	•	Rollins Research Ltd	806-353-7886, cell- 806-654-2376	•	•	•	

CR	CV	PR	US	BK	←Courts **ROBERTSON**	Recorder→	UC	RE	TX	VS
		•		•	Abstracts/Trustees of Texas	888-452-0331	•	•	•	
	•		•	•	Carma Austin	254-634-1701	•		•	
		•			DeedSearcher Title Research Services	281-375-8480	•	•	•	
	•	•			Guaranty Title Co of Robertson County Inc	979-828-4688	•	•	•	•

CR	CV	PR	US	BK	←Courts ROCKWALL	Recorder→	UC	RE	TX	VS
		•		•	Abstracts/Trustees of Texas	888-452-0331	•	•	•	
•	•				Accu-Source Inc	940-627-4944				
					David C Bayoud	214-824-9944		•		
•	•	•	•	•	CRRG Inc	800-687-9030	•	•	•	•
•	•		•		Dataprompt Corporation	214-395-2530				
		•			DeedSearcher Title Research Services	281-375-8480	•	•	•	
•	•	•			Nell Watkins & Associates	972-226-8811	•	•	•	•
•		•			Princeton Data Search Inc	469-474-1025		•	•	
•	•	•	•	•	Quick Search	214-358-2840	•	•	•	•
•	•	•	•	•	Security Information Service Inc [SOP]	214-637-4055	•	•	•	•
•	•	•	•	•	Taylor Research & Investigations [SOP]	972-991-5045	•	•	•	•
•	•		•	•	Texsearch #A09479 [SOP]	903-786-4636	•	•	•	
					TOB Public Records Research	214-358-4744	•	•	•	
•	•	•			Watkins Investigations [SOP]	972-926-6011	•	•	•	

CR	CV	PR	US	BK	←Courts RUNNELS	Recorder→	UC	RE	TX	VS
•	•	•	•	•	MS Document Services Inc	800-292-3868	•	•	•	•
•	•	•			Surety Title Co of Ballinger	325-365-5713	•	•	•	•

CR	CV	PR	US	BK	←Courts RUSK	Recorder→	UC	RE	TX	VS
		•			DeedSearcher Title Research Services	281-375-8480	•	•	•	
	•	•			M & M Title / Mitchell Co	318-798-1198	•	•	•	

CR	CV	PR	US	BK	←Courts SABINE	Recorder→	UC	RE	TX	VS
					See adjoining counties for retrievers or call court/recorder directly.					

CR	CV	PR	US	BK	←Courts SAN AUGUSTINE	Recorder→	UC	RE	TX	VS
					See adjoining counties for retrievers or call court/recorder directly.					

CR	CV	PR	US	BK	←Courts SAN JACINTO	Recorder→	UC	RE	TX	VS
•	•	•		•	Courthouse Specialists	800-925-4225	•	•	•	
		•			DeedSearcher Title Research Services	281-375-8480	•	•	•	

CR	CV	PR	US	BK	←Courts SAN PATRICIO	Recorder→	UC	RE	TX	VS
•	•	•	•	•	Condor Inv [SOP]	361-881-8977	•	•	•	•
•	•	•	•	•	Corpus Christi Court Services	361-815-8202	•	•	•	
•	•	•	•	•	FYII Acct [SOP]	563-299-5683	•	•	•	•
•	•	•	•	•	Shawver & Associates	800-364-2333	•	•	•	•
•	•	•	•	•	Texas Civil Process [SOP]	800-976-9595	•	•	•	•

CR	CV	PR	US	BK	←Courts SAN SABA	Recorder→	UC	RE	TX	VS
					See adjoining counties for retrievers or call court/recorder directly.					

CR	CV	PR	US	BK	←Courts SCHLEICHER	Recorder→	UC	RE	TX	VS
					Benton Abstract & Title Co	325-853-2600 x19	•	•	•	

CR	CV	PR	US	BK	←Courts SCURRY	Recorder→	UC	RE	TX	VS
•	•	•	•	•	Davick Services	800-658-6656	•	•	•	
		•			DeedSearcher Title Research Services	281-375-8480	•	•	•	
•	•	•	•	•	MS Document Services Inc	800-292-3868	•	•	•	•
		•	•		Snyder Abstract & Title Co Inc	325-573-6339	•	•	•	

CR	CV	PR	US	BK	←Courts SHACKELFORD	Recorder→	UC	RE	TX	VS
	•	•			Albany Abstract Co	325-762-3077	•	•	•	•
•	•	•	•	•	MS Document Services Inc	800-292-3868	•	•	•	•

CR	CV	PR	US	BK	←Courts SHELBY	Recorder→	UC	RE	TX	VS
	•	•			M & M Title / Mitchell Co	318-798-1198	•	•	•	

CR	CV	PR	US	BK	←Courts SHERMAN	Recorder→	UC	RE	TX	VS
					See adjoining counties for retrievers or call court/recorder directly.					

CR	CV	PR	US	BK	←COURTS	SMITH	RECORDER→	UC	RE	TX	VS
•	•		•		Dataprompt Corporation		214-395-2530				
		•			DeedSearcher Title Research Services		281-375-8480	•	•	•	
	•	•			M & M Title / Mitchell Co		318-798-1198	•	•	•	
•	•	•	•	•	Private Eyes		903-882-5697	•	•	•	•
•	•				Research & Demographic Solutions LLC		817-706-7726				
	•	•		•	Smith County Title Co		903-581-6400	•	•	•	

CR	CV	PR	US	BK	←COURTS	SOMERVELL	RECORDER→	UC	RE	TX	VS
•	•	•			B & B Info Search		817-774-1310				
•	•	•	•	•	Mendenhall Information Services		940-696-0758	•	•	•	•

CR	CV	PR	US	BK	←COURTS	STARR	RECORDER→	UC	RE	TX	VS
		•			DeedSearcher Title Research Services		281-375-8480	•	•	•	
•	•	•	•	•	Professional Civil Process (McAllen) [SOP]		800-880-4223	•	•	•	•
•	•	•	•	•	Shawver & Associates		800-364-2333	•	•	•	•

CR	CV	PR	US	BK	←COURTS	STEPHENS	RECORDER→	UC	RE	TX	VS
•	•	•	•	•	MS Document Services Inc		800-292-3868	•	•	•	•
					Stephens County Abstract		254-559-9089	•	•	•	

CR	CV	PR	US	BK	←COURTS	STERLING	RECORDER→	UC	RE	TX	VS
		•			Sterling Title Co		325-378-2405	•	•	•	

CR	CV	PR	US	BK	←COURTS	STONEWALL	RECORDER→	UC	RE	TX	VS
					Caprock Title Co.		432-687-3232				
		•			Consolidated Abstract Co		940-989-3566	•	•	•	•
•	•	•	•	•	Davick Services		800-658-6656	•	•	•	

CR	CV	PR	US	BK	←COURTS	SUTTON	RECORDER→	UC	RE	TX	VS
					See adjoining counties for retrievers or call court/recorder directly.						

CR	CV	PR	US	BK	←COURTS	SWISHER	RECORDER→	UC	RE	TX	VS
•	•	•	•	•	Davick Services		800-658-6656	•	•	•	
	•	•	•	•	Rollins Research Ltd		806-353-7886, cell- 806-654-2376	•	•	•	

CR	CV	PR	US	BK	←COURTS	TARRANT	RECORDER→	UC	RE	TX	VS
•	•	•	•	•	A+ Super Search Inc		800-687-5553	•	•	•	•
		•		•	Abstracts/Trustees of Texas		888-452-0331	•	•	•	
•	•				Accu-Source Inc		940-627-4944				
	•	•			Ameristar Information Network		800-920-9270		•	•	•
•	•	•	•	•	ASA (Attorney Service Associates) [SOP]		972-394-1175	•	•	•	•
•	•	•	•	•	Asset Control Inc		877-277-3812	•	•	•	•
•	•	•	•	•	Attorney's Service Bureau of Texas [SOP]		888-522-5297	•	•	•	•
					David C Bayoud		214-824-9944		•		
•	•	•	•	•	Bray & Freeman LP [SOP]		817-596-9255	•	•	•	•
•	•	•	•	•	Certified Process Service [SOP]		800-717-3463	•	•	•	•
•	•	•			Courthouse Specialists		800-925-4225	•	•	•	
•	•				Crimecheck Research Services		281-288-6930				
•	•	•	•	•	CRRG Inc		800-687-9030	•	•	•	•
•	•				Data Screen Inc		817-294-7671				
•	•		•		Dataprompt Corporation		214-395-2530				
		•			DeedSearcher Title Research Services		281-375-8480	•	•	•	
•	•	•	•	•	DFW Court Services [SOP]		800-436-0516	•	•	•	
•	•	•	•	•	ETC Investigations		888-560-4001	•	•	•	•
•	•				First Advantage		800-687-0894				
•	•		•	•	FP Resources		866-989-8999				
•	•		•	•	G.A. Public Record Services Inc		800-760-2468 x314				
•	•		•	•	General Information Services		800-447-0798	•	•		
•	•		•	•	Hart & Associates Inc		866-429-4044				
•	•	•	•	•	Info2go		817-656-1997	•	•	•	•

•	•				Inquest Investigations, LLC	903-893-2020	•		•	
•	•	•	•	•	Kimmons Security Services Inc [SOP]	281-679-0070	•	•	•	•
		•			Land Records of Texas	800-678-8016	•	•	•	
•	•		•	•	Lone Star Investigations & Recovery Inc	800-887-3890	•	•	•	•
•	•	•	•	•	Mendenhall Information Services	940-696-0758	•	•	•	•
•	•	•	•	•	MS Document Services Inc	800-292-3868	•	•	•	•
•	•		•		Murray Research	817-295-4820				
•	•	•	•	•	PADIC Inc [SOP]	940-665-6130	•	•	•	•
•	•	•	•	•	Private Eyes	903-882-5697	•	•	•	•
•	•	•	•	•	Professional Civil Process (Austin) [SOP]	800-950-7493	•	•	•	•
•	•	•	•	•	Quick Search	214-358-2840	•	•	•	•
•	•	•	•	•	Reliable Courier [SOP]	214-637-4800			•	•
•	•				Research & Demographic Solutions LLC	817-706-7726				
•	•	•	•	•	Security Information Service Inc [SOP]	214-637-4055	•	•	•	•
•	•	•	•	•	Segovia & Associates [SOP]	877-573-7833		•		•
•	•				Spearhead Research - On Target Information	512-295-7298				
•	•		•	•	Spectrum Screening Inc	800-222-8199	•		•	
•	•	•	•	•	Taylor Research & Investigations [SOP]	972-991-5045	•	•	•	•
•	•				Tex Research	817-472-5997, cell- 682-551-5306				
•	•	•	•	•	Texas Industrial Security Inc	214-634-2791			•	
•	•		•	•	Texsearch #A09479 [SOP]	903-786-4636	•	•	•	
		•			Title Info	817-244-7757		•	•	
					TOB Public Records Research	214-358-4744	•	•	•	

CR	CV	PR	US	BK	←COURTS **TAYLOR**	RECORDER→	UC	RE	TX	VS
		•		•	Abstracts/Trustees of Texas	888-452-0331	•	•	•	
		•			Big Country Title	325-698-9195	•	•	•	•
		•			DeedSearcher Title Research Services	281-375-8480	•	•	•	
•	•	•	•	•	MS Document Services Inc	800-292-3868	•	•	•	•
•	•	•			Texas Research	325-646-2890	•	•	•	

CR	CV	PR	US	BK	←COURTS **TERRELL**	RECORDER→	UC	RE	TX	VS
					See adjoining counties for retrievers or call court/recorder directly.					

CR	CV	PR	US	BK	←COURTS **TERRY**	RECORDER→	UC	RE	TX	VS
	•	•			Brownfield Abstract & Title Co.	806-637-9595	•	•	•	
•	•	•	•	•	Davick Services	800-658-6656	•	•	•	

CR	CV	PR	US	BK	←COURTS **THROCKMORTON**	RECORDER→	UC	RE	TX	VS
•	•	•	•	•	Mendenhall Information Services	940-696-0758	•	•	•	•
•	•	•	•	•	Superior Process Service [SOP]	888-230-2663				

CR	CV	PR	US	BK	←COURTS **TITUS**	RECORDER→	UC	RE	TX	VS
	•		•	•	Joe Gillenwater [SOP]	870-772-2923	•	•	•	
	•	•			Titus County Title Company	903-577-0333	•	•	•	•

CR	CV	PR	US	BK	←COURTS **TOM GREEN**	RECORDER→	UC	RE	TX	VS
•	•				Accu-Source Inc	940-627-4944				
		•			DeedSearcher Title Research Services	281-375-8480	•	•	•	
•	•	•	•	•	MS Document Services Inc	800-292-3868	•	•	•	•
•	•				Research & Demographic Solutions LLC	817-706-7726				
•	•	•	•		Surety Title Co of San Angelo	325-658-7588	•	•	•	•
•	•		•	•	Texsearch #A09479 [SOP]	903-786-4636	•	•	•	

CR	CV	PR	US	BK	←COURTS **TRAVIS**	RECORDER→	UC	RE	TX	VS
		•		•	Abstracts/Trustees of Texas	888-452-0331	•	•	•	
•	•		•		American Background Checks	512-497-7988	•		•	
•	•	•	•	•	Americorp Research Inc	800-620-0015	•	•	•	•
	•	•	•	•	Ameritle Abstract & Research Inc	800-856-1228	•	•	•	
•	•		•		Bar Nunn Research Specialists	512-497-5584				
	•	•	•		John Blackburn	210-867-0399	•	•	•	

CR	CV	PR	US	BK	←Courts	Recorder→	UC	RE	TX	VS
•	•	•	•	•	Blumberg Excelsior Corporate Services Inc (Texas)	800-252-3050	•	•	•	•
	•		•	•	Capitol Services Inc (Texas)	800-345-4647	•		•	
	•	•	•	•	Central Tejas Research & Title Services	512-469-6026	•	•	•	
•	•	•	•	•	Countywide Research Services [SOP]	512-922-1676	•	•	•	•
•	•	•	•	•	CPS (Capitol Process Service) [SOP]	800-856-0216	•	•	•	•
•	•		•		Dataprompt Corporation	214-395-2530				
		•			DeedSearcher Title Research Services	281-375-8480	•	•	•	
•	•	•	•	•	DFW Court Services [SOP]	800-436-0516	•	•	•	
					Executec Services	512-345-5402	•	•	•	
•	•				First Advantage	800-687-0894				
•	•		•	•	G.A. Public Record Services Inc	800-760-2468 x314				
•	•	•	•	•	John C Dunaway & Company [SOP]	512-835-5888	•	•	•	•
•	•	•	•	•	Kimmons Security Services Inc [SOP]	281-679-0070	•	•	•	•
		•			Land Records of Texas	800-678-8016	•	•	•	
•	•	•	•	•	Lawyer's Aid Service	888-474-2112	•	•	•	•
•	•	•	•	•	MS Document Services Inc	800-292-3868	•	•	•	•
•	•	•	•	•	Professional Civil Process (Austin) [SOP]	800-950-7493	•	•	•	•
•	•	•	•	•	Profile Information Services	512-472-9380	•	•	•	•
•	•	•	•	•	Promesa Enterprises Inc	800-474-4420	•	•	•	•
•	•	•	•	•	Property Research & Documentation Service Inc	210-520-7884	•	•	•	•
•	•	•		•	Research N More	512-868-5828	•	•	•	•
•	•	•	•	•	Research Network	512-469-1740	•	•	•	•
•	•				Spearhead Research - On Target Information	512-295-7298				
•	•		•	•	Spectrum Screening Inc	800-222-8199	•		•	
•	•		•	•	Sterling Research	512-670-9334	•	•	•	•
•	•	•	•	•	Taylor Research & Investigations [SOP]	972-991-5045	•	•	•	•
•	•		•	•	Texsearch #A09479 [SOP]	903-786-4636	•	•	•	
•	•	•	•	•	Weeks and Associates LLC [SOP]	512-472-9989	•		•	•

CR	CV	PR	US	BK	←Courts	TRINITY	Recorder→	UC	RE	TX	VS
					East Texas Public Records		936-632-7385		•		
	•	•			Trinity County Abstract		936-642-1698	•	•	•	

CR	CV	PR	US	BK	←Courts	TYLER	Recorder→	UC	RE	TX	VS
		•			DeedSearcher Title Research Services		281-375-8480	•	•	•	
•	•	•	•		Professional Civil Process (Austin) [SOP]		800-950-7493	•	•	•	•

CR	CV	PR	US	BK	←Courts	UPSHUR	Recorder→	UC	RE	TX	VS
•	•		•		Dataprompt Corporation		214-395-2530				
		•			DeedSearcher Title Research Services		281-375-8480	•	•	•	

CR	CV	PR	US	BK	←Courts	UPTON	Recorder→	UC	RE	TX	VS
		•		•	Abstracts/Trustees of Texas		888-452-0331	•	•	•	
	•	•			Southwest Abstract & Title Co		432-693-2242	•	•	•	

CR	CV	PR	US	BK	←Courts	UVALDE	Recorder→	UC	RE	TX	VS
		•			Land Records of Texas		800-678-8016	•	•	•	

CR	CV	PR	US	BK	←Courts	VAL VERDE	Recorder→	UC	RE	TX	VS
		•			DeedSearcher Title Research Services		281-375-8480	•	•	•	
	•	•			Southwest Abstract Co Inc		830-775-8508	•	•	•	•

CR	CV	PR	US	BK	←Courts	VAN ZANDT	Recorder→	UC	RE	TX	VS
•	•		•		Dataprompt Corporation		214-395-2530				
		•			DeedSearcher Title Research Services		281-375-8480	•	•	•	
•	•	•			Elliott & Waldron Abstract & Title Co of Canton		903-567-4127	•	•	•	•
•		•			Princeton Data Search Inc		469-474-1025		•	•	
•	•	•	•	•	Private Eyes		903-882-5697	•	•	•	•
•	•	•	•	•	Taylor Research & Investigations [SOP]		972-991-5045	•	•	•	•

CR	CV	PR	US	BK	←COURTS VICTORIA	RECORDER→	UC	RE	TX	VS
•	•	•	•	•	All State Document Services	888-246-8180	•	•	•	•
•	•	•	•	•	Condor Inv [SOP]	361-881-8977	•	•	•	•
•	•		•		Dataprompt Corporation	214-395-2530				
		•			DeedSearcher Title Research Services	281-375-8480	•	•	•	
•	•				Research & Demographic Solutions LLC	817-706-7726				
•	•	•	•	•	Shawver & Associates	800-364-2333	•	•	•	•

CR	CV	PR	US	BK	←COURTS WALKER	RECORDER→	UC	RE	TX	VS
•	•	•	•	•	All State Document Services	888-246-8180	•	•	•	•
•	•	•		•	Courthouse Specialists	800-925-4225	•	•	•	
•	•				Crimecheck Research Services	281-288-6930				
		•			DeedSearcher Title Research Services	281-375-8480	•	•	•	
•	•	•			Metro Research & Inv [SOP]	936-441-2294	•	•	•	•
•	•	•	•	•	PM Clinton International Investigation [SOP]	866-686-6864	•	•	•	

CR	CV	PR	US	BK	←COURTS WALLER	RECORDER→	UC	RE	TX	VS
•	•	•	•	•	All State Document Services	888-246-8180	•	•	•	•
•	•	•		•	Courthouse Specialists	800-925-4225	•	•	•	
		•			DeedSearcher Title Research Services	281-375-8480	•	•	•	
	•	•	•	•	Garza-McNamee Agency Inc	888-262-6221	•	•	•	
		•			Land Records of Texas	800-678-8016	•	•	•	
•	•		•	•	Mach 5 Couriers Inc [SOP]	800-593-2023				
•	•	•	•	•	PM Clinton International Investigation [SOP]	866-686-6864	•	•	•	
•	•	•	•	•	The Research Staff Inc	800-822-3584	•	•	•	

CR	CV	PR	US	BK	←COURTS WARD	RECORDER→	UC	RE	TX	VS
	•	•			Pioneer-Ward County Abstract Co	432-943-5561	•	•	•	

CR	CV	PR	US	BK	←COURTS WASHINGTON	RECORDER→	UC	RE	TX	VS
		•		•	Abstracts/Trustees of Texas	888-452-0331	•	•	•	
•	•	•	•	•	All State Document Services	888-246-8180	•	•	•	•
		•			Botts Title Co	254-697-6962	•	•	•	•
		•			DeedSearcher Title Research Services	281-375-8480	•	•	•	

CR	CV	PR	US	BK	←COURTS WEBB	RECORDER→	UC	RE	TX	VS
					Border Title Group	956-791-5810	•	•	•	
•	•	•	•	•	Condor Inv [SOP]	361-881-8977	•	•	•	•
•	•		•		Dataprompt Corporation	214-395-2530				
		•			DeedSearcher Title Research Services	281-375-8480	•	•	•	
•	•	•	•	•	Shawver & Associates	800-364-2333	•	•	•	•

CR	CV	PR	US	BK	←COURTS WHARTON	RECORDER→	UC	RE	TX	VS
•	•	•	•	•	All State Document Services	888-246-8180	•	•	•	•
		•			DeedSearcher Title Research Services	281-375-8480	•	•	•	
		•			Land Records of Texas	800-678-8016	•	•	•	
•	•	•	•	•	The Research Staff Inc	800-822-3584	•	•	•	

CR	CV	PR	US	BK	←COURTS WICHITA	RECORDER→	UC	RE	TX	VS
		•		•	Abstracts/Trustees of Texas	888-452-0331	•	•	•	
		•			DeedSearcher Title Research Services	281-375-8480	•	•	•	
•	•	•	•	•	Mendenhall Information Services	940-696-0758	•	•	•	•
•	•	•	•	•	Superior Process Service [SOP]	888-230-2663				
•	•	•	•	•	Texas Detective.com [SOP]	940-592-7000	•	•	•	•
•	•		•	•	Texsearch #A09479 [SOP]	903-786-4636	•	•	•	

CR	CV	PR	US	BK	←COURTS WILBARGER	RECORDER→	UC	RE	TX	VS
•	•		•		Dataprompt Corporation	214-395-2530				
•	•	•	•	•	Mendenhall Information Services	940-696-0758	•	•	•	•
•	•	•	•	•	Superior Process Service [SOP]	888-230-2663				
•	•	•			T.A.B.B.S. Investigations & Process Service [SOP]	580-477-3292	•	•	•	•

CR	CV	PR	US	BK	←Courts	Recorder→	UC	RE	TX	VS
•	•	•	•	•	Texas Detective.com [SOP]	940-592-7000	•	•	•	•

CR	CV	PR	US	BK	←Courts **Willacy**	Recorder→	UC	RE	TX	VS
•	•		•		American Background Checks	512-497-7988	•		•	
•	•	•	•	•	Professional Civil Process (McAllen) [SOP]	800-880-4223	•	•	•	•
	•	•	•	•	Valley Abstract & Trustee Services	956-571-1119	•	•	•	

CR	CV	PR	US	BK	←Courts **Williamson**	Recorder→	UC	RE	TX	VS
		•		•	Abstracts/Trustees of Texas	888-452-0331	•	•	•	
		•			American Abstract & Title Co Inc	254-526-9525		•	•	•
•	•	•	•	•	Americorp Research Inc	800-620-0015	•	•	•	•
	•		•	•	Carma Austin	254-634-1701	•		•	
•	•		•		Bar Nunn Research Specialists	512-497-5584				
	•	•	•		John Blackburn	210-867-0399	•	•	•	
	•	•	•	•	Central Tejas Research & Title Services	512-469-6026	•	•	•	
•	•	•	•	•	Countywide Research Services [SOP]	512-922-1676	•	•	•	•
•	•	•	•	•	CPS (Capitol Process Service) [SOP]	800-856-0216	•	•	•	•
		•			DeedSearcher Title Research Services	281-375-8480	•	•	•	
					Executec Services	512-345-5402	•	•	•	
•	•				First Advantage	800-687-0894				
•	•	•	•	•	John C Dunaway & Company [SOP]	512-835-5888	•	•	•	•
•	•	•	•	•	MS Document Services Inc	800-292-3868	•	•	•	•
•	•	•	•	•	Promesa Enterprises Inc	800-474-4420	•	•	•	•
•	•	•	•	•	Property Research & Documentation Service Inc	210-520-7884	•	•	•	•
•	•	•		•	Research N More	512-868-5828	•	•	•	•
•	•	•	•	•	Research Network	512-469-1740	•	•	•	•
•	•				Spearhead Research - On Target Information	512-295-7298				
•	•		•	•	Spectrum Screening Inc	800-222-8199	•		•	
•	•		•	•	Sterling Research	512-670-9334	•	•	•	•
•	•	•	•	•	Taylor Research & Investigations [SOP]	972-991-5045	•	•	•	•
•	•		•	•	Texsearch #A09479 [SOP]	903-786-4636	•	•	•	
•	•	•	•	•	Weeks and Associates LLC [SOP]	512-472-9989	•		•	•

CR	CV	PR	US	BK	←Courts **Wilson**	Recorder→	UC	RE	TX	VS
		•		•	Abstracts/Trustees of Texas	888-452-0331	•	•	•	
•	•	•	•	•	Best Process Service [SOP]	210-930-7417	•	•	•	•
•	•				Crimecheck Research Services	281-288-6930				
		•			Land Records of Texas	800-678-8016	•	•	•	
•	•	•	•	•	Property Research & Documentation Service Inc	210-520-7884	•	•	•	•

CR	CV	PR	US	BK	←Courts **Winkler**	Recorder→	UC	RE	TX	VS
	•	•	•	•	Stewart Title of Midland Inc	432-687-3355		•		

CR	CV	PR	US	BK	←Courts **Wise**	Recorder→	UC	RE	TX	VS
•	•				Accu-Source Inc	940-627-4944				
•	•	•			B & B Info Search	817-774-1310				
•	•	•	•	•	Bray & Freeman LP [SOP]	817-596-9255	•	•	•	•
•	•				Crimecheck Research Services	281-288-6930				
•	•		•		Dataprompt Corporation	214-395-2530				
		•			DeedSearcher Title Research Services	281-375-8480	•	•	•	
•	•	•	•	•	ETC Investigations	888-560-4001	•	•	•	
•	•	•	•	•	Info2go	817-656-1997	•	•	•	•
		•			Land Records of Texas	800-678-8016	•	•	•	
•	•	•	•	•	Mendenhall Information Services	940-696-0758	•	•	•	•

CR	CV	PR	US	BK	←Courts **Wood**	Recorder→	UC	RE	TX	VS
•	•		•		Dataprompt Corporation	214-395-2530				
		•			DeedSearcher Title Research Services	281-375-8480	•	•	•	
•	•	•	•	•	Private Eyes	903-882-5697	•	•	•	•

CR	CV	PR	US	BK	←COURTS YOAKUM	RECORDER→	UC	RE	TX	VS
•	•	•	•	•	Davick Services	800-658-6656	•	•	•	
		•			Yoakum County Abstract Co	806-456-2615		•	•	

CR	CV	PR	US	BK	←COURTS YOUNG	RECORDER→	UC	RE	TX	VS
•	•	•	•	•	ETC Investigations	888-560-4001	•	•	•	
•	•	•	•	•	Mendenhall Information Services	940-696-0758	•	•	•	•

CR	CV	PR	US	BK	←COURTS ZAPATA	RECORDER→	UC	RE	TX	VS
					Border Title Group	956-791-5810	•	•	•	
		•			DeedSearcher Title Research Services	281-375-8480	•	•	•	

CR	CV	PR	US	BK	←COURTS ZAVALA	RECORDER→	UC	RE	TX	VS
•	•	•			Border Legal Services [SOP]	830-773-0525			•	•
					Border Title - Zavala Abstract Co.	830-374-3218		•	•	
					Border Title Group	956-791-5810	•	•	•	

[SOP] = PERFORMS SERVICE OF PROCESS

COURT RECORDS

CODE	GOVERNMENT AGENCY	TYPE OF INFORMATION
CR	Criminal Court	Municipal, county and state level criminal cases
CV	Civil Court	Municipal, county and state level civil cases
PR	Probate Court	Wills and estate cases
US	US District Court	Federal civil and criminal cases
BK	Bankruptcy Court	United States bankruptcy cases

COUNTY RECORDS - RECORDINGS

CODE	GOVERNMENT AGENCY	TYPE OF INFORMATION
UC	UCC Filing Office	Uniform Commercial Code and other personal property liens
RE	Real Estate Recording Office	Real property transactions and liens
TX	Tax Filing Office(s)	Federal and state tax liens, judgment liens
VS	Vital Records Office	Vital statistics—birth, death, marriage, divorce

 = PRRN Member. *A retriever you can trust!*

Utah

COURT RECORDS RETRIEVED — CAPITAL - SALT LAKE COUNTY — RECORDED RECORDS RETRIEVED

CR	CV	PR	US	BK	←COURTS	BEAVER	RECORDER→	UC	RE	TX	VS
•	•	•	•	•	All-Search		800-227-3152	•	•	•	•
	•	•	•	•	D W Moore & Assoc Inc		801-266-6585	•	•	•	•
	•	•			Security Title of Beaver County		435-438-2354	•	•	•	
CR	**CV**	**PR**	**US**	**BK**	**←COURTS**	**BOX ELDER**	**RECORDER→**	**UC**	**RE**	**TX**	**VS**
•	•	•	•	•	All-Search		800-227-3152	•	•	•	•
	•	•	•	•	D W Moore & Assoc Inc		801-266-6585	•	•	•	•
•	•	•			Mower Services [SOP]		888-317-7458	•	•	•	
•	•	•	•	•	Quick Data Services Inc		800-720-6167	•	•	•	•
	•	•			The Home Abstract & Title Co Inc		800-699-7861	•	•	•	
•	•				Wasatch Investigations Inc [SOP]		800-970-8220				
CR	**CV**	**PR**	**US**	**BK**	**←COURTS**	**CACHE**	**RECORDER→**	**UC**	**RE**	**TX**	**VS**
•	•	•	•	•	All-Search		800-227-3152	•	•	•	•
	•	•	•	•	D W Moore & Assoc Inc		801-266-6585	•	•	•	•
•	•	•			Hickman Land Title		800-365-7760	•	•	•	•
•	•	•			Mower Services [SOP]		888-317-7458	•	•	•	
•	•	•	•	•	Quick Data Services Inc		800-720-6167	•	•	•	•
					Reliance Abstract Company - UT		800-207-1523	•	•	•	
•	•				Wasatch Investigations Inc [SOP]		800-970-8220				
CR	**CV**	**PR**	**US**	**BK**	**←COURTS**	**CARBON**	**RECORDER→**	**UC**	**RE**	**TX**	**VS**
	•	•	•	•	D W Moore & Assoc Inc		801-266-6585	•	•	•	•
•	•	•			Southeastern Utah Title		435-637-4455	•	•	•	•
CR	**CV**	**PR**	**US**	**BK**	**←COURTS**	**DAGGETT**	**RECORDER→**	**UC**	**RE**	**TX**	**VS**
	•	•	•	•	D W Moore & Assoc Inc		801-266-6585	•	•	•	•
CR	**CV**	**PR**	**US**	**BK**	**←COURTS**	**DAVIS**	**RECORDER→**	**UC**	**RE**	**TX**	**VS**
•	•	•	•	•	All-Search		800-227-3152	•	•	•	•
•	•	•	•	•	Beehive Attorney Service [SOP]		800-779-0379			•	
	•	•	•	•	D W Moore & Assoc Inc		801-266-6585	•	•	•	•
•	•	•	•	•	DataTrace Online Inc, PI# 100008 [SOP]		800-748-5335	•	•	•	•
•	•	•			Hickman Land Title		800-365-7760	•	•	•	•
•	•	•	•	•	Quick Data Services Inc		800-720-6167	•	•	•	•
					Reliance Abstract Company - UT		800-207-1523	•	•	•	
	•	•			The Home Abstract & Title Co Inc		800-699-7861	•	•	•	
•	•				Wasatch Investigations Inc [SOP]		800-970-8220				
CR	**CV**	**PR**	**US**	**BK**	**←COURTS**	**DUCHESNE**	**RECORDER→**	**UC**	**RE**	**TX**	**VS**
•	•	•	•	•	All-Search		800-227-3152	•	•	•	•
	•	•	•	•	D W Moore & Assoc Inc		801-266-6585	•	•	•	•
CR	**CV**	**PR**	**US**	**BK**	**←COURTS**	**EMERY**	**RECORDER→**	**UC**	**RE**	**TX**	**VS**
	•	•	•	•	D W Moore & Assoc Inc		801-266-6585	•	•	•	•
•	•	•			Southeastern Utah Title		435-637-4455	•	•	•	•
CR	**CV**	**PR**	**US**	**BK**	**←COURTS**	**GARFIELD**	**RECORDER→**	**UC**	**RE**	**TX**	**VS**
•	•	•	•	•	All-Search		800-227-3152	•	•	•	•
	•	•	•	•	D W Moore & Assoc Inc		801-266-6585	•	•	•	•
•	•	•			Security Title Co of Garfield County		435-676-8808	•	•	•	•

CR	CV	PR	US	BK	←COURTS	GRAND	RECORDER→	UC	RE	TX	VS
	•	•	•	•	D W Moore & Assoc Inc		801-266-6585	•	•	•	•
•	•	•			Southeastern Utah Title		435-637-4455	•	•	•	•

CR	CV	PR	US	BK	←COURTS	IRON	RECORDER→	UC	RE	TX	VS
	•	•	•	•	D W Moore & Assoc Inc		801-266-6585	•	•	•	•

CR	CV	PR	US	BK	←COURTS	JUAB	RECORDER→	UC	RE	TX	VS
•	•	•	•	•	All-Search		800-227-3152	•	•	•	•
	•	•	•	•	D W Moore & Assoc Inc		801-266-6585	•	•	•	•
•	•	•			Juab Title & Abstract Co		435-623-0387	•	•	•	

CR	CV	PR	US	BK	←COURTS	KANE	RECORDER→	UC	RE	TX	VS
	•	•	•	•	D W Moore & Assoc Inc		801-266-6585	•	•	•	•
•	•	•			Southern Utah Title Co		435-644-5891	•	•	•	•

CR	CV	PR	US	BK	←COURTS	MILLARD	RECORDER→	UC	RE	TX	VS
•	•	•	•	•	All-Search		800-227-3152	•	•	•	•
	•	•	•	•	D W Moore & Assoc Inc		801-266-6585	•	•	•	•
•	•	•			Juab Title & Abstract Co		435-623-0387	•	•	•	
•	•	•			Utah Title & Abstract		435-896-5429	•	•	•	

CR	CV	PR	US	BK	←COURTS	MORGAN	RECORDER→	UC	RE	TX	VS
•	•	•	•	•	All-Search		800-227-3152	•	•	•	•
	•	•	•	•	D W Moore & Assoc Inc		801-266-6585	•	•	•	•
•	•	•	•	•	Quick Data Services Inc		800-720-6167	•	•	•	•
	•	•			The Home Abstract & Title Co Inc		800-699-7861	•	•	•	

CR	CV	PR	US	BK	←COURTS	PIUTE	RECORDER→	UC	RE	TX	VS
•	•	•	•	•	All-Search		800-227-3152	•	•	•	•
	•	•	•	•	D W Moore & Assoc Inc		801-266-6585	•	•	•	•
•	•	•			Security Title Co of Garfield County		435-676-8808	•	•	•	•
•	•	•			Utah Title & Abstract		435-896-5429	•	•	•	

CR	CV	PR	US	BK	←COURTS	RICH	RECORDER→	UC	RE	TX	VS
	•	•	•	•	D W Moore & Assoc Inc		801-266-6585	•	•	•	•
•	•	•			Hickman Land Title		800-365-7760	•	•	•	•
•	•	•			Mower Services [SOP]		888-317-7458	•	•	•	

CR	CV	PR	US	BK	←COURTS	SALT LAKE	RECORDER→	UC	RE	TX	VS
•	•	•	•	•	All-Search		800-227-3152	•	•	•	•
•	•	•	•	•	Beehive Attorney Service [SOP]		800-779-0379			•	
	•	•	•	•	D W Moore & Assoc Inc		801-266-6585	•	•	•	•
•	•	•	•	•	DataTrace Online Inc, PI# 100008 [SOP]		800-748-5335	•	•	•	•
•	•	•			Hickman Land Title		800-365-7760	•	•	•	•
•	•	•	•	•	Quick Data Services Inc		800-720-6167	•	•	•	•
					Reliance Abstract Company - UT		800-207-1523	•	•	•	
•	•		•	•	Secure Data Corporation		801-595-1510	•		•	
•	•				Wasatch Investigations Inc [SOP]		800-970-8220				
•					Western Reporting		800-466-1996				

CR	CV	PR	US	BK	←COURTS	SAN JUAN	RECORDER→	UC	RE	TX	VS
•	•				Attorney Service New Mexico [SOP]		505-326-7486				
	•	•	•	•	D W Moore & Assoc Inc		801-266-6585	•	•	•	•
•	•	•			Southeastern Utah Title		435-637-4455	•	•	•	•

CR	CV	PR	US	BK	←COURTS	SANPETE	RECORDER→	UC	RE	TX	VS
•	•	•	•	•	All-Search		800-227-3152	•	•	•	•
	•	•	•	•	D W Moore & Assoc Inc		801-266-6585	•	•	•	•
•	•	•			Juab Title & Abstract Co		435-623-0387	•	•	•	

CR	CV	PR	US	BK	←Courts — SEVIER	Recorder→	UC	RE	TX	VS
•	•	•	•	•	All-Search	800-227-3152	•	•	•	•
	•	•	•	•	D W Moore & Assoc Inc	801-266-6585	•	•	•	•
•	•	•			Utah Title & Abstract	435-896-5429	•	•	•	

CR	CV	PR	US	BK	←Courts — SUMMIT	Recorder→	UC	RE	TX	VS
•	•	•	•	•	All-Search	800-227-3152	•	•	•	•
•	•	•	•	•	Beehive Attorney Service [SOP]	800-779-0379			•	
	•	•	•	•	D W Moore & Assoc Inc	801-266-6585	•	•	•	•
•	•	•	•	•	Quick Data Services Inc	800-720-6167	•	•	•	•

CR	CV	PR	US	BK	←Courts — TOOELE	Recorder→	UC	RE	TX	VS
•	•	•	•	•	All-Search	800-227-3152	•	•	•	•
•	•	•	•	•	Beehive Attorney Service [SOP]	800-779-0379			•	
	•	•	•	•	D W Moore & Assoc Inc	801-266-6585	•	•	•	•
•	•	•	•	•	Quick Data Services Inc	800-720-6167	•	•	•	•
•	•				Wasatch Investigations Inc [SOP]	800-970-8220				

CR	CV	PR	US	BK	←Courts — UINTAH	Recorder→	UC	RE	TX	VS
•	•	•	•	•	All-Search	800-227-3152	•	•	•	•
	•	•	•	•	D W Moore & Assoc Inc	801-266-6585	•	•	•	•

CR	CV	PR	US	BK	←Courts — UTAH	Recorder→	UC	RE	TX	VS
•	•	•	•	•	All-Search	800-227-3152	•	•	•	•
•	•	•	•	•	Beehive Attorney Service [SOP]	800-779-0379			•	
	•	•	•	•	D W Moore & Assoc Inc	801-266-6585	•	•	•	•
•	•	•	•	•	DataTrace Online Inc, PI# 100008 [SOP]	800-748-5335	•	•	•	•
•	•	•			Juab Title & Abstract Co	435-623-0387	•	•	•	
•	•	•	•	•	Quick Data Services Inc	800-720-6167	•	•	•	•
					Reliance Abstract Company - UT	800-207-1523	•	•	•	
•	•				Wasatch Investigations Inc [SOP]	800-970-8220				

CR	CV	PR	US	BK	←Courts — WASATCH	Recorder→	UC	RE	TX	VS
•	•	•	•	•	All-Search	800-227-3152	•	•	•	•
	•	•	•	•	D W Moore & Assoc Inc	801-266-6585	•	•	•	•
•	•	•	•	•	Quick Data Services Inc	800-720-6167	•	•	•	•

CR	CV	PR	US	BK	←Courts — WASHINGTON	Recorder→	UC	RE	TX	VS
•	•	•	•	•	All-Search	800-227-3152	•	•	•	•
	•	•	•	•	D W Moore & Assoc Inc	801-266-6585	•	•	•	•

CR	CV	PR	US	BK	←Courts — WAYNE	Recorder→	UC	RE	TX	VS
	•	•	•	•	D W Moore & Assoc Inc	801-266-6585	•	•	•	•
•	•	•			Utah Title & Abstract	435-896-5429	•	•	•	

CR	CV	PR	US	BK	←Courts — WEBER	Recorder→	UC	RE	TX	VS
•	•	•	•	•	All-Search	800-227-3152	•	•	•	•
•	•	•	•	•	Beehive Attorney Service [SOP]	800-779-0379			•	
	•	•	•	•	D W Moore & Assoc Inc	801-266-6585	•	•	•	•
•	•	•			Hickman Land Title	800-365-7760	•	•	•	•
•	•	•	•	•	Quick Data Services Inc	800-720-6167	•	•	•	•
					Reliance Abstract Company - UT	800-207-1523	•	•	•	
	•	•			The Home Abstract & Title Co Inc	800-699-7861	•	•	•	
•	•				Wasatch Investigations Inc [SOP]	800-970-8220				

Vermont

Vermont has 14 counties and 246 towns/cities which have 246 recording offices. There is **no county recording** in this state. All recording is done at the city/town level. Many towns are so small that their mailing addresses are in different towns. Watch for these 4 towns that have the same names as cities - Barre, Newport, Rutland, and St. Albans. Watch for 11 cities or towns that bear the same name as a Vermont county - Addison, Bennington, Chittenden, Essex, Franklin, Grand Isle, Orange, Rutland, Washington, Windham, and Windsor.

COURT RECORDS RETRIEVED — CAPITAL - WASHINGTON COUNTY — RECORDED RECORDS RETRIEVED

CR	CV	PR	US	BK	←COURTS		RECORDER→	UC	RE	TX	VS
					ADDISON						
•	•	•	•	•	New England Recovery Inc [SOP]	800-922-7376		•	•	•	•
•	•	•	•	•	Title Search Services Inc	802-867-4447		•	•	•	•
•	•	•	•	•	Vermont Land Records Research	802-985-9723		•	•	•	•
					BENNINGTON						
•	•	•	•	•	New England Recovery Inc [SOP]	800-922-7376		•	•	•	•
•	•	•	•	•	Title Search Services Inc	802-867-4447		•	•	•	•
					CALEDONIA						
•	•	•	•	•	Countryside Paralegal Services	802-888-2150		•	•	•	•
•	•	•	•	•	New England Recovery Inc [SOP]	800-922-7376		•	•	•	•
					CHITTENDEN						
•	•	•	•	•	Inquisitive Research Corporation	732-321-0041		•	•	•	•
•	•	•	•	•	New England Recovery Inc [SOP]	800-922-7376		•	•	•	•
•	•	•	•	•	Title Search Services Inc	802-867-4447		•	•	•	•
•	•	•	•	•	Vermont Land Records Research	802-985-9723		•	•	•	•
•	•				VPS [SOP]	802-496-6863					
					ESSEX						
•	•	•	•	•	Countryside Paralegal Services	802-888-2150		•	•	•	•
•	•	•	•	•	New England Recovery Inc [SOP]	800-922-7376		•	•	•	•
					FRANKLIN						
•	•	•	•	•	Countryside Paralegal Services	802-888-2150		•	•	•	•
•	•	•	•	•	New England Recovery Inc [SOP]	800-922-7376		•	•	•	•
•	•	•	•	•	Title Search Services Inc	802-867-4447		•	•	•	•
					GRAND ISLE						
•	•	•	•	•	New England Recovery Inc [SOP]	800-922-7376		•	•	•	•
•	•	•	•	•	Title Search Services Inc	802-867-4447		•	•	•	•
					LAMOILLE						
•	•	•	•	•	Countryside Paralegal Services	802-888-2150		•	•	•	•
•	•	•	•	•	New England Recovery Inc [SOP]	800-922-7376		•	•	•	•
					ORANGE						
•	•	•	•	•	New England Recovery Inc [SOP]	800-922-7376		•	•	•	•
					ORLEANS						
•	•	•	•	•	Countryside Paralegal Services	802-888-2150		•	•	•	•
•	•	•	•	•	New England Recovery Inc [SOP]	800-922-7376		•	•	•	•

CR	CV	PR	US	BK	←COURTS RUTLAND	RECORDER→	UC	RE	TX	VS
•	•	•	•	•	Inquisitive Research Corporation	732-321-0041	•	•	•	•
•	•	•	•	•	New England Recovery Inc [SOP]	800-922-7376	•	•	•	•
•	•	•	•	•	Title Search Services Inc	802-867-4447	•	•	•	•

CR	CV	PR	US	BK	←COURTS WASHINGTON	RECORDER→	UC	RE	TX	VS
•	•	•	•	•	New England Recovery Inc [SOP]	800-922-7376	•	•	•	•
•	•				VPS [SOP]	802-496-6863				

CR	CV	PR	US	BK	←COURTS WINDHAM	RECORDER→	UC	RE	TX	VS
•	•	•	•	•	Margaret H Knoras	802-885-4375	•	•	•	•
•	•	•	•	•	New England Recovery Inc [SOP]	800-922-7376	•	•	•	•

CR	CV	PR	US	BK	←COURTS WINDSOR	RECORDER→	UC	RE	TX	VS
•	•	•	•	•	Margaret H Knoras	802-885-4375	•	•	•	•
•	•				MSI Inv [SOP]	603-298-8060				
•	•	•	•	•	New England Recovery Inc [SOP]	800-922-7376	•	•	•	•

COURT RECORDS

CODE	GOVERNMENT AGENCY	TYPE OF INFORMATION
CR	Criminal Court	Municipal, county and state level criminal cases
CV	Civil Court	Municipal, county and state level civil cases
PR	Probate Court	Wills and estate cases
US	US District Court	Federal civil and criminal cases
BK	Bankruptcy Court	United States bankruptcy cases

COUNTY RECORDS - RECORDINGS

CODE	GOVERNMENT AGENCY	TYPE OF INFORMATION
UC	UCC Filing Office	Uniform Commercial Code and other personal property liens
RE	Real Estate Recording Office	Real property transactions and liens
TX	Tax Filing Office(s)	Federal and state tax liens, judgment liens
VS	Vital Records Office	Vital statistics—birth, death, marriage, divorce

Editor's Tip: Remember the first rule about public record searching-- Simply because your state or county has certain rules, regulations and practices regarding the accessibility and content of public records, does not mean that another state or county adheres to the same rules.

Virginia

Virginia has 95 counties and 41 independent cities. 26 cities have separate filing offices. Charles City and James City are counties, not cities. The City of Franklin is not in or adjacent to Franklin County. The City of Richmond is not in Richmond County. The City of Roanoke is not in Roanoke County. 15 independent cities share the Clerk of Circuit Court with the county - Bedford, Covington (Alleghany County), Emporia (Greenville County), Fairfax, Falls Church (Arlington or Fairfax County), Franklin (Southhampton County), Galax (Carroll County), Harrisonburg (Rockingham County), Lexington (Rockbridge County), Manassas and Manassas Park (Prince William County), Norton (Wise County), Poquoson (York County), South Boston (Halifax County), and Williamsburg (James City County).

COURT RECORDS RETRIEVED — CAPITAL - RICHMOND CITY — RECORDED RECORDS RETRIEVED

CR	CV	PR	US	BK	←Courts ACCOMACK	Recorder→	UC	RE	TX	VS
•	•	•			Judith Ayres	757-336-5313	•	•	•	•
•	•				Innovative Enterprises Inc	888-777-9435				

CR	CV	PR	US	BK	←Courts ALBEMARLE	Recorder→	UC	RE	TX	VS
	•	•			Blue Ridge Title, Div of Chicago Title Ins Co	434-295-7196	•	•	•	
	•				E Title & Abstract LLC	540-727-0515	•	•	•	
					Fact Finders Ltd	866-672-0666	•	•	•	
•	•				Innovative Enterprises Inc	888-777-9435				

CR	CV	PR	US	BK	←Courts ALEXANDRIA	Recorder→	UC	RE	TX	VS
•	•		•	•	ABA Services	720-344-1259	•	•	•	
•	•	•	•	•	ALIASS [SOP]	800-747-0820	•	•	•	•
•	•	•	•	•	Alliance Legal Services Inc [SOP]	703-644-8571	•	•	•	•
					Amarisearch Inc	703-267-6827	•	•	•	
•	•	•	•	•	CorpAssist Inc - DC Office	800-438-2996	•	•	•	•
					Direct Title Solutions Inc	540-450-0740	•	•	•	
•	•	•	•	•	Enterprise Title Company Inc	703-351-8066	•	•	•	•
					Estate Title & Escrow Inc	703-385-5850	•	•	•	
		•			Examiner's Title LC	703-491-0805		•		
	•	•	•	•	Federal Research LLC [SOP]	800-846-3190	•	•	•	•
•	•	•	•	•	Fitzgerald Servaites Inc	202-257-7775	•	•	•	•
•	•	•	•	•	Infoline Inc	888-284-4581	•	•	•	•
•	•	•	•	•	InfoNation Inc - Virginia [SOP]	888-346-9090	•	•	•	
•	•				Innovative Enterprises Inc	888-777-9435				
•	•	•	•	•	Mohr Information Services LLC	540-678-8775	•	•	•	
•	•		•	•	National Background Investigations Inc	800-798-0079			•	
•	•	•	•	•	Security Consultants Inc	202-686-3953			•	•

CR	CV	PR	US	BK	←Courts ALLEGHANY	Recorder→	UC	RE	TX	VS
•	•				Innovative Enterprises Inc	888-777-9435				
•	•	•	•	•	Law Offices of Joan C Singleton	540-839-5009	•	•	•	•

CR	CV	PR	US	BK	←Courts AMELIA	Recorder→	UC	RE	TX	VS
•	•	•			Abstracts by Starkey Inc	804-305-6022	•	•	•	•
•	•	•			Dominion Abstract & Title Agency	804-794-9037	•	•	•	
•	•				Innovative Enterprises Inc	888-777-9435				
•	•	•	•	•	UCC Retrievals, Inc	804-559-5919	•		•	

CR	CV	PR	US	BK	←Courts AMHERST	Recorder→	UC	RE	TX	VS
•	•	•			Berry & Maddox	434-263-4886	•	•	•	•
•	•				Innovative Enterprises Inc	888-777-9435				

CR	CV	PR	US	BK	←COURTS		RECORDER→	UC	RE	TX	VS
					APPOMATTOX						
•	•				Innovative Enterprises Inc		888-777-9435				
					ARLINGTON						
•	•		•	•	ABA Services		720-344-1259	•	•	•	
•	•	•	•	•	ALIASS [SOP]		800-747-0820	•	•	•	•
•	•	•	•	•	Alliance Legal Services Inc [SOP]		703-644-8571	•	•	•	•
					Amarisearch Inc		703-267-6827	•	•	•	
•	•	•	•	•	Capitol District Information [SOP]		800-494-5225	•	•	•	
•	•	•	•	•	CorpAssist Inc - DC Office		800-438-2996	•	•	•	•
					Direct Title Solutions Inc		540-450-0740	•	•	•	
•	•	•	•	•	Enterprise Title Company Inc		703-351-8066	•	•	•	•
					Estate Title & Escrow Inc		703-385-5850	•	•	•	
		•			Examiner's Title LC		703-491-0805	•	•		
	•	•	•	•	Federal Research LLC [SOP]		800-846-3190	•	•	•	•
•	•	•	•	•	Fitzgerald Servaites Inc		202-257-7775	•	•	•	•
•	•	•	•	•	Infoline Inc		888-284-4581	•	•	•	•
•	•	•	•	•	InfoNation Inc - Virginia [SOP]		888-346-9090	•	•	•	
•	•				Innovative Enterprises Inc		888-777-9435				
•	•	•	•	•	Investigative Consultants Inc		202-237-1500	•	•	•	•
•	•	•	•	•	Mohr Information Services LLC		540-678-8775	•	•	•	
•	•		•	•	National Background Investigations Inc		800-798-0079			•	
•	•	•	•	•	Security Consultants Inc		202-686-3953			•	•
•	•	•	•	•	Washington Document Service (DC)		800-728-5201	•	•	•	•
					AUGUSTA						
•	•				Innovative Enterprises Inc		888-777-9435				
					BATH						
•	•				Innovative Enterprises Inc		888-777-9435				
•	•	•	•	•	Law Offices of Joan C Singleton		540-839-5009	•	•	•	•
					BEDFORD						
•	•	•			Deeds Inc		540-563-5699	•	•	•	
•	•				Innovative Enterprises Inc		888-777-9435				
					BEDFORD CITY						
•	•				Innovative Enterprises Inc		888-777-9435				
					BLAND						
•	•				Innovative Enterprises Inc		888-777-9435				
•	•	•			Diana L Johnson		540-921-1958	•	•	•	•
					New Century Title		276-223-1207		•	•	
					BOTETOURT						
		•			Betsy Biesenbach		540-982-7892	•	•	•	
•	•	•			Deeds Inc		540-563-5699	•	•	•	
•	•				Innovative Enterprises Inc		888-777-9435				
					BRISTOL						
•	•				Innovative Enterprises Inc		888-777-9435				
					BRUNSWICK						
•	•				Innovative Enterprises Inc		888-777-9435				
					BUCHANAN						
•	•				Innovative Enterprises Inc		888-777-9435				
					BUCKINGHAM						
•	•				Innovative Enterprises Inc		888-777-9435				
•	•	•	•	•	UCC Retrievals, Inc		804-559-5919	•		•	

CR	CV	PR	US	BK	←COURTS	BUENA VISTA	RECORDER→	UC	RE	TX	VS
•	•					Innovative Enterprises Inc	888-777-9435				

CR	CV	PR	US	BK	←COURTS	CAMPBELL	RECORDER→	UC	RE	TX	VS
•	•					Innovative Enterprises Inc	888-777-9435				

CR	CV	PR	US	BK	←COURTS	CAROLINE	RECORDER→	UC	RE	TX	VS
						Amarisearch Inc	703-267-6827	•	•	•	
•	•	•				American Dream Title LLC	540-903-1481 or 804-994-0245	•	•	•	
						Fact Finders Ltd	866-672-0666	•	•	•	
•	•	•	•	•		Greater Richmond Abstract & Title Inc	804-266-2101	•	•	•	
•	•					Innovative Enterprises Inc	888-777-9435				
						Johnson Title & Abstract Inc	540-368-8104	•	•	•	
	•					Margene Libertino Inc	540-785-9930	•	•	•	
•	•	•	•	•		UCC Retrievals, Inc	804-559-5919	•		•	

CR	CV	PR	US	BK	←COURTS	CARROLL	RECORDER→	UC	RE	TX	VS
•	•					Innovative Enterprises Inc	888-777-9435				
						New Century Title	276-223-1207		•	•	

CR	CV	PR	US	BK	←COURTS	CHARLES CITY	RECORDER→	UC	RE	TX	VS
•	•	•	•	•		Greater Richmond Abstract & Title Inc	804-266-2101	•	•	•	
•	•					Innovative Enterprises Inc	888-777-9435				
•	•	•	•	•		UCC Retrievals, Inc	804-559-5919	•		•	

CR	CV	PR	US	BK	←COURTS	CHARLOTTE	RECORDER→	UC	RE	TX	VS
•	•					Innovative Enterprises Inc	888-777-9435				

CR	CV	PR	US	BK	←COURTS	CHARLOTTESVILLE	RECORDER→	UC	RE	TX	VS
	•	•				Blue Ridge Title, Div of Chicago Title Ins Co	434-295-7196	•	•	•	
						Fact Finders Ltd	866-672-0666	•	•	•	
•	•					Innovative Enterprises Inc	888-777-9435				

CR	CV	PR	US	BK	←COURTS	CHESAPEAKE	RECORDER→	UC	RE	TX	VS
•	•		•	•		Data-Tec Research Inc	757-424-3606; Fax- same				
•	•		•	•		Dominion Record Search	757-566-8233	•	•	•	•
•	•					Innovative Enterprises Inc	888-777-9435				
	•		•	•		Research & Retrieval Services Inc	757-463-0030	•	•	•	

CR	CV	PR	US	BK	←COURTS	CHESTERFIELD	RECORDER→	UC	RE	TX	VS
•	•	•				Abstracts by Starkey Inc	804-305-6022	•	•	•	•
•	•	•				Dominion Abstract & Title Agency	804-794-9037	•	•	•	
•	•	•	•	•		Greater Richmond Abstract & Title Inc	804-266-2101	•	•	•	
•	•					Innovative Enterprises Inc	888-777-9435				
•	•	•	•	•		The Pettit Company	800-752-6158	•	•	•	
•	•	•	•	•		UCC Retrievals, Inc	804-559-5919	•		•	

CR	CV	PR	US	BK	←COURTS	CLARKE	RECORDER→	UC	RE	TX	VS
						Direct Title Solutions Inc	540-450-0740	•	•	•	
						Estate Title & Escrow Inc	703-385-5850	•	•	•	
•	•					Innovative Enterprises Inc	888-777-9435				
	•	•				Shenandoah Title Services Inc	540-667-1393	•	•	•	

CR	CV	PR	US	BK	←COURTS	CLIFTON FORGE	RECORDER→	UC	RE	TX	VS
•	•					Innovative Enterprises Inc	888-777-9435				
•	•	•	•	•		Law Offices of Joan C Singleton	540-839-5009	•	•	•	•

CR	CV	PR	US	BK	←COURTS	COLONIAL HEIGHTS	RECORDER→	UC	RE	TX	VS
•	•	•				Abstracts by Starkey Inc	804-305-6022	•	•	•	•
•	•	•	•	•		Greater Richmond Abstract & Title Inc	804-266-2101	•	•	•	
•	•					Innovative Enterprises Inc	888-777-9435				
•	•	•	•	•		The Pettit Company	800-752-6158	•	•	•	

CR	CV	PR	US	BK			UC	RE	TX	VS
•	•	•	•	•	UCC Retrievals, Inc	804-559-5919	•		•	

CR	CV	PR	US	BK	←Courts COVINGTON	Recorder→	UC	RE	TX	VS
•	•				Innovative Enterprises Inc	888-777-9435				
•	•	•	•	•	Law Offices of Joan C Singleton	540-839-5009	•	•	•	•

CR	CV	PR	US	BK	←Courts CRAIG	Recorder→	UC	RE	TX	VS
•	•				Innovative Enterprises Inc	888-777-9435				
•	•	•			Diana L Johnson	540-921-1958	•	•	•	•

CR	CV	PR	US	BK	←Courts CULPEPER	Recorder→	UC	RE	TX	VS
•	•	•			American Dream Title LLC	540-903-1481 or 804-994-0245	•	•	•	
					Atlantic Title & Research	540-439-1800	•	•	•	
	•				E Title & Abstract LLC	540-727-0515	•	•	•	
					Fact Finders Ltd	866-672-0666	•	•	•	
•	•				Innovative Enterprises Inc	888-777-9435				
					Raines Record Research Inc	540-937-2005		•		•

CR	CV	PR	US	BK	←Courts CUMBERLAND	Recorder→	UC	RE	TX	VS
•	•				Innovative Enterprises Inc	888-777-9435				
•	•	•	•	•	UCC Retrievals, Inc	804-559-5919	•		•	

CR	CV	PR	US	BK	←Courts DANVILLE	Recorder→	UC	RE	TX	VS
•	•				Innovative Enterprises Inc	888-777-9435				

CR	CV	PR	US	BK	←Courts DICKENSON	Recorder→	UC	RE	TX	VS
•	•				Innovative Enterprises Inc	888-777-9435				

CR	CV	PR	US	BK	←Courts DINWIDDIE	Recorder→	UC	RE	TX	VS
•	•	•			Abstracts by Starkey Inc	804-305-6022	•	•	•	•
•	•	•	•	•	Greater Richmond Abstract & Title Inc	804-266-2101	•	•	•	
•	•				Innovative Enterprises Inc	888-777-9435				
•	•	•	•	•	UCC Retrievals, Inc	804-559-5919	•		•	

CR	CV	PR	US	BK	←Courts EMPORIA	Recorder→	UC	RE	TX	VS
•	•				Innovative Enterprises Inc	888-777-9435				

CR	CV	PR	US	BK	←Courts ESSEX	Recorder→	UC	RE	TX	VS
•	•				Innovative Enterprises Inc	888-777-9435				
•	•	•	•	•	Investigative Consultants Inc	202-237-1500	•	•	•	•
•	•	•	•	•	UCC Retrievals, Inc	804-559-5919	•		•	

CR	CV	PR	US	BK	←Courts FAIRFAX	Recorder→	UC	RE	TX	VS
•	•		•	•	ABA Services	720-344-1259	•	•	•	
•	•	•	•	•	ALIASS [SOP]	800-747-0820	•	•	•	•
•	•	•	•	•	Alliance Legal Services Inc [SOP]	703-644-8571	•	•	•	•
					Amarisearch Inc	703-267-6827	•	•	•	
					Atlantic Title & Research	540-439-1800	•	•	•	
•	•	•	•	•	CorpAssist Inc - DC Office	800-438-2996	•	•	•	•
					Direct Title Solutions Inc	540-450-0740	•	•	•	
•	•	•	•	•	Docu-Search of Washington DC	202-737-5707	•	•	•	•
•	•	•	•	•	Enterprise Title Company Inc	703-351-8066	•	•	•	•
					Estate Title & Escrow Inc	703-385-5850	•	•	•	
		•			Examiner's Title LC	703-491-0805	•	•		
	•	•	•	•	Federal Research LLC [SOP]	800-846-3190	•	•	•	•
•	•	•	•	•	Fitzgerald Servaites Inc	202-257-7775	•	•	•	•
•	•				For The Record In Virginia	703-862-9105			•	
•	•	•	•	•	Hylind Search Company Inc (Maryland) [SOP]	888-449-5463	•	•	•	•
•	•	•	•	•	Infoline Inc	888-284-4581	•	•	•	•
•	•	•	•	•	InfoNation Inc - Virginia [SOP]	888-346-9090	•	•	•	
•	•				Innovative Enterprises Inc	888-777-9435				
•	•	•	•	•	Investigative Consultants Inc	202-237-1500	•	•	•	•

CR	CV	PR	US	BK	←Courts	Recorder→	UC	RE	TX	VS
•	•	•	•	•	Mohr Information Services LLC	540-678-8775	•	•	•	
•	•		•	•	National Background Investigations Inc	800-798-0079			•	
•	•	•	•	•	Security Consultants Inc	202-686-3953			•	•
•	•	•	•	•	Washington Document Service (DC)	800-728-5201	•	•	•	•

CR	CV	PR	US	BK	←Courts **Fairfax City**	Recorder→	UC	RE	TX	VS
•	•	•	•	•	ALIASS [SOP]	800-747-0820	•	•	•	•
•	•	•	•	•	CorpAssist Inc - DC Office	800-438-2996	•	•	•	•
					Direct Title Solutions Inc	540-450-0740	•	•	•	
•	•				For The Record In Virginia	703-862-9105			•	
•	•				Innovative Enterprises Inc	888-777-9435				
•	•	•	•	•	Investigative Consultants Inc	202-237-1500	•	•	•	•
•	•	•	•	•	Mohr Information Services LLC	540-678-8775	•	•	•	
•	•		•	•	National Background Investigations Inc	800-798-0079			•	

CR	CV	PR	US	BK	←Courts **Falls Church**	Recorder→	UC	RE	TX	VS
					Direct Title Solutions Inc	540-450-0740	•	•	•	
•	•	•	•	•	Enterprise Title Company Inc	703-351-8066	•	•	•	•
•	•				Innovative Enterprises Inc	888-777-9435				
•	•		•	•	National Background Investigations Inc	800-798-0079			•	

CR	CV	PR	US	BK	←Courts **Fauquier**	Recorder→	UC	RE	TX	VS
•	•	•	•	•	ALIASS [SOP]	800-747-0820	•	•	•	•
					Amarisearch Inc	703-267-6827	•	•	•	
					American Dream Title LLC	540-903-1481 or 804-994-0245	•	•	•	
					Atlantic Title & Research	540-439-1800	•	•	•	
	•				E Title & Abstract LLC	540-727-0515	•	•	•	
					Estate Title & Escrow Inc	703-385-5850	•	•	•	
		•			Examiner's Title LC	703-491-0805	•	•		
					Fact Finders Ltd	866-672-0666	•	•	•	
•	•	•	•	•	InfoNation Inc - Virginia [SOP]	888-346-9090	•	•	•	
•	•				Innovative Enterprises Inc	888-777-9435				
					Raines Record Research Inc	540-937-2005		•		•

CR	CV	PR	US	BK	←Courts **Floyd**	Recorder→	UC	RE	TX	VS
•	•	•			Deeds Inc	540-563-5699	•	•	•	
•	•				Innovative Enterprises Inc	888-777-9435				
•	•	•			Diana L Johnson	540-921-1958	•	•	•	•

CR	CV	PR	US	BK	←Courts **Fluvanna**	Recorder→	UC	RE	TX	VS
	•	•			Blue Ridge Title, Div of Chicago Title Ins Co	434-295-7196	•	•	•	
					Fact Finders Ltd	866-672-0666	•	•	•	
•	•				Innovative Enterprises Inc	888-777-9435				
•	•	•	•	•	UCC Retrievals, Inc	804-559-5919	•		•	

CR	CV	PR	US	BK	←Courts **Franklin**	Recorder→	UC	RE	TX	VS
•	•	•			Deeds Inc	540-563-5699	•	•	•	
•	•				Innovative Enterprises Inc	888-777-9435				

CR	CV	PR	US	BK	←Courts **Franklin City**	Recorder→	UC	RE	TX	VS
•	•				Innovative Enterprises Inc	888-777-9435				

CR	CV	PR	US	BK	←Courts **Frederick**	Recorder→	UC	RE	TX	VS
					Direct Title Solutions Inc	540-450-0740	•	•	•	
•	•				Innovative Enterprises Inc	888-777-9435				
•	•	•	•	•	Investigative Consultants Inc	202-237-1500	•	•	•	•
•	•	•	•	•	Mohr Information Services LLC	540-678-8775	•	•	•	
	•	•			Shenandoah Title Services Inc	540-667-1393	•	•	•	

CR	CV	PR	US	BK	←Courts	Fredericksburg	Recorder→	UC	RE	TX	VS
						Amarisearch Inc	703-267-6827	•	•	•	
						Amcor Title LLC	540-752-2246	•	•	•	
•	•	•				American Dream Title LLC	540-903-1481 or 804-994-0245	•	•	•	
						Fact Finders Ltd	866-672-0666	•	•	•	
•	•					Innovative Enterprises Inc	888-777-9435				
						Johnson Title & Abstract Inc	540-368-8104	•	•	•	
	•					Margene Libertino Inc	540-785-9930	•	•	•	

CR	CV	PR	US	BK	←Courts	Galax	Recorder→	UC	RE	TX	VS
•	•					Innovative Enterprises Inc	888-777-9435				

CR	CV	PR	US	BK	←Courts	Giles	Recorder→	UC	RE	TX	VS
•	•					Innovative Enterprises Inc	888-777-9435				

CR	CV	PR	US	BK	←Courts	Gloucester	Recorder→	UC	RE	TX	VS
						Hixson Enterprises	757-898-9865; cell- 876-0018	•	•	•	
•	•					Innovative Enterprises Inc	888-777-9435				
•	•	•	•	•		UCC Retrievals, Inc	804-559-5919	•		•	

CR	CV	PR	US	BK	←Courts	Goochland	Recorder→	UC	RE	TX	VS
•	•	•				Abstracts by Starkey Inc	804-305-6022	•	•	•	•
•	•	•	•	•		Greater Richmond Abstract & Title Inc	804-266-2101	•	•	•	
•	•					Innovative Enterprises Inc	888-777-9435				
•	•	•	•	•		UCC Retrievals, Inc	804-559-5919	•		•	

CR	CV	PR	US	BK	←Courts	Grayson	Recorder→	UC	RE	TX	VS
•	•					Innovative Enterprises Inc	888-777-9435				
						New Century Title	276-223-1207		•	•	

CR	CV	PR	US	BK	←Courts	Greene	Recorder→	UC	RE	TX	VS
	•	•				Blue Ridge Title, Div of Chicago Title Ins Co	434-295-7196	•	•	•	
	•					E Title & Abstract LLC	540-727-0515	•	•	•	
						Fact Finders Ltd	866-672-0666	•	•	•	
•	•					Innovative Enterprises Inc	888-777-9435				

CR	CV	PR	US	BK	←Courts	Greensville	Recorder→	UC	RE	TX	VS
•	•					Innovative Enterprises Inc	888-777-9435				

CR	CV	PR	US	BK	←Courts	Halifax	Recorder→	UC	RE	TX	VS
•	•					Innovative Enterprises Inc	888-777-9435				

CR	CV	PR	US	BK	←Courts	Hampton	Recorder→	UC	RE	TX	VS
•	•		•	•		Data-Tec Research Inc	757-424-3606; Fax- same				
•	•		•	•		Dominion Record Search	757-566-8233	•	•	•	•
•	•					Innovative Enterprises Inc	888-777-9435				
•	•	•	•	•		Nikki A O'Connell	757-877-8469	•	•	•	
	•		•	•		Research & Retrieval Services Inc	757-463-0030	•	•	•	

CR	CV	PR	US	BK	←Courts	Hanover	Recorder→	UC	RE	TX	VS
•	•	•				Abstracts by Starkey Inc	804-305-6022	•	•	•	•
						Amarisearch Inc	703-267-6827	•	•	•	
•	•	•				American Dream Title LLC	540-903-1481 or 804-994-0245	•	•	•	
•	•	•				Dominion Abstract & Title Agency	804-794-9037	•	•	•	
•	•	•	•	•		Greater Richmond Abstract & Title Inc	804-266-2101	•	•	•	
•	•					Innovative Enterprises Inc	888-777-9435				
•	•	•	•	•		The Pettit Company	800-752-6158	•	•	•	
•	•	•	•	•		UCC Retrievals, Inc	804-559-5919	•		•	

CR	CV	PR	US	BK	←Courts	Harrisonburg	Recorder→	UC	RE	TX	VS
•	•					Innovative Enterprises Inc	888-777-9435				
•	•	•	•	•		Doris Pye [SOP]	540-433 8134	•	•	•	•

CR	CV	PR	US	BK	←Courts	HENRICO	Recorder→	UC	RE	TX	VS
•	•	•			Abstracts by Starkey Inc		804-305-6022	•	•	•	•
					Amarisearch Inc		703-267-6827	•	•	•	
•	•	•			Dominion Abstract & Title Agency		804-794-9037	•	•	•	
•	•	•	•	•	Greater Richmond Abstract & Title Inc		804-266-2101	•	•	•	
•	•				Innovative Enterprises Inc		888-777-9435				
•	•	•	•	•	The Pettit Company		800-752-6158	•	•	•	
•	•	•	•	•	UCC Retrievals, Inc		804-559-5919	•		•	

CR	CV	PR	US	BK	←Courts	HENRY	Recorder→	UC	RE	TX	VS
•	•				Innovative Enterprises Inc		888-777-9435				

CR	CV	PR	US	BK	←Courts	HIGHLAND	Recorder→	UC	RE	TX	VS
•	•				Innovative Enterprises Inc		888-777-9435				
•	•	•	•	•	Law Offices of Joan C Singleton		540-839-5009	•	•	•	•

CR	CV	PR	US	BK	←Courts	HOPEWELL	Recorder→	UC	RE	TX	VS
•	•	•			Abstracts by Starkey Inc		804-305-6022	•	•	•	•
•	•	•	•	•	Greater Richmond Abstract & Title Inc		804-266-2101	•	•	•	
•	•				Innovative Enterprises Inc		888-777-9435				
•	•	•	•	•	The Pettit Company		800-752-6158	•	•	•	
•	•	•	•	•	UCC Retrievals, Inc		804-559-5919	•		•	

CR	CV	PR	US	BK	←Courts	ISLE OF WIGHT	Recorder→	UC	RE	TX	VS
					Carr Title		757-647-7873				
•	•				Innovative Enterprises Inc		888-777-9435				
	•		•	•	Research & Retrieval Services Inc		757-463-0030	•	•	•	

CR	CV	PR	US	BK	←Courts	JAMES CITY	Recorder→	UC	RE	TX	VS
•	•		•	•	Data-Tec Research Inc		757-424-3606; Fax- same				
•	•		•	•	Dominion Record Search		757-566-8233	•	•	•	•
					Hixson Enterprises		757-898-9865; cell- 876-0018	•	•	•	
•	•				Innovative Enterprises Inc		888-777-9435				
•	•	•	•	•	Nikki A O'Connell		757-877-8469	•	•	•	
	•		•	•	Research & Retrieval Services Inc		757-463-0030	•	•	•	

CR	CV	PR	US	BK	←Courts	KING AND QUEEN	Recorder→	UC	RE	TX	VS
•	•				Innovative Enterprises Inc		888-777-9435				
•	•	•	•	•	UCC Retrievals, Inc		804-559-5919	•		•	

CR	CV	PR	US	BK	←Courts	KING GEORGE	Recorder→	UC	RE	TX	VS
•	•	•			American Dream Title LLC		540-903-1481 or 804-994-0245	•	•	•	
					Fact Finders Ltd		866-672-0666	•	•	•	
•	•				Innovative Enterprises Inc		888-777-9435				
					Johnson Title & Abstract Inc		540-368-8104	•	•	•	
	•				Margene Libertino Inc		540-785-9930	•	•	•	
•	•	•	•	•	UCC Retrievals, Inc		804-559-5919	•		•	

CR	CV	PR	US	BK	←Courts	KING WILLIAM	Recorder→	UC	RE	TX	VS
•	•	•			Abstracts by Starkey Inc		804-305-6022	•	•	•	•
•	•	•	•	•	Greater Richmond Abstract & Title Inc		804-266-2101	•	•	•	
•	•				Innovative Enterprises Inc		888-777-9435				
•	•	•	•	•	UCC Retrievals, Inc		804-559-5919	•		•	

CR	CV	PR	US	BK	←Courts	LANCASTER	Recorder→	UC	RE	TX	VS
•	•				Innovative Enterprises Inc		888-777-9435				

CR	CV	PR	US	BK	←Courts	LEE	Recorder→	UC	RE	TX	VS
•	•				Innovative Enterprises Inc		888-777-9435				

CR	CV	PR	US	BK	←Courts	LEXINGTON	Recorder→	UC	RE	TX	VS
•	•				Innovative Enterprises Inc		888-777-9435				

CR	CV	PR	US	BK	←COURTS LOUDOUN	RECORDER→	UC	RE	TX	VS
•	•		•	•	ABA Services	720-344-1259	•	•	•	
•	•	•	•	•	ALIASS [SOP]	800-747-0820	•	•	•	•
					Amarisearch Inc	703-267-6827	•	•	•	
					Atlantic Title & Research	540-439-1800	•	•	•	
•	•	•	•	•	CorpAssist Inc - DC Office	800-438-2996	•	•	•	•
					Direct Title Solutions Inc	540-450-0740	•	•	•	
•	•	•	•	•	Enterprise Title Company Inc	703-351-8066	•	•	•	•
					Estate Title & Escrow Inc	703-385-5850	•	•	•	
		•			Examiner's Title LC	703-491-0805	•	•		
	•	•	•	•	Federal Research LLC [SOP]	800-846-3190	•	•	•	•
•	•	•	•	•	Fitzgerald Servaites Inc	202-257-7775	•	•	•	•
•	•	•	•	•	Infoline Inc	888-284-4581	•	•	•	•
•	•	•	•	•	InfoNation Inc - Virginia [SOP]	888-346-9090	•	•	•	
•	•				Innovative Enterprises Inc	888-777-9435				
•	•	•	•	•	Mohr Information Services LLC	540-678-8775	•	•	•	

CR	CV	PR	US	BK	←COURTS LOUISA	RECORDER→	UC	RE	TX	VS
•	•	•			Abstracts by Starkey Inc	804-305-6022	•	•	•	•
	•	•			Blue Ridge Title, Div of Chicago Title Ins Co	434-295-7196	•	•	•	
	•				E Title & Abstract LLC	540-727-0515	•	•	•	
					Fact Finders Ltd	866-672-0666	•	•	•	
•	•				Innovative Enterprises Inc	888-777-9435				
					Johnson Title & Abstract Inc	540-368-8104	•	•	•	
•	•	•	•	•	UCC Retrievals, Inc	804-559-5919	•		•	

CR	CV	PR	US	BK	←COURTS LUNENBURG	RECORDER→	UC	RE	TX	VS
•	•				Innovative Enterprises Inc	888-777-9435				

CR	CV	PR	US	BK	←COURTS LYNCHBURG	RECORDER→	UC	RE	TX	VS
•	•				Innovative Enterprises Inc	888-777-9435				

CR	CV	PR	US	BK	←COURTS MADISON	RECORDER→	UC	RE	TX	VS
	•				E Title & Abstract LLC	540-727-0515	•	•	•	
					Fact Finders Ltd	866-672-0666	•	•	•	
•	•				Innovative Enterprises Inc	888-777-9435				

CR	CV	PR	US	BK	←COURTS MANASSAS	RECORDER→	UC	RE	TX	VS
•	•	•	•	•	CorpAssist Inc - DC Office	800-438-2996	•	•	•	•
					Direct Title Solutions Inc	540-450-0740	•	•	•	
•	•				Innovative Enterprises Inc	888-777-9435				
•	•	•	•	•	Investigative Consultants Inc	202-237-1500	•	•	•	•

CR	CV	PR	US	BK	←COURTS MANASSAS PARK	RECORDER→	UC	RE	TX	VS
					Direct Title Solutions Inc	540-450-0740	•	•	•	
•	•				Innovative Enterprises Inc	888-777-9435				
•	•	•	•	•	Investigative Consultants Inc	202-237-1500	•	•	•	•

CR	CV	PR	US	BK	←COURTS MARTINSVILLE	RECORDER→	UC	RE	TX	VS
•	•				Innovative Enterprises Inc	888-777-9435				

CR	CV	PR	US	BK	←COURTS MATHEWS	RECORDER→	UC	RE	TX	VS
					Hixson Enterprises	757-898-9865; cell- 876-0018	•	•	•	
•	•				Innovative Enterprises Inc	888-777-9435				
•	•	•	•	•	UCC Retrievals, Inc	804-559-5919	•		•	

CR	CV	PR	US	BK	←COURTS MECKLENBURG	RECORDER→	UC	RE	TX	VS
•	•				Innovative Enterprises Inc	888-777-9435				

CR	CV	PR	US	BK	←COURTS MIDDLESEX	RECORDER→	UC	RE	TX	VS
•	•				Innovative Enterprises Inc	888-777-9435				

CR	CV	PR	US	BK	←Courts		Recorder→	UC	RE	TX	VS
•	•	•	•	•	UCC Retrievals, Inc		804-559-5919	•		•	
CR	**CV**	**PR**	**US**	**BK**	**←Courts**	**Montgomery**	**Recorder→**	**UC**	**RE**	**TX**	**VS**
•	•	•			Deeds Inc		540-563-5699	•	•	•	
	•	•	•	•	Federal Research LLC [SOP]		800-846-3190	•	•	•	•
•	•				Innovative Enterprises Inc		888-777-9435				
•	•	•			Diana L Johnson		540-921-1958	•	•	•	•
CR	**CV**	**PR**	**US**	**BK**	**←Courts**	**Nelson**	**Recorder→**	**UC**	**RE**	**TX**	**VS**
•	•	•			Berry & Maddox		434-263-4886	•	•	•	•
	•	•			Blue Ridge Title, Div of Chicago Title Ins Co		434-295-7196	•	•	•	
•	•				Innovative Enterprises Inc		888-777-9435				
CR	**CV**	**PR**	**US**	**BK**	**←Courts**	**New Kent**	**Recorder→**	**UC**	**RE**	**TX**	**VS**
•	•	•			Abstracts by Starkey Inc		804-305-6022	•	•	•	•
•	•	•	•	•	Greater Richmond Abstract & Title Inc		804-266-2101	•	•	•	
					Hixson Enterprises		757-898-9865; cell- 876-0018	•	•	•	
•	•				Innovative Enterprises Inc		888-777-9435				
•	•	•	•	•	UCC Retrievals, Inc		804-559-5919	•		•	
CR	**CV**	**PR**	**US**	**BK**	**←Courts**	**Newport News**	**Recorder→**	**UC**	**RE**	**TX**	**VS**
•	•		•	•	Data-Tec Research Inc		757-424-3606; Fax- same				
•	•		•	•	Dominion Record Search		757-566-8233	•	•	•	•
•	•				Innovative Enterprises Inc		888-777-9435				
•	•	•	•	•	Nikki A O'Connell		757-877-8469	•	•	•	
	•		•	•	Research & Retrieval Services Inc		757-463-0030	•	•	•	
CR	**CV**	**PR**	**US**	**BK**	**←Courts**	**Norfolk**	**Recorder→**	**UC**	**RE**	**TX**	**VS**
•	•		•	•	Data-Tec Research Inc		757-424-3606; Fax- same				
•	•		•	•	Dominion Record Search		757-566-8233	•	•	•	•
•	•				Innovative Enterprises Inc		888-777-9435				
	•		•	•	Research & Retrieval Services Inc		757-463-0030	•	•	•	
CR	**CV**	**PR**	**US**	**BK**	**←Courts**	**Northampton**	**Recorder→**	**UC**	**RE**	**TX**	**VS**
•	•	•			Judith Ayres		757-336-5313	•	•	•	•
•	•				Innovative Enterprises Inc		888-777-9435				
CR	**CV**	**PR**	**US**	**BK**	**←Courts**	**Northumberland**	**Recorder→**	**UC**	**RE**	**TX**	**VS**
					Innovative Enterprises Inc		888-777-9435				
CR	**CV**	**PR**	**US**	**BK**	**←Courts**	**Norton**	**Recorder→**	**UC**	**RE**	**TX**	**VS**
•	•				Innovative Enterprises Inc		888-777-9435				
CR	**CV**	**PR**	**US**	**BK**	**←Courts**	**Nottoway**	**Recorder→**	**UC**	**RE**	**TX**	**VS**
•	•				Innovative Enterprises Inc		888-777-9435				
•	•	•	•	•	UCC Retrievals, Inc		804-559-5919	•		•	
CR	**CV**	**PR**	**US**	**BK**	**←Courts**	**Orange**	**Recorder→**	**UC**	**RE**	**TX**	**VS**
•	•	•			American Dream Title LLC		540-903-1481 or 804-994-0245	•	•	•	
	•				E Title & Abstract LLC		540-727-0515	•	•	•	
					Estate Title & Escrow Inc		703-385-5850	•	•	•	
					Fact Finders Ltd		866-672-0666	•	•	•	
•	•				Innovative Enterprises Inc		888-777-9435				
					Johnson Title & Abstract Inc		540-368-8104	•	•	•	
CR	**CV**	**PR**	**US**	**BK**	**←Courts**	**Page**	**Recorder→**	**UC**	**RE**	**TX**	**VS**
					Fact Finders Ltd		866-672-0666	•	•	•	
•	•				Innovative Enterprises Inc		888-777-9435				
	•	•			Shenandoah Title Services Inc		540-667-1393	•	•	•	
CR	**CV**	**PR**	**US**	**BK**	**←Courts**	**Patrick**	**Recorder→**	**UC**	**RE**	**TX**	**VS**
•	•				Innovative Enterprises Inc		888-777-9435				

CR	CV	PR	US	BK	←Courts	Petersburg	Recorder→	UC	RE	TX	VS
•	•	•			Abstracts by Starkey Inc		804-305-6022	•	•	•	•
•	•	•	•	•	Greater Richmond Abstract & Title Inc		804-266-2101	•	•	•	
•	•				Innovative Enterprises Inc		888-777-9435				
•	•	•	•	•	The Pettit Company		800-752-6158	•	•	•	
•	•	•	•	•	UCC Retrievals, Inc		804-559-5919	•		•	

CR	CV	PR	US	BK	←Courts	Pittsylvania	Recorder→	UC	RE	TX	VS
•	•				Innovative Enterprises Inc		888-777-9435				

CR	CV	PR	US	BK	←Courts	Poquoson	Recorder→	UC	RE	TX	VS
•	•		•	•	Dominion Record Search		757-566-8233	•	•	•	•
•	•				Innovative Enterprises Inc		888-777-9435				

CR	CV	PR	US	BK	←Courts	Portsmouth	Recorder→	UC	RE	TX	VS
•	•		•	•	Data-Tec Research Inc		757-424-3606; Fax- same				
•	•				Innovative Enterprises Inc		888-777-9435				
	•		•	•	Research & Retrieval Services Inc		757-463-0030	•	•	•	

CR	CV	PR	US	BK	←Courts	Powhatan	Recorder→	UC	RE	TX	VS
•	•	•			Abstracts by Starkey Inc		804-305-6022	•	•	•	•
•	•	•			Dominion Abstract & Title Agency		804-794-9037	•	•	•	
•	•	•	•	•	Greater Richmond Abstract & Title Inc		804-266-2101	•	•	•	
•	•				Innovative Enterprises Inc		888-777-9435				
•	•	•	•	•	The Pettit Company		800-752-6158	•	•	•	
•	•	•	•	•	UCC Retrievals, Inc		804-559-5919	•		•	

CR	CV	PR	US	BK	←Courts	Prince Edward	Recorder→	UC	RE	TX	VS
•	•				Innovative Enterprises Inc		888-777-9435				

CR	CV	PR	US	BK	←Courts	Prince George	Recorder→	UC	RE	TX	VS
•	•	•			Abstracts by Starkey Inc		804-305-6022	•	•	•	•
	•	•	•	•	Federal Research LLC [SOP]		800-846-3190	•	•	•	•
•	•	•	•	•	Greater Richmond Abstract & Title Inc		804-266-2101	•	•	•	
•	•				Innovative Enterprises Inc		888-777-9435				
•	•	•	•	•	UCC Retrievals, Inc		804-559-5919	•		•	

CR	CV	PR	US	BK	←Courts	Prince William	Recorder→	UC	RE	TX	VS
•	•		•	•	ABA Services		720-344-1259	•	•	•	
•	•	•	•	•	ALIASS [SOP]		800-747-0820	•	•	•	•
					Amarisearch Inc		703-267-6827	•	•	•	
					Atlantic Title & Research		540-439-1800	•	•	•	
•	•	•	•		Bob Lessemun Investigations Inc [SOP]		703-580-6611	•	•	•	•
•	•	•	•	•	CorpAssist Inc - DC Office		800-438-2996	•	•	•	•
					Direct Title Solutions Inc		540-450-0740	•	•	•	
•	•	•	•	•	Enterprise Title Company Inc		703-351-8066	•	•	•	•
					Estate Title & Escrow Inc		703-385-5850	•	•	•	
		•			Examiner's Title LC		703-491-0805	•	•		
	•	•	•	•	Federal Research LLC [SOP]		800-846-3190	•	•	•	•
•	•	•	•	•	Fitzgerald Servaites Inc		202-257-7775	•	•	•	•
•	•	•	•	•	Infoline Inc		888-284-4581	•	•	•	•
•	•	•	•	•	InfoNation Inc - Virginia [SOP]		888-346-9090	•	•	•	
•	•				Innovative Enterprises Inc		888-777-9435				
•	•	•	•	•	Investigative Consultants Inc		202-237-1500	•	•	•	•
•	•				Investigative Research Specialists LLC [SOP]		703-753-4468				
•	•	•	•	•	Mohr Information Services LLC		540-678-8775	•	•	•	
•	•		•	•	National Background Investigations Inc		800-798-0079			•	
•	•	•	•	•	Security Consultants Inc		202-686-3953			•	•

CR	CV	PR	US	BK	←Courts	Pulaski	Recorder→	UC	RE	TX	VS
•	•				Innovative Enterprises Inc		888-777-9435				
•	•	•			Diana L Johnson		540-921-1958	•	•	•	•

CR	CV	PR	US	BK	←Courts	Radford	Recorder→	UC	RE	TX	VS
•	•				Innovative Enterprises Inc		888-777-9435				
•	•	•			Diana L Johnson		540-921-1958	•	•	•	•

CR	CV	PR	US	BK	←Courts	Rappahannock	Recorder→	UC	RE	TX	VS
•	•				Innovative Enterprises Inc		888-777-9435				
					Raines Record Research Inc		540-937-2005		•		•

CR	CV	PR	US	BK	←Courts	Richmond	Recorder→	UC	RE	TX	VS
•	•				Innovative Enterprises Inc		888-777-9435				
•	•				Innovative Enterprises Inc		888-777-9435				
•	•		•	•	WestLaw CourtEXPRESS (DC) [SOP]		800-542-3320				

CR	CV	PR	US	BK	←Courts	Richmond City	Recorder→	UC	RE	TX	VS
•	•	•			Abstracts by Starkey Inc		804-305-6022	•	•	•	•
•	•	•			Dominion Abstract & Title Agency		804-794-9037	•	•	•	
	•	•	•	•	Federal Research LLC [SOP]		800-846-3190	•	•	•	•
•	•	•	•	•	Greater Richmond Abstract & Title Inc		804-266-2101	•	•	•	
•	•	•	•	•	The Pettit Company		800-752-6158	•	•	•	
•	•	•	•	•	UCC Retrievals, Inc		804-559-5919	•		•	
•	•	•	•	•	Washington Document Service (DC)		800-728-5201	•	•	•	•

CR	CV	PR	US	BK	←Courts	Roanoke	Recorder→	UC	RE	TX	VS
		•			Betsy Biesenbach		540-982-7892	•	•	•	
•	•	•			Deeds Inc		540-563-5699	•	•	•	
•	•				Innovative Enterprises Inc		888-777-9435				
•	•		•	•	Securitec Screening Solutions Inc		540-725-1571				

CR	CV	PR	US	BK	←Courts	Roanoke City	Recorder→	UC	RE	TX	VS
		•			Betsy Biesenbach		540-982-7892	•	•	•	
•	•	•			Deeds Inc		540-563-5699	•	•	•	
•	•				Innovative Enterprises Inc		888-777-9435				
•	•		•	•	Securitec Screening Solutions Inc		540-725-1571				

CR	CV	PR	US	BK	←Courts	Rockbridge	Recorder→	UC	RE	TX	VS
•	•				Innovative Enterprises Inc		888-777-9435				

CR	CV	PR	US	BK	←Courts	Rockingham	Recorder→	UC	RE	TX	VS
•	•				Innovative Enterprises Inc		888-777-9435				
•	•	•	•	•	Doris Pye [SOP]		540-433 8134	•	•	•	•

CR	CV	PR	US	BK	←Courts	Russell	Recorder→	UC	RE	TX	VS
•	•				Innovative Enterprises Inc		888-777-9435				

CR	CV	PR	US	BK	←Courts	Salem	Recorder→	UC	RE	TX	VS
		•			Betsy Biesenbach		540-982-7892	•	•	•	
•	•	•			Deeds Inc		540-563-5699	•	•	•	
•	•				Innovative Enterprises Inc		888-777-9435				
•	•		•	•	Securitec Screening Solutions Inc		540-725-1571				

CR	CV	PR	US	BK	←Courts	Scott	Recorder→	UC	RE	TX	VS
•	•				Innovative Enterprises Inc		888-777-9435				

CR	CV	PR	US	BK	←Courts	Shenandoah	Recorder→	UC	RE	TX	VS
•	•				Innovative Enterprises Inc		888-777-9435				
	•	•			Shenandoah Title Services Inc		540-667-1393	•	•	•	

CR	CV	PR	US	BK	←Courts	**SMYTH**	Recorder→	UC	RE	TX	VS
•	•				Innovative Enterprises Inc		888-777-9435				
					New Century Title		276-223-1207		•	•	

CR	CV	PR	US	BK	←Courts	**SOUTH BOSTON**	Recorder→	UC	RE	TX	VS
•	•				Innovative Enterprises Inc		888-777-9435				

CR	CV	PR	US	BK	←Courts	**SOUTHAMPTON**	Recorder→	UC	RE	TX	VS
					Carr Title		757-647-7873				
•	•				Innovative Enterprises Inc		888-777-9435				
•	•	•	•	•	UCC Retrievals, Inc		804-559-5919	•		•	

CR	CV	PR	US	BK	←Courts	**SPOTSYLVANIA**	Recorder→	UC	RE	TX	VS
					Amarisearch Inc		703-267-6827	•	•	•	
					Amcor Title LLC		540-752-2246	•	•	•	
•	•	•			American Dream Title LLC		540-903-1481 or 804-994-0245	•	•	•	
	•				E Title & Abstract LLC		540-727-0515	•	•	•	
					Estate Title & Escrow Inc		703-385-5850	•	•	•	
					Fact Finders Ltd		866-672-0666	•	•	•	
•	•				Innovative Enterprises Inc		888-777-9435				
					Johnson Title & Abstract Inc		540-368-8104	•	•	•	
	•				Margene Libertino Inc		540-785-9930	•	•	•	

CR	CV	PR	US	BK	←Courts	**STAFFORD**	Recorder→	UC	RE	TX	VS
					Amarisearch Inc		703-267-6827	•	•	•	
					Amcor Title LLC		540-752-2246	•	•	•	
•	•	•			American Dream Title LLC		540-903-1481 or 804-994-0245	•	•	•	
					Atlantic Title & Research		540-439-1800	•	•	•	
•	•	•	•	•	Enterprise Title Company Inc		703-351-8066	•	•	•	•
					Estate Title & Escrow Inc		703-385-5850	•	•	•	
					Fact Finders Ltd		866-672-0666	•	•	•	
•	•	•	•	•	Fitzgerald Servaites Inc		202-257-7775	•	•	•	•
•	•				Innovative Enterprises Inc		888-777-9435				
					Johnson Title & Abstract Inc		540-368-8104	•	•	•	
	•				Margene Libertino Inc		540-785-9930	•	•	•	

CR	CV	PR	US	BK	←Courts	**STAUNTON**	Recorder→	UC	RE	TX	VS
•	•				Innovative Enterprises Inc		888-777-9435				

CR	CV	PR	US	BK	←Courts	**SUFFOLK**	Recorder→	UC	RE	TX	VS
•	•		•	•	Data-Tec Research Inc		757-424-3606; Fax- same				
•	•		•	•	Dominion Record Search		757-566-8233	•	•	•	•
•	•				Innovative Enterprises Inc		888-777-9435				
	•		•	•	Research & Retrieval Services Inc		757-463-0030	•	•	•	

CR	CV	PR	US	BK	←Courts	**SURRY**	Recorder→	UC	RE	TX	VS
					Carr Title		757-647-7873				
•	•				Innovative Enterprises Inc		888-777-9435				

CR	CV	PR	US	BK	←Courts	**SUSSEX**	Recorder→	UC	RE	TX	VS
•	•				Innovative Enterprises Inc		888-777-9435				
•	•	•	•	•	UCC Retrievals, Inc		804-559-5919	•		•	

CR	CV	PR	US	BK	←Courts	**TAZEWELL**	Recorder→	UC	RE	TX	VS
•	•				Innovative Enterprises Inc		888-777-9435				

CR	CV	PR	US	BK	←Courts	**VIRGINIA BEACH**	Recorder→	UC	RE	TX	VS
•	•		•	•	Data-Tec Research Inc		757-424-3606; Fax- same				
•	•		•	•	Dominion Record Search		757-566-8233	•	•	•	•
•	•				Innovative Enterprises Inc		888-777-9435				
	•		•	•	Research & Retrieval Services Inc		757-463-0030	•	•	•	

CR	CV	PR	US	BK	←COURTS	WARREN	RECORDER→	UC	RE	TX	VS
•	•	•	•	•	Enterprise Title Company Inc		703-351-8066	•	•	•	•
					Fact Finders Ltd		866-672-0666	•	•	•	
•	•				Innovative Enterprises Inc		888-777-9435				
	•	•			Shenandoah Title Services Inc		540-667-1393	•	•	•	

CR	CV	PR	US	BK	←COURTS	WASHINGTON	RECORDER→	UC	RE	TX	VS
•	•				Innovative Enterprises Inc		888-777-9435				

CR	CV	PR	US	BK	←COURTS	WAYNESBORO	RECORDER→	UC	RE	TX	VS
•	•				Innovative Enterprises Inc		888-777-9435				

CR	CV	PR	US	BK	←COURTS	WESTMORELAND	RECORDER→	UC	RE	TX	VS
•	•				Innovative Enterprises Inc		888-777-9435				
•	•	•	•	•	UCC Retrievals, Inc		804-559-5919	•		•	

CR	CV	PR	US	BK	←COURTS	WILLIAMSBURG	RECORDER→	UC	RE	TX	VS
•	•		•	•	Data-Tec Research Inc		757-424-3606; Fax- same				
•	•		•	•	Dominion Record Search		757-566-8233	•	•	•	•
					Hixson Enterprises		757-898-9865; cell- 876-0018	•	•	•	
•	•				Innovative Enterprises Inc		888-777-9435				
	•		•	•	Research & Retrieval Services Inc		757-463-0030	•	•	•	

CR	CV	PR	US	BK	←COURTS	WINCHESTER	RECORDER→	UC	RE	TX	VS
					Direct Title Solutions Inc		540-450-0740	•	•	•	
•	•				Innovative Enterprises Inc		888-777-9435				
•	•	•	•	•	Mohr Information Services LLC		540-678-8775	•	•	•	
	•	•			Shenandoah Title Services Inc		540-667-1393	•	•	•	

CR	CV	PR	US	BK	←COURTS	WISE	RECORDER→	UC	RE	TX	VS
•	•				Innovative Enterprises Inc		888-777-9435				

CR	CV	PR	US	BK	←COURTS	WYTHE	RECORDER→	UC	RE	TX	VS
•	•				Innovative Enterprises Inc		888-777-9435				
					New Century Title		276-223-1207		•	•	

CR	CV	PR	US	BK	←COURTS	YORK	RECORDER→	UC	RE	TX	VS
•	•		•	•	Data-Tec Research Inc		757-424-3606; Fax- same				
•	•		•	•	Dominion Record Search		757-566-8233	•	•	•	•
					Hixson Enterprises		757-898-9865; cell- 876-0018	•	•	•	
•	•				Innovative Enterprises Inc		888-777-9435				
•	•	•	•	•	Nikki A O'Connell		757-877-8469	•	•	•	
	•		•	•	Research & Retrieval Services Inc		757-463-0030	•	•	•	

Editor's Tip: This section of the directory is not organized to promote search firms that are statewide, regional, or national in coverage. A limited list of larger firms who are PRRN members is listed in the back of the book. Screening companies are included

An expanded resource of search firms, distributors, and screening firms is BRB Publication's website at www.brbpub.com. Click the "Find A Record Vendor" tab. Both sources contain information on firms that use online resources to obtain public record index information.

Virgin Islands

COURT RECORDS RETRIEVED — **CAPITAL - CHARLOTTE AMALIE** — **RECORDED RECORDS RETRIEVED**

CR	CV	PR	US	BK	←COURTS ST. CROIX RECORDER→	UC	RE	TX	VS
•	•	•	•	•	Dennis R Sheraw & Associates Inc [SOP]....800-967-6379	•	•	•	•
•	•		•	•	GPS & Associates - Florida....866-813-8131	•		•	•

CR	CV	PR	US	BK	←COURTS ST. JOHN RECORDER→	UC	RE	TX	VS
•	•	•	•	•	Dennis R Sheraw & Associates Inc [SOP]....800-967-6379	•	•	•	•
•	•		•	•	GPS & Associates - Florida....866-813-8131	•		•	•

CR	CV	PR	US	BK	←COURTS ST. THOMAS RECORDER→	UC	RE	TX	VS
•	•	•	•	•	Dennis R Sheraw & Associates Inc [SOP]....800-967-6379	•	•	•	•
•	•		•	•	GPS & Associates - Florida....866-813-8131	•		•	•

[SOP] = PERFORMS SERVICE OF PROCESS

Editor's Tip: Only Call a Retriever For the Records They Retrieve. If you call for a criminal record from a retriever who only does work at the recorder's office, then you are wasting your time and the retriever's time.

COURT RECORDS

CODE	GOVERNMENT AGENCY	TYPE OF INFORMATION
CR	Criminal Court	Municipal, county and state level criminal cases
CV	Civil Court	Municipal, county and state level civil cases
PR	Probate Court	Wills and estate cases
US	US District Court	Federal civil and criminal cases
BK	Bankruptcy Court	United States bankruptcy cases

COUNTY RECORDS - RECORDINGS

CODE	GOVERNMENT AGENCY	TYPE OF INFORMATION
UC	UCC Filing Office	Uniform Commercial Code and other personal property liens
RE	Real Estate Recording Office	Real property transactions and liens
TX	Tax Filing Office(s)	Federal and state tax liens, judgment liens
VS	Vital Records Office	Vital statistics—birth, death, marriage, divorce

Washington

COURT RECORDS RETRIEVED — CAPITAL - THURSTON COUNTY — RECORDED RECORDS RETRIEVED

CR	CV	PR	US	BK	←COURTS ADAMS	RECORDER→	UC	RE	TX	VS
	•				AM-PM Services [SOP]	509-765-1776	•	•	•	•
•	•		•	•	ASAP Legal Messenger [SOP]	253-640-1312		•		
•	•	•	•	•	Quik Check Records Inc	503-876-6477	•	•	•	•
•	•	•	•	•	Trident Investigative Service Inc [SOP]	888-277-3238	•	•	•	•
•	•	•	•	•	Washington Court Records Service	509-448-5012	•	•	•	•

CR	CV	PR	US	BK	←COURTS ASOTIN	RECORDER→	UC	RE	TX	VS
•	•	•	•	•	Gem State Inv [SOP]	208-746-4152	•	•	•	•
•	•		•	•	Ryan Myers	208-882-6678	•	•	•	
•	•	•	•	•	Quik Check Records Inc	503-876-6477	•	•	•	•
					Rat Dog Research LLC	208-765-4598	•	•	•	
•	•	•	•	•	Trident Investigative Service Inc [SOP]	888-277-3238	•	•	•	•
•	•	•	•	•	Washington Court Records Service	509-448-5012	•	•	•	•

CR	CV	PR	US	BK	←COURTS BENTON	RECORDER→	UC	RE	TX	VS
•	•		•	•	American Legal Process & Messenger Service Inc [SOP]	509-946-0807	•	•	•	
•	•	•			Information Retrieval Services	800-769-3051	•	•	•	
•	•	•	•	•	Pronto Process & Messenger Service [SOP]	509-547-1122	•	•	•	
•	•	•	•	•	Quik Check Records Inc	503-876-6477	•	•	•	•
•	•	•	•	•	Trident Investigative Service Inc [SOP]	888-277-3238	•	•	•	•
•	•	•	•	•	Washington Court Records Service	509-448-5012	•	•	•	•

CR	CV	PR	US	BK	←COURTS CHELAN	RECORDER→	UC	RE	TX	VS
	•				AM-PM Services [SOP]	509-765-1776	•	•	•	•
•	•		•	•	ASAP Legal Messenger [SOP]	253-640-1312		•		
					Miller & Assoc Information Services Inc	253-752-5500	•	•	•	
•	•				Patterson Investigations Inc [SOP]	509-884-7531				
•	•	•	•	•	Quik Check Records Inc	503-876-6477	•	•	•	•
•	•	•	•	•	Trident Investigative Service Inc [SOP]	888-277-3238	•	•	•	•
•	•	•	•	•	Washington Court Records Service	509-448-5012	•	•	•	•

CR	CV	PR	US	BK	←COURTS CLALLAM	RECORDER→	UC	RE	TX	VS
•	•	•	•	•	Quik Check Records Inc	503-876-6477	•	•	•	•
•	•	•	•	•	Trident Investigative Service Inc [SOP]	888-277-3238	•	•	•	•
•	•	•	•	•	Washington Court Records Service	509-448-5012	•	•	•	•

CR	CV	PR	US	BK	←COURTS CLARK	RECORDER→	UC	RE	TX	VS
•	•	•	•	•	Barrister Support Service [SOP]	503-246-8934				
•	•	•	•	•	Burton-Dukes Legal Support LLC [SOP]	360-254-0878	•	•	•	•
•	•	•	•	•	Data Research Inc (Oregon)	800-992-1983	•	•	•	
•	•	•	•	•	Franchise Profiles LLC	360-566-0438	•	•	•	•
•	•	•	•	•	Lawyer's Legal Service LLC [SOP]	800-224-7911	•	•	•	•
					Linda's Property Information Service	503-659-6186	•	•	•	
•	•				Prospective Renters Verification Service	503-655-0888	•	•	•	•
•	•	•	•	•	Quik Check Records Inc	503-876-6477	•	•	•	•
	•	•			Timely Documents	360-944-1082	•	•	•	
•	•	•	•	•	Trident Investigative Service Inc [SOP]	888-277-3238	•	•	•	•
•	•		•	•	Vancouver Legal Messengers Inc [SOP]	888-695-3654	•	•	•	•
•	•	•	•	•	Washington Court Records Service	509-448-5012	•	•	•	•

CR	CV	PR	US	BK	←COURTS COLUMBIA	RECORDER→	UC	RE	TX	VS
•	•	•	•	•	Pronto Process & Messenger Service [SOP]	509-547-1122	•	•	•	
•	•	•	•	•	Trident Investigative Service Inc [SOP]	888-277-3238	•	•	•	•

CR	CV	PR	US	BK	←COURTS COWLITZ	RECORDER→	UC	RE	TX	VS
•	•	•	•	•	Burton-Dukes Legal Support LLC [SOP]	360-254-0878	•	•	•	•
					Frank Paine Records Search & Retrieval	888-739-8760	•	•	•	
•	•	•	•	•	Lawyer's Legal Service LLC [SOP]	800-224-7911	•	•	•	•
•	•	•	•	•	Quik Check Records Inc	503-876-6477	•	•	•	•
•	•	•	•	•	Trident Investigative Service Inc [SOP]	888-277-3238	•	•	•	•
•	•		•	•	Vancouver Legal Messengers Inc [SOP]	888-695-3654	•	•	•	•
•	•	•	•	•	Washington Court Records Service	509-448-5012	•	•	•	•

CR	CV	PR	US	BK	←COURTS DOUGLAS	RECORDER→	UC	RE	TX	VS
	•				AM-PM Services [SOP]	509-765-1776	•	•	•	•
•	•		•	•	ASAP Legal Messenger [SOP]	253-640-1312		•		
•	•				Patterson Investigations Inc [SOP]	509-884-7531				
•	•	•	•	•	Quik Check Records Inc	503-876-6477	•	•	•	•
•	•	•	•	•	Trident Investigative Service Inc [SOP]	888-277-3238	•	•	•	•
•	•	•	•	•	Washington Court Records Service	509-448-5012	•	•	•	•

CR	CV	PR	US	BK	←COURTS FERRY	RECORDER→	UC	RE	TX	VS
•	•	•	•	•	Quik Check Records Inc	503-876-6477	•	•	•	•
•	•	•	•	•	Trident Investigative Service Inc [SOP]	888-277-3238	•	•	•	•
•	•	•	•	•	Washington Court Records Service	509-448-5012	•	•	•	•

CR	CV	PR	US	BK	←COURTS FRANKLIN	RECORDER→	UC	RE	TX	VS
•	•		•	•	American Legal Process & Messenger Service Inc [SOP]	509-946-0807	•	•	•	
	•				AM-PM Services [SOP]	509-765-1776	•	•	•	•
•	•	•	•	•	Information Retrieval Services	800-769-3051	•	•	•	•
•	•	•	•	•	Pronto Process & Messenger Service [SOP]	509-547-1122	•	•	•	
•	•	•	•	•	Quik Check Records Inc	503-876-6477	•	•	•	•
•	•	•	•	•	Trident Investigative Service Inc [SOP]	888-277-3238	•	•	•	•
•	•	•	•	•	Washington Court Records Service	509-448-5012	•	•	•	•

CR	CV	PR	US	BK	←COURTS GARFIELD	RECORDER→	UC	RE	TX	VS
•	•	•	•	•	Gem State Inv [SOP]	208-746-4152	•	•	•	•
•	•	•	•	•	Quik Check Records Inc	503-876-6477	•	•	•	•
•	•	•	•	•	Trident Investigative Service Inc [SOP]	888-277-3238	•	•	•	•
•	•	•	•	•	Washington Court Records Service	509-448-5012	•	•	•	•

CR	CV	PR	US	BK	←COURTS GRANT	RECORDER→	UC	RE	TX	VS
	•				AM-PM Services [SOP]	509-765-1776	•	•	•	•
•	•				Patterson Investigations Inc [SOP]	509-884-7531				
•	•	•	•	•	Quik Check Records Inc	503-876-6477	•	•	•	•
•	•	•	•	•	Trident Investigative Service Inc [SOP]	888-277-3238	•	•	•	•
•	•	•	•	•	Washington Court Records Service	509-448-5012	•	•	•	•

CR	CV	PR	US	BK	←COURTS GRAYS HARBOR	RECORDER→	UC	RE	TX	VS
•	•	•	•	•	ABC Legal Services Inc [SOP]	800-736-7295	•	•	•	•
					Frank Paine Records Search & Retrieval	888-739-8760	•	•	•	
•	•	•	•	•	Quik Check Records Inc	503-876-6477	•	•	•	•
•	•	•	•	•	Trident Investigative Service Inc [SOP]	888-277-3238	•	•	•	•
•	•	•	•	•	Washington Court Records Service	509-448-5012	•	•	•	•

CR	CV	PR	US	BK	←COURTS ISLAND	RECORDER→	UC	RE	TX	VS
•	•	•	•	•	ABC Legal Services Inc [SOP]	800-736-7295	•	•	•	•
•	•				Diligenz Inc	800-858-5294	•		•	
•	•	•			Madrona Research Inc	360-647-8126	•	•	•	•
	•				Mask Research Services	425-361-2235		•	•	
•	•	•	•	•	Trident Investigative Service Inc [SOP]	888-277-3238	•	•	•	•

CR	CV	PR	US	BK	←Courts	Recorder→	UC	RE	TX	VS
•	•	•	•	•	Washington Court Records Service	509-448-5012	•	•	•	•

CR	CV	PR	US	BK	←Courts **JEFFERSON**	Recorder→	UC	RE	TX	VS
•	•				Diligenz Inc	800-858-5294	•		•	
•	•	•	•	•	Quik Check Records Inc	503-876-6477	•	•	•	•
•	•	•	•	•	Trident Investigative Service Inc [SOP]	888-277-3238	•	•	•	•
•	•	•	•	•	Washington Court Records Service	509-448-5012	•	•	•	•

CR	CV	PR	US	BK	←Courts **KING**	Recorder→	UC	RE	TX	VS
•	•	•	•	•	ABC Legal Services Inc [SOP]	800-736-7295	•	•	•	•
•	•		•	•	ASAP Legal Messenger [SOP]	253-640-1312		•		
•	•	•	•	•	Attorneys' Information Bureau Inc	206-622-1909	•	•	•	•
•	•				Diligenz Inc	800-858-5294	•		•	
•	•				Wesley W Ewart, PI [SOP]	800-646-1143				
					HK Partners Research	808-291-2071	•	•	•	•
•	•	•			Information Retrieval Services	800-769-3051	•	•	•	
•	•		•	•	McGowan & Clark Inv	425-396-5680	•	•	•	•
					Miller & Assoc Information Services Inc	253-752-5500	•	•	•	
•	•	•	•	•	N W Legal Support Inc [SOP]	800-729-9426	•	•	•	•
•	•	•	•	•	North Sound Professional Research	425-267-9070	•	•	•	•
•	•	•	•	•	North West Legal Support	800-729-9426		•	•	
•	•	•	•	•	Personal Background Investigations, Inc	800-949-9982			•	
•	•	•	•	•	Quik Check Records Inc	503-876-6477	•	•	•	•
•	•	•	•	•	Seattle Process Service Inc [SOP]	800-842-8913				
•	•	•	•	•	Select Information Business Services	425-444-7877	•	•	•	•
•	•	•	•	•	Trident Investigative Service Inc [SOP]	888-277-3238	•	•	•	•
•	•		•	•	Unisearch Inc (Washington)	800-722-0708	•		•	•
•	•	•	•	•	Washington Court Records Service	509-448-5012	•	•	•	•

CR	CV	PR	US	BK	←Courts **KITSAP**	Recorder→	UC	RE	TX	VS
•	•	•	•	•	ABC Legal Services Inc [SOP]	800-736-7295	•	•	•	•
•	•		•	•	ASAP Legal Messenger [SOP]	253-640-1312		•		
•	•	•	•	•	Attorneys' Information Bureau Inc	206-622-1909	•	•	•	•
					Miller & Assoc Information Services Inc	253-752-5500	•	•	•	
•	•	•	•	•	Personal Background Investigations, Inc	800-949-9982			•	
•	•	•	•	•	Quik Check Records Inc	503-876-6477	•	•	•	•
•	•	•	•	•	Trident Investigative Service Inc [SOP]	888-277-3238	•	•	•	•
•	•	•	•	•	Washington Court Records Service	509-448-5012	•	•	•	•

CR	CV	PR	US	BK	←Courts **KITTITAS**	Recorder→	UC	RE	TX	VS
	•				AM-PM Services [SOP]	509-765-1776	•	•	•	•
•	•	•	•	•	Quik Check Records Inc	503-876-6477	•	•	•	•
•	•	•	•	•	Trident Investigative Service Inc [SOP]	888-277-3238	•	•	•	•
•	•	•	•	•	Washington Court Records Service	509-448-5012	•	•	•	•

CR	CV	PR	US	BK	←Courts **KLICKITAT**	Recorder→	UC	RE	TX	VS
•	•	•	•	•	Quik Check Records Inc	503-876-6477	•	•	•	•
•	•	•	•	•	Trident Investigative Service Inc [SOP]	888-277-3238	•	•	•	•
•	•		•	•	Vancouver Legal Messengers Inc [SOP]	888-695-3654	•	•	•	•
•	•	•	•	•	Washington Court Records Service	509-448-5012	•	•	•	•

CR	CV	PR	US	BK	←Courts **LEWIS**	Recorder→	UC	RE	TX	VS
•	•	•	•	•	ABC Legal Services Inc [SOP]	800-736-7295	•	•	•	•
•	•				Diligenz Inc	800-858-5294	•		•	
					Frank Paine Records Search & Retrieval	888-739-8760	•	•	•	•
•	•	•	•	•	Quik Check Records Inc	503-876-6477	•	•	•	•
•	•	•	•	•	Trident Investigative Service Inc [SOP]	888-277-3238	•	•	•	•
•	•		•	•	Unisearch Inc (Washington)	800-722-0708	•		•	•
•	•	•	•	•	Washington Court Records Service	509-448-5012	•	•	•	•

CR	CV	PR	US	BK	←COURTS LINCOLN	RECORDER→	UC	RE	TX	VS
	•				AM-PM Services [SOP]	509-765-1776	•	•	•	•
•	•	•	•	•	Quik Check Records Inc	503-876-6477	•	•	•	•
•	•	•	•	•	Trident Investigative Service Inc [SOP]	888-277-3238	•	•	•	•
•	•	•	•	•	Washington Court Records Service	509-448-5012	•	•	•	•

CR	CV	PR	US	BK	←COURTS MASON	RECORDER→	UC	RE	TX	VS
•	•	•	•	•	ABC Legal Services Inc [SOP]	800-736-7295	•	•	•	•
					Miller & Assoc Information Services Inc	253-752-5500	•	•	•	
•	•	•	•	•	Quik Check Records Inc	503-876-6477	•	•	•	•
•	•	•	•	•	Trident Investigative Service Inc [SOP]	888-277-3238	•	•	•	•
•	•		•	•	Unisearch Inc (Washington)	800-722-0708	•		•	•
•	•	•	•	•	Washington Court Records Service	509-448-5012	•	•	•	•

CR	CV	PR	US	BK	←COURTS OKANOGAN	RECORDER→	UC	RE	TX	VS
•	•				Patterson Investigations Inc [SOP]	509-884-7531				
•	•	•	•	•	Quik Check Records Inc	503-876-6477	•	•	•	•
•	•	•	•	•	Trident Investigative Service Inc [SOP]	888-277-3238	•	•	•	•
•	•	•	•	•	Washington Court Records Service	509-448-5012	•	•	•	•

CR	CV	PR	US	BK	←COURTS PACIFIC	RECORDER→	UC	RE	TX	VS
•	•	•	•	•	Quik Check Records Inc	503-876-6477	•	•	•	•
•	•	•	•	•	Trident Investigative Service Inc [SOP]	888-277-3238	•	•	•	•
•	•		•	•	Vancouver Legal Messengers Inc [SOP]	888-695-3654	•	•	•	•
•	•	•	•	•	Washington Court Records Service	509-448-5012	•	•	•	•

CR	CV	PR	US	BK	←COURTS PEND OREILLE	RECORDER→	UC	RE	TX	VS
•	•	•	•	•	Quik Check Records Inc	503-876-6477	•	•	•	•
•	•	•	•	•	Trident Investigative Service Inc [SOP]	888-277-3238	•	•	•	•
•	•	•	•	•	Washington Court Records Service	509-448-5012	•	•	•	•

CR	CV	PR	US	BK	←COURTS PIERCE	RECORDER→	UC	RE	TX	VS
•	•	•	•	•	ABC Legal Services Inc [SOP]	800-736-7295	•	•	•	•
•	•		•	•	ASAP Legal Messenger [SOP]	253-640-1312		•		
•	•	•	•	•	Attorneys' Information Bureau Inc	206-622-1909	•	•	•	•
•	•				Diligenz Inc	800-858-5294	•		•	
•	•	•	•	•	Hoover Professional Investigations [SOP]	253-272-5090	•	•	•	•
•	•		•	•	McGowan & Clark Inv	425-396-5680	•	•	•	•
					Miller & Assoc Information Services Inc	253-752-5500	•	•	•	
•	•	•	•	•	N W Legal Support Inc [SOP]	800-729-9426	•	•	•	•
•	•	•	•	•	North West Legal Support	800-729-9426		•	•	
•	•	•	•	•	Personal Background Investigations, Inc	800-949-9982			•	
•	•	•	•	•	Quik Check Records Inc	503-876-6477	•	•	•	•
•	•	•	•	•	Seattle Process Service Inc [SOP]	800-842-8913				
•	•	•	•	•	Trident Investigative Service Inc [SOP]	888-277-3238	•	•	•	•
•	•		•	•	Unisearch Inc (Washington)	800-722-0708	•		•	•
•	•	•	•	•	Washington Court Records Service	509-448-5012	•	•	•	•

CR	CV	PR	US	BK	←COURTS SAN JUAN	RECORDER→	UC	RE	TX	VS
•	•				Paper Chase LLC [SOP]	360-378-3345				
•	•	•	•	•	Quik Check Records Inc	503-876-6477	•	•	•	•
•	•	•	•	•	Trident Investigative Service Inc [SOP]	888-277-3238	•	•	•	•
•	•	•	•	•	Washington Court Records Service	509-448-5012	•	•	•	•

CR	CV	PR	US	BK	←COURTS SKAGIT	RECORDER→	UC	RE	TX	VS
•	•	•			4th Corner Network Inc [SOP]	800-321-2455	•		•	•
•	•	•	•	•	ABC Legal Services Inc [SOP]	800-736-7295	•	•	•	•
•	•				Diligenz Inc	800-858-5294	•		•	
•	•	•			Information Retrieval Services	800-769-3051	•	•	•	
•	•	•			Madrona Research Inc	360-647-8126	•	•	•	•

CR	CV	PR	US	BK	←Courts	Recorder→	UC	RE	TX	VS
					Miller & Assoc Information Services Inc	253-752-5500	•	•	•	
•	•	•	•	•	Quik Check Records Inc	503-876-6477	•	•	•	•
•	•	•	•	•	Trident Investigative Service Inc [SOP]	888-277-3238	•	•	•	•
•	•		•	•	Unisearch Inc (Washington)	800-722-0708	•		•	•
•	•	•	•	•	Washington Court Records Service	509-448-5012	•	•	•	•

CR	CV	PR	US	BK	←Courts SKAMANIA	Recorder→	UC	RE	TX	VS
•	•	•	•	•	Burton-Dukes Legal Support LLC [SOP]	360-254-0878	•	•	•	•
•	•	•	•	•	Lawyer's Legal Service LLC [SOP]	800-224-7911	•	•	•	•
•	•	•	•	•	Quik Check Records Inc	503-876-6477	•	•	•	•
•	•	•	•	•	Trident Investigative Service Inc [SOP]	888-277-3238	•	•	•	•
•	•		•	•	Vancouver Legal Messengers Inc [SOP]	888-695-3654	•	•	•	•
•	•	•	•	•	Washington Court Records Service	509-448-5012	•	•	•	•

CR	CV	PR	US	BK	←Courts SNOHOMISH	Recorder→	UC	RE	TX	VS
•	•	•	•	•	ABC Legal Services Inc [SOP]	800-736-7295	•	•	•	•
•	•		•	•	ASAP Legal Messenger [SOP]	253-640-1312		•		
•	•	•	•	•	Attorneys' Information Bureau Inc	206-622-1909	•	•	•	•
•	•				Diligenz Inc	800-858-5294	•		•	
•	•	•			Information Retrieval Services	800-769-3051	•	•	•	
•	•		•	•	McGowan & Clark Inv	425-396-5680	•	•	•	•
					Miller & Assoc Information Services Inc	253-752-5500	•	•	•	
•	•	•	•	•	N W Legal Support Inc [SOP]	800-729-9426	•	•	•	•
•	•	•	•	•	North Sound Professional Research	425-267-9070	•	•	•	•
•	•	•	•	•	North West Legal Support	800-729-9426		•	•	
•	•	•	•	•	Personal Background Investigations, Inc	800-949-9982			•	
•	•	•	•	•	Quik Check Records Inc	503-876-6477	•	•	•	•
•	•	•	•	•	Seattle Process Service Inc [SOP]	800-842-8913				
•	•	•	•	•	Select Information Business Services	425-444-7877	•	•	•	•
•	•	•	•	•	Trident Investigative Service Inc [SOP]	888-277-3238	•	•	•	•
•	•		•	•	Unisearch Inc (Washington)	800-722-0708	•		•	•
•	•	•	•	•	Washington Court Records Service	509-448-5012	•	•	•	•

CR	CV	PR	US	BK	←Courts SPOKANE	Recorder→	UC	RE	TX	VS
•	•	•	•	•	ewaprocess.com [SOP]	509-325-0001	•	•	•	•
•	•	•	•	•	N W Legal Support Inc [SOP]	800-729-9426	•	•	•	•
•	•	•	•	•	North West Legal Support	800-729-9426		•	•	
•	•		•	•	Quik Check Records Inc	503-876-6477	•	•	•	•
					Rat Dog Research LLC	208-765-4598	•	•	•	
•	•	•	•	•	Trident Investigative Service Inc [SOP]	888-277-3238	•	•	•	•
•	•	•	•	•	Washington Court Records Service	509-448-5012	•	•	•	•

CR	CV	PR	US	BK	←Courts STEVENS	Recorder→	UC	RE	TX	VS
•	•	•	•	•	Quik Check Records Inc	503-876-6477	•	•	•	•
					Rat Dog Research LLC	208-765-4598	•	•	•	
•	•	•			Stevens County Title	509-684-4589	•	•	•	
•	•	•	•	•	Trident Investigative Service Inc [SOP]	888-277-3238	•	•	•	•
•	•	•	•	•	Washington Court Records Service	509-448-5012	•	•	•	•

CR	CV	PR	US	BK	←Courts THURSTON	Recorder→	UC	RE	TX	VS
•	•	•	•	•	ABC Legal Services Inc [SOP]	800-736-7295	•	•	•	•
•	•	•	•	•	AccuFacts Research Corporation	800-898-5583	•		•	
•	•	•	•	•	Attorneys' Information Bureau Inc	206-622-1909	•	•	•	•
•	•				Diligenz Inc	800-858-5294	•		•	
•	•	•	•	•	Fairchild Record Search Ltd [SOP]	800-547-7007	•		•	•
					Frank Paine Records Search & Retrieval	888-739-8760	•	•	•	
•	•	•	•	•	Hoover Professional Investigations [SOP]	253-272-5090	•	•	•	•
					Miller & Assoc Information Services Inc	253-752-5500	•	•	•	
•	•	•	•	•	Personal Background Investigations, Inc	800-949-9982			•	
•	•	•	•	•	Quik Check Records Inc	503-876-6477	•	•	•	•

CR	CV	PR	US	BK	←Courts	Recorder→	UC	RE	TX	VS
•	•	•	•	•	Trident Investigative Service Inc [SOP]	888-277-3238	•	•	•	•
•	•		•	•	Unisearch Inc (Washington)	800-722-0708	•		•	•
•	•	•	•	•	Washington Court Records Service	509-448-5012	•	•	•	•

CR	CV	PR	US	BK	←Courts WAHKIAKUM	Recorder→	UC	RE	TX	VS
•	•	•	•	•	Trident Investigative Service Inc [SOP]	888-277-3238	•	•	•	•
•	•		•	•	Vancouver Legal Messengers Inc [SOP]	888-695-3654	•	•	•	•

CR	CV	PR	US	BK	←Courts WALLA WALLA	Recorder→	UC	RE	TX	VS
•	•		•	•	American Legal Process & Messenger Service Inc [SOP]	509-946-0807	•	•	•	
•	•	•	•	•	Pronto Process & Messenger Service [SOP]	509-547-1122	•	•	•	
•	•	•	•	•	Quik Check Records Inc	503-876-6477	•	•	•	•
•	•	•	•	•	Trident Investigative Service Inc [SOP]	888-277-3238	•	•	•	•
	•	•			Walla Walla Title Co	509-525-8660	•	•	•	•
•	•	•	•	•	Washington Court Records Service	509-448-5012	•	•	•	•

CR	CV	PR	US	BK	←Courts WHATCOM	Recorder→	UC	RE	TX	VS
•	•	•			4th Corner Network Inc [SOP]	800-321-2455	•		•	•
•	•	•	•	•	ABC Legal Services Inc [SOP]	800-736-7295	•	•	•	•
•	•				Diligenz Inc	800-858-5294	•		•	
•	•	•			Madrona Research Inc	360-647-8126	•	•	•	•
•	•	•	•	•	Trident Investigative Service Inc [SOP]	888-277-3238	•	•	•	•

CR	CV	PR	US	BK	←Courts WHITMAN	Recorder→	UC	RE	TX	VS
•	•	•	•	•	Gem State Inv [SOP]	208-746-4152	•	•	•	•
•	•		•	•	Ryan Myers	208-882-6678	•	•	•	
•	•	•	•	•	Quik Check Records Inc	503-876-6477	•	•	•	•
•	•	•	•	•	Trident Investigative Service Inc [SOP]	888-277-3238	•	•	•	•
•	•	•	•	•	Washington Court Records Service	509-448-5012	•	•	•	•

CR	CV	PR	US	BK	←Courts YAKIMA	Recorder→	UC	RE	TX	VS
•	•		•	•	American Legal Process & Messenger Service Inc [SOP]	509-946-0807	•	•	•	
•	•	•			Information Retrieval Services	800-769-3051	•	•	•	
•	•	•	•	•	Legal Couriers Inc [SOP]	888-450-9453	•	•	•	•
•	•	•	•	•	Quik Check Records Inc	503-876-6477	•	•	•	•
•	•	•	•	•	Trident Investigative Service Inc [SOP]	888-277-3238	•	•	•	•
•	•	•	•	•	Washington Court Records Service	509-448-5012	•	•	•	•

[SOP] = Performs service of process

= PRRN Member. *A retriever you can trust!*

Editor's Tip: At the back of this directory is a short list of search firms who are Public Record Retriever Network "Associate Members." These Associate Members utilize retrievers to obtain documents outside their local area of coverage. The Associate Members are statewide, regional, or national in scope, and are not listed in the county sections.

West Virginia

COURT RECORDS RETRIEVED					CAPITAL - KANAWHA COUNTY		RECORDED RECORDS RETRIEVED			
CR	**CV**	**PR**	**US**	**BK**	**←COURTS** — **BARBOUR**	**RECORDER→**	**UC**	**RE**	**TX**	**VS**
•	•	•	•	•	DMI [SOP]	304-842-2946	•	•	•	•
•	•	•	•	•	Lester E Howard	304-669-1447 cell; 304-592-2190 ofc	•	•	•	•
•	•		•	•	JH Records Research	304-531-4681			•	
					Liberty Record Search Inc	304-863-5542	•	•	•	
	•	•	•	•	Marjorie Croson aka The Croson Agency	304-727-2555	•	•	•	•
•	•	•	•	•	Vanhorn & Vanhorn Inc [SOP]	304-623-1362	•	•	•	•
CR	**CV**	**PR**	**US**	**BK**	**←COURTS** — **BERKELEY**	**RECORDER→**	**UC**	**RE**	**TX**	**VS**
•	•		•		JH Records Research	304-531-4681			•	
					Liberty Record Search Inc	304-863-5542	•	•	•	
	•	•	•	•	Marjorie Croson aka The Croson Agency	304-727-2555	•	•	•	•
					Paralegal Services (Berkeley Springs)	304-676-5550	•	•	•	
•	•				PAT Research	304-725-4845			•	
•					Whiting Background & Legal Services	304-372-6499 or 304-532-1613			•	
CR	**CV**	**PR**	**US**	**BK**	**←COURTS** — **BOONE**	**RECORDER→**	**UC**	**RE**	**TX**	**VS**
•	•	•	•	•	American Investigations [SOP]	304-343-3346	•	•	•	•
					Liberty Record Search Inc	304-863-5542	•	•	•	
	•	•	•	•	Marjorie Croson aka The Croson Agency	304-727-2555	•	•	•	•
CR	**CV**	**PR**	**US**	**BK**	**←COURTS** — **BRAXTON**	**RECORDER→**	**UC**	**RE**	**TX**	**VS**
•	•	•	•	•	DMI [SOP]	304-842-2946	•	•	•	•
					Liberty Record Search Inc	304-863-5542	•	•	•	
	•	•	•	•	Marjorie Croson aka The Croson Agency	304-727-2555	•	•	•	•
CR	**CV**	**PR**	**US**	**BK**	**←COURTS** — **BROOKE**	**RECORDER→**	**UC**	**RE**	**TX**	**VS**
•	•		•	•	JH Records Research	304-531-4681			•	
					Liberty Record Search Inc	304-863-5542	•	•	•	
	•	•	•	•	Marjorie Croson aka The Croson Agency	304-727-2555	•	•	•	•
•	•				River Research Service	304-670-3622	•	•	•	
CR	**CV**	**PR**	**US**	**BK**	**←COURTS** — **CABELL**	**RECORDER→**	**UC**	**RE**	**TX**	**VS**
•	•		•		Accu-Check Information Services	304-375-4802	•		•	
•	•	•			Accurate Research & Information Svcs	304-252-0863			•	
•	•	•	•	•	American Investigations [SOP]	304-343-3346	•	•	•	•
•	•	•	•		Daniel Agency	606-324-6029	•	•	•	•
					Liberty Record Search Inc	304-863-5542	•	•	•	
	•	•	•	•	Marjorie Croson aka The Croson Agency	304-727-2555	•	•	•	•
•	•				West Virginia Records Research	304-633-6964				
•					Whiting Background & Legal Services	304-372-6499 or 304-532-1613			•	
CR	**CV**	**PR**	**US**	**BK**	**←COURTS** — **CALHOUN**	**RECORDER→**	**UC**	**RE**	**TX**	**VS**
					Liberty Record Search Inc	304-863-5542	•	•	•	
	•	•	•	•	Marjorie Croson aka The Croson Agency	304-727-2555	•	•	•	•
CR	**CV**	**PR**	**US**	**BK**	**←COURTS** — **CLAY**	**RECORDER→**	**UC**	**RE**	**TX**	**VS**
					Liberty Record Search Inc	304-863-5542	•	•	•	
	•	•	•	•	Marjorie Croson aka The Croson Agency	304-727-2555	•	•	•	•

CR	CV	PR	US	BK	←Courts	Doddridge	Recorder→	UC	RE	TX	VS
•	•		•		Accu-Check Information Services		304-375-4802	•		•	
•	•	•	•	•	DMI [SOP]		304-842-2946	•	•	•	•
•	•	•	•	•	Lester E Howard		304-669-1447 cell; 304-592-2190 ofc	•	•	•	•
•	•		•	•	JH Records Research		304-531-4681			•	
					Liberty Record Search Inc		304-863-5542	•	•	•	
	•	•	•	•	Marjorie Croson aka The Croson Agency		304-727-2555	•	•	•	•
•	•	•	•	•	Vanhorn & Vanhorn Inc [SOP]		304-623-1362	•	•	•	•

CR	CV	PR	US	BK	←Courts	Fayette	Recorder→	UC	RE	TX	VS
•	•		•		Accu-Check Information Services		304-375-4802	•		•	
•	•	•			Accurate Research & Information Svcs		304-252-0863			•	
					Liberty Record Search Inc		304-863-5542	•	•	•	
	•	•	•	•	Marjorie Croson aka The Croson Agency		304-727-2555	•	•	•	•
•					Whiting Background & Legal Services		304-372-6499 or 304-532-1613			•	

CR	CV	PR	US	BK	←Courts	Gilmer	Recorder→	UC	RE	TX	VS
					Liberty Record Search Inc		304-863-5542	•	•	•	
	•	•	•	•	Marjorie Croson aka The Croson Agency		304-727-2555	•	•	•	•

CR	CV	PR	US	BK	←Courts	Grant	Recorder→	UC	RE	TX	VS
•	•		•	•	JH Records Research		304-531-4681			•	
	•	•	•	•	Marjorie Croson aka The Croson Agency		304-727-2555	•	•	•	•

CR	CV	PR	US	BK	←Courts	Greenbrier	Recorder→	UC	RE	TX	VS
•	•		•		Accu-Check Information Services		304-375-4802	•		•	
•	•	•			Drema Sharp		304-799-6509; Fax- same	•	•	•	•
					Liberty Record Search Inc		304-863-5542	•	•	•	
	•	•	•	•	Marjorie Croson aka The Croson Agency		304-727-2555	•	•	•	•

CR	CV	PR	US	BK	←Courts	Hampshire	Recorder→	UC	RE	TX	VS
•	•		•	•	JH Records Research		304-531-4681			•	
•	•	•	•	•	Marjorie Croson aka The Croson Agency		304-727-2555	•	•	•	•

CR	CV	PR	US	BK	←Courts	Hancock	Recorder→	UC	RE	TX	VS
•	•		•	•	JH Records Research		304-531-4681			•	
					Liberty Record Search Inc		304-863-5542	•	•	•	
	•	•	•	•	Marjorie Croson aka The Croson Agency		304-727-2555	•	•	•	•
•	•				River Research Service		304-670-3622	•	•	•	

CR	CV	PR	US	BK	←Courts	Hardy	Recorder→	UC	RE	TX	VS
•	•		•	•	JH Records Research		304-531-4681			•	
	•	•	•	•	Marjorie Croson aka The Croson Agency		304-727-2555	•	•	•	•

CR	CV	PR	US	BK	←Courts	Harrison	Recorder→	UC	RE	TX	VS
•	•	•	•	•	DMI [SOP]		304-842-2946	•	•	•	•
•	•	•	•	•	Lester E Howard		304-669-1447 cell; 304-592-2190 ofc	•	•	•	•
•	•		•	•	JH Records Research		304-531-4681			•	
					Liberty Record Search Inc		304-863-5542	•	•	•	
	•	•	•	•	Marjorie Croson aka The Croson Agency		304-727-2555	•	•	•	•
•	•	•	•	•	Vanhorn & Vanhorn Inc [SOP]		304-623-1362	•	•	•	•

CR	CV	PR	US	BK	←Courts	Jackson	Recorder→	UC	RE	TX	VS
•	•		•		Accu-Check Information Services		304-375-4802	•		•	
•	•	•	•	•	American Investigations [SOP]		304-343-3346	•	•	•	•
					Liberty Record Search Inc		304-863-5542	•	•	•	
	•	•	•	•	Marjorie Croson aka The Croson Agency		304-727-2555	•	•	•	•
•					Whiting Background & Legal Services		304-372-6499 or 304-532-1613			•	

CR	CV	PR	US	BK	←Courts	**Jefferson** Recorder→	UC	RE	TX	VS
•	•		•		Accu-Check Information Services	304-375-4802	•		•	
•	•		•	•	JH Records Research	304-531-4681			•	
					Liberty Record Search Inc	304-863-5542	•	•	•	
	•	•	•	•	Marjorie Croson aka The Croson Agency	304-727-2555	•	•	•	•
•	•				PAT Research	304-725-4845			•	
•					Whiting Background & Legal Services	304-372-6499 or 304-532-1613			•	

CR	CV	PR	US	BK	←Courts	**Kanawha** Recorder→	UC	RE	TX	VS
•	•		•		Accu-Check Information Services	304-375-4802	•		•	
•	•	•			Accurate Research & Information Svcs	304-252-0863			•	
•	•	•	•	•	American Investigations [SOP]	304-343-3346	•	•	•	•
•	•	•	•		Daniel Agency	606-324-6029	•	•	•	•
					Liberty Record Search Inc	304-863-5542	•	•	•	
	•	•	•	•	Marjorie Croson aka The Croson Agency	304-727-2555	•	•	•	•
•	•				West Virginia Records Research	304-633-6964				
•					Whiting Background & Legal Services	304-372-6499 or 304-532-1613			•	

CR	CV	PR	US	BK	←Courts	**Lewis** Recorder→	UC	RE	TX	VS
•	•	•	•	•	DMI [SOP]	304-842-2946	•	•	•	•
•	•	•	•	•	Lester E Howard	304-669-1447 cell; 304-592-2190 ofc	•	•	•	•
•	•		•	•	JH Records Research	304-531-4681			•	
					Liberty Record Search Inc	304-863-5542	•	•	•	
	•	•	•	•	Marjorie Croson aka The Croson Agency	304-727-2555	•	•	•	•
•	•	•	•	•	Vanhorn & Vanhorn Inc [SOP]	304-623-1362	•	•	•	•

CR	CV	PR	US	BK	←Courts	**Lincoln** Recorder→	UC	RE	TX	VS
•	•	•	•	•	American Investigations [SOP]	304-343-3346	•	•	•	•
•	•	•	•		Daniel Agency	606-324-6029	•	•	•	•
					Liberty Record Search Inc	304-863-5542	•	•	•	
	•	•	•	•	Marjorie Croson aka The Croson Agency	304-727-2555	•	•	•	•

CR	CV	PR	US	BK	←Courts	**Logan** Recorder→	UC	RE	TX	VS
					Liberty Record Search Inc	304-863-5542	•	•	•	
	•	•	•	•	Marjorie Croson aka The Croson Agency	304-727-2555	•	•	•	•

CR	CV	PR	US	BK	←Courts	**Marion** Recorder→	UC	RE	TX	VS
•	•	•	•	•	DMI [SOP]	304-842-2946	•	•	•	•
•	•	•	•	•	Lester E Howard	304-669-1447 cell; 304-592-2190 ofc	•	•	•	•
•	•		•	•	JH Records Research	304-531-4681			•	
					Liberty Record Search Inc	304-863-5542	•	•	•	
	•	•	•	•	Marjorie Croson aka The Croson Agency	304-727-2555	•	•	•	•
•	•	•	•	•	Vanhorn & Vanhorn Inc [SOP]	304-623-1362	•	•	•	•

CR	CV	PR	US	BK	←Courts	**Marshall** Recorder→	UC	RE	TX	VS
•	•		•	•	JH Records Research	304-531-4681			•	
					Liberty Record Search Inc	304-863-5542	•	•	•	
	•	•	•	•	Marjorie Croson aka The Croson Agency	304-727-2555	•	•	•	•

CR	CV	PR	US	BK	←Courts	**Mason** Recorder→	UC	RE	TX	VS
•	•	•	•	•	DMI [SOP]	304-842-2946	•	•	•	•
					Liberty Record Search Inc	304-863-5542	•	•	•	
	•	•	•	•	Marjorie Croson aka The Croson Agency	304-727-2555	•	•	•	•
		•			Paralegal Services Point Pleasant	304-675-4008	•	•	•	•

CR	CV	PR	US	BK	←Courts	**McDowell** Recorder→	UC	RE	TX	VS
					Liberty Record Search Inc	304-863-5542	•	•	•	
	•	•	•	•	Marjorie Croson aka The Croson Agency	304-727-2555	•	•	•	•

CR	CV	PR	US	BK	←Courts	**Mercer**	Recorder→	UC	RE	TX	VS
					Liberty Record Search Inc		304-863-5542	•	•	•	
	•	•	•	•	Marjorie Croson aka The Croson Agency		304-727-2555	•	•	•	•

CR	CV	PR	US	BK	←Courts	**Mineral**	Recorder→	UC	RE	TX	VS
•	•		•	•	JH Records Research		304-531-4681			•	
	•	•	•	•	Marjorie Croson aka The Croson Agency		304-727-2555	•	•	•	•

CR	CV	PR	US	BK	←Courts	**Mingo**	Recorder→	UC	RE	TX	VS
•	•		•		Accu-Check Information Services		304-375-4802	•		•	
					Liberty Record Search Inc		304-863-5542	•	•	•	
	•	•	•	•	Marjorie Croson aka The Croson Agency		304-727-2555	•	•	•	•

CR	CV	PR	US	BK	←Courts	**Monongalia**	Recorder→	UC	RE	TX	VS
•	•	•			Accurate Research & Information Svcs		304-252-0863			•	
•	•	•	•	•	DMI [SOP]		304-842-2946	•	•	•	•
•	•		•	•	JH Records Research		304-531-4681			•	
					Liberty Record Search Inc		304-863-5542	•	•	•	
	•	•	•	•	Marjorie Croson aka The Croson Agency		304-727-2555	•	•	•	•

CR	CV	PR	US	BK	←Courts	**Monroe**	Recorder→	UC	RE	TX	VS
					Liberty Record Search Inc		304-863-5542	•	•	•	
	•	•	•	•	Marjorie Croson aka The Croson Agency		304-727-2555	•	•	•	•

CR	CV	PR	US	BK	←Courts	**Morgan**	Recorder→	UC	RE	TX	VS
					Liberty Record Search Inc		304-863-5542	•	•	•	
	•	•	•	•	Marjorie Croson aka The Croson Agency		304-727-2555	•	•	•	•
•	•				Connie Miller		304-258-8554			•	
					Paralegal Services (Berkeley Springs)		304-676-5550	•	•	•	

CR	CV	PR	US	BK	←Courts	**Nicholas**	Recorder→	UC	RE	TX	VS
•	•		•		Accu-Check Information Services		304-375-4802	•		•	
					Liberty Record Search Inc		304-863-5542	•	•	•	
	•	•	•	•	Marjorie Croson aka The Croson Agency		304-727-2555	•	•	•	•

CR	CV	PR	US	BK	←Courts	**Ohio**	Recorder→	UC	RE	TX	VS
•	•	•	•	•	Confidential Services [SOP]		800-752-4581	•	•	•	•
•	•		•	•	JH Records Research		304-531-4681			•	
					Liberty Record Search Inc		304-863-5542	•	•	•	
	•	•	•	•	Marjorie Croson aka The Croson Agency		304-727-2555	•	•	•	•
•	•				River Research Service		304-670-3622	•	•	•	

CR	CV	PR	US	BK	←Courts	**Pendleton**	Recorder→	UC	RE	TX	VS
	•	•	•	•	Marjorie Croson aka The Croson Agency		304-727-2555	•	•	•	•

CR	CV	PR	US	BK	←Courts	**Pleasants**	Recorder→	UC	RE	TX	VS
•	•		•		Accu-Check Information Services		304-375-4802	•		•	
					Liberty Record Search Inc		304-863-5542	•	•	•	
	•	•	•	•	Marjorie Croson aka The Croson Agency		304-727-2555	•	•	•	•

CR	CV	PR	US	BK	←Courts	**Pocahontas**	Recorder→	UC	RE	TX	VS
					Liberty Record Search Inc		304-863-5542	•	•	•	
	•	•	•	•	Marjorie Croson aka The Croson Agency		304-727-2555	•	•	•	•
•	•	•			Drema Sharp		304-799-6509; Fax- same	•	•	•	•

CR	CV	PR	US	BK	←Courts	**Preston**	Recorder→	UC	RE	TX	VS
•	•	•	•	•	DMI [SOP]		304-842-2946	•	•	•	•
•	•		•	•	JH Records Research		304-531-4681			•	
					Liberty Record Search Inc		304-863-5542	•	•	•	
	•	•	•	•	Marjorie Croson aka The Croson Agency		304-727-2555	•	•	•	•

CR	CV	PR	US	BK	←COURTS	PUTNAM	RECORDER→	UC	RE	TX	VS
•	•		•		Accu-Check Information Services		304-375-4802	•		•	
•	•	•	•	•	American Investigations [SOP]		304-343-3346	•	•	•	•
					Liberty Record Search Inc		304-863-5542	•	•	•	
	•	•	•	•	Marjorie Croson aka The Croson Agency		304-727-2555	•	•	•	•
•	•				West Virginia Records Research		304-633-6964				
•					Whiting Background & Legal Services		304-372-6499 or 304-532-1613			•	

CR	CV	PR	US	BK	←COURTS	RALEIGH	RECORDER→	UC	RE	TX	VS
•	•		•		Accu-Check Information Services		304-375-4802	•		•	
•	•	•			Accurate Research & Information Svcs		304-252-0863			•	
					Liberty Record Search Inc		304-863-5542	•	•	•	
	•	•	•	•	Marjorie Croson aka The Croson Agency		304-727-2555	•	•	•	•
•					Whiting Background & Legal Services		304-372-6499 or 304-532-1613			•	

CR	CV	PR	US	BK	←COURTS	RANDOLPH	RECORDER→	UC	RE	TX	VS
•	•	•	•	•	DMI [SOP]		304-842-2946	•	•	•	•
					Liberty Record Search Inc		304-863-5542	•	•	•	
	•	•	•	•	Marjorie Croson aka The Croson Agency		304-727-2555	•	•	•	•
•	•	•			Drema Sharp		304-799-6509; Fax- same	•		•	•

CR	CV	PR	US	BK	←COURTS	RITCHIE	RECORDER→	UC	RE	TX	VS
•	•		•		Accu-Check Information Services		304-375-4802	•		•	
•	•	•	•	•	DMI [SOP]		304-842-2946	•	•	•	•
					Liberty Record Search Inc		304-863-5542	•	•	•	
	•	•	•	•	Marjorie Croson aka The Croson Agency		304-727-2555	•	•	•	•
•					Professional Services of America Inc		304-485-1278				

CR	CV	PR	US	BK	←COURTS	ROANE	RECORDER→	UC	RE	TX	VS
					Liberty Record Search Inc		304-863-5542	•	•	•	
	•	•	•	•	Marjorie Croson aka The Croson Agency		304-727-2555	•	•	•	•

CR	CV	PR	US	BK	←COURTS	SUMMERS	RECORDER→	UC	RE	TX	VS
					Liberty Record Search Inc		304-863-5542	•	•	•	
	•	•	•	•	Marjorie Croson aka The Croson Agency		304-727-2555	•	•	•	•

CR	CV	PR	US	BK	←COURTS	TAYLOR	RECORDER→	UC	RE	TX	VS
•	•	•	•	•	DMI [SOP]		304-842-2946	•	•	•	•
•	•	•	•	•	Lester E Howard		304-669-1447 cell; 304-592-2190 ofc	•	•	•	•
•	•		•	•	JH Records Research		304-531-4681			•	
					Liberty Record Search Inc		304-863-5542	•	•	•	
	•	•	•	•	Marjorie Croson aka The Croson Agency		304-727-2555	•	•	•	•
•	•	•	•	•	Vanhorn & Vanhorn Inc [SOP]		304-623-1362	•	•	•	•

CR	CV	PR	US	BK	←COURTS	TUCKER	RECORDER→	UC	RE	TX	VS
•	•	•	•	•	DMI [SOP]		304-842-2946	•	•	•	•
•	•		•	•	JH Records Research		304-531-4681			•	
	•	•	•	•	Marjorie Croson aka The Croson Agency		304-727-2555	•	•	•	•

CR	CV	PR	US	BK	←COURTS	TYLER	RECORDER→	UC	RE	TX	VS
•	•		•		Accu-Check Information Services		304-375-4802	•		•	
•	•	•	•	•	DMI [SOP]		304-842-2946	•	•	•	•
•	•		•	•	JH Records Research		304-531-4681			•	
					Liberty Record Search Inc		304-863-5542	•	•	•	
	•	•	•	•	Marjorie Croson aka The Croson Agency		304-727-2555	•	•	•	•

CR	CV	PR	US	BK	←COURTS UPSHUR	RECORDER→	UC	RE	TX	VS
•	•	•	•	•	DMI [SOP]	304-842-2946	•	•	•	•
•	•		•	•	JH Records Research	304-531-4681			•	
					Liberty Record Search Inc	304-863-5542	•	•	•	
	•	•	•	•	Marjorie Croson aka The Croson Agency	304-727-2555	•	•	•	•
•	•	•	•	•	Vanhorn & Vanhorn Inc [SOP]	304-623-1362	•	•	•	•

CR	CV	PR	US	BK	←COURTS WAYNE	RECORDER→	UC	RE	TX	VS
•	•	•	•		Daniel Agency	606-324-6029	•	•	•	•
					Liberty Record Search Inc	304-863-5542	•	•	•	
	•	•	•	•	Marjorie Croson aka The Croson Agency	304-727-2555	•	•	•	•
•	•				West Virginia Records Research	304-633-6964				

CR	CV	PR	US	BK	←COURTS WEBSTER	RECORDER→	UC	RE	TX	VS
•	•	•	•	•	DMI [SOP]	304-842-2946	•	•	•	•
	•	•	•	•	Marjorie Croson aka The Croson Agency	304-727-2555	•	•	•	•

CR	CV	PR	US	BK	←COURTS WETZEL	RECORDER→	UC	RE	TX	VS
•	•		•		Accu-Check Information Services	304-375-4802	•		•	
•	•	•	•	•	DMI [SOP]	304-842-2946	•	•	•	•
•	•		•	•	JH Records Research	304-531-4681			•	
					Liberty Record Search Inc	304-863-5542	•	•	•	
	•	•	•	•	Marjorie Croson aka The Croson Agency	304-727-2555	•	•	•	•

CR	CV	PR	US	BK	←COURTS WIRT	RECORDER→	UC	RE	TX	VS
•	•		•		Accu-Check Information Services	304-375-4802	•		•	
					Liberty Record Search Inc	304-863-5542	•	•	•	
	•	•	•	•	Marjorie Croson aka The Croson Agency	304-727-2555	•	•	•	•

CR	CV	PR	US	BK	←COURTS WOOD	RECORDER→	UC	RE	TX	VS
•	•		•		Accu-Check Information Services	304-375-4802	•		•	
•	•	•	•	•	DMI [SOP]	304-842-2946	•	•	•	•
					Liberty Record Search Inc	304-863-5542	•	•	•	
	•	•	•	•	Marjorie Croson aka The Croson Agency	304-727-2555	•	•	•	•
•					Professional Services of America Inc	304-485-1278				
•	•				West Virginia Records Research	304-633-6964				
•					Whiting Background & Legal Services	304-372-6499 or 304-532-1613			•	

CR	CV	PR	US	BK	←COURTS WYOMING	RECORDER→	UC	RE	TX	VS
					Liberty Record Search Inc	304-863-5542	•	•	•	
	•	•	•	•	Marjorie Croson aka The Croson Agency	304-727-2555	•	•	•	•

[SOP] = PERFORMS SERVICE OF PROCESS

 = PRRN Member. *A retriever you can trust!*

Wisconsin

COURT RECORDS RETRIEVED — CAPITAL - DANE COUNTY — RECORDED RECORDS RETRIEVED

CR	CV	PR	US	BK	←COURTS ADAMS RECORDER→	Phone	UC	RE	TX	VS
		•			Boles-Wallner Abstract & Title	715-423-6940	•	•	•	
					Central Wisconsin Title	608-297-2789		•	•	

CR	CV	PR	US	BK	←COURTS ASHLAND RECORDER→	Phone	UC	RE	TX	VS
•					Affirm Background Screening Inc	715-682-2601				
	•	•	•	•	Phillips Land Title Co Inc	715-339-2230	•	•	•	

CR	CV	PR	US	BK	←COURTS BARRON RECORDER→	Phone	UC	RE	TX	VS
•	•				Chippewa Valley Civil Process [SOP]	715-289-3922; cell 715-559-3922				
	•	•			Guaranty Title Services Inc	715-235-3393	•	•	•	

CR	CV	PR	US	BK	←COURTS BAYFIELD RECORDER→	Phone	UC	RE	TX	VS
•					Affirm Background Screening Inc	715-682-2601				

CR	CV	PR	US	BK	←COURTS BROWN RECORDER→	Phone	UC	RE	TX	VS
•	•	•	•	•	Attorney's Process & Investigative Services [SOP]	800-236-5202	•	•	•	•
	•	•			Bay Title & Abstract Inc	920-431-6100	•	•	•	
					Document Search Services	800-526-2157		•		
•	•	•	•	•	Lowery Professional Services Corp [SOP]	920-830-2114	•	•	•	•

CR	CV	PR	US	BK	←COURTS BUFFALO RECORDER→	Phone	UC	RE	TX	VS
•	•				Advanced Private Inv [SOP]	608-785-2744				
		•		•	The Title Co Inc (Eau Claire)	800-848-4853	•	•	•	

CR	CV	PR	US	BK	←COURTS BURNETT RECORDER→	Phone	UC	RE	TX	VS
					Burnett County Abstract Co	715-349-2269	•	•	•	

CR	CV	PR	US	BK	←COURTS CALUMET RECORDER→	Phone	UC	RE	TX	VS
•	•	•	•	•	Attorney's Process & Investigative Services [SOP]	800-236-5202	•	•	•	•
	•	•			Bay Title & Abstract Inc	920-431-6100	•	•	•	
					Document Search Services	800-526-2157		•		
					Fox Cities Title Co	920-731-5494		•	•	

CR	CV	PR	US	BK	←COURTS CHIPPEWA RECORDER→	Phone	UC	RE	TX	VS
•	•				Chippewa Valley Civil Process [SOP]	715-289-3922; cell 715-559-3922				
	•	•			Guaranty Title Services Inc	715-235-3393	•	•	•	
		•		•	The Title Co Inc (Eau Claire)	800-848-4853	•	•	•	

CR	CV	PR	US	BK	←COURTS CLARK RECORDER→	Phone	UC	RE	TX	VS
		•			Boles-Wallner Abstract & Title	715-423-6940	•	•	•	
		•		•	The Title Co Inc (Eau Claire)	800-848-4853	•	•	•	

CR	CV	PR	US	BK	←COURTS COLUMBIA RECORDER→	Phone	UC	RE	TX	VS
	•	•	•	•	Priority Records Search LLC [SOP]	608-544-9991	•	•	•	•
	•	•			Stewart Title Services Inc, Wisconsin	800-523-3060	•	•	•	•

CR	CV	PR	US	BK	←COURTS CRAWFORD RECORDER→	Phone	UC	RE	TX	VS
	•	•	•	•	The Title Co Inc (Prairie Du Chien WI)	888-918-4853	•	•	•	•

CR	CV	PR	US	BK	←Courts	Dane	Recorder→	UC	RE	TX	VS
•	•				Angel P I's [SOP]		800-973-3832				
•	•	•	•	•	Attorney's Process & Investigative Services [SOP]		800-236-5202	•	•	•	•
	•	•			Bay Title & Abstract Inc		920-431-6100	•	•	•	
•	•	•	•	•	Dane County Legal Notice [SOP]		800-720-6871	•		•	
					Document Search Services		800-526-2157		•		
•	•	•	•	•	Gregg Investigations, Inc of Madison [SOP]		800-866-1976	•			•
•	•		•	•	Infotrack Information Services Inc		800-275-5594	•	•	•	
•	•	•	•	•	Paul C Klumb Agency LLC		414-254-1335	•	•	•	•
	•	•	•	•	Priority Records Search LLC [SOP]		608-544-9991	•	•	•	•
•	•	•		•	Southeast Wisconsin Process [SOP]		262-650-8904	•	•	•	•
	•	•			Stewart Title Services Inc, Wisconsin		800-523-3060	•	•	•	•

CR	CV	PR	US	BK	←Courts	Dodge	Recorder→	UC	RE	TX	VS
					Document Search Services		800-526-2157		•		
•	•		•	•	Infotrack Information Services Inc		800-275-5594	•	•	•	
•	•	•	•	•	Paul C Klumb Agency LLC		414-254-1335	•	•	•	•
•	•	•		•	Southeast Wisconsin Process [SOP]		262-650-8904	•	•	•	•
	•	•			Stewart Title Services Inc, Wisconsin		800-523-3060	•	•	•	•

CR	CV	PR	US	BK	←Courts	Door	Recorder→	UC	RE	TX	VS
•	•	•	•	•	Attorney's Process & Investigative Services [SOP]		800-236-5202	•	•	•	•
	•	•			Bay Title & Abstract Inc		920-431-6100	•	•	•	
					Document Search Services		800-526-2157		•		

CR	CV	PR	US	BK	←Courts	Douglas	Recorder→	UC	RE	TX	VS
	•	•	•	•	Abstract & Title Services of Carlton Inc [SOP]		888-331-3966	•	•	•	
					Document Search Services		800-526-2157		•		

CR	CV	PR	US	BK	←Courts	Dunn	Recorder→	UC	RE	TX	VS
•	•				Chippewa Valley Civil Process [SOP]		715-289-3922; cell 715-559-3922				
					Dunn County Abstract & Title Inc		800-628-5727		•	•	
	•	•			Guaranty Title Services Inc		715-235-3393	•	•	•	
		•			The Title Co Inc (Eau Claire)		800-848-4853	•	•	•	

CR	CV	PR	US	BK	←Courts	Eau Claire	Recorder→	UC	RE	TX	VS
•	•				Chippewa Valley Civil Process [SOP]		715-289-3922; cell 715-559-3922				
	•	•			Guaranty Title Services Inc		715-235-3393	•	•	•	
		•		•	The Title Co Inc (Eau Claire)		800-848-4853	•	•	•	

CR	CV	PR	US	BK	←Courts	Florence	Recorder→	UC	RE	TX	VS
	•	•			Florence County Abstract		715-528-3272	•	•	•	•
•	•				Shadow Process Service [SOP]		800-626-7578				
					Superior Title & Abstract		906-774-9010		•	•	

CR	CV	PR	US	BK	←Courts	Fond du Lac	Recorder→	UC	RE	TX	VS
•	•	•	•	•	Backgrounds Plus		920-457-5745	•	•	•	•
	•	•			Bay Title & Abstract Inc		920-431-6100	•	•	•	
					Document Search Services		800-526-2157		•		
•	•	•		•	Southeast Wisconsin Process [SOP]		262-650-8904	•	•	•	•
	•	•			Stewart Title Services Inc, Wisconsin		800-523-3060	•	•	•	•

CR	CV	PR	US	BK	←Courts	Forest	Recorder→	UC	RE	TX	VS
•	•				Shadow Process Service [SOP]		800-626-7578				

CR	CV	PR	US	BK	←Courts	Grant	Recorder→	UC	RE	TX	VS
	•	•	•	•	The Title Co Inc (Prairie Du Chien WI)		888-918-4853	•	•	•	•

CR	CV	PR	US	BK	←Courts	Green	Recorder→	UC	RE	TX	VS
•	•	•			Ekum Abstract & Title		608-328-8221	•	•	•	
•	•	•	•	•	Gregg Investigations Inc of Janesville [SOP]		800-866-1976	•		•	•

CR	CV	PR	US	BK	Name	Phone	UC	RE	TX	VS
•	•	•	•	•	Stewart & Associates Inc - Rockford [SOP]	815-961-0150	•	•	•	•
	•	•			Stewart Title Services Inc, Wisconsin	800-523-3060	•	•	•	•

CR	CV	PR	US	BK	←Courts **Green Lake**	Recorder→	UC	RE	TX	VS
		•			Green Lake Title & Abstract Co	920-294-6070	•	•	•	
	•	•			Stewart Title Services Inc, Wisconsin	800-523-3060	•	•	•	•

CR	CV	PR	US	BK	←Courts **Iowa**	Recorder→	UC	RE	TX	VS
					Iowa County Title	608-935-3834		•	•	

CR	CV	PR	US	BK	←Courts **Iron**	Recorder→	UC	RE	TX	VS
•					Affirm Background Screening Inc	715-682-2601				
	•	•			Associate Title - Iron County	906-932-6340	•	•	•	

CR	CV	PR	US	BK	←Courts **Jackson**	Recorder→	UC	RE	TX	VS
•	•				Advanced Private Inv [SOP]	608-785-2744				
		•			Boles-Wallner Abstract & Title	715-423-6940	•	•	•	

CR	CV	PR	US	BK	←Courts **Jefferson**	Recorder→	UC	RE	TX	VS
					Document Search Services	800-526-2157		•		
•	•	•	•	•	Gregg Investigations, Inc of Madison [SOP]	800-866-1976	•			•
•	•		•	•	Infotrack Information Services Inc	800-275-5594	•	•	•	
•	•	•	•	•	Paul C Klumb Agency LLC	414-254-1335	•	•	•	•
•	•	•		•	Southeast Wisconsin Process [SOP]	262-650-8904	•	•	•	•
	•	•			Stewart Title Services Inc, Wisconsin	800-523-3060	•	•	•	•

CR	CV	PR	US	BK	←Courts **Juneau**	Recorder→	UC	RE	TX	VS
		•			Boles-Wallner Abstract & Title	715-423-6940	•	•	•	

CR	CV	PR	US	BK	←Courts **Kenosha**	Recorder→	UC	RE	TX	VS
•	•	•			AGH Professional Inv [SOP]	262-884-4688		•		•
•	•	•	•	•	Attorney's Process & Investigative Services [SOP]	800-236-5202	•	•	•	•
					Document Search Services	800-526-2157		•		
•	•	•	•	•	ESI Associates [SOP]	262-652-6361	•	•	•	•
•	•	•			Great Minds/Search Associates	414-321-3375	•	•	•	
•	•		•	•	Infotrack Information Services Inc	800-275-5594	•	•	•	
•	•	•	•	•	Myhre Process [SOP]	414-271-9574				•
•	•	•	•	•	Paul C Klumb Agency LLC	414-254-1335	•	•	•	•
•	•	•			PeopleSearch	877-835-1983	•	•	•	•
•	•	•		•	Southeast Wisconsin Process [SOP]	262-650-8904	•	•	•	•
	•	•			Stewart Title Services Inc, Wisconsin	800-523-3060	•	•	•	•
•	•				WERC - Wisconsin Employee & Renter Check LLC	414-967-9342			•	

CR	CV	PR	US	BK	←Courts **Kewaunee**	Recorder→	UC	RE	TX	VS
•	•	•	•	•	Attorney's Process & Investigative Services [SOP]	800-236-5202	•	•	•	•
	•	•			Bay Title & Abstract Inc	920-431-6100	•	•	•	
					Document Search Services	800-526-2157		•		

CR	CV	PR	US	BK	←Courts **La Crosse**	Recorder→	UC	RE	TX	VS
•	•				Advanced Private Inv [SOP]	608-785-2744				
		•	•	•	The Title Co Inc (La Crosse)	800-788-4853	•	•	•	

CR	CV	PR	US	BK	←Courts **Lafayette**	Recorder→	UC	RE	TX	VS
•	•	•			Ekum Abstract & Title	608-328-8221	•	•	•	
	•	•			Lafayette County Abstract	608-776-3338	•	•	•	

CR	CV	PR	US	BK	←Courts **Langlade**	Recorder→	UC	RE	TX	VS
•	•				Shadow Process Service [SOP]	800-626-7578				

CR	CV	PR	US	BK	←Courts **Lincoln**	Recorder→	UC	RE	TX	VS
•	•				Shadow Process Service [SOP]	800-626-7578				

CR	CV	PR	US	BK	←Courts	Manitowoc	Recorder→	UC	RE	TX	VS
•	•	•	•	•	Attorney's Process & Investigative Services [SOP]		800-236-5202	•	•	•	•
•	•	•	•	•	Backgrounds Plus		920-457-5745	•	•	•	•
	•	•			Bay Title & Abstract Inc		920-431-6100	•	•	•	
					Document Search Services		800-526-2157		•		
	•	•			Evans Title Companies		920-684-1261	•	•	•	•

CR	CV	PR	US	BK	←Courts	Marathon	Recorder→	UC	RE	TX	VS
		•			Boles-Wallner Abstract & Title		715-423-6940	•	•	•	
•	•				Shadow Process Service [SOP]		800-626-7578				

CR	CV	PR	US	BK	←Courts	Marinette	Recorder→	UC	RE	TX	VS
•	•	•	•	•	Attorney's Process & Investigative Services [SOP]		800-236-5202	•	•	•	•
	•	•			Bay Title & Abstract Inc		920-431-6100	•	•	•	
					Document Search Services		800-526-2157		•		

CR	CV	PR	US	BK	←Courts	Marquette	Recorder→	UC	RE	TX	VS
					Central Wisconsin Title		608-297-2789		•	•	

CR	CV	PR	US	BK	←Courts	Menominee	Recorder→	UC	RE	TX	VS
	•	•			Bay Title & Abstract Inc		920-431-6100	•	•	•	

CR	CV	PR	US	BK	←Courts	Milwaukee	Recorder→	UC	RE	TX	VS
•	•	•	•	•	Attorney's Process & Investigative Services [SOP]		800-236-5202	•	•	•	•
					Document Search Services		800-526-2157		•		
•	•	•	•	•	🏛ESI Associates [SOP]		262-652-6361	•	•	•	•
•	•	•			🏛Great Minds/Search Associates		414-321-3375	•	•	•	
•	•		•	•	🏛Infotrack Information Services Inc		800-275-5594	•	•	•	
•	•		•	•	Interstate Reporting Co Inc (IRC)		262-251-6590	•		•	
•	•	•	•	•	🏛Klitzke & Assoc Inc/Klitzke Services Group		262-521-9502	•	•	•	•
•	•	•	•	•	Myhre Process [SOP]		414-271-9574	•		•	•
•	•	•	•	•	🏛Paul C Klumb Agency LLC		414-254-1335	•	•	•	•
•	•	•		•	Southeast Wisconsin Process [SOP]		262-650-8904	•	•	•	•
	•	•			Stewart Title Services Inc, Wisconsin		800-523-3060	•	•	•	•
•	•		•	•	Verified Inc		866-265-9426				
•	•				WERC - Wisconsin Employee & Renter Check LLC		414-967-9342			•	

CR	CV	PR	US	BK	←Courts	Monroe	Recorder→	UC	RE	TX	VS
•	•				Advanced Private Inv [SOP]		608-785-2744				

CR	CV	PR	US	BK	←Courts	Oconto	Recorder→	UC	RE	TX	VS
•	•	•	•	•	Attorney's Process & Investigative Services [SOP]		800-236-5202	•	•	•	•
	•	•			Bay Title & Abstract Inc		920-431-6100	•	•	•	

CR	CV	PR	US	BK	←Courts	Oneida	Recorder→	UC	RE	TX	VS
•	•				Shadow Process Service [SOP]		800-626-7578				

CR	CV	PR	US	BK	←Courts	Outagamie	Recorder→	UC	RE	TX	VS
•	•	•	•	•	Attorney's Process & Investigative Services [SOP]		800-236-5202	•	•	•	•
	•	•			Bay Title & Abstract Inc		920-431-6100	•	•	•	
					Document Search Services		800-526-2157		•		
					Fox Cities Title Co		920-731-5494		•	•	
•	•	•	•	•	Lowery Professional Services Corp [SOP]		920-830-2114	•	•	•	•
•	•	•			Wisconsin Title of Shawano Inc		715-823-3600	•	•	•	

CR	CV	PR	US	BK	←Courts	Ozaukee	Recorder→	UC	RE	TX	VS
•	•	•	•	•	Attorney's Process & Investigative Services [SOP]		800-236-5202	•	•	•	•
					Document Search Services		800-526-2157		•		
•	•	•			🏛Great Minds/Search Associates		414-321-3375	•	•	•	
•	•		•	•	🏛Infotrack Information Services Inc		800-275-5594	•	•	•	
•	•		•	•	Interstate Reporting Co Inc (IRC)		262-251-6590	•		•	

CR	CV	PR	US	BK			UC	RE	TX	VS
•	•	•	•	•	Myhre Process [SOP]	414-271-9574	•		•	•
•	•	•	•	•	Paul C Klumb Agency LLC	414-254-1335	•	•	•	•
•	•	•		•	Southeast Wisconsin Process [SOP]	262-650-8904	•	•	•	•
	•	•			Stewart Title Services Inc, Wisconsin	800-523-3060	•	•	•	•
•	•				WERC - Wisconsin Employee & Renter Check LLC	414-967-9342			•	

CR	CV	PR	US	BK	←COURTS **PEPIN**	RECORDER→	UC	RE	TX	VS
					Dunn County Abstract & Title Inc	800-628-5727		•	•	
	•	•			Guaranty Title Services Inc	715-235-3393	•	•	•	
		•		•	The Title Co Inc (Eau Claire)	800-848-4853	•	•	•	

CR	CV	PR	US	BK	←COURTS **PIERCE**	RECORDER→	UC	RE	TX	VS
•	•	•	•	•	Avalon Information Services	715-222-4095		•	•	•
	•	•			Guaranty Title Services Inc	715-235-3393	•	•	•	
•	•	•			St Croix Valley Title Services Inc	715-425-1519	•	•	•	
		•		•	The Title Co Inc (Eau Claire)	800-848-4853	•	•	•	

CR	CV	PR	US	BK	←COURTS **POLK**	RECORDER→	UC	RE	TX	VS
•	•	•	•	•	Avalon Information Services	715-222-4095		•	•	•
					Guaranty Title Services Osceola	888-620-7243	•	•	•	

CR	CV	PR	US	BK	←COURTS **PORTAGE**	RECORDER→	UC	RE	TX	VS
		•			Boles-Wallner Abstract & Title	715-423-6940	•		•	

CR	CV	PR	US	BK	←COURTS **PRICE**	RECORDER→	UC	RE	TX	VS
	•	•	•	•	Phillips Land Title Co Inc	715-339-2230	•	•	•	

CR	CV	PR	US	BK	←COURTS **RACINE**	RECORDER→	UC	RE	TX	VS
•	•	•			AGH Professional Inv [SOP]	262-884-4688		•		•
•	•	•	•	•	Attorney's Process & Investigative Services [SOP]	800-236-5202	•	•	•	•
					Document Search Services	800-526-2157		•		
•	•	•	•	•	ESI Associates [SOP]	262-652-6361	•	•	•	•
•	•	•			Great Minds/Search Associates	414-321-3375	•	•	•	
•	•		•	•	Infotrack Information Services Inc	800-275-5594	•	•	•	
•	•		•	•	Interstate Reporting Co Inc (IRC)	262-251-6590	•		•	
•	•	•	•	•	Myhre Process [SOP]	414-271-9574	•		•	•
•	•	•	•	•	Paul C Klumb Agency LLC	414-254-1335	•	•	•	•
•	•	•		•	Southeast Wisconsin Process [SOP]	262-650-8904	•	•	•	•
	•	•			Stewart Title Services Inc, Wisconsin	800-523-3060	•	•	•	•
•	•				WERC - Wisconsin Employee & Renter Check LLC	414-967-9342			•	

CR	CV	PR	US	BK	←COURTS **RICHLAND**	RECORDER→	UC	RE	TX	VS
	•	•	•	•	The Title Co Inc (Prairie Du Chien WI)	888-918-4853	•	•	•	•
		•			Wisconsin Title of Richland Center Inc	800-236-4596	•	•	•	•

CR	CV	PR	US	BK	←COURTS **ROCK**	RECORDER→	UC	RE	TX	VS
•	•				Angel P I's [SOP]	800-973-3832				
•	•	•	•	•	Gregg Investigations Inc of Janesville [SOP]	800-866-1976	•		•	•
•	•	•	•	•	Stewart & Associates Inc - Rockford [SOP]	815-961-0150	•	•	•	•
	•	•			Stewart Title Services Inc, Wisconsin	800-523-3060	•	•	•	•

CR	CV	PR	US	BK	←COURTS **RUSK**	RECORDER→	UC	RE	TX	VS
•	•				Chippewa Valley Civil Process [SOP]	715-289-3922; cell 715-559-3922				
					Sawyer County Abstract & Title	715-634-9444	•	•	•	

CR	CV	PR	US	BK	←COURTS **SAUK**	RECORDER→	UC	RE	TX	VS
	•	•	•	•	Priority Records Search LLC [SOP]	608-544-9991	•	•	•	•
	•	•			Stewart Title Services Inc, Wisconsin	800-523-3060	•	•	•	•

CR	CV	PR	US	BK	←COURTS **SAWYER**	RECORDER→	UC	RE	TX	VS
					Sawyer County Abstract & Title	715-634-9444	•	•	•	

CR	CV	PR	US	BK	←COURTS SHAWANO	RECORDER→	UC	RE	TX	VS
•	•	•	•	•	Attorney's Process & Investigative Services [SOP]	800-236-5202	•	•	•	•
	•	•			Bay Title & Abstract Inc	920-431-6100	•	•	•	
•	•	•			Wisconsin Title of Shawano Inc	715-823-3600	•	•	•	

CR	CV	PR	US	BK	←COURTS SHEBOYGAN	RECORDER→	UC	RE	TX	VS
•	•	•	•	•	Backgrounds Plus	920-457-5745	•	•	•	•
•	•	•			Great Minds/Search Associates	414-321-3375	•	•	•	
•	•	•		•	Southeast Wisconsin Process [SOP]	262-650-8904	•	•	•	•
	•	•			Stewart Title Services Inc, Wisconsin	800-523-3060	•	•	•	•
•	•		•	•	Verified Inc	866-265-9426				

CR	CV	PR	US	BK	←COURTS ST. CROIX	RECORDER→	UC	RE	TX	VS
•	•	•	•	•	Avalon Information Services	715-222-4095		•	•	•
•	•	•	•	•	Capitol Lien Records & Research [SOP]	800-845-4077	•	•	•	•
	•	•			Guaranty Title Services Inc	715-235-3393	•	•	•	
•	•	•			St Croix Valley Title Services Inc	715-425-1519	•	•	•	
•	•	•	•	•	Twin Cities Research	651-714-0002	•	•	•	•

CR	CV	PR	US	BK	←COURTS TAYLOR	RECORDER→	UC	RE	TX	VS
•	•	•			Gowley Abstract	715-748-4790	•	•	•	

CR	CV	PR	US	BK	←COURTS TREMPEALEAU	RECORDER→	UC	RE	TX	VS
•	•				Advanced Private Inv [SOP]	608-785-2744				
		•	•	•	The Title Co Inc (La Crosse)	800-788-4853	•	•	•	

CR	CV	PR	US	BK	←COURTS VERNON	RECORDER→	UC	RE	TX	VS
•	•				Advanced Private Inv [SOP]	608-785-2744				
	•	•	•	•	The Title Co Inc (Viroqua)	800-538-4853	•	•	•	

CR	CV	PR	US	BK	←COURTS VILAS	RECORDER→	UC	RE	TX	VS
	•	•			Northern Title of Vilas County	715-479-6459	•	•	•	
•	•				Shadow Process Service [SOP]	800-626-7578				

CR	CV	PR	US	BK	←COURTS WALWORTH	RECORDER→	UC	RE	TX	VS
•	•	•			Great Minds/Search Associates	414-321-3375	•	•	•	
•	•	•	•	•	Gregg Investigations Inc of Janesville [SOP]	800-866-1976	•		•	•
•	•		•	•	Infotrack Information Services Inc	800-275-5594	•	•	•	
•	•	•	•	•	Myhre Process [SOP]	414-271-9574	•		•	•
•	•	•	•	•	Paul C Klumb Agency LLC	414-254-1335	•	•	•	•
•	•	•		•	Southeast Wisconsin Process [SOP]	262-650-8904	•	•	•	•
	•	•			Stewart Title Services Inc, Wisconsin	800-523-3060	•	•	•	•

CR	CV	PR	US	BK	←COURTS WASHBURN	RECORDER→	UC	RE	TX	VS
					Sawyer County Abstract & Title	715-634-9444	•	•	•	

CR	CV	PR	US	BK	←COURTS WASHINGTON	RECORDER→	UC	RE	TX	VS
					Document Search Services	800-526-2157		•		
•	•	•			Great Minds/Search Associates	414-321-3375	•	•	•	
•	•		•	•	Infotrack Information Services Inc	800-275-5594	•	•	•	
•	•		•	•	Interstate Reporting Co Inc (IRC)	262-251-6590	•		•	
•	•	•	•	•	Myhre Process [SOP]	414-271-9574	•		•	•
•	•	•	•	•	Paul C Klumb Agency LLC	414-254-1335	•	•	•	•
•	•	•		•	Southeast Wisconsin Process [SOP]	262-650-8904	•	•	•	•
	•	•			Stewart Title Services Inc, Wisconsin	800-523-3060	•	•	•	•
•	•		•	•	Verified Inc	866-265-9426				
•	•				WERC - Wisconsin Employee & Renter Check LLC	414-967-9342			•	

CR	CV	PR	US	BK	←COURTS WAUKESHA	RECORDER→	UC	RE	TX	VS
•	•	•	•	•	Attorney's Process & Investigative Services [SOP]	800-236-5202	•	•	•	•
					Document Search Services	800-526-2157		•		
•	•	•			Great Minds/Search Associates	414-321-3375	•	•	•	
•	•		•	•	Infotrack Information Services Inc	800-275-5594	•	•	•	
•	•		•	•	Interstate Reporting Co Inc (IRC)	262-251-6590	•		•	
•	•	•	•	•	Klitzke & Assoc Inc/Klitzke Services Group	262-521-9502	•	•	•	•
•	•	•	•	•	Myhre Process [SOP]	414-271-9574	•		•	•
•	•	•	•	•	Paul C Klumb Agency LLC	414-254-1335	•	•	•	•
•	•	•		•	Southeast Wisconsin Process [SOP]	262-650-8904	•	•	•	•
	•	•			Stewart Title Services Inc, Wisconsin	800-523-3060	•	•	•	•
•	•		•	•	Verified Inc	866-265-9426				
•	•				WERC - Wisconsin Employee & Renter Check LLC	414-967-9342			•	

CR	CV	PR	US	BK	←COURTS WAUPACA	RECORDER→	UC	RE	TX	VS
	•	•			Bay Title & Abstract Inc	920-431-6100	•	•	•	
	•	•			Stewart Title Services Inc, Wisconsin	800-523-3060	•	•	•	•
•	•	•			Wisconsin Title of Shawano Inc	715-823-3600	•	•	•	

CR	CV	PR	US	BK	←COURTS WAUSHARA	RECORDER→	UC	RE	TX	VS
		•			Boles-Wallner Abstract & Title	715-423-6940	•	•	•	

CR	CV	PR	US	BK	←COURTS WINNEBAGO	RECORDER→	UC	RE	TX	VS
•	•	•	•	•	Attorney's Process & Investigative Services [SOP]	800-236-5202	•	•	•	•
	•	•			Bay Title & Abstract Inc	920-431-6100	•	•	•	
					Document Search Services	800-526-2157		•		
					Fox Cities Title Co	920-731-5494		•	•	
•	•	•	•	•	Lowery Professional Services Corp [SOP]	920-830-2114	•	•	•	•
	•	•			Stewart Title Services Inc, Wisconsin	800-523-3060	•	•	•	•

CR	CV	PR	US	BK	←COURTS WOOD	RECORDER→	UC	RE	TX	VS
		•			Boles-Wallner Abstract & Title	715-423-6940	•	•	•	

Editor's Tip: Remember the first rule about public record searching: Simply because your state or county has certain rules, regulations and practices regarding the accessibility and content of public records, does not mean that another state or county adheres to the same rules.

Wyoming

COURT RECORDS RETRIEVED — CAPITAL - LARAMIE COUNTY — RECORDED RECORDS RETRIEVED

CR	CV	PR	US	BK	←COURTS ALBANY RECORDER→	UC	RE	TX	VS
	•	•	•	•	Daniel E Peel 970-377-8500	•	•	•	

CR	CV	PR	US	BK	←COURTS BIG HORN RECORDER→	UC	RE	TX	VS
	•	•			Heritage Escrow LLC 307-765-9399	•	•	•	•
•	•				Process Service of Wyoming [SOP] 307-266-1979				

CR	CV	PR	US	BK	←COURTS CAMPBELL RECORDER→	UC	RE	TX	VS
					See adjoining counties for retrievers or call court/recorder directly.				

CR	CV	PR	US	BK	←COURTS CARBON RECORDER→	UC	RE	TX	VS
•	•				Process Service of Wyoming [SOP] 307-266-1979				

CR	CV	PR	US	BK	←COURTS CONVERSE RECORDER→	UC	RE	TX	VS
•	•				Process Service of Wyoming [SOP] 307-266-1979				

CR	CV	PR	US	BK	←COURTS CROOK RECORDER→	UC	RE	TX	VS
					First American Title Co of Crook Cty 307-283-1844	•	•	•	
•	•	•	•	•	Legal Support Services Inc 800-583-0365	•	•	•	•

CR	CV	PR	US	BK	←COURTS FREMONT RECORDER→	UC	RE	TX	VS
•	•				Process Service of Wyoming [SOP] 307-266-1979				

CR	CV	PR	US	BK	←COURTS GOSHEN RECORDER→	UC	RE	TX	VS
					First American Torrington 307-532-5642		•	•	

CR	CV	PR	US	BK	←COURTS HOT SPRINGS RECORDER→	UC	RE	TX	VS
•	•				Process Service of Wyoming [SOP] 307-266-1979				

CR	CV	PR	US	BK	←COURTS JOHNSON RECORDER→	UC	RE	TX	VS
•	•				Process Service of Wyoming [SOP] 307-266-1979				

CR	CV	PR	US	BK	←COURTS LARAMIE RECORDER→	UC	RE	TX	VS
	•	•	•	•	Daniel E Peel 970-377-8500	•	•	•	

CR	CV	PR	US	BK	←COURTS LINCOLN RECORDER→	UC	RE	TX	VS
•	•	•			Bontecou Investigative Services Inc [SOP] 307-733-2637	•	•	•	
	•	•			Land Title Co 800-289-9920		•	•	

CR	CV	PR	US	BK	←COURTS NATRONA RECORDER→	UC	RE	TX	VS
	•	•	•	•	Daniel E Peel 970-377-8500	•	•	•	
	•	•			Petroleum Title Service Inc 307-235-6237	•	•	•	
•	•				Process Service of Wyoming [SOP] 307-266-1979				

CR	CV	PR	US	BK	←COURTS NIOBRARA RECORDER→	UC	RE	TX	VS
•	•				Process Service of Wyoming [SOP] 307-266-1979				

CR	CV	PR	US	BK	←COURTS PARK RECORDER→	UC	RE	TX	VS
•	•	•			Bontecou Investigative Services Inc [SOP] 307-733-2637	•	•	•	
•	•	•			Grizzly Investigative Services [SOP] 307-587-8395	•	•	•	

CR	CV	PR	US	BK	←COURTS PLATTE RECORDER→	UC	RE	TX	VS
					First American Wheatland 307-322-2133		•	•	

CR	CV	PR	US	BK	←COURTS	SHERIDAN	RECORDER→	UC	RE	TX	VS
	•	•	•	•	Daniel E Peel		970-377-8500	•	•	•	
	•	•	•		Sheridan County Title		307-672-6478	•	•	•	

CR	CV	PR	US	BK	←COURTS	SUBLETTE	RECORDER→	UC	RE	TX	VS
•	•	•			Bontecou Investigative Services Inc [SOP]		307-733-2637	•	•	•	

CR	CV	PR	US	BK	←COURTS	SWEETWATER	RECORDER→	UC	RE	TX	VS
•	•	•	•	•	Pioneer National Title Insurance		307-875-9833	•	•	•	

CR	CV	PR	US	BK	←COURTS	TETON	RECORDER→	UC	RE	TX	VS
•	•	•			Bontecou Investigative Services Inc [SOP]		307-733-2637	•	•	•	
	•	•			Land Title Co		800-289-9920		•	•	

CR	CV	PR	US	BK	←COURTS	UINTA	RECORDER→	UC	RE	TX	VS
					Uinta Title		307-789-1777		•	•	

CR	CV	PR	US	BK	←COURTS	WASHAKIE	RECORDER→	UC	RE	TX	VS
•	•				Process Service of Wyoming [SOP]		307-266-1979				

CR	CV	PR	US	BK	←COURTS	WESTON	RECORDER→	UC	RE	TX	VS
					Weston County Title		307-746-2001		•	•	

[SOP] = PERFORMS SERVICE OF PROCESS

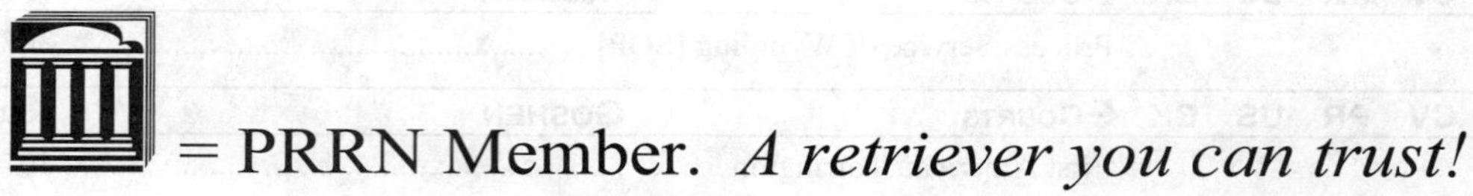

COURT RECORDS

CODE	GOVERNMENT AGENCY	TYPE OF INFORMATION
CR	Criminal Court	Municipal, county and state level criminal cases
CV	Civil Court	Municipal, county and state level civil cases
PR	Probate Court	Wills and estate cases
US	US District Court	Federal civil and criminal cases
BK	Bankruptcy Court	United States bankruptcy cases

COUNTY RECORDS - RECORDINGS

CODE	GOVERNMENT AGENCY	TYPE OF INFORMATION
UC	UCC Filing Office	Uniform Commercial Code and other personal property liens
RE	Real Estate Recording Office	Real property transactions and liens
TX	Tax Filing Office(s)	Federal and state tax liens, judgment liens
VS	Vital Records Office	Vital statistics—birth, death, marriage, divorce

Local Document Retriever Profiles

Information Found In The Retriever Profiles Section

The 2597 retriever profiles that follow are listed in alphabetical order. Individuals are listed by last name; companies are listed by the first letter of the company name.

Each Profile Contains...

- Retriever name and the logo if a PRRN Member in 2007 at time this Directory printed
- Address and telephone numbers, including fax when available
- Web page address; email address
- Summary of types of records retrieved
- Local retrieval area — a list of counties each services directly
- Other geographic areas serviced through correspondents
- Year established
- Project turnaround times
- Billing and payment terms
- If they perform service of process
- Additional information, including special areas of expertise

Although the usual billing practices used by each of the retrieval companies are indicated, no information about actual pricing is included. Fees are subject to private negotiation and depend on the type and extent of any given project.

Hints and Tips on Using the Profiles Section

Alphabetical Rules

As mentioned above, individual names are alphabetized by last name first, unless the name appears as part of a company name, in which case it is alphabetized by the first letter of the company name.

If the word "The" appears to be a definitive connected part of the company name, you may find the company in the "T" section.

Branch offices of larger retriever firms are listed individually. Usually the firm name is followed by the branch office name or locale in parenthesis, along with that branch's corresponding retrieval area.

Read for Specialties and Expertise

Each retriever was given the opportunity to submit a twenty-five word statement indicating what they do best. Take a moment and read this statement before calling a retriever. This will give you a much better idea of their service and expertise.

Listed at the end of this section are PRRN Associate Members who offer regional or national search or screening services only.

Some Retrievers Are Mobile

Don't be alarmed if you don't get a live person when calling a retriever. Many retrievers are on the job at the local courthouse or recorder's office. Some may carry a cell phone. As a general rule, retrievers will return calls as they are able. We provide all the telephone numbers for each entry in this Profile section. The previous section—the Index—only had the main telephone number.

Only Call a Retriever for the Records They Retrieve

Please review which categories of records are retrieved by a company prior to making a telephone call. For example, if a company only searches records at the recorder's office, you are wasting your time and the retriever's time to ask for a criminal or civil record from a court record repository.

Coverage Area Claimed in the County Index

Entries in this publication are based on the responses of each retrieval company. A county entry is shown when a retriever states to us that he, she or a true payroll employee visits that particular jurisdiction, and not a friend, another retriever, or correspondent.

Companies that offer only online indexing to these counties have been excluded, to the best of our knowledge. However, there are many companies that offer both hands-on and electronic retrieval.

Coverage Area By Correspondents or Networks

Keep in mind that many companies provide service in areas beyond the counties listed. When a retriever has the capability of offering expanded geographic coverage, the area is indicated in its Retriever Profile under **Correspondent Relationships**.

Searching Records at State Agencies

The retrievers located in or near a state capital often offer expertise in searching records at state agencies, for example where corporate and UCC records are located. If you need records retrieved or searched from a state agency, start with those firms with a physical presence in the capital, or if the firm states this expertise in the profile.

A & A Legal Service Inc
210 Fell St #17, San Francisco, CA 94102
Phone: 650-697-9431 - **Fax:** 650-697-4640
www.aalegalservice.com **email:** general@aalegalservice.com

Types of Records Retrieved: Criminal, Civil and Probate courts; Federal courts; Real Estate; Tax Liens/Judgments; UCC records; Vital records

Local Retrieval Area: CA-Alameda, Contra Costa, Marin, San Francisco, San Mateo, Santa Clara. **Correspondent Relationships:** nationwide.

Add'l Information: Established 1978. Normal turnaround time- 2-3 days. Expedited service available. Most projects billed by the hour; they charge mileage and/or per copy. First project may require prepayment. Credit cards accepted. A & A Legal Service Inc is accurate, trustworthy and reliable. Their researchers are well trained and keep updated on court procedures. A licensed PI in CA. Performs service of process.

A & A Screening Solutions LLC
PO Box 608, Mobile, AL 36601
Phone: 877-999-9318; 251-432-6100 - **Fax:** 877-999-9319; 251-432-6103
www.aaverify.com **email:** rbw@aaverify.com

Types of Records Retrieved: Criminal, Civil and Probate courts; Federal courts; UCC records; Tax Liens/Judgments

Local Retrieval Area: AL-Baldwin, Mobile. **Correspondent Relationships:** nationwide. Real time online access to all AL counties.

Add'l Information: Established 1996. Normal turnaround time- same day to 72 hours. Projects billed by number of names searched. Fees may vary. First project may require prepayment. Credit cards accepted. Payment terms can be net 30 days. They specialize in criminal record retrieval, civil/criminal investigations, service of process, pre-employment screening/tenant screening & background checks for pre-employment and tenant screening. They serve process all along the Gulf Coast in AL & MS. A licensed PI in AL. Performs service of process.

A & C Research
6185 Magnolia Ave #257, Riverside, CA 92506-2524
Phone: 951-301-6956 - **Fax:** 951-301-6823 aandcresearch@mchsi.com

Types of Records Retrieved: Criminal and Civil courts

Local Retrieval Area: CA-Orange, Riverside, San Bernardino

Add'l Information: Established 2001. Normal turnaround time- 24 hours. Projects billed by number of names searched. Will file/record documents for clients. Will bill weekly or bi-monthly with a net 30 days. They have over 20 years combined experience. They specialize in performing searches personally i.e., no online or database searches. Federal archives retrieval for Central and Southern Divisions.

A & M Attorney Services Inc
4647 Long Beach Blvd #D2, Long Beach, CA 90805-6976
Phone: 562-426-8306 - **Fax:** 562-426-6384 macy@amattorneyservice.com

Types Records Retrieved: Criminal, Civil and Probate courts; Federal courts

Local Retrieval Area: CA-Los Angeles, Orange

Add'l Information: Established 1959. Normal turnaround time- 1-4 days. Projects billed by the hour. Credit cards accepted. They specialize in process service. Performs service of process.

A & S Abstracting
1602 Little Cake Rd, Columbia, KY 42728
Phone: 270-250-1203 - **Fax:** 270-384-4805

Types of Records Retrieved: Real Estate; Tax Liens/Judgments

Local Retrieval Area: KY-Adair

Add'l Information: Established 2003. First project may require prepayment. They specialize in real estate.

A All State Tracers Company
6180C Hixson Pike #105, Hixson, TN 37343-3030
Phone: 423-605-0155 - **Fax:** 423-842-8011 cham7854_@bellsouth.net

Types of Records Retrieved: Criminal, Civil and Probate courts; US District/Bankruptcy courts; Real Estate; Tax Liens/Judgments; UCC records; Vital records

Local Retrieval Area: AL-De Kalb, Jackson; GA-Bartow, Catoosa, Chattooga, Cherokee, Clayton, Cobb, Dawson, De Kalb, Douglas, Floyd, Forsyth, Fulton, Gilmer, Gordon, Gwinnett, Henry, Murray, Paulding, Pickens, Polk, Whitfield; TN-Bedford, Bledsoe, Blount, Bradley, Cannon, Coffee, Cumberland, Davidson, Decatur, Dekalb, Franklin, Grundy, Hamilton, Knox, Lincoln, Loudon, McMinn, Marion, Meigs, Monroe, Polk, Rhea, Roane, Rutherford, Sequatchie, Van Buren, Warren, White, Williamson, Wilson. **Correspondent Relationships:** nationwide.

Add'l Information: Established 1990. Turnaround time- 24-72 hours. Projects billed by number of names searched. First project may require prepayment. Credit cards accepted. Will file/record documents for clients. They specialize in real estate, mortgages, UCCs, suits, tax liens/judgments, corporate filings, skiptracing, asset info. They perform title searches & current owner searches. Also performs criminal searches in 6 TN counties.

A California Process & Attorney Service
206 S "D" St, San Bernardino, CA 92401
Phone: 909-381-5185 - **Fax:** 909-885-5199
www.youbeenserved.com **email:** stephanie@youbeenserved.com

Types of Records Retrieved: Criminal, Civil and Probate courts; Federal courts; Real Estate; Tax Liens/Judgments; UCC records; Vital records

Local Retrieval Area: CA-Los Angeles, Orange, Riverside, San Bernardino. **Correspondent Relationships:** nationwide.

Add'l Information: Established 1985. Normal turnaround time- 1-3 days. Projects billed by the hour. First project may require prepayment. Will file/record documents for clients. They specialize in civil and real estate searches, process service and all attorney support services, including mobile photocopying and notary service. Performs service of process.

A Data Source
7909 Walerga Rd #112-205, Antelope, CA 95843
Phone: 916-726-4636 - **Fax:** 916-726-4902 adatas@aol.com

Types of Records Retrieved: Criminal, Civil and Probate courts; Federal courts; Real Estate; UCC records; Vital records

Local Retrieval: CA-Placer, Sacramento. **Correspondents:** nationwide.

Add'l Information: Established 1996. Normal turnaround time- 24-48 hours. Credit cards accepted. Will file/record documents for clients. They specialize in UCC, corporate, court and real property research, pre-employment screening, business and individual background profiles. Antelope, CA is located in Sacramento County.

A David Research
122 Calistoga Rd #243, Santa Rosa, CA 95409
Phone: 707-479-2779 - **Fax:** 707-535-2040 office@workingthecourts.com

Types of Records Retrieved: Criminal, Civil and Probate courts; Real Estate; Tax Liens/Judgments; UCC records; Vital records

Local Retrieval Area: CA-Napa, Sonoma

Add'l Information: Established 1991. Normal turnaround time- 24 hours. Projects billed by number of names searched. They have 15 years daily experience. Know who, what and exactly where to find it. Forensic searches done in both counties. 2,000,000/3,000,000 E & O insurance.

A J Info
6 Frederick St, East Brunswick, NJ 08816
Phone: 732-766-9268 or 732-353-6835 - **Fax:** 732-390-0988
www.ajinfosearch.com **email:** ramani@ajinfosearch.com

Types of Records Retrieved: Criminal, Civil and Probate courts; Federal courts; Real Estate; Tax Liens/Judgments; UCC records; Vital records

Local Retrieval Area: NY-New York, Richmond

Add'l Information: Established 2004. Normal turnaround time- within 24 hours. Projects billed by number of names searched. First project may require prepayment. Credit cards accepted. They specialize in civil, criminal courts, Federal courts, real estate, tax liens/judgments, UCC records, bankruptcy and probate.

A P Legal Support Services

2522 N Calvert St, Baltimore, MD 21218
Phone: 800-273-9928; 410-366-9109 - **Fax:** 410-366-9403
www.aplegalsupport.com **email:** craig@aplegelsupport.com

Types of Records Retrieved: Criminal, Civil and Probate courts; Federal courts; Real Estate; Tax Liens/Judgments; UCC records; Vital records

Local Retrieval Area: MD-Anne Arundel, Baltimore, Baltimore City, Carroll, Harford, Howard, Montgomery, Prince George's

Add'l Information: Established 1969. Normal turnaround time- 24-48 hours. Same day service available. Projects billed by the hour. First project may require prepayment. Will file/record documents for clients. In addition to document services and process service, they provide asset and property searches, online service, and witness and defendant locates. Call with any questions and to inquire about other services. Performs service of process.

A Public Record Expert Inc

5028 Lakehurst Ct, Palmetto, FL 34221
Phone: 941-504-7734 - **Fax:** 941-723-3989

Types of Records Retrieved: Criminal, Civil and Probate courts; Federal courts; Real Estate; Tax Liens/Judgments; UCC records

Local Retrieval Area: FL-Charlotte, De Soto, Hardee, Hillsborough, Manatee, Pinellas, Sarasota. **Correspondent Relationships:** Virginia.

Add'l Information: Established 2001. Normal turnaround time- 12-48 hours. Projects billed by number of names searched. Bulk rate discounts are available. Will file/record documents for clients. Payment net 30 days. They specialize in UCCs, tax liens, judgments, pending suits, mortgage retrievals and title searches. They are a notary & certified signing agent.

A Public Record Search Inc

PO Box 1119, Covington, LA 70434-1119
Phone: 985-892-5194 - **Fax:** 985-898-0837 lds@skycom1.com

Types of Records Retrieved: Civil and Probate courts; Real Estate; Tax Liens/Judgments; UCC records

Local Retrieval Area: LA-St. Tammany Parish. **Correspondent Relationships:** Jefferson, Livingston, Orleans, St Bernard, St Charles, Tangipahoa, Washington parishes.

Add'l Information: Established 1960. Normal turnaround time- 5 working days. Fee basis will vary by type of project. First project may require prepayment. Will file/record documents for clients. They specialize in document retrieval, metes and bounds, lot and block abstracting, property tax research and ownerships.

A Scott Broadhurst Associates

12 Main St, Dover, MA 02030
Phone: 617-536-3486 - **Fax:** 508-785-2852

Types of Records Retrieved: Criminal, Civil and Probate courts; Federal courts; Real Estate; Tax Liens/Judgments; UCC records

Local Retrieval Area: MA-Middlesex, Norfolk, Suffolk, Worcester

Add'l Information: Established 1988. Normal turnaround time- 24-48 hours. Expedited service is available. Projects billed by number of names searched. Will file/record documents for clients. They specialize in real estate, current owner, mortgage and assignment searches and document retrieval as well as UCC and court record searches. They are fully insured.

A Short Abstract Co

PO Box 657, Cavalier, ND 58220
Phone: 701-265-4176 - **Fax:** 701-265-4176

Types of Records Retrieved: Real Estate; Tax Liens/Judgments

Local Retrieval Area: ND-Pembina

Add'l Information: Established 1920. Normal turnaround time- 1-2 weeks depending on the order. Fee basis will vary by type of project. First project may require prepayment. Will file/record documents for clients. Out-of-state orders require prepayment. They specialize in title searches and abstracts of title.

A Very Private Eye Inc

220 S Orange Ave #2700, Orlando, FL 32801-6400
Phone: 407-273-6646 - **Fax:** 407-324-2527
www.averyprivateeye.com **email:** crahn@intellistar.net

Types of Records Retrieved: Criminal, Civil and Probate courts; Federal courts; Real Estate; Tax Liens/Judgments; UCC records; Vital records

Local Retrieval Area: FL-Brevard, Lake, Orange, Osceola, Polk, Seminole

Add'l Information: Established 1996. Normal turnaround time- 24 hours. Projects billed by the hour. First project may require prepayment. Credit cards accepted. They specialize in electronic sweeps, backgrounds, intelligence, covert equipment, domestics, locates, formal government wiretapping export. They are 25 year law enforcement veterans. They cover all of Central FL, both civil and criminal investigations. A licensed PI in FL. Performs service of process.

A Very Private Eye Research & Inv. Corp

20165 N 67th Ave #122A, Glendale, AZ 85308
Phone: 623-572-2665 - **Fax:** 623-572-2651 vimpi@worldnet.att.net

Types of Records Retrieved: Criminal, Civil and Probate courts; Federal courts; Real Estate; Tax Liens/Judgments; UCC records

Local Retrieval Area: AZ-Maricopa. **Correspondent Relationships:** Pinal, Pima, Cochise, Coconino, AZ counties.

Add'l Information: Established 2000. Normal turnaround time- 1-2 days. May be longer depending on court requirements-will advise clients. Projects billed by number of names searched. Projects billed by number of records located. Depends on assignments. First project may require prepayment. They specialize in birth/adoptee, witness & missing heir locates, background checks, asset, civil & criminal investigations. A licensed PI in AZ.

A.D.I. Litigation Support Services

323 6th St, Marysville, CA 95901
Phone: 530-743-4245 - **Fax:** 530-743-4250
www.nationwidelegal.com **email:** lonny.hord@nationwidelegal.com

Types of Records Retrieved: Criminal, Civil and Probate courts; Real Estate; Tax Liens/Judgments; Vital records

Local Retrieval Area: CA-Butte, Colusa, Sutter, Yuba

Add'l Information: Established 1990. Normal turnaround time- 1-2 days. Projects billed by the hour. First project may require prepayment. Formerly known as A.D.I. Investigative, they specialize in SOP and record retrieval. Insured. Celebrating 14th year serving Yuba, Sutter, Butte, and eastern Colusa counties. Also provides subpoena preparation and legal photocopy services. Performs service of process.

A.G.O. Legal Process Service

PO Box 16143, Las Cruces, NM 88004
Phone: 505-526-4303 - **Fax:** 505-526-4303

Types of Records Retrieved: Criminal, Civil and Probate courts; Real Estate; Tax Liens/Judgments; UCC records; Vital records

Local Retrieval: NM-Dona Ana, Grant, Hidalgo, Lincoln, Luna; TX-El Paso

Add'l Information: Established 1992. Normal turnaround time- 1-4 days. Expedited service available. Projects billed by the hour. All projects require prepayment. Performs service of process.

A/M Investigations

25 Congress St, Portland, ME 04101
Phone: 207-838-3111 - **Fax:** 207-772-5455 nmmpi007@yahoo.com

Types of Records Retrieved: Federal courts

Local Retrieval Area: ME-Cumberland. **Correspondent Relationships:** Maine, with personal service to Androscoggin, Sagadahoc, Waldo, York.

Add'l Information: Established 1988. Normal turnaround time- 24-48 hours for nearby counties; northern counties require more. Projects billed by the hour. All projects require prepayment. Many searches require fees to Clerk up front. Specialize in process service throughout Maine, 1 mile from civil and federal courthouse in Cumberland, Kennebec, Androscoggin, Sagadahoc, York, Knox and Waldo. Call for rates. A licensed PI in ME. Performs service of process.

A+ Super Search Inc

1245 Hurstview Dr #100, Hurst, TX 76053
Phone: 800-687-5553; 817-268-3224 - **Fax:** 800-687-5554; 817-285-9956
www.callsupersearch.com **email:** dwelch@callsupersearch.com

Types of Records Retrieved: Criminal, Civil and Probate courts; Federal courts; Real Estate; Tax Liens/Judgments; UCC records; Vital records

Local Retrieval: TX-Collin, Dallas, Denton, Ellis, Hood, Johnson, Tarrant

Add'l Information: Established 1990. Normal turnaround time- 24-48 hours. Projects billed by number of names searched. First project may require prepayment. Will file/record documents for clients. MasterCard and Visa credit cards only accepted. They specialize in court record research and legal document filings and retrieval. They also specialize in the UCC department. Will also go the National Archives.

A1 Background Screening

416 Classic Dr, Tallmadge, OH 44278
Phone: 330-940-2454 - **Fax:** 330-940-2454
a1background@neo.rr.com

Types of Records Retrieved: Criminal and Civil courts; Federal courts

Local Retrieval Area: OH-Cuyahoga, Medina, Portage, Stark, Summit. **Correspondent Relationships:** statewide.

Add'l Information: Established 2006. Normal turnaround time- 24-48 hours. Projects billed by number of names searched. First project may require prepayment. Will invoice, net 30 days. They are accurate and timely.

A1 Cleveland Service Agency Inc

PO Box 93447, Cleveland, OH 44101-5447
Phone: 888-212-5614; - **Fax:** 888-212-0896
www.clevelandservice.com **email:** phil@clevelandservice.com

Types of Records Retrieved: Criminal, Civil and Probate courts; Federal courts; Real Estate; Tax Liens/Judgments; UCC records; Vital records

Local Retrieval: OH-Cuyahoga, Lake. **Correspondents:** statewide.

Add'l Information: Established 2000. Normal turnaround time- 1-3 business days. Expedited service available. Projects billed by the hour. All projects require prepayment. Credit cards accepted. They specialize in "Getting the job done right". They are prior military and law enforcement professionals providing superior legal support services to Northeast Ohio. A licensed PI in OH. Performs service of process.

A-1 Document Service LLC

PO Box 50507, Sparks, nv 89435
Phone: 775-544-7993 - **Fax:** 775-626-1609
www.a-1ds.com **email:** a-1docsvc@charter.net

Types of Records Retrieved: Civil and Probate courts; Federal courts; Real Estate; Tax Liens/Judgments; UCC records; Vital records

Local Retrieval Area: NV-Washoe

Add'l Information: Established 2005. Normal turnaround time- 24-48 hours. Projects billed by number of names searched. Payment due upon receipt. They provide title abstracting, document research and retrieval, recording and mobile notary.

A1 Inv

PO Box 357, 114 N West St #204 (45801), Lima, OH 45802
Phone: 419-229-1955, 419-229-2872 - **Fax:** 419-222-4137
www.a1investigations.net **email:** a1invest@wcoil.com

Types of Records Retrieved: Criminal and Civil courts

Local Retrieval Area: OH-Allen, Auglaize, Hancock, Hardin, Mercer, Putnam, Van Wert

Add'l Information: Established 1997. All projects require prepayment. They also provide skiptracing, private investigations, and is a examiner and consultant for computer voice stress analyzer. A licensed PI in OH. Performs service of process.

A-1 Unisource Screening & Information

8280 Utica Ave, Rancho Cucamonga, CA 91730
Phone: 800-525-6972; 909-980-3311 - **Fax:** 909-980-5566
www.unisourcescreening.com **email:** info@unisourcescreening.com

Types of Records Retrieved: Criminal and Civil courts; Federal courts

Local Retrieval Area: CA-Alameda, El Dorado, Glenn, Kern, Los Angeles, Orange, Riverside, Sacramento, San Bernardino, San Diego, San Francisco, San Mateo, Santa Barbara, Ventura. **Correspondents:** nationwide.

Add'l Information: Established 1986. Normal turnaround time- 24-72 hours. Projects billed by number of names searched. They conduct drug testing and background screening nationally. With over 14 years investigative experience, they are dedicated to "Providing Safe Environments" for employers and employees nationally.

AAA Abstract & Title Co Inc (Texas)

PO Box 38, 1 Planter St, Emory, TX 75440
Phone: 903-473-2233 - **Fax:** 903-474-9483 rca@verizon.net

Types of Records Retrieved: Civil and Probate courts; Real Estate; Tax Liens/Judgments **Local Retrieval Area:** TX-Rains

Add'l Information: Established 1965. Normal turnaround time- variable depending on project. Fee basis varies by type of transaction. First project may require prepayment. Will file/record documents for clients. Performs service of process.

AAA Abstract Co Inc (Oklahoma)

118 W Olive St, Stilwell, OK 74960
Phone: 918-696-2770 - **Fax:** 918-696-5869 aaaabstract@alltel.net

Types of Records Retrieved: Criminal, Civil and Probate courts; Federal courts; Real Estate; Tax Liens/Judgments; UCC records; Vital records

Local Retrieval Area: OK-Adair

Add'l Information: Established 1965. Normal turnaround time- 1-10 days. Projects billed by number of records located. All projects require prepayment. Will file/record documents for clients. Personal checks are accepted. They specialize in abstracts by photocopies of actual documents, increasing accuracy of abstract and usefulness to examining attorney. They also do closings.

AAA Process Service Inc

PO Box 21788, St Louis, MO 63109-0788
Phone: 888-350-5809; 314-351-7979 - **Fax:** 314-752-5785
www.havepaperswilltravel.com **email:** andersonispy@aol.com

Types of Records Retrieved: Criminal, Civil and Probate courts; Federal courts; Real Estate; Tax Liens/Judgments; UCC records; Vital records

Local Retrieval Area: IL-Madison, Monroe, St. Clair; MO-Franklin, Jefferson, St. Charles, St Louis City, St. Louis. **Correspondent Relationships:** statewide.

Add'l Information: Established 1998. Normal turnaround time- 3-5 days. Expedited service available. Projects billed by the hour. All projects require prepayment. Credit cards accepted. A licensed PI in MO. Performs service of process.

AAA Research

1548 Strong Highway, El Dorado, AR 71730
Phone: 870-310-3528 - **Fax:** 870-862-4770

Types of Records Retrieved: Criminal, Civil and Probate courts; Real Estate; UCC records; Tax Liens/Judgments; Vital records

Local Retrieval Area: AR-Ashley, Bradley, Calhoun, Chicot, Clark, Cleveland, Columbia, Dallas, Drew, Grant, Hempstead, Howard, Lafayette, Lincoln, Little River, Nevada, Ouachita, Pike, Sevier, Union; LA-Claiborne, Morehouse, Ouachita, Union. **Correspondent Relationships:** Garland, Hot Spring, Pulaski, Saline counties, AR.

Add'l Information: Established 1997. Normal turnaround time- 24-48 hours. Fee depends on quantity per county. They specialize in all types of records in Southern Arkansas and far northern Louisiana counties, and are expanding into Texarkana and Northern Louisiana.

AAA Search Excellence Inc

3099 Deltona Blvd, Spring Hill, Fl 34606
Phone: 352-688-6751 - **Fax:** 352-666-1449

Types of Records Retrieved: Civil and Probate courts; Real Estate; Tax Liens/Judgments; UCC records

Local Retrieval Area: FL-Alachua, Bay, Brevard, Charlotte, Citrus, Clay, Collier, Duval, Hernando, Indian River, Lee, Marion, Monroe, Okaloosa, Pasco, Pinellas, Polk, Sarasota, Seminole, Walton

Add'l Information: Established 1994. Normal turnaround time- 24-48 hours. Projects billed by number of names searched. Will file/record documents for clients. They provide document retrievals, current owner searches, full searches and document filings. Call for full information. Has 24-48 hour turnaround. Other counties serviced.

AAA VTS Investigations

79 W Monroe St #1122, Chicago, IL 60603
Phone: 800-203-4160; 312-782-7361 - **Fax:** 312-782-2838
www.pichicago.com **email:** lisah@pichicago.com

Types of Records Retrieved: Criminal, Civil and Probate courts; Federal courts; Real Estate; Tax Liens/Judgments; UCC records; Vital records

Local Retrieval Area: IL-Cook, De Kalb, Du Page, Kane, Kendall, Lake, McHenry, Will. Also retrieve from the Federal Archive Center in Chicago

Add'l Information: Established 1980. Normal turnaround time- 24-48 hours. Rush service accepted. Projects billed by number of names searched. Credit cards accepted. Will file/record documents for clients. Personal checks accepted. Formerly VTS, they are a licensed, insured Illinois detective agency providing document retrieval in Chicago metro area since 1979. They cover all of Northern IL. Cook county experts. Has a daily standing appointment at Chicago Federal Archives Ctr. A licensed PI in IL. Performs service of process.

Aaron Anderson Agency

PO Box 2065, Escondido, CA 92033-2065
Phone: 760-751-0101 - **Fax:** 760-751-0599 apvti@yahoo.com

Types of Records Retrieved: Criminal and Civil courts; Federal courts; Tax Liens/Judgments

Local Retrieval Area: CA-San Diego. **Correspondents:** nationwide.

Add'l Information: Established 1993. Normal turnaround time- 1-2 days. Projects billed by number of names searched. Monthly payment. They specialize in civil, criminal and workers' compensation. All searches are "hands on." Owner is a retired US Probation/Parole Officer now licensed as a California Private Investigator. A licensed PI in CA.

ABA Services

1156 W Thornbury Pl, Highlands Ranch, CO 80129
Phone: 720-344-1259 - **Fax:** 720-344-1265 karl-long@comcast.net

Types of Records Retrieved: Criminal and Civil courts; Federal courts; Real Estate; Tax Liens/Judgments; UCC records

Local Retrieval Area: CO-Arapahoe, Denver, Douglas, Jefferson; DC-District of Columbia; VA-Alexandria, Fairfax, Loudoun, Prince William

Add'l Information: Established 2004. Normal turnaround time- 24-72 hours. Projects billed by number of names searched. Payment due net 15 days. A complete court retrieval research and document retrieval services.

ABC Investigators Inc

PO Box 1981, Crowley, LA 70527
Phone: 800-738-7300; 307-783-6131 - **Fax:** 337-783-7070
www.abcinvestigators.com **email:** pete@abcinvestigators.com

Types of Records Retrieved: Criminal, Civil and Probate courts; Federal courts; Real Estate; Tax Liens/Judgments; UCC records

Local Retrieval Area: LA-Acadia, Jefferson Davis, Lafayette, St. Landry, Vermilion Parishes. **Correspondent Relationships:** nationwide.

Add'l Information: Established 1982. Normal turnaround time- same week. Projects billed by the hour. First project may require prepayment. Will file/record documents for clients. They are a certified legal investigative firm, a CLI. A licensed PI in LA. Performs service of process.

ABC Legal Services Inc

633 Yesler Way, Seattle, WA 98104-2725
Phone: 800-736-7295; 206-839-1195 - **Fax:** 800-536-0797
www.abclegal.com **email:** research@abclegal.com

Types of Records Retrieved: Criminal, Civil and Probate courts; Federal courts; Real Estate; Tax Liens/Judgments; UCC records; Vital records

Local Retrieval Area: WA-Grays Harbor, Island, King, Kitsap, Lewis, Mason, Pierce, Skagit, Snohomish, Thurston, Whatcom. **Correspondent Relationships:** nationwide.

Add'l Information: Established 1974. Normal turnaround time- 1-2 days. Billing depends on the nature of the project. Credit cards accepted. Will file/record documents for clients. They will also invoice. Personal checks are accepted. They are online with SCOMIS, PACER and CourtLink, which allows them instant access to court index records. A licensed PI in WA. Performs service of process.

ABC Services Inc Court Services

2 E Minnesota St, Le Center, MN 56057-1502
Phone: 507-357-6320 - **Fax:** 507-357-6056 tba@frontiernet.net

Types of Records Retrieved: Criminal and Civil courts; Federal courts

Local Retrieval Area: MN-Aitkin, Anoka, Beltrami, Benton, Big Stone, Blue Earth, Brown, Carlton, Carver, Cass, Chippewa, Chisago, Clearwater, Cook, Cottonwood, Crow Wing, Dakota, Dodge, Faribault, Fillmore, Freeborn, Goodhue, Grant, Hennepin, Houston, Isanti, Itasca, Jackson, Kanabec, Kandiyohi, Kittson, Koochiching, Lac Qui Parle, Lake, Le Sueur, Lincoln, Lyon, Mahnomen, Marshall, Martin, McLeod, Meeker, Mille Lacs, Morrison, Mower, Murray, Nicollet, Nobles, Norman, Olmsted, Pennington, Pine, Pipestone, Polk, Pope, Ramsey, Redwood, Renville, Rice, Rock, Roseau, Scott, Sherburne, Sibley, St. Louis, Steele, Stevens, Swift, Todd, Traverse, Wabasha, Wadena, Waseca, Washington, Watonwan, Wilkin, Winona, Wright, Yellow Medicine. **Correspondents:** statewide.

Add'l Information: Established 1991. Normal turnaround time- 8-24 hours. Projects billed by number of names searched. Monthly billing. They have been in business for over 10 years; the owner was deputy court administrator for six years. They also offer statewide unlawful detainers. Will retrieve court records statewide via their network.

ABC Services Inc Real Estate Svcs

2 E Minnesota St, Le Center, MN 56057-1502
Phone: 507-357-6320 - **Fax:** 507-357-6056 tba@frontiernet.net

Types of Records Retrieved: Criminal and Civil courts; Federal courts; Real Estate; Tax Liens/Judgments; UCC records

Local Retrieval Area: MN-Anoka, Blue Earth, Brown, Carver, Dakota, Dodge, Freeborn, Hennepin, Le Sueur, McLeod, Mower, Nicollet, Olmsted, Ramsey, Rice, Scott, Sherburne, Sibley, Steele, Waseca, Washington. **Correspondent Relationships:** statewide.

Add'l Information: Established 1991. Normal turnaround time- 8-24 hours. Projects billed by number of names searched. Monthly billing. They have been in business for over 10 years; the owner was deputy court administrator for six years. They also offer statewide unlawful detainers. Will retrieve real estate, UCC, and tax lien records for select MN counties.

Abeln Abstract & Title Co

PO Box 92, 47 W 7th St, Dubuque, IA 52004-0092
Phone: 563-582-7148 - **Fax:** 563-582-5298

Types of Records Retrieved: Civil and Probate courts; Real Estate; Tax Liens/Judgments; UCC records; Vital records

Local Retrieval Area: IA-Dubuque

Add'l Information: Established 1890. Normal turnaround time- 2-3 days. Projects billed by number of names searched. A charge for time is also included. Will file/record documents for clients. They specialize in real estate and personal lien searches.

Aberdeen Investigations, Inc

172 Wolverine Cr, Thunder Bay, ON P7C 5Z2
Phone: 807-626-4074 - **Fax:** 807-475-6915 rperkins@tbaytel.net

Types of Records Retrieved: Civil and Probate courts; Real Estate; Tax Liens/Judgments

Local Retrieval Area: CANADA-Ontario, Thunder Bay

Add'l Information: Established 1981. Normal turnaround time- 24 hours. Projects billed by the hour. Will file/record documents for clients. Payment due upon receipt of invoice. They specialize in Thunder Bay, Ontario, and northwestern Ontario. They are a full service investigation company that services all of Northwestern Ontario. In business since 1981. A licensed PI in ONTARIO, CANADA. Performs service of process.

Able Atlanta Research

3904 N Darid Hills Rd, Decatur, GA 30033
Phone: 404-502-2024 - **Fax:** 770-987-3782

Types of Records Retrieved: Criminal and Civil courts; UCC records; Tax Liens/Judgments

Local Retrieval Area: GA-Barrow, Clayton, De Kalb, Fulton, Gwinnett, Hall, Henry, Rockdale, Walton. **Correspondent Relationships:** Cobb, Cherokee, Forsyth.

Add'l Information: Established 2003. Normal turnaround time- 24-48 hours. Projects billed by number of names searched. Will bill 30 days net.

Abstract & Data Search Services

513 E McKinley Ave, Mishawaka, IN 46545
Phone: 888-457-5344; 574-256-5344 - **Fax:** 574-256-7350
www.adss1.com **email:** datasearch@ameritech.net

Types of Records Retrieved: Civil courts; Probate courts; Federal courts; Real Estate; UCC records; Tax Liens/Judgments; Vital records

Local Retrieval Area: IN-Elkhart, La Porte, Marion, St. Joseph

Add'l Information: Established 1988. Normal turnaround time- same or next day. Bill monthly and special arrangements are available. First project may require prepayment. Will file/record documents for clients. Their main objectives are solid communications, consistent turnaround times and top quality research.

Abstract & Guaranty Co

812 Manvel Ave, Chandler, OK 74834-3858
Phone: 405-258-1244 - **Fax:** 405-258-1657

Types of Records Retrieved: Civil and Probate courts; Real Estate; Tax Liens/Judgments; UCC records **Local Retrieval Area:** OK-Lincoln

Add'l Information: Established 1900. Normal turnaround time- 48 hours. Fee basis will vary by the type of project. All projects require prepayment. Will file/record documents for clients.

Abstract & Title Co

PO Box 182, Albion, IL 62806
Phone: 618-445-2554 - **Fax:** 618-445-2938 abstractandtitle@direcway.com

Types of Records Retrieved: Real Estate

Local Retrieval Area: IL-Clark, Clay, Coles, Crawford, Cumberland, Edwards, Effingham, Franklin, Gallatin, Hamilton, Jackson, Jasper, Jefferson, Johnson, Lawrence, Marion, Massac, Perry, Pope, Randolph, Richland, Saline, Union, Wabash, Wayne, White, Williamson. **Correspondent Relationships:** Gibson and Posey counties IN.

Add'l Information: Established 1974. Normal turnaround time- 36 hours. Projects billed by number of names searched. Will file/record documents for clients. Terms: net 15-30 days. They specialize in all the above services along with full real estate searches and preparation of Complete Abstracts of Title in all listed counties.

Abstract & Title Guaranty Co

326 5th Ave S, Clinton, IA 52732-4511
Phone: 563-243-2027 - **Fax:** 563-243-6108
www.abstractco.com **email:** atgc@abstractco.com

Types of Records Retrieved: Criminal, Civil and Probate courts; Real Estate; Tax Liens/Judgments; UCC records; Vital records

Local Retrieval Area: IA-Clinton, Jackson

Add'l Information: Established 1893. Normal turnaround time- 2-3 days. Expedited service available. Fee basis varies by type of transaction. Will file/record documents for clients.

Abstract & Title Inc

PO Box 246, 413 D St, Fairbury, NE 68352
Phone: 402-729-2771 - **Fax:** 402-729-6366 abstractandtitle@netscape.net

Records Retrieved: Real Estate; Tax Liens/Judgments; UCC records

Local Retrieval: NE-Clay, Fillmore, Gage, Jefferson, Saline, Seward, Thayer

Add'l Information: Established 1964. Normal turnaround time- 24 hours. Projects billed by number of names searched. Projects billed by number of records located. Fee basis is per description of one ownership. First project may require prepayment. Will file/record documents for clients. They specialize in abstracting, title insurance, closing and research. They have been in business over 30 years and have a 100-year title plant.

Abstract & Title Services Inc

PO Box 26, 503 W Main, Anamosa, IA 52205
Phone: 319-462-4828 - **Fax:** 319-462-4958

Types of Records Retrieved: Criminal, Civil and Probate courts; Real Estate; Tax Liens/Judgments; UCC records; Vital records

Local Retrieval Area: IA-Jones

Add'l Information: Established 1857. Normal turnaround time- 1-5 days. Projects are billed by predetermined fees, extra for additional research or excessive copies. Will file/record documents for clients. They have the most complete set of records for Jones County; excellent turnaround time.

Abstract & Title Services of Carlton Inc

PO Box 556, 199 Chestnut, Carlton, MN 55718
Phone: 888-331-3966; 218-384-3450 - **Fax:** 218-384-3451
www.abstracttitle.net **email:** info@abstracttitle.net

Types of Records Retrieved: Civil and Probate courts; Federal courts; Real Estate; Tax Liens/Judgments; UCC records

Local Retrieval Area: MN-Aitkin, Carlton, Pine, St. Louis; WI-Douglas

Add'l Information: Established 1993. Normal turnaround time- 24 hours depending on travel time. Projects billed by number of names searched. Projects billed by the hour. First project may require prepayment. Will file/record documents for clients. They specialize in real estate & searches for UCC, court judgment, tax lien, probate records & bankruptcy docs. Access US Bankruptcy & judgment records in Duluth. Licensed closers & abstractors. Special orders OK. Aitkin cty office phone- 877-751-5528. Performs service of process.

Abstract &Title Co

PO Box 720, 299 N Main St, Watford City, ND 58854-0720
Phone: 701-842-3366 - **Fax:** 701-444-2709 abstract@rtc.coop

Types of Records Retrieved: Civil and Probate courts; Real Estate; Tax Liens/Judgments; UCC records; Vital records

Local Retrieval Area: ND-McKenzie

Add'l Information: Established 1954. Normal turnaround time- variable depending on project. Projects billed by number of names searched. Projects billed by the hour. First project may require prepayment. Will file/record documents for clients. Personal checks are accepted.

Abstract Art Corporation

217 E Houston St, # 5E, New York, NY 10002
Phone: 212-228-1850 - **Fax:** 212-228-0114
www.abstractartnyc.com **email:** ximena@abstractartnyc.com

Types of Records Retrieved: Civil courts; Federal courts; Real Estate; Tax Liens/Judgments; UCC records

Local Retrieval Area: NY-Bronx, Kings, New York, Queens, Richmond

Add'l Information: Established 2003. Normal turnaround time- 24-48 hours. Projects billed by number of names searched. All projects require prepayment. Will file/record documents for clients. Accurate Search Corp will guarantee superior service in the New York City area abstracting and record retrieval industry. Twenty years experience and a great team of qualified abstractors.

Abstract Art Inc

PO Box 1749, Clinton, NC 28329
Phone: 910-592-2972 - **Fax:** 910-592-4942

Types of Records Retrieved: Real Estate; Tax Liens/Judgments; UCC records; Vital records

Local Retrieval Area: NC-Cumberland, Harnett, Johnston, Sampson, Wayne
Add'l Information: Established 1995. Normal turnaround time- 24 hours. Projects billed by number of names searched. First project may require prepayment. Will file/record documents for clients.

Abstract Associates of Lancaster Inc

1903 Lititz Pike, Lancaster, PA 17601-3805
Phone: 717-581-5841 - **Fax:** 717-581-5845
www.abstractassociates.com **email:** bstull@abstractassociates.com

Types of Records Retrieved: Real Estate; Tax Liens/Judgments; Probate courts; UCC records; Vital records

Local Retrieval Area: PA-Berks, Chester, Dauphin, Lancaster, Lebanon, York. **Correspondent Relationships:** nationwide.

Add'l Information: Established 1992. Normal turnaround time- 1 week. Expedited service available. Fee basis will vary by the type of project. First project may require prepayment. They specialize in deed and lien searches, financing statements, and document retrieval. Performs service of process.

Abstract Enterprises Inc

628 Spruce St, Scranton, PA 18503
Phone: 570-963-5290 - **Fax:** 570-983-0093

Types of Records Retrieved: Civil and Probate courts; Real Estate; Tax Liens/Judgments; UCC records; Vital records

Local Retrieval Area: PA-Lackawanna

Add'l Information: Established 1990. Normal turnaround - 3 days. Fee basis will vary by the type of project. Will file/record documents for clients.

Abstract One

31162 Dogwood Acres Rd, Dagsboro, DE 19939
Phone: 302-732-9027 - **Fax:** 302-732-9029 abstract1@mchsi.com

Types of Records Retrieved: Criminal, Civil and Probate courts; Real Estate; Tax Liens/Judgments; UCC records; Vital records

Local Retrieval Area: PA-York. **Correspondents:** nationwide.

Add'l Information: Established 1986. Normal turnaround time- 24-48 hours. Projects billed by number of names searched. Projects billed by the hour. Fee basis will vary by the type of project. First project may require prepayment. Will file/record documents for clients. Terms: net 30 days. They specialize in lien searches (one or more owner property reports), criminal checks, UCC reports, judgments and full title searches.

Abstracting & Legal Research Inc

PO Box 127, Alexandria, LA 71309-0127
Phone: 318-473-9979 - **Fax:** 318-449-9739
www.alrinc-la.com **email:** alrinc@cox-internet.com

Types of Records Retrieved: Criminal, Civil and Probate courts; Federal courts; Real Estate; Tax Liens/Judgments; UCC records; Vital records

Local Retrieval Area: LA-Allen, Avoyelles, Evangeline, Grant, Natchitoches, Rapides, Sabine, St. Landry, Vernon Parishes. **Correspondent Relationships:** statewide.

Add'l Information: Established 1989. Normal turnaround time- 48 hours for direct parishes and over 48 hours for the remainder of state. Projects billed by number of names searched. Projects billed by the hour. First project may require prepayment. They specialize in parish records.

Abstracting US Inc

PO Box 944, Nashua, NH 03061
Phone: 603-598-4106 x208 - **Fax:** 603-598-4108
www.abstractingus.com **email:** info@abstractingus.com

Types of Records Retrieved: Civil courts; Federal courts; Real Estate; Tax Liens/Judgments; UCC records; Vital records

Local Retrieval Area: NH-Belknap, Carroll, Cheshire, Coos, Grafton, Hillsborough, Merrimack, Rockingham, Strafford, Sullivan. **Correspondent Relationships:** MA, CT.

Add'l Information: Established 2006. Normal turnaround time- 3-5 days. Projects billed by number of records located. First project may require prepayment. Specialize in retrieval of business/individual, small claims/civil judgments, evictions, state/federal tax liens/releases. Along with UCC filings, vital records and archived bankruptcy court files.

Abstractor Associates Inc

18044 13 Mile Rd #200, Roseville, MI 48066
Phone: 586-778-7554 - **Fax:** 586-778-9730
www.abstractorassociates.com **email:** michele@abstractorassociates.com

Types of Records Retrieved: Civil and Probate courts; Federal courts; Real Estate; Tax Liens/Judgments; UCC records; Vital records

Local Retrieval Area: MI-Macomb, St. Clair, Washtenaw, Wayne. **Correspondents:** Oakland, Genesee, Lapeer, Saginaw, Shiawassee.

Add'l Information: Established 1990. Normal turnaround time- 24-48 hours. Expedited service available. Projects billed by number of names searched. Projects billed by the hour. They specialize in title research (current owner to full 60 year searches). They also do asset lien searches, litigation research, document retrieval, commercial and cell tower searches.

Abstracts by Godail

251 Florida Blvd #212, Baton Rouge, LA 70801
Phone: 800-660-7318; 225-343-0351 - **Fax:** 800-660-7469; 225-343-1341

Types of Records Retrieved: Civil and Probate courts; Federal courts; Real Estate; Tax Liens/Judgments; UCC records

Local Retrieval Area: LA-Ascension Parish, Assumption Parish, East Baton Rouge Parish, Livingston Parish, Pointe Coupee Parish, Rapides Parish, St. Landry Parish, West Baton Rouge Parish. **Correspondents:** statewide.

Add'l Information: Established 1981. Normal turnaround time- 1-2 days. Projects billed by the hour. First project may require prepayment. Will file/record documents for clients. They have been established for over 22 years. Covers all Louisiana at added cost.

Abstracts by Starkey Inc

4031-B Clinton Ave, Richmond, VA 23227
Phone: 804-305-6022 - **Fax:** 866-272-6673
www.abstractsbystarkey.com **email:** mail@abstractsbystarkey.com

Types of Records Retrieved: Criminal, Civil and Probate courts; Real Estate; Tax Liens/Judgments; UCC records; Vital records

Local Retrieval Area: VA-Amelia, Chesterfield, Colonial Heights, Dinwiddie, Goochland, Hanover, Henrico, Hopewell, King William, Louisa, New Kent, Petersburg, Powhatan, Prince George, Richmond City

Add'l Information: Established 2005. Normal turnaround time- 24 hours. Expedited service available. Projects billed by number of records located. First project may require prepayment. Abstracts by Starkey is a progressive and energetic company dedicated to advancing the field of records research. They offer two-way portable faxing and emailing capabilities.

Abstracts of McIntosh County Inc

PO Box 154, Ashley, ND 58413-0154
Phone: 701-288-3618 - **Fax:** 701-288-3508 grosslo@drtel.net

Types of Records Retrieved: Criminal, Civil and Probate courts; Real Estate; Tax Liens/Judgments; UCC records; Vital records

Local Retrieval Area: ND-McIntosh

Add'l Information: Established 1984. Normal turnaround time- 1-3 days. Projects billed by number of names searched. Projects billed by number of records located. First project may require prepayment. Will file/record documents for clients. They specialize in researching all records on file in the county offices. They have many records in-house.

Abstracts/Trustees of Texas

PO Box 9932, 4505 Spicewood Springs Rd #303, Austin, TX 78766
Phone: 888-452-0331; 512-340-0331 - **Fax:** 888-452-3442; 512-340-0226
www.atotx.com **email:** orders@atotx.com

Types of Records Retrieved: Real Estate; Tax Liens/Judgments; UCC records; Probate courts; Bankruptcy court

Local Retrieval Area: TX-Atascosa, Austin, Bastrop, Bexar, Blanco, Brazoria, Brazos, Burleson, Burnet, Caldwell, Collin, Colorado, Comal, Coryell, Dallas, Denton, Ector, Falls, Fayette, Fort Bend, Freestone, Frio, Galveston, Gillespie, Gonzales, Grayson, Grimes, Guadalupe, Harris, Hays, Hidalgo, Hill, Howard, Jefferson, Johnson, Karnes, Kaufman, Kendall, Kerr, Lampasas, Lavaca, Lee, Limestone, Llano, McLennan, Medina, Midland, Milam, Montgomery, Potter, Robertson, Rockwall, Tarrant, Taylor, Travis, Upton, Washington, Wichita, Williamson, Wilson. **Correspondent Relationships:** the balance of Texas and the USA.

Add'l Information: Established 1986. Normal turnaround time- 24-72 hours. Projects billed by number of names searched. Fees vary depending upon volume. First project may require prepayment. Will file/record documents for clients. They specialize in property searches and foreclosures.

Abstrax

315 Meigs Rd #A178, Santa Barbara, CA 93109
Phone: 805-683-9606 - **Fax:** 805-967-6525 rpfols@juno.com

Types of Records Retrieved: Criminal, Civil and Probate courts; Federal courts; Real Estate; Tax Liens/Judgments; UCC records; Vital records

Local Retrieval Area: CA-Santa Barbara, Ventura

Add'l Information: Established 1993. Normal turnaround time- 24-48 hours. Projects billed by number of names searched. Contract services available. First project may require prepayment. Will file/record documents for clients. Terms: net 45 days.

Acadia Legal Support

PO Box 191, Frankfort, ME 04438-0191
Phone: 207-223-5285 - **Fax:** 207-223-3904 acadialegal@gwi.net

Types of Records Retrieved: Criminal, Civil and Probate courts; Federal courts; UCC records; Real Estate; Tax Liens/Judgments; Vital records

Local Retrieval Area: ME-Hancock, Penobscot, Waldo

Add'l Information: Established 1997. Normal turnaround time- 1-2 days. Expedited service available. Projects billed by number of names searched. First project may require prepayment. They promise fast, efficient, dependable service to the mid-coast region. Performs service of process.

ACBS

5910 Hamilton Blvd, Allentown, PA 18106
Phone: 866-530-2227; - **Fax:** 610-530-5665
www.acbsi.com **email:** info@acbsi.com

Types of Records Retrieved: Criminal and Civil courts; Real Estate; Tax Liens/Judgments; UCC records

Local Retrieval Area: PA-Carbon, Lehigh, Northampton, Schuylkill. **Correspondent Relationships:** statewide in PA, NJ.

Add'l Information: Established 1929. Normal turnaround time- 24-36 hours. Projects billed by number of records located. Will file/record documents for clients. Will invoice monthly. Their real estate department has a comprehensive selection of business and real estate search reports and flood certification reports with life of loan, accessible via Internet ordering.

Access Information

234 Columbine St #310, Denver, CO 80206-4711
Phone: 800-827-7607; 303-778-7677 - **Fax:** 303-778-7691
www.access-information.com **email:** ai@access-information.com

Types of Records Retrieved: Criminal, Civil and Probate courts; Federal courts; Real Estate; Tax Liens/Judgments; UCC records; Vital records

Local Retrieval Area: CO-Arapahoe, Boulder, Broomfield, Denver, Douglas, Jefferson. **Correspondents:** most of Colorado and nationwide.

Add'l Information: Established 1981. Normal turnaround time- same or next day. Projects billed by the hour. First project may require prepayment. Credit cards accepted. Will file/record documents for clients. They specialize in document research and retrieval, as well as court monitoring and insurance records.

Access Information Services Inc - NY

1773 Western Ave, Albany, NY 12203
Phone: 800-388-1598; 518-452-1873 - **Fax:** 800-388-1599; 518-452-0822
accessin@sprynet.com

Types of Records Retrieved: Criminal and Civil courts; Federal courts; Real Estate; Tax Liens/Judgments; UCC records

Local Retrieval Area: NY-Albany, Rensselaer, Saratoga, Schenectady. **Correspondent Relationships:** nationwide.

Add'l Information: Established 1994. Normal turnaround time- 24-36 hours. Projects billed by number of names searched. First project may require prepayment. Credit cards accepted. Will file/record documents for clients. They specialize in UCC preparation, filing and searching. Will search any public record nationwide. Performs service of process.

Access Information Svcs - AZ Katie Anderson

PO Box 90585, Tucson, AZ 85752
Phone: 520-405-8737 - **Fax:** 520-844-1759 katieand@earthlink.net

Types of Records Retrieved: Criminal and Civil courts

Local Retrieval Area: AZ-Apache, Cochise, Coconino, Gila, Graham, Greenlee, La Paz, Maricopa, Mohave, Navajo, Pima, Pinal, Santa Cruz, Yavapai, Yuma. **Correspondent Relationships:** statewide.

Add'l Information: Established 1992. Normal turnaround time- within 24 hours of ordering. Projects billed by number of names searched. She specializes in felony, misdemeanor, and civil cases in Arizona.

Access Louisiana Inc

400 Travis St #504, Shreveport, LA 71101
Phone: 800-489-5620; 318-227-9730 - **Fax:** 800-705-8953; 318-222-3053

Types of Records Retrieved: Civil and Probate courts; Federal courts; Real Estate; Tax Liens/Judgments; UCC records

Local Retrieval Area: LA-Bienville, Bossier, Caddo, Claiborne, DeSoto, Red River, Webster. **Correspondent Relationships:** Louisiana, Texas, Florida extensively.

Add'l Information: Established 1991. Normal turnaround time- 24-48 hours. Projects billed by number of names searched. They offer a discount for volume. Will file/record documents for clients. Personal checks are accepted. They provide registered agent services for Louisiana and all corp services and filings with the Sec. of State. They are online with the UCC system and corporate database with the Sec. of State. Registered agent services for Louisiana.

Access Research

PO Box 33325, San Diego, CA 92163
Phone: 619-231-8947 - **Fax:** 619-231-9338
www.accessresearchsd.com **email:** newrequest@accessresearchsd.com

Types of Records Retrieved: Criminal, Civil and Probate courts; Federal courts; Tax Liens/Judgments; UCC records; Vital records

Local Retrieval Area: CA-Alameda, Butte, Contra Costa, Fresno, Imperial, Kern, Lake, Los Angeles, Marin, Monterey, Orange, Riverside, Sacramento, San Bernardino, San Diego, San Francisco, San Mateo, Santa Clara, Ventura. **Correspondent Relationships:** nationwide.

Add'l Information: Established 1995. Normal turnaround time- 24-48 hours. Expedited service available. Projects billed by number of names searched. Payment due net 30 days. They specialize in fast, accurate background research and document retrieval in every California county.

Access RI Public Information

1 Richmond Sq #125B, Providence, RI 02906
Phone: 877-999-7474; 401-421-5700 - **Fax:** 401-421-5701
www.ri-pi.com **email:** accessri@cox.net

Types of Records Retrieved: Criminal, Civil and Probate courts; Federal courts; Tax Liens/Judgments; UCC records; Vital records

Local Retrieval Area: RI-Bristol, Kent, Newport, Providence, Washington. **Correspondent Relationships:** statewide.

Add'l Information: Established 1994. Normal turnaround time- 24 hours or same-day service. Projects billed by the hour. 1-hr minimum on most jobs. Orders submitted with multiple names for statewide criminal searches will be billed per name. First project may require prepayment. Will file/record documents for clients. They specialize in comprehensive personal background and corporate due diligence profiling as well as document procurement and document filing. Located in downtown Providence. A licensed PI in RI. Performs service of process.

Accessible Document Retrieval

525 N Fulton St, Fresno, CA 93728-3401
Phone: 559-779-5491 - **Fax:** 559-443-0073 lovetra.sullivant@amail.com

Types of Records Retrieved: Criminal, Civil and Probate courts; Federal courts; Real Estate; Tax Liens/Judgments; UCC records; Vital records

Local Retrieval Area: CA-Fresno, Madera

Add'l Information: Established 1992. Normal turnaround time- 24 hours, except weekends, holidays. Some archived courts records may take longer. Projects billed by number of names searched. Fee basis varies by type of project. Will file/record documents for clients. Per agreement. They specialize in all types of court records research and county recorder records in Fresno and Madera Counties CA. All work is "hands on" from actual public records.

Accountable Process Servers Inc

PO Box 588, Cambridge, MN 55008-0588
Phone: 612-991-7849 - **Fax:** 763-689-4191 lynxamanda@msn.com

Types of Records Retrieved: Criminal, Civil and Probate courts; Federal courts; Real Estate; Tax Liens/Judgments

Local Retrieval Area: MN-Anoka, Chisago, Hennepin, Isanti, Ramsey, Sherburne, Washington

Add'l Information: Established 1986. Normal turnaround time- 1-2 days. Billed by project. Will file/record documents for clients. Will invoice; terms net 30 days. They specialize in current owner searches, document retrievals, filing, full searches, criminal and civil record searches, and process serving. Performs service of process.

Accu-Check Information Services

PO Box 1002, Parkersburg, WV 26102
Phone: 304-375-4802 - **Fax:** 304-375-2018 mlsandy@charter.net

Types of Records Retrieved: Criminal and Civil courts; US District court; UCC records; Tax Liens/Judgments

Local Retrieval Area: OH-Washington; WV-Cabell, Doddridge, Fayette, Greenbrier, Jackson, Jefferson, Kanawha, Mingo, Nicholas, Pleasants, Putnam, Raleigh, Ritchie, Tyler, Wetzel, Wirt, Wood

Add'l Information: Established 1999. Normal turnaround time- 24-48 hours. Expedited service available. Projects billed by number of names searched. First project may require prepayment. Monthly billing. Accu-Check Information Services is owned and operated by professional record researcher of over 10 years experience. They believe their clients deserve excellent and accurate customer service.

AccuFacts Research Corporation

PO Box 514, Olympia, WA 98507-0514
Phone: 800-898-5583; 360-956-3990 - **Fax:** 800-473-0148; 360-956-1398
www.accufactsresearch.com **email:** cynthia@accufactsresearch.com

Types of Records Retrieved: Criminal, Civil and Probate courts; Federal courts; Tax Liens/Judgments; UCC records

Local Retrieval Area: WA-Thurston. **Correspondents:** nationwide.

Add'l Information: Established 1994. Normal turnaround time- 4 hours. Projects billed by number of names searched. Charges are per jurisdiction/per name searched. Will file/record documents for clients. Terms: net 30 days. They specialize in obtaining Superior Court records at all counties in Washington, and UCC and corporate services nationwide. Online access to US District & Bankruptcy courts nationwide.

Accufax: Authentic Document Retrieval

PO Box 177, 1463D Gravel Pike, Perkiomenville, PA 18074-0177
Phone: 800-336-1001; 215-234-0700 - **Fax:** 215-234-0905
www.accufax.cc **email:** sd@accufax.cc

Types of Records Retrieved: Criminal and Civil courts; Federal courts; Real Estate; Tax Liens/Judgments; UCC records; Vital records

Local Retrieval Area: DE-Kent, New Castle, Sussex; NJ-all counties; PA-all counties; MD-all counties. **Correspondent Relationships:** nationwide.

Add'l Information: Established 1986. Normal turnaround time- 12-24 hours. Projects billed by number of names searched. Fees are by county searched. First project may require prepayment. Credit cards accepted. Will file/record documents for clients. Authentic, genuine file retrieval and a full-service background screener, courthouse retrieval includes federal courts and state agencies. 21 years consecutive, uninterrupted operations.

Accurate Abstracting Services LLC

PO Box 701363, Louisville, KY 40270
Phone: 502-585-4017 - **Fax:** 502-585-4018 amandac@iglou.com

Types of Records Retrieved: Bankruptcy court; Real Estate; Tax Liens/Judgments; UCC records

Local Retrieval Area: KY-Bullitt, Clark, Jefferson, Nelson, Oldham, Spencer. **Correspondent Relationships:** KY, IN, OH.

Add'l Information: Established 2005. Normal turnaround time- 24-48 hours. Projects billed by number of names searched. Payment due net 30 days. They are a professional title reporting company specializing in full and current owner searches. Will perform lien/judgment searches as well as real estate document retrieval and filings.

Accurate Abstracts by Delores Dios

46 Chelsea Rd, Clifton, NJ 07012-1609
Phone: 201-207-0628 - **Fax:** 973-256-0757
www.accurateabstracts.com **email:** matt.dios@accurateabstracts.com

Types of Records Retrieved: Real Estate; Tax Liens/Judgments; Probate courts; UCC records

Local Retrieval Area: NJ-Atlantic, Bergen, Burlington, Camden, Cape May, Cumberland, Essex, Gloucester, Hudson, Hunterdon, Mercer, Middlesex, Monmouth, Morris, Ocean, Passaic, Salem, Somerset, Sussex, Union, Warren

Add'l Information: Established 1974. Normal turnaround time- 3 days. Projects billed by number of names searched. Projects billed by number of records located. First project may require prepayment. Will file/record documents for clients. Payment due upon receipt. She specializes in court record searches, real estate and environmental searches, foreclosures and tax sales. Voice mail: 973-837-1959.

Accurate Background Check

108 N Magnolia Ave #202, Ocala, FL 34475
Phone: 877-611-2277; 352-291-1155 - **Fax:** 877-913-2277; 352-854-8917
www.AccurateBackgroundCheck.com
email: LolaGonzalez@AccurateBackgroundCheck.com

Types of Records Retrieved: Criminal, Civil and Probate courts; Federal courts; Real Estate; Tax Liens/Judgments; Vital records

Local Retrieval Area: FL-Alachua, Citrus, Levy, Marion, Pasco, Sumter. **Correspondent Relationships:** statewide.

Add'l Information: Established 1999. Normal turnaround time- 24 hours. Projects billed by number of names searched. First project may require prepayment. Credit cards accepted. They specialize in criminal, misdemeanor civil searches, drug screening, credit reports, warranty deeds, tenant screening, polygraphs & investigations. Their staff includes a licensed PI. They also do workers comp, electronic fingerprinting & retrieval. A licensed PI in FL. Performs service of process.

Accurate Background Inc

6 Orchard #200, Lake Forest, CA 92630-8306
Phone: 800-784-3911; 949-609-0155 - **Fax:** 800-784-3593; 949-609-0166
www.accuratebackground.com **email:** caldrich@accuratebackground.com

Types of Records: Criminal and Civil courts; Federal District courts

Local Retrieval Area: CA-Los Angeles, Orange, Riverside, San Bernardino, San Diego, San Francisco, San Mateo, Santa Clara, Ventura; AZ-Maricopa; NV-Clark. **Correspondent Relationships:** nationwide.

Add'l Information: Established 1997. Normal turnaround time- 24-48 hours. Projects billed by number of names searched. Credit cards accepted. Credit accounts accepted. They are a national wholesaler of criminal and civil court searches for pre-employment screeners. Online computer ordering and electronic transfers are featured.

Accurate Background Services LLC

829 Bethel Rd #132, Columbus, OH 43235
Phone: 614-205-0743 - **Fax:** 614-840-0141
www.absllc.info **email:** hillabs@sbcglobal.net

Types of Records Retrieved: Criminal, Civil and Probate courts; Federal courts; Real Estate; Tax Liens/Judgments; UCC records; Vital records

Local Retrieval Area: OH-Delaware, Fairfield, Franklin, Licking, Pickaway

Add'l Information: Established 2005. Normal turnaround time- 24-72 hours. Expedited services available. Projects billed by number of names searched. Will invoice, net 30 days. ABS's mission is to provide customers with the most accurate, affordable background information available. They offer on-site fingerprinting, electronic searches and will file or retrieve documents. A licensed PI in OH.

Accurate Confidential Research Inc

12973 SW 112th St #317, Miami, FL 33186
Phone: 305-386-6677 - **Fax:** 305-383-2514 accurate247@aol.com

Types of Records Retrieved: Criminal, Civil and Probate courts; Federal courts; Real Estate; Tax Liens/Judgments; UCC records; Vital records

Local Retrieval Area: FL-Broward, Dade, Palm Beach. **Correspondent Relationships:** nationwide.

Add'l Information: Established 1984. Normal turnaround time- 24 hours. Projects billed by number of names searched. Payment terms are net 30 days. First project may require prepayment. Credit cards accepted. Will file/record documents for clients. They do all of their court/real estate research ON-SITE. They use old fashioned methods for accuracy; can retrieve any document. They use microfilm, microfiche and ledger books. A licensed PI in FL.

Accurate Data

805 Fox St Box 73, Elizabethtown, NC 28337
Phone: 910-862-4949 - **Fax:** 910-862-4101 bcampbell6@ec.rr.com

Types of Records Retrieved: Civil and Probate courts; Tax Liens/Judgments; UCC records

Local Retrieval Area: NC-Columbus, Cumberland, Robeson, Sampson

Add'l Information: Established 2005. Normal turnaround time- 1-3 days. Projects billed by number of names searched. First project may require prepayment. Credit cards accepted. They have over 20 years experience in searching civil and criminal records on the state level. Worked in the court system as a deputy clerk from 1977-1998.

Accurate Records Research LLC

1801 Todd Way, Meridian, ID 83642
Phone: 208-888-2857 - **Fax:** 208-288-4371 recresrch@cableone.net

Types of Records Retrieved: Criminal and Civil courts; Federal District courts; Real Estate; Tax Liens/Judgments; UCC records

Local Retrieval Area: ID-Ada, Bannock, Boise, Canyon, Gem, Latah, Payette. **Correspondent Relationships:** All counties in Idaho.

Add'l Information: Established 1998. Normal turnaround time- 24-48 hours. Projects billed by number of names searched. Will file/record documents for clients. Net 30 days. They specialize in criminal background checks and current owner searches.

Accurate Research & Closing Services

10415 Olympia Fields Dr, Bakersfield, CA 93312
Phone: 661-302-5110 or 5105 - asinks-gholaw@earthlink.net

Types of Records Retrieved: Criminal, Civil and Probate courts; Real Estate; Tax Liens/Judgments; UCC records

Local Retrieval Area: CA-Kern

Add'l Information: Established 1991. Normal turnaround time- 24-48 hours. Will file/record documents for clients. Has extensive knowledge of escrow, title and banking industry. Is a member for 15 years with the National Notary Assoc Certified Loan Signing Agent/Paralegal. Licensed process server on staff. Performs service of process.

Accurate Research & Information Svcs

PO Box 152, Mabscott, WV 25871
Phone: 304-252-0863 - **Fax:** 304-252-0909 clvia1@charter.net

Types of Records Retrieved: Criminal, Civil and Probate courts; Tax Liens/Judgments

Local Retrieval Area: WV-Cabell, Fayette, Kanawha, Monongalia, Raleigh. **Correspondent Relationships:** statewide.

Add'l Information: Established 2000. Normal turnaround time- 24-48 hours. Projects billed by number of names searched. First project may require prepayment. They specialize in local court records and can provide quick turnaround in Raleigh, Cabell, and Fayette counties due to their offices in Beckley and in Huntington.

Accurate Source.com Inc

1185 Dundas St E, #215, Mississauga, Ontario, CANADA L4Y 2C6
Phone: 877-635-8551; 905-829-0755 - **Fax:** 800-404-4677
https://www.accuratesource.com/home/ **email:** info@accuratesource.com

Types of Records Retrieved: Criminal and Civil courts; Driver Records & Abstracts; SINs; Reference checks

Local Retrieval Area: Canada-Alberta, British Columbia, Manitoba, New Brunswick, Newfoundland, Northwest Territories, Nova Scotia, Ontario, Prince Edward, Saskatchewan, Yukon. **Correspondents:** Canada.

Add'l Information: Established 1995. Normal turnaround time- 48-72 hours. Projects billed by number of names searched. Credit cards accepted. Payment due net 15-30 days. They are a public records retrieval and service corp engaged in providing private sector wholesale prices and service in research for entire Canada, including driver records/abstracts, SINs, ref checks.

Accurate Source.com Inc

PO Box 3488, Fullerton, CA 92831
Phone: 800-978-8950; 714-449-0961 - **Fax:** 800-978-8951; 714-449-9581
https://www.accuratesource.com/home/ **email:** info@accuratesource.com

Types of Records Retrieved: Criminal and Civil courts; Federal courts; Tax Liens/Judgments; UCC records

Local Retrieval Area: CA-Los Angeles, Orange, Riverside, San Bernardino, San Diego, Ventura. **Correspondent Relationships:** statewide and Canada.

Add'l Information: Established 1995. Normal turnaround time- 12-48 hours. Projects billed by number of names searched. Credit cards accepted. Payment terms are net 15-30 days. They are a public records retrieval and services company providing the private sector with wholesale prices and exceptional service. Performs service of process.

AccuScreen Systems

1038 Main St, Baton Rouge, LA 70802
Phone: 800-383-6476; 225-343-8378 - **Fax:** 225-383-6445
www.accuscreensystems.com **email:** bruce@accuscreensystems.com

Types of Records: Criminal and Civil courts; Federal District court

Local Retrieval Area: LA-East Baton Rouge Parish, West Baton Rouge Parish. **Correspondent Relationships:** LA parishes of St. Tammany, Lafayette, Rapides.

Add'l Information: Established 1974. Normal turnaround time- 2 days. Projects billed by number of names searched. First project may require prepayment. Monthly billing available. They specialize in criminal background checks, investigative services, pre-employment screening and drug testing. A licensed PI in LA. Performs service of process.

AccuSearch Inc

2338 W Royal Palm Rd, Suite J, Phoenix, AZ 85021-9339
Phone: 800-462-7019; 602-249-3466 - **Fax:** 800-632-2104; 602-249-0821
www.accusearch.biz **email:** info@accusearch.biz

Types of Records Retrieved: Criminal, Civil and Probate courts; Federal courts; Real Estate; Tax Liens/Judgments; UCC records

Local Retrieval Area: AZ-Apache, Coconino, Gila, Graham, Greenlee, La Paz, Maricopa, Mohave, Navajo, Pima, Pinal, Yavapai. **Correspondent Relationships:** statewide.

Add'l Information: Established 1989. Normal turnaround time- 24-48 hours. Projects billed by number of names searched. Credit cards accepted. Will file/record documents for clients. Payment terms are net 30 days. Checks accepted. Volume discounts available. A licensed, bonded, insured PI agency searching all Arizona counties & records. Statewide searches cover all 15 Arizona counties. Corporate filings, document retrieval, state agent service, UCCs and other filings. A licensed PI in AZ.

Accu-Source Inc

PO Box 1661, Decatur, TX 76234
Phone: 940-627-4944 - **Fax:** 817-887-5553
www.accu-source.com **email:** sales@accu-source.com

Types of Records Retrieved: Criminal and Civil courts

Local Retrieval Area: TX-Bexar, Collin, Dallas, Denton, Grayson, Gregg, Harris, Hunt, Johnson, Kaufman, Lamar, Nueces, Parker, Rockwall, Tarrant, Tom Green, Wise. **Correspondent:** nationwide (for criminal).

Add'l Information: Established 1986. Normal turnaround time- 24-48 hours for local counties, usually less than 2 hrs. Projects billed by number of names searched. First project may require prepayment. Credit cards accepted. Terms are net 30 days. Pay Pal payments are also accepted. They specialize in pre-employment background processing, automated plate and VIN searches. Please note their fast turnaround times and online services on criminal records and credit header searches.

AccuTech Legal Support Services

PO Box 12037, San Diego, CA 92101
Phone: 800-275-7189; 619-232-9905 - **Fax:** 619-232-5928
accubob1@msn.com

Types of Records Retrieved: Criminal, Civil and Probate courts; Federal courts; Real Estate; Tax Liens/Judgments; UCC records; Vital records

Local Retrieval Area: CA-San Diego. **Correspondents:** statewide.

Add'l Information: Established 1986. Normal turnaround time- 1-4 days. Projects billed by number of names searched. Projects billed by number of records located. First project may require prepayment. Credit cards accepted. Will file/record documents for clients. Terms: net 30 days. MasterCard and Visa accepted. They specialize in court research and record retrieval. A general attorney service and can scan documents to CD-ROM. Performs service of process.

Ace Background Check Inc

6158 Sierra Trl, Clinton, OH 44216
Phone: 800-731-9221; 330-882-4284 - **Fax:** 330-882-4292
www.acebackground.com **email:** jabologa@msn.com

Types of Records Retrieved: Criminal, Civil and Probate courts; Federal courts; Real Estate; Tax Liens/Judgments; UCC records; Vital records

Local Retrieval Area: OH-Ashtabula, Belmont, Carroll, Columbiana, Coshocton, Cuyahoga, Erie, Geauga, Guernsey, Harrison, Holmes, Huron, Jefferson, Knox, Lake, Licking, Lorain, Medina, Muskingum, Portage, Richland, Stark, Trumbull, Tuscarawas, Wayne. **Correspondent Relationships:** statewide.

Add'l Information: Established 2002. Normal turnaround time- 24-72 hours. Expedited service available. Projects billed by number of names searched. Credit cards accepted. Will file/record documents for clients. Will invoice net 30 days. With the mission of providing their clients with the most accurate, affordable background information available, Ace offers one-stop search to extensive employment, tenant/character profile screenings in the State of Ohio. Covers WV for criminal search.

ACME Research

44272 Rail Rd, Guthrie, MN 56461-9728
Phone: 218-224-3239 - **Fax:** 218-224-4005 acme@paulbunyan.net

Types of Records Retrieved: Criminal, Civil and Probate courts; Federal courts; Real Estate; Tax Liens/Judgments; UCC records; Vital records

Local Retrieval Area: MN-Beltrami, Cass, Hubbard

Add'l Information: Established 1991. Normal turnaround time- 72 hours. Projects billed by the hour. First project may require prepayment. Personal checks accepted. They specialize in personal injury investigation. A licensed PI in MN. Performs service of process.

Acme Research

Michigan City, IN 46360
Phone: 219-878-9950, fax-same

Types of Records Retrieved: Criminal courts

Local Retrieval Area: IN-Elkhart, Marshall, St. Joseph. **Correspondent Relationships:** Adams County, IL for criminal records only.

Add'l Information: Established 1989. Normal turnaround time- 24 hours. Projects billed by number of names searched. First project may require prepayment. Will bill established customers on 15th and end of month. Their work is very accurate with fast turnaround time; is a paralegal and has been in government, ran for county clerk. Fax contact suggested.

ACMS Process Service

PO Box 26604, Tucson, AZ 85726
Phone: 520-629-0303 - **Fax:** 520-628-8339 acms2serve@cox.net

Types of Records Retrieved: Criminal, Civil and Probate courts; Federal courts; Real Estate; Tax Liens/Judgments; UCC records; Vital records

Local Retrieval Area: AZ-Pima, Pinal, Santa Cruz. **Correspondent Relationships:** Cochise and Graham counties AZ.

Add'l Information: Established 1975. Normal turnaround time- 2-3 days. Expedited service available. Projects billed by number of names searched. First project may require prepayment. ACMS Process Service prides itself in its customer service and customer satisfaction. They are fast efficient and professional. Performs service of process.

Action Legal Support Services

5528 N Palm #123, Fresno, CA 93704
Phone: 559-432-3337 - **Fax:** 559-432-1140
www.actionlegalsupport.com **email:** action@attitude.com

Types of Records Retrieved: Criminal, Civil and Probate courts; Federal courts

Local Retrieval Area: CA-Fresno, Kern, Madera, Merced, Stanislaus, Tulare. **Correspondent Relationships:** Fresno, Kern, Kings, Madera, Merced, Stanislaus, Tulare counties CA.

Add'l Information: Established 1968. Normal turnaround time- within 1 week. Projects billed by number of names searched. Projects billed by number of records located. Projects billed by the hour. First project may require prepayment. Will file/record documents for clients. They have more than 35 years in business and are members of CAPPS and NAPPS. Performs service of process.

Action Professional Services

115 E 11th #212, Sioux Falls, SD 57104
Phone: 888-335-3090; 605-335-3090
http://action.business-direct.com **email:** action@willinet.net

Types of Records Retrieved: Criminal and Civil courts; Real Estate; Tax Liens/Judgments; UCC records

Local Retrieval Area: SD-Lincoln, Minnehaha

Add'l Information: Established 1983. Normal turnaround time- 4 days. Projects billed by number of names searched. First project may require prepayment. Credit cards accepted. They specialize in service of process and collections. Performs service of process.

Action Services & Research Inc

25 Falconer St #2, North Tonawanda, NY 14120
Phone: 877-553-7504; 716-692-5032 - **Fax:** 716-692-5039
www.actionlegal.biz **email:** mike@actionlegal.biz

Types of Records Retrieved: Criminal, Civil and Probate courts; Federal courts; Real Estate; Tax Liens/Judgments; UCC records; Vital records

Local Retrieval Area: NY-Erie, Niagara. **Correspondent Relationships:** New York.

Add'l Information: Established 1985. Normal turnaround time- 1-2 days depending on project. Projects billed by number of names searched. First project may require prepayment. Credit cards accepted. Will file/record documents for clients. Action Services knows the business and progressively work at being the best, so you are the best. Performs service of process.

Active Detective Bureau Inc

4239 Hamilton Ave, Cincinnati, OH 45223
Phone: 800-405-4006; 513-541-6600 - **Fax:** 513-541-6690
www.adbsecurity.com **Types of Records Retrieved:** Criminal, Civil and Probate courts; Federal courts; Real Estate; Tax Liens/Judgments; Vital records

Local Retrieval Area: KY-Boone, Campbell, Kenton; OH-Butler, Clermont, Hamilton, Warren

Add'l Information: Established 1976. Normal turnaround time- 2-3 days. Expedited service available. Projects billed by number of records located. Projects billed by the hour. First project may require prepayment. Process service requires pre-payment. They specialize in legal service of process, investigative services, commercial & domestic surveillance, as well as security services. A licensed PI in OH & IN. Performs service of process.

AD Services (ADS)

38750 Paseo Padre Pky #A1, Fremont, CA 94536-6169
Phone: 800-827-9101; 510-795-1111 - **Fax:** 510-793-2222

Types of Records Retrieved: Criminal, Civil and Probate courts; Real Estate; Tax Liens/Judgments; Vital records

Local Retrieval Area: CA-Alameda, Contra Costa, San Joaquin, San Mateo, Santa Clara, Stanislaus

Add'l Information: Established 1972. Normal turnaround time- 2-5 days. Projects billed by the hour. All individuals must prepay, all companies are invoiced. They specialize in process servicing. Performs service of process.

Adair County Abstract Company

230 Public Square, PO Box 86, Greenfield, IA 50849
Phone: 800-798-6129; 641-743-6129 - **Fax:** 641-743-6129

Types of Records Retrieved: Civil and Probate courts; Real Estate; Tax Liens/Judgments; UCC records

Local Retrieval Area: IA-Adair

Add'l Information: Established 1875. Normal turnaround time- 1-2 days. They charge a flat rate per project. Will file/record documents for clients.

Adams County Abstract Co

PO Box 790, Hettinger, ND 58639
Phone: 701-567-2224 - **Fax:** 701-567-2910

Types of Records Retrieved: Real Estate; Tax Liens/Judgments; UCC records

Local Retrieval Area: ND-Adams

Add'l Information: Established 1907. Normal turnaround time- 7-10 days full title. Fee basis will vary by the amount of time to perform the search. First project may require prepayment. Will file/record documents for clients. They will also invoice. They specialize in title and mineral searches.

Adams Freelance Title

1875 Kentucky Hwy 1781, Waynesburg, KY 40489
Phone: 606-365-8108 - **Fax:** 606-365-8108

Types of Records Retrieved: Real Estate; Tax Liens/Judgments

Local Retrieval Area: KY-Boyle, Garrard, Lincoln, Rockcastle

Add'l Information: Established 1997. Normal turnaround time- 48 hours. First project may require prepayment. She specializes in abstractor/title searches and document retrieval.

Adams Investigations

8146 Ivy St, Dexter, IA 50070-7507
Phone: 888-844-0624; 515-523-1081
www.investigatorlady.com **email:** Nic@investigatorlady.com

Types of Records Retrieved: Criminal, Civil and Probate courts; Federal courts; Real Estate; Tax Liens/Judgments; UCC records; Vital records

Local Retrieval Area: IA-Dallas, Polk. **Correspondent Relationships:** O'Brien, Sioux counties IA.

Add'l Information: Established 1995. Normal turnaround time- 24-48 hours. Projects billed by number of names searched. Projects billed by the hour. All projects require prepayment. Credit cards accepted. Will file/record documents for clients. They specialize in location of people and assets, fraud detection, witness location, identity theft, legal research, hidden assets, witness interviews, fraud and insurance. A licensed PI in IA. Performs service of process.

Adams Land Title (Hastings)

PO Box 1347, 422 N Hastings Ave #102, Hastings, NE 68901
Phone: 402-463-4198 - **Fax:** 402-463-6480
adamslt@alltel.net

Types of Records Retrieved: Real Estate; Tax Liens/Judgments; Probate courts; Federal courts

Local Retrieval Area: NE-Adams, Buffalo, Clay, Fillmore, Franklin, Hall, Hamilton, Kearney, Nuckolls, Webster, York. **Correspondent Relationships:** Nebraska.

Add'l Information: Established 1979. Normal turnaround time- 1 week. Projects billed by number of records located. First project may require prepayment. Will file/record documents for clients.

Roy Adams

3998 Acorn Dr, Harrison, AR 72601
Phone: 870-741-0489

Types of Records Retrieved: Real Estate; Tax Liens/Judgments; Criminal and Civil courts (rarely)

Local Retrieval Area: AR-Baxter, Benton, Boone, Caroll, Madison, Newton (rarely), Washington

Add'l Information: Established 1999. Normal turnaround time- 24-48 hours. Projects billed by number of names searched. Fee depends on nature of search. First project may require prepayment. He specializes in real estate in northwest AR, but can also perform UCC and Tax Lien/Judgment searches. Rarely does court searches. Rarely visits Newton County.

Adit Research Inc

3512 35th Ave S, Minneapolis, MN 55406
Phone: 888-721-5220; 612-721-5220 - **Fax:** 612-721-5224
aditresearch@yahoo.com

Types of Records Retrieved: Criminal, Civil and Probate courts; Federal courts; Real Estate; Tax Liens/Judgments; UCC records; Vital records

Local Retrieval Area: MN-Anoka, Carver, Dakota, Hennepin, Ramsey, Scott, Sherburne, Washington; SD-Butte, Custer, Fall River, Lawrence, Meade, Pennington, Shannon. **Correspondent Relationships:** MN & SD.

Add'l Information: Established 2002. Normal turnaround time- 24-48 hours. Projects billed by number of names searched. First project may require prepayment. They specialize in document retrieval, UCC, state and federal tax liens, real estate and civil and criminal background checks. Do the entire state of MN for criminal and civil searches.

ADM & Associates Inc

3059 Madison Ln, Chelsea, AL 35043
Phone: 800-242-5999; 205-678-4713 - **Fax:** 205-678-4714
adminc1@bellsouth.net

Types of Records Retrieved: Criminal courts; Federal courts

Local Retrieval Area: AL-Jefferson, Shelby

Add'l Information: Established 1993. Normal turnaround time- 1 day. Projects billed by number of names searched. First project may require prepayment. ADM specializes in criminal record research for Alabama, Birmingham Municipal, and Alabama Federal Courts; these searches are returned next morning. A licensed PI in AL.

Advanced Background Check Inc

1221 Wilmington Av #211, Dayton, OH 45420
Phone: 888-264-4018; 937-296-9585 - **Fax:** 800-414-6212; 937-296-9608
www.abcheck.com **email:** dmachowsky@abcheck.com

Types of Records Retrieved: Criminal, Civil and Probate courts; Federal courts; Real Estate; Tax Liens/Judgments; UCC records; Vital records; Mortgages and Deeds

Local Retrieval Area: OH-Butler, Cuyahoga, Delaware, Franklin, Hamilton, Lorain, Lucas, Montgomery, Summit, Warren. **Correspondent Relationships:** nationwide.

Add'l Information: Established 1993. Normal turnaround time- 24-48 hours. Projects billed by number of names searched. First project may require prepayment. Credit cards accepted. Will file/record documents for clients. They specialize in civil, criminal, federal and probate court searches. Also real estate, tax liens/judgments, UCC records and vital records.

Advanced Background Services

PO Box 17162, Indianapolis, IN 46217
Phone: 317-884-4600 - **Fax:** 317-884-4601
www.advancedbackground.com **email:** info@advancedbackground.com

Types of Records Retrieved: Criminal and Civil courts; Federal courts; Real Estate; Tax Liens/Judgments

Local Retrieval Area: IN-Marion. **Correspondent Relationships:** nationwide, especially in Allen, Lake, Johnson and St. Joseph counties, IN.

Add'l Information: Established 2000. Normal turnaround time- 24-48 hours. Depending on size of request. First project may require prepayment. Advanced Background Svcs specializes in all levels of criminal record searches - metro, county, state, federal. Their expert services also include reports on SSNs, driver records, civil court and bankruptcy. Will do real estate & liens Marion county only.

Advanced Collection Services Inc

PO Box 127, Geneva, IN 46740-0127
Phone: 260-827-8189 - **Fax:** 260-824-1553
www.visitacs.com **email:** jmyers@visitacs.com

Types of Records Retrieved: Criminal and Civil courts; Tax Liens/Judgments; Real Estate; Vital records

Local Retrieval Area: IN-Adams, Huntington, Wells. **Correspondent Relationships:** Wabash, Miami, Jay, Whitley, Dekalb, Steuben, Lagrange, Grant, Delaware counties in NE Indiana.

Add'l Information: Established 1997. Normal turnaround time- 24-48 hours. Projects billed by number of names searched. First project may require prepayment. Monthly invoice. ACS Inc is in their Indiana courts daily for criminal & civil background checks. Also performs title searches. Contact them for specialized case information and fast turnaround. Add'l phone 260-824-1553.

Advanced Private Inv

PO Box 3024, 2107 Main St, La Crosse, WI 54601
Phone: 608-785-2744 - **Fax:** 608-784-0149
www.advancedprivateinvestigations.com **email:** apimark@charter.net

Types of Records Retrieved: Criminal and Civil courts

Local Retrieval Area: WI-Buffalo, Jackson, La Crosse, Monroe, Trempealeau, Vernon

Add'l Information: Established 2001. Normal turnaround time- 2 days. First project may require prepayment. They also provide court filings, subpoena preparation, photocopying, skiptracing, and private investigations. A licensed PI in WI, MN. Performs service of process.

Advanced Research & Inv. LLC

PO Box 6503, Gulfport, MS 39506
Phone: 888-896-9305; 228-896-9305 - **Fax:** 228-896-9310
www.arinvestigations.com **email:** ari@cableone.net

Types of Records Retrieved: Civil and Probate courts; Probate courts; Federal courts; Real Estate; Tax Liens/Judgments; UCC records; Vital records

Local Retrieval Area: MS-Hancock, Harrison, Jackson, Pearl River, Stone

Add'l Information: Established 2003. Normal turnaround time- same day to 48 hours. Projects are billed by flat fees. Add'l charge for same-day rush service. First project may require prepayment. All projects require payment upon receipt of information. They are a full service investigative agency providing record retrieval, process service, surveillance, judgment recovery, photography, and asset location and recovery. A licensed PI in MS. Performs service of process.

Advanced Surveillance Group Inc

40 Macomb Pl #201, Mount Clemens, MI 48043-5615
Phone: 888-677-9700; 586-493-0300 - **Fax:** 586-783-3939
www.asginvestigations.com **email:** info@asginvestigations.com

Types of Records Retrieved: Criminal, Civil and Probate courts; Federal courts; Real Estate; UCC records; Vital records

Local Retrieval Area: MI-Genesee, Macomb, Oakland, Wayne. **Correspondent Relationships:** Manistee, Mason, Lake, Oceana, Muskegon counties OR.

Add'l Information: Established 1995. Normal turnaround time- 48 hours. Projects billed by number of names searched. Projects billed by number of records located. First project may require prepayment. Credit cards accepted. Will file/record documents for clients. They are in most state, federal and county offices within Metro-Detroit almost daily. Very competitive prices. Performs service of process.

Advanced Title Co LLC

277 Reservoir Ave #101, Meriden, CT 06451
Phone: 203-634-0721 - **Fax:** 775-307-8750
www.advtitlellc.com **email:** advtitlellc@aol.com

Types of Records: Real Estate; Tax Liens/Judgments; UCC records

Local Retrieval Area: CT-Hartford, Middlesex, New Haven. **Correspondent Relationships:** CT, DE, MA, ME, NH, RI.

Add'l Information: Established 1998. Normal turnaround time- 24-48 hours. Projects billed by number of names searched. Will file/record documents for clients. They specialize in document retrievals and filings, mortgage/deed searches, current owner searches, recording updates, 2 owner searches and PMM searches.

Advantage Background Services Inc

3888 Pearl Rd, Cleveland, OH 44109
Phone: 800-355-2650; 216-635-2638 - **Fax:** 440-842-9123
absbackgrounds@aol.com

Types of Records Retrieved: Criminal and Civil courts; Federal District courts

Local Retrieval Area: CA-Alameda, San Francisco, Santa Clara; OH-Butler, Cuyahoga, Geauga, Hamilton, Lake, Montgomery, Summit. **Correspondent Relationships:** CA, OH, FL, NC, TX, VA, WI.

Add'l Information: Established 2000. Normal turnaround time- 48-72 hours. Projects billed by number of names searched. First project may require prepayment. They specialize in retrieving court copies and also offer the following services; workers compensation, motor vehicle reports, education and employment verifications.

Advantage Research Corporation

2230 Malvern Ave #F, Hot Springs, AR 71901-8000
Phone: 501-262-5575 - **Fax:** 800-262-0013
www.advantageresearchcorp.com **email:** search@advantageresearchcorp.com

Types of Records Retrieved: Criminal, Civil and Probate courts; Federal courts; Real Estate; Tax Liens/Judgments; UCC records; Vital records

Local Retrieval Area: AR-Benton, Clark, Faulkner, Garland, Hot Spring, Jefferson, Miller, Pulaski, Saline, Sebastian, Washington. **Correspondent Relationships:** statewide.

Add'l Information: Normal turnaround time- 24 hours. Projects billed by number of names searched. Credit cards accepted. Will file/record documents for clients. Payment terms are net 30 days.

AEGIS Consulting & Investigations Inc

3420 Mountain Meadows Rd, Helena, MT 59601
Phone: 888-742-3447; 406-458-5369 - **Fax:** 406-458-6431
http://aegisinvestigations.com **email:** lswaegis@aol.com

Types of Records Retrieved: Criminal, Civil and Probate courts; Federal courts; Tax Liens/Judgments; UCC records; Vital records

Local Retrieval Area: MT-Broadwater, Cascade, Gallatin, Jefferson, Lewis and Clark, Missoula, Yellowstone. **Correspondent Relationships:** statewide; they do almost all of their statewide work themselves.

Add'l Information: Established 1995. Normal turnaround time- 24-48 hours. Federal records take a maximum of 2 days. Projects billed by number of names searched. First project may require prepayment. Credit cards accepted. Will file/record documents for clients. Please call to establish account. They specialize in fraud & private investigations, public records searches/retrieval, registered agent representation, public record filing, pre-employment screening (MT), background & asset investigations, litigation support. A licensed/bonded PI in MT, WA.

Affirm Background Screening Inc

310 Stuntz Ave #306, Ashland, WI 54806
Phone: 715-682-2601 - **Fax:** 866-216-6456
support@affirmbackgrounds.com

Types of Records Retrieved: Criminal courts.

Local Retrieval Area: KS-Johnson, MI-Gogebic, MO-Cass; WI-Ashland, Bayfield, Iron. **Correspondent Relationships:** nationwide

Add'l Information: Established 1996. Normal turnaround time- 24-48 hours. Projects billed by number of names searched. A national wholesale criminal records company with on-site criminal searches and MVRs.

Affordable Pearlegal Inc
2395 Menlo, Clovis, CA 93611
Phone: 800-958-2144; 559-824-1387 - **Fax:** 559-298-4539
pearlegalinc@yahoo.com

Types of Records Retrieved: Criminal, Civil and Probate courts; Federal courts; Real Estate; Tax Liens/Judgments; UCC records; Vital records

Local Retrieval Area: CA-Fresno, Kings, Madera, Tulare. **Correspondent Relationships:** Central CA area

Add'l Information: Established 1998. Normal turnaround time- 24 hours. Projects billed by number of names searched. Projects billed by number of records located. Projects billed by the hour. Will invoice. On a daily basis, Affordable Pearlegal specializes in volume data abstract and retrieval in Fresno Superior and Federal courts and Fresno Recorders office.

AFX Corp Inc
131 Prominence Ct #220, Dawsonville, GA 30534
Phone: 706-867-6794 - **Fax:** 800-201-0620
www.afxc.com **email:** dave22@afxc.com

Types of Records Retrieved: Civil courts; Real Estate; Tax Liens/Judgments

Local Retrieval Area: GA-Dawson

Add'l Information: Established 1998. Normal turnaround time- 72 hours. Projects billed by number of names searched. All projects require prepayment. They specialize in real estate title search services.

Agency-One Inv
1332 Ashley Square, Winston-Salem, NC 27103
Phone: 800-557-5500; 336-760-4000 - **Fax:** 336-760-4155
www.a1investigations.com **email:** a1investigations@aol.com

Types of Records Retrieved: Criminal and Civil courts; Federal courts; Real Estate; Tax Liens/Judgments; UCC records; Vital records

Local Retrieval Area: NC-Davidson, Davie, Forsyth, Guilford, Rockingham, Rowan, Stokes, Surry, Yadkin

Add'l Information: Established 1977. Normal turnaround time- 48 hours. Projects billed by the hour. All projects require prepayment. Credit cards accepted. Will file/record documents for clients. They will also invoice. They specialize in criminal, civil judgment, probate and property searches. A licensed PI in NC, SC. Performs service of process.

AGH Professional Inv
PO Box 085133, Racine, WI 53408
Phone: 262-884-4688 - **Fax:** 262-884-4689
aghpi@wi.rr.com

Types of Records Retrieved: Criminal, Civil and Probate courts; Real Estate; Vital records

Local Retrieval Area: WI-Kenosha, Racine

Add'l Information: Established 1992. Normal turnaround time- 48 hours. First project may require prepayment. Will file/record documents for clients. They specialize in skiptracing and public records. A licensed PI in WI. Performs service of process.

Ahern Research
Box 662, Mountain Ranch, CA 95246
Phone: 209-754-9709
www.mendopartners.com **email:** dahern@mcn.org

Types of Records Retrieved: Criminal, Civil and Probate courts; Federal courts; Real Estate; Tax Liens/Judgments; UCC records; Vital records

Local Retrieval Area: CA-Amador, Calaveras

Add'l Information: Established 2003. Normal turnaround time- 1 day. All projects require prepayment. Credit cards accepted. They are a background checking firm, Mt Ranch CA, also offering competitive Intel, other info gathering, special projects with emphasis on business/financial background information in CA, NY and MA.

Airborn Civil Process & Inv
PO Box 131381, Houston, TX 77219
Phone: 888-933-6863; 713-523-0471 - **Fax:** 713-523-9112
www.claimyourmoney.net **email:** tillman@pdisinc.com

Types of Records Retrieved: Criminal, Civil and Probate courts; Federal courts; Real Estate; Tax Liens/Judgments; UCC records; Vital records

Local Retrieval Area: TX-Brazos, Fort Bend, Harris

Add'l Information: Established 1998. Normal turnaround time- 24 hours. Projects billed by the hour. All projects require prepayment. Credit cards accepted. Will file/record documents for clients. When you need diligence, call them. They are your local hands on document retrievers. A licensed PI in TX. Performs service of process.

Al Bernardi Backgrounds Process Service
PO Box 1272, Manhattan, KS 66505
Phone: 785-456-8821 - **Fax:** 785-456-8821
albpi@wamego.net

Types of Records Retrieved: Criminal and Civil courts; Real Estate; Tax Liens/Judgments; UCC records

Local Retrieval Area: KS-Dickinson, Geary, Riley

Add'l Information: Established 1996. Normal turnaround time- 24 hours. Projects billed by number of names searched. Invoices at the end of the month.

AL McLeroy Inv
PO Box 5052, 5601 Remington Way (72916), Ft. Smith, AR 72913
Phone: 479-484-0444, Fax- same

Types of Records Retrieved: Criminal, Civil and Probate courts; Federal District courts; Real Estate; UCC records; Vital records

Local Retrieval Area: AR-.Crawford, Logan, Scott, Sebastian. **Correspondent Relationships:** Western Arkansas, Eastern Oklahoma.

Add'l Information: Established 1968. Normal turnaround time- 48 hours. Expedited service available. Projects billed by the hour. First project may require prepayment. A licensed PI in AR. Performs service of process.

Al Smith Private Inv
PO Box 5079, Lakeland, FL 33807
Phone: 863-295-1375 - **Fax:** 863-534-9483
alsmith@gate.net

Types of Records Retrieved: Criminal, Civil and Probate courts; Real Estate; Tax Liens/Judgments; UCC records; Vital records

Local Retrieval Area: FL-Hardee, Highlands, Polk. **Correspondent Relationships:** nationwide.

Add'l Information: Established 1989. Normal turnaround time- 24 hours. Projects billed by the hour. First project may require prepayment. Credit cards accepted. Will file/record documents for clients. Al Smith is a 260yr veteran of county law enforcement and private investigations. General investigations provided in addition to document retrieval. A licensed PI in FL. Performs service of process.

AlaDocs Inc
911 2nd Ave N, Birmingham, AL 35203
Phone: 205-251-8200 - **Fax:** 205-251-9007
www.aladocs.com **email:** rick@aladocs.com

Types of Records Retrieved: Civil and Probate courts; Real Estate; Tax Liens/Judgments; UCC records

Local Retrieval Area: AL-Autauga, Baldwin, Barbour, Bibb, Blount, Bullock, Butler, Calhoun, Chambers, Cherokee, Chilton, Choctaw, Clarke, Clay, Cleburne, Coffee, Colbert, Conecuh, Coosa, Covington, Crenshaw, Cullman, Dale, Dallas, De Kalb, Elmore, Escambia, Etowah, Fayette, Franklin, Geneva, Greene, Hale, Henry, Houston, Jackson, Jefferson, Lamar, Lauderdale, Lawrence, Lee, Limestone, Lowndes, Macon, Madison, Marengo, Marion, Marshall, Mobile, Monroe, Montgomery, Morgan, Perry, Pickens, Pike, Randolph, Russell, St Clair, Shelby, Sumter, Talladega, Tallapoosa, Tuscaloosa, Walker, Washington, Wilcox, Winston. **Correspondent Relationships:** statewide.

Add'l Information: Established 2001. Normal turnaround time- 1-3 days. Projects billed by number of names searched. Credit cards accepted. Will file/record documents for clients. Terms are net 30 with approved credit. They specialize in title work, real estate filings and document retrieval, also UCC and probate courts records. They have 9 employees to cover the state; may use correspondents in some counties at times.

Alaska Court Services

PO Box 212041, Anchorage, AK 99521-2041
Phone: 907-258-3211 - **Fax:** 907-279-0754
www.alaska-court.com **email:** arturos@alaska.net

Types of Records Retrieved: Criminal and Civil courts; Federal courts

Local Retrieval Area: AK-Anchorage, Fairbanks North Star, Kenai Peninsula, Kodiak Island, Valdez-Cordova. **Correspondent Relationships:** Eagle River, Wasilla, Palmer, Chugiak, Eklutna, Girdwood, Bird Creek, Hope, North Pole.

Add'l Information: Established 1087. Normal turnaround time- 3-5 days. Expedited service available. Projects billed by number of names searched. Formerly Anchorage & Matzu Process Service, they specialize in process service in south central Alaska. A licensed PI in AK. Performs service of process.

Alaska Public Records Search LLC

PO Box 210587, 8200 Pioneer Dr, Anchorage, AK 99521-0587
Phone: 800-808-5105; 907-333-5105 - **Fax:** 907-333-5155
www.alaskapublicrecords.com **email:** info@alaskapublicrecords.com

Types of Records Retrieved: Criminal and Civil courts; Federal courts; Real Estate; Tax Liens/Judgments; UCC records

Local Retrieval Area: AK-Aleutian Islands East & West, Anchorage Borough, Bristol Bay Borough, Fairbanks North Star, Juneau, Kenai Peninsula, Lake And Peninsula, Matanuska-Susitna, North Slope, Valdez-Cordova. **Correspondent Relationships:** statewide and nationwide.

Add'l Information: Established 1993. Normal turnaround time- 24-72 hours. Projects billed by number of names searched. First project may require prepayment. Will file/record documents for clients. Credit accounts accepted, terms are net 15 days. They specialize in UCC, asset/lien, litigation, real property, corporate, filing services, licensing/registrations. They cover all federal, state and county level agencies in Alaska including Lake & Peninsula district. They are registered agents. A licensed PI in AK. Performs service of process.

Albany Abstract Co

PO Box 817, Albany, TX 76430
Phone: 325-762-3077 - **Fax:** 325-762-2102

Types of Records Retrieved: Civil and Probate courts; Real Estate; Tax Liens/Judgments; UCC records; Vital records

Local Retrieval Area: TX-Shackelford

Add'l Information: Established 1922. Normal turnaround time- up to 1 week. Fee basis will vary by the type of project. All projects require prepayment. Will file/record documents for clients.

Albert Lea Abstract Co

205 S Washington Ave, Albert Lea, MN 56007
Phone: 507-373-9001 - **Fax:** 507-373-2528
alac@smig.net

Types of Records Retrieved: Real Estate; Tax Liens/Judgments; Probate courts; UCC records; Vital records

Local Retrieval Area: MN-Freeborn, Mower

Add'l Information: Established 1976. Normal turnaround time- 2 days. Projects billed by number of names searched. All projects require prepayment. Will file/record documents for clients. They specialize in title searching, closings and 1031 exchanges.

Albright Abstract & Title Guaranty

PO Box 467, Newkirk, OK 74647
Phone: 877-362-2525; 580-362-2525 - **Fax:** 580-362-3390

Types of Records Retrieved: Civil and Probate courts; Real Estate; Tax Liens/Judgments

Local Retrieval Area: OK-Kay

Add'l Information: Established 1899. Normal turnaround time- 2-5 days. Fee is determined on a "per name plus time" basis. First project may require prepayment. Will file/record documents for clients. Payment due upon delivery. They specialize in title insurance statewide, abstracts and lien reports in Kay county.

Aldridge & Associates

PO Drawer 90, Smithville, MS 38870-0090
Phone: 662-651-7376 - **Fax:** 662-651-6060
jerryaldridge@yahoo.com

Types of Records Retrieved: Criminal, Civil and Probate courts; Federal courts; Real Estate; Tax Liens/Judgments; UCC records; Vital records

Local Retrieval Area: AL-Lamar; MS-Calhoun, Chickasaw, Clay, Itawamba, Lee, Lowndes, Monroe, Pontotoc, Union

Add'l Information: Established 1997. Normal turnaround time- 48 hours. Projects billed by number of names searched. Projects billed by the hour. First project may require prepayment. Will file/record documents for clients. They specialize in criminal court records, background screening, real estate, legal service of process, notary signing agent, private investigations, probate & pre-employment/tenant screening. They also offer attorney services. A licensed PI in MS. Performs service of process.

Alfalfa Guaranty Abstract Co

201 S Grand Ave., PO Box 224, Cherokee, OK 73728
Phone: 580-596-3394 - **Fax:** 580-596-3395

Types of Records Retrieved: Civil and Probate courts; Real Estate; Tax Liens/Judgments; UCC records; Vital records

Local Retrieval Area: OK-Alfalfa

Add'l Information: Established 1989. Normal turnaround time- 1-2 days. Projects billed by the hour. Will file/record documents for clients. If amount is over $500.00, payment is made before abstracter leaves office.

ALIASS

10560 Main St #405, Fairfax, VA 22030
Phone: 800-747-0820; 703-934-6777 - **Fax:** 703-383-3246
www.american-legal.com **email:** aals@american-legal.com

Types of Records Retrieved: Criminal, Civil and Probate courts; Federal courts; Real Estate; Tax Liens/Judgments; UCC records; Vital records

Local Retrieval Area: DC-District of Columbia; MD-Montgomery, Prince George's; VA-Alexandria City, Arlington, Fairfax, Fairfax City, Fauquier, Loudoun, Prince William. **Correspondent Relationships:** Maryland and Virginia.

Add'l Information: Established 1998. Normal turnaround time- 2 days. Projects billed by the hour. First project may require prepayment. Credit cards accepted. Will file/record documents for clients. Personal checks are accepted. They do service of process for the entire Metropolitan DC area, MD, VA and courthouse research. A licensed PI in VA. Performs service of process.

All American Document Services

15 NE 4th St, Ft Lauderdale, FL 33301-3237
Phone: 954-761-7292 - **Fax:** 954-761-7294
www.allamericandocs.com **email:** customerservice@allamericandocs.com

Types of Records Retrieved: Criminal, Civil and Probate courts; Federal courts; Real Estate; Tax Liens/Judgments; UCC records; Vital records

Local Retrieval Area: FL-Broward, Dade, Palm Beach. **Correspondent Relationships:** statewide.

Add'l Information: Established 1996. Normal turnaround time- 72 hours. Expedited service available. Projects billed by number of names searched. Projects billed by number of records located. Projects billed by the hour. First project may require prepayment. Credit cards accepted. All American's services include current owner searches, judgments, liens, bankruptcy and civil/criminal searches at county/state/federal levels. They provide experienced, accurate and honest service. All American is licensed and insured.

All Penn Abstract Co

15 Public Square #200, Wilkes-Barre, PA 18701
Phone: 570-823-5410 - **Fax:** 570-822-2774

Types of Records Retrieved: Real Estate; Tax Liens/Judgments; Probate courts; UCC records

Local Retrieval Area: PA-Luzerne

Add'l Information: Established 1987. Normal turnaround time- 7 to 10 days. They charge a flat rate per project. Will file/record documents for clients. They specialize in real estate, closings and property searches.

All Phase Reports

4403 Golfwood Blvd, Tampa, FL 33634-7323
Phone: 813-885-9822 - **Fax:** 813-885-9822
Types of Records Retrieved: Criminal, Civil and Probate courts; Federal courts; Real Estate; Tax Liens/Judgments; UCC records; Vital records
Local Retrieval Area: FL-Hillsborough, Pasco, Pinellas, Polk. **Correspondents:** Broward, Dade, Lee, Orange, Osceola counties.
Add'l Information: Established 1992. Normal turnaround time- 24-48 hours. Expedited service available. Fees are per name per court. Fees can be negotiated per project. Will file/record documents for clients. First 4 payments required to establish "Good Will" to pay. A paralegal owned/operated company using expertise/technology searching both online and manual data. A recent addition, All Phase Investigations & Reports is a full service private investigation firm. A licensed PI in FL. Performs service of process.

All Search Title Co

PO Box 544, Grayson, KY 41143
Phone: 606-474-4253 - **Fax:** 606-474-2615
Types of Records Retrieved: Real Estate; Tax Liens/Judgments
Local Retrieval Area: KY-Bath, Boyd, Carter, Elliott, Fleming, Floyd, Greenup, Johnson, Lawrence, Lewis, Martin, Mason, Menifee, Montgomery, Morgan, Rowan
Add'l Information: Established 1985. Normal turnaround time- 48 hours. Will do monthly billings. First project may require prepayment. Will file/record documents for clients. They specialize in real estate title searches and also perform witness closings.

All Secure Inc

PO Box 1166, Belgrade, MT 59714-1166
Phone: 406-388-7505; cell- 406-920-1931 - **Fax:** 406-388-3480
rorobi2@msn.com
Types of Records Retrieved: Criminal and Civil courts; Bankruptcy court; Real Estate; Tax Liens/Judgments; UCC records
Local Retrieval Area: MT-Gallatin
Add'l Information: Established 2004. Normal turnaround time- 24-72 hours, up to 1 week for out of state criminal records. Projects billed by number of names searched. First project may require prepayment. Will file/record documents for clients. Account's excepted. Formerly P.I.I.-Professional Investigation & Inquiry, they specialize in criminal background checks. Also real estate/lien/asset searches and civil record search. Also a full private investigation service. A licensed PI in MT.

All State Document Services

2418 N Krenek, Crosby, TX 77532
Phone: 888-246-8180; 281-462-2730 - **Fax:** 888 236 0863; 281-462-2731
tjmatt@aol.com
Types of Records Retrieved: Criminal, Civil and Probate courts; Federal courts; Real Estate; Tax Liens/Judgments; UCC records; Vital records
Local Retrieval Area: TX-Austin, Brazoria, Brazos, Calhoun, Chambers, Colorado, Fort Bend, Galveston, Hardin, Harris, Jackson, Jefferson, Liberty, Matagorda, Montgomery, Orange, Victoria, Walker, Waller, Washington, Wharton. **Correspondent Relationships:** nationwide.
Add'l Information: Established 1998. Normal turnaround time- 24-48 hours. Projects billed by number of names searched. First project may require prepayment. Credit cards accepted. Invoice monthly. All State Documents established in 1998, the owner is a 20 year plus record research & retrieval individual. Has professionalism and accurate knowledge of research provided for state & county needs.

All The Facts

2620 Centenary Blvd Bldg 2 #210, Shreveport, LA 71104
Phone: 866-401-5676; 318-222-5676 - **Fax:** 318-425-8524
www.all-the-facts.com **email:** allfacts@xspedius.net
Types of Records Retrieved: Criminal, Civil and Probate courts; Federal courts; Real Estate; Tax Liens/Judgments; UCC records; Vital records
Local Retrieval Area: LA-Bossier, Caddo. **Correspondents:** statewide.
Add'l Information: Established 1995. Normal turnaround time- 6-12 hours. Out of area: 24-48 hours. Projects billed by number of names searched. Will file/record documents for clients. Billing is monthly. Terms are net 30 days. They also provide sex offender information as well as medicare/medicaid fraud, GSA list of excluded persons, pre-employment, pre-leasing credit reports, private investigations and 24 hour mobile notary services. A licensed PI in LA. Performs service of process.

Allen Abstract & Title

3 West Side Court Sq, Alton, MO 65606
Phone: 417-778-6665 - **Fax:** 417-778-7880
Types of Records Retrieved: Real Estate; Tax Liens/Judgments
Local Retrieval Area: MO-Oregon
Add'l Information: First project may require prepayment. They specialize in Oregon County real estate related records.

Stephanie Allen

917 Round Bottom Rd, Milford, OH 45150
Phone: 513-658-1647 - **Fax:** 513-248-0646
Types of Records Retrieved: Civil and Probate courts; Real Estate; Tax Liens/Judgments; UCC records **Local Retrieval Area:** OH-Clermont
Add'l Information: Established 2000. Normal turnaround time- 24-48 hours. Expedited service available. Projects billed by number of names searched. Payment due upon completion. She is a sole proprietor and does all title searches and document retrieval personally. Has been performing these services for 13 years in Clermont County, the last 5 years independently.

Alliance Legal Services Inc

PO Box 523078, Springfield, VA 22152-5080
Phone: 703-644-8571 - **Fax:** 703-644-8572
www.alliancelegalservices.com **email:** alliance.express@verizon.net
Types of Records Retrieved: Criminal, Civil and Probate courts; Federal courts; Real Estate; Tax Liens/Judgments; UCC records; Vital records
Local Retrieval Area: VA-Arlington, Alexandria, Fairfax. **Correspondent Relationships:** Washington DC and Maryland.
Add'l Information: Established 1993. Normal turnaround time- 24-72 hours depending on agency where records are stored. Projects billed by the hour. First project may require prepayment. Will file/record documents for clients. They provide private investigations and process serving, including filings and document retrieval. A licensed PI in VA. Performs service of process.

Alliance Title & Escrow Corp

PO Box 644, 78 N Main, Driggs, ID 83422
Phone: 800-214-1418; 208-354-2285 - **Fax:** 208-354-2811
www.alliancetitle.com **Types of Records Retrieved:** Federal courts; Real Estate; Tax Liens/Judgments; UCC records
Local Retrieval Area: ID-Teton
Add'l Information: Fees vary by type of project. Will file/record documents for clients. Alliance Title & Escrow Corp has 22 offices throughout Idaho, Montana, Washington and Wyoming.

Allied Investigative Services

PO Box 5063, Anderson, SC 29623-5012
Phone: 800-302-0861; 864-231-8446 - **Fax:** 864-224-3175
www.alliedinvestigative.com **email:** bonnie@alliedinvestigative.com
Types of Records Retrieved: Criminal and Civil courts
Local Retrieval Area: SC-Anderson
Add'l Information: Established 2002. First project may require prepayment. They also provide court filings, photocopying, skiptracing, private investigations, and research on questioned documents. A licensed PI in SC. Performs service of process.

Allington International

19885 Detroit Rd #314, Cleveland, OH 44116-1815
Phone: 866-729-8555; - **Fax:** 866-470-0506 allingtoninc@abjel.net
Types of Records Retrieved: Criminal, Civil and Probate courts; Federal courts; Real Estate; Tax Liens/Judgments; UCC records; Vital records

Local Retrieval Area: OH-Ashtabula, Cuyahoga, Geauga, Lake, Lorain, Medina, Stark, Summit, Trumbull. **Correspondents:** nationwide.

Add'l Information: Established 1989. Normal turnaround time- 1 business days. Credit cards accepted. Will file/record documents for clients. Terms: net 30 days. They specialize in employment screening programs, drug testing, criminal and court record searches, motor vehicle information, workers' compensation claims, shopping services, security consulting and due diligence investigations.

All-Search

1108 E South Union Av, Midvale, UT 84047-2904
Phone: 800-227-3152; 801-984-8160 - **Fax:** 801-984-8170
www.all-search.com **email:** brad@all-search.com

Types of Records Retrieved: Criminal, Civil and Probate courts; Federal courts; Real Estate; Tax Liens/Judgments; UCC records; Vital records

Local Retrieval Area: UT-Beaver, Box Elder, Cache, Davis, Duchesne, Garfield, Juab, Millard, Morgan, Piute, Salt Lake, Sanpete, Sevier, Summit, Tooele, Uintah, Utah, Wasatch, Washington, Weber. **Correspondent Relationships:** nationwide and Canada.

Add'l Information: Established 1983. Normal turnaround time- 1-2 days for Utah; 1-4 days nationwide. Projects billed by number of names searched. Credit cards accepted. Will file/record documents for clients. Will invoice. They specialize in corporate document retrieval and corporate filings. All liens searched, all jurisdictions. They also are a registered agent for Utah corporations. Also, complete real estate research.

Alma Abstract & Title Co

310 N State St, Alma, MI 48801
Phone: 989-463-8325 - **Fax:** 989-463-2363
www.almaabstract.com **email:** dedicated@almaabstract.com

Types of Records Retrieved: Real Estate; Tax Liens/Judgments; Probate courts; UCC records; Vital records

Local Retrieval Area: MI-Gratiot, Montcalm

Add'l Information: Established 1980. Normal turnaround time- 1 week. Fee basis will vary by type of project. Will file/record documents for clients. They specialize in real estate.

Alpha Attorney Service

1010 2nd Ave #120B, San Diego, CA 92101-4961
Phone: 619-235-8008 - **Fax:** 619-235-0580 joewestt@msn.com

Types of Records Retrieved: Criminal, Civil and Probate courts; Federal courts; Real Estate; Tax Liens/Judgments; UCC records; Vital records

Local Retrieval Area: CA-San Diego. **Correspondent Relationships:** Orange and Imperial Counties, California.

Add'l Information: Established 1990. Normal turnaround time- 1-2 days. Projects billed by number of names searched. Will file/record documents for clients. They specialize in process serving, records search, copy service, rush filings and fax filings. Their office is 2 blocks from the San Diego central courthouse. Performs service of process.

Alpha Court Records & Research

1326 Osceola Ave, St Paul, MN 55105
Phone: 651-699-2222 - **Fax:** 651-699-9004
miriamleone11@msn.com

Types of Records Retrieved: Criminal courts

Local Retrieval Area: MN-Anoka, Benton, Big Stone, Blue Earth, Brown, Carlton, Carver, Cass, Chippewa, Chisago, Cook, Cottonwood, Dakota, Dodge, Faribault, Fillmore, Freeborn, Goodhue, Grant, Hennepin, Houston, Isanti, Itasca, Jackson, Kanabec, Kandiyohi, Kittson, Lac Qui Parle, Lake, Le Sueur, Lincoln, Lyon, Mahnomen, Marshall, Martin, McLeod, Meeker, Mille Lacs, Mower, Murray, Nicollet, Nobles, Norman, Olmstead, Pennington, Pine, Pipestone, Polk, Pope, Ramsey, Redwood, Renville, Rock, Roseau, Scott, Sherburne, Sibley, St. Louis, Steele, Stevens, Swift, Wabasha, Waseca, Washington, Watonwan, Wilkin, Winona, Wright, Yellow Medicine

Add'l Information: Established 1992. Normal turnaround time- same day or following day. Work assigned by 11AM (CT) will be returned same day. Projects billed by number of names searched. Credit cards accepted. Will file/record documents for clients. Terms: net 30 days. They have specialized in criminal background searches (felonies, misdemeanors & alcohol/drug-related traffic) since 1992.

Alpha Information Inc

10153 Riverside Dr #590, Tuluca Lake, CA 91602
Phone: 800-900-1471; - **Fax:** 800-900-1488 kbanks@alphainformation.com

Types of Records Retrieved: Criminal and Civil courts

Local Retrieval Area: CA-Fresno, Los Angeles, Marin, Orange, Riverside, San Bernardino, San Diego, Ventura. **Correspondent Relationships:** San Luis Obispo, San Francisco counties CA.

Add'l Information: Established 1991. Normal turnaround time- 24-36 hours. Projects billed by number of names searched. Will invoice two times monthly. They have over 15 years experience and have their own researchers going to courts daily. They do large volume searches. They can report directly on a client's website. They provide volume discounts.

Alpha Omega USA Information Brokers LLC

1055 W College Ave #148, Santa Rosa, CA 95401
Phone: 866-636-6342; - **Fax:** 866-326-6342
www.alphaomegausa.com **email:** usa@alphaomegausa.com

Types of Records Retrieved: Criminal courts

Local Retrieval Area: CA-Sonoma. **Correspondents:** nationwide.

Add'l Information: Established 1994. Normal turnaround time- 48-72 hours. Projects billed by number of names searched. They provide nationwide criminal records for pre-employment and process serving in Placer county in CA. Performs service of process.

Alpha Record Search & Retrieval

PO Box 2156, Los Angeles, CA 90078
Phone: 323-851-5701 - **Fax:** 323-851-6611 finderjm@pacbell.net

Types of Records Retrieved: Criminal, Civil and Probate courts; Federal courts; Real Estate; Tax Liens/Judgments; UCC records; Vital records

Local Retrieval Area: CA-Los Angeles

Add'l Information: Established 1997. Normal turnaround time- per agreement. Expedited service available. Fees are by mutually agreed terms and vary by assignment. First project may require prepayment. They specialize in complicated, unusual assignments. They have over 20 years experience with all public record file systems in the 5-county area. Experience counts! A licensed PI in CA.

Alpha-Omega Investigations

3307 S College Ave #200-8, Ft Collins, CO 80525
Phone: 866-510-8200; 970-282-8200 - **Fax:** 970-282-8803
www.alpha-omega-investigations.com **email:** alpha-omega@qwest.net

Types of Records Retrieved: Criminal, Civil and Probate courts; Federal courts; Real Estate; Tax Liens/Judgments; UCC records; Vital records

Local Retrieval Area: CO-Boulder, Larimer, Weld

Add'l Information: Established 1990. Normal turnaround time- 48 hours. Expedited service available. Projects billed by number of names searched. First project may require prepayment. Credit cards accepted. Will invoice PRRN members. They have a record retrieval service available in Larimer, Weld and Boulder counties. Statewide Colorado available through state association. Performs service of process.

Alstate Process Service Inc

60 Burt Dr, Deer Park, NY 11729
Phone: 631-667-1800 - **Fax:** 631-667-0302
www.alstateprocessservice.com **email:** office@alstateprocessservice.com

Types of Records Retrieved: Criminal, Civil and Probate courts; Federal courts; Real Estate; Tax Liens/Judgments; UCC records; Vital records

Local Retrieval Area: NY-Bronx, Kings, Nassau, New York, Queens, Richmond, Suffolk. **Correspondent Relationships:** statewide.

Add'l Information: Established 1980. Normal turnaround time- 48 hours. Fee basis will vary by the type of project. Will file/record documents for clients. Will bill. A licensed PI in NY. Performs service of process.

Alternative Investigative & Attorney Services

7657 Winnetka Ave #545, Canoga Park, CA 91306
Phone: 818-402-0800 - **Fax:** 818-341-8804 altinv1000@aol.com

Types of Records Retrieved: Criminal, Civil and Probate courts; Federal courts; Real Estate; Tax Liens/Judgments; UCC records; Vital records

Retrieval Area: Los Angeles, Orange, San Bernardino, Riverside, Ventura

Add'l Information: Established 1992. Normal turnaround time- 24 hours depending on the court. Projects billed by the hour. Charge by volume. First project may require prepayment. Will file/record documents for clients. Discounts for volume. They have "FLAT FEE" service of process, no attempt/mileage on routine work, specialize in real estate loan documents, and is a "traveling" notary public-statewide document signing. A licensed PI in CA. Performs service of process.

AM Search & Retrieve

336 E Perry St, Versailles, IN 47042-9478

Phone: 812-689-0672 - **Fax:** 812-689-5832

Types of Records Retrieved: Criminal, Civil and Probate courts; Real Estate; Tax Liens/Judgments; UCC records

Local Retrieval Area: IN-Dearborn, Ohio, Ripley

Add'l Information: Established 1994. Normal turnaround time- less than 48 hours. Projects billed by number of names searched. First project may require prepayment. Will file/record documents for clients. They specialize in criminal background checks, UCC searches and current owner real estate searches.

Amarisearch Inc

4085 Chain Bridge Rd #G5, Fairfax, VA 22030-4111

Phone: 703-267-6827 - **Fax:** 703-267-6825

www.amarisearch.com **email:** info@amarisearch.com

Records Retrieved: Real Estate; Tax Liens/Judgments; UCC records

Local Retrieval Area: VA-Alexandria, Arlington, Caroline, Fairfax, Fauquier, Fredericksburg, Hanover, Henrico, Loudoun, Prince William, Spotsylvania, Stafford. **Correspondent Relationships:** Metro Atlanta, GA; Metro Richmond, VA.

Add'l Information: Established 2001. Normal turnaround time- 24-48 hours. Projects billed by number of names searched. Also charged by property address. Will file/record documents for clients. They will invoice monthly.

Heidi Ambrose

PO Box 372, Idaho City, ID 83631

Phone: 208-392-6709; Fax- same

Types of Records Retrieved: Criminal, Civil and Probate courts; Real Estate; Tax Liens/Judgments; Vital records

Local Retrieval Area: ID-Boise

Add'l Information: Established 2003. Normal turnaround time- 24-48 hours. Billing depends on nature of the request.

Amcor Title LLC

87 Summer Breeze Ln, Fredericksburg, VA 22406

Phone: 540-752-2246 - **Fax:** 540-752-4271 RDACRDAC@Adelphia.net

Records Retrieved: Real Estate; Tax Liens/Judgments; UCC records

Local Retrieval Area: VA-Fredericksburg, Spotsylvania, Stafford

Add'l Information: Established 2001. Normal turnaround time- 24-48 hours. Will file/record documents for clients. Payment due upon receipt, net 30 days. Searches include: Current and full owner searches, UCC/judgments, document retrievals, recordings, updates, courthouse research needs, quick turnaround time and highest efficiency, competitively priced.

American Abstract

24 Woodbine Ave #20, Northport, NY 11768

Phone: 631-262-1826 - **Fax:** 631-262-1927

www.nationalabstract.com **email:** info@nationalabstract.com

Types of Records Retrieved: Federal courts; Real Estate; Tax Liens/Judgments; UCC records; Vital records

Local Retrieval Area: NY-Bronx, Kings, Nassau, New York, Queens, Richmond, Suffolk, Westchester. **Correspondents:** nationwide.

Add'l Information: Established 1996. Normal turnaround time- 24-48 hours. Projects billed by number of names searched. First project may require prepayment. Will file/record documents for clients. Payment terms are net 30 days. Located on Long Is, NY, they provide a large nationwide network of real estate services.

American Abstract & Title

814 Avenue F, Fort Madison, IA 52627-2817

Phone: 319-372-8110 - **Fax:** 319-372-2628

Types of Records Retrieved: Civil and Probate courts; Real Estate; Tax Liens/Judgments; UCC records; Vital records

Local Retrieval Area: IA-Lee

Add'l Information: Established 1978. Normal turnaround time- variable. Projects billed by number of names searched. Fee may be based per year searched. Will file/record documents for clients.

American Abstract & Title Co Inc

2501-B E Elms Rd, Killeen, TX 76542

Phone: 254-526-9525 - **Fax:** 254-526-9518 staff@americanabstract.org

Types of Records Retrieved: Real Estate; Tax Liens/Judgments; Probate courts; UCC records

Local Retrieval Area: TX-Bell, Coryell, Williamson. **Correspondent Relationships:** statewide.

Add'l Information: Established 1978. Normal turnaround time- 5-7 days. Fee basis will vary by the type of project. All projects require prepayment. Will file/record documents for clients. They specialize in closing loans including commercial and single family (1-4 family).

American Abstract Company

PO Box 1565, 138 W Main, Purcell, OK 73080

Phone: 405-527-7575 - **Fax:** 405-527-7574

Types of Records Retrieved: Civil and Probate courts; Real Estate; Tax Liens/Judgments; UCC records

Local Retrieval Area: OK-McClain

Add'l Information: Normal turnaround time- 1-2 days. Projects billed by number of names searched. Projects billed by number of records located. Projects billed by the hour. Credit cards accepted.

American Abstractors Inc

PO Box 97, Broomall, PA 19008

Phone: 610-353-5375 - **Fax:** 610-356-3245 nathanlautar@comcast.net

Types of Records Retrieved: Criminal, Civil and Probate courts; Federal courts; Real Estate; Tax Liens/Judgments; UCC records; Vital records

Local Retrieval Area: PA-Chester, Delaware, Lancaster, Montgomery, Philadelphia

Add'l Information: Established 1999. Normal turnaround time- 24-48 hours. Projects billed by number of names searched. Projects billed by number of records located. First project may require prepayment. Formerly known as American Abstractors. A licensed PI in PA, DE. Performs service of process.

American Background Checks

403 Whitetail Dr, Manchaca, TX 78652-4716

Phone: 512-497-7988 - **Fax:** 512-282-3813 abchecks@austin.rr.com

Types of Records Retrieved: Criminal and Civil courts; Federal District courts; Tax Liens/Judgments; UCC records

Local Retrieval Area: TX-Travis, Williamson. **Correspondent Relationships:** nationwide.

Add'l Information: Established 1998. Normal turnaround time- 24-48 hours. Projects billed by number of names searched. clients billed monthly; 30 days net. They specialize in wholesale criminal and civil searches in TX and the US. Has 20 years legal experience. A licensed PI in TX.

American Detective Agency

111 N Harrison Ave, Oklahoma City, OK 73104-1817

Phone: 800-219-9120; 405-636-4222 - **Fax:** 405-632-7667

www.americanpi.net **email:** lwatson@americanpi.net

Types of Records Retrieved: Criminal, Civil and Probate courts; Federal courts; Real Estate; Tax Liens/Judgments; UCC records; Vital records

Local Retrieval Area: OK-Canadian, Cleveland, Oklahoma. **Correspondent Relationships:** TX, MO, KS.

Add'l Information: Normal turnaround time- 24 hours. Projects billed by number of names searched. Projects billed by the hour. First project may require prepayment. Credit cards accepted. They specialize in full service investigating with emphasis on criminal defense, insurance and workers compensation. A licensed PI in OK, TX. Performs service of process.

American Dream Title LLC

26532 N Anna Dr, Ruther Glen, VA 22546
Phone: 540-903-1481 or 804-994-0245 - **Fax:** 804-994-0479
americandreamtitle@yahoo.com

Types of Records Retrieved: Criminal, Civil and Probate courts; Real Estate; Tax Liens/Judgments; UCC records

Local Retrieval Area: VA-Caroline, Culpeper, Fauquier, Fredericksburg, Hanover, King George, Orange, Spotsylvania, Stafford

Add'l Information: Established 2003. Normal turnaround time- next day. Projects billed by number of names searched. Projects billed by the hour. Payment due net 30 days. They are an independent title examiner with over 20 years experience. They are about service, excellence and reliability with the flexibility to meet your needs. Call John Rutledge.

American Heritage Abstract

104A N Lincoln St, Desloge, MO 63601
Phone: 573-431-1359 - **Fax:** 573-431-2137 ahaco@sbcglobal.net

Types of Records Retrieved: Civil and Probate courts; Real Estate; Tax Liens/Judgments; UCC records

Local Retrieval Area: MO-Iron, Madison, St. Francois, Washington. **Correspondent Relationships:** St. Genevieve, Jefferson, St. Louis, St. Charles, Bollinger counties, MO.

Add'l Information: Established 1984. Normal turnaround time- 1 week. Projects billed by number of names searched. Projects billed by number of records located. Projects billed by the hour. Will file/record documents for clients. Personal checks are accepted. They specialize in title insurance, land title searches, real estate closing and escrow disbursing.

American Investigations

1120 Main St, Charleston, WV 25302-1108
Phone: 304-343-3346 - **Fax:** 304-343-2211 jkjpi@charterinternet.com

Types of Records Retrieved: Criminal, Civil and Probate courts; Federal courts; Real Estate; Tax Liens/Judgments; UCC records; Vital records

Local Retrieval: WV-Boone, Cabell, Jackson, Kanawha, Lincoln, Putnam

Add'l Information: Normal turnaround time- 2 days. Projects billed by the hour. A licensed PI in WV. Performs service of process.

American Legal Process & Messenger Svc

PO Box 729, Richland, WA 99352
Phone: 509-946-0807 - **Fax:** 866-858-1909
www.eamericanlegal.com **email:** cj@eAmericanLegal.com

Types of Records Retrieved: Criminal and Civil courts; Federal courts; Real Estate; Tax Liens/Judgments; UCC records

Local Retrieval Area: WA-Benton, Franklin, Walla Walla, Yakima. **Correspondent Relationships:** Washington State.

Add'l Information: Established 2004. Projects billed by number of names searched. Projects billed by the hour. Billed by type of task. First project may require prepayment. Will file/record documents for clients. Their staff has over 30 years experience in locating information, document retrieval, and finding people who don't want to be found. A licensed PI in WA. Performs service of process.

American Legal Services

225 S Civic Dr #216, Palm Springs, CA 92262
Phone: 760-323-5445 - **Fax:** 760-323-5509 als@amlegal.net

Types of Records Retrieved: Criminal, Civil and Probate courts; Federal courts; Real Estate; Tax Liens/Judgments

Local Retrieval Area: CA-Riverside. **Correspondents:** nationwide.

Add'l Information: Established 1991. Normal turnaround time- 24-48 hours. Fee basis varies by type of project. They also charge per page if they do any copies. First project may require prepayment. They specialize in record document photocopying and process serving. Can retrieve records from the Joshua Tree Branch in San Bernardino County. Performs service of process.

American Legal Solution Inc

7060 Nova Dr #107, Davie, FL 33317
Phone: 954-791-1415 - **Fax:** 954-791-1530 americanlegal@comcast.net

Types of Records Retrieved: Criminal, Civil and Probate courts; Federal courts; Real Estate; Tax Liens/Judgments; UCC records; Vital records

Local Retrieval Area: FL-Broward, Collier, Dade, Monroe, Palm Beach. **Correspondent Relationships:** nationwide, Canada, Puerto Rico.

Add'l Information: Established 2001. Normal turnaround time- 24-48 hours. Projects billed by number of names searched. Projects billed by number of records located. Projects billed by the hour. First project may require prepayment. They specialize in court research & retrieval of case litigations, from Circuit, Federal & District Court of Appeals, including civil, criminal, domestic & multidistrict cases. Also search public records for properties, judgments, liens & UCC.

American Research Unlimited Inc

PO Box 362, Carthage, MO 64836
Phone: 417-358-6494 - **Fax:** 417-359-5734 amru@ecarthage.com

Types of Records Retrieved: Criminal, Civil and Probate courts; Real Estate; Tax Liens/Judgments; UCC records; Vital records

Local Retrieval Area: KS-Bourbon, Cherokee, Crawford, Labette; MO-Barton, Bates, Cedar, Christian, Dade, Greene, Jasper, Lawrence, McDonald, Newton, Vernon

Add'l Information: Established 1984. Normal turnaround time- 1-2 days. They charge a flat rate per search. Will file/record documents for clients. Personal checks accepted. Will bill regular clients. They have 10 years experience in public records research. Very timely turnaround with a staff of experienced researchers; competitive prices.

American Title & Abstract Specialists Inc

217 N Kansas, Liberal, KS 67901
Phone: 620-624-9111 - **Fax:** 620-624-6610
www.amtitles.com **email:** amt@swko.net

Types of Records Retrieved: Criminal, Civil and Probate courts; Real Estate; Tax Liens/Judgments; UCC records; Vital records

Local Retrieval Area: KS-Grant, Haskell, Johnson, Morton, Seward, Stevens

Add'l Information: Established 1992. Normal turnaround time- 1-3 days. Fee basis varies by type of transaction. Will file/record documents for clients. They specialize in title ins, abstracting & closings. They give prompt & efficient service. They write for First American Title & Commonwealth. Have a branch office at 206 E. Grant, Ulysses, KS 67888; 620-356-2100; 356 2161 Fax. Manager is Evelyn Hacker.

American Title & Escrow of Big Horn County

207 N Center Ave, Hardin, MT 59034
Phone: 406-665-3797 - **Fax:** 406-665-1099 hardin@amtitlemontana.com

Types of Records Retrieved: Civil and Probate courts; Real Estate; Tax Liens/Judgments; UCC records

Local Retrieval Area: MT-Big Horn. **Correspondent Relationships:** southeastern Montana.

Add'l Information: Normal turnaround time- up to 5 days. Expedited service available. Projects billed by the hour. Will file/record documents for clients. They specialize real estate and title searches.

American Title & Escrow of Musselshell County

226 Main St, PO Box 838, Roundup, MT 59072
Phone: 406-323-3165 - **Fax:** 406-323-3311
www.amtitlemontana.com **email:** roundup@amtitlemontana.com

Types of Records: Real Estate; Tax Liens/Judgments; UCC records

Local Retrieval Area: MT-Musselshell

Add'l Information: Established 1988. Normal turnaround time- 3-5 days. Fee basis varies by type of transaction.

American Title Company of Lenawee

142 N Winter St, Adrian, MI 49221-2043
Phone: 517-263-4040 - **Fax:** 517-265-2533 atcl@tc3net.com

Types of Records Retrieved: Real Estate

Local Retrieval Area: MI-Lenawee

Add'l Information: Established 1979. Normal turnaround time- 1 week. Fee basis will vary by type of project. Will file/record documents for clients. They specialize in real estate.

American-First Abstract Co

111 E Comanche St, Norman, OK 73069
Phone: 405-321-7577 - **Fax:** 405-321-3833
www.americanfirst.com **email:** chawkins@americanfirst.com

Types of Records Retrieved: Civil and Probate courts; Real Estate; Tax Liens/Judgments; UCC records

Local Retrieval Area: OK-Cleveland

Add'l Information: Established 1963. Normal turnaround time- 3-5 days. Fee basis will vary by the type of project. First project may require prepayment. They specialize in real estate title searches.

Americorp Research Inc

2700 Pecan St West #427, Pflugerville, TX 78660
Phone: 800-620-0015; 512-989-6854 - **Fax:** 800-620-0016; 512-989-6858
anne@capitollien.com

Types of Records Retrieved: Criminal, Civil and Probate courts; Federal courts; Real Estate; Tax Liens/Judgments; UCC records; Vital records

Local Retrieval Area: TX-Bastrop, Bell, Hays, Travis, Williamson. **Correspondent Relationships:** nationwide.

Add'l Information: Established 1999. Normal turnaround time- 24-48 hours. Projects billed by number of records located. All projects require prepayment. Credit cards accepted. Will file/record documents for clients. They specialize in Secretary of State Texas UCCs and corporate filings. Filings can be faxed for same day filing.

Ameristar Information Network

500 S Nolen Dr #100, Southlake, TX 95092
Phone: 800-920-9270; 817-912-0600 - **Fax:** 800-920-9271; 817-912-3140
www.ameristarusa.com **Types of Records Retrieved:** Civil and Probate courts; Real Estate; Tax Liens/Judgments; Vital records

Local Retrieval Area: TX-Collin, Dallas, Denton, Tarrant. **Correspondent Relationships:** nationwide for property research.

Add'l Information: Established 1989. Normal turnaround time- 24-72 hours. Projects billed by number of names searched. Will file/record documents for clients.

Ameritex Legal Support

PO Box 96134, Houston, TX 77213
Phone: 888-670-7575; 713-670-7575 - **Fax:** 713 670 7501
www.ameritexlegal.com **email:** rharris90@houston.rr.com

Types of Records: Criminal, Civil and Probate courts; Federal courts

Area: TX-Brazoria, Fort Bend, Galveston, Harris, Liberty, Montgomery

Add'l Information: Established 1990. Normal turnaround time- 1-3 days. Projects billed by the hour. First project may require prepayment. Credit cards accepted. They specialize in process serving and records retrieval, including medical records retrieval. Will also file records. A licensed PI in TX.

Amerititle Abstract & Research Inc

6300 Hillcroft #114, Houston, TX 77081
Phone: 800-856-1228; 713-772-7870 - **Fax:** 713-772-7922
www.atitle.net **email:** kmorris@atitle.net

Types of Records Retrieved: Civil and Probate courts; Federal courts; Real Estate; Tax Liens/Judgments; UCC records

Local Retrieval Area: TX-Brazoria, Collin, Dallas, Denton, Fort Bend, Galveston, Harris, Montgomery, Travis. **Correspondents:** Texas.

Add'l Information: Established 1986. Normal turnaround time- 24-48 hours. First project may require prepayment.

Amma H General Ltd

PO Box 226, Beaufort, SC 29901-0226
Phone: 843-263-5677 or 843-525-9890 - **Fax:** 843-525-6923
ammagen1@yahoo.com

Types of Records Retrieved: Criminal, Civil and Probate courts; Real Estate; Tax Liens/Judgments; UCC records

Local Retrieval Area: SC-Beaufort, Hampton, Jasper

Add'l Information: Established 1986. Normal turnaround time- 48 hours. Projects billed by number of names searched. First project may require prepayment. Amma H General has been a leader in the R.A.C.E. for the past 15 years. Each clients assignment is treated with reliability, accuracy, confidentiality and expediency.

AM-PM Services

PO Box 1776, Moses Lake, WA 98837
Phone: 509-765-1776 - **Fax:** 509-766-5776

Types of Records Retrieved: Civil courts; Real Estate; Tax Liens/Judgments; UCC records; Vital records

Local Retrieval Area: WA-Adams, Chelan, Douglas, Franklin, Grant, Kittitas, Lincoln

Add'l Information: Established 1977. Normal turnaround time- 3 days or less. Projects billed by the hour. One hour minimum. Mileage is at 50 cents per mile. First project may require prepayment. Will file/record documents for clients. Money orders and cashier checks accepted. Special orders may require downpayment. They specialize in process serving and document retrieval, and will go to the Canadian border. Performs service of process.

Anderson Abstract Co

PO Box 8, Tekamah, NE 68061-0008
Phone: 402-374-1476 - **Fax:** 402-374-1478 randerson@huntel.net

Types of Records Retrieved: Criminal, Civil and Probate courts; Real Estate; Tax Liens/Judgments; UCC records

Local Retrieval Area: NE-Burt

Add'l Information: Established 1905. Normal turnaround time- 2 days. Projects billed by number of names searched. Add'l fee for copies, etc. Will file/record documents for clients. Payment due upon receipt of invoice. They have provided record search, title insurance and abstracting services for over 90 years. In the Nebraska 402 area code, may dial (800) 246-1476.

Anderson County Abstract Co

PO Box 847, 519 N Church St, Palestine, TX 75801
Phone: 903-729-5871 - **Fax:** 903-729-1160

Types of Records Retrieved: Real Estate; Tax Liens/Judgments; UCC records; Vital records

Local Retrieval Area: TX-Anderson

Add'l Information: Established 1900. Normal turnaround time- 1 week to 10 days. Fee basis varies by type of transaction. First project may require prepayment. Will file/record documents for clients. They specialize in title policies and abstracting. Specialize in marriage/divorce and death searches.

H Ray Anderson

618 F Ave, Lawton, OK 73501
Phone: 580-355-4450 - **Fax:** 580-250-1482 hraypi@aol.com

Types of Records Retrieved: Criminal, Civil and Probate courts; Federal courts; Real Estate; Tax Liens/Judgments; UCC records

Local Retrieval Area: OK-Comanche, Cotton, Jefferson, Stephens, Tillman. **Correspondent areas:** Comanche, Cotton, other Southwestern OK areas.

Add'l Information: Established 1990. Normal turnaround time- 24 hours. Projects billed by the hour. Criminal searches are a flat rate. Credit cards accepted. Will file/record documents for clients. Personal checks are accepted. He specializes in workers' compensation, defense, personal injuries, custody and asset searches. A licensed PI in OK.

Andrea's Abstracting aka ASAP Services

PO Box 253, Pleasant Hill, MO 64080
Phone: 816-987-6300 - **Fax:** 816-987-6302 asap@kcweb.net

Types of Records Retrieved: Civil and Probate courts; Federal courts; Real Estate; Tax Liens/Judgments

Local Retrieval Area: MO-Cass, Clay, Jackson. **Correspondent Relationships:** Platte, Bates, Johnson, Henry counties MO; Johnson, Wyandotte counties KS.

Add'l Information: Established 1998. Normal turnaround time- 24 hours. Projects billed by number of names searched. First project may require prepayment. Will file/record documents for clients. They specialize in residential and real estate abstracting along with Federal District and Bankruptcy courts. Performs service of process.

Andrews Agency Inc

736-B N Magnolia Ave, Orlando, FL 32803-3809
Phone: 407-649-2085 - **Fax:** 407-649-3053

Types of Records Retrieved: Criminal, Civil and Probate courts; Federal courts; Real Estate; Tax Liens/Judgments; UCC records; Vital records

Local Retrieval: FL-Brevard, Lake, Orange, Osceola, Seminole, Volusia

Add'l Information: Established 1983. Normal turnaround time- 24 hours. Projects billed by the hour. Credit cards accepted. MasterCard, Visa, American Express and Discover accepted. They specialize in process serving. A licensed PI in FL. Performs service of process.

Sharron Andrews

230 Grant St, Independence, CA 93526
Phone: 760-878-2038 - **Fax:** 760-878-2038

Types of Records Retrieved: Criminal, Civil and Probate courts; Real Estate; Tax Liens/Judgments; UCC records; Vital records

Local Retrieval Area: CA-Inyo

Add'l Information: Established 1978. Normal turnaround time- 1-2 days. Projects billed by the hour. First project may require prepayment. Will file/record documents for clients. She will invoice companies.

Angel P I's

500 State St, Ottawa, IL 61350
Phone: 800-973-3832; 815-228-3694 - **Fax:** 800-708-9336; waterboypi@yahoo.com

Types of Records Retrieved: Criminal and Civil courts

Local Retrieval Area: IL-Boone, Bureau, De Kalb, Grundy, Kendall, La Salle, Lee, Livingston, Logan, Marshall, Menard, Ogle, Peoria, Putnam, Sangamon, Tazewell, Winnebago, Woodford; WI-Dane, Rock. **Correspondent Relationships:** Other counties in northern and central Illinois, and far South Central Wisconsin.

Add'l Information: Established 2001. First project may require prepayment. They also provide court filings, skiptracing, subpoenas, photocopying, and private investigations. A licensed PI in IL. Performs service of process.

Annette Sanders Research

637 Edenderry Dr, Vacaville, CA 95688-8552
Phone: 707-449-3620 - **Fax:** 707-449-3655 netsand@compuserve.com

Types of Records Retrieved: Criminal and Civil courts

Local Retrieval Area: CA-Napa, Solano

Add'l Information: Established 1996. Normal turnaround time- 4-24 hours. Projects billed by number of names searched. Will customize billing method. Will invoice monthly. She offer fast, accurate service; she lives minutes from the court house and can return results faster than others. Has been a researcher for 10 years.

API

PO Box 40, Lake Park, GA 31636
Phone: 229-559-4717 - **Fax:** 229-559-0040

Types of Records Retrieved: Criminal, Civil and Probate courts; Tax Liens/Judgments; Limited Real Estate

Local Retrieval Area: FL-Hamilton, Jefferson, Leon, Madison, Suwanee; GA-Atkinson, Berrien, Brooks, Clinch, Colquitt, Cook, Echols, Lanier, Lowndes, Thomas, Tift

Add'l Information: Established 1986. Normal turnaround time- 24-48 hours. Projects billed by number of names searched. Projects billed by the hour. Fees depend on nature of the job. They are an expert in Georgia counties within 60 miles of Valdosta, including border counties in Florida. Is a PI.

Applicant Insight Ltd

PO Box 458, New Port Richey, FL 34656-0458
Phone: 800-771-7703; - **Fax:** 800-890-6454
www.ainsight.com **Types of Records Retrieved:** Criminal and Civil courts; Federal courts; UCC records

Local Retrieval Area: FL-Pasco, Pinellas. **Correspondent Relationships:** nationwide, hands-on.

Add'l Information: Established 1990. Normal turnaround time- 1-3 business days. Projects billed by number of names searched. Credit cards accepted. Invoiced monthly. They do in-depth interviews of the supervisor to whom the applicant reported. Statewide, they have an interactive web site for orders and retrievals at www.ainsight.com. A licensed PI in FL.

Applicant Profile Services

1231 8th St #222, West Des Moines, IA 50265
Phone: 515-727-7964 - **Fax:** 515-727-7965
www.applicantprofileservices.com **email:** info@applicantprofileservices.com

Types of Records Retrieved: Criminal, Civil and Probate courts; Federal courts; Real Estate; Tax Liens/Judgments; UCC records; Vital records

Local Retrieval Area: IA-Boone, Dallas, Greene, Grundy, Guthrie, Hamilton, Hardin, Jasper, Madison, Marshall, Polk, Story, Warren, Webster, Wright. **Correspondent Relationships:** statewide.

Add'l Information: Established 1993. Normal turnaround time- 24-48 hours. Projects billed by number of names searched. They specialize in pre-employment screening, real estate title search work, current owner searches, document retrieval, and mortgage recordings. Also provides skiptracing services, tenant background checks, asset recovery. Performs service of process.

Applied Research & Investigation

1415 20th Ave., Beaver Falls, PA 15010
Phone: 800-594-0008; 724-847-1116 - **Fax:** 724-847-7268
michael.yaria@verizon.net

Types of Records Retrieved: Criminal, Civil and Probate courts

Local Retrieval Area: OH-Columbiana; PA-Allegheny, Beaver

Add'l Information: Established 2001. Normal turnaround time- 1-2 days. Projects billed by number of names searched. First project may require prepayment. They are a comprehensive pre-employment screening service focused on healthcare, manufacturing and engineering/technical fields. Reference available.

APSCREEN Inc

PO Box 80639, Rancho Santa Margarita, CA 92688-0639
Phone: 800-277-2733; 949-646-4003 - **Fax:** 888-277-2733; 949-646-5160
www.apscreen.com **email:** tomlawson@apscreen.com

Types of Records Retrieved: Criminal, Civil and Probate courts; Federal courts; Real Estate; Tax Liens/Judgments; UCC records; Vital records

Local Retrieval Area: CA-Kern, Los Angeles, Orange, Riverside, San Bernardino, San Diego, Santa Barbara, Ventura. **Correspondent Relationships:** worldwide.

Add'l Information: Established 1980. Normal turnaround time- 24-48 hours. Projects billed by number of names searched. Credit cards accepted. They specialize in asset searches, document retrieval, research, fraud examinations, due diligence, permissible purpose credit reporting (licensed credit bureau), expert testimony, employment/tenant screening.

Arbor Abstracting Co

110 9th St, Honesdale, PA 18431
Phone: 570-253-0472 - **Fax:** 570-253-6214 titleins@ptd.net

Types of Records Retrieved: Criminal, Civil and Probate courts; Real Estate; Tax Liens/Judgments; UCC records

Local Retrieval Area: PA-Pike, Wayne

Add'l Information: Established 1983. Normal turnaround time- 24-48 hours. Expedited service available. They charge a flat rate per project. Will file/record documents for clients. Payment expected upon presentation of file. They specialize in real estate, title insurance and settlement services. They will file/record UCC and real estate documents on behalf of clients in Wayne County only.

Arbuckle Searches

1003 N King, Harrisonville, MO 64701
Phone: 816-550-9106 - **Fax:** 815-642-9147 arbucklesearches@earthlink.net

Types of Records Retrieved: Civil courts; Real Estate; Tax Liens/Judgments

Local Retrieval Area: MO-Cass, Johnson

Add'l Information: Established 2001. Normal turnaround time- 24-48 hours. Projects billed by number of names searched. They have over 3 years experience with record retrievals, provides mortgage/single property searches with a 24-48 hours turnaround time.

ARC Document Research Inc

205 W Randolph St #1401, Chicago, IL 60606-1815
Phone: 312-346-4895 - **Fax:** 312-346-4947
www.arcdocumentresearchinc.net **email:** arcdocs@aol.com

Types of Records: Real Estate; Tax Liens/Judgments; UCC records

Local Retrieval Area: IL-Cook, Du Page, Kane, Lake, McHenry, Sangamon, Will, Winnebago. **Correspondent Relationships:** Illinois.

Add'l Information: Established 1997. Normal turnaround time- 48-72 hours. Projects billed by number of names searched. First project may require prepayment. Will file/record documents for clients. They specialize in real estate searches.

Archives Retrieval Service of GA

85 Highland Park Way, Sharpsburg, GA 30277
Phone: 770-252-5510 - **Fax:** 770-252-1542 arsdocuments@aol.com

Types of Records Retrieved: Criminal, Civil and Probate courts; Federal courts; Real Estate; Tax Liens/Judgments; UCC records

Local Retrieval Area: GA-Cherokee, Clayton, Coweta, De Kalb, Fayette, Fulton, Gwinnett, Henry. **Correspondent Relationships:** Georgia.

Add'l Information: Established 1998. Normal turnaround time- 24-48 hours. Projects billed by number of records located. They specialize in professional research in bankruptcy, civil and criminal courts, real estate and tax liens and judgments throughout the entire state of Georgia.

Arenae Abstract & Title Co

PO Box 727, Standish, MI 48658-0727
Phone: 989-846-6560 - **Fax:** 989-846-6633

Types of Records Retrieved: Criminal, Civil and Probate courts; Real Estate; Tax Liens/Judgments; UCC records; Vital records

Local Retrieval Area: MI-Arenac

Add'l Information: Normal turnaround time- up to 1 week. Projects billed by the hour. All projects require prepayment. Will file/record documents for clients. They specialize in title insurance.

Argus Services Inc

123 W Madison St #1650, Chicago, IL 60602-4589
Phone: 800-297-3377; 312-922-6766 - **Fax:** 312-786-9508
ops@argus-services.com

Types of Records Retrieved: Criminal, Civil and Probate courts; Federal courts; Tax Liens/Judgments; Vital records

Local Retrieval Area: IL-Cook, De Kalb, Du Page, Kane, Kendall, Lake, McHenry, Will, Winnebago. **Correspondent Relationships:** all counties in the US for criminal records.

Add'l Information: Established 1991. Normal turnaround time- 24 hours; same day available in Chicago metro area. Projects billed by number of names searched. Projects billed by the hour. Net 20 days. First project may require prepayment. Credit cards accepted. Located in downtown Chicago 1 block from the Cook Cty Offices & 4 blocks from the Fed Bldg. Licensed private detective agency in IL, offering many kinds of criminal checks in the Chicago area. Also IL St Police Livescan vendors for fingerprinting. A licensed PI in IL. Performs service of process.

Arizona Research & Retrieval Services Inc

24810 S Lakewood Dr, Chandler, AZ 85248
Phone: 888-500-7767; 480-802-5918 - **Fax:** 602-532-7764
www.azretrieval.com **email:** info@azretrieval.com

Types of Records Retrieved: Criminal, Civil and Probate courts; Federal courts; Real Estate; Tax Liens/Judgments; UCC records; Vital records

Local Retrieval Area: AZ-Apache, Cochise, Coconino, Gila, Graham, Greenlee, La Paz, Maricopa, Mohave, Navajo, Pima, Pinal, Santa Cruz, Yavapai, Yuma; NV-Clark. **Correspondents:** statewide in Arizona.

Add'l Information: Established 1998. Normal turnaround time- 24-48 hours. Expedited service available. Projects billed by number of names searched. First project may require prepayment. Terms are net 15 days. They specialize in research and retrieval of county/federal court and county recorder records throughout AZ and in Clark County (Las Vegas) NV. A licensed PI in AZ (pending).

Arkansas Corporate Research & Service Co

323 Center St #1202, Little Rock, AR 72201
Phone: 501-374-3843 - **Fax:** 501-374-3836 acrsc@swbell.net

Types of Records Retrieved: Criminal and Civil courts; Federal courts; UCC records

Local Retrieval Area: AR-Faulkner, Lonoke, Pulaski, Lonoke. **Correspondent Relationships:** statewide.

Add'l Information: Established 1995. First project may require prepayment. They provide court record and UCC services for entire state of Arkansas.

Victoria J Armes

263 Whippoorwill Rd, Mooresville, NC 28117
Phone: 704-663-4085 - **Fax:** 704-663-7801 lakehideaway4u@yahoo.com

Types of Records Retrieved: Civil courts; Bankruptcy court; Real Estate; Tax Liens/Judgments; UCC records

Local Retrieval Area: NC-Cabarrus, Catawba, Iredell, Lincoln, Rowan. **Correspondent Relationships:** Durham, Johnston, Orange, Wake counties.

Add'l Information: Established 1985. Normal turnaround time- 24 hours. Projects billed by number of names searched. First project may require prepayment. Will file/record documents for clients. She specializes in real estate title searches. She has 30 years experience. Licensed PI in NC, GA.

Armstrong Document Retrieval

8711 Rosewood Dr, Prairie Village, KS 66207-2223
Phone: 913-341-1991 - **Fax:** 913-341-1667 armdoc@kc.rr.com

Types of Records Retrieved: Criminal and Civil courts; Federal courts; Real Estate; Tax Liens/Judgments; UCC records

Local Retrieval Area: KS-Johnson, Wyandotte; MO-Clay, Jackson, Platte

Add'l Information: Established 1988. Normal turnaround time- 24-48 hours. Projects billed by number of names searched. First project may require prepayment. Will file/record documents for clients. Prepayment required if copy charges are over $50.00. They do daily document retrieval from the two Federal Archives in K.C., one of which has closed case files from New York and New Jersey.

Rachel Arnold

1 Public Sq #200, Shelbyville, TN 37160 **Phone:** 931-684-1672

Types of Records Retrieved: Criminal and Civil courts; Tax Liens/Judgments **Local Retrieval Area:** TN-Bedford

Add'l Information: Established 2005. Normal turnaround time- 24 hours. Projects billed by number of names searched. First project may require prepayment. She is at the courthouse daily. Call for fax number.

Arrow Background Services LLC

41549 Burnt Mill Dr, Hollywood, MD 20636-2301
Phone: 301-475-7802 - **Fax:** 301-475-7803
janneszokoly@verizon.net

Types of Records Retrieved: Criminal courts; Federal District courts

Local Retrieval Area: MD-Anne Arundel, Baltimore, Baltimore City, Carroll, Harford, Howard, Montgomery, Prince George's. **Correspondent Relationships:** statewide, including eastern shore.

Add'l Information: Established 1995. Normal turnaround time- 24 hours. Projects billed by number of names searched. First project may require prepayment. They specialize in court record retrievals and Maryland State Department of Assessment and Taxation retrievals and filings.

ASA (Attorney Service Associates)

PO Box 116874, Carrollton, TX 75011
Phone: 972-394-1175 - **Fax:** 972-492-4552
www.asainfo.com **email:** asasearch@sprintmail.com

Types of Records Retrieved: Criminal, Civil and Probate courts; Federal courts; Real Estate; Tax Liens/Judgments; UCC records; Vital records

Local Retrieval Area: TX-Collin, Dallas, Denton, Tarrant. **Correspondent Relationships:** statewide.

Add'l Information: Established 1991. Normal turnaround time- 24-48 hours. Expedited service available. Projects billed by number of names searched. Will file/record documents for clients. Terms: net 15 days, 5% late fee. They specialize in courthouse/public records research and retrieval services in Texas. A licensed PI in TX. Performs service of process.

ASAP Legal Messenger

6824 W 19th St #215, Tacoma, WA 98466
Phone: 253-640-1312 andyigor@ix.netcom.com

Records Retrieved: Criminal and Civil courts; Federal courts; Real Estate

Local Retrieval Area: WA-Adams, Chelan, Douglas, King, Kitsap, Pierce, Snohomish. **Correspondent Relationships:** Washington and Oregon.

Add'l Information: Established 1990. Normal turnaround time- 3 days. Projects billed by number of names searched. First project may require prepayment. Performs service of process.

ASAP Process Service

PO Box 607, 230 E 1st Ave, Lisbon, IA 52253
Phone: 877-455-2490; 319-455-2490 - **Fax:** 319-455-5041
rcook10672@aol.com

Types of Records Retrieved: Criminal, Civil and Probate courts; Federal courts; Real Estate; Vital records

Local Retrieval Area: IA-Cedar, Iowa, Jackson, Johnson, Jones, Linn

Add'l Information: Established 1996. Normal turnaround time- 3-4 days. Expedited service available. Projects billed by the hour. All projects require prepayment. They also provide court filings, subpoena preparation, photocopying, and skiptracing. Performs service of process.

Ascension Title Services Inc

PO Box 117, Gonzales, LA 70707 (311 E Cornerview, Prairieville, LA)
Phone: 225-647-8051 - **Fax:** 225-647-8064
ascensiontitle@ats.brcoxmail.com

Types of Records Retrieved: Civil and Probate courts; Real Estate; Tax Liens/Judgments; UCC records

Local Retrieval Area: LA-Ascension, Iberville, St. James Parishes. **Correspondent Relationships:** statewide.

Add'l Information: Established 1992. Normal turnaround time- 2-3 days. Fee basis varies by type of transaction. First project may require prepayment. Will file/record documents for clients.

Ashley Abstract Co

113 W Main St, PO Box 365, Ashley, ND 58413
Phone: 701-288-3584 - **Fax:** 701-288-2110

Types of Records Retrieved: Civil courts; Real Estate; Tax Liens/Judgments; UCC records; Vital records

Local Retrieval Area: ND-McIntosh

Add'l Information: Established 1901. Normal turnaround time- 24 hours. Projects billed by number of names searched. Projects billed by number of records located. All projects require prepayment. Will file/record documents for clients.

ASK Services Inc

42180 Ford Rd #101, Canton, MI 48187
Phone: 888-416-1313; - **Fax:** 734-983-9041
www.ask-services.com **email:** publicrecords@ask-services.com

Types of Records Retrieved: Criminal and Civil courts; Federal courts; Real Estate; Tax Liens/Judgments; UCC records

Local Retrieval Area: OH-Cuyahoga, Delaware, Fairfield, Franklin, Hamilton, Licking, Lucas, Madison. **Correspondent Relationships:** MI, IN, NC, SC and nationwide.

Add'l Information: Established 2000. Normal turnaround time- 24-48 hours. Projects billed by number of names searched. Credit cards accepted. Specializing in title searches, retrievals and recordings as well as criminal, civil, UCC and lien related records. They are your ONE source for all public records. A licensed PI in MI, NC.

ASK Services Inc (Indiana)

136 E Market St, Indianapolis, IN 43204
Phone: 888-416-1313; - **Fax:** 734-983-9041
www.ask-services.com **email:** publicrecords@ask-services.com

Types of Records Retrieved: Criminal and Civil courts; Federal courts; Real Estate; UCC records; Tax Liens/Judgments

Local Retrieval Area: IN-Allen, DeKalb, Elkhart, Hamilton, Hendricks, Johnson, Lake, La Porte, Marion, Morgan, Porter, St. Joseph, Steuben. **Correspondent Relationships:** nationwide.

Add'l Information: Established 2000. Normal turnaround time- 24-48 hours. Projects billed by number of names searched. Credit cards accepted. Will file/record documents for clients. Specializing in title searches, retrievals and recordings as well as criminal, civil, UCC and lien related records. They are your ONE source for all public records. A licensed PI in MI, NC.

ASK Services Inc (Michigan)

42180 Ford Rd, Canton, MI 48187
Phone: 888-416-1313; - **Fax:** 800-742-7051; 734-983-9041
www.ask-publicrecords.com **email:** publicrecords@ask-services.com

Types of Records Retrieved: Criminal, Civil and Probate courts; Federal courts; Real Estate; Tax Liens/Judgments; UCC records; Vital records

Local Retrieval Area: MI-all counties. **Correspondents:** nationwide.

Add'l Information: Established 1985. Normal turnaround time- 24-48 hours. Expedited service available. Projects billed by number of names searched. Projects billed by the hour. Credit cards accepted. Will file/record documents for clients. Specializing in title searches, retrievals and recordings as well as criminal, civil, UCC and lien related records. They are your ONE source for all public records. A licensed PI in MI.

ASK Services Inc (North Carolina)

5 W Hargett St #803, Raleigh, NC 27601-1357
Phone: 888-416-1313; - **Fax:** 734-983-9041
www.ask-services.com **email:** publicrecords@ask-services.com

Types of Records Retrieved: Criminal, Civil and Probate courts; Federal courts; Real Estate; Tax Liens/Judgments; UCC records; Vital records

Local Retrieval Area: NC-Chatham, Durham, Harnett, Johnston, Lee, Orange, Wake. **Correspondent Relationships:** nationwide.

Add'l Information: Established 1998. Normal turnaround time- 24-48 hours. Expedited service available. Projects billed by number of names searched. Projects billed by the hour. Credit cards accepted. Will file/record documents for clients. They specialize in civil, criminal and bankruptcy searches, also UCC, tax liens searches and filings for all counties covered. Will complete expedited real property/title searches. A licensed PI in MI.

Asset Control Inc

1300 Fulton Pl #300, Denton, TX 76201
Phone: 877-277-3812; 940-891-1919 - **Fax:** 877-277-3829
www.assetcontrol.net **email:** info@assetcontrol.net

Types of Records Retrieved: Criminal and Civil courts; Federal courts; Real Estate; Tax Liens/Judgments; UCC records; Vital records

Local Retrieval Area: DC-Washington; IL-Cook; TX-Bexar, Collin, Dallas, Denton, Harris, Hidalgo, Tarrant. **Correspondents:** nationwide.

Add'l Information: Established 1994. Normal turnaround time- 24-48 hours. Projects billed by number of names searched. Credit cards accepted. Net 30 days on monthly bills. A licensed PI in TX.

Asset Protection Associates Inc

PO Box 310, Little Switzerland, NC 28749
Phone: 828-765-9359 - **Fax:** 828-765-9369
www.asset-protectionassociates.com
email: swilson@asset-protectionassociates.com

Types of Records Retrieved: Criminal and Civil courts

Local Retrieval Area: NC-Mitchell, Yancey

Add'l Information: Normal turnaround time- 24-48 hours. Expedited service available at add'l charge. Projects billed by the hour. First project may require prepayment. Will invoice. Payment due net 30 days. They are a full service investigative firm serving the business, legal and financial communities since 1978. A licensed PI in NC.

Asset Protection Investigations, Inc

PO Box 2426, Beaufort, SC 29902
Phone: 843-525-9664 - **Fax:** 843-521-4667 i@charter.net

Types of Records Retrieved: Criminal, Civil and Probate courts; Real Estate; Tax Liens/Judgments

Local Retrieval Area: SC-Beaufort, Colleton, Hampton, Jasper

Add'l Information: Established 1995. Normal turnaround time- 48-72 hours. Expedited service available. Projects billed by the hour. A licensed PI in SC, GA. Performs service of process.

ASSIST International

212 W 29th St Front, New York, NY 10001-5288
Phone: 800-382-7747; 212-244-2074 - **Fax:** 212-594-1939
www.assistintl.net **email:** assistnyc@aol.com

Types of Records Retrieved: Criminal, Civil and Probate courts; Federal courts; Real Estate; Tax Liens/Judgments; UCC records; Vital records

Local Retrieval Area: NY-Bronx, Kings, New York, Orange, Putnam, Queens, Richmond, Rockland, Suffolk, Westchester. **Correspondent Relationships:** nationwide.

Add'l Information: Established 1981. Normal turnaround time- immediate to 5 days. Projects billed by number of names searched. They are a full service investigation agency specializing in locates, investigations and surveillance. Online computer searches are available. A licensed PI in NJ, NY. Performs service of process.

Assist Investigations

1223 Wilshire Blvd #943, Santa Monica, CA 90403
Phone: 310-451-2204 - **Fax:** 310-395-7355
www.assistinvestigations.com **email:** btb@assistinvestigations.com

Types of Records Retrieved: Criminal, Civil and Probate courts; Federal courts; Real Estate; Tax Liens/Judgments; UCC records; Vital records

Local Retrieval Area: CA-Los Angeles, Orange

Add'l Information: Established 1998. Normal turnaround time- 24-72 hours. Projects billed by number of names searched. Projects billed by the hour. First project may require prepayment. Will invoice. They have over 15 years experience conducting public record research in Southern CA. They specialize in real estate documents and court records research. A licensed PI in CA, Lic# 21703.

Associate Title - Iron County

205 Harrison St, Ironwood, MI 49938
Phone: 906-932-6340 - **Fax:** 906-932-4350
www.peninsula.net **email:** associated@pentitle.net

Types of Records Retrieved: Civil and Probate courts; Real Estate; Tax Liens/Judgments; UCC records

Local Retrieval Area: MI-Gogebic; WI-Iron

Add'l Information: Established 1937. Normal turnaround time- 1-2 days. Fee basis varies by type of transaction. All projects require prepayment. Will file/record documents for clients. They are an agent for the insurance companies. They also are title searchers, abstractors, do real estate closings and construction disbursements.

Associated Abstracting Services of MN

PO Box 39047, Edina, MN 55439
Phone: 612-819-6115 - **Fax:** 952-842-0812
www.aasom.com **email:** info@aasom.com

Types of Records Retrieved: Civil courts; Federal courts; Real Estate; Tax Liens/Judgments; UCC records

Local Retrieval Area: MN-Anoka, Benton, Blue Earth, Carver, Chisago, Hennepin, Isanti, LaSueur, Mille Lacs, Nicollet, Rice, Scott, Sherburne, Stearns, Steele, Wright

Add'l Information: Established 1985. Normal turnaround time- 24-48 hours. Projects billed by number of names searched. First project may require prepayment. Terms: net 30 days. AASM has over 20 years of experience.

Associated Attorney Services

123 W Padre St, #E, Santa Barbara, CA 93105
Phone: 805-898-0022 - **Fax:** 805-898-0012

Types of Records Retrieved: Criminal, Civil and Probate courts; Federal courts; Real Estate; Tax Liens/Judgments; UCC records; Vital records

Local Retrieval Area: CA-Santa Barbara. **Correspondents:** California.

Add'l Information: Established 1965. Normal turnaround time- 24 hours. Projects billed by number of names searched. Projects billed by number of records located. First project may require prepayment. They specialize in process service. Performs service of process.

Associated Investigative Services Inc

30 S 9th St, Allentown, PA 18102
Phone: 610-351-9911 - **Fax:** 610-351-9913
www.associnv.com **email:** aisinc@rcn.com

Types of Records Retrieved: Criminal, Civil and Probate courts; Federal courts; Real Estate; Tax Liens/Judgments; UCC records

Local Retrieval Area: PA-Lehigh

Add'l Information: Established 1995. Normal turnaround time- 48 hours. Projects billed by number of names searched. Credit cards accepted. They specialize in being a full service investigative agency serving the Lehigh Valley (Allentown) Bethlehem/Eastern area of PA. They are licensed, bonded and insured. A licensed PI in PA. Performs service of process.

Associated Peninsula Title & Abstract Co

PO Box 516, 945 First St, Menominee, MI 49858
Phone: 906-863-7871 - **Fax:** 906-863-1363
cindybehnke@menomineeabstract.com

Types of Records Retrieved: Criminal, Civil and Probate courts; Real Estate; Tax Liens/Judgments; UCC records; Vital records

Local Retrieval Area: MI-Menominee

Add'l Information: Established 1970. Normal turnaround time- 2-3 days. Projects billed by the hour. $120.00 minimum for Title Insurance; $50.00 minimum for searches. First project may require prepayment. Will file/record documents for clients. Terms: net 30 days. They specialize in title insurance, title searches (letter reports), closings and escrows.

Associated Professional Services

PO Box 4068, New Bedford, MA 02740-4068
Phone: 800-849-7870; 508-995-5901 - **Fax:** 508-998-4926
asscprosvc@verizonmail.com

Types of Records Retrieved: Criminal, Civil and Probate courts; Federal courts; Real Estate; Tax Liens/Judgments; UCC records; Vital records

Local Retrieval Area: MA-Barnstable, Bristol, Plymouth. **Correspondent Relationships:** Rhode Island.

Add'l Information: Established 1979. Normal turnaround time- 24-48 hours. First project may require prepayment. Will file/record documents for clients. They are a private investigation firm. Their retrieval unit is dedicated to record retrieval and exist as an adjunct to our core services. A licensed PI in MA. Performs service of process.

Associated Services

PO Box 5437, Harrisburg, PA 17110
Phone: 717-938-1550 - **Fax:** 717-938-5546
www.assocservlimited.com **email:** assocser1@aol.com

Types of Records Retrieved: Criminal, Civil and Probate courts; Federal courts; Real Estate; Tax Liens/Judgments; UCC records

Local Retrieval Area: PA-Cumberland, Dauphin, York. **Correspondent Relationships:** Lancaster county PA.

Add'l Information: Established 1989. Normal turnaround time- 24-48 hours. Fee basis varies by project. Will file/record documents for clients. Net 30 days. They specialize in criminal background checks, current owner searches, civil and UCC searches, service of process and court filings. Performs service of process.

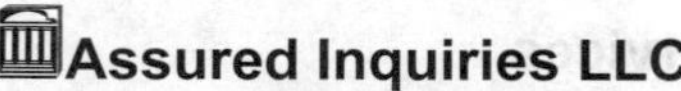

Assured Inquiries LLC

PO Box 87, 19 Bunker Hill Rd, New Castle, DE 19720-0087
Phone: 888-644-0004; 302-324-1190 - **Fax:** 302-324-0177
www.assuredinquiries.com **email:** louis.dempsey@verizon.net

Types of Records Retrieved: Criminal, Civil and Probate courts; Federal courts; Real Estate

Local Retrieval Area: DE-New Castle

Add'l Information: Established 2002. Normal turnaround time- 3 business days. Expedited service available. First project may require prepayment. They provide general investigative services including pre-employment screening and security consultation in Delaware. Over 31 years experience in law enforcement and corporate security management. A licensed PI in DE. Performs service of process.

Assured Realty

2nd & Norwegian St, Pottsville, PA 17901
Phone: 570-622-1366 - **Fax:** 570-622-4216

Types of Records Retrieved: Civil and Probate courts; Real Estate; Tax Liens/Judgments; UCC records

Local Retrieval Area: PA-Schuylkill

Add'l Information: Established 1984. Normal turnaround time- variable depending on search. Charges vary depending on type of search. First project may require prepayment. Assured Realty takes pride in its experienced staff and over 25 years in business - providing real estate title search and title insurance services.

Assured Title Company

801 S Woodlawn Ave, O'Fallon, MO 63366
Phone: 636-240-0833 - **Fax:** 636-240-0786
www.assuredtitle.net/index.html **email:** bscheidegger@landam.com

Types of Records Retrieved: Criminal, Civil and Probate courts; Real Estate; Tax Liens/Judgments; UCC records

Local Retrieval Area: MO-Franklin, Jefferson, Lincoln, Montgomery, St. Charles, St. Louis, St. Louis City, Warren. **Correspondent Relationships:** Pike, Camden, Miller, Ralls counties, MO.

Add'l Information: Established 1977. Normal turnaround time- 5 working days. Projects billed by number of names searched. Will file/record documents for clients. They specialize in record searching for title insurance & real estate closings. Add'l office in St Charles, 636-940-5406.

ATACO Inc

109 E Evans St #B, West Chester, PA 19380-2660
Phone: 800-220-2039; 610-436-6510 - **Fax:** 610-436-8112
www.atlantictitleabstract.com **email:** edougherty@landam.com

Types of Records Retrieved: Real Estate

Local Retrieval Area: PA-Berks, Bucks, Chester, Delaware. **Correspondent Relationships:** Pennsylvania and Delaware.

Add'l Information: Established 1987. Normal turnaround time- 2-3 days for lien searches, up to 2 weeks for all other searches. Expedited service available. Fee basis will vary by the type of project. Will file/record documents for clients. They specialize in real estate and abstracting.

Atlanta Attorney Services

2814 Spring Rd #120, Atlanta, GA 30339-3047
Phone: 800-804-4078; 404-303-7899 - **Fax:** 404-303-7890
www.aaslegal.com **email:** ddreeman@aaslegal.com

Types of Records Retrieved: Criminal, Civil and Probate courts; Federal courts; Tax Liens/Judgments; UCC records

Local Retrieval Area: GA-Clayton, Cobb, De Kalb, Forsyth, Fulton, Gwinnett. **Correspondent Relationships:** nationwide.

Add'l Information: Established 1996. Normal turnaround time- 48 hours. Expedited service available. Projects billed by number of names searched. Credit cards accepted. Will file/record documents for clients. They specialize in court searches, document retrieval, service of process, court filings and bankruptcy services. Performs service of process.

Atlanta Legal Services Inc

3070 Presidential Pky #148, Atlanta, GA 30340-3712
Phone: 877-302-4136; 404-876-8098 - **Fax:** 404-876-8099
www.atlantalegalservices.com **email:** info@atlantalegalservices.com

Types of Records Retrieved: Criminal, Civil and Probate courts; Federal courts; Real Estate; Tax Liens/Judgments; UCC records; Vital records

Local Retrieval Area: GA-Clayton, Cobb, De Kalb, Douglas, Forsyth, Fulton, Gwinnett, Paulding, Rockdale

Add'l Information: Established 1993. Normal turnaround time- 24 hours. Expedited service available. Projects billed by number of names searched. Projects billed by the hour. Flat rate per county (plus) time if over 30 minutes. First project may require prepayment. Credit cards accepted. Will invoice. They are a full litigation support service, providing process service, record retrieval and research and court filings. A licensed PI in GA. Performs service of process.

Atlanta Title Abstractors

3410 Bold Springs Rd, Monroe, GA 30656
Phone: 770-267-2727 - **Fax:** 770-267-6554

Types of Records Retrieved: Civil and Probate courts; Federal courts; Real Estate; Tax Liens/Judgments; UCC records

Local Retrieval Area: GA-Barrow, Clark, Clayton, Cobb, De Kalb, Douglas, Fayette, Fulton, Gwinnett, Hall, Jackson, Madison, Morgan, Newton, Oconee, Oglethorpe, Rockdale, Spalding. **Correspondent Relationships:** IN, SC, FL, NJ, AL, MS, TN, GA.

Add'l Information: Established 1985. Normal turnaround time- 48 hours. Projects billed by number of names searched. First project may require prepayment. They specialize in current owner of property, full owner of property, UCC by name, probate of name, civil by full name and tax liens by name/address.

Atlantic Coast Abstract Co

PO Box 1247, Freehold, NJ 07728
Phone: 732-431-1099 - **Fax:** 732-431-4338
www.atlanticcoastabstract.com
email: customerservice@atlanticcoastabstract.com

Types of Records Retrieved: Real Estate

Local Retrieval Area: NJ-Burlington, Mercer, Middlesex, Monmouth, Ocean, Somerset, Union

Add'l Information: Established 1947. Normal turnaround time- 24-48 hours. Depending on nature of request. Will file/record documents for clients. ACA has 165 years title experience, strives to provide clients with all their abstracting needs at competitive prices without sacrificing customer service. Branch offices in Monmouth, Mercer, and Middlesex.

Atlantic Investigations

315 W Ponce de Leon Ave, Suite 800, Decatur, GA 30030
Phone: 800-216-9877; 404-378-0700 - **Fax:** 404-378-1030
www.atlanticinvestigations.com **email:** jasonbeeker@aol.com

Types of Records Retrieved: Criminal, Civil and Probate courts; Federal courts; Real Estate; Tax Liens/Judgments; UCC records; Vital records

Local Retrieval Area: GA-De Kalb. **Correspondents:** Georgia.

Add'l Information: Established 1963. Normal turnaround time- 2-7 days. Projects billed by the hour. First project may require prepayment. Credit cards accepted. Visa and MasterCard accepted. They have provided investigative services for more than 40 years. Services include extensive database access and surveillance. A licensed PI in GA. Performs service of process.

Atlantic Title & Research

6184 Library Ln, Bealeton, VA 22712
Phone: 540-439-1800 - **Fax:** 540-439-1700 talkmac@aol.com

Records Retrieved: Real Estate; Tax Liens/Judgments; UCC records

Local Retrieval Area: VA-Culpeper, Fairfax, Fauquier, Loudoun, Prince William, Stafford. **Correspondent Relationships:** statewide.

Add'l Information: Established 2002. Normal turnaround time- 24-48 hours. Projects billed by number of names searched. First project may require prepayment. Credit cards accepted. Terms agreed on individual basis They specialize in real estate, tax liens/judgments and UCC records. They have nearly 20 years of experience.

Atlas Abstract Co

125 N Broadway, Holdenville, OK 74848
Phone: 405-379-3311 - **Fax:** 405-379-3349

Types of Records Retrieved: Civil and Probate courts; Real Estate; Tax Liens/Judgments

Local Retrieval Area: OK-Hughes

Add'l Information: Established 1904. Normal turnaround time- varied by project. Will file/record documents for clients. They specialize in Hughes county real estate.

Atlas Research Services Inc

16163 Nordhoff St #246, North Hills, CA 91343
Phone: 818-920-6376 - **Fax:** 818-920-6434 atlasrsch@socal.rr.com

Records Retrieved: Criminal and Civil courts; Federal District courts

Local Retrieval Area: CA-Alameda, Calaveras, Contra Costa, Fresno, Humboldt, Kern, Los Angeles, Monterey, Napa, Orange, Placer, Riverside, San Bernardino, San Diego, San Joaquin, Santa Barbara, Santa Clara, Santa Cruz, Siskiyou, Solano, Sonoma, Ventura, Yolo. **Correspondent Relationships:** all of California.

Add'l Information: Established 1996. Normal turnaround time- 24-48 hours. Charge by number of records located after 5 recorded cases. Credit cards accepted. Terms: net 25 days. They specialize in criminal background investigations. Online ordering available.

Atoka Abstract Co Inc

308 E Court St, Atoka, OK 74525
Phone: 580-889-7316 - **Fax:** 580-889-7317

Records Retrieved: Real Estate; Tax Liens/Judgments; UCC records

Local Retrieval Area: OK-Atoka

Add'l Information: Established 1977. Normal turnaround time- variable depending on project. Projects billed by the hour. Will file/record documents for clients.

ATT Investigations Inc

PO Box 25831, Fort Lauderdale, FL 33320
Phone: 800-733-4405; 954-733-4005 - **Fax:** 954-677-0562
customerservice@attloss.com

Types of Records Retrieved: Criminal, Civil and Probate courts; Federal courts; Real Estate; Tax Liens/Judgments; UCC records; Vital records

Local Retrieval Area: FL-Broward, Dade, Hillsborough, Lake, Marion, Orange, Osceola, Palm Beach, Pasco, Pinellas, Seminole, Volusia. **Correspondent Relationships:** nationwide.

Add'l Information: Established 1994. Normal turnaround time- 2-3 days. Projects billed by number of names searched. Projects billed by number of records located. Credit cards accepted. They provide extensive public record retrieval in all courts and recorders offices. A licensed PI in FL.

ATT Loss Prevention Inc

PO Box 1681, Torrington, CT 06790
Phone: 877-556-9613; - **Fax:** 877-556-9614 customerservice@attloss.com

Types of Records Retrieved: Criminal, Civil and Probate courts; Federal courts; Real Estate; Tax Liens/Judgments; UCC records; Vital records

Local Retrieval Area: CT-Fairfield, Hartford, Litchfield, Middlesex, New Haven, New London, Tolland, Windham. **Correspondents:** nationwide.

Add'l Information: Established 1994. Normal turnaround time- 2-3 days. Will bill depending on the nature of the project. First project may require prepayment. Credit cards accepted. One of the oldest and most reliable local companies in the state, they provide extensive public record retrieval in all courts, recorders offices and motor vehicle records nationwide.

Attorney Civil Process Service

425 Austin Ave #2102, Waco, TX 76701
Phone: 254-755-6447 - **Fax:** 254-754-4050

Records Retrieved: Criminal, Civil and Probate courts; Federal courts

Local Retrieval Area: TX-Bell, Bosque, Falls, Hill, McLennan

Add'l Information: Established 1986. Normal turnaround time- 2-3 days. Projects billed by number of names searched. All projects require prepayment. They specialize in service of process, court records search, skiptracing and videotape depositions. Performs service of process.

Attorney Service Bureau

PO Box 382, Pomona, NY 10970
Phone: 845-638-1323 - **Fax:** 845-638-3831
attorneyservicebureau@yahoo.com

Types of Records Retrieved: Criminal, Civil and Probate courts; Federal courts; Real Estate; Tax Liens/Judgments; UCC records; Vital records

Local Retrieval Area: NY-Orange, Rockland, Westchester. **Correspondent Relationships:** nationwide.

Add'l Information: Established 1980. Normal turnaround time- 7 working days. Same day service available. Projects billed by number of names searched. Projects billed by number of records located. Projects billed by the hour. All projects require prepayment. Will file/record documents for clients. They specialize in Tri-State Metro-Mid Hudson areas of NY, NJ and CN. They serve process service and public record investigations. A licensed PI in NY. Performs service of process.

Attorney Service New Mexico

418 W Broadway #A, Farmington, NM 87401
Phone: 505-326-7486 - **Fax:** 505-326-3492 mduncan@co.san-juan.nm.us

Types of Records Retrieved: Criminal and Civil courts

Local Retrieval Area: AZ-Apache; CO-Archuleta, La Plata, Montezuma; NM-Cibola, McKinley, Rio Arriba, San Juan; UT-San Juan

Add'l Information: Established 2000. All projects require prepayment. They also provide court filings, subpoena preparation, photocopying, and skiptracing. The specialize in Indian reservations in the Four Corners area. Performs service of process.

Attorney Service of California-Monterey

270 El Dorado St, Monterey, CA 93940
Phone: 888-306-2194 - **Fax:** 831-465-9632

Types of Records Retrieved: Criminal, Civil and Probate courts; Real Estate; Tax Liens/Judgments; UCC records; Vital records

Local Retrieval Area: CA-Monterey

Add'l Information: Established 1972. Normal turnaround time- 1-2 days. Projects billed by number of names searched. First project may require prepayment. Will file/record documents for clients. They specialize in process service and investigations and court research. Also has an office in Watsonville and in Monterey County. Performs service of process.

Attorney Service of California-Santa Cruz

PO Box 1436, Santa Cruz, CA 95061
Phone: 888-306-2194; - **Fax:** 831-465-9632

Types of Records Retrieved: Criminal, Civil and Probate courts; Real Estate; Tax Liens/Judgments; UCC records; Vital records

Local Retrieval Area: CA-Monterey, Santa Cruz. **Correspondent Relationships:** nationwide.

Add'l Information: Established 1972. Normal turnaround time- 1-2 days. Expedited service available. Projects billed by number of names searched. Projects billed by the hour. Will file/record documents for clients. They specialize in process service and investigations and court research. Also has an office in Watsonville. Performs service of process.

Attorney Service of Merced

PO Box 2351, 2440 M St (95340), Merced, CA 95344
Phone: 209-383-3233 - **Fax:** 209-383-0311

Types of Records Retrieved: Criminal, Civil and Probate courts; Federal courts; Real Estate; Tax Liens/Judgments; UCC records; Vital records

Retrieval Area: CA-Madera, Mariposa, Merced, San Joaquin, Stanislaus

Add'l Information: Established 1982. Normal turnaround time- up to 3 days. Projects billed by number of names searched. First project may require prepayment. Credit cards accepted. Will file/record documents for clients. They specialize in process serving. Performs service of process.

Attorney Service of San Luis Obispo

860 Walnut St, San Luis Obispo, CA 93401
Phone: 850-543-8919
www.firstlegalsupport.com **email:** dh@firstlegalsupport.com

Types of Records Retrieved: Criminal, Civil and Probate courts; Federal courts; Real Estate; Tax Liens/Judgments; UCC records; Vital records

Local Retrieval Area: CA-San Luis Obispo, Santa Barbara. **Correspondent Relationships:** statewide.

Add'l Information: Established 1973. Projects billed by number of names searched. Billing varies depending on project. First project may require prepayment. They specialize in document management and litigation support. Performs service of process.

Attorney Services of Kentucky

PO Box 221408, Louisville, KY 40252
Phone: 502-327-6677 - **Fax:** 502-412-1955

Types of Records Retrieved: Criminal, Civil and Probate courts; Federal courts; Real Estate; Tax Liens/Judgments; UCC records; Vital records

Local Retrieval Area: KY-Bullitt, Fayette, Franklin, Hardin, Jefferson, Kenton, Meade, Nelson, Oldham, Shelby. **Correspondent Relationships:** Clark, Floyd, Hancock counties IN.

Add'l Information: Established 1993. Turnaround time- 24 hours. Projects billed by the hour. First project may require prepayment. They specialize in witness and defendant locates, asset searches, records research, KY employment search and driver's licenses. Performs service of process.

Attorney Services of Northeast Ohio

221 Springside Dr, Akron, OH 44333
Phone: 800-804-7787; 330-376-8100 x2 - **Fax:** 330-376-0110
www.asneo.us **email:** AttorneyServicesNEO@yahoo.com

Types of Records Retrieved: Criminal, Civil and Probate courts; Federal courts; Real Estate; Tax Liens/Judgments; Vital records

Local Retrieval Area: OH-Cuyahoga, Geauga, Lake, Lorain, Mahoning, Medina, Portage, Stark, Summit, Trumbull, Wayne

Add'l Information: Established 1972. Normal turnaround time- variable depending on project. Projects billed by the hour. First project may require prepayment. Will file/record documents for clients. After 20 years experience, they can often times advise of local procedures or acquire documents quickly, while others less experienced might not be as successful. They specialize in accomplishing rush, priority, same day orders. Performs service of process.

Attorney's Aid Inc of Sacramento

50 Fullerton Ct #201, Sacramento, CA 95825-5205
Phone: 916-648-1559 - **Fax:** 916-648-1583

Types of Records Retrieved: Criminal, Civil and Probate courts; Federal courts; Real Estate; UCC records; Vital records

Local Retrieval Area: CA-Alameda, Contra Costa, El Dorado, Fresno, Placer, Sacramento, San Joaquin, Shasta, Sonoma, Stanislaus, Sutter, Yolo. **Correspondent Relationships:** statewide.

Add'l Information: Established 1974. Normal turnaround time- 2 days. Projects billed by the hour. Will file/record documents for clients. Prepayment required if you are not with a law firm/private attorney or insurance company. They specialize in document reproduction, onsite and in-house. Performs service of process.

Attorney's Diversified Services-Bakersfield

701 H St, Bakersfield, CA 93304
Phone: 800-842-6334; 661-323-2377 - **Fax:** 661-323-3376
www.attorneysdiversified.com **email:** rallison@attorneysdiversified.com

Types of Records Retrieved: Criminal, Civil and Probate courts; Federal courts; Tax Liens/Judgments; UCC records

Local Retrieval Area: CA-Kern

Add'l Information: Normal turnaround time- routine 72 hours. Projects billed by number of names searched. Projects billed by the hour. First project may require prepayment. Credit cards accepted. Will file/record documents for clients. They specialize in document management and litigation support. Performs service of process.

Attorney's Diversified Services-Fresno

741 N Fulton St, Fresno, CA 93728
Phone: 800-842-2695; 559-233-1475 - **Fax:** 559-486-4119
www.attorneysdiversified.com **Types of Records Retrieved:** Criminal, Civil and Probate courts; Federal courts; Real Estate; Tax Liens/Judgments; UCC records; Vital records

Local Retrieval Area: CA-Fresno, Inyo, Kings, Madera, Mariposa, Merced, Mono, Monterey, San Benito, Santa Cruz, Tulare

Add'l Information: Normal turnaround time- routine 72 hours. Projects billed by number of names searched. Projects billed by the hour. First project may require prepayment. Credit cards accepted. They specialize in document management and litigation support. Performs service of process.

Attorney's Diversified Services-Modesto

948 11th St. #A, Modesto, CA 95354
Phone: 800-473-0273; 209-576-0273 - **Fax:** 209-576-0238
www.attorneysdiversified.com **Types of Records Retrieved:** Criminal, Civil and Probate courts; Federal courts; Real Estate; Tax Liens/Judgments; UCC records; Vital records

Local Retrieval Area: CA-Stanislaus, Tuolumne. **Correspondent Relationships:** nationwide.

Add'l Information: Established 1969. Normal turnaround time- routine 72 hours. Projects billed by number of names searched. Projects billed by the hour. First project may require prepayment. Credit cards accepted. Will file/record documents for clients. They specialize in document management and litigation support. Performs service of process.

Attorney's Diversified Services-Oakland

3640 Grand Ave #211, Oakland, CA 94610
Phone: 800-800-6788; 510-835-9176 - **Fax:** 510-835-0510
www.attorneysdiversified.com **Types of Records Retrieved:** Criminal, Civil and Probate courts; Federal courts; Real Estate; Tax Liens/Judgments; UCC records; Vital records

Local Retrieval Area: CA-Alameda, Contra Costa

Add'l Information: Normal turnaround time- routine 72 hours. Projects billed by number of names searched. Projects billed by the hour. First project may require prepayment. Credit cards accepted. They specialize in document management and litigation support. Performs service of process.

Attorney's Diversified Services-Redding

2395 Bechelli Lane #C, Redding, CA 96002
Phone: 800-473-1228; 530-241-1228 - **Fax:** 530-241-1508
www.attorneysdiversified.com **Types of Records Retrieved:** Criminal, Civil and Probate courts; Federal courts; Real Estate; Tax Liens/Judgments; UCC records; Vital records

Local Retrieval Area: CA-Butte, Del Norte, Glenn, Lassen, Modoc, Plumas, Shasta, Siskiyou, Tehama, Trinity

Add'l Information: Normal turnaround time- routine 72 hours. Projects billed by number of names searched. Projects billed by the hour. First project may require prepayment. Credit cards accepted. They specialize in document management and litigation support. Performs service of process.

Attorney's Diversified Services-Sacramento

1424 21st St, Corporate Office, Sacramento, CA 95814
Phone: 800-266-4624; 916-441-4396 - **Fax:** 916-443-1162
www.attorneysdiversified.com **email:** g_singley@yahoo.com

Types of Records Retrieved: Criminal, Civil and Probate courts; Federal courts; Real Estate; Tax Liens/Judgments; UCC records; Vital records

Local Retrieval Area: CA-Alpine, Colusa, El Dorado, Nevada, Placer, Sacramento, Sierra, Solano, Sutter, Yolo, Yuba

Add'l Information: Normal turnaround time- routine 72 hours. Projects billed by number of names searched. Projects billed by the hour. First project may require prepayment. Credit cards accepted. They specialize in document management and litigation support. Performs service of process.

Attorney's Diversified Services-San Diego

2535 Camino Del Rio S #324, San Diego, CA 92108
Phone: 800-566-9501; 619-839-3400 - **Fax:** 619-839-3414
www.attorneysdiversified.com **Types of Records Retrieved:** Criminal, Civil and Probate courts; Federal courts; Real Estate; Tax Liens/Judgments; UCC records; Vital records

Local Retrieval Area: CA-Imperial, Orange, Riverside, San Diego. **Correspondent Relationships:** statewide.

Add'l Information: Normal turnaround time- routine 72 hours. Projects billed by number of names searched. Projects billed by the hour. First project may require prepayment. Credit cards accepted. Will file/record documents for clients. They specialize in document management and litigation support. Performs service of process.

Attorney's Diversified Services-San Francisco

1453 Mission St #510, San Francisco, CA 94103
Phone: 800-775-3455; 415-437-6177 - **Fax:** 415-437-6175
www.attorneysdiversified.com **Types of Records Retrieved:** Criminal, Civil and Probate courts; Federal courts; Real Estate; Tax Liens/Judgments; UCC records; Vital records

Local Retrieval Area: CA-San Francisco, San Mateo, Santa Clara. **Correspondent Relationships:** statewide.

Add'l Information: Established 1969. Normal turnaround time- routine 72 hours. Projects billed by number of names searched. Projects billed by the hour. First project may require prepayment. Credit cards accepted. Will file/record documents for clients. They specialize in document management and litigation support. Performs service of process.

Attorney's Diversified Services-Santa Rosa

2421 Mendocino Ave 2nd Fl, Santa Rosa, CA 95403
Phone: 800-473-5455; 707-545-5455 - **Fax:** 707-545-5454
www.attorneysdiversified.com **Types of Records Retrieved:** Criminal, Civil and Probate courts; Federal courts; Real Estate; Tax Liens/Judgments; UCC records; Vital records

Retrieval Area: CA-Humboldt, Lake, Marin, Mendocino, Napa, Sonoma

Add'l Information: Normal turnaround time- routine 72 hours. Projects billed by number of names searched. Projects billed by the hour. All projects require prepayment. Credit cards accepted. Due upon receipt of invoice. They specialize in document management and litigation support. Performs service of process.

Attorney's Diversified Services-Stockton

306 E. Main #304, Stockton, CA 95202
Phone: 800-343-2108; 209-948-6110 - **Fax:** 209-948-0806
www.attorneysdiversified.com **Types of Records Retrieved:** Criminal, Civil and Probate courts; Federal courts; Real Estate; Tax Liens/Judgments; UCC records; Vital records

Local Retrieval Area: CA-Amador, Calaveras, San Joaquin

Add'l Information: Normal turnaround time- routine 72 hours. Projects billed by number of names searched. Projects billed by the hour. First project may require prepayment. Credit cards accepted. They specialize in document management and litigation support. Performs service of process.

Attorney's Diversified Services-Ventura

1891 Goodyear Ave #620, Ventura, CA 93003-6431
Phone: 800-933-8014; 805-644-8014 - **Fax:** 805-658-6336
www.attorneysdiversified.com **Types of Records Retrieved:** Criminal, Civil and Probate courts; Federal courts; Real Estate; Tax Liens/Judgments; UCC records; Vital records

Retrieval Area: CA-Los Angeles, San Luis Obispo, Santa Barbara, Ventura

Add'l Information: Normal turnaround time- routine 72 hours. Projects billed by number of names searched. Projects billed by the hour. First project may require prepayment. Credit cards accepted. They specialize in document management and litigation support. Performs service of process.

Attorneys' Information Bureau Inc

516 3rd Ave, C603 King County Courthouse, Seattle, WA 98104
Phone: 206-622-1909 - **Fax:** 206-622-2911 attysinfob@aol.com

Types of Records Retrieved: Criminal, Civil and Probate courts; Federal courts; Real Estate; Tax Liens/Judgments; UCC records; Vital records

Local Retrieval Area: WA-King, Kitsap, Pierce, Snohomish, Thurston. **Correspondent Relationships:** statewide.

Add'l Information: Established 1923. Normal turnaround time- 24 hours, same day is available for a higher fee. Fee basis varies by type of transaction. First project may require prepayment. Credit cards accepted. They can search all of Washington court records through an online system.

Attorneys Messenger Service

PO Box 15363, 1407 S Vista Ave, Boise, ID 83715
Phone: 208-345-2905 - **Fax:** 208-345-8740

Types of Records Retrieved: Criminal, Civil and Probate courts; Federal courts; Real Estate; Tax Liens/Judgments; UCC records; Vital records

Local Retrieval Area: ID-Ada, Bannock, Canyon, Elmore, Gem, Owyhee, Twin Falls. **Correspondent Relationships:** statewide.

Add'l Information: Established 1977. Normal turnaround time- 1-3 days. Expedited service available. Flat fee. First project may require prepayment. Will file/record documents for clients. They perform a variety of services at reasonable rates including skiptracing. They specialize in full-service in Ada and Canyon counties; for other counties, call for coverage information. Performs service of process.

Attorneys' Personal Services

P.O. Box 7710, 544 Plasters Ave NE, Atlanta, GA 30357
Phone: 800-245-0122; 404-872-1200 - **Fax:** 404-872-4578
www.aps-ga.com **email:** esmith@aps-ga.net

Types of Records Retrieved: Criminal, Civil and Probate courts; Federal courts; Real Estate; Tax Liens/Judgments; UCC records; Vital records

Local Retrieval Area: GA-Clayton, Cobb, De Kalb, Fulton, Gwinnett. **Correspondent Relationships:** Georgia.

Add'l Information: Established 1983. Normal turnaround time- same day. Projects billed by the hour. A mileage fee is also added. First project may require prepayment. Credit cards accepted. Will file/record documents for clients. APS specializes in court research and process service. Goes to the Federal Records Center. A licensed PI in GA. Performs service of process.

Attorney's Process & Investigative Services

205 Doty St #202, Green Bay, WI 54301
Phone: 800-236-5202; 920-435-8317 - **Fax:** 920-436-7585
www.api-inc.com **email:** api@api-inc.com

Types of Records Retrieved: Criminal, Civil and Probate courts; Federal courts; Real Estate; Tax Liens/Judgments; UCC records; Vital records

Local Retrieval Area: WI-Brown, Calumet, Dane, Door, Kenosha, Kewaunee, Manitowoc, Marinette, Milwaukee, Oconto, Outagamie, Ozaukee, Racine, Shawano, Waukesha, Winnebago. **Correspondent Relationships:** statewide in Wisconsin.

Add'l Information: Established 1975. Normal turnaround time- 72 hours. Expedited service available. Projects billed by number of records located. First project may require prepayment. They specialize in Eastern Wisconsin; they have a branch offices in Milwaukee. A licensed PI in WI. Performs service of process.

Attorney's Process & Research Service Inc

279 Washington Ave, Albany, NY 12206
Phone: 800-640-7863; 518-465-8951 - **Fax:** 518-465-0449
deborahaberline@gmail.com

Types of Records Retrieved: Civil courts; Federal courts; Tax Liens/Judgments; UCC records

Local Retrieval Area: NY-Albany, Columbia, Rensselaer, Saratoga, Schenectady, Warren, Washington. **Correspondents:** statewide.

Add'l Information: Established 1977. Normal turnaround time- same day or next day. Projects billed by the hour. First project may require prepayment. They specialize in document retrieval throughout the state of New York, court record research, nationwide service of process and state agency, and corporate records. A licensed PI in NY. Performs service of process.

Attorney's Service Bureau of Texas

900 Jackson St #750, Dallas, TX 75202
Phone: 888-522-5297; 214-522-5297 - **Fax:** 214-393-0210
asb-texas@sbcglobal.net

Types of Records Retrieved: Criminal, Civil and Probate courts; Federal courts; Real Estate; Tax Liens/Judgments; UCC records; Vital records

Local Retrieval Area: TX-Collin, Dallas, Denton, Tarrant. **Correspondent Relationships:** statewide, nationwide and Canada.

Add'l Information: Established 1986. Normal turnaround time- same day to 24 hours. Expedited service available. Projects billed by number of names searched. Projects billed by number of records located. Projects billed by the hour. With established credit will invoice. They have extensive experience in all state, federal & county courts including Bankruptcy Courts, and all Secretary of State records, and have long term experience with all Federal Records Centers & National Archives facilities. Performs service of process.

Attorneys Services & Legal Inv

936 2nd Ave, Columbus, GA 31901
Phone: 706-322-3554 or 322-3224 - **Fax:** 706-323-0182
www.aslllc.com **email:** attysvclglinv@aol.com

Types of Records Retrieved: Criminal and Civil courts; Bankruptcy courts; Real Estate; Tax Liens/Judgments; UCC records

Local Retrieval Area: AL-Chambers, Lee, Russell; GA-Chattahoochee, Harris, Marion, Muscogee, Stewart

Add'l Information: Established 1992. Normal turnaround time- 48-72 hours. Expedited service available. Projects billed by number of names searched. First project requires prepayment. Accept check or money orders. A legal support company that specialize perfecting Service of Process serving Nationwide. Please call for quotes. The company also specialize in computer forensic, surveillance, criminal/civil background and provides criminal defense investigation. A licensed PI in GA. Performs service of process.

Attorney's Services Inc

400 W Capitol #1248, Little Rock, AR 72201
Phone: 888-376-6267; 501-376-2300 - **Fax:** 501-376-7925
myersas@swbell.net

Types of Records Retrieved: Criminal, Civil and Probate courts; Federal courts; Real Estate; Tax Liens/Judgments; UCC records; Vital records

Local Retrieval Area: AR-Pulaski. **Correspondents:** nationwide.

Add'l Information: Established 1963. Normal turnaround time- 1 week. Expedited service available. Projects billed by the hour. All projects require prepayment. Will file/record documents for clients. Terms: net 30 days. They specialize in records research/retrieval, process service, courier service, general private investigation, expert consultation/witness (investigative techniques and negligent security). A licensed PI in AR. Performs service of process.

Attorney's Title Co

PO Box 407, Concordia, KS 66901-0407
Phone: 785-243-1357 - **Fax:** 785-243-1359
www.condraylaw.com **email:** condraylaw@condraylaw.com

Types of Records Retrieved: Criminal, Civil and Probate courts; Real Estate; Tax Liens/Judgments; UCC records

Retrieval Area: KS-Clay, Cloud, Mitchell, Ottawa, Republic, Washington

Add'l Information: Established 1989. Normal turnaround time- 2-3 days. Projects billed by the hour. First project may require prepayment. Will file/record documents for clients. They provide quality searches in a timely manner. The searcher is a full time title insurance representative and record retriever.

Attorney's Title Ins. Fund Inc

2355 Stanford Ct, Naples, FL 34112
Phone: 239-774-2627 - **Fax:** 239-774-0063
www.thefund.com **email:** mmiller@thefund.com

Types of Records Retrieved: Civil courts; Real Estate; Tax Liens/Judgments; UCC records; Vital records

Local Retrieval Area: FL-Collier

Add'l Information: Established 1955. Normal turnaround time- 1-3 days. Fee basis will vary by the type of project. First project may require prepayment. Will file/record documents for clients. Formerly Lawyers' Abstract Service Inc, they specialize in land records and title information.

Auburn Abstract & Title Company LLC

910 13th St, Auburn, NE 68305
Phone: 402-274-4321 - **Fax:** 402-274-4323

Types of Records Retrieved: Real Estate; Tax Liens/Judgments; Probate courts; UCC records

Local Retrieval Area: NE-Nemaha. **Correspondent Relationships:** Richardson and Johnson counties.

Add'l Information: Established 1925. Normal turnaround time- 1-2 days. Projects billed by number of names searched. All projects require prepayment. They prefer prepay request, but will invoice. Personal checks are accepted.

Audrain County Title Co

PO Box 599, Mexico, MO 65265
Phone: 573-581-5136 - **Fax:** 573-581-8752
actc@audraincountyabstract.com

Types of Records Retrieved: Civil and Probate courts; Real Estate; Tax Liens/Judgments; UCC records

Local Retrieval Area: MO-Audrain

Add'l Information: Established 1895. Normal turnaround time- 2-3 days. Fee varies by project type. Will file/record documents for clients. Terms: net 30 days from date of billing. They specialize in real estate searches.

Eileen Augatis

731 Washington Ave, Woodbury, NJ 08096
Phone: 609-472-6513 - **Fax:** 856-845-3060
www.emaxabstract.com **email:** emaxabstract@comcast.net

Types of Records Retrieved: Criminal and Civil courts; Real Estate; Tax Liens/Judgments; UCC records

Local Retrieval Area: NJ-Camden, Gloucester

Add'l Information: Established 1986. Normal turnaround time- same day-24-48 hours. Projects billed by number of names searched. Invoices by month or by job. They provide fast reliable "hands-on" servicing of property & foreclosure searches, county level UCCs, criminal and civil record searches. They are E & O insured.

Aurico Reports Inc

116 W Eastman #101, Arlington Heights, IL 60004
Phone: 866-255-1852; 847-890-4033 - **Fax:** 847-259-0283
www.auricoinvestigations.com **email:** info@auricoinvestigations.com

Types of Records Retrieved: Federal courts; Real Estate; Tax Liens/Judgments; UCC records; Vital records

Local Retrieval Area: IL-Cook. **Correspondent Relationships:** nationwide and international.

Add'l Information: Established 1994. Normal turnaround time- 48-72 hours. Expedited service available. Projects billed by number of names searched. Projects billed by the hour. AKA Aurico Investigations, they specialize public records nationally/internationally, also corporate, legal, insurance, personal investigation svcs, surveillance, security consulting, protective svcs - everything you need, Chicago particularly. A licensed PI in IL. Performs service of process.

Aurora County Land Title Company

PO Box 443, Plankinton, SD 57368
Phone: 605-942-7558 - **Fax:** 605-942-7901 acltco@siouxvalley.net

Types of Records Retrieved: Criminal, Civil and Probate courts; Bankruptcy court; Real Estate; Tax Liens/Judgments

Local Retrieval Area: SD-Aurora

Add'l Information: Established 2000. Normal turnaround time- 3-4 days. First project may require prepayment. They specialize in real estate and mortgage loan closings.

Carma Austin

PO Box 10364, Killeen, TX 76547-0364
Phone: 254-634-1701 - **Fax:** 254-634-1588 carma4tx@aol.com

Types of Records Retrieved: Civil courts; Federal courts; Tax Liens/Judgments; UCC records

Local Retrieval Area: TX-Bastrop, Bell, Brazos, Burleson, Burnet, Caldwell, Coryell, Falls, Hays, Lampasas, McLennan, Milam, Robertson, Williamson

Add'l Information: Established 1996. Normal turnaround time- 48 hours. Projects billed by number of names searched. First project may require prepayment. Will file/record documents for clients. Over 12 years experience. Most counties can be done next day.

Autauga Abstract

140 W Main St, Prattville, AL 36067
Phone: 334-361-0606 - **Fax:** 334-361-8402

Types of Records Retrieved: Real Estate; Tax Liens/Judgments; Probate courts; UCC records

Local Retrieval Area: AL-Autauga, Elmore

Add'l Information: Established 1975. Normal turnaround time- 24-48 hours. Projects billed by the hour. First project may require prepayment. Will file/record documents for clients. Personal checks are accepted.

AV Investigations Inc

PO Box 95, Geneva, IL 60134
Phone: 630-443-3617 - **Fax:** 630-443-3618
www.avInvestigations.com **email:** tvincent@ameritech.net

Types of Records Retrieved: Criminal, Civil and Probate courts; Real Estate; Tax Liens/Judgments; UCC records; Vital records

Local Retrieval Area: IL-De Kalb, Du Page, Kane, Kendall. **Correspondent Relationships:** nationwide.

Add'l Information: Established 1998. Normal turnaround time- 24-48 hours. Projects billed by number of names searched. First project may require prepayment. Will file/record documents for clients. They specialize in pre-employment background screening, process serving, skiptracing, general investigations and document retrieval. A licensed PI in IL. Performs service of process.

Avalon Information Services

194 135th St, Deer Park, WI 54007
Phone: 715-222-4095 - **Fax:** 715-269-5347 avaloninfo@amerytel.net

Types of Records Retrieved: Criminal, Civil and Probate courts; Federal courts; Real Estate; Tax Liens/Judgments; Vital records

Local Retrieval Area: MN-Anoka, Carver, Dakota, Hennepin, Ramsey, Scott, Sherburne, Washington; WI-Pierce, Polk, St Croix

Add'l Information: Established 1998. Normal turnaround time- same day. Projects billed by number of names searched. Terms are net 30 days. They specialize in criminal and civil searches, also document retrieval, all public records, and real estate land searches.

Avalon/Tracy Bowers

1821 Emerald Bay Dr, Reno, NV 89521
Phone: 775-853-3003 - **Fax:** 775-853-3007 nvsearch@charter.net

Types of Records Retrieved: Criminal, Civil and Probate courts; Federal courts; Real Estate; Tax Liens/Judgments; UCC records; Vital records

Local Retrieval Area: NV-Carson City, Churchill, Clark, Douglas, Elko, Humboldt, Lyon, Storey, Washoe

Add'l Information: Established 1996. Normal turnaround time- 24 hours. Expedite service available. Projects billed by number of names searched. First project may require prepayment. Payment due net 30 days. They conduct Nevada searches, retrievals and filings on all types and they also offer a mobile notary public and signing agent service.

Avritt & Avritt

PO Box 671, 103 W Main St, Lebanon, KY 40033
Phone: 270-692-4270 - **Fax:** 270-692-0520

Types of Records Retrieved: Civil and Probate courts; Real Estate; Tax Liens/Judgments; UCC records; Vital records

Local Retrieval Area: KY-Marion

Add'l Information: Established 1980. Normal turnaround time- 3-4 days. Projects billed by the hour. First project may require prepayment. Will file/record documents for clients.

Ronald J Axelrod

PO Box 275, Morris Plains, NJ 07950-0275
Phone: 973-538-4606 - **Fax:** 973-267-4606

Types of Records Retrieved: Real Estate; Tax Liens/Judgments; Probate courts; UCC records

Local Retrieval Area: NJ-Morris, Somerset. **Correspondent Relationships:** Sussex, Bergen, Warren NJ counties.

Add'l Information: Established 1979. Normal turnaround time- Varies depending on type of job; contact office to discuss time frame. First project may require prepayment. Will file/record documents for clients. A 3rd generation company in business since 1979, specializing in title searches, title abstracts & UCC/judgment searches along with boundary/location deeds & filing of original docs. Somerset City office # 908-722-4606.

Axis Research Inc

900 Old Roswell Lakes Pky #310, Roswell, GA 30076
Phone: 877-795-1005; 678-795-1005 - **Fax:** 877-795-1002; 678-795-1002
www.axisresearch.com **email:** axisrinc@bellsouth.net

Types of Records Retrieved: Criminal, Civil and Probate courts; Federal courts; Real Estate; Tax Liens/Judgments; UCC records

Local Retrieval Area: GA-Bartow, Cherokee, Clayton, Cobb, De Kalb, Douglas, Fayette, Forsyth, Fulton, Gwinnett, Hall, Henry, Paulding, Pickens, Spalding; NC-Cabarrus, Catawba, Gaston, Lincoln, Mecklenburg, Rowan, Union. **Correspondent Relationships:** nationwide.

Add'l Information: Established 1996. Normal turnaround time- 24 hours in Metro Atlanta, Raleigh or Charlotte; 1-3 days in other counties. Projects billed by number of names searched. Will file/record documents for clients. Axis specializes in public records research and corporate document preparation. They have access to all counties in GA and most in NC.

Jerry Axton

12216 Clark Bayou Rd, Moss Point, MS 39562
Phone: 228-475-1739 - **Fax:** 228-475-4822 axtonj@bellsouth.net

Types of Records Retrieved: Criminal, Civil and Probate courts; Real Estate; Tax Liens/Judgments; Vital records

Local Retrieval Area: MS-George, Jackson. **Correspondent Relationships:** Hancock & Harrison, MS counties.

Add'l Information: Established 2000. Normal turnaround time- 24-48 hours. Projects billed by number of names searched. Terms are net 30 days. He specializes in civil, criminal checks, property, probate, tax liens and judgments. He is also a process server. Retrieves documents, case law decisions, and files in 2 counties. Researches case histories for publishers and legal professionals. Performs service of process.

Judith Ayres

3487 Accomack St, Chincoteague Island, VA 23336
Phone: 757-336-5313 - **Fax:** 757-336-1357 jhayres@verizon.net

Types of Records Retrieved: Criminal, Civil and Probate courts; Real Estate; Tax Liens/Judgments; UCC records; Vital records

Local Retrieval Area: MD-Somerset, Wicomico, Worcester; VA-Accomack, Northampton

Add'l Information: Established 1991. Normal turnaround time- 24-48 hours. Expedited service available. Fee basis will vary by type of project. First project may require prepayment. Will file/record documents for clients. She specializes in real estate, UCC searches, criminal and litigation. She also performs searches from the 1600's to the present. Her pager (and voice number) is 757-990-0314.

B & B Info Search

4400 Ascot Dr, Cleburne, TX 76033
Phone: 817-774-1310 - **Fax:** 817-517-7295 bbinfo@digitex.net

Types of Records Retrieved: Criminal, Civil and Probate courts

Local Retrieval Area: TX-Bosque, Ellis, Erath, Hill, Hood, Johnson, Navarro, Palo Pinto, Parker, Somervell, Wise. **Correspondent Relationships:** Anderson, Freestone counties.

Add'l Information: Established 1996. Normal turnaround time- 48 hours. Projects billed by number of names searched. Volume discount with multiple counties. Billed by 1st of month, payment by 15th of month. They have 25 years of professional Law Enforcement experience. A criminal research specialist. They are celebrating their 10th year in business. A licensed PI in TX.

B & B Investigative Services

11 Whitman Blvd, Englishtown, NJ 07726
Phone: 732-446-7482 - **Fax:** 732-446-3886

Types of Records Retrieved: Criminal and Civil courts

Local Retrieval Area: NJ-Essex, Hudson, Mercer, Middlesex, Monmouth, Ocean, Somerset, Union

Add'l Information: Established 1995. Normal turnaround time- 24 hours. Projects billed by number of names searched. Will bill monthly. They specialize in the New Jersey area. They expedite with 100% accuracy.

B & B Reporting Inc

PO Box 191, 106 W Laurel, Scottsboro, AL 35768
Phone: 256-574-2524 - **Fax:** 256-259-4323
www.bbreporting.com **email:** adminstrator@bbreporting.com

Types of Records Retrieved: Criminal, Civil and Probate courts; Federal courts; Real Estate; Tax Liens/Judgments; UCC records; Vital records

Local Retrieval Area: AL-Calhoun, De Kalb, Jackson, Madison, Marshall; TN-Shelby. **Correspondent Relationships:** Alabama, nationwide.

Add'l Information: Established 1985. Normal turnaround time- 1 day. Projects billed by number of names searched. First project may require prepayment. Will file/record documents for clients. They will also invoice monthly. They specialize in state and federal court searches and criminal and civil searches nationwide. They perform MVRs nationwide, in Canada and Puerto Rico. Performs service of process.

B & G Ltd of Hollidaysburg

416 Allegheny St, Hollidaysburg, PA 16648-2026
Phone: 814-695-8414 - **Fax:** 814-695-8496

Types of Records Retrieved: Criminal, Civil and Probate courts; Real Estate; Tax Liens/Judgments; UCC records

Local Retrieval Area: PA-Bedford, Blair, Cambria, Centre, Clearfield, Huntingdon

Add'l Information: Established 1984. Normal turnaround time- 24-48 hours. Projects billed by number of names searched. First project may require prepayment. Will file/record documents for clients. They specialize in real estate and abstracting.

B & J/Barristers' Aide Inc

PO Box 88, Eugene, OR 97440
Phone: 541-687-0747 - **Fax:** 541-687-0429 www.barristersaide.com

Types of Records Retrieved: Criminal, Civil and Probate courts; Federal courts; Vital records

Local Retrieval Area: OR-Lane

Add'l Information: Established 1976. Normal turnaround time- next day. Projects billed by number of names searched. Projects billed by the hour. Charges will include costs. First project may require prepayment. Will file/record documents for clients. Performs service of process.

B & R Services for Professionals

235 S 13th St, Philadelphia, PA 19107
Phone: 800-503-7400; 215-546-7400 - **Fax:** 215-985-0169
www.brservices.com **email:** fredb@concentric.net

Types of Records Retrieved: Criminal, Civil and Probate courts; Federal courts; Real Estate; Tax Liens/Judgments; UCC records; Vital records

Local Retrieval Area: PA-Bucks, Chester, Delaware, Montgomery, Philadelphia. **Correspondent Relationships:** Dauphin.

Add'l Information: Established 1967. Normal turnaround time- 24-48 hours. Projects billed by number of names searched. Projects billed by number of records located. Projects billed by the hour. First project may require prepayment. Will file/record documents for clients. They specialize in court filings, record retrieval, process service, court reporting and private investigation. A licensed PI in PA. Performs service of process.

Background Data Services LLC

140 N Clifton Ave, Aldan, PA 19018
Phone: 610-284-2834, cell- 610-529-2200 - **Fax:** 610-284-9917
www.backgrounddataservices.com
email: info@backgrounddataservices.com

Types of Records Retrieved: Criminal, Civil and Probate courts; Federal courts; Tax Liens/Judgments; UCC records; Vital records

Local Retrieval Area: PA-Bucks, Chester, Delaware, Montgomery, Philadelphia. **Correspondent Relationships:** nationwide.

Add'l Information: Established 2006. Normal turnaround time- 48 hours. Projects billed by number of names searched. All projects require prepayment. They also provide expert pre-employment/tenant screening, background checks, verifications, due diligence searches and more.

Background Hound LLC

PO Box 20875, Baltimore, MD 21219
Phone: 410-484-6887 - **Fax:** 410-484-6889
www.backgroundhound.com **email:** moreynz@aol.com

Types of Records Retrieved: Criminal and Civil courts; Federal courts; UCC records; Tax Liens/Judgments

Local Retrieval Area: MD-Anne Arundel, Baltimore, Baltimore City, Carroll, Howard, Prince George's. **Correspondent Relationships:** statewide in Maryland.

Add'l Information: Established 2004. Normal turnaround time- 1 to 3 days; expedited service available. Projects billed by number of names searched. Projects billed by number of records located. Credit cards accepted. Founded by legal professionals, Background Hound provides quality research and retrieval at reasonable prices.

Background Information Services

1800 30th St #204, Boulder, CO 80301
Phone: 303-442-3960 - **Fax:** 303-442-1004
www.bisi.com **email:** john@bisi.com

Records Retrieved: Criminal and Civil courts; Federal courts; UCC records

Local Retrieval Area: CO-Boulder. **Correspondents:** nationwide.

Add'l Information: Established 1988. Normal turnaround time- 1 day for MVRs. In-state CBI is 1 day. Database results are immediate. Projects billed by number of names searched. Terms: net 15 to 30 days. They have their own database of civil, criminal (nationwide), domestic relations, UCC, Secretary of State and Department of Revenue records. They also specialize in pre-employment and tenant screening as well as MVRs, credit checks, workers compensation.

Background Research Agency Inc

PO Box 1850, 1820 Hwy 20 #132-188, Conyers, GA 30012
Phone: 770-788-1885 - **Fax:** 770-788-1277 gasearches@aol.com

Types of Records Retrieved: Criminal and Civil courts; Tax Liens/Judgments

Local Retrieval Area: GA-143 of 159 counties. **Correspondent Relationships:** nationwide.

Add'l Information: Established 1998. Normal turnaround time- 24-48 hours. Projects billed by number of names searched. Terms are net 30 days. They provide criminal, civil and tax lien research in numerous counties in GA. All research is accurate, hands-on and generally returned within 24-48 hours. A licensed PI in GA.

Backgrounds Express LLC

55 N 3rd St, Memphis, TN 38103-2304
Phone: 888-811-4667; 901-578-3287 - **Fax:** 888-811-4668; 901-578-7889
www.backgrounds-express.com **email:** expressBE@aol.com

Types of Records Retrieved: Criminal and Civil courts; Federal courts

Local Retrieval Area: TN-Shelby

Add'l Information: Established 1991. Normal turnaround time- same day. Projects billed by number of names searched. Projects billed by the hour. First project may require prepayment. Credit cards accepted. They specialize in pre-employment and tenant investigations. They visit Memphis government agencies once daily and maintain a database of forcible detainer cases. A licensed PI in TN. Performs service of process.

Backgrounds Plus

PO Box 624, Sheboygan, WI 53082-0624
Phone: 920-457-5745 - **Fax:** 920-457-5745 backplus@gmail.com

Types of Records Retrieved: Criminal, Civil and Probate courts; Federal courts; Real Estate; Tax Liens/Judgments; UCC records; Vital records

Local Retrieval Area: WI-Fond du Lac, Manitowoc, Sheboygan

Add'l Information: Established 1993. Normal turnaround time- 1-2 business days. Projects billed by number of records locates plus mileage. They do research for private investigators, attorneys, business firms and the public.

Judy J Badon/Public Records Specialists

10928 Ansley Ave, Baton Rouge, LA 70816
Phone: 225-291-5537 - **Fax:** 225-291-5856 jjbad@cox.net

Types of Records Retrieved: Criminal, Civil and Probate courts; Federal courts; Real Estate; Tax Liens/Judgments; UCC records; Vital records

Retrieval Area: LA-East Baton Rouge Parish, West Baton Rouge Parish

Add'l Information: Established 1995. Normal turnaround time- 24 hours-3 business days. Projects billed by the hour. Terms are net 15 days. (30 day credit on approval). First project may require prepayment. Will file/record documents for clients. They specialize in filings, search & retrieval, criminal, civil, judgments, tax liens, bankruptcy, CDV's & one/last owner property searches. They also collect judgments, tax liens, bankruptcies, mortgages, etc. by the record or name.

Virginia Balentine

5600 Critchlow Rd SE, Elizabeth, IN 47117
Phone: 812-267-5497-cell - **Fax:** 812-737-2038 vkbalentine@verizon.net

Types of Records Retrieved: Real Estate

Local Retrieval Area: IN-Clark, Floyd, Harrison. **Correspondent Relationships:** Jackson, Jennings, Scott, Washington counties, IN; Bullitt, Orange, Shelby, Meade counties, KY.

Add'l Information: Established 1998. Normal turnaround time- 24-48 hours. Invoice per each order or as discussed. Specializes in mortgages/assignments/releases, general document retrieval, certified copies, walk-in recordings, comparable sales, new home owners, vesting deed & TX-ID#, ownership report, full copy, signature page, front pg, legal disc, recording info.

Balkin Information Services

295 Hurstbourne Rd, Rochester, NY 14609
Phone: 585-482-1506 - **Fax:** 585-654-5235
www.balkininfo.com **email:** rbalkin@balkininfo.com

Types of Records Retrieved: Criminal, Civil and Probate courts; Federal courts; Real Estate; Tax Liens/Judgments; UCC records

Local Retrieval Area: NY-Monroe. **Correspondent Relationships:** surrounding counties: Wayne, Ontario, Livingston, Genesee, Orleans.

Add'l Information: Established 1978. Normal turnaround time- 72 hours. Projects billed by the hour. First project may require prepayment. Credit cards accepted. Credit cards accepted through PayPal. Servicing corporations, law firms, and consulting since 1978, they provide full public records services, document delivery as well as research. They provide access to online and printed resources.

Banko Document Retrieval

100 S 5th St #300, Minneapolis, MN 55402-1237
Phone: 800-969-2377; - **Fax:** 800-486-2377
www.banko.com **Types of Records Retrieved:** Bankruptcy court

Local Retrieval Area: CA-Los Angeles, San Diego; FL-Dade; Also covers the boroughs of New York (Bronx, Brooklyn, Kings, Manhattan, Queens and Staten Island). **Correspondent Relationships:** every Federal bankruptcy court in the US, including Puerto Rico and Virgin Islands.

Add'l Information: Established 1989. Normal turnaround time- 2-5 days. Projects billed by number of names searched. Accounts are set-up and invoices are sent. They offer online ordering and delivery, order confirmation, shipping logs, status reports, and saving completed orders for up to 60 days (unless original copy is sent). Does death certificate searches.

Banta Abstract Co

108 E Washington St, PO Box 240, Osceola, IA 50213-0240
Phone: 641-342-2029, Fax- same - **Fax:** 641-342-2544

Types of Records Retrieved: Real Estate; Tax Liens/Judgments

Local Retrieval Area: IA-Clarke

Add'l Information: Established 1869. Normal turnaround time- 3 days. They charge a flat rate per project. First project may require prepayment. Will file/record documents for clients. They specialize in real estate title.

Bar Nunn Research Specialists

1204 Parker Pl, Cedar Park, TX 78613
Phone: 512-497-5584 - **Fax:** 512-260-1079 debbienunn2001@austin.rr.com

Records Retrieved: Criminal and Civil courts; Federal District court

Local Retrieval Area: TX-Bell, Guadalupe, Hays, Travis, Williamson

Add'l Information: Established 2002. Normal turnaround time- 24 hours or less. Projects billed by number of names searched. Payment due net 30 days. She is an independent contractor.

Barbour Title Co

P.O. Box 541, Winfield, KS 67156
Phone: 866-379-0430; 620-221-0430 - **Fax:** 866-379-2839; 620-221-2839
www.barbourtitle.com **email:** firstcontact@barbourtitle.com

Types of Records Retrieved: Criminal, Civil and Probate courts; Real Estate; Tax Liens/Judgments; UCC records; Vital records

Local Retrieval Area: KS-Cowley, Sumner

Add'l Information: Established 1915. Normal turnaround time- 24-48 hours. Projects billed by number of names searched. First project may require prepayment. Will file/record documents for clients. Associated with Rogers Abstract and Title Co, 620-326-7460, 116 E Harvey St, Wellington. KS

Barefoot Private Investigations

1011 E Morehead St #110, Charlotte, NC 28204-2890
Phone: 704-377-1000 - **Fax:** 704-343-9226
www.barefootpi.com **email:** barefoot@barefootpi.com

Types of Records Retrieved: Criminal, Civil and Probate courts; Federal courts; Real Estate; Tax Liens/Judgments; UCC records

Local Retrieval Area: NC-Gaston, Mecklenburg

Add'l Information: Established 1986. Normal turnaround time- 48 hours. Projects billed by number of names searched. Projects billed by number of records located. Projects billed by the hour. First project may require prepayment. Credit cards accepted. Will file/record documents for clients. They specialize in all types of private investigative work, including courthouse research, surveillance, personal injury and criminal defense. A licensed PI in NC, SC. Performs service of process.

Barnes Information Svcs LLC

42363 Garfield Rd #380902, Clinton Township, MI 48038
Phone: 248-232-3842 - **Fax:** 320-205-3842
www.barnesinfo.com **email:** prrn@barnesinfo.com

Types of Records Retrieved: Criminal, Civil and Probate courts; Federal courts; Real Estate; Tax Liens/Judgments; UCC records; Vital records

Local Retrieval Area: MI-Oakland, Macomb, Wayne

Add'l Information: Established 2004. Normal turnaround time- 48-hr turnaround; 24-hr rush available. Projects billed by number of names searched. First project may require prepayment. Credit cards accepted. Call first before faxing. Specializes in public records retrieval and background profiles on business and individuals. Professional information scientists with over 15 years experience in public and private sectors.

James M Barnes Jr

PO Box 639, Marion, AL 36756

Phone: 334-683-6060 - **Fax:** 334-683-9242 jmbarnes@pinebelt.net

Types of Records Retrieved: Criminal, Civil and Probate courts; Real Estate; Tax Liens/Judgments; UCC records; Vital records

Local Retrieval Area: AL-Perry

Add'l Information: Established 1983. Normal turnaround time- 3 days. Fee basis will vary by the type of the project. First project may require prepayment. Will file/record documents for clients. Terms: net 30 days. He is an attorney in general practice. Performs service of process.

Sharisa Barnes

864 Rosewood Dr, Twin Falls, ID 83301

Phone: 208-308-5496; Fax- same sLb864@hotmail.com

Types of Records Retrieved: Criminal and Civil courts

Local Retrieval Area: ID-Twin Falls

Add'l Information: Established 2004. Normal turnaround time- 24 hours. Projects billed by number of names searched. First project may require prepayment. She specializes in the Twin Falls County area.

Barney Abstract & Title Co

PO Box 546, 2222 2nd Ave #100 (68847), Kearney, NE 68848

Phone: 308-234-5548 - **Fax:** 308-236-9240

Types of Records Retrieved: Civil and Probate courts; Real Estate; Tax Liens/Judgments; UCC records; Vital records

Local Retrieval Area: NE-Buffalo

Add'l Information: Established 1888. Turnaround time- up to 2 weeks. Fee basis varies by type of transaction. Will file/record documents for clients.

Barnone Bailbonds & Investigations

PO Box 2632, 104 S Broad St, Globe, AZ 85502

Phone: 800-607-8200; 928-425-3270 - **Fax:** 928-425-3270

haughbarnone@aol.com

Types of Records Retrieved: Criminal, Civil and Probate courts; Real Estate; Tax Liens/Judgments; UCC records; Vital records

Local Retrieval Area: AZ-Gila

Add'l Information: Established 2000. Normal turnaround time- can be hours. Projects billed by number of records located. Needs retainer. Barnone is an experienced public record retrieval company that knows its way around the court house. Also provides bailbond and private investigation services. Excellent service provided. A licensed PI in AZ. Performs service of process.

Barrett Title Co

PO Box 467, Baxter Springs, KS 66713-0467

Phone: 620-856-3531 - **Fax:** 620-856-3408 barrettdonna@hotmail.com

Types of Records Retrieved: Criminal, Civil and Probate courts; Real Estate; Tax Liens/Judgments; UCC records; Vital records

Local Retrieval Area: KS-Cherokee

Add'l Information: Established 1994. Normal turnaround time- 48-72 hours. Projects billed by number of names searched. Projects billed by the hour. Will file/record documents. They are a law office and title company.

Barrister Support Service

8700 SW 26th #L, Portland, OR 97219

Phone: 503-246-8934 - **Fax:** 503-246-0098

www.barristersupport.com **Types of Records Retrieved:** Criminal, Civil and Probate courts; Federal courts

Local Retrieval Area: OR-Clackamas, Multnomah, Washington; WA-Clark. **Correspondent Relationships:** nationwide.

Add'l Information: Established 1983. Normal turnaround time- 7-10 days. Expedited service available. Projects billed by the hour. First project may require prepayment. Will file/record documents for clients. They specialize in service of process. Performs service of process.

Barry County Abstract & Title

PO Box 427, Cassville, MO 65625

Phone: 417-847-3224 - **Fax:** 417-847-3118 bcat@mo-net.com

Types of Records Retrieved: Real Estate; Tax Liens/Judgments; Probate courts; UCC records **Local Retrieval Area:** MO-Barry

Add'l Information: Established 1935. Normal turnaround time- 5-10 days. Expedited service available. Projects billed by number of names searched. First project may require prepayment. Will file/record documents for clients. They have the only complete set of real estate records for Barry County and take pride in the services they provide.

Barry Shuster Information Services, A Div of Search-It Inc

PO Box 79578, North Dartmouth, MA 02747

Phone: 877-852-2507; 508-999-5436 - **Fax:** 877-852-7531; 508-990-2655

ucclien@rcn.com

Types of Records Retrieved: Criminal, Civil and Probate courts; Federal courts; Real Estate; Tax Liens/Judgments; UCC records; Vital records

Local Retrieval Area: FL-Palm Beach; MA-Barnstable, Berkshire, Bristol, Dukes, Essex, Franklin, Hampden, Hampshire, Middlesex, Nantucket, Norfolk, Plymouth, Suffolk, Worcester; RI-Bristol, Kent, Newport, Providence, Washington. **Correspondent Relationships:** nationwide.

Add'l Information: Established 1981. Normal turnaround time- same day to 1 week. Projects billed by number of names searched. Fee basis will vary by jurisdiction. First project may require prepayment. Will file/record documents for clients. Payment due upon receipt of completed work. They specialize in property searches (chain of title) & state/federal tax liens. They also provide UCC. Litigation and judgments, motor vehicle & pre-employment record retrieval, also resident agent services in MA & RI.

Cindy Bartkis

RR 1 Box 137 H, Susquehanna, PA 18847

Phone: 570-756-3093 - **Fax:** 570-756-2560

Types of Records Retrieved: Criminal, Civil and Probate courts; Real Estate; Tax Liens/Judgments; UCC records; Vital records

Local Retrieval Area: PA-Susquehanna

Add'l Information: Established 1985. Normal turnaround time- 48 hours. Projects billed by number of names searched. Projects billed by number of records located. Will file/record documents for clients. She specializes in real estate record searches.

Barton County Abstract & Title Co

2010 Forest, Great Bend, KS 67530-4093

Phone: 620-793-3781 - **Fax:** 620-793-5475

Types of Records Retrieved: Civil and Probate courts; Real Estate; Tax Liens/Judgments; UCC records **Local Retrieval Area:** KS-Barton

Add'l Information: Established 1874. Normal turnaround time- 24-48 hours. Projects billed by the hour. First project may require prepayment. Will file/record documents for clients. They specialize in title insurance and special ownership searches.

Barton County Title Co

122 W 10th St, Lamar, MO 64759

Phone: 417-682-3100 - **Fax:** 417-682-3975

Types of Records Retrieved: Criminal, Civil and Probate courts; Real Estate; Tax Liens/Judgments; UCC records; Vital records

Local Retrieval Area: MO-Barton

Add'l Information: Established 1989. Normal turnaround time- about one week. Fee basis will vary by the type of project. Will file/record documents for clients.

BAST Research Services Inc

405 Main St #308, Houston, TX 77002-1837
Phone: 713-721-7077 - **Fax:** 713-721-7747
www.bastresearch.com **email:** bast@mail.bastresearch.com

Types of Records Retrieved: Civil and Probate courts; Federal courts; Real Estate; Tax Liens/Judgments; UCC records

Local Retrieval Area: TX-Brazoria, Fort Bend, Galveston, Harris, Montgomery. **Correspondent Relationships:** nationwide.

Add'l Information: Established 1993. Normal turnaround time- 24-48 hours; 3-5 days for 50 year and asset searches. Expedited service available. Fees will vary by the type of search. First project may require prepayment. They specialize in real estate title, ownership/lien reports for home equity/improvement lending & 50 year chain of title searches for environmental site assessments; UCC, tax lien, judgment & litigation searches, mortgage/assignment & document research.

Baxter County Abstract Co

617 S Baker, Mountain Home, AR 72653
Phone: 870-425-8989 - **Fax:** 870-425-9080 bxtitle@cox.net

Types of Records Retrieved: Real Estate; Probate Courts

Local Retrieval Area: AR-Baxter

Add'l Information: Established 1982. Normal turnaround time- 5 days. Expedited service available. Fee basis will vary by type of project. First project may require prepayment. Will file/record documents for clients. Payment due within 10 days of service. They specialize in real estate, abstracts, and title insurance.

Baxter Research Inc

500 Lansdale Ave, San Francisco, CA 94127-1618
Phone: 415-333-5402 - **Fax:** 415-333-6244 timothy@baxterresearch.net

Types of Records Retrieved: Criminal and Civil courts; Federal courts

Local Retrieval Area: CA-Alameda, Contra Costa, Marin, Monterey, San Francisco, San Mateo, Santa Clara, Santa Cruz, Sonoma. **Correspondent Relationships:** Los Angeles, Napa, Monterey, Placer, Sacramento, Santa Barbara, Santa Cruz, Santa Clara, Solano, Yolo, San Joaquin, San Luis Obispo, San Bernardino, Kings, Fresno, Tulare, Madera, Lake, Kern, Ventura counties CA; Cook county, IL.

Add'l Information: Established 1993. Normal turnaround time- 24 hours. Projects billed by number of names searched. Credit cards accepted. They bill monthly with a net 30 days. They are experienced California researchers. Timely, competent, responsive. Official records only, hands on, in the courts daily. Secure web access.

Bay Area Records

544 Golden Gate Ave, Mezz., San Francisco, CA 94102
Phone: 888-934-3848; 415-440-9100 - **Fax:** 415-440-9200
www.bayarearecords.com **email:** commune@probusresearch.com

Types of Records Retrieved: Criminal, Civil and Probate courts; Federal courts; Real Estate; Tax Liens/Judgments; UCC records

Local Retrieval Area: CA-Alameda, Contra Costa, Marin, San Francisco, San Mateo, Santa Clara. **Correspondent Relationships:** most California counties.

Add'l Information: Established 1985. Normal turnaround time- same day to 2 days. Projects billed by number of names searched. Hourly charge for special projects. First project may require prepayment. Terms: net 30 days. They specialize in complex litigation case file, regulatory, business and library research. They also provide fax filings and super rush research and document retrievals. Performs service of process.

Bay City Abstract & Title

2228 Ave G, Bay City, TX 77414-5003
Phone: 979-245-6321 - **Fax:** 979-245-1323

Types of Records Retrieved: Real Estate; Tax Liens/Judgments; Probate courts; UCC records **Local Retrieval Area:** TX-Matagorda

Add'l Information: Established 1936. Normal turnaround time- 14 days. Projects billed by number of names searched. First project may require prepayment. Will file/record documents for clients.

Bay County Abstract Co

612 Adams St, Bay City, MI 48708-5832
Phone: 989-895-9910 - **Fax:** 989-895-5631

Types of Records Retrieved: Real Estate; Tax Liens/Judgments; Probate courts; UCC records

Local Retrieval Area: MI-Arenac, Bay, Clare, Gladwin, Huron, Isabella, Lapeer, Midland, Sanilac, Saginaw, Tuscola

Add'l Information: Established 1974. Normal turnaround time- 3-4 days. Fee basis will vary by type of project. Will file/record documents for clients. They require out of town clients to prepay. They specialize in real estate searches.

Bay State Corporate Services Inc

6 Beacon St #510, Boston, MA 02108
Phone: 617-742-8484 - **Fax:** 617-742-8482
www.baystatecorp.com **email:** scryan@baystatecorp.com

Types of Records Retrieved: Civil and Probate courts; Real Estate; Tax Liens/Judgments; UCC records; Vital records

Local Retrieval Area: MA-Middlesex, Suffolk. **Correspondent Relationships:** nationwide.

Add'l Information: Established 1998. Normal turnaround time- 24 hours. Expedited service available. Projects billed by number of names searched. Will file/record documents for clients. Terms are net 30 days. They are located one block from the MA SOS and within minutes of Boston city clerk, US District court, US Bankruptcy court and all Suffolk county government offices.

Bay Title & Abstract Inc

345 S Monroe Ave, Green Bay, WI 54301
Phone: 920-431-6100 - **Fax:** 920-431-6101
www.baytitle.com **Types of Records Retrieved:** Civil and Probate courts; Real Estate; Tax Liens/Judgments; UCC records

Local Retrieval Area: WI-Brown, Calumet, Dane, Door, Fond du Lac, Kewaunee, Manitowoc, Marinette, Menominee, Oconto, Outagamie, Shawano, Waupaca, Winnebago. **Correspondent Relationships:** Manitowoc county.

Add'l Information: Normal turnaround time- 24 hours. Projects billed by number of names searched. Will file/record documents for clients. Personal checks are accepted.

Bayou Investigations Inc

PO Box 92825, Lafayette, LA 70509
Phone: 800-256-9009; 337-235-2322 - **Fax:** 337-234-5417
www.bayouinvestigations.com **email:** steve@bayouinvestigations.com

Types of Records Retrieved: Criminal and Civil courts; Federal courts; UCC records

Local Retrieval Area: LA-Acadia Parish, Evangeline Parish, Iberia Parish, Jefferson Davis Parish, Lafayette Parish, St. Landry Parish, St. Martin Parish, St. Mary Parish, Vermilion Parish. **Correspondents:** Louisiana.

Add'l Information: Established 1986. Normal turnaround time- 72 hours. Projects billed by the hour. Will file/record documents for clients. They specialize in research, investigations, surveillance and process service. A licensed PI in LA. Performs service of process.

David C Bayoud

6207 Bryan Parkway, Dallas, TX 75214
Phone: 214-824-9944 - **Fax:** 214-824-4350
dbayou@hotmail.com

Types of Records Retrieved: Real Estate

Local Retrieval Area: TX-Collin, Dallas, Denton, Ellis, Rockwall, Tarrant

Add'l Information: Established 1981. Normal turnaround time- 24 hours. Projects billed by number of names searched. Projects billed by number of records located. First project may require prepayment.

Bayshore Research & Retrieval

888 N 1st St #211, San Jose, CA 95112
Phone: 408-298-1354 - **Fax:** 408-291-5931 p.hooks.brr@sbcglobal.net

Types of Records Retrieved: Criminal, Civil and Probate courts; Federal courts; Real Estate; Tax Liens/Judgments; UCC records; Vital records

Local Retrieval Area: CA-San Mateo, Santa Clara

Add'l Information: Established 1987. Turnaround time- same day to 24 hours. Projects billed by number of names searched. Will file/record documents for clients. Monthly billing available. They customize their services & prices to fit the specific needs of each of their clients. Super rush requests and large copy/document retrieval jobs welcomed. Large volume requests accepted. Recordings/Filings done daily. Performs service of process.

BBI LLC

PO Box 6222, Evansville, IN 47719-0222
Phone: 812-985-0832; cell- 812-774-7500 - **Fax:** 812-985-0832
bbakerinv@aol.com

Types of Records Retrieved: Criminal, Civil and Probate courts; Federal courts; Real Estate; Tax Liens/Judgments; UCC records; Vital records

Retrieval Area: IN-Gibson, Posey, Vanderburgh, Warrick; KY-Henderson

Add'l Information: Established 1996. Normal turnaround time- Will discuss on an individual basis. Will discuss on an individual basis. Will discuss on an individual basis. BBI's services include document retrieval, process service, surveillance, workers comp surveillance, MVRs, background checks, court filing, skip-tracing and photocopying, videography and digital photography. A licensed PI in IN.

Bearak Reports

1257 Worcester Rd #308, Framingham, MA 01701
Phone: 800-331-5677; 508-788-6660 - **Fax:** 508-788-6642
www.bearak.com **email:** info@bearak.com

Records Retrieved: Criminal, Civil and Probate courts; Federal courts; Real Estate; Tax Liens/Judgments; UCC corporate records; Vital records

Local Retrieval Area: MA-Barnstable, Berkshire, Bristol, Essex, Franklin, Hampshire, Middlesex, Norfolk, Plymouth, Suffolk, Worcester. **Correspondent Relationships:** nationwide.

Add'l Information: Established 1992. Normal turnaround time- 1-5 business days. Expedite service available. Projects are billed at a flat rate or time and expenses. First project may require prepayment. Credit cards accepted. Terms: net 30 days with credit approval. They specialize in nationwide asset searches, public record research, retrieval services and pre-employment screening services. Will retrieve DMV and Criminal records.

Leslie Bearce

1075 Capistrano Ct, San Luis Obispo, CA 93405
Phone: 805-704-5699 - **Fax:** 805-541-2615 leslieb930@aol.com

Types of Records Retrieved: Criminal, Civil and Probate courts; Real Estate; Tax Liens/Judgments; UCC records; Vital records

Local Retrieval Area: CA-San Luis Obispo

Add'l Information: Established 1995. Normal turnaround time- 24-48 hours. Projects billed by number of names searched.

Joyce Beasley

4812 N Yorkshire Ct, Bloomington, IN 47404
Phone: 812-325-2379 - **Fax:** 425-799-0811

Types of Records Retrieved: Criminal, Civil and Probate courts; Tax Liens/Judgments; UCC records

Local Retrieval Area: IN-Lawrence, Monroe, Morgan, Owen

Add'l Information: Established 1999. Normal turnaround time- 24 hours. Projects billed by number of names searched. She specializes in the 4 county area around Bloomington, IN.

Beauregard Abstract Co

108 W 1st St, PO Box 280, DeRidder, LA 70634
Phone: 337-463-7090 - **Fax:** 337-463-7094

Types of Records Retrieved: Real Estate; Tax Liens/Judgments; Probate courts; UCC records

Local Retrieval Area: LA-Beauregard Parish

Add'l Information: Established 1913. Normal turnaround time- 24 hours. Projects billed by number of names searched. First project may require prepayment. Will file/record documents for clients. Terms: net 30 days. They have a tract index covering entire Beauregard Parish real estate, and have all records on microfilm, with last 10 years on computer.

Beaver County Abstract Co

PO Box 928, 118 Douglas St, Beaver, OK 73932
Phone: 580-625-4423 - **Fax:** 580-625-3643

Types of Records Retrieved: Civil and Probate courts; Real Estate; Tax Liens/Judgments; UCC records; Vital records

Local Retrieval Area: OK-Beaver

Add'l Information: Established 1979. Normal turnaround time- 3-4 days. Projects billed by the hour. Will file/record documents for clients.

Beckham County Abstract

PO Box 80, Sayre, OK 73662 **Phone:** 580-928-3143 - **Fax:** 580-928-5000

Types of Records Retrieved: Criminal, Civil and Probate courts; Real Estate; Tax Liens/Judgments; UCC records; Vital records

Local Retrieval Area: OK-Beckham

Add'l Information: Established 1907. Normal turnaround time- 1 week. Projects billed by number of names searched. Projects billed by number of records located. Projects billed by the hour. First project may require prepayment. Will file/record documents for clients. Personal checks are accepted. They specialize in situations affecting mineral or surface matters in Beckham County.

Bedgood Abstract & Title Co (Goliad)

PO Box 12, 325 S Market St, Goliad, TX 77963
Phone: 361-645-3145 - **Fax:** 361-645-3256
www.bedgoodtitle.com **Types of Records Retrieved:** Civil and Probate courts; Real Estate; Tax Liens/Judgments; UCC records

Local Retrieval Area: TX-Goliad

Add'l Information: Established 1987. Normal turnaround time- 1-2 days. Fee basis will vary by the type of project. First project may require prepayment. Will file/record documents for clients. They also have offices in Port Lavaca, Port O'Connor, and Victoria.

Bedgood Abstract & Title Co (Port Lavaca)

PO Box 143, 416 E Railroad Ave, Port Lavaca, TX 77979
Phone: 361-552-6761, 361-573-1785 - **Fax:** 361-575-7581
www.bedgoodtitle.com **Types of Records Retrieved:** Civil and Probate courts; Real Estate; Tax Liens/Judgments; UCC records

Local Retrieval Area: TX-Calhoun

Add'l Information: Established 1897. Normal turnaround time- 1-2 days. Fee basis will vary by the type of project. First project may require prepayment. Will file/record documents for clients. They also have offices in Goliad, Port O'Connor, and Victoria.

Beehive Attorney Service

5258 Pinemont Dr #210, Murray, UT 84123
Phone: 800-779-0379; beehiveattorney@hotmail.com

Types of Records Retrieved: Criminal, Civil and Probate courts; Federal courts; Tax Liens/Judgments

Local Retrieval Area: UT-Davis, Salt Lake, Summit, Tooele, Utah, Weber

Add'l Information: Established 2005. Normal turnaround time- 1-3 days. Projects billed by number of names searched. First project may require prepayment. Credit cards accepted. Will file/record documents for clients. They specialize in the populated counties around Salt Lake area. Performs service of process.

Bell Investigative Services Inc

PO Box 848395, Pembroke Pines, FL 33084
Phone: 954-454-4859 - **Fax:** 954-458-8493 bellinv@inv.com

Types of Records Retrieved: Criminal, Civil and Probate courts; Federal courts; Real Estate; Tax Liens/Judgments; UCC records; Vital records

Local Retrieval Area: FL-Brevard, Broward, Collier, Dade, Hillsborough, Lee, Monroe, Orange, Palm Beach, Pinellas, Seminole, St Lucie, Volusia

Add'l Information: Established 1997. Normal turnaround time- same day to 36 hours. Projects billed by number of names searched. First project may require prepayment. Payment due by 15th of month. They specialize in background investigations for the purposes of pre-employment screening and secret shopper, executive protection, surveillance, and other services. A licensed PI in FL.

Benchmark Investigations

32158 Camino Capistrano #A-415, San Juan Capistrano, CA 92675
Phone: 800-248-7721; 949-248-7721 - **Fax:** 949-248-0208
www.benchmarkinvestigations.com **email:** zimmerpi@pacbell.net

Types of Records Retrieved: Criminal, Civil and Probate courts; Federal courts; Real Estate; Tax Liens/Judgments; UCC records; Vital records

Local Retrieval Area: CA-Los Angeles, Orange, San Diego

Add'l Information: Established 1989. Normal turnaround time- 1-2 days. Projects billed by the hour. First project may require prepayment. Credit cards accepted. A full service private investigation agency specializing in asset, process service and court records searching. A licensed PI in CA. Performs service of process.

Bent County Abstract & Title

PO Box 183, Las Animas, CO 81054
Phone: 719-456-0381 - **Fax:** 719-456-0791

Types of Records Retrieved: Real Estate; Tax Liens/Judgments

Local Retrieval Area: CO-Bent, Prowers

Add'l Information: Established 1902. Normal turnaround time- 3-5 days. Fee basis will vary by the type of project. Will file/record documents for clients. They specialize in ownership and encumbrance reports, title insurance, and abstract updates.

Bentley Title Co

PO Box 104, Hermitage, MO 65668
Phone: 417-745-6626 - **Fax:** 417-745-6160 bentleytitle@yahoo.com

Records Retrieved: Real Estate; Tax Liens/Judgments; UCC records

Local Retrieval Area: MO-Hickory

Add'l Information: Established 1890. Normal turnaround time- 3-5 days. Fee basis varies by type of transaction. Will file/record documents for clients. A $75.00 cancellation fee applies.

Benton Abstract & Title Co

106 W Redwood, Eldorado, TX 76936
Phone: 325-853-2600 x19

Records Retrieved: Real Estate; Tax Liens/Judgments; UCC records

Local Retrieval Area: TX-Schleicher

Add'l Information: Established 1916. Normal turnaround time- 1-2 days. Fee basis varies by type of transaction. First project may require prepayment. Will file/record documents for clients. They have their own complete set of land title records covering Schleicher county, in digital form available over the internet. Company established in 1916.

Benton County Abstract Co

PO Box 128, 411 Dewey St, Foley, MN 56329-0128
Phone: 320-968-7278 - **Fax:** 320-968-6487

Types of Records Retrieved: Civil and Probate courts; Federal courts; Real Estate; Tax Liens/Judgments; UCC records; Vital records

Local Retrieval Area: MN-Benton

Add'l Information: Established 1911. Normal turnaround time- same day. Projects billed by number of names searched. Projects billed by number of records located. Will file/record documents for clients. Personal checks are accepted. They specialize in owners encumbrance reports, abstracting and name searches.

Benton County Title Co

112 E. 4th St, Vinton, IA 52349
Phone: 319-472-2369 - **Fax:** 319-472-2360
www.bctco.com **email:** cjuhl@bctco.com

Records Retrieved: Criminal, Civil and Probate courts; Federal District courts; Real Estate; Tax Liens/Judgments; UCC records; Vital records

Local Retrieval Area: IA-Benton

Add'l Information: Established 1863. Normal turnaround time- 2 days. Projects billed by number of names searched. First project may require prepayment. Will file/record documents for clients. They are a title company providing searches and abstracts in real estate, including liens and taxes, escrow closing and appraisals.

Lyndalee Berger

PO Box 7745, Loveland, CO 80537
Phone: 970-669-7691

Types of Records Retrieved: Civil courts; Real Estate; Tax Liens/Judgments

Local Retrieval Area: CO-Larimer, Weld

Add'l Information: Established 1992. Normal turnaround time- 2-3 days. Projects billed by the hour. Payment minimum charge-1 hr, in advance.

Bergman Records Access

988 Stearns Dr #1, Los Angeles, CA 90048
Phone: 323-939-1632 - **Fax:** 310-481-6720 jscottbergman@sbcglobal.net

Types of Records Retrieved: Criminal, Civil and Probate courts; Federal courts; Real Estate; Tax Liens/Judgments; UCC records; Vital records

Local Retrieval Area: CA-Los Angeles, Orange. **Correspondent Relationships:** San Francisco, CA; Las Vegas, NV.

Add'l Information: Established 1997. Normal turnaround time- 24 hours. Projects billed by number of names searched. Projects billed by the hour. First project may require prepayment. Will file/record documents for clients. They specialize in all around reliable and accurate support in public record and asset information acquisition. A pager number to reach them is 323-969-6690. Performs service of process.

Berry & Maddox

PO Box 354, Lovingston, VA 22949
Phone: 434-263-4886 - **Fax:** 434-263-4285

Types of Records Retrieved: Criminal, Civil and Probate courts; Real Estate; Tax Liens/Judgments; UCC records; Vital records

Local Retrieval Area: VA-Amherst, Nelson

Add'l Information: Established 1983. Normal turnaround time- 2 days. Projects billed by the hour. First project may require prepayment. Will file/record documents for clients.

Best Legal Services Inc

1617 JFK Blvd #1045, Philadelphia, PA 19103
Phone: 800-562-9620; 215-567-7777 - **Fax:** 215-561-4546

Types of Records Retrieved: Criminal and Civil courts; Federal courts; Real Estate; Tax Liens/Judgments; UCC records; Vital records

Local Retrieval Area: NJ-Burlington, Camden, Gloucester; PA-Berks, Bucks, Chester, Dauphin, Delaware, Lancaster, Montgomery, Philadelphia. **Correspondent Relationships:** Lehigh, Allegheny, Lancaster, Dauphin, Luzerne, York counties PA.

Add'l Information: Established 1981. Normal turnaround time- 2 days. Projects billed by number of names searched. First project may require prepayment. Will file/record documents for clients. Will invoice. They specialize in serving legal papers, document filings, skiptracing and provide access to the Federal Record Ctr in Philadelphia for states of PA, MD, DE, DC and VA. They provide nationwide service through their correspondent relationship with NAPPS. Performs service of process.

Best Process Service

6 Gallery Ct, San Antonio, TX 78209
Phone: 210-930-7417 - **Fax:** 877-227-9390
www.bestprocessservice.com **email:** bestprocess@satx.rr.com

Types of Records Retrieved: Criminal, Civil and Probate courts; Federal courts; Real Estate; Tax Liens/Judgments; UCC records; Vital records

Local Retrieval Area: TX-Atascosa, Bandera, Bexar, Comal, Frio, Guadalupe, Kerr, Medina, Wilson. **Correspondents:** statewide.

Add'l Information: Established 1999. Normal turnaround time- 12-24 hours. Expedited service available. Projects billed by the hour. First project may require prepayment. Credit cards accepted. Credit card done by PayPal request. They are an expanding company that does, online research, records research, skip tracing, missing persons location, background checks and document retrieval. Performs service of process.

Bettendorf Abstract Co

1987 Spruce Hills Dr, Bettendorf, IA 52722
Phone: 563-359-3646 - **Fax:** 563-359-3647

Types of Records Retrieved: Criminal, Civil and Probate courts; Real Estate; Tax Liens/Judgments; UCC records; Vital records

Local Retrieval Area: IA-Scott

Add'l Information: Established 1982. Normal turnaround time- up to 7 days. Projects billed by the hour. First project may require prepayment. Will file/record documents for clients. They specialize in real estate and abstracting. Performs service of process.

Bexar Professional

2186 Jackson Keller, #330, San Antonio, TX 78213
Phone: 210-228-0083 - **Fax:** 210-228-0066 bexarpro@swbell.net

Types of Records Retrieved: Criminal, Civil and Probate courts; Federal courts; Real Estate; Tax Liens/Judgments; UCC records; Vital records

Local Retrieval Area: TX-Bexar. **Correspondent Relationships:** Texas.

Add'l Information: Established 1987. Normal turnaround time- same day to next day. Projects billed by number of names searched. Projects billed by number of records located. Projects billed by the hour. First project may require prepayment. Will file/record documents for clients. They specialize in process service. Performs service of process.

BG Criminal Research

PO Box 795, Waco, TX 76703-0795
Phone: 254-755-6808 - **Fax:** 254-753-5980

Types of Records Retrieved: Criminal and Civil courts; Federal courts; Tax Liens/Judgments; UCC records

Local Retrieval Area: TX-Bell, Coryell, McLennan

Add'l Information: Established 1994. Normal turnaround time- 24 to 48 hours. Projects billed by number of names searched. Will bill every two weeks or monthly. They specialize in criminal record information. A licensed PI in TX.

Betsy Biesenbach

1948 Belleville Rd SW, Roanoke, VA 24015
Phone: 540-982-7892 - **Fax:** 540-982-7892

Types of Records Retrieved: Real Estate; Tax Liens/Judgments; Probate courts; UCC records

Local Retrieval Area: VA-Botetourt, Roanoke, Roanoke City, Salem City

Add'l Information: Established 1986. Normal turnaround time- 24 hours for Roanoke City, Roanoke County and Salem City, and 48 hours for all others. Projects billed by number of names searched. Projects billed by number of records located. Will file/record documents for clients. She specializes in title examinations and document retrieval.

Big Country Title

400 Pine St #765, Abilene, TX 79601
Phone: 325-698-9195 - **Fax:** 325-698-1864

Types of Records Retrieved: Real Estate; Tax Liens/Judgments; Probate courts; UCC records; Vital records

Local Retrieval Area: TX-Callahan, Taylor

Add'l Information: Normal turnaround time- 2 days. Projects billed by number of names searched. First project may require prepayment. Will file/record documents for clients. They specialize in divorce and death searches, title insurance and abstracting.

Big Spring Abstract & Title Co Inc

208 W 3rd St, Big Spring, TX 79720
Phone: 432-267-1604 - **Fax:** 432-267-1815 tpaige@moutonlaw.com

Records Retrieved: Real Estate; Tax Liens/Judgments; Probate courts

Local Retrieval Area: TX-Glasscock, Howard

Add'l Information: Established 1986. Normal turnaround time- 2-3 days. Fee basis will vary by the type of project. First project may require prepayment.

BirthCertificate.com

601 Van Ness Av #E, San Francisco, CA 94102
Phone: 888-934-3848; 415-440-9100 - **Fax:** 415-440-9200
www.birthcertificate.com **email:** commune@probusresearch.com

Types of Records Retrieved: Vital records

Local Retrieval Area: CA-Alameda, Contra Costa, Marin, San Francisco, San Mateo, Santa Clara. **Correspondent Relationships:** nationwide.

Add'l Information: Established 1985. Normal turnaround time- same day to 2 days. Projects billed by number of names searched. Hourly charge for special projects. First project may require prepayment. Terms- net 30 days. They specialize in nationwide vital records retrieval. The company provides direct service in San Francisco Bay area counties, also same day services electronically in states of Texas and Ohio.

Bismarck Title Co

PO Box 1811, 421 N 4th St, Bismarck, ND 58502
Phone: 701-222-4247 - **Fax:** 701-221-3039
www.bismarcktitle.com **email:** orderdesk@BismarckTitle.com

Types of Records Retrieved: Criminal, Civil and Probate courts; Real Estate; Tax Liens/Judgments; UCC records

Local Retrieval Area: ND-Burleigh, Morton. **Correspondent Relationships:** abstract companies throughout North Dakota.

Add'l Information: Established 1987. Normal turnaround time- 24 hours. Fee basis is per base rate plus name. Will file/record documents for clients.

Bison Security Group

3402 - 8 St. SE, Calgary, Alberta, Canada, CAN T2G 2S7
Phone: 800-661-2245, 866-245-2083; 403-262-4545 - **Fax:** 403-266-3827
www.bsgcorp.com **email:** info@bsgcorp.com

Types of Records Retrieved: Criminal and Civil courts; Real Estate; Tax Liens/Judgments; Vital records

Local Retrieval Area: CANADA-Alberta. **Correspondent Relationships:** Edmonton, Red Deer, Lethbridge, Alberta; also in British Columbia, Western Canada.

Add'l Information: Established 1980. Normal turnaround time- 24-48 hours, if local. Projects billed by number of names searched. Projects billed by the hour. All projects require prepayment. They specialize in due diligence, corporate/commercial crime investigations, loss prevention, insurance, polygraph. Performs service of process.

Bi-State Title Search (Div of Bi-State Ind.)

10024 Office Center Ave #100, St Louis, MO 63128-1392
Phone: 866-450-7399; - **Fax:** 314-843-1238
www.bistate.info **email:** bsts@bistate.info

Types of Records Retrieved: Criminal, Civil and Probate courts; Real Estate; Tax Liens/Judgments; UCC records

Local Retrieval Area: IL-Adams, Bond, Clinton, Jackson, Jersey, Macoupin, Madison, Monroe, Montgomery, Perry, Randolph, St. Clair, Sangamon, Union, Washington; KS-Atchison, Douglas, Franklin, Jefferson, Johnson, Leavenworth, Miami, Wyandotte; MO-Audian, Bates, Buchanan, Callaway, Cass, Clark, Clay, Clinton, Crawford, Dent, Franklin, Gasconade, Henry, Jackson, Jefferson, Johnson, Knox, Lafayette, Lewis, Lincoln, Marion, Monroe, Montgomery, Pike, Platte, Ralls, Ray, St. Charles, Ste. Genevieve, St. Francois, St. Louis, St. Louis City, Scotland, Warren, Washington. **Correspondent in** remainder of Missouri, Kansas, Illinois, Indiana.

Add'l Information: Established 2000. Normal turnaround time- 24-48 hours. Projects billed by number of names searched. Credit cards accepted. Invoice monthly and per search. Payment is net 30 days. Missouri based company established in Illinois, Kansas and Indiana for public record searching and retrieval.

Bit O' Blarney

9835 Rolling Meadows Ln, Salinas, CA 93907
Phone: 831-663-6945 - **Fax:** 831-663-1119 mja@bitoblarney.com

Types of Records Retrieved: Criminal and Civil courts

Local Retrieval Area: CA-Monterrey

Add'l Information: Established 1999. Normal turnaround time- 1-2 days. Fee basis depends upon type of project. First project may require prepayment. They specialize in backgrounding, court retrieval, and cats.

Bitterroot Research

PO Box 1422, Hamilton, MT 59840
Phone: 406-363-4408 - **Fax:** 406-363-4408

Records Retrieved: Real Estate; Tax Liens/Judgments; UCC records

Local Retrieval Area: MT-Ravalli

Add'l Information: Established 1993. Normal turnaround time- 1-5 days. Projects billed by number of names searched. Projects billed by the hour.

First project may require prepayment. Will file/record documents for clients. They specialize in water rights, mineral rights and easements.

Black Hawk County Abstract Co

614 Sycamore St, Waterloo, IA 50703-4726
Phone: 319-291-4000 - **Fax:** 319-291-3929
www.blackhawkabstract.com **email:** order@blackhawkabstract.com

Types of Records Retrieved: Civil and Probate courts; Real Estate; Tax Liens/Judgments; UCC records

Local Retrieval Area: IA-Black Hawk

Add'l Information: Established 1878. Normal turnaround time- 24-48 hours. Projects billed by number of names searched. Projects billed by the hour. Fees negotiated with volume. First project may require prepayment. Will file/record documents for clients. They specialize in complete real estate title searches, current ownership and lien reports within 24 hours with few exceptions on any real estate within Black Hawk county.

John Blackburn

PO Box 50263, Austin, TX 78763
Phone: 210-867-0399 - **Fax:** 707-885-3658 john03@flash.net

Types of Records Retrieved: Civil and Probate courts; Federal district courts; UCC records; Real Estate; Tax Liens/Judgments

Local Retrieval Area: TX-Bell, Bexar, Bosque, Hays, McLennan, Travis, Williamson. **Correspondent Relationships:** Blanco, Burnet, Caldwell, Comal, Falls, Guadalupe, Johnson, Kerr, Lampasas, Lee, Limestone, Somervell.

Add'l Information: Established 1995. Normal turnaround time- 24-48 hours. Projects billed by number of names searched. Will file/record documents for clients. Invoices once a month.

Blaine County Abstract

PO Box 368, 100 W Main, Watonga, OK 73772
Phone: 580-623-7248 or 7257 - **Fax:** 580-623-7268 bca@watonga.net

Types of Records Retrieved: Civil and Probate courts; Real Estate; Tax Liens/Judgments; UCC records

Local Retrieval Area: OK-Blaine

Add'l Information: Normal turnaround time- 1 week. Projects billed by rate schedules. Personal checks are accepted. They specialize in abstracts, title insurance, closings, deed preparation and record searches.

Blaine County Title Co

PO Box 1328, 411 Ohio St, Chinook, MT 59523
Phone: 406-357-3884 - **Fax:** 406-357-2884
bctitle@ttc-cmc.net

Types of Records Retrieved: Criminal, Civil and Probate courts; Real Estate; Tax Liens/Judgments; UCC records; Vital records

Local Retrieval Area: MT-Blaine

Add'l Information: Turnaround time- 3 days. Projects billed by the hour. 1st project may require prepayment. Will file/record documents for clients.

Sallie Blount

509 N Rogers St, Waxahachie, TX 75165
Phone: 972-824-1414 - **Fax:** 214-975-1174 sallieblount@sbcglobal.net

Types of Records Retrieved: Criminal and Civil courts

Local Retrieval Area: TX-Ellis

Add'l Information: Established 1999. Normal turnaround time- less than 48 hours. Projects billed by number of names searched. Invoice monthly; terms net 30 days. She provides civil and criminal records in less than 2 days. Other services are available on a as needed basis, including county recorder records. A licensed PI in TX.

Blue Line Investigations

6600 Stage Rd #107, PMB 602, Bartlett, TN 38134
Phone: 901-266-7100 - **Fax:** 901-266-7121 blueln1@bellsouth.net

Types of Records Retrieved: Criminal courts

Local Retrieval Area: AR-Crittenden, Pulaski; MS-Desoto, Marshall, Oktibbeha, Panola, Tate, Tunica; TN-Dyer, Fayette, Henderson, Lauderdale, Obion, Shelby, Tipton, Weakley. **Correspondent Relationships:** nationwide researcher network who perform criminal background checks.

Add'l Information: Established 1996. Normal turnaround time- same day for Shelby County, TN; 48 hours for other counties; 48-72 other counties. Projects billed by number of names searched. Terms: net 30 days. Specializes in the Memphis area, including AR, MS as well as TN. A licensed PI in TN.

Blue Marble Logistics LLC

800 King St, Wilmington, DE 19801
Phone: 302-661-4390 - **Fax:** 302-661-4398
www.bluemarblelog.com **email:** research@bluemarblelog.com

Types of Records Retrieved: Criminal and Civil courts; Federal courts; Real Estate; Tax Liens/Judgments; UCC records

Local Retrieval Area: DE-Kent, New Castle; PA-Chester, Delaware, Philadelphia. **Correspondent Relationships:** Sussex, DE, and nationwide.

Add'l Information: Established 2003. Normal turnaround time- 24 hours. Expedited service available. Projects billed by number of names searched. First project may require prepayment. Credit cards accepted. They focus on detail, accuracy, and quick turnaround times. Documents can be scanned and emailed for speed and convenience. Performs service of process.

Blue Ridge Title, Div of Chicago Title Ins Co

218 5th St NE, Charlottesville, VA 22902
Phone: 434-295-7196 - **Fax:** 434-979-7208 whiteb@ctt.com

Types of Records Retrieved: Civil and Probate courts; Real Estate; Tax Liens/Judgments; UCC records

Local Retrieval Area: VA-Albemarle, Charlottesville City, Fluvanna, Greene, Louisa, Nelson. **Correspondent Relationships:** Augusta, Orange, Madison counties VA.

Add'l Information: Established 1973. Normal turnaround time- 1-2 days in Albemarle; 3-5 days in other counties. Fee basis varies by type of transaction. First project may require prepayment. Will file/record documents for clients. They specialize in real estate and title searches.

Blumberg Excelsior Corporate Services Inc

52 S Pearl St, 2nd Fl, Albany, NY 12207
Phone: 800-999-0850; 518-436-0855 - **Fax:** 800-835-7137
www.blumberg.com **email:** slb@blumb.com

Types of Records Retrieved: Criminal, Civil and Probate courts; Federal courts; Real Estate; Tax Liens/Judgments; UCC records; Vital records

Local Retrieval Area: NY-Albany, Columbia, Greene, Rensselaer, Schenectady. **Correspondent Relationships:** nationwide and international.

Add'l Information: Established 1972. Normal turnaround time- 24 hours. Projects billed by number of names searched. First project may require prepayment. Credit cards accepted. They specialize in corporate filings, document retrieval, trademark searches and filings and litigation and lien packages. Performs service of process.

Blumberg Excelsior Corporate Svcs Inc (NYC)

62 White St, 2nd Fl, New York, NY 10013
Phone: 800-221-2972; 212-431-5000 - **Fax:** 888-692-9256
www.blumberg.com **email:** slb@blumb.com

Types of Records Retrieved: Tax Liens/Judgments; UCC records

Local Retrieval Area: NY-Bronx, Kings, New York, Queens, Richmond. **Correspondent Relationships:** nationwide.

Add'l Information: Established 1975. Normal turnaround time- 1-2 days. Projects billed by number of names searched. First project may require prepayment. Credit cards accepted. Will file/record documents for clients. House accounts available. They specialize in trademark, copyright, nationwide and international incorporation services. Will search for and file UCC documents.

Blumberg Excelsior Corporate Svcs Inc (Texas)

814 San Jacinto Blvd #303, Austin, TX 78701
Phone: 800-252-3050; 512-478-6620 - **Fax:** 512-478-0001
www.blumberg.com **email:** blumberg@texas.net

Types of Records Retrieved: Criminal, Civil and Probate courts; Federal courts; Real Estate; Tax Liens/Judgments; UCC records; Vital records

Local Retrieval Area: TX-Travis. **Correspondents:** nationwide.

Add'l Information: Established 1975. Normal turnaround time- 24 hours. Projects billed by number of names searched. Projects billed by number of records located. First project may require prepayment. Credit cards accepted. Will file/record documents for clients. They specialize in research, retrieval and filing of any type of public record.

BMC Abstract

1026 Division Rd, Jasper, IN 47546
Phone: 812-661-2484 - **Fax:** 812-482-4912 bmcabstracts@gmail.com
Types of Records Retrieved: Real Estate; Tax Liens/Judgments
Local Retrieval Area: IN-Daviess, Dubois, Perry, Pike, Spencer
Add'l Information: Established 2002. Normal turnaround time- 48 hours or less. Projects billed by the hour. Charges a flat fee for specific real estate services. First project may require prepayment. Will file/record documents for clients. BMC specializes in real estate; current owner searches, etc. They can also retrieve court records in Dubois County only.

Bob Lessemun Investigations Inc

4893 Prince William Pky #201, Woodbridge, VA 22192
Phone: 703-580-6611 - **Fax:** 703-670-8668
www.lessemun.com **email:** blessemun@yahoo.com
Records Retrieved: Criminal, Civil and Probate courts; Federal district courts; Real Estate; Tax Liens/Judgments; UCC records; Vital records
Local Retrieval Area: VA-Prince William. **Correspondent Relationships:** Alexandria, Arlington, Fairfax, Winchester counties VA.
Add'l Information: Established 1999. Turnaround time- 24 hours. Projects billed by number of names searched. First project may require prepayment. Is a licensed private investigator operating throughout Northern VA with 38 years investigative experience specializing in crime, domestic, civil, process serving, tracing missing persons and deadbeats. He is professional and dedicated. A licensed PI in VA. Performs service of process.

Bodo PI

PO Box 32821, Laughlin, NV 89028
Phone: 877-381-7009 - **Fax:** 877-381-7009
www.BodoPI.com **email:** bodo@bodopi.com
Types of Records Retrieved: Criminal, Civil and Probate courts; Federal courts; Real Estate; Tax Liens/Judgments; UCC records; Vital records
Local Retrieval Area: AZ-Mohave; NV-Clark (Goes to Bullhead City, AZ and Laughlin, NV). **Correspondent Relationships:** nationwide.
Add'l Information: Established 1979. Normal turnaround time- 24 hours. Projects billed by the hour. Will invoice, payment terms are net 30 days. Credit cards accepted. Will file/record documents for clients. They are a full service investigative agency specializing in background inquires, asset inquiries and locate inquires-nationwide. A licensed PI in AZ, CA, NV. Performs service of process.

Todd Boehr

133 East De la Guerra St #150, Santa Barbara, CA 93101
Phone: 805-452-7579 - **Fax:** 805-456-3813 www.crimicheck.com
Types of Records Retrieved: Criminal and Civil courts
Local Retrieval Area: CA-Santa Barbara, Ventura
Add'l Information: Established 1991. Normal turnaround time- usually same day. Projects billed by number of names searched. First project may require prepayment. Terms: net 30 days. Specializing in Santa Barbara and Ventura court and county records. He has been providing research and retrieval services since 1993.

Boerger Investigative Services LLC

1350 W 5th Ave #330, Columbus, OH 43212
Phone: 877-754-8295; 614-481-0777 - **Fax:** 614-481-0778
www.ohioprocessserver.com **Types of Records Retrieved:** Criminal, Civil and Probate courts; Federal courts; Real Estate; Tax Liens/Judgments; UCC records; Vital records
Retrieval Area: OH-Athens, Cuyahoga, Delaware, Fairfield, Franklin, Lake, Licking, Madison, Marion, Richland, Stark, Summit, Union, Wyandot
Add'l Information: Established 1998. Normal turnaround time- 48-72 hours. Expedited service available. Projects billed by number of names searched. All projects require prepayment. Credit cards accepted. Will file/record documents for clients. They are a full-service litigation support and investigative agency serving all of Ohio. Prompt, efficient and professional service with process service and records retrieval within 48 hours. A licensed PI in OH. Performs service of process.

Boles-Wallner Abstract & Title

214 W Grand Ave, Wisconsin Rapids, WI 54495-0575
Phone: 715-423-6940 - **Fax:** 715-423-6912
Types of Records Retrieved: Real Estate; Tax Liens/Judgments; Probate courts; UCC records
Local Retrieval Area: WI-Adams, Clark, Jackson, Juneau, Marathon, Portage, Waushara, Wood
Add'l Information: Established 1987. Normal turnaround time- 48 hours. Projects billed by number of records located. First project may require prepayment.

Bollinger Attorney Service

PO Box 3296, Palm Springs, CA 92263-3296
Phone: 760-329-2504 http://home.att.net/~DennisBollinger/
email: dennisbollinger@worldnet.att.net
Types of Records Retrieved: Criminal, Civil and Probate courts; Federal courts; Real Estate; Tax Liens/Judgments; UCC records; Vital records
Local Retrieval Area: CA-Imperial, Riverside, San Bernardino. **Correspondent Relationships:** worldwide.
Add'l Information: Established 1972. Normal turnaround time- 24 hours. Expedited service available. Projects billed by number of records located. First project may require prepayment. Will file/record documents for clients. Fax on request. They specialize in court filings, investigations, process serving-evasive, record searches from all agencies and paralegal JD services. Performs service of process.

Bollinger County Abstract Co

PO Box 889, Marble Hill, MO 63764
Phone: 573-238-2823 - **Fax:** 573-238-2819
www.bocoabst.com **email:** bocoabst@hotmail.com
Types of Records Retrieved: Criminal, Civil and Probate courts; Real Estate; Tax Liens/Judgments; UCC records
Local Retrieval Area: MO-Bollinger
Add'l Information: Established 1907. Normal turnaround time- 7-10 days. Projects billed by the hour. First project may require prepayment. Will file/record documents for clients. Payment acceptance may vary. They specialize in land title and geographic land locations. They also do real estate closing.

Bombet Cashio & Associates

11220 N Harrells Ferry Rd, Baton Rouge, LA 70816
Phone: 800-256-5333; 225-275-0796 - **Fax:** 225-272-3631
www.bombet.com **email:** buddy@bombet.com
Types of Records Retrieved: Criminal, Civil and Probate courts; Federal courts; Real Estate; Tax Liens/Judgments; UCC records; Vital records
Local Retrieval Area: LA-Ascension, Bossier, Caddo, East Baton Rouge, Iberville, Jefferson, Orleans, St. Charles, St. John the Baptist, St. Tammany, West Baton Rouge Parishes. **Correspondent Relationships:** worldwide.
Add'l Information: Established 1967. Normal turnaround time- 24-48 hours. Projects billed by the hour. Net 30 days. All projects require prepayment. Credit cards accepted. Will file/record documents for clients. They specialize in general investigations, research and process service. They have been in business since 1967. Have staff statewide. A licensed PI in LA. Performs service of process.

Bon Homme Title Co

PO Box 276, Tyndall, SD 57066
Phone: 605-589-3572 - **Fax:** 605-589-3093
Types of Records Retrieved: Real Estate; Tax Liens/Judgments
Local Retrieval Area: SD-Bonhomme
Add'l info: 1st project may require prepayment. They specialize in real estate.

Bond Title

102 E Main, Greenville, IL 62246
Phone: 618-664-1872 - **Fax:** 618-664-1873 buchmillerlaw@sbcglobal.net

Types of Records Retrieved: Civil and Probate courts; Bankruptcy court; Real Estate; Tax Liens/Judgments; Vital records

Local Retrieval Area: IL-Bond, Clinton, Fayette, Macoupin, Madison, Montgomery, St. Clair

Add'l Information: Established 1870. Normal turnaround time- Nov. to March- 1-2 days. April to October- 1 week. Projects billed by number of names searched. First project may require prepayment. They have been in business since 1870 and they have title insurance policies. PI in IL.

Bontecou Investigative Services Inc

PO Box 2448, 350 E Broadway, Jackson, WY 83001
Phone: 307-733-2637 - **Fax:** 307-733-5873
www.wyominginvestigator.com **email:** bisinc@earthlink.net

Types of Records Retrieved: Criminal, Civil and Probate courts; Real Estate; Tax Liens/Judgments; UCC records

Local Retrieval Area: WY-Lincoln, Park, Sublette, Teton. **Correspondent Relationships:** statewide.

Add'l Information: Established 1884. Normal turnaround time- 3-5 business days. Projects billed by number of names searched. Projects billed by the hour. First project may require prepayment. Will file/record documents for clients. They specialize in background searches civil litigation, investigation & surveillance and process service. They also provide court filings, subpoena preparation, photocopying, skiptracing. A licensed PI in WY. Performs service of process.

Boone County Abstract Co

814 8th St, Boone, IA 50036 **Phone:** 515-432-3633 - **Fax:** 515-432-3634

Types of Records Retrieved: Criminal, Civil and Probate courts; Real Estate; Tax Liens/Judgments; UCC records; Vital records

Local Retrieval Area: IA-Boone

Add'l Information: Normal turnaround time- up to 1 week. Projects billed by number of names searched. Will file/record documents for clients. They specialize in real estate.

Border Legal Services

909 Austin St, Eagle Pass, TX 78852-5205
Phone: 830-773-0525 - **Fax:** 830-757-1069 borderlegalprocess@yahoo.com

Types of Records Retrieved: Criminal, Civil and Probate courts; Tax Liens/Judgments; Vital records

Local Retrieval Area: TX-Maverick, Dimmit, Zavala

Add'l Information: Established 1997. Normal turnaround time- 2 days. Projects billed by the hour. First project may require prepayment. They also do business under the name of "Professional Civil Process." Performs service of process.

Border Title - Zavala Abstract Co

215 N 1st Ave, Crystal City, TX 78839
Phone: 830-374-3218 - **Fax:** 830-374-9374

Types of Records Retrieved: Real Estate; Tax Liens/Judgments

Local Retrieval Area: TX-Zavala

Add'l Information: Established 1958. Normal turnaround time- up to 1 week. Fee basis will vary by the type of project. First project may require prepayment. Formerly Zavala County Abstract Co; became part of the Border Title Group in 2005-6.

Border Title Group

5901 McPherson Rd #6C, Laredo, TX 78041
Phone: 956-791-5810 - **Fax:** 956-791-5555
www.bordertitle.com **email:** batco@bordertitle.com

Records Retrieved: Real Estate; Tax Liens/Judgments; UCC records

Local Retrieval Area: TX-Brooks, Dimmit, Jim Hogg, Jim Wells, La Salle, Maverick, Webb, Zapata, Zavala

Add'l Information: Normal turnaround time- 7-10 working days. Fee basis varies according to the type of project. All projects require prepayment. They have a branch office at 6019 McPherson Rd in McPherson, 956-717-8339, also offices in Crystal City, Carrizo Springs, Eagle Pass, and Alice.

Border Title Group

1000 Crown Ridge Blvd #E, Eagle Pass, TX 78852
Phone: 830-773-0555 - **Fax:** 830-773-6886

Types of Records Retrieved: Real Estate; Tax Liens/Judgments; Probate courts; UCC records **Local Retrieval Area:** TX-Maverick

Add'l Information: Established 1992. Normal turnaround time- 3-4 days. Projects billed by number of names searched. All projects require prepayment. Will file/record documents for clients.

Border Title Group, FKA Elliott & Waldron Abstract

PO Box 248, Carrizo Springs, TX 78834
Phone: 830-876-2926 - **Fax:** 830-876-5077
www.bordertitle.com **email:** ballen@bordertitle.com

Types of Records Retrieved: Real Estate; Tax Liens/Judgments

Local Retrieval Area: TX-Dimmit. **Correspondent Relationships:** They have offices in Laredo, Alice, Eagle Pass, Carrie Springs, Crystal City. Also have correspondents in Webb, LaSalle, Jim Wells, Jim Hogg, Zapata, Brooks, Dimmit, Maverick and Zavala.

Add'l Information: Established 1955. Normal turnaround time- 1-5 days. Fee basis will vary by the type of project. First project may require prepayment. Border Title Group is a computerized title plant with an imaged database of the counties they are active in. For a fee their plant can be accessed through www.bordertitle.com.

Bosic & Bosic

PO Box 1024, Huntington Beach, CA 92647-1024
Phone: 951-788-1988; Fax- same

Types of Records Retrieved: Criminal, Civil and Probate courts; Real Estate; Tax Liens/Judgments; Vital records

Local Retrieval Area: CA-Orange, Riverside, San Bernardino. **Correspondent Relationships:** Los Angeles and San Diego counties, but can retrieve records throughout most of CA.

Add'l Information: Established 1980. Turnaround time- 1-2 days. Projects billed by the hour. First project may require prepayment. Will file/record documents for clients. A licensed PI in CA. Performs service of process.

Botts & Assoc

2537 Spring Place Rd SE, Cleveland, TN 37323
Phone: 423-479-7714 - **Fax:** 423-472-0211 aebotts@aol.com

Types of Records Retrieved: Criminal and Civil courts; Federal courts; Real Estate; UCC records; Tax Liens/Judgments; Vital records

Local Retrieval Area: TN-Bradley, Loudon, McMinn, Meigs, Monroe, Polk, Rhea. **Correspondent Relationships:** statewide.

Add'l Information: Established 1994. Turnaround time- 3 days. Expedited service available. Projects billed by the hour. First project may require prepayment. They provide professional investigations, service of process as well as record checks. A licensed PI in TN. Performs service of process.

Botts Title Co

300 E 1st St, Cameron, TX 76520
Phone: 254-697-6962 - **Fax:** 254-697-2952

Types of Records Retrieved: Real Estate; Tax Liens/Judgments; Probate courts; UCC records; Vital records **Local Retrieval Area:** TX-Austin, Burleson, Colorado, Fayette, Milam, Washington

Add'l Information: Normal turnaround time- 2-5 days. Fees vary by project. First project may require prepayment. They are familiar with all records maintained at the county courthouse. The sell title insurance.

Botts Title Co

200 S Grimes, Giddings, TX 78942
Phone: 979-542-3636 - **Fax:** 979-542-5604

Types of Records Retrieved: Civil and Probate courts; Federal courts; Real Estate; Tax Liens/Judgments **Local Retrieval Area:** TX-Lee

Add'l Information: Established 1906. Normal turnaround time- 2-3 days. Fee basis will vary by the type of project. First project may require prepayment. Will file/record documents for clients.

Brabston Legal Investigations Inc

PO Box 91711, Mobile, AL 36691-1711
Phone: 251-666-5666 - **Fax:** 251-661-8807
www.survsol.com/bli.htm **email:** alpi@survsol.com

Types of Records Retrieved: Civil and Probate courts; Federal courts; Tax Liens/Judgments; UCC records

Local Retrieval Area: AL-Baldwin, Clarke, Mobile. **Correspondent Relationships:** Alabama.

Add'l Information: Established 1986. Normal turnaround time- 2-3 days. Projects billed by number of names searched. First project may require prepayment. Will file/record documents for clients. They are online with Alabama State Judicial Computer. A licensed PI in AL, FL. Performs service of process.

Lisa Bracey-Farris

1219 Walker Rd, Goodlettsville, TN 37072
Phone: 615-859-7135; cell- 615-943-4118 - **Fax:** 615-859-3982
farris05@bellsouth.net

Types of Records Retrieved: Real Estate; Tax Liens/Judgments

Local Retrieval Area: TN-Davidson, Sumner

Add'l Information: Established 1999. Normal turnaround time- 24 hours. Projects billed by the hour. Will invoice. Her specialty is current owner searches. She is a paralegal with a BS in addition to a paralegal certification from an ABA approved school. Cell phone- is 615-943-4118. Performs service of process.

Bradley Enterprises LLC

7716 Mary Eve Rd, Shreveport, LA 71106-6015
Phone: 318-868-4906 - **Fax:** 318-219-3000 bellcla@aol.com

Types of Records Retrieved: Criminal, Civil and Probate courts; Federal courts; Real Estate; Tax Liens/Judgments; UCC records

Local Retrieval Area: LA-Bossier Parish, Caddo Parish

Add'l Information: Established 1993. Normal turnaround time- 24-48 hours. Fee basis varies by type of project. Terms are net 15 days. Will file/record documents for clients. Terms: net 15 days. They specialize in oil and gas searches, RE titles, abstracts, criminal and bankruptcy court searches.

Branda Agency

PO Box 781444, Wichita, KS 67278
Phone: 800-310-8174; 316-634-0000 - **Fax:** 316-636-4406
www.effectivedetective.com **email:** dbranda@aol.com

Types of Records Retrieved: Criminal, Civil and Probate courts; Federal courts; Real Estate; Tax Liens/Judgments; UCC records; Vital records

Retrieval Area: KS-Butler, Harvey, Kingman, Reno, Sedgwick, Sumner

Add'l Information: Established 1983. Normal turnaround time- county court records in 48 hours; federal records depend on nature of file. Projects billed by number of names searched. All projects require prepayment. Will file/record documents for clients. Visit the web site for additional services. A licensed PI in KS. Performs service of process.

Attorney Leonard Brashear

PO Box 677, Hyden, KY 41749
Phone: 606-672-3577 - **Fax:** 606-672-2142

Types of Records Retrieved: Criminal, Civil and Probate courts; Real Estate; Tax Liens/Judgments; UCC records

Local Retrieval Area: KY-Leslie

Add'l Information: Established 1982. Normal turnaround time- up to 1 week. Projects billed by the hour. All projects require prepayment. Will file/record documents for clients.

Jerry M Braud

1312 Park Dr, Thibodaux, LA 70301
Phone: 985-447-1227 - **Fax:** 985-447-1227

Types of Records Retrieved: Criminal, Civil and Probate courts; Federal District courts; Real Estate; Tax Liens/Judgments; UCC records

Local Retrieval Area: LA-Lafourche Parish

Add'l Information: Established 1965. Turnaround time- 1-2 days. Projects billed by the hour. First project may require prepayment. Will file/record documents for clients. Will invoice. She has been in business for over 40 years. She specializes in real estate, mineral and all public record searches.

BraveWolf's Background Investigations

300 Bayou Blvd #215, Pensacola, FL 32503
Phone: 850-791-6279 - **Fax:** 850-607-7190
www.superpages.com **email:** apacheindians37@hotmail.com

Types of Records Retrieved: Criminal, Civil and Probate courts; Federal courts; Real Estate; UCC records

Local Retrieval Area: FL-Escambia

Add'l Information: Established 2006. Normal turnaround time- 1-2 days. Projects billed by number of names searched. Will accept checks and money orders. They specialize in background checks and criminal history/criminal records.

Bray & Freeman LP

PO Box 123991, Ft. Worth, TX 76121
Phone: 817-596-9255 - **Fax:** 817-834-1179 georgebray@charter.net

Types of Records Retrieved: Criminal, Civil and Probate courts; Federal courts; Real Estate; Tax Liens/Judgments; UCC records; Vital records

Local Retrieval Area: TX-Collin, Dallas, Denton, Hood, Jack, Johnson, Palo Pinto, Parker, Tarrant, Wise. **Correspondent:** national and international.

Add'l Information: Established 1992. Normal turnaround time- 3 days. Projects billed by the hour. First project may require prepayment. Will file/record documents for clients. They specialize in personnel matters for corporation. Several areas they cover are internal theft, fraud, drug use and thefts. They work complex domestic issues and with automobile dealerships. They also do due diligence and asset searches. A licensed PI in TX. Performs service of process.

Bremer County Abstract Co

218 E Bremer Ave, Waverly, IA 50677
Phone: 319-352-2710 - **Fax:** 319-352-0675

Types of Records Retrieved: Civil courts; Federal District courts; Probate courts; Real Estate; Tax Liens/Judgments; UCC records; Vital records

Local Retrieval Area: IA-Bremer

Add'l Information: Normal turnaround time- 3 days. Projects billed by number of names searched. Fee may also be based per claim. All projects require prepayment. Will file/record documents for clients.

Bridge Service Corp

277 Broadway #1710, New York, NY 10007-2001
Phone: 800-225-2736; 212-267-8600 - **Fax:** 888-267-8680; 212-267-8687
www.bridgeservice.com **email:** info@bridgeservice.com

Types of Records Retrieved: Civil and Probate courts; Federal courts; Real Estate; Tax Liens/Judgments; UCC records

Local Retrieval Area: NY-Bronx, Kings, New York, Queens. **Correspondent Relationships:** nationwide.

Add'l Information: Established 1994. Normal turnaround time- 1-3 days. Expedited service available. Projects billed by number of names searched. Projects billed by the hour. First project may require prepayment. Credit cards accepted. Will file/record documents for clients. They specialize in all filing and search services in 4 of the 5 counties which comprise New York City in all courts, agencies and government offices.

Brill Title Company

240 W Main Plaza, West Plains, MO 65775
Phone: 417-256-2951 - **Fax:** 417-256-0284

Types of Records Retrieved: Civil and Probate courts; Real Estate; Tax Liens/Judgments; UCC records

Local Retrieval Area: MO-Howell

Add'l Information: Established 1895. Tturnaround time- 2-3 days. Projects billed by number of names searched. They specialize in title insurance.

J Stephen Broadway

310 Market St E, Fayetteville, TN 37334-3024
Phone: 931-433-5979 - **Fax:** 931-433-7297

Types of Records Retrieved: Criminal, Civil and Probate courts; Real Estate; Tax Liens/Judgments; UCC records; Vital records

Retrieval Area: TN-Franklin, Giles, Lawrence, Lincoln, Marshall, Moore

Add'l Information: Established 1982. Normal turnaround time- 2-3 days. Charges vary depending on type of search. First project may require prepayment. Will file/record documents for clients.

Brown County Abstract Co (Nebraska)

127 W 3rd St, Ainsworth, NE 69210

Phone: 402-387-2718 - **Fax:** 402-387-2342 cmizner@threeriver.com

Types of Records Retrieved: Civil and Probate courts; Real Estate; Tax Liens/Judgments; UCC records

Local Retrieval Area: NE-Blaine, Brown, Keya Paha, Rock

Add'l Information: Established 1981. Normal turnaround time- 2-7 days. Fee basis includes a charge by the hour; there is a minimum. Will file/record documents for clients. Payment due upon service. Will charge fee if cancelled. They specialize in title certificates and title insurance.

Brown County Abstract Co (Texas)

201 S Broadway St, Brownwood, TX 76801

Phone: 325-646-6591 - **Fax:** 325-643-5086

Types of Records Retrieved: Civil and Probate courts; Real Estate; Tax Liens/Judgments; UCC records

Local Retrieval Area: TX-Brown

Add'l Information: Normal turnaround time- 1 week. Projects billed by the hour. There is a possibility of a retainer required. First project may require prepayment. A retainer may be required. They specialize in oil and gas searches.

Brown County Title Co

112 S 7th St, Hiawatha, KS 66434

Phone: 785-742-4194 - **Fax:** 785-742-7103 .

Types of Records Retrieved: Criminal, Civil and Probate courts; Real Estate; Tax Liens/Judgments; UCC records

Local Retrieval Area: KS-Brown

Add'l Information: Established 1991. Normal turnaround time- 5-10 days. Projects billed by number of names searched. First project may require prepayment. Will file/record documents for clients.

Brown, Creighton & Peckham Attorneys

PO Box 46, Atwood, KS 67730

Phone: 785-626-3295 - **Fax:** 785-626-9448

Types of Records Retrieved: Criminal, Civil and Probate courts

Local Retrieval Area: KS-Rawlins

Add'l Information: Established 1980s. Normal turnaround time- 1-5 days. Projects billed by number of names searched. Projects billed by the hour. First project may require prepayment. Visits the courts twice weekly.

Pat Brown

610 Pappas Ave, Holcomb, KS 87851

Phone: 620-277-2065 - **Fax:** 620-277-2065 pbrown6785@sbcglobal.net

Types of Records Retrieved: Criminal courts

Local Retrieval Area: KS-Finney

Add'l Information: Established 2003. Normal turnaround time- 24-48 hours. Projects billed by number of names searched. First project may require prepayment. She specializes in Finney County and Garden City, KS area. Has credentials to do criminal checks in Finney Co. for the US Office of Personnel Mgmt.

Brownfield Abstract & Title Co

305B W Broadway, Brownfield, TX 79316

Phone: 806-637-9595 - **Fax:** 806-637-7560 bfldabst@aol.com

Types of Records Retrieved: Civil and Probate courts; Real Estate; Tax Liens/Judgments; UCC records

Local Retrieval Area: TX-Terry

Add'l Information: Established 1985. Normal turnaround time- 2-3 days. It may average 1-2 weeks for difficult tracts. Projects billed by number of records located. Projects billed by the hour. Personal checks are accepted. They specialize in abstracts of title, title insurance and closing services. They also have complete computerized services.

Brule County Abstract Co

PO Box 378, Chamberlain, SD 57325

Phone: 605-734-4275, fax-same malarson@lbjtitle.intranets.com

Types of Records Retrieved: Civil and Probate courts; Real Estate; Tax Liens/Judgments

Local Retrieval Area: SD-Brule, Buffalo, Jackson, Lyman. **Correspondent Relationships:** nationwide.

Add'l Information: Established 1975. Normal turnaround time- up to 2 weeks. Fee basis varies by type of transaction. They specialize in land records. They will file/record real estate documents on behalf of clients on a same or next day basis.

Bryant Information Services

109 Lee St, Brighton, TN 38011

Phone: 901-475-1276 - **Fax:** 901-475-1277 bryantinfo@covingtones.com

Types of Records Retrieved: Criminal, Civil and Probate courts; Federal courts; Real Estate; Tax Liens/Judgments; UCC records

Local Retrieval Area: TN-Crockett, Fayette, Gibson, Hardeman, Haywood, Lauderdale, Obion, Shelby, Tipton

Add'l Information: Established 1998. Normal turnaround time- 24-48 hours. Projects billed by number of names searched. Will file/record documents for clients. They have a 30 day billing cycle. Bryant Information Services will meet your research needs; accuracy, timely and with integrity. A hands-on research firm providing up-to-the-minute information.

BSG Connecticut Search, LLC

PO Box 57, 1924 Straits Turnpike, Middlebury, CT 06762

Phone: 203-758-2493 - **Fax:** 203-841-1069

www.bsgctsearch.com **email:** info@bsgctsearch.com

Types of Records Retrieved: Real Estate; Tax Liens/Judgments; UCC records; Corporate Filings

Local Retrieval Area: CT-Fairfield, Hartford, Litchfield, New Haven

Add'l Information: Established 2003. Normal turnaround time- 2-5 business days. Expedited service available. Projects billed by number of names searched. First project may require prepayment. Will file/record documents for clients. BSG is a full service title abstracting and document filing and retrieval company, providing fast, dependable service, competitive prices.

Dan & Jackie Buck

162 Anthony Rd, Glen Gardner, NJ 08826

Phone: 908-537-2475 - **Fax:** 908-537-2978 guinnessgirl@comcast.net

Types of Records Retrieved: Criminal, Civil and Probate courts; Real Estate; Tax Liens/Judgments; UCC records; Vital records

Local Retrieval Area: NJ-Hunterdon, Morris, Somerset, Warren

Add'l Information: Established 1979. Normal turnaround time- 24-48 hours. Projects billed by number of records located. Will file/record documents for clients. Subsequent projects are individually invoiced. They are fourth generation family owned and operated title searchers and abstractors with more than 30 years experience.

Budget Document Retrieval & Information

215 W Grape St #15, San Diego, CA 92101-1935

Phone: 866-805-6288; 619-235-6288 - **Fax:** 619-235-6288

budgetretrieval@cs.com

Types of Records Retrieved: Civil courts; Real Estate; Tax Liens/Judgments; Vital records

Local Retrieval Area: CA-San Diego

Add'l Information: Established 2001. Normal turnaround time- 24-48 hours. Projects billed by number of names searched. First project may require prepayment. They are located near all downtown courthouses and county assessors office.

Buffalo Land Abstract Inc

103 N Kemp Ave, Tishomingo, OK 73460

Phone: 800-631-1880; 580-371-9375 - **Fax:** 580-371-2771

Types of Records Retrieved: Civil and Probate courts; Real Estate; Tax Liens/Judgments; UCC records

Local Retrieval Area: OK-Johnston

Add'l Information: Established 1989. Tturnaround time- 2-5 days. They charge per page or per certificate. Specialize in closings and title insurance.

B Scott Buffington

PO Box 745, 115 Main St, Magee, MS 39111
Phone: 601-849-4267 - **Fax:** 601-849-9600

Records Retrieved: Real Estate; Tax Liens/Judgments; UCC records

Local Retrieval Area: MS-Covington, Forrest, Jefferson Davis, Lamar, Simpson, Smith

Add'l Information: Turnaround time- 1-2 days. Fee basis varies by type of transaction. First project may require prepayment. He is in general practice.

Rebecca Bulls

4488 Hyndsver Rd, Martin, TN 38237
Phone: 731-799-3066; Fax- same cricket000136@yahoo.com

Records Retrieved: Criminal, Civil and Probate courts; Federal courts

Local Retrieval Area: IL-Williamson; KY-Ballard, Calloway, Carlisle, Graves, Hickman, Marshall, Mc Cracken; TN-Henry, Obion, Weakley

Add'l Information: Established 2004. Normal turnaround time- 24-72 hours. Projects billed by number of names searched. First project may require prepayment. She specializes in the far western Kentucky area, also NW TN; she is also a federal investigator. 2nd phone number is 618-982-2305

Burnett County Abstract Co

25084 State Rd 35, Siren, WI 54872-9002
Phone: 715-349-2269 - **Fax:** 715-349-7604

Records Retrieved: Real Estate; Tax Liens/Judgments; UCC records

Local Retrieval Area: WI-Burnett

Add'l Information: Established 1906. Normal turnaround time- 3 days. Projects billed by number of names searched. Projects billed by number of records located. Projects billed by the hour. Will invoice with a prepaid deposit. They specialize in real estate title searches.

Burr Investigation

PO Box 6486, Boise, ID 83707
Phone: 800-582-5441; 208-342-3463 - **Fax:** 208-342-8097
www.burrinternational.com **email:** 76233.475@compuserve.com

Types of Records Retrieved: Criminal, Civil and Probate courts; Federal courts; Real Estate; Tax Liens/Judgments; UCC records; Vital records

Local Retrieval Area: ID-Ada, Adams, Blaine, Boise, Canyon, Cassia, Elmore, Gem, Gooding, Minidoka, Owyhee, Twin Falls, Valley. **Correspondent Relationships:** nationwide and international.

Add'l Information: Established 1975. Normal turnaround time- several days. Projects billed by the hour. All projects require prepayment. They have 25 years combined law enforcement and investigative experience. A licensed PI in ID-Ada. Performs service of process.

Burton-Dukes Legal Support LLC

PO Box 820861, Vancouver, WA 98682
Phone: 360-254-0878 - **Fax:** 360-254-6390
www.burtonprofessional.com **email:** info@burtonprofessional.com

Types of Records Retrieved: Criminal, Civil and Probate courts; Federal courts; Real Estate; Tax Liens/Judgments; UCC records; Vital records

Local Retrieval Area: OR-Clackamas, Multnomah, Washington; WA-Clark, Cowlitz, Skamania. **Correspondent Relationships:** Pacific, Lewis counties, WA; Clatsop, Columbia counties OR.

Add'l Information: Established 2002. Normal turnaround time- 24-48 hours. Expedited service available. Projects billed by number of names searched. Also trip fee plus copy charges. First project may require prepayment. Credit cards accepted. Will file/record documents for clients. They specialize in document retrieval, investigations and business support services. Also do court document filing, foreclosure postings and field services. They are local process servers. A licensed PI in WA, OR. Performs service of process.

Business Connections

810 Main St, Red Bluff, CA 96080
Phone: 530-527-6229 - **Fax:** 530-529-2645
www.bcconnects.com **email:** business@bcconnects.com

Types of Records Retrieved: Criminal and Civil courts; Federal courts; Tax Liens/Judgments; UCC records; Vital records

Local Retrieval Area: CA-Butte, Fresno, Glenn, Merced, Modoc, Shasta, Tehama. **Correspondent Relationships:** California except Tulare, Alpine, San Luis Obispo, Colusa, Sierra.

Add'l Information: Normal turnaround time- 24-48 hours. Projects billed by number of names searched. Credit cards accepted. Will file/record documents for clients. Terms are net 30 days. They specialize in deeds, bankruptcies, liens, UCCs-fixture filings, judgments and county and city building permit searches. They also do service of process in Tehama County only. Performs service of process.

Business Intelligence Inc

350 S Oyster Bay Rd, Syosset, NY 11791
Phone: 516-938-1525 x107 - **Fax:** 516-938-0010
www.businessintell.com **email:** info@businessintell.com

Types of Records Retrieved: Criminal, Civil and Probate courts; Federal courts; Real Estate; Tax Liens/Judgments; UCC records; Vital records

Local Retrieval Area: NY-Kings, Nassau, New York, Queens, Suffolk, Westchester. **Correspondent Relationships:** nationwide.

Add'l Information: Established 1998. Normal turnaround time- 48 hours. Projects billed by number of names searched. First project may require prepayment. Credit cards accepted. Will file/record documents for clients. Business Intelligence Inc provides full-service due diligence, employment screening, litigation support, computer system intelligence, special research and public record retrieval, usually of business information. A licensed PI in NY. Performs service of process.

Butcher & Associates Ltd

1531 County Lane, Bismarck, ND 58503
Phone: 701-224-1541 - **Fax:** 701-224-1097
www.northdakotapi.com **email:** dina.wtba@midconetwork.com

Types of Records Retrieved: Criminal, Civil and Probate courts; Federal courts; Real Estate; Tax Liens/Judgments; UCC records; Vital records

Local Retrieval Area: MN-Clay; ND-Burleigh, Cass, Morton. **Correspondent Relationships:** North Dakota and nationwide.

Add'l Information: Established 1982. Normal turnaround time- 24-48 hours. Projects billed by number of names searched. Fee basis varies by type of transaction. First project may require prepayment. Will file/record documents for clients. They are former FBI agents that specialize in private investigations, pre-employment screening & state & county record retrieval. Voter registration records are only available for Clay County, MN. Criminal, civil & UCC records are available for all of ND. A licensed PI in ND. Performs service of process.

C & S Research
450 Harding Rd, Yuba City, CA 95993-5116
Phone: 530-415-3161 - **Fax:** 530-673-0264
sherryherkal@hotmail.com

Types of Records Retrieved: Criminal, Civil and Probate courts; Federal courts; Real Estate; Tax Liens/Judgments; UCC records; Vital records

Local Retrieval Area: CA-Alameda, Butte, Colusa, Contra Costa, El Dorado, Mendocino, Nevada, Placer, Plumas, Sacramento, Shasta, Sierra, Sutter, Tehama, Yolo, Yuba. **Correspondents:** Northern California.

Add'l Information: Established 1997. Normal turnaround time- 12-36 hours. Projects billed by number of names searched. Projects billed by number of records located. Will file/record documents for clients. Will bill once or twice per month, Their goal is to give their clients fast and accurate service at a quality price. In Law enforcement and record searching since 1988. Visits all courts daily.

C W Lynn Abstract Co Inc
121 N 7th St, Salina, KS 67401
Phone: 785-823-3706 - **Fax:** 785-823-7922

Types of Records Retrieved: Civil and Probate courts; Real Estate; Tax Liens/Judgments; UCC records

Local Retrieval Area: KS-Saline

Add'l Information: Established 1867. Normal turnaround time- 2-3 days. Charges vary by purchase price or mortgage amount. Will file/record documents for clients. They specialize in title insurance.

C.C.I.
PO Box 2383, Fargo, ND 58108
Phone: 701-235-4842 - **Fax:** 701-235-4842

Types of Records Retrieved: Criminal, Civil and Probate courts; Federal courts; Real Estate; Tax Liens/Judgments; UCC records

Local Retrieval Area: MN-Clay; ND-Cass

Add'l Information: Established 1995. Normal turnaround time- 48 hours. Projects billed by number of names searched. Payment due upon receipt by client. They specialize in civil, criminal, insurance investigation and surveillance. A licensed PI in ND. Performs service of process.

Cal Info Inc
316 W 2nd St #1102, Los Angeles, CA 90012
Phone: 213-687-8710 - **Fax:** 213-687-8778
www.calinfo.net **email:** califola@aol.com

Types of Records Retrieved: Criminal, Civil and Probate courts; Federal courts; Real Estate; Tax Liens/Judgments; UCC records; Vital records

Local Retrieval Area: CA-Los Angeles, Orange. **Correspondent Relationships:** nationwide.

Add'l Information: Established 1957. Normal turnaround time- same day. Projects billed by the hour. First project may require prepayment. Credit cards accepted. They are a research and retrieval firm whose expertise includes law, business, government documents and the sciences with offices in Los Angeles, CA and Washington, DC.

Cal Info Inc
12 Bay Reach, Rehoboth Beach, DE 19971
Phone: 202-537-8901 - **Fax:** 202-537-8902
www.calinfo.net **email:** haugerjs@aol.com

Records Retrieved: Criminal, Civil and Probate courts; Federal courts

Local Retrieval Area: DC-District of Columbia. **Correspondent Relationships:** nationwide.

Add'l Information: Established 1987. Normal turnaround time- same day. Projects billed by the hour. First project may require prepayment. Credit cards accepted. They specialize in research and document retrieval with offices in Washington, DC and Los Angeles, CA, 213-687-8710.

Cal Search
PO Box 9552, San Diego, CA 92169
Phone: 858-488-7572 - **Fax:** 858-488-7592
www.calsearch.com **email:** calsearch@calsearch.com

Types of Records Retrieved: Criminal, Civil and Probate courts; Federal courts; Tax Liens/Judgments; UCC records; Vital records

Local Retrieval Area: CA-Alameda, Butte, Contra Costa, Fresno, Los Angeles, Marin, Merced, Monterey, Orange, Riverside, Sacramento, San Bernardino, San Diego, San Francisco, San Mateo, Santa Barbara, Santa Clara, Santa Cruz, Stanislaus, Ventura. **Correspondent Relationships:** all of California and nationwide.

Add'l Information: Established 1995. Normal turnaround time- 24-48 hours. Expedited service available. Projects billed by number of names searched. Payment due net 30 days. Visa/MC accepted. They specialize in fast and accurate background research & Document retrieval in every CA county. Also specialize in criminal, civil, federal, tax liens, judgments, probate and bankruptcy.

Cal Title-Search Inc
1005 12th St #E, Sacramento, CA 95814
Phone: 800-482-1497; 916-448-1397 - **Fax:** 916-448-1698
caltitlesearch@hotmail.com

Types of Records Retrieved: Civil and Probate courts; Federal courts; Real Estate; Tax Liens/Judgments; UCC records; Vital records

Local Retrieval Area: CA-Sacramento. **Correspondent Relationships:** nationwide.

Add'l Information: Established 1979. Normal turnaround time- 24 hours for state records, 2-3 days for county records. Projects billed by number of names searched. First project may require prepayment. Will file/record documents for clients.

California Backgrounds
7081 N Marks Ave #104, Fresno, CA 93711
Phone: 559-274-9784 - **Fax:** 559-274-9038

Types of Records Retrieved: Criminal courts

Local Retrieval Area: CA-Fresno, Kern, Kings, Madera, San Joaquin, Tulare

Add'l Information: Established 1998. Normal turnaround time- 24 hours. Projects billed by number of names searched. Payment due upon receipt of monthly invoice. All requests are processed at the courts public access. No databases used.

California Criminal Research
4195 Chino Hills Pky #317, Chino Hills, CA 91709
Phone: 909-590-9177 - **Fax:** 775-854-0081
www.calcriminalresearch.com
email: customer_support@calcriminalresearch.com

Types of Records Retrieved: Criminal, Civil and Probate courts

Local Retrieval Area: CA-Los Angeles, Orange, San Diego

Add'l Information: Established 1989. Normal turnaround time- 24 hours or less. Projects billed by number of names searched. All projects require prepayment. Since 1989, CCR has specialized in criminal record searches, civil and probate courts for Southern California. All work completed within 24 hours. Professional staff and highest standards and accuracy in the industry. Performs service of process.

Callahan Lawyers Service
PO Box 632, 50 Main St, 07601, Hackensack, NJ 07602
Phone: 877-767-2245; 201-489-2245 - **Fax:** 201-489-8093
www.processandbail.com **email:** dan@processandbail.com

Types of Records Retrieved: Criminal, Civil and Probate courts; Federal courts; Vital records

Local Retrieval Area: NJ-Bergen, Essex, Hudson, Morris, Passaic, Sussex. **Correspondent Relationships:** Morris and Hudson.

Add'l Information: Established 1965. T turnaround time- 2-3 days. Expedited service available. Fee basis is per job. First project may require prepayment. Credit cards accepted. Will file/record documents for clients. Large enough to serve you, small enough to care. Performs service of process.

Camp County Land Abstract Co

PO Box 99, 103 North Ave, Pittsburg, TX 75686-0099
Phone: 903-856-3676 - **Fax:** 903-856-0470
Types of Records Retrieved: Civil and Probate courts; Real Estate; UCC records; Vital records **Local Retrieval Area:** TX-Camp
Add'l Information: Established 1981. Normal turnaround time- 1-7 days. Fee basis will vary by the type of project. First project may require prepayment. Will file/record documents for clients. They specialize in land searches, title policies, and real estate closings.

Campbell Abstract Co

PO Box 425, 7 NW 2nd St, Buffalo, MN 55313-0425
Phone: 763-682-1252 - **Fax:** 763-682-5810 karen@campbellabstract.com
Types of Records Retrieved: Civil and Probate courts; Federal courts; Real Estate; Tax Liens/Judgments
Local Retrieval Area: MN-Wright
Add'l Information: Established 1925. Normal turnaround time- 2-3 days. Projects billed by number of names searched. Projects billed by number of records located. First project may require prepayment. Will file/record documents for clients. Terms: net 30 days. They specialize in abstracts of title, owners and encumbrances and tract checks.

Campbell Abstract Inc

417 N 8th St, Garden City, KS 67846-5302
Phone: 620-275-7441 - **Fax:** 620-275-8658 cs.gardencity.ks@firstam.com
Types of Records Retrieved: Civil and Probate courts; Real Estate; Tax Liens/Judgments; UCC records
Local Retrieval Area: KS-Finney
Add'l Information: Established 1978. Normal turnaround time- 1-3 days. Projects billed by the hour. First project may require prepayment. Will file/record documents for clients.

Campbell County Abstract & Title

PO Box 315, Herreid, SD 57632
Phone: 605-437-2222, Fax- same
Types of Records Retrieved: Real Estate; Tax Liens/Judgments
Local Retrieval Area: SD-Campbell
Add'l Information: Established 1920. First project may require prepayment. They specialize in real estate.

Tina Campbell

PO Box 4, Kimbolton, OH 43749
Phone: 740-492-0228, cell- 740-260-1194 - **Fax:** 740-492-0441
Types of Records Retrieved: Criminal, Civil and Probate courts; Real Estate; Tax Liens/Judgments; UCC records
Local Retrieval Area: OH-Coshocton, Guernsey, Hocking, Licking, Morgan, Muskingum, Noble, Perry. **Correspondent Relationships:** 25 counties throughout SE Ohio.
Add'l Information: Established 2000?. Normal turnaround time- 24-48 hours. Projects billed by number of names searched. Negotiable; billing may depend on nature of the request.

Cape Girardeau County Abstract & Title

PO Box 878, Cape Girardeau, MO 63702-0878
Phone: 573-335-5890 - **Fax:** 573-335-6381
www.capetitle.com **email:** ktanner@capetitle.com
Types of Records Retrieved: Civil and Probate courts; Federal District courts; Real Estate; Tax Liens/Judgments; UCC records
Local Retrieval Area: MO-Cape Girardeau
Add'l Information: Established 1903. Normal turnaround time- 3 days. Projects billed by number of names searched. Projects billed by number of records located. Will file/record docs for clients. They specialize in land title record searches title insurance, escrow and complete closing services.

Capital City Assurance Group

1616 E Indian School Rd #102, Phoenix, AZ 85016-8602
Phone: 602-728-0100 - **Fax:** 602-728-0500
www.ccaginvestigations.com **email:** louie@ccaginvestigations.com
Types of Records Retrieved: Criminal, Civil and Probate courts; Federal courts; Real Estate; Tax Liens/Judgments; Vital records
Local Retrieval Area: AZ-Maricopa. **Correspondents:** nationwide.
Add'l Information: Established 1995. Normal turnaround time- 48 hours or less. Expedited service available. Projects billed by number of names searched. First project may require prepayment. Billed weekly with 15 day net. They provide service without limitations in a timely and reader friendly manner, to include criminal history checks as well as employment verifications. A licensed PI in AZ. Performs service of process.

Capital Connection

417 E Virginia St #1, Tallahassee, FL 32301
Phone: 850-224-8870 - **Fax:** 800-342-8062; 850-222-1222
www.capitalconnection.com **email:** mycapitalconnection@yahoo.com
Types of Records Retrieved: Criminal and Civil courts; Federal courts; Real Estate; Tax Liens/Judgments; UCC records
Local Retrieval Area: FL-Gadsden, Jefferson, Leon, Wakulla. **Correspondent Relationships:** nationwide.
Add'l Information: Established 1983. Normal turnaround time- 1-2 days. Projects billed by number of names searched. First project may require prepayment. Credit cards accepted. Will bill service companies, attorneys and CPA's. Filing, retrieval and corporate supply company specializing in 1 day incorporations, registered agent service, UCC searches, complete corporate book and out of state retrievals. Performs service of process.

Capital Investigative Services Inc

3127 SW Huntoon #12, Topeka, KS 66604
Phone: 800-633-7136; 785-232-1515 - **Fax:** 785-232-9170
www.cis-pi.com **Types of Records Retrieved:** Criminal and Civil courts
Local Retrieval Area: KS-Dickinson, Douglas, Ellsworth, Franklin, Geary, Harvey, Jackson, Jefferson, Lyon, Marion, McPherson, Osage, Pottawatomie, Rice, Riley, Saline, Shawnee, Wabaunsee. **Correspondent Relationships:** all of NE Kansas.
Add'l Information: First project may require prepayment. They also provide court filings, photocopying, and private investigations. Licensed PI in KS.

Capitol City Network

1191 Spruce Tree Cir, Sacramento, CA 95831
Phone: 916-395-2917 - **Fax:** 916-429-2823 ccnis@sbcglobal.net
Types of Records Retrieved: Criminal, Civil and Probate courts; Federal courts; Real Estate; Tax Liens/Judgments; UCC records; Vital records
Local Retrieval Area: CA-Sacramento. **Correspondents:** nationwide.
Add'l Information: Established 1985. Normal turnaround time- 2-24 hours. Fee basis varies by type of transaction. First project may require prepayment. Will file/record documents for clients. They specialize in legislative analysis/bill tracking and asset searches. They do all Secretary of State filings for California. Obtain all business defendant filings for Sacramento County daily. Check web site for more information.

Capitol Corporate Services Inc (AZ)

815 N 1st Ave #4, Phoenix, AZ 85003
Phone: 800-255-4052; 602-254-4489 - **Fax:** 800-752-0098; 602-258-5833
www.capitolservices.com **email:** capserv@capitolservices.com
Types of Records Retrieved: Civil and Probate courts; Federal courts; Tax Liens/Judgments; UCC & corporate records
Local Retrieval Area: AZ-Maricopa. **Correspondent Relationships:** Arizona, nationwide.
Add'l Information: Established 1985. Normal turnaround time- 24 hours in Maricopa; 2-4 days in other Arizona counties. Projects billed by number of names searched. They sometimes charge by the hour depending on search. First project may require prepayment. Credit cards accepted. Will file/record documents for clients. They specialize in UCC, tax lien and judgments searches and corporate document filing, retrieval and registered agent services.

Capitol Corporate Services Inc (California)

455 Capitol Mall Complex #217, Sacramento, CA 95814
Phone: 800-327-4842; 916-444-6787 - **Fax:** 800-770-1332; 916-444-6178
www.capitolservices.com **email:** tsartell@capitolservices.com

Types of Records Retrieved: Civil courts; Federal courts; Tax Liens/Judgments; UCC & corporate records

Local Retrieval Area: CA-Sacramento. **Correspondents:** nationwide.

Add'l Information: Established 1996. Normal turnaround time- next day. Projects billed by number of names searched. First project may require prepayment. Credit cards accepted. Will file/record documents for clients. They specialize in UCC searches and filings, corporation document filing and retrieval and registered agent services.

Capitol Corporate Services Inc (Louisiana)

8550 United Plaza Blvd, Bldg 2, #305, Baton Rouge, LA 70809
Phone: 800-408-1262; 225-922-4693 - **Fax:** 888-234-5859; 225-922-4694
www.capitolservices.com **email:** info-batonrouge@capitolservices.com

Types of Records Retrieved: Civil courts; Federal courts; Tax Liens/Judgments; UCC & corporate records

Local Retrieval Area: LA-East Baton Rouge Parish. **Correspondent Relationships:** nationwide.

Add'l Information: Established 1996. Normal turnaround time- within 24 hours. Projects billed by number of names searched. First project may require prepayment. Credit cards accepted. Will file/record documents for clients. They do except check payments. They are a public research company specializing in Lien searches. Also provides corporate records from Secretary of State.

Capitol Corporate Services Inc (Nevada)

202 S Minnesota, Carson City, NV 89703
Phone: 800-899-0490; 775-884-0490 - **Fax:** 888-231-4790; 775-884-0493
www.capitolservices.com **email:** mellis@capitolservices.com

Records Retrieved: Tax Liens/Judgments; UCC & corporate records

Local Retrieval Area: NV-Carson City. **Correspondents:** nationwide.

Add'l Information: Established 1991. Normal turnaround time- 1-2 days for the listed counties; 3-5 days for network counties. Next day for state records. Projects billed by number of names searched. First project may require prepayment. Credit cards accepted. Will file/record documents for clients. They specialize in UCC searches and filings, corporation document filings and retrieval as well as county tax lien, judgment and pending litigation searches.

Capitol District Information

471 H St NW #LWR, Washington, DC 20001-2617
Phone: 800-494-5225; 202-265-1516 - **Fax:** 800-494-7512; 202-265-5006
www.capitoldistrict.com **email:** info@capitoldistrict.com

Types of Records Retrieved: Criminal, Civil and Probate courts; Federal courts; Real Estate; Tax Liens/Judgments; UCC records; Corporate records

Local Retrieval Area: DC-District of Columbia; MD-Anne Arundel, Baltimore, Baltimore City, Montgomery, Prince George's; VA-Arlington. **Correspondent Relationships:** nationwide.

Add'l Information: Established 1988. Normal turnaround time- 2-48 hours. Projects billed by number of names searched. Projects billed by the hour. Credit accounts available. Call for price/time quote. First project may require prepayment. Credit cards accepted. Will invoice most companies. They specialize in research/retrieval of legal/financial documents at federal, state and local levels. Emphasis on federal courts and agencies. Also offer services at federal libraries (Library of Congress and National Library of Medicine). Performs service of process.

Capitol Lien Records & Research

1010 Dale St, St Paul, MN 55117-5603
Phone: 800-845-4077; 651-488-0100 - **Fax:** 800-845-4080; 651-488-0200
www.capitollien.com **email:** tony@capitollien.com

Types of Records Retrieved: Criminal, Civil and Probate courts; Federal courts; Real Estate; Tax Liens/Judgments; UCC records; Vital records

Local Retrieval Area: MN-all counties; WI-St. Croix. **Correspondent Relationships:** nationwide.

Add'l Information: Established 1990. Normal turnaround time- 1-3 days. Projects billed by number of names searched. Projects billed by number of records located. First project may require prepayment. Credit cards accepted. Will file/record documents for clients. Terms: net 30 days after first order. Personal checks are accepted. They have access to UCC electronic filings online for all 50 states. Performs service of process.

Capitol Services (California)

1225 8th St., Suite 580, Sacramento, CA 95814
Phone: 916-443-0657 - **Fax:** 916-443-1908
www.cutredtape.com **email:** capserve@cwo.com

Types of Records Retrieved: UCC records

Local Retrieval Area: CA-Sacramento

Add'l Information: Established 1982. Normal turnaround time- 3-4 working days. First project may require prepayment. Credit cards accepted. They provide document filing and retrieval at the California Secretary of State's office in Sacramento.

Capitol Services Inc (New York)

40 Colvin Ave #200, Albany, NY 12206
Phone: 800-662-0171; 518-453-0171 - **Fax:** 800-662-0275; 518-453-0275
www.capitolservices.com **email:** lfrank@capitolservices.com

Types of Records Retrieved: Federal courts; Tax Liens/Judgments; UCC and corporate records

Local Retrieval Area: NY-Albany, Rensselaer. **Correspondent Relationships:** nationwide.

Add'l Information: Established 1993. Normal turnaround time- next day. Projects billed by number of names searched. First project may require prepayment. Credit cards accepted. Will file/record documents for clients. They are a full service UCC and corporate search and filing service.

Capitol Services Inc (Texas)

800 Brazos #1100, Austin, TX 78701
Phone: 800-345-4647; 512-474-8377 - **Fax:** 800-432-3622; 512-476-3678
www.capitolservices.com **email:** jrobinson@capitolservices.com

Types of Records Retrieved: Civil courts; Federal courts; Tax Liens/Judgments; UCC & corporate records

Local Retrieval Area: TX-Dallas, Harris, Travis. **Correspondent Relationships:** nationwide.

Add'l Information: Established 1978. Normal turnaround time- next day. Projects billed by number of names searched. First project may require prepayment. Credit cards accepted. Will file/record documents for clients. They specialize in UCC, tax lien, judgment and pending litigation searches, expedited UCC filings and corporation document filing and retrieval.

Caprock Title Co

511 W Ohio Ave #100, Midland, TX 79701
Phone: 432-687-3232 - **Fax:** 432-687-3240 caprock@apex2000.net

Types of Records Retrieved: Civil and Probate courts; Real Estate; Tax Liens/Judgments

Local Retrieval Area: NM-Eddy, Lea; TX-Dickens, Kent, King, Stonewall. **Correspondent Relationships:** West Texas, Southeast, New Mexico.

Add'l Information: Established 1984. Normal turnaround time- up to 1 week. Fee basis will vary by the type of project. First project may require prepayment. They specialize in oil & gas, mineral interests and working interests.

Carbon County Abstract & Title

PO Box 787, 105 N Broadway, Red Lodge, MT 59068
Phone: 406-446-1090 - **Fax:** 406-446-1091
www.ccatco.com **email:** ccatco@montana.net

Records Retrieved: Real Estate; Tax Liens/Judgments; UCC records

Local Retrieval Area: MT-Carbon

Add'l Information: Established 1981. Normal turnaround time- 2-3 days. Fees vary by project. Will file/record documents for clients.

Cardinal Title LLC

1000 Mid Rivers Mall Dr, St Peters, MO 63376
Phone: 636-397-4300 - **Fax:** 636-397-4646
www.cardtitle.com **email:** sandy@cardtitle.com

Types of Records Retrieved: Criminal and Civil courts; Real Estate

Local Retrieval Area: MO-St. Charles, St. Louis, St. Louis City

Add'l Information: Established 2004. Normal turnaround time- 24-48 hours. Charge by search. Payment due 15 day net. They specialize in title searches, title policies, letter reports, informational binders, document retrieval, civil and criminal searches.

Caribbean Investigative Network

62 St Johns Rd, Pembroke, Bermuda, BER HM07
Phone: 441-292-2626 - **Fax:** 441-292-8341
www.carib.bm **email:** carib@ibl.bm

Types of Records Retrieved: Criminal, Civil and Probate courts; Real Estate; Vital records

Local Retrieval Area: Bermuda. **Correspondent Relationships:** Caribbean Islands-Aruba, Anquilla, Antigua, British Virgin Island, Bahamas, Barbados, Cayman Islands, Curacao, Dominica, Grenada, Jamaica, Montserrat, Nevis, St Lucia, St Kitts, St Vincent, Trinidad, Turks & Caicos Islands.

Add'l Information: Established 1982. Normal turnaround time- 5 business days. Projects billed by number of names searched. A licensed PI in BER. Performs service of process.

Carly J Carman Abstracting Service

2046 Independence Sq, Iuka, MS 38852-1006
Phone: 662-424-2233 - **Fax:** 662-423-1410 carly_carman@yahoo.com

Types of Records Retrieved: Civil and Probate courts; Real Estate; Tax Liens/Judgments; UCC records

Local Retrieval Area: MS-Tishomingo

Add'l Information: Established 1997. Normal turnaround time- 24-48 hours. Projects billed by number of records located. First project may require prepayment. Will file/record documents for clients. They specialize in retrieval of real estate records and in performing current owner/possessory abstract of title searches. Performs service of process.

Carmona & Associates

PO Box 992600, 1726 Tehama St (96001), Redding, CA 96099
Phone: 530-246-1010 - **Fax:** 530-246-1313

Types of Records Retrieved: Criminal and Civil courts; Real Estate; Tax Liens/Judgments; UCC records; Vital records

Local Retrieval Area: CA-Shasta, Siskiyou, Tehama

Add'l Information: Established 1988. Normal turnaround time- 2-3 days. Expedited service available. Projects billed by number of names searched. Projects billed by the hour. First project may require prepayment. They specialize in insurance defense investigations. A licensed PI in CA. Performs service of process.

Carolina Investigative Research (SC)

106D Fountain Brook Circle, Cary, NC 27511
Phone: 800-328-8981; 919-460-7799 - **Fax:** 919 460 5338
www.cir-nc.com **email:** ann@cir-nc.com

Types of Records Retrieved: Criminal, Civil and Probate courts; Federal courts; Real Estate; Tax Liens/Judgments; UCC records; Vital records

Local Retrieval Area: SC-Abbeville, Anderson, Cherokee, Florence, Greenville, Greenwood, Lancaster, Laurens, Richland, Spartanburg, York. **Correspondent Relationships:** NC, SC, GA, AL, FL, TN, VA.

Add'l info: Established 1998. Turnaround time- 24-48 hours. Projects billed by number of names searched. First project may require prepayment. Credit cards accepted. Will file/record documents for clients. They specialize in public record searches including criminal, civil, federal, real estate, UCCs, pre-employment and tenant screening. A licensed PI in NC, SC.

Carolina Investigative Research Inc

106D Fountain Brook Circle, Cary, NC 27511
Phone: 800-328-8981; 919-460-7799 - **Fax:** 919-460-5338
www.cir-nc.com **email:** ann@cir-nc.com

Types of Records Retrieved: Criminal, Civil and Probate courts; Real Estate; Tax Liens/Judgments; UCC records; Vital records

Local Retrieval Area: NC-Buncombe, Chatham, Cumberland, Durham, Harnett, Hoke, Johnston, Lee, Moore, Wake. **Correspondent Relationships:** nationwide, specializing in GA, NC, SC, AL, FL, TN, VA.

Add'l Information: Established 1998. Normal turnaround time- 48 hours. Projects billed by number of names searched. First project may require prepayment. Credit cards accepted. Will file/record documents for clients. They are licensed private investigators who specialize in employment screening. They also perform all types of public record searches, including all types of real estate searches. A licensed PI in NC, SC. Performs service of process.

Terry Carpenter

4191 Stanley Valley Rd, Church Hill, TN 37642
Phone: 423-357-1125 - **Fax:** 423-357-6054 t.carpenter@juno.com

Types of Records Retrieved: Criminal and Civil courts; Tax Liens/Judgments; UCC records

Local Retrieval Area: TN-Hawkins, Sullivan, Washington

Add'l Information: Established 1996. Normal turnaround time- 24-48 hours. fees depend on the nature of the request. First project may require prepayment.

Carr Title

26433 Collosse Rd, Carrsville, VA 23315
Phone: 757-647-7873 - **Fax:** 757-569-0486 carrtitle@aol.com

Types of Records Retrieved: Real Estate; Tax Liens/Judgments

Local Retrieval Area: VA-Isle of Wight, Southampton, Surry

Add'l Information: Established 2003. Normal turnaround time- 24-48 hours depending on search. First project may require prepayment. Will file/record documents for clients. They specialize in real estate.

Carroll Abstract Co

4 W Benton St, Carrollton, MO 64633
Phone: 660-542-1364 - **Fax:** 660-542-1764

Types of Records Retrieved: Criminal, Civil and Probate courts; Real Estate; Tax Liens/Judgments

Local Retrieval Area: MO-Carroll

Add'l Information: Established 1904. First project may require prepayment. They specialize in court records and real estate.

Ruth Joane Carson

PO Box 461, Southfield, MI 48037
Phone: 888-895-3697; 248-980-4323 lunamaiden2003@yahoo.com

Types of Records Retrieved: Criminal, Civil and Probate courts; Federal courts; Real Estate; Tax Liens/Judgments; Vital records

Local Retrieval Area: MI-Macomb, Oakland, Wayne. **Correspondent Relationships:** nationwide.

Add'l Information: Established 2005. Projects billed by number of names searched. Projects billed by number of records located. She specializes in the Detroit area.

Carter Investigations

PO Box 492, Pocatello, ID 83204-0492
Phone: 208-232-3592 - **Fax:** 208-232-0444 carterpi@msn.com

Types of Records Retrieved: Criminal, Civil and Probate courts; Federal courts; Real Estate; Tax Liens/Judgments; UCC records; Vital records

Local Retrieval Area: ID-Bannock, Bingham, Bonneville, Power. **Correspondent Relationships:** Northern Idaho.

Add'l Information: Established 1988. Normal turnaround time- 24-48 hours. Projects billed by number of names searched. First project may require prepayment. Will file/record documents for clients. Payment method negotiable. They specialize in child custody, domestic work, insurance, process serving and repossessions. Performs service of process.

Case Services Inc

PO Box 2343, South Bend, IN 46680
Phone: 877-291-6868; 574-291-0480 - **Fax:** 574-291-0855
www.casepi.com **email:** casey@casepi.com

Types of Records Retrieved: Criminal, Civil and Probate courts; Federal courts; Real Estate; Tax Liens/Judgments; UCC records; Vital records

Local Retrieval Area: IN-Elkhart, La Porte, Marshall, St. Joseph; MI-Berrien, Cass. **Correspondent Relationships:** nationwide.

Add'l Information: Established 1986. Normal turnaround time- 48-hour rush service available. Projects billed by number of names searched. First project may require prepayment. Credit cards accepted. Will file/record documents for clients. They are a full service investigative agency specializing in attorney litigation investigations, and corporate background investigations, fraud investigations and security assessment. Also does pre-employment screening. A licensed PI in IN. Performs service of process.

Don W Caskey

702 N Circle, Baytown, TX 77520
Phone: 281-422-7527 - **Fax:** 281-422-1405

Types of Records Retrieved: Criminal, Civil and Probate courts; Real Estate; Tax Liens/Judgments; UCC records; Vital records

Local Retrieval Area: TX-Chambers, Liberty

Add'l info: Established 1992. Turnaround time- 24-48 hours. Projects billed by number of names searched. Will file/record documents for clients. Due upon receipt of statement. Visits courthouses daily. Includes docket book searches. Serving Chambers & Liberty counties since 1991.

Cass County Abstract Co (North Dakota)

PO Box 826, Fargo, ND 58107
Phone: 701-232-3341 - **Fax:** 701-232-7851

Records Retrieved: Real Estate; Tax Liens/Judgments; UCC records

Local Retrieval Area: MN-Clay; ND-Cass

Add'l Information: Established 1910. Normal turnaround time- 2 days. Fee basis will vary by type of search. Will file/record documents for clients. They specialize in real estate.

Cass County Abstract Co Inc (Iowa)

518 Chestnut St, Atlantic, IA 50022
Phone: 712-243-2136 - **Fax:** 712-243-4360 nancy@cassabstract.com

Types of Records Retrieved: Criminal, Civil and Probate courts; Federal courts; Real Estate; Tax Liens/Judgments; UCC records; Vital records

Local Retrieval Area: IA-Cass

Add'l Information: Established 1948. Normal turnaround time- 1-10 days. Fee basis will vary by the type of project. Will file/record documents for clients. They have a full title plant in their office back to 1800's. Huge advantage over "courthouse only" searchers.

M B Cassell

PO Box 235, Finley, ND 58230-0235
Phone: 701-524-1961 - **Fax:** 701-524-1961

Types of Records Retrieved: Civil courts; Real Estate; Tax Liens/Judgments

Local Retrieval Area: ND-Steele

Add'l Information: Established 1890. Normal turnaround time- 1-3 days. Projects billed by number of names searched. Projects billed by number of records located.

Cassia County Abstract Co

PO Box 548, Burley, ID 83318
Phone: 208-678-8347 - **Fax:** 208-678-8348 ccatitle@pmt.org

Types of Records Retrieved: Real Estate; Tax Liens/Judgments; Probate courts; UCC records **Local Retrieval Area:** ID-Cassia

Add'l Information: Established 1904. Normal turnaround time- 2 days. Projects billed by the hour. All projects require prepayment. Will file/record documents for clients. Some projects require prepayment. They specialize in title insurance and real estate closing.

Cattaraugus Abstract Corp

406 Erie St, Little Valley, NY 14755
Phone: 800-559-1242; 716-938-9109 - **Fax:** 716-938-6259
cattabs@yahoo.com

Types of Records Retrieved: Civil and Probate courts; Real Estate; Tax Liens/Judgments; UCC records **Local Retrieval Area:** NY-Cattaraugus

Add'l Information: Established 1964. Turnaround time- 48 hours. Projects billed by number of names searched. Will file/record documents for clients.

CB Research

3047 Cribbens Ave, Boise, ID 83713
Phone: 208-376-3312 - **Fax:** 208-377-3760 ccbrooks@netzero.net

Types of Records Retrieved: Criminal and Civil courts; Federal District courts; Real Estate; Tax Liens/Judgments; UCC records; Vital records

Local Retrieval Area: ID-Ada, Canyon

Add'l Information: Established 1989. Normal turnaround time- 24-48 hours. Expedited service available. Projects billed by number of names searched. Fees vary by type of search required. First project may require prepayment. Will file/record documents for clients. Monthly invoice or by prior agreement. They offer accurate searches, quick turnaround and competitive rates. They have been family owned and operated since 1989 and are continuing to strive for excellence. They also handle MVRs. A licensed PI in ID. Performs service of process.

CCB Researchers Ltd

437 Lincoln, Urbana, OH 43078
Phone: 937-653-4466 - **Fax:** 937-652-0266

Types of Records Retrieved: Criminal, Civil and Probate courts; Federal courts; Real Estate; UCC records; Tax Liens/Judgments

Local Retrieval Area: OH-Auglaize, Champaign, Clark, Darke, Delaware, Franklin, Greene, Logan, Madison, Mercer, Miami, Montgomery, Preble, Shelby, Union

Add'l Information: Established 2000. Normal turnaround time- 24-48 hours. Projects billed by number of names searched. Volume discounts available. Will file/record documents for clients. They specialize in the Columbus area eastward to the Indiana border, including cities of Dayton, Delaware, Springfield, Bellefontaine and Sidney.

Cedar Ridge Abstracts

239 Hatwood Farm Rd, Abbeville, SC 29620
Phone: 864-366-9239 - **Fax:** 864-366-2383

Types of Records Retrieved: Real Estate; Tax Liens/Judgments; Criminal and Civil courts **Local Retrieval Area:** SC-Abbeville

Add'l Information: Established 1970s. Normal turnaround time- 24-48 hours. Billing depends on records sought. First project may require prepayment. Will file/record documents for clients.

Centennial Abstract of Pratt

126 E 3rd St, Pratt, KS 67124-2710
Phone: 620-672-5928 - **Fax:** 620-672-7334

Types of Records Retrieved: Civil and Probate courts; Real Estate; Tax Liens/Judgments; UCC records

Local Retrieval Area: KS-Pratt. **Correspondent Relationships:** Barber, Kiowa, Stafford counties KS.

Add'l Information: Established 1984. Normal turnaround time- 3-5 days. Projects billed by number of names searched. First project may require prepayment. Will file/record documents for clients. They specialize in real estate records, also civil & probate court record retrieval.

Centennial Coverages Inc (Colorado)

PO Box 441433, 16748 C E Smoky Hill Rd #227, Aurora, CO 80044-1433
Phone: 800-338-8221; 303-400-3990 - **Fax:** 303-400-3322
centennial@speakeasy.net

Types of Records Retrieved: Criminal, Civil and Probate courts; Federal courts; Real Estate; Tax Liens/Judgments; UCC records; Vital records

Local Retrieval Area: CO-Adams, Arapahoe, Boulder, Denver, Douglas, El Paso, Elbert, Jefferson, Larimer. **Correspondents:** nationwide.

Add'l Information: Established 1986. Normal turnaround time- 2-10 days. Fee basis will vary with type of search. Fee is by the hour on chain-of-title searches First project may require prepayment. Will file/record documents for clients. Terms: net 10 days. They specialize in real estate searches, UCC searches, skiptracing, civil and criminal court searches, asset investigations, real estate chain-of-title, investigative background reports and nationwide UCC article 9 work.

Centennial Title & Abstract Co

G4137 Fenton Road, Burton, MI 48529
Phone: 810-238-5100 - **Fax:** 810-238-5270
www.centennialtitle.com **email:** ctac@centennialtitle.com

Types of Records Retrieved: Real Estate; Tax Liens/Judgments

Retrieval Area: MI-Genesee, Livingston, Saginaw, Shiawassee, Tuscola

Add'l Information: Established 1980. Normal turnaround time- 1-2 days. Fee basis will vary by the project. First project may require prepayment. They specialize in real estate transactions and title searches. .

Central Arkansas Title

212 S Main St, Malvern, AR 72104
Phone: 501-332-3770 - **Fax:** 501-337-0729
www.centralarkansastitle.com **email:** shodge@centralarkansastitle.com

Types of Records Retrieved: Real Estate; Tax Liens/Judgments; UCC records; Vital records **Local Retrieval Area:** AR-Hot Spring

Add'l Information: Established 1983. Normal turnaround time- 3 days. Projects billed by number of names searched. Fee basis will vary by the type of project. First project may require prepayment. Will file/record documents for clients. They specialize in real estate records.

Central Indiana Paralegal Service Inc

55 Monument Cir #422, Indianapolis, IN 46204
Phone: 317-636-1311 - **Fax:** 800-321-1600; 317-636-1426
www.cips1.com **email:** cips1@cips1.com

Types of Records Retrieved: Civil and Probate courts; Federal courts; Tax Liens/Judgments; UCC records

Local Retrieval Area: IN-Marion. **Correspondent Relationships:** Indiana.

Add'l Information: Established 1992. Normal turnaround time- 2-3 days. Projects billed by number of names searched. Will file/record documents for clients. Terms: net 30 days. They specialize in public record research and document filing & retrieval at Indiana Secretary of State and Indiana Counties, plus all federal, state, & local government offices located in Marion County. A licensed PI in IN.

Central Legal Services

PO Box 150, Bend, OR 97709-0150
Phone: 800-599-8133; 541-389-8133 - **Fax:** 541-388-5033
mlong@empnet.com

Types of Records Retrieved: Criminal, Civil and Probate courts; Real Estate; Tax Liens/Judgments; UCC records; Vital records

Local Retrieval Area: OR-Crook, Deschutes, Jefferson

Add'l Information: Established 1977. Normal turnaround time- 48 hours. Expedited service available. Projects billed by number of names searched. Will file/record documents for clients. Remit upon invoice. They will file/record UCC and real estate documents on behalf of clients on a same or next day basis in Deschutes County only. PI license# 1998022. A licensed PI in OR. Performs service of process.

Central New York Abstract Corp

PO Box 268, 24 Elizabeth St, Utica, NY 13503
Phone: 315-724-1614 - **Fax:** 315-724-0563

Types of Records Retrieved: Civil and Probate courts; Real Estate; Tax Liens/Judgments; UCC records

Local Retrieval Area: NY-Cayuga, Herkimer, Madison, Oneida

Add'l Information: Established 1904. Normal turnaround time- 1-2 days for reports; 1-2 weeks for abstracts. Projects billed by number of names searched. Projects billed by number of records located. First project may require prepayment. Will file/record documents for clients.

Central Tejas Research & Title Services

807 Brazos #607, Austin, TX 78701
Phone: 512-469-6026 - **Fax:** 512-469-6053
www.centraltejasresearch.com **email:** orders@centraltejasresearch.com

Types of Records Retrieved: Civil and Probate courts; Federal courts; Real Estate; Tax Liens/Judgments; UCC records

Local Retrieval Area: TX-Bastrop, Caldwell, Hays, Travis, Williamson

Add'l Information: Established 2004. Normal turnaround time- 24-48 hours. Projects billed by number of names searched. Payment due net 30 days. They specialize in document retrieval, document filings, probate & bankruptcy courts; historical deed chains, owner lien encumbrance reports, easements, restrictions & right of ways, Deed of Trust assignment and other real estate related research.

Central Valley Records Service Inc

2101 Ottawa Ct, Modesto, CA 95356
Phone: 209-524-3849 - **Fax:** 209-525-8786 cvrs@sbcglobal.net

Types of Records Retrieved: Criminal and Civil courts; Bankruptcy court; Tax Liens/Judgments; UCC records; Vital records

Local Retrieval Area: CA-Merced, San Joaquin, Stanislaus. **Correspondent Relationships:** Tuolumne county, CA.

Add'l Information: Established 1989. Normal turnaround time- 24 hours in Stanislaus & San Joaquin; 24-48 hours in Merced County. Projects billed by number of names searched. Will file/record documents for clients. Monthly billing available.

Central Wisconsin Title

PO Box 117, Montello, WI 53949
Phone: 608-297-2789 - **Fax:** 608-297-9387

Types of Records Retrieved: Real Estate; Tax Liens/Judgments

Local Retrieval Area: WI-Adams, Marquette

Add'l Information: Established 1993. First project may require prepayment. They specialize in real estate.

Cerro Gordo Abstract Co

305 N Federal Ave #2, Mason City, IA 50401
Phone: 641-423-1145 - **Fax:** 641-423-0289
bmoreau@cerrogordoabstract.com

Types of Records Retrieved: Criminal, Civil and Probate courts; Federal courts; Real Estate; Tax Liens/Judgments; UCC records; Vital records

Local Retrieval Area: IA-Cerro Gordo

Add'l Information: Normal turnaround time- 1-2 days. Projects billed by number of names searched. Fee basis may also be per description. Will file/record documents for clients. They specialize in real estate.

Certified Judicial Process Service & Legal Support

41 Watchung Plaza #131, Montclair, NJ 07042-4117
Phone: 877-217-3783; 973-332-4016 - **Fax:** 973-833-0251
www.certifiedjudicial.com **email:** certifiedjudicial@gmail.com

Types of Records Retrieved: Criminal, Civil and Probate courts; Federal courts; Real Estate; Tax Liens/Judgments; UCC records; Vital records

Local Retrieval Area: NJ-Bergen, Essex, Hudson, Mercer, Middlesex, Morris, Passaic, Union. **Correspondent Relationships:** nationwide.

Add'l Information: Established 1999. Normal turnaround time- 1-5 days. Projects billed by the hour. All projects require prepayment. Credit cards accepted. They specialize in pre-employment and tenant screening, process service, court filings, legal research, skiptracing, notary service and fingerprinting. A licensed PI in CO. Performs service of process.

Certified Process & Information Services

1058 W 36th Pl, Yuma, AZ 85365-4583
Phone: 928-341-0756 - **Fax:** 928-783-1230 locator@cybertrails.com

Types of Records Retrieved: Criminal, Civil and Probate courts; Federal courts; Real Estate; Tax Liens/Judgments; UCC records; Vital records

Local Retrieval Area: AZ-Yuma

Add'l Information: Established 1996. Normal turnaround time- 2-3 days. Projects billed by number of names searched. Projects billed by the hour. All projects require prepayment. They specialize in skiptracing as well as document retrieval. A licensed PI in AZ. Performs service of process.

Certified Process Service

PO Box 496508, Garland, TX 75049
Phone: 800-717-3463; 972-303-6282 - **Fax:** 972-226-6480
www.texassubpoena.com **email:** keith@texassubpoena.com

Types of Records Retrieved: Criminal, Civil and Probate courts; Federal courts; Real Estate; Tax Liens/Judgments; UCC records; Vital records

Local Retrieval Area: TX-Collin, Dallas, Tarrant. **Correspondent Relationships:** Texas.

Add'l Information: Established 1990. Normal turnaround time- 24 hours. Projects billed by the hour. All projects require prepayment. Credit cards accepted. Will file/record documents for clients. Formerly known as Texas Subpoena & Process Service, they specialize in investigations and document retrieval. A licensed PI in TX. Performs service of process.

Cestero & Co Inc

PO Box 194511, San Juan, PR 00919-4511
Phone: 866-456-6672; 787-764-7229 - **Fax:** 787-766-0881
www.puertoricoproserve.com **email:** rcestero@coqui.net

Types of Records Retrieved: Criminal and Civil courts; Federal courts; Real Estate; UCC records; Tax Liens/Judgments; Vital records

Local Retrieval Area: Puerto Rico

Add'l Information: Established 1994. Normal turnaround time- 48-72 hours. Projects billed by the hour. First project may require prepayment. Will file/record documents for clients. Mr. Reinaldo E. Cestero is a licensed private investigator who provides Asset Identification, Service of Process, Accident and Civil case investigations. He is bilingual and provides reports in English or Spanish. Document retrieval is also provided. A licensed PI in PR. Performs service of process.

Cfacts

650 Smithfield St #1850, Pittsburgh, PA 15222
Phone: 800-233-4747; 412-232-3232 - **Fax:** 800-332-2317; 412-232-0903
www.cfacts.com **email:** inquire@cfacts.com

Types of Records Retrieved: Civil and Probate courts; Federal courts; Real Estate; Tax Liens/Judgments; UCC records

Local Retrieval Area: PA-Allegheny, Beaver, Butler, Washington, Westmoreland. **Correspondent Relationships:** nationwide.

Add'l Information: Established 1984. Normal turnaround time- 48 hours. Projects are billed by the number of addresses searched. Will file/record documents for clients. Terms are 15 days. Cfacts offers a full complement of title & closing services. They emphasize single-source convenience, local resources and personalized attention. They have been in operation since 1984.

Chaffee Title and Escrow Inc

225 "G" St, Salida, CO 81201
Phone: 719-539-2215 - **Fax:** 719-539-2588 chaffeetitle@amigo.net

Records Retrieved: Real Estate; Tax Liens/Judgments; UCC records

Local Retrieval Area: CO-Chaffee

Add'l Information: Established 1968. Normal turnaround time- 3 days. Fee basis will vary by the type of project. Will file/record documents for clients. They specialize in real estate searching.

Chambers Investigations

606 49th St W, Bradenton, FL 34209
Phone: 800-792-1107; 941-798-3804 - **Fax:** 941-795-1075 slipinn@aol.com

Types of Records Retrieved: Criminal, Civil and Probate courts; Real Estate; Tax Liens/Judgments; UCC records; Vital records

Local Retrieval Area: FL-Manatee, Sarasota. **Correspondent Relationships:** nationwide.

Add'l Information: Established 1982. Turnaround time- 24 hours. Projects billed by the hour. All projects require prepayment. Credit cards accepted. MasterCard, Visa accepted. They specialize in private investigations and intelligence information such as non-public phones, cellular and hidden assets. Also civil and criminal investigations and surveillance.

Charles F Edgar & Associates Inc

2724 10th Ave SW, Huntsville, AL 35805-4136
Phone: 256-539-7761 - **Fax:** 256-539-7768 searches@cfedgar.com

Types of Records Retrieved: Criminal, Civil and Probate courts; Federal courts; Real Estate; Tax Liens/Judgments; UCC records

Local Retrieval Area: AL-22 Counties; TN-10 Counties

Add'l Information: Established 1974. Normal turnaround time- 24-48 hours. Projects billed by number of names searched. Will file/record documents for clients. Terms: net 30 days. For over 20 years this firm handles civil and criminal investigations, surveillance, background investigations, public record checks, video depositions and process services. Does only real estate, tax liens & probate in the TN counties. A licensed PI in AL. Performs service of process.

Charles Jones Inc

PO Box 8488, Trenton, NJ 08650-8488
Phone: 800-792-8888; 609-538-1000 - **Fax:** 800-883-0677; 609-883-0677
www.charlesjones.com **email:** info@charlesjones.com

Types of Records Retrieved: Civil and Probate courts; Federal courts; Real Estate; Tax Liens/Judgments; UCC records

Local Retrieval Area: NJ-Atlantic, Bergen, Burlington, Camden, Cape May, Cumberland, Essex, Gloucester, Hudson, Hunterdon, Mercer, Middlesex, Monmouth, Morris, Ocean, Passaic, Salem, Somerset, Sussex, Union, Warren. **Correspondent Relationships:** Mid-Atlantic states.

Add'l Information: Established 1911. Normal turnaround time- 1-10 days. Projects billed by number of names searched. Projects billed by number of records located. First project may require prepayment. Credit cards accepted. Will file/record documents for clients. Charles Jones Inc. has been an information services leader for over 90 years. Services include statewide lien searches and certified patriot name searches.

Charlson & Wilson Bonded Abstractors

1213 Hylton Heights Rd #121, Manhattan, KS 66502
Phone: 785-537-2900 - **Fax:** 785-537-2904
www.charlsonandwilson.com **email:** info@charlsonandwilson.com

Types of Records Retrieved: Civil and Probate courts; Real Estate; Tax Liens/Judgments; UCC records

Local Retrieval Area: KS-Riley. **Correspondent Relationships:** Pottawatomie County, KS.

Add'l Information: Established 1930. Normal turnaround time- 3-5 days. Projects billed by the hour. All projects require prepayment. Will file/record documents for clients. Specialize in any kind of title search.

Chautauqua County Abstract Co inc

121 W Main St, Sedan, KS 67361
Phone: 620-725-3215 - **Fax:** 620-725-5569

Types of Records Retrieved: Criminal, Civil and Probate courts; Real Estate; Tax Liens/Judgments; UCC records; Vital records

Local Retrieval Area: KS-Chautauqua

Add'l Information: Established 1994. Normal turnaround time- 2-3 days. Fee basis varies by type of transaction. First project may require prepayment. Will file/record documents for clients. They specialize in abstract and title searching.

Cheboygan Title

228 N Main St, Cheboygan, MI 49721
Phone: 866-627-7150; 231-627-3131 - **Fax:** 231-627-5191
www.cheboygantitle.com **email:** service@cheboygantitle.com

Types of Records Retrieved: Real Estate; Tax Liens/Judgments; UCC records; Vital records **Local Retrieval Area:** MI-Cheboygan

Add'l Information: Established 1981. Normal turnaround time- 2-5 days. Fee basis will vary by type of project. First project may require prepayment. They specialize in land title searches. They purchased the former Cheboygan Straits Area Title company in 2004.

Checkered Past Inc

PO Box 1369, Lafayette, IN 47905
Phone: 765-474-3905 - **Fax:** 765-474-3795 checkeredpastinc@hotmail.com
Types of Records Retrieved: Criminal and Civil courts; Federal District courts; Real Estate; Tax Liens/Judgments; UCC records
Local Retrieval Area: IN-Boone, Hamilton, Hendricks, Tippecanoe
Add'l Information: Established 1997. Normal turnaround time- 24-48 hours. Projects billed by number of names searched. Fees vary by type of project. They specialize in civil and criminal courts; driving records, real estate, tax liens and UCC records.

Cheri's Court Service

PO Box 56827, Riverside, CA 92517
Phone: 951-684-6499, cell- 951-233-1037 - **Fax:** 951-684-6491
cheriscourtservice@sbcglobal.net
Types of Records Retrieved: Criminal, Civil and Probate courts
Local Retrieval Area: CA-Riverside, San Bernardino
Add'l Information: Established 2002. Normal turnaround time- 24 hours unless in storage or out to court. Projects billed by number of names searched. First project may require prepayment. Will file/record documents for clients. Their company is customer friendly. They pride themselves on customer service. They try to go above and beyond their customer request for complete customer satisfaction.

Cherokee Capitol Abstract Title & Closing

107-109 E Delaware St, Tahlequah, OK 74464
Phone: 918-456-8851 - **Fax:** 918-456-8322 ccabst@swbell.com
Types of Records Retrieved: Criminal, Civil and Probate courts; Real Estate; Tax Liens/Judgments; UCC records; Vital records
Local Retrieval Area: OK-Cherokee
Add'l Information: Established 1903. Normal turnaround time- within same day of request. Projects billed by number of records located. First project may require prepayment. Will file/record documents for clients. Lenders may send loan documents via fax at 918-456-7681.

Chesapeake Services

PO Box 470, 202 Anchor Ln., Chester, MD 21619
Phone: 800-834-7938; 410-643-3731 - **Fax:** 410-643-4814
tony@friend.ly.net
Types of Records Retrieved: Criminal, Civil and Probate courts; Real Estate; Tax Liens/Judgments; UCC records; Vital records
Retrieval Area: MD-Anne Arundel, Caroline, Kent, Queen Anne's, Talbot
Add'l Information: Established 1983. Normal turnaround time- 24-48 hours. Projects billed by number of names searched. Charge by hour for research work. First project may require prepayment. Will file/record documents for clients. Payment net 30 days. They have access to a statewide Court computer system. They can communicate with accounts through Internet e-mail online with State Motor Vehicle Administrations. A licensed PI in MD. Performs service of process.

Cheyenne County Abstract

1024 Jackson St, Sidney, NE 69162
Phone: 308-254-5636 - **Fax:** 308-254-6159 cheycoabs@qwest.net
Types of Records Retrieved: Civil and Probate courts; Federal courts; Real Estate; Tax Liens/Judgments; UCC records
Local Retrieval Area: NE-Cheyenne
Add'l Information: Established 1907. Turnaround time- 3-5 days. Projects billed by number of records located. Will file/record documents for clients.

Cheyenne County Abstract Co

PO Box 9, 130 S 1st E, Cheyenne Wells, CO 80810
Phone: 719-767-5585 - **Fax:** 719-767-5029 ccabst@rebeltec.net
Types of Records Retrieved: Real Estate; Tax Liens/Judgments; Probate courts; UCC records
Local Retrieval Area: CO-Cheyenne
Add'l Information: Established 1907. Normal turnaround time- up to 1 week. Projects billed by number of names searched. Projects billed by the hour. Will file/record documents for clients. Terms: net 30 days. They specialize in real estate title.

Chicagoland Detective Services Inc

2223 W Lyndale Dr #R1, Chicago, IL 60647-3205
Phone: 877-426-4278; 312-661-0702 or 773-772-2651 - **Fax:** 312-661-0734 or 773-772-7319 www.falconpi.com **email:** falconpi@aol.com
Types of Records Retrieved: Criminal, Civil and Probate courts; Federal courts; Real Estate; Tax Liens/Judgments; UCC records; Vital records
Local Retrieval Area: IL-Cook, Du Page, Kane, Lake. **Correspondent Relationships:** nationwide.
Add'l Information: Established 1988. Normal turnaround time- 2 days. Projects billed by the hour. First project may require prepayment. Credit cards accepted. Formerly Don C Haworth & Assoc, they provide record retrievals as well as investigation services to the business, insurance, and legal communities. A licensed PI in IL. Performs service of process.

Chilvers Abstract & Title Co

PO Box 204, Pierce, NE 68767
Phone: 402-329-4525 - **Fax:** 402-329-4845
Types of Records Retrieved: Real Estate; Tax Liens/Judgments; Probate courts; UCC records **Local Retrieval Area:** NE-Pierce, Wayne
Add'l Information: Normal turnaround time- 1-3 days. Fee bases is a flat rate and per record. They specialize in title insurance.

Darlene Chiota

PO Box 1849, Erie, PA 16507-0849
Phone: 814-454-7589 - **Fax:** 814-454-7589
Types of Records Retrieved: Criminal and Civil courts; Federal courts; Real Estate; Tax Liens/Judgments; UCC records
Local Retrieval Area: PA-Erie
Add'l Information: Established 1982. Normal turnaround time- 24-48 hours. Turnaround time is up to 1 week for title searches. Projects billed by number of names searched. Projects billed by number of records located. Will file/record documents for clients. She requests prepayment for copies, but will invoice for services. She specializes in current owner searches and criminal records.

Chippewa Valley Civil Process

PO Box 188, Chippewa Falls, WI 54729
Phone: 715-289-3922; cell 715-559-3922 - **Fax:** 715-289-3922
Types of Records Retrieved: Criminal and Civil courts
Local Retrieval Area: WI-Barron, Chippewa, Dunn, Eau Claire, Rusk
Add'l Information: Established 1998. Normal turnaround time- 2-5 business days. First project may require prepayment. Will file/record documents for clients. They provide service of process, court filing and skiptracing services. They also provide most other law firm support services. Please call them for prices. Performs service of process.

Choctaw County Abstract & Title

PO Box 636, Hugo, OK 74743
Phone: 580-326-9616 - **Fax:** 580-326-6782
Types of Records Retrieved: Civil and Probate courts; Real Estate; Tax Liens/Judgments; UCC records
Local Retrieval Area: OK-Choctaw
Add'l Information: Established 1978. Normal turnaround time- 1 week. Fee basis will vary by the type of project. First project may require prepayment. Will file/record documents for clients. Clients may make payments upon receipt.

Chouteau County Abstract Co

Box 578, Fort Benton, MT 59442
Phone: 406-622-3221 - **Fax:** 406-622-3221 ccac@mtintouch.net
Types of Records Retrieved: Civil and Probate courts; Real Estate; Tax Liens/Judgments **Local Retrieval Area:** MT-Chouteau
Add'l Info: Normal turnaround time- 2-4 days. Projects billed by the hour.

Chreyton Research

10811 Tanglewood Trail, Concord Township, OH 44077
Phone: 440-354-0316 - **Fax:** 440-354-2677
chretyonresearch@yahoo.com

Types of Records Retrieved: Criminal, Civil and Probate courts; Federal courts; Real Estate; Tax Liens/Judgments; UCC records; Vital records

Local Retrieval Area: OH-Geauga, Lake

Add'l Information: Established 2004. Normal turnaround time- 24 hours or less. Expedited service available. Projects billed by number of names searched. Will invoice, payment due net 30 days.

CIBMS

600 Saw Mill Rd, PO Box 26775, West Haven, CT 06516-0966
Phone: 800-922-0002; 203-931-2000 - **Fax:** 203-931-2075
www.cibms.com **email:** asimeone@cbct.com

Types of Records Retrieved: Real Estate; Tax Liens/Judgments

Local Retrieval Area: CT-Fairfield, Hartford, Litchfield, Middlesex, New Haven, New London, Tolland, Windham

Add'l Information: Established 1929. Normal turnaround time- 3 business days. Payable upon receipt. First project may require prepayment. Will file/record documents for clients. Payment by check accepted. They are a major supplier of title searches, appraisals, document recording and retrieval, flood certification, credit reporting and collection services to the financial industry. For info, add extension #248 to phone number.

Citizen's Title Co

115 N Spring St, Searcy, AR 72143
Phone: 501-268-5571 - **Fax:** 501-268-7378

Types of Records Retrieved: Criminal, Civil and Probate courts; Real Estate; Tax Liens/Judgments; UCC records

Local Retrieval Area: AR-White

Add'l Information: Established 1963. Normal turnaround time- up to 1 week. Fee basis will vary by type of project. First project may require prepayment. Will file/record documents for clients. They specialize in land title and title insurance.

City Abstract

PO Box 257, Scottsbluff, NE 69363
Phone: 308-632-4021 - **Fax:** 308-635-2896

Types of Records Retrieved: Real Estate; Tax Liens/Judgments

Local Retrieval Area: NE-Banner, Scotts Bluff

Add'l Information: Established 1984. First project may require prepayment. They specialize in real estate.

CIV, Inc

7512 Dr Phillips Blvd #50, Orlando, FL 32819
Phone: 407-352-4188, 407-433-1612 civ@cfl.rr.com

Types of Records Retrieved: Criminal, Civil and Probate courts; Federal courts; Real Estate; Tax Liens/Judgments; UCC records; Vital records

Local Retrieval Area: FL-Lake, Orange, Osceola, Seminole. **Correspondent Relationships:** statewide.

Add'l Information: Established 1993. Normal turnaround time- 48 hours. Projects billed by number of names searched. Projects billed by number of records located. Volume discounts. First project may require prepayment. They specialize in record search and retrieval services throughout Florida.

Civil Claims Service

PO Box 33898, Juneau, AK 99803
Phone: 907-364-2714 tshanley@gci.net

Types of Records Retrieved: Criminal, Civil and Probate courts; Federal courts; Real Estate; Tax Liens/Judgments; UCC records; Vital records

Local Retrieval Area: AK-Haines, Juneau, Ketchikan Gateway, Sitka, Skagway-Hoonah-Angoon, Wrangell-Petersburg

Add'l Information: Established 1982. Normal turnaround time- 24-48 hours. Expedited service available. The billing method is dependant on nature of the job. They specialize in civil process service, investigations, and repossessions. A licensed PI in AK. Performs service of process.

Clarifacts Inc

130 N Central Ave #309, Phoenix, AZ 85004
Phone: 800-318-0553; 602-258-8858 - **Fax:** 602-258-7177
www.clarifacts.com **email:** kevin@clarifacts.com

Types of Records Retrieved: Criminal courts

Local Retrieval Area: AZ-Maricopa

Add'l Information: Established 2001. Normal turnaround time- 24-48 hours. Projects billed by number of names searched. Monthly billings. Professional, reliable researchers located just blocks from the courthouse of the nation's 4th most-populated county. A licensed PI in AZ.

Clark Abstract & Title Co

PO Box 253, Clark, SD 57225
Phone: 605-532-3812 - **Fax:** 605-532-3812

Types of Records Retrieved: Real Estate; Tax Liens/Judgments; Probate courts; UCC records; Vital records

Local Retrieval Area: SD-Clark

Add'l Information: Established 1980. Normal turnaround time- 2-3 days. Fee basis varies by type of transaction. Will file/record documents for clients. Payment due on delivery. Abstracts of title, title insurance and title reports are our main business.

Clark County Abstract & Title Co Inc

310 Clay St, Arkadelphia, AR 71923
Phone: 870-246-2821 - **Fax:** 870-246-9501

Types of Records Retrieved: Criminal, Civil and Probate courts; Real Estate; Tax Liens/Judgments; UCC records

Local Retrieval Area: AR-Clark

Add'l Information: Established 1907. Normal turnaround time- 3 days. Expedited service available. Fee basis will vary by type of project. First project may require prepayment. Will file/record documents for clients.

Clarke Investigations Inc

1405 Ridgecrest Rd, Edmond, OK 73013
Phone: 405-844-7300 - **Fax:** 405-844-8196
clarkeinvestigations@hotmail.com

Types of Records Retrieved: Criminal, Civil and Probate courts; Federal courts; Real Estate; Tax Liens/Judgments; UCC records; Vital records

Local Retrieval Area: OK-Bryan, Caddo, Canadian, Carter, Cherokee, Cleveland, Comanche, Creek, Custer, Delaware, Dewey, Ellis, Garfield, Garvin, Grady, Greer, Harmon, Harper, Jackson, Jackson, Kay, Kingfisher, Kiowa, Lincoln, Logan, Mayes, McClain, Muskogee, Noble, Oklahoma, Okmulgee, Payne, Roger Mills, Rogers, Texas, Tillman, Tulsa, Wagoner, Washington, Woodward. **Correspondent Relationships:** statewide.

Add'l Information: Established 1996. Normal turnaround time- 24-48 hours. Projects billed by number of names searched. Will file/record documents for clients. Will invoice monthly. They specialize in aircraft ownership and pilot licensing nationwide and also do Oklahoma DMV histories and license plate registrations. They also do work for abstractors. Daily, hands-on service to all Oklahoma counties. A licensed PI in OK. Performs service of process.

Brad Clarkson

169 N Meridian Rd, Glen Carbon, IL 62034
Phone: 618-288-7599 - **Fax:** 618-288-7599
http://clarksondiversified.com **email:** clarkson@clarksondiversified.com

Types of Records Retrieved: Criminal, Civil and Probate courts; Federal courts; Real Estate; Tax Liens/Judgments; UCC records; Vital records

Local Retrieval Area: IL-Madison, St. Clair; MO-St. Charles, St. Louis, St. Louis City. **Correspondent Relationships:** Sangamon, Macon, Shelby counties, IL.

Add'l Information: Established 1993. Normal turnaround time- 1-3 days, depending on court. Expedited service available. Projects billed by number of names searched. First project may require prepayment. He specializes in civil and criminal courts, Eastern Missouri & Southern Illinois Federal courts, real estate, tax liens, UCC records and probate.

Clay County Abstract Co

403 Center Ave #600, Moorhead, MN 56560-1975
Phone: 218-233-1358 - **Fax:** 218-233-1359

Types of Records Retrieved: Civil and Probate courts; Federal courts; Real Estate; Tax Liens/Judgments; UCC records

Local Retrieval Area: MN-Clay; ND-Cass. **Correspondent Relationships:** Becker, Otter Tail, Norman, Polk, Red Lake, Wilkin, Mahnomen, Marshall, Kittson, Roseau counties.

Add'l Information: Established 1832. Normal turnaround time- 5-10 days. Projects billed by number of names searched. Personal checks are accepted. They are across the river from Fargo, North Dakota. Performs service of process.

Clay County Title

121 W Kidder St #104, Vermillion, SD 57069-3085
Phone: 605-624-2068 - **Fax:** 605-624-9640

Types of Records Retrieved: Real Estate; Tax Liens/Judgments

Local Retrieval Area: SD-Clay

Add'l Information: First project may require prepayment. They specialize in real estate.

Clayton County Abstract Co

126 S Main, Elkader, IA 52043
Phone: 563-245-1430 - **Fax:** 563-245-1490
abstract@alpinecom.net

Types of Records Retrieved: Criminal, Civil and Probate courts; Real Estate; Tax Liens/Judgments; UCC records; Vital records

Local Retrieval Area: IA-Clayton

Add'l Information: Established 1878. Normal turnaround time- 24-48 hours. Fee basis will vary by the type of project. Will file/record documents for clients.

Clayton Title Services Inc

PO Box 327, 8 Main St, Clayton, NM 88415
Phone: 505-374-9789 - **Fax:** 505-374-8381

Types of Records Retrieved: Civil and Probate courts; Real Estate; Tax Liens/Judgments; UCC records; Vital records

Local Retrieval Area: NM-Union

Add'l Information: Established 1978. Normal turnaround time- 5-10 days. Fee basis will vary by the type of project. First project may require prepayment. They specialize in abstracts, title insurance, closings, oil and gas searches, mineral searches.

Clear Creek-Gelpin Abstract & Title Corp

PO Box 545, 619 5th St, Georgetown, CO 80444
Phone: 303-569-2391 - **Fax:** 303-569-2670
www.ccgat.com **email:** rjonas@ccgat.com

Types of Records Retrieved: Real Estate

Local Retrieval Area: CO-Clear Creek, Gilpin

Add'l Information: Established 1966. Normal turnaround time- 3-5 days. Fee basis will vary by the type of project. First project may require prepayment. Will file/record documents for clients. They specialize in real estate and title matters.

Clear Title Co

140 S Washington St, La Grange, TX 78945-2629
Phone: 979-968-5885 - **Fax:** 979-968-6082
www.cleartitlecompany.com **email:** cleartitle@cmaaccess.com

Types of Records Retrieved: Criminal, Civil and Probate courts; Real Estate; Tax Liens/Judgments; UCC records; Vital records

Local Retrieval Area: TX-Fayette

Add'l Information: Normal turnaround time- up to 1 week as court is not computerized. Fee basis will vary by the type of project. First project may require prepayment. Will file/record documents for clients.

Clear Title Search Inc

39 Busbin Ln, Colbert, GA 30628
Phone: 706-340-6278 - **Fax:** 706-742-5508

Types of Records Retrieved: Real Estate; Civil and Probate courts; Tax Liens/Judgments

Local Retrieval Area: GA-Oconee, Oglethorpe

Add'l Information: Established 1981. Normal turnaround time- 24-48 hours. Search fee depends on scope of the search. First project may require prepayment. Will file/record documents for clients. They specialize in commercial as well as residential real estate. Experts in their area.

Cleveland & Carl Inv

PO Box 5358, Central Point, OR 97502-0054
Phone: 800-888-6629; 541-535-6005 gcwrightjr@aol.com

Types of Records Retrieved: Criminal, Civil and Probate courts; Federal courts; Real Estate; Tax Liens/Judgments; UCC records; Vital records

Local Retrieval Area: CA-Siskiyou; OR-Jackson, Josephine, Klamath, Lane, Polk. **Correspondent Relationships:** statewide and California.

Add'l Information: Established 1983. Normal turnaround time- up to 3 days. Expedited service available. Projects billed by number of names searched. Projects billed by the hour. First project may require prepayment. Will bill for established clients. A licensed PI in OR, CA. Performs service of process.

Clinton Abstract Co Inc

519 Gary Blvd, Clinton, OK 73601
Phone: 580-323-3025 - **Fax:** 580-323-0524

Types of Records Retrieved: Civil and Probate courts; Real Estate; Tax Liens/Judgments; UCC records

Local Retrieval Area: OK-Custer

Add'l Information: Established 1941. Normal turnaround time- 2 days. Copy charges will be added to the fee. Will file/record documents for clients. Personal checks are accepted. They are a licensed abstractor in Custer County.

Clovis Title & Abstract Ltd

420 Mitchell St, Clovis, NM 88101
Phone: 505-762-4403 - **Fax:** 505-762-4404

Types of Records Retrieved: Criminal, Civil and Probate courts; Federal courts; Real Estate; Tax Liens/Judgments; UCC records

Local Retrieval Area: NM-Curry

Add'l Information: Established 1908. Normal turnaround time- 24 hours to 2 days. Projects billed by number of names searched. Will file/record documents for clients. Personal checks are accepted. They specialize in title searches, abstracts of title, title insurance, lien searches and criminal searches. They also do loan closing on new loans or refinances. They also search for financing statements in Curry County, NM.

CLUSO Inc

PO Box 227503, Dallas, TX 75222-7503
Phone: 866-30-CLUSO; 214-999-1140 - **Fax:** 214-853-4423
www.cluso.com **email:** sales@cluso.com

Types of Records Retrieved: Criminal and Civil courts

Local Retrieval Area: TX-Dallas. **Correspondents:** nationwide.

Add'l Information: Established 1999. Normal turnaround time- 24-hours. First project may require prepayment. CLUSO Inc provides courthouse research for the Dallas/Ft. Worth area every day. They also offer national and international background services, including pre-employment and tenant screening.

CMT Abstract

380 Catherine St, Somerville, NJ 08876
Phone: 908-722-6565 - **Fax:** 908-722-5011 staff@cmtabstract.com

Types of Records Retrieved: Real Estate; Tax Liens/Judgments; Probate courts; UCC records **Local Retrieval Area:** NJ-Somerset

Add'l Information: Established 1986. Normal turnaround time- 24 hours. Fee basis will vary by type of project. Will file/record documents for clients. They perform title, judgments, and UCC searches, and property searches at the county level.

CN Search LLC

239 Baileyville Rd, Middlefield, CT 06455
Phone: 860-349-3772 - **Fax:** 860-349-8581 cnsearchct@comcast.net

Types of Records Retrieved: Criminal and Civil courts; Federal courts; Real Estate; Tax Liens/Judgments; UCC records

Local Retrieval Area: CT-Fairfield, Hartford, Litchfield, Middlesex, New Haven, New London, Tolland, Windham. **Correspondent Relationships:** nationwide and Canada.

Add'l Information: Established 1986. Normal turnaround time- 24 hours for courts; other times vary with jurisdiction. Projects billed by number of names searched. First project may require prepayment. Payment due upon receipt of invoice. Perform UCC, corporate searches and record retrievals. Visits Sec of State daily. Will search courts statewide. Performs UCC, tax lien and current owner searches at CT towns.

Coast to Coast Abstracting

1529 Chepacket St, Brandon, FL 33511-1831
Phone: 813-748-3699 - **Fax:** 727-499-7536 abstractor@tampabay.rr.com

Types of Records Retrieved: Real Estate; Tax Liens/Judgments; Probate courts; UCC records

Local Retrieval Area: FL-Citrus, Hernando, Hillsborough, Lee, Manatee, Pasco, Pinellas, Polk, Sarasota, Sumter

Add'l Information: Established 2004. Normal turnaround time- 24-48 hours. Billed according to search or services ordered. Will invoice. They specialize in document retrieval & recordings; also bringdowns, current owner & full searches. They have 6 years experience.

Coast to Coast Research Network

PO Box 268, 7 Poplar Circle, Center Barnstead, NH 03225
Phone: 603-776-5985 - **Fax:** 603-776-5986 ctcrn@aol.com

Types of Records Retrieved: Criminal, Civil and Probate courts; Federal courts; Real Estate; Tax Liens/Judgments; UCC records; Vital records

Local Retrieval Area: NH-all counties

Add'l Information: Established 1987. Normal turnaround time- 24-72 hours. Projects billed by number of names searched. Will file/record documents for clients. Terms are net 30 days. They specialize in UCC, corporate searches, property title updates on current owner, tax liens, voter registration and real estate assessment records found in towns and cities, also criminal and civil searches in all courts.

Coastal Office Dimensions

PO Box 744, Pensacola, FL 32591-0744
Phone: 850-637-1058 - **Fax:** 877-866-0687 CoastalSGL@aol.com

Types of Records Retrieved: Criminal, Civil and Probate courts; Federal courts; Real Estate; Tax Liens/Judgments; UCC records; Vital records

Local Retrieval Area: FL-Escambia, Monroe, Santa Rosa

Add'l Information: Established 1995. Normal turnaround time- 24-48 hours. Projects billed by number of names searched. Projects billed by number of records located. First project may require prepayment. They specialize in pre-employment searches, including felony and misdemeanor, federal criminal and federal civil. They also provide document retrieval and fillings in Escambia & Santa Rosa Counties.

Coastal Research

PO Box 7343, Arroyo Grande, CA 93421
Phone: 805-710-4926 - **Fax:** 805-473-1431 coastalresearch1@aol.com

Types of Records Retrieved: Criminal and Civil courts; Real Estate; Tax Liens/Judgments

Local Retrieval Area: CA-Kern, Riverside, San Bernardino, San Diego, San Luis Obispo, Santa Barbara, Ventura. **Correspondents:** statewide.

Add'l Information: Established 2004. Normal turnaround time- 24-48 hours. Projects billed by number of names searched. First project may require prepayment. Credit cards accepted. They personally go to courthouses daily

Coit Enterprises

2560 Newport Ave #A, Omaha, NE 68112-3326
Phone: 402-451-0462 - **Fax:** 402-451-3949
www.coitenterprises.com **email:** terry@terrycoit.com

Types of Records Retrieved: Criminal, Civil and Probate courts; Federal courts; Real Estate; Tax Liens/Judgments

Local Retrieval Area: IA-Mills, Pottawattamie; NE-Dodge, Douglas, Sarpy, Washington

Add'l Information: Established 1994. Normal turnaround time- next day for Douglas, Pottawattamie, and Sarpy counties; 2-7 business days for others counties. Projects billed by number of names searched. Also may charge by jurisdiction. Will file/record documents for clients. Will bill monthly. Professional, personalized service provided by the owners. Not all services and retrievals listed are available in all counties.

Coke County Abstract Co

PO Box 69, 3 E 6th St, Robert Lee, TX 76945
Phone: 325-453-2049 - **Fax:** 325-453-2345

Types of Records Retrieved: Criminal, Civil and Probate courts; Real Estate; Tax Liens/Judgments; UCC records; Vital records

Local Retrieval Area: TX-Coke

Add'l Information: Established 1938. Normal turnaround time- 1-2 days. Fee basis will vary by the type of project. First project may require prepayment. Will file/record documents for clients.

Coleman County Title Co

PO Box 865, 108 W Liveoak St, Coleman, TX 76834-0865
Phone: 325-625-4628 - **Fax:** 325-625-4417

Types of Records Retrieved: Real Estate; Tax Liens/Judgments; Probate courts; UCC records **Local Retrieval Area:** TX-Coleman

Add'l Information: Normal turnaround time- up to 5 days. Projects billed by the hour. First project may require prepayment. Will file/record documents for clients.

Colfax County Title & Abstract Co

1109 C St, Schuyler, NE 68661
Phone: 402-352-2027 - **Fax:** 402-352-2027

Types of Records Retrieved: Civil and Probate courts; Real Estate; Tax Liens/Judgments

Local Retrieval Area: NE-Butler, Colfax. **Correspondents:** nationwide.

Add'l Information: Established 1988. Normal turnaround time- 2 days. Projects billed by number of names searched. Will file/record documents for clients. Personal checks are accepted.

Collective Intelligence Inc

14622 Ventura Blvd #419, Sherman Oaks, CA 91403
Phone: 800-436-1969; 818-788-7015 - **Fax:** 818-788-1220
www.collintel.com **email:** erika@collintel.com

Types of Records Retrieved: Criminal, Civil and Probate courts; Federal courts; Vital records

Local Retrieval Area: CA-Los Angeles, Orange, Riverside, San Bernardino, San Diego, San Luis Obispo, Santa Barbara, Ventura. **Correspondent Relationships:** statewide.

Add'l Information: Established 2001. Normal turnaround time- 24-48 hours. Projects billed by number of names searched. Projects billed by the hour. Credit cards accepted. A private investigation/research company providing on-site record search & retrieval. They offer expedient & accurate results with services available at the county, state & federal levels. Prices vary by area & service. A licensed PI in CA. Performs service of process.

Collier Abstracts Inc

107 N Main St, Smith Center, KS 66967-0254
Phone: 785-282-3351 - **Fax:** 785-282-6998

Types of Records Retrieved: Civil and Probate courts; Real Estate; Tax Liens/Judgments; UCC records

Local Retrieval Area: KS-Smith

Add'l Information: Established 1930. Normal turnaround time- up to 1 week. Fee basis varies by type of transaction. Will file/record documents for clients. They request prepayment from out of state clients, but will invoice established customers.

Collier Connections

309 Co Rd 530, Jackson, MO 63755
Phone: 573-576-3035 - **Fax:** 573-833-6166
Records Retrieved: Real Estate; Tax Liens/Judgments; UCC records
Local Retrieval Area: MO-Bollinger, Cape Girardeau, Perry, Scott, St. Francois, Ste. Genevieve, Stoddard
Add'l Information: Established 2000. Normal turnaround time- 24-48 hours. Projects billed by number of names searched. Will file/record documents for clients. They invoice 2 weeks to 30 day net. The principal of the company has worked 10 years at the Cape Girardeau County Recorder's Office. She is very skilled in land records & retrieval services.

Traci Collins

715 S Cleveland, Colby, KS 67704 **Phone:** 785-672-2719
Types of Records Retrieved: Criminal and Civil courts
Local Retrieval Area: KS-Thomas. **Correspondent Relationships:** Logan, McPherson, Saline, KS
Add'l Information: Established 2006. Turnaround time- 24 hours. Projects billed by number of names searched. First project may require prepayment.

Colonial Valley Abstract Co

216 E Market St, York, PA 17403
Phone: 717-848-2871 - **Fax:** 717-845-6161 cva@blazenet.net
Records Retrieved: Real Estate; Tax Liens/Judgments; UCC records
Local Retrieval Area: PA-Adams, Franklin, Lancaster, York
Add'l Information: Normal turnaround time- 5 days. Fee basis will vary by the type of project. First project may require prepayment. They specialize in real estate.

Colorado County Abstract Co

PO Box 428, 315 Walnut St, Columbus, TX 78934
Phone: 979-732-2213 - **Fax:** 979-732-6096 joan.ewabst@sbcglobal.net
Records Retrieved: Real Estate; Tax Liens/Judgments; UCC records
Local Retrieval Area: TX-Colorado
Add'l Information: Normal turnaround time- 2-3 days. Fee basis will vary by the type of project. First project may require prepayment. Will file/record documents for clients.

Colorado Records Search Inc

2223 S Raleigh St, Denver, CO 80219
Phone: 800-645-7712; 303-797-6831 - **Fax:** 800-988-2303; 303-797-8329
colorecord@msn.com
Types of Records Retrieved: Criminal, Civil and Probate courts; Federal courts; Real Estate; Tax Liens/Judgments; UCC records; Vital records
Local Retrieval Area: CO-Adams, Arapahoe, Archuleta, Baca, Boulder, Broomfield, Cheyenne, Clear Creek, Delta, Denver, Douglas, Eagle, El Paso, Elbert, Fremont, Garfield, Gilpin, Gunnison, Jefferson, La Plata, Larimer, Las Animas, Mesa, Montezuma, Montrose, Morgan, Ouray, Park, Pitkin, Pueblo, Rio Grande, Routt, San Miguel, Teller, Weld. **Correspondent Relationships:** statewide and elsewhere.
Add'l Information: Established 1986. Normal turnaround time- 24-48 hours. Projects billed by number of names searched. They specialize in public record retrieval, service of process, UCC tax liens/judgments, corporate filing and is a registered agent. Performs service of process.

Colorado Records Sooner

3210 Huron Peak Ave, Superior, CO 80027
Phone: 303-494-2132 - **Fax:** 303-494-2133 sooner93@aol.com
Types of Records Retrieved: Civil courts; Real Estate, Tax Liens/Judgments; UCC records
Local Retrieval Area: CO-Adams, Arapahoe, Boulder, Broomfield, Denver, Douglas, El Paso, Grand, Jefferson, Larimer, Weld
Add'l Information: Established 1993. Normal turnaround time- 24 hours or less. Projects billed by number of names searched. First project may require prepayment. They specialize in limited title/O&E reports, document retrieval and recordings with or without date.

Colton & Associates Inc

PO Box 15433, Clearwater, FL 33766-5433
Phone: 800-704-6699; 727-789-0485 - **Fax:** 727-734-8413
www.intelligencesource.com **email:** gregg@intelligencesource.com
Types of Records Retrieved: Criminal, Civil and Probate courts; Federal courts; Real Estate; Tax Liens/Judgments; UCC records; Vital records
Local Retrieval Area: FL-Hillsborough, Pasco, Pinellas. **Correspondent Relationships:** nationwide for criminal and civil records only.
Add'l Information: Established 1988. Normal turnaround time- 2 business days. Projects billed by number of names searched. First project may require prepayment. Will file/record documents for clients. Terms: net 10 days. They specialize in statewide criminal histories for CO, FL and TX as well as loss prevention, claims investigations, employment screening, process service, and business intelligence. A licensed PI in FL. Performs service of process.

Comanche Abstract & Title Co

PO Box 41, 120 E Main, Coldwater, KS 67029
Phone: 620-582-2125 - **Fax:** 620-582-2125
Types of Records Retrieved: Criminal, Civil and Probate courts; Real Estate; Tax Liens/Judgments; UCC records
Local Retrieval Area: KS-Comanche
Add'l Information: Established 1950. Normal turnaround time- 7-10 days. Projects billed by number of names searched. Projects billed by number of records located. Personal checks are accepted. They specialize in title searches, ownership, mineral interest, leasehold, oil and gas searches, and certificates of title and abstracts.

Comanche County Abstract Co

PO Box 747, 106 N Austin St, Comanche, TX 76442
Phone: 325-356-2564 - **Fax:** 325-356-3066
Types of Records Retrieved: Criminal, Civil and Probate courts; Real Estate; Tax Liens/Judgments; UCC records; Vital records
Local Retrieval Area: TX-Comanche
Add'l Information: Normal turnaround time- 2-5 days. Fee basis will vary by type of project. First project may require prepayment. Will file/record documents for clients.

Commercial Process Serving Inc

674 County Sq Dr #107, Ventura, CA 93003
Phone: 800-382-0088; 805-650-9291 - **Fax:** 805-658-8170
www.comproserve.net **Types of Records Retrieved:** Criminal, Civil and Probate courts
Local Retrieval Area: CA-Santa Barbara, Ventura. **Correspondent Relationships:** Los Angeles, Orange, Santa Barbara, San Bernardino, Riverside, San Diego counties.
Add'l Information: Established 1992. Normal turnaround time- varied, depending on project. Projects billed by the hour. First project may require prepayment. Personal checks accepted. They specialize in court filings, fax filings, process serving and deposition interpreting (English/Spanish). They also offer reprographics, digital scanning, subpoena preparation, deposition officer assignment. Performs service of process.

Commonwealth Investigative Agency

137 N 5th St #2, Allentown, PA 18102-4151
Phone: 610-433-2325 - **Fax:** 610-821-8627
www.commonwealthdetectives.com **email:** ja0071944@aol.com
Types of Records Retrieved: Criminal, Civil and Probate courts; Federal courts; Real Estate; Tax Liens/Judgments; UCC records; Vital records
Local Retrieval Area: PA-Berks, Bucks, Lehigh, Luzerne, Northampton
Add'l Information: Normal turnaround time- 1-3 days. Projects billed by the hour. First project may require prepayment. They are a full service private investigations firm. A licensed PI in PA.

Community Title Co

302 N University Dr, Nacogdoches, TX 75961
Phone: 936-559-7900 - **Fax:** 936-559-7977 www.communitytitle.com

Types of Records Retrieved: Criminal, Civil and Probate courts; Real Estate; Tax Liens/Judgments; UCC records; Vital records

Local Retrieval Area: TX-Angelina, Nacogdoches. **Correspondent Relationships:** San Augustine and Sabine counties.

Add'l Information: Normal turnaround time- up to 1 week. Projects billed by the hour. First project may require prepayment. Payment due upon receipt of bill. Formerly East Texas Title & Abstract Co. Now has a branch office in Lufkin, 936-634-1600.

Comparable Sales Research

7 N Cascade #C, Montrose, CO 81401
Phone: 970-249-2118 - **Fax:** 970-249-6482 lynnv@montrose.net

Records Retrieved: Real Estate; Tax Liens/Judgments; UCC records

Local Retrieval Area: CO-Delta, Montrose, Ouray. **Correspondent Relationships:** Gunnison county CO.

Add'l Information: Established 1991. Normal turnaround time- 24 to 36 hours. Projects billed by number of records located. First project may require prepayment. Will file/record documents for clients. They have available a comprehensive comparable sales database. They can tailor a commercial, single family or vacant comparable report for you for the 3 counties they serve. Several types of reports & statistical reports are available. Call for info.

Compass Investigations

10 S New River Dr East, Ft Lauderdale, FL 33301
Phone: 954-527-5722 - **Fax:** 954-527-4451
www.compassinvestigations.net **email:** sheri@compassinvestigations.net

Types of Records Retrieved: Criminal, Civil and Probate courts; Federal courts; Real Estate; Tax Liens/Judgments; UCC records; Vital records

Local Retrieval Area: FL-Broward, Dade, Palm Beach. **Correspondent Relationships:** Florida.

Add'l Information: Established 1986. Normal turnaround time- same day. Projects billed by number of names searched. Projects billed by the hour. First project may require prepayment. Will file/record documents for clients. They specialize in record research, surveillance and process service. Their office is located next to the courthouse. A licensed PI in FL. Performs service of process.

Compex Legal Services

2040 North Loop W #200, Houston, TX 77018-8113
Phone: 713-861-3900 - **Fax:** 713-864-0439
www.compexlegal.com **email:** cservice@compexlegal.com

Types of Records Retrieved: Criminal, Civil and Probate courts; Federal courts; Vital records

Local Retrieval Area: TX-Fort Bend, Galveston, Harris, Jefferson, Montgomery. **Correspondent Relationships:** Bexar, Cameron, Dallas, Hidalgo, Jefferson, Tarrant.

Add'l Information: Established 1974. Normal turnaround time- 2-3 days. Projects billed by number of records located. Projects billed by the hour. All projects require prepayment. Formerly MRS Datascope Inc, they specialize in record retrieval for pretrial discovery, complete litigation support services, court reporters and legal video. They also do business and medical searches. Performs service of process.

Complete Corporate Services of Alaska

PO Box 33735, 4009 Diane Rd, Juneau, AK 99803
Phone: 907-790-4956 - **Fax:** 907-790-4954 sharon2@gci.net

Types of Records Retrieved: Criminal, Civil and Probate courts; Federal courts; Real Estate; Tax Liens/Judgments; UCC records

Local Retrieval Area: AK-Anchorage, Haines, Juneau, Ketchikan Gateway, Prince of Wales-Outer Ketchikan, Sitka, Skagway-Hoonah-Angoon, Wrangell-Petersburg Boroughs. **Correspondent Relationships:** Alaska.

Add'l Information: Established 1991. Normal turnaround time- same day for most records. Fee basis will vary by the type of project. All projects require prepayment. Will file/record documents for clients. They also will accept personal checks. Located in the capitol city, they specialize in searches at the State level also at UCC central. Does searches and recording of corporate records. They also provide service to Southern Alaska. Current owner searches a specialty. Performs service of process.

Compu-Fact Research Inc

4 Silkrose Ct, St Peters, MO 63376-7769
Phone: 636-477-1115, 618-239-0677 - **Fax:** 636-477-1115
compufact@hotmail.com

Types of Records Retrieved: Criminal, Civil and Probate courts; Real Estate; Tax Liens/Judgments; UCC records

Local Retrieval Area: IL-Madison, St. Clair; MO-Greene. **Correspondent Relationships:** IL-Cook, Kankakee, Madison, Sangamon; MO-St. Louis; NE-Dawes, Douglas, Lancaster.

Add'l Information: Established 1994. Normal turnaround time- 1-2 days. Projects billed by number of names searched. First project may require prepayment. They specialize in public record retrieval.

Concord Commercial Services

5213 Streamwood Ln, Plano, TX 75093
Phone: 972-931-7431 - **Fax:** 267-295-8632 mrude@sbcglobal.net

Types of Records Retrieved: Real Estate

Local Retrieval Area: IL-Cook; TX-Collin, Dallas. **Correspondent Relationships:** nationwide.

Add'l Information: Established 1994. Normal turnaround time- 24-48 hours. Projects billed by number of names searched.

Concord Search & Retrieval Inc

10 Ferry St #427C, Concord, NH 03301
Phone: 877-273-1119; 603-856-0087 - **Fax:** 877-647-5734; 603-856-0099
www.concordsearch.net **email:** greg@concordsearch.net

Types of Records Retrieved: Civil and Probate courts; Federal courts; Real Estate; Tax Liens/judgment; UCC records; Vital records

Local Retrieval Area: NH-Belknap, Cheshire, Coos, Hillsborough, Merrimack, Rockingham, Strafford, Sullivan. **Correspondent Relationships:** nationwide.

Add'l Information: Established 2002. Normal turnaround time- 24-48 hours. Projects billed by number of names searched. Will file/record documents for clients. Will invoice. They provide fast reliable UCC, tax lien, litigation and real property searches in New Hampshire.

Condello Associates, Accusearch

5082 E Hampden Ave #157, Denver, CO 80222
Phone: 888-756-9687; 303-756-9687 - **Fax:** 303-758-5486
www.coloradoinvestigations.com **email:** acusearch9@aol.com

Types of Records Retrieved: Criminal, Civil and Probate courts; Federal courts; Real Estate; Tax Liens/Judgments; UCC records; Vital records

Local Retrieval Area: CO-Adams, Arapahoe, Boulder, Broomfield, Denver, Jefferson, Larimer, Weld. **Correspondent Relationships:** statewide.

Add'l Information: Established 1978. Normal turnaround time- 48 hours. Expedited service available. Projects billed by number of names searched. First project may require prepayment. Credit cards accepted. Will file/record documents for clients. Payment terms are net 30 days. They specialize in locating individuals, process service, court record research/retrieval and general investigation for the legal community and general public nationwide. In business since 1978. A licensed PI in CO. Performs service of process.

Condor Inv

PO Box 181293, 317 Peoples St #400, Corpus Christi, TX 78480-1293
Phone: 361-881-8977 - **Fax:** 361-884-1658

Types of Records Retrieved: Criminal, Civil and Probate courts; Federal courts; Real Estate; Tax Liens/Judgments; UCC records; Vital records

Local Retrieval Area: TX-Aransas, Bee, Brooks, Calhoun, Duval, Jim Wells, Kleberg, Nueces, Refugio, San Patricio, Victoria, Webb. **Correspondent Relationships:** Nueces, San Patricio, Aransas, Jim Wells, Duval, Kleberg.

Add'l Information: Established 1987. Normal turnaround time- 24-48 hours. Projects billed by the hour. First project may require prepayment. Credit cards accepted. They specialize in service of civil process. They also have investigators available for background, surveillance, statements and skiptracing. A licensed PI in TX. Performs service of process.

Confi-Chek

1821 Q St, Sacramento, CA 95814
Phone: 800-821-7404; 916-443-4822 - **Fax:** 800-758-5859; 916-443-7420
www.confi-chek.com **Types of Records Retrieved:** Criminal, Civil and Probate courts; Federal courts; Real Estate; Tax Liens/Judgments; UCC records; Vital records
Local Retrieval Area: CA-Sacramento. **Correspondent Relationships:** via national online data.
Add'l Information: Established 1987. Normal turnaround time- same day if online. Projects billed by number of names searched. First project may require prepayment. Credit cards accepted. They specialize in online services and people locator information. They also do National credit header titles and judgments. A licensed PI in CA.

Confidential Background Services

1344 Westminster Place, Birmingham, AL 35235
Phone: 205-447-1539 - **Fax:** 205-853-4535
Types of Records Retrieved: Criminal, Civil and Probate courts; Federal courts; Real Estate; Tax Liens/Judgments; UCC records; Vital records
Local Retrieval Area: AL-Jefferson, Shelby, St Clair. **Correspondent Relationships:** statewide in criminal, traffic, civil.
Add'l Information: Established 1986. Normal turnaround time- 24 hours. Projects billed by number of names searched. First project may require prepayment. Will file/record documents for clients. They specialize in law enforcement background, state licensed. Also pre-law degree. Do pre-employment screening. All inquiries kept strictly confidential. Authorized to get state criminal record searches covering a 10 year period. A licensed PI in AL. Performs service of process.

Confidential Investigations

5531 Memorial Rd, Allentown, PA 18104
Phone: 800-969-4827; 610-821-9112 - **Fax:** 610-366-0529
www.confidentialinv.com **email:** worldwideci@aol.com
Types of Records Retrieved: Criminal and Civil courts; Federal courts; Real Estate; Tax Liens/Judgments; UCC records; Vital records
Local Retrieval Area: PA-Berks, Carbon, Lehigh, Monroe, Northampton. **Correspondent Relationships:** nationwide.
Add'l Information: Established 1988. Normal turnaround time- 24 hours. Projects billed by the hour. First project may require prepayment. Invoice net 30 days. They specialize in commercial crime, theft fraud, workers' compensation and background checks. A licensed PI in PA & NJ. Performs service of process.

Confidential Services

1156 Alum Creek Dr, Columbus, OH 43209-2715
Phone: 800-752-4581; 614-552-4646 - **Fax:** 614-252-5359
Types of Records Retrieved: Criminal, Civil and Probate courts; Federal courts; Real Estate; Tax Liens/Judgments; UCC records; Vital records
Local Retrieval Area: OH-Athens, Clermont, Cuyahoga, Delaware, Franklin, Hamilton, Lucas, Medina; WV-Ohio. **Correspondents:** nationwide.
Add'l Information: Established 1988. Normal turnaround time- 24-72 hours. Projects billed by number of names searched. Projects billed by number of records located. Projects billed by the hour. First project may require prepayment. Credit cards accepted. They specialize in unsolved criminal cases, child custody/endangerment, skiptracing, locate services and complete asset protection throughout Ohio. They are the largest full service agency in Ohio. They also do process service nationwide. A licensed PI in OH. Performs service of process.

Sherry Conley

225 Simpson Ridge Rd, Wiliamstown, KY 41097
Phone: 859-824-6001, Fax- same
Types of Records Retrieved: Criminal and Civil courts
Local Retrieval Area: KY-Boone, Campbell, Fayette, Grant, Kenton, Owen, Pendleton, Scott
Add'l Information: Established 2001. Normal turnaround time- 24-48 hours. Projects billed by number of names searched. First project may require prepayment. She is an expert in the county courts in the Lexington-Frankfort-Covington triangle.

Connecticut Investigative Services

4 Research Dr #402, Shelton, CT 06484
Phone: 888-676-1472; 203-402-7306 - **Fax:** 203-732-3592
www.ctinvestigativeservices.com
email: contact@ctinvestigativeservices.com
Types of Records Retrieved: Criminal, Civil and Probate courts; Federal courts; Real Estate; Tax Liens/Judgments; UCC records; Vital records
Local Retrieval Area: CT-Fairfield, New Haven
Add'l Information: Established 2005. Normal turnaround time- 24 hours. Projects billed by number of records located. First project may require prepayment. Credit cards accepted. Connecticut Investigative Services and our investigators can provide law firms, insurance companies, large and small corporations, private agencies and citizens with professional investigative services. A licensed PI in CT.

Jeanetta, Conner

1765 Beckham Rd, Smith Grove, KY 42171
Phone: 270-746-4465 - **Fax:** 270-563-4112
Types of Records Retrieved: Real Estate; Tax Liens/Judgments
Local Retrieval Area: KY-Barren, Metcalfe, Warren
Add'l Information: Established 1997. First project may require prepayment. She specializes in real estate.

Consolidated Abstract Co

PO Box 569, Aspermont, TX 79502
Phone: 940-989-3566 - **Fax:** 940-989-2032
Types of Records Retrieved: Real Estate; Tax Liens/Judgments; Probate courts; UCC records; Vital records
Local Retrieval Area: TX-Stonewall
Add'l Information: Normal turnaround time- 1-2 days. Fee basis will vary by the type of project. First project may require prepayment.

Contemporary Information Corp

42913 Capital Dr #101, Lancaster, CA 93535
Phone: 800-754-0009; 661-284-2731 - **Fax:** 800-677-8494; 661-284-2737
www.continfo.com **email:** wbower@continfo.com
Types of Records Retrieved: Criminal and Civil courts; US District court; Tax Liens/Judgments
Local Retrieval Area: AZ-Maricopa, Pinal; CA-Alameda, Contra Costa, Imperial, Kern, Los Angeles, Monterey, Orange, Riverside, Sacramento, San Benito, San Bernardino, San Diego, San Francisco, San Mateo, Santa Barbara, Santa Clara, Santa Cruz, Ventura. **Correspondent Relationships:** AZ, CA, NM, NV, OR, WA.
Add'l Information: Established 1986. Normal turnaround time- 24-48 hours. Projects billed by number of names searched. Credit cards accepted. CIC has the largest eviction db on west coast, reaching to 47 states.

Contemporary Realty Solutions Inc

1056 W Jericho Turnpike, Smithtown, NY 11787
Phone: 631-979-5677 - **Fax:** 631-979-1042
www.contemporaryrealty.com **email:** jgirardi@contemporaryrealty.com
Records Retrieved: Real Estate; Tax Liens/Judgments; UCC records
Local Retrieval Area: NY-Nassau, Suffolk. **Correspondent Relationships:** nationwide.
Add'l Information: Established 1999. Normal turnaround time- 2-3 days. Projects billed by number of names searched. Will file/record documents for clients. Terms are net 30 days.

Nina N Cooper

620 Fulmar Dr, Suisun City, CA 94585
Phone: 707-758-6165 - **Fax:** 707-428-5712
ninacooper_research@comcast.net
Types of Records Retrieved: Criminal, Civil and Probate courts; Tax Liens/Judgments; Vital records
Local Retrieval Area: CA-Butte, Napa, Nevada, Sacramento, Sierra, Solano, Sutter, Yolo, Yuba. **Correspondent Relationships:** Alameda, Contra Costa, Butte, Nevada, Sacramento, Sutter, Yolo, Yuba, CA counties.

Add'l Information: Established 1999. Normal turnaround time- 24-48 hours. Projects billed by number of names searched. Payment terms are net 30 days. They specialize in criminal, civil and probate records. County recorder records inclusive of vital records, tax liens, UCC and voter registration, serving above counties in CA. Offering personalized service for reliability, accuracy and expediency.

Copper Range Abstract & Title Agency

707 Shelden Ave, Houghton, MI 49931
Phone: 906-482-7903 - **Fax:** 906-482-7977
www.copperrangetitle.com **email:** crat@chartermi.net

Types of Records Retrieved: Real Estate; Tax Liens/Judgments; Probate courts; Federal courts; UCC records; Vital records

Local Area: MI-Baraga, Houghton, Iron, Keweenaw, Marquette, Ontonagon

Add'l Information: Established 1976. Normal turnaround time- 2 days. Fee basis will vary by type of project. Will file/record documents for clients. They specialize in real estate, sale and loan closings, title insurance and searches and construction loan disbursing.

Corley Research

1642 N Lake Dr, Lexington, SC 29072
Phone: 803-331-3309 - **Fax:** 803-358-6594
www.corleyresearch.com **email:** tara@corleyresearch.com

Types of Records Retrieved: Criminal and Civil courts

Local Retrieval Area: SC-Anderson, Beaufort, Charleston, Florence, Greenville, Lexington, Pickens, Richland, Sumter, York. **Correspondent Relationships:** Darlington, Marlboro, Dillon, Chester, Marion, Jasper and Lee counties, SC

Add'l Information: Established 2004. Normal turnaround time- 24 hours. Projects billed by number of names searched. All projects require prepayment. Corley research is a courthouse researcher specializing in county criminal records.

Christy Corley

7740 Rogers Rd East, Pine Bluff, AR 71603
Phone: cell- 870-672-2957, 870-357-8714; fax-same

Types of Records Retrieved: Criminal and Civil courts; Bankruptcy court; Real Estate; Tax Liens/Judgments; Vital records

Local Retrieval Area: AR-Arkansas, Bradley, Cleveland, Drew, Grant, Jefferson, Lincoln

Add'l Info: Established 1999. Turnaround time- 24-48 hours. Projects billed by number of names searched. She specializes in real estate retrieval; in addition to county courthouse, she can access municipal records.

Cornell Abstract Co

1811 Hill Ave, Spirit Lake, IA 51360
Phone: 712-336-3845 - **Fax:** 712-336-1402
www.cornellabstract.com **email:** info@cornellabstract.com

Types of Records Retrieved: Real Estate; Tax Liens/Judgments; Probate courts; UCC records

Local Retrieval Area: IA-Dickinson

Add'l Information: Established 1947. Normal turnaround time- variable depending on project. They try to turn abstracts in 24-48 hours. Fee basis will vary by the type of project. Will file/record documents for clients. They specialize in real estate and closings.

Cornerstone Title Research

22109 Senna Hills Dr, San Antonio, TX 78266
Phone: 210-354-7102 - **Fax:** 305-704-3866 ctr@satx.rr.com

Types of Records Retrieved: Criminal, Civil and Probate courts; Real Estate; Tax Liens/Judgments; UCC records; Vital records

Local Retrieval Area: TX-Bexar, Comal. **Correspondent Relationships:** Atascosa, Bandera, Bastrop, Brazoria, Caldwell, Callahan, Cameron, Cooke, Frio, Guadalupe, Hays, Hidalgo, Jones, Kendall, Lubbock, Hockley, Medina, Real, Starr, Taylor, Throckmorton, Travis, Uvalde, Willacy, Williamson, Wilson counties in TX.

Add'l Information: Established 1996. Normal turnaround time- 1-2 days. Projects billed by number of names searched. Projects billed by the hour. First project may require prepayment. Will file/record documents for clients. They specialize in quality, affordable abstracting and public records retrieval and they support the survey industry with deed research and 50-year chains of title.

CorpAmerica Inc - Corp. Service Co

30 Old Rudnick Ln, Dover, DE 19901
Phone: 888-736-4300; 302-736-4300 - **Fax:** 302-736-5620

Types of Records Retrieved: Criminal and Civil courts; Real Estate; Tax Liens/Judgments; UCC records

Local Retrieval Area: DE-Kent, New Castle, Sussex. **Correspondent Relationships:** nationwide.

Add'l Information: Established 1989. Normal turnaround time- 1-2 days depending upon state systems time frame. Projects billed by number of names searched. First project may require prepayment. Credit cards accepted. Will file/record documents for clients. Credit cards are subject to 5% rush fee. They specialize in forming corporations and providing registered agent service in all states and in retrieving SOS records. Complete UCC and public records services for Delaware, including MVR records. Now part of Lexis-Nexis Document Solutions.

CorpAssist Inc - DC Office

1090 Vermont Ave NW #910, Washington, DC 20005
Phone: 800-438-2996; 202-371-8090 - **Fax:** 202-371-1945
www.corpassist.com **email:** corpdc@aol.com

Types of Records Retrieved: Criminal, Civil and Probate courts; Federal courts; Real Estate; Tax Liens/Judgments; UCC records; Vital records

Local Retrieval Area: DC-District of Columbia; MD-Montgomery, Prince George's; VA-Alexandria City, Arlington, Fairfax, Fairfax City, Loudoun, Manassas City, Prince William. **Correspondent Relationships:** nationwide (National Registered Agents, Inc).

Add'l Information: Established 1992. Normal turnaround time- 24-48 hours. Projects billed by number of names searched. Projects billed by the hour. First project may require prepayment. Will file/record documents for clients. Terms: net 15 days for service companies. They provide research services at all federal agencies and courts in addition to the traditional UCCs, tax liens, judgments, real estate, judgments, etc. They also search corporate records. Also provide Registered Agent services worldwide.

CorpAssist Inc - Baltimore

836 Park Ave #B 2nd Fl, Baltimore, MD 21201
Phone: 800-536-9778; 410-225-2995 - **Fax:** 410-225-2996
www.corpassist.com **email:** kerry@corpassist.com

Types of Records Retrieved: Criminal and Civil courts; Federal courts; Real Estate; Tax Liens/Judgments; UCC records

Local Retrieval Area: MD-Anne Arundel, Baltimore, Baltimore City, Howard. **Correspondent Relationships:** nationwide (National Registered Agents, Inc).

Add'l Information: Established 1992. Normal turnaround time- 24-72 hours. Projects billed by number of names searched. Projects billed by number of records located. Net 15 days. First project may require prepayment. Credit cards accepted. Will file/record documents for clients. They provide research at the Federal level, state level and listed county level. They specialize in registered agent services on a nationwide basis. They are affiliated with National Registered Agents Inc. They do not do commercial real estate research.

Corporate Access Inc

236 E 6th Ave, Tallahassee, FL 32303
Phone: 800-969-1666; 850-222-2666 - **Fax:** 850-222-1666
www.user.talstar.com/cai/ **email:** cai@talstar.com

Types of Records Retrieved: Criminal, Civil and Probate courts; Federal courts; Real Estate; Tax Liens/Judgments; UCC records; Vital records

Local Retrieval Area: FL-Bay, Calhoun, Franklin, Gadsden, Gulf, Jefferson, Leon, Liberty, Wakulla; GA-Thomas. **Correspondents:** nationwide.

Add'l Information: Established 1994. Normal turnaround time- 24-48 hours. Projects billed by number of names searched. First project may require prepayment. Credit cards accepted. Will file/record documents for clients. Corporate Access will file and retrieve anything that is publicly available. Performs service of process.

Corporate Research Solutions Inc

2900 Bristol St #D201, Costa Mesa, CA 92626
Phone: 800-486-0757; - **Fax:** 800-486-0859
www.crslink.com **email:** sprewitt@crslink.com

Types of Records Retrieved: Criminal and Civil courts; Federal courts; Real Estate; Tax Liens/Judgments; UCC records; Vital records

Local Retrieval Area: CA-Los Angeles, Orange. **Correspondent Relationships:** nationwide.

Add'l Information: Established 2002. Normal turnaround time- 24 hours. Expedited service available. Projects billed by number of names searched. Will invoice after completion of project. They are a full service company providing public record research, filing services and document retrievals. They provide personalized and consistent service.

Corporate Screening Services

16530 Commerce Ct, Cleveland, OH 44130
Phone: 800-229-8606; 440-816-0500 - **Fax:** 440-243-4204
www.corporate-screening.com **email:** tfeher@corporatescreening.com

Types of Records Retrieved: Criminal, Civil and Probate courts; Federal courts; UCC records

Local Retrieval Area: OH-Cuyahoga, Lake, Lorain, Medina. **Correspondent Relationships:** nationwide.

Add'l Information: Established 1987. Normal turnaround time- 24-72 hours. Projects billed by number of names searched. Credit cards accepted. Bill monthly. They specialize in screening of UCC and court records in the Cleveland area. A licensed PI in OH.

Corpus Christi Court Services

4228 FM 1069, Aransas Pass, TX 78336
Phone: 361-815-8202 - **Fax:** 361-758-0177
sgage@cccsvcs.com

Types of Records Retrieved: Criminal, Civil and Probate courts; Federal courts; Real Estate; Tax Liens/Judgments; UCC records

Local Retrieval Area: TX-Aransas, Bee, Duval, Goliad, Jim Wells, Kleberg, Live Oaks, Nueces, Refugio, San Patricio. **Correspondent Relationships:** most Texas counties and nationwide.

Add'l Information: Established 1986. Normal turnaround time- 36 hours or less. 2-hour expedited service available. Projects billed by number of names searched. Projects billed by the hour. First project may require prepayment. Will file/record documents for clients. They specialize in personalized and professional processing of your document filing, retrieval and research requests. They are locally owned and operated for 17 years.

Thomas E Corsi

52 Edna Pl, Buffalo, NY 14218-1326
Phone: 716-863-7797 - **Fax:** 716-828-1620 tcorsi@msn.com

Types of Records Retrieved: Real Estate

Local Retrieval Area: NY-Genesee, Cattaraugus, Chautauqua, Erie, Livingston, Niagara, Orleans, Wyoming. **Correspondent Relationships:** Steuben county.

Add'l Information: Established 1996. Normal turnaround time- 24-48 hours. Projects billed by number of names searched. Will file/record documents for clients. Will invoice. Terms, net 30 days. Specializes in current owner/last owner/property reports and institutional lender/two-owner searches. Forte is quick turnaround time.

Teresa L Coty

722 Florence Ave, Ft Wayne, IN 46808
Phone: 260-420-1015 - **Fax:** 260-420-1432 tlcoty@yahoo.com

Types of Records Retrieved: Criminal Courts

Local Retrieval Area: IN-Allen.

Add'l Information: Established 2001. Normal turnaround time- 24-48 hours. Projects billed by number of names searched. Specializes in felony and misdemeanor searches.

Cottonwood County Abstract Company

900 3rd Ave, PO Box 336 (56101-0336), Windom, MN 56101
Phone: 507-831-1504 - **Fax:** 507-831-3675

Types of Records Retrieved: Real Estate; Tax Liens/Judgments

Local Retrieval Area: MN-Cottonwood

Add'l Information: Established 1965. Normal turnaround time- variable depending on project. Expedited service available for add'l charge. Projects billed by number of names searched. Projects billed by number of records located. All projects require prepayment. Personal checks are accepted. They specialize in abstracting, name searches, judgment searches, tax and bankruptcy searches.

Couch Title and Abstract

119 N Jennings Ave, Anthony, KS 67003
Phone: 620-842-5512, Fax- same

Types of Records Retrieved: Criminal and Civil courts; Real Estate; Tax Liens/Judgments **Local Retrieval Area:** KS-Harper

Add'l Information: Normal turnaround time- 24-48 hours. Billing depends on nature of the request. First project may require prepayment. Will file/record documents for clients. They specialize in Harper County which is on the Oklahoma border south of Wichita.

Countryside Paralegal Services

13 Depot Street Extension, Hyde Park, VT 05655
Phone: 802-888-2150 - **Fax:** 802-888-2183
jmcountryside@pshift.com

Types of Records Retrieved: Criminal, Civil and Probate courts; Federal courts; Real Estate; Tax Liens/Judgments; UCC records; Vital records

Local Retrieval Area: VT-Caledonia, Essex, Franklin, Lamoille, Orleans. **Correspondent Relationships:** statewide.

Add'l Information: Normal turnaround time- 48-72 hours. Projects billed by number of names searched. Projects billed by the hour. First project may require prepayment. Will file/record documents for clients.

County Court Retrievers Inc

4970 Sparks Ave, San Diego, CA 92110-1361
Phone: 909-307-0814
www.countyretrievers.com **email:** rlowe@countyretrievers.com

Types of Records Retrieved: Real Estate

Local Retrieval Area: CA-San Diego.

Add'l Information: Established 1997. First project may require prepayment. They specialize in the retrieval & recording of real estate information & documents, including current owner searches & title policies. With more that 25 years of combined experience in the mortgage industry they are able to provide up-to-the minute info.

County Courthouse Retrieval

PO Box 532288, Indianapolis, IN 46253 **Phone:** 765-485-0233

Types of Records Retrieved: Criminal, Civil and Probate courts; Bankruptcy court; Real Estate; Tax Liens/Judgments; UCC records

Local Retrieval Area: IN-Benton, Boone, Clinton, Hendricks, Montgomery, Tippecanoe

Add'l Information: Established 2002. Normal turnaround time- 1-2 business days. Projects billed by number of names searched. First project may require prepayment. Payment due 30 days net for existing clients. Call first for fax number, NO UNSOLICTED FAXES. Specializing in document retrieval and real estate searches: current owner, full title searches and foreclosures at the county level. Ask about discounted rates for bulk orders.

County House Research Inc

42 S 15th St #1200, Philadelphia, PA 19102-2212
Phone: 866-594-1177; 215-717-7433 - **Fax:** 866-872-7610; 215-717-7437
www.countyhouseresearch.com **email:** info@countyhouseresearch.com

Types of Records Retrieved: Criminal and Civil courts; Federal courts; Tax Liens/Judgments

Local Retrieval Area: NJ-Camden; PA-Philadelphia. **Correspondent Relationships:** All counties in Delaware, D.C., Maine, Massachusetts, New Jersey, Pennsylvania.

Add'l Information: Established 1996. Normal turnaround time- 24-48 hours. Most counties searched daily. Projects billed by number of names searched. First project may require prepayment. Credit cards accepted. Payments due net 30 days. They specialize in same day searches, using the Flexible Research System technology and with the abilities of "FRS Connect" can provide access to CT, DC, DE, GA, MA, ME, NC, NH, NJ, PA, SC. Fully staffed office. Federal courts for PA districts.

County Wide Abstract & Title Co Inc

PO Box 98, (4 S Elm St), Dexter, MO 63841
Phone: 573-624-2436 - **Fax:** 573-624-5376 countywd@midwest.net

Types of Records Retrieved: Real Estate; Tax Liens/Judgments; Probate courts; UCC records

Local Retrieval Area: MO-Stoddard

Add'l Information: Established 1972. Normal turnaround time- 2 days. Projects billed by number of records located. First project may require prepayment. Will file/record documents for clients. Serving Stoddard county since 1972.

Countywide Research Services

30111 Carmel Bay Ct, Georgetown, TX 78628
Phone: 512-922-1676 - **Fax:** 512-869-8185 ramona.batts@verizon.net

Types of Records Retrieved: Criminal, Civil and Probate courts; Federal courts; Real Estate; Tax Liens/Judgments; UCC records; Vital records

Local Retrieval Area: TX-Bell, Bexar, Burnet, Travis, Williamson

Add'l Information: Established 1997. Normal turnaround time- 24-48 hours. Expedited service available. Projects billed by number of names searched. First project may require prepayment. Will file/record documents for clients. They specialize in current property searches & lien searches, 50 year chain or title searches, preforeclosure title searches, STLs, FTLs, AJs, UCCs, criminal & civil litigation and asset searches. They offer notary. A licensed PI in TX. Performs service of process.

Court Data Research Services

PO Box 1184, Tulsa, OK 74101
Phone: 918-745-2231 - **Fax:** 918-745-2234 jphager1@sbcglobal.net

Types of Records Retrieved: Criminal, Civil and Probate courts; Federal courts; Real Estate; Tax Liens/Judgments; UCC records

Local Retrieval Area: OK-Rogers, Tulsa. They also offer criminal and real estate searches in Creek county. **Correspondent Relationships:** Oklahoma.

Add'l Information: Established 1981. Normal turnaround time- 24 hours. Projects billed by number of names searched. Projects billed by the hour. Flat rate available per court also. Hands on court work and copy (document) retrieval. First project may require prepayment. Will file/record documents for clients. Payment due upon receipt of invoice. They specialize in court searches, title, criminal, bankruptcy searches and federal/USDC searches.

Court Data Search

6 Sycamore Way, Mt Arlington, NJ 07856
Phone: 973-770-1170 - **Fax:** 973-770-1170

Types of Records Retrieved: Criminal and Civil courts

Local Retrieval Area: NJ-Bergen, Essex, Hudson, Middlesex, Monmouth, Morris, Passaic, Somerset, Sussex, Union

Add'l Information: Established 1987. Normal turnaround time- 48 hours. Projects billed by number of names searched. They specialize in criminal and civil judgment checks.

Court Explorers Inc

111 John Street, #645, New York, NY 10038
Phone: 212-608-1585 - **Fax:** 212-608-1586
www.courtexplorers.com **email:** tcollins@courtexplorers.com

Types of Records Retrieved: Criminal, Civil and Probate courts; Federal courts; Real Estate; Tax Liens/Judgments; UCC records; Vital records

Local Retrieval Area: NY-Bronx, Dutchess, Kings, Nassau, New York, Orange, Queens, Richmond, Suffolk, Westchester. **Correspondent Relationships:** nationwide.

Add'l Information: Established 1995. Normal turnaround time- 1-3 days. Projects billed by number of names searched. First project may require prepayment. Credit cards accepted. Will file/record documents for clients. They specialize in all public record searches. Performs service of process.

Court Record Consultants

11024 Balboa Blvd PMB 128, Granada Hills, CA 91344-5007
Phone: 818-366-1906 - **Fax:** 818-366-1985
www.crconsultants.net **email:** cbucknam@crconsultants.net

Types of Records Retrieved: Criminal, Civil and Probate courts; Federal courts; Real Estate; Tax Liens/Judgments; UCC records; Vital records

Local Retrieval Area: CA-Alameda, Contra, Costa, Fresno, Kern, Los Angeles, Marin, Monterey, Orange, Riverside, Sacramento, San Benito, San Bernardino, San Diego, San Francisco, San Luis Obispo, Santa Barbara, Santa Clara, Stanislaus, Ventura. **Correspondents:** statewide.

Add'l Information: Established 1985. Normal turnaround time- 1-3 days. Projects billed by number of names searched. Projects billed by the hour. First project may require prepayment. Credit cards accepted. Will file/record documents for clients. They specialize in pre-employment screening, private investigation and real estate research. A licensed PI in CA. Performs service of process.

Court Record Research Inc

405 Main St #550, Houston, TX 77002-1876
Phone: 800-552-3353; 713-227-3353 - **Fax:** 888-395-8055; 713-236-1970
https://www.courtrecords.com **email:** angela@courtrecords.com

Types of Records Retrieved: Criminal, Civil and Probate courts; Federal courts; Real Estate; Tax Liens/Judgments; UCC records; Vital records

Local Retrieval Area: TX-Brazoria, Fort Bend, Galveston, Harris, Montgomery. **Correspondent Relationships:** Austin, Brazos, Chambers, Colorado, Grimes, Madison, Polk, San Jacinto, Walker, Waller, Wharton and Washington counties, TX.

Add'l Information: Established 1974. Normal turnaround time- 1-3 days. Harris county same day service available. Expedited service available. Projects billed by the hour. Will also work on retainer. First project may require prepayment. Credit cards accepted. Will file/record documents for clients. They do public record document retrieval and provide searches in all public databases. A licensed PI in TX. Performs service of process.

Court Services of Iowa Inc

980 NE 134th Ave, Alleman, IA 50007
Phone: 515-965-5722 - **Fax:** 515-965-5674 kroberts@prairieinet.net

Types of Records Retrieved: Civil courts; Real Estate; Tax Liens/Judgments; UCC records

Local Retrieval Area: IA-all counties. **Correspondents:** statewide.

Add'l Information: Established 2002. Normal turnaround time- 24-48 hours. Expedited service available. Projects billed by number of names searched. They invoice per search completed. They have been business since 2002, and have 2 full-time and 3 part-time searchers on staff. Rush orders accepted at no extra charge.

CourtCheckers

315 W Los Olivos St #8, Santa Barbara, CA 93105
Phone: 805-898-7084 - **Fax:** 805-898-7094 courtcheckers@cox.net

Types of Records Retrieved: Criminal, Civil and Probate courts; Bankruptcy court; Real Estate; Tax Liens/Judgments; UCC records; Vital records

Local Retrieval Area: CA-San Luis Obispo, Santa Barbara, Ventura

Add'l Information: Established 1994. Normal turnaround time- 24 hours. Will file/record documents for clients. Monthly billing. They specialize in 24-hour turnaround, accurate and professional filing as well as research and information retrieval. Performs service of process.

Courtesy Title

PO Box 493, Jamestown, KY 42629
Phone: 270-343-4486 - **Fax:** 270-343-4487

Types of Records Retrieved: Real Estate; Tax Liens/Judgments

Local Retrieval Area: KY-Russell

Add'l Information: Established 2000. First project may require prepayment. They specialize in real estate.

Courthouse Abstractors

PO Box 1172, Cumming, GA 30028

Phone: 770-271-9002 - **Fax:** 877-726-8950 cortabs@charter.net

Types of Records Retrieved: Civil courts; Federal courts; Real Estate; Tax Liens/Judgments; UCC records

Local Retrieval Area: GA-Barrow, Bartow, Cherokee, Clayton, Cobb, Dawson, De Kalb, Douglas, Forsyth, Fulton, Gordon, Gwinnett, Hall, Lumpkin, Whitfield

Add'l Information: Established 1997. Normal turnaround time- 24-48 hours. Projects billed by number of names searched. Will file/record documents for clients. They specialize in servicing surrounding metro Atlanta counties and North Georgia.

Courthouse Concepts Inc

16 W Center, Fayetteville, AR 72701

Phone: 877-750-3660; 479-582-3660 - **Fax:** 877-750-7379; 479-582-3662

www.courthouseconcepts.com **Types of Records Retrieved:** Criminal, Civil and Probate courts; Federal courts; Real Estate; Tax Liens/Judgments; UCC records; Vital records

Local Retrieval Area: AR-Benton, Carroll, Conway, Crawford, Faulkner, Franklin, Johnson, Madison, Pope, Pulaski, Sebastian, Washington. **Correspondent Relationships:** nationwide.

Add'l Information: Established 2000. Normal turnaround time- 24 hours. Projects billed by number of names searched. Will invoice monthly. They specialize in information retrieval to include current owner, document retrieval, criminal, civil and application screening.

Courthouse Filings Inc

544 Shenondoah Pk, Conroe, TX 77302

Phone: 936-273-6427 - **Fax:** 936-273-2067

www.courthousefilings.com **email:** orders@courthousefilings.com

Types of Records Retrieved: Criminal, Civil and Probate courts; Real Estate; Tax Liens/Judgments; UCC records; Vital records

Local Retrieval Area: TX-Montgomery

Add'l Information: Established 2001. Normal turnaround time- 24 hours. All orders received by noon are processed that day. Projects billed by number of records located. A family owned business specializing in providing owner research and document retrieval on a 24 hours turnaround basis in Montgomery County, Texas.

Courthouse Specialists

9800 Northwest Fwy, Ste 400, Houston, TX 77092

Phone: 800-925-4225; 713-683-0491 - **Fax:** 713-683-0493

www.courth.com **email:** orders@courth.com

Types of Records Retrieved: Criminal, Civil and Probate courts; Bankruptcy court; Real Estate; Tax Liens/Judgments; UCC records

Local Retrieval Area: TX-Brazoria, Chambers, Collin, Dallas, Denton, Fort Bend, Galveston, Harris, Liberty, Montgomery, San Jacinto, Tarrant, Walker, Waller. **Correspondent Relationships:** nationwide.

Add'l Information: Established 1982. Normal turnaround time- 24-48 hours. Projects billed by number of names searched. Projects billed by the hour. First project may require prepayment. Credit cards accepted. Will file/record documents for clients. They specialize in chain of title, ownership searches, lien searches, 50-year environmental searches, expert testimony and educational instruction with proprietary databases.

CourthouseData

3608 N Steele Blvd #140, Fayetteville, AR 72703

Phone: 479-582-0900 - **Fax:** 479-582-5869

www.courthousedata.com **email:** order@courthousedata.com

Types of Records Retrieved: Criminal, Civil and Probate courts; Federal courts; Real Estate; Tax Liens/Judgments; UCC records

Local Retrieval Area: AR-Benton, Boone, Carroll, Clark, Cleburne, Conway, Crawford, Faulkner, Franklin, Garland, Grant, Hot Spring, Jefferson, Johnson, Logan, Lonoke, Madison, Montgomery, Newton, Perry, Polk, Pope, Pulaski, Saline, Scott, Sebastian, Van Buren, Washington, White, Yell. **Correspondent Relationships:** statewide.

Add'l Information: Established 2001. Normal turnaround time- same day or within 48 hours. Projects billed by number of names searched. Projects billed by number of records located. Agreement required for a title plant subscription. First project may require prepayment. Credit cards accepted. All major credit cards and all orders can be placed online and delivered online. CourthouseData is a real estate information services company, a Division of Data Trace, that has imaged and indexed over 5 million public records. They provide fast, accurate public record and title research throughout Arkansas.

Coyne Search Service Inc

5911 Bristol Emilie Rd, Levittown, PA 19057-2605

Phone: 215-547-1853 - **Fax:** 215-547-1855

coynesearch@comcast.net

Types of Records Retrieved: Criminal, Civil and Probate courts; Federal courts; Real Estate; Tax Liens/Judgments; UCC records; Vital records

Local Retrieval Area: NJ-Burlington, Camden, Mercer; PA-Bucks, Chester, Delaware, Montgomery, Philadelphia

Add'l Information: Established 1984. Normal turnaround time- 24-48 hours. They charge per name and per index. Will file/record documents for clients. Monthly billing can be arranged for certain services. Billed upon completion. They retrieve records from the US Coast Guard-Philadelphia, Federal Records Center and the New Jersey Superior Court Record Center.

Coyote

17890 Fantail Cir, Reno, NV 89506

Phone: 775-972-6530 - **Fax:** 775-972-6683 cltvcoyote@aol.com

Types of Records Retrieved: Federal courts; Real Estate; Tax Liens/Judgments; UCC records

Local Retrieval Area: NV-Carson City, Storey, Washoe

Add'l Information: Established 1998. Normal turnaround time- 24 hours. Projects billed by number of names searched. All projects require prepayment. Will file/record documents for clients. Monthly billing is available for established clients. She will also do notary loan signings. Will travel beyond her coverage area if needed for signings, with pre-agreement.

CPS (Capitol Process Service)

PO Box 1323, Georgetown, TX 78627

Phone: 800-856-0216; 512-930-7378 - **Fax:** 512-863-7477

austincps@cox-internet.com

Types of Records Retrieved: Criminal, Civil and Probate courts; Federal courts; Real Estate; Tax Liens/Judgments; UCC records; Vital records

Local Retrieval Area: TX-Travis, Williamson. **Correspondent Relationships:** nationwide.

Add'l Information: Established 1988. Normal turnaround time- 24 hours. Fees are charged by case. Performs service of process.

Crawford County Abstract Co (Iowa)

PO Box 277, 1317 Broadway, Denison, IA 51442

Phone: 712-263-5626 - **Fax:** 712-263-8773

Types of Records Retrieved: Criminal, Civil and Probate courts; Real Estate; Tax Liens/Judgments; UCC records; Vital records

Local Retrieval Area: IA-Crawford

Add'l Information: Established 1993. Normal turnaround time- 1-3 days. Projects billed by number of names searched. Projects billed by number of records located. Will file/record documents for clients. Terms: net 30 days.

Crawford County Abstract Co Inc (Arkansas)

PO Box 426, 424 Main St, Van Buren, AR 72956

Phone: 479-474-2711 - **Fax:** 479-474-2954

crawfordcountyabstract@hotmail.com

Types of Records Retrieved: Criminal, Civil and Probate courts; Real Estate; Tax Liens/Judgments

Local Retrieval Area: AR-Crawford

Add'l Information: Established 1972. Normal turnaround time- 2 days. Projects billed by number of names searched. Will file/record documents for clients. They specialize in real estate.

Crawford County Title Co

600 W Washington St, Cuba, MO 65453-1221
Phone: 573-885-6470 - **Fax:** 573-885-2758 wepllc@fidnet.com
Types of Records Retrieved: Real Estate; Tax Liens/Judgments
Local Retrieval Area: MO-Crawford. **Correspondent Relationships:** Franklin, Dent, Phelps, Gasconade counties MO.
Add'l Information: Established 1967. Normal turnaround time- 1 week. Fee basis varies by type of transaction. Will file/record documents for clients.

Crawford Cty Title, Roscommon Cty Title

PO Box 581, Grayling, MI 49738
Phone: 989-348-9832 - **Fax:** 989-348-7511
mferrigan@landcoenterprises.com
Records Retrieved: Real Estate; Tax Liens/Judgments; UCC records
Local Retrieval Area: MI-Crawford, Kalkaska, Roscommon. **Correspondent Relationships:** Oscoda, Otsego, Grand Traverse and Charlevoix.
Add'l Information: Established 1971. Normal turnaround time- up to 1 week. Fee basis will vary by the type of project. All projects require prepayment. Will file/record documents for clients. They require a prepayment for all out of area transactions. They specialize in title insurance. Additional phone is 517-821-4544 and Fax: 517-821-3844.

Diane Crawley

195 Melody Ridge Rd, Russellville, KY 42276
Phone: 270-847-0177 dicrawley@cebridge.net
Types of Records Retrieved: Criminal courts
Local Retrieval Area: KY-Logan
Add'l Information: Established 2004. Normal turnaround time- 2 days or less. Projects billed by number of names searched. First project may require prepayment. She specializes in Logan County, KY criminal records.

Credit Bureau of Eudora Inc (CBE)

PO Box 545, Eudora, KS 66025-0545
Phone: 785-542-1771 - **Fax:** 785-542-1661
www.eudoraks.com/ksrental/index.htm **email:** cbe@sunflower.com
Types of Records Retrieved: Criminal, Civil and Probate courts; Federal courts; Real Estate; Tax Liens/Judgments; UCC records; Vital records
Local Retrieval Area: KS-Douglas, Johnson, Leavenworth, Shawnee. **Correspondent Relationships:** Kansas and nationwide.
Add'l Information: Established 1993. Normal turnaround time- 24-48 hours. Expedited service available. Projects billed by number of names searched. Projects billed by the hour. With a maximum flat rate of $200.00 will go anywhere in Kansas. Credit cards accepted. Will file/record documents for clients. All projects require prepayment retainer or credit card on website. CBE specializes in rent-screens, skiptraces, research & document retrieval. They daily update their specialized regional/local databases and have a sex offender database for 24 states. The principal is a licensed private investigator. A licensed PI in KS. Performs service of process.

Credit Bureau of Valley City

PO Box 912, 135 Fourth St NW, Valley City, ND 58072
Phone: 701-845-3912 - **Fax:** 701-845-0220 cbvcmen@daktel.com
Types of Records Retrieved: Criminal, Civil and Probate courts; Real Estate; Tax Liens/Judgments; UCC records; Vital records
Local Retrieval Area: ND-Barnes
Add'l Information: Established 1990. Normal turnaround time- 2-3 days. Fee basis will vary by the type of project. First project may require prepayment. They request that all out of county clients prepay.

Credit Control Inc/Resource Confidential

500 S Salina #102, Syracuse, NY 13202
Phone: 800-886-7407; 315-475-4191 - **Fax:** 315-484-3389
n.bernardo@creditneeds.com
Types of Records Retrieved: Criminal, Civil and Probate courts; Federal courts; Real Estate; Tax Liens/Judgments; UCC records; Vital records
Local Retrieval Area: NY-Albany, Broome, Fulton, Herkimer, Madison, Oneida, Onondaga, Oswego, Rensselaer, Saratoga, Schenectady, Warren, Washington. **Correspondent Relationships:** nationwide. The also offer service to southern New York including NYC.
Add'l Information: Established 1990. Normal turnaround time- 24-48 hours. Projects billed by number of names searched. Credit cards accepted. Will file/record documents for clients. Will bill bi-monthly. Whatever your particular search requirements might be, they have the experienced staff to provide you with the specific results you need. Performs service of process.

Credit Lenders Service Agency Inc

PO Box 508, Cherry Hill, NJ 08003
Phone: 856-787-9005 - **Fax:** 800-648-0401
www.creditlenders.com **email:** keithm@creditlenders.com
Types of Records Retrieved: Federal courts; Real Estate; Tax Liens/Judgments; UCC records
Local Retrieval Area: NJ-Bergen, Burlington, Camden, Mercer, Middlesex, Morris, Ocean, Somerset; PA-Lackawanna, Monroe, Pike, Wayne. **Correspondent Relationships:** nationwide.
Add'l Information: Established 1983. Normal turnaround time- 24-48 hours. Projects billed by number of names searched. Projects billed by number of records located. First project may require prepayment. Will file/record documents for clients. They specialize in real estate searching. They are also a title company.

Crime Checkers

PO Box 57, Dixon Springs, TN 37057
Phone: 615-735-0010 - **Fax:** 615-735-0081 crimchckrs@comcast.net
Types of Records Retrieved: Criminal and Civil courts; Tax Liens/Judgments; UCC records
Local Retrieval Area: TN-Rutherford, Wilson
Add'l Information: Established 1995. Normal turnaround time- 24 hours. Projects billed by number of names searched. First project may require prepayment. Credit cards accepted. Credit cards accepted thru PayPal.

Crimecheck Research Services

PO Box 8333, The Woodlands, TX 77387-8333
Phone: 281-288-6930 - **Fax:** 281-296-8261
crimecheckresearchsvcs2003@yahoo.com
Types of Records Retrieved: Criminal and Civil courts
Local Retrieval Area: TX-Angelina, Atascosa, Bandera, Bell, Bosque, Brazos, Caldwell, Collin, Comal, Ellis, Gonzales, Guadalupe, Hays, Hill, Hood, Johnson, Montgomery, Potter, Randall, Tarrant, Walker, Wilson, Wise. **Correspondent Relationships:** nationwide.
Add'l Information: Established 1995. Normal turnaround time- 24-48 hours. Projects billed by number of names searched. Payment due upon receipt of invoice. They specialize in criminal and civil record research and pre-employment screening.

Criminal Background Investigations

PO Box 2363, Angleton, TX 77516
Phone: 979-848-0632 - **Fax:** 979-549-0695 sramsower@sbcglobal.net
Types of Records Retrieved: Criminal and Civil courts
Local Retrieval Area: TX-Brazoria, Galveston
Add'l Information: Established 1992. Normal turnaround time- if faxed over by 8 AM, 24 hours same day. Projects billed by number of names searched. Monthly billing for NAPBS members. Will invoice monthly. Started researching criminal records in 1992. Visits the courthouse daily and obtains all information from the courthouse. Does not use online databases to perform searches. 24-hr turnaround. A founding member of NAPBS.

Criminal Information Network Inc

PO Box 54961, Cincinnati, OH 45254
Phone: 888-923-0271; 513-474-8800 - **Fax:** 513-474-8801
Types of Records Retrieved: Criminal and Civil courts
Local Retrieval Area: KY-Boone, Campbell, Kenton; OH-Clermont, Hamilton. **Correspondent Relationships:** nationwide.
Add'l Information: Turnaround time- 24 hours. Projects billed by number of names searched. Will invoice bi-monthly. They specialize in accurate criminal records and MVRs from KY, and also OH and other state MVRs.

Criminal Research & Inv

15614 Dr Martin Luther King Jr Blvd #B, Dover, FL 33527-4214
Phone: 888-243-5252; 813-708-0007 - **Fax:** 888-698-3929
customerservice@criscreening.com

Types of Records Retrieved: Criminal and Civil courts; Federal courts; Tax Liens/Judgments

Local Retrieval Area: FL-Hillsborough, Pasco, Pinellas, Polk. **Correspondent Relationships:** statewide and nationally.

Add'l Information: Established 1996. Normal turnaround time- 24-48 hours. Projects billed by number of names searched. Will bill, net 15 days. CRI specializes in criminal, civil (local and federal), motor vehicle records, and social security traces. Has correspondent relationships nationwide

David and Marvin Criqui

PO Box 189, 101 Leonard St, Onaga, KS 66521
Phone: 785-889-4659 - **Fax:** 785-889-4659

Types of Records Retrieved: Criminal, Civil and Probate courts; Tax Liens/Judgments; Vital records

Local Retrieval Area: KS-Atchison, Brown, Doniphan, Douglas, Jackson, Jefferson, Leavenworth, Marshall, Nemaha, Pottawatomie, Riley, Shawnee, Wabaunsee. **Correspondent Relationships:** Eastern Kansas including Shawnee County.

Add'l Information: Established 1997. Normal turnaround time- 48 hours or less in almost all cases. Projects billed by number of names searched. First project may require prepayment. CIS Investigations as it is sometimes known visits the courts every 2 days and does work for some of the biggest companies in the business. Dave Criqui cellphone is 785-224-1152

Crisp & Associates

PO Box 31070, Savannah, GA 31410
Phone: 912-898-9973 - **Fax:** 912-898-5044
www.crispandassociates.com **email:** jwcrisp@bellsouth.net

Types of Records Retrieved: Criminal, Civil and Probate courts; Federal courts; Tax Liens/Judgments; UCC records

Local Retrieval Area: GA-Bryan, Chatham, Effingham, Liberty

Add'l Information: Established 1992. Normal turnaround time- 48 hours. They specialize in process service and investigations. A licensed PI in GA, SC. Performs service of process.

Crockett County Abstract Co

PO Drawer E, 1108 Ave E, Ozona, TX 76943
Phone: 325-392-2232 - **Fax:** 325-392-2839

Records Retrieved: Real Estate; Tax Liens/Judgments; UCC records

Local Retrieval Area: TX-Crockett

Add'l Information: Normal turnaround time- 2-3 days. Fee basis will vary by the type of project. First project may require prepayment.

Marjorie Croson aka The Croson Agency

804 Monmouth St, St Albans, WV 25177
Phone: 304-727-2555 - **Fax:** 304-727-1353

Types of Records Retrieved: Civil and Probate courts; Federal courts; Real Estate; Tax Liens/Judgments; UCC records; Vital records

Local Retrieval Area: WV-all counties. **Correspondents:** nationwide.

Add'l Information: Established 1958. Normal turnaround time- Search may take 24-48 hours. For faster service, please fax your order for fee quote. No work will begin until they receive your final approval via fax. They accept no verbal orders. Projects billed by number of names searched. Hands on searches in remote WV counties are available at an hourly rate plus expenses. First project may require prepayment. Will file/record documents for clients. Terms net 30 days. Retired legal investigators providing support services to legal & financial communities since 1958. Their office is 15 minutes from the WV Sec of ST & the local USDC & Bankruptcy courts. If there is a delay in promised TAT you are kept informed of status.

David Cross

PO Box 70, Albany, KY 42602
Phone: 606-387-6638 - **Fax:** 606-387-6639

Types of Records Retrieved: Criminal and Civil courts; Real Estate; Tax Liens/Judgments **Local Retrieval Area:** KY-Clinton

Add'l Information: Established 1984. First project may require prepayment. He is an attorney and performs searches on a very limited basis.

Laura Cross

4859 Geranium, Oakland, CA 94619
Phone: 510-336-0865 - **Fax:** 510-336-9688 crosslaura@hotmail.com

Types of Records Retrieved: Criminal and Civil courts; Federal courts; Tax Liens/Judgments; Vital records

Local Retrieval Area: CA-Alameda, Contra Costa, Marin, San Francisco, San Mateo, Santa Clara. **Correspondent Relationships:** Santa Cruz, Monterey, Napa, Sacramento, Yolo, Placer, Solano, Kern, San Joaquin counties CA.

Add'l Information: Established 1994. Normal turnaround time- 24 hours but often same day service. Projects billed by number of names searched. Terms: net 30 days.

Crossland Abstract

213 Matthews Ave, Villas, NJ 08251
Phone: 609-465-2220 - **Fax:** 609-886-6066

Types of Records Retrieved: Criminal and Civil courts; Real Estate; Tax Liens/Judgments

Local Retrieval Area: NJ-Cape May

Add'l Information: Established 2002. Normal turnaround time- 24 hours. Projects billed by number of names searched. First project may require prepayment. Will file/record documents for clients.

Crossroads Research

9833 S Power Pl, Terra Haute, IN 47802
Phone: 812-299-0809 - **Fax:** 812-299-0808 crossroadsresearch@verizon.net

Types of Records Retrieved: Criminal and Civil courts

Local Retrieval Area: IN-Clay, Knox, Parke, Sullivan, Vermillion, Vigo IL-Clark, Crawford, Edgar, Lawrence. **Correspondent Relationships:** statewide and Illinois.

Add'l Information: Normal turnaround time- 2-3 days. First project may require prepayment. Specializes in the Terra Haute, Indiana area but they have a top notch national network for criminal records.

Crow Wing County Abstract Co

PO Box 378, Brainerd, MN 56401
Phone: 218-829-7368 - **Fax:** 218-829-8586

Records Retrieved: Real Estate; Tax Liens/Judgments; UCC records

Local Retrieval Area: MN-Crow Wing

Add'l Information: Established 1915. Normal turnaround time- 2-7 days. Projects billed by number of names searched. Projects billed by the hour. Will file/record documents for clients. They specialize in land title.

CRRG Inc

PO Box 40526, Ft Worth, TX 76140-0526
Phone: 800-687-9030; 817-459-0075 - **Fax:** 800-687-7658
www.crrginc.com **email:** crrg1@msn.com

Types of Records Retrieved: Criminal, Civil and Probate courts; Federal courts; Real Estate; Tax Liens/Judgments; UCC records; Vital records

Local Retrieval Area: TX-Collin, Dallas, Denton, Ellis, Johnson, Kaufman, Parker, Rockwall, Tarrant. **Correspondent Relationships:** nationwide.

Add'l Information: Established 1994. Normal turnaround time- same day if order in by 10AM. Projects billed by number of names searched. First project may require prepayment. Credit cards accepted. Will file/record documents for clients. Invoice monthly. They are a national search firm, specializing in every kind of courthouse research in every county in the country. A licensed PI in TX.

Crummey Investigations Inc
PO Box 510405, Melbourne Beach, FL 32951-0130
Phone: 321-724-0518 - **Fax:** 321-728-0274
www.crummey-p-i.com **email:** bev@cfl.rr.com

Types of Records Retrieved: Criminal, Civil and Probate courts; Real Estate; Tax Liens/Judgments; UCC records; Vital records

Local Retrieval Area: FL-Brevard, Indian River, Orange

Add'l Information: Established 1985. Normal turnaround time- 24 hours. Projects billed by the hour. First project may require prepayment. Credit cards accepted. Will file/record documents for clients. Personal checks are accepted. They specialize in missing persons. A licensed PI in FL. Performs service of process.

Crump Investigative Services
120 Bean Hill, Endicott, NY 13760
Phone: 607-785-2661 - **Fax:** 607-785-2661 klcrump@aol.com

Types of Records Retrieved: Criminal, Civil and Probate courts; Federal courts; Real Estate; Tax Liens/Judgments; UCC records; Vital records

Local Retrieval Area: NY-Broome, Chemung, Tioga, Tompkins

Add'l Information: Established 1998. Normal turnaround time- 3 days. Expedited services. Projects billed by number of records located. First project may require prepayment. They specialize in general investigations, worker's comp, video surveillance and process services. A licensed PI in NY. Performs service of process.

Crutchfield & Associates
21350 Nordhoff St #112, Chatsworth, CA 91311
Phone: 818-349-4836 - **Fax:** 818-349-4856
www.pi4stars.com **email:** cindy@pi4stars.com

Types of Records Retrieved: Criminal and Civil courts; Real Estate; Tax Liens/Judgments; UCC records

Local Retrieval Area: CA-Los Angeles, Orange, San Bernardino, San Diego, Ventura. **Correspondent Relationships:** nationwide, Mexico, Canada.

Add'l Information: Established 1978. Normal turnaround time- 24 hours to 1 month depending on court. Projects billed by number of names searched. Fees depend on case file activity. First project may require prepayment. They specialize in criminal background checks, surveillance, driving records, credit checks with a signed release and asset searches. A licensed PI in CA. Performs service of process.

Crystal Clear Copy Service
8241 Mesa Ave, Oakhill, CA 92344
Phone: 760-947-5699 - **Fax:** 760-949-1389 crystalclearcopy@gmail.com

Types of Records Retrieved: Civil courts; Federal courts

Local Retrieval Area: CA-Orange, Riverside, San Bernardino. **Correspondent Relationships:** statewide.

Add'l Information: Established 1990. Normal turnaround time- 10 days. Expedited service available. Fee basis will vary by the type of project. They specialize in photocopy. Performs service of process.

CSC - Corporation Service Company
2711 Centerville Rd #400, Wilmington, DE 19808-1645
Phone: 800-927-9800; 302-636-5400 - **Fax:** 302-636-5454
https://www.incspot.com/public/index.html **email:** selias@cscinfo.com

Types of Records Retrieved: Criminal, Civil and Probate courts; Federal courts; Real Estate; Tax Liens/Judgments; UCC records; Vital records

Local Retrieval Area: DC-District of Columbia; DE-Kent, Sussex; IL-Cook; MA-South Middlesex, Suffolk; NV-Carson City; NJ-Mercer; OR-Marion. **Correspondent Relationships:** nationwide.

Add'l Information: Established 1899. Normal turnaround time- 24-48 hours. Projects billed by number of names searched. They also charge by index. First project may require prepayment. Credit cards accepted. Wilmington, DE is the corporate headquarters of the national SCS network, specializing in UCC and corp services. Also see CSC NYC and CSC Minnesota for other local doc retrieval services. Performs service of process.

CSC Minnesota
380 Jackson St #418, St Paul, MN 55101-3899
Phone: 800-327-1886; 651-227-7575 - **Fax:** 800-603-0266; 651-225-9244
jcilmi@cscinfo.com

Types of Records Retrieved: Civil and Probate courts; Federal courts; Real Estate; Tax Liens/Judgments; UCC records; Vital records

Local Retrieval Area: MN-Anoka, Carver, Dakota, Hennepin, Ramsey, Scott, Sherburne, Washington, Wright. **Correspondent Relationships:** nationwide.

Add'l Information: Established 1966. Normal turnaround time- 24-72 hours. Projects billed by number of names searched. Will file/record documents for clients. Will invoice monthly. Formerly US Corporate Services, they specialize in handling the needs of credit and banking professionals as they pertain to UCCs and the requisite due diligence associated with lending.

CSC New York City
1133 Avenue of the Americas #3100, New York, NY 10036-6710
Phone: 800-221-0770; 212-299-9100 - **Fax:** 212-299-9102
https://www.incspot.com/public/index.html

Types of Records Retrieved: Criminal, Civil and Probate courts; Federal courts; Real Estate; Tax Liens/Judgments; UCC records; Vital records

Local Retrieval Area: NY-Kings, New York, Queens. **Correspondent Relationships:** nationwide.

Add'l Information: Established 1899. Normal turnaround time- 1-2 days. Projects billed by number of names searched. First project may require prepayment. They are part of the CSC network of offices, specializing in UCC and corporate matters.

CSI Investigations
102 Chainlake Dr, Halifax, Nova Scotia, Canada, CAN B3S 1A7
Phone: 866-245-2089, 888-818-5251; 902-450-0697
Fax: 888-450-0875; 902-484-5379
www.csiinvest.com **email:** csihalifax@csiinvest.com

Types of Records Retrieved: Criminal, Civil and Probate courts; Federal District court; Real Estate; Tax Liens/Judgments; UCC records

Local Retrieval Area: CANADA-New Brunswick, Newfoundland, Nova Scotia, Prince Edward Island.. **Correspondent Relationships:** All Provinces and internationally.

Add'l Information: Established 1995. Normal turnaround time- 24-48 hours; 3-5 days for remote areas. Projects billed by number of names searched. Projects billed by the hour. Civil records search fee is by the hour; criminal by number of names searched. They provide clients with the most trusted professional investigative services in the country. Their internationally-recognized investigators and high level of customer service has made them the top investigative firm in Canada. A licensed PI in Nova Scotia. Performs service of process.

CSRA Background Verification Inc
519 Pleasant Home Rd #C-2, Augusta, GA 30907
Phone: 706-869-8882 - **Fax:** 706-869-9689
www.csrabv.com **email:** charles@csrabv.com

Types of Records Retrieved: Criminal, Civil and Probate courts; Federal courts; Real Estate; Tax Liens/Judgments; UCC records

Local Retrieval Area: GA-Burke, Columbia, McDuffie, Richmond; SC-Aiken. **Correspondent Relationships:** Jefferson, Johnson, Washington, Glasscock, Hancock, Warren, Lincoln, Taliaferro, Wilkes counties GA.

Add'l Information: Established 1993. Normal turnaround time- 12-48 hours. Projects billed by number of names searched. First project may require prepayment. Bills monthly. They specialize in pre-employment background checks and current owner/title searches. They provide a full array of courthouse records retrieval.

Cumberland Research
162 Langford Rd, Carthage, TN 37030
Phone: 615-735-6558 - **Fax:** 615-735-6558 CMBRR@comcast.net

Types of Records Retrieved: Criminal and Civil courts

Local Retrieval Area: TN-Macon, Smith, Sumner, Trousdale

Add'l Information: Established 2000. Normal turnaround time- 24 hours. Projects billed by number of names searched. First project may require prepayment. They specialize in criminal and civil searches in Macon, Smith, Sumner, and Trousdale counties in TN. Results usually in 24 hours.

Cumberland Title
43 Ashley Dr, Liberty, KY 42539
Phone: 606-787-8743
Types of Records Retrieved: Real Estate; Tax Liens/Judgments
Local Retrieval Area: KY-Taylor
Add'l Information: First project may require prepayment. They specialize in real estate.

Current River Abstract
129 State St, Doniphan, MO 63935
Phone: 573-996-2907 - **Fax:** 573-996-2909
Types of Records Retrieved: Real Estate; Tax Liens/Judgments
Local Retrieval Area: MO-Ripley
Add'l Information: Established 1993. First project may require prepayment. They specialize in real estate.

Currier Abstract Company
PO Box 540, Artesia, NM 88211-0540
Phone: 505-746-9823 - **Fax:** 505-746-9661
Types of Records Retrieved: Civil and Probate courts; Real Estate; Tax Liens/Judgments; UCC records
Local Retrieval Area: NM-Eddy
Add'l Info: Established 1940. Normal turnaround time- 1 week. Fee basis will vary by the type of project. Land title business in Eddy County, NM.

CuTitle Services Inc
PO Box 487, Clayton, NM 88415
Phone: 505-374-8517 - **Fax:** 505-374-8294
Types of Records Retrieved: Real Estate; Tax Liens/Judgments
Local Retrieval Area: NM-Harding

Cygneture Title Inc
13432 Elmwood Dr #1, Baxter, MN 56425
Phone: 218-828-0122 - **Fax:** 218-828-0873
Types of Records Retrieved: Criminal courts; Probate courts; Real Estate; Tax Liens/Judgments; UCC records
Local Retrieval Area: MN-Cass, Crow Wing, Morrison, Todd, Wadena
Add'l Information: Established 1988. Normal turnaround time- 1-10 days depending on types of records retrieved. Fee basis will vary by type of project. First project may require prepayment. Will file/record documents for clients. They will also invoice. They specialize in real estate.

Cynthia H Miller, Paralegal
931 Watch Creek Dr, Cincinnati, OH 45230
Phone: 513-368-2855 - **Fax:** 513-624-0858 cctn.cincy@off.res.com
Types of Records Retrieved: Civil courts; Real Estate; Tax Liens/Judgments; UCC records
Local Retrieval Area: OH-Butler, Clermont, Hamilton, Warren
Add'l Information: Established 1990. Normal turnaround time- 2-3 days. Projects billed by number of names searched. Terms are net 30 days. She specializes in searching records for UCCs, federal, state, civil suits and judgments, obtains copies and file documents. Is also insured.

Cynthia-Renee's Professional Business Svc
1715 Fillmore St, Davenport, IA 52804
Phone: 563-324-9445 - **Fax:** 563-326-0437 cindi4@mchsi.com
Types of Records Retrieved: Criminal, Civil and Probate courts; Federal courts; Real Estate; Tax Liens/Judgments; UCC records; Vital records
Local Retrieval Area: IA-Clinton, Muscatine, Scott; IL-Rock Island
Add'l Information: Established 2002. Normal turnaround time- 1-2 days. Billing varies due to type of job. First project may require prepayment. They specialize in the Quad Cities areas; services include expert process service, paralegal service, investigative services, court fillings, records retrieval, document delivery and notary. Holds a masters degree and paralegal certificate. A licensed PI in IL. Performs service of process.

D & B Legal Services Inc
PO Box 7471, Overland Park, KS 66207
Phone: 913-963-1279 - **Fax:** 913-385-9992
www.bdiinvestigations.com **email:** billpowell@kc.rr.com
Types of Records Retrieved: Criminal, Civil and Probate courts; Federal courts; Real Estate; Tax Liens/Judgments; UCC records; Vital records
Local Retrieval Area: KS-Johnson, Wyandotte; MO-Cass, Clay, Jackson, Platte. **Correspondent Relationships:** Shawnee, Douglas counties, KS; Johnson, Lafayette counties MO.
Add'l Information: Established 2000. Normal turnaround time- 24 hours. Projects billed by number of names searched. First project may require prepayment. D & B Legal Services, they have been in the legal field for 22 years and know their way around the courts. A licensed PI in KS, MO. Performs service of process.

D & D Retrieval Services
2 Canton St #110, Stoughton, MA 02072
Phone: 781-297-0933 - **Fax:** 781-297-0988 dndretrieval@aol.com
Types of Records Retrieved: Criminal, Civil and Probate courts; Federal courts; Real Estate; Tax Liens/Judgments; UCC records
Retrieval Area: MA-Bristol, Essex, Middlesex, Norfolk, Plymouth, Suffolk
Add'l Information: Established 1998. Normal turnaround time- 8-48 hours if received by 8AM EST. Projects billed by number of names searched. Large projects require prepayment. They specialize in public record research, document retrieval, filing services, UCC searches, corporate document retrieval, civil and criminal court searches, state and federal tax lien and bankruptcy retrieval.

D D Hamilton Title Co
301 W Washington, Marshfield, MO 65706
Phone: 417-859-2078 - **Fax:** 417-859-2020
Types of Records Retrieved: Civil and Probate courts; Real Estate; Tax Liens/Judgments; UCC records
Local Retrieval Area: MO-Webster, Wright
Add'l Information: Established 1893. Normal turnaround time- 48 hours. Projects billed by number of names searched. Projects billed by number of records located. Will file/record documents for clients. They specialize in land title and civil judgments.

D K Abstract
2095 W Vanhook St, Milan, TN 38358
Phone: 731-686-9363 - **Fax:** 731-686-9309
Types of Records Retrieved: Criminal, Civil and Probate courts; Federal courts; Real Estate; Tax Liens/Judgments; UCC records; Vital records
Local Retrieval Area: TN-Benton, Carroll, Chester, Crockett, Decatur, Dyer, Fayette, Gibson, Hardeman, Hardin, Haywood, Henderson, Henry, Humphreys, Lake, Lauderdale, McNairy, Madison, Obion, Perry, Stewart, Tipton, Weakley
Add'l Information: Established 1989. Normal turnaround time- 48 hours. They charge by search. Personal checks are accepted. They do bankruptcy searches in Madison County only.

D W Moore & Assoc Inc
4849 S State St #2, Salt Lake City, UT 84107-4821
Phone: 801-266-6585 - **Fax:** 801-266-6031
www.dwmoore.com **email:** david@dwmoore.com
Types of Records Retrieved: Civil and Probate courts; Federal courts; Real Estate; Tax Liens/Judgments; UCC records; Vital records

Local Retrieval Area: UT-Beaver, Box Elder, Cache, Carbon, Daggett, Davis, Duchesne, Emery, Garfield, Grand, Iron, Juab, Kane, Millard, Morgan, Piute, Rich, Salt Lake, San Juan, Sanpete, Sevier, Summit, Tooele, Uintah, Utah, Wasatch, Washington, Wayne, Weber

Add'l Information: Established 1987. Normal turnaround time- 3-5 days. Projects billed by the hour. They specialize in research and historical investigation, environmental review and education services. Also offers genealogical services

D.G.I. LLC

PO Box 1182, 8444 Kingston Dr, Newburgh, IN 47630

Phone: 812-853-3222 - **Fax:** 812-853-3222 d.gainer@adelphia.net

Types of Records Retrieved: Criminal and Civil courts; Federal courts; Real Estate; Tax Liens/Judgments; UCC records; Vital records

Local Retrieval Area: IN-Posey, Spencer, Vanderburgh, Warrick; KY-Henderson. **Correspondent Relationships:** nationwide.

Add'l Information: Established 1993. Normal turnaround time- 48 hours. Expedited service available for add'l fee. Projects billed by number of names searched. Projects billed by the hour. First project may require prepayment. Will file/record documents for clients. Terms: net 10 days. They specialize in general investigations, surveillance, photographics and time-lapse video, accident reconstruction; serving Metro Evansville, IN. They will do other nearby counties on demand. A pager number is: 812-467-9220. A licensed PI in IN. Performs service of process.

Daggett Abstract Co

PO Box 389, Marianna, AR 72360

Phone: 870-295-3434 x16 - **Fax:** 870-295-3445 daggettabstract@aol.com

Types of Records Retrieved: Criminal, Civil and Probate courts; Real Estate; Tax Liens/Judgments; UCC records

Local Retrieval Area: AR-Lee

Add'l Information: Established 1873. Normal turnaround time- 1 day to 1 week. Fee basis will vary by type of project. All projects require prepayment. Credit cards accepted. Visa accepted. They specialize in title search and land ownership.

Daily Journal Corporation

915 E 1st St, Los Angeles, CA 90012

Phone: 800-952-5232; 213-229-5300 - **Fax:** 213-680-3682

www.dailyjournal.com **email:** searches@dailyjournal.com

Types of Records Retrieved: Criminal, Civil and Probate courts; Federal courts; Real Estate; Tax Liens/Judgments; UCC records

Local Retrieval Area: CA-Los Angeles, Orange, Riverside, San Bernardino, San Diego, Ventura. **Correspondent Relationships:** California.

Add'l Information: Established 1888. Normal turnaround time- 3-5 business days. Expedited service available. Projects billed by number of names searched. First project may require prepayment. Fees due upon receipt of invoice. They will record legal notices and coordinate publication of legal notices. They will also file/record UCC documents, also FBN searches, and credit cards are accepted

The Daily News & Chandler Reports

193 Jefferson Ave, Memphis, TN 38103

Phone: 901-523-1561 - **Fax:** 901-526-5813

www.memphisdailynews.com **email:** info@memphisdailynews.com

Types of Records Retrieved: Criminal, Civil and Probate courts; Real Estate

Local Retrieval Area: TN-Fayette, Shelby, Tipton

Add'l Information: Established 1886. Will file/record documents for clients. The Daily News provides public records searches on real estate, business, people and the courts. Chandler Reports provides value-added, highly analyzed real estate data covering specific properties and the entire market.

Dakota County Abstract Co

1250 N Hwy 55, Hastings, MN 55033

Phone: 651-437-5600 - **Fax:** 651-437-8876 www.dcatitle.com

Types of Records Retrieved: Real Estate; Tax Liens/Judgments; Probate courts; UCC records

Local Retrieval Area: MN-Dakota. **Correspondents in:** Minnesota.

Add'l Information: Established 1957. Turnaround time- 1-5 days. Projects billed by number of names searched. Projects billed by number of records located. All projects require prepayment. Will file/record documents for clients. They will also invoice. They specialize in title searches.

Dana Caughey Document Retrieval Service

11 Country Ln, East Peoria, IL 61611

Phone: 309-694-4407 - **Fax:** 309-694-4528 wct@insightbb.com

Types of Records Retrieved: Criminal, Civil and Probate courts; Federal courts; Real Estate; Tax Liens/Judgments; UCC records

Local Retrieval Area: IL-Peoria, Tazewell, Woodford. **Correspondent Relationships:** Fulton, Knox, Mason, Marshall, Sangamon, and Woodford counties IL.

Add'l Information: Established 1998. Normal turnaround time- 24-48 hours. Expedited service available. Projects billed by number of names searched. Monthly or Bi-Weekly billing. They specialize in criminal/civil searches at county and Federal levels, real estate, UCC, and tax liens/judgments.

Dane County Legal Notice

139 W Wilson St #106, Madison, WI 53703

Phone: 800-720-6871; 608-251-1181 - **Fax:** 608-251-8999

Types of Records Retrieved: Criminal, Civil and Probate courts; Federal courts; Tax Liens/Judgments; UCC records

Local Retrieval Area: WI-Dane

Add'l Information: Established 1977. Turnaround time- 24-48 hours. Projects billed by number of names searched. Projects billed by the hour. Hourly plus mileage anywhere in WI. Will file/record documents for clients. Will extend credit to PRRN members. They specialize in process service and records retrieval. A licensed PI in WI.

Daniel Agency

PO Box 342, Ashland, KY 41105

Phone: 606-324-6029 - **Fax:** 606-324-6029

Records Retrieved: Criminal, Civil and Probate courts; Federal District courts; Real Estate; Tax Liens/Judgments; UCC records; Vital records

Local Area: KY-Boyd, Carter, Elliott, Floyd, Greenup, Johnson, Lawrence, Martin, Morgan, Pike, Rowan; WV-Cabell, Kanawha, Lincoln, Wayne

Add'l Information: Established 1981. Turnaround time- 2-3 days. Projects billed by the hour. First project may require prepayment. The company is a multi-faceted real estate research and consulting firm providing abstracts of title, right-of-way & easement acquisition, real estate & mineral acquisition and leasing and acquisition investigation. They are bonded.

Darren J Harper & Associates

5000 W Esplanade Ave #196, Metairie, LA 70006

Phone: 800-962-4907; 504-888-5262 - **Fax:** 504-341-1966

x1212djh@yahoo.com

Types of Records Retrieved: Civil courts; Federal courts; Real Estate; Tax Liens/Judgments

Local Retrieval Area: LA-Jefferson, Orleans Parishes. **Correspondent Relationships:** East Baton Rouge, LA.

Add'l Information: Established 1990. Normal turnaround time- 4 days. Projects billed by the hour. Will file/record documents for clients. Will invoice. Performs service of process.

Data Quest Ltd

180 Lincoln St #501, Boston, MA 02111-2400

Phone: 800-292-9797; 617-437-0030 - **Fax:** 877-362-7272; 617-437-0034

www.dataquestonline.com **email:** tturgeon@dataquestonline.com

Types of Records Retrieved: Criminal, Civil and Probate courts; Federal courts; Real Estate; Tax Lien/Judgments; UCC records; Vital records

Local Retrieval Area: MA-Bristol, Essex, Middlesex, Norfolk, Plymouth, Suffolk, Worcester. **Correspondents:** Statewide and nationally.

Add'l Information: Established 1981. Normal turnaround time- 24-48 hours. Billing depends on nature of request. First project may require prepayment. Credit cards accepted. Data Quest Ltd is a licensed private investigations agency which provides all types of court document research and public record retrieval throughout the United States. A licensed PI in MA. Performs service of process.

Data Reporting Corp

330 Roberts St #203, East Hartford, CT 06108-3654
Phone: 800-570-7750; 860-282-0685 - **Fax:** 800-672-8635; 860-290-3731

Types of Records Retrieved: Criminal, Civil and Probate courts; Federal courts; Real Estate; Tax Liens/Judgments; UCC records

Local Retrieval Area: CT-Fairfield, Hartford, Litchfield, Middlesex, New Haven, New London, Tolland, Windham. **Correspondent Relationships:** nationwide.

Add'l Information: Normal turnaround time- same day to 3-5 days. Projects billed by the hour. Has flat rate by entity name. First project may require prepayment. Performs service of process.

Data Research Inc (Oregon)

8130 SW Beaverton Hillsdale Hwy, Portland, OR 97225-1845
Phone: 800-992-1983; 503-296-0760 - **Fax:** 800-992-1984; 503-296-0766
mail@drius.com

Types of Records Retrieved: Criminal, Civil and Probate courts; Federal courts; Real Estate; Tax Liens/Judgments; UCC records

Local Retrieval Area: OR-Benton, Clackamas, Columbia, Coos, Crook, Curry, Deschutes, Douglas, Hood River, Jackson, Jefferson, Klamath, Lane, Lincoln, Linn, Marion, Multnomah, Polk, Wasco, Washington, Yamhill; WA-Clark. **Correspondent Relationships:** nationwide.

Add'l Information: Established 1989. Normal turnaround time- 24-72 hours. Projects billed by number of names searched. Will file/record documents for clients. Small company with friendly experienced staff providing timely accurate service. They specialize in records retrieval/research, filings/recordings and litigation.

Data Screen Inc

PO Box 16839, Fort Worth, TX 76162
Phone: 817-294-7671 - **Fax:** 817-294-0773 datascreen@mesh.net

Types of Records Retrieved: Criminal and Civil courts

Local Retrieval Area: TX-Tarrant. **Correspondent Relationships:** statewide and nationwide.

Add'l Information: Established 1991. Normal turnaround time- 24-48 hours. Projects billed by number of names searched. Will bill clients. For over 14 years they have specialized in criminal record checks, MVRs and North Texas Federal Records facility access as well as statewide checks and services throughout Texas, and the nation. A licensed PI in TX.

Data-Find

PO Box 575, Glasco, NY 12432
Phone: 845-246-3263 - **Fax:** 845-247-0126 tschirmer@hvc.rr.com

Types of Records Retrieved: Criminal, Civil and Probate courts; Real Estate; Tax Liens/Judgments; UCC records

Local Retrieval Area: NY-Ulster

Add'l Information: Established 1996. Normal turnaround time- 48 hours. Projects billed by number of names searched. Projects billed by number of records located. First project may require prepayment. Will file/record documents for clients. Payment due upon receipt. They specialize in previous owner and tax searches for Ulster County.

Datalink Investigative Services

PO Box 755, White Pine, TN 37890
Phone: 865-674-0030 - **Fax:** 865-674-0076
www.datalinksvcs.com **email:** dis@planetc.com

Types of Records Retrieved: Criminal and Civil courts

Local Retrieval Area: TN-Cocke, Hamblen, Jefferson

Add'l Information: Established 1998. Normal turnaround time- 24-48 hours. Projects billed by number of names searched. First project may require prepayment. Invoice on a monthly basis. They specialize in criminal and civil records searches; serving the Tennessee area since 1998. A licensed PI in TN. Performs service of process.

Dataprompt Corporation

402 Valencia St, Dallas, TX 75223-1124
Phone: 214-395-2530 - **Fax:** 972-838-1446
dataprompt@msn.com

Types of Records Retrieved: Criminal and Civil courts; US District court

Local Retrieval Area: TX-Anderson, Bee, Bell, Bexar, Bowie, Brazos, Collin, Cooke, Coryell, Dallas, Denton, Erath, Fannin, Grayson, Gregg, Harris, Henderson, Hopkins, Howard, Hunt, Johnson, Kaufman, Kleberg, Lamar, Limestone, Lubbock, McLennan, Nueces, Parker, Rockwall, Smith, Tarrant, Travis, Upshur, Van Zandt, Victoria, Webb, Wilbarger, Wise, Wood. **Correspondent Relationships:** statewide.

Add'l Information: Established 1993. Normal turnaround time- next day. Projects billed by number of names searched. Terms: net 30 days. They do criminal and civil searches, specializing in remote counties within Texas. A licensed PI in TX.

DataSearch

PO Box 3195, 1531 Vista Ln #C, Clarksville, TN 37043
Phone: 866-645-2562; 931-645-2562 - **Fax:** 866-645-1173; 931-645-1173
gibbsdatasearch@charter.net

Types of Records Retrieved: Criminal courts; Tax Liens/Judgments

Local Retrieval Area: TN-Cheatham, Montgomery, Robertson, Stewart

Add'l Information: Established 1999. Normal turnaround time- 24-48 hours in Montgomery. 1 day per week in Stewart County. Projects billed by number of names searched. Invoices at the end of the month. She has been doing research since 1999.

DataSearch Inc

PO Box 15406, Sacramento, CA 95851
Phone: 800-452-3282; 916-925-3282 - **Fax:** 916-922-5199
datasearch@sbcglobal.net

Types of Records Retrieved: Criminal, Civil and Probate courts; Federal courts; Real Estate; Tax Liens/Judgments; UCC records; Vital records

Local Retrieval Area: CA-Sacramento. **Correspondents:** nationwide.

Add'l Information: Established 1930. Normal turnaround time- 24-48 hours. Projects billed by number of names searched. First project may require prepayment. Credit cards accepted. Will file/record documents for clients. They specialize in UCC, Corporate, LP, LLC and business name filing and document retrieval services. They have access to DMV (nationwide), courthouse records and county recorder records.

Data-Search of Arkansas

PO Box 21042, Little Rock, AR 72221
Phone: 501-868-4814 - **Fax:** 501-868-4815 wilmax@hughes.net

Records Retrieved: Criminal and Civil courts; Federal courts; UCC records

Local Retrieval Area: AR-Faulkner, Garland, Jackson, Jefferson, Lee, Lonoke, Ouachita, Pulaski, Saline, White. **Correspondents:** statewide.

Add'l Information: Established 1981. Normal turnaround time- 24-48 hours. Projects billed by number of names searched. Terms are net 30 days. First project may require prepayment. Same day turnaround in most cases.

Data-Tec Research Inc

4024 Tanglewood Tr, Chesapeake, VA 23325-2252
Phone: 757-424-3606; Fax- same ljvanderhoff@cox.net

Types of Records Retrieved: Criminal and Civil courts; Federal courts

Local Retrieval Area: VA-Chesapeake City, Hampton City, James City, Newport News, Norfolk, Portsmouth, Suffolk, Virginia Beach; Williamsburg, York. **Correspondent Relationships:** Virginia.

Add'l Information: Established 1987. Normal turnaround time- 12-48 hours. Projects billed by number of names searched. First project may require prepayment. Personal checks accepted. They specialize in court record searches in southeast Virginia, also tax liens and judgments in above counties except for James City and York.

DataTrace Online Inc, PI# 100008

PO Box 95322, South Jordan, UT 84095-0322
Phone: 800-748-5335; 801-253-2400 - **Fax:** 801-253-2478
https://www.datatraceonline.com **email:** scott@datatraceonline.com

Types of Records Retrieved: Criminal, Civil and Probate courts; Federal courts; Real Estate; Tax Liens/Judgments; UCC records; Vital records

Local Retrieval Area: UT-Davis, Salt Lake, Utah. **Correspondent Relationships:** statewide and nationwide.

Add'l Information: Established 1983. Normal turnaround time- 24-48 hours. Expedited service available. Projects billed by number of names searched. Projects billed by the hour. Credit cards accepted. Service agreement required for billing. They specialize in online employment/tenant screening, background checks, due diligence, skip tracing & asset searches, public record research & retrieval, investigations and process service. A licensed PI in UT. Performs service of process.

Davenport Background Searches

1174 N Yellowstone Hwy, Rexburg, ID 83440
Phone: 208-356-5036 kendalld2@prodigy.net

Types of Records Retrieved: Criminal and Civil courts; Real Estate; Tax Liens/Judgments

Local Retrieval Area: ID-Madison

Add'l Information: Established 1999. Normal turnaround time- 24-48 hours. Projects billed by number of names searched. First project may require prepayment. She specializes in beautiful Madison County Idaho. Can also file and research building permits and construction related needs.

Davick Services

PO Box 1274, Shallowater, TX 79363-1274
Phone: 800-658-6656; 806-832-4349 - **Fax:** 512-233-1768
www.davickservices.com **email:** dbloys@door.net

Types of Records Retrieved: Criminal, Civil and Probate courts; Federal courts; Real Estate; Tax Liens/Judgments; UCC records

Local Retrieval Area: NM-Curry, De Baca, Lea, Quay, Roosevelt; TX-Andrews, Armstrong, Bailey, Borden, Briscoe, Castro, Cochran, Cottle, Crosby, Dawson, Deaf Smith, Dickens, Ector, Fisher, Floyd, Gaines, Garza, Glasscock, Hale, Hockley, Howard, Kent, King, Knox, Lamb, Lubbock, Lynn, Martin, Midland, Mitchell, Motley, Nolan, Oldham, Parmer, Potter, Randall, Scurry, Stonewall, Swisher, Terry, Yoakum

Add'l Information: Established 1989. Normal turnaround time- 24-48 hours. Projects billed by number of names searched. First project may require prepayment. Will file/record documents for clients. Personal checks accepted. Providing accurate public records research into Lubbock County, TX & 37 surrounding counties, insured & experienced. Mobile abstracting & research offices mean your orders are received, processed and retrieved direct from the courthouse in record time.

David Lung & Assoc

2977 Hwy K, #119, Ofallon, MO 63366
Phone: 888-477-2664; 636-262-1082
www.davelung.com **email:** dave@davelung.com

Types of Records Retrieved: Criminal and Civil courts

Local Area: MO-Franklin, Jefferson, Lincoln, St. Charles, St. Louis, Warren

Add'l Information: Established 1994. First project may require prepayment. They also provide court filings, skiptracing, private investigation and bank account info. Performs service of process.

David Smith Detective Agency

3018 Hill Creek Dr, Augusta, GA 30909
Phone: 877-793-9426; 706-793-8279 davidp3407@aol.com

Types of Records Retrieved: Criminal, Civil and Probate courts; Federal courts; Tax Liens/Judgments; UCC records

Local Retrieval Area: GA-Burke, Columbia, Jefferson, Lincoln, McDuffie, Richmond; SC-Aiken, Edgefield, Saluda

Add'l Information: Established 1975. Normal turnaround time- 1-2 days. Expedited service available. Will file/record documents for clients. A licensed PI in GA, SC. Performs service of process.

Daviess County Land Title LLC

106 N Market St, Gallatin, MO 64640
Phone: 660-663-2155 - **Fax:** 660-663-2156

Types of Records Retrieved: Civil and Probate courts; Real Estate; Tax Liens/Judgments; UCC records

Local Retrieval Area: MO-Caldwell, Clinton, Daviess, DeKalb

Add'l Information: Established 1972. Turnaround time- 3 days. Projects billed by number of records located. First project may require prepayment. Will file/record documents for clients. They specialize in real estate searches. Will not perform civil court record searches in Davies County.

Davis and Assoc.

PO Box 1023, Pryor, OK 74362 **Phone:** 918-825-5223 - **Fax:** 918-825-5273

Types of Records Retrieved: Criminal and Civil courts

Local Retrieval Area: OK-Craig, Delaware, Mayes, Rogers

Add'l Information: Established 1995. First project may require prepayment. They also provide court filings, skiptracing, and private investigations A licensed PI in OK. Performs service of process.

Dawes County Abstract Co

PO Box 70, Chadron, NE 69337
Phone: 308-432-4840 - **Fax:** 308-432-4338 dcat@panhandle.net

Types of Records Retrieved: Real Estate; Tax Liens/Judgments; Probate courts; UCC records

Local Retrieval Area: NE-Dawes, Sheridan, Sioux

Add'l Information: Established 1982. Normal turnaround time- 3 days. Projects billed by number of names searched. First project may require prepayment. They specialize in title insurance and oil and gas reports. They will file/record UCC and real estate documents on behalf of clients on a same or next day in Dawes and Sheridan counties only.

Lori A Day

1047 Donal Dr, Mansfield, OH 44907
Phone: 419-544-4740 - **Fax:** 419-756-4293 loriday1959@aol.com

Types of Records Retrieved: Real Estate

Local Retrieval Area: OH-Richland

Add'l Information: Established 1990. Normal turnaround time- 24-48 hours. Projects billed by number of names searched. Invoices at the end of the month. Specializes in real estate work only. Cover 1 county only to insure quick turnaround times. 25 years experience, many references upon requests.

Dayton Hayes Inc

373 Glen Cove Dr, Avondale Estates, GA 30002
Phone: 404-418-8323 - **Fax:** 404-296-5472 daytonhayes@earthlink.net

Types of Records Retrieved: Criminal and Civil courts: Real Estate; Tax Liens/Judgments; UCC records

Local Retrieval Area: GA-Cobb, De Kalb, Fulton, Gwinnett

Add'l Information: Established 2006. Normal turnaround time- 24 hours. Projects billed by number of names searched. Projects billed by the hour. First project may require prepayment. Payment due after search completed. He has been conducting searches for 5 years.

DBU Investigations

7814 Soledad Dr, Houston, TX 77083-4977
Phone: 281-564-9043 or 832-283-6518 - **Fax:** 281-494-0951
www.dbuinvestigations.com **email:** TWF@DBUinvestigations.com

Types of Records Retrieved: Criminal and Civil courts; Federal courts; Tax Liens/Judgments; UCC records

Local Retrieval Area: TX-Harris. **Correspondents:** nationwide.

Add'l Information: Established 2000. Normal turnaround time- 24-72 hours. Credit cards accepted. They specialize in access to criminal records- felony and misdemeanor. They also offer civil/family records, including a wide variety of lawsuits, tax, divorce/paternity case information, also general investigations, security svcs and consulting. A licensed PI in TX.

DCW & Associates

7400 Center Ave #209, Huntington Beach, CA 92647
Phone: 800-899-0442; 714-892-0442 - **Fax:** 714-892-3543
www.dcwpi.com **email:** info@dcwpi.com

Types of Records Retrieved: Criminal, Civil and Probate courts; Federal courts; Real Estate; Tax Liens/Judgments; UCC records; Vital records

Local Retrieval Area: CA-Alpine, El Dorado, Fresno, Kern, Lake, Los Angeles, Nevada, Orange, Placer, Riverside, San Bernardino, San Diego, San Luis Obispo, Santa Barbara, Sierra, Sonoma, Ventura. **Correspondent Relationships:** NV-Las Vegas, TX- Dallas, CO-Denver, Durango.

Add'l Information: Established 1987. Normal turnaround time- 24-48 hours. Projects billed by number of names searched. Projects billed by the hour. First project may require prepayment. Credit cards accepted. They conduct research/retrieval on a nationwide bases for a flat fee plus court costs. A licensed PI in CA. Performs service of process.

DDI Inc

218 W Pike St, Covington, KY 41011
Phone: 866-954-3000; 859-431-3011 - **Fax:** 866-431-1541; 859-392-8583
www.ddi-incorporated.com **email:** sales@ddi-incorporated.com
Types of Records Retrieved: Criminal, Civil and Probate courts; Federal courts; Real Estate; Tax Liens/Judgments; UCC records; Vital records
Local Retrieval Area: IN-Dearborn; KY-Boone, Campbell, Kenton; OH-Hamilton. **Correspondent Relationships:** IN, KY, OH, TN, MS.
Add'l Information: Established 1997. Normal turnaround time- 24-30 hours. Expedited service available. Projects billed by number of names searched. First project may require prepayment. Credit cards accepted. Will file/record documents for clients. They are a licensed registered and insured company that provides regional access to county courts. They are a FRS user and Clearstar user. A licensed PI in KY, OH. Performs service of process.

DDR (Delaware Document Retrieval)

4 East 7th St, Wilmington, DE 19801
Phone: 800-343-1742; 302-658-9971 - **Fax:** 302-658-9951
www.parcelsinc.com **email:** info@parcelsinc.com
Types of Records Retrieved: Criminal, Civil and Probate courts; Federal courts; Real Estate; Tax Liens/Judgments; UCC records
Local Retrieval Area: DE-Kent, New Castle, Sussex. **Correspondent Relationships:** Philadelphia, PA.
Add'l Information: Established 1981. Normal turnaround time- same day. Projects billed by number of names searched. First project may require prepayment. Credit cards accepted. Will file/record documents for clients. Visa, MasterCard and American Express accepted. They specialize in any type of search, document retrieval, filings, service of process, Secretary of State work and CD-rom briefs. They visit SOS, DMV, and Supreme Court regularly. Second web address is www.virtualdocket.com. Performs service of process.

De Baca Abstract Inc

PO Drawer 330, 811 N 4th, Fort Sumner, NM 88119
Phone: 505-355-2431 - **Fax:** 505-355-2850 debacabstract@plateautel.net
Records Retrieved: Civil and Probate courts; Real Estate; UCC records
Local Retrieval Area: NM-De Baca
Add'l Information: Established 1917. Normal turnaround time- 1 week. Projects billed by number of names searched. Projects billed by number of records located. First project may require prepayment. Will file/record documents for clients.

Dealey Abstract & Title Company

311 West Ave, Holdrege, NE 68949
Phone: 308-995-4622 - **Fax:** 308-995-6103 jdealey@charterinternet.com
Types of Records Retrieved: Real Estate; Tax Liens/Judgments; Probate courts; UCC records
Local Retrieval Area: NE-Phelps
Add'l Information: Established 1986. Normal turnaround time- 24-48 hours. Fee basis will vary by type of project.

Dean Research Group

9336 Greyhawk Dr, Ft Wayne, IN 46835
Phone: 260-485-4648 - **Fax:** 260-485-4651 fairrisdean@aol.com
Types of Records Retrieved: Criminal and Civil courts; Real Estate; Tax Liens; UCC records
Local Retrieval Area: IN-Adams, Allen, DeKalb, Huntington, Kosciusko, LaGrange, Miami, Noble, Steuben, Wabash, Wells, Whitley
Add'l Information: Established 2000. Normal turnaround time- 24-48 hours. Projects billed by number of names searched. Will invoice at the end of the month. She performs all types of public record searches hands-on, criminal, civil, state & federal tax lien searches and document retrieval in Northeast Indiana counties.

Debra Smith Research

6477 Walker Ln, Bonners Ferry, ID 83805-8541
Phone: 208-267-5605 - **Fax:** 208-267-1503 cory_deb@verizon.net
Types of Records Retrieved: Criminal and Civil courts; Real Estate; Tax Liens/Judgments; UCC records; Vital records
Local Retrieval Area: ID-Bonner, Boundary
Add'l Information: Established 1999. Normal turnaround time- 24-48 hours. First project may require prepayment. Will file/record documents for clients. Is a specialist hands-on retriever for extreme northern Idaho. Performs service of process.

Decatur County Abstract

308 State St, Atwood, KS 67730-9719
Phone: 785-626-3885 - **Fax:** 785-626-9481
Types of Records Retrieved: Criminal, Civil and Probate courts; Real Estate; Tax Liens/Judgments; UCC records; Vital records
Local Retrieval Area: KS-Decatur, Rawlins
Add'l Information: Established 1985. Normal turnaround time- 1-3 days. Projects billed by number of records located. Projects billed by the hour. Will file/record documents for clients. Personal checks are accepted. They specialize in real estate titles and title insurance.

Deception Control Inc

1835 S Perimeter Rd #125, Fort Lauderdale, FL 33309
Phone: 800-776-1660; 954-771-6900 - **Fax:** 954-776-7687
www.deception.com **email:** dci@deception.com
Types of Records Retrieved: Criminal and Civil courts; Real Estate; Tax Liens/Judgments; Vital records
Local Retrieval Area: FL-Broward, Dade, Palm Beach. **Correspondent Relationships:** nationwide.
Add'l Information: Established 1975. Normal turnaround time- 24-72 hours. Projects billed by number of names searched. First project may require prepayment. They specialize in pre-employment screening of employees to include retrieval, drug screening, polygraph testing & application verification. They now have a Windows-based system which makes them easy to access for pre-employment screening. A licensed PI in FL.

Decker Document Retrieval

814 S Covell Ave, Sioux Falls, SD 57104
Phone: 605-336-8402 - **Fax:** 605-336-8402
Types of Records Retrieved: Criminal, Civil and Probate courts; Federal courts; Real Estate; Tax Liens/Judgments; UCC records; Vital records
Local Retrieval Area: SD-Brookings, Lincoln, Minnehaha
Add'l Information: Established 1987. Normal turnaround time- 24-48 hours. Projects billed by number of names searched. Will file/record documents for clients. Press *51 when faxing.

Deeds Inc

3738 Williamson Rd, Roanoke, VA 24012
Phone: 540-563-5699 - **Fax:** 540-362-7833 gail@deedsinc.com
Types of Records Retrieved: Criminal, Civil and Probate courts; Real Estate; Tax Liens/Judgments; UCC records
Local Retrieval Area: VA-Bedford, Botetourt, Floyd, Franklin, Montgomery, Roanoke, Roanoke City, Salem City. **Correspondent in:** Richmond.
Add'l Information: Established 1991. Normal turnaround time- 24-48 hours unless otherwise states. Projects billed by number of names searched. Trip fees to outside counties are charged. Will file/record documents for clients. Terms: net 30 days. They specialize in title work, document retrieval, UCC retrieval and tax liens. Note- Bedford City title records located in Bedford County, Please confirm exact location of search prior to request for work.

Deeds Plus Abstract Services Inc

PO Box 114, Wyalusing, PA 18853
Phone: 570-746-3844 - **Fax:** 570-746-3699
www.lesliewizelman.com **email:** lwizelman@epix.net
Records Retrieved: Real Estate; Tax Liens/Judgments; UCC records
Local Retrieval Area: PA-Bradford
Add'l Information: Established 1983. Normal turnaround time- 24-48 hours depending on project and workload. Projects billed by number of names

searched. Terms are net 10 days, after which interest accrues. First project may require prepayment. Credit cards accepted. Will file/record documents for clients. They specialize in complete real estate and mortgage closings, including the issuing of title insurance. Closings and settlements are completed promptly and professionally with quality service.

DeedSearcher Title Research Services

4407 FM 1489, Brookshire, TX 77423
Phone: 281-375-8480 - **Fax:** 281-375-8481
www.deedsearcher.com **email:** deedsearcher@aol.com

Types of Records Retrieved: Real Estate; Tax Liens/Judgments; Probate courts; UCC records

Local Retrieval Area: TX-Anderson, Angelina, Atascosa, Austin, Bastrop, Bee, Bell, Bexar, Brazoria, Brazos, Brooks, Burleson, Burnett, Caldwell, Calhoun, Cameron, Camp, Cherokee, Collin, Colorado, Comal, Coryell, Dallas, Denton, Dewitt, Ector, El Paso, Ellis, Fannin, Fayette, Fort Bend, Galveston, Goliad, Grayson, Gregg, Grimes, Guadalupe, Harris, Hays, Hidalgo, Hood, Houston, Jackson, Jefferson, Jim Hogg, Jim Wells, Johnson, Kaufman, Kendall, Knox, LaSalle, Lavaca, Lubbock, Madison, Marion, Matagorda, McLennan, Midland, Milam, Montgomery, Nacogdoches, Nueces, Ochiltree, Orange, Palo Pinto, Panola, Parker, Pecos, Potter, Randall, Refugio, Robertson, Rockwall, Rusk, San Jacinto, Scurry, Smith, Starr, Tarrant, Taylor, Tom Green, Travis, Tyler, Upshur, Val Verde, Van Zandt, Victoria, Walker, Waller, Washington, Webb, Wharton, Wichita, Williamson, Wise, Wood, Zapata. **Correspondent Relationships:** Texas.

Add'l Information: Established 1994. Normal turnaround time- 6-24 hours. Projects billed by number of names searched. Will file/record documents for clients. Terms are net 30 days. They specialize in providing expedient real estate property searches statewide with a commitment to accuracy and complete customer satisfaction. They have competitive fees and have a 24 hour FAX. Document copies provided with every order. Licensed PI in TX.

Deines Inc

PO Box 750441, Las Vegas, NV 89136-0441
Phone: 702-453-9859 - **Fax:** 702-437-1558 deinesinc@cox.net

Types of Records Retrieved: Criminal, Civil and Probate courts; Federal courts; Real Estate; Tax Liens/Judgments; UCC records

Local Retrieval Area: NV-Clark, Washoe

Add'l Information: Established 1999. Normal turnaround time- 24 hours. Projects billed by number of names searched. Payments due net 30 days. They specialize in fast document filing and retrieval of most types of documents located in Clark County, NV. Has been in business since 1999.

Delaware Attorney Services

2000 Pennsylvania Ave #207, Wilmington, DE 19806
Phone: 800-457-9560; 302-429-0657 - **Fax:** 302-429-0656

Types of Records Retrieved: Criminal and Civil courts; Federal courts; Real Estate; Tax Liens/Judgments; UCC records; Vital records

Local Retrieval Area: DE-Kent, New Castle, Sussex

Add'l Information: Established 1985. Normal turnaround time- 2-5 days. Expedited service available. Projects billed by number of names searched. Will file/record documents for clients. Terms: net 30 days. They specialize in skiptracing and process service. Performs service of process.

Delaware County Abstract Co (Iowa)

304 E Main St, Manchester, IA 52057
Phone: 563-927-4858 - **Fax:** 563-927-1028 dcabstract@iowatelecom.net

Types of Records Retrieved: Criminal, Civil and Probate courts; Real Estate; Tax Liens/Judgments; UCC records; Vital records

Local Retrieval Area: IA-Delaware

Add'l Information: Established 1906. Normal turnaround time- 1-2 days. Projects billed by number of names searched. Projects billed by the hour. Will file/record documents for clients. They request prepayment from individuals, but will invoice businesses and established customers. They specialize in real estate lien searches.

Delaware County Abstract Co (Oklahoma)

330 S 5th St, Jay, OK 74346
Phone: 918-253-4425 - **Fax:** 918-253-6224

Types of Records Retrieved: Civil and Probate courts; Real Estate; Tax Liens/Judgments; UCC records

Local Retrieval Area: OK-Delaware

Add'l Information: Established 1907. Normal turnaround time- 2-3 days. Fee basis is determined per search. Will file/record documents for clients. They specialize in title insurance and will also do divorce searches.

Delmarva Abstractors

PO Box 376, 4 Kiowa Rd, Cambridge, MD 21613
Phone: 410-228-6044 - **Fax:** 410-228-6044

Types of Records Retrieved: Criminal, Civil and Probate courts; Real Estate; Tax Liens/Judgments; UCC records

Local Retrieval Area: MD-Caroline, Dorchester, Queen Anne's, Talbot

Add'l Information: Normal turnaround time- 24-48 hours. Projects billed by number of names searched. They specialize in title searches and current owner searches. Performs service of process.

Delta County Title Co

PO Box 127, Cooper, TX 75432
Phone: 903-395-4116 - **Fax:** 903-395-2106 delta_title@hotmail.coom

Types of Records Retrieved: Criminal, Civil and Probate courts; Real Estate; Tax Liens/Judgments; UCC records; Vital records

Local Retrieval Area: TX-Delta

Add'l Information: Established 1914. Normal turnaround time- variable depending on project. Projects billed by the hour. First project may require prepayment. Will file/record documents for clients. They have an attorney on staff. Performs service of process.

Kathleen Demmitt

3006 S Bannock St #408, Englewood, CO 80110
Phone: 303-781-0605, Fax- same searcher10@mail.com

Types of Records Retrieved: Criminal, Civil and Probate courts; Federal courts; Vital records **Local Retrieval Area:** CO-Denver

Add'l Info: Established 1998. Normal turnaround time- 24-48 hours. Projects billed by number of names searched. Will file/record documents for clients. She specializes in probate, federal and county criminal record searches.

Dennis R Sheraw & Associates Inc

5131 Estate Welcome, Christiansted, St Croix, VI 00820-4962
Phone: 800-967-6379; 340-773-3110 - **Fax:** 340-773-3113
www.islands.vi/~sheraw/ **email:** sheraw@islands.vi

Types of Records Retrieved: Criminal, Civil and Probate courts; Federal courts; Real Estate; Tax Liens/Judgments; UCC records; Vital records

Local Retrieval Area: VI-St. Croix, St. John, St. Thomas. Call for availability of other Caribbean islands. **Correspondents:** nationwide.

Add'l Information: Established 1983. Normal turnaround time- 1 week. Projects billed by the hour. First project may require prepayment. They specialize in civil investigation for attorneys and insurance companies. They cover the entire Caribbean. A licensed PI in Virgin Islands. Performs service of process.

DeReign & DeReign Attorneys at Law

PO Box 108, Caruthersville, MO 63830-0108
Phone: 573-333-4666 - **Fax:** 573-333-2641 dereign@semo.net

Types of Records Retrieved: Civil and Probate courts; Real Estate; Tax Liens/Judgments; UCC records

Local Retrieval Area: MO-Pemiscot

Add'l Information: Established 1930. Normal turnaround time-1-3 days. Fee basis will vary by the type of project. They specialize in title probate.

Desha Abstract & Title Co LLC

PO Box 261, McGehee, AR 71654
Phone: 870-222-5001 - **Fax:** 870-222-5504 smithanddrake@ipa.net

Types of Records Retrieved: Criminal, Civil and Probate courts; Real Estate; Tax Liens/Judgments; UCC records

Local Retrieval Area: AR-Desha

Add'l Information: Established 1930. Normal turnaround time- 1 week. Projects billed by the hour. First project may require prepayment. Will file/record documents for clients. They specialize in real estate, civil judgments and probate. They will file/record real estate documents on behalf of clients.

DeSoto Abstract & Title Co (FL)

11 N Polk Ave, Arcadia, FL 34266
Phone: 863-494-3656 - **Fax:** 863-494-3481 desoabst@earthlink.net

Types of Records Retrieved: Criminal, Civil and Probate courts; Real Estate; Tax Liens/Judgments; UCC records; Vital records

Local Retrieval Area: FL-De Soto. **Correspondent Relationships:** Charlotte, Lee, Hardee, Highlands counties.

Add'l Information: Established 1889. Normal turnaround time- 3-5 days. Projects billed by number of records located. Will file/record documents for clients. They specialize in title insurance and O & E searches.

Detailed Investigations

PO Box 5, Winslow, NJ 08095
Phone: 609-704-1801 - **Fax:** 609-704-2980
admin@detailedinvestigations.info

Types of Records Retrieved: Criminal and Civil courts

Local Retrieval Area: NJ-Atlantic, Bergen, Burlington, Camden, Cape May, Cumberland, Essex, Gloucester, Hudson, Hunterdon, Mercer, Middlesex, Monmouth, Morris, Ocean, Passaic, Salem, Somerset, Sussex, Union, Warren

Add'l Information: Established 1985. Normal turnaround time- 24-36 hours. Projects billed by number of names searched. A sole proprietorship since 1985, they specialize in detailed criminal record retrieval throughout New Jersey. A licensed PI in NJ.

Deuel County Abstract Co

PO Box 737, Clear Lake, SD 57226-0737
Phone: 605-874-8597 - **Fax:** 605-874-8598 dcabstco@itctel.com

Types of Records Retrieved: Criminal, Civil and Probate courts; Real Estate; Tax Liens/Judgments; UCC records; Vital records

Local Retrieval Area: SD-Deuel

Add'l Information: Established 1889. Normal turnaround time- 10 days. Fee basis will vary by the type of project. All projects require prepayment. Will file/record documents for clients. They specialize in title insurance.

Deuel County Abstract Co (Nebraska)

171 Vincent Ave, Chappell, NE 69129
Phone: 308-874-2212 - **Fax:** 308-874-3491 paliklaw@earthlink.net

Types of Records Retrieved: Civil and Probate courts; Real Estate; Tax Liens/Judgments; UCC records

Local Retrieval Area: NE-Cheyenne, Deuel, Garden, Keith, Kimball, Morrill, Scotts Bluff

Add'l Information: Normal turnaround time- 3-4 days. Charges may vary depending on projects. Will file/record documents for clients. They are an attorneys' office; they can retrieve UCC records from the state. They can provide real estate closing services if needed. Performs service of process.

Devine & Co Inc

PO Box 1149, Minot, ND 58702
Phone: 701-852-6800 - **Fax:** 701-852-6806 devine@minot.ndak.net

Types of Records Retrieved: Criminal, Civil and Probate courts; Federal District courts; Real Estate; Tax Liens/Judgments

Local Retrieval Area: ND-Ward. **Correspondent Relationships:** 22 other counties; NW North Dakota.

Add'l Information: Established 1903. Normal turnaround time- 1-2 days. Projects billed by number of names searched. Abstracting has per item charge. All projects require prepayment. Will file/record documents for clients. They will also invoice. They specialize real estate closings, title insurance, title searches, title memorandums and abstracts.

Dewey County Abstract Co

PO Box 157, Taloga, OK 73667
Phone: 580-328-5556 - **Fax:** 580-328-5484

Types of Records Retrieved: Criminal, Civil and Probate courts; Federal courts; Real Estate; Tax Liens/Judgments; UCC records

Local Retrieval Area: OK-Dewey

Add'l Info: Established 1896. Turnaround time- less than 1 week. Projects billed by number of names searched. Projects billed by the hour. Fee basis will vary by the type of project. Will file/record documents for clients.

DFW Court Services

PO Box 50071, Dallas, TX 75250
Phone: 800-436-0516; 214-747-1756 - **Fax:** 888-318-8569; 214-747-1758
www.dfwcourtservices.com **email:** dfwcourt@yahoo.com

Types of Records Retrieved: Criminal, Civil and Probate courts; Federal courts; Real Estate; Tax Liens/Judgments; UCC records

Local Retrieval Area: TX-Bexar, Collin, Dallas, Denton, Grayson, Harris, Tarrant, Travis. **Correspondent Relationships:** statewide.

Add'l Information: Established 1993. Normal turnaround time- 24 hours for Tarrant and Dallas Counties, 48-72 hours for all other counties. Expedited service available. Projects billed by number of names searched. Credit cards accepted. Will file/record documents for clients. They specialize in all public records on county, state and federal basis, including document retrieval and court filings in these courts. They also have extensive experience with the Federal Record Center and National Archive facility. A licensed PI in TX. Performs service of process.

Diamond Abstractors Inc

PO Box 751501, Las Vegas, NV 89136-1501
Phone: 702-355-0364 - **Fax:** 702-437-1558 diamondinc@cox.net

Types of Records Retrieved: Criminal, Civil and Probate courts; Federal courts; Real Estate; Tax Liens/Judgments; UCC records; Vital records

Local Retrieval Area: NV-Clark, Washoe. **Correspondents:** statewide.

Add'l Information: Established 2004. Normal turnaround time- 24 hours. Projects billed by number of names searched. Will file/record documents for clients. Payment due net 30 days. They offer competitive pricing, fast turn-around, accuracy and volume discounts. A licensed PI in NV.

Dickey County Abstract & Title

PO Box 339, Ellendale, ND 58436
Phone: 701-349-3450 - **Fax:** 701-349-2453

Types of Records Retrieved: Criminal, Civil and Probate courts; Federal courts; Real Estate; Tax Liens/Judgments; UCC records; Vital records

Local Retrieval Area: ND-Dickey

Add'l Information: Established 1961. Normal turnaround time- variable depending on project. Projects billed by number of names searched. Fee basis will vary by the type of project. Will file/record documents for clients. Payment due upon delivery of invoice.

George L Dickinson

PO Box 1761, Chicago, IL 60690
Phone: 708-307-4792 - **Fax:** 815-806-8359 gdickinson@earthlink.net

Types of Records Retrieved: Criminal and Civil courts; Federal courts

Local Retrieval Area: IL-Cook. **Correspondent Relationships:** DeKalb, DuPage, Kane, Lake, McHenry counties IL.

Add'l Information: Established 1986. Normal turnaround time- 24 hours. Projects billed by number of names searched. Projects billed by the hour. First project may require prepayment. Net 30 days. They also perform workers' comp record searches.

Diligent Detective Agency Inc

PO Box 581, Clifton, IL 60927 diligent@prairienet.net
Phone: 877-694-3332; 815-694-3332 - **Fax:** 815-694-3351

Types of Records Retrieved: Criminal, Civil and Probate courts; Federal courts; Real Estate; Tax Liens/Judgments; Vital records

Local Retrieval Area: IL-Champaign, Ford, Iroquois, Kankakee, Vermilion

Add'l Information: Established 1991. Normal turnaround time- 48 hours. Expedited service available. Projects billed by number of names searched. Projects billed by number of records located. First project may require prepayment. A licensed PI in IL. Performs service of process.

Diligenz Inc

6500 Harbour Heights Pky, Mukilteo, WA 98275
Phone: 800-858-5294; - **Fax:** 800-345-6059
www.diligenz.com **email:** chritg@diligenz.com

Types of Records Retrieved: Criminal and Civil courts; Tax Liens/Judgments; UCC records

Local Retrieval Area: WA-Island, Jefferson, King, Lewis, Pierce, Skagit, Snohomish, Thurston, Whatcom. **Correspondents:** nationwide.

Add'l Information: Established 1991. Normal turnaround time- 24 hours. Projects billed by number of names searched. Credit cards accepted. Will file/record documents for clients. They specialize in UCC searches and filing, also Corporate Good Standing searches, Federal/state Tax Liens/Judgments, corporate document retrieval, Bankruptcy searches, business credit reports, litigation searches, flood determinations.

Direct Corporate Services Inc

12043 Warwick Cr., Parish, FL 34219

Phone: 800-783-7904; - **Fax:** 941-776-9812 directcorp@tampabay.rr.com

Types of Records Retrieved: Criminal, Civil and Probate courts; Federal courts; Real Estate; Tax Liens/Judgments; UCC records

Local Retrieval Area: FL-Alachua, Bay, Brevard, Broward, Charlotte, Collier, Dade, De Soto, Escambia, Flagler, Hendry, Hernando, Hillsborough, Indian River, Lake, Lee, Leon, Manatee, Marion, Martin, Monroe, Okaloosa, Okeechobee, Orange, Osceola, Palm Beach, Pasco, Pinellas, Polk, Santa Rosa, Sarasota, Seminole, St. Lucie, Sumter, Volusia, Walton. **Correspondent Relationships:** statewide.

Add'l Information: Established 1985. Normal turnaround time- 24-48 hours. Expedited service available. Projects billed by number of names searched. First project may require prepayment. Will file/record documents for clients. Terms: net 30 days. They specialize in complete research for UCC, federal and state tax liens, judgments and litigation. They also do bulk projects and current owner searches. Title searches are done in Pinellas and Hillsborough counties only.

Direct Title Solutions Inc

12 N Braddock St, Winchester, VA 22601-4120

Phone: 540-450-0740 - **Fax:** 540-450-0744 info@dtsadvantage.com

Records Retrieved: Real Estate; Tax Liens/Judgments; UCC records

Local Area: VA-Alexandria, Arlington, Clarke, Fairfax, Fairfax City, Falls Church City, Frederick, Loudoun, Manassas City, Manassas Park City, Prince William, Winchester; DC-Washington. **correspondents:** nationwide.

Add'l Information: Established 2000. Normal turnaround time- 24 hours or less. Projects billed by number of names searched. Fees negotiated with volume. First project may require prepayment. Will file/record documents for clients. They specialize in all types of real estate search services in the Washington, DC and Northern VA areas.

DiSearch

3417 Quail Ridge Ln, Matthews, NC 28104

Phone: 704-846-6335 - **Fax:** 704-846-8178 disearch99@carolina.rr.com

Types of Records Retrieved: Civil and Probate courts; Real Estate; Tax Liens/Judgments; UCC records

Local Retrieval Area: NC-Mecklenburg, Union. **Correspondent Relationships:** statewide.

Add'l Information: Established 1999. Normal turnaround time- 1-2 days. Projects billed by number of names searched. First project may require prepayment. Will file/record documents for clients. Payment due net 30 days. They specialize in property/real estate. They are a professional hands-on service in all local courts.

Divide Abstract Co

206 N Main St, Crosby, ND 58730

Phone: 701-965-6352, 701-965-2222 - **Fax:** 701-965-6353

Types of Records Retrieved: Real Estate; Tax Liens/Judgments

Local Retrieval Area: ND-Divide

Add'l Information: Established 1900. First project may require prepayment. They specialize in real estate.

DJ Records

PO Box 753597, Memphis, TN 38175-3597

Phone: 901-795-6450 - **Fax:** 901-362-8320 JLucyDJR@aol.com

Types of Records Retrieved: Criminal courts

Local Retrieval Area: TN-Shelby

Add'l Information: Established 1996. Normal turnaround time- 24 hours. Projects billed by number of names searched. Will bill once a month.

DL Investigations & Attorney Support

3507 N Central #203, Phoenix, AZ 85012

Phone: 602-285-9901 - **Fax:** 602-285-0445

Types of Records Retrieved: Criminal, Civil and Probate courts; Federal courts; Real Estate; Tax Liens/Judgments; UCC records; Vital records

Local Retrieval Area: AZ-Maricopa. **Correspondent Relationships:** Pinal, Pima, Coconino counties AZ.

Add'l Information: Established 1994. Normal turnaround time- 24 hours. Projects billed by number of names searched. Projects billed by number of records located. Projects billed by the hour. First project may require prepayment. Will file/record documents for clients. Payment due upon completion of work. A licensed PI in AZ. Performs service of process.

DLS (Demovsky Lawyer Service - Albany)

100 State St #220, Albany, NY 12207

Phone: 518-449-8411 - **Fax:** 518-449-2467

Types of Records Retrieved: Criminal, Civil and Probate courts; Federal courts; Real Estate; Tax Liens/Judgments; UCC records

Local Retrieval Area: NY-Albany, Rensselaer, Schenectady. **Correspondent Relationships:** nationwide.

Add'l Information: Established 1983. Normal turnaround time- 72 hours. Projects billed by the hour. Charges may be varied depending on project. Will file/record documents for clients. First project requires prepayment. They specialize in corporate law. Performs service of process.

DLS (Demovsky Lawyer Service - New York)

401 Broadway #510, New York, NY 10013

Phone: 800-443-1058; 212-925-1220 - **Fax:** 212-941-0235

www.dlsny.com **email:** info@dlsny.com

Types of Records Retrieved: Criminal, Civil and Probate courts; Federal courts; Real Estate; Tax Liens/Judgments; UCC records; Vital records

Local Retrieval Area: NJ-Bergen, Essex; NY-Bronx, Kings, Nassau, New York, Queens, Richmond, Rockland, Westchester. **Correspondent Relationships:** New York, New Jersey, Connecticut, also nationally, internationally.

Add'l Information: Established 1983. Normal turnaround time- 24 hours. Projects billed by the hour. First project may require prepayment. They specialize in detail-oriented personal service. Can retrieve MVRs nationwide, as well as specializing in NY. Also do process serving nationwide. Performs service of process.

DLS Background Services Inc

30141 Antelope Rd PMB #231, Menifee, CA 92584

Phone: 951-301-8584 - **Fax:** 951-672-2234 dlsbackground@comcast.net

Types of Records Retrieved: Criminal and Civil courts; Federal courts; Tax Liens/Judgments; UCC records

Local Retrieval Area: CA-Amador, Los Angeles, Marin, Placer, Riverside, Santa Clara, Solano, Tehama, Tulare, Tuolumne. **Correspondent Relationships:** nationwide.

Add'l Information: Established 1998. Normal turnaround time- 24-48 hours. Projects billed by number of names searched. First project may require prepayment. Credit cards accepted. They specialize in criminal and civil record research throughout the whole State of California with nationwide correspondence; other searches available include MVR report and employment/education verification. They offer quick and thorough turnaround.

DMI

413 High St #300, Bridgeport, WV 26330

Phone: 304-842-2946 - **Fax:** 304-842-5826

www.dmiauctions.com **email:** dmi@dmiauctions.com

Types of Records Retrieved: Criminal, Civil and Probate courts; Federal courts; Real Estate; Tax Liens/Judgments; UCC records; Vital records

Local Retrieval Area: WV-Barbour, Braxton, Doddridge, Harrison, Lewis, Marion, Mason, Monongalia, Preston, Randolph, Ritchie, Taylor, Tucker, Tyler, Upshur, Webster, Wetzel, Wood. **Correspondent Relationships:** West Virginia.

Add'l Information: Established 1978. Normal turnaround time- 24-48 hours. Projects billed by number of names searched. Credit cards accepted. Will file/record documents for clients. Has 22+ years experience. Performs service of process.

Shelly and James Dobler

207 Bob Hayes Rd, Jonesboro, TN 37659
Phone: 423-753-4885 - **Fax:** 423-753-4885
Types of Records Retrieved: Criminal and Civil courts
Local Retrieval Area: TN-Carter, Sullivan, Unicoi, Washington
Add'l Information: Established 2000. Normal turnaround time- within 24 hrs if received by 8AM. First project may require prepayment. They specialize in civil and criminal court records.

Doc Hunters

812 Pinellas St, Clearwater, FL 33756-3429
Phone: 727-518-6700 - **Fax:** 727-518-6886
www.dochunters.com **email:** orders@dochunters.com
Types of Records Retrieved: Real Estate; Current Owner Searches; UCC records; Tax Liens/Judgments
Local Retrieval Area: FL-Hillsborough, Pinellas. **Correspondent Relationships:** nationwide.
Add'l Information: Established 2001. Normal turnaround time- 48 hours for title work, 3-5 days for document retrieval. Expedited service available. Projects billed by number of names searched. Billing can be customized. Will do large orders or projects. Will file/record documents for clients. Specialize in Nationwide Title Searches, Document Retrieval & Recordings. Competitive pricing, experienced, insured, live customer service. Client can submit orders, view order status & download online. Experienced abstracting & vendor management company.

Doc*U*Search Inc

PO Box 777, Concord, NH 03302-0777
Phone: 800-332-3034; 603-224-2871 - **Fax:** 877-524-3034; 603-224-2794
www.docusearchinc.com **email:** info@docusearchinc.com
Types of Records Retrieved: Criminal, Civil and Probate courts; Federal courts; Real Estate; Tax Liens/Judgments; UCC records; Vital records
Local Retrieval Area: NH-Belknap, Carroll, Cheshire, Coos, Grafton, Hillsborough, Merrimack, Rockingham, Strafford, Sullivan.
Correspondent Relationships: nationwide.
Add'l Information: Established 1977. Normal turnaround time- usually 48 hours. Fee basis will vary by type of search. Will file/record documents for clients. Credit accounts accepted. They specialize in UCC, corporate, real estate abstracts, court documents, tax lien, current owner, and specific mortgage/assignment searches in all New England states.

Docket Detective LLC

404 W South St, Carlisle, PA 17013
Phone: 717-249-7053 - **Fax:** 717-249-9397
dawnflower@comcast.net
Types of Records Retrieved: Criminal and Civil courts
Local Retrieval Area: PA-Adams, Beaver, Cambria, Cumberland, Dauphin, Lancaster, Lebanon, Perry, Sullivan, Union, York
Add'l Information: Established 1995. Normal turnaround time- 20 hours or less. Projects billed by number of names searched. With 11 years experience, The Docket Detective LLC provides reliable, fast turnaround service for clients and understands the importance of every search as a degreed, seasoned HR professional.

Docu-File USA Inc

1609 S Boston Ave, Tulsa, OK 74119-4415
Phone: 877-742-4994; 918-742-4994 - **Fax:** 800-722-8889; 918-742-4228
www.docufileusa.com **email:** info@docufileusa.com
Types of Records Retrieved: Real Estate
Local Retrieval Area: OK-Creek, Rogers, Tulsa. **Correspondent Relationships:** nationwide.
Add'l Information: Established 1997. Normal turnaround time- 24 hours. Projects billed by number of names searched. First project may require prepayment. Will file/record documents for clients. They specialize in real estate record checks, including 40 years searches. They have 20 years experience in title business.

Document Depot Express

18738 Jersey Ave, Artesia, CA 90701
Phone: 562-860-2907, cell- 562-706-2031 - **Fax:** 562-865-8207
docdepotexpress@aol.com
Types of Records Retrieved: Real Estate; Tax Liens/Judgments; Vital records
Local Retrieval Area: CA-Los Angeles, Orange, Riverside, San Bernardino, San Diego. **Correspondent Relationships:** Southern California.
Add'l Information: Established 1999. Normal turnaround time- 24 hours. Projects billed by number of names searched. All projects require prepayment. Will file/record documents for clients. Payment terms are net 30 days. They specialize in real estate record research, document retrieval, current owner and deed reports.

Document Recording & Retrieval Services

55 S Valle Verde #235-192, Henderson, NV 89012
Phone: 702-558-6207 - **Fax:** 702-617-9548
www.drrsvcs.com **email:** customerservice@drrsvcs.com
Types of Records Retrieved: Real Estate; Vital records
Local Retrieval Area: NV-Clark, Washoe. **Correspondent Relationships:** nationwide.
Add'l Information: Established 2000. Normal turnaround time- 48 hours. Projects billed by number of names searched. First project may require prepayment. Will file/record documents for clients. They specialize in document recording of assignments in all recording districts. They do expedient retrieval of records nationwide.

Document Research Service

6002 E Cambridge Av, Scottsdale, AZ 85257
Phone: 480-947-5493 - **Fax:** 480-947-5496 jjohn32@cox.net
Types of Records Retrieved: Real Estate; Tax Liens/Judgments; UCC records; Vital records; Police reports
Local Retrieval Area: AZ-Maricopa
Add'l Information: Established 1999. Normal turnaround time- 24-48 hours, depending upon project. Projects billed by number of names searched. Or per project or report. Payment due upon receipt. They specialize in current owner/mortgage abstracts and obtaining local and nationwide police reports. A licensed PI in AZ.

Document Retrieval Inc

6307 Red Haven Rd, Columbia, MD 21045-4475
Phone: 443-995-7488 - **Fax:** 410-312-9989 a_carels@yahoo.com
Types of Records Retrieved: Real Estate
Local Retrieval Area: MD-Anne Arundel, Baltimore, Baltimore City, Calvert, Carroll, Cecil, Charles, Frederick, Harford, Howard, Montgomery, Prince George's, Queen Anne's, St. Mary's
Add'l Information: Established 1999. Normal turnaround time- 24-48 hours if electronic, 3-5 days if courthouse retrieval. Projects billed by number of names searched. First project may require prepayment. Document Retrieval Inc started in 1999. They specialize in land record recording and retrieval, but will pull legal documents as well. They have the ability to pull records from home as well as from the courthouses. Also a process server. Performs service of process.

Document Retrieval Network Inc

101 Data Farm Rd, Falmouth, KY 41040
Phone: 859-654-2890 - **Fax:** 859-654-2892
www.docret.com **email:** nathan@docret.com
Records Retrieved: Real Estate; Tax Liens/Judgments; UCC records
Local Retrieval Area: KY-Boone, Campbell, Fayette, Grant, Harrison, Jefferson, Kenton, Pendleton; NY-Bronx, Kings, Nassau, Queens, Suffolk; OH-Butler, Clermont, Hamilton, Montgomery, Warren. **Correspondent Relationships:** OH, NY, NJ, PA, KY, WV, ME, CT & MA.
Add'l Information: Established 1999. Normal turnaround time- 24-48 hours. Projects billed by number of names searched. First project may require

prepayment. Will file/record documents for clients. They specialize in high volume real estate document retrieval and title searches.

Document Retrieval Service

613 SW 112th St, Oklahoma City, OK 73170
Phone: 877-902-9377; 405-235-3653 - **Fax:** 877-903-9377; 405-235-2691
www.drsok.com **email:** steve@drsok.com

Types of Records Retrieved: Criminal, Civil and Probate courts; Federal courts; Real Estate; Tax Liens/Judgments; UCC records; Vital records; Corporate filings; Secretary of State documents

Local Retrieval Area: OK-77 counties. **Correspondent Relationships:** statewide.

Add'l Info: Established 1970. Turnaround time- 24 hours Oklahoma County and Secretary of State, all other counties 48 hours or more. Projects billed by number of names searched. Bulk discounts are given. Will file/record documents for clients. Payment is due on receipt. They specialize in corporate retrieval and filings at the Secretary of State. They also search all (77) counties in Oklahoma for UCC filings, State and Federal tax liens, pending suits and judgments as well as real property searches.

Document Search Services

422 Memory Ct, Green Bay, WI 54301
Phone: 800-526-2157; 920-437-6040 shinegb@aol.com

Types of Records Retrieved: Real Estate

Local Retrieval Area: WI-Brown, Calumet, Dane, Dodge, Door, Douglas, Fond du Lac, Jefferson, Kenosha, Kewaunee, Manitowoc, Marinette, Milwaukee, Outagamie, Ozaukee, Racine, Washington, Waukesha, Winnebago. **Correspondent Relationships:** statewide.

Add'l Information: Normal turnaround time- 3-5 days. Projects billed by number of names searched. Bill within 15-30 days. Will file/record documents for clients. They specialize in providing document retrieval of mortgage and assignment copies in all Wisconsin counties.

Documents 5280

2623 W 119th Ave, Westminster, CO 80234
Phone: 303-438-8967 - **Fax:** 866-232-6478 documents5280@msn.com

Records Retrieved: Real Estate; Tax Liens/Judgments; UCC records

Local Retrieval Area: CO-Adams, Arapahoe, Boulder, Broomfield, Denver, Douglas, Jefferson

Add'l Information: Established 2004. Normal turnaround time- 24-72 hours. Expedited service available. Projects billed by number of names searched. Payment due-net 30 days. Invoice sent with each job. They specialize in real estate document search/retrieval in the Metro Denver area. Expect professional and accurate work completed on time and at a fair rate.

DocumentServe Express

1800 3rd Ave #612, Rock Island, IL 61201
Phone: 309-786-2220 - **Fax:** 309-786-2221
www.documentserve.com **email:** documentserve@mchsi.com

Types of Records Retrieved: Criminal, Civil and Probate courts; Federal courts; Real Estate; Tax Liens/Judgments; UCC records; Vital records

Local Retrieval Area: IA-Scott; IL-Rock Island

Add'l Information: Established 1997. Normal turnaround time- 48-72 hours. Expedited service available. May charge by number of records searched. First project may require prepayment. Credit cards accepted. Please call to schedule service and payment. DocumentServe Express provides Federal, State and Municipal court and record services that are dependable, fast and responsive to our clients. DocumentServe Express services Illinois and Iowa. A licensed PI in IA Lic# 747, IL Lic# 115-001662. Performs service of process.

Docu-Search California

14252 Culver Dr #A802, Irvine, CA 92604
Phone: 800-466-9450; 714-836-8664 - **Fax:** 888-466-9459; 714-836-8871

Types of Records Retrieved: Criminal, Civil and Probate courts; Federal courts; Real Estate; Tax Liens/Judgments; UCC records; Vital records

Local Retrieval Area: CA-Los Angeles, Orange, Riverside, San Bernardino. **Correspondent Relationships:** statewide.

Add'l Information: Established 1990. Normal turnaround time- 1-3 days. Projects billed by number of names searched. First project may require prepayment. Will file/record documents for clients.

Doc-U-Search Hawaii

1188 Bishop St #2212, Honolulu, HI 96813
Phone: 808-523-1200 - **Fax:** 808-533-3686

Types of Records Retrieved: Criminal and Civil courts; Federal courts; Real Estate; Tax Liens/Judgments; UCC records

Local Retrieval Area: HI-Hawaii, Honolulu, Kalawao, Kauai, Maui

Add'l Info: Established 1986. Normal turnaround time- 1-2 days. Expedited service available. Projects billed by number of names searched. First project may require prepayment. Will file/record documents for clients.

Docu-Search of Washington DC

806 7th St NW #301-A, Washington, DC 20001
Phone: 202-737-5707 - **Fax:** 202-737-5708

Types of Records Retrieved: Criminal, Civil and Probate courts; Federal courts; Real Estate; Tax Liens/Judgments; UCC records; Vital records

Local Retrieval Area: DC-District of Columbia, MD-Montgomery, Prince George's, VA-Fairfax

Add'l Information: Established 1991. Normal turnaround time- 48 hours. Fee depends upon type of project. First project may require prepayment. Will file/record documents for clients. They specialize in real estate searches, land tax liens, and UCC in the city of Washington, DC. A cell phone contact number for the company is 202-276-0119.

DocuSearch Services

1036 Shady Fork Rd, Chattanooga, TN 37421
Phone: 423-894-2425 - **Fax:** 423-894-3572 hendersonlarry@juno.com

Records Retrieved: Real Estate; Tax Liens/Judgments; UCC records

Local Retrieval Area: GA-Catoosa, Chattooga, Cherokee, Cobb, Floyd, Gordon, Murray, Walker, Whitfield; TN-Hamilton

Add'l Information: Established 1996. Normal turnaround time- 12-24 hours. Projects billed by number of names searched. Prefer 30-60 payment cycles. They are a document retrieval resource pledging timeliness and accuracy. Very competitive fees.

Docx

1111 Alderman Dr #350, Alpharetta, GA 30005
Phone: 866-729-8099; - **Fax:** 770-753-2730
www.docx.com **email:** docxacct@docx.com

Types of Records Retrieved: Real Estate; UCC records

Local Retrieval Area: GA-Cobb, De Kalb, Fulton. **Correspondent Relationships:** nationwide contractors every county nationwide.

Add'l Information: Normal turnaround time- 3-5 business days. Projects billed by number of names searched. First project may require prepayment. Will file/record documents for clients. Payment due upon receipt for established clients. They offer image delivery, certified copies, online ordering, 1 day turnaround on "information only" requests, and online status reporting.

Dody Fuhrmann-Private Investigator

PO Box 50507, Sparks, NV 89435-0507
Phone: 775-544-7993 - **Fax:** 775-626-1609 dodyf4@charter.net

Types of Records Retrieved: Criminal, Civil and Probate courts; Federal courts; Real Estate; Tax Liens/Judgments; UCC records; Vital records

Local Retrieval Area: NV-Washoe

Add'l Information: Established 2006. Normal turnaround time- 24-48 hours. Projects billed by number of names searched. First project may require prepayment. They provide criminal court searches in Washoe County, NV. Volume discounts available. A licensed PI in NV.

Dominion Abstract & Title Agency

PO Box 72607, Richmond, VA 23235
Phone: 804-794-9037 - **Fax:** 804-379-6232 saabgirl1@netzero.com

Types of Records Retrieved: Criminal, Civil and Probate courts; Real Estate; Tax Liens/Judgments; UCC records

Local Retrieval Area: VA-Amelia, Chesterfield, Hanover, Henrico, Powhatan, Richmond City

Add'l Information: Established 1985. Normal turnaround time- 24-48 hours. Projects billed by number of names searched. First project may require prepayment. Will file/record documents for clients.

Dominion Record Search

2416 Little Creek Dam Rd, Toano, VA 23168
Phone: 757-566-8233 - **Fax:** 757-566-8291
joan.hanchey@verizon.net

Types of Records Retrieved: Criminal and Civil courts; Federal courts; Real Estate; Tax Liens/Judgments; UCC records; Vital records

Local Retrieval Area: VA-Chesapeake, Hampton, James City, Newport News, Norfolk, Poquoson, Suffolk, Virginia Beach, Williamsburg, York

Add'l Information: Established 2001. Normal turnaround time- 24 hours. Projects billed by number of names searched. End of the month billing cycle. Dominion Record Search represents the Old Dominion state in the greater Hampton Roads and Tidewater areas. Requests are searched in civil courts, federal courts, district and circuit courts.

Lorina Dominquez

610 Hickory St, Carlsbad, NM 88220-4522
Phone: 505-887-3489; Fax- same

Types of Records Retrieved: Criminal and Civil courts

Local Retrieval Area: NM-Eddy

Add'l Information: Normal turnaround time- 1-2 days. First project may require prepayment. Her cell phone is 505-361-0015. She specializes in criminal court records, also civil.

Don Martin & Assoc.

103 N Main, #3, Kokomo, IN 46901
Phone: 765-452-1760 - **Fax:** 765-236-1770
www.indianapi.com **email:** dmartin@indianapi.com

Types of Records Retrieved: Criminal and Civil courts

Local Retrieval Area: IN-Cass, Grant, Howard, Miami, Tipton, Wabash

Add'l Information: Established 2003. Normal turnaround time- 3-5 days. First project may require prepayment. They also provide court filings, court record retrieval, skiptracing and private investigations. A licensed PI in IN. Performs service of process.

Larry R Dorning PC

111 W Main St, Hohenwald, TN 38462-1404
Phone: 931-796-5959 - **Fax:** 931-796-5950

Records Retrieved: Real Estate; Tax Liens/Judgments; UCC records

Local Retrieval Area: TN-Hickman, Lawrence, Lewis, Maury, Perry, Wayne

Add'l Information: Established 1975. Normal turnaround time- 48 hours. Charges vary depending on type of search. Will file/record documents for clients. He specializes in real estate record searches. He will file documents in Lewis County only.

Dotter Abstract & Associates

506 Main St, Walsenburg, CO 81089
Phone: 719-738-1730 - **Fax:** 719-738-1012

Types of Records Retrieved: Real Estate; Tax Liens/Judgments; UCC records; Vital records

Local Retrieval Area: CO-Huerfano, Las Animas

Add'l Information: Established 1982. Normal turnaround time- 2-3 days. Fee basis will vary by the type of project. First project may require prepayment. Will file/record documents for clients. They specialize in real estate title and insurance.

Dora Doty

106 Ruggles Ave, St Clairsville, OH 43950
Phone: 740-695-4917 - **Fax:** 740-699-0676

Types of Records Retrieved: Criminal, Civil and Probate courts; Real Estate; Tax Liens/Judgments; UCC records; Vital records

Retrieval Area: OH-Belmont, Guernsey, Harrison, Jefferson, Monroe, Noble

Add'l Information: Established 1990. Normal turnaround time- 24-48 hours. Projects billed by number of names searched. Will file/record documents for clients. She specializes in title and lien work. 35 years experience.

Douglas County Abstract & Title Co

PO Box 97, Ava, MO 65608
Phone: 417-683-4701 - **Fax:** 417-683-5980

Types of Records Retrieved: Criminal, Civil and Probate courts; Real Estate; Tax Liens/Judgments

Local Retrieval Area: MO-Douglas

Add'l Information: Established 1950. Turnaround time- 5 working days. Fee basis will vary by type of project. Will file/record documents for clients.

Douglas County Abstract Co

117 7th Ave E, Alexandria, MN 56308-1807
Phone: 320-763-3426 - **Fax:** 320-762-2455 dcac@rea-alp.com

Types of Records Retrieved: Civil and Probate courts; Real Estate; Tax Liens/Judgments

Local Retrieval Area: MN-Douglas, Pope. **Correspondents:** statewide.

Add'l Information: Normal turnaround time- 1 week. Projects billed by number of names searched. Charges vary depending on project. First project may require prepayment. Will file/record documents for clients. They also invoice. They specialize in abstracts, closings and title insurance.

Douglas County Abstract Co Inc

PO Box 167, 110 E Sale St, Tuscola, IL 61953
Phone: 217-253-3214 - **Fax:** 217-253-3022

Types of Records Retrieved: Real Estate; Tax Liens/Judgments; Probate courts; UCC records **Local Retrieval Area:** IL-Douglas

Add'l Information: Established 1896. Normal turnaround time- 1-3 days. Projects billed by the hour. First project may require prepayment. Will file/record documents for clients. They are Chicago Title agents.

Douglas County Title Co (Oregon)

629 SE Main St, Roseburg, OR 97470
Phone: 541-672-3388 - **Fax:** 541-672-8110
www.douglascountytitle.com **email:** lorries@douglascountytitle.com

Types of Records Retrieved: Criminal, Civil and Probate courts; Real Estate; Tax Liens/Judgments; UCC records; Vital records

Local Retrieval Area: OR-Douglas

Add'l Information: Established 1879. Normal turnaround time- 2-3 days. Projects billed by the hour. All projects require prepayment. Will file/record documents for clients. They specialize in real estate and escrow collections.

Douglas County Title Inc (South Dakota)

PO Box 310, 722 Main St, Armour, SD 57313
Phone: 605-724-2235 - **Fax:** 605-724-2419

Types of Records Retrieved: Civil and Probate courts; Real Estate; Tax Liens/Judgments **Local Retrieval Area:** SD-Douglas

Add'l Information: Established 1953. Normal turnaround time- 4 days. Fee basis varies by type of transaction. They specialize in abstracts and title insurance. They also file/record real estate documents on behalf of clients on a same or next day basis.

Dovolos & Associates

PMB 207 - 5021 Vernon Ave S #207, Edina, MN 55436-2102
Phone: 952-920-9999 dovolos@msn.net

Types of Records Retrieved: Criminal and Civil courts; Federal bankruptcy; Tax Liens/Judgments; UCC records; Vital records

Local Retrieval Area: MN-Anoka, Carver, Dakota, Hennepin, Ramsey, Scott, Washington. **Correspondents:** nationwide and Canada.

Add'l Information: Established 1968. Normal turnaround time- 24-36 hours. Projects billed by number of names searched. First project may require prepayment. They are a full service licensed private investigative agency. A licensed PI in MN. Performs service of process.

Dr Dave's Docs

PO Box 251183, Glendale, CA 91225
Phone: 818-246-3087 - **Fax:** 818-265-5006 dhatch1@earthlink.net

Types of Records Retrieved: Real Estate

Local Retrieval Area: CA-Los Angeles, Orange, Riverside, San Bernardino, San Diego, Santa Barbara, Ventura

Add'l Information: Established 1999. Normal turnaround time- 24-72 hours. Projects billed by number of names searched. First project may require prepayment. Terms are net 30 days. Will do walk-in recording of docs.

Drake Land Title Co

PO Box 998, 167 W Main, Warsaw, MO 65355-0998

Phone: 660-438-5188 - **Fax:** 660-438-6644 drakeland@earthlink.net

Types of Records Retrieved: Civil and Probate courts; Real Estate; Tax Liens/Judgments; UCC records

Local Retrieval Area: MO-Benton

Add'l Information: Established 1886. Normal turnaround time- variable depending on project. Projects billed by number of names searched. First project may require prepayment. Will file/record documents for clients. They specialize in title insurance. 150 year title plant.

Drew County Abstract & Title Co

PO Box 533, Monticello, AR 71657

Phone: 870-367-6607 - **Fax:** 870-367-6560

www.drewcountytitle.com **email:** drewabst@seark.net

Types of Records Retrieved: Criminal, Civil and Probate courts; Real Estate; Tax Liens/Judgments; UCC records

Local Retrieval Area: AR-Drew

Add'l Information: Established 1982. Fee basis will vary by type of project. All projects require prepayment. Will file/record documents for clients. They specialize in title insurance and loan closings.

DRP Paralegal Services Inc

PO Box 625, Mercer, PA 16137-0625

Phone: 724-699-5528 - **Fax:** 724-662-5932

Types of Records Retrieved: Criminal, Civil and Probate courts; Real Estate; Tax Liens/Judgments; UCC records

Local Retrieval Area: PA-Mercer

Add'l Information: Established 1998. Normal turnaround time- 28-48 hours. Projects billed by number of names searched. Projects billed by number of records located. Will file/record documents for clients. Will bill upon completion. Is a full-service paralegal service with over 12 years of experience, specializing in title searches, lien checks and criminal/civil record checks. Second phone is 724-662-5933.

Duke City Process Service & Inv

PO Box 16166, Albuquerque, NM 87191-6166

Phone: 888-335-9889; 505-275-0994 - **Fax:** 505-275-7327

amy@comcast.net

Types of Records Retrieved: Criminal, Civil and Probate courts; Federal courts; Real Estate; Tax Liens/Judgments; Vital records

Local Retrieval Area: NM-Bernalillo, Cibola, Dona Ana, Los Alamos, Sandoval, Santa Fe, Taos, Torrance, Valencia. **Correspondent Relationships:** statewide.

Add'l Information: Established 1974. Normal turnaround time- 3-4 days. Expedited service available. Projects billed by the hour. First project may require prepayment. Will file/record documents for clients. Three decades of experience in New Mexico's economic center, and now offers the same great service statewide. Can access the 2nd Judicial district court of NM. A licensed PI in NM. Performs service of process.

Jonathan Duke

PO Box 433, Paducah, KY 42003

Phone: 270-596-7509 - **Fax:** 270-538-5395 duke_42003@hotmail.com

Types of Records Retrieved: Criminal and Civil courts

Local Retrieval Area: KY-Ballard, McCracken

Add'l Information: Established 2004. Normal turnaround time- 24-48 hours. Projects billed by number of names searched. First project may require prepayment. Will bill regular customers. He specializes in court records from courts near Paducah, KY.

Dunn County Abstract & Title Inc

815 7th St E, Menomonie, WI 54751

Phone: 800-628-5727; 715-235-0875 - **Fax:** 715-235-9690 dcat@wwt.net

Types of Records Retrieved: Real Estate; Tax Liens/Judgments

Local Retrieval Area: WI-Dunn, Pepin

Add'l Information: Established 1940. Normal turnaround time- 1-2 days for Dunn county. For Pepin county 1 week to 10 days. Fee basis varies by type of transaction. First project may require prepayment. They specialize in title work and closings.

E Title & Abstract LLC

10831 Dutch Hollow Rd, Rixeyville, VA 22737

Phone: 540-727-0515 - **Fax:** 540-727-0519 etitleabstract@aol.com

Types of Records Retrieved: Civil courts; Real Estate; Tax Liens/Judgments; UCC records

Local Retrieval Area: VA-Albemarle, Culpeper, Fauquier, Greene, Louisa, Madison, Orange, Spotsylvania

Add'l Information: Established 2003. Normal turnaround time- 24-48 hours. Projects billed by number of names searched. Will invoice with a net 10 days. E Title & Abstract is a quality title research company in the North Central area of Virginia committed to being of service.

Eagle Communications

4568 Mayfield Rd #213, Cleveland, OH 44121

Phone: 216-297-3200 - **Fax:** 216-297-3203 miker@wingsinfonet.com

Types of Records Retrieved: Criminal, Civil and Probate courts; Federal courts; Real Estate; Tax Liens/Judgments; UCC records; Vital records

Local Retrieval Area: OH-Ashtabula, Cuyahoga, Franklin, Geauga, Hamilton, Lake, Lorain, Mahoning, Portage, Stark, Summit, Trumbull. **Correspondent Relationships:** all 88 Ohio counties; most counties nationwide; Canada, Puerto Rico.

Add'l Information: Established 1990. Normal turnaround time- 24-48 hours. Projects billed by number of names searched. Billing dependent on type of search. Will file/record documents for clients. Terms: net 10 days. They specialize in real estate (current owner & full searches), UCCs, FTL, STL, JL, PS (lien searches), pre-employment screening, business & individual (due diligence) background screening/profiles, felony, misd & civil searches. They file/record records. Performs service of process.

EAGLE i Communications

7800 Lonesome Harbor Ave, Las Vegas, NV 89131-5001

Phone: 702-658-3912 - **Fax:** 702-658-4860

www.eagleprocessservers.com **email:** retrieve@vail.net

Types of Records Retrieved: Civil and Probate courts; Federal courts; Real Estate; Tax Liens/Judgments; UCC records

Local Retrieval Area: CA-Los Angeles, Orange; NV-Clark. **Correspondent Relationships:** statewide.

Add'l Information: Established 1996. Normal turnaround time-24-72 hours. Projects billed by number of names searched. Terms: net 30 days. They specialize in civil litigation, UCCs, liens and all recorded documents as well as retrieval from the US Bankruptcy Central District of California & US District Court, Central District. Also includes Clark County, NV.

Eagle Process Servers

PO Box 1582, 138 Bluffs Dr, Eagle, CO 81631

Phone: 970-331-7712 - **Fax:** 303-845-8748

http://eagleprocessservers.com **email:** retrieve@vail.net

Types of Records Retrieved: Criminal, Civil and Probate courts; Federal courts; Real Estate; Tax Liens/Judgments; UCC records; Vital records

Local Retrieval Area: CO-Eagle. **Correspondents:** nationwide.

Add'l Information: Established 1966. Normal turnaround time- 24 hours to 2 weeks depending on the records. Projects billed by number of names searched. Projects billed by number of records located. Projects billed by the hour. All projects require prepayment. Formerly Research Specialists & Investigators, Eagle is a full time background public records company. They also do tenant screening, employment screening & service of process. Also the web post of CO process servers directory.

East Arkansas Title Co

PO Box 408, Helena, AR 72342-0408
Phone: 870-338-8306 - **Fax:** 870-338-8307
Types of Records Retrieved: Civil and Probate courts; Real Estate; Tax Liens/Judgments; UCC records
Local Retrieval Area: AR-Phillips
Add'l Information: Established 1937. Normal turnaround time- 3-5 days. Projects billed by the hour. First project may require prepayment.

East Tex Records Research

PO Box 2652, Lufkin, TX 75902
Phone: 936-414-1193 - **Fax:** 801-981-6523
www.masterwebs.com/eastex/ **email:** eastexrecords@yahoo.com
Types of Records Retrieved: Criminal, Civil and Probate courts; Federal District courts; Real Estate; Tax Liens/Judgments; UCC records
Local Retrieval Area: TX-Angelina, Nacogdoches. **Correspondent Relationships:** most of East and Central Texas areas.
Add'l Information: Established 1994. Normal turnaround time- 2-36 hours, most CV/CR orders rec'd by e-mail or by 10 AM are completed on same day. Expedited service available. Projects billed by number of names searched. Terms are net 30 days. Credit cards accepted. Will file/record documents for clients. Terms net 30 days. Accurate and timely reports result from concerted attention to detail & over 17 years experience. Searches are performed "hands on" at the courts (including USDC TX East Div.) not by databases. 2nd fax number- 936-824-3724.

East Texas Public Records

PO Box 152555, Lufkin, TX 75915
Phone: 936-632-7385 - **Fax:** 936-632-7385
meredithsmith@consolidated.net
Types of Records Retrieved: Real Estate
Local Retrieval Area: TX-Angelina, Trinity
Add'l Information: Established 1997. Normal turnaround time- 24-72 hours. Projects billed by number of names searched. Will invoice. Will file/record documents for clients. They specialize in real estate searches. They have been in business since 1997. Fax is same as phone.

Eastern Oregon Title Inc

PO Box 1084, 1601 Adams Ave, La Grande, OR 97850
Phone: 541-963-8561 - **Fax:** 541-963-2391
www.eotitle.com **email:** chris@eotitle.com
Types of Records Retrieved: Criminal and Civil courts; Real Estate; Tax Liens/Judgments; UCC records
Local Retrieval Area: OR-Union
Add'l Information: Established 1974. Normal turnaround time- 3-4 days. Projects billed by the hour. First project may require prepayment. Will file/record documents for clients. Terms: net 30 days. They specialize in title, escrow and collections.

Eastland Title Co

PO Box 680, 69 W Franklin St, Hillsboro, TX 76645
Phone: 254-582-2762 - **Fax:** 254-582-2760 eastlandtitle@hillsboro.net
Types of Records Retrieved: Criminal, Civil and Probate courts; Real Estate; Tax Liens/Judgments; UCC records; Vital records
Local Retrieval Area: TX-Hill
Add'l Information: Established 1898. Normal turnaround time- up to 1 week. Fee basis will vary by the type of project. Will file/record documents for clients. Prepayment requirement on first project for title searches.

Eaton Abstract Company

122 S Van Buren St, Newton, IL 62448
Phone: 618-783-8474 - **Fax:** 618-783-3199
Types of Records Retrieved: Criminal, Civil and Probate courts; Real Estate; Tax Liens/Judgments; UCC records
Local Retrieval Area: IL-Jasper
Add'l Information: Established 1941. Normal turnaround time- 24-48 hours. Projects billed by number of names searched. Projects billed by number of records located. First project may require prepayment. Will file/record documents for clients. They specialize in complete title service searches.

Donna Eccles

4207 Thompson Rd, Sulphur, LA 76665
Phone: 337-558-6627 - **Fax:** 337-558-6627 deccles4207@aol.com
Types of Records Retrieved: Criminal records at the District court only
Local Retrieval Area: LA-Calcasieu
Add'l Information: Established 1996. Normal turnaround time- 24-48 hours. First project may require prepayment. Specializes in criminal searches in Calcasieu Parish; all searches confidential.

Ed Knight Information Service

6651 Cameron Rd, Morrow, GA 30260
Phone: 800-282-6418; - **Fax:** 800-282-6416
www.edknight.com **email:** ekis@edknight.com
Types of Records Retrieved: Criminal, Civil and Probate courts; Federal courts; Real Estate; Tax Liens/Judgments; UCC records
Local Retrieval Area: GA-Clayton, Henry. **Correspondents:** statewide.
Add'l Information: Established 1972. Normal turnaround time- 1-2 days. Projects billed by number of names searched. First project may require prepayment. Will file/record documents for clients. Payment due net 30 days from invoice. They specialize in lien searches in metropolitan Atlanta, but will drive to any county in Georgia for a reasonable fee. They are online with the Georgia Clerks Authority.

Eddy County Abstract Co

116 N Canyon St, Carlsbad, NM 88220
Phone: 800-348-1232; 505-887-2828 - **Fax:** 505-887-0824
Types of Records Retrieved: Civil and Probate courts; Real Estate; Tax Liens/Judgments; UCC records
Local Retrieval Area: NM-Eddy. **Correspondents:** worldwide.
Add'l Information: Established 1891. Normal turnaround time- 12-24 hours. Fees depend on type of service. Will file/record documents for clients. They specialize in loan closing and mineral searches, and are fully computerized.

Edgar County Title Co

206 W Washington St, Paris, IL 61944
Phone: 217-465-5821 - **Fax:** 217-463-7265
www.edgarcountytitle.com **email:** requests@edgarcountytitle.com
Types of Records Retrieved: Civil and Probate courts; Real Estate; Tax Liens/Judgments; UCC records; Vital records
Local Retrieval Area: IL-Edgar
Add'l Information: Established 1977. Normal turnaround time- 1-5 days. Projects billed by number of names searched. Will file/record documents for clients. Billing upon completion.

Edith Wiggins & Marvin Singer

1725 Taylor St #1A, San Francisco, CA 94133
Phone: 415-771-9369 - **Fax:** 415-441-8519
www.mesinger.com **email:** maemsi@mesinger.com
Types of Records Retrieved: Criminal, Civil and Probate courts; Federal courts; Tax Liens/Judgments; UCC records
Local Retrieval Area: CA-San Francisco, San Mateo
Add'l Info: Turnaround time- 1 day or less. Projects billed by number of names searched. Terms: net 30 days. They provide criminal pre-employment background checks and a variety of public record search svcs.

Edmunds County Abstract Co

PO Box 128, Ipswich, SD 57451-0128
Phone: 605-426-6041 - **Fax:** 605-426-6400
Types of Records Retrieved: Civil and Probate courts; Real Estate; Tax Liens/Judgments **Local Retrieval Area:** SD-Edmunds
Add'l Information: Established 1929. Normal turnaround time- 3-5 days. Projects billed by number of names searched. Projects billed by number of

records located. Projects billed by the hour. All projects require prepayment. Will file/record documents for clients.

EHS Research Services

253 Garth Rd, Scarsdale, NY 10583
Phone: 914-472-5848 - **Fax:** 914-725-3613 ehsshap316@cs.com
Types of Records Retrieved: Criminal, Civil and Probate courts; Federal courts; Real Estate; Tax Liens/Judgments; UCC records
Local Retrieval Area: NY-New York, Putnam, Rockland, Westchester
Add'l Information: Established 1992. Normal turnaround time- 48-72 hours. Projects billed by the hour. They specialize in locating people and assets and conducts surveillance. A licensed PI in NY. Performs service of process.

Ekum Abstract & Title

PO Box 263, 912 18th Ave (53566), Monroe, WI 53566-0263
Phone: 608-328-8221 - **Fax:** 608-328-8223
www.ekum.com **email:** ekum@ekum.com
Types of Records Retrieved: Criminal, Civil and Probate courts; Real Estate; Tax Liens/Judgments; UCC records
Local Retrieval Area: WI-Green, Lafayette. **Correspondent Relationships:** Lafayette county WI.
Add'l Information: Established 1897. Normal turnaround time- 1-2 days. Projects billed by number of names searched. They specialize in real estate and maintain their own in-house records of real estate in tract indexes. All other county records are 1 block away.

Elder & Ryan Abstracts LLC

30 Courthouse Sq #403, Rockville, MD 20850
Phone: 301-854-1200 - **Fax:** 301-854-1212 jamie@elderabstracts.com
Types of Records Retrieved: Criminal, Civil and Probate courts; Federal courts; Real Estate; Tax Liens/Judgments; UCC records; Vital records
Local Retrieval Area: MD-Montgomery
Add'l Information: Established 1985. Normal turnaround time- 6-24 hours. Projects billed by number of names searched. Will file/record documents for clients. Payment due net 30 days. They specialize in title abstracts and local document retrieval.

ELH Contracting Inc Independent Land & Title Abstractor

PO Box 35, Dayton, TX 77535
Phone: 409-832-5793 - **Fax:** 409-866-3546 leehill@sbcglobal.net
Types of Records Retrieved: Criminal, Civil and Probate courts; Federal courts; Real Estate; Tax Liens/Judgments; UCC records; Vital records
Local Retrieval Area: TX-Chambers, Hardin, Jefferson, Liberty, Orange
Add'l Information: Established 1989. Normal turnaround time- 24-48 hours. Projects billed by number of names searched. Invoices at the end of month. They specialize in civil and criminal records, probate, tax liens/judgments, real estate, UCCs, vital records, dba/assumed names, abstracting and general retrieval and filings.

Elk County Abstract & Title Co

PO Box 458, 144 E Randolph, Howard, KS 67349-0458
Phone: 620-374-2500 - **Fax:** 620-374-2555
Types of Records Retrieved: Criminal, Civil and Probate courts; Real Estate; Tax Liens/Judgments; UCC records; Vital records
Local Retrieval Area: KS-Elk
Add'l Information: Established 1900. Normal turnaround time- 1-2 days. Fee basis varies by type of transaction. All projects require prepayment. Will file/record documents for clients. They specialize in title insurance and abstracts.

Elliott & Waldron Abstr Co of Palo Pinto

403 S Oak Ave, Mineral Wells, TX 76067
Phone: 940-325-6564 - **Fax:** 940-325-1036 ew@cox-internet.com
Types of Records Retrieved: Real Estate; Tax Liens/Judgments; Probate courts; UCC records
Local Retrieval Area: TX-Palo Pinto
Add'l Information: Established 1959. Normal turnaround time- 2 days. Fee basis will vary by the type of project. First project may require prepayment. Will file/record documents for clients.

Elliott & Waldron Abstract & Title Co of Canton

681 W Dallas St, Canton, TX 75103
Phone: 903-567-4127 - **Fax:** 903-567-1757 cfreeman@aaa-camm.com
Types of Records Retrieved: Criminal, Civil and Probate courts; Real Estate; Tax Liens/Judgments; UCC records; Vital records
Local Retrieval Area: TX-Van Zandt. **Correspondent Relationships:** Dallas, Kaufman, Rains, Smith, Wood, Rockwell, Hunt counties.
Add'l Information: Established 1960. Normal turnaround time- 1-3 days. Fee basis will vary by the type of project. Will file/record documents for clients. Payment due upon completion. They are fast and accurate. They specialize in title examination, real estate closing and title policy issues.

Elliott & Waldron Abstract Co - Pecos

PO Box 490, 306 S Nelson St, Fort Stockton, TX 79735-0490
Phone: 432-336-5214 - **Fax:** 432-336-7869
Records Retrieved: Real Estate; Tax Liens/Judgments; UCC records
Local Retrieval Area: TX-Pecos
Add'l Information: Normal turnaround time- up to 1 week. Fee basis will vary by the type of project. First project may require prepayment. Will file/record documents for clients.

Elliott & Waldron Title & Abstract

1819 N Turner #B, Hobbs, NM 88240
Phone: 505-393-7706 - **Fax:** 505-393-7725
www.ewtitle.com **email:** james@ewtitle.com
Types of Records Retrieved: Civil and Probate courts; Real Estate; Tax Liens/Judgments; UCC records
Local Retrieval Area: NM-Lea
Add'l Information: Established 1979. Normal turnaround time- variable depending on project. Fee basis will vary by type of project. Will file/record documents for clients. Terms: net 30 days.

Ellis County Abstract & Title Co

110 E 12th St, Hays, KS 67601
Phone: 785-625-2316 - **Fax:** 785-625-6349
Types of Records Retrieved: Criminal, Civil and Probate courts; Real Estate; Tax Liens/Judgments; UCC records; Vital records
Local Retrieval Area: KS-Ellis, Rooks
Add'l Information: Normal turnaround time- 2-3 days. Projects billed by number of names searched. Will file/record documents for clients. They specialize in abstract, title insurance and certificates.

Cynthia Ellis

229 Davis Dr, Sycamore, IL 60178-8796
Phone: 815-895-9527 - **Fax:** 815-895-1775 cindypotthoff@comcast.net
Types of Records Retrieved: Criminal, Civil and Probate courts
Local Retrieval Area: IL-De Kalb, Kane, Kendall, Madison, Sangamon, Will, Winnebago
Add'l Information: Established 1997. Normal turnaround time- within 24 hours. Projects billed by number of names searched. Her services are completed in less than 24 hours.

Ellyson Abstract & Title Co of Brewster

PO Box 418, Alpine, TX 79830
Phone: 432-837-5801 - **Fax:** 432-837-3509
Types of Records Retrieved: Civil and Probate courts; Real Estate; Tax Liens/Judgments; UCC records; Vital records
Local Retrieval Area: TX-Brewster, Jeff Davis, Presidio
Add'l Information: Normal turnaround time- 2 days. Fee basis will vary by the type of project. First project may require prepayment. Will file/record documents for clients.

Elman Resources

478 E Altamonte Dr #108-286, Altamonte Springs, FL 32701
Phone: 407-834-5344, cell- 407-221-8485 - **Fax:** 407-834-6748
caelman@aol.com

Types of Records Retrieved: Criminal and Civil courts

Local Retrieval Area: FL-Lake, Marion, Orange, Osceola, Seminole, Volusia. **Correspondent Relationships:** Martin, Polk, Brevard, Monroe, Palm Beach, Hernando, Hillsborough, Pinellas, Duval, Flagler, Lee, Pasco, Sarasota, St Johns.

Add'l Information: Established 1997. Normal turnaround time- 24-48 hours. Projects billed by number of names searched. First project may require prepayment. Formerly Elman Searches, they specialize in criminal and civil searches. Requests accepted via fax, phone or email. Initial project guaranteed satisfaction.

Elson & Fulton Abstractors

203 NE Idaho St, Leon, IA 50144
Phone: 641-446-4621 - **Fax:** 641-446-4888 enf@grm.net

Types of Records Retrieved: Criminal, Civil and Probate courts; Real Estate; Tax Liens/Judgments; UCC records; Vital records

Local Retrieval Area: IA-Decatur

Add'l Information: Established 1875. Normal turnaround time- 7-14 days. Fee basis varies by type of transaction. Will file/record documents for clients. Payment due on completion of work.

Emerald Coast Protective Services Inc

PO Box 9949, Panama City Beach, FL 32417
Phone: 877-234-6252; 850-234-6252 - **Fax:** 850-234-8006
www.emeraldpi.net **email:** rpeak@knology.net

Types of Records Retrieved: Criminal, Civil and Probate courts; Federal courts; Real Estate; Tax Liens/Judgments; UCC records; Vital records

Local Retrieval Area: FL-Bay, Gulf, Jackson, Walton. **Correspondent Relationships:** statewide.

Add'l Information: Established 1997. Normal turnaround time- 48 hours. Projects billed by the hour. First project may require prepayment. Credit cards accepted. Will file/record documents for clients. They provide investigative services for Northwest Florida in civil process service and foreclosure sales. A licensed PI in FL. Performs service of process.

Emmons County Abstract & Title

PO Box 428, Linton, ND 58552
Phone: 701-254-4261 - **Fax:** 701-254-4261

Records Retrieved: Real Estate; Tax Liens/Judgments; UCC records

Local Retrieval Area: ND-Emmons

Add'l Information: Established 1963. Normal turnaround time- 1-5 days. Fee basis will vary by the type of project. Terms: net 30 days. They specialize in title searches and abstracting.

Employee Assurance Inc

10744 Ayrshire Dr, Tampa, FL 33626
Phone: 888-640-9847; - **Fax:** 888-640-9846;
www.employeeassurance.com **email:** eai@tampabay.rr.com

Types of Records Retrieved: Criminal and Civil courts; Bankruptcy court

Local Retrieval Area: FL-Hillsborough, Pasco, Pinellas. **Correspondent Relationships:** nationwide.

Add'l Information: Established 1996. Normal turnaround time- 48 hours. Employee Assurance provides county criminal record searches nationwide at very competitive prices. They have a 24-48 hour turnaround time and highly-trained network of court researchers.

English Research & Retrieval Inc

3631 10th St #203, Riverside, CA 91501
Phone: 951-328-9995 - **Fax:** 951-328-9997 callmenglish@msn.com

Types of Records Retrieved: Criminal, Civil and Probate courts; Federal courts; Real Estate; Tax Liens/Judgments; UCC records; Vital records

Local Retrieval Area: CA-Los Angeles, Orange, Riverside, San Bernardino, San Luis Obispo, Santa Barbara, Ventura. **Correspondent Relationships:** West Los Angeles, CA.

Add'l Information: Established 2003. Normal turnaround time- 24 hours. Expedited service available. Projects billed by number of names searched. Projects billed by number of records located. Projects billed by the hour. First project may require prepayment. Credit cards accepted. Terms are net 30 days. The specialize in research and retrieval from all county, state and federal agencies and archives. Daily filing provided in Riverside County. Orders accepted by email. Performs service of process.

Enterprise Title Company Inc

4343 Lee Hwy #202, Arlington, VA 22207-3241
Phone: 703-351-8066 - **Fax:** 703-351-8069 ncc-1701@verizon.net

Types of Records Retrieved: Criminal, Civil and Probate courts; Federal courts; Real Estate; Tax Liens/Judgments; UCC records

Local Retrieval Area: DC-District of Columbia; MD-Montgonery, Prince George's; VA-Alexandria City, Arlington, Fairfax, Falls Church City, Loudoun, Prince William, Stafford, Warren. **Correspondent Relationships:** Virginia and Maryland.

Add'l Information: Established 1984. Projects billed by number of names searched. Projects billed by the hour. Charges depends on search. First project may require prepayment. They also provide research in the federal agencies in Washington, DC, such as the Library of Congress, the Patent & Trademark Office, and the SEC and US Archives.

Jo Ann Entwisle

16340 West 143rd St, Lockport, IL 60441
Phone: 815-838-2871 joentwisl@sbcglobal.net

Types of Records Retrieved: Criminal and Civil courts

Local Retrieval Area: IL-Will

Add'l Information: Established 1996. Normal turnaround time- 24-48 hours. Projects billed by number of names searched.

Equisearch

PO Box 21838, 410 Kingswood Dr, Lexington, KY 40522-1838
Phone: 859-268-1206 - **Fax:** 859-254-0799

Types of Records Retrieved: Civil courts; Federal courts; Real Estate; Tax Liens/Judgments; UCC records

Local Retrieval Area: KY-Anderson, Bourbon, Boyle, Clark, Fayette, Franklin, Garrard, Jessamine, Lincoln, Madison, Mercer, Montgomery, Scott, Woodford. **Correspondent Relationships:** Kentucky.

Add'l Information: Established 1987. Normal turnaround time- 24-48 hours. Projects billed by number of names searched. Fee basis will vary by type of project. First project may require prepayment. Will file/record documents for clients. Payment due upon completion of job. They specialize in KY Secretary of state records and Eastern Dist. KY federal court records, as well as 14 eastern KY county courts.

Equity Process Management

PO Box 4906, Missoula, MT 59806
Phone: 888-721-3337; 406-721-3337 - **Fax:** 406-721-0372
www.equityprocess.com **email:** equity@centric.net

Types of Records Retrieved: Criminal, Civil and Probate courts; Federal courts; Tax Liens/Judgments; UCC records; Vital records

Local Retrieval Area: MT-Cascade, Deer Lodge, Flathead, Gallatin, Hill, Lake, Lewis & Clark, Missoula, Powell, Ravalli, Silver Bow. **Correspondent Relationships:** statewide.

Add'l Info: Established 1992. Turnaround time- 1-3 days. Expedited service available. Projects billed by the hour. First project may require prepayment. Credit cards accepted. They specialize in no limits on servicing the clients needs. A licensed PI in MT. Performs service of process.

Equity Title Search

137 N Larchmont #545, Los Angeles, CA 90004
Phone: 323-965-0759 - **Fax:** 323-965-1247 email@equitytitlesearch.com

Types of Records Retrieved: Criminal, Civil and Probate courts; Real Estate; Vital records

Local Retrieval Area: CA-Alameda, Los Angeles, Orange, Riverside, San Francisco. **Correspondent Relationships:** Florida, New Jersey, Illinois, Colorado.

Add'l Information: Established 1973. Normal turnaround time- 24 hours. Expedited service available. Fees vary by complexity of the project. First project may require prepayment. They specialize in locating people and assets. A licensed PI in CA. Performs service of process.

ESI Associates

723 58th St #101, Kenosha, WI 53140
Phone: 262-652-6361 - **Fax:** 262-658-4610 esi_assoc@hotmail.com

Types of Records Retrieved: Criminal, Civil and Probate courts; Federal courts; Real Estate; Tax Liens/Judgments; UCC records; Vital records; Voter Registration records

Local Retrieval Area: WI-Kenosha, Milwaukee, Racine. **Correspondent Relationships:** Walworth, Waukesha counties WI.

Add'l Information: Established 1983. Normal turnaround time- 24 hours. Projects billed by number of records located. First project may require prepayment. Credit cards accepted. They have 20 years experience in real estate, criminal, civil and document retrieval. A licensed PI in WI. Performs service of process.

Espanola Abstract Co

PO Box 1282, 224 Los Alamos Hiway, Espanola, NM 87532
Phone: 505-753-2248 - **Fax:** 505-753-4392

Types of Records Retrieved: Civil and Probate courts; Real Estate; Tax Liens/Judgments; UCC records; Vital records

Local Retrieval Area: NM-Rio Arriba. **Correspondent Relationships:** courtesy closings throughout New Mexico.

Add'l Information: Established 1947. Normal turnaround time- 10-14 days. Charges vary depending on project. Payment is due upon delivery. They are the only local title company with records dating back to county's inception. They will file UCC and real estate documents on behalf of clients twice a week.

Espy Investigative Services

PO Box 968, Ripon, CA 95366
Phone: 877-843-3779; 209-609-2676 - **Fax:** 209-599-6454
www.espypi.com **email:** espypi@aol.com

Types of Records Retrieved: Criminal, Civil and Probate courts; Federal courts; Real Estate; Tax Liens/Judgments; UCC records; Vital records

Local Retrieval Area: CA-Alameda, Contra Costa, San Joaquin, Santa Clara, Stanislaus

Add'l Information: Established 2003. Normal turnaround time- 3-5 business days. Expedition available in 2 days. Projects billed by number of names searched. All projects require prepayment. Espy is a full service private investigative agency. Their mission is to provide attorneys, businesses and private individuals with pertinent information quickly and accurately. A licensed PI in CA.

Esquire Assist Ltd

300 N 2nd St #630, Harrisburg, PA 17101
Phone: 717-232-9398 - **Fax:** 717-232-6248
www.esquireassist.com **email:** assist@esquireassist.com

Types of Records Retrieved: Criminal, Civil and Probate courts; Federal courts; Real Estate; Tax Liens/Judgments; UCC records; Vital records

Local Retrieval Area: PA-Dauphin. **Correspondent Relationships:** statewide for judgments/liens and UCC searches.

Add'l Information: Established 1988. Normal turnaround time- 24-48 hours, same day items (state corp records, etc). Projects billed by number of names searched. They also bill by the hour for large jobs. First project may require prepayment. Will file/record documents for clients. Accounts for established clients. Visa/MC accepted. They provide state level corporate/UCC document filing and searching, PA corp bureau and upper level courts, and also registered agent services for PA. Will search Dauphin courts on special request only.

Esquire Express Inc

1501 NW 29th St, Miami, FL 33142
Phone: 800-439-8744; 305-530-9580 - **Fax:** 305-530-8414
www.esquireexpress.com **email:** esqexpress@aol.com

Types of Records Retrieved: Criminal, Civil and Probate courts; Federal courts; Real Estate; Tax Liens/Judgments; UCC records; Vital records

Local Retrieval Area: FL-Broward, Dade, Palm Beach. **Correspondent Relationships:** Leon, Gadsden, Escambia, Santa Rosa, Hillsborough, Pinellas and nationwide.

Add'l Information: Established 1990. Normal turnaround time- 24 hours. Expedited service available. Projects billed by the hour. First project may require prepayment. Credit cards accepted. Will file/record documents for clients. MasterCard, Visa and American Express accepted. They specialize in civil, criminal, bankruptcy and public records retrieval throughout South Florida. Courier service. A licensed PI in FL. Performs service of process.

Essex County Paralegals Inc

PO Box 7076, 37 Northern Ave, Beverly, MA 01915
Phone: 800-922-4752; 978-921-5300 - **Fax:** 800-928-4752; 978-921-5398
don@essexparalegals.com

Types of Records Retrieved: Civil and Probate courts; Federal courts; Real Estate; Tax Liens/Judgments; UCC records

Local Retrieval Area: MA-Essex, Middlesex, Worcester

Add'l Information: Established 1995. Normal turnaround time- 24-72 hours. Fees are per subject/jurisdiction. First project may require prepayment. Terms: net 30 days. They specialize in real estate current owner searches, also UCCs, tax liens, judgments and litigation searches.

Estate Title & Escrow Inc

4041 University Dr #302, Fairfax, VA 22030
Phone: 703-385-5850 - **Fax:** 703-385-8787 michele@estatetitle.com

Records Retrieved: Real Estate; Tax Liens/Judgments; UCC records

Local Retrieval Area: DC-District of Columbia; VA-Alexandria City, Arlington, Clarke, Culpeper, Fairfax, Fauquier, Loudoun, Prince William, Spotsylvania, Stafford. **Correspondent Relationships:** Virginia, Maryland.

Add'l Information: Established 1984. Normal turnaround time- 2-3 days. Payment due upon receipt of invoice. Will file/record documents for clients. Payment due upon receipt of invoice. They specialize in providing title evidence in real estate transactions, tax liens and other liens, UCC and court records. They are a full service title insurance company and agent who underwrites through several major underwriters.

Patricia L Estes-Howell

101 Medina Hwy, Humboldt, TN 38343
Phone: 731-784-1050 - **Fax:** 731-784-2634

Types of Records Retrieved: Criminal and Civil courts

Local Retrieval Area: TN-Benton, Chester, Crockett, Dyer, Gibson, Hardeman, Haywood, Henderson, Lake, Lauderdale, Madison, McNairy, Obion, Weakley

Add'l Information: Established 1999. Normal turnaround time- 4 days or less. Projects billed by number of names searched. First project may require prepayment. She is a criminal background screening specialist in far western Tennessee except for the 3 county Memphis area.

Estherville Abstract Co

119 N 6th St, Estherville, IA 51334-2228
Phone: 712-362-3148 - **Fax:** 712-362-8042 evabstco@mchsi.com

Types of Records Retrieved: Criminal, Civil and Probate courts; Real Estate; Tax Liens/Judgments; UCC records; Vital records

Local Retrieval Area: IA-Emmet

Add'l Information: Established 1937. Normal turnaround time- 2 days. They charge a flat rate per search. Will file/record documents for clients. They specialize in abstracting and real estate transactions.

Kim Estrada

875 Peak View Way, Prescott, AZ 86303
Phone: 928-273-2835 - **Fax:** 928-445-4437 azestrada@cableone.net

Types of Records Retrieved: Criminal and Civil courts; Tax Liens/Judgments; UCC records

Local Retrieval Area: AZ-Yavapai

Add'l Information: Established 1995. Normal turnaround time- 24-48 hours. Projects billed by number of names searched. Some projects may be charged per hour. Will file/record documents for clients. Specializing in criminal, civil, UCC, tax lien and judgment searches. Searches done on-site.

ETC Investigations

PO Box 123407, Ft Worth, TX 76121-3407
Phone: 888-560-4001; 817-560-4005 - **Fax:** 817-886-2214
www.etcinvestigations.com **email:** snoop@etcinvestigations.com

Types of Records Retrieved: Criminal, Civil and Probate courts; Federal courts; Real Estate; Tax Liens/Judgments; UCC records

Local Retrieval Area: TX-Cooke, Denton, Ellis, Erath, Hill, Hood, Jack, Johnson, Montague, Palo Pinto, Parker, Tarrant, Wise, Young. **Correspondent Relationships:** nationwide.

Add'l Information: Established 1990. Normal turnaround time- 2-3 days. Projects billed by number of names searched. First project may require prepayment. Credit cards accepted. They specialize in court research, including retrieval from the Federal Records Center serving Texas, Oklahoma, Arkansas and Louisiana. Their priority service is Process Service in Tarrant and Parker counties. A licensed PI in TX.

Ethical Equations

Box 88 Cassville Station, Jackson, NJ 08527
Phone: 732-928-4130 - **Fax:** 732-928-2743
www.ethicalequations.com **email:** jack@ethicalequations.com

Types of Records Retrieved: Criminal and Civil courts

Local Retrieval Area: NJ-Mercer, Monmouth, Ocean; PA-Philadelphia

Add'l Information: Established 2000. Normal turnaround time- 24-48 hours. Projects billed by number of names searched. First project may require prepayment. They are a private investigations and document retrieval firm operating in the NJ coastal counties, Central NJ and Philadelphia areas. Quick and accurate retrievals and turnarounds. A licensed PI in NJ, NY.

Etna Abstract Corp

PO Box 462, 355 W Main St, Malone, NY 12953
Phone: 518-483-7204 - **Fax:** 518-483-7204

Types of Records Retrieved: Real Estate; Tax Liens/Judgments; Probate courts; UCC records

Local Retrieval Area: NY-Franklin

Add'l Information: Established 1977. Normal turnaround time- 1-2 weeks. Projects billed by number of names searched. Projects billed by number of records located. Fee basis will vary per abstract. All projects require prepayment. Will file/record documents for clients. They specialize in abstracts of title.

Euchner Research LLC

PO Box 81, Calhoun, GA 30703-0081
Phone: 678-614-1816 johneuchner@earthlink.net

Records Retrieved: Criminal, Civil and Probate courts; Federal District courts; Real Estate; Tax Liens/Judgments/UCC records; Vital records

Local Retrieval Area: GA-Floyd, Gordon

Add'l Information: Established 2002. Normal turnaround time- 24 hours. Projects billed by number of names searched. Will file/record documents for clients. Payment due net 30 days. They are a research and retrieval firm specializing in public records searches and retrieval for the banking, mortgage, investigative and legal industries.

Eufaula Abstract & Title Co Inc

PO Box 548, Eufaula, OK 74432
Phone: 918-689-2241 - **Fax:** 918-689-2248

Records Retrieved: Real Estate; Tax Liens/Judgments; UCC records

Local Retrieval Area: OK-McIntosh

Add'l Information: Normal turnaround time- 10-12 working days after receipt of order. Projects billed by the hour. Will file/record documents for clients. They specialize in abstracting and title insurance.

Euler Abstract & Title Co

PO Box 326, 137 S Main, Troy, KS 66087
Phone: 785-985-3562 - **Fax:** 785-985-2322

Types of Records Retrieved: Criminal, Civil and Probate courts; Real Estate; Tax Liens/Judgments

Local Retrieval Area: KS-Doniphan

Add'l Information: Established 1895. Normal turnaround time- 3 days. Fee basis varies by type of transaction. Will file/record documents for clients. They specialize in abstracting and title insurance and own a title plant which includes all land title records for Doniphan County. They have been in business for over 40 years. Their staff includes 3 attorneys. Performs service of process.

Evans Title Companies

PO Box 6, 823 Jay St, Manitowoc, WI 54221
Phone: 920-684-1261 - **Fax:** 920-684-6581
www.firstam.com **email:** tkunesh@firstam.com

Types of Records Retrieved: Civil and Probate courts; Real Estate; Tax Liens/Judgments; UCC records; Vital records

Local Retrieval Area: WI-Manitowoc. **Correspondent Relationships:** Outagamie, Winnebago, Calumet, Waupaca, Portage, Brown, Shawano, Marquette, Waushara, Green Lake.

Add'l Information: Established 1898. Normal turnaround time- 2-3 days. Projects billed by number of names searched. First project may require prepayment. Will file/record documents for clients.

Everhart & Everhart Abstractors

PO Box 37, Toledo, IL 62468
Phone: 217-849-2671 - **Fax:** 217-849-2671 everhart@rr1.net

Records Retrieved: Real Estate; Tax Liens/Judgments; UCC records

Local Retrieval Area: IL-Clark, Coles, Cumberland, Effingham

Add'l Information: Established 1881. Normal turnaround time- 3-4 days. Projects billed by number of names searched. Projects billed by number of records located. Projects billed by the hour. Will file/record documents for clients. Personal checks are accepted. They specialize in title insurance and abstracts, and also perform judgment/lien, UCC and other record searches. There may be additional charges for Clark County searches due to distance from their home office.

Evident

PO Box 2002, Saskatoon, Saskatchewan, Canada, CAN F7K 3S7
Phone: 866-245-2084; 306-933-3388 - **Fax:** 306-933-0114
www.evident.ca **email:** discover@evident.ca

Types of Records Retrieved: Criminal and Civil courts; Federal District court; Real Estate; Tax Liens/Judgments

Local Retrieval Area: CANADA-Saskatchewan. **Correspondent Relationships:** All Provinces.

Add'l Information: Established 2005. Normal turnaround time- depends on nature of the job. Projects billed by number of names searched. They are experts on Saskatchewan and corporate affairs there. Part of the Investigations Canada Group. A licensed PI in Saskatchewan. Performs service of process.

ewaprocess.com

621 W Mallon Ave #301, Spokane, WA 99201-2181
Phone: 509-325-0001 - **Fax:** 509-328-3226
www.ewaprocess.com **email:** myrnaallen@comcast.net

Types of Records Retrieved: Criminal, Civil and Probate courts; Federal courts; Real Estate; Tax Liens/Judgments; UCC records; Vital records

Local Retrieval Area: WA-Spokane. **Correspondents:** statewide.

Add'l Information: Established 1979. Normal turnaround time- 48 hours. Projects billed by number of names searched. First project may require prepayment. Will file/record documents for clients. Formerly known as A & A Attorney Services Inc, they are specialists in their Spokane area and Pend Oreille, Adams, Lincoln, Stevens, Whitman counties WA and Kootenai county ID. Performs service of process.

Wesley W Ewart, PI

PO Box 95828, Seattle, WA 98145
Phone: 800-646-1143; 425-646-1143 - **Fax:** 425-454-2611
http://wesleyewart.aiass.org **email:** on-point@worldnet.att.net

Types of Records Retrieved: Criminal and Civil courts

Local Retrieval Area: WA-King. **Correspondents:** Washington state.

Add'l Information: Established 1995. Normal turnaround time- 1 week. Projects billed by the hour. First project may require prepayment. They specialize in process service, surveillance and witness location. A licensed PI in WA. Performs service of process.

Thomas E Ewinger Jr

3900 Old Tasso Rd NE, Cleveland, TN 37312-5827
Phone: 423-614-5290 - **Fax:** 423-614-5299

Types of Records Retrieved: Real Estate; Tax Liens/Judgments; Probate courts; UCC records; Vital records

Retrieval Area: TN-Anderson, Bledsoe, Blount, Bradley, Hamilton, Knox, Loudon, Marion, McMinn, Meigs, Monroe, Polk, Rhea, Roane, Sequatchie

Add'l Information: Established 1979. Normal turnaround time- 24-48 hours. Projects billed by number of names searched. All projects require prepayment. They specialize in title abstracts, deed copies, updates, recordings, current owner & 20 year and 30 years searches.

Exacta Search & Document Retrieval

1821 N 22nd St, Springfield, IL 62702
Phone: 217-528-3677 - **Fax:** 217-528-2458 exactasearch@insightbb.com

Types of Records Retrieved: Criminal, Civil and Probate courts; Real Estate; Tax Liens/Judgments; UCC records

Local Retrieval Area: IL-Cass, Champaign, Christian, De Witt, Fulton, Logan, Macon, Macoupin, Mason, McLean, Menard, Montgomery, Morgan, Peoria, Piatt, Sangamon, Schuyler, Scott, Tazewell, Woodford. **Correspondent Relationships:** DuPage, Will, Kane, Kendall counties, IL.

Add'l Information: Established 2006. Normal turnaround time- 24-48 hours. Expedited service available. Projects billed by number of names searched. Exacta Search is a full service company that has 16 years of experience in the public records system. They offer quality service at reasonable prices.

Examiner's Title LC

1617 Mount High St, Woodbridge, VA 22192-2421
Phone: 703-491-0805 - **Fax:** 703-497-0408 pyianilos@aol.com

Types of Records Retrieved: Real Estate; UCC records; Probate courts

Local Retrieval Area: VA-Alexandria, Arlington, Fairfax, Fauquier, Loudoun, Prince William. **Correspondent Relationships:** Frederick, City of Winchester, Culpeper, Stafford counties VA.

Add'l Information: Established 1997. Normal turnaround time- 24-48 hours. Same day turnaround in many cases. Projects billed by number of names searched. Call for info on regular invoicing, payment terms. They perform document retrieval for current owner searches (as well as regular title searches) for the local neighboring counties of Northern Virginia. They can e-mail their reports to clients as they wish.

Excel Abstract Services

PO Box 70, 322 S Julianna St, Bedford, PA 15522-0070
Phone: 814-623-5213 - **Fax:** 814-623-1602 excelabstract@earthlink.net

Types of Records Retrieved: Criminal and Civil courts; Federal courts; Real Estate; Tax Liens/Judgments; UCC records

Local Retrieval Area: PA-Bedford.. **Correspondent Relationships:** Cambria, Somerset, Indiana, Clearfield.

Add'l Information: Established 1960. Normal turnaround time- 24 hours. Expedited service available. Fees based on type of report. Will file/record documents for clients. Terms: net 30 days. They specialize in property reports, current owner searches, title searches, lien searches, criminal searches and closings.

EX-CEL Investigations

PO Box 22124, St Petersburg, FL 33742
Phone: 800-317-7626; 727-527-5440
www.ex-celpi.com **email:** excel@digital.net

Types of Records Retrieved: Criminal, Civil and Probate courts; Federal courts; Real Estate; Tax Liens/Judgments; UCC records; Vital records

Local Retrieval Area: FL-Hillsborough, Pinellas. **Correspondent Relationships:** Pasco and Hernando.

Add'l Information: Established 1974. Normal turnaround time- 48 hours. Projects billed by number of names searched. Projects billed by the hour. Copy expenses added to the fee. All projects require prepayment. Will file/record documents for clients. Terms: net 15 days. They specialize in process service, background checks, locates and video surveillance. They also do traffic and boat record searches. A licensed PI in FL. Performs service of process.

Excel Search Inc

6704 Mountain Lake Ln, Cumming, GA 30040
Phone: 770-844-1201 - **Fax:** 770-205-2623 excelsearch@adelphia.net

Types of Records Retrieved: Criminal, Civil and Probate courts; Federal courts; Real Estate; Tax Liens/Judgments; UCC records; Vital records

Local Retrieval Area: GA-Barrow, Cherokee, Clarke, Clayton, Cobb, Dawson, De Kalb, Forsyth, Fulton, Gwinnett, Hall, Henry, Jackson, Madison, Morgan, Newton, Oconee, Oglethorpe, Rockdale, Walton. **Correspondent Relationships:** Georgia.

Add'l Information: Established 1982. Normal turnaround time- 12-48 hours. Projects billed by number of names searched. Fees for some counties can vary. A rush request may make rate higher. Will file/record documents for clients. Bill upon completion. They specialize in UCC searches and filing, tax liens, suits, judgments, court records retrieval and title searches.

Executec Services

6404 Sumac Dr, Austin, TX 78731
Phone: 512-345-5402 - **Fax:** 512-345-3932
www.ExecutecServices.com **email:** gwen@executecservices.com

Records Retrieved: Real Estate; Tax Liens/Judgments; UCC records

Local Retrieval Area: TX-Bastrop, Travis, Williamson

Add'l Information: Established 1989. Normal turnaround time- 24-48 hours. Projects billed by number of names searched. First project may require prepayment. Will file/record documents for clients. They specialize in property records including warranty and trust deeds, assignments, liens, foreclosures, plats, etc. They only do document filing in Travis County.

Executive Attorney Service Inc

201 N Figueroa St #535, Los Angeles, CA 90012
Phone: 213-482-6680 - **Fax:** 213-482-6688
www.EASSITE.com **email:** Silvia@eassite.com

Types of Records Retrieved: Criminal, Civil and Probate courts; Federal courts; Real Estate; Tax Liens/Judgments; UCC records; Vital records

Local Area: CA-Los Angeles, Orange, Riverside, San Bernardino, Ventura

Add'l Information: Established 1966. Normal turnaround time- variable depending on project. Projects billed by number of names searched. Projects billed by the hour. First project may require prepayment. Credit cards accepted. Will file/record documents for clients. They specialize in service of writs, court filing, service of process, skiptracing and small claims. Performs service of process.

Executive Investigative Services

PO Box 13308, Overland Park, KS 66282-3308
Phone: 800-764-9484; 913-764-9484 - **Fax:** 913-764-9484
http://kansascityprocessservers.org/default.aspx **email:** TLosh@msn.com

Types of Records Retrieved: Criminal and Civil courts; Federal courts; Real Estate; Tax Liens/Judgments; UCC records

Local Retrieval Area: KS-Franklin, Douglas, Johnson, Leavenworth, Miami, Wyandotte; MO-Clay, Platte. **Correspondent Relationships:** Miami, Douglas, Leavenworth, Franklin, Anderson, Jefferson, Atchison, Geary KS.

Add'l Information: Established 1990. Normal turnaround time- 1-2 days. Projects billed by the hour. First project may require prepayment. They serve an area within 100 miles of Kansas City, Either side of the KS or MO state line. Call for price quote. Performs service of process.

E-Z Messenger Attorney Service Inc

10 W Madison, Phoenix, AZ 85003
Phone: 800-380-8081; 602-258-8081 - **Fax:** 602-258-8864
www.e-zmessenger.com **email:** ronezell@e-zmessenger.com

Types of Records Retrieved: Criminal, Civil and Probate courts; Federal courts; UCC records; Vital records

Local Retrieval Area: AZ-Maricopa

Add'l Info: Established 1973. Normal turnaround time- 48 hours. Expedited service available. Projects billed by number of names searched. All projects require prepayment. A licensed PI in AZ. Performs service of process.

E-Z Messenger Attorney Service Inc

65 E Pennington St, Tucson, AZ 85701
Phone: 800-264-8436; 520-623-8436, 520-628-9737 - **Fax:** 520-624-1819
www.helpaz.com **email:** ronezell@e-zmessenger.com

Types of Records Retrieved: Criminal, Civil and Probate courts; Federal courts; Real Estate; Tax Liens/Judgments; UCC records

Local Retrieval Area: AZ-Cochise, Pima, Santa Cruz

Add'l Information: Established 1973. Normal turnaround time- 48 hours. Expedited service available. Projects billed by number of names searched. Projects billed by the hour. All projects require prepayment. Will file/record documents for clients. Formerly E-Z Messenger Attorney Service Inc, they are a full attorney service. They also have offices in Phoenix to cover Maricopa County and northern parts of AZ. A licensed PI in AZ. Performs service of process.

Fact Finders Ltd

125 Chapman St, Orange, VA 22960
Phone: 866-672-0666; 540-672 0666 - **Fax:** 540-672-6276
http://factfindersltd.com **email:** theperfectsearch@factfindersltd.com

Records Retrieved: Real Estate; Tax Liens/Judgments; UCC records

Local Retrieval Area: VA-Albemarle, Caroline, Charlottesville, Culpeper, Fauquier, Fluvanna, Fredericksburg, Greene, Louisa, King George, Madison, Orange, Page, Spotsylvania, Stafford, Warren

Add'l Information: Established 2001. Normal turnaround time- less than 72 hours. Projects billed by number of names searched. Fees dependant on volume. Payment due upon receipt of invoice. A family owned and operated business, they promise their searches will be timely and efficient. Also offering signature settlement services & real estate settlements.

Fact Finders of Nebraska

609 S Ash, North Platte, NE 69101
Phone: 308-534-8956 - **Fax:** 308-534-5884
2newport@nque.com

Types of Records Retrieved: Criminal and Civil courts; Real Estate; Tax Liens/Judgments; UCC records

Local Retrieval Area: NE-Adams, Buffalo, Dawson, Gosper, Hall, Kearney, Lincoln, Phelps, Red Willow. **Correspondent Relationships:** Custer, Cheyenne, counties NE.

Add'l Information: Established 1997. Normal turnaround time- 1-3 working days. Charge billed per name per county. Will file/record documents for clients. Terms are net 30 days. Monthly billing. Fact Finders provides personal services. They personally go to the courthouses. They have the capabilities to do bulk document retrievals. Have been in business 10 years.

Fairbanks Title Agency

714 3rd Ave, Fairbanks, AK 99701
Phone: 907-456-6626 - **Fax:** 907-452-5406

Types of Records Retrieved: Real Estate; Tax Liens/Judgments

Local Retrieval Area: AK-Barrow, Fairbanks Recording District, Fort Gibbon, Kotzebue, Manley Hot Springs, Mount McKinley, Nenana, Nome, Nulato, Rampart

Add'l Information: Established 1976. Normal turnaround time- 24 hours. Projects billed by the hour. All projects require prepayment. Will file/record documents for clients. They specialize in title insurance searches and escrow closings in Fairbanks Recording District and statewide.

Fairchild Record Search Ltd

PO Box 1368, 3400 Capitol Blvd S #101, Olympia, WA 98507
Phone: 800-547-7007; 360-786-8775 - **Fax:** 800-433-3404; 360-943-6656
www.recordsearch.com **email:** renee@recordsearch.com

Types of Records Retrieved: Criminal, Civil and Probate courts; Federal courts; Tax Liens/Judgments; UCC records; Vital records

Local Retrieval Area: WA-Thurston. **Correspondent Relationships:** nationwide and Canada.

Add'l Information: Established 1980. Normal turnaround time- 1-2 days. Projects billed by number of names searched. First project may require prepayment. Credit cards accepted. They will file/record UCC documents on behalf of clients on a same or next day basis. They are a registered agent service. Performs service of process.

Fairview Abstract Co

PO Box 60, Fairview, OK 73737
Phone: 580-227-4524 - **Fax:** 580-227-3607

Types of Records Retrieved: Criminal, Civil and Probate courts; Real Estate; Tax Liens/Judgments; UCC records; Vital records

Local Retrieval Area: OK-Major

Add'l Information: Established 1917. Turnaround time- 1 week. Projects billed by the hour. Will file/record documents for clients. Terms: net 30 days. They specialize in abstracting, title insurance and escrow closings.

Faith to Faith Legal Productions LLC

10062 High Pines Dr, Baton Rouge, LA 70809-5915
Phone: 225-751-9202 - **Fax:** 225-751-9203 f2flp@cox.net

Types of Records Retrieved: Criminal, Civil and Probate courts; Federal courts; Real Estate; Tax Liens/Judgments; UCC records

Local Retrieval Area: LA-Ascension, Assumption, East Baton Rouge, Iberville, Livingston, Pointe Coupee, West Baton Rouge. **Correspondent Relationships:** East Feliciana, West Feliciana.

Add'l Information: Established 1995. Turnaround time- 24-48. Expedited service available. Projects billed by number of names searched. Net 30 days. They specialize in the areas of document retrievals, real estate, abstracting, real estate notarial closings, and criminal and civil background checks.

Faithful Abstract

2 Broad St, Elizabeth, NJ 07201 **Phone:** 908-351-9398 **Fax:** 732-557-4618

Types of Records Retrieved: Civil and Probate courts; Real Estate; Tax Liens/Judgments; UCC records

Local Retrieval Area: NJ-Ocean, Union

Add'l Information: Established 1980. Normal turnaround time- 1-5 days. Fee basis will vary by the type of project. First project may require prepayment. Will file/record documents for clients. They have more than 20 years of abstract and title experience.

Falcon Research & Settlement

4181 Brookville St, Hawthorn, PA 16230
Phone: 800-828-4081; 814-365-5455 - **Fax:** 814-365-5019
www.falconsettlement.com
email: customerservice@falconsettlement.com

Types of Records Retrieved: Criminal and Civil courts; Bankruptcy court; Real Estate; Tax Liens/Judgments; UCC records

Local Retrieval Area: PA-Armstrong, Butler, Cameron, Clarion, Clearfield, Elk, Forest, Indiana, Jefferson, McKean, Mercer, Potter, Venango, Warren

Add'l Information: Established 1986. Normal turnaround time- up to 1 week. Projects billed by number of names searched. Fee basis will vary by the type of project. Will file/record documents for clients. Will invoice at the end of the month. They have served the real estate and banking business for over 20 years with quick turnaround times and thorough top quality work in Western Pennsylvania.

Fall River Abstract Co

PO Box 1157, 141 S Chicago St, Hot Springs, SD 57747
Phone: 605-745-5187 - **Fax:** 605-745-5482 frtitlco@gwtc.net
Records Retrieved: Real Estate; Tax Liens/Judgments; Probate courts
Local Retrieval Area: SD-Fall River, Shannon
Add'l Information: Established 1943. Normal turnaround time- 24-48 hours. Projects billed by the hour. Terms are net 30 days after billing. First project may require prepayment. Will file/record documents for clients.

Fallon County Abstractor

PO Box 827, Baker, MT 59313
Phone: 406-778-3929 - **Fax:** 406-778-3928
Types of Records Retrieved: Real Estate; Tax Liens/Judgments
Local Retrieval Area: MT-Fallon
Add'l Information: Established 1913. First project may require prepayment. They specialize in real estate.

Falls County Title Co Inc

122 Bridge St, Marlin, TX 76661-2829
Phone: 254-883-2112 - **Fax:** 254-883-6260
Types of Records Retrieved: Civil and Probate courts; Real Estate; Tax Liens/Judgments; UCC records; Vital records
Local Retrieval Area: TX-Falls
Add'l Information: Established 1995. Normal turnaround time- 1 week. Fee basis will vary by the type of project. All projects require prepayment.

FarVision Consulting Title Co

4751 Rte 10, Barboursville, WV 25504
Phone: 304-733-5086 - **Fax:** 304-733-5087
Types of Records Retrieved: Real Estate; Tax Liens/Judgments
Local Retrieval Area: KY-Boone, Bracken
Add'l Information: Established 1993. First project may require prepayment. They specialize in real estate.

Farwell Abstract Co Inc

402 3rd St, Farwell, TX 79325
Phone: 806-481-9992 - **Fax:** 806-481-9060
Types of Records Retrieved: Criminal, Civil and Probate courts; Real Estate; Tax Liens/Judgments
Local Retrieval Area: TX-Bailey, Parmer
Add'l Information: Established 1907. Normal turnaround time- 72 hours. Projects billed by the hour. Will file/record documents for clients. They specialize in title insurance.

Faxxon Legal Information Services Inc

1 W Old State Capitol Plaza #805, Myers Bldg, Springfield, IL 62701
Phone: 800-932-9966; 217-522-3280 - **Fax:** 800-229-7028; 217-522-3570
www.faxxon.com **email:** wjstokes@faxxon.com
Types of Records Retrieved: Criminal, Civil and Probate courts; Federal courts; Real Estate; Tax Liens/Judgments; UCC records; Vital records
Local Retrieval Area: IL-Sangamon. **Correspondent Relationships:** nationwide, especially Central IL area.
Add'l Information: Established 1995. Normal turnaround time- 24 hours. Projects billed by number of names searched. First project may require prepayment. Credit cards accepted. Will file/record documents for clients. An expert in the field of public record searching since 1982, they specialize in IL state records - Sec of State, UCCs, etc. Also specialize in real estate and personal abstracting.

Fayette Professional Services

56 E Main St, Uniontown, PA 15401
Phone: 412-439-1450 fayette1@gmail.com
Types of Records Retrieved: Criminal, Civil and Probate courts; Real Estate; Tax Liens/Judgments; UCC records
Local Retrieval Area: PA-Fayette, Greene, Washington, Westmoreland
Add'l Information: Established 1976. Normal turnaround time- same day in Fayette County only. Fee basis will vary by type of project. Will file/record documents for clients. Terms: net 30 days. Specialize in real estate closing (witness only). They take pride in their excellent service. Same day or 24-hour return of reports.

FBIG Investigations

225 - 17 Fawcett Rd, Coquitlam, British Columbia, Canada, CAN V3K 6V2
Phone: 866-245-2082, 888-540-0456; 604-540-0455 - **Fax:** 604-540-0454
www.fbig.ca **email:** web3@fbig.ca
Types of Records Retrieved: Criminal and Civil courts; Federal District court; Real Estate; Tax Liens/Judgments
Local Retrieval Area: CANADA-British Columbia. **Correspondent Relationships:** All Provinces.
Add'l Information: Established 1988. Normal turnaround time- 24-48 hours. Projects billed by number of names searched. First project may require prepayment. In addition to expert document retrieval and investigations services in BC, they have a screening firm known as HRscreening.com. FBIG is part of Investigations Canada Group. A licensed PI in British Columbia. Performs service of process.

Federal Research LLC

1023 15th St NW #401, Washington, DC 20005
Phone: 800-846-3190; - **Fax:** 202-783-0145
www.federalresearch.com **email:** inquiries@federalresearch.com
Types of Records Retrieved: Civil and Probate courts; Federal courts; Real Estate; Tax Liens/Judgments; UCC records; Vital records
Local Retrieval Area: DC-District of Columbia; MD-Anne Arundel, Baltimore, Baltimore City, Harford, Howard, Montgomery, Prince George's; VA-Alexandria City, Arlington, Fairfax, Loudoun, Prince William, Richmond City. **Correspondent Relationships:** nationwide.
Add'l Information: Established 1985. Normal turnaround time- 3-5 days. Expedited service available. Fee may be based per index. Federal searches are per hour. Credit cards accepted. Will file/record documents for clients. Visa, MasterCard and American Express accepted In addition to nationwide UCC and corporate searches, they specialize in intellectual property searches and filings, document authentication, federal agency and Library of Congress work, embassies, also copyright/trademarks. Federal agent services. Performs service of process.

R L Ferrelle

109 Chinese Fir Ct, Pooler, GA 31322-4038
Phone: 912-330-9923 - **Fax:** 912-330-9923 b422chattlamga@earthlink.net
Types of Records Retrieved: Criminal and Civil courts; Federal courts
Local Retrieval Area: GA-Chatham, Effingham
Add'l Information: Established 1996. Normal turnaround time- 24-48 hours. Projects billed by number of names searched. Terms are net 30 days. They specialize in being prompt, reliable, accurate with 10 years of experience. Phone calls returned promptly. Also do hospital liens and UCCs.

Ferret Diversified Services Inc

PO Box 661, 210 Skokie Valley Rd, Highland Park, IL 60035
Phone: 847-579-0007 - **Fax:** 847-831-3203
www.ferretdiv.com **email:** ferretdiv@aol.com
Types of Records Retrieved: Criminal, Civil and Probate courts; Real Estate
Local Retrieval Area: IL-Adams, Carroll, Champaign, Coles, Cook, De Kalb, Du Page, Henry, Jackson, Jo Daviess, Kane, Kendall, Lake, Lee, Logan, Madison, Mercer, Ogle, Pike, Rock Island, Sangamon, Stephenson, Union, Whiteside, Will, Winnebago. **Correspondents:** nationwide.
Add'l Information: Established 1997. Normal turnaround time- same day if received by 3 PM CST. Payment due net 15 days. They specialize in providing criminal background information and other screening services. A licensed PI in IL.

Fidelifacts

42 Broadway, New York, NY 10004
Phone: 800-678-0007; - **Fax:** 800-509-8496; 212-248-5619
www.fidelifacts.com **email:** tnorton@fidelifacts.com

Types of Records Retrieved: Criminal, Civil and Probate courts; Federal courts; Real Estate; Tax Liens/Judgments; UCC records; Vital records

Local Retrieval Area: NJ-Atlantic, Bergen, Burlington, Camden, Cape May, Cumberland, Essex, Gloucester, Hudson, Hunterdon, Mercer, Middlesex, Monmouth, Morris, Ocean, Passaic, Salem, Somerset, Sussex, Union, Warren; NY-Bronx, Dutchess, Kings, Nassau, New York, Orange, Putnam, Queens, Richmond, Rockland, Suffolk, Ulster, Westchester. **Correspondent Relationships:** nationwide.

Add'l Information: Established 1956. Normal turnaround time- 2-10 days. Projects billed by number of names searched. First project may require prepayment. They specialize in criminal records checks and credit checks plus employment background investigations nationwide. A licensed PI in NJ, NY.

Fidelity Abstract & Title Co

PO Box 247, 115 N Main, Howard, SD 57349

Phone: 605-772-5632 - **Fax:** 605-772-5648 fatc@alliancecom.net

Types of Records Retrieved: Civil and Probate courts; Real Estate; Tax Liens/Judgments; UCC records

Local Retrieval Area: SD-Miner

Add'l Information: Established 1947. Normal turnaround time- depends on nature of project. Projects billed by the hour. First project may require prepayment. Will file/record documents for clients. They specialize in title insurance and abstracting. Faxing them is suggested.

Fidelity Home Abstract Inc

3 Landmark Ctr, East Stroudsburg, PA 18301

Phone: 800-224-5601; 570-424-5600 - **Fax:** 570-424-9860

Types of Records Retrieved: Civil and Probate courts; Real Estate; Tax Liens/Judgments; UCC records

Local Retrieval Area: PA-Carbon, Monroe, Northampton, Pike, Wayne. **Correspondent Relationships:** Nebraska and Pennsylvania.

Add'l Information: Normal turnaround time- 10 days. Expedited service available. Projects billed by number of records located. Terms: net 30 days. They specialize in abstracting.

File Finders Public Record Research Inc/dba Filefinders

PO Box 210265, Chula Vista, CA 91921

Phone: 619-656-6068 - **Fax:** 619-482-8042 www.filefindersonline.com

email: customersupport@filefindersonline.com

Types of Records Retrieved: Criminal and Civil courts; Federal courts; Tax Liens/Judgments

Local Retrieval Area: CA-San Diego. **Correspondents:** nationwide.

Add'l Information: Established 1994. Normal turnaround time- 6-8 hours initial results; 24-48 hours hit results. Projects billed by number of names searched. First project may require prepayment. Credit cards accepted. Large projects may require a down payment. They are a full service public record research and screening company specializing in public record searches, credit information, credential and education verification, and reference checking. Rush service available - turnaround time of 1-3 hours.

Financial Dimensions

1400 Lebanon Church Rd, Pittsburgh, PA 15236

Phone: 800-858-9808; 412-650-1700 - **Fax:** 800-858-9810

www.financialdimensions.com **email:** bill@financialdimensions.com

Types of Records Retrieved: Criminal and Civil courts; Federal courts; Real Estate; Tax Liens/Judgments; UCC records

Local Retrieval Area: PA-Allegheny. **Correspondents:** nationwide.

Add'l Information: Established 1986. Normal turnaround time- 24-48 hours. Projects billed by number of names searched. They invoice monthly. Will file/record documents for clients. They specialize in mortgage document retrieval, recording and servicing nationwide.

Fink Abstract Co

PO Box 418, 622 Madison St, Fredonia, KS 66736

Phone: 620-378-2351 - **Fax:** 620-378-4425

Types of Records Retrieved: Civil and Probate courts; Real Estate; Tax Liens/Judgments; UCC records; Vital records

Local Retrieval Area: KS-Wilson

Add'l Information: Established 1904.Turnaround time- 2-3 days. Fee basis varies by type of transaction. First project may require prepayment.

Finley Abstract & Title Co

PO Box 397, 309 Jefferson Street, Oskaloosa, KS 66066

Phone: 785-863-2271 - **Fax:** 785-863-2065

finley_abstract@msn.com

Types of Records Retrieved: Civil and Probate courts; Real Estate; Tax Liens/Judgments; UCC records **Local Retrieval Area:** KS-Jefferson

Add'l Information: Established 1889. Normal turnaround time- 2-3 days. Projects billed by the hour. First project may require prepayment. Will file/record documents for clients.

Finney Land Co

PO Box 2471, Durango, CO 81302

Phone: 970-259-5691 - **Fax:** 970-259-4279 Finney@frontier.net

Records Retrieved: Criminal, Civil and Probate courts; State District courts; Real Estate; Tax Liens/Judgments; UCC records; Vital records

Local Retrieval Area: CO-Archuleta, La Plata, Montezuma

Add'l Information: Established 1988. Normal turnaround time- 1-2 days. Projects billed by the hour. Payment due upon receipt, no work done until last job paid. First project may require prepayment. Will file/record documents for clients. They specialize in oil and gas.

Margaret Fiorillo

151 N Vermillion St #4, Paxton, IL 60957-1381

Phone: 217-379-3359

Types of Records Retrieved: Criminal and Civil courts; Real Estate; Tax Liens/Judgments; UCC records; Vital records

Local Retrieval Area: IL-Ford

Add'l Information: Established 1994. Turnaround time- 24 hours. Projects billed by number of names searched. Will file/record documents for clients. She specializes in criminal record searches. Performs service of process.

First Abstract & Loan Co

601 W Main, Cherokee, IA 51012

Phone: 712-225-3612 - **Fax:** 712-225-1033

Types of Records Retrieved: Criminal, Civil and Probate courts; Real Estate; Tax Liens/Judgments; UCC records

Local Retrieval Area: IA-Cherokee

Add'l Information: Established 1950. Normal turnaround time- 2 weeks. Fee basis will vary by type of project. Will file/record documents for clients.

First Advantage

10501 N Central Expy #309, Dallas, TX 75231

Phone: 800-687-0894; 214-360-9122 - **Fax:** 800-600-1408; 214-360-0775

www.backgroundsystems.com **email:** beverly@natcrime.com

Types of Records Retrieved: Criminal and Civil courts

Local Retrieval Area: TX-Bexar, Collin, Dallas, Denton, Harris, Tarrant, Travis, Williamson. **Correspondent Relationships:** nationwide, especially in 375 counties nearby.

Add'l Information: Established 1980. Normal turnaround time- 24 hours. Payment due upon receipt of invoice. First Advantage provides high-quality, reliable pre-employment and background screening to national corporate clients and well over 100 independent school districts and municipalities. A licensed PI in TX.

First American Title & Escrow (Libby)

120 W 6th St, Libby, MT 59923

Phone: 800-282-5630; 406-293-3721 - **Fax:** 406-293-3723

Types of Records Retrieved: Criminal, Civil and Probate courts; Real Estate; Tax Liens/Judgments; UCC records; Vital records

Local Retrieval Area: MT-Lincoln

Add'l Information: Established 1990. Turnaround time- next day. Fee basis varies by type of transaction. Will file/record documents for clients.

First American Title & Escrow (Polson)
PO Box 910, 210 2nd St E, Polson, MT 59860
Phone: 800-331-2349; 406-883-5258 - **Fax:** 406-883-3056
cs.polson.mt@firstam.com
Types of Records Retrieved: Criminal, Civil and Probate courts; Real Estate; Tax Liens/Judgments; UCC records
Local Retrieval Area: MT-Lake
Add'l Information: Established 1975. Normal turnaround time- next day. Fee basis varies by type of transaction. Will file/record documents for clients. Will bill.

First American Title Co
111 N Main St, Poplar Bluff, MO 63901
Phone: 573-686-1495 - **Fax:** 573-686-3804
Types of Records Retrieved: Civil and Probate courts; Real Estate; Tax Liens/Judgments; UCC records
Local Retrieval Area: MO-Butler
Add'l Information: Normal turnaround time- 1-3 days. Projects billed by number of names searched. Projects billed by number of records located. First project may require prepayment. Personal checks are accepted.

First American Title Co
PO Box 899, Ennis, MT 59729-0899
Phone: 800-570-5337; 406-843-5337 alongfellow@firstam.com
Types of Records Retrieved: Real Estate
Local Retrieval Area: MT-Madison
Add'l Information: Established 1922. Normal turnaround time- 1-3 days. Projects billed by the hour. First project may require prepayment. Will file/record documents for clients.

First American Title Co (Colorado)
102 Grand Ave #B, Delta, CO 81416-2058
Phone: 970-874-8286 - **Fax:** 970-874-4762
Records Retrieved: Real Estate; Tax Liens/Judgments; UCC records
Local Retrieval Area: CO-Delta, Montrose, Ouray
Add'l Information: Established 1985. Normal turnaround time- 3-5 days. Fee basis will vary by the type of project. Terms: net 30 days. They specialize in title insurance and full closing services.

First American Title Co (Thomspon Falls)
Box 850, 1211 Main St, Thompson Falls, MT 59873
Phone: 406-827-3591 - **Fax:** 406-827-3848
Types of Records Retrieved: Real Estate; Tax Liens/Judgments; UCC records; Probate courts; Federal District courts
Local Retrieval Area: MT-Sanders
Add'l Information: Normal turnaround time- 3-5 days. Projects billed by the hour. First project may require prepayment.

First American Title Co of Crook Cty
PO Box 190, Sundance, WY 82729-0190
Phone: 307-283-1844 - **Fax:** 307-283-1855 lfoster@firstam.com
Records Retrieved: Real Estate; Tax Liens/Judgments; UCC records
Local Retrieval Area: WY-Crook
Add'l Information: Established 1981. Normal turnaround time- 1-2 days. Projects billed by number of names searched. Projects billed by the hour. First project may require prepayment. They specialize in title insurance, abstracts and certificates of titles. Will search civil and probate courts in connection with real estate only.

First American Title Co of Montana Inc
304 N Kendrick Ave, Glendive, MT 59330-1716
Phone: 406-365-5482 - **Fax:** 406-365-5835 mherring@firstam.com
Types of Records Retrieved: Civil and Probate courts; Real Estate; Tax Liens/Judgments; UCC records
Local Retrieval Area: MT-Dawson, McCone
Add'l Information: Normal turnaround time- 1 week or less. Projects billed by number of names searched. Project billed according to amount of mortgage, etc. Will file/record documents for clients.

First American Title Ins Co
2233 Lee Rd #101, Winter Park, FL 32789
Phone: 407-740-7131 - **Fax:** 407-691-5300 www.firstam.com
Types of Records Retrieved: Civil and Probate courts; Federal courts; Real Estate; Tax Liens/Judgments; UCC records; Vital records
Local Retrieval Area: FL-Brevard, Duval, Flagler, Lake, Marion, Orange, Osceola, Polk, Seminole, Volusia
Add'l Information: Established 1883. Normal turnaround time- 3 working days. Projects billed by the hour. They specialize in serving Central Florida and have a computer database of real estate for Orange, Seminole, Lake, Osceola and Volusia counties.

First American Title Insurance Company (IL)
351 Sabella St, Central IL Division, Pekin, IL 61554
Phone: 309-347-6126 - **Fax:** 309-347-4523
Types of Records Retrieved: Civil and Probate courts; Real Estate; Tax Liens/Judgments; UCC records; Vital records
Local Retrieval Area: IL-Cass, Fulton, Mason, Menard, Schuyler
Add'l Information: Established 1948. Normal turnaround time- recording same day received; 5 working days for searches. Expedited service available. Projects billed by number of names searched. Will file/record documents for clients. They are a full service title company. They also prepare documents, closings, search of real estate and circuit clerk records.

First American Title Insurance of Oregon
454 Commercial St, Coos Bay, OR 97420
Phone: 800-235-0119; 541-269-0119 - **Fax:** 541-269-0470
Types of Records Retrieved: Civil and Probate courts; Real Estate; Tax Liens/Judgments; UCC records; Vital records
Local Retrieval Area: OR-Coos. **Correspondent Relationships:** courtesy signing throughout Oregon.
Add'l Information: Normal turnaround time- 1-2 days. Projects billed by the hour. Their hourly rate varies. First project may require prepayment. Will file/record documents for clients. They specialize in title insurance and escrow services.

First American Title Mineral County
PO Box 548, 305 W 3rd Ave, Superior, MT 59872
Phone: 406-822-3391 - **Fax:** 406-822-3396
Types of Records Retrieved: Civil and Probate courts; Real Estate; Tax Liens/Judgments
Local Retrieval Area: MT-Mineral. **Correspondent Relationships:** nationwide.
Add'l Information: Established 1984. They specialize in real estate, transactions, title searches and escrows.

First American Title of Preston
PO Box 148, 28 W Oneida St, Preston, ID 83263
Phone: 208-852-2810 - **Fax:** 208-852-2811
Types of Records Retrieved: Real Estate; Tax Liens/Judgments; UCC records; Vital records, Civil and Probate courts
Local Retrieval Area: ID-Franklin
Add'l Information: Established 1996. Normal turnaround time- 1-2 days. Projects billed by the hour.

First American Torrington
PO Box 39, Torrington, WY 82240
Phone: 307-532-5642 - **Fax:** 307-532-3001
Types of Records Retrieved: Real Estate; Tax Liens/Judgments
Local Retrieval Area: WY-Goshen
Add'l Information: Established 1977. First project may require prepayment. They specialize in real estate.

First American Wheatland
PO Box 722, Wheatland, WY 82201
Phone: 307-322-2133 - **Fax:** 307-322-2213
Types of Records Retrieved: Real Estate; Tax Liens/Judgments

Local Retrieval Area: WY-Platte
Add'l Information: Established 1992. First project may require prepayment. The specialize in real estate.

1st Choice Abstracting
79 Axworthy Ln, Goshen, NY 10924-5019
Phone: 845-313-6437 - **Fax:** 845-294-9532
firstchoiceabstracting@yahoo.com
Types of Records Retrieved: Criminal and Civil courts; Real Estate; Tax Liens/Judgments; UCC records;
Local Area: NY-Dutchess, Orange, Putnam, Rockland, Sullivan, Westchester
Add'l Information: Projects billed by number of names searched. First project may require prepayment. They are friendly, fast, reliable with reasonable rates.

First Choice Research
6151 Miramar Pky #307, Miramar, FL 33023
Phone: 888-878-1595; 954-964-1260 - **Fax:** 954-964-8283
www.firstchoiceresearch.com **email:** jloriga@firstchoiceresearch.com
Types of Records Retrieved: Criminal, Civil and Probate courts; Federal courts; Tax Liens/Judgments; UCC records
Local Retrieval Area: FL-all counties. **Correspondent Relationships:** nationwide.
Add'l Information: Established 1995. Normal turnaround time- 24-48 hours or upon assignment. Projects billed by number of names searched. End of month billing. They specialize in record retrieval, criminal, civil, federal, UCC searches, judgments/liens and statewide and nationwide criminal searches. Is also a pre-employment company. A licensed PI in FL.

First Choice Title Service LLC
23 Bussing Ct, Timonium, MD 21093-2009
Phone: 410-960-6493 - **Fax:** 410-252-9209
firstchoicetitle@comcast.net
Types of Records Retrieved: Real Estate
Retrieval Area: MD-Allegany, Anne Arundel, Baltimore County, Baltimore City, Calvert, Caroline, Carroll, Cecil, Charles, Dorchester, Frederick, Garrett, Harford, Howard, Kent, Montgomery, Prince George, Queen Anne's, Summerset, St. Mary's, Talbot, Washington, Wicomico, Worchester
Add'l Information: Established 1996. Normal turnaround time- 24-72 hours. Projects billed by number of names searched. They pride themselves in their thorough work and quick request turn-around time. They cover all of Maryland in a timely dependable manner. Low-rate pricing. Cell phone # is 410-960-6493.

First Coast Inv
PO Box 10673, Jacksonville, FL 32247
Phone: 904-398-4076 - **Fax:** 904-346-0329 jakiseer1@iwon.com
Types of Records Retrieved: Criminal, Civil and Probate courts; Federal courts; Tax Liens/Judgments; Vital records
Local Retrieval Area: FL-Clay, Duval, Nassau. **Correspondent Relationships:** Miami and Orlando.
Add'l Information: Established 1979. Normal turnaround time- 24-48 for criminal records. Fees are based on a county schedule. Surveillance required deposit. They specialize in background investigations and Motor Vehicle Record checks. A licensed PI in FL. Performs service of process.

First Gunnison Title & Escrow
113 E Georgia, Gunnison, CO 81230
Phone: 800-530-9598; 970-641-4600 - **Fax:** 970-641-4071
www.firstgunnison.com **email:** service@firstgunnison.com
Types of Records Retrieved: Real Estate; Tax Liens/Judgments
Local Retrieval Area: CO-Gunnison, Hinsdale
Add'l Information: Established 1994. Normal turnaround time- 24 hours. Projects billed by the hour. First project may require prepayment. Will file/record documents for clients. They specialize in real estate records. 21st century technology with a small town touch.

First Idaho Title Co
469 Washington, Montpelier, ID 83254
Phone: 208-847-1300 - **Fax:** 208-847-1314 fitc@dcdi.net
Types of Records Retrieved: Real Estate; Tax Liens/Judgments; UCC records, Civil and Probate courts;
Local Retrieval Area: ID-Bear Lake
Add'l Information: Established 1980. Normal turnaround time- 1 week. Fees vary by project. Will file/record documents for clients.

First Insurance Agency of Hoxie Inc
700 Main St, Hoxie, KS 67740-0108
Phone: 800-569-0198; 785-675-3252 - **Fax:** 785-675-3811
econard@ruraltel.net
Types of Records Retrieved: Criminal, Civil and Probate courts; Federal courts; Real Estate; Tax Liens/Judgments; UCC records
Local Retrieval Area: KS-Decatur, Gove, Graham, Sheridan, Thomas. **Correspondent Relationships:** Gove, Thomas, Decatur counties KS.
Add'l Information: Established 1976. Normal turnaround time- 1 day for Sheridan County; 2-3 days for surrounding counties. Projects billed by number of records located. Projects billed by the hour. Will file/record documents for clients. Personal checks are accepted. They specialize in record searches.

First Investigative Consultants, PI# 6949
2529 Foothill Blvd #212, La Cresenta, CA 91214
Phone: 800-900-4342; 818-957-1958 - **Fax:** 800-842-4004; 818-957-4910
www.fic-ca.com **email:** infosvcs@earthlink.net
Types of Records Retrieved: Criminal, Civil and Probate courts; Federal courts; Real Estate; Tax Liens/Judgments; UCC records; Vital records
Local Retrieval Area: CA-Los Angeles, Orange, Riverside, San Bernardino, San Diego, Ventura. **Correspondent Relationships:** California.
Add'l Information: Established 1977. Normal turnaround time- 24-72 hours. Projects billed by number of names searched. Projects billed by the hour. Fee basis depends on type of search. First project may require prepayment. Credit cards accepted. Terms: net 30 days. They specialize in insurance investigations, pre-trial preparation, attorney services (service of process), information services, locate investigations, backgrounds, fraud, workers' compensation, surveillance. A licensed PI in AZ, CA, NV. Performs service of process.

First Mason Title Co
PO Box 1219, 100 Broad St, Mason, TX 76856
Phone: 325-347-6388 - **Fax:** 325-347-5418 jacklee@tstar.net
Types of Records Retrieved: Civil and Probate courts; Real Estate; Tax Liens/Judgments; UCC records; Vital records
Local Retrieval Area: TX-Mason
Add'l Information: Normal turnaround time- 2-5 days. Projects billed by the hour. Charges may also be a set fee depending on the project. All projects require prepayment. Will file/record documents for clients.

First Quality Research Co
31239 Bridgegate Dr, Zephyrhills, FL 33544
Phone: 813-862-2778 - **Fax:** 813-862-2782
Types of Records Retrieved: Criminal and Civil courts
Local Retrieval Area: FL-Bay, Columbia, Hillsborough, Leon, Martin, Nassau, Orange, Palm Beach, Pasco, Polk, Putnam, Seminole, St. Johns, St. Lucie, Union, Walton
Add'l Information: Established 2002. Normal turnaround time- 24-48 hours. Projects billed by number of names searched. Casual requests allowed.

First Securities Corp in Aurora
1220 L St, Aurora, NE 68818
Phone: 402-694-6926 - **Fax:** 402-694-6927
Types of Records Retrieved: Criminal, Civil and Probate courts; Real Estate; Tax Liens/Judgments; UCC records; Vital records
Local Retrieval Area: NE-Hamilton
Add'l Information: Established 1932. Normal turnaround time- 3-4 days. Fee basis varies by type of transaction. Will file/record documents for clients. Terms: net 30 days. They specialize in title searches.

First State Abstract

101 E Front St #101, Lonoke, AR 72086-3237
Phone: 501-676-2486 - **Fax:** 501-676-2444
Types of Records Retrieved: Civil and Probate courts; Real Estate; Tax Liens/Judgments; UCC records **Local Retrieval Area:** AR-Lonoke
Add'l Information: Established 1953. Normal turnaround time- 3-4 days. Fee basis will vary by type of project. All projects require prepayment. Will file/record documents for clients. They specialize in title insurance.

First Title Services

PO Box 1288, Tucumcari, NM 88401
Phone: 505-461-1300 - **Fax:** 505-461-2946
Types of Records Retrieved: Real Estate; Tax Liens/Judgments
Local Retrieval Area: NM-Harding

Randy Fish

PO Box 107, Uniontown, KY 42461
Phone: 270-822-4412; cell- 270-952-0731
Types of Records Retrieved: Criminal, Civil and Probate courts
Local Retrieval Area: KY-Henderson, Union
Add'l Information: Established 1992. Normal turnaround time- 24-48 hours. Projects billed by number of names searched. Will invoice after first job paid. Specializes in felony and misdemeanor lookups. Call before faxing.

Fisher/Jones Title Co (Anson)

PO Box 149, 1312 Commercial Ave, Anson, TX 79501
Phone: 325-823-3236 - **Fax:** 325-823-3224
Types of Records Retrieved: Criminal, Civil and Probate courts; Real Estate; Tax Liens/Judgments; UCC records; Vital records
Local Retrieval Area: TX-Jones
Add'l Information: Established 1901. Normal turnaround time- 1-2 days. Fee basis will vary by the type of project. First project may require prepayment. Will file/record documents for clients. Their main office is in Roby in Fisher County.

Fisher/Jones Title Co (Roby)

PO Box 428, W Hiway 180, Roby, TX 79543
Phone: 325-776-2471 - **Fax:** 325-776-2886
Types of Records Retrieved: Criminal, Civil and Probate courts; Real Estate; Tax Liens/Judgments; UCC records; Vital records
Local Retrieval Area: TX-Fisher
Add'l Information: Established 1901. Normal turnaround time- 1-2 days. Fee basis will vary by the type of project. First project may require prepayment. Will file/record documents for clients.

Fitzgerald Servaites Inc

7308 Langsford Ct, Springfield, VA 22153
Phone: 202-257-7775 - **Fax:** 703-912-4840
www.fsiresearch.com **email:** fsiresearch@aol.com
Types of Records Retrieved: Criminal, Civil and Probate courts; Federal courts; Real Estate; Tax Liens/Judgments; UCC records; Vital records
Local Retrieval Area: DC-District of Columbia; MD-Montgomery, Prince George's; VA-Alexandria City, Arlington, Fairfax, Loudoun, Prince William, Stafford
Add'l Information: Established 1997. Turnaround time- 24 hours. Projects billed by number of names searched. Projects billed by the hour. All projects are invoiced. They specialize in providing accurate, expeditious litigation research within the Washington, DC metropolitan region.

Judith A Fitzgerald

421 Manono St, Kailua, HI 96734
Phone: 808-263-2120 - **Fax:** 808-263-5823 heyjude831@aol.com
Types of Records Retrieved: Criminal, Civil and Probate courts; Federal courts; Real Estate; Tax Liens/Judgments; UCC records
Local Retrieval Area: HI-Hawaii, Honolulu, Kauai, Maui
Add'l Information: Established 1982. Normal turnaround time- variable depending on project. Projects billed by the hour. Terms: net 30 days. She specializes in real property asset searches & lien searches statewide, is a retired certified Real Estate Appraiser & a certified polygraph examiner. Court record searches for Oahu only (City & county of Honolulu) & criminal convictions statewide.

Flagler County Abstract Co

PO Box 398, Bunnell, FL 32110
Phone: 386-437-4151 - **Fax:** 386-437-1913
www.flaglercountyabstract.com **email:** fcac@flaglercountyabstract.com
Types of Records Retrieved: Real Estate; Tax Liens/Judgments; Probate courts; UCC records
Local Retrieval Area: FL-Flagler, St. Johns, Volusia
Add'l Information: Established 1917. Normal turnaround time- 24 hours. Projects billed by number of names searched. All projects require prepayment. They have been established since 1917 and specialize in titles. Another address for their web site is www.fcac.earthmax.net. Performs service of process.

Fleming Attorney Service

PO Box 3882, Phoenix, AZ 85030
Phone: 800-776-3301; 602-253-1155 - **Fax:** 602-253-5841
www.flemingattorneyservices.com
email: admin@flemingattorneyservices.com
Types of Records Retrieved: Criminal, Civil and Probate courts; Federal courts; Real Estate; Tax Liens/Judgments; UCC records
Local Retrieval Area: AZ-Maricopa. **Correspondents:** statewide.
Add'l Information: Established 1964. Normal turnaround time- next day for court searches; 2-3 days for UCC and tax records. Projects billed by number of names searched. Projects billed by the hour. First project may require prepayment. Will file/record documents for clients. They specialize in process servicing, asset searches, and skiptracing. A licensed PI in AZ. Performs service of process.

Glenn A Fleming

PO Box 772, Belle Chasse, LA 70037
Phone: 504-393-0988 - **Fax:** 504-433-5101
Types of Records Retrieved: Criminal and Civil courts; Real Estate; Tax Liens/Judgments; UCC records
Local Retrieval Area: LA-Plaquemines Parish
Add'l Information: Established 1990. Normal turnaround time- 1-3 days. Fee basis varies by type of transaction. First project may require prepayment. Will file/record documents for clients. He specializes in real estate transfer searches, mortgage searches, tax searches and title abstracts.

Flink Findzum Lawyers Service

31 Pleasant Pl, Oceanport, NJ 07757
Phone: 800-380-5434; 732-219-5433 - **Fax:** 732-219-5466
mpagan4750@aol.com
Types of Records Retrieved: Criminal and Civil courts; Federal courts; Real Estate; Tax Liens/Judgments; UCC records; Vital records
Local Retrieval Area: NJ-All counties
Add'l Information: Established 1987. Normal turnaround time- 1-2 days. Expedited service available. Projects billed by number of names searched. Projects billed by number of records located. Projects billed by the hour. First project may require prepayment. Will file/record documents for clients. A licensed PI in NJ. Performs service of process.

Florence County Abstract

PO Box 86, Florence, WI 54121
Phone: 715-528-3272 - **Fax:** 715-528-4707
Types of Records Retrieved: Civil and Probate courts; Real Estate; Tax Liens/Judgments; UCC records; Vital records
Local Retrieval Area: WI-Florence
Add'l Information: Established 1950. Normal turnaround time- 24-48 hours. Projects billed by number of names searched. Will file/record documents for clients. They have the a complete in-house tract index and judgment index to serve Florence County.

Florida Filing & Search Services Inc

155 Office Plaza Dr #A, Tallahassee, FL 32301
Phone: 800-435-9371; 850-216-0457 - **Fax:** 850-216-0460
www.floridafiling.com **email:** paul@floridafiling.com

Types of Records Retrieved: Civil courts; Federal courts; Tax Liens/Judgments; UCC records

Local Retrieval Area: FL-Gadsden, Jackson, Jefferson, Leon, Wakulla. **Correspondent Relationships:** nationwide.

Add'l Information: Established 1990. Normal turnaround time- 24-48 hours. Projects billed by number of names searched. Will file/record documents for clients. Will use PayPal. They specialize in UCC, state and federal tax liens, judgments, pending suits & corporate document filing & retrieval. Registered agent services.

Florida Information Associates Inc

PO Box 11144, Tallahassee, FL 32302-3144
Phone: 850-878-0188 - **Fax:** 850-656-2126
www.fia-research.com **email:** etfia@earthlink.net

Types of Records Retrieved: Civil courts; Federal courts

Local Retrieval Area: FL-Leon

Add'l Information: Established 1985. Normal turnaround time- 2-3 days. Expedited service available. Projects billed by number of names searched. Projects billed by the hour. They offer flexible charging for large requests. First project may require prepayment. They research and retrieve for state executive, judicial & legislative agencies at the state capital, including legislative intent, corporations, UCC, motor vehicle records, regulatory/licensure agencies and administrative proceedings.

Florida Records Research

1200 Lastrada Ln, Naples, FL 34103
Phone: 239-435-1189 - **Fax:** 239-435-1089 Leedmc@earthlink.net

Types of Records Retrieved: Criminal, Civil and Probate courts; Federal courts; Real Estate; Tax Liens/Judgments; UCC records; Vital records

Local Retrieval Area: FL-Collier, Hendry, Lee

Add'l Information: Established 1980. Normal turnaround time- 24-48 hours, may vary. Projects billed by number of names searched. Projects billed by the hour. Depends upon the project. First project may require prepayment. They are a fully experienced examiner in business for over 20 years. Researches counties is Southwest Florida. Also do locations and social security number traces, etc. Is experienced, insured and professional.

Florida Research & Filing Services Inc

1211 Circle Dr, Tallahassee, FL 32301
Phone: 850-656-6446 - **Fax:** 850-942-6446
www.myfloridaresearch.com **email:** lydia@myfloridaresearch.com

Types of Records Retrieved: Civil courts; Federal courts; Real Estate; Tax Liens/Judgments; UCC records

Local Retrieval Area: FL-Leon. **Correspondent Relationships:** nationwide.

Add'l Information: Established 2003. Normal turnaround time- 24 hours. Projects billed by number of names searched. First project may require prepayment. Will file/record documents for clients. They specialize in corporate document retrieval/filings, registered agent services and UCC, tax liens, judgments and pending litigation searches. Over 10 years experience in the industry.

Margaret Flowers

3640 N. Woodford, Decatur, IL 62526
Phone: 217-877-2105 - **Fax:** 217-877-2105 marghappy@insightbb.com

Types of Records Retrieved: Criminal and Civil courts

Local Retrieval Area: IL-De Witt, Logan, Macon, Moultrie, Sangamon

Add'l Information: Established 1994. Normal turnaround time- 24-48 hours. Projects billed by number of names searched. She will bill monthly. They specialize in quality record and retrieval service.

For The Record In Virginia

9105 Lyon Park Ct, Burke, VA 22015
Phone: 703-862-9105 - **Fax:** 703-323-3685 dzigninglady1@yahoo.com

Types of Records Retrieved: Criminal courts

Local Retrieval Area: VA-Fairfax, Fairfax City

Add'l Information: Established 1989. Normal turnaround time- 24-72 hours. Expedited service available. Projects billed by number of names searched. Projects billed by the hour. Fee basis varies by type of project. Will accept check payments. First project may require prepayment. Continual monthly projects invoiced; searches and verifications invoiced. They specialize in background/pre-employment, criminal searches, federal/state tax lien information, new business listings filed with the court, judgments and document prepared retrieval. Is a licensed VA Private Investigator. A licensed PI in VA.

For The Record Inc

PO Box 19302, Raleigh, NC 27619
Phone: 919-836-7559 - **Fax:** 919-828-2876
www.myftr.com **email:** info@myftr.com

Types of Records Retrieved: Criminal and Civil courts; Federal courts

Local Retrieval Area: NC-Wake. **Correspondents:** nationwide.

Add'l Information: Established 1996. Normal turnaround time- same day if received before 11AM EST. Projects billed by number of names searched. Monthly billing. They specialize in electronic searching of all 100 NC counties, featuring a direct link to the statewide criminal court computer system by computer terminals located in the Wake County courthouse.

For The Record Title & Court Services

12614 Grand Teton Dr, Bakersfield, CA 93312
Phone: 661-703-9610 - **Fax:** 661-589-1895 fortherecord@earthlink.net

Types of Records Retrieved: Criminal, Civil and Probate courts; Real Estate; Tax Liens/Judgments; UCC records; Vital records

Local Retrieval Area: CA-Kern. **Correspondent Relationships:** statewide.

Add'l Information: Established 1995. Normal turnaround time- 24-48 hours. Expedited service available. Projects billed by number of names searched. First project may require prepayment. Will file/record documents for clients. Terms are net 30. They specialize in title searches, judgments/liens and document recording/filing. They can do signups and notary. A mobile phone number to reach them is 661-703-9610. Also can file petitions, business and publish.

Forbes Public Research Inc

PO Box 332, East Schodack, NY 12063-0332
Phone: 518-732-2961 - **Fax:** 518-732-2963
eforbespublicr@nycap.rr.com

Types of Records Retrieved: Civil courts; Federal courts; Real Estate; Tax Liens/Judgments; UCC records

Local Retrieval Area: MA-Hampden; NY-Albany, Saratoga, Schenectady, Warren. **Correspondent Relationships:** nationwide.

Add'l Info: Established 2000. Turnaround time- 24-48 hours. Expedited service available. Projects billed by number of names searched. First project may require prepayment. Payment due within 30 days. They are known to be one of the fastest and most economical public research teams in litigation and real estate. Will also search Mass. at town court level. Provides records from bankruptcy and US District Courts nationwide.

Ford Abstract Corp

221 N Franklin St, Greensburg, IN 47240
Phone: 812-663-2190 - **Fax:** 812-222-2190
www.fordabstractcorp.com **Types of Records Retrieved:** Civil and Probate courts; Real Estate; Tax Liens/Judgments; UCC records

Local Retrieval Area: IN-Decatur. **Correspondent Relationships:** Rush, Franklin, Ripley counties IN.

Add'l Information: Established 1940. Normal turnaround time- 5 days. They charge a flat rate per project. Will file/record documents for clients.

Ford County Title Co Inc

205 Gunsmoke St, Dodge City, KS 67801
Phone: 620-227-2349 - **Fax:** 620-227-8052

Types of Records Retrieved: Civil and Probate courts; Real Estate; Tax Liens/Judgments; UCC records **Local Retrieval Area:** KS-Ford, Gray

Add'l Information: Normal turnaround time- 48 hours. Billing depends on nature of request. First project may require prepayment. Will file/record documents for clients. Ford Title is mentioned by the courts as a record retriever. Service to Gray County will take a couple days longer. Part of the First American Network. They are sometimes hesitant to do criminal record searches.

Ford Data Research

PO Box 236, Richmond, TX 77406
Phone: 281-238-9400 - **Fax:** 281-238-0575
www.cfordinvestigations.com **email:** forddataresearch@aol.com

Types of Records Retrieved: Criminal and Civil courts

Local Retrieval Area: TX-Fort Bend

Add'l Information: Established 2002. Normal turnaround time- Usually same day. Projects billed by number of names searched. Billing at end of month. Owner has12 years experience as a researcher for private investigators and attorneys. They conduct pre-employment investigations and record retrieval service. Affiliated with Charles Ford Investigations.

Fort Enterprises Process Srv & Investigation

PO Box 56589, North Pole, AK 99705
Phone: 907-488-7766 - **Fax:** 907-451-0132 fepsi@gci.net

Types of Records Retrieved: Criminal, Civil and Probate courts; Federal courts; Real Estate; Tax Liens/Judgments; UCC records; Vital records

Local Retrieval Area: AK-Fairbanks North Star Borough. **Correspondent Relationships:** statewide.

Add'l Information: Established 1984. Normal turnaround time- 2 days to 2 weeks. Billing methods depends on project. Also bill by monthly retainer and special arrangements. First project may require prepayment. Will file/record documents for clients. Monthly billing to approved credit. They specialize in field work and locating persons who are not "in the system." Exercises proper care and diligence in retrieval and researching public records. A licensed PI in AK. Performs service of process.

Foster County Abstract & Title

105 10th Ave N, Carrington, ND 58421
Phone: 701-652-3164 - **Fax:** 701-652-3165

Types of Records Retrieved: Civil and Probate courts; Real Estate; Tax Liens/Judgments; UCC records; Vital records

Local Retrieval Area: ND-Foster. **Correspondent Relationships:** statewide.

Add'l Information: Established 1962. Normal turnaround time- 1-2 days. Projects billed by number of records located. First project may require prepayment. Will file/record documents for clients. They are a full-service title company - compiling abstracts of title, searches, document recording and retrieval services.

Foster Inv

PO Box 863, Normal, IL 61761
Phone: 800-526-0307; 309-862-3473 - **Fax:** 309-862-0197
www.fosterinvestigations.com **email:** mark@fosterinvestigations.com

Types of Records Retrieved: Criminal, Civil and Probate courts; Real Estate; Tax Liens/Judgments; UCC records; Vital records

Local Retrieval Area: IL-McLean

Add'l Information: Established 1994. Normal turnaround time- 1-2 days. Fee varies according to the nature of the project. First project may require prepayment. They offer more than nine years experience in their area. A licensed PI in IL. Performs service of process.

Four Corners Abstract

370 East Ave, Rochester, NY 14604
Phone: 800-724-3668; 585-454-2263 - **Fax:** 585-454-6163
www.fourcornersabstract.com **email:** s.walrath@fourcornersabstract.com

Types of Records Retrieved: Real Estate; Tax Liens/Judgments; UCC records; Probate courts; Bankruptcy court

Local Retrieval Area: NY-Albany, Broome, Cayuga, Chenango, Columbia, Delaware, Erie, Fulton, Genesee, Greene, Herkimer, Livingston, Madison, Monroe, Montgomery, Niagara, Oneida, Onondaga, Ontario, Orleans, Oswego, Rensselaer, Saratoga, Schenectady, Seneca, Tioga, Wayne, Yates. **Correspondent Relationships:** nationwide.

Add'l Information: Established 1980. Normal turnaround time- 1-3 working days. Fees are calculated on a per order basis. First project may require prepayment. Will file/record documents for clients. They specialize in title insurance, settlement services, defaults services, document recording, and tax searches.

4th Corner Network Inc

110 Prospect St, Bellingham, WA 98225-4402
Phone: 800-321-2455; 360-671-2455 - **Fax:** 888-861-0287; 360-734-1286
www.4thcorner.com **email:** robin@4thcorner.com

Types of Records Retrieved: Criminal, Civil and Probate courts; Tax Liens/Judgments; UCC records; Vital records

Local Retrieval Area: WA-Skagit, Whatcom

Add'l Information: Established 1978. Normal turnaround time- 1-3 days for Whatcom County; 2-5 days for Skagit County. Fee basis depends upon the type of project. Credit cards accepted. Will file/record documents for clients. Terms: net 30 days. They specialize in a wide variety of record retrieval, filings, etc. Performs service of process.

Fowler Abstract & Title Inc

110 N Main, Wakeeney, KS 67672
Phone: 785-743-6422 - **Fax:** 785-743-5769 fowler@ruraltel.net

Types of Records Retrieved: Criminal, Civil and Probate courts; Real Estate; Tax Liens/Judgments; UCC records; Vital records

Local Retrieval Area: KS-Trego. **Correspondent Relationships:** Ness, Gove, Graham counties KS.

Add'l Information: Established 1975. Normal turnaround time- 1-2 days. Projects billed by the hour. Will file/record documents for clients. Personal checks are accepted.

Fox Cities Title Co

PO Box 2547, Appleton, WI 54912-2547
Phone: 920-731-5494 - **Fax:** 920-731-5493 foxcitiestitle@tds.net

Types of Records Retrieved: Real Estate; Tax Liens/Judgments

Local Retrieval Area: WI-Calumet, Outagamie, Winnebago. **Correspondent Relationships:** Waupaca, Brown counties, WI.

Add'l Information: Established 1978. Normal turnaround time- 3-5 days. Projects are billed by the number of parcels searched. First project may require prepayment. Will file/record documents for clients. They are a full service title insurance company with on-site legal staff and a licensed real estate broker, specializing in "for sale by owner" transactions.

Fox Hunt

PO Box 742342, Houston, TX 77274
Phone: 713-772-8018 - **Fax:** 713-772-8774
www.foxhuntland.com **email:** bryan@foxhuntland.com

Records Retrieved: Real Estate; Tax Liens/Judgments; UCC records

Local Retrieval Area: TX-Brazoria, Fort Bend, Harris, Montgomery

Add'l Information: Established 1982. Normal turnaround time- 24-48 hours. Projects billed by number of names searched. First project may require prepayment. They are in their 24th year of business. They pride themselves in being able to customize their service to fit their client's needs.

FP Resources

4100 Spring Valley #250, Dallas, TX 75224
Phone: 866-989-8999; 972-991-8999 - **Fax:** 972-702-0776
www.fpstaff.net **email:** yamarino@fpstaff.net

Types of Records Retrieved: Criminal and Civil courts; Federal District courts

Local Retrieval Area: TX-Bexar, Collin, Dallas, Denton, Fort Bend, Harris, Montgomery, Tarrant. **Correspondent Relationships:** nationwide.

Add'l Information: Normal turnaround time- 24-48 hours. Projects billed by number of names searched. Billings go out weekly for searches done the previous week. They specialize in many different pre-employment searches. They have a web based program. Their prices are competitive and they have a quick turnaround time.

Franchise Profiles LLC

4712 NE 138th St, Vancouver, WA 98686
Phone: 360-566-0438 - **Fax:** 360-397-0196
franchiseprof@yahoo.com

Types of Records Retrieved: Criminal, Civil and Probate courts; Federal courts; Real Estate; Tax Liens/Judgments; UCC records; Vital records

Local Retrieval Area: WA-Clark. **Correspondent Relationships:** Washington state and nationwide.

Add'l Information: Established 2004. Normal turnaround time- 48 hours or less. Projects billed by number of names searched. Billing methods depends on size and nature of the request. All projects require prepayment. Net 15 days. Their services also include financial/business profiling, employment screening, interviews, tenant screening, banking and asset verification. They specialize in Washington County Court records.

Frank Paine Records Search & Retrieval

179 Bay Rd, Winlock, WA 98596
Phone: 888-739-8760; 360-785-0477 - **Fax:** 360-785-9937
fnpaine2@yahoo.com

Records Retrieved: Real Estate; Tax Liens/Judgments; UCC records

Local Retrieval Area: WA-Cowlitz, Grays Harbor, Lewis, Thurston

Add'l Information: Established 1998. Normal turnaround time- 24-48 hours. Projects billed by number of names searched. Net 10 days. They specialize in current owner search for property, last vesting deed, legal description, parcel number, OPEN mortgages, assignments, judgments, liens, land improvement values and taxes.

Franklin Civil Process

2661 Jack Rd, Chambersburg, PA 17201
Phone: 717-263-0041 - **Fax:** 717-263-6423

Types of Records Retrieved: Criminal, Civil and Probate courts; Federal courts; Real Estate; Tax Liens/Judgments; UCC records; Vital records

Local Retrieval Area: PA-Adams, Cumberland, Franklin, Fulton. **Correspondent Relationships:** statewide.

Add'l Information: Established 1991. Normal turnaround time- 48 hours. Expedited service available. Projects billed by the hour. First project may require prepayment. In business since 1991. Licensed private investigator in the state of PA with connections worldwide. Process service statewide with expedited service available. PALI and NAPS Members. A licensed PI in PA. Performs service of process.

Franklin County Abstract Co (Iowa)

121 1st Ave NE, Hampton, IA 50441
Phone: 641-456-4551 - **Fax:** 641-456-2359

Types of Records Retrieved: Criminal, Civil and Probate courts; Real Estate; Tax Liens/Judgments; UCC records; Vital records

Local Retrieval Area: IA-Franklin

Add'l Information: Established 1979. Turnaround time- 2-3 days. Fee basis varies by type of transaction. Will file/record documents for clients.

Fraser Abstracting

141 N Main St #203, Brewer, ME 04412
Phone: 207-947-6344 - **Fax:** 207-990-3843 fraserabst@aol.com

Types of Records Retrieved: Real Estate; Tax Liens/Judgments; Probate courts; UCC records

Local Retrieval Area: ME-Hancock, Penobscot, Piscataquis, Waldo

Add'l Information: Established 1989. Normal turnaround time- 48 hours. Projects billed by the hour. First project may require prepayment. Statements due upon receipt.

Frazee Abstract & Title, Inc

301 N Main, Syracuse, KS 67878
Phone: 800-736-7832; 620-384-7828 - **Fax:** 620-384-6759
frazee1@pld.com

Types of Records Retrieved: Criminal, Civil and Probate courts; Real Estate; Tax Liens/Judgments; UCC records; Vital records

Local Retrieval Area: KS-Grant, Hamilton, Kearny, Stanton

Add'l Information: Established 1979. Normal turnaround time- 1 day for Hamilton County, 2 days for Stanton and Grant counties and 3 days for Kearney County. Projects billed by number of names searched. Will file/record documents for clients. Payment due on receipt of statement. They will file/record UCC and real estate documents on behalf of clients on a same or next day basis in Hamilton and Grant counties only.

Frazier & Associates

308 S School St, Ukiah, CA 95482-4826
Phone: 707-462-8559 - **Fax:** 707-462-8579 sfrazier@pacific.net

Types of Records Retrieved: Criminal, Civil and Probate courts; Tax Liens/Judgments; UCC records; Vital records

Local Retrieval Area: CA-Mendocino. **Correspondents:** nationwide.

Add'l Information: Established 1988. Normal turnaround time- 2-3 days. Expedited service available for an additional charge. Projects billed by number of names searched. Projects billed by the hour. First project may require prepayment. Credit cards accepted. Will file/record documents for clients. Visa, MasterCard, American Express and Discover accepted. They specialize in public record searches, fax filings, attorney support services.

Fred Phillips Research Inc

10080 Timberline Ct, San Diego, CA 92131-1420
Phone: 858-735-3431 - **Fax:** 858-777-5537
bestresearch@aol.com

Types of Records Retrieved: Criminal, Civil and Probate courts; Federal courts; Real Estate; Tax Liens/Judgments; UCC records;

Local Retrieval Area: CA-San Diego

Add'l Information: Established 1994. Normal turnaround time- 12-48 hours. Projects billed by number of names searched. Pay after names are searched. They specialize in criminal and civil records research that is fast, reliable, efficient and reasonably prices. Serving the San Diego County area.

Fredericksburg Titles Inc

203 W Austin St, Fredericksburg, TX 78624
Phone: 830-997-3852 - **Fax:** 830-997-0193
www.fredericksburgtitles.com/ **email:** fbgtitle@ktc.com

Types of Records Retrieved: Criminal, Civil and Probate courts; Real Estate; Tax Liens/Judgments; UCC records

Local Retrieval Area: TX-Gillespie

Add'l Information: Established 1986. Normal turnaround time- 1-10 days depending on project. Fee basis will vary by the type of project. All projects require prepayment. Will file/record documents for clients. They specialize in title searches and lien searches.

Freelance Abstracting Service

507 W Third St, Iuka, MS 38852
Phone: 662-424-3636 - **Fax:** 662-423-2048 youngjan@bellsouth.net

Types of Records Retrieved: Criminal, Civil and Probate courts; Real Estate; Tax Liens/Judgments; UCC records

Local Retrieval Area: AL-Colbert; MS-Alcorn, Benton, Itawamba, Lee, Pontotoc, Prentiss, Tishomingo, Tippah; TN-Hardin, McNairy

Add'l Information: Established 1988. Normal turnaround time- 1-2 days. Projects billed by number of names searched. Fee basis depends upon type of project. First project may require prepayment. Will file/record documents for clients. Payment due upon completion. Independent title abstractor & record retriever. Company provides hands-on professional title searches & abstracts, public record retrievals, witness loan closings, foreclosures & other real estate services. They have over 18 years hands on experience. Performs service of process.

Irene Friend

406 Old Hwy 11, Beattyville, KY 41311
Phone: 606-464-2638 - **Fax:** 606-464-2638

Records Retrieved: Real Estate; Tax Liens/Judgments; UCC records

Local Retrieval Area: KY-Breathitt, Estill, Lee, Owsley, Powell, Wolfe

Add'l Information: Established 1985. Normal turnaround time- 1-2 days. Fee basis varies by type of transaction. All projects require prepayment. She specializes in researching coal, oil, and mineral rights.

Fritcher Abstract Co

605 Cayuga St, Storm Lake, IA 50588
Phone: 712-732-2732 - **Fax:** 712-732-2444

Types of Records Retrieved: Criminal, Civil and Probate courts; Real Estate; Tax Liens/Judgments; Vital records

Local Retrieval Area: IA-Buena Vista

Add'l Information: Established 1942. Normal turnaround time- up to 4 days. Fee basis is "per search". Will file/record documents for clients. Terms: net 30 days.

Froese Title Research

288 Cape Split Rd, Addison, ME 04606

Phone: 207-483-2282 - **Fax:** 800-561-5134 froesetitle@hotmail.com

Types of Records Retrieved: Criminal, Civil and Probate courts; Real Estate; Tax Liens/Judgments; UCC records

Local Retrieval Area: ME-Hancock, Penobscot, Washington

Add'l Information: Established 1990. Normal turnaround time- 24 hours. Projects billed by number of names searched. Payment due upon receipt of search results. They have two full-time abstractors/record retrievers with combined experience of over 35 years.

Frontier Private Process Service (Flagstaff)

PO Box 1863, Flagstaff, AZ 86002

Phone: 800-711-8511; - **Fax:** 928-779-1044

Types of Records Retrieved: Criminal, Civil and Probate courts; Real Estate; Tax Liens/Judgments; UCC records

Local Retrieval Area: AZ-Coconino. **Correspondents:** Arizona.

Add'l Information: Established 1963. Normal turnaround time- 48 hours. Projects billed by number of names searched. First project may require prepayment. Will file/record documents for clients. They specialize in process serving, skiptracing, and record retrieval. A licensed PI in AZ. Performs service of process.

Frontier Private Process Service (Phoenix)

1145 W McDowell Rd, Phoenix, AZ 85007

Phone: 800-860-0858; 602-258-0022 - **Fax:** 602-258-9550

www.frontierpps.com **email:** receptionist@frontierpps.com

Types of Records Retrieved: Criminal, Civil and Probate courts; Federal courts; Real Estate; Tax Liens/Judgments; UCC records; Vital records

Local Retrieval Area: AZ-Maricopa. **Correspondents:** Arizona.

Add'l Information: Established 1963. Normal turnaround time- 48 hours; recorders may take 1 week. Projects billed by number of names searched. First project may require prepayment. Will file/record documents for clients. They specialize in process service, skiptracing, record retrieval, court and probate bonds. A licensed PI in AZ. Performs service of process.

Ft Lauderdale-Miami Courthouse Research Inc

4796 SW 110th Ave, Ft Lauderdale, FL 33328

Phone: 954-434-6819 - **Fax:** 954-434-5862

Records Retrieved: Real Estate; Tax Liens/Judgments; UCC records

Local Retrieval Area: FL-Broward, Clay, Nassau, Orange, Palm Beach

Add'l Information: Established 1991. Normal turnaround time- 24 hours. Projects billed by number of names searched. Will file/record documents for clients. Billing every 2 weeks. Their title services cover Broward, Clay, Nassau and Orange counties. They provide title reports and current owner reports. They have 15 years experience, are accurate and timely.

Peg Fuoti

35 English Lane, Egg Harbor Twp, NJ 08234

Phone: 609-625-9401 - **Fax:** 609-653-8066

Records Retrieved: Real Estate; Tax Liens/Judgments; UCC records

Local Retrieval Area: NJ-Atlantic

Add'l Information: Established 1980. Normal turnaround time- 2-7 days. Fee basis will vary by the type of project. She specializes in title searches. They will file/record real estate documents on behalf of clients.

Furnas Valley Title

PO Box 776, Oxford, NE 68967

Phone: 308-824-3304 - **Fax:** 308-824-3342 frnscott1-larry@atcjet.net

Types of Records Retrieved: Criminal, Civil and Probate courts; Real Estate; Tax Liens/Judgments

Local Retrieval Area: NE-Furnas, Harlan

Add'l Info: Established 2002. Normal turnaround time- 48 hours. First project may require prepayment. They specialize in real estate closings, title ins-residential, agriculture and commercial and escrow services.

Future Security Concepts

16217 W 144th St, Olathe, KS 66062

Phone: 800-398-3051; 913-782-1766 - **Fax:** 913-782-5281

www.futuresecurityconcepts.com

email: june@futuresecurityconcepts.com

Types of Records Retrieved: Criminal and Civil courts; Federal courts; Tax Liens/Judgments; UCC records

Local Retrieval Area: KS-Douglas, Johnson, Leavenworth, Shawnee, Wyandotte. **Correspondent Relationships:** all Texas, Kansas.

Add'l Information: Established 1993. Normal turnaround time- within 24 hours. Expedited service available. Projects billed by number of names searched. Billing at end of month. They specialize in criminal searches by name in all KS and TX counties. They can do criminal searches nationwide by county; call for price quote. Specialize in criminal searches nationwide.

FYI Investigations

PO Box 21, Perry Hall, MD 21128

Phone: 877-475-7083; 410-529-4442 - **Fax:** 410-529-6819

www.fyi-investigations.com **email:** PI@FYI-Investigations.com

Types of Records Retrieved: Criminal, Civil and Probate courts; Real Estate; Tax Liens/Judgments; UCC records

Local Retrieval Area: MD-Baltimore, Harford. **Correspondent Relationships:** Anne Arundel county, MD.

Add'l Information: Established 1999. Normal turnaround time- 1-3 days. Projects billed by number of names searched. First project may require prepayment. They specialize in investigations, paralegal services and document retrieval in Harford County. A licensed PI in MD.

FYI Screening Inc

PO Box 29698, Columbus, OH 43229

Phone: 800-809-2419; 614-890-9908

www.fyiscreening.com **email:** info@fyiscreening.com

Types of Records Retrieved: Criminal courts

Local Retrieval Area: OH-Franklin. **Correspondents:** nationwide.

Add'l Information: Established 1994. Normal turnaround time- 2-3 business days. Projects billed by number of names searched. All projects require prepayment. Credit cards accepted. They are a licensed investigation company and specialize in on-site criminal background searches. They deliver timely, accurate information and adhere to the highest professional standards. A licensed PI in OH.

FYII Acct

226 Sandpiper Dr, Portland, TX 78374

Phone: 563-299-5683 - **Fax:** 703-991-7411 research@fyii.org

Types of Records Retrieved: Criminal, Civil and Probate courts; Federal courts; Real Estate; Tax Liens/Judgments; UCC records; Vital records; Voter registration records

Local Retrieval Area: IA-Cedar, Johnson, Linn, Muscatine, Polk, Scott; IL-Rock Island; TX-Nueces, San Patricio. **Correspondent Relationships:** Iowa and nationwide.

Add'l Information: Established 2001. Normal turnaround time- same day or 24 hours. Projects billed by number of names searched. Will file/record documents for clients. Invoices 1st of each month. They specialize in criminal and background checks. They have low prices and quick turnaround time. Performs service of process.

G & L Research Associates

PO Box 11765, Jacksonville, FL 32239
Phone: 904-743-4116 - **Fax:** 904-743-0022
glresearch@comcast.net

Types of Records Retrieved: Criminal and Civil courts; Federal courts; Real Estate; Tax Liens/Judgments; UCC records

Local Retrieval Area: FL-Clay, Duval, Nassau, St. Johns

Add'l Information: Established 1996. Normal turnaround time- 24-48 hours. Projects billed by number of names searched. Will file/record documents for clients. Terms: net 30 days. They specialize in 4 part UCC, tax lien and judgments searches, also expedited criminal background checks.

G.A. Public Record Services Inc

3200 W Pleasant Run Rd #420, Lancaster, TX 75146
Phone: 800-760-2468 x314; 469-727-0457
Fax: 800-669-1642; 469-727-0461
www.gaprs.biz **email:** parrington@gaprs.com

Types of Records Retrieved: Criminal and Civil courts; Federal courts

Local Retrieval Area: NY-Bronx, Erie, Kings, New York, Queens, Suffolk; TX-Collin, Dallas, Denton, Harris, Tarrant, Travis; GA-Barrow. **Correspondent Relationships:** nationwide.

Add'l Information: Established 1989. Normal turnaround time- 24-72 hours. Projects billed by number of names searched. Credit cards accepted. Since 1993, they have specialized in on-site, county level criminal record searches nationwide. GA is one of the largest search firms in the nation. A licensed PI in TX.

Tracy A Gabehart, Paralegal

3413 E Hebron Ln, Shephardsville, KY 40165-8949
Phone: 502-957-6459 - **Fax:** 502-957-6479 tcuevas007@aol.com

Types of Records Retrieved: Criminal and Civil courts; Tax Liens/Judgments

Local Retrieval Area: KY-Bullitt, Hardin, Jefferson, Nelson; IN-Clark, Floyd. **Correspondent Relationships:** nearby Louisville, KY area and IN.

Add'l Info: Established 1992. Turnaround time- 24-48 hours. Projects billed by number of names searched. Fee basis varies upon volume. Monthly billing. They have 15 years experience in background research and information retrieval, with an average 24 hour turnaround time. Specializes in 7-year felony-misdemeanor searches on circuit and district levels. Pager #: 502-672-1505. Cell #: 502-643-1633. A licensed PI in KY.

Gadsden Abstract Co

120 S Madison St, Quincy, FL 32351
Phone: 850-627-6811 - **Fax:** 850-627-6440

Types of Records Retrieved: Civil and Probate courts; Real Estate; Tax Liens/Judgments **Local Retrieval Area:** FL-Gadsden

Add'l Information: Established 1967. Normal turnaround time- 1-5 days. Projects billed by number of names searched. Projects billed by the hour. They specialize in real estate.

Ginger Galloway

PO Box 233, Cedarville, OH 45314
Phone: 937-241-8442 - **Fax:** 937-766-9873
crthseservs@yahoo.com

Types of Records Retrieved: Criminal, Civil and Probate courts; Real Estate; Tax Liens/Judgments; UCC records

Local Retrieval Area: OH-Brown, Champaign, Clark, Clinton, Fayette, Greene, Highland, Madison. **Correspondent Relationships:** Ross, Warren counties, OH.

Add'l Information: Established 1970. Normal turnaround time- 24-72 hours for real estate records and 72 hours for all others. She specializes in title exams.

Gamble Legal Research

302 Timberhill Ct, Knoxville, TN 37934
Phone: 865-966-3364 - **Fax:** 865-966-8260
ferretoutinfo@charter.net

Types of Records Retrieved: Criminal and Civil courts; Federal courts; Tax Liens/Judgments; UCC records

Local Retrieval Area: TN-Anderson, Blount, Knox, Loudon, Roane, Sevier

Add'l Information: Established 2000. Normal turnaround time- 12-48 hours. Projects billed by number of names searched. Will bill monthly, payment due net 30 days. She has 9 years experience, having owned her own business for 6 years. She provides accurate, expedient results and stays in close communication with her customers.

Gamma Investigative Research Inc

PO Box 10981, Fairfield, NJ 07004-6981
Phone: 800-878-9393; 973-227-1415 - **Fax:** 973-882-0960
www.priveye.com **email:** gamma@priveye.com

Types of Records Retrieved: Criminal, Civil and Probate courts; Federal courts; Real Estate; Tax Liens/Judgments; UCC records

Local Retrieval Area: NJ-Bergen, Hudson, Passaic, Sussex, Union, Warren. **Correspondent Relationships:** nationwide.

Add'l Information: Established 1981. Normal turnaround time- 24-48 hours. The online is almost immediate. Projects billed by the hour. First project may require prepayment. They access New Jersey courts and state criminal through online systems. They also specialize in field investigations, skiptraces, background, asset investigations and surveillance. A licensed PI in NJ. Performs service of process.

Catherine J Garbus

PO Box 504, Tunkhannock, PA 18657
Phone: 570-836-6749 - **Fax:** 570-836-8894

Types of Records Retrieved: Criminal, Civil and Probate courts; Real Estate; Tax Liens/Judgments; UCC records; Vital records

Local Retrieval Area: PA-Wyoming. **Correspondent Relationships:** Susquehanna and Lackawannock.

Add'l Information: Established 1987. Normal turnaround time- 24 hours. Projects billed by number of names searched. Charges vary depending on type of search. First project may require prepayment. Will file/record documents for clients. Monthly billing.

Daniel E Gardner, dba SCIPRIS

430 S Dunn St #213, Bloomington, IN 47401
Phone: 812-335-0746 - **Fax:** 812-335-0746 scipris@sbcglobal.net

Types of Records Retrieved: Criminal, Civil and Probate courts; Real Estate; Tax Liens/Judgments; UCC records; Vital records

Local Retrieval Area: IN-Monroe

Add'l Information: Established 1995. Normal turnaround time- 24-48 hours. Projects billed by number of names searched. Payment due upon completion of project. Will file/record documents for clients. Now known as South Central IN Public Record Information Svc, they specialize in criminal felony and misdemeanor records, current owner searches, title searches, and abstracting.

Garland Smith Abstract Co

PO Box 329, 132 E Lamar St, Jasper, TX 75951
Phone: 409-384-2571 - **Fax:** 409-384-4762

Types of Records Retrieved: Real Estate; Tax Liens/Judgments; Probate courts; UCC records; Vital records

Local Retrieval Area: TX-Jasper, Newton

Add'l Information: Established 1908. Normal turnaround time- 48 hours. Fees vary by project. Will file/record documents for clients.

Garza-McNamee Agency Inc

PO Box 19893, Houston, TX 77224-9893
Phone: 888-262-6221; 713-465-9877 - **Fax:** 713-932-1973

vmcnameec@sbcglobal.net

Types of Records Retrieved: Civil and Probate courts; Federal courts; Real Estate; Tax Liens/Judgments; UCC records

Local Retrieval Area: TX-Brazoria, Fort Bend, Galveston, Harris, Montgomery, Waller. **Correspondent Relationships:** Bexar, Dallas, Tarrant, Travis counties TX.

Add'l Information: Established 1981. Normal turnaround time- maximum 3 working days. Expedited service available if agreed in advance. Projects billed by number of names searched. Projects billed by the hour. "Standard" reports by name, otherwise by the hour. Will file/record documents for clients. Invoiced and net 30 days. They specialize in mortgage company updates, full title searches, real property problem analysis, other miscellaneous searches for people or corporations in Texas.

Brenda L Gaskill

34 Buttermilk Way, Buzzards Bay, MA 02532
Phone: 508-759-3156 blgaskill@aol.com

Types of Records Retrieved: Criminal, Civil and Probate courts; Real Estate; Tax Liens/Judgments; UCC records; Vital records

Local Retrieval Area: MA-Barnstable, Bristol, Plymouth

Add'l Information: Established 2004. Normal turnaround time- 2-3 business days. Projects billed by number of names searched. First project may require prepayment. She provides dependable, reliable service in court record retrieval, real estate, tax liens but is not limited to the above.

Gates Land Title Corp

222 W Van Buren St, Columbia City, IN 46725
Phone: 260-244-5127 - **Fax:** 260-244-7423

Types of Records Retrieved: Civil and Probate courts; Real Estate; Tax Liens/Judgments; UCC records; Vital records

Local Retrieval Area: IN-Whitley

Add'l Information: Established 1908. Normal turnaround time- 1 week. Fee basis varies by type of transaction. Will file/record documents for clients.

Marcia A Gazoorian

PO Box 53, Worcester, MA 01613-0053
Phone: 508-754-9503 - **Fax:** 508-754-9503 magparalegal@verizon.net

Types of Records Retrieved: Civil and Probate courts; Federal courts; Real Estate; Tax Liens/Judgments; UCC records

Local Retrieval Area: MA-Worcester

Add'l Information: Established 1990. Normal turnaround time- 2 days. Expedited service available. Projects billed by number of names searched. Projects billed by the hour. First project may require prepayment. Will file/record documents for clients. Requires immediate reimbursement of costs expended. She specializes in document search and investigation at Worcester Bankruptcy Court. Offering paralegal services since 1976.

G-Docs Abstracting LLC

12939 Hwy 21, Desoto, MO 63020
Phone: 636-586-4242 - **Fax:** 636-586-3619
www.g-docs.net **email:** stephm@g-docs.net

Types of Records Retrieved: Bankruptcy court; Real Estate; Tax Liens/Judgments; UCC records

Local Retrieval Area: MO-Boone, Camden, Crawford, Franklin, Gasconade, Howell, Jasper, Jefferson, Laclede, Lincoln, Miller, Newton, Phelps, Pulaski, St. Charles, Ste. Genevieve, St. Louis, St. Louis City, Texas, Washington. **Correspondent Relationships:** nationwide.

Add'l Information: Normal turnaround time- 24-72 hours. Projects billed by number of names searched. They specialize in current owner searches and document retrieval throughout Missouri and across the US. They offer expert 45-years searches. Preparation and recording of releases, assignments, etc.

Gem State Inv

1521 17th Ave, Lewiston, ID 83501-6154
Phone: 208-746-4152 - **Fax:** 208-746-5078 debbie_singleton@msn.com

Types of Records Retrieved: Criminal, Civil and Probate courts; Federal courts; Real Estate; Tax Liens/Judgments; UCC records; Vital records

Local Retrieval Area: ID-Benewah, Clearwater, Idaho, Latah, Lewis, Nez Perce; WA-Asotin, Garfield, Whitman. **Correspondent Relationships:** Northern Idaho and Eastern Washington.

Add'l Information: Established 1981. Turnaround time- variable depending on project. Fee basis varies by type of transaction. First project may require prepayment. Will file/record documents for clients. They specialize in insurance fraud. Licensed PI in ID. Performs service of process.

Genco Services

PO Box 16334, Baton Rouge, LA 70893
Phone: 225-218-4511 - **Fax:** 225-223-6402
http://gencoservices.org **email:** gensvc@aol.com

Types of Records Retrieved: Criminal, Civil and Probate courts; Federal courts; Real Estate; Tax Liens/Judgments; UCC records; Vital records

Local Retrieval Area: LA-East Baton Rouge, Iberville, West Baton Rouge Parishes. **Correspondent Relationships:** Mississippi County MO.

Add'l Info: Established 1987. Turnaround time- 24-48 hours. Expedited service available. Charges are by name and court searched, plus copy expenses. 1st project may require prepayment. Performs service of process.

Genealogical Researcher

18 Main St, East Hampton, CT 06424
Phone: 860-365-0580 - **Fax:** 860-365-0580 gdgmemos@snet.net

Types of Records Retrieved: Criminal, Civil and Probate courts; Real Estate; Tax Liens/Judgments; Vital records

Local Retrieval Area: CT-Fairfield, Hartford, Litchfield, Middlesex, New Haven, New London, Tolland, Windham. **Correspondent Relationships:** New Haven, Fairfield, Litchfield, CT counties.

Add'l Information: Established 1995. Normal turnaround time- 2-3 days. Expedited service available. Projects billed by the hour. First project may require prepayment. Credit cards accepted. Specialize in document and genealogical research for the legal and real estate professionals.

General Corporate Investigations - GCI

PO Box 2657, Cincinnati, OH 45201
Phone: 800-735-7992; 859-491-5341 - **Fax:** 859-491-5420
www.gcicorp.net **email:** gciadmin@gcicorp.net

Types of Records Retrieved: Criminal, Civil and Probate courts; Federal courts; Real Estate; Tax Liens/Judgments; UCC records; Vital records

Local Retrieval Area: KY-Boone, Campbell, Kenton; OH-Butler, Clermont, Hamilton, Montgomery, Warren. **Correspondent Relationships:** Ohio, Kentucky, Indiana.

Add'l Information: Established 1982. Normal turnaround time- 2 days. Projects billed by the hour. First project may require prepayment. They specialize in surveillance, activity, background and asset checks, financial investigations, subrogation, locations and pre-employment. A licensed PI in OH, KY, IN, TN. Performs service of process.

General Information Services

12770 Coit Rd #1200, Dallas, TX 75251
Phone: 800-447-0798; 214-207-8629
www.geninfo.com **email:** dbartley@geninfo.com

Types of Records Retrieved: Criminal and Civil courts; Federal courts; Real Estate; UCC records

Local Retrieval Area: TX-Collin, Dallas, Denton, Harris, Tarrant. **Correspondent Relationships:** California, Colorado, New York, Ohio, South Carolina.

Add'l Info: Established 1966. Turnaround time- 24-48 hours. Projects billed by number of names searched. Will invoice monthly. They specialize in pre-employment background investigations, criminal record research, credit and MVR reports and mortgage/title services. A licensed PI in TX.

General Investigations LLC

510 Christopher, Warrensburg, MO 64093
Phone: 660-747-8900 - **Fax:** 815-301-9620 gijohn_llc@hotmail.com

Types of Records Retrieved: Criminal, Civil and Probate courts; Real Estate; Tax Liens/Judgments; UCC records; Vital records

Local Retrieval Area: MO-Benton, Henry, Johnson, Pettis, Saline. **Correspondent Relationships:** Cass, Carroll, St. Clair, Bates, Lafayette counties MO.

Add'l Information: Established 1997. Normal turnaround time- next day. Projects billed by number of names searched. First project may require prepayment. Will file/record documents for clients. Net 15 days. John has a masters degree in criminal justice and a real estate license. Performs service of process.

Geo G Smith & Son Inc

108 E Morrison, Fayette, MO 65248
Phone: 660-248-2467 - **Fax:** 660-248-3731

Types of Records Retrieved: Criminal, Civil and Probate courts; Real Estate; Tax Liens/Judgments; UCC records; Vital records

Local Retrieval Area: MO-Howard

Add'l Information: Established 1915. Normal turnaround time- 1-5 days. Projects billed by number of names searched. Fee may also be based per page. First project may require prepayment. Will file/record documents for clients. Personal checks are accepted. They specialize in abstracting and title insurance.

GHI Abstracting Inc

110 Jardin Cir, Highland, IL 62249
Phone: 618-971-5780 or 618-654-7253 - **Fax:** 618-654-1741
getdocs@charter.net

Records Retrieved: Real Estate; Tax Liens/Judgments; UCC records

Local Retrieval Area: IL-Madison, St. Clair

Add'l Information: Established 2002. Normal turnaround time- 24-48 hours. Projects billed by number of names searched. Payment within 30 days of service. She specializes best prices for property searches ranging from document pulls to 100 year searches.

GHS Inc - Record Research

3019 63rd Ave N, Brooklyn Center, MN 55429
Phone: 763-566-2125, cell- 612-210-9716 - **Fax:** 763-566-2588
ghsresearch@comcast.net

Types of Records Retrieved: Criminal and Civil courts; Real Estate; Tax Liens/Judgments

Local Retrieval Area: MN-Anoka, Carver, Chisago, Dakota, Freeborn, Hennepin, Mower, Nicollet, Olmsted, Ramsey, Rice, Scott, Sherburne, Washington. **Correspondent Relationships:** statewide.

Add'l Information: Established 1998. Normal turnaround time- 24-48 hours. Projects billed by number of names searched. First project may require prepayment. In addition to local court records, they provide remortgage and real estate services, also vital records from some counties. Retreivels civil records from all MN counties.

Connie Giandalia

18850 Wigwam Pl, Independence, MO 64056
Phone: 816-217-1849 - **Fax:** 816-796-1130

Types of Records Retrieved: Civil and Probate courts; Federal courts; Real Estate; Tax Liens/Judgments; UCC records

Local Retrieval Area: KS-Wyandotte; MO-Clay, Jackson

Add'l Information: Established 2003. Normal turnaround time- 24-48 hours. Projects billed by number of names searched. First project may require prepayment. Credit cards accepted. She specializes in real estate, probate and federal courts, tax liens/judgments, filing/recording documents, document retrieval and notary services. Has 20 years experience in the mortgage industry.

Gietzen & Associates Inc

1302 N Marion St, Tampa, FL 33602-2917
Phone: 813-223-3233 - **Fax:** 813-223-9717
www.gietzen.com **Types of Records Retrieved:** Criminal, Civil and Probate courts; Federal courts; Real Estate; Tax Liens/Judgments

Local Retrieval Area: FL-Hillsborough, Pasco, Pinellas, Polk. **Correspondent Relationships:** nationwide.

Add'l Information: Established 1990. Normal turnaround time- 1 day. Projects billed by the hour. First project may require prepayment. Credit cards accepted. Will file/record documents for clients. They specialize in financial and general investigations, process and court reporting. A licensed PI in FL. Performs service of process.

Jack Gilland

611 W 18th St, Connersville, GA 47331-2218
Phone: 765-825-6461; Fax- same

Types of Records Retrieved: Criminal courts; Tax Liens/Judgments

Local Retrieval Area: IN-Fayette, Franklin, Union

Add'l Information: Established 1996. Normal turnaround time- 24-48 hours. Projects billed by number of names searched. He is the recommended court records expert in Fayette and Union Counties.

Joe Gillenwater

1415 Mangan, Texarkana, AR 71854
Phone: 870-772-2923 - **Fax:** 870-773-0108

Types of Records Retrieved: Civil courts; Federal courts; Real Estate; Tax Liens/Judgments; UCC records

Local Retrieval Area: AR-Columbia, Hempstead, Howard, Lafayette, Little River, Miller, Nevada; TX-Bowie, Cass, Franklin, Morris, Red River, Titus

Add'l Information: Established 1993. Normal turnaround time- 24-48 hours. Fees are plus copy charge. First project may require prepayment. Will file/record documents for clients. Terms: net 20 days. He will file/record UCC documents on behalf of clients. Contact for quote on other counties in NE Texas, SW Arkansas or Northern Louisiana. Performs service of process.

Gion Law Office

PO Box 101, Regent, ND 58650-0101
Phone: 701-563-4354 - **Fax:** 701-563-4497

Types of Records Retrieved: Criminal, Civil and Probate courts; Real Estate; Tax Liens/Judgments; UCC records; Vital records

Local Retrieval Area: ND-Adams, Bowman, Grant, Hettinger, Slope, Stark

Add'l Information: Established 1980. Normal turnaround time- 5-7 days. Projects billed by the hour. First project may require prepayment. They specialize in general law practice.

Roger Gladden Law Office

PO Box 219, Oxford, GA 30054-0219
Phone: 404-550-0749; Fax- same rglad1@juno.com

Types of Records Retrieved: Criminal, Civil and Probate courts; Real Estate; Tax Liens/Judgments; UCC records

Local Retrieval Area: GA-Newton, Rockdale, Walton

Add'l Information: Established 1977. Normal turnaround time- 1-3 days. Projects billed by number of names searched. Projects billed by number of records located. First project may require prepayment. They specialize in criminal and civil searches in Newton, Rockdale and Walton counties. Performs service of process.

Gladwin County Abstract Company

111 E Cedar Ave #1, Gladwin, MI 48624-2262
Phone: 989-426-7411 - **Fax:** 989-426-2411
www.titlepeople.com **email:** info@titlepeople.com

Types of Records Retrieved: Real Estate; Tax Liens/Judgments; Probate courts; UCC records

Local Retrieval Area: MI-Gladwin. **Correspondent Relationships:** Bay, Clare, Roscommon, Midland, Ogemaw, Saginaw counties MI.

Add'l Information: Established 1877. Normal turnaround time- 1 week unless requested sooner. Projects billed by number of names searched. Projects billed by number of records located. First project may require prepayment. Will file/record documents for clients. Personal checks are accepted. They specialize in closings, searches, abstracts, escrow services, and 1031 exchanges.

Glaze Research

710 Friar Tuck Ln, Macon, GA 31220
Phone: 478-476-0539, 478-256-6696 - **Fax:** 478-476-4846

Types of Records Retrieved: Criminal, Civil and Probate courts; Federal courts; Real Estate; Tax Liens/Judgments; Vital records

Retrieval Area GA-Bibb, Crawford, Houston, Jones, Monroe, Peach, Twiggs

Add'l Information: Established 1983. Normal turnaround time- 24-48 hours. Projects billed by number of names searched. Real Estate search fee determined by nature of the search. First project may require prepayment. A family-owned business, they are insured and focus on accuracy. Searches include fed bankruptcy and current owner real estate.

Global Investigative & Legal Service

1214 E Cornerview St #6, Gonzales, LA 70723
Phone: 888-644-2066; 225-644-2066 - **Fax:** 225-644-4589
hvicknair@globalinvestigative.com

Types of Records Retrieved: Criminal and Civil courts; Federal courts

Local Retrieval Area: LA-Ascension, Assumption, Avoyelles, Beauregard, East Baton Rouge, Grant, Iberia, Jefferson, Jefferson Davis, Lafourche, Livingston, Natchitoches, Orleans, Rapides, Sabine, St. Charles, St. James, St. John the Baptist, Terrebonne, Vermillion, Vernon, West Baton Rouge. **Correspondent Relationships:** statewide.

Add'l Information: Established 1995. Normal turnaround time- 24-48 hours. Projects billed by number of names searched. Credit cards accepted. They pride themselves on honesty and integrity. They are a comprehensive investigation firm, specializing in surveillance, process service and public record research. A licensed PI in LA. Performs service of process.

Global Securities Information

1100 13th St NW #300, Washington, DC 20005-4051
Phone: 202-572-1997 - **Fax:** 202-628-1133
www.gsionline.com **email:** gsi.info@thomson.com

Records Retrieved: Criminal, Civil and Probate courts; Federal courts

Local Retrieval Area: DC-District of Columbia. **Correspondent Relationships:** NY, CA, IL, TX, MD, VA, DE, PA, FL, TN.

Add'l Information: Established 1988. Normal turnaround time- same day. Projects billed by the hour. They specialize in document retrieval from all federal and state courts and government agencies, specifically SEC filings. Now part of WestLaw.

Global Title Reporting Services Inc

4125 Santa Terrasa Pl, Las Vegas, NV 89121
Phone: 702-248-0593 - **Fax:** 702-248-5475
www.globaltrs.net **email:** customer_service@globaltrs.net

Records Retrieved: Real Estate; Tax Liens/Judgments; UCC records

Local Retrieval Area: NV-Clark. **Correspondents:** nationwide.

Add'l Information: Established 2002. Normal turnaround time- 24-72 hours. Projects billed by number of names searched. Will file/record documents for clients. Net 30 days. They are a full-service company specializing in nationwide current owner reports; E&O coverage; 24-72 hour turnarounds.

GMV Research

1225 Dana Dr #C, Fairfield, CA 94533-3517
Phone: 707-228-8708 - **Fax:** 707-421-1219 gerardimvana@sbcglobal.net

Types of Records Retrieved: Criminal, Civil and Probate courts; Tax Liens/Judgments; Vital records

Local Retrieval Area: CA-Contra Costa, Napa, Shasta, Solano. **Correspondent Relationships:** San Joaquin, Kern counties, CA.

Add'l Information: Established 2005. Normal turnaround time- 2-3 days. Projects billed by number of names searched. Projects billed by number of records located. First project may require prepayment. They offer pre-employment screening & attorney support services. They provide hands on in person searches, record retrieval & filing services. With over 10 years experience working in the courts, you can count on fast, accurate service with GMV Research.

Linda Gonzales

PO Box 345, Tucson, AZ 85702
Phone: 520-603-6360 - **Fax:** 520-670-0034 Lygonz@hotmail.com

Types of Records Retrieved: Criminal, Civil and Probate courts; Federal courts; Real Estate; Tax Liens/Judgments; UCC records; Vital records

Local Retrieval Area: AZ-Pima

Add'l Information: Established 1988. Normal turnaround time- 24 hours. Projects billed by number of names searched. Will file/record documents for clients. She specializes in criminal name searches for employment screening, insurance, etc.

Gotcha Attorney Services Inc

PO Box 1240, Aquebogue, NY 11931-1240
Phone: 800-698-2748; 631-751-1450 www.gotchaattorneyservices.com
email: seth@gotchaattorneyservices.com

Types of Records Retrieved: Criminal, Civil and Probate courts; Federal courts; Real Estate; Tax Liens/Judgments; UCC records

Local Retrieval Area: NY-Nassau, Suffolk. **Correspondent Relationships:** nationwide and international.

Add'l Information: Established 1989. Normal turnaround time- 4 hours to 2 days. Projects billed by the hour. First project may require prepayment. Will file/record documents for clients. Formerly known as Gotcha Legal Process Service Inc. Performs service of process.

Gowley Abstract

PO Box 326, Medford, WI 54451
Phone: 715-748-4790 - **Fax:** 715-748-6826

Types of Records Retrieved: Criminal, Civil and Probate courts; Real Estate; Tax Liens/Judgments; UCC records

Local Retrieval Area: WI-Taylor

Add'l Information: Established 1931. First project may require prepayment. They specialize in court records and real estate.

GPS & Associates - Florida

PO Box 1465, Zephyrhills, FL 33539-1465
Phone: 866-813-8131; - **Fax:** 866-813-8132
www.gpsassociatesinc.com **email:** backgrounds@gpsassociatesinc.com

Types of Records Retrieved: Criminal and Civil courts; Federal courts; Tax Liens/Judgments; UCC records; Vital records

Local Retrieval Area: FL-Citrus, Dade, Hernando, Hillsborough, Palm Beach, Pasco, Pinellas, Polk, Orange; VI-St. Croix, St. John, St. Thomas; Puerto Rico. **Correspondent Relationships:** nationwide, Puerto Rico, Guam, Virgin Islands.

Add'l Information: Established 1991. Normal turnaround time- 24-48 hours. Projects billed by number of names searched. They will invoice every 30 days. They specialize in background screening and document retrieval as a nationwide pre-employment service. Specialties include VI driving and criminal records, and Puerto Rico. Also do investigative work. A licensed PI in FL, TN.

Graham Abstract & Title Co

121 W 2nd St, Portales, NM 88130
Phone: 505-356-8505 - **Fax:** 505-356-8508 grahamtitle@yucca.net

Types of Records Retrieved: Civil and Probate courts; Federal courts; Real Estate; Tax Liens/Judgments; UCC records

Local Retrieval Area: NM-Roosevelt

Add'l Information: Established 1998. Normal turnaround time- 1-5 days. Fee basis will vary by the type of project. Will file/record documents for clients. They specialize in escrow, title insurance, closings, mineral searches and escrow collection services.

Grand Forks Abstract & Title Co

PO Box 6326, Grand Forks, ND 58206-6326
Phone: 701-772-3484 - **Fax:** 701-795-1957 orderdesk@gfabstract.com

Types of Records Retrieved: Civil courts; Real Estate; Tax Liens/Judgments; UCC records

Local Retrieval Area: ND-Grand Forks, MN-Pennington

Add'l Information: Established 1930. Normal turnaround time- 48 hours. Projects billed by number of names searched. First project may require prepayment. Will file/record documents for clients. They specialize in title insurance and abstracting.

Grand Traverse Title Co

116 Boardman Ave, Traverse City, MI 49684
Phone: 231-946-5686 - **Fax:** 231-929-5486

Types of Records Retrieved: Real Estate; Tax Liens/Judgments; Probate courts; UCC records

Local Retrieval Area: MI-Grand Traverse. **Correspondent Relationships:** Antrim, Kalkaska counties MI.

Add'l Information: Established 1927. Normal turnaround time- 2-3 days. Fee basis will vary by type of project. First project may require prepayment. They specialize in title insurance.

Grand Valley Associates

PO Box 2932, Grand Junction, CO 81502
Phone: 970-256-9300 - **Fax:** 970-257-7174

www.grandvalleyassociates.com **Types of Records Retrieved:** Criminal, Civil and Probate courts; Real Estate; Tax Liens/Judgments; UCC records

Local Retrieval Area: CO-Delta, Garfield, Mesa, Montrose

Add'l Information: Established 1993. Projects billed by number of names searched. Projects billed by the hour. First project may require prepayment. Credit cards accepted. They specialize in investigations, process serving and collections. Performs service of process.

Grant County Abstract & Title Co

210 E 5th Ave, Milbank, SD 57252
Phone: 605-432-5461 - **Fax:** 605-432-7517 gctitle@tnics.com

Types of Records Retrieved: Civil and Probate courts; Real Estate; Tax Liens/Judgments; UCC records **Local Retrieval Area:** SD-Grant

Add'l Information: Established 1909. Normal turnaround time- 1 week to 10 days. Projects billed by number of records located. All projects require prepayment. They specialize in real estate titles.

Grant County Abstract Co (Indiana)

200 S Washington, Marion, IN 46952
Phone: 765-664-7371 - **Fax:** 765-664-0766

Types of Records Retrieved: Civil and Probate courts; Real Estate; Tax Liens/Judgments; UCC records **Local Retrieval Area:** IN-Grant

Add'l Information: Established 1946. Normal turnaround time- variable depending on project. Projects billed by number of names searched. Projects billed by the hour. Will file/record documents for clients. They specialize in title insurance.

Grant County Abstract Co (Oklahoma)

PO Box 25, Medford, OK 73759
Phone: 580-395-2854 - **Fax:** 580-395-2854

Types of Records Retrieved: Civil and Probate courts; Real Estate; Tax Liens/Judgments; UCC records **Local Retrieval Area:** OK-Grant

Add'l Info: Established 1893. Turnaround time- 1-2 days. Projects billed by number of records located. First project may require prepayment.

K Maxwell Graves Jr

PO Box 607, Meadville, MS 39653
Phone: 601-384-2733 - **Fax:** 601-384-5568 mgraves@telepak.net

Types of Records Retrieved: Criminal, Civil and Probate courts; Real Estate; Tax Liens/Judgments; UCC records

Local Retrieval Area: MS-Franklin. **Correspondent Relationships:** adjacent counties.

Add'l Information: Normal turnaround time- 1 working day. Projects billed by the hour. Will file/record documents for clients. They accept personal checks. He specializes in general law practice. Performs service of process.

Graystone Investigations Inc

PO Box 5091, Macon, GA 31208-5091
Phone: 478-743-5551 - **Fax:** 478-743-5121 graystoneinv@aol.com

Types of Records Retrieved: Criminal, Civil and Probate courts; Federal courts; Real Estate; Tax Liens/Judgments; UCC records; Vital records

Local Retrieval Area: GA-Bibb, Crawford, Forsyth, Houston, Jones, Monroe, Peach. **Correspondent Relationships:** Kentucky, Indiana, Tennessee, South Carolina, Georgia, Florida, Alabama.

Add'l Information: Established 1991. Normal turnaround time- 3-5 days. Projects billed by the hour. Fees will include mileage when applicable. First project may require prepayment. They specialize in background investigation, surveillance, and defense case searches. A licensed PI in GA, FL, TN, KY, AL, & SC. Performs service of process.

Great Divide Title

390 Boulder Dr #100, Pagosa Springs, CO 81147-9889
Phone: 970-731-7700 - **Fax:** 970-731-7740 gdtpagosa@yahoo.com

Types of Records Retrieved: Real Estate; Tax Liens/Judgments; Probate courts; UCC records

Local Retrieval Area: CO-Archuleta

Add'l Information: Established 1980. Normal turnaround time- 3 days to 1 week. Projects billed by the hour. Will file/record documents for clients. Out of town clients are charged a setup fee and must prepay. They specialize in real estate and title matters.

Great Lake Search

332 Maple St, Kingsford, MI 49802
Phone: 906-774-4654 - **Fax:** 906-776-0974 jfblatz@charter.net

Types of Records Retrieved: Criminal, Civil and Probate courts

Local Retrieval Area: MI-Dickinson, Iron. **Correspondent Relationships:** Marquette, Delta, Menominee, MI.

Add'l Information: Established 1994. Normal turnaround time- 48 hours. Projects billed by number of names searched. First project may require prepayment. He is a retired sheriff deputy of 30 years, can interrupt court codes, etc. Search fee of $15.00 per search per court per time.

🏛Great Minds/Search Associates

7740 W Forest Home Ave, Greenfield, WI 53220-3386
Phone: 414-321-3375 - **Fax:** 414-321-3377
www.greatminds.us **email:** greatminds@ameritech.net

Types of Records Retrieved: Criminal, Civil and Probate courts; Real Estate; Tax Liens/Judgments; UCC records

Local Retrieval Area: WI-Kenosha, Milwaukee, Ozaukee, Racine, Sheboygan, Walworth, Washington, Waukesha

Add'l Information: Established 1991. Normal turnaround time- 24-48 hours. Projects billed by number of names searched. Fee depends on type of search. First project may require prepayment. Formerly known as Great Minds Research and Two Great Minds, they specialize in real estate title searches, letter/title reports, in-home loan closings, days, nights and weekends. A licensed PI in WI.

Great Northern Title & Abstract Inc

155 W Baraga #201, Marquette, MI 49855
Phone: 906-228-6100 - **Fax:** 906-228-4015

Types of Records Retrieved: Real Estate; Tax Liens/Judgments; Probate courts; UCC records

Local Retrieval Area: MI-Marquette

Add'l Information: Established 1983. Normal turnaround time- 1 week. Projects billed by the hour. First project may require prepayment. They specialize in title insurance and abstracts of title.

🏛Greater Richmond Abstract & Title Inc

4801 Hermitage Rd #101, Richmond, VA 23227
Phone: 804-266-2101 - **Fax:** 804-266-2810

Types of Records Retrieved: Criminal, Civil and Probate courts; Federal courts; Real Estate; Tax Liens/Judgments; UCC records

Local Retrieval Area: VA-Caroline, Charles City, Chesterfield, Colonial Heights, Dinwiddie, Goochland, Hanover, Henrico, Hopewell, King William, New Kent, Petersburg, Powhatan, Prince George, Richmond City

Add'l Information: Established 1997. Normal turnaround time- 12-24 hours. Projects billed by number of names searched. Will file/record documents for clients. Invoice after projects are completed. They perform title examinations from current owners to full title searches. Retrieve all documents of public record from criminal records to insurance rate filings.

Green Lake Title & Abstract Co

510 Lake St, Green Lake, WI 54941
Phone: 920-294-6070 - **Fax:** 920-294-3630 gltitle@voyager.net
Types of Records Retrieved: Real Estate; Tax Liens/Judgments; Probate courts; UCC records
Local Retrieval Area: WI-Green Lake. **Correspondent Relationships:** Fond du Lac, Marquette, Waushara counties WI.
Add'l Information: Established 1984. Normal turnaround time- 1-2 days. Fee basis varies by type of transaction. First project may require prepayment. Will file/record documents for clients.

Greene County Abstract Company Inc

102 S Wilson Ave, Jefferson, IA 50129
Phone: 515-386-2191 - **Fax:** 515-386-4509
Types of Records Retrieved: Criminal, Civil and Probate courts; Real Estate; Tax Liens/Judgments; UCC records; Vital records
Local Retrieval Area: IA-Greene
Add'l Information: Established 1900. Turnaround time- 1-7 days. Projects billed by number of names searched. Projects billed by number of records located. Fee may also be based on a combination of valuation and clerical. All projects require prepayment. Will file/record documents for clients.

Alex Greene

PO Box 5674, Texarkana, TX 75505
Phone: 903-794-1371 - **Fax:** 903-794-9141
Types of Records Retrieved: Criminal courts; Tax Liens/Judgments
Local Retrieval Area: AR-Hempstead, Little River, Miller
Add'l Information: Established 1990. Normal turnaround time- 8 hours. Expedited service available. Projects billed by number of names searched. per court. He faxes copies of all records.

Greer Guaranty Abstract Co

111 N Oklahoma Ave, Mangum, OK 73554
Phone: 580-782-3121 - **Fax:** 580-782-3121
Types of Records Retrieved: Civil and Probate courts; Real Estate; Tax Liens/Judgments; UCC records; Vital records
Local Retrieval Area: OK-Greer
Add'l Information: Established 1900. Normal turnaround time- 1-2 days. Charges are set fees. Will file/record documents for clients.

Gregg Investigations Inc of Janesville

PO Box 669, 210 Dodge St, Janesville, WI 53547-0669
Phone: 800-866-1976; 608-755-1976 - **Fax:** 608-755-5853
www.gregginvestigations.com **email:** lisa@gregginvestigations.com
Types of Records Retrieved: Criminal, Civil and Probate courts; Federal courts; Tax Liens/Judgments; UCC records; Vital records
Local Retrieval Area: WI-Rock, Green, Walworth
Add'l Information: Established 1979. Normal turnaround time- same day. Projects billed by number of names searched. Projects billed by the hour. Credit cards accepted. Their specialty is "Information Services". They also work with DOT records, boats, city directory library, bartenders and bowlers. A licensed PI in WI & IL. Performs service of process.

Gregg Investigations, Inc of Madison

PO Box 6155, 6320 Monona Dr, Madison, WI 53716-0155
Phone: 800-866-1976; 608-256-1074 - **Fax:** 800-377-5853; 608-755-5853
www.gregginvestigations.com **email:** lisa@gregginvestigations.com
Types of Records Retrieved: Criminal, Civil and Probate courts; Federal courts; UCC records; Vital records
Local Retrieval Area: WI-Dane, Jefferson. **Correspondent Relationships:** Wisconsin.
Add'l Information: Established 1979. Normal turnaround time- same day. Projects billed by number of names searched. Projects billed by the hour. Credit cards accepted. They specialize in "Information Services". They also work with DOT records, boats, city directory, library, bartenders and bowlers. A licensed PI in WI, IL. Performs service of process.

Gregg Investigations, Inc of Rockford

401 W State St #607, Rockford, IL 61101-1228
Phone: 800-866-1976; 608-755-1976 - **Fax:** 800-377-5853; 608-755-5853
www.gregginvestigations.com **email:** lisa@gregginvestigations.com
Types of Records Retrieved: Criminal, Civil and Probate courts; Federal courts; Real Estate; Tax Liens/Judgments; UCC records; Vital records
Local Retrieval Area: IL-Winnebago. **Correspondent Relationships:** Wisconsin.
Add'l Information: Established 1999. Normal turnaround time- same day. Projects billed by number of names searched. Credit accounts accepted. They specialize in "Information Services" near Rockford, IL, with offices in So. WI at Madison & Janesville. A licensed PI in IL, WI. Performs service of process.

Gregory Abstract & Title Co Inc

124 W Main, Osborne, KS 67473
Phone: 785-346-5445 - **Fax:** 785-346-5446
Types of Records Retrieved: Criminal, Civil and Probate courts; Real Estate; Tax Liens/Judgments; UCC records
Local Retrieval Area: KS-Osborne
Add'l Information: Established 1930. Normal turnaround time- 12-24 hours or less. Projects billed by number of names searched. Will file/record documents for clients. Payment due upon receipt of requested information.

Gregory County Title Co

PO Box 352, Burke, SD 57523
Phone: 605-775-2943; Fax- same
Types of Records Retrieved: Civil and Probate courts; Real Estate; Tax Liens/Judgments
Local Retrieval Area: SD-Gregory
Add'l Information: Established 1949. Normal turnaround time- 10 days. Fee basis will vary by the type of project. All projects require prepayment. Will file/record documents for clients. They specialize in real estate.

Joe C Griffin

PO Box 237, Ackerman, MS 39735
Phone: 662-285-6080 - **Fax:** 662-285-6089 jgriffin@telapex.com
Types of Records Retrieved: Criminal, Civil and Probate courts; Real Estate; Tax Liens/Judgments; UCC records; Vital records
Local Retrieval Area: MS-Choctaw
Add'l Information: Established 1979. Normal turnaround time- 1-2 days. Projects billed by the hour. First project may require prepayment. He specializes in marriage/divorce and property searches.

Grizzly Investigative Services

800 South Fork Rd, Cody, WY 82414
Phone: 307-587-8395 - **Fax:** 307-587-5855 grizly@wtp.net
Types of Records Retrieved: Criminal, Civil and Probate courts; Real Estate; Tax Liens/Judgments; UCC records
Local Retrieval Area: WY-Park. **Correspondent Relationships:** Washakie County, WY.
Add'l Information: Established 1997. Normal turnaround time- 72 hours. First project may require prepayment. They also provide private investigation services. Performs service of process.

Groesbeck Abstract & Title Co d/b/a Limestone County Title Company

PO Box 127, Groesbeck, TX 76642
Phone: 254-729-3806 - **Fax:** 254-729-5655
www.limestonetitle.com **email:** service@limestonetitle.com
Types of Records Retrieved: Real Estate; Tax Liens/Judgments; Probate courts; UCC records; Vital records
Local Retrieval Area: TX-Limestone. **Correspondents:** statewide.
Add'l Information: Established 1892. Normal turnaround time- 3-4 days. Fee basis will vary by the type of project. First project may require prepayment. Will file/record documents for clients. They specialize in real property records.

Grue Abstract Co

PO Box 559, Webster, SD 57274
Phone: 605-345-3891 - **Fax:** 605-345-4051

Types of Records Retrieved: Civil and Probate courts; Real Estate; Tax Liens/Judgments; UCC records; Vital records

Local Retrieval Area: SD-Day

Add'l Information: Normal turnaround time- 5-10 days. Fee basis will vary by the type of project. Will file/record documents for clients. They specialize in land title.

Gary Grusha

1244 Cedarwood Dr, Mineral Ridge, OH 44440
Phone: 330-544-9424 - **Fax:** 330-544-3753 ggrusha@sbcglobal.net

Types of Records Retrieved: Criminal, Civil and Probate courts; Federal courts; Real Estate; Tax Liens/Judgments; UCC records; Vital records

Local Retrieval Area: OH-Columbiana, Mahoning, Trumbull

Add'l Information: Established 1990. Normal turnaround time- 24 hours. Projects billed by number of names searched. End of the month billings. They provide searches on your forms or ours. They have 3 people who do searches. They also work as abstractors.

Gryder Express Tracking Service Inc

PO Box 937, W Palm Beach, FL 33402
Phone: 561-535-1495, cell- 561-584 2079 - **Fax:** 561-337-9155
www.robert.davis.pi-agency.us **email:** robert.davis@pi-agency.us

Types of Records Retrieved: Criminal, Civil and Probate courts; Federal courts; Real Estate; Tax Liens/Judgments; UCC records; Vital records

Local Retrieval Area: CO-Denver, FL-Palm Beach

Add'l Information: Established 2002. Normal turnaround time- 24-48 hours. Expedited service available. Projects billed by number of records located. All projects require prepayment. They are able to go to both counties. A licensed PI in CO.

Guaranty Abstract Co (Colorado)

PO Box 859, 311 S Main St, Lamar, CO 81052
Phone: 719-336-3261 - **Fax:** 719-336-8106

Types of Records Retrieved: Real Estate; Tax Liens/Judgments; Probate courts; UCC records

Local Retrieval Area: CO-Bent, Prowers

Add'l Information: Established 1927. Normal turnaround time- 1-3 days. Fee basis is determined on "per name/description" or "flat rate." First project may require prepayment. Will file/record documents for clients. They specialize in real estate and title matters.

Guaranty Abstract Co (Silverton)

PO Box 718, 415 Main St, Silverton, TX 79257
Phone: 806-823-2354 - **Fax:** 806-823-2354

Types of Records Retrieved: Civil and Probate courts; Real Estate; Tax Liens/Judgments; UCC records

Local Retrieval Area: TX-Briscoe

Add'l Info: Turnaround time- 2-3 days. Projects billed by the hour. First project may require prepayment. Will file/record documents for clients.

Guaranty Abstract Co of Jackson County Inc

116 W Main, Edna, TX 77957
Phone: 361-782-3591 - **Fax:** 361-782-3649

Types of Records Retrieved: Civil and Probate courts; Real Estate; Tax Liens/Judgments; UCC records

Local Retrieval Area: TX-Jackson

Add'l Information: Established 1992. Normal turnaround time- 24-48 hours. Fees vary by project. Will file/record documents for clients.

Guaranty Abstract of Stigler

PO Box 278, 101 E Main St, Stigler, OK 74462
Phone: 918-967-8876 - **Fax:** 918-967-2191

Types of Records Retrieved: Civil and Probate courts; Real Estate; Tax Liens/Judgments; UCC records

Local Retrieval Area: OK-Haskell

Add'l Information: Normal turnaround time- 1 week. 2 weeks on abstracts. Projects billed by the hour. All projects require prepayment. Will file/record documents for clients. They specialize in land records.

Guaranty Land Title

2000 Forum Blvd #5, Columbia, MO 65203-5460
Phone: 573-874-4912 - **Fax:** 573-874-4916
www.guarantytitle.com **Types of Records Retrieved:** Civil and Probate courts; Real Estate; Tax Liens/Judgments; UCC records; Vital records

Local Retrieval Area: MO-Audrain, Boone, Caldwell, Callaway, Camden, Chariton, Clinton, Cole, Cooper, Crawford, Daviess, DeKalb, Dent, Howard, Laclede, Livingston, Macon, Maries, Miller, Moniteau, Monroe, Morgan, Osage, Pettis, Phelps, Pulaski, Randolph, Saline, St. Louis, St. Louis City

Add'l Information: Established 1991. Normal turnaround time- next day to 2 days. Projects billed by number of names searched. First project may require prepayment. Will file/record documents for clients. They specialize in land title searches and UCC searches in 30 key Missouri counties. Centralized ordering and billing.

Guaranty Research Svcs Inc

115 Winwood Dr #210, Lebanon, TN 37087
Phone: 800-697-8534; 615-466-5400 - **Fax:** 800-887-7872; 615-444-6240
www.guarantyresearch.com **email:** swright@guarantyresearch.com

Types of Records Retrieved: Criminal and Civil courts; Federal courts; Tax Liens/Judgments

Local Retrieval Area: TN-Davidson, Rutherford, Sumner, Williamson, Wilson. **Correspondent Relationships:** nationwide and 250 foreign countries.

Add'l Information: Established 1996. Normal turnaround time- 24-48 hours. Projects billed by number of names searched. Credit cards accepted. Will bill monthly. GRS provides full service employment and tenant screening; plus expert doc retrieval locally.

Guaranty Title Co (Centerville)

PO Box 449, Centerville, TX 75833
Phone: 903-536-2133 - **Fax:** 903-536-7643

Types of Records Retrieved: Civil and Probate courts; Real Estate; Tax Liens/Judgments; UCC records; Vital records

Local Retrieval Area: TX-Leon. **Correspondent Relationships:** statewide.

Add'l Information: Normal turnaround time- up to 1 week. Fee basis will vary by the type of project. First project may require prepayment. Will file/record documents for clients.

Guaranty Title Co (New Mexico)

108 N Canyon, PO Box 430, Carlsbad, NM 88221-0430
Phone: 505-887-3593 - **Fax:** 505-885-5204
www.guarantytitlenm.com **email:** docs@guarantytitlenm.com

Types of Records Retrieved: Civil and Probate courts; Real Estate; Tax Liens/Judgments; UCC records

Local Retrieval Area: NM-Eddy

Add'l Information: Established 1940. Normal turnaround time- 1 week. Fee basis will vary by the type of project. Will file/record documents for clients. The same family has owned and operated this business in Eddy County for over 60 years.

Guaranty Title Co of Grimes County

PO Box 1540, Navasoto, TX 77688
Phone: 936-825-7322 - **Fax:** 936-825-8512

Types of Records Retrieved: Civil and Probate courts; Real Estate; Tax Liens/Judgments; UCC records

Local Retrieval Area: TX-Grimes

Add'l Information: Normal turnaround time- 2-3 weeks. Fee basis will vary by the type of project. First project may require prepayment.

Guaranty Title Co of Robertson County Inc

PO Box 481, Franklin, TX 77856
Phone: 979-828-4688 - **Fax:** 979-828-3803
Types of Records Retrieved: Civil and Probate courts; Real Estate; Tax Liens/Judgments; UCC records; Vital records
Local Retrieval Area: TX-Robertson
Add'l Information: Established 1975. Normal turnaround time- up to 1 week. Fee basis will vary by the type of project. First project may require prepayment. Will file/record documents for clients.

Guaranty Title Services Inc

PO Box 69, Menomonie, WI 54751
Phone: 715-235-3393 - **Fax:** 715-235-0624
www.titleservice.com **Types of Records Retrieved:** Civil and Probate courts; Real Estate; Tax Liens/Judgments; UCC records
Local Retrieval Area: WI-Barron, Chippewa, Dunn, Eau Claire, Pepin, Pierce, St. Croix. **Correspondent Relationships:** Fond du Lac, Marathon, Door, Dodge, Green Lake, Polk counties WI.
Add'l Information: Established 1885. Normal turnaround time- 24 hours. Projects billed by number of names searched. Projects billed by number of records located. First project may require prepayment. Will file/record documents for clients. Personal checks accepted.

Guaranty Title Services Osceola

PO Box 126, Osceola, WI 54020
Phone: 888-620-7243; 715-294-2624 - **Fax:** 715-755-3535
www.titleservice.com **email:** gtsosceola@titleservice.com
Records Retrieved: Real Estate; Tax Liens/Judgments; UCC records
Local Retrieval Area: WI-Polk. **Correspondent Relationships:** Burnett, Barron, St. Croix, Pierce.
Add'l Information: Established 1882. Normal turnaround time- 2-7 days. Projects billed by number of names searched. Projects billed by number of records located. Will file/record documents for clients. Payment due upon receipt. Formerly known as Oakey & Oakey Abstract Co, they specialize in DOT searches for new road set ups, title searches and full abstracting.

Guardian Investigations & Document Svc Inc

637 N 3rd Ave #8, Phoenix, AZ 85003
Phone: 602-257-0897 - **Fax:** 602-257-1038
www.guardian-ids.com **email:** info@guardian-ids.com
Types of Records Retrieved: Criminal, Civil and Probate courts; Federal courts; Real Estate; Tax Liens/Judgments; UCC records
Local Retrieval Area: AZ-Maricopa. **Correspondent Relationships:** Pima, Pinal, Yavapai, Coconino, Mohave, Santa Cruz counties, AZ.
Add'l Information: Established 2002. Normal turnaround time- 24-48 hours. Projects billed by number of names searched. All projects require prepayment. Formerly Arizona One Investigations, they merged with L & L Paper Chase; they now provide expert criminal record searches and screening. A licensed PI in AZ.

Guardian Title

222 E Ayer St, Ironwood, MI 49938
Phone: 906-932-3244 - **Fax:** 906-932-3270
guardiantitle@charterinternet.com
Types of Records Retrieved: Real Estate
Local Retrieval Area: MI-Gogebic, Ontonagon
Add'l Info: established 1996. Turnaround time- 24-48 hours. Billing depends on nature of request. Will file/record documents for clients. Guardian is a private company mentioned by the county administrators office.

Jerry Guffey

62 Public Square, Leitchfield, KY 42754
Phone: 270-259-4828 - **Fax:** 270-259-8161
Types of Records Retrieved: Real Estate; Tax Liens/Judgments; Probate courts; UCC records; Vital records
Local Retrieval Area: KY-Breckenridge, Butler, Edmonson, Grayson, Hardin, Hart, Ohio
Add'l Information: Established 1975. Normal turnaround time- 2-4 days. Expedited service available. Projects billed by number of names searched. Will file/record documents for clients. Will mail statement with findings. He specializes in real estate searches.

Guiles & O'Hear LLC

163 Glenwood St, Moblie, AL 36606
Phone: 251-478-8245 - **Fax:** 251-476-0512 guilesohearllc@comast.net
Types of Records Retrieved: Civil and Probate courts; Real Estate; Tax Liens/Judgments; UCC records; Vital records
Local Retrieval Area: AL-Baldwin, Mobile
Add'l Information: Established 1998. Normal turnaround time- 24 hours. Projects billed by number of names searched. They invoice at the end of the month. They have 5 abstractors with 20 years of experience. They do title searches "current owner", full title searches, document retrieval and document filings.

Gulf Coast AccuSearch

808 Travis St #1101, Houston, TX 77002
Phone: 713-228-6600; cell- 713-542-3047 - **Fax:** 832-201-5368
www.gulfcoastaccusearch.com
email: krodgers@gulfcoastaccusearch.com
Types of Records Retrieved: Criminal, Civil and Probate courts; Federal courts; Real Estate; Tax Liens/Judgments; UCC records; Vital records
Local Retrieval Area: TX-Brazoria, Fort Bend, Harris, Matagorda, Montgomery. **Correspondent Relationships:** Harris & Montgomery counties, TX.
Add'l Information: Established 2001. Normal turnaround time- 24-48 hours. Projects billed by the hour. First project may require prepayment. Credit cards accepted. Gulf Coast AccuSearch is a private investigation company licensed by the State of TX that specializes in background research and document retrieval. A licensed PI in TX.

Gulf Coast Records

10985 Peppertree Ln, Port Richey, FL 34668
Phone: 727-580-4873 - **Fax:** 727-863-6396 gulfcoastrecords@verizon.net
Types of Records Retrieved: Criminal, Civil and Probate courts; Federal courts; Real Estate, Tax Liens/Judgments; UCC records; Vital records
Local Retrieval Area: FL-Hernando, Hillsborough, Manatee, Pasco, Pinellas, Polk, Sarasota
Add'l Information: Established 1996. Normal turnaround time- 24 hours. Projects billed by number of names searched. First project may require prepayment. Will file/record documents for clients. Prepayment required on files larger than 50 pages. They specialize in criminal and civil record checks. They also perform current owner searches and obtain mortgage documents. They also obtain court case copies.

Michelle Gump

21454 Schwier Rd, Sunman, IN 47041
Phone: 812-537-8877 - **Fax:** 812-532-3296
Types of Records Retrieved: Criminal and Civil courts
Local Retrieval Area: IN-Dearborn
Add'l Information: Established 2005. Normal turnaround time- Next day. Projects billed by number of names searched. She provides daily, in person access to the clerk's office.

Guthrie County Abstract

110 N 4th St, PO Box 39, Guthrie Center, IA 50115
Phone: 641-332-2339; Fax- 641-332-2340 abstrct@netins.net
Types of Records Retrieved: Civil and Probate courts; Real Estate; Tax Liens/Judgments; UCC records; Vital records
Local Retrieval Area: IA-Guthrie
Add'l Information: Established 1954. Normal turnaround time- 1-2 days. Fee basis varies by type of transaction. First project may require prepayment. Will file/record documents for clients.

Guzman Title Research Inc

4726 Oakley Rd, North Port, FL 34288-2359
Phone: 941-423-5310 - **Fax:** 941-423-5320 guzman4726@yahoo.com
Types of Records Retrieved: Civil and Probate courts; Real Estate; Tax Liens/Judgments; UCC records

Local Retrieval Area: FL-Charlotte, De Soto, Lee, Sarasota

Add'l Information: Established 1988. Normal turnaround time- 24 hours. Projects billed by number of names searched. Projects billed by the hour. Fees depend on type of service requested. Will file/record documents for clients. They specialize in real estate title reports, UCC searches, judgments, liens, US tax liens and real estate tax information. The owner has more than 30 years experience.

H S Black Abstractor Inc

PO Box 717, 415 Commerce St, Childress, TX 79201
Phone: 940-937-3681 - **Fax:** 940-937-3682

Types of Records Retrieved: Civil and Probate courts; Real Estate; Tax Liens/Judgments; UCC records; Vital records

Local Retrieval Area: TX-Childress

Add'l Information: Established 1920. Turnaround time- 2-3 days. Fee basis will vary by the type of project. Will file/record documents for clients.

Haakon County Abstract Co

Box 40, Philip, SD 57567-0040
Phone: 605-859-2461 - **Fax:** 605-859-3461

Records Retrieved: Real Estate; Tax Liens/Judgments; UCC records

Local Retrieval Area: SD-Haakon. **Correspondent Relationships:** Pennington, Jackson, Stanley counties SD.

Add'l Information: Established 1999. Normal turnaround time- 2-3 days. Projects billed by the area searched. First project may require prepayment. Will file/record documents for clients. Personal checks are accepted. Credit accounts not accepted. They specialize in real estate title searches for abstracts or title insurance.

Haber Investigations

1702-L Meridian Ave #333, San Jose, CA 95125
Phone: 800-382-6333; 408-978-2325 - **Fax:** 408-266-1119
haberpeye@earthlink.net

Types of Records Retrieved: Criminal, Civil and Probate courts; Federal courts; Real Estate; Tax Liens/Judgments; UCC records; Vital records

Local Retrieval Area: CA-Santa Clara. **Correspondents:** worldwide.

Add'l Info: Established 1987. Normal turnaround time- 2 hours. Projects billed by number of names searched. All projects require prepayment. Terms: net 30 days. He has 30 years police and investigative experience, a law degree and a criminology degree, and teaches a hands-on workshop. Cali PI #12519. A licensed PI in CA. Performs service of process.

Hale Investigative Services/Process

PO Box 720426, 6564 Bayboro Ct, Orlando, FL 32872-0426
Phone: 800-882-5137; 407-275-6969 - **Fax:** 407-275-9171
www.hale-pi.com **email:** halepi@hale-pi.com

Types of Records Retrieved: Criminal, Civil and Probate courts; Federal courts; Real Estate; Tax Liens/Judgments; UCC records; Vital records

Local Retrieval Area: FL-Brevard, Lake, Orange, Osceola, Polk, Seminole, Volusia. **Correspondent Relationships:** statewide.

Add'l Information: Established 1985. Normal turnaround time- 24-48 hours. Expedited service available. Projects billed by number of names searched. They do individual considerations. Credit cards accepted. Will file/record documents for clients. Checks accepted, upon approval They specialize in surveillance and counter electronic surveillance. They investigate civil, criminal, domestic and industrial cases, also property, tax searches. They also have a division that can serve legal documents anywhere in the US or Florida. A licensed PI in FL. Performs service of process.

Haley Title Co Inc

320 S Main St, Ottawa, KS 66067
Phone: 785-242-2457 - **Fax:** 785-242-6830

Types of Records Retrieved: Criminal, Civil and Probate courts; Real Estate; Tax Liens/Judgments; UCC records

Local Retrieval Area: KS-Franklin

Add'l Information: Established 1945. Normal turnaround time- 1-2 days. Fee basis varies by type of transaction.

Hamilton & Johnson Abstract Inc

PO Box 85, Wahoo, NE 68066 **Phone:** 402-443-3081 - **Fax:** 402-443-4120

Types of Records Retrieved: Real Estate; Tax Liens/Judgments; Probate courts; UCC records **Local Retrieval Area:** NE-Saunders

Add'l Information: Established 1962. Normal turnaround time- 24 business hours. Projects billed by number of names searched. Will file/record documents for clients.

Sue P Hamm

PO Box 46, Aurora, NC 27806 **Phone:** 252-322-5015 - **Fax:** 252-322-7205

Types of Records Retrieved: Civil courts; Real Estate; Tax Liens/Judgments; UCC records; Vital records

Local Retrieval Area: NC-Beaufort, Craven, Lenoir, Pamlico, Pitt

Add'l Information: Established 1990. Normal turnaround time- 24-48 hours. Fee basis will vary by the type of project. She specializes in real estate, civil action and lien searches. Cell phone is 252-635-7694.

Hancock County Abstract Co

130 E 8th St, Garner, IA 50438
Phone: 641-923-2454 - **Fax:** 641-923-3381

Types of Records Retrieved: Real Estate; Tax Liens/Judgments; Probate courts; UCC records **Local Retrieval Area:** IA-Hancock

Add'l Information: Established 1903. Turnaround time- 2-3 days. Projects billed by number of records located. Will file/record documents for clients.

Hand County Abstract & Title Co

PO Box 368, 114 E 3rd St, Miller, SD 57362
Phone: 605-853-2194 - **Fax:** 605-853-3606 title.office@midconetwork.com

Records Retrieved: Real Estate; Tax Liens/Judgments; UCC records

Local Retrieval Area: SD-Hand

Add'l Information: Turnaround time- 1 week. Projects billed by the hour.

Hannaford Abstract & Title Co

222 E Main St, Marion, KS 66861
Phone: 620-382-2130 - **Fax:** 620-382-2253 hanorder@stewart.com

Types of Records Retrieved: Criminal, Civil and Probate courts; Real Estate; Tax Liens/Judgments; UCC records; Vital records

Local Retrieval Area: KS-Marion

Add'l Information: Established 1871. Normal turnaround time- 3 days. Projects billed by number of names searched. Fee basis varies by type of transaction. First project may require prepayment. Will file/record documents for clients. They specialize in title insurance, title searches, escrow closings and certificates of title.

Sharon K Hannaman Abstracter

PO Box 246, Blue Earth, MN 56013
Phone: 507-526-5144

Types of Records Retrieved: Real Estate; Tax Liens/Judgments

Local Retrieval Area: MN-Faribault

Add'l Information: Established 1990. Normal turnaround time- 1-2 weeks. Projects billed by number of names searched. Projects billed by number of records located. First project may require prepayment.

Harbor City Research Inc

201 N Charles St #900, Baltimore, MD 21201-4113
Phone: 800-445-6029; 410-539-0400 - **Fax:** 800-331-1566; 410-659-0517
www.hcrsearch.com **email:** orders@hcrsearch.com

Types of Records Retrieved: Civil and Probate courts; Federal courts; Real Estate; Tax Liens/Judgments; UCC records

Local Retrieval Area: MD-Anne Arundel, Baltimore, Baltimore City, Harford, Howard, Montgomery, Prince George's. **Correspondent Relationships:** nationwide.

Add'l Information: Established 1985. Normal turnaround time- 1-2 days. Projects billed by number of names searched. Projects billed by number of records located. First project may require prepayment. Will file/record documents for clients.

Hardin County Abstract Co

Main Street Courthouse, PO Box 158, Elizabethtown, IL 62931
Phone: 618-287-7944 - **Fax:** 618-287-7833

Types of Records Retrieved: Criminal, Civil and Probate courts; Real Estate; Tax Liens/Judgments; Local UCC records; Vital records

Local Retrieval Area: IL-Hardin County. **Correspondent Relationships:** Pope County.

Add'l Information: Established 1920. Normal turnaround time- 3 days or less. Projects billed by number of names searched. Projects billed by number of records located. First project may require prepayment. Will file/record documents for clients. Issuing agents for Chicago Title Insurance Company in Hardin and Pope Counties. Other services provided--real estate closings and document filing.

Harding County Abstract

PO Box 86, 202 4th St West, Buffalo, SD 57720
Phone: 605-375-3422 - **Fax:** 605-375-3403

Types of Records Retrieved: Real Estate; Tax Liens/Judgments

Local Retrieval Area: SD-Harding

Add'l Information: Established 1950. Normal turnaround time- 24-48 hours. First project may require prepayment. They specialize in real estate but may be able to access courts by special request.

Dudley P Hardy PA

PO Drawer 1030, Starke, FL 32091
Phone: 904-964-5701 - **Fax:** 904-964-2304 dudleyph@earthlink.net

Types of Records Retrieved: Civil and Probate courts; Real Estate; Tax Liens/Judgments; UCC records

Local Retrieval Area: FL-Bradford. **Correspondent Relationships:** Union, Clay, Alachua counties FL.

Add'l Information: Established 1966. Turnaround time- 2-3 days depending on the project. Projects billed by number of records located. Payment due upon receipt of invoice. They specialize in all types of title searches.

Harlan County Abstract

PO Box 695, Alma, NE 68920
Phone: 308-928-2343 - **Fax:** 308-928-2612

Types of Records Retrieved: Real Estate; Tax Liens/Judgments

Local Retrieval Area: NE-Harlan

Add'l Information: Established 1969. First project may require prepayment. They specialize in real estate.

Harmon Document Retrieval Service

PO Box 1794, Jefferson City, MO 65102
Phone: 573-635-6690 - **Fax:** 573-635-2339 jchdrs@aol.com

Types of Records Retrieved: Civil & Criminal courts; Federal District courts

Local Retrieval Area: MO-Boone, Callaway, Camden, Cole, Miller, Moniteau, Morgan, Osage. **Correspondent Relationships:** various states.

Add'l Information: Established 1978. Normal turnaround time- 1 day. Projects billed by number of names searched. Credit cards accepted. Will file/record documents for clients. Billed monthly. Specialize in statewide criminal searches (thru MSHP-CRID) & public record retrieval. They will file/record UCC documents same or next day, also serve summons & subpoenas. Make daily runs to Div of Workers Comp & Dept of Revenue for driving records. Performs service of process.

Penny Harmon

4560 Chestateek Heights Rd, Gainesville, GA 30506
Phone: 404-580-3099 - **Fax:** 770-887-2834 harm7249@bellsouth.net

Types of Records Retrieved: Real Estate; Criminal, Civil and Probate courts; Tax Liens/Judgments; UCC records

Local Retrieval Area: GA-Forsyth, Hall

Add'l Information: Established 2002. Normal turnaround time- 24-48 hours. Fees depend on nature of request. First project may require prepayment. She is a specialist in Forsyth and Hall counties. Will not do municipal court record search.

Nancy Harris

1408 Luna St, Las Curces, NM 88001-4357
Phone: 877-461-6700; 505-647-0290 - **Fax:** 928-437-1215
believe58@juno.com

Types of Records Retrieved: Criminal and Civil courts; Federal District courts; Tax Liens/Judgments; UCC records

Local Retrieval Area: NM-Dona Ana, Los Alamos, Rio Arriba, San Miguel, Santa Fe

Add'l Information: Established 1992. Normal turnaround time- 24-48 hours. Projects billed by number of names searched. Projects billed by number of records located. Projects billed by the hour. First project may require prepayment. Will file/record documents for clients. They specialize in real estate, title searches, criminal background searches, mortgage data, retrieval, judicial judgment assistance and locating missing persons. They also search in the Department of Insurance. Performs service of process.

Harrison County Title

14048 Main St, Bethany, MO 64424-1966
Phone: 660-425-3523 - **Fax:** 660-425-6698

Types of Records Retrieved: Civil and Probate courts; Real Estate; Tax Liens/Judgments; UCC records

Local Retrieval Area: MO-Harrison

Add'l Information: Established 1947. Normal turnaround time- variable depending on project. Fee varies depending on project. Will file/record documents for clients. Formerly known as Harrison County Abstract Co. They specialize in lien and real estate searches.

Harrison County Title & Guaranty

114 N 2nd Ave, Logan, IA 51546
Phone: 712-644-2703 - **Fax:** 712-644-2557

Types of Records Retrieved: Criminal, Civil and Probate courts; Real Estate; Tax Liens/Judgments

Local Retrieval Area: IA-Harrison

Add'l Information: Established 1981. Normal turnaround time- 1 week. Projects billed by number of records located. Will file/record documents for clients. Payment due upon receipt of billing.

Harry W Hawley Inc

4 Court St, Delhi, NY 13753
Phone: 607-746-3860 - **Fax:** 607-746-3339
www.hwhawleyrealty.com **email:** info@hwhawleyrealty.com

Types of Records Retrieved: Civil and Probate courts; Federal courts; Real Estate; Tax Liens/Judgments; UCC records

Local Retrieval Area: NY-Delaware. **Correspondent Relationships:** Otsego, Schoharie, Chenango counties.

Add'l Information: Established 1971. Normal turnaround time- 3-10 days. Fee basis will vary by type of project. Will file/record documents for clients. Personal checks and/or cash is accepted. Credit accounts are not accepted. They specialize in abstracts, appraisals, title searches, title insurance, witness closings and escrow services.

Hart & Associates Inc

PO Box 606, Euless, TX 76039-0606
Phone: 866-429-4044; - **Fax:** 877-446-3775
www.hartassocinc.com **email:** hart@hartassocinc.com

Records Retrieved: Criminal and Civil courts; Federal District courts

Local Retrieval Area: TX-Dallas, Denton, Tarrant. **Correspondent Relationships:** nationwide.

Add'l Information: Established 1996. Normal turnaround time- 24-72 hours. Projects billed by number of names searched. Projects billed by number of records located. Projects billed by the hour. First project may require prepayment. Net 30 days. They specialize in pre-employment screening as well as commercial, residential rental property screening. Services include employee drug testing, interviews, evaluations and profiles and document retrieval. A licensed PI in TX.

Harvey Public Records Inc

PO Box 11397, Waco, TX 76716
Phone: 254-662-6265 - **Fax:** 254-662-6266
www.harveypublicrecords.com **email:** info@harveypublicrecords.com

Types of Records Retrieved: Criminal, Civil and Probate courts; Federal courts; Real Estate; Tax Liens/Judgments; UCC records; Vital records

Local Retrieval Area: TX-Bell, McLennan

Add'l Information: Established 1984. Normal turnaround time- 24-48 hours. Projects billed by number of names searched. Will file/record documents for clients. Family owned and operated.

Haskell Abstract & TItle Co

306 N 1st St, Haskell, TX 79521
Phone: 940-864-2604 - **Fax:** 940-864-2840 hat@valornet.com

Types of Records Retrieved: Criminal, Civil and Probate courts; Real Estate; Tax Liens/Judgments; UCC records; Vital records

Local Retrieval Area: TX-Haskell

Add'l Information: Normal turnaround time- 1-2 days. Fee basis will vary by the type of project. First project may require prepayment. Will file/record documents for clients. They specialize in real estate closings, deed preparation, land/lien searches. They are a law office.

Haskell County Abstract & Title

PO Box 636, 109 S Inman, Sublette, KS 67877
Phone: 620-675-2322 - **Fax:** 620-675-2025

Types of Records Retrieved: Criminal, Civil and Probate courts; Real Estate; Tax Liens/Judgments; UCC records; Vital records

Local Retrieval Area: KS-Haskell

Add'l Information: Established 1980. Normal turnaround time- 2 days. Projects billed by number of names searched. Projects billed by the hour. Document filing/rec fees must accompany documents. Will file/record documents for clients. They specialize in abstracts and title insurance, and closing services.

Attorney John A Hatcher

101 W College St, Booneville, MS 38829
Phone: 662-728-9444 - **Fax:** 662-728-9440

Types of Records Retrieved: Criminal, Civil and Probate courts; Real Estate; Tax Liens/Judgments; UCC records; Vital records

Local Retrieval Area: MS-Prentiss. **Correspondent:** nationwide.

Add'l Information: Established 1992. Normal turnaround time- 1-2 days. Projects billed by the hour. First project may require prepayment. Will file/record documents for clients. He is an attorney in general practice. Performs service of process.

Hatfield Process Service

1669 Jefferson, Kansas City, MO 64108
Phone: 816-842-9800 - **Fax:** 816-842-9801
www.hatfieldprocess.com **email:** service@hatfieldprocess.com

Types of Records Retrieved: Criminal, Civil and Probate courts; Federal courts; Real Estate; Tax Liens/Judgments; UCC records; Vital records

Local Retrieval Area: KS-Douglas, Johnson, Shawnee, Wyandotte; MO-Buchanan, Cass, Clay, Jackson, Platte. **Correspondent Relationships:** Boone, Cole counties.

Add'l Information: Established 1976. Normal turnaround time- 1-2 days. Expedited service available. Projects billed by the hour. First project may require prepayment. Will file/record documents for clients. Hatfield Process Service (HPS) is on e of Kansas City's oldest legal services firms. Only experienced investigators are used for their document research and retrieval. Please visit www.hatfieldprocess.com. A licensed PI in KS, MO. Performs service of process.

William Patrick Hauser

PO Box 1900, Barbourville, KY 40906
Phone: 606-546-3811 - **Fax:** 606-546-3050

Types of Records Retrieved: Real Estate; Tax Liens/Judgments

Local Retrieval Area: KY-Knox

Add'l Information: Established 1979. Normal turnaround time- 2-3 days. First project may require prepayment. He is an attorney and performs searches on a very limited basis.

Hawaii Real Property Research

PO Box 622, Kaaawa, HI 96730
Phone: 808-396-7581 - **Fax:** 808-396-4452
www.hawaiiresearch.com **email:** hawaiiresearch@hawaii.rr.com

Types of Records Retrieved: Real Estate; Tax Liens/Judgments; Probate courts; Federal courts; UCC records; Vital records

Local Retrieval Area: HI-Hawaii, Honolulu, Kalawao, Kauai, Maui. **Correspondent Relationships:** statewide.

Add'l Information: Established 1995. Normal turnaround time- 48 hours. Expedited service available. Projects billed by number of names searched. Projects billed by number of records located. First project may require prepayment. Credit cards accepted. Escrow billing accepted. They specialize in real estate research, title records, (Bureau of Conveyance) tax office records, building permits, market research, and mailing lists.

Hawk Investigations

1647 Butler Plank Rd #12, Glenshaw, PA 15116-1704
Phone: 412-487-9274 - **Fax:** 412-487-9260
www.hawk-investigations.com **email:** hawk17@earthlink.net

Types of Records Retrieved: Criminal, Civil and Probate courts; Federal courts; Real Estate; Tax Liens/Judgments; UCC records; Vital records

Local Retrieval Area: PA-Allegheny, Armstrong, Beaver, Butler, Fayette, Indiana, Lawrence, Washington, Westmoreland

Add'l Information: Established 1989. Normal turnaround time- 2-3 days. Projects billed by the hour. First project may require prepayment. Will file/record documents for clients. They specialize in record retrieval and all types of investigations in Pittsburgh and surrounding areas. March, 2005 they will be able to handle all of PA electronic connection to all county criminal records. A licensed PI in PA. Performs service of process.

Hawkeye Legal Services

2731 Douglas Ave, Des Moines, IA 50310
Phone: 515-276-3984 - **Fax:** 515-271-0664 pagepi@msn.com

Types of Records Retrieved: Criminal, Civil and Probate courts; Federal courts; UCC records; Vital records

Local Retrieval Area: IA-Dallas, Greene, Jasper, Madison, Mahaska, Marion, Polk, Story, Warren. **Correspondent Relationships:** nationwide.

Add'l Information: Established 1990. Normal turnaround time- 48 hours. First project may require prepayment. Will file/record documents for clients. Pre-payment of private parties, invoice to attorneys, other investigators & process servers. Formerly Page-Hawkeye Legal Services, they now also provide court filings, skiptracing, and private investigations. They have 20 years of experience, full-time office staff. A licensed PI in IA. Performs service of process.

Hawkins & EZmessenger Inc

10 W Madison St, Phoenix, AZ 85003-2122
Phone: 602-452-1800 - **Fax:** 602-271-4517
www.helpaz.com **email:** tmacdonald@hawkinsandcampbell.com

Types of Records Retrieved: Criminal, Civil and Probate courts; Federal courts; Real Estate; Tax Liens/Judgments; UCC records; Vital records

Local Retrieval Area: AZ-Coconino, Maricopa. **Correspondent Relationships:** Arizona.

Add'l Information: Established 1948. Normal turnaround time- 24 hours. Projects billed by the hour. First project may require prepayment. Will file/record documents for clients. They specialize in litigation support, process serving, paper investigation, and skiptracing by licensed experienced professionals. Has an office in Flagstaff, 928-226-7221 A licensed PI in AZ. Performs service of process.

Hayes Inv

325 Claypool-Alvaton Rd, Bowling Green, KY 42103
Phone: 270-781-7488 - **Fax:** 270-781-7488 jkjwhayes@bellsouth.net
Types of Records Retrieved: Criminal and Civil courts
Local Retrieval Area: KY-Allen, Barren, Butler, Edmonson, Logan, Simpson, Warren
Add'l Information: Established 2002. Normal turnaround time- 24 hours. First project may require prepayment. They also provide court filings, subpoena preparation, photocopying, private investigations, witness locates, statements, pre-employment screening, surveillance and service of process. Performs service of process.

Tommy Hayes

PO Box 748, McKee, KY 40447 **Phone:** 606-287-8891 **Fax:** 606-287-8428
Types of Records Retrieved: Real Estate
Local Retrieval Area: KY-Jackson
Add'l Information: Established 1987. First project may require prepayment. He specializes in real estate.

Becky Headrick

Route 1, Box 111, Richards, MO 64778 **Phone:** 417-321-0745
Types of Records Retrieved: Criminal and Civil courts
Local Retrieval Area: KS-Bourbon
Add'l Information: Established 2000?. Projects billed by number of names searched. First project may require prepayment. She performs searches in Bourbon County Kansas, but lives just across the border in Missouri.

Heart O' Texas Research

2901 Cumberland Ave, PO Box 1613 (76703), Waco, TX 76707
Phone: 254-752-2057 - **Fax:** 254-752-8201 vrgnweb@aol.com
Types of Records Retrieved: Real Estate; Tax Liens/Judgments
Local Retrieval Area: TX-Bell, Bosque, Coryell, Falls, McLennan
Add'l Information: Established 1986. Normal turnaround time- 24-96 hours. Projects billed by number of names searched. First project may require prepayment. Terms: 30 days net. They specialize in real estate, environmental, and other public record research. They do a full title report (real property only) from last owner forward. Their report includes complete deed info, all open liens, 10 year state & fed tax lien check, etc.

Heartland Document Retrieval

9921 W 71st, Merriam, KS 66203
Phone: 888-221-2778 orders only; 913-362-6190 - **Fax:** 888-221-2778 orders only; 913-722-6367
www.heartlanddocuments.com **email:** patty@heartlanddocuments.com
Types of Records Retrieved: Criminal, Civil and Probate courts; Federal courts; Real Estate; Tax Liens/Judgments; UCC records; Vital records
Local Retrieval Area: KS-Douglas, Franklin, Johnson, Leavenworth, Miami, Shawnee, Wyandotte. **Correspondent Relationships:** Kansas, Oklahoma.
Add'l Information: Established 2000. Normal turnaround time- 48 hours for non-certified copies. Projects billed by number of names searched. Payment due net 30 days. They provide fast and accurate service in Kansas and Oklahoma. Specializes in current owner searches. Toll-free numbers are for orders only!

Heartland Information Services

527 Marquette Ave #900, Minneapolis, MN 55402-1312
Phone: 800-967-1882; 612-371-9255 - **Fax:** 800-695-9531; 612-371-9262
www.heartlandinfo.com **email:** skolar@heartlandinfo.com
Types of Records Retrieved: Criminal, Civil and Probate courts; Federal courts; Real Estate; Tax Liens/Judgments; UCC records; Vital records
Local Retrieval Area: MN-Anoka, Carver, Dakota, Hennepin, Ramsey, Scott, Washington. **Correspondent Relationships:** nationwide.
Add'l Information: Established 1991. Normal turnaround time- 24-72 hours. Projects billed by number of names searched. Projects billed by the hour. Credit cards accepted. Will file/record documents for clients. Terms: net 15 days. They are a licensed and bonded private investigative agency. A licensed PI in MN. Performs service of process.

Heartland Investigations Inc

PO Box 453, Benton, IL 62812
Phone: 877-684-6313; 618-438-4900 - **Fax:** 618-438-4805
www.heartlandinvestigations.com
email: kevin@heartlandinvestigations.com
Types of Records Retrieved: Criminal, Civil and Probate courts; Federal courts; Real Estate; Tax Liens/Judgments; UCC records; Vital records
Local Retrieval Area: IL-Alexander, Franklin, Gallatin, Hamilton, Hardin, Jackson, Jefferson, Johnson, Massac, Perry, Pope, Pulaski, Randolph, Saline, Union, White, Williamson
Add'l Information: Established 1986. Normal turnaround time- 42-72 hours. Projects billed by the hour. Credit cards accepted. Will invoice. Heartland is a fully licensed investigation team that has a proven professional track record. They provide services ranging from fire investigation to surveillance. Also has an office at PO Box 1096, Murphysboro, IL 62966. A licensed PI in IL. Performs service of process.

Heartland Title Company

404 N Fisk, Brownwood, TX 76801
Phone: 325-646-0509 - **Fax:** 325-643-5059 heartlandtitle@juno.com
Types of Records Retrieved: Real Estate; Tax Liens/Judgments; Probate courts; UCC records; Mortgage records
Local Retrieval Area: TX-Brown
Add'l Information: Established 1975. Normal turnaround time- 5 days. Projects billed by number of names searched. Projects billed by the hour. First project may require prepayment. Will file/record documents for clients. Their searches are made by attorneys with many years of experience.

Heather Gilbert Title Abstract & Closing Svc

520 3rd St, Waynesburg, PA 15370
Phone: 724-998-5954 - **Fax:** 724-627-7480 hlgilbert@alltel.net
Types of Records Retrieved: Criminal, Civil and Probate courts; Real Estate; Tax Liens/Judgments; UCC records; Vital records
Local Retrieval Area: PA-Fayette, Greene, Washington
Add'l Info: Established 1999. Turnaround time- 24 hours. Projects billed by number of names searched. Projects billed by the hour. Payment due net 30 days. They specialize in being a full service title search company which includes surface, coal, oil and gas. Commercial searches available.

Hebert Land Services

PO Box 772, Poteau, OK 74953
Phone: 918-647-9524 - **Fax:** 918-647-9522 jabear1@alltel.net
Types of Records Retrieved: Civil and Probate courts; Real Estate; Tax Liens/Judgments; UCC records; Vital records
Local Retrieval Area: AR-Crawford, Franklin, Logan, Pope, Scott, Sebastian, Yell; OK-Haskell, Latimer, Le Flore, Pittsburg, Sequoyah. **Correspondent Relationships:** nationwide.
Add'l Info: Established 1981. Normal turnaround time- 1-2 days. Fee basis is determined "per hour/day". First project may require prepayment. Will file/record documents for clients. They specialize in oil and gas.

Hedlund Abstract

PO Box 188, Hugo, CO 80821
Phone: 719-743-2353 - **Fax:** 719-743-2349
Types of Records Retrieved: Civil court; Real Estate; Tax Liens/Judgments; older UCC records **Local Retrieval Area:** CO-Lincoln
Add'l Information: Normal turnaround time- 1-2 days. First project may require prepayment. They are a title company.

Held Abstract & Title Co Inc

10 Railroad St, Williamsport, IN 47993-0068
Phone: 765-762-2457 - **Fax:** 765-762-2458
Types of Records Retrieved: Criminal, Civil and Probate courts; Real Estate; Tax Liens/Judgments; UCC records
Local Retrieval Area: IN-Benton, Fountain, Warren
Add'l Information: Established 1890. Normal turnaround time- 48 hours. Fee basis will vary by type of project. All projects require prepayment. Will file/record documents for clients.

Helena Abstract & Title Co

PO Box 853, 6th & Fuller, Helena, MT 59624
Phone: 406-442-5080 - **Fax:** 406-442-6179
Types of Records Retrieved: Civil and Probate courts; US District courts; Real Estate; Tax Liens/Judgments; UCC records
Local Retrieval Area: MT-Lewis and Clark. **Correspondent Relationships:** statewide non-Real Estate.
Add'l Information: Established 1935. Normal turnaround time- 2-5 days. Fee basis varies by type of transaction. Will file/record documents for clients. They specialize in real estate searches.

Hempstead County Abstract & Title

401 S Washington, Hope, AR 71801
Phone: 870-777-2351 - **Fax:** 870-777-6033 wrwpa@sbcglobal.net
Types of Records Retrieved: Criminal, Civil and Probate courts; Real Estate; Tax Liens/Judgments; UCC records
Local Retrieval Area: AR-Hempstead
Add'l Information: Established 1891. Normal turnaround time- 1 week. Projects billed by number of records located. Will file/record documents for clients. Credit accounts not accepted. They specialize in title insurance, land titles and abstracts.

Barbara K Henritze

807 Brooklawn Dr, Boulder, CO 80303-2729
Phone: 303-499-3750 barbara@henritze.com
Types of Records Retrieved: Criminal, Civil and Probate courts; Federal courts; Real Estate; Tax Liens/Judgments; UCC records; Vital records
Local Retrieval Area: CO-Adams, Boulder, Broomfield, Denver, Jefferson
Add'l Information: Established 1986. Normal turnaround time- 2 days. Projects billed by the hour. First project may require prepayment. Will file/record documents for clients. She specializes in 50 year environmental title chains.

Henry County Abstract Co (Iowa)

300 S Adams St, Mt Pleasant, IA 52641
Phone: 319-385-9017 - **Fax:** 319-385-9017
Types of Records Retrieved: Criminal, Civil and Probate courts; Real Estate; Tax Liens/Judgments; UCC records; Vital records
Local Retrieval Area: IA-Henry
Add'l Information: Established 1978. Normal turnaround time- 2-3 days. Fee basis will vary by the type of project. Billing upon completion.

Henry County Abstract Co (Missouri)

101 N Main St, Clinton, MO 64735
Phone: 660-885-6168 - **Fax:** 660-885-3945
Types of Records Retrieved: Real Estate; Probate Courts
Local Retrieval Area: MO-Henry
Add'l Information: Normal turnaround time- 5-7 days. Fee basis will vary by the type of project. Will file/record documents for clients. They specialize in title searches and closings.

Heritage Escrow LLC

PO Box 72, Greybull, WY 82426-0072
Phone: 307-765-9399 - **Fax:** 307-765-9599 hesjd00@tctwest.net
Types of Records Retrieved: Civil and Probate courts; Real Estate; Tax Liens/Judgments; UCC records; Vital records
Local Retrieval Area: WY-Big Horn
Add'l Information: Established 1992. Normal turnaround time- 24-48 hours. Projects billed by number of names searched. Heritage Escrow LLC is a full service closing company that is expanding into title searches, ownership and encumbrance reports, title preliminary and soon offering title insurance.

Rick Hessig

404 Hidden Oak Way, Louisville, KY 40222-4894
Phone: 502-583-2453 - **Fax:** 502-339-8828 rickhessig@aol.com
Types of Records Retrieved: Criminal, Civil and Probate courts; Federal courts; Tax Liens/Judgments; UCC records; Vital records
Local Retrieval Area: KY-Jefferson; IN-Clark, Floyd. **Correspondent Relationships:** nationwide.
Add'l Information: Normal turnaround time- up to 1 week. Rush service available. A licensed PI in IN. Performs service of process.

Hettinger-Sioux County Abstractors Inc

Box 160, Mott, ND 58646
Phone: 701-824-3148 - **Fax:** 701-824-3148
Types of Records Retrieved: Civil courts; Federal courts; Real Estate; Tax Liens/Judgments; UCC records; Vital records
Local Retrieval Area: ND-Hettinger, Sioux
Add'l Information: Established 1989. Projects are billed by the amount of entries. Will file/record documents for clients. They specialize in real estate title work.

Hickman Land Title

PO Box 386, Logan, UT 84323-0386
Phone: 800-365-7760; 435-752-0582 - **Fax:** 435-752-0584
www.landtitleco.com **email:** hlt@landtitleco.com
Types of Records Retrieved: Criminal, Civil and Probate courts; Real Estate; Tax Liens/Judgments; UCC records; Vital records
Local Retrieval Area: UT-Cache, Davis, Rich, Salt Lake, Weber
Add'l Information: Established 1904. Normal turnaround time- 1-2 days. Projects billed by the hour. They are a licensed title insurance company in the state of Utah.

Attorney John O Hicks III

PO Box 64, 105 Main St, Calhoun, KY 42327
Phone: 270-273-5749 - **Fax:** 270-273-9855
Types of Records Retrieved: Civil and Probate courts; Real Estate; Tax Liens/Judgments; UCC records
Local Retrieval Area: KY-Daviess, McLean, Muhlenberg. **Correspondent Relationships:** statewide.
Add'l Information: Established 1977. Normal turnaround time- 2 days for McLean County; up to 1 week for Muhlenberg and Daviess counties. Fee basis varies by type of transaction. First project may require prepayment.

Susan Hicks

1607 Thornton Pl, Henderson, KY 42420
Phone: 270-724-2093 - **Fax:** 270-831-2710
Types of Records Retrieved: Criminal, Civil and Probate courts
Local Retrieval Area: KY-Henderson
Add'l Info: Established 1997. Turnaround time- 24 hours. First project may require prepayment. She specializes in accuracy and fast turnaround.

Hidalgo County Abstract

PO Box 188, Lordsburg, NM 88045
Phone: 505-542-9181 - **Fax:** 505-542-9190 hcacinc@aznex.net
Types of Records Retrieved: Real Estate; Tax Liens/Judgments
Local Retrieval Area: NM-Hidalgo
Add'l Information: Established 1962. Normal turnaround time- 1 week. Projects billed by number of names searched. Will file/record documents for clients. A deposit is required. They specialize in land searches. They are a licensed title escrow agent in NM.

High Plains Land & Title

PO Box 878, Dodge City, KS 67801
Phone: 620-225-6574 - **Fax:** 620-225-6575
Types of Records Retrieved: Civil and Probate courts; Real Estate; Tax Liens/Judgments
Local Retrieval Area: KS-Clark, Edwards, Ford, Gray, Hodgeman, Meade
Add'l Information: Normal turnaround time- usually within 72 hours. Billing depends on nature of request. First project may require prepayment. Will file/record documents for clients. High Plains is mentioned by the courts as a document retriever. Is an expert in the area.

High Sierra Courier Service

100 Washington St #103, Reno, NV 89503
Phone: 877-812-8444; 775-322-8444 - **Fax:** 775-322-4501
hscourier@softcom.net

Types of Records Retrieved: Criminal, Civil and Probate courts; Federal courts; Tax Liens/Judgments; UCC records; Vital records

Local Retrieval Area: NV-Carson City, Douglas, Washoe

Add'l Information: Established 1996. Normal turnaround time- 3-5 days. Expedited service available. Flat fee and costs. First project may require prepayment. Performs service of process.

Hill County Title Co

PO Box 1688, 309 3rd St, Havre, MT 59501
Phone: 406-265-7624 - **Fax:** 406-265-8385 title@hillcountytitle.com

Types of Records Retrieved: Civil and Probate courts; Real Estate; Tax Liens/Judgments; UCC records; Vital records

Local Retrieval Area: MT-Hill

Add'l Information: Established 1890. Normal turnaround time- 2-3 days. Projects billed by the hour. Will file/record documents for clients.

Linda Catherine Hill

2674 Pentley Pl, Kettering, OH 45429
Phone: 937-294-7961 - **Fax:** 937-296-9609 lchill1997@aol.com

Types of Records Retrieved: Criminal courts

Local Retrieval Area: OH-Greene, Montgomery

Add'l Information: Established 1995. Normal turnaround time- 24-48 hours. Projects billed by number of names searched. Monthly billing. She has been doing record retrieval for 10 years. All searches are conducted hands-on in a quick, yet thorough manner, giving you the most accurate information available.

Hill-N-Dale Abstracters Inc

PO Box 547, 20 Scotchtown Ave, Goshen, NY 10924
Phone: 845-294-5110 - **Fax:** 845-294-9581
john@hillndaleabstracters.com

Types of Records Retrieved: Real Estate

Local Retrieval Area: NY-Orange, Sullivan, Ulster

Add'l Information: Established 1959. Normal turnaround time- 2-3 days. Projects billed by number of names searched. Will file/record documents for clients. They specialize in foreclosure searches, last owner searches, full searches and title insurance.

Hinsdale Title Co

PO Box 69, 0324 N Silver, Lake City, CO 81235
Phone: 970-944-2614 - **Fax:** 970-944-4444
www.hinsdaletitle.com **email:** mail@hinsdaletitle.com

Records Retrieved: Real Estate; Tax Liens/Judgments; Probate courts

Local Retrieval Area: CO-Hinsdale

Add'l Information: Established 1978. Normal turnaround time- 3-5 days. Projects billed by the hour. First project may require prepayment. Will file/record documents for clients. They specialize in real estate.

Hi-Tech Investigative

1209 Lincoln Ave, Evansville, IN 47714-1043
Phone: 812-477-1400 - **Fax:** 812-477-6250

Types of Records Retrieved: Criminal and Civil courts; Federal courts

Local Retrieval Area: IN-Gibson, Posey, Spencer, Vanderburgh, Warrick. **Correspondent Relationships:** Henderson, KY.

Add'l Information: Established 1976. Normal turnaround time- 24-48 hours. Projects billed by number of names searched. First project may require prepayment. Credit cards accepted. Will file/record documents for clients. Terms: net 15 days. They are a full service investigative agency, investigations, drug testing, paper & pencil testing and record retrieval. A licensed PI in IN. Performs service of process.

Hixson Enterprises

800 Dandy Loop Rd, Yorktown, VA 23692
Phone: 757-898-9865; cell- 876-0018 - **Fax:** 757-872-4717
hixson@infionline.net

Records Retrieved: Real Estate; Tax Liens/Judgments; UCC records

Local Retrieval Area: VA-Gloucester, James City, Mathews, New Kent, Williamsburg, York

Add'l Information: Established 1990. Normal turnaround time- 1 day. Projects billed by number of names searched. Projects billed by the hour. Charges by the hour are for 60 year searches. Will file/record documents for clients. Payment due upon presentation of statement. They specialize in old land records in York County and do some genealogy research. A cell phone number to reach them is 757-876-0018.

HK Partners Research

PO Box 622, Kaaawa, HI 96730
Phone: 808-291-2071 - **Fax:** 808-396-4452 hkpresearch@hotmail.com

Types of Records Retrieved: Real Estate; Tax Liens/Judgments; UCC records; Vital records

Local Retrieval Area: AZ-Maricopa; HI-Honolulu; WA-King

Add'l Information: Normal turnaround time- 5 business days. Expedited service available. Projects billed by number of names searched. Projects billed by number of records located. First project may require prepayment. Credit cards accepted. They specialize in real estate research, title records, HI Bureau of Conveyance tax office records, building permits, market research and mailing lists.

Hodgeman County Abstract & Title Ins Co Inc

PO Box 487, 112 E Bramley, Jetmore, KS 67854-0487
Phone: 620-357-8328 - **Fax:** 620-357-6221

Types of Records Retrieved: Criminal, Civil and Probate courts; Real Estate; Tax Liens/Judgments; UCC records

Local Retrieval Area: KS-Hodgeman

Add'l Information: Established 1973. Normal turnaround time- 1-2 days. Fee basis varies by type of transaction. All projects require prepayment. Will file/record documents for clients. They specialize in closings, abstracts and title insurance.

Hogan Land Title Co

1605 E Sunshine St, Springfield, MO 65804-1312
Phone: 417-882-3000 - **Fax:** 417-823-2620
www.hogantitle.com **Types of Records Retrieved:** Civil and Probate courts; Real Estate; Tax Liens/Judgments

Local Retrieval Area: MO-Christian, Greene, Stone, Taney

Add'l Information: Established 1955. Normal turnaround time- 3 days. Fee basis varies by type of transaction. They will file/record real estate documents on behalf of clients on a same or next day basis. Also has offices in Branson West and Branson.

Holden Abstract Co

PO Box 67, 202 W Wood St, Albany, MO 64402
Phone: 660-726-3417 - **Fax:** 660-726-3487 abstract@labanymo.net

Types of Records Retrieved: Civil and Probate courts; Real Estate; Tax Liens/Judgments; UCC records

Local Retrieval Area: MO-Gentry

Add'l Information: Established 1868. Normal turnaround time- variable depending on project. Fee basis is per document. Will file/record documents for clients. Payment must be paid in advance for the file/record of UCC and real estate documents. They specialize in title searches, abstracts and title insurance.

Holifield Investigation Agency

PO Box 8, 95 Main St, Bisbee, AZ 85603
Phone: 800-427-1294; 520-432-7364 - **Fax:** 520-432-7044

Types of Records Retrieved: Criminal, Civil and Probate courts; Real Estate; Tax Liens/Judgments

Local Retrieval Area: AZ-Cochise

Add'l Information: Established 1998. Normal turnaround time- 24 hours. Projects billed by the hour. First project may require prepayment. Will file/record documents for clients. They specialize in background investigations, insurance claims, missing persons, and surveillance. A licensed PI in AZ.

Hollenbeck Title Co

PO Box 215, Vienna, MO 65582
Phone: 573-422-3633 - **Fax:** 573-422-3213

Types of Records Retrieved: Real Estate; Tax Liens/Judgments; Probate courts; UCC records **Local Retrieval Area:** MO-Maries

Add'l Information: Established 1893. Normal turnaround time- 48 hours. Projects billed by number of names searched. Projects billed by number of records located. First project may require prepayment. Will file/record documents for clients.

Hollerbach and Assoc Inc

1400 Tower Life Building, San Antonio, TX 78205
Phone: 800-580-8485; 210-226-2556 - **Fax:** 800-580-7663; 210-224-7663
www.hollerbach.com **email:** jhollerbach@hollerbach.com

Types of Records Retrieved: Criminal, Civil and Probate courts; Federal courts; Real Estate; Tax Liens/Judgments; UCC records; Vital records

Local Retrieval Area: TX-Bexar, Dallas, Harris. **Correspondent Relationships:** statewide in Texas, also Mexico.

Add'l Information: Established 1985. Normal turnaround time- 24-48 hours. Billing method depends on nature of project. Credit cards accepted. Will file/record documents for clients. Hollerbach & Associates is a team of research and service professionals committed to providing fast, accurate, and cost-effective courthouse records research.

Hollis Search

123 Nodaway St, Oregon, MO 64473
Phone: 660-446-2730 - **Fax:** 660-446-2750

Types of Records Retrieved: Criminal, Civil and Probate courts; Real Estate; Tax Liens/Judgments

Local Retrieval Area: MO-Andrew, Atchison, Buchanan, Caldwell, Clay, Clinton, Daviess, De Kalb, Gentry, Harrison, Holt, Nodaway, Platte, Worth

Add'l Information: Established 2000. Normal turnaround time- 24-48 hours. Projects billed by number of names searched. First project may require prepayment. Will file/record documents for clients. They specialize in counties north of Kansas City.

Holt County Title Co

PO Box 256, 105 S Washington St, Oregon, MO 64473
Phone: 660-446-2371 - **Fax:** 660-446-2371

Types of Records Retrieved: Real Estate; Tax Liens/Judgments

Local Retrieval Area: MO-Holt

Add'l Information: Established 1940s. Normal turnaround time- 24-48 hours. First project may require prepayment. Will file/record documents for clients. They specialize in Holt County real estate.

Home Abstract Co

PO Box 520, Martin, SD 57551
Phone: 605-685-6525 - **Fax:** 605-685-6558

Types of Records Retrieved: Civil courts; Real Estate; Tax Liens/Judgments

Local Retrieval Area: SD-Bennett

Add'l Information: Established 1924. Normal turnaround time- 2 weeks. First project may require prepayment. They specialize in real estate.

HomeHistories.com

5806 Severna Pl, Harrisburg, PA 17111
Phone: 717-754-0283 - **Fax:** 866-271-8286;
www.home-histories.com **email:** stefhoover@gmail.com

Records Retrieved: Civil and Probate courts; Real Estate; Vital records

Local Retrieval Area: PA-Dauphin, Lebanon

Add'l Information: Established 1992. Normal turnaround time- 24-48 hours. Projects billed by the hour. All projects require prepayment. Forensic genealogy research & document retrieval; estate & probate, obituary, property searches; state library & archives; county & upper level courts; free quotes.

Honolulu Information Service, Inc

PO Box 2390, 1136 Union Mall #301, Honolulu, HI 96804
Phone: 808-524-4488 - **Fax:** 808-524-4499
www.honinfo.com **email:** info@honinfo.com

Types of Records Retrieved: Criminal, Civil and Probate courts; Federal courts; Real Estate; Tax Liens/Judgments; UCC records; Vital records

Local Retrieval Area: HI-Hawaii, Honolulu, Kauai, Maui. **Correspondent Relationships:** nationwide.

Add'l Information: Established 1982. Normal turnaround time- 48 hours. Expedited service available. Projects billed by number of names searched. First project may require prepayment. Credit cards accepted. Will file/record documents for clients. Terms: net 10 days. Established in 1982, Honolulu Information Services Inc offers a full spectrum of public record filing, search, and retrieval services for the State of Hawaii. Performs service of process.

Hons Investigations

311 S 4th St #204, Grand Forks, ND 58201
Phone: 800-450-4667; 701-775-7704 - **Fax:** 701-775-8062
www.honsinvestigations.com **email:** pi@honsinvestigations.com

Types of Records Retrieved: Criminal and Civil courts

Local Retrieval Area: ND-Barnes, Benson, Bottineau, Bowman, Burleigh, Cass, Cavalier, Dickey, Dunn, Eddy, Emmons, Grand Forks, McLean, Mercer, Morton, Mountrail, Pembina, Pierce, Ramsey, Richland, Rolette, Stark, Stutsman, Walsh, Ward, Williams. **Correspondents:** statewide.

Add'l Information: Established 1992. Normal turnaround time- 24 hours. Projects billed by number of names searched. First project may require prepayment. Credit cards accepted. Volume discounts available. They do statewide criminal history checks through ND Bureau of Criminal Investigations with 1-2 day turnaround. A licensed PI in ND, MN, MT. Performs service of process.

Hood & Whalen

137 E Pike St, Cynthiana, KY 41031
Phone: 859-234-4321; Fax- same

Types of Records Retrieved: Civil and Probate courts; Real Estate; Tax Liens/Judgments; UCC records; Vital records

Local Retrieval Area: KY-Harrison. **Correspondent Relationships:** surrounding counties.

Add'l Information: Established 1984. Normal turnaround time- 3-4 days. Projects billed by the hour. First project may require prepayment. They are a general practice law firm.

Hooks Title & Abstract

PO Box 2190, Kountze, TX 77625
Phone: 409-246-3447 - **Fax:** 409-246-3559
www.hookstitle.com **email:** hooks@hookstitle.com

Types of Records Retrieved: Civil and Probate courts; Real Estate; Tax Liens/Judgments; UCC records **Local Retrieval Area:** TX-Hardin

Add'l Information: Established 1902. Normal turnaround time- 2-5 days. Fees vary by project. Will file/record documents for clients. They have an in-house title plant.

Hoover Professional Investigations

3202 E "M", Tacoma, WA 98404-4027
Phone: 253-272-5090 - **Fax:** 253-272-5090
hooverinvestigations@netzero.com

Types of Records Retrieved: Criminal, Civil and Probate courts; Federal courts; Real Estate; Tax Liens/Judgments; UCC records; Vital records

Local Retrieval Area: WA-Pierce, Thurston. **Correspondent Relationships:** King, Kitsap, Mason, Snohomish counties Washington.

Add'l Information: Established 1964. Normal turnaround time- 1-7 days. Projects billed by the hour. First project may require prepayment. Will file/record documents for clients. Specialize in all phases of investigations since 1964. Electronic debugging service and intelligence gathering. A licensed PI in WA. Performs service of process.

Horger Barnwell & Reid LLP

PO Drawer 329, 1459 Amelia St, Orangeburg, SC 29116
Phone: 803-531-3000 - **Fax:** 803-531-3030 rhorger@hbrllp.com
Types of Records Retrieved: Civil and Probate courts; Federal courts; Real Estate; Tax Liens/Judgments; UCC records; Vital records
Local Retrieval Area: SC-Bamberg, Calhoun, Dorchester, Orangeburg. **Correspondent Relationships:** statewide.
Add'l Information: Established 1950. Normal turnaround time- 2-3 days. Projects billed by the hour. First project may require prepayment. Will file/record docs for clients. They do worker's comp and corporate law.

Hornthal Riley Ellis & Maland

PO Box 220, 301 E Main St, Elizabeth City, NC 27907-0220
Phone: 252-335-0871 - **Fax:** 252-335-4760 www.hrem.com
Types of Records Retrieved: Criminal, Civil and Probate courts; Federal courts; Real Estate; Tax Liens/Judgments; UCC records; Vital records
Local Retrieval Area: NC-Camden, Chowan, Dare, Gates, Hertford, Pasquotank, Perquimans, Tyrrell, Washington
Add'l Information: Established 1900. Normal turnaround time- 48 hours. Projects billed by the hour. Fee basis varies by type of transaction. Will file/record documents for clients. They are a full service law firm. They specialize in litigation, real estate, corporate practice and criminal practice. They also have an Outer Banks office, 252-441-0871.

Horvath Enterprises Inc

PO Box 52, 105 Park Ave, Milaca, MN 56353
Phone: 320-982-3253 - **Fax:** 320-982-2572 tph02@maxminn.com
Types of Records Retrieved: Criminal and Civil courts; Tax Liens/Judgments; UCC records
Local Retrieval Area: MN-Anoka, Becker, Benton, Chisago, Clay, Douglas, Isanti, Kanabec, Mille Lacs, Morrison, Otter Tail, Pine, Sherburne, Stearns, Todd, Wadena, Washington, Wright
Add'l Information: Established 1994. Normal turnaround time- 1-2 days. Projects billed by number of names searched. First project may require prepayment. Will bill monthly. They make your job easier with their 1-2 day turnaround and monthly billing.

Hotopp Public Record Searches

4021 S Whitehorse Rd, Nashville, IN 47448
Phone: 812-342-2163 - **Fax:** 812-342-6395 hotopp@hsonline.net
Types of Records Retrieved: Civil courts; Real Estate; Tax Liens/Judgments; UCC records
Local Retrieval Area: IN-Bartholomew, Brown, Jackson, Johnson, Monroe. **Correspondent Relationships:** Marion and Shelby County.
Add'l Information: Established 1999. Normal turnaround time- 24-48 hours. Projects billed by number of names searched. Projects billed by number of records located. First project may require prepayment. Will file/record documents for clients. Billing upon search completion. In business since 1999, they are known for their fast turnaround, 24-28 hours in most cases.

Houston Court Services Inc

1201 Louisiana St #210, Houston, TX 77002-5609
Phone: 713-655-0555
www.mach5couriers.com **email:** info@mach5couriers.com
Types of Records Retrieved: Criminal, Civil and Probate courts; Federal courts; Real Estate; Tax Liens/Judgments; UCC records; Vital records
Local Retrieval Area: TX-Brazoria, Brazos, Fort Bend, Harris, Montgomery. **Correspondent Relationships:** the Southern states.
Add'l Information: Established 1988. Normal turnaround time- 24-72 hours. Expedited service available. Projects billed by number of names searched. Credit cards accepted. Will file/record documents for clients. Payment due upon receipt. They specialize in servicing legal documents and court record retrieval on a nationwide basis. They also provide courier/messenger service and same day and overnight service. A licensed PI in TX. Performs service of process.

Howard County Abstract & Title Co

115 S Park Pl, Cresco, IA 52136-1632
Phone: 563-547-4944 - **Fax:** 563-547-5197
Types of Records Retrieved: Civil and Probate courts; US District court; Real Estate; Tax Liens/Judgments; UCC records
Local Retrieval Area: IA-Howard
Add'l Information: Established 1972. Turnaround time- 1-2 days. Projects billed by number of names searched. File/record real estate documents on behalf of clients will be submitted with filing fees advanced. 1st project may require prepayment. Will file/record documents for clients.

Lester E Howard

Rte. 3, Box 245, Bridgeport, WV 26330
Phone: 304-669-1447 cell; 304-592-2190 ofc
Types of Records Retrieved: Criminal, Civil and Probate courts; Federal courts; Real Estate; Tax Liens/Judgments; UCC records; Vital records
Local Retrieval Area: WV-Barbour, Doddridge, Harrison, Lewis, Marion, Taylor. **Correspondent Relationships:** statewide WV.
Add'l Information: Established 1980. Normal turnaround time- 12-48 hours. Projects billed by number of names searched. Negotiable; billing will depend on the types of records searched, volume, etc. First project may require prepayment. Based out of Harrison County, he offers 25+ years of investigative and retrieval experience and in all types of records. For add'l fee, he will visit any West Virginia county. A licensed PI in WV.

HR Plus

2902 Evergreen Pky #100, Evergreen, CO 80439
Phone: 800-332-7587; 303-670-8177 - **Fax:** 303-670-8906
www.hrplus.com **email:** information@hrplus.com
Types of Records Retrieved: Criminal courts
Local Retrieval Area: CO-Denver, Larimer. **Correspondents:** nationwide.
Add'l Information: Established 1989. Normal turnaround time- 1-2 days. Expedited service available. Projects billed by number of names searched. Projects are billed monthly, net 10 days. They specialize in criminal record retrieval.

Hubbard-Kavanaugh Title Co

106 S Fisher, Versailles, MO 65084
Phone: 573-378-4411 - **Fax:** 573-378-6385
Types of Records Retrieved: Civil and Probate courts; Real Estate; Tax Liens/Judgments; UCC records; Vital records
Local Retrieval Area: MO-Morgan
Add'l Information: Normal turnaround time- 24 hours. Projects billed by number of records located. Will file/record documents for clients. They specialize in land titles, only complete set of records outside of the county courthouse. Have been in business for over 125 years.

Huddleston & Huddleston Law Firm

PO Box 807, 307 W Main St, Warsaw, KY 41095
Phone: 859-567-2818 **Fax:** 859-567-2404
Types of Records Retrieved: Real Estate; Tax Liens/Judgments; Probate courts; UCC records
Local Retrieval Area: KY-Gallatin
Add'l Information: Established 1980. Normal turnaround time- 2-3 days. Projects billed by the hour. Will file/record documents for clients. He is the prosecuting attorney for the county.

Huffman Research

27520 E 15th St, Hayward, CA 94544
Phone: 510-537-4261 - **Fax:** 510-217-3615 huffmanresearch@prodigy.net
Types of Records Retrieved: Criminal and Civil courts
Local Retrieval Area: CA-Alameda
Add'l Information: Established 1995. Normal turnaround time- 24-48 hours. Projects billed by number of names searched. Payment terms are net 30 days. First project may require prepayment. They bill monthly. They specialize in prompt, efficient and thorough service at competitive prices. Volume rate discounts are available.

Hughes Legal Support

7 Eva Ln, Cranston, RI 02921
Phone: 800-783-7690; 401-944-8980 - **Fax:** 401-944-3314
www.rhodeislandprocess.com **email:** hughes_legal_support@usa.net

Types of Records Retrieved: Criminal, Civil and Probate courts; Federal courts; Real Estate; Tax Liens/Judgments; UCC records

Local Retrieval Area: RI-Bristol, Kent, Newport, Providence, Washington. **Correspondent Relationships:** nationwide.

Add'l Information: Established 1982. Normal turnaround time- 1 business day. Projects billed by the hour. First project may require prepayment. Will file/record documents for clients. They are a RI company providing litigation support and document retrieval to the RI community since 1982 Performs service of process.

Human Arts Consulting

6420 Escondido Dr #4C, El Paso, TX 79912
Phone: 800-493-2641; 915-751-1532 - **Fax:** 915-751-1578
humanarts@aol.com

Types of Records Retrieved: Criminal and Civil courts; Federal courts

Local Retrieval Area: TX-El Paso. **Correspondent Relationships:** nationwide and Canada.

Add'l Information: Established 1995. Normal turnaround time- 24-36 hours. Projects billed by number of names searched. Net 20 days. First project may require prepayment. They specialize in training in human resources management issues (e.g. sexual harassment prevention, management leadership, documenting employee behavior, team building). Also write policies & company handbooks for employees. SSN Verification & Skiptrace.

Bill Hundemer

12326 Buttermilk Rd, Knoxville, TN 37932
Phone: 865-670-1740, 670-604-6031 - **Fax:** 865-690-7735

Types of Records Retrieved: Criminal, Civil and Probate courts; Federal courts; Real Estate; Tax Liens/Judgments; UCC records

Local Retrieval Area: TN-Anderson, Blount, Cumberland, Knox, Loudon, McMinn, Monroe, Morgan, Polk, Putnam, Roane, Sevier

Add'l Information: Established 2001. Normal turnaround time- 24-28 hours. Projects billed by number of names searched. First project may require prepayment. He specializes in Knoxville and the counties west and southwest of Knoxville.

Hunter & Oelke

PO Box 792, Dalhart, TX 79022
Phone: 800-350-1288; 806-244-5632 - **Fax:** 806-244-2863
hunterok@xit.net

Types of Records Retrieved: Civil and Probate courts; Real Estate; Tax Liens/Judgments

Local Area: TX-Dallam, Hartley. **Correspondent Relationships:** Texas.

Add'l Information: Established 1977. Normal turnaround time- 3-4 days. Projects billed by the hour. First project may require prepayment. They specialize in Real Estate Law. They are a general practice law office. They will also file/record UCC documents on behalf of clients on a same or next day basis, and specialize in estate work.

Huron Shores Abstract & Title

206 S 3rd Street, Rogers City, MI 49779
Phone: 989-734-3344 - **Fax:** 989-734-4920

Types of Records Retrieved: Real Estate; Tax Liens/Judgments; Probate courts; UCC records

Local Retrieval Area: MI-Alpena, Presque Isle. **Correspondent Relationships:** Cheboygan and Montmorency counties MI.

Add'l Information: Established 1990. Normal turnaround time- 4 days. Fee basis will vary by the type of project. Will file/record documents for clients. Terms: net 30 days. They specialize in title insurance, oil, gas and mineral research.

Huron Title Co

PO Box 563, Huron, SD 57350
Phone: 605-352-6157 - **Fax:** 605-352-7354

Types of Records Retrieved: Civil and Probate courts; Real Estate; Tax Liens/Judgments; UCC records

Local Retrieval Area: SD-Beadle

Add'l Information: Established 1949. Normal turnaround time- 5-10 days. Fee basis will vary by the type of project. Will file/record documents for clients. Payment due upon completion of order. They specialize in land title searches.

Huron Title Co (Michigan)

330 Michigan St, Port Huron, MI 48060
Phone: 800-878-4853; 810-987-2141 - **Fax:** 810-987-1317
www.hurontitle.com **Types of Records Retrieved:** Civil and Probate courts; Real Estate; Tax Liens/Judgments; UCC records

Local Retrieval Area: MI-St. Clair

Add'l Information: Established 1970. Normal turnaround time- 5 days. Fee basis will vary by type of project. First project may require prepayment. Will file/record documents for clients. They specialize in real estate and title insurance.

Hylind Search Company Inc (Delaware)

304 S State St, Dover, DE 19901-6730
Phone: 888-243-6857; 302-744-9023 - **Fax:** 888-243-6859; 302-744-9025
www.hylindsearch.com **email:** hylindde@concentric.net

Types of Records Retrieved: Criminal, Civil and Probate courts; Federal courts; Real Estate; Tax Liens/Judgments; UCC records; Vital records

Local Retrieval Area: DE-Kent, New Castle, Sussex. **Correspondent Relationships:** nationwide.

Add'l Information: Established 2000. Normal turnaround time- 24-48 hours. Expedited service available. Projects billed by number of names searched. Will file/record documents for clients. Invoicing available. They are a national search & filing service that specializes in searching, filing & document retrieval of corporate, UCC, real estate & resident agent services. They are online agents for the State of DE & can perform same day searches & filings. Performs service of process.

Hylind Search Company Inc (Maryland)

245 W Chase St, Baltimore, MD 21201-4823
Phone: 888-449-5463; 410-468-3333 - **Fax:** 888-597-7377; 410-468-0808
www.hylindsearch.com **email:** info@hylindsearch.com

Types of Records Retrieved: Criminal, Civil and Probate courts; Federal courts; Real Estate; Tax Liens/Judgments; UCC records; Vital records

Local Retrieval Area: DC-Washington; MD-Allegany, Anne Arundel, Baltimore, Baltimore City, Calvert, Caroline, Carroll, Cecil, Charles, Dorchester, Frederick, Garrett, Harford, Howard, Kent, Montgomery, Prince George's, St Mary's, Talbot, Washington, Wicomico, Worcester; VA-Fairfax. **Correspondent Relationships:** nationwide.

Add'l Information: Established 1996. Normal turnaround time- 48 hours or less. Projects billed by number of names searched. Fees are per index searched. Credit cards accepted. Will file/record documents for clients. Terms: net 30 days. They tailor their asset/lien searches to the client's needs. They offer competitive pricing & volume discounts. Online ordering & expedited services are available. They have a location in Dover, DE as well. They have a quick turnaround & reasonable fees. Performs service of process.

I L Research

3089 N Main St, Milan, TN 38358
Phone: 731-686-0526 - **Fax:** 731-723-0055
Types of Records Retrieved: Criminal and Civil courts
Local Retrieval Area: TN-Gibson, Madison
Add'l Information: Established 1994. Normal turnaround time- 24-48 hours. Projects billed by number of names searched. First project may require prepayment. She will search both courts in Gibson County.

ICDI Inc

460 W Central Pkwy, Altamont Springs, FL 32714-2415
Phone: 407-622-2532 - **Fax:** 407-622-2535 icdi@cfl.rr.com
Types of Records Retrieved: Civil and Probate courts; Federal courts; Real Estate; Tax Liens/Judgments; UCC records
Local Retrieval Area: FL-Brevard, Orange, Osceola, Seminole, Volusia. **Correspondent Relationships:** Lake County FL.
Add'l Information: Established 1992. Normal turnaround time- 24-48 hours. Projects billed by number of names searched. First project may require prepayment. Will file/record documents for clients. Payment due on receipt. They specialize in several counties online, and to counties physically in courthouse records.

ICORP Services & Solutions

710 S 11th St #2B, Philadelphia, PA 19147-1971
Phone: 888-512-8257; 215-922-2851 - **Fax:** 267-200-0885
www.icorpss.com **email:** walt@buckslegal.com
Types of Records Retrieved: Criminal, Civil and Probate courts; Federal courts; Real Estate; Tax Liens/Judgments; UCC records; Vital records
Local Retrieval Area: PA-Bucks, Delaware, Montgomery, Philadelphia. **Correspondent Relationships:** New Jersey.
Add'l Information: Established 1998. Normal turnaround time- 24-48 hours. Projects billed by number of names searched. Monthly or individual search billing available. First project may require prepayment. Credit cards accepted. Will file/record documents for clients. Please call before sending orders. Formerly Bucks Legal Svcs, they retrieve records in NJ or southeast PA. Documents can be copied or scanned; returns faxed, mailed or emailed. Also searches the NARA and Philadelphia federal courts. Performs service of process.

Idaho Title & Trust Co

260 W Grand, PO Box 802, Arco, ID 83213
Phone: 208-527-8517 - **Fax:** 208-527-3930 ittarco@atcnet.net
Types of Records Retrieved: Civil and Probate courts; Real Estate; Tax Liens/Judgments; UCC records
Local Retrieval Area: ID-Butte
Add'l Information: Established 1987. Normal turnaround time- 48 hours. Fees vary by project. Only title company in Butte County, ID. They have been there since 1920. Performs service of process.

Idealogic

20 Eglinton Ave W #1300, Toronto, Ontario, Canada, CAN M4R 1K8
Phone: 866-506-9900; 416-506-9900 - **Fax:** 866-506-0700; 416-506-0700
www.idealogic.com **email:** ideal@idealogic.com
Types of Records Retrieved: Civil courts; Bankruptcy court; Real Estate; Tax Liens/Judgments; UCC records; Vital records
Local Retrieval Area: CANADA-Ontario, Canada. **Correspondent Relationships:** provinces in Canada.
Add'l Information: Established 1980. Normal turnaround time- same or next day. Projects billed by number of names searched. Projects billed by the hour. First project may require prepayment. Credit cards accepted. Will file/record documents for clients. They specialize in Canadian corporate information, civil and bankruptcy courts, motor vehicle, real estate, PPSA and trademark work for all provinces. Member and director of NPRRA. Performs service of process.

IGB Associates Inc

1181 Shipwatch Circle, Tampa, FL 33602
Phone: 813-226-8810 - **Fax:** 813-226-8710
Igrantbu@aol.com
Types of Records Retrieved: Civil courts; Federal courts; Real Estate; Tax Liens/Judgments; UCC records
Local Retrieval Area: FL-Broward, Dade, Duval, Hillsborough, Manatee, Orange, Pasco, Pinellas, Polk, Sarasota. **Correspondents:** nationwide.
Add'l Information: Established 1993. Normal turnaround time- 24-48 hours. Projects billed by number of names searched. First project may require prepayment. Will file/record documents for clients. Terms: net 10 days. They specialize in current owner & title searches (abstracting), bankruptcy, US Federal courts, county courts, and property searches. They can acquire Social Security, address verification and address changes. They carry E & O Insurance.

Karl Iggers

PO Box 1001, Buffalo, NY 14205
Phone: 716-812-2587 aa262@ustrackers.com
Types of Records Retrieved: Real Estate; Tax Liens/Judgments; UCC records; Vital records
Local Retrieval Area: NY-Erie, Monroe, Niagara
Add'l Information: Established 1999. Normal turnaround time- 72 hours. Projects billed by the hour. First project may require prepayment.

Ike L Hoy PE (Control Systems)

10640 S Forestline Ave, Inverness, FL 34452-9260
Phone: 850-259-4650 captcasino@aol.com
Types of Records Retrieved: Criminal, Civil and Probate courts; Federal courts; Real Estate; Tax Liens/Judgments; UCC records; Vital records
Local Retrieval Area: AL-Baldwin, Covington, Escambia, Geneva, Mobile; FL-Bay, Holmes, Okaloosa, Santa Rosa, Walton, Washington. **Correspondent Relationships:** statewide.
Add'l Information: Established 1975. Normal turnaround time- 24-72 hours. If order is received in AM, will send in PM. Projects billed by number of names searched. Projects billed by number of records located. First project may require prepayment. Credit cards accepted. He is a registered professional engineer. He has 25 years in research and development and is a Florida notary public.

Iles & Bond Inc

210 W Clinton Ave, Oaklyn, NJ 08107
Phone: 856-854-9580 - **Fax:** 856-854-9582 ilesandbond@comcast.net
Types of Records Retrieved: Criminal courts; Real Estate; UCC records
Local Retrieval Area: PA-Philadelphia
Add'l Information: Established 2000. Normal turnaround time- 4-6 hours. Fees negotiated with volume. Will file/record documents for clients. They also offer records from the Department of Records. They have a 22-year library of county Dept. of Records data in-house on microfilm.

ILS Research Inc

1512 N Church St, Route 309, Hazleton, PA 18202
Phone: 570-454-3535 - **Fax:** 570-454-5436 ilsresearch@epix.net
Types of Records Retrieved: Criminal, Civil and Probate courts; Federal courts; Real Estate; Tax Liens/Judgments; UCC records; Vital records
Local Retrieval Area: PA-Armstrong, Beaver, Bedford, Butler, Cambria, Cameron, Carbon, Clarion, Columbia, Crawford, Cumberland, Elk, Fayette, Forest, Greene, Indiana, Jefferson, Lackawanna, Lawrence, Luzerne, McKean, Schuylkill, Venango, Warren, Westmoreland. **Correspondent Relationships:** PA, DE, NJ.
Add'l Information: Established 1988. Normal turnaround time- 24-48 hours. Projects billed by number of names searched. Billing with each job completed. First project may require prepayment. Will file/record documents for clients. Net 30 days. They specialize in criminal & civil

background searches, real estate closings, current owner searches & document retrieval of estates, bankruptcies, UCCs, deeds & mortgages. Performs service of process.

In Search of Inc

247 Wayne Ave, Cliffside, NJ 07010
Phone: 201-224-3063 - **Fax:** 201-224-0761 iso.search@verizon.net
Types of Records Retrieved: Criminal, Civil and Probate courts; Federal courts; Real Estate; Tax Liens/Judgments; UCC records; Vital records
Local Retrieval Area: NJ-Bergen, Essex, Hudson, Passaic, Union
Add'l Information: Established 1992. Normal turnaround time- 24-48 hours. Projects billed by number of names searched. Will file/record documents for clients. Terms are net 30 days. They specialize in fast reliable and cost-effective public information, retrieval and filing.

Incognito Services

234 Marshall St, Upstairs #3, Redwood City, CA 94063-1550
Phone: 650-363-9100 - **Fax:** 650-363-9200
www.incognitoservices.com **Types of Records Retrieved:** Criminal and Civil courts; Real Estate
Local Retrieval Area: CA-San Mateo. **Correspondent Relationships:** California; the West Coast;, International.
Add'l Information: Established 1980. Normal turnaround time- 48 hours. Expedited service available. Projects billed by the hour. They add mileage and copy costs. First project may require prepayment. Credit cards accepted. Will file/record documents for clients. They specialize in investigations, electronic countermeasures equipment and service, including covert video equipment, and installations. They also offer surety+bail, bail bond, notary public services and bail fugitive recovery services. A licensed PI in CA. Performs service of process.

Incorporating Services Ltd

3500 S DuPont Hwy, Dover, DE 19901
Phone: 800-346-4646; 302-531-0855 - **Fax:** 302-531-3150
www.incserv.com **email:** admin@incserv.com
Types of Records Retrieved: Civil courts; Federal courts; Real Estate; Tax Liens/Judgments; UCC records; Vital records
Local Retrieval Area: DE-Kent, New Castle, Sussex. **Correspondent Relationships:** nationwide and Canada.
Add'l Information: Established 1972. Normal turnaround time- 1-2 working days. Projects billed by number of names searched. Projects billed by number of records located. First project may require prepayment. Credit cards accepted. Will file/record documents for clients. Certified checks, money orders or cash are accepted. Providing blue ribbon service for over 31 years, specializing in registered agent services, corporate and UCC searches, retrievals and filings. Located in Dover, DE and providing nationwide services.

Independence County Abstract Co

150 S Broad St, Batesville, AR 72501
Phone: 870-793-3333 - **Fax:** 870-793-3343
independence@cox-Internet.com
Types of Records Retrieved: Real Estate; Tax Liens/Judgments; Probate courts; UCC records
Local Retrieval Area: AR-Independence
Add'l Info: Established 1950. Turnaround time- 5-10 days. Expedited service available. Projects billed by the hour. A minimum charge also applies. Will file/record documents for clients. They specialize in real estate.

Independent Abstract & Title

600 Whitehead St #204, Key West, FL 33040
Phone: 305-294-5105 - **Fax:** 305-294-5354 intitle@bellsouth.net
Types of Records Retrieved: Criminal, Civil and Probate courts; Real Estate; Tax Liens/Judgments; UCC records
Local Retrieval Area: FL-Monroe
Add'l Information: Established 1984. Normal turnaround time- 48 hours. They charge a flat rate per project. First project may require prepayment. Will file/record documents for clients. They specialize in title insurance. In a county which is only partly computerized, Independent Abstract & Title fills the niche for accurate and fast searches. They are located adjacent to Monroe County Courthouse & have been in business since 1984.

Independent Abstracting Service Inc

299 Coon Rapids Blvd NW #212, Coon Rapids, MN 55433-5870
Phone: 763-792-6800 - **Fax:** 763-792-6820
www.independentabstracting.com
email: holly@independentabstracting.com
Types of Records Retrieved: Real Estate; Tax Liens/Judgments; Probate courts; UCC records; Vital records
Local Retrieval Area: MN-Anoka, Carver, Chisago, Dakota, Hennepin, Isanti, Ramsey, Scott, Sherburne, Washington, Wright. **Correspondent Relationships:** St. Louis County.
Add'l Information: Established 1986. Normal turnaround time- 3-5 days. Fee basis will vary by type of project. First project may require prepayment. They are a real estate services company providing document retrieval, ownership & encumbrance reports, lien reports, chain of title, abstract updates and title insurance.

Independent Research Assoc

PO Box 677988, 359 Portstewart Dr, 32828, Orlando, FL 32867-7988
Phone: 407-832-8580 - **Fax:** 407-823-8939 SLLina2@gmail.com
Types of Records Retrieved: Civil and Probate courts; Federal courts; Real Estate; Tax Liens/Judgments; UCC records
Local Retrieval Area: FL-Brevard, Orange, Osceola, Seminole, Volusia
Add'l Information: Established 1979. Normal turnaround time- 24 hours. Projects billed by number of names searched. Will file/record documents for clients. They specialize in rapid return of official records - UCCs, tax liens, etc.

Independent Research Inc

2963 Wyndwicke Dr, St Joseph, MI 49085
Phone: 269-429-9873 - **Fax:** 269-429-5693
independent@sbcglobal.net
Types of Records Retrieved: Criminal and Civil courts
Local Retrieval Area: MI-Berrien, Genesee, Ingham, Kalamazoo, Kent, Macomb, Oakland, Saginaw, Washtenaw, Wayne. **Correspondent Relationships:** criminal/civil all counties in MI.
Add'l Information: Established 1990. Normal turnaround time- 1-2 days. Expedited service available. Projects billed by number of names searched. Projects billed by number of records located. First project may require prepayment. Credit accounts are payable net 30 days. They specialize in criminal searches in Michigan and numerous other states.

Independent Research LLC

12649 W Warren Ave, Lakewood, CO 80228
Phone: 303-969-8608 - **Fax:** 303-969-9363
www.independentresearchofcolorado.com
email: searchcolorado@netscape.net
Types of Records Retrieved: Criminal, Civil and Probate courts; Federal courts; Real Estate; Tax Liens/Judgments; UCC records; Vital records
Local Retrieval Area: CO-all counties. **Correspondent Relationships:** statewide.
Add'l Information: Established 1982. Normal turnaround time- 24 hours. Projects billed by number of names searched. First project may require prepayment. Will file/record documents for clients. Terms: net 30-60 days. They offer discounts for multiple/similar names searched. They also provide E & O searches in all Colorado counties. They are online with Sec of State Statewide database for all UCCs - same day results with copies. Can order via Internet or website.

Indepth Profiles Inc

PO Box 55713, Tulsa, OK 74155
Phone: 800-364-8319; 918-610-0192 - **Fax:** 800-416-9504; 918-610-1183
www.indepthprofiles.com **email:** sales@indepthprofiles.com
Types of Records Retrieved: Criminal and Civil courts; Federal courts
Local Retrieval Area: OK-Tulsa. **Correspondent Relationships:** nationwide, Canada and other countries.

Add'l Information: Established 1985. Normal turnaround time- 24-72 hours. Projects are billed by the number of searches. Credit cards accepted. They specialize in all phases of pre-employment screening, background investigations and criminal record retrieval nationwide.

Infiniti Title Agency Inc

33 E Main St #2, Moorestown, NJ 08057
Phone: 856-727-0818 - **Fax:** 856-727-5173
www.infinitytitle.com **email:** jgreene@infinitytitle.com

Types of Records Retrieved: Real Estate; Tax Liens/Judgments

Local Retrieval Area: NJ-Burlington. **Correspondent Relationships:** New Jersey, Eastern Pennsylvania.

Add'l Information: Established 1942. Normal turnaround time- 24 hours. Fee basis will vary by the type of project. Will file/record documents for clients. Formerly known as Burlington County Abstract, they specialize in real estate records throughout New Jersey; now also in eastern PA.

Info Quest Inc

812 S Poplar Dr, Surfside Business Ctr, #8, Surfside Beach, SC 29587
Phone: 800-507-9628; 843-233-9675 - **Fax:** 800-588-1152; 843-233-9676
www.in-foquest.com/ **email:** Billstanton@sc.rr.com

Types of Records Retrieved: Criminal courts

Local Retrieval Area: SC-Horry. **Correspondent Relationships:** nationwide.

Add'l Information: Established 1995. Normal turnaround time- 24-72 hours. Projects billed by number of names searched. Projects billed by number of records located. First project may require prepayment. Credit cards accepted. They specialize in criminal records retrieval, pre-employment background checks, rental background checks and credit reports. They conduct nationwide pre-employment screening.

Info Search Inc

PO Box 40221, Indianapolis, IN 46240
Phone: 317-251-6290 - **Fax:** 317-251-1755 info-search@prodigy.net

Types of Records Retrieved: Criminal, Civil and Probate courts; Federal courts; Real Estate; Tax Liens/Judgments; UCC records; Vital records

Local Retrieval Area: IN-Hamilton, Hendricks, Marion

Add'l Information: Established 1996. Normal turnaround time- 24 hours (criminal); 24-36 (other). Projects billed by number of names searched. First project may require prepayment. Will file/record documents for clients. Invoice net 30 days. They specialize in criminal, civil and bankruptcy court searches.

Info2go

5305 Grand Mesa Dr, Fort Worth, TX 76137
Phone: 817-656-1997 - **Fax:** 817-656-3099
www.debsinfo2go.us **email:** deb@debsinfo2go.us

Types of Records Retrieved: Criminal, Civil and Probate courts; Federal courts; Real Estate; Tax Liens/Judgments; UCC records; Vital records

Local Retrieval Area: TX-Dallas, Denton, Tarrant, Wise

Add'l Information: Established 2003. Normal turnaround time- 24 hours, Tarrant; 48 hours for other counties. Projects billed by number of names searched. First project may require prepayment. Will accept PayPal. Info2go retrieves public records in the DFW area and manually searches newspapers and archives, including the Federal Records Center and NARA Fort Worth.

InfoCorp Investigative Services LLC

PO Box 120, Lewis Center, OH 43035
Phone: 866-657-8003; 614-785-1669 - **Fax:** 614-340-7179
www.infocorponline.com **email:** infocorpllc@aol.com

Types of Records Retrieved: Criminal, Civil and Probate courts; Federal courts; Tax Liens/Judgments; UCC records; Vital records

Local Retrieval Area: OH-Delaware, Franklin. **Correspondent Relationships:** statewide.

Add'l Information: Established 2002. Normal turnaround time- 48-72 hours. Expedited service available. Projects billed by number of names searched. Credit cards accepted. Will invoice. They offer pre-employment screening, fingerprinting (manual & web check prints), public record research & retrieval, process svc, professional license, education verification, private investigation, surveillance, locates, notary assignments & field calls. A licensed PI in OH. Performs service of process.

InfoFax

PO Box 2, 1161 Hollis St, Halifax, Nova Scotia, CN B2J 2L4
Phone: 902-425-4444 - **Fax:** 888-878-7772; 902-429-9990
www.infofax.ca **email:** infofax@hfx.earthlink.ca

Types of Records Retrieved: Criminal and Civil courts; Real Estate; Tax Liens/Judgments

Local Retrieval Area: Canada-New Brunswick, Newfoundland, Nova Scotia, Prince Edward Island

Add'l Information: Established 1995. Normal turnaround time- 24-48 hours. Billing methods depends on nature of request. First project may require prepayment. They provide expert public record search services in the Maritime Provinces.

Infoline Inc

1012 14th St NW #900, Washington, DC 20005
Phone: 888-284-4581; 202-783-3538 - **Fax:** 877-404-2262; 202-393-0933
www.infolineinc.com **email:** requests@infolineinc.com

Types of Records Retrieved: Criminal, Civil and Probate courts; Federal courts; Real Estate; Tax Liens/Judgments; UCC records; Vital records

Local Retrieval Area: DC-District of Columbia; MD-Anna Arundel, Baltimore, Baltimore City, Calvert, Charles, Frederick, Howard, Montgomery, Prince George's; VA-Alexandria City, Arlington, Fairfax, Loudoun, Prince William. **Correspondent Relationships:** nationwide.

Add'l Information: Established 1989. Normal turnaround time- same day or by requested deadline. Credit cards accepted. Will file/record documents for clients. Visa and MasterCard accepted. Infoline Inc specializes in research and retrieval from federal, state and bankruptcy courts as well as Capitol Hill and federal/state agencies. Case monitoring available. They provide real & personal property abstracting svcs throughout MD, VA, DC.

Infomax

PO Box 15744, Rio Rancho, NM 87174
Phone: 505-994-0370 - **Fax:** 505-994-0338
www.infomaxnm.com **email:** submit@infomaxnm.com

Types of Records Retrieved: Criminal, Civil and Probate courts; Federal courts; Real Estate; Tax Liens/Judgments; UCC records; Vital records

Local Retrieval Area: NM-Bernalillo, Chaves, Cibola, Colfax, Curry, DeBaca, Dona Ana, Eddy, Grant, Guadalupe, Hidalgo, Lea, Lincoln, Los Alamos, Luna, McKinley, Otero, Quay, Rio Arriba, Roosevelt, San Juan, San Miguel, Sandoval, Santa Fe, Sierra, Socorro, Taos, Torrance, Union, Valencia. **Correspondent Relationships:** New Mexico and nationwide.

Add'l Information: Established 1988. Normal turnaround time- 12-48 hours. Projects billed by number of names searched. First project may require prepayment. Will file/record documents for clients. They specialize in lien and asset searches, background investigations, pre-employment screening and real property abstracting. A licensed PI in NM.

InfoNation Inc - Virginia

9910 Broadview Dr, Fairfax, VA 22030-2007
Phone: 888-346-9090; 703-278-9090 - **Fax:** 703-278-9184
www.infonationinc.com **email:** info4usa@aol.com

Types of Records Retrieved: Criminal, Civil and Probate courts; Federal courts; Real Estate; Tax Liens/Judgments; UCC records

Local Retrieval Area: VA-Alexandria City, Arlington, Fairfax, Fauquier, Loudoun, Prince William. **Correspondent Relationships:** nationwide.

Add'l Information: Established 1997. Normal turnaround time- 24-48 hours. Projects billed by the hour. Credit cards accepted. Will file/record documents for clients. They specialize in skiptracing, asset location, courthouse research, real estate and pre-employment checks. Performs service of process.

Infopoint Research

2815 Derek Dr #111, Lake Charles, LA 70607
Phone: 888-457-0501, 409-729-1944 - **Fax:** 409-729-1179
www.infopointresearch.com **email:** support@infopointresearch.com

Types of Records Retrieved: Criminal courts

Local Retrieval Area: LA-Calcasieu; TX-Hardin, Jefferson, Orange. **Correspondent Relationships:** TX, LA, OK, MS, AR.

Add'l Information: Established 2001. Normal turnaround time- 24-48 hours. Projects billed by number of names searched. Credit cards accepted. Does monthly invoicing. Infopoint specializes in criminal record research at wholesale prices. To view pricing and coverage, please visit website.

InfoRetrieval Services

PO Box 268, Georgetown, DE 19947
Phone: 302-337-0548 - **Fax:** 302-337-8730
www.inforetrieval.net **email:** info@inforetrieval.net

Types of Records Retrieved: Criminal and Civil courts; Federal courts

Local Retrieval Area: DE-Kent, New Castle, Sussex. **Correspondent Relationships:** MD, PA, NJ.

Add'l Information: Established 1993. Normal turnaround time- 24 hours. Projects billed by number of names searched. Fees vary by depth of search requested (standard search vs. pull and read entire file). Credit cards accepted. Jobs billed at month's end. Since 1993, specializing in service of process and complete in-depth criminal searches for attorneys/investigators with subject report/ copies of relevant sections of records. All names hand searched by owner. A licensed PI in DE. Performs service of process.

Information Inc

PO Box 382, Hermitage, TN 37076
Phone: 615-884-8000 - **Fax:** 615-889-6492
http://hometown.aol.com/publicrecordstn **email:** InfomanTN@aol.com

Types of Records Retrieved: Criminal and Civil courts; Federal District court; Vital records; Tax Liens/Judgments

Local Retrieval Area: TN-Davidson

Add'l Information: Established 1991. Normal turnaround time- 2 hours - 72 hours. Expedited service available. Projects billed by number of names searched. First project may require prepayment. They operate a criminal database available online containing criminal history to 01/01/87. For a free demonstration, just call us. Will not be undersold!

Information Management Systems Inc

PO Box 2924, 114 W Main St #202, New Britain, CT 06050
Phone: 888-403-8347; 860-229-1119 - **Fax:** 888-403-8402; 860-225-5524
www.imswebb.com **email:** info@imswebb.com

Types of Records Retrieved: Criminal, Civil and Probate courts; Federal courts; Real Estate; Tax Liens/Judgments; UCC records; Vital records

Local Retrieval Area: CT-Fairfield, Hartford, Litchfield, Middlesex, New Haven, New London, Tolland, Windham. **Correspondent Relationships:** Domestic and International.

Add'l Information: Established 1989. Normal turnaround time- same day. Projects billed by number of names searched. Fees vary by project volume. Credit cards accepted. Will file/record documents for clients. They specialize in public and business record retrieval and asset locates. They also provide nationwide background investigation, MVRs and due diligence services; criminal/civil records and more. Document retrieval and delivery. Performs service of process.

Information Network Associates Inc

5235 N Front St, Harrisburg, PA 17110-1717
Phone: 800-443-0824; 717-599-5505 - **Fax:** 717-599-5507
www.ina-inc.com **email:** records@ina-inc.com

Types of Records Retrieved: Criminal, Civil and Probate courts; Federal courts; Real Estate; Tax Liens/Judgments; UCC records; Vital records

Local Retrieval Area: PA-Cumberland, Dauphin, Lebanon, York. **Correspondent Relationships:** nationwide.

Add'l Information: Established 1986. Normal turnaround time- 24-48 hours. Projects billed by number of records located. Credit cards accepted. Will file/record documents for clients. Payment due upon receipt of invoice. They specialize in asset searches, state level searches and employment screening/background investigations. A licensed PI in PA. Performs service of process.

Information Protective Services Inc (IPS)

PO Box 800383, Houston, TX 77280
Phone: 888-720-3784; 713-460-8884 - **Fax:** 713-460-9399
crnix@houston.rr.com

Types of Records Retrieved: Criminal and Civil courts

Local Retrieval Area: TX-Fort Bend, Harris, Jim Wells, Kleberg. **Correspondent Relationships:** nationwide, especially in Texas.

Add'l Info: Established 1995. Turnaround time- 24-48 hours. Projects billed by number of names searched. Terms: net 30 days, with approved credit. They specialize in pre-employment screening and third party administrator for drug testing on a nationwide level. A licensed PI in TX.

Information Reporting Services Inc

2101 Hennepin Ave #201, Minneapolis, MN 55405
Phone: 612-870-8770 - **Fax:** 612-870-8765
www.inforeport.com **email:** dahl@inforeport.com

Types of Records Retrieved: Criminal, Civil and Probate courts; Federal courts; Tax Liens/Judgments

Local Retrieval Area: MN-Anoka, Blue Earth, Carver, Dakota, Goodhue, Hennepin, Olmsted, Ramsey, Scott, Washington, Winona, Wright. **Correspondent Relationships:** nationwide.

Add'l Information: Established 1989. Normal turnaround time- 24-48 hours. Projects billed by number of names searched. Monthly billing available. They specialize in background screening for corporations. Search capabilities include entire State of MN. Their searches are hands-on. Their results are typed, reviewed and returned to you the same day. A licensed PI in MN, WI.

Information Retrieval Services

15220 OK Mill Rd, Snohomish, WA 98290-4504
Phone: 800-769-3051; 425-334-2052 - **Fax:** 425-397-6519
inforetrieval@comcast.net

Types of Records Retrieved: Criminal, Civil and Probate courts; Real Estate; Tax Liens/Judgments; UCC records

Retrieval Area: WA-Benton, Franklin, King, Skagit, Snohomish, Yakima

Add'l Information: Established 1992. Normal turnaround time- 24 hours. Will file/record documents for clients. Monthly billing statements. They have over 25 years experience in local courts. They are a small company with the ability to focus on your individual needs. Cell # 425-238-4622.

Information Search Inc

PO Box 33657, Palm Beach Gardens, FL 33420-3657
Phone: 561-624-5115 - **Fax:** 561-694-8281
www.infohotline.com **email:** info@infohotline.com

Types of Records Retrieved: Criminal, Civil and Probate courts; Federal courts; Real Estate; Tax Liens/Judgments; UCC records; Vital records

Local Retrieval Area: FL-Martin, Palm Beach, St. Lucie. **Correspondent Relationships:** Florida and nationwide.

Add'l Information: Established 1995. Normal turnaround time- 3 days. Call for expedited service. Call for pricing options. First project may require prepayment. Will file/record documents for clients. Call for details. May negotiate for larger contracts. They source, discover, verify or retrieve critical information for clients in the solution of their business problems in addition to public records retrieval. Filing of documents requires prepayment. PI in FL. A licensed PI in FL.

Information Searches Inc

11809 S 104th E Ave, Bixby, OK 74008
Phone: 918-369-8126 - **Fax:** 918-369-8127
isiok_inc@yahoo.com

Types of Records Retrieved: Criminal and Civil courts; Federal courts

Local Retrieval Area: OK-Adair, Atoka, Carter, Creek, Grady, Mayes, McIntosh, Muskogee, Nowata, Okmulgee, Osage, Rogers, Tulsa, Washington. **Correspondent Relationships:** statewide.

Add'l Information: Established 1998. Normal turnaround time- 24-72 hours. Projects billed by number of names searched. They will invoice. They do felony, misdemeanor, civil, motor vehicle, workman's comp and bankruptcy checks for future employers and real estate companies.

Information Services (Colorado)

PO Box 2085, Durango, CO 81302
Phone: 970-385-4897 - **Fax:** 970-259-9454
www.frontier.net/~dkgis/ **email:** dkgis@frontier.net

Types of Records Retrieved: Real Estate; Tax Liens/Judgments; UCC records; Vital records

Local Retrieval Area: CO-La Plata, Mesa

Add'l Information: Established 1995. Normal turnaround time- 24 hours. Projects billed by the hour. First project may require prepayment. Will file/record documents for clients.

Infotrack Information Services Inc

111 Deerlake Rd #105, Deerfield, IL 60015-4986
Phone: 800-275-5594; 847-444-1177 - **Fax:** 800-275-5595; 847-444-1166
www.infotrackinc.com **email:** skaplan@infotrackinc.com

Types of Records Retrieved: Criminal and Civil courts; Federal courts; Real Estate; Tax Liens/Judgments; UCC records

Local Retrieval Area: AZ-Maricopa, Pima, Pinal; FL-Broward, Charlotte, Collier, Duval, Escambia, Hillsborough, Indian River, Lake, Lee, Leon, Manatee, Dade, Nassau, Okaloosa, Orange, Osceola, Palm Beach, Pasco, Pinellas, Polk, Sarasota, Volusia, Walton; IL-Adams, Bond, Boone, Brown, Bureau, Calhoun, Carroll, Cass, Champaign, Christian, Clinton, Coles, Cook, Cumberland, De Kalb, De Witt, Douglas, Du Page, Edgar, Effingham, Fayette, Ford, Franklin, Fulton, Greene, Grundy, Hancock, Henderson, Henry, Iroquois, Jackson, Jefferson, Jersey, Jo Daviess, Johnson, Kane, Kankakee, Kendall, Knox, Lake, La Salle, Lee, Livingston, Logan, McDonough, McHenry, McLean, Macon, Macoupin, Madison, Marion, Marshall, Mason, Menard, Mercer, Monroe, Montgomery, Morgan, Moultrie, Ogle, Peoria, Perry, Piatt, Pike, Putnam, Randolph, Rock Island, St. Clair, Sangamon, Schuyler, Scott, Shelby, Stark, Stephenson, Tazewell, Union, Vermilion, Warren, Washington, Whiteside, Will, Williamson, Winnebago, Woodford; IN-Lake, La Porte, Marion, Porter; MO-Lincoln, Franklin, Jefferson, St. Charles, St. Louis County, St. Louis City, Warren; WI-Dane, Dodge, Jefferson, Kenosha, Milwaukee, Ozaukee, Racine, Walworth, Washington, Waukesha. **Correspondent Relations:** nationwide.

Add'l Information: Established 1990. Normal turnaround time- 1-2 days. Projects billed by number of names searched. Credit cards accepted. Will file/record documents for clients. They specialize in pre-employment, tenant screening, title services, investigative, litigation support and wholesale criminal research. A licensed PI in IL.

Infotrackers Inc

800 N Rainbow Blvd #123, Las Vegas, NV 89107
Phone: 702-948-7055 - **Fax:** 702-948-7056
www.infotrackersinc.com **email:** infotrackers@aol.com

Types of Records Retrieved: Criminal, Civil and Probate courts; Federal courts; Real Estate; Tax Liens/Judgments; UCC records

Local Retrieval Area: NV-Clark

Add'l Information: Established 2002. Normal turnaround time- 2-5 hours for information w/o copies, 1-3 days for District Courts; 1 day for Recorders Office (plain copies); 1-3 weeks for certified copies. Projects billed by number of names searched. Projects billed by the hour. First project may require prepayment. Accepts checks by fax or phone. They provide the business community with personal records research, court research and investigative services. All requests are handled with prompt and professional response. A licensed PI in NV.

Innovative Enterprises Inc

12695 McManus Blvd., #4-B, Newport News, VA 23602
Phone: 888-777-9435; 757-875-9500 - **Fax:** 888-777-9436; 757-877-4242
www.knowthefacts.com **email:** info@knowthefacts.com

Types of Records Retrieved: Criminal and Civil courts

Local Retrieval Area: VA-all counties. **Correspondents:** nationwide.

Add'l Information: Established 1996. Normal turnaround time- next business day. Expedited service available. Projects are billed on a per-search basis. First project may require prepayment. Credit cards accepted. Terms are net 30 days. Using their proprietary research database, they provide identifiers for 85% - 90% of the Virginia cases reported by their competitors as "name match only".

INPRO

14870 Granada Ave #323, Apple Valley, MN 55124-5514
Phone: 952-891-3617 - **Fax:** 952-891-3618
www.inprousa.com **email:** inprousa@mac.com

Types of Records Retrieved: Criminal and Civil courts; Federal courts; Tax Liens/Judgments; UCC records; Vital records

Local Retrieval Area: MN-Carver, Dakota, Hennepin, Ramsey, Scott. **Correspondent Relationships:** statewide.

Add'l Information: Established 1994. Normal turnaround time- 24-48 hours. Expedited service available. Projects billed by the hour. Some projects may require prepayment. Terms: net 15 days. PayPal is accepted. They specialize in providing prompt and professional investigative search and retrieval services. A licensed PI in MN, WI. Performs service of process.

Inquest

464 Monterrey Ave, Los Gatos, CA 95030
Phone: 408-395-1300 - **Fax:** 408-395-8466
www.inquestscreening.com **email:** info@inquestscreening.com

Types of Records Retrieved: Criminal and Civil courts

Local Retrieval Area: CA-Alameda, Contra Costa, Sacramento, San Mateo, Santa Clara, Santa Cruz. **Correspondent Relationships:** nationwide.

Add'l Information: Established 1999. Normal turnaround time- 2-48 hours. Projects billed by number of names searched. Terms: net 30 days. Inquest is a full service pre-employment screening company that specializes in criminal records retrieval in the Silicon Valley, CA.

Inquest Investigations, LLC

1201 W Washington St, Sherman, TX 75092
Phone: 903-893-2020 - **Fax:** 903-892-6211
www.inquestinvestigations.com **email:** inquest@texoma.net

Types of Records Retrieved: Criminal and Civil courts; Tax Liens/Judgments; UCC records

Local Retrieval Area: TX-Collin, Dallas, Denton, Grayson, Gregg, Nueces, Tarrant. **Correspondent Relationships:** nationwide.

Add'l Information: Established 1998. Normal turnaround time- 24-72 hours. Projects billed by number of names searched. Will file/record documents for clients. They specialize in criminal, civil, skiptrace and property research as well as nationwide pre-employment screening and MVR retrieval. A licensed PI in TX.

Inquisitive Research Corporation

416 Main St 2nd Fl, Metuchen, NJ 08840
Phone: 732-321-0041 - **Fax:** 732-321-0085
www.iqresearch.com **email:** info@iqresearch.com

Types of Records Retrieved: Criminal, Civil and Probate courts; Federal courts; Real Estate; Tax Liens/Judgments; UCC records; Vital records

Local Retrieval Area: NJ-all counties; NY-Bronx, Kings, Nassau, New York, Queens, Richmond, Suffolk, Westchester; PA-Bucks, Chester, Delaware, Montgomery, Northampton, Philadelphia; VT-Chittenden, Rutland. **Correspondent Relationships:** NY, PA & VT.

Add'l Information: Established 1992. Normal turnaround time- 24-48 hours. Projects billed by number of names searched. First project may require prepayment. Credit cards accepted. Will file/record documents for clients. Their specialties are: mortgage/assignment document retrieval/research in NJ, NY, PA & VT. Documents are e-mailed back fast!

Insight Public Record Research Corp

PO Box 891571, Temecula, CA 92589
Phone: 800-615-8111; - **Fax:** 800-889-1932;
www.iprrc.com **email:** sbovy@iprrc.com

Records Retrieved: Criminal and Civil courts; Federal District courts

Local Retrieval Area: CA-Orange, Riverside, San Bernardino, San Diego

Add'l Information: Established 2006. Normal turnaround time- 24-48 hours. Projects billed by number of names searched. Projects billed by number of records located. First project may require prepayment. Credit cards accepted. They are a national wholesaler of criminal court searches for pre-employment screeners. Online ordering and customized processing featured.

Insured Titles Inc

1724 Fairview Av, Missoula, MT 59806
Phone: 406-728-7900 - **Fax:** 406-728-5892
www.insuredtitles.com **email:** info@insuredtitles.com

Types of Records Retrieved: Real Estate; Tax Liens/Judgments; Probate courts; UCC records

Local Retrieval Area: MT-Missoula. **Correspondent Relationships:** Missoula County MT.

Add'l Information: Established 1975. Normal turnaround time- 3-5 days. Projects billed by number of names searched. Will file/record documents for clients. They specialize in real estate record searches, also title and escrow closings.

Integrity Abstracting

410 8th Ave, Crystal City, MO 63019-1503
Phone: 314-807-6359 - **Fax:** 636-937-1177
www.integrityabs.com **email:** integrity1000@yahoo.com

Types of Records Retrieved: Civil and Probate courts; Real Estate

Local Retrieval Area: MO-Jefferson, St. Charles, St. Louis

Add'l Information: Established 2000. Normal turnaround time- 24 hours. Expedited service available. Projects billed by number of names searched. Projects billed by number of records located. Will bill monthly/semi-monthly. They are dedicated to quick, accurate customer service in title searches and document retrieval. They offer exclusive cooperation with interested companies. Does criminal record searches on a limited basis. Performs service of process.

Integrity Check

PO Box 1301, Beaumont, TX 77704
Phone: 409-962-1991 - **Fax:** 801-337-7410
yosko@ijntb.net

Types of Records Retrieved: Criminal and Civil courts

Local Retrieval Area: TX-Chambers, Hardin, Jefferson, Orange

Add'l Information: Established 2005. Normal turnaround time- 24-48 hours. Expedited service available. Projects billed by number of names searched. First project may require prepayment. They offer comprehensive background checks, criminal and civil record retrieval for pre-employment and tenant screenings. A licensed PI in TX.

Integrity Check LLC

2250 E Chemise Dr, Meridian, ID 83646
Phone: 877-887-1226; 208-887-1226 - **Fax:** 877-887-3934; 208-887-9801
www.integritycheckllc.com **email:** scompton@integritycheckllc.com

Types of Records Retrieved: Criminal, Civil and Probate courts; Federal courts; Real Estate; Tax Liens/Judgments; UCC records; Vital records

Local Retrieval Area: ID-Ada, Boise, Canyon, Elmore, Gem. **Correspondent Relationships:** statewide.

Add'l Information: Established 2004. Normal turnaround time- 24-48 hours. Projects billed by number of names searched. First project may require prepayment. They are a full service background investigation and document retrieval company servicing Idaho and the northwest. They are experienced and professional. A licensed PI in ID.

Integrity Records Access

325 S 3rd St, PMB 184, Las Vegas, NV 89101
Phone: 702-296-9145 - **Fax:** 702-441-7008
integrityra@cox.net

Types of Records Retrieved: Criminal, Civil and Probate courts; Federal courts; Real Estate; Tax Liens/Judgments; UCC records; Vital records

Local Retrieval Area: NV-Clark. **Correspondent:** nationwide.

Add'l Information: Established 1996. Normal turnaround time- 24-48 hours. Projects billed by number of names searched. Projects billed by the hour. If extensive searches, it moves to hourly charges. First project may require prepayment. Will file/record documents for clients. Terms: net 30 days. They specialize in state & federal court research & retrieval, also filing & searching at recorders' offices across the US. They provide retrieval services from the Federal Records Ctr in Laguna Niguel, CA. Extensive contacts throughout the Southwest.

Intelysis Corp (Ziegler & Assoc.)

1230 Parkway Ave, #304, West Trenton, NJ 08628
Phone: 800-489-1239; 609-538-0508 - **Fax:** 609-637-9403
www.ziegler-inv.com **email:** zieglerandassociates@verizon.net

Records Retrieved: Criminal and Civil courts; Real Estate; Vital records

Local Retrieval Area: NJ-Mercer. **Correspondent Relationships:** nationwide, Canada, International (criminal records).

Add'l Information: Established 1995. Normal turnaround time- 10 business days for statewide criminal records; other records 2 days. Projects billed by number of names searched. First project may require prepayment. They specialize in statewide criminal searches, computer forensics, fire/arson/explosion investigations, international searches and employee screening. They do Canadian wide criminal record searches. A licensed PI in NJ, PA.

Inter-County Abstract

926 Court St, Honesdale, PA 18431-1871
Phone: 570-253-4734 - **Fax:** 570-253-1359

Types of Records Retrieved: Civil courts; Real Estate

Local Retrieval Area: PA-Wayne. **Correspondent Relationships:** Lackawanna.

Add'l Information: Established 1979. Turnaround time- 1 week. Projects billed by number of names searched. Charges are also based on title insurance. All projects require prepayment. Will file/record documents for clients. They specialize in information certificates for real estate abstracts.

International Investigators Inc

3216 N Pennsylvania St, Indianapolis, IN 46205-3414
Phone: 800-403-8111; 317-925-1496 - **Fax:** 317-926-1177
www.iiiweb.net **email:** info@iiiweb.net

Types of Records Retrieved: Criminal, Civil and Probate courts; Federal courts; Real Estate; Tax Liens/Judgments; UCC records; Vital records

Local Retrieval Area: IN-Boone, Hamilton, Hancock, Hendricks, Johnson, Marion, Shelby. **Correspondents:** nationwide & international.

Add'l Information: Established 1960. Normal turnaround time- 1-4 days. Projects billed by the hour. First project may require prepayment. Credit cards accepted. They specialize in international insurance fraud, loss prevention, corporate request and attorney assistance. Also do skiptracing, investigations, surveillance, countermeasures sweeps and covert video systems. A licensed PI in IN. Performs service of process.

Interquest Information Services

PO Box 2082, Cape Girardeau, MO 63702
Phone: 800-455-1655; 573-339-1505 - **Fax:** 573-332-2786
www.interqst.com **email:** tbarnhart@interqst.com

Types of Records Retrieved: Criminal and Civil courts; Federal courts; Real Estate; Tax Liens/Judgments; UCC records; Vital records

Local Retrieval Area: MO-Cape Girardeau. **Correspondent Relationships:** nationwide.

Add'l Information: Established 1989. Normal turnaround time- 24-72 hours. Projects billed by number of names searched. First project may require prepayment. Credit cards accepted. Will file/record documents for clients. Terms: net 30 days for established accounts. They specialize in employment screening, drug & tenant screening, skiptracing, and general information research for business, industrial and legal use. Also credit reports, driving records and social security trace.

Interstate Reporting Co Inc (IRC)

W177N9886 Rivercrest Dr #104, Germantown, WI 53022-4500
Phone: 262-251-6590 - **Fax:** 262-251-0929 ircinc@execpc.com

Types of Records Retrieved: Criminal and Civil courts; Federal courts; Tax Liens/Judgments; UCC records

Retrieval Area: WI-Milwaukee, Ozaukee, Racine, Washington, Waukesha

Add'l Information: Established 1984. Normal turnaround time- 48-72 hours. Projects billed by the hour. First project may require prepayment. They specialize in asset reports, pre-employment background reports, also insurance fraud, public assistance, and worker's compensation investigations. Statewide electronic access to criminal records. A licensed PI in WI.

Intra-Lex Investigations Inc

505 5th St #331, Sioux City, IA 51101
Phone: 712-233-1639 - **Fax:** 712-255-1127 ilex@iw.net

Types of Records Retrieved: Criminal and Civil courts; Federal courts; Real Estate; Tax Liens/Judgments; UCC records

Local Retrieval Area: IA-Woodbury; NE-Dakota. **Correspondent Relationships:** other Nebraska counties.

Add'l Information: Established 1983. Normal turnaround time- 24 hours. Projects billed by number of names searched. Projects billed by the hour. Mileage charges will be added. A minimum fee applies. Will file/record documents for clients. Payment in full 30 days from date of service. They are a full line investigation agency, multi-state licensed, bonded and insured. A licensed PI in IA, NE. Performs service of process.

Intricate Solutions Inc

1525 Highway 53 East, Dawsonville, GA 30534
Phone: 866-640-5210; 706-265-6235 - **Fax:** 706-265-6234
www.4ebi.com **email:** intricatesolutions@yahoo.com

Types of Records Retrieved: Criminal courts

Local Retrieval Area: GA-Dawson, Lumpkin. **Correspondent Relationships:** nationwide.

Add'l Information: Established 2001. Normal turnaround time- guaranteed 24-hr return. Projects billed by number of names searched. Will bill to accepted clients. EBI - Employee Background Investigators - provides criminal records for Dawson and Lumpkin counties, also Georgia (also MT, NM, RI, WA, WI) statewide criminal history, with signed release.

Introspect Investigations USA Inc

752A Hempstead Turnpike #205, Franklin Square, NY 11010
Phone: 800-847-7177; 516-292-4130 - **Fax:** 516-292-4135
www.introspectusa.com **email:** introusa@aol.com

Types of Records Retrieved: Criminal, Civil and Probate courts; Federal courts; Real Estate; Tax Liens/Judgments; UCC records

Local Retrieval Area: NY-Kings, Nassau, New York, Queens. **Correspondent Relationships:** nationwide.

Add'l Information: Established 1984. Normal turnaround time- 3 days. Expedited service available. Projects billed by number of names searched. First project may require prepayment. They specialize in public record research, background investigations, asset investigations, pre-employment screening, DMV records and general investigations. Special request considered. A licensed PI in NY. Performs service of process.

Investigate-Claims.com

8 Tudor Ct, Buffalo, NY 14068
Phone: 716-689-6577 - **Fax:** 716-689-4721
www.investigate-claims.com **email:** ferraribuffalony@att.net

Types of Records Retrieved: Criminal, Civil and Probate courts; Federal courts; Real Estate; Tax Liens/Judgments; UCC records; Vital records

Local Retrieval Area: NY-Erie, Niagara. **Correspondent Relationships:** nationwide network of retrievers.

Add'l Information: Established 1978. Normal turnaround time- 3-5 business days; expedited service by request. Can perform NY statewide court record search in 24 hours. Projects billed by number of names searched. Projects billed by the hour. All projects require prepayment. Credit cards accepted. Net due 30 days for insurance companies. AMBest co-rated them as Qualified Spec. Investigator. They are a Licensed PI and Independent Adjuster. Also is notary public. Operates PublicRecordWorld.com and www.investigate-claims.com. Online direct to NY MVRs. A licensed PI in NY. Performs service of process.

Investigative Consultant Service

3337 Earhart Rd, Mt Juliet, TN 37122
Phone: 615-885-1126 - **Fax:** 615-885-1641
phillipdsutton@bellsouth.net

Types of Records Retrieved: Criminal, Civil and Probate courts; Federal courts; UCC records; Vital records

Local Retrieval Area: TN-Davidson, Wilson

Add'l Information: Established 1997. Normal turnaround time- 3 days or less, depending on type of search performed. Billing method varies by type of searches and volume. First project may require prepayment. Credit cards accepted. In addition to record retrieval, they provide background investigations for pre-employment, employee theft cases, also copyright investigations. A licensed PI in TN.

Investigative Consultants Inc

2020 Pennsylvania Ave NW #813, Washington, DC 20006
Phone: 202-237-1500 - **Fax:** 202-237-8642
www.icioffshore.com **email:** dberlin@icioffshore.com

Types of Records Retrieved: Criminal, Civil and Probate courts; Federal courts; Real Estate; Tax Liens/Judgments; UCC records; Vital records

Local Retrieval Area: DC-District of Columbia; MD-Howard, Montgomery, Prince George's; VA-Arlington, Essex, Fairfax, Fairfax City, Frederick, Manassas City, Manassas Park City, Prince William. **Correspondent Relationships:** nationwide.

Add'l Information: Established 1977. Normal turnaround time- 4 hours to 4 days. Projects billed by the hour. Retainer of 80% of all fees is required. All projects require prepayment. Credit cards accepted. Wire transfers and firm checks only. They specialize in assisting attorneys who practice in the field of complex federal and state litigation. A licensed PI in DC, WI.

Investigative Information Inc

27852 Ashland Ave, Harrison Township, MI 48045
Phone: 586-491-6125 - **Fax:** 586-783-5242 vojo8665@juno.com

Types of Records Retrieved: Criminal and Civil courts; Real Estate; Tax Liens/Judgments

Local Retrieval Area: MI-Genesee, Macomb, Oakland, Saginaw, St. Clair, Wayne. **Correspondent Relationships:** Saginaw, Genesee, St Clair counties MI.

Add'l Info: Established 1997. Turnaround time- 24-48 hours. Projects billed by number of names searched. Billed monthly. They provide investigative information on criminal and civil litigation in the Detroit Metropolitan area. Clients receive accurate information and fast turnaround time.

Investigative Legal Services Inc

PO Box 3551, Orlando, FL 32802-3551
Phone: 888-426-7436; 407-426-7433 - **Fax:** 407-426-6968
www.processfl.com **email:** donatils@aol.com

Types of Records Retrieved: Criminal, Civil and Probate courts; Federal courts; Real Estate; Tax Liens/Judgments; UCC records; Vital records

Local Retrieval Area: FL-Lake, Orange, Osceola, Seminole. **Correspondent Relationships:** nationwide including Puerto Rico.

Add'l Information: Established 1992. Normal turnaround time- 5 days. Projects billed by the hour. First project may require prepayment. Will file/record documents for clients. Personal checks are accepted. He was a practicing trial lawyer for over 30 years. A licensed PI in FL. Performs service of process.

Investigative Research Consultants Inc

191 N Wacker Dr #2350, Chicago, IL 60606
Phone: 888-578-8600; 312-578-8600 - **Fax:** 888-578-1320; 630-681-9243
www.irc-web.com **email:** brad@irc-web.com

Types of Records Retrieved: Criminal and Civil courts

Local Retrieval Area: IL-Cook, Du Page. **Correspondents:** statewide.

Add'l Information: Established 1996. Normal turnaround time- 24 hours. Projects billed by number of names searched. First project may require prepayment. Credit cards accepted. A licensed PI in IL. Performs service of process.

Investigative Research Specialists LLC

PO Box 903, Bristow, VA 20136-0903

Phone: 703-753-4468 - **Fax:** 703-468-4536

www.corporateresearchers.com **email:** lwz@corporateresearchers.com

Types of Records Retrieved: Criminal and Civil courts

Local Retrieval Area: VA-Prince William

Add'l Information: Established 1991. Normal turnaround time- 3-5 business days. Projects billed by the hour. First project may require prepayment. They provide public record research and investigative due diligence to attorneys, investors and corporations. A licensed PI in VA. Performs service of process.

Investigative Resources

PO Box 70209, Staten Island, NY 10307-0209

Phone: 212-571-2500 - **Fax:** 718-967-0688 joepiny@yahoo.com

Types of Records Retrieved: Criminal and Civil courts; Federal courts; Real Estate; Tax Liens/Judgments; UCC records

Local Retrieval Area: NY-Bronx, Kings, New York, Queens, Richmond. **Correspondent Relationships:** the Northeast.

Add'l Information: Established 1978. Normal turnaround time- as soon as 4 hours. Emergency Expedited service available. Billing depends upon volume. First project may require prepayment. Will file/record documents for clients. They specialize in locating Department of Motor Vehicle records within one hour. They also have a 2nd office. A licensed PI in NY. Performs service of process.

Investigative Solutions

PO Box 250, Atwater, OH 44201-0250

Phone: 330-947-2911 - **Fax:** 330-947-2799 moore.dennis@sbcglobal.net

Types of Records Retrieved: Criminal, Civil and Probate courts; Federal courts; Tax Liens/Judgments; UCC records; Vital records

Local Retrieval Area: OH-Ashland, Ashtabula, Columbiana, Cuyahoga, Erie, Geauga, Holmes, Huron, Lake, Lorain, Mahoning, Medina, Ottawa, Portage, Sandusky, Stark, Summit, Trumbull, Tuscarawas, Wayne. **Correspondent Relationships:** nationwide.

Add'l Information: Established 1987. Normal turnaround time- 1-7 days. Billing generally based upon the type of search requested. Volume discounts available. First project may require prepayment. They specialize in polygraph.

Investigative Survelliance Group

1828 Cason Trail, Murfreesboro, TN 37128

Phone: 615-895-0268 - **Fax:** 615-893-7892

www.courthousesearch.com **email:** sales@courthousesearch.com

Types of Records Retrieved: Criminal, Civil and Probate courts; Federal courts; Real Estate; Tax Liens/Judgments; UCC records; Vital records

Local Retrieval Area: TN-Davidson, Rutherford, Wilson. **Correspondent Relationships:** elsewhere in the state.

Add'l Information: Established 1999. Normal turnaround time- 1-2 days. Projects billed by the hour. Billing method depends on nature of project. First project may require prepayment. Credit cards accepted. They can assist you in any way; feel free to contact them. Tennessee statewide process service. Also see www.isgsiu.com A licensed PI in TN. Performs service of process.

InVision Research

6083 N Figarden Dr PMB 136, Fresno, CA 93722

Phone: 559-271-3170 - **Fax:** 559-271-3150 bonita200@juno.com

Types of Records Retrieved: Criminal courts

Local Retrieval Area: CA-Fresno, Kern, Kings, Madera, Placer, Sacramento, San Francisco, San Joaquin, San Mateo, Tulare, Yolo

Add'l Information: Established 1999. Normal turnaround time- 24 hours. Projects billed by number of names searched. First project may require prepayment. Bills monthly. All orders are processed hands on at local courts using public access systems.

Iosco County Abstract Office Ltd

432 W Lake St, Tawas City, MI 48764-0420

Phone: 989-362-3231 - **Fax:** 989-362-7844

Types of Records Retrieved: Civil and Probate courts; Real Estate; Tax Liens/Judgments; UCC records; Vital records

Local Retrieval Area: MI-Iosco

Add'l Information: Established 1869. Normal turnaround time- 5 working days or less. Projects billed by number of names searched. Projects billed by number of records located. Projects billed by the hour. First project may require prepayment. A setup fee is required for abstracts and searches only. Personal checks are accepted. They specialize in title insurance and closings. A licensed PI in ND.

Iowa County Abstract Company

PO Box 226, Marengo, IA 52301

Phone: 319-642-7321 - **Fax:** 319-642-1231

Types of Records Retrieved: Criminal, Civil and Probate courts; Real Estate; Tax Liens/Judgments; UCC records

Local Retrieval Area: IA-Iowa

Add'l Info: Established 1914. Turnaround time- 2-3 days for personal lien searches, and 3-4 days for a full written search. Fee basis is per transaction. Will file/record documents for clients. Personal checks are accepted.

Iowa County Title

141 N Iowa St, Dodgeville, WI 53533

Phone: 608-935-3834 - **Fax:** 608-935-9165

Types of Records Retrieved: Real Estate; Tax Liens/Judgments

Local Retrieval Area: WI-Iowa

Add'l Information: Established 1954. First project may require prepayment. They specialize in real estate.

Iowa Title & Guaranty Co

115 S 2nd St, #4 Park Plaza Bldg, Maquoketa, IA 52060

Phone: 563-652-6081 - **Fax:** 563-652-3544

Types of Records Retrieved: Civil and Probate courts; Real Estate; Tax Liens/Judgments; UCC records; Vital records

Local Retrieval Area: IA-Jackson

Add'l Information: Established 1952. Normal turnaround time- 1-3 days. Fee basis will vary by the type of project.

Iowa Title & Realty Co

101 N Main St, Charles City, IA 50616-2014

Phone: 641-228-1515 - **Fax:** 641-228-7538

Types of Records Retrieved: Real Estate; Tax Liens/Judgments; Probate courts; UCC records; Vital records

Local Retrieval Area: IA-Floyd

Add'l Information: Normal turnaround time- 1-7 days. Fee basis will vary by the type of project. First project may require prepayment.

Iowa Title Co

312 1st St SE, Cedar Rapids, IA 52401

Phone: 319-365-1478 - **Fax:** 319-365-1340

www.iowatitle.com **Types of Records Retrieved:** Criminal, Civil and Probate courts; Federal courts; Real Estate; Tax Liens/Judgments; UCC records; Vital records

Local Retrieval Area: IA-Linn. **Correspondent Relationships:** statewide.

Add'l Information: Established 1867. Normal turnaround time- 24-48 hours. Fee basis varies by type of transaction. Will file/record documents for clients. They request prepayment from individuals, but will invoice companies. Iowa Title Co, formerly United Title Services Inc, specialize in abstracts, flood and credit.

Terri Irwin

4383 Warmstone Path, Douglasville, GA 30135

Phone: 770-920-9957 - **Fax:** 770-920-3772 irwint@bellsouth.net

Types of Records Retrieved: Criminal, Civil and Probate courts; Tax Liens/Judgments **Local Retrieval Area:** GA-Douglas

Add'l Information: Established 1998. Normal turnaround time- 24 hours. Projects billed by number of names searched. Monthly billing. She specializes in 7-year superior and state court searches, felony and misdemeanor. Guarantees next day turnaround. Specializing in Douglas County for 8 years.

Isabella County Abstract

209 E Broadway, Mt Pleasant, MI 48858
Phone: 989-773-3241 - **Fax:** 989-773-6221
www.ibttitle.com **email:** isabellaabstract@ibttitle.com

Records Retrieved: Real Estate; Tax Liens/Judgments; Vital records

Local Retrieval Area: MI-Clare, Isabella, Mecosta, Montcalm

Add'l Information: Established 1930. Normal turnaround time- 1 week. Projects billed by number of records located. Will file/record documents for clients. Personal checks are accepted. They occasionally do civil and criminal court record searches.

Island Legal

PO Box 785, Hilo, HI 96721
Phone: 808-756-7404 - **Fax:** 866-861-9863
www.island-legal.com **email:** info@island-legal.com

Types of Records Retrieved: Criminal, Civil and Probate courts; Federal courts; Real Estate; Tax Liens/Judgments; UCC records; Vital records

Local Retrieval Area: HI-Hawaii, Honolulu, Kauai, Maui

Add'l Information: Established 2006. Normal turnaround time- 2 days. Expedited service available. Projects billed by the hour. First project may require prepayment. They are a mobile notary service, process server and has a passion for public records research.

Itasca County Abstract Co

430 NE 3rd Av, Grand Rapids, MN 55744
Phone: 218-326-9601 - **Fax:** 218-326-4348 annsmith@firstam.com

Types of Records Retrieved: Civil and Probate courts; Real Estate; Tax Liens/Judgments; UCC records; Vital records

Local Retrieval Area: MN-Itasca

Add'l Information: Established 1927. Normal turnaround time- 24 hours for name and UCC searches. 5 to 10 days for owner's and encumbrance reports and abstracts. Projects billed by number of names searched. Projects billed by number of records located. First project may require prepayment. Will file/record documents for clients. Personal checks are accepted. They specialize in complete title service.

Izard County Abstract Co

PO Box 579, Hiway 9 and 69, Melbourne, AR 72556
Phone: 870-368-4818 - **Fax:** 870-368-5511

Types of Records Retrieved: Real Estate; Tax Liens/Judgments; Probate courts; UCC records **Local Retrieval Area:** AR-Izard

Add'l Information: Normal turnaround time- 3-5 days. Fee basis will vary by the type of project. Will file/record documents for clients. They specialize in real estate.

J & A Land Searching

3588 S Lexus Ave, Springfield, MO 65807-8688
Phone: 417-887-1049 - **Fax:** 417-887-1049 jandalandsearch@sbcglobal.net

Records Retrieved: Real Estate; Tax Liens/Judgments; UCC records

Local Retrieval Area: MO-Greene

Add'l Information: Established 1997. Normal turnaround time- 24 hours. Projects billed by number of names searched. Will file/record documents for clients. They specialize in current owner searches, institutional searches, and full searches with a very quick turnaround time and very competitive pricing. .

J & J Enterprises - MO

10012 Steamboat Run, Jefferson City, MO 65101
Phone: 573-395-4205 - **Fax:** 573-395-3378 J2ent@aol.com

Types of Records Retrieved: Criminal and Civil courts; Federal District court; Real Estate; Tax Liens/Judgments; UCC records

Local Retrieval Area: MO-Boone, Callaway, Cole, Gasconade, Maries, Miller, Osage, Phelps, Pulaski

Add'l Information: Established 1996. Normal turnaround time- 24-48 hours. Projects billed by number of names searched. Billing by job or monthly. Credit cards accepted. Will file/record documents for clients. They specialize in Missouri state criminal searches and current owner searches. Federal criminal records retrieved from MO East & West Districts. Performs service of process.

J & J Research

33 Wilshore Dr, Bossier City, LA 71111
Phone: 318-752-8320 - **Fax:** 318-747-7690 jmurray@jandjresearch.com

Types of Records Retrieved: Criminal and Civil courts

Local Retrieval Area: LA-Bossier, Caddo Parishes

Add'l Information: Established 1994. Normal turnaround time- 24 hours. Projects billed by number of names searched. All projects require prepayment. Can bill by invoice 1st monthly. They also do searches in the Shreveport City Court and Bossier City Court. They do fast, accurate work with a goal of trying hard to net return a "name match only" report. Their work is hands on with case files pulled when needed. A licensed PI in LA.

J B Data & Research, LLC

502 S 19th Ave #103, Bozeman, MT 59718-6827
Phone: 406-585-3323 - **Fax:** 877-856-2803; 406-585-3323
www.eEllis.Net/JBData.htm **email:** jbdata@ellis.net

Types of Records Retrieved: Criminal, Civil and Probate courts; Bankruptcy court; Real Estate; Tax Liens/Judgments; UCC records

Local Retrieval Area: MT-Beaverhead, Broadwater, Cascade, Fergus, Flathead, Gallatin, Jefferson, Lake, Lewis & Clark, Lincoln, Madison, Missoula, Park, Ravalli, Sanders, Silver Bow, Yellowstone. **Correspondent Relationships:** Call for availability of service to all other MT counties.

Add'l Information: Established 1999. Normal turnaround time- 24-48 hours. Projects billed by number of names searched. Projects billed by number of records located. First project may require prepayment. Will file/record documents for clients. They do property searches for larger counties in Montana, along with criminal/civil, judgment, and other searches. They collect bulk civil records in 55 counties.

J C Humphrey Abstract Co

217 W Broadway, PO Box 84 (73702), Enid, OK 73701
Phone: 580-237-3136 - **Fax:** 580-237-1948
www.enidabstract.com **email:** toddh@enidabstract.com

Types of Records Retrieved: Civil and Probate courts; Real Estate; Tax Liens/Judgments; UCC records

Local Retrieval Area: OK-Garfield. **Correspondent Relationships:** Grant County, Oklahoma.

Add'l Information: Established 1930. Normal turnaround time- 1-2 days. Projects billed by number of records located. First project may require prepayment. Will file/record documents for clients. They specialize in abstracting.

J H L Enterprises

7775 York Rd, Parma, OH 44130

Phone: 440-845-2823 - **Fax:** 440-845-2823 j.belter@sbcglobal.net

Types of Records Retrieved: Criminal and Civil courts; Federal courts; Real Estate; Tax Liens/Judgments; UCC records

Local Retrieval Area: OH-Cuyahoga, Medina, Wayne

Add'l Information: Established 1988. Normal turnaround time- 24-48 hours. Projects billed by number of names searched. First project may require prepayment. Will invoice monthly. They specialize in civil, criminal, UCC, tax liens and US District and Bankruptcy court searches.

Jackson County Abstract Co

PO Box 756, Altus, OK 73521

Phone: 580-482-1235 - **Fax:** 580-482-9180

www.jacksoncountyabstractok.com **Types of Records Retrieved:** Civil and Probate courts; Real Estate; Tax Liens/Judgments; UCC records

Local Retrieval Area: OK-Jackson

Add'l Information: Established 1948. Normal turnaround time- variable depending on project. Projects billed by the hour. First project may require prepayment. Will file/record documents for clients. They specialize in abstracts.

Jackson County Land Title Services, Inc

508 3rd St, Newport, AR 72112

Phone: 870-523-8976 - **Fax:** 870-523-3969

Types of Records Retrieved: Civil and Probate courts; Real Estate; Tax Liens/Judgments; UCC records

Local Retrieval Area: AR-Jackson

Add'l Information: Established 1960. Normal turnaround time- up to 10 days. Projects billed by the hour. They specialize in real estate abstracting and title insurance.

Jackson Information Services Inc

23710 Tuscany, Eastpoint, MI 48021

Phone: 586-242-4122 - **Fax:** 586-218-4591

jacksoninfoservices@yahoo.com

Types of Records Retrieved: Criminal, Civil and Probate courts; Federal courts; Real Estate; Tax Liens/Judgments; UCC records

Local Retrieval Area: MI-Macomb, Oakland, St. Clair, Wayne

Add'l Information: Established 2004. Normal turnaround time- 24-48 hours. Projects billed by number of names searched. Will invoice bi-weekly or monthly. Will accept credit cards via PayPal. Jackson Information Services is committed to providing fast, accurate and on-time service, from pre-employment screening to document filings and retrievals.

Karen Jackson

181 Snyder Rd NE, Millegeville, GA 31061 **Phone** 478-452-9390; fax- same

Types of Records Retrieved: Criminal and Civil courts; Tax Liens/Judgments

Local Retrieval Area: GA-Baldwin

Add'l Information: Established 1984. Normal turnaround time- 24 hours. Projects billed by number of names searched. First project may require prepayment. She is the acknowledged expert in Baldwin County courts.

Jacobs & Associates CPD Inc

901 East Wood St, Decatur, IL 62521

Phone: 800-445-1675; 217-429-2711 - **Fax:** 217-429-2718

www.jacobscpd.com **email:** phil@jacobscpd.com

Types of Records Retrieved: Criminal, Civil and Probate courts; Federal courts; Real Estate; Tax Liens/Judgments; UCC records; Vital records

Local Retrieval Area: IL-Champaign, Coles, De Witt, Douglas, Logan, McLean, Macon, Mason, Moultrie, Piatt, Sangamon, Shelby. **Correspondent Relationships:** nationwide by ex-FBI agents.

Add'l Information: Established 1970. Normal turnaround time- 1-3 days. Same day if received by noon central time. Projects billed by number of names searched. Will file/record documents for clients. Terms: net 30 days. They specialize in forensic sciences, criminal and civil investigations and process service. A licensed PI in IL. Performs service of process.

James F Havill Attorney at Law PC

401 E South St, Washington, IN 47501

Phone: 812-254-0050 - **Fax:** 812-254-7633

Types of Records Retrieved: Civil and Probate courts; Real Estate; Tax Liens/Judgments; UCC records; Vital records

Local Retrieval Area: IN-Daviess. **Correspondent Relationships:** Knox, Martin, Pike counties.

Add'l Information: Established 1971. Normal turnaround time- 1 week to 10 days. Personal checks are accepted. They specialize in title opinions and title insurance.

James M Sweeney & Associates Inc

320 Leclaire St, Davenport, IA 52801-1721

Phone: 800-494-5922; 563-323-5922 - **Fax:** 563-323-5441

www.inquirehire.com **email:** inbox@inquirehire.com

Types of Records Retrieved: Criminal, Civil and Probate courts; Federal courts; Tax Liens/Judgments; UCC records; Vital records

Local Retrieval Area: IA-Scott; IL-Rock Island. **Correspondent Relationships:** nationwide.

Add'l Information: Established 1994. Normal turnaround time- 24-48 hours. Projects billed by number of names searched. Credit cards accepted. Will file/record documents for clients. Payment due upon receipt. They specialize in criminal checks in state and federal courts, drivers' licenses, workers' compensation records, bankruptcy and reference checks. An alternate web address is www.sweeneyinc.com. A licensed PI in IA, IL. Performs service of process.

Janke Abstract Co

PO Box 114, St Paul, NE 68873

Phone: 308-754-4251 - **Fax:** 308-754-4444 jankeabco@qwest.net

Types of Records Retrieved: Civil and Probate courts; Real Estate; Tax Liens/Judgments; UCC records

Local Retrieval Area: NE-Greeley, Hall, Howard, Merrick, Nance, Sherman. **Correspondent Relationships:** Howard, Merrick, Greeley, Hall, Sherman and Nance counties.

Add'l Information: Established 1980. Normal turnaround time- 2-3 days. Projects billed by number of names searched. Projects billed by number of records located. Projects billed by the hour. First project may require prepayment. Will file/record documents for clients. They specialize in real estate.

Jay Portland Abstract Inc Co

PO Box 1237, Portland, IN 47371

Phone: 260-726-6466 - **Fax:** 260-726-6627

Types of Records Retrieved: Civil and Probate courts; Real Estate; Tax Liens/Judgments; UCC records; Vital records

Local Retrieval Area: IN-Jay

Add'l Information: Established 1978. Normal turnaround time- 5 days. Projects billed by number of names searched. Projects billed by the hour. All projects require prepayment. Will file/record documents for clients. They will also invoice. They specialize in abstracting and title insurance.

JB Acree Research

7922 N County Rd 675 W, Brazil, IN 47834

Phone: 812-443-2443 - **Fax:** 812-443-2443

Types of Records Retrieved: Criminal and Civil courts; Federal courts; UCC records; Real Estate; Tax Liens/Judgments

Local Retrieval Area: IN-Clay, Fountain, Parke, Putnam, Vermillion, Vigo

Add'l Information: Established 2001. Normal turnaround time- 2-4 days. Will file/record documents for clients. Acree specializes in Terra Haute and the region just north.

Jean Randall Process Service

561 Louis Dr, Novato, CA 94945
Phone: 866-386-5777; 415-897-2361 - **Fax:** 415-897-2305
jeanrandallps@aol.com

Types of Records Retrieved: Criminal, Civil and Probate courts; Real Estate; Tax Liens/Judgments; UCC records

Local Retrieval Area: CA-Contra Costa, Marin, Solano, Sonoma

Add'l Information: Established 1978. Normal turnaround time- 1 day. Projects billed by number of names searched. First project may require prepayment. Will file/record documents for clients. Personal checks accepted. She also specializes in fictitious business name filing searches, process service and notary. Performs service of process.

Jeff City Filing Inc

222 E Dunklin #102, Jefferson City, MO 65101
Phone: 573-634-3894 - **Fax:** 573-634-5159 jeffcityfiling@earthlink.net

Types of Records Retrieved: Criminal, Civil and Probate courts; Real Estate; Tax Liens/Judgments; UCC records; Vital records; Corporate filing/retrieval with Mo. Sec. of State

Local Retrieval Area: MO-Cole

Add'l Information: Established 1986. Normal turnaround time- 24-48 hours. Projects billed by number of names searched. Will file/record documents for clients. Terms: net 30 days. Specializing in filings/retrievals at the MO Sec of State's office, Cole Co, & other local offices, includes corp records, UCCs, apostilles, tax clearances, criminal records, DMV, county/supreme court services, etc. Also providing Registered Agent svcs. Performs service of process.

Jeff Davis County Abstract Co

PO Box 813, 309 State St, Fort Davis, TX 79734
Phone: 432-426-3288 - **Fax:** 432-426-3844

Types of Records Retrieved: Civil and Probate courts; Real Estate; Tax Liens/Judgments; UCC records

Local Retrieval Area: TX-Jeff Davis. **Correspondent Relationships:** adjoining counties.

Add'l Information: Normal turnaround time- 2 days. Projects billed by the hour. First project may require prepayment. Will file/record documents for clients. They specialize in title work.

Jefferson County Abstract

122 N Court St, Fairfield, IA 52556-2811
Phone: 641-472-5052 - **Fax:** 641-472-1944
jeffcoab@lisco.com

Types of Records Retrieved: Criminal, Civil and Probate courts; Real Estate; Tax Liens/Judgments; UCC records; Vital records

Local Retrieval Area: IA-Jefferson. **Correspondent Relationships:** Van Buren County IA.

Add'l Information: Established 1800. Normal turnaround time- 1-2 days. Fee basis varies by type of transaction. First project may require prepayment. Will file/record documents for clients. They specialize in complete land records, updated daily in Jefferson County.

Jerauld County Abstract Co Inc

Box 341, 210 E Main St, Wessington Springs, SD 57382
Phone: 605-539-1541 - **Fax:** 605-539-1541

Types of Records Retrieved: Civil and Probate courts; Real Estate; Tax Liens/Judgments; UCC records

Local Retrieval Area: SD-Jerauld

Add'l Information: Established 1991. Normal turnaround time- variable depending on project. Projects billed by number of records located. Specializes in title insurance and abstracting.

Jess Barker Document Research/Retrieval

209A S Macoupin St, Gillespie, IL 62033-1605
Phone: 888-316-3773; 217-839-3219 - **Fax:** 877-522-7537; 217-839-2901
www.documentresearch.biz **email:** documentretrieval@frontiernet.net

Types of Records Retrieved: Real Estate; Criminal, Civil and Probate courts; Federal courts; Tax Liens/Judgments; UCC records; Vital records

Local Retrieval Area: CA-San Mateo, Santa Clara, Tulare; IL-Macoupin, Madison, Sangamon, St. Clair; MO-Jackson, St. Charles, St. Louis; OR-Multnomah, Washington. **Correspondent Relationships:** Illinois.

Add'l Information: Established 1993. Normal turnaround time- 24-48 hours. Projects billed by number of names searched. Will file/record documents for clients. They specialize in real estate current owner searches. They also do UCC, Lien and court record searches. The principal has an M.A. in Legal Studies focusing on law-related research and writing. Current owner searches/call for quote.

JG Weiss Research & Retrieval

5433 S Dorchester #1-N, Chicago, IL 60615
Phone: 773-241-6923 - **Fax:** 773-241-5012 jgweiss@sbcglobal.net

Types of Records Retrieved: Criminal, Civil and Probate courts; Federal courts; Real Estate; Tax Liens/Judgments; UCC records; Vital records

Local Retrieval Area: IL-Cook, Du Page, Kane, Lake, Will. **Correspondent Relationships:** statewide.

Add'l Information: Established 1997. Normal turnaround time- 24 hours. Expedited service available. Projects are billed by the type of job done. First project may require prepayment. They specialize in title/property reports, document retrieval, judgments/liens and document recording. Competitive fees. Has E & O Insurance. No subcontracting. Has 6 years experience.

JH Records Research

216 Stone Gate Cir, Morgantown, WV 26505
Phone: 304-531-4681 - **Fax:** 304-598-7108 juli.hatcher@gmail.com

Types of Records Retrieved: Criminal and Civil courts; Federal courts; Tax Liens/Judgments

Local Retrieval Area: WV-Barbour, Berkeley, Brooke, Doddridge, Grant, Hampshire, Hancock, Hardy, Harrison, Jefferson, Lewis, Marion, Marshall, Mineral, Monongalia, Ohio, Preston, Taylor, Tucker, Tyler, Upshur, Wetzel

Add'l Information: Established 2005. Normal turnaround time- 24-48 hours. Projects billed by number of names searched. Regular clients billed monthly. Reliable and accurate, they provide searches from court records.

Jireh Business Information Solutions Inc

8775 Norwin Ave PMB 194, North Huntingdon, PA 15642-2744
Phone: 724-863-7270 - **Fax:** 724-863-7271
www.jbizinfo.com **email:** info@jkizinfo.com

Types of Records Retrieved: Civil and Probate courts; Real Estate; Tax Liens/Judgments

Retrieval Area: PA-Armstrong, Beaver, Bedford, Blair, Butler, Cambria, Fayette, Greene, Indiana, Lawrence, Somerset, Washington, Westmoreland

Add'l Information: Established 2001. Projects billed by number of names searched. Projects billed by number of records located. Projects billed by the hour. They will bill monthly. Terms are net 30 days w/10 day grace period. They furnish land title information, public records research and background screening services in ten southwestern PA counties. Professionalism, integrity and confidentiality are their highest priorities.

JM Search Services Inc

7787 SW 86th St #102-E, Miami, FL 33143
Phone: 800-393-7563; 305-273-7766 - **Fax:** 305-273-8855
jamie.milton@prodigy.net

Types of Records Retrieved: Criminal, Civil and Probate courts; Federal courts; Real Estate; Tax Liens/Judgments; UCC records

Local Retrieval Area: FL-Broward, Dade, Palm Beach

Add'l Information: Established 1991. Normal turnaround time- 24-48 hours. Expedited service available. Projects billed by number of names searched. Projects billed by the hour. Payment due upon receipt of invoice. They specialize in asset/lien, due diligence, civil/criminal, US District Ct, bankruptcy and real property searches. They also perform historical and biographical research for news publications and organizations. Will file documents in Dade County only.

JMB Title Abstracting

103 Kendall Pond Rd, Windham, NH 03087
Phone: 603-505-1910 - **Fax:** 603-537-1044 j.bastian_7@comcast.net
www.abstractorconnection.com

Types of Records Retrieved: Criminal, Civil and Probate courts; Real Estate

Local Retrieval Area: MA-Essex, Middlesex; NH-Hillsborough, Rockingham. **Correspondent Relationships:** MA & NH.

Add'l Information: Established 2003. Fee based on number of names searched. First project may require prepayment. Full services. Process Svc.

John C Dunaway & Company

PO Box 202102, Austin, TX 78720

Phone: 512-835-5888 - **Fax:** 512-835-2136 texaspi@swbell.net

Types of Records Retrieved: Criminal, Civil and Probate courts; Federal courts; Real Estate; Tax Liens/Judgments; UCC records; Vital records

Local Retrieval Area: TX-Bastrop, Hays, Travis, Williamson. **Correspondent Relationships:** nationwide and Canada.

Add'l Information: Established 1978. Normal turnaround time- 24-48 hours. Projects billed by number of names searched. Will file/record documents for clients. They bill at the end of the month. They are a full service investigations company assisting employers by helping them avoid potential claims exposure and to better evaluate the risks inherent when hiring personnel. A licensed PI in TX. Performs service of process.

John E Jones Jr Land Title & Appraisal

PO Box 105, 231 S Broad St, Metter, GA 30439

Phone: 912-685-3047 - **Fax:** 912-685-3393

www.jlta.net **email:** info@jlta.net

Types of Records Retrieved: Real Estate; Tax Liens/Judgments; Probate courts; Federal courts; UCC records; Vital records

Local Retrieval Area: GA-Candler. **Correspondent Relationships:** Eastern and Southern Georgia.

Add'l Information: Established 1982. Normal turnaround time- 1-4 days. Expedited service available. Projects billed by number of names searched. Fee basis will vary by type of search plus costs of copies. First project may require prepayment. They specialize in appraisal, title, UCC, lien and judgment, federal court, and bankruptcy searches. Can do appraisals in adjoining or nearby counties.

John H Rider Abstracts of Title

PO Box 256, 300 W Marion, Corydon, IA 50060

Phone: 641-872-1966 - **Fax:** 641-872-2468

Types of Records Retrieved: Criminal, Civil and Probate courts; Real Estate; Tax Liens/Judgments; UCC records

Local Retrieval Area: IA-Wayne

Add'l Information: Normal turnaround time- 2-3 days. Fee basis varies by type of transaction. First project may require prepayment. Will file/record documents for clients.

John Roberson Inv

246 Outback Ridge Tr, Jasper, GA 30143

Phone: 800-325-0914; 706-301-5687 - **Fax:** 706-301-5686

www.robersoninvestigations.com **email:** jri@mindspring.com

Types of Records Retrieved: Criminal, Civil and Probate courts; Federal courts; Real Estate; Tax Liens/Judgments; UCC records; Vital records

Local Retrieval Area: GA-Clayton, Cobb, Coweta, Dawson, De Kalb, Fannin, Fayette, Fulton, Gilmer, Gwinnett, Hall, Henry, Pickens, Spalding. **Correspondent Relationships:** nationwide.

Add'l Information: Established 1984. Normal turnaround time- 2 days. Projects billed by the hour. First project may require prepayment. Will file/record documents for clients. Payment due upon receipt. They are specialists and experts in skiptrace and asset location. A licensed PI in GA. Performs service of process.

John The Abstractor

PO Box 239, Santa Rosa, NM 88435

Phone: 505-472-1197 - **Fax:** 505-472-1197 jrmccormack@plaueautel.net

Types of Records Retrieved: Real Estate; Tax Liens/Judgments; UCC records; Probate courts; US District court

Local Retrieval Area: NM-Guadalupe

Add'l Information: Normal turnaround time- 3 business days or less. Projects billed by number of names searched. Charge by flat fee also. Will file/record documents for clients.

John V Eriksson Group Inc

1203 El Dorado, Houston, TX 77062

Phone: 281-488-0018 - **Fax:** 281-488-0018 Jerik1@aol.com

Types of Records Retrieved: Criminal, Civil and Probate courts; Federal courts; Real Estate; Tax Liens/Judgments; UCC records; Vital records

Local Retrieval Area: TX-Brazoria, Fort Bend, Galveston, Harris, Montgomery. **Correspondent Relationships:** Travis, Williamson, Hayes, Bexar counties TX.

Add'l Information: Established 1996. Normal turnaround time- 1-2 days. Projects billed by number of names searched. Projects billed by the hour. Fee basis varies by type of project. First project may require prepayment. They specialize in background and asset searches. Licensed Private Investigator, and Certified Fraud Examiner. A licensed PI in TX.

Johnson County Abstract

PO Box 627, Vienna, IL 62995-0627

Phone: 618-658-3721 - **Fax:** 618-658-3700 johnsoncoabs@verizon.net

Types of Records Retrieved: Civil and Probate courts; Real Estate; Tax Liens/Judgments; UCC records; Vital records

Local Retrieval Area: IL-Johnson

Add'l Information: Established 1800. Normal turnaround time- 2-3 business days. Projects billed by number of records located. Will file/record documents for clients. Personal checks are accepted. They specialize in title insurance through Chicago Title Insurance Company.

Johnson Title & Abstract Inc

410 Westwood Office Park, Fredricksburg, VA 22401

Phone: 540-368-8104 - **Fax:** 540-368-8105 johnsontitle@aol.com

Records Retrieved: Real Estate; Tax Liens/Judgments; UCC records

Local Retrieval Area: VA-Caroline, Fredericksburg City, King George, Louisa, Orange, Spotsylvania, Stafford

Add'l Info: Established 1993. Turnaround time- 24-48 hours. Projects billed by number of names searched. Will file/record documents for clients. Payment due upon receipt of title work. She performs witness closings.

Diana L Johnson

1501 Wenonah Ave, Pearisburg, VA 24134

Phone: 540-921-1958 - **Fax:** 540-921-0004

Types of Records Retrieved: Criminal, Civil and Probate courts; Real Estate; Tax Liens/Judgments; UCC records; Vital records

Local Retrieval Area: VA-Bland, Craig, Floyd, Montgomery, Pulaski, Radford City

Add'l Information: Established 1986. She charges a flat fee per name. Craig and Floyd counties may be more if you order a quick return. First project may require prepayment. She specializes in Bland, Montgomery, Pulaski, Radford; she visits Craig and Floyd counties irregularly.

Johnston & Associates

PO Box 1183, Albertville, AL 35950-0019

Phone: 256-673-0855 - **Fax:** 815-377-6850

http://paralegalone.tripod.com **email:** jeffjohnson1977@msn.com

Types of Records Retrieved: Criminal, Civil and Probate courts; Real Estate; Tax Liens/Judgments; UCC records

Local Retrieval Area: AL-Blount, Etowah, Madison, Marshall

Add'l Information: Established 2000. Normal turnaround time- 24-48 hours. Projects billed by number of names searched. 10-day billing. They specialize in full-service paralegal services and document retrieval and real estate title abstracting.

Jones & Associates Inc

1611 S Utica Av, PMB 117, Tulsa, OK 74104-4909

Phone: 918-583-4779 - **Fax:** 918-587-8571 jones007@cox.net

Types of Records Retrieved: Criminal, Civil and Probate courts; Federal courts; Real Estate; Tax Liens/Judgments; UCC records; Vital records

Local Retrieval Area: OK-Tulsa. **Correspondent Relationships:** Oklahoma.

Add'l Information: Established 1976. Normal turnaround time- 24-72 hours. Projects billed by number of records located. Projects billed by the hour. Projects billed per time involved and copy costs. All projects require prepayment. Will file/record documents for clients. They specialize in private investigation, process service, medical research, document retrieval, and legal research. Will retrieve all types of records. A licensed PI in OK. Performs service of process.

Jones & Renfrow Abstracters

802 9th, Heatly Building, Paducah, TX 79248
Phone: 806-492-3573 - **Fax:** 806-492-3574

Types of Records Retrieved: Real Estate; Tax Liens/Judgments; Probate courts; UCC records; Vital records

Local Retrieval Area: TX-Cottle, King, Motley

Add'l Information: Established 1910. Normal turnaround time- 1-2 days. Fee basis will vary by the type of project. First project may require prepayment.

Jones Abstract & Title Co Inc

313 Warren St, Huntington, IN 46750
Phone: 866-356-5663; 260-356-2122 - **Fax:** 260-356-4533
www.jonesabstract.com **email:** jonesabstract@jonesabstract.com

Types of Records Retrieved: Civil and Probate courts; Real Estate; Tax Liens/Judgments; UCC records

Local Retrieval Area: IN-Huntington. **Correspondent Relationships:** most of the state through an alliance of title companies, also Ohio, Kentucky, Wisconsin.

Add'l Information: Established 1877. Normal turnaround time- 3-5 days. Fee basis will vary by the type of project. First project may require prepayment. Will file/record documents for clients. They specialize in title searching.

Jones County Title Company

PO Box 508, Murdo, SD 57559
Phone: 605-669-3004 - **Fax:** 952-960-0090 alfuoss@gwtc.net

Types of Records Retrieved: Criminal, Civil and Probate courts; Real Estate; Tax Liens/Judgments; UCC records; Vital records

Local Retrieval Area: SD-Jackson, Jones. **Correspondent Relationships:** Mellette county, SD.

Add'l Information: Established 1998. Normal turnaround time- 48-72 hours. First project may require prepayment. Will file/record documents for clients. They specialize in real estate, title searches and reports.

Reba Jones

95 Big Buck Trail, Jackson, GA 30233
Phone: 478-994-4501 - **Fax:** 478-994-2501

Types of Records Retrieved: Criminal, Civil and Probate courts

Local Retrieval Area: GA-Butts, Lamar, Monroe, Pike, Upson

Add'l Information: Established 2005. Normal turnaround time- 24-48 hours. Projects billed by number of names searched. First project may require prepayment. She specializes in court records from counties just northeast of Macon, GA.

JR Investigations

PO Box 4175, Des Moines, IA 50333
Phone: 515-288-4682 - **Fax:** 515-288-3295
www.jrinvestigations.com **email:** vixxenn@msn.com

Types of Records Retrieved: Criminal, Civil and Probate courts; Federal courts; Real Estate; Tax Liens/Judgments; UCC records; Vital records

Local Retrieval Area: IA-Jasper, Madison, Polk, Warren. **Correspondent Relationships:** statewide.

Add'l Information: Established 1987. Normal turnaround time- 24 hours. First project may require prepayment. Will file/record documents for clients. Billed at end of the month. They specialize in pre-employment screening, workers' compensation, surveillance, accident investigations, process service and real estate research/abstracting. A licensed PI in IA. Performs service of process.

JRW Documents & Lien Services LLC

PO Box 5491, Yuma, AZ 85366
Phone: 928-314-3993 - **Fax:** 928-314-0951 jrwdocs@aol.com

Types of Records Retrieved: Federal courts; Real Estate; Tax Liens/Judgments; UCC records

Local Retrieval Area: AZ-Yuma; also retrieve bankruptcy records for LaPaz and Mohave counties

Add'l Information: Established 2000. Normal turnaround time- 24-48 hours. Projects billed by number of names searched. Will file/record documents for clients. Net 30 days. Require payment for first time customers. Cell phone number is 928-210-8804. They specialize in real estate.

Juab Title & Abstract Co

PO Box 246, Nephi, UT 84648
Phone: 435-623-0387 - **Fax:** 435-623-1000
www.juabtitle.com **email:** tina@juabtitle.com

Types of Records Retrieved: Criminal, Civil and Probate courts; Real Estate; Tax Liens/Judgments; UCC records

Local Retrieval Area: UT-Juab, Millard, Sanpete, Utah

Add'l Information: Established 1901. Normal turnaround time- 1-2 days. Charges vary according to project. All projects require prepayment. They specialize in real estate. They will file/record UCC and real estate documents on behalf of clients on a same or next day basis in Juab County ONLY.

Judd Law Office

PO Box 415, Burkesville, KY 42717
Phone: 270-864-3144 - **Fax:** 270-864-3144

Types of Records Retrieved: Real Estate; Tax Liens/Judgments

Local Retrieval Area: KY-Cumberland

Add'l Information: First project may require prepayment. They specialize in real estate.

Judicial Process & Support Inc

19 W Flagler St #312, Miami, FL 33130
Phone: 800-852-5002; 305-347-3353 - **Fax:** 305-347-3354
www.judicialsupport.com **email:** maria@judicialsupport.com

Types of Records Retrieved: Criminal, Civil, Probate courts; Federal courts

Local Retrieval Area: FL-Broward, Dade. **Correspondents:** nationwide.

Add'l Information: Established 2000. Normal turnaround time- 3 days. Expedited service available. Projects billed by number of names searched. Projects billed by number of records located. Projects billed by the hour. All projects require prepayment. Established clients can pay net 30 days. They are a litigation support company. The president has been in the legal field for over 18 years. They are assigned on a daily basis to complex matters and can accomplish your projects effectively and efficiently. A licensed PI in PI #A2300228. Performs service of process.

Judicial Research & Retrieval Services (Ft Lauderdale)

1 E Broward Blvd #106, Ft Lauderdale, FL 33301
Phone: 954-832-0111 - **Fax:** 954-832-0993
www.judicialresearch.com **Types of Records Retrieved:** Criminal, Civil and Probate courts; Federal courts; Real Estate; Tax Liens/Judgments; UCC records; Vital records

Local Retrieval Area: FL-Broward. **Correspondents:** nationwide.

Add'l Information: Normal turnaround time- 24-48 hours. Projects billed by number of names searched. Projects billed by the hour. First project may require prepayment. Credit cards accepted. Will file/record documents for clients. They specialize in civil litigation, public records and bankruptcy. A licensed PI in FL.

Judicial Research & Retrieval Services (GA)

70 Spring St SW, Atlanta, GA 30303
Phone: 800-529-1338; 404-525-9400 - **Fax:** 404-522-9600
www.judicialresearch.com **Types of Records Retrieved:** Criminal courts; Probate courts; Federal courts; Real Estate; Tax Liens/Judgments; UCC records; Vital records

Local Retrieval Area: GA-Clayton, Cobb, De Kalb, Fulton, Gwinnett. **Correspondent Relationships:** nationwide.

Add'l Information: Normal turnaround time- 24-48 hours. Projects billed by number of names searched. Projects billed by the hour. First project may require prepayment. Credit cards accepted. Will file/record documents for clients. They specialize in civil litigation, public records, and bankruptcy.

Judicial Research & Retrieval Services (Jacksonville)

140 W Monroe St #220, Jacksonville, FL 32202
Phone: 904-356-9110

www.judicialresearch.com **Types of Records Retrieved:** Criminal, Civil and Probate courts; Federal courts; Real Estate; Tax Liens/Judgments; UCC records; Vital records

Local Retrieval Area: FL-Duval, Nassau, St. Johns. **Correspondent Relationships:** nationwide.

Add'l Information: Established 1996. Normal turnaround time- 24-48 hours. Projects billed by number of names searched. Projects billed by the hour. First project may require prepayment. Credit cards accepted. Will file/record documents for clients. They specialize in civil litigation, public records and bankruptcy.

Judicial Research & Retrieval Services (Miami)

17 NW Miami Ct, Miami, FL 33128-1829
Phone: 305-379-3900 - **Fax:** 305-379-4460

www.judicialresearch.com **Types of Records Retrieved:** Criminal, Civil and Probate courts; Federal courts; Real Estate; Tax Liens/Judgments; UCC records; Vital records

Local Retrieval Area: FL-Dade, Escambia, Gadsden, Lee, Leon. **Correspondent Relationships:** nationwide.

Add'l Information: Established 1996. Normal turnaround time- 24-48 hours. Projects billed by number of names searched. Projects billed by the hour. First project may require prepayment. Credit cards accepted. Will file/record documents for clients. They specialize in civil litigation, public records and bankruptcy. A licensed PI in FL. Performs service of process.

Judicial Research & Retrieval Services (Orlando)

62 W Washington St, Orlando, FL 32801
Phone: 407-999-7717 - **Fax:** 407-999-5220

www.judicialresearch.com **Types of Records Retrieved:** Criminal, Civil and Probate courts; Federal courts; Real Estate; Tax Liens/Judgments; UCC records; Vital records

Local Retrieval Area: FL-Orange, Osceola, Seminole. **Correspondent Relationships:** nationwide.

Add'l Information: Established 1996. Normal turnaround time- 24-48 hours. Projects billed by number of names searched. Projects billed by the hour. First project may require prepayment. Credit cards accepted. Will file/record documents for clients. They specialize in civil litigation, public records and bankruptcy. A licensed PI in FL.

Judicial Research & Retrieval Services (Palm Beach)

328 Banyan Blvd #A, West Palm Beach, FL 33401
Phone: 561-659-7677 - **Fax:** 561-659-6061

www.judicialresearch.com **Types of Records Retrieved:** Criminal, Civil and Probate courts; Federal courts; Real Estate; Tax Liens/Judgments; UCC records; Vital records

Local Retrieval Area: FL-Palm Beach, St Lucie. **Correspondent Relationships:** nationwide.

Add'l Information: Normal turnaround time- 24-48 hours. Projects billed by number of names searched. Projects billed by the hour. First project may require prepayment. Credit cards accepted. Will file/record documents for clients. They specialize in civil litigation, public records and bankruptcy.

Judicial Research & Retrieval Services (Tampa)

711 N Florida Ave #227, Tampa, FL 33602
Phone: 813-228-7200 - **Fax:** 813-228-7400

www.judicialresearch.com **Types of Records Retrieved:** Criminal, Civil and Probate courts; Federal courts; Real Estate; Tax Liens/Judgments; UCC records; Vital records

Local Retrieval Area: FL-Hillsborough, Pasco, Pinellas, Polk. **Correspondent Relationships:** nationwide.

Add'l Information: Established 1996. Normal turnaround time- 24-48 hours. Projects billed by number of names searched. Projects billed by the hour. First project may require prepayment. Credit cards accepted. Will file/record documents for clients. They specialize in civil litigation, public records and bankruptcy.

Justifacts Credential Verification Inc

8085 Saltsburg Rd #100, Pittsburgh, PA 15239
Phone: 800-356-6885; 412-798-4790 - **Fax:** 412-798-5249

www.justifacts.com **email:** ayoder@justifacts.com

Types of Records Retrieved: Criminal courts

Local Retrieval Area: PA-Allegheny, Armstrong, Butler, Westmoreland. **Correspondent Relationships:** nationwide.

Add'l Info: Established 1984. Turnaround time- 24-48 hours. Projects billed by number of names searched. Will invoice monthly. They are a nationwide background information service specializing in comprehensive personnel profiles. They verify employment, credit, driving, education, workers' compensation, criminal/civil records and professional licenses.

Kamber Agency

247 N Main St #126, Fort Bragg, CA 95437
Phone: 707-961-5464 - **Fax:** 707-961-1581

www.kamberagency.com **email:** kkamber@adelphia.net

Types of Records Retrieved: Criminal and Civil courts

Local Retrieval Area: CA-Mendocino

Add'l Information: Established 2000. Turnaround time- 5 days. Expedited service available at add'l charge. First project may require prepayment. PayPal accepted. Private investigation specializing in criminal defense, civil litigation support, insurance defense, missing persons & public record retrieval. A licensed PI in CA #15517. Performs service of process.

Kansas Investigative Services Inc

970 N Santa Fe, Wichita, KS 64214
Phone: 888-889-3340; 316-267-1356 - **Fax:** 316-267-5476
kisinc@swbell.net

Types of Records Retrieved: Criminal, Civil and Probate courts; Federal courts; Real Estate; Tax Liens/Judgments; UCC records; Vital records

Local Retrieval Area: KS-Butler, Reno, Sedgwick

Add'l Information: Established 1976. Normal turnaround time- 2 hours for criminal and civil records, 4-24 hours for real estate in Sedgwick; 1-3 days for Butler or Reno. Projects billed by number of names searched. Projects billed by the hour. Charges are by the trip. Flat fees are available for all searches. First project may require prepayment. Will file/record documents for clients. They also service surrounding Kansas counties on 1-2 weekly trips. Sedgwick County searched daily, both A.M. and P.M. Toll-free number is available 24 hours. A licensed PI in KS. Performs service of process.

Karnes Land Title Co Inc

108 N Panna Maria Ave, Karnes City, TX 78118
Phone: 830-780-2221 - **Fax:** 830-780-2236

Types of Records Retrieved: Civil and Probate courts; Real Estate; Tax Liens/Judgments; UCC records; Vital records

Local Retrieval Area: TX-Karnes. **Correspondent Relationships:** adjoining counties.

Add'l Information: Normal turnaround time- 1 week. Fee basis will vary by the type of project. First project may require prepayment.

KasparNet LLC

3613 Reserve Commons Dr, Medina, OH 44256-8179
Phone: 800-886-7534; 330-725-7534 - **Fax:** 800-845-1610; 330-722-4969
www.kasparassociates.com **email:** larryc@kasparassociates.com

Types of Records Retrieved: Civil and Probate courts; Bankruptcy courts; Real Estate; Tax Liens/Judgments; UCC records

Local Retrieval Area: OH-Cuyahoga, Medina, Portage, Summit. **Correspondent Relationships:** statewide.

Add'l Information: Established 1980. Normal turnaround time- 24-72 hours. Projects billed by number of names searched. Will file/record documents for clients. They will invoice. Formerly known as Kaspar & Associates Inc, they specialize in real estate title research in all 88 Ohio counties.

Kaufman Information Resources Inc

14 Scenic Dr, Dayton, NJ 08810-1495
Phone: 732-438-1967 - **Fax:** 732-438-1971 kaufmaninc@aol.com

Types of Records Retrieved: Civil courts; Federal courts; Real Estate; Tax Liens/Judgments; UCC records; Vital records

Local Retrieval Area: NJ-Mercer, Middlesex, Monmouth, Somerset, Union. **Correspondent Relationships:** New Jersey.

Add'l Information: Established 1995. Normal turnaround time- 3 days. Projects billed by number of names searched. First project may require prepayment. Will file/record documents for clients. Terms: net 30 days. They specialize in UCC, corporate records, state and federal tax liens, and federal, state, county and local courts and retrieve records from Department of Treasury.

Kay's Rapid Record Research

33359 Manning St, Yucaipa, CA 92399
Phone: 909-790-2073 - **Fax:** 909-790-8914 maxeykrrr@verizon.net

Records Retrieved: Criminal, Civil and Probate courts; Federal courts; Real Estate; Tax Liens/Judgments; UCC records; Vital records; Archives

Local Retrieval Area: CA-Riverside, San Bernardino

Add'l Information: Established 1991. Normal turnaround time- 1-2 days. Expedited service available. Projects billed by number of names searched. First project may require prepayment. After 1st project, billed by invoice. They have 16 years covering all courts & recorders in jurisdiction including bankruptcy and archives. Daily filing service, document retrieval & quick turnaround. Dependable, reliable always. E&O insurance. Orders received by email, fax, mail, courier.

KC Court Research Inc

PO Box 4288, Olathe, KS 66063
Phone: 913-239-8995 - **Fax:** 913-239-9901 kccourt@kc.rr.com

Types of Records Retrieved: Criminal, Civil and Probate courts; Federal courts; Real Estate; Tax Liens/Judgments; UCC records

Local Retrieval Area: KS-Johnson, Wyandotte; MO-Jackson

Add'l Information: Established 1999. Normal turnaround time- 48 hours. Projects billed by number of names searched. First project may require prepayment. net 30 days. They specialize in Johnson & Wyandotte Counties, also Kansas Federal Courts and Missouri Western District statewide. They also specialize in all document retrieval from federal records center in Lee's Summit and Kansas City, MO.

Keating & Walker

1 Beekman St #406, New York, NY 10038
Phone: 800-466-2730; 212-964-6444 - **Fax:** 212-964-5508
www.keatingandwalker.com **email:** johnwalker@keatingandwalker.com

Types of Records Retrieved: Civil and Probate courts; Federal courts

Local Retrieval Area: NY-Bronx, Kings, Nassau, New York, Queens, Richmond, Westchester. **Correspondent Relationships:** nationwide.

Add'l Information: Established 1992. Normal turnaround time- 24 hours. Projects billed by number of names searched. First project may require prepayment. They specialize in the NY city and suburban NYC area. Performs service of process.

Kellerman Investigations Ltd

6611 State Rte 162, Maryville, IL 62062
888-402-6662; 618-288-6662; cell- 618-410-3943 - **Fax:** 618-288-6668
www.kellermaninvestigations.com/ **email:** klaxon_greg@yahoo.com

Records Retrieved: Criminal, Civil and Probate courts; Federal courts

Local Retrieval Area: IL-Madison, St. Clair. **Correspondent Relationships:** Sangamon and Logan counties, IL.

Add'l Information: Established 1987. Normal turnaround time- less that 24 business hours. Projects billed by number of names searched. Will file/record documents for clients. They are near the Madison County Courthouse in Illinois making their turnaround time reliably fast. Licensed and insured investigative agency, license #'s 115-001758/117-001201. A licensed PI in IL. Performs service of process.

Keppler Legal Research

768 W Celeste Ave, Fresno, CA 93704-1813
Phone: 559-431-2591 - **Fax:** 559-431-2591 mikekeppler@hotmail.com

Types of Records Retrieved: Criminal and Civil courts; Federal courts

Local Retrieval Area: CA-Fresno, Kings, Madera, Tulare

Add'l Information: Established 1992. Normal turnaround time- 24 hours. Projects billed by number of names searched. Will file/record documents for clients. Invoices on the 15th of each month. They specialize in criminal and civil research, bankruptcy, and federal civil.

Kern Attorney Service Inc

1614 W Temple St, Los Angeles, CA 90026
Phone: 800-675-5376; 213-483-4900 - **Fax:** 213-483-7777
www.kernattysvc.com **Records Retrieved:** Criminal, Civil and Probate courts; Federal courts; Real Estate; Tax Liens/Judgments; Vital records

Local Retrieval Area: CA-Los Angeles, Orange, Riverside, San Bernardino, San Diego, Ventura

Add'l Information: Established 1971. Normal turnaround time- 1-3 days. Expedited service available. Projects billed by number of names searched. All projects require prepayment. Credit cards accepted. Will file/record documents for clients. Has branch offices in Orange and Ventura Counties. Performs service of process.

Kevin W McClain Investigations Ltd

PO Box 1434, Centralia, IL 62801
Phone: 877-532-1152; 618-532-1152 - **Fax:** 618-545-0375
www.kevinwmcclain.com **email:** ispy4u@accessus.net

Types of Records Retrieved: Criminal, Civil and Probate courts; Federal courts; Real Estate; Tax Liens/Judgments; UCC records; Vital records

Local Retrieval Area: IL-Clinton, Cook, Effingham, Franklin, Jefferson, Madison, Marion, St. Clair, Washington, Williamson. **Correspondent Relationships:** nationwide.

Add'l Information: Established 1994. Normal turnaround time- 24-48 hours. Expedited service available. Projects billed by number of names searched. Projects billed by number of records located. Projects billed by the hour. First project may require prepayment. Credit cards accepted. Will file/record documents for clients. They are a full service investigative agency, specializing in civil, criminal, workers compensation, process serving, nationwide background checks and online access in IL statewide in criminal history. They have a paralegal on staff. A licensed PI in IL, IN. Performs service of process.

Keys Paper Chase

2743 E 105 North, Idaho Falls, ID 83401
Phone: 208-523-9680; Fax- same

Types of Records Retrieved: Criminal and Civil courts; Real Estate; Tax Liens/Judgments; UCC records

Local Retrieval Area: ID-Bonneville, Fremont, Jefferson, Madison

Add'l Information: Established 2006. Normal turnaround time- 24-48 hours. Projects billed by number of names searched. First project may require prepayment.

Keystone Intelligence Network Inc

1704 Locust St, Philadelphia, PA 19103
Phone: 215-545-1111 - **Fax:** 215-545-1773 truthfinder@netcarrier.com
Types of Records Retrieved: Criminal, Civil and Probate courts; Federal courts; Real Estate; Tax Liens/Judgments; UCC records; Vital records
Local Retrieval Area: PA-Montgomery, Philadelphia; NJ-Camden, Gloucester
Add'l Information: Normal turnaround time- 1 day. Projects billed by the hour. First project may require prepayment. Credit cards accepted. They are a private investigating firm, performing various services for clients such as law firms & private individuals.

Kidder County Abstract Co

114 Mitchell Ave S, Box 108, Steele, ND 58482
Phone: 701-475-2432
Records Retrieved: Real Estate; Tax Liens/Judgments; UCC records
Local Retrieval Area: ND-Kidder
Add'l Information: Normal turnaround time- 2 days. Projects billed by number of names searched. Payment due upon receipt of invoice. Will file/record documents for clients.

Kiefer Title Co

21 S Main St, Perryville, MO 63775-2522
Phone: 573-547-7755 - **Fax:** 573-547-7788 ktcmary@powrup.net
Records Retrieved: Real Estate; Tax Liens/Judgments; Probate courts
Local Retrieval Area: MO-Perry
Add'l Information: Established 1991. Normal turnaround time- 3 days. They charge a flat rate per project. First project may require prepayment. Will file/record documents for clients.

Kimmons Security Services Inc

2000 Dairy Ashford #430, Houston, TX 77077-5737
Phone: 281-679-0070 - **Fax:** 281-679-0080
www.kimmonssecurity.com **email:** rob@kimmonssecurity.com
Types of Records Retrieved: Criminal, Civil and Probate courts; Federal courts; Real Estate; Tax Liens/Judgments; UCC records; Vital records
Local Retrieval Area: TX-Brazoria, Dallas, Fort Bend, Galveston, Harris, Montgomery, Tarrant, Travis. **Correspondent Relationships:** most Texas counties and many counties nationwide.
Add'l Information: Established 1982. Normal turnaround time- 24-48 hours. Projects billed by number of names searched. Projects billed by the hour. First project may require prepayment. Credit cards accepted. Will file/record documents for clients. Personal checks are accepted. Billing after each assignment. They specialize in asset investigations and public record searches. They also have nationwide capabilities for multitude of information databanks. They are an investigative and security company. A licensed PI in TX. Performs service of process.

King Investigations Inc

PO Box 799, Altus, OK 73522
Phone: 580-477-1676 - **Fax:** 580-477-1828
www.kinginvestigations.net **email:** helenking@kinginvestigations.net
Types of Records Retrieved: Criminal, Civil and Probate courts; Federal District court; Real Estate; Tax Liens/Judgments
Retrieval Area: OK-Comanche, Greer, Harmon, Jackson, Kiowa, Tillman
Add'l Information: Established 1996. Normal turnaround time- 48 hours. Projects billed by number of names searched. First project may require prepayment. Will file/record documents for clients. They specialize in locates, pre-employment, background information, real estate searches, civil-criminal searches and market research. Helen also has a BS degree in criminal justice management & ethics. A licensed PI in OK.

Vickie King Paralegal

PO Box 1340, Whitley City, KY 42653
Phone: 606-376-5931 - **Fax:** 606-376-4401 vickygking@yahoo.com
Types of Records Retrieved: Real Estate
Local Retrieval Area: KY-Mc Creary
Add'l Information: Established 1994. First project may require prepayment. She specializes in real estate.

Patrick King

4538 Halifax Rd, El Monte, CA 91731-1539
Phone: 626-452-0838 - **Fax:** 626-452-0838
www.paddyking.com **email:** kilgore211@juno.com
Types of Records Retrieved: Civil and Probate courts; Federal courts; Real Estate; Tax Liens/Judgments; Vital records
Local Retrieval Area: CA-Los Angeles
Add'l Information: Established 1990. Normal turnaround time- 1 day. Projects billed by number of names searched. First project may require prepayment. Will file/record documents for clients. His number one goal is customer satisfaction. They can do everything from court filings to serving papers and interviewing people if it aids in getting the information. If required he can do Orange and San Bernardino counties in CA. Performs service of process.

Kingman Abstract & Title Co Inc

221 N Main, Kingman, KS 67068
Phone: 620-532-2011 - **Fax:** 620-532-5383
Types of Records Retrieved: Civil and Probate courts; Real Estate; Tax Liens/Judgments
Local Retrieval Area: KS-Kingman
Add'l Information: Established 1889. Normal turnaround time- 24-48 hours. Projects billed by the hour. They specialize in title insurance, escrow and closings. They will file/record real estate documents on behalf of clients.

King-Reed & Assoc Ltd

85 Scarsdale Rd #309, Toronto, ON M3B 2R2
Phone: 877-695-6575; 416-449-8677 - **Fax:** 416-449-9889
www.king-reed.com **email:** king@king-reed.com
Types of Records Retrieved: Civil and Probate courts; Federal courts; Tax Liens/Judgments; UCC records; Vital records
Local Retrieval Area: CANADA-Ontario, Toronto. **Correspondent Relationships:** affiliates across Canada for national service through Investigations Canada.
Add'l Information: Established 1984. Projects billed by number of names searched. Projects billed by the hour. First project may require prepayment. Will file/record documents for clients. They specialize in due diligence inquiries, full record searches, surveillance, general investigations. Has 10 offices in Ontario. A licensed PI in CANADA.

Kings Title & Abstract Co (Anderson)

223 W 9th St, Anderson, IN 46016-1366
Phone: 800-317-1515; 765-643-3019 - **Fax:** 765-644-0362
www.kingstitle.com **email:** anderson@kingstitle.com
Types of Records Retrieved: Civil and Probate courts; Real Estate; Tax Liens/Judgments; UCC records
Local Retrieval Area: IN-Madison
Add'l Information: Established 1974. Normal turnaround time- 24-48 hours. Projects billed by number of names searched. Projects billed by number of records located. Projects billed by the hour. First project may require prepayment. They specialize in right of way and railroad research.

Kings Title & Abstract Co (Marion)

201 W 3rd St, Marion, IN 46952
Phone: 800-662-1299; 765-662-1111 - **Fax:** 765-662-2018
www.kingstitle.com **email:** marion@kingstitle.com
Types of Records Retrieved: Civil and Probate courts; Real Estate; Tax Liens/Judgments; UCC records
Local Retrieval Area: IN-Grant. **Correspondent Relationships:** surrounding counties.
Add'l Information: Established 1974. Normal turnaround time- 24-48 hours. Projects billed by number of names searched. Projects billed by number of records located. Projects billed by the hour. First project may require prepayment. Will file/record documents for clients. They specialize in right of way and railroad research.

Kings Title & Abstract Co (Muncie)

3100 N. Oakwood, Muncie, IN 47304-2212
Phone: 800-294-1566; 765-288-1566 - **Fax:** 765-288-1642
www.kingstitle.com **email:** muncie@kingstitle.com

Types of Records Retrieved: Civil and Probate courts; Real Estate; Tax Liens/Judgments; UCC records

Local Retrieval Area: IN-Delaware

Add'l Information: Established 1974. Normal turnaround time- 24-48 hours. Projects billed by number of names searched. Projects billed by number of records located. Projects billed by the hour. First project may require prepayment. Will file/record documents for clients. They specialize in railroad research.

Kings Title & Abstract Co (Richmond)

100 S 5th St, Richmond, IN 47374-4223
Phone: 800-757-7762; 765-962-6541 - **Fax:** 765-966-3719
www.kingstitle.com **email:** richmond@kingstitle.com

Types of Records Retrieved: Civil and Probate courts; Real Estate; Tax Liens/Judgments; UCC records

Local Retrieval Area: IN-Wayne

Add'l Information: Established 1961. Normal turnaround time- 24-48 hours. Projects billed by number of names searched. Projects billed by number of records located. Projects billed by the hour. First project may require prepayment. They specialize in right of way and railroad research.

Kings Title & Abstract Co (Rushville)

111 W 3rd St, Rushville, IN 46173-1839
Phone: 877-932-5757; 765-932-5757 - **Fax:** 765-932-2168
www.kingstitle.com **email:** rushville@kingstitle.com

Types of Records Retrieved: Civil and Probate courts; Real Estate; Tax Liens/Judgments; UCC records

Local Retrieval Area: IN-Rush. **Correspondent Relationships:** statewide.

Add'l Information: Established 1974. Normal turnaround time- 24-48 hours. Projects billed by number of names searched. Projects billed by number of records located. Projects billed by the hour. First project may require prepayment. Will file/record documents for clients. They are the area's leader in title & closing services.

Kings Title & Abstract Co (Shelbyville)

1 Howard St, Shelbyville, IN 46176-2616
Phone: 317-398-0424 - **Fax:** 317-392-0174
www.kingstitle.com **email:** shelbyville@kingstitle.com

Types of Records Retrieved: Civil and Probate courts; Real Estate; Tax Liens/Judgments; UCC records

Local Retrieval Area: IN-Hancock, Shelby

Add'l Information: Established 1974. Normal turnaround time- 24-48 hours. Projects billed by number of names searched. Projects billed by number of records located. Projects billed by the hour. First project may require prepayment. They specialize in right of way and railroad research.

Kings Title & Abstract Co (Winchester)

125 S Main St, PO Box 25, Winchester, IN 47394
Phone: 800-280-6322; 765-584-9882 - **Fax:** 765-584-2302
www.kingstitle.com **email:** winchester@kingstitle.com

Types of Records Retrieved: Civil and Probate courts; Real Estate; Tax Liens/Judgments; UCC records

Local Retrieval Area: IN-Randolph. **Correspondent Relationships:** Jay and Darke counties OH.

Add'l Info: Established 1970. Turnaround time- 24-48 hours. Projects billed by number of names searched. Will file/record documents for clients. Payment due upon project completion. They specialize in right of way, railroad research, title and abstracts research and insured escrow closings.

Kings Title & Closing Services

1111 Broad St, New Castle, IN 47362
Phone: 800-860-2990; 765-593-2167 - **Fax:** 765-593-2168
www.kingstitle.com **email:** statewide@kingstitle.com

Types of Records Retrieved: Civil and Probate courts; Bankruptcy court; Real Estate; Tax Liens/Judgments; UCC records; Vital records

Local Retrieval Area: IN-Allen, Blackford, Decatur, Delaware, Fayette, Franklin, Grant, Henry, Jay, Madison, Randolph, Rush, Shelby, Wayne. **Correspondent Relationships:** IN, OH, KY, IL.

Add'l Information: Established 1974. Normal turnaround time- 24-48 hours. Projects billed by the hour. First project may require prepayment. Will file/record documents for clients. They specialize in utility right of way/railroad research. They service the entire state with searches, title insurance, and closings.

Kiowa County Abstract Co

PO Box 128, 1304 Goff, Eads, CO 81036
Phone: 719-438-5811 - **Fax:** 719-438-5926

Records Retrieved: Real Estate; Tax Liens/Judgments; Vital records

Local Retrieval Area: CO-Kiowa

Add'l Information: Established 1907. Normal turnaround time- 1-2 days. Fee basis will vary by the type of project. Will file/record documents for clients. They specialize in real estate title.

Kiowa County Abstract Company

108 E 4th St, Hobart, OK 73651
Phone: 580-726-5283 - **Fax:** 580-726-3545 kcac@itlnet.net

Types of Records Retrieved: Civil and Probate courts; Real Estate; Tax Liens/Judgments; UCC records

Local Retrieval Area: OK-Kiowa

Add'l Information: Established 1901. Normal turnaround time- variable depending on project. Fees vary by project type or search location. They will accept personal checks. They are a full title service company.

Jimmie Kirby

185 Trisdale Ln, Gainesboro, TN 38562
Phone: 931-858-8786, cell- 931-267-2418

Types of Records Retrieved: Criminal and Civil courts; Real Estate; Tax Liens/Judgments

Local Retrieval Area: TN-Clay, Fentress, Jackson, Overton, Putnam, Smith, White, Wilson

Add'l Information: Normal turnaround time- 1-2 days usually. First project may require prepayment. Specializes in NE Tennessee.

Terry Kirkland

215 Walnut St, Monticello, KY 42633
Phone: 606-348-8645

Types of Records Retrieved: Real Estate; Tax Liens/Judgments

Local Retrieval Area: KY-Wayne

Add'l Information: Established 1992. First project may require prepayment. Terry specializes in real estate.

KJB Court Services

710 S College Rd #11, Lafayette, LA 70503
Phone: 225-274-6453 - **Fax:** 866-574-0482
Brian.KJBCourtServices@gmail.com

Types of Records Retrieved: Criminal and Civil courts

Local Retrieval Area: LA-East Baton Rouge, Iberville, Livingston, Orleans, West Baton Rouge, West Feliciana

Add'l Information: Established 1991. Normal turnaround time- 24 hours. Projects billed by number of names searched. All projects require prepayment. They specialize in accurate and timely records retrieval for criminal and civil information in East/West Baton Rouge, Livingston, Ascension, Iberville & Orleans Parishes.

KJK Abstract Co

38 Alpine Way, Raritan, NJ 08869
Phone: 908-725-6336 - **Fax:** 908-253-9228

Records Retrieved: Real Estate; Tax Liens/Judgments; UCC records

Local Retrieval Area: NJ-Somerset

Add'l Information: Established 1985. Normal turnaround time- 5-10 days. Fee basis will vary by type of project. Will file/record documents for clients. They specialize in real estate searches.

Klitzke & Assoc Inc/Klitzke Services Group

PO Box 144, Genessee Depot, WI 53127-0144
Phone: 262-521-9502 - **Fax:** 262-521-9503
www.klitzke.biz **email:** kklitzke@wi.rr.com

Types of Records Retrieved: Criminal, Civil and Probate courts; Federal courts; Real Estate; Tax Liens/Judgments; UCC records; Vital records

Local Retrieval Area: WI-Milwaukee, Waukesha

Add'l Information: Established 1994. Normal turnaround time- 24-48 hours. Projects billed by number of names searched. Credit cards accepted. $2.00 per page for copies. Statewide criminal record searches in 50 states and in more that 120 foreign countries. Also driver records, asset searches and locate people. More that 15,000 confidential databases. Licensed PI in WI.

KLK Research

51 Eldorado Dr, Moscow Mills, MO 63362
Phone: 636-366-7055 - **Fax:** 636-356-4557
www.geocities.com/klk_research/index.htm
email: klkresearch@centurytel.net

Types of Records Retrieved: Criminal and Civil courts

Local Retrieval Area: IL-St Clair; MO-St Charles, St Louis, St Louis City

Add'l Information: Established 1998. Normal turnaround time- 24 hours. Projects billed by number of names searched. Payment due net 30 days. They specialize in criminal and civil background searches for pre-employment, and tenant screening.

Judi Knecht

4817 Bowfield Dr, Antioch, TN 37013
Phone: 615-832-8255 - **Fax:** 615-833-3082 judi_knecht@comcast.net

Types of Records Retrieved: Real Estate; UCC records; Tax Liens/Judgments

Local Retrieval Area: TN-Davidson, Hamilton, Knox, Rutherford, Shelby, Williamson. **Correspondent Relationships:** throughout most of Tennessee.

Add'l Information: Established 2002. Normal turnaround time- 24-48 hours. Projects are billed by the number of properties searches. She provides current-owner searches that are accurate and prompt, at reasonable rates. All reports are typed. No per-page fee for emailing results.

Charles M Kneisley

1602 Sewanee Dr, West Columbia, SC 29169-6054
Phone: 803-936-1200 - **Fax:** 803-936-1201 ckneisley@sc.rr.com

Types of Records Retrieved: Criminal, Civil and Probate courts; Federal courts; Real Estate; Tax Liens/Judgments; UCC records

Local Retrieval Area: SC-Lexington, Richland. **Correspondent Relationships:** Sumter, Kershaw, Orangeburg, Charleston, Calhoun, Aiken counties.

Add'l Information: Established 1990. Normal turnaround time- 24-48 hours. Projects billed by number of names searched. Will file/record documents for clients. Monthly billing. They specialize in retrieving statewide criminal histories from the SC Law Enforcement Division. They have been in business for 14 years.

Margaret H Knoras

23 East Lane, Springfield, VT 05156
Phone: 802-885-4375 - **Fax:** 802-885-2405 peggyk@vermontel.net

Types of Records Retrieved: Criminal, Civil and Probate courts; Federal courts; Real Estate; Tax Liens/Judgments; UCC records; Vital records

Local Retrieval Area: VT-Windham, Windsor. **Correspondent Relationships:** statewide.

Add'l Information: Established 1996. Normal turnaround time- 48 hours. Projects billed by number of names searched. Will file/record documents for clients.

Know It All Background Research Services

1950 Street Rd #211, Bensalem, PA 19020
Phone: 888-281-9535; 215-245-1975 - **Fax:** 215-352-4469
www.screenmyapplicants.com **email:** research@screenmyapplicants.com

Records Retrieved: Criminal and Civil courts; Federal District courts

Local Retrieval Area: DE-Kent, New Castle, Sussex; PA-Philadelphia. **Correspondent Relationships:** nationwide.

Add'l Information: Established 1999. Normal turnaround time- 24-48 hours. Projects billed by number of names searched. Know It All has been serving the industry since 1999. They are dedicated to providing outstanding customer service and quick, accurate results.

Knox County Abstract

105 S First St, Edina, MO 63537 **Phone:** 660-397-3259

Types of Records Retrieved: Civil courts; Real Estate; Tax Liens/Judgments

Local Retrieval Area: MO-Knox

Add'l Information: Established 1970. First project may require prepayment. Will file/record documents for clients. They specialize in Knox County real estate.

Kolling & Associates

3576 W FR 182, Brookline, MO 65619
Phone: 417-889-4092 - **Fax:** 417-889-4026 coachmkoll@aol.com

Types of Records Retrieved: Criminal, Civil and Probate courts; Federal courts; Real Estate; Tax Liens/Judgments; UCC records; Vital records

Local Retrieval Area: MO-Christian, Greene. **Correspondent Relationships:** nationwide.

Add'l Information: Established 1997. Normal turnaround time- 24-36 hours or less. Projects billed by number of names searched. First project may require prepayment. Credit cards accepted. Requires pre-paid check. They specialize in criminal record checks statewide and county, credit reports, MVRs (all 50 states), educational employment, and license verifications, as well as tracing, verification, and finding SSNs.

Kossuth Abstract & Title Co

113 N Hall St, Algona, IA 50511-2318
Phone: 515-295-3745 - **Fax:** 515-295-7633

Types of Records Retrieved: Civil and Probate courts; Real Estate; Tax Liens/Judgments

Local Retrieval Area: IA-Kossuth

Add'l Information: Established 1850. Normal turnaround time- 2-3 days. Will file/record documents for clients.

Kotner Abstract & Title

1333 B Locust St, Eldorado, IL 62930
Phone: 618-273-7611 - **Fax:** 618-273-7611

Types of Records Retrieved: Civil and Probate courts; Real Estate; Tax Liens/Judgments; UCC records

Local Retrieval Area: IL-Saline

Add'l Information: Established 1978. Normal turnaround time- 24 hours. Projects billed by number of names searched. Projects billed by number of records located. Projects billed by the hour. He specializes in title abstracts and title insurance in Saline County. He is a policy issuing agent for 1st American Title and Nat. Land Title Insurance Companies. Will file/record UCC and real estate documents for clients in Saline County only.

Krayer Detective Agency Inc

107 N Apple St, Dunmore, PA 18512
Phone: 800-249-3704; 570-347-5754 - **Fax:** 570-347-4913
www.krayerdetective.com **email:** krayer@aol.com

Types of Records Retrieved: Criminal and Civil courts

Local Retrieval Area: PA-Bradford, Columbia, Lackawanna, Luzerne, Monroe, Pike, Susquehanna, Wayne, Wyoming

Add'l Information: Established 1987. First project may require prepayment. They also provide court filings, subpoena preparation, skiptracing, private investigations, and repossessions. A licensed PI in PA. Performs service of process.

Kroes Detective Agency

7301 E 22nd St, Tucson, AZ 85710
Phone: 800-249-0694; 520-886-8397 - **Fax:** 877-428-6939; 520-886-0949
jimkroes@cs.com

Types of Records Retrieved: Criminal, Civil and Probate courts; Federal courts; Real Estate; Tax Liens/Judgments; UCC records

Local Retrieval Area: AZ-Pima. **Correspondents:** nationwide.

Add'l Information: Established 1970. Normal turnaround time- 24-48 hours. Projects billed by number of names searched. First project may require prepayment. They have 24 years experience, knowledge and equipment in debugging services. They also perform pre-employment screening, all types of investigation and process serving. A licensed PI in AZ. Performs service of process.

Kroll Background America

1900 Church St #400, Nashville, TN 37203
Phone: 800-697-7189; 615-320-9800 - **Fax:** 800-845-2183; 615-321-9585
https://www.baionline.net **email:** moutlaw@krollworthode.com

Types of Records Retrieved: Criminal courts; Real Estate; Tax Liens/Judgments

Local Retrieval Area: TN-Davidson, Rutherford; MD-Baltimore, Baltimore City, Carroll, Harford. **Correspondent Relationships:** nationwide. Kroll has offices in Hampstead MD 800-673-9089, Nashville TN 800-697-7189.

Add'l Information: Established 1983. Normal turnaround time- 24 hours in Maryland, other areas 3-5 days. Projects billed by number of names searched. Will bill monthly. They specialize in pre-employment background investigations, including criminal records nationwide, MVRs, credit histories and reference checking. Maryland statewide criminal records within 24 hours; TN statewide convictions only searches. A licensed PI in FL, MD, TN.

Kroll Document Filing & Retrieval Services

1900 Church St #400, Nashville, TN 37203
Phone: 800-324-2050; 615-321-2050 - **Fax:** 800-788-0835; 615-329-3343
https://www.baionline.net **email:** documentservices@kroll.com

Types of Records Retrieved: Criminal, Civil and Probate courts; Federal courts; Real Estate; Tax Liens/Judgments; UCC records; Vital records; DMV records

Local Retrieval Area: TN-Cheatham, Davidson, Robertson, Rutherford, Sumner, Williamson, Wilson. **Correspondent Relationships:** nationwide.

Add'l Information: Established 1979. Normal turnaround time- 1-3 days. Projects billed by number of names searched. First project may require prepayment. Credit cards accepted. Will file/record documents for clients. They specialize in corporate work, state/county UCCs, tax liens/judgments and real property. They visit the TN Secretary of State office four times a day. They provide registered agent services. Performs service of process.

KY Data Search Inc

1374 Ouerbacker Ct, Louisville, KY 40208
Phone: 502-637-4658 - **Fax:** 502-637-4495 springbooks@insightbb.com

Types of Records Retrieved: Civil courts; Federal District courts; Real Estate; Tax Liens/Judgments; UCC records

Local Retrieval Area: KY-Bullitt, Franklin, Hardin, Henry, Jefferson, Meade, Nelson, Oldham, Shelby, Spencer

Add'l Information: Established 1989. Normal turnaround time- 48 hours. Projects billed by number of names searched. Will file/record documents for clients. Terms: net 30 days. Formerly Kentucky Data Search, they specialize in current owner searches, UCCs, lien searches and litigation searches.

KY Search & Retrieval Services

1413 Pine Meadow Rd, Lexington, KY 40504
Phone: 859-252-6874 - **Fax:** 859-231-0808

Types of Records Retrieved: Civil courts; Federal courts; Real Estate; Tax Liens/Judgments; UCC records

Local Retrieval Area: KY-Anderson, Bourbon, Boyle, Clark, Fayette, Fleming, Franklin, Garrard, Harrison, Jessamine, Lincoln, Madison, Mercer, Montgomery, Scott, Woodford

Add'l Information: Established 1990. Normal turnaround time- 48-72 hours. Projects billed by number of names searched. Payment by check only. They provide public record searches at federal, local and KY SOS specializing in UCC/Tax/Corporate records.

Chet Kylander

PO Box 1772, Nashville, IN 47448
Phone: 812-988-9522 - **Fax:** 812-988-4099

Types of Records Retrieved: Criminal and Civil courts; Tax Liens/Judgments

Local Retrieval Area: IN-Bartholomew, Brown, Decatur, Jackson, Jennings, Johnson, Shelby

Add'l Information: Turnaround time- 8-24 hours. First project may require prepayment. They specialize in the areas of Jackson, Jennings and Shelby.

Kyle & Kyle (Michelle Kyle)

7015 Eagle View Ct, St Louis, MO 63129
Phone: 314-846-7728 - **Fax:** 314-846-9925 kylenkyleri@aol.com

Types of Records Retrieved: Criminal, Civil and Probate courts; Federal courts; Real Estate; Tax Liens/Judgments; UCC records

Local Retrieval Area: MO-St. Charles, St. Louis, St. Louis City

Add'l Information: Established 1987. Normal turnaround time- 24-48 hours. Projects billed by number of names searched. Will file/record documents for clients. Will Bill. They specialize in court records, judgments, pre-employment screening, UCCs and tax lien records. Nineteen years experience in the area.

KYMRON Research LLC

PO Box 655, Jonesboro, GA 30237
Phone: 770-703-7301 - **Fax:** 770-703-7302 kymmorrow@netzero.net

Types of Records Retrieved: Criminal and Civil courts

Local Retrieval Area: GA-Carroll, Cherokee, Clayton, Cobb, De Kalb, Douglas, Fayette, Fulton, Gwinnett, Muscogee. **Correspondent Relationships:** Carroll, Cherokee, Douglas, Hall, Henry, Rockdale counties, GA.

Add'l Information: Established 1992. Normal turnaround time- 24-48 hours. Projects billed by number of names searched. Will file/record documents for clients. Payment due within 30 days of billing. They specialize in record retrieval from county, state and superior courts and criminal and civil background checks. Performs service of process.

L & J Research

PO Box 211874, Chula Vista, CA 91921-1874
Phone: 619-829-2083 - **Fax:** 619-397-5594 ljresearch@cox.net

Types of Records Retrieved: Criminal and Civil courts; Federal courts; Tax Liens/Judgments; UCC records; Vital records

Local Retrieval Area: CA-San Diego

Add'l Information: Established 1995. Normal turnaround time- 24-48 hours. Check or money order only accepted. Invoice on the 1st & 15th of each month. They specialize in public record retrieval at all court levels.

L Fay Hedden Abstract Office Inc

214 N 7th St, Vincennes, IN 47591-2114
Phone: 812-882-5273 - **Fax:** 812-882-9886

Types of Records Retrieved: Civil and Probate courts; Real Estate; Tax Liens/Judgments; UCC records; Vital records

Local Retrieval Area: IN-Knox

Add'l Information: Established 1939. Normal turnaround time- 5-10 days. Projects billed by number of names searched. Projects billed by number of records located. They specialize in real estate title.

L L Lesko Inc

1072 SE Floresta Dr, Port St Lucie, FL 34983
Phone: 772-879-2625 - **Fax:** 800-944-9811; 772-879-0068
www.leskotitle.com **email:** iva@adelphia.net

Records Retrieved: Real Estate; Tax Liens/Judgments; UCC records

Retrieval Area: FL-Brevard, Indian River, Martin, Palm Beach, St. Lucie

Add'l Information: Established 1996. Normal turnaround time- within 24 hours. Projects billed by number of names searched. First project may require prepayment. Terms: net 30 days. They specialize in title and abstract research, O/E reports, title search reports, UCCs.

Deborah Labhart

320 N Kirscher Ln, Placentia, CA 92870

Phone: 714-993-0185 - **Fax:** 714-993-5264 deborahlabhart@sbcglobal.net

Types of Records Retrieved: Criminal and Civil courts

Local Retrieval Area: CA-Orange. **Correspondent Relationships:** San Diego, Riverside, San Bernardino counties CA.

Add'l Information: Established 1981. Normal turnaround time- 24-48 hours. Projects billed by number of names searched. Payment is net 30 days. She specializes in background screening info and civil/criminal court records.

Lacey Pioneer Abstract Company Inc

PO Box 788, Anadarko, OK 73005

Phone: 405-247-5152 - **Fax:** 405-247-5777 lacey-pioneer@classicnet.net

Types of Records Retrieved: Criminal, Civil and Probate courts; Real Estate; Tax Liens/Judgments; UCC records; Vital records

Local Retrieval Area: OK-Caddo

Add'l Information: Established 1901. Normal turnaround time- 1-2 days. Projects billed by number of names searched. Will file/record documents for clients. Personal checks are accepted. They specialize in closings, title insurance and title searches. They also prepare abstract of titles.

LaCrosse Abstract & Title LLC

PO Box 636, 110 W 8th, La Crosse, KS 67548

Phone: 800-256-6911; 785-222-2712 - **Fax:** 785-222-3340 stull1@gbta.net

Types of Records Retrieved: Criminal, Civil and Probate courts; Real Estate; Tax Liens/Judgments; UCC records

Local Retrieval Area: KS-Rush

Add'l Information: Established 1994. Normal turnaround time- up to 1 week. Fee basis varies by type of transaction. Will file/record documents for clients.

Lafayette County Abstract

330 Main St, Darlington, WI 53530

Phone: 608-776-3338 - **Fax:** 608-776-4798

www.lafayettecountytitle.com **Types of Records Retrieved:** Civil and Probate courts; Real Estate; Tax Liens/Judgments; UCC records

Local Retrieval Area: WI-Lafayette

Add'l Information: Normal turnaround time- 1-2 days. Fee basis varies by type of transaction. All projects require prepayment. They specialize in abstracts, title insurance and closing service.

Lafayette County Abstract & Title Inc

PO Box 943, 113 E 3rd St, Lewisville, AR 71845

Phone: 870-921-4263 - **Fax:** 870-921-5262 lafabs@aol.com

Types of Records Retrieved: Criminal, Civil and Probate courts; Real Estate; Tax Liens/Judgments; UCC records; Vital records

Local Retrieval Area: AR-Lafayette

Add'l Information: Established 1939. Normal turnaround time- 1 week. Projects billed by the hour. Will file/record documents for clients. They accept personal checks. They specialize in anything to do with real estate.

Lafayette County Land Title Co

545 S 13 Hwy, PO Box 128, Lexington, MO 64067

Phone: 660-259-4631 - **Fax:** 660-259-3142

Types of Records Retrieved: Real Estate; Probate Courts

Local Retrieval Area: MO-Lafayette

Add'l Information: Established 1860. Normal turnaround time- 2-3 days. Fee basis will vary by type of project. They specialize in real estate title.

LaGrange Title Company

127 W Spring, LaGrange, IN 46761

Phone: 260-463-3232 - **Fax:** 260-463-3232 lagrangetitle@earthlink.net

Types of Records Retrieved: Criminal, Civil and Probate courts; Real Estate; Tax Liens/Judgments; UCC records; Vital records

Local Retrieval Area: IN-LaGrange

Add'l Information: Established 1947. Normal turnaround time- 3 business days. Projects billed by number of names searched. Will file/record documents for clients. The only locally owned title company, serving LaGrange County since 1947.

Lake County Abstract & Title Co

314 1st St E Suite 101, Polson, MT 59860

Phone: 800-823-6225; 406-883-6226 - **Fax:** 406-883-2586

www.lctitles.com **email:** info@lctitles.com

Types of Records Retrieved: Civil and Probate courts; Real Estate; Tax Liens/Judgments; UCC records; Vital records

Local Retrieval Area: MT-Lake

Add'l Information: Established 1923. Normal turnaround time- 3 days. Projects billed by the hour.

Lake County Abstract Co Inc

PO Box 369, 830 N Michigan Ave #501, Baldwin, MI 49304

Phone: 231-745-3432 - **Fax:** 231-745-7660

www.lcac.com **email:** leeannr@lcac.com

Types of Records Retrieved: Criminal, Civil and Probate courts; Real Estate; Tax Liens/Judgments; UCC records; Vital records

Local Retrieval Area: MI-Lake, Osceola

Add'l Information: Established 1913. Normal turnaround time- up to 1 week. Expedited service available. Fee basis will vary by type of project. Will file/record documents for clients. They will invoice. They specialize in real estate.

Lake Michigan Title Co

11 W Main St, Hartford, MI 49057 269-637-8595 - **Fax:** 269-637-1857

Types of Records Retrieved: Real Estate; Tax Liens/Judgments; Probate courts; UCC records

Local Retrieval Area: MI-Allegan, Berrien, Van Buren

Add'l Information: Normal turnaround time- up to 1 week. Fee basis will vary by the type of project. They specialize in title insurance.

LaMoure County Abstract Co

PO Box 596, 103 S Main St, LaMoure, ND 58458-0596

Phone: 701-883-4246 - **Fax:** 701-883-4475 abstract@drtel.net

Types of Records Retrieved: Real Estate; Tax Liens/Judgments

Local Retrieval Area: ND-La Moure

Add'l Information: Established 1900. Normal turnaround time- 2-5 days. Fee basis will vary by type of project. First project may require prepayment. Will file/record documents for clients. They specialize in abstracts of title and title memorandums.

Land America Lawyers Title

727 Clinton St #100, Fort Wayne, IN 46802-1801

Phone: 260-424-2929 - **Fax:** 260-424-0037

Types of Records Retrieved: Civil and Probate courts; Real Estate; Tax Liens/Judgments; UCC records; Vital records

Local Retrieval Area: IN-Boone, Clinton, DeKalb, Hamilton, Hancock, Henry, Huntington, Johnson, Kosciusko, Lagrange, Madison, Marion, Morgan, Noble, Steuben, Wabash, Wells, Whitley

Add'l Information: Established 1978. Turnaround time- 2-3 days. Fee basis varies by type of transaction. Will file/record documents for clients.

Land Grant Title Group Inc

420 S 2nd St, Elkhart, IN 46516

Phone: 888-563-4768; 574-295-1620 - **Fax:** 888-563-4760; 574-295-8302

www.mylandgrant.com **email:** wecare@mylandgrant.com

Types of Records Retrieved: Civil and Probate courts; Federal courts; Real Estate; Tax Liens/Judgments; UCC records

Local Retrieval Area: IN-Elkhart, Kosciusko, LaGrange, Marshall, St. Joseph. **Correspondent Relationships:** LaGrange and Marion counties IN.

Add'l Information: Established 1996. Normal turnaround time- 3 business days. Projects billed by number of names searched. Projects billed by number of records located. First project may require prepayment. Will file/record documents for clients. They will also invoice. They specialize in title insurance, land record searches and escrow closings.

Land Records of Texas

1945 Walnut Hill Ln, Irving, TX 75038
Phone: 800-678-8016; 972-580-8575 - **Fax:** 800-678-8017; 972-518-2412
https://www.fntic.com/services/l_records.htm **email:** jakins@fnf.com

Types of Records Retrieved: Real Estate; Tax Liens/Judgments; Probate courts; UCC records

Local Retrieval Area: TX-Atascosa, Austin, Bandera, Bastrop, Bexar, Brazoria, Brazos, Caldwell, Chambers, Collin, Dallas, Denton, Ellis, Fayette, Fort Bend, Frio, Grimes, Guadalupe, Harris, Hays, Hill, Hunt, Johnson, Kaufman, Medina, Parker, Tarrant, Travis, Uvalde, Waller, Wharton, Wilson, Wise. **Correspondent Relationships:** nationwide.

Add'l Information: Established 1983. Normal turnaround time- 1-5 days. Projects billed by the hour. First project may require prepayment. Will file/record documents for clients. They specialize in pre-foreclosure reports, trustee services and current owner searches.

Land Title & Abstract

247 W Cedar Ave, Gladwin, MI 48624
Phone: 989-426-0011 - **Fax:** 989-426-7141
www.ltabstract.com **email:** pattie@ltabstract.com

Types of Records Retrieved: Real Estate; Tax Liens/Judgments; Probate courts; UCC records; Vital records

Local Retrieval Area: MI-Clare, Gladwin

Add'l Information: Established 1987. Normal turnaround time- 2-3 days. Fee basis may vary by the type of project. First project may require prepayment. Will file/record documents for clients. They specialize in title insurance and closings.

Land Title Co

PO Box 651, Jackson, WY 83001
Phone: 800-289-9920; 307-733-4713 - **Fax:** 307-733-6186
landtitle@onewest.net

Types of Records Retrieved: Civil and Probate courts; Real Estate; Tax Liens/Judgments

Local Retrieval Area: WY-Lincoln, Teton. **Correspondents:** statewide.

Add'l Information: Turnaround time- 1-2 days. Projects billed by number of names searched. Will file/record documents for clients. Net 30 days.

Land Title Corp

116 W 5th St, Tipton, IA 52772
Phone: 563-886-6915 - **Fax:** 563-886-1238

Types of Records Retrieved: Real Estate; Tax Liens/Judgments; Probate courts; UCC records

Local Retrieval Area: IA-Cedar

Add'l Information: Established 1987. Normal turnaround time- up to 3 days. Fee basis will vary by the type of project. First project may require prepayment. Payment due upon completion.

Land Title Guarantee Co

533 E Hopkins, Aspen, CO 81611
Phone: 970-925-1678 - **Fax:** 970-925-6243
www.ltgc.com **email:** dharris@ltgc.com

Types of Records Retrieved: Real Estate; Tax Liens/Judgments; UCC records; Vital records **Local Retrieval Area:** CO-Pitkin

Add'l Information: Established 1993. Normal turnaround time- 2 days. Projects billed by number of records located. Projects billed by the hour. All projects require prepayment. Main office is in Glenwood Springs, CO (970-945-2610).

Land Title Inc

1900 Silver Lake Rd #200, New Brighton, MN 55112
Phone: 651-638-1900 - **Fax:** 651-638-1994

Types of Records Retrieved: Civil courts; Real Estate; Tax Liens/Judgments; UCC records

Local Retrieval Area: MN-Anoka, Chisago, Dakota, Hennepin, Ramsey, Washington. **Correspondent Relationships:** statewide.

Add'l Information: Established 1985. Normal turnaround time- 2-3 days. Projects billed by number of names searched. Will file/record documents for clients. Personal checks accepted. They specialize in distressed property and foreclosure information.

Land Title of America Group

3700 US Hwy 1 S, St Augustine, FL 32086-7150
Phone: 904-797-9600 - **Fax:** 904-794-4744
www.titlecompany.tv **email:** patti@ltoag.com

Types of Records Retrieved: Real Estate; Tax Liens/Judgments; Probate courts; UCC records; Vital records

Local Retrieval Area: FL-Clay, Duval, Flagler, Nassau, Putnam, St. Johns

Add'l Information: Established 1979. Normal turnaround time- variable depending on project. Fee basis will vary by the type of project. Will file/record documents for clients. They specialize in real estate title work.

Landmark Abstract & Information Services

PO Box 504, Hernando, MS 38632
Phone: 901-268-3200 bill.garrett@mac.com

Types of Records Retrieved: Real Estate; Tax Liens/Judgments; Probate courts; UCC records

Local Retrieval Area: MS-De Soto. **Correspondent Relationships:** Tate, Marshall, Tunica, Hinds, Rankin, Madison counties MS.

Add'l Info: Established 1991. Turnaround time- 24-48 hours. Projects billed by number of names searched. Projects billed by the hour. First project may require prepayment. Will file/record documents for clients.

Landmark Title Co of Madison County

PO Box 160, Madisonville, TX 77864
Phone: 936-348-5618 - **Fax:** 936-348-5604

Types of Records Retrieved: Civil and Probate courts; Real Estate; Tax Liens/Judgments; UCC records

Local Retrieval Area: TX-Madison

Add'l Information: Normal turnaround time- 2-4 days. Fee basis will vary by the type of project. First project may require prepayment.

Landmark Title Inc (Clovis NM)

PO Box 1326, 117 E 4th St, Clovis, NM 88102-1326
Phone: 505-763-3904 - **Fax:** 505-763-6610 landmark@plateautel.net

Types of Records Retrieved: Civil and Probate courts; Real Estate; Tax Liens/Judgments; UCC records **Local Retrieval Area:** NM-Curry

Add'l Information: Established 1989. Normal turnaround time- 48 hours. Projects billed by number of names searched. First project may require prepayment. Will file/record documents for clients. Will invoice.

Landmark Title Roswell

109 W 3rd St, Roswell, NM 88201
Phone: 505-622-5340 - **Fax:** 505-622-5346 ltr@drn.com

Types of Records Retrieved: Civil and Probate courts; Real Estate; Tax Liens/Judgments; UCC records

Local Retrieval Area: NM-Chaves

Add'l Information: Established 1992. Normal turnaround time- variable depending on project. Fee basis will vary by the type of project. First project may require prepayment.

Landmark Title Service - MI

10315 E Grand River, Brighton, MI 48116
Phone: 810-227-1733 - **Fax:** 810-227-1570 landmark@covad.net

Types of Records Retrieved: Civil and Probate courts; Real Estate; Tax Liens/Judgments; UCC records; Vital records

Local Retrieval Area: MI-Livingston, Oakland, Washtenaw

Add'l Information: Normal turnaround time- 3 days. Fee basis will vary by the type of project. First project may require prepayment. They specialize in title insurance and escrow closings.

LaPeer County Abstract & Title Co Inc

68 N Nepressing St, LaPeer, MI 48446-2145
Phone: 810-664-9951 - **Fax:** 810-664-8331
Types of Records Retrieved: Real Estate; Tax Liens/Judgments; Probate courts; UCC records; Vital records
Local Retrieval Area: MI-Lapeer
Add'l Information: Established 1940. Normal turnaround time- 1 week. Projects billed by number of names searched. Projects billed by number of records located. They specialize in real estate.

LaPrade Services Inc

PO Box 5218, 31 Corlies Ave, Poughkeepsie, NY 12602-5218
Phone: 845-473-0468 - **Fax:** 845-473-1667
Types of Records Retrieved: Criminal, Civil and Probate courts; Real Estate; Tax Liens/Judgments; UCC records; Vital records
Local Retrieval Area: NJ-Sussex, Warren; NY-Dutchess, Orange, Putnam, Ulster. **Correspondent Relationships:** Westchester, NYC, Long Island, Sullivan, Rockland counties.
Add'l Information: Established 1985. Normal turnaround time- 2-4 days. Expedited service available. Fee basis will vary by the type of project. They may require a retainer. They have the county contract for social services and handle 200 court papers a week. Performs service of process.

Margaret Laratta

95 Blossom Dr, Toms River, NJ 08753
Phone: 732-349-1301 - **Fax:** 732-341-7224
Types of Records Retrieved: Real Estate; Tax Liens/Judgments; Probate courts; UCC records
Local Retrieval Area: NJ-Ocean
Add'l Information: Established 1967. Normal turnaround time- 1-2 days. Projects billed by number of names searched. Projects billed by the hour. Will file/record documents for clients. They will invoice. Their alternate fax number is 732-929-1058.

Larson Abstract Co

70 First Ave SE, Little Falls, MN 56345
Phone: 320-632-5667 - **Fax:** 320-632-4583
Types of Records Retrieved: Real Estate; Tax Liens/Judgments; Probate courts; UCC records; Vital records
Local Retrieval Area: MN-Morrison
Add'l Information: Established 1923. Normal turnaround time- 10 days. Fee basis will vary by type of project. All projects require prepayment. They will also invoice. They specialize in real estate.

LaSalle Process Servers LP

29 S LaSalle St #956, Chicago, IL 60603
Phone: 800-815-3801; 312-263-0620 - **Fax:** 312-263-0622
www.lasalleprocessservers.com **email:** lps956@aol.com
Types of Records Retrieved: Criminal, Civil and Probate courts; Federal courts; Real Estate; Tax Liens/Judgments
Local Retrieval Area: IL-Cook, Du Page, Kane, Lake, McHenry, Will. **Correspondent Relationships:** nationwide.
Add'l Information: Established 1944. Normal turnaround time- same day to 1 day. If archives need to be searched, time averages 1-2 weeks. Projects billed by the hour. Copy expenses will be added to the fee. First project may require prepayment. Process service is their specialty. Check out their website for services provided. Performs service of process.

Lassen Attorney/Investigative Services

PO Box 909, Susanville, CA 96130
Phone: 530-251-2399 - **Fax:** 530-251-5494 johncapi@yahoo.com
Types of Records Retrieved: Criminal and Civil courts
Local Retrieval Area: CA-Lassen, Modoc, Plumas, Sierra
Add'l Information: Established 1994. Normal turnaround time- 2-3 days. Projects billed by the hour. A licensed PI in CA. Performs service of process.

Law In Motion

560 Ash St, San Diego, CA 92101
Phone: 619-232-1291 - **Fax:** 619-232-0910 lawinmotionsd@yahoo.com
Types of Records Retrieved: Criminal, Civil and Probate courts; Federal courts; Real Estate; Tax Liens/Judgments; UCC records; Vital records
Local Retrieval Area: CA-San Diego. **Correspondent Relationships:** Calif.
Add'l Information: Established 1988. Normal turnaround time- 3-4 days. Expedited service available. Projects billed by the hour. Some cases require fees in advance. First project may require prepayment. Will file/record documents for clients. Terms: net 10 days. They also work with the Assessor's office and search fictitious business name. They do nationwide process serving. Performs service of process.

Noel D Law Jr

450 W 7th St #141, Tulsa, OK 74119
Phone: 918-599-0988 - **Fax:** 918-599-0986 TCRAY76@yahoo.com
Types of Records Retrieved: Real Estate; UCC records
Local Retrieval Area: OK-Canadian, Cherokee, Cleveland, Craig, Creek, Delaware, Lincoln, Logan, Mayes, McClain, Muskogee, Noble, Nowata, Oklahoma, Okmulgee, Osage, Ottawa, Pawnee, Payne, Rogers, Tulsa, Wagoner, Washington
Add'l Information: Established 1995. Normal turnaround time- 24-48 hours. Projects billed by number of names searched. Will file/record documents for clients. They specialize in title searches. Has over 25 years experience. Business is across the street from Tulsa County Courthouse.

Lawrence County Title

1300 15th St, Lawrenceville, IL 62439
Phone: 618-943-4464 - **Fax:** 618-943-4299 lct5@verizon.net
Types of Records Retrieved: Criminal, Civil and Probate courts; Real Estate; Tax Liens/Judgments; UCC records; Vital records
Local Retrieval Area: IL-Crawford, Lawrence, Richland, Wabash
Add'l Information: Established 1988. Normal turnaround time- 24-48 hours for liens and judgment searches, and 1 to 2 weeks for abstracts and title insurance. Projects billed by number of names searched. Projects billed by number of records located. Projects billed by the hour. A charge per page and length of period (years) searched will be added to the fee. Will file/record documents for clients. Some clients are required to pay a retainer. Personal checks are accepted. They will file/record UCC and real estate documents on behalf of clients on a same or next day basis in Lawrence County only.

Lawyers' Abstract Co

220 S Main St, Holly Point #A, Butler, PA 16001
Phone: 724-283-3510 - **Fax:** 724-283-2258
Types of Records Retrieved: Civil and Probate courts; Real Estate; Tax Liens/Judgments; UCC records
Local Retrieval Area: PA-Armstrong, Butler, Westmoreland. **Correspondent Relationships:** Lawrence, Mercer, Crawford, Clarion, Beaver, Westmoreland, Armstrong counties.
Add'l Information: Normal turnaround time- 2-14 days. Projects billed by the hour. They will also invoice. First project may require prepayment. They will also invoice. Personal checks are accepted. They specialize in title searching and title insurance. The company is owned by Butler County Lawyers and has been in business since 1965. They have the largest title plant in Butler County.

Lawyer's Aid Service

PO Box 848, 408 W 17th St, Austin, TX 78767-0848
Phone: 888-474-2112; - **Fax:** 888-474-4218
www.LawyersAidService.com
email: MainDesk@LawyersAidService.com
Types of Records Retrieved: Criminal, Civil and Probate courts; Federal courts; Real Estate; Tax Liens/Judgments; UCC records; Vital records
Local Retrieval Area: TX-Travis. **Correspondent Relationships:** most Texas counties.
Add'l Information: Established 1980. Normal turnaround time- 24 hours. Projects billed by the hour. Court fees add'l. Will file/record documents for clients. Payment terms are net 10 days, pay simultaneously if large fees are advanced. They specialize in retrievals and filings in virtually all federal,

state, local agencies and courts in Austin, plus corporate outfits and registered agent service. Visits the Sec of State for corporate and other records, lawyers preferred.

Lawyers Investigating Service

PO Box 8479, Portland, ME 04104
Phone: 888-244-5685; 207-775-5685 - **Fax:** 207-893-1475
www.lawyersinvestigatingservice.com **email:** aeglis@aol.com

Types of Records Retrieved: Criminal, Civil and Probate courts; Federal courts; Real Estate; Tax Liens/Judgments; UCC records; Vital records

Local Retrieval Area: ME-Androscoggin, Cumberland, Kennebec, Lincoln, Oxford, Sagadahoc, York. **Correspondents:** statewide in Maine.

Add'l Information: Established 1975. Normal turnaround time- 5-7 days. Expedited service available. Projects billed by the hour. All projects require prepayment. They are a full-service nationally-recognized investigative agency, licensed, bonded, and insured. A licensed PI in ME. Performs service of process.

Lawyer's Legal Service LLC

PO Box 9007, 3301 SW Barbur Blvd #200, Portland, OR 97207
Phone: 800-224-7911; 503-224-7911 - **Fax:** 503-224-9611
lls@easystreet.com

Types of Records Retrieved: Criminal, Civil and Probate courts; Federal courts; Real Estate; Tax Liens/Judgments; UCC records; Vital records

Local Retrieval Area: OR-Clackamas, Clatsop, Columbia, Hood River, Marion, Multnomah, Washington, Yamhill; WA-Clark, Cowlitz, Skamania. **Correspondent Relationships:** Oregon and Southwest Washington.

Add'l Information: Established 1982. Normal turnaround time- 1st attempt within 4 days; 3 attempts within 10 days. Expedited service available. Projects billed by number of names searched. Projects billed by number of records located. Projects billed by the hour. First project may require prepayment. Will file/record documents for clients. Payment in advance for first time requests; 15 days net on all accounts. Their process services include rush and difficult services. Commission for out-of-state subpoenas in all OR counties. Specialties include investigations, document retrieval, and on or off site photocopy. Established in 1982. A licensed PI in OR. Performs service of process.

Lawyer's Resource

7528 Pershing Blvd #B, PMB 103, Kenosha, WI 53142
Phone: 888-218-8361; 847-263-9214 - **Fax:** 847-263-1676
www.lawyersresource.net **email:** wendy@lawyersresource.net

Types of Records Retrieved: Criminal, Civil and Probate courts; Real Estate; Tax Liens/Judgments; UCC records; Vital records

Local Retrieval Area: IL-Lake

Add'l Information: Established 1996. Normal turnaround time- 24 hours, often same day. Projects billed by number of names searched. Projects billed by the hour. First project may require prepayment. Credit cards accepted. Will file/record documents for clients. They conduct criminal, civil & property-related searches, document retrieval and court filings daily. They collect court data weekly to be used for marketing purposes. They service high-volume accounts without compromising quality or turnaround time.

LC Limited Inc

2865 Punto Alto Ct, Indianapolis, IN 46227-6146
Phone: 317-887-9688 - **Fax:** 317-887-5049 lclimitedinc@aol.com

Records Retrieved: Criminal and Civil courts; Federal District courts

Local Retrieval Area: IN-Boone, Hamilton, Hendricks, Marion. **Correspondent Relationships:** statewide.

Add'l Information: Established 2003. Normal turnaround time- 8-24 hours. Projects billed by number of names searched. Will invoice on 1st of month. They specialize in criminal research.

Leelanau Title Co

PO Box 10, Suttons Bay, MI 49682
Phone: 231-271-6191 - **Fax:** 231-271-3516

Types of Records Retrieved: Real Estate; Tax Liens/Judgments; Probate courts; UCC records

Local Retrieval Area: MI-Leelanau

Add'l Information: Established 1970. Normal turnaround time- 2-3 days. Fee basis will vary by transactions. First project may require prepayment. They specialize in real estate, title searches, and abstracts.

Legal 1 Document Retrieval

437 Golden Isles Dr #12G, Hallandale, FL 33009-7558
Phone: 954-455-5220 - **Fax:** 954-455-5787 legal1doc@msn.com

Types of Records Retrieved: Criminal, Civil and Probate courts; Federal courts; Real Estate; Tax Liens/Judgments; UCC records; Vital records

Local Retrieval Area: FL-Broward, Dade, Orange, Palm Beach, Seminole, Volusia. **Correspondent Relationships:** Volusia, Seminole, Orange, Hillsborough, Pinellas, Lee counties FL.

Add'l Information: Established 1998. Normal turnaround time- 24-48 hours. Projects billed by number of names searched. They perform the research, abstracting searches, recordings and document retrieval from most of the public records in South Florida. They also have a reliable network along Florida's east coast. A licensed PI in FL. Performs service of process.

Legal Abstract Co

301 E 2nd St, Muscatine, IA 52761
Phone: 563-263-3171 - **Fax:** 563-263-5206 legalabstractco@machlink.com

Types of Records Retrieved: Civil and Probate courts; Real Estate; Tax Liens/Judgments; UCC records; Vital records

Local Retrieval Area: IA-Muscatine

Add'l Information: Established 1937. Normal turnaround time- up to 1 week. Fee basis will vary by the type of project. Will file/record documents for clients. Have been serving Muscatine for over 50 years with computerized record keeping.

Legal Beagles Inc

PO Box 886, New Castle, DE 19720
Phone: 800-743-9897; 302-322-9897 - **Fax:** 302-322-8418
legalbegls@aol.com

Types of Records Retrieved: Criminal, Civil and Probate courts; Federal courts; Real Estate; Tax Liens/Judgments; UCC records; Vital records

Local Retrieval Area: DE-New Castle

Add'l Info: Established 1992. Turnaround time- 48 hours or less. Projects billed by number of names searched. First project may require prepayment. Service of Process always requires prepayment. They specialize in public records research; majority of research is criminal records searches for pre-employment screening. Performs service of process.

Legal Couriers Inc

PO Box 825, Yakima, WA 98907-0825
Phone: 888-450-9453; 509-453-1134 - **Fax:** 509-575-6680
legalcouriers@yahoo.com

Types of Records Retrieved: Criminal, Civil and Probate courts; Federal courts; Real Estate; Tax Liens/Judgments; UCC records; Vital records

Local Retrieval Area: WA-Yakima

Add'l Information: Established 1966. Normal turnaround time- 24 hours. Projects billed by number of names searched. Will bill clients. They perform the following services: process service, document retrieval, skiptracing, federal fax filings, document research, monitoring of trustee sales, full attorney services. They have 35 years of experience. Performs service of process.

Legal Data Resources

2816 W Summerdale, Chicago, IL 60625
Phone: 800-735-9207; 773-561-2468 - **Fax:** 773-561-2488
www.ldrsearch.com **email:** info@ldrsearch.com

Types of Records Retrieved: Criminal, Civil and Probate courts; Federal courts; Real Estate; Tax Liens/Judgments; UCC records; Vital records

Local Retrieval Area: IL-Cook, Du Page, Lake, Will. **Correspondent Relationships:** Counties near Chicago including McHenry County.

Add'l Information: Established 1990. Normal turnaround time- 24 hours. Projects billed by number of names searched. Projects billed by the hour. Credit cards accepted. Will file/record documents for clients. Personal checks are accepted. Legal Data Resources is the premier information provider in the Chicago Metro region. They access all courts & government agencies. Daily service to the National Archives/Great Lakes Region. Also specializes in real estate abstracting.

Legal Document Search & Signing Services

882 Cascade Dr, Sunnyvale, CA 94087
Phone: 408-483-0061 - **Fax:** 408-973-7261 legaldocs4u@comcast.net
Types of Records: Criminal and Civil courts; Tax Liens/Judgments; Vital records **Local Retrieval Area:** CA-San Mateo, Santa Clara
Add'l Information: Established 2000. Normal turnaround time- 24-48 hours. Expedited service available. Projects billed by the hour. All projects require prepayment. They specialize in self-help legal documents, prompt and accurate public record research and loan signing services. They are a bonded legal document assistant in Santa Clara County. Performs service of process.

Legal Eagle Inc / Eagle Search & Service

17330 W Center Rd #110-310, Omaha, NE 68130-2392
Phone: 402-342-4427 - **Fax:** 402-691-8824 LegalEagleWMR@cox.net
Types of Records Retrieved: Criminal, Civil and Probate courts; Federal courts; Real Estate; Tax Liens/Judgments; UCC records; Vital records
Local Retrieval Area: IA-Pottawattamie; NE-Douglas, Sarpy. **Correspondent Relationships:** Washington, Cass, Saunders counties NE.
Add'l Info: Established 1986. Turnaround time- 24-48 hours. Projects billed by number of names searched. First project may require prepayment. Will file/record documents for clients. They have been in business since 1986, Statewide Neb. criminal history checks, they also handle all your document filing needs. Notary on staff. Performs service of process.

Legal Express

15 S Weber #D, Colorado Springs, CO 80903
Phone: 719-578-0407 - **Fax:** 719-635-9802
www.legalexpressco.homestead.com **email:** legalexpressco@hotmail.com
Types of Records Retrieved: Criminal, Civil and Probate courts; Real Estate; Tax Liens/Judgments; Vital records
Local Retrieval Area: CO-El Paso, Teller
Add'l Information: Established 1967. Normal turnaround time- 2 working days. Projects billed by number of names searched. Will file/record documents for clients. Performs service of process.

Legal Investigations

8612 Malmaison Way, Knoxville, TN 37923-7142
Phone: 865-970-4444 tedhembree@bellsouth.net
Types of Records Retrieved: Criminal, Civil and Probate courts; Federal courts; Real Estate; UCC records
Local Retrieval: TN-Knox. **Correspondents:** other Tennessee counties.
Add'l Information: Established 1982. Normal turnaround time- 1-3 working days. Projects billed by the hour. First project may require prepayment. Will file/record documents for clients. They specialize in personal injury investigation searches and automotive safety. All East Tennessee served on a per case basis. A licensed PI in TN. Performs service of process.

Legal Net Process Service

1444 Montana Ave #210, El Paso, TX 79902
Phone: 915-532-7871 - **Fax:** 915-533-8039
Types of Records Retrieved: Criminal, Civil and Probate courts; Federal courts; Tax Liens/Judgments; UCC records; Vital records
Local Retrieval Area: NM-Dona Ana; TX-El Paso, Hudspeth
Add'l Information: Established 1992. Normal turnaround time- 1 day in El Paso; 2-3 days in other counties. Projects billed by number of names searched. Fee basis will vary by type of project. First project may require prepayment. Will file/record documents. Performs service of process.

Legal Recording of Rochester Inc

16 E Main St #6, Rochester, NY 14614-1803
Phone: 585-232-6710 - **Fax:** 585-232-1475 legalrecording@frontiernet.net
Types of Records Retrieved: Criminal, Civil and Probate courts; Federal courts; Real Estate; Tax Liens/Judgments; UCC records
Local Retrieval Area: NY-Monroe
Add'l Information: Established 1970. Normal turnaround time- 24-48 hours. Projects billed by number of names searched. Projects billed by number of records located. First project may require prepayment. Credit cards accepted. Will file/record documents for clients. Cost of copies and disbursements for filing fees require prepayment. They specialize in real property tax searches for lenders, criminal searches and real estate DBA searches, as well as civil court record retrieval.

Legal Research Associates Inc

PO Box 3091, Tustin, CA 92781-3091
Phone: 714-734-9337 - **Fax:** 714-734-9441 **email:** lratim@cox.net
https://www.legalresearchassociates.com/home_main.php
Types of Records Retrieved: Criminal, Civil and Probate courts; Federal courts; Real Estate; Tax Liens/Judgments; UCC records; Vital records
Local Retrieval Area: CA-Los Angeles, Orange, Riverside, San Bernardino. **Correspondent Relationships:** nationwide.
Add'l Information: Established 1993. Normal turnaround time- 24-48 hours. Projects billed by number of names searched. Projects billed by number of records located. Projects billed by the hour. All projects require prepayment. Credit cards accepted. Will bill bi-weekly or monthly. Performs service of process.

Legal Research Services

128 S Governor's Blvd, Dover, DE 19901
Phone: 302-672-9411 - **Fax:** 302-672-9277 collenaw@yahoo.com
Types of Records Retrieved: Criminal and Civil courts; Real Estate; Tax Liens/Judgments; UCC records; Vital records
Local Retrieval Area: DE-Kent, New Castle, Sussex
Add'l Information: Established 1993. Normal turnaround time- 24-36 hours. Projects billed by number of names searched. First project may require prepayment. Needs deposit for 1st time and big orders. Cell-302-363-7112.

Legal Research Solutions

3209 Warner Dr, Springfield, IL 62703 217-585-0668 - Fax: 217-529-1482
Types of Records: Criminal courts; Bankruptcy; Tax Liens/Judgments
Local Retrieval Area: IL-Morgan, Sangamon; **Correspondents:** statewide
Add'l Information: Established 1995. Projects billed by number of names searched. Provides accurate up-to-date criminal info throughout IL.

Legal Support Services Inc

19 Nickel Pl, Spearfish, SD 57783
Phone: 800-583-0365; 605-642-7146 - **Fax:** 605-642-5941
lls_ii@yahoo.com
Types of Records Retrieved: Criminal, Civil and Probate courts; Federal courts; Real Estate; Tax Liens/Judgments; UCC records; Vital records
Local Retrieval Area: SD-Brown, Lawrence, Meade, Minnehaha, Pennington; WY-Crook. **Correspondents:** South Dakota, Wyoming.
Add'l Information: Established 1980. Normal turnaround time- same day to 72 hours. Projects billed by number of names searched. Will file/record documents for clients. They specialize in record searches and filings in federal, state and county agencies including Secretary of State in both South Dakota and Wyoming.

LegalEase Inc

139 Fulton St #1013, New York, NY 10038
Phone: 800-393-1277; 212-393-9070 - **Fax:** 212-393-9796
www.legaleaseinc.com **email:** info@legaleaseinc.com
Types of Records Retrieved: Civil and Probate courts; Federal courts; Tax Liens/Judgments
Local Retrieval Area: NY-Bronx, Kings, Nassau, New York, Queens, Westchester. **Correspondent Relationships:** nationwide.
Add'l Information: Established 1985. Normal turnaround time- 24-72 hours. Expedited service available. Projects billed by number of names searched. Projects billed by the hour. Volume searches will be charged by the hour. First project may require prepayment. Credit cards accepted. They specialize in document retrieval (federal and state courts) online

information retrieval, and public record research. Rush service a specialty. Performs service of process.

Legalese

1754 36th St, Sacramento, CA 95816-6613
Phone: 916-453-2860 - **Fax:** 916-453-2875 jeffs@cwo.com
Types of Records Retrieved: Criminal, Civil and Probate courts; Federal courts; Real Estate; Tax Liens/Judgments; UCC records; Vital records
Local Retrieval Area: CA-El Dorado, Placer, Sacramento, San Joaquin, Sutter, Yolo, Yuba. **Correspondent Relationships:** California
Add'l Information: Established 1980. Normal turnaround time- 2 days. Projects billed by number of names searched. First project may require prepayment. Will file/record documents for clients. They specialize in UCC, corporation and county records. Performs service of process.

LegalNet Inc

2510 W 237th St #110, Torrance, CA 90505
Phone: 888-530-3100; 310-530-2200 - **Fax:** 310-530-1014
www.legalnetinc.com **Types of Records Retrieved:** Criminal, Civil and Probate courts; Federal courts; Real Estate; Tax Liens/Judgments; UCC records; Vital records
Local Retrieval Area: CA-Los Angeles, Orange. **Correspondent Relationships:** Ventura, San Diego, Riverside, San Bernardino.
Add'l Information: Established 1971. Normal turnaround time- routine 72 hours. Expedited service available. Projects billed by number of names searched. Projects billed by the hour. All projects require prepayment. Credit cards accepted. Will file/record documents for clients. Generally a process server and mobile copy service, their standard service includes all Courts in LA and Orange Counties. Premium service includes San Bernardino, Riverside, Ventura and San Diego Counties. Performs service of process.

LegalTrieve Information Services

18 Oliver St #204, North Easton, MA 02356
Phone: 508-238-4227 - **Fax:** 508-238-4678 legaltrieve@email.msn.com
Types of Records Retrieved: Criminal, Civil and Probate courts; Federal courts; Real Estate; Tax Liens/Judgments; UCC records
Local Retrieval Area: MA-Bristol, Essex, Middlesex, Norfolk, Plymouth, Suffolk. **Correspondent Relationships:** nationwide.
Add'l Information: Established 1995. Normal turnaround time- 1-3 business days. Projects billed by number of names searched. First project may require prepayment. Will file/record documents for clients. Large projects require prepayment. Payment due upon receipt for smaller projects. They specialize in public record research, document retrieval and asset searches.

LegalWorks Inc

PO Box 435, Clinton, NY 13323-0435
Phone: 800-853-6756; 315-737-9800 - **Fax:** 315-737-0055
http://legal-works.com **email:** gregg@legal-works.com
Types of Records Retrieved: Criminal, Civil and Probate courts; Federal courts; Real Estate; Tax Liens/Judgments; UCC records; Vital records
Local Retrieval Area: NY-Herkimer, Madison, Oneida
Add'l Information: Established 1982. Normal turnaround time- 24 hours. Projects billed by number of names searched. First project may require prepayment. Credit cards accepted. They specialize in proficient expertise, progressive technologies and premier service via integrity, diligence and timeliness. Performs service of process.

Lehr's Process Service

1017 SW 86th Way, Gainesville, FL 32607-4949
Phone: 352-331-1010 - **Fax:** 352-332-3895
www.lehrsprocessservice.com **email:** steve@lehrsprocessservice.com
Types of Records Retrieved: Criminal, Civil and Probate courts; Federal District courts; Real Estate; Tax Liens/Judgments; UCC records; Vital records; Voter registration records
Local Retrieval Area: FL-Alachua, Marion
Add'l Information: Established 1994. Normal turnaround time- 24-72 hours. Projects billed by number of names searched. Will file/record documents for clients. Will invoice due to cost of copies. Performs service of process.

Len Page Paralegal/Research Services

PO Box 128, West Wareham, MA 02576-0128
Phone: 508-967-2504 - **Fax:** 775-514-1742 len.page@lpprs.com
Types of Records Retrieved: Criminal, Civil and Probate courts; Federal courts; Real Estate; Tax Liens/Judgments; UCC records; Vital records
Local Retrieval Area: MA-Barnstable, Bristol, Norfolk, Plymouth. **Correspondent Relationships:** Suffolk, Dukes counties MA.
Add'l Information: Established 2003. Normal turnaround time- 24-72 hours. Projects billed by number of names searched. Projects billed by number of records located. Projects billed by the hour. LPPRS being a provider to the legal community, conducts research, filings and retrieval of pertinent information from public resources. LPPRS prides itself in providing excellent quality work.

Lenmark Personal Services

PO Box 211, Eureka, MO 63025
Phone: 636-677-3831 - **Fax:** 636-677-3831 Trailhorse1@Juno.com
Types of Records Retrieved: Criminal, Civil and Probate courts; Federal courts; Real Estate
Local Retrieval Area: MO-Franklin, Jefferson, St. Charles, St. Louis. **Correspondent Relationships:** St Louis, MO extended area.
Add'l Information: Established 1977. Normal turnaround time- 48 hours or less. Billing method depends on project. Rural counties are 50 miles to courthouse, basic rates will be higher because of fluctuating gas prices. First project may require prepayment. Will file/record documents for clients. They specialize in credit and collection services. They will perform record retrieval in outlying counties, away from the St. Louis area, though rates are slightly higher than urban charges. Performs service of process.

Lenow International Inc

1503 Union Ave #210, Memphis, TN 38104
Phone: 901-726-0735 www.lenowinternational.com
Types of Records Retrieved: Criminal, Civil and Probate courts; Federal courts; Tax Liens/Judgments; UCC records; Vital records
Local Retrieval Area MS-De Soto; TN-Shelby. **Correspondents:** statewide.
Add'l Info: Established 1977. Normal turnaround time- 24 hours. Projects billed by the hour. First project may require prepayment. Will file/record documents for clients. They specialize in locating records when limited information is available. A licensed PI in TN. Performs service of process.

Dawn Curran Letcher

125 Main St, Carlisle, KY 40311
Phone: 859-289-3745 - **Fax:** 859-289-3746
Types of Records Retrieved: Real Estate; Tax Liens/Judgments
Local Retrieval Area: KY-Carlisle
Add'l Information: Established 1991. First project may require prepayment. Will file/record documents for clients. They perform real estate services on a limited basis only.

Lewis County Abstract (Idaho) d/b/a Lewis County Title

PO Box 36, Nezperce, ID 83543
Phone: 208-937-2621 - **Fax:** 208-937-2621 dmjjd@camasnet.com
Types of Records Retrieved: Criminal, Civil and Probate courts; Real Estate; Tax Liens/Judgments
Local Retrieval Area: ID-Lewis
Add'l Information: Established 1911. Normal turnaround time- 1-2 days. Fee basis will vary by the type of project. They specialize in providing title insurance. Also legal and accounting available.

Lewis County Abstract (Missouri)

307 Lewis St., Canton, MO 63435
Phone: 573-288-4461 - **Fax:** 573-288-4463
Types of Records Retrieved: Real Estate; Tax Liens/Judgments; Probate courts; UCC records
Local Retrieval Area: MO-Clark, Lewis, Marion, Ralls
Add'l Information: Established 1920. Normal turnaround time- 24 hours. Projects billed by number of records located. Personal checks are accepted.

Lexington Title Corp

301 Gibson Rd, Lexington, SC 29072
Phone: 803-957-1243 - **Fax:** 803-957-9359
Types of Records Retrieved: Civil and Probate courts; Real Estate; Tax Liens/Judgments; UCC records
Local Retrieval Area: SC-Aiken, Calhoun, Edgefield, Fairfield, Kershaw, Lexington, Newberry, Orangeburg, Richland, Saluda
Add'l Information: Established 1985. Normal turnaround time- 24-48 hours. Fee basis varies by type of transaction. Terms: net 15 days. They specialize in title abstracts and title insurance.

LG Services LLC

507 Poplar St, East Dublin, GA 31027
Phone: 478-290-3808, 478-274-8622 lgservices@nlamerica.com
Types of Records Retrieved: Criminal, Civil and Probate courts
Local Retrieval Area: GA-Laurens. **Correspondent Relationships:** statewide; 12 counties on regular basis.
Add'l Information: Established 2005. Normal turnaround time- 48 hours or less. Projects billed by number of names searched. LG Services gives extra scrutiny to identifier information, making sure of name matches. They also do work for Lighthouse Information Services, 770-516-9152, for 12 counties east of Dublin, Laurens County.

Margene Libertino Inc

11609 Bend Bow Dr, Fredericksburg, VA 22407-7491
Phone: 540-785-9930 - **Fax:** 540-785-9933
Types of Records Retrieved: Civil courts; Real Estate; Tax Liens/Judgments; UCC records
Local Retrieval Area: VA-Caroline, Fredericksburg City, King George, Spotsylvania, Stafford
Add'l Information: Established 1991. Normal turnaround time- 24-48 hours. Projects billed by number of names searched. Will file/record documents for clients. Payment due upon receipt of invoice. Her cell number is 540-850-8408

Liberty Alliance

22707 LaPalma Ave, Yorba Linda, CA 92887
Phone: 800-630-2880; 714-696-5410 - **Fax:** 800-630-2808; 714-696-5421
http://liberty-alliance.com/index1.php **Types of Records Retrieved:** Criminal and Civil courts
Local Retrieval Area: CA-Los Angeles, Orange, Riverside, San Bernardino, San Diego, Ventura. **Correspondent Relationships:** nationwide.
Add'l Information: Established 2000. Normal turnaround time- 24-72 hours. Projects billed by number of names searched. Projects billed by number of records located. Projects billed by the hour. First project may require prepayment. Credit cards accepted. Liberty Alliance is a service provider to all; call and speak to a live representative. They also specialize in background screening. A licensed PI in CA. Performs service of process.

Liberty Corporate Services Inc

1040 Rock-N-Creek Rd, Leesville, SC 29070
Phone: 888-875-1280; 803-604-0264 - **Fax:** 888-875-4223; 803-604-0834
libertycorp@starband.net
Types of Records Retrieved: Civil and Probate courts; Federal courts; Real Estate; UCC records; Tax Liens/Judgments
Local Retrieval Area: SC-Abbeville, Aiken, Anderson, Beaufort, Berkeley, Calhoun, Charleston, Colleton, Darlington, Dorchester, Florence, Georgetown, Greenville, Greenwood, Hampton, Horry, Jasper, Kershaw, Laurens, Lee, Lexington, Newberry, Oconee, Orangeburg, Pickens, Richland, Saluda, Spartanburg, Sumter, York. **Correspondent Relationships:** nationwide.
Add'l Information: Established 1995. Normal turnaround time- 1-5 days. Fee basis is by name and location by county. Will file/record documents for clients. Credit accounts are accepted. They are a full service company with a UCC/Corporate division. Their real estate division handles filings, lost mortgage retrievals, and land record searches.

Liberty Record Search Inc

#1 Lubeck Hills, Washington, WV 26181
Phone: 304-863-5542 - **Fax:** 304-863-5670
www.libertyrecordsearch.com **email:** lrsinc@casinternet.net
Records Retrieved: Real Estate; Tax Liens/Judgments; UCC records
Local Retrieval Area: OH-Athens, Carroll, Columbiana, Gallia, Jefferson, Meigs, Washington; WV-Barbour, Berkeley, Boone, Braxton, Brooke, Cabell, Calhoun, Clay, Doddridge, Fayette, Gilmer, Greenbrier, Hancock, Harrison, Jackson, Jefferson, Kanawha, Lewis, Lincoln, Logan, McDowell, Marion, Marshall, Mason, Mercer, Mingo, Monongalia, Monroe, Morgan, Nicholas, Ohio, Pleasants, Pocahontas, Preston, Putnam, Raleigh, Randolph, Ritchie, Roane, Summers, Taylor, Tyler, Upshur, Wayne, Wetzel, Wirt, Wood, Wyoming
Add'l Info: Established 1992. Turnaround time- 24-48 hours depending on county of search. Projects billed by number of names searched. Billed monthly with net due the 15th. They specialize in property searches.

Liberty Record Search of NJ Inc

470 Ridgedale Ave #3, East Hanover, NJ 07936
Phone: 973-887-8808 - **Fax:** 973-887-8801 lrsnj@optonline.net
Types of Records Retrieved: Civil and Probate courts; Real Estate; Tax Liens/Judgments; UCC records
Local Retrieval Area: NJ-Atlantic, Bergen, Cumberland, Burlington, Camden, Cape May, Essex, Gloucester, Hudson, Hunterdon, Mercer, Middlesex, Monmouth, Morris, Ocean, Passaic, Salem, Somerset, Sussex, Union, Warren. **Correspondent Relationships:** statewide.
Add'l Information: Established 1996. Normal turnaround time- 24-48 hours. Projects billed by number of names searched. Will file/record documents for clients. Monthly billing; net due by the 15th. The specialize in expert service with quick turnaround in all of New Jersey.

LIDA Credit Agency Inc

450 Sunrise Hwy, Rockville Centre, NY 11570
Phone: 516-678-4600 - **Fax:** 516-678-4611 lidacredit@digizip.com
Types of Records Retrieved: Criminal, Civil and Probate courts; Federal courts; Real Estate; Tax Liens/Judgments; UCC records; Vital records
Local Retrieval Area: NY-Nassau, Queens, Suffolk. **Correspondent Relationships:** nationwide.
Add'l Information: Established 1920. Normal turnaround time- 8-48 hours. Projects billed by number of records located. All projects require prepayment. Credit cards accepted. They specialize in public record research, background reports, commercial and individual, credit reports and general investigations.

Lighthouse Information Services

1025 Rose Creek Dr #620-212, Woodstock, GA 30189
Phone: 770-516-9152 - **Fax:** 770-516-9151
wbpeacock@lighthouseinfoserv.com
Types of Records Retrieved: Criminal and Civil courts; Federal courts
Local Retrieval Area: GA-Appling, Atkinson, Bacon, Baldwin, Bartow, Ben Hill, Berrien, Bleckley, Brantley, Bulloch, Camden, Candler, Charlton, Chatham, Cherokee, Clinch, Cobb, Coffee, Colquitt, Cook, De Kalb, Dodge, Dougherty, Emanuel, Fulton, Glynn, Gwinnett, Irwin, Jeff Davis, Jefferson, Jenkins, Johnson, Lanier, Laurens, Lee, Lowndes, McIntosh, Montgomery, Pierce, Pulaski, Screven, Stephens, Telfair, Terrell, Tift, Treutlen, Turner, Twiggs, Ware, Washington, Wheeler, Wilcox, Worth. **Correspondent Relationships:** statewide.
Add'l Info: Established 1998. Turnaround time- 24-48 hours. Projects billed by number of names searched. Will invoice monthly. With over a decade of industry experience, they cover each county in GA, go directly to each courthouse, technologically superior to competition, accuracy is priority. They are a NAPBS Member. Performs service of process.

Lightning Legal Services LLC

PO Box 9132, Albany, NY 12209
Phone: 518-463-1049 - **Fax:** 518-463-3681
www.lightninglegal.info **email:** kgunner@lightninglegal.info
Types of Records Retrieved: Probate courts; Federal courts; Tax Liens/Judgments; UCC records; Vital records

Local Retrieval Area: NY-Albany, Rensselaer, Saratoga, Schenectady. **Correspondent Relationships:** nationwide.

Add'l Information: Established 1993. Normal turnaround time- variable. Billing method depends on project. First project may require prepayment. Will file/record documents for clients. They specialize in corporate services, including the preparation & filing of corporate documents in NY & other states. They have prompt reliable document filing and retrieval. Also NY UCC, tax lien searches, death records, and DMV. Performs service of process.

Lightning Records Inc

341 Emmons, Wyandotte, MI 48192

Phone: 734-285-2495 - **Fax:** 734-285-2809 lightning_records@yahoo.com

Types of Records Retrieved: Civil courts; Federal District courts; Real Estate; Tax Liens/Judgments; UCC records

Local Retrieval Area: MI-Oakland, Washtenaw, Wayne

Add'l info: Established 2001. Normal turnaround time- 24-48 hours. Projects billed by number of names searched. Call for payment information. This company is operated by an abstractor with over 14 years of experience in South East Michigan. Fast turnaround and reasonable prices.

Lincoln Abstract Co

PO Box 37, Star City, AR 71667

Phone: 870-628-3144 - **Fax:** 870-628-3348 lincolnabstract@centurytel.net

Types of Records Retrieved: Real Estate; Tax Liens/Judgments; UCC records; Probate courts

Local Retrieval Area: AR-Lincoln. **Correspondent Relationships:** Bradley, Cleveland, Drew, Desha, Jefferson counties AR.

Add'l Information: Established 1930. Normal turnaround time- 48 hours. Projects billed by the hour. Billed by the job. All projects require prepayment. They are experts at Lincoln County, AR record books. They have the only title plant in Lincoln County, AR.

Lincoln County Abstract & Title Co (NM)

PO Box 2335, Ruidoso, NM 88355-2335

Phone: 800-635-4692; 505-258-5959 - **Fax:** 505-258-9010

lcatc@zianet.com

Types of Records Retrieved: Civil and Probate courts; Real Estate; Tax Liens/Judgments; UCC records

Local Retrieval Area: NM-Lincoln

Add'l Information: Established 1989. Turnaround time- variable depending on project. Projects billed by number of names searched. Projects billed by number of records located. They specialize in title insurance.

Lincoln Home Title (KS)

113 S 5th St, Lincoln, KS 67455

Phone: 785-524-4228 - **Fax:** 785-524-3042

www.landhometitle.com **Types of Records Retrieved:** Civil and Probate courts; Real Estate; Tax Liens/Judgments; UCC records

Local Retrieval Area: KS-Lincoln

Add'l Information: Established 1935. Normal turnaround time- 2-3 days. Fee basis varies by type of transaction. First project may require prepayment. Will file/record documents for clients. Formerly Lincoln County Abstract & Title Co.

Lincoln Investigations Inc DBA Bay Point Legal Service

820 Park Row #652, Salinas, CA 93901

Phone: 800-383-0897; 831-422-3007; alt fax- 831-417-2115 - **Fax:** 831-455-0848 lincolnpi@aol.com

Types of Records Retrieved: Criminal, Civil and Probate courts; Real Estate; Tax Liens/Judgments; UCC records; Vital records

Local Retrieval Area: CA-Monterey, San Benito, Santa Cruz. **Correspondent Relationships:** statewide.

Add'l Information: Established 1997. Normal turnaround time- 72 hours. Expedited service available. Projects billed by number of names searched. Projects billed by number of records located. Projects billed by the hour. First project may require prepayment. Will file/record documents for clients. They are a full service investigative firm. They also are a full scale process service and document retrieval and research company. A licensed PI in CA. Performs service of process.

Lincoln Trail Title

2935 Dolphine #101, Elizabethtown, KY 42701

Phone: 270-765-5566 - **Fax:** 270-769-3267

Types of Records Retrieved: Real Estate; Tax Liens/Judgments

Local Retrieval Area: KY-Larue

Add'l Information: Established 1984. First project may require prepayment. They specialize in real estate.

Lincoln Trail Title Services Inc

PO Box 111, 2935 Dolphin Dr, Elizabethtown, KY 42702

Phone: 270-765-5566 - **Fax:** 270-769-3267

Types of Records Retrieved: Civil and Probate courts; Real Estate; Tax Liens/Judgments; UCC records

Local Retrieval Area: KY-Hardin

Add'l Information: Established 1986. Normal turnaround time- 3-5 days. Projects billed by the hour. First project may require prepayment.

Lincoln-Evans Advanced Land & Title

203 N 2nd Ave, Ozark, MO 65721-7450

Phone: 417-581-8251 - **Fax:** 417-581-8280

Records Retrieved: Real Estate; Tax Liens/Judgments; UCC records

Local Retrieval Area: MO-Christian, Greene, Taney

Add'l Information: Established 1993. Normal turnaround time- 3 days. Projects billed by number of names searched. Projects billed by number of records located. Will file/record documents for clients. They will accept cashiers checks. Terms are net 30 days. They specialize in title and escrow closings. The phone number for their Taney and Greene, MO office is 417-889-1818.

Linda's Property Information Service

12208 SE 22nd Ave, Milwaukie, OR 97222

Phone: 503-659-6186 - **Fax:** 503-654-7104 hotrodmomma56@msn.com

Records Retrieved: Real Estate; Tax Liens/Judgments; UCC records

Local Retrieval Area: OR-Clackamas, Multnomah, Washington; WA-Clark

Add'l Information: Established 2003. Normal turnaround time- 24-48 hours depending on county and weather in fall. Projects billed by number of names searched. Will send invoice and prefers to be paid by weekly every 2 weeks. Has been an abstractor for 3 years and is sole owner. Does all work personally. Prides herself on quick and accurate work.

Lindsey and Suyak Investigations LLC

PO Box 9537, Owensboro, KY 42302

Phone: 270-281-0213 **Fax:** 270-281-0311 wesearchforyou@omuonline.net

Types of Records Retrieved: Criminal, Civil and Probate courts; US District court; Real Estate; Tax Liens/Judgments; UCC records

Local Retrieval Area: KY-Daviess, Hancock, Ohio

Add'l Info: Established 2001. Turnaround time- 24 hours. Projects billed by the hour. Occasionally there is a mileage charge. Will invoice net 20 days. A one-member LLC able to do investigations, surveillance and record checks. Will serve process. Has a BS degree in Criminal Justice and is retired Navy (legal). KY PI Lic. #115; insured in accordance with KRS 329A. A licensed PI in KY. Performs service of process.

Troy Lindsey

301 Bufford Rd, Brunswick, GA 31523

Phone: 912-265-4405; Fax- same

Types of Records Retrieved: Criminal and Civil courts; Us District court

Local Retrieval Area: GA-Camden, Glynn, McIntosh

Add'l Information: Established 1994. Normal turnaround time- 48 hours or less. He specializes in felony and 7-year searches; visits US District court for felonies. Call first to be certain he can retrieve in Camden or Mc Intosh Counties in a timely manner.

Linn County Abstract Co

PO Box 98, 108 S 5th St, Mound City, KS 66056
Phone: 888-795-2949; 913-795-2949 - **Fax:** 913-795-2449
smittylcac@earthlink.net

Types of Records Retrieved: Criminal, Civil and Probate courts; Real Estate; Tax Liens/Judgments; UCC records

Local Retrieval Area: KS-Bourbon, Linn

Add'l Information: Established 1973. Normal turnaround time- 1 day. Basis for fees varies by project. Will file/record documents for clients.

Linn County Title

118 N Main St, Burkfield, MO 64628
Phone: 660-258-2260 - **Fax:** 660-258-7287

Types of Records Retrieved: Real Estate; Tax Liens/Judgments

Local Retrieval Area: MO-Linn

Add'l Information: Established 1976. First project may require prepayment. They specialize in real estate.

Liquori Investigations

6539 Turtlemound Rd, New Smyrna Beach, FL 32169
Phone: 386-423-4235 - **Fax:** 386-428-9110 wliquori@cfl.rr.com

Types of Records Retrieved: Criminal, Civil and Probate courts; Federal courts; Real Estate; Tax Liens/Judgments; UCC records; Vital records

Local Retrieval Area: FL-Orange, Seminole, Volusia

Add'l Information: Established 1987. Normal turnaround time- 24-48 hours. Projects billed by number of names searched. First project may require prepayment. A licensed PI in FL.

LLG Enterprises

911 N Birch Ct, Oak Grove, MO 64075
Phone: 816-625-0947 - **Fax:** 816-625-0948 lgraves@llgenterprises.net

Types of Records Retrieved: Criminal courts

Local Retrieval Area: KS-Douglas, Johnson, Sedgwick, Shawnee, Wyandotte; MO-Barton, Boone, Buchanan, Callaway, Cape Girardeau, Clay, Dunklin, Howell, Jackson, Montgomery, Osage, Perry, Pettis, Platte, Randolph, St. Charles, Stoddard. **Correspondent Relationships:** Kansas and Missouri statewide criminal record repository.

Add'l Information: Established 1997. Projects billed by number of names searched. Will file/record documents for clients. End of month billing due in 14 days. They specialize in hands-on county criminal research. They visit each courthouse daily. 24-hour turnaround.

LNS Research Co.

335 S SR 415, New Smyrna, FL 32186
Phone: 386-428-1936 - **Fax:** 386-409-0336 lnsresearch@bellsouth.net

Types of Records Retrieved: Criminal courts

Local Retrieval Area: FL-Flagler, Seminole, Volusia

Add'l Information: Established 1999. Normal turnaround time- 24 hours. Projects billed by number of names searched. First project may require prepayment. They special in criminal records throughout Florida, with online access to a number of courts other than the hands-on counties listed above.

Locke-Neosho Abstracts Inc

PO Box 178, 219 S Main, Erie, KS 66733
Phone: 620-244-3641 - **Fax:** 620-244-3234
admin@lockeneosho.kscoxmail.com

Types of Records Retrieved: Civil and Probate courts; Federal courts; Real Estate; Tax Liens/Judgments; UCC records

Local Retrieval Area: KS-Neosho

Add'l Information: Established 1930. Normal turnaround time- up to 1 week. Fee basis varies by type of transaction. They request prepayment from out of area clients.

Logan County Abstract Co

Box 45, Napoleon, ND 58561
Phone: 701-754-2200 - **Fax:** 701-754-2749

Types of Records Retrieved: Civil courts; Real Estate; Tax Liens/Judgments; UCC records

Local Retrieval Area: ND-Logan

Add'l Information: Normal turnaround time- 1-2 days. Projects billed by number of records located.

Logan Registration Service Inc

PO Box 161644, Sacramento, CA 95816
Phone: 916-457-5787 - **Fax:** 800-524-4111; 916-457-5789
www.loganreg.com **email:** joan@loganreg.com

Types of Records Retrieved: Sec of State Corporate records

Local Retrieval Area: CA-Sacramento. **Correspondent Relationships:** nationwide DMV records.

Add'l Information: Established 1976. Normal turnaround time- 24-48 hours. Online immediately. Projects are billed by the number of records run. Terms: net 30 days. Court records are online only. They specialize in all types of California DMV records, online and manual access. Also, manual retrieval of UCC and Sec of State records . They also obtain DMV records from most of the US.

Lone Star Investigations & Recovery Inc

PO Box 701688, Dallas, TX 75370
Phone: 800-887-3890; 972-774-0037 - **Fax:** 972-774-9612

Types of Records Retrieved: Criminal, Civil and Probate courts; Federal courts; Real Estate; Tax Liens/Judgments; UCC records; Vital records

Local Retrieval Area: TX-Collin, Dallas, Denton, Tarrant. **Correspondent Relationships:** Travis and Williamson counties TX.

Add'l Information: Established 1996. Normal turnaround time- 24-48 hours. May search by either number of names or by number of records located. First project may require prepayment. Will file/record documents for clients. Will bill. They are a licensed private investigator with 25-plus years banking/financial experience, and record research and asset lien searches. A licensed PI in TX.

Lone Star Legal

340 Division St, San Francisco, CA 94103-4810
Phone: 415-255-8550 - **Fax:** 415-255-8549
www.lonestarlegal.com **email:** jon@lonestarlegal.com

Types of Records Retrieved: Criminal, Civil and Probate courts; Federal courts; Real Estate; Tax Liens/Judgments; UCC records; Vital records

Local Retrieval Area: CA-Alameda, San Francisco, San Mateo

Add'l Information: Established 1989. Normal turnaround time- 2 days. Projects billed by the hour. First project may require prepayment. Credit cards accepted. They specialize in complex and routine court research, complete litigation copying and on-site copying. Large volume specialists. We also offer scanning, imaging and digital printing.

Lorain County Title Co

424 Middle Ave, Elyria, OH 44035
Phone: 440-284-5100 - **Fax:** 440-284-5161
www.lctc.com **email:** lctc@lctc.com

Types of Records Retrieved: Civil and Probate courts; Federal courts; Real Estate; Tax Liens/Judgments; UCC records; Vital records

Local Retrieval Area: OH-Cuyahoga, Erie, Lorain

Add'l Information: Established 1952. Normal turnaround time- 3 days. Projects billed by number of names searched. Fee basis varies by type of transaction. First project may require prepayment. Will file/record documents for clients. Payment due upon delivery, terms are net 10 days.

Lord Investigations, LLC

PO Box 2509, Eagle, ID 83616-9118
Phone: 208-939-4040 lordinvestigative@msn.com

Types of Records Retrieved: Criminal, Civil and Probate courts; Federal courts; UCC records

Local Area: ID-Ada, Boise, Canyon, Elmore, Gem, Valley, Washington

Add'l Information: Established 1990. Normal turnaround time- 72 hours. Projects billed by the hour. They specialize in civil and criminal investigations (plaintiff and defense), sub rosa surveillance, locates and security consulting. A licensed PI in ID & UT. Performs service of process.

Los Angeles County Document Services Inc

1914 N Verdugo Rd #6, Glendale, CA 91208

Phone: 818-241-1990 - **Fax:** 818-550-1509 glenn@ladocs.biz

Types of Records Retrieved: Real Estate; Tax Liens/Judgments

Local Retrieval Area: CA-Los Angeles, Orange, Riverside, San Bernardino, San Diego, Ventura

Add'l Information: Established 2001. Normal turnaround time- 24 hours. Projects billed by number of names searched. Payment due net 30 days. They specialize in 100% accurate title/current owner searches. They do document retrieval and recordings in Los Angeles, San Bernardino, Riverside, Orange, San Diego and Ventura counties.

Loss Prevention Associates Inc

9550 Warner Ave #250, Fountain Valley, CA 92708

Phone: 714-593-2323 - **Fax:** 714-593-2383

www.lpassociates.com **email:** bkelsheimer@lpassociates.com

Records Retrieved: Criminal, Civil and Probate courts; Federal courts

Local Retrieval Area: CA-Los Angeles, Orange, Riverside, San Bernardino, San Diego. **Correspondent Relationships:** nationwide.

Add'l Information: Established 1995. Normal turnaround time- 24-48 hours. Projects billed by number of names searched. Will bill monthly/bi-monthly. Loss Prevention Associates is a nationwide leader in security consulting, investigations and pre-employment/tenant background screening. They can provide their clients a decisive advantage in the business world. A licensed PI in CA.

Lowery Professional Services Corp

1809 N Linwood Ave, Appleton, WI 54914-2404

Phone: 920-830-2114

Types of Records Retrieved: Criminal, Civil and Probate courts; Federal courts; Real Estate; Tax Liens/Judgments; UCC records; Vital records

Local Retrieval Area: WI-Brown, Outagamie, Winnebago

Add'l Information: Established 1985. Normal turnaround time- 1-4 days depending on project. Expedited service available. Projects billed by number of names searched. Projects billed by number of records located. First project may require prepayment. They provide physical searches and retrieval of public records at city, county, state and federal locations. They also provide court filings and service of documents, skip tracing, property verification, pre-employment screenings and database searches. Performs service of process.

Lowry Document Service

2384 Statler Terrace, Deltona, FL 32738

Phone: 386-789-6193 - **Fax:** 386-789-3801 milow4@peoplepc.com

Types of Records Retrieved: Criminal, Civil and Probate courts; Real Estate; Tax Liens/Judgments; UCC records; Vital records

Local Retrieval Area: FL-Flagler, Seminole, Volusia

Add'l Information: Established 1995. Normal turnaround time- 24-48 hours. Projects billed by number of names searched. Will file/record documents for clients. They have a paralegal background and have a notary service.

Linda Lucia

385 Bayou Bank Ln, Franklin, LA 70538

Phone: 337-923-4271; Fax- same lucia3392@bellsouth.net

Types of Records Retrieved: Criminal and Civil courts

Local Retrieval Area: LA-St. Mary

Add'l Information: Established 2000?. Turnaround time- 24-36 hours. All projects require prepayment. She does document search on a part time basis but can give you very personalized service for St Mary Parrish court.

Lucy and Tyler Public Records Services

622 N Thompson St, Raritan, NJ 08869

Phone: 908-725-4356 - **Fax:** 908-429-1749

Types of Records Retrieved: Criminal courts; Real Estate

Retrieval Area: NJ-Somerset; TN-Davidson, Hamilton, Knox, Williamson

Add'l Information: Established 1991. Normal turnaround time- 24-48 hours. Projects billed by number of names searched. Projects billed by number of records located. Will invoice. Payment due net 30 days. They specialize in employment screening and real estate searches in Tennessee counties. They are a private investigator in Tennessee. Also cover entire state of New Jersey, on-site record searching of civil and criminal searches. A licensed PI in TN.

Lueken Document Research Inc

9864 Diamond Point Dr, St Louis, MO 63123

Phone: 314-631-5928 - **Fax:** 314-638-8082 LuekenDoc@earthlink.net

Types of Records Retrieved: Criminal, Civil and Probate courts; Federal courts; Real Estate; Tax Liens/Judgments; UCC records; Vital records

Local Retrieval Area: MO-St. Louis, St. Louis City

Add'l Information: Established 1983. Normal turnaround time- next day. Same day for filings. Projects billed by number of names searched. Will file/record documents for clients. They specialize in checks for EPA and ERISA liens.

Lutek Investigations LLC

PO Box 161, Hartford, CT 06141

Phone: 860-729-3310 - **Fax:** 860-216-1754

www.lutekpi.com **email:** sitek@lutekpi.com

Types of Records Retrieved: Criminal, Civil and Probate courts; Federal courts; Real Estate; Tax Liens/Judgments; UCC records; Vital records

Local Retrieval Area: CT-Fairfield, Hartford, Litchfield, Middlesex, New Haven, New London, Tolland, Windham

Add'l Information: Established 2002. Normal turnaround time- within 48 hours. Expedited service available. Projects billed by the hour. First project may require prepayment. They are a full service detective agency available to retrieve records within their work territory. A licensed PI in CT. Performs service of process.

Lyman County Title Co

PO Box 187, Kennebec, SD 57544

Phone: 605-869-2269 - **Fax:** 605-869-2236

Types of Records Retrieved: Civil and Probate courts; Real Estate; Tax Liens/Judgments; UCC records

Local Retrieval Area: SD-Lyman

Add'l Information: Normal turnaround time- up to 2 weeks. Fee basis varies by type of transaction. They specialize in land records.

Lynch Abstracting

PO Box 129, Bloomfield, IA 52537

Phone: 641-664-3188 - **Fax:** 641-664-3186

Types of Records Retrieved: Criminal, Civil and Probate courts; Real Estate; Tax Liens/Judgments; UCC records; Vital records

Local Retrieval Area: IA-Davis

Add'l Information: Established 1975. Normal turnaround time- 3-4 days. Fee basis will vary by the type of project. Will file/record documents for clients. They specialize in title searches on real estate and personal lien searches in Davis County.

Lenn R Lynch

PO Box 6856, Americus, GA 31709

Phone: 229-942-7331

Types of Records Retrieved: Real Estate; Tax Liens/Judgments

Local Retrieval Area: GA-Bacon, Dougherty, Lee, Randolph, Schley, Sumter, Terrell, Webster

Add'l Information: Established 1991. Normal turnaround time- 24-48 hours. Fee charge is determined by the nature of the job and mileage. First project may require prepayment. Will file/record documents for clients. He specializes in real estate, title searches, tax liens, and filings mostly for attorney firms. He can visit criminal courts by special arrangement.

Patricia Lynch

5383 E State Rd 56, DuBois, IN 47527
Phone: 812-678-4416 or 812-678-4809
www.lynchpersohn.zoomshare.com **email:** pdlynch62@hotmail.com
Types of Records Retrieved: Criminal and Civil courts; Bankruptcy court; Real Estate; Tax Liens/Judgments
Local Retrieval Area: IN-Dubois, Martin, Spencer, Warrick. **Correspondent Relationships:** Southwestern Indiana.
Add'l Information: Established 2003. Normal turnaround time- 24-72 hours. Projects billed by number of names searched. First project may require prepayment. She and partner Patricia Persohn provide expert court coverage and are expanding into real estate types of searches.

Lynne J Cox Paralegal

1631 Fisher St, Munster, IN 46321
Phone: 800-510-3009; 219-838-1890 - **Fax:** 800-510-3009; 219-838-1890
LegaLynne1@msn.com
Types of Records Retrieved: Criminal, Civil and Probate courts; Federal courts; Real Estate; Tax Liens/Judgments; UCC records
Local Retrieval Area: IL-Cook; IN-Lake. **Correspondent Relationships:** Lake, DeKalb, DuPage, Kane, Kendall, McHenry, IL; Porter, LaPorte, Marion, IN.
Add'l Information: Established 1997. Normal turnaround time- 24-48 hours. Projects billed by number of names searched. As trained and credentialed paralegals, they provide on-site court and county record searches which are accurate, timely and meet the highest legal and ethical standards.

Lyon County Title Co Inc

109 S Marshall St, Rock Rapids, IA 51246
Phone: 712-472-3758 - **Fax:** 712-472-3758
Records Retrieved: Real Estate; Tax Liens/Judgments; Probate courts
Local Retrieval Area: IA-Lyon
Add'l Information: Normal turnaround time- 1-3 days. Fee basis will vary by the type of project. First project may require prepayment.

M & D Records Research

648 Forsythe, Toledo, OH 43605
Phone: 419-693-5649 - **Fax:** 419-693-4211
mdrecordsresearch@buckeye-express.com
Types of Records Retrieved: Criminal, Civil and Probate courts; Federal courts; Real Estate; Tax Liens/Judgments; UCC records; Vital records
Local Retrieval Area: OH-Lucas, Wood
Add'l Information: Established 1990. Normal turnaround time- 24-48 hours. Projects billed by number of names searched. Projects billed by number of records located. Charges are quoted by job. Will file/record documents for clients.

M & J Abstractors

416 Hillcrest Ct, Lansing, KS 66043
Phone: 913-727-3588 - **Fax:** 913-351-0175 jmenzell@kc.rr.com
Types of Records Retrieved: Civil and Probate courts; Federal District courts; Real Estate; Tax Liens/Judgments; UCC records
Local Retrieval Area: KS-Johnson, Leavenworth; MO-Clay, Jackson, Platte, Wyandotte.
Add'l Information: Established 1999. Normal turnaround time- 24-72 hours. Projects billed by number of names searched. First project may require prepayment. Will file/record documents for clients. They specialize in accurate searches in a timely manner. Please feel free to contact their company with any questions.

M & M Legal Services

PO Box 364, La Grande, OR 97850
Phone: 541-963-8219; Fax- same
Types of Records Retrieved: Criminal, Civil and Probate courts; Real Estate; Tax Liens/Judgments; Vital records
Local Retrieval Area: OR-Baker, Union, Wallowa
Add'l Information: Established 1979. Normal turnaround time- 1 day for Union County; 1-2 days for Baker County; 4 days for Wallowa County. Projects billed by the hour. They request prepayment from out of state clients, but will invoice established customers. A licensed PI in OR. Performs service of process.

M & M Search Service

17 W Jefferson St #007, Rockville, MD 20850-4201
Phone: 301-251-9545 - **Fax:** 301-251-6785
www.mandmsearchservice.com **email:** info@mandmsearchservice.com
Types of Records Retrieved: Civil and Probate courts; Federal courts; Real Estate; Tax Liens/Judgments; UCC records; Vital records
Local Retrieval Area: DC-District of Columbia; MD-Montgomery, Prince George's. **Correspondent Relationships:** DC area.
Add'l Information: Established 1985. Normal turnaround time- 8 hours for court records and UCCs. Full 60-year real estate search: 2 to 3 days. They charge by the hour for Commercial searches only. They charge by the property or address First project may require prepayment. Credit cards accepted. Will file/record documents for clients. A full-service real estate title and abstract company, they specialize in real estate and UCC searches.

M & M Title / Mitchell Co

2412 E 70th St, Shreveport, LA 71105
Phone: 318-798-1198 - **Fax:** 318-798-1191
Types of Records Retrieved: Civil and Probate courts; Real Estate; Tax Liens/Judgments; UCC records
Local Retrieval Area: LA-Bienville Parish, Bossier Parish, Caddo Parish, Claiborne Parish, De Soto Parish, Lincoln Parish, Webster Parish; TX-Cass, Harrison, Henderson, Marion, Panola, Rusk, Shelby, Smith. **Correspondent Relationships:** Southern Louisiana.
Add'l Information: Established 1960. Normal turnaround time- variable, depending on project. Projects billed by the hour. First project may require prepayment. Formerly DeSoto Abstract, they specialize in oil, gas and environmental assessment.

M C Associates

766 Robinhood Dr, Newark, OH 43055
Phone: 740-366-1922 - **Fax:** 740-366-1922
mmcordova@yahoo.com
Types of Records Retrieved: Criminal, Civil and Probate courts; Federal courts; Real Estate; Tax Liens/Judgments; UCC records; Vital records
Local Retrieval Area: OH-Delaware, Fairfield, Franklin, Hamilton, Knox, Licking, Montgomery, Muskingum, Pickaway, Ross, Union
Add'l Information: Established 1994. Normal turnaround time- 24-48 hours. Expedited service available. Projects billed by number of names searched. Will file/record documents for clients. They specialize in real property searches, document retrieval, real property tax, & property ownership verification. They also do federal & state tax liens, mortgages, judgments, criminal searches, civil searches, state & federal tax liens & UCCs. Performs service of process.

Mach 5 Couriers Inc

1201 Louisiana #210, Houston, TX 77002
Phone: 800-593-2023; 713-754-8239, 713-754-8244 - **Fax:** 713-655-1219
www.mach5couriers.com **email:** james@mach5couriers.com
Types of Records Retrieved: Criminal and Civil courts; Federal courts
Local Retrieval Area: TX-Brazoria, Chambers, Fort Bend, Galveston, Harris, Jefferson, Montgomery, Waller
Add'l Information: Established 1985. Normal turnaround time- 24-48 hours. First project may require prepayment. They also specialize in courier service, 24/7. Performs service of process.

MacIntire & Associates (Tucson)

3906 W Ina Rd #200, Tucson, AZ 85741
Phone: 800-641-2737; 520-622-2737 - **Fax:** 866-363-6143; 520-792-2764
www.macintireandassociates.com
email: info@macintireandassociates.com

Types of Records Retrieved: Criminal, Civil and Probate courts; Federal courts; Tax Liens/Judgments; UCC records

Local Retrieval Area: AZ-Apache, Cochise, Coconino, Gila, Graham, Greenlee, LaPaz, Maricopa, Mohave, Navajo, Pima, Pinal, Santa Cruz, Yavapai, Yuma. **Correspondents:** nationwide and international.

Add'l Information: Established 1979. Normal turnaround time- 48 hours. Expedited service available. Projects billed by number of names searched. Projects billed by the hour. Prepayment required for volume requests. First project may require prepayment. Credit cards accepted. Payment is a flat fee and due upon completion. They have extensive background in criminal defense, personal injury, surveillance and employment screening services. A licensed PI in AZ.

Mackinac Abstract & Title

291 Stockbridge, PO Box 322, St Ignace, MI 49781
Phone: 906-643-7452 - **Fax:** 906-643-0026

Types of Records Retrieved: Real Estate; Tax Liens/Judgments; Probate courts; UCC records

Local Retrieval Area: MI-Chippewa, Luce, Mackinac

Add'l Information: Established 1979. Normal turnaround time- 3-10 business days. Fee basis will vary by type of project. They specialize in real estate and tax record searches, title insurance and abstracts of title.

Macon County Title

PO Box 562, Macon, MO 63552-0562
Phone: 660-385-6474 - **Fax:** 660-385-6629

Types of Records Retrieved: Civil and Probate courts; Real Estate; Tax Liens/Judgments; UCC records; Vital records

Local Retrieval Area: MO-Macon

Add'l Information: Normal turnaround time- next day. Projects billed by number of names searched. Will file/record documents for clients. Formerly A Verne Baker Abstract Co, they specialize in title searches.

Madrona Research Inc

PO Box 29001, Bellingham, WA 98228
Phone: 360-647-8126 - **Fax:** 360-650-0819 marlenesmi@comcast.net

Types of Records Retrieved: Criminal, Civil and Probate courts; Real Estate; Tax Liens/Judgments; UCC records; Vital records

Local Retrieval Area: WA-Island, Skagit, Whatcom

Add'l Information: Established 1994. Normal turnaround time- 24 hours. Will file/record documents for clients. They specialize real estate owner reports and lien/judgment searches.

Maggie M & Associates

2 Bordeaux Ct, Petaluma, CA 94954
Phone: 707-778-7304 - **Fax:** 707-762-3282
www.maggiemassoc.com **email:** maggiemassoc@comcast.net

Records Retrieved: Criminal, Civil and Probate courts; Bankruptcy court; Real Estate; Tax Liens/Judgments; UCC records; Vital records

Local Retrieval Area: CA-Alameda, Contra Costa, El Dorado, Fresno, Marin, Merced, Napa, San Francisco, Santa Clara, Shasta, Sonoma

Add'l Information: Established 1996. Normal turnaround time- 24-48 hours. Projects billed by number of names searched. First project may require prepayment. Will file/record documents for clients. The competent & thorough abstractors leave no stone unturned. The team specializes in UCCs, tax liens/judgments superior/civil courts & retrieve new business listing in the San Francisco Bay area counties. List is maintained & updated on a weekly basis.

Mahaffey Law Office

PO Box 367, 304 Estelle St, Wrens, GA 30833
Phone: 706-547-4090 - **Fax:** 706-547-0502

Types of Records Retrieved: Criminal and Civil courts

Local Retrieval Area: GA-Glascock

Add'l Information: Projects billed by the hour. First project may require prepayment. Recommended by the Superior Court clerk as able to perform court record searches.

Mahaska Title - Johnson Abstract Co

121 High Ave E, Oskaloosa, IA 52577
Phone: 641-673-5666 - **Fax:** 641-673-9224
www.mtja.net **email:** mtja@mtja.net

Types of Records Retrieved: Criminal, Civil and Probate courts; Real Estate; Tax Liens/Judgments; UCC records; Vital records

Local Retrieval Area: IA-Mahaska

Add'l Information: Established 1980. Normal turnaround time- 1-2 days. Also billed according to assessed value and flat rates. First project may require prepayment. Will file/record documents for clients. The Mahaska Title Johnson Abstract staff has 80+ years of experience and provides the best service in Mahaska County. Also includes full service closing dept.

Mahnomen County Abstract Co

210 N Main, Mahnomen, MN 56557
Phone: 218-935-5227 - **Fax:** 218-935-5227

Types of Records Retrieved: Real Estate **Retrieval Area:** MN-Mahnomen

Add'l Information: Established 1987. Normal turnaround time- 48 hours. Projects billed by number of names searched. Projects billed by number of records located. Will send invoice. Press *51 when faxing. They specialize in title searches, owner and encumbrance reports, registered property abstracts, continuation of existing abstracts, preparation of new abstracts.

Maine Public Record Services

PO Box 514, Moody, ME 04054
Phone: 207-646-9065 - **Fax:** 207-646-9065 mepub@verizon.net

Types of Records Retrieved: Civil and Probate courts; Federal District courts; Real Estate; Tax Liens/Judgments; UCC records

Local Retrieval Area: ME-Cumberland, York

Add'l Information: Established 1993. Normal turnaround time- 24-48 hours. Will file/record documents for clients. Terms net 30 days. They specialize in document & information retrieval, current owner, two owner & PMM reports, walk in recording services, UCC searches & special requests. Established in 1993.

Mainline Researchers Inc

PO Box 741, 213 S Center St (15931), Ebensburg, PA 15931-0741
Phone: 814-472-7913 - **Fax:** 814-472-7936 mresearchers@verizon.net

Types of Records Retrieved: Criminal and Civil courts; Real Estate; Tax Liens/Judgments; UCC records

Local Retrieval Area: PA-Cambria. **Correspondent Relationships:** most Western Pennsylvania counties.

Add'l Information: Established 1971. Normal turnaround time- 24 hours. 60 year title searches take longer. Projects billed by number of names searched. Charges vary depending on type of search. Will file/record documents for clients. Billed monthly; terms are net 10 days.

Majestic Research Services Inc

931 Polk St NW, Marietta, GA 30064-2054
Phone: 678-355-5393 - **Fax:** 678-355-6762 majestic_1@msn.com

Types of Records Retrieved: Real Estate; Tax Liens/Judgments; Probate courts; UCC records

Local Retrieval Area: GA-Bartow, Cherokee, Clayton, Cobb, Coweta, DeKalb, Douglas, Fulton, Fayette, Gwinnett, Henry, Paulding

Add'l Information: Established 2000. Normal turnaround time- 24-48 hours. Projects billed by number of names searched. Will file/record documents for clients. Payment terms net 30 days.

Johanna E Malki

11041 NE 10th Ave, Biscayne Park, FL 33161
Phone: 305-899-0273 - **Fax:** 305-899-2092 bdrfl@mindspring.com
Types of Records Retrieved: Bankruptcy court; Real Estate; Tax Liens/Judgments; UCC records **Local Retrieval Area:** FL-Broward, Dade
Add'l Information: Established 1995. Normal turnaround time- 24-48 hours. Projects billed by number of names searched. First project may require prepayment. Will file/record documents for clients. She is a Notary Public in the State of Florida since 1971.

Management Information Services

1836 W 25th St #2A, Cleveland, OH 44113-3152
Phone: 216-241-4282 - **Fax:** 216-241-3227
www.managementinfoservices.com
email: mis@management nfoservices.com
Records Retrieved: Criminal and Civil courts; Federal District courts
Local Retrieval Area: OH-Ashtabula, Cuyahoga, Geauga, Lake, Lorain. **Correspondent Relationships:** nationwide.
Add'l Information: Established 1995. Normal turnaround time- 1-4 days. Projects billed by number of names searched. Net 30 days. They specialize in pre-employment screening. Services include: criminal checks, employment verification and Ohio drivers license.

Manistee Abstract & Title Co

63 Maple St, Manistee, MI 49660
Phone: 231-723-3397 - **Fax:** 231-723-5382
Types of Records Retrieved: Criminal, Civil and Probate courts; Real Estate; Tax Liens/Judgments; UCC records; Vital records
Local Retrieval Area: MI-Manistee
Add'l Information: Established 1947. Normal turnaround time- 3-5 days. Fee basis will vary by type of project. All projects require prepayment. They will also invoice. They specialize in real estate.

Marathon Research LLC

2072 Defoors Ferry Rd #L-3, Atlanta, GA 30318
Phone: 678-570-7163 - **Fax:** 770-234-4274 ardesmond@aol.com
Types of Records Retrieved: Criminal, Civil and Probate courts; Federal courts; Real Estate; Tax Liens/Judgments; UCC records; Vital records
Local Retrieval Area: GA-Cobb, De Kalb, Fulton
Add'l Information: Established 2001. Normal turnaround time- 3 days. Expedited service available. Projects billed by number of names searched. Projects billed by number of records located. Projects billed by the hour. Credit cards accepted. Preferred payment method is PayPal. Their specialties are real estate and lost heirs.

Marias Title Company

PO Box 589, Shelby, MT 59474-0589
Phone: 406-434-5156 - **Fax:** 406-434-5157 title@3rivers.net
Types of Records Retrieved: Civil and Probate courts; Real Estate; Tax Liens/Judgments; UCC records; Vital records
Local Retrieval Area: MT-Liberty, Toole
Add'l Information: Established 1915. Normal turnaround time- 8 days. Projects billed by the hour. All projects require prepayment. Will file/record documents for clients. They will file/record UCC and real estate documents on behalf of clients if filing fees are included with the request, payable to the County.

Maricopa Research

12467 W Palm Ln, Avondale, AZ 85323
Phone: 623-935-0572 - **Fax:** 623-535-4197 lilmel89@yahoo.com
Types of Records Retrieved: Civil courts; Bankruptcy court; Real Estate; Tax Liens/Judgments; UCC records; Vital records
Local Retrieval Area: AZ-Maricopa
Add'l Information: Established 1999. Normal turnaround time- 3-5 days. Projects billed by the hour. First project may require prepayment.

Marietta Abstract Co

PO Box 287, 305 W Main St, Marietta, OK 73448
Phone: 580-276-2231 - **Fax:** 580-276-2771
Types of Records Retrieved: Civil and Probate courts; Real Estate; Tax Liens/Judgments; UCC records; Vital records
Local Retrieval Area: OK-Love
Add'l Information: Established 1906. Normal turnaround time- varied by project. Projects billed by the hour. All projects require prepayment. Will file/record documents for clients.

Marilyn Smolinsky & Associates

1119 Round Pointe Dr, Haverstraw, NY 10927
Phone: 845-634-5770 - **Fax:** 845-634-5791 mtsmolinsky@optonline.net
Types of Records Retrieved: Criminal, Civil and Probate courts; Real Estate; UCC records
Local Retrieval Area: NY-Rockland
Add'l Information: Established 1988. Normal turnaround time- 24 hours. Projects billed by number of names searched. Will file/record documents for clients. Payment due upon delivery. They specialize in property searches for title insurance companies. They perform title and witness only closings, document retrieval and filings. In business since 1988.

Marion County Abstract Co (Arkansas)

PO Box 388, Yellville, AR 72687
Phone: 870-449-4218 - **Fax:** 870-449-4220
Types of Records Retrieved: Criminal, Civil and Probate courts; Real Estate; Tax Liens/Judgments; UCC records
Local Retrieval Area: AR-Marion
Add'l Information: Established 1967. Normal turnaround time- 24-72 hours. Fee basis will vary by type of project. All projects require prepayment. Will file/record documents for clients. They have more than 35 years experience in real estate.

Marion County Abstract Co (Missouri)

PO Box 2, Palmyra, MO 63461
Phone: 800-952-5314; 573-769-2212 - **Fax:** 573-769-4916
harla@marioncountyabstract.com
Types of Records Retrieved: Criminal, Civil and Probate courts; Real Estate; Tax Liens/Judgments; UCC records; Vital records
Local Retrieval Area: IL-Adams, Pike; MO-Clark, Lewis, Macon, Marion, Monroe, Pike, Ralls, Shelby
Add'l Information: Established 1900. Normal turnaround time- 4-5 days. Fee basis will vary by the type of project. Invoice sent with report. Will file/record documents for clients. Payment due upon completion They specialize in title insurance, title searches and abstracting, closings and escrow services, and 1031 exchanges.

Marion County Title Services

303 S 2nd St, Knoxville, IA 50138-2212
Phone: 641-842-3518 - **Fax:** 641-842-3528
Types of Records Retrieved: Criminal, Civil and Probate courts; Real Estate; Tax Liens/Judgments; UCC records; Vital records
Local Retrieval Area: IA-Marion
Add'l Info: Established 1902. Turnaround time- 1-2 days. Fee basis varies by type of transaction. First project may require prepayment.

Theresa Marrinan

52 Fairlane Dr, Springfield, KY 40069
Phone: 859-336-5425 - **Fax:** 859-336-5408
Types of Records Retrieved: Real Estate; Tax Liens/Judgments
Local Retrieval Area: KY-Washington
Add'l Info: First project may require prepayment. She specializes in real estate; works on a limited basis only. After hours phone is 859-336-3581.

Marshall County Abstract Co

PO Box 50, Madill, OK 73446
Phone: 580-795-7388 - **Fax:** 580-795-7389
Types of Records Retrieved: Real Estate

Local Retrieval Area: OK-Carter, Johnston, Marshall

Add'l Information: Established 1920. Normal turnaround time- 2 days. Fee basis will vary by the type of project. First project may require prepayment. Will file/record documents for clients. They only retrieve court records from Johnston, Marshall and Love counties.

Marshall County Abstract Company

23 S Center St, Marshalltown, IA 50158-2850
Phone: 641-752-5358 - **Fax:** 641-754-1763 meac@marshallnet.com

Types of Records Retrieved: Criminal, Civil and Probate courts; Federal courts; Real Estate; Tax Liens/Judgments; UCC records; Vital records

Local Retrieval Area: IA-Marshall

Add'l Information: Established 1950. Normal turnaround time- 2 days. Fee basis will vary by type of project.

Marshall Land & Title Co Inc

PO Box 898, Britton, SD 57430
Phone: 605-448-5796 - **Fax:** 605-448-2894 mlt@venturecomm.net

Types of Records Retrieved: Real Estate; Tax Liens/Judgments; Probate courts; UCC records; Vital records

Local Retrieval Area: SD-Marshall

Add'l Information: Established 1894. Normal turnaround time- 3-4 days. Fee basis is based on evaluation of project. First project may require prepayment. Will file/record documents for clients. They specialize in abstracts, title insurance, and real estate transaction closings.

Martha's Retrieval

Route 1 Box 39, Leoti, KS 67861
Phone: 620-375-2251 - **Fax:** 620-375-2251

Types of Records Retrieved: Criminal and Civil courts; Real Estate

Local Retrieval Area: KS-Greeley, Wallace, Wichita

Add'l Information: Established 1993. Normal turnaround time- 24-48 hours. Bills per name per county searched. First project may require prepayment. She is the document retrieval expert in this three county area.

Martin Abstract Co (Warren)

PO Box 970, Warren, AR 71671
Phone: 870-226-7487 - **Fax:** 870-226-2685

Types of Records Retrieved: Criminal, Civil and Probate courts; Real Estate; Tax Liens/Judgments; UCC records

Local Retrieval Area: AR-Bradley, Cleveland

Add'l Information: Established 1965. Normal turnaround time- up to 7 days. Projects billed by number of names searched. First project may require prepayment. Credit cards accepted. They specialize in title insurance, record checks and real estate closing.

Martin Title & Closing Services

602 Dequeen St, Mena, AR 71953
Phone: 479-394-1963 - **Fax:** 479-394-1995

Types of Records Retrieved: Criminal, Civil and Probate courts; Real Estate; Tax Liens/Judgments; UCC records

Local Retrieval Area: AR-Polk

Add'l Info: Established 1904. Normal turnaround time- 2-3 days. Fee basis will vary by the type of project. First project may require prepayment.

Mary Lindsey Research

11643 Pride Port Hudson Rd, Zachary, LA 70791
Phone: 225-654-6576 - **Fax:** 225-658-0029 maryblindsey@cs.com

Types of Records Retrieved: Civil courts; Federal courts

Retrieval Area: LA-East Baton Rouge, West Baton Rouge, West Feliciana

Add'l Information: Established 1984. Normal turnaround time- 24 hours. Projects billed by the hour. First project may require prepayment. She is a research librarian who specializes in online database, Internet, and library research. She can provide LA state agency records, e.g. DEQ, Dept of Natural Resources, and LA Public Service Commission.

Maryland Research & Abstract Co

25 W Chesapeake Ave #214, Baltimore, MD 21204-4820
Phone: 410-823-1944 - **Fax:** 410-823-7254 mrac@radicus.net

Records Retrieved: Civil and Probate courts; Real Estate; UCC records

Local Retrieval Area: MD-Baltimore, Harford

Add'l Information: Established 1989. Normal turnaround time- 1 week. Projects billed by number of names searched. Fee may be charged per property. They specialize in real estate title searches.

Mashburn's Background Screening

65 Frazier Rd, Leoma, TN 38468
Phone: 931-852-2713 - **Fax:** 931-852-4033
vmashburn@lorettotel.net

Types of Records Retrieved: Criminal and Civil courts; Tax Liens/Judgments

Local Retrieval Area: TN-Decatur, Giles, Hardin, Hickman, Lawrence, Lewis, Lincoln, Maury, Perry, Wayne

Add'l Information: Established 2000. Normal turnaround time- 24-48 hours; Decatur may take longer. Projects billed by number of names searched. First project may require prepayment. Is an expert in South Central Tennessee records; also provides data for background screening purposes.

Mask Research Services

PO Box 1499, Granite Falls, WA 98252
Phone: 425-361-2235 - **Fax:** 425-361-2209 amynay@comcast.net

Types of Records Retrieved: Civil courts; Real Estate; Tax Liens/Judgments

Local Retrieval Area: WA-Island

Add'l Information: Established 2000. Normal turnaround time- 48 hours. Projects billed by number of names searched. Projects billed by number of records located. Fees negotiated with volume. Will file/record documents for clients. They specialize in real estate current ownership.

Mason County Abstract & Title Inc

5734 W Deren Rd, Ludington, MI 49431-9795
Phone: 231-843-2645 - **Fax:** 231-843-3305

Records Retrieved: Real Estate; Tax Liens/Judgments; UCC records

Local Retrieval Area: MI-Mason

Add'l Information: Established 1892. Normal turnaround time- variable depending on project. Projects billed by number of names searched. Projects billed by number of records located. Projects billed by the hour. Will file/record documents for clients. They specialize in searches covering real estate in Mason County, MI.

Massachusetts Document Retrieval

PO Box 529, North Easton, MA 02356-0529
Phone: 617-249-0323 - **Fax:** 800-699-0249
www.mass-doc.com **email:** services@mass-doc.com

Types of Records Retrieved: Civil and Probate courts; Bankruptcy court; Real Estate; Vital records

Local Retrieval Area: MA-Middlesex, Suffolk. **Correspondent Relationships:** Bristol, Essex, Worcester, Norfolk, Plymouth, Hampden counties, MA.

Add'l Information: Established 1997. Normal turnaround time- varied with request, project, size/scope; usually 24-48 hours. Projects billed by number of names searched. Projects billed by the hour. All projects require prepayment. Specialize in heir researching, vital records research including divorce, missing persons and genealogical projects. Other search services include wills/probate and naturalization records.

Masscourtresearch

28 Craig St, Milton, MA 02186
Phone: 617-696-2178 - **Fax:** 617-696-7814
www.masscourtresearch.com **email:** masscourt.research@verizon.net

Types of Records Retrieved: Criminal and Civil courts; Federal courts; Tax Liens/Judgments

Local Retrieval Area: MA-Middlesex, Suffolk

Add'l Information: Established 1995. Normal turnaround time- 48 hours. 30 day billings. They are hands-on court researcher at the Superior Courts and all District courts in Suffolk and Middlesex counties.

Massey Abstract Inc

PO Box 211, Covington, IN 47932-0211
Phone: 765-793-3451 - **Fax:** 765-793-0668 lmassey@masseyabstract.com
Types of Records Retrieved: Civil and Probate courts; Real Estate; Tax Liens/Judgments; UCC records
Local Retrieval Area: IN-Fountain, Vermillion, Warren
Add'l Information: Established 1950. Normal turnaround time- 5 working days. Projects billed by number of names searched. First project may require prepayment. Will file/record documents for clients. They specialize in title searches.

Master File Inc

7925 Clayton Road #200, St Louis, MO 63117
Phone: 866-242-0469; 314-862-6049 - **Fax:** 314-863-8300
www.masterfile-stlouis.com **email:** sjw@mail.masterfile-stlouis.com
Types of Records Retrieved: Civil and Probate courts; Federal courts; Real Estate; Tax Liens/Judgments; UCC records
Local Retrieval Area: IL-Madison, St. Clair; MO-Jefferson, St. Charles, St. Louis, St. Louis City. **Correspondent Relationships:** MO and Southern IL.
Add'l Information: Established 1991. Normal turnaround time- 24-36 hours. Fee basis varies by type of project. Terms are net 15 days. First project may require prepayment. Credit cards accepted. Will file/record documents for clients. Terms: net 30 days. They specialize in court and recorder searches. Performs service of process.

Matrix Info Services

4348 Carter Creek #103, Bryan, TX 77802
Phone: 979-846-3593 - **Fax:** 979-846-7005 charlesstipe90@hotmail.com
Types of Records Retrieved: Criminal, Civil and Probate courts; Federal courts; Real Estate; Tax Liens/Judgments; UCC records; Vital records
Local Retrieval Area: TX-Brazos
Add'l Information: Established 1994. Normal turnaround time- 2-3 days. Expedited service available. Projects billed by number of names searched. First project may require prepayment. Will file/record documents for clients. In business in the same area for 5 years; Texas process server #SCH-1672. Mobile notary, skiptracing, and database services also available. Performs service of process.

Mayes County Abstract

PO Box 967, Pryor, OK 74362
Phone: 918-825-3074 - **Fax:** 918-825-3571
Types of Records Retrieved: Civil and Probate courts; Real Estate; Tax Liens/Judgments; UCC records; Vital records
Local Retrieval Area: OK-Mayes
Add'l Information: Established 1910. Normal turnaround time- 1-2 days. Projects billed by the hour.

William "Bill" H Maynard

4984 Cindy Circle NW, PMB 289, Cleveland, TN 37312
Phone: 423-472-9858 - **Fax:** 423-614-5484
Records Retrieved: Real Estate; Tax Liens/Judgments; UCC records
Local Retrieval Area: TN-Blount, Bradley, Hamilton, Knox, Loudon, McMinn, Meigs, Monroe, Polk, Rhea, Roane
Add'l Information: Established 1997. Normal turnaround time- 24-48 hours. Projects billed by number of records located. Payment due at time of invoicing or monthly statement. They service southeast Tennessee for Real Estate. 11 counties along the I-75 corridor from Hamilton to Knox counties. Specialize in current owner and full (30-40 year) searches. Cell number is 423-715-5310.

MBE

4080 Hampshire Ct, Allentown, PA 18104
Phone: 610-395-2202 - **Fax:** 610-530-7198 maronercol@rcn.com
Types of Records Retrieved: Criminal courts
Local Retrieval Area: PA-Berks, Bucks, Lehigh, Montgomery, Northampton, Philadelphia. **Correspondent Relationships:** New Jersey.
Add'l Information: Established 1997. Normal turnaround time- 24 hours. Projects billed by number of names searched. Will bill monthly.

MBK Consulting

60 N Harding Rd, Columbus, OH 43209-1524
Phone: 614-239-8977 - **Fax:** 614-239-0599
www.mbkcons.com **email:** mbkcons@netexp.net
Types of Records Retrieved: Real Estate; Tax Liens/Judgments; Probate courts; Federal courts; UCC records; Vital records
Local Retrieval Area: OH-Franklin. **Correspondent Relationships:** other counties in Ohio.
Add'l Information: Established 1991. Normal turnaround time- 24-48 hours. Projects billed by number of names searched. Project rates available. First project may require prepayment. Will file/record documents for clients. Large projects require prepayment. They specialize in historical and genealogical research as well as general public record retrieval. They also do title examinations.

McAllister & Associates Inc

PO Box 12082, 16 Northtown Dr #200-D, Jackson, MS 39236-2082
Phone: 601-977-0406 - **Fax:** 601-977-8464 rustymcallister@aol.com
Types of Records Retrieved: Criminal, Civil and Probate courts; Federal courts; Tax Liens/Judgments; Vital records
Local Retrieval Area: MS-Hinds, Madison, Rankin. **Correspondent Relationships:** Mississippi.
Add'l Information: Established 1979. Normal turnaround time- variable depending on project. Projects billed by the hour. First project may require prepayment. They will also invoice. They are a general investigative agency. Charges mileage plus hourly for Sunflower, Sharkey, Issaquena, Yazoo, Holmes, Humphreys, and Washington counties which are beyond their usual retrieval area. A licensed PI in MS. Performs service of process.

McBrayer McGinnis Leslie & Kirkland

PO Box 280, Main & Harrison St, Greenup, KY 41144
Phone: 606-473-7303 - **Fax:** 606-473-9003 brucemac@zoominternet.net
Types of Records Retrieved: Criminal, Civil and Probate courts; Federal courts; Real Estate; Tax Liens/Judgments; UCC records; Vital records
Local Retrieval Area: KY-Boyd, Carter, Fayette, Franklin, Greenup, Lawrence, Lewis
Add'l Information: Established 1960. Normal turnaround time- 2 days. Projects billed by the hour. Or billing by arrangement. Credit cards accepted. Will file/record documents for clients. Net 30 days.

McCarthy Abstract Co

PO Box 528, O'Neill, NE 68763
Phone: 402-336-2860 - **Fax:** 402-336-4489
Types of Records Retrieved: Real Estate; Tax Liens/Judgments; Probate courts; UCC records
Local Retrieval Area: NE-Boyd, Holt, Wheeler
Add'l Information: Established 1983. Normal turnaround time- 3-5 days in Holt county. Projects billed by the hour. First project may require prepayment. Will file/record documents for clients. They specialize in real estate records, abstracts, title insurance, and real estate closings.

McCook County Abstract & Title Ins

PO Box 506, Salem, SD 57058
Phone: 605-425-2612 - **Fax:** 605-425-3277
Types of Records Retrieved: Criminal, Civil and Probate courts; Real Estate; Tax Liens/Judgments; UCC records; Vital records
Local Retrieval Area: SD-McCook
Add'l Information: Established 1900. Normal turnaround time- 1 week. Fee basis is set by state law. All projects require prepayment. They specialize in title insurance.

McCormick Detective Agency

PO Box 444, Breckenridge, CO 80424
Phone: 970-453-6378 - **Fax:** 970-453-6852 mda444brek@aol.com
Types of Records Retrieved: Criminal and Civil courts; Real Estate; Tax Liens/Judgments; UCC records
Local Retrieval Area: CO-Clear Creek, Lake, Park, Summit. **Correspondent Relationships:** Denver, CO.
Add'l Information: Established 1977. Normal turnaround time- 1 day. Projects billed by the hour. Will file/record documents for clients. Will bill at the first of the month. They specialize in trial preparation for civil and criminal cases. A licensed PI in CO. Performs service of process.

McCoy Investigations (CAPI# 18621)

PO Box 174, Carmichael, CA 95609
Phone: 800-287-6789; 916-481-3525 - **Fax:** 916-481-5293
www.mccoyinvestigations.com **email:** nancy@mccoyinvestigations.com
Types of Records Retrieved: Criminal and Civil courts
Local Retrieval Area: CA-Sacramento. **Correspondents:** nationwide.
Add'l info: Established 1993. Normal turnaround time- 24-72 hours. Projects billed by number of records located. First project may require prepayment. They specialize in screening services for the business community, nationwide. They use "On-Hands" researchers to check criminal records nationwide. They also provide driving records, SS traces, credit reports, employment verification, education and civil. A licensed PI in CA.

Jean McCullough

PO Box 70, c/o Superior Court Clerk Office, Carnesville, GA 30521
Phone: 706-491-9595
Types of Records Retrieved: Criminal and Civil courts; Real Estate; Tax Liens/Judgments
Local Retrieval Area: GA-Franklin
Add'l Information: First project may require prepayment. She is recommended by the Superior Court clerk. You may also leave a message for her through the Superior Court clerk office 706-384-2514, PO Box 70.

Lisa McDonald

1825 Highway 90 West, Mauk, GA 31058
Types of Records Retrieved: Criminal and Civil courts; Tax Liens/Judgments
Local Retrieval Area: GA-Taylor
Add'l Information: Established 2002. Normal turnaround time- 24 hours. Projects billed by number of names searched. First project may require prepayment. Daily access to the Taylor County Superior Ct. Call court.

Sheri McDowell

PO Box 10, Broadus, MT 59317
Phone: 406-436-2885 - **Fax:** 406-436-2885 mcd@rangeweb.net
Types of Records Retrieved: Criminal, Civil and Probate courts
Local Retrieval Area: MT-Powder River
Add'l Information: Established 2000. Normal turnaround time- 24-48 hours. First project may require prepayment. She specializes in court records.

McGinley Search & File Service Corp

722 Bristol Ct, Greenwood, IN 46143-3161
Phone: 317-807-0760 - **Fax:** 317-807-0767 bmcginleydavis@yahoo.com
Types of Records Retrieved: Civil courts; Federal courts; Real Estate; Tax Liens/Judgments; UCC records
Local Retrieval Area: IN-all counties except Switzerland. **Correspondent Relationships:** statewide, also Illinois and Michigan.
Add'l Information: Established 1992. Normal turnaround time- 24-72 hours. Projects billed by number of names searched. Will file/record documents for clients. From Indianapolis, they specialize in assisting various professionals in filing, searching and retrieval of documents in all local, county, state and district offices statewide. They do not search criminal indexes. A licensed PI in IN.

McGowan & Clark Inv

7810 Fairway Ave SE #1201, Snoqualmie, WA 98065-9020
Phone: 425-396-5680 - **Fax:** 425-396-5681 raymcgowan@comcast.net
Types of Records Retrieved: Criminal and Civil courts; Federal courts; Real Estate; Tax Liens/Judgments; UCC records; Vital records; Property records
Local Retrieval Area: WA-King, Pierce, Snohomish. **Correspondent Relationships:** statewide.
Add'l Information: Established 1993. Normal turnaround time- 24 hours. Expedited service available. Projects billed by number of names searched. Terms: net 30 days. For 13 years they have been accessing all of Washington's public records through physical retrieval, courthouse & county databases, along with online access.

Paul Kevin McGriff

133 W South Mountain Ave, Phoenix, AZ 85041
Phone: 602-309-7138 pkmcgriff@yahoo.com
Types of Records Retrieved: Criminal, Civil and Probate courts; Federal courts; Real Estate; Tax Liens/Judgments; UCC records; Vital records
Local Retrieval Area: AZ-Maricopa. **Correspondents:** statewide.
Add'l Information: Established 2006. Normal turnaround time- 1 week. Projects billed by number of names searched. Projects billed by number of records located. Projects billed by the hour. First project may require prepayment. Credit cards accepted. A licensed PI in CO.

McGuire Research Associates

107 Danielson Pike, Scituate, RI 02857
Phone: 401-647-7881 - **Fax:** 401-647-4693 lmcguire12@cox.net
Types of Records Retrieved: Civil and Probate courts; Federal courts; Real Estate; Tax Liens/Judgments; UCC records
Local Retrieval Area: RI-Bristol, Kent, Newport, Providence, Washington. **Correspondent Relationships:** Bristol County MA.
Add'l Information: Established 1989. Normal turnaround time- 24 hours at state agencies, 24-48 hours at town offices. Projects billed by number of names searched. Will file/record documents for clients. Terms: net 30 days. They specialize in filings in Rhode Island, at the state or town level. They cover all thirty-nine (39) towns.

McHenry County Abstract & Title Co

PO Box 420, Towner, ND 58788
Phone: 701-537-5723 - **Fax:** 701-537-5723
Types of Records Retrieved: Criminal, Civil and Probate courts; Federal courts; Real Estate; Tax Liens/Judgments; UCC records
Local Retrieval Area: ND-McHenry, Sheridan
Add'l Information: Established 1986. Normal turnaround time- 24 hours. Fee basis varies by the type of project First project may require prepayment. Will file/record documents for clients. They specialize in title abstracting and document retrieval.

McHugh Abstract Co

PO Box 151, Langdon, ND 58249
Phone: 701-256-2851 - **Fax:** 701-256-2852
Types of Records Retrieved: Civil courts; Federal courts; Real Estate; Tax Liens/Judgments; UCC records; Vital records
Local Retrieval Area: ND-Cavalier
Add'l Information: Established 1970. Normal turnaround time- 2-5 days. Fee based on nature of project. Will file/record documents for clients.

McIver Abstract & Title Co

317 NW Front St, Ashdown, AR 71822 **Phone:** 870-898-3502
Types of Records Retrieved: Real Estate
Local Retrieval Area: AR-Little River
Add'l Information: Established 1930. Normal turnaround time- 3-4 days. Fee basis will vary by type of project. First project may require prepayment. They specialize in real estate and title work.

Mark McKee, PI

12608 Rohan Ct, Oklahoma City, OK 73170
Phone: 405-636-1976 peaeye007@aol.com
Types of Records Retrieved: Criminal, Civil and Probate courts; Federal courts; Real Estate; Tax Liens/Judgments; UCC records; Vital records
Local Retrieval Area: OK-Canadian, Cleveland, McClain, Oklahoma. **Correspondent Relationships:** Oklahoma, Texas.
Add'l Information: Established 1984. Normal turnaround time- 24-48 hours. Projects billed by number of names searched. First project may require prepayment. Will file/record documents for clients. Service and application agreement may be required. Call before faxing. They specialize in background checks, insurance fraud, asset locating, collections, skiptracing, process serving, and public & private record retrieval. A licensed PI in OK, AR. Performs service of process.

McKesson Title Corp

407 N Center St, Plymouth, IN 46563
Phone: 800-261-8437; 574-936-2555 - **Fax:** 574-935-5515
http://mckessontitle.com **email:** info@mckessontitle.com
Records Retrieved: Real Estate; Tax Liens/Judgments; UCC records
Local Retrieval Area: IN-Elkhart, Fulton, Kosciusko, La Porte, Marshall, Pulaski, St Joseph, Starke
Add'l Information: Established 1919. Normal turnaround time- varied; rush service available on request. Fees vary depending on project. Personal or cashier checks are accepted. They specialize in title insurance and escrow closings, 1031 tax exchanges and home owners insurance. They are celebrating the 88th year in business, being the oldest family-owned title company in Indiana. A licensed PI in IN. Performs service of process.

McLean County Abstract Inc

PO Box 370, 615 Main Ave, Washburn, ND 58577
Phone: 701-462-3244 - **Fax:** 701-462-8444
Types of Records Retrieved: Criminal, Civil and Probate courts; Federal courts; Real Estate; Tax Liens/Judgments; UCC records; Vital records
Local Retrieval Area: ND-McLean
Add'l Information: Established 1991. Normal turnaround time- 2 weeks. Fee basis will vary by type of project. All projects require prepayment. Will file/record documents for clients. They will also invoice.

McPheron Info Services

PO Box 190, Lebanon, IN 46052
Phone: 765-482-1650, cell- 765-894-0107 - **Fax:** 765-482-6409
www.mcpheroninformation.com **email:** info.mcpheron@insightbb.com
Types of Records Retrieved: Criminal, Civil and Probate courts; Real Estate; UCC records; Tax Liens/Judgments; Vital records
Local Retrieval Area: IN-Bartholomew, Boone, Brown, Carroll, Clinton, Decatur, Decatur, Fayette, Fountain, Hamilton, Hancock, Hendricks, Henry, Howard, Johnson, Madison, Marion, Montgomery, Randolph, Rush, Shelby, Tippecanoe, Tipton, Union, Wayne. **Correspondent Relationships:** Indiana counties of Allen, Blackford, Dekalb, Grant, Huntington, Jackson, Jennings, LaGrange, Lake, Lawrence, Monroe, Morgan, Posey, Vanderburgh, Vigo, Warrick, Wells.
Add'l Information: Established 1995. Normal turnaround time- 24-72 hours. Projects billed by number of names searched. Fees may depend on nature of the request. First project may require prepayment. They are a full service document retrieval company, specializing in current owner searches, judgments, pending suits, mortgage-deed retrieval.

McQueen Abstract Company

PO Box 549, 521 S Main, Hugoton, KS 67951
Phone: 620-544-2311 - **Fax:** 620-544-8029 glen@pld.com
Types of Records Retrieved: Criminal, Civil and Probate courts; Real Estate; Tax Liens/Judgments; UCC records
Local Retrieval Area: KS-Stevens
Add'l Information: Established 1974. Normal turnaround time- 3-5 days. Projects billed by the hour.

Tim McQuinn

116 S Third St, Monticello, IN 47960
Phone: 574-583-9360 - **Fax:** 574-583-8305
Types of Records Retrieved: Criminal and Civil courts
Local Retrieval Area: IN-White
Add'l Information: Established 1995. Normal turnaround time- 24 hours usually. First project may require prepayment. He specializes in just White County courts.

Meade County Title

PO Box 520, 121 E Carthage, Meade, KS 67864
Phone: 620-873-2756 - **Fax:** 620-873-2756
Types of Records Retrieved: Civil and Probate courts; Real Estate; Tax Liens/Judgments; UCC records
Local Retrieval Area: KS-Meade. **Correspondent Relationships:** Clark County KS.
Add'l Information: Established 1966. Normal turnaround time- 2-3 days. Fee basis varies by type of transaction. First project may require prepayment. Will file/record documents for clients. Payment due upon receipt of report.

Meade County Title Clark County

PO Box 221, Ashland, KS 67831
Phone: 800-725-7802; - **Fax:** 620-635-2716
Types of Records Retrieved: Civil and Probate courts; Real Estate; Tax Liens/Judgments; UCC records; Vital records
Local Retrieval Area: KS-Clark. **Correspondent Relationships:** Meade County, KS.
Add'l Information: Normal turnaround time- 2-3 days. Fee basis varies by type of transaction. First project may require prepayment.

Meador Investigations

PO Box 157, Lincoln, IL 62656
Phone: 888-688-9944; 217-732-1585 - **Fax:** 888-688-9944; 217-732-1585
www.pi-pro.com **email:** admin@pi-prom.com
Types of Records Retrieved: Criminal, Civil and Probate courts; Federal courts; Real Estate; Tax Liens/Judgments; UCC records; Vital records
Retrieval Area: IL-Logan, Macon, Menard, Peoria, Sangamon, Tazewell
Add'l Information: Established 1999. Projects billed by number of names searched. They are a licensed private investigations agency specializing in process service and background investigations. A licensed PI in IL. Performs service of process.

Gwen Meairs

PO Box 915, Sublette, KS 67877 **Phone:** 620-629-0551
Types of Records Retrieved: Criminal, Civil and Probate courts
Local Retrieval Area: KS-Haskell
Add'l Information: Established 2000?. Normal turnaround time- 24-48 hours. Projects billed by number of names searched. First project may require prepayment. She provides fast turnaround and expert service.

Medina Retrieval Service

271 NE 45th St, Ft Lauderdale, FL 33334
Phone: 954-560-9077 - **Fax:** 954-958-0871
www.mrssearch.com **email:** gmedina@mrssearch.com
Types of Records Retrieved: Criminal, Civil and Probate courts; Federal courts; Real Estate
Local Retrieval Area: FL-Broward, Dade, Palm Beach. **Correspondent Relationships:** Leon County, FL.
Add'l Information: Established 2002. Normal turnaround time- 1-2 days dependant on time request is received and availability of documents. Expedited service available for $25 charge. Projects billed by the hour. First project may require prepayment. Credit cards accepted. Will bill major firms. They are a legal document retrieval service for Broward, Miami-Dade and Palm Beach counties. They focus on Federal and State/County courts.

Medlin Research Company

PO Box 159, Louisburg, KS 66053-0159
Phone: 913-206-4615 - **Fax:** 913-837-4975 wtmedlin@yahoo.com

Types of Records Retrieved: Criminal, Civil and Probate courts; Federal courts; Real Estate; Tax Liens/Judgments; UCC records

Local Retrieval Area: KS-Johnson, Miami; MO-Cass. **Correspondent Relationships:** Platte, Clay counties MO.

Add'l Information: Established 1999. Normal turnaround time- 24-36 hours. Projects billed by number of names searched. Payment due at the end of the month. They offer criminal, civil, UCC, tax liens, Federal criminal and bankruptcy searches. They also do current owner searches on property (residential only). Pager # is 913-259-1626.

Jesse Melcher, Attny

PO Box 345, Mt Olivet, KY 41064
Phone: 606-724-5322 - **Fax:** 606-724-2612 jpmelcher@yahoo.com

Types of Records Retrieved: Real Estate; Tax Liens/Judgments

Local Retrieval Area: KY-Robertson

Add'l Information: Established 1999. First project may require prepayment. He specializes in real estate.

MEM Consulting

1083 N Collier Blvd #137, Marco Island, FL 34145
Phone: 239-394-2893 - **Fax:** 239-394-1893 mmosser1@earthlink.net

Types of Records Retrieved: Criminal, Civil and Probate courts; Federal courts; Real Estate; Tax Liens/Judgments; UCC records; Vital records

Local Retrieval Area: FL-Collier. **Correspondent Relationships:** Lee, FL county.

Add'l Information: Established 1998. Normal turnaround time- 24-72 hours. Projects billed by number of names searched. First project may require prepayment. She is a private investigation company who performs civil and criminal record retrieval and all types at criminal investigations. A licensed PI in FL. Performs service of process.

Menard Title & Abstract Co Inc

121 Court St, Clarendon, AR 72029
Phone: 870-747-3712 - **Fax:** 870-747-5488

Types of Records Retrieved: Criminal, Civil and Probate courts; Real Estate; Tax Liens/Judgments; Vital records

Local Retrieval Area: AR-Monroe

Add'l info: Normal turnaround time- up to 2 weeks. Fee basis will vary by the type of project. They specialize in real estate and title insurance.

Mendenhall Information Services

4245 Kemp Blvd #304, Wichita Falls, TX 76308
Phone: 940-696-0758 - **Fax:** 940-689-8408 mendenhallsvcs@aol.com

Types of Records Retrieved: Criminal, Civil and Probate courts; Federal courts; Real Estate; Tax Liens/Judgments; UCC records; Vital records

Local Retrieval Area: TX-Archer, Baylor, Childress, Clay, Collin, Cooke, Dallas, Denton, Erath, Foard, Grayson, Hardeman, Haskell, Hood, Jack, Johnson, Knox, Montague, Palo Pinto, Parker, Somervell, Tarrant, Throckmorton, Wichita, Wilbarger, Wise, Young; OK-Comanche, Cotton, Jackson, Stephens, Tillman

Add'l Information: Established 1999. Normal turnaround time- 24-72 hours. Projects billed by number of names searched. First project may require prepayment. Will file/record documents for clients. A licensed PI in TX.

Mendo-Lake Paralegals

435 N Main St, Lakeport, CA 95453
Phone: 707-263-8755 - **Fax:** 707-263-0298 mlpara@sbcglobal.net

Types of Records Retrieved: Criminal, Civil and Probate courts; Real Estate; Tax Liens/Judgments; UCC records; Vital records

Local Retrieval Area: CA-Lake

Add'l Information: Established 1988. Normal turnaround time- 2-3 days. Projects billed by number of names searched. First project may require prepayment. Will file/record documents for clients. Will bill established clients. They specialize in real property research.

Mercer County Abstract Co Inc

PO Box 1003, Hazen, ND 58545
Phone: 701-748-2190 - **Fax:** 701-748-2191

Types of Records Retrieved: Civil courts; Real Estate; Tax Liens/Judgments

Local Retrieval Area: ND-Mercer. **Correspondent Relationships:** North Dakota.

Add'l Information: Established 1991. Normal turnaround time- 2 days. Projects billed by number of names searched. First project may require prepayment. Will file/record documents for clients. They specialize in title insurance, title searches, closing search title memos, abstracts, closings and oil & gas searches.

Mercury Service Inc

PO Box 46196, Station D, Vancouver, BC, Canada, CAN V6J 5G5
Phone: 604-228-9993 - **Fax:** 604-224-8682 ahmsi@telus.net

Types of Records Retrieved: Criminal, Civil and Probate courts; Federal courts; Real Estate; UCC records; Corporate records

Local Retrieval Area: CANADA-British Columbia, Canada. **Correspondent Relationships:** Alberta, Ontario, Quebec provinces.

Add'l Information: Established 1972. Normal turnaround time- 4 hours on database searches; 24 hours for "hand" searches. Projects billed by number of names searched. Projects billed by the hour. First project may require prepayment. They specialize in business backgrounds (individuals and companies), accident investigation (legal), forensic photography and tracing people. A licensed PI in British Columbia.

Merkel Abstract & Title

216 N Broadway, PO Box 767, Hartington, NE 68739-0767
Phone: 402-254-3547 - **Fax:** 402-254-3547

Types of Records Retrieved: Real Estate, Probate courts; Federal courts

Local Retrieval Area: NE-Cedar

Add'l Information: Established 1991. Normal turnaround time- 2-4 days. Projects billed by number of names searched. Projects billed by number of records located. First project may require prepayment.

Merola Services

PO Box 54, Michigan City, IN 46361-0054
Phone: 219-878-9699 - **Fax:** 800-272-7717; 219-878-9698
www.merolaservices.com **email:** info@merolaservices.com

Types of Records Retrieved: Criminal and Civil courts; Federal courts; Real Estate; Tax Liens/Judgments; UCC records; Vital records

Local Retrieval Area: NY-Albany, Onondaga. **Correspondent Relationships:** FL, OH, CT. Access entire eastern seaboard for DMV records.

Add'l Information: Established 1988. Normal turnaround time- same day to 2 days. Projects billed by number of names searched. First project may require prepayment. Credit cards accepted. Payment due upon receipt. They specialize in retrieval of certified documents at NYS DMV (and elsewhere EC), insurance (auto-nationwide) and police reports, asset searches, background & pre-employment searches as well as civil and criminal searches at the state and federal level.

Merola Services (Indiana)

PO Box 54, Michigan City, IN 46361
Phone: 219-878-9699 - **Fax:** 219-878-9698
www.merolaservices.com **email:** info@merolaservices.com

Types of Records Retrieved: Criminal and Civil courts; Federal courts; Real Estate; Tax Liens/Judgments; UCC records; Vital records

Local Retrieval Area: IN-La Porte. **Correspondent Relationships:** FL, OH, CT. They access the entire eastern seaboard for DMV records.

Add'l Information: Established 1988. Normal turnaround time- same day to 2 days. Projects billed by number of names searched. First project may require prepayment. Credit cards accepted. Payment due upon receipt. They specialize in retrieval of certified documents at NYS DMV (and elsewhere EC), insurance (auto-nationwide) and police reports, asset searches, background & pre-employment searches as well as civil and criminal searches at the state and federal level.

Merritt & Henry LLC

155 S Main St, Madison, GA 30650

Phone: 706-342-9668 - **Fax:** 706-342-9843

Types of Records Retrieved: Criminal, Civil and Probate courts; Real Estate; Tax Liens/Judgments; UCC records

Local Retrieval Area: GA-Greene, Morgan, Putnam

Add'l Information: Established 1987. Normal turnaround time- 48 hours. Projects billed by number of names searched. Projects billed by the hour. All projects require prepayment. Credit cards accepted. Will file/record documents for clients. Personal checks accepted. He specializes in real estate searches. He also does file/record UCC and real estate documents of behalf of clients on same or next day basis in Morgan.

Metro Clerking Inc

134 N La Salle #1320, Chicago, IL 60602

Phone: 312-263-2977 - **Fax:** 312-263-2985 samantha@metroclerking.com

Types of Records Retrieved: Criminal, Civil and Probate courts; Federal courts; Real Estate; Tax Liens/Judgments; UCC records; Vital records; Workers Comp records

Local Retrieval Area: IL-Cook, Du Page, Kane, Lake, McHenry, Will

Add'l Information: Established 1985. Normal turnaround time- 24 hours. Expedited service available. Projects billed by number of names searched. First project may require prepayment. Will file/record documents for clients. They have an attorney on staff to cover court matters in State & Federal Courts. They also do searches in the Federal Records Center, in Chicago, which houses archived District Court files from MI, WI, OH, IN, IA and IL. Will do IL workers' comp searches.

Metro Legal Services

330 S 2nd Ave #150, Minneapolis, MN 55401

Phone: 800-488-8994; 612-332-0202 - **Fax:** 612-332-5215

www.metrolegal.com **email:** service@metrolegal.com

Types of Records Retrieved: Criminal, Civil and Probate courts; Federal courts; Real Estate; Tax Liens/Judgments; UCC records; Vital records

Local Retrieval Area: MN-Anoka, Carver, Dakota, Hennepin, Ramsey, Scott, Sherburne, Washington, Wright. **Correspondent Relationships:** nationwide.

Add'l Information: Established 1969. Normal turnaround time- 24 hours. Expedited service available. Projects billed by number of names searched. First project may require prepayment. Will file/record documents for clients. They have a trained staff of over 100, they are uniquely capable of providing document retrievals, public record searches and filings in the State of Minnesota. A licensed PI in MN. Performs service of process.

Metro Research & Inv

219 Sunset Blvd, Conroe, TX 77303

Phone: 936-441-2294 - **Fax:** 936-539-1236 metro@wt.net

Types of Records Retrieved: Criminal, Civil and Probate courts; Real Estate; Tax Liens/Judgments; UCC records; Vital records

Local Retrieval Area: TX-Harris, Montgomery, Walker

Add'l info: Established 1990. Turnaround time- 24 hours. Projects billed by number of names searched. Projects billed by number of records located. Projects billed by the hour. First project may require prepayment. They a full service investigative firm specializing in civil rights investigations and pre-employment backgrounds. Also conduct all aspects of civil and criminal investigations including title and tax research, specialist in asset investigations. A licensed PI in TX. Performs service of process.

Metropolis Group

10061 Riverside Dr #230, Toluca Lake, CA 91602

Phone: 818-861-7099 - **Fax:** 818-861-7088 liesel36@pacbell.net

Types of Records Retrieved: Criminal and Civil courts; Federal courts

Local Retrieval Area: CA-Los Angeles, San Diego, Ventura. **Correspondent Relationships:** nationwide.

Add'l Information: Established 1994. Normal turnaround time- 48 hours. Projects billed by number of names searched. Projects billed by the hour. Charge by number in criminal searches; hourly for document retrieval. Credit cards accepted. Will bill once account is established and agreement signed. Normal turnaround is 1-2 days. Volume discounts. Searches can be returned via web or fax. Quality research in a timely efficient manner since 1995. A licensed PI in CA.

Metropolitan Title Co (Hastings)

202 S Broadway St #1, Hastings, MI 49058-1886

Phone: 269-945-9447 - **Fax:** 269-945-5350

www.metropolitantitle.com/branches/branch.asp?BranchID=9 **Types of Records Retrieved:** Criminal, Civil and Probate courts; Real Estate; Tax Liens/Judgments; UCC records; Vital records

Local Retrieval Area: MI-Barry

Add'l Information: Established 1989. Normal turnaround time- 3 days. Fee basis will vary by the type of project. They specialize in real estate title work.

Michael Anderson Company

325 N Center St #200, Northville, MI 48167-2768

Phone: 800-992-9936; 248-596-9711 - **Fax:** 800-992-9937; 248-596-9719 MichaelAnderson@ameritech.net

Types of Records Retrieved: Criminal, Civil and Probate courts; Federal courts; Real Estate; Tax Liens/Judgments; UCC records; Vital records

Local Retrieval Area: MI-Livingston, Macomb, Oakland, Washtenaw, Wayne. **Correspondent Relationships:** statewide.

Add'l Information: Established 1997. Normal turnaround time- 24-48 hours. Projects billed by number of names searched. Will invoice upon completion of order. They are professional, dependable and confidential. Also offer pre-employment screening and statewide searching for corporate information, UCCs, MVRs and real estate.

Michael B Fixman & Associates

PO Box 490036, 72 Hancock St, Everett, MA 02149

Phone: 800-434-9626; 617-387-1100

www.constableservices.com **email:** fixman@constableservices.com

Types of Records Retrieved: Criminal, Civil and Probate courts; Federal courts; Real Estate; Tax Liens/Judgments; UCC records; Vital records

Local Retrieval Area: MA-Essex, Middlesex, Suffolk. **Correspondent Relationships:** Massachusetts and other New England states upon request.

Add'l info: Established 1957. Normal turnaround time- 1 day. Projects billed by the hour. All projects require prepayment. Will file/record documents for clients. Personal checks are accepted. He is a private detective licensed in MA and NH, a process server and a licensed/bonded constable. A licensed PI in MA, NH. Performs service of process.

Michael's Legal Research

PO Box 2558, Darien, GA 31305

Phone: 912-269-5532 - **Fax:** 912-437-3510 mcgrathbus@earthlink.net

Types of Records Retrieved: Real Estate; UCC records

Local Retrieval Area: GA-Brantley, Camden, Glynn, Long, McIntosh

Add'l Information: Established 1998. Normal turnaround time- 24-48 hours (primary); 48-72 hours (secondary). Billed by the type of real estate abstract, i.e. full, limited or update. Will file/record documents for clients. Residential and commercial real estate title abstracting, full searches. Developer & limited recordation of documents, document retrieval, liens and judgment searches in McIntosh & Glenn counties only. They are a member of NALA.

Michiana Info LLC

PO Box 4021, South Bend, IN 46634

Phone: 574-277-8909 - **Fax:** 574-277-6489

Types of Records Retrieved: Criminal, Civil and Probate courts; Bankruptcy; Tax Liens/Judgments

Local Retrieval Area: IN-Elkhart, La Porte, St. Joseph

Add'l Information: Established 1991. Normal turnaround time- 24 hours or less. Projects billed by number of names searched. First project may require prepayment. In addition to document retrieval, they can act as agents at sheriff sales throughout northern-most Indiana.

Michiana Searches Inc
28916 Kehres St, Elkhart, IN 46514-9563
Phone: 574-266-4652, 574-536-7135 - **Fax:** 574-266-8399
conduit2me@comcast.net

Types of Records Retrieved: Civil courts; Real Estate; Tax Liens/Judgments; UCC records

Local Retrieval Area: IN-Elkhart, St. Joseph

Add'l Information: Established 1993. Normal turnaround time- no more than 48 hours unless notified. Projects billed by number of names searched. Will file/record documents for clients. Terms: net 10 days. She specializes in foreclosures, UCC, court record searching, real estate/ title searches and genealogy.

Michigan Court Reports
2813 Brandon St, Flint, MI 48503 **phone:** 810-210-4741 **fax:** 810-233-9363
mhansard@michigancourtreports.com

Types of Records Retrieved: Criminal and Civil courts

Local Retrieval Area: MI-Genesee, Lapeer, St. Clair.

Correspondent Relationships: Monroe, Lenawee, Wayne, Oakland, Macomb, Washtenaw and Livingston counties, MI.

Add'l Information: Established 1999. Normal turnaround time- 24-48 hours. Expedited service available. Projects billed by number of names searched. Volume discounts available. They provide consistent accurate and timely results. Excellent communication and thorough reports. Will accept and return results via web/email.

Michigan Search Company
181 Helen St, Garden City, MI 48135-2787
Phone: 734-427-7224 - **Fax:** 734-427-1218 Michigansearchco@aol.com

Types of Records Retrieved: Civil courts; Federal courts; Real Estate; Tax Liens/Judgments; UCC records

Local Retrieval Area: MI-Allegan, Barry, Berrien, Branch, Calhoun, Cass, Dickinson, Eaton, Genesee, Grand Traverse, Hillsdale, Ingham, Isabella, Jackson, Kalamazoo, Kent, Livingston, Macomb, Midland, Oakland, Ottawa, Saginaw, St Joseph, Van Buren, Wayne, Washtenaw, Wexford. **Correspondent Relationships:** Allegan, Barry, Berrien, Branch, Calhoun, Cass, Dickinson, Eaton, Genesee, Grand Traverse, Hillsdale, Ingham, Isabella, Jackson, Kalamazoo, Kent, Livingston, Macomb, Midland, Oakland, Ottawa, Saginaw, St Joseph, Van Buren, Wayne, Washtenaw, Wexford.

Add'l Information: Established 1992. Normal turnaround time- 48 hours. Expedited service available. Projects billed by number of names searched. Will file/record documents for clients. They specialize in UCC & lien searches, civil record checks, good standings, name reservations and corporate documents.

Mid-America Reporting Co LLC
PO Box 145, Nesbit, MS 38651-0145
Phone: 662-487-0932 - **Fax:** 662-487-0934
www.marcinfo.com **email:** customerservice@marcinfo.com

Types of Records Retrieved: Criminal, Civil and Probate courts; Real Estate; Tax Liens/Judgments; UCC records; Vital records

Local Retrieval Area: MS-De Soto, Lafayette, Panola, Tunica. **Correspondent Relationships:** statewide.

Add'l Information: Normal turnaround time- typically 24-48 hours. Fees vary depending upon request. Will file/record documents for clients. Mid-America Reporting Company, LLC., specializes in on-site court searches, document retrieval and filings.

Midland Title and Abstract Co
612 Adams St, Bay City, MI 48708
Phone: 989-839-1003 - **Fax:** 989-895-0580

Types of Records Retrieved: Civil and Probate courts; Federal courts; Real Estate; Tax Liens/Judgments; UCC records; Vital records

Local Retrieval Area: MI-Isabella, Midland

Add'l Information: Established 1987. Normal turnaround time- 2-3 days. Fee basis will vary by the type of project. They require out of town clients to prepay. They specialize in title insurance.

Mid-South Legal Services
PO Box 610008, 215 Richard Arrington Jr. Blvd. North #505, Birmingham, AL 35261 **Phone:** 800-340-9855; 205-326-0900 - **Fax:** 205-326-0600
www.midsouthlegal.com **Types of Records Retrieved:** Criminal, Civil and Probate courts; Federal courts; Tax Liens/Judgments; UCC records; Vital records

Local Retrieval Area: AL-Jefferson, Shelby, St Clair, Talladega, Tuscaloosa, Walker

Add'l Info: Established 1983. Turnaround time- 24-48 hours. Fees vary depending upon request. Credit cards accepted. They specialize in process service, document retrieval, and skiptracing. Performs service of process.

Mid-South Subpoena Service
100 N Main #3033, Memphis, TN 38103
Phone: 800-737-8542; 901-528-9116 - **Fax:** 901-528-9118
www.privateinvestigatortn.com/ **email:** charles@midsouthsubpoena.com

Types of Records Retrieved: Criminal, Civil and Probate courts; Federal courts; Real Estate; Tax Liens/Judgments; UCC records; Vital records

Local Retrieval Area: TN-Fayette, Hardeman, Lauderdale, Madison, Meigs, Shelby, Tipton. **Correspondent Relationships:** West Tennessee.

Add'l info: Established 1982. Normal turnaround time- 2-3 days. Expedited service available. Projects billed by the hour. First project may require prepayment. They are a notary service. They also do document retrieval and asset searches. A licensed PI in TN, NC. Performs service of process.

Midstate Legal Support Services
PO Box 7, Utica, NY 13503
Phone: 315-797-8609 - **Fax:** 315-797-0270

Types of Records Retrieved: Criminal, Civil and Probate courts; Federal courts; Real Estate; Tax Liens/Judgments; UCC records; Vital records

Local Retrieval Area: NY-Oneida

Add'l Information: Established 1984. Normal turnaround time- 72 hours. Projects billed by number of names searched. Projects billed by number of records located. First project may require prepayment. Invoicing is available. They specialize in judgment enforcement, process service, auto repossessions, foreclosure bidding and bank repossessions (homes secured, etc). Performs service of process.

Mid-State Records
134 Ewingville Dr, Franklin, TN 37064
Phone: 615-791-1123 - **Fax:** 615-591-7733 mem-o-ries@home.com

Types of Records Retrieved: Criminal and Civil courts; Tax Liens/Judgments

Local Retrieval Area: TN-Rutherford, Williamson. **Correspondent Relationships:** Maury, Sumner, and Wilson Counties, TN.

Add'l Information: Established 2000?. Normal turnaround time- 24-48 hours. Projects billed by number of names searched. First project may require prepayment. Mid-States may be better known by the owner's name, Carolyn Blankenship.

Midwest Abstract Co
8070 Washington Village Dr, Centerville, OH 45458
Phone: 800-606-9488; 937-228-2292 - **Fax:** 937-228-0640
midwestabstract2@netzero.net

Records Retrieved: Real Estate; Tax Liens/Judgments; UCC records

Local Retrieval Area: OH-Montgomery. **Correspondent Relationships:** Miami, Darke, Clark, Preble, Warren, Butler, Clermont, Green counties.

Add'l Information: Established 1984. Normal turnaround time- 5-7 days. Projects billed by number of names searched. The fee basis is per examination. They specialize in "ALL" real estate title examinations.

Midwest Backgrounds Inc
101 N Park Ave #200, Herrin, IL 62948
Phone: 618-942-8808 - **Fax:** 618-942-8810
www.mbiworldwide.com **email:** info@mbiworldwide.com

Types of Records Retrieved: Criminal courts; Federal courts

Local Retrieval Area: IL-Franklin, Williamson. **Correspondent Relationships:** nationwide.

Add'l Information: Established 1998. Normal turnaround time- 24-72 hours. Projects billed by number of names searched. All projects require prepayment. Credit cards accepted. They specialize in employee screening. Orders may be placed via fax, secure website, mail, phone or email.

Midwest Investigative Services Inc

6077 Far Hills Ave #215, Dayton, OH 45459-1923
Phone: 800-227-9740; 937-433-9903 - **Fax:** 937-433-9918
misi@earthlink.net
Records Retrieved: Criminal and Civil courts; Federal courts; Vital records
Local Retrieval Area: OH-Greene, Miami, Montgomery, Warren
Add'l Information: Established 1989. Normal turnaround time- 1-3 days. Expedited service available. Projects are billed by court search. They will invoice. They specialize in pre-employment screening, civil and criminal investigations, process service, corporate investigations, locator service and witness interviews. A licensed PI in OH. Performs service of process.

Midwest Security Group LLC

1803 Lincolnway West, Mishawaka, IN 46544
Phone: 800-311-5498; 574-256-7140 - **Fax:** 574-256-7160
Types of Records Retrieved: Criminal and Civil courts; Tax Liens/Judgments
Local Retrieval Area: IN-Elkhart, La Porte, Lake, St. Joseph. **Correspondent Relationships:** statewide.
Add'l Information: Established 1996. Normal turnaround time- 24-48 hours. Projects billed by number of names searched. In addition to record retrieval in NW Indiana, they are a full-service background screening firm, statewide and national.

Steven P Mielke

116 E Market St, Celina, OH 45822
Phone: 419-586-2323 - **Fax:** 419-586-2154 mielkelaw@yahoo.com
Types of Records Retrieved: Criminal, Civil and Probate courts; Real Estate; Tax Liens/Judgments; UCC records
Local Retrieval Area: OH-Auglaize, Mercer, Van Wert
Add'l Information: Normal turnaround time- 3 days. Fee basis will vary by type of project. First project may require prepayment. Will file/record documents for clients. They specialize in real estate record searches.

Sarah B Migues

5503 Old LA 25, New Iberia, LA 70560
Phone: 337-364-8509 - **Fax:** 337-364-8509 tmigues@bellsouth.net
Types of Records Retrieved: Criminal and Civil courts
Local Retrieval Area: LA-Iberia, St. Martin, St. Mary, Vermilion Parishes
Add'l Information: Normal turnaround time- 2-12 hours depending on the parish. First project may require prepayment. Will file/record documents for clients. Sarah Migues cell phone number is 337-519-9851. She is recommended for index searches by the Iberia Clerk of Court.

Milestone Legal Support

1550 Larimer St #504, Denver, CO 80202
Phone: 800-317-9221; 303-794-6364 f2flp@cox.net
Types of Records Retrieved: Criminal, Civil and Probate courts; Federal courts; Real Estate; Tax Liens/Judgments; UCC records; Vital records
Local Retrieval Area: CO-Boulder, Denver. **Correspondent Relationships:** NAPPS members in all states.
Add'l Information: Established 1987. Normal turnaround time- 24 hours. Projects billed by number of names searched. Projects billed by the hour. All projects require prepayment. Will file/record documents for clients. They specialize in process service and court record retrieval. A licensed PI in CO. Performs service of process.

Mill Creek Investigation Agency PC

992 Cottage St NE, Salem, OR 97301
Phone: 877-378-1581; 503-378-1581 - **Fax:** 503-585-4384
tnlinv@comcast.net
Types of Records Retrieved: Criminal, Civil and Probate courts; Real Estate
Local Retrieval Area: OR-Marion, Polk
Add'l Information: Established 1990. Normal turnaround time- 2 days if information is furnished by 3:00 pm. Projects billed by number of names searched. First project may require prepayment. The Mill Creek Investigation Agency engages in public record research and litigation support in civil and criminal cases in Oregon courts. A licensed PI in OR.

Mill Creek Title Service

PO Box 911, Plainfield, IN 46168
Phone: 317-714-7190 - **Fax:** 317-539-6804
www.millcreektitle.com **email:** dave@millcreektitle.com
Types of Records Retrieved: Real Estate; Tax Liens/Judgments; UCC records; Vital records
Local Retrieval Area: IN-Boone, Carroll, Clinton, Fountain, Hendricks, Johnson, Monroe, Montgomery, Morgan, Owen, Parke, Putnam, Tippecanoe, Vermillion, Warren
Add'l Information: Established 2002. Normal turnaround time- 1-2 days. Rush "immediate service" available. First project may require prepayment. Will file/record documents for clients. Mill Creek is a local title company servicing central and western counties in Indiana. 24-48 hr turnaround times, E&O insurance, and competitive prices.

Millennial Investigative Agency

10604 Quail Ridge Dr, St Augustine, FL 32095
Phone: 888-299-7574; 904-819-9700 - **Fax:** 904-826-1071
www.stevenkbrown.com **Types of Records Retrieved:** Criminal, Civil and Probate courts; Federal courts; Real Estate; Tax Liens/Judgments; UCC records; Vital records
Local Retrieval Area: FL-Clay, Duval, St. Johns
Add'l Information: Established 1984. Normal turnaround time- 48 hours. Expedited service available. Projects billed by number of names searched. All projects require prepayment. Credit cards accepted. They specialize in retrieval of all public records available, criminal, civil, filings, recordings, bankruptcy and federal. They have been in business for 20 years. A licensed PI in FL.

Miller & Assoc Information Services Inc

6001 N Westgate Blvd, Tacoma, WA 98406-2526
Phone: 253-752-5500 - **Fax:** 253-752-5538 orderdesk@millerinfo.com
Records Retrieved: Real Estate; Tax Liens/Judgments; UCC records
Local Retrieval Area: WA-Chelan, King, Kitsap, Mason, Pierce, Skagit, Snohomish, Thurston
Add'l Information: Established 1996. Normal turnaround time- 6-12 business hours. Charges are per address/name. Will file/record documents for clients. Terms: net 30 days. They specialize in current owner searches. All research is supervised by a senior title researcher with 25 years experience. Carries E & O insurance.

Miller & Johnson PLLC

PO Box 49, 766 W King St, Boone, NC 28607
Phone: 828-264-1125 - **Fax:** 828-262-3544
Types of Records Retrieved: Civil and Probate courts; Real Estate; Tax Liens/Judgments; UCC records
Local Retrieval Area: NC-Ashe, Avery, Watauga
Add'l Information: Established 1988. Normal turnaround time- 2 days. Projects billed by the hour. First project may require prepayment. Will file/record documents for clients. They specialize in real estate, foreclosures, corporations and estate planning.

Miller Abstract & Title Co

401 E 4th St #101, PO Box 107, Minden, NE 68959
Phone: 308-832-0969 - **Fax:** 308-832-0969 millerabstract@yahoo.com
Types of Records Retrieved: Real Estate; Tax Liens/Judgments; Probate courts; UCC records
Local Retrieval Area: NE-Kearney. **Correspondent Relationships:** Phelps, Franklin, Buffalo counties.
Add'l Information: Established 1991. Normal turnaround time- 1-4 days. Fee basis is per search. Will file/record documents for clients. Personal checks are accepted. They specialize in title insurance, abstracting and limited title reports.

Miller Abstracts

2555 Monroeville Blvd, Monroeville, PA 15146
Phone: 412-607-4952 - **Fax:** 412-824-7141 millerabstracts@msn.com
Types of Records Retrieved: Criminal, Civil and Probate courts; Real Estate; Tax Liens/Judgments; UCC records
Local Retrieval Area: PA-Allegheny, Westmoreland
Add'l Information: Established 2003. Normal turnaround time- 1-3 days for title searches, document retrieval 1 day. Expedited service available for $50.00 surcharge. Projects billed by number of names searched. First project may require prepayment. She is an independent abstractor with 7 years experience. Accurate title search reports that are easy to understand. Documents in PDF. format. Immediate cell phone access during business hours. Professional liability insurance.

Connie Miller

77 Fairfax St, Berkeley Springs, WV 25411
Phone: 304-258-8554 - **Fax:** 304-258-7319
Types of Records Retrieved: Criminal and Civil courts; Tax Liens/Judgments
Local Retrieval Area: WV-Morgan
Add'l Information: Established 1999. Normal turnaround time- 24-48 hours. Projects billed by number of names searched. First project may require prepayment. She is an expert in Morgan county court records.

G Scott Miller

103 N Union St #A, Delaware, OH 43015-1709
Phone: 740-363-1324 - **Fax:** 740-548-5443 gsm@rrohio.com
Types of Records Retrieved: Civil and Probate courts; Real Estate; Tax Liens/Judgments; UCC records
Local Retrieval Area: OH-Delaware
Add'l Information: Established 1985. Normal turnaround time- 24 hours. Fee basis will vary by the type of project. Will file/record documents for clients. He is an attorney.

Gail L Miller

208 N Commercial, Mankato, KS 66956
Phone: 785-378-3128 - **Fax:** 785-378-3543
Types of Records Retrieved: Criminal, Civil and Probate courts; Tax Liens/Judgments
Local Retrieval Area: KS-Jewell, Republic
Add'l Information: Established 1987. Normal turnaround time- 1-7 days. Projects billed by the hour. Personal checks are accepted. Credit accounts are not accepted.

Mimbres Valley Abstract & Title Co

PO Drawer 2849, 920 S Diamond Ave (88030), Deming, NM 88031
Phone: 505-546-8896 - **Fax:** 505-546-9697 mvat@zianet.com
Types of Records Retrieved: Criminal, Civil and Probate courts; Real Estate; Tax Liens/Judgments; UCC records; Vital records
Local Retrieval Area: NM-Luna
Add'l info: Normal turnaround time- 2-5 days. Fee basis is determined per name or per legal description. They specialize in title searches.

Minor Services Inc - Excel Legal Search

4886 Woodhurst Way, Stone Mountain, GA 30088
Phone: 770-987-0942, 770-789-8543 - **Fax:** 770-987-8884
pat4142@bellsouth.net
Types of Records Retrieved: Criminal and Civil courts; Tax Liens/Judgments; UCC records
Local Retrieval Area: GA-Clayton, De Kalb, Fulton, Henry, Rockdale. **Correspondent Relationships:** Forsyth, Hall, Cobb, Barrow.
Add'l Information: Established 1992. Normal turnaround time- 24-48 hours. Projects billed by number of names searched. Often known as simply Excel Legal Search, they specialize in efficient affordable service and quick turnaround. Voice mail phone number is 770-987-0942 or 770-789-8543.

Missaukee Title Co

PO Box 480, Lake City, MI 49651
Phone: 231-839-4563 - **Fax:** 231-839-5642
missaukee_title@chartermi.net
Types of Records Retrieved: Real Estate
Local Retrieval Area: MI-Missaukee
Add'l Information: Established 1980. Normal turnaround time- 2 day Expedited service available. Projects billed by number of records located. First project may require prepayment.

Mississippi County Abstract & Loan Co

105 E Court St, Charleston, MO 63834
Phone: 573-683-4671 - **Fax:** 573-683-6898 misscoabst@sbcglobal.net
Types of Records Retrieved: Civil and Probate courts; Real Estate; Tax Liens/Judgments
Local Retrieval Area: MO-Mississippi
Add'l Information: Established 1974. Normal turnaround time- 3-5 days. Fee basis will vary by type of project. First project may require prepayment. Will file/record documents for clients. They specialize in title insurance.

Mitchell County Abstract Co

519 Main St, Osage, IA 50461
Phone: 641-732-4571 - **Fax:** 641-732-5550 abstract@osage.net
Types of Records Retrieved: Criminal, Civil and Probate courts; Real Estate; Tax Liens/Judgments; UCC records
Local Retrieval Area: IA-Mitchell
Add'l Information: Established 1945. Normal turnaround time- 3-5 days. They charge a flat rate per project. All projects require prepayment.

Mitchell McNutt & Sams PA

PO Box 7120, Tupelo, MS 38802
Phone: 662-842-3871 - **Fax:** 662-842-8450
www.mitchellmcnutt.com **Types of Records Retrieved:** Civil and Probate courts; Federal courts; Real Estate; Tax Liens/Judgments; UCC records; Vital records
Retrieval Area: MS-Alcorn, Lafayette, Lee, Lowndes, Pontotoc, Union
Add'l Information: Established 1902. Normal turnaround time- 1-2 days. Projects billed by the hour. They specialize in insurance investigations.

MJS Inv.

51 Cherokee Circle, Thomasville, GA 31757
Phone: 229-226-1292 - **Fax:** 229-226-8724
Types of Records Retrieved: Criminal and Civil courts
Local Retrieval Area: GA-Thomas
Add'l Information: Established 1991. Normal turnaround time- 24 hours. Projects billed by number of names searched. First project may require prepayment. See specializes in Thomas county court records.

MJT Research

3902 N US 35, LaPorte, IN 46350
Phone: 219-326-7637 or 219-363-2070 - **Fax:** 219-325-9083
mjtslater@comcast.net
Types of Records Retrieved: Criminal and Civil courts; Federal courts; Real Estate; Tax Liens/Judgments; UCC records; Vital records
Local Retrieval Area: IN-Elkhart, Lake, La Porte, Marshall, Porter, St. Joseph. **Correspondent Relationships:** Knox, Allen, Vigo, Putnam, Monroe counties IN. Retrieves criminal records from nearly all IN counties.
Add'l Information: Established 1994. Normal turnaround time- 48 hours or less. Projects billed by number of names searched. Bill at end of month. They specialize in criminal background screening but can do any public record searches.

MLQ Attorney Services

2000 Riveredge Pky NW #885, Atlanta, GA 30326-4694
Phone: 800-446-8794; 770-984-7007 - **Fax:** 800-984-7049; 770-984-7049
www.mlqattorneyservices.com **email:** mmarks@mlqattorneyservices.com
Types of Records Retrieved: Criminal, Civil and Probate courts; Federal courts; Real Estate; Tax Liens/Judgments; UCC records; Vital records

Local Retrieval Area: GA-Cobb, De Kalb, Fulton, Gwinnett; MD-Anne Arundel, Frederick, Montgomery, Prince George's. **Correspondent Relationships:** nationwide.

Add'l Information: Established 1982. Normal turnaround time- 24-48 hours. Expedited service available. Projects billed by the hour. First project may require prepayment. Credit cards accepted. MLQ Attorney Services is a one stop legal support service. UCC, title document retriever and service of process. Performs service of process.

MO Data Inc

1152 S 20th St, Ozark, MO 65721
Phone: 417-299-2469 - **Fax:** 417-581-1492
modatainc@yahoo.com

Types of Records Retrieved: Civil courts; Real Estate; Tax Liens/Judgments; UCC records

Local Retrieval Area: MO-Christian, Greene, Stone, Taney, Webster

Add'l Information: Established 1996. Normal turnaround time- 24-48 hours. Projects billed by number of names searched. First project may require prepayment. Will file/record documents for clients. They specialize in current owner and refinance searches. Would prefer customers to use email as primary contact, but fax can also be used as secondary contact number.

Mobile Abstracting Services

8174 Sunbonnet Dr, Fair Oaks, CA 95628
Phone: 916-965-6544 - **Fax:** 916-459-4913
www.faqsforyou.com **email:** info@faqsforyou.com

Records Retrieved: Real Estate; Tax Liens/Judgments; UCC records

Retrieval Area: CA-El Dorado, Placer, Sacramento, Sutter, Yolo, Yuba

Add'l Information: Established 2004. Normal turnaround time- 24-48 hours. Expedited service available for extra charge. Projects billed by number of names searched. Projects billed by number of records located. First project may require prepayment. Will file/record documents for clients. Payment due net 30 days. Formerly known as Nisonger Abstracting Services, with their mobile abstracting service they can save you hours of waiting. Is fully insured; references available on request.

Models with Brains

3000 F Danville Blvd #408, Alamo, CA 94507
Phone: 925-838-3899 - **Fax:** 925-215-8402 Cherie@modelswithbrains.com

Records Retrieved: Real Estate; Tax Liens/Judgments; UCC records

Local Retrieval Area: CA-Alameda, Contra Costa, Placer, Sacramento, San Francisco, San Mateo, Santa Clara, Solano. **Correspondent Relationships:** Pima county, AZ; counties of CA.

Add'l Information: Established 1998. Normal turnaround time- 48 hours. Projects billed by number of names searched. First project may require prepayment. Credit cards accepted. Will file/record documents for clients. With over 7 years experience, they provide fast, accurate, reliable service as well as affordable pricing.

Jodi Moellering

427 Converse, Oakley, KS 67748
Phone: 785-672-3979 - **Fax:** 785-672-2697 jodimm@sbcglobal.net

Types of Records Retrieved: Criminal and Civil courts

Local Retrieval Area: KS-Logan. **Correspondent Relationships:** McPherson, Saline, Thomas, KS.

Add'l Information: Established 2000?. Normal turnaround time- 24 hours. Projects billed by number of names searched. First project may require prepayment. She can also cover Thomas County courts.

Mohave County Process Service

PO Box 4357, Kingman, AZ 86402-4357
Phone: 800-692-5881; 928-692-9088 - **Fax:** 928-757-9088
process@citlink.net

Types of Records Retrieved: Criminal and Civil courts; Tax Liens/Judgments

Local Retrieval Area: AZ-Mohave

Add'l Information: Established 1993. Normal turnaround time- 24 hours. Projects billed by number of names searched. First project may require prepayment. They specialize in process service. Also do skip tracing nationwide electronically. Performs service of process.

Mohr Information Services LLC

47 S Cameron St #1, Winchester, VA 22601-4782
Phone: 540-678-8775 - **Fax:** 540-678-1696
www.mohrinformation.com **email:** orders@mohrinformation.com

Types of Records Retrieved: Criminal, Civil and Probate courts; Federal courts; Real Estate; Tax Liens/Judgments; UCC records

Local Retrieval Area: DC-District of Columbia; FL-Hernando, Hillsborough, Pasco, Pinellas, Polk; MD-Anne Arundel, Baltimore, Baltimore City, Frederick, Howard, Montgomery, Prince George's, Washington; VA-Alexandria City, Arlington, Fairfax, Fairfax City, Frederick, Loudoun, Prince William, Winchester City

Add'l Information: Established 1992. Normal turnaround time- 24-48 hours. Projects billed by number of names searched. Credit cards accepted. Will file/record documents for clients. Will submit an invoice upon completion of research requested and require prompt payment. They specialize in criminal, civil, UCC, judgments, and property searches. Most research completed within 24 hours. Quality research, very reasonable. A licensed PI in VA, FL.

Molloy & Company Inc dba Judicial Courier

422 N Church Ave, Tucson, AZ 85701
Phone: 520-792-0250 - **Fax:** 520-792-0278
www.judicialcourier.com **email:** craig@judicialcouries.com

Types of Records Retrieved: Criminal, Civil and Probate courts; Federal courts; Real Estate; Tax Liens/Judgments; UCC records; Vital records

Local Retrieval Area: AZ-Pima. **Correspondent Relationships:** statewide.

Add'l Information: Established 1987. Normal turnaround time- 48 hours. Expedited service available. Projects billed by the hour. First project may require prepayment. They specialize in process serving, court running and skip tracing. Performs service of process.

Molly Ply Investigations

PO Box 61, Redfield, AR 72132
Phone: 501-397-2620, Fax-same
www.mollyplyinvestigations.com **email:** mollyply@cei.net

Types of Records Retrieved: Criminal, Civil and Probate courts; Tax Liens/Judgments; UCC records

Local Retrieval Area: AR-Jefferson, Pulaski

Add'l Information: Established 1997. Normal turnaround time- 24-48 hours. Rush service available. Projects billed by number of names searched. First project may require prepayment. Credit cards accepted. She specializes in criminal record searches, also skiptraces, domestics, adoptions, locates, surveillance. Cell phone # 501-416-9385. A licensed PI in AR.

Monroe County Abstract & Title Co Inc

229 N Main St, Paris, MO 65275
Phone: 660-327-4109 - **Fax:** 660-327-4331 hendlaw@dstream.net

Types of Records Retrieved: Criminal, Civil and Probate courts; Real Estate; Tax Liens/Judgments; UCC records

Local Retrieval Area: MO-Monroe. **Correspondent Relationships:** Ralls, Marion, Shelby counties MO.

Add'l Information: Established 1900. Normal turnaround time- 3 days. Projects billed by number of names searched. A fee for the length of the search may also be added to the per name charge. Will file/record documents for clients. They provide complete title service, abstracting, title insurance, document preparation, escrow and closings.

Monroe County Title Co

PO Box 188, 231 S Main St, Waterloo, IL 62298
Phone: 618-939-8292 - **Fax:** 618-939-3931

Types of Records Retrieved: Real Estate

Local Retrieval Area: IL-Monroe

Add'l Information: Established 1930. Normal turnaround time- 5 days. Projects billed by number of names searched. Personal checks are accepted. They specialize in insured real estate title searches.

Monroe Title Insurance Corp (Albany)

, 32 N. Russell Rd., Albany, NY 12206
Phone: 800-966-6763; 518-462-6566 - **Fax:** 518-462-0625
www.monroetitle.com/offices.asp?office=albany
email: comments@monroetitle.com

Types of Records Retrieved: Federal courts; Real Estate; Tax Liens/Judgments; UCC records

Local Retrieval Area: NY-Albany, Rensselaer

Add'l Information: Established 1922. Normal turnaround time- 48 hours. Projects billed by number of names searched. Projects billed by number of records located. First project may require prepayment. Credit cards accepted. They have 20 offices statewide. The 800 number is direct to their state customer service administrator.

Monroe Title Insurance Corp (Rochester)

47 W Main St, Rochester, NY 14614
Phone: 800-966-6763; 585-232-2070 - **Fax:** 585-232-4988
www.monroetitle.com **Types of Records Retrieved:** Real Estate; Tax Liens/Judgments; Probate courts; Federal courts; UCC records

Local Retrieval Area: NY-Albany, Allegany, Broome, Cayuga, Chatauqua, Chemung, Erie, Fulton, Genesee, Livingston, Madison, Monroe, Montgomery, Niagara, Oneida, Onondaga, Ontario, Orleans, Oswego, Otsego, Rensselaer, Saratoga, Schenectady, Schuyler, Seneca, Steuben, Tioga, Tompkins, Warren, Washington, Wayne, Wyoming, Yates. **Correspondent Relationships:** NY-Cattaraugus, Chenango, Clinton, Columbia, Cortland, Delaware, Essex, Franklin, Greene, Hamilton, Herkimer, Jefferson, Lewis, Schoharie, St. Lawrence counties.

Add'l Information: Established 1922. Normal turnaround time- 48 hours. Projects billed by number of names searched. Projects billed by number of records located. All projects require prepayment. Credit cards accepted. Will file/record documents for clients. They will also invoice.

Montana Abstract & Title Co

2961 Nevada Ave, Butte, MT 59701-1116
Phone: 406-533-0433 - **Fax:** 406-533-0430 mtabstract@aol.com

Types of Records Retrieved: Criminal, Civil and Probate courts; Federal courts; Real Estate; Tax Liens/Judgments; UCC records; Vital records

Local Retrieval Area: MT-Deer Lodge, Granite, Silver Bow

Add'l Information: Established 1902. Normal turnaround time- variable with each project. Projects billed by the hour. They specialize in title insurance.

Montana Abstract Co Inc

PO Box 128, Scobey, MT 59263
Phone: 406-487-5961

Types of Records Retrieved: Civil and Probate courts; Federal courts; Real Estate; Tax Liens/Judgments; Vital records

Local Retrieval Area: MT-Daniels

Add'l Information: Established 1982. Normal turnaround time- 1 week. Projects billed by number of records located. Projects billed by the hour. First project may require prepayment. They specialize in title insurance and abstract updating.

Montezuma-Dolores Title Co

236 W North St, Cortez, CO 81321
Phone: 970-565-8491 - **Fax:** 970-565-7050 mdtitle@charter.net

Records Retrieved: Real Estate; Tax Liens/Judgments; UCC records

Local Retrieval Area: CO-Dolores, Montezuma

Add'l Information: Normal turnaround time- 5-7 days. Projects billed by the hour. Personal checks are accepted. Specialize in real estate title searches.

Montgomery County Abstract & Title Co

106 N Sturgeon St, Montgomery City, MO 63361
Phone: 573-564-2298 - **Fax:** 573-564-6158

Types of Records Retrieved: Criminal, Civil and Probate courts; Real Estate; Tax Liens/Judgments; UCC records

Local Retrieval Area: MO-Montgomery

Add'l Information: Established 1950. Normal turnaround time- 5-10 days. Fee basis will vary by the type of project. Will file/record documents for clients. They will invoice. They maintain a complete set of in-house record books for Montgomery County.

Montgomery County Abstract Co

PO Box 743, Independence, KS 67301-0743
Phone: 620-331-1440 - **Fax:** 620-331-4760

Types of Records Retrieved: Civil and Probate courts; Real Estate; Tax Liens/Judgments; UCC records

Local Retrieval Area: KS-Montgomery

Add'l Information: Established 1940. Normal turnaround time- 1-2 days. Fee basis varies by type of transaction. First project may require prepayment. Will file/record documents for clients.

Moody County Abstract Co

218 2nd Ave E, Flandreau, SD 57028
Phone: 605-997-3723 - **Fax:** 605-997-3872

Types of Records Retrieved: Civil and Probate courts; Real Estate; Tax Liens/Judgments; UCC records

Local Retrieval Area: SD-Moody

Add'l Information: Established 1900. Normal turnaround time- 1 week. Fee basis will vary by the type or project. First project may require prepayment. They specialize in title insurance and record searches.

Moon Abstract Co

421 Commercial St, Emporia, KS 66801
Phone: 620-342-1917 - **Fax:** 620-342-6888
www.moonabstract.com **email:** info@moonabstract.com

Types of Records Retrieved: Civil and Probate courts; Real Estate; Tax Liens/Judgments; UCC records

Local Retrieval Area: KS-Chase, Coffey, Greenwood, Lyon, Morris. **Correspondent Relationships:** Chase, Coffey, Greenwood, Morris, Osage.

Add'l Information: Established 1934. Normal turnaround time- "as soon as possible" for Lyon County and 1 week for other counties served. Projects billed by number of names searched. Projects billed by number of records located. Fee basis varies by type of transaction. Will file/record documents for clients. Statement sent when order completed. They specialize in long term escrow holdings, title insurance, closings and searches.

Attorney Reed Moore Jr

PO Box 235, 109 2nd St, Tompkinsville, KY 42167
Phone: 270-487-6262 - **Fax:** 270-487-8000 reedmoorejr@mcksi.com

Types of Records Retrieved: Civil and Probate courts; Real Estate; Tax Liens/Judgments; UCC records

Local Retrieval Area: KY-Barren, Monroe

Add'l Information: Established 1981. Normal turnaround time- 2-3 days. Fee basis varies by type of transaction. First project may require prepayment.

Moore Mowdy & Youngblood

PO Box 540, Atoka, OK 74525-0540
Phone: 580-889-5656 - **Fax:** 580-889-7149 mylf@mail.atoka.net

Types of Records Retrieved: Real Estate

Local Retrieval Area: OK-Atoka, Bryan, Coal, Johnston, Pushmataha

Add'l info: Established 1953. Turnaround time- 48 hours. Projects billed by the hour. They specialize in probate and real estate record searches.

Moore Title & Escrow Inc

1215 E Hoffer St, Kokomo, IN 46902-5728
Phone: 888-289-1301; 765-459-3183 - **Fax:** 765-459-3188
www.mooretitle.com **email:** mte@mooretitle.com

Types of Records Retrieved: Civil and Probate courts; Real Estate; Tax Liens/Judgments; UCC records; Vital records

Local Retrieval Area: IN-Howard, Tipton

Add'l Information: Established 1899. Normal turnaround time- 2-3 days. Fee basis varies by type of transaction. Will file/record documents for clients. They have a branch office in Tipton, 800-845-9644, 765-675-2704, 118 W Madison.

Heather Moore

3850 Spring Valley Rd, Cumberland, TN 37050
Phone: 931-413-5594; cell- 931-721-7284 - **Fax:** 931-413-5594

Types of Records Retrieved: Criminal and Civil courts; Tax Liens/Judgments; Real Estate

Local Retrieval Area: TN-Houston

Add'l Information: Established 2001. Normal turnaround time- 24-48 hours. Projects billed by number of names searched. First project may require prepayment. She provides expert court search services; her real estate service is limited to current owner searches only.

Conrad Mord

PO Drawer 311, Tylertown, MS 39667
Phone: 601-876-2611 - **Fax:** 601-876-4379

Types of Records Retrieved: Criminal, Civil and Probate courts; Real Estate; Tax Liens/Judgments; UCC records; Vital records

Local Retrieval Area: MS-Amite, Pike, Walthall

Add'l Information: Normal turnaround time- 1 day in Walthall; 2-3 days in other counties. Projects billed by the hour. First project may require prepayment. He is an attorney in general practice, including real estate and family law.

Morgan/Brooks Resources Inc

115 E Travis St #1140, San Antonio, TX 78205-1606
Phone: 210-476-0500 - **Fax:** 210-476-0503

Types of Records Retrieved: Real Estate; Tax Liens/Judgments; Probate courts; Federal courts; UCC records

Local Retrieval Area: TX-Bexar, Comal

Add'l Information: Established 1991. Normal turnaround time- 24-48 hours; 50-year and asset searches take 3-5 days. Projects billed by the hour. First project may require prepayment. Will file/record documents for clients. Morgan/Brooks has more than 40 years experience in title research, providing timely, accurate and detailed title information to a variety of businesses.

Morrilton Abstract Co

110 S Chestnut, Morrilton, AR 72110
Phone: 501-354-2611 - **Fax:** 501-354-4634

Types of Records Retrieved: Civil and Probate courts; Real Estate; Tax Liens/Judgments; UCC records

Local Retrieval Area: AR-Conway

Add'l Information: Normal turnaround time- 1 week. Fee basis will vary by the type of project. All projects require prepayment. They will also invoice. They specialize in title and real estate research.

Morris Abstracting

700 Ponderosa Way, Ocilla, GA 31774
Phone: 229-831-7535, cell-229-848-2709 - **Fax:** 229-831-2735

Types of Records Retrieved: Real Estate; Tax Liens/Judgments

Retrieval Area: GA-Benn Hill, Berrien, Colquitt, Cook, Tift, Turner, Worth

Add'l Information: Established 1982. Normal turnaround time- 24-48 hours. Fee depends on nature of job and county visited. First project may require prepayment. They specialize in real estate searches and are capable of visiting the courts in special circumstances.

Melissa F Morris

10854 US Highway 29, Andalusia, AL 36420
Phone: 334-222-1986 - **Fax:** 334-222-1986
cmmorris@alaweb.com

Types of Records Retrieved: Civil and Probate courts; Real Estate; Tax Liens/Judgments; UCC records

Local Retrieval Area: AL-Conecuh, Covington, Escambia

Add'l Information: Established 1996. Normal turnaround time- 24-48 hours. Projects billed by number of names searched. First project may require prepayment. Will file/record documents for clients. She specializes in real estate, UCC, lien and judgment searches. She has over 10 years experience as an assistant to a Real Estate Attorney.

Morrissey Morrissey & Dalluge

PO Box 597, Tecumseh, NE 68450
Phone: 402-335-3344 - **Fax:** 402-335-3345

Types of Records Retrieved: Real Estate

Local Retrieval Area: NE-Johnson

Add'l Information: Established 1960. Normal turnaround time- 1 week. Projects billed by the hour. First project may require prepayment. Credit cards accepted. They specialize in probate and real estate.

Mosley Abstract & Title Insurance Co

PO Box 2124, Fort Smith, AR 72902
Phone: 479-782-3054 - **Fax:** 479-782-5432 www.mosleyabst.com

Types of Records Retrieved: Real Estate; Tax Liens/Judgments

Local Retrieval Area: AR-Crawford, Franklin, Sebastian

Add'l Information: Established 1953. Normal turnaround time- 2 days. Projects billed by number of names searched. Fee basis varies by type of project. All projects require prepayment. Will file/record documents for clients. They specialize in real estate.

Alice S Mosley

PO Box 164, 35570 CR 39 N, Stapleton, AL 36578
Phone: 251-937-8468 - **Fax:** 251-580-0292 mosley0292@bellsouth.net

Types of Records Retrieved: Criminal, Civil and Probate courts; Real Estate; Tax Liens/Judgments; UCC records

Local Retrieval Area: AL-Baldwin. **Correspondent Relationships:** Mobile and Baldwin counties AL.

Add'l info: Established 1981. Normal turnaround time- 24-36 hours. Projects billed by number of names searched. First project may require prepayment. Will file/record documents for clients. They can search any Alabama county online for criminal and civil cases. Performs service of process.

Mountain States Title Services

1975 Oro Fino Gulch, Helena, MT 59624
Phone: 406-443-0521 - **Fax:** 406-443-7973 harwellco@aol.com

Types of Records Retrieved: Criminal and Civil courts; Real Estate; Tax Liens/Judgments; UCC records

Local Retrieval Area: MT-Broadwater, Jefferson, Lewis and Clark, Powell

Add'l Information: Established 1981. Normal turnaround time- 24-48 hours. Projects billed by number of names searched. Special billing for oil, gas and mineral reports. First project may require prepayment. They specialize is mineral reports, oil & gas reports, ownership & encumbrance reports, and right-of-way title reports.

Mountain View Abstract Co

PO Box 130, Mountain View, AR 72560
Phone: 870-269-8410 - **Fax:** 870-269-6901

Types of Records Retrieved: Civil and Probate courts; Real Estate; Tax Liens/Judgments; UCC records

Local Retrieval Area: AR-Stone

Add'l Information: Established 1947. Normal turnaround time- 1-2 weeks. Fee basis will vary by the type of project. All projects require prepayment. They will invoice. They specialize in real estate and title work.

Mountrail County Abstract & Title Co

PO Box 519, Stanley, ND 58784 **Phone:** 701-628-2886

Types of Records Retrieved: Civil and Probate courts; Federal courts; Real Estate; Tax Liens/Judgments; UCC records

Local Retrieval Area: ND-Burke, McKenzie, Mountrail, Ward, Williams

Add'l Information: Established 1972. Normal turnaround time- 1-5 days. Fee basis will vary by type of project.

Mower Services

PO Box 2041, Pocatello, ID 83206
Phone: 888-317-7458; 208-237-0116 - **Fax:** 208-775-3019

Types of Records Retrieved: Criminal, Civil and Probate courts; Real Estate; Tax Liens/Judgments; UCC records

Local Retrieval Area: ID-Blaine, Oneida; UT-Box Elder, Cache, Rich. **Correspondent Relationships:** statewide.

Add'l Information: Established 1994. Normal turnaround time- 1-5 days. Expedited service available. Projects billed by number of records located. First project may require prepayment. They specialize in foreclosure notices and process service. Performs service of process.

Mozark Investigations

PO Box 61, 10891 State Route BB, Rolla, MO 65402
Phone: 866-308-1411; 573-308-1411 - **Fax:** 573-368-4307
www.mozark.com **email:** bobjones@mozark.com

Types of Records Retrieved: Criminal, Civil and Probate courts; Real Estate; Tax Liens/Judgments; UCC records; Vital records

Local Retrieval Area: MO-Camden, Carter, Crawford, Dent, Franklin, Gasconade, Iron, Maries, Miller, Phelps, Pulaski, Reynolds, Shannon, St. Francois, Texas, Washington

Add'l Information: Established 1997. Normal turnaround time- 3-5 days. Expedited service available. Projects billed by number of names searched. Projects billed by number of records located. Projects billed by the hour. All projects require prepayment. Credit cards accepted. Also provides services related to investigations, bail bonds, collections, accredited/certified computer investigations, national and special criminal records. A licensed PI in MO. Performs service of process.

Mr Holmes Inv

PO Box 3176, Jackson, MS 39207-3176
Phone: 601-859-7955 - **Fax:** 601-859-0455 mrholmes@netdoor.com

Types of Records Retrieved: Criminal, Civil and Probate courts; Federal courts; Real Estate; Tax Liens/Judgments; UCC records; Vital records

Local Retrieval Area: MS-Hinds, Madison, Rankin

Add'l Information: Established 1990. Normal turnaround time- 24-30 hours. Projects billed by number of names searched. Projects billed by the hour. All projects require prepayment. Will file/record documents for clients. They specialize in criminal, civil, liens (state tax, judgments & federal tax), federal, criminal & civil courts, bankruptcy court and UCCs (state & county level) in the above listed counties in MS each day. Performs service of process.

MS Document Services Inc

PO Box 49850 (707 West Ave #204), Austin, TX 78765
Phone: 800-292-3868; 512-474-8973 - **Fax:** 800-292-2103; 512-474-1639
www.msdocs.com **email:** mindy@msdocs.com

Types of Records Retrieved: Criminal, Civil and Probate courts; Federal courts; Real Estate; Tax Liens/Judgments; UCC records; Vital records

Local Retrieval Area: NY-Jefferson, Monroe, Onondaga, Oswego; TX-Bastrop, Bexar, Blanco, Brown, Burnet, Caldwell, Callahan, Coleman, Collin, Comal, Comanche, Dallas, Denton, Eastland, Fisher, Hays, Harris, Jones, Lee, Mitchell, Nolan, Palo Pinto, Parker, Runnels, Scurry, Shackelford, Stephens, Tarrant, Taylor, Tom Green, Travis, Williamson. **Correspondent Relationships:** Texas and New York.

Add'l Information: Established 1997. Normal turnaround time- varied. Some documents retrieved immediately; most 24-48 hours. Projects billed by number of names searched. First project may require prepayment. Will file/record documents for clients. Specialize in abstracting, insurance, and filing services in New York, Texas, and throughout the Federal Court System. Prompt, accurate service, built to your needs. Get substantial savings in time and money for Travis County Texas and Texas Sec of State.

MSI Inv

PO Box 5342, West Lebanon, NH 03784
Phone: 603-298-8060 - **Fax:** 603-298-6080
www.msipi.com **email:** msi@vermontel.net

Types of Records Retrieved: Criminal and Civil courts

Local Retrieval Area: NH-Belknap, Cheshire, Grafton, Sullivan; VT-Windsor. **Correspondent Relationships:** NH, VT.

Add'l Information: Established 1984. Normal turnaround time- 24-72 hours. Projects billed by number of names searched. First project may require prepayment. They specialize in criminal and civil record retrieval daily from Vermont and New Hampshire county courts. A licensed PI in NH, VT. Performs service of process.

MT Corporate Services

PO Box 1165, 407 E King St, East Helena, MT 59635
Phone: 406-227-7665 - **Fax:** 406-227-7991
mtcorpserv@hotmail.com

Types of Records Retrieved: Criminal, Civil and Probate courts; Federal courts; Real Estate; Tax Liens/Judgments; UCC records

Local Retrieval Area: MT-Broadwater, Lewis and Clark. **Correspondent Relationships:** Has relationships with courts and clerks statewide.

Add'l Information: Established 1999. Normal turnaround time- 24-48 hours. Projects billed by number of names searched. Will file/record documents for clients. Will advance costs not exceeding $25.00. Terms are net 30 days. They can assist with Montana contractor & insurance licensing, and obtain insurance good standing certificates. A corporate registered agent. Cell-406-431-3353. Also handle motor vehicle registrations; will search motor vehicle/drivers license records.

Mt Pleasant Abstract & Title Inc

116 Court St #A, Mt Pleasant, MI 48858
Phone: 989-773-3651 - **Fax:** 989-773-0751
palexander@mtpleasantabstract.com

Types of Records Retrieved: Civil and Probate courts; Real Estate; Tax Liens/Judgments; UCC records

Local Retrieval Area: MI-Alcona, Alpena, Antrim, Cheboygan, Clare, Crawford, Gladwin, Gratiot, Iosco, Isabella, Kalkaska, Lake, Mecosta, Midland, Missaukee, Montcalm, Montmorency, Newaygo, Ogemaw, Osceola, Otsego, Presque Isle, Roscommon,

Add'l Information: Normal turnaround time- 1 week. Fee basis will vary by type of project. They specialize in real estate and title insurance.

David Mulberry

4050 Lakespur Circle S, Palm Beach Gardens, FL 33410
Phone: 800-704-1287; 561-624-0526 - **Fax:** 561-624-0576
www.PalmBeachPI.com **email:** david@palmbeachpi.com

Types of Records Retrieved: Criminal, Civil and Probate courts; Federal courts; Real Estate; Tax Liens/Judgments; UCC records; Vital records

Local Retrieval Area: FL-Palm Beach. **Correspondent Relationships:** Florida.

Add'l info: Established 1979. Normal turnaround time- variable, depending on project. Projects billed by the hour. First project may require prepayment. Credit cards accepted. Will file/record documents for clients. He is a private investigator and certified process server with over 30 years of investigative experience. Licensed PI in FL. Performs service of process.

Mulholland Investigations & Security

221 E Adams St, Jacksonville, FL 32202
Phone: 904-354-7989 - **Fax:** 904-354-7922
www.mulhollandinvestigation.com **email:** miscwork@bellsouth.net

Types of Records Retrieved: Criminal, Civil and Probate courts; Federal courts; Real Estate; Tax Liens/Judgments; UCC records; Vital records

Local Retrieval Area: FL-Baker, Clay, Duval, Nassau, St. Johns

Add'l Information: Normal turnaround time- 24-48 hours. Projects billed by number of names searched. Projects billed by the hour. Credit cards accepted. Only Visa and MasterCard accepted. Their offices are 2 blocks from the Duval County Courthouse, 3 from the sheriff's office, and walking distance to Middle Dist. of Florida Federal courthouse. A licensed PI in FL. Performs service of process.

Mullen Abstract Co

PO Box 567, 119 SW 2nd St, Walnut Ridge, AR 72476
Phone: 870-886-2452 - **Fax:** 870-886-5929

Types of Records Retrieved: Criminal, Civil and Probate courts; Real Estate; Tax Liens/Judgments; UCC records

Local Retrieval Area: AR-Lawrence

Add'l Information: Established 1975. Normal turnaround time- 3-5 days. Fee basis will vary by the type of project. They specialize in real estate abstracting and title insurance

Mullins Abstract

211 N Main, Rushville, IN 46173
Phone: 765-932-3182; Fax- same

Types of Records Retrieved: Criminal, Civil and Probate courts; Real Estate; Tax Liens/Judgments

Local Retrieval Area: IN-Rush

Add'l Information: Belling depends on nature of the project. First project may require prepayment. Will file/record documents for clients. They specialize in real estate for Rush County but will also search court records.

Donna Mundwiller

118 E 4th St, Hermann, MO 65041
Phone: 573-486-2925 - **Fax:** 573-486-2059

Types of Records Retrieved: Criminal, Civil and Probate courts; Real Estate; Tax Liens/Judgments; UCC records; Vital records

Local Retrieval Area: MO-Gasconade

Add'l Information: Established 1965. Normal turnaround time- variable depending on project. Projects billed by the hour. All projects require prepayment. She specializes in genealogy searches.

Murray County Abstract Inc

1020 W 2nd, Sulphur, OK 73086
Phone: 800-687-2988; 580-622-5294 - **Fax:** 580-622-2866
mcat@brightok.net

Types of Records Retrieved: Civil and Probate courts; Real Estate; Tax Liens/Judgments; UCC records

Local Retrieval Area: OK-Murray

Add'l Information: Established 1935. Normal turnaround time- 24 hours. Projects billed by the hour. First project may require prepayment. They specialize in abstracting, title insurance, escrow closings and title reports.

Murray Research

808 Redbud Rd, Burleson, TX 76028
Phone: 817-295-4820 - **Fax:** 817-426-4212
murrayresearch@murrayresearch.com

Records Retrieved: Criminal and Civil courts; Federal District courts

Local Retrieval Area: TX-Cameron, Dallas, Denton, Hidalgo, Hill, Johnson, Kleberg, Lamar, Parker, Tarrant. **Correspondent Relationships:** statewide.

Add'l Information: Established 1998. Normal turnaround time- 4-24 hours. Projects billed by number of names searched. Payment due net 30 days. Murray Research is a licensed and insured private investigation company specializing in courthouse research where speed, accuracy and price matter, including retrieval from the Federal Records Center serving Texas, Oklahoma, Arkansas and Louisiana. A licensed PI in TX.

Musselman Abstract Co

PO Box 1072, 216 E 4th St, Bartlesville, OK 74005
Phone: 918-336-6410 - **Fax:** 918-336-4880
www.musselmanabstract.com **email:** mussabst@fullnet.net

Types of Records Retrieved: Civil and Probate courts; Real Estate; Tax Liens/Judgments; UCC records

Local Retrieval Area: OK-Washington

Add'l Information: Established 1907. Normal turnaround time- 24 hours. Fee basis will vary by the type of project.

Mutual Abstract Corporation

132 Nassau St #812, New York, NY 10038
Phone: 212-964-4686 - **Fax:** 212-385-0758 rshul@aol.com

Types of Records Retrieved: Bankruptcy court; Tax Liens/Judgments; Real Estate; UCC records

Local Retrieval Area: NY-Bronx, Kings, Nassau, New York, Queens, Westchester. **Correspondent Relationships:** nationwide.

Add'l Information: Established 1964. Normal turnaround time- 2-4 days. Expedited service available. Projects billed by number of names searched. Fees may vary. First project may require prepayment. Will file/record documents for clients. They specialize in cooperative apartment lien searches, UCC searching and filing. They also search mechanics liens, tax liens and pending suits.

Myaer & Co Inc

PO Box 189, Mohall, ND 58761
Phone: 701-756-6487 - **Fax:** 701-756-6186

Types of Records Retrieved: Real Estate; Tax Liens/Judgments; UCC records

Local Retrieval Area: ND-Renville

Add'l Information: Established 1996. Normal turnaround time- 10 days. Fee basis will vary by type of project. Will file/record documents for clients.

Myers Investigations Inc

3205 E Thompson Rd, Indianapolis, IN 46227
Phone: 800-788-8018; 317-865-1006 - **Fax:** 317-882-7204
www.myerspi.com **email:** dmyers@myerspi.com

Types of Records Retrieved: Criminal and Civil courts; Tax Liens/Judgments; UCC records; Vital records

Local Retrieval Area: IN-Bartholomew, Boone, Delaware, Hamilton, Hancock, Hendricks, Johnson, Madison, Marion, Monroe, Putnam, Shelby. **Correspondent Relationships:** Indiana, Kentucky, Ohio, Michigan.

Add'l Information: Established 1995. Normal turnaround time- 24 hours or less. Projects billed by number of names searched. First project may require prepayment. Will file/record documents for clients. Net 10 days after pre-paid case. They specialize in legal investigations, locates, process service, background investigations, and witness interviews. A licensed PI in IN. Performs service of process.

Carrie J Myers

866 Conestoga Dr, Moscow, ID 83843
Phone: 208-883-7963 - **Fax:** 208-883-7963 jnmyers@verizon.net

Types of Records Retrieved: Criminal and Civil courts; Federal courts; Real Estate; Tax Liens/Judgments; UCC records

Local Retrieval Area: ID-Latah

Add'l Information: Established 1998. Normal turnaround time- 24 hours. Projects billed by number of names searched. Will file/record documents for clients. Payment due within one month of job completion. They provide fast and accurate full property searches and document retrievals at very reasonable rates. Specialize in background checks at discounted prices. Has 7 years experience.

Martha Myers

Route 1, Box 39, Leoti, KS 67861
Phone: 620-375-2251; Fax- same

Types of Records Retrieved: Criminal and Civil courts; Tax Liens/Judgments

Local Retrieval Area: KS-Greeley, Wallace, Wichita

Add'l Information: Established 1996. Normal turnaround time- 24-48 hours. Projects billed by number of names searched. Charge is by name per county. First project may require prepayment. She is centrally located in her 3 county area.

Ryan Myers

215 E Henley St #301, Moscow, ID 83843
Phone: 208-882-6678 - **Fax:** 208-883-7963
ryanmealmyers@yahoo.com

Types of Records Retrieved: Criminal and Civil courts; Federal courts; Real Estate; Tax Liens/Judgments; UCC records

Local Retrieval Area: ID-Latah, Nez Perce; WA-Asotin, Whitman

Add'l Information: Established 1999. Normal turnaround time- 48 hours. Projects billed by number of names searched. Payment due within 30 days of completion.

Myhre Process

740 N Plankinton Ave, Milwaukee, WI 53203
Phone: 414-271-9574 - **Fax:** 414-271-4018

Types of Records Retrieved: Criminal, Civil and Probate courts; Federal courts; Tax Liens/Judgments; UCC records; Vital records

Local Retrieval Area: WI-Kenosha, Milwaukee, Ozaukee, Racine, Walworth, Washington, Waukesha. **Correspondent Relationships:** Wisconsin.

Add'l Information: Established 1971. Normal turnaround time- usually same day; maximum 1 day. Projects billed by the hour. Fee may include incurred costs. First project may require prepayment. They specialize in process serving, skiptracing & notary. Performs service of process.

N F Field Abstract Co
PO Box 697, Fergus Falls, MN 56538
Phone: 218-736-6844 - **Fax:** 800-736-5988; 218-736-5988
www.nffield.com **Types of Records Retrieved:** Civil and Probate courts; Real Estate; Tax Liens/Judgments; UCC records
Local Retrieval Area: MN-Otter Tail
Add'l Information: Established 1910. Normal turnaround time- 5-10 days. Projects billed by number of names searched. Fee may also be based per entry. All projects require prepayment. They will also invoice. They specialize in title insurance and closings.

N W Legal Support Inc
200 W Thomas St #140, Seattle, WA 98119-4215
Phone: 800-729-9426; 206-223-9426 - **Fax:** 800-916-9475; 206-223-9475
www.nwlegal.com **email:** evennes@nwlegal.com
Types of Records Retrieved: Criminal, Civil and Probate courts; Federal courts; Real Estate; Tax Liens/Judgments; UCC records; Vital records
Local Retrieval Area: WA-King, Pierce, Snohomish, Spokane. **Correspondent Relationships:** Washington statewide.
Add'l Information: Established 1989. Normal turnaround time- 48 hours. Projects billed by the hour. First project may require prepayment. Credit cards accepted. Will file/record documents for clients. Terms: net 10 days. They do process service, provide messenger services and investigations. Also has offices in Everett 425-258-9338 and Spokane 509-342-6482. Performs service of process.

NACM/Colorado
777 S Wadsworth Blvd Bldg 2-100, Lakewood, CO 80226-4300
Phone: 800-451-7868; 303-837-1280 - **Fax:** 303-830-7808
www.nacmcolorado.com **email:** sharonl@nacmcolorado.com
Types of Records Retrieved: UCC records
Local Retrieval Area: CO-Denver
Add'l Information: Established 1896. Normal turnaround time- 3-4 hours. Projects billed by number of names searched. Projects billed by number of records located. All projects require prepayment. Credit cards accepted. They are a credit reporting association that can provide business and corporate information for KS, NE, NM, AZ, CO, MT, and WY

Nancy Durbin Court Research
PO Box 1341, Salem, IL 62881
Phone: 618-267-0472 cell; 618-548-8296 - **Fax:** 618-548-8296
Types of Records Retrieved: Criminal, Civil and Probate courts; Federal courts; Real Estate; Tax Liens/Judgments; UCC records; Vital records
Local Retrieval Area: IL-Clay, Clinton, Fayette, Jefferson, Marion
Add'l Information: Established 1994. Normal turnaround time- 1-3 days. Expedited service available. Projects billed by the hour. First project may require prepayment. Formerly known as Nancy Durbin Process Service, she specializes in South Central Illinois. Call before faxing. A licensed PI in IL. Performs service of process.

Napa-Sonoma Connection
2678 Monticello Rd, Napa, CA 94558
Phone: 707-952-6426 - **Fax:** 707-257-2191 napa-conoma@sonic.net
Types of Records Retrieved: Criminal, Civil and Probate courts; Real Estate; Tax Liens/Judgments; UCC records; Vital records
Local Retrieval Area: CA-Napa, Sonoma
Add'l Information: Established 1992. Normal turnaround time- 24 hours. Projects billed by number of names searched. Is a research expert with years of experience in the Napa-Sonoma area.

National Abstract
7557 S State St, Lowville, NY 13367-1512
Phone: 800-535-3477; 315-376-3911 - **Fax:** 315-376-8305
nac1@telenet.net
Types of Records Retrieved: Civil and Probate courts; Real Estate; Tax Liens/Judgments; UCC records
Local Retrieval Area: NY-Lewis. **Correspondent Relationships:** Herkimer, Jefferson, Oneida, St Lawrence counties.
Add'l Information: Established 1920. Normal turnaround time- 24 hours for court records, taxes, UCCs; 24-48 hours for real estate searches. Projects billed by number of names searched. Will file/record documents for clients. They specialize in title insurance.

National Background Investigations Inc
PO Box 966, Stevensville, MD 21666
Phone: 800-798-0079; 410-604-6200 - **Fax:** 877-472-4676; 410-604-2496
www.nationalbackground.com **email:** research@nationalbackground.com
Types of Records Retrieved: Criminal and Civil courts; Federal courts; Tax Liens/Judgments
Local Retrieval Area: DE-all counties; MD-Allegany, Anne Arundel, Baltimore, Baltimore City, Calvert, Caroline, Carroll, Cecil, Charles, Dorchester, Frederick, Garrett, Harford, Howard, Kent, Montgomery, Prince George's, Queen Anne's, St Mary's Somerset, Talbot, Washington, Wicomico, Worcester; NJ-Atlantic, Bergen, Burlington, Camden, Cape May, Cumberland, Essex, Gloucester, Hudson, Hunterdon, Mercer, Middlesex, Monmouth, Morris, Ocean, Passaic, Salem, Somerset, Sussex, Union, Warren; VA-6 counties near DC; DC-District of Columbia. **Correspondent Relationships:** nationwide.
Add'l Information: Established 1996. Normal turnaround time- 24-48 hours. Projects billed by number of names searched. Credit cards accepted. Will file/record documents for clients. Terms: net 15 days. They are a regional firm with collective team experience of over 30 years in public record retrieval, including title searching.

National Corporate Research Ltd
615 S Dupont Hwy, Dover, DE 19901-4517
Phone: 800-483-1140; 302-734-1450 - **Fax:** 302-734-1476
www.nationalcorp.com **email:** info@nationalcorp.com
Types of Records Retrieved: Civil courts; Federal courts; Real Estate; Tax Liens/Judgments; UCC records
Local Retrieval Area: DE-Kent. **Correspondents:** nationwide.
Add'l Information: Established 1994. Normal turnaround time- next day. Projects billed by number of names searched. First project may require prepayment. AMEX cards accepted. They invoice for each indices and jurisdiction searched. They specialize in UCC and corporate searches at the Delaware Secretary of State office, to which they are connected online.

National Document
2601 N 3rd St #202, Phoenix, AZ 85004
Phone: 800-829-5578; 602-274-5578 - **Fax:** 800-837-5573; 602-274-5573
www.nationaldoc.com **email:** werelistening@natldoc.com
Types of Records Retrieved: Criminal, Civil and Probate courts; Federal courts; Real Estate; Tax Liens/Judgments; UCC records
Local Retrieval Area: AZ-Maricopa. **Correspondent Relationships:** Arizona, nationwide.
Add'l Information: Established 1985. Normal turnaround time- same day to 48 hours. Projects billed by number of names searched. Projects billed by the hour. First project may require prepayment. Credit cards accepted. Will file/record documents for clients. Net 30 days, or as agreed to. National Document is a nationwide public record company specializing in the retrieval and filing of county and state documents. They are a licensed private investigative firm. A licensed PI in AZ.

National Information Access Bureau (NIAB)
PO Box 30326, Honolulu, HI 96820
Phone: 800-787-6422; 808-455-2900 - **Fax:** 808-455-2951
www.publicrecords-hawaii.com **email:** brendadey@earthlink.net
Types of Records Retrieved: Criminal and Civil courts; Federal courts; Real Estate; Vital records

Local Retrieval Area: HI-Honolulu. **Correspondents:** statewide.

Add'l Information: Established 1995. Normal turnaround time- 24-48 hours. Projects billed by number of names searched. First project may require prepayment. They specialize in criminal background histories and MVRs. Performs service of process.

National Information Agency

3206 S Hopkins Ave #240, Titusville, FL 32780
Phone: 321-543-9381 - **Fax:** 321-383-8929
www.infoagency.com **email:** search@infoagency.com

Types of Records Retrieved: Criminal, Civil and Probate courts; bankruptcy court; Real Estate; Tax Liens/Judgments; UCC records; Vital records

Local Retrieval Area: FL-Brevard. **Correspondents:** nationwide.

Add'l Information: Established 1998. Normal turnaround time- 1-2 days. Expedited service available. Projects billed by the hour. First project may require prepayment. Credit cards accepted. NIA specializes in record retrieval, foreclosure representation, process service, civil and criminal, probate, real estate, tax liens/judgments, vital records and property records. A licensed PI in FL. Performs service of process.

National Investigative Services Inc

1325 W Sunshine St, PMB 228, Springfield, MO 65807-2344
Phone: 417-831-2500

Types of Records Retrieved: Criminal, Civil and Probate courts; Federal courts; Real Estate; Tax Liens/Judgments; UCC records; Vital records

Local Retrieval Area: MO-Barry, Barton, Cedar, Christian, Dade, Dallas, Douglas, Greene, Hickory, Jasper, Laclede, Lawrence, McDonald, Miller, Newton, Ozark, Phelps, Polk, Stone, Taney, Vernon, Webster, Wright

Add'l info: Established 1989. Normal turnaround time- 2 days. Projects billed by number of names searched. First project may require prepayment. Will file/record documents for clients. They specialize in record retrieval and process serving in 23 MO counties. Performs service of process.

National Pre-Employment Research

PO Box 2272, Stockbridge, GA 30281
Phone: 770-389-6607 - **Fax:** 770-389-5297
nationalpr@bellsouth.net

Types of Records Retrieved: Criminal and Civil courts

Local Retrieval Area: GA-Appling, Baldwin, Bibb, Bleckley, Brantley, Bryan, Bulloch, Burke, Butts, Camden, Chatham, Clarke, Columbia, Coweta, Effingham, Evans, Glascock, Glynn, Greene, Habersham, Henry, Jasper, Lamar, Laurens, Liberty, McDuffie, McIntosh, Madison, Marion, Meriwether, Monroe, Morgan, Muscogee, Newton, Oconee, Peach, Pierce, Pike, Putnam, Richmond, Rockdale, Spalding, Talbot, Taliaferro, Tattnall, Taylor, Troup, Twiggs, Upson, Walton, Ware, Wayne; TN-Carter, Cumberland, Davidson, Fayette, Franklin, Giles, Hawkins, Haywood, Lauderdale, Lawrence, Lewis, Marion, Maury, McMinn, Meigs, Morgan, Polk, Sevier, Tipton, Union. **Correspondent Relationships:** nationwide.

Add'l info: Established 2002. Payment method may depend on nature of job. First project may require prepayment. National Pre-Employment Research has 10 years experience in the pre-employment area. They specialize in criminal record information in the South, and driver information across the nation. They also provide locates. Performs service of process.

National Research Associates Inc

2138 Silas Deane Hwy #102, Rocky Hill, CT 06067-2317
Phone: 860-529-3006 - **Fax:** 860-529-4375

Types of Records Retrieved: Criminal, Civil and Probate courts; Federal courts; Real Estate; Tax Liens/Judgments; UCC records; Vital records

Local Retrieval Area: CT-Fairfield, Hartford, Litchfield, Middlesex, New Haven, New London, Tolland, Windham. **Correspondent Relationships:** nationwide, Canada, Puerto Rico.

Add'l Information: Established 1980. Normal turnaround time- 24-48 hours. Projects billed by number of names searched. First project may require prepayment. Will file/record documents for clients. They provide background searches for employment purposes, due diligence, asset investigations, current owner searches, two owner searches and mortgage/deed searches. They also complete searches at Sec of State & Municipal Offices throughout CT.

National Search Solutions LLC

3736 Braewood Cir, Las Vegas, NV 89120
Phone: 702-431-9100 - **Fax:** 702-431-9120 marc248@cox.net

Types of Records Retrieved: Criminal, Civil and Probate courts; Federal courts; Real Estate; Tax Liens/Judgments; UCC records; Vital records

Local Retrieval Area: NV-Clark

Add'l Information: Established 1999. Normal turnaround time- 12-24 hours. Projects billed by number of names searched. First project may require prepayment. They offer the quickest turn-around, along with accurate information and lowest prices. "Need we say more?"

National Service Information Inc (Indiana)

320 N Meridian #817, Indianapolis, IN 46204
Phone: 317-266-0040 - **Fax:** 317-266-8453
www.nsii.net **email:** search@nsii.net

Types of Records Retrieved: Criminal, Civil and Probate courts; Federal courts; Real Estate; Tax Liens/Judgments; UCC records; Vital records

Local Retrieval Area: IN-Hamilton, Hancock, Hendricks, Johnson, Marion. **Correspondent Relationships:** IN, OH, KY and nationwide.

Add'l Information: Established 1989. Normal turnaround time- 1-3 days. Fee basis varies by project. They are online with Ohio and Indiana Secretary of State databases and can provide microfilm copies. They also perform corporate work. Performs service of process.

National Service Information Inc (Ohio)

145 Baker St, Marion, OH 43302
Phone: 800-235-0337; 740-387-6806 - **Fax:** 800-382-1256; 740-382-1256
www.nsii.net **email:** search@nsii.net

Types of Records Retrieved: Criminal, Civil and Probate courts; Federal courts; Tax Liens/Judgments; UCC records; Vital records

Local Retrieval Area: KY-Franklin; OH-Cuyahoga, Delaware, Franklin, Hamilton, Lucas, Marion, Montgomery, Summit. **Correspondent Relationships:** Ohio, Indiana, Kentucky, nationwide.

Add'l Information: Established 1989. Normal turnaround time- 1-3 days. Fee basis will vary by type of project. They are online with OH and IN Secretary of State databases and can provide microfilm copies. They also perform corporate work and maintain online databases (w/images) of UCC/Corporate for CA, IN, OH, & PA.

Nationwide Environmental Title Research

2055 E Rio Salada Pky, Tempe, AZ 85281
Phone: 800-324-4956; 480-967-6752 - **Fax:** 480-966-9422
www.netronline.com **email:** brett@netronline.com

Types of Records Retrieved: Real Estate

Local Retrieval Area: AZ-Coconino, Maricopa, Mohave, Pima, Pinal, Yavapai. **Correspondent Relationships:** nationwide.

Add'l Information: Established 1993. Normal turnaround time- 5-7 days. Flat fee per project is available. Credit cards accepted. Terms: net 10 days. They specialize in providing historical property information (environmental title searches) throughout the country, to satisfy one of the requirements for the land owner defense to CERCLA liability.

Nationwide Information Services Inc

52 James Street, Albany, NY 12207
Phone: 800-873-3482; 518-449-8429 - **Fax:** 800-234-8522
nis@broadviewnet.net

Types of Records Retrieved: Criminal, Civil and Probate courts; Federal courts; Real Estate; Tax Liens/Judgments; UCC records; Vital records; Corporate records

Local Retrieval Area: NY-Albany. **Correspondents:** nationwide.

Add'l Information: Established 1980. Normal turnaround time- 24-48 hours. Expedited service available. Projects billed by number of names searched. First project may require prepayment. Credit cards accepted. Will file/record documents for clients. Performs service of process.

Navarro County Abstract Co

PO Box 685, Corsicana, TX 75151
Phone: 903-874-3768 - **Fax:** 903-874-6204

Records Retrieved: Real Estate; Tax Liens/Judgments; Probate courts

Local Retrieval Area: TX-Navarro

Add'l Information: Normal turnaround time- variable depending on project. Fee basis will vary by type of project.

NC Corporate Connection Inc

2605 Scribe Ct, Raleigh, NC 27615
Phone: 888-844-8360; 919-844-3360 - **Fax:** 919-844-8364
krozar@nc.ri.com

Types of Records Retrieved: Civil and Probate courts; Federal courts; Real Estate; Tax Liens/Judgments; UCC records; Vital records

Local Retrieval Area: NC-Alamance, Cabarrus, Catawba, Chatham, Durham, Franklin, Gaston, Granville, Harnett, Johnston, Lincoln, Mecklenburg, Nash, Orange, Rowan, Union, Wake. **Correspondent Relationships:** nationwide.

Add'l Information: Established 1999. Normal turnaround time- 24-48 hours. Projects billed by number of names searched. Will invoice for all projects. They specialize in civil and criminal court, probate courts, federal courts, superior courts, liens/judgments, UCC, vital records and last owner searches. They also do Secretary of State filings and searches.

Nebraska Default & Title Services Inc

11313 Davenport St, Omaha, NE 68154
Phone: 866-866-5100; 402-614-3580 - **Fax:** 402-614-9613
www.ndtsi.com **email:** title@ndtsi.com

Types of Records Retrieved: Real Estate; Tax Liens/Judgments; Probate courts; Federal courts

Local Retrieval Area: NE-Cass, Dodge, Douglas, Lancaster, Sarpy, Saunders, Washington. **Correspondent Relationships:** statewide.

Add'l Information: Established 2004. Normal turnaround time- 3 days without book & page, a couple hours if supplied with book & page. Projects billed by number of names searched. They are a cutting edge title company that does more than search. They are a "cradle to grave" title company with the newest technology.

Nebraska Title Company

629 Court St, Beatrice, NE 68310
Phone: 402-228-2233 - **Fax:** 402-228-4543

Types of Records Retrieved: Civil and Probate courts; Federal courts; Real Estate; Tax Liens/Judgments; UCC records

Local Retrieval Area: NE-Gage. **Correspondent Relationships:** Lancaster county NE.

Add'l Information: Established 1948. Normal turnaround time- 36 hours. Projects billed by number of names searched. First project may require prepayment. Will file/record documents for clients.

Nell Watkins & Associates

6417 Faircove Circle, Garland, TX 75043
Phone: 972-226-8811 - **Fax:** 972-226-8811 nellw@tx.rr.com

Types of Records Retrieved: Criminal, Civil and Probate courts; Real Estate; Tax Liens/Judgments; UCC records; Vital records

Local Retrieval Area: TX-Dallas, Kaufman, Rockwall. **Correspondent Relationships:** nationwide.

Add'l Information: Established 1994. Normal turnaround time- 24-48 hours. Projects billed by number of names searched. In Dallas county, charge by hourly rate. They specialize in background, asset and locate investigations. 25 years experience in court record research/retrieval. Licensed PI in TX.

Nemaha County Abstract & Title Co

507 Main St., Seneca, KS 66538
Phone: 785-336-2137 - **Fax:** 785-336-2537

Types of Records Retrieved: Civil and Probate courts; Real Estate; Tax Liens/Judgments; UCC records; Vital records

Local Retrieval Area: KS-Nemaha

Add'l info: Established 1994. Normal turnaround time- 1-2 days. Fee basis varies by type of transaction. First project may require prepayment.

Joe Y Nerio

1832 Cordova Av, Colton, CA 92324
Phone: 909-824-9358 - **Fax:** 909-824-8012

Types of Records Retrieved: Criminal, Civil and Probate courts; Federal courts; Vital records

Local Retrieval Area: CA-Riverside, San Bernardino, San Diego. **Correspondent Relationships:** Los Angeles, Orange counties CA.

Add'l Information: Established 1994. Normal turnaround time- 1-3 days. Projects billed by number of names searched. Projects billed by the hour. First project may require prepayment. He specializes in criminal record searches. Does searches at the US National Archives and Record Administration Pacific Region or NARA.

Ness County Abstract

HC 61, Box 2A, Ness City, KS 67560
Phone: 785-798-3846

Types of Records Retrieved: Criminal and Civil courts; Real Estate; Tax Liens/Judgments

Local Retrieval Area: KS-Ness

Add'l Information: Normal turnaround time- 24-48 hours. Billing depends on nature of the request. First project may require prepayment. Will file/record documents for clients. They specialize in Ness County real estate and are very familiar with the area.

Net Check Investigations

26523 N Huntswood Ln, Santa Clarita, CA 91387
Phone: 888-638-2432; 661-250-3188 - **Fax:** 661-250-3198
netcheckpi@yahoo.com

Types of Records Retrieved: Criminal, Civil and Probate courts; Federal courts; Real Estate; UCC records

Local Retrieval Area: CA-Los Angeles

Add'l Information: Established 1997. Normal turnaround time- 24-48 hours. Projects billed by number of names searched. Will invoice monthly. They specialize in criminal, civil, property record searches in one to three days. Volume discounts. Also does surveillance, behavioral assessments, profiling, pre-employment, domestic violence/stalking prevention. A licensed PI in CA, AZ.

Tim Neuroth

PO Box 484, Webster City, IA 50595-0484
Phone: 515-832-3156 - **Fax:** 515-832-9153

Types of Records Retrieved: Criminal, Civil and Probate courts; Real Estate; Tax Liens/Judgments; UCC records; Vital records

Local Retrieval Area: IA-Hamilton

Add'l Information: Established 1989. Normal turnaround time- 1-2 days. Projects billed by the hour. First project may require prepayment. He will accept personal checks.

Nevada Land Services

PO Box 1169, 363 Erie Main St, Tonopah, NV 89049
Phone: 800-233-4999; 775-482-5641 - **Fax:** 775-482-8935
sjroper@cowcountytitle.com

Types of Records Retrieved: Real Estate; Tax Liens/Judgments; UCC records

Local Retrieval Area: NV-Churchill, Esmeralda, Eureka, Humboldt, Lander, Lincoln, Mineral, Nye, Pershing

Add'l Information: Established 1990. Normal turnaround time- 10 days. Projects billed by number of names searched. Will file/record documents for clients. Personal checks are accepted.

New Century Title

140 S 4th St, Witheville, VA 24382
Phone: 276-223-1207 - **Fax:** 276-223-1807
nct@newcenturytitle.net

Types of Records Retrieved: Real Estate; Tax Liens/Judgments

Local Retrieval Area: VA-Bland, Carroll, Grayson, Smyth, Wythe

Add'l Information: Established 1999. Normal turnaround time- 24-48 hours. First project may require prepayment. Will file/record documents for clients. They handle all types of real estate research for their 5-county area in SW Virginia. They also provide real estate closings and title insurance.

New England Abstract LLC

6 N. Main St, Wallingford, CT 06492
Phone: 203-430-7712 - **Fax:** 815-301-8506
www.newenglandabstract.com **email:** jharlow@newenglandabstract.com

Types of Records Retrieved: Civil and Probate courts; Federal courts; Real Estate; Tax Liens/Judgments; UCC records; Vital records

Local Retrieval Area: CT-Fairfield, Hartford, Litchfield, Middlesex, New Haven. **Correspondent Relationships:** statewide.

Add'l Information: Established 2002. Normal turnaround time- 24-48 hours. Expedited service available. Projects billed by number of names searched. Billing done on client terms. They are a locally-owned and operated title search and document retrieval firm covering all of CT. Search and pricing options available upon inquiry. Cell phone is 203-430-7712.

New England Recovery Inc

PO Box 1025, Barre, VT 05641
Phone: 800-922-7376; 802-433-6111 - **Fax:** 802-433-6742
chrisdupre1@aol.com

Types of Records Retrieved: Criminal, Civil and Probate courts; Federal courts; Real Estate; Tax Liens/Judgments; UCC records; Vital records

Local Retrieval Area: VT-Addison, Bennington, Caledonia, Chittenden, Essex, Franklin, Grand Isle, Lamoille, Orange, Orleans, Rutland, Washington, Windham, Windsor

Add'l Information: Established 1985. Normal turnaround time- 2-4 days. They charge a base fee and per hour. They also charge extra for the copy charges. First project may require prepayment. Will file/record documents for clients. Will discuss with clients terms for billings. They specialize in hidden asset searches and location of missing persons. A licensed PI in NH, VT. Performs service of process.

Newell & Associates Inc

PO Box 1624, Meridian, MS 39302
Phone: 601-693-7700 - **Fax:** 601-483-7954 newellcan@aol.com

Types of Records Retrieved: Criminal and Civil courts; Real Estate; Tax Liens/Judgments; UCC records

Local Retrieval Area: MS-Choctaw, Lauderdale, Lowndes, Neshoba. **Correspondent Relationships:** statewide.

Add'l Information: Established 2000. Normal turnaround time- Same day in Lauderdale County if received before 10:00 AM; 24 hours elsewhere. Projects billed by number of names searched. First project may require prepayment. Will file/record documents for clients. Must pre-pay for process service. Newell & Associates Inc is a service support company that is motivated to provide accurate and expedient customer service. Can also retrieve records from Oktibbeha, Neshoba, and other nearby counties. Performs service of process.

NH Background Investigations LLC

PO Box 1064, Nashua, NH 03061
Phone: 603-598-4106 - **Fax:** 603-598-4108
www.preemploymentsearch.com **email:** rod@preemploymentsearch.com

Types of Records Retrieved: Criminal, Civil and Probate courts; Federal courts; Real Estate; Tax Liens/Judgments; UCC records; Vital records; DMV records

Retrieval Area: MA-Middlesex, Suffolk; NH-Belknap, Carroll, Cheshire, Coos, Grafton, Hillsborough, Merrimack, Rockingham, Strafford, Sullivan

Add'l Information: Established 1994. Normal turnaround time- 12-24 hours. Projects billed by number of names searched. Credit cards accepted. Clients are billed monthly. They specialize in pre-employment screening, criminal record searches, background investigations and corporate due-diligence reports. They are a subsidiary of Gagnon & Wendt, A NH PI Agency. A licensed PI in NH.

Jake Nichols

PO Box 441, Plentywood, MT 59254
Phone: 406-765-1651 (Fax- same), alt phone- 406-765-1806

Types of Records Retrieved: Real Estate; Tax Liens/Judgments

Local Retrieval Area: MT-Daniels, Roosevelt, Sheridan

Add'l Information: Established 1957. Normal turnaround time- variable depending on project. Projects billed by the hour. First project may require prepayment. He specializes in mineral searches.

NNBS Inc

3536 Calvert St, Rockford, TN 37853-3926
Phone: 865-977-8808 - **Fax:** 865-977-8223
http://anytimeservices.com **email:** dossier@anytimeservices.com

Types of Records Retrieved: Real Estate; Tax Liens/Judgments; Probate courts; UCC records; Vital records

Local Retrieval Area: TN-Anderson, Blount, Jefferson, Knox, Loudon, Roane, Sevier, Union. **Correspondent Relationships:** KY, AL, GA, MS & TN.

Add'l Information: Established 2001. Normal turnaround time- 24-72 hours. They only charge by the hour on probate and will searches, others charged by order. Credit cards accepted. Will file/record documents for clients. Discounts for volume/monthly orders. NNSB Inc provides residential and commercial searches in a six state area. Continually growing, offer nationwide services for loan closings.

Nodaway County Abstract Co

501 N Market St, Maryville, MO 64468-1616
Phone: 660-582-2332 - **Fax:** 660-582-8145 mail@nodabstract.com

Types of Records Retrieved: Civil and Probate courts; Real Estate; Tax Liens/Judgments

Local Retrieval Area: MO-Nodaway

Add'l Information: Established 1980. Normal turnaround time- 3 days or less. Projects billed by number of names searched. They specialize in complete searches of land records.

Melinda Nolan

1388 N Bend Rd, Stanton, KY 40380
Phone: 606-663-4141 - **Fax:** 606-663-2710

Types of Records Retrieved: Criminal, Civil and Probate courts; Real Estate; Tax Liens/Judgments

Local Retrieval Area: KY-Powell

Add'l Information: Established 1997. Normal turnaround time- Same day, usually. Projects billed by number of names searched. First project may require prepayment. Fax to "Attention Melinda Nolan" only.

Nor-Cal Court Research

PO Box 246, Orland, CA 95963
Phone: 530-865-3525 - **Fax:** 530-865-8066 lefdalbarbara@snowcrest.net

Types of Records Retrieved: Criminal and Civil courts

Local Retrieval Area: CA-Butte, Glenn, Humboldt, Shasta, Tehama. **Correspondent Relationships:** Oregon, Washington.

Add'l Information: Established 1997. Normal turnaround time- 12-24 hours. Projects billed by number of names searched. Terms are net 30 days. They specialize in court record retrieval.

Norcal Public Records Service

21430 Perimeter Rd, Grass Valley, CA 95949
Phone: 408-221-6654 - **Fax:** 408-559-4818

Types of Records Retrieved: Criminal and Civil courts; Real Estate; Tax Liens/Judgments; UCC records

Local Retrieval Area: CA-Nevada, Placer, Sonoma. **Correspondent Relationships:** other California counties.

Add'l Information: Established 1993. Normal turnaround time- 1-3 days. Projects billed by number of names searched. Will file/record documents for clients. Terms: net 15 days. They are specialist in county court, federal court, and county recorder research. Fax ordering is encouraged. Reports are faxed back at no charge.

North American Security Solutions
2844 E River Rd, Dayton, OH 45439-1538
Phone: 888-898-6277; 937-890-4300 - **Fax:** 937-890-4301
www.nassinc.com **email:** tgeiselman@nassinc.com

Types of Records Retrieved: Criminal and Civil courts; Federal courts; Real Estate; Tax Liens/Judgments

Local Retrieval Area: OH-Clark, Darke, Greene, Miami, Montgomery, Preble

Add'l Information: Established 1997. Normal turnaround time- 1-3 days. Projects billed by the hour. Credit cards accepted. A licensed PI in OH.

North Country Process Inc
PO Box 101126, Anchorage, AK 99510
Phone: 907-274-2023 - **Fax:** 907-274-2823

Types of Records Retrieved: Criminal, Civil and Probate courts; Federal courts; UCC records; Real Estate; Tax Liens/Judgments

Local Retrieval Area: AK-Anchorage, Fairbanks North Star, Kenai Peninsula, Ketchikan Gateway, Matanuska-Susitna

Add'l info: Established 1987. Turnaround time- 1-2 days. Expedited service available. Projects billed by the hour. All projects require prepayment. Their hands-on coverage includes these areas: Anchorage, Ft Richardson, Elmendorf AFB, Eagle River, Chugiak, Wasilla, Palmer, Talkeetna, Big Lake, Kenai, Soldotna, Nikiski, Seward, Homer, Fairbanks, North Pole, Ketchikan, Elison AFB and Girdwood. Performs service of process.

North Florida Abstract & Title Company
PO Box 838, Monticello, FL 32345
Phone: 850-997-2670 - **Fax:** 850-997-3412 nfabstract@cs.com

Types of Records Retrieved: Criminal, Civil and Probate courts; Real Estate; Tax Liens/Judgments; UCC records; Vital records

Local Retrieval Area: FL-Jefferson

Add'l Information: Established 1972. Normal turnaround time- 1 week. Fee basis will vary by the type of project. They specialize in real estate searches.

North Missouri Title
PO Box 787, Kirksville, MO 63501
Phone: 660-665-4711 - **Fax:** 660-627-0625

Types of Records Retrieved: Real Estate; Tax Liens/Judgments

Local Retrieval Area: MO-Adair

Add'l Information: First project may require prepayment. They specialize in real estate.

North Pacific Legal
PO Box 193, 895 Commercial Ave, Coos Bay, OR 97420
Phone: 541-888-5118 - **Fax:** 541-269-5294

Types of Records Retrieved: Criminal, Civil and Probate courts; Tax Liens/Judgments **Local Retrieval Area:** OR-Coos

Add'l Information: Established 1987. Normal turnaround time- variable depending on project. Projects billed by the hour. They specialize in process service and trustee sales. Performs service of process.

North Sound Professional Research
PO Box 12088, Everett, WA 98206-2088
Phone: 425-267-9070 - **Fax:** 425-267-9070
www.northsoundproresearch.com
email: info@northsoundproresearch.com

Types of Records Retrieved: Criminal, Civil and Probate courts; Federal courts; Real Estate; Tax Liens/Judgments; UCC records; Vital records

Local Retrieval Area: WA-King, Snohomish. **Correspondent Relationships:** nationwide.

Add'l Information: Established 2005. Normal turnaround time- 24-72 hours. Projects billed by the hour. First project may require prepayment. NSPR is a fully licensed and insured investigation agency specializing in background investigations. A licensed PI in WA.

North Vernon Abstract Co Inc
PO Box 368, North Vernon, IN 47265
Phone: 812-346-2259 - **Fax:** 812-346-6056 nvabstract@seidata.com

Types of Records Retrieved: Civil and Probate courts; Real Estate; Tax Liens/Judgments; UCC records

Local Retrieval Area: IN-Jennings. **Correspondent Relationships:** Jackson, Jefferson, Scott, Ripley Bartholomew, Decatur counties.

Add'l Information: Established 1969. Normal turnaround time- variable, depending on project. Projects billed by number of names searched. Will file/record documents for clients. Personal checks accepted.

North Winds Investigations Inc
PO Box 1654, Rogers, AR 72757
Phone: 800-530-4514; 479-925-1612 - **Fax:** 479-925-2819
nwi@cox-internet.com

Types of Records Retrieved: Criminal, Civil and Probate courts; Federal courts; Real Estate; Tax Liens/Judgments; UCC records; Vital records

Local Retrieval Area: AR-Benton, Crawford, Pulaski, Sebastian, Washington. **Correspondent Relationships:** Arkansas.

Add'l Information: Established 1986. Normal turnaround time- 2-3 days. Projects billed by the hour. First project may require prepayment. Will file/record documents for clients. They specialize in worker's compensation, liability surveillance, skiptracing, fire cause and origin, product liability, background searches and complete asset searches as well as polygraph exams and process service. A licensed PI in AR, MO, MS, OK, TN. Performs service of process.

Northeast Colorado Title Co LLC
PO Box 110, 206 N 3rd St, Sterling, CO 80751
Phone: 970-522-7130 - **Fax:** 970-522-7382
northeast_colorado_title@hotmail.com

Types of Records Retrieved: Criminal and Civil courts; Real Estate; Tax Liens/Judgments; UCC records

Local Retrieval Area: CO-Logan

Add'l Information: Established 1996. Normal turnaround time- 48 hours. Projects billed by number of names searched. First project may require prepayment. Will file/record documents for clients.

Northeast Criminal Research
16 Cutler Rd, Litchfield, NH 03052
Phone: 603-880-6805 - **Fax:** 603-880-6805 northeast_research@yahoo.com

Types of Records Retrieved: Criminal, Civil and Probate courts; Federal courts; Vital records

Local Retrieval Area: NH-Hillsborough, Merrimack, Rockingham, Strafford

Add'l Information: Established 2005. Normal turnaround time- 24 hours. Projects billed by number of names searched. Flat rate for name searches. Will bill post project; payment by check or electronic transfer. They specialize in criminal research, highly experienced in civil/probate records, retrieval of vital records & Fed court records. Formerly with large NH PI agency. They provide their clients with a 5 day a week walk-in service at all covered courts.

Northeast Investigations Inc
201 W Genesee St #200, Fayetteville, NY 13066
Phone: 888-796-1051; 315-682-1160 - **Fax:** 315-682-1157
jcalver945@aol.com

Types of Records Retrieved: Criminal, Civil and Probate courts; Federal courts; Real Estate; Tax Liens/Judgments; UCC records; Vital records

Local Retrieval Area: NY-Albany, Broome, Cayuga, Cortland, Erie, Herkimer, Jefferson, Lewis, Madison, Monroe, Oneida, Onondaga, Oswego. **Correspondent Relationships:** most of NY State, including Albany and Erie counties.

Add'l Information: Established 1989. Normal turnaround time- 3-4 days to 1 week. Projects billed by number of names searched. Projects billed by the hour. First project may require prepayment. Credit cards accepted. Will take checks upon assignment for new customers. They are a full service company, specializing in investigations. They offer the insurance fraud hotline via their toll-free number. Record retrieval and trial preparation work a specialty. A licensed PI in NY. Performs service of process.

Northeast Nebraska Court Research
Box 842, 1007 Tenth St, Stanton, NE 68779
Phone: 402-439-2469 - **Fax:** 402-439-2468 nncr_carla@yahoo.com

Types of Records Retrieved: Criminal and Civil courts; Real Estate; Tax Liens/Judgments; Vital records

Local Retrieval Area: NE-Madison, Stanton

Add'l Information: Established 1994. Normal turnaround time- 24 hours, sometimes less. Projects billed by number of names searched. Monthly billing. Services include state/federal tax liens, property searches & delinquent tax lien lists. Can do 6 counties for property searches. Is a member of Nebraska Gov backgrounds website for all 93 counties.

Northeast Nebraska Title & Escrow

PO Box 991, Norfolk, NE 68702-0991
Phone: 402-371-1221 - **Fax:** 402-371-7800

Types of Records Retrieved: Civil and Probate courts; Real Estate; Tax Liens/Judgments; UCC records; Vital records

Local Retrieval Area: NE-Knox, Madison, Pierce

Add'l Information: Established 1990. Normal turnaround time- 1-3 days. Fee basis is a flat rate and per record. They specialize in title insurance.

Northern Arizona Investigations

PO Box 1326, Flagstaff, AZ 86002
Phone: 800-657-2747; 928-779-2823 - **Fax:** 928-779-1044
tamaraofnai@yahoo.com

Types of Records Retrieved: Criminal, Civil and Probate courts; Real Estate; Tax Liens/Judgments; UCC records

Local Retrieval Area: AZ-Coconino, Navajo

Add'l Information: Established 1989. Normal turnaround time- 24-48 hours in Coconino County; 48-72 hours in Navajo County. Projects billed by number of names searched. First project may require prepayment. Will file/record documents for clients. They specialize in skiptracing, process serving and civil and criminal investigations. A licensed PI in AZ. Performs service of process.

Northern Intermountain Security Inc

PO Box 4793, Ketchum, ID 83340
Phone: 208-726-2705 - **Fax:** 208-726-5802

Types of Records Retrieved: Criminal, Civil and Probate courts; Real Estate; Tax Liens/Judgments; UCC records; Vital records

Local Retrieval Area: ID-Blaine, Camas, Gooding, Jerome, Lincoln, Twin Falls. **Correspondent Relationships:** surrounding counties.

Add'l Information: Established 1994. Normal turnaround time- 24 hours. Expedited service available. Projects billed by number of records located. Performs service of process.

Northern Title of Vilas County

Box 877, Eagle River, WI 54521
Phone: 715-479-6459 - **Fax:** 715-477-2515

Types of Records Retrieved: Civil and Probate courts; Real Estate; Tax Liens/Judgments; UCC records

Local Retrieval Area: WI-Vilas

Add'l Information: Established 1975. Normal turnaround time- 2 days. Projects billed by number of names searched. Standard fees are charged for searches. They specialize in title, closing and escrow services.

Northshore Paralegal Services Inc

130 Centre St, Danvers, MA 01923
Phone: 800-883-6020; 978-750-6020 - **Fax:** 888-844-8135; 978-750-8135
www.nsps.com **email:** tlannon@nsps.com

Types of Records Retrieved: Criminal, Civil and Probate courts; Federal courts; Real Estate; Tax Liens/Judgments; UCC and corporate records; Vital records

Local Retrieval Area: MA-Barnstable, Berkshire, Bristol, Essex, Franklin, Hampden, Hampshire, Middlesex, Nantucket, Norfolk, Plymouth, Suffolk, Worcester. **Correspondent Relationships:** nationwide.

Add'l Information: Established 1987. Normal turnaround time- 1-2 business days. Expedited service available. Projects billed by number of names searched. First project may require prepayment. Credit cards accepted. Will file/record documents for clients. Payment due upon receipt of report/invoice. They specialize in current owner searches, corporate retrieval and filings, resident agent, court searches, UCC retrieval and filings on state and town levels. Performs service of process.

Northwest Abstract & Title Inc

PO Box 1265, Williston, ND 58802
Phone: 800-798-6723; 701-774-8829 - **Fax:** 701-774-9004
nwat@nemontel.net

Types of Records Retrieved: Civil courts; Real Estate; Tax Liens/Judgments; UCC records

Local Retrieval Area: ND-Burke, Dunn, Williams

Add'l Information: Established 1987. Normal turnaround time- 3 days. Projects billed by the hour. First project may require prepayment. Will file/record documents for clients. They specialize in abstracts, title insurance, real estate closings, escrow services and oil and gas titles.

Northwest Kansas Abstract & Title Co Inc

117 E 9th St, Goodland, KS 67735
Phone: 785-899-5641, cell- 785-821-3748 - **Fax:** 785-899-5670

Types of Records Retrieved: Criminal and Civil courts; Real Estate; Tax Liens/Judgments

Local Retrieval Area: KS-Sherman

Add'l Information: Established 1985. Normal turnaround time- 24-48 hours. Projects billed by number of names searched. Real estate search fees depend on nature of the request. Will file/record documents for clients. May be able to visit other counties in far NW Kansas.

NR&C

24 Preble St 2nd Fl, Portland, ME 04101
Phone: 207-791-2852 - **Fax:** 207-791-2858
www.nationwideresearch.com **email:** nrcinfo@maine.rr.com

Types of Records Retrieved: Criminal, Civil and Probate courts; Federal courts; Real Estate; Tax Liens/Judgments; UCC records

Local Retrieval Area: ME-Cumberland, Franklin, Kennebec, Oxford, York; NH-Carroll, Cheshire, Hillsborough, Merrimack, Rockingham. **Correspondent Relationships:** nationwide and international.

Add'l Information: Established 1997. Normal turnaround time- 24-48 hours. Projects billed by the hour. They specialize in litigation monitoring services, national bankruptcy information, due diligence and document retrieval.

NU West Investigations

5717 W Glendale Ave, Glendale, AZ 85301
Phone: 623-937-9676 - **Fax:** 623-937-8706
www.nuwestinvestigations.com **email:** royce_fowler@hotmail.com

Types of Records Retrieved: Criminal, Civil and Probate courts; Federal courts; Real Estate; Tax Liens/Judgments; UCC records; Vital records

Local Retrieval Area: AZ-Maricopa

Add'l Information: Established 1996. Normal turnaround time- 48 hours. Expedited service available. Projects billed by the hour. All projects require prepayment. Credit cards accepted. An investigative firm with full service, process service, fingerprinting, photographs, mystery shopping, court document retrieval, surveillance, background checks, debuggings and locates. Performs service of process.

NW Missouri Information Services

PO Box 8222, St Joseph, MO 64508-6334
Phone: 816-233-4779 - **Fax:** 816-233-6934 nwmis@csimokan.com

Types of Records Retrieved: Criminal, Civil and Probate courts; Federal courts; Real Estate; Tax Liens/Judgments; UCC records; Vital records

Local Retrieval Area: MO-Andrew, Atchison, Buchanan, Clay, Clinton, DeKalb, Holt, Jackson, Nodaway, Platte

Add'l Information: Established 1980. Normal turnaround time- 1-4 days depending on county. Projects billed by number of names searched. Fee basis will vary by the type and location (distance) of project. First project may require prepayment. Will file/record documents for clients. They specialize in real estate, civil and criminal records as well as process service and missing persons. Northwest Missouri Info Svcs performs the document retrieval; phone is 816-233-4779. Orders are NOT accepted by e-mail. A licensed PI in KS, MO. Performs service of process.

O & E Specialties Inc
140 Whitaker Rd, Lutz, FL 33549
Phone: 813-948-1354 - **Fax:** 813-948-1355
www.floridatitlesearch.com **email:** info@floridatitlesearch.com

Types of Records Retrieved: Civil courts; Real Estate; Tax Liens/Judgments; UCC records; Vital records

Local Retrieval Area: FL-Hillsborough, Pasco, Pinellas, Polk. **Correspondent Relationships:** statewide.

Add'l Information: Established 1986. Normal turnaround time- 4-12 hours. Projects billed by number of names searched. Credit cards accepted. They search Florida public records, specializing in ownership & encumbrance property reports. Cover 65 Florida counties.

O H Vivell Title Co
506 N Main St, Carrollton, IL 62016-0031
Phone: 217-942-3733 - **Fax:** 217-942-3207 ohvivell@earthlink.net

Types of Records Retrieved: Criminal, Civil and Probate courts; Real Estate; Tax Liens/Judgments; UCC records; Vital records

Local Retrieval Area: IL-Greene. **Correspondent Relationships:** Calhoun.

Add'l Information: Established 1891. Normal turnaround time- variable depending on project. Projects billed by number of records located. First project may require prepayment. Will file/record documents for clients.

Oberdier Search Services
5191 Wyandot Rd, Nevada, OH 44849
Phone: 740-361-7530 - **Fax:** 775-255-5839 crtrnr1@aol.com

Types of Records Retrieved: Civil and Probate courts; Real Estate; Tax Liens/Judgments; UCC records

Local Retrieval Area: OH-Allen, Crawford, Marion, Morrow, Wyandot. **Correspondent Relationships:** state of Ohio.

Add'l Information: Established 1992. Normal turnaround time- 24-72 hours. Projects billed by number of names searched. Will file/record documents for clients. Terms: net 30 days. She specializes in UCCs, federal & state tax liens, judgments, fixture filings, residential property searches & delinquent tax information. Document retrieval of court records available. Filing of UCCs, mortgages & deeds also available. E & O insurance.

Betty O'Brien
c/o County Clerk & Recorder, 320 W Main, Rm 5, Grangeville, ID 83530
Phone: 208-983-2751

Types of Records Retrieved: Criminal, Civil and Probate courts

Local Retrieval Area: ID-Idaho

Add'l Information: Established 2000. Normal turnaround time- 1-2 days. Projects billed by number of names searched. First project may require prepayment. She is intimately involved with the clerks office on a daily basis.

Rosemary O'Brien
8207 17th Ave, Adelphi, MD 20783
Phone: 301-434-4044; cell- 301-807-1809 - **Fax:** 301-434-9144
rosemary.obrien@verizon.net

Types of Records Retrieved: Criminal, Civil and Probate courts; Federal courts; Real Estate; Tax Liens/Judgments; UCC records; Vital records

Retrieval Area: MD-Anne Arundel, Howard, Montgomery, Prince George's

Add'l Information: Established 2000. Normal turnaround time- 3-5 days. Expedited service available. Hourly rate charged plus costs with a minimum of 1/2 hours. She is an independent paralegal, provide legal services for attorneys, i.e., physically search & retrieve documents from various state & county & federal offices. Also does Motor Vehicle record searches. Cell # is 301-807-1809 or 807-1721. Performs service of process.

Nikki A O'Connell
155 Princess Margaret Dr, Newport News, VA 23602
Phone: 757-877-8469 - **Fax:** 757-877-8469 searchvasenikki@aol.com

Types of Records Retrieved: Criminal, Civil and Probate courts; Federal courts; Real Estate; Tax Liens/Judgments; UCC records

Local Retrieval Area: VA-Hampton, James City, Newport News, York

Add'l Information: Normal turnaround time- 24-48 hours. Projects billed by number of names searched. Fees also determined by number of indexes. Will file/record documents for clients. Personal checks accepted. She specializes in UCC, judgment, tax liens, suits & property/title searches. She also does credit & construction reporting & document filings. Would consider search requests for Gloucester, Isle of Wight, Norfolk, Virginia Beach & Surry counties.

Ogemaw County Abstract Co
111 N 3rd St, West Branch, MI 48661
Phone: 989-345-0110 - **Fax:** 989-345-2907

Types of Records Retrieved: Real Estate; Tax Liens/Judgments

Local Retrieval Area: MI-Ogemaw

Add'l info: Established 1902. turnaround time- 3-5 business days. Projects billed by number of names searched. Or charge by legal descriptions First project may require prepayment. Will file/record documents for clients. Pre-payment required for searches. In business since 1902, they have the records in their office to provide fast and efficient service.

Ogemaw Title Co
PO Box 939, Standish, MI 48658-0939 **Phone:** 989-345-7240

Types of Records Retrieved: Criminal, Civil and Probate courts; Real Estate; Tax Liens/Judgments; UCC records; Vital records

Local Retrieval Area: MI-Arenac, Ogemaw

Add'l Information: Established 1987. Normal turnaround time- up to 1 week. Expedited service available. Fee basis will vary by the type of project. Will file/record documents for clients. They request prepay on out of area transactions. They specialize in title insurance and closing.

Ohio Title
250 S Prospect St, Ravenna, OH 44266
Phone: 330-297-7003 - **Fax:** 330-296-9644

Types of Records Retrieved: Civil and Probate courts; Real Estate; Tax Liens/Judgments; UCC records; Vital records

Local Retrieval Area: OH-Portage

Add'l Information: Established 1954. Normal turnaround time- 24 hours for most searches, and full real estate title searches average 3 working days. Fee basis will vary by type of project. Will file/record documents for clients. Personal checks are accepted.

Okeechobee Abstract & Title Ins Inc
207 NW 2nd St, Okeechobee, FL 34972-4115
Phone: 863-763-3710 - **Fax:** 863-763-3787

Types of Records Retrieved: Criminal, Civil and Probate courts; Real Estate; Tax Liens/Judgments; UCC records

Local Retrieval Area: FL-Glades, Okeechobee. **Correspondent Relationships:** Palm Beach, Martin, St. Lucie, Broward, Dade, Monroe counties.

Add'l Information: Established 1943. Normal turnaround time- same day for name and UCC searches; 2-3 days for real estate commitments. Projects billed by number of names searched. They are a family owned company that has been in business for over 50 years.

Okfusee Abstract & Title Co
320 W Broadway St, PO Box 66, Okemah, OK 74859
Phone: 918-623-0565 - **Fax:** 918-623-4022

Types of Records Retrieved: Civil and Probate courts; Real Estate; Tax Liens/Judgments; UCC records; Vital records

Local Retrieval Area: OK-Okfuskee
Add'l Information: Established 1991. Normal turnaround time- 2-3 days. Projects billed by the hour. Will file/record documents for clients.

Oklahoma Court Explorers

PO Box 2453, Muskogee, OK 74402
Phone: 918-360-4798 - **Fax:** 918-687-1899 jgann74401@yahoo.com
Types of Records Retrieved: Criminal and Civil courts; Federal courts; Real Estate; Tax Liens/Judgments
Local Retrieval Area: OK-Cherokee, Mayes, McIntosh, Muskogee, Rogers, Tulsa, Wagoner
Add'l Information: Established 1998. Normal turnaround time- 24-48 hours. Projects billed by number of names searched. First project may require prepayment. Will file/record documents for clients. Any information or documents you need will be obtained and returned to you as quickly as possible at a competitive price.

Theresa Olaires

12 Eastwind Dr, Buena Park, CA 90621
Phone: 714-595-4729 - **Fax:** 714-670-2156 tolairesresearch@yahoo.com
Types of Records Retrieved: Criminal, Civil and Probate courts; Federal courts; Real Estate; Tax Liens/Judgments; UCC records; Vital records
Local Retrieval Area: CA-Los Angeles, Orange
Add'l Information: Established 2001. Normal turnaround time- 1-2 days. Orders received after 10AM requesting same day turnaround is considered rush. Projects billed by number of names searched. Will charge by the hour on special projects. First project may require prepayment. Terms are net 15 days. They specialize in servicing other search companies in their document filings, UCCs, tax liens, judgments, property and all types of litigation searches. All searches are performed in person.

Oliver County Abstract

Box 105, Center, ND 58530
Phone: 701-794-3496 - **Fax:** 701-794-3476
Types of Records Retrieved: Civil and Probate courts; Federal courts; Real Estate; Tax Liens/Judgments; UCC records
Local Retrieval Area: ND-Mercer, Oliver
Add'l Information: Established 1910. Normal turnaround time- variable depending on project. Projects billed by the hour. A base rate is charged in addition to the hourly rate. First project may require prepayment. Professional credit extended to clients whose accounts are current. They specialize in title abstracts, lien searches and title memorandums.

Oliver, Yaskiw & Associates

Unit 15 - 1599 Dugald Rd, Winnipeg, Manitoba, Canada, CAN R2J 0H3
Phone: 866-245-5045; 204-942-8002 - **Fax:** 204-942-8220
www.oliveryaskiw.com **email:** goliver@oliveryaskiw.com
Types of Records Retrieved: Criminal, Civil and Probate courts; Federal court; Real Estate; UCC records; Tax Liens/Judgments; Vital records
Local Retrieval Area: CANADA-Manitoba. **Correspondent Relationships:** All Provinces.
Add'l Information: Established 1994. Normal turnaround time- 48 hours or less. Projects billed by number of names searched. Fee depends on nature of the request. Also has an office in Thunder Bay, Ontario (807-622-2221), and in Brandon, Manitoba. Part of the Investigations Canada group. A licensed PI in Manitoba. Performs service of process.

Olson & Humboldt County Abstract

PO Box 276, 503 Sumner Ave, Humboldt, IA 50548
Phone: 515-332-1593 - **Fax:** 515-332-3672
Types of Records Retrieved: Criminal, Civil and Probate courts; Real Estate; Tax Liens/Judgments; UCC records; Vital records
Local Retrieval Area: IA-Humboldt
Add'l Information: Established 1975. Normal turnaround time- 7-10 days. Projects billed by number of names searched. Fee basis depends upon type of project. First project may require prepayment. Will file/record documents for clients. They specialize in title searches.

Omni Data Retrieval Inc

20890 Kenbridge Ct, Lakeville, MN 55044
Phone: 952-985-7220 - **Fax:** 952-985-7211
www.omnidataretrieval.com **email:** sales@omnidataretrieval.com
Types of Records Retrieved: Criminal and Civil courts; US District court; Tax Liens/Judgments
Local Retrieval Area: MN-all counties. **Correspondents:** nationwide.
Add'l Information: Normal turnaround time- 24 hours. Payment due net 15 days from date of invoice. Credit cards accepted. They specialize in criminal background searches. Also have office in Rochester, 507-529-3693.

On the Record Inc

700 Youngstown-Warren Rd, Niles, OH 44446
Phone: 330-652-4109 - **Fax:** 330-652-4283
www.ontherecordonline.com/index.htm
email: webmaster@ontherecord.com
Types of Records Retrieved: Criminal, Civil and Probate courts; Federal courts; Real Estate; Tax Liens/Judgments; UCC records; Vital records
Local Retrieval Area: OH-Ashland, Ashtabula, Belmont, Carroll, Columbiana, Cuyahoga, Erie, Geauga, Harrison, Holmes, Huron, Jefferson, Lake, Lorain, Mahoning, Medina, Portage, Richland, Stark, Summit, Trumbull, Tuscarawas, Wayne. **Correspondent Relationships:** Ohio.
Add'l Information: Established 1999. Normal turnaround time- 24-48 hours. Charge by search type. Credit cards accepted. Will file/record documents for clients. Specialize in title abstracting, current owner (42-60 yrs), pre judicial reports, UCC/document retrieval, commercial real estate div & pre-employment div. Title attorneys on staff. Online ordering/tracking. Visit their website & real estate closing dept.

One Legal, Inc

504 Redwood Blvd #223, Novato, CA 94947
Phone: 800-938-8815; 415-491-0606 - **Fax:** 415-884-9954
www.onelegal.com **email:** support@onelegal.com
Records Retrieved: Criminal, Civil and Probate courts; Federal courts
Local Retrieval Area: CA-Alameda, Contra Costa, Fresno, Imperial, Kern, Kings, Los Angeles, Madera, Marin, Merced, Monterey, Napa, Orange, Placer, Riverside, Sacramento, San Bernardino, San Diego, San Francisco, San Joaquin, San Luis Obispo, San Mateo, Santa Barbara, Santa Clara, Santa Cruz, Solano, Sonoma, Stanislaus, Tulare, Ventura, Yolo. **Correspondent Relationships:** California, nationwide generally.
Add'l Information: Established 1990. Normal turnaround time- 3-5 days. Projects billed by the hour. Credit cards accepted. Will file/record documents for clients. Formerly Fax & File Legal Services Inc, they specialize in filing state court documents the same day and process service. They have 17 branches throughout California. Performs service of process.

Oneida Valley Abstract

PO Box 29, Court St, Wampsville, NY 13163
Phone: 315-363-1444 - **Fax:** 315-363-9547
Types of Records Retrieved: Real Estate; Tax Liens/Judgments; Probate courts; UCC records
Local Retrieval Area: NY-Madison
Add'l Information: Established 1986. Normal turnaround time- 48 hours. Fee basis will vary by years searched. Will file/record documents for clients. Personal checks are accepted.

Onistagrawa Abstracting Corp

PO Box 777, Middleburgh, NY 12122-0777
Phone: 518-827-8088 - **Fax:** 518-827-6566 oacorp@midtel.net
Types of Records Retrieved: Criminal, Civil and Probate courts; Real Estate; Tax Liens/Judgments
Local Retrieval Area: NY-Columbia, Delaware, Fulton, Greene, Montgomery, Otsego, Schenectady, Schoharie
Add'l Information: Established 1987. Normal turnaround time- 1-3 days for current owner, judgments, probate, simple deed/mortgage searches and full abstracts. Projects billed by number of names searched. The fee basis for real estate is figured on a per parcel basis.

Oplinger Abstract & Title Inc

PO Box 133, 155 Euclid St, Olivet, SD 57052
Phone: 605-387-2335 - **Fax:** 605-387-2337
Types of Records Retrieved: Criminal, Civil and Probate courts; Real Estate; Tax Liens/Judgments; UCC records; Vital records
Local Retrieval Area: SD-Hutchinson
Add'l Information: Established 1948. Normal turnaround time- 5 days. Projects billed by the hour. All projects require prepayment.

Orange Abstractor Services Co

222 Greenwich Ave, Goshen, NY 10924
Phone: 845-294-3331 - **Fax:** 845-294-8748 ngill2@hvc.rr.com
Types of Records Retrieved: Criminal, Civil and Probate courts; Federal courts; Real Estate; Tax Liens/Judgments; UCC records
Local Retrieval Area: NY-Orange
Add'l Information: Established 1984. Normal turnaround time- 1-14 days. Fee basis will vary by type of project. Will file/record documents for clients. Terms: net 30 days.

Orange County Abstract & Title Co Inc

204 E Main St, Paoli, IN 47454
Phone: 812-723-3044 - **Fax:** 812-723-3044
Types of Records Retrieved: Civil and Probate courts; Real Estate; Tax Liens/Judgments; UCC records
Local Retrieval Area: IN-Orange
Add'l Information: Established 1974. Normal turnaround time- 24-72 hours. Projects billed by number of names searched. Projects billed by the hour. First project may require prepayment. Personal checks accepted. They specialize in title searches and lien searches. They have been in business for 30 years.

Orange Paper Placers Inc

PO Box 22, 26 Scotchtown Ave, Goshen, NY 10924
Phone: 845-294-7810 - **Fax:** 845-294-3511
Types of Records Retrieved: Criminal, Civil and Probate courts; Real Estate; Tax Liens/Judgments; UCC records; Vital records
Retrieval Area: NY-Dutchess, Orange, Putnam, Rockland, Sullivan, Ulster
Add'l Information: Established 1976. Normal turnaround time- 4 days. Expedited service available. Projects billed by number of names searched. All projects require prepayment. They specialize in court services, getting judges signatures on court documents, etc. Performs service of process.

Dora Orum

4485 Andrews Ave, Fresno, CA 93726
Phone: 559-251-5193
Types of Records Retrieved: Criminal, Civil and Probate courts; Federal courts; Real Estate; Tax Liens/Judgments; UCC records; Vital records
Local Retrieval Area: CA-Fresno
Add'l Information: Established 1986. Normal turnaround time- 1-2 days. Fee basis is per search. First project may require prepayment. Will file/record documents for clients. She specializes in abstracting and public record searching in superior or federal court, which includes fictitious business name searches. Second contact person is Loretta Reyna at 559-253-0963; Fax 559-253-0363.

Kim Osborne

716 Cloud Springs Rd, Rossville, GA 30741
Phone: 706-935-4202 - **Fax:** 706-965-7431
Types of Records Retrieved: Criminal and Civil courts
Local Retrieval Area: GA-Catoosa
Add'l Information: Established 2000. Normal turnaround time- 24-48 hours. Projects billed by number of names searched. First project may require prepayment. She is an expert at Superior Court in Catoosa County.

Robert Osborne

43 Thomas Cove, Jackson, TN 38305
Phone: 731-664-6234 - **Fax:** 731-664-7710
Records Retrieved: Criminal and Civil courts; Tax Liens/Judgments
Local Retrieval Area: TN-Madison
Add'l Information: Established 1980s. Normal turnaround time- 24048 hours. Projects billed by number of names searched. More years of experience than anyone in the area.

Oscoda County Abstract Inc

PO Box 127, Mio, MI 48647
Phone: 989-826-5832 - **Fax:** 989-826-3294 ocainc@i2k.com
Types of Records Retrieved: Civil and Probate courts; Real Estate; Tax Liens/Judgments; UCC records
Local Retrieval Area: MI-Oscoda
Add'l Information: Established 1978. Normal turnaround time- 24 hours. Fee basis depends upon type of project. All projects require prepayment. Will file/record documents for clients. They specialize in title insurance.

William J O'Shea, PI

17895 Rt 37, West Frankfort, IL 62896
Phone: 618-937-3895 - **Fax:** 618-937-2805 osheas@midwest.net
Types of Records Retrieved: Criminal, Civil and Probate courts; Federal courts; Tax Liens/Judgments; Vital records
Local Retrieval Area: IL-Franklin, Williamson. **Correspondent Relationships:** Southern IL area.
Add'l Information: Established 1983. Normal turnaround time- 24-48 hours. Projects billed by number of names searched. All projects require prepayment. Credit cards accepted. Will file/record documents for clients. Volume billing available. He specializes in insurance investigation, video/still photography, process service, skiptracing, and So. IL Federal District Court records. A licensed PI with 17 years experience, also 20 years experience with the Chicago Police Dept. A licensed PI in IL. Performs service of process.

Otoe County Title Co

PO Box 488, Nebraska City, NE 68410
Phone: 402-873-5501 - **Fax:** 402-873-5622
Types of Records Retrieved: Criminal, Civil and Probate courts; Real Estate; Tax Liens/Judgments; UCC records
Local Retrieval Area: NE-Cass, Nemaha, Otoe
Add'l Information: Established 1965. Normal turnaround time- 1-2 days. They charge a flat fee per project. First project may require prepayment. Will file/record documents for clients. They specialize in title records.

Ouren Title Inc

1009 7th St, PO Box 229, Harlan, IA 51537-0229
Phone: 712-755-2174 - **Fax:** 712-755-3865
ourentitleinc@harlannet.com
Types of Records Retrieved: Real Estate; Tax Liens/Judgments; Probate courts; Vital records
Local Retrieval Area: IA-Shelby
Add'l Information: Established 1895. Normal turnaround time- 24 hours. Projects billed by number of names searched. Projects billed by number of records located. Will file/record documents for clients. Payment due upon receipt of billing. They specialize in preparing abstracts record ownership and lien reports. Can retrieve bankruptcy records if recorded in Recorders Office.

Owens & Associates Inv

2245 San Diego Ave #225, San Diego, CA 92110-2942
Phone: 800-297-1343; 619-297-1343 - **Fax:** 619-297-7622
www.owenspi.com **email:** wayne@owenspi.com
Types of Records Retrieved: Criminal, Civil and Probate courts; Federal courts; Real Estate; Tax Liens/Judgments; UCC records; Vital records
Local Retrieval Area: CA-San Diego. **Correspondents:** nationwide.
Add'l Information: Established 1988. Normal turnaround time- 24-48 hours. Projects billed by number of names searched. Projects billed by the hour. First project may require prepayment. Credit cards accepted. They offer on-site criminal and civil searches nationwide and worldwide full service investigations by former FBI agents and other law enforcement officers. A licensed PI in CA. Performs service of process.

Ozark Inv

3761 Spencer Creek Rd, Camdenton, MO 65020
Phone: 888-685-5366; 573-346-5366 - **Fax:** 417-532-9728
Types of Records Retrieved: Criminal and Civil courts
Local Retrieval Area: MO-Benton, Camden, Dallas, Hickory, Laclede, Miller, Morgan, Pulaski
Add'l Information: Established 1996. First project may require prepayment. The also provide court record retrieval, and private investigations Performs service of process.

P & A Research Service

10155 June Rd, St James, LA 70086
Phone: 225-279-2118 - **Fax:** 225-473-3723 ankum@cox.net
Types of Records Retrieved: Criminal and Civil courts; Federal courts; Real Estate; Tax Liens/Judgments; UCC records
Local Retrieval Area: LA-Ascension, Lafourche, St. Charles, St. James, St. John the Baptist
Add'l Information: Established 1994. Normal turnaround time- 12-24 hours; same day for Ascension if received by 4 PM. First project may require prepayment. Credit cards accepted. Will file/record documents for clients. Invoice on a monthly basis. They specialize in civil and criminal investigations, pre-employment screening and record retrieval. They are also a process server along the Louisiana area. Performs service of process.

P.S.P.S. Legal Support Services Inc

PO Box 520155, Winthrop, MA 02152
Phone: 617-846-7130 - **Fax:** 617-846-1017 ILQQK4DOE@worldnet.att.net
Types of Records Retrieved: Criminal, Civil and Probate courts; Federal courts; Real Estate; Tax Liens/Judgments; UCC records; Vital records; Voter registration records
Local Retrieval Area: MA-Essex, Middlesex, Suffolk. **Correspondent Relationships:** Norfolk and Plymouth counties MA
Add'l Information: Established 1995. Normal turnaround time- 2 days. Projects billed by number of names searched. Projects billed by the hour. Fees negotiated with volume. First project may require prepayment. Credit cards accepted. They specialize in background investigations, real estate due diligence, RE title abstracts, rule 4c process service and all manner of protective services. A licensed PI in MA. Performs service of process.

PAC Data LLC

PO Box 549, Milan, IN 47031
Phone: 812-654-3207 - **Fax:** 812-654-3649 pacubert@ureach.com
Types of Records Retrieved: Criminal and Civil courts; Real Estate; Tax Liens/judgment; Vital records
Local Retrieval Area: IN-Bartholomew, Brown, Dearborn, Decatur, Fayette, Franklin, Greene, Hamilton, Jackson, Jefferson, Jennings, Johnson, Lawrence, Marion, Monroe, Ohio, Perry, Porter, Ripley, Rush, Scott, Shelby, Steuben, Switzerland, Union, Wayne. **Correspondents in:** all counties in Indiana, Illinois, Kentucky, Ohio, and Tennessee.
Add'l Information: Established 1997. Normal turnaround time- within 48 hours usually. Projects billed by number of names searched. First project may require prepayment. They specialize in SE Central Indiana and southern counties near the border with state of Ohio, but can reach most anywhere in the state.

PAC Research

1840 41st Ave 102-243, Capitola, CA 95010
Phone: 831-475-7780 - **Fax:** 831-475-7781 peggy@pacresearch.net
Types of Records Retrieved: Criminal and Civil courts; Federal courts; Tax Liens/Judgments; UCC records
Local Retrieval Area: CA-Santa Clara, Santa Cruz
Add'l Information: Established 1997. Normal turnaround time- 24-48 hours. Projects billed by number of names searched. Fee basis depends upon type of project. Will file/record documents for clients. Terms net 30 days. End of month billing They are a family operation that provides quick turnaround, accurate results, and exceptional personalized service.

Walter J Pace

125 Linden St, Everett, MA 02149
Phone: 617-389-6730 - **Fax:** 617-389-5936 searchlink@webtv.net
Types of Records Retrieved: Criminal and Civil courts
Local Retrieval Area: MA-Middlesex, Suffolk
Add'l Information: Established 1996. Normal turnaround time- 24-48 hours. Projects billed by number of names searched. Terms are net 30 days. He specializes in criminal and civil court record searches and document retrieval.

Pacific Corporate & Title Services (Sacramento)

914 S St, Sacramento, CA 95814
Phone: 800-230-4988; 916-558-4988 - **Fax:** 800-230-2217; 916-441-2217
www.paccorp.com **email:** info@paccorp.com
Types of Records Retrieved: Civil and Probate courts; Federal courts; Real Estate; Tax Liens/Judgments; UCC records; Vital records
Local Retrieval Area: CA-Alameda, Contra Costa, El Dorado, Fresno, Los Angeles, Marin, Monterey, Napa, Orange, Placer, Riverside, Sacramento, San Bernardino, San Diego, San Francisco, San Joaquin, San Mateo, Santa Clara, Santa Cruz, Solano, Sonoma, Stanislaus, Yolo. **Correspondent Relationships:** nationwide.
Add'l Information: Established 1987. Normal turnaround time- 1-2 days. Projects billed by number of names searched. First project may require prepayment. Credit cards accepted. Will file/record documents for clients. Terms: Net 30 days for clients. They specialize in UCC, title and publishing and filing services. They also have 10 branch offices throughout California. They are registered agents.

Pacific NW Title of Alaska

3201 C St #110, Anchorage, AK 99503
Phone: 907-561-5122 - **Fax:** 907-261-2275
www.aktitle.com **email:** info@aktitle.com
Types of Records Retrieved: Real Estate; Tax Liens/Judgments
Local Retrieval Area: AK-Anchorage, Bethel, Bristol Bay, Iliamna, Kvichak, Valdez-Cordova. **Correspondent Relationships:** statewide.
Add'l Information: Normal turnaround time- 24 hours. Projects billed by the hour. All projects require prepayment. Will file/record documents for clients. They also have a branch in Eagle River, 907-696-5426.

Pacific Photocopy & Research (Ft. Lauderdale)

33 NE 2nd St #207, Ft Lauderdale, FL 33301-1036
Phone: 954-764-5646 - **Fax:** 954-764-5447
www.pacificphotocopy.com **email:** Legal@pacificphotocopy.com
Types of Records Retrieved: Criminal, Civil and Probate courts; Federal courts; Real Estate; Tax Liens/Judgments; UCC records; Vital records
Local Retrieval Area: FL-Broward. **Correspondents:** nationwide.
Add'l Information: Established 1972. Normal turnaround time- 2 days, 1 day, and Same Day options available. Fee basis will vary by the type of project. First project may require prepayment. Credit cards accepted. They specialize in bankruptcy court records as well as records in all departments of the circuit court.

Pacific Photocopy & Research (Jacksonville)

33 NE 2nd St #207, Ft Lauderdale, FL 33301-1036
Phone: 904-355-1062 - **Fax:** 904-355-0958
www.pacificphotocopy.com **email:** Legal@pacificphotocopy.com
Types of Records Retrieved: Criminal, Civil and Probate courts; Federal courts; Real Estate; Tax Liens/Judgments; UCC records; Vital records
Local Retrieval Area: FL-Baker, Bradford, Citrus, Clay, Columbia, Duval, Flagler, Hamilton, Marion, Nassau, Putnam, St Johns, Sumter, Suwannee, Union. **Correspondent Relationships:** nationwide.

Add'l Information: Established 1972. Normal turnaround time- 1 hour to availability of the file. Fee basis will vary by the type of project. All projects require prepayment. Will file/record documents for clients. They specialize in bankruptcy court records. Performs service of process.

Pacific Photocopy & Research (Miami)

33 N 2nd St #207, Fort Lauderdale, FL 33301
Phone: 305-371-7694 - **Fax:** 305-371-9657
www.pacificphotocopy.com **email:** Legal@pacificphotocopy.com

Types of Records Retrieved: Criminal, Civil and Probate courts; Federal courts; Real Estate; Tax Liens/Judgments; UCC records; Vital records

Local Retrieval Area: FL-Dade, Highlands, Indian River, Martin, Monroe, Okeechobee, St. Lucie. **Correspondents:** Florida and nationwide.

Add'l Information: Established 1972. Normal turnaround time- 1 hour to availability of the file. Fee basis will vary by the type of project. First project may require prepayment. Credit cards accepted. Will file/record documents for clients. They specialize in bankruptcy court records.

Pacific Photocopy & Research (Orlando)

129-9 Los Alamitos Ct, Orlando, FL 32837-6333
Phone: 407-425-7234 - **Fax:** 407-425-7218
www.pacificphotocopy.com **email:** Legal@pacificphotocopy.com

Types of Records Retrieved: Criminal, Civil and Probate courts; Federal courts; Real Estate; Tax Liens/Judgments; UCC records; Vital records

Local Retrieval Area: FL-Orange, Osceola, Seminole. **Correspondent Relationships:** nationwide.

Add'l Information: Established 1972. Normal turnaround time- same or next day. Fee basis will vary by the type of project. First project may require prepayment. Credit cards accepted. Will file/record documents for clients. They specialize in bankruptcy court records.

Pacific Photocopy & Research (Pensacola)

33 NE 2nd St #207, Fort Lauderdale, FL 33301
Phone: 850-435-3183 - **Fax:** 850-435-3185
www.pacificphotocopy.com **email:** Legal@pacificphotocopy.com

Types of Records Retrieved: Criminal, Civil and Probate courts; Federal courts; Real Estate; Tax Liens/Judgments; UCC records; Vital records

Local Retrieval Area: FL-Bay, Escambia, Okaloosa, Santa Rosa, Walton, Washington. **Correspondent Relationships:** nationwide.

Add'l info: Established 1972. Turnaround time- 24-48 hours depending on availability of file. Fee basis will vary by type of project. First project may require prepayment. Credit cards accepted. They specialize in bankruptcy court records and Federal court records as well as all County court records, including civil and criminal. Performs service of process.

Pacific Photocopy & Research (Tampa)

33 NE 2nd St #207, Ft Lauderdale, FL 33301
Phone: 813-221-6828 - **Fax:** 813-221-6678
www.pacificphotocopy.com **email:** Legal@pacificphotocopy.com

Types of Records Retrieved: Criminal, Civil and Probate courts; Federal courts; Real Estate; Tax Liens/Judgments; UCC records; Vital records

Local Retrieval Area: FL-Charlotte, Collier, Desoto, Glades, Hardee, Hendry, Hernando, Hillsborough, Lee, Manatee, Pasco, Pinellas, Polk, Sarasota. **Correspondent Relationships:** nationwide.

Add'l Information: Established 1982. Normal turnaround time- 1 hour to availability of the file. Fee basis will vary by the type of project. First project may require prepayment. Credit cards accepted. They specialize in bankruptcy court records.

Pacific Photocopy & Research (W. Palm Beach)

33 NE 2nd St #207, Fort Lauderdale, FL 33301
Phone: 561-832-3878 - **Fax:** 561-832-8035
www.pacificphotocopy.com **email:** Legal@pacificphotocopy.com

Types of Records Retrieved: Criminal, Civil and Probate courts; Federal courts; Real Estate; Tax Liens/Judgments; UCC records; Vital records

Local Retrieval Area: FL-Palm Beach. **Correspondents:** nationwide.

Add'l Information: Established 1972. Normal turnaround time- 1 hour to availability of the file. Fee basis will vary by type of project. First project may require prepayment. Credit cards accepted. Will file/record documents for clients. They specialize in bankruptcy court records.

Pacific Research & Retrieval Inc

28 N 1st St #700, San Jose, CA 95113-1210 **Phones:** 800-222-7040; 408-295-6800 - **Fax:** 408-295-6895 **email-** pacrsch@aol.com

Types of Records Retrieved: Criminal, Civil and Probate courts; Federal courts; Real Estate; Tax Liens/Judgments; UCC records; Vital records

Local Retrieval Area: CA-Alameda, Contra Costa, Marin, San Francisco, San Mateo, Santa Clara. **Correspondent Relationships:** nationwide.

Add'l Information: Established 1992. Normal turnaround time- 24 hours, but specializes in 1-2 hour service. Projects billed by number of names searched. Projects billed by the hour. Fees negotiable with volume. First project may require prepayment. Credit cards accepted. Will file/record documents for clients. Payment due net 30 days. They specialize in 1-2 HR rushes, also difficult document intensive research assignments, large copy or file is "unavailable" jobs. Regular and fax filings in state and federal courts. Performs service of process.

Pacific Security Intelligence

PO Box 2256, Portola, CA 96122
Phone: 530-832-0259 - **Fax:** 530-832-0209
www.pacificsecurityintelligence.com **email:** frank-psi@sbcglobal.net

Types of Records Retrieved: Criminal, Civil and Probate courts; Federal courts; Real Estate; Tax Liens/Judgments; UCC records; Vital records

Local Retrieval Area: NV-Carson City, Churchill, Clark, Douglas, Elko, Esmeralda, Eureka, Humboldt, Lander, Lincoln, Lyon, Mineral, Nye, Pershing, Storey, Washoe, White Pine

Add'l Information: Established 2003. Normal turnaround time- Washoe county, 7 hours, Clark county, 8 hours. Projects billed by number of names searched. First project may require prepayment. The Safe Group provides civil and criminal record searches in Nevada and security and investigations. A licensed PI in CA, NV.

Pacificsearch & Information

656 5th Ave #C, San Diego, CA 92101
Phone: 619-702-3334 - **Fax:** 619-702-3336 jgatto2457@aol.com

Types of Records Retrieved: Criminal, Civil and Probate courts; Federal courts; Real Estate; Tax Liens/Judgments; UCC records; Vital records

Local Retrieval Area: CA-Los Angeles, Orange, San Diego. **Correspondent Relationships:** Los Angeles and Orange counties.

Add'l Information: Established 1997. Normal turnaround time- 24 hours. Projects billed by number of names searched. Will file/record documents for clients.

PADIC Inc

1609 E Broadway, Gainesville, TX 76240
Phone: 940-665-6130 - **Fax:** 940-665-7486
www.padic.com **email:** padic@ntin.net

Types of Records Retrieved: Criminal, Civil and Probate courts; Federal courts; Real Estate; Tax Liens/Judgments; UCC records; Vital records

Local Retrieval Area: TX-Collin, Cooke, Dallas, Denton, Ellis, Grayson, Tarrant. **Correspondent Relationships:** nationwide.

Add'l Information: Established 1991. Normal turnaround time- 48 hours. Projects billed by number of names searched. First project may require prepayment. They specialize in document retrieval, asset searches, environmental investigations, surveillance, witness location and statements, computer database research and insurance defense investigation. A licensed PI in TX. Performs service of process.

Page County Abstract & Title Company

118 N 16th St, PO Box 180, Clarinda, IA 51632
Phone: 712-542-3613 - **Fax:** 712-542-2629 pagecoabst@iowatelecom.net

Types of Records Retrieved: Civil and Probate courts; Real Estate; Tax Liens/Judgments; UCC records

Local Retrieval Area: IA-Page

Add'l Information: Established 1989. Normal turnaround time- 48 hours. Fee basis will vary by the type of project. Will file/record documents for clients. Personal checks are accepted. They specialize in searching county records and abstracting real estate titles.

Pallorium Inc

PO Box 155, Brooklyn, NY 11230
Phone: 212-969-0286 - **Fax:** 212-858-5720
www.pallorium.com **email:** pallorium@pallorium.com

Types of Records Retrieved: Criminal, Civil and Probate courts; Real Estate; Tax Liens/Judgments; Vital records

Local Retrieval Area: NY-Bronx, Kings, Nassau, New York, Queens, Richmond, Suffolk, Westchester. **Correspondent Relationships:** San Antonio and Los Angeles, USA. Also Toronto, Canada, Hong Kong, Bangkok, Thailand, all of Israel, and add'l countries.

Add'l Information: Established 1980. Normal turnaround time- 1-3 days. Projects billed by the hour. First project may require prepayment. Terms: net 30 days. They maintain an online investigative support system with criminal, voter, credit, MVR, corporate telephone, and other records. They also maintain an online network of 850+ investigative agencies. They have offices in USA, Canada, Israel and Hong Kong. A licensed PI in CA, LA, NY, TX. Performs service of process.

Palmer & Murrie Abstract Co Inc

PO Box 337, 506 N. Market St, Marion, IL 62959
Phone: 618-993-3866 - **Fax:** 618-993-3015
www.palmermurrie.com **Types of Records Retrieved:** Real Estate; Tax Liens/Judgments; UCC records

Local Retrieval Area: IL-Franklin, Jefferson, Johnson, Massac, Saline, Union, Williamson. **Correspondent Relationships:** Jackson, Galatin, Hamilton, Hardin, Pope, Pulaski counties.

Add'l info: Established 1962. Normal turnaround time- 5-6 working days. Projects billed by number of names searched. Projects billed by number of records located. Projects billed by the hour. Personal checks are accepted.

Palmer Abstract Inc

19 1st Ave NW, Waukon, IA 52172
Phone: 563-568-3488 - **Fax:** 563-568-5055

Types of Records Retrieved: Criminal, Civil and Probate courts; Real Estate; Tax Liens/Judgments; UCC records; Vital records

Local Retrieval Area: IA-Allamakee

Add'l Information: Established 1925. Normal turnaround time- 48 hours. Projects billed by number of names searched. Projects billed by number of records located. Projects billed by the hour.

Palmer Investigative Services

PO Box 10760, Prescott, AZ 86304-0760
Phone: 800-280-2951; 928-778-2951 - **Fax:** 800-215-7049; 928-445-7204
www.palmerinvestigative.com **email:** magnum@cableone.net

Types of Records Retrieved: Criminal, Civil and Probate courts; Federal courts; Real Estate; Tax Liens/Judgments; UCC records

Local Retrieval Area: AZ-Yavapai. **Correspondent Relationships:** Coconino, Maricopa, Mohave counties AZ. Can retrieve adoption records.

Add'l info: Established 1980. Turnaround time- 48 hours. Expedited service available. Excessive document retrieval is charged by the hour; per name for initial search. All projects require prepayment. Credit cards accepted. Will file/record documents for clients. Regular clients may arrange for credit. They specialize in investigations, legal process serving and drug and alcohol testing. They can retrieve UCC, recorder and Secretary of State records. A licensed PI in AZ. Performs service of process.

Palo Alto County Abstract Co

1009-1011 Broadway St, Emmetsburg, IA 50536
Phone: 712-852-4313 - **Fax:** 712-852-4313

Types of Records Retrieved: Criminal, Civil and Probate courts; Federal District courts; Real Estate; Tax Liens/Judgments; UCC records

Local Retrieval Area: IA-Palo Alto

Add'l Information: Established 1800. Normal turnaround time- variable depending on project. Fee basis will vary by the type of project. Will file/record documents for clients.

Palo Verde Research

15260 Shamrock Dr, Ft Myers, FL 33912
Phone: 239-481-9434 - **Fax:** 239-481-9890
info@paloverderesearch.com

Types of Records Retrieved: Criminal, Civil and Probate courts; Real Estate; Tax Liens/Judgments; UCC records

Local Retrieval Area: FL-Charlotte, Collier, Hendry, Lee

Add'l Information: Established 1993. Normal turnaround time- 24-48 hours. Projects billed by number of names searched. First project may require prepayment. They specialize in real estate records.

Paper Chase LLC

PO Box 2331, 690 Larson St, Friday Harbor, WA 98250
Phone: 360-378-3345 - **Fax:** 360-378-9732
paperchase@centurytel.net

Types of Records Retrieved: Criminal and Civil courts

Local Retrieval Area: WA-San Juan

Add'l Information: Established 1993. Normal turnaround time- 1-2 days. Fee basis varies by type of transaction. First project may require prepayment. Will file/record documents for clients. Located in the county seat of Friday Harbor, we offer a variety of courthouse services as well as county wide service of process. Performs service of process.

Paper Trail Information Services Inc

PO Box 4715, Lafayette, IN 47905
Phone: 866-623-7238; 765-471-4999 - **Fax:** 866-901-6008; 765-471-2666
papertrailinfo@aol.com

Types of Records Retrieved: Criminal and Civil courts

Local Retrieval Area: IN-Boone, Hamilton, Hendricks, Putnam, Tippecanoe

Add'l info: Established 2003. Turnaround time- 24-48 hours. Expedited service available. Projects billed by number of names searched. First project may require prepayment. They specialize in criminal & civil courts.

Paragon Document Research Inc

PO Box 65216, St Paul, MN 55165
Phone: 800-892-4235; 651-222-6844 - **Fax:** 800-847-7369; 651-222-2281
www.banc.com/pdrstore/ **email:** paragoninc@qwest.net

Types of Records Retrieved: Criminal and Civil courts; Federal courts; Real Estate; Tax Liens/Judgments; UCC records

Local Retrieval Area: MN-All counties. **Correspondent Relationships:** nationwide (state and county level), Canada, International.

Add'l Information: Established 1990. Normal turnaround time- 24-48 hours. Expedited service available. Projects billed by number of names searched. Research projects are billed by the hour. First project may require prepayment. Credit cards accepted. Will file/record documents for clients. Will bill clients on a monthly basis. They specialize in notification letter processing, UCC e-filing, corporate documents and registered agent services nationwide. They offer nationwide MVR service/real property searches, background profiles and detective referral services. A licensed PI in MN. Performs service of process.

Paralegal Enterprises Inc

401 W First St #2-D, Greenville, NC 27835
Phone: 252-758-6622 - **Fax:** 252-758-6622

Types of Records Retrieved: Civil and Probate courts; Real Estate; Tax Liens/Judgments; UCC records; Vital records

Local Retrieval Area: NC-Greene, Pitt

Add'l Information: Established 1991. Normal turnaround time- 48 hours. Projects billed by number of names searched. Projects billed by the hour. Fee basis will vary with portions of tracts of land. First project may require prepayment. Will file/record documents for clients. They specialize in real estate searches.

Paralegal Field Research Service

330 Clematis St #209, West Palm Beach, FL 33401
Phone: 800-256-7459; 561-832-5770 - **Fax:** 561-832-1857
www.pfrsinvestigations.com **email:** shapka@adelphia.net

Records Retrieved: Criminal, Civil and Probate courts; Federal courts

Local Retrieval Area: FL-Palm Beach. **Correspondent Relationships:** Florida.

Add'l Information: Established 1989. Normal turnaround time- variable depending on project. Projects billed by number of names searched. Projects billed by number of records located. Projects billed by the hour. All projects require prepayment. Credit cards accepted. Will file/record documents for clients. They specialize in criminal investigations and mitigation investigations (Capital cases). Mobile phone # is: 561-714-8255. A licensed PI in FL. Performs service of process.

Paralegal Resource Center Inc

4 Faneuil Hall Marketplace, Boston, MA 02109
Phone: 866-742-1939; 617-742-1939 - **Fax:** 617-742-1417
www.paralegalboston.com **email:** prc@paralegalboston.com

Types of Records Retrieved: Criminal, Civil and Probate courts; Federal courts; Real Estate; Tax Liens/Judgments; UCC records; Vital records; Corporate documents

Local Retrieval Area: MA-Essex, Middlesex, Norfolk, Plymouth, Suffolk, Worcester. **Correspondents:** outside Greater Boston and New England.

Add'l Information: Established 1976. Normal turnaround time- 1-3 business days. Expedited service available. Projects billed by number of names searched. Projects billed by number of records located. Projects billed by the hour. First project may require prepayment. Will file/record documents for clients. They specialize in UCC, corporate records, state & federal tax lien searches & document retrieval of all court records at all Massachusetts courthouses & public records at state agencies. They also provide permanent & temporary paralegal staffing.

Paralegal Services (Berkeley Springs)

1787 Spohrs Rd, Berkeley Springs, WV 25411
Phone: 304-676-5550 - **Fax:** 304-258-4287 pperry21@cox.net

Records Retrieved: Real Estate; Tax Liens/Judgments; UCC records

Local Retrieval Area: WV-Berkeley, Morgan

Add'l Information: Established 1989. Normal turnaround time- 24-48 hours. Expedited service available. Projects billed by number of names searched. First project may require prepayment. Will file/record documents for clients. They will bill monthly. They specialize in real estate title work, with 20 years of experience. They also assist in civil and criminal litigation, trial preparation and summarizing depositions.

Paralegal Services Inc

PO Box 118, 100 Hillcrest Dr, Marion, NC 28752
Phone: 828-606-8297 - **Fax:** 828-659-2502 unc45mom@aol.com

Types of Records Retrieved: Criminal, Civil and Probate courts; Federal courts; Real Estate; Tax Liens/Judgments; UCC records; Vital records

Local Retrieval Area: NC-Buncombe, Henderson, McDowell, Mitchell, Polk, Rutherford

Add'l Information: Established 1995. Normal turnaround time- 6-12 hours. Projects billed by number of names searched. Will file/record documents for clients. Terms are net 30 days. Above phone number is the primary number (cell number) and the other local number is 828-659-3508.

Paralegal Services of Buffalo

424 Main St Rm 1133, Buffalo, NY 14202-3611
Phone: 716-822-3279 - **Fax:** 716-853-0184
www.paralegalservicesofbuffalo.com **email:** para@adelphia.net

Types of Records Retrieved: Criminal, Civil and Probate courts; Federal courts; Real Estate; Tax Liens/Judgments; UCC records; Vital records

Local Retrieval Area: NY-Erie, Niagara. **Correspondents:** nationwide.

Add'l Information: Established 1976. Normal turnaround time- 1 day. Projects billed by number of names searched. First project may require prepayment. Will file/record documents for clients. They specialize in criminal records, civil searches, real estate related and document retrieval in all courts. They also retrieve DMV insurance, title and license information. They have been in business since 1976.

Paralegal Services of North Carolina Inc

120 Penmarc Dr #118, Raleigh, NC 27603
Phone: 919-821-7762 - **Fax:** 919-832-6378
www.psnc.net **email:** psnc@bellsouth.net

Types of Records Retrieved: Criminal, Civil and Probate courts; Federal courts; Real Estate; Tax Liens/Judgments; UCC records; Vital records

Local Retrieval Area: NC-Alamance, Chatham, Cumberland, Durham, Franklin, Guilford, Harnett, Johnston, Nash, Orange, Wake, Wayne. **Correspondent Relationships:** statewide.

Add'l Information: Established 1988. Normal turnaround time- 1-3 days. Projects billed by number of names searched. Invoice due in 30 days. First project may require prepayment. Will file/record documents for clients. They specialize in real property, asset/lien searches, probate and process service, and Secretary of State filings and information searches. They cover every county in North Carolina either hands on or by agent. A licensed PI in NC. Performs service of process.

Paralegal Services Point Pleasant

RR 2 Box 65, Point Pleasant, WV 25550-4775
Phone: 304-675-4008 - **Fax:** 304-675-4008
masoncoclerk@eurekanet.com

Types of Records Retrieved: Real Estate; Tax Liens/Judgments; Probate courts; UCC records; Vital records

Local Retrieval Area: WV-Mason

Add'l Information: Established 1988. Normal turnaround time- 24-48 hours. Projects billed by number of names searched. Net 10 days from receipt of invoice. Will file/record documents for clients. Specialize in Real Estate.

Parasearch Inc

222 Jefferson Blvd, Warwick, RI 02888
Phone: 401-732-2490 - **Fax:** 800-739-7740; 401-739-7708
www.para-search.com **email:** richd@para-search.com

Types of Records Retrieved: Criminal, Civil and Probate courts; Federal courts; Real Estate; Tax Liens/Judgments; UCC records

Local Retrieval Area: RI-Kent, Newport, Providence, Washington. **Correspondent Relationships:** nationwide.

Add'l Information: Established 1987. Normal turnaround time- 24-48 hours. Projects billed by number of names searched. First project may require prepayment. Terms: net 30 days. They specialize in UCC searches, state, cities, towns corporate document filings and procurement.

Parasec (California)

640 Bercut Dr #A, Sacramento, CA 95814
Phone: 800-533-7272; 916-441-1001 - **Fax:** 800-603-5868; 916-447-6091
www.parasec.com **email:** parasec@parasec.com

Types of Records Retrieved: Criminal, Civil and Probate courts; Federal courts; Real Estate; Tax Liens/Judgments; UCC records; Vital records

Local Retrieval Area: CA-Los Angeles, Orange, Sacramento. **Correspondent Relationships:** nationwide.

Add'l Information: Established 1977. Normal turnaround time- 24-72 hours. Projects billed by number of names searched. Projects billed by number of records located. Projects billed by the hour. Credit cards accepted. Will file/record documents for clients. Personal checks are accepted. They specialize in UCC, corporate, limited partnership, real estate and litigation. They are qualified to do business in all 50 states & act as Agent for Service of Process in all states.

Parasec (Nevada)

318 N Carson St, #208, Carson City, NV 89701
Phone: 888-972-7273; 775-883-0104 - **Fax:** 888-886-7168; 775-883-0340
www.parasec.com **email:** nv@parasec.com

Types of Records Retrieved: Civil courts; Federal District courts; Tax Liens/Judgments; UCC records

Local Retrieval Area: NV-Carson City, Douglas. **Correspondent Relationships:** nationwide.

Add'l Information: Established 1996. Normal turnaround time- 24-72 hours. Projects billed by number of names searched. For credit card payment, VISA, MC, AmEx only. First project may require prepayment. Credit cards accepted. Will file/record documents for clients. They specialize in Nevada document filing, retrieval, and searching except for real estate documents.

Parker Legal Services

1379 E Riviera Dr, Mobile, AL 36605

Phone: 251-476-7464 - **Fax:** 251-473-7309 wkp1@aol.com

Types of Records Retrieved: Criminal, Civil and Probate courts; Federal courts; Real Estate; Tax Liens/Judgments; UCC records; Vital records

Local Retrieval Area: AL-Baldwin, Mobile

Add'l Information: Established 1995. Normal turnaround time- 24-48 hours. Projects billed by number of names searched. Projects billed by number of records located. First project may require prepayment. Will file/record documents for clients. They specialize in legal research, process service, civil and criminal investigations as well as loss prevention and process service. A licensed PI in FL. Performs service of process.

Susan Parker

PO Box 708, Union City, TN 38261

Phone: 731-884-9994 - **Fax:** 731-884-2774 sptitlesearches@gmail.com

Types of Records Retrieved: Civil and Probate courts; Federal courts; Real Estate; Tax Liens/Judgments; UCC records

Local Retrieval Area: KY-Fulton, Hickman, TN-Benton, Carroll, Crockett, Dyer, Gibson, Haywood, Henry, Humphreys, Lake, Lauderdale, Madison, Obion, Stewart, Tipton, Weakley

Add'l Information: Established 1991. Normal turnaround time- 1-2 days. Projects billed by number of names searched. Will file/record documents for clients. She has searched courthouse records for over 20 years. Staff brings 30 years of combined experience. Also handle witness real estate closings.

Parrish Research

1447 Alabama St, Navarre, FL 32566-7100

Phone: 850-936-1240 - **Fax:** 850-939-7282

parrishresearch@mchsi.com

Types of Records Retrieved: Criminal, Civil and Probate courts; Federal courts; Real Estate; Tax Liens/Judgments; UCC records; Vital records

Local Retrieval Area: AL-Baldwin, Clarke, Coffee, Conecuh, Covington, Dale, Escambia, Geneva, Henry, Houston, Jefferson, Mobile, Monroe, Pike, St Clair, Shelby, Tuscaloosa; FL-Bay, Calhoun, Escambia, Franklin, Gadsden, Gulf, Holmes, Jackson, Leon, Liberty, Okaloosa, Santa Rosa, Wakulla, Walton, Washington

Add'l Information: Established 1999. Normal turnaround time- 24 hours. Projects billed by number of records located. Payment due when project completed.

Parsley Enterprises Inc

4527 S 450 W, Trafalgar, IN 46181

Phone: 317-878-9979 - **Fax:** 317-878-5514 parcelli@aol.com

Types of Records Retrieved: Civil courts; Real Estate; Tax Liens/Judgments

Local Retrieval Area: IN-Bartholomew, Brown, Decatur, Hancock, Jackson, Jennings, Johnson, Marion, Scott, Shelby

Add'l Information: Normal turnaround time- 24-hours. Projects billed by number of names searched. First project may require prepayment. They specialize in mortgage and assignment retrieval.

PAT Research

PO Box 305, Charlestown, WV 25414

Phone: 304-725-4845 - **Fax:** 304-728-3969 patdickeus@aol.com

Records Retrieved: Criminal and Civil courts; Tax Liens/Judgments

Local Retrieval Area: WV-Berkeley, Jefferson

Add'l Information: Normal turnaround time- 1-2 days. Projects billed by number of names searched. Monthly billing available. They specialize in local court records.

Patricia Chambers Inv

PO Box 211, Canyon, TX 79015

Phone: 806-258-7555, cell- 806-671-5221 - **Fax:** 806-258-7635

pchambers@wtrt.net

Types of Records Retrieved: Criminal, Civil and Probate courts; Federal courts; Real Estate; Tax Liens/Judgments; UCC records

Local Retrieval Area: TX-Deaf Smith, Potter, Randall

Add'l info: Established 1990. Normal turnaround time- 24 hours, exception on Holidays. Projects billed by number of names searched. First project may require prepayment. Billed monthly. They have been business since 1990. Conduct civil, criminal & background investigations. They provide public record searches made in person at county, district, and federal levels. NAPBS member. A licensed PI in TX. Performs service of process.

Patterson Investigations Inc

PO Box 893, Wenatchee, WA 98807

Phone: 509-884-7531 - **Fax:** 509-884-7531

Types of Records Retrieved: Criminal and Civil courts

Local Retrieval Area: WA-Chelan, Douglas, Grant, Okanogan

Add'l Information: Established 1994. First project may require prepayment. They also provide court filings, photocopying, skiptracing, private investigations, and asset searches. A licensed PI in WA. Performs service of process.

Patton Investigative Agency Inc

PO Box 1321, Jensen Beach, FL 34958

Phone: 772-398-1227

www.flaprivateinvestigations.com **email:** pattonpi@adelphia.net

Types of Records Retrieved: Criminal, Civil and Probate courts; Real Estate; Tax Liens/Judgments; UCC records; Vital records

Local Retrieval Area: FL-Martin, Okeechobee, St Lucie

Add'l Information: Established 2003. Normal turnaround time- 24-48 hours. Expedited service available. Projects billed by number of names searched. First project may require prepayment. Full service private investigative agency specializing in domestic relations. Principles have extensive background in legal, police (law enforcement) and certified public accountant fields. A licensed PI in FL. Performs service of process.

Paul C Klumb Agency LLC

1100 W Wells St #1807, Milwaukee, WI 53233

Phone: 414-254-1335 - **Fax:** 888-755-6415 pklumb@msn.com

Types of Records Retrieved: Criminal, Civil and Probate courts; Federal courts; Real Estate; Tax Liens/Judgments; UCC records; Vital records

Local Retrieval Area: WI-Dane, Dodge, Jefferson, Kenosha, Milwaukee, Ozaukee, Racine, Walworth, Washington, Waukesha. **Correspondent Relationships:** national and international.

Add'l Information: Established 1994. Normal turnaround time- 48 hours. Expedited service available. Projects billed by number of names searched. Projects billed by the hour. First project may require prepayment. Credit cards accepted. Will file/record documents for clients. They prefer payment by credit card. Specializes in competitive intelligence, municipal records, hidden assets, informal business relationships, video GPS or electronic surveillance and digital imaging. Also, he is certified for paint inspection and risk assessor. E&O insured. Notary. A licensed PI in WI.

Paul Maisano Designs

6770 Berwick Dr, Clarkston, MI 48346

Phone: 248-625-6366 - **Fax:** 248-625-5098

www.paulmaisanodesigns.com **email:** vickey@paulmaisanodesigns.com

Types of Records Retrieved: Civil and Probate courts; Federal courts; Real Estate; Tax Liens/Judgments; UCC ecords

Local Retrieval Area: MI-Bay, Calhoun, Clinton, Eaton, Genesee, Ingham, Jackson, Kalamazoo, Kent, Lapeer, Livingston, Macomb, Monroe, Oakland, Ottawa, Saginaw, Shiawassee, St. Clair, Washtenaw, Wayne. **Correspondent Relationships:** statewide, and IN,OH,KY,IA,MO, KS,CO.

Add'l info: Established 2001. Normal turnaround time- 24-48 hours. Projects billed by number of names searched. Will file/record documents for clients. Net 10 days after bill. They provide public record document retrieval for all of MI including current owner, UCC & fixtures, tax liens, and judgments. They also do filings. Any volume. Accurate, reliable results.

Pawnee County Abstract Co

637 G St, Pawnee City, NE 68420
Phone: 402-852-2035 - **Fax:** 402-852-2035
Types of Records Retrieved: Criminal, Civil and Probate courts; Real Estate; Tax Liens/Judgments; UCC records
Local Retrieval Area: NE-Pawnee
Add'l Information: Established 1976. Turnaround time- variable depending on project. Projects billed by number of names searched. Projects billed by number of records located. Will file/record documents for clients.

PC Abstracting

79 Axworthy Ln, Goshen, NY 10924-5019
Phone: 845-699-6107 - **Fax:** 845-294-9532 pcabstracting@yahoo.com
Types of Records Retrieved: Criminal and Civil courts; Real Estate; Tax Liens/Judgments; UCC records
Local Retrieval Area: NY-Dutchess, Orange, Putnam, Rockland, Sullivan, Westchester
Add'l Information: Established 1999. Normal turnaround time- 24 hours. Projects billed by number of names searched. First project may require prepayment. They are friendly, fast, reliable with reasonable rates.

PDQ Legal Services Inc

7720 E Evans Rd #107, Scottsdale, AZ 85260
Phone: 480-556-6660 - **Fax:** 480-556-6661
www.pdqlegal.com **email:** bmadanick@pdqlegal.com
Types of Records Retrieved: Criminal courts
Local Retrieval Area: AZ-Apache, Cochise, Coconino, Gila, Graham, Greenlee, La Paz, Maricopa, Mohave, Navajo, Pima, Pinal, Santa Cruz, Yavapai, Yuma. **Correspondent Relationships:** statewide.
Add'l Information: Established 1996. Normal turnaround time- 24 hours. Possible same day if received by 9am MST. Projects billed by number of names searched. They specialize in a fast, true prehire program that included speed, accuracy & economy. Their goal is to win your confidence daily through the quality and timeliness of every background request. They have researchers in the courthouse daily. A licensed PI in AZ.

Pearl Information Services

110 Park St, Portland, ME 04101
Phone: 207-775-5889 - **Fax:** 207-512-1399
www.pearlinformation.com **email:** pearl@maine.rr.com
Types of Records Retrieved: Criminal, Civil and Probate courts; Federal courts; Real Estate; Tax Liens/Judgments; UCC records; Vital records
Local Retrieval Area: ME-Androscoggin, Cumberland, Kennebec, Knox, Sagadahoc, York
Add'l Information: Established 2000. Normal turnaround time- 48-72 hours. Expedited service available. Projects billed by number of names searched. Projects billed by the hour. First project may require prepayment. Credit cards accepted. They provide business research including competitive intelligence, asset searches, corporate profiles, employment screening and due diligence.

Pebble Beach Enterprises

PO Box 2346, Bakersfield, CA 93303
Phone: 661-301-7979 - **Fax:** 661-326-0361 ahashim@adavcoinc.com
Types of Records Retrieved: Civil and Probate courts; Real Estate; Tax Liens/Judgments; Vital records
Local Retrieval Area: CA-Kern
Add'l Information: Established 2004. Normal turnaround time- same day. Projects billed by number of names searched. Will file/record documents for clients. They specialize in document recording and retrieval. Licensed PI. A licensed PI in CA, FL.

Jean Peck

1735 N Park Ave, Fremont, NE 68025
Phone: 402-721-4143 - **Fax:** 402-753-9255
Types of Records Retrieved: Criminal, Civil and Probate courts; Real Estate; Tax Liens/Judgments; UCC records; Vital records
Local Retrieval Area: NE-Dodge, Saunders, Washington; TX-Hidalgo (from Nov-April [956-381-9203])
Add'l Information: Established 1996. Normal turnaround time- 24 hours. Projects billed by number of names searched. Will file/record documents for clients. Statements sent end of month. Performs service of process.

Richard Peek Jr Attny

PO Box 8, Smithland, KY 42081
Phone: 270-928-4523 - **Fax:** 270-928-2717 peeklaw@heis.net
Types of Records Retrieved: Real Estate; Tax Liens/Judgments
Local Retrieval Area: KY-Livingston
Add'l Information: Established 1974. First project may require prepayment. He specializes in real estate.

Daniel E Peel

155 W Harvard St #101, Fort Collins, CO 80525
Phone: 970-377-8500 - **Fax:** 970-377-8502 danpeel@qwest.net
Types of Records Retrieved: Civil and Probate courts; Federal courts; Real Estate; Tax Liens/Judgments; UCC records
Local Retrieval Area: CO-Larimer, Weld; WY-Albany, Laramie, Natrona, Sheridan; other CO and WY counties are available by arrangement. **Correspondent Relationships:** correspondents in Rocky Mt. region.
Add'l Information: Established 1982. Normal turnaround time- 24-48 hours, or by arrangement. Net 30 days. They specialize in current owner searches in CO, WY and OR. Other searches by arrangement.

Pellish & Pellish Attorneys at Law

809 W Market St, Pottsville, PA 17901
Phone: 570-622-2338 - **Fax:** 570-622-2339
www.pellishlaw.com **email:** rpellish@pellishlaw.com
Types of Records Retrieved: Criminal, Civil and Probate courts; Real Estate; Tax Liens/Judgments; UCC records; Vital records
Local Retrieval Area: PA-Schuylkill
Add'l Information: Established 1978. Normal turnaround time- 1-14 days. Projects billed by the hour. First project may require prepayment. Personal checks are accepted. They specialize in assured, accurate and prompt service. They have an experienced staff.

Penncorp Service Group Inc

600 N 2nd St #500, Harrisburg, PA 17101
Phone: 800-544-9050; 717-234-2300 - **Fax:** 800-264-1137; 717-238-8232
penncorp@ezonline.com
Types of Records Retrieved: Civil and Probate courts; Federal courts; Real Estate; Tax Liens/Judgments; UCC records; Vital records
Local Retrieval Area: PA-Cumberland, Dauphin. **Correspondent Relationships:** nationwide and Canada.
Add'l Information: Established 1987. Normal turnaround time- 24 hours. If certification is needed, allow 3-7 days. Projects billed by number of names searched. Credit cards accepted. Will file/record documents for clients. Personal checks accepted. They specialize in working with the Pennsylvania State Corp. Bureau and Dept. of Transportation. All state search requests are completed within 24 hours or less.

Pennington County Abstract Co

PO Box 508, Thief River Falls, MN 56701
Phone: 218-681-2527 - **Fax:** 218-681-2528
www.pcabstract.com **Types of Records Retrieved:** Federal courts; Real Estate; Tax Liens/Judgments
Local Retrieval Area: MN-Marshall, Pennington
Add'l Information: Normal turnaround time- variable depending on project. Fee basis will vary by type of project. They provide abstracting, searches, title insurance, and closing services.

Penninsula Title & Abstract Corp

15 S 4th St, Crystal Falls, MI 49920
Phone: 906-875-6618 - **Fax:** 906-875-4382
Records Retrieved: Real Estate; Tax Liens/Judgments; UCC records
Local Retrieval Area: MI-Iron, Ontonagon
Add'l Information: Established 1974. Normal turnaround time- 1 day. Fee basis will vary by type of project. All projects require prepayment. Will file/record documents for clients. They specialize in real estate.

PeopleSearch

PO Box 873, Waukegan, IL 60079
Phone: 877-835-1983; 847-360-0360 - **Fax:** 847-623-3501
peoplesearch@comcast.net
Types of Records Retrieved: Criminal, Civil and Probate courts; Real Estate; Tax Liens/Judgments; UCC records; Vital records
Local Retrieval Area: IL-Lake; WI-Kenosha. **Correspondent Relationships:** McHenry county, IL.
Add'l Information: Established 1995. Normal turnaround time- 24 hours. Usually same day. Projects billed by number of names searched. First project may require prepayment. Credit cards accepted. They have 30 years genealogical research experience, adoption research and do skiptracing, missing relatives, etc, as well as 13+ years of background/courthouse research. Principal of company is a Confidential Intermediary for State of Illinois.

Peregrine Investigation & Research

PO Box 3601, Boulder, CO 80307-3601
Phone: 303-324-7442 - **Fax:** 303-499-9834 pmclean@cris.com
Types of Records Retrieved: Criminal, Civil and Probate courts; Federal courts; Real Estate; Tax Liens/Judgments; UCC records; Vital records
Local Retrieval Area: CO-Adams, Arapaho, Boulder, Denver, Douglas, Jefferson, Weld. **Correspondent Relationships:** Larimer, Archuletta, Weld, El Paso counties.
Add'l Information: Established 1979. Normal turnaround time- 1-2 days. Projects billed by number of names searched. Projects billed by the hour. First project may require prepayment. Will file/record documents for clients. They specialize in real estate research and document retrieval. They find those who default on consumer and commercial loans and in background and asset searches. Performs service of process.

Perkins County Abstract Co

PO Box 157, Bison, SD 57620
Phone: 605-244-5544, Fax-same
Types of Records Retrieved: Criminal, Civil and Probate courts; Real Estate; Tax Liens/Judgments; UCC records
Local Retrieval Area: SD-Perkins
Add'l info: Established 1949. Turnaround time- 2 weeks. Will provide expedited service. Projects billed by number of names searched. Projects billed by the hour. First project may require prepayment. Will file/record documents for clients. They specialize in abstracts and title insurance.

Permian Court Reporters Inc

605 W Texas Ave, Midland, TX 79701
Phone: 432-683-3032 - **Fax:** 432-683-5324
Types of Records Retrieved: Criminal and Civil courts; Federal courts
Local Retrieval Area: TX-Ector, Midland
Add'l Information: Established 1974. Normal turnaround time- 2 days. Projects billed by number of names searched. Projects billed by the hour. First project may require prepayment. Odessa customers may call 432-620-9887. Performs service of process.

Shirley Perrone

9722 Deerpath Circle, Marcy, NY 13403
Phone: 315-733-6126 - **Fax:** 315-733-7333
Types of Records Retrieved: Criminal, Civil and Probate courts; Federal courts; Tax Liens/Judgments
Local Retrieval Area: NY-Oneida
Add'l Information: Established 1991. Normal turnaround time- 24 hours. Projects billed by number of names searched. Monthly billing available. Fifteen years experience as a record retriever. He provides federal court services in Northern District of NY. He provides county court services in Oneida County Court.

Marilyn Person

819 W 3rd, Pierre, SD 57501
Phone: 605-224-8168 - **Fax:** 605-945-2440
personmj@msn.com
Types of Records Retrieved: Criminal, Civil and Probate courts; Federal courts; Tax Liens/Judgments; UCC records; Vital records; Good Standings at State Level; Secretary of State Filings
Local Retrieval Area: SD-Hughes, Stanley, Sully. **Correspondent Relationships:** Lincoln, Minnehaha, Pennington.
Add'l Information: Established 1980. Normal turnaround time- 24-48 hours. Projects billed by number of names searched. Fees are based upon project. They will invoice. Will file/record documents for clients. She acts as registered agent for corporations. She will do any type of filings or searches needed at the state level at State Capitol in Pierre, SD.

Personal Background Investigations, Inc

307 29th ST NE #130, Puyallup, WA 98372
Phone: 800-949-9982; 253-770-4935 - **Fax:** 253-770-4908
pbiinc@comcast.net
Types of Records Retrieved: Criminal, Civil and Probate courts; Federal courts; Tax Liens/Judgments
Local Retrieval Area: WA-King, Kitsap, Pierce, Snohomish, Thurston. **Correspondent Relationships:** statewide.
Add'l Information: Established 1990. Normal turnaround time- 24-48 hours for most records. Fee basis varies by type of transaction. First project may require prepayment. Will invoice business accounts. They specialize in pre-employment screening. They have direct online capabilities for several northwest states, and statewide access in several others, also national SSN, DMV and credit.

Pete Costanzo Private Inv

5130 E Charleston Blvd #5 PMB 70, Las Vegas, NV 89142-1034
Phone: 702-459-1640 - **Fax:** 702-459-4723
Types of Records Retrieved: Criminal, Civil and Probate courts; Federal courts; Real Estate, UCC records; Tax Liens/Judgments
Local Retrieval Area: NV-Clark
Add'l Information: Established 1999. Normal turnaround time- 1-2 days. Projects billed by number of records located. First project may require prepayment. They specialize in general private investigations and locates. A licensed PI in NV.

Marilyn Peterson

810 S Pinkham St, Visalia, CA 93292
Phone: 559-732-2135 - **Fax:** 559-635-4612 amstarlet@aol.com
Types of Records Retrieved: Civil and Probate courts; Real Estate; Tax Liens/Judgments; UCC records; Vital records
Local Retrieval Area: CA-Kings, Tulare
Add'l Information: Established 1987. Normal turnaround time- 24 hours or less. Projects billed by number of names searched. Projects billed by the hour. First project may require prepayment. Will file/record documents for clients. Net 30 days She is a certified notary public and will travel to handle loan documents and other signings in her area. Will retrieve large scale record orders in Fresno County. Performs service of process.

Petroleum Title Service Inc

3603 Hawthorne Ave, Casper, WY 82604
Phone: 307-235-6237 - **Fax:** 307-577-4966
Types of Records Retrieved: Civil and Probate courts; Real Estate; Tax Liens/Judgments; UCC records
Local Retrieval Area: WY-Natrona
Add'l Information: Established 1962. Normal turnaround time- 1 week. Mileage expenses will be added to the fee. All billing is done on per case basis. Will file/record documents for clients. They prepare abstracts of title, title certificates and any research pertaining to title information on surface,

minerals, research for ownership for probates, leasehold checks or any type of title research across the State of Wyoming.

Shelia Pettit

469 Old Stagecoach Rd, Carrollton, GA 30116
Phone: 770-832-9273 - **Fax:** 770-830-9301 pettit_s@bellsouth.net
Types of Records Retrieved: Criminal and Civil courts
Local Retrieval Area: GA-Carroll, Coweta, Heard, Haralson, Polk, Troup
Add'l Information: Normal turnaround time- 48-72 hours. Projects billed by number of names searched. Will invoice monthly. She has been working in deed room for almost 4 years. She collects criminal, civil & liens. She has a 2-3 day turnaround time unless weather or courthouse closing prevents it.

PFC Information Services Inc

6114 LaSalle Ave #638, Oakland, CA 94611
Phone: 510-653-5061 - **Fax:** 510-653-0842
www.pfcinformation.com **email:** lpeterson@pfcinformation.com
Types of Records Retrieved: Criminal, Civil and Probate courts; Federal courts; Real Estate; Tax Liens/Judgments; UCC records; Vital records
Local Retrieval Area: CA-Alameda, San Francisco. **Correspondent Relationships:** Marin, Santa Clara, Contra Costa, San Mateo.
Add'l Information: Established 1987. Normal turnaround time- 24 hours. Projects billed by number of names searched. Projects billed by the hour. Credit cards accepted. Personal checks are accepted. They specialize in asset searches, corporate profiles, locating people, employment screening, competitor intelligence and due diligence research.

PHB Minerals

PO Box 50216, 838 Senora Av, Billings, MT 59105
Phone: 406-248-8838 - **Fax:** 406-248-8838 phbeddow@bresnan.net
Records Retrieved: Criminal, Civil and Probate courts; Federal District courts; Real Estate; Tax Liens/Judgments; UCC records; Vital records
Local Retrieval Area: MT-Yellowstone. **Correspondent Relationships:** Wyoming & Montana as needed.
Add'l Information: Established 1978. Normal turnaround time- 24-48 hours; for instant counties- 48 or more hours depending on travel time. Projects billed by number of names searched. Projects billed by the hour. Travel expenses are added for outlying counties. First project may require prepayment. Will file/record documents for clients. Payment due upon delivery. Travel billed for outlying counties. Invoice net 15 days. They specialize in current owner, encumbrance reports, complete memorandum of title, mineral search, civil and criminal record search and retrieval of records. Also visits Carbon, Big Horn, Stillwater, and Musselshell counties by special request.

Phelps Employer Services

PO Box 9147, Mesa, AZ 85214-9147
Phone: 800-347-9918; 480-807-9799 - **Fax:** 800-494-7950; 480-807-5530
http://phelpsemployerservice.com/default.aspx **email:** rhoste@msn.com
Types of Records Retrieved: Criminal courts; Federal courts; Real Estate
Local Retrieval Area: AZ-Maricopa. **Correspondents:** statewide.
Add'l Information: Established 1986. Normal turnaround time- 24-48 hours. Expedited service available. Projects billed by number of names searched. Projects billed by number of records located. First project may require prepayment. They specialize in credit reports, driving records, drug screening, pre-employment screening and retrieving state and county records. A licensed PI in AZ.

Philip D Smith & Associates

338 Harris Hill Rd., Buffalo, NY 14221
Phone: 716-631-2100 - **Fax:** 716-632-7838
www.pdsainc.com **email:** smith@pdsainc.com
Types of Records Retrieved: Criminal and Civil courts; Federal courts; Tax Liens/Judgments; UCC records
Local Retrieval Area: NY-Erie, Monroe, Niagara
Add'l info: Established 1986. Turnaround time- 48 hours. Projects billed by the hour. First project may require prepayment. They specialize in the Buffalo NY area. A licensed PI in NY. Performs service of process.

Phillips County Abstract Co

53 South 2 nd Sy. East, P.O. Box 250, Malta, MT 59538
Phone: 406-654-1413
Types of Records Retrieved: Real Estate; Tax Liens/Judgments
Local Retrieval Area: MT-Phillips
Add'l Information: First project may require prepayment. They specialize in real estate.

Phillips Land Title Co Inc

174 N Avon Ave, Phillips, WI 54555
Phone: 715-339-2230 - **Fax:** 715-339-4975
Types of Records Retrieved: Civil and Probate courts; Federal courts; Real Estate; Tax Liens/Judgments; UCC records
Local Retrieval Area: WI-Ashland, Price. **Correspondent Relationships:** Ashland County WI.
Add'l Information: Established 1978. Normal turnaround time- 2 days. Fee basis varies by type of transaction. First project may require prepayment.

Phoenix Document Service Inc

13191 Starkey Rd #6, Largo, FL 33773-1438
Phone: 727-581-2552 - **Fax:** 727-581-2589
www.phoenixdocument.com **email:** kurt@phoenixdocument.com
Types of Records Retrieved: Civil courts; Federal courts; Real Estate; Tax Liens/Judgments; UCC records
Local Retrieval Area: FL-Alachua, Baker, Bay, Brevard, Charlotte, Citrus, Collier, Dade, Escambia, Flagler, Hernando, Highlands, Hillsborough, Indian River, Lake, Lee, Leon, Manatee, Marion, Martin, Monroe, Nassau, Okaloosa, Orange, Palm Beach, Pasco, Pinellas, Polk, Putnam, St. Johns, St. Lucie, Santa Rosa, Sarasota, Seminole, Volusia, Walton; NJ-Bergen, Essex, Middlesex, Monmouth, Morris, Ocean, Passaic, Union. **Correspondent Relationships:** check website for extended areas.
Add'l Information: Established 2000. Normal turnaround time- 24 hours. Projects billed by number of names searched. Will file/record documents for clients. Will invoice client. They are a full service public records research & retrieval company. They have been serving the needs of the settlement & title industry since 2000. Let their friendly staff assist you today.

Phoenix Research Inc

100 Lyming Farm Rd, Mt Orab, OH 45154
Phone: 800-260-1092; - **Fax:** 800-260-3997
www.hrliability.com **email:** bbrown@hrliability.com
Types of Records Retrieved: Criminal courts
Local Retrieval Area: IN-Dearborn; KY-Boone, Campbell, Kenton, Union; OH-Butler, Clermont, Hamilton, Warren. **Correspondents:** nationwide.
Add'l Information: Established 1997. Normal turnaround time- 48-72 hours. Projects billed by number of names searched. Use their software and receive a discount. Volume discounts available. First project may require prepayment. Credit cards accepted. Prepayment discount available. Credit card required for NY O.C.A. search requests. They specialize in criminal record histories, training seminars, public speaking and due diligence issues. They are published authors on background investigations and privacy issues. They are a wholesale company and don't provide retail screening svcs.

Photo Abstract Co

22 E Central Ave, Miami, OK 74354
Phone: 918-542-1871 - **Fax:** 918-542-9748
Types of Records Retrieved: Civil and Probate courts; Real Estate; Tax Liens/Judgments; UCC records; Vital records
Local Retrieval Area: OK-Ottawa
Add'l Information: Established 1917. Normal turnaround time- 1-3 days. Projects billed by number of records located. They will file/record real estate documents on behalf on clients.

PI Inc

PO Box 1584, Sequin, TX 78155
Phone: 800-359-5131; 830-303-3373 - **Fax:** 800-730-0050; 830-303-3374
edward@the-cia.net

Types of Records Retrieved: Criminal courts
Local Retrieval Area: TX-Bexar, Caldwell, Comal, Guadalupe, Harris, Hays
Add'l Information: Established 1965. Normal turnaround time- 48 hours. Projects billed by type and quantity involved. Net 30 days; invoice weekly. They specialize in criminal records and pre-employment screening. We can retrieve MVR records in any state. A licensed PI in TX.

Pierce County Abstract

216 S Main Ave, Rugby, ND 58368
Phone: 701-776-7777, Fax-same

Types of Records Retrieved: Civil and Probate courts; Real Estate; Tax Liens/Judgments; UCC records
Local Retrieval Area: ND-Pierce
Add'l Information: Normal turnaround time- 2 weeks. Fee basis will vary by type of project. There is a set fee for abstracting. Will file/record documents for clients.

PII Inc

1337 Wabash Ave, Springfield, IL 62704
Phone: 217-483-8845 - **Fax:** 217-483-5491
www.piidetective.com **email:** pennell@piidetective.com

Types of Records Retrieved: Criminal, Civil and Probate courts; Federal courts; Real Estate; Tax Liens/Judgments; UCC records; Vital records
Local Retrieval Area: IL-Adams, Cass, Christian, Coles, Effingham, Logan, Macon, Macoupin, Mason, Menard, Montgomery, Morgan, Moultrie, Sangamon, Scott, Shelby
Add'l Information: Established 1991. Normal turnaround time- 2-3 days. Expedited service available. Projects billed by the hour. First project may require prepayment. Credit cards accepted. PII is a retired police officer with a solid background working with public records. A licensed PI in IL. Performs service of process.

Pinnacle Records

4000 Faxon Ave, Memphis, TN 38122-5217
Phone: 901-324-9163 - **Fax:** 901-324-4685
pinnaclerecords@midsouth.rr.com

Types of Records Retrieved: Criminal and Civil courts
Local Retrieval Area: TN-Shelby
Add'l Information: Established 1997. Normal turnaround time- same day in many cases. Projects billed by number of names searched. Fee basis depends upon type of project. They specialize in background searches for both felonies and misdemeanors.

Pioneer Abstract Co of McAlester Inc

PO Box 926, 101 E Carl Albert Pky (74501), McAlester, OK 74502
Phone: 918-423-0817 - **Fax:** 918-423-1202
pioneerabstract@ureach.com

Types of Records Retrieved: Criminal, Civil and Probate courts; Real Estate; Tax Liens/Judgments
Local Retrieval Area: OK-Pittsburg
Add'l Information: Normal turnaround time- 3 days. Projects billed by the hour. First project may require prepayment. Credit cards accepted. Will file/record documents for clients. They specialize in real estate closings, title insurance abstract updates and title searches.

Pioneer National Title Insurance

122 W Railroad Ave, Green River, WY 82935
Phone: 307-875-9833 - **Fax:** 307-875-5025
pioneertitle@sweetwaterhsa.com

Types of Records Retrieved: Criminal, Civil and Probate courts; Federal courts; Real Estate; Tax Liens/Judgments; UCC records
Local Retrieval Area: WY-Sweetwater
Add'l Information: Established 1982. Normal turnaround time- 24-48 hours. Projects billed by number of names searched. Payment due upon receipt of invoice. Will file/record documents for clients. They specialize in full complete of title services including closings and escrows.

Pioneer-Ward County Abstract Co

407 S Allen Ave, Monahans, TX 79756
Phone: 432-943-5561 - **Fax:** 432-943-3716

Types of Records Retrieved: Civil and Probate courts; Real Estate; Tax Liens/Judgments; UCC records
Local Retrieval Area: TX-Ward
Add'l Information: Normal turnaround time- 2-3 days. Projects billed by the hour. First project may require prepayment.

Pipestone County Abstract Co LLC

PO Box 335, Pipestone, MN 56164
Phone: 507-825-5833 - **Fax:** 507-825-5833

Types of Records Retrieved: Criminal, Civil and Probate courts; Real Estate; Tax Liens/Judgments; UCC records
Local Retrieval Area: MN-Pipestone
Add'l info: Established 1995. Turnaround time- 2-3 days. Projects billed by number of names searched. Projects billed by number of records located. Will file/record documents for clients. They specialize in real estate recordings and complete abstracting. They also offer closing services.

Pittsburgh Information & Research Co

PO Box 99181, Pittsburgh, PA 15233
Phone: 412-766-3832 - **Fax:** 412-761-5391 pirc@comcast.net

Types of Records Retrieved: Criminal, Civil and Probate courts; Federal courts; Real Estate; Tax Liens/Judgments; UCC records; Vital records
Local Retrieval Area: PA-Allegheny, Beaver, Berks, Blair, Bucks, Butler, Chester, Cumberland, Dauphin, Delaware, Erie, Lackawanna, Lancaster, Lehigh, Luzerne, Monroe, Philadelphia, Washington, Westmoreland, York. **Correspondent Relationships:** Pennsylvania.
Add'l Information: Established 1984. Normal turnaround time- 24-48 hours for verbal report. Fees are by name/index. First project may require prepayment. Will file/record documents for clients. Terms: net 30 days. They specialize in complete coverage of every jurisdiction contained within Pennsylvania, including federal and state offices. A licensed PI in PA. Performs service of process.

Platte County Title & Escrow Co

PO Box 946, 2511 15th St, Columbus, NE 68602
Phone: 402-563-4519 - **Fax:** 402-564-0588

Types of Records Retrieved: Criminal, Civil and Probate courts; Real Estate; Tax Liens/Judgments; UCC records; Vital records
Local Retrieval Area: NE-Platte. **Correspondent Relationships:** Boone, Nance, Butler, Merrick counties.
Add'l Information: Normal turnaround time- 1 week. Fee basis varies by type of transaction. Will file/record documents for clients. They specialize in escrow closings.

Platte Title Co

PO Box 788, Platte, SD 57369
Phone: 605-337-3824 - **Fax:** 605-337-3811

Types of Records Retrieved: Real Estate; Tax Liens/Judgments
Local Retrieval Area: SD-Charles Mix
Add'l Information: First project may require prepayment. They specialize in real estate.

PLM Court Research

PO Box 2903, Ranchos De Taos, NM 87557
Phone: 505-758-4467 - **Fax:** 505-758-4629
Nica@LaPlaza.org

Types of Records Retrieved: Criminal, Civil and Probate courts
Local Retrieval Area: NM-Taos
Add'l Information: Established 2001. Normal turnaround time- 24-48 hours. Projects billed by number of names searched. First project may require prepayment. They specialize in court searches in the Taos area. Performs service of process.

Plymouth County Abstract

126 Central Ave SE, Le Mars, IA 51031
Phone: 712-546-4564 - **Fax:** 712-546-4124
Types of Records Retrieved: Real Estate; Tax Liens/Judgments; Probate courts; UCC records
Local Retrieval Area: IA-Plymouth
Add'l Information: Normal turnaround time- 2-7 days. Fee basis will vary by type of project. Personal checks are accepted.

PM Clinton International Investigation

7201 Westview, Houston, TX 77055
Phone: 866-686-6864; 713-686-6864 - **Fax:** 713-686-6891
pmclinton@houston.rr.com
Types of Records Retrieved: Criminal, Civil and Probate courts; Federal courts; Real Estate; Tax Liens/Judgments; UCC records
Local Retrieval Area: TX-Brazoria, Chambers, Fort Bend, Galveston, Harris, Montgomery, Walker, Waller
Add'l Information: Established 1988. Normal turnaround time- 1-3 days. Expedited service available. Projects billed by number of names searched. Projects billed by the hour. All projects require prepayment. Credit cards accepted. They are a results oriented firm. They work for some of the largest firms in the US to the smallest. They give all their clients 110%. A licensed PI in TX. Performs service of process.

Poindexter & Associates Inc

PO Box 37284, Raleigh, NC 27627
Phone: 800-373-2804; 919-859-5294 - **Fax:** 919-834-7039
www.poindexter-associates.com
email: DetectiveOne@poindexter-associates.com
Types of Records Retrieved: Criminal and Civil courts
Local Retrieval Area: NC-Chatham, Cumberland, Durham, Franklin, Granville, Harnett, Johnston, Rowan, Vance, Wake, Warren. **Correspondent Relationships:** DC, NC, VA.
Add'l Information: Established 1995. Normal turnaround time- 24-48 hours. Projects billed by the hour. First project may require prepayment. Credit cards accepted. Will file/record documents for clients. They have a direct T1 connection to NC statewide criminal, civil and DMV records with instantaneous access. They are licensed detective agencies in NC, VA & DC. A licensed PI in NC, VA, DC & FL. Performs service of process.

Poinsett County Abstract Co

409 Court St, Harrisburg, AR 72432
Phone: 870-578-5914 - **Fax:** 870-578-5808
Types of Records Retrieved: Criminal, Civil and Probate courts; Real Estate; Tax Liens/Judgments; UCC records
Local Retrieval Area: AR-Poinsett
Add'l Information: Established 1912. Normal turnaround time- 1 week. Fee basis will vary by the type of project. Will file/record documents for clients. They are a full service title company.

Maureen H Poole

PO Box 1664, Spring Hill, TN 37174-1664
Phone: 931-294-2988 - **Fax:** 931-294-3032
sankar2@bellsouth.net
Types of Records Retrieved: Civil and Probate courts; Federal District courts; Real Estate; Tax Liens/Judgments; UCC records
Local Retrieval Area: TN-Bedford, Coffee, Davidson, Franklin, Giles, Hickman, Lawrence, Lewis, Lincoln, Marshall, Maury, Moore, Rutherford, Wayne, Williamson, Wilson; AL-Colbert, Franklin, Lauderdale, Limestone, Madison, Marion, Morgan. She will search other AL and TN counties upon request. **Correspondent Relationships:** can provide statewide services on request.
Add'l Information: Established 1998. Normal turnaround time-24-48 hours. Expedited service available. Projects billed by number of names searched. Fees vary with type of search. Will file/record documents for clients. Terms: net 30 days. They also will do searches in other north Alabama and south central Tennessee counties on request. Filing services, notary, and closing services available.

Pott County Researchers

317 Club House Dr, Shawnee, OK 74801
Phone: 405-395-4460 - **Fax:** 405-395-4461
pottcoresearch@gmail.com
Types of Records Retrieved: Criminal and Civil courts
Local Retrieval Area: OK-Pottawatomie
Add'l Information: Established 2006. Normal turnaround time- 24-36 hours. Projects billed by number of names searched. First project may require prepayment. Does monthly invoices. Has nine (9) years experience conducting criminal and civil record searches. They are a 3 partner company; one has been a licensed Private Investigator for 6 years. A licensed PI in TN.

Pottawatomie County Abstract Co

PO Box 218, Westmoreland, KS 66549-0218
Phone: 785-457-3441 - **Fax:** 785-457-3612 pottcoab@kansas.net
Types of Records Retrieved: Civil and Probate courts; Real Estate; Tax Liens/Judgments; UCC records; Vital records
Local Retrieval Area: KS-Pottawatomie
Add'l Information: Normal turnaround time- 2-3 days. Fee basis varies by type of transaction. First project may require prepayment. They will file/record UCC and real estate documents on behalf of clients, if they did the closings or title work.

Potter & Co

PO Box 650, White Sulphur Springs, MT 59645
Phone: 406-547-3355 - **Fax:** 406-547-3445
Types of Records Retrieved: Criminal, Civil and Probate courts; Real Estate; Tax Liens/Judgments; UCC records; Vital records
Local Retrieval Area: MT-Meagher
Add'l Information: Established 1922. Normal turnaround time- 1 week. Projects billed by the hour. Will file/record documents for clients. They specialize in real estate and land title work.

Potter County Land & Abstract Inc

PO Box 203, Gettysburg, SD 57442
Phone: 605-765-2858 - **Fax:** 605-765-2252
Types of Records Retrieved: Criminal, Civil and Probate courts; Real Estate; Tax Liens/Judgments; Vital records
Local Retrieval Area: SD-Potter
Add'l Information: Established 1884. Normal turnaround time- 5 days. Projects billed by the hour. All projects require prepayment. They specialize in real estate.

Powell Court Service

14083 Quinnault Rd, Apple Valley, CA 92307
Phone: 888-976-9355; 760-912-6119 - **Fax:** 760-240-7951
spcourtservice@hotmail.com
Types of Records Retrieved: Criminal, Civil and Probate courts; Federal courts; Real Estate; Tax Liens/Judgments; UCC records; Vital records
Local Retrieval Area: CA-Alameda, Los Angeles, Orange, Riverside, San Bernardino, Santa Clara
Add'l Information: Established 2000. Normal turnaround time- 24-48 hours. Expedited service available. Projects billed by number of names searched. Projects billed by number of records located. Will invoice. They specialize in document research, retrieval, filing in the areas listed above.

Powell's Backtracking

112 Lake Lynn Dr, Harvey, LA 70058
Phone: 504-342-2052 - **Fax:** 504-342-2752 powellbt@bellsouth.net
Records Retrieved: Criminal and Civil courts; Federal District courts
Retrieval Area: LA-Jefferson, Orleans, St. Bernard, St. Tammany Parishes
Add'l Information: Established 1995. Normal turnaround time- 24-36 hours. Fees are per court search or per property. First project may require prepayment. Payment due upon billing. They specialize in criminal and civil searches. A licensed PI in LA. Performs service of process.

Powers Abstract Co Inc

PO Box 707, 635 Delaware St, Perry, OK 73077
Phone: 580-336-4068 - **Fax:** 580-336-4060
Types of Records Retrieved: Criminal, Civil and Probate courts; Federal courts; Real Estate; Tax Liens/Judgments; UCC records
Local Retrieval Area: OK-Noble
Add'l Information: Established 1971. Normal turnaround time- 5-7 days. Fee basis will vary by the type of project. First project may require prepayment. Will file/record documents for clients. They specialize in real estate and titles.

Poweshiek Abstract Co Inc

PO Box 683, 833 Main St, Grinnell, IA 50112
Phone: 641-236-8668 - **Fax:** 641-236-0614
poweshiekabtstract@hotmail.com
Types of Records Retrieved: Criminal, Civil and Probate courts; Federal courts; Real Estate; Tax Liens/Judgments; UCC records; Vital records
Local Retrieval Area: IA-Poweshiek
Add'l Information: Established 1950. Normal turnaround time- 1 business week. Projects billed by number of names searched. First project may require prepayment.

Prairie Abstract & Title

203 S Logan Ave, Terry, MT 59349
Phone: 406-635-5472 - **Fax:** 406-635-5472
Types of Records Retrieved: Criminal, Civil and Probate courts; Real Estate; Tax Liens/Judgments; UCC records; Vital records
Local Retrieval Area: MT-Prairie
Add'l Information: Established 1915. Normal turnaround time- 2-3 days. Projects billed by the hour. First project may require prepayment. Will file/record documents for clients.

Pre-Check, The Pre-Check Company

14701 Detroit Ave #LL70, PO Box 771264, Lakewood, OH 44107
Phone: 800-268-2435; 216-226-7700 - **Fax:** 216-226-0777
www.pre-check.com **email:** info@pre-check.com
Types of Records Retrieved: Criminal and Civil courts; US District court
Local Retrieval Area: OH-Ashtabula, Columbiana, Cuyahoga, Franklin, Geauga, Greene, Hancock, Lake, Lorain, Lucas, Madison, Mahoning, Medina, Pickaway, Portage, Stark, Summit, Trumbull, Wood. **Correspondent Relationships:** nationwide.
Add'l Information: Established 1992. Normal turnaround time- 2-4 days. Projects billed by number of names searched. Credit cards accepted. Net 30 days. They specialize in comprehensive pre-employment background checks, offer comprehensive drug testing solutions, including 90-day hair tests, alcohol & oral fluids for "under the influence" detection.

Precision Quest

PO Box 6088, Marion, OH 43302
Phone: 740-383-3753 - **Fax:** 740-383-5543 precisionquest@adelphia.net
Types of Records Retrieved: Criminal, Civil and Probate courts; Real Estate; Tax Liens/Judgments; UCC records; Vital records
Retrieval Area: OH-Crawford, Delaware, Franklin, Marion, Morrow, Union
Add'l Information: Established 1997. Normal turnaround time- 24 hours. Projects billed by number of names searched. Will file/record documents for clients. Payment terms net 30 days. They specialize in current owner and second owner searches, UCC, criminal, mortgage, suits, judgments and Federal & State tax liens. Performs service of process.

Precision Research & Information

PO Box 3162, Quail Valley, CA 92587
Phone: 951-244-8118 - **Fax:** 951-244-8777
www.pri-cal.com **email:** earl@pri-cal.com
Types of Records Retrieved: Criminal, Civil and Probate courts; Federal courts; Tax Liens/Judgments; UCC records; Vital records
Local Retrieval Area: CA-Riverside, San Bernardino
Add'l Information: Established 1995. Normal turnaround time- 12-24 hours. Projects billed by number of names searched. Payment terms are net 30 days. All searches are conducted at the county seat. Record retrieval depends upon the location of file.

Preferred Land Title

PO Box 708, Farmington, MO 63640
Phone: 800-310-6721; 573-756-6721 - **Fax:** 573-756-0519
Types of Records Retrieved: Real Estate; Tax Liens/Judgments; Probate courts; UCC records
Retrieval Area: MO-Madison, St. Francois, Ste. Genevieve, Washington
Add'l Information: Established 1906. Normal turnaround time- 3-5 working days. Projects billed by number of names searched. Projects billed by the hour. Fee basis is per chain of title. All projects require prepayment. Will file/record documents for clients. Personal checks are accepted. They maintain complete geographical indexed title plants for each county they do business in.

Premier Corporate Services MN

590 Park St #6, St Paul, MN 55103-1846
Phone: 800-227-1256; 651-225-9500 - **Fax:** 800-227-1263; 651-225-9579
www.premiercorp.com **email:** suej@premiercorp.com
Types of Records Retrieved: Criminal and Civil courts; Federal courts; Real Estate; Tax Liens/Judgments; UCC records
Local Retrieval Area: MN-Hennepin, Ramsey. **Correspondent Relationships:** nationwide.
Add'l Information: Established 1991. Normal turnaround time- 48 hours. Credit cards accepted. Will file/record documents for clients. Formerly Unisearch Inc (Minnesota) they specialize in Minnesota but can certainly obtain corporate and other documents nationwide.

Premiere Investigations

767 S State Rd 7 #22-C, Margate, FL 33068
Phone: 954-974-1139 - **Fax:** 954-956-7508
www.premierepi.com **email:** info@pinvestigations.com
Types of Records Retrieved: Criminal, Civil and Probate courts; Federal courts; Real Estate; Tax Liens/Judgments; UCC records; Vital records
Local Retrieval Area: FL-Broward, Dade, Palm Beach
Add'l Info: Established 1997. Turnaround time- 2-5 days. Expedited service available. Projects billed by number of names searched. Projects billed by the hour. First project may require prepayment. Will file/record documents for clients. They specialize in domestic cases, accident investigations, worker's comp, surveillance, insurance fraud, locates (skiptrace), witness statements, asset and background searches, and process service. Se habla espanol. A licensed PI in FL. Performs service of process.

PreSearch Background Services

PO Box 50134, Colorado Springs, CO 80949-0134
Phone: 719-533-1880 - **Fax:** 719-260-7172, 719-535-0223
presearch@adelphia.net
Types of Records Retrieved: Criminal courts
Local Retrieval Area: CO-El Paso. **Correspondents:** nationwide.
Add'l Information: Established 1995. Normal turnaround time- 24 hours. Will file/record documents for clients. Invoiced monthly for services rendered. Presearch Background Services specializes in hands-on document retrieval for El Paso county, CO. Normal turnaround time is 24 hours. The company also provides criminal & civil retrieval services in all CO statewide courts, with access to online sources.

Presidio County Abstract

PO Box 1357, 212 N Highland Ave, Marfa, TX 79843
Phone: 432-729-4264 - **Fax:** 432-729-3286
www.bigbendabstract.com **email:** psabstract@sbcglobal.net
Types of Records Retrieved: Criminal, Civil and Probate courts; Federal courts; Real Estate; Tax Liens/Judgments; UCC records
Local Retrieval Area: TX-Brewster, Presidio
Add'l Information: Established 1968. Normal turnaround time-1-2 days. Projects billed by the hour. All projects require prepayment. They specialize in escrow closings, title searches and abstracting.

Presley's Title & Abstract Co, Inc

309 N Pine St, Brewton, AL 36426

Phone: 888-544-8006; - **Fax:** 251-867-2968 dpreley@hotmail.com

Types of Records Retrieved: Civil and Probate courts; Federal courts; Real Estate; Tax Liens/Judgments; UCC records; Vital records

Local Retrieval Area: AL-Clarke, Conecuh, Covington, Escambia, Monroe

Add'l Information: Established 1996. Normal turnaround time- 24-48 hours. Fees are by type of projects. Terms: net 30 days. She specializes in title searches, UCC, lien & judgments and mineral reports. She has worked for 20 years with the same Title and Abstract Company.

Presque Isle Title Inc

159 N 3rd St, Rogers City, MI 49779-1608

Phone: 989-734-2816 - **Fax:** 989-734-3896

Types of Records Retrieved: Civil and Probate courts; Real Estate; Tax Liens/Judgments; UCC records

Local Retrieval Area: MI-Presque Isle

Add'l Information: Normal turnaround time- 48-72 hours. Fee basis will vary by type of project. All projects require prepayment. Will file/record documents for clients. They specialize in title/mortgage insurance.

Prestige Legal Services

14620 N Nebraska Ave #101A, Tampa, FL 33613

Phone: 800-784-7572; 813-264-1889 - **Fax:** 813-264-5539

www.plsprocess.com **email:** dean@plsprocess.com

Types of Records Retrieved: Criminal, Civil and Probate courts; Federal courts; Real Estate; Tax Liens/Judgments; UCC records; Vital records

Local Retrieval Area: FL-Citrus, Hernando, Hillsborough, Pasco, Pinellas, Sumter. **Correspondent Relationships:** Florida.

Add'l Information: Established 1991. Normal turnaround time- 24-48 hours. Projects billed by the hour. Credit cards accepted. Will invoice. They have over 30 years experience. A licensed PI in FL. Performs service of process.

Prewitt-Rogers Abstract Co

203 E Hale Ave, Osceola, AR 72370

Phone: 870-563-2137 - **Fax:** 870-563-3558 susylvia@msn.com

Types of Records Retrieved: Civil and Probate courts; Real Estate; Tax Liens/Judgments; UCC records

Local Retrieval Area: AR-Mississippi. **Correspondent Relationships:** Chickasawba district of Mississippi County.

Add'l Information: Established 1923. Normal turnaround time- 2-5 days. Projects billed by number of names searched. Projects billed by number of records located. Will file/record documents for clients. Personal checks are accepted. They specialize in abstracts of title, title insurance, title searches, commitments and insurance policy. Also witness signings and recordings.

Price One Inv

128 Cameron Dr, Nicholasville, KY 40356

Phone: 859-881-4452, cell- 859-608-5100 - **Fax:** 859-881-0349

Types of Records Retrieved: Criminal and Civil courts; Real Estate

Local Retrieval Area: KY-Bath, Bourbon, Bracken, Fayette, Fleming, Harrison, Jessamine, Nicholas. **Correspondent Relationships:** 28 counties in central Kentucky.

Add'l Information: Established 2000?. First project may require prepayment. They specialize in courts and real estate searches. Call for additional county coverage,

Primetime Research Inc

83 Hanover St #8, Manchester, NH 03101

Phone: 866-737-2714; 603-666-4687 - **Fax:** 866-621-0754; 603-621-0754

www.ptrionline.com **email:** lschofield@primetimeresearch.com

Types of Records Retrieved: Criminal and Civil courts

Local Retrieval Area: MA-Essex, Franklin, Hampden, Hampshire, Middlesex, Norfolk, Suffolk, Worcester; NH-Belknap, Cheshire, Hillsborough, Merrimack, Rockingham, Strafford; RI-Bristol, Kent, Newport, Providence, Washington

Add'l Information: Established 1998. Normal turnaround time- 8-48 hours. (8AM EST cutoff). Projects billed by number of names searched. Terms are net 30 days. Formerly Primetime Research Inc, they specialize in customer service, they also are web enabled and insured.

Princeton Data Search Inc

PO Box 1162, Kaufman, TX 75142

Phone: 469-474-1025 - **Fax:** 972-932-2217

www.princetondatasearch.net **email:** pds@princetondatasearch.net

Types of Records Retrieved: Criminal courts; Probate courts; Real Estate; Tax Liens/Judgments

Local Retrieval Area: TX-Dallas, Henderson, Hunt, Kaufman, Rockwall, Van Zandt. **Correspondent Relationships:** Texas, Louisiana, Arkansas.

Add'l Information: Established 2001. Normal turnaround time- 24-48 hours. Criminal records are billed monthly. They obtain felony and misdemeanor records in person for almost all of the counties served, with a quick turnaround time and low price. They also complete document retrievals and current owner searches.

Priority Abstract LLC

4250 Veterans Memorial Hwy #4000, Holbrook, NY 11741

Phone: 888-941-1234; 631-981-4400 - **Fax:** 631-981-5514

www.priorityabstract.com **email:** arlenenelson@arlenenelson.com

Types of Records Retrieved: Criminal, Civil and Probate courts; Federal courts; Real Estate; Tax Liens/Judgments; UCC records; Vital records

Local Retrieval Area: NY-Bronx, Kings, Nassau, New York, Queens, Richmond, Suffolk. **Correspondent Relationships:** nationwide.

Add'l info: Established 1994. Turnaround time- 2 days. Fee basis depends on type of project. First project may require prepayment. Will file/record documents for clients. Will bill; terms net 30 days. They specialize in foreclosure litigation and service of process. Performs service of process.

Priority Process Service

Rt 1 Box 51, Newberry, IN 47449

Phone: 866-464-2192; 812-863-4129 - **Fax:** 812-863-4130

www.angelfire.com/in/HSI/ **email:** jimhart@smithville.net

Types of Records Retrieved: Criminal and Civil courts; Real Estate; Tax Liens/Judgments; UCC records

Local Retrieval Area: IN-Brown, Clay, Daviess, Dubois, Greene, Knox, Lawrence, Martin, Monroe, Orange, Owen, Pike, Sullivan, Vigo. **Correspondent Relationships:** Brown, Daviess, Greene, Lawrence, Martin, Monroe, Orange, Owen, Sullivan Vigo, Dubois, Knox, Pike and Clay counties Indiana.

Add'l Information: Established 1983. Normal turnaround time- 2 days. Expedited service available. Projects billed by number of names searched. Monthly invoice - due within 30 days. They specialize in process serving, criminal record searches and document retrieval. A licensed PI in IN. Performs service of process.

Priority Records Search LLC

S8386 Hemlock Rd, North Freedom, WI 53951-9760

Phone: 608-544-9991 - **Fax:** 608-544-9941 prsllc@chorus.net

Types of Records Retrieved: Civil and Probate courts; Federal courts; Real Estate; Tax Liens/Judgments; UCC records; Vital records

Local Retrieval Area: WI-Columbia, Dane, Sauk. **Correspondent Relationships:** statewide, nationwide.

Add'l Information: Established 2001. Normal turnaround time- 24-48 hours. Expedited service available. Projects billed by number of names searched. Payment due upon receipt. Their business is a records search and retrieval service. They have all the resources to give accurate and timely responses to their clients and customers, with personal attention and professional confidentiality. Performs service of process.

Private Eyes

15684 CR 472, Tyler, TX 75706

Phone: 903-882-5697 - **Fax:** 903-882-5697 sandieslaton@yahoo.com

Types of Records Retrieved: Criminal, Civil and Probate courts; Federal courts; Real Estate; Tax Liens/Judgments; UCC records; Vital records

Local Retrieval Area: TX-Dallas, Henderson, Hill, Kaufman, Palo Pinto, Parker, Smith, Tarrant, Van Zandt, Wood. **Correspondent Relationships:** SD, AL, LA, OK and Lubbock, Rockwall, Houston and Ellis, TX counties.

Add'l Information: Established 2001. Normal turnaround time- 24-48 hours. Expedited service available for a fee. Projects billed by the hour. Mileage is also charged. First project may require prepayment. Credit cards accepted. Retainer required They have 5 years experience as a licensed PI, specializing in legal research, licensed realtor, investigative reporting, DWI transcriptionist. Their motto is "We find what you can't". A PI in TX.

Private Eyes Inc

190 N Wiget Ln #220, Walnut Creek, CA 94598
877-292-3330; 925-927-3333 x4279 - **Fax:** 877-292-3330; 925-927-3330
www.privateeyesinc.com **email:** stacey@privateeyesinc.com

Types of Records Retrieved: Criminal and Civil courts; Real Estate; Tax Liens/Judgments; UCC records

Local Retrieval Area: CA-Alameda, Contra Costa, Solano

Add'l Information: Established 2003. Normal turnaround time- 8-12 business hours. Projects billed by number of names searched. Along with their competitive pricing their clients have told them they are thrilled with their consistently fast turnaround time and accurate reports.

PRN Abstract & Title Co

123 N 3rd St, Wahpeton, ND 58074
Phone: 701-642-3781 - **Fax:** 701-642-3852
richlandabstract@702com.net

Types of Records Retrieved: Criminal, Civil and Probate courts; Real Estate; Tax Liens/Judgments; UCC records; Vital records

Local Retrieval Area: MN-Wilkin; ND-Richland. **Correspondent Relationships:** North Dakota and Minnesota.

Add'l Information: Established 1922. Normal turnaround time- 1 week or less. Projects billed by number of names searched. First project may require prepayment. Will file/record documents for clients. They specialize in real estate records, taxes, judgments and UCC searches.

Pro Facto Inc

9300 Batesville Pike, Jacksonville, AR 72076
Phone: 501-988-5340 - **Fax:** 501-988-5874 profacto@centurytel.net

Types of Records Retrieved: Criminal and Civil courts; Federal courts; Real Estate; Tax Liens/Judgments; UCC records

Local Retrieval Area: AR-Faulkner, Hot Spring, Lonoke, Pulaski, Saline

Add'l Information: Established 1989. Normal turnaround time- 1-2 days. Expedited service available. Fee basis will vary by the type of search. Will file/record documents for clients. Will invoice by project or monthly. They specialize in quick turnaround and good communication with clients. They have provided quality searches and retrieval services since 1989.

Pro Search Inc

91 Dora St, Stamford, CT 06902
Phone: 203-348-6994 cell- 203-969-5566 - **Fax:** 203-276-1899

Types of Records Retrieved: Real Estate; Tax Liens/Judgments; UCC records; Land records 9035

Local Retrieval Area: CT-Fairfield. **Correspondents in:** Connecticut.

Add'l Information: Established 1988. Normal turnaround time- 3-5 days. Projects billed by number of names searched. They search the records in the towns in Fairfield county.

Probus Research

601 Van Ness Ave #E, San Francisco, CA 94102
Phone: 888-934-3848; 415-440-9100 - **Fax:** 415-440-9200
www.probusresearch.com **email:** commune@probusresearch.com

Types of Records Retrieved: Criminal, Civil and Probate courts; Federal courts; Real Estate; Tax Liens/Judgments; UCC records; Vital records

Local Retrieval Area: CA-Alameda, Contra Costa, Marin, San Francisco, San Mateo, Santa Clara. **Correspondent Relationships:** most California counties, also Texas, Ohio.

Add'l Info: Established 1985. Turnaround time- same day to 2 days. Projects billed by number of names searched. Charge by the hour on special projects. First project may require prepayment. Terms: net 30 days for established clients. Specializes in complex litigation case file, regulatory, business and library research. Pprovides fax filings and super rush research and document retrievals, plus online access to various public record databases. Integrated document ordering. Performs service of process.

Process Service Network

19524 Nordhoff St #10, Northridge, CA 91324-2439
Phone: 800-417-7623; 818-772-4795 - **Fax:** 818-772-4798
www.processnet1.com **email:** processnet@sbcglobal.net

Types of Records Retrieved: Criminal, Civil and Probate courts; Federal courts; Real Estate; Tax Liens/Judgments; Vital records

Local Retrieval Area: CA-Los Angeles, Orange, Riverside, San Bernardino, Ventura. **Correspondent Relationships:** Kern, Santa Barbara, San Diego counties CA.

Add'l Information: Established 1978. Normal turnaround time- 1 day. Projects billed by number of names searched. All projects require prepayment. Credit cards accepted. Will file/record documents for clients. Visa, MasterCard and American Express accepted. They specialize in court filings, document retrieval, hard-to-serve process, and international service of process. Performs service of process.

Process Service of Wyoming

224 South Park, Casper, WY 82601
Phone: 307-266-1979 - **Fax:** 307-265-7747
www.wyomingprocessserver.com
email: bob@wyomingprocessserver.com

Types of Records Retrieved: Criminal and Civil courts

Local Retrieval Area: WY-Big Horn, Carbon, Converse, Fremont, Hot Springs, Johnson, Natrona, Niobrara, Washakie. **Correspondent Relationships:** statewide.

Add'l Information: Established 2001. First project may require prepayment. They also provide court filing, subpoena preparation, photocopying, skiptracing, private investigations. Performs service of process.

Process Serving Unlimited

PO Box 1884, 1832 Gippy Ln (29407), Charleston, SC 29402
Phone: 843-728-2732 - **Fax:** 843-766-0618

Types of Records Retrieved: Criminal and Civil courts; Federal District courts

Local Retrieval Area: SC-Charleston

Add'l Information: Established 1984. Normal turnaround time- 2 days. Projects billed by number of names searched. Projects billed by the hour. First project may require prepayment. Will file documents in Charleston County only. Call before faxing. Performs service of process in Berkley, Charleston, and Dorchester Counties SC. Performs service of process.

ProCom Services Corp

2427 S MacArthur Blvd, Springfield, IL 62704-4505
Phone: 217-525-7600 - **Fax:** 217-544-1005
www.pro-comservices.com **email:** cbsiprocom@aol.com

Types of Records Retrieved: Criminal, Civil and Probate courts; Federal courts; Tax Liens/Judgments; UCC records; Vital records

Local Retrieval Area: IL-Sangamon. **Correspondent Relationships:** Sangamon, IL.

Add'l Information: Established 1924. Normal turnaround time- 24 hours. Projects billed by number of names searched. First project may require prepayment. Monthly billing available. Specializing in collection services, mortgage reporting, tenant screening and employment screening.

Professional Background Searches LLC

PO Box 551707, Davie, FL 33355
Phone: 954-394-8680 - **Fax:** 509-691-9433
SHERIMAYOR@BELLSOUTH.NET

Types of Records Retrieved: Criminal and Civil courts; Federal courts

Local Retrieval Area: FL-Dade, Broward, Palm Beach

Add'l Information: Established 2005. Normal turnaround time- 12-48 hours. Projects billed by number of names searched. First project may require prepayment. Goes directly into each courthouse to provide the most current and accurate information. Regular service to Florida Southern District federal courts. Provides document and microfiche retrieval at all locations; does not use online databases. E&O insured.

Professional Background Services Inc

612 Smithfield Rd #18, North Providence, RI 02904
Phone: 401-714-8433 - **Fax:** 401-354-8885
www.pbsincorporated.com **email:** info@pbsincorporated.com

Types of Records Retrieved: Criminal, Civil and Probate courts; Federal courts; Real Estate; Tax Liens/Judgments; UCC records; Vital records

Local Retrieval Area: RI-Bristol, Kent, Newport, Providence, Washington

Add'l Information: Established 2004. Normal turnaround time- 24-72 hours. Projects billed by number of names searched. First project may require prepayment. They are a full service background screening company. They provide up-to-date and accurate information. They perform criminal/civil, credit history, MVR, tenant screening and professional certifications.

Professional Choice Services

32055 Tiboe Plaza, Springfield, LA 70462
Phone: 225-294-3703 - **Fax:** 225-294-7499
www.professionalchoiceservices.com **email:** bethbordelon@bellsouth.net

Types of Records Retrieved: Criminal, Civil and Probate courts; Real Estate; Tax Liens/Judgments; UCC records; Vital records

Local Retrieval Area: LA-Livingston, St Tammany, Tangipahoa

Add'l Information: Established 1995. Normal turnaround time- 48 hours. Expedited service available. Projects billed by the hour. First project may require prepayment. Will file/record documents for clients. They specialize in document recording, retrieval and research services. Notary public certified signing agent.

Professional Civil Process (Austin)

510 S Congress #110, Austin, TX 78704-1246
Phone: 800-950-7493; 512-477-3500 - **Fax:** 512-477-8700
www.pcpusa.com **email:** austin@pcpusa.net

Types of Records Retrieved: Criminal, Civil and Probate courts; Federal courts; Real Estate; Tax Liens/Judgments; UCC records; Vital records

Local Retrieval Area: TX-Austin, Bexar, Cameron, Dallas, Denton, El Paso, Fort Bend, Galveston, Harris, Houston, Nueces, Tarrant, Travis, Tyler. **Correspondent Relationships:** Texas.

Add'l Information: Established 1978. Normal turnaround time- 2-3 days. Expedited service available. Projects billed by the hour. First project may require prepayment. Will file/record documents for clients. They have expanded their business to cover all Texas. Performs service of process.

Professional Civil Process (McAllen)

4307 N 10th St #G-2, McAllen, TX 78504-3019
Phone: 800-880-4223; 956-630-4223 - **Fax:** 956-630-4182

Types of Records Retrieved: Criminal, Civil and Probate courts; Federal courts; Real Estate; Tax Liens/Judgments; UCC records; Vital records

Local Retrieval Area: TX-Cameron, Hidalgo, Starr, Willacy. **Correspondent Relationships:** Texas.

Add'l Information: Established 1992. Normal turnaround time- 5 working days. Expedited service available. Projects billed by the hour. All projects require prepayment. Credit cards accepted. They will invoice to NAPPS members only. Their specialties include medical records. Performs service of process.

Professional Courier Service

124 Lyon NW, Grand Rapids, MI 49503
Phone: 616-451-4445 - **Fax:** 616-451-4459 csmith@pcscourier.com

Types of Records Retrieved: Criminal and Civil courts; Federal courts; UCC records; Vital records

Local Retrieval Area: MI-Kent

Add'l Information: Established 1978. Normal turnaround time- 24-48 hours. Expedited service available. Projects billed by the hour. A flat fee is also charged in addition to the per hour fee. First project may require prepayment. Credit cards accepted. Will file/record documents for clients.

Professional Paralegal Services Inc

25 Mill Run Dr, Comer, GA 30629
Phone: 706-783-2648 - **Fax:** 706-783-2009 gaparalegalsvc@yahoo.com

Types of Records Retrieved: Criminal and Civil courts; Real Estate

Local Retrieval Area: GA-Barrow, Clarke, Elbert, Greene, Madison, Morgan, Oconee, Oglethorpe, Putnam, Walton

Add'l Information: Established 1993. Normal turnaround time- varies by job. All projects require prepayment. Will file/record documents for clients. They also provide skiptracing, court filings, court records retrieval, process serving, title searches, deed filings. Performs service of process.

Professional Services of America Inc

601 Avery St #500, Parkersburg, WV 26101
Phone: 304-485-1278 - **Fax:** 304-485-9286
www.psa-inc.com **email:** jzotti@psa-inc.com

Types of Records Retrieved: Criminal courts

Local Retrieval Area: IL-Cook, Du Page; WV-Ritchie, Wood

Add'l Information: Established 1989. Normal turnaround time- 48 hours areas served. Projects billed by number of names searched. First project may require prepayment. They specialize in criminal background checks and social security number trace. They are also a staffing, screening and out-sourcing services company.

Professional Services of New Mexico Inc

PO Box 51554, Albuquerque, NM 87181
Phone: 505-271-2291 - **Fax:** 505-271-2313

Types of Records Retrieved: Criminal courts; Probate courts; Federal courts

Local Retrieval Area: NM-Bernalillo, Sandoval

Add'l Information: Established 1989. Normal turnaround time- 48 hours. Projects billed by number of names searched. Projects billed by the hour. First project may require prepayment. They specialize in search and retrieval of public records.

Professional Support Services of Siouxland

3318 Dearborne Blvd, Sioux City, IA 51104
Phone: 712-233-2382 searchne1@aol.com

Types of Records Retrieved: Criminal, civil and probate courts; Federal courts; Real Estate; Tax Liens/Judgments; UCC records; Vital records

Local Retrieval Area: IA-Woodbury; NE-Dakota; SD-Union

Add'l info: Established 1971. Turnaround time- If requested by 8AM CST, same day; otherwise 36-48 hours. Projects billed by number of names searched. Projects billed by number of records located. Certain projects may be billed by the hour. Service billed upon completion, payable on receipt of detailed report. 1st project may require prepayment. Payment/ Statements billed monthly. Is a consultant and resource for wholesale information retrieval companies who wish to expand into retail markets. Provides full support and detail outline to raise wholesale rate by expanding to retail revenue per search over 400%. A licensed PI in IA.

Profile Information Services

816 Congress Ave #1280, Austin, TX 78701
Phone: 512-472-9380 - **Fax:** 512-472-9551
www.profileinfo.com **email:** profileinfo@sbcglobal.net

Types of Records Retrieved: Criminal, Civil and Probate courts; Federal courts; Real Estate; Tax Liens/Judgments; UCC records; Vital records

Local Retrieval Area: TN-Blount, Knox, Loudon; TX-Anderson, Travis. **Correspondent Relationships:** nationwide and Canada.

Add'l Info: Established 1993. Normal turnaround time- 48-72 hours. Projects billed by number of names searched. First project may require prepayment. They specialize in background verification, asset searches, and corporate, personal financial verification and fraud investigations. Owner Herbert J Cleveland is a certified fraud examiner and PI. A licensed PI in TN.

Promesa Enterprises Inc

5316 W Highway 290 #500, Austin, TX 78735
Phone: 800-474-4420; 512-891-6060 - **Fax:** 512-891-6161
www.integratedscreening.com **email:** info@promesa.com

Types of Records Retrieved: Criminal, Civil and Probate courts; Federal courts; Real Estate; Tax Liens/Judgments; UCC records; Vital records

Local Retrieval Area: TX-Bastrop, Hays, Travis, Williamson. **Correspondent Relationships:** nationwide.

Add'l Information: Established 1994. Normal turnaround time- 24-72 hours. Projects billed by number of names searched. Projects billed by the hour. First project may require prepayment. Terms: net 30 days. They specialize in pre-employment screening, which includes criminal & civil litigation, also litigation support, pre & post lending decision making, and asset search/verification for individuals nationwide. A licensed PI in TX.

Pronto Process & Messenger Service

PO Box 1194, 114 N 5th Ave, Pasco, WA 99301
Phone: 509-547-1122 - **Fax:** 509-547-5472
pmessen896@charterinternet.com

Types of Records Retrieved: Criminal, Civil and Probate courts; Federal courts; Real Estate; Tax Liens/Judgments; UCC records

Local Retrieval Area: WA-Benton, Columbia, Franklin, Walla Walla

Add'l Information: Established 1981. Normal turnaround time- 1-2 days. Expedited service available. Projects billed by number of names searched. First project may require prepayment. Performs service of process.

Property Research & Documentation Svc Inc

158 Park Rd #11 N, Gonzales, TX 78629
Phone: 210-520-7884 - **Fax:** 210-520-7885 PropResearch@aol.com

Types of Records Retrieved: Criminal, Civil and Probate courts; Federal courts; Real Estate; Tax Liens/Judgments; UCC records; Vital records

Local Retrieval Area: TX-Atascosa, Bandera, Bexar, Caldwell, Comal, DeWitt, Gonzales, Guadalupe, Hays, Kendall, Kerr, Lavaca, Medina, Travis, Williamson, Wilson. **Correspondent Relationships:** Bell, Cameron, Hidalgo, Nueces counties.

Add'l Information: Established 1988. Normal turnaround time- 24-48 hours. Projects billed by number of names searched. Projects billed by the hour. First project may require prepayment. Will file/record documents for clients. Terms: net 15 days for new clients, otherwise net 30. Specializing in subject/adjoiner research for surveyors/engineers; Chains-of title for Environmental Site Assessments, Phase I; city, county, state & federal abstracting, retrieval & recording services. Now with offices in Gonzales & San Antonio.

ProSearch Information Retrieval

69333 County Rd 384, South Haven, MI 49090-7771
Phone: 269-637-5145; Cell- 269-214-0856 - **Fax:** 269-639-8400
www.prosearchinfo.com **email:** office@prosearchinfo.com

Types of Records Retrieved: Criminal, Civil and Probate courts; Federal courts; Real Estate; Tax Liens/Judgments; UCC records; Vital records

Retrieval Area: MI-Allegan, Berrien, Cass, Kalamazoo, Kent, Van Buren

Add'l Information: Established 1996. Normal turnaround time- 24 hours. Projects billed by number of names searched. Terms: net 15 days. They specialize in title and property searches & closings, civil and criminal searches and document retrieval. Expedited services and volume discounts available; call for details and charges. Notary Public.

Prospective Renters Verification Service

PO Box 69, Eagle Creek, OR 97022-0069
Phone: 503-655-0888 - **Fax:** 503-655-0900

Types of Records Retrieved: Criminal and Civil courts; Real Estate; Tax Liens/Judgments; UCC records; Vital records

Local Retrieval Area: OR-Multnomah; WA-Clark. **Correspondent Relationships:** Oregon and Washington.

Add'l Information: Established 1991. Normal turnaround time- 2 hours or less. Projects billed by number of names searched. Monthly billing available. Subscription agreement required. They specialize in tenant and employee screening.

Pro-Tech Investigations LLC

PO Box 6133, Laurel, MS 39441-6133
Phone: 877-685-5655; 601-649-3800 - **Fax:** 601-649-3899
www.proinvestigating.com **email:** jcsj@bellsouth.net

Types of Records Retrieved: Criminal, Civil and Probate courts; Federal courts; Real Estate; Tax Liens/Judgments

Local Retrieval Area: MS-Clarke, Covington, Forrest, Greene, Hancock, Harrison, Jasper, Jefferson Davis, Jones, Lamar, Marion, Pearl River, Perry, Smith, Stone, Wayne

Add'l Information: Established 1997. Normal turnaround time- 24 hours. Projects billed by number of names searched. Will file/record documents for clients. Net 30 days. They specialize in pre-employment screening, background checks, records research, property searches, property abstracting, notary services and document retrieval. A licensed PI in MS.

Provest - Ohio

644 Lynn St #824, Cincinnati, OH 45203
Phone: 800-519-6331; 513-621-1017 - **Fax:** 513-632-3832
paulapi5@aol.com

Types of Records Retrieved: Civil and Probate courts; Federal courts; Real Estate; Tax Liens/Judgments

Local Retrieval Area: OH-Ashland, Brown, Butler, Clermont, Crawford, Cuyahoga, Darke, Delaware, Erie, Fairfield, Fayette, Franklin, Geauga, Greene, Hamilton, Huron, Knox, Lake, Licking, Lorain, Lucas, Madison, Marion, Medina, Montgomery, Morrow, Ottawa, Pickaway, Portage, Preble, Richland, Sandusky, Seneca, Stark, Summit, Union, Warren, Wayne, Wood, Wyandot. **Correspondents:** Ohio and nationwide.

Add'l Information: Established 1996. Normal turnaround time- 1 day or same day service. Projects billed by number of names searched. All projects require prepayment. Formerly Legal Ease Inc, they now provide statewide court record retrieval, filings, process service, and investigative research to clients nationwide. Has Ohio offices in Toledo, Columbus and Cleveland, Performs service of process.

PST Abstracting Inc

38 Ivy Rd, Rocky Point, NY 11778
Phone: 631-744-0759 - **Fax:** 631-744-7120 pstabstracting@aol.com

Types of Records Retrieved: Civil and Probate courts; Federal courts; Real Estate; Tax Liens/Judgments; UCC records

Local Retrieval Area: NY-Nassau, Suffolk

Add'l Information: Established 1995. Normal turnaround time- less than 48 hours. Projects billed by number of names searched. Discounts given for multiple searches ordered. Will file/record documents for clients. A full service information and retrieval corp that includes records, UCC, mortgages, deeds, judgments, etc. They have an excellent turnaround time.

Public Chex Inc

4160 High Gables E, Cumming, GA 30041-2009
Phone: 770-889-5662 - **Fax:** 770-889-1132 pchex@adelphia.net

Types of Records Retrieved: Criminal and Civil courts; Federal courts; Real Estate; Tax Liens/Judgments; UCC records

Local Retrieval Area: GA-Bartow, Cherokee, Cobb, Dawson, De Kalb, Forsyth, Fulton, Gwinnett, Hall

Add'l Information: Established 1999. Normal turnaround time- 24-36 hours. Projects billed by number of names searched. Will file/record documents for clients.

Public Information Resource

PO Box 509, Readfield, ME 04355-0509
Phone: 800-675-6350; 207-685-3500 - **Fax:** 207-685-3338
keepar@adelphia.net

Types of Records Retrieved: Real Estate; Tax Liens/Judgments; UCC records; Vital records

Local Retrieval Area: ME-Androscoggin, Cumberland, Franklin, Kennebec, Knox, Lincoln, Oxford, Penobscot, Sagadahoc, Somerset, Waldo, York. **Correspondent Relationships:** Maine and New Brunswick, Canada.

Add'l Information: Established 1985. Normal turnaround time- same day to 48 hours. Projects billed by number of names searched. Projects billed by the hour. First project may require prepayment. Will file/record documents for clients. Personal checks are accepted. They take UCC-11's to the State Department daily. They file UCCs, articles of incorporation, annual reports and obtain Certificates of Good Standing. (CGS).

Public Record Services

PO Box 11565, Montgomery, AL 36111
Phone: 334-262-0350 - **Fax:** 334-263-0167 m.gewin@worldnet.att.net
Types of Records Retrieved: Criminal, Civil and Probate courts; Federal courts; Real Estate; Tax Liens/Judgments; UCC records; Vital records
Local Retrieval Area: AL-Autauga, Baldwin, Barbour, Bibb, Blount, Bullock, Butler, Calhoun, Chambers, Cherokee, Chilton, Choctaw, Clarke, Clay, Cleburne, Coffee, Colbert, Conecuh, Coosa, Covington, Crenshaw, Cullman, Dale, Dallas, De Kalb, Elmore, Escambia, Etowah, Fayette, Franklin, Geneva, Greene, Hale, Henry, Houston, Jackson, Jefferson, Lamar, Lauderdale, Lawrence, Lee, Limestone, Lowndes, Macon, Madison, Marengo, Marion, Marshall, Mobile, Monroe, Montgomery, Morgan, Perry, Pickens, Pike, Randolph, Russell, St Clair, Shelby, Sumter, Talladega, Tallapoosa, Tuscaloosa, Walker, Washington, Wilcox, Winston. **Correspondent Relationships:** statewide.
Add'l info: Established 1974. Projects billed by number of names searched. Projects billed by the hour. Will file/record documents for clients. The only Alabama firm covering all record sources. Performs service of process.

Public Records Abstract

142 Koenig Rd, Bernville, PA 19506
Phone: 484-256-6416
Types of Records Retrieved: Criminal and Civil courts; Federal courts; Real Estate; Tax Liens/Judgments; UCC records; Vital records
Local Retrieval Area: PA-Berks
Add'l Information: Established 1998. Normal turnaround time- 24-48 hours. Will file/record documents for clients. They will invoice bi-monthly. They specialize in all courthouse records.

Public Records Info Service

PO Box 91109, Tucson, AZ 85752
Phone: 520-797-0486 - **Fax:** 520-575-8644 perhach@earthlink.net
Types of Records Retrieved: Criminal and Civil courts
Local Retrieval Area: AZ-Coconino, Maricopa, Pima; NV-Clark
Add'l Information: Established 1989. Normal turnaround time- 24-48 hours. Projects billed by number of names searched. Will bill at end of month.

Public Records Research

403-C N Jefferson Ave, Cookeville, TN 38501
Phone: 931-520-8902 - **Fax:** 931-520-1911 shawngp@excite.com
Types of Records Retrieved: Criminal, Civil and Probate courts; Federal courts; Real Estate; Tax Liens/Judgments; UCC records; Vital records
Local Retrieval Area: TN-Cumberland, DeKalb, Overton, Putnam. **Correspondent Relationships:** Van Buren, Warren, White counties TN.
Add'l Information: Established 1997. Normal turnaround time- 1-3 days. Projects billed by number of names searched. First project may require prepayment.

Public Records Research Inc (Florida)

11350 178th Rd No, Jupiter, FL 33478
Phone: 561-746-0850 - **Fax:** 561-745-2450 publicrr@adelphia.net
Types of Records Retrieved: Criminal, Civil and Probate courts; Federal courts; Real Estate; Tax Liens/Judgments; UCC records
Local Retrieval Area: FL-Martin, Palm Beach
Add'l Information: Established 1986. Normal turnaround time- 48 hours. Projects billed by number of names searched. Projects billed by number of records located. Projects billed by the hour. First project may require prepayment. Will file/record documents for clients. They have over 30 years experience searching court records. They are very customer orientated and very knowledgeable and have reasonable rates.

Pulaski County Abstract - IN

117 Main St, Winamac, IN 46996
Phone: 574-946-3841 - **Fax:** 574-946-7330
Types of Records Retrieved: Criminal and Civil courts; Real Estate; Tax Liens/Judgments
Local Retrieval Area: IN-Pulaski
Add'l Information: Normal turnaround time- 24-48 hours. Projects billed by number of names searched. First project may require prepayment. Will file/record documents for clients. They specialize in Pulaski County exclusively.

Pulaski County Abstract Company - IL

232 Main St, Mound City, IL 62963
Phone: 618-748-9233, Fax- same
Types of Records Retrieved: Civil and Probate courts; Real Estate; Tax Liens/Judgments; UCC records; Vital records
Local Retrieval Area: IL-Pulaski
Add'l Information: Established 1960. Normal turnaround time- 2-14 days. Fee basis will vary by complexity and time of the job. Personal checks are accepted. They specialize in real estate transactions and court records.

Pure Again

37861 Town Hall, Harrison Township, MI 48045
Phone: 586-465-4359, cell- 586-484-3242 - **Fax:** 586-465-5727
steve@totheworld.com
Types of Records Retrieved: Criminal courts (Macomb county only); Real Estate; Tax Liens/Judgments; UCC records
Local Retrieval Area: MI-Macomb, Oakland, Wayne
Add'l Information: Established 1994. Normal turnaround time- 24-48 hours. Expedited service available. Projects billed by number of names searched. They take pride in everything they do. They work efficiently and exactly. Has been a record retriever for 12 years without complaints. Also does commercial searches in Wayne County.

Purintun Abstract

103 Second St SE, De Smet, SD 57231
Phone: 605-854-3401; Fax- same
Types of Records Retrieved: Real Estate; Tax Liens/Judgments; UCC records; Probate courts
Local Retrieval Area: SD-Kingsbury
Add'l Information: Established 1906. Normal turnaround time- 1-10 days. First project may require prepayment. Will file/record documents for clients. He specializes in real estate.

Pushmataha County Abstract Co

Box 849, Antlers, OK 74523
Phone: 580-298-3189 - **Fax:** 580-298-2322
Types of Records Retrieved: Civil and Probate courts; Real Estate; Tax Liens/Judgments
Local Retrieval Area: OK-Pushmataha
Add'l Information: Established 1988. Normal turnaround time- 3-7 days. Projects billed by number of names searched. Projects billed by number of records located. Projects billed by the hour. All projects require prepayment. They specialize in abstracting and title insurance.

Putnam County Abstract

PO Box 303, 107 S 16th St, Unionville, MO 63565
Phone: 660-947-3105 - **Fax:** 660-947-3105
Records Retrieved: Real Estate; Tax Liens/Judgments; UCC records
Local Retrieval Area: MO-Putnam, Sullivan
Add'l Information: Established 1967. Normal turnaround time- 1 week. Fee basis varies by type of transaction. Will file/record documents for clients.

Doris Pye

250 Hartman Dr, Harrisonburg, VA 22802
Phone: 540-433 8134 - **Fax:** 540-433 8134
dapye@adelphia.net
Types of Records Retrieved: Criminal, Civil and Probate courts; Federal courts; Real Estate; Tax Liens/Judgments; UCC records; Vital records
Local Retrieval Area: VA-Harrisonburg City, Rockingham
Add'l Information: Established 1991. Normal turnaround time- 48 hours. Projects billed by number of names searched. First project may require prepayment. Will file/record documents for clients. Please email all requests to dapye@adelphia.net. They specialize in ABA certified paralegal services, jury consulting, process service, and document retrieval. A licensed PI in VA. Performs service of process.

Pyramid Abstract

PO Box 127, 222 Center Ave, Oakley, KS 67748
Phone: 785-672-4285 - **Fax:** 785-672-3122

Types of Records Retrieved: Criminal and Civil courts; Real Estate; Tax Liens/Judgments **Local Retrieval Area:** KS-Logan

Add'l Information: First project may require prepayment. Will file/record documents for clients. They specialize in real estate but can do court searches when asked.

Pyramid Research

907 Kent Dr, David, CA 95616
Phone: 530-867-1568 - **Fax:** 530-750-3302 rdelao@sbcglobal.net

Types of Records Retrieved: Criminal and Civil courts; Tax Liens/Judgments

Local Retrieval Area: CA-Contra Costa, Solano, Yolo

Add'l Information: Established 2005. Normal turnaround time- 24 hours on name searches. Projects billed by name depending on volume. They specialize in in-person research. They are prompt and professional.

Quality Abstractors Inc

129 W Patrick St #11, Frederick, MD 21701
Phone: 301-695-9329 - **Fax:** 301-695-5016
www.quality-titles.com **email:** requests@quality-titles.com

Types of Records Retrieved: Criminal, Civil and Probate courts; Real Estate; Tax Liens/Judgments; UCC records

Local Retrieval Area: MD-Frederick, Washington

Add'l Information: Established 1966. Normal turnaround time- 1-14 days. Projects billed by number of names searched. Personal checks are accepted. They have been in the land title abstracting business for more than 25 years. They are the largest abstracting company in Frederick County, MD.

Quality Business Information

PO Box 2645, Elk Grove, CA 95759
Phone: 916-684-0444 - **Fax:** 916-684-4950
qbinfocoy@aol.com

Types of Records Retrieved: Criminal and Civil courts

Local Retrieval Area: CA-Amador, Calaveras, El Dorado, Nevada, Placer, Sacramento, San Joaquin, Solano, Stanislaus, Yolo. **Correspondent Relationships:** statewide.

Add'l Information: Established 1989. Normal turnaround time- 48 hours. Projects billed by number of names searched. Terms: net 30-60 days. No databases are used. Researchers personally go to all courthouses on a daily basis. Many counties researched by private investigators. They have over 50 years experience with court research. A licensed PI in CA.

Quality Research Service Inc

814 Barbara Dr, Craig, CO 81625
Phone: 970-824-4144, cell- 970-629-0388 - **Fax:** 970-824-4144
bjohnson@gct21.net

Types of Records Retrieved: Real Estate; Tax Liens/Judgments; UCC records; Mineral interests

Local Retrieval Area: CO-Moffat, Rio Blanco, Routt. **Correspondent Relationships:** Routt, Rio Blanco counties CO.

Add'l Information: Established 2002. Normal turnaround time- 24-36 hours. Results returned by fax. Projects billed by number of names searched. Big projects such as chain of title for mineral/surface ownership are billed by hour or by day rate. Payment due within 30 days. They specialize in searches, document retrieval, county loan closings, document filings & oil & gas minerals search. Also provided title searches for mineral ownership. She is a retired county clerk with 24 years experience. Cell phone# is 970-629-0388.

Quantum Recording Services

6610 Lear Nagle Rd #257, North Ridgeville, OH 44039-3288
Phone: 440-327-5604, 440-554-0040 - **Fax:** 440-327-5604
www.qrs.50megs.com **email:** Qrscrystal@alltel.net

Types of Records Retrieved: Criminal and Civil courts; Real Estate; Tax Liens/Judgments; Vital records

Local Retrieval Area: OH-Cuyahoga, Lorain, Medina. **Correspondent Relationships:** elsewhere in Ohio.

Add'l Information: Established 2004. Normal turnaround time- same day for request received by 10 am (EST) otherwise 24 hours. Projects billed by number of names searched. First project may require prepayment. They specialize in document retrieval on Northeastern OH. You name the document, they will find it. Also, they provide recording services and Notary services.

Queen City Paralegal

3901 Belfast Ave, Cincinnati, OH 45236-1633
Phone: 513-984-4345 - **Fax:** 513-984-4342
gayle_lunken@hotmail.com

Types of Records Retrieved: Civil and Probate courts; Real Estate; Tax Liens/Judgments

Local Retrieval Area: OH-Butler, Clermont, Hamilton, Warren

Add'l Information: Established 1993. Normal turnaround time- 24-48 hours. Will bill monthly or per project. Will file/record documents for clients. They specialize in 42 year and current owner real estate searches, as well as E.P.A. (environmental) and commercial title examinations. They also have loan closing availability.

Quest & Assoc Inc

2517 Wenzell Ave, Pittsburgh, PA 15216
Phone: 412-563-1007 - **Fax:** 412-563-6869
quest78820@earthlink.net

Types of Records Retrieved: Criminal, Civil and Probate courts; Federal courts; Real Estate; Tax Liens/Judgments; UCC records

Local Retrieval Area: PA-Allegheny. **Correspondent Relationships:** Pennsylvania; sub-contractors for nationwide searches.

Add'l Information: Established 1990. Normal turnaround time- 24-72 hours. Projects billed by number of names searched. Will file/record documents for clients. Billed last business day of month. They specialize in all public record searches.

Quest Discovery Service

2025 Gateway Place #330, San Jose, CA 95110
Phone: 408-441-7000 - **Fax:** 408-441-7070
www.questds.com **email:** becky@questds.com

Types of Records Retrieved: Civil and Probate courts; Federal courts; Real Estate; Tax Liens/Judgments; UCC records; Vital records

Local Retrieval Area: CA-all counties. **Correspondent Relationships:** Nevada and nationally.

Add'l Information: Established 1966. Normal turnaround time- 4 days. Projects billed by number of names searched. Projects billed by number of records located. First project may require prepayment. Will file/record documents for clients. Terms: net 30 days. Formerly Valley Copy Svc. An attorney service with 8 branch offices, they prepare subpoenas, serve process and copy medical employment and other records throughout CA. Performs service of process.

Quest Research (Arkansas)

101 S Spring St #220, Little Rock, AR 72201
Phone: 501-374-4712 - **Fax:** 501-374-3029
www.questresearch.info **email:** questark@sprynet.com

Types of Records Retrieved: Criminal, Civil and Probate courts; Federal courts; Real Estate; Tax Liens/Judgments; UCC records; Vital records

Local Retrieval Area: AR-Arkansas, Clark, Conway, Faulkner, Garland, Grant, Hot Spring, Jefferson, Lonoke, Monroe, Montgomery, Perry, Prairie,

Pulaski, Saline. **Correspondent Relationships:** statewide, AR, TX, OK, MO, TN, KY, MS, AL, GA, FL.

Add'l Information: Established 1982. Normal turnaround time- 1-3 days. Projects billed by number of names searched. First project may require prepayment. Will file/record documents for clients. Payment due upon receipt of invoice. They specialize in corporate retrieval, filing service, lien searches title searches, and document retrieval. They provide these services in all 75 Arkansas counties through a combination of employees and correspondents. Established in 1982.

Quick Data Services Inc

50 W 3900 S #2B, Salt Lake City, UT 84107
Phone: 800-720-6167; 801-268-4407 - **Fax:** 800-720-6168; 801-268-4415
lquick@quickdatastaff.com

Types of Records Retrieved: Criminal, Civil and Probate courts; Federal courts; Real Estate; Tax Liens/Judgments; UCC records; Vital records

Local Retrieval Area: UT-Box Elder, Cache, Davis, Morgan, Salt Lake, Summit, Tooele, Utah, Wasatch, Weber. **Correspondents:** statewide.

Add'l Information: Established 1995. Normal turnaround time- same day or next day. Expedited service available. Projects billed by number of names searched. First project may require prepayment. Will file/record documents for clients. Terms: net 30 days. They specialize in state level UCC searches & filings, corporate document filing and registered agent services. They also do county level UCC, tax lien and judgment searches, property reports and certified copy retrieval.

Quick Search

4155 Buena Vista St, Dallas, TX 75204-7518
Phone: 214-358-2840 - **Fax:** 214-358-6057
www.quicksi.com **email:** dwolter@quicksi.com

Types of Records Retrieved: Criminal, Civil and Probate courts; Federal courts; Real Estate; Tax Liens/Judgments; UCC records; Vital records

Local Retrieval Area: TX-Collin, Cooke, Dallas, Denton, Ellis, El Paso, Fannin, Grayson, Hunt, Johnson, Kaufman, Montague, Rockwall, Tarrant. **Correspondent Relationships:** nationwide.

Add'l Information: Established 1991. Normal turnaround time- 4-72 hours. Projects billed by number of names searched. Credit cards accepted. Will file/record documents for clients. Terms: net 30 days. They specialize all types of retrieval. Check their website at www.quicksi.com. Customers can send and receive orders by online system, data transfer, email, or fax. A licensed PI in TX.

Quick Search Title Services

3420 Elm St, St Charles, MO 63301
Phone: 636-723-1888 qusearch@aol.com

Records Retrieved: Criminal, Civil and Probate courts; Bankruptcy court; Real Estate; Tax Liens/Judgments; UCC records; Vital records

Local Retrieval Area: MO-St. Charles, St. Louis City, St. Louis. **Correspondent Relationships:** Franklin, Jefferson, Lincoln counties.

Add'l Information: Established 1995. Normal turnaround time- 6-8 hours. Will file/record documents for clients. Quick Search Title Svcs offers quick and accurate title search services with superior customer service.

Quickfacts

134 Hill St, Woodstock, IL 60098
Phone: 815-236-8874 - **Fax:** 815-308-5027
myillinoissearcher@comcast.net

Types of Records Retrieved: Criminal and Civil courts; Real Estate; Tax Liens/Judgments; UCC records

Local Retrieval Area: IL-McHenry. **Correspondent Relationships:** Illinois.

Add'l Information: Established 1993. Normal turnaround time- 24-48 hours. Projects billed by number of names searched. Will file/record documents for clients. Will invoice with a net 30 days. Melissa Flavin specializes in local court criminal cases and does civil searches incidentally. Has more that 13 years experience in public record document retrieval and research.

Quik Check Records Inc

PO Box 440, Willamina, OR 97396-0440
Phone: 503-876-6477 - **Fax:** 503-876-6877
info@quikcheckrecords.com

Types of Records Retrieved: Criminal, Civil and Probate courts; Federal courts; Real Estate; Tax Liens/Judgments; UCC records; Vital records

Local Retrieval Area: OR-Baker, Benton, Clackamas, Clatsop, Columbia, Coos, Crook, Curry, Deschutes, Douglas, Gilliam, Grant, Harney, Hood River, Jackson, Jefferson, Josephine, Klamath, Lake, Lane, Lincoln, Linn, Malheur, Marion, Morrow, Multnomah, Polk, Sherman, Tillamook, Umatilla, Union, Wallowa, Washington, Wheeler, Yamhill; WA-Adams, Asotin, Benton, Chelan, Clallam, Clark, Cowlitz, Douglas, Ferry, Franklin, Garfield, Grant, Grays Harbor, Jefferson, King, Kitsap, Kittitas, Lewis, Lincoln, Mason, Okanogan, Pacific, Pend Oreille, Pierce, San Juan, Skagit, Skamania, Snohomish, Spokane, Stevens, Thurston, Walla Walla, Whitman, Yakima. **Correspondent Relationships:** Nationwide and especially OR, WA, CA, NV.

Add'l Information: Established 1996. Normal turnaround time- 24 hours; can depend on search type and requirements. Expedited service available. Projects billed by number of names searched. Projects billed by the hour. Volume discounts available. Will file/record documents for clients. Terms net 15 days of invoice. They specialize in civil and criminal research, land records research, document recording, and they copy medical records from physicians, hospitals and clinics. They have been providing Washington and Oregon public records since 1996.

Quinn and Woodall Attnys

PO Box 1549, Cadiz, KY 42211
Phone: 270-522-3481 - **Fax:** 270-522-3483

Types of Records Retrieved: Real Estate; Tax Liens/Judgments

Local Retrieval Area: KY-Trigg

Add'l Information: First project may require prepayment. They specialize in real estate; is a law firm; they perform search services on a limited basis.

Quirk Associates

368 Washington St, Dedham, MA 02026
Phone: 781-326-1202 - **Fax:** 781-326-0916

Types of Records Retrieved: Real Estate; Tax Liens/Judgments; Probate courts; UCC records; Vital records

Local Retrieval Area: MA-Middlesex, Norfolk, Suffolk. **Correspondent Relationships:** Plymouth, Essex, Bristol counties.

Add'l Information: Established 1988. Normal turnaround time- within 1 week. The fee basis will vary with the type of search. They specialize in real estate record searches.

R & B Research & Recording Inc

208 S Blvd #A, Evanston, IL 60202
Phone: 847-477-7510 - **Fax:** 847-492-9241 rbresearch@sbcglobal.net

Types of Records Retrieved: Real Estate; UCC records

Local Retrieval Area: IL-Cook, Du Page, Kane, Lake, McHenry, Will. **Correspondent Relationships:** statewide.

Add'l Information: Established 2002. Normal turnaround time- 1-3 days. Projects billed by number of names searched. payment due net 30 days. They are a document retrieval/recording company. They provide quick turnaround in the Chicago land area. Also provide coverage for State of IL.

R & D Research Services

108 Central Ave NW, Orange City, IA 51041
Phone: 712-737-8741 - **Fax:** 712-737-8629
www.certifiedabstractandtitle.com **email:** vanroeke@frontiernet.net

Types of Records Retrieved: Criminal, Civil and Probate courts; Federal courts; Real Estate; Tax Liens/Judgments; UCC records; Vital records

Local Retrieval Area: IA-Buena Vista, Cherokee, Clay, Dickinson, Lyon, O'Brien, Osceola, Plymouth, Sioux, Woodbury. **Correspondent Relationships:** nationwide.

Add'l Information: Established 1999. Normal turnaround time- 24-48 hours. Projects billed by number of names searched. All projects require prepayment. They specialize in far northwest Iowa counties. Also abstracting, appraisals, mortgage broker and witness closing. A licensed PI in IA. Performs service of process.

R & R Search Inc

24 Lowell Mason Rd, Medfield, MA 02052
Phone: 508-359-2400 - **Fax:** 508-359-7682
www.randrsearch.com **email:** orders@randrsearch.com

Types of Records Retrieved: Criminal, Civil and Probate courts; Federal courts; Real Estate; Tax Liens/Judgments; UCC records; Vital records

Local Retrieval Area: MA-Barnstable, Berkshire, Bristol, Dukes, Essex, Franklin, Hampden, Hampshire, Middlesex, Nantucket, Norfolk, Plymouth, Suffolk, Worcester. **Correspondent Relationships:** nationwide.

Add'l Information: Established 1997. Normal turnaround time- 24-48 hours. Projects billed by number of names searched. First project may require prepayment. They specialize in Massachusetts and nationwide public record research, document retrieval, filing services, UCC searches, corporate document retrieval, court searches, tax lien searches and real property searches.

R A Heales & Associates Ltd

7935 E Prentice Ave #301, Englewood, CO 80111
Phone: 800-225-7043; 303-721-6300 - **Fax:** 303-721-6340
www.heales-pi.com **Types of Records Retrieved:** Criminal, Civil and Probate courts; Federal courts; Real Estate; Tax Liens/Judgments; UCC records; Vital records

Local Retrieval Area: CO-Adams, Arapahoe, Boulder, Denver, Douglas, El Paso, Jefferson. **Correspondent Relationships:** Minnesota and Colorado.

Add'l Information: Established 1974. Normal turnaround time- 2-3 days. Projects billed by the hour. First project may require prepayment. Credit cards accepted. Will file/record documents for clients. Personal checks are accepted. Also has offices in Minneapolis and Cross Lake Minnesota. Is Past President of Prof. PI Association of Colorado; served on Board of Directors of the NCISS.

R Frier Title Services

6315 Winner Ave, Baltimore, MD 21215
Phone: city- 410-627-1991; county- 410-977-6667 - **Fax:** 410-358-7527
ralphfrier@earthlink.net

Types of Records Retrieved: Real Estate; Tax Liens/Judgments

Local Retrieval Area: MD-Baltimore City and County.. **Correspondent Relationships:** statewide.

Add'l Information: Established 1995. Normal turnaround time- 1-2 days. Projects billed by number of names searched. Formerly Action Abstracts, they specialize in document retrieval statewide and title abstracts in Baltimore county. Fully insured, thorough and on time.

R Miller & Associates LLC

PO Box 40579, Albuquerque, NM 87196
Phone: 800-395-1992; 505-345-4100 - **Fax:** 505-345-4374
www.rmalocate.com **email:** rmalocate@aol.com

Types of Records Retrieved: Criminal, Civil and Probate courts; Federal courts; Real Estate; Tax Liens/Judgments; UCC records

Local Retrieval Area: NM-Bernalillo

Add'l Information: Established 1982. Normal turnaround time- 24-48 hours. Projects billed by number of names searched. Bill monthly. The do general investigations, background screening, missing persons, asset searches and record retrieval. They are licensed and bonded and have 25 years experience. A licensed PI in NM. Performs service of process.

R T Boxold & Associates LLC

PO Box 212855, Royal Palm Beach, FL 33411
Phone: 561-371-3855 - **Fax:** 206-666-4314
www.boxold.net **email:** rtb2002@bellsouth.net

Types of Records Retrieved: Criminal, Civil and Probate courts; Federal courts; Real Estate; Tax Liens/Judgments; UCC records; Vital records

Local Retrieval Area: FL-Broward, Dade, Hendry, Martin, Okeechobee, Palm Beach

Add'l Information: Established 2004. Normal turnaround time- 3-5 days. Expedited service available. Projects billed by the hour. All projects require prepayment. He is a private investigator with extensive experience in applicant background and police compliance investigations. A licensed PI in FL. Performs service of process.

Raban's Record Search & Inv

PO Box 1105, St Johns, AZ 85936
Phone: 928-337-4250 - **Fax:** 928-337-4250 dcraban@frontier.net

Types of Records Retrieved: Criminal, Civil and Probate courts; Real Estate; Tax Liens/Judgments; UCC records

Local Retrieval Area: AZ-Apache

Add'l Information: Established 1992. Normal turnaround time- 24 hours; guaranteed 48. Projects billed by number of names searched. First project may require prepayment. Will file/record documents for clients. They specialize in Apache County AZ as a document retriever, process server, and attorney service. They will also accept and file documents, confirm and return. FedEx service available. Performs service of process.

Raines Record Research Inc

10072 Dulaney Rd, Rixeyville, VA 22737
Phone: 540-937-2005 - **Fax:** 540-937-3848 rainesrecordrsch@aol.com

Types of Records Retrieved: Real Estate; Vital records

Local Retrieval Area: VA-Culpeper, Fauquier, Rappahannock

Add'l Information: Established 2000. Normal turnaround time- 24-48 hours. Fees negotiated with volume. Will file/record documents for clients. They specialize in document retrieval and abstracting and get them to clients as soon as possible. Services include vital records, deeds, wills, judgments, and UCC searches.

RAM Services

PO Box 8356, Newport Beach, CA 92658-8356
Phone: 714-792-2860 - **Fax:** 714-792-2860
ramservices@pacbell.net

Types of Records Retrieved: Criminal, Civil and Probate courts; Federal courts; Real Estate; Tax Liens/Judgments; UCC records; Vital records

Local Retrieval Area: CA-Orange

Add'l Information: Established 1983. Normal turnaround time- 24 hours to 2 weeks. A licensed PI in CA. Performs service of process.

Ramsey Paralegal/Process

18 S Bradley Branch Rd #12, Arden, NC 28704
Phone: 828-687-9974; send faxes to Attn. Don Ramsey - **Fax:** 828-650-6678
dram12@hotmail.com

Types of Records Retrieved: Criminal, Civil and Probate courts; Federal courts; Real Estate; Tax Liens/Judgments; UCC records; Vital records

Local Retrieval Area: NC-Buncombe, Burke, Cherokee, Cleveland, Haywood, Henderson, Jackson, Macon, Madison, McDowell, Polk, Rutherford, Swain, Transylvania, Yancey

Add'l Information: Established 1989. Turnaround time- 1-2 days. Expedited service available. Fee varies. First project may require prepayment. They specialize in data searches, locate persons, SOP & record retrievals and buys mortgage and business notes. Performs service of process.

Ranger Recovery

PO Box 1184, Woodstock, NY 12498
Phone: 845-679-2957 - **Fax:** 845-679-5889
http://ronsafe.webjogger.net **email:** rangerrecovery@yahoo.com

Types of Records Retrieved: Criminal, Civil and Probate courts; Real Estate; Tax Liens/Judgments; UCC records; Vital records

Local Retrieval Area: NY-Ulster. **Correspondent Relationships:** Greene, Dutchess, Columbia counties NY and DE counties.

Add'l Information: Established 1986. Normal turnaround time- less than 1 week. Projects billed by number of names searched. Projects billed by number of records located. Projects billed by the hour. First project may require prepayment. Will file/record documents for clients. A licensed PI in NY. Performs service of process.

Ransom County Title Co

PO Box 511, 7 Fourth Ave W, Lisbon, ND 58054

Phone: 701-683-5511; Fax- same

Types of Records Retrieved: Real Estate; Tax Liens/Judgments

Local Retrieval Area: ND-Ransom

Add'l Information: Established 1953. Normal turnaround time- 1 week. Projects billed by number of names searched. Projects billed by number of records located. Fee basis will vary by the type of project. First project may require prepayment. Will file/record documents for clients.

Rapid Document Service

211 S Lincoln Way, Galt, CA 95632

Phone: 209-745-0999 - **Fax:** 800-225-0036; 209-745-0908

dseitz@softcom.net

Types of Records Retrieved: Criminal, Civil and Probate courts; Federal courts; Real Estate; Tax Liens/Judgments; UCC records; Vital records

Local Retrieval Area: CA-Alameda, Amador, Calaveras, Contra Costa, El Dorado, Fresno, Madera, Marin, Merced, Napa, Placer, Sacramento, San Francisco, San Joaquin, San Mateo, Santa Clara, Solano, Stanislaus, Sutter, Yolo. **Correspondent Relationships:** Putnam, White counties TN.

Add'l Information: Established 2001. Normal turnaround time- 12-48 hours. Projects billed by number of names searched. They invoice monthly. They specialize in felony, misdemeanor and civil searches.

Rapid Documents

2512 Dave Dietz Dr, Cookville, TN 38506

Phone: 931-372-6948 - **Fax:** 931-372-2948 dseitz@softcom.net

Types of Records Retrieved: Criminal, Civil and Probate courts; Real Estate; Tax Liens/Judgments; UCC records; Vital records

Local Retrieval Area: TN-Putnam, White

Add'l Information: Normal turnaround time- 12-48 hours. Projects billed by number of names searched.

Rapid Record Retrieval

PO Box 677, Monument Beach, MA 02553-0677

Phone: 508-759-8622 - **Fax:** 508-759-9657

www.rapidrecordretrieval.com **email:** lori@rapidrecordretrieval.com

Types of Records Retrieved: Criminal and Civil courts

Local Retrieval Area: MA-Barnstable, Bristol, Norfolk, Plymouth; RI-Bristol, Kent, Newport, Providence, Washington. **Correspondent Relationships:** New Hampshire.

Add'l Information: Established 1999. Normal turnaround time- 2 business days. Projects billed by number of names searched. First project may require prepayment. Terms: net 15 days.

Rapid Research

1271 Washington Ave #580, San Leandro, CA 94577

Phone: 510-777-9461 - **Fax:** 510-291-9659

jimdammann@sbcglobal.net

Types of Records Retrieved: Criminal and Civil courts

Local Retrieval Area: CA-Alameda, San Mateo. **Correspondent Relationships:** California.

Add'l Information: Established 1994. Normal turnaround time- 1 day. Projects billed by number of names searched. They specialize in criminal records for pre-employment screening companies; courts are visited daily.

RASCAL

28465 Old Town Front St #318, Temecula, CA 92590

Phone: 951-693-0165 - **Fax:** 951-693-4056

www.ranchoattorneyservice.com **email:** ranchoattysvc@aol.com

Types of Records Retrieved: Criminal, Civil and Probate courts; Real Estate; Tax Liens/Judgments

Local Retrieval Area: CA-Riverside, San Diego. **Correspondent Relationships:** Los Angeles, Orange, Ventura, San Bernardino, Riverside, San Diego.

Add'l Information: Established 1988. Normal turnaround time- 1-5 days. Projects billed by number of names searched. Projects billed by the hour. First project may require prepayment. They accept personal checks. They specialize in service of process in those "hard to reach" places. They also specialize in "search and serves." A licensed PI in CA PI# 24790. Performs service of process.

Rat Dog Research LLC

204 Bruce Dr, Coeur D' Alene, ID 83814

Phone: 208-765-4598 - **Fax:** 208-666-8872 ratdogresearch@hotmail.com

Records Retrieved: Real Estate; Tax Liens/Judgments; UCC records

Local Retrieval Area: ID-Kootenai; WA-Asotin, Spokane, Stevens. **Correspondent Relationships:** Ada, Bannock, Benewah, Bingham, Bonner, Bonneville, Boundary, Canyon, Cassia, Fremont, Gem, Gooding, Idaho, Jefferson, Jerome, Kootenai, Latah, Lewis, Lincoln, Madison, Minidoka, Nez Perce, Owyhee, Payette, Twin Falls, Washington.

Add'l Information: Established 1996. Normal turnaround time- 24 hours. Projects billed by number of names searched. Will file/record documents for clients. Monthly billing. They specialize in searches in northern Idaho and eastern Washington State. They offer over 20 years of mortgage underwriting experience.

Ray County Land Title

203 W Main, Richmond, MO 64085

Phone: 816-470-6500 - **Fax:** 816-776-8265

Types of Records Retrieved: Real Estate; Tax Liens/Judgments

Local Retrieval Area: MO-Ray

Add'l Information: Established 1997. First project may require prepayment. They specialize in real estate.

RCC & Associates Inc

PO Box 201, N Grafton, MA 01536

Phone: 508-839-3234 - **Fax:** 508-839-0199 rccsearch@aol.com

Types of Records Retrieved: Criminal, Civil and Probate courts; Federal courts; Tax Liens/Judgments

Local Retrieval Area: MA-Middlesex, Suffolk, Worcester

Add'l Information: Established 1999. Normal turnaround time- 24 hours. Projects billed by number of names searched. Payment due net 30 days. They are a retrieval company offering services with the highest level of integrity, quality and efficiency.

Real County Title Co

PO Box 298, Leakey, TX 78873

Phone: 830-232-5303 - **Fax:** 830-232-5399

Types of Records Retrieved: Civil and Probate courts; Real Estate; Tax Liens/Judgments; UCC records

Local Retrieval Area: TX-Real

Add'l Information: Normal turnaround time- 1-2 days. Fee basis will vary by the type of project. Will file/record documents for clients. They specialize in title insurance, title runs and real estate closings.

Real Data

204 Jordan St, Jefferson City, MO 65109-1239

Phone: 573-893-4898 - **Fax:** 573-893-6282

Types of Records Retrieved: Real Estate; Tax Liens/Judgments

Local Retrieval Area: MO-Audrain, Boone, Callaway, Camden, Cole, Cooper, Crawford, Gasconade, Maries, Marion, Morgan, Osage, Pettis, Phelps, Pulaski, Ralls, Randolph

Add'l info: Established 1984. Normal turnaround time- 48 hours. Fee basis will vary per county. Will file/record documents for clients. They specialize in residential real estate searches, deed filing, and document retrievals.

Real Estate Data Inc

3073 Rt 148, Marion, IL 62959-8878
Phone: 618-964-1907 - **Fax:** 618-964-1366

Records Retrieved: Real Estate; Tax Liens/Judgments; UCC records

Local Retrieval Area: IL-Franklin, Johnson, Williamson

Add'l info: Established 1982. Turnaround time- 3 days. Projects billed by number of names searched. Will file/record documents for clients. They specialize in real estate searches and issuance of title policies.

Real Estate Loan Services

5751 Uptain Rd #524, Chattanooga, TN 37411-5675
Phone: 423-855-0581 - **Fax:** 423-894-3184

www.rels-corp.com **Types of Records Retrieved:** Civil and Probate courts; Real Estate; Tax Liens/Judgments; UCC records

Local Retrieval Area: TN-Bledsoe, Bradley, Grundy, Hamilton, McMinn, Marion, Meigs, Monroe, Polk, Rhea, Sequatchie. **Correspondent Relationships:** Georgia.

Add'l info: Normal turnaround time- 24-72 hours. Projects billed by number of records located. First project may require prepayment. Will file/record documents for clients. They specialize in title openings and closing.

Real Estate Loan Services of TN Inc

1100 Kermit Dr #204, Nashville, TN 37217
Phone: 800-475-2334; 615-367-2300 - **Fax:** 615-399-9491

Types of Records Retrieved: Civil and Probate courts; Federal courts; Real Estate; Tax Liens/Judgments; UCC records

Local Retrieval Area: TN-Cannon, Cheatham, Cumberland, Davidson, DeKalb, Dickson, Fentress, Giles, Hickman, Houston, Humphreys, Jackson, Lawrence, Lewis, Macon, Marshall, Maury, Montgomery, Overton, Perry, Pickett, Putnam, Robertson, Rutherford, Smith, Stewart, Sumner, Trousdale, Wayne, White, Williamson, Wilson. **Correspondent Relationships:** Kentucky and Alabama.

Add'l info: Established 1975. Turnaround time- 24-48 hours. Projects billed by number of records located. Fees are based on the number of property addresses searched. All projects require prepayment. Will file/record documents for clients. They specialize in appraisals, property reports, commitments for title insurance, closing documents (prepared, closing, escrow service, foreclosure sales) and other courthouse related services.

Real Land Abstract Inc

3545 Wolf Rd, Taylor Mill, KY 41015
Phone: 859-291-1140 - **Fax:** 859-291-0112 realand@fuse.net

Types of Records Retrieved: Civil and Probate courts; Real Estate; Tax Liens/Judgments; UCC records

Retrieval Area: KY-Boone, Campbell, Kenton; OH-Clermont, Hamilton

Add'l Information: Established 2003. Normal turnaround time- 24-48 hours. First project may require prepayment. Will file/record documents for clients. They specialize in real estate titles.

Real Property Resources

8015 Mountain Road Pl, NE #105, Albuquerque, NM 87110
Phone: 505-232-3555 - **Fax:** 505-294-3244 orders@rprnm.com

Types of Records Retrieved: Civil and Probate courts; Real Estate; Tax Liens/Judgments; UCC records

Local Retrieval Area: NM-Bernalillo, Cibola, Dona Ana, Los Alamos, McKinley, Sandoval, San Juan, Santa Fe, Valencia,. **Correspondent Relationships:** nationwide.

Add'l Information: Established 1999. Normal turnaround time- 48 hours or less for current owner searches. Projects billed by number of names searched. Will file/record documents for clients. Billing is included in delivery of all orders. Their services include but are not limited to real estate research, document retrieval, generation of title reports, document filing, retrieval of taxes & assessments, etc. They are also a mobile notary public/signing agent.

Reality Check Inc

PO Box 2233, East Peoria, IL 61611-2233
Phone: 309-699-1846 - **Fax:** 309-699-5862 realitychecksrus@hotmail.com

Types of Records Retrieved: Criminal and Civil courts; Federal courts; Real Estate; Tax Liens/Judgments; UCC records

Local Retrieval Area: IL-Peoria, Tazewell

Add'l Information: Established 1998. Normal turnaround time- 24-48 hours. Projects billed by number of names searched. Will do monthly invoicing. They specialize in federal, civil and criminal searches, also title abstracting. Highest quality and accurate researching at low price. OEM clearance credentials. Illinois notary.

Realty Inc

406 Commercial St, Oswego, KS 67356
Phone: 620-795-4511 - **Fax:** 620-795-4759

Types of Records Retrieved: Criminal and Civil courts; Real Estate; Tax Liens/Judgments

Local Retrieval Area: KS-Labette

Add'l Information: Established 1949. Normal turnaround time- 24 hours. First project may require prepayment. Will file/record documents for clients. They specialize in real estate but can do court searches when asked.

Realty Settlement Inc

915 Liberty St, Meadville, PA 16335
Phone: 814-336-1802 - **Fax:** 814-336-5881

Types of Records Retrieved: Civil courts; Real Estate; Tax Liens/Judgments; UCC records

Local Retrieval Area: PA-Crawford, Mercer, Venango

Add'l Information: Normal turnaround time- up to 7 days. Fee basis will vary by the type of project. Will file/record documents for clients. They specialize in title insurance.

Realty Title Co Inc

201 6th Ave South, Lewistown, MT 59457
Phone: 406-535-2326 - **Fax:** 406-535-5184 rtc@midrivers.com

Types of Records Retrieved: Criminal, Civil and Probate courts; Real Estate; Tax Liens/Judgments; UCC records; Vital records

Local Retrieval Area: MT-Fergus, Judith Basin, Petroleum

Add'l info: Established 1890. Normal turnaround time- 2-3 days. Projects billed by the hour. They specialize in title insurance and long-term escrows.

Record Access

327 E 2nd St #225, Los Angeles, CA 90012-4210
Phone: 888-621-1491; 213-617-1828 - **Fax:** 213-625-1792
recordaccess@yahoo.com

Types of Records Retrieved: Criminal, Civil and Probate courts; Federal courts; Tax Liens/Judgments; UCC records

Local Retrieval Area: CA-Los Angeles, Orange. **Correspondent Relationships:** nationwide.

Add'l Information: Established 1996. Normal turnaround time- same to next day. Fee may be by number of names searched or by the hour. First project may require prepayment. They specialize in name searches in all government offices and research of public records and documents.

Record Data Inc (Arkansas)

11501 Huron Ln, Little Rock, AR 72211
Phone: 501-223-0949 - **Fax:** 501-223-0944

Types of Records Retrieved: Civil and Probate courts; Federal courts; Real Estate; Tax Liens/Judgments; UCC records

Local Retrieval Area: AR-all counties. **Correspondents in:** Tennessee.

Add'l Information: Established 1986. Normal turnaround time- variable depending upon search requirements. Fee basis varies by project. Formerly Wilson & Associates, RDI provides accurate, timely real estate records retrieval statewide in Arkansas and Tennessee.

Record Data Inc (Tennessee)

100 Winners Circle #110, Brentwood, TN 37027
Phone: 615-221-0021 - **Fax:** 615-221-0053

Types of Records Retrieved: Civil and Probate courts; Federal courts; Real Estate; Tax Liens/Judgments; UCC records

Local Retrieval Area: TN-all counties. **Correspondent in:** Arkansas.

Add'l Information: Established 1986. Normal turnaround time- variable depending on search. Fee basis will vary with type of search. Formerly Wilson & Associates, RDI provides accurate, timely real estate records retrieval statewide in Arkansas and Tennessee.

Record Finders

PO Box 3242, Brownsville, TX 78523
Phone: 956-571-5378 - **Fax:** 956-350-5120 recordfinders@gmail.com

Types of Records Retrieved: Criminal, Civil and Probate courts; Federal courts; Real Estate; Tax Liens/Judgments; UCC records; Vital records

Local Retrieval Area: TX-Cameron, Hidalgo

Add'l info: Established 1998. Normal turnaround time- 24-48 hours. Projects billed by number of names searched. Charge is per index when multiple indexes are searched. Will file/record documents for clients. Will bill per order or at end of month, They specialize in 50 year chain of title searches.

Record Information Services

PO Box 894, Elburn, IL 60119
Phone: 630-557-1000 - **Fax:** 630-557-1001
www.public-record.com **email:** jmetcalf@public-record.com

Types of Records Retrieved: Criminal, Civil and Probate courts; Federal courts; Real Estate; Tax Liens/Judgments; UCC records; Vital records

Local Retrieval Area: IL-Cook, De Kalb, Du Page, Kane, Kendall, Lake, McHenry, Will

Add'l Information: Established 1993. Normal turnaround time- 24 hours. Fees are on project by project basis. All projects require prepayment. Credit cards accepted. They specialize in bankruptcies, judgments, foreclosures, new businesses, homeowners lists, criminal, misdemeanors, felonies, foreclosure sales, building permits, state & federal tax liens, DUIs, divorce, mortgages, foreclosures & property tax liens.

Record Retrieval of Indianapolis

2516 E 17th St, Indianapolis, IN 46218-4302
Phone: 317-383-1306 - **Fax:** 317-383-1306
www.angelfire.com/in4/alvinesper/ **email:** alvinbrenda1@netzero.com

Types of Records Retrieved: Criminal, Civil and Probate courts; Federal courts; Real Estate; Tax Liens/Judgments; UCC records; Vital records

Local Retrieval Area: IN-Marion. **Correspondent Relationships:** nationwide.

Add'l Information: Established 1992. Normal turnaround time- 24-48 hours. Projects billed by number of names searched. Projects billed by the hour. All projects require prepayment. Will file/record documents for clients. Call before faxing. They specialize in service of process and record retrieval, investigations. A licensed PI in IN. Performs service of process.

Record Retrieval Services Inc

5100 Eldorado Pky #102, McKinney, TX 75070-7295
Phone: 866-569-8343; 972-569-8343 - **Fax:** 866-693-0066; 972-569-8363
rrsinc@comcast.net

Types of Records Retrieved: Criminal and Civil courts; Real Estate; Tax Liens/Judgments

Local Retrieval Area: TX-Collin, Dallas. **Correspondents:** statewide.

Add'l Information: Established 1996. Normal turnaround time- 24-48 hours. Projects billed by number of names searched. Invoice monthly. They specialize in fast, accurate, competitively-priced in-person searches at the court house or title plants. They are a licensed PI, real estate broker and property/casualty agent with general liability and errors & omissions insurance. A licensed PI in TX.

Record Search America Inc

5481 Kendal St, Boise, ID 83706
Phone: 208-375-1906 - **Fax:** 208-322-5469
www.researchforyou.com **email:** sby@researchforyou.com

Types of Records Retrieved: Real Estate; Tax Liens/Judgments; Probate courts; Federal courts; UCC records

Local Retrieval Area: ID-Ada, Bannock, Canyon, Caribou, Gem, Latah, Payette. **Correspondent Relationships:** all of Idaho (44 counties), 17 counties in NV, 36 counties in OR, 18 counties in UT, 30 counties in MT, 38 counties in WA.

Add'l Information: Established 1991. Normal turnaround time- 24 hours. Projects billed by number of names searched. First project may require prepayment. Credit cards accepted. Will file/record documents for clients. They have a trained land title researcher in every county for ID, NV, OR, MT, UT and WA for real estate searches with a 24 hour turnaround time. They have a private investigation license and can obtain Idaho DMV and criminal court records A licensed PI in ID.

Record Time Research

6072 Lotus Ln, Lufkin, TX 75904
Phone: 936-632-5150 - **Fax:** 936-632-5150 elbel@cox-internet.com

Types of Records Retrieved: Real Estate

Local Retrieval Area: TX-Angelina, Nacogdoches. **Correspondent Relationships:** Angelina County TX.

Add'l Information: Established 1998. Normal turnaround time- 24-48 hours. Will file/record documents for clients. They specialize in current owner searches conducted in several East TX counties. Call for more information.

Record-Check Services Inc

4515 Poplar #527, Memphis, TN 38117
Phone: 800-530-7226; 901-761-9979 - **Fax:** 901-761-3409
www.recordcheckservices.com **email:** orders@recordcheckservices.com

Types of Records Retrieved: Criminal, Civil and Probate courts; Federal courts; Real Estate; Tax Liens/Judgments; UCC records; Vital records

Local Retrieval Area: MS-Benton, De Soto, Marshall; TN-Fayette, Shelby, Tipton. **Correspondent Relationships:** nationwide and Puerto Rico. They routinely search all of TN, KY, MS, MO, AL.

Add'l Information: Established 1985. Normal turnaround time- 1-3 days. Expedited service available. Projects billed by number of names searched. Projects billed by the hour. Fees depend on type of search. First project may require prepayment. Will file/record documents for clients. A Division of Strategic Research, they specialize in multi-state and multi-county projects. They have a combined 55 years of real estate experience in-house.

Records Quest

1607 S Ironton St, Aurora, CO 80012
Phone: 303-369-0693 - **Fax:** 303-755-0597 danballan@comcast.net

Types of Records Retrieved: Real Estate; Tax Liens/Judgments; UCC records; Vital records

Local Retrieval Area: CO-Adams, Arapahoe, Boulder, Broomfield, Denver, Douglas, El Paso, Jefferson, Larimer, Mesa, Weld

Add'l Information: Established 1999. Normal turnaround time- 4 hours. Projects billed by number of names searched. Will invoice. They specialize in 24 hours or less document retrieval. O & E. Recording and e-mail capabilities. They have competitive rates and can handle high volume. He has 11 years experience.

Records Research & Retrieval

375 Cedar Grove Rd, Dresden, ME 04342
Phone: 207-737-2903; cell- 207-504-2444 sldoucette@earthlink.net

Records Retrieved: Criminal, Civil and Probate courts; Bankruptcy court; Real Estate; Tax Liens/Judgments; UCC records; Vital records

Local Retrieval Area: ME-Cumberland, Kennebec, Lincoln, Sagadahoc

Add'l Information: Established 1995. Normal turnaround time- 24-48 hours. Projects billed by number of names searched. First project may require prepayment. Will file/record documents for clients. Also have access to electronic bankruptcy filing in Maricopa County, AZ.

Records Research Inc (California)

PO Box 19300, Sacramento, CA 95819
Phone: 800-952-5766; - **Fax:** 800-870-6877
www.recordsresearch.com **email:** tech@recordsresearch.com

Types of Records Retrieved: Criminal and Civil courts; Real Estate; UCC records; Tax Liens/Judgments, MVR; Secretary of State

Local Retrieval Area: CA-Sacramento

Add'l Information: Established 1981. Normal turnaround time- varied depending on state. Check website for details. Projects billed by number of names searched. They specialize in instant retrieval of California MVRs. Other states are also available.

Records Research Inc (Nebraska)

PO Box 6169, 6003 Old Cheney Rd, Lincoln, NE 68506
Phone: 402-476-3869, 402-323-3828- direct line - **Fax:** 402-486-4949
swest@nebtitlelincoln.com

Records Retrieved: Federal courts; Tax Liens/Judgments; UCC records

Local Retrieval Area: NE-Lancaster. **Correspondent:** statewide.

Add'l info: Established 1981. Turnaround time- 24 hours to 48 hours. Projects billed by number of names searched. First project may require prepayment. Will file/record documents for clients. They specialize in UCC searches statewide as well as corporate filings. Performs service of process.

Records Research of Knoxville

7725 Devonshire Dr, Knoxville, TN 37919
Phone: 865-693-3589 - **Fax:** 865-693-5716
recordsresearchknox@comcast.net

Types of Records Retrieved: Criminal and Civil courts; Federal courts; Real Estate; Tax Liens/Judgments; UCC records

Local Retrieval Area: TN-Anderson, Blount, Knox, Sevier, Union

Add'l Information: Established 1996. Normal turnaround time- 24-48 hours. Projects billed by number of names searched. Projects billed by the hour. First project may require prepayment. Will file/record documents for clients. Billing schedule may be applicable. They specialize in criminal searches and civil searches, local & federal. They have an excellent turnaround time.

Records Research of Mesa County

935 Bader Dr, Grand Junction, CO 81501
Phone: 866-321-6611; 970-241-6470 - **Fax:** 970-241-6282
www.gardnerbusiness.com **email:** asgardner@gardnerbusiness.com

Types of Records Retrieved: Criminal, Civil and Probate courts; Federal courts; Real Estate; Tax Liens/Judgments; UCC records; Vital records

Local Retrieval Area: CO-Mesa

Add'l Information: Established 1996. Normal turnaround time- 24-48 hours. Projects billed by the hour. Credit cards accepted. Will invoice customers meeting their standards. They specialize in routine research and investigations as well as those that others cannot accomplish. Primary investigator has an LLB and PE. Performs service of process.

Records Retrieval Service

5505 Old US 23 #450, Brighton, MI 48114
Phone: 810-220-0810 - **Fax:** 810-220-0910 dnidz@hotmail.com

Types of Records Retrieved: Criminal, Civil and Probate courts; Federal courts; Real Estate; Tax Liens/Judgments; UCC records; Vital records

Local Retrieval Area: MI-Bay, Calhoun, Genesee, Ingham, Kalamazoo, Kent, Livingston, Macomb, Midland, Monroe, Oakland, Ottawa, Saginaw, Washtenaw, Wayne. **Correspondent Relationships:** statewide.

Add'l Information: Established 1997. Normal turnaround time- 1-3 days. Projects billed by number of names searched. Will file/record documents for clients. They provide court research for criminal & civil histories through direct contact with the courts. They will file documents in Genesee, Livingston & Washtenaw Counties only. They are capable of providing statewide county & state searches. A licensed PI in MI.

Records Search & Report Service

PO Box 82, Hominy, OK 74035
Phone: 918-885-4724, 918-885-9955 - **Fax:** 918-885-4049
cbbfcl@aol.com

Types of Records Retrieved: Real Estate; Tax Liens/Judgments; Probate courts; Federal courts; UCC record; Vital records

Local Retrieval Area: OK-Adair, Cherokee, Craig, Creek, Delaware, Haskell, Kay, Lincoln, Logan, Mayes, McIntosh, Muskogee, Noble, Nowata, Okfuskee, Okmulgee, Osage, Ottawa, Pawnee, Payne, Rogers, Sequoyah, Tulsa, Wagoner, Washington. **Correspondent Relationships:** Oklahoma.

Add'l Information: Established 2003. Normal turnaround time- 24-48 hours. Projects may be billed by the hour or by number of names searched. First project may require prepayment. They specialize in ownership of surface, minerals, oil & gas lease holds, real estate, also liens/judgments and record retrieval.

RecordSearch Inc

4301 Chaucer Ln, Columbus, OH 43220
Phone: 614-905-0085 - **Fax:** 614-224-5843

Types of Records Retrieved: Civil and Probate courts; Real Estate; Tax Liens/Judgments; UCC records **Local Retrieval Area:** OH-Franklin

Add'l Information: Established 1990. Normal turnaround time- 24-48 hours. Projects billed by number of names searched. Projects billed by number of records located. Projects billed by the hour. First project may require prepayment. Credit cards accepted. Will file/record documents for clients. Terms are net 30 days. They specialize mostly in the following: real estate searches, current owner, back title and full. They carry E & O Insurance.

Reda's Attorney Service

70 Osborne Ave, Mount Sinai, NY 11766
Phone: 631-331-0700 - **Fax:** 631-474-0592 search01@optonline.net

Types of Records Retrieved: Criminal courts; Real Estate; Tax Liens/Judgments; UCC records

Local Retrieval Area: NY-Nassau, Suffolk

Add'l Information: Established 1986. Normal turnaround time- 24 hours for Suffolk County and 48 hours for Nassau County. Expedited service available. Projects billed by number of names searched. Fee basis will vary by the type of search. First project may require prepayment. Will file/record documents for clients. They specialize in title and variance searches.

Redi-Info Information Services

PO Box 12145, Oklahoma City, OK 73157
Phone: 888-320-6805; - **Fax:** 405-917-5961
www.redi-info.com **email:** customerservice@redi-info.com

Types of Records Retrieved: Criminal and Civil courts

Local Retrieval Area: OK-Adair, Alfalfa, Atoka, Beaver, Beckham, Blaine, Bryan, Caddo, Canadian, Carter, Cherokee, Cleveland, Comanche, Cotton, Craig, Creek, Custer, Delaware, Dewey, Ellis, Garfield, Garvin, Grant, Greer, Harmon, Harper, Haskell, Hughes, Jackson, Jefferson, Johnston, Kay, Kingfisher, Kiowa, Latimer, Leflore, Lincoln, Logan, Love, Major, Marshall, Mayes, McClain, McCurtain, McIntosh, Murray, Muskogee, Noble, Nowata, Okfuskee, Oklahoma, Okmulgee, Osage, Ottawa, Pawnee, Payne, Pittsburg, Pontotoc, Pottawatomie, Pushmataha, Roger Mills, Rogers, Seminole, Sequoyah, Stephens, Texas, Tillman, Tulsa, Wagoner, Washington, Washita, Woods, Woodward. **Correspondents:** nationwide.

Add'l Information: Established 1992. Normal turnaround time- 24-48 hours. Projects billed by number of names searched. Account billing. They specialize in Oklahoma court records.

Red's Rapid Research

1148 Miller Ct, Rio Dell, CA 95562
Phone: 707-764-8836 - **Fax:** 707-764-8811
wendy@redsrapidresearch.com

Types of Records Retrieved: Criminal and Civil courts; Real Estate; Tax Liens/Judgments; UCC records; Vital records

Local Retrieval Area: CA-Del Norte, Humboldt

Add'l Information: Established 1998. Normal turnaround time- 24 hours. Expedited service available. Projects billed by number of names searched. Credit cards accepted. Will file/record documents for clients. Payment terms are net 30. Performing hands on record searches daily, Red's Rapid Research provides the most-accurate and up-to-date information with the fastest possible turnaround time.

David Reed

315 W 4th St, Emporium, PA 15834

Phone: 814-486-9327 - **Fax:** 814-486-0464 reeddavidjohn@yahoo.com

Types of Records Retrieved: Criminal, Civil and Probate courts; Real Estate; Tax Liens/Judgments; UCC records; Vital records

Local Retrieval Area: PA-Cameron, Elk, McKean, Potter

Add'l Information: Established 1980. Normal turnaround time- 24-48 hours. Fee is determined by an established schedule. First project may require prepayment. Will file/record documents for clients. Requests that individuals prepay, but will invoice attorneys and companies. He specializes in oil and gas ownership searches. Performs service of process.

Regier Title Co

129 E Broadway #100, Newton, KS 67114

Phone: 316-283-2750 - **Fax:** 316-283-5680

Types of Records Retrieved: Civil and Probate courts; Real Estate; Tax Liens/Judgments; UCC records

Local Retrieval Area: KS-Harvey

Add'l Information: Normal turnaround time- 2-3 days. Fee basis varies by type of transaction. First project may require prepayment. Will file/record documents for clients.

Registry Research

PO Box 448, South Egremont, MA 01258

Phone: 413-528-3919 - **Fax:** 413-528-0907

Types of Records Retrieved: Real Estate; Probate Courts

Local Retrieval Area: MA-Berkshire

Add'l Information: Established 1988. Normal turnaround time- 2 weeks. Projects billed by the hour. First project may require prepayment. A downpayment is required. They specialize in title abstracts and historical or genealogical documentation in Southern Berkshire.

Reliable Abstract

PO Box 141, Locust Grove, GA 30248

Phone: 678-614-0715 - **Fax:** 770-898-1596

www.reliableabstractcompany.com

email: bene@reliableabstractcompany.com

Types of Records Retrieved: Civil and Probate courts; Real Estate; Tax Liens/Judgments

Local Retrieval Area: GA-Butts, Henry, Spalding. **Correspondent Relationships:** in other Central Georgia counties.

Add'l Information: Established 1998. Normal turnaround time- 24-48 hours. Projects billed by number of names searched. First project may require prepayment. Will file/record documents for clients. Due upon completion of project. They specialize in full and limited title searches.

Reliable Courier

2797 Irving Blvd #110, Dallas, TX 75207-2310

Phone: 214-637-4800 - **Fax:** 214-637-4803 courier2@swbell.net

Types of Records Retrieved: Criminal, Civil and Probate courts; Federal courts; Tax Liens/Judgments; Vital records

Local Retrieval Area: TX-Dallas, Ellis, Tarrant

Add'l Information: Established 1990. Normal turnaround time- 2 days. Projects billed by the hour. Credit cards accepted. A licensed PI in TX. Performs service of process.

Reliable Document Retrieval Inc

2111 20th St, Sacramento, CA 95818

Phone: 916-438-3000 - **Fax:** 916-438-3001

www.reliabledocs.com **email:** orders@reliabledocs.com

Types of Records Retrieved: Real Estate; Tax Liens/Judgments; UCC records; Secretary of State

Local Retrieval Area: CA-El Dorado, Placer, Sacramento, San Joaquin, Yolo. **Correspondent Relationships:** CA statewide, OR, WA, NV, TX, UT, AZ.

Add'l Information: Established 1998. Normal turnaround time- 1-3 days. Projects billed by number of names searched. Fee basis depends upon type of project. First project may require prepayment. Will file/record documents for clients. Terms are net 30 days. They specialize in real estate research, document retrieval & current owner. Secretary Of State, walk-in recordings in 7 states.

Reliable Record Research

3874 Taylorview Ln, Idaho Falls, ID 83406

Phone: 208-522-9886; cell-208-569-5825 - **Fax:** 208-522-9010

Types of Records Retrieved: Criminal, Civil and Probate courts; Real Estate; Tax Liens/Judgments; UCC records; Vital records

Local Retrieval Area: ID-Bingham, Bonneville, Jefferson, Madison

Add'l Information: Established 1993. Normal turnaround time- 24-48 hours. Piece rate; fee depends on nature of search. Will file/record documents for clients. They specialize in all types of records except Fed courts; over a decade of experience in their coverage area.

Reliable Title Co of NH

PO Box 84, Epsom, NH 03234

Phone: 603-798-5230 - **Fax:** 603-798-5231

www.nhtitle.com **email:** dave@nhtitle.com

Types of Records Retrieved: Real Estate; Tax Liens/Judgments; Probate courts; UCC records

Local Retrieval Area: NH-Rockingham

Add'l Information: Established 1990. Normal turnaround time- 24 hours. Projects billed by number of names searched. Will invoice for services. They offer full abstract services in Rockingham County, from current owner searches to commercial projects, from asset searches to document recordings.

Reliable Title Search Inc

5600 Palm Dr, Fort Pierce, FL 34982

Phone: 772-489-9650 - **Fax:** 772-489-9651

Records Retrieved: Real Estate; Tax Liens/Judgments; UCC records

Local Retrieval Area: FL-Indian River, Martin, Okeechobee, Palm Beach, St. Lucie

Add'l Information: Established 1995. Normal turnaround time- 24 hours. Projects billed by number of names searched. Will invoice. Will file/record documents for clients.

Reliance Abstract Company - AZ

70 S Val Vista Dr #605, Gilbert, AZ 85296

Phone: 800-207-1523; 480-926-6312 - **Fax:** 800-207-1526; 480-926-6311

relianceabstract@yahoo.com

Records Retrieved: Real Estate; Tax Liens/Judgments; UCC records

Local Retrieval Area: AZ-Maricopa, Mohave, Pima, Pinal, Yavapai. **Correspondent Relationships:** statewide.

Add'l Information: Established 1982. Normal turnaround time- 24 hours. Expedited service available Projects billed by number of names searched. Projects billed by number of records located. Payment due upon receipt of product or service. They specialize in land records research & reports, current owner searches, deed reports, deed of trust, assignments & reconveyance research & retrieval, UCC research & retrieval and document recording & filing.

Reliance Abstract Company - UT

1275 N University Ave #8, Provo, UT 84604

Phone: 800-207-1523; 801-375-1800 - **Fax:** 800-207-1526; 801-371-0514

relianceabstract@yahoo.com

Records Retrieved: Real Estate; Tax Liens/Judgments; UCC records

Local Retrieval Area: UT-Cache, Davis, Salt Lake, Utah, Weber. **Correspondent Relationships:** statewide.

Add'l Information: Established 1982. Normal turnaround time- 24 hours. Expedited service available. Projects billed by number of names searched. Projects billed by number of records located. Payment due upon receipt of product or service. They specialize in land records research and reports, current owner searches, deed reports, deed of trust, assignments &

reconveyance research & retrieval, UCC research & retrieval and document recording & filing.

Reliance Title Services

725 S Clinton St, Iowa City, IA 52244

Phone: 319-354-6505 - **Fax:** 319-354-9705 kstoner@reliancetitle.com

Types of Records Retrieved: Criminal, Civil and Probate courts; Real Estate; Tax Liens/Judgments; UCC records; Vital records

Local Retrieval Area: IA-Johnson

Add'l Information: Established 1987. Normal turnaround time- 24 hours for court searches, and 2 working days for real estate. Will file/record documents for clients.

Relyea Services Inc

1524 Central Av, Albany, NY 12205

Phone: 800-854-4111; - **Fax:** 800-854-4112 relyeaserv@aol.com

Types of Records Retrieved: Criminal, Civil and Probate courts; Federal courts; Real Estate; Tax Liens/Judgments; UCC records; Vital records

Local Retrieval Area: NY-Albany, Rensselaer, Saratoga, Schenectady. **Correspondent Relationships:** every court in the nation.

Add'l Information: Established 1991. Normal turnaround time- same day. Projects billed by number of names searched. Will file/record documents for clients. They specialize in court record retrieval, UCC searching and filing and corporate work. Performs service of process.

Reno/Carson Messenger Service Inc

185 Martin St, Reno, NV 89509-2827

Phone: 800-222-4249; 775-322-2424 - **Fax:** 775-322-3408

www.renocarson.com **email:** pete1@callat6.com

Types of Records Retrieved: Criminal, Civil and Probate courts; Federal courts; Real Estate; Tax Liens/Judgments; UCC records; Vital records

Local Retrieval Area: NV-Carson City, Churchill, Douglas, Lyon, Storey, Washoe. **Correspondent Relationships:** Northern Nevada; El Dorado and Placer CA counties.

Add'l Information: Established 1982. Normal turnaround time- 24 hours to 3 days. Projects billed by number of names searched. Projects billed by number of records located. Projects billed by the hour. First project may require prepayment. Credit cards accepted. Will file/record documents for clients. They specialize in process service. Performs service of process.

Renville County Abstract Co

PO Box 86, Olivia, MN 56277

Phone: 320-523-5328 - **Fax:** 320-523-5321 rencoabst@rswb.coop

Types of Records Retrieved: Real Estate; Tax Liens/Judgments

Local Retrieval Area: MN-Redwood, Renville

Add'l Information: Established 1988. Normal turnaround time- 2 days. Fee basis will vary by type of project. First project may require prepayment. Will file/record documents for clients. Payment due on receipt of work. They specialize in real estate title searches and abstracts.

Research & Demographic Solutions LLC

606 Elington Dr, Grapevine, TX 76051

Phone: 817-706-7726 - **Fax:** 817-488-2026

mgardiner@rdsresearch.com

Types of Records Retrieved: Criminal and Civil courts

Local Retrieval Area: TX-Brazoria, Brazos, Cameron, Collin, Comal, Dallas, Denton, El Paso, Grayson, Gregg, Hays, Hidalgo, Johnson, Nueses, Parker, Parmer, Smith, Tarrant, Tom Green, Victoria

Add'l Information: Established 1998. Normal turnaround time- 24 hours or less. Projects billed by number of names searched. Bill once a month. RDS concentrates on several Texas counties to provide fast, reliable results. Rates are low and competitive. Fax or email requests.

Research & Investigative Associates

PO Box 1321, Eureka, CA 95502

Phone: 707-444-8767 pitracy6682@pacbell.net

Types of Records Retrieved: Criminal, Civil and Probate courts; Real Estate; Tax Liens/Judgments; UCC records; Vital records

Local Retrieval Area: CA-Del Norte, Humboldt

Add'l Information: Established 1983. Normal turnaround time- 48 hours for verbal request; 5 days on complex requests. Projects billed by the hour. First project may require prepayment. A 50% retainer is required. Personal checks are accepted. They specialize in investigation, locates, background and trial preparation. They are a full service agency. They also do worker's comp. A licensed PI in CA. Performs service of process.

Research & Retrieval Inc

1301 Manhattan Ave #E, Hermosa Beach, CA 90254

Phone: 800-707-8771; 310-798-8100 - **Fax:** 310-798-9394

http://researchandretrieval.com **email:** order@researchandretrieval.com

Types of Records Retrieved: Criminal, Civil and Probate courts; Federal courts; Real Estate; Tax Liens/Judgments; UCC records

Local Retrieval Area: CA-Los Angeles, Orange, Riverside, Sacramento, San Bernardino, San Diego, San Francisco, Santa Clara. **Correspondent Relationships:** nationwide.

Add'l Information: Established 1990. Normal turnaround time- same day to 24 hours. Projects billed by number of names searched. Terms are net 30 days. Will file/record documents for clients. They specialize in providing public record research & document retrieval from all county, state and federal agencies & archives. Same day service at no extra cost. You can order via email- order@researchandretrieval.com.

Research & Retrieval Services Inc

800 Seahawk Cir #105, Virginia Beach, VA 23452-7818

Phone: 757-463-0030 - **Fax:** 757-463-0040

www.researchandretrievals.com **email:** dbeloff@cox.net

Types of Records Retrieved: Civil courts; Federal courts; Real Estate; Tax Liens/Judgments; UCC records

Local Retrieval Area: VA-Chesapeake, Hampton, Isle of Wight, James City, Newport News, Norfolk, Portsmouth, Suffolk, Virginia Beach, Williamsburg, York

Add'l Information: Established 1995. Normal turnaround time- 24-48 hours. Projects billed by number of names searched. Projects billed by number of records located. First project may require prepayment. Will file/record documents for clients. Payment due upon receipt of job. They specialize in knowing the many idiosyncrasies of each individual courthouse.

Research Associates

27999 Clemens Rd, Cleveland, OH 44145

Phone: 800-225-9693; 440-892-1000 - **Fax:** 440-892-9439

www.raiglobal.com **email:** info@raiglobal.com

Types of Records Retrieved: Criminal, Civil and Probate courts; Federal courts; Real Estate; Tax Liens/Judgments; UCC records; Vital records

Local Retrieval Area: OH-Cuyahoga, Lorain, Lake, Summit

Add'l Information: Normal turnaround time- 5-7 days. First project may require prepayment.

Research by Robin

4025B Blake Ave, El Mendorf AFB, AK 99506

Phone: 907-929-7850 - **Fax:** 866-841-9674; 907-929-7850

robinnxn@infostations.com

Types of Records Retrieved: Criminal, Civil and Probate courts; Federal courts; Real Estate; Tax Liens/Judgments; UCC records; Vital records

Local Retrieval Area: AK-Anchorage. **Correspondent Relationships:** Palmer, AK (weather permitting-April thru October).

Add'l Information: Established 2001. Normal turnaround time- Usually 24 hours. (If in by 4:30 AM will be faxed back by 4:30 PM unless file/cases in archives). Projects billed by number of names searched. Projects billed by number of records located. Payment due upon receipt of invoice (month billing). Alaska lists all cases statewide, can "search" statewide but retrieve only in Anchorage and Palmer counties.

The Research Connection Inc of NH

1 Old Loudon Rd, Concord, NH 03301-7810

Phone: 800-540-5064; 603-226-8600 - **Fax:** 603-228-6440

www.theresearchconnection.com **email:** researchnh@comcast.net

Types of Records Retrieved: Criminal and Civil courts; Federal courts; Real Estate; Tax Liens/Judgments; UCC records; Vital records

Local Retrieval Area: NH-Belknap, Carroll, Cheshire, Coos, Grafton, Hillsborough, Merrimack, Rockingham, Strafford, Sullivan

Add'l Information: Established 1989. Normal turnaround time- 3-5 business days. Projects billed by number of names searched. First project may require prepayment. Will file/record documents for clients. They specialize in obtaining UCC/tax lien and corporate searches at the Secretary of State's office, and town and county searching.

Research Express

3055 Crawfordville Hwy, Crawfordville, FL 32327

Phone: 850-926-5665 - **Fax:** 850-926-4166

Types of Records Retrieved: Real Estate

Local Retrieval Area: FL-Bay, Calhoun, Columbia, Dixie, Franklin, Gadsden, Gilchrist, Gulf, Hamilton, Holmes, Jackson, Jefferson, Lafayette, Leon, Liberty, Madison, Suwannee, Taylor, Union, Wakulla, Washington

Add'l Information: Established 1996. Normal turnaround time- 24 hours. Expedited service available. First project may require prepayment. Will file/record documents for clients. Terms: net 30 days. They specialize in property searches. They also perform witness location, closings after property search and mortgage recordings. The cellular phone number is 850-926-5665.

Research For You

10929 Firestone Blvd #158, Norwalk, CA 90650

Phone: 626-974-4484 - **Fax:** 626-974-4934 srchlady12@yahoo.com

Types of Records Retrieved: Criminal, Civil and Probate courts; Federal courts; Real Estate; Tax Liens/Judgments; UCC records; Vital records

Local Retrieval Area: CA-Los Angeles, Orange

Add'l Information: Established 1996. Normal turnaround time- 24 hours. Projects billed by number of names searched. First project may require prepayment. Will file/record documents for clients. Terms: net 30 days. They specialize in locating documents from only partial information in courts and county offices. Same day fax results available. All research is performed in-person.

Research Information Consultants

4939 Fuller Dr, Columbus, OH 43214

Phone: 614-286-6303 - **Fax:** 614-430-0104 lpahdopony@aol.com

Types of Records Retrieved: Civil and Probate courts; Real Estate; Tax Liens/Judgments; UCC records

Local Retrieval Area: OH-Delaware, Franklin

Add'l Information: Established 1996. Normal turnaround time- 48 hours. Projects billed by number of names searched. First project may require prepayment. Will file/record documents for clients. They offer over 15 years experience in document retrieval, R-O-W Research, archaeology/surveying research, oil gas and mineral & title abstracts. E & O insurance guaranteed on all title work.

Research Information Services LLC

2741 39th St, Topeka, KS 66617

Phone: 800-522-3884; 785-235-6767 - **Fax:** 800-327-6987; 785-235-1919

www.ristoday.com **email:** ris@ristoday.com

Types of Records Retrieved: Criminal and Civil courts; Federal courts; Tax Liens/Judgments; UCC records

Local Retrieval Area: KS-all counties. **Correspondents:** nationwide.

Add'l Information: Established 1960. Normal turnaround time- 48 hours. Projects billed by number of names searched. Will invoice monthly or by project. Specializing in criminal background checks for over 40 years. Offers quick access to court records in Kansas, Colorado, Florida, Maryland, Pennsylvania, and Wisconsin.

Research N More

PO Box 2623, Georgetown, TX 78627-2623

Phone: 512-868-5828 - **Fax:** 512-868-5847

http://researchnmore.7p.com **email:** researchnmore@verizon.net

Records Retrieved: Criminal, Civil and Probate courts; Bankruptcy court; Real Estate; Tax Liens/Judgments; UCC records; Vital records

Local Retrieval Area: TX-Bell, Travis, Williamson

Add'l Information: Established 2001. Normal turnaround time- 24-48 hours. Projects billed by number of names searched. Projects billed by the hour. First project requires prepayment. They also provide comprehensive reports, I.e. current owner; deed chains, deed of trust assignments, foreclosure research, new business mailing lists and more. Have been in business since 2001.

Research Network

807 Brazos #312, Austin, TX 78701

Phone: 512-469-1740 - **Fax:** 512-469-9305 researchnetwork@austin.rr.com

Types of Records Retrieved: Criminal, Civil and Probate courts; Federal courts; Real Estate; Tax Liens/Judgments; UCC records; Vital records

Local Retrieval Area: TX-Bastrop, Hays, Travis, Williamson

Add'l Information: Established 1997. Normal turnaround time- same day to 36 hours. Projects billed by number of names searched. Projects billed by the hour. Flat fees are charged on certain searches. First project may require prepayment. Will file/record documents for clients. They specialize in all public records, including criminal, property and state record searches. A licensed PI in TX.

Research North Inc of Alpena

537 W Chisholm #400, Alpena, MI 49707-0637

Phone: 888-876-1010; - **Fax:** 888-876-1401

www.researchnorth.com **email:** info@researchnorth.com

Types of Records Retrieved: Criminal, Civil and Probate courts; Federal courts; Real Estate; Tax Liens/Judgments; UCC records; Vital records

Local Retrieval Area: MI-Alpena, Presque Isle

Add'l Information: Established 1981. Normal turnaround time- 24-48 hours. Projects are billed by time and material. All projects require prepayment. They specialize in investigative services for the insurance industry, legal community and business and industrial groups. Performs service of process.

Research North Inc of Marquette

220 W Washington #320, Marquette, MI 49855-4331

Phone: 888-876-1010; - **Fax:** 888-876-1401

www.researchnorth.com **email:** info@researchnorth.com

Types of Records Retrieved: Criminal, Civil and Probate courts; Federal courts; Real Estate; Tax Liens/Judgments; UCC records; Vital records

Local Retrieval Area: MI-Delta, Marquette

Add'l Information: Established 1981. Normal turnaround time- 24-48 hours. Projects billed by the hour. Projects are billed by time and material. All projects require prepayment. Will file/record documents for clients. They specialize in investigative services for the insurance industry, legal community and business and industrial groups. A licensed PI in MI, OH and WI. Performs service of process.

Research North Inc of Petoskey

207 Michigan, Petoskey, MI 49770-2607

Phone: 888-876-1010; - **Fax:** 888-876-1401

www.researchnorth.com **email:** info@researchnorth.com

Types of Records Retrieved: Criminal, Civil and Probate courts; Federal courts; Real Estate; Tax Liens/Judgments; UCC records; Vital records

Local Retrieval Area: MI-Charlevoix, Emmet. **Correspondent Relationships:** Alpena, Grand Traverse, Ingham, Marquette counties MI.

Add'l info: Established 1981. Turnaround time- 24-48 hours. Projects are billed by time and material. All projects require prepayment. Will file/record documents for clients. They specialize in investigative services for the insurance industry, legal community and business as well as industrial groups. Licensed PI in MI, OH, WI. Performs service of process.

Research North Inc of Traverse City

207 Michigan St (Corporate Office), Petoskey, MI 49770

Phone: 888-876-1010; - **Fax:** 888-876-1401

www.researchnorth.com **email:** info@researchnorth.com

Types of Records Retrieved: Probate courts; Federal courts

Local Retrieval Area: MI-Grand Traverse, Leelanau

Add'l Information: Established 1981. Normal turnaround time- 24-48 hours. Projects are billed by time and material All projects require prepayment. They specialize in investigative services for the insurance industry, legal community and business and industrial groups. A licensed PI in MI. Performs service of process.

Research Specialists Inc

16 Denise Dr, Thornton, PA 19373
Phone: 610-358-2507 or 724-5353 - **Fax:** 610-361-2030
research@icdc.com

Types of Records Retrieved: Criminal and Civil courts; Federal courts; Tax Liens/Judgments; UCC records

Local Retrieval Area: DE-Kent, New Castle, Sussex; PA-Bucks, Chester, Delaware, Montgomery

Add'l Information: Normal turnaround time- same day to 24 hours. Credit cards accepted. The do statewide vital records searches in PA and DE.

Research Unlimited LLC

PO Box 86075, Tucson, AZ 85754
Phone: 520-624-7024 - **Fax:** 520-770-0807 suzyatresearch@aol.com

Types of Records Retrieved: Criminal, Civil and Probate courts; Federal courts; Real Estate; Tax Liens/Judgments; UCC records; Vital records

Local Retrieval Area: AZ-Pima, Cochise, Santa Cruz

Add'l Information: Established 1992. Normal turnaround time- 24 hours. Projects billed by number of names searched. Will file/record documents for clients. They specialize in real estate records, superior court record retrieval and background searches in the Tucson and Pima county areas.

ResearchSource for Hard-to-Find Information

1255 New Hampshire Ave NW #521, Washington, DC 20036-2352
Phone: 202-778-0002 - **Fax:** 202-331-1585 crichter@researchsource.com

Types of Records Retrieved: Civil courts; Federal courts; National Archives

Local Retrieval Area: DC-Washington

Add'l Information: Established 1996. Normal turnaround time- 24 hours for Federal filings. Projects billed by the hour. First project may require prepayment. Payment due upon receipt of invoice. Specializes in research and retrieval at US district, appellate, and special courts including Tax & Federal Claims, also Library of Congress, National Archives, Patent Office, regulatory agencies.

Resource Management Specialists

1311 Fort Crook Rd South, #103, Bellevue, NE 68005
Phone: 877-476-3337; 402-682-9305 - **Fax:** 877-314-2110; 402-682-0016
www.rmspecialists.com **email:** rms@rmspecialists.com

Types of Records Retrieved: Criminal courts

Local Retrieval Area: NE-Buffalo, Douglas, Hall, Lancaster, Lincoln, Sarpy. **Correspondent Relationships:** nationwide.

Add'l Information: Established 1998. Normal turnaround time- 24-48 hours. Projects billed by number of names searched. Will invoice. They specialize in fast accurate criminal court records retrieval in both felony and misdemeanor searches.

Resource Reporting Ltd

30 Courthouse Sq #206, Rockville, MD 20850
Phone: 877-268-7810; 301-838-9200 - **Fax:** 240-358-0296
processmd@aol.com

Types of Records Retrieved: Criminal, Civil and Probate courts; Federal courts; Real Estate; Tax Liens/Judgments; UCC records; Land record/Title Abstracting

Local Retrieval Area: MD-Frederick, Montgomery, Washington. **Correspondents in:** Maryland, Virginia, DC (District of Columbia).

Add'l Information: Established 1983. Normal turnaround time- 24-72 hours. Projects billed by the hour. Projects are also billed by a flat rate. First project may require prepayment. Credit cards accepted. Will file/record documents for clients. They specialize in document retrieval, investigative services, genealogical research, document retrieval, asset identification, surveillance, real property title current owner searches, database information research & service of process in MD, VA, DC, PA. A licensed PI in MD. Performs service of process.

Reynolds Professional Service Inc

4801 E Independence Blvd #700, Charlotte, NC 28212-5408
Phone: 800-814-8662; 704-338-1775 - **Fax:** 704-338-1686
www.reynoldsprofessionalservice.com
email: reynoldsproserv@mindspring.com

Records Retrieved: Criminal and Civil courts; Federal courts; Vital records

Local Retrieval Area: NC-Cabarrus, Cleveland, Davidson, Gaston, Iredell, Lincoln, Mecklenburg, Rowan, Stanly; SC-York. **Correspondent Relationships:** North Carolina.

Add'l Information: Established 1990. Normal turnaround time- 48 hours. Projects billed by the hour. First project may require prepayment. They specialize in process serving and location of missing witnesses and defendants, private investigation, mystery shopping, and they perform filing and issuance services applicable to state and federal courts. A licensed PI in NC, PI#2216. Performs service of process.

Dawn Richards

482 Evergreen St, Dresden, TN 38225
Phone: 731-364-2456 - **Fax:** 731-364-6765

Types of Records Retrieved: Criminal and Civil courts

Local Retrieval Area: TN-Weakley

Add'l Information: Established 1996. Normal turnaround time- 24-48 hours. Projects billed by number of names searched. First project may require prepayment. She promises expert service in Weakley County.

Richardson Abstract Co Inc

521 Marsh St, Kinsley, KS 67547
Phone: 620-659-2592 - **Fax:** 620-659-2730 susanploger@sbcglobal.net

Types of Records Retrieved: Civil and Probate courts; Real Estate; Tax Liens/Judgments; UCC records

Local Retrieval Area: KS-Edwards

Add'l Information: Normal turnaround time- same day. Projects billed by the hour. Will file/record documents for clients. Personal checks are accepted. They specialize in title insurance and abstracts.

Ridgerunner Record Search Inc

2201 Holly, Fayetteville, AR 72703-1214
Phone: 479-443-4928 - **Fax:** 479-251-1955

Types of Records Retrieved: Criminal and Civil courts; Federal courts; Tax Liens/Judgments; UCC records

Local Retrieval Area: AR-Benton, Washington. **Correspondent Relationships:** Has working relationships in Northwest Arkansas.

Add'l Information: Established 1990. Normal turnaround time- same day to 24 hours. Projects billed by number of names searched. Individual company billing. Ridgerunner Record Search Inc is a public record search and retrieval service with background search experience of 44 years.

Right On Time Documents Inc

622 Belgium Dr, Hermitage, TN 37076
Phone: 615-885-8672 - **Fax:** 615-884-1369
www.rightontimedocs.com **email:** rotdocuments@earthlink.net

Types of Records Retrieved: Real Estate; Tax Liens/Judgments; UCC records; Probate courts; Bankruptcy court

Local Retrieval Area: TN-Cheatham, Davidson, Dickson, Hamilton, Knox, Montgomery, Robertson, Rutherford, Shelby, Sullivan, Sumner, Williamson, Wilson. **Correspondent Relationships:** statewide.

Add'l Information: Established 2000. Normal turnaround time- 24-48 hours; rural counties 72 hours. Projects billed by number of names searched. First project may require prepayment. This company's products include retrieval of Deeds of Trust, chain of assignments, releases, walk in recordings, current owner searches and bring down report with recording. They have excellent turnaround time.

Right Staff Ltd

PO Box 513, Canal Winchester, OH 43110
Phone: 614-833-3401 - **Fax:** 614-834-3272 rightstaffltd@juno.com

Types of Records Retrieved: Criminal and Civil courts

Local Retrieval Area: OH-Franklin. **Correspondents:** statewide.

Add'l Information: Established 1995. Normal turnaround time- 24 hours. Projects billed by number of names searched. Payment due net 30 days. Right Staff provides background checks that include a trace, searching all counties dating back 7 years and motor vehicle records.

RightTrack Services

563 E Olmstead Ave, Evansville, IN 47711

Phone: 812-421-0866 - **Fax:** 812-423-1156 rwtracks@aol.com

Types of Records Retrieved: Criminal and Civil courts; Federal courts; Real Estate; Tax Liens/Judgments; UCC records

Retrieval Area IN-Gibson (by special request), Posey, Vanderburgh, Warrick

Add'l Information: Established 1997. Normal turnaround time- 24-48 hours. Projects billed by number of names searched. Payment due net 30 days. They specialize in criminal & civil searches, tax liens, UCC, bankruptcy and mortgage retrieval. Has 9+ years experience. Will do Gibson County under special circumstances.

Rigoli Searches

14604 W 68th St, Shawnee, KS 66216-2146

Phone: 913-908-8863

Types of Records Retrieved: Criminal and Civil courts; Real Estate; Tax Liens/Judgments; UCC records

Local Retrieval Area: KS-Johnson, Leavenworth; MO-Clay, Platte. **Correspondent Relationships:** Eastern Kansas or Western Missouri.

Add'l Information: Established 2004. Normal turnaround time- 24-48 hours. Projects billed by number of names searched. Will invoice. They provide accurate and prompt abstracting services including current owner searches, UCC/FLS/SLS, document retrieval and walk-in recordings.

Ringgold County Abstract Co Inc

109 W Madison St #104, Mount Ayr, IA 50854

Phone: 641-464-3902 - **Fax:** 641-464-2265

Types of Records Retrieved: Criminal, Civil and Probate courts; Real Estate; Tax Liens/Judgments; UCC records; Vital records

Local Retrieval Area: IA-Ringgold

Add'l Information: Established 1986. Normal turnaround time- 3-5 days. Fee basis will vary by the type of project. First project may require prepayment. Will file/record documents for clients. They have a tract index beginning in 1856 and runs to current date.

Rio Grande Mineral Title

PO Box 489, 580 Columbia Ave, Del Norte, CO 81132

Phone: 719-657-3366 - **Fax:** 719-657-2395 rgmt@fone.net

Types of Records Retrieved: Real Estate; Tax Liens/Judgments; UCC records

Local Retrieval Area: CO-Mineral, Rio Grande. **Correspondent Relationships:** Saguache, Alamosa, Conejos counties CO.

Add'l Information: Established 1893. Normal turnaround time- 48 hours. Projects billed by number of names searched. Personal checks accepted.

Ripley County Abstract

118 Washington St, Doniphan, MO 63935

Phone: 573-996-3115 - **Fax:** 573-996-7211

Types of Records Retrieved: Civil court; Real Estate; Tax Liens/Judgments

Local Retrieval Area: MO-Ripley

Add'l Information: Normal turnaround time- 24-48 hours. Billing depends on nature of request. Will file/record documents for clients. They specialize in county real estate.

RIQ and Associates Inc

PO Box 494, 473 Eaglestone Dr, Castle Rock, CO 80104

Phone: 720-529-5736 - **Fax:** 720-529-8120 riq_company@msn.com

Types of Records Retrieved: Criminal and Civil courts; Federal District courts; Real Estate; Tax Liens/Judgments; UCC records; Vital records

Local Retrieval Area: CO-Adams, Arapahoe, Boulder, Broomfield, Clear Creek, Custer, Denver, Douglas, Eagle, El Paso, Elbert, Fremont, Gilpin, Jefferson, Larimer, Morgan, Park, Pueblo, Summit, Teller, Weld. **Correspondent Relationships:** Arizona, Colorado.

Add'l Information: Established 2002. Normal turnaround time- 24-48 hours. Projects billed by number of records located. First project may require prepayment. Quantity discounts available. He specializes in public record search and retrieval in accurate and timely manner. Also do real estate closings and is a certified signing agent.

Risk Assessment Group

PO Box 27443, Tempe, AZ 85285

Phone: 866-777-1114; 480-777-1114 - **Fax:** 866-777-0004; 480-777-3776

https://www.riskassessmentgroup.com/home.aspx

email: brad@ragrp.com

Types of Records Retrieved: Criminal courts

Local Retrieval Area: AZ-Maricopa. **Correspondents:** nationwide.

Add'l Information: Established 2000. Normal turnaround time- same day. Projects billed by number of names searched. Will file/record documents for clients. Bill monthly. A licensed PI in AZ, #1002339.

Risk Mitigation Services Inc

404 W Avalon Ave #103, PO Box 2129 (35662), Muscle Shoals, AL 35661

Phone: 866-633-9339; 256-383-1180 - **Fax:** 866-633-9309; 256-314-0488

riskms@bellsouth.net

Types of Records Retrieved: Criminal, Civil and Probate courts; Federal courts; Tax Liens/Judgments; UCC records

Local Retrieval Area: AL-Colbert, Lauderdale, Lawrence

Add'l Information: Established 1999. Normal turnaround time- less than 24 hours. Projects billed by number of names searched. Will file/record documents for clients. Monthly billing. Performs service of process.

River Enterprises

15 Russell Ln, Casscoe, AK 72026

Phone: 870-672-1732 - **Fax:** 870-241-1044 riverent@earthlink.net

Types of Records Retrieved: Civil and Probate courts; Federal courts; Real Estate; Tax Liens/Judgments; UCC records; Vital records

Local Retrieval Area: AR-Arkansas (Northern District), Jefferson, Lonoke, Monroe, Prairie

Add'l Information: Established 2001. Normal turnaround time- 24-48 hrs. Billing method depends on nature of request. First project may require prepayment. They specialize in title searches and current owner searches. Their search area in Arkansas County is the Northern District.

River Research Service

2237 Marianna St, Wellsburg, WV 26070

Phone: 304-670-3622 - **Fax:** 740-422-0377 vmlough@msn.com

Types of Records Retrieved: Criminal and Civil courts; Real Estate; Tax Liens/Judgments; UCC records

Local Retrieval Area: OH-Harrison, Jefferson; WV-Brooke, Hancock, Ohio

Add'l Information: Established 2002. Normal turnaround time- 24-48 hours. Projects billed by number of names searched. First project may require prepayment. The company performs checks on criminal and civil cases/people. Along with doing tax liens, title searches on real estate and UCC checks.

RJI Services Inc

2219 W Olive Blvd #295, Burbank, CA 91506

Phone: 800-344-4754; 818-846-5038 - **Fax:** 818-846-5977

www.rji.com **email:** rafael@rji.com

Types of Records Retrieved: Criminal, Civil and Probate courts; Federal courts; Real Estate; Tax Liens/Judgments; UCC records; Vital records

Local Retrieval Area: CA-Alameda, Contra Costa, Los Angeles, Orange, Riverside, San Diego, San Francisco, Ventura. **Correspondent Relationships:** nationwide.

Add'l Information: Established 1988. Normal turnaround time- 1-3 days. Projects billed by number of names searched. Will file/record documents for clients. Terms: net 30 days. They specialize in hands on research and record retrieval of criminal, civil, UCC, tax liens and bankruptcy records at the local and federal courts. A full service investigative company. A licensed PI in CA. Performs service of process.

Roberts County Title
516 2nd Ave East, Sisseton, SD 57262
Phone: 605-698-7272 - **Fax:** 605-698-7890
Types of Records Retrieved: Real Estate; Tax Liens/Judgments
Local Retrieval Area: SD-Roberts
Add'l Information: Established 1954. Normal turnaround time- 2 days to 2 weeks. First project may require prepayment. Will file/record documents for clients. They specialize in real estate.

Rocksprings Abstract & Title Co
PO Box 1062, 116 N Wells St, Rocksprings, TX 78880
Phone: 830-683-2185 - **Fax:** 830-683-4185
Types of Records Retrieved: Civil and Probate courts; Real Estate; Tax Liens/Judgments; UCC records; Vital records
Local Retrieval Area: TX-Edwards
Add'l Information: Established 1930. Normal turnaround time- variable depending on project. Fee basis will vary by the type of project. First project may require prepayment. Will file/record documents for clients.

Rogers County Abstract Co
PO Box 38, 119 S Missouri Ave (74017), Claremore, OK 74018
Phone: 918-341-0525 - **Fax:** 918-341-2117
Types of Records Retrieved: Civil and Probate courts; Real Estate; Tax Liens/Judgments; UCC records; Vital records
Local Retrieval Area: OK-Rogers
Add'l Information: Established 1907. Normal turnaround time- 3-4 days. Fee basis will vary by the type of project. Will file/record documents for clients. They specialize in title insurance and closings.

Rogers Investigations & Research
PO Box 1825, Carlsbad, CA 92018
Phone: 800-935-6654; 760-930-0700 - **Fax:** 760-438-5028
www.rogersinvestigations.com **email:** brogers@rogersinvestigations.com
Types of Records Retrieved: Criminal, Civil and Probate courts; Federal courts; Real Estate; Tax Liens/Judgments; UCC records; Vital records
Local Retrieval Area: CA-Orange, San Diego. **Correspondent Relationships:** nationwide.
Add'l Information: Established 1981. Normal turnaround time- 24 hours. Projects billed by number of names searched. Projects billed by number of records located. Projects billed by the hour. First project may require prepayment. Credit cards accepted. They specialize in research, surveillance, locate missing persons and professional counter measures. A licensed PI in CA.

Rolette County Abstract Inc
PO Box 549, Rolla, ND 58367
Phone: 701-477-3149 - **Fax:** 701-477-0375 abstract@utma.com
Types of Records Retrieved: Criminal, Civil and Probate courts; Real Estate; Tax Liens/Judgments; UCC records; Vital records
Local Retrieval Area: ND-Rolette
Add'l info: Established 1902. Normal turnaround time- 1-2 weeks. Fee basis will vary by the type of project. Will file/record documents for clients.

Rollins Research Ltd
6412 Alpine Lane, Amarillo, TX 79109
Phone: 806-353-7886, cell- 806-654-2376 rollinsresearch@cox.net
Types of Records Retrieved: Civil and Probate courts; Federal courts; Real Estate; Tax Liens/Judgments; UCC records
Local Retrieval Area: TX-Armstrong, Carson, Castro, Dallam, Deaf Smith, Donley, Gray, Hartley, Hutchinson, Moore, Oldham, Potter, Randall, Roberts, Swisher
Add'l Information: Established 1987. Normal turnaround time- 24-72 hours for Potter and Randall Counties; 24-120 hours for all other counties. Projects billed by number of names searched. Add'l mileage charges may be applied for local court record searches in counties other than Potter & Randall. First project may require prepayment. Will file/record documents for clients. She specializes in title runs for foreclosures or second liens, UCC, asset searches and home equity loans. She does criminal record searches in Potter and Randall counties only.

Roosevelt County Abstract Co Inc
PO Box 176, Wolf Point, MT 59201
Phone: 406-653-2800 - **Fax:** 406-653-2803
Types of Records Retrieved: Civil and Probate courts; Real Estate; Tax Liens/Judgments; UCC records
Local Retrieval Area: MT-Roosevelt
Add'l Information: Established 1919. Normal turnaround time- 4 days. Projects billed by the hour. Will file/record documents for clients. Billing mailed with completed job. They specialize in title insurance.

Susan K Rosenbaum
PO Box 4, Genoa, NE 68640-0004
Phone: 888-459-8700; 402-560-6759 - **Fax:** 888-459-8700
rosenbaumsusan@msn.com
Types of Records Retrieved: Criminal and Civil courts; Tax Liens/Judgments
Local Retrieval Area: NE-Antelope, Boone, Butler, Colfax, Dodge, Hall, Hamilton, Howard, Knox, Lancaster, Madison, Merrick, Nance, Pierce, Platte, Polk, Saunders, Seward, York
Add'l Information: Established 1989. Normal turnaround time- 24-48 hours. Invoice monthly or per search.

Betty M Rowell, CLA
PO Box 989, Blackshear, GA 31516-0989
Phone: 912-449-0849 - **Fax:** 912-449-0849
Types of Records Retrieved: Civil and Probate courts; Real Estate; Tax Liens/Judgments; UCC records
Local Retrieval Area: GA-Brantley, Pierce, Ware
Add'l Information: Established 1991. Normal turnaround time- 24-48 hours. Projects billed by number of names searched. She specializes in real estate matters. She will file/record UCC and real estate documents on behalf of clients in Ware & Pierce Counties only.

Royal Title Services
108 N Lebanon St, Lebanon, IN 46052
Phone: 800-773-7279; 765-482-2270 - **Fax:** 765-483-3549
www.royaltitle.com **email:** lebanon@royaltitle.com
Types of Records Retrieved: Criminal and Civil courts; Real Estate; Tax Liens/Judgments; UCC records; Vital records
Local Retrieval Area: IN-Boone. **Correspondent Relationships:** Indiana.
Add'l Information: Established 1950. Normal turnaround time- 24-48 hours. Projects billed by number of names searched. Will file/record documents for clients. They specialize in title searching and closings.

Rucar Business Information Center
100 Gran Bolevar Paseos #112 MSC 369, San Juan, PR 00926-5955
Phone: 787-645-1659 - **Fax:** 787-293-1071
rub_00926@hotmail.com
Types of Records Retrieved: Criminal and Civil courts; Federal courts; Real Estate; Tax Liens/Judgments; UCC records; Vital records
Local Retrieval Area: Puerto Rico, Dominican Republic. **Correspondent Relationships:** Puerto Rico.
Add'l Information: Established 1998. Normal turnaround time- 10 days or less. Projects billed by number of names searched. First project may require prepayment. The specialize in all types of records, ins inspections, claims process & medical record copies. They also process claims and have a surveillance department . Do criminal and MVRs searches in the Dominican Republic with ID's. A licensed PI in PR.

David M Rumancik
1681 Cadbury St NW, Massillon, OH 44646
Phone: 330-837-7737 - **Fax:** 330-837-7737 venariyy@aol.com
Types of Records Retrieved: Criminal, Civil and Probate courts; Real Estate; Tax Liens/Judgments; UCC records

Local Retrieval Area: OH-Carroll, Holmes, Stark, Summit, Trumbull, Tuscarawas, Wayne; PA-Crawford, Mercer, Venango

Add'l info: Established 1979. Turnaround time- 24 hours and up depending on the service requested. Fee depends on type of search. All projects require prepayment. Will file/record documents for clients. He specializes in real estate titles, oil & gas titles, oil & gas research, easement & right of way research for utility companies, criminal & misdemeanor background checks on individuals for employment purposes and lien searches.

Runnymeade Research Inc

20 S. Tollgate Rd, Owings Mills, MD 21117
Phone: 410-998-9886 - **Fax:** 443-431-0217
www.runnymeaderesearch.com **email:** orders@runnymeaderesearch.com

Types of Records Retrieved: Real Estate

Local Retrieval Area: MD-Anne Arundel, Baltimore, Baltimore City, Carroll, Howard. **Correspondent Relationships:** statewide in Maryland.

Add'l Information: Established 2001. Normal turnaround time- 3-5 days. Expedited service available. Projects billed by number of names searched. Payment due upon receipt. They offer accurate, fast, personal service at their guaranteed lowest cost in Maryland. All new clients will receive their first order "Free". Call for details.

Rus B Robison & Associates Inc

PO Box 720560, Oklahoma City, OK 73172-0560
Phone: 405-603-2932 - **Fax:** 405-722-2422
www.robisonpi.com **email:** rbr@robisonpi.com

Types of Records Retrieved: Criminal, Civil and Probate courts; Federal courts; Real Estate; Tax Liens/Judgments; UCC records

Local Retrieval Area: OK-Canadian, Cleveland, McClain, Oklahoma

Add'l Information: Established 1972. Normal turnaround time- 1-2 business days. Projects billed by number of names searched. Certain projects can also be billed by the hour. First project may require prepayment. Will file/record documents for clients. Will accept immediate bank account payments, but not credit cards, through Pay Pal. They have numerous legal proprietary databases for added access. A licensed PI in OK. Performs service of process.

Russell Abstract

PO Box 6, 6 S Main St, Greenfield, MO 65661
Phone: 417-637-2414 - **Fax:** 417-637-2214

Records Retrieved: Real Estate; Tax Liens/Judgments; Probate courts

Local Retrieval Area: MO-Dade

Add'l Information: Established 1850. Normal turnaround time- 3-5 business days. Fee basis will vary by type of project. First project may require prepayment. Will file/record documents for clients. They specialize in title searches; title plant dating back to 1849. Also do real estate escrow closings and title insurance.

Russell-Surles Title Inc

337 Market St, Baird, TX 79504
Phone: 325-854-1115 - **Fax:** 325-854-1459

Types of Records Retrieved: Criminal, Civil and Probate courts; Real Estate; Tax Liens/Judgments; UCC records

Local Retrieval Area: TX-Callahan

Add'l Information: Normal turnaround time- variable depending on project. Projects billed by number of names searched. Will file/record documents for clients. Personal checks are accepted.

Ryco Information Services Inc

7591 Morgan Rd #1, Liverpool, NY 13090
Phone: 800-240-7926; 315-461-8308 - **Fax:** 315-461-4501
www.rycoinfo.com **email:** searches@rycoinfo.com

Types of Records Retrieved: Civil and Probate courts; Real Estate; Tax Liens/Judgments; UCC records

Local Retrieval Area: NY-All counties. **Correspondents:** nationwide.

Add'l Information: Established 1992. Normal turnaround time- 24-48 hours; updates in 48 hours; full search in 48-72 hours. By order Will file/record documents for clients. Net 30 days. Established 13 years ago, Ryco provides professional, accurate, and timely property information. Their knowledgeable staff maintains all requirements in the property abstract industry. Can also do counties in Virginia.

S & G Information Services

4558 S 150 West, La Porte, IN 46350
Phone: 219-898-5610-cell, 219-325-3473; Fax- same

Types of Records Retrieved: Criminal courts; US District court

Local Retrieval Area: IN-La Porte, Lake, Porter, St. Joseph

Add'l Information: Established 2004. Normal turnaround time- 24-48 hours. Projects billed by number of names searched. First project may require prepayment. They are experts at criminal records in Northwest Indiana.

Sac County Abstract Co

PO Box 98, 420 Main, Sac City, IA 50583
Phone: 712-662-7317 - **Fax:** 712-662-4090 mgreen@pionet.net

Types of Records Retrieved: Criminal, Civil and Probate courts; Real Estate; Tax Liens/Judgments; UCC records; Vital records

Local Retrieval Area: IA-Sac

Add'l Information: Normal turnaround time- 2-3 days. Fee basis will vary by the type of project. First project may require prepayment. Will file/record documents for clients.

Sacandaga Abstract Corp

8 Fremont St, Gloversville, NY 12078
Phone: 518-773-2828 - **Fax:** 518-725-9875

Types of Records Retrieved: Real Estate; Tax Liens/Judgments; Probate courts; UCC records

Local Retrieval Area: NY-Fulton, Montgomery

Add'l Information: Established 1986. Normal turnaround time- 1-5 days. Projects billed by number of names searched. Projects billed by number of records located. First project may require prepayment. Will file/record documents for clients. Personal checks are accepted. Their company offers fast and efficient abstracting work at reasonable prices.

Alice E Sackman

10617 N Ash St, Hayden, ID 83835
Phone: 208-964-0209 - **Fax:** 208-762-4757 thesackmans@roadrunner.com

Types of Records Retrieved: Criminal and Civil courts; Real Estate; Tax Liens/Judgments; UCC records

Local Retrieval Area: ID-Kootenai

Add'l Information: Established 1998. Normal turnaround time- 24 hours. Projects billed by number of names searched. First project may require prepayment. They specialize in high quality, accurate work delivered within 24 hours at an affordable price. Most orders are returned the same day. Been in business since 1998.

SafeHire

2637 Spring St, Eureka, CA 95501
Phone: 707-442-5043 - **Fax:** 707-443-5798
www.safehire.info **email:** sandybowman@sbcglobal.net

Types of Records Retrieved: Criminal, Civil and Probate courts; Tax Liens/Judgments; UCC records; Vital records

Local Retrieval Area: CA-Humboldt. **Correspondent Relationships:** Riverside, Siskiyou & Ventura counties, CA, WA, CO, NC, UT, PA, VA, OK, NM, RI, TX & WI.

Add'l Information: Established 1998. Normal turnaround time- within 24 hours. Projects billed by number of names searched. Will invoice 1st of the month. Safehire, a small business woman owned business, in operation since 1998, provides fast & reliable results, mainly to other public record search firms.

Saguache County Abstract & Investment

PO Box 157, Saguache, CO 81149

Phone: 719-655-2611 - **Fax:** 719-655-2326

Types of Records Retrieved: Real Estate; Tax Liens/Judgments

Local Retrieval Area: CO-Saguache

Add'l Information: Established 1905. Normal turnaround time- 2-5 days. Projects billed by number of records located. Will file/record documents for clients. Out of state clients prepay, in-state terms are net 30 days. They specialize in all related title insurance company searches and closings.

Salem Title Corporation

54 Courthouse Sq, Salem, IN 47167

Phone: 812-883-5806 - **Fax:** 812-883-5229 salemtitlecorp@yahoo.com

Records Retrieved: Real Estate; Tax Liens/Judgments; UCC records

Local Retrieval Area: IN-Clark, Crawford, Floyd, Harrison, Jackson, Lawrence, Orange, Scott, Washington

Add'l Information: Established 1954. Normal turnaround time- 2 day for judgment or UCC searches, and 3-5 days for complete title searches. Fee basis will vary by the type of project. First project may require prepayment. Will file/record documents for clients. Personal checks are accepted. They maintain a title plant in their office. They are a full service title company. A licensed PI in IN.

Salyer & Assoc.

114 W Main, McArthur, OH 45651

Phone: 740-596-5291 - **Fax:** 740-596-3700

Types of Records Retrieved: Criminal, Civil and Probate courts; Real Estate; Tax Liens/Judgments; UCC records; Vital records

Local Retrieval Area: OH-Jackson, Vinton. **Correspondent Relationships:** Athens, Hocking, Meigs and Ross counties Ohio.

Add'l Information: Established 1995. Normal turnaround time- variable depending on search. Charges vary depending on the type of search. Will file/record documents for clients. They are attorneys and specialize in real estate record searches.

Judi Sampson

PO Box 137, Kimbolton, OH 43749

Phone: 740-439-1202 - **Fax:** 740-432-8166

Types of Records Retrieved: Criminal and Civil courts; Real Estate; Tax Liens/Judgments; UCC records

Local Retrieval Area: OH-Ashland, Athens, Belmont, Carroll, Coshocton, Gallia, Guernsey, Harrison, Hocking, Jackson, Jefferson, Knox, Licking, Meigs, Monroe, Muskingum, Noble, Perry, Richland, Stark, Tuscarawas, Vinton, Washington, Wayne/

Add'l Information: Established 1996. Normal turnaround time- 24-48 hours. Projects billed by number of names searched. Billing depends on types of records searched. First project may require prepayment. She and her family staff specialize in court records; real estate services include current owner searches, deed or mortgage searches.

San Juan County Abstract & Title

111 N Orchard Ave, Farmington, NM 87401

Phone: 505-325-2808 - **Fax:** 505-327-7483

www.sanjuantitle.com **email:** admin@sanjuantitle.com

Types of Records Retrieved: Criminal, Civil and Probate courts; Real Estate; Tax Liens/Judgments; UCC records; Vital records

Local Retrieval Area: NM-San Juan

Add'l Information: Established 1946. Normal turnaround time- 1-3 days. Fee basis will vary by the type of project. A minimum fee is involved. Payment due upon delivery of order.

Sanborn County Realty & Title

PO Box 127, 207 S Dumont Ave, Woonsocket, SD 57385-0127

Phone: 605-796-4417 - **Fax:** 605-796-4248 scrtmpp@santel.net

Types of Records Retrieved: Civil and Probate courts; Real Estate; Tax Liens/Judgments

Local Retrieval Area: SD-Sanborn

Add'l Information: Established 1982. Normal turnaround time- 7-10 days. The fee basis is a flat fee. First project may require prepayment. Will file/record documents for clients. Personal checks and cash are accepted. They specialize in abstracts and title insurance. They also search liens and real estate taxes. They also have a real estate closing service. They will file/record real estate documents of behalf of clients.

Sandhills Abstracting

218 N Main St, Gordon, NE 69343

Phone: 308-282-1140 - **Fax:** 308-282-1240 cginkens@broncs.net

Types of Records Retrieved: Criminal, Civil and Probate courts; Real Estate; Tax Liens/Judgments; UCC records; Vital records

Local Retrieval Area: NE-Cherry, Sheridan

Add'l Information: Established 1987. Normal turnaround time- 1 week. Projects billed by number of names searched. Projects billed by number of records located. Projects billed by the hour. Will file/record documents for clients. Personal checks are accepted. They specialize in records from Sheridan County, but will provide service to Cherry county for add'l fee.

Sandhills Title

PO Box 181, Valentine, NE 69201

Phone: 402-376-2639 - **Fax:** 402-376-1180 suznbee1@yahoo.com

Types of Records Retrieved: Criminal, Civil and Probate courts; Real Estate; Tax Liens/Judgments

Local Retrieval Area: NE-Brown, Cherry, Keya Paha, Thomas

Add'l Information: Established 1995. Normal turnaround time- 1-2 days in Cherry County; other counties up to 1 week. Projects billed by number of names searched. Projects billed by the hour. First project may require prepayment. Will file/record documents for clients. They specialize in record and title searches. Will file documents in Cherry County only.

SanDiver & Associates

3009 Washington St, Commerce, TX 75428

Phone: 903-886-2909 - **Fax:** 903-886-2909 jsands9612@earthlink.net

Types of Records Retrieved: Criminal, Civil and Probate courts; Real Estate; Tax Liens/Judgments; UCC record; Vital records

Local Retrieval Area: TX-Delta, Hopkins, Hunt

Add'l Information: Established 1980. Normal turnaround time- 24 hours. Expedited service available. Projects billed by number of names searched. Do monthly billings. SanDiver & Associates was formed as a partnership July 1980. Both owners have been active in the business with changes in ownership. They do general investigations. A licensed PI in TX.

Sargents Title Co

625 S Grand Traverse St, Flint, MI 48502

Phone: 810-767-2355 - **Fax:** 810-767-2430

www.sargentstitle.com **Types of Records Retrieved:** Real Estate

Local Retrieval Area: MI-Genesee. **Correspondent Relationships:** 21 counties in SE Michigan area.

Add'l Information: Established 1968. Normal turnaround time- 3-5 days. Projects billed by the hour. Fee basis depends upon type of project. Will file/record documents for clients. They specialize in title insurance.

SAS Associates Inc

1423 Brown St, Bettendorf, IA 52722

Phone: 800-373-0727; 563-359-0408 - **Fax:** 563-359-0830

www.sasassociates.com **email:** sas@netexpress.net

Types of Records Retrieved: Criminal and Civil courts

Local Retrieval Area: IA-Jackson, Polk, Scott; IL-Henry, Mercer, Rock Island. **Correspondent Relationships:** statewide and IL, MN, WS, NE, NV, ND, SD, OH, PA, IL.

Add'l Information: Established 1984. Normal turnaround time- 3-4 days. Projects billed by number of names searched. Projects billed by the hour.

First project may require prepayment. Credit cards accepted. Net 10 days upon receipt of invoice. Specialize in background investigations including criminal & civil searches. Document retrieval & filings, general investigations for businesses and process servers. Licensed investigations in Iowa and Illinois. In business since 1984. A licensed PI in IA, IL. Performs service of process.

Sathre Title & Abstracting Inc

315 5th St NW #2, Bemidji, MN 56601-3021
Phone: 218-751-4565 - **Fax:** 218-751-7991 title@paulbunyan.net
Records Retrieved: Real Estate; Tax Liens/Judgments; UCC records
Local Retrieval Area: MN-Beltrami
Add'l Information: Established 1914. Normal turnaround time- variable depending on project. Fee basis will vary by type of project. Will file/record documents for clients. They specialize in real estate and property reports.

Sawyer County Abstract & Title

PO Box 169, Hayward, WI 54843
Phone: 715-634-9444 - **Fax:** 715-634-9445
www.sawyercountytitle.com **email:** sawyercountytitle@centurytel.net
Records Retrieved: Real Estate; Tax Liens/Judgments; UCC records
Local Retrieval Area: WI-Rusk, Sawyer, Washburn
Add'l Information: Normal turnaround time- 48 hours. Projects billed by number of names searched. Projects billed by number of records located. Projects billed by the hour. Personal checks are accepted.

SCC Information Services Inc

PO Box 494, Lexington, SC 29071
Phone: 803-957-1243 - **Fax:** 803-957-9359 menlow@alltel.net
Types of Records Retrieved: Civil and Probate courts; Real Estate; Tax Liens/Judgments; UCC records
Local Retrieval Area: SC-Aiken, Edgefield, Lexington, Newberry, Saluda
Add'l Information: Established 1995. Normal turnaround time- 24-48 hours. Projects billed by number of names searched. Projects billed by number of records located. Terms: net 30 days.

Schaeffer Papers

100 N Main #220B, Memphis, TN 38103
Phone: 800-848-6119; 901-725-9555 - **Fax:** 901-578-7424
suelynch@memphismoonlighters.com
Types of Records Retrieved: Criminal, Civil and Probate courts; Federal courts; Real Estate; Tax Liens/Judgments; Vital records
Local Retrieval Area: MS-De Soto, Tunica; TN-Blount, Davidson, Knox, Shelby, Sumner. **Correspondent Relationships:** Fayette, Tipton counties.
Add'l Information: Established 1988. Normal turnaround time- 24-72 hours. Projects billed by number of names searched. Projects billed by number of records located. Incurred expenses will be added to the fee. By the hour fees are for out of county or state. Flat fee charged for Shelby County Service of Process. All projects require prepayment. Will file/record documents for clients. Personal checks are accepted. They specialize in civil court matters and process service. They are also abstractors. Also do title searches for all of Tennessee and North Mississippi. Performs service of process.

Schillinger & Keith Abstract & Settlement

840 Philadelphia St #201, Indiana, PA 15701
Phone: 800-275-2959; 724-465-9520 - **Fax:** 724-465-9583
snkinc@adelphia.net
Types of Records Retrieved: Criminal, Civil and Probate courts; Real Estate; Tax Liens/Judgments; UCC records
Local Retrieval Area: PA-Indiana
Add'l Information: Established 1993. Normal turnaround time- 24 hours. Charges vary depending on type of search. They do monthly invoicing. Will file/record documents for clients. Due within 10 days of billing. They are a title insurance agent for Stewart Title Ins. and Lawyers Title Ins Co.

Kathleen Schloesser

403 Wayne St, Bethany, PA 18431
Phone: 570-253-5368 - **Fax:** 570-253-5367 momaK8@ptd.net
Types of Records Retrieved: Criminal, Civil and Probate courts; Real Estate; Tax Liens/Judgments; UCC records
Local Retrieval Area: PA-Wayne
Add'l Information: Established 1981. Normal turnaround time- 24 hours. Projects billed by number of names searched. Will file/record documents for clients. Net 5 days. She specializes in real estate searches, current owner, 60 year and real estate closings.

Jacqueline Schoeneberg

2848 S Quail Av, Springfield, MO 65807
Phone: 417-889-6390 - **Fax:** 417-882-8973 schonanny@aol.com
Types of Records Retrieved: Criminal courts
Local Retrieval Area: MO-Greene
Add'l Information: Established 1999. Normal turnaround time- 24 hours. Projects billed by number of names searched. Monthly billing. They do daily hands-on service with a 24 hour turnaround.

Bill Scholly

PO Box 1, Buckshead, GA 30625
Phone: 706-342-4166; Fax- same
Types of Records Retrieved: Criminal, Civil and Probate courts; US District court; Tax Liens/Judgments
Local Retrieval Area: GA-Greene, Jasper, Morgan, Putnam
Add'l Information: Established 2000. Normal turnaround time- 24-48 hours. Projects billed by number of names searched. Projects billed by the hour. First project may require prepayment. Name pronounced Show-lay. He specializes in court research including the federal court in Athens.

Paul Scholtes

PO Box 1262, West Palm Beach, FL 33402
Phone: 561-385-8163 - **Fax:** 561-745-4404
paulscholtes@hotmail.com
Types of Records Retrieved: Criminal, Civil and Probate courts; Federal courts; Real Estate; Tax Liens/Judgments; UCC records; Vital records
Local Retrieval Area: FL-Palm Beach. **Correspondent Relationships:** Broward, Dade, Martin, Palm Beach, St. Lucie counties FL.
Add'l Information: Established 1990. Normal turnaround time- variable depending on project. Projects billed by the hour. All projects require prepayment. Will file/record documents for clients. They specialize in private investigating, process serving and most other legal services. A licensed PI in FL. Performs service of process.

Schurger Land Title Co

119 S 2nd St, Decatur, IN 46733
Phone: 260-724-4408 - **Fax:** 260-724-4446
Types of Records Retrieved: Criminal and Civil courts; Real Estate; Tax Liens/Judgments; UCC records
Local Retrieval Area: IN-Adams
Add'l Information: Established 1871. Normal turnaround time- 24-72 hours. First project may require prepayment. Will file/record documents for clients. They have been the experts in Adams County spanning 3 centuries.

Scotland County Abstract & Title Inc

205 E Monroe St, Memphis, MO 63555
Phone: 660-465-7052 - **Fax:** 660-465-7452 scat@nemr.com
Records Retrieved: Real Estate; Tax Liens/Judgments; Probate courts
Local Retrieval Area: MO-Clark, Knox, Schuyler, Scotland
Add'l Information: Established 1981. Normal turnaround time- 3 days. Projects billed by number of records located. Will file/record documents for clients. They specialize in title insurance and title searches.

Scott Abstract

220 N Dewey St, North Platte, NE 69101
Phone: 308-532-8535 - **Fax:** 308-532-6559
Types of Records Retrieved: Criminal, Civil and Probate courts; Real Estate; Tax Liens/Judgments; UCC records; Vital records
Local Retrieval Area: NE-Frontier, Hayes, Hooker, Lincoln, Logan, McPherson, Thomas

Add'l Information: Established 1984. Normal turnaround time- 3 days for Lincoln County, and longer for other counties. Fee basis varies by type of transaction. They will file/record UCC and real estate documents on behalf of clients on a same or next day basis in Lincoln county only.

Scott County Abstract & Title Co Inc

310 Court St, Scott City, KS 67871
Phone: 620-872-3470 - **Fax:** 620-872-7105 sc@wbsnet.org

Types of Records Retrieved: Civil and Probate courts; Federal courts; Real Estate; Tax Liens/Judgments; UCC records; Vital records

Local Retrieval Area: KS-Scott

Add'l Info: Established 1972. Normal turnaround time- 24-48 hours. Projects billed by number of names searched. First project may require prepayment. Will file/record documents for clients. Personal checks accepted.

Scott Investigation

PO Box 7704, St Cloud, MN 56302
Phone: 800-357-7862; 320-363-7559 - **Fax:** 320-363-8512
piscott@aol.com

Types of Records Retrieved: Criminal, Civil and Probate courts; Real Estate; Tax Liens/Judgments; UCC records; Vital records

Local Retrieval Area: MN-Benton, Stearns. **Correspondent Relationships:** Central Minnesota.

Add'l Information: Established 1992. Normal turnaround time- 24-48 hours. Expedited service available. Projects billed by the hour. First project may require prepayment. They are a full service private detective agency specializing in personal injury, background checks, skip tracing and process service. A licensed PI in MN. Performs service of process.

Screencorp Inc

4859 E Skinner Dr, Cave Creek, AZ 85331
Phone: 602-739-7289 - **Fax:** 480-515-9895
www.pre-employmentscreens.com **email:** email@pre-employmentscreens.com

Types of Records Retrieved: Criminal courts

Local Retrieval Area: AZ-Maricopa. **Correspondents:** nationwide.

Add'l Information: Established 1994. Normal turnaround time- 24-36 hours. Projects billed by number of names searched. Will do monthly invoicing. They do pre-employment background checks provided to client companies on job applicants. This is all they do. They have a rapid turnaround, very affordable pricing and comprehensive information. A licensed PI in AZ.

Search & Find

PO Box 1053, LaGrange, GA 30241
Phone: 706-884-9801 - **Fax:** 706-812-9407
www.search-and-find-usa.com **email:** snf1996@aol.com

Records Retrieved: Criminal and Civil courts; Tax Liens/Judgments

Local Retrieval Area: GA-Catoosa, Clayton, Coweta, Fayette, Harris, Heard, Henry, Muscogee, Newton, Rockdale, Troup, Walker, Walton. **Correspondent Relationships:** statewide.

Add'l Information: Normal turnaround time- 24-48 hours. Projects billed by number of names searched. First project may require prepayment. Credit cards accepted. They have been in business since 1994. Their staff is there to care for all your needs in the area of criminal & civil research.

Search & Genealogy Services

281 Glenn Rd, Murphysboro, IL 62966
Phone: 618-529-1024
www.sgservices.bravepages.com **email:** timjuli@earthlink.net

Types of Records Retrieved: Criminal, Civil and Probate courts; Real Estate; Tax Liens/Judgments; UCC records; Vital records

Local Retrieval Area: IL-Jackson, Perry, Union

Add'l Information: Established 2000. Normal turnaround time- next day in most cases. Expedited service available. Projects billed by number of names searched. Projects billed by the hour. First project may require prepayment. Credit cards accepted. Search & Genealogy Services retrieves documents in-person in several southern Illinois counties, conducts nationwide people searches, locates missing heirs and conducts genealogical research.

Search & Retrieve

PO Box 1496, Parker, CO 80138
Phone: 303-587-7852 www.searchandretrieve.com
email: jeannecollins@searchandretrieve.com

Records Retrieved: Criminal, Civil and Probate courts; Federal courts; Real Estate; Tax Liens/Judgments; UCC records; Vital records

Local Retrieval Area: CO-Arapahoe, Denver, Douglas, Jefferson.

Add'l Information: Normal turnaround time-48 hours. Projects billed by number of records located. First project may require prepayment. In business since 2005. Will file documents locally.

Search 4 U

3602 Valley St, Catlettsburg, KY 41129
Phone: 606-739-5050 - **Fax:** 606-405-3104

Records Retrieved: Criminal and Civil courts; Tax Liens/Judgments

Local Retrieval Area: KY-Boyd

Add'l Information: Normal turnaround time- 24-48 hours. First project may require prepayment.

Search Company International

1535 Grant St #140, Denver, CO 80203-1843
Phone: 800-727-2120; 303-863-1800 - **Fax:** 800-956-1200; 303-863-7767
www.searchcompanyintl.com **email:** find-it@searchcompanyintl.com

Types of Records Retrieved: Criminal, Civil and Probate courts; Federal courts; Real Estate; Tax Liens/Judgments; UCC records; Corporate filings; Federal Records Center documents

Local Retrieval Area: CO-Adams, Arapahoe, Boulder, Broomfield, Clear Creek, Delta, Denver, Douglas, Eagle, El Paso, Elbert, Fremont, Garfield, Gilpin, Jefferson, Larimer, Mesa, Pueblo, Teller, Weld. **Correspondent Relationships:** Colorado and nationwide.

Add'l Information: Established 1979. Normal turnaround time- 24-48 hours. Projects billed by number of names searched. First project may require prepayment. Personal checks are accepted. They are online with CO's Sec of State. They have the Sec of State microfilm library & all CO UCC filings. They specialize in UCC, tax liens/judgments, real estate, litigation (State/Fed), corporate filing. They can e-mail results & take orders online. Performs service of process.

Search Company of North Dakota LLC

1008 E Capitol Ave, Bismarck, ND 58501-1930
Phone: 701-223-1848 - **Fax:** 701-223-1850
www.searchcompanynd.com **email:** michael@searchcompanynd.com

Types of Records Retrieved: Criminal, Civil and Probate courts; Federal courts; Real Estate; Tax Liens/Judgments; UCC records; Vital records

Local Retrieval Area: ND-Burleigh, Cass, Morton. **Correspondent Relationships:** North Dakota.

Add'l Information: Established 1984. Normal turnaround time- 24-72 hours. Projects billed by number of names searched. Will file/record documents for clients. They have 18 years of public record experience in North Dakota at the city, county, state and federal levels. They also provide registered agent services. A licensed PI in ND. Performs service of process.

Search International Inc

22 Commonwealth Av, Erlanger, KY 41018-1798
Phone: 859-342-0456 - **Fax:** 859-342-0457

Types of Records Retrieved: Criminal and Civil courts; Federal courts; Real Estate; Tax Liens/Judgments; UCC records

Local Retrieval Area: KY-Boone, Campbell, Grant, Kenton, Pendleton; OH-Clermont, Hamilton

Add'l Information: Established 1995. Normal turnaround time- 24-48 hours. Projects billed by number of names searched. First project may require prepayment. Will file/record documents for clients. They specialize in felony, misdemeanor, UCC searches, civil, tax liens. They also cover federal courts in Southwest Ohio. They are court research specialists.

Search Network Ltd (Iowa)

1503 42nd St #210, West Des Moines, IA 50266
Phone: 800-383-5050; 515-223-1153 - **Fax:** 800-383-5060; 515-223-2814
www.searchnetworkltd.com **email:** lharken@searchnetworkltd.com

Types of Records Retrieved: Civil courts; Federal courts; Real Estate; Tax Liens/Judgments; UCC records

Local Retrieval Area: IA-Polk. **Correspondent Relationships:** nationwide and Canada.

Add'l Information: Established 1965. Normal turnaround time- same day for state UCC; County; 2-4 days. Projects billed by number of names searched. Projects billed by the hour. First project may require prepayment. Terms: net 30 days. They specialize in UCC lien filing and search services, also corporate document filings and retrieval. Onsite UCC database for Iowa and Kansas.

Search Network Ltd (Kansas)

700 SW Jackson #100, Topeka, KS 66603
Phone: 800-338-3618; 785-235-5777 - **Fax:** 785-235-5788
www.searchnetworkltd.com/searchnetworkltd/
email: lharken@searchnetworkltd.com

Types of Records Retrieved: Civil courts; Federal courts; Real Estate; Tax Liens/Judgments; UCC records; Vital records

Local Retrieval Area: KS-Shawnee. **Correspondent Relationships:** nationwide, especially Kansas, Missouri.

Add'l Information: Established 1965. Normal turnaround time- same day for state UCC; County; 2-4 days. Projects billed by number of names searched. First project may require prepayment. Will file/record documents for clients. Terms: net 30 days. They specialize in corporate & UCC lien filing and retrieval. They are online with Kansas for UCC records, and provide an onsite database for Kansas and Iowa from their Iowa office. They have correspondents in all KS counties

Search NY Inc

111 John St, 6th Fl, New York, NY 10038
Phone: 212-608-2546 - **Fax:** 212-566-5901
www.searchnyinc.com **email:** pnuzio@searchnyinc.com

Types of Records Retrieved: Criminal, Civil and Probate courts; Federal courts; Real Estate; Tax Liens/Judgments; UCC records; Vital records

Local Retrieval Area: NY-Bronx, Dutchess, Kings, Nassau, New York, Orange, Queens, Richmond, Rockland, Suffolk, Westchester. **Correspondent Relationships:** nationwide.

Add'l Information: Established 1983. Normal turnaround time- 24-72 hours. Projects billed by number of names searched. First project may require prepayment. Credit cards accepted. Will file/record documents for clients. They specialize in all public record searches. Performs service of process.

Search One Services

6746 Axtel Dr, Columbus, OH 43110-8429
Phone: 614-834-5603 - **Fax:** 614-834-5605 searchone@sbcglobal.net

Types of Records Retrieved: Civil courts; Federal courts; Real Estate; Tax Liens/Judgments; UCC records

Local Retrieval Area: OH-Cuyahoga, Delaware, Fairfield, Franklin, Greene, Hamilton, Licking, Miami, Pickaway. **Correspondent Relationships:** Cuyahoga, Summit, Stark, Miami counties.

Add'l Information: Established 1996. Normal turnaround time- same day to 48 hours. Projects billed by number of names searched. Terms: net 30 days. They search UCCs, tax liens, judgments, federal and bankruptcy courts. They do document retrievals and Franklin filings; No correspondent fees. Rapid Franklin County service.

Search Services

116 Byron Pl, Raleigh, NC 27609
Phone: 919-801-3010 - **Fax:** 919-781-3706
www.registeredagent.com **email:** searchsvcs@yahoo.com

Types of Records Retrieved: Civil courts; Federal courts; Tax Liens/Judgments; UCC records; Vital records

Local Retrieval Area: NC-Durham, Wake

Add'l Information: Established 1978. Normal turnaround time- 24-48 hours. Projects billed by number of names searched. Will file/record documents for clients. Terms are net 30 days. Record research specialist in the Raleigh, NC area. Is a registered Agent.

Searcher Girls

PO Box 8573, Hamilton, NJ 08650-0573
Phone: 800-292-2757; - **Fax:** 800-292-2858
www.searchergirls.net **email:** 1search@searchergirls.net

Types of Records Retrieved: Criminal, Civil and Probate courts; Federal courts; Real Estate; Tax Liens/Judgments; UCC records

Local Retrieval Area: NJ-Atlantic, Bergen, Burlington, Camden, Essex, Gloucester, Hudson, Hunterdon, Mercer, Middlesex, Monmouth, Morris, Ocean, Passaic, Somerset, Union. **Correspondents in:** New Jersey.

Add'l Information: Established 1995. Normal turnaround time- 24-48 hours. Projects billed by number of names searched. Projects billed by the hour. Credit cards accepted. Will file/record documents for clients. They assist attorneys who practice in the field of complex federal and state litigation and develop computer programs and solutions.

Searches by SKW

14355 Bradford Ct, Waverly, NE 68462
Phone: 402-786-2184 - **Fax:** 402-786-2185 skw3@alltel.net

Types of Records Retrieved: Criminal and Civil courts; Federal District courts; Tax Liens/Judgments

Local Retrieval Area: NE-Lancaster

Add'l info: Established 1995. Normal turnaround time- 24-48 hours. Projects billed by number of names searched. First project may require prepayment. They specialize in background checks by name for misdemeanor or felony judgments. Also can check for state or federal tax liens.

Searching Registration Service

PO Box 15824, Sacramento, CA 95852-1824
Phone: 800-488-0238; 916-452-8231 - **Fax:** 800-488-0231; 916-451-2322

Types of Records Retrieved: Real Estate; UCC records; Vital records

Local Retrieval Area: CA-Sacramento

Add'l Information: Established 1946. Projects billed by number of names searched. First project may require prepayment. Terms: net 10 days. They specialize in driver/license and vehicle registration searches.

SearchLink LLC

299 Commonwealth Ave, Buffalo, NY 14216
Phone: 716-873-8315 - **Fax:** 716-873-2534
www.searchlink.org **email:** searchlink@searchlink.org

Types of Records Retrieved: Criminal, Civil and Probate courts; Federal courts; Real Estate; Tax Liens/Judgments; UCC records

Local Retrieval Area: NY-all counties. **Correspondents:** nationwide.

Add'l Information: Established 1991. Normal turnaround time- 24-48 hours. Projects billed by number of names searched. Will file/record documents for clients. Terms net 30 days. Formerly NY Criminal Search, they specialize in criminal record searches in Erie, Monroe, Niagara and Westchester Counties, also UCC searches, tax liens and judgments. Can do any search statewide.

Searchtec

211 N 13th St #600, Philadelphia, PA 19107
Phone: 877-2SEARCH; 215-963-0888 x111 - **Fax:** 215-851-8775
www.searchtec.com **email:** info@searchtec.com

Types of Records Retrieved: Civil and Probate courts; Federal courts; Real Estate; Tax Liens/Judgments; UCC records

Local Retrieval Area: NJ-Burlington, Camden, Gloucester, Mercer; PA-Bucks, Chester, Delaware, Montgomery, Philadelphia. **Correspondent Relationships:** nationwide.

Add'l Information: Established 1990. Normal turnaround time- 24-48 hours. Charge by product. Credit cards accepted. Will file/record documents for clients. They specialize in public record searches, corp svcs appraisals, title ins & settlements, witness closings & filing records. They combine advanced technology with a knowledgeable staff to provide svcs to those in the legal, real estate, etc. industries.

Searchtec (Carolinas)

2 Office Park Ct #103, Columbia, SC 29223
Phone: 800-528-8790; 803-699-6130 - **Fax:** 800-542-7499; 803-699-6178
www.searchtec.com **email:** ndac@searchtec.com

Types of Records Retrieved: Criminal, Civil and Probate courts; Federal courts; Real Estate; Tax Liens/Judgments; UCC records; Vital records

Local Retrieval Area: NC-78 counties; SC-all counties. **Correspondent Relationships:** nationwide.

Add'l Information: Established 1990. Normal turnaround time- 24 hours - 3 days. Projects billed by number of names searched. First project may require prepayment. Will file/record documents for clients. Terms: net 15 days. Formerly National Data Access Corp, their quality work is surpassed only by their superb customer service. Recently acquired by SearchTec, Inc their combined companies make them a leader in their industry. Has office in Raleigh, NC at 4208 Six Forks Rd. Performs service of process.

SearchWorks Inc

6917 W 76th St, Overland Park, KS 66204
Phone: 913-383-0940 - **Fax:** 913-383-8561

Types of Records Retrieved: Civil courts; Federal courts; Real Estate; Tax Liens/Judgments; UCC records

Local Retrieval Area: KS-Douglas, Johnson, Wyandotte; MO-Cass, Clay, Jackson, Johnson, Platte

Add'l Information: Established 1989. Normal turnaround time- 2 days. Projects billed by number of names searched. Will file/record documents for clients. Payment due net 30 days. They specialize in real estate; current-owner forward showing open liens and UCC, tax liens, and litigation.

Seattle Process Service Inc

17404 161st Ave SE, Renton, WA 98058-9142
Phone: 800-842-8913;
www.seattleprocessservice.com **email:** seattleprocess@qwest.net

Types of Records Retrieved: Criminal, Civil and Probate courts; Federal courts

Local Retrieval Area: WA-King, Pierce, Snohomish

Add'l Information: Established 1980. Normal turnaround time- approximately 5 business days. Projects billed by the hour. First project may require prepayment. Formerly Seattle Process Service Inc serving in downtown Seattle; has routine coverage in the Greater Seattle Metropolitan area. Big enough to get the job done and small enough to offer personal attention. Performs service of process.

Sebia LLC Investigations

PO Box 12629, 4960 S. Gilbert Rd, #1-484, Chandler, AZ 85248
Phone: 877-814-0307; 602-445-6463 - **Fax:** 602-218-7269
www.sebia.biz **email:** pr@sebia.biz

Types of Records Retrieved: Criminal, Civil and Probate courts; Federal courts; Real Estate; Tax Liens/Judgments; UCC records

Local Retrieval Area: AZ-Maricopa, Pinal

Add'l Information: Established 2005. Normal turnaround time- 1-2 days. Expedited service available. Projects billed by number of names searched. Projects billed by number of records located. First project may require prepayment. Credit cards accepted. They specialize in civil and criminal investigations, conduct background checks and skiptracing locates. A licensed PI in AZ. Performs service of process.

Secrest Legal Services

4515 Prentice St #102, Dallas, TX 75206
Phone: 214-696-3959 abbey2@aol.com

Types of Records Retrieved: Criminal, Civil and Probate courts; Federal courts; Real Estate; Tax Liens/Judgments; UCC records

Local Retrieval Area: TX-Dallas. **Correspondents:** nationwide and Canada.

Add'l info: Established 1992. Normal turnaround time- 24 hours. Projects billed by number of names searched. First project may require prepayment. Will file/record documents for clients. They specialize in UCC, county and federal court searches. Filing mortgages and assignment of liens in mass quantity is also a service provided. Owner operated and managed.

Secretarial Outsource Services

1303 Catherine St, Pekin, IL 61554
Phone: 309-347-3736 - **Fax:** 309-347-4571

Types of Records Retrieved: Criminal and Civil courts

Local Retrieval Area: IL-Tazewell

Add'l Information: Established 1992. Normal turnaround time- 24 hours. Projects billed by number of names searched. First project may require prepayment.

Secure Data Corporation

508 E South Temple #A28, Salt Lake City, UT 84102-1018
Phone: 801-595-1510 - **Fax:** 801-595-8366

Types of Records Retrieved: Criminal and Civil courts; Federal courts; Tax Liens/Judgments; UCC records

Local Retrieval Area: UT-Salt Lake

Add'l Information: Established 1997. Normal turnaround time- 24-48 hours. Projects billed by number of names searched. All projects require prepayment. They specialize in pre-employment screening.

Securitec Screening Solutions Inc

2374 Idavere Rd, Roanoke, VA 24015
Phone: 540-725-1571 - **Fax:** 540-400-0953
www.securitecscreening.com **email:** michael@securitecscreening.com

Types of Records Retrieved: Criminal and Civil courts; Federal courts

Local Retrieval Area: VA-Roanoke, Roanoke City, Salem. **Correspondent Relationships:** nationwide.

Add'l Information: Normal turnaround time- 24-48 hours. Projects billed by number of names searched. They offer local document retrieval services and nationwide screening services at wholesale prices. They perform statewide or regional record retrieval for some document types.

Security Abstract & Title Co

510 Main St, Miles City, MT 59301
Phone: 800-728-5022; 406-234-3415 - **Fax:** 406-234-3447

Types of Records Retrieved: Civil and Probate courts; Real Estate; Tax Liens/Judgments; UCC records

Local Retrieval Area: MT-Carter, Custer, Garfield. **Correspondent Relationships:** various throughout Montana.

Add'l Information: Established 1929. Normal turnaround time- as much as 2 weeks. Projects billed by the hour. First project may require prepayment. Will file/record documents for clients. They specialize in title insurance.

Security Abstract & Title Inc

114 N 1st Ave, Winterset, IA 50273
Phone: 515-462-1691 - **Fax:** 515-462-3927

Types of Records Retrieved: Criminal, Civil and Probate courts; Federal courts; Real Estate; Tax Liens/Judgments; UCC records; Vital records

Local Retrieval Area: IA-Madison

Add'l Information: Established 1901. Normal turnaround time- 2-5 days. Projects billed by number of names searched. Projects billed by the hour. First project may require prepayment. Will file/record documents for clients. Will also visit federal courts for Madison County related information.

Security Abstract Co

PO Box 673, 222 S Sully, Clarendon, TX 79226
Phone: 806-874-3511 - **Fax:** 806-874-3298

Types of Records Retrieved: Criminal, Civil and Probate courts; Real Estate; Tax Liens/Judgments; UCC records; Vital records

Local Retrieval Area: TX-Armstrong, Donley, Hall. **Correspondent Relationships:** statewide.

Add'l Information: Established 1987. Normal turnaround time- 2-3 weeks. Projects billed by number of names searched. They specialize in extensive property reports.

Security Abstract Co (Arkansas)

101 N Washington, Magnolia, AR 71753
Phone: 870-234-1291 - **Fax:** 870-234-5590 secabco@seark.net

Types of Records Retrieved: Civil and Probate courts; Real Estate; Tax Liens/Judgments; UCC records

Local Retrieval Area: AR-Columbia. **Correspondent Relationships:** Union County AR.

Add'l Information: Normal turnaround time- 2-3 days for civil, criminal and UCC searches, 5-7 days for real estate and probate. Fee basis will vary by the type of project. Will file/record documents for clients. They specialize in title insurance.

Security Abstract Co (Missouri)

305 Main, New Madrid, MO 63869
Phone: 573-748-2372 - **Fax:** 573-748-2376 jeaneavann@sbcglobal.net

Types of Records Retrieved: Criminal, Civil and Probate courts; Real Estate; Tax Liens/Judgments; Vital records

Local Retrieval Area: MO-New Madrid

Add'l Information: Established 1945. Normal turnaround time- 1 week or less. Projects billed by number of names searched. All projects require prepayment. Personal checks are accepted.

Security Abstract Company

214 E Washington St, Norton, KS 67654-2150
Phone: 785-877-2141 - **Fax:** 785-877-2185

Types of Records Retrieved: Criminal, Civil and Probate courts; Real Estate; Tax Liens/Judgments; UCC records; Vital records

Local Retrieval Area: KS-Norton

Add'l Information: Established 1949. Normal turnaround time- 24 hours. Projects billed by the hour. Payment due on completion of project. They specialize in abstracts, title insurance, home loans and investments.

Security Consultants Inc

5020 45th St NW, Washington, DC 20016-4043
Phone: 202-686-3953 - **Fax:** 202-686-0264
www.dcbackground.com **email:** sci@dcbackground.net

Types of Records Retrieved: Criminal, Civil and Probate courts; Federal courts; Tax Liens/Judgments; Vital records

Local Retrieval Area: DC-District of Columbia; MD-Anne Arundel, Baltimore, Harford, Howard, Montgomery, Prince George's; VA-Alexandria, Arlington, Fairfax, Prince William

Add'l Information: Established 1992. Normal turnaround time- 8 hours in DC; 12 business hours in other jurisdictions. Projects billed by number of names searched. Terms: net 30 days. They specialize in on-site searches in Washington, DC/Baltimore/Northern Virginia metro areas. SCI was founded by a former CIA Station Chief, a former Federal Investigator with 25 yrs experience later joined the firm.

Security Enforcement Inc

117 N Long Beach Rd, Rockville Ctr, NY 11570
Phone: 800-924-2896 (NY); 516-678-0344, cell- 800-924-2896
www.securityenforcementinc.net
email: securityenforcementinc@hotmail.com

Types of Records Retrieved: Criminal, Civil and Probate courts; Federal courts; Real Estate; Tax Liens/Judgments; UCC records; Vital records

Local Retrieval Area: NY-Nassau, Suffolk. **Correspondent Relationships:** Westchester, Kings, Queens, Richmond, New York City.

Add'l Information: Established 1986. Normal turnaround time- variable, depending on project. First project may require prepayment. Will file/record documents for clients. Personal checks accepted. They specialize in the NYC metro area. A licensed PI in NY. Performs service of process.

Security Essentials LLC

34 S Main St #3, Chagrin Falls, OH 44022-3200
Phone: 440-247-7808 purban1@msn.com

Types of Records Retrieved: Criminal and Civil courts; Federal courts; Tax Liens/Judgments

Local Retrieval Area: OH-Cuyahoga, Geauga, Lake, Summit

Add'l Information: Established 1997. Normal turnaround time- 24-48 hours. Expedited service available. Projects billed by number of names searched. First project may require prepayment. Terms are net 10 days. They conduct background investigations on persons and businesses. Forms in compliance with the Fair Credit Reporting Act are provided to clients at no cost. Expect professional and thorough service. A licensed PI in OH.

Security First Title Co

205 W Stephenson, Freeport, IL 61032
Phone: 815-235-2900 - **Fax:** 815-235-9955
www.securityfirsttitlecompany.com **email:** sec1title@aol.com

Types of Records Retrieved: Criminal, Civil and Probate courts; Bankruptcy courts; Real Estate; Tax Liens/Judgments; UCC records

Local Retrieval Area: IL-Boone, Carroll, Jo Daviess, Lee, Ogle, Stephenson, Whiteside, Winnebago

Add'l Information: Established 1999. Normal turnaround time- 48 hours. Projects billed by number of names searched. Projects billed by number of records located. Will file/record documents for clients. They specialize in Northwestern Illinois.

Security Information Service Inc

PO Box 1661, Decatur, TX 76234-6149
Phone: 214-637-4055 - **Fax:** 214-481-0555
www.SecurityInfoService.com **email:** Sales@SecurityInfoService.com

Types of Records Retrieved: Criminal, Civil and Probate courts; Federal courts; Real Estate; Tax Liens/Judgments; UCC records; Vital records

Local Retrieval Area: TX-Collin, Cooke, Dallas, Denton, Ellis, Grayson, Hunt, Johnson, Kaufman, Rockwall, Tarrant. **Correspondent Relationships:** nationwide and international.

Add'l Information: Established 1967. Normal turnaround time- 1-3 days. Projects billed by number of names searched. Projects billed by number of records located. Projects billed by the hour. All projects require prepayment. Credit cards accepted. They specialize in pre-employment investigations, loss prevention, process service. Experience in theft by fraud/embezzlement, due diligence/financial risk analysis, litigation/legal support, conflict of interest/bribery, etc. Texas' oldest PI firm. A licensed PI in TX. Performs service of process.

Security Land Title Co

607 1st Ave West, Box 113, Spencer, IA 51301
Phone: 712-262-1074 - **Fax:** 712-262-1082 sltc@ncn.net

Types of Records Retrieved: Criminal, Civil and Probate courts; Real Estate; Tax Liens/Judgments; UCC records

Local Retrieval Area: IA-Clay **Add'l Information:** Established 1858. Normal turnaround time- variable depending on project. They charge a flat fee per project. Will file/record documents for clients.

Security Search & Abstract Co Inc

926 Pine St, Philadelphia, PA 19107
Phone: 800-345-9494; 215-592-0660 - **Fax:** 800-343-4284; 215-592-1277
www.securitysearchabstract.com **email:** abarone@securitysearchabstract.com

Types of Records Retrieved: Civil courts; Federal courts; Real Estate; Tax Liens/Judgments; UCC records

Local Retrieval Area: DE-New Castle; NJ-Monmouth, Ocean; PA-Berks, Bucks, Chester, Delaware, Lancaster, Lehigh, Montgomery, Northampton, Philadelphia, Schuylkill. **Correspondent Relationships:** nationwide.

Add'l Information: Established 1962. Normal turnaround time- 24-48 hours. Projects billed by number of names searched. First project may require prepayment. They are a nationwide full service public records research company with title plants in Philadelphia, Bucks, Chester, Delaware and Montgomery counties.

Security Services Inc (SSI)

1009 N Sheridan Rd, Peoria, IL 61606
Phone: 800-383-4312; 309-674-4321 - **Fax:** 309-674-9357
www.securityservicesinc.us **email:** info@securityservicesinc.us
Types of Records Retrieved: Criminal and Civil courts; Federal courts
Local Retrieval Area: IL-Fulton, Knox, Marshall, McLean, Peoria, Stark, Tazewell, Woodford
Add'l Information: Established 1957. Normal turnaround time- 1-3 working days. Projects billed by the hour. Established clients are billed by the hour plus expenses. First project may require prepayment. A licensed PI in IL. Performs service of process.

Security Title Canon City

804 Main St, Canon City, CO 81212-3741
Phone: 800-526-7805; 719-275-3304 - **Fax:** 719-269-3353
www.stgco.com **Types of Records Retrieved:** Real Estate
Local Retrieval Area: CO-Custer, Fremont. **Correspondents:** statewide.
Add'l Information: Established 1946. Normal turnaround time- 1-2 days. They specialize in real estate and title matters.

Security Title Co of Garfield County

PO Box 177, Panguitch, UT 84759
Phone: 435-676-8808 - **Fax:** 435-676-2421 sectitle@color-country.net
Types of Records Retrieved: Criminal, Civil and Probate courts; Real Estate; Tax Liens/Judgments; UCC records; Vital records
Local Retrieval Area: UT-Garfield, Piute
Add'l Information: Established 1978. Normal turnaround time- 3-5 days. Projects billed by the hour. Will file/record documents for clients. They specialize in recreational properties.

Security Title of Beaver County

P.O. Box 819, Beaver, UT 84713
Phone: 435-438-2354 - **Fax:** 435-438-5805
Types of Records Retrieved: Civil and Probate courts; Real Estate; Tax Liens/Judgments; UCC records **Local Retrieval Area:** UT-Beaver
Add'l Information: Established 1977. Normal turnaround time- 24 hours. Projects billed by number of names searched. All projects require prepayment. Will file/record documents for clients.

Sedgwick County Title Co

114 W 1st St, Julesburg, CO 80737
Phone: 970-474-2696 - **Fax:** 970-474-2293
Records Retrieved: Real Estate; Tax Liens/Judgments; UCC records
Local Retrieval Area: CO-Sedgwick
Add'l Information: Established 1993. Normal turnaround time- 24 hours. Projects billed by number of names searched. All projects require prepayment. Will file/record documents for clients. They specialize in closings and notary services. They also do O & E's, mineral searches and title searches.

Carol Seewald

6101 Sequioa Rd NW #A6, Albuquerque, NM 87120
Phone: 505-831-5713 - **Fax:** 505-831-5713
Types of Records Retrieved: Real Estate; Tax Liens/Judgments; UCC records
Local Retrieval Area: NM-Bernalillo, Sandoval, Santa Fe, Socorro, Torrance, Valencia
Add'l Information: Normal turnaround time- 24-48 hours. Projects billed by number of names searched. First project may require prepayment. Will file/record documents for clients. Performs service of process.

Segars & Holly

1231 Curtis Dr, Iuka, MS 38852
Phone: 662-423-1006 - **Fax:** 662-423-1091
Types of Records Retrieved: Criminal, Civil and Probate courts; Real Estate; Tax Liens/Judgments; UCC records; Vital records
Local Retrieval Area: MS-Alcorn, Prentiss, Tishomingo
Add'l Information: Established 1992. Normal turnaround time- 1-2 days. Fee basis varies by type of project. First project may require prepayment. Will file/record documents for clients. Payment due upon receipt of statement. He is an attorney in general and real estate practice. Performs service of process.

Segovia & Associates

2020 E Pioneer Pky #100 PMB 5, Arlington, TX 76010-6806
Phone: 877-573-7833; - **Fax:** 877-221-6008
www.segoviaandassociates.com **email:** info@segoviaandassociates.com
Types of Records Retrieved: Criminal, Civil and Probate courts; Federal courts; Real Estate; Vital records
Local Retrieval Area: TX-Dallas, Tarrant. **Correspondent Relationships:** Johnson, Parker, Wise, Ellis, Denton counties TX; TX Sec of State.
Add'l Information: Established 1996. Normal turnaround time- 24 hours or less. Projects billed by number of names searched. All projects require prepayment. Credit cards accepted. Check by Telephone/Fax They specialize in service of process, document retrieval, legal and courthouse research and photocopying. Former private investigator with ten (10) years experience in the industry. Performs service of process.

Select Information Business Services

12025 215th Pl SE, Snohomish, WA 98296
Phone: 425-444-7877 - **Fax:** 253-540-1824 or 425-848-8400
www.selectinfobiz.com **email:** cbowers@selectinfobiz.com
Types of Records Retrieved: Criminal, Civil and Probate courts; Federal courts; Real Estate; Tax Liens/Judgments; UCC records; Vital records
Local Retrieval Area: WA-King, Snohomish. **Correspondent Relationships:** statewide.
Add'l Information: Established 2003. Normal turnaround time- 24-72 hours. First project may require prepayment. They file, retrieve & abstract, including public record info & the recorder, federal and state courts, Everett & Seattle planning offices & vital stats, real property, litigation & screening support. Over 20-yrs experience; efficient & professional.

Serunian Inv

211 Marginal Way, PMB 114, Portland, ME 04101
Phone: 207-773-2660 - **Fax:** 207-773-4369
Types of Records Retrieved: Criminal and Civil courts
Local Retrieval Area: ME-Cumberland, York
Add'l Information: Established 1985. Normal turnaround time- 24 hours. Projects billed by number of names searched. First project may require prepayment. Will file/record documents for clients. They specialize in public record retrieval, private investigator/detective, service of process, notary public, pre-employment screening, mystery shopper and background investigations. Criminal searches a specialty; in business since 1985. A licensed PI in ME. Performs service of process.

Service Abstract Company of Randolph County

208 E Everett St, Pocahontas, AR 72455
Phone: 870-892-4538 - **Fax:** 870-892-0302
servabst@cox-Internet.com
Types of Records Retrieved: Criminal, Civil and Probate courts; Federal courts; Real Estate; Tax Liens/Judgments; UCC records
Local Retrieval Area: AR-Randolph
Add'l Information: Established 1979. Normal turnaround time- variable depending on project. Projects billed by number of records located. Projects billed by the hour. Fee basis will vary by the type of project. Will file/record documents for clients. Personal checks accepted. They specialize in title insurance, abstracts and loan closings. A licensed PI in AR. Performs service of process.

Services For Lawyers

221 N Olive St, Media, PA 19063
Phone: 610-566-9165 - **Fax:** 610-566-9166
lawyerserv@aol.com
Types of Records Retrieved: Criminal, Civil and Probate courts; Federal courts; Real Estate; Tax Liens/Judgments; Vital records
Local Retrieval Area: PA-Chester, Delaware, Montgomery
Add'l Information: Established 1990. Normal turnaround time- 24-48 hours. Billing method depends on project. They specialize in civil and criminal

searches and document retrieval. Located next to Delaware county courthouse. A short drive to Chester and Montgomery counties.

Services Rendered Inc

7186 Manchester Rd, St Louis, MO 63143
Phone: 888-434-8200; 314-644-3955 - **Fax:** 314-645-4291
www.lgr-sri.com **email:** larry@lgr-sri.com

Types of Records Retrieved: Criminal, Civil and Probate courts; Federal courts; UCC records; Vital records

Local Retrieval Area: IL-Madison, Monroe, St Clair; MO-Franklin, Jefferson, St Charles, St Louis City, St Louis. **Correspondent Relationships:** nationwide in USA, also in Europe, Canada, Australia.

Add'l Information: Established 1989. Normal turnaround time- 3 day; 24-hr. rush service and 48-hr. priority service available. Projects billed by number of names searched. First project may require prepayment. They specialize in finding individuals and their assets. Performs service of process.

Servico Inc

283 Washington Ave, Albany, NY 12206
Phone: 518-463-4179 - **Fax:** 518-463-3752
www.servico.com **email:** inc@servico.com

Types of Records Retrieved: Criminal, Civil and Probate courts; Federal courts; Real Estate; Tax Liens/Judgments; UCC records; Vital records; Corporate records

Local Retrieval Area: NY-Albany, Schenectady. **Correspondent Relationships:** New York.

Add'l Information: Established 1924. Normal turnaround time- 1-5 business days. Projects billed by number of names searched. Credit cards accepted. They require prepayment for corporation filings. A licensed PI in NY. Performs service of process.

Seva Services

501 W Broadway #A231, San Diego, CA 92101
Phone: 619-253-7932 - **Fax:** 858-490-9009 triguru@sbcglobal.net

Types of Records Retrieved: Civil and Probate courts; Federal courts; Real Estate; Tax Liens/Judgments; Vital records

Local Retrieval Area: CA-San Diego

Add'l Information: Established 1990. Normal turnaround time- 48 hours. Projects billed by number of names searched. Projects billed by the hour. First project may require prepayment. They specialize in accurate abstracting of all types of court cases. Will retrieve all public records.

Seve Company

PO Box 14286, Charleston, SC 29422
Phone: 843-762-4520 - **Fax:** 843-762-4593
www.sevecompany.com **email:** info@sevecompany.com

Types of Records Retrieved: Real Estate; Tax Liens/Judgments; UCC records

Local Retrieval Area: SC-Charleston. **Correspondent Relationships:** statewide.

Add'l Information: Established 2002. Normal turnaround time- 48-72 hours. Projects billed by number of names searched. Terms are net 30 days. They are a South Carolina public records and document research and retrieval company.

Seyfried Support Services

PO Box 2882, Carmichael, CA 95609-2882
Phone: 916-359-5275 - **Fax:** 916-359-5276 seycheck@surewest.net

Types of Records Retrieved: Criminal, Civil and Probate courts; Federal courts; Real Estate; Tax Liens/Judgments; UCC records; Vital records

Local Retrieval Area: CA-El Dorado, Placer, Sacramento, Sutter, Yolo, Yuba

Add'l Information: Established 1991. Normal turnaround time- 24 hours. Projects billed by number of names searched. Will do monthly billings. They specialize in rapid turnaround. They are an experienced and accurate data retriever.

Seyler Retrieval

278 Mountain Rd, Wildbraham, MA 01095-1750
Phone: - **Fax:** 413-599-1470 seylersnj@msn.com

Types of Records Retrieved: Criminal, Civil and Probate courts; Federal district courts; UCC (before 06/00)

Local Retrieval Area: MA-Berkshire, Franklin, Hampden, Hampshire

Add'l Information: Established 1997. Normal turnaround time- 24 hours if docket copy clears, 48 hours if docket copy required. Projects billed by number of names searched. First project may require prepayment. Will invoice monthly. They are a small emerging retrieval company offering excellent personal prompt and reliable service at flexible pricing. Also do mass housing and small claims searches.

Shadow Process Service

PO Box 1499, Rhinelander, WI 54501
Phone: 800-626-7578; 715-369-5944 - **Fax:** 715-369-2405

Types of Records Retrieved: Criminal and Civil courts

Local Retrieval Area: WI-Forest, Florence, Langlade, Lincoln, Marathon, Oneida, Vilas. **Correspondent Relationships:** Eau Claire, La Crosse.

Add'l Information: Established 1987. Normal turnaround time- 3-5 days. First project may require prepayment. Specializing in process service, they also provide court filings. A licensed PI in WI. Performs service of process.

Shadow Trackers Investigative Services Inc

217 E Pine Ave, Meridian, ID 83642-2332
Phone: 208-895-0074 - **Fax:** 208-884-8257
www.shadowtrackers.com **email:** ron@shadowtrackers.com

Types of Records Retrieved: Criminal & Civil courts; Federal courts; Tax Liens/Judgments

Local Retrieval Area: ID-Ada, Canyon. **Correspondent Relationships:** Idaho and nationwide.

Add'l Information: Established 1992. Normal turnaround time- 72 hours or less. 24 hours for Ada County. Projects billed by number of names searched. First project may require prepayment. Credit cards accepted. They are a full service PI firm. Voted leading PI firm in USA by PI Magazine. A licensed PI in ID. Performs service of process.

Sharp County Abstract Co Inc

PO Box 81, Ash Flat, AR 72513
Phone: 870-994-7314 - **Fax:** 870-994-2880

Types of Records Retrieved: Criminal, Civil and Probate courts; Real Estate; Tax Liens/Judgments; UCC records

Local Retrieval Area: AR-Sharp

Add'l Information: Established 1896. Normal turnaround time- 10 days. Expedited service available. Fee basis will vary by the type of project. Will file/record documents for clients. They specialize in title insurance, escrow and closings.

Sharp Law Firm

PO Box 906, Mt Vernon, IL 62864
Phone: 618-242-0246 - **Fax:** 618-242-8950
www.sharptitle.com **email:** sheryl@lotsharp.com

Types of Records Retrieved: Real Estate; Tax Liens/Judgments

Local Retrieval Area: IL-Clinton, Edwards, Franklin, Hamilton, Jefferson, Marion, Wayne, Williamson

Add'l Information: Established 1974. Normal turnaround time- 3-5 days. Projects billed by the hour. Will file/record documents for clients. They specialize in real estate searches.

Drema Sharp

Route 1, Box 304, Marlinton, WV 24954
Phone: 304-799-6509; Fax- same form@meer.net

Types of Records Retrieved: Criminal, Civil and Probate courts; Real Estate; UCC records; Tax Liens/Judgments; Vital records

Local Retrieval Area: WV-Greenbrier, Pocahontas, Randolph

Add'l Information: Established 2000?. Normal turnaround time- 24 hours. Projects billed by number of names searched. First project may require prepayment. Her name is pronounced dream-ah. She will perform all types of local searches including deed searches.

Shawver & Associates

6262 Weber Rd #112, Corpus Christi, TX 78413-4030
Phone: 800-364-2333; 361-880-8968 - **Fax:** 361-880-8971
www.stxpi.com **email:** dshawver@stxpi.com

Types of Records Retrieved: Criminal, Civil and Probate courts; Federal courts; Real Estate; Tax Liens/Judgments; UCC records; Vital records

Local Retrieval Area: TX-Aransas, Bee, Brooks, Cameron, Duval, Hidalgo, Jim Wells, Kleberg, Nueces, Refugio, San Patricio, Starr, Victoria, Webb. **Correspondent Relationships:** Texas.

Add'l Information: Established 1986. Normal turnaround time- 2 days for areas within a 50 mile radius. Projects billed by the hour. First project may require prepayment. They specialize in finding the missing, litigation support, and insurance fraud investigations. A licensed PI in TX.

Shelby County Land Title Corp

PO Box 473, 236 E Main St, Shelbyville, IL 62565
Phone: 217-774-2623 - **Fax:** 217-774-3702

Types of Records Retrieved: Criminal, Civil and Probate courts; Real Estate; Tax Liens/Judgments; UCC records; Vital records

Local Retrieval Area: IL-Shelby

Add'l info: Established 1920. Turnaround time- 2 days. Projects billed by number of records located. Will file/record documents for clients. Payment due after work is completed. They specialize in mortgage closings.

Shenandoah Title Services Inc

2113 Valley Ave, Winchester, VA 22601-2753
Phone: 540-667-1393 - **Fax:** 540-667-0464 titles@shentel.net

Types of Records Retrieved: Civil and Probate courts; Real Estate; Tax Liens/Judgments; UCC records

Local Retrieval Area: VA-Clarke, Frederick, Page, Shenandoah, Warren, Winchester City

Add'l Information: Established 1988. Normal turnaround time- 3-5 days. Expedited service available. Fee basis will vary by type of project. Will file/record documents for clients. They specialize in real estate searches.

Shepp Johnman & Associates Inv

2723 37 Ave NE #121, Calgary, Alberta, Canada, CAN T1Y 5R8
Phone: 877-258-9073; 403-250-8947 - **Fax:** 403-250-9205
www.sheppjohnman.com **email:** roger_maslen@compuserve.com

Types of Records Retrieved: Criminal and Civil courts

Local Retrieval Area: CANADA-Alberta. **Correspondent Relationships:** British Columbia, Canada.

Add'l info: Established 1975. Projects billed by the hour. All projects require prepayment. They specialize in record retrieval in Calgary and southern Alberta. A licensed PI in Alberta, BC. Performs service of process.

Sheridan County Title

23 S Main St, Sheridan, WY 82801
Phone: 307-672-6478 - **Fax:** 307-672-8310

Types of Records Retrieved: Civil and Probate courts; Federal courts; Real Estate; Tax Liens/Judgments; UCC records

Local Retrieval Area: WY-Sheridan

Add'l Information: Established 1976. Normal turnaround time- 2 days. Projects billed by the hour. First project may require prepayment. Will file/record documents for clients.

Sherlock Research

PO Box 2629, Akron, OH 44309
Phone: 330-882-4690 - **Fax:** 330-882-4686

Types of Records Retrieved: Criminal, Civil and Probate courts; Federal courts; Real Estate; Tax Liens/Judgments; UCC records; Vital records

Retrieval Area: OH-Cuyahoga, Medina, Portage, Stark, Summit, Wayne

Add'l info: Established 1989. Turnaround time- 1 week upon payment. Expedited service available. Projects billed by number of names searched. Projects billed by number of records located. Projects billed by the hour. Down payment up front, balance due upon completion. They are coroner trained investigative reporter owned firm. Can find in OH, Midwest, northeast, DC. Will interview officials for cases. Good at assets location.

Sherman County Abstract

214 E 10th St, Goodland, KS 67735
Phone: 785-890-7507

Types of Records Retrieved: Criminal and Civil courts; Real Estate; Tax Liens/Judgments **Local Retrieval Area:** KS-Sherman

Add'l Information: Normal turnaround time- 24-48 hours. Billing methods depends on nature of request. First project may require prepayment. Will file/record documents for clients. They are specialists in the Sherman County area.

Valerie Shickel

PO Box 846, Essex, CT 06426
Phone: 860-767-2269 - **Fax:** 860-767-7621 vshickel@netscape.net

Types of Records Retrieved: Civil and Probate courts; Real Estate; Tax Liens/Judgments; UCC records; Vital records

Local Retrieval Area: CT-Middlesex, New Haven, New London

Add'l Information: Established 1984. Normal turnaround time- 24-48 hours. Fees are based on a per search basis. First project may require prepayment. Will file/record documents for clients. Billed by project. She specializes in 40 to 60 year land and probate record searches and document retrieval in Middlesex and New London Counties.

Shinkowsky Investigations

316 Fawn Ridge N, Harrisburg, PA 17110
Phone: 800-276-0202; 717-540-0631 - **Fax:** 800-996-1246
www.harrisburgpi.com **email:** records@harrisburgpi.com

Types of Records Retrieved: Criminal, Civil and Probate courts; Federal courts; Real Estate; Tax Liens/Judgments; UCC records; Vital records

Local Retrieval Area: PA-Dauphin, Lancaster, Northumberland. **Correspondent Relationships:** nationwide.

Add'l Information: Established 2002. Normal turnaround time- 24-48 hours. Expedited service available. Projects billed by number of names searched. First project may require prepayment. Credit cards accepted. They specialize in state agency records, corporation bureau filings, court filings and litigation support services. They conduct background/pre-employment investigations and skip tracing/locates. Notary Public services available. A licensed PI in PA.

Shore One Title Abstract Services

PO Box 537, 403 N Main St, Hurlock, MD 21643
Phone: 410-943-8637 - **Fax:** 410-943-0028

Types of Records Retrieved: Criminal, Civil and Probate courts; Real Estate; Tax Liens/Judgments; UCC records

Local Retrieval Area: MD-Caroline, Dorchester, Talbot. **Correspondent Relationships:** Eastern Shore counties.

Add'l Information: Established 1996. Normal turnaround time- 24-48 hours. Fee basis will vary with type of search. Will file/record documents for clients. Payment due upon completion/settlement. They specialize in title searches, full searches, and P and J's.

Simmons Agency Inc

190 High St 2nd Fl, Boston, MA 02210
Phone: 800-237-8230; 508-771-4477 - **Fax:** 508-771-5353
www.simmonsagency.com **email:** simmons.agency@verizon.net

Types of Records Retrieved: Criminal, Civil and Probate courts; Federal courts; Real Estate; Tax Liens/Judgments; Vital records

Local Retrieval Area: MA-Barnstable, Middlesex, Norfolk, Plymouth, Suffolk. **Correspondent Relationships:** Essex, Hampden, Worcester counties MA.

Add'l Information: Established 1937. Normal turnaround time- 1-3 days. Projects billed by the hour. First project may require prepayment. They are experienced private investigators capable of performing in-depth background and due diligence investigations. Many areas covered, see the web site. A licensed PI in MA. Performs service of process.

Faith Simpson

20663 Becky Dr, McCalla, AL 35111
Phone: 205-381-0788 - **Fax:** 205-477-6708 faithsroe@aol.com

Types of Records Retrieved: Real Estate; Tax Liens/Judgments; Probate courts; UCC records

Local Retrieval Area: AL-Jefferson. **Correspondent Relationships:** Shelby and Tuscaloosa counties AL.

Add'l Information: Established 1994. Normal turnaround time- 48 hours. Projects billed by number of names searched. First project may require prepayment. Will file/record documents for clients. Will bill weekly or monthly. Will also send bill with returned documents on report. She specializes in probate, UCC, tax liens, real estate, mortgage and deed, assignment retrieval, property reports, estate, wills, voter registration and notary search. Cell phone number is 205-381-0788. Email is faithsroe@aol.com. Performs service of process.

SingleSource Services Corp

2320 S 3rd St #7, Jacksonville Beach, FL 32250
Phone: 800-713-3412; 904-241-1821 - **Fax:** 877-835-5787; 904-241-0601
https://www.singlesourceservices.com/default.aspx
email: checkit@singlesourceservices.com

Types of Records Retrieved: Criminal and Civil courts; Tax Liens/Judgments; UCC records

Local Retrieval Area: FL-Duval. **Correspondent Relationships:** especially North Carolina, Ohio, Texas, Georgia, New Jersey, Delaware, South Carolina, Virginia, Tennessee, Kentucky, also national and international.

Add'l Information: Established 1993. Normal turnaround time- 48 hours requested; most results in 24 hours or less. Projects billed by number of names searched. Fees vary according to work type and volume. First project may require prepayment. Terms: net 30 days. They also feature web-based applicant tracking, employee assessments and full-service background screening. Researchers deal directly with the client. HRIS system and payroll. A licensed PI in FL.

Law Offices of Joan C Singleton

PO Box 116, Courthouse Rd, Warm Springs, VA 24484
Phone: 540-839-5009 - **Fax:** 540-839-2986

Types of Records Retrieved: Criminal, Civil and Probate courts; Federal courts; Real Estate; Tax Liens/Judgments; UCC records; Vital records

Local Retrieval Area: VA-Alleghany, Bath, Clifton Forge City, Covington City, Highland

Add'l Information: Established 1985. Normal turnaround time- 24 hours. Projects billed by the hour. Will file/record documents for clients.

Sittig Services

PO Box 1379, Eunice, LA 70535
Phone: 337-580-3334 - **Fax:** 866-756-4447

Records Retrieved: Criminal, Civil and Probate courts; Federal courts

Local Retrieval Area: LA-Acadia, Evangeline, Lafayette, St. Landry

Add'l Information: Established 2005. Normal turnaround time- no more that 72 hours. Expedited service available. Projects billed by the hour. Invoices are due and payable upon receipt. Sittig Services performs service of process, in-person retrieval of civil, criminal and federal records and nationwide electronic records retrieval. Expedited service is also available. A licensed PI in LA. Performs service of process.

Skimerhorn Inv

444 N Jackson Ave, Bradley, IL 60915
Phone: 815-933-0843 - **Fax:** 815-933-0843 JVS54@comcast.net

Types of Records Retrieved: Criminal, Civil and Probate courts; Real Estate; Tax Liens/Judgments; UCC records; Vital records

Local Retrieval Area: IL-Kankakee. **Correspondent Relationships:** Iroquois County, Illinois.

Add'l Information: Established 1990. Normal turnaround time- 1-2 days. Expedited service available. Fees are per name searched, per class of record. Process service on case-by-case basis per paper served, per name. First project may require prepayment. May be billed monthly. They specialize in skiptracing, asset searches and conduct missing person checks. They also specialize in lis pendens, misc. liens, mechanics liens, judgments and civil & criminal investigations. A licensed PI in IL. Performs service of process.

Bobbie Slice

128 Stoney Pointe Dr, Chapin, SC 29036
Phone: 803-932-7013 - **Fax:** 803-753-9963 bobbieslice@yahoo.com

Types of Records Retrieved: Criminal, Civil and Probate courts; Federal courts; Real Estate; Tax Liens/Judgments; UCC records

Local Retrieval Area: SC-Lexington, Newberry, Richland

Add'l Information: Established 2000. Normal turnaround time- 24 hours. Projects billed by number of names searched. Will bill monthly. They specialize in court record research and information and document retrieval. Professional and accurate reporting. No outsourcing or offsite online databases used, does physical searches.

Slover Investigations

PO Box 6515, Chandler, AZ 85246-6515
Phone: 480-917-3708 - **Fax:** 480-917-2603
www.sloverpi.com **email:** sloverpi@msn.com

Types of Records Retrieved: Criminal, Civil and Probate courts; Federal courts; Tax Liens/Judgments; UCC records

Local Retrieval Area: AZ-Maricopa

Add'l Information: Established 1988. Normal turnaround time- 1-2 days. Projects billed by number of names searched. Projects billed by the hour. First project may require prepayment. They specialize in criminal records checks, motor vehicle, watercraft and aircraft searches, skiptracing, personal injury, asset, background, and pre-employment investigations. A licensed PI in AZ.

Smith County Title Co

5040 Kinsey Dr, Tyler, TX 75703
Phone: 903-581-6400 - **Fax:** 903-581-6445

Types of Records Retrieved: Civil and Probate courts; Real Estate; Tax Liens/Judgments; UCC records

Local Retrieval Area: TX-Smith

Add'l Information: Established 1923. Normal turnaround time- 1-3 days. Projects billed by number of names searched. Projects billed by the hour. Will file/record documents for clients. Personal checks accepted. Formerly Smith County Title Co.

Cheryl Smith

692 New Liberty Rd, New Bern, NC 28562
Phone: 252-633-3890 - **Fax:** 252-633-3890

Types of Records Retrieved: Real Estate; UCC records

Local Retrieval Area: NC-Craven, Jones, Pamlico

Add'l Information: Established 1986. Normal turnaround time- 1-3 days. Projects billed by the hour. Will file/record documents for clients. Personal checks are accepted. She specializes in title examinations.

Pam Smith

PO Box 83, Rock Island, TN 38581
Phone: 931-686-2804 - **Fax:** 931-686-8911

Records Retrieved: Criminal and Civil courts; Tax Liens/Judgments

Local Retrieval Area: TN-Cannon, Coffee, Dekalb, Grundy, Overton, Putnam, Warren, White, Van Buren

Add'l Information: Established 1988. Normal turnaround time- up to 48 hours. Projects billed by number of names searched. Search fee may also depend on nature of the request. She has been in the public record field for 18 years and works closely with all the court clerks in the offices she visits.

SMS Searches

1212 Avery Ct, St Louis, MO 63122
Phone: 314-691-1593 - **Fax:** 314-965-8531 smssearches@charter.net

Types of Records Retrieved: Criminal, Civil and Probate courts; Federal courts; Real Estate; UCC records; Vital records; Tax Liens/Judgments

Local Retrieval Area: MO-St Charles, St Louis County, St Louis City

Add'l Information: Established 1996. Normal turnaround time- 8-48 hours. Fee basis varies by project. Net 30 days. They specialize in current owner to

45 years ownership for real estate; deed reports; recordings, signature signing by notary, all document retrieval. Criminal & civil searches.

Snyder Abstract & Title Co Inc

1816 26th St, Snyder, TX 79549
Phone: 325-573-6339 - **Fax:** 325-573-8112 satco1@sbcglobal.net
Types of Records Retrieved: Real Estate; Tax Liens/Judgments; UCC records; Probate courts; Federal District courts
Local Retrieval Area: TX-Borden, Scurry
Add'l Information: Normal turnaround time- 2-3 days. Fee basis will vary by the type of project. First project may require prepayment. Will file/record documents for clients. They provide title insurance, abstracts, abstractor's certificates and searches.

Somerset Abstract Co Ltd

PO Box 374, Somerset, PA 15501
Phone: 814-445-9525 - **Fax:** 814-443-2255
Types of Records Retrieved: Civil courts; Real Estate; Tax Liens/Judgments
Local Retrieval Area: PA-Somerset
Add'l info: Turnaround time- up to 1 week. Fee basis is per transaction. Will file/record documents for clients. They specialize in real estate.

Camelia Soprano

251 Bayou Bank Ln, Franklin, LA 70538
Phone: 337-923-4273 - **Fax:** 337-923-2207
Records Retrieved: Criminal and Civil courts; Tax Liens/Judgments
Local Retrieval Area: LA-St. Mary, St. Martin
Add'l Information: Normal turnaround time- 24 hours in St Mary parish; St Martin Parish may be 48-72. Projects billed by number of names searched. There may be a surcharge for St Martin Parish only. First project may require prepayment. She regularly searches St Mary Parish court records including Morgan City Court searches. St Martin Parish is not visited as frequently.

Leslie or Mike Sosa

100 Frazer Ct, Folsom, CA 95630-7718
Phone: 916-984-7654 - **Fax:** 916-984-0910 or 916-984-0970
www.pub-info.com **email:** leslie@pub-info.com
Records Retrieved: Real Estate; Tax Liens/Judgments; UCC records
Local Retrieval Area: CA-Alameda, El Dorado, Kings, Marin, Merced, Monterey, Placer, Sacramento, San Mateo, Santa Clara, Santa Cruz, Siskiyou, Solano
Add'l info: Established 1977. Turnaround time- 24 hours. Projects are billed by the number of names or properties searches. First project may require prepayment. Will file/record documents for clients. Large copy orders may require prepayment. They have 23 years of experience in providing fast and accurate reports, specializing in title searches.

Source Documents & Information Inc

404 S Dr Martin Luther King Jr Ave, Clearwater, FL 33756
Phone: 727-447-8844 - **Fax:** 727-447-8414
www.sourcedocsinfo.com **email:** Sam@sourcedocsinfo.com
Records Retrieved: Real Estate; Tax Liens/Judgments; UCC records
Local Retrieval Area: FL-Brevard, Broward, Dade, Hernando, Hillsborough, Manatee, Orange, Palm Beach, Pasco, Pinellas, Polk, Sarasota. **Correspondent Relationships:** statewide in FL, GA, NC, SC, MD, VA, Washington, DC.
Add'l Information: Established 1999. Normal turnaround time- 1-3 days. Expedited 1-day service available. Projects billed by number of names searched. Will file/record documents for clients. Payment upon order completion. They specialize in document retrieval of mortgages, deeds, assignments, satisfactions, liens, etc. Will provide photocopy, certified copies or recording info. Walk-in recordation service. Offers current owner searches in FL, GA, VA & MD.

Source Resources

PO Box 88, Cookeville, TN 38503
Phone: 800-678-8774; 931-537-3642 - **Fax:** 800-537-3297
www.sourceresources.com **email:** info@sourceresources.com
Types of Records Retrieved: Criminal, Civil and Probate courts; Federal courts; Real Estate; Tax Liens/Judgments; UCC records
Local Retrieval Area: TN-Cumberland, DeKalb, Jackson, Macon, Overton, Putnam, Roane, Smith, White. **Correspondent Relationships:** nationwide.
Add'l Information: Established 1985. Normal turnaround time- 1-7 working days. Projects billed by number of names searched. All projects require prepayment. Credit cards accepted. They specialize in extended court filings and court searches nationwide, electronically. They also search public record information on individuals and businesses. A licensed PI in TN. Performs service of process.

South Central Missouri Title Co

600 N Main, Mountain Grove, MO 65711-1758
Phone: 417-926-6163 - **Fax:** 417-926-6146 wctc@getgoin.net
Types of Records Retrieved: Civil and Probate courts; Real Estate; Tax Liens/Judgments; UCC records
Local Retrieval Area: MO-Douglas
Add'l Information: Established 1989. Normal turnaround time- 1-2 weeks. Projects billed by number of names searched. First project may require prepayment. Formerly known as Wright County Title, they specialize in real estate records, chains of title and encumbrances.

South Central Title Agency Inc

35096 Kenai Spur Hwy, Soldotna, AK 99669
Phone: 907-262-4494 - **Fax:** 907-262-3925
sctitle@alaska.net
Types of Records Retrieved: Real Estate; Tax Liens/Judgments
Local Retrieval Area: AK-Kenai Peninsula, Seward. **Correspondent Relationships:** statewide.
Add'l info: Normal turnaround time- 24 hours. Projects billed by the hour. All projects require prepayment. Will file/record documents for clients.

South East Arizona Legal Support

PO Box 1223, Bisbee, AZ 85603
Phone: 520-432-9032 - **Fax:** 520-432-3384
www.seazlegalsupport.com **email:** 2seals@cableone.net
Types of Records Retrieved: Criminal, Civil and Probate courts; Federal courts; Real Estate; Tax Liens/Judgments; UCC records; Vital records
Local Retrieval Area: AZ-Cochise. **Correspondents:** nationwide.
Add'l Information: Established 1995. Normal turnaround time- 24-48 hours. Projects billed by number of names searched. Projects billed by number of records located. First project may require prepayment. Terms are net 30 days. Past due invoices are subject to late fees. They are a public record provider, pre-employment screening firm and real estate searches. All research is performed by "hands on" researchers at the courthouse and county recorders.

South Eastern Data

501A E Mt Vernon St, Somerset, KY 42501
Phone: 606-679-1688 - **Fax:** 606-679-1677 sedata@alltel.net
Types of Records Retrieved: Real Estate; Tax Liens/Judgments
Local Retrieval Area: KY-Adair, Casey, Clay, Clinton, Garrard, Jackson, Knox, Laurel, Lincoln, Madison, Mc Creary, Pulaski, Rockcastle, Russell, Wayne, Whitley
Add'l info: Established 1984. Normal turnaround time- 24 hours for current owner. First project may require prepayment. They specialize in real estate.

South Florida Legal Services of Naples

PO Box 8456, Naples, FL 34101
Phone: 239-332-7000 - **Fax:** 239-337-2100 sflsnaples@aol.com
Types of Records Retrieved: Criminal, Civil and Probate courts; Federal courts; Real Estate; Tax Liens/Judgments; Vital records
Local Retrieval Area: FL-Charlotte, Collier, Hendry, Lee. **Correspondent Relationships:** Florida and nationwide.
Add'l Information: Established 1992. Normal turnaround time- 2 days. Expedited service available. Fee is based on the nature of the search. First project may require prepayment. The specialize in the area of Ft Myers, Florida. A licensed PI in FL. Performs service of process.

South Florida Title Research Inc dba SFTR

12527 Central Ave NE #330, Minneapolis, MN 55434
Phone: 866-398-7387; - **Fax:** 866-329-7387
www.sftr.net **email:** info@sftr.net

Types of Records Retrieved: Criminal, Civil and Probate courts; Federal courts; Real Estate; Tax Liens/Judgments; UCC records

Local Retrieval Area: FL-Broward, Dade, Martin, Palm Beach. **Correspondent Relationships:** statewide.

Add'l Information: Established 1987. Normal turnaround time- 24 hours. Projects billed by number of records located. net 30 days. They specialize in current owner searches and environmental searches (statewide). Main office at 13833 Wellington Trace #121, West Palm Beach, FL 33414.

South Plains Abstract Co

PO Box 418, 408 N 1st St, LaMesa, TX 79331
Phone: 806-872-3023 - **Fax:** 806-872-2904

Records Retrieved: Real Estate; Tax Liens/Judgments; UCC records

Local Retrieval Area: TX-Dawson **Add'l Information:** Normal turnaround time- 2 days. Fee basis will vary by the type of project. All projects require prepayment. Will file/record documents for clients.

South Ridge Abstract & Title Co

229 S Commerce Ave, Sebring, FL 33870
Phone: 863-385-2521 - **Fax:** 863-382-6438 sratseb@ct.net

Types of Records Retrieved: Civil and Probate courts; Real Estate; Tax Liens/Judgments; UCC records

Local Retrieval Area: FL-Highlands

Add'l Information: Established 1948. Normal turnaround time- 7-10 working days. Projects billed by number of names searched. First project may require prepayment. Will file/record documents for clients. Invoice sent with results. They maintain an in-house title plant. A licensed PI in FL.

South Texas Title and Trustee Services

530 Lake Dr, Harlingen, TX 78550
Phone: 956-412-3413 - **Fax:** 956-412-0103 mmedley@rgv.rr.com

Types of Records Retrieved: Criminal, Civil and Probate courts; Federal courts; Real Estate; Tax Liens/Judgments; UCC records; Vital records

Local Retrieval Area: TX-Cameron, Hidalgo

Add'l Information: Established 1993. Normal turnaround time- 24 hours. Projects billed by number of names searched. Will file/record documents for clients. Payment due upon receipt. Formerly Valley Court Services, they are an experienced company specializing in title abstracting and trustee sales for Cameron and Hidalgo counties.

Southeast Nebraska Abstract

1524 Stone St, Falls City, NE 68355
Phone: 402-245-4222 - **Fax:** 402-245-3859

Types of Records Retrieved: Criminal, Civil and Probate courts; Real Estate; Tax Liens/Judgments; UCC records

Local Retrieval Area: NE-Richardson

Add'l Information: Established 1973. Normal turnaround time- 24-48 hours. Fee basis will vary by the type of project. Will file/record documents for clients. Depends on project.

Southeast Wisconsin Process

419 N Grand Ave, Waukesha, WI 53186
Phone: 262-650-8904 - **Fax:** 262-650-8921

Records Retrieved: Criminal, Civil and Probate courts; Bankruptcy court; Real Estate; Tax Liens/Judgments; UCC records; Vital records

Local Retrieval Area: WI-Dane, Dodge, Fond du Lac, Jefferson, Kenosha, Milwaukee, Ozaukee, Racine, Sheboygan, Walworth, Washington, Waukesha. **Correspondent Relationships:** statewide.

Add'l Information: First project may require prepayment. They offer instant email notification and status by the web. Performs service of process.

Southeastern Utah Title

PO Box 855, Price, UT 84501
Phone: 435-637-4455 - **Fax:** 435-637-4459
www.southeasttitle.com **email:** setitle@emerytelcom.net

Types of Records Retrieved: Criminal, Civil and Probate courts; Real Estate; Tax Liens/Judgments; UCC records; Vital records

Local Retrieval Area: UT-Carbon, Emery, Grand, San Juan

Add'l Information: Established 1949. Normal turnaround time- 24 hours. Fee basis will vary by the type of project. First project may require prepayment. Will file/record documents for clients.

Southern Abstract & Title Co

PO Box 507, 16 NW Martin Luthur King Ave, Idabel, OK 74745
Phone: 580-286-2288 - **Fax:** 580-286-7885

Types of Records Retrieved: Civil and Probate courts; Real Estate; Tax Liens/Judgments; UCC records; Vital records

Local Retrieval Area: OK-McCurtain **Add'l Information:** Normal turnaround time- 2-3 weeks. Projects billed by the hour. Fee is also determined per abstract. Clients pay before searches are released.

Southern California Strategic Research

249 N Brand Blvd #314, Glendale, CA 91023
Phone: 323-257-4472 - **Fax:** 323-257-8613 weplatz@aol.com

Types of Records Retrieved: Criminal, Civil and Probate courts; Federal courts; Real Estate; Tax Liens/Judgments; UCC records; Vital records

Local Retrieval Area: CA-Los Angeles, Orange, Riverside, San Bernardino, Santa Barbara, Ventura. **Correspondent Relationships:** statewide.

Add'l Information: Established 2003. Normal turnaround time- 1-3 days for index; 1-7 days for documents depending on the courts. Projects billed by the hour. Special flat rates for bulk searches are available. Association of individually licensed private investigators with over 50 years combined experience in investigations throughout southern California. Due diligence, litigation support and background investigations. A licensed PI in CA.

Southern Courthouse Ventures

PO Box 81483, 2078 Beechwood Dr, Conyers, GA 30013
Phone: 678-413-4697 - **Fax:** 678-413-4626 jimreyscv@aol.com

Types of Records Retrieved: Civil courts; Bankruptcy court; Real Estate; Tax Liens/Judgments; UCC records

Local Retrieval Area: GA-Baldwin, Banks, Barrow, Bartow, Bibb, Butts, Carroll, Catoosa, Chattooga, Cherokee, Clarke, Clayton, Cobb, Coweta, Crawford, Dawson, DeKalb, Douglas, Fannin, Fayette, Floyd, Forsyth, Franklin, Fulton, Gilmer, Gordon, Greene, Gwinnett, Habersham, Hall, Hancock, Haralson, Henry, Jackson, Jasper, Jones, Lamar, Lumpkin, Macon, Madison, Monroe, Morgan, Murray, Newton, Oconee, Oglethorpe, Paulding, Peach, Pickens, Pike, Polk, Putnam, Rabun, Rockdale, Spalding, Stephens, Towns, Union, Walton, Walker, White, Whitfield

Add'l Information: Established 1990. Normal turnaround time- 24-48 hours. Charge by number of searches requested. Will file/record documents for clients. Some projects require prepayment. Terms: net 30 days. They do hand delivered filings. Three major bankruptcy courts covered. Statewide index access and 24 hours service available upon request.

Southern Land & Title LLC

1136 Forrest Ave, Gadsden, AL 35901
Phone: 256-543-1361 - **Fax:** 256-543-1377 solandtitle@microxl.com

Types of Records Retrieved: Civil and Probate courts; Federal courts; Real Estate; Tax Liens/Judgments; UCC records

Local Retrieval Area: AL-Calhoun, Cherokee, Cleburne, De Kalb, Etowah, Jefferson, Madison, Marshall, Randolph, St Clair, Shelby, Talladega. **Correspondent Relationships:** Alabama, Georgia and Tennessee.

Add'l Information: Established 1998. Normal turnaround time- 48 hours. Projects billed by number of names searched. Payment due upon completion. Will file/record documents for clients. They provide comprehensive research and service in the public document retrieval business. They provide UCC, tax lien, judgment and litigation searches. They also provide deed, mortgages and tax assessment information on real estate transactions.

Southern Montana Abstract & Title

PO Box 390, 15 S Idaho St, Dillon, MT 59725
Phone: 406-683-4445 - **Fax:** 406-683-4393
Types of Records Retrieved: Civil and Probate courts; Real Estate; Tax Liens/Judgments; UCC records; Vital records
Local Retrieval Area: MT-Beaverhead
Add'l Information: Established 1917. Normal turnaround time- 5 days. Fee basis varies by type of transaction.

Southern Process Service

2000 Whittle Springs Rd, Knoxville, TN 37917
Phone: 865-525-3124
www.southernprocess.com **email:** jim@southernprocess.com
Types of Records Retrieved: Criminal, Civil and Probate courts; Federal courts; Real Estate **Local Retrieval Area:** TN-Knox
Add'l Information: Established 1993. Normal turnaround time- 48 hours or less; same day service for an add'l fee. Projects billed by number of names searched. Will invoice attorneys only. First project may require prepayment. Call before faxing. They are court appointed and bonded for service of process. Performs service of process.

Southern Research Company

2850 Centenary Blvd, Shreveport, LA 71104
Phone: 888-772-6952; 318-227-9700 - **Fax:** 888-429-5604; 318-424-1801
www.southernresearchinc.com **email:** tjo@southernresearchinc.com
Types of Records Retrieved: Criminal, Civil and Probate courts; Federal courts; Real Estate; Tax Liens/Judgments; UCC records
Local Retrieval Area: LA-Bossier, Caddo Parishes. **Correspondent Relationships:** Louisiana and nationwide.
Add'l Information: Established 1956. Normal turnaround time- same day to 48 hours. Clients are normally billed by the number of names searched per court. Special projects are billed by the hour. First project may require prepayment. Will file/record documents for clients. They specialize in employment & tenant screening, localized court documents & field investigation searches. A licensed PI in LA.

Southern Research Enterprises

24 Jeffery Ln NE, Cartersville, GA 30121
Phone: 770-387-9439 - **Fax:** 770-387-0664
www.sre-abstractor.com **email:** nena@sre-abstractor.com
Types of Records Retrieved: Criminal, Civil and Probate courts; Federal courts; Real Estate; Tax Liens/Judgments; UCC records; Vital records
Local Retrieval Area: GA-Bartow, Catoosa, Chattooga, Cherokee, Cobb, Coweta, Dade, Dawson, Douglas, Fannin, Floyd, Fulton, Gilmer, Gordon, Lumpkin, Murray, Paulding, Pickens, Walker, Whitfield;. **Correspondent Relationships:** statewide.
Add'l Information: Established 2001. Normal turnaround time- 24-48 hours. Expedited service available. Projects billed by number of names searched. Projects billed by number of records located. Projects are billed by the number of addresses or legal descriptions. First project may require prepayment. Will provide monthly billing with proof of estimated cost. Can invoice individual jobs. They specialize in real estate record retrieval, all secure forms from current to 150 years, federal/state tax liens, UCC and judgments. Fast, accurate and reliable; has E&O coverage. Will go the extra mile. Performs service of process.

Southern Utah Title Co

44 N Main St, Kanab, UT 84741
Phone: 435-644-5891 - **Fax:** 435-644-8136
www.titlesearch.net **email:** sutico@xpressweb.com
Types of Records Retrieved: Criminal, Civil and Probate courts; Real Estate; Tax Liens/Judgments; UCC records; Vital records
Local Retrieval Area: UT-Kane
Add'l Information: Established 1948. Normal turnaround time- 1 week or less. Fee basis will vary by the type of project. All projects require prepayment. Will file/record documents for clients.

Southwest Abstract & Title Co

PO Box 1149, 902 SW D Ave (73501), Lawton, OK 73502
Phone: 405-355-3680 - **Fax:** 580-248-1849
donj@swatco.net
Types of Records Retrieved: Civil and Probate courts; Real Estate; Tax Liens/Judgments; UCC records
Local Retrieval Area: OK-Comanche
Add'l Information: Normal turnaround time- 2-4 days. Fee basis will vary by the type of project. Will file/record documents for clients. They specialize in abstracts of title, closing services and title insurance.

Southwest Abstract & Title Co

PO Box 13, 1006 Rankin Ave, Rankin, TX 79778
Phone: 432-693-2242 - **Fax:** 432-693-2249
Types of Records Retrieved: Civil and Probate courts; Real Estate; Tax Liens/Judgments; UCC records
Local Retrieval Area: TX-Upton
Add'l Information: Established 1915. Normal turnaround time- 2-3 days. Fee basis will vary by the type of project. Will file/record documents for clients.

Southwest Abstract & Title Company

PO Box 559, Bowman, ND 58623
Phone: 701-523-2922 - **Fax:** 701-523-2922
swabstract1@ndsupernet.com
Types of Records Retrieved: Civil and Probate courts; Federal courts; Real Estate; Tax Liens/Judgments; UCC records
Local Retrieval Area: ND-Bowman, Slope
Add'l Information: Normal turnaround time- 1-3 days. Projects billed by the hour. First project may require prepayment. Will file/record documents for clients. Prepayment dependant on job. They specialize in abstracting, title search, title insurance and closings. They have 24 years experience in the business.

Southwest Abstract Co Inc

PO Box 1175, Del Rio, TX 78841
Phone: 830-775-8508 - **Fax:** 830-775-9183
www.southwestabstract.com **email:** requests@southwestabstract.com
Types of Records Retrieved: Civil and Probate courts; Real Estate; Tax Liens/Judgments; UCC records; Vital records
Local Retrieval Area: TX-Val Verde
Add'l info: Established 1910. Turnaround time- 2 days. Projects billed by number of names searched. Fee basis will vary by the type of project. All projects require prepayment. Will file/record documents for clients.

Southwest Tax & Accounting

PO Box 1367, Elkhart, KS 67950
Phone: 620-697-2422 - **Fax:** 620-697-4757
http://swtero.com **email:** tryman@elkhart.com
Types of Records Retrieved: Criminal and Civil courts
Local Retrieval Area: KS-Morton
Add'l info: Established 1988. Normal turnaround time- 24-48 hours. Projects billed by number of names searched. First project may require prepayment. They specialize in court records and are very familiar with the area.

Southwestern Title Agency of Western Nebraska

711 E 1st St, Ogallala, NE 69153
Phone: 308-284-4001 - **Fax:** 308-284-8319 jmartinosky@hotmail.com
Types of Records Retrieved: Civil and Probate courts; Real Estate; Tax Liens/Judgments
Local Retrieval Area: NE-Arthur, Chase, Dundy, Keith, Perkins. **Correspondent Relationships:** Perkins and Keith counties.
Add'l Information: Established 1969. Normal turnaround time- 2 days. Projects billed by the hour. Will file/record documents for clients. They do not accept personal checks. Formerly known as Southwestern Title & Abstract Co, they specialize in title insurance and real estate.

Sparks Searches

1286 S Riverbend Ct, Nixa, MO 65714
Phone: 417-725-4851 - **Fax:** 417-725-7765 gjs1286@aol.com
Types of Records Retrieved: Real Estate; Tax Liens/Judgments
Local Retrieval Area: MO-Christian, Douglas, Stone, Taney
Add'l Information: Established 1995. Normal turnaround time- 12-24 hours. Projects billed by number of names searched. Will file/record documents for clients.

Spearhead Research - On Target Information

PO Box 244, Buda, TX 78610
Phone: 512-295-7298 - **Fax:** 512-295-7308
smichelle@spearheadresearch.com
Types of Records Retrieved: Criminal and Civil courts
Local Retrieval Area: TX-Bexar, Comal, Hays, Tarrant, Travis, Williamson. **Correspondent Relationships:** statewide.
Add'l info: Established 1998. Normal turnaround time- 24 to 48 hours most request results returned. Expedited service available. Projects billed by number of names searched. Will file/record documents for clients. Invoices are sent monthly due upon receipt, with a max net 30 days. Research work is done hands-on - very accurate and detailed by experienced researchers. Excellent turnaround times. Most Texas Counties are covered.

Spears & Jones Attorneys

113 S Market St, Benton, AR 72015
Phone: 501-315-5335 - **Fax:** 501-315-6475 spearsandjones2@yahoo.com
Types of Records Retrieved: Criminal, Civil and Probate courts; Real Estate; Tax Liens/Judgments; UCC records
Local Retrieval Area: AR-Grant, Saline
Add'l Information: Established 2000. Normal turnaround time- 48-72 hours. Projects billed by number of names searched. First project may require prepayment. Will file/record documents for clients. They also do real estate title searches with tax info and witness closings.

Special Investigations Inc

984 Logan St #1, Noblesville, IN 46060
Phone: 317-773-7900 - **Fax:** 317-773-3752
www.indianainvestigator.com
email: investigator@indianainvestigator.com
Types of Records Retrieved: Criminal, Civil and Probate courts; Federal courts; Real Estate; Tax Liens/Judgments; UCC records; Vital records
Local Retrieval Area: IN-Boone, Hamilton, Marion
Add'l Information: Established 1996. Normal turnaround time- 3-5 days. Expedited service available. Projects billed by the hour. They specialize in insurance, civil/domestic matters, service of process as well as document retrieval. A licensed PI in IN. Performs service of process.

Special Private Investigations Inc

72 Indian Lakes NE, Sparta, MI 49345
Phone: 800-577-3783; 616-887-8574 - **Fax:** 616-887-8775 spi@iserv.net
Types of Records Retrieved: Probate courts; Federal courts
Local Retrieval Area: MI-Kent
Add'l Information: Established 1989. Normal turnaround time- 2 days for civil cases and probate. Projects billed by the hour. First project may require prepayment. They specialize in vehicle and driver license registrations for the State of Michigan and statewide criminal conviction searches. A licensed PI in MI.

Specialized Investigations

9255 Corbin Ave #200, Northridge, CA 91324
Phone: 800-714-3728; 818-909-9607 - **Fax:** 818-782-3012
www.specialpi.com **email:** si@specialpi.com
Types of Records Retrieved: Criminal, Civil and Probate courts; Federal courts; Real Estate; Tax Liens/Judgments; UCC records; Vital records
Local Retrieval Area: CA-Los Angeles. **Correspondent Relationships:** Kern, Riverside, San Bernardino, San Diego, Santa Barbara, Orange, Ventura counties CA.
Add'l Information: Established 1982. Normal turnaround time- 1-7 working days. Projects billed by number of names searched. Projects billed by the hour. Can charge a flat rate if discussed beforehand. First project may require prepayment. Credit cards accepted. Terms: net 30 days. They specialize in insurance fraud, surveillance, background checks, asset searches, trial preparation and skiptracing as well as labor and employment law investigations. A licensed PI in CA. Performs service of process.

Specialty Services

8491 Hospital Dr, PMB 151, Douglasville, GA 30134
Phone: 770-942-8264 - **Fax:** 770-942-5355
Types of Records Retrieved: Criminal and Civil courts; Federal courts; Real Estate; Tax Liens/Judgments; UCC records
Local Retrieval Area: GA-Carroll, Coweta, De Kalb, Douglas, Fulton, Paulding. **Correspondent Relationships:** Alabama.
Add'l Information: Established 1991. Normal turnaround time- 24-72 hours. Projects billed by number of names searched. Projects billed by the hour. Billed monthly, due upon receipt (late fees after 30 days). They specialize in record retrieval from county, state and federal courts. Criminal and civil backgrounds for pre-employment screening, litigation support, insurance fraud investigation assistance, asset reports, UCC searches, etc. Performs service of process.

Spectrum Screening Inc

PO Box 685055, Austin, TX 78768-5055
Phone: 800-222-8199; 512-459-2181 - **Fax:** 512-459-2182
www.spectrumscreening.net **email:** stacey@spectrumscreening.net
Types of Records Retrieved: Criminal and Civil courts; Federal courts; Tax Liens/Judgments; UCC records
Local Retrieval Area: TX-Bexar, Collin, Dallas, Denton, Fort Bend, Galveston, Harris, Hays, Tarrant, Travis, Williamson. **Correspondents:** statewide in TX, GA, MO, VA, NC, TN, AL, AR, KY, CA, CO.
Add'l Information: Established 1992. Normal turnaround time- 24-72 hours depending on the project. Projects billed by number of names searched. First project may require prepayment. Will file/record documents for clients. They specialize in criminal/civil/federal court research.

Spencer Investigations LLC

PO Box 3141, 3063 Hwy 126 #7, Blountville, TN 37617
Phone: 423-323-1100 - **Fax:** 866-359-1639
www.spencerinvestigations.com **email:** pi@spencerinvestigations.com
Types of Records Retrieved: Criminal, Civil and Probate courts; Bankruptcy court; Real Estate; Tax Liens/Judgments; UCC records
Local Retrieval Area: TN-Sullivan, Washington
Add'l Information: Established 2006. Normal turnaround time- 1-3 business days. Projects billed by number of names searched. All projects require prepayment. Credit cards accepted. They are a PI company that provides many investigative services in civil, criminal or other business capacities in TN. A licensed PI in TN. Performs service of process.

SPI

5650 S Archer, Chicago, IL 60638
Phone: 773-581-1400 - **Fax:** 773-581-6900
Types of Records Retrieved: Criminal and Civil courts; Federal courts
Local Retrieval Area IL-Cook, DuPage, Will. **Correspondents:** nationwide.
Add'l Information: Established 1983. Normal turnaround time- 24-48 hours. Projects billed by number of names searched. Fees negotiated with volume. First project may require prepayment. Security Professionals Inc specialize in pre-employment screening, Illinois drivers' abstracts, social security verification, criminal background checks and workers' compensation checks. Performs service of process.

SPI

72 Indian Lakes Rd, Sparta, MI 49345
Phone: 800-577-3783; 616-887-5261 - **Fax:** 616-887-8775 spi@iserv.net
Types of Records Retrieved: Probate courts; Federal courts

Local Retrieval Area: MI-Kent

Add'l Information: Established 1990. Normal turnaround time- Call for turnaround times. First project may require prepayment. They also provide court filings, photocopying as well as computer searches of MI Sec of State records. A licensed PI in MI. Performs service of process.

Spiller Abstract

122 E Belknap, PO Box I, Jacksboro, TX 76458
Phone: 940-567-2271 - **Fax:** 940-567-3999

Types of Records Retrieved: Civil and Probate courts; Real Estate; Tax Liens/Judgments; UCC records

Local Retrieval Area: TX-Jack

Add'l Information: Established 1888. Normal turnaround time- 3 days to 1 week. Fees vary by project. They specialize in real estate records.

Spink County Abstract

502 N Main St, Redfield, SD 57469
Phone: 605-472-2011 - **Fax:** 605-472-2001

Types of Records Retrieved: Real Estate; Tax Liens/Judgments

Local Retrieval Area: SD-Spink

Add'l Information: First project may require prepayment. Will file/record documents for clients. They specialize in real estate.

Springdale Realty

PO Box 40, Ord, NE 68862
Phone: 308-728-3569 - **Fax:** 308-728-3587

Types of Records Retrieved: Real Estate; Tax Liens/Judgments

Local Retrieval Area: NE-Valley

Add'l Information: Established 2001. First project may require prepayment. They specialize in real estate.

Spyglass Research

PO Box 528499, Chicago, IL 60652-8499
Phone: 773-581-0180 - **Fax:** 773-581-0181
spyglasspreemployment@comcast.net

Types of Records Retrieved: Criminal, Civil and Probate courts; Federal courts; Real Estate; Tax Liens/Judgments; UCC records; Vital records

Local Retrieval Area: IL-Cook, Du Page, Kane, Lake, Will. **Correspondent Relationships:** surrounding counties.

Add'l Information: Established 1992. Normal turnaround time- 24-48 hours. Projects billed by number of names searched. Will file/record documents for clients. They will bill monthly. They take a one on one relationship with each client. No client is to small or big for us. A licensed PI in IL. Performs service of process.

SRA Investigations Inc

1456 Ellis Ave, Jackson, MS 39204-2204
Phone: 800-530-7115 x4197; 601-960-4194 - **Fax:** 601-360-0521
arouchon@jam.rr.com

Types of Records Retrieved: Criminal and Civil courts

Local Retrieval Area: MS-Hinds, Madison, Rankin

Add'l Information: Established 2000. All projects require prepayment. They also provide court filings, subpoena preparation, skiptracing, and private investigations. Performs service of process.

SRS Private Investigations Inc

52 Mission Cir #122, PMB 152, Santa Rosa, CA 95409
Phone: 707-537-1091 - **Fax:** 707-537-1095 srspi@prodigy.net

Types of Records Retrieved: Criminal, Civil and Probate courts; Real Estate; Tax Liens/Judgments; UCC records; Vital records

Local Retrieval Area: CA-Sonoma

Add'l Information: Established 1980. Normal turnaround time- 3 days. Expedited service available. Projects billed by the hour. First project may require prepayment. Credit cards accepted. They specialize in full range investigative services that include backgrounds, locates, asset searches, security surveys, witness statements and much more. A licensed PI in CA. Performs service of process.

SRT Investigations

PO Box 35403, Tulsa, OK 74153
Phone: 918-481-6045 - **Fax:** 918-491-9774 srti@cox.net

Types of Records Retrieved: Real Estate; Tax Liens/Judgments

Local Retrieval Area: OK-Creek, Muskogee, Nowata, Oklahoma, Okmulgee, Osage, Rogers, Tulsa, Wagoner, Washington. **Correspondent Relationships:** statewide.

Add'l info: Established 1987. Turnaround time- 24 hours. Projects billed by number of names searched. Projects billed by the hour. First project may require prepayment. Will file/record documents for clients. They specialize in record searches, title searches, chain of owner searches. Offer a 24 hour turnaround time on most searches. A licensed PI in OK.

St Croix Valley Title Services Inc

PO Box 750, 109 N Main St, River Falls, WI 54022
Phone: 715-425-1519 - **Fax:** 715-425-2569

Types of Records Retrieved: Criminal, Civil and Probate courts; Real Estate; Tax Liens/Judgments; UCC records

Local Retrieval Area: WI-Pierce, St. Croix

Add'l Information: Normal turnaround time- 1-2 days. Fee basis varies by type of transaction. First project may require prepayment. Will file/record documents for clients.

St Joseph County Abstract Office Inc

PO Box 217, Centreville, MI 49032
Phone: 269-467-6075 - **Fax:** 269-467-4314

Types of Records Retrieved: Criminal, Civil and Probate courts; Real Estate; Tax Liens/Judgments; UCC records; Vital records

Local Retrieval Area: MI-Cass, St. Joseph

Add'l Information: Normal turnaround time- 3 days. Projects billed by the hour. Will file/record documents for clients. They specialize in title and real estate.

St Paul Abstract & Title

710 Howard Ave, St Paul, NE 68873
Phone: 308-754-4922 - **Fax:** 308-754-4922 sdecamp@cornhusker.net

Types of Records Retrieved: Real Estate; Tax Liens/Judgments, Probate courts; Federal courts

Local Retrieval Area: NE-Adams, Buffalo, Hall, Howard

Add'l Information: Established 1991. Normal turnaround time- 24-48 hours. Bill per search jobs. Will file/record documents for clients. All projects are billed and payable within 2 weeks.

ST Sayers & MS Chiarkas

RR #3 Box 91A, Sunbury, PA 17801
Phone: 570-286-9831 - **Fax:** 570-286-8774 SayersChiarkas@aol.com

Types of Records Retrieved: Criminal, Civil and Probate courts; Real Estate; Tax Liens/Judgments

Local Retrieval Area: PA-Montour, Northumberland, Snyder, Union. **Correspondent Relationships:** Pennsylvania.

Add'l Information: Established 1975. Normal turnaround time- 24-48 hours. Projects billed by number of names searched. Charges vary depending on type of search. Will file/record documents for clients. All searches are insured against errors and omissions.

St Vrain Resources

11939 Manchester Rd #264, St Louis, MO 63131
Phone: 314-645-1710 - **Fax:** 314-645-1707

Types of Records Retrieved: Criminal, Civil and Probate courts; Federal courts; Tax Liens/Judgments; Vital records

Retrieval Area: MO-Jefferson, Franklin, St. Louis, St. Louis City, St Charles

Add'l info: Established 1984. Normal turnaround time- 24-72 hours. Projects billed by the hour. Charge by the mile also. First project may require prepayment. They specialize in conducting investigation, research and documentation, especially US military records and federal district court of appeals searches. A licensed PI in MO. Performs service of process.

Stafford County Abstract & Title Co

PO Box 265, 205 E 4th Ave, St John, KS 67576
Phone: 620-549-3579 - **Fax:** 620-549-6594

Types of Records Retrieved: Civil and Probate courts; Real Estate; Tax Liens/Judgments; UCC records; Vital records

Local Retrieval Area: KS-Stafford

Add'l Information: Established 1933. Normal turnaround time- up to 1 week. Projects billed by the hour. Payment due at time of completion of work. Will file/record documents for clients. They specialize in courthouse and record searches.

Stallings Search Services

2832 Azalea Pl, Nashville, TN 37204
Phone: 615-781-2323 - **Fax:** 615-781-6821 stallingssearch@aol.com

Types of Records Retrieved: Criminal, Civil and Probate courts; Federal courts; Real Estate; Tax Liens/Judgments; UCC records; Vital records

Local Retrieval Area: TN-Anderson, Carroll, Cheatham, Davidson, Dickson, Hamilton, Knox, Montgomery, Robertson, Rutherford, Shelby, Sumner, Washington, Williamson, Wilson. **Correspondents:** statewide.

Add'l Information: Established 1997. Normal turnaround time- 24-48 hours. Projects billed by number of names searched. Will file/record documents for clients. Net 30 day invoicing. Over 23 years combined experience in public records and the title industry. Quick turnarounds, typed reports and optional e-mailed reports. All searches are on-site.

Stan Duby Investigations

PO Box 208, Salinas, CA 93902
Phone: 800-953-0435; 831-675-0435 - **Fax:** 831-675-8552
pvti@sbcglobal.net

Types of Records Retrieved: Criminal, Civil and Probate courts; Tax Liens/Judgments; UCC records; Vital records

Local Retrieval Area: CA-Monterey. **Correspondents:** nationwide.

Add'l Information: Established 1992. Normal turnaround time- 24-48 hours. Projects billed by number of names searched. First project may require prepayment. Will file/record documents for clients. Payments are net 20 days. They are licensed investigators specializing in background checks and locates. A licensed PI in CA. Performs service of process.

Stanton Co Abstract

PO Box 86, Stanton, NE 68779
Phone: 402-439-2142 - **Fax:** 402-439-2145

Types of Records Retrieved: Real Estate; Tax Liens/Judgments

Local Retrieval Area: NE-Stanton

Add'l Information: Established 1981. Normal turnaround time- 1-3 days. Fee basis is flat rate plus per record and mileage. Will file/record documents for clients. Payment due upon receipt of invoice. They specialize in title insurance, title searches, abstracts, closings and escrows.

Star Security & Inv

7034 Indianapolis Blvd, Hammond, IN 46324
Phone: 219-554-0100 - **Fax:** 219-554-0101
www.starsecurity.org **email:** staray@aol.com

Types of Records Retrieved: Criminal and Civil courts; Federal courts; Real Estate; Tax Liens/Judgments; UCC records; Vital records

Local Retrieval Area: IN-Jasper, Lake, La Porte, Newton, Porter

Add'l Information: Established 1989. Normal turnaround time- 2-3 days. Expedited service available. Fees vary. Credit cards accepted. Will invoice. A licensed PI in IN. Performs service of process.

Starhill Technical Services

R1, Box 51E, Bloomfield, IN 47424
Phone: 812-384-7840 - **Fax:** 812-384-8091 starhill@airnwire.com

Types of Records Retrieved: Criminal and Civil courts; Real Estate; UCC records; Tax Liens/Judgments

Local Retrieval Area: IN-Greene, Lawrence, Monroe, Owen

Add'l Information: Established 2002. Normal turnaround time- maximum 48 hours. Projects billed by number of names searched. Check due on project completion. They specialize in independent title search services, current owner, full title, document retrievals, judgment and lien searches. E&O insured.

Starke County Abstract Title & Guaranty

14 E Washington St, Knox, IN 46534
Phone: 574-772-3733 - **Fax:** 574-772-7603

Types of Records Retrieved: Criminal, Civil and Probate courts; Real Estate; Tax Liens/Judgments; UCC records

Local Retrieval Area: IN-Starke

Add'l Information: Established 1876. Normal turnaround time- 3-5 days. Fee basis will vary by type of project. Will file/record documents for clients. They specialize in record searching.

State Capital Title & Abstract Co

830 Bear Tavern Rd, Trenton, NJ 08628-1020
Phone: 800-876-8994; 609-771-4301 - **Fax:** 609-771-0821
www.statecapital.net **email:** info@statecapital.net

Types of Records Retrieved: Federal courts

Local Retrieval Area: NJ-Mercer

Add'l Information: Established 1925. Normal turnaround time- 24-48 hours. Will invoice monthly. They are the oldest and largest provider of certified corporate searches in NJ. They provide full filing services in Trenton and comprehensive foreclosure services.

State Information Bureau

842 E Park Ave #B, Tallahassee, FL 32301
Phone: 800-881-1742; 850-561-3990 - **Fax:** 800-948-1543; 850-561-3995
www.stateinformationbureau.com
email: info@stateinformationbureau.com

Types of Records Retrieved: Criminal, Civil and Probate courts; Federal courts; Real Estate; Tax Liens/Judgments; UCC records; Vital records

Local Retrieval Area: FL-Gadsden, Jefferson, Leon, Wakulla. **Correspondent Relationships:** major Florida counties.

Add'l Information: Established 1986. Normal turnaround time- 24-48 hours for Leon County. Fee basis will vary by type of project. First project may require prepayment. They are a licensed private investigative agency that specializes in obtaining information from state records. A licensed PI in FL. Performs service of process.

Statewide Recovery Inc

PO Box 6513, Great Falls, MT 59406
Phone: 406-761-4843 - **Fax:** 406-452-1365

Records Retrieved: Criminal, Civil and Probate courts; Federal District courts; Real Estate; Tax Liens/Judgments; UCC records; Vital records

Local Retrieval Area: MT-Cascade, Lewis & Clark

Add'l Information: Established 1987. Normal turnaround time- 3-5 days. Expedited service available. Projects billed by number of names searched. Projects billed by number of records located. Projects billed by the hour. First project may require prepayment. Performs service of process.

Statewide Recovery Inc

PO Box 6513, Great Falls, MT 59406
Phone: 406-761-4843 - **Fax:** 406-452-1365 repoplus@montana.com

Types of Records Retrieved: Criminal and Civil courts

Local Retrieval Area: MT-Cascade, Chouteau, Flathead, Glacier, Hill, Pondera, Teton, Toole

Add'l Information: Established 2004. All projects require prepayment. They also provide court filings, photocopying, and collections/repossessions. Performs service of process.

Staton Abstract & Title Co

PO Box 168, 516 Washington St, Chillicothe, MO 64601
Phone: 660-646-1421 - **Fax:** 660-646-1441

Types of Records Retrieved: Civil and Probate courts; Real Estate; Tax Liens/Judgments; UCC records; Vital records

Local Retrieval Area: MO-Livingston

Add'l Information: Established 1890. Normal turnaround time- 3 days. Fee basis varies by type of transaction. Will file/record documents for clients.

Steele County Abstract Co

PO Box 413, 125 W Bridge St, Owatonna, MN 55060
Phone: 507-451-6487 - **Fax:** 507-444-6262 scabstract@smig.net
Types of Records Retrieved: Real Estate; Tax Liens/Judgments
Local Retrieval Area: MN-Steele
Add'l Information: Established 1984. Normal turnaround time- 4 days. Projects billed by number of names searched. First project may require prepayment. Will file/record documents for clients.

Steele Investigation Agency

PO Box 1635, Bradenton, FL 34206-1635
Phone: 941-758-5890 - **Fax:** 941-755-1100 sia@fali.com
Types of Records Retrieved: Criminal, Civil and Probate courts; Real Estate; Tax Liens/Judgments; UCC records; Vital records
Local Retrieval Area: FL-Manatee, Sarasota. **Correspondents:** nationwide.
Add'l Information: Established 1981. Normal turnaround time- 3 days. Expedited service available. Projects billed by the hour. First project may require prepayment. They specialize in online Florida records, and are a full service investigative agency including, but not limited to asset location, criminal, civil, background, video, photograph, missing persons and surveillance. A licensed PI in FL. Performs service of process.

Steelman Abstracting Co

PO Box 544, Salem, MO 65560
Phone: 573-729-6183 - **Fax:** 573-729-1042 steelabs@fident.com
Types of Records Retrieved: Civil and Probate courts; Real Estate; Tax Liens/Judgments
Local Retrieval Area: MO-Dent
Add'l Information: Normal turnaround time- 2 weeks. Projects billed by number of records located. First project may require prepayment. Will file/record documents for clients. They specialize in title insurance.

Stehlik Law Office

653 G St, Pawnee City, NE 68420
Phone: 402-852-2973 - **Fax:** 402-852-2940
www.stehliklaw.com **email:** stehliklaw@stehliklaw.com
Types of Records Retrieved: Criminal, Civil and Probate courts; Real Estate; Tax Liens/Judgments; UCC records
Local Retrieval Area: NE-Pawnee
Add'l Information: Established 1971. Normal turnaround time- 24 hours. Projects billed by the hour. Will file/record documents for clients. Personal checks are accepted. They specialize in general law and abstracting.

Stephens County Abstract

100 N Baylor, Cook Building, Breckenridge, TX 76424
Phone: 254-559-9089 - **Fax:** 254-559-8935
Records Retrieved: Real Estate; Tax Liens/Judgments; UCC records
Local Retrieval Area: TX-Stephens
Add'l Information: Established 1895. Normal turnaround time- 2 days. Fee basis will vary by the type of project. All projects require prepayment.

Stephens County Abstract Co

919 W Main St, Duncan, OK 73533
Phone: 580-255-2525 - **Fax:** 580-255-3844
Types of Records Retrieved: Civil and Probate courts; Real Estate; Tax Liens/Judgments; UCC records
Local Retrieval Area: OK-Stephens
Add'l Information: Established 1907. Normal turnaround time- 4-5 days. Fee basis is per page and time. Will file/record documents for clients. Payment due when service is delivered.

Pat Stephens

2109 Agnew, Bonham, TX 75418
Phone: 903-583-5215 - **Fax:** 903-640-0206
Types of Records Retrieved: Real Estate; Tax Liens/Judgments; Probate courts; Federal courts; UCC records
Local Retrieval Area: OK-Bryan; TX-Collin, Fannin, Grayson, Hunt, Lamar. **Correspondent Relationships:** OK, TX.
Add'l Information: Normal turnaround time- 2-3 days. Projects billed by number of names searched. Projects billed by number of records located. She specializes in abstracting deeds and also 50 year title commercial searches and foreclosure sale documents.

Sterling Pacific Investigations Ltd

PO Box 38033, 794 Fort St, Victoria, BC V8W 3N2
Phone: 250-652-0541 - **Fax:** 250-652-0851
www.sterlingpacificinv.bc.ca **email:** spi@pacificcoast.net
Types of Records Retrieved: Criminal, Civil and Probate courts
Local Retrieval Area: CANADA-British Columbia. **Correspondent Relationships:** across Canada.
Add'l Information: Established 1988. Projects billed by the hour. First project may require prepayment. They specialize in court record retrieval and insurance claims in Victoria and the Vancouver Island area. A licensed PI in British Columbia. Performs service of process.

Sterling Research

14303 Richard Walker Blvd, Austin, TX 78728
Phone: 512-670-9334 - **Fax:** 512-670-9334 grocamora@austin.rr.com
Types of Records Retrieved: Criminal and Civil courts; Federal courts; Real Estate; Tax Liens/Judgments; UCC records; Vital records
Local Retrieval Area: TX-Bell, Travis, Williamson. **Correspondent Relationships:** nationwide.
Add'l Information: Established 2002. Normal turnaround time- 24-48 hours. Projects billed by number of names searched. First project may require prepayment. They specialize in UCCs, fixtures, State & Federal tax liens, judgments, civil, criminal, bankruptcy, vital statistics, driving records, corporate and UCC fillings.

Sterling Title Co

609 4th St, PO Box 2, Sterling City, TX 76951
Phone: 325-378-2405 - **Fax:** 325-378-2750 sharicope@aol.com
Types of Records Retrieved: Real Estate; Tax Liens/Judgments; Probate courts; UCC records **Local Retrieval Area:** TX-Sterling
Add'l Information: Established 1992. Normal turnaround time- 2-3 days. Projects billed by number of names searched. Projects billed by the hour. All projects require prepayment. Will file/record documents for clients.

Steve Knight Services

PO Box 1282, Jeffersonville, IN 47131-1282
Phone: 812-364-4461 - **Fax:** 812-283-9811
Types of Records Retrieved: Criminal, Civil and Probate courts; Federal courts; Real Estate; Tax Liens/Judgments; UCC records; Vital records
Local Retrieval Area: IN-Clark, Floyd, Harrison
Add'l Information: Established 1989. Normal turnaround time- 24 hours or as soon as possible. Projects billed by the hour. $20.00 per hour-two hour minimum. All projects require prepayment. Steve Knight Services is a licensed private detective agency. They do investigations-background, missing persons, skip trace, assets and judgment recovery. A PI in IN.

Stevens County Title

PO Box 349, 280 S Oak St, Colville, WA 99114
Phone: 509-684-4589 - **Fax:** 509-684-5448
Types of Records Retrieved: Criminal, Civil and Probate courts; Real Estate; Tax Liens/Judgments; UCC records
Local Retrieval Area: WA-Stevens
Add'l Information: Normal turnaround time- 24-48 hours. Projects billed by the hour. First project may require prepayment. Will file/record documents for clients. They specialize in title searches.

Stewart & Associates Inc - Rockford

308 W State St, Stewart Sq #175, Rockford, IL 61101
Phone: 815-961-0150 - **Fax:** 815-235-1290
www.bwstewart.com **email:** brians@bwstewart.com
Types of Records Retrieved: Criminal, Civil and Probate courts; Federal courts; Real Estate; Tax Liens/Judgments; UCC records; Vital records

Local Retrieval Area: IL-Boone, Carroll, De Kalb, Jo Daviess, Lee, Ogle, Stephenson, Whiteside, Winnebago; WI-Green, Rock. **Correspondent Relationships:** statewide.

Add'l Information: Established 1987. Normal turnaround time- 1-2 business days. Fee basis negotiated by volume of project. First project may require prepayment. Credit cards accepted. Will file/record documents for clients. They are an Illinois, Iowa, and Wisconsin licensed private detective agency that specializes in investigative services, records and background services. A licensed PI in IL, IA, WI. Performs service of process.

Stewart Title Co

PO Box 913, 131 W 5th St, Leadville, CO 80461
Phone: 719-486-2688 - **Fax:** 719-486-8352

Types of Records Retrieved: Real Estate; Tax Liens/Judgments; Probate courts; UCC records; Vital records **Local Retrieval Area:** CO-Lake

Add'l Information: Established 1965. Normal turnaround time- 1 week to 10 days. Fee basis will vary by the type of project. First project may require prepayment. They specialize in real estate title searches.

Stewart Title of Arkansas

200 E Central, Bentonville, AR 72712
Phone: 479-273-2111 - **Fax:** 479-273-9247
www.stewart.com **email:** jay.hubert@stewart.com

Types of Records Retrieved: Civil and Probate courts; Real Estate; Tax Liens/Judgments; UCC records

Local Retrieval Area: AR-Benton, Washington

Add'l Information: Established 1893. Normal turnaround time- 3 days for UCC and taxes and 5 days for real estate. Projects billed by the hour. Flat fee for closing. Will file/record documents for clients. All projects require prepayments or down payments. They specialize in title insurance and escrow services to include 1099's.

Stewart Title of Midland Inc

206 N Main St, Midland, TX 79701
Phone: 432-687-3355 - **Fax:** 432-687-3358
www.stewartmidland.com **email:** chejones@stewart.com

Records Retrieved: Civil and Probate courts; Federal courts; Real Estate

Local Retrieval Area: TX-Culberson, Loving, Martin, Midland, Reagan, Reeves, Winkler

Add'l Information: Established 1986. Normal turnaround time- variable depending on project. Projects billed by number of names searched. Projects billed by number of records located. Projects billed by the hour. First project may require prepayment. Will file/record documents for clients. They will also invoice. Personal checks are accepted. They specialize in title examinations, mineral take off and name searches, abstracts and title insurance.

Stewart Title Services Inc, Wisconsin

5150 N Port Washington Rd #121, Milwaukee, WI 53217
Phone: 800-523-3060; 414-967-3060 - **Fax:** 414-967-0744
www.stewarttitleservices.com **email:** dnelson@stewart.com

Types of Records Retrieved: Civil and Probate courts; Real Estate; UCC records; Tax Liens/Judgments; Vital records

Local Retrieval Area: WI-Columbia, Dane, Dodge, Fond du lac, Green, Green Lake, Jefferson, Kenosha, Milwaukee, Ozaukee, Racine, Rock, Sauk, Sheboygan, Walworth, Washington, Waukesha, Waupaca, Winnebago

Add'l Information: Established 1998. Normal turnaround time- 24-48 hours. Projects billed by number of names searched. Net 30 days. Stewart Title Svcs - a wholly-owned subsidiary of Stewart Title Corp - provides clear, accurate property reports by either email, fax of Sureclose.

Lori Stewart

515 Longbranch Rd, Hohenwald, TN 38462
Phone: 931-796-2565 - **Fax:** 931-796-2566

Types of Records Retrieved: Criminal, Civil and Probate courts

Local Retrieval Area: TN-Lewis

Add'l Information: Established 1977. Normal turnaround time- 24 hours. Projects billed by number of names searched. First project may require prepayment. She specializes in courthouse research in Lewis County.

Marilyn Stewart

161 Gregory St, Forrest City, AR 72335
Phone: 870-633-0149, cell 870-270-7286 mellonstew@yahoo.com

Types of Records Retrieved: Criminal, Civil and Probate courts; Real Estate; Tax Liens/Judgments

Local Retrieval Area: AR-Cross, Crittenden (rarely) Lee, St Francis

Add'l Information: Established 2000. Normal turnaround time- 24-48 hours; Crittenden County (Marion City) may be longer. Projects billed by number of names searched. All projects require prepayment. Fax to "Attn. Marilyn" at 870-261-1723. She specializes in St Francis County. She will perform real estate searches if they are "short." Call to determine is she can do Crittenden County (Marion City) in a timely manner.

Stillwater Abstract

PO Box 806, 21 4th St, Columbus, MT 59019
Phone: 406-322-5216 - **Fax:** 406-322-4465

Types of Records Retrieved: Civil and Probate courts; Real Estate; Tax Liens/Judgments; UCC records

Local Retrieval Area: MT-Stillwater

Add'l Information: Normal turnaround time- 2-3 days. Fee basis depends on the project. Will file/record documents for clients.

Story Countpitle Co

1013 6th St, Nevada, IA 50201
Phone: 515-382-4127 - **Fax:** 515-382-4358

Records Retrieved: Real Estate; Tax Liens/Judgments; UCC records

Local Retrieval Area: IA-Story

Add'l Information: Normal turnaround time- 3-5 days. Fee basis will vary by the type of project. Will file/record documents for clients. They specialize in real estate title.

Donna Stovall

32 Pearl Rd, Rocky Point, NY 11778-9689
Phone: 631-744-5834 - **Fax:** 631-744-9379 dstovalsuffolk@aol.com

Types of Records Retrieved: Criminal and Civil courts; Real Estate; Tax Liens/Judgments; UCC records **Local Retrieval Area:** NY-Suffolk

Add'l Information: Established 1986. Normal turnaround time- 24-48 hours. Fee basis will vary by type of project. First project may require prepayment. Will file/record documents for clients. Will bill monthly. She also does judgment searches. Performs service of process.

Strander Abstract Inc

PO Box 622, Crookston, MN 56716
Phone: 218-281-1191 - **Fax:** 218-281-3212 stranderabstract@qwest.net

Types of Records Retrieved: Real Estate; Tax Liens/Judgments

Local Retrieval Area: MN-Polk

Add'l Information: Established 1886. Normal turnaround time- 1 week. Projects billed by number of names searched. Will file/record documents for clients.

Street Abstract Co

PO Box 306, 118 N Main, Yates Center, KS 66783
Phone: 620-625-2421 - **Fax:** 620-625-3631

Types of Records Retrieved: Criminal, Civil and Probate courts; Real Estate; Tax Liens/Judgments; UCC records

Retrieval Area: KS-Allen, Coffey, Greenwood, Neosho, Wilson, Woodson

Add'l Information: Established 1964. Normal turnaround time- 48 hours. Fee basis varies by type of transaction. First project may require prepayment. Will file/record documents for clients.

Marg Strein

204 W Mary St, Old Forge, PA 18518
Phone: 570-457-3939 - **Fax:** 570-457-3939 mar24g@aol.com

Types of Records Retrieved: Civil courts; Real Estate; Tax Liens/Judgments; Mortgage; Discovery

Local Retrieval Area: PA-Lackawanna, Luzerne

Add'l Information: Normal turnaround time- 24-48 hours. varied. First project requires prepayment. Database includes real estate searches - mortgages/assignments, current owner-deeds. Verification/extraction of information in Lackawanna/Luzerne counties. Specializes in civil records and litigation research.

Lori Stroebel
PO Box 1478, Hailey, ID 83333 **Phone:** 208-481-0806 - **Fax:** 208-788-1759
Records Retrieved: Criminal and Civil courts; Tax Liens/Judgments
Local Retrieval Area: ID-Blaine
Add'l Information: Established 2003. Normal turnaround time- 24-48 hours. Fee depends on nature of the job. First project may require prepayment.

Strother-Wilbourn Land Title Co
308 E Market Ave, Searcy, AR 72143
Phone: 501-268-8273 - **Fax:** 501-268-3275
www.strotherwilbourn.com **email:** wtitle@cablelynx.com
Types of Records Retrieved: Civil and Probate courts; Real Estate; Tax Liens/Judgments; UCC records **Local Retrieval Area:** AR-White
Add'l Information: Established 1918. Normal turnaround time- 5-10 days. Fee basis will vary by the type of project. They specialize in title insurance.

Stroud Research & Sales
PO Box 214, Stinnett, TX 79083
Phone: 806-878-3195; cell- 806-886-3731 - **Fax:** 806-878-3723
rstroud@amaonline.com
Types of Records Retrieved: Criminal, Civil and Probate courts; Bankruptcy court; Tax Liens/Judgments; Vital records
Local Retrieval Area: TX-Hutchinson
Add'l Information: Established 2000. Normal turnaround time- 24 hours. Expedited service available. Projects billed by number of names searched. Billings at the 1st of the month. Has access to District court 24 hours a day. Charges per name; if copies are requested there is a $1.00 per page charge.

Stutsman County Abstract
223 3rd Ave SW, Jamestown, ND 58401
Phone: 701-252-4870 - **Fax:** 701-252-4960 abstract@daktel.com
Records Retrieved: Real Estate; Tax Liens/Judgments; UCC records
Local Retrieval Area: ND-La Moure, Stutsman. **Correspondent Relationships:** working relationship with all ND abstract companies.
Add'l Information: Established 1901. Normal turnaround time- 2-5 days. Fee basis will vary by type of project. First project may require prepayment. Will file/record documents for clients.

Suburban Record Research
12 Main St, Dover, MA 02030
Phone: 617-536-3486 - **Fax:** 508-785-2852
Types of Records Retrieved: Criminal, Civil and Probate courts; Federal courts; Real Estate; Tax Liens/Judgments; UCC records
Local Retrieval Area: MA-Middlesex, Norfolk, Suffolk, Worcester
Add'l Information: Established 1982. Normal turnaround time- 24-48 hours. Expedited service available. Projects billed by number of names searched. Will file/record documents for clients. They specialize in real estate, current owner, mortgage and assignment searches and document retrieval as well as UCC and court record searches. They are fully insured.

Sugarbaker Investigations
PO Box 15498, Brooksville, FL 34604
Phone: 352-684-9388 - **Fax:** 352-684-9173 sugarbaker@bellsouth.net
Types of Records Retrieved: Criminal, Civil and Probate courts; Federal courts; UCC records; Vital records
Local Retrieval Area: FL-Broward, Dade, Hernando, Hillsborough, Manatee, Marion, Orange, Pasco, Pinellas, Polk, Sarasota, Seminole, Volusia. **Correspondent Relationships:** nationwide.
Add'l Information: Established 1985. Normal turnaround time- 24-48 hours. Projects billed by the hour. First project may require prepayment. They specialize in automobile product liability and general litigation support. They have been in business for over 19 years. They retrieve records from all states in the USA, also in Canada. A licensed PI in FL.

Sullivan County Abstract Co
217 E 3rd St, Milan, MO 63556
Phone: 660-265-3744 - **Fax:** 660-265-4908 scac@nemr.net
Types of Records Retrieved: Criminal, Civil and Probate courts; Federal courts; Real Estate; Tax Liens/Judgments; UCC records; Vital records
Local Retrieval Area: MO-Sullivan. **Correspondent Relationships:** Putnam, Grundy, Linn, Adair counties.
Add'l Information: Established 1975. Normal turnaround time- 2 days. Fee basis will vary by the type of project. All projects require prepayment. Will file/record documents for clients. They specialize in title insurance.

SumData
1203 Ranch Rd, McPherson, KS 67460
Phone: 620-241-5448 - **Fax:** 620-241-5448 sumdata05@sbcglobal.net
Types of Records Retrieved: Criminal, Civil and Probate courts; Real Estate; Tax Liens/Judgments; UCC records
Local Retrieval Area: KS-Harvey, Marion, McPherson, Reno, Rice, Saline
Add'l Information: Established 2004. Normal turnaround time- 24-48 hours. Projects billed by number of names searched. First project may require prepayment. Specialize in retrieval of real estate records, UCCs, judgments/tax liens & bankruptcy in Reno, McPherson, Saline, Harvey & Marion counties, KS. Criminal/civil background searches in McPherson, Saline & Harvey counties, KS.

Summit Documents
PO Box 1603, Owensboro, KY 42301
Phone: 270-281-5406 - **Fax:** 270-281-5406
Types of Records Retrieved: Criminal, Civil and Probate courts; Federal courts; Real Estate; Tax Liens/Judgments; UCC records; Vital records
Local Retrieval Area: IN-Perry, Spencer, Warrick; KY-Daviess, Hancock, Henderson, Ohio, Webster
Add'l Information: Established 1995. Normal turnaround time- 24-48 hours. Projects billed by number of names searched. Projects billed by the hour. Will file/record documents for clients. They specialize in local court and KY Federal Court record retrieval in the Owensboro area, both Kentucky and Indiana; offers a variety of investigative services as well.

Sumpter & Associates LLC
4425-C Treat Blvd #298, Concord, CA 94521
Phone: 925-671-7755 - **Fax:** 925-671-2095
www.sumpterassociates.com **email:** sales@sumpterassociates.com
Types of Records Retrieved: Criminal and Civil courts; Real Estate; Tax Liens/Judgments; UCC records; Vital records
Local Retrieval Area: CA-Alameda, Contra Costa, Solano
Add'l info: Established 2001. Normal turnaround time- 24-48 hours. Projects billed by number of names searched. Will file/record documents for clients. They have over 16 years in the public record search and retrieval business. They also provide corporate, fictitious name, and MVR records.

Sunshine Research Inc
1501 S Pinellas Ave #3H, Tarpon Springs, FL 34689
Phone: 888-786-1242; 727-939-9039 - **Fax:** 888-785-7451; 727-934-2939
www.sunshineresearch.com **email:** info@sunshineresearch.com
Types of Records Retrieved: Criminal and Civil courts; Federal District courts; UCC records
Local Retrieval Area: FL-Hillsborough, Pasco, Pinellas, Manatee. **Correspondent Relationships:** LA-Jefferson, Orleans; NY-Kings, Queens, Richmond, Suffolk, Nassau, New York City.
Add'l Information: Established 1997. Normal turnaround time- 24 hours. Projects billed by number of names searched. First project may require prepayment. Credit cards accepted. They are a fully Internet-based, full-service pre-employment screening firm. They offer nationwide searches. A licensed PI in FL.

Sunstate Research Associates Inc
143 Whetherbine Way W, Tallahassee, FL 32301
Phone: 800-621-7234; - **Fax:** 850-656-5454
Types of Records Retrieved: Civil courts; Federal courts; Tax Liens/Judgments; UCC records
Local Retrieval Area: FL-Gadsden, Jefferson, Leon, Wakulla. **Correspondent Relationships:** Pinellas and Hillsborough counties.
Add'l Information: Established 1990. Normal turnaround time- same or next day for Secretary of State; 1-3 days for remainder of their service area. Projects billed by number of names searched. First project may require prepayment. Personal checks are accepted. They specialize in filing and retrieval of UCC documents from the FL Secured Transaction Registry and corporate documents from the Florida Secretary of State. They also search federal and state tax liens and judgment files with the SOS.

Superior Information Services, LLC
PO Box 8787, Trenton, NJ 08650-0787
Phone: 800-848-0489; 609-883-7000 - **Fax:** 609-883-1413
www.superiorinfo.com/TagX/Home/ **email:** lmartin@superiorinfo.com
Types of Records Retrieved: Civil courts; Federal courts; Tax Liens/Judgments; UCC records **Local Retrieval Area:** NJ-all counties
Add'l Information: Established 1987. Normal turnaround time- 3-5 business days depending on location. Service fee by case or file. Credit cards accepted. In addition to their online judgment database, Superior provides direct hands-on access to case documents in all federal and state courts located in NJ, and UCC documents filed at the state & county levels in NJ. They also offer NJ corporate services.

Superior Process Service
409 E Summit Ave, Electra, TX 76360
Phone: 888-230-2663; 940-495-2663 glenthe5@aol.com
Records Retrieved: Criminal, Civil and Probate courts; Federal courts
Local Retrieval Area: TX-Archer, Baylor, Clay, Foard, Hardeman, Haskell, Jack, Knox, Montague, Throckmorton, Wichita, Wilbarger. **Correspondent Relationships:** statewide in Texas.
Add'l Information: Established 1990. Normal turnaround time- 2-4 days. Expedited service available. Projects billed by number of names searched. First project may require prepayment. Performs service of process.

Superior Subpoena Service
PO Box 2002, 126 S Wood Ave, Linden, NJ 07036
Phone: 908-392-6229 - **Fax:** 908-486-0332
Types of Records Retrieved: Criminal, Civil and Probate courts; Federal courts; Real Estate; Tax Liens/Judgments; UCC records
Local Retrieval Area: NJ-Essex, Hudson, Middlesex, Union. **Correspondent Relationships:** New Jersey.
Add'l Information: Established 1978. Normal turnaround time- variable depending on project. Expedited service available. Projects billed by the hour. Billed by job also. First project may require prepayment. Will file/record documents for clients. They can access almost all records in most of NJ. The principle of the company is also a constable. They also do service of process, summons & complaints, subpoenas, also special assignments and courier tasks, hand deliveries. Performs service of process.

Superior Title & Abstract
PO Box 766, Iron Mountain, MI 49801-0766
Phone: 906-774-9010 - **Fax:** 906-774-8994
www.baytitle.com **email:** ckallal@baytitle.com
Types of Records Retrieved: Real Estate; Tax Liens/Judgments
Local Retrieval Area: MI-Dickinson; WI-Florence. **Correspondent Relationships:** all counties in Michigan upper peninsula.
Add'l Information: Established 1975. Normal turnaround time- 24-48 hours. Will file/record documents for clients. The specialize in real estate closings, escrow and title work.

Sure Search
35 Boyce Rd, Pine Bush, NY 12566
Phone: 845-744-4243 - **Fax:** 845-744-6469 smills@hvc.rr.com
Types of Records Retrieved: Criminal and Civil courts; Real Estate; Tax Liens/Judgments; UCC records
Local Retrieval Area: NY-Duchess, Orange, Putnam, Rockland, Suffolk, Sullivan, Westchester. **Correspondent Relationships:** statewide.
Add'l Information: Established 1991. Normal turnaround time- 24-48 hours. Projects billed by number of names searched. First project may require prepayment. Will file/record documents for clients. They offer NY statewide criminal searches.

Surette Investigations
PO Box 116, Litchfield, ME 04350
Phone: 207-268-3419 - **Fax:** 207-268-3420
www.suretteinvestigations.com **email:** kevin@suretteinvestigations.com
Types of Records Retrieved: Criminal, Civil and Probate courts; Real Estate; Tax Liens/Judgments; UCC records; Vital records
Local Retrieval Area: ME-Androscoggin, Kennebec, Lincoln, Sagadahoc. **Correspondent Relationships:** Massachusetts and New Hampshire.
Add'l Information: Established 1992. Normal turnaround time- 24-48 hours. Expedited service available. Projects billed by number of names searched. Flat rate. First project may require prepayment. They specialize in full service security consulting and investigations. A licensed PI in ME, MA, NH. Performs service of process.

Surety Title Co
PO Box 551, 523 Central Av, New Rockford, ND 58356
Phone: 701-947-2446 - **Fax:** 701-947-2443
Types of Records Retrieved: Civil and Probate courts; Real Estate; Tax Liens/Judgments; UCC records
Local Retrieval Area: ND-Benson, Eddy, Griggs
Add'l Information: Established 1925. Normal turnaround time- 5 days. Fee basis will vary by the type of project. Will file/record documents for clients. Payment is based on individual basis.

Surety Title Co of Ballinger
PO Box 31, 803 Hutchings, Ballinger, TX 76821-0031
Phone: 325-365-5713 - **Fax:** 325-365-3897
Types of Records Retrieved: Criminal, Civil and Probate courts; Real Estate; Tax Liens/Judgments; UCC records; Vital records
Local Retrieval Area: TX-Runnels. **Correspondent Relationships:** add'l offices in Kendall, San Angelo, San Saba, Kimble, Real, Concho, Tom Green counties.
Add'l Information: Normal turnaround time- 1-2 days. Fee basis will vary by the type of project. First project may require prepayment.

Surety Title Co of San Angelo
136 W Twohig, San Angelo, TX 76903
Phone: 325-658-7588 - **Fax:** 325-655-3743
Types of Records Retrieved: Criminal, Civil and Probate courts; Federal courts; Real Estate; Tax Liens/Judgments; UCC records; Vital records
Local Retrieval Area: TX-Tom Green. **Correspondent Relationships:** various Texas counties including offices in Kendall, San Angelo, San Saba, Kimble, Real, Concho, Runnels counties.
Add'l Information: Established 1886. Normal turnaround time- 1-2 days. Fee basis will vary by the type of project. First project may require prepayment. Will file/record documents for clients. They have a fully equipped title plant with three abstractors.

Sutherlin Associated Services
300 Carlsbad Village Dr #108A-354, Carlsbad, CA 92008-2999
Phone: 760-433-1555 - **Fax:** 760-433-6155 sutherlinassoc3@aol.com
Types of Records Retrieved: Criminal, Civil and Probate courts; Federal courts; Real Estate; Tax Liens/Judgments; UCC records

Local Retrieval Area: CA-San Diego. **Correspondent Relationships:** network affiliations nationwide.

Add'l Information: Established 1986. Normal turnaround time- 24-48 hours. Expedited service available. Charges are by the number of names searched or hourly depending on project. Credit cards accepted. They do bi-monthly invoicing, terms are net 15 days. Prepayment is required for some projects. They are licensed private investigators since 1986, doing nationwide background checks and pre-employment screening, workplace investigations, due diligence and witness locations/statements. A PI in CA.

Sutton & Associates Investigations Inc

1 Chick Springs Rd #201C, Greenville, SC 29609

Phone: 864-232-9007 - **Fax:** 864-271-3898 wecucarol@aol.com

Types of Records Retrieved: Criminal, Civil and Probate courts; Federal courts; Real Estate; Tax Liens/Judgments; UCC records; Vital records

Local Retrieval Area: SC-Anderson, Greenville, Pickens, Spartanburg. **Correspondent Relationships:** SC.

Add'l Information: Established 1978. Normal turnaround time- 2 days. Expedited service available. Projects billed by the hour. All projects require prepayment. They are an investigation firm who has been in business for 25 years. Specialize in investigations, locating, document retrieval & pre-employment backgrounds. Licensed PI in SC. Performs service of process.

Sweet Grass Title Co

118 W 1st Ave, PO Box 1067, Big Timber, MT 59011

Phone: 406-932-4888 - **Fax:** 406-932-5378

Types of Records Retrieved: Civil and Probate courts; Real Estate; Tax Liens/Judgments

Local Retrieval Area: MT-Golden Valley, Sweet Grass, Wheatland

Add'l Information: Established 1960. Normal turnaround time- variable depending on project. Fee basis varies by type of transaction. They provide title insurance and related products, mineral reports and abstracts and closing services.

Kathy Swenson, PI

36250 Cross St, Pearl River, LA 70452-5962

Phone: 985-863-8151 - **Fax:** 985-863-3603 swensonk007@bellsouth.net

Types of Records Retrieved: Criminal, Civil and Probate courts; Real Estate; Tax Liens/Judgments; UCC records

Local Retrieval Area: LA-St. Tammany Parish

Add'l Information: Established 1986. Normal turnaround time- 24-48 hours. Will file/record documents for clients. She specializes in criminal record research and retrieval, property record research & retrieval (including title/current owner forward). A licensed PI in LA. Performs service of process.

SWF Private Inv

3626 Tami Ami Tr, Pt Charlotte, FL 33952

Phone: 941-764-9156 - **Fax:** 941-764-6200

www.swfpi.com **email:** jimg@swfpi.com

Types of Records Retrieved: Criminal, Civil and Probate courts; Federal courts; Real Estate; Tax Liens/Judgments; UCC records; Vital records

Local Retrieval Area: FL-Charlotte, Lee, Sarasota. **Correspondent Relationships:** nationwide.

Add'l Information: Established 2000. Normal turnaround time- 1-3 days turnaround; 48-hour guaranteed expedited service. Dependant on number of searches and method of search. First project may require prepayment. Terms negotiable. Will accept check by fax. Willing to go the extra mile, they also provide security and private eye services as well as pre-employment and tenant screening. A PI in FL. Performs service of process.

Swift Attorney Service

500 Allerton St #105, Redwood City, CA 94063

Phone: 800-987-9438; 650-364-9612 - **Fax:** 650-364-3305

www.swiftattorneyservice.com **email:** swiftattysvc@hotmail.com

Types of Records Retrieved: Criminal, Civil and Probate courts; Federal courts; Real Estate; UCC records; Tax Liens/Judgments; Vital records

Local Retrieval Area: CA-Alameda, Contra Costa, San Mateo, Santa Clara, San Francisco. **Correspondent Relationships:** statewide.

Add'l Information: Established 1976. Normal turnaround time- call for turnaround time. Projects billed by number of names searched. Projects billed by number of records located. Projects billed by the hour. First project may require prepayment. Additional services include medical records, locates, skiptraces, writ services and private investigations. A licensed PI in CA. Performs service of process.

SWP Searches

119 S Hopkins, Grand Haven, MI 49417

Phone: 616-847-6989 - **Fax:** 616-850-9802 spyle@i2k.com

Types of Records Retrieved: Criminal, Civil and Probate courts; Federal courts; Real Estate; Tax Liens/Judgments; UCC records; Vital records

Local Retrieval Area: MI-Allegan, Kent, Muskegon, Ottawa

Add'l Information: Established 1998. Normal turnaround time- 24-48 hours. Projects billed by number of names searched. First project may require prepayment. Will file/record documents for clients. They specialize in any type of search. Performs service of process.

Synerfax Inc

460 State St #301, Rochester, NY 14608

Phone: 800-245-3013; 585-546-1640 - **Fax:** 585-546-1683

www.synerfax.com **email:** charlie@synerfax.com

Types of Records Retrieved: Criminal and Civil courts; Federal courts

Local Retrieval Area: NY-Allegany, Bronx, Cayuga, Courtland, Erie, Hamilton, Kings, Monroe, Montgomery, Nassau, New York, Niagara, Onondaga, Ontario, Orleans, Queens, Richmond, Wayne. **Correspondent Relationships:** nationwide.

Add'l Information: Established 1997. Normal turnaround time- 1-2 days. Projects billed by number of names searched. Payment due net 30 days. An information services company providing pre-employment background checking. Specializing in criminal record searches in Monroe, Ontario, Wayne, Erie, Niagara, Onondaga, as well as all NY Counties affiliated with the NY Office of Court Admin. (NYOCA).

Dona Szymaszek

22032 Chestnut Ridge, Kildeer, IL 60047

Phone: 847-540-7425 - **Fax:** 847-438-4980 tomszymaszek@aol.com

Types of Records Retrieved: Criminal, Civil and Probate courts; Real Estate; Tax Liens/Judgments; UCC records; Vital records

Local Retrieval Area: IL-Lake, McHenry

Add'l Information: Established 1999. Normal turnaround time- 24 hours. Expedited service available. Projects billed by number of names searched. First project may require prepayment. She is a paralegal with ten (10) years experience in document retrieval and searches in the Circuit Courts and County Recorders of Lake and McHenry counties in Illinois.

T.A.B.B.S. Investigations & Process Service

1509 N Main - PMB 112, Altus, OK 73521
Phone: 580-477-3292 - **Fax:** 580-477-3257
www.tabbs.net **email:** tonya@tabbs.net

Types of Records Retrieved: Criminal, Civil and Probate courts; Real Estate; Tax Liens/Judgments; UCC records; Vital records

Local Retrieval Area: OK-Comanche, Greer, Harmon, Jackson, Kiowa, Tillman; TX-Hardeman, Wilbarger. **Correspondent Relationships:** Oklahoma City, Norman; all 77 Oklahoma counties.

Add'l Information: Established 1999. Normal turnaround time- 24-72 hours. Projects billed by number of records located. Credit cards accepted. Will file/record documents for clients. They specialize in locates, pre-employment, background, workman's comp, criminal/civil courts, insurance fraud, domestic, child custody, civil, process service and public record retrieval. A licensed PI in OK. Performs service of process.

Tactical Private Inv

PO Box 12457, Lake Charles, LA 70611
Phone: 800-779-4893; 337-855-6470 - **Fax:** 337-855-0168
www.tacticalpi.8m.com **email:** spyguytwo@aol.com

Types of Records Retrieved: Criminal, Civil and Probate courts; Federal courts; Real Estate; Tax Liens/Judgments; UCC records; Vital records

Local Retrieval Area: LA-Calcasieu. **Correspondent Relationships:** Lafayette, Baton Rouge, Orleans parishes LA.

Add'l Information: Established 1989. Normal turnaround time- 1-2 days. Expedited service available. Projects billed by the hour. All projects require prepayment. They are a Louisiana's premier investigative firm. A licensed PI in LA. Performs service of process.

The Talon Group

32 E Bacon St, Hillsdale, MI 49242-1636
Phone: 517-437-7345 - **Fax:** 517-439-1659

Types of Records Retrieved: Real Estate; Tax Liens/Judgments; Probate courts; Vital records

Local Retrieval Area: MI-Branch, Calhoun, Hillsdale. **Correspondent Relationships:** adjoining counties.

Add'l Information: Normal turnaround time- up to 1 week. Fee basis will vary by type of project. They specialize in real estate and title research. They will file/record real estate documents on behalf of clients on a same or next day basis.

Talone & Associates

423 S 15th St, Philadelphia, PA 19146
Phone: 800-553-5189; 215-546-6080 - **Fax:** 215-546-2412

Types of Records Retrieved: Criminal, Civil and Probate courts; Federal courts; Real Estate; Tax Liens/Judgments; UCC records; Vital records

Local Retrieval Area: NJ-Burlington, Camden, Gloucester; PA-Bucks, Chester, Delaware, Lancaster, Lehigh, Montgomery, Philadelphia. **Correspondent Relationships:** surrounding NJ and PA counties.

Add'l Information: Established 1987. Normal turnaround time- 2-3 days. Projects billed by number of names searched. Projects billed by the hour. Charge by hour if it is a protracted search. First project may require prepayment. Will file/record documents for clients. Terms: net 30 days. They specialize in prompt, professional service, with expedited same/next day service available. A licensed PI in NJ, PA. Performs service of process.

Tama County Abstract

PO Box 2, 123 W High St, Toledo, IA 52342
Phone: 888-561-9061; 641-484-4386 - **Fax:** 641-484-5449

Types of Records Retrieved: Criminal, Civil and Probate courts; Federal courts; Real Estate; Tax Liens/Judgments; UCC records; Vital records

Local Retrieval Area: IA-Tama

Add'l info: Established 1949. Normal turnaround time- 1-2 days. Fee basis varies by type of transaction. Will file/record documents for clients. If accounts are paid in a timely fashion, they won't require prepayment.

Tammy L Listen Investigations

3950 Connie Ln, Edmond, OK 73634
Phone: 405-340-4843 - **Fax:** 405-340-9610 tllisten@aol.com

Types of Records Retrieved: Criminal and Civil courts; Federal courts; Real Estate; Tax Liens/Judgments; UCC records; Vital records

Local Retrieval Area: OK-Caddo, Canadian, Cleveland, Grady, Lincoln, Logan, McClain, Oklahoma, Pottawatomie. **Correspondents:** statewide.

Add'l Information: Established 1996. Normal turnaround time- 24-48 hours. Expedited service available. Projects billed by number of names searched. Will invoice. This is a one person company, service oriented, with a bachelor's degree in education. She takes her work very serious and prides herself in doing the best job possible. Female owned. A licensed PI in OK. Performs service of process.

Taya Gordon Research

PO Box 514, Hull, GA 30646 **Phone:** 706-546-6598 - **Fax:** 706-369-9733

Types of Records Retrieved: Criminal, Civil and Probate courts; Real Estate; Tax Liens/Judgments; UCC records

Local Retrieval Area: GA-Clarke, Jackson, Madison, Oconee, Oglethorpe

Add'l Information: Established 1999. Normal turnaround time- 24-48 hours. Projects billed by number of names searched. First project may require prepayment. She specializes in document retrieval, title exams, witness/notary closings, also offering certified copies and reasonable rates.

Taylor Abstract & Title Inc

PO Box 305, 114 W 5th St, Larned, KS 67550
Phone: 620-285-2026 - **Fax:** 620-285-2753 titledoc@sbcglobal.net

Types of Records Retrieved: Criminal, Civil and Probate courts; Real Estate; Tax Liens/Judgments; UCC records

Local Retrieval Area: KS-Pawnee, Stafford

Add'l Information: Established 1896. Normal turnaround time- 2 days; Stafford county may take longer. Fee basis varies by type of transaction. First project may require prepayment. Will file/record documents for clients. They specialize in abstract and title insurance.

Taylor Research & Investigations

7417 Whispering Pines Dr, Dallas, TX 75248-3061
Phone: 972-991-5045 - **Fax:** 972-503-3302
www.dallasprivateeye.com **email:** jhtj@swbell.net

Types of Records Retrieved: Criminal, Civil and Probate courts; Federal courts; Real Estate; Tax Liens/Judgments; UCC records; Vital records

Local Retrieval Area: TX-Bell, Collin, Dallas, Denton, Ellis, Hunt, Johnson, Kaufman, Parker, Rockwall, Tarrant, Travis, Van Zandt, Williamson. **Correspondent Relationships:** TX, LA, OK.

Add'l Information: Established 1992. Normal turnaround time- 24 hours. Projects billed by the hour. First project may require prepayment. Credit cards accepted. They are a full service investigative and research company with expeditious, efficient results. Performs service of process.

Teeters Abstract & Title Co

PO Box 645, 517 Main, Goodland, KS 67735
Phone: 785-890-7138 - **Fax:** 785-890-6644

Types of Records Retrieved: Civil and Probate courts; Real Estate; Tax Liens/Judgments; UCC records

Local Retrieval Area: KS-Sherman

Add'l Information: Established 1885. Normal turnaround time- 2 days. First project may require prepayment. Will file/record documents for clients. They specialize in real estate searches.

TenantSafe Inc

310 2nd St, Lakewood, NJ 08701
Phone: 888-502-0135; 732-364-5710 - **Fax:** 732-370-1785
www.tenantsafe.net **email:** info@tenantsafe.net

Types of Records Retrieved: Criminal courts

Local Retrieval Area: NJ-Atlantic, Bergen, Burlington, Camden, Cape May, Cumberland, Essex, Gloucester, Hudson, Hunterdon, Mercer, Middlesex, Monmouth, Morris, Ocean, Passaic, Salem, Somerset, Sussex, Union, Warren

Add'l Information: Established 2001. Normal turnaround time- 1-2 business days. Full service tenant & employment screening company. Searches are performed on a national level. Statewide-county level criminal searches. Eviction data also available.

TENSTAR Corporation (Baton Rouge)

10985 N Harrell's Ferry Rd #200, Baton Rouge, LA 70816
Phone: 800-864-5154; 225-928-3877 - **Fax:** 225-273-8987
www.tenstarcorporation.com **email:** tenstarco@aol.com

Types of Records Retrieved: Criminal, Civil and Probate courts; Federal courts; Real Estate; Tax Liens/Judgments; UCC records; Vital records

Local Retrieval Area: LA-Ascension, Avoyelles, Concordia, East Baton Rouge, East Feliciana, Iberville, Livingston, Pointe Coupee, St. Helena, West Baton Rouge, West Feliciana. **Correspondent Relationships:** Louisiana and Mississippi statewide.

Add'l Information: Established 1989. Normal turnaround time- 48 hours. Expedited service available for add'l fee. Projects billed by number of names searched. Projects billed by the hour. Flat rates apply to some services. First project may require prepayment. Credit cards accepted. Will file/record documents for clients. Personal checks and bank wires accepted. They specialize in research, retrieval, recording, corporate services, notary services, abstracting, process service, litigation support, paralegal services, court reporting, investigations, risk management & claims adjusting. All services are statewide. A licensed PI in LA. Performs service of process.

TENSTAR Corporation (Crowley)

607 N Parkerson Ave, Crowley, LA 70527
Phone: 800-960-2214; 337-839-1833 - **Fax:** 337-839-8120
www.tenstarcorporation.com **email:** tenstarco@aol.com

Types of Records Retrieved: Criminal, Civil and Probate courts; Federal courts; Real Estate; Tax Liens/Judgments: UCC records; Vital records

Local Retrieval Area: LA-Acadia, Jefferson Davis. **Correspondent Relationships:** Louisiana, Missouri

Add'l Information: Established 1989. Normal turnaround time- 48 hours. 24-hour Expedited service available for an extra charge. Projects billed by number of names searched. Projects billed by the hour. First project may require prepayment. Credit cards accepted. Flat rates apply to some services. Personal checks and bank wires accepted. They specialize in research, retrieval, recording, corporate services, notary services, abstracting, process service, litigation support, paralegal services, court reporting, investigations, risk management & claims adjusting. All services are statewide. A licensed PI in LA. Performs service of process.

TENSTAR Corporation (Jackson)

1040 Hiway 49 South, #F- Box 104, Richland, MS 39218
Phone: 800-864-5154; - **Fax:** 225-273-8987
www.tenstarcorporation.com **email:** tenstarco@aol.com

Types of Records Retrieved: Criminal, Civil and Probate courts; Federal courts; Real Estate; Tax Liens/Judgments; UCC records; Vital records

Local Retrieval Area: MS-Adams, Claiborne, Copiah, George, Hancock, Harrison, Hinds, Holmes, Jackson, Jefferson, Jones, Lawrence, Lincoln, Madison, Rankin, Simpson, Warren, Yazoo. **Correspondent Relationships:** Louisiana and Mississippi statewide.

Add'l Information: Established 1989. Normal turnaround time- 48 hours. 24-hour Expedited service available for an extra charge. Projects billed by number of names searched. Projects billed by the hour. Flat rates apply to some services. Credit cards accepted. Will file/record documents for clients. Personal checks and bank wires accepted. They specialize in research, retrieval, recording, corporate services, notary services, abstracting, process service, litigation support, paralegal services, court reporting, investigations, risk management & claims adjusting. All services are statewide. A licensed PI in LA. Performs service of process.

TENSTAR Corporation (Main Office)

PO Box 82535, Lafayette, LA 70598
Phone: 800-960-2214; 337-839-1833 - **Fax:** 337-839-8120
www.tenstarcorporation.com **email:** tenstarco@aol.com

Types of Records Retrieved: Criminal, Civil and Probate courts; Federal courts; Real Estate; Tax Liens/Judgments; UCC records; Vital records

Local Retrieval Area: LA-Allen, Beauregard, Calcasieu, Caldwell, Cameron, Catahoula, East Carroll, Evangeline, Franklin, Grant, Iberia, Jackson, La Salle, Lafayette, Lincoln, Madison, Morehouse, Ouachita, Rapides, Richland, St. Landry, St. Martin, St. Mary, Tensas, Union, Vermilion, Vernon, West Carroll, Winn. **Correspondent Relationships:** Louisiana and Mississippi statewide.

Add'l Information: Established 1989. Normal turnaround time- 48 hours. 24-hour Expedited service available for an extra charge. Projects billed by number of names searched. Projects billed by the hour. Flat rates apply to some services. Credit cards accepted. Will file/record documents for clients. Personal checks and bank wires accepted. They specialize in research, retrieval, recording, corporate services, notary services, abstracting, process service, litigation support, paralegal services, court reporting, investigations, risk management & claims adjusting. All services are statewide. A licensed PI in LA. Performs service of process.

TENSTAR Corporation (New Orleans)

650 Poydras St #1400, New Orleans, LA 70130
Phone: 800-864-5154; 504-524-4267 - **Fax:** 504-524-9727
www.tenstarcorporation.com **email:** tenstarco@aol.com

Types of Records Retrieved: Criminal, Civil and Probate courts; Federal courts; Real Estate; Tax Liens/Judgments; UCC records; Vital records

Local Retrieval Area: LA-Assumption, Jefferson, Lafourche, Orleans, Plaquemines, St. Bernard, St. Charles, St. James, St. John the Baptist, St. Tammany, Tangipahoa, Terrebonne, Washington. **Correspondent Relationships:** Louisiana and Mississippi statewide.

Add'l Information: Established 1989. Normal turnaround time- 48 hours. Expedited service available. Projects billed by number of names searched. Projects billed by the hour. Flat rates apply to some services. First project may require prepayment. Credit cards accepted. Will file/record documents for clients. They specialize in research, retrieval, recording corporate services, notary services, abstracting, process service, litigation support, paralegal services, court reporting, investigations, risk management & claims adjusting. All services are statewide. A licensed PI in LA. Performs service of process.

TENSTAR Corporation (Shreveport)

6658 Youree Dr #22, Shreveport, LA 71105
Phone: 800-960-2214; - **Fax:** 337-839-8120
www.tenstarcorporation.com **email:** tenstarco@aol.com

Types of Records Retrieved: Criminal, Civil and Probate courts; Federal courts; Real Estate; Tax Liens/Judgments; UCC records; Vital records

Local Retrieval Area: LA-Bienville, Bossier, Caddo, Claiborne, DeSoto, Natchitoches, Red River, Sabine, Webster. **Correspondent Relationships:** Louisiana and Mississippi statewide.

Add'l Information: Normal turnaround time- 48 hours. 24-hour Expedited service available for an extra charge. Projects billed by number of names searched. Projects billed by the hour. Flat rates apply to some services. Credit cards accepted. Personal checks and bank wires accepted. They specialize in research, retrieval, recording, corporate services, notary services, abstracting, process service, litigation support, paralegal services, court reporting, investigations, risk management & claims adjusting. All services are statewide. A licensed PI in LA. Performs service of process.

TENSTAR Corporation (Tupelo)

1020 N Gloster St, Tupelo, MS 38801
Phone: 800-864-5154; - **Fax:** 225-273-8987
www.tenstarcorporation.com **email:** tenstarco@aol.com

Types of Records Retrieved: Criminal, Civil and Probate courts; Federal courts; Real Estate; Tax Liens/Judgments; UCC records; Vital records

Local Retrieval Area: MS-Chickasaw, Grenada, Itawamba, Lee, Monroe, Montgomery, Pontotoc, Prentiss, Tippah, Union, Webster, Yalobusha. **Correspondent Relationships:** Louisiana and Mississippi statewide.

Add'l Information: Established 1989. Normal turnaround time- 48 hours. 24-hour Expedited service available for an extra charge. Projects billed by number of names searched. Projects billed by the hour. Flat rates apply to some services. Credit cards accepted. Will file/record documents for clients. Personal checks and bank wires accepted. They specialize in research, retrieval, recording, corporate services, notary services, abstracting, process service, litigation support, paralegal services, court reporting, investigations, risk management & claims adjusting. All services are statewide. A licensed PI in LA. Performs service of process.

Territorial Title

PO Box 987, 919 Douglas Ave, Las Vegas, NM 87701
Phone: 505-425-3563 - **Fax:** 505-425-9637
www.territorialtitle.com **email:** questions@territorialtitle.com

Types of Records Retrieved: Real Estate; Tax Liens/Judgments; Probate courts; UCC records; Vital records

Local Retrieval Area: NM-Guadalupe, Mora, San Miguel

Add'l Information: Normal turnaround time- 1 week for San Miguel, 4 weeks for Mora, and 2 weeks for Guadalupe. Projects billed by the hour. Will file/record documents for clients. They specialize in title insurance and closings.

Teter Security Assoc Inc

PO Box 8212, Saginaw, MI 48608
Phone: 800-726-5959; gatpi@aol.com

Types of Records Retrieved: Criminal, Civil and Probate courts; Federal courts; Tax Liens/Judgments

Local Retrieval Area: MI-Bay, Midland, Saginaw

Add'l Information: Established 1983. Normal turnaround time- 48 hours. Projects billed by number of names searched. First project may require prepayment. They specialize in pre-employment investigations, background investigations, surveillance, and records research. A licensed PI in MI.

Tex Research

5225 Rio Bravo Dr, Arlington, TX 76017
Phone: 817-472-5997, cell- 682-551-5306 - **Fax:** 817-466-2889
ddtexx@sbcglobal.net

Types of Records Retrieved: Criminal and Civil courts

Local Retrieval Area: TX-Collin, Tarrant. **Correspondents in:** Texas.

Add'l Information: Established 1999. Normal turnaround time- 24-48 hours. Projects billed by number of names searched. Billed 1st of month, payment due net 15 days. They specialize in criminal and civil record searches. Collin & Tarrant County records can be returned same day.

Texas Abstract Services

1340 Prince St, Houston, TX 77008
Phone: 866-290-3743; 713-221-1757 - **Fax:** 713-221-1756
txabstra@swbell.net

Records Retrieved: Real Estate; Tax Liens/Judgments; Probate courts

Local Retrieval Area: TX-Fort Bend, Harris. **Correspondent Relationships:** nationwide.

Add'l Information: Established 1985. Normal turnaround time- 1-3 days. Flat fee per order, quoted in advance. First project may require prepayment. Will file/record documents for clients. They are a full service abstract company, specializing in searches for home equity and home improvement loans, right-of-ways, oil and gas research as well as environmental property assessments.

Texas Civil Process

1650 S Brownlee Blvd, Corpus Christi, TX 78404
800-976-9595; 361-887-9595; cell- 361-946-3217 - **Fax:** 361-887-9597
www.texascivilprocess.net **email:** bddeel.tcp@interconnect.net

Types of Records Retrieved: Criminal, Civil and Probate courts; Federal courts; Real Estate; Tax Liens/Judgments; UCC records; Vital records

Local Retrieval Area: TX-Aransas, Bee, Duval, Jim Wells, Kleberg, Live Oak, Nueces, Refugio, San Patricio. **Correspondent Relationships:** Bexar, Travis, Harris, Tarrant, Dallas, McMullen, Cameron, Hidalgo, Williamson, Taylor.

Add'l Information: Established 1980. Normal turnaround time- 24-48 hours. Projects billed by number of names searched. First project may require prepayment. Invoices are net 30 days. They specialize in process service, record research and skiptracing. Licensed private investigator on staff. Is a mobile notary and state-certified supreme court process server. A licensed PI in TX. Performs service of process.

Texas Detective.com

PO Box 851, Iowa Park, TX 76367
Phone: 940-592-7000 - **Fax:** 940-592-1013
www.texasdetective.com **email:** records@texasdetective.com

Types of Records Retrieved: Criminal, Civil and Probate courts; Federal courts; Real Estate; Tax Liens/Judgments; UCC records; Vital records

Local Retrieval Area: TX-Archer, Clay, Wichita, Wilbarger. **Correspondent Relationships:** nationwide.

Add'l Information: Established 1996. Normal turnaround time- 72 hours. Expedited service available. Projects billed by number of names searched. All projects require prepayment. Credit cards accepted. PayPal payments accepted. They are a licensed private investigator (#A10709) who takes care of your needs. For peace of mind leave the search to them. A licensed PI in TX. Performs service of process.

Texas Industrial Security Inc

703 McKinney Ave #106, Dallas, TX 75202-1003
Phone: 214-634-2791 - **Fax:** 214-634-2793
www.txsecurity.com **email:** dclines@sbcglobal.net

Types of Records Retrieved: Criminal, Civil and Probate courts; Federal courts; Tax Liens/Judgments

Local Retrieval Area: TX-Bexar, Dallas, Tarrant

Add'l Information: Normal turnaround time- 2-5 days. Projects billed by number of records located. Projects billed by the hour. All projects require $100.00 retainer fee per case. They specialize in criminal, civil and domestic cases. Also do background investigation and surveillance.

Texas Research

2301 Austin Ave, Brownwood, TX 76804
Phone: 325-646-2890 - **Fax:** 325-646-3035
elling40@hotmail.com

Types of Records Retrieved: Criminal, Civil and Probate courts; Real Estate; Tax Liens/Judgments; UCC records

Local Retrieval Area: TX-Bee, Brown, Lubbock, Taylor

Add'l Information: Normal turnaround time- 24 hours for civil and criminal records; all other records 2-3 days. Projects billed by number of names searched. Fee varies dependent on type of search. Other area counties available on a special order basis. Also specializes in real estate in Brown, Callahan, Coleman, Comanche, Eastland, McCulloch, Mills, San Saba, Taylor and other Central Texas counties.

TexDirect

342 N Ridge, New Braunfels, TX 78132
Phone: 830-964-5233 - **Fax:** 830-964-5234
mproue@satx.rr.com

Types of Records Retrieved: Criminal, Civil and Probate courts; Real Estate; Tax Liens/Judgments; UCC records

Local Retrieval Area: TX-Bexar, Caldwell, Comal, Gonzales, Guadalupe, Hays. **Correspondent Relationships:** statewide.

Texsearch #A09479

2895 Gage Rd, Sherman, TX 75092-4950
Phone: 903-786-4636 - **Fax:** 903-786-3363
www.texsearch.net **email:** serena@texsearch.net

Types of Records Retrieved: Criminal and Civil courts; Federal courts; Real Estate; Tax Liens/Judgments; UCC records

Local Retrieval Area: TX-Bell, Bexar, Cameron, Collin, Comal, Cooke, Dallas, Denton, Ector, Fannin, Grayson, Gregg, Guadalupe, Harris, Hays, Hidalgo, Kaufman, McLennan, Midland, Nueces, Potter, Randall, Rockwall, Tarrant, Tom Green, Travis, Wichita, Williamson. **Correspondent Relationships:** statewide.

Add'l Information: Established 1997. Normal turnaround time- 24 hours or less. Projects billed by number of names searched. They accept payments via PayPal (www.paypal.com) and bill monthly. First project may require prepayment. Will file/record documents for clients. Billed monthly payable 30 days net. A licensed investigative company that specializes in public record retrieval in any TX county, at county, state level. Services include court record searches, real estate, asset/lien, property ownership, motor vehicle ownership & driving records. A licensed PI in TX. Performs service of process.

Thalken Title Co

PO Box 307, 520 N Spruce, Ogallala, NE 69153
Phone: 308-284-3972 - **Fax:** 308-284-6802

Types of Records Retrieved: Civil courts; Real Estate; Tax Liens/Judgments; UCC records

Local Retrieval Area: NE-Arthur, Chase, Cherry, Deuel, Garden, Grant, Keith, Perkins, Sheridan. **Correspondent Relationships:** Banner, Cheyenne, Kimball, Morrill counties NE.

Add'l Information: Established 1962. Normal turnaround time- 1 day for Keith; 2-5 days for the other counties. Fee basis varies by type of transaction. First project may require prepayment. Will file/record documents for clients. They specialize in title insurance searches. Will file/record real estate documents if fees are attached and made out to correct county clerk.

The Amherst Group

4804 Arlington Ave #A, Riverside, CA 92504
Phone: 800-521-0237; 951-785-5777 - **Fax:** 951-785-5888
www.amherst-group.com **email:** amherst@pe.net

Types of Records Retrieved: Criminal, Civil and Probate courts; Federal courts; Real Estate; Tax Liens/Judgments; UCC records; Vital records

Local Retrieval Area: CA-Alameda, Contra Costa, Imperial, Los Angeles, Marin, Napa, Orange, Riverside, Sacramento, San Bernardino, San Diego, San Francisco, Santa Barbara, Santa Clara, Sonoma, Ventura. **Correspondent Relationships:** nationwide.

Add'l Information: Established 1982. Normal turnaround time- 24-48 hours. Projects billed by number of names searched. Credit cards accepted. Terms: net 20 days. They specialize in national criminal, credit and motor vehicle records. They also have a national service offering background checks, tenant screening and general information services.

The Berkana Firm LLC

123 N College Ave #200, Ft Collins, CO 80524
Phone: 970-669-2179 - **Fax:** 970-212-4739
www.theberkanafirm.com **email:** lisa@theberkanafirm.com

Types of Records Retrieved: Criminal, Civil and Probate courts; Federal courts; Real Estate; Tax Liens/Judgments; UCC records; Vital records

Local Retrieval Area: CO-Larimer, Weld

Add'l info: Established 2006. Turnaround time- 3 days. Expedite services available for additional fees. Projects billed by number of names searched. First project may require prepayment. Credit cards accepted. Quantity discounts available. They specialize in litigation investigations, corporate, licensing/registration, civil and criminal. Statewide Colorado available. Thorough and professional Performs service of process.

The Copy Shop of Aberdeen

115B E Commerce St, Aberdeen, MS 39730
Phone: 662-369-4428 - **Fax:** 662-369-4112 copyshop@aberdeen.ms

Types of Records Retrieved: Civil courts; Federal courts

Local Retrieval Area: MS-Monroe

Add'l Information: Established 2001. Normal turnaround time- Same day. Expedited service available, add 10%. Projects billed by number of records located. Projects billed by the hour. First project may require prepayment. Credit cards accepted. Their primary focus is copy service (plus color), including litigation copying. Owner is former legal secretary (3 years) and medical researcher (18 years).

The Daily Report

310 H St, Bakersfield, CA 93304-2914
Phone: 800-803-6127; 661-322-3226 - **Fax:** 661-322-9084
www.thedailyreport.com **email:** annem@thedailyreport.com

Types of Records Retrieved: Civil and Probate courts; Real Estate; Tax Liens/Judgments; UCC records; Vital records

Local Retrieval Area: CA-Kern

Add'l Information: Established 1907. Normal turnaround time- 2 days. Projects billed by the hour. Credit cards accepted. Will file/record documents for clients. They specialize in legal advertising. They also search at the municipal court level, superior court and county recorder's office. The web site offers a searchable database with up-to-date information at www.thedailyreport.com.

The Discovery Group Inc

1595 Main St, Southhaven, MS 38671
Phone: 662-280-1576 - **Fax:** 662-280-1607 jf1534@aol.com

Types of Records Retrieved: Criminal, Civil and Probate courts; Federal courts; Tax Liens/Judgments; UCC records; Vital records

Local Retrieval Area: AR-Crittenden; MS-Coahoma, De Soto, Lafayette, Marshall, Quitman, Tate, Tunica; TN-Shelby. **Correspondent Relationships:** nationwide.

Add'l Information: Established 1996. Normal turnaround time- 24-48 hours. First project may require prepayment. Credit cards accepted. They specialize fast, reliable record searching services. Full service in all types of record retrieval. A licensed PI in TN.

The Docket Clerk LLC

77 Tunxis Ave, Bloomfield, CT 06002-2005
Phone: 866-758-2683; 860-242-2684 - **Fax:** 860-242-2646
www.thedocketclerk.com **email:** admin@thedocketclerk.com

Types of Records Retrieved: Criminal, Civil and Probate courts; Federal courts; Real Estate; Tax Liens/Judgments; UCC records; Vital records

Local Retrieval Area: CT-all counties. **Correspondents:** nationwide.

Add'l Information: Established 1999. Normal turnaround time- same day/24 hours. Projects billed by number of names searched. First project may require prepayment. Will file/record documents for clients. Terms are net 30 days. They specialize in researching and obtaining publicly filed documents, performing due diligence, litigation/judgment searches, background investigations and pre-employment services. They also provide nationwide document retrieval and brokering svcs.

The Fatman Intl Private Detective Service

6638 Cascade Rd SE, Grand Rapids, MI 49546-6896
Phone: 616-949-1790 - **Fax:** 616-949-4800
www.fatmanpi.com **email:** superprivateye@prodigy.net

Types of Records Retrieved: Criminal, Civil and Probate courts; Federal courts; Real Estate; Tax Liens/Judgments; UCC records; Vital records

Local Retrieval Area: MI-Barry, Calhoun, Kent, Ottawa. **Correspondent Relationships:** worldwide.

Add'l Information: Established 1955. Normal turnaround time- 1-2 days. Fee basis varies by type of transaction. First project may require prepayment. Will file/record documents for clients. They ask for a retainer. They specialize in investigations. They have an office in Europe, located in Wassenaar, The Netherlands. A licensed PI in MI. Performs service of process.

The Gordon Company of Colby

450 N Franklin, Colby, KS 67701-0489
Phone: 785-462-7555 - **Fax:** 785-462-2099
ggordon@st-tel.net

Types of Records Retrieved: Criminal, Civil and Probate courts; Real Estate; Tax Liens/Judgments; UCC records

Local Retrieval Area: KS-Thomas

Add'l Information: Established 1885. Normal turnaround time- 24 hours. Projects billed by number of names searched. Projects billed by number of records located. Projects billed by the hour. Will file/record documents for clients. Personal checks are accepted. Will invoice at time of provided service. They specialize in title insurance searches, abstracts, certificates of title and appraisals.

The Henry Agency

7527 Farm Gate Dr, Charlotte, NC 28215
Phone: 704-526-5030 piworking@aol.com
Records Retrieved: Criminal, Civil and Probate courts; Federal District courts; Real Estate; Tax Liens/Judgments; UCC records; Vital records
Local Retrieval Area: NC-Cabarrus, Gaston, Iredell, Lincoln, Mecklenburg, Stanly, Union. **Correspondent Relationships:** statewide and SC.
Add'l Information: Established 1981. Normal turnaround time- 2 days. Expedited service available. Projects billed by number of names searched. All projects require prepayment. They specialize in general investigations, record retrieval and SOP. A licensed PI in NC. Performs service of process.

The Home Abstract & Title Co Inc

2380 Washington Blvd #200, Ogden, UT 84401
Phone: 800-699-7861; 801-621-7861 - **Fax:** 801-621-7850
Types of Records Retrieved: Civil and Probate courts; Real Estate; Tax Liens/Judgments; UCC records
Local Retrieval Area: UT-Box Elder, Davis, Morgan, Weber
Add'l Information: Established 1908. Normal turnaround time- 48 hours. Projects billed by number of names searched. First project may require prepayment. Will file/record documents for clients. Terms: net 15 days. Personal checks are accepted. They specialize in title insurance and escrow closing service. They have a Utah certified residential appraiser of counsel.

The Legal Source Attorney Services

PO Box 1542, Chico, CA 95927
Phone: 800-786-8163; 530-895-8163 - **Fax:** 530-891-6616
Types of Records Retrieved: Criminal and Civil courts
Local Retrieval Area: CA-Butte, Colusa, Glenn, Lassen, Nevada, Plumas, Sacramento, Shasta, Sutter, Tehama, Yuba. **Correspondent Relationships:** California, Nevada, Oregon.
Add'l Information: Established 1980. Normal turnaround time- 7 to 15 days for remote counties. Expedited service available. Projects billed by number of records located. Charge is by location and by the page. First project may require prepayment. Terms: net 30 days. They prepare subpoenas to retrieve and photocopy records. They are a registered process server and certified notary public. also specialize in workers' comp records.

The McDowell Agency Inc

1714 University Ave W, St Paul, MN 55104
Phone: 651-644-3880 - **Fax:** 651-644-3877
www.mcdowellagency.com **email:** kmf@mcdowellagency.com
Types of Records Retrieved: Criminal, Civil and Probate courts; Federal courts; Real Estate; Tax Liens/Judgments; UCC records; Vital records
Local Retrieval Area: MN-Dakota, Hennepin, Ramsey, Washington
Add'l Information: Established 1984. Normal turnaround time- 24-72 hours. Projects billed by number of names searched. Credit cards accepted. Will file/record documents for clients. Volume discounts. They are a full service licensed private detective agency with over 20 years of experience, specializing in pre-employment screening and courthouse record retrieval. A licensed PI in MN. Performs service of process.

The Paper Chase - CO

PO Box 520, Greeley, CO 80632
Phone: 970-350-1008 - **Fax:** 970-352-1828 cmason123@comcast.net
Types of Records Retrieved: Criminal, Civil and Probate courts; Federal courts; Real Estate; Tax Liens/Judgments; UCC records; Vital records
Local Retrieval Area: CO-Boulder, Larimer, Weld
Add'l Information: Established 1988. Normal turnaround time- 24-48 hours. Projects billed by the hour. Will file/record documents for clients. They specialize in counties north of Denver. Performs service of process.

The Paper Chase - KY

2709 Kenwood Dr, Hopkinsville, KY 42240
Phone: 270-886-0367; Fax-same
Types of Records Retrieved: Criminal and Civil courts
Local Retrieval Area: KY-Christian
Add'l Information: Normal turnaround time- 24-48 hours. First project may require prepayment. She specializes in Christian County records.

The Partnership

1617 Fannin St #3015, Houston, TX 77002-7643
Phone: 877-558-9928; 713-695-9928 - **Fax:** 877-914-6671; 713-697-6671
jmbrum@swbell.net
Types of Records Retrieved: Criminal and Civil courts; US District court; UCC records; Tax Liens/Judgments
Local Retrieval Area: TX-Galveston, Hardin, Harris, Jefferson, Montgomery, Orange
Add'l Information: Established 1979. Normal turnaround time- 24-48 hours. They invoice once a month. They specialize in criminal and civil county court records. Mobile phone is 713-825-9953. A licensed PI in CA. Performs service of process.

The Pettit Company

12807 Rossmere Ct, Midlothian, VA 23113
Phone: 800-752-6158; 804-379-2462 - **Fax:** 800-236-2859; 804-379-3217
www.pettitcompany.com **email:** orders@pettitcompany.com
Types of Records Retrieved: Criminal, Civil and Probate courts; Federal courts; Real Estate; Tax Liens/Judgments; UCC records
Local Retrieval Area: VA-Chesterfield, Colonial Heights City, Hanover, Henrico, Hopewell City, Petersburg City, Powhatan, Richmond City. **Correspondent Relationships:** nationwide.
Add'l Information: Established 1994. Normal turnaround time- 1-2 days. Projects billed by number of names searched. Will file/record documents for clients. Terms: net 30 days. They specialize in providing quick, accurate and inexpensive personal service. They also offer filing services nationwide. Call to discuss special needs.

The Public Record Source

PO Box 6212, Peoria, AZ 85385-6212
Phone: 623-773-3997 - **Fax:** 623-773-2861 azsherri@aol.com
Types of Records Retrieved: Criminal, Civil and Probate courts; Tax Liens/Judgments; UCC records; Vital records
Local Retrieval Area: AZ-all counties. **Correspondents:** nationwide.
Add'l Information: Established 1997. Normal turnaround time- 24 hours. Projects billed by number of names searched. First project may require prepayment. They specialize in public record research, have been doing research since 1985. A licensed PI in AZ pending.

The R M Jaqua Abstract Co

Box 665, St Francis, KS 67756
Phone: 785-332-3041 - **Fax:** 785-332-2595
Types of Records Retrieved: Criminal, Civil and Probate courts; Federal courts; Real Estate; Tax Liens/Judgments; UCC records
Local Retrieval Area: KS-Cheyenne
Add'l Information: Established 1886. Normal turnaround time- within 48 hours. Projects billed by number of names searched. Will file/record documents for clients. Personal checks accepted.

The Records Reviewer Inc

243 Wimbledon Lake Dr, Plantation, FL 33324-2445
Phone: 305-934-4920 - **Fax:** 954-252-2245 recrev@bellsouth.net
Types of Records Retrieved: Criminal, Civil and Probate courts; Federal courts; Real Estate; Tax Liens/Judgments; UCC records
Local Retrieval Area: FL-Broward, Dade, Palm Beach
Add'l Information: Established 1984. Normal turnaround time- 48 hours or less. Expedited service available. Projects billed by number of names searched. They may bill by the 1/4 hour. First project may require prepayment. They specialize in bankruptcy, environmental searches,

criminal searches current owner searches and due diligence. They also record documents in Dade, Broward and Palm Beach, Fl counties.

The Research Staff Inc

5718 Hewitt St, Houston, TX 77092-5125
Phone: 800-822-3584; 713-688-3584 - **Fax:** 713-688-1121 or 713-686-4980
www.researchstaffonline.com **email:** carla@researchstaffonline.com

Types of Records Retrieved: Criminal, Civil and Probate courts; Federal courts; Real Estate; Tax Liens/Judgments; UCC records

Local Retrieval Area: TX-Austin, Brazoria, Brazos, Chambers, Fort Bend, Galveston, Hardin, Harris, Jefferson, Liberty, Matagorda, Montgomery, Orange, Waller, Wharton. **Correspondent Relationships:** Texas.

Add'l Information: Established 1985. Normal turnaround time- 24-48 hours. Expedited service available. Projects billed by number of names searched. First project may require prepayment. Credit cards accepted. Will file/record documents for clients. Since 1985 they have specialized in property reports (all kinds), specific name searches, UCC, T/L, A/J, business closings, asset searches and courts (all levels). Will design reports for special projects.

The Right Search

810 E Aldrich, MPB 413, Bolivar, MO 65613
Phone: 417-852-7097 - **Fax:** 417-852-1200 rtbarr@centurytel.net

Types of Records Retrieved: Civil and Probate courts; Real Estate; Tax Liens/Judgments; UCC records

Local Retrieval Area: MO-Benton, Greene, Hickory, Polk, St. Clair

Add'l Information: Established 1998. Normal turnaround time- same day/24 hours depending on when request received. Invoices monthly. In business for 10 years with 4 employees, they do title searches and offer excellent turnaround time. They do UCC Federal/State tax liens, current owner, deed reports, and document retrieval; licensed & E&O covered. Specialize in 40-yr or more searches.

The Searchers-NKA Hackman Abstracts Inc

1050 NW 96th Pl, Chiefland, FL 32626
Phone: 352-493-0101 - **Fax:** 352-493-8004 searchers_34602@yahoo.com

Types of Records Retrieved: Real Estate; Tax Liens/Judgments; Probate courts; UCC records

Local Retrieval Area: FL-Alachua, Citrus, Dixie, Gilchrist, Hernando, Levy, Marion, Pasco, Sumter, Taylor, Volusia

Add'l Information: Established 2000. Normal turnaround time- 24-36 hours. Projects are billed by the type of search requested. First project may require prepayment. Will file/record documents for clients. They do full title search, current owner, deed reports and document retrieval. Also do tax liens, judgment, commercial searches and UCC searches at reasonable fees.

The Title Co Inc (Eau Claire)

3408 Oakwood Mall Dr, Eau Claire, WI 54701
Phone: 800-848-4853; 715-838-2800 - **Fax:** 877-838-2810; 715-838-2810
www.titleco.com **email:** mike@titleco.com

Types of Records Retrieved: Real Estate; Tax Liens/Judgments; Probate courts; UCC records

Local Retrieval Area: WI-Buffalo, Chippewa, Clark, Dunn, Eau Claire, Pepin, Pierce. **Correspondent Relationships:** WI, MN, IA.

Add'l Information: Established 1985. Normal turnaround time- variable, depending on project. Projects billed by number of names searched. Title insurance search fees are preset. First project may require prepayment. Credit cards accepted. Will file/record documents for clients. Visa, MasterCard and Discover are accepted. They specialize in title insurance and title reports.

The Title Co Inc (Iowa)

PO Box 256, Sibley, IA 51249-0256
Phone: 712-754-2284 - **Fax:** 712-754-3195 titleco@hickorytech.net

Types of Records Retrieved: Real Estate; Tax Liens/Judgments; UCC records; Probate courts; Federal District courts

Local Retrieval Area: IA-Osceola

Add'l info: Established 1967. Normal turnaround time- 1-3 days. Fee basis will vary by the type of project. First project may require prepayment. Will file/record documents for clients. They specialize in abstracts.

The Title Co Inc (La Crosse)

750 N 3rd St #A, La Crosse, WI 54601
Phone: 800-788-4853; 608-791-2000 - **Fax:** 888-791-2015; 608-791-2015
www.titleco.com **email:** mike@titleco.com

Types of Records Retrieved: Real Estate; Tax Liens/Judgments; Probate courts; Federal courts; UCC records

Local Retrieval Area: MN-Houston; WI-La Crosse, Trempealeau. **Correspondent Relationships:** Wisconsin and Iowa.

Add'l Information: Normal turnaround time- variable, depending on project. Projects billed by number of names searched. Title insurance fees are preset. First project may require prepayment. Credit cards accepted. They are branch office that visits both WI and MN, and specialize in title insurance and reports.

The Title Co Inc (Prairie Du Chien WI)

PO Box 408, 124 E Blackhawk Ave, Praire Du Chien, WI 53821
Phone: 888-918-4853; 608-326-7330 - **Fax:** 877-918-4853; 608-326-7631
www.titleco.com **email:** pdc@titleco.com

Types of Records Retrieved: Civil and Probate courts; Federal courts; Real Estate; Tax Liens/Judgments; UCC records; Vital records

Local Retrieval Area: IA-all counties with a few exceptions; WI-Crawford, Grant, Richland

Add'l Information: Normal turnaround time- variable, depending on project. Projects billed by number of names searched. Title insurance search fees are preset. First project may require prepayment. Credit cards accepted. They specialize in title insurance and reports in SW Wisconsin, all of Iowa.

The Title Co Inc (Viroqua)

210 N Main St, Viroqua, WI 54665
Phone: 800-538-4853; 608-637-3700 - **Fax:** 877-637-3700; 608-637-3799
www.titleco.com **email:** mike@titleco.com

Types of Records Retrieved: Civil and Probate courts; Federal courts; Real Estate; Tax Liens/Judgments; UCC records

Local Retrieval: WI-Vernon. **Correspondent Relationships:** WI, MN, IA.

Add'l Information: Normal turnaround time- variable, depending on project. Projects billed by number of names searched. Title insurance search fees are preset. First project may require prepayment. Credit cards accepted. They specialize in title insurance and reports.

Thomas Legal Support Service

PO Box 80, Walport, OR 97394
Phone: 541-563-3345 - **Fax:** 541-563-4046 tai-pi@pioneer.net

Types of Records Retrieved: Criminal and Civil courts

Local Retrieval Area: OR-Lane (coastal areas-Florence), Lincoln, Tillamook

Add'l Information: Established 2001. First project may require prepayment. They also provide court filings, photocopying, skiptracing, and private investigations. For Lane county, they serve only the Pacific coast area. A licensed PI in OR. Performs service of process.

Thomas Research Services

1019 Tekamah Ln, Papillion, NE 68046
Phone: 402-339-7291 - **Fax:** 402-339-0051

Types of Records Retrieved: Criminal and Civil courts; Federal courts; Tax Liens/Judgments; UCC records **Local Retrieval Area:** IA-Harrison, Mills, Pottawattamie; NE-Cass, Douglas, Otoe, Sarpy, Washington. **Correspondent Relationships:** Audubon, Cass, Davis, Dodge, Shelby, Saunders counties IA.

Add'l Information: Established 1993. Normal turnaround time- 24-48 hours. Expedited service available. Projects billed by number of names searched. Will file/record documents for clients. Personal checks accepted. Special interest of genealogy. She is compiling a book on Audubon county, IA cemetery inscriptions, and performs research for maiden and other married names. She also goes to the federal building in Douglas County. Performs service of process.

Julie L Thomas

7645 N Crestview Rd, Stillman Valley, IL 61084

Phone: 815-234-4172 - **Fax:** 815-234-4172 julieilresearch@rockford.com

Types of Records Retrieved: Criminal and Civil courts

Local Retrieval Area: IL-Boone, De Kalb, Jo Daviess, Kane, Kendall, Ogle, Stephenson, Winnebago. **Correspondent Relationships:** Du Page, Lake, McHenry, Will counties IL.

Add'l Information: Established 1994. Normal turnaround time- same day if requested before 8AM CST in most cases. Projects billed by number of names searched. Will file/record documents for clients. Will bill at end of month. Will file UCC & real estate documents in Boone, Ogle, Stephenson, and Winnebago counties only, on same or next day basis.

Thompson & Hollingsworth PA

116 E 2nd St, Forest, MS 39074

Phone: 601-469-3411 - **Fax:** 601-469-3020

Types of Records Retrieved: Criminal, Civil and Probate courts; Real Estate; Tax Liens/Judgments; UCC records; Vital records

Local Retrieval Area: MS-Scott, Smith

Add'l Information: Established 1947. Normal turnaround time- 1 day. Projects billed by the hour. First project may require prepayment. They are in general practice. They specialize in marriage/divorce searches.

Thompson Research

4024 Braddock St, Martinez, GA 30907

Phone: 706-860-4181 - **Fax:** 706-228-4464

Types of Records Retrieved: Real Estate; Tax Liens/Judgments

Local Retrieval Area: GA-Burke, Lincoln, McDuffie, Richmond

Add'l Information: Established 1995. Normal turnaround time- same day to 24 hours. Flat rate per county. Will file/record documents for clients. They are real estate specialists fully E&O insured. Excellent fast turnaround time, and will do filings.

Deborah W Thompson

268 Bush St #3326, San Francisco, CA 94104

Phone: 415-272-5773 - **Fax:** 866-387-2280 abstractordeb@gmail.com

Types of Records Retrieved: Criminal and Civil courts; Real Estate; Tax Liens/Judgments; UCC records

Local Retrieval Area: CA-San Francisco; NY-Kings, New York, Queens

Add'l Information: Established 2003. Normal turnaround time- 24-48 hours. Expedited service available. Projects billed by number of names searched. Negotiable. They pride themselves on delivering accurate and speedy service with a smile. Providing document retrieval, current owner searches, recordings and civil and criminal searches. Ask about their other services.

Ticor Title Roseburg

PO Box 59, Roseburg, OR 97470

Phone: 800-660-1146; 541-673-1146 - **Fax:** 541-673-2118

www.ticortitlenw.com **Types of Records Retrieved:** Criminal, Civil and Probate courts; Real Estate; Tax Liens/Judgments; UCC records

Local Retrieval Area: OR-Douglas

Add'l Information: Established 1985. Normal turnaround time- 2-3 days. First project may require prepayment. Formerly Key Title, they specialize in real estate, title insurance, escrow services, 1031 exchanges, lender insurance and escrow collections.

Timely Documents

15406 NE 47th Circle, Vancouver, WA 98682-6093

Phone: 360-944-1082 - **Fax:** 877-463-6809;

www.timelydocuments.com **email:** kris@timelydocuments.com

Types of Records Retrieved: Civil and Probate courts; Real Estate; Tax Liens/Judgments; UCC records

Local Retrieval Area: OR-Clackamas, Multnomah, Washington; WA-Clark. **Correspondent Relationships:** Oregon, Washington, and Idaho.

Add'l Information: Established 2001. Normal turnaround time- 1-4 days. Projects billed by number of names searched. As contract bidded. They perform accurate, reliable real estate and court records searches of all types in most counties in Oregon and Washington states. They specialize in research, retrieval and recording.

Tippecanoe Title Services Inc

415 Columbia St, Lafayette, IN 47901

Phone: 888-423-2457; 765-423-2457 - **Fax:** 765-742-0194

www.tiptitle.com **email:** tts@tiptitle.com

Types of Records Retrieved: Criminal, Civil and Probate courts; Real Estate; Tax Liens/Judgments; UCC records

Local Retrieval Area: IN-Benton, Boone, Carroll, Cass, Clinton, Fountain, Hamilton, Hendricks, Howard, Jasper, Marion, Montgomery, Newton, Parke, Tippecanoe, Vermillion, Warren, White

Add'l Information: Established 1987. Normal turnaround time- 3-4 days for Tippecanoe; 5-7 days for other counties. Projects billed by the hour. Will file/record documents for clients. They specialize in land title insurance, real estate closings and title searches.

Title Abstracts & Document Services

9 Spyglass Dr, Aiken, SC 29803

Phone: 803-649-2500, Fax- same deannaromeo_tads@bellsouth.net

Types of Records Retrieved: Criminal, Civil and Probate courts; Federal courts; Real Estate; Tax Liens/Judgments; UCC records; Vital records

Local Retrieval Area: SC-Aiken, Allendale, Bamberg, Barnwell, Edgefield, Lexington, Newberry, Orangeburg, Richland. **Correspondent Relationships:** SC, NC, GA.

Add'l Information: Established 1990. Normal turnaround time- 24-48 hours. Projects billed by number of names searched. First project may require prepayment. Invoices monthly. Their company offers professional & detail perfect work. All reports are typed out on computer for easier reading and understanding.

Title Company of Denver

2200 S Valley Hwy #B, Denver, CO 80222-5035

Phone: 303-369-5443 www.tcod.com

Types of Records Retrieved: Real Estate; Tax Liens/Judgments

Local Retrieval Area: CO-Adams, Arapahoe, Boulder, Broomfield, Denver, Douglas, El Paso, Elbert, Jefferson, Larimer, Weld

Add'l Information: Established 1994. Normal turnaround time- 7 days. Retainer and fee agreement required prior to searches. They specialize in title underwriting and legal services.

The Title Company

PO Box 1304, 213 E 4th Ave, Mitchell, SD 57301

Phone: 605-996-4900 - **Fax:** 605-996-3270

Types of Records Retrieved: Civil courts; Real Estate; Tax Liens/Judgments

Local Retrieval Area: SD-Davison, Hanson

Add'l Information: Established 1800s. First project may require prepayment. They specialize in real estate.

Title Court Service

1305 Franklin St #501, Oakland, CA 94612

Phone: 510-763-0975 - **Fax:** 510-763-0802

www.titlecourt.com **email:** tcsala@pacbell.net

Types of Records Retrieved: Civil and Probate courts; Federal courts; Real Estate; Tax Liens/Judgments; UCC records; Vital records

Local Retrieval Area: CA-all counties. **Correspondent Relationships:** statewide; all US Bankruptcy Courts.

Add'l Information: Established 1978. Normal turnaround time- 24-48 hours. Projects billed by number of names searched. First project may require prepayment. Credit cards accepted. Will file/record documents for clients. They specialize in court research and document retrieval in all the CA counties, document recordings, building and safety permits and current owner searches.

Title Express Inc

4940 Davy Crockett Pky, Morristown, TN 37813

Phone: 423-587-9886 - **Fax:** 423-587-5682 titleexpress@charter.net

Types of Records Retrieved: Criminal, Civil and Probate courts; Real Estate; Tax Liens/Judgments; UCC records

Local Retrieval Area: TN-Claiborne, Cocke, Greene, Hamblen, Hawkins, Jefferson, Sevier

Add'l Information: Established 1995. Normal turnaround time- 48 hours. Projects billed by number of names searched. First project may require prepayment. Will file/record documents for clients. They specialize in real estate title examinations and litigation research.

Title Guaranty & Trust of Chattanooga

617 Walnut St, Chattanooga, TN 37402
Phone: 423-266-5751 - **Fax:** 423-266-3525

Types of Records Retrieved: Civil and Probate courts; Federal courts; Real Estate; Tax Liens/Judgments; UCC records

Local Retrieval Area: AL-Cherokee, De Kalb, Houston; GA-Catoosa, Chattooga, Dade, Fannin, Gilmer, Gordon, Murray, Walker, Whitfield; TN-Bledsoe, Bradley, Coffee, Franklin, Grundy, Hamilton, Loudon, McMinn, Marion, Meigs, Monroe, Polk, Rhea, Sequatchie, Van Buren,. **Correspondent Relationships:** nationwide.

Add'l Information: Established 1887. Normal turnaround time- 2 days. Projects billed by the hour. First project may require prepayment. Will file/record documents for clients. They specialize in title insurance. They have a second office at: 7042 Lee Hwy #102, Chattanooga, TN 37321 (423-892-7914, fax 423-855-1288).

Title Info

10103 Westridge Rd, Ft. Worth, TX 76126-1709
Phone: 817-244-7757 - **Fax:** 817-244-7455

Records Retrieved: Real Estate; Tax Liens/Judgments; Probate courts

Local Retrieval Area: TX-Collin, Dallas, Denton, Johnson, Parker, Tarrant. **Correspondent Relationships:** Ellis, Ft. Bend, Harris, Hood, Travis, Williamson counties TX.

Add'l info: Established 1985. Turnaround time- 24 hours. Projects billed by number of names searched. Net 30 days. They specialize in property searches, environmental chains of title, judgment and tax lien searches.

Title Information Services

2304 Ash St, Billings, MT 59101-0505
Phone: 800-443-7874; 406-256-7224 - **Fax:** 406-248-6478
www.dwwtitles.com   **email:** dwwtitles@dwwtitles.com

Types of Records Retrieved: Civil and Probate courts; Real Estate; Tax Liens/Judgments; UCC records; Vital records

Local Retrieval Area: MT-Yellowstone

Add'l Information: Established 1952. Normal turnaround time- 24 hours days. Out of county can be done in 1 week. Charges vary per service. Will file/record documents for clients. They specialize in abstracts of title and mineral title research and O&E reports.

Title Runners

3083 1/2 Calle Mariposa, Santa Barbara, CA 93105-2740
Phone: 805-569-6939 - **Fax:** 805-569-6962   hancey@silcom.com

Types of Records Retrieved: Bankruptcy court; Real Estate; Tax Liens/Judgments; UCC records; Vital records

Local Retrieval Area: CA-Santa Barbara. **Correspondent Relationships:** Kern county, CA.

Add'l Information: Established 1988. Normal turnaround time- 24-48 hours. Expedited service available. Projects billed by number of names searched. Projects billed by the hour. Fees depend on the type of search. Will file/record documents for clients. Projects estimates over $300.00 require 50% prepayment of estimated final cost, otherwise payment is net 30 days of invoice date. They specialize in title searches for 50 year environmental chains, parcel validity studies, lot book reports and lien searches.

Title Search Services Inc

2349 West Rd, Dorset, VT 05251
Phone: 802-867-4447 - **Fax:** 802-867-5506
www.vermontlandrecords.com   **email:** tss@sover.net

Types of Records Retrieved: Criminal, Civil and Probate courts; Federal courts; Real Estate; Tax Liens/Judgments; UCC records; Vital records

Local Retrieval Area: VT-Addison, Bennington, Chittenden, Franklin, Grand Isle, Rutland. **Correspondent Relationships:** Essex, Caledonia, Windham, Windsor.

Add'l Information: Established 1997. Normal turnaround time- 24-48 hours. Projects billed by number of names searched. Projects billed by the hour. First project may require prepayment. Will file/record documents for clients. Please visit my web site, www.vermontlandrecords.com, for more information on the complete services they provide for the State of VT. They are the VT independent title abstractors' league. They also perform "full" 40-year title searches for VT attorneys.

Title Searches by Liz Aulis

3306 Atlantic Ave, Raleigh, NC 27604-1642
Phone: 919-878-0227; cell- 919-395-7433 - **Fax:** 919-882-1289
lzardbeth@nc.rr.com

Types of Records Retrieved: Criminal, Civil and Probate courts; Federal courts; Real Estate; Tax Liens/Judgments; UCC records; Vital records

Local Retrieval Area: NC-Durham, Franklin, Granville, Orange, Person, Vance, Wake, Warren

Add'l Information: Established 2005. Normal turnaround time- 48 hours. Projects billed by number of names searched. All filing fees require prepayment. Monthly statements or invoice sent with results. She goes to the counties herself and does the job right the first time.

Titles of Dakota Inc (Dupree)

PO Box 100, Dupree, SD 57623-0100
Phone: 605-365-5247 - **Fax:** 605-365-5248   tidak@dakota2k.net

Types of Records Retrieved: Criminal, Civil and Probate courts; Real Estate; Tax Liens/Judgments; UCC records

Local Retrieval Area: SD-Dewey, Ziebach. **Correspondent Relationships:** Dewey, Stanley, Sully counties SD.

Add'l Information: Normal turnaround time- 1 week. Fee basis will vary by the type of project. Will file/record documents for clients. They specialize in title insurance and abstracting.

Titles of Dakota Inc (Fort Pierre)

PO Box 278, Fort Pierre, SD 57532-0278 **Phone:** 800-794-2725; 605-223-2727 - **Fax:** 605-223-9237   tidak@dakota2k.net

Types of Records Retrieved: Real Estate; Tax Liens/Judgments; Probate courts; UCC records

Local Retrieval Area: SD-Stanley, Sully. **Correspondent Relationships:** Ziebach, Dewey, Hyde, Sully counties SD.

Add'l Information: Normal turnaround time- 1 week. Fee basis will vary by the type of project. Will file/record documents for clients. They specialize in title insurance and abstracting. Also has an office in Onida.

Titles of Dakota Inc (Timber Lake)

PO Box 402, Timber Lake, SD 57656-0402 **Phone:** 605-365-5247
Fax: 605-365-5248   raymond.tidak@midconetwork.com

Types of Records Retrieved: Civil and Probate courts; Real Estate; Tax Liens/Judgments

Local Retrieval Area: SD-Dewey. **Correspondent Relationships:** Ziebach, Sully, Stanley counties SD.

Add'l Information: Normal turnaround time- 1 week. Fee basis will vary by the type of project. Will file/record documents for clients. They specialize in title insurance and abstracting.

Titleworks

6 Reeders Village Dr, Helena, MT 59601-9684
Phone: 406-442-4450 - **Fax:** 406-442-4450   titleworks@hotmail.com

Types of Records Retrieved: Criminal, Civil and Probate courts; US District court; Real Estate; Tax Liens/Judgments

Local Retrieval Area: MT-Broadwater, Cascade, Deer Lodge, Jefferson, Lewis and Clark, Meagher, Missoula, Powell

Add'l Information: Established 1994. Normal turnaround time- 24-48 hours. Projects billed by number of names searched. Will file/record documents for clients. Terms: net 30 days. They search all real estate public records, provide ownership and encumbrance reports, lot book reports, mortgage searches, title searches, document retrieval, witness closings & loan closings. Custom orders accepted. Cell # 406-431-1389.

Titus County Title Company

103 N Madison Ave, Mt Pleasant, TX 75455
Phone: 903-577-0333 - **Fax:** 903-577-1666

Types of Records Retrieved: Civil and Probate courts; Real Estate; Tax Liens/Judgments; UCC records; Vital records

Local Retrieval Area: TX-Titus

Add'l Information: Established 1992. Normal turnaround time- 2-3 days. Fee basis will vary by the type of project. First project may require prepayment. Will file/record documents for clients.

TJM & Associates

65 Norfield Rd, Weston, CT 06883
Phone: 800-749-4254; 203-227-8360 - **Fax:** 203-221-0852
tjma@optonline.net

Types of Records Retrieved: Criminal, Civil and Probate courts; Federal courts; Real Estate; Tax Liens/Judgments; UCC records; Vital records

Retrieval Area: CT-Fairfield, Hartford, Litchfield, Middlesex, New Haven

Add'l Information: Established 1988. Normal turnaround time- 24-48 hours. Expedited service available. Projects billed by number of names searched. Project fees available for large projects. First project may require prepayment. Will file/record documents for clients.

TMC

201 Ave B, #9, Knoxville, TN 37920
Phone: 865-609-7675 - **Fax:** 866-250-4232; 206-350-2014
mintzco@msn.com

Types of Records Retrieved: Real Estate; Criminal, Civil and Probate courts; Tax Liens/Judgments

Local Retrieval Area: TN-Anderson, Blount, Knox, Rutherford, Union, Washington. **Correspondent Relationships:** GA, NC, SC, TN

Add'l Information: Established 2002. Projects billed by number of names searched. First project may require prepayment. Will file/record documents for clients. They specialize in retrieval of recorded documents including mortgages, assignments, deeds, UCCs, liens in GA, NC, SC, TN; hands-on in eastern TN; does all specialties in Anderson, Blount, and Knox counties. Does real estate in all of TN and GA.

TOB Public Records Research

4430 Shady Hill, Dallas, TX 75229
Phone: 214-358-4744 - **Fax:** 214-358-4489 jeantom10@sbclobal.net

Records Retrieved: Real Estate; Tax Liens/Judgments; UCC records

Local Retrieval Area: TX-Collin, Dallas, Denton, Ellis, Kaufman, Rockwall, Tarrant. **Correspondents:** All counties in Texas and Oklahoma.

Add'l Information: Established 1994. Normal turnaround time- 3-5 days. Billed by the job-1 fee. Will file/record documents for clients. Payment due net 30 days. Specializes in 50 year chain for cell tower leases, commercial deed searches & property search for home equity loans, current owner updates, also property, lien and environmental searches.

Toby Nason Detective & Security Agency

44 Main St, Waterville, ME 04901
Phone: 207-873-7512 - **Fax:** 207-872-2436 nason@dialmaine.com

Records Retrieved: Criminal, Civil and Probate courts; Federal courts

Local Retrieval Area: ME-Androscoggin, Aroostook, Cumberland, Franklin, Hancock, Kennebec, Knox, Lincoln, Oxford, Penobscot, Piscataquis, Sagadahoc, Somerset, Waldo, Washington, York

Add'l Information: Established 1962. Normal turnaround time- 24 hours. Projects billed by the hour. All projects require prepayment. Will file/record documents for clients. They can visit any county in Maine upon request. A licensed PI in ME, FL. Performs service of process.

Tom Baxley Law Office

12837 Magnolia St, PO Box 670, Blakely, GA 39823
Phone: 229-723-3426 - **Fax:** 229-723-6464

Types of Records Retrieved: Criminal and Civil courts

Local Retrieval Area: GA-Early

Add'l Information: Projects billed by the hour. First project may require prepayment. Is recommended by the Superior Court clerk. Baxley has a woman who specializes in court record searches.

Toma Abstract Inc

410 Broad St, Hazelton, PA 18201-6107
Phone: 570-454-7899 - **Fax:** 570-454-5999 tomaabstract@epix.net

Types of Records Retrieved: Civil and Probate courts; Real Estate; Tax Liens/Judgments; UCC records

Local Retrieval Area: PA-Carbon, Columbia, Luzerne, Monroe, Montour, Schuylkill

Add'l Information: Established 1985. Normal turnaround time- never more than 2 weeks. Projects billed by number of names searched. Projects billed by the hour. They specialize in title searching and title insurance.

Top Flight Solutions

550 N McCarran Blvd #294, Sparks, NV 89431
Phone: 775-331-6490 - **Fax:** 775-331-3086 topflight@dslextreme.com

Types of Records Retrieved: Real Estate; Tax Liens/Judgments; UCC records; Vital records

Local Retrieval Area: NV-Carson City, Churchill, Douglas, Storey, Washoe

Add'l Information: Established 1997. Normal turnaround time- 2-3 days. Expedited service available. Projects billed by number of names searched. Discounts for volume requests. Will file/record documents for clients. Will invoice, net is 30 days. They are familiar with all types of public records since 1992.

Torri's Legal Services

PO Box 18647, Washington, DC 20036
Phone: 800-990-7378; 202-296-0222 - **Fax:** 202-296-4584
www.torrilegalservices.com **email:** tlsnc@erols.com

Records Retrieved: Criminal, Civil and Probate courts; Federal courts

Local Retrieval Area: DC-District of Columbia; MD-Baltimore City. **Correspondent Relationships:** nationwide.

Add'l Information: Established 1991. Normal turnaround time- 1 day. Expedited service available. Projects billed by number of names searched. Projects billed by number of records located. Projects billed by the hour. First project may require prepayment. Will file/record documents for clients. They specialize in skiptracing, process serving, asset searches, filing and court house record research. They also service numerous counties in Maryland and the Baltimore area. A licensed PI in DC. Performs service of process.

Total Access

PO Box 2368, Clovis, CA 93613
Phone: 559-325-1169 - **Fax:** 559-325-2910
www.yourtotalaccess.com **email:** darrylynn@yourtotalaccess.com

Types of Records Retrieved: Criminal and Civil courts; Bankruptcy court; Tax Liens/Judgments; UCC records; Vital records

Local Retrieval Area: CA-Fresno, Kern, Kings, Madera, Tulare

Add'l Information: Established 1996. Normal turnaround time- if received by 9:00AM PT, returned by 7PM PT. Expedited service (via phone 4 hours) available. Projects billed by number of names searched. Invoices bi-monthly or monthly. They have served employers and background reporting agencies since 1996. Their timeliness is only second to their accuracy. Pre-employment criminal is their specialty.

Town & Country Abstract Co (Arkansas)

102 W War Eagle Ave, Huntsville, AR 72740
Phone: 479-738-2055 - **Fax:** 479-738-1747

Types of Records Retrieved: Real Estate; Tax Liens/Judgments; Probate courts; UCC records

Local Retrieval Area: AR-Madison

Add'l info: Established 1977. Normal turnaround time- 1-2 days. Fee basis will vary by the type of project. First project may require prepayment. Will file/record documents for clients. They specialize in title insurance.

Town & Country Abstract Co (Missouri)

101 S Main, Huntsville, MO 65259
Phone: 660-277-3467 - **Fax:** 660-277-3939 tca@cvalley.net

Types of Records Retrieved: Civil and Probate courts; Real Estate; Tax Liens/Judgments; UCC records

Local Retrieval Area: MO-Randolph. **Correspondents:** nationwide.

Add'l Information: Established 1929. Normal turnaround time- 24-48 hours. Projects billed by number of names searched. Projects billed by the hour. First project may require prepayment. Will file/record documents for clients. Personal checks are accepted. They have the only complete set of land records for Randolph County, MO.

Towner County Abstract Co

PO Box 265, Cando, ND 58324
Phone: 701-968-3006 - **Fax:** 701-968-3009

Types of Records Retrieved: Real Estate; Tax Liens/Judgments

Local Retrieval Area: ND-Towner **Add'l Information:** Established 1991. Normal turnaround time- 2 weeks. Projects billed by number of records located. Fee basis is per entry. First project may require prepayment.

TPQ Associates

1136 Pine Grove Dr, Alpharetta, GA 30004
Phone: 770-475-0743 - **Fax:** 770-740-2088 peghussing@comcast.net

Types of Records Retrieved: Criminal and Civil courts; Real Estate; Tax Liens/Judgments; UCC records

Local Retrieval Area: GA-Clayton, Cobb, DeKalb, Forsyth, Fulton, Gwinnett, Hall

Add'l Information: Established 1999. Normal turnaround time- 24 hours. Projects billed by number of names searched. Payment terms are net 30 days. They are honest, accurate and reliable.

Trace Investigations

PO Box 2603, Bloomington, IN 47402
Phone: 812-334-8857 - **Fax:** 812-334-2274
www.traceinvestigations.com **email:** dcjcli@insightbb.com

Types of Records Retrieved: Criminal, Civil and Probate courts; Real Estate; Tax Liens/Judgments; UCC records; Vital records

Local Retrieval Area: IN-Monroe. **Correspondent Relationships:** Indiana for legal investigations and service of process.

Add'l Information: Established 1990. Normal turnaround time- 24-48 hours. Type of search determines billing. First project may require prepayment. Terms: net 30 days. Credit cards by Pay Pal accepted. They specialize in legal investigations, service of process, public record retrieval and skiptracing. They retrieve Indiana MVRs online. Requests must comply with permissible purposes pursuant to the DPPA. A licensed PI in IN, #PD58900651. Performs service of process.

Track' Um Private Investigations

PO Box 4, Wilkesboro, NC 28651
Phone: 877-634-9106; 336-903-1700 - **Fax:** 336-903-1701
www.carolinapi.com **email:** Hayden@CarolinaPI.com

Types of Records Retrieved: Criminal, Civil and Probate courts; Federal courts; Real Estate; Tax Liens/Judgments; UCC records; Vital records

Local Retrieval Area: NC-Alexander, Alleghany, Ashe, Caldwell, Catawba, Iredell, Surry, Watauga, Wilkes, Yadkin

Add'l Information: Established 1997. Normal turnaround time- 2 days. Projects billed by the hour. First project may require prepayment. Will file/record documents for clients. They specialize in domestic investigations, process service, record retrieval, locate investigations, insurance investigations and witness interviews. A licensed PI in NC. Performs service of process.

Colleen Tracy

1395 S 100 W, LaGrange, IN 46761
Phone: 260-463-4044 - **Fax:** 260-463-4198

Types of Records Retrieved: Criminal and Civil courts; Real Estate; Vital records; Tax Liens/Judgments

Local Retrieval Area: IN-LaGrange, Noble, Steuben

Add'l Information: Established 1990. Normal turnaround time- 24-48 hours. First project may require prepayment. Will file/record documents for clients. She specializes in full 7-year searches. In addition to court and real estate services, she is a notary and will file/record documents.

Traill County Abstract

PO Box 69, Hillsboro, ND 58045
Phone: 701-636-4880 - **Fax:** 701-636-4880

Types of Records Retrieved: Civil courts; Real Estate; Tax Liens/Judgments; UCC records

Local Retrieval Area: ND-Trail

Add'l Information: Established 1995. Normal turnaround time- 48 hours. First project may require prepayment. Will file/record documents for clients. They are the only abstract company in Traill County.

Trax

17 Joy St, Barrington, RI 02806
Phone: 401-245-3004 - **Fax:** 401-245-9443

Types of Records Retrieved: Criminal, Civil and Probate courts; Federal courts; Real Estate; Tax Liens/Judgments; UCC records; Vital records

Local Retrieval Area: RI-Bristol, Kent, Newport, Providence, Washington

Add'l Information: Established 1983. Normal turnaround time- 24 hours. Expedited service available. Projects billed by number of names searched. Terms are net 30 days. First project may require prepayment. Will file/record documents for clients. Terms: net 14 days. Licensed PI RI State Constable. Skip tracing, asset research. ALL courts researched, title/abstract research (real estate) & RI/MA MVR records, trace plate & VIN MVR title & ins research. Also, check addresses, obtain statements, photos & measurements. A licensed PI in RI. Performs service of process.

Treasure Coast Title Co

500 Virginia Ave, Fort Pierce, FL 34982
Phone: 772-461-7190 - **Fax:** 772-468-8461

Types of Records Retrieved: Real Estate; Tax Liens/Judgments; Probate courts; UCC records

Local Retrieval Area: FL-Indian River, Martin, Okeechobee, St. Lucie

Add'l Information: Established 1905. Normal turnaround time- 7 days. Fee basis will vary by the type of project. They specialize in residential and commercial title searches. They will file/record UCC and real estate documents on behalf of clients if part of a closing.

Trenton Abstract and Title Co LLC

910 Main St, Trenton, MO 64683-2052
Phone: 660-359-2100 - **Fax:** 660-339-7115
www.trentonabstract.com **email:** trentonabstract@grundycc.net

Types of Records Retrieved: Real Estate; Tax Liens/Judgments

Local Retrieval Area: MO-Daviess, Grundy, Livingston, Mercer

Add'l Information: Established 1869. Normal turnaround time- 3 days. First project may require prepayment. Will file/record documents for clients. Specializing in real estate foreclosures. Oldest abstract/title company in Grundy County.

Tri County Investigations

1122 Briarwood Pl, Salinas, CA 93901
Phone: 831-758-3124 - **Fax:** 831-758-0655
bettylyn@comcast.net

Types of Records Retrieved: Criminal, Civil and Probate courts; Real Estate; Tax Liens/Judgments; UCC records; Vital records

Local Retrieval Area: CA-Monterey, San Benito, Santa Cruz

Add'l Information: Established 1987. Normal turnaround time- 24 hours. Projects billed by number of names searched. Will file/record documents for clients. Monthly billing. They specialize in court record searches and document retrieval of records in the Monterey, Santa Cruz and San Benito counties, CA area. Cell # 831-594-8639.

Tri County Title & Escrow Co

258 N State St, Osceola, NE 68651
Phone: 402-747-2141 - **Fax:** 402-747-2151 tri@alltel.net

Types of Records Retrieved: Real Estate; Tax Liens/Judgments; Probate courts; UCC records

Local Retrieval Area: NE-Platte, Polk

Add'l Information: Established 1983. Normal turnaround time- 1 week. Fee basis varies by type of transaction. First project may require prepayment.

Will file/record documents for clients. They specialize in title insurance searches.

Tri-County Abstract & Title Guaranty

122 17th Ave North, St Cloud, MN 56303

Phone: 800-892-2399; 320-253-2096 - **Fax:** 320-253-4536

Records Retrieved: Real Estate; UCC records; Tax Liens/Judgments

Local Retrieval Area: MN-Benton, Mille Lacs, Morrison, Sherburne, Stearns, Wright. **Correspondent Relationships:** statewide.

Add'l Information: Established 1973. Normal turnaround time- 1-10 business days. Projects billed by number of names searched. Projects billed by number of records located. Will file/record documents for clients. Personal checks are accepted. They do abstracting in six counties, have 2 licensed abstractors, and store records for 5 counties.

Tri-County Land Title

110 S Jefferson St, Berne, IN 46711

Phone: 260-589-3139 - **Fax:** 260-589-3130

Types of Records Retrieved: Civil and Probate courts; Real Estate; Tax Liens/Judgments; UCC records; Vital records

Local Retrieval Area: IN-Adams, Jay, Wells

Add'l Information: Established 1986. Normal turnaround time- 1-5 days. Projects billed by number of records located. All projects require prepayment. Will file/record documents for clients. They specialize in real estate closings and title insurance.

Tri-County Legal Process Service

PO Box 309, 64060 Old Bend-Redmond Hwy #2, Bend, OR 97709

Phone: 800-600-6315; 541-317-5680 - **Fax:** 541-317-0143

www.pjprocessplus.com **email:** pjhelikson@pjprocessplus.com

Types of Records Retrieved: Criminal and Civil courts

Local Retrieval Area: OR-Crook, Deschutes, Jefferson

Add'l Information: Established 1991. First project may require prepayment. They also provide photocopying, skiptracing, DMV, assessor records and background checks. Performs service of process.

Tri-County Process Serving

417 W Fort St, Boise, ID 83702

Phone: 800-473-3454; 208-344-4132 - **Fax:** 208-338-1530

tcps@rmci.net

Types of Records Retrieved: Criminal, Civil and Probate courts; Federal courts; Real Estate; Tax Liens/Judgments; UCC records

Local Retrieval Area: ID-Ada, Boise, Canyon, Elmore, Gem, Payette, Valley. **Correspondent Relationships:** Twin Falls, Gooding, Jerome, Bonneville, Madison, Jefferson, Power, most counties in northern Idaho.

Add'l Information: Established 1976. Normal turnaround time- variable depending on project. Projects billed by number of names searched. Will file/record documents for clients. They specialize in process service and skiptracing. Performs service of process.

Tri-County Title Abstracts Inc

1003 K St NW #215, Washington, DC 20001

Phone: 202-737-6116 - **Fax:** 202-737-6117 tricountytitle@verizon.net

Types of Records Retrieved: Civil and Probate courts; Real Estate; Tax Liens/Judgments; UCC records

Local Retrieval Area: DC-District of Columbia. **Correspondent Relationships:** Montgomery county MD.

Add'l Information: Established 1993. Normal turnaround time- 48-72 hours. Projects billed by number of names searched. Projects billed by number of records located. They charge per transaction for title searches. First project may require prepayment. Will file/record documents for clients. They specialize in UCC, real estate, title searches, judgments, liens, court records, corporate standing and all research activities related to document retrieval and recording.

TRI-County Title LLC

PO Box 128, Washington, MO 63090

Phone: 636-239-7800 - **Fax:** 636-239-4002

Types of Records Retrieved: Criminal, Civil and Probate courts; Real Estate; Tax Liens/Judgments; UCC records

Local Retrieval Area: MO-Franklin

Add'l Information: Established 1983. Normal turnaround time- 7 working days. Fee basis will vary by type of project. Fee may be based per tract of land and/or per owner as required. First project may require prepayment. Will file/record documents for clients. Payment due upon receipt. They specialize in title insurance, closings and title searches.

Trident Investigative Service Inc

PO Box 1950, Renton, WA 98057-1950

Phone: 888-277-3238; 206-772-9646 - **Fax:** 206-772-9647

www.tridentseattle.com **email:** mike@tridentseattle.com

Types of Records Retrieved: Criminal, Civil and Probate courts; Federal courts; Real Estate; Tax Liens/Judgments; UCC records; Vital records

Local Retrieval Area: WA-Adams, Asotin, Benton, Chelan, Clallam, Clark, Columbia, Cowlitz, Douglas, Ferry, Franklin, Garfield, Grant, Grays Harbor, Island, Jefferson, King, Kitsap, Kittitas, Klickitat, Lewis, Lincoln, Mason, Okanogan, Pacific, Pend Oreille, Pierce, San Juan, Skagit, Skamania, Snohomish, Spokane, Stevens, Thurston, Wahkiakum, Walla Walla, Whatcom, Whitman, Yakima. **Correspondents:** nationwide.

Add'l Information: Established 1991. Normal turnaround time- 1-2 days. Projects billed by the hour. Fee varies depending on type of search. First project may require prepayment. Credit cards accepted. They specialize in investigative and data research. A licensed PI in OR, WA, AK. Performs service of process.

Trinity County Abstract

PO Box 249, Groveton, TX 75845

Phone: 936-642-1698 - **Fax:** 936-642-1697 trinitycoabst@consolidated.net

Types of Records Retrieved: Civil and Probate courts; Real Estate; Tax Liens/Judgments; UCC records

Local Retrieval Area: TX-Trinity

Add'l Information: Established 1981. Normal turnaround time- 5-10 working days. Commitments and land searches take 15 working days. Projects billed by number of names searched. First project may require prepayment. Will file/record documents for clients. Personal checks are accepted. Payment upon completion. They specialize in land title searches and title insurance.

Tripp & Todd Title Company

134 E 3rd St, Winner, SD 57580-1804

Phone: 605-842-0334 - **Fax:** 605-842-3088 tttco@gwtc.net

Types of Records Retrieved: Civil and Probate courts; Real Estate; Tax Liens/Judgments; UCC records; Vital records

Local Retrieval Area: SD-Todd, Tripp

Add'l Information: Established 1994. Normal turnaround time- 5 business days. Fee basis will vary by the type of project. First project may require prepayment.

TriState Courier

827 King St, Wilmington, DE 19801

Phone: 800-783-0945; 302-654-4264 - **Fax:** 302-654-3479

www.tristatecourier.com **email:** docs@tristatecourier.com

Types of Records Retrieved: Criminal and Civil courts; Federal courts; Real Estate; Tax Liens/Judgments; UCC records

Local Retrieval Area: DE-New Castle. **Correspondent Relationships:** NY, TX, FL, CA, DC, MS, MO, OH & TN.

Add'l Information: Established 1993. Normal turnaround time- 24-48 hours. Expedited service available. Projects billed by number of names searched. First project may require prepayment. Credit cards accepted. They specialize in the fastest service offered in New Castle county. TriState is reliable, honest and accurate. Performs service of process.

Triwest Investigative Services

1441 Huntington Dr #1930, South Pasadena, CA 91030

Phone: 323-254-5151 - **Fax:** 323-258-1627 triwestinv@earthlink.net

Types of Records Retrieved: Criminal, Civil and Probate courts; Federal courts; Tax Liens/Judgments; Vital records

Local Retrieval Area: CA-Los Angeles. **Correspondent Relationships:** southern and Bay area of California; also Oregon, Texas, Florida.

Add'l Information: Established 1995. Normal turnaround time- 24-48 hours. Projects billed by the hour. First project may require prepayment. They specialize in corporate and personal due diligence. They have a library of public record indices and proprietary databases to support complex research. A licensed PI in CA. Performs service of process.

Troy Title Co LLC

15 Ellis Ave, Troy, MO 63379-1151
Phone: 636-528-2220 - **Fax:** 636-528-3953
www.troytitle.com **email:** janet@troytitle.com

Types of Records Retrieved: Civil and Probate courts; Real Estate; Tax Liens/Judgments

Local Retrieval Area: MO-Lincoln, Montgomery, Pike, Warren. **Correspondent Relationships:** St Charles County MO.

Add'l Information: Established 1985. Normal turnaround time- 2-3 days. Projects billed by number of names searched. Will file/record documents for clients. Personal checks are accepted. They specialize in real estate title searches, closings and construction escrows.

Trumbull County Abstract Co

PO Box 1268, 174 N Park Ave, Warren, OH 44482
Phone: 330-399-1891 - **Fax:** 330-399-1892 tcac@usawebnet.net

Records Retrieved: Real Estate; Tax Liens/Judgments; Probate courts

Local Retrieval Area: OH-Trumbull

Add'l Information: Established 1898. Normal turnaround time- 3 days. Charges vary by project. All projects require prepayment. Will file/record documents for clients. They specialize in abstracting and real estate title.

Tseng Document Retrieval

12640 Bloomfield Ave #90, Norwalk, CA 90650
Phone: 562-863-3415 - **Fax:** 562-863-3415 tsenglisa_755@hotmail.com

Records Retrieved: Real Estate; Tax Liens/Judgments; UCC records

Local Retrieval Area: CA-Los Angeles, Orange, Riverside, San Bernardino, San Diego, Ventura

Add'l info: Established 1998. Turnaround time- 24-48 hours. Projects billed by number of names searched. All projects require prepayment. They do mini current owner searches, current owner searches, title searches, legal testing, filling fictitious business and recording and they are excellent, prompt of their work and they have been doing this for 6 years.

TSI - Title Services LLC

7 Woodstone Plza #7, Hattiesburg, MS 39402-8342
Phone: 800-736-9331; 601-264-3500 - **Fax:** 601-264-6622
www.tsititle.com **email:** perry@tsititle.com

Types of Records Retrieved: Real Estate; Tax Liens/Judgments; UCC records

Local Retrieval Area: MS-Forrest, Lamar, Perry

Add'l Information: Normal turnaround time- 2 days. Fee basis varies by type of transaction. First project may require prepayment. Term are net 30 days. A Mississippi residential and commercial title company, they specialize in real estate transactions. Visit their web site.

Taylor Tucker

PO Box 7, Louisville, MS 39339
Phone: 662-773-9254 - **Fax:** 662-773-9255 tucker9254@bellsouth.net

Types of Records Retrieved: Civil and Probate courts; Real Estate; Tax Liens/Judgments; UCC records; Vital records

Local Retrieval Area: MS-Winston

Add'l Information: Established 1979. Normal turnaround time- 2 days. Projects billed by the hour. First project may require prepayment. Will file/record documents for clients. He is an attorney in general practice.

Turek Paralegal Services

PO Box 1575, Gainesville, GA 30503
Phone: 770-540-7891 cell, 706-548-6842 - **Fax:** 706-583-8350

Types of Records Retrieved: Criminal and Civil courts; Real Estate; Tax Liens/Judgments

Local Retrieval Area: GA-Banks, Barrow, Clarke, Dawson, Elbert, Habersham, Hall, Jackson, Lumpkin, Madison, Oconee, Oglethorpe, Rockdale, Walton, White, Wilkes

Add'l Information: Established 1995. First project may require prepayment. They specialize in rural counties east and northeast of Atlanta.

Turner County Abstract

205 N Main St, Parker, SD 57053
Phone: 605-297-5555

Types of Records Retrieved: Real Estate; Tax Liens/Judgments

Local Retrieval Area: SD-Turner

Add'l info: 1st project may require prepayment. They specialize in real estate.

Barbara Tweedle

PO Box 9, Rosedale, MS 38769
Phone: 662-759-3048, 662-759-3762 - **Fax:** 662-759-3467

Types of Records Retrieved: Criminal, Civil and Probate courts; Real Estate; Tax Liens/Judgments; UCC records

Local Retrieval Area: MS-Bolivar

Add'l Information: Normal turnaround time- 1-2 days. Projects billed by number of names searched. All projects require prepayment. She specializes in records at the Rosedale courts. A fax number is available upon request.

24 Hour Record Retriever & Abstract Inc

44 E Bridge St #203, Oswego, NY 13126-2108
Phone: 800-294-3740; 315-342-8363 - **Fax:** 800-451-5028; 315-342-9058
www.24rra.com **email:** twentyfourhour@mac.com

Types of Records Retrieved: Criminal, Civil and Probate courts; Real Estate; Tax Liens/Judgments; UCC records

Local Retrieval Area: NY-Cayuga, Jefferson, Monroe, Onondaga, Oswego

Add'l Information: Established 2003. Normal turnaround time- 24 hours-court records, 24-48 hours-Real Estate searches. Expedited service available. Projects billed by number of names searched. Credit cards accepted. Invoiced weekly, monthly, or per order. They do accept PayPal. They provide timely, quality service for county court records, real estate searches, abstracts, bankruptcy and lien searches. Criminal records available within 24 hours and title insurance underwritten by Land America & First American Title Ins Co. Performs service of process.

Twin Cities Research

PO Box 28636, St Paul, MN 55128
Phone: 651-714-0002 - **Fax:** 651-714-0003
twincitiesresearch@hotmail.com

Types of Records Retrieved: Criminal, Civil and Probate courts; Federal courts; Real Estate; Tax Liens/Judgments; UCC records; Vital records

Local Retrieval Area: MN-Anoka, Benton, Blue Earth, Brown, Carlton, Carver, Chippewa, Chisago, Cook, Cottonwood, Dakota, Dodge, Faribault, Goodhue, Hennepin, Isanti, Itasca, Jackson, Kanabec, Kandiyohi, Lac Qui Parle, Lake, Le Sueur, McLeod, Martin, Meeker, Mille Lacs, Nicollet, Pine, Ramsey, Redwood, Renville, St. Louis, Scott, Sherburne, Sibley, Washington, Watonwan, Wright, Yellow Medicine; WI-St Croix

Add'l Information: Established 1989. Normal turnaround time- 24-48 hours. Projects billed by number of names searched. Projects are billed by the type of research required. First project may require prepayment. Will file/record documents for clients. They do invoice monthly. They have been serving the Twin Cities metro area for the past 17 years. Their service includes all matters of public record, but they will do their best to meet any research needs you may have. A cell phone number to reach them is 612-840-9846.

Twin City Title Co Inc

2409 Summerhill Rd, Texarkana, TX 75501
Phone: 903-793-7671 - **Fax:** 903-792-2847

Types of Records Retrieved: Civil and Probate courts; Real Estate; Tax Liens/Judgments; UCC records

Local Retrieval Area: TX-Bowie

Add'l info: Normal turnaround time- 7 days. Projects billed by the hour. All projects require prepayment. Will file/record documents for clients.

Twin Oaks Research

4814 W Woodlawn St, Dunnellon, FL 34433
Phone: 352-465-7844 - **Fax:** 352-465-7846
twinoaksresearch@earthlink.net

Types of Records Retrieved: Criminal, Civil and Probate courts; Real Estate; Tax Liens/Judgments; UCC records

Local Retrieval Area: FL-Alachua, Citrus, Levy. **Correspondent Relationships:** Marion, Hernando counties FL.

Add'l Information: Established 1997. Normal turnaround time- 24 hours. Projects billed by number of names searched. They have provided excellent service for ten years, at a reasonable rate. The North West Central Florida searching professionals.

UCC Direct Services - Albany

187 Wolf Rd, Suire 101, Albany, NY 12205
Phone: 800-342-3676; - **Fax:** 800-962-7049; 518-434-1521
www.uccdirectservices.com **email:** uds_albany@uccdirect.com

Types of Records Retrieved: Civil courts; Federal courts; Real Estate; Tax Liens/Judgments; UCC records; Secretary of State records

Local Retrieval Area: NY-Albany. **Correspondents:** nationwide.

Add'l Information: Established 1935. Normal turnaround time- 2-3 days. Projects billed by number of names searched. Fee may be based on location searched. First project may require prepayment. Credit cards accepted. Will file/record documents for clients. They have provided public record retrieval services since 1935; offering services including UCC/lien and corporate document search, retrieval, preparation and filing.

UCC Retrievals, Inc

7288 Hanover Green Dr, Mechanicsville, VA 23111
Phone: 804-559-5919 - **Fax:** 804-559-5920
www.uccretrievals.com **email:** traci@uccretrievals.com

Types of Records Retrieved: Criminal, Civil and Probate courts; Federal courts; Tax Liens/Judgments; UCC records

Local Retrieval Area: VA-Amelia, Buckingham, Caroline, Charles City, Chesterfield, Colonial Heights, Cumberland, Dinwiddie, Essex, Fluvanna, Gloucester, Goochland, Hanover, Henrico, Henry, Hopewell, King and Queen, King George, King William, Louisa, Mathews. Middlesex, New Kent, Nottoway, Petersburg, Powhatan, Prince George, Richmond, Southampton, Sussex, Westmoreland. **Correspondents:** statewide.

Add'l Information: Established 1989. Normal turnaround time- 48 hours. They offer same or next day service at Secretary of State's office for searches and corporate filings. Projects billed by number of names searched. Will file/record documents for clients. They specialize in all Virginia Counties and Secretary of State, for research, retrieval and filing of public records throughout Virginia. They are located in the capitol. They will act as a registered agent for you.

UCC Search Inc

PO Box 9315, 1012 Marquez Pl #106B (87505), Santa Fe, NM 87504-9315
Phone: 800-453-9404; 505-983-4228 - **Fax:** 800-642-6382; 505-983-1169
uccsearchinc@msn.com

Types of Records Retrieved: Civil courts; Federal courts; Real Estate; Tax Liens/Judgments; UCC records

Local Retrieval Area: NM-Santa Fe. **Correspondents in:** New Mexico.

Add'l Information: Established 1985. Normal turnaround time- 2 days. Projects billed by number of names searched. Terms: net 30 days. 1 1/2% per month interest for late payment. They specialize in customer satisfaction and quick turnaround. They also retrieve corporate records at the state level and file corporate paperwork.

Uinta Title

1048 Main St, Evanston, WY 82930
Phone: 307-789-1777 **Fax:** 307-789-8549

Types of Records Retrieved: Real Estate; Tax Liens/Judgments

Local Retrieval Area: WY-Uinta

Add'l Information: Established 1960. First project may require prepayment. They specialize in real estate.

Undercover LLC

140 Limestone St, Bowling Green, KY 42101
Phone: 270-784-2070 - **Fax:** 270-783-9460

Types of Records Retrieved: Criminal, Civil and Probate courts; Real Estate; Tax Liens/Judgments

Local Retrieval Area: KY-Crittenden, Warren

Add'l Information: Established 1994. Normal turnaround time- 48 hours or less. Projects billed by number of names searched. Can bill monthly. First project may require prepayment. No credit cards accepted. They specialize in court records and real estate title searches.

Union Abstract Co

200 N Jefferson Ave #214, El Dorado, AR 71730
Phone: 870-863-6053 - **Fax:** 870-864-0094

Types of Records Retrieved: Civil and Probate courts; Real Estate; Tax Liens/Judgments; UCC records

Local Retrieval Area: AR-Union

Add'l Information: Established 1940. Normal turnaround time- 1 day. Projects billed by the hour. All projects require prepayment.

Union County Abstract & Title Co

PO Box 40, Elk Point, SD 57025-0040
Phone: 605-356-3180 - **Fax:** 605-356-3112

Types of Records Retrieved: Criminal, Civil and Probate courts; Real Estate; Tax Liens/Judgments; UCC records; Vital records

Local Retrieval Area: SD-Union

Add'l Information: Established 1940. Normal turnaround time- 24-48 hours. Projects billed by the hour. Fee for copies additional. They specialize in title searches, lien searches, abstracting and title insurance. They are a licensed abstractor for Union County, South Dakota.

Union County Title Co

1 W Union St, Liberty, IN 47353-1349
Phone: 765-458-7148 - **Fax:** 765-458-6331 unioncountytitle@aol.com

Types of Records Retrieved: Civil courts; Real Estate; Tax Liens/Judgments; UCC records

Local Retrieval: IN-Fayette, Franklin, Union, Wayne; OH-Butler, Preble.

Correspondent Relationships: elsewhere in Indiana.

Add'l Information: Established 1994. Normal turnaround time- 24 hours. Projects billed by number of names searched. Invoices are done at the end of the month.

Union-Speer Abstract Co

22 S Park St, Sapulpa, OK 74066
Phone: 918-224-4540 - **Fax:** 918-224-4549

Types of Records Retrieved: Civil and Probate courts; Real Estate; Tax Liens/Judgments; UCC records

Local Retrieval Area: OK-Creek

Add'l Information: Established 1904. Normal turnaround time- variable depending on project. Fee basis is per page.

Unisearch Inc (California)

1903 21st St, Sacramento, CA 95814-6813
Phone: 800-769-1864; 916-456-4111 - **Fax:** 800-769-1868; 916-456-4068
www.unisearch.com **email:** gales@unisearch.com

Types of Records Retrieved: Criminal and Civil courts; Federal courts; Tax Liens/Judgments; UCC records

Local Retrieval Area: CA-Sacramento. **Correspondent Relationships:** nationwide; affiliates with National Registered Agents Inc.

Add'l Information: Established 1995. Normal turnaround time- 1-2 days. Projects billed by number of names searched. First project may require prepayment. Credit cards accepted. Will file/record documents for clients. Payment due net 30 days. They specialize in searching, filing and retrieving public documents nationwide. An extensive range of UCC/Lien and Corporate services to the legal, financial and business community in all 50 states as well as internationally.

Unisearch Inc (Nevada)

10 Bodie Dr, Carson City, NV 89705
Phone: 800-260-1131; 775-884-2700 - **Fax:** 800-260-8118
www.unisearch.com **email:** vickij@unisearch.com

Types of Records Retrieved: Criminal, Civil and Probate courts; Federal courts; Tax Liens/Judgments; UCC records

Local Retrieval Area: NV-Carson City, Douglas, Storey, Washoe. **Correspondent Relationships:** nationwide with affiliates of National Registered Agents Inc.

Add'l Information: Established 1991. Normal turnaround time- 1-2 days. Projects billed by number of names searched. Credit cards accepted. Will file/record documents for clients. Online access to over 40 states' records and UCC records on microfilm for 12 states. A licensed PI in NV. Performs service of process.

Unisearch Inc (Ohio)

2545 Hilliard Rome Rd PMB 232, Hilliard, OH 43026-9471
Phone: 877-208-7783; 614-853-3355 - **Fax:** 877-440-5104; 614-878-3264
www.unisearch.com **email:** amya@unisearch.com

Types of Records Retrieved: Civil courts; Federal courts; Tax Liens/Judgments; UCC records

Local Retrieval Area: OH-Franklin. **Correspondent Relationships:** all states, counties nationwide.

Add'l Information: Established 1991. Normal turnaround time- 24-48 hours. Projects are billed per name searched. Credit cards accepted. Will file/record documents for clients. They have offices in 7 states and are online to over 30 state offices, and have UCC microfilm for 12 states. They also obtain corporate documents nationwide.

Unisearch Inc (Oregon)

3533 Fairview Industrial Dr SE, Salem, OR 97302-1155
Phone: 800-554-3113; 503-399-9500 - **Fax:** 800-554-3114; 503-378-7870
www.unisearch.com **email:** lorettam@unisearch.com

Types of Records Retrieved: Civil courts; Federal courts; Tax Liens/Judgments; UCC records

Local Retrieval Area: OR-Marion. **Correspondents:** nationwide.

Add'l Information: Established 1991. Normal turnaround time- 1-2 days. Projects billed by number of names searched. Copy costs and disbursements are added to the search charge. Credit cards accepted. Will file/record documents for clients. They specialize in UCC, corporate and registered agent services throughout the United States. They also search/retrieve/file documents with the Oregon Secretary of State.

Unisearch Inc (Washington)

1780 Barnes Blvd SW, Tumwater, WA 98512-0410
Phone: 800-722-0708; 360-956-9500 - **Fax:** 800-531-1717; 360-956-9504
www.unisearch.com **email:** wendyb@unisearch.com

Types of Records Retrieved: Criminal and Civil courts; Federal courts; Tax Liens/Judgments; UCC records; Vital records

Local Retrieval Area: WA-King, Lewis, Mason, Pierce, Skagit, Snohomish, Thurston. **Correspondent Relationships:** nationwide.

Add'l Information: Established 1991. Normal turnaround time- 24-48 hours. Projects billed by number of names searched. Copy costs and disbursements are added to search charge. Credit cards accepted. Will file/record documents for clients. They have online access to over 30 states' records. They have microfilm for 12 states. A licensed PI in NV.

United Attorneys' Services

601 University Ave #134, Sacramento, CA 95825
Phone: 916-457-3000

Types of Records Retrieved: Criminal, Civil and Probate courts; Federal courts; Real Estate; Tax Liens/Judgments; UCC records; Vital records

Local Retrieval Area: CA-Placer, Sacramento, San Joaquin, Yolo. **Correspondent Relationships:** Solano, El Dorado, Nevada counties.

Add'l Information: Established 1980. Normal turnaround time- 4 days. Projects billed by number of names searched. Personal checks are accepted.

United Legal Services

217 N Harvey #102, Oklahoma City, OK 73102
Phone: 888-232-8432; 405-232-8432 - **Fax:** 405-232-8442
alongi100@aol.com

Types of Records Retrieved: Criminal, Civil and Probate courts; Federal courts; Real Estate; Tax Liens/Judgments; UCC records

Local Retrieval Area: OK-Canadian, Cleveland, Grady, Lincoln, Logan, McClain, Oklahoma, Pottawatomie. **Correspondent Relationships:** Oklahoma.

Add'l Information: Established 1970. Normal turnaround time- 48 hours for close counties. Contract areas average 3-4 days. Projects billed by the hour. First project may require prepayment. Personal checks are accepted. Performs service of process.

United Risk Partners LLC

2222 Lunt Ave, Elk Grove Village, IL 60007
Phone: 877-593-9995; 847-593-9995 x303 - **Fax:** 847-593-9996
www.unitedriskpartners.com **email:** direction@unitedriskpartners.com

Types of Records Retrieved: Criminal, Civil and Probate courts; Federal courts; Real Estate; Tax Liens/Judgments; UCC records; Vital records

Local Retrieval Area: IL-Champaign, Cook, De Kalb, Du Page, Kane, Kendall, Lake, Madison, McHenry, Rock Island, Sangamon, Will. **Correspondent Relationships:** nationwide.

Add'l Information: Established 2002. Normal turnaround time- 24-48 hours depending on clerk except for archived cases. Projects billed by number of names searched. Projects billed by number of records located. Projects billed by the hour. First project may require prepayment. Time efficient, cost-effective public records research, document retrieval, video surveillance and litigation service. A licensed PI in IL.

Universal Information Research

PO Box 8154, Mission Hills, CA 91346
Phone: 800-363-9813; 818-894-6226 - **Fax:** 888-307-3433; 818-894-0868
www.piagency.com **email:** piagency@piagency.com

Types of Records Retrieved: Criminal, Civil and Probate courts; Federal courts; Real Estate; UCC records; Vital records

Local Retrieval Area: CA-Alameda, Los Angeles, Marin, Orange, Riverside, San Bernardino, San Diego, San Francisco, Santa Clara, Ventura. **Correspondent Relationships:** Ventura, Marin, Alameda, Santa Clara, San Francisco, also nationwide.

Add'l Information: Established 1994. Normal turnaround time- 48-72 hours. Projects billed by the hour. They do monthly billings. Credit cards accepted. Will file/record documents for clients. MasterCard, Visa and American Express accepted. They are a full service company. They specialize in court record searches and subpoena files. They also take statements, conduct activity checks and do surveillance. A licensed PI in CA. Performs service of process.

Upper State Title Corp

PO Box 2205, Anderson, SC 29625-2205
Phone: 864-260-4649 or 864-260-4063

Types of Records Retrieved: Real Estate; Tax Liens/Judgments; Probate courts; UCC records

Local Retrieval Area: SC-Abbeville, Anderson, Greenville, Greenwood, Laurens, McCormick, Oconee, Pickens, Spartanburg

Add'l Information: Normal turnaround time- 2-3 days. Projects billed by number of names searched. Projects billed by number of records located. Projects billed by the hour. All projects require prepayment.

Upstate Investigations

2418 Hwy 72 / 221 East, Greenwood, SC 29649
Phone: 864-277-0757 - **Fax:** 253-322-9230
www.UpstateInvestigations.com **email:** wbensel@InfoAve.net

Records Retrieved: Criminal and Civil courts; Tax Liens/Judgments

Local Retrieval Area: SC-Abbeville, Greenwood, McCormick

Add'l Information: Established 1995. Normal turnaround time- 24-48 hours. Projects billed by number of names searched. First project may require prepayment. Will file/record documents for clients. They are an all around investigative agency. A licensed PI in SC. Performs service of process.

Urban Abstract Inc

6727 Eagle Creek Dr, Liberty Township, OH 45011
Phone: 513-755-8527 - **Fax:** 513-755-8591 urbanabstract@adelphia.net

Records Retrieved: Civil and Probate courts; Real Estate; UCC records

Local Retrieval Area: OH-Butler, Clermontk Hamilton, Montgomery, Warren

Add'l Information: Established 1984. Normal turnaround time- 24-48 hours. Projects billed by number of names searched. First project may require prepayment. Will file/record documents for clients. She specializes in current owner, 42 year, 62 year, commercial real estate, and foreclosure sale searches. Provides prompt, accurate service covering Butler, Warren, Hamilton, Montgomery, Clermont, OH counties.

Urban Title Search Services Inc

609 W Main St, Ashland, OH 44805
Phone: 419-289-0437 - **Fax:** 419-282-0437 urbantitle@zoominternet.net

Types of Records Retrieved: Criminal, Civil and Probate courts; Real Estate; Tax Liens/Judgments; UCC records; Vital records

Local Retrieval Area: OH-Ashland, Holmes, Richland, Wayne

Add'l Information: Established 1990. Normal turnaround time- 24-48 hours. Projects billed by number of names searched. First project may require prepayment. Will file/record documents for clients.

US Background Screening Inc

638 Lindero Canyon Rd #136, Oak Park, CA 91377
Phone: 866-777-1322; - **Fax:** 866-777-1323
www.usbscorp.net **email:** andrew@usbscorp.net

Types of Records Retrieved: Criminal and Civil courts

Local Retrieval Area: CA-Los Angeles. **Correspondents:** nationwide.

Add'l Information: Established 1947. Normal turnaround time- 48 hours. Projects billed by number of names searched. First project may require prepayment. Credit cards accepted. Will invoice bi-monthly. They are a wholesale felony and misdemeanor research firm. They conduct research in every county in US. They service many of the largest background screening companies in the US. Statewide searches are available in addition to the county levels.

US Document Retrieval Service Inc

11 Park Pl #1512, New York, NY 10007
Phone: 800-595-0145; 212-528-0777 - **Fax:** 800-595-3212; 212-528-1620
www.usretrieval.com **email:** orders@usretrieval.com

Types of Records Retrieved: Criminal, Civil and Probate courts; Federal courts; Real Estate; Tax Liens/Judgments; Vital records

Local Retrieval Area: NJ-Atlantic, Bergen, Camden, Essex, Hudson, Middlesex, Monmouth, Morris, Ocean, Union; NY-Bronx, Kings, Nassau, New York, Orange, Queens, Richmond, Rockland, Suffolk, Westchester. **Correspondent Relationships:** nationwide.

Add'l Information: Established 1998. Normal turnaround time- within 24 hours. Projects billed by the hour. First project may require prepayment. Credit cards accepted. Will file/record documents for clients. Payment due upon receipt. They specialize in complex research and retrieval in all state & federal courts, including New York, New Jersey, and lower Connecticut. Eighteen years experience with the NY state court system.

US Legal Support of Lubbock

PO Box 11564, Lubbock, TX 79408
Phone: 877-947-8500; 806-747-8500 - **Fax:** 806-741-0947
ayoung@nts-online.net

Types of Records Retrieved: Criminal, Civil and Probate courts; Real Estate; Tax Liens/Judgments; UCC records; Vital records

Local Retrieval Area: TX-Lubbock. **Correspondent Relationships:** has a network within Texas.

Add'l Information: Established 1988. Normal turnaround time- 1-3 days. Fee basis varies by type of transaction. First project may require prepayment. Will file/record documents for clients. They have process servers who will do record retrieval, filing, court searches, and more. Call for quote. Performs service of process.

Utah Title & Abstract

PO Box 337, 109 E 200 N, Richfield, UT 84701
Phone: 435-896-5429 - **Fax:** 435-896-6095 uttitle@xmission.com

Types of Records Retrieved: Criminal, Civil and Probate courts; Real Estate; Tax Liens/Judgments; UCC records

Local Retrieval Area: UT-Millard, Piute, Sevier, Wayne

Add'l Information: Established 1981. Normal turnaround time- as much as 2-3 weeks. Projects billed by the hour. All projects require prepayment.

V & A Research LLC

6198 Co Rd 33, Skipperville, AL 36374
Phone: 334-774-7092 - **Fax:** 334-774-7092

Types of Records Retrieved: Real Estate; Tax Liens/Judgments; Probate courts; UCC records

Local Retrieval Area: AL-Coffee, Dale, Geneva, Henry, Houston

Add'l Information: Established 1995. Normal turnaround time- 24-48 hours. If search takes longer, will notify client. Fees based upon type of search requested. Will file/record documents for clients. Payment due upon receipt of invoice. They research probate, tax, real estate, marriage and estate records, specializing in title searches, UCC/lien searches, updates and document recordings.

Valley Abstract & Trustee Services

1408 Palm Valley Dr East, Harlingen, TX 78552
Phone: 956-571-1119 - **Fax:** 956-412-1117 valleyabstract@aol.com

Types of Records Retrieved: Civil and Probate courts; Federal courts; Real Estate; Tax Liens/Judgments; UCC records

Local Retrieval Area: TX-Cameron, Hidalgo, Willacy

Add'l Information: Established 1998. Normal turnaround time- 24-48 hours. Projects billed by number of names searched. They specialize in providing quality title abstracting (focusing on foreclosure work) and trustee services in the Rio Grande Valley of TX.

Valley County Abstract Company

431 2nd Ave S, Glasgow, MT 59230
Phone: 406-228-2350 - **Fax:** 406-228-2350

Types of Records Retrieved: Criminal, Civil and Probate courts; Real Estate; Tax Liens/Judgments; UCC records; Vital records

Local Retrieval Area: MT-Valley

Add'l Information: Established 1950. Normal turnaround time- variable depending on project. Projects billed by the hour. They specialize in mineral searches and title insurance.

Valley Security Inc

3136 Hwy 70, Thatcher, AZ 85552
Phone: 928-428-2142 - **Fax:** 928-428-6653

Types of Records Retrieved: Criminal, Civil and Probate courts; Real Estate; Tax Liens/Judgments; Vital records

Local Retrieval Area: AZ-Cochise, Graham, Greenlee

Add'l Information: Established 2000. First project may require prepayment. They provide document retrieval and messenger service to and from attorneys and courts. They do not service Southern Cochise County. Performs service of process.

Valley Title Services Inc
PO Box 141, 306 W Pike St, Vevay, IN 47043
Phone: 812-427-2135 - **Fax:** 812-427-2139
Types of Records Retrieved: Civil and Probate courts; Real Estate; Tax Liens/Judgments; UCC records
Local Retrieval Area: IN-Switzerland
Add'l Information: Normal turnaround time- normally 36-48 hours. Will file/record documents for clients.

Valverde Abstract Co Inc
PO Box 5, 304 Main St, Center, NE 68724
Phone: 402-288-4466 - **Fax:** 402-288-4426
Types of Records Retrieved: Criminal, Civil and Probate courts; Real Estate; Tax Liens/Judgments
Local Retrieval Area: NE-Knox
Add'l Information: Established 1987. Normal turnaround time- 48 hours. Projects billed by the hour. First project may require prepayment. Will file/record documents for clients.

Van Buren Abstract Co
PO Box 218, 405 Dodge St, Keosauqua, IA 52565
Phone: 319-293-7760 - **Fax:** 319-293-6431
Types of Records Retrieved: Criminal, Civil and Probate courts; Real Estate; Tax Liens/Judgments; UCC records; Vital records
Local Retrieval Area: IA-Van Buren
Add'l info: Established 1930. Normal turnaround time- 2-3 days. Fee basis will vary by the type of project. First project may require prepayment.

Van Buren County Abstract Office
207 Paw Paw St, Paw Paw, MI 49079
Phone: 269-657-4250 - **Fax:** 269-657-3207 vbcao@aol.com
Types of Records Retrieved: Criminal, Civil and Probate courts; Real Estate; Tax Liens/Judgments; UCC records; Vital records
Local Retrieval Area: MI-Van Buren
Add'l Information: Established 1800. Normal turnaround time- 2-3 days. Expedited service available. Fee basis will vary by type of project. All projects require prepayment. They specialize in real estate matters.

Kevin Van Tilburg
6760 Fleetfoot Rd, Celina, OH 45822
Phone: 419-733-0478 - **Fax:** 419-942-6538
Types of Records Retrieved: Criminal and Civil courts; Real Estate; Tax Liens/Judgments
Local Retrieval Area: OH-Darke, Defiance, Fulton, Hancock, Hardin, Henry, Paulding, Putnam, Shelby, Van Wert, Wood
Add'l Information: Established 1990s. Normal turnaround time- 24-72 hours. Projects billed by number of names searched. First project may require prepayment. He specializes in Northwest Ohio.

Vance Title Research
777 Ivy Hill, Harlan, KY 40831-1536
Phone: 606-574-1912, cell- 606-273-2460 - **Fax:** 606-573-7912
lsvance@hotmail.com
Records Retrieved: Real Estate; Tax Liens/Judgments; UCC records
Local Retrieval Area: KY-Bell, Clay, Harlan, Knott, Knox, Laurel, Leslie, Letcher, Perry, Whitley
Add'l Information: Established 2001. Normal turnaround time- 24-48 hours. Projects billed by number of names searched. First project may require prepayment. She specializes in real estate.

Vancouver Legal Messengers Inc
412 W 12th St #C, Vancouver, WA 98660-2801
Phone: 888-695-3654; 360-695-3654 - **Fax:** 360-695-3894
www.vanlegal.com **email:** vlm@vanlegal.com
Types of Records Retrieved: Criminal and Civil courts; Federal courts; Real Estate; Tax Liens/Judgments; UCC records; Vital records
Local Retrieval Area: OR-Clackamas, Multnomah, Washington; WA-Clark, Cowlitz, Klickitat, Pacific, Skamania, Wahkiakum. **Correspondent Relationships:** worldwide.
Add'l Information: Established 1995. Normal turnaround time- 2-3 days. Expedited service available. Projects billed by number of names searched. Projects billed by the hour. First project may require prepayment. VLM can file legal documents with local, state and federal court systems, also deliver documents to the County Clerk, Auditor, Recorder or other municipal offices. Performs service of process.

Vanhorn & Vanhorn Inc
PO Box 1742, Clarksburg, WV 26302
Phone: 304-623-1362 - **Fax:** 304-623-1363
www.vanhornpi.com **email:** info@vanhornpi.com
Types of Records Retrieved: Criminal, Civil and Probate courts; Federal courts; Real Estate; Tax Liens/Judgments; UCC records; Vital records; Voter registration records
Local Retrieval Area: WV-Barbour, Doddridge, Harrison, Lewis, Marion, Taylor, Upshur. **Correspondent Relationships:** Roanoke, VA.
Add'l info: Established 1979. Turnaround time- 1-3 days. Projects billed by number of names searched. Fees negotiated with volume. First project may require prepayment. Will file/record documents for clients. They specialize in civil and criminal courts, probate courts, federal courts, real estate, tax liens and judgments, UCC records, vital records and voter registration records. A licensed PI in VA, WV. Performs service of process.

Variety International Processing Inc
100 E Linton Blvd #202A, Delray Beach, FL 33483
Phone: 877-245-6994; 561-243-6994 - **Fax:** 561-265-3476
stangooden@bellsouth.net
Types of Records Retrieved: Criminal and Civil courts
Local Retrieval Area: FL-Broward, Dade, Palm Beach, St. Lucie
Add'l Information: Established 2001.

Varoga & Shallett
3303 Louisiana #240, Houston, TX 77006
Phone: 713-522-0101 - **Fax:** 713-522-0440
Types of Records Retrieved: Criminal, Civil and Probate courts; Federal courts; Real Estate; Tax Liens/Judgments; UCC records; Vital records
Local Retrieval Area: TX-Harris. **Correspondent Relationships:** Alameda, Contra Costa, Marin, San Francisco, San Mateo, Santa Clara counties CA.
Add'l Information: Established 1995. Normal turnaround time- 1 day. Projects billed by the hour. They specialize in search strategy design as well as drafting and monitoring FOIA and Open Records Act requests.

VeriCorp Inc
PO Box 436054, Louisville, KY 40253-6054
Phone: 502-413-5313 - **Fax:** 502-413-5313
www.vericorp.org **email:** gdewitt@vericorp.org
Types of Records Retrieved: Criminal and Civil courts
Local Retrieval Area: KY-Fayette, Jefferson, Oldham, Shelby. **Correspondent Relationships:** national and worldwide.
Add'l Information: Established 1996. Normal turnaround time- 24-36 hours. Projects billed by number of names searched. First project may require prepayment. Credit cards accepted. Invoice terms are net 15 days. Full-service company with electronic data communication capability. Provides Internet based ASP for clients and Internet order/delivery. Automated processing system available for screening companies and court researchers.

Verifi LLC
PO Box 519, Harrison, TN 37341
Phone: 423-344-0133 - **Fax:** 423-344-0602 verifi@bellsouth.net
Types of Records Retrieved: Criminal and Civil courts; Federal courts; Real Estate; Tax Liens/Judgments; UCC records
Local Retrieval Area: GA-Burke, Catoosa, Chattooga, Columbia, Dade, Gilmer, McDuffie, Murray, Richmond, Walker, Warren, Whitfield; SC-Aiken, Allendale, Barnwell, Edgefield, Lexington, Richland; TN-Anderson, Blunt, Bledsoe, Bradley, Cumberland, Hamilton, Knox, Loudon, Marion,

McMinn, Meigs, Monroe, Morgan, Polk, Putnam, Rhea, Roane, Sequatchie, Sevier

Add'l Information: Established 1993. Normal turnaround time- 24-72 hours depending on courthouse. Projects billed by number of names searched. First project may require prepayment. Will file/record documents for clients. Monthly billing for most accounts. 17 years experience; will tailor service to fit your needs; former Experian manager.

Verified Credentials Inc

20890 Kenbridge Ct, Lakeville, MN 55044
Phone: 800-473-4934; 952-985-7200 - **Fax:** 952-985-7218
www.verifiedcredentials.com **Types of Records Retrieved:** Criminal, Civil and Probate courts; Federal courts; Real Estate; Tax Liens/Judgments; UCC records; Vital records

Local Retrieval Area: MN-Anoka, Carver, Chisago, Dakota, Goodhue, Hennepin, Ramsey, Rice, Scott, Sherburne, Stearns, Washington, Wright. **Correspondent Relationships:** nationwide.

Add'l Information: Established 1984. Normal turnaround time- 24 hours. Projects billed by number of names searched. Credit cards accepted. They specialize in employment background screening. They have 20 years of criminal record searching experience.

Verified Inc

9800 Bluemound Rd, Milwaukee, WI 53226
Phone: 866-265-9426; 414-727-1718 - **Fax:** 414-727-5510
www.verifiedinc.com **email:** adam@verifiedinc.com

Types of Records Retrieved: Criminal and Civil courts; Federal courts

Local Retrieval Area: WI-Milwaukee, Sheboygan, Washington, Waukesha. **Correspondent Relationships:** statewide.

Add'l Information: Established 2002. Normal turnaround time- 24-72 hours. Records in a vault can take 1 week. Projects are billed by the number of names searches, plus court copy fees. First project may require prepayment. Credit cards accepted. Will invoice monthly. Verified Inc provides employment screening services to employers across the country. They comply with FCRA requirements. Their attorney reviews all records before they release results.

Veritas Information Services

9 Alton St, Arlington, MA 02474
Phone: 781-643-7811 - **Fax:** 781-643-1136
www.veritasinfo.com **email:** michael@veritasinfo.com

Types of Records Retrieved: Real Estate; Genealogical Searches

Local Retrieval Area: MA-Middlesex, Norfolk, Suffolk. **Correspondent Relationships:** Essex, Barnstable, Bristol, Worcester counties.

Add'l info: Established 1994. Turnaround time- 48 hours; longer for real estate. Projects billed by the hour. First project may require prepayment. Will file/record documents for clients. They specialize in real estate title examinations, including resolution of lost or disputed ownerships.

Vermont Land Records Research

460 Acorn Ln, Shelburne, VT 05482-6395
Phone: 802-985-9723 - **Fax:** 802-985-9723
www.vermontlandrecords.com **email:** ddf@together.net

Types of Records Retrieved: Criminal, Civil and Probate courts; Federal courts; Real Estate; Tax Liens/Judgments; UCC records: Vital records

Local Retrieval Area: VT-Addison, Chittenden. **Correspondent Relationships:** all of Vermont.

Add'l Information: Established 1995. Normal turnaround time- 48 hours. Projects billed by the hour. Will file/record documents for clients. They specialize in real estate/land records.They file documents in Chittenden County only. A member of VITAL - Vermont Land Records group.

Vinita Title Co

PO Box 306, Vinita, OK 74301 **Phone:** 918-256-2617 - **Fax:** 918-256-3412
www.vinitatitle.com **email:** vtc@vinitatitle.com

Types of Records Retrieved: Real Estate; Tax Liens/Judgments; UCC records; Vital records **Local Retrieval Area:** OK-Craig

Add'l Information: Established 1972. Normal turnaround time- 48 hours. Projects billed by number of names searched. All projects require prepayment. Will file/record documents for clients.

Vinson Detective Agency TN

2008 E Magnolia Ave, Knoxville, TN 37917
Phone: 888-525-5047; 865-525-5047 - **Fax:** 865-525-7960
www.vinsonguard.com **email:** operations@vinsonguard.com

Types of Records Retrieved: Criminal, Civil and Probate courts; Federal courts; Real Estate; Tax Liens/Judgments; UCC records; Vital records

Local Retrieval Area: TN-Anderson, Blount, Jefferson, Knox, Sevier

Add'l Information: Normal turnaround time- 3-5 days. Projects billed by number of names searched. First project may require prepayment. Credit cards accepted. Performs service of process.

Vio-Com-Data Research

6295 N Anna St, Fresno, CA 93710-5305
Phone: 559-438-1058 - **Fax:** 559-438-1158 Kricha4634@aol.com

Types of Records Retrieved: Criminal, Civil and Probate courts; Federal courts; Real Estate

Local Retrieval Area: CA-Fresno, Kern, Kings, Madera, Tulare, Ventura. **Correspondent Relationships:** nationwide.

Add'l Information: Established 1996. Normal turnaround time- 24 hours in Fresno and Madera; 48 hours for other counties. Projects billed by number of names searched. Will file/record documents for clients. Monthly billing available. Terms are net 45 days. They have over 30 years experience in criminal research. Lowest prices and best service, can beat any other prices in the area. Cell number is 559-974-1961.

VIP Services LLC

1312-C Ashley River Rd, Charleston, SC 29407
Phone: 888-249-9947; 843-402-6868 - **Fax:** 843-402-0149
www.vip-servicesllc.com **email:** vips-viper@msn.com

Types of Records Retrieved: Criminal, Civil and Probate courts; Federal courts; Real Estate; Tax Liens/Judgments; UCC records

Local Retrieval Area: SC-Bamberg, Berkley, Calhoun, Charleston, Dorchester, Lexington, Orangeburg

Add'l Information: Established 1994. Normal turnaround time- 24-48 hours. Expedite service available. Projects billed by the hour. Plus court costs. Credit cards accepted. Paid prior to issuance but after retrieval. They are a full service regional investigation and research company. Full time staff in coastal and midlands regions. Experts in property and real-estate records. A licensed PI in SC.

VISTA Inc

29516 Southfield Rd, Southfield, MI 48076-2029
Phone: 248-559-3500 - **Fax:** 248-559-4757
www.vistapi.com **email:** gporter@vistapi.com

Types of Records Retrieved: Criminal, Civil and Probate courts; Federal courts; Real Estate; Tax Liens/Judgments; UCC records; Vital records

Local Retrieval Area: MI-Macomb, Monroe, Oakland, Washtenaw, Wayne. **Correspondent Relationships:** Michigan.

Add'l info: Established 1976. Normal turnaround time- 1-2 weeks depending on the county. Projects billed by number of names searched. Projects billed by the hour. First project may require prepayment. May require retainer if not affiliated with national PI organization. They specialize in defense sub rosa. They also have the capability to retrieve documents in most European venues. A licensed PI in MI. Performs service of process.

Robert Vollrath

PO Box 010068, Miami, FL 33101-0068
Phone: 305-343-9344 - **Fax:** 305-444-1563 robvoll@bellsouth.net

Types of Records Retrieved: Criminal, Civil and Probate courts; Federal courts; Real Estate; Tax Liens/Judgments; UCC records; Vital records

Local Retrieval Area: FL-Dade

Add'l Information: Established 1983. Normal turnaround time- 1 week. Projects billed by the hour. All projects require prepayment. He is a licensed private investigator who specializes in process service. A licensed PI in FL. Performs service of process.

VPS
311 Hiddenwood Rd, Fayston, VT 05673
Phone: 802-496-6863 - **Fax:** 802-496-6865 vpsdcain@madriver.com
Types of Records Retrieved: Criminal and Civil courts
Local Retrieval Area: VT-Chittenden, Washington
Add'l Information: Established 1997. All projects require prepayment. They also provide court filings, subpoena preparation, photocopying, skiptracing, videography, photography, and state public record searches. Performs service of process.

W.E. Works Office/Attorney Support
2373 Apache Dr, Bishop, CA 93514
Phone: 760-873-3788 - **Fax:** 760-873-4208
www.weworks.com/wwnpage2.html **email:** weworks98@yahoo.com
Types of Records Retrieved: Criminal and Civil courts; Bankruptcy court; Real Estate; Tax Liens/Judgments; Vital records
Local Retrieval Area: CA-Inyo, Mono
Add'l Information: Established 1997. Normal turnaround time- 1-2 days. Expedited service available. Projects billed by the hour. First project may require prepayment. They have a mobile photocopier and are a mobile Notary Public; certified notary signing agent. Member of CAPPS, NAPPS, NNA. Performs service of process.

Wabash Valley Abstract Co Inc
PO Box 1350, 2 1/2 N Broadway #203, Peru, IN 46970
Phone: 765-472-4351 - **Fax:** 765-472-4352
www.wvaco.com **Types of Records Retrieved:** Civil and Probate courts; Real Estate; Tax Liens/Judgments; UCC records
Local Retrieval Area: IN-Miami
Add'l Information: Established 1929. Normal turnaround time- 5-7 days. Projects billed by number of records located. Payments are also based on the premium and search time.

Wabasha County Abstract Co
100 W Main St, Wabasha, MN 55981
Phone: 651-565-3391 - **Fax:** 651-565-0227 wababst@wabasha.net
Types of Records Retrieved: Civil and Probate courts; Federal courts; Real Estate; Tax Liens/Judgments; UCC records; Vital records
Local Retrieval Area: MN-Wabasha
Add'l Information: Established 1976. Normal turnaround time- 2 days. Projects billed by number of names searched. Payment upon receipt of invoice. They specialize in posting abstract of title, preparing owner & encumbrance reports, name searches, real estate tax searches, preparation of new abstracts and research of real estate records. Also do title insurance.

Wagoner County Abstract Co
PO Box 188, 219 E Cherokee, 74467, Wagoner, OK 74477
Phone: 918-485-2215 - **Fax:** 918-485-9162 avcfi@aol.com
Types of Records Retrieved: Civil and Probate courts; Real Estate; Tax Liens/Judgments; UCC records **Local Retrieval Area:** OK-Wagoner
Add'l Information: Established 1907. Normal turnaround time- 2-3 days. Projects billed on per case basis. Personal checks and cash are accepted. They have serviced Wagoner County since 1907.

Wakeman Process Service Inc
22283 Main Street, Hayward, CA 94541 **Phone:** 510-886-7667
Fax: 510-886-1523 wakeman_process@hotmail.com
Records Retrieved: Criminal, Civil and Probate courts; Federal courts
Local Retrieval Area: CA-Alameda, Contra Costa, San Francisco, San Mateo, Santa Clara. **Correspondent Relationships:** nationwide.
Add'l Information: Established 1967. Normal turnaround time- 3-5 business days depending on size of job. Projects billed by number of names searched. Projects billed by number of records located. First project may require prepayment. All records copied on microfilm copier and reproduced according to request. Also offer subpoena preparation and service. Performs service of process.

Walla Walla Title Co
PO Box 1058, 102 W Main St #100, Walla Walla, WA 99362
Phone: 509-525-8660 - **Fax:** 509-529-4716
Types of Records Retrieved: Civil and Probate courts; Real Estate; Tax Liens/Judgments; UCC records; Vital records
Local Retrieval Area: WA-Walla Walla
Add'l Information: Established 1970. Normal turnaround time- 1-2 days. Fee basis is determined on "per job". Out of area clients are asked to prepay. They specialize in real estate matters.

Walsh Investigative Services
PO Box 524, Fishkill, NY 12524-0524
Phone: 845-896-3566 - **Fax:** 845-896-3584
www.walshinvestigative.com **email:** hwalsh@walshinvestigative.com
Types of Records Retrieved: Criminal, Civil and Probate courts; Federal courts; Real Estate; Tax Liens/Judgments; UCC records; Vital records
Local Retrieval Area: NY-Columbia, Dutchess, Orange, Putnam, Rockland, Sullivan, Ulster, Westchester. **Correspondent Relationships:** New York County, Long Island, Albany.
Add'l Information: Established 1988. Normal turnaround time- 1-2 days. Expedited service available. Projects billed by the hour. First project may require prepayment. Will file/record documents for clients. They specialize in all types of record retrieval, all types of investigations and all types of searches performed. A licensed PI in NY. Performs service of process.

🏛Walt J Grant Title Services
222 Brandon Rd, Norristown, PA 19403
Phone: 610-631-7672 - **Fax:** 610-631-7614 granwax@comcast.net
Types of Records Retrieved: Criminal, Civil and Probate courts; Federal courts; Real Estate; Tax Liens/Judgments; UCC records; Vital records
Local Retrieval Area: PA-Montgomery
Add'l Information: Established 1990. Normal turnaround time- 12-24 hours. Projects billed by number of names searched. Billed at the end of month. Company has 2 persons working in the courthouse and home office. Working with attorneys, title companies, banks and individuals.

🏛Walters Document Service
3102 E 1st, Wichita, KS 67214
Phone: 316-682-5629 - **Fax:** 316-682-1476 ljwalt@southwind.net
Types of Records Retrieved: Criminal, Civil and Probate courts; Federal courts; Real Estate; Tax Liens/Judgments; UCC records
Local Retrieval Area: KS-Butler, Cowley, Harvey, Reno, Sedgwick, Sumner
Add'l Information: Established 2005. Normal turnaround time- 24-48 hours. Projects billed by number of names searched. Will invoice client. They conduct document retrievals, service of process, skiptracing and private investigations. Has work experience of 20 years as a private investigator and 7 years as an insurance investigator. A licensed PI in KS. Performs service of process.

Walworth County Abstract & Title
PO Box 418, Selby, SD 57472-0418
Phone: 605-649-7772 - **Fax:** 605-649-7204
Types of Records Retrieved: Civil and Probate courts; Real Estate; Tax Liens/Judgments; UCC records
Local Retrieval Area: SD-Walworth
Add'l info: Established 1895. Normal turnaround time- 2 days. Projects billed by number of records located. Will file/record documents for clients.

Ward Abstracting Services

25 Windsong Dr, Roanoke Rapids, NC 27870-8112

Phone: 252-535-3440 mhl1959@aol.com

Types of Records Retrieved: Criminal, Civil and Probate courts; Real Estate; Tax Liens/Judgments; UCC records; Vital records

Local Retrieval Area: NC-Halifax, Northampton, Warren. **Correspondent Relationships:** They may search nearby counties upon request such as Edgecombe, Nash, Franklin, Vance, others.

Add'l Information: Established 1986. Normal turnaround time- 24 hours; most performed the same day. Projects billed by number of names searched. All projects require prepayment. Has 25 years experience in courthouse real estate searches and record searches that include civil, probate, UCC, vitals, tax liens and real estate.

Larry M Warner

PO Box 601, Crossville, TN 38557 **Phone:** 931-484-1611

Records Retrieved: Criminal courts; Real Estate; Tax Liens/Judgments

Local Retrieval Area: TN-Clay, Cumberland, Fentress, Overton, Pickett, Putnam, White

Add'l Information: Established 1974. Normal turnaround time- 1-2 days. Fee basis will vary with type of search. He is an attorney. For real estate, they can only provide records from Cumberland county.

Warren County Abstract Company

215 W Salem Ave, Indianola, IA 50125-2420

Phone: 515-961-7479 - **Fax:** 515-961-7470

Types of Records Retrieved: Real Estate; Tax Liens/Judgments; Probate courts; UCC records; Vital records

Local Retrieval Area: IA-Warren

Add'l Information: Established 1970. Normal turnaround time- 24 hours for most abstract continuations and 1 week for title abstracts. Projects billed by number of names searched. Projects billed by number of records located. Personal checks are accepted.

Wasatch Investigations Inc

1271 South, 2430 West, Syracuse, Roy, UT 84075

Phone: 800-970-8220; 801-773-8220 - **Fax:** 801-773-8229

Types of Records Retrieved: Criminal and Civil courts

Retrieval Area UT-Box Elder, Cache, Davis, Salt Lake, Tooele, Utah, Weber

Add'l Information: Established 2003. First project may require prepayment. The also provide court filings, subpoena preparation, photocopying, skiptracing, private and fire investigations. A licensed PI in UT. Performs service of process.

Washington County Title

35 W Idaho St, Weiser, ID 83672

Phone: 208-414-1455 - **Fax:** 208-414-1487

Types of Records Retrieved: Criminal, Civil and Probate courts; Real Estate; Tax Liens/Judgments; UCC records

Local Retrieval Area: ID-Washington

Add'l Information: Established 1980. Normal turnaround time- 24 hours. Projects billed by number of names searched. Projects billed by number of records located. First project may require prepayment. Will file/record documents for clients. They specialize in Washington County and can meet you needs.

Washington County Title Co

158 Main Ave, PO Box 397, Akron, CO 80720

Phone: 970-345-2256 - **Fax:** 970-345-2953

Records Retrieved: Real Estate; Tax Liens/Judgments; UCC records

Local Retrieval Area: CO-Washington

Add'l Information: Established 1887. Normal turnaround time- 1 week. Projects billed by number of names searched. Terms are net 30 days. First project may require prepayment. Will file/record documents for clients. Title insurance and abstracting.

Washington Court Records Service

PO Box 30291, Spokane, WA 99223

Phone: 509-448-5012 - **Fax:** 509-448-8221

Types of Records Retrieved: Criminal, Civil and Probate courts; Federal courts; Real Estate; Tax Liens/Judgments; UCC records; Vital records

Local Retrieval Area: WA-Adams, Asotin, Benton, Chelan, Clallam, Clark, Cowlitz, Douglas, Ferry, Franklin, Garfield, Grant, Grays Harbor, Island, Jefferson, King, Kitsap, Kittitas, Klickitat, Lewis, Lincoln, Mason, Okanogan, Pacific, Pend Oreille, Pierce, San Juan, Skagit, Skamania, Snohomish, Spokane, Stevens, Thurston, Walla Walla, Whitman, Yakima; OR-Baker, Benton, Clackamas, Clatsop, Columbia, Coos, Crook, Curry, Deschutes, Douglas, Gilliam, Grant, Hood River, Jackson, Jefferson, Josephine, Klamath, Lane, Lincoln, Linn, Marion, Morrow, Multnomah, Polk, Sherman, Tillamook, Umatilla, Union, Wallowa, Washington, Wheeler, Yamhill; MT-Beaverhead, Blaine, Broadwater, Carbon, Carter, Cascade, Dawson, Fergus, Flathead, Gallatin, Wibaux. **Correspondent Relationships:** WA, MT, ID, OR.

Add'l Information: Normal turnaround time- negotiable. Projects billed by number of names searched. Projects billed by the hour. Will file/record documents for clients. Bill twice monthly unless otherwise arranged. They have over 20 years experience with personal court visit research, they take pride in accurate service in a timely manor, using efficient, dependable researchers. Nationwide correspondence are abundant.

Washington Document Service (DC)

1023 15th St NW 12th Floor, Washington, DC 20005

Phone: 800-728-5201; 202-628-5200 - **Fax:** 800-385-3823

www.wdsdocs.com **email:** wdsdocs@worldnet.att.net

Types of Records Retrieved: Criminal, Civil and Probate courts; Federal courts; Real Estate; Tax Liens/Judgments; UCC records; Vital records

Local Retrieval Area: DC-District of Columbia; MD-Montgomery; VA-Arlington, Fairfax, Richmond City. **Correspondent Relationships:** nationwide and Canada.

Add'l Information: Established 1979. Normal turnaround time- same day. Projects billed by the hour. First project may require prepayment. Credit cards accepted. Visa, MasterCard and American Express accepted. They specialize in court research and obtaining documents nationwide including the Supreme Court and all state, federal and bankruptcy courts. They also search public agencies including the Securities and Exchange Commission. Case monitoring available.

Washita Valley Abstract Co

PO Box 458, Chickasha, OK 73023

Phone: 405-224-6111 - **Fax:** 405-222-4429

Types of Records Retrieved: Civil and Probate courts; Real Estate; Tax Liens/Judgments; UCC records

Local Retrieval Area: OK-Grady

Add'l Information: Established 1907. Normal turnaround time- 2-3 days. Fee basis is time. They specialize in complete abstracting, title insurance and loan closing services. Also do mineral ownership.

Watertown Title & Escrow Co

PO Box 1444, 20 S Maple St, Watertown, SD 57201

Phone: 605-886-8406 - **Fax:** 605-882-3473

Types of Records Retrieved: Real Estate; Tax Liens/Judgments; Probate courts; UCC records; Vital records **Local Retrieval Area:** SD-Codington

Add'l Information: Normal turnaround time- 2-5 days. Fee basis varies by type of transaction.

Watkins Investigations

746 Colonel Dr #2E, Garland, TX 75043

Phone: 972-926-6011 - **Fax:** 972-926-6022 rlw@myexcel.com

Types of Records Retrieved: Criminal, Civil and Probate courts; Real Estate; Tax Liens/Judgments; UCC records

Local Retrieval Area: TX-Dallas, Kaufman, Rockwall

Add'l Information: Established 1999. Normal turnaround time- 24-48 hours. Invoice monthly. They specialize in background investigations, public record research, locates, asset investigations, process service, surveillance. A licensed PI in TX. Performs service of process.

Kathi Watson

PO Box 45, Canton, NC 28716
Phone: 828-648-5830 - **Fax:** 828-648-0060 mycroft111@yahoo.com
Types of Records Retrieved: Criminal, Civil and Probate courts; Real Estate; Tax Liens/Judgments; UCC records; Vital records
Local Retrieval Area: NC-Haywood, Jackson. **Correspondent Relationships:** Western NC depending on nature of project.
Add'l Information: Established 1978. Normal turnaround time- 24-48 hours. Projects billed by number of names searched. All projects require prepayment. Credit cards accepted. Will file/record documents for clients. PayPal.com is used for Credit Card use. She specializes in real estate and title searches. Other counties available depending on need and cost.

Wayne County Abstract

103 Sycamore St, Greenville, MO 63944
Phone: 573-224-3616 - **Fax:** 573-224-3196 wayneabs@alltel.com
Types of Records Retrieved: Civil and Probate courts; Real Estate; Tax Liens/Judgments
Local Retrieval Area: MO-Wayne
Add'l Information: Established 1905. First project may require prepayment. They specialize in any real estate-related records. Also do title insurance, closings and record searches.

We Search Information Retrieval

PO Box 20646, St Petersburg, FL 33742
Phone: 727-656-6977 - **Fax:** 727-577-0158 wesearchinfo@aol.com
Types of Records Retrieved: Criminal and Civil courts; Real Estate
Local Retrieval Area: FL-Pinellas. **Correspondents:** nationwide.
Add'l Information: Established 2005. Normal turnaround time- 2-8 hours. Expedited service available. Projects billed by number of names searched. Specializing in same day rush service.

We Search ReSearch Inc

PO Box 125, 316 N Main St, Avilla, IN 46710
Phone: 800-251-8167; 260-897-2336 - **Fax:** 260-897-4489; 260-897-3988
Types of Records Retrieved: Criminal, Civil and Probate courts; Federal courts; Real Estate; Tax Liens/Judgments; UCC records
Local Retrieval Area: IN-Adams, Allen, Benton, Blackford, Boone, Carroll, Cass, Clinton, DeKalb, Delaware, Elkhart, Fayette, Fountain, Fulton, Grant, Hamilton, Hancock, Hendricks, Henry, Howard, Huntington, Jasper, Jay, Johnson, Kosciusko, La Porte, LaGrange, Lake, Madison, Marion, Marshall, Miami, Montgomery, Newton, Noble, Porter, Pulaski, Randolph, Rush, Shelby, St Joseph, Starke, Steuben, Tippecanoe, Tipton, Union, Wabash, Warren, Wayne, Wells, White, Whitley
Add'l Information: Established 1997. Normal turnaround time- 24-48 hours. Projects billed by number of records located. Will file/record documents for clients. Will invoice on a monthly basis, except when requested a different billing method. They specialize in felony and misdemeanor searches, civil charge searches, UCC, mortgages, judgments, tax liens, deed searches and bankruptcy searches. They have been in service for 10 years.

Weber Abstract Co

PO Box 263, Madison, SD 57042
Phone: 605-256-4640 - **Fax:** 605-256-3835
www.weberabstract.com **email:** info@weberabstract.com
Types of Records Retrieved: Civil and Probate courts; Real Estate; Tax Liens/Judgments; UCC records; Vital records
Local Retrieval Area: SD-Lake
Add'l Information: Established 1949. Normal turnaround time- 1 day to 2 weeks. Fee basis is set by law. First project may require prepayment. They specialize in title work.

David V Weber, Attorney

849 Brookfield Pky, Augusta, GA 30907-3157
Phone: 706-860-8160 dvweber@bellsouth.net
Types of Records Retrieved: Real Estate
Local Retrieval Area: GA-Burke, Columbia, Richmond
Add'l Information: Established 1976. Normal turnaround time- usually up to 3 days. Fee basis will vary by the type of project. He specializes in title searches.

Webster County-Butler & Rhodes Abstract

628 Central Ave, Fort Dodge, IA 50501-3812
Phone: 515-573-3341 - **Fax:** 515-573-8806
Types of Records Retrieved: Criminal, Civil and Probate courts; Real Estate; Tax Liens/Judgments; UCC records; Vital records
Local Retrieval Area: IA-Webster
Add'l Information: Normal turnaround time- 1-2 days. Fee basis will vary by the type of project. First project may require prepayment.

Webster's Research Inc

PO Box 7565, Rapid City, SD 57709
Phone: 605-718-5472 - **Fax:** 605-718-3914 lwebster@rushmore.com
Types of Records Retrieved: Criminal, Civil and Probate courts; Federal courts; Real Estate; Tax Liens/Judgments; UCC records
Local Retrieval Area: SD-Butte, Custer, Fall River, Lawrence, Meade, Pennington. **Correspondent Relationships:** statewide.
Add'l Information: Established 2000. Normal turnaround time- 24-48 hours. Projects billed by number of names searched. Will file/record documents for clients. Invoice with the job, payment due within 30 days. They specialize in real estate, record searches and filing in all federal, state and county agencies in South Dakota, including Secretary of State.

Weeks and Associates LLC

316 W 12th St #308, Austin, TX 78701
Phone: 512-472-9989 - **Fax:** 512-494-1133
www.carlweeks.com **email:** cw@carlweeks.com
Types of Records Retrieved: Criminal, Civil and Probate courts; Federal courts; Tax Liens/Judgments; UCC records; Vital records
Local Retrieval Area: TX-Travis, Williamson. **Correspondent Relationships:** Dallas, Harris, Bexar, Tarrant counties TX.
Add'l Information: Established 1992. Normal turnaround time- 2 business days. Expedited service available. Projects billed by number of names searched. All projects require prepayment. Credit cards accepted. They specialize in full service legal support, document service records from all State of TX agencies, medical & business records, deposition by written questions and business records affidavit. A licensed PI in TX. Performs service of process.

Weissinger & Hunter

PO Box 215, Rolling Fork, MS 39159
Phone: 662-873-6258 - **Fax:** 662-873-6903
Types of Records Retrieved: Criminal, Civil and Probate courts; Real Estate; Tax Liens/Judgments; UCC records; Vital records
Local Retrieval Area: MS-Issaquena, Sharkey
Add'l Information: Normal turnaround time- 2 days. Projects billed by the hour. First project may require prepayment. They are a law firm that will do public record searching.

Welch & Ekman

PO Box 107, 321 Briggs Ave S #2, Park River, ND 58270
Phone: 701-284-7833 - **Fax:** 701-284-7832
Types of Records Retrieved: Criminal, Civil and Probate courts; Real Estate; Tax Liens/Judgments; UCC records; Vital records
Local Retrieval Area: ND-Cavalier, Pembina, Walsh
Add'l Information: Established 1992. Normal turnaround time- 1 day. Projects billed by the hour.

Welliver & Associates LLC

22431 Antonio Pky #B160-435, Rancho Santa Margarita, CA 92688
Phone: 800-569-5677; 949-459-5919 - **Fax:** 949-459-5922
www.4quicksearch.com **email:** welliver@4quicksearch.com
Types of Records Retrieved: Criminal courts; Federal courts

Local Retrieval Area: CA-Los Angeles, Orange, Riverside, San Bernardino, San Diego, Ventura. **Correspondent Relationships:** nationwide.

Add'l Information: Established 1989. Normal turnaround time- 24 hours. Projects billed by number of names searched. Credit cards accepted. They specialize in retail loss prevention, internal theft, investigations and bank account searches (judgments required). A licensed PI in CA. Performs service of process.

Wells Abstract Co

PO Box 732, 119 S 10th, Hannibal, MO 63401
Phone: 573-221-0644 - **Fax:** 573-221-7303

Types of Records Retrieved: Civil and Probate courts; Real Estate; Tax Liens/Judgments; UCC records

Local Retrieval Area: MO-Audrain, Knox, Lewis, Macon, Marion, Monroe, Ralls, Randolph, Shelby

Add'l Information: Established 1900. Normal turnaround time- 2 days. Projects billed by number of records located. Will file/record documents for clients. Personal checks accepted.

Wells County Abstract

523 Railroad St South, Fessenden, ND 58438
Phone: 701-547-3433

Types of Records Retrieved: Real Estate; Tax Liens/Judgments

Local Retrieval Area: ND-Wells **Add'l Information:** First project may require prepayment. They specialize in real estate.

Weltner Phillips Law Office

PO Box 303, Mankato, KS 66956
Phone: 785-378-3172 - **Fax:** 785-378-3203 rweltmer@uscenter.net

Types of Records Retrieved: Criminal, Civil and Probate courts; Real Estate; Tax Liens/Judgments; UCC records

Local Retrieval Area: KS-Jewell. **Correspondent Relationships:** Mitchell, Republic, Smith counties KS.

Add'l Information: Normal turnaround time- 24 hours. Projects billed by the hour. Will file/record documents for clients. They accept personal checks. They also operate Weltner Phillips Abstract and Title Co. which specializes in title searches, abstracts, and title insurance. They have been in business over 65 years.

WERC - Wisconsin Employee & Renter Check

4141 N Bartlett Ave, Milwaukee, WI 53211
Phone: 414-967-9342 - **Fax:** 414-967-9346
www.wercinc.com **email:** aaronswerc@yahoo.com

Records Retrieved: Criminal and Civil courts; Tax Liens/Judgments

Local Retrieval Area: WI-Kenosha, Milwaukee, Ozaukee, Racine, Washington, Waukesha. **Correspondent Relationships:** subcontractors statewide.

Add'l Information: Established 1993. Normal turnaround time- 24 hours. Projects billed by number of names searched. First project may require prepayment. Credit cards accepted. Net 30 days after receipt of invoice. Formerly Cryaar Inv, they specialize in statewide criminal background checks and renter checks.

West Central Abstracting Co

202 Junius Ave, Fergus Falls, MN 56537
Phone: 218-736-5685 - **Fax:** 218-739-4610
westcen@prtel.com

Types of Records Retrieved: Real Estate; Tax Liens/Judgments; Probate courts; UCC records; Vital records

Local Retrieval Area: MN-Otter Tail

Add'l Information: Established 1988. Normal turnaround time- 3-5 days. Fee basis is per entry.

West Central Process Service

511 E 2nd St, Starbuck, MN 56381
Phone: 320-239-2665, cell- 320-808-6968

Types of Records Retrieved: Criminal and Civil courts

Local Retrieval Area: MN-Douglas, Grant, Pope, Stevens

Add'l info: Established 1977. Turnaround time- 24-48 hours. Billing may depend on the nature of job, volume. First project may require prepayment. They specialize in West Central Minnesota. Rush service available; investigations and security available. Performs service of process.

West Coast MCI

PO Box 627, Martinez, CA 94553 **Phone:** 925-372-8909

Types of Records Retrieved: Criminal, Civil and Probate courts; Federal courts; Real Estate; Tax Liens/Judgments; UCC records; Vital records

Local Retrieval Area: CA-Contra Costa, Solano. **Correspondent Relationships:** the bay area of Northern California.

Add'l Information: Established 1982. Normal turnaround time- 24-48 hours. Projects billed by the hour. First project may require prepayment. They specialize in hands-on searching and investigation since 1982. A licensed PI in CA. Performs service of process.

West Star Inv

1029 First St, Henderson, KY 42420
Phone: 270-826-4030, cell- 270-869-4071 - **Fax:** 270-827-5328
weststar@lightpower.net

Types of Records Retrieved: Criminal and Civil courts

Local Retrieval Area: KY-Henderson, Hopkins, Webster

Add'l Information: Normal turnaround time- not known. First project may require prepayment. Additional services may be available; call for availability of searches in other western Kentucky counties.

West Virginia Records Research

PO Box 2222, Huntington, WV 25722
Phone: 304-633-6964 - **Fax:** 304-697-0996
www.wvrecords.com **email:** william.alan@worldnet.att.net

Types of Records Retrieved: Criminal and Civil courts

Local Retrieval Area: WV-Cabell, Kanawha, Putnam, Wayne, Wood. **Correspondent Relationships:** Fayette, Raleigh, Boone, Pleasants, Jackson, Roane counties WV.

Add'l Information: Established 1998. Normal turnaround time- 24-36 hours. Projects billed by number of names searched. Net 15 days. Regular clients billed monthly. They specialize in protecting clients from costly mistakes. Since 1998, reliable and accurate, they provide background checks from court records. Discount rates available. Go online: www.wvrecords.com.

Wayne K Westblade, Attny

PO Box 1407, Syracuse, KS 67878
Phone: 620-384-5352 - **Fax:** 620-384-7694

Types of Records Retrieved: Criminal, Civil and Probate courts

Local Retrieval Area: KS-Hamilton

Add'l Information: Established 2000. Normal turnaround time- 24-48 hours. All projects require prepayment. They are a law firm but willing to search court records when needed.

Westchester Court Services-Fox Advertising Inc

PO Box 352, Tarrytown, NY 10591
Phone: 914-948-5200 - **Fax:** 914-948-5501

Types of Records Retrieved: Criminal, Civil and Probate courts; Federal courts; Tax Liens/Judgments; UCC records

Local Retrieval Area: NY-Rockland, Westchester. **Correspondent Relationships:** New York City, Queens, King, Bronx, Brooklyn, Staten Island, Long Island.

Add'l Information: Established 1937. Normal turnaround time- variable, depending on project. Projects billed by number of records located. Will file/record documents for clients. They retrieve records in only Rockland and Westchester Counties but do filings in Dutchess, Orange, Putnam, Rockland, Sullivan, Ulster, Westchester. Performs service of process.

Western Attorney Services

75 Columbia Sq, San Francisco, CA 94103-4099
Phone: 415-487-4140 - **Fax:** 415-864-6238

Records Retrieved: Criminal, Civil and Probate courts; Federal courts

Local Retrieval Area: CA-Alameda, Contra Costa, Marin, Monterey, San Francisco, San Mateo, Santa Clara, Solano, Sonoma. **Correspondent Relationships:** nationwide.

Add'l info: Turnaround time- same day. Call for fee charges. First project may require prepayment. They specialize in civil case record searches.

Western Kentucky Title

1135 Tennevue, Paducah, KY 42003
Phone: 270-898-9666 - **Fax:** 270-898-9667

Types of Records Retrieved: Real Estate; Tax Liens/Judgments

Local Retrieval Area: KY-Ballard, Calloway, Carlisle, Graves, Marshall, Mc Cracken

Add'l info: Established 1994. 1st project may require prepayment. They specialize in real estate. Has 2nd office in Murray, KY call 270-759-3760.

Western Nebraska Inv

PO Box 401, North Platte, NE 69103-0401
Phone: 308-534-9003 - **Fax:** 308-696-0009 wni804@hamilton.net

Types of Records Retrieved: Criminal and Civil courts; Real Estate; Tax Liens/Judgments; UCC records

Local Retrieval Area: NE-Custer, Dawson, Keith, Lincoln, Perkins

Add'l Information: Established 2000. Normal turnaround time- 24 hours. First project may require prepayment. They also provide photocopying, skiptracing, private investigations and interviews. Covers central and western Nebraska. A licensed PI in NE. Performs service of process.

Western Reporting

1787 Fort Union Blvd #107, Salt Lake City, UT 84121-2872
Phone: 800-466-1996; 801-281-2000 - **Fax:** 800-351-4558; 801-281-2005
www.westernreporting.com
email: customerservice@westernreporting.com

Types of Records Retrieved: Criminal courts; Probate courts

Local Retrieval Area: UT-Salt Lake. **Correspondents in:** Western US.

Add'l Information: Established 1993. Normal turnaround time- 4-24 hours. Projects billed by number of names searched. First project may require prepayment. Set up accounts of check by phone. They are a screening firm, they do tenant, employment and business screening statewide and nationally. They have reports that include criminal, credit, eviction, bad check and all verifications.

Westlaw Court Express

633 W 5th St #2300, Los Angeles, CA 90071
Phone: 800-766-3320; - **Fax:** 213-680-7813
www.courtexpress.com **email:** lsolancho@courtexpress.com

Types of Records Retrieved: Criminal, Civil and Probate courts; Federal courts; Real Estate; Tax Liens/Judgments; UCC records; Vital records

Local Retrieval Area: CA-Los Angeles, Orange, Sacramento, San Diego, San Francisco, San Mateo, Santa Clara. **Correspondent Relationships:** nationwide.

Add'l Information: Established 1981. Normal turnaround time- same or next day. Projects billed by the hour. First project may require prepayment. Credit cards accepted. Will file/record documents for clients. MasterCard, Visa accepted. They specialize in obtaining legal and financial documents from any source in the country. Provide online name/case searching and docket sheets.

WestLaw CourtEXPRESS (DC)

1100 13th St NW #300, Washington, DC 20005
Phone: 800-542-3320; 202-737-7111 - **Fax:** 202-628-1133
http://courtexpress.westlaw.com
email: WestlawCourtExpress@thomson.com

Types of Records Retrieved: Criminal and Civil courts; Federal courts; Supreme Court records

Local Retrieval Area: CA-Los Angeles; DC-District of Columbia; MD-Montgomery; NY-New York; VA-Arlington, Fairfax, Richmond. **Correspondent Relationships:** nationwide.

Add'l Information: Established 1979. Normal turnaround time- 24-48 hours. Projects billed by the hour. Credit cards accepted. They specialize in online searches and ordering of documents from any court USA court and from government agencies and various international courts. Also specialize in case monitoring and Freedom of Information Act requests. Performs service of process.

Weston County Title

PO Box 548, New Castle, WY 82701
Phone: 307-746-2001 - **Fax:** 307-746-2217

Types of Records Retrieved: Real Estate; Tax Liens/Judgments

Local Retrieval Area: WY-Weston

Add'l Information: Established 1996. First project may require prepayment. They specialize in real estate.

Derrick Wetherell

429 W 24th St #1E, New York, NY 10011
Phone: 646-216-9831 - **Fax:** 646-216-9831
dweth123@netscape.net

Types of Records Retrieved: Criminal, Civil and Probate courts; Federal courts; Real Estate; Tax Liens/Judgments; UCC records; Vital records

Local Retrieval Area: NY-New York, Putnam, Westchester

Add'l Information: Established 2005. Normal turnaround time- 24 hours in most cases. Projects billed by the hour. Fraud examiner formerly with top firm provides all aspects of public records retrieval, investigation and analysis. Several years experience, competitive rates.

Wetherill Law Office

215 Main St, Rockport, IN 47635
Phone: 812-649-2221 - **Fax:** 812-649-2222 wethlaw@sbcglobal.net

Types of Records Retrieved: Criminal, Civil and Probate courts; Real Estate; Tax Liens/Judgments; UCC records; Vital records

Local Retrieval Area: IN-Spencer

Add'l Information: Established 1970. Normal turnaround time- variable depending on search. Charges vary with the type of record. They specialize in record searches, deeds and title insurance. Has 36 years experience.

The Wethersfield Group

110 Haverhill Rd #308, Amesbury, MA 01913
Phone: 978-388-5551 - **Fax:** 978-388-4449
www.thewethersfieldgroup.com
email: thewethersfieldgroup@yahoo.com

Types of Records Retrieved: Criminal and Civil courts

Local Retrieval Area: MA-Essex, Middlesex. **Correspondent Relationships:** statewide.

Add'l Information: Established 1996. Normal turnaround time- Superior courts: 12-24 hours, District courts: varies according to court procedures, usually 48 hours. Projects are billed by the number of names searched and per court. Net due upon receipt of invoice. They are reliable, diligent, hands-on court researchers. Secure custom in-house computer program for volume processing and accurate, timely search results. Excellent court relationships. Responsive client communication.

WF Greenberg & Co LLC

7040 Seminole Pratt Whitney Rd #25-169, Loxahatchee, FL 33470-5717
Phone: 888-770-9008; 305-770-4437 - **Fax:** 800-770-4496; 786-248-3000
http://bgss.com **email:** bill@bgss.com

Types of Records Retrieved: Criminal, Civil and Probate courts; Federal courts; Real Estate; Tax Liens/Judgments; UCC records; Vital records; Property records

Local Retrieval Area: FL-Broward, Dade, Palm Beach. **Correspondent Relationships:** Florida.

Add'l Information: Established 1987. Normal turnaround time- 8-24 hours. Projects billed by number of names searched. Projects billed by the hour. All projects require prepayment. Credit cards accepted. Will file/record documents for clients. They specialize in the service of legal papers, current owner and other property searches, investigation, surveillance and document retrieval. A licensed PI in FL. Performs service of process.

Wheels of Justice Inc

657 Mission St #502, San Francisco, CA 94105
Phone: 800-649-1198; 415-546-6000 - **Fax:** 888-649-1199; 415-546-6199
www.proserver.com **email:** woj@proserver.com

Types of Records Retrieved: Civil and Probate courts; Federal courts; Real Estate; Tax Liens/Judgments; UCC records; Vital records

Local Retrieval Area: CA-Alameda, Contra Costa, Marin, San Francisco, San Mateo, Santa Clara. **Correspondent Relationships:** nationwide.

Add'l Information: Established 2000. Normal turnaround time- 24-48 hours. Expedited service available. Projects billed by number of names searched. Projects billed by the hour. First project may require prepayment. Credit cards accepted. They are a San Francisco based litigation support company with an experienced staff. They offer court research, court filings, service of process and skiptracing. Performs service of process.

Whiteside Abstract & Title Insurance

132 N State St, St Ignace, MI 49781
Phone: 906-643-9292 - **Fax:** 906-643-9806 whiteside@sault.com

Types of Records Retrieved: Real Estate; Tax Liens/Judgments; Probate courts; UCC records **Local Retrieval Area:** MI-Mackinac

Add'l Information: Normal turnaround time- 3-10 days. Fee basis will vary by type of project. First project may require prepayment. They specialize in real estate and title insurance.

Whiting Background & Legal Services

HC 88 Box 72B, Statts Mill, WV 25279
Phone: 304-372-6499 or 304-532-1613 - **Fax:** 304-372-6812
patonaw@yahoo.com

Types of Records Retrieved: Criminal courts; Tax Liens/Judgments

Local Retrieval Area: WV-Berkeley, Cabell, Fayette, Jackson, Jefferson, Kanawha, Putnam, Raleigh, Wood

Add'l info: Established 2002. Normal turnaround time- 24 hours or less. Projects billed by number of names searched. Will invoice monthly. They have been in business since 2002. They have been in civil and criminal law for 25 years. Civil, criminal, tax liens and civil verifications performed.

Wilma Whitney

303 E Ramon, Sharon Springs, KS 67758
Phone: 785-852-4932 grandma7@aol.com

Types of Records Retrieved: Criminal, Civil and Probate courts; Real Estate; Tax Liens/Judgments

Local Retrieval Area: KS-Cheyenne, Logan, Sherman, Thomas, Wallace

Add'l Information: Established 1990. Normal turnaround time- 24 hours in Wallace; other counties 2-5 days. Projects billed by number of names searched. Mileage charged for visits to counties other than Wallace. First project may require prepayment. She specializes in Wallace county in NW Kansas but she will travel to Cheyenne, Sherman, Logan and Thomas by special request. Call for fax number.

Wieder Young Research

501 Burnt Mills Ave, Silver Spring, MD 20901
Phone: 301-681-7206 - **Fax:** 301-593-1583 wiederyoung@comcast.net

Types of Records Retrieved: Criminal and Civil courts; Federal courts; Tax Liens/Judgments

Local Retrieval Area: MD-Baltimore, Baltimore City, Calvert, Carroll, Charles, Frederick, Harford, Howard, Montgomery, Prince George's, Washington. **Correspondent Relationships:** Washington, DC.

Add'l Information: Established 1990. Normal turnaround time- 24-36 hours. Projects billed by number of names searched. Formerly Wieder Young & Assoc Inc; new name adopted for 2007, still same great service. All of their searches are performed at the courthouse. They do not search State of Maryland web databases.

The Wilki Group Inc

2303 Randal Rd #307, Carpentersville, IL 60110-3448
Phone: 847-204-7339 - **Fax:** 847-930-0364
www.thewilkigroup.com **email:** info@thewilkigroup.com

Types of Records Retrieved: Real Estate; UCC records

Local Retrieval Area: IL-Cook, Du Page, Kane, McHenry, Will

Add'l Information: Established 2002. Normal turnaround time- 24-48 hours. Projects billed by number of records located. The Wilki Group is a public record retrieval/court filing company that services Northeastern IL.

Wilkin County Abstract

PO Box 910, Wahpeton, ND 58075
Phone: 701-642-3781 - **Fax:** 701-642-3852 richlandabstract@702com.net

Types of Records Retrieved: Criminal, Civil and Probate courts; Real Estate; Tax Liens/Judgments; UCC records

Local Retrieval Area: MN-Wilkin. **Correspondent Relationships:** Traverse, Stevens, Ottertail, Grant, Clay counties MN.

Add'l Information: Established 1922. Normal turnaround time- 1 week or less. Projects billed by number of names searched. Will file/record documents for clients. They are escrow agents and title insurance agents representing Old Republic and Stewart Title Insurance Company as well as Chicago Title.

Jacquie Willems

405 Normal St, Lindsborg, KS 67456
Phone: 785-227-4775 - **Fax:** 785-227-8792

Types of Records Retrieved: Criminal and Civil courts

Local Retrieval Area: KS-McPherson, Saline. **Correspondent Relationships:** Logan, Thomas, KS

Add'l Information: Established 2006. Normal turnaround time- 24-48 hours. Projects billed by number of names searched. First project may require prepayment.

William C Brown & Co

631 Walnut St, Reading, PA 19601
Phone: 610-373-1516 - **Fax:** 610-373-7360
Wm.C.Brown@juno.com

Types of Records Retrieved: Criminal, Civil and Probate courts; Real Estate; Tax Liens/Judgments; UCC records

Local Retrieval Area: PA-Berks

Add'l Information: Established 1972. Normal turnaround time- 1-2 days. Fee basis will vary by the type of project. First project may require prepayment. They specialize in title searches.

William R Young Law Office Inc

PO Box 472, Eddyville, KY 42038
Phone: 270-388-0807 - **Fax:** 270-388-0307 wryoung2@bellsouth.net

Records Retrieved: Real Estate; Tax Liens/Judgments; Probate courts

Local Retrieval Area: KY-Caldwell, Crittenden, Livingston, Lyon, Marshall, Trigg

Add'l Information: Established 1970. Normal turnaround time- 5 days or less. First project may require prepayment. He specializes in court records and real estate.

George Williams

PO Box 63, 113 A Main St, Quitman, MS 39355
Phone: 601-776-2111 - **Fax:** 601-776-2112

Types of Records Retrieved: Criminal, Civil and Probate courts; Real Estate; Tax Liens/Judgments; UCC records

Local Retrieval Area: MS-Clarke

Add'l Information: Normal turnaround time- 2-3 days. Projects billed by the hour. First project may require prepayment. He is an attorney.

Williamson Abstract Co

PO Box 43, Greenfield, IA 50849
Phone: 641-743-2175 - **Fax:** 641-743-6201

Types of Records Retrieved: Real Estate; Tax Liens/Judgments; UCC records; Vital records

Local Retrieval Area: IA-Adair

Add'l Information: Established 1960. Normal turnaround time- 2-5 days. Fee basis will vary by the type of search. Will file/record documents for clients. They require a retainer and will accept personal checks. They specialize in abstract and real estate searches.

John Wilmot

515 Vaughn Rd, Athens, GA 30606
Phone: 706-546-7411 - **Fax:** 706-354-4177
thewilmotcompany@hotmail.com

Types of Records Retrieved: Criminal, Civil and Probate courts; US District court; Real Estate; Tax Liens/Judgments; UCC records; Vital records

Local Retrieval Area: GA-Clarke, Jackson, Madison, Oconee, Oglethorpe,

Add'l Information: Established 1979. Normal turnaround time- 24-48 hours. Projects billed by number of names searched. They are a complete title company and will provide personalized, in-depth service.

Wilson Abstract Co

215 W Washington, Macomb, IL 61455
Phone: 309-833-2049 - **Fax:** 309-833-5311 wlnabst@macomb.com

Types of Records Retrieved: Real Estate; Tax Liens/Judgments; Probate courts; UCC records; Vital records

Local Retrieval Area: IL-Fulton, Hancock, Henderson, McDonough, Schuyler, Warren

Add'l Information: Normal turnaround time- 2 days for a judgment search; 4 days for title work. Projects billed by the hour. Travel expenses will be included in the fee. All projects require prepayment. They have been in business for over 54 years.

Todd Wilson PC

PO Box 325, Elwood, NE 68937
Phone: 308-785-2550 - **Fax:** 308-785-2852
http://toddwilsonpc.taxwisepartner.com **email:** toddwilsonpc@actjet.net

Types of Records Retrieved: Criminal, Civil and Probate courts; Federal courts; Real Estate; Tax Liens/Judgments; UCC records

Local Retrieval Area: NE-Gosper. **Correspondent Relationships:** Dawson, Furnas, Frontier, Phelps counties, NE.

Add'l Information: Established 1998. First project may require prepayment. They specialize in court and real estate records. They can help with any and all correspondence from the IRS.

Patricia Winters

2757 Jacob Dr, Thompsons Station, TN 37179
Phone: 615-595-2670 - **Fax:** 615-599-7344

Records Retrieved: Criminal and Civil courts; Tax Liens/Judgments

Local Retrieval Area: TN-Maury. **Correspondent Relationships:** Rutherford, Sumner, Williamson, Wilson, TN

Add'l Information: Established 2004. Normal turnaround time- 24 hours. Projects billed by number of names searched. First project may require prepayment. Excellent turnaround time. She operates as a correspondent of Mid-State records.

Wisconsin Title of Richland Center Inc

PO Box 436, 161 N Central Ave, Richland Center, WI 53581
Phone: 800-236-4596; 608-647-4596 - **Fax:** 608-647-8033

Types of Records Retrieved: Real Estate; Tax Liens/Judgments; Probate courts; UCC records; Vital records

Local Retrieval Area: WI-Richland

Add'l Information: Normal turnaround time- 1-2 days. Fee basis varies by type of transaction. First project may require prepayment.

Wisconsin Title of Shawano Inc

110 W North Water St, New London, WI 54961-1208
Phone: 715-823-3600 clintonville@wititleinc.com

Types of Records Retrieved: Criminal, Civil and Probate courts; Real Estate; Tax Liens/Judgments; UCC records

Local Retrieval Area: WI-Outagamie, Shawano, Waupaca. **Correspondent Relationships:** Ashland, Fond du Lac, Appleton, Richland Center, Stevens Point, Washburn, Wausau, Waupaca, WI.

Add'l Information: Normal turnaround time- 1-2 days. Fee basis varies by type of transaction. First project may require prepayment. They specialize in quality service with a fast and accurate turnaround time.

Wise Land & Abstract Co Inc

PO Box 608, 1117 Kirkman St, Lake Charles, LA 70601
Phone: 337-436-3419 - **Fax:** 337-439-3451 wiseland@suddenlinkmail.com

Types of Records Retrieved: Criminal, Civil and Probate courts; Federal courts; Real Estate; Tax Liens/Judgments; UCC records; Vital records

Area: LA-Beauregard Parish, Calcasieu Parish, Jefferson Davis Parish

Add'l Information: Established 1992. Normal turnaround time- variable depending on project. Fee basis will vary by the type of project. Will file/record documents for clients. Formerly known as Pelican Land & Abstract Co Inc, they specialize in oil, gas and leasing research and in residential and commercial abstracts of title and right-of-way research.

WNC Search Service

PO Box 637, Candler, NC 28715
Phone: 828-768-0062 - **Fax:** 828-665-9701 xstchn@bellsouth.net

Types of Records Retrieved: Criminal and Civil courts; Federal courts; Real Estate; Tax Liens/Judgments; UCC records

Local Retrieval Area: NC-Buncombe, Haywood, Henderson, Madison, McDowell, Polk, Rutherford, Transylvania

Add'l Information: Established 2001. Normal turnaround time- 48-72 hours. Projects billed by number of names searched.

Woelfel & Assoc Inc

2011 Mall St #D, Collinsville, IL 62234
Phone: 888-297-7180; 618-345-3411 - **Fax:** 618-345-9337
www.woelfelassociates.com **email:** woelfel@woelfelassociates.com

Types of Records Retrieved: Criminal, Civil and Probate courts; Federal courts; Real Estate; Tax Liens/Judgments; UCC records

Retrieval Area: IL-Adams, Bond, Calhoun, Clay, Clinton, Fayette, Jersey, Macoupin, Madison, Marion, Randolph, St. Clair; MO-St Charles, St Louis

Add'l Information: Established 1995. Normal turnaround time- 12-48 hours. Projects billed by the hour. First project may require prepayment. They are a fully service agency, offering civil and criminal investigation as well as surveillance, process service and skiptracing. A licensed PI in IL. Performs service of process.

Elaine Wolf

561 Village Sq, Hazelwood, MO 63042
Phone: 314-731-1839 - **Fax:** 314-731-1464 werica28@aol.com

Records Retrieved: Criminal, Civil and Probate courts; Vital records

Local Retrieval Area: MO-St. Charles, St. Louis

Add'l info: Established 1995. Normal turnaround time- 24-48 hours; 1-day expedited service available. Projects billed by number of names searched. She specializes in civil and criminal record searches, including the Federal District Court/Eastern District of Missouri. She also does National Labor Relations Board filings and will consider any projects not listed here.

Patricia Wolff

PO Box 146, Wayzata, MN 55391
Phone: 952-270-0095
www.businessmaven.com **email:** paw952@gmail.com

Types of Records Retrieved: Criminal, Civil and Probate courts; Federal courts; Real Estate; Tax Liens/Judgments; UCC records; Vital records

Local Retrieval Area: MN-Anoka, Carver, Dakota, Scott, Wright. **Correspondent Relationships:** Counties near the Twin Cities area.

Add'l Information: Established 2002. Normal turnaround time- 24 hours. Projects billed by the hour. First project may require prepayment. Formerly located in CO and named Business Maven, Investigative Consultants LLC provides research and investigation services for attorneys, businesses and nonprofits. Expertise in federal, state and local public records research, FOIA and Open Records Act. Performs service of process.

Kathy Wolken

4838 N Campbell Ave, Tucson, AZ 85718-5930
Phone: 520-615-7665 - **Fax:** 520-615-7965 kmwolken@msn.com

Types of Records Retrieved: Criminal, Civil and Probate courts; Federal courts; Tax Liens/Judgments

Local Retrieval Area: AZ-Pima

Add'l Information: Established 1993. Normal turnaround time- less that 24 hours excluding weekends and holidays. Will file/record documents for clients. They bill monthly. Specialized in document retrieval and research for attorneys. A licensed PI in AZ.

Wolz Corporate USA

36 S 18th Ave #D, Brighton, CO 80601
Phone: 303-655-9659 - **Fax:** 303-942-7322
www.wolzcorporate.com **email:** eric@wolzcorporate.com

Types of Records Retrieved: Criminal, Civil and Probate courts; Federal courts; Tax Liens/Judgments; UCC records

Local Retrieval Area: CO-Adams, Arapahoe, Boulder, Broomfield, Denver, Jefferson. **Correspondent Relationships:** statewide.

Add'l Information: Established 2004. Normal turnaround time- 24-48 hours. Projects billed by number of names searched. First project may require prepayment. Featuring regular access to Colorado Sec of State, Wolz Corporate USA provides reliable timely local retrieval services to all types of companies at reasonable rates, including nationwide registered agent services.

Wood & Tait Inc

PO Box 6180, 64-5249 Kauakea Rd, Kamuela, HI 96743
Phone: 800-774-8585; 808-885-5090 - **Fax:** 888-630-0500
www.woodtait.com **email:** jwood@woodtait.com

Types of Records Retrieved: Criminal, Civil and Probate courts; Federal courts; Real Estate

Local Retrieval Area: HI-Hawaii, Honolulu, Kauai, Maui. **Correspondent Relationships:** close relationships with search firms nationwide.

Add'l Information: Established 1984. Normal turnaround time- 2-3 working days. Customized pricing offered. First project may require prepayment. Credit cards accepted. All major credit cards accepted. They specialize Private investigations in finding property tax records, business registrations, professional and occupational licenses and bankruptcies. A licensed PI in HI. Performs service of process.

Woodard & Bohse Law Office

121 W 3rd St, Dover, OH 44622
Phone: 330-343-8848 or 8849 - **Fax:** 330-343-3496

Types of Records Retrieved: Criminal, Civil and Probate courts; Real Estate; Tax Liens/Judgments; UCC records; Vital records

Retrieval Area: OH-Carroll, Coshocton, Harrison, Holmes, Tuscarawas

Add'l Information: Established 1945. Normal turnaround time- 1 week. Projects billed by number of records located. Projects billed by the hour. First project may require prepayment. They will accept personal checks. They specialize in real estate, accounts receivable, probate and estates. Performs service of process.

Woods County Abstract Corp

PO Box 686, Alva, OK 73717
Phone: 580-327-1746 - **Fax:** 580-327-1780

Types of Records Retrieved: Criminal, Civil and Probate courts; Real Estate; Tax Liens/Judgments; UCC records

Local Retrieval Area: OK-Woods

Add'l Information: Normal turnaround time- 1-5 days. Fee basis will vary by the type of project. They specialize in title work, special certificates and abstracting.

Woodward County Abstract Co

PO Box 508, Woodward, OK 73802
Phone: 580-256-3344 - **Fax:** 580-256-4530

Types of Records Retrieved: Civil and Probate courts; Real Estate; Tax Liens/Judgments; UCC records

Local Retrieval Area: OK-Harper, Woodward

Add'l Information: Normal turnaround time- 2-3 days. They specialize in abstracts of title and title insurance.

Worcester Record Search Inc

4 Jill Circle, Shrewsbury, MA 01545
Phone: 508-842-7282 - **Fax:** 508-842-2236 wrsearch@aol.com

Types of Records Retrieved: Criminal, Civil and Probate courts; Federal courts; Real Estate; Tax Liens/Judgments; UCC records; Vital records

Local Retrieval Area: MA-Franklin, Hampden, Hampshire, Worcester

Add'l Information: Established 1992. Normal turnaround time- 24 hours. Projects billed by number of names searched. Will file/record documents for clients. They file, search, abstract and retrieve public records in each court, land registry and municipal office in the 4 counties of Central MA and the Pioneer Valley.

Worth County Abstract Co Inc

PO Box 64, 736 Central Ave, Northwood, IA 50459
Phone: 641-324-1761 - **Fax:** 641-324-1761 wcac@qwest.net

Types of Records Retrieved: Civil and Probate courts; Real Estate; Tax Liens/Judgments; UCC records; Vital records

Local Retrieval Area: IA-Worth

Add'l Information: Established 1901. Normal turnaround time- 1-3 days. Projects billed by the hour. First project may require prepayment.

WP Mortensen & Associates

PO Box 2619, Dublin, CA 94568
Phone: 925-828-6440 - **Fax:** 800-891-7510 seektruth1@sbcglobal.net

Types of Records Retrieved: Criminal, Civil and Probate courts; Federal Courts; Real Estate; Tax Liens/Judgments; UCC records; Vital records

Local Retrieval Area: CA-Alameda, Contra Costa

Add'l Information: Established 1996. Normal turnaround time- less than 6 days. Projects billed by the hour. Is a PI in CA.

Wright Research

PO Box 1590, Caldwell, ID 83606
Phone: 208-455-2450 - **Fax:** 208-455-2462 swrightresearch@msn.com

Types of Records Retrieved: Criminal, Civil and Probate courts; Tax Liens/Judgments; UCC records; Vital records

Local Retrieval Area: ID-Ada, Canyon

Add'l Information: Established 1997. Normal turnaround time- same day guaranteed 24 hours. Projects billed by number of names searched. Will file/record documents for clients. Will do the work and bill the company at the end of the month.

Jerry Wright

PO Box 261, Marion, KY 42064
Phone: 270-965-2721 - **Fax:** 270-965-2767

Types of Records Retrieved: Criminal courts

Local Retrieval Area: KY-Crittenden

Add'l Information: Normal turnaround time- 24 hours - 3 days. Projects billed by number of names searched.

XL Professional Services Inc

PO Box 3045, San Diego, CA 92014-6045

Types of Records Retrieved: Criminal, Civil and Probate courts; Federal courts; Real Estate; Tax Liens/Judgments; UCC records; Vital records

Local Retrieval Area: CA-Los Angeles, Riverside, San Diego. **Correspondent Relationships:** nationwide.

Add'l Information: Established 1989. Normal turnaround time- 1-3 days. Projects billed by number of names searched. Projects billed by number of records located. Projects billed by the hour. First project may require prepayment. Will file/record documents for clients. Payment due upon receipt on work. They specialize in civil court research, filing of court documents & service of process. They also deal with workers compensation, County Recorders & Court of Appeals & family law at Superior & Municipal Court levels. They can do this nationwide. Performs service of process.

Xpedite Wholesale Criminal Research

3091 W Galbraith Rd #308, Cincinnati, OH 45239

Phone: 800-325-3609; 513-522-8764 - **Fax:** 513-728-4411

www.xpediteonline.com **email:** tirvin@xpediteonline.com

Records Retrieved: Criminal and Civil courts; Federal District courts

Local Retrieval Area: KY-Boone, Campbell, Kenton; OH-Butler, Clermont, Franklin, Hamilton, Warren. **Correspondent Relationships:** nationwide and international.

Add'l Information: Established 1988. Normal turnaround time- 24-48 hours. Projects billed by number of names searched. First project may require prepayment. Credit cards accepted. They specialize in criminal research.

XpertSearch Inc

PO Box 403, Flagler Beach, FL 32136

Phone: 732-229-6688 - **Fax:** 775-248-6436

www.xpertsearch.com **email:** research@xpertsearch.com

Types of Records Retrieved: Criminal and Probate courts; Federal courts; Real Estate; Tax Liens/Judgments; UCC records; Vital records

Local Retrieval Area: FL-Flagler, Orange, Seminole, St. Johns, Volusia; NJ-Monmouth, Ocean. **Correspondents:** nationwide and international.

Add'l Information: Normal turnaround time- 24-48 hours. Projects billed by number of names searched. Credit cards accepted. They specialize in criminal research and pre-employment screening, but are capable of retrieving any public record of any kind nationwide or worldwide.

Xpress Research

PO Box 3004, Jeffersonville, IN 47131

Phone: 812-923-7202; cell- 812-207-4284 - **Fax:** 812-923-7209

robb@xpressresearch.com

Types of Records Retrieved: Criminal and Civil courts

Local Retrieval Area: IN-Clark, Floyd, Harrison, Jefferson, Scott, Washington; KY-Bullitt, Fayette, Hardin, Henry, Jefferson, Larue, Nelson, Oldham, Shelby, Spencer, Trimble. **Correspondents:** Kentucky statewide.

Add'l Information: Established 1993. Normal turnaround time- 24-48 hours. First project may require prepayment. They specialize in courts in far South Central Indiana along the Ohio River, also northern Kentucky counties bordering on Indiana.

Yahnke Professional Services & Investigations

2112 W Galena Blvd #8-235, Aurora, IL 60506

Phone: 630-966-9774; Fax- same

www.ypsandi.com **email:** toni@ypsandi.com

Types of Records Retrieved: Criminal, Civil and Probate courts; Federal courts; Real Estate; Tax Liens/Judgments; UCC records; Vital records

Local Retrieval Area: IL-De Kalb, Du Page, Kane, Kendall, Will. **Correspondent Relationships:** Cook county, IL. Is also police chief of Maple Park, IL.

Add'l info: Established 2004. Turnaround time- 48-72 hours. Expedited service available at double rate. Projects billed by number of names searched. First project may require prepayment. They specialize in process service, first run papers (free if not served), court records searches, skiptracing, surveillance, private investigations. State registered firearms and control tactics training. Licensed PI in IL. Performs service of process.

Yoakum County Abstract Co

PO Box 457, Plains, TX 79355

Phone: 806-456-2615 - **Fax:** 806-456-2625 ycac@crosswind.net

Records Retrieved: Real Estate; Tax Liens/Judgments; Probate courts

Local Retrieval Area: TX-Yoakum

Add'l Information: Established 1984. Normal turnaround time- 2-3 days. Fee basis varies by type of project. Will file/record documents for clients.

York County Title Co

PO Box 572, 608 N Grant Ave, York, NE 68467

Phone: 402-362-4405 - **Fax:** 402-362-4421

www.yorkcountytitleco.com **email:** yctc@alltel.net

Types of Records Retrieved: Criminal, Civil and Probate courts; Real Estate; Tax Liens/Judgments; UCC records

Local Retrieval Area: NE-York

Add'l Information: Established 1969. Normal turnaround time- 24 hours. Fee basis varies by type of transaction. Will file/record documents for clients. Project may require prepayment. They will file UCC and real estate documents if prepaid.

Beth Young

1012 Lumber Ave, Elliott, IA 51532

Phone: 712-767-2510 - **Fax:** 712-767-2510 jon_beth@netins.net

Types of Records Retrieved: Criminal courts; Real Estate; Tax Liens/Judgments

Local Retrieval Area: IA-Cass, Montgomery

Add'l Information: Established 1995. Normal turnaround time- 48 hours. Projects billed by number of names searched. First project may require prepayment. Will file/record documents for clients. They also do title and abstract searches.

Zap! Courier Service

90 S Swan St, Albany, NY 12210

Phone: 518-449-3361 - **Fax:** 518-449-1332 zapalbany@aol.com

Types of Records Retrieved: Civil courts; Federal courts

Local Retrieval Area: NY-Albany, Rensselaer, Saratoga, Schenectady. **Correspondent Relationships:** New York City and Washington, DC.

Add'l Information: Established 1977. Normal turnaround time- 24 hours depending on court turnaround. Projects billed by number of names searched. Projects billed by the hour. Will file/record documents for clients. They work closely with the Public Service Commission, Department of State, Insurance Department and New York State Legislature.

John A Zapf

PO Box 1006, 628 W Broad St, Bethlehem, PA 18016-1006

Phone: 610-868-5101 - **Fax:** 610-691-1216 jazapf@verizon.net

Types of Records Retrieved: Civil and Probate courts; Real Estate; Tax Liens/Judgments; UCC records

Local Retrieval Area: PA-Lehigh, Northampton

Add'l Information: Established 1976. Normal turnaround time- 48 hours. Projects billed by number of names searched. Will file/record documents for clients. They specialize in real estate title searches and abstracts as well as current owner, UCC< and lien searches.

Zero Investigations Inc

2816 E 51st St #300, Tulsa, OK 74105-1743
Phone: 866-400-9376; 918-492-7741 - **Fax:** 918-492-7677
www.zeroinvestigationsinc.com/index.asp
email: info@zeroinvestigationsinc.com

Types of Records Retrieved: Criminal, Civil and Probate courts; Federal courts; Real Estate; Tax Liens/Judgments; UCC records; Vital records

Local Retrieval Area: OK-Creek, Rogers, Tulsa. **Correspondent Relationships:** nationwide correspondent network.

Add'l Information: Established 2000. Normal turnaround time- 24-48 hours. Projects billed by number of names searched. Credit cards accepted. They specialize in nationwide employment screening services, process service and document retrieval. Private investigations, drug & alcohol testing, hair follicle, DNA paternity testing and instant drug testing products. A licensed PI in OK. Performs service of process.

Zook Search Inc, L.A. California

12640 Bloomfield Ave #86, Norwalk, CA 90650
Phone: 562-484-1638 - **Fax:** 562-929-0148
www.zooksearch.com **email:** la@zooksearch.com

Types of Records Retrieved: Criminal, Civil and Probate courts; Federal courts; Real Estate; Tax Liens/Judgments; UCC records; Vital records

Local Retrieval Area: CA-Los Angeles, Orange

Add'l Information: Established 2001. Normal turnaround time- 24 hours. Expedited service available. Projects billed by number of names searched. First project may require prepayment. Accurate & Efficient document retrieval and filing services in the New York City, Los Angeles and San Francisco metropolitan areas. They have errors & omissions insurance.

Zook Search Inc, S.F. California

1230 Market St #333, San Francisco, CA 94102
Phone: 415-387-1029 - **Fax:** 415-387-1030
www.zooksearch.com **email:** dana@zooksearch.com

Types of Records Retrieved: Criminal, Civil and Probate courts; Federal courts; Real Estate; Tax Liens/Judgments; UCC records; Vital records

Local Retrieval Area: CA-Alameda, Marin, San Francisco. **Correspondent Relationships:** Has a branch in New York City and Los Angeles.

Add'l Information: Established 2001. Normal turnaround time- 24 hours. Same day expedited service available. Projects billed by number of names searched. First project may require prepayment. Accurate and efficient document retrieval and filing services in New York City, Los Angeles and San Francisco metro areas. 24 hour turnaround and Error & Omissions Insurance.

Zook Search Inc, NYC

285 22nd St #2, Brooklyn, NY 11215
Phone: 718-369-3879 - **Fax:** 718-369-0849
www.zooksearch.com **email:** ny@zooksearch.com

Types of Records Retrieved: Criminal, Civil and Probate courts; Federal courts; Real Estate; Tax Liens/Judgments; UCC records; Vital records

Local Retrieval Area: NY-Bronx, Kings, New York, Queens. **Correspondent Relationships:** Has a branch in San Francisco Bay area, also Los Angeles and Orange Counties.

Add'l Information: Established 2001. Normal turnaround time- 24 hours. Same day expedited service available. Projects billed by number of names searched. First project may require prepayment. Will file/record documents for clients. Payment is net 30 days. Accurate and efficient document retrieval and filing services in New York City, Los Angeles, and San Francisco metro areas. 24 hour turnaround and Error & Omissions Insurance.

 = PRRN Member. *A retriever you can trust!*

Public Record Retriever Network 2007 Associate Members

(Includes PRRN Members not Listed in the Local Retrievers Section)

The following companies are PRRN Associate Members who provide statewide or regional services, either as a search firm or screening firm such as pre-employment screening or tenant screening company. For local retrievers companies, see the previous sections. Many local document retrieval companies who are standard PRRN members are also search firms or screening firms, and they can be found in these previous sections. Search firms and screening firms can also be found at www.brbpub.com and www.brbpub.com/pubrecsites_ven.asp.

Also, the BRB book *Public Records Online* contains listing on hundreds of additional companies that offer online or other electronic access to public record information.

2007 PRRN Member Search Firms, Distributors, Publishers, Gateways, Database Companies—

ADAM Safeguard

PO Box 1210, Toms River, NJ 08754
Phone: 800-722-2326, 732-286-0800 **Fax:** 732-286-9201
www.adamsafeguard.com/home.htm
email- dld@adamsafeguard.com **Founded:** 1973
Memberships: IALEIA, IACP, PRRN
Clientele restrictions: Agreement required.
Pre-Employment Screening Services: Credit Reports, Drug Testing - Outsourced, Workers Compensation History, Criminal Records, Education/Employment, Licenses/Registrations/Permits
Distribution Methods to Client: Dial-Up (Other than Internet), Email
ADAM Safeguard is the only company to provide a "How-to" book to all registered clients. The owner of ADAM Safeguard is co-author of "25 Essential Lessons in Employee Management" and "Don't Hire a Crook!" ADAM Safeguard conducts pre-employment background checks for all types of businesses. Ordering is processed by fax, phone, and mail as well as HireCheck software for direct access via modem.

AccuQuick Abstracting

600 Ridge Rd, North Arlington, NJ 07031
Phone: 201-991-5656 **Fax:** 201-991-2322
www.accuquickabstracting.com **email-** info@accuquickabstracting.com **Founded:** 2003
Memberships: PRRN, NALTEA, WISE
Clientele restrictions: Casual requestors permitted.
Applications: Real Estate Transactions, Legal Compliance, Filing/Recording Documents, Asset/Lien Searching/Verification,
Products & Information Categories: Real Estate/Assessor, Litigation/Judgments/Tax Liens, Uniform Commercial Code, Criminal Information (DE, FL, GA, MD, NY, NJ, PA, VA)
Special Distribution Methods to Client: Email, Internet
AccuQuick Abstracting, Inc. specializes in current owner searches, doc retrieval, recordings, commercial, foreclosures and many other categories of searches and mortgage recording with a turnaround time of 24-48 hours. Through their network of experienced professionals they provide the search and/or document you need accurately, quickly, and economically, with quality control on every order before delivery. Our customer-oriented staff is always available by phone, email, or fax during all business hours. Carries $1M in E&O insurance.

Advanced Reporting

PO Box 12398, Salem, OR 97309
Phone: 888-375-0451, 503-375-0451 **Fax:** 503-364-0195
www.advrep.com **email-** ddeckelmann@advrep.com
Parent Company: MaPS Credit Union. **Founded:** 1984
Memberships: PRRN, NAR, SHRM, NAPBS
Clientele restrictions: Service agreement required
Pre-Employment Screening Services: Credit Reports, Criminal Records, Bankruptcy, Education/Employment
Tenant Screening Services: Credit Reports, Criminal Records, Forcible Detainer Check, Litigation/Judgments
Distribution Methods to Client: Email, Gateway via Another Online Service
Advanced Reporting specializes in mortgage credit reporting, tenant screening, and pre-employment screening. Their services are available online, and criminal records are searched in real time.

Affiliated Background Searches Inc

12733 Lake City Way, #204, Seattle, WA 98125
Phone: 800-420-4233, 206-365-0887 **Fax:** 509-692-7298
www.backgroundfacts.com **email-** support@backgroundfacts.com
Founded: 1999 **Memberships:** PRRN, NAPBS
Clientele restrictions: Statement of purpose required.

Applications: Background Info - Business, Background Info - Individuals, Asset/Lien Searching/Verification, Employment Screening, Tenant Screening

Products & Information Categories:
Criminal Information, Driver and/or Vehicle, Litigation/Judgments/Tax Liens, Education/Employment (FL, WA, US)
Credit Information, Bankruptcy (US)

Pre-Employment Screening Services: Credit Reports, Criminal Records, MVRs, Bankruptcy , Education/Employment, Former Employer Interviews, Licenses/Registrations/Permits

Tenant Screening Services: Credit Reports, Criminal Records , Litigation/Judgments , MVRs

Special Distribution Methods to Client: Internet

Affiliated Background Searches has over 30 years experience in employee benefits relations and since 1999 they have provided nationwide pre-employment screening services. Key note is service. All clients receive personal account representatives, fast turnaround, and flexible plan packages to suit their needs, all at affordable cost.

American Screening LLC

PO Box 1444, Hebron, CT 06248
Phone: 888-251-4044, 860-228-0111 **Fax:** 860-228-0065
www.americanscreening.com **email-** info@americanscreening.com
Parent Company: Datafind Systems. **Founded:** 1991
Memberships: NAPBS, PRRN
Clientele restrictions: Signed agreement required

Applications: Background Info - Individuals, Collections, Employment Screening, Locating People/Businesses, Tenant Screening

Products & Information Categories:
Addresses/Telephone Numbers, Bankruptcy, Credit Information, Criminal Information (CT, US)
Corporate/Trade Name Data, Education/Employment, Litigation/Judgments/Tax Liens (CT, US)
Driver and/or Vehicle (AL,AZ,AR,CA,DE,FL,GA,IA,ID,IL,IN,KS,KY,LA, MD,ME,MI,MN,MO,MT,ND,ND,NE,NH,NJ,NM,NV,NY,OH,OK,RI,SC,SD, TN,TX,UT,VA,VT,WV,WY)
Foreign Country Information (CD, CAN)

Proprietary Databases or Gateways:
DB Name: CT Judicial
- Criminal Information (CT)

Gateway Name: Trans Union
- Credit Information (CT, US)

Pre-Employment Screening Services: Bankruptcy, Local Document Retrieval, Credit Reports, MVRs , Criminal Records, Drug Testing - Outsourced, Education/Employment

Tenant Screening Services: Credit Reports, Criminal Records , Litigation/Judgments , Local Document Retrieval

Special Distribution Methods to Client: Dial-Up (Other than Internet), Email, Gateway via Another Online Service

American Screening Services, which reaches nationwide, services the human resource industry by screening potential employees, and also provides public record searches for locating people and businesses. Their staff is comprised of highly-trained experts in all facets of the public records retrieval. They provide the highest quality information via databases and physical hand searches and in complete compliance with the FCRA.

Ascertain Screening & Investigations

110 N High St #201, Gahanna, OH 43230
Phone: 800-858-2901, 614-858-0100 **Fax:** 614-418-9617
www.ascertainsi.com **email-** info@ascertainsi.com
Founded: 2005
Memberships: PRRN, NAPBS, ASIS, SHRM, HRACO
Clientele restrictions: Casual requesters permitted.

Applications: Background Info - Individuals, Employment Screening, Legal Compliance, Tenant Screening,

Products & Information Categories:
Addresses/Telephone Numbers, Criminal Information, Education/Employment, Licenses/Registrations/Permits, (OH, US)
Bankruptcy, Litigation/Judgments/Tax Liens (OH, US)
Aviation, Credit Information (US)
Driver and/or Vehicle (OH)

Pre-Employment Screening Services: Bankruptcy, Credit Reports, Criminal Records, Education/Employment , Former Employer Interviews, Licenses/Registrations/Permits , MVRs

Tenant Screening Services: Credit Reports, Criminal Records , Forcible Detainer Check , Litigation/Judgments

Special Distribution Methods to Client: Email, Gateway via Another Online Service, Internet

The founders and associates at Ascertain have over 40 years experience in investigative projects and criminal research, and possess backgrounds in law enforcement, security and the U.S. Military. The promise thorough review of results prior to delivery; unparalelled personal service; competitive pricing; dependable turnaround; attention to detail; integrity and experience of owners who are key in day-to-day operations.

Buffalo Employment Screening

PMB 350, 333 S State St #V, Lake Oswego, OR 97034-3961
Phone: 866-391-6296, 503-699-3340 **Fax:** 971-223-5131
www.bfloscreen.com **email-** info@bfloscreen.com
Memberships: 1993, **Clientele restrictions:** Agreement required for wholesale services.

Applications: Background Info - Individuals, Employment Screening, Litigation, Risk Management, Government Document Retrieval

Products & Information Categories:
Criminal Information, Litigation/Judgments/Tax Liens (CO, CT, IL, ME, MN, MO, NC, NE, OK, OR, SC, SD, TX, WA, WI, US)

Pre-Employment Screening Services: Criminal Records, Education/Employment, Drug Testing - Outsourced, Licenses/Registrations/Permits , Local Document Retrieval

Buffalo Employment Screening specializes in pre-employment criminal searches, SSN verifications, and overseeing drug screening especially in Oregon and Washington states but overall, they have nationwide reach, particularly for criminal records and civil judgments, and they can customize services to fit your exact needs.

Confi-Data LLC

5124 Stage Rd, Memphis, TN 38134
Phone: 888-382-4410, 901-881-6039 **Fax:** 901-382-4233
www.confi-data.com **email-** info@confi-data.com **Founded:** 2005

Memberships: PRRN, NAPBS
Clientele restrictions: Casual requesters permitted.

Pre-Employment Screening Services: Bankruptcy, Credit Reports, Criminal Records, Education/Employment , Former Employer Interviews, Licenses/Registrations/Permits , MVRs

Tenant Screening Services: Credit Reports, Criminal Records , Forcible Detainer Check , Former Landlord Interviews

Distribution Methods to Client: Email, Gateway via Another Online Service

Through customized services, Confi-Data, LLC provides prompt, quality data to both employers and individuals. Company has grown to become a reliable and efficient provider of advanced background services. Features include desktop delivery and 24/7 delivery for all services. Would appreciate an opportunity to show you how their experience and service can meet your needs.

Creative Services Inc

64 Pratt St, Mansfield, MA 02048
Phone: 800-227-0002, 508-339-5451 **Fax:** 508-339-2352
www.creativeservices.com
email- info@creativeservices.com
Branch Offices: Cranston, RI, 800-227-0002; Fax: 508-339-2352
Founded: 1976

Memberships: PRRN, ASIS, INOA, NAFI, SHRM, NEHRA, NAPBS
Clientele restrictions: Client agreement/user certification required.

Applications: Background Info - Business, Background Info - Individuals, Employment Screening, Tenant Screening, Fraud Prevention/Detection

Products & Information Categories:
Credit Information (US, MA, RI)
Criminal Information (US, MA, RI)
Driver and/or Vehicle (MA, RI)
Licenses/Registrations/Permits (CT, FL, MA, NJ, RI)
Military Svc (US)
Workers Compensation (MA, RI)

Pre-Employment Screening Services: Credit Reports, Bankruptcy, Criminal Records, Drug Testing - Outsourced , Education/Employment, Former Employer Interviews, Licenses/Registrations/Permits

Special Distribution Methods to Client: Internet

Creative Services (CSI) is a full-service pro-active pre-employment screening and security consulting firm. Will help you prevent loss at all levels. Compliance with employment laws, driver/privacy rules, and FCRA. Investigative thinking applied to every case; understand their clients needs and provide customized reporting, superior customer service, comprehensive and factual data, and meet sensitive time lines.

easyBackgrounds.com

PO Box 952, Newfields, NH 03856
Phone: 800-538-6525, 603-778-1820 **Fax:** 603-772-0316
www.easybackgrounds.com
email- suzannem@easybackgrounds.com
Founded: 1995
Memberships: NAPBS, PRRN

Clientele restrictions: Casual requesters permitted.

Applications: Background Info - Individuals, Employment Screening,

Products & Information Categories:
Criminal Information, Education/Employment (NH, US, Intl)
Workers Compensation (NH, US)

Pre-Employment Screening Services: Bankruptcy, Credit Reports, Criminal Records, Education/Employment , Licenses/Registrations/Permits, MVRs, Workers' Compensation History

Special Distribution Methods to Client: Email, Internet

EasyBackgrounds provides background screening services for employment purposes using state of the art web-based tracking. Their a la carte services include criminal record research, verifications of education, verification of past employment and credentials, reference interviews, also driver history, civil records checks, sex offender registry, and more. Workers comp records from most states. Easybackground's services and pricing are straightforward, making the screening process easy for users.

Employment Screening Resources

7110 Redwood Blvd Ste C, Novato, CA 94945
Phone: 888-999-4474, 415-898-0044 **Fax:** 415-680-1627
www.ESRcheck.com **email-** esr@ESRcheck.com
Founded: 1996

Memberships: SHRM,

Clientele Restrictions: Must be ongoing account

Pre-Employment Screening Services: Drug Testing - Outsourced, Credit Reports, Former Employer Interviews, Workers Compensation History

Special Distribution Methods to Client: Email, Internet

Employment Screening Resources (ESR) combines investigative, legal and public record research experience to provide pre-employment background reports to human resources and security departments. ESR provides services nationally as well as to California employers who need to comply with complicated California regulations. In compliance with the Fair Credit Reporting Act, ESR reports highlight and summarize important information, not merely providing raw data or computer printouts. The status of all reports is available in real time, 24/7 on the secured ESRnet online reporting system. ESR offers support, training and consultation in safe hiring procedures as well as HR help desk. ESR also offers a turnaround time guarantee.

Ernst Publishing Co, LLC

PO Box 318, 1937 Delaware Turnpike #B Clarksville, NY 12041
Phone: 800-345-3822,
www.ernstpublishing.com **email-** lrcanier@ernst.cc
Parent Company: Ernst Publishing Co, LLC.
Founded: 1992
Memberships: AIIP, SIIA, NPRRA, PRRN
Clientele restrictions: None reported

Applications: Lending/Leasing, Legal Compliance, Filing/Recording Documents, General Business Information, Real Estate Transactions

Proprietary Databases or Gateways:
Database Name: Uniform Commercial Code Filing Guide
‣ Uniform Commercial Code Filing Guide (US)

Database Name: Real Estate Recording Guide
‣ Real Estate/Assessor (US)

Special Distribution Methods to Client: Database, Internet, Publication/Directory

The Uniform Commercial Code Filing Guide™ is a practical "How To" reference for the preparation, filing and searching of Article 9 Financing Statements nationwide. This Guide provides information re: fees, forms, facts for all 4,316 filing jurisdictions and is designed for the high-volume filer. Included are sections hosting the Model Act, Filing Fundamentals, Purchase Money Secured Interest and Definitions. Subscription is annual with quarterly updates; a newsletter is provided in non-updating months. The new Revised Article 9 Alert assists filers and searchers to function in the new Revision environment. They also publish the Real Estate Recording Guide and National Release Guide and offer a database and web-based product, National Online Mortgage Assistance Database Program.

Full Disclosure LLC

2836 Portobello Ct, Waldorf, MD 20603
Phone: 877-214-4717,
www.full-disclosure.org **email-** fdenman@full-disclosure.org
Founded: 2006
Memberships: PRRN,
Clientele restrictions: Casual requesters permitted.
Applications: Background Info - Individuals, Employment Screening, Fraud Prevention/Detection, Risk Management,

Products & Information Categories:
Education/Employment, Criminal Information, Credit Information (MD,DC,VA,US)
Addresses/Telephone Numbers, Driver and/or Vehicle, Workers Compensation (MD,DC,VA)

Pre-Employment Screening Services: Bankruptcy, Credit Reports, Criminal Records, Education/Employment , Former Employer Interviews, Licenses/Registrations/Permits, MVRs

Special Distribution Methods to Client: Email

Full Disclosure is fully compliant with all aspects of the Fair Credit Reporting Act (FCRA), providing services that meet clients needs including state, federal and county criminal record checks.

GLG Inv

7312 Baylor Dr, Baylor, IN 46819
Phone: 260-747-9448 **Fax:** 260-747-5235
http://glginvestigations.com/default.aspx
email- kb9tui@hotmail.com
Founded: 2006
Memberships: PRRN

Clientele restrictions: Casual requesters permitted.

Applications: Asset/Lien Searching/Verification, Background Info - Business, Employment Screening, Fraud Prevention/Detection, Litigation

Products & Information Categories:
Criminal Information, Litigation/Judgments/Tax Liens, Workers Compensation, Bankruptcy, Education/Employment (IN)
Corporate/Trade Name Data, Driver and/or Vehicle (IN)

Special Distribution Methods to Client: Email

GLG specializes in litigation support, fraud and signal piracy investigating, conducting surveillance for investigations and special projects, service of process, even perform statewide document retrieval for many document types including real estate, and can provide you with personalized, accurate and legal service.

Merlin Information Services

215 S Complex Dr, Kalispell, MT 59901
Phone: 800-367-6646, 406-755-8550 **Fax:** 406-755-8568
www.merlindata.com **email-** Support@merlindata.com
Founded: 1991
Memberships: ACA, CAC, CAPPS, NARM, SCRIA, NCSEA
Clientele restrictions: Casual requesters permitted

Applications: Locating People/Businesses, Asset/Lien Searching/Verification, Background Info - Business, Collections, Fraud Prevention/Detection

Proprietary Databases or Gateways:
Database Name: Merlin Cross Directory
‣ Addresses/Telephone #s, Credit Data, Driver and/or Vehicle, Vital Records, Voter Registration (US)

Gateway Name: National FlatRate, Collector's FlatRate
‣ Civil/Criminal Indexes, UCC, Aviation/Vessels, MVRs, Real Estate/Assessor, Litigation/Judgments/Tax Liens, Addresses/Telephone #s, Corp./Trade Name Data, SSN, Bankruptcy, Credit Information, Licenses/Registration/Permits, Vital Records, Voter Regis. (US)

Gateway Name: Merlin Super Header
‣ Addresses/Telephone #s, SSNs, Credit Information, Vital Statistics (US)

Gateway Name: QuikInfo.net FlatRate
‣ Civil/Criminal (CA), UCC, Aviation/Vessels, Real Estate/Assessor, Criminal Data, Driver and/orVehicle, Wrokers' Comp, Addresses/Telephone Numbers, Corporation/Trade Name Data, SSN, Bankruptcy, Licenses/Registration/Permits, Vital Records, Voter Regis. (US)

Database Name: Nat'l Fictitious Business Names
‣ Corporation/Trade Names, Addresses/Telephone #s (CA, US)

Database Name: CA Criminal Indexes, CA Brides/Grooms, CA Birth/Death Indexes, many other CA databases
‣ UCC (Filing Index), Civil/Criminal Indexes, Vital Records, Licenses/Reg./Permits, Real Estate/Assessor, Litigation/Judgments/Tax Liens, Wills/Probate (CA)

Gateway Name: Link to America, DOB File
‣ Addresss/Phone #s, Credit Data, Driver and/or Vehicle, Real Estate/Assessor, Vital Statistics, Voter Registration (US)

Database Name: Nat'l People Finder/Credit Headers/Criminal/Property
‣ Addresses/Phone #s, Real Estate/Assessor, Litigation/Judgments/Tax Liens, Criminal Data, Credit Data, Vital Statistics (US)

Special Distribution Methods to Client: CD-ROM, Dial-Up (Other than Internet), Internet, Magnetic Tape

Merlin Information Services provides access to public records on the Internet. Their search and retrieval site and their software assists in obtaining results not found through traditional access. Merlin's extensive California databases are the most current and complete available. Their wide selection of national databases The Merlin Cross-Directory, Link to America, and Nat'l FlatRate round out their extensive skiptracing and investigative tools, helping you locate people, assets, neighbors, associates.

Missouri Record Service Inc

1406 Missouri Blvd, #F, Jefferson City, MO 65109
Phone: 573-893-4428 **Fax:** 573-893-2396
email- mrsi@earthlink.net
Founded: 2000
Memberships: PRRN,
Clientele restrictions: Casual requesters permitted.

Applications: Asset/Lien Searching/Verification, Background Info - Individuals, Employment Screening, Legal Compliance, Fraud Prevention/Detection

Products & Information Categories:
Criminal Info, Driver and/or Vehicle, Litigation/Judgments/Tax Liens (MO) Education/Employment, Licenses/Registrations/Permits, Workers Compensation (MO)

Special Distribution Methods to Client: Email

Missouri Record Service Inc specializes in expert Missouri statewide record checks in background checks for employment purposes.

Motznik Information Services

8301 Briarwood St #100, Anchorage, AK 99518-3332
Phone: 907-344-6254 **Fax:** 907-344-1759
www.motznik.com **email-** lori@motznik.com
Founded: 1974
Memberships: NFIB
Clientele restrictions: Casual requesters permitted

Applications: Direct Marketing, Locating People/Businesses, Real Estate Transactions, Government Document Retrieval, Filing/Recording Documents

Proprietary Databases or Gateways:
Database Name: Motznik Online Svc
‣ Addresses/Telephone Numbers, Bankruptcy, Licenses/Registrations/Permits, Litigation/Judgments/Tax Liens, Criminal Information, Corporate/Trade Name Data, Uniform Commercial Code, Real Estate/Assessor, Voter Registration, Driver and/or Vehicle (AK)

Database Name:
‣ Vessels (AK, US)

Special Distribution Methods to Client: CD-ROM, Database, Dial-Up (Other than Internet), Disk, Email, FTP, Lists/Labels, Magnetic Tape

Formerly Motznik Computer Services, they offer a comprehensive online information research system that provides access to a wide selection of Alaska public files. Their files are cumulative and, in some cases, is the only source for many historical records dating back to 1972. Motznik also provides mailing lists and reports for analysis. Has most CDS files for Alaska. Many of their current databases are for sale and can be delivered in many formats.

NAPS Inc

1920 3rd Ave North, Bessemer, AL 35020
Phone: 866-425-9671, 205-425-6277 **Fax:** 205-425-5129
www.nationalaps.com **email-** customerservice@nationalaps.com
Founded: 1997
Memberships: PRRN, NAPBS, CDIA
Clientele restrictions: Casual requesters permitted.
Pre-Employment Screening Services: Credit Reports, Criminal Records, Drug Testing - Outsourced, Education/Employment , Former Employer Interviews, Profile/Aptitude Testing, Workers' Comp History
Tenant Screening Services: Credit Reports, Criminal Records , MVRs

Special Distribution Methods to Client: Dial-Up (Other than Internet), Gateway via Another Online Service, Internet

NAPS employment and screening services include criminal histories, workers' comp claims history, SSN verification/name matches, driving records, credit reports, drug screening, employment and education verifications, OIG/Medicare sanctions, homeland security terrorist watch list search, sex offender search. They provide state of the art online submission and retrieval, XML software interface and excel spreadsheet submission interface plus traditional service from experienced professionals.

Owens OnLine Inc

6501 N Himes Ave #104, Tampa, FL 33614
Phone: 800-745-4656, 813-877-2008 **Fax:** 813-877-1826
www.owens.com **email-** email@owens.com
Founded: 1992
Clientele restrictions: Casual requesters permitted

Applications: Background Info - Business, Background Info - Individuals, Risk Management, Competitive Intelligence, Employment Screening

Products & Information Categories:
Bankruptcy (US, itl) Education/Employment (US, itl)
Uniform Commercial Code (US) Criminal Information (US, Itl)
Vital Records (US, itl) Voter Registration (US, itl)

Proprietary Databases or Gateways:
Gateway Name: Owens OnLine

‣ Credit Information (US, Itl)

Gateway Name: Owens OnLine
‣ Foreign Country Information (Itl)

Special Distribution Methods to Client: Email, FTP, Internet

Owens OnLine specializes in international background checks and credit reports on businesses and individuals, and in Intl. criminal checks. They provide worldwide coverage and also offer FreeDirectories.com where over 1 billion people, companies, and public records can be found free of charge.

PreemploymentDirectory.com

22701 Woodlake Ln, Lake Forest, CA 92630
Phone: 949-770-5264 **Fax:** 949-597-0977
www.workplaceviolence911.com/docs/preemploymenthome.htm
email- wbnixon@aol.com
Branch Offices: Long Beach, CA, 562-590-0512; Fax: 562-590-9412
Parent Company: Nat'l Inst. For Prevention of Workplace Violence.
Founded: 1994
Memberships: PRRN, NAPBS, PIHRA, SHRM, ATAP, ASIS
Clientele restrictions: None **Applications:** Background Info - Business, Competitive Intelligence, General Business Information, Employment Screening, Current Events

Proprietary Databases or Gateways:
DB Name: Background Screening Directory
‣ Addresses/Telephone Numbers (US, CA)

Special Distribution Methods to Client: Publication/Directory

PreemploymentDirectory.com helps employers meet the critical need to know whom they are hiring and who is on their payroll. Is a comprehensive online directory of background screening firms designed to make it easy for employers to quickly find a company to meet their screening needs. A one-stop timesaving source; search the directory alphabetically, geographically by state or internationally, or search the Vendor Showcase for vendors and suppliers to the industry. A comprehensive tool to support your business workplace security effort to provide a safe workplace.

Private Security & Investigations Inc

PO Box 6047, 316 Broad St, Rome, GA 30162
Phone: 877-235-7574, 706-413-3729 **Fax:** 706-235-6452
www.psibackgroundcheck.com **email-** info@psibackgroundcheck.com **Founded:** 1998
Memberships: PRRN, NAPBS, BBB, CHE
Clientele restrictions: Casual requesters permitted.

Applications: Employment Screening, Tenant Screening, Background Info - Individuals, Fraud Prevention/Detection, Risk Management

Proprietary Databases or Gateways:
Gateway Name: PSI Proprietary Database
‣ Criminal Information (GA)

Pre-Employment Screening Services: Credit Reports, Criminal Records, Education/Employment, Former Employer Interviews , Local Document Retrieval, Bankruptcy, MVRs
Tenant Screening Services: Credit Reports, Criminal Records , Former Landlord Interviews , Local Document Retrieval

Special Distribution Methods to Client: Email

PSI is a nationwide pre-employment screening company that specializes in background investigations. Their staff is well trained and educated, each holding college degrees in various disciplines. They offer a free 30-day trial of their services. They offer access to Georgia criminal records via the state's repository which can only be acced via a law-enforcement agency, with same-day to 24-hr turnaround time. PSI maintains a personal relationship with each client to facilitate a positive working environment, and is committed to listening to clients and providing an integrated team solution to any concerns, all helping you make better informed hiring decisions.

Public Record Research System

PO Box 27869, Tempe, AZ 85285
Phone: 800-929-3811, 480-829-7475 **Fax:** 480-829-8505
www.brbpub.com **email-** brb@brbpub.com
Parent Company: BRB Publications Inc.
Founded: 1989
Memberships: PRRN, NAPBS
Clientele restrictions: Casual requesters permitted

Applications: General Business Info, Government Document Retrieval, Risk Management, Locating People/Businesses, Competitive Intelligence

Proprietary Databases or Gateways:
Database Name: PRRS
‣ Addresses/Telephone Numbers, Legislation/Regulations (US, AZ)

Gateway Name: PRRS
‣ News/Current Events (US)

Special Distribution Methods to Client: CD-ROM, Database, Disk, Internet, Lists/Labels, Publication/Directory

The Public Record Research System is a series of in-depth databases formatted into books, CDs and online. BRB is recognized as the nation's leading research and reference publisher of public record related information. The principals of the parent company are directors of the Public Record Retriever Network. Over 26,000 government and private enterprises are analyzed in-depth regarding regulations and access of public records and public information.

Recordscheck.net

PO Box 8542, Coral Springs, FL 33075
Phone: 954-575-2240 **Fax:** 954-827-0508
www.recordscheck.net **email-** webmaster@recordscheck.net
Parent Company: First Data Source.
Founded: 2000 **Memberships:** PRRN
Restrictions: Casual requesters permitted.
Applications: Background Info - Individuals, Fraud Prevention/Detection, Employment Screening, Locating People/Businesses, Tenant Screening

Products & Information Categories:
Addresses/Telephone Numbers, Criminal Information, Corporate/Trade Name Data (FL, US)
Vital Records (CA, CO, CT, FL, ID, KY, ME, MN, NV, OH, TX, UT)
Aviation, Vessels (US)
Proprietary Databases or Gateways:
Gateway Name: USA Business Profiles
‣ Corporate/Trade Name Data (US)

Gateway Name: Firearms Registration; DEA Registration
‣ Licenses/Registrations/Permits (FL, US)

Gateway Name: Pilots, Planes Registrations
‣ Aviation (US)

Gateway Name: Merchant Vessels
‣ Vessels (US)

Gateway Name: Sex Offenders Database
‣ Criminal Information (US)

Gateway Name: Peoplefinder
‣ Addresses/Telephone Numbers (US)

Special Distribution Methods to Client: Email, Gateway via Another Online Service, Internet

Since the late 1990s, RecordsCheck.net has been a driving force behind many online public record research groups and businesses. They provide XML feeds fro a variety of public records. All searches are instant and our XML feeds can be integrated into your existing web applications. Compiling and providing fresh data to both corporate and consumer clients is their specialty. Gathering data from various government and private sources as well as proprietary databases, providing clients with current and accurate data.

RUI Inc

3730 E Clement Rd, Boise, ID 83704
Phone: 866-759-8883, 208-323-8883 **Fax:** 208-323-8884
email- search@ruiinc.info **Founded:** 2002
Memberships: PRRN

Clientele restrictions: Casual requesters permitted.

Applications: Asset/Lien Searching/Verification, Background Info - Business, Background Info - Individuals, Filing/Recording Documents, Tenant Screening

Products & Information Categories:
Bankruptcy, Corporate/Trade Name Data, Criminal Information, Tenant History, Trademarks, Associations/Trade Groups (US, ID)

Driver and/or Vehicle, Vital Records, Workers Compensation (ID, MT) Litigation/Judgments/Tax Liens, Real Estate/Assessor, Uniform Commercial Code (ID, MT, OR, WA, UT, WY, NV)

Special Distribution Methods to Client: Automated Telephone Look-Up, Dial-Up (Other than Internet), Email, Internet

RUI features 24-48 hour turnaround in most jurisdictions. Key employees have been recruited from government offices, and trained in the use of the most current techniques. They prefer to email results so that clients receive results without delay.

United State Homeland Investigations

PO Box 359, Mount Vernon, VA 22121
Phone: 703-780-2057 **Fax:** 703-340-1695
www.ushii.com **email-** inquiries@ushii.com
Branch Offices: Alexandria, VA; Boston, MA; Denver, CO
Founded: 2003

Memberships: PRRN, ABI, NAWBO, SHRM, NAPBS, WIPP
Clientele restrictions: Casual requestors permitted.

Pre-Employment Screening Services: Credit Reports, Criminal Records, MVRs, Education/Employment , Licenses/Registrations/ Permits, Profile/Aptitude Testing, Drug Testing - Outsourced
Tenant Screening Services: Credit Reports, Criminal Records , Forcible Detainer Check , Litigation/Judgments

Distribution Methods to Client: Email, Gateway via Another Online Service

USHI is a women-owned screening corporation in the DC Metro area. Experienced personnel include former federal law enforcement, legal professionals, and research experts. USHI unique attributes include screening outsourcing, 24/7 client assistance, 24/7 access to screening reports, international capabilities, industry-leading security for confidential information, and risk management services. Conducts real-time searches, especially on criminal records. Clients include government agencies, no-profits, corporations, small businesses and individuals.

PRRN - The Public Record Retriever Network

PRRN - The Public Record Retriever Network - is the largest membership organization representing professionals in the public record industry. With more than 750 members in 50 states, Puerto Rico, Canada and elsewhere in North America retrieving documents from local government agencies in over 2,000 counties, boroughs, parishes and provinces, PRRN Members are recognized as the nation's leaders in local public record searching and document retrieval.

Visit www.brbpub.com to find a PRRN Member by state and county or parish. With over 18,000 hits monthly, this site gives great to PRRN Members.

Who Is Eligible For Membership?

Any firm eligible to be listed in *The Directory of Local Court and County Record Retrievers* is eligible for annual membership. Once a member, continued membership depends on the firm maintaining the standards expressed in the Code of Professional Conduct and Terms of Membership.

What is PRRN's Mission?

The mission of PRRN is to promote development within the public document retrieval industry of—

- Standards of professional conduct, and
- Improved marketing and sales practices

What is the PRRN Code of Public Record Retriever Standards?

Members of PRRN commit their organization to a set standard Record Retrieval and of Professional Conduct. These standards are summarized starting on page 654.

The Benefits of PRRN Membership

New Business Opportunities

The PRRN Membership roster is strongly promoted to business entities that use public records and hire public record retrievers. For example:

PRRN Members are exclusively profiled on the *Public Record Research System*, an Internet subscription product.

The public may do a query to exclusively find PRRN members at www.brbpub.com/prrn.

The PRRN Member listings are prominently featured in *The Directory of Local Court and County Record Retrievers* and in the CD-ROM version of the directory.

Network With Other Professionals

PRRN Members can rely upon the assurance and pledge from other PRRN members when looking for a record retriever to service a client need outside of their local retrieval area. The PRRN **Member Logo** can be used in member's advertising and promotional materials.

The **PRRN Membership Kit** that each member receives includes a printed roster of all members. Throughout the year PRRN members may view or download the updated roster from the web site.

The PRRN Directors **monitor problems or disputes** members may have with other members or non-members.

Educational Benefits

PRRN Members receive the Public Record Retrieval Industry Standards Manual (PRRISM). This 32-page document is a training aid and is full of useful information regarding:

- Taking the order, preparing the report
- Standards, guaranties, and disclaimers
- Pricing and invoicing, how to handle billing and receivables problems

PRRN Members receive the PRRN newsletter, SOURCES. This newsletter features articles relevant to the public record retrieval industry, and how to increase your business or to operate more efficiently.

Throughout the year, PRRN members are notified when events affect the business public record retrievers. The directors monitor legislation and get involved when necessary to lobby legislative committees and licensing boards.

PRRN Members will receive a 10% discount on single book purchases from BRB Publications.

Features of the PRRN Members Only Web Page

Search for a PRRN Member. You can find a PRRN member by searching in a specific county or by state. This is the same service open to the general public, and a source of new business for many members.

Download PRRN Forms For Your New Client and Credit Needs. You can download three important PRRN-approved forms. (Sample forms are included in this package.)

- New Account/Credit Application – For a Business
- New Account/Credit Application – For an Individual
- Personal Guarantee Authorization to Release Information

The forms are available on the web site in either MS Word or PDF. You can modify the MS Word forms by adding your company information and logo, or editing the text, or you can print the PDF versions and paste your address or logo onto the forms. Also, the PRRN Logo can be downloaded from this location. You can use the PRRN logo on any forms or your company advertising pieces.

Download Current Roster of PRRN Members. This is a PDF file of approximately 70 pages. The roster is updated weekly, adding new members and making changes as necessary. You are free to download and print the file, or keep it on your system as a viewable PDF file.

Download Memos and Newsletters. Previous editions of Sources and copies of email memos can be found here.

The Bulletin Board. The PRRN Bulletin Board is a forum to help PRRN members with particular questions or needs. Once a topic or "discussion" is initiated, all additional member comments are saved and viewable. We ask that you please identify yourself when you participate. We want to make this site as easy and functional as possible and are very interested in your feedback and comments, if you have the time and interest.

By the way, the PRRN Members Bulletin Board is NOT meant to promote or market services. Members attempting to use the Bulletin Board as a means of self-promotion will have their passwords deleted by the Directors.

Terms of Membership in PRRN

PRRN is a service by BRB Publications, Inc. for the purpose of promoting standards in the retrieval industry. The principals of BRB, Carl Ernst and Michael Sankey, serve as the Directors of PRRN.

PRRN members agree to follow the highest standards of ethics and conduct in all their dealings with other members and with clients. These standards not only include those explicitly listed in the Code of Professional Conduct, but also include such matters as paying invoices to other firms in a timely fashion and not accepting projects which members are not competent to complete correctly or in a timely manner.

The members of PRRN may communicate with the Directors at any time, using the Retriever Satisfaction Survey or any other means, concerning problems or disputes with other members or with clients. The Directors may, at their sole discretion, use such information to inform members about such disputes, including but not limited to failure to pay invoices and failure to complete project on time or correctly. At the request of any member, the Directors may mediate disputes among members.

Once you are a PRRN Member, your continued membership depends on your maintaining the standards expressed in the Code of Professional Conduct and the Terms of Membership. The Directors of PRRN may, at their sole discretion and without notice, cancel the membership of any member that, in their opinion, has not met the spirit of these terms. Fees will not be returned upon cancellation of membership.

Members agree explicitly not to hold the Directors or any other members liable in any way for reporting or taking action on problems or disputes communicated to them in good faith.

Membership Fees

The annual fee for PRRN membership is based on the number of counties you service hands-on on a regular basis. The fee is $10.00 per county. The minimum fee is $25.00. The maximum fee is $200.00.

A PRRN "Associate Membership" – available to search firms, screening firms, and other public record-related companies that do not retrieve county or court documents in person – is available for $39.00 per year.

For questions or for a PRRN application, please contact BRB Publications, PO Box 27869, Tempe AZ 85285, phone 800-929-3811, fax: 800-929-4981 or visit www.brbpub.com/PRRN.

PRRN Code of Public Record Retriever Standards©

Part of the PRRN mission is establishing industry standards for public record retrieval. These standards apply to all members within the specific part of the industry they serve.

1. Definitions

In order to establish standards, it is first necessary to make certain that all retrievers are using a common language. The industry segments for the purpose of this Code of Standards are defined as follows:

Public Record Retriever (PRR)—PRRs search specific requested categories of public records, usually in order to obtain documentation for legal compliance, lending, hiring, screening, or litigation support. The retriever or his/her personnel goes directly to the agency to look up the information. A retriever may be relied upon for strong knowledge in a local area, whereas a search generalist has a breadth of knowledge and experience in a wider geographic range. A PRR may also be known as an **Abstractor**.

PRRs do not review or interpret the results or issue reports in the sense that investigators or CRA's do. Instead PRRs return copies of documents if requested, and/or report the findings of their searches. A search will usually involve some form of manual intervention, which may include on-site access to a courthouse or other government agency, but which may be automated to some extent, such as access to PACER or another agency with direct access indexes.

Beyond the local coverage of most PRRs, **Retriever Companies** are a type of PRR that offers record retrieval services on a state, regional, or national basis**. Retriever Companies** use a network of retrievers and/or correspondents. When the term PRR is used in this document, the term is also meant to include Retriever Companies. When a local PRR is hired by another PRR or Retriever Company, the PRR may also be known as an **Independent Contractor.**

Retail Screening Companies—Companies that provide background checks use public records and other information to prepare an overall report about a subject for an end-user, e.g. employer or property owner. When a Screening Company performs services for employers or property owners, the Screening Company must comply with the **Federal Fair Credit Reporting Act (FCRA),** under which the Screening Company is considered to be a **Consumer Reporting Agency (CRA).**

There are several types of Screening Companies. The two with which we are primarily concerned are:

Employment Screener—Provides applicant and employee background screening services to employers.

Tenant Screener—Provides tenant background screening services to property owners.

The responsibility of the Retail Screening Company is to review the results of public record research to determine what is reportable to the end-user.

Retail Search Firms—These Search Firms furnish public records to a variety of clients as an intermediary, or to end-users. Search firms obtain public records from numerous sources including Wholesale Distributors and Gateways (see below), government sources, PRRs, and other search firms.

Wholesale Distributors—Are automated public record firms who combine public sources of bulk data and/or provide online access to supply information to retail Screening Companies. Examples include:

Primary Distributors collect or buy public record information from its original source and reformat the information in some useful way, usually to create a proprietary database of information.

Gateways provide their customers with seamless, automated access to other Distributors' data or to government sources. Gateways thus provide "one-stop shopping" for multiple geographic areas and/or categories of information.

Companies can be both Primary Distributors and Gateways.

Private Investigators—PIs use public records as tools (rather than as ends in themselves) in order to create an overall, comprehensive "picture" of an individual or company for a particular purpose. PIs interpret the information they have gathered in order to identify further investigation options. PIs summarize their results in a report compiled from all the sources used. Many Private Investigators also provide FCRA-compliant employment and tenant screening services as well as public record retrieval. In addition, an investigator may be licensed and may perform the types of services traditionally thought of as detective work, such as surveillance.

More Industry Terms:

FCRA—The federal Fair Credit Reporting Act and related FTC rules.

Subject—The applicant or employee about whom background information is being gathered.

Customer—Direct customer or client of a PRR or a Retriever Company, but not an End-User.

End-User—The entity that ultimately ends up with the search results (e.g. the customer of the attorney, title company, or the employer or property owner customer of a Screening Company).

Result—An item of information obtained that may pertain to a Subject.

Negative or Derogatory Information—Information unearthed during the performance of public record retrieval that could later be classified as adverse to the Subject under FCRA or other law.

Review—To look at Results obtained from other sources for the purpose of determining whether the information is Reportable to an end-user. PRRs do not perform a review; their clients do.

Reportable—This term refers to which Results can be reported to an end-user, after a Review. The standard for what is "Reportable" is whether the information complies with applicable law, such as the FCRA. PRRs do not determine what is Reportable.

Identifiers—Facts about the Subject used to analyze a public record for the purpose of determining if the record is about the Subject. Examples are full name, DOB, SSN, sex, address, and hair color.

Matching Logic—Using the Identifiers given with a search request in order to determine if the record found does, in fact, belong to the Subject. Retail Screening Companies are always responsible to determine the level of matching logic that will meet FCRA rules before reporting a Result. Stricter matching logic should be applied to Negative or Derogatory Information.

Three levels of matching logic are: **Partial Name Match Logic**—Matching Logic that requires only a partial match of the Subject's name to a Result; **Name Match Only**—Results of a search that uses the full Subject name as a match; **Strict Match Logic**—Match logic that requires a minimum of two and when possible three Subject Identifiers before reporting.

Match—A Result is the Matching Logic the Retail Screening Company determines is about the Subject.

2. General Standard

A Public Record Retriever (PRR) shall work diligently and use reasonable care in the performance of this work in order to provide the highest possible level of service and accuracy. All searches will be conducted directly by the PRR or by researchers that are under the PRR's direct and immediate supervision and control. Order taking follows standard, written procedures that assure the Customer has provided complete and accurate Identifiers to the PRR. **Report preparation is standardized to include all the information taken on the order as well as a clear explanation of the Results and the procedures, as outlined in** ***Section*** *7 Reporting the Logistics of the Search,* used in obtaining them. **Report preparation does not include a determination of what is Reportable to a Customer's client or end-user.** Disclaimers are used appropriately to put the Customer on notice about the extent of any guaranties and the constraints on obtaining information from government agencies. Pricing and invoicing methods are understandable and ethical.

3. Legal Compliance

The PRR agrees to perform public record searches in a manner consistent with that prescribed by the local, state, or federal offices and courts in which it searches. A PRR also agrees the searches will be performed legally in the manner prescribed by said offices and courts. At no time will the PRR obtain or convey to a Customer any information that was obtained through illegal or unethical means. A PRR agrees to obtain any business license that is required under applicable local city or county laws or regulations.

4. Timeliness

A PRR agrees that public record search services provided for the Customer are to be completed in an agreed upon timeframe starting from receipt of each individual search requested by the Customer. Unless otherwise agreed with the Customer, the PRR begins the search as soon as possible after the receipt of the order, and immediately transmits any Results obtained to the Customer. In the event that there is a delay caused by the need of a court clerk to obtain files, the PRR will track the progress daily, make all necessary effort to obtain the information as soon a possible, and keep the Customer informed.

5. Performing the Search

The PRR uses only the most current, official, due-diligence-compliant source from the government agency when conducting a search. If not, the PRR will disclose the fact up front to the Customer. The PRR will fully divulge the source of information (i.e., court clerk, online service, correspondent, etc.), and the manner in which the search was conducted, (i.e. microfiche, court computer, submission to the clerk, etc.).

The following pertains to performing a search of an individual Subject name:

A. In searching a common name on an index with no DOBs or other comparable ID, the PRR should use reasonable care to investigate any name matches or near name matches listed on the index with no middle initial. If such cannot be eliminated as a match by a clerk check or other valid means, the PRR should pull and examine the files in question to search for more Identifiers. If this further examination is not reasonable to do, then the PRR must inform the Customer.

B. The Customer determines the minimum scope of each search, and the PRR should never assume a default depth of the search. If the timeframe to be researched has not been transmitted with the request, or if it is not mutually agreed upon in writing, the PRR should seek clarification from the Customer prior to performing the research.

C. For every Subject name to search in each court requested – and unless instructions are given otherwise – the PRR is expected to search at least 7 years, but not less than the depth of records readily available at that court or per specific request. The PRR shall do so without spending additional access fees unless specifically authorized to spend those fees. **In all cases, all history possibly relating to the Subject, regardless of the age of the record, disposition or offense, must be reported unless otherwise agreed with the Customer.** Thus, if a default 7-year search is requested, and 12 years are available at no additional court cost in the same index, a 12-year history is expected, unless prior instruction is given. In that same court, if an additional 20 years is available by searching through ledger books, that search is not performed unless the Customer separately authorizes such a search. In a different court, if only 5 years are available on a public index and the remaining years are in ledger books or only through the court staff, the PRR is expected to search whatever source and record material is required to deliver the depth of search, unless otherwise specified by the Customer, up to the default minimum of 7 years.

D. The PRR recognizes a "Name Match Only" record report constitutes a problem for the Customer in that it presents an uncertainty. As such, the PRR must give best efforts in searching for any type of ID on the record. If none can be found, the name should not be cleared; rather the PRR will submit to the Customer a "Name Match Only" report including an express statement that no Identifiers of any kind could be found in the file or agency database. In addition, if the PRR determines in its judgment that a record with only a partial name match may in fact be about the Subject, the PRR is encouraged to report the record as a "Name Match Only" record. In other words, the basic reporting rule for a PRR to follow is: **let the Customer decide what is reportable to the End-User.**

6. Reporting the Search

The PRR will report the search results in a clear, concise, legible manner that can be easily understood by the Customer. This includes refraining from the use of locally acceptable abbreviations that may not be understood outside the area.

The PRR will refrain from passing on any record information they themselves do not understand until the PRR gets any such data clarified and understood before including that data in a report.

The PRR will report only verifiable facts that can be substantiated by available court records. The researcher should refrain from guessing or "dubbing in" key case information.

The PRR will report the existence of any additional records found in the course of research that may match to the Subject, unless instructions otherwise given. This holds true regardless of the record's location, and regardless of whether it is listed under an alias.

The PRR will report the existence of any AKA's or other ID variations found in the course of research on any given Subject.

In reporting on a record where the name or ID given to search differs in any way from that which was found in the court or government office, the PRR should include a statement acknowledging this discrepancy so there is no question as to whether it was intentional or accidental.

Reporting Results to a CRA—It is not the responsibility of the PRR or the Retriever Company to Review the Results of a search to determine what information is Reportable, per the FCRA, to a CRA. The PRR reports the results of a search to the CRA; the CRA determines what is Reportable to the End-User.

7. Reporting the Logistics of the Search

The PRR agrees to supply as part of each public record search the following information:

A. Full name of subject, property address checked, and other Identifiers as supplied by the Customer.

B. Specific agency(s), name(s) and indices checked.

C. Date the search was completed.

D. The period the research covers, meaning how far back the records in the file, index or database go AND the through date (date through which records have been posted, i.e., the currency of records) on the government office system.

Logistics of results in the event a criminal record is located at a court—If a criminal record is found and in addition to the information specified above, the PRR agrees to provide the following information, if known:

A. Exact full name as listed in docket or index, and the docket or index number.

B. All Identifiers listed in docket or index including address, date of birth, SSN, or any other relatable Identifier.

C. The original charges and date of charge listed in docket or index.

D. The final disposition as listed in docket or index, including conviction charge, level of charge (felony, misdemeanor, indictable, violation, petty misdemeanor, etc), all sentencing information listed and any subsequent and pertinent information pertaining to the docket or index.

E. If requested in advance by the Customer and possible to obtain, the actual code sections that were charged as well as any relevant subsequent history (i.e. expunged, pardoned, dismissed, etc.).

F. If requested in advance by the Customer and possible to obtain, the PRR will request and provide copies of the court records and/or documents that support the information reported above. The PRR and Customer will determine, in advance, a reasonable pricing scheme for those copies.

8. Correcting Information

In the event a PRR discovers that information was given to a Customer in error, it is the absolute professional obligation of the PRR to correct any mistake or error as soon as humanly possible despite any embarrassment or difficulty it may create. All parties should understand that mistakes and errors are always possible when it comes to public records despite taking every reasonable effort to be factual and correct, but that the failure to correct the errors if and when discovered is a gross violation of a researcher's ethical duties.

9. Audits

Retriever Companies and Search Firms will conduct various procedures to audit the PRRs they use and advise their Customers of the general nature of those procedures. Retriever Companies and PRRs acknowledge that Customers reserve the right to periodically send names that are known to have "hits," or to direct identical searches to multiple PRRs in order to test the PRR and to establish that the Customer has exercised due diligence in the selection of a PRR. A Customer will not advise a Retriever Company or PRR ahead of time when a test is being conducted.

10. Confidentiality

The PRR agrees that all information provided by the Customer shall be maintained by the PRR in strict confidence and disclosed only to individuals whose duties reasonably relate to the legitimate business purposes for which the information is submitted. The PRR will not sell or otherwise distribute to third parties any information received, except as otherwise required by law or agreed upon in writing between the PRR and the Customer.

Code of Professional Conduct

The Public Record Retriever Network (PRRN) Code consists of ten guidelines according to which each member of the Network conducts its business.

Competency Guidelines

The Competency Guidelines refer to each of the types of record a PRRN member is proficient in retrieving

1. We know where each type of local public record is maintained.
2. We access these agencies regularly.
3. We understand the contents of the documents we retrieve.
4. We search records ourselves in those agencies that do not conduct searches for the public.
5. We maintain good relationships with agency personnel.

Customer Service Guidelines

The Customer Service Guidelines refer to the way in which each member of PRRN is expected to serve its clients.

1. We return calls promptly.
2. We complete projects as promised.
3. We explain our charges in advance.
4. We will expedite results, on request.
5. We will explain how agencies maintain their records, on request.

Retriever Satisfaction Survey

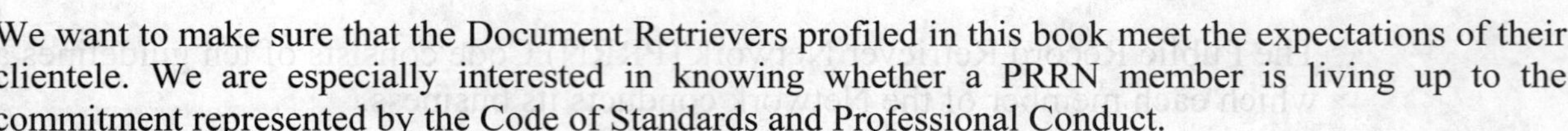

We want to make sure that the Document Retrievers profiled in this book meet the expectations of their clientele. We are especially interested in knowing whether a PRRN member is living up to the commitment represented by the Code of Standards and Professional Conduct.

Therefore, we are providing a separate survey form for you to communicate to us your experience, positive or negative, with Document Retrievers. This form, known as *The Retriever Satisfaction Survey*, appears on the next page. To request a copy of this form, call 800-929-3811. You may choose to have it faxed or mailed to you.

Negative comments will be held in confidence by BRB Publications. Based on your input, we reserve the right to exclude from future editions any firms who fail to maintain an acceptable standard of professional conduct.

Retriever Satisfaction Survey

for readers of the 2007 *Directory of Local Court and County Record Retrievers*

Instructions

1. Make a copy of this form so you can use it again.
2. Report exceptional (good or bad) service you received from a public record retriever.
3. Enter all information that you think useful in assessing the performance of the retriever. The source of negative comments will be kept in confidence.
4. **FAX to Michael Sankey, BRB Publications, 1-800-929-3810.**

Date: ____________________ This is a ☐ positive report or a ☐ negative report.

Your Name	
Company	
Address	
City, State, ZIP	
Telephone Number	
Type of Company (Why you use retrievers)	

Retrieval Firm Name	
Address	
City, State, ZIP	
Telephone Number	

Summarize Your Favorable Comments or Negative Concerns:

____

____

____

____

____

____

General Questions about the Retrieval Firm:

Please answer Yes, No, Usually, or DK (for don't know) based upon your experience with this firm:

Is this firm a member of the Public Record Retriever Network? .... ______
How many times have you used this firm during the past six months? .... ______
Is the firm knowledgeable about the kinds of information it retrieves for you? .... ______
Is the firm always available when you need their services? .... ______
Does the firm perform within the turnaround times stated in our publication? .... ______
Will this firm expedite work on request? .... ______
Does this firm access all the agencies marked for it in the County Index? .... ______
Is billing timely and accurate? .... ______
Does this firm cover all the counties listed in its profile? .... ______
Is all the information in this company's profile accurate? .... ______
If not, what information is wrong?

____

____

____

If you cannot fax, then mail to BRB Publications, PO Box 27869, Tempe, AZ 85285

To Be Included in the Next Edition...

If you are a document retriever, you need to be listed in this book. What's more, it is a free listing. Here is what you need to be included in the next issue.

On the facing page is a blank questionnaire where you provide your company information and details about your record retrieval services, coverage area, and any related services you may provide such as document filing/recording, process service, investigative services, or more. *

A retriever is a company, branch office, or individual that meets the following criterion: you or employees under your direct supervision go to court offices, courts, or other government agencies on a regular basis to search public records or retrieve documents.

Public Record Retriever Application Instructions

Section 1. Local Retrieval Area In this section, list ONLY the county names where you or your FICA employees regularly visit in person. The purpose here is to present your company as an expert for a given area and not merely someone who can "get anything from anywhere." (For counties where you use another retriever - a "correspondent" - or where you use an online source to access records, these can be mentioned in Section 6.)

If you list more than 20 counties, please attach a statement to your profile explaining how you cover all these counties, for example, "we have twenty employees in cars" or "we do a circuit every two days." To avoid complaints, we need you to provide us with evidence that your true employees are regularly visiting - in person - those counties. 1099 people are not included. We may need to call to discuss this.

Sections 2-5. Profile Items Let us know the types of records you can retrieve in person; if or when you require prepayment; if you are licensed PI; your standard billing and payment methods. These details enhance your profile and should cut down on nuisance calls.

Section 6. Expanded Coverage Retrieval Area This is where you can indicate the geographic region if you use other retrievers, correspondents, sub-contractors, etc. Typical answers are "statewide" or listing the counties, states, foreign countries, etc. Here you can show coverage with 1099 people.

Section 7. Your 25-word Company Description Here you can describe your company's special features, advantages to clients, or other important facts - in 25 words or less. Typical items to mention are specialized services, online databases you may use, length of your experience, etc. One exception: we cannot print information about your rates. If you are not sure what to include, say what you do best.

Fill out the questionnaire, review, then return it either by fax or mail as soon as possible to BRB Publications. If you have questions, feel free to call BRB Publications at 800-929-3811.

---

* In addition to your free listing in this book, if you also wish to become a member of the PRRN (Public Record Retriever Network), please indicate so on your questionnaire. Details about PRRN membership and PRRN membership fees are on previous pages. Only PRRN members are featured on BRB websites that receive over 18,000 hits per month and appear in other packaged products sold to large public record provider companies. In short, as a PRRN member you will receive greater exposure. With more than 750 members in 50 states and elsewhere in North America retrieving documents from local government agencies in over 2,000+ counties, boroughs, parishes and provinces, PRRN Members are recognized as the nation's leaders in local public record searching and document retrieval.

Local Court & County Record Retriever Book
Retriever & Abstractor Questionnaire

New ____________

Office us only: ☐ Access ☐Q&A ☐ Cert ☐ Kit .

Basic Information About Your Company List full company name. ☐ Check here to be included as a PRRN member*

Contact Name ______________________ Telephone: ______________

Firm Name ______________________ Toll Free Phone ______________

Address ______________________ Local Fax ______________

City ______________ State____ Zip__________ Toll-free Fax ______________

Web address ______________________ Cell phone ______________

Email (your best email address for contacting you) ______________________

In what year did you start doing business? __________ If you perform litigation Service of Process, check here ☐

1. Local Retrieval Area List ONLY the COUNTIES where YOUR wage-earning employees retrieve records IN-PERSON.
(Do NOT list online or electronic retrieval here. Do NOT list third parties or 1099 people here)

2. TYPES of Records You Retrieve IN-PERSON

A. County Court Records

☐ Civil ☐ Criminal ☐ Probate

B. Federal Court Records

☐ US District ☐ Bankruptcy

C. County Recorded Records

☐ UCCs ☐ Real Estate ☐ Tax Liens/Judgments ☐ Vital Records

D. Other Services

☐ You can file/record documents for clients ☐ You are a licensed PI (in what state(s): ________

3. Usual Turnaround Time for Document Retrieval Explain turnaround times in days or hours; also expedited services:

4. Billing Methods ☐ Bill by # of names searched ☐ Bill by the hour ☐ Bill by # or records located

5. Payment Terms ☐ All projects require prepayment ☐ First project may require prepayment

☐ Will accept credit cards Other payment terms: ______________________

6. Extended Services Extended services using correspondents, independent contractors or others not under your direct control

☐ Yes, we can conduct services beyond our local area (using correspondents) If you use correspondents, list their counties/states/nationwide:

☐ Check this box if you offer electronic record retrieval on a statewide/regional/national basis.

7. 25-word Company Description Describe your company, services, and special features in 25 words or less.

Questionnaire completed by: Date:

FAX to 800-929-4981 or mail to BRB Publications, PO Box 27869, Tempe AZ 85285

BRB Publications, PO Box 27869, Tempe AZ 85285 Phone: 800-929-3811 www.brbpub.com

* to become a PRRN member and receive add'l benefits, a PRRN member application and payment must be included. See PRRN section

Notes

Additional BRB Titles and Information

The Social Security Number Validator-CD

Updated Monthly   Printed on Demand   price $29.00

Enhance your verification process. *The SSN Validator* provides cost-effect assurance of verifying identity and fighting fraud. Simply enter the 9-digit SSN and you know within seconds if the number is valid. The CD also identifies the year and state of issue - geographic and chronological due to when and where the individual obtained the SSN.

College and University Student Records-CD

Updated Monthly   Printed on Demand   Price $29.00

A must for backgrounding. This comprehensive resource is used to verify college attendance and degrees. The CD gives you the direct connection to over 6,000 accredited schools PLUS over 750 bogus schools and diploma mills are red flagged. Includes how to get copies of transcripts, reach alumni associations, and when colleges outsource verification to vendors.

Ultimate County Locator *With Adjoining County Search*-CD

Updated Monthly   Printed on Demand   Price $29.00

Accurately locate the correct county for public record searching. Simply type in a ZIP Code or one of the 90,000 Place Names (cities, towns, burgs) in this powerful index. Shows when ZIP Codes cross county lines (10,000 combinations) or when a ZIP is a PO Box drop. Also has an "adjoining county locator" tool with population figures.

The MVR Book

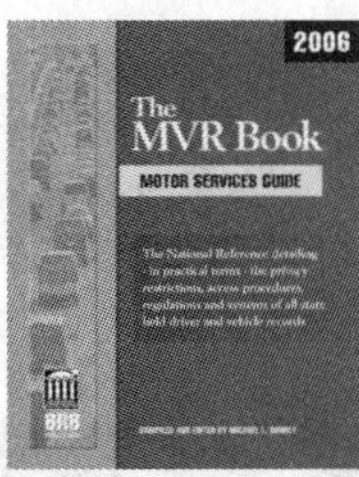

ISBN # 1-879792-86-6   Pub. 1/07   Pages 384   Price $23.95

The New 2007 Version is Ready to Ship! Description: The national reference detailing — in practical terms — the privacy restrictions, access procedures, regulations, and database systems of all state-held driver and vehicle records. For all states.

The MVR Decoder Digest

ISBN # 1-879792-87-7   Pub 1/07   Pages 448   Price $23.95

The New 2007 Version is Ready to Ship! Description: The companion to *The MVR Book*. Translates the codes and abbreviations of violations and licensing categories that appear on motor vehicle records. For all states.

BRB Publications, Inc.
PO Box 27869 • Tempe, AZ 85285-7869
Phone: 800-929-3811 • Fax: 1-800-929-4981
www.brbpub.com